THE INDIANA COMPANION TO
TRADITIONAL CHINESE LITERATURE

THE

Indiana Companion

TO

TRADITIONAL
CHINESE LITERATURE

WILLIAM H. NIENHAUSER, JR.
Editor and Compiler

CHARLES HARTMAN
Associate Editor for Poetry

Y. W. MA
Associate Editor for Fiction

STEPHEN H. WEST
Associate Editor for Drama

INDIANA UNIVERSITY PRESS • BLOOMINGTON

The preparation and the publication of this volume were assisted by
grants from the Tools Program and the Publications Program of the
National Endowment for the Humanities, a federal agency.

Library of Congress Cataloging in Publication Data
Main entry under title:

The Indiana companion to traditional Chinese Literature.

Bibliography: p.
Includes indexes.
Contents: pt. 1. Essays. — pt. 2. Entries.
1. Chinese literature—Bio-bibliography. 2. Chinese
literature—History and criticism—Addresses, essays,
lectures. I. Nienhauser, William H. Jr.
Z3108.L5153 1985 [PL2264]   895.1′09   83-49511
ISBN 0-253-32983-3

1 2 3 4 5 89 88 87 86

*This volume is dedicated to
my parents*

Contents

Preface

Before the ink on these pages dries it will have been over seven years since the project began. The impetus for the work may lie in the opening line of Georges Margouliès' *Histoire de la littérature chinoise*—"La littérature chinoise a été jusqu'ici et de nos jours reste encore absolument en dehors des horizons littéraires du lecteur européen"—since it seems his claim holds as true today as it did when he wrote it in 1949. To trace the history and the goals of this project, however, it is necessary to return even beyond the time of Margouliès to the year 1705, for it was then that Ts'ao Yin 曹寅 (1658-1712) received from the K'ang-hsi Emperor the edict to print the *Ch'üan T'ang shih* 全唐詩 (Complete T'ang Poetry). For the next year and a half Ts'ao was beset by deadlines from his printers and from the court, his staff was riddled by infirmity, illness, and death, the project slowed while a particular textual source was sought, etc. Yet the compilation which resulted from this project, despite a number of problems with the text, has proved an important starting point for research into T'ang poetry for several centuries.

The *Indiana Companion to Traditional Chinese Literature* was initiated not by royal command, but at the suggestion of my colleague and friend Joseph S. M. Lau. Moreover, the work went on without sponsorship by any formal association or society (although the various agencies, institutions, and foundations mentioned below have been generous with their support). And it was not completed quite so quickly as Ts'ao Yin's compilation. It has rather been the efforts of an international group of nearly two hundred scholars (Ts'ao Yin had only a handful of collaborators) who have made possible the completion of this volume.

The work was originally modeled on the Oxford Companions. Soon it became apparent that the entries in most of the Oxford volumes were more concise than what would be most useful for readers of Chinese traditional literature. We also wanted to provide the reader with a good basic bibliography for each of the subjects discussed. Employing the tables of contents in the draft literature volume of the *Tz'u-hai*, my first project assistant, Ms. Sharon S. J. Hou 侯師娟 , and I compiled a draft list of about seven hundred entries. We concentrated on authors, works, and genres. As an introduction to the entries, we conceived of a series of essays on major types of traditional literature such as drama, fiction, criticism, poetry, prose, and rhetoric. Later, essays on Buddhist literature, Taoist literature, women's literature, and popular literature were added. The essays were to introduce the educated Western reader to the genres which approximate what we know as "fiction" or "poetry" in the West, as well as to provide an overview for the more specialized student. Thus in the essay on fiction the reader would encounter discussions of such terms as *hsiao-shuo* 小說 and *chih-kuai* 志怪 which he could explore further under the entries for those subjects.

The draft contents were then sent to a number of scholars in the field for their comments. Three in particular agreed to serve as associate editors: Charles Hartman 蔡涵墨 (for poetry), Y. W. Ma 馬幼垣 (for fiction), and Stephen H. West 奚如谷 (for drama). Their intelligence, devotion, humor, and flexibility were crucial to setting the project in motion. At this early stage we also received advice from several other scholars concerning the scope and design of the project: special thanks to F. W. Mote, Nathan Sivin, Herbert Franke, and David R. Knechtges—their detailed responses to the draft table of contents helped to shape the final version. John Gallman, the director of Indiana University Press, provided me with a contract for the volume within weeks of its conception. His courage and belief in the project was also instrumental to setting it in motion and certainly contributed to funding from the National Endowment for the Humanities beginning in 1980. NEH has been our chief benefactor throughout the project, generously underwriting two summers of research for each of the associate editors and allowing me to reduce or eliminate my own teaching during several semesters. Their patience and their guidance also merit our sincere thanks.

The real "authors" of this volume are of course the contributors—approximately 170 from a dozen nations. Some were particularly cooperative—Edward H. Schafer was the first to submit an entry, and Jerry Schmidt, Sharon S. J. Hou, Edmond Yee, Bill Schultz, and Wilt Idema seemed always willing to add another assignment to their list of entries. I have been pleased with the congeniality and dedication of scores of my past associates and especially of colleagues I have never met except through correspondence related to this project. For some time I was afraid that attempting to work with so many scholars would result in Alexander Pope's dilemma: "Companions have I enough, friends few" ("Letter to Gay"). Not so. Although I cannot imagine myself involved in a project of this magnitude again for some time, I must admit that the group of individuals who worked with me on the *Companion* proved to me that such cooperative ventures can still be accomplished.

Helmut Martin organized and directed a workshop on the *Companion* in June 1982 in Schwerte, West Germany. Thanks to a grant from the Alexander von Humbolt Foundation, he and I had been able to meet with Dr. Joachim Wiercimok of the Deutsche Forschungsgemeinschaft during the spring of 1981 to plan the gathering. The Schwerte Workshop brought more than a dozen distinguished European scholars together with the editors of the *Companion* for a review of the project to date and the four hundred entries then on hand; it resulted in a rewriting or reassigning of nearly two hundred entries. It also allowed me the opportunity to meet with N. G. D. Malmqvist, the genial editor of the *Descriptive Handbook of Chinese Literary Works from 1900-1949*, and to benefit from his experience in working on this complementary tome. The week spent in Schwerte was without question the single most influential event of the entire compilation period, and this is attributable to the careful planning of Professor Martin, his staff at Ruhr University (Bochum), and our mentor at the sponsoring Deutsche Forschungsgemeinschaft, Dr. Wiercimok.

Debts are also owed the Association for Asian Studies, which provided seed monies, the American Council of Learned Societies and Dr. Jason Parker, for funding two meetings of the editorial staff and a trip to the Harvard-Yenching Library among other things, and the Research Committee of the Graduate School and the College of Letters and Science of the University of Wisconsin, which provided continous support in various forms. A special thanks to Linda Bock of the Dean's Office, Letters and Science, who was instrumental in raising the matching funds for the National Endowment for the Humanities grant and who was always ready with encouragement when I most needed it, to Walt Keough, who helped put together the original proposal, to Robert Perkl, who administered a complex series of grants for us, to Donna Jahnke, who was ever ready with answers concerning grant regulations, and to Tai-loi Ma, FARE, University of Chicago, who through regular assistance put the FARE collection "at my fingertips." The grant monies which did not in some form underwrite activities of the editorial staff were earned by a sequence of project assistants beginning with Sharon S. J. Hou, which included Jenny K. C. Li 黎國珍 , Sin-sing Kong 江先聲 , and Beth Po-hui Chuang 莊博蕙. Besides writing several entries for which authors were not to be found, Sin-sing Kong translated the dozen or so entries we received in Chinese and coordinated the project during the spring of 1983 when I was in Taiwan. Beth Chuang was particularly helpful with the typing and proofreading of the Chinese characters. Support for her early assistance came from the National Science Foundation of the Republic of China, which also underwrote other expenses related to the composition of the essay on prose. Meei-chyn Wang 王美琴 also began to work on the *Companion* while I was in Taipei and she has continued to offer advice and assistance since that time. Dr. David Te-wei Wang 王德威 of National Taiwan University has regularly provided suggestions and assistance for the past year and a half. Asanuma Shigeru 淺沼茂 served as a reference person for questions concerning Japanese romanization. Naomi Galbreath was an effective liaison person who succeeded in calling in entries from a number of dilatory contributors. Caitlin McManus and Christine Pheley typed most of the manuscripts onto the Wang Workstation we used to typeset the text. My wife, Judith Brockway Nienhauser, typed editorial changes and supervised the pasteup of the Chinese characters. Christa Cutter and Cui Shuqin also worked on the pasteup and final editing. Ron Gray and Chan Chiuming helped with the indexes. Cheryl Arn provided various types of secretarial assistance. Teresa Nealon has, among other tasks, kept the skein of purse strings to the supporting agencies untangled for the past seven years. And students of several classes at the University of Wisconsin and National Taiwan University read parts of the manuscript and offered useful suggestions.

Several individuals contributed to our "gifts and match fund," thus facilitating the completion of the project. We should like to especially thank Stephen Tse, Lester Kissel, Stanley Ginsberg, Kelly and Eva Knight, Thomas Rohlich, and Nancy A. Wang.

Finally, my sincere thanks to those people who actually "made" the book, to William Kasdorf, whose expertise in computer typesetting has guided us throughout, to Joan Leffler and Steve Caldwell of Administrative Data Processing, who aided in a number of ways related to the Wang Workstation, to Tarry Curry of Indiana University Press, who coordinated the final steps of production, and especially to Lynn Lightfoot, my very patient editor at Indiana University Press, who good-naturedly but carefully nudged and nurtured the manuscript through what has seemed to be an interminable series of corrections, additions, and changes.

Without the help of these several hundred people, the *Companion* could not have been completed. Only the errors and omissions remain the responsibility of the editor alone.

WILLIAM H. NIENHAUSER, JR.
München, 14 July 1984

List of Contributors

AB   Anne Birrell
AED Albert E. Dien 丁愛博, Stanford University
AH   Andrew Hsieh 謝正光, Grinnell College
AL   André Lévy 雷威安, University of Paris
ALo Andrew Lo, University of London
AP   Andrew H. Plaks 蒲安迪, Princeton University
AR   Adele Rickett 李又安, University of Maryland
AJP Angela Jung Palandri 榮之穎, University of Oregon
AY   Anthony C. Yu 余國藩, University of Chicago

BL   C. Bradford Langley 龍伯德, Colby College
BTW Baitao Wu 吳白陶, Nanjing University
BU   Beth Upton

CB   Cyril Birch 白之, University of California, Berkeley
CC   Chris Connery, Princeton University
CF   Craig Fisk 費維廉, University of Chicago
CFL Ch'i-fang Li 李齊芳, Tamkang University
CH   Charles Hartman 蔡涵墨, State University of New York, Albany
CHP Ching-Hsi Perng 彭鏡禧, National Taiwan University
CHW Ching-hsien Wang 王靖獻, University of Washington
CIT Ching-i Tu 涂經詒, Rutgers University
CLC Cynthia L. Chennault
CLP Chia-lin Pao 鮑家麟, University of Arizona
CM   Colin Mackerras 馬克林, Griffith University
CSC C. S. Chang 張春樹, University of Michigan
CSG C. S. Goodrich 顧傳習, University of California, Santa Barbara
CW   C. Witzling
CY   Cordell Yee 余定國, University of Wisconsin
CYi Chan Ying 詹鍈, Honan University
CYC Clara Yü Cuadrado, University of Maryland

DB   Daniel Bryant 白潤德, University of Victoria
DG   Donald Gjertson 周宗德, University of Massachusetts
DH   Donald Holzman, École des Hautes Études, Paris

DJ Dale Johnson 章道犖, Oberlin College
DL David Lattimore, Brown University
DLM David L. McMullen 麥大維, Cambridge University
DN Douglas Nielson, University of California, Berkeley
DP David Pollack, University of Rochester
DR David Roy 芮效衛, University of Chicago
DW Douglas Wilkerson 魏道格, Yale University

EB Elizabeth Bernard, University of California, Berkeley
ES Edward H. Schafer 薛愛華, University of California, Berkeley
EY Edmond Yee 余卓豪, Pacific Lutheran Theological Seminary

GD Günther Debon 德博, University of Heidelberg
GL Gaylord Kai Loh Leung 梁錫華, Chinese University of Hong Kong
GM Göran Malmqvist 馬悅然, Stockholm University

HC Hu Chi 胡忌, Nanking University
HF Herbert Franke 傅海博, University of Munich
HH Harriet Halbert, University of Washington
HHF Hans Frankel 傅漢思, Yale University
HI   Hideo Iwaki 岩城秀夫, Yamaguchi University
HK Heike Kotzenberg, University of Bonn
HLL Hsüeh-lun Lo 駱雪倫
HM Helmut Martin 馬漢茂, University of Bochum
HSK Hsin-sheng Kao 高信生
HW Hartmut Walravens, Hamburg

IT   Issei Tanaka 田仲一成, Tokyo University

JA Joseph R. Allen, Washington University
JB Judith Boltz 鮑菊隱, University of California, Berkeley
JC J. Cavanaugh 甘乃元, Far East Research Library, Minneapolis
JCS James C. T. Shu 許經田, Tsing-hua University
JDS J. D. Schmidt, University of British Columbia
JEC J. Creutz 甘靈寧, University of Michigan
JH James M. Hargett 何瞻, University of Colorado
JK Jon Kowallis 寇志明, University of California, Berkeley
JL James J. Y. Liu 劉若愚, Stanford University
JLo John Louton, University of Washington
JM John Marney 馬約翰, Oakland University
JoM John Minford, Chinese University of Hong Kong
JoW John Wang 王靖宇, Stanford University
JP Jordan Paper, York University
JPD J. P. Diény 桀溺, École Pratique des Hautes Études, Paris
JR Jeffrey Riegel, University of California, Berkeley
JS Jonathan Spence 史景遷, Yale University

JTW   J. Timothy Wixted 魏世德, Arizona State University
JW   Jason Chia-sheng Wang 王家聲, National Sun Yat-sen University
JWW   Jan W. Walls, University of Victoria

KCL   K. C. Leung 梁啟昌, San Jose State University
KD   Kenneth Dewoskin 杜志豪, University of Michigan
KH   Kenneth Ho 何沛雄, University of Hong Kong
KIC   Kang-i Sun Chang 孫康宜, Yale University
KK   Karl S. Y. Kao 高辛勇, Yale University
KS   Kristopher Schipper 施舟人, École Pratique des Hautes Études, Paris

LLC   Li-li Chen 陳荔荔, Tufts University

MCh   Madeline Chu 朱陳曼麗, Oberlin College
MC   Marie Chan, University of Arizona
MD   Milena Doleželová 米列娜, University of Toronto
MF   Michael B. Fish 癈林, University of Oregon
MH   Marlon Hom 譚雅倫, University of California, Los Angeles
MRS   Michael R. Stas
MS   Madeline Spring 司馬德琳 University of Colorado
MSD   Michael S. Duke 杜邁可, University of British Columbia
MSH   Ming-shui Hung 洪銘水, Brooklyn College
MSP   Ming-sun Poon, Chinese University of Hong Kong
MW   Marsha Wagner 魏瑪莎, China Institute in America, New York
MWe   Maxine Belmont Weinstein 白曼馨, University of Pennsylvania

OL   Oscar Lee 李厚承, Columbia University

PA   Pedro Acosta 柯彼得, Yale University
PH   Patrick Hanan 韓南, Harvard University
PHC   Po-hui Chuang 莊博蕙, University of Wisconsin
PHL   Peter H. Lee 李鶴株, University of Hawaii
PL   Peter Li 李培瑞, Rutgers University
PLC   P. L. Chan 陳炳良, University of Hong Kong
PR   Paul Ropp 羅溥洛, Memphis State University
PS   Phillip Sun 孫述宇, Chinese University of Hong Kong
PTH   Pi-twan Huang 黃碧端, National Sun Yat-sen University
PWK   Paul W. Kroll, University of Colorado
PY   Pauline R. Yu 余寶琳, University of Minnesota

RB   Richard Bodman 包瑞車, St. Olaf College
RCH   Richard C. Hessney, Brooklyn College
REH   Robert E. Hegel 何谷理, Washington University
RES   Richard E. Strassberg 韓祿伯, University of California, Los Angeles
RH   Robert Henricks, Dartmouth University
RMH   Richard M. W. Ho 何文滙, Chinese University of Hong Kong

xv

RIN   Rod Ivan Nelson
RJC   Robert Joe Cutter 高德耀, University of Wisconsin
RL   Richard J. Lynn 林理彰
RM   Richard B. Mather 馬瑞志, University of Minnesota
RS   Robert Strauss 司徒博, University of Munich
RVF   Rainer von Franz 傅浪士, University of Bonn

SB   Susan Blader 裴玄德, Dartmouth University
SD   Stephen Durrant 杜潤德, University of Utah
SFL   S. F. Lai 賴瑞和, Princeton University
SH   Sharon S. J. Hou 侯師娟, Pomona College
SHS   Stuart H. Sargent 薩進德, University of Maryland
SI   Sohei Itoh 伊藤漱平, Tokyo University
SKW   Siu-kit Wong 黃兆傑, Hong Kong University
SL   Shuen-fu Lin 林順夫, University of Michigan
SLD   Shu-leung Dang 鄧仕樑, Chinese University of Hong Kong
SLY   Shiao-ling Yü 余孝玲, Ohio State University
SM   Stanley Mickel 米凱樂, Wittenberg University
SO   Stephen Owen 宇文所安Harvard University
SOH   Stephen O'Harrow, University of Hawaii
SRB   Stephen R. Bokenkamp, University of California, Berkeley
SSK   Sin-sing Kong 江先聲, University of Wisconsin
SSW   Shirleen S. Wong 黃秀魂, University of California, Los Angeles
SW   Stephen H. West 奚如谷, University of Arizona
SY   Sarah Yim

TCY   Tao-chung Yao 姚道中, University of Arizona
TFC   Tsai-fa Cheng 鄭再發, University of Wisconsin
TIJ   Tsung-i Jao 饒宗頤, Chinese University of Hong Kong
TLM   Tai-loi Ma 馬泰來, University of Chicago
TP   Timoteus Pokora 鮑格洛, Prague University
TS   Tamotsu Satō 佐藤保, Ochanomizu University
TTC   Tse-tsung Chow 周策縱, University of Wisconsin
TW   Timothy Wong 黃宗泰, Arizona State University

VC   Victoria Cass 鄧爲寧, University of Minnesota
VHM   Victor H. Mair 梅維恆, University of Pennsylvania
VK   Volker Klöpsch 呂福克, National Taiwan University

WD   William Dolby 杜爲廉, Edinburgh University
WH   William Hennessey 韓亞布, University of Illinois
WHN   William H. Nienhauser, Jr. 倪豪士, University of Wisconsin
WI   Wilt Idema 伊維德, University of Leiden
WJ   W. J. F. Jenner 詹納爾, University of Leeds
WK   Wolfgang Kubin, Freie Universität, Berlin
WLW   W. L. Wong 黃維樑, Chinese University of Hong Kong

WMC   Wing-ming Chan 陳永明, State University of New York, Albany
WO   Werner Oberstenfeld, University of Bochum
WaS   Wayne Schlepp 施文林, University of Toronto
WS   Wilfried Spaar 石磊, University of Wisconsin
WS   William Schultz 舒威霖, University of Arizona

YHC   Ying-hsiung Chou 周英雄, Chinese University of Hong Kong
YHJ   Yün-hua Jan 冉雲華, McMaster University
YPC   Yupi Chen 陳毓羆, Academy of Social Sciences, Beijing
YSY   Ying-shih Yü 余英時, Yale University
YWM   Y. W. Ma 馬幼垣, University of Hawaii

XLW   Xinlei Wu 吳新雷, Nanjing University

A Note on Using This Book

A typical author entry gives a brief biographical background, followed by an introduction and a brief analysis of the major works of the author. Concluding remarks generally contain an assessment of the author's place in literary history. Every entry has a tripartite bibliography (including works through late 1984), listing editions (especially those which are most reliable and most accessible), translations (into English, French, German, and Japanese), and studies. In the present edition only a few Russian works are included—for further reference see the bibliographic studies by Jeanne Kelly and Helmut Martin in *CLEAR*, v. 3 and 6 respectively and Gilbert Rozman, ed., *Soviet Studies of Premodern China* (Ann Arbor, 1985).

Discussion of a particular work will usually be found in the entry for its author. When authorship of a work is uncertain or it is the only major work by its author, discussion of it is entered by title. Besides entries for authors, works, and genres, there are also a few more general entries such as the series on Chinese literature in Japanese translation, Chinese literature in Korean translation, etc.

We have tried not to slight the women writers of traditional Chinese literature. Aside from the essay on women's literature, there are entries for Ch'en Tuan-sheng, Chu Shu-chen, Hsüeh T'ao, Ku T'ai-ch'ing, Li Ch'ing-chao, Ts'ai Yen, Yeh Hsiao-wan, and Yü Hsüan-chi.

When the reader can find additional information on a subject by consulting another entry or essay, he is referred to it either by an asterisk—"Ch'ü Yüan*" means "q.v. Ch'ü Yüan"—or by the word "see" in parentheses followed by the referenced entry: e.g., Yen Yü (see *Ts'ang-lang shih-hua*). Chinese characters are given for an author's names and the titles of his or her works only in the entry devoted to that author or title. With the exception of Ts'ao Hsüeh-ch'in (Ts'ao Chan), all authors are cited by their *ming* 名 (given name). In each entry the *tzu* 字 (style or courtesy name), *hao* 號 (pen name or literary name), and other specialized names are given.

Abbreviated titles cited in the bibliographies can be identified by referring to the list of oft-cited works; for the Chinese or Japanese original of a journal title or a journal abbreviation, see the list of journals.

Only four other bibliographic reference works are cited in the Studies section of the entry bibliographies: Howard L. Boorman's *Biographical Dictionary of Republican China* (New York, 1967)—cited as *BDRC*, Herbert Franke's *Sung Biographies* (Wiesbaden, 1976)—*SB*, L. Carrington Goodrich and Chaoying Fang's *Dictionary of Ming Biography, 1368-1644* (New York, 1976)—*DMB*, and Arthur Hummel's *Eminent Chinese of the Ch'ing Period* (Washington, D.C., 1943-1944)—*ECCP*. For a listing which includes a number of other important reference works, see the general bibliography.

Several other Chinese terms need commentary. *Nien-p'u* 年譜 refers to the stark, chronological "biography" which is still today a standard Chinese biographic genre. *Chüan* (or *ch.*) 卷 (roll or scroll) is the most common means by which traditional Chinese texts were divided. Ages of authors are generally given according to their Western reckoning.

The abbreviations "HY" and "TT," especially common in entries on Taoist subjects, refer to the *Tao-tsang tzu-mu yin-te* 道藏子目引得 (Combined Indices to the Authors and Titles of Books in the Two Collections of Taoist Literature), Harvard-Yenching Institute Sinological Index Series, No. 25, and to the fascicle (i.e., *chüan*) number of the *Tao-tsang* respectively (see also the Taoist Literature essay). Other rather standard abbreviations used are *c.* (*circa*), ch. (chapter), coll. (collator), comm. (commentator), comp. (compiler), *fl.* (*floruit*), ed. (editor, if preceded by a person's name, otherwise edition), trans. (translator).

There is frequent reference to the various examinations of the literati. The civil-service examination system can be said to have begun in the late seventh century. Three levels of examination—the *hsiu-ts'ai* 秀才 (cultivated talents), the *chü-jen* 舉人 (recommended man), and the *chin-shih* 進士 (presented scholar)—were held. Candidates in the T'ang came from the national universities or were recommended by local officials. The capital examinations (*chih-shih*) were held annually until 1067 and triennially in subsequent years. In the early T'ang an average of twenty-five scholars were successful in the examinations each year. This figure grew to approximately one hundred in the late T'ang and to more than double that in succeeding dynasties.

At present there is no standard translation for the titles of the official positions assumed by the literati upon completion of the examinations. Charles O. Hucker is compiling *A Dictionary of Official Titles in Imperial China* and he was kind enough to provide us with translations for those titles which occur in *Companion* entries. For a brief description of these positions and the original Chinese terms, see the corresponding entry in Hucker.

Journals

AcA—*Acta Asiatica: Bulletin of the Institute of Eastern Culture* (Tokyo)
Aichi Kenritsu Daigaku Bungakubu roshuū (gogaku, bungaku) 愛知縣立大學文學部論集　（語學文學.）
Aichi Kenritsu Joshi Daigaku kiyō 愛知縣立女子大學紀要
Altorientalische Forschungen
AM—*Asia Major, New Series*
Annual of the China Society of Singapore
AO—*Archiv Orientalni*
AOr—*Acta Orientalia* (Copenhagen)
ArA—*Artibus Asiae*
AS—*Asiatische Studien*
Asian Culture Quarterly

BEFEO—*Bulletin l'Ecole Francaise d' Extrême-Orient*
Biburia (Tenri toshokan)—see *Tenri biburia* ビブリア（天理圖書館）
BIHP—*Bulletin of the Institute of History and Philology*—see CYYY
BMFEA—*Bulletin of the Museum of Far Eastern Antiquities*
BSOAS—*Bulletin of the School of Oriental and African Studies*
BSSCR—*Bulletin of the Society for the Study of Chinese Religions*
BSYS—*Bulletin of Sung-Yüan Studies*
Bulletin de l'Université l'Aurore
Bungaku 文學 (Hiroshima University Studies, Literature Department)
Bunka 文化

Cahiers d'histoire mondiale
CC—*Chinese Culture*
Ch'ang-liu yüeh-k'an 暢流月刊
Che-chiang yüeh-k'an 浙江月刊
Che-hsüeh yen-chiu 哲學研究
Chen-li 眞理
Chi-lin Shih-ta hsüeh-pao (Che-hsüeh she-hui k'o-hsüeh) 吉林師大學報　（哲學社會科學）
Ch'i-ta chi-k'an 齊大季刊
Chiang-hai hsüeh-k'an 江海月刊
Chiao-hsüeh yü yen-chiu 敎學與研究
China aktuel

JOURNALS

China Review

CL—Chinese Literature

Chinese Studies in History

Ch'ing-hua chou-k'an 清華週刊

Ch'ing-hua hsüeh-pao—see THHP

Ch'ing-shih wen-ti 清史問題

CHINOPERL

CHINOPERL Papers—see CHINOPERL

Chü-hsüeh yüeh-k'an 劇學月刊

Chü-pen 劇本

Ch'ü-hsüeh chi-k'an 曲學季刊　(Taipei)

Chūgoku bungakuhō 中國文學報

Chūgoku bungaku kenkyū 中國文學研究

Chūgoku bungaku ronshū 中國文學論集

Chūgoku bungei zadankai nōto 中國文藝座談會ノート

Chūgoku bunka to shakai 中國文化と社會

Chūgoku chūsei bungaku kenkyū 中國中世文學研究

Chūgoku gogaku 中國語學

Chūgoku kankei ronsetsu shiryō 中國關係論說資料

Chūgoku koten bungaku zenshū geppō 中國古典文學全集月報

Chūgoku koten kenkyū 中國古典研究

Ch'un wen-hsüeh 純文學

Chung-ho (yüeh-k'an) 中和 (月刊)

Chung-hua hsüeh-yüan 中華學苑

Chung-hua wen-hua fu-hsing yüeh-k'an 中華文化復興月刊

Chung-hua wen-shih lun-ts'ung 中華文史論叢

Chung-kuo shih chi-k'an

Chung-kuo yü-wen 中國語文

Chung-shan hsüeh-shu wen-hua chi-k'an 中山學術文化季刊

Chung-shan Ta-hsüeh hsüeh-pao (She-hui k'o-hsüeh) 中山大學學報 (社會科學)

Chung-shan Ta-hsüeh Yü-yen li-shih hsüeh yen-chiu-so chou-k'an 中山大學語言歷史學研究所週刊

Chung-wai wen-hsüeh 中外文學

Chung-yang jih-pao 中央日報

Chūtetsubun gakkai hō 中哲文學會報

Chūyō Daigaku bungakubu kiyō 中央大學文學部紀要

Cina

CLEAR—Chinese Literature: Essays, Articles, Reviews

Comparative Literature

CYYY—Chung-yang yen-chiu yüan: Yü-yen li-shih yen-chiu-so chi-k'an 中央研究院：歷史語言研究所 集刊　(Bulletin of the Institute of History and Philology, Academic Sinica [Taiwan])

The Denver Quarterly

Fu-jen Ta-hsüeh jen-wen hsüeh-pao 輔仁大學人文學報

Fukui kōhyō kōtō semmon gakkō kenkyū kiyō (Jimbun shakai kagaku)　福井工業高等專門學校研究 紀要 (人文社會科學)

Fu-nü tsa-chih 婦女雜誌.

Geibun kenkyū 藝文研究
Gumma Daigaku kiyō 群馬大學紀要

Han-hsüeh 漢學
Heidelberger Jahrbücher
Hiroshima Daigaku Bungakubu kiyō 廣島大學文學部紀要
HJAS—Harvard Journal of Asiatic Studies
Ho-pei Ta-hsüeh hsüeh-pao 河北大學學報
Hokkaidō Daigaku Bungakubu kiyō 北海道大學文學部紀要
Hsi-chü i-shu 戲劇藝術
Hsi-ch'ü yen-chiu 戲曲研究
Hsiang-kang Ta-hsüeh Chung-wen hsüeh-hui hui-k'an 香港大學中文學會會刊
Hsiao-shuo yüeh-pao 小說月報
Hsien-tai p'ing-lun 現代評論
Hsien-tai wen-hsüeh 現代文學
Hsin chien-she 新建設
Hsin-chu shih-chuan hsüeh-pao 新竹師專學報
Hsin-ya hsüeh-pao 新亞學報
Hsin-ya Shu-yüan Chung-kuo wen-hsüeh-hsi nien-k'an 新亞書院中國文學系年刊
Hsing-tao jih-pao 星島日報 , "Su wen-hsüeh" 俗文學
Hsüeh-heng 學衡
Hsüeh-i 學藝
Hsüeh-shu chi-k'an 學術季刊
Hsüeh-shu lun-wen chi-k'an 學術論文季刊
Hsüeh-shu yen-chiu 學述研究
Hsüeh-wen tsa-chih 學文雜誌
Hsüeh yüan 學苑
Hua-kuo 華國
Hua-nan Shih-yüan hsüeh-pao 華南師院學報
Hung-lou meng *hsüeh-k'an* 紅樓夢學刊

I-lin ts'ung-lu 藝林叢錄
Isis

JA—Journal asiatique
JAOS—Journal of the American Oriental Society
JAS—Journal of Asian Studies
JCL—Journal of Chinese Linguistics
JCLTA—Journal of the Chinese Language Teachers Association
JCP—Journal of Chinese Philosophy
Jen-sheng tsa-chih 人生雜誌 *(The Youngsun)*
Jen-wen hsüeh-pao 人文學報
JHKBRAS—Journal of the Hong Kong Branch of the Royal Asiatic Society
JICS—Journal of the Institute of Chinese Studies of the Chinese University of Hong Kong

Jimbun kenkyū 人文研究
Jimbun ronsō 人文論叢
JNCBRAS—Journal of the North China Branch of the Royal Asiatic Society
Jōnan kangaku 城南漢學
JOS—Journal of Oriental Studies
JOSA—Journal of the Oriental Society of Australia
Journal of Chinese Philosophy
Journal of the Australasian Universities Language and Literature Association
Journal of the Chinese University of Hong Kong

Kambun Gakkai kaihō 漢文學會會報
Kambun kyōshitsu 漢文教室
Kangakkai zasshi 漢學會雜誌
Kan-su Shih-ta hsüeh-pao (Che-hsüeh she-hui k'o-hsüeh) 甘肅師大學報（哲學社會科學）
Kenkyū 研究
Kōbe Gaidai ronsō 神戸外大論叢
Kokubungaku Kambungaku ronsō
Kokugo kokubun 國語國文
Ko-yao chou-k'an 歌謠週刊 (Folksongs Weekly of National Peking University)
Ku-chin 古今
Ku-kung chi-k'an 故宮季刊
Ku-kung t'u-shu chi-k'an 故宮圖書季刊
Ku-kung wen-hsien 故宮文獻
Ku-tai wen-hsüeh li-lun yen-chiu 古代文學理論研究
Ku-tien wen-hsüeh lun-ts'ung 古典文學論叢 (Tsinan)
Kuang-ming jih-pao 光明日報
Kuo-ch'uan yüeh-k'an 國專月刊
Kuo-hsüeh hui-p'ien 國學滙篇
Kuo-li Cheng-chih Ta-hsüeh hsüeh-pao 國立政治大學學報
Kuo-li Chung-shan Ta-hsüeh Wen-shih yen-chiu-so yüeh-k'an 國立中山大學文史研究所月刊
Kuo-li Chung-yang t'u-shu-kuan kuan-k'an 國立中央圖書館館刊
Kuo-li Pei-p'ing t'u-shu-kuan kuan-k'an 國立北平圖書館館刊
Kuo-li Pien-i-kuan kuan-k'an 國立編譯館館刊
Kuo-li T'ai-wan Shih-fan Ta-hsüeh Kuo-wen yen-chiu-so chi-k'an 國立臺灣師範大學國文研究所集刊
Kuo-shih-kuan kuan-k'an 國史館館刊
Kuo-wen chou-pao 國聞週報
Kuo-wen hsüeh-pao 國文學報
Kuo-wen yüeh-k'an 國文月刊
Kyūshū Chūgoku gakkaihō 九州中國學會報

LEW—Literature East and West
Li-shih yen-chiu 歷史研究
Lien-ho Shu-yüan hsüeh-pao 聯合書院學報
Ling-nan hsüeh-pao 嶺南學報
Lun hsüeh 論學

Mélanges publiés par l'Institut des Hautes Etudes Chinoise
Michigan Papers in Chinese Studies
Ming-pao yüeh-k'an 明報月刊
Mitteilungen des Instituts für Orientforschung der Deutschen Akademie der Wissenschaften zu Berlin
MS—Monumenta Serica
MTB—Memoirs of the Research Department of the Tōyō Bunko

NAAB—New Asia Academic Bulletin
Nagoya Daigaku Bungakubu kenkyū ronshū 名古屋大學文學部研究論集
Nan-k'ai Ta-hsüeh Jen-wen k'o-hsüeh chiao-hsüeh yü yen-chiu hui-k'an 南開大學人文科學教學與研究會刊

Nan-k'ai Ta-hsüeh hsüeh-pao (Che-hsüeh she-hui k'o-hsüeh) 南開大學學報（哲學社會科學）
Nan-yang Ta-hsüeh Chung-kuo yü-wen hsüeh-hui nien-k'an 南洋大學中國語文學會年刊
Nan-yang Ta-hsüeh hsüeh-pao 南洋大學學報
The New China Review
Nihon Chūgoku Gakkai-hō 日本中國學會報

Ochanomizu Joshi Daigaku Jimbunkagaku kiyō お茶の水女子大學人文科學紀要
OE—Oriens Extremus
Orient / Wort
Oriental Art
Ōtani gakuhō 大谷學報

Papers on China, East Asian Research Center, Harvard University
Papers on Far Eastern History
Parerga
Pei-ching Ta-hsüeh Yen-chiu-so Kuo-hsüeh yüeh-k'an 北京大學研究所國學月刊
Pei-p'ing Pei-hai t'u-shu-kuan yüeh-k'an 北平北海圖書館月刊
Perspectives
PMLA—Publications of the Modern Language Association of America

Renditions
Revue de littérature comparée
Ritsumeikan bungaku 立命館文學
Ritsumeikan Daigaku ronsō 立命館大學論叢

Selected Papers in Asian Studies (Western Conference of the Association of Asian Studies)
Shan-hsi Shih-fan Hsüeh-yüan hsüeh-pao 山西師範學院學報
Shan-hsi Shih-yüan hsüeh-pao (She-hui k'o-hsüeh) 山西師院學報（社會科學）
Shan-tung wen-hsüeh 山東文學
She-hui k'o-hsüeh yen-chiu 社會科學研究
Sheng-liu 勝流
Shibun 斯文
Shien 史淵
Shigaku kenkyū 史學研究

Shih-chieh wen-k'u 世界文庫
Shih-hsüeh nien-pao 史學年報
Shih-k'an 詩刊
Shimmatsu shōsetsu kenkyū 清末小說研究
Shinagaku 支那學
Shinagaku kenkyū 支那學研究
Shosetsu 敍說
Shu ho jen 書和人
Shūkan tōyōgaku 集刊東洋學
Shu-mu chi-k'an 書目季刊
Signs: Journal of Women in Culture and Society
Sinica
Sinologica
Society for the Study of Chinese Religions, Bulletin
Ssu-ch'uan Ta-hsüeh hsüeh-pao 四川大學學報
Ssu-ch'uan wen-hsien 四川文獻
St. Anthony Papers
Studia Serica
Sui-pi 隨筆

Ta-kung pao 大公報 (Tientsin), "T'u-shu fu-k'an" 讀書副刊
Ta-lu tsa-chih 大陸雜誌
T'ai-nan Shih-chuan hsüeh-pao 臺南師專學報
T'ai-wan Sheng-li Shih-fan Ta-hsüeh yen-chiu chi-k'an 臺灣省立師範大學研究集刊
Tan-chiang hsüeh-pao 淡江學報
Tenri biburia 天理ビブリア
Tenri Daigaku gakuhō 天理大學學報
THHP—Tsing Hua hsüeh-pao 清華學報 (Tsing Hua Journal of Chinese Studies, new series)
THM—T'ien-hsia Monthly
TkR—Tamkang Review
Tōhōgaku 東方學
Tōhōgakuhō 東方學報
Tōhō shūkyō 東方宗教
Tōhoku Daigaku Bungakubu kenkyū nempō 東北大學文學部研究年報
Tōkai Daigaku kiyō (Bungakubu) 東海大學紀要 (文學部)
Tōkō 東光
Tōkyō Gakugei Daigaku kenkyū hōkoku
Tōkyō Shinagakuhō 東京支那學報
Tōyō bunka 東洋文化
Tōyō bunka fukukan 東洋文化復刊
Tōyō bunka kenkyūjo kiyō 東洋文化研究所紀要
Tōyō bunko shohō 東洋文庫書報
Tōyō no bunka to shakai 東洋の文化と社會
Tōyōshi kenkyū 東洋史研究
Tōyō shisō no kenkyū 東洋思想の研究
TP—T'oung Pao

Tu-shu 讀書
T'u-sha-kuan hsüeh-pao 圖書館學報
Tung-fang tsa-chih 東方雜誌
Tung-hai hsüeh-pao 東海學報
Tung-pei Jen-min Ta-hsüeh Jen-wen k'o-hsüeh hsüeh-pao 東北人民大學人文科學學報
Tung-Wu wen-shih hsüeh-pao 東吳文史學報
T'ung-sheng yüeh-k'an 同聲月刊
Tz'u-hsüeh chi-k'an 詞學季刊

Wen-che chi-k'an 文哲季刊
Wen-hsien 文獻
"*Wen-hsüeh i-ch'an*" 文學遺產 , *Kuang-ming jih-pao* 光明日報
Wen hsüeh i-ch'an hsüan-chi 文學遺產選集
Wen-hsüeh i-chian tseng-k'an 文學遺產增刊
Wen-hsüeh nien-pao 文學年報
Wen-hsüeh p'ing-lun 文學評論 , 1956-   [Peking]
Wen-hsüeh p'ing-lun 文學評論 , 1975-   [Taipei]
Wen-hsüeh p'ing-lun ts'ung-k'an 文學評論叢刊
Wen-hsüeh shih-chieh chi-k'an 文學世界季刊
Wen-hsüeh tsa-chih 文學雜誌
Wen-i lun-ts'ung 文藝論叢
Wen-i pao 文藝報
Wen-i yüeh-k'an 文藝月刊
Wen-shih 文史
Wen-shih-che 文史哲
Wen-shih-che hsüeh-pao 文史哲學報
Wen-shih tsa-chih 文史雜誌
Wen-t'an 文壇
Wen-wu 文物
Wen-wu ts'an-k'ao tzu-liao 文物參考資料
Wu-han Ta-hsüeh wen che chi-k'an 武漢大學文哲季刊

YCGL—Yearbook of Comparative and General Literature
Yamaguchi Daigaku bungaku zasshi 山口大學文學雜誌
Yasō 野草
Yen-ching hsüeh-pao 燕京學報
Yokohama Shiritsu Daigaku kiyō (Jimbunkagaku) 橫濱市立大學紀要 （人文科學）
Yu-shih hsüeh-chih 幼獅學誌
Yu-shih wen-i 幼獅文藝
Yu-shih yüeh k'an 幼獅月刊
Yü-wen hsüeh-hsi 語文學習

ZDMG—Zeitschrift der Deutschen Morgenländischen Gesellschaft
Zengaku kenkyū 禪學研究
ZAS—Zentralasiatische Studien

Oft-cited Works

Aoki, *Gikyokushi*—Aoki Masaru 青木正兒. *Shina kinsei gikyokushi* 支那近世戲曲史. Tokyo, *1930*.

———, *Shindai*—*Shindai bungaku hyōron shi* 清代文學評論史. Tokyo, 1950; included in *Aoki Masaru zenshū* 青木正兒全集, Tokyo, 1969, v. 1, pp. 389-581.

Ayling, *Collection*—Alan Ayling and Duncan Mackintosh, trans. *A Collection of Chinese Lyrics.* London, 1965.

———, *Further Collection*—Alan Ayling and Duncan Mackintosh, trans. *A Further Collection of Chinese Lyrics.* London, 1969.

Bauer, *Golden Casket*—Wolfgang Bauer and Herbert Franke, eds. *The Golden Casket.* Christopher Levenson, translator. Baltimore, 1967.

BDRC—*Biographical Dictionary of Republican China.* Howard L. Boorman, ed. 4v. New York, 1967-1971.

Birch, *Anthology*—Cyril Birch. *Anthology of Chinese Literature.* 2v. New York, 1965.

Bodman, "Poetics"—Richard Bodman. "Poetics and Prosody in Early Medieval China: A Study and Translation of Kūkai's *Bunkyō hifuron.*" Unpublished Ph.D. dissertation, Cornell University, 1978.

Bryant, "Selected Ming Poems"—Bryant, Daniel, "Selected Ming Poems," *Renditions*, 8 (Autumn 1977), 85-91.

Bynner, *Jade Mountain*—Witter Bynner and Kiang Kang-hu. *The Jade Mountain.* 1929. Rpt. New York, 1972.

Chang, *Evolution*—Kang-i Sun Chang. *The Evolution of Chinese Tz'u Poetry, From Late T'ang to Northern Sung.* Princeton, 1980.

Chao, *Pi-t'an*—Chao Ching-shen 趙景深. *Hsi-ch'ü pi-t'an* 戲曲筆談. Shanghai, 1963.

Chaves, *Mei Yao-ch'en*—Jonathan Chaves. *Mei Yao-ch'en and the Development of Early Sung Poetry.* New York and London, 1976.

Chen-pen—*Ssu-k'u ch'üan-shu chen-pen* 四庫全書珍本.

Cheng, *Su-wen-hsüeh*—Cheng Chen-to 鄭振鐸. *Chung-kuo su-wen-hsüeh shih* 中國俗文學史. Changsha, 1938.

Chien, *Sung-shih*—Ch'ien Chung-shu 錢鍾書. *Sung shih hsüan-chu* 宋詩選註. Peking, 1958.

Chin, *Chi-ku-ko*—Chin Meng-hua 金夢華. *Chi-ku-ko liu-shih-chung ch'ü hsü-lu* 汲古閣六十種曲敘錄. Taipei, 1969.

Chinese Approaches—*Chinese Approaches to Literature: From Confucius to Liang Ch'i-ch'ao.* Adele Austin Rickett, ed. Princeton, 1978.

Chinese Fiction—*Critical Essays on Chinese Fiction.* Winston L. Y. Yang and Curtis P. Adkins, eds. Hong Kong, 1980.

Chinese Narrative—*Chinese Narrative: Critical and Theoretical Essays.* Andrew H. Plaks, ed. Princeton, 1977.

Chow, "Shih"—Chow Tse-tsung. "The History of the Chinese Word *Shih* (Poetry)," in *Wen-lin: Studies in the Chinese Humanities*, Chow Tse-tsung, ed., Madison, Wisconsin, 1968, pp. 151-209.

Ch'u Tz'u—Hawkes, David. *Ch'u Tz'u: The Songs of the South.* London, 1959.

Ch'üan Sung tz'u—*Ch'üan Sung tz'u* 全宋詞. T'ang Kuei-chang 唐圭璋, ed. 5v. Shanghai, 1965.

Ch'üan T'ang shih—*Ch'üan T'ang shih* 全唐詩. 12v. Peking, 1960.

Ch'üan T'ang wen—*Ch'in-ting Ch'üan T'ang wen* 欽定全唐文. 20v. Taipei, 1961. Facsimile reproduction of 1814 edition.

Chung-kuo ku-tien hsiao-shuo yen-chiu chuan-chi 中國古典小說研究專集, v. 1-5 (Taipei, 1979-1982).

Confucian Personalities—Confucian Personalities. Arthur F. Wright and Denis Twitchett, eds. Stanford, 1962.

Critical Essays—Critical Essays on Chinese Literature, William H. Nienhauser, Jr., ed. Hong Kong, 1976.

Davis, *Penguin*—A. R. Davis, ed. *The Penguin Book of Chinese Verse.* Translations by Robert Kotewall and Norman L. Smith. Baltimore, 1962.

Debon, *Ts'ang-lang*—Günther Debon. *Ts'ang-lang's Gespräche über die Dichtung, Ein Beitrag zur chinesischen Poetik.* Wiesbaden, 1962.

Demiéville, *Anthologie*—Paul Demiéville. *Anthologie de la poésie chinoise classique.* Paris, 1962.

Diény, *Dix-neuf*—Jean-Pierre Diény. *Les Dix-neuf poémes ancien.* Paris, 1963.

———, *Origines—Aux origines de la poésie classique en Chine.* Leiden, 1968.

DMB—Dictionary of Ming Biography (1368-1644). L. Carrington Goodrich, ed. 2v. New York and London, 1976.

Dolby, *Eight*—William Dolby. *Eight Chinese Plays.* London and New York, 1978.

———, *History—A History of Chinese Drama.* London, 1976.

ECCP.—Eminent Chinese of the Ch'ing Period (1644-1912). Arthur W. Hummel, ed. 2v. Washington, D.C., 1943-1944; rpt. in 1v. Taipei, 1964.

Edwards, "A Classified Guide"—E. D. Edwards, "A Classified Guide to the Thirteen Classes of Chinese Prose," *BSOAS,* 12 (1948), 770-788.

Frankel, *Palace Lady*—Hans H. Frankel. *The Flowering Plum and the Palace Lady.* New Haven, 1976.

———, "Yüeh-fu"—"Yüeh-fu Poetry," in *Studies in Chinese Literary Genres.* Cyril Birch, ed. Berkeley, 1974, pp. 69-107.

Frodsham, *Anthology*—J. D. Frodsham and Cheng Hsi. *An Anthology of Chinese Verse: Han Wei Chin and the Northern and Southern Dynasties.* Oxford, 1967.

———, *Murmuring*—J. D. Frodsham. *The Murmuring Stream, The Life and Works of the Chinese Nature Poet Hsieh Ling-yün (385-433), Duke of K'ang-le.* Kuala Lumpur, 1967.

Fu, *Ch'ing*—Fu Hsi-hua 傅惜華. *Ch'ing-tai tsa-chü ch'üan-mu* 清代雜劇全目. Peking, 1981.

———, *Ch'uan-ch'i*—Fu Hsi-hua. *Ming-tai ch'uan-ch'i ch'üan-mu* 明代傳奇全目. Peking, 1959.

———, *Ming tsa-chü—Ming-tai tsa-chü ch'üan-mu* 明代雜劇全目. Peking, 1958.

Fu, *Shih-jen*—Fu Hsüan-ts'ung 傅璇琮. *T'ang-tai shih-jen ts'ung-k'ao* 唐代詩人叢考. Peking, 1980.

Fu, *Yüan*—Fu Hsi-hua. *Yüan-tai tsa-chü ch'üan-mu* 元代雜劇全目. Peking, 1957.

Ginsberg, Stanley M. *A Bibliography of Criticism on T'ang and Sung Tz'u Poetry.* Madison, 1975.

Graham, *Lament*—William T. Graham. *The Lament for the South: Yü Hsin's Ai Chiang-nan fu.* New York, 1980.

Graham, *Late T'ang*—A. C. Graham. *Poems of the Late T'ang.* Middlesex and Baltimore, 1965.

Gundert, *Lyrik*—Wilhelm Gundert, ed. *Lyrik des Ostens: China.* München, 1958.

Hanan, *Vernacular Story*—Patrick Hanan. *The Chinese Vernacular Story.* Cambridge, Mass., 1981.

Hawkes, *Ch'u Tz'u*—David Hawkes. *Ch'u Tz'u, The Songs of the South.* London, 1959.

———, "Quest"—"The Quest of the Goddess," *AM,* 13 (1967), 71-94; rpt. *Literary Genres,* pp. 42-68.

Hervouet, *Sung*—Yves Hervouet, ed. *A Sung Bibliography (Bibliographie des Sung).* Hong Kong, 1978.

Hightower, "Ch'ü Yüan"—James R. Hightower. "Ch'ü Yüan Studies," in *Silver Jubilee,* pp, 192-223.

———, *Topics—Topics in Chinese Literature.* Cambridge, Mass., 1950.

Ho, *Ch'ing tz'u*—Ho Kuang-chung 賀光中. *Lun Ch'ing tz'u* 論清詞. Singapore, 1956.

Holzman, *Poetry and Politics*—Donald Holzman. *Poetry and Politics, The Life and Works of Juan Chi.* Cambridge, 1976.

Hsi-ch'ü lun-chu—Chung-kuo ku-tien hsi-ch'ü lun-chu chi-ch'eng 中國古典戲曲論著集成. Chung-kuo hsi-ch'ü yen-chiu-yüan 中國戲曲研究院, comp. 10v. Peking, 1959.

Hsia, *Novel*—C. T. Hsia. *The Classic Chinese Novel: A Critical Introduction.* New York, 1968.

Hsü, *Anthologie*—S. N. Hsü. *Anthologie de la littérature chinoise des origines à nos jours.* Paris, 1933.

Hughes, *Two Chinese Poets*—Ernest Richard Hughes. *Two Chinese Poets: Vignettes of Han Life and Thought.* Princeton, 1960.

Hung, *Ming*—Josephine Huang Hung. *Ming Drama.* Taipei, 1966.

Idema and West, *Chinese Theater*—Wilt Idema and Stephen H. West. *Chinese Theater 1100-1450: A Source Book.* Wiesbaden, 1982.

Iriya—Iriya Kyōju Ogawa Kyōju taikyū kinen Chūgoku bungaku gogaku ronshū 入矢教授小川教授退休記念中國文學語學論集. Tokyo, 1974.

Jao, "Chan-kuo"—Jao Tsung-i 饒宗頤, "Chan-kuo wen-hsüeh" 戰國文學, *BIHP*, 48 (1977), 153-176.

Knechtges, *Han Rhapsody*—David R. Knechtges. *The Han Rhapsody: A Study of the* Fu *of Yang Hsiung (53 B.C.-A.D. 18)*. Cambridge, England, 1976.

———, *Wen xuan*—*Wen xuan or Selections of Refined Literature. Volume One: Rhapsodies on Metropolises and Capitals*. Princeton, 1982.

Ku-pen—*Ku-pen hsi-ch'ü ts'ung-k'an* 古本戲曲叢刊. I: *ch'u-chi* 初集, Shanghai, 1954; II: *erh-chi* 二集, 1955; III: *san-chi* 三集, 1957; IV: *ssu-chi* 四集, 1958.

Kung, "Ming ch'i-tzu"—Kung, Hsien-tsung 龔顯宗. "Ming ch'i-tzu shih-wen chi ch'i lun-p'ing chih yen-chiu" 明七子詩文及其論評之研究. Unpublished Ph.D. dissertation, Chung-kuo Wen-hua Hsüeh-yüan, 1979. The fullest and most detailed study of the Ming Archaists.

———, "Ming-tai ch'i-tz'u"—"Ming-tai ch'i-tzu-p'ai shih-lun chih yen-chiu" 明代七子派詩論之研究, *T'ai-nan Shih-chuan hsüeh-pao*, 8 (1975), 41-65; 9 (1976), 169-187. A condensed version of the above.

Kuo, *P'i-p'ing shih*—Kuo Shao-yü 郭紹虞. *Chung-kuo wen-hsüeh p'i-p'ing shih* 中國文學批評史. Shanghai, 1964.

———, *Sung shih-hua*—*Sung shih-hua chi-i* 宋詩話輯佚. Peking, 1937.

Lin, *Transformation*—Lin Shuen-fu. *The Transformation of the Chinese Lyrical Tradition: Chiang K'uei and Southern Sung Tz'u Poetry*. Princeton, 1978.

Literary Genres—*Studies in Chinese Literary Genres*. Cyril Birch, ed. Berkeley, 1974.

Liu, *Buddhist and Taoist*—Liu Ts'un-yan. *Buddhist and Taoist Influences on Chinese Novels*. Wiesbaden, 1962.

———, *Middlebrow*—*Chinese Middlebrow Fiction from the Ch'ing and Early Republican Periods*. Liu Ts'un-yan, ed. Hong Kong, 1984.

Liu-ch'ao wen—*Ch'üan shang-ku San-tai Ch'in Han San-kuo Liu-ch'ao wen* 全上古三代秦漢三國六朝文. Yen K'o-chün 嚴可均, ed. 4v. Rpt. Taipei, 1961.

Liu, *Chinese Theories*—James J. Y. Liu. *Chinese Theories of Literature*. Chicago, 1975.

Liu, *Classical Prose*—Shih Shun Liu, trans. *Chinese Classical Prose: The Eight Masters of the T'ang-Sung Period*. Hong Kong, 1979.

Liu, *London Libraries*—Liu Ts'un-yan. *Chinese Popular Fiction in Two London Libraries*. Hong Kong, 1967.

Liu, *Lyricists*—James J. Y. Liu. *Major Lyricists of the Northern Sung (A.D. 960-1126)*. Princeton, 1974.

Liu-shih—*Liu-shih-chung ch'ü* 六十種曲. Mao Chin 毛晉, comp. N.p., 1800.

Lo, *Lun-wen hsüan*—Lo Lien-t'ien 羅聯添, ed. *Chung-kuo wen-hsüeh shih lun-wen hsüan* 中國文學史論文選. 4v. Taipei, 1979.

Margouliès, *Anthologie*—Georges Margouliès. *Anthologie raisonnée de la littérature chinoise*. Paris, 1948.

———, *Kou-wen*—ed. and trans., *Le Kou-wen chinois; recueil de textes avec introduction et notes*. Paris, 1925.

———, *Prose*—*Histoire de la littérature chinoise: prose*. Paris, 1949.

Mather, *New Account*—Richard B. Mather. *Shih-shuo hsin-y : A New Account of Tales of the World*. Minneapolis, 1976.

McMullen, "Literary Theory"—David L. McMullen. "Historical and Literary Theory in the Mid-Eighth Century," in *Perspectives on the T'ang*, Arthur F. Wright and Denis Twitchett, ed. New Haven, 1973, pp. 307-342.

Miao, *Studies*—Ronald C. Miao, ed. *Studies in Chinese Poetry and Poetics*. V. 1. San Francisco, 1978.

Min, "Ming-tai"—Min, Tse 敏澤. "Ming-tai ch'ien-hou ch'i-tzu te shih-wen li-lun" 明代前後七子的詩文理論, *Wen-hsüeh p'ing-lun ts'ung-k'an* (Peking), 3 (1979), 65-92.

Nan-pei-ch'ao shih—*Ch'üan Han San-kuo Chin Nan-pei-ch'ao shih* 全漢三國晉南北朝詩. Ting Fu-pao 丁福保, ed. 6v. Rpt. Taipei, 1968.

Nienhauser, *Liu*—William H. Nienhauser, Jr. *et al. Liu Tsung-yüan*. New York, 1973.

———, *Critical Essays*—William H. Nienhauser, Jr., ed. *Critical Essays on Chinese Literature*. Hong Kong, 1976.

Ogawa, *Sangen*—Ogawa Yōichi 小川陽. *Sangen Nihaku honji ronkō shūsei* 三言二拍本事論考集成. Tokyo, 1981.

Ogawa, *Tōdai*—*Tōdai no shijin—sono denki* 唐代の詩人 —その傳記. Ogawa Tamaki 小川環樹, comp. Tokyo, 1975.

Orchid Boat—*Orchid Boat*. Kenneth Rexroth and Ling Chung, trans. New York, 1972.

Owen, "Deadwood"—Stephen Owen. "Deadwood: The Barren Tree from Yü Hsin to Han Yü," *CLEAR*, 1.2 (July 1979), 157-179.

———, *Early T'ang*—*The Poetry of the Early T'ang*. New Haven, 1977.

———, *High T'ang*—*The Great Age of Chinese Poetry: The High T'ang*. New Haven, 1981.

———, *Meng Chiao*—*The Poetry of Meng Chiao and Han Yü*. New Haven, 1975.

Pai-san—*Han Wei Liu-ch'ao pai-san ming-chia chi* 漢魏六朝百三名家集. Chang P'u 張溥, ed. 4v. Taipei, 1963.

Perspectives—*Perspectives on the T'ang*. Denis Twitchett and Hans H. Frankel, eds. New Haven, 1973.

PPTSCC—*Pai-pu ts'ung-shu chi-ch'eng* 百部叢書集成. Also known as *Ts'ung-shu chi-ch'eng cheng-pien* 叢書集成正編. Rpt. Taipei, 1965-1970.

SB—*Sung Biographies*. Herbert Franke, ed. 4v. Wiesbaden, 1976.

Schafer, *Golden Peaches*—Edward H. Schafer. *The Golden Peaches of Samarkand: A Study of T'ang Exotics*. Berkeley, 1963.

———, *Vermilion Bird*—*The Vermilion Bird: T'ang Images of the South*. Berkeley, 1967.

Self and Society—*Self and Society in Ming Thought*. Wm. Theodore de Bary, ed. New York, 1970.

Sheng-Ming—*Sheng-Ming tsa-chü* 盛名雜劇. Shen T'ai 沈泰, ed. 20v. (contains 30 works). N.p., 1918; rpt. Taipei, 1963. Photolithographic reprint of the Sung-fen shih 誦芬室 edition.

Silver Jubilee—*Silver Jubilee Volume of the Zimbun kagaku Kenkyusyo*. Kyoto, 1954.

SKCS.—*Ssu-k'u ch'üan-shu* 四庫全書.

SPPY—*Ssu-pu pei-yao* 四部備要. Shanghai, 1927-1937; rpt. Taipei, 1966.

SPTK—*Ssu-pu ts'ung-k'an* 四部叢刊. Chang Yüan-chi 張元濟, ed. 3 series. Shanghai, 1919-1937.

Sunflower—*Sunflower Splendor: Three Thousand Years of Chinese Poetry*. Wu-chi Liu and Irving Yu-cheng Lo, eds. Garden City, N. Y., 1975.

Sung Bibliography—*A Sung Bibliography*. Yves Hervouet, ed. Hong Kong, 1978.

Suzuki, *Kan Gi*—Suzuki Shūji 鈴木修次. *Kan Gi shi no kenkyū* 漢魏の研究. Tokyo, 1967.

Suzuki, *Todai*—Suzuki Shūji. *Todai shijin ron* 唐代詩人論. 2v. Tokyo, 1973.

T'an, *San-yen*—T'an, Cheng-pi 譚正璧, ed. *San-yen Liang-p'ai tzu-liao* 三言二拍資料. 2v. Shanghai, 1980 (preface dated 1963).

T'ang, *Tz'u-hua*—*Tz'u-hua ts'ung-pien* 詞話叢編. T'ang Kuei-chang 唐圭璋, ed., 1935; rpt. Taipei, 1967.

T'ang-jen hsiao-shuo—*T'ang-jen hsiao-shuo* 唐人小說. Wang P'i-chiang 汪辟疆, ed. Shanghai, 1955.

T'ang-shih yen-ch'iu—*T'ang-shih yen-chiu lun-wen chi* 唐詩研究論文集 Peking, 1959.

T'ang-wen shih-i—*T'ang-wen shih-i* 唐文拾遺. Lu Hsin-yüan 陸心源, ed. 3v. Taipei, 1962.

Traditional Chinese Stories—*Traditional Chinese Stories: Themes and Variations*. Y. W. Ma and Joseph S. M. Lau, eds. New York, 1978.

TSCC, see *PPTSCC* and *TSCCCP*.

TSCCCP—*Ts'ung-shu chi-ch'eng ch'u-pien* 叢書集成初編. Shanghai, 1935-1937.

Tseng, "Ch'ing-tai tsa-chü"—Tseng Yung-i 曾永義. "Ch'ing-tai tsa-chü kai-lun" 清代雜劇概論, in his *Chung-kuo ku-tien hsi-chü lun-chi* 中國古典戲劇論集. Taipei, 1976, pp. 117-243.

———, *Ming tsa-chü*—*Ming-tai tsa-chü kai-lun* 明代雜劇概論. Taipei, 1978.

Waley, *Chinese Poems*—Arthur Waley. *Chinese Poems: Selected from 170 Chinese Poems, More Translations from the Chinese, The Temple and The Book of Songs*. London, 1946.

———, *Po Chü-i*—*The Life and Times of Po Chü-i*. London, 1949.

———, *The Temple*—*The Temple, and Other Poems*. New York, 1926.

———, *Translations*—*Translations from the Chinese*. New York, 1941.

Watson, *Early*—Burton Watson. *Early Chinese Literature*. New York and London, 1962.

———, *Lyricism*—*Chinese Lyricism*. New York, 1971.

———, *Rhyme-Prose*—*Rhyme-Prose: Poems in the Fu Form from the Han and the Six Dynasties Periods*. New York and London, 1971.

Wen-lin—*Wen-lin: Studies in the Chinese Humanities*. Chow Tse-tsung, ed. Madison, Wis., 1968.

West, *Vaudeville*—Stephen H. West. *Vaudeville and Narrative: Aspects of Chin Theater*. Wiesbaden, 1977.

Wu, *Ch'ang-chou*—Wu Hung-i 吳宏一. *Ch'ang-chou tz'u-hsüeh yen-chiu* 常州詞學研究. Taipei, 1970.

Wu, *Ch'ing-tai*—Wu Hung-i. *Ch'ing-tai shih-hsüeh ch'u-t'an* 清代詩學初探. Taipei, 1977.

Yagisawa, *Gekisakuka*—Yagisawa Hajime 八木澤元. *Mindai gekisakuka kenkyū* 明代劇作家研究. Tokyo, 1959.

Yang, *Fifty Songs*—Richard Fu-sen Yang and Charles R. Metzger. *Fifty Songs from the Yüan: Poetry of 13th Century China*. London, 1967.

Yee, "Love"—Edmond Yee. "Love Versus Neo-Confucian Orthodoxy: An Evolutionary and Critical Study of *Yü-tsan chi* by the Ming Dramatist Kao Lien." Unpublished Ph.D. dissertation, University of California, Berkeley, 1977.

Yeh, "Ch'ang-chou"—Yeh Chia-ying [Chao Yeh Chia-ying]. "The Ch'ang-chou School of *Tz'u* Criticism," in *Chinese Approaches to Literature from Confucius to Liang Ch'i-ch'ao*, Adele Austin Rickett, ed., Princeton, 1978, pp. 151-188.

Yokota, "Mindai"—Yokota, Terutoshi 横田輝俊 "Mindai bunjin kessha no kenkyū" 明代文人 結社 の研究 , *Hiroshima Daigaku bungakubu kiyō*, 35 (1975), 10-20.

———, "Mindai bungakuron"—"Mindai bungakuron no tenkai" 明代文學論的展開 , Pt. I. *Hiroshima Daigaku bungakubu kiyō*, 37 (1977).

Yoshikawa, *Gen-Min*—Yoshikawa, Kōjirō 吉川幸次郎 . *Gen-Min shi gaisetsu* 元明詩概說 . Tokyo, 1963.

———, *Sung*—*Introduction to Sung Poetry*. Burton Watson, translator. Cambridge, Mass, 1967.

Yüan-ch'ü hsüan—*Yüan-ch'ü hsüan* 元曲選 . Tsang Mao-hsün 臧懋循 , comp. 4v. Peking, 1961.

Yüan-ch'ü hsüan wai-pien—*Yüan-ch'ü hsüan wai-pien* 元曲選外編 . Sui Shu-sen 隋樹森 , ed. Peking, 1959.

Yüan Ming tsa-chü—*Yüan Ming tsa-chü* 元明雜劇 . Peking, 1958.

von Zach, *Anthologie*—Erwin von Zach. *Die Chinesische Anthologie*. Cambridge, Mass., 1958.

von Zach, *Han Yü*—*Han Yü's poetische Werke*. Cambridge, Mass, 1952.

General Bibliography

Anthologie de la poésie chinoise classique. Paul Demiéville, ed. Paris, 1962.

Bailey, Roger B. *Guide to Chinese Poetry and Drama*. Boston, 1973.

Beasley, W. G. and E. G. Pulleyblank, ed. *Historians of China and Japan*. London, 1961.

Bibliography of Asian Studies. Ann Arbor, 1956— (Annual).

Birch, Cyril, ed. *Studies in Chinese Literary Genres*. Berkeley, 1974.

Bishop, John L., ed. *Studies in Chinese Literature*. Cambridge, Mass., 1965.

Chang, Ch'un-shu. *Premodern China: A Bibliographical Introduction*. Ann Arbor, 1971.

Chang, Ch'ün 章群. *Min-kuo hsüeh-shu lun-wen so-yin* 民國學術論文索引. Taipei, 1954.

Chang, Hsiang 張相. *Shih tz'u ch'ü yü-tz'u hui shih* 詩詞曲語辭滙釋. Shanghai, 1953.

Chang, Hsin-chang. *Chinese Literature, Volume 2: Nature Poetry*. New York, 1977.

———. *Chinese Literature, Volume 1: Popular Fiction and Drama*. Edinburgh, 1973.

Chang, Kang-i Sun. *The Evolution of Chinese Tz'u Poetry, From Late T'ang to Northern Sung*. Princeton, 1980.

Chang, P'u 張溥; Yin Meng-lun 殷孟倫, annot. *Han Wei Liu-ch'ao pai-san chia chi t'i-tz'u chu* 漢魏六朝百三家集題辭注. Peking, 1981.

Chen, Charles K. H. (陳澄之). *A Biographical and Bibliographical Dictionary of Chinese Authors* (中國著作家辭典). Hanover, N. H., 1971; *Supplement* (2 v.), 1976.

Ch'en, Nai-ch'ien 陳乃乾. *Shih-ming pieh-hao so-yin* 室名別號索引. Peking, 1957.

Cheng, Chen-to 鄭振鐸. *Chung-kuo su-wen-hsüeh shih* 中國俗文學史. Changsha, 1938.

Chiang, Liang-fu 姜亮夫. *Li-tai ming-jen nien li pei chuan tsung-piao* 歷代名人年里碑傳總表. Taipei, 1965.

Ch'ien, Ch'ien-i 錢謙益. *Lieh-ch'ao shih-chi hsiao-chuan* 列朝詩集小傳. Peking, 1961.

Chow, Tse-tsung, ed. *Wen-lin: Studies in the Chinese Humanities*. Madison, 1968.

Chu, Tung-jun 朱東潤. *Chung-kuo wen-hsüeh p'i-p'ing shih ta-kang* 中國文學批評史大綱. 1943 (?); rpt. Hong Kong, 1959.

Ch'üan-kuo po- so-shih lun-wen fen-lei mu-lu 全國博碩士論文分類目錄. Wang Mo-li 王茉莉 and Lin Yü-ch'üan 林玉泉, compilers. Taipei, 1977. The section on Chinese literature runs from pp. 344-368.

Chūgoku kankei ronsetsu shiryō 中國關係論說資料 (The Collected Articles on China), 1- (1964-). Selected articles relating to Chinese studies from various scholarly journals published in Japan; published annually, in four parts: Part 1: Philosophy and Religion, Part 2: Literature and Language, Part 3: History and Social Studies I, and Part 4: History and Social Studies II.

Chung-kuo hsi-ch'ü yen-chiu-yüan 中國戲曲研究院, ed. *Chung-kuo ku-tien hsi-ch'ü lun-chu chi-ch'eng* 中國古典戲曲論著集成. 10v. Peking, 1960.

Chung-kuo k'o-hsüeh-yüan li-shih yen-chiu-so 中國科學院歷史研究所, Pei-ching ta-hsüeh li-shih-hsi 北京大學歷史系. *Chung-kuo shih-hsüeh lun-wen so-yin* 中國史學論文索引, 2v. Peking, 1957.

Chung-kuo k'o-hsüeh yüan wen-hsüeh yen-chiu-so 中國科學院文學研究所. *Chung-kuo wen-hsüeh shih* 中國文學史. 3v. Peking, 1962. *Chung-kuo ku-tien wen-hsüeh ming-chu t'i-chieh* 中國古典文學名著題解. Chung-kuo ch'ing-nien ch'u-pan she 中國青年出版社, eds. Peking, 1980. A handy introductory reference tool.

Chung-kuo ku-tien wen-hsüeh yen-chiu lun-wen so-yin (1949-1966) 中國古典文學研究論文索引. Revised edition. Hong Kong, 1980.

Chung-kuo ku-tien wen-hsüeh yen-chiu lun-wen so-yin (1967.1-1979.12) 中國古典文學研究論文索引. Peking, 1982.

Chung-kuo li-tai ming-jen tz'u-tien 中國歷代名人辭典 . Nan-ching ta-hsüeh li-shih hsi 南京大學歷史系 , ed. Nan-ch'ang, 1982.

Chung-kuo li-tai nien-p'u tsung-lu 中國歷代年譜綜錄. Yang Tien-hsün 楊殿勳 , ed. Peking, 1980.

Chung-kuo li-tai shih-wen pieh-chi lien-ho shu mu 中國歷代詩文別集聯合書目 . Wang Min-hsin 王民信 , ed. 5v. to date. Taipei, 1981-1982. Through Five Dynasties; v. 5 contains an index to authors.

Chung-kuo she-hui k'o-hsüeh yüan li-shih yen-chiu-so 中國社會科學院歷史研究所 . *Chung-kuo shih-hsüeh lun-wen so-yin: Ti-erh pien (1937-1949)* 中國史學論文索引: 第二編 . Hong Kong, 1980.

Chung-kuo ta pai-k'o ch'üan-shu 中國大百科全書 . *Chung-kuo wen-hsüeh chüan* 中國文學卷 . Peking, forthcoming.

———, *Hsi-ch'ü ch'ü-i* 戲曲曲藝 . Peking and Shanghai, 1983.

Chung-kuo wen-hsüeh ku-chi hsüan-chieh 中國文學古籍選介 . Wei K'ai 魏凱 , Yin T'ung-san 陰通三 , and Shih Lin 石林 , comps. Tai-yüan, 1981.

"Classics of the Chinese Tradition," in *A Guide to Oriental Classics*, William Theodore de Bary *et al.*, eds., 2nd. ed., New York and London, 1975, pp. 143-215. Annotated bibliography for the classical, major philosophical works, novels, and a general section on poetry. Still useful.

Cordier, Henri. *Bibliotheca Sinica: Dictionnaire bibliographique des ouvrages relatifs à l'Empire Chinois.* 5v. Paris, 1922-1924; rpt. Taipei, 1966.

Crump, James I. *Chinese Theater in the Days of Kubulai Khan.* Tucson, 1980.

Cumulative Bibliography of Asian Studies, 1941-1970. 14v. Boston, 1969-72.

Debon, Günther, ed. *Ostasiatisches Literaturen*, v. 23 of *Neues Handbuch der Literaturwissenschaft.* Wiesbaden, 1984.

Doctoral Dissertations on China, 1971-1975: A Bibliography of Studies in Western Languages. Frank J. Shulman, compiler. Seattle and London, 1978.

Doctoral Dissertations on China, A Bibliography of Studies in Western Languages, 1945-1970. Leonard H. D. Gordon and Frank J. Shulman, compilers. Seattle, 1972.

Dolby, William. *A History of Chinese Drama.* London, 1976.

École des Hautes Études en Sciences Sociales. *Révue bibliographique de sinologie.* Paris, 1957- .

Feifel, Eugen. *Geschichte der chinesischen Literatur.* Hildesheim, 1967.

Franke, Herbert. *Sinologie.* Bern, 1953.

Frankel, Hans. *The Flowering Plum and the Palace Lady: Interpretations of Chinese Poetry.* New Haven, 1976.

Fu, Hsi-hua 傅惜華 . *Ch'ing-tai tsa-chü ch'üan-mu* 清代雜劇全目 . Peking, 1981.

———. *Ming-tai ch'uan-ch'i ch'üan-mu* 明代傳奇全目 . Peking, 1959.

———. *Ming-tai tsa-chü ch'üan-mu* 明代雜劇全目 . Peking, 1958.

———. *Yüan-tai tsa-chü ch'üan-mu* 元代雜劇全目 . Peking, 1957.

Fu, Hsüan-tsung 傅璇琮 . *T'ang-tai shih-jen ts'ung-k'ao* 唐代詩人叢考 . Peking, 1980.

Fujino, Iwatomo 藤野岩友 , *et al. Chūgoku bungaku shōjiten* 中國文學小事典 . Tokyo, 1972.

"Gakkai tembō" 學界展望 , in *Nippon Chūgoku-Gakkai-ho.*

Giles, Herbert A. *A Chinese Biographical* Dictionary. Shanghai, 1898; rpt. Taipei, 1962.

Ginsberg, Stanley M. *A Bibliography of Criticism on T'ang and Sung Tz'u Poetry.* Madison, 1975.

Goodrich, L. Carrington, ed. *Dictionary of Ming Biography, 1368-1644.* 2v. New York and London, 1976.

Gordon, Leonard H. and Frank J. Shulman. *Doctoral Dissertations on China:* A Bibliography of Studies in Western Languages, 1945-1970. Seattle, 1972.

Hanan, Patrick. *The Chinese Short Story: Studies in Dating, Authorship, and Composition.* Cambridge, Mass., 1973.

———. *The Chinese Vernacular Story.* Cambridge, Mass., 1981.

Hatano, Tarō 波多野太郎 . *Chūgoku bungakushi kenkyū: Shōsetsu gikyoku ronkō* 中國文學研究小說戲曲論考 . Tokyo, 1974.

Heibonsha 平凡社 , ed. *Ajia rekishi jiten* アジア歴史事典 , 10v. Tokyo, 1959-62.

Hervouet, Yves, ed. *A Sung Bibliography (Bibliographie des Sung).* Hong Kong, 1978.

Hightower, James R. *Topics in Chinese Literature: Outlines and Bibliographies.* Cambridge, Mass., 1953. Hiraoka, Takeo 平岡武夫 , ed. *Tōdai kenkyū no shiori* 唐代研究のしおり (The T'ang Civilization Reference Series). 12v. Originally published by the Research Institute for Humanistic Studies of Kyoto University; rpt. Tokyo, 1977.

Hiraoka, Takeo and Imai Kiyoshi 今井清 . *Tōdai no sambunsakka* 唐代の散文作家 . Kyoto, 1954.

Hiraoka, Takeo and Ichihara Kōkichi 市原亨吉 . *Tōdai no shijin* 唐代の詩人 . Kyoto, 1960.

Hsia, Ch'eng-t'ao 夏承燾 . *T'ang-Sung tz'u-jen nien-p'u* 唐宋詞人年譜 . Peking, 1961. Revised edition: Shanghai, 1979.

Hsia, C. T. *The Classic Chinese Novel: A Critical Introduction.* New York, 1968.

Hsin, Wen-fang 辛文房 (*fl.* 1304). *T'ang ts'ai-tzu chuan* 唐才子傳. Peking, 1965.

Hu, Yü-chin 胡玉縉. *Ssu-k'u ch'üan-shu tsung-mu t'i-yao pu-cheng* 四庫全書總目提要補正. Wang Hsin-fu 王欣夫, ed. Shanghai, 1964.

Huang, Li-chen 黃立振. *Pa-pai chung ku-tien wen-hsüeh chu-tso chieh-shao* 八百種古典文學著作介紹. Chengchow, 1982.

Huang, Lin 黃霖 and Han T'ung-wen 韓同文, comp. and comm. 1982. *Chung-kuo li-tai hsiao-shuo lun-chu hsüan* 中國歷代小說論著選. Nan-ch'ang.

Hucker, Charles O. *China: A Critical Bibliography.* Tucson, 1962.

———. *A Dictionary of Official Titles in Imperial China.* Stanford, 1985.

Hummel, Arthur W., ed. *Eminent Chinese of the Ch'ing Period, 1644-1912.* 2v. Washington, D. C., 1943-44.

Idema, Wilt and Stephen H. West. *Chinese Theater, 1100-1450: A Source Book.* Wiesbaden, 1982.

Iriya, Yoshitaka 入矢義高. *Mindai shi-bun* 明代詩文. Tokyo, 1978.

Jao, Tsung-i 饒宗頤. *Tz'u chi k'ao* 詞籍考. Hong Kong, 1963.

Kao, Yü-man 高宇讏. *Wen-hsüeh i-ch'an so-yin (1954. 3-1966.6)* 文學遺產索引. Peking, 1981.

Kondō, Haruo 近藤春雄. *Chūgoku gakugei daijiten* 中國學藝大事典. Tokyo, 1978.

Kuo-chia ch'u-pan-chü pan-pen t'u-shu-kuan 國家出版局版本圖書館, ed. *Ku-chi mu-lu* 古籍目錄. Peking, 1981.

Kuo-hsüeh lun-wen so-yin 國學論文索引. Peking (1st issue: 1929, comp. by Wang Chung-min 王重民; 2nd issue: 1931, comp. by Hsü Hsü-ch'ang 徐緒昌; 3rd issue: 1934, comp. by Liu Hsiu-yeh 劉修業; 4th issue; 1936, comp. by Liu Hsiu-yeh; 5th issue: 1955, 2v., comp. by Hou Chih-chung 侯直忠); rpt. Taipei, 1967 (4 issues, in 3 vols.; the 5th issue excluded).

Kuo-li Chung-yang t'u-shu-kuan 國立中央圖書館. *Chung-kuo chin erh-shih nien wen-shih-che lun-wen fen-lei so-yin* 中國近二十年文史哲論文分類索引. Taipei, 1970.

Kuo-li Chung-yang t'u-shu-kuan 國立中央圖書館, ed. *Ming-jen chuan-chi tzu-liao so-yin* 明人傳記資料索引. Taipei, 1965.

Kuo-li T'ai-wan ta-hsüeh t'u-shu-kuan 國立臺灣大學圖書館. *Chuang-wen ch'i-k'an lun-wen fen-lei so-yin* 中文期刊論文分類索引. Taipei, 1960.

Kuo, Shao-yü 郭紹虞, comp. *Chung-kuo li-tai wen-lun hsüan* 中國歷代文論選. Hong Kong, 1979.

———. *Chung-kuo wen-hsüeh p'i-p'ing shih* 中國文學批評史. Shanghai, 1964.

Kyōto daigaku jimbunkagaku kenkyūjo 京都大學人文科學研究所. *Tōyōgaku bunken ruimoku* 東洋學文獻類目 (*Tōyōshi kenkyū bunken ruimoku* 東洋史研究文獻類目). 1934-1957, annual or semi-annual; thereafter, annual, Kyoto.

Lang, David M. and D. R. Dudley, eds. *The Penguin Companion to Classical, Oriental and African Literature* (v. 4 of *Penguin Companion to World Literature*). Harmondsworth, Middlesex, England, 1969.

Leslie, Donald, *et al.*, ed. *Essays on the Sources for Chinese History.* Canberra, 1973.

Li, T'ien-yi. *Chinese Fiction: A Bibliography of Books and Articles in Chinese and English.* New Haven, 1968.

———. *The History of Chinese Literature: A Selected Bibliography.* New Haven, 1970.

Liang, T'ing-ts'an 梁廷燦. *Li-tai ming-jen sheng-tsu nien-piao* 歷代名人生卒年表. Shanghai, 1933.

Liu, James J. Y. *Chinese Theories of Literature.* Chicago, 1975.

———. *The Art of Chinese Poetry.* Chicago, 1962.

———. *Major Lyricists of the Northern Sung, A. D. 960-1126.* Princeton, 1974.

Liu, K'ai-yang 劉開揚. *T'ang-shih lun-wen chi* 唐詩論文集. Peking, 1961.

Liu, Ta-chieh 劉大杰. *Chung-kuo wen-hsüeh fa-chan shih* 中國文學發展史. 3v. Shanghai, 1973.

Lo, Chin-t'ang 羅錦堂. *Chung-kuo hsi-ch'ü tsung-mu hui-pien* 中國戲曲總目彙編. Hong Kong, 1966.

Lo, Irving Yucheng and William Schultz, editors. *Waiting for the Unicorn: Poems of China's Last Dynasty (1644-1911).* Bloomington, Indiana, 1985. Translations of works by eighty Ch'ing-dynasty poets.

Lo, Ken-tse 羅根澤. *Chung-kuo wen-hsüeh p'i-p'ing shih* 中國文學批評史. 3v. Shanghai, 1958-62.

Lu, Hsün 魯迅. *Chung-kuo hsiao-shuo shih-lüeh* 中國小說史略; in *Lu Hsün ch'üan-chi* 魯迅全集, v. 9. Peking, 1973.

Lu, Tan-an 陸澹安. *Hsiao-shuo tz'u-yü hui-shih* 小說詞語滙釋. Shanghai, 1964; rpt. Hong Kong, 1968.

Lust, John. *Index Sinicus: A Catalogue of Articles Relating to China in Periodicals and Other Collective Publications, 1920-1955.* Cambridge, England, 1964.

Lynn, Richard John. *Chinese Literature: A Draft Bibliography in Western European Languages.* Canberra, 1979.

Lyrik des Ostens: China. Wilhelm Gundert, ed. Munich, 1958.

Mackerras, Colin. "Modern Chinese Scholarship on Theatre History: A Bibliographical Essay," *Papers on Far Eastern History,* 13 (1976), 163-190.

Maeno, Naoaki 前野直彬 . *Chūgoku bungakushi* 中國文學史 . Tokyo, 1975.

———. *Sō-shi kanshō jiten* 宋詩鑑賞辭典 . Tokyo, 1977.

———. *Tō-shi kanshō jiten* 唐詩鑑賞辭典 . Tokyo, 1970. Margouliès, Georges. *Histoire de la littérature chinoise: prose.* Paris, 1949.

McMullen, David L. *Concordances and Indexes to Chinese Texts.* London, 1972.

Miao, Ronald, ed. *Studies in Chinese Poetry and Poetics.* 3v. San Francisco, 1978.

Nienhauser, William H., Jr., ed. *Critical Essays on Chinese Literature.* Hong Kong, 1976.

Nunn, Godfrey Raymond. *Asia: A Selected and Annotated Guide to Reference Works.* Cambridge, Mass., 1971.

Ogawa, Tamaki 小川環樹 , ed. *Tōdai no shijin—sono denki* 唐代の詩人 — その傳記 . Tokyo, 1975.

Ōta, Tatsuo 太田辰夫 . *Hakki bunjin denki sōgō sakuin kō* 八旗文人傳記綜合索引稿 . Tokyo, 1975.

Owen, Stephen. *The Great Age of Chinese Poetry: The High T'ang.* New Haven, 1980.

———. *The Poetry of the Early T'ang.* New Haven, 1977.

Paper, Jordon D. *Guide to Chinese Prose.* Boston, 1973.

Pei-ching ta-hsüeh Chung-kuo yü-yen wen-hsüeh hsi 北京大學中國語言文學系 . *Chung-kuo wen-hsüeh shih* 中國文學史 . 4v. Peking, 1959.

Rickett, Adele Austin, ed. *Chinese Approaches to Literature from Confucius to Liang Ch'i-ch'ao.* Princeton, 1978.

Shang-hai i-shu yen-chiu-so 上海藝術研究所 and Chung-kuo hsi-chü-chia hsieh-hui Shang-hai fen-hui 中國戲劇家協會上海分會 , eds. *Chung-kuo hsi-ch'ü ch'ü-i tz'u-tien* 中國戲曲曲藝詞典 . Shang-hai, 1981.

Shang-hai t'u-shu-kuan 上海圖書館 . *Chung-kuo ts'ung-shu tsung-lu* 中國叢書綜錄 . 3v. Peking, 1959, 1961, 1962.

Shih, Chung-wen. *The Golden Age of Chinese Drama: Yüan Tsa-chü.* Princeton, 1976.

Shirakawa, Shizuka 白川靜 . *Chūgoku no kodai bungaku* 中國の古代文學 . 2v. Tokyo, 1977.

Ssu-k'u ch'üan-shu tsung-mu 四庫全書總目 . Chi Yün 紀昀 (1724-1805), *et al.*, comp. Shanghai, 1930; rpt. Taipei, 1969 (10 v.).

Sun, K'ai-ti 孫楷第 . *Chung-kuo t'ung-su hsiao-shuo shu-mu* 中國通俗小說書目 . Peking, 1933.

Suzuki, Shūji 鈴木修次 , *et al. Bungaku gairon* 文學概論 . and *Bungakushi* 文學史 ; in *Chūgoku bunka sōsho* 中國文化叢書 . Tokyo, 1973.

———. *Tōdai shijin ron* 唐代詩人論 . 2v. Tokyo, 1973.

T'an, Cheng-pi 譚正璧 . *Chung-kuo wen-hsüeh-chia ta tz'u-tien* 中國文學家大辭典 . Rpt. Hong Kong, 1961.

———. *Hua-pen yü ku-chü* 話本與古劇 . Shanghai, 1957.

T'ang-shih yen-chiu chuan-chu, lun-wen mu-lu so-yin, 1949-1981 唐史研究專著，論文目錄索引 . Chinese Department, Shansi Normal University, eds. Hsi-an, 1982.

Teng, Ssu-yü and Knight Biggerstaff. *An Annotated Bibliography of Selected Chinese Reference Works.* Cambridge, Mass., 1971.

Ting, Nai-tung and Ting Hsu Lee-hsia. *Chinese Folk Narratives: A Bibliographical Guide.* San Francisco, 1975.

Tōhōgaku kankei chosho ronbun mokuroku 東方學關係著書論文目錄 . Tōhō Gakkai 東方學會 , ed.

Tsang, Li-ho 臧勵龢 , *et al.,* eds. *Chung-kuo jen-ming ta tz'u-tien* 中國人名大辭典 . Hong Kong, 1981.

Tsien, Tsuen-hsuin and James K. M. Cheng. *China: An Annotated Bibliography of Bibliographies.* Boston, 1978.

Wan, Man 萬曼 . *T'ang-chi hsü-lu* 唐集敍錄 . Peking, 1980.

Wang, Chung-min 王重民 . *Ch'ing-tai wen-chi pien-mu so-yin* 清代文集編目索引 . Peking, 1935.

Wang, Pao-hsien 王寶先 . *Li-tai ming-jen nien-p'u tsung-mu* 歷代名人年譜總目 . Taichung, 1965.

Wang, Ying 王鍈 . *Shih tz'u ch'ü yü-tz'u li-shih* 詩詞曲語辭例釋 . Peking, 1980.

Watson, Burton. *Chinese Lyricism: Shih Poetry from the Second to the Twelfth Century.* New York, 1971.

———. *Chinese Rhyme-Prose: Poems in the Fu form from the Han and Six Dynasty Periods.* New York, 1971.

West, Stephen H. *Vaudeville and Narrative: Aspects of Chin Theater.* Wiesbaden, 1977.

Wilkinson, Endymion. *The History of Imperial China: A Research Guide.* Cambridge, Mass., 1973.

Wong, Kai-chee, *et al. A Research Guide to English Translation of Chinese Verse: Han Dynasty to T'ang Dynasty.* Hong Kong, 1977.

Yamane, Yukio 山根幸夫 . *Zōtei Nihon genson Minjin bunshū mokuroku* 增訂日本現存明人文集目錄 Tokyo, 1978.

Yang, Chia-lo 楊家駱, ed. *Chung-kuo wen-hsüeh pai-k'o ch'üan-shu* 中國文學百科全書. 4v. Taipei, 1971 (fifth printing).

Yang, Kuo-hsiung 楊國雄 and Li Shu-t'ien 黎樹添. *Hsien-tai lun-wen chi wen-shih-che lun-wen so-yin* 現代論文集文史哲論文索引. Hong Kong, 1979.

Yang, Winston L. Y. *et al. Classical Chinese Fiction: A Guide to Its Study and Appreciation: Essays and Bibliographies.* Boston, 1978.

Yoshikawa, Kōjirō 吉川幸次郎 and Kurokawa Yōichi 黑川洋一, eds. *Chūgoku bungakushi* 中國文學史. Tokyo, 1974.

Yoshikawa, Kōjirō. *Introduction to Sung Poetry.* Burton Watson, trans. Cambridge, Mass., 1967.

Yü, Chia-hsi 余嘉錫. *Ssu-k'u ch'üan-shu t'i-yao pien-cheng* 四庫全書提要辨證. 1937; rpt. Taipei, 1959; revised ed. Peking, 1958. Yü, Ping-ch'üan 余秉權. *Chung-kuo shih-hsüeh lun-wen yin-te* 中國史學論文引得, 1902-1962 (*Chinese History: Index to Learned Articles*). Hong Kong, 1963.

Yu, Ping-kuen. *Chinese History: Index to Learned Articles, Volume II, 1905-1964 (Based on Collections in American and European Libraries).* Cambridge, Mass., 1970.

Yüan, Hsing-p'ei 袁行霈 and Hou Chung-i 侯忠義, ed. *Chung-kuo wen-yen hsiao-shuo shu-mu* 中國文言小說書目. Peking, 1981.

Yüan, T'ung-li. *China in Western Literature: A Continuation of Cordier's* Bibliotheca Sinica. New Haven, 1958.

Major Chinese Dynasties and Periods

Hsia	c. 2100–c. 1600 B.C.
Shang	c. 1600–c. 1028 B.C.
Chou	c. 1027–256 B.C.
Western Chou	c. 1027–771 B.C.
Eastern Chou	c. 770–256 B.C.
Spring and Autumn	722–468 B.C.
Warring States	403–221 B.C.
Ch'in	221–207 B.C.
Han	206 B.C.–A.D. 220
Former Han	206 B.C.–A.D. 8
Latter Han	A.D. 25–220
Hsin	A.D. 9–25
Three Kingdoms	220–265
Wei	220–265
Shu	221–263
Wu	222–280
Six Dynasties (Wu, Eastern Chin, Liu Sung, Southern Ch'i, Southern Liang, and Southern Ch'en)	222–589
Chin	265–420
Western Chin	265–317
Eastern Chin	317–420
Southern Dynasties	420–589
Former (Liu) Sung	420–479
Southern Ch'i	479–502
Southern Liang	502–557
Southern Ch'en	557–589
Northern Dynasties	386–581
Northern Wei	386–534
Eastern Wei	534–550
Western Wei	535–577
Northern Ch'i	550–577
Northern Chou	557–581
Sui	581–618

DYNASTIES AND PERIODS

T'ang	618–907
Five Dynasties	907–960
Liao	916–1125
Sung	960–1279
Northern Sung	960–1126
Southern Sung	1127–1279
Chin (Jurchen)	1115–1234
Yüan	1260–1368
Ming	1368–1644
Ch'ing	1644–1911

PART I
ESSAYS

BUDDHIST LITERATURE

Jan Yün-hua

I. Introduction

OF all religious literature written in Chinese, the body of Buddhist literature is the largest and the most varied in theme and style. It has a long history. The earliest known Chinese translations of foreign literature are of Buddhist texts, and they inspired subsequent Chinese texts, compilations, and exegeses. This literature has had a dominant impact on all East Asian Buddhists and further influenced the cultures and literatures of China, Korea, and Japan.

According to a recently revised catalogue of the Chinese Buddhist canon, the *Ta-tsang ching* 大藏經 published in Japan consists of 2,500 works in nearly 10,000 fascicles. It is therefore impossible to give a detailed description of the canon. One can, however, introduce the various styles of Buddhist literature in chronological order and point out their literary value and significance. For convenience of reference, a number is given to each title when it is mentioned for the first time. A "T" before the number refers to the *Taishō-shinshū daizōkyō* 大正新修大藏經, published in Japan; an "HTC" refers to the *Hsü Tsang-ching* 續藏經 reprinted in Taiwan.

II. Translated Scriptures

When Buddhism spread to China, the followers of this new and foreign faith were eager to learn all they could about it. As the number of believers grew, the demand for religious scripture increased. The translation of Buddhist texts into Chinese was a consequence of this demand, and translations of Buddhist scriptures form the core of the canon.

The major translations of Buddhist texts from Indic and Central Asian languages into Chinese took place towards the middle of the second century A.D. Among the few foreign missionaries who first traveled to China and rendered some Buddhist texts into Chinese, the leading translators were An Shih-kao 安世高 (*fl.* 148-170), of the Parthian royal lineage, and Chih-lou chia-ch'an 支婁迦讖, a Scythian. The former was responsible for the introduction of the Abhidharmic and the meditative texts of the Hīnayāna school of Buddhism; while the latter rendered Mahāyāna scriptures. Their translations introduced a new view of life. The ideas that life is suffering, that all phenomena are impermanent, that salvation is possible only by forsaking family life, and that meditation is the highest experience possible in religious practice were all important to the Chinese mind as well as for literary philosophy.

The translations of Buddhist canons from foreign languages into Chinese continued to flourish during the third century A.D. Among a number of the translators, Chih-

1

ch'ien 支謙 and Fa-hu法護, or Dharmarakṣa, were prominent. The former translated a number of important canons like the *Vimalakīrtinirdeśa* 維摩詰經 (T474), *T'ai-tzu jui-ying peng-ch'i ching* 太子瑞應本起經 (T185), and *Ta-ming-tu ching* 大明度經 (T225), all of which are important doctrinally as well as literarily. Fa-hu was the most distinguished translator during the period and there are more than a hundred works and translations ascribed to him. Some of these works like the *Cheng-fa-jua ching* 正法華經 (T263), or the *Lotus sutra*, the *P'u-yao ching* 普曜經 (T186 Skt. *Lalitavistara*), and the *Kuang-tsan ching* 光讚經 (T222 Skt. *Pañcaviṁśatisāhasrikā-sūtra*), were the authoritative scriptures of Chinese Buddhism till the fifth century. The ideal Buddhist layman was Vimalakīrti, who had a tremendous influence on Chinese literature and art at large. The concept of Emptiness (*śūnyatā*) was the central philosophy of Mahāyāna Buddhism and it also influenced Chinese literary thought. The *Lotus sutra* was one of those scriptures that had the strongest impact on the Chinese mind and became a great inspiration for Chinese and other East Asian Buddhists in their religious cultivation, literary compositions, and artistic creations. The description of the Bodhisattvas' careers in the *T'ai-tzu jui-ying peng-ch'i ching* and the *P'u-yao ching* introduced a new type of heroic narrative. However, as Chinese Buddhism was still in the formative period, its followers were comparatively few in number, and knowledge of the Indian religion was still unsystematic. Linguistic preparation and translation techniques were not fully developed. Consequently, the quality and influence of the early Chinese translations were limited.

China underwent a drastic change during the fourth century when the heartland of its civilization was conquered by foreign rulers, forcing the Chinese elite to flee to the South. Thereafter, China suffered from incessant wars and political instability. Social and cultural institutions broke down; economic order was destroyed. This painful experience unexpectedly helped Buddhism, since its teachings on suffering and impermanence, combined with the friendly relationships between some high priests and the ruling houses, attracted many followers to Buddhism. Among the new converts were a number of learned members who had distinguished themselves as scholars before their conversions and consequently brought a new standard of scholarship to the study and understanding of Buddhism. Tao-an 道安(d. 285), his disciple Hui-yüan慧遠(334-416), and their associates were well-educated, able writers, thinkers, and organizers. Along with other leading Buddhists of the period, they made Buddhism more respectable in the eyes of the Chinese elite and the masses at large. The literary efforts of these Buddhist leaders include prefaces to the translated canons, treatises on doctrinal matters and religio-political controversies, personal correspondence, and poems. Most of their works are now recognized as classics of Chinese Buddhism.

Buddhist translations done around A.D. 400 ushered in a new era. Eminent translators and distinguished assistants were active at different centers in China. Sanghabhadra衆賢(*fl.* 383), Kumārajīva 鳩摩羅什 (*fl.* 385-409), and Buddhabhadra覺賢(d. 429) all contributed to these new achievements in translation. These new groups of translators possessed a more advanced knowledge of Mahāyāna Buddhism. They were also fortunate to have more learned Chinese assistants. This better understanding of Indian Buddhism and related languages, together with the better native assistants, made their translations more accurate, elegant, and readable than earlier works. Thus, many of these translations replaced the older translations of the same text, and became the preferred readings in China. They also had significant influence on Chinese literature.

From a literary viewpoint, many of the translations done during this period are quite sophisticated works, especially those by Kumārajīva and his associates. Their version of the *Lotus sutra*, the *Miao-fa lien-hua ching* 妙法蓮華經 (T262), not only contained the profound doctrines that became the essence of several Chinese and Japanese Buddhist schools, but the parables, such as the "Burning House" or the "Runaway Son," in Chapters 3 and 4 became well-known pieces of literature. The chapter on Kuan-yin, or Avalokiteśvara (ch. 24), as the Savior is also an important piece of Buddhist literature. Their translation of *Vimalakīrtinirdeśa*, the *Wei-mo-chieh so-shuo ching* 維摩詰所說經 (T475), besides being a work of religious doctrines, is structurally a novel. The work describes the dramatic encounters between Buddha's disciples and Vimalakīrti, the learned lay Buddhist. This work had a deep and long-lasting influence on Chinese poetry, storytelling, and painting. The long and short versions of *Pan-jo po-lo-mi-ching* 般若波羅密經 (T223, 227), translated by Kumārajīva and his assistants, are still standard scriptures among Chinese Buddhists. They are systematic expositions of the Māhayāna doctrine of emptiness (*k'ung* 空, *śūnyatā*), an essential but difficult concept. Some sections of this lengthy scripture, like the *Ching-kang ching* 金剛經 (T235) or the *Hsin-ching* 心經 (T250), remain the preferred renderings despite other subsequent translations.

Kumārajīva's contribution was not limited to the translation of scriptures, but extended to the rendering of philosophical texts. His work *Ta-chih-tu lun* 大智度論 (T1509), a gigantic and magnificent treatise in 100 chapters, expounded comprehensively the philosophy and practice of Mahāyāna Buddhism. His version of the *Chung lun* 中論 (T1564), or *Mādhyamakaśāstra*, the *Shih-erh-men lun* 十二門論, or *Dvādāsanikayāśāstra* (T1568), and the *Pai-lun* 百論, or *Satakaśāstra* (T1569), laid down the foundation of the *San-lun* 三論 School and strongly influenced other Buddhist philosophies. There seems no doubt that the efforts and contributions of Kumārajīva and his associates put Chinese Buddhists in an advantageous position, since this was the first time they began systematically to possess a comprehensive knowledge of Buddhist philosophy and practice.

Other contemporaries include Buddhabhadra, Guṇabhadra, Guṇavṛdhi, and others who worked in South China. They translated important Buddhist scriptures, disciplinary texts, and philosophical treatises. In Northwest China Dharmaksema 曇無讖 (*fl.* 385-433) was the outstanding translator. Buddhabhadra's translation of the *Avataṁsaka, Hua-yen ching* 華嚴經 (T278), is a text full of imagination, and two chapters of this text, "Ming-nan p'in" 明難品 and "Ju-fa-chieh p'in" 入法界品, are well known for their literary qualities. Guṇabhadra's version of the *Laṅkāvatārasūtra, Leng-chia a-po-to-lo pao-ching* 楞伽阿跋多羅寶經 (T670), and Dharmaksema's translation of *Mahāparinirvānasūtra*, or *Ta-pan nieh-p'an ching* 大般涅槃經 (T374), both greatly affected Chinese Buddhist thought; the philosophy of these two texts is still regarded as the pillar of several Chinese Buddhist schools. Apart from the doctrinary literature, there are other texts equally important to the Buddhist religion: Dharmaksema's translation *Fo so-hsing tsan* 佛所行讚 (T192) is the Chinese version of the *Buddhacarita* composed by the great Indian poet, Aśvaghoṣa, and Fa-yün's 法雲 (467-529) *Fo pen-hsing ching* 佛本行經 (T193) is a poetic translation of the *Career of the Enlightened*. This work comprises verses in five-line, seven-line, and four-line styles, which are often free from the restriction of rhyme. Some sections of the work contain vivid descriptions, and this thirty-one-chapter book of verse seems to be the longest poetic work in medieval China. Other works on the previous lives of the Buddhas, like the *Tsa pi-yü ching* 雜譬喩經 (T207-208) and the *Pai-yü ching* 百喩經 (T209), are full of Indian parables and folklores. Their influence on Chinese storytelling is well known.

III. The Chinese Writings

Apart from translation from foreign languages, Chinese Buddhists also wrote their own original works. The number of these writings increased with the progess of time, eventually outnumbering the translated canons, especially after the twelfth century, when Buddhism declined in India. The Chinese writings included treatises on doctrinal problems, exegeses of translated scriptures, prefaces, personal correspondence, and travel accounts of pilgrims. The earliest extant native Chinese Buddhist work is the *Mou-tzu li-huo lun* 牟子理惑論, now more or less recognized as a work of the third century. It discussed a number of controversies between Buddhism and Chinese tradition. The essay, written from a Buddhist point of view, successfully defended the author's religion against the points objected to by his opponents. Among other extant treatises, the *Chao lun* 肇論, or the *Book of Chao* (T1858), is a collection of essays by Seng-chao 僧肇 (c. 374-414), a close associate of Kumārajīva with a gifted mind for philosophy and literature. In this short work, the author discussed some of the most difficult problems in Buddhist philosophy using both Buddhist and Taoist terminology. The work is regarded as a milestone in the Chinese understanding of Buddhism. Of the texts composed by the Chinese exegetes, Tao-an's *Jen-pen-yü-sheng ching chu* 人本欲生經註 (T1693), Tao-sheng's 道生 (d. 434) *Fa-hua ching shu* 法華經疏 (HTC v. 150), and the *Chu Wei-mo ching* 註維摩 經 (T1775) by Seng-chao and his friends are still regarded as the best of their kind. Although exegetic works are by their very nature rather dry and disjointed, the sparkling sentences and insights in these works compensate for those shortcomings.

The prefaces to translated scriptures played a significant role in the spread of Buddhism. Because of the foreign flavor, unusual grammatical structure, and strange ideas contained in the translated literature, it was rather difficult to attract Chinese readers, especially during the early centuries. The Chinese writers of the prefaces were usually distinguished men of letters, who strove to make the translated texts more understandable and acceptable to their readers. It is remarkable that they were so often able to summarize a voluminous translation and its complicated meanings within such limited space. It was by this technique of introduction that Buddhism was more readily and speedily accepted by the Chinese. Important prefaces written during the early centuries of Chinese Buddhism were collected and edited by Seng-yu 僧祐 (445-518) in *Ch'u san-tsang chi chi* 出三藏記集 (T2145). The record of travels is another form of Chinese Buddhist literature. The earliest extant work of this kind is the *Fo-kuo chi* 佛國記 (A Record of Buddhist Kingdoms) by Fa-hsien 法顯 (fl. 399-416). It has been translated into other languages, and its importance for South and Southeast Asian history and culture is well known.

IV. New Era of Scholarship

The high standards of translation and the native Chinese writings of Kumārajīva and Seng-chao inspired a new era of Buddhist scholarship in China. Hundreds of translators and exegetes flourished during the following centuries. Among the translators, the works by Paramārtha眞諦(499-569) are the most distinguished by a foreign missionary. It was this monk who began to introduce the *Vijñaptimātratā* 唯識 school of Buddhist philosophy to China. Another missionary, Bodhiruci菩提流支 (*fl.* 508-535), translated Vasubandhu's commentary on the Pure Land scripture, the *Wu-liang-shou ching wu-pi-t'i-she yüan-sheng chieh* 無量壽經優波提舍願生偈 (T1524), which ultimately inspired the Pure Land Buddhist movement in East Asia.

The greatest Chinese Buddhist translator was Hsüan-tsang玄奘(600-664), who spent seventeen years in India and brought a number of Buddhist Sanskrit works back to China, many of which he translated. The six-hundred-chapter translation of the *Mahāprajñāpāramitāsūtra* 大般若波羅密多經 (T220) is respected as the best-translated text in the *Ta-tsang ching.* He was also responsible for translating philosophical treatises such as the *Vijñaptimātratā* and the *Abhidharmakośa,* as well as Buddhist logical texts. Apart from the translations, his autobiographical narratives of his experiences in India and Central Asia were carefully recorded by his disciple Pien-chi辯機, and are known as the *Ta-t'ang hsi-yü chi*大唐西域記 (Buddhist Records of the Western World). The work not only enriched Chinese knowledge of the "Western World" but also had a considerable impact on the Chinese novel and on storytelling. Another great Chinese translator and traveler was I-tsing義淨(635-717), who followed in the steps of Hsüan-tsang, and visited India and Southeast Asia, bringing back and translating a number of scriptures into Chinese. The *Chin-kuang-ming tsui-sheng-wang ching* 金光明最勝王經 (Golden Light Sutra) (T665) and books on the monastic disciplines of the Sarvāstivādin school along with his travel accounts and biographical writings are important.

Tantric or exoteric Buddhism became popular in India in the seventh century. By the eighth century, three Indian missionaries, Śubhakarasimha善無畏(637-735), Vajrabodhi 金剛智 (671-741), and Amoghavajra不空(705-774), went to the T'ang court, and introduced this latest form of Buddhism to the Chinese through the translation of new scriptures and religious rituals. However, the influence of these Tantric texts seems quite limited as far as Chinese literature is concerned.

Apart from translations, Chinese Buddhists continued their efforts in recording their own religious experiences. This finally led to the formation of the Chinese schools of Buddhism. After the establishment of the schools, their followers read only a few prescribed texts from the translations along with original writings by the Chinese masters. As a consequence of this trend, Chinese compositions became more influential, and in some cases, like that of Ch'an Buddhism, Chinese compositions finally replaced translated texts as scriptures. These Chinese compositions took many forms: historical, sectarian, exegetic, philosophical, poetic, and popular literature. All of these genres flourished in Chinese Buddhist literature. Chronologically speaking, biography and hagiography came soon after the exegetic writings already mentioned. Centuries after the spread of Buddhism, Buddhist scholars began to work on biographies, partly to record the great achievement of their brethren and partly to gain the respect of the Chinese elite. The *Ming-seng chuan*名僧傳 by Pao-ch'ang寶唱(*fl.* 495-516), and especially the *Kao-seng chuan** 高僧傳(T2059) by Hui-chiao慧皎(497-554) led to a series of biographical histories of Chinese Buddhism. Although this form of historical literature was composed in the mode of Chinese biographies, the religious sentiment, personal touches, and hagiographical flavor made Buddhist biographies differ from their official Chinese counterpart. The Chinese Buddhist historians also compiled religious chronicles: the *Li-tai san-pao chi* 歷代三寶記 (T2034) by Fei Ch'ang-fang 費長房 (*fl.* sixth century), the *Fo-tsu t'ung-chi* 佛祖統記 (T2035) by Chi-p'an 志磐 (*fl.* 1250-1269), and the *Fo-tsu li-tai t'ung-tsai* 佛祖歷代通載 (T2036) by Nien-ch'ang 念常 (1282-1342?).

V. Sectarian Writings

The sectarian movement transformed in many ways the Buddhist religion from its Indian origin to a native Chinese entity. At first, Chinese monks who studied certain translated texts wrote exegeses on them; later, they extracted ideas from the translated texts, harmonizing them with their own experiences and systematizing them in original writings. Some of these ideas were the central theme of the Indian texts; others were new points highlighted by the Chinese writers. The earliest major sectarian movement in China was probably the Pure Land. T'an-luan 曇鸞 (476-542) compiled the *Ching-t'u lun chu* 淨土論註 (T1819) which laid the foundation for the movement. His works were further carried on by Tao-ch'o 道綽 (562-645), Shan-tao 善導 (613-681?), and their followers. The emphasis on the visualization of Amitābha and the recitation of the Buddha's name, as well as on pictures of Heaven and hells, had great influence on Chinese popular literature and art. Although this movement stressed practices rather than literature, its impact on religious literature should not be underestimated. There was a continuous growth of Pure Land literature from the T'ang period until recent times.

The T'ien-t'ai School was another pillar of Chinese Buddhism. It was founded by Hui-ssu 慧思 (515-577) and Chih-i 智顗 (538-597). The former wrote an autobiographical account, the *Li-shih-yüan wen* 立誓願文 (T1933) and a meditative guide, the *Ta-ch'eng chih-kuan fa-men* 大乘止觀法門 (T1924). However, it was through the works of Chih-i that the school became firmly established. Some of Chih-i's works like the *Fa-hua wen-chü* 法華文句 are annotative; others like the *Fa-hua hsüan-i* 法華玄義 (T1716) are exegetic and renotative and *Mo-ha chih-kuan* 摩訶止觀 (T1911) is an original work which laid the foundation of the school on both theoretical and practical levels. Through the prolific writings and organizational efforts made by Chih-i and his disciples, T'ien-t'ai Buddhism became a major school in East Asia. Other great thinkers and writers of the school including Ch'an-jan 湛然 (711-782), Chih-li 知禮 (960-1028), and Chih-hsü 智旭 (1599-1655) contributed to the development of the school.

Contemporary with the formation of T'ien-t'ai, the San-lun tsung 三論宗 School was established by Chi-tsang 吉藏 (549-623). Unlike most of the other schools, the works of Chi-tsang are largely philosophical and closer to an Indian outlook. These works, expositions of Mādhyimaka philosophy like the *San-lun hsüan-i* 三論玄義 (T1852), the *Ta-ch'eng hsüan-lun* 大乘玄論 (T1853), and the *Erh-t'i i* 二諦義 (T1854), are philosophically oriented and completely free from the disjointedness of exegetic writing. His works are highly respected for their profound philosophy and literary skill.

The Hua-yen School is the latest school of Chinese Buddhist philosophy. The theoretical frame of the school was established through the writings of Fa-tsang 法藏 (643-712) and Ch'eng-kuan 澄觀 (738-839). The former is well known for his original thought; the latter systematized that thought with great literary skill. Commentaries and books written by these two Hua-yen masters, like the *Hua-yen ching t'an-hsüan chi* 華嚴經探玄

記(T7133) and the *Hua-yen ching Chuan-chi* 華嚴經傳記 (2073) by Fa-tsang and the *Hua-yen ching shu* 華嚴經疏 (T1735) and the *Sui-shu yen-i ch'ao* 隨疏演義鈔 (T1736) by Ch'eng-kuan, are classic exegeses of Chinese and Buddhist wisdom containing sayings, texts, and lore. The writings of other masters of the school also influenced Chinese thought. The *Yüan-jen lun* 原人論 (T1886) and *Ch'an-yüan chu-ch'uan-chi tu-hsü* 禪源諸詮集都序 (T2015), both by Tsung-mi 宗密 (780-841), are important philosophical essays.

The most influential and significant sectarian writings were done by the followers of the Ch'an Buddhist Schools. Traditionally this school claimed that it was founded by Bodhidharma 菩提達摩 (*fl*. 470-516), and there was a shadowy lineage of patriarchs variably mentioned before the eighth century. Thereafter, a number of schools appeared claiming to be the legitimate successors of the founder, Bodhidharma. This struggle for legitimacy produced a polemic literature, written in the forms of dialogues, hagiography (on dialogues and hagiography, see *Ch'an yü-lu*), and discursive treatises. Some attention should be given to the discursive works. Among the manuscripts discovered in Tun-huang, many belonged to Ch'an Buddhism. One of them, the *Erh-ju ssu-hsing lun* 二入四行論 (T2009), is attributed to Bodhidharma and set the tone of Ch'an Buddhism, which ultimately developed into a great tradition. Other treatises attributed to Tao-hsin 道信 (580-651) and Hung-jen 弘忍 (602-675) are also important for an understanding of the early history and thought of the Ch'an movement. When the sectarian Ch'an struggle began in the eighth century, more new treatises and forged "old" documents appeared. Of them, the *Kuan-hsin lun* 觀心論 (T2833) and the *Ta-ch'eng an-hsin ju-tao fa* 大乘安心入道法 are attributed to the so-called Northern School, the *Wu-hsin lun* 無心論 (T2831) to the Southern School, and the *Chüeh-kuan lun* 絕觀論 to the Ox-head School. Among the later Ch'an treatises, the *Tun-wu yao-men* 頓悟要門 (HTC v. 110) by Hui-hai (*fl*. eighth century) and the *Ch'uan-hsin fa-yao* 傳心法要 (T2012a) by Hsi-yün 希運 (d. 850) are important treatises for Ch'an philosophy. The records of Ma-tsu 馬祖 and his disciples contained description of dramatic actions and conversations. The most scholarly and voluminous work of the Ch'an school is the *Tsung-ching lu* 宗鏡錄 (T2016) compiled by Yen-shou 延壽 (904-975) in one hundred chapters. It is a systematical analysis and harmonization of Buddhist philosophy and Ch'an practice. Quotations from various authoritatively translated texts, Chinese writings, sayings, and hymns by Ch'an masters were skillfully put together into a coherent system. The book is a treasury of Chinese Buddhism yet to be explored fully. Among all Ch'an writings, only the *Liu-tsu t'an-ching* 六祖壇經 (Platform Sutra of the Sixth Patriarch) (T2007) attributed to Hui-neng 慧能 (d.713), attained to the stature of an authoritative scripture for Ch'an in China, Son in Korea, and Zen in Japan. It records the personal experiences of the patriarch along with his thought and teachings. A number of translations are available in European languages.

VI. Popular and Poetic Works

Apart from dialogues and treatises, some Ch'an Buddhists also wrote a considerable amount of hymns and poetry. These Ch'an contributions may be classified into the following categories: hymns, songs, and verses for transmitting the Teaching. Religious hymns existed in China long before the Ch'an Buddhists. The hymns attributed to Wang-ming 忘名 and Master Tui 兌 are well-known early examples. However, the flourishing of Ch'an stimulated a new impulse for poetic composition as a means of religious expression. The *Hsin-hsin ming* 信心銘 (T2010), attributed to Tao-hsin, and the *Cheng-tao ko* 證道歌 (T2014), attributed to the Master of Yung-chia (Hsüan-chüeh 玄覺 665-713), are good examples of influential religious hymns. Religious songs seem to have been very popular in China during the T'ang. A number of such songs written by Ch'an Buddhists were discovered in the Tun-huang manuscripts. These songs were composed under the titles of *Wu-keng chuan* 五更轉, *Shih-erh shih* 十二時, *Hsing-lu nan* 行路難, etc. Originally, they were for popular entertainment, but Ch'an monks took over the form and composed new songs to express their religious experiences and inspirations. Verses for transmitting the Ch'an teachings were highly valued by Ch'an monks during the late T'ang and Sung period, but the literary quality of these verses is less than one might expect.

Although Ch'an monks contributed much to popular literature, they by no means monopolized the field. The Pure Land teachings were the most popular faith among Chinese masses, and this school contributed much to religious ritual and poetry. The ritualistic works known as *ch'an-fa* 懺法, or "confessional cermonies," claimed to originate with the Buddhist patron, Emperor Wu of the Liang dynasty (r. 502-549). A work called *Tz'u-pei tao-ch'ang ch'an-fa* 慈悲道場懺法 (T1909), attributed to the Masters of Religion of the Liang dynasty, is probably the earliest extant ritual if the attribution is valid. The Pure Land monks compiled new texts to serve their religious needs. The *Chuan-ching hsing-tao yüan wang-sheng ching-t'u fa-shih tsan* 轉經行道願往生淨土法事讚 (T1979) by Shan-tao and the *Ching-t'u wu-hui nien-fo lüeh fa-shih-i-tsan* 淨土五會念佛略法事儀讚 (T1983) by Fa-chao 法照 (*fl.* eighth century) are representative of these Pure Land efforts. Probably because of the Pure Land success in religious rituals, other schools followed suit compiled ritualistic texts on certain scriptures which they considered essential for their own respective school. The *Yüan-chüeh ching tao-ch'ang hsiu-cheng i* 圓覺經道場修證儀 (HTC v. 128) by Tsung-mi, the *Fa-hua san-mei ch'an-i* 法華三昧懺儀 (T1941), and the *Chin-kuang-ming tsui-sheng ch'an-i* 金光明最勝懺儀 (T1946) by Chih-li are examples from the Hua-yen and T'ien-t'ai schools. These ritualistic works contained sets of intricate liturgies for the worship of various Buddhas and Bodhisattvas. They contain imaginative descriptions of heavens and hells, stories about the retribution of good and bad deeds, karma and rebirth. Even some of the dry manuals used for meditative guides often contained summaries in verse, which could be intoned in the prescribed rite and easily memorized. It seems likely that such religious rituals are related to the development of the *pien-wen* 變文 literature (see *Tun-huang wen-hsüeh*).

Both *pien-wen* and *yün-wen* 韻文 have been popular topics of recent scholarship. However, most pieces mentioned in these recent publications do not exactly belong to *pien-wen*. Only those works which have the works *pien-wen* in the titles can be properly called *pien-wen*. The rest are certainly popular writings, but not necessarily *pien-wen*. Stories from Buddhist scriptures like the *Fa-hua ching* or the *Wei-mo ching* or on ideal heroes like the Buddha and his previous existences or on Mu-lien 目連 are typical Buddhist *pien-wen*, because they all originated in Buddhist scripture and were recreated for the popularization of the religion. Other pieces on traditional Chinese heroes gradually appeared: the stories of Wang Ling 王陵, Wu Tzu-hsü 伍子胥, and Meng Chiang-nü 孟姜女. The secularization of popular Buddhist literature did not mean that the secular writings completely took over the religious works, however. During the later period, especially in Ming and Ch'ing times, a popular religious literature still prevailed, known as *pao-*

*chüan*寶卷(precious scrolls). Apart from Buddhist topics, other *pao-chüan* deal with Taoist or popular-entertainment topics. The *yün-wen* or rhymed literature, discovered at Tun-huang have been edited by Wang Chung-min, Jen Erh-pei, Jao Tsung-i, Pa-chow, and others. The influence of the *pien-wen* and *yün-wen* of the T'ang period on *ku-tzu-tz'u** and *chu-kung-tiao** has been firmly established.

Buddhism was also influential in the development of the early Chinese novel (see *Hsi-yu chi, Jou-p'u t'uan, Feng-shen yen-i*) and of drama. The conversion of Chinese intellectuals to Buddhism not only advanced Chinese understanding of the religion but also brought some branches of native Chinese literature into contact with Buddhism. Apart from historiography, which has already been mentioned, some Buddhists used poetry to express their religious sentiments and experiences. The poems written by Chih-tun支遁(314-366) and Hui-yüan (334-416) are the best example of early Chinese Buddhist poetry. Although some of these early poems are expressions of religious experiences, their literary quality is also high. Buddhism also influenced the reevaluation of the Chinese landscape in Chinese poetry which took place in the fourth and fifth centuries as best exemplified in the works of Hsieh Ling-yün.* When poetry became the prime form of Chinese literature during the T'ang, some monk-poets adopted poetry as the principal medium for their religious expression. Wang Fan-chih* (T2863) and Han-shan* are two distinguished representatives. Their poems influenced many Ch'an Buddhists and other poets at large, such as Wang Wei,* Chiao-jan,* Kuan-hsiu,* and Ch'i-chi* brought Buddhist poetry into a new state: though they still wrote about religious life and thought, in the eyes of later literary critics their poetry was excellent literature in its own right. Poetic aesthetic and skill replaced religious sentiment as the chief element in these works. From the Sung period onward poems written by Buddhist monks became a regular feature in Chinese literature. These Buddhist poetic compositions are impressive both in quality and quantity. A recent publication, *Ch'an-men i-shu*禪門逸書 , collected 140 works of Buddhist poetry in its first series, and more works are expected in the forthcoming series of the same publication. The new emphasis on literary quality rather than on religious content was not only recognized by literary critics, but also openly acknowledged by some Buddhist poets themselves. They called their poetic work *Wai-chi*外集(Secular Collections) to distinguish them from the *Nei-hsüeh*內學(Religious Learning). Among the later Buddhist poets, the achievements of Tao-ch'ien道潛, or Ts'ai-liao tzu參寥子(b. 1102), Te-hung德洪(1071-1128), and Ch'i-sung契嵩(1107-1172) are outstanding. The last two are also well known for their prose writings in *ku-wen** style. Poetic criticism also owes a debt to Buddhism—contributions by Chiao-jan and Yen Yü (see *Ts'ang-lang shih-hua*) were particularly noteworthy.

VII. *Ta-tsang ching*

Chinese Buddhist literature has been collected and published mainly in various edition of the *Ta-tsang ching*, which comprises both translated scriptures and Chinese writings. The collection is voluminous, an accumulation of Buddhist efforts in China for the last two thousand years. The standard edition, the *Taishō shihshū daizōkyō*, for example, contains thirty-two large volumes in fine print of translated canons. It includes Hinayana, Mahayana, and Tantric scriptures, along with various accounts of the lives

9

of the Buddha. The books of monastic discipline and philosophical treatises are also included in these volumes. Works written in Chinese comprise 24 volumes (33-55 and 85). This includes the exegesis of translated scriptures and treatises as well as books of monastic discipline, (v. 33-43) sectarian writings of Chinese Buddhist schools (44-48), historical works (49-52), encyclopedias and interreligious writings (53-54), catalogues and supplements (55-86). Many works in this collection are not extant in other languages, even though they were originally translated from Sanskrit or Pali. A few of these works have been translated into European languages, but most of the collection remains for open scholarly exploration.

VIII. The Influence

The introduction of Buddhism into China not only propagated a new religion, it also transmitted Indian literature and civilization to the Chinese. The introduction, assimilation, and transformation of this new religion and its foreign civilization inevitably influenced Chinese life and culture in many ways and to a deep degree. As far as Chinese literature is concerned, the influence of Buddhism may be summarized as follows: (1) Buddhism brought with it a number of ideas to China, a number of ideas that were destined to become dominant factors in the Chinese attitude towards life and death, society and cosmos. The ideas of impermanence (*anitya*) and suffering (*duhkha*), *karma* and rebirth, paradises and hells, emptiness and reality, bondage and liberation, were all essential to the development of Chinese literary thought. (2) When during the T'ang dynasty translation of Buddhist literature from the Indic languages into Chinese flourished, the popular form of literature prevalent was *pien-wen*, and Chinese poetry was dominated by lines with a fixed number of syllables and rigid rhythmns. This form was incapable of dealing with the Indian Buddhist literature, so different in style and rich in content. Under these circumstances, the translation of Buddhist works brought in new styles of writing that were freer, longer, more elegant, varied, and interconnected. At first, these new styles were only used for translations, but gradually they spread to Chinese compositions as well. Finally these styles went beyond Buddhist literature and influenced Chinese writings at large. Among the new styles introduced by Buddhist translations was the interfusion of prose and verse narratives which became the predominant stylistic feature of Chinese short stories and novels. (3) To the Chinese, Buddhism was a new and complete way of life: the renunciation of household, the striving for *nirvana* through monastic life, the compassionate Bodhisattva, and the hope for a new and happier life in a future existence were all new to the Chinese. These new ideas opened up Chinese thinking and provided new materials for Chinese literature. Because of this, many writers were able to free themselves and their writings from the rigid structure of Chinese society and Confucian dogma. (4) This freedom in writing about new ways of life and new problems went deep into the psychological spheres of Chinese consciousness. The Buddhist analyses of psychic function and experiences and the emphasis on systematic personal cultivation of mind provided Chinese writers with a new and subjective world, one that merged with the love of nature in traditional Chinese poetry to reach far beyond this society and life, thus enriching the imaginative powers of Chinese literature. This was true not only for literature created by Buddhist writers; it also transformed other genres such as historiography and poetry, which had existed before the spread of Buddhism in China. In other words, Buddhism restructured old literary forms even as it was introducing new ones. (5) Buddhists also brought new subject matter and terminology to Chinese literature. Strange animals and birds, gods and goddesses, flowers and plants, demons and spirits, peoples and tribes, transmigrations and retributions, oceans and mountains, ideas and ideals were all new items. Buddhism also brought a number of new terms and phrases into Chinese literature, many of which still exist in modern Chinese usage. Some are no longer connected with Buddhism but have become idiomatic expressions and phrases in literary compositions.

To recapitulate: Chinese Buddhist literature comprises both canonical and other collections. The canonical literature comprises Chinese translations of Indian scriptures, books on monastic discipline, philosophical treatises, ritual manuals, and a few hagiographies. The Chinese canon also includes native Chinese compositions, which constitute the foundations of Chinese Buddhism. Other forms of literature such as historiography and hagiography, dialogues and treatises, religious geography and encyclopedias, poetry and popular writings are also prominent in the canon. Some branches of Buddhist literature extended beyond the religious realm and were absorbed in the mainstream of Chinese literature. Buddhism influenced virtually all Chinese literary thought, styles, and forms. It provided new subject matters and terminology, expanded the psychological dimensions of the Chinese mind, and enriched the Chinese power of imagination.

EDITIONS:

Ch'an-men i-shu 禪門逸書, Ming-fu 明復, ed. 1980. Taipei, lst Series.

Ch'ang, Jen-hsia 常任俠, compiler. Fo-ching wen-hsüeh ku-shih hsüan 佛經文學故事選. Peking, 1958.

Demiéville, P. and Hubert Durt, et al., ed. 1978. Répertoire du canon bouddhique Sino-Japonaise édition de Taishō, Fasc. annexe du Hōbōgirin. Tokyo-Paris.

Hsü, Ti-shan 許地山, et al., ed. 1933. Combined Indices to the Authors and Titles of Books and Chapters in Four Collections of Buddhist Literature. 3v. Peiping; rpt. Taipei, 1966.

Hsü Tsang-ching 續藏經. 1971. Rpt. Taipei.

Mizuno, Kogen   , et al., ed. 1977. Butten kaidai jiten 佛典解題事典. Tokyo.

Taishō shinshū daizōkyō 大正新修大藏經 1924-1929. v. 1-55. Tokyo.

Taishō shinshū daizōkyō sakuin 大正新修大藏經索引. 1978- .

TRANSLATIONS:

Beal, Samuel. 1871. A Catena of Buddhist Scriptures from the Chinese. London.

Chavannes, Édouard. 1910-1934. Cinq cents contes et apologues. Extraits du Tripitaka chinois et tr. en francais. Paris.

Iriya, Yoshitaka 入矢義高 et al. 1975. Bukkyo bungaku shū 佛教文學集. Tokyo. Contains lightly annotated versions of pien-wen 變文, yin-yüan 因緣, p'i-yü 譬諭, and ling-yen 靈驗; with an introduction to this literature in the backmatter.

Robinson, Richard H. 1954. Chinese Buddhist Verse. Rpt. 1980. Westport, Conn.

Waley, Arthur. 1960. Ballads and Stories from Tun-huang. London.

STUDIES:

Chang, Man-t'ao 張曼濤, ed. 1977-1978. Hsien-tai fo-chiao hsüeh-shu ts'ung-k'an 現代佛教學術叢刊. Taipei. Vols. 10 and 17 contain the Ta-tsang ching yen-chiu hui-pien 大藏經研究彙編, v. 19 the Fo-chiao yü Chung-kuo wen-hsüeh 佛教與中國文學, and v. 60 the Fo-tien i-shu yü chu-lu k'ao-lüeh 佛典譯述與著錄考略.

Ch'en, Kenneth K.S. 1973. The Chinese Transformation of Buddhism. Princeton.

Cheng, Chen-to 鄭振鐸. 1938. Chung-kuo su-wen-hsüeh shih 中國俗文學史. 2v. Shanghai.

———. 1927. "Fo-ch'ü hsü-lu" 佛曲敍錄, in Cheng's (ed.) *Chung-kuo wen-hsüeh yen-chiu* 中國文學研究, Shanghai (rpt. Shanghai, 1981), v. 2, pp. 1-19 (separate pagination).

Gjertson, D. E. 1981. "The Early Chinese Buddhist Miracle Tale," *JAOS*, 101, 287-302.

Hirano, Kenshō   . 1978. *Tōdai bungaku to Bukkyō no kenkyū* 唐代文學と佛教の研究. Kyoto.

Hsia, C. T. 1968. *The Classical Chinese Novel*. New York.

Hsiang, Ta 向達. 1957. *T'ang-tai Ch'ang-an yü Hsi-yü wen-ming* 唐代長安與西域文明. Peking.

Hu, Shih 胡適. 1959. *Pai-hua wen-hsüeh-shih* 白話文學史. Rpt. Hong Kong.

Jao, Tsung-i 饒宗頤. 1971. *Airs de Touen-houang*. Paris.

Jen, Erh-pei 任二北. 1957. *Tun-huang ch'ü chiao-lu* 敦煌曲初錄. Shanghai.

———. 1955. *Tun-huang ch'ü ch'u-t'an* 敦煌曲初探. Shanghai.

Kaji, T. 加地哲定. 1979. *Chūgoku bukkyō bungakū kenkyu* 中國佛教文學研究. Tokyo.

Kanaoka, S. 金岡照光. 1971. *Tonko nō bungakū* 敦煌の文學. Tokyo.

Liu, Tsun-yan. 1962. *Buddhist and Taoist Influence on Chinese Novels*. Wiesbaden.

Menśikov, L. N. 1980. "Les paraboles bouddhiques dans la littérature chinoise," *BEFEO*, 67, 303-336.

Pachow 巴宙, ed. 1965. *Tun-huang yün-wen chi* 敦煌韻文集. Kao-hsiung.

Sawada, Mizuho 澤田瑞穗. 1975. *Bukkyō to Chūgoku bungaku* 佛教と中國文學. Tokyo.

———. 1975. *Zoko Hōkan no kenkyū* 增補寶卷の研究. Tokyo.

Sun, K'ai-ti 孫楷第. 1956. *Su-chiang shuo-hua yü pai-hua hsiao-shuo* 俗講說話與白話小說. Shanghai.

Tanaka, R. 田中良昭, *et al.* 1980. *Tonko Butten to Zen* 敦煌佛典と禪. Tokyo.

Wang, Chung-min 王重民. 1954. *Tun-huang ch'ü-tzu-tz'u chi* 敦煌曲子詞集. Shanghai.

———, *et al.*, ed. 1957. *Tun-huang pien-wen chi* 敦煌變文集. 2v. Peking.

DRAMA

Stephen H. West

As a prelude, there are two major points to be made about dramatic literature. The first is that drama has two lives—one in the eyes of the audience, the other in the hands of the reader. While this essay is concerned primarily with drama as literature, it is impossible to separate stage from text. Techniques of performance, the layout of the stage, and the highly symbolic nature of both costuming and dramatic gesture had enormous influence on dramatic literature. Conversely, the conservative adaptation of traditional legends and historical anecdotes by playwrights strengthened the symbolic mode of Chinese drama and its consequent presentation on stage.

The second point is that scarcely any form of Chinese theater had (or has) catholic appeal; the history of drama in China is a history of regional theater and regional literature. There has been a long dialectic between northern and southern values in the development of structure, language, and even role types, dating back to the eleventh century. Indeed, despite many shared characteristics, regional variation is the most striking fact to emerge from a comparison of dramatic forms. Variations aside, all forms of Chinese drama share the following characteristics: first, it is music drama, and the music is drawn from many native and foreign sources; second, the dramas may be staged as fragments (i.e., in one or more scenes); third, the major literary form is poetry (i.e., lyrics); and fourth, all dramas rely on "role types," Theophastrian characters rather than mimetic, representational characters.

There are three major traditions of Chinese theater that have made a significant impact on theater history and on the history of dramatic literature. These are the northern *tsa-chü*,* also called *pei-ch'ü* 北曲 (northern songs) or *Yüan-ch'ü* 元曲 (Yüan songs), which flourished from the thirteenth to the middle of the fifteenth century; the southern tradition, including *nan-hsi*,* also called *Wen-chou tsa-chü* 溫州雜劇, *ch'uan-ch'i*,* and *K'un-ch'ü*,* dating from the early fourteenth century to the middle of the seventeenth; and the *p'i-huang* 皮黃, or *ching-chü*,* which flourished from the middle of the seventeenth century to beginning of the present century. Of course, some of these traditions, especially the *K'un-ch'ü* and *ching-chü*, continue to the present day, carried on by small groups of amateurs and fostered as national traditions. Our discussion will focus on the two earlier traditions, since *ching-chü* is primarily a performance devoted to spectacle, dance, gesture, and song; a marvelous theatrical form, it is a weak literary art.

The earliest history of Chinese drama is clouded in obscurity and seems vaguely related to religious sacrifice and shamanistic ceremony, predominantly dance. There has been a long and intimate history between the stage and the temple, especially in rural China (Van der Loon, 1977). Archaeological evidence from the eleventh to the fourteenth centuries suggests that the stages were a regular feature of local temples, particularly those dedicated to earth, agriculture, or weather deities (Ting Ming-i, 1972; Liu Nien-tz'u, 1974; West, 1979; and Idema and West, 1982, pp. 89-91). This is not surprising since the temple was, and continues to be, the center of Chinese village (and urban neighborhood) life. The corpus of extant plays and the titles of lost plays from this same period, however, suggest that drama was overwhelmingly secular in nature. The temple was the center of ordinary as well as religious life, and while acting troupes certainly performed on festival days, the greater part of their repertoire was secular, even bawdy, entertainment. There was evidently little sense of what Westerners consider sacred about religious sites, and consequently little sense of blasphemy in performing raucous and spectacular shows at such temples.

The rise of typical Chinese drama—that is, drama that includes alternating sung lyrics and spoken prose, recited passages, and acrobatic interludes—was tied to two major developments. The first was the influence of what the Chinese term *shuo-ch'ang wen-hsüeh* 說唱文學 (prosimetric literature—see essay on Popular Literature); the term literally means "literature that is both spoken and sung." The second was the emergence of large metropolitan centers in the heartland of China: in the capitals of Pien-liang (modern Kaifeng), Wu-lin or Lin-an (modern Hangchow), and Ta-tu (modern Peking), and in the important regional metropolises of P'ing-yang in Shansi, Tung-p'ing in Shantung, and Chin-ting in Hopeh.

Prosimetric literature is a term coined by the modern scholar Yeh Te-chün (1979) to describe the long tradition of performing literature that begins with the *pien-wen* tales (see *Tun-huang wen-hsüeh*) of the T'ang and continues to modern "national theater" (*kuo-chü* 國劇 or *wo-kuo hsi-chü* 我國戲曲). This form is marked by alternating prose and rhymed passages—either chanted or sung to musical accompaniment. It is performed (with rare exceptions) by a single storyteller, told in the third-person point of view, and is in the form of a unilinear narrative.

From this literature, drama borrowed the basic structure of alternating sung and spoken passages, the use of a unilinear narrative plot (in *tsa-chü*), and the introduction of characters on stage by a process of self- description which is a simple substitution of the first for the third-person description of narrative forms. Another feature borrowed from prosimetric literature is the use of long passages to describe scenery and background. A storyteller, of course, has to create a mental landscape as background for his characters. When this is carried over into drama, the lyrics of which also describe scenery and setting, it obviates the need for elaborate stage sets. The audience, through generations or even centuries of custom, had simply become accustomed to the creation of a mental landscape through language and imagery.

One particularly influential genre of prosimetric literature, *chu-kung-tiao** (all keys and modes), developed during the early Sung period (roughly 1050). This coincided with the development of large entertainment districts in the great cities of China. These centers were called *wa-she* 瓦舍, *wa-tzu* 瓦子, or *wa-chieh* 瓦解, terms that literally mean "tile markets," but connoted large pleasure precincts, a floating netherworld that centered around enormous government-controlled and operated theaters, some holding hundreds of people (Idema and West, 1982, pp. 10-102).

Of the tens of hundreds of entertainments held in these centers, the All Keys and Modes and the Farce Play (called *tsa-chü** or *yüan-pen*) were the two protodramatic forms that directly influenced the formation of traditional Chinese music drama. The All Keys and Modes was a long narrative ballad, written in the form of suites of arias interspersed with bits of prose dialogue. The two extant *chu-kung-tiao*—*Liu Chih-yüan chu-kung-tiao** and *Tung Chieh-yüan Hsi-hsiang-chi chu-kung-tiao**—show a musical structure that appears to be a transitional form between *tz'u** music and *ch'ü** arias. That is, the earlier *tz'u* form is marked by a single song of two stanzas, followed in the *chu-kung-tiao* by a coda (*wei-sheng* 尾聲); the latter *ch'ü* suites are constituted of several songs of a single stanza, all belonging to a single mode, arranged in a roughly pre-determined sequence, followed by a coda (Cheng Ch'ien, 1951). The All Keys and Modes uses both types of musical arrangements.

The advantage of this latter model to narrative is obvious; its adaptation into *tsa-chü* drama was fortuitous. Each of the four acts of the *tsa-chü* is hung upon a skeleton of one long suite of music written to a single mode, utilizes the same rhyme throughout, and is sung by a single person. The close relationship of the musical structure and the use of a single singing lead point to the influence of the All Keys and Modes.

The variety show of the pleasure precincts also featured farce performances. In the Northern and Southern Sung dynasties, they were also called *tsa-chü*. The term *tsa-chü* was used in three senses. First, it referred to the entire variety show that was held in the pleasure precincts; second, it referred to the farce skit that was but one constituent of that long variety performance; third, it referred to the full-fledged Northern style music drama. The multiple use of the term is somewhat confusing, but also indicative of the close relationship between farce plays and later drama (see *tsa-chü*).

In the Chin, such variety shows and farce skits were called *yüan-pen*, a term that literally means, "scripts from the entertainer's guilds." Despite the difference in names in the Sung and Chin, the performance was basically the same: a four-part presentation framed by a musical prelude and postlude. This four-part performance began with a solo entertainment that, depending on the audience, was made up of either some kind of enconium or of jests and japes. This was followed by a main piece in two parts, one a slapstick farce involving the *fu-ching* role (as butt) and the *fu-mo* role (as knave) and the other a more serious drama involving other role types, either as singers or as players in a complicated drama (Idema and West, 1982, pp. 172-204; West, 1977, pp. 1-47; Tanaka, 1968). The final portion was usually a parody of country hicks, modelled on the bumpkins of Hopeh and Shantung who stumbled wide-eyed into the metrocapitals of North China. This four-part staging was probably the origin of the four-act structure of *tsa-chü* drama.

More important for the development of drama, however, was the appearance of troupes in these variety shows composed of role types (see *chiao-se*) instead of characters. These role types were based on *kinds* of roles played and stipulated both the performances and the professional training of entertainers. Variety troupes were composed of five role types:

mo-ni 末泥	: manager;
yin-hsi 引戲	: play leader;
fu-ching 付（副）淨	: second clown/butt;
fu-mo 付（副）末	: second male/knave;
ku 孤	: official (usually venal).

In early variety shows, the *fu-ching*/*fu-mo* team seems to have received the star billing, but as the musical aspect of Chinese theater grew, availing itself of the musical format of the *chu-kung-tiao,* the *mo-ni* and *yin-hsi* evolved, respectively, into the male and female singing leads, and became the star performers and most important members of later dramatic troupes, especially of northern *tsa-chü.*

Yüan *tsa-chü* was the most strictly regulated form of Chinese drama and the closest to the folk tradition. Severe restrictions in both the staging and the music led to particular literary characteristics. The major restrictions of (1) four acts per drama, with the option of a wedge, (2) one singing role per play, and (3) strict organization of musical arrangement, all exercised some influence of *tsa-chü* drama as literature.

The four-act structure clearly allowed only for a unilinear plot, one usually comprised of either four or five major scenes. This stereotyped plot development is akin in some respects to the traditional couplet structure of regulated verse (see *shih*): *ch'i* 起, *ch'eng* 承, *chuan* 轉, and *ho* 合, or "begin, continue, turn/twist, and resolve." In virtually every drama in the *tsa-chü* style, the second and third act are the high points of action, when both lyricism and action are at their peak. The fourth act, with some minor exceptions, is usually shorter than the other three (especially in the earliest editions of texts), and is devoted to restoring harmony in the social, judicial, or ethical world.

The convention of one singing lead per play can be thought of as a limitation, but in reality it simply allows the play to develop along different lines than one in which several characters/role types sing. The playwright is, for instance, free to focus his energies on the lyrics sung by one character. This has the effect of subordinating dramatic action to lyricism. This results in the underdevelopment of secondary characters, but it also allows for an ever-deepening psychological portrayal of the inner world of the major lead (Perng, 1978, pp. 85-146, esp. 109-120). This single character becomes the focus of interest in the drama, and his or her mind the mirror in which the reflected action of the play is seen.

In some plays the subordination of secondary characters to speaking roles clearly limits dramatic potential. For instance, in such plays as Ma Chih-yüan's* *Han-kung ch'iu* 漢宮秋 (Sorrow in the Han Palace) and Pai P'u's* *Wu-t'ung yü* 梧桐雨 (Rain on the Wu-t'ung Tree) the female characters, Wang Chao-chün and Yang Kuei-fei, certainly deserve a place in drama commensurate with their stature in legend and in other literature. Yet, despite their popularity, they remain backdrops or ironic foils to imperial grief, and the royal male presence dominates center stage.

There are even plays in which the main character either does not sing at all or is limited to one or two of the acts. For instance, in the first two acts of Kuan Han-ch'ing's* *Tan-tao hui* 單刀會 (A Single Sword Meeting), the male *role type* appears first in two separate characters to testify to the valor and martial prowess of the great Kuan Yü before his appearance on stage. Such character switching serves some dramatic purpose—here the first descriptions serve as testimony to the powers of a man already deified in the popular mind and provide an ironic background for this, Kuan Yü's last brilliant and prideful stroke before his lust for vengeance and his impetuosity bring the bravest knight of China to his death. (Although his death is not mentioned in the play, the incident of the single sword meeting occurs in the legend just before he meets his death.)

In addition to this limitation to a single singer, the stiff musical requirements also demand one modal suite per act. The mode used depended on the order of the acts—

there were stipulations about which modes belonged to which acts. Moreover, within each of these modal suites, the sequence of individual songs was also prescribed. Each of the modes was also thought to create its own special mood—heroic, sentimental, etc.—and when coupled with the stipulation of a single rhyme per suite, this resulted in a highly unified and integrated poetic structure for each act. The playwright capitalized on this unity to structure his work. Since each act was presented (usually) as a single scene or incident, only one theme or emotion was consistently stressed in an act. Thus, each drama was usually made up of four major scenes, each tightly structured by musical and metrical requirements, and there was only cursory (if any) development and subplots.

It is obvious that this form of staging and musical structure leaves little room for action. Any action in drama usually took place in farce interludes based on the old knave-and-butt routines or in displays of martial arts or acrobatics. Such interludes took place both between acts and at specific points in the actual performance, either allowing the singer to rest between acts or providing comedy or spectacle as relief for more serious action. Still, it is clear that the general absence of action leads to a consequent emphasis on lyricism as the major vehicle of dramatic interest. This has resulted in a dense, colloquial lyric poetry that is the hallmark of *tsa-chü* and later drama.

Yüan *tsa-chü* is one of two early forms of drama—the other is *nan-hsi*—that is close to folk traditions, and as long as it survived in the entertainment districts of the major cities, it remained a truly anonymous form. Because of its relationship to folk tradition and the survival rate of its scripts, Yüan theater has the largest known range of themes. Yet, despite its abundant thematic corpus, there is no standard classification of drama, as for instance, between comedy and tragedy in the West, and consequently there are no stipulated esthetic standards by which to compose or criticize *tsa-chü* or other forms. The lack of any serious consideration of dramatic form at the period of its flourishing is in marked contrast to the history of drama in the Western world and points to the different place that drama occupies in the classical canon of each civilization. Drama and the epic were the central forms of literature in the Greek world; both were considered inferior literature in the polite world of the classical Chinese.

There have been several attempts to categorize *tsa-chü* by various methods, although few have been made to draw thematic categories for either *ch'uan-ch'i* or *p'i-huang* plays. This suggests that once the general fund of themes of a strongly conventional tradition has been described for an earlier form, it is no longer necessary to repeat the process. This is especially true in the case of drama, where many plays on the same theme and with nearly or exactly the same title exist in the same time period. Moreover, the tradition in drama is to adapt earlier plays for production rather than create ones on new topics. Therefore, because of this predilection for adaptation and because the thematic boundaries of drama actually shrank with time, a thematic description of *tsa-chü* has general relevance for all other forms of drama as well.

Dramatic and literary historians, of course, categorize drama on the basis of form, as in this and other essays in this compendium. Another method of identifying plays is by their function or use. For instance, a distinction is often drawn between performable plays (*ch'ang-shang*場上: "on stage plays") and closet drama (*an-t'ou*案頭: "desktop dramas").

The most common way to describe the corpus of Yüan theater, however, is by topic. The earliest form of classification was the system of popular designations found in the *Ch'ing-lou chi,* a record of sing-song girls in the Yüan. In this work, we find five different kinds of dramas performed by the actresses:

1) *chia-t'ou* 駕頭   "plays about emperors";
2) *hua-tan* 花旦   "flowered female leads" (probably romances involving women of pleasure);
3) *juan-mo-ni* 軟末泥   "weak male leads";
4) *kuei-yüan* 閨怨   "boudoir laments";
5) *lü-lin* 綠林   "greenwood plays" (about bandits, especially those of the *Shui-hu chuan** legend).

In a later Ming-dynasty work (late fifteenth century), the *T'ai-ho cheng-yin-p'u* of Chu Ch'üan,* there are three more popular categories mentioned:

6) *chün-ch'en* 君臣   "lords and ministers";
7) *t'o-po* 脫膊   "bare arms" (martial arts plays);
8) *shen-fo* 神佛   "spirits and Buddhas."

Except for the category of "bare arms", all of these classifications are based on types of characters portrayed. To this list, Chu added twelve categories of his own:

1) *shen-hsien tao-hua* 神仙道化   "spiritual transcendence and transformation with the Tao";
2) *yin-chu lo-tao* 隱居樂道   "living in seclusion, rejoicing in the Tao" (also known as *lin-ch'üan ch'iu-ho* 林泉丘壑, "forest, springs, hills, and valleys");
3) *p'i-pao chien-tu* 披袍秉笏   "folding the robe, grasping the plaque" (also known as "lord and minister plays");
4) *chung-ch'en lieh-shih* 忠臣烈士   "loyal ministers and ardent men of worth";
5) *hsiao-i lien-chieh* 孝義廉節   "filiality and righteousness, incorruptibility and integrity";
6) *ch'ih-chien ma-ch'an* 叱奸罵讒   "rebuking treachery and cursing slander";
7) *chu-ch'en ku-tzu* 逐臣孤子   "banished ministers and orphaned sons";
8) *po-tao kan-pang* 鐐刀趕棒   "wielding blades and plying staffs";
9) *feng-hua hsüeh-yüeh* 風花雪月   "windy blossoms, snowy moonlight" (romantic plays);
10) *pei-huan li-ho* 悲歡離合   "grief and happiness at separation and reunion";
11) *yen-hua fen-tai* 烟花粉黛   "misty blossoms, powder and mascara" (love stories about courtesans);
12) *shen-t'ou kuei-mien* 神頭鬼面   "spirit-heads and ghostly faces."

The demarcation between several of these categories is unclear and they seem, in fact, to overlap. Seven of the twelve categories—1, 2, 5, 6, 8, 9, and 10—are based on content or theme, while the other five are tied primarily to the position, or status, of the characters involved. A modern classification by Lo Chin-t'ang (1960) lists altogether eight major categories: historical plays, social plays, household plays, love plays, plays about illicit romance, plays about eremites, Taoist and Buddhist plays, and plays about spirits and marvels.

From the standpoint of dramatic history, the rise of classification schemes in the Ming went hand in glove with the rising censorship of drama and with drama's slow climb up the social ladder. Earlier thematic classification, especially that in the *Ch'ing-*

lou chi, is molded by the context in which it is found. The *Ch'ing-lou chi* was, after all, a text about performers, and each of the five categories found there represents a performer's specialty. Chu Ch'üan, of course, is notorious for his efforts to ascribe the legitimate values of literati art to drama (Idema and West, 1982, pp. 135-169). His schema is partially based on that of the *Ch'ing-lou chi,* but the categories he created himself tend to be didactic and moralistic in their conception, and they reflect the rise in status of drama in general and *tsa-chü* in particular. This rise and the subsequent literati indulgence in drama as legitimate art also drew the attention of censors—either official or self-appointed. Gradually, through legal promulgation in the Ming and Ch'ing eras, the kinds of plays that could be performed were severely restricted (see Wang Hsiao-chuan, 1958). For instance, no plays about emperors, no plays with lewd or lascivious themes, and no plays that preached rebellious dissatisfaction with government policies were allowed on stage. These proscriptions were, of course, theoretical and the extent of their enforcement is unknown.

Love stories were the major interest of post-Yüan drama, and the earlier corpus of stories, which abounded in the freer atmosphere linked primarily to a popular audience, shrank considerably. This was undoubtedly also due to the predilections of dramatists, who tended to adapt earlier plays and earlier sources rather than strive for original creations.

Ch'uan-ch'i drama differs from *tsa-chü* in several respects. First, *ch'uan-ch'i* is a southern form. Its predecessor was the *nan-hsi* of the Southern Sung and Yüan. The shape of *nan-hsi* was unknown until the present century, when three texts that belonged to the dispersed collectanea *Yung-lo ta-tien* (see *lei-shu*) were found in London. This early form of drama, later to develop into *ch'uan-ch'i,* was noted for its earthy and sometimes vulgar language. Its musical lyrics are often indistinguishable from prose passages, and it used primarily folk tunes. Many of the plays were banned outright, probably because of their critical portrayal of the gentry-official class.

Ch'uan-ch'i supplanted *nan-hsi* as a viable form primarily due to the popularity of Kao Ming's* *P'i-p'a chi* 琵琶記. Like its predecessor, the *ch'uan-ch'i* also used southern music, although its lyrics were more sophisticated and polished. There was quite a bit of freedom in terms of musical arrangements, and while this form used primarily southern melodies, it was also free to mix northern and southern tunes together.

Another difference from northern *tsa-chü* was length: *ch'uan-ch'i* could range from 10 to 240 acts, and the average play had 30 to 50 acts. The dramas still continued to be divided into two major sections and the denouement of part one, like the third act of the *tsa-chü,* was usually the point of highest action. The play was introduced by a prologue (*chia-men* 家門) of two *tz'u* stanzas, which usually gave a generalized statement about the theme or incident that was central to the play.

In contrast to the strict rule of one modal suite per act in northern *tsa-chü,* the musical structure of *ch'uan-ch'i* was quite free. A suite usually consisted of an introduction (*yin-tzu* 引子), sequential songs (*kuo-ch'ü* 過曲), and a coda. A mode might be switched any time during an act, and in fact often was, usually to match a shift of emphasis or change of emotion within a scene.

Moreover, as contrasted to the single singing lead of *tsa-chü,* any player may sing in *ch'uan-ch'i,* although the male lead (*sheng* 生) and female lead (*tan* 旦) are usually predominant. The only requirement is that all characters must sing songs appropriate to

19

their roles. The *sheng* and *tan*, for instance, sing songs classified as *sheng-tan ch'ü*, or "songs for male and female leads," and the comic and the villain sing only *ching-ch'ou ch'iang*淨丑腔 (clown and comic melodies). These song types could not be intermixed.

Because of the kind of music used, the number of acts, the interchangeable use of modes, and the ability of every character to sing, *ch'uan-ch'i* is quite a bit freer in form than *tsa-chü* and perhaps a bit more realistic in its presentation of complex action. However, by the time *ch'uan-ch'i* rose to popularity the pool of playwrights was restricted primarily to the literati. Instead of using the new freedom to explore different dramatic possibilities, they simply exploited to the fullest the lyric potential of the music. Fond of erudition, they were inclined to fret over the language and style of the poetry of a play. Moreover, they severely limited the popular appeal of the plays by using drama much as they did other forms of literature—for venting their private frustrations, hopes, and desires through social and political allegory (cf. Wang Chiu-ssu and K'ang Hai). This private use of dramatic form was quite distinct from the popular themes of Yüan drama, which, although generally expressive of deep emotion, tended to be more collective and generalized than later literati drama. Although the new literati playwrights adopted, in some cases, a multilinear plot development, the plays generally lacked any organizational thread to bring all elements to a satisfactory conclusion, so that the integrity of the story was not consistently maintained throughout. (It should be pointed out that the great plays—"Mu-tan t'ing" [see T'ang Hsien-tsu], the "Ch'ang-sheng tien" [see Hung Sheng], etc.—were generally far better and more successful in maintaining unity and interest than the vast majority of *ch'uan-ch'i*.) Some playwrights resorted to the technique of a material symbol as a unifying factor, for instance the thorn hairpin in the drama of the same name, the engraved box in *Ch'ang-sheng tien*, or the peach blossom fan of its namesake drama (*T'ao-hua shan*, see K'ung Shang-jen). As one critic, Tseng Yung-i, has put it, "These artifacts are like a shuttle of a loom; back and forth they thread the fabric of such plays . . . and it is this method, indeed, which becomes the special characteristic of the structure of the *ch'uan-ch'i*" (1975, p. 4).

K'un-ch'ü is in reality simply a form of *ch'uan-ch'i* that is distinguished from the rest only by its use of music from the *K'un-shan*崑山 region of China. As far as literature is concerned, *K'un-ch'ü* shows the same general characteristics as *ch'uan-ch'i*. It dominated the Chinese stage until the middle of the seventeenth century, when it was gradually replaced by another form, the *p'i-huang-hsi*, better known in the West as Peking Opera (see *ching-chü*).

Peking Opera is of little literary interest. It is usually a fragmented and incomplete performance that uses single acts from a variety of sources. While it adapts these random acts from both *ch'uan-ch'i* and *tsa-chü*, it neglects all of their original conventions and formats of singing, prose, and recited sections. It makes no use of the modal suites of either earlier dramatic tradition and is entirely haphazard in its arrangements of scenes. Since it is primarily a musical and kinetic performance, its written text is terse in the extreme and of minimal value.

Dramatic literature, then, revolves around the texts left from the northern *tsa-chü* and southern *ch'uan-ch'i* traditions. From these works can be deduced some of the special shared characteristics that set Chinese drama apart from other traditions in the world, notably those of the Western tradition.

Tseng Yung-i (1975, pp. 1-45) has identified three salient features of the Chinese tradition: that it is symbolic rather than representational; that it tends toward hyperbole in presentation; that it creates an intentional distance between the action on stage and the audience. In addition to these three features, it should also be kept in mind that drama, like other performing literatures in China, was heavily didactic and served the double purpose of education and entertainment (Tseng Yung-i, 1975, pp. 36-37).

There are clear reasons why the Chinese theater went primarily in the direction of the symbolic rather than the mimetic and representational (a feature it shared with most Oriental theater, see Irwin, 1972, pp. 11-14, 17-19). The first is the structure of, and limited space on, the Chinese stage. The first physical locations for performances were simply cleared areas around which an audience gathered. The common phrase *hua-ti tso-ch'ang* 畫地作場 (to mark off the ground and perform) is used in earlier texts, and the recurrent use of the word *ch'ang* 場 (a square of cleared earth) derives from the practice of performing in the public square or the cleared area in a temple courtyard. Later, this square of earth was elevated, awnings were added, and finally the back portion of the stage was closed off to the public. In the end, three sides of the stage were shut to public view, or were crowded with musicians and extras (Feng Yüan-chün, 1956, pp. 1-120; Idema and West, 1982, pp. 185-191).

A single cloth hanging divided the back and front portions of the stage, leaving two doorways through which players entered and exited. No realistic scenery was allowed on stage (a holdover from the oral narrative tradition). A piece of large cloth might do for a city wall, a cart, or a mountain; a table could function as a judge's dais, a bed, a raised platform, or even—a table. Props were generally hand-held and were used for their symbolic value: a horsewhip for cavalry riders, a tally for Confucian officials.

Since the stage was devoid of scenery and props and was a small and restricted area, movement and nonlinguistic references on stage were limited. This also influenced characterization (through role types, facial makeup, and costuming), music (and poetic lyrics), spoken dialogue, and the kinetic actions of pantomime, gesture, and spectacle.

Role types (see *chiao-se*) were originally named on the basis of their status or their characteristics. For instance, in early farces one finds the *ku*, or official, the *tan*, or female, the *suan*, or scholar, and the *mo* and *ching*, or knave and butt. Later, in the *tsa-chü* of the Yüan period, one finds four major roles: *cheng-mo*, male lead, *cheng-tan*, female lead, *ching*, or comic-cum-villain, and *ch'ou*, or clown. Because of the rise of music drama, the *mo* and *tan* were the major roles of *tsa-chü*. Southern drama added the *sheng*, or young male. To these five roles, Peking Opera added the *liu* 流, "flag bearers," *wu* 武, bullies who stood on the sides of the major performance, and the *shang-hsia shou*, "upper and lower hands," the armies of government forces (upper hands) and the bands of anti-government gangs (lower hands). All of these last types were involved with some kind of acrobatic or martial art performance.

These role types were not meant to portray realistic characters, but to be exemplary models of human conduct, personifications of moral traits. There is a strong tendency, in Chinese literature in general, to stress the universal and repetitive in human nature rather than the specific and unique personality of an individual. One has only to look, for instance, at historical biography or characters from popular legend to see that the tendency is to introduce only a limited number of incidents that capture the moral essence of the individual—that is, what is symbolic or exemplary in that individual's social and ethical existence, or what allows him to be categorized according to the extrinsic moral criteria of the Confucian ethical tradition.

The same holds true for the role types of drama: They are meant to represent moral and social kinds rather than unique personalities. This is partially attributable to the overtly didactic element in Chinese entertainment. Since the dramatist found himself in the same position as the storyteller in regard to consensual values, he had to strive to uphold the ancient tradition that "good and evil should be clearly discriminated and that the upright are praised and the vile excoriated," while telling a story that could arouse human interest. This is clear in early drama, where the *sheng* and the *tan* invariably portray characters who are good, learned, loyal, upright, and ritually proper in their deportment and the *ching* and *ch'ou* are either comic, crafty, or villainous. In the farce plays, strong conventions were woven about such characters: the official, for instance, was either the shining paragon of justice or a venal and corrupt worm, the *suan* usually a headstrong examination-bound student who sacrifices his one moment of freedom from family authority to pursue a courtesan.

This tendency toward character as symbol led easily to satire and allegory, especially when drama passed into the hands of the literati in the Ming. They were trained in the arts of polite literature, which dealt heavily with social criticism and political allegory, and they incorporated these ideals (as well as their private grievances) into drama. It was easy, given the already heavily symbolic nature of characters on stage, to turn them into participants in a broad political allegory.

This trend was strengthened by the proliferation of role types over time. They became more and more specialized and were divided into many subcategories. For instance, the earliest reference to the female role is by the name *chuang-tan* 裝旦, which means "one who [temporarily] costumes as the female." By the Yüan, the *tan* was a full-fledged type, and soon afterward was broken into several smaller categories: the *erh-tan*, "second female lead," the *t'ieh-tan* or "added female," and the *hua-tan*, or "painted female role." Later, these role types fragmented even further. The *se-tan* 色旦, or "colored female role", played women of bad character or prostitutes; the *kuei-men tan* 閨門旦, or "inner chamber female role," played a young maiden not yet sent out to marriage. The *ch'ing-i* 青衣, or "green robe," of Peking Opera played a middle-aged *Hausfrau*.

These later subdivisions, based on the *moral quality* of character, had their own associated gesture and costume. For instance, the backchamber role had to be "elegant and solemn" in her posture and have a singing voice that was both "lilting and elegant," that is, a voice suitable to a young virginal maiden. The green robe, on the other hand, had to be able to portray "spirited yet resolute" gestures and sing and speak in a cultured but authoritative tone. It is obvious, then, that the gestures and songs became more stereotyped and symbolic with the passage of time. The influence of these stage conventions is reflected in the descriptive lyrics and dialogue of extant texts.

The emphasis on universal traits also led to stipulated makeup for role types. This phenomenon goes back at least as far as the puppet and shadow plays of Northern and Southern Sung and the farce plays of North China. According to *Tu-ch'eng chi-sheng* (see *Tung-ching meng Hua lu*):

> The noble and upright [characters of shadow plays] are carved with an upright demeanor, the wicked and evil with an ugly mien. That was probably to put the praise of the good and the censure of the evil into the. "eye entertainments" of the marketplace commoner (Idema and West, 1982, p. 80).

The farce plays of Sung and Chin also clearly show that the *ching* role had a limed face striped with black, and in Yüan drama Li K'uei, the hero of the Water Margin stories (see *Shui-hu chuan*), often goes to great lengths to describe his black countenance. By the advent of the Ming there is clear indication that there was a distinction between black, red, white, green, and pied facial makeup—a convention systematized and regularized in the stylized makeup and masks of the Peking Opera.

Different colors, of course, represented different qualities of characters. Black usually signified great loyalty and righteousness; white, treachery; blue, arrogant tyranny; green, fierce violence. Some of these colors themselves stem from earlier prosimetric and narrative traditions. For instance, red is the color of bravery and loyalty, and is usually associated with the great martial hero, Kuan Yü, who is described in the earliest source (the *tsa-chü*, the *San-kuo p'ing-hua* [see *p'ing-hua*], and the *San-kuo chih yen-i**) as "nine-feet tall, with a long two-foot beard, and a face [red as] a jujube. His lips are like painted rouge, with cinnabar phoenix eyes, and reclining silkworm brows."

Besides color, other facial role markers included exaggerated, stylized expressions and beards of varying lengths or no beard at all. Generally, the more solemn or serious a character, the more beard; characters of expansive loyalty, for instance, are usually full-bearded while the comic and flippant roles are bare-faced.

Costuming was likewise a way of indexing character types. The earliest archaeological evidence shows conventional forms of dress for the knave and butt of the farce skit (West, 1977, pp. 38-45; Idema and West, 1982, pp. xii-xv; Maeda, 1979, for summaries of early costuming), and wall murals and figurines from the Yüan period all point to a developing tradition of highly systematized modes of costuming. In the *Mai-wang-kuan* editions of Yüan *tsa-chü* (see *tsa-chü*) some of the earlier texts still list the costumes to be worn by major roles. Feng Yüan-chün has divided these costumes into six classifications:

> Those that show the differences between native Chinese and non-Chinese roles; those that show differences between military and civil roles; those that show differences between noble and base roles; those that show differences between rich and poor; those that show differences between young and old; those that show differences between good and evil (Feng Yüan-chün, 1956, pp. 74-82).

Sometimes, the traditions of popular romances and the stylized conventions of makeup and costuming distort history. For instance, Chu-ko Liang 諸葛亮 (181-234) is known in history as a staunch Confucian advisor to the emperor. But in the popularizations of the Three Kingdoms' legends, he has been turned into a Taoist wizard. In the Yüan play *Po-wang shao-t'un* 博望燒屯 (*Mai-wang-kuan* ed.), he appears on stage carrying Taoist paraphernalia, wearing Taoist robes, and donning a full beard. His antagonist, Chou Chin, is presented "in the flower of his bravery" and is wearing no beard. This destroys historical accuracy, because we know that Chou Chin was the elder of the pair by seven years. But he died at thirty-six, while Chu-ko Liang lived to be fifty-four, so he is represented, anachronistically, on stage as the older and more mature figure.

These elements of staging, costuming, makeup, and their associated gestures and song performances clearly lead to a process of exaggerating the dominant characteristics of each role type. Systemization and stylization simply exaggerate their particular moral or ethical quality to the exclusion of individuating characteristics. Hyperbole functions as the handmaiden of symbolism.

The heavily symbolic nature of the Chinese theater also allowed a certain artistic distance to develop between the audience and the play. The intimate nature of the Chinese stage has already been noted. The earliest audiences pressed around the cleared space on all sides, and even later, when stages were raised and closed off on one or more sides, the physical distance between the audience and the action was slight. However, the audience was fluid and there was (and still is) a constant flow of people in and out of the theater. The typical audience of Chinese music drama was mobile, noisy, and heavily involved in the stagecraft—for instance, this description of the theater during the Ch'ing period:

> All of the theater parks have tea service, but no wine, so they are called "tea halls" or "tea parks." . . . There is much tea-conversation and an intermingled sea of people. When the various performers ascend the stage to each perform his or her speciality, then the drums and gongs clang and bang. The sounds of shouting "marvelous, marvelous" are often like ten thousand crows vying in their chattering (quoted in Tseng, 1975, p. 32).

Moreover, a play was constantly interrupted between acts and during scenes by non-dramatic performances: farce skits introduced for comic relief, acrobatics, swordplay, walking on ropes, etc. Therefore, there was little sense of the progression of a story or a plot. There was, instead, a heavy emphasis on providing pleasure and entertainment through spectacle. In such situations, the audience probably did not identify with the characters as is done, for instance, in modern (post-Renaissance) theater in the West—as real people undergoing real experience. The Chinese dramatist was not interested in mimetic verisimilitude, but rather with character as the embodiment of generalized philosophical or moral truth.

This does not mean that the audience was incapable of sympathy or empathy with those characters. Rather they saw the role types of Chinese drama as projections of their own hopes, their own sense of justice, tragedy, or humor in a highly stylized form. Furthermore, these symbolic presentations of abstract moral principles were also effective as didacticism, presenting typical human responses to typical situations, teaching correct behavior in a highly ritualized and authoritarian social world. Chinese drama deals in universal truths in action, not with particularized and idiosyncratic psychological states.

This lack of attention to mimetic action on stage led to several characteristics of drama both as stagecraft and as literature. First, there is relatively little attention to plot development. The focus of the stage performance was music—the arias sung by one or more lead singers. In turn, the lyrics of these arias became the focus of literary appreciation. Second, drama abounds in the anachronistic use of locations, places, people, and official ranks. Third, any consistency of tone disappears through the constant interruption of plot by elements of spectacle. And if no need was felt for a continuous, tightly woven plot or for consistency of tone on stage, their influence was certainly not to be felt in the literary text. There is no consistently "tragic" or comic tone in the majority of dramas, and elements of each are mixed indiscriminately in a single play. Moreover, since compilers of scripts kept them primarily as curiosity pieces or as texts of a lower order of literature, they did not feel inclined to correct the anachronisms or to rewrite the play, as literature, in a more consistent tone. What the editors did labor over were the lyrics of the songs—a natural predilection, given the dominant position of the poetic lyric in the Chinese literary tradition.

Such a fluid audience and fragmented performance also placed severe restrictions on theme and plot. The reader of Chinese drama cannot help being impressed by the predilection for imitation and adaptation of earlier or contemporary stories and the importance of history and popular legend as source material. Dramatists inevitably picked well-worn stories for their plays, and there are clear reasons for this choice. Music was the center of Chinese drama; therefore the author expended his energy on the lyrics and the actors devoted theirs to singing and the associated gestures of dance and proper hand movement. Moreover, the audience paid closest attention to the songs, finding the music and dance to be their major source of entertainment.

This accounts in part for the fluid nature of the audience—if they knew the story beforehand, then they could concentrate on the quality of the performance. They could walk into the middle of a play, know the story thoroughly, pick up on the action in the proper place, and let the judgment rest on the quality of the star's voice. This does not demand close attention to plot. If, in fact, the audience has to concentrate on the unravelling of a complex and new story, their attention will be diverted from the musical performance. Therefore, authors tended to select stories that had passed through years, even centuries, of storytellers' mouths.

Stylization, as noted above, leads easily to allegory, and historical figures and events provided many incidents that could be used to indirectly vent grievances and make ironic references to, or even pointed satire about, contemporary events or people. In Yüan theater, this kind of reference was highly generalized and can be seen as a collective expression. Such upright though diverse characters as Judge Pao and the bandits of the Liang-shan Marshes (see *Shui-hu chuan*) provided hope for an audience used to injustices of various kinds, as did stories of retribution levied in the hereafter by ghosts and spirits against the evil and corrupt. When drama began to be the province of the literati, the allegory became more pointed and specific. Ministers and eunuchs in power were criticized by analogy with historical example, and figures from antiquity mouthed political criticism meant for the current court. (see especially K'ang Hai and Wang Chiu-ssu entries).

As stressed above, plot structure was not a primary concern of the dramatist. In real terms, only a few of the major dramas achieved complete integrity in their development of plot. The causes for this haphazard treatment of story-line have been suggested above—the influence of the prosimetric narrative and the predominant emphasis on poetic lyricism. Lyricism, and the expansion of the world of the drama through one or more character's minds, led to a symbolic but emotionally charged characterization. Plot itself was usually dependent on the unfolding of a single story in unilinear progression; any movement in the direction of subplot was severely restricted or, in fact, left unresolved. Suspense and countermotion in plot were seldom-used devices. Chinese drama was also extraordinarily free in its flow across space and time, and there are none of the severe restrictions of the nature of the three unities of the classical Western tradition. Therefore, to a person nurtured on the tightly controlled drama based on the Greek model, Chinese drama may seem distracted, loose, and uncontrolled to the point of haphazard presentation. However, the true beauty of the Chinese tradition lies in the complex emotions presented through lyrical exposition.

In some respects, lyrics do the work done by dialogue in Western drama. First, as noted above, they are heavily descriptive. The stage was bare of scenery, and the long descriptions of setting, natural scenery, or seasonal symbols serve to decorate the stage in the mind of the audience. They are also used to describe a past or present situation that has some bearing on the incidents that unfold on stage. They also describe stage actions that might otherwise be unclear without verbal commentary.

But the most important use of lyrics is the description of complex states of interior psychology. The singer is the mirror of the play's action and its development. In the earlier tradition of the *tsa-chü*, and to some extent in the later *ch'uan-ch'i* plays, this elevates the lead player to the level of commentator and center of consciousness. Lead players not only present their own psychological and emotional responses to situations, but feel free to interpret or comment on the actions and motives of other characters. Rhetorically, then, the singers provide both moral commentary and a psychological exposition of their own interior state. Therefore, while the character may not be said to develop through progressive plot action as "round" or "dynamic" characters do in Western drama, there are still ever-deepening levels of psychological interest, expecially as related to a general concept of moral or social types.

The role of prose (*pin-pai* 賓白) in drama, which is often overlooked, is varied. The earliest dramatic texts (published during the first third of the fourteenth century) omitted dialogue from the script, keeping only stage directions and cue lines. This had led some people to speculate that playwrights wrote only the poetic lyrics and that the prose dialogue was added by actors at the time of performance. Since, however, the cue lines often parallel those of later editions of the same dramas, there does not seem to be much evidence for this brief. It is not known, however, how dialogue was performed in Yüan plays. In the later traditions, especially *ch'uan-ch'i* and Peking Opera, the spoken portions of the text bear no resemblance to everyday language. Whether used as ordinary dialogue, as intrusive speech in the arias themselves, or to recite poetry, aphorisms, or doggerel, prose has its own repertoire of performance. In this later drama, it is usually highly stressed and modulated and is performed often to the accompaniment of gongs, drums, or clappers. It is, in reality, a form of singing. There is strong evidence that prose in early Yüan plays was performed far closer to ordinary speech, but in the later tradition, prose is really a recitation, an extension of the singing parts. Functionally, as in other forms of performing literature, prose is used to advance the plot while the lyrics repeat the action through the eyes of the singer or expand the emotional dimensions of scenes just carried out in dialogue. Dramatic criticism has tended to downplay the role of prose in drama, but the common expression from Peking Opera, "a thousand catties of spoken text, four taels of singing," demonstrates the importance of the prose sections to the drama as a whole.

Dramatic criticism has generally tended to concentrate on the musical and poetic aspects of the theater to the exclusion of other elements. The first work of secondary nature to be produced were the so-called *yüeh-p'u* 樂譜 (musical formularies). These were repositories of the songs of drama, arranged according to mode. They were meant as guides for composition of lyrics and included the complex metrical patterns of each song, including markings for "main characters"—characters used for the base prosodic structure and for padding works—characters that were used at the head or in the middle of arias, where they functioned as extra-metrical beats. The major contribution of such works today, since the music is now lost, is that they have preserved melodies and lyrics that have been lost in other forms and some earlier versions of lyrics in later editions. Sometimes, as in the case of Chu Ch'üan's* *T'ai-ho cheng-yin-p'i,* the formularies will also include guidelines for playwrights about how to create verse. This was the case in the *Chung-yüan yin-yün,** where there are listed "ten rules on the composition of lyrics" that provide guidelines for such things as the correct kinds of language to use in composition, the kind of dialect, the proper sociolect, etc.

The most important later formularies were the *Sheng-shih hsin-sheng* 盛世新聲, the *Tz'u-lin chai-yen* 詞林摘艷, and the *Yung-hsi yüeh-fu* 雍熙樂府. All three of these formularies are Ming compilations and collect the songs of Yüan *ch'ü,* primarily those of drama. The works are indispensable sources for the textual study of early drama.

Dramatic criticism is also a fairly recent development. Drama was not, until the Ming dynasty, a legitimate scholarly pursuit and was primarily considered a literature of amusement, even when written by the scholar. There were indeed few writers who considered themselves specialists in drama. Critics of these early times either concentrated on the musical aspects of drama or were content to record scattered and unsystematic comments on drama much like the popular form of poetic criticism, the *shih-hua.** Even then, their discussions were likely to concentrate on the language of drama, the metrical requirements, or the style of the poetry (i.e., style in the sense of "atmosphere" [*feng-ko*]). The major works of such criticism have recently been collected in an important work entitled *Chung-kuo ku-tien hsi-ch'ü lun-chu chi-ch'eng* 中國古典戲曲論著集成 (A Compendium of Essays on Classical Chinese Theater). Two exceptions to the haphazard and unsystematic writings of these early critics can be found in Wang Chi-te* and Li Yü* (1611-1679), who between them wrote the most complete discussions of drama. Wang Chi-te's *Ch'ü-lü* is a discussion of both the dramatic and lyric *ch'ü* (i.e., the *san-ch'ü*). It is a long work of some forty-odd sections, but only four of them are entirely devoted to drama, and only fragments of a few more mention dramatic works. None of Wang's discussions of drama are systematic enough to gain a clear impression of what his own ideas and concepts of drama were. The systematic study of drama begins with Li Yü, who considered theater in a holistic sense as a art comprising both literature and stagecraft. He paid attention not only to the lyrics and prose passages of drama, but also to the way that dance, song, and gesture were preformed on stage. Li Yü, however, had some failings as a critic, and he did not maintain strict boundaries to the categories he created (Tseng, 1976, pp. 2-3).

The modern study of drama began with the groundbreaking work of Wang Kuo-wei,* who in 1912 wrote the first modern treatise on drama. Since that time, the study of drama has flourished first in China, and then, in the 1920s and 1930s, in Japan, where Aoki Masaru, Yoshikawa Kōjirō, and Tanaka Kenji have been at the forefront of the study of stage literature. In the past thirty years, such eminent writers as Chou I-pai, Hu Chi, Chao Ching-shen, and Feng Yüan-chun in the People's Republic of China and Cheng Ch'ien and Tseng Yung-i in the Republic of China have contributed to the ever-growing body of modern historical and critical work on the Chinese theater.

EDITIONS:

(Most editions will be listed under separate entries, see, especially, *tsa-chü, ch'uan-ch'i, K'un-ch'ü,* and *ching-chü.*)

Ku-pen. 1954-1958. *Ku-pen hsi-ch'ü ts'ung-k'an wei-yüan-hui* 古本戲曲叢刊委員會, ed. *Ku-pen hsi-ch'ü ts'ung-k'an* (I, IV, IX). Shanghai. The most complete collection of dramas available; generally photolithographic reproductions of the best texts available, after original manuscripts. A variorum edition.

Fu, Ao 傅傲. 1962. *Chung-kuo li-tai hsi-ch'ü hsüan* 中國歷代戲曲選. Shanghai. A punctuated selection of representative dramas from the Yüan through the Ch'ing, with annotations in modern Chinese.

Hu, Chi 胡忌. 1959, 1960, 1962. *Ku-tai hsi-ch'ü hsüan-chi* 古代戲曲選集. Peking. A very short selection of acts from the most famous *tsa-chü* and *ch'uan-ch'i* dramas of the Yüan and Ming periods.

TRANSLATIONS:

(Translations of dramas are generally either individual works or are generic groupings. These works have been listed under specific entries—i.e., *tsa-chü,* etc. Only translations that incorporate more than one kind of drama are listed here.)

Dolby, William. 1977. *Eight Chinese Plays.* New York.

Iriya, Yoshitaka 入矢義高, *et al.* 1971. *Gikyokushu* 戲曲集. 2v., in *Chūgoku kotenbungaku taikei* 中國古典文學大系, v. 52 and 53. Tokyo.

STUDIES:

Aoki, Masaru 青木正兒. 1937. *Shina kinsei gikyokushi* 支那近世戲曲史. Tokyo. Translated as *Chung-kuo chin-shih hsi-ch'ü shih* 中國近世戲曲史, Wang Ku-lu 王古魯, trans. Peking, 1958.

Chang, Chiang-ts'ai 張江裁. 1934. *Ch'ing-tai Yen-tu li-yüan shih-liao* 清代燕都梨園史料. Peking. A collection of Ch'ing *pi-chi* or miscellaneous records on theater life.

Chang, Keng 張庚 and Kuo Han-ch'eng 郭漢城. 1981. *Chung-kuo hsi-ch'ü t'ung-shih* 中國戲曲通史. 3v. Peking.

Chang, Ti-hua 張棣華. 1976. *Shan-pen chü-ch'ü ching-yen lu* 善本劇曲經眼錄. Taipei. A detailed description of the editions of dramas in Taiwan's libraries that were seen by the writer. An accurate account of extant manuscripts of good quality.

Chao, Ching-shen 趙景深. 1957. *Yüan Ming nan-hsi k'ao-lüeh* 元明南戲考略. Peking.

———. 1959. *Ming Ch'ing ch'ü-t'an* 明清曲談. Shanghai.

———. 1959. *Tu-ch'ü hsiao-chi* 讀曲小記. Peking.

———. 1962. *Hsi-ch'ü pi-t'an* 戲曲筆談. Peking.

Ch'en, Chih-hsien 陳志憲. n.d. *Ku-tien hsi-ch'ü yen-chiu lun-wen-chi* 古典戲曲研究論文集. Hong Kong.

Ch'en, Wan-nai 陳萬鼐. 1956. *Yüan Ming Ch'ing chü-ch'ü shih* 元明清劇曲史. Taipei.

Cheng, Chen-to 鄭振鐸. 1957. "*Sheng-shih hsin-sheng* yü *Tz'u-lin chai-yen*" 盛世新聲與詞林摘艷, in *Chung-kuo wen-hsüeh yen-chiu* 中國文學研究, Peking, pp. 971-1005. Along with the next entry, the two best works on traditional formularies.

———. 1957a. "*Tz'u-lin chai-yen* li te hsi-ch'ü tso-chia chi san-ch'ü tso-chia k'ao" 詞林摘艷裏的戲曲作家及散曲作家考, in *ibid.*, pp. 640-752.

Cheng, Ch'ien 鄭騫. 1951. "*Tung Hsi-hsiang* yü ts'u chi Nan-pei ch'ü te kuan-hsi" 董西廂與詞及南北曲的關係., *Wen-shih-che hsüeh-pao,* 2, 113-137.

Ch'i Ju-shan Hsien-sheng i-chu pien-yin wei-yüan-hui 齊如山先生遺著編印委員會, eds. 1964. *Ch'i Ju-shan ch'üan-chi* 齊如山全集. Taipei.

Chou, I-pai 周貽白. 1934. *Chung-kuo hsi-chü-shih lüeh* 中國戲劇史略. Shanghai.

———. 1953. *Chung-kuo hsi-chü-shih* 中國戲劇史. 3v. Peking. The single most authoritative, complete, and accurate history of Chinese drama in any language.

———. 1958. *Chung-kuo hsi-chü-shih chiang-tso* 中國戲劇史講座. Peking.

———. 1960. *Chung-kuo hsi-ch'ü lun-chi* 中國戲曲論集. Peking.

———. 1962. *Hsi-ch'ü yen-ch'ang lun-chu chi-shih* 戲曲演唱論著輯釋. Peking. Annotations to and discussions of four major works of dramatic criticism.

Chuang, I-fu 莊一符. 1982. *Ku-tien hsi-ch'ü ts'un-mu hui-k'ao* 古典戲曲存目彙考. 3v. Shanghai. An exhaustive bibliography of *tsa-chü* and *ch'uan-ch'i* from Sung-Yüan to modern times.

Chung-kuo hsi-ch'ü yen-chiu-yüan 中國戲曲研究院, ed. 1960. *Chung-kuo ku-tien hsi-ch'ü lun-chu chi-ch'eng* 中國古典戲曲論著集成. 10v. Peking. A meticulously collated collection of the major works of dramatic criticism. Each work has been evaluated in terms of sources and editions, and has been meticulously compared and collated, with all variant readings recorded in the notes.

Chung-kuo ta pai-k'o ch'üan-shu, Hsi-ch'ü ch'ü-i 中國大百科全書, 戲曲曲藝. Peking and Shanghai, 1983.

Crump, J. I. 1980. *Chinese Theater in the Days of Kublai Khan.* Tucson.

Dolby, William. 1976. *A History of Chinese Drama.* London.

———. "The Origins of Chinese Puppetry," *BSOAS,* 41 (1978), 97-120.

Fu, Hsi-hua 傅惜華. 1957. *Ku-tien hsi-ch'ü sheng-yüan lun-chu ts'ung-pien* 古典戲曲聲樂論著叢編. Peking.

Gimm, Martin. 1966. *Das Yüan-fu tsa-lu des Tuan An-chieh; Studien zur Geschichte von Musik, Schauspiel un Tanz in der T'ang Dynastie.* Wiesbaden.

Hsi-chü pao 戲劇報 editorial board, ed. 1962. *Li-shih-chu lun chi* 歷史劇論集. Shanghai.

———. 1980. *Hsi-ch'ü yen-chiu* 戲曲研究. Chi-lin.

Idema, Wilt. 1978. "Stage and Court in China: The Case of Hung-wu's Imperial Theater," *JOS,* 16, 63-78.

Idema, Wilt and Stephen West. 1982. *Chinese Theater from 1100-1450: A Source Book.* Wiesbaden.

Irwin, Vera. 1972. *Four Classical Asian Plays.* Baltimore. Contains excellent essays on the staging of Chinese drama in the context of Asian drama.

Iwaki, Hideo 岩城秀夫. 1972. *Chōku gikyoku engeki kinkyu* 中國戲曲演劇研究. Tokyo.

Jen, Pan-t'ang 任半塘. 1958. *T'ang hsi-nung* 唐戲弄. Peking.

Li, Hsiao-ts'ang 李嘯倉. 1953. *Sung Yüan chi-i tsa-k'ao* 宋元伎藝雜考. Shanghai.

Liu, Nien-tz'u 劉念慈. 1974. "Ts'ung chien-kuo hou fa-hsien-te i-hsieh wen-wu k'an Chin Yüan tsa-chü tsai P'ing-yang ti-ch'ü te fa-chan" 從建國後發現的一些文物看金元雜劇在平陽地區的發展, in *Wen-shih lun-ts'ung* 文史論叢, Hong Kong, pp. 388-404.

Lo, Chin-t'ang 羅錦堂. 1966. *Chung-kuo hsi-ch'u tsung-mu hui-pien* 中國戲曲總目彙編. Hong Kong.

———. 1977. *Chin-t'ang lun-ch'ü* 錦堂論曲. Taipei.

———. 1960. *Hsien-ts'un Yüan-jen tsa-chü pen-chih-k'ao* 現存元人雜劇本事考. Taipei.

Van der Loon, Piet. 1977. "Les Origines Rituelles du Theater Chinois," *JA,* 265, 141-168.

Mackerras, Colin, ed. 1983. *Chinese Theater from its Origins to the Present Day.* Honolulu.

———. 1976. "Modern Chinese Scholarship on Theater History," *Papers on Far Eastern History,* 13, 163-190.

Maeda, Robert. 1974. "Some Sung, Chin, and Yüan Representations of Actors," *ArA,* 41, 132-156.

Perng, Ching-hsi. 1978. *Double Jeopardy: A Critique of Seven Yüan Courtroom Dramas.* Ann Arbor.

Sun, K'ai-ti 孫楷第. 1953. *K'uei-lei-hsi k'ao-yüan* 傀儡戲考原. Shanghai.

———. 1965. *Ts'ang-chou-chi* 滄州集. Peking. The collected works of Sun, including many essays on drama and on early Chinese drama.

T'an, Cheng-pi 譚正璧. 1957. *Hua-pen yü ku-chü* 話本與古劇. Shanghai.

T'ang, Ts'ao-yüan 湯草元 and T'ao Hsiung 陶雄, eds. 1981. *Chung-kuo hsi-ch'ü-i tz'u-tien* 中國戲曲曲藝詞典. Shanghai.

Ting, Ming-i 丁明夷. 1972. "Shan-hsi chung-nan-pu te Sung Yüan hsi-t'ai" 山西中南部的宋元戲台, in *Wen-wu,* 4 (1972), 46-56; translated by Stephen H. West, "Stages Unearthed in South-Central Portion of Shansi, *Journal of Chinese Archaeology,* 1 (1979), 25-47.

Tseng, Yung-i 曾永義. 1975. *Chung-kuo ku-tien hsi-ch'ü lun-chi* 中國古典戲劇論集. Taipei. A collection of thoughtful essays on such topics as the characteristics of Chinese drama, its symbolic nature, and the categorization of drama.

———. 1976. *Shou hsi-ch'ü* 說戲曲. Taipei. Includes discussions of the difference between "substantive" and fictional topics, and on such diverse topics as the role of the spirit world in Chinese drama.

Tung, Mei-k'an 董每戡. 1983. *Shuo-chü* 說劇. Peking. A collection of essays on various aspects of the history of Chinese drama.

Wang, Hsiao-chuan 王曉傳. 1958. *Yüan Ming Ch'ing san-tai chin-hui hsiao-shuo hsi-ch'ü shih-liao* 元明清三代禁毀小說戲曲史料. Peking.

Wang, Kuo-wei 王國維. 1957. *Wang Kuo-wei hsi-ch'ü lun-wen-chi* 王國維戲曲論文集. Peking. The collected writings of the father of modern criticism of Chinese drama.

Wang, P'ei-lun 王沛綸, ed. 1975. *Hsi-ch'ü tz'u-tien* 戲曲辭典. Taipei.

West, Stephen H. 1977. *Vaudeville and Narrative: Aspects of Chin Theater.* Wiesbaden.

Wu, Kuo-ch'in 吳國欽. 1980. *Chung-kuo hsi-ch'ü shih man-hua* 中國戲曲史漫話. Shanghai.

Yao, Christina Shu-hwa. 1983. "*Cai-zi jia-ren:* Love Drama During the Yuan, Ming and Qing Periods." Unpublished Ph.D. dissertation, Stanford University.

Yeh, Te-chün 葉德均. 1953. *Sung Yüan Ming chiang-ch'ang wen-hsüeh-shih* 宋元明講唱文學史. Shanghai.

———. 1979. *Hsiao-shuo hsi-ch'ü ts'ung-k'ao* 小說 戲曲叢考. 2v. Peking. A collection of essays on Chinese drama and fiction.

Yüan Ming Ch'ing hsi-ch'ü yen-chiu lun-wen-chi 元 明清戲曲研究論文集. 1957,1959. V. 1 and 2. Peking.

—SHW

FICTION

Y.W. Ma

FICTION, in the present context, may be defined as a composition written mainly in prose that creates an imaginative rather than factual reality. This permits the exclusion of drama and narrative poetry. It not only creates an imaginative reality, but brings about a reality which is the result of a conscious act on the part of the author. This helps to draw lines between fiction on the one hand and parables, folklore, and various components of mythology on the other. Function should not be a measuring standard either; whether a composition entertains, instructs, persuades, or arouses should not affect its being classified as fiction. Similarly, formalistic elements such as situation, plot, character, theme, and point of view can be useful in analysis, but their existence or non-existence should have little to do with identifying a work as fiction. History and fiction share many such elements, for example. To use them as criteria as evidence that a work is fictional, therefore, would overstress the differences between otherwise markedly distinguished genres.

Of course, the presentation of an imaginative reality does not exclude the use of fact. Both fictional works heavily dependent upon historical sources and fictional works with unambiguous disclaimers of being fiction are by no means rare. In a novel as factual as the *Tung-Chou lieh-kuo chih* 東周列國志 (Records of the Many States of the Eastern Chou Dynasty) or a work of history as event-oriented as the *T'ung-chien chi-shih pen-mo* 通鑑紀事本末 (The Comprehensive Mirror for Aid in Government Topically Arranged), it is the authorial intention and the physical form in which the work is cast that really count. Fiction is therefore more subject matter presented in a prescribed way than a type of literature easily definable by extrinsic factors. There are, needless to say, no hard and fast rules; a work like *T'ai-wan wai-chi* 臺灣外紀 [Informal Records of Taiwan] has equally been claimed by the historian and the scholar of fiction.

In the case of Chinese fiction, much of the confusion is caused by the use of an ancient term for a late literary development. Unlike its modern English equivalent with its Latin root meaning "to make," the Chinese term *hsiao-shuo,** which goes back to a reference in the *Chuang-tzu*, did not originally mean much more than "small talk," which included but was not limited to rumors and word-of-mouth. These were trivial matters in comparison with political annoucements, philosophical deliberations, and moralistic remarks. While the provenance of the *Chuang-tzu* chapter concerned is disputed, the long list of works in the "I-wen chih" chapter of the *Han-shu* (see Pan Ku) labelled *hsiao-shuo* makes it clear that use of the term was already established during the Former Han. None of the works listed survived even until the T'ang period, but judging from their titles and from the few extant fragments, it seems clear that they were miscellaneous writings on different subjects considered to be less significant in those days, that few if any of them could have been conscious creations of imaginative reality, and that as a group they were denied the dignity of being considered one of the nine Han schools of learning. Such ancient references should be registered to clarify the early connotations of *hsiao-shuo* and other similar terms, but they should not be cited as evidence of the early development of fiction in China.

Another source of confusion is the desire, particularly strong among literary historians, to trace the development of a tradition far beyond what can be proved on concrete evidence. The quality and the attractiveness of a tradition are often seen as in direct proportion to its complexity and the length of its history. National pride too has much to do with this sentiment—few nations care to be thought of as having short cultural histories. As a result of this, there have been enthusiastic remarks about the narrative techniques of the *Tso-chuan*,* the *Chan-kuo ts'e*,* and other pre-Ch'in texts, on the fictional quality of Ssu-ma Ch'ien's* *Shih-chi*,* and on the excellence of the *Yen Tan-tzu*ardt as a fine example of the earliest fiction. Cases like the *Yen Tan-tzu* involve problems in dating rather than deliberate intention to establish the beginnings of Chinese fiction in a period lacking definitive evidence of those beginnings. But to search for fictional (or for that matter narrative) elements in ancient texts is such a deliberate act. It would at least be a misrepresentation of authorial intention and the function of the work concerned to see the skillful use of dialogues, vivid descriptions of characters and events, careful planning of presentational order, and the artful expressions of viewpoints as evidence of fictional elements. All this is essential to the function of recording, and most of the ancient texts, save pure philosophical discussion and various forms of poetry, have the obligation to "record." Historical texts particularly should be seen from this perspective. If they do not record, they fail to serve their raison d'etre in the first place; the so-called fictional elements are but presentational techniques to record. Whether later fiction writers made use of the techniques used in *Shih-chi* and similar texts is an entirely different matter. While it is legitimate to find out whether a certain fiction writer was under the influence of *Shih-chi* or other early texts, it is erroneous to say that the business of fiction writing started with Ssu-ma Ch'ien and his colleagues.

The failure to separate mythology from fiction generates another confusion, and this confusion was initiated by no less influential an authority than Lu Hsün 鲁迅 (Chou Shu-jen 周樹人, 1881-1936), whose *Chung-kuo hsiao-shuo shih-lüeh* 中國小說史略 (A Short History of Chinese Fiction) has an entire chapter on how fiction is supposed to have been originated from passages in ancient sources like the *Mu T'ien-tzu chuan*,* the *Shan-hai ching*,* and the *Ch'u-tz'u*.* This theory has been upheld religiously by students of Chinese literature for the better part of the century. Many early texts defy clearcut classification, and it is often possible to place them equally well in different generic categories. But fiction is not and cannot be one of these categories. A good example of this is the Bible, which is at once history, mythology, and religion. There are numerous instances of fictional (or fictitious) elements in the Bible. Should a history of fiction in the Western world begin with the Bible? Obviously not. The confusion of the Chinese case is apparently caused by the abundance of imaginary passages in these early texts. These passages are imaginary (not imaginative) by present standards, but to the ancients the world was not much different from what was described in the *Shan-hai ching*! What really can be gained by tracing the history of Chinese fiction far back into a period in which disciplines were not clearly distinguished and many books served multifunctional purposes? It may be argued that the abundance of mythological elements in these early works with their involvement with collective thought and the subconscious inspired and encouraged later fiction writers to incorporate imaginative components in their creations and, if the evidence is there, even provided them the source materials to work with. This, however, does not mean that mythology marks the beginning of Chinese fiction.

The Six Dynasties is the first period that provides a host of concrete examples of prose compositions which consciously create imaginative reality, with or without the use of historical sources. Until proven otherwise, imaginative works like *Shen-i ching* 神異經 (The Classic of Deities and Marvels) and *Han Wu-ti nei-chuan,** traditionally assigned to the Han period, should be regarded as written by Six Dynasties writers. Nothing is really lost by beginning a history of Chinese fiction with the Six Dynasties.

Fictional works from the Six Dynasties through the May Fourth Movement of 1919 can be categorized in a number of ways, each of which illustrates certain characteristics of traditional Chinese fiction. One possibility is to divide fiction into stories and novels according to the physical form and chapter division. A story can be as short as a few dozen words (examples can be found in the *Shih-shuo hsin-yü*) or, like "Mai-yu lang tu-chan hua-k'uei" 賣油郎獨佔花魁 (in *Hsing-shih heng-yen*—see Feng Meng-lung), as long as twenty thousand words. Irrespective of its length, a story is an unbroken narrative with no formal divisional device.

Novels are expected to be long, and most of them range from forty to one hundred chapters. If we do not count sequels, Chang Ch'un-fan's 張春帆 *Chiu-wei kuei* 九尾龜 (Nine-tailed Tortoise), with its 192 chapters, is probably the longest traditional novel. The shortest novels are not much different from stories with respect to length. *Ch'ih po-tzu chuan* 痴婆子傳 (Story of a Silly Woman), in two *chüan* (not chapters), has about 11,000 words. *Ju-i chün chuan* 如意君傳 (The Perfect Companion), about 9,000 words, and *Ch'un-meng so-yen* 春夢瑣言 (Trifling Story of a Spring Dream), less than 4,000, are even shorter and do not have formal chapter divisions. (Incidentally, all three are Ming erotic novels.) This brings an inevitable question. Why should these short pieces of the average length of T'ang tales and without chapter divisions be considered novels? This has much to do with the point discussed above. In defining Chinese fiction and its groupings, authorial intention and the physical form of the work involved must be considered. Works like *Ch'un-meng so-yen* are too slim for regular chapter divisions, but complete with prefaces and issued separately, they were intended to be individual books. In the case of the *Ch'ih po-tzu chuan*, it has both a preface and a table of contents.

Moreover, why shouldn't these short novels or works of intermediate length like the *Ta-T'ang San-tsang ch'ü-ching shih-hua* 大唐三藏取經詩話, the *Hsüan-ho i-shih,** and the several well-known historical *p'ing-hua** be classified as novelettes after the Western practice of using length (say, 15,000-30,000 words) as a major criterion in identifying a middle group between the story and the novel? Given the importance of the physical form in distinguishing the story from the novel, length by itself is not significant, and there is no practical need to establish an in-between group. Despite their relative shortness, the aforementioned samples neatly fit the categorization of novels discussed later and should thus be treated as such. Even the term short novel is unnecessary. Incidentally, many of the works which may be called novelettes are early attempts at composing full-scale novels. They are intermediate only in this respect, and not in terms of length or complexity.

Having settled the distinction between the story and the novel, further classification can be attempted. The story, because of its moderate length and relative simplicity, is easier to categorize. One suggestion is to divide the traditional stories with respect to length, language, form, period, and context into (1) *pi-chi*,* note-form jottings popular from the Six Dynasties to the early Republican days—however, not all *pi-chi* writings are fiction; (2) *ch'uan-ch'i*,* classical-language tales, generally on unusual events, popular in the T'ang and Sung periods, with a considerable revival in the Ming and Ch'ing periods, although the later stories lack the vitality of their precursors; (3) *pien-wen* (see *Tun-huang wen-hsüeh*), T'ang and Five Dynasties popularized religious—mostly Buddhist—stories (with a few exceptions on historical or contemporary topics) from the Tun-huang caves, which served as the genesis, directly or indirectly, of later storytelling genres and various types of chantefable literature; (4) *hua-pen*,* stories in the vernacular (some in simple classical language) of Sung-Ming times originating directly or indirectly from professional storytelling, including later stories fashioned by the literati after the established conventions; and (5) *kung-an*, broadly referring to any stories of the aforesaid types that narrate crime cases solved by legal, and sometimes detective, means, or more specifically referring to stories in a group of collections labeled as *kung-an* in the Wan-li period of the Ming dynasty.

When it comes to the novel, the demarcation is even less clearcut, and there have not been many attempts at classification, let alone convincing ones. A commendable, though generally unnoticed, scheme is the one advanced by Sun K'ai-ti in his *Chung-kuo t'ung-su hsiao-shuo shu-mu* 中國通俗小說書目 (A Bibliography of Popular Chinese Fiction), in which post-Yüan novels, along with colloquial-story collections, are grouped into:

1) *chiang-shih* 講史 (historical novels);
2) *hsiao-shuo* B (A was used for stories and story collections) for non-historical novels are divided into:
   i) *yen-fu* 烟粉 (romantic novels), with five subdivisions:
      a) *jen-ch'ing* 人情 (novels of manners), e.g., *Chin P'ing Mei** and *Hung-lou meng**;
      b) *hsia-hsieh* 狹邪 (novels about brothels), e.g., *Hua-yüeh hen* 花月痕 (The Flower and the Moon) and *Hai-shang hua lieh-chuan* 海上花列傳 (Lives of Shanghai Singsong Girls);
      c) *ts'ai-tzu chia-jen* 才子佳人 (beau-and-beauty novels), e.g., *Yü Chiao Li* and *Hao-ch'iu chuan;*
      d) *ying-hsuing erh-nü* 英雄兒女 (knight-errant novels), e.g., *Yeh-sou p'u-yen* 野叟曝言 (A Rustic's Idle Talk) and *Erh-nü ying-hsiung chuan;*
      e) *wei-hsieh* 猥褻 (pornographic novels), e.g., *Jou p'u-t'uan** and *Chu-lin yeh-shih* 株林野史 (Unofficial History of the Bamboo Grove).
   ii) *ling-kuai* 靈怪 (novels of the supernatural), e.g., *Hsi-yu chi* and *Feng-shen yen-i.*
   iii) *shuo kung-an* 說公案 (chivalry/or detective novels), with two subdivisions:
      a) *hsia-i* 俠義 (novels of the heroic), e.g., *Shui-hu chuan** and *San-hsia wu-i**;
      b) *ching-ch'a* 精察 (detective novels), e.g., *Chiu-ming ch'i-yüan* (see Wu Wo-yao) and *Li-kung-an ch'i-wen* 李公案奇聞 (Cases of Lord Li).
   iv) *feng-yü* 諷諭 (allegorical novels), with two subdivisions:

a) *feng-tzu* 諷刺(novels of satire), e.g., *Ju-lin wai-shih** and *Lao-ts'an yu-chi*;*

b) *ch'üan-chieh* 勸戒(novels of admonition), e.g., *Hsing-shih yin-yüan chuan* 醒世姻緣傳(Marriage that Awakens the World) and *Ch'i-lu teng.**

No classification can be perfect, but a good classification, based on in-depth analysis, can present in a plain summary the complexity of the issues concerning the nature of traditional Chinese novels. Although Sun K'ai-ti's scheme has its share of weaknesses and errors, it is, with all its problems, detailed enough to capture the diversity of the genre and, through the proportional number of works registered in the complete list, a reflection of the relative popularity of each category. No one has given the problem more thought. What needs to be done next is not the application of Western critical methods to Chinese novels, as the comparatists advocate, but a careful reading of the lesser known Chinese novels to identify their distinguishable or even unique features. Western theories can best be, on occasion, suggestive and inspirational to the student of the Chinese novel, but they do not seem to be able to provide a universal doctrine or model as some critics have claimed.

Modern research on traditional Chinese novels has focused on half a dozen major novels, with the *Hung-lou meng* receiving the lion's share even among these favored few. (About one-fifth of the monographs and articles published on Chinese fiction in the past eight decades discuss the *Hung-lou meng*.) This results in the standard attitude of taking the characteristics seen in these few works as representative of traditional Chinese novels as a whole. This view is as incomplete as it is distorted. If a comprehensive understanding of the novels produced in pre-modern China is desired, the first step should be an overall classification system, with less emphasis on value judgment and more on as broad a coverage as possible. To avoid some of the ambiguities of Sun K'ai-ti's scheme, categorization should be based on differences in kind and not on differences in degree, and, as far as possible, the same criteria should apply to novels of the same type when it comes to further grouping. In this way, a unified approach can be adopted to reveal the range of diversity, the historical trend (works within each unit should be chronologically arranged), and the characteristics (both unique and universal) of pre-modern Chinese novels.

Besides the story-novel classifications, attention should also be paid to the problem of language. As mentioned above, with the exception of the *hua-pen*, few stories can be regarded as written in the vernacular. Since it seems unlikely that people in the T'ang period carried out their daily communication in the compact, laconic, allusion-laden language seen in the *pien-wen* pieces, these stories from the Tun-huang caves should be placed in the classical-language group. Conversely, vernacular is the predominant medium for the novels. Classical-language novels probably constitute less than one percent of the novels produced in pre-modern China. One such novel which is seldom read but comes easily to mind is Ch'en Ch'iu's 陳球 *Yen-shan wai-shih* 燕山外史 written in parallel prose. The artificiality of its language, particularly in the dialogues, illustrates the wisdom of the traditional novelists who produced their wares either in the vernacular or in a combination of the vernacular and a simple classical language (e.g., *San-kuo chih yen-i**).

The choice of the classical-language or the vernacular, the story form or the novel, and the option of generic types within the story or the novel also present themselves in a neat historical pattern. Only a few pre-Yüan works have ever been labeled as novels, and most of them have serious dating problems—one such case is the *Hsüan-ho i-shih.** The few works which can be reasonably assigned to the Yüan period are generically transitional. Thus the traditional novel is practically a concern of the Ming and Ch'ing dynasties alone. With the increased complexity of the structure and presentation demanded by the novel (vis-à-vis the story) this later development of the novel conforms with the growth pattern of fiction in other national literatures. In the Chinese case, however, it is more than the evolutionary necessity of developing from simple to complex; the growth of the novel, predominantly in the vernacular, was under the direct influence of the singular type of story written in the vernacular, the *hua-pen*.

The rise of the *hua-pen*, with its specific circumstantial factors, and the formal features of *hua-pen* stories are well-researched topics. What needs to be pointed out here is that the advent of the *hua-pen* led to the growth of this new genre itself and to the foundations of the novel. The stock phrases of the storyteller and interpolated passages in rhyme are links between *hua-pen* and the novel. These, however, are minor in comparison with the influence of the device used by professional storytellers in dividing their stories at suitably critical points to guarantee the return of the audience on the formal feature of chapter division in the novel. Chapter division is of course a universal feature of the novel, but in the Chinese novel it is more than a convenience—it is a required formality. Towards the end of each chapter, the reader, confronted with an unexpected twist or with an event truncated at a critical point, is asked to turn to the next chapter for a resolution. Except for the few examples intended to be novels without the necessary length of the genre (e.g., *Ju-i chün chuan*), this formula was religiously followed by virtually all Ming and Ch'ing novelists. On occasion there are a few end-of-chapter announcements of surprises which are unfulfilled or even forgotten in the succeeding chapters. Such characteristics, along with other storytelling conventions, invite disapproval, particularly from critics familiar with Western fiction and its critical tradition. Fortunately this kind of misconstruction has been countered. Although excessive loyalty to the conventions inherited from professional storytelling is not to be blindly defended, the concern here is not evaluation of these techniques but examination of them as one of the surest roads to understanding the rise of the Chinese novel.

The connection between *hua-pen* and the novel is direct and lineal. Although most of the extant early *hua-pen* stories cannot possibly be in an original, unaltered form, a significant number can be taken as reasonable representations of the actual storytelling presentations. With its origin in such a background, the reliance of the novel on storytelling conventions is inevitable, if not desirable; it is only the extent, not the presence, of such a reliance that needs to be explained.

This phenomenon has much to do with the respect for tradition and the conformist spirit of Chinese thought. To draw on tradition was always a cherished way to conduct business. By modeling on a past golden age and certain of its great masters, the leaders of the *ku-wen** movement in the mid-T'ang elevated the art of prose writing to a new height in charm and clarity, while a superficially similar movement in the Ming period, conducted by the mediocre with far less insight and ingenuity, ended up in blind alleys of imitation. The issue is thus whether the tradition has been a role, but what that role is. Wanton use of conventions, like ignoring the crisis that has ended a previous chapter in its sequel, merits censure. But to attack the presence of storytelling conventions in the novel is to demand a completely severed relationship between the novel and the very source to which it owes its existence.

Literary creation, even in its most private moments, is a challenge. For the traditional Chinese writer, one form of the challenge is in satisfying the rules of the genre in which he wrote. This preliminary hurdle is not easy to clear, for the rules are many and varied—recall the demanding regulations that qualify a poem to be a *lü-shih* (see *shih*). But the *lü-shih* regulations, already complicated by Western standards, pale in comparison with the mind-numbing rules of *san-ch'ü* or the technical rigors of *hui-wen shih* 迴文詩 (palindromes). Readers are also shocked in their initial contacts with Yüan drama to learn that the playwrights had to observe so many seemingly unreasonable rules. But the poets and their readers, the playwrights and their audiences, did not complain. To master these rules was a challenge to the writers, and the ability of the writers to master these rules ensured the appreciation of the audience. The adoption of storytelling conventions in the novel does not belong to the same level of rigidity and sophistication, but it is of the same nature and mentality. It reflects the conformist spirit of the Chinese writers and the expectations of their audience.

The transition from *hua-pen* to the novel has not been adequately studied, but the available materials, notably the *p'ing-hua** examples published in the Yüan period and the possibly earlier *Ta-T'ang San-tsang ch'ü-ching shih-hua*, if thoroughly examined in this respect, seem to reveal the character of the connection and certain details of the evolution. The sectioning of these relatively simple narratives is similar to those seen in the early editions of the *San-kuo chih yen-i*. The growth from the stories to sectioning of longer narratives to the full chapter division of the novel is logical, although as far as available materials are concerned the development is not a strictly lineal one. Here is a pattern which may be called atavistic linearity.

A general survey returns to the T'ang *pien-wen*. The direct descendants of *pien-wen* are chantefables like *pao-chuan* 寶卷 and *ku-tzu-tz'u*.* Its influence on *hua-pen* was mainly technical, rather than thematic or generic. The oral presentation of *pien-wen* was enhanced by the attendant series of pictures known as *pien-hsiang* 變相, which of course could be independent. There are a few extant examples of pairing *pien-wen* and *pien-hsiang*, and the effectiveness of such a coupling deeply influenced later works. Available evidence, however, reveals no similar pairing in popular literary genres of the Sung period. The illustrated Yüan *p'ing-hua*, published in the early 1320s, stand as a rather isolated phenomenon, if they are not seen from a broad historical perspective. The time gap between them and the *pien-wen* was several centuries, and the subsequent examples were by no means immediate descendents either.

The earliest full-sized novel is either the *San-kuo chih yen-i* or the *Shui-hu chuan*, but there are no known editions of either novel, extant or otherwise, before the Chia-ching period (1522-1566) of the Ming dynasty. None of the few Chia-ching samples of these two novels are illustrated. But when illustration, mostly on every page, eventually became fashionable in the Wan-li period (1573-1620), the format and layout were strikingly close to those of the several Yüan *p'ing-hua*.

The sectional titles of the *p'ing-hua* texts generally coordinate with the illustrations, which in turn reflect the contents of the pages concerned. The earliest known *San-kuo chih yen-i* is divided into 240 sections (not chapters) but has no illustrations. Many of the novels published in the later Wan-li period, however, including different editions of the *San-kuo chih yen-i,* have clearly marked chapters and page-by-page illustrations, each with individual captions, which can be argued as reminiscent of the earlier more general sectional titles. This is specially clear in those published in the Chien-yang 建陽 and Chien-an 建安 areas of Fukien, the same areas that produced the Yüan *p'ing-hua.*

Wan-li is the golden age of vernacular fiction in general, and novels in particular, and there are many examples to demonstrate the various transitional stages. In post Wan-li publications, illustrations play a lesser role. But the extant fiction of the centuries from the T'ang through the Wan-li period, centuries during which several major generic types of fiction took shape, suffice to suggest a historical relationship between the early and later genres. Yet the inconsistencies of the relationships between divisions of text, illustrations, and length of narratives indicate that the history of Chinese fiction, though generally following a chronological scheme, is still rather elusive. The discussion here is admittedly preliminary, and is offered as a basis for further investigation. Present knowledge of textual history, the business practices of the major publishing concerns, and interests of the leading publishers and editors is far from sufficient to resolve the problem.

While the novel owes its origin to *hua-pen,* the indebtedness is mainly limited to form. The Chia-ching period, which saw the advent of the novel, was also a watershed for the *hua-pen,* which was still to undergo considerable transformation, but at a more rapid pace than its earlier developments. The products of this second period of *hua-pen* evolution, erroneously labeled by modern scholars *ni hua-pen* 擬話本 (imitation *hua-pen*), bear little witness to the contemporary development of the novel. Except for the possibility that some *hua-pen* materials may have been included in several early novels of long evolutionary history like *Shui-hu chuan* and *Hsi-yu chi,* and the rare cases of outright textual liftings such as those contributed to the making of the *Chin P'ing Mei,* direct connections between *hua-pen* stories and Ming novels are almost beyond detection. This kind of connection in various forms of borrowing (enlargements, condensation, combination, etc.), was common among *pi-chi, ch'uan-ch'i, hua-pen,* and *kung-an,* irrespective of their differences in language and in degree of elaboration. This shows that the development of the story and the growth of the novel were rather independent of each other even after the appearance of novels. The relationship and mutual influence of novels and plays were much greater than those between novels and stories.

In any case, since novels began to appear in increasing quanity, stories became secondary in importance. *Hua-pen* stories produced by Ming writers, whether or not they can be labeled as imitations of earlier pieces, lack the charming colloquialism, swift tempo, and surprise twists of events that characterize their precursors. Instead, the story moved towards pedestrian didacticism and earthy concerns, in the guise of worn-out plots. In the skillful hands of Feng Meng-lung,* Ling Meng-ch'u,* Li Yü (1611-1680),* and a few others, the *hua-pen* form could still work its magic. But even these masters failed to attain the captivating qualities of the early works. They did not live in the age of the early professional storytellers and their creative processes had little to do with live audiences, the very blood of the early *hua-pen* stories.

Conscious preservation of a stagnated form can only delay, not prevent, its demise. For *hua-pen,* this inevitable deterioration was aggravated by senseless bifurcation of the form through a multiplication of the subplots of the preamble, or by a heedless overproduction as evidenced by numerous collections of the late Ming. Although literary historians relish the fortuitous survival of *Liu-shih chia hsiao-shuo** and the *San-yen* series (see Feng Meng-lung), the almost total disappearance of *hua-pen,* early in the Ch'ing, except for the anthology *Chin-ku ch'i-kuan,** was to some extent a blessing in disguise.

The decline of *ch'uan-ch'i* started even earlier; some purists put it as early as the Sung period. Nevertheless, from the Sung through the Ch'ing, there are a few outstanding *ch'uan-ch'i* stories, usually constituents of some of the commendable collections that appeared infrequently. Liu Fu's 劉斧 *Ch'ing-so kao-i* 清瑣高議 (Remarkable Opinions under the Green Latticed Window), Ch'ü Yu's *Chien-teng hsin-hua,** P'u Sung-ling's* *Liao-chai chih-i,* Chi Yün's* *Yüeh-wei ts'ao-t'ang pi-chi,* and Hsüan Ting's 宣鼎 *Yeh-yü ch'iu-teng lu* 夜雨秋燈錄 (Writings Done in the Rainy Nights and Under the Autumn Lamp) are some examples. They are good works in their own right; but they were too few and too infrequent to sustain the genre as a major form of fiction in these years.

This does not mean that there had been an irrevocable decline in the importance and the quality of the *ch'uan-ch'i.* A good writer like Ch'ü Yu might be able to bring about a revival, and for a genius like P'u Sung-ling there was always room for innovation. Although differences from age to age can be discerned (such as the predominance of contempory themes in T'ang stories and the preoccupation with ghosts and spirits in Ch'ing stories), Chinese tale writers were basically tradition bound, and major changes are occasional.

It is from this viewpoint that the greatness of P'u Sung-ling can be appreciated. One of his many innovations was to allow his supernatural heroines (notably fox-spirits) to live on happily with their lovers. Considering that since the beginning of Chinese fiction in the Six Dynasties the union of a human being (usually the male) and his protean lover (usually a female-animal spirit) were rarely permitted a happy ending, and that when the end came, usually in violent tragedy or in helpless despair, the one who suffered most was the female, P'u Sung-ling's departure is dramatic indeed. Tradition is nevertheless tradition. After P'u Sung-ling, who had many imitators, there were few bold enough to continue challenging it, and the sad fate of the otherworldly beauties returned as norm. With this kind of stagnation, the decline of the *ch'uan-chi* was inevitable.

Pi-chi, despite its enormous quantity, did not fare much better. It can even be argued that after the Six Dynasties there is not a single collection which matches the *Shih-shuo hsin-yü** in charm and influence. From the T'ang onward, although fictional *pi-chi* continued to be written, the emphasis shifted progressively to the historical and the philological type. The casual form of *pi-chi* gave utmost liberty to the recorders and commentators of minor events and permitted scholars to jot down their observations. The majority of the *pi-chi* collections from the T'ang through the Ch'ing now serve mainly as source materials for historians (including literary historians) and philologists.

The development of traditional fiction can therefore be seen as two-staged. Although the bulk of stories were written in the Ming and Ch'ing dynasties, most of the memorable ones were composed earlier. The decline of the story form, in terms of quality, coincided with the rapid growth of the full-sized novel. While it may be a simplification to say that the novel replaced the story in popularity, the changes in the *pi-chi,* the most common type of story, noted above suggest that the fictional mainstream shifted to the long narratives once the presentational techniques and publishing channels were available.

Although the history of the novel is much shorter than that of the story it poses more serious problems because of the length and complexity of the long narrative. While physical features are generally sufficient to distinguish the different types of stories, novels are physically homogeneous. Other standards are needed to distinguish their types. This recalls the categorization scheme of Sun K'ai-ti discussed above.

The main problem with Sun's system is the inconsistency of including all the historical novels in one huge group while breaking the rest into four groups, three of them with several subdivisions. This ignores the quantity, not counting the enormous output of the late Ch'ing, of historical novels: about one out of five novels can be so classified. Moreover, Sun arranges the historical novels chronologically according to their contents. His method may serve well in compiling a handy bibliographical index, but fails to accord the historical novel the chronology by date of composition given the rest. Noting the central role played by the nation in the historical novels, it would be possible to divide them into three thematic categories: dynasty-building, national security, and dynastic chronicle, with items arranged according to their dates of composition.

Another problem of the Sun K'ai-ti categorization is the classification of knight-errant novels under *yen-fen* 胭粉 and of novels as diverse as *Shui-hu chuan* and *Chiu-ming ch'i-yüan* under one main heading (although assigned to different subdivisions), *shuo kung-an*. Although the misclassification of knight-errant novels is not a serious issue, the misuse of old terms is. Terms like *yen-fen* and *shuo kung-an* are inseparably associated with Sung professional storytelling and by extension with the rise of vernacular fiction. But Ming and Ch'ing novels bear little resemblance to the immediate products of the earlier storytellers. Such an application of earlier terms of specific meaning to substantially different later writings, similar to identifying Han or even pre-Ch'in *hsiao-shuo* titles as fiction, points to one persistent problem in studying and in understanding Chinese fiction: the indiscriminate applications of key terms with restricted intent, applications which have proved an obstacle in discerning the growth of Chinese fiction, its scope, and its nature.

Important though it is to the understanding of Chinese fiction, categorization of Ming and Ch'ing novels obviously cannot be adequately treated here; considerations of space aside, the groundwork for such a comprehensive classification has yet to be laid. It should ideally be the end product of systematic analyses, with criteria uniformly applied, of these novels from different perspectives—historical, textual, generic, formalistic, aesthetic, structural, thematic, and contextual—and should not be approached merely as an end in itself.

The most valuable insight offered by Sun K'ai-ti in his initiatory categorization is the recognition of the importance of history. This helps identify the largest group of novels published before the boom of the late Ch'ing days. The role of history actually goes far beyond this. To classify a novel as historical, the use of verifiable facts as the central narrative framework has to be determined, otherwise there would be little meaning in the exercise. And the proportion of the use of the past to the present as the time background of the novels must be considered. Although no detailed enumeration has been done, it would seem that, before the popularity of *ts'ai-tzu chia-jen** novels in the late Ming period, a setting in the past with at least token reference to some well-known historical personages and events seems to have been the norm. From the time of the *ts'ai-tzu chia-jen* novels to the eve of the late Ch'ing boom, possibly one-third of all novels used contemporary settings (including the recent past, say, a mid-Ch'ing novelist's using an early-Ch'ing time frame). In novels published in the late Ch'ing period, past settings constitute a negligible minority.

The use of the past, however, can be rather deceptive. One example is the anonymous Ch'ing novel *Tz'u-yün t'ai-tzu tsou-kuo* 慈雲太子走國 (Prince Tz'u-yün on the Run), in which a young crown prince, the future Sung Emperor Hui-tsung (r. 1101-1125), is constantly threatened by palace intrigues and assassination plots and only manages after many near escapes to return to the palace in triumph with the help of loyal ministers and daring knight-errants. Even though the novel uses historical characters, there is not a shred of truth in the plot line. Yet Sun K'ai-ti routinely classifies it as a historical novel. Perhaps it is easier to identify the non-historical nature of a novel cast in a seemingly possible historical environment but peopled mainly by fictitious characters, such as *Chin P'ing Mei* (also set in the Hui-tsung reign) and *Ju-lin wai-shih* (set in Ming times), than to dismiss as non-historical a novel of fictitious events involving eminent historical figures. Whether the past is used as a bona-fide setting or just as a pretext, history is involved in perhaps eighty percent of the novels published before the late Ch'ing boom.

But why is there such a heavy reliance on the past in the first place? For those who try their hand at writing genuine historical novels, the presence of an enormous amount of readily available historical literature makes the job easier and to some extent defines the historicity of the resultant works. The falsified historical game is something else and can be explained in a number of ways. One is certainly laziness: it is easier to ride on the historical wagon. The more substantial the book, the more unlikely it is that the reader will check its historical reliability, and the more freedom the writer can enjoy in permitting his imagination to roam.

The practice of individual writers composing chain novels also bestows legitimacy upon these works of falsified history. At the end of the *Tz'u-yün t'ai-tzu tsou-kuo*, the reader is reminded that this is a continuation of the *Wu-hu p'ing-nan* 五虎平南 (Five Tigers Pacifying the South) and is urged to continue reading the saga of Yüeh Fei 岳飛 (1103-1141) (presumably meaning the more popular *Shuo Yüeh ch'üan-chuan* 說岳全傳 [The Life of Yüeh Fei] rather than its obscure Ming antecedents) for the events that follow. This is a stark claim to being a constituent of a family of better-known and better-written novels. *Wu-hu p'ing-nan* itself is a sequel of *Wu-hu p'ing-hsi* 五虎平西 (Five Tigers Pacifying the West), which lines up legitimately with a whole cluster of novels on the Yang family generals 楊家將, the Hu family generals 呼家將, and Ti Ch'ing 狄青 (1008-1057), and by extension with an even larger group of virtually countless dramas and chantefables. There are understandably vast differences in historicity among these novels, and the less carefully written ones can always shelter in the reputation of the better members of the chain.

The use of the past in *Chin P'ing Mei* and *Ju-lin wai-shih* obviously belongs to a different category. The reason for the use of the past in non-historical novels range from derivative (*Chin P'ing Mei* owes its origin to an episode in the *Shui-hu chuan*), to protective (especially when a novel like *Ju-lin wai-shih* closely reflects the contemporary scene), to tradition-bound (the Chinese preference for indirect reference in using the past to represent the present), to contextual, (to place the extravagant fantasy of the

Feng-shen yen-i in a period less remote than the Chou dynasty is to lessen its claim of credibility), to thematic (the theme of women's liberation left little choice but for *Ching-hua yüan* to be placed in the time of Empress Wu Tse-t'ien), to merely convenient (whether historical events and figures are mentioned or not, to set the time background vaguely in the past gives the novelist more liberty than he would enjoy in writing about the present; one example is the *P'ing Shan Leng Yen*). With such a heavy use of history in the making of both historical and non-historical novels, a good knowledge of Chinese history and documentary sources becomes a prerequisite for a sound understanding of Ming and Ch'ing novels.

Although this dominance of history was first softened by the usually contemporary settings of the *ts'ai-tzu chia-jen* novels of the late Ming and early Ch'ing days, the structure of these novels is so formulistic and their link with the real world is so tenuous that the actual breakthrough did not occur until the business of fiction writing underwent fundamental changes in the late Ch'ing period. When this happened, the past was effectively replaced by the present. Keenly associated with political, social, and intellectual issues of the rapidly changing environments, these novels constitute the "relevant" literature of the day. Even those on more relaxed matters such as Ch'en Sen's 陳森 (*c.* 1796-*c.* 1870) *P'in-hua pao-chien* 品花寶鑑 (A Mirror for Evaluating the Flowers), Wei Hsiu-jen's 魏秀仁 (1819-1874) *Hua-yüeh hen*, and Han Pang-ch'ing's 韓邦慶 (1856-1894) *Hai-shang hua lieh-chuan*—all of which have been criticized as being little more than guides to the Peking and Shanghai brothels—could be realistic to the level of being factual. Such proximity between the subject matter and the immediate readership had never been attempted before, and this proximity by necessity meant a close observation of the matter represented. With almost every aspect of life changing rapidly during the late Ch'ing, an appreciation of the novels produced at that time requires a tremendous amount of historical knowledge. An explanatory index to the thinly disguised characters in the *Nieh-hai hua* (there are quite a few such lists) reads like a who's who in China at the turn of the century, Although this may be an extreme example it is by no means an isolated one. Despite the common use of the present in these later novels, the key to their understanding is still history.

While it is difficult, if not impossible, to name one novel on contemporary matters composed before the middle of the Wan-li period, it is equally difficult to credit the early novels to any individual without relying on shaky evidence such as hearsay, second- or third-hand information, or the uncritical acceptance of the labels of the early editions, labels which might be a hundred years or more later than the alleged dates of composition. Unfortunately, the two earliest full-sized novels *San-kuo chih yen-i* and *Shui-hu chuan* belong to this category. (Although *San-kuo chih yen-i* has been customarily regarded as the earlier of the two, probably because it treats an earlier era, the question has never been properly addressed). In the absence of indisputable firsthand information, Lo Kuan-chung's* authorship of the *San-kuo chih yen-i* and Shih Nai-an's authorship of the *Shui-hu chuan* (or for that matter Lo's involvement in the making of the *Shui-hu chuan*) cannot be taken seriously. These two novels are the products of long and complicated evolutionary cycles. Even among extant editions, there are numerous, vastly different, versions, most of which should be treated individually on an equal basis. Until the relationships among these versions have been clarified, it is simply inappropriate to treat one version as if it alone stands for the novel, or to attribute it to an individual who would then be considered the sole author of the whole cluster of compositions.

Every early novel developed out of an evolutionary cycle, and the attribution of any of them should be viewed with doubt. It would not even be surprising if Lo Kuan-chung were found to have had nothing to do with fiction writing! It is strange that students of Chinese fiction find it easy to believe in the evolutionary nature of these early novels, but difficult to accept the idea of composite authorship. Individual authorship can only refer to the situation where it can be shown that before an individual worked on a certain novel (a novel of evolutionary nature, that is), the accumulative efforts of his predecessors had not produced anything more substantial and coherent than some isolated story cycles, and that this individual then edited, compiled, and modified these materials into something which can be accepted as a novel. One such possiblity is the *Hsi-yu chi;* although Wu Ch'eng-en's authorship is still not absolutely beyond dispute, there should not be much doubt that a single author is responsible for the extant one-hundred chapter version of the the novel. For evolutionary novels like *San-kuo chih yen-i, Shui-hu chuan,* and the twenty-chapter version of the *P'ing-yao chuan,* to search for an editer-compiler who gave the work an orderly totality and a thematic coherence out of the relatively individually developed cyclical units seems to make better sense. To assign these novels to composite authorship really does not compromise their glamor at all.

For those who do not have enough faith in the working of composite authorship, there is an almost perfect set of records of such a cycle. The performance of the legendary mid-nineteenth century Ch'ing chantefable storyteller Shih Yü-k'un (see *San-hsia wu-i*) has been recorded in great detail in more than one well-preserved, though incomplete, set of manuscripts known as the *Lung-t'u kung-an* (not to be confused with the late Ming *kung-an* story collection of the same name). When the storytelling version was edited to be a regular narrative text, this stage is again adequately recorded in several manuscript sets (*Lung-t'u erh-lu*). Further editorial work resulted in a prose novel for formal circulation, *Chung-lieh hsia-i chuan,* the first edition of which is still available. But this novel is known to the general public in a later edition by the title *San-hsia wu-i* and Shih Yü-k'un is duly credited as the author. Later, the Confucian philologist Yü Yüeh brought out a revised version of his own, *Ch'i-hsia wu-i,* and this version is still associated with Shih Yü-k'un's name. Through this fortunate preservation of the complete cycle, one can easily see that composite authorship is not difficult to understand. It becomes clear that to attribute any of the texts produced in the later stages of the evolutionary cycle to a single author is unfair. Moreover, the instance cited is a simple evolutionary cycle involving only one level of language and structure in each stage. For a novel like *Shui-hu chuan,* with different levels of complexity and developed over a much longer period of time, the process has to be far more complicated and the contribution of any individual much less.

Novels of composite authorship are of a limited number. They require a favorable combination of several necessary factors: the suitability and adaptability of the context, a chance to run the full course of the cycle, cross-fertilization with other traditions and genres, the devotion of capable editor-compilers, the availability of printed media, and the acceptance of the readership. The much greater complexity of the novel in comparison with other genres of popular literature means that more often than not the novel represents the culmination of the evolution rather than one of the intermediate stages. Some cycles, in spite of their popularity, simply did not make it that far. Those of Meng Chiang-nü 孟姜女 and Tung Yung 董永, for instance, never reach the complexity of producing novels. Even the time-honored cycles of the Eight Immortals have not been able to produce anything more complicated than a few thin minor novels.

If it is agreed that none of the traditional attributions should be accepted unless they are backed up by unquestionable contemporary evidence demonstrably identified with the extant texts, then the late Ming publisher-novelists constitute the first major group of known writers that was responsible for the transmission of the bulk of the Ming novels. Yü Hsiang-tou 余象斗 and Hsiung Ta-mu 熊大木, both active in Fukien in the Wan-li period and after, are representatives of this important but scarcely studied group. Most of what they brought out were either pure historical novels or non-historical novels with a strong, though usually imaginary, identification with the past. Since historical materials cannot remain entirely devoid of changes and elaborations in passing down from generation to generation, some of these novels might have significant evolutionary backgrounds; but most of them clearly do not belong to the same category as *Shui-hu chuan* and *San-kuo chih yen-i* with their slow, stage-by-stage, cyclical growth. In a word, most of the novels brought out by these publisher-novelists can be reasonably taken as compositions of individual authors, although it is still difficult to define the actual role played by Yü Hsiang-tou, Hsiung Ta-mu, and other similar figures in the making of each individual novel. Should they best be described as part author, editor-author, full author, or mere publisher? Individually, few of these novels can be critically acclaimed (students of minor, neglected novels are often tempted to exaggerate the value, both historical and literary, of their subjects); collectively, they, together with the multitude of *ts'ai-tzu chia-jen* novels, stand for the majority of Ming novels. If this numerical weight is given its due, these minor novels, rather than the illustrious few, should be regarded as the novels generally known to the Ming public. Works like *Hsi-yu chi* and *Chin P'ing Mei* represent the height of Ming achievement of fiction writing, but because they represent such a small percentage of the total corpus, they cannot be seen as representative of Ming novels as a whole.

Even though many of the novels brought out by these publisher-novelists can be regarded as works of individual authorship, their dependence on historical materials still placed some restrictions on these authors. Much more creative freedom can be seen beginning with the *ts'ai-tzu chia-jen* novels. With the lesser dependence on history came the increasing testimony of individuality. Professionalism decreased accordingly, but it was not until the late Ch'ing period that the next major group of novelists who could make a living, no matter how humbly, on fiction writing, e.g., Li Po-yüan and Wu Chien-jen, can be seen.

Non-historical novels of individual authorship share one common feature with similar novels of other national literatures; the first novel of any author is almost inevitably autobiographical to some extent and writing it usually takes a fairly long period of time. *Ching-hua yüan** and *Hung-lou meng** are two good examples of this phenomenon. Both Li Ju-chen and Ts'ao Hsüeh-ch'in* were so absorbed in the making of these two novels that one produced no other fictional work, the other could not even complete the one at hand. Even in the work of the late Ch'ing novelists who supported themselves by their writing, many of their early works are still openly autobiographical. Liu E's *Lao-ts'an yu-chi* serves as a good example.

Until the late Ch'ing period, fiction writing had little commercial value. Although figures like Yü Hsiang-tou and Ling Meng-ch'u were professionals, they did not make a living mainly on fiction writing; what they wrote and published was part of the regular business activities of their publishing concerns. In this sense, Yü Hsiang-tou must have been a very busy man, witness the profuse variety of works brought out by his companies. They include, but are not limited to, novels, popular encyclopedias, rhyme guides, dictionaries, almanacs, geomantic manuals, and examination digests. For those writers who completed just one or two novels (or for that matter story collections), commercial reward, if any, was in most cases negligible.

Confucian rejection of fiction as a legitimate literary genre and Confucian dominance of the ever-important civil-service examinations had immense negative effects on the growth and image of fiction throughout the ages. Thus, those who chose to write fiction used pseudonyms (particularly if they wrote only one or two works) or justified their writing as intended to provide moral instruction or serve as an awful warning of the consequences of vice (an excuse widely used for novels with erotic elements) or even claimed that what they wrote was not fiction but reporting of fact. That Ts'ao Hsüeh-ch'in's authorship of a novel as popular as the *Hung-lou meng* was not established until the 1920s is one index of the degree to which Confucian disapproval of fiction affected the genre, its practitioners, and its very history. The authors' reluctance to be reputed to write fiction further lessened the effect of commercial considerations in the production of novels. Only a few writers had a direct financial interest in the companies that brought out their novels, like Yü Hsiang-tou and others who must have been significantly benefited by the publication of their works, or Ts'ai Tung-fan 蔡東藩 (1877-1945), who composed a mammoth set of historical novels covering almost the full range of Chinese history. In general commercial considerations had little effect on the writing of novels. Anyway, most of these are historical novels, whose reliance on historical sources, traditional conventions, and the relationship with contextually related novels should have had at least as much influence on their production as commercial considerations. That, however, does not imply that authors of highly personalized novels did not heed the response of their audience. Ts'ao Hsüeh-ch'in sought the advice of readers of his preliminary drafts, and the resultant seemingly ceaseless rounds of revisions (a key factor which inhibited the novel's completion) show that an author could be obsessively concerned with the response of his readers.

The concern for quality and that for financial reward ran against each other in the late Ch'ing period when well over one thousand novels were produced in just a few decades (almost double the total of all previous titles in the vernacular). This boom was made possible by two factors. The unprecedented rate and degree of change in society provided a great number of topics: the deterioration of traditional systems, outrageous corruption, the incompetence of the ruling class, the impact of Western thought and technology, the conflicting solutions for saving China. Few novelists were drawn to the worn-out historical plots or the *ts'ai-tzu chia-jen* framework. Despite the attractiveness of the topics and the generally high competency of the writers, most late Ch'ing novels, including the highly acclaimed ones, are relatively carelessly written. Generally without either the spontaneity of the *Shui-hu chuan* or the polish of the *Hung-lou meng*, they are usually hastily composed, without the benefit of revision, and sometimes even without an overall plan.

This has much to do with the second factor which brought about the boom in the first place. Western and, later, Japanese influences made newspapers and periodicals indispenable parts of urban life, especially in coastal cities like Shanghai. Most carried serialized fiction, a practice still current in Taiwan and Hong Kong newspapers (but no longer in mainland newspapers). Perhaps more than ninety percent of late Ch'ing novels were first written in this form. Only a small fraction of the better-written ones were reissued in book form. Even where this was possible, the chance for authorial revision was rare. Serialized publication was a hazardous procedure that demanded daily the production of fixed-length installments, each of which should have something substantial to say and should encourage the reader to read on without exposing too many upcoming events. But the continiuation of the serial depended on not only its popularity with the readership but also on the continued existence of the publication itself, and so many late Ch'ing newspapers and periodicals were surprisingly short-lived.

With the authorial concern for quality on the one hand, and the possible negative effect of commercial consideration on the other, what were the guides of fiction writing in China? If one has in mind the kind of well-thought-out, constructive criticism, book reviews included, that serves to bring fiction writing to a higher level of excellence, then the reply has to be rather negative: there were few guides of this sort. Even Chin Sheng-t'an, whose critical insight has recently been lavishly praised inside and outside China, did not succeed in formulating fiction criticism more coherent than itemized guidelines in the front matter and isolated notes scattered throughout the text. At least one can say, whatever value can be found in the comments of Chin Sheng-t'an, his predecessors, and his followers, that they fail to produce the kind of systematic theories that are evident in other major genres. For example, even high school students in China can enumerate the principles advocated by the T'ung-ch'eng school of prose writing, the Chiang-hsi school of Sung poetry, or the Wu-chiang school of Ming *ch'uan-ch'i* drama, and name the key practitioners of each school. As to fiction criticism, the best that can be presented as a school is still that of Chin Sheng-t'an and his major followers (Mao Tsung-kang,* Wang Wang-ju 王望如, etc.), but what they mutually upheld is not easily summarized.

There is a temptation to see a fairly well-defined tradition of fiction criticism running from Li Chih* (Li Cho-wu) and Chung Hsing 鍾惺(Chung Po-ching 鍾伯敬, 1574-1624), the eminent predecessors of Chin Sheng-t'an, through Chin himself and his followers. In terms of form, the answer is the affirmative. They all share an obsession with marginal and interlinear notes and, especially after Chin Sheng-t'an, with presenting reading guidelines as part of the front matter. One may even add Feng Meng-lung and Ling Meng-ch'u, whose notes are scattered throughout their *San-yen* and *Erh-p'o* volumes. But in terms of content these materials are of little value, particularly the notes, which express idiosyncratic preference for certain characters or episodes, make cheap jokes, and remind the reader of morals to be drawn from the story—i.e., they do little to advance the art of fiction writing.

There are many texts of a wide range of novels with commentaries attributed to Li Cho-wu and Chung Po-ching, but virtually none of the attributions has been verified, despite all that has been written about the fiction criticism of Li Chih in general and his understanding of the *Shui-hu chuan* in particular (fortunately, no scholarly attention has been given to Chung Po-ching in this respect). Take the *Shui-hu* as an illustration.

There are two *Shui-hu* versions, each with a different number of chapters, each with a commentary attributed to Li Chih. The commentaries, alas, are entirely different. The truth must be either that one of the commentaries is authentic or that both are forgeries. The sad fact is that literary critics are almost as a rule poor bibliographers and incompetent philologists. Some just pick up either set of the Li Cho-wu commentaries available to them and completely ignore the other in talking about Li's viewpoint of the novel. Others dismiss one set as a forgery and elaborate Li's view on the basis of the other, without bothering to establish the authenticity of that set. Or in maintaining the usability of one set, it may be claimed that the thought expressed therein is consistent with that seen in other verifiable works of Li Cho-wu. But it is a good imitator's duty to closely study the style and thought of his subject before he embarks on the work. The key trouble is that the majority of commentaries associated with annotated Ming novels are attributed to Li Cho-wu and Chung Po-ching. Before clearing up these textual and philological problems, there is simply no way to talk about criticism of fiction in Ming China. And without clarifying Ming criticism of fiction, it is easy to overpraise the contributions of Chin Sheng-t'an and his followers.

Turning to the state of the art and the way fiction was understood by the immediate and traditional readership, there are a number of prefaces and postfaces scattered in the almost countless Ming and Ch'ing novels and story collections which may prove helpful. Again, if it is wrong to talk about Ming and Ch'ing novels by relying only on the several major works, it is equally wrong to pay attention only to the prefaces and the postfaces of the key titles. Materials from every available work should be given equal attention in the initial analysis. To gather these materials is surely a formidable task. Fortunately, this work has been enthusiastically pursued by mainland Chinese researchers recently and quite a few impressive collections have already been made available. This is admittedly a vast and exceedingly divergent corpus, and a comprehensive analysis would not be a simple job. It should, however, bring out many overlooked aspects of Chinese fiction.

Serious study of traditional Chinese fiction is a young discipline, only slightly more than half a century old. There are still many fundamental facts unknown, especially when compared with other genres. While there are numerous problems waiting the attention of historians and textual scholars, there is still room for critics, once they have been made aware of the pitfalls (e.g., Li Cho-wu's *Shui-hu* commentaries), to carry out their share of the task. The study of fiction, however, must be kept distinct from politics. It is not necessary to condemn Sung Chiang simply because he crushes Fang La who is considered the leader of a peasant revolution and not a mere bandit chieftain. Similarily, to praise Chin Sheng-t'an should not make it necessary to find a strained way to explain that he really intended to protect Sung Chiang in attacking him. Since fiction studies have always been given high priority in China since 1949, it would be interesting to speculate on advances in the field had not so much talent and effort been wasted in supporting the current party line through "scholarship." Perhaps now with circumstances much improved, it is time not only for the historian-textual specialist and the critic to join hands, but also for scholars in China to exchange their research results with those outside in the hope of avoiding the communication gaps of the past. If this can be done, the state of modern understanding of traditional Chinese fiction can make great progress in just a few decades.

FICTION

BIBLIOGRAPHY:

Since the essay is basically a personal statement of one researcher's concept of traditional Chinese fiction, and since most of the ideas have to be developed further, no references are cited in the text as in the other essays. The following is a minimal reading list for a basic understanding of the genre. References pertinent to individual authors and titles are given in the entries devoted to them.

A-ying 阿英 [Ch'ien Hsing-ts'un 錢杏邨]. 1958. *Wan-Ch'ing hsiao-shuo shih* 晚清小說史. Revised edition. Peking.

Chia, Wen-chao 賈文昭 and Hsü Chao-hsün 徐召勛. 1982. *Chung-kuo ku-tien hsiao-shuo i-shu hsin-shang* 中國古典小說藝術欣賞. Hofei.

Doleželová-Velingerová, Milena. 1980. *The Chinese Novel at the Turn of the Century.* Toronto.

Hanan, Patrick. 1973. *The Chinese Short Story: Studies in Dating, Authorship, and Composition.* Cambridge, Mass.

———. 1981. *The Chinese Vernacular Story.* Cambridge, Mass.

Hegel, Robert E. 1981. *The Novel in Seventeenth-Century China.* New York.

Hsia, C. T. 夏志清. 1968. *The Classic Chinese Novel: A Critical Introduction.* New York.

Idema, Wilt Lukas. 1974. *Chinese Vernacular Fiction: The Formative Period.* Leiden.

Hu, Shih-ying 胡士瑩. 1980. *Hua-pen hsiao-shuo kai-lun* 話本小說概論. 2v. Peking.

Lévy, André. 1981. *Le conte en langue vulgaire du XVIIe siècle.* Paris.

Lu Hsün 魯迅 [Chou Shu-jen 周樹人]. 1981. *Chung-kuo hsiao-shuo shih lüeh* 中國小說史略. Vol. 9 of *Lu Hsün ch'üan-chi* 魯迅全集. Peking. The only annotated edition of the classic study, which is available in a range of widely different editions.

Ma, Y. W. 馬幼垣, and Joseph S. M. Lau 劉紹銘. 1978. *Traditional Chinese Stories: Themes and Variations.* New York. Read front matter for an explanation of the types of short stories.

Ma, Y. W. 1975. "The Chinese Historical Novel: An Outline of Themes and Context," *JAS,* 34.2 (February), 277-294.

Maeno, Naoaki 前野直彬. 1975. *Chūgoku shōsetsu shikō* 中國小說史考. Tokyo.

Ōsaka shiritsu daigaku Chūgoku bungaku kenkyūshitsu 大阪市立大學中國文學研究室. 1965. *Chūgoku no hachi dai shōsetsu* 中國の八大小說. Tokyo.

Pei-ching ta-hsüeh chung-wen hsi 北京大學中文系. 1978. *Chung-kuo hsiao-shuo shih* 中國小說史. Peking.

Plaks, Andrew. 1977. *Chinese Narrative: Critical and Theoretical Essays.* Princeton.

Sawada, Mizuo 澤田瑞穗. *Sō Mei Shin shōsetsu sōkō* 宋明清小說叢考. Tokyo, 1982.

Sun, K'ai-ti 孫楷第. 1957. *Chung-kuo t'ung-su hsiao-shuo shu-mu* 中國通俗小說書目. Revised edition. Peking. Only comprehensive guide of this kind.

Tarumoto, Teruo 樽本照雄. 1983. *Shimmatsu shōsetsu kandan* 清末小說閒談. Kyoto.

Tseng, Tsu-yin 曾祖蔭 et al. 1982. *Chung-kuo li-tai hsiao-shuo hsü-pa hsüan-chu* 中國歷代小說序跋選注. Chang-chiang 長江.

Uchida, Michio 內田道夫. 1970. *Chūgoku shōsetsu no sekai* 中國小說の世界. Tokyo.

———. 1977. *Chūgoku shōsetsu kenkyū* 中國小說研究. Tokyo.

Yüan, Hsing-pei 袁行霈 and Hou Chung-i 侯忠義. 1981. *Chung-kuo wen-yen hsiao-shuo shu-mu* 中國文言小說書目. Peking. Companion to Sun K'ai-ti's guide.

48

LITERARY CRITICISM

Craig Fisk

O F all the major genres of Chinese writing, literary criticism is certainly the least well known. Its history is long, however, and holds interest both as an independent field of study and because some acquaintance with it increases sensitivity to the history of the literature as well as an awareness of its characteristics. Among the very general differences between Chinese criticism and Western criticism, taken as a whole, the three most important concern imitation, fictionality, and genres. In China there were no concepts comparable to Aristotelian mimesis or Christian figura, both of which are bound to the representation of action in time. Rather, the object of representation is mood at a point in time and the correspondences between mind and the state of the surrounding world. Fictionality is not a concern for essentially similar reasons. Although the fantastical, the unreal, and impersonation all have their place in Chinese literature, the literary work is generally understood by the critic as if it were personal history. Lastly, Chinese literary criticism until very recent centuries was concerned almost exclusively with poetry. Dramatic theory had no part in the formation of early criticism as it did in the West; indeed, there is no dramatic corpus of a date comparable to Greek or Roman drama.

Although the earliest critical writing in China dates from the early third century (Holzman, 1978), from before that time there are statements and ideas that merit some attention as backgrounds to later criticism. The earliest remarks that shed light on the uses of poetry are contained in the *Shih-ching*,* which dates from the first half of the first millennium B.C. Most of these lyrics, songs, chants, and hymns have the anonymity of oral tradition. But some have authors who say that their intent was to express sorrow, inform others of their will, praise beauty and goodness, criticize a ruler, or dwell nostalgically on the sages of earlier times. These motivations were shared by the literarily self-conscious lyric poem from the third century A.D. onwards, except that the latter added an idea of poetry as a medium of spiritual self-cultivation.

The several centuries following the period of *Shih-ching* witnessed the development of political and social views on poetry that are evident throughout the Confucian Classics and other ancient texts. The *Li chi* (see *ching*), for example, says that every five years officials of the feudal lords were made to recite songs of the people as a gauge of the political climate. The bibliographical essay in the *Han-shu* also makes the claim that in ancient times rulers employed "song collectors" to measure the efficacy of their policies (Diény, 1968). And the statement that "song expresses the will" (詩言志) in the *Shu-ching* (see *ching*) was often cited in later centuries as authority for the argument that poetry has a political and collective, not an emotional and individual voice (Chow, 1979).

As for early social uses of poetry, historical sources such as the *Tso-chuan** and the *Kuo-yü** make it apparent that the cultivated man was expected to be well-versed in the *Shih-ching* as a mark of social polish. Passages taken out of context and bearing more or less established interpretations formed the elements of sophisticated repartee.

Confucius took this practice a step further by using these social commonplaces as philosophical exempla. In *Lun-yü* 1.15 he praises his disciple Tzu-kung for having acquired the ability to grasp a point when it is made to him in the form of alluding to an image from one of the *Shih-ching* songs. But the *Lun-yü* is also concerned that educated young men be able to use these songs socially. *Lun-yü* 17.8 says that "With the *Songs* you can raise issues, understand others, take your place among men, and express grievances."

The *Lun-yü* also develops a number of philosophical concepts that are reflected in later literary criticism. Most important among these are that literary documents mirror the character of the age that produced them, that crafted language is necessary to effective presentation of ideas and that there should always be a fine balance between form and content. The latter idea calls for some explanation, since literature, culture, text, pattern, and what we mean by "form" here are all interrelated. A central tenet of Confucian thought is that it is the function of culture to regulate and give shape to the basic substance of man and society. By the same token, cultivated, literary writing shapes the basic substance of human expression. It is possible, at the one extreme, for expression to be raw and untutored; or, conversely, to be overly studied, at which point substance is sacrificed. Translated into literary critical terms, Confucian thinking simultaneously justifies the artificiality of literary language and stands ready to criticize art for art's sake.

It may also be mentioned in passing that Confucian distaste for the supernatural and fictitious played no small part in preventing the legitimation of prose fiction in China until the critical realists of the European nineteenth century became known. Even then the novel could only become literarily acceptable by a twist on Confucian views and at the expense of poetry, which lost its status at the same time that Confucian bureacracy and traditional education were devalued.

In sum, the earliest interpretive practices in China were not concerned with either the literariness of literature, the concept of individual expression, or the integrity of the literary work. Aesthetics was indivisible from the *ethos* as a whole.

Several Han-dynasty developments had more impact on literary criticism than has usually been recognized. First was the appearance of literary commentary, a highly Confucian form that evolved from interpretive schools using the *Shih-ching.* The Chi, Lu, Han, and Mao schools all competed for official recognition and essentially still used the Songs of the *Shih-ching* as exempla. The Mao Commentary to the *Shih-ching* and Cheng Hsüan's 鄭玄(127-200) interpretations based on it established commentary as a critical genre.

The Han dynasty was also the first heavily text-oriented culture. The *Lun-heng*論衡 of Wang Ch'ung王充(27-97) distinguished among four types of learned men: the specialist in one classic, the teacher who knows many texts old and new, the political thinker who goes further in his use of broad knowledge in action, and the philosopher-writer who develops new ideas through the medium of writing. The last of these is the role that Wang Ch'ung ascribes to Confucius. The *Han-shu* also includes the new, text-oriented critical genres of bibliographical, biographical, and literary historical writing.

Finally, the emergence in the Han dynasty of the *fu** and study of the *Ch'u-tz'u,** the shamanistic quest literature of the South from which the *fu* partly grew, had several ramifications for aesthetics and literary criticism. For one thing, the use of imperson-ation in this poetry led to the broader notion of personae, or voices through which the literary man could cast himself alternately as such things as peasant, courtesan, fish-erman, hermit, or poet of the past. Poetry was thus no longer purely non-fictive. It had new synthetic and eclectic possibilities. Also, the highly cultivated descriptive language of the ode helped establish the artificial dialect of poetic language—actually a polyphony of poetic languages. And the imagistic consistency, logical continuity, and sheer volume of writing in the *fu* form made it impossible to disregard the unity and style of individual literary "works."

Although the *fu* stimulated the concept of writing as a craft in which the broadly educated man could creatively express himself and was commonly practiced, as the historical essay in the bibliography to the *Han-shu* bears witness, there were also fre-quently expressed doubts, for example by Yang Hsiung* and Emperor Hsüan, as to the Confucian propriety of the form (Knechtges, 1976). Consequently, one last critical aspect of the Han dynasty is the application of Confucian allegory to the *fu* to justify its existence. From this, literary criticism became attuned to the broader, more spec-ulative elements of story in allegorical interpretation.

The first work strictly devoted to literary criticism is generally considered to be Ts'ao P'i's* "Lun wen" 論文(Essay on Literature) in his *Tien lun* 典論(Classical Essays). The book itself is no longer extant, but the "Essay on Literature" was preserved in the *Wen-hsüan.** The work provides short criticism of each of the Chien-an ch'i-tzu (see Ch'en Lin), who were the leading contemporary writers, as well as of Ch'ü Yüan,* Chia I,* and other earlier poets. It also includes remarks on the characteristics of four genres: bureaucratic written proposals, personal letters and essays, the epigraph, and poetic writing in the lyric or ode forms. In the latter section Ts'ao P'i puts forward his theory of *ch'i* 氣(vital force) in literary works. The quality of the work is a reflection of the "vital force" of its author, a concept that remains important in later poetry criticism.

After this there gradually come to be more and more writings concerned exclusively with literary criticism during the Six Dynasties. Two factors are important here. One is the making of literary anthologies, to which critical essays largely historical in form were often appended (Rickett, 1975). The other is the influence of abstract, binary modes of thought from early Chinese Buddhism. Chung Jung's *Shih-p'in** and Liu Hsieh's *Wen-hsin tiao-lung** from the early sixth century mention a number of earlier Six Dynasties works of criticism about which very little is known. These include such works as the "Wen fu" by Lu Chi* and the *Wen-chang chih* by Chih Yü.*

Lu Chi's "Wen fu" was preserved in the *Wen-hsüan*. This elaborate, poetic essay on literature might best be described as a rhapsody on the metaphysics, craft, and psychology of literary composition. Chih Yü's work appears to have been a literary anthology with an appended critical essay (Allen, 1976). From fragments preserved in other works it seems it was concerned with general evaluations. From this period there are also some fragments of texts by Shen Yüeh* and Wang Pin 王斌 on metrics.

With Liu Hsieh's *Wen-hsin tiao-lung* and Chung Jung's *Shih-p'in* in the early sixth century, literary criticism becomes a substantial and completely independent enterprise. The considerable reputations of both men are based solely on their literary criticism, and both works are remarkable in size and quality. The fifty chapters of the *Wen-hsin tiao-lung* are equally divided between discussions of all the major literary genres and discussions of what might best be called the dynamics of literary works, i.e., their form, style, use of material, and rhetorical structure. Given the size of the *Wen-hsin tiao-lung*, it has proven difficult for scholars to point to themes that dominate Liu Hsieh's critical thought (Gibbs, 1970). Nevertheless, Liu Hsieh seems to be simultaneously motivated by both Confucian and Buddhist ideas, because he argues for the use of the Confucian Classics as models for contemporary writing, yet takes a strongly Buddhist influenced approach to the abstract analysis that goes into his technical chapters. Secondly, even though he wants writers to take the Confucian Classics as models and to be diverse in their generic capabilities, Liu Hsieh's technical chapters clearly show that his conception of literature is dominated by the lyric poetry and odes of the early third through the early fifth centuries. Perhaps it is best to say that the *Wen-hsin tiao-lung* is a moderately conservative book of criticism written in a period when the distinction between literary and nonliterary writing was not yet so sharp, and that it redefined the classics *as* literature.

In this respect Chung Jung's *Shih-p'in* seems much more modern simply because it restricts itself to criticism of the lyric. Chung Jung says in his preface that he limited his compass because the lyric combined the best features of all other forms of composition. The central argument in Chung Jung's views on poetry is that the essence of poetry consists in "expressing states of mind" 詩言志. That is, poetry is a personal reflection that should not be adulterated by overly studied literary features such as metrics and classical allusions. But Chung Jung's critical views are also very much centered on the landscape lyric and artful description that gives the impression of finding the poet's emotions mirrored in the landscape. Thus the poets in his top rank are all distinguished by their ability to express emotion, those in the second rank by at least artful description, and those in the lowest rank by their inability to stand out in either regard. There is, however, much controversy over the standing accorded some poets—T'ao Ch'ien,* for example, is in the second group, although most other traditional and modern critics would consider him among the best in the first rank (see *Shih-p'in*).

Until recently the literary criticism that survives from the T'ang dynasty was largely ignored, in part because the interests of the criticism seemed to clash with dominant interpretations of T'ang poetry and in part because T'ang criticism was often contained in less well-known sources, such as the early ninth-century *Bunkyō hifuron** (i.e., *Wen-ching mi-fu lun*) by the Japanese monk Kūkai and Chi Yu-kung's twelfth-century *T'ang-shih chi-shih.** From the earlier part of the T'ang there are works such as Wu Ch'ing's 吳兢 (670-749) *Yüeh-fu ku-t'i yao-chieh* 樂府古題要解 (Explanations of Old Ballads), Yüan Ching's 元兢 *Ku-chin shih-jen hsiu-chü* 古今詩人秀句 (Beautiful Lines by Ancient and Modern Poets) and Li Chiao's* (644-713) *P'ing shih ko* 評詩格 (Poetic Modes). Wu Ching's work was concerned with relating older ballad themes to a T'ang audience of poets who might want to use them, Yüan Ching's appears to have been largely a collection of striking couplets from earlier poets, and Li Chiao's study served as a rather mechanical introduction to the topoi of early eighth-century poetry.

Of greater interest both for their broad aesthetic concerns and for their relevance to High T'ang poetry are Wang Ch'ang-ling's* *Shih ko* and Chiao-jan's* *Shih-shih* from the late eighth century. Both emphasize the artfulness of making emotive and descriptive language seem to merge together in the lyric and the use of the lyric as an instrument of personal reflection. In this they are fairly close to Chung Jung's *Shih-p'in*. In addition, Wang Ch'ang-ling's *Shih ko* expounds a phenomenology of the creative process that suggests the poet achieves a privileged position in the world through his ability to deftly manipulate the power of words. Chiao-jan's *Shih-shih* on the other hand, is especially concerned with the intellectual craft of poetry, which has as its object, however, the appearance of total naturalness and effortlessness in its finished product.

From the late T'ang Ssu-k'ung T'u's* *Erh-shih ssu shih-p'in* and Chang Wei's 張爲 *Shih-jen chu-k'o t'u* 詩人主客圖 (Masters and Schools Among the Poets) are the most important critical works. Ssu-k'ung T'u distinguishes among twenty-four varieties of taste in poetry—such as "powerful," "tranquil," "fine and delicate," "profound," "archaic," "classically elegant" and so on—and describes the character of each in twelve lines of verse. Ssu-k'ung T'u is also known for some of his critical letters, especially the *Yü Li Sheng lun-shih shu* 與李生論詩書 (Letter to Li Sheng on Poetry), which uses the metaphors of vinegar and salt to speak of significance beyond taste or interest beyond words.

Chang Wei's *Masters and Schools Among the Poets* separates Mid- and Late T'ang poets into six movements with a star poet as the "master" in each case. These six movements are described as: (1) Transforming Teachings of the Great Way (with Po Chü-i* as its master), (2) Archaic and Profound (Meng Yü-ch'ing 孟雲卿), (3) Clear, Strange, and Elegant (Li I 李益), (4) Clear, Strange, and Bitter (Meng Chiao*), (5) Learned and Lofty (Pao Jung 包融), and (6) Clear, Strange, and Beautiful (Wu Yüan-heng 武元衡).

It should also be mentioned in passing that much important T'ang criticism is to be found in the letters of authors such as Han Yü,* Liu Tsung-yüan,* and Po Chü-i,* especially as concerns arguments about literary movements and interpretations of views on earlier literature. Epigraphs and prefaces are often also important vehicles for critical statements of this type. The T'ang, particularly from the mid-eighth century onwards, was a period of much more literarily self-conscious poets and essayists, rather than of critics per se.

Sung-dynasty criticism is marked by the flourishing of poetry criticism in the new *shih-hua** form that collects a writer's critical insights and remarks in loose chronological and topical order of the subject matter. The typical author of *shih-hua* was an older scholar who had spent many years collecting information on poetry, discussing poems with friends in leisurely conversation, and jotting down occasional insights. Hence, the character of remarks in the *shih-hua* ranges from pithy to extremely casual and tangential. Rarely is there anything like a unifying theme or theory in these works, although most reflect strongly held personal opinions.

The poet and essayist Ou-yang Hsiu* started the form around 1070 with his *Liu-i shih-hua* a work largely devoted to the transparent style of Mei Yao-ch'en.* At about the same time Wang An-shih* completed the *Ssu-chia shih hsüan* 四家詩選 (Anthology of Four Poets), which included Tu Fu,* Ou-yang Hsiu, Han Yü and Li Po.* Much of the poetry criticism over the course of the next century was written under the heading of the opposition between Ou-yang Hsiu's interest in naturalness of tone and Wang An-shih's interest in strikingness of style. Critical writing in support of the former, the Yüan-yu 元祐 Group, included Ou-yang Hsiu's *Liu-i shih-hua*, critical remarks of Su Shih collected by later followers, Hui-hung's 惠洪 (1071-1128) *Leng-chai yeh-hua* 冷齋夜話 (Evening Discourses from a Cold Studio), Hsü I's 許顗 (*tzu*, Yen-chou 彥周, *fl.* 1110) *Yen-chou* *shih-hua*, Chu Pien's 朱弁(d. 1154) *Feng-yeh t'ang shih-hua* 風月堂詩話 (Criticism of Poetry from the Hall of Wind and Moonlight), and Wu K'o's 吳可(*fl.* 1126) *Ts'ang-hai shih-hua* 藏海詩話. Critical writing that supported the emphasis on striking style, the Shao-shu 紹述 Group, included Yeh Meng-te's 葉夢得(1077-1148) *Shih-lin shih-hua* 石林詩話 (Criticism of Poetry by the Scholar of Stone Forest, and poetry criticism by the writers associated with the Kiangsi School,* such as Lü Pen-chung 呂本中(*fl.* 1119), who were followers of the poet Huang T'ing-chien,* even though Huang T'ing-chien himself was critical of Wang An-shih.

Another leading aspect of poetry criticism in the eleventh and twelfth centuries is its overriding concern with the work of the T'ang poet Tu Fu. Because of the technical brilliance of Tu Fu's poetry, his work was of special interest to Wang An-shih, who placed him first in his *Anthology of Four Poets,* and to the Shao-shu Group. But there was sufficient diversity to the character of Tu Fu's poetry that it became the touchstone for both sides. Far more remarks were devoted to Tu Fu than to any other poet in the poetry criticism of this period, as witnessed by collections such as Hu Tzu's *T'iao-hsi yü-yin ts'ung-hua,** Ts'ai Meng-pi's 蔡夢弼(*fl.* 1247) *Ts'ao-t'ang shih-hua* 草堂詩話 (Criticism of the Poet of the Grass Cottage), and Chang Chieh's 張戒(*fl.* 1135) *Sui-han t'ang shih-hua* 歲寒堂詩話 (Criticism of Poetry by a Man in a Cold Season). Ko Li-fang's 葛立方(d. 1164) *Yün-yü yang-ch'iu* 韻語陽秋 (Annals of Verse), dating from the early twelfth century, also gives more space to Tu Fu than to any other poet in what is probably the most extensive collection of criticism by any Sung author. What most attracted critics about Tu Fu was his skill in the blending of feeling and landscape, in the application of allusions, in creating semantic/syntactic twists, and in casting himself into the role of voice of the people (Fisk, 1980).

Among late Sung works of poetry criticism, four stand out. Chiang K'uei's* *Pai-shih tao-jen shih-shuo* 白石道人詩說 (Criticism of Poetry from White Rock), Yen Yü's *Ts'ang-lang shih-hua** (Criticism of Poetry by a Hermit on the Azure Stream), and Yang Wan-li's* (Criticism of Poetry from the Studio of Sincerity) all emphasize the superiority of genius over poetic craft. Of these Yen Yü's work is the one that most influenced later critics through its use of Zen Buddhist metaphors, its belief that "penetration of the spirit" into one's subject produced enlightened poetry, and its emphasis on the poets of the High T'ang as the touchstone for criticism. A fourth thirteenth-century work, Fan Hsi-wen's 范晞文(*fl.* 1279) *Tui-ch'uang yeh-hua* 對床夜話 (Night Dialogues), summarizes the key elements on the technical side of Sung poetic criticism. These include the aesthetics of blending the abstract and the concrete, or feeling and scene in the central couplets of the lyric; the fascination with the alchemy of borrowing and playing upon imagery and ideas, often discussed under the rubric of "changing the bones and extracting the embryo" (Fisk, 1977) and the poetics of word placement and verbal surprise, known as focusing attention on the "verse eye."

The Sung was very much an age of poetry criticism. Among the best introductions to the mass of writing on poetry from this period are three collections of criticism, each of which has a different type of focus. Hu Tzu's *T'iao-hsi yü-yin ts'ung-hua* is organized by poets in chronological order, Juan Yüeh's 阮閱(*fl.* 1126) *Shih-hua tsung-kuei* 詩話總龜 (General Compendium of Poetry Criticism) by common topics in poetry, and Wei Ch'ing-chih's *Shih-jen yü-hsieh* by technical devices and poets.

A common concern in poetry criticism of the Ming and Ch'ing dynasties is with the art of reading and theories of appreciation. Critics are no longer seriously writing for contemporary poets in a prescriptive mode, as was at least partially still the case in the Sung dynasty. Rather, critics assume that the canon of Six Dynasties, High T'ang, and Northern Sung poets established by the Sung can in no way be excelled by contemporary writing, and so their criticism is retrospective and eclectic, seeking to refine the techniques of appreciation.

Li Tung-yang's* *Lu-t'ang shih-hua* 麓堂詩話 (Criticism of Poetry from a Hall at the Foot of the Mountain), written at the turn of the sixteenth century, goes so far as to emphasize the visual and aural pleasures of perceiving poetry in his theory of "form and sound." Wang Fu-chih's* *Chiang-chai shih-hua* also emphasizes the art of reading, while refining older ideas such as feeling and scene and unobtrusive use of allusions. Hu Ying-lin's* *Shih-sou* 詩藪 (Art of Poetry) from the same period provides an excellent historical treatment of poetry, highlighting the differences of movements, styles, and interpretations of the past that form the pattern of literary history.

The *shen-yün* 神韻 (divine harmony) theory of Wang Shih-chen (1634-1711)* from the early seventeenth century says that reading aloud imperceptibly leads to an experience of pure harmony and pleasure that is the object of literature. The *ling-hsing* 靈性 (mind and spirit) theory of Yüan Mei's* late eighteenth-century *Sui-yüan shih-hua* 隨園詩話 (Criticism of Poetry from the Garden of Leisure) says that it is necessary to ride freely with movements of states of mind in the experience of poetry and to not get tangled in the verbal surface of the poem. But such theories at best only provide ambiguous confirmation of the pleasures of reading, while it is the occasional insights into the style and character of earlier poetry that have more substance. Perhaps for that reason critical works such as Chao I's* *Ou-pei shih-hua* 甌北詩話 (Criticism of Poetry from the Northern Wastes) or Yeh Hsieh's* *Yüan shih* 原詩 (Origins of Poetry) are ultimately much more satisfying. The former work emphasizes the broad range and character of a limited group of major poets, including Li Po, Tu Fu, and Han Yü from the T'ang; Su Shih* and Lu Yu from the Sung; Yüan Hao-wen* from the Chin; Kao Ch'i* from the Ming, and Wu Wei-yeh* and Cha Shen-hsing* from the Ch'ing. Yeh Hsieh's *Yüan shih*, on the other hand, is the fairly organic exposition of a phenomenology of feeling in poetry.

It is only possible to mention very briefly a few of the works relevant to criticism of prose writing, the song lyric, arias and opera, and the novel (see also essays on drama, fiction, and prose). Two works on prose from the twelfth and thirteenth centuries merit notice, although there are some scattered remarks on prose techniques in T'ang and earlier Sung dynasty authors. The first is Ch'en K'uei's 陳騤 (1128-1203) *Wen-tse,* * which thinks highly of the simple, pithy ancient prose of the pre-Ch'in period and is distinguished by its attention to analysis of style, rhetoric, and the use of language. The other is Li T'u's 李塗 (fl. 1147) *Wen-chang ching-i* 文章精義 (Essential Meaning of Prose), which has something of a Neo-Confucian flavor because its author was a second-generation disciple of Chu Hsi.

*Ku-wen** style is well discussed by the section on prose in Liu Hsi-tsai's 劉熙載 (1813-1881) *I kai* 藝概 (Introduction to the Arts). Hsüeh Fu-ch'eng's 薛福成 (1838-1894) *Lun-wen chi-yao* 論文集要 (Collection of Essential Ideas on Prose) from the same period gathers useful material by Ch'ing authors on ancient prose style, providing an understanding of the key ideas of the T'ung-ch'eng p'ai.*

Criticism of the *tz'u** began in the late Sung dynasty. Wang Cho's 王灼 (fl. 1162) *Pi-chi man-chih* 碧雞漫志 (Idle Records from the Azure Stream) is the earliest. It discusses

55

the development, lyrics, and associated anecdotes for songs from the T'ang and Sung dynasties. Wang Cho's taste is for the work of Su Shih. He also discusses some of the musical aspects of the song, as does Chang Yen 張炎 (1248-1320) in *Tz'u yüan* 詞源 (Wellspring of the Lyric), written slightly later. Chang Yen wrote partly against the current popularity of Chou Pang-yen* and in order to promote poets such as Ch'in Kuan (1049-1100) and Chiang K'uei.* Much of Ming and Ch'ing criticism on the lyric involves the carryover of critical concepts from the literary lyric and musical concepts that need not concern us here. The *Tz'u-yüan ts'ung-t'an* 詞苑叢談 (Collected Discourses from the Garden of the Lyric) by Hsü Ch'iu 徐釚 (1636-1708) is a vast collection of this material covering evaluation, theory, and anecdotes from earlier periods arranged according to topics.

Early opera criticism is mainly concerned with the composition of free arias and not with broader questions of literary structure or performance. The *Chung-yüan yin-yün* by Chou Te-ch'ing (c. 1270-after 1324) of the Yüan dynasty, for example, includes in its second part a discussion of ten techniques in the composition of arias. From the early Ming, the first part of Chu Ch'üan's* *T'ai-ho cheng-yin p'u* offers brief critiques of the styles of one hundred some authors of opera and free arias from the Yüan and early Ming. Hsü Wei's* *Nan tz'u hsü-lu* 南詞敘錄 (Description of the Art of Southern Libretti) discusses literary and musical sides of the Southern Aria and operas. The *Chü-lü* 曲律 (Methodology of the Aria) by his disciple Wang Chi-te 王驥德 (d. 1623) is a systematic and general introduction to the opera and free aria, while Lü T'ien-ch'eng's 呂天成 (1573-1619) *Ch'ü-p'in* 曲品 (Evaluation of Arias) provides fairly exhaustive criticism of all Southern Arias and drama up to the late sixteenth century. Finally, perhaps the best general introduction to opera, especially on its structure and composition, is the section on lyrics and arias in Li Yü's* (1611-1680) *Hsien-ch'ing ou-chi* 閒情偶寄 (Sojourn in Leisure).

Criticism of the novel in China before the modern period dates mainly from the late Ming and the Ch'ing dynasties. It is very voluminous but rarely takes on the shape of independent work, found rather as stray remarks or as a commentary to a specific novel such as was the case with the early Ch'ing critic Chin Sheng-t'an,* whose critical editions of the *Shui-hu chuan** and the *Hsi-hsiang chi** are both well known. His method is to introduce the novel with a "reading approach" essay, to give general critical commentary at the head of each chapter and to interlace the text with running commentary. A roughly similar method is followed in other novel criticism from the Ch'ing, most notably the *Chih-yen chai ts'ung-p'ing Shih-t'ou chi* 脂硯齋重評石頭記 (Red Inkstone Commentary to the Dream of the Red Chamber).

BIBLIOGRAPHY:
Allen, Joseph Roe, III. 1976. "Chih Yü's Discussion of Different Types of Literature: A Translation and Brief Comment," in *Parerga 3: Two Studies in Chinese Literary Criticism*, Seattle, pp. 1-36.
Aoki, Masaru 青木正兒. 1943. *Shina bungaku shisōshi* 支那文學思想史. Tokyo.
———. 1949. *Shina bungaku geijitsu kō* 支那文學藝術考. Rpt. Tokyo.
———. 1969. *Shindai bungaku hihyō shi* 清代文學批評, in *Aoki Masaru zenshū* 青木正兒全集,

Tokyo, v. 1, pp. 393-581.
Bodman, Richard Wainwright. 1978. "Poetics and Prosody in Early Mediaeval China: A Study and Translation of Kūkai's *Bunkyō hifuron*." Unpublished Ph.D dissertation, Cornell University.
Chang, Chien 張健. 1969. *Chu Hsi te wen-hsüeh p'i-p'ing yen-chiu* 朱熹的文學批評研究. Taipei.
———, ed. 1978. *Nan Sung wen-hsüeh p'i-p'ing tzu-liao hui-pien* 南宋文學批評資料彙編. Taipei.
Ch'en, Shih-hsiang. 1951. "In Search of the Beginnings of Chinese Literary Criticism," in

Semitic and Oriental Studies, Walter J. Fischel, ed., pp. 45-63. Berkeley and Los Angeles.

Chow, Tse-tsung. 1979. "Ancient Chinese Views on Literature, the *Tao,* and Their Relationship," *CLEAR,* 1.1 (January), 3-29.

Chu, Tung-jun 朱東潤. 1960. *Chung-kuo wen-hsüeh p'i-p'ing shih ta-kang* 中國文學批評史大綱. 1944; rpt. Taipei.

———— *et al.* 1971. *Chung-kuo wen-hsüeh p'i-p'ing chia yü wen-hsüeh p'i-p'ing* 中國文學批評家與文學批評. 4v. Taiwan Hsüeh-sheng shu-chü, comp. Taipei.

Chung-kuo ku-tai wen-hsüeh li-lun hsüeh-hui 中國古代文學理論學會, ed. 1979-1981. *Ku-tai wen-hsüeh li-lun yen-chiu* 古代文學理論研究. 4v. Shanghai.

Chung-kuo ku-tien hsi-ch'u lun-chu chi-ch'eng 中國古典戲曲論著集成. 1959-60. 10v. Chung-kuo hsi-ch'ü yen-chiu-yüan 中國戲曲研究院, comp. Peking.

Debon, Günther, tr. 1962. *Ts'ang-Lang's Gespräche über die Dichtung: Ein Beitrag zur Chinesischen Poetik.* Wiesbaden.

Diény, Jean Pierre. 1968. *Aux origines de la poésie classique en Chine. Etude sur la poésie a l'époque des Han.* Leiden.

Fisk, Craig. 1980. "The Alterity of Chinese Literature in Its Critical Contexts," *CLEAR,* 2.1 (January), 87-99.

———. 1976. "Formal Themes in Mediaeval Chinese and Modern Western Literary Theory: Mimesis, Intertextuality, Figurativeness, and Foregrounding." Unpublished Ph.D. dissertation. University of Wisconsin, Madison.

———. 1980. "On the Dialectics of the Strange and Sublime in the Historical Reception of Tu Fu," in *Proceedings of the Ninth Congress of the International Comparative Literature Association,* v. 2, pp. 75-82. Innsbruck.

———. 1977. "The Verse Eye and the Self-animating Landscape in Chinese Poetry," *TkR,* 8.1 (April), 123-153.

Fu, Keng-sheng 傅庚生. 1947. *Chung-kuo wen-hsüeh p'i-p'ing t'ung-lun* 中國文學批評通論. Shanghai.

Funatsu, Tomihiko 船津富彥. 1977. *Chūgoku shiwa no kenkyū* 中國詩話の研究. Tokyo.

Gibbs, Donald Arthur. 1970. "Literary Theory in the *Wen-hsin tiao-lung.*" Unpublished Ph.D. dissertation, University of Washington.

———. 1972. "Notes on the Wind: The Term "Feng" in Chinese Literary Criticism," in *Transition and Permanence: Chinese History and Culture,* David C. Buxbaum and Frederick W. Mote, eds., pp. 285-293. Hong Kong.

Golygina, Kirina Ivanovna. 1971. *Teoriya izyashchuoi slovesnosti v Kitae [The Theory of Literature in China].* Moscow.

Hanan, Patrick. 1981. *The Chinese Vernacular Story.* Esp. "Feng's Life and Ideas," pp. 75-97, "Ling Mengchu," pp. 140-164, and "Dramatic and Fictional Theory," pp. 145-148. Cambridge, Mass.

Hayashida, Shinnosuke 林田慎之助. 1979. *Chūgoku chūsei bungaku hyōron shi* 中國中世文學評論史. Tokyo.

Hightower, James Robert. 1962. "Literary Criticism through the Six Dynasties," in *Topics in Chinese Literature,* rev. ed., pp. 42-48. Cambridge, Mass.

Holzman, Donald. 1978. "Confucius and Ancient Chinese Literary Criticism," in *Chinese Approaches to Literature,* Adele Rickett, ed., pp. 21-41. Princeton.

Hsia, C. T. 1976. "Yen-fu and Liang Ch'i-ch'ao as Advocates of New Fiction," in *Journal of Oriental Studies,* 14, 133-149.

Huang, Ch'i-fang 黃啓方. 1978. *Pei Sung wen-hsüeh p'i-p'ing tzu-liao hui-pien* 北宋文學批評資料彙編. Taipei.

Knechtges, David R. 1976. *The Han Rhapsody, A Study of the Fu of Yang Hsiung, 53 B.C.-A.D. 18.* Cambridge.

K'o, Ch'ing-ming 柯慶明 and Tseng Yung-i 曾永義, eds. 1978. *Liang Han Wei Chin Nan-pei-ch'ao wen-hsüeh p'i-p'ing tzu-liao hui-pien* 兩漢魏晉南北朝文學批評資料彙編. Taipei.

Ku-tai wen-hsüeh li-lun yen-chiu ts'ung-k'an 古代文學理論研究叢刊. 1979. V. 1. Shanghai.

Kuo, Shao-yü 郭紹虞, ed. 1979. *Chung-kuo li-tai wen-lun hsüan* 中國歷代文論選. 3v. Hong Kong.

———. 1961. *Chung-kuo wen-hsüeh p'i-p'ing shih* 中國文學批評史. Shanghai.

Legge, James. 1960. "The Great Preface," in *The Chinese Classics,* v. 4: *The She King [The Book of Poetry].* Rpt. pp. 34-37. Hong Kong.

Liao, Wei-ch'ing 廖蔚卿. 1978. *Liu-ch'ao wen-lun* 六朝文論. Taipei.

Lin, Ming-te 林明德, ed. 1979. *Chin-tai wen-hsüeh p'i-p'ing tzu-liao hui-pien* 金代文學批評資料彙編. Taipei.

Liu, James J. Y. 1962. *The Art of Chinese Poetry.* Chicago, 1962.

———. 1975. *Chinese Theories of Literature.* Chicago and London, 1975.

———. 1972. "Prolegomena to a Study of Traditional Chinese Theories of Literature," *LEW,* 16.3 (September), 935-949.

———. 1966. "Towards a Chinese Theory of Poetry," *YCGL*, 15, 159-165.

———. 1977. "Towards a Synthesis of Chinese and Western Theories of Literature," *JCP*, 4.1, 1-24.

Liu, Wei-ping. 1967. "A Study of the Development of Chinese Poetic Theories in the Ch'ing Dynasty (1644-1911)." Unpublished Ph.D. dissertation, University of Sydney.

Lo, Ken-tse 羅根澤. 1962. *Chung-kuo wen-hsüeh p'i-p'ing shih* 中國文學批評史. Shanghai.

Lo, Lien-t'ien 羅聯添, ed. 1978. *Sui T'ang Wu-tai wen-hsüeh p'i-p'ing tzu-liao-pien* 隋唐五代文學批評資料彙編. Taipei.

Ma, Yau-woon. 1970. "Confucius as a Literary Critic: A Comparison with the Early Greeks," in *Essays in Chinese Studies Dedicated to Professor Jao Tsung-i*, pp. 13-45. Hong Kong.

Martin, Helmut. 1980. "Chinesische Literaturkritik: Die heutige Bedeutung des traditionellen Literaturbegriffes sowie Forschungsstand und Quellensituation der Literaturkritikgeschichte," *OE*, 27.1, 115-129.

———. 1966. *Li Li-weng über das Theater.* Heidelberg, 1966.

———. 1973. *So-yin pen Ho-shih li-tai shih-hua* 索引本何氏歷代詩話 [Index to the Ho Collection of Twenty-eight Shih-jua]. 2v. Taipei.

———. 1973. "A Transitional Concept of Chinese Literature 1897-1917: Liang Ch'i-chao on Poetry Reform, Historical Drama and the Political Novel," *OE*, 20, 175-217.

Matsushita, Tadashi 松下忠. 1978. *Min Shin no san-shisetsu* 明清の三詩説. Tokyo.

McMullen, David. 1973. "Historical and Literary Theory in the Mid-Eighth Century," in *Perspectives on the T'ang*, Arthur F. Wright and Denis Twitchett, eds., pp. 307-342. New Haven and London.

Miao, Ronald. 1972. "Literary Criticisim at the End of the Eastern Han," *LEW*, 16, 1013-1034.

———, ed. 1978. *Studies in Chinese Poetry and Poetics.* V. 1. San Francisco.

Rickett, Adele Austin. 1975. "The Anthologist as Literary Critic in China," *LEW*, 19, 146-165.

———, ed. 1978. *Chinese Approaches to Literature from Confucius to Liang Ch'i-ch'ao.* Princeton.

———. 1973. "The Personality of the Chinese critic," in *The Personality of the Critic* [Yearbook of Comparative Criticism, v. 6], Joseph P. Strelka, ed., pp. 111-134. University Park, Penn., and London.

———. 1968. "Technical Terms in Chinese Literary Criticism," *LEW*, 12 (1968), 141-147.

San-wen yü lun-p'ing chih pu 散文與論評之部. 1979. In *Chung-kuo ku-tien wen-hsüeh yen-chiu ts'ung-k'an* 中國古典文學研究叢刊, K'o Ch'ing-ming 柯慶明 and Lin Ming-te 林明德, eds. Taipei. Contains several articles on literary criticism.

Shih, Vincent Yuchung, tr. 1959. *The Literary Mind and the Carving of Dragons.* New York.

Suzuki, Shuji 鈴木修次. 1977. *Chūgoku kodai bungaku ron—Shi kei no bungeisei* 中國古代文學論—詩經の文藝性. Tokyo.

Tōkei, Ferenc. 1971. *Genre Theory in China in the 3rd-6th Centuries (Liu Hsieh's Theory on Poetic Genres).* Budapest.

Tseng, Yung-i 曾永義. 1978. *Yüan-tai wen-hsüeh p'i-p'ing tzu-liao hui-pien* 元代文學批評資料彙編. 2v. Taipei.

Wang, John. 1972. *Chin Sheng-t'an.* New York.

Watson, Burton. 1958. "Ssu-ma Ch'ien's Theory of Literature," in *Ssu-ma Ch'ien: Grand Historian of China*, pp. 154-158. New York.

Wixted, John Timothy. 1982. *Poems on Poetry, Literary Criticism by Yüan Hao-wen (1190-1257).* Wiesbaden.

Wong, Wai-leung. 1976. "Chinese Impressionistic Criticism: A Study of the Poetry-Talk (Shih-hua tz'u-hua) Tradition." Unpublished Ph.D. dissertation. Ohio State University.

Wu, Hung-i 吳宏一 and Yeh Ch'ing-ping, eds. 1979. *Ch'ing-tai wen-hsüeh p'i-p'ing tzu-liao hui-pien* 清代文學批評資料彙編. 2v. Taipei.

Yeh, Ch'ing-ping 葉慶炳 and Shao Hung 邵紅, eds. 1979. *Ming-tai wen-hsüeh p'i-p'ing tzu-liao hui-pien* 明代文學批評資料彙編. 2v. Taipei.

Yip, Wai-lim. 1970. "Yen Yü and the Poetic Theories in the Sung Dynasty," *TKR*, 1.2 (October), 183-200.

Yu, Pauline. 1978. "Chinese and Symbolist Poetic Theories," *Comparative Literature*, 30, 291-312.

POETRY

Charles Hartman

I. The Verse Forms

THE history of poetry in China gains in comprehensibility if one adopts a somewhat broader definition of verse than has been usual among historians of Chinese literature. For the purposes of this essay, verse is defined as discourse possessing both rhythm and rhyme. There is no general term in Chinese to cover such a broad range of linguistic phenomena. The Chinese, on the contrary, have preferred to concentrate on the origin and development of individual verse forms. This preference has tended to minimize those features that are common to all Chinese verse forms and to ignore the often considerable cross-fertilization across genre lines. The most important verse forms in China have been:

1) the ancient *shih** (odes) of the *Shih-ching,**
2) the Han *yüeh-fu** (Music-Bureau) poetry and its continuation as "old style-poetry" 古體詩,
3) the *lü-shih* 律詩 (regulated verse) of the T'ang and after,
4) the *sao* 騷 (elegiac) poetry of the state of Ch'u (see *Ch'u-tz'u*), its later imitations, and continuation as *fu** (prose poem),
5) the *tz'u** (lyric) beginning in the T'ang, and
6) the *ch'ü** (aria) beginning in the Yüan.

II. The Ancient Odes

The origins of *shih* poetry are usually traced to the *Shih-ching* 詩經 (The Classic of Poetry), an anthology of about three hundred verse texts composed between 1100 and 600 B.C. This anthology probably existed in much its present state during the lifetime of Confucius (551-479 B.C.), who legend relates compiled the work from a collection of over three thousand poems. The present text, and its oldest commentary, date from the Han period (206 B.C.-A.D. 220). This is the *Mao Shih Cheng chien* 毛詩鄭箋 (The Mao [Edition of the *Classic of*] *Poetry* with Commentary by Cheng [Hsüan]).

Although the *Shih-ching* is the earliest monument in the Chinese poetic tradition, its sophistication betrays the long-standing use of verse for a wide variety of social and political occasions. Many bronze inscriptions, for instance, contain versified passages that were recited at various court rituals, and the diction of these recitations often shows affinity with that of the *Shih-ching* (Yü, 1936). And the *I-ching* (The Classic of Change—see *ching*) has at least twenty passages of gnomic versified incantations, many of which are similar to *Shih-ching* formulations (Waley, 1933).

59

Although the diversity of non-*Shih-ching* Chou verse confirms the catholicity of this anthology's compiler(s), later Confucian scholars were unanimous as to the collection's moralistic purpose and value. Their views are articulated in the "Ta hsü"大序(Great Preface) to the anthology which, whatever period it may date from (estimates range from fifth century B.C. to third century A.D.), summarized traditional Confucian notions of the function of poetry in society. Popular song, arising from the illiterate population, was taken as a mirror that reflected the efficacy of the sovereign's government. Beneficent administration gave rise to joyous sounds, malevolent government caused sounds of sorrow. The court of a sagacious sovereign, in turn, used this collected corpus of popular song both as a repository of formulas with which to versify their own political issues and as a source of inspiration for court ritual verses. These latter, having undergone a metamorphosis at the hands of court musicians, were disseminated to the populace, there to work their influence as an impetus to civil virtue. Such was the concept of *feng*風(verse criticism), the first of the so-called *liu-i*六義(six principles [of poetry]) outlined in the "Great Preface."

The Mao Commentary in the edition of Cheng Hsüan (*Mao Shih Cheng chien*) is the repository of exegesis that interpreted individual *Shih-ching* poems as critical comments on specific political situations of the early Chou period. These are the infamous "allegorical" readings of the *Shih-ching*, which have come under attack since the May Fourth Movement in 1919. Whatever their relation to Western allegory and whatever feelings the modern reader may have toward them, the Mao readings were the accepted interpretations of the *Shih-ching* for over two thousand years. They were the background against which traditional ideas about poetry were formed and against which contemporary performance was measured.

The "Great Preface" summarizes these interpretations and related notions about the purpose of poetry in the enigmatic slogan "Poetry expresses intention" (詩言志). Comparison of pre-Ch'in passages relating to this phrase has demonstrated beyond doubt that "intention" meant an official's opinion on a political matter presented at court in verse form either by the official himself or by musically trained technicians (Chu, 1945; Chow, 1968, pp. 151-166). This close union of poetry and politics was to remain central to the Chinese poetic tradition, for those authors who existed as officials of the Confucian state (and most did) were required, in theory at least, to uphold and continue the traditions of those whose poetry had "expressed their intentions."

This emphasis on the important role of poetry in the conduct of social and political life was (and still is) a central feature of the Chinese poetic tradition. It is probably in fact a misnomer to speak of a Chinese "poet" at all. It is doubtful if any Chinese writer of poetry viewed himself as principally a "poet" in the Western sense of the word—an individual whose primary function is to compose poetry. In China, skill in writing poetry is *not* a polite accomplishment of the true gentleman: it is a requirement for admission to that status. And this conviction was institutionalized on a permanent and regular basis in the early T'ang dynasty when compositions in two verse genres (the *fu* and the *shih*) became required components of civil-service examinations.

This institutionalization of poetry, both ideally as a distinguishing characteristic of the accomplished gentleman and practically as a required skill of the successful official, narrowly defined the audience for traditional Chinese poetry. Just as the *Shih-ching* formed the standard curriculum for Confucius and other mid-Chou diplomats, so did it, along with selections from later poetry, form part of the examination-syllabus for government service. Although this curriculum varied from period to period, it was remarkably consistent for any single generation of authors. These shared a uniform education and common career goals that, taken together, defined them as a social and literary group—the literati—that formed a distinctive class more enduring and more cohesive than any similar group in the Western tradition.

Both the fastidiousness with which Chinese commentators specify the circumstances of composition (as well as the audience for individual poems) and the detailed specificity of the often editor-supplied titles to Chinese poems testify to the extremely narrow audiences for which most Chinese poems were written. The modern reader may question as totally unverifiable the details of specific Mao-Cheng attributions for individual *Shih-ching* poems; he may observe conflicting Ming and Ch'ing explications of T'ang political allegory and lament the fixation of the Chinese commentator with "historical background." Yet to dismiss either as "far-fetched" is a serious error. This very insistence of the commentarial tradition on the historical specificity of the poem, although often no longer verifiable, signals the probability that these scholars, who were of course poets was well as commentators, are likely to have *composed* their own poetry in the same way they read the poetry of others. The specificity of Chinese commentary is almost as old as Chinese poetry itself. It is both a reflection of the specificity of the poet and a mark of the homogeneity of this poetic tradition.

A by-product of this cohesiveness, this unity of purpose between poet and audience, was the pervasive practice of imitation as an accepted part of the Chinese literary tradition. It has been written that "Chinese literature is a literature of centos" (Granet, 1934, p. 58). The pejorative connotation of the word in English (*cento*—"a piece of patchwork, a composition formed by joining scraps from other authors") should not be allowed to cloud the validity of the observation. For, given the homogeneous nature of the Chinese body poetic, all drew from a common (and therefore limited) font of literary precedent. Originality did not consist of devising new formulations but rather of displaying virtuosity at juxtaposing old formulas. The author worked with sources as well-known to his audience as to himself. Traditional Chinese poetry is a poetry of technique, a poetry where no attempt is made to camouflage the visibility of the artistic process, which is open to the full view of all who share the common tradition. These features also help to explain the bookish and scholastic aura that permeates much Chinese verse, even if most of this aura disappears when the verse is translated into another language. The close symbiosis in China between text and commentary, essential for the literati's education in the prevailing state orthodoxy, was reflected in their attitude toward the study and composition of poetry. The more typical Chinese poem, rather than being a direct expression of firsthand experience of nature, is more likely to be a bookish encounter with earlier poems on a similar theme. Of course, the greatest poets of the language—T'ao Ch'ien,* Tu Fu,* Su Shih*—succeeded because of their ability to fuse their own direct experience with the scholasticism of the tradition. Such poetry sustained and rejuvenated the tradition but was the exception that proved the rule. And in time, the poetic texts of these authors, replete with commentary, became the school texts of later generations.

III. *The Songs of Ch'u*

A modern scholar surveying the past three thousand years of Chinese poetry receives a curious and unsettling impression: the tradition so often and so thoroughly resculpted its own past (to provide justification for contemporary political and literary needs) that it became increasingly shorn of rough edges and odd pieces. It turned eventually into a museum collection of monuments seemingly preselected and precut to fit into a limited number of historically orthodox configurations. The impression, while valid in some respects, is a distortion of an obviously once multifarious tradition caused by the Chinese predilection for anthologies and the ancillary tendency to ignore for purposes of literary history poetry that is not in standard anthologies. A large amount of all pre-T'ang poetry survives in only three anthologies—the *Shih-ching*, the *Ch'u-tz'u*,* and the *Wen-hsüan*.* The dominant poetic genre during the four centuries of the Han dynasty was the *fu*, variously translated "rhyme-prose," "rhapsody," "prose-poetry," "verse-essay." The word seems originally to have signified a type of chanting used by officials of the Chou dynasty to present political "intentions" at court. Towards the end of the Warring States period, this technique evolved into a genre, the earliest *fu* being those in the "*Fu* Chapter" of the *Hsün-tz'u* (see *Chu-tzu pai-chia*). Although these verses show stylistically similar ties to the *Shih-ching* and demonstrate the formal link between the two genres, the key link seems to have been their common purpose, which was to present "criticism" (風). This is the meaning of Pan Ku's* famous statement that the "*fu* is a development of the old poetry" (賦者古詩之流) and the implication behind Liu Hsieh's (*c.* 465-522, see *Wen-hsin tiao-lung*) belief that the change from *shih* through *fu* to the *sao* poetry of the *Ch'u-tz'u* represented a continuous line of development (Jao, 1977, p. 161; Chu, 1945, pp. 31-32).

The *Ch'u-tz'u* is an anthology of poetry written in the *sao* tradition of the southern state of Ch'u. The major figure associated with the collection is Ch'ü Yüan* (*c.* 340-278 B.C.), the reputed author of the volume's first text, the "Li sao" (Encountering Sorrow), a long narrative poem of 187 couplets. The compiler of the *Ch'u-tz'u* and its first and most famous commentator was Wang I 王逸 (d. A.D. 158).

In all senses that were important to the Chinese critical mind, the "Li sao" and, to a much lesser extent, the other major texts in the *Ch'u-tz'u* anthology formed a complementary antithesis to the *Shih-ching*. Formally, the two collections are quite different: the *Shih-ching* poems are mostly short lyrical expressions; the *Ch'u-tz'u* texts are long expositions with emphasis on narrative and dramatic modes. Yet the real antitheses are much deeper. Against the impersonality of the *Shih-ching*, the "Li sao" assumes major importance as the first Chinese poem to articulate the personality of its author. Scholars may argue about how this personality—or better, persona—compares with what little is known of the historical Ch'ü Yüan (Hawkes, 1959; Hightower, 1954), yet this should not cloud the fact that the "Li sao" presents a vivid picture of a specific individual with a particular problem.

It has long been a commonplace of Chinese literary history to affiliate the *Shih-ching* with a northern and the *Ch'u-tz'u* with a southern tradition of Chou poetry. Recently, more perspicacious scholars have pointed out the inadequacies of this schema by emphasizing both the intensely regional nature of Warring States literature and the formal elements the *Shih-ching* and *Ch'u-tz'u* have in common (Jao, 1977; Fei, 1980).

Ideologically, both corpuses share the belief that "poetry expresses intentions," although in the latter text this is now localized in the plight of a single individual and so fused with his own emotions.

So pervasive is this tone of lamentation in the *Ch'u-tz'u* that many scholars have translated the title as *Elegies of Ch'u* and seen in the word *tz'u*鰷 a generic designation for "elegy" (Hsü, 1971; Tökei, 1967). This character of the *Ch'u-tz'u* mode as an outpouring of lamentation links this collection to a small but historically important group of songs preserved in the standard histories, sometimes called "Ch'u songs" (Hightower, 1950, p. 53), the essential nature of which was an *"improvisation pathétique:* the poet, in a tragic or very moving situation, frees himself from the feelings that oppress him; he sings, playing sometimes a musical instrument or asking a beloved friend to accompany him" (Diény, 1968, pp. 44-45). The best-known of these improvisations occurs in the eighth chapter of the *Shih-chi** (Records of the Historian) where Liu Pang (256-195 B.C.), first emperor of Han, passes through his native village of P'ei on his return to the capital:

> He gave a banquet in the palace of P'ei and invited all his friends, the old and the young, to come and feast with him. And he formed a group of 120 young men from P'ei and taught them to sing. Flushed with the wine, Kao-tsu took the lute and sang a song which he made:
>
> A great wind arose, the clouds flew up and away;
> my majesty now grown to the sea's edges, I return to my old home;
> Yet where shall I find brave men to guard the four quarters?
>
> Commanding the young men to take up his song, Kao-tsu rose to dance, when he was struck by a powerful feeling of sadness and tears streamed down his face.

In addition to being one of the most moving passages in the *Shih-chi*, this account explains much about the character of early Han poetry. The Han founders were natives of Ch'u, and the influence of this region's cultural life was especially strong during the early years of the dynasty. These facts doubtless explain the noticeable shamanistic element in Han ritual and the popularity of the *Ch'u-tz'u* during these years (Kaltenmark, 1963, p. 430). Most significantly, however, this *Shih-chi* account once again places the highest echelons of the court, whose patronage and ritual were always powerful molders of artistic life, in direct contact with a poetry that was inseparable from a living tradition of music and dance. These poems were popular, direct, and very much tied to the specific situation of the author: "without an understanding of the circumstances which occasioned them, they are all but meaningless" (Watson, 1962, p. 285). This poetry and music was adapted for use in the official rites of the Han dynasty. Liu Pang's *improvisation pathétique* became the official voice of Han, and the Confucian distinctions between formal court music and popular song passed into obscurity.

IV. The Music Bureau

The great Han Emperor Wu's (r. 141-87 B.C.) policy of cultural pluralism and assimilation sparked a liberalization of court music and a revitalization of poetry by establishing the Yüeh-fu 樂府 (Music Bureau, in existence *c.* 114-7 B.C.), an official government institution responsible for all musical functions at the Han court (Loewe, 1973). The Han Music Bureau reflected a cosmopolitan mixture of voices from many provinces, with considerable input of foreign music and poetic themes from beyond the far corners of the empire (Diény, 1968, pp. 54-64). At the time of its dissolution in 7 B.C., the Music Bureau had over 900 employees. They collected popular songs, adapted and orchestrated these songs, orchestrated song-texts composed by famous poets, and composed song-texts for existing tunes—all for use at court functions. Although relatively few of these Han Music Bureau works survive, they are important links between the pre-Ch'in traditions of the *Ch'u-tz'u* (and the "Ch'u songs") and the medieval poetry of the post-Han period (Diény, 1968, pp. 101-164; Frankel, 1974; Frodsham, 1967, pp. 1-8).

Yet the renaissance was short-lived. What was a living, vital tradition for the Han founders was already losing this force by the middle of the second century B.C. (Diény, 1968, p. 44). The very court luxury and opulence that made the Music Bureau a necessity spelled doom for the spontaneity the poetry had once drawn from its popular roots. The "Ch'u songs" thrived in a milieu where each member of the group could sing and dance; the Music Bureau was created by people who would rather watch others than participate themselves. By the end of the Former Han, the *improvisation pathétique* had disappeared among upper classes, as had likewise a taste for the *Ch'u-tz'u* (Hawkes, 1967). The practitioners of the Han Music Bureau purified for their royal audiences the popular poetry they had once known directly, reducing it to set formulas and motifs. The result of this process, toward the end of the Former Han, was the "five-character old-style poem" (*wu-yen ku-shih* 五言古詩), the most enduring and versatile of Chinese poetic forms.

The gradual genesis of the pentasyllabic *ku-shih* is implied in the earliest major collection in that form, the anonymous *Ku-shih shih-chiu shou** (Nineteen Old Poems) preserved in the early sixth-century *Wen-hsüan.* The maturity of these poems, evident in their sure mastery of the new form, betrays a considerable prehistory, as does the wide divergence of opinion concerning their date of composition (second century B.C. to second century A.D.). The first poem in the series is as follows:

> Going on always on and on;
> alive, but parted from you,
> Gone ten thousand miles and more,
> each to a far edge of the sky.
>
> The road is hard and long
> with nothing sure about meeting again.
> Tartar horses lean to the northern wind,
> Viet birds nest on southern boughs.
>
> Days advance, the parting grows long,
> days advance, the sash grows loose.
> Floating clouds hide the bright sun—
> the wanderer can think of no return.
>
> Loving you I became old,
> suddenly the time is late—
> Enough, I speak no more;
> try hard to stay well.

The pensive melancholy and brooding of Liu Pang's "A Great Wind Arose," characteristic of the *improvisation pathétique,* is heightened in this poem: yet the immediacy and urgency are gone, replaced by the careful control and restraint that are earmarks of literati composition. The earliest commentary to the poem (by Li Shan 李善 [*fl.* 660] in the *Wen-hsüan*) interprets the separation between the speaker and his/her lover as a metaphor for alienation between minister and ruler. This suggests that whatever natural imagery is new in *Nineteen Old Poems* has already been categorized and transposed to stand for archetypal moral values based on *Shih-ching* and *Ch'u-tz'u* exegesis. Direct textual links demonstrate that the author knew the old anthologies well ("Alive, but parted from you" echoes a *Ch'u-tz'u* "Nine Songs" line; "The road is hard and long" echoes a line from *Shih-ching* Mao No. 129—Diény, 1963; Watson, 1971, pp. 20-23). In other words, *Nineteen Old Poems* stands at that juncture in literary history when when literate authors begin to realign a popular genre by integrating its new music, meter, and motifs to coincide with the allegorical structure of the tradition's existing poetic corpus. Or, as Diény expressed the idea in reverse, *Nineteen Old Poems*, "gathering the heritage of the past, announced the future" (Diény, 1963). Before discoursing on this future, it is necessary to define the distinction between literati and popular poetry. As implied above, the distinction turns not so much on the social class of the author as on the size and composition of his intended audience. A large, educationally diffuse audience forced the Chinese author to adopt a more colloquial diction and the looser, hypotactic syntax characteristic of "popular" poetry. Writing to a single friend or to a small group of colleagues, however, he could rely on their homogeneous educational background to draw upon a shared knowledge of allusion, precedent, and textual exegesis and so construct a much tighter, paratactic poem. Of course, nothing prohibited an author from writing both types of poetry or from mixing elements of each to achieve a desired stylistic effect. In fact, the degree to which such cross-fertilization was acceptable is an important definer of period-style in Chinese poetry. It is useful to conceptualize these two types of poetry as two idealized foci of an ellipse, which, as they move closer together or farther apart, define the contours of the Chinese verse of any given period.

There is also an important related concept: as the "homogeneous educational background" of the literati changed over time, so did the intelligibility of previous poetry and its relation to the living poetic tradition. The young Chinese scholar acquired the basic lexical building blocks of his poetic vocabulary not from his spoken language but from memorizing a set corpus of prose and verse prescribed by educational custom or law. He shared this "language" with others who had memorized the same texts and began poetic composition by patching together small pieces of this memorization corpus much as seventeenth-century European schoolboys crafted snippets of memorized Vergil and Horace into Latin verse of their own. But changing canons of orthodoxy and literary taste forced periodic revisions in this "memorization corpus." For example, a T'ang reader would have recognized contemporary textual use of many Han *fu* by virtue of their inclusion in the *Wen-hsüan*, but a reader in the Ch'ing dynasty, when the *Wen-hsüan* was no longer memorized, would miss the connection. On the other hand, a quotation from *Meng-tzu* in an early medieval poem would have been an arcane reference (and therefore perhaps jocular or pedantic) for its original audience but would have been recognized at once by a Ch'ing reader. Thus did the texture of a poem change over time and produce difficulties for that literati society where custom and decorum dictated that memorizer and poet be invariably linked in the same person and where that person's first attempts at "poetry" were undertaken long before his required course of memorization was finished.

There were two responses to this situation: the commentary and the anthology. The first provided its reader with the "memorization corpus" of the poem's original audience and so preserved the basic intelligibility of the text. This explains the nature of the *tsu* 祖, literally "ancestors," that constitute the majority of later Chinese commentary to earlier poetry and which modern readers mistakenly call "allusions," "textual borrowings," or "references." They are rather that small part of the "memorization corpus" applicable to the poetic line in question which was probably known by the original, intended audience but perhaps not by the audience for whom the commentary was written. The second response, that of the anthology, provided the memorizer/poet with a manageable "memorization corpus" for use in his own verse. Chinese anthologies, especially in the post-T'ang periods, are thus attempts not simply to preserve old poems but to provide a rigidly defined program of earlier verse for memorization and imitation. They are thus important barometers to measure changes in contemporary taste and to understand the critical positions of their compilers.

V. The Poetry of Emotion

Early medieval times did introduce an important new concept, however, not about how to compose, but about the purpose of poetry. Literary theory through the Han seems not to have questioned the old dictum "Poetry expresses intention"; by definition, poetry was an activity of the public domain. The *Shih-ching* is impersonal, the *Ch'u-tz'u* is personal; yet, although both concern political "intentions," neither is private, neither is concerned with emotions that do not relate in some way to the body politic and its health. The emergence of a totally private poetry is rooted in the breakdown of political order before the collapse of the Han and in the quest for spiritual meaning known as the *Hsüan-hsüeh* 玄學 (Dark Learning) of the third century (Chu Tzu-ch'ing, 1945, pp. 35-36; Balazs, 1964). This transition is signaled in the famous phrase from Lu Chi's* 陸機 (261-303) "Wen fu" 文賦 (Prose-poem on Literature), "Poetry is based on emotion [expressed in] patterned splendor" (詩緣情而綺靡 ; Hsü, 1980). This formulation constituted a broadening, not a contradiction, of the older tradition that "poetry expresses intention" (詩言志). Six Dynasties' critical texts support this interpretation of the relationship between the old and new view of poetry (Chu, 1945, pp. 35-38; Holzman, 1974). Representative is the statement of Liu Hsieh from the poetry chapter ("Ming-shih" 明詩) of his *Wen-hsin tiao-lung**: "A human is endowed with the seven emotions. When these encounter the physical world they are stirred up; and thus stirred by the physical world, he sings forth his intentions. [This process] is totally spontaneous" (人稟七情, 應物斯感, 感物吟志, 莫非自然). To see in these two Chinese views of poetry a hypothetical antithesis between "didactic value" and the "legitimate expression of feeling" (Graham, 1980, p. 22) interjects pejorative notions recently attached to the Western tradition of "didactic" literature into a culture that had quite other ideas and thus considerably muddles the history of post-Han poetry.

A key figure in the emergence of the new poetry was Juan Chi* (210-263), whose long series of eighty-two "*Yung-huai shih* 詠懷詩 (Poems that Sing My Innermost Thoughts) utilized the tension of maintaining a proper poetic balance between private sentiment and public pronouncement to expand the personal lament of the *yüeh-fu* into poetry of philosophical comment (Holzman, 1976). Juan Chi's series still "expresses intentions" by commenting on the contemporary political scene; it is also "based on emotion" because its author does not stand, as did the *Shih-ching* author, emotionally aloof from his opinions. Juan Chi uses the interplay between his own feelings and "outside" events to discourse on the abstract significance of both. While still rooted in the specificity of the occasion (the political event), his poetry is no longer bound and confined to it. Significantly, this blending of old and new is mirrored in Juan Chi's style: while retaining the allegorical framework of earlier tradition, he was the first major author fully to embrace the pentasyllabic *ku-shih* form and to reject the *yüeh-fu* influence still so prominent in the generation before him—Ts'ao Ts'ao 曹操 (155-220), Ts'ao Chih* (192-232), and the authors of the Chien-an period (196-220) (von den Steinen, 1939; Watson, 1971, pp. 33-51).

The final step in this transition from poetry as impersonal public pronouncement to poetry as private meditation was effected by T'ao Ch'ien* (365-427), who wrote in his autobiographical "Wu-liu Hsien-sheng chuan" 五柳先生傳 (Master of the Five Willows) that he "often wrote literature to amuse himself and to reveal his own intentions" (常著文章自娛，頗示己志). Significantly, T'ao Ch'ien still here links the composition of literature to "intention," but his admission that his main purpose was to "amuse himself" manifests a weakening of the traditional association of literature to social values. And this softening of the old commitment cleared the way for poetry solely concerned with the inner and private life of the author, for poetry as an exercise in self-expression, and finally for poetry as a technical exercise.

The unrelenting honesty with which T'ao Ch'ien faced the major questions of life and death lends his poetry a directness quite uncharacteristic of his contemporaries and unusual in Chinese verse before the Sung when his reputation became established. He uses two major voices. One is a highly philosophical tone (something he shares with Juan Chi) that is a direct inheritance from the poetic passages in the pre-Ch'in Taoist Classics. The second is a cultivated rusticity (actually a mirror-image of the first voice), which articulated for the first time in Chinese poetry the pleasures of "retirement" not as a civilized way to endure exile but as a genuine alternative to public service. T'ao Ch'ien was also the last major poet unaffected by Buddhism, a trait that helped endear him to the Neo-Confucian Sung scholars. He thus stands as a natural counterpart to his younger contemporary Hsieh Ling-yün* (385-433) whose work was much more representative of the poetry of the age (Frodsham, 1967a).

The Six Dynasties witnessed a fundamental innovation in poetic form. In the centuries immediately after the introduction of Buddhism to China, the necessity of reproducing the exact intonation of Sanskrit mantras in Chinese spurred research into the phonology of the Chinese language, which led in turn to the realization of the phonemic nature of pitch and the "discovery" of the "four tones." According to tradition, Shen Yüeh* (441-513) was the first author to devise from this discovery a system for arranging these tones to form regulated patterns throughout the poem. The basic unit was the couplet. The "four tones" were divided into two contrasting categories—

"even" (平) and "uneven" (仄). The poet was required to manipulate his couplets so that the second line formed a complementary, mirror image of the first:

(line 1): uneven uneven even   even   uneven
(line 2): even   even   uneven uneven even

This system was, in effect, an extension of parallelism down to the most basic phonic level of the line. Previously, parallelism had been confined to syntactic parallelism between couplets ("Tartar horses lean to the northern wind,/Viet birds nest on southern branches"). But now, the tonal parallelism of "regulated verse" enabled the poet to coordinate the syntactic and semantic parallelism, in which his ideas had traditonally been expressed, with a purely rhythmic and formal parallelism that depended solely on sound. This probably explains both the immediate popularity of the new form and the lasting feeling of the Chinese poet for "regulated verse" as the quintessence of all verse genres.

It was to be over two centuries, however, before the potential of "regulated verse" to achieve this perfect coordination of form and content was realized in practice. Its more immediate result in the end of the Six Dynasties period was to encourage a development that most later critics regarded as pernicious; the immediate preoccupation of writers with the formal techniques of versification encouraged poetry as a technical exercise and intensified a tendency toward the composition of erotic verse as emotional outlet. The bifurcation of the old Chinese social conception of poetry opened the door for the making of verse that had meaning *only* as articulation of pure emotion, a verse without moral-allegorical import and thus shorn of its traditional relation to society. Known usually as *kung-t'i shih** (palace-style poetry) and gathered in the sixth-century anthology *Yü-t'ai hsin-yung,** this poetry was condemned by the Confucian critics of later centuries as frivolous and licentious because it appropriated and expanded the old images of sexual love while abandoning their traditional moral-political associations (Hightower, 1950, pp. 46-47; Watson, 1971, pp. 90-108). Thus shorn of its allegorical meaning, love poetry turned into erotic verse.

VI. The T'ang Synthesis

The T'ang dynasty (618-907), generally acknowledged as the golden age of Chinese poetry, partially resolved the conflicts that had arisen during the Six Dynasties concerning the nature and purpose of poetry. Already in the Liang dynasty (502-557), critics had reacted against the languid boudoir poetry of the times and advocated a return to the classical principle that "poetry expresses intention." Although such a return was hardly possible, its advocacy did encourage a movement to emphasize the considerable points of convergence rather than the points of conflict between the poetry of "intention" and that of "emotion." Gradually a synthesis emerged which is best expressed in K'ung Ying-ta's 孔穎達 (574-648) commentary to the "Great Preface" of the *Shih-ching*: intentions are produced when emotions respond to outside stimuli (Chu, 1945, pp. 38-40).

During the first hundred years of the T'ang, the Six Dynasties poetic style lingered on and underwent a slow process of adapting to new social conditions and absorbing foreign influences that came from the military expansion of the seventh century (Owen, 1977; Ogawa, 1960). Poetry in the Six Dynasties was very much an aristocratic affair, the domain of small and increasingly inbred coteries of literati-officials who obtained political office as a birthright. The adoption in the late seventh century of a unified examination system that required the composition of *fu* and *shih* and considerably expanded the "memorization corpus" to include the *Wen-hsüan* and selected pre-Ch'in classics had a major impact on Chinese poetry. The most immediate results were two-fold: it enlarged the social base of "poets" to include anyone who had studied for the examinations and, more important, it specified in detail the "memorization corpus," which, though now enlarged, was known by all who studied for the government examinations. The T'ang author thus knew exactly what he could expect his audience to know of earlier literature. Of course, these expectations were only a starting point, the least-common-denominator for the T'ang educated. The literary giants of the age ranged far beyond these basic beginnings in the demands they placed on their readers. Yet this fundamental base was always there, and as a result, the homogeneity between poet and audience was closer during T'ang than at any other period in Chinese history. And the resulting confidence and facility of expression is a major reason for the greatness of T'ang poetry.

Much of the homogeneity developed during the seventh century when poetic activity seems to have centered around the court in Ch'ang-an. The court poetry of most cultures is notorious for the rigidity of its conventions and for its concern with the niceties of acceptable poetic themes. The Chinese court poetry of the early T'ang is no exception. And yet the upper echelons of capital society proved the ideal literary surrounding in which to experiment with the yet unrealized potential of regulated verse because these experimenters of the seventh century were quite different from the originators of the sixth. The great T'ang Emperor T'ai-tsung (r. 627-650) himself, though from the Northwest, was a devotee of "southern" writings as typified in the *Yü-tai hsin-yung.* This commingling of the plain directness of the northern Chinese spirit with the refined formalism of the Six Dynasties southern tradition made possible K'ung Ying-ta's synthesis between "intention" and "emotion." It also made possible the conservative experimentation that finally resulted, toward the beginning of the eighth century, in the adoption of official guidelines for regulated verse. Although seldom read with enjoyment today, this early T'ang verse established normative standards in which the more famous authors of the eighth and ninth centuries were schooled and against which they often rebelled. Thus the political union of the country under the T'ang dynasty in the early seventh century formed the basis for an eventual intellectual and literary reunification that was the source of much of the vitality in T'ang literature.

The emergence in the early eighth century of a new social class of poets from slightly humbler origins than the aristocrats of the seventh coincided with the final perfection of regulated verse forms and with the apogee of T'ang political and cultural influence in East Asia. This was the reign of the T'ang Emperor Hsüan-tsung (713-756) and the age of the great T'ang poets Wang Wei* (699-761), Li Po* (701-762), and Tu Fu* (712-770). The major achievement of Wang Wei was to amalgamate the ideals of Buddhist meditative verse with the imagery of Chinese landscape poetry to produce a style of Buddhist contemplative verse that was not alien to Chinese readers. The rising popularity of the Ch'an school of Buddhism, its most quintessentially Chinese manifestation, in the mid-eighth century provided Wang Wei's verse with a sophisticated and receptive audience that understood and imitated his achievement. This "Ch'an landscape" verse exerted a profound influence on later authors, even Confucian ones, and its style and techniques became the basis for several Sung schools of poetry and criticism.

Li Po and Tu Fu have been paired together since the early ninth century as the twin culminations of T'ang poetry, their respective arts contrasting yet complementing each other in accordance with the bipolar archetype so beloved of the Chinese critic. Li Po was the social outsider, perhaps even the son of a convict exiled to Central Asia, whose dazzling displays of verbal magic and spontaneous composition delighted the audiences of Ch'ang-an. He was apparently a somewhat eccentric character, a rambler, and a practicing Taoist, who lacked the unrelenting Confucian will to succeed. Although there is some serious religious poetry and much poetry of social commentary and criticism in his corpus, a handful of his private poems that display a distinctive fusion of alcohol, moonlight, and madness have been widely anthologized in later times and mistakenly taken as representative. He favored the relative stylistic freedom of the "old style" and the *yüeh-fu* forms.

Tu Fu, on the other hand, was the son of a wealthy and cultured family: his grandfather had been one of the leading poets of his day. Tu Fu was well-educated, well-traveled, and well-schooled in the poetry of the Six Dynasties and early T'ang. He was the consummate craftsman of regulated verse who plodded and struggled with the formidable demands of the "new poetry." These labors, however, made Tu Fu the master of many styles both in regulated and non-regulated forms, and it was this formal mastery, combined with an acute sense of the significance of the historical events through which he lived, that justify the claim that Tu Fu was China's greatest poet. For Tu Fu, unlike Li Po, was tormented by the Confucian compulsion to make himself and his poetry of use to the state. While this compulsion resulted in a frustrated, almost pathetic official career, it resulted in a unique awareness of the collective identity of the Chinese as a people (one could almost say as a nation) and of their ability to endure and preserve this identity in the face of overwhelming political upheavals and personal suffering. The poetry Tu Fu wrote during the An Lu-shan Rebellion chronicles the horrors of these years with a gift for direct observation and an ability to relate without maudlinness his own personal suffering to that of the country. Yet these gifts would have no literary avail without his mastery of the earlier poetic tradition. Tu Fu's poetry escapes the bookishness of the tradition not by evading it but by mastering it to such a degree that his erudition fuses imperceptibly with the immediacy of his own experience. This poetry is the most perfect realization of that goal articulated at the beginning of the dynasty by K'ung Ying-ta, the most perfect synthesis ever achieved between "intention" and "emotion." Kenneth Rexroth called Tu Fu "the greatest non-epic, non-dramatic poet who has survived in any language." Despite the considerable qualifications, the statement is probably true. Tu Fu is the only Chinese poet with an incontestable claim to be included among the greatest names of world literature: Homer, Virgil, Dante, Shakespeare, Goethe . . . Tu Fu.

Although Tu Fu's poetry was little known during his lifetime, it began to exert a powerful influence on the writers of the late eighth century. So broad had been his range of styles that his corpus contained the prototypes of most later stylistic developments in *shih* poetry. The highly allusive, ambiguous, and syntactically dense style of Li Shang-yin* (812-858) can be traced to the poetry of Tu Fu's later years. The "New *Yüeh-fu*" poetry of Po Chü-i* (772-846) and Yüan Chen* (779-831) is prefigured in Tu Fu's narrative ballads of the An Lu-shan Rebellion years.

VII. The Sung and After

The enormous popularity of poetry in the T'ang and the resulting dynamic growth in the cumulative body of Chinese verse provided the basis for the fragmentation of this unified poetic world that had made possible the greatness of T'ang poetry. The history of Chinese poetry from the beginning of the Sung dynasty (960-1279) until modern times is a history of an ever-increasing array of "schools," each with its own tenets, anthology, and poetic style. This development is best understood as a "safety valve" that although it fragmented forever the earlier unity of the poetic world, preserved the traditional literati method of composition. The "memorization corpus" was only a common starting point. The major T'ang poets all showed great ingenuity in modifying and enlarging this basic common corpus of accepted referents, in adapting diction from their spoken language, and in imitating their contemporaries. As the body of prior poetry grew, so did the amount of referential material the budding poet was required to master. The Sung "schools" were an attempt to cope with this problem by limiting the amount of earlier material the student had to master to a standard body of canonical texts plus the corpus of one or two T'ang poets. The great Sung poets of the eleventh century—Mei Yao-ch'en* (1002-1060), Ou-yang Hsiu* (1007-1072), Su Shih* (1037-1101), and Wang An-shih* (1021-1086)—were the last poets ever to command a mastery of the entirety of the Chinese poetic tradition. The increasing proliferation of "schools" and the popularity of the *shih-hua** and poetic handbooks in the Southern Sung (1127-1279) changed forever the way the Chinese poet viewed his own work in relation to the work of the past. It also changed his attitude toward other contemporary poets. The factiousness that was so evident a characteristic of Chinese political life now dominated Chinese poetic life. The past was divided into various "streams" (*p'ai*派) that flowed each in its own channel to contemporary times. And because each contemporary poet mastered the poetry of his own stream, he could be assured of his own poetry being fully comprehended only by fellow members of his school (Yoshikawa, 1967; Debon, 1962; Hightower, 1950, pp. 84-89).

This process accelerated in the Yüan dynasty (1260-1368) as Mongol discontinuation of the traditional examination system for recruiting officials further eroded the homogeneous educational base of the literati. At the same time, as schools of poetry proliferated, the use of the colloquial language increased and the repertoire of acceptable poetic themes grew dramatically as some poets reacted against the tendency of each "stream" to trickle off into increasingly narrow byways or to flow into catchbasins of stagnant poetizing. Furthermore, the reconstruction of state orthodoxy on Neo-Confucian lines in the early Ming (1368-1644) ill assorted with the critical tenets of many schools founded on the aesthetics of Ch'an Buddhism (Tu, 1976; Debon, 1962; Lynn, 1975). This is reflected in the changed emphasis in the Ming-Ch'ing examination system from poetry to the *pa-ku wen** (eight-legged essay). The age-old dispute between "intention" and "emotion" continued to replay itself out in new guises, for instance in the controversies between the Archaist (*ni-ku* 公安) and the Kung-an (擬古) schools in the mid-Ming period. The almost perfect conformity between the history of Ming-Ch'ing poetry and the history of Ming-Ch'ing literary criticism makes it possible to understand why the highest accolade possible for a Ch'ing poet was that he "developed his own style" and belonged to no school (Aoki, 1950; Wu, 1977).

VIII. An Underlying Pattern

The history of the other major poetic genres in China, the *tz'u* and the *ch'ü*, sheds considerable light on the underlying forces that also governed the development of the *shih* genre. It may be useful at this point to recall the six major traditions of verse writing in China: (1) the ancient "odes," (2) old style poetry, (3) regulated verse, (4) the *sao-fu*, (5) the *tz'u*, and (6) the *ch'ü*. Of course, each of these genres continued to develop, influencing and being influenced by the others in the periods after it first flourished. The *fu*, for instance, continued as an important genre through the Sung, its style greatly influenced by regulated verse and prose forms. Even the *Shih-ching* continued until modern times to serve as a conscious model for certain types of ritual, eulogistic verse.

Yet there is an underlying rhythm to the historical development of each of these six forms that coincides with the traditional Confucian notion that poetry must be useful. Remembering the distinction formulated above between "popular" and "literati" poetry, it is remarkable that each of the six forms passed through a similar three-step process: (1) emergence as a popular song form (usually by virtue of Chinese conquest of, or contact with, non-Chinese peoples) and adoption by the literati as written song-texts; (2) allegorization by the literati on the pattern of already allegorized forms to express their "intentions," (3) fossilization of the form once its full allegorical potential had been extracted.

Traditional Chinese scholars seem to have been aware of the general outlines of this process. Chu Hsi 朱熹 (1130-1200) and Feng Meng-lung* (1574-1646), for instance, were both aware of the popular origins of the "odes of the states" in the *Shih-ching*. Likewise, there are numerous cases of literati composing song-texts not only in imitation of, but directly *for,* a popular audience—the "Chiu ko" 九詠 (Nine Songs) of Ch'ü Yüan according to legend, the "Chu-chih tz'u" 竹枝詞 (Bamboo Branch Tunes) of Liu Yü-hsi* (772-842) according to fact. It is also suggestive that the emergence of new song forms among the populace often coincided with periods of extensive Chinese contact with non-Chinese peoples by virtue of either conquering or being conquered, in other words, in periods when a more cosmopolitan culture prevailed: the Western Chou (early *shih*), the Warring States (*sao-fu*), the Former Han (*yüeh-fu, ku-shih*), and the Yüan (*ch'ü*). The coincidence is perhaps startling enough to suggest that the history of Chinese poetry is somewhat less self-contained than hitherto presumed. The history of the *tz'u* form is important in this regard. Recent research on the Tun-huang manuscripts has thrown into perspective the long "prehistory" of this form, detailing its popular roots, which extend well back into the Six Dynasties period, and revealing a long period of gestation at semi-literate levels of society before its emergence as a full, literate form in the late

T'ang. The *tz'u* is the only form for which enough documentation exists to trace in detail its evolution from popular poetry to fossilized allegory.

The literati penchant for allegory and allegoresis is well-known. Sooner or later they composed allegorically in each form, and then posited allegorical readings back to the beginning of the form. The *Shih-ching*, for instance, because it contains texts spanning a period of over five hundred years, reveals this process most clearly: although the Mao-Cheng interpretations of the "odes of the states" may be allegoresis, many of the "folksongs" in the *hsiao-ya* 小雅 section are genuine political allegories composed during the early Spring and Autumn period (Watson, 1962, p. 220). On the other hand, the Ch'ang-chou School of *tz'u* criticism of the late eighteenth century was a fascinating attempt to rejuvenate interest in the *tz'u* form by insisting (rightly or wrongly?) on the allegorical pedigree of the form and by raising its most clearly allegorical authors to the status of aesthetic models for contemporary imitation.

Fossilization of the form occurred when all of the new images, themes, and techniques it brought into the literati's repertoire have been adapted to express their own "intentions," when its classical examples have entered into their "memorization corpus," and when the form has lost all contact with its popular origins. It is clear from this scenario that a given form's greatest potential for successful aesthetic utilization by the literati occurred during the second stage. During this time, the form still remained close enough to its popular origins for an author to incorporate new material into the form. Nor was he confined to existing traditions governing the use of the allegorical mode. He was free to experiment as he wished. Again, the history of the *tz'u* provides the clearest examples of this dynamic interaction between popular and literati poetry. The form flourished when the music was still performed, when authors such as Wei Chuang* (836-910) and Liu Yung* (987-1053) could still find direct inspiration from more popular manifestations of the form, and when authors such as Li Yü* (937-978) and Su Shih were still free to devise their own allegorical frameworks based on the form's popular imagery.

BIBLIOGRAPHY:

Allen, Joseph Roe, III. 1982. "Early Chinese Narrative Poetry: The Definition of a Tradition." Unpublished Ph.D. dissertation, University of Washington.

Aoki, 1950, *Shindai*.

Balazs, Etienne. 1964. "Political Philosophy and Social Crisis at the End of the Han Dynasty" and "Nihilistic Revolt or Mystical Escapism," in *Chinese Civilization and Bureaucracy: Variations on a Theme*, H.M. Wright, tr., pp. 187-254. New Haven.

Chow, 1968, "Shih."

Chu, Tzu-ch'ing 朱自清. 1945. *Shih-yen-chih pien* 詩言志辨 [A Study of "Poetry Expresses Intention"]. Shanghai.

Debon, 1962, *Ts'ang-lang*.

Diény, 1963, *Dix-neuf*.

Diény, 1968, *Origines*.

Fei, P'u-hsien 裴普賢. 1980. "*Shih-ching* pi-chiao yen-chiu. Ch'u-tz'u p'ien" [*Shih-ching* Comparative Studies. The *Ch'u-tz'u*]. *Chung-wai wen-hsüeh*, 8.8 (January) 28-54.

Frankel, 1979, "Yüeh-fu."

Frodsham, 1967, *Anthology*.

Frodsham, 1967a, *Murmuring*.

Graham, 1980, *Lament*.

Granet, Marcel. 1934. *La pensée chinoise*. Paris.

Hawkes, 1959, *Ch'u Tz'u*. Hawkes, 1967, "Quest."

Hightower, 1950, *Topics*.

Hightower, 1954, "Ch'ü Yüan."

Holzman, Donald. 1974. "Literary Criticism in China in the Early Third Century A.D.," *AS* 28, 111-149.

Holzman, 1976, *Poetry and Politics*.

Hsü, Fu-kuan 徐復觀. 1971. "Hsi-Han wen-hsüeh lun-lüeh" 兩漢文學論略 [A Synopsis of Western Han Literature], *Hsin-ya shu-yüan hsüeh-shu nien-k'an*, 13, 99-121.

———. 1980. *"Lu Chi 'Wen-fu' shu-shih ch'u-kao"* 陸機文賦疏釋初稿 (A Draft Commentary on Lu Chi's "*Fu* on Literature"), *Chung-wai wen-hsüeh*, 9, 6-41.

Jao, 1977, "Chan-kuo."

Kaltenmark, Max. 1963. "Les Danses sacrées en Chine," in *Les dances sacrées*, pp. 413-450. Paris.

Loewe, Michael. 1973. "The Office of Music, c. 114 to 7 B.C.," *BSOAS*, 36, 340-351.

Lynn, Richard John. 1975. "Orthodoxy and Enlightenment: Wang Shih-chen's Theory of Poetry and Its Antecedents," in *The Unfolding of Neo-Confucianism*, Wm. Theodore de Bary, ed., pp. 217-269. New York.

Morino, Shigeo 森野繁夫. 1976. *Rokuchō shi no kenkyū* 六朝詩の研究. Tokyo.

Ogawa, Tamaki. 1960. "The Song of Ch'ih-le, Chinese Translations of Turkic Folk Songs and Their Influence on Chinese Poetry," *AA* 1, 43-55.

Owen, 1977, *Early T'ang.*

von den Steinen, Diether. 1939-40. "Poems of Ts'ao Ts'ao," *MS*, 4, 125-181.

Suzuki, Shūji 鈴木修次. 1976. *Tōshi* 唐詩. Tokyo.

Tökei, F. 1967. *Naissance de l'élégie chinoise.* Paris.

Tu, Sung-po 杜松柏. 1976. *Ch'an-hsüeh yü T'ang-Sung shih-hsüeh* 禪學與唐宋詩學 [Ch'an and T'ang-Sung Poetics]. Taipei.

Waley, Arthur. 1933. "The Book of Changes," *BMFEA*, 5, 121-142.

Watson, Burton. 1962. *Early Chinese Literature.* New York.

———. 1971. *Chinese Lyricism. Shih Poetry from the Second to the Twelfth Century.* New York.

Wu, 1977, *Ch'u-t'an.*

Yu, Pauline. 1983. "Allegory, Allegoresis and the *Classic of Poetry*," *HJAS*, 43.2 (December), 373-412.

Yü, Hsing-wu 于省吾. 1936. *Shuang-chien-ch'ih Shih-ching hsin-cheng* 雙劍誃詩經新證 [New Textual Evidence for the *Shih-ching*]. Peking, 1936.

Yoshikawa, 1967, *Sung.*

POPULAR LITERATURE

PART I: FOLK LITERATURE

Victor H. Mair and Maxine Belmont Weinstein

U NTIL this century, the preservation and study of folk literature in China had been hampered by a number of factors. Perhaps the chief of these was the overwhelming bias of the literati against anything written in the vernacular. Consequently, a sharp dichotomy existed between what was writable and what was sayable. Indeed, two separate Chinese languages developed, the *wen-yen* 文言(classical) and the *pai-hua* 白話(colloquial or "unadorned"). Because of this opposition between that which was *su* 俗(vulgar) and that which was *ya* 雅(elegant), there was little hope for any widespread public recognition of the worth of folk literature. As the elite themselves were wont to put it, vernacular literature was "not fit for sophisticated salons" (*pu teng ta-ya chih t'ang* 不登大雅之堂).

Chinese scholars have long been aware of the existence of dialects and, indeed, of different languages that were spoken within the territory controlled by the Han people. During the final years of the Former Han dynasty Yang Hsiung* even wrote a book on this subject entitled *Fang-yen* 方言. Reliable records dating from the Warring States period show that dialects already were a significant factor in the intercourse carried out within the vast area we now know as China. Naturally, all these linguistic groupings had their own local cultures and folk traditions. A few of these have been noted in such historical works as the *Tso-chuan*,* the *Shih-chi*,* and the *Hou-Han shu* 後漢書. But strict adherence to a primarily ideographic writing system keyed to a single standard language has always proved to be a drawback to the faithful and ready transcription of non-elite, non-Han texts (oral or otherwise).

There is little evidence for the use of vernacular language in any ancient Chinese writings. Although reference is made to "vulgar" or "rustic" speech (*su-yü* 俗語 or *li-yü* 俚語), except in extremely rare instances, it has not been recorded. It was once widely held that the *Shih-ching*,* and the *Ch'u-tz'u*,* included many dialectical and colloquial elements, but there has as yet been no convincing demonstration of this. One of the difficulties in providing such a demonstration is the fact that both collections were submitted to repeated redaction and would appear to have been at least partially regularized according to Han standards. Thus it is possible to learn from them something of the content of early folk literature, but it is not in anything resembling its pristine form.

The earliest texts in which a few of the grammatical features of colloquial Chinese begin to appear with some frequency are late Han Buddhist translations. Certain Six Dynasties ballads and anecdotes display a limited amount of colloquial usage. Colloquial expressions are also scattered in T'ang poetry and become even more evident in Sung *tz'u** and Yüan *ch'ü** (Chu, 1961). But the first full-length literary texts in the vernacular date from the latter half of the T'ang and the Five Dynasties periods (see *Tun-huang wen-hsüeh*). Other early texts of substantial length written in the vernacular are the dialogues of Zen (Ch'an) masters called *Ch'an yü-lu*.* The famous *Tsu-t'ang chi* 祖堂集 (Collection from the Hall of Patriarchs), compiled in 952, is a good example of this type of text. It is probable that vernacular Chinese initially came to be used as a fully functioning written language in a Buddhist context because of the socio-religious doctrines and institutions of that imported faith. By the Sung, though still decisively rejected by the vast majority of the literati, vernacular Chinese was accepted as a medium for written narrative by some members of the burgeoning urban bourgeoisie. Vernacular Chinese also appeared in historical works such as the *San-ch'ao pei-meng hui-pien* 三朝北盟會編 (Compilation of Materials on the Northern Alliances of the Three Courts) by Hsü Meng-hsin 徐夢華 (1124-1205). Yüan drama were written in a lively colloquial and, in the Ming and Ch'ing, authors unabashedly wrote entire novels in vernacular Chinese. There were even a few iconoclastic critics such as Chin Sheng-t'an* and Li Yü (1611-1680)* who actively promoted the disintegration of the barriers between "vulgar" and "elegant."

Thus, for many centuries, China was poised on the verge of the sort of linguistic revolution—allowing the use of vernacular languages, rather than Latin, in literary works—that Europe experienced at the end of the Middle Ages under the leadership of such men as Dante (1265-1321) and Luther (1483-1546). In China, however, this movement toward the unification of speech and writing did not come to full fruition until the end of the second decade of the twentieth century. It was only then that the economic and political configuration of society had been sufficiently transformed to allow for the complete acceptance of vernacular Chinese as a legitimate medium for written expression. Two of the most important figures in this movement were Hu Shih 胡適 (1891-1962) and Ch'en Tu-hsiu 陳獨秀 (1879-1942).

With the ascension of vernacular Chinese came a whole series of efforts to re-examine and reassess China's literary past. Hu Shih wrote his landmark *Pai-hua wen-hsüeh shih* 白話文學史 (History of Vernacular Literature) where he presented the idea that folk and popular literature had always been the most vital components of the Chinese literary scene. All new and dynamic literary trends were initiated by the people, then gradually taken up by the literati, and finally became stale and rigid. Cheng Chen-to 鄭振鐸 (1898-1958) broke new ground in many directions with the publication of his *Chung-kuo su-wen-hsüeh shih* 中國俗文學史 (History of Chinese Popular Literature). Energetic efforts to collect and record oral traditions throughout China were made by Ku Chieh-kang 顧頡剛 (b. 1895), Chou Tso-jen 周作人 (1885-1968), Liu Pan-nung 劉半農 (1891-1934), Lou Tzu-k'uang 婁子匡, and many other modern scholars. These efforts have continued and, in some areas, have been expanded since the founding of the People's Republic.

The reconstruction of China's literary past has required intense scrutiny of historical records coupled with comparative studies of existing local traditions. Fortunately, new materials have come to light from many different places. Much popular literature has been preserved in Japan, Russia, England, and elsewhere outside of China. Even more fortuitous have been the discoveries of old texts at various archaeological sites within China. Relying on all of these disparate types of sources, it is now possible to piece together a rough picture of folk literature (referred to as *p'ing-min wen-hsüeh* 平民文學, *min-chien wen-i* 民間文藝, and other terms) in China before the twentieth century.

One very large area for investigation is that of mythology. Although it has been seriously fragmented and euhemerized, the extant corpus of native Chinese myth (*shen-hua* 神話, Yüan, 1957, 1963; Bodde, 1961; Münke, 1976) can tell us much about the beliefs of the common man in ancient China. Among the most significant works for this sort of investigation are the *Shu-ching* 書經 (see *ching*), the *Shih-ching*,* the *Shan-hai ching*,* and the *Huai-nan-tzu* 淮南子. In spite of the fact that her neighbors (the Mongols, Tibetans, Lolos, Indians, and various Siberian and Central Asian peoples) possess long and beautiful epics, none remain in China. This is not to say, however, that China never had an epic tradition or the beginnings of one. Indeed, the fragmented condition of her mythology indicates that the rationalizing instincts of the literati may have prevented it from achieving a coherent corpus of texts.

A closely related type of literature is that known as legend (*ch'uan-shuo* 傳說). The dividing line between history and legend is quite fuzzy and there are a number of interesting works which seem to embrace a bit of both. These include the *Mu T'ien-tzu chuan*,* the *Han Wu-ti nei-chuan*,* the *Wu-Yüeh ch'un-ch'iu*,* and so on. Many of the well-known Chinese legends date from the Han period or the early part of the Six Dynasties. A number of legendary tales may be found in the Taoist canon, the *Tao-tsang*.*

Another important area for study is that of folksongs (*min-ko*;* Hu, 1925). Occasionally there are early songs preserved in classical writings, but we cannot be certain to what extent thay have been rewritten by the various editors who have transmitted them. Two examples are the "K'ang-ch'ü erh-t'ung yao" 康衢兒童謠 (Child's Song of the Highway) which purports to derive from the time of the semi-mythical Emperor Yao, and the "Chi-jang ko" 擊壤歌 (Pushpin Song), supposed to have been sung by old men as they rested from work and expressive of the bucolic harmony they enjoyed. Both of these songs, unfortunately, are to be found in works dating from after the Han, respectively the *Lieh-tzu* 列子 (see *Chu-tzu pai-chia*) and the *Kao-shih chuan* 高士傳 (Accounts of Aloof Scholars). Songs of this nature have often been incorporated in the history books because they were liable to be manufactured or manipulated for political advantage. This was particularly true of the *t'ung-ko/yao* 童歌／謠 (boys' songs), *shih-yao* 詩妖 (prophecies of evil), and the *ch'an-wei* 讖緯 (verifications of prophecies). Nevertheless, folksongs are one of the few types of early popular literature for whose existence there is substantial evidence.

In contrast to our knowledge of ancient folksongs, it is essential to note that virtually nothing is known about professional storytelling (*shuo-shu* 說書 or *shuo-hua* 說話) in China before T'ang times (Chen, 1936, 1958; Ma, 1976). No documentable proof has yet been adduced to demonstrate its existence. Yet surely people must have told stories to each other informally if not professionally. There is some indirect evidence for this in the Six Dynasties *chih-kuai** collections of anecdotes about anomalous events. A tradition of brief oral narrative is also reflected in the Chinese Buddhist collections of tales from the same period and from the T'ang such as Wang Yen's 王琰 *Ming-hsiang chi* 冥祥記 (Notes on Netherworld Phenomena) and Shih Tao-shih's 釋道世 *Fa-yüan chu-lin*.* Buddhist preachers were fond of including apologues and parables in their sermons; this too must have contributed to the growth of storytelling in China. The Chinese narrative tradition was further enriched by the translation of *Hsien-yü ching* 賢愚經(Sutra of the Wise and the Foolish), which was brought to China from Khotan by a group of Chinese monks. Already during the Warring States period, Chuang-tzu and Han Fei-tzu had demonstrated a flair for the use of allegory and fable (*yü-yen**). Rhetoricians during that period were also fond of using parables to drive home a political point. Again, however, we must emphasize that it was only in the Sung that professional storytelling as a form of entertainment became sufficiently popular for us to be able to document it now.

Another category of folk literature that has come down to us are jokes (Wang, 1975). Pre-Han writings such as the *Mencius* and the *Chuang-tzu* are not lacking in jokes, but the earliest joke collections per se are Han-tan Ch'un's 邯鄲淳 *Hsiao-lin* 笑林(Forest of Laughs), dating from the Wei period during the Three Kingdoms, and Hou Pai's 侯白 *Ch'i-yen lu* 啓顏錄(Tales to Crack a Smile By) of the Sui period (see *Ku-chi*). The collection of humorous anecdotes continued, and remnants of lost joke books from medieval times may be found in encyclopedias. During the late Ming and early Ch'ing, joke books became quite popular, and scholars such as Li Chih (1527-1602)* and Yü Yüeh 俞樾(1821-1907) included jokes among their miscellaneous writings. The most famous of all Chinese joke books, Feng Meng-lung's* *Hsiao-fu* 笑府(Treasury of Jokes), dates from this period. Although the *Treasury of Jokes* formed the basis of the *Hsiao-lin kuang-chi* 笑林廣記(Expanded Forest of Jokes) which continued to circulate in China, the *Treasury of Jokes* itself survived only in Japan, where it was widely read, admired, and imitated.

Some of the jokes in these collections are no longer intelligible, for they refer to bygone events or use local dialects. In others, the lampooning of officials, stupid peasants, quack physicians, cuckolded husbands, and misers evokes as much laughter today as ever. Stock characters in these collections and in twentieth-century collections include the stupid son-in-law who inadvertently insults his father-in-law and mortifies his wife, the trickster Hsü Wen-ch'ang 徐文長, and the teacher who is outwitted by mischievous students. Many of the humorous stories in Chinese collections are similar to jokes of other nations and can be found in folklore indices. Others are best appreciated within the context of Chinese social relations. Jokes collected in China by twentieth-century folklorists frequently bear close resemblance to jokes recorded in the *Treasury of Jokes* and other early joke books. Although the occasions for and targets of humor may be ephemeral, good jokes thus seem to persist in the tradition (Kao, 1946).

Other early types of folk literature for which there is evidence from as early as pre-Ch'in times are *mi* 謎(riddles) and *yen-yü* 諺語(proverbs), also called *su-yen* 俗諺 or *li-yen* 俚諺(Ch'ien, 1959). Chinese riddles often describe a written character or make allusion to a well-known work of literature. These became especially popular beginning in the Six Dynasties. It is curious that many riddles deal with people who are afflicted with various sorts of diseases and infirmities. There were, in addition, conundrums reserved for special occasions, such as the *teng-mi* 燈謎(lantern riddles) asked in conjunction with the Lantern Festival (fifteenth day of the first month). Proverbs, when rhymed, might be call *yao-yen* 謠諺. Though their use has declined somewhat in the past fifty years, the Chinese language is still liberally peppered with such figures of speech, witness the propensity for *ch'eng-yü* 成語(set phrases), *hsieh-hou-yü* 歇後語(two-part allegorical sayings), *ko-yen* 格言(maxims), *chen-yen* 箴言(admonitions), and the like.

From the above survey, it would appear that the Chinese people have always delighted in the exchange of tales, anecdotes, legends, jokes, and other "hearsay" in casual conversation. References to casual storytelling may be found an historical records, in religious writings, in notebooks (*pi-chi**) kept by scholars, and in other literary genres. Detailed scrutiny of these varied sources and of the many collections of Chinese folktales compiled in the twentieth century has scarcely begun.

One of the most urgent tasks facing the twentieth-century folklorist has been the classification of forms of casual storytelling (Aarne and Thompson, 1961). General agreement with regard to the use of terms denoting major genres of oral literature facilitates communication between scholars as well as the organization of texts collected in the field into anthologies. Moreover, scholars adhering to the theories of the Finnish school have regarded such classification as a prerequisite to the serious study of historical and geographical variations in individual tales.

No universal consensus with regard to the defining characteristics of genres of casual storytelling has been reached. Some folklorists, indeed, prefer to ignore the issue altogether, arguing that their informants are blissfully unaware of whether the stories they tell are myths, legends, or märchen. Others argue that the folklorists should try to formulate rules by which natives distinguish different types of stories through storytelling behavior, if not in terminology, much as a linguist might go about formulating a grammar. However, most folklorists and editors of anthologies continue to characterize stories as märchen, legends, fables, myths, anecdotes, or humorous tales, however inadequate this type of classification may be.

Such terms are thus inevitably used to refer to Chinese tales and merit brief definitions. Märchen are told for amusement. They are frequently not set in any specific time or place and may often be identified with tales known in many different countries. They adhere to a plot structure familiar all over the world, in which the youngest and weakest proves to be the smartest and kindest, and in which wondrous objects and beings aid the hero or heroine. Legends concern specific customs, people, or places. They are sometimes migratory, told about more than one place or historical figure. The narrator of a legend attempts to convince the audience that the story he or she tells is a true one. Fables are similar to legends but tend to be more didactic in intent and often employ animals as characters that speak and behave like human beings. Myths are stories of the gods' exploits in remote times. They are frequently concerned with origins of peoples and their rituals. Anecdotes relate unusual adventures of ordinary mortals in their quests for fame and fortune. Humorous tales are told to provoke laughter.

Although such distinctions are generally adequate for the purpose of classifying a huge and perhaps otherwise intractable body of literature, they nonetheless pose problems for the student of Chinese literature in search of categories that are supposed to be mutually exclusive. A single Chinese tale may seem to be myth, legend, *and* märchen to the reader who notes that it concerns gods (myth), yet also alludes to a specific place (legend) *and* embodies the narrative structure of a märchen. The distinction between myth and legend is difficult if the major criterion is the distinction between gods and mortals, for in traditional China humans could become members of the celestial bureaucracy through a process of reverse euhemerization. Problems such as these can sometimes be resolved if the student can obtain clear information about the rhetorical purposes of the narrator. Was the story told to entertain, to offer testimony to a belief questioned by some segments of society, or to teach its audience about the exploits of gods and culture heroes in a timeless past? One should remember that a given plot or episode can form the basis of a myth, märchen, or legend, or even a joke, depending upon how the narrator places it in time and space and what rhetorical framework he uses.

Folklorists have found many Chinese tales, especially märchen and humorous tales, to be similar to tales told in other parts of the world. Wolfram Eberhard began the task of classifying Chinese tales in accordance with the Aarne-Thompson type index, and Nai-tung Ting has recently produced an expanded type index of Chinese tales. Such indices are essential to the study of the transmission of tales across linguistic and cultural boundaries as well as in the delineation of local variations of internationally known tales. A brief perusal of these indices suggests an extensive exchange of tales between China and its neighbors and attests to the universal appeal of many folktales.

Nonetheless, even tales which circulate internationally may undergo changes as they are told to and by Chinese, as for example, a story about a wicked priest might become a story about a wicked monk or one about a princess might become one about the daughter of a high official. The vast majority of stories told in China, especially legends and myths, have been shaped by beliefs and cultural institutions peculiarly Chinese to the extent that they resist classification as international tale types and are best understood within the contexts of these beliefs and institutions. Such stories include popular tales of young men bewitched by women who are actually foxes in disguise, stories of the exploits of Taoist immortals, stories of filial sons and loyal generals, and others (Eberhard, 1965; Wilhelm, 1971).

Folktales reflect the fears and aspirations of their narrators and audiences. In many tales, unfilial behavior, excessive greed, or failure to pay heed to omens harbingers a descent into poverty, while proper behavior leads to prosperity. Rewards and punishments may not take effect until another reincarnation, however. Such tales both promise that rewards and punishments are delivered in an orderly manner and explain why evil men may nonetheless come upon good fortune and honest men meet with disaster. Here Buddhist didactic literature, especially its emphasis on the notion of *pao-ying* 報 應 (recompense), has had an important impact on the belief structure which undergirds many Chinese tales.

Romantic love is the theme of some of the most popular Chinese folktales, many of which have inspired novels, ballads, and plays. Probably the earliest and best-known Chinese märchen is the charming story of the patient love between the Herd-boy and the Weaving Maid (*niu-lang chih-nü* 牛郎織女). Marriages in traditional China were arranged by go-betweens, and many of these stories tell how two young people fall in love, are unable to marry, and die from unhappiness. In other stories, however, women who are either daughters of powerful men or immortals in disguise play surprisingly active roles in choosing their mates. Because young people were discouraged by their parents from forming romantic attachments, many of them must have found these stories encouraging and gratifying.

Finally, many of the humorous stories show how the powerful can be made to look ridiculous. In a large number of these stories, the teacher, ideally respected by his students, is the butt of practical jokes. In others, common people outwit magistrates and young people outwit their elders. Still, in all fairness it must be added that in other stories the victims of tricksters are innocent. Such victims include the young men and women tricked into accepting deformed partners by clever matchmakers.

The Chinese folktale deserves extensive study for the insights it promises into almost all aspects of Chinese culture, but especially for an understanding of all genres of literature. Professional storytellers and writers of plays and novels drew upon the fund of folklore for source material, and they delivered their products to audiences deeply familiar with folklore. Although study of the ways in which folktales are modified and manipulated by professional storytellers and by writers is tedious, it nonetheless promises greater understanding of familiar literary works.

BIBLIOGRAPHY

Aarne, Antti and Stith Thompson. 1961. *The Types of the Folktale: A Classification and Bibliography.* Folklore Fellows Communications, v. 75, no. 184. Helsinki.

Blyth, R. H. 1959. *Oriental Humour.* Tokyo.

Bodde, Derk. 1961. "The Myths of Ancient China," in *Mythologies of the Ancient World*, S. Kramer, ed., pp. 367-408. New York.

Chang, Ch'ang-kung 張長弓. 1948. *Ku-tzu ch'ü yen* 鼓子曲言. Shanghai.

Chao, Ching-shen 趙景深. 1960. *Ku-tzu hsüan* 鼓子選. Shanghai, 1957; rpt. Peking.

———. 1969. *Min-chien ku-shih ts'ung-hua* 民間故事叢話, in *Chung-shan Ta-hsüeh min-su ts'ung-shu* 中山大學民俗叢書, v. 12. Taipei.

———. 1937. *Ta-ku yen-chiu* 大鼓研究. Shanghai.

Chao, Shu-li 趙樹理, et al. 1950. *Ta-chung wen-i lun-chi* 大眾文藝論叢. Peking.

Ch'en, Ju-heng 陳汝衡. 1936. *Shuo-shu hsiao-shih* 說書小史. Shanghai.

———. 1958. *Shuo-shu shih-hua* 說書史話. Peking.

Cheng, Chen-to. 1959. *Chung-kuo su-wen-hsüeh shih.* 2v. Shanghai, 1938; rpt. Peking.

Chiang, Tsu-i 蔣祖怡. 1973 (?). *Chung-kuo jen-min wen-hsüeh shih* 中國人民文學史. Shanghai, 1951; rpt. Hong Kong.

Ch'ien, Nan-yang 錢南楊. 1969. *Mi-shih* 謎史, in *Chung-shan ta-hsüeh min-su ts'ung-shu*, v. 27. Taipei.

Chu, Tzu-ch'ing 朱自清. 1961. *Chung-kuo ko-yao* 中國歌謠. Peking, 1957; rpt. *Su-wen-hsüeh ts'ung-k'an* 俗文學叢刊, series 1, no. 7, Taipei.

Chung, Ching-wen 鍾敬文, ed. 1950. *Min-chien wen-i hsin lun-chi* 民間文藝新論集. Peking.

Dorson, Richard, ed. 1972. *Folklore and Folklife, an Introduction.* Chicago.

Eberhard, Wolfram, ed. and tr. 1965. *Folktales of China.* Rev. ed., Chicago.

———. 1970. "The Past and Present State of the Folklore Movement in China," revised and translated version of "Früherer und jetziger Stand der Volkskundebewegung Chinas," *Zeitschrift für Ethnologie*, 55 (1934), 316-325, reprinted in the author's *Studies in Chinese Folklore and Related Essays*, pp. 113-127. Bloomington, Indiana.

———. 1969. "Selected Bibliography of Chinese Folklore," *Chinoperl*, 1, 38-51.

———. 1970. *Studies in Taiwanese Folktales.* Berkeley and Taipei.

———. 1981. "Thoughts on Chinese Folk Theatre Performances," *OE*, 28, 1-14.

Fu, Hsi-hua 傅惜華. 1953. *Ch'ü-i lun-ts'ung* 曲藝論叢. Shanghai.

———. 1962. *Pei-ching ch'uan-t'ung ch'ü-i tsung-lu* 北京傳統曲藝總錄. Peking.

Hu, Huai-ch'en 胡懷琛. 1925. *Chung-kuo min-ko yen-chiu* 中國民歌研究. Shanghai.

Hu, Shih 胡適. 1928. *Pai-hua wen-hsüeh shih*, v. 1. Shanghai.

Izushi, Yoshihiko 石誠諺. 1973. *Shina shinwa dentō no kenkyū* 支那神話傳說研究. Tokyo.

Jagendorf, M. A. and Virginia Weng, tr. and ed. 1980. *The Magic Boat and Other Chinese Folk Stories.* New York.

Jameson, R. D. 1932. *Three Lectures on Chinese Folklore.* Peiping.

Kao, George, ed. 1946. *Chinese Wit and Humor.* New York.

Ko-yao chou-k'an 歌謠週刊 (Folksongs Weekly of National Peking University). 1932-1937. Facsimile reproduction Taipei, 1970.

Kuan, Te-tung 關德棟. 1962. *Chü-i lun-chi* 曲藝論集. Shanghai, 1958; rpt. Peking.

Levy, Howard S., tr. 1974. *China's Dirtiest Trickster: Folklore about Hsü Wen-ch'ang (1521-1593).* Arlington, Virginia.

———. 1974. *Chinese Sex Jokes in Traditional Times.* Taipei.

Li, Chia-jui 李家瑞. 1974. *Pei-p'ing su-ch'ü lüeh* 北平俗曲略. Peking: Academia Sinica, 1933; rpt. Taipei.

Lieberman, Frederic, comp. 1979. *Chinese Music: Annotated Bibliography.* New York, 1970; 2nd ed., rev. and enl., New York.

Liu, Fu 劉復 and Li Chia-jui 李家瑞. 1932. *Chung-kuo su-ch'ü tsung-mu kao* 中國俗曲總目稿. 2v. Peking.

Lou, Tzu-k'uang 婁子匡 and Chu Chieh-fan 朱介凡. 1963. *Wu-shih nien lai-te Chung-kuo su-wen-hsüeh* 五十年來的中國俗文學. *Hsien-tai Chung kuo wen-hsüeh shih ts'ung-shu* 現代中國文學史叢書. Taipei.

Ma, Kuo-fan 馬國凡. 1978. *Ch'eng-yü* 成語. Hu-ho-kao-t'e, Inner Mongolia.

Ma, Y. W. 1976. "The Beginnings of Professional Storytelling in China: A Critique of Current Theories and Evidence," in *Études d'histoire et de littérature offertes au Professeur Jaroslav Prusek,* pp. 227-245. Paris.

Mei, Tsu-lin 梅祖麟. 1980. "*San-ch'ao pei-meng hui-pien* li te pai-hua tzu-liao 三朝北盟會編裡的白話資料 (Vernacular Dialogues Preserved in the *San-ch'ao Pei-meng Hui-pien*)," *Chung-kuo shu-mu chi-k'an,* 14.2 (December), 27-52. With English summary.

Münke, Wolfgang. 1976. *Die Klassische chinesische Mythologie.* Stuttgart.

Pellowski, Anne. 1977. *The World of Storytelling.* New York.

Pian, Rulan Chao. 1974. "Primary Sources of Materials from the Chinese Oral Tradition: An Interim Bibliography," *Chinoperl,* 4, 78-84.

Pimpaneau, Jacques. 1978. *Chanteurs, conteurs, bateleurs: Littérature orale et spectacles populaires en Chine.* Paris.

Propp, Vladimir I. 1968. *Morphology of the Folktale.* Laurence Scott, tr. 2nd ed., rev. Louis A. Wagner, ed. Austin.

Ranke, Kurt, *et al.*, ed. 1979. *Enzyklopädie des Märchens: Handworterbuch zur historischen und vergleichenden Erzählforschung.* v. 2, Columns 1286-1364. Berlin. Articles by Wolfram Eberhard, Helwig Schmidt-Glintzer, André Lévy, and Nai-tung Ting.

Shih-chieh shu-chü 世界書局, ed. 1961. *Chung-kuo hsiao-hua-shu (144-chung)* 中國笑話書 (144 種). *Chung-kuo hsüeh-shu ming-chu, su-wen-hsüeh ts'ung-k'an* 中國學術名著俗文學叢刊, 1. Taipei. Taken from Wang Li-ch'i, *q.v.*

Smith, Arthur Henderson. 1964. *Proverbs and Common Sayings from the Chinese.* Rpt. New York.

Thompson, Stith. 1979. *The Folktale.* Rpt. New York.

Ting, Nai-tung and Lee-hsi Hsu Ting. 1975. *Chinese Folk Narratives: A Bibliographical Guide.* San Francisco.

———. 1978. *A Type Index of Chinese Folktales in the Oral Tradition and Major Works of Non-Religious Classical Literature.* Helsinki.

Wang, Li-ch'i 王利器, comp. 1975. *Li-tai hsiao-hua chi* 歷代笑話集. Shanghai, 1956; rpt. Hong Kong.

Weisstein, Ulrich. 1973. "Thematology [Stoffgeschichte]," in *Comparative Literature and Literary Theory: Survey and Introduction,* William Riggan, in collaboration with the author, translators, pp. 124-149. Bloomington, Indiana. Wilhelm, Richard, tr. 1971. *Chinese Folktales.* Ewald Osers, tr. [from the German]. London.

Yang, Yin-shen 楊蔭深. 1961. *Chung-kuo su-wen-hsüeh kai-lun* 中國俗文學概論. *Su-wen-hsüeh ts'ung-k'an,* series 1, no. 7. Rpt. Taipei.

Yeh, Te-chün 葉德均. 1979. "Ko-yao tzu-liao hui-lu" 歌謠資料彙錄, in Yeh's *Hsi-ch'ü hsiao-shuo ts'ung-k'ao* 戲曲小說叢考, Peking, v. 2, pp. 757-835.

Yü, Hui-yung 王會泳. 1957. *Shan-tung ta-ku* 山東大鼓. Peking.

Yüan, K'o 袁珂. 1957. *Chung-kuo ku-tai shen-hua* 中國古代神話. Shanghai.

———. 1963. *Shen-hua ku-shih hsin-pien* 神話故事新編. Peking.

PART II: PROSIMETRIC LITERATURE
W. L. Idema

Despite the high prestige of literature in Chinese culture throughout its long history, the overwhelming majority of the population remained illiterate until well into the twentieth century. While the Chinese population as a whole supported education avidly—certainly since the Sung dynasty when the myth that any poor student might by perseverance and intelligence rise through the examination system to the highest positions in the state established itself in popular lore—yet illiteracy at the beginning of this century was generally estimated to be eighty percent, and if a minimally defined literacy may have been higher among the male population, female illiteracy may safely be assumed to have been more than ninety percent.

Chinese traditional literature therefore has always been the preserve of a tiny minority, except for those forms of literature that were orally composed and transmitted or were meant for performance before an audience. By their nature, all such forms of literature were composed in the vernacular of their time and place, but one should be aware that every vernacular as a rule had its own "literary" register. Through the ages China has known a very rich and variegated popular literature of myths, legends, fairytales, humorous tales, jokes, riddles, proverbs, and songs of many kinds. In contrast to these relatively short and simple forms, there also arose longer and more complex forms of performative literature (mainly, but not exclusively, the domain of professional artists) like drama and storytelling. The many different genres of professional storytelling nowadays are usually collectively designated as *shuo-shu* 說書 (literally "telling books"); they constitute the major ingredient of *ch'ü-i* 曲藝 (theatrical entertainments with the exception of drama and acrobatics) and provide the bulk of the corpus of *su-wen-hsüeh* 俗文學 (popular literature).

Storytelling is of course a universal human characteristic. But in China, as in other traditional cultures, there were also professional artists who told stories for a living. It is not unlikely that storytelling was one of the many arts of the *yu* 優, the entertainers at the feudal courts during the Chou dynasty. In writings of the T'ang dynasty there are scattered, meager references to professional storytelling. But the earliest systematic descriptions first appeared in the Sung. The capital diaries for Kaifeng and Hangchow like the *Tung-ching meng Hua lu** contain descriptions of the pleasure precincts of these metropolises, cataloguing the amusements offered and listing the most famous artists, both male and female (who often used fanciful or picturesque stage-names). The best-known description of Sung-dynasty storytelling is found in the *Tu-ch'eng chi-sheng* (see *Tung-ching meng Hua lu*) which divides the Hangchow storytellers of its time into four schools, according to subject-matter. Exactly which four schools has been a matter of extensive scholarly debate, but Hu Shih-ying's (1980) solution is probably the best. According to him, the *Tu-ch'eng chi-sheng* distinguishes the following four schools:

1. *Chiang shih-shu* 講史書 (explicating history books), tales on the fall and rise of dynasties in Chinese history, and the wars connected with these great events of state;

2. *Shuo t'ieh-chi-erh* 說鐵騎兒 (telling of iron-clad cavalry), tales from the recent wars between the Sung and the Chin dynasties;

3. *Shuo ching* 說經 (telling the sutras), tales on religious subjects, both of a serious and a comic nature;

4. *Hsiao-shuo* (stories), tales of romantic love and miracles, tales of crime and incorrupt judges (*kung-an* 公案 [courtcases]), tales of noble brigands and their exploits, and tales of a sudden and spectacular rise in fortune.

The *Tsui-weng t'an-lu* 醉翁談錄, most likely a source-book for the (amateur) storyteller, which in its present form dates from the Yüan dynasty, lists in its "Hsiao-shuo k'ai-p'i" 小說開闢 (The Origin of *Hsiao-shuo*) over one hundred titles, representative of the storytellers' repertoire. These stories derived from a great variety of sources—canonical historiography, T'ang-dynasty *ch'uan-ch'i*, popular lore, recent crimes and scandals—and many of them survived into later ages, because they remained favorites with storytellers and their audiences, and were adapted for the stage or were written up into *p'ing-hua*,* novels, or *hua-pen*.* The Sung-dynasty sources do not allow conclusions to be drawn as to what extent the differentiation according to subject matter was paralleled by one according to length and format, but whereas some probably told their stories as all prose narratives, others employed a prosimetric form of one kind or another, as in later ages.

In the Ming and Ch'ing dynasties, professional storytellers were an omnipresent feature of Chinese society. Our information, however, even if gradually increasing in quantity and quality, remains scattered and scarce. The main reason for this is that storytelling, a far more modest entertainment than drama, only very rarely captured the fancy of the nation's elite, the literati, whose writings are our major source for the knowledge of China's past up to the present century. Ever since the Yüan dynasty, however, the literati have doted on drama, composing plays and writing extensive critical tracts on drama, playwrights, actors and actresses.

Most storytellers started out in their profession by being apprenticed to an established performer. Quite often storytelling was a family trade, transmitted through a number of generations. However, there were also artists who had entered the profession without any formal training. One was Liu Ching-t'ing 柳敬亭 (c. 1590-after 1669), possibly China's most famous storyteller. Liu performed in the main cities of the Kiangnan area. His tales ingratiated him with Tso Liang-yü 左良玉 (1598-1645), one of the generals who supported the Ming in 1645 during an attempt to organize resistance against the Manchus. Liu's status with Tso Liang-yü raised him for a moment to a position of minor political importance. During his lifetime Liu Ching-t'ing also attracted the attention of such literary luminaries as Ch'ien Ch'ien-i,* and Wu Wei-yeh,* and after his death was immortalized by K'ung Shang-jen,* who gave him a subsidiary role in his *T'ao-hua shan*. Some storytellers performed for extended periods of time at a fixed location, others were itinerant artists. Storytellers could also be summoned to private residences to perform: Liu Ching-t'ing in his heyday had to be booked ten days in advance.

If Liu Ching-t'ing was an exception in attracting literati attention, it does not follow that all genres of storytelling equally appealed to the same low-class public. Each genre had its own audience, as is already brought out in one of the Hangchow diaries, the *Hsi-hu Lao-jen fan-sheng-lu* (see *Tung-ching meng Hua lu*): "If one recites *Yai-tz'u* 涯詞, one only draws the young playboys; those who listen to *t'ao-chen* 淘眞 are all village people." (Unfortunately, nothing else about the other properties of these two genres is known.) Another example of a close relation between a specific genre of storytelling and a specific audience is provided by the *tzu-ti shu*,* which during the eighteenth and nineteenth centuries in Peking was especially practiced by Manchu amateurs. Also, within each genre the level of each performer and his or her repertoire could vary widely, and the character of the audience would change accordingly.

The genres of storytelling can on the basis of form be divided into two broad categories, the prose narrative and the chantefable. The prose narrative is known by different names in different regions: *shuo-shu, p'ing-shu* 評書, or *p'ing-hua* 評話. The performers were men, who told their stories alone, without accompaniments, their only requisites being two pieces of dry-sounding wood and a fan. These performers made no use of completely written-out texts, which allowed them to adapt each performance to the composition and mood of the audience. They might be in the possession of *ti-pen* 底本 (source-books), containing the barest outlines of stories, and poems, lyrics, and descriptive pieces of parallel prose, to be inserted wherever the occasion allowed it. Perhaps the *Tsui-weng t'an-lu* is an early example of such a *ti-pen*. It has also been argued that the *p'ing-hua** and *hua-pen** originally served as (or derived from) such source-books. However, since the early fifties a number of partial and complete performances of prose narratives have been recorded on tape, transcribed, edited, and printed. The best known example is *Wu Song* 武松 (2v., Nanking, 1959), which presents the saga of one of the heroes from the *Shui-hu chuan*,* as recounted by Wang Shao-t'ang 王少堂 (1887-1968), a great master of Yangchow *p'ing-hua* as heir to a rich family tradition.

In contrast to the prose narrative, the chantefable or prosimetric forms of storytelling had both male and female performers, who might rely on completely written-out texts. In the prosimetric forms, the story is told alternately in passages of prose, which are spoken, and rhymed metrical passages, which are chanted or sung (the prose passages may of course contain poems, lyrics, and descriptive set pieces in parallel prose, which are all recited). The modern Chinese term for this type of literature is therefore *shuo-ch'ang wen-hsüeh* 說唱文學 (speak-and-sing literature). In many of these prosimetric forms of storytelling metrical rhymed passages predominate. The prose passages are occasionally dispensed with altogether. It is therefore not correct to say that China knew no epic poetry, as an enormous amount of it has been preserved. However it differs from the European case rather in that in China epic poetry makes no appearance in the earliest beginnings of literature and that it never became the most highly valued literary genre and an expression of the most cherished ideals of the nation's elite.

Many modern scholars have argued for an Indian origin of the chantefable form. They point to the example of the Buddhist sutras, in which prose sections alternate with *gatha* and hold that Buddhist monks played an essential role in the origin and development during T'ang times of *pien-wen* (see *Tun-huang wen-hsüeh*), the earliest prosimetric form of which examples have been preserved. However, the *gatha* in Chinese sutras are metrically different from the verse section of *pien-wen* and rarely rhyme. The exclusive link between monks and *pien-wen* has also been denied recently. It would appear, therefore, that it is premature to exclude the possibility of an indigenous origin of the chantefable in China.

The original motive for writing down the texts of prosimetric forms of storytelling is a matter of some speculation. If some scholars assume they were put in writing by their authors for the benefit of performers (who might either read them out or memorize them), other scholars will argue that the storytellers who practiced prosimetric forms were capable of oral composition, and incline to the view that the texts are recordings of performances for the benefit of those listeners who wanted to be able to read the stories they fancied. However, once written texts circulated, they were used both for public performance and for private reading, and whereas some texts may have been primarily composed for the first purpose, other texts apparently were from the outset primarily intended for the second. As materials for private readings, these texts found their main public among the modestly literate segments of society. Most of their authors also came from that group, although occasionally individual literati also used the chantefable. The number of preserved prosimetric texts from the T'ang dynasty until well into the sixteenth century is very limited, and most of these are archaeological discoveries of this century (see *Tun-huang wen-hsüeh, Liu Chih-yüan chu-kung-t'iao, tz'u-hua* [doggerel story]). But from the Wan-li period (1573-1620) onwards, there exists a voluminous body of texts that rapidly expands with each subsequent century.

The singers of prosimetric form of storytelling performed singly or were accompanied by one or more instrumentalists in the chanted or sung sections. On the basis of the nature of the versified sections, prosimetric literature can be divided into two broad groups: (a) texts in which the prose passages alternate with songs or song-suites written to *tz'u,** or *ch'ü** tunes; (b) texts in which the verse sections are mostly or exclusively written in lines of equal length (five syllables, seven syllables, or ten syllables).

The best-known representatives of the first group date from the twelfth to the fourteenth centuries. In the *ku-tzu-tz'u** the narrative is carried forward in prose, while the intervening songs, each to the same *tz'u* tune, comment on the preceding action. Of this genre only two texts remain, one from *c.* 1200, another from the early Ming. In the *chu-kung-tiao** the prose-passages only occupy a small part of the text, which mainly consists of song-suites written to *ch'ü* tunes. This genre originated by the late eleventh century, flourished during the twelfth and thirteenth, to fade away during the fourteenth century. It excelled in the ironic treatment of romantic love. Unfortunately, only one complete example of the form has come down to us, together with some fragments of a few more titles. Another form of chantefable literature belonging to this group from the same period is the narrative *huo-lang-erh* 貨郎兒(pedlars' songs). The only example of this genre to be found is provided by the final act of the anonymous Yüan-dynasty *tsa-chü Hou-lang tan* 貨郎旦(A Pedlar: A Female Lead). Of course, there also existed (and continued to exist) long and short chantefable forms of this group in later times.

The overwhelming majority of chantefable texts belong to the second group. Confusingly enough, the pentasyllabic, heptasyllabic, and decasyllabic lines employed in their versified sections are also called *tz'u*詞. Even though the pentasyllabic and heptasyllabic lines are of the same length as the lines in *shih** poetry, they do not follow the prosodic rules of *shih* poetry. In these *tz'u*-passages the even lines rhyme as in *shih* poetry, but whereas *shih*-poets were expected to adhere to the rhyme-classes prescribed by the rhyme-books, the authors of prosimetric literature rhyme by ear. The major genres within the second group are *pien-wen, tz'u-hua, ku-tz'u*鼓詞(drum rhymes, see also *ta-ku*), *t'an-tz'u,** and *pao-chüan*寶卷(precious scrolls), and it will cause no surprise that the element *tz'u* occurs in a number of these names.

The *pien-wen*, dating from the eighth to tenth centuries, constitute the earliest preserved examples of Chinese prosimetric literature. In their versified sections they do not yet employ the decasyllabic line, but in all other respects they show a striking similarity to the other chantefable forms in the second group despite a gap of over four centuries between the most recent *pien-wen* and the earliest preserved *tz'u-hua* texts. This fact suggests a continuous tradition from T'ang to Ming throughout the Sung and Yüan dynasties.

Tz'u-hua appears to have been the general designation of prosimetric texts of the second group in Yüan and Ming times until well into the sixteenth century. In the Kiangnan area the same texts may in those years have been designated as *t'ao-chen*陶 眞. Until recently, the only known examples of *tz'u-hua* were sixteenth-century imitations of the form by literary men, but in 1967 sixteen *tz'u-hua*, printed in or around the Ch'eng-hua period (1465-1488), were discovered. The versified sections of *tz'u-hua* employ heptasyllabic and decasyllabic lines, as is the case with later genres in this group.

From around 1600 various contemporary genres of chantefable literature of the second group are distinguished, not so much on the basis of formal criteria of the written-out text, but rather on the basis of dialect, manner of performance, and nature of the contents. The long prosimetric narratives divided into many chapters that were performed in North China are known as *ku-tz'u*. The genre supposedly derives its name from the fact that at some stage of its development the performer accompanied himself on a drum. The performers of *ku-tz'u* were mainly men, and the genre is said to excel in descriptions of battle-scenes. Within *ku-tz'u* there existed a great variety of local and personal styles of performance. In North China during the Ch'ing dynasty shorter forms like *ta-ku** and *tzu-ti-shu* also flourished.

The general designation of the long prosimetric narratives as performed in Central and South China since the seventeenth century is *t'an-tz'u*彈詞(plucking rhymes), as the performance was accompanied by string instruments. *T'an-tz'u* were mostly performed by women. A peculiarity of *t'an-tz'u* singing was that in performance the text might be distributed over a number of artists. The preferred subject matter of *t'an-tz'u* is said to be extremely complicated melodramatic love stories—many *t'an-tz'u* authors were women. As with *ku-tz'u* there existed a great variety of local *t'an-tz'u* styles. Special mention should perhaps be made of the *mu-yü shu*木魚書 (wooden-fish books) that, hailing from Kwangtung province, are written in the Cantonese dialect.

Pao-chüan is the name of the long prosimetric narrative texts with a Buddhist inspiration, originally often performed by nuns. Various Buddhist and syncretist sects also employed the *pao-chüan* format to propagate their teachings. But the *pao-chüan* format also came to be used to treat popular stories that have no ostensible religious significance. The same development can be seen in *tao-ch'ing*道情(Taoist sentiments), which originally preached religious Taoism.

The subjects of prosimetric literature are extremely varied. Many texts derived their materials from popular lore, well-known story-cycles, or myth and legend. There also existed a continuous reciprocal borrowing between the various forms of vernacular literature like drama, fiction, and storytelling. Any subject that gained popularity in one of these forms would quickly be transposed into the others. Stories developed by generations of storytellers were adapted for the stage and written up into novels or *hua-pen*, which then in turn might be reworked again into one or more of the many varieties of prosimetric literature. These texts might again become the basis for other plays or novels. In this process, the stories concerned would be continuously changed and developed, according to the dictates of the form, the fashions of the time, and the talent of each individual writer.

A good example of this process of reciprocal borrowing of subject materials is provided by the tale of the love-affair of Chang Chün-jui and Ts'ui Ying-ying. The first version of the story, the "Ying-ying chuan" by Yüan Chen* was a T'ang-dynasty *ch'uan-ch'i*. It was adapted in Sung times both as a *ku-tzu-tz'u* and a *chu-kung-tiao*. The *chu-kung-tiao* in turn served as the basis of Wang Shih-fu's adaptation for the stage as a five-act *tsa-chü* play, the *Hsi-hsiang-chi*. This was not only again reworked into *ch'uan-ch'i* plays and adapted in the many forms of regional drama, but also rewritten as prosimetric text, e.g. as *ku-tz'u* and *tzu-ti shu*.

Another example of this continuous reciprocal borrowing is provided by the development of the legend of Judge Pao. Pao Cheng (999-1062) established during his lifetime a reputation as a sagacious and incorrupt judge, and by the Southern Sung he had become a popular figure with storytellers to judge by the "Hsiao-shuo k'ai-p'i" of *Tsui-weng t'an-lu*. In *tsa-chü* of the Yüan and early Ming dynasties he makes his appearance in many courtroom plays. No fewer than eight of the fifteenth-century *tz'u-hua* feature him. By the end of the sixteenth century, his many adventures were organized into a one-hundred-chapter novel, which was later reorganized into a collection of independent cases in its editions as *Lung-t'u kung-an*, the most popular example of *kung-an* fiction. A *hua-pen* concerning Judge Pao that was included in Feng Meng-lung's* *San-yen* was later, in Ch'ing times, developed into a short novel entitled *Ch'ing-feng-cha* 清風閘 (Clear Breeze Lock), and Pao Cheng was also assigned a major role in the military romances on the eleventh century general Ti Ch'ing 狄青, such as *Wan-hua lou* 萬花樓 and *Wu-hu p'ing-hsi* 五虎平西 (Five Tigers Pacify the West). In the nineteenth century, the *tzu-ti shu* artist Shih Yü-k'un 石玉昆 (c. 1810-1870) excelled in performing stories from *Lung-t'u kung-an*. Shih Yü-k'un created a distinctive personal style known as *Shih-p'ai shu* (Shih-school Texts), and various manuscript versions of *Shih-p'ai shu* of cases of Judge Pao and the adventures of his underlings survive. These prosimetric versions in turn served as the basis of the novel *San-hsia wu-i*.* Serialization of the Judge Pao stories on television in Taiwan in recent years testifies to the continuing popularity of these materials.

The two examples adduced above all demonstrate that some subjects displayed a remarkable vitality as they were reworked and reworked century after century. Some subjects remained popular in prosimetric literature from the T'ang dynasty until the present century. Examples are the tales of Tung Yung 董永 and of Meng Chiang-nü 孟姜女. The tale of Tung Yung celebrates filial piety and has very much the characteristics of a fairytale. When his father dies, Tung Yung finds himself so poor that he has to indenture himself for a three-year period to a rich local squire in order to provide for a decent burial. Moved by his filial piety, Heaven sends down an immortal maiden to assist him. Her miraculous weaving skills free him of his debts within a month, and having given birth to a son (the famous scholar Tung Chung-shu*), she returns to her original abode. The development of this legend can be followed from Han times onward, and its first preserved prosimetric version is a Tun-huang *pien-wen*. In Yüan and Ming times the subject inspired *tsa-chü* and *ch'uan-ch'i*. During the Ch'ing it remained popular in regional drama and was also treated as a *pao-chüan* and a *t'an-tz'u*.

Meng Chiang-nü is portrayed as a paragon of wifely devotion. During the cruel reign of the First Emperor of the Ch'in, Meng Chiang-nü's husband is drafted for building the Great Wall. He soon dies of physical exhaustion and is buried in the wall. When Meng Chiang-nü comes to the labor site to bring her husband winter clothes, she is overcome with grief at the news of his death and weeps until the wall collapses on the place where he was buried, enabling her to take her husband's bones home for burial. The earliest preserved prosimetric version of the legend is again (a fragment of) a *pien-wen*. From more recent centuries we have versions as *ku-tz'u*, *tzu-ti shu*, *t'an-tz'u*, and *pao-chüan*.

It should also be borne in mind that almost all of the popular story-cycles known from a version in a novel or a play were also treated, and often in far greater detail, in many varieties of chantefable. The saga of the wars between the states of Ch'u, Wu, and Yüeh in the sixth and fifth centuries B.C., which provided some of the most stirring pages of early historical works like *Tso-chuan** and *Shih-chi** and later inspired Liang Ch'en-yü* to write his *Wan-sha chi*, had already in T'ang times given rise to the *Wu Tzu-hsü pien-wen* 伍子胥變文, which narrates how Wu Tzu-hsü manages to avenge himself on the state of Ch'u by serving Wu, but is ordered to commit suicide when his advice to guard against Yüeh is not heeded. Some incidents from the wars following the downfall of the Ch'in dynasty, between Liu Pang, the eventual founder of the Han dynasty, and his initially spectacularly successful opponent, Hsiang Yü, are also treated in *pien-wen*. The turmoil at the end of the Han, resulting in the tripartition of the realm, which are the subject of the classic novel *San-kuo chih yen-i*, were also already a favorite subject of T'ang and Sung storytellers. The wars accompanying the founding of the T'ang dynasty, together with the campaigns in which Hsüeh Jen-kuei 薛仁貴 and his descendants distinguished themselves during the first century of the dynasty's existence, was not only repeatedly reworked as fiction (see *Sui T'ang yen-i*), but also incorporated into *tz'u-hua* and later prosimetric forms. The troubles that brought about the end of the T'ang, the continuous warfare that plagued the Five Dynasties, the founding of the Sung dynasty, and its campaigns against northern and western foes (in which the generals of the Yang 楊 family were given a preeminent role), all of which were recounted in a series of novels from the sixteenth century and later and were perennially popular on stage, also already provided stories to *chu-kung-tiao* and *tz'u-hua*. The enormous popularity of Pao Cheng, the honest judge, had its counterpart in the perhaps even greater popularity of the adventures of the noble bandits from Liang-shan Marsh, headed by Sung Chiang, that found their classic expression in the novel *Shui-hu chuan.** The wars accompanying the partial conquest of China by the Chin dynasty were already popular with Southern Sung storytellers as noted above; eventually these tales came to focus on Yüeh Fei 岳飛(1103-1141), who had been successful in the field against the Jürched but was treasonably murdered in prison to achieve a shameful peace. His career became the subject of many plays and novels (for example, the *Shuo Yüeh ch'üan-chuan* 說岳全傳 by Ch'ien Ts'ai 錢彩), in which he is treated as a paragon of loyalty, as in the *t'an-tz'u*, *tzu-ti shu*, *Shih-p'ai shu*, etc., devoted to this subject. Later history continued to provide new subject-matter in the lives of brave generals, who defended the population against foreign invasion and internal rebellion, noble swords-men, honest judges, and emperors travelling through their realm incognito, who all came to the aid of the poor and downtrodden.

Love stories were also popular. Two examples beyond the *Hsi-hsiang chi* story might be mentioned in order to suggest the diversity of theme and treatment. One of the most popular romances was the tale of Liang Shan-po 梁山伯 and Chu Ying-t'ai 祝英台. Chu Ying-t'ai is an educated girl, who in male attire goes for study to Hangchow and there befriends Liang Shan-po. For three years Liang shares a room with Chu, without realizing her true sex. When her father wants her to return home, she urges Liang Shan-po to come and ask for "her sister" in marriage. After her departure, Liang Shan-po is brought to realize the true state of affairs; but when he visits the Chu's, his proposal is refused, since Chu Ying-t'ai has already been promised to someone else. Liang Shan-po returns home, pines away, and dies. On her wedding day, Chu Ying-t'ai visits his grave, it opens up, and she jumps into it, after which it closes again. From the grave a pair of butterflies are seen to emerge. This tale, which was also very popular in regional drama, was treated in various chantefable forms, including *ku-tz'u*, *t'an-tz'u*, and *mu-yü-shu*.

The legend of the white snake relates how on a rainy day on the bank of Hangchow's West Lake the apothecary shop assistant Hsü Hsien 許仙 meets an attractive young widow, Madame Pai 白. They soon marry; Madame Pai repeatedly lavishes gifts on her new husband, which land him in trouble as they turn out to be stolen. Yet each time she has a convincing explanation. When he visits the famous Chin-shan Monastery, the abbot Fa-hai 法海 deduces from his aura that he is bewitched and sets out to exorcise the danger. Madame Pai turns out to be a thousand-year-old white snake (*pai-she* 白蛇), which the abbot buries below Hangchow's famous Lei-feng Pagoda. The tale is known as a *hua-pen* from Ming times; in Ch'ing *ch'uan-ch'i* and chantefable versions Madame Pai is allowed, before being incarcerated below the pagoda, to give birth to a son who will win highest honors in the examinations. Among the prosimetric treatments of this theme are *ku-tz'u*, *pao-chüan*, and *t'an-tz'u*. As Madame Pai only acts out of love, without any intention of stealing Hsü's vitality, the *t'an-tz'u* is known as *I-yao chuan* 義妖傳 (The Righteous Witch).

Religious legends and fables also often provide themes for chantefable literature. Among *pien-wen*, the various versions of the tale of Mu-lien 目蓮, the disciple of the Buddha who searches through all the hells to find his sinful mother and save her from her tortures, occupy a prominent position. In early *pao-chüan* the Chinese legend of Kuan-yin is an important subject. The legend of the pilgrimage of Hsüan-tsang, or Tripitaka, to the Western Paradise, which found its classic expression in Wu Ch'eng-en's *Hsi-yu-chi*,* remained popular with authors of prosimetric literature.

During the final years of the Ch'ing dynasty reformists and revolutionaries also employed prosimetric forms, especially the *t'an-tz'u*, in order to propagate their views more widely. The most conspicuous example is the *K'eng-tzu kuo-pien t'an-tz'u* 庚子國變彈詞 (*T'an-tz'u* on the Disturbances of the Year K'eng-tzu) by Li Pao-chia,* which deals with the Boxer Rebellion. The famous female revolutionary Ch'iu Chin 秋瑾 (1875-1907) discussed the position of women in traditional Chinese society in her unfinished *t'an-tz'u* entitled *Ching-wei shih* 精衛石 (Stones of the Ching-wei Bird). Other *t'an-tz'u* intro-duced European female revolutionaries as examples to their Chinese readership and audience.

Despite the great popularity of storytelling as entertainment, to a modern reader the literary value of most prosimetric texts would appear to be slight. In general histories of Chinese literature they are often treated perfunctorily at best. The most notable exception is the *Hsi-hsiang chi chu-kung-tiao,** which is given due attention as a masterwork of Chin-dynasty literature. *Pien-wen* are also given some attention. However, many general histories of Chinese literature, both Chinese and Western, remain completely silent on the subject of the voluminous prosimetric literature from the Ch'ing dynasty. At the present, the study of chantefable texts is still in its infancy. Prosimetric literature has not benefited to the same degree as drama and fiction from the reevaluation of traditional vernacular literature since the May Fourth Movement. For all the labors of scholars like A Ying, Chao Ching-shen, Cheng Chen-to, Fu Hsi-hua, Lu Kung, T'ang Cheng-pi and Yeh Te-chün, Hatano Tarō, and Sawada Mizuho, the study of prosimetric literature has scarcely advanced beyond the stage of collection and cataloguing. The major genres have been characterized and the development of a number of very popular stories has been traced, but critical analyses of individual works are still exceedingly scarce. It is therefore quite imaginable that continued research will generate standards of evaluation that may allow a clearer discrimination between texts of greater and lesser artistic merit, allowing the best works in this genre to be assigned their rightful place in Chinese literary history. If the bulk of the texts in the chantefable form should indeed turn out to be undistinguished as works of literature, study of them would still be interesting for the light they may shed on the values and feelings of the moderately literate groups in Chinese society (e.g., women) who wrote them and read them. Moreover, prosimetric literature had a major influence, perhaps even greater than that of drama, on the illiterate masses. Prosimetric texts are one of the very few segments of traditional Chinese literature that did not originate from the tiny circumscribed cultural elite of literati. Study of them is therefore significant because they transcend the normally accepted bounds of literature.

EDITIONS:

The most extensive collection of prosimetric texts, both manuscripts and printed editions, is held by the Fu Ssu-nien Library of the Academia Sinica, Taiwan.

COLLECTIVE EDITIONS:

A, Ying 阿英, ed. 1960. *Wan-Ch'ing wen-hsüeh ts'ung-ch'ao Shuo-ch'ang wen-hsüeh chüan* 晚清文學叢鈔說唱文學卷. 2v. Peking.

Fu, Hsi-hua 傅惜華, ed. 1955. *Hsi-hsiang-chi shuo-ch'ang chi* 西廂記說唱集. Shanghai.

———. 1958. *Pai-she-chuan chi* 白蛇傳集. Peking.

Lu, Kung 路工, ed. 1955. *Liang Chu ku-shih shuo-ch'ang chi* 梁祝故事說唱集. Shanghai.

———. 1958. *Meng Chiang-nü wan-li hsün-fu chi* 孟姜女萬里尋夫集. Peking.

———, and Fu Hsi-hua, eds. 1975. *Shih-wu kuan hsi-ch'ü tzu-liao hui-pien* 十五貫戲曲資料彙編. Peking.

P'u, Sung-ling 蒲松齡. 1962. *P'u Sung-ling chi* 蒲松齡集. Lu Ta-huang 路大荒, ed. 2v. Peking.

Also includes some prosimetric texts.

Shang-hai chiao-yü ch'u-pan-she 上海教育出版社, ed. *Chung-wei min-chien ku-shih hsüan* 中外民間故事選. Shanghai, 1982.

Tu, Ying-t'ao 杜穎陶. 1957. *Tung Yung Ch'en-hsiang ho-chi* 董永沈香合集. Shanghai.

———, ed. 1957. *Yüeh Fei ku-shih hsi-ch'ü shuo-ch'ang chi* 岳飛故事戲曲說唱集. Shanghai.

TRANSLATIONS:

Idema, Wilt and Stephen H. West. 1982. *Chinese Theatre 1100–1450, A Source Book*. Wiesbaden. Contains a translation of Act IV of *Huo-lang-tan*, pp. 278–298.

Qiu, Jin. 1976. *Pierre de l'oiseau Jingwei*. Catherine Gipoulon, tr. Paris. Retranslated into German as *Die Steine des Vogels Jingwei*. Munich, 1977. Translation of *Ching-wei-shih*, preceded by biographical study of Ch'iu Chin.

STUDIES:

A, Ying. 1979. *A Ying wen-chi* 阿英文集. 2v. Hong Kong. Collected articles by the leading expert on late Ch'ing literature.

Chao, Ching-shen 趙景深. *Ch'ü-i ts'ung-t'an* 曲藝叢談. Peking, 1982. A collection of articles on various forms of prosimetric literature.

Ch'en, Ju-heng 陳汝衡. 1936. *Shuo-shu hsiao-shih* 說書小史. Shanghai.

———. 1958. *Shuo-shu shih-hua* 說書史話. Peking.

———. 1979. *Sung-tai shuo-shu shih* 宋代說書史. Shanghai.

———. 1979. *Shuo-shu i-jen Liu Ching-t'ing* 說書藝人柳敬亭. Shanghai.

Cheng, Chen-to 鄭振鐸. 1959. *Chung-kuo su-wen-hsüeh shih* 中國俗文學史. Rpt. Peking. A history of folksongs and prosimetric literature by the leading authority during the first half of this century on traditional vernacular literature.

———. 1957. *Chung-kuo wen-hsüeh yen-chiu* 中國文學研究. 3v. Peking. Collected articles, including those on prosimetric literature.

Cheung, Samuel Hung-nin. "The Use of Verse in the Dun-huang bian-wen," *JCL,* 8.1 (January 1980), 149-162.

Chung-kuo hsi-ch'ü ch'ü-i tz'u-tien 中國戲曲曲藝詞典. 1981. Shanghai.

Chung-kuo ta pai-k'o ch'üan-shu, Hsi-ch'ü ch'ü-i 中國大百科全書, 戲曲曲艺. Peking and Shanghai, 1983.

Dudbridge, Glen. 1978. *The Legend of Miao-shan.* London. Traces the development of the Chinese legend of Kuan-yin, including *pao-chüan* versions.

Eberhard, Wolfram. 1970. "Notes on Chinese Storytellers," in *Fabula,* 11, 1-31.

Fu, Hsi-hua. 1954. *Chü-i lun-ts'ung* 曲藝論叢. Shanghai.

———. 1962. *Pei-ching ch'uan-t'ung ch'ü-i tsung-lu* 北京傳統曲藝總錄. Peking.

Hanan, Patrick. 1973. "The *Yün-men chuan:* from Chantefable to Short Story," *BSOAS,* 36, 299-308.

Hatano, Tarō 波多野太郎. 1974. *Chūgoku bungakushi kenkyū* 中國文學史研究. Tokyo. Collected articles, including those on prosimetric literature.

Hrdlickova, Vera. 1965. "The Professional Training of Chinese Storytellers and the Storytellers' Guilds," *AO,* 33, 225-298.

Hu, Shih-liang 胡士瑩. 1957. *Liu Ching-t'ing p'ing-chuan* 柳敬亭評傳. Shanghai.

Johnson, David. 1981. "Chinese Popular Literature and Its Contexts," *CLEAR,* 3, 225-233.

Kuan, Te-tung 關德棟. 1958. *Ch'ü-i lun-chi* 曲藝論集. Peking. Collected articles.

Lévy, André. 1969. "Un texte burlesque du XVIe siècle dans le style de la chantefable,"

BEFEO, 56, 119-124.

———. 1973. "La ballade de l'heroine francaise, Notes pour servir a l'histoire de Madame Roland en Chine," *Revue de Littérature Comparée,* 67.2, 177-192.

Li, Shih-yü 李世瑜. *Pao-chüan tsung-lu* 寶卷綜錄. Peking, 1961.

Lou, Tzu-k'uang 婁子匡 and Chu Chieh-fan 朱介凡. 1963. *Wu-shih-nien lai te Chung-kuo su-wen-hsüeh* 五十年來的中國俗文學. Taipei.

Ma, Yau-woon. 1976. "The Beginnings of Professional Storytelling in China: A Critique of Current Theories and Evidence," in *Études d'histoire et de littérature chinoises offertes au Professeur Jaroslav Prusek,* Yves Hervouet, ed., pp. 227-245. Paris.

Owan, Gail K. "A Study of *Hua Guan Suo zhuan:* A Prosimetric Narrative Printed in 1478." Unpublished Ph.D. dissertation, University of Chicago, 1982.

Pimpaneau, Jacques. 1978. *Chanteurs, conteurs, bateleurs, littérature orale et spectacle populaires en Chine.* Paris. The only general introduction to the subject in a western language. Contains many illuminating translations, profusely illustrated but weak on bibliography.

Prusek, Jaroslav. 1970. "Chui-tzu-shu, Folk Songs from Honan," in his *Chinese History and Literature,* pp. 170-198. Dordrecht.

Sawada, Mizuho 澤田瑞穗. 1976. *Bōken no kenkyū* 寶卷の研究. Nagoya, 1963; rev. and expanded edition.

Tseng, Yung-i 曾永義. 1980. *Shuo su-wen-hsüeh* 說俗文學. Taipei. Collected articles.

Wang, Ch'iu-kuei. 1978. "The Formation of the Early Versions of the Meng Chiang-nü Story," *TkR,* 9, 111-140.

———. 1977. "The Tun-huang Versions of the Meng Chiang-nü Story," *Asian Culture Quarterly,* 5.4, 67-81.

———. 1979. "The *Hsiao-shih Meng Chiang Chung-lieh Chen-chieh Hsien-liang Pao-chüan—* An Analytical Study," *Asian Culture Quarterly,* 7.4, 46-72.

———. 1981. "From Pao-chüan to Ballad, A Study of Literary Adaptation as Exemplified by Two Versions of the Meng Chiang-nü Story," *Asian Culture Quarterly,* 9.1, 48-65.

Yeh, Te-chün 葉德均. 1957. *Sung Yüan Ming chiang-ch'ang wen-hsüeh shih* 宋元明講唱文學史. Shanghai.

———. 1979. *Hsi-ch'ü hsiao-shuo ts'ung-k'ao* 戲曲小說叢考. 2v. Peking. Collected articles, including those on prosimetric literature.

PROSE

William H. Nienhauser, Jr.

I. Introduction

ONE of the first obstacles to presenting traditional Chinese prose to the Western reader is the term *prose* itself. The English word is derived from the Latin *prorsa oratio*, "straightforward talk," or *prorsus*, "straightforward" (as opposed to verse, from *vertere*, "to turn"), and the greatest virtue of prose is clarity—George Orwell claimed good prose is "like a windowpane." Unfortunately, the term has taken on negative connotations in English: a "prosy" old fellow, a "prosaic" problem, or a preacher "prosing" away for hours. As a result prose has been much neglected in Western criticism. This attitude has influenced studies of Chinese literature in the West, so that there are few works on prose.

Nothing could be further from the Chinese case, where *wen*文, the crucial morpheme common to the various terms which approximate our word *prose*, is exalted as one of the pillars of Chinese society. The earliest meaning of *wen* (Archaic Chinese: 夊, *miwun*) was "drawn lines" or "fine patterns" (Thern, 1966, p. 53). It came to mean successively "refined or polished," "ornamentation" (as opposed to "substance"), "rhymed prose," and finally "literature in general." The term which comes closest to our notion of prose ("the ordinary form of written language" or "all discourse not patterned into recurrent metric units") is *wen-chang* 文章, which may have had this meaning as early as the third century of our era (Fang, 1951, p. 560, n. 1).

In the modern West a common distinction between prose and poetry is language: prose tends to reflect ordinary speech, whereas poetry employs a special kind of condensed, charged language. Poetry is also often rhymed and exhibits a rhythm.

Not so in traditional China. Although very early prose may reflect to a certain extent the then contemporary vernacular, later texts do not. The medium of most prose until the early twentieth century was *wen-yen* 文言, an artificial written language. Moreover, when a young student began to study prose, he took care to note the figures of speech, imagery, and rhythm of his models. Then he memorized the passage, rehearsed it, and finally performed it for his teacher. A sense of rhythm comparable to that found in the prose masters of Rome and Greece is found in most Chinese authors and styles (Ch'i, 1982). Many rhetorical devices were also common to both prose and poetry. Moreover, until the ninth century the distinction between *wen*文(belles lettres) and *pi*筆(utilitarian literary works) was more significant than that between prose and verse (Lo, 1982, p. 121).

The most admired prose writers composed a terse, laconic style which could be differentiated from poetry primarily by the lack of a fixed rhythm, by its use of grammatical particles, and of course by rhyme. Indeed, some schemes of traditional Chinese literature divide all texts into *yün-wen* 韻文 (rhymed literature) and *wu yün-wen* 無韻文 (unrhymed literature). Another distinction between prose and verse can be seen in the close ties between poetic genres and music, at least in the formative stages (see *tz'u* or *ch'ü*, for example).

There are numerous traditional classifications of prose, but most confuse genre (histories, philosophic works) with the reception of the text (the Confucian Classics) or their style (*ku-wen*) haphazardly.

Contemporary ideas of the history of Chinese prose have been influenced by the predominance of T'ung-ch'eng p'ai* adherents among early and mid-twentieth-century scholars who compiled many of the literary histories and anthologies available today. Under their guidance, *san-wen* 散文 (*san* refers to a relaxed, irregular, and independent style, thus "free prose," or even "essay") has been elevated to a position of prominence. Although persuasion is at the heart of most of these essays, there are a number of lyrical pieces. Unfortunately, this emphasis on the essay has caused the neglect of the other major forms of Chinese prose—philosophical, historical, and documentary—a neglect which will not be totally rectified in this study.

Hsieh Fang-te 謝枋得 (1226-1289), the compiler of the *Wen-chang kuei-fan* 文章規範 (Models for Prose Writing) divided Chinese prose (although he too conceived it as consisting primarily of *san-wen*) into *fang-tan wen* 放膽文 (pieces of plucked up courage—i.e., didactic), and *hsiao-hsin wen* 小心文 (pieces of careful detail), types which approximate the formal and informal essay of the contemporary West, but his classification had little subsequent influence. The basic distinction remains that of stylistic categories between (1) formalized, euphuistic works and (2) pieces which emphasize clarity and content. The modern labels for referring to these styles are *p'ien-wen** (parallel prose) and *ku-wen** (ancient-style prose).

Reaching a zenith in the sixth and seventh centuries, *p'ien-wen* established early a connection to the court: written by courtiers during the Six Dynasties and preserved for posterity in the royally sponsored *Wen-hsüan,** *p'ien-wen* gradually lost favor among the literati beginning in the eighth century, but generally remained the style of court documents for centuries thereafter. Not long after—in Han Yü's era—*p'ien-wen* began to be referred to as *shih-wen* 時文 (contemporary prose), in contrast to *ku-wen*. It became the most common style for lyrical pieces and was used in examinations during part of the Sung and the entire Ming. *San-wen,* on the other hand, became the medium of argumentation employed by reformers and "new men," members of the local elites whose clans were attempting to climb the social ladders of T'ang and Sung China, but who had no close court ties. There are of course exceptions to this generalization, but basically when the literary stage was set up close to the court *p'ien-wen* dominated, whereas during periods in which most of the literary activity took place at some distance beyond the palace walls, *san-wen* was the norm. This was true even in the Ming as *san-wen* became somewhat stultified through an overemulation of earlier models, since by this time *pai-hua wen* 白話文 (vernacular prose) in *yü-lu* 語錄 (analecta) and in fiction had to some extent begun to supplant *san-wen*. The euphuistic, emotive style of *p'ien-wen* and the lean, discursive prose of *ku-wen* have also been associated throughout Chinese history with North and South China respectively (Liu, 1983).

Thus in *p'ien-wen* itself the emphasis is on the aesthetic and the lyrical, and although many of the genres which regularly employed the style (*lei* 誄 [elegies], *piao* 表 [memorials], *hsi* [military dispatches]) were ostensibly practical in nature, the overall communication of ideas or information was often little more than what is found in a modern Western legal or administrative document. It is no coincidence that many of these genres involved court or other rituals. Thus, like its parent genre, the *fu,** later *p'ien-wen* often fell short of any practical goals, all the while delighting the senses (see the two examples translated in Hightower, 1966, for example). Ronald C. Egan (1979, p. 345) can claim that the three main styles of *p'ien-wen* in the early sixth century were "circumambulatory," "allusive and blindly parallel," and "sensual"—they are *patterned* (文) rather than disposed towards straightforwardness.

Ku-wen pieces, however, can be generally identified as didactic. In fact, Margouliès' (1926, "Introduction," p. iv) definition stipulates that a *ku-wen* piece must have (1) a complete and unique independence and sense, (2) an absolute unity of action with little or no superfluous detail, and (3) the presence of a philosophical or moral idea. Although not bound by the intricate prosody of the *p'ien-wen* style, *ku-wen* from the time of its greatest early exponents such as Han Yü* incorporated parallel couplets. Indeed, on occasion differentiating the two styles is difficult: Liu Tsung-yüan* has been claimed as both one of the major figures in the revival of *ku-wen* and a *p'ien-wen* author of note (Sun, 1962, p. 587), and some of the best-known works of Ou-yang Hsiu,* the major figure in establishing *ku-wen* as the stylistic norm during the eleventh century, are in *p'ien-wen*. It was rather genres (more than individuals) which determined the style to be used. Thus Liu Tsung-yüan's contemporary renown was based on court documents he wrote in the *p'ien-wen* style during his youth, but his fame has endured because of the *ku-wen* he wrote during his years in exile (a classic example of the applicability of *p'ien-wen* to court life and the role of *ku-wen* as a medium of the disenchanted). Moreover, some of the Southern genres such as the *sao*騷 (lamentation) used by Liu in exile required *p'ien-wen*.

As in Western criticism (since Aristotle noted that prose was not "destitute of rhythm"), Chinese scholars have often commented on the rhythm of prose. The basic unit of prose is generally accepted to be a four-word (or four-graph) phrase or sentence. Although on the surface this parallels nicely the *paeon* which Western critics have claimed is the base rhythm of classical Western prose (Saintsbury, 1912, p. 1), actually it is a much more "natural" configuration (witness the usual length of an aphorism). Besides, because of the impact of parallelism on Chinese prose of all sorts, there is a tendency for primary rhythm (that based on syntactical and thought patterns) to be more in concert with secondary rhythm (that based on sound and prosody) than is the case in the West. A more regular rhythm and attention to oral presentation, therefore, was able to perform another important function by substituting for punctuation and paragraphing, which were unknown in traditional prose.

II. Genres

Although most early anthologies of prose and works of literary criticism spoke to the question of genres (Hightower, 1957), the theory which has exerted the most influence on modern critics is that of Yao Nai 姚鼐 (1732-1815). Yao was a *ku-wen* advocate and a member of the T'ung-ch'eng p'ai and his generic categories thus reflect this bias.

But it is not a matter of genre alone which determined style, since many genres appear in both *ku-wen* and *p'ien-wen* collections. Moreover, while genre titles remained fixed, their contents often varied considerably over time (Nienhauser, 1977). Nevertheless, Yao's generic theories, as embodied in his *Ku-wen tz'u-lei tsuan*,* deserve mention. Yao divided Chinese prose into thirteen genres (and a host of subgenres):

1. *lun pien* 論辯 (essays and arguments);
2. *hsü pa* 序跋 (prefaces and colophons);
3. *tsou i* 奏議 (memorials and deliberations);
4. *shu tu* 書牘 (letters);
5. *tseng-hsü* 贈予 (compositions presented at parting);
6. *chao ling* 詔令 (edicts and orders);
7. *chuan chuang* 傳狀 (biographies and obituaries);
8. *pei chih* 碑誌 (epitaphs and necrologies);
9. *tsa-chi* 雜記 (miscellaneous records);
10. *chen ming* 箴銘 (admonitions and inscriptions);
11. *sung tsan* 頌贊 (eulogies and panegyrics);
12. *tz'u fu* 辭賦 (prose poetry);
13. *ai chi* 哀記 (elegies and funeral orations).

Class one, *lun pien*, owes its origin to the pre-Ch'in philosophers. It includes *shuo* 說 (discourses), *tui-wen* 對 (questions and answers), *kao* (investigations), and *yü* (parables), and was a favorite of the T'ang *ku-wen* writers, as Liu Tsung-yüan's "Pu-she-che shuo" 捕蛇者說 (Discourse of the Snake-catcher), "Ta-wen" 答問 (Answering Questions), "Feng-chien lun" 封建論 (On Feudalism), and "*Lun-yü* pien" 論語辯 (A Discussion of the *Analects of Confucius*) may serve to illustrate. *Hsü pa*, Yao's second category, consists of the kinds of commentaries on a work that are placed in either front or back matter: prefaces, colophons, abstracts, introductions, appraisals, summaries, etc. Several of its generic types (*tu* 讀 [on reading . . .], *t'i-hou* 題後 [postfaces on having read . . .]) also first became popular under the T'ang. *Tsou i*, the third category, includes the dozens of types of communications addressed by ministers to their sovereigns. The origins of this type of prose can be found in the *Shu-ching* (Book of Documents—see *ching*). Letters (*shu tu*), the fourth corpus, includes two basic varieties: those from inferior to superior and those between equals. Traditional Chinese letters were to a certain extent considered public documents; they often dealt with weighty topics in quite formal terms and were circulated among a much larger audience than just the author and his addressee (the correspondence between Han Yü and Liu Tsung-yüan may serve as an example). The composition presented at parting (*tseng-hsü*) is primarily a T'ang genre. *Hsü* literally means preface and they were generally written to introduce poems written at parting. But often the poems were never written down and the *hsü* stood alone. Li Po's collected works contain many of these parting pieces. The sixth class, edicts and orders (*chao-ling*), were also derived from *Shu-ching* prototypes. Although a few early works of this type (see *Wen-hsüan*, *ch.* 35 and 36) are well known, most of the authors of such pieces enjoyed only a contemporary reputation in court circles. Epitaphs and necrologies (*pei chih*) have a very ancient provenance and were probably originally carved on wooden tablets in the ancestral hall. Although several pre-T'ang works in these genres are well known, it was Han Yü who elevated the form to a high literary art—his "Liu Tzu-hou mu-chih ming" 柳子厚墓誌銘 (Inscription on Liu Tsung-yüan's Tomb Tablet) is one of the best-known pieces. These works often combined a *p'ien-wen*-style prose with verse. Yao's ninth category, miscellaneous records (*tsa-chi*), suggests some of the difficulties inherent in any classification of Chinese prose. Under this rubric he includes *chi* 紀(historical records), *chi* 記(records, often of an occasion, some of which were quite mundane), *chih* 志(chronicle), *ching* 經(treatise), *lu* 錄(notes), and *t'i* 題(here a "dedicatory address or inscription") in short a repository for those genres which proved difficult to classify. The nature of most of these works is historical. Two literary exceptions are the "note" (*lu*) which should include *yü-lu* 語錄 (*analecta*), a genre which was originated by the Buddhists (see *Ch'an yü-lu*) and subsequently recorded the words of Neo-Confucian scholars in a relatively vernacular prose, and the record (*chi*) which provides a forum for many informal essays and engendered an important subgenre, the *yu-chi* 遊記(record of an excursion), made famous by Liu Tsung-yüan's pieces written during his exile in the South. Although most admonitions and inscriptions (*chen ming*) failed to achieve literary repute, Yüan Chieh's* works in a subgenre, *kuei* 規(lesson or admonition), are notable. These forms have a long ancestry which stretches into the era of bronze inscriptions. The eulogies and panegyrics (*sung tsan*), Yao's eleventh category, claim a line of descent from the *sung* in the *Shih-ching*.* More often these works were at least partly in verse, and some of the subgenres Yao notes are *generally* verse compositions. The twelfth category, prose poetry (*tz'u* is sometimes differentiated from *fu* by its more limited subject matter and indeed existed as a separate genre in the Han), originated in the *Ch'u-tz'u** and rhetorical writings of pre-Ch'in times. Although its form and style in any given period reflect to a certain extent the prevailing literary trend of the times (during the T'ang, for example, the *lü-fu* 律賦 [regulated prose poem] was current), it normally consisted of a prose preface, a verse body, and a coda. Such prose prefaces were common in other poetic genres, however, and the basic form remains poetic (see essay on Poetry). The prose poetry of the Han is usually seen as the apotheosis of the genre, although it was written in every era. Yao's final category, elegies and funeral orations, contains nearly a score of ritualistic subgenres such as *chi wen* 祈文(petition), *chu* 祝(an invocation), *kao-wen* 告文(an announcement [to the spirits]), and *shang-liang wen* 上梁文(a laudatory composition written for the setting up of the main crossbeam of a new building).

These thirteen classes (Edwards, 1948) are condensed from over twice as many categories (many included as subcategories in Yao's classification) found in the *Wen-hsüan* and *Wen-hsin tiao-lung*.* That the question of generic division was problematic is evident from the numerous works on the subject, especially during the Ming. And although Yao emphasizes *ku-wen*-oriented genres (classes 1, 4, 5, 7, 9), he also includes *p'ien-wen* types (classes 3, 6, 10, and 11) and even *fu*.

III. Historical Development

A. Pre-Ch'in Era

"The earliest use of connected writing . . . was as an aid to memory," claims Arthur Waley (1935, p. 101). In traditional China memorization of all texts, especially the "sacred," was required. Thus it is not surprising that poetry, with its close ties to ritual and its comparative (vis-à-vis prose) adaptability to memorization, was recorded much earlier than prose and that the earliest prose exhibits some qualities—parallelism and rhyme—which made it easier to memorize. The first Chinese "books"—the *I-ching*, the *Shu-ching*, and the *Shih-ching*—were sacred and closely connected with the court. The *Shih-ching* is a collection of verse, but the other two texts serve to illustrate the very early association between parallel prose and the court. Indeed, for this early era the court held a virtual monopoly on written literature.

This early state of patterned, elegant court prose was followed by the development of two types (Liu Shen-shu, 1978): (1) a prose which alleged to record speech and therefore used a simpler style and more logical arguments, although it was not without rhetorical flourishes, and (2) a statutory or legal prose, found primarily in the ritual texts. Other critics have chosen to categorize prose under different schemes, such as the two basic types Jao Tsung-i discerns (1977, p. 164): style-oriented (rhetoricians and Taoists) and substance-oriented (Confucians, Mohists and Legalists), the former having the most influence on later prose. Fu Ssu-nien 傅斯年 (1896-1950) has taken a chronological approach and claimed that recorded speech (*chi-yen* 記言—as in the *Lun-yü* 論語) was the earliest type of Chinese prose, followed by the composition of essays (*chu-lun* 著論—as in the *Hsün-tzu* 荀子) and the writing of books (成書—as in the *Lü-shih ch'un-ch'iu*), although he admits there are some problems in fitting Taoist texts to this scheme. His theory may serve to draw our attention briefly to the relationship between the spoken and written languages during the Chou. Lo Ken-tse (1957, "Preface," p. 19), among others, has argued that the written and spoken languages were quite close during this period, citing the *Lun-yü* and *Kuo-yü* as examples. But what seems more probable is the conception originated by Cheng Hsüan 鄭玄 (127-200), the Latter Han commentator, which was also popular with Ch'ing scholars (see Waley, 1938, p. 126, n. 4 and pp. 242-243, and Chou, 1956), that Confucius (and other literate men in the Chou period) spoke two languages—one an elegant, formal, archaic, and somewhat contrived (*ya-yen* 雅言) official tongue, the other his native, regional dialect. This formal language seems to have been similar to the regional vernaculars in its syntax but different in vocabulary and pronunciation. Moreover, the scribal tendencies for simplification (once in writing, ambiguity is reduced, allowing for some abbreviation; the difficulty of carving in the durable mediums of bronze, bone, wood, and bamboo also urged conciseness) probably augmented the differences between "speech" as recorded in the *Lun-yü* and similar texts and that of everyday life. In other words, even at this early period, there was a form of "ancient-style prose" similar to what later became known as *ku-wen*. The perception among the ancient Chinese that such a bifurcation existed or had developed, however, may not have come until the end of the Former Han.

The corpus of extant pre-Ch'in prose is rather substantial. Yen K'o-chün's *Ch'üan Shang-ku San-tai Ch'in Han San-kuo Liu-ch'ao wen** (Preface, fol. 6a) includes 16 *chüan* of works by 206 individuals (although it should be noted that a fair percentage of the pieces he includes may well be spurious). Almost all of these works can be classified as either philosophy or history, but they served as the model for various *literary* genres in the eras succeeding. Both types of prose (philosophical and historical) show a predilection for recording "direct speech" and for the dramatic form (Watson, 1962, p. 23).

Attempts to explain the rise of prose in terms of socio-economic change (Liu Ta-chieh, 1962, v. 1, pp. 61-65) are unconvincing. Related to this trend has been the view, derived from Pan Ku,* that various philosophic schools are historically tied to social or professional groups—the Taoists originating from the historians, the Confucians from the officials in charge of education, etc. A recent and somewhat refined explication in this line is that of Lo Ken-tse (1957, p. 17).

Elsewhere in this volume a claim is made that oracle-bone and bronze inscriptions represent the earliest extant Chinese prose. Indeed, literary styles (parallelism) and genres (the admonitions on Yü's bathtub) can be traced to these earliest "writings." Although many of the inscriptions are rhymed and resemble the sung頌(hymns) in the Shih-ching, some are closer to the prose found in the Shu-ching (Ch'en, 1965, p. 87). To a certain extent the related argument that the bronze inscriptions represent the only Chou prose that was intended to be read as literature (Ch'en, p. 87) seems valid.

The Shu-ching itself is not generally read even today as literature, but in the "P'an-keng"盤庚 section it may contain one of the earliest passages capable of being labeled a piece of "prose" (Feng Ch'i-yung, 1962, p. 1). Moreover, its style has exerted an enormous influence on the documentary style in government and diplomatic pieces (Margouliès [1926, Introduction, p. 1] notes that in the 1920s presidential decrees still employed formulae from the Shu-ching).

The second major historical work of importance is the Tso-chuan. Stylistically it, along with the Mencius and the Chuang-tzu, has had a greater impact on subsequent prose than any other early work. It was appreciated as a classic in historical style very early (Liu Ta-chieh, p. 61, notes Liu Chih-chi's* [660-721] praise for this work and certainly Ssu-ma Ch'ien* was influenced by it), but Chin Sheng-t'an's comments on the Tso-chuan as one of the major works in traditional literature may well mark the apotheosis of its literary reputation. Its lapidary and laconic prose has been called "san-wen" (Margouliès, 1949, p. 17), and it is well represented in later anthologies of prose (for example, over two-thirds of the Chou selections in the Ku-wen kuan-chih are from the Tso-chuan).

The Lun-yü became a model for many later philosophical works—Yang Hsiung's Fa-yen法言 and its imitations, and the yü-lu of the Sung and subsequent eras, to name but two major descendants. Moreover, certain of its stylistic formulae have given rise to traditional means of argumentation or even subgenres (such as the form "in ancient times people did such and such, today they do so and so" [invariably the practices of "ancient times" are superior]). Modern collections of informal essays suggest that some of the passages in the Lun-yü (such as the last section in Book XI in which Confucius and his disciples discuss what they would do, if they were free to choose any style of life) are the earliest hsiao-p'in wen小品文(informal essays—cf. Tao, 1934, pp. 1-3).

The Mo-tzu has been exalted as the earliest organized exposition of doctrine and a model of logical style. Yet its literary value is not high. Burton Watson (1962, p. 154) assails its uninspired arguments and its flat, repetitious style; Arthur Waley is less kind (1935, p. 163), viewing the work as "devoid of a single passage that could possibly be said to have wit, beauty or force." Nevertheless the clarity of style and argument Mo-tzu achieved has many admirers.

The Chuang-tzu is, as noted above, one of the three Chou prose works which greatly influenced later writing. Chuang-tzu was the second great Taoist writer of antiquity, and his style is vigorous and unique. But the qualities which most impressed later admirers and imitators are his skepticism and his use of allegory, analogy, and satire.

Another corpus from the South, the *Ch'u-tzu*,* though normally considered verse, did much to establish the basic line and couplet of subsequent *p'ien-wen* prose. Because of the political interpretations given the major pieces in this collection almost from the time of their composition, these works have escaped the admonitions directed at subsequent parallel prose.

The *Mencius* is a compilation roughly contemporary with the *Ch'u-tz'u* and the *Chuang-tzu*. It is a model of straightforward, expository prose which also emphasized the use of analogy (Lau, 1970, Appendix 5, pp. 235-263). Its reception was enhanced after Han Yü* (768-824) praised both its content and expression.

The *Hsün-tzu* contains the prototypes (see, for example, *chüan* 1 and 17) of the Chinese essay (Hightower, 1953, p. 8). This text marks the replacement of the dialogue form (*Lun-yü* and *Mencius*) in Confucianism; the arguments are tighter than those in the *Mo-tzu*. The style of the *Hsün-tzu* (Watson, 1963, p. 133) is "consciously literary," with a rich diction cast in balanced, symmetrical forms. The work was written not for a small group of the initiated, as the *Lun-yü* and most other early philosophical works had been (Watson, 1962), but as an attempt to proselytize among a much larger audience. This no doubt reflects the change in readership from a small, court-based elite in the early Chou to a much larger audience of a broader social base.

Aside from the influence of the *Hsün-tzu* on the essay, other works such as the *Tso-chuan*, the *Han-fei-tzu*, the *Lü-shih ch'un-ch'iu*, and the *Chan-kuo ts'e* helped to establish a fairly uniform prose style (the last of these works embodied the culmination of stylized, rhetorical argumentation) which became that of Ssu-ma Ch'ien, and through him the basic expository medium of the last two millennia.

Because the changes noted above in readership, style, and genres of Chou prose had taken place by the early third century B.C., it may be more fruitful to think of 300 B.C. (with the popularity of the proto-*fu* in Ch'u concurrent) as the watershed in literary development than to follow the usual political division (i.e., the establishment of the Ch'in in 256 B.C.). Ch'en Chu (1965) takes a first step in this direction by dividing the early history of prose as follows: (1) an early era in which literature served the government needs lasting through the Shang and early Chou dynasties; (2) a period of gradual transition to literature based in learning which coincides with the Spring and Autumn Period; and (3) the Warring States years during which literature based itself in learning.

B. Han Dynasty

Early Han prose is a legacy of the persuaders of the late Chou (T'ai, 1979, p. 217). In the late Warring States two schools of Confucian scholars existed: one group of pure scholars, each specializing in a single classic; the other, Confucian "statesmen," "counselors," or "persuaders." Lu Chia陸賈 (c. 228-c. 140 B.C.), a statesman, left two major works, the *Hsin-yü* 新語(New Speeches) and the *Ch'u Han ch'un-ch'iu*楚漢春秋 (Spring and Autumn Annals of Ch'u and Han). Each is a depiction of the rise of Han, the former philosophical, the latter, which served as the source of the accounts of the relations between Hsiang Yü and Liu Pang in the *Shih-chi*,* historical. They represented an important step toward incorporating the rhetoric of oral persuasion into written literature. In the works of Chia I,* another Confucian persuader, these written techniques of persuasion become codified. His "Kuo Ch'in lun" 過秦論 (Essay on the Faults of Ch'in) depicts the moral and resultant political failures of Ch'in. This piece marked a continued development of the style of logical argument seen in the *Hsün-tzu* and may be considered the earliest discursive essay. Other works in the small extant corpus (less than a dozen pieces) of Chia I are also prototypes and thus significant. His "Tiao Ch'ü Yüan fu" 悼屈原賦 (Prose-poem Lamenting Ch'ü Yüan) established a tradition in which exiled writers adopted the pose of Ch'ü Yüan* and a style modeled on the collection of works attributed to him. And his "Shang-shu ch'en cheng-shih" 上疏陳政事 (Presented Letter in Political Affairs) is the first work to sustain a political plea (it notes social-political weaknesses of the Han and suggests solutions) to such length—it is a small monograph.

In opposition to these Confucian statesmen-literati are the compilers of the *Huai-nan-tzu* 淮南子 (scholars at the court of Liu An 劉安 [d. 122 B.C.], King of Huai-nan) and Ch'ao Ts'o 鼂錯 (200-154 B.C.), a courtier and an outspoken Legalist who opposed the reestablishment of a feudal system and the power it brought the Han princes. Only a few of Ch'ao's works remain, all official in nature. These writings, such as his "Shang-shu yen ping-shih" 上書言兵事 (Memorial Speaking of Military Matters), became models for later court correspondence. The *Huai-nan tzu* is an eclectic collection of treatises on many topics, with a preference for Taoism evident. The work is unique in containing some of the earliest passages on cosmology.

Although the extant corpus by Tsou Yang 鄒陽 (206-129 B.C.) is relatively small, one of his memorials has become representative of the early Han persuasive writings. Tsou was a rhetorician who served first King Wu (Liu P'i 劉濞) and then King Hsiao of Liang 梁孝王 during the unsettled years of the mid-second century B.C. While in Liang he was slandered. Imprisoned and about to be executed, he composed the "Yü-chung shang-shu tzu-ming" 獄中上書自鳴 (A Memorial to Explain Myself, Written in Prison [150 B.C.]). This work not only won him reinstatement at court, but also exercised influence on the early *fu* (many were written by literati in this same court). It is noted for its "circular argumentation," which involved allusion to more than forty historical figures or events, and for its extensive parallelism. Works such as this led Yao Nai to pair *shu* (letters or memorials) and *shui* 說 (persuasive speeches) in his anthology (Chang, 1982, pp. 36f.)

Ssu-ma Hsiang-ju* (179-117 B.C.) was the first Han author to base both his livelihood and his literature on aesthetic considerations. He was more court literatus than literate statesman. Mainly noted for the word magic of his *fu*—he is the master of this genre—he also incorporated some of the conventions of persuasive writing into his prefaces and codas. His two extant prose writings also stress diction over persuasive rhetoric, although their subjects remain political in nature.

The most influential writer of the Han, and one of the major stylists in the entire prose tradition, was Ssu-ma Ch'ien* (*c.* 145-*c.* 90 B.C.), a historian. His influence was twofold. First, in the *Shih-chi* (Records of the Grand Historian) he established the clear, vivid style that became the standard for all later biographical writing, historical and fictional. His categorization of biographies according to more generalized headings such as *Yu-hsia* 遊俠 (Wandering Knights) encouraged the subsequent use of types in

101

biographical accounts and led to a conscious shaping and selection of source material to conform with these parameters. Second, his "Pao Jen An shu"報任安書(Letter in Reply to Jen An) and autobiographical postface to the *Shih-chi* established the personal letter and the autobiography as forms which became the models for literary works which give vent to the author's personal feelings. Indeed, Ssu-ma Ch'ien felt all literature was the product of suffering and frustration. His legacy was a prose with a vigorous, regular cadence, sometimes incorporating parallel structure but not bound by it, which was to characterize Former Han style.

Another historian of importance to the development of prose was Pan Ku* (A.D. 32-92) the author of the first dynastic history, the *Han-shu*漢書(History of the Han). In contrast to Ssu-ma Ch'ien, whose study led him often to Chou-dynasty documents, Pan Ku labored over Former Han sources, which may partly account for the salient features of his style—cadenced and elaborately structured, it became the model for most subsequent histories (Margouliès, 1929, p. 79). He also wrote many *fu* and the "Feng Yen-jan shan ming"封燕然山銘 (Inscription for the Demarcation of Yen-jan Mountain [As a Part of the Empire]). The latter set the pattern for later *ming*—a long prose introduction followed by a tetrametric section which borrows heavily from the *Shih-ching*.

Another genre, the *pei*碑(epitaph), was established by Ts'ai Yung* (133-192). This genre is similar in construction to the *ming*—a prose introduction followed by the actual inscription to be placed on the stele in a tetrameter reminiscent of the "Sung" section of the *Shih-ching*. Ts'ai made his reputation (and presumably some profit) from the *pei* he wrote early in life, but his large extant prose corpus is more varied than that of any other Han writer. It includes *sung*頌(eulogies), *fu*, various types of letters, memorials, inscriptions, admonitions, dialogues, and essays. In this corpus of nearly 150 pieces, Ts'ai Yung developed the allusive and euphuistic *p'ien-wen* style which was to dominate Chinese prose for nearly a millennium.

To a certain extent Ts'ai Yung was a transitional figure, helping to codify the numerous genres which developed during the Han, while offering a style which began to dominate prose in the Chien-an period (A.D. 196-220). The *fu*, *ming*, and *sung* were established in the writings of Han literati as embellished writings, whereas *lun*, *pien*, and *shu* exhibited a plainer style. Throughout the Latter Han, however, parallel structures found their way into this latter group. At the same time diction had grown less archaic (there were fewer "philologists" among the Latter Han literati [Liu, 1904, p. 26]).

C. Period of Disunion (220-589)

Following the fall of the Han, literature came to be seen (see *Wen-hsin tiao-lung*,* "Tsung-shu" 總術 chapter, for example) as consisting of two types of works: *wen*文(literally "pattern" and by extension "rhymed writings") and *pi*筆(literally "writing brush," thus "unrhymed, utilitarian writings"). A formal distinction between prose and poetry came later, in the T'ang (Lo, 1982, p. 121). It may also be seen as a literature of the court, genteel and often intended for oral presentation (ritual texts, prayers, memorials, etc.); thus the oral devices such as rhyme, parallelism, and tonal patterns are quite fitting.

In addition to the role of the court and the aristocracy in this insider's literature, three other factors were of importance to the development of prose. First, there was a simplification of the spoken language to accommodate the Central Asian tribes who ruled much of North China during these four centuries. This resulted in marked differences between the vernacular and written Chinese. Second, the Buddhists—this was an era in which Confucianism played a minor role—in translating their scriptures from Sanskrit into Chinese created a style heavily influenced by Sanskrit syntax. This style, in combination with their aims of proselytism, was to be held up as a model for prose reforms by the T'ang and Sung Neo-Confucian *ku-wen* writers. Third, the lush, ornate, literary style of the South—the *Ch'u-tz'u* is the prototype—which encouraged personal plaint rather than social statement, played a major role in genre and subject selection and generally set the tone for the literature of this period.

The literary legacy of the aristocrats in the *Wen-hsüan** has caused this period to be seen as one dominated by *p'ien-wen*, or parallel prose (Ch'en, 1965, ch. 2), an era in which *wen*文 (literary embellishment) gradually overcame *chih*質 (content). In terms of content, there were three types of prose which played a larger role than in the Han: landscape depiction, lyrical portrayals of the author's emotions, and *yung-wu*詠物 (still life) descriptions.

The first author of note is the founder of the Wei Kingdom, Ts'ao Ts'ao曹操 (155-220). His work set the tone for the prose of much of the third century (Feng Ch'i-yung, 1962, p. 23). A number of petitions, memorials, and mandates have been attributed to him, including one ("Hsiu-hsüeh ling" 修學令) urging the study of literature in order to re-instill the ethics and morality shattered by the warfare at the end of the Han. His best-known work is the "Jang-hsien tzu-ming pen-chih ling" 讓縣自明本志令 (Mandate Clarifying My Intention in Giving Up My Prefectural Post), written in 210 near the end of his life. Written in a clear, "classical" style, it pleads his loyalty to the Han dynasty in a brief account of key events in his career followed by an emotion-filled appeal.

The prose of his sons, Ts'ao P'i* and Ts'ao Chih,* is also of note. In letters like Ts'ao P'i's "Yü Wu Chih shu" 與吳質書 (Letter to Wu Chih) and Ts'ao Chih's "Yü Yang Te-tsu shu" 與楊德祖書 (Letter to Yang Te-tsu) they took up the topics of friendship and literature, rehearsing both in the "confessional" (*shu-ch'ing*抒情) style which typified the prose of the era. Yet literature was not yet merely *mei-t'an*美談 (beautiful words), as Ts'ao Chih had described a friend's comments on writing. In his famous "Lun-wen"論文 (On Literature—the only extant piece of a collection entitled *Tien-lun*典論), Ts'ao P'i stresses the relationship between literature and the orderly management of the state, calls for classical elegance in court writings, and advocates *li*麗 (euphuistic beauty) only in poetry (*shih** and *fu**). Some of their writings, such as Ts'ao Chih's "Chi-t'ien shuo" 籍田說 (Discourse on Registered Lands), a dialogue between Ts'ao and a retainer who was helping him cultivate his fields which compares agriculture to politics, seem to have influenced Han Yü and Liu Tsung-yüan's political allegories. Ts'ao Chih's "Ch'en shen-chü piao" 陳番舉表 (Memorial on Careful Promotions), begins with a long theoretical statement of the care needed in appointing officials and ends with a personal, almost poetic statement. Similar in structure is Chu-ko Liang's 諸葛亮 (181-234) "Ch'ien ch'u-shih piao" 前出師表 (First Memorial on Sending Out the Troops). Together they established the memorial format of discursive or descriptive introduction followed by emotional appeal.

Li Mi's李密(224-287) famous "Ch'en ch'ing piao" 陳情表(Memorial Expressing My Emotions), in which Li depicts the love he has for his critically ill grandmother and asks to be dismissed to care for her, is purely a lyrical document. It is also one of the few pieces from this period to be included in anthologies made during the Ming and Ch'ing eras.

Wang Hsi-chih's王羲之(303-379) "Lan-t'ing chi hsü" 蘭亭集序 (Preface to the Orchid Pavilion Collection), exhibits the relaxed style and interest in the landscape which typifies prose in the next period, the Eastern Chin. Aside from his masterpiece, which already shows the influence of *p'ien-wen*, Wang left a number of prose works and dozens of *t'ieh*帖(informal letters and notes) such as those collected in *Shu-fa yao-lu* 書法要錄 (Essential Notes on Calligraphy). This latter corpus exhibits both narrative and lyric styles, is in the *ch'ing-t'an*清談 (pure talk) mode, and contains some of the earliest examples of *hsiao-p'in* (informal essays).

At the end of the Eastern Chin T'ao Ch'ien* was the major literary figure. His prose such as "Kuei-ch'ü lai hsi tz'u" 歸去來兮辭 (On Returning Home), "T'ao-hua yüan chi" 桃花源記 (Record of the Peach-blossom Fount), and "Wu-liu Hsien-sheng chuan"五柳先生傳 (Biography of Mr. Five Willows), are notable for their vigorous style and for their influence on later prose. "Mr. Five Willows" has been cited by Lu Hsün as one of the sources of the style and format of T'ang *ch'uan-ch'i** tales.

Three other influential prose works are Li Tao-yüan's *Shui-ching chu,** which contains landscape descriptions afterwards seen as the precursors of the landscape essay (see also *yu-chi*), Yang Hsüan-chih's *Lo-yang chieh-lan chi,** which in its depiction of contemporary Lo-yang society marks an early use of satire, and Yen Chih-t'ui's* *Yen-shih chia-hsün*, which employs a simple, intimate, moving style in a work intended as a guide for the author's children.

But the simple style of Yen Chih-t'ui was not typical of the times. The euphuistic, allusive, parallel prose of *p'ien-wen* was by the fifth century dominant in South China. Among the best known *p'ien-wen* pieces of the time are works such as Pao Chao's* "Teng Ta-lei kan yü mei shu" 登大雷岸與妹書 (A Letter to My Younger Sister Having Climbed Great Thunder Bank), which consists of descriptions of the surrounding landscape, vistas portrayed in couplets of four-character lines followed by Pao's emotional reaction to the scene, K'ung Chih-kuei's孔稚珪(448-501) "Pei-shan i-wen" 北山移文 (Dispatch from North Mountain), in which K'ung wryly calls on the mountain spirits of North Mountain (modern Tzu-chin shan紫金山 northwest of Nanking) to block the path of Chou Yü 周顒 who was travelling to a post by way of the region where Chou had lived in reclusion (the work implies criticism of such pseudo-hermits); and Wu Chün's吳均(469-520) letters.

But the supreme *p'ien-wen* artist was Yü Hsin.* He is best known for his *fu* of which fifteen are extant—the *magnum opus* is "Ai Chiang-nan fu" 哀江南賦 (Lament for the South, A Prose-poem—see Graham, 1980). But the numerous *p'ien-wen* court documents he wrote served as models for the T'ang officialdom. The thirty-some grave-tablet inscriptions and other epitaphs he wrote testify to his contemporary fame.

Aside from the euphuistic, lyrical *p'ien-wen* writings, there were also biographical-narrative and discursive prose. Hsi K'ang's* numerous *lun* or the works of Buddhists such as Mou-tzu's牟子(fl. mid-fifth century) "Chih-huo lun" 治惑論 (The Dispositions of Error) may represent the latter group; Juan Chi's* "Ta-jen Hsien-sheng chuan" 大人

先生傳 (The Great Man), which in the tradition of the Han *fu* affords three interlocutors the occasion to question the Great Man, or Fu Hsüan's* "Ma Chün chuan" 馬鈞傳 (Biography of Ma Chün) are examples of the former. In the Buddhist apologetic literature may be seen precursors for the *ku-wen* defense of Confucianism several centuries later. The pseudo-biographies had a direct influence on the development of the *ch'uan-ch'i* tale in the T'ang dynasty.

Although various paradigms have been proposed for classifying prose of the third through the sixth centuries, refined literary embellishment and the expression of personal, usually sorrowful, emotions—both part of the legacy of the *Ch'u-tz'u*—are the major media in both poetry and prose of this era. The major exceptions to this norm can be found in the *chih-kuai** (records of anomalies) and the historical works such as Ch'en Shou's 陳壽 (233-297) *San-kuo chih* 三國志 (Records of the Three Kingdoms) and Fan Yeh's (398-445) *Hou Han-shu* 後漢書 (History of the Latter Han Dynasty—see Egan, 1979, pp. 344-345).

Two anthologies have been responsible for transmitting the large corpus of belletristic prose of the Period of Disunion: the sixth-century *Wen-hsüan*, which along with the *Ch'u-tz'u* and the *Shih-ching** became the basis for all literary education under the subsequent T'ang dynasty, and the massive eighteenth-century *Ch'üan Shang-ku San-tai Ch'in Han San-kuo Liu-ch'ao wen*.

D. Sui and T'ang Dynasties

The periodization that divides the late Six Dynasties from the Sui and T'ang is a political one. The developments in prose and poetry suggest the end of the seventh century would be a more logical date for a new literary era.

In the Sui, *p'ien-wen* continued its dominance, despite some attacks on the trifling subjects and overemphasis on style in the preceding Ch'i and Liang reigns. Much of the remaining prose is in the form of rescripts. The major authors are Chiang Tsung,* who left nine of the shorter, "still life" *fu* which were then in vogue (Marney, 1971, pp. 174ff.), in addition to a few court documents and funerary pieces, and Chih-i 知顗 (532-597), founder of the T'ien-t'ai School of Buddhism, whose correspondence with Prince Chin 晉王 (later Emperor Yang) and essays such as "Ching-t'u shih-i lun" 淨土十疑論 (Essay on Ten Doubts about Pure Land) are of interest. Chih-i and other Buddhists were invited to the Sui capital at Ch'ang-an in a conciliatory attempt thereby to win over an important segment of the former Southern intelligentsia.

But the return of the cultural center of China to the North led rapidly to a reaction against things "Southern"—especially following the T'ang takeover in 618. K'ung Ying-ta 孔穎達 (574-648) working with Yen Shih-ku 顏師古 (581-645) and others were ordered to establish a "correct" edition of the Confucian Classics, which had—it was felt—been misinterpreted by unorthodox scholars from the various Southern Dynasties (Kano, 1965, pp. 336ff.). Their work resulted in the *Wu-ching cheng-i* 五經正義 (Converted Significance of the Five Classics) in 180 *chüan*, which actually incorporated many Southern concepts.

More successful in opposing Southern influence—and thus its literature—were the historians of the seventh century such as Li Yen-shou 李延壽 (7th century), who in his

Pei-shih 北史 (History of the Northern Dynasties) wrote, "Southerners are simple and terse [in their work on the Classics], obtaining [only] their blossoms and flowers [i.e., the essence]; Northern scholarship is profound but disorderly, reaching through [even] to their twigs and branches [i.e., into details]" 南人約簡　得其英華　北學深蕪　得其枝葉, or Ling-hu Te-fen 令孤德棻 (583-666), the major historian from the aristocratic families of the Northwest, who attacked Yü Hsin's writings as *yin* 淫 (licentious) in his biography of Yü for the *Chou-shu* 周書 (History of the Chou Dynasty).

These historians, along with Liu Chih-chi* in the generation to follow, were precursors of later neo-classical movements in literature. But these developments had to await the eighth and ninth centuries. During the seventh, *p'ien-wen* prose continued to hold sway.

Some scholars have identified "three changes" in the development of T'ang prose: (1) a more sophisticated handling of flowery diction and parallelism in the writings of Wang Po* and the other *Ch'u T'ang Ssu-chieh* (Four Worthies of the Early T'ang—see Yang Chiung), (2) the early eighth century reduction of prosodic and grammatical parallelism in the writings of Chang Yüeh* and Su T'ing* and their reverence of Han prose as a model, and (3) the *ku-wen yün-tung* of the late eighth and ninth centuries (Lo, 1982, p. 122; Chang, 1962, pp. 428-429ff.). However, it seems more useful to see the major development as the creation of *san-wen* 散文 (prose with lines of no fixed length, or "free prose") to rival *p'ien-wen*. This process is closely related to the gradual rise of a new gentry during the T'ang and early Sung which was based at first on success in the civil-service examinations and a lower-level official career as a base of power—in contrast to the traditional aristocrats of the northwest and northeast. This new gentry was therefore in opposition to the aristocrat-dominated court. Their writings took their legitimacy and their function from the Confucian Classics, and they opposed the (aristocratic) literature and society of the Southern Dynasties.

In modern times their movement has been called the *ku-wen yün-tung* 古文運動 (ancient-style prose movement), a part of a larger mood, *fu-ku* 復古 (return to antiquity), which dominated eighth- and ninth-century literature. Thus *p'ien-wen*, which remained the style of court writings throughout the T'ang, and *san-wen*—the stylistic designation of *ku-wen* writings—were complementary. They are closely tied to genres, allowing a single writer to use both styles depending on his position and aim. In rescripts, memorials, formal official correspondence, and funerary inscriptions *p'ien-wen* remained the norm. Many *ku-wen* genres were renovated from classical times—for example, the *shuo* 說 (discourse) and *tui* 對 (response), the former derived from the *Chuang-tzu* and the latter from the rhetorical tradition of the Warring States via the *fu*. Others such as the *hsü* 序 (preface) and the *chuan* 傳 ("biography" or often "pseudo-biography") were transformed in the hands of *ku-wen* writers. The ties between genre and style can be seen clearly in the works of Liu Tsung-yüan,* who before his exile in 805 was noted as a powerful courtier and a *p'ien-wen* master and thereafter served only in the provinces while establishing himself as a master of *ku-wen*, or in the dichotomy between the verse of Po Chü-i,* which clearly evinces a *fu-ku* spirit, and the over three hundred rescripts of his long career which were all written in *p'ien-wen*. Many authors are claimed by adherents to both *p'ien-wen* and *ku-wen* for this reason. And it is necessary to recall that all T'ang literati cultivated the euphuistic style of the *fu*, since the *chin-shih* examination required them to write a prose-poem on a set theme and rhyme.

The seventh-century historians noted above were the forerunners of the *ku-wen* movement. Following them Ch'en Tzu-ang,* Li Hua,* Hsiao Ying-shih,* Liang Su,* Liu Mien柳冕 (*fl.* 790), and Tu-ku Chi* are usually cited as the *ku-wen* proponents of the next century. Examples of *san-wen* are often traced to Yüan Chieh* and Tu Fu,* although Tu Fu has left only three or four works (two *shuo* and two *shu*述[reflections or narratives]) which could be so judged. Yet although there are some important theoretical and practical *ku-wen* pieces in the corpora of these men, the key figures of this school, and of T'ang prose in general, began writing only at the turn of the ninth century.

This pair, Han Yü and Liu Tsung-yüan, produced the writings which shaped *san-wen* until the present day. Han Yü was—with Ssu-ma Ch'ien and Ou-yang Hsiu*—one of the three most significant writers in the history of Chinese prose. Like Ssu-ma Ch'ien's, his work in genres such as the *lun, shuo, chuan, hsü,* and the various epistolary genres became a standard. In a letter to his student Li I李翊 he set up writings of the Three Ancient Ages (Hsia, Shang, and Chou) and the Two Han Dynasties (Former and Latter) as the only work worthy of consideration. He especially stressed the Confucian Classics as the sole source of literary inspiration and style. Yet although he advocated a lucid style like the Classics, he did not condone imitation: "Imitate their intent, don't imitate their language" 師其意不師其辭 ("Ta Li Cheng-fu shu" 答李正夫書 [Letter in Reply to Li Cheng-fu]). In the logical structure of his discursive pieces Han Yü demonstrates a debt to Buddhist apologists of the Southern Dynasties. But among his best-known works (see also *ku-wen*) is the "Lun Fo-ku piao" 論佛骨表 (Memorial Discussing the Buddha's Bone), condemning Buddhist influence over the court. Pseudo-biographies such as "Mao Ying chuan" 毛穎傳 (Biography of Fur-point), iconoclastic textual criticism such as "Tu *Hsün*" 讀荀 (On Reading *Hsün-tzu*), discursive essays such as "Yüan Tao" 原道 (On the Origin of the Way), and numerous *mu-chih ming* 墓誌銘 (grave-tablet inscriptions) such as "Liu Tzu-hou mu-chih ming" 柳子厚墓誌銘 (Grave-tablet Inscription for Liu Tsung-yüan) are among his best writings. The last mentioned were pieces done for a commission and mark a first step towards the creation in the fourteenth and fifteenth centuries of a group of writers who were able to earn a living from their literary output alone.

Liu Tsung-yüan is noted for his landscape essays, especially the "Yung-chou pa-chi"永州八記 (Eight Records of Excursions in Yung Prefecture). These pieces begin by setting the scene in precise terms ("one-hundred paces east of such-and-such we find . . ."), and proceed through a lush prose description of some isolated but lovely scenes, to Liu's reflections thereupon. Their antecedents are the landscape letters of Pao Chao *et al.* during the Period of Disunion, the *Shui-ching chu,** Yüan Chieh's writings about the scenes around neighboring Tao-chou 道州, and Hsieh Ling-yün's* nature poetry, which is similarly structured. Ultimately these records derive from the tradition of the literature of Ch'u (see *Ch'u-tz'u*) in both style (*p'ien-wen*) and intent (personal plaint). The other group of writings for which Liu is known, are his allegories and fables, such as "Sung Ch'ing chuan"宋清傳 (Biography of Sung Ch'ing), "Discourse of a Snake-catcher," and "Chung-shu Kuo T'o-to chuan" 種樹郭橐駝傳 (Biography of Camel Kuo the Gardener). They won him recognition as co-founder of the ancient-style prose movement and also have some relationship to the development of the *chuan-ch'i** tale during the T'ang.

The relationship between T'ang fiction and ancient-style prose is still a subject of controversy. It is true that Han, Liu, and their followers wrote fictional works and that the *ch'uan-ch'i* and *ku-wen* rose almost concurrently. But rather than arguing that *ch'uan-ch'i* influenced ancient-style writers (Ma, 1967, pp. 207-211), it would seem that both were the result of the iconoclastic attitudes of historians like Liu Chih-chi in the late seventh century which led to a call for a style based on the Classics (i.e., *ku-wen*) and a distinction between history and non-history or fiction.

Following Han, who had a number of disciples, and Liu, there is a bifurcation of the *ku-wen* movement into wings. One group, which included Fan Tsung-shih 樊宗師 (d. 821), Huang-fu Shih 皇甫湜 (c. 777-c. 830), and Sun Ch'iao 孫樵 (fl. 860-888), overemphasized the concept of *ch'i* (the strange or the unconventional) which Han Yü had advocated. The other, consisting in part of P'i Jih-hsiu,* Lu Kuei-meng,* and Lo Yin,* tried to adhere too closely in style and intent (Han Yü had warned against this) producing writings which were unnatural and almost unintelligible (Ts'en, 1957, pp. 179-180). Correspondingly the influence of ancient-style prose declined in the late T'ang.

In contrast, *p'ien-wen* remained the standard for all court and many official documents. Wang Po,* Yang Chiung,* Su T'ing,* Yang Yen 楊炎 (727-781), Ch'ang Kun 常袞, Lu Chih,* Li Te-yü 李德裕, Ling-hu Ch'u 令狐楚 (766-837), Weng T'ing-yün,* Li Shang-yin,* Ssu-k'ung T'u,* Ku Yün 顧雲 (d. 894) and Hsü Hsüan 徐鉉 (916-991) are its noted practitioners. Aside from court documents (Li Shang-yin alone left nearly three hundred), the prefaces to literary collections of this time were generally written in *p'ien-wen*. Indeed, in the late T'ang there is seemingly a connection between the rise of the *tz'u** and *p'ien-wen*, probably because both were court genres.

E. Sung and Yüan Dynasties

The style which carries through the Five Dynasties and the early Sung was known as Hsi-k'un 西崑, after the anthology *Hsi-k'un ch'ou-ch'ang chi,** and owed a great debt to Li Shang-yin. It also influenced the selections in the early Sung anthology, *Wen-yüan ying-hua** 文苑英華 (982), which was intended as a sequel to the *Wen-hsüan* and included works from the Liang through the T'ang. As a result an anthology to represent *ku-wen* interests was soon compiled—the *T'ang wen ts'ui** (1011). Together with the *Ch'üan T'ang wen** these collections are the most important extant sources for T'ang prose.

The Hsi-k'un authors—Yang I, Liu Yün 劉筠 (971-1031), and Ch'ien Wei-yen* are the trio most commonly named—seem to have had close ties to court and the old aristocracy. In opposition to them, and according to some critics representing the "new men" of locally based gentry, writers such as Wang Yü-ch'eng* and Shih Chieh 石介 (1005-1045) attempted to promote *ku-wen*. The ancient-style prose movement, if such a label is valid for this era, found itself divided into two groups. One influenced by early Sung moralists emphasized the *Tao* to the neglect of style. The other looked primarily to stylistic reform. But neither produced a political or literary figure capable of challenging the dominance of Hsi-k'un.

By the mid-eleventh century the time was ripe for change. The Hsi-k'un writers had died and there were no successors. *Ku-wen* had been promoted at court intermittently for several decades. And the local gentry had lodged themselves firmly in the upper levels of officialdom. All that was missing was a leader. When Ou-yang Hsiu* returned to K'ai-feng to work with the commission compiling a new T'ang history, he was nearly fifty years old, at the height of his literary skills, and on good terms with many of the most powerful men at court. Thus in 1057 when he was to supervise the *chin-shih* examinations, he made it known that he would give weight to the substance, not the style, of the examination papers. This encouraged the candidates with a pre-dilection for *ku-wen* and for a time brought ancient-style prose to influence even court writings. More important, the notoriety caused by this examination drew many young literati to the style. The completion of the *Hsin T'ang-shu* 新唐書 (New T'ang History) in 1060—for which Ou-yang wrote or supervised all sections but the biographies—further extended the influence of *ku-wen*. Moreover, because Ou-yang Hsiu held up the then relatively unknown Han Yü as his model, he in effect laid the foundation for Han's subsequent reputation. All the major prose writers of the Sung, including philosophers such as Chu Hsi 朱熹 (1130-1200) and historians like Ssu-ma Kuang 司馬光 (1019-1086), were influenced by Ou-yang's ancient style.

Aside from the *Hsin T'ang-shu*, Ou-yang's works included the *Hsin Wu-tai shih* 新五代史 (New History of the Five Dynasties), also in an elegant but laconic style; the "Tsui-weng T'ing chi" 醉翁亭記 (Record of the Old Tippler's Pavilion); the "Liu-i Chü-shih chuan" 六一居士傳 (Biography of the Retired Scholar, "Six Ones" [an autobiographical sketch—Ou-yang numbered himself (an old man) among his five favorite pastimes: *one* large library, *one* thousand ancient inscriptions, *one* zither, *one* chess set, and *one* pot of wine]); the "Hsien-shan T'ing chi" 峴山亭記 (Record of the Pavilion on Mount Hsien); and his numerous discursive writings, some of which were submitted to the emperor and resulted in an occasional loss of favor. Ou-yang's style has been called "cleaner" (清新) than that of Han Yü. In a manner typical of the Sung, an interest in the mundane and the details of day-to-day life can be seen in works like the "Record of the Old Tippler's Pavilion." These records differ from their T'ang predecessors in that they populate the landscapes they depict and that they interject philosophical or historical comments throughout. Ou-yang Hsiu himself felt records of a place need not depict the scenes visible therefrom—this should be left for the reader to experience himself (see his comments in "Hsien-shan T'ing chi," for example: 宜其覽者自得之 "One ought to allow those who come to sightsee to obtain them [the views] for themselves").

The sweeping changes caused by his prose (even Japanese authors writing in Chinese took his works as models) may be attributed to Ou-yang Hsiu's political prominence, to his literary skill, and perhaps even to the development of printing and the growth in literacy during the eleventh century. It may have also been augmented by the success of his students.

The most outstanding of these disciples was Su Shih.* Although his political career never reached the heights of his master's, he is unquestionably the greatest writer of the Sung, excelling in poetry and prose. His prose style was fluid but dynamic. Philosophically he was more eclectic than the Neo-Confucian Ou-yang Hsiu. Su admired Liu Tsung-yüan, and his writings, thought, and career parallel somewhat those of the other great T'ang essayist. *Meng-tzu, Chuang-tzu,* and the *Chan-kuo ts'e** also exerted considerable influence on Su Shih's writings (Feng, 1962, p. 34). As might be surmised from this list of models, his strength was in discursive pieces, many of which discussed famous historical figures ("Fan Li lun" 范蠡論 [On Fan Li], for example). The depiction of a landscape in works such as the two "Ch'ih-pi fu" 赤壁賦 (Prose-poems on the Red Cliff) is often blended with a revelation of his mood, presented in sensuous, rhythmical style.

Even more than Ou-yang Hsiu, Su broke down the structure of landscape writings which, since the letters of the Period of Disunion, had consisted of an opening which set the scene, a description of it, and a coda which expressed the emotional or intellectual reaction of the author, interweaving emotion and comment throughout pieces such as "Fang-ho T'ing chi" 放鶴亭記 (Record of Crane-Releasing Pavilion) and the Red Cliff pair of pieces, probably his masterpiece. Although in official circles the reputation of Ou-yang Hsiu's prose remained paramount, Su Shih's style set the standard for more private and purely literary prose.

Ou-yang Hsiu, Su Shih, Han Yü, Liu Tsung-yüan, and four other eleventh-century writers—Tseng Kung,* Wang An-shih,* Su Hsün,* and Su Ch'e*—are jointly acclaimed the "T'ang-Sung pa-ta chia" 唐宋八大家 (Eight Masters of T'ang and Sung [Prose]). Despite some fine pieces of prose by Tseng and Wang, the fame of these latter four owes more to the historical happenstance that they were linked with their more famous brothers (literally in one case—Su Ch'e was Su Shih's younger brother) by later critics than to their own accomplishments.

Besides six of the Eight Masters and Ssu-ma Kuang's *Tzu-chih t'ung-chien* 資治通鑑 (Comprehensive Mirror for Aid in Government), a mammoth history of the Warring States down to the end of the Five Dynasties, the Northern Sung also saw the rise of the *sui-pi** and *yü-lu* genres. The former included various types of notes, colophons, and miscellaneous writings which can be linked to later *hsiao-p'in wen*, while the latter recorded conversations of the great Neo-Confucian thinkers in a style close to the vernacular. In addition, fiction written in a style much closer to the spoken language (*pien-wen*—see *Tun-huang wen-hsüeh, hua-pen,** and *p'ing-hua**) arose, diminishing the attention paid, but not eliminating, traditional classical-language fiction (*chih-kuai* and *ch'uan-ch'i*). *P'ien-wen* did not disappear either—some of Li Ch'ing-chao's* pieces, such as her "*Chin-shih lu* hou-hsü" 金石錄後序 (Postface to the *Record of Bronze and Stone Inscriptions*), are written in an elegant parallel style. Even Ou-yang Hsiu and Su Shih contributed to maintaining the style (Chang, 1960, pp. 521-526 and 528-539).

When the court fled before the Chin armies to Hangchow and the South in the 1120s it was following a general trend which had seen the major population centers of China shift from the North in the seventh century to the Lower Yangtze Region in the eleventh and twelfth centuries. More and more literati came from that area. But the Southern Sung failed to produce any major figure in prose. Works by Yüeh Fei 岳飛 (1103-1141), Hu Ch'üan 胡銓 (1102-1180), Wen T'ien-hsiang 文天祥 (1236-1282), Yang Wan-li,* Lu Yu,* and others are cited in historical accounts, but none are accorded the status of a major force in Sung prose. A collection of *Northern* Sung Neo-Confucian writings, the *Chin-ssu lu* 近思錄 (Reflections on Things at Hand), edited by Chu Hsi 朱熹 (1130-1200) and Lü Tsu-ch'ien 呂祖謙 (1137-1181), is considered a highpoint of *Southern* Sung prose. These judgments were surely influenced by the low regard that Neo-Confucians, such as the great prose anthologists of the T'ung-ch'eng p'ai who did much to shape modern taste, had for this feckless reign. Despite Ou-yang Hsiu's efforts, *shih-wen* 時文 (contemporary-style prose), synonymous with *p'ien-wen*, was used in the examinations and the parallel style enjoyed a minor revival.

Li Liu 李劉 (*chin-shih*, 1214) and Hung Mai* were among the best-known stylists, and Hung also composed a study of the form—the *Jung-chai ssu-liu ts'ung-t'an* 容齋四六叢談 (Collected Conversations on the Four-six Style by Hung Mai). The *p'ien-wen* of this era maintained only metrical, not tonal and grammatical, parallelism in reflecting the general Sung penchant for simplification. This style was used especially in the *ch'i*啟(a type of letter), a popular genre. The most important accomplishment of this era was the collection of Sung (primarily *Northern* Sung) prose into anthologies such as Lü Tsu-ch'ien's (1137-1181) *Sung-wen chien*宋文鑑(A Key to Sung Prose) or Hsieh Fang-te's *Wen-chang kuei-fan*. Despite the lack of a noted writer, a great deal was written in the twelfth and thirteenth centuries lending its weight, together with the brilliance of the Northern Sung, to the acceptance of the Sung as the dynasty most often associated with prose in the traditional scheme which linked one era to a single genre (Han *shih*漢史 [history], T'ang *shih*唐詩, Yüan *ch'ü*,* and Sung *wen*宋文 [prose]).

There is no collection "complete Sung prose," in part because the size of the corpus would be too unwieldy, but also owing to the better availability of printed editions of the collected works of the major writers.

The Liao regime produced some authors noted for rescripts, and their style is often compared to the Four Worthies of Early T'ang. The succeeding Chin followed the *ku-wen* traditions of the northern Sung. Chao Ping-wen* and Yüan Hao-wen* are the best of this era from which so much prose is no longer extant. Chao is noted for a series of essays he wrote on various dynasties and for his numerous memorials and colophons. He used many genres which Han Yü had employed—*yüan* and *shuo*, for example. Yüan, because of his contemporary fame, was called on to preface a number of collections. He also left many *chi* (records) and colophons. Yang Yün-i楊雲翼(1170-1228), who worked on the classics and compiled a sequel to the *Tzu-chih t'ung-chien*, Liu Chung劉中(*fl.* 1210), a *ku-wen* stylist who taught Wang Jo-hsü,* and Li Chün-min李俊民(*fl.* 1217), whose work is noted for its stylistic purity and tranquil tone, also merit mention.

Under the Yüan dynasty the Mongols continued the Chin veneration of *ku-wen*—*p'ien-wen* was virtually ignored until the early Ch'ing. Several styles or schools have been discerned in Yüan prose. Aside from a basic North-South division, there are two southern groups, one north of the Yangtze and the other in modern Chekiang and Kiangsi (Wu, 1934, pp. 6ff.). The latter has the most significance to literary history. There is also a certain affinity between Northern writers and the fundamentalist Neo-Confucian philosophy and between Southerners and Taoism (Sun, 1981, pp. 219-252).

Wu Ch'eng吳澄(1249-1333) was a native of Ch'ung-jen崇仁(modern Kiangsi), the same region which produced Ho Chung何中, his teacher, and Yao Sui姚燧(1238-1314), another literatus noted for his court prose. He was a noted classicist and essayist. In his "Pieh Chao Tzu-ang hsü"別趙子昂序 (Composition Presented to Chao Tzu-ang on Parting) he argued that one's prose style is a natural emanation of one's character—only noble personalities can produce great prose. His "Sung Ho T'ai-hsü pei-yu hsü" 送何太虛北遊序 (Composition Presented at Seeing Off Ho T'ai-hsü [Chung] on a Northern Journey) is an essay which notes the "importance of travel to gaining an understanding of people," but attacks those who travelled for personal gain. Wu's student Yü Chi虞集(1272-1348), another Southerner and a major poet of the era, is generally considered the best prose writer of the Yüan. The "Shang-chih Chai shuo" 尚志齋說 (Discourse of the Study Where High Purpose Is Valued), written for his brother, argues the importance of a higher goal for study than the mere quest of knowledge. His disciple, Su T'ien-chüeh, a Mongol known for his biographical writings, was the compiler of the *Kuo-ch'ao wen-lei*,* the main source of Yüan prose. Liu Yin劉因 (1249-1293) may be the best essayist among the northern literati. Raised in a strict Neo-Confucian family, his best-known works are "Hsiao-tzu T'ien Chün mu-piao" 孝子田君墓表 (Funerary Inscription on T'ien Chün, A Filial Son) which depicts the cruelty of the Mongol conquest, and "Wang-ch'uan t'u chi" 輞川圖記 (Record of the Wang River Paintings) which criticizes Wang Wei* as a man who lost his integrity.

Another important part of Yüan prose was the historical writings. Three dynastic histories—the Chin, Liao, and Sung—were composed by the Yüan historians. The Sung history, which was based closely on its documentary sources, is considered dry and difficult to read and the Liao is criticized for the coarseness of its style. Only the history of the Chin, based on Yüan Hao-wen's work, is comparable in style to other important dynastic histories (Chan, 1981, pp. 82 and 91).

In general the prose of the Yüan was written in a clear, practical style. Some *pei* (epitaphs) and the famous *Yüan mi shih* 元秘史 (A Secret History of the Yüan) were written in the vernacular language. Aside from official documents (Chavannes, 1904, 1906, and 1908), many pieces were of a more private nature than in the T'ang and Sung. Although *p'ien-wen* was not widely written, a continued concern with the purely formal aspects of prose can be seen in Wang Ch'ung-yün's 王充耘 advocacy of the *pa-pi t'i* 八比體 (eight-pairs style), a precursor of the Ming *pa-ku wen*, during the first decades of the fourteenth century.

F. Ming and Ch'ing Dynasties

In the Ming dynasty the development of prose is broken into a number of schools associated with historical periods. It may also be seen as bifurcated into groups dominated by the court and those independent of the government. Already the Southern Sung Neo-Confucians such as Chu Hsi had become disillusioned with a government which professed to be Neo-Confucian itself but remained feckless and corrupt. These scholars no longer sought government positions, but set themselves up in private academies or under the aegis of a provincial patron. They also turned inward, seeking the *li* 理 (principle) in things.

The first period of Ming prose is dominated by courtiers such as Sung Lien* and Liu Chi.* Sung was noted for his biographical writings such as "Ch'in-shih lu" 秦士錄 (Notes on a Gentleman from Ch'in), "Tu Huan hsiao-chuan" 杜環小傳 (A Biographical Sketch of Tu Huan), and "Wang Mien chuan" 王冕傳 (Biography of Wang Mien). His *P'u-yang jen-wu chi* 浦陽人物記 (A Record of Personages from P'u-yang, *c.* 1350), a collection of twenty-nine biographies of men from his native locale, is praised as being in the tradition of Ou-yang Hsiu's historical work. Sung's official historiographical accomplishments as one of the directors of the *Yüan-shih* 元史 (History of the Yuan) project has met with much harsher evaluations. Liu Chi is best known for a collection of nearly two hundred essays known as the *Yü-li tzu* 郁離子 (Master of Civilized Enlightenment) in a style which mixes historical allusion, fable, and sarcasm and is reminiscent of similar late T'ang *ku-wen* collections.

Wang Wei 王褘 (1323-1374), a native of Chin-hua 金華 (modern Chekiang), which had produced so many scholars in the thirteenth and fourteenth centuries, was one of the compilers of the *Yüan-shih* 元史 (History of the Yüan). He was also noted for his numerous court writings which blended parallel passages with *ku-wen* syntax and diction and which became the basis of Ming documentary style.

In the fifteenth century a style known as *T'ai-ko t'i* or "Secretariat Style" dominated prose. Although not *p'ien-wen*, this type of writing emphasized long, parallel lines—content was virtually ignored. The "Three Yangs"—Yang Shih-ch'i 楊士奇 (1365-1444), Yang Jung楊榮(1371-1440), and Yang P'u楊溥(1372-1446)—who also established the Grand Secretariat as an important government institution, were its chief practitioners This period also witnessed the first important anthology of Ming prose, the *Ming wen heng.**

Beginning in the latter decades of the fifteenth century with Li Tung-yang,* and continuing especially in the writers later known as the "Ch'ien ch'i-tzu"前七子(Former Seven Masters), there was a movement to return to antiquity as the source of literary inspiration. This "group"—Ho Ching-ming* and Li Meng-yang* are the most noted "members"—consisted of seven independent literati with similar literary ideas who were dubbed "Ch'ien-ch'i-tzu" by an association of later writers who called themselves the "Hou ch'i-tzu"後七子 (Latter Seven Masters). In contrast to the *ku-wen yün-tung* these Former Masters advocated study and imitation of both content and style—*fa*法(rules) was a key term—of the classical models: the High T'ang era in poetry and the Ch'in and Han dynasties for prose. This tendency reached its zenith in the work of Li P'an-lung,* the central figure in the "Hou ch'i-tzu" of the mid-sixteenth century. His writings are mosaics of phrases and diction borrowed from Han and pre-Han texts set in a very unnatural syntax. The result is an almost unintelligible, if "classic," style.

Reactions to this archaicism came from several directions. T'ang Shun-chih,* Mao K'un茅坤(1512-1601), and Kuei Yu-kuang* held up as models the prose of the Eight Masters of the T'ang and Sung (Mao K'un had first grouped them in an anthology he edited), but they opposed imitation as such, seeking rather the *pen-se*本色(basic spirit) of the writings of their models. Wang Shih-chen* (1526-1590) believed the *fa* of prose was something which could not be observed—it was internal. He felt inspiration must be the source of all literature.

Another association of literati—the Kung-an P'ai 公安派, named for the hometown of its most illustrious members—was built around Yüan Hung-tao* and his brothers during the late sixteenth and early seventeenth centuries. Yüan's pastoral landscapes—rural settings or gardens animated by scenes from day-to-day life—set the relaxed tone. "Hu-ch'iu chi"虎丘記(Record of Tiger Hill) is one of the best, depicting the festivities of the Mid-Autumn Festival there. These men sought only *hsing-ling*性靈(personality and innate sensibility) in their writings and emphasized originality. They also developed the informal essay into a major form for a brief period—recognition of their accomplishments awaited the acclaim of the modern essayists of the 1930s. Chang Tai's* work in this genre is also praised in part because of the patriotic sentiment infused in his landscape essays. But the contemporary influence of these men was not great and many of their works were banned in the early Ch'ing.

Although the Ming is known as an era without *p'ien-wen*, formalism is dominant in *pa-ku wen*, which became the standard for examination essays in 1487. Using a type of metrically parallel prose and a rigidly defined structure of eight sections, a preface, and a conclusion, this style became an accepted genre in the Ming and its structure certainly influenced both other genres and interpretations of earlier prose (Chang, 1978a, p. 1329).

113

Two other genre developments of the Ming are noteworthy. Hsü Hung-tsu 徐宏祖(1586-1641, better known by his *hao*, Hsia-k'o 霞客), left a voluminous corpus of *yu-chi* 遊記(travel records). An overview of landscape writings through the centuries normally notes the danger sensed by Ch'ü Yüan, the serenity found by Hsieh Ling-yün on his excursions in the mountains, and the reluctant acceptance of the beauties of Southern Hunan by Liu Tsung-yüan.* Hsü differed by spending much of his life wandering through the mountains and rivers in many remote regions of China. And he did so by choice. As a result he identified with the landscape much more than his predecessors— 尋山如訪友 "I search out a mountain as I would visit a friend," and 遠山含笑 " [those] distant mountains on the point of breaking into a smile." His style is similar to that of Liu Tsung-yüan, but there is little personal reflection on any subject but the landscape itself.

The development of Ming fiction—in both the classical and vernacular languages— is an important part of an overview of Ming prose. There was a revival of *ch'uan-ch'i* tales (see *Ch'ien-teng hsin-hua*), which were more successful as a showcase for the other literary forms they included (from poetry to texts on the successful erection of a building) than as integral works of fiction. The novel came of age during the sixteenth and seventeenth centuries and no doubt borrowed from and in turn reinfluenced a number of related prose genres including *pa-ku wen*, landscape descriptions, and the informal essay. Kuei Yu-kuang's personal essays, for example, are said to have incorporated fictional techniques of characterization through dialogue.

The second important anthology of Ming prose, the *Ming wen hai* 明文海(Ocean of Prose from the Ming), in 48 *chüan*, was compiled during the early Ch'ing by Huang Tsung-hsi 黃宗羲(1610-1695). It was no doubt shaped by current literary tastes which differed little from those of the late Ming. Huang himself held ideas on motivations similar to those of the Kung-an p'ai—but he also stressed learning as the basis of writing.

Other early Ch'ing essayists in the *ku-wen* tradition include Kuei Yu-kuang's grandson, Kuei Chuang 歸莊(1614-1673), Ku Yen-wu,* Hou Fang-yü 侯方域(1618-1655), Shao Ch'ang-heng 邵長蘅(1637-1704), and Ch'üan Tsu-wang 全祖望(1705-1755). During these years there was also a revival of *p'ien-wen*—Yu T'ung,* Ch'en Wei-sung,* and Mao Ch'i-ling 毛奇齡(1623-1716) were the best-known adherents. But Ch'ing *p'ien-wen* offered few innovations. Most authors imitated one earlier era and traditional historiography divides them into various schools such as the Liu-ch'ao p'ai 六朝派(Six Dynasties School) or the [Wan] T'ang p'ai [晚]唐派([late] T'ang School). Yüan Mei* may be the only exception— his *p'ien-wen* writings revitalized the style. But the tour de force of Ch'ing *p'ien-wen* is Huang Chih-chün's 黃之雋(1668-1748) "*Hsiang-hsieh chi* tzu-hsü" 香屑集自序 (Author's Preface to the *Fragrant-Powder Collection*), a long work (nearly three thousand words) in which every phrase has been culled verbatim from the prose of T'ang-dynasty authors.

Since it could be dangerous to address current or recent history, it is no surprise that the eighteenth century was dominated by the T'ung-ch'eng p'ai,* a school named after the hometown of its leaders, Fang Pao,* Liu Ta-k'uei,* and Yao Nai (see *Ku-wen tzu-lei tsuan*), the most influential of the trio. They advocated a return to ancient prose models of pre-Han, Han, T'ang, and Sung and stressed a balance of *i* 義 and *fa* 法. The significance of these terms varies from writer to writer, but generally they are concerned with substance and form respectively. Some of the works of writers of this school are noteworthy: Fang's "Yü-chung tsa-chi" 獄中雜記 (Miscellaneous Notes from Prison), which revealed the horrendous conditions in which prisoners lived and the corruption of their jailors, or Yao Nai's "Teng T'ai-shan chi" 登泰山記 (Record of Climbing Mount T'ai), which includes some elegant descriptions of the mountain and a sunrise. But they generally pale in comparison to the works of the T'ang and Sung. The school's real significance lies in its systemization of prose through anthologies (both Fang and Yao edited collections of prose), theoretical works which laid down rigid guidelines for writing, and a number of students. At least two other groups, the contemporary Yang-hu p'ai 陽湖派 (Lake Yang School) and the "Hsiang-hsiang p'ai" 湘鄉派 (Hsiang Province School) of the nineteenth century are seen as offshoots.

However, the ponderous didacticism of T'ung-ch'eng theory and the overall lack of grandeur in both their own writings and their assessment of current social and political problems invited criticism. Juan Yüan 阮元 (1764-1849), the noted classicist and member of the Han School of Learning, agreed that the classics should be the source of literature, but saw in them much parallel prose. His argument, that only Six Dynasties and subsequent parallel prose was devoid of proper substance, marks his contribution as uniquely original in the history of Ch'ing *p'ien-wen.*

Kung Tzu-chen* also opposed the formalization of rigid rules of prose in the T'ung-ch'eng School. In one of his best-known pieces, "Ping-mei Kuan chi" 病梅舘記 (A Record of Diseased Plum-tree Hall) he describes how he replanted three hundred plum trees which had been bound and potted so as to grow into miniature *bonsai* plants—the attack on literati and artists who relish such bent, restricted forms seems to be a veiled critique of T'ung-ch'eng regimentation (suggested perhaps more strongly by the alternate title, "Liao mei shuo" 療梅說 [Discourse on Treating Plum Trees]).

It would be remiss not to note that two of the most accomplished prose writers of the eighteenth century toiled in the genre of fiction. P'u Sung-ling's (see *Liao-chai chih-i*) classical-language tales modernized the literary language. Ts'ao Hsüeh-ch'in's* various styles in the *Hung-lou meng,** China's greatest novel, mark perhaps the apogee of traditional prose.

The Ch'ing also witnessed the compilation of the *Ku-wen kuan-chih,* an anthology of prose with an influence on subsequent students of prose comparable to that of the *T'ang-shih san-pai shou* in verse.

In the latter half of the nineteeth century Liang Ch'i-ch'ao* and Lin Shu* are noteworthy. Liang's fluid style and his talent for creating a mood and persuasion are evident in his numerous writings of which "Shao-nien Chung-kuo shuo" 少年中國說 (A Discourse on the Youthful China) is representative. Lin Shu, who left several important studies of traditional essayists and their writings, is primarily known for the elegant prose in which he rendered nearly two hundred Western literary works. Despite the rise of other genres such as the *cha-chi* 札記 (notation book) and *fang-chih* 方志 (local gazetteer) during the Ch'ing, Lin Shu's translations provide a fitting climax to this survey, for although they had some influence on modern writers of fiction such as Lao She 老舍 (1899-1966), they were essentially outdated only a few years after they were completed. The late Ch'ing was an iconoclastic era, one in which the newly fashioned "newspaper prose" became more popular than the classics themselves. Two final impacts of traditional prose have been the literary historical surveys of the 1920s and 1930s compiled in large measure by followers of the T'ung-ch'eng School which shaped the modern assessment of the history of Chinese prose and the popularity of the *tsa-wen* 雜文 (essays) by Lu Hsün 魯迅 (1881-1936) and others.

BIBLIOGRAPHY:

Anthologies mentioned in the text which have their own separate entries are not noted herein. See also bibliographies under *ku-wen* and *p'ien-wen*.

An-huei jen-min ch'u-pan-she 安徽人民出版社, ed. 1963. *T'ung-ch'eng p'ai yen-chiu lun-wen-chi* 桐城派研究論文集. Hofei.

Bauer, Wolfgang, 1964. "Icherleben und Autobiographie im älteren China," *Heidelberger Jahrbücher*, 8, 12-40.

Baum, P. F. 1952. *The Other Harmony of Prose: An Essay in English Prose Rhythm*. Durham.

Chan, Hok-lam. 1981. "Chinese Official Historiography at the Yüan Court: the Composition of the Liao, Chin, and Sung Histories," in *China Under Mongol Rule*, John D. Langlois, Jr., ed., pp. 56-92. Princeton.

Chang, Ch'i-wen 張起文, ed. 1962. *T'ang-tai san-wen hsüan-chu* 唐代散文選注. Shanghai; rpt. Hong Kong, 1977.

Chang, Eva Yueh-wah. 1982. "A Study of the 'Shu' (letters) of the Han Dynasty (206 B.C.-A.D. 220)." Unpublished Ph.D. dissertation, University of Washington.

Chang, Hui-chih 張撝之, ed. 1979. *T'ang-tai san-wen hsüan-chu* 唐代散文選注. Shanghai.

Chang, Hsü 張須. 1978. "Wei-Chin Sui-T'ang wen" 魏晉隋唐文, in Lo, *Lun-wen hsüan*, pp. 443-448.

———. 1978a. "Sung Yüan Ming Ch'ing wen lun" 宋元明清文論, in Lo, *Lun-wen hsüan*, pp. 1327-1334.

Chang, Jen-ch'ing 張仁青. 1960. *Chung-kuo p'ien-wen fa-chan shih* 中國駢文發展史. 2v. Taipei.

Chang, P'u 張溥, ed. 1963. *Han-Wei Liu-ch'ao pai-san ming-chia chi* 漢魏六朝百三名家集. 4v. Rpt. Taipei.

———. 1961. *Han Wei Liu-ch'ao pai-san chia chi t'i-tz'u chu* 漢魏六朝百三家集題辭注. Hong Kong.

Chang, Shun-hui 張舜徽. 1963. *Ch'ing-jen wen-chi pieh-lu* 清人文集別錄. 2v. Rpt. Peking, 1980.

Chavannes, Edouard. 1904, 1905, 1908. "Inscriptions et pièces de chancellerie chinoises de l'epoque mongole," *TP*, 5, 6, and 9, 357-447, 1-42, and 297-428.

Ch'en, Chu 陳柱. 1965. *Chung-kuo san-wen shih* 中國散文史. Taipei.

Ch'en, Chung-fan 陳中凡, ed. 1957. *Han-Wei Liu-ch'ao san-wen hsüan* 漢魏六朝散文選. Shanghai.

Ch'en, Hung-ch'ih 陳鴻墀, ed. 1962. *Ch'üan T'ang wen chi-shih* 全唐文紀事. 3v. Rpt. Shanghai.

Ch'en, Shao-t'ang 陳少棠. 1982. *Wan-Ming hsiao-p'in lun-hsi* 晚明小品論析. Taipei.

Ch'en, Yü-kuang 陳宇光, ed. 1981. *T'ang-wen hsüan-chu* 唐文選注. Peking.

Ch'en, Yin-k'o 陳寅恪. 1937. "Han Yü and the T'ang Novel," *HJAS*, 2, 38-43.

Cheng, Chen-to 鄭振鐸, ed. 1937. *Wan-Ch'ing wen-hsüan* 晚清文選. Shanghai.

Ch'i, Fa-jen 戚法仁. 1957. "Hsü-yen" 序言, in *Hsien Ch'in san-wen hsüan-chu* 桐城文派評述, Peking, pp. 1-22.

Ch'i, Kung 啓功. 1982. *Shih wen sheng-lü lun k'ao* 詩文聲律論稿. Taipei.

Chiang, Po-ch'ien 蔣伯潛 and Chiang Tsu-i 蔣祖怡. 1941. *P'ien-wen yü san-wen* 駢文與散文. Shanghai.

Ch'ien, Mu 錢穆. 1963. "Chung-kuo san-wen" 中國散文, in *Chung-kuo wen-hsüeh yen-chiang chi* 中國文學演講集, pp. 36-46. Hong Kong.

———. 1964. "Han-tai chih san-wen" 漢代之散文(lecture recorded by Hsieh Cheng-kuang 謝正光), *Hsin-ya shu-yüan Chung-kuo wen-hsüeh hsi nien-k'an*, 2 (June), 36-47.

Ch'ien, Tung-fu 錢多父. 1979. *T'ang-Sung ku-wen yün-tung* 唐宋古文運動. Shanghai.

Chih, Wei-ch'eng 支偉成. N.d. *Ko-t'i wen-hsüan* 各體文選. Shanghai.

Chin, Chü-hsiang 金秬香. 1967. *P'ien-wen kai-lun* 駢文概論. Rpt. Taipei.

Chin, Chung-shu 金中樞. 1963. "Sung-tai ku-wen yün-tung chi fa-chan yen-chiu" 宋代古文運動及發展研究, *Hsin-ya hsüeh-pao*, 5.2, 80-95.

Chou, Tsu-mo 周祖謨. 1956. "Ts'ung wen-hsüeh yü-yen te kai nien lun Han-yü te ya-yen, wen-yen, ku-wen teng wen-t'i" 從文學語言的概念論漢語的雅言, 文言, 古文等問題, *Pei-ching Ta-hsüeh hsüeh-pao (Jen-wen k'o-hsüeh)*, 1, 127-135.

Chu, Chien-hsin 朱劍心, ed. 1936. *Wan-Ming hsiao-p'in-wen hsüan* 晚明小品文選, v. 1. Shanghai.

Chu, Hsüan 朱玄. 1974. *Yao Hsi-pao hsüeh-chi* 姚惜抱學記. Taipei.

Ch'ü, Tui-chih 瞿兌之. 1975 (rpt.). *Chung-kuo wen-hsüeh pa-lun: P'ien-wen lun* 中國文學八論: 駢文論. Taipei.

Ch'ü, Tui-yüan 瞿蛻園, ed. 1979. *Han Wei Liu-ch'ao fu hsüan* 漢魏六朝賦選. Rpt. Shanghai.

Chung-kuo ch'ing-nien ch'u-pan-she 中國青年出版社, ed. 1964. *Ku-wen hsüan-tu* 古文選讀. Peking; rpt. 1979.

Chung-kuo Jen-min Ta-hsüeh Yü-wen hsi Wen-hsüeh-shih chiao-yen shih 中國人民大學語文系文學史教研室, ed. 1962. *Li-tai wen-hsüan* 歷代文選. Peking.

Chung-kuo ku-tien san-wen yen-chiu lun-wen-chi 中國古典散文研究論文集. 1959 and 1969. V. 1. Peking: Jen-min wen-hsüeh ch'u-pan-she pien-chi-pu 人民文學出版社編輯部, ed.; v. 2. Hong Kong: Chung-kuo yü-wen hsüeh-she 中國語文學社, ed.

Edwards, E. D. 1948. "A Classified Guide to the Thirteen Classes of Chinese Prose," *BSOAS*, 12, 770-788.

Egan, Ronald C. 1979. "The Prose Style of Fan Yeh," *HJAS*, 39.2 (December), 339-401.

Fairbank, J. K. and S. Y. Teng. 1940. "On The Types and Uses of Ch'ing Documents," *HJAS*, 5, 1-71.

Fang, Achilles, trans. and annot. 1951. "Rhymeprose on Literature, the *Wen-fu* of Lu Chi (A.D. 261-303)," *HJAS*, 14, 527-566.

Fang, Hsiao-yüeh 方孝岳. 1975. *Chung-kuo wen-hsüeh pa-lun: San-wen lun* 中國文學八論: 散文論. Rpt. Taipei.

Feng, Ch'i-yung 馮其庸 *et al.* 1962. "Ch'ien-yen" 前言, in *Chung-kuo li-tai wen-hsüan* 中國歷代文選, 2v., Peking, pp. 1-46.

Franke, Herbert. 1974. "Literary Parody in Traditional Chinese Literature: Descriptive Pseudo-Biographies," *OE*, 21, 23-31.

Fu, Ssu-nien 傅斯年. 1919. "Chung-kuo wen-hsüeh shih fen-ch'i chih yen-chiu" 中國文學史分期之研究, *Hsin-ch'ao*, 1 (February), 323-328.

Fu, Tseng-hsiang 傅增湘, ed. 1943. *Sung-tai Shu wen chi-ts'un* 宋代蜀文輯存. Rpt. Hong Kong, 1971.

Graham, William T. 1980. *The Lament for the South, Yü Hsin's "Ai Chiang-nan fu."* Cambridge, England.

Henricks, Robert G. 1976. "Hsi K'ang (223-263): His Life, Literature and Thought." Unpublished Ph.D. dissertation, University of Wisconsin, Madison.

Hightower, James Robert. 1953. "Early Expository Prose: The Philosophers," in *Topics*, pp. 7-13.

———. 1958. "Preface" to von Zach, *Anthologie*.

———. 1953. "Parallel Prose," in *Studies in Chinese Literature*, John L. Bishop, ed., Cambridge, Mass., pp. 38-41.

———. 1953a. "Some Characteristics of Parallel Prose," *ibid.*, pp. 108-139.

———. 1957. "The *Wen hsüan* and Genre Theory," *HJAS*, 20, 512-533.

Ho, Chieh 何潔, ed. 1877. *Ming-wen tsai* 明文在. 2v. Chiang-su shu-chü.

Hoshikawa, Kiyotaka, ed. 1963 and 1967. *Ko-bun shimpo* 古文眞寶. 3v. Tokyo.

Hu-nan jen-min ch'u-pan-she 湖南人民出版社, ed. 1980. *Li-tai yu-chi hsüan* 歷代游記選.

Hung, Ming-shui. 1974. "Yüan Hung-tao and the Late Ming Literary and Intellectual Movement." Unpublished Ph.D. dissertation, University of Wisconsin, Madison.

Huo, Jan 霍然. 1961. "Ku-tien san-wen te fan-wei wen-t'i" 古典散文的範圍問題, *Wen-hsüeh i-ch'an*, 314, *Kuang-ming jih-pao*, May 21.

Itō, Masafumi 伊藤正文 and Itsukai Tomoyoshi 一海知義, trans. 1970. *Kan Gi Rikuchō Tō Sō sambunsen* 漢魏六朝唐宋散文選. Tokyo. Contains a "Kaisetsu" 解說 (pp. 377-393) by Itō.

Iriya, Yoshitaka 入矢義高, ed. 1971. *Kinsei zuihitsu shū* 近世隨筆集. Tokyo. Contains translations of selected passages from the *sui-pi* 隨筆 (occasional jottings) of the Sung dynasty and selected passages from Hsieh Chao-che's 謝肇淛 *Wu tsa-tsu* 五雜組 (translated by Iriya Yoshitaka), as well as selections from Chou Liang-kung's 周亮工 *Shu-ying* 書影 and Yü Yüeh's 俞樾 *Ch'un-tsai t'ang sui-pi* 春在堂隨筆 (Translated by Iwaki Hideo 岩城秀夫), and selections from Li Chih's 李贄 *Fen-shu* 焚書 (translated by Mizoguchi Yūzō 溝口雄三).

Jao Tsung-i 饒宗頤. 1977. "Chan-kuo wen-hsüeh" 戰國文學, *CYYY*, 48.1 (March), 153-175.

Jen-min chiao-yü ch'u-pan-she 人民教育出版社, ed. 1962. *Ku-tai san-wen hsüan* 古代散文選. Peking; rpt. 1980.

Kano, Naoaki 狩野直喜. 1965. *Chūgoku tetsugakushi* 中國哲學史. Rpt. Tokyo.

Kao, Ming 高明, general editor. 1957-1960. *Chung-hua wen-hui* 中華文彙. 8v. Taipei. V. 1: *Hsien-Ch'in wen-hui* 先秦文彙, Li Yüeh-kang 李曰剛, ed.; v. 2: *Liang Han San-kuo wen-hui* 兩漢三國文彙, Lin Yin 林尹, ed.; v. 3: *Liang Chin Nan-pei-ch'ao wen-hui* 兩晉南北朝文彙, Pa Hu-t'ien 巴壺天 and Tai P'ei-chih 戴培之, eds.; v. 4: *Sui T'ang Wu-tai wen-hui* 隋唐五代文彙, Chang Shou-p'ing 張壽平, ed.; v. 5: *Sung wen-hui* 宋文彙, Fang Yüan-jao 方遠堯, ed.; v. 6: *Liao Chin Yüan wen-hui* 遼金元文彙, Chiang Ying-lung 江應龍, ed.; v. 7: *Ming wen-hui* 明文彙, Yüan Huan-jo 袁奐若, ed.; v. 8: *Ch'ing wen-hui* 清文彙, Chu Hsiu-hsia 祝秀俠 and Yüan Shuai-nan 袁帥南, eds.

Kao, Pu-ying 高步瀛, ed. 1976. *T'ang-Sung wen chü-yao* 唐宋文舉要. 3v. Rpt. Hong Kong.

Knechtges, David R., trans. and annot. 1982. *Wen Xuan, or Selections of Refined Literature*. V. 1. Princeton. Contains excellent front matter.

K'o, Ch'ing-ming 柯慶明 and Lin Ming-te 林明德, eds. 1978. *Chung-kuo ku-tien wen-hsüeh yen-chiu ts'ung-k'an: San-wen yü lun-p'ing chih-pu* 中國古典文學研究叢刊：散文與論評之部. Taipei.

Krause, F. E. A. 1922. *Tseng Kung: Ein Beitrag aus der Literatur der Sung-Zeit*. Heidelberg.

K'ung, Te-ch'eng 孔德成. 1974. *Ming Ch'ing san-wen hsüan-chu* 明清散文選注. Taipei.

Kuo, Shang-hou 過商侯, ed. 1975. *Ku-wen p'ing-chu* 古文評註. Rpt. T'ai-chung.

Kuo-yü jih-pao she *Ku-chin wen-hsüan pien-chi-shih* 國語日報社古今文選編輯室, ed. 1978. *T'ang-Sung pa-ta-chia wen-hsüan* 唐宋八大家文選. Taipei.

Li, Chao-lo 李兆洛. *P'ien-t'i wen-ch'ao* 駢體文鈔. *SPPY*.

Li, Chi. 1974. *The Travel Diaries of Hsü Hsia-k'o*. Hong Kong.

Li, K'ai 李凱, ed. 1981. *Wei-Chin Nan-pei-ch'ao san-wen hsüan-chiang* 魏晉南北朝散文選講. Wuhan.

Li, Pin 李賓, ed. 1964. *Pa-tai wen-ch'ao* 八代文鈔. 16v. Taipei.

Liang, Ch'i-ch'ao 梁啟超. 1959. *Intellectual Trends in the Ch'ing Period* 清代學術概論, Immanuel C. Y. Hsü, trans. and annot. Cambridge, Mass.

Liang Jung-jo 梁容若 *et al*. eds. 1957-. *Ku-chin wen-hsüan* 古今文選. 5v. Taipei.

Linberg, G. D. 1971-1972. "The Prose *fu* of the Sung Dynasty in Historical Perspective," *TkR*, 2.3/3.1 (October/April), 279-294.

Liu, James T. C. 1967. *Ou-yang Hsiu: An Eleventh Century Neo-Confucianist*. Stanford, California.

Liu, James J. Y. 1979. "Classical Prose," in *Essentials of Chinese Literary Art*. North Scituate, Massachusetts, pp. 33-48.

Liu, Lin-sheng 劉麟生. 1934. *P'ien-wen hsüeh* 駢文學. Shanghai.

Liu, P'an-sui 劉盼遂 and Kuo Yü-heng 郭預衡, eds. 1980. *Chung-kuo li-tai san-wen hsüan* 中國歷代散文選. 2v. Peking.

Liu, Shen-shu 劉申叔. 1978. "Lun-wen tsa-chi" 論文雜記, in Lo, *Lun-wen hsüan*, pp. 1-32.

Liu, Shih-p'ei 劉師培. 1904. "Lun-wen tsa-chi" 論文雜記, rpt. in Lo, *Lun-wen hsüan*, v. 1, 1978, pp. 1-32.

———. 1983. "Nan-pei wen-hsüeh pu-t'ung lun" 南北文學不同論, in *Wen-lun shih-chien* 文論十箋, Ch'eng Ch'ien-fan 程千帆, ed., Harbin, pp. 81-125.

Liu, Shih Shun. 1979. *Chinese Classical Prose: The Eight Masters of the T'ang-Sung Period*. Hong Kong.

Liu, Ta-chieh 劉大杰. 1962. *Chung-kuo wen-hsüeh fa-chan shih* 中國文學發展史. 2nd ed. 3v. Rpt. Hong Kong.

———. 1958. "Liu Tsung-yüan chi ch'i san-wen" 柳宗元及其散文, *Wen-hsüeh i-ch'an*, 219, *Kuang-ming jih-pao*, July 27.

Liu, Ta-pai 劉大白. 1935. "T'ung-ch'eng-p'ai kuei-hua-wen ho pa-ku-wen te kuan-hsi" 桐城派鬼話文和八股文的關係, in *Chung-kuo hsin wen-hsüeh ta-hsi* 中國新文學大系, Chao Chia-pi 趙家璧, ed., Shanghai; rpt. Hong Kong, 1962, v. 6, pp. 96-100.

Lo, Ken-tse 羅根澤, ed. 1957. *Hsien-Ch'in san-wen hsüan* 先秦散文選. Ch'i Fa-jen 戚法仁. annot. Peking.

———. 1955. "Hsien-Ch'in san-wen fa-chan kai-k'uang" 先秦散文發展概況, in *Wen-hsüeh i-ch'an tseng-k'an*, v. 1, Peking.

Lo, Lien-t'ien 羅聯添. 1982. "T'ang Sung ku-wen te fa-chan yü yen-pien" 唐宋古文的發展與演變, in *Chung-kuo wen-hsüeh te fa-chan kai-shu* 中國文學的發展概述, pp. 121-183. Taipei.

Lu, Ch'ien 盧前. 1937. *Pa-ku hsiao-shih* 八股小史. Shanghai.

Lu, Hsün 魯迅. 1957. "Hsiao-p'in wen te wei-chi" 小品文的危機, in *Lu Hsün ch'üan-chi* 魯迅傳記, Peking, v. 4, pp. 440-443.

Lü, Tsu-ch'ien 呂祖謙, ed., 1886. *Sung wen-chien* 宋文鑑. 4v. Chiang-su shu-chü.

Lung, Yü-ch'un 龍宇純. 1963. "Hsien-Ch'in san-wen chung te yün-wen" 先秦散文中的韻文, *Ch'ung-chi hsüeh-pao*, 2.2 (May), 137-168, 3.1 (November), 55-87.

McCaskey, M. 1971. "Categorization of Chinese Literature: Prose," in *Languages and Linguistics: Working Papers*, No. 2 (Georgetown University School of Language and Linguistics), pp. 35-50.

McMullen, David. 1973. "Historical and Literary Theory in the Mid-Eighth Century," *Perspectives*, pp. 307-342.

Ma, Y. W. 1967. "Prose Writings of Han Yü and Ch'uan-ch'i Literature," *JOS*, 7 (1969), 195-223.

Maeno, Naoaki 前野直彬, ed. 1961-1962. *Bunshō kihan* 文章軌範. 2v. Tokyo.

Margouliès, Georges, ed. and trans. 1925. *Le Kou-wen chinois; recueil de textes avec introduction et notes*. Paris.

———. 1926. Appendix III (Notes bibliographiques sur les différents recueils de Kou-wen), cxi-cxvi.

———, ed. and trans. 1929. *Évolution de la prose artistique chinoise*. München.

———. 1949. *Histoire de la littérature chinoise: prose*. Paris.

Marney, John. 1971. "Emperor Chien-wen of the Liang Dynasty: His Life and Literature." Unpublished Ph.D. dissertation, University of Wisconsin.

Matsueda, Shigeo 松枝茂夫, ed. 1969. *Kiroku bungaku shū* 記錄文學集. Tokyo. Contains translations of selected passages from various *pi-chi** ranging from the *Hsi-ching tsa-chi** to Yü Cheng-hsieh's 兪正燮 *K'uei-ssu ts'un-kao*癸巳存考 of the Ch'ing dynasty.

Miki, Katsumi 三木克己, *et al.*, trans. 1965. *Chūgoku sambunsen: Denki-hen, shokan-hen, zatsubun hen* 中國散文選傳記篇書翰篇雜文篇. Tokyo.

Mou, Jun-sun 牟潤孫. 1968. "T'ang-ch'u nan-pei hsüeh-jen lun-hsüeh chih i-ch'ü chi ch'i ying-hsiang" 唐初南北學人論學之異趣及其影響 (The Differences of Academic Approaches Between the Northern and Southern Scholars in the Early T'ang Period and Their Influence), *JICS*, 1 (September), pp. 50-88.

Nienhauser. 1973. *Liu Tsung-yüan*.

———. 1977. "A Structural Reading of the *Chuan* in the *Wen-yüan ying-hua*, *JAS*, 36.3 (May), 443-456.

Nivison, David. 1966. *The Life and Thought of Chang Hsüeh-ch'eng (1738-1801)*. Stanford.

Okamura, Shigeru 岡村繁. 1980. "Hen bun" 駢文, in *Chung-kuo wen-hsüeh kai-lun* 中國文學概論, Hung Shun-lung 洪順隆, trans., Taipei, pp. 145-161.

Olbricht, Peter. 1957. "Die Biographie in China," *Saeculum*, 8, 224-235.

P'eng, Chao-sun 彭兆蓀, ed. 1936. *Nan-pei-ch'ao wen-ch'ao* 南北朝文鈔. 2v. Taipei.

Phelan, Timothy S. 1976. "Yao Nai's Classes of *Ku-wen* Prose: A Translation of the Introduction," *Parerga*, 3, 39-65.

Quirin, Michael. 1980. "Beiträge zur Erforschung von Liu Zhiji's *Shi Tong*." Unpublished M.A. thesis, Universität Bonn.

Rotours, Robert des. 1975. *Les Inscriptions Funéraires de Ts'ouei Mien*崔沔*(673-739), de sa Femme née Wang* 王*(685-734), et de Ts'ouei Yeoufou*崔祐甫 *(721-780)*. Paris: Ecole Francaise d'è Extréme-Orient.

Saintsbury, George. 1912. *A History of English Prose Rhythm*. London.

Schwartz, Ernst. 1973. *Der Ruf der Phönixflöte, Klassische chinesische Prosa*. 2v. Berlin. Free translations of over one hundred selections from Chou through Republican times.

Shen, Ping 申丙, ed. 1969. *T'ang-Sung san-wen hsüan-chu* 唐宋散文選注. Taipei.

Ssu-ch'uan Shih-fan Hsüeh-yüan Chung-wen-hsi ku-tien wen-hsüeh chiao-yen-tsu 四川師範學院中文系古典文學教研組, ed. 1981. *Chung-kuo li-tai wen-hsüan* 中國歷代文選. 2v. Peking.

Sun, Mei 孫梅, ed. 1962. *Ssu-liu ts'ung-hua*四六叢話. Rpt. Taipei.

Su, T'ien-chüeh 蘇天爵, ed. 1877. *Yüan wen lei* 元文類. 2v. Chiang-su shu-chü.

Sun, K'o-k'uan. 1981. "Yü Chi and Southern Taoism during the Yüan Period," in *China Under Mongol Rule*, John D. Langlois, Jr., ed., pp. 212-253. Princeton.

Sung, Yin-ku 宋蔭谷. 1969. "Lüeh-t'an wo-kuo ku-tai cheng-lun san-wen" 略談我國古代政論散文, in *Chung-kuo ku-tien san-wen yen-chiu lun-wen chi* 中國古典散文研究論文集, v. 2, pp. 13-19.

Suzuki, Torao 鈴木虎雄. 1960. *Bembunshi josetsu* 駢文史序說. Kyoto.

T'ai, Ching-nung 台靜農. 1951. "Chung-kuo wen-hsüeh yu yü-wen fen-li hsing-ch'eng te liang ta chu-liu" 中國文學由語文分離形成的兩大主流, *Ta-lu tsa-chih*, 2.9-10 (May).

———. 1979. "Lun liang Han san-wen te yen-pien" 論兩漢散文的演變, in Lo, *Lun-wen hsüan*, v. 1, pp. 217-227.

T'an, Chia-chien 譚家健. 1957. "Lüeh-t'an *Meng-tzu* san-wen te i-shu t'e-cheng" 略談孟子散文的藝術特徵, *Wen-hsüeh i-ch'an*, 173 and 174, *Kuang-ming jih-pao*, September 8 and 15.

T'ao, Ying-ch'iu 陶英秋. *Hsiao-p'in wen-hsüan*小品文選. 2v. Shanghai, 1934.

Thern, K. L. 1966. *Postface of the* Shuo-wen Chieh-tzu, *The First Comprehensive Chinese Dictionary*. Madison, Wisconsin.

Ts'ai, I-chung 蔡義忠. 1977. *Chung-kuo pa-ta san-wen-chia* 中國八大散文家. Taipei.

Tsang, Li-ho 臧勵龢, ed. 1969. *Han-Wei Liu-ch'ao wen* 漢魏六朝文. Rpt. Taipei.

Ts'en, Chung-mien 岑仲勉. 1957. "Wen-tzu yu p'ien-li pien-wei san-t'i" 文字由駢儷變爲散體, in his *Sui T'ang shih* 隋唐史. Peking, pp. 175-180.

Tseng, Yü 曾燠, ed. 1961. *Kuo-ch'ao p'ien-t'i cheng-tsung p'ing-pen* 國朝駢體正宗評本. Rpt. Taipei.

Tu, Ching-i. 1974-1975. "The Chinese Examination Essay: Some Literary Considerations," *MS*, 31, 393-406.

Tung, Kao 董誥, *et al.*, eds. 1972. *Ch'in-ting Ch'üan T'ang wen* 欽定全唐文. 20v. N.p., 1814; rpt. Taipei.

Twitchett, Denis. 1962. "Lu Chih (754-805): Imperial Adviser and Court Official," *Con-*

fucian Personalities, Arthur F. Wright and Denis Twitchett, eds. Stanford.

———. 1962. "Problems of Chinese Biography," in *Confucian Personalities,* Arthur F. Wright and Twitchett, eds., Stanford.

Waley, Arthur. 1938. *The Analects of Confucius.* London.

———. 1949. *The Life and Times of Po Chü-i, 772-846 A.D.* London.

———. 1935. *The Way and Its Power.* London.

———. 1956. *Yüan Mei, Eighteenth Century Chinese Poet.* London.

Wang, Jao 王瑤. 1956. "Hsü Yü yü p'ien-t'i" 徐庾與駢體, in his *Chung-kuo wen-hsüeh shih lun-chi* 中古文學史論集. Shanghai, pp. 158-163.

Wang, John. 1977. "Early Chinese Narrative: The *Tso-chuan* as Example," in *Chinese Narrative,* pp. 3-20.

Wang, Jung-ch'u 王榮初 and Ts'ai I-p'ing 蔡一平, eds. 1980. *Ch'ing-tai san-wen hsüan-chu* 清代散文選注. Shanghai.

Wang, Shui-chao 王水照. 1962. "Sung-tai san-wen te feng-ko" 宋代散文的風格, *Wen-hsüeh i-ch'an,* 439, *Kuang-ming jih-pao,* November 11.

———, comp. and comm. 1964. *Sung-tai san-wen hsüan-chu* 宋代散文選注. Peking.

Wang, Wen-ju 王文濡, ed. 1965. *Ch'ing wen-hui* 清文滙. Rpt. Taipei.

———, ed. 1967. *Chin-tai wen p'ing-chu* 近代文評註. Rpt. Taipei.

———, ed. 1981. *T'ang-wen p'ing-chu tu-pen* 唐文評註讀本. Taipei.

Watson, Burton. 1962. *Early Chinese Literature.* New York.

———, trans. 1963. *Hsün-tzu, Basic Writings.* New York.

———, trans. 1968. *Records of the Grand Historian of China.* 2v. New York.

Wei, Ch'i-hsien 魏齊賢 and Yeh Fen 葉棻, eds. 1964. *Wu-pai chia po-fang ta-ch'üan wen-ts'ui* 五百家播芳大全文粹. Rpt. Taipei.

Wu, Ch'i-ning 吳契寧 *et al.,* eds. 1936. *Liang Han san-wen hsüan* 西漢散文選. Peking; rpt. Shanghai 1946 and Taipei 1956.

Wu, K'ai-sheng 吳闓生, ed. 1970. *Ku-wen fan* 古文範. Rpt. Taipei.

Wu, Mei 吳梅. 1934. *Liao-Chin-Yüan wen-hsüeh-shih* 遼金元文學史. Shanghai.

Wu, Tseng-ch'i 吳增祺, ed. 1910. *Han-fen lou ku-chin wen-ch'ao* 涵芬樓古今文鈔. 14v. Shanghai; rpt. Taipei, 1970.

Yang, Yin-shen 楊蔭深, ed. 1937. *Ku-wen-chia chuan-chi wen-hsüan* 古文家傳記文選. Shanghai.

Yao, Hsüan 姚鉉. *T'ang-wen ts'ui* 唐文粹. 2v. *SPTK.*

Yao, Nai 姚鼐. *Ku-wen-tz'u lei-tsuan.* *

Yeh, Lung 葉龍. 1975. *T'ung-ch'eng-p'ai wen-hsüeh-shih* 桐城派文學史. Hong Kong.

Yen, Chi-ch'eng 嚴既澄. 1927. "Yün-wen yü p'ien-t'i wen" 韻文與駢體文, in *Chung-kuo wen-hsüeh yen-chiu* 中國文學研究, Cheng Chen-to 鄭振鐸, ed., v. 2, pp. 1-15 (separate pagination). Rpt. Shanghai, 1981.

Yen, K'o-chün 嚴可均, ed. 1961. *Ch'üan Shang-ku San-tai Ch'in-Han San-kuo Liu-ch'ao wen* 全上古三代秦漢三國六朝文. 4v. Rpt. Taipei.

Yin, Meng-lun 殷孟倫, annot. 1960. *Han Wei Liu-ch'ao pai-san chia chi t'i-tz'u chu* 漢魏六朝百三家集題辭注. Peking.

Yokota, Terutoshi 横田輝俊. 1976. "Mindai no kobun to hachikōbun" 明代の古文と八股文, *Hiroshima daigaku bungakubu kiyō,* 36, 1-23.

Yoshikawa, Kōjirō 吉川幸次郎. 1966. "Chūgoku bunsho ron" 中國文章論, in *Chūgoku sambun ron* 中國散文論. Tokyo, pp. 11-73.

von Zach, *Anthologie.*

RHETORIC

Karl S. Y. Kao

I. Introduction

THE development of rhetoric in China passed through stages parallel to those of Western rhetoric: originating in the technique of public address, it gradually came to be applied to more purely literary texts. Both the close relationship of rhetoric and poetry in the Middle Ages and the shift of focus to figures in the later European treatises on rhetoric sharpened the distinction between persuasive rhetoric and "ornamental" rhetoric. A similar division can be perceived in the Chinese tradition, although the circumstances under which the division took place differed from those in the West. Before taking up this main topic, ornamental (or literary) rhetoric, it is necessary to survey the kinds of writing in which rhetorical concerns (both persuasive and ornamental) are prominent.

The earliest examples of persuasive discourse are found in the speeches attributed to the Shang and Chou rulers and their military commanders, such as their charges against the enemy and the exhortations to their own troops. These speeches as preserved in the *Shu-ching* 書經 are either forensic or deliberative in nature. During the Warring States period a highly rhetorical form of oratory was practiced by political counsellors and diplomatic agents. Such speeches survive only in later recreations, and it is uncertain whether the original oratorical models were delivered extempore or were planned compositions (written or memorized). As in the West, rhetorical persuasion became one primary model of philosophical discourse. Thus in extant written texts, rhetorical discourse appears in various forms, ranging from philosophical expositions to sophistic arguments to debates over military and political policies. Different kinds of philosophical discourses can be found in the *chu-tzu pai-chia** writings, while histories and quasi-historical texts like *Kuo-yü,** *Tso-chuan,** and *Chan-kuo ts'e** are especially important as repositories of persuasions by political counsellors and strategic advisors. After the unification of the various states under the Ch'in, interstate diplomacy and free competition of ideologies—conditions comparable to the Greek democracy that encouraged the flourishing of oratory—no longer existed. In the Han and subsequent dynasties, rhetoric as persuasion and argumentation appeared primarily in the political counsellors' deliberation over the policies of the state and the ministers' remonstration with their emperors; thus, it often manifested itself as an art of "criticism by indirection." Many such persuasions are preserved in dynastic histories like *Shih-chi** and *Han-shu* (see Pan Ku). In addition, discursive genres such as *lun* 論 (Chia I's* "Kuo Ch'in lun" 過秦論, Huan K'uan's 桓寬 [*fl.* 73 B.C.] *Yen t'ieh lun* 塩鐵論), and official writings like the *piao* 表, the *shang-shu* 上書, and the *tsan* 贊 can be considered rhetorical in that they argue, deliberate, or praise with the intention of influencing the hearer's attitude.

Besides the political function, rhetoric in the Han also found a literary outlet in the *fu*,* a genre characterized by its display of epideictic discourse (Knechtges, 1976), thus launching rhetoric's influx into literature. As the taste for ornamentation grew, literary prose evolved into a highly patterned form known as *p'ien-wen*,* a form that reached its peak of development in the Six Dynasties and still stands as the most florid and "rhetorical" of all Chinese writings. Archaizing writers of the T'ang and Sung spent much of their energy combating its influence. This conflict between ancient-style prose and parallel prose intensified debate over the relative merit of the "ornate" and "plain" styles (華麗 vs. 樸實 , or 文 vs. 質), an issue that had been central to the traditional discussion of literature. At the same time, there was in the T'ang a growing interest in specific rhetorical devices: rules of parallelism were codified, and some poets reveled in the composition of the so-called *tsa-t'i shih* 雜體詩 (poems of miscellaneous forms), forms distinguished mainly by their employment of certain figures in the poem. After the T'ang, in the *tz'u** and *ch'ü*,* poetry became more "rhetorical" in its use of allotropic variations as the chief mode of composition. With *ch'ü* particularly, adaptation of, and variation on, existing expressions gradually became the prominent device (see *yin-yung* 引用, no. 26 in the list of figures below); and operatic songs of *tsa-chü** and *ch'uan-ch'i** plays were also characterized by an elaborated syntactic figuration (Schlepp, 1970). Meanwhile, testing of literary skills in the civil-service examinations had its effect on the development of rhetoric in both poetry and prose. Careful instructions on how to compose examination poetry and essays were laid down, and the prescriptive regulation reached its height in the Ming and Ch'ing *chih-lü* 制律 poetry and *chih-i* 制義 prose, the latter otherwise known as *pa-ku wen*.* The formal rules spelled out for this prose form, combined with the restricted nature of its contents, so burdened the writings with decorum that *pa-ku wen* gradually became a term to be uttered with disdain; the literary revolution of the May Fourth Movement was in fact partly a reaction against the *pa-ku* tradition. However, the nature of ornamentation in this form represents a different kind of rhetorical stylization than that in *p'ien-wen*. As the latter is largely characterized by ornamentation related to the use of diction, *pa-ku wen* is rhetorical in its formal, structural elaboration.

II. The Sources

Rhetoric as a discipline has never been clearly established in China. The "four subjects" of cultivation in the Confucian "curriculum" include the art of speech (言語 ; see *Lun-yü* 論語, XI. 3), but neither Confucius nor other philosophers of the Warring States period ever treated the subject in the same fashion as Aristotle or Cicero and Quintilian did. Some of the philosophical texts contain sections on the subject of persuasion and argumentation, normally with an emphasis on the psychological factors of the interlocutor and the moral principles involved. The most important of these are the sections in *Han-fei-tzu* entitled "Nan-yen" 難言 (ch. 3), "Shuo-nan" 說難 (ch. 13) and "Shuo-lin" 說林 (chs. 22-23) and the chapter "Fei-hsiang" 非相 (ch. 5) in *Hsün-tzu*. A more technical treatment is found in the chapters constituting the so-called "Mo-ching" 墨經 portion of *Mo-tzu* 墨子, particularly the chapters "Ching, I" 經上 and "Hsiao-ch'ü" 小取 , where figures like *pi* 辟 (metaphor/analogy) and *mou* 侔 (substitution by synonyms or equivalents) are mentioned as a part of the process of argumentation.

Discussions of ornamental or literary rhetoric, particularly of figures of speech, are found early in texts of literary criticism, such as in the *Lun-heng* 論衡 and *Wen-hsin tiao-lung*.* The discourses on poetry that developed from the T'ang through the Ch'ing also make frequent reference to specific figures. Material collected in Wei Ch'ing-chih's *Shih-jen yü-hsieh** and Kūkai's *Bunkyō hifuron** are useful sources for rules and examples of composition and figurations. During the Sung, treatises on the specific devices of prose writing started to appear, of which Ch'en K'uei's *Wen-tse** is an eminent example. The most important texts on both prose and poetic rhetoric produced over the period from the Sung to the Yüan include: Yen Yü's *Ts'ang-lang shih-hua*,* Hu Tzu's *T'iao-hsi yü-yin ts'ung-hua*,* Hung Mai's *Jung-tsai sui-pi* and its sequels, and Ch'en I-tseng's 陳繹曾 (*fl.* 1329) *Wen-shuo* 文說. During the Ming and Ch'ing the flourishing of various schools of prose writing also resulted in treatises and anthologies dealing with prose rhetoric. Some of those that contain references to specific figures are: Hsü Shih-tseng's *Wen-t'i ming-pien*,* T'ang Piao's 唐彪 (late Ch'ing) *Tu-shu tso-wen p'u* 讀書作文譜, Chang Hsüeh-ch'eng's 章學誠 (1783-1801) *Wen-shih t'ung-i* 文史通義, Yü Yüeh's 俞樾 (1821-1906) *Ku-shu i-i chu-li* 古書疑義舉例, and Lin Shu's* *Wei-lu lun-wen* 畏廬論文. As for the material related to the composition of poetry and essays for examinations, they are conveniently collected in Liang Chang-chu's 梁章鉅 (1775-1849) two compilations: *Shih-lü ts'ung-hua* 試律叢話 and *Chih-i ts'ung-hua* 制義叢話 (Cheng Tze-yü, 1965). The single most important study on Chinese rhetoric from a systematic perspective which gives a relatively consistent, comprehensive taxonomy of figures is the *Hsiu-tz'u-hsüeh fa-fan* (1932) by Ch'en Wang-tao, who studied rhetoric in the Waseda University and was influenced by the Western approach. More recent works on Chinese rhetoric have based themselves on Ch'en, of which Huang Ch'ing-hsüan offers the most comprehensive collection of examples, particularly from the modern vernacular literature which supplement Ch'en's classical ones. There are others, such as Cheng Tien, Yang Shu-ta, and Chang Wen-chih, who reject the Western models and methodologies and maintain an indigenous approach; the merits of these works lie mainly in their efforts to put together the traditional materials and examples rather than in cogent analyses. The works of Chin Chao-tzu and Hsü Chin-t'ing attempt a synthesis of Western and Chinese rhetorics, but they suffer from a lack of consistency and clarity.

III. Western Rhetoric as a Methodological Model

In dealing with Chinese rhetoric, it is apparent that while the notion of figurative language is an eminent one in the tradition, well evidenced by the attention paid to the *shih-ko* 詩格 and *wen-fa* 文法, the concept of rhetoric as such (i.e., an organized study of discourse in general) does not exist independent of literary criticism and generic discussion. To sort out what might be properly considered as rhetoric, it may be useful to look briefly at the model established in the classical rhetoric in the West. Rhetoric was originally conceived and taught with the pragmatic purpose of moving the interlocutor to adapt an attitude or act in favor of the speaker's cause. Classical rhetoric is divided into three branches, each corresponding to a type of discourse: (1) *deliberative*, which advises, exhorts, or dissuades; (2) *judicial*, or *forensic*, which accuses or defends; and (3) *epideictic*, or *demonstrative*, which blames, commemmorates, or praises. Some

Latin treatises divide a speech into five components: (1) *Invention,* the devising of subjects, methods of arguments, and persuasion; (2) *Arrangement,* or *Disposition,* the ordering and distribution of the main parts of the speech; (3) *Style,* or *Elocution,* the choice and adaptation of suitable words, sentences, and their organization; (4) *Memory,* memorization of the speech; and (5) *Delivery,* the regulation of voice, gesture, etc., at the presentation. Different emphases have been placed on different parts by individual theorists. Thus only Style remains a constant component, and rhetorical treatises of the sixteenth and seventeenth centuries often concentrate on the discussion of figures, the essential elements of Style. Gradually, the persuasive function came to be replaced by an emphasis on literary, aesthetic function.

Each of the five components is further divided into subcategories. In relation to *Arrangement* (*Disposition*), for instance, a more elaborated scheme would include seven sections (introduction, narration, exposition, proposition, confirmation, refutation, and conclusion). *Style* (*Elocution*), originally a matter concerned with the appropriateness of language (linguistic decorum) in the three branches of rhetoric, is also divided into three contrasting types: the grand, the middle, and the low (or plain) style, based on the degree of ornamentation employed. Figures of speech and prose rhythm are the most important ornaments, for their effectiveness in imparting aesthetic pleasure. There are two kinds of figure: figures of words and figures of thought. The former is in turn divided into two subtypes: *trope* (the use of a word in a sense different from its normal one, such as metaphor) and *scheme* (in which words have their ordinary meaning but are placed in non-ordinary syntactic arrangement, such as asyndeton). *Figure of thought* is a large-scale figure manifested on a higher level of the text, such as allegory (sometimes it is considered the same as trope). The distinction between figure of thought and figure of words is often ambiguous, and specific examples often overlap.

From the modern point of view, rhetoric is concerned only with the linguistic mechanism of composition. Because they are either pre-verbal or are acts performed after the formation of the discourse, Invention, Memory, and Delivery are excluded from rhetoric; thus only Disposition and Elocution are left over from the classical model. The notion of the mechanism of verbalization, although not without ambiguity, can also be used as a rough criterion to distinguish rhetorical materials in Chinese sources, with these materials further differentiated as dispositional or elocutional. According to this, then, Liu Hsieh's topic of "Shen-ssu" 神思(spirit and imagination), for instance, is not a matter of rhetoric, while his sections titled "Li-tz'u" 麗辭, "Sheng-lü" 聲律, "Chang-chu"章句, "Pi hsing" 比興, etc., may contain elements of it. The differentiation of compositional cause and literary effect is also pertinent. For example, Yao Nai's eight factors of style—*shen, li, ch'i, wei, ke, lü, sheng, se* (神 , 理 , 氣 , 味 , 格 , 律 , 聲 , 色 , roughly, "spirit, reason/argument, air/entelechy, flavor, figures, rules, sound/rhythm, color/diction"—see his preface to the *Ku-wen-tz'u lei-ts'uan**)—fall into two groups; the first four terms being either pre-verbal or about the stylistic effect of the language and hence not rhetoric, while the last four, about the compositional cause and choice of figures in the process, are rhetorical. As for the elocutional and the dispositional elements, the distinction is less equivocal: the latter is related to the formal structure of parts, and the former to the actualization of the discourse in language. In the following, there will be an examination of how the elocutional and dispositional devices are manifested in Chinese.

IV. Application of the Model

In disposition the structural organization can be seen from two perspectives: linear and hierarchical. Linear structure involves both the arrangement of parts and sections and the development from section to section; and hierarchical structure is revealed through the coherence (or consistency) of the constituents considered as a whole. The Chinese view of the problem, like that of classical rhetoric of the West, sees the question mainly from the linear perspective, but a hierarchical conception is not entirely lacking. One of the earliest views on the hierarchical organization is found in Liu Hsieh's conception of *chang*章(paragraphs) and *chü*句(clauses) as constituents making up the whole of the *p'ien*篇(ch. 34, "Chang chü"章句: cf. ch. 43, "Fu-hui"附會, which deals with coherence). But the most rigorous prescription for organization is epitomized in the rules of *pa-ku wen*, which as noted above, is rigidly structured such that each section is to perform a definite function. A description of the *pa-ku wen* structure may serve as a Chinese model of rhetorical organization.

An essay in the *pa-ku* genre normally expounds on a given theme set forth by a quotation from the Confucian classics (which serves as the "topic," the *t'i*題 of the essay) and the ideas expressed by the writer must conform with the orthodox exegesis (such as Chu Hsi's朱熹). The essay consists of five sections: (1) *p'o-t'i*破題, referring to the topic or the theme as indicated by the quotation; (2) *ch'eng-t'i*承題, elaboration of the theme sentence; (3) *ch'i-chiang*起講, presenting the overall ideas; (4) *t'i-pi*提比(also called *ju-shou*入手), beginning the exposition, which proceeds in four subsections—*hsü-pi*虛比, "empty" pair; *chung-pi*中比, middle pair; *hou-pi*后比, hind pair; *su-pi*束比, concluding pair (sometimes omitted)—and (5) *ta-chieh*大結, summation. Of these the "middle pair" is the most crucial and the *ta-chieh* must sum up the entire piece, sometimes with an allusion to what follows the theme sentence in the source text. The form is called *pa-ku*八股(eight-legged) because section (4), *t'i-pi*, contains four pairs or eight strands of parallel prose sentences. However, *hsü-pi* and *su-pi* always comprise parallel sentences, and when *su-pi* is omitted there are only three pairs or "six legs" to the section (it is also possible to have an essay with ten, twelve, even twenty, "legs"). Many *fa*法(devices) are prescribed for the presentation of not only the content and the expression of these sections and subdivisions but also the transition and cross-sentential relationship, including how to "generate" one sentence from another. Often the *fa* are strategies of dealing with the way the topic of the theme is given (only half a sentence quoted, two sentences joined in parallelism, incomplete sentences put together, etc.—a variety of more than forty ways). Optional and obligatory rules are given regarding the exposition by *fan*反(posing the opposite view), and the use of allusion and metaphor (or analogy) for the explanatory purpose. Each section has its preferred device of presentation (T'ang Piao lists more than thirty for *ch'eng-t'i*, such as "open and shut" [開闔], "creation suspense" [故作疑案], "pointing to the opposite" [反題說], etc., while devices of parallel prose, including variation of tones for euphonic effect, are required in the *pa-ku* subsections. The overall development, more generally, is regulated by the four stages of *ch'i, ch'eng, chuan, ho* 起承轉合 (inception, continuation, transition, and conclusion), which is taken from the terminology of discourse on poetry. The total number of words in an essay is also prescribed, the usual range being from 450 to 600 words.

With respect to their function in poetry, the rules for linear structure are normally more lax. In regulated verse (see *shih**), parallelism governs the internal structure of the four (or at least the inner two) couplets, while the connection between the couplets—designated metaphorically as *shou-lien*首聯, *han-lien*頷, *ching-lien*頸, and *wei-lien*尾(head, chin, neck, and tail couplets)—is governed by the notion of *ch'i, ch'eng, chuan, ho* which is a formalization of semantic connectivity and may be flexibly manifested in a number of ways. (The body metaphor of structure occurs also in Western rhetoric, in Longinus).

V. Major Figures in Chinese Rhetoric

A list of tropes and schemes is below. But a few important ones—metaphor, parallelism and others related to them—call for a brief discussion here. The recent revival of interest in rhetoric in the West has been directed mainly to figures of speech, and inquiries in this area are a corollary of studies in stylistics and poetics in general. Prompted probably by the Russian Formalists' notion of defamiliarization as an essential characteristic of literary language, modern poetics sees in figures the preeminence of literary language, figures being usually thought of as a departure from the normal usage and hence defamiliarizing. Other disciplines such as philosophy, psychology, and psychoanalytical approaches to literature have also taken an increasing interest in the problems of figuration in language. The discussion here is largely limited to the manifestation of figurative language in traditional Chinese literature.

Since Aristotle metaphor has been identified as the most important and powerful of all figures in the West. Its operation is perceived as a deviation, i.e., a word or an expression used with a meaning different from its normal usage. Metaphor is also seen as a substitution, or a "transferring to one thing a name which designates something else." As such it is a substitution based on equivalence (synonymity, antonymity) which has been recognized as one of the two fundamental operations in literary language in the modern theory of poetics (the other is metonymic operation—substitution based on contiguity, Jakobson, 1960). The equivalent principle of metaphoric relationship has been applied to the study of T'ang poetry, where it is shown to be a principle underlying not only the level of imagery but the structural level of the poem as a whole (Kao and Mei, 1978). In that sense, the metaphoric process (or paradigmatic process as opposed to the syntagmatic progress of metonymy) can be considered a basic organizing principle of Chinese poetry too.

Called *p'i-yü* 譬喻 or *pi-yü* 比喻, metaphor in the Chinese tradition is closely related to two literary forms: it underlies the parables (or analogies) used as a mode of explanation in the early philosophical texts, and it is also the basis of the poetic modes, *pi*比 and *hsing*興, associated with the exegeses of the *Shih-ching** poems. Metaphor, or *p'i-yü*, thus has to be understood from these two perspectives. To consider its connection with *hsing* and *pi* first, the operation of this trope in terms of semiotic association will be redescribed. A metaphoric operation may be seen as a "semic identity" between the two terms implied in a metaphoric relation, *semes* or *semantic features* being the "meaning components" of an expression. The two terms to be put in a metaphoric relationship—or tenor and vehicle—share certain meaning components which constitute the ground of comparison; metaphor then is an identification that brings to the fore the latent semes shared by the two terms. Thus, "the FEROCITY of a lion" and "the FEROCITY of Achilles" "Achilles is a lion"; or "the WHITENESS & COOLNESS of jade" and "the WHITENESS & COOLNESS of Yang Kuei-fei's arm" "Yang Kuei-fei's jade arm." From this description, a metaphor is a trope of comparison rather than substitution, and the notion of a comparison is central to both the *hsing* and the *pi* modes (which can be seen to derive eventually from the idea of correspondence or *lei* 類). However, in the *Shih-ching* as well as the Chinese poetic tradition in general, *hsing* takes precedence over *pi* as a poetic mode, the latter being the same as *pi-yü* in terms of linguistic mechanism. Generally speaking, *hsing* is distinguished from *pi-yü* (as well as *pi*) in two respects: (1) the "vehicle" (normally a natural phenomenon or an external situation) is always given first, with the function of *evoking* the "tenor" (normally a human phenomenon or an internal situation) and (2) the "semic identity" between the two terms is often cryptic and ambiguous or equivocal to the uninitiated (*Wen-hsin tiao-lung:* " [the point of comparison is visible as] in the twilight of dawn, but not in the full light of the day" 明而未融; ch. 36, "Pi hsing" 比興). In other words, the "pointer" that serves to signal the semic identity (or qualities to be compared) is implicit rather than explicit, and the metaphoric relation, instead of linguistically determined, is culturally determined by the exegetic tradition. As a result of (1), a *hsing* comparison always points to a co-presence of both phenomena or situations instead of a mere highlighting of the qualities and attributes (or foregrounding of certain semes) as in a metaphor. Inherent in (2) is a sense of indeterminacy of the relationship which, even with the mediation of the traditional interpretation, remains only partially resolved. Both the notion of co-presence and the sense of indeterminacy presumed in a *hsing* relationship are central to the Chinese conception of literature. Later poetic theories of the *ch'ing* 情 and *ching* 景 correspondence, for instance, in their taking the poem to be a manifestation where an analogical relationship between the *ch'ing* and *ching* is revealed is essentially a theory based on the *hsing* mode of comparison.

A different use of analogical mode in Chinese tradition is seen in the parables and fables, or *yü-yen,** incorporated in the philosophical expositions of the early prose. *Yü-yen* as analogy departs from *hsing* in the question of determinacy and presence. While *hsing* is characterized by the ambiguity in making latent the potential semic identity, *yü-yen* operates by identifying more than one point of comparability in the two situations (or states) in question. And while an equal value of reference is placed on the two situations in *hsing*, a *yü-yen* may have to do with its eventual loss of ground to historical allusion as a mode of analogical patterning of experiences and as a model of signification in Chinese tradition, where history, or what is thought to be history, is valued over fiction. It may be the same desire for a basis in historicity, that leads religious Taoism to invest the True Man 眞人 of Chuang-tzu's *yü-yen*, for instance, with a reality so much sought in the later cult of immortality. (This seems to be an existential version of the epistemic leap from metaphor to reality, which has a parallel in the linguistic device of "literalization" of metaphor in literature; see below).

To return to the question of metaphor in general, it may be said that all natural languages seem to show a metaphoric quality and that metaphor occupies an important position in our conceptualization and understanding of the world. Many of our experiences, insofar as they are expressed verbally, are structured and presented in metaphoric terms which in turn contribute to condition our understanding and perception and may also reveal our world view. The conception of time, for instance, is often presented in spatial terms, such as expressed in the common injunction in English, "One must look ahead to the future!" Compare this with Ch'en Tzu-ang's* lines: "In front, I see no men of the past;/behind me, there are no new comers" 前不見古人，後不見來者（登幽州台歌）"Teng Yu-chou T'ai ko" where time is also spatialized but in such a manner that it contrasts sharply with the English expression in point of view and conception the ("men of the past" are sages or the "worthies" of Yen 燕, where the Yu-chou Tower is located). To understand and explain one dimension or domain of reality in terms of another is a mental act very often performed in the use of human languages, and Chinese poses no exception. The polar contrast observed in "the shade and the sunlight," or yin and yang, for example, is applied to many areas of human and physical realities. A quick glance at the Erh-ya 爾雅 and Shuo-wen chieh-tzu 說文解字 definitions of most of their entries will show the fundamentally metaphoric nature of Chinese vocabulary (the metaphors of course are mostly so dead and ossified in their extended usage as to make their metaphoric origin quite insensible).

Closely associated with metaphor in paired contrast, as suggested above, is metonymy. Metonymy is considered a subtype of chieh-tai 借代 in Chinese, and in terms of frequency, chieh-tai is much more prominent than pi-yü. Huang Ch'ing-hsüan (1975, pp. 259-261) gives 163 chieh-tai epithets and kennings for the moon (although many of them are in fact metaphors, the number left is still impressive). The figure reveals a way of perception characterized by the tendency to situate things in their spatial and temporal context, or to keep the relation of cause and consequence, material and manifestation, in a well-established track of association.

If metaphor is the master figure in the West, parallelism, or tui-ou 對偶(parison, isocolon), is its counterpart in the Chinese tradition. In the Chinese context parallelism is a rigorously defined figuration of language that has much to do with the language's monosyllabic nature. It is basically a syntactic figure, but it operates over the various levels of the language simultaneously (syntax, semantics, and phonology) and may pertain to various ranges of syntagmatic segments (phrases, sentences, couplets). Pervasive in all belletristic writings, it is dominant in the fu and also becomes the chief generic feature of parallel prose, or p'ien-wen, as well as regulated verse. As it appears in a poetic couplet, parallelism requires a matching syntax (or positioning of the shih-tzu 實字 and hsü-tzu 虛字) between the two lines which brings on at the same time an alignment in semantic categorization (in the sense of synonymity and antonymity, hyponymity and superordination as well as other experiential criteria; see Wang Li, 1962). Like p'i-yü and chieh-tai, the scheme of parallelism includes many subtypes and variations such as ts'o-tsung 錯綜, hsiang-ch'ien 鑲嵌, and ts'eng-ti 層遞(see list below). Twenty-nine types of parallelism and antitheses are given in Bunkyō hifuron (Frankel, 1976).

Finally a few literary phenomena related to figurative language might be mentioned. As with parallelism, a figure can sometimes be so dominant that it becomes a distinctive feature for certain genres. The Wen-hsüan* in its generic classification has included the form tui-wen 對問 and she-lun 設論(chüan 45) which may be seen to have a basic structure modeled on the scheme of she-wen 設問(cf. also Ch'ü Yüan's* "T'ien wen" 天問), while lien-chu 連珠 (Wen-hsüan, chüan 55) is a subtype of ting-chen 頂眞(note the selection in Wen-hsüan is an anaphoric type, i.e., repetition of the same phrase at the beginning of successive verses, which is a variant of anadiplosis, or lien-huan 連環). The intentional exploration of some of the figures by the T'ang poets like P'i Jih-hsiu* and Liu Yü-hsi* has contributed to the so-called *tsa-t'i shih* (verse of miscellaneous forms) including *hui-wen* 廻文, *lien-chü* 聯句, *li-ho* 離合, *fan-fu* 反復, *shuang-sheng* 雙聲 and *tieh-yün* 疊韻.

A comparable phenomenon is narrative expansion of metaphoric mechanism into the allegoric genres of the parable and fable used in texts like *Chuang-tzu* and *Lieh-tzu* 列子. Besides the actual incorporation of allegory in a narrative (e.g., the "six thieves" episode in the late Ming novel *Hsi-yu pu,** ch. 14) there is also the elaboration of sterotyped expressions such as *jen-sheng-ju-meng* 人生如夢 in tales like the "Miao-chu po-chen" 廟祝柏枕 (Cypress Pillow of the Temple Curate) of the *chih-kuai** type and other pillow-stories like "Chen-chung chi" 枕中記 of the T'ang (cf. the use of rhetorical topoi in Medieval and Renaissance poetry). This kind of elaboration can be shown to be based on the techniques of "literalization of metaphor." One of the most striking examples of such narrative uses of figure is found in *Hsi-yu pu* where, besides the literalization of the trope "life is like a dream," characters are linguistically "derived;" e.g., the character called Hsiao Yüeh-wang 小月王 (Little Moon King) is created "anagramatically" from the components of the word *ch'ing* 情 (passion, feeling) (see *hsi-tzu* 析字, no. 29, below). Many of the stories in P'u Sung-ling's *Liao-chai chih-i** and Shen Ch'i-feng's 沈起鳳 (b. 1741) *Hsieh-tou* 諧鐸 contain such narrativized instances of figures. Similarly, syntactic figures like *ts'eng-ti* 層遞 (gradation, no. 12) often appear on a textual level as a device of intensification (one of the most common methods of sustaining the reader's interest in the *wu-hsia hsiao-shuo* 武俠小說 [stories of gallants and heroes] is the successive introduction of characters who are increasingly more powerful and more skillful). Antithetical parallelism can also be transformed to the larger scale of narration as a way of organizing the events and episodes in both narrative and drama (e.g., the juxtaposition of different locales and the contrast of moods in *P'i-p'a chi**). In this connection we should mention that traditional commentators of vernacular diction like Chin Sheng-t'an* have accumulated a set of critical terms (often metaphorical) to describe the narrative techniques and devices (e.g., *ts'ao-she hui-hsien* 草蛇灰線 "the dim traces of a grass snake," i.e., the use of recurrent motifs; *heng-yün tuan-shan* 橫雲斷山 "intruding clouds severing the mountain," i.e., interruption of an event or topic to be picked up later). These may be considered, in a sense, figures of thought.

VI. Conclusion

It should be emphasized that systematic study of Chinese rhetoric has just begun. The discussion above has tried to suggest some procedures and has touched on a few questions, but many tasks, including the preliminary ones, remain. The first step is sifting through the traditional sources for related material (Cheng Tien and Tan Ch'üan-chi, 1980, have greatly facilitated this), after which there should be a more rigorous analysis and description of the figures and the construction of taxonomy based on the nature of the language. An investigation of how figurative language is related to the operation of literary work, both in the context of a period and that of an individual's corpus, can then begin.

VII. Appendix: Rhetorical Figures

A few words of explanation are in order. Generally the distinction between schemes and tropes (conceiving one as primarily a matter of syntactic figuration and the other that of semantic transference), with the items belonging to the former listed before those belonging to the latter, has been maintained. This distinction, however, is sometimes difficult to keep and there are overlappings. At the end of the list some devices are included which may not be figures properly speaking, but they have been traditionally treated as types of *hsiu-tz'u-ke* 修辭格 and might be useful for discourse on traditional literature. Many of the figures and illustrative examples are taken from Ch'en Wang-tao and other modern works, sometimes modified for the present purpose. Subtypes are given under main entries, but this practice is not consistently observed. The definition of figures is given in a traditional way, and the distinction between "expression" (form of expression) and "content" (form of content) is adhered to, but loosely; a more rigorous system of description has yet to be worked out. For some of the entries, comparable names or equivalents from Western classical rhetoric are suggested but it should be understood that the similarity of mechanism does not always entail similarity of function or status (e.g., irony), and some Chinese figures in fact are defined functionally rather than operationally.

1. *She-wen* 設問 (hyopophora): an exposition or emotive expression that uses a question-and-answer format; subdividable into two types—
   (a) *T'i-wen* 提問, in which the question format is used for an exposition purpose: 何以守位？曰仁（易〞繫辭傳〞）. By what means can one safeguard the position? The answer is *jen*.
   (b) *Chi-wen* 激問, in which the question functions like an exclamatory expression and no answer is expected, as in a rhetorical question: 誰能思不歌？誰能飢不食？（子夜歌）. Who can refrain from singing when stirred by longing?/who would abstain from food when hungry?

2. *T'iao-t'o* 跳脫 (aposiopesis, interruption; cf. anapodoton): an expression or statement that stops halfway, with the unuttered portion understood: 五年 . . . 諸侯及將相相與尊漢王爲皇帝。

   …漢王三讓，不得已，曰 ‘〞諸君必以爲便…便國家…〞 甲午，乃卽皇帝位氾水之 陽（史記〞漢高祖 本紀〞）. In the fifth year . . . the lords of various states and generals and ministers all deferred to the Prince of Han [Liu Pang], wishing to make him emperor . . . The Prince of Han declined several times, but could not extract himself. So he said, "If you gentlemen insist that this . . . will benefit the country . . . ." So on the day of *chia-wu* he ascended the throne at the city north to the Ssu River.

3. *Tao-chuang* 倒裝 (anastrophe): a reversal or unusual arrangement of words: 香豆啄餘鸚鵡粒 （杜甫："秋興八首之八"）fragrant grains, pecked (and) left-over, parrot kernels (where "fragrant grains" and "parrot" are syntactically reversed, as 鸚鵡啄餘香豆粒, "the parrot pecked and left the fragrant grain-kernels," would be the normal order). Related to this scheme is the device called *hsüan-tsao* 旋造, a "twisted" construction: 泉甘酒洌（歐陽修"醉翁亭記"）The spring is sweet, the wine cool . . . (where the stative verbs *lieh* 洌, "cool," and *kan* 甘, "sweet," are predicated of "wrong" subjects due to a syntactic inversion).

4. *Fei-pai* 飛白 (cf. barbarismus): unintended deviation in a spoken expression intentionally retained in a written form, such as Chou Ch'ang's 周倉 stuttered speech in his remonstration against Han Kao-tsu's 漢高祖 intention to replace the heir-apparent with a different son: "臣期期以爲不可"（史記."張著列傳"）"I am di . . . di . . . deeply convinced it should not be done . . ."

5. *Ts'ang-tz'u* 藏詞 (cf. ellipsis): a reference to a word or phrase which forms a part of a set expression by mentioning only the other portion of the expression; something like a "syntagmatic metonymy." According to whether it is the beginning or the ending portion that

is meant but unexpressed, the figure is subdivided into *ts'ang-t'ou-yü* 藏頭語 and *hsieh-hou-yü* 歇後語, besides which there is also a related device called *p'i-chieh-yü* 譬解語:

(a) *Ts'ang-t'ou-yü*, hiding the beginning portion, as implied in the use of the phrase *erh-li* 而立, ". . . and was established," to mean "thirty years old," because Confucius said, "I . . . at age thirty, established myself," 吾 [. . .] 三十而立. (論語 "爲政").

(b) *Hsieh-hou-yü*, hiding the ending portion, such as using the phrase *niu-tou-ma* 牛頭馬 to refer to the word *mien* 面, "face," based on the set expression *niu-tou ma-mien* 牛頭馬面 (ox-headed and horse-faced). This device is rather important in the colloquial language.

(c) *P'i-chieh-yü*, an "explanatory formula" in which the intended term, instead of being left out, is hidden in a pun that forms part of the expression. Like (a) and (b), this is also often used playfully and mostly in the colloquial language: 豬八戒的脊梁—悟能之背 Chu Pa-chieh's spine, i.e., the back of Wu-neng (which is a circumlocutory way of saying *wu-neng chih pei* 無能之輩 or "useless man/bunch of men" by punning on *wu-neng chih pei* 悟能之背).

6. *Lien-chi* 連及: use of a character not appropriate for the context but "tugged on" due to its close association with the word intended (as part of a compound or a set expression): 潤之以風雨 (易. "繫辭傳") Moisten it with *wind* and rain.

7. *Hsiang-ch'ien* 鑲嵌 or *p'ing-tzu-fa* 拼字法 (diacope): an "inlaying" or interlacing of a set phrase in another set phrase, i.e., a "dovetailing." This is an effective way of turning cliches into something fresh: 歡喜 (happy and joyous) + 天地 (heaven and earth) = 歡天喜地 (exuberantly happy). 花柳 (flower and willow) + 明暗 (light and dark) = 柳暗花明又一村 (the willow grove shadowy, the flowers brighten up: another village ahead). 綺羅 (silk and gauze) + 愁恨 (sorrowful and grievous) = 愁羅恨綺 (silk is sadness; gauze, grief).

8. *Fu-tz'u* 複辭 (ploce; cf. anatanaclasis, polyptoton): a repetition of the same character in close interval with a change of meaning or syntactic function: 老吾老以及人之老 (孟子. "梁惠王上") treat-with-respect-due-to-the-elders the elders of our own families and in extension, the elders of other families.

9. *Tui-ou* 對偶 or *tui-chang* 對仗 (parallelism, antithesis, parison): conjoining of expressions with contrasting or similar meanings by syntactic and often tonal coordinations: 雲從龍，風從虎 (易. "文言") "Clouds follow the dragon; winds follow the tiger." This is part of a literary device that is frequent in the Chinese language at all levels and in all genres. The next entry lists some of its variations.

10. *Ts'o-tsung* 錯綜: variations of parallelism, seen in three subtypes:

(a) *Hu-wen* 互文: synonymous substitution for a parallel expression: 仁有數．義有長短大小 (禮記 "表記") *Jen* shows in several forms: *i* comes in various shapes and sizes.

(b) *Chiao-ts'o* 交錯: variation in syntactic positioning: 裙拖六幅湘江水，鬢聳巫山一段雲 (李商隱 "贈鄭相井歌姬") skirt trails six scenes (of) Hsiang River's waters; tresses curl up Wu Mountain's one strand (of) clouds.

(c) *Ts'o-tui* 蹉對: similar to the above, but the parallel characters are transported to form a "mis-match" (cf. *hsüan-tsao* in 3): 春殘葉密花枝少，睡起茶多酒盞疏 (王安石 "晚春詩") spring wearing out, leaves grow dense, flowers few; waking up, tea there is plenty, wine cups scanty (where 多, "plenty," and 疏, "scanty," in line 2 are inversed in their match with 少, "few," and 密, "dense," in line 1).

11. *Ting-chen* 頂眞 (anadiplosis, redouble): a repetition of the last character or phrase of a line (or clause) in a series of lines. There are two kinds:

(a) *Lien-chu* 聯珠: the repetition is carried on continuously between consecutive clauses: 幽泉怪石．無遠不到，到則披草而坐．傾壺而醉．醉則更相枕以臥．臥而夢 . . . (柳宗元 "始得西山宴遊記") . . . The secluded springs and strange-looking rocks, however distant they were, there was none that we did not reach; reaching them, we would flatten the grass to sit and pour out the wine jug to get drunk; drunk, we pillowed on each other to sleep; to sleep was to dream . . .

(b) *Lien-huan* 連環: when the repetition occurs only after an intervention of a longer sequence of words: 昭明有融，高朗令終，令終有俶，公尸嘉告，其告維何？籩豆靜嘉，朋友攸攝，攝以威儀，威儀孔時，君子有孝子‥(詩 大雅 "旣醉")

131

> May their shining light beam mildly upon you;
> High fame and good end to all you do.
> That good end is well assured;
> The impersonator of the Ancient tells a lucky story.
>
> The lucky story, what is it.
> 'Your bowls and dishes are clean and good;
> The friends that helped you
> Helped with perfect manners.
>
> Perfect manners, irreproachable;
> My lord will have pious sons, . . .'
>
> (adapted from Waley)

12. *Ts'eng-ti* 層遞(gradation, climax; cf. auxesis): a succession of at least three related expressions so arranged as to show either a mounting or a descending in their import. Somewhat similar to *lien-chu* (11.b) this also looks like a sorites: 天時不如地利. 地利不如人和 （孟子. " 公孫丑下") The temporal circumstances are less crucial than the spatial factors; the spatial factors not as decisive as human endeavors.

13. *Mo-chuang* 摹狀 or *mo-ni* 模擬(cf. onomatopoeia): formation of a modifier or a predicate expression by reduplication of a character, usually suggestive of some properties of the subject: 車轔轔. 馬蕭蕭. 行人弓箭各在腰 （杜甫. " 兵車行") War chariots rattling *lin-lin,*/the horses whinnying *siao-siao;*/each traveler with bow and arrows on his belt.

14. *Wan-ch'u* 婉曲 or *wei-wan* 委婉(cf. periphrasis, euphemism): a circumlocuted way of presenting a subject or suggesting something (cf. *t'iao-t'o*, 2). This is subdivided into three types:
    (a) *Hung-t'o* 烘托: hinting at the subject by elimination of alternatives; sometimes considered as a use of foil: 新來瘦. 非關病酒. 不是悲秋 （李清照. " 鳳凰台上憶吹簫") Lately I have grown thin:/ and it's not due to too much wine,/ nor is it from grieving over the autumn.
    (b) *Shan-shuo* 閃爍: hedging: 孟武伯問子路仁乎 ? 子曰. 不知也. （論語. " 公冶長") The Earl of Meng-wu asked [Confucius] whether Tzu-lu was *jen* (benevolent). The master said, "That I do not know."
    (c) *Wan-chuan* 婉轉: euphemism and observation of taboos, such as referring to the death of a high-ranking person metaphorically as "the collapse of the mountain range" 山陵崩.

15. *Ching-tse* 警策(apothegm, cf. paradox): a "striking" statement. Sometimes the assertion of a truth in a seemingly self-contradictory expression: 善游者溺. 善騎者墮（文子. " 符言") A good swimmer is bound to be drowned; a skillful equestrian bound to fall.

16. *Ying-ch'eng* 映襯(cf. oxymoron, antithesis): juxtaposition of antonyms within the same phrase or clause. There are two kinds,
    (a) *Fan-ying* 反映: two antonyms put in a predication relation or one term used as modifier of the other: 雅的這樣俗 （儒林外史. ch. 29) So very vulgarly refined.
    (b) *Tui-cheng* 對襯: an antithetical parallelism functionally defined, i.e., one term used as a foil for another: 一將功成萬骨枯. （曹松. " 己亥歲二首之一 ") The aim of a general accomplished; tens of thousands of men turned into dry bones.

17. *Shuang-kuan* 雙關 or *hsieh-yin* 諧隱(paronomasia, cf. syllepsis, zeugma, antanoclasis): playing on the sound and meaning of characters to produce a double-entendre. This is most prominent in the songs of Wu （吳聲歌) where punnings on the names of objects abound, e.g., *p'i*匹(as in 布匹 , "bolt of fabric," and 匹偶 , "couple, man and wife") and *kuan*關(as in 關門 , "close the door," and 關心 , "concern the heart"): 裊晴絲 [情思] 飛來閑庭院 (湯顯祖 牡丹亭sc. 10) The gently wavering gossamer threads [thoughts of love] waft to the leisurely courtyard.

18. *Pi-yü* 比喻 or *p'i-yü* 譬喻(metaphor, simile): essentially a device of explanation in Chinese usage (by comparison, examples, etc.), this trope can be seen as the perception or understanding of one thing in terms of another, but instead of substitution, it emphasizes comparison. It is normally subdivided into three major types, depending on how the tenor is expressed:
    (a) *Ming-yü* 明喻(simile): the tenor explicitly related to the vehicle by a particle: 以若所爲 . 求若所欲 .猶緣木而求魚也(孟子. " 梁惠王上 ") Hoping to achieve what you want by means of what you have done is like going up a tree to seek fish.

(b) *Yin-yü*隱喻 (metaphor properly speaking): no particle is supplied to indicate the relationship between the tenor and the vehicle: 嗟怨之水，特結憤泉 (庾信．"擬連珠") The water of grievance gathers and turns into a spring of anger.

(c) *Chieh-yü*借喻 or *an-pi*暗比 (cryptic metaphor): both the tenor and the ground are omitted while the vehicle itself tends to become a symbol. In the example below, the "pine and cypress" are symbolic of a superior man or *chün-tzu*君子 (tenor), specifically about his holding fast to principles under trying circumstances (ground). 歲寒然後知松柏之後凋也 (論語．"子罕") Only when the year turns cold does one realize the pine and cypress are the last to lose their leaves.

Ch'en K'uei in his *Wen-tse* mentions the construction of metaphoric expressions by distinguishing ten types of *yü* which include (a) and (b) above and others that are either combinations and extensions of basic comparative device of metaphor or metaphoric mode based on other criteria (e.g. *tui-yü* 對喻 is a metaphor couched in parallelism; *chien-yü*簡喻 is based on structure, and *hsü-yü*虛喻 on referentiality). A closer analysis of the various criteria implied in his classification might reveal more of the Chinese conception of metaphor, shedding light on how it functions and what its motivation is.

19. *Chieh-tai*借代 (metonymy, synecdoche; cf. kenning, epithet): using the name of one thing for that of something else associated with it by way of contiguity of part-whole and species-genus relationships. The two major subtypes, *p'ang-chieh*旁借 and *tui-tai*對代, correspond to synecdoche and metonymy respectively and each is further dividable into other varieties:

(a) *P'ang-chieh* (metonymy): substitution of a characteristic or trait of an entity for the entity itself, the location for the entity, the author or producer for the entity, the tool or material for the entity (they may sometimes overlap): 紈袴不餓死．儒冠多誤身 (杜甫．"贈韋左丞") The 'silk trousers' [i.e., the wealthy] never die from hunger;/a 'scholar's cap' [i.e., a literatus' career] often leads one astray.

(b) *Tui-tai* (synecdoche): substitution of the whole for the part (and vice versa), the specific for the general (and vice versa), the concrete for the abstract (and vice versa) and cause for effect (and vice versa): 過盡千帆皆不是．斜暉脈脈水悠悠 (溫庭筠．"望江南") Thousands of sails have passed by—none is it;/the sunset glows as if full of feeling and the water flows into the distance. 被堅執銳．義不如公．(史記．"項羽本紀") "In wearing the firm [i.e., armor] and holding the sharp [i.e., weapon], I, Yi, am not your equal."

20. *Pi-ni*比擬 (cf. personification): a type of metaphor involving the presentation of the animate in terms of the inanimate (and vice versa) or the human in terms of non-human (and vice versa). According to whether the comparison is that of the inanimate with the animate (or human) or the human with the non-human (or inanimate), two subtypes are recognized:

(a) *Ni-jen*擬人: personification of inanimate or insentient things: 蠟炬成灰淚始乾 (李商隱．"無題詩") The candle stops shedding tears only when it turns into ashes.

(b) *Ni-wu*擬物: comparison of a human with an inanimate object: 姑山半峯雪．瑤水一枝蓮 (白居易．"女道士") [She is] the snow on the side of the Ku Mountain;/a lotus standing amidst the Jasper Pool. 姑山半峯雪，瑤水一枝蓮．

21. *Nien-lien*拈連: a type of metaphor created by extending the predicative verb of one subject (or object) to another adjacent to it: 午睡醒來，愁未醒 (張先．"天仙子") Emerging from the afternoon nap,/but not from sorrows.

22. *Kan-hsing*感興: a situation (or a set of events) evoking another situation, the two being understood to entertain a metaphoric relationship but the point of comparison remains unspecified. Basically the *hsing* mode as used in the *Shih ching*, this is not a trope in the normal sense (see discussion above): 野有死麕．白茅包之；有女懷春．吉士誘之 (詩國風．"野有死麕") In the wilds there is a dead doe; With white rushes we cover her. There was a lady longing for the spring; A fine knight seduced her. (tr. A. Waley)

23. *K'ua-shih* 夸飾 or *k'ua-chang*誇張 (hyperbole, overstatement): an exaggerated or extravagant expression not to be taken literally: 力拔山兮．氣蓋世．(項羽．"垓下歌") My strength can uproot a mountain; my valor holds the world under its sway.

24. *Tao-fan*倒反 (cf. irony): an expression used with a meaning opposed to its literal or habitual usage; subdivided into two kinds:

133

(a) *Tao-tz'u* 倒辭: usually an endearment expressed by a seemingly antagonistic term, such as calling a beloved person *yüan-chia* 冤家 "my adversary" or *k'e-tseng-ts'ai* 可憎材 "you hateful person."

(b) *Fan-yü* 反語 (cf. sarcasm): an affirmative expression or statement meant to have an opposite intent, such as in the Jester Meng's 優孟 remark below, made when he heard that King Chuang of Ch'u 楚莊王 intended to bury his favorite horse with the funeral ritual normally accorded a high-ranking official. "馬者王之所愛也." 以楚國堂堂之大．何求不得？ 而以大夫之禮葬之？薄！請以人君禮葬之．(史記 " 滑稽列傳 ") "The horse is very dear to the King and with a grand state like Ch'u, what could not be asked and obtained? To bury it with the rite of a great official? No, it's inadequate. I propose to bury it with a funeral rite accorded a king."

Sarcasm or irony has never been prominent in the Chinese tradition. When criticism is called for, it is the *feng* 諷 mode, or "indirect criticism," that is normally preferred, for it avoids affronting the addressee.

25. *Chuan-p'in* 轉品 (anthimeria): using one part of speech to function as another, a rather common trope in Chinese language for its fluidity in such transferences: 夏雨雨人 (說苑. " 貴德 ") Summer rain rains on a person.

26. *Yin-yung* 引用 (adaptation): adaptation of phrases or clauses with or without variation: 欲待曲終尋問取．人不見． 數峯青 (蘇軾. " 江城子 ") Hoping to approach her after the music ended,/ but then she was gone;/several peaks stood green (an adaptation of 曲終人不見. 江上數峯青 (錢起. " 省試湘靈鼓瑟詩 ").

This device, like most of following entries, is not a figure of speech but it represents a phenomenon or device first advocated theoretically by Huang T'ing-chien* and gradually grew pervasive in the late *tz'u* and particularly late *ch'ü* in which almost all the lines in a poem are *yin-yung* adaptations, the extreme form of it being the practice of *chi-chü* 集句, or "collection of lines," as seen in some of the southern dramas, at the conclusion of a scene.

27. *Yin-ching* 引經 (argumentum adverecundiam): an appeal to the authority of canonical texts by actual citation. The locus classicus sometimes is given but need not always be: 仁之興義. 敬之與和． 相反而相成．易曰. " 天下同歸而殊途．一致而百慮." (漢書 " 藝文志 ") Regarding *jen* and *i*, *ching* and *ho*, the terms in each pair exist in opposition yet bring each other to completion. The *I-ching* says, "The world goes different ways but returns to the same source; it has hundreds of concerns but all attend to one goal."

In its specific usage, this device refers to the practice during the Warring States period of citing the classics (the *Shih, Shu, I*, etc.) which in the Han extended to include other canonical texts (*Lun-yü, Lao-tzu*, etc.). The pre-Ch'in practice of quoting from the *Shih* is important for its social, political, and diplomatic function, and there are different ways of going about it (quoting a passage out of its context, for instance, is a permissible practice). *Yin-ching* always uses the source in a positive light, unlike *chi-ku* (next entry) in which early material may be cited either with a positive or negative interpretation (Wang Li, 1962).

28. *Chi-ku* 稽古 or *yung-shih* 用事 (allusion, cf. exemplum): a reference to incidents, stories, or events contained in an earlier text (again the source need not always be given): 故士或自盛以囊. 或鑿坏以遁. (楊雄 " 解嘲 ") Therefore, a *shih* may 'hide himself in a sack,' or 'escape by digging through the wall' (the first allusion referring to Fan Chü's 范睢 escape; the second to Yen Ho's 顏闔 flight from an offer of official position; see 史記, "范睢、蔡澤列傳" and 淮南子, "積俗訓").

Use of allusion is a prominent phenomenon in Chinese literature; historical allusions are used to relate the present to the past and to give meaning to the current events (Kao and Mei, 1978; Lattimore, 1973).

29. *Hsi-tzu* 析字 (cf. anagram, paronomasia): a play on the shape of a character (radicals and components), its sound (phonological figuration), or its meaning (synonymity, etymology), largely related to the peculiar qualities of Chinese orthography. It is divided into three types, each with subdivisions:

(a) *Hua-hsing* 化形: related to the character formation,

  (i) *Li-ho* 離合: a dissection of a character into its components, such as calling a "soldier"兵(*ping*) a *ch'iu-pa*丘八, referring to the surname Chang張 as *kung ch'ang* 弓長, or as in the following song that puns on Tung Cho's董卓 name:千里草何青青; 十日卜,不得生 (後漢書 "五行志") (a thousand *li* of grass,/how green it is;/for ten days the prognostications have indicated,/it will not live).

(ii) *Tseng-sun*增損: reference to a character by "substitution" and "addition," such as the tour de force play on the surname of Wang Hsin王昕 in the following: 有言則 誦, 近犬便狂, 加頸足 而為馬 ，施角尾而為羊 (北齊書 "徐之材傳") When given a "word"言, he/it [王] is prone to "cheat/lie (?)"詿[cf.詿]; put next to a "dog"犬/犭, it turns "mad"狂; applying a neck and feet, it becomes a "horse"馬; and added horns and a tail, it changes into a "goat"羊.

(b) *Hsieh-yin*諧音: phonological punning:

(i) *Chieh-yin*借音 (cf. syllepsis): a homonymic pun pointing to a semantic association: 談 笑有鴻儒．往來無白丁 (劉禹錫．"陋室銘") Among his friends are learned scholars,/of his acquaintances, none is a commoner (where the first syllable of *hung-ju*鴻儒, "learned scholars," is a homonym of 紅, "red," which contrasts semantically with the 白, "white," of *pai-ting*白丁, "commoners").

(ii) *Ch'ieh-chiao*切腳: reference to the sound of a word or character by means of its *fan-ch'ieh* 反切 representation. 遺我新蒲入突欒 (王廷珪．" 甯公瑞惠蒲團 ") He bestowed on me new rush to make *t'u-luan*/mats (where 突欒 *t'u-luan* is a phonetic spelling that conflates to yield 團, *t'uan*, i.e., "mats").

(iii) *Shuang-fan*雙反: an application of (ii) in both normal order and reverse order to yield a two-character compound. 或謂後主名叔寶．反語為少福．亦敗亡之徵云．(南史" 陳後主紀 ") It was said that the Last Emperor's name Shu-pao (/siuk päu/) in *fan-yü* [i.e., *shuang-fan*] would be *shao-fu* (/siau b'iuk/) ("lack of blessings"), which was portentous of his downfall.

Such plays on words, like *li-ho* above, occur often in the folk tradition and reflect a system of belief in which omens and portents (e.g. as recorded in the "天文志" and "五行志" of *Han-shu*, are conceived as "signs" or signals pointing to the correspondence between different domains of reality such as between the "heavenly pattern"天文 and the "human pattern"人文).

(c) *Yen-i*衍義: a play that explores various semantic paradigms of the language (synonymity, antonymity, polarity, etymological categories):

(i) *Ch'ien-fu*牽附: generation of an expression based on polar relationship of lexes, such as Lin Chih-yang's "invention" of the titles *Yu chuan*右傳(lit., "right transmission") and *Shao tzu*少子(lit., "young master") by the association with *Tso-chuan* (lit., "left transmission") and *Lao-tzu* (lit., "old master"—李汝珍. 鏡花緣 , chs. 22, 31).

(ii) *Tai-huan*代換: direct replacement of characters by synonyms, as the replacement between the two lines, 天聲動北陬 — 神威震坎隅 (cited in 郎瑛 . 七修類稿 , 49) Heaven's voices shook the northern corner—Divine forces agitate the north nook.

(iii) *Sou-tzu*廋辭 or *yin-yü*隱語: a transference of linguistic codes by etymological recombination (cf. *li-ho*, 29, a, i, above); the best known example of this probably is the decoding of 黃絹幼歸外孫韲臼 (yellow-silk, young-woman, daughter's-son, garlic-mortar) to read as 絕妙好辭 (absolutely wonderful exquisite expressions), where each of the last four characters is seen to be composed of two parts which match the compounds in the original string: silk-colored, girl-young, daughter-son, mortar-peppery (see the anecdote in *Shih-shuo hsin-yü*,* ch. 11, "捷悟").

30. *Hui-wen*廻文(cf. palindrome): strings of characters or lines of a poem arranged to yield grammatically well-formed sentences or meaningful expressions read either forward or backward: 碧峯千點數鷗輕 (蘇軾 "題金山寺") Blue peaks, a thousand dots; several gulls [floating] lightly (when read from left to right, i.e., downward from the top in traditional printing). Light gulls, several dots; a thousand peaks, [all] blue (when read from right to left, or upward from the bottom).

This has become the curio par excellence of Chinese language and is often used as an example to show its monosyllabic constituency and its syntactic flexibility. The verse form based on the palindromic construction is called *hui-wen shih* 廻文詩; several varieties have evolved. The most complex is the *hsüan-chi t'i* 璇璣體 in which strings of characters arranged in rows and columns (or a single string coiling on itself to form a disc-shaped block) yield numerous "poems" by changing the point of inception and the direction of reading. Examples of various kinds of palindromic verse can be found in *Hui-wen lei-chü* 廻文類聚.

BIBLIOGRAPHY:

Brooke-Rose, Christine. 1958. *A Grammar of Metaphor.* London.

Chang, Hsin-chang. *Allegory and Courtesy in Spenser; A Chinese View.* Edinburgh, 1955.

Chang, Hsüeh-ch'eng 章學誠. *Wen shih t'ung-i* 文史通義. *SPPY.*

Chang, Wen-chih 張文治. 1937. *Ku-shu hsiu-tz'u li* 古書修辭例. Shanghai.

Chang, Yen 張嚴. 1975. *Hsiu-tz'u lun-shuo yü fang-fa* 修辭論說與方法. Taipei.

Chao, I 趙翼. 1960. *Kai-yü ts'ung-k'ao* 陔餘叢考. Rpt. Taipei.

Ch'en, Chieh-pai 陳介白. *1931. Hsiu-tz'u-hsüeh* 修辭學. Shanghai.

Ch'en, I-tseng 陳繹曾. 1972. *Wen-shuo* 文說. Rpt. Taipei.

Ch'en, K'uei 陳騤. 1962. *Wen-tse* 文則. Rpt. Peking.

Ch'en, Wang-tao 陳望道 1964. *Hsiu-tz'u-hsüeh fa-fan* 修辭學發凡. 1932, rpt. Hong Kong.

Cheng, Tien and T'an Ch'üan-chi 譚全基, comp. 1980. *Chung-kuo hsiu-tz'u-hsüeh tzu-liao hui-pien* 中國修辭學資料滙編. Peking. Makes available a comprehensive collection of excerpts from practically all relevant traditional sources except for the standard, book-length treatises like the *Wen-hsin tiao-lung** and *Shih-jen yü-hsieh.**

Cheng, Tzu-yü 鄭子瑜. 1965. *Chung-kuo hsiu-tz'u-hsüeh te pien-ch'ien* 中國修辭學的變遷. Tokyo.

*Chiao-jan.** *Shih shih* 詩式. *SPTK.*

Ch'ien, Ta-hsin 錢大昕. 1963. *Shih-chia-chai yang-hsin lu* 十駕齋養薪錄. Rpt. Taipei.

Chin, Chao-tzu 金兆梓. 1932. *Shih-yung kuo-wen hsiu-tz'u hsüeh* 實用國文修辭學. Shanghai.

Chou, Hui 周煇. *Ch'ing-po tsa-chih* 清波雜誌. *Chih-pu-tsu-chai ts'ung-shu.*

Chung, Jung 鍾嶸. 1958. *Shih-p'in.** Peking.

Culler, Jonathan. 1975. *Structuralist Poetics.* Ithaca.

Curtius, E. R. 1967. *European Literature and the Latin Middle Ages.* W.R. Trask, tr. Rpt. Princeton.

Dubois, J. *et al.* 1970. *Rhetorique generale.* Paris.

Ducrot, Oswald and T. Todorov. 1979. *Encyclopedic Dictionary of the Sciences of Language.* Catherine Porter, tr. Baltimore.

Fan, Heng 范梈. *Mu-t'ien chin-yü* 木天禁語. *TSCCCP.*

Fang, P'eng-ch'eng 方鵬程. 1975. *Hsien-Ch'in ho-tsung lien-heng shuo-fu ch'uan-po te yen-chiu* 先秦合縱連橫說服傳播的研究. Taipei.

Frankel, Hans H. 1976. *The Flowering Plum and the Palace Lady.* New Haven.

Hsieh, Chen 謝榛. *Ssu-ming shih-hua* 四溟詩話. *TSCCCP.*

Hsü, Chin-t'ing 徐芹庭. 1970. *Hsiu-tz'u-hsüeh fa-wei* 修辭學發微. Taipei.

Hsü, Shih-tseng 徐師曾. 1965. *Wen-t'i ming-pien hsü shuo* 文體明辨序說. Hong Kong.

Hu, Chen-heng 胡震亨. *T'ang-yin kuei-ch'ien.** *SKCS.*

Hu, Shih. 1928. *Development of the Logical Method in Ancient China.* Third ed. Shanghai.

Hu, Tzu 胡仔. *T'iao-hsi yü-yen ts'ung-hua.** *SPPY.*

Huang, Ch'ing-hsüan 黃慶宣. 1975. *Hsiu-tz'u-hsüeh* 修辭學. Taipei.

Hung, Mai.** *Jung-chai sui-pi* 容齋隨筆. *SPTK.*

Jakobson, Roman. 1960. "Linguistics and Poetics," in *Style in Language,* T. Sebeok, ed., pp. 350-377. Cambridge, Mass.

Jakobson, Roman and Morris Halle. 1971. *Fundamentals of Language.* The Hague.

Jen, Fang 任昉. *Wen-chang yüan-ch'i* 文章緣起. *TSCCCP.*

Kao, Yu-kung and Mei Tsu-lin. 1971. "Syntax, Diction and Imagery in T'ang Poetry," *HJAS,* 30, 49-136.

———. 1978. "Meaning, Metaphor, and Allusion in T'ang Poetry," *HJAS,* 38, 281-356.

Knechtges, David. 1976. *The Han Rhapsody: A Study of the Fu of Yang Hsiung.* Cambridge, England.

Ku, Yen-wu.** *Jih chih lu* 日知錄. *SPPY.*

Kuei, Yu-kuang.** 1972. *Wen-chang chih-nan* 文章指南. Rpt. Taipei.

Kūkai 空海. 1975. *Bunkyō hifuron.** Peking.

Kuo, Shao-yü 郭紹虞. 1979. *Han-yü yü-fa hsiu-tz'u hsin-t'an* 漢語語法修辭新探. Peking.

Lanham, Richard. 1968. *A Handlist of Rhetorical Terms.* Berkeley.

Lattimore, David. "Allusion and T'ang Poetry" in *Perspectives,* pp. 405-439.

Li, Ch'i-ch'ing 李耆卿. *Wen-chang ching-i* 文章精義. *SKCS.*

Li, T'iao-yuan 李調元. *Yü-ts'un shih-hua* 雨村詩話. *TSCCCP.*

Liang, Chang-chu 梁章鉅, comp. 1976. *Chih-i ts'ung-hua* 制義叢話. Rpt. Taipei.

———, comp. 1976. *Shih-lü ts'ung-hua* 試律叢話. Rpt. Taipei.

Liang, Shao-jen 梁紹壬. *Liang-pan ch'iu-yü-an sui-pi* 兩般秋雨盦隨筆, in *Ch'ing-tai pi-chi ts'ung-k'an* 清代筆記叢刊.

Lin, Shu.* 1921. *Wei-lu lun-wen* 畏廬論文 (i.e., *Ch'un-chüeh-chai lin-wen* 春覺齋論文). Shanghai.

Liu, Chih-chi.* *Shih-t'ung* 史通. *SPPY.*

Liu, Hsiang.* *Shuo-yüan* 說苑. *SPTK.*

Liu, Hsieh. *Wen-hsin tiao-lung* 文心雕龍.*

Liu, James J. Y. 1962. *The Art of Chinese Poetry.* Chicago.

———. 1975. *Chinese Theories of Literature.* Chicago.

Murphy, James J., ed. 1972. *A Synoptic History of Classical Rhetoric.* New York.

Oliver, Robert T. 1971. *Communication and Culture in Ancient India and China.* Syracuse, N.Y.

Owen, Stephen. 1984. *Omen of the World.* Madison, Wis.

———. 1979. "Transparencies: Reading the T'ang Lyric," *HJAS,* 39, 231-251.

——— and Walter L. Reed. 1979. "A Motive for Metaphor," *Criticism,* 21.4 (Fall), 287-306.

Puttenham, George. 1936. *The Arte of English Poesie.* Gladys D. Willcock and Alice Walker, eds. Cambridge, England.

Richards, I. A. 1936. *The Philosophy of Rhetoric.* New York.

Sacks, Sheldon, ed. 1979. *On Metaphor.* Chicago.

Schlepp, Wayne. 1970. *San-ch'ü, Technique and Imagery.* Madison, Wisconsin.

Shao, Po 邵博. *Wen-chien hou-lu* 聞見後錄. *TSCCCP.*

Shibles, Warren, ed. 1972. *Essays on Metaphor.* Whitewater, Wisconsin.

T'ang, Piao 唐彪. *Tu-chu tso-wen p'u* 讀書作文譜. Rpt. Taipei, 1976.

T'ang, Yüeh 唐鉞. 1933. *Hsiu-tz'u-ko* 修辭格. 1923, rpt. Shanghai.

Todorov, Tzvetan. 1967. *Littérature et signification.* Paris.

Tuve, Rosemond. 1947. *Elizabethan and Metaphysical Imagery: Renaissance Poetics and Twentieth Century Critics.* Chicago.

Wang, C. H. 1974. *The Bell and the Drum.* Berkeley.

Wang, Chung 汪中. *Shu hsüeh* 述學. *Huang Ch'ing ching-chieh* 皇清經解.

———. *Lun-heng* 論衡. *SPTK.*

Wang, Jo-hsü.* *Hu-nan i-lao chi* 滹南遺老集. *SPTK.*

Wang, Li 王力. 1957. *Han-yü shih-lü hsüeh* 漢語詩律學. Peking.

Wei, Ch'ing-chih 魏慶之. 1958. *Shih-jen yü-hsieh.** Shanghai.

Wilson, Thomas. 1974. *Arte of Rhetorique.* G.H. Mair, ed. 1560, rpt. Oxford.

Wu, Na 吳訥. 1965. *Wen-chang pien-t'i hsü shuo* 文章辨體序說. Hong Kong.

Yang, Shen 楊慎. *Tan-ch'ien tsung-lu* 丹鉛總錄. *SKCS.*

Yang, Shu-ta 楊樹達. 1954. *Chung-kuo hsiu-tz'u-hsüeh* 中國修辭學 (i.e., *Han-wen wen-yen hsiu-tz'u-hsüeh* 漢文文言修辭學). 1933, rpt. Peking.

Yen, Yü 嚴羽. *Ts'ang-lang shih-hua.** *TSCCCP.*

Yü, Cheng-hsieh 俞正燮. *K'uei-ssu ch'un-kao* 癸巳存稿. *TSCCCP.*

Yü, Yüeh 俞樾. *Ku-shu i-i chü-li* 古書疑義舉例. *Huang-Ch'ing ching-chieh.*

TAOIST LITERATURE

PART I: THROUGH THE T'ANG DYNASTY
Stephen Bokenkamp

A. Introduction

THE literature of the Taoist religion displays a diversity in all respects commensurate with that of Chinese letters as a whole. Within the pages of the Taoist texts preserved for us in both canonical and extra-canonical sources can be found examples of narrative, verse, commentary, technical and descriptive writing, song, and even, in the form of liturgical performance, proto-drama. These writings stem from a succession of organized religious movements, originating with the Way of the Celestial Master 天師道 of Chang Tao-ling 張道陵, who received a revelation from the deified Lao-tzu 老子, traditionally in A.D. 142. Originally intended for transmission within a limited circle of initiates, these texts, through the missionary impetus of the religion and the mechanisms of dissemination made possible by imperial sponsorship, became widely known and exercised a profound influence on Chinese society and literature.

The very diversity of Taoist writings and of the social entities which produced them has led to a still unresolved controversy regarding the exact definition of Taoism. Attempts to firmly place the origins of Taoism have been confused by the tendency of Taoist writers to trace their ancestry not only to the mythological figures of China's past, but also to the shadowy magi of the Han known from such historical works as the *Shih-chi** and the *Han-shu* (see Pan Ku). Rather than enter into this controversy, the definition proposed by Michel Strickmann (1979), who suggests that the word "Taoist" be restricted to the Celestial Masters and their lineal descendants, will be adopted here. This decision is dictated by the material to be covered, for it is in relation to the Celestial Master movement that the earliest unique texts of Taoism are found—those texts that survive only in the Ming *Tao-tsang** 道藏 (Taoist Canon) and others, like those found at Tun-huang (see *Tun-huang wen-hsüeh*), which at one time were part of the Taoist canon. Thus, only brief mention will be accorded the pre-Han philosophical works found in the canon (see also *ching*).

Taoist literature will be treated here under five headings: (1) Revelation and Ritual, (2) Hagiography, (3) Historical and Topographical Monographs, (4) Philosophical and Alchemical Treatises, and (5) Exegeses and Encyclopedic Compilations. These general categories, it should be noted, by no means exhaust the variety of literary genres to be found in Taoist writings. Further, despite the proliferation of Taoist studies in the last decades, the enormity of the task—almost fifteen hundred titles are collected in the *Tao-tsang* alone—is such that Taoist studies may be said to be yet in its infancy. The present survey encompasses only a portion of the identified pre-Sung Taoist texts, selected both for their importance within the Taoist religion and for their influence on Chinese literature as a whole.

B. Revelation and Ritual

Taoism has been, from the beginning, a revealed religion. The scriptures of Taoism were generally viewed as "translations" into profane language of the powerful divine writs which inhere in the cosmos and are revealed to an elect few to aid them and their followers in attaining to their rightful positions in the immutable celestial order. Given this view of the written word as a central creative force everywhere immanent in the natural order of things, the authors of revealed literature spoke with the voice of divine authority, expressing themselves in a diversity of styles.

The prototypal Taoist revelation was that of the *Wu-ch'ien wen* 五千文 (Five Thousand [character] Classic). Better known as the *Tao-te-ching* (see *ching*), this text was granted Yin Hsi 尹喜, guardian of the passes, by Lao-tzu, deified in Taoism as the Most High Lord Lao. The *Hsiang-erh chuan* 想爾傳 (Hsiang-erh Commentary), a Celestial Master commentary to the *Tao-te-ching* attributed to the grandson of Chang Tao-ling, Chang Lu 張魯, provides insight into the use of this text in the early church as a mystic manual of physical and moral cultivation (Jao, 1956). This was the first scripture bestowed on the aspiring Taoist novitiate.

Documentation is scant for the formative years of Taoism, and the few texts which seem to date from this period have not yet fully yielded up their secrets to modern scholarship. Controversy remains concerning the exact nature of the relationships between one of the earliest surviving texts of Taoism, the lengthy *T'ai-p'ing ching* 太平經 (The Scripture of Great Peace, TT 746-755, HY 1093), the Way of Great Peace 太平道 of Chang Chüeh 張角 (*fl.* 180) in Eastern China, and the Way of the Celestial Master of Chang Tao-ling which began in Szechwan. The Scripture of Great Peace may preserve elements of two earlier Han-dynasty T'ai-p'ing books, one presented to the throne by Kan Chung-k'e 甘忠可 (*c.* 32-7 B.C.) and another revealed to Kan Chi 干吉 and sponsored before the Emperor Shun of the Han (r. A.D. 125-144) by Kung Ch'ung 宮崇. It contains additions made as late as the sixth century A.D. The earliest sections of the extant Scripture of Great Peace are written in the form of a colloquy between a divine emissary, the Celestial Master, and his disciples, the Six Perfected 六眞人. The pronouncements of the Celestial Master range over a variety of topics pertaining to the religious community he addresses, from the establishment of the perfect state based on cosmological principles to morals and techniques for long life.

No text has yet been identified as that bestowed on Chang Tao-ling by the "newly appeared" (新出) Lao-tzu, although later revelations sometimes claim that distinction. Indeed, the early church may not have been based on revelatory scripture as such. Taoist historical references to Lao-tzu's epiphany speak of Chang Tao-ling's investiture as Celestial Master rather than the transmission of a text. Scriptures which have been identified as including materials dating from the early years of the Celestial Master movement do not claim divine transmission, stemming rather from priests who speak with authority on the conditions and practices of the church. Such works regularly contain as their focus lists of *lu* 籙 (protective deities) which were bestowed on communicants in the church. It has been argued that the earliest documents of the Celestial Master movement were no more than this, charts and their accompanying registers bearing the name of deities and the twenty-four parish centers (Schipper, 1975). An abundance of such material can be found in a group of texts possibly stemming from the lost *Cheng-i fa-wen* 正一法文 (Ch'en Kuo-fu, 1963). One likely text, the *Cheng-i fa-wen t'ien-shih-chiao chieh-k'e ching* 正一法文天師教戒科經 (Text of the Law of Right Unity; Scripture of the Teachings, Precepts, and Ordinances of the Celestial Master, TT 563, HY 788) written *c.* 250, primarily concerns itself with the metaphysical underpinnings of the "true Way" 眞道, its importance to the welfare of the state, and priorities in the maintenance of ecclesiastical order. For the instruction of the laity, the text includes such easily memorized formulas as a set of five precepts and a "Teaching of the Celestial Master" 天師教 in seven-syllable verse reminiscent of the *Huang-t'ing ching* 黃庭經 (Scripture of the Yellow Court, see below).

Another class of writings important to the early church were the *lü* 律 (statutes) invoked in the Taoist's dealings with the unseen world both privately, in the meditation chamber, and in collective ritual. The canon contains the *Hsüan-tu lü-wen* 玄都律文 (Text of the Statutes of the Mystical Capital, TT 78, HY 188), a list of regulations governing the living Taoist's moral and ritual conduct and the *Nü-ch'ing kuei-lü* 女青鬼律 (The Demon Statutes of Nü-ch'ing, TT 563, HY 789) containing a list of unruly spirits and demons which may be controlled through knowledge of their appearance and "true names." The titles of these works are mentioned in early texts, though the date of our received versions has not been established with certainty.

A version of the Celestial Master rite of sexual and spiritual union, known as the *ho ch'i* 合氣 (union of breaths), in which the spirit registers of male and female devotees were joined, is found in the *Huang-shu kuo-tu i* 黃書過度儀 (The Yellow Writings—Ritual for Crossing Over, TT 1009, HY 1284). The theoretical foundations of this sexual rite are based on the *Lo shu* 河圖 (Lo [River] Writings), cosmological speculations on the supposed movement of the sun through a magic square made up of the numbers from one to nine arranged in columns of three so that the sum of each column or row is always fifteen, and similar computations involving the eight trigrams of the *I-ching* (see *ching*). Further amplifications of this system, which coordinates the movements of the sexual partners with the intricate mechanisms of the cosmos, can be found in another work, the *Tung-chen huang-shu* 洞眞黃書 (Yellow Writings of Cavern Perfection, TT 1031, HY 1332).

During the third and early fourth centuries, scores of new scriptures were written dealing with alchemy, herbalism, and new forms of meditation. These came to be called collectively the *T'ai-ch'ing Ching* 太淸經 (T'ai-ch'ing Scriptures) after the Heaven of Grand Clarity 太淸天 to which the practitioners of their methods aspired. Among these texts is the *Huang-t'ing [wai-ching] ching* 黃庭外景經 (Scripture [on the Outer Phosphors] of the Yellow Court; Schipper, 1975), a rhymed meditation on the palaces and powers of the body which, through an elaborate system of correspondences, are co-extensive with those of the heavens. Such meditations, employing terms such as *ts'un-ssu* 存思 (retentive contemplation) and *shou* 守 (preservation), were meant to strengthen such correspondences through the absorption of lunar, solar, and stellar essences, sometimes visualized in the guise of deities, to recharge and vitalize the adept. These texts often employ alchemical imagery to describe the refining of the spiritual elements in the crucible of the body. Through such practice, the meditant becomes one with the incorruptible, eternal forces of the cosmos. This form of meditation, inherited from Han *fang-shih*,* came to dominate Taoist practice. The *Ling-pao wu-fu hsü* 靈寶五符序 (Five Talismans of the Numinous Treasure with Preface, TT 183, HY 388), in addition to further clarifying such practices, is augmented with lists of corporeal deities drawn from the Han *wei shu* 緯書(weft texts, apocrypha appended to the Classics [*ching**]) and contains detailed instructions for the preparation of herbal potions, procedures for harvesting divine mushrooms, and a lengthy account of a visit to a cavern-heaven 洞天 within a holy mountain. The most convenient guide to these scriptures and at least some of the practices associated with them is the *Pao p'u-tzu* 抱朴子(The Master Who Embraces Simplicity, TT 868-873, HY 1177, 1179) of Ko Hung* (283-343). Enough of the texts mentioned by Ko have survived to show that this marked the beginnings of a revolution in Taoism, prefiguring the remarkable southern revelations which were to follow.

The first fully documented Taoist revelations occurred in the Eastern Chin capital of Chien-k'ang建康(modern Nanking) and the nearby prefectural town of Chü-jung句容 during the years 364-370. These were the Shang-ch'ing上清 Revelations, granted to Yang Hsi楊羲(330-*c.* 386) by a group of Perfected from the Heaven of Upper Clarity 上清天. The Perfected appeared to Yang in midnight visions, dictating to him full-scale scriptures, biographies of the Perfected, and supplementary instruction. Some of the more earthly forces inspiring Yang may be gauged in the fact that these revealed materials included re-workings of both the *Huang-t'ing ching*—the *Huang-t'ing nei-ching ching* (Scripture on the Inner Phosphors of the Yellow Court; Schipper, 1975)—and the early Buddhist *Erh-shih-ssu chang-ching*二十四章經 (Sutra of the Twenty-four Stanzas). Yang was directed to pass these materials on to his patrons, Hsü Mi許謐(303-373) and his son Hsü Hui許翽(341-*c.*370). The texts of the Shang-ch'ing Revelations in the hands of Yang Hsi and the Hsüs were later collected and annotated by T'ao Hung-ching陶弘景(456-536). T'ao arranged the miscellaneous portions of the transcripts in his *Chen-kao*眞誥(Declarations of the Perfected, TT 637-640, HY 1010). This is our primary source for the Shang-ch'ing Scriptures, many of which survive elsewhere in the canon (see Strickmann, 1981; Robinet, 1981).

The materials bestowed on Yang concern themselves primarily with visionary meditation practice and forms of meditative alchemy, all imbued with a vision of the stars as the incorruptible gem-palaces and physical embodiments of the celestial hierarchy— the ultimate goals of man's spiritual quest. Thus, for example, the *Pa-su chen-ching*八素眞經(The Perfect Scripture of the Eight Immaculates, TT 194, HY 426) makes known a method for visualizing the divinities of the five planets and absorbing their luminous effluents. Mastery of such practices was of considerable urgency, for, according to such scriptures as the *Hou-sheng lieh-chi* 後聖列紀 (Annals of the Latter-day Sage, TT 198, HY 142), the apocalypse was close at hand and only a favored few would survive to be received by the Savior Li Hung李弘. For the adept's survival in the chaotic last days, Lord Li himself had sanctioned a talisman and apotropaic incantations for warding off the demon armies of the six heavens, northern abode of earth-bound dead. These are preserved in the *Shen-hu yin-wen* 神虎隱文 (The Concealed Text of the Spirit Tiger, TT 1031, HY 1323). The adept, however, need not live through the destruction of the old order. The *Tzu-wen*紫文(The Purple Text, TT 120, HY 255) and other scriptures of the Shang-ch'ing corpus describe deadly elixirs, products of both operative alchemy and meditative practice, which could ensure the practitioner's immediate transferral to the heavenly realms.

One of the more enduring aspects of these texts was the vast quantity of inspired verse which the Perfected dictated to Yang. Poetry had from the beginning occupied an important place in Taoist texts and ritual. Hymns, rhymed incantation, and esoteric verse are all to be found among the scriptures predating the Shang-ch'ing Revelations. Now, in the Shang-ch'ing Scriptures, verse was shown to be the chosen method of communication with and among the higher powers, and poetic excellence was a sure sign of divine inspiration. Elements, both thematic and stylistic, of Yang's poetry can be traced in generations of secular poets (Schafer, 1980).

Some thirty years after the last of Yang Hsi's visions, a new canon of revealed matter appeared in Chü-jung. This was the work of Ko Ch'ao-fu 葛巢甫 (*fl.* 400), a nephew of Ko Hung. Ko did not personally claim to be the beneficiary of a revelation, holding instead that the texts he revealed to a select group of disciples were the result of revelations granted his third-century ancestor Ko Hsüan 葛玄. Drawing together materials from the Shang-ch'ing Scriptures, from texts of the T'ai-ch'ing tradition, and elements of certain Buddhist scriptures circulating in south China, Ko Ch'ao-fu constructed a compelling body of texts which even reproduced samples of the celestial script in which the scriptures had been written across the heavens at creation. In addition, the Ling-pao ching 靈寶經 (Numinous Treasure Scriptures), as they were known, introduced a new Taoist cosmology, extensive communal liturgies for the salvation of the living and the dead, and a series of precepts and observances for the laity.

In the Ling-pao Scriptures the three classes of works revealed in the south—the T'ai-ch'ing, Shang-ch'ing, and Ling-pao scriptures—were classified as the Three Caverns 三洞. This tripartite division was to become the basic organizing principle of the first, and all subsequent, Taoist canons (see *Tao-tsang*). This is not to say that the canon was closed; revelations continued and new scriptures were constantly being written. In northern China, for instance, K'ou Ch'ien-chih 寇謙之 (d. 448) became the recipient of revelations from the Most High Lord Lao and his "great-great grandson" Li P'u-wen 李普文. K'ou appropriated the title Celestial Master and was so known at the court of the T'o-pa Wei, which briefly adopted Taoism as its official religion. K'ou's single surviving scripture is a reformational diatribe against the excesses of the Way of the Celestial Master—sexual rites, rice-levies for priests, and millenarianism.

Meanwhile, in southern China, apocalyptic concerns continued to be expressed in revelations dealing with salvation and survival in the final days, including such works as the early fifth-century *Tung-yüan shen-chou ching* 洞元神呪經 (Scripture of Spirit-spells of the Cavernous Abyss, TT 170-173, HY 335). The first portion of this scripture (*chüan* 1; the remaining chapters were written at least by the end of the T'ang) gives an account of plague, drought, and flood demons, and their control through incantation. Subsequent revelations tended to associate themselves with one or more of the three traditions sanctioned in the Three Caverns of the canon. Texts listed as unrevealed in the primary scriptures were duly revealed and new scriptures made known.

The sixth through the mid-seventh centuries saw the creation of a series of lengthy scriptures modeled closely on Buddhist sutras. These scriptures may be viewed as part of an overall Taoist strategy to annex Buddhism as but a foreign branch of China's indigenous faith. There are such oddities as the sage Hai-k'ung chih-tsang 海空智藏 whose name renders into perfect Sanskrit—an epithet of the Buddha—and who sits beneath a tree in a strange land answering the questions of seekers of religious truths (TT 20-22, HY 9). The majority of these scriptures, such as the *Pen-hsiang ching* 本相經 (Scripture of the Original Images, TT 764-765, HY 1123), and the *Pen-chi ching* 本際經 (Scripture of the Original Junctures, TT 758, HY 1103), now survive only in fragmentary form in the canon. Fortunately, copies of these works also survive in manuscripts from Tun-huang. Such texts, with their long discussions of "Tao-nature" 道性 (cf. Buddha-nature 佛性), karmic retribution, and other Buddhist ideological constructs, were at the center of Buddho-Taoist polemics. At some point, most likely in the latter half of the seventh century, they seem to have been systematically purged of Buddhist elements or dropped from the canon.

The initial burst of Taoist revelation, spanning over four hundred years, came to an end at about the same time—coinciding with Taoism's increasing prestige as the predominant faith of the ruling house during the T'ang. The T'ang may be called the great age of Taoist scholasticism, a tendency fostered by the court through the establishment of official exams on Taoist scriptures. Prolonged official sponsorship meant tighter controls on Scriptural production. It was not until after the T'ang that Taoism was again to enjoy an efflorescence of revelatory exuberance such as it had known during this formative period.

C. Hagiography

Taoist hagiography extends from what might more properly be called theogony down to simple factual stories of holy men. It is an integral part of a long tradition of narratives recounting the lives of sages, recluses, and transcendents. This tradition was by no means static. Augmented by both a continuing oral tradition and the imaginations of the "inspired," these tales were repeated and elaborated from text to text. The most fecund source of such elaborations was the Taoist tendency to invoke the authority of various sages of antiquity, often providing further information regarding their secret practices and other worldly careers to vouchsafe the authenticity of revealed scripture. Thus, Wang Tzu-ch'iao 王子喬, who first appears as a *hsien* 仙 (transcendent) in the Han portions of the *Ch'u-tz'u** and is provided with a biography in the *Lieh-hsien chuan*,* appeared in his exalted status to Yang Hsi as the Youth of Mount T'ung-po 桐柏山童子 "capped in a lotus crown and dressed in vermilion garb with white pearls sewn into the hems." The more recent information concerning Wang's posthumous status and activities was supplemented in later scriptures and finally collected in an expanded work which must once have graced a temple wall together with the illustrations of its author, the Taoist priest and painter Ssu-ma Ch'eng-chen* (647-735).

The best-known hagiographies dealing with Taoist figures are those which were always more or less in the public domain; works such as the *Lieh-hsien chuan, Shen-hsien chuan,** *Sou-shen chi,** and the *Sou-shen hou-chi* (see *Sou-shen chi*). These collections do not treat exclusively of Taoist figures, drawing their material from local and Buddhist traditions as well, but they make use of Taoist sources and were in turn often quoted in Taoist works. Frequently studied, they are often mistakenly seen as the only sources for glossing literary references to Taoist figures. The case of Wang Tzu-ch'iao, outlined above, suggests at once that this is not the case.

Further, it is in Taoist scriptures that there is a greater richness of narrative detail and closer portrayal of particulars of aspect and costume, for intimate knowledge of a celestial being betokened scriptural authenticity and a close familiarity with physical appearance allowed the adept to recognize the figures of his visions. The influence that the prose stylizations resulting from these concerns wrought on subsequent poetry, the fictional *ch'uan-ch'i*,* and painting remains to be fully assessed.

The paramount figure of Taoist hagiography is Lao-tzu. Numerous hagiographical notices of this deity can be found in the texts of all lineages, and many separate scriptures are attributed to him. Three works stand out. The earliest of these, the late second-century *Lao-tzu pien-hua ching* 老子變化經 (Scripture of the Transformations of Lao-tzu), surviving only in a Tun-huang manuscript, presents Lao-tzu as a personified supreme principle who manifested himself under differing names to the sage-kings of antiquity, culminating in five appearances between A.D. 132 and 155 in the Ch'eng-tu area (Of-uchi, 1978). This text was produced by a messianic movement that operated in the same area and contemporaneously with the early Way of the Celestial Masters, but was apparently unrelated. The *Lao-tzu hua-hu ching* 老子化胡經 (Scripture of Lao-tzu's Conversion of the Western Barbarians), written by Wang Fou 王浮 in the late third or early fourth century, related the already circulating tale of Lao-tzu's appearance to the barbarians as the Buddha to expound the tenets of Taoism in a fashion they could understand. This highly controversial text underwent a number of recensions, including Buddhist versions, and was repeatedly invoked in Buddho-Taoist polemic over such matters as imperial patronage, the authenticity of Taoist versions of Buddhist scripture, etc. The fragments of this text surviving in Tun-huang manuscript seem to stem from the T'ang ten-*chüan* recension and include such later additions as Lao-tzu's transformation into Mani (216-274), the eponymous Persian founder of the Manichaean religion which reached China early in the eighth century. The *Lao-chün pien-hua wu-chi ching* 老君變化無極經 (Scripture of the Illimitable Transformations of Lord Lao [-tzu], TT 875, HY 1186) was composed during the Liu-Sung dynasty. This scripture portrays Lao-tzu not as a revolutionary messiah but as a legitimizer of kings whose appearance was to inaugurate an era of Grand Peace for the Sung restoration of Han rule. Lao-tzu was to manifest himself once again in this guise, more successfully, at the founding of the T'ang.

In addition to information on the careers of a variety of transcendents and magi, now found scattered in the *Chen-kao* (TT 637-640, HY 1010) along with T'ao Hung-ching's copious annotations, Yang Hsi received from the Perfected six complete biographies of more exalted personages. Unfortunately, the only biographies from Yang's hand to survive intact are the *P'ei-chün chüan* 裴君傳 (Tradition of Lord P'ei—found in the *Yun-ch'i ch'i-chien** (TT 677-702, HY 1026, ch. 105) and the *Hou-sheng lieh-chi*. A rewritten T'ang version of another, the *Wei fu-jen chuan* 魏夫人傳 (Tradition of Lady Wei) is collected in the *T'ai-p'ing kuang-chi.** Stylistically, these works are simply scriptures in which biographical information figures somewhat more prominently than technical matters. The didactic intent of these works can be seen in their emphasis on the texts and practices favored by their subjects, and the appended oral instructions meant to aid the recipient of the text. Later works in this style include the *Tzu-yang chen-jen nei-chuan* 紫陽眞人內傳 (Inner Traditions of the Perfected of Tzu-yang, TT 152, HY 303), a fuller account dating from the late fourth century of one of the Perfected present in the Yang Hsi revelations, and the *Han Wu-ti nei chuan*.* T'ang contributions to the genre include Tu Kuang-t'ing's* *Yung-ch'eng chi-hsien lu* 墉城集仙錄 (Records of the Assembled Transcendents of Yung-ch'eng, TT 560-561, HY 782), a collective biography of the female divinities of Taoism beginning with yet another transformation of Lao-tzu—as his own mother, the Primal Sovereign Mother of the Sage 聖母元君—as well as the Queen Mother of the West and the Perfected of her retinue. This work, like Ssu-ma Ch'eng-chen's biography of Wang Tzu-ch'iao, draws on earlier scriptural materials and is primarily concerned with the iconology and attributes of the divinities themselves rather than the practices they sponsored.

Hagiographical sections of the Ling-pao Scriptures are of a different sort, being more heavily influenced by the Buddhist *avadāna* literature which was widely translated in the third and fourth centuries. Ko Ch'ao-fu's account of the previous lives of Ko Hsüan found in the *Ling-pao pen-hsing yin-yüan ching* 靈寶本行因緣經 (Numinous Treasure Scripture of the Original Activities and Causalities [of the Transcendents], TT 758, HY 1107) is particularly interesting in that it contains perhaps the earliest popular reference to the Buddhist belief in rebirth as an animal. Such accounts of a sage or deity's repeated appearances in history can be traced back to tales of the Five Emperors in the Han weft texts and accounts of the deified Lao-tzu's transformations.

The frequent appearance of new scriptures claiming a lineal descent extending to this or that sage or deity and substantiated by new and sometimes contradictory accounts of his life seems to have led to the rapid obsolescence of Taoist hagiographical works. Only one of the collective biographies written through the T'ang period has come down to us intact. Collective biographies, which can be reconstructed in part from later collections, were of basically two types. The first dealt with a single master-discipline lineage, such as the *Lou-kuan hsien-shih pen-ch'i nei-chuan* 樓觀先師本起內傳 (Inner Traditions of the Origins and Activities of the Former Masters of the Storied Observatory—on Mount Chung-nan 終南山, near Ch'ang-an). The first chapter of this work was purportedly revealed to Liang Ch'en 梁諶 in 305, the second added during the Northern Chou by Wei Chieh 韋節, and the third by Yin Wen-ts'ao 尹文操 (d. 688). The second type, exemplified by Ma Shu's 馬樞 (522-581) comprehensive *Tao-hsüeh chuan* 道學傳 (Traditions of Students of the Tao; citations collected in Ch'en, 1963), was comprehensive in scope. The single surviving biographical collection, Tu Kuang-t'ing's *Shen-hsien kan-yü chuan* 神仙感遇傳 (Traditions of Meetings with the Divine Transcendents, TT 328, HY 592), falls into this category. Tu's work is a collection of tales concerning little-known figures, mostly of the T'ang period, who shared the distinction of having come into contact with transcendents, either through their Taoist practice or by virtue of their character. Here the Taoist hagiographical tradition merges with T'ang *ch'uan-ch'i** literature and the Buddhist miracle tale. Some of Tu's tales are known from other sources, for many became the subject of subsequent literary productions.

D. Historical and Topographical Monographs

While quasi-historical accounts of Taoist lineages survive in many scriptures, only a handful of separate pre-Sung historical monographs have come down to us. Avowedly partisan in nature, these few works provide a needed corrective to the skewed view of Taoism presented in the official histories.

The earliest monograph dealing with the religion as a whole was the *San-t'ien nei-chieh ching* 三天內解經 (Scripture of the Inner Explanations of the Three Heavens, TT 876, HY 1196), composed during the Liu-Sung dynasty by a Taoist surnamed Hsü 徐. The first chapter of this work outlines the history of Taoism from the golden age of antiquity through its "re-establishment" by Chang Tao-ling down to the present dynasty which "abounds in men of the Tao." Hsü was primarily concerned with establishing the primacy of Taoism over Buddhism and his account provides little information concerning the development of the various lineages seen in the scriptural legacy. A more cautious and carefully documented treatment of the Shang-ch'ing tradition and the diffusion of the Yang Hsi revelations forms *chüan* 19 and 20 of T'ao Hung-ching's *Chen-kao.* Unfortunately, this sort of careful scholarship was not elsewhere emulated.

The most prolific recorder of the Taoist heritage was Tu Kuang-t'ing. Working at the end of the T'ang period, Tu was responsible for collecting vast quantities of Taoist scriptural and epigraphic material, most probably for collection in the library of the Former Shu 前蜀 kingdom, which he served late in his life. Only a few works from his voluminous writings will be mentioned here. The most patently historical of Tu's writings is the *Li-tai ch'ung-tao chi* 歷代崇道記 (Record of the Veneration of the Tao Through the Ages, TT 329, HY 593) which records chronologically Taoist epiphanies, portents, and the honors bestowed on the religion under various emperors through the ages. The greater part of these records relate to the T'ang, with special attention to the divine favors shown to Li Lung-chi (T'ang Hsüan-tsung), preeminent among the T'ang emperors who supported Taoism. Epigraphic records inform Tu's *Tao-chiao ling-yan chi* 道教靈驗記 (TT 325-326, HY 590), a collection of marvels, which prefigures the *T'ai-p'ing kuang chi* in its categorical organization (see *Tu Kuang-t'ing*).

From the beginning Taoist texts have been concerned with the sacred geography of the Central Kingdom. As in popular religion and the state cult, the focus of this interest was the holy mountain, abode of saints and transcendents, and provider of numinous herbs and healing waters. For the Taoist, the rugged exterior of certain mountains masked a grander mystery—cavern-heavens within. Access to the five sacred marchmounts was provided through mere possession of the talismanic *Wu-yüeh chen-hsing t'u* 五嶽眞形圖 (Charts of the True Form of the Five Holy Mountains), another early text which knew many recensions. An interlocking system of thirty-six cavern-heavens and ten major ones was detailed in the materials bestowed on Yang-hsi (see the *Chen-kao*). This system formed the basis of Tu Kuang-t'ing's spare listing of the cavern-heavens and sacred places of China, the *Tung-t'ien fu-ti yüeh-tu ming-shan chi* 洞天福地嶽瀆名山記 (Record of Cavern-heavens, Blessed Spots, Holy Mountains, Conduits and Mountains of Renown, TT 331, HY 599). Tu was not the only Taoist impelled by the destruction of the Huang Ch'ao rebellion and the disorders presaging the end of the T'ang into collecting information pertaining to Taoism. Li Ch'ung-chao 李冲昭, visiting the southern marchmount, Mount Heng 衡山, was dismayed at the loss of records following the disorders. In 902, Li composed his *Nan-yüeh hsiao-lu* 南嶽小錄 (TT 201, HY 453), a record of the temples, peaks, and cavern-heavens of the mountain drawn from epigraphic records and scripture.

E. Philosophical and Alchemical Treatises

Philosophical works collected in the Taoist canon include the traditional classics of Chinese thought as well as later, doctrinal works. Such early philosophical works as the *Chuang-tzu* and *Lieh-tzu* were admitted to the canon under Li Lung-chi, Emperor Hsüan-tsung of the T'ang, who instituted a separate civil-service examination on these texts, and himself wrote a commentary to the *Lao-tzu* (TT 677, HY 355). The preeminent importance of Taoist-inspired commentaries to many of these texts is indicative of the influence wrought by Taoist scholarship on Chinese intellectual currents, for, since the T'ang, many of these classics have been viewed as somehow inherently "Taoist." While these texts clearly did not emanate from a single pre-Han Taoist school, modern understanding of them has been largely conditioned by a very real school of Taoist scholarship.

The canon also includes such minor philosophical works as the *Kuei-ku-tzu* 鬼谷子 (TT 671, HY 1019) and the *Kuan-yin-tzu* 關尹子 (TT 347, HY 667). The attribution of such texts to figures already celebrated in Taoist scripture leads one to suspect that Taoist scholars were not content with merely culling the existing classics for passages in support of the antiquity of their religion. For instance, the pastiche-text *K'ang-sang-tzu* 亢桑子 (TT 348, HY 669), attributed to a disciple of Lao-tzu known from the *Chuang-tzu*, was "restored" by Wang Shih-yüan and, under his patronage, briefly granted canonical status in 742 under the exalted title *Perfected Scripture of the Penetrating Numina* 洞靈眞經.

Equally informative on the philosophical underpinnings of the religion are the essays of individual Taoists. While there are bibliographic references to a number of such works, only a handful survive. Li Lung-chi's patronage of Taoism was particularly productive of such essays, several of which are known to have been formally presented to the throne. Wu Yün's 吳筠 (d. 778) *Hsüan-kang lun* 玄綱論 (Treatise on the Mystic Mainstay, TT 727, HY 1046), together with his letter of presentation and the emperor's grateful acknowledgment of receipt, is extant. Wu Yün is known primarily as an influential Taoist poet and close friend of Li Po,* but his collected works (TT 726-727, HY 1045) contain, in addition, other essays on the pursuit of the Tao.

Perhaps more influential by virtue of his high station were the treatises of Ssu-ma Ch'eng-chen, twelfth patriarch in the established lineage of Shang-ch'ing. Among his works preserved in the canon is the *Shang-ch'ing han-hsiang chien-chien t'u* 上清含象劍鑑圖 (Diagrams of the Upper Clarity Swords and Mirrors Bearing Simulacra, TT 196, HY 431), is a text which accompanied his presentation of spiritually potent Taoist swords and mirrors to the throne. This detailed discussion is perhaps the best source on the iconography of such apotropaic treasures. Another of Ssu-ma's works, the *Tso-wang lun* 坐忘論 (Treatise on Sitting in Forgetfulness, TT 104, HY 1030), is, in its discussion of Taoist transcendence, a close cognate to T'ang *Ch'an* 禪 treatises.

Although often employed as an encyclopedic work for its extensive citation of Taoist scripture, the early seventh-century *Tao-chiao i-shu* 道教義樞 (The Pivot of Meaning of Taoism, TT 762-763, HY 1121) of Meng An-pai 孟安排 is in fact an expository work on Taoist doctrine and practice. Originally organized under thirty-seven terms (one and one-half of its ten *chüan* are now lost), it provides first the meaning of the heading and then a long analysis. This work is particularly valuable in that it preserves quotations from earlier Taoist essays as well as scriptural citations.

While they are not strictly treatises, another sort of expository writing deserves mention here—written transcripts of a master's teachings. Foremost of such works is the *Tao-men ching-fa* 道門經法(Initiatory Scriptures and Doctrine, TT 762, HY 1120), which purports to record Master P'an Shih-cheng's 潘師正 (585-682) instructional dialogue with Li Chih 李治 (Kao-tsung, r. 649-683) in 679. Parts of this text are in dialogue; the remainder contains a list of brief explanations of Taoist concepts and terminology such as might have been offered to a Taoist novitiate—even one of imperial status.

Another element of traditional Chinese cosmological investigation which played a part in the formation of Taoism was the art of alchemy. As noted already, the recondite and allusive language of alchemy suffused Taoist ritual and meditation texts beginning at least with the T'ai-ch'ing scriptures.

The earliest known alchemical work, and by far the most influential, is the *Chou-i ts'an-t'ung-ch'i* 周易參同契(TT 621-629, HY 996-1005), written in the mid-second century and attributed to Wei Po-yang魏伯陽. This text gives an explanation, in verse and prose, of the process by which the cyclically transformed elixir 還丹 may be produced in stages derived from the hexagrams of the *I ching*. It is not, however, a laboratory manual. The arcane terminology used here to describe the accelerated cosmic merging of *yin* and *yang* has been exploited in countless Taoist meditational and ritual texts such as that explaining the Celestial Master rite of sexual union.

Ko Hung's *Pao-p'u-tzu*, a defense of the possibility of attaining transcendence directed at Ko's contemporaries in the upper-class southern society of the Six Dynasties, contains two *chüan* on operative alchemy culled from early alchemical texts. These books were bestowed on Ko by his master Cheng Yin 鄭隱. While Ko himself states that he possessed insufficient funds to test the elixirs himself, the information he records preserves much that was subsequently lost in the esoteric lines of alchemical transmission.

Among the highest of the Shang-ch'ing elixirs was the elixir formula originally appended to the biography of Lord Mao revealed to Yang Hsi, now surviving in the canon as a separate work, the *T'ai-chi chen-jen chiu-chuan huan-tan yao-chüeh* 太極眞人九轉還丹要訣(TT 586, HY 888). According to the T'ang Taoist Chia Sung's 賈嵩biography of T'ao Hung-ching (TT 151, HY 300), T'ao himself attempted to prepare this elixir for Liang Wu-ti 梁武帝 between 504 and 506. Still, aside from Ko Hung's meager collection, the only pre-Sung landmark *collection* of alchemical recipes discovered to date is the *Tan-ching yao-chüeh* 丹經要訣 (TT 677-702, HY 1026, ch. 71) attributed to Sun Ssu-mo孫思邈 (c. 650), author of the important medical text, the *Pei-chi ch'ien-chin fang* 備急千金方 (TT 799, HY 1154).

F. Exegeses and Encyclopedic Compilations

Throughout the history of the Taoist religion, the auricular transmission of knowledge from master to disciple has been stressed. Texts were bestowed on disciples in a formal ceremony, accompanied by secret oral instructions in the meaning and use of scripture. Scriptural revelations were conceived of as occurring in a similar manner, with the deity becoming in effect the master of his human disciple. Due to the importance accorded them, oral instructions were often recorded in writing and, somewhat paradoxically, became an important literary genre. The majority of early Taoist textual exegesis, then, is divinely inspired. Not surprisingly, even divine commentators seem to have owed a debt to the methodology of Han scholarship, employing, for instance, paronomastic glosses worthy of Hsü Shen 許慎. Like divinely inspired commentary, the work of Taoist scholars was generally intended for lineal transmission.

Perhaps the most meticulous commentator on the Taoist scriptural records of the pre-Sung period was T'ao Hung-ching, best known outside Taoist circles for his *Shen-nung pen-ts'ao ching chi-chu* 神農草本集註. T'ao's annotated collection of Yang-Hsü manuscript remains, the *Chen-kao*, has already been noted. In addition, T'ao copied a selection of these manuscripts most suited to the instruction of the practicing Taoist together with oral instruction originally appended to the biographies of the Perfected into his *Teng-chen yin-chüeh* 登眞隱訣 (TT 193, HY 421). The commentary to this work, now surviving only in part, is even more detailed that that found in the *Chen-kao*. Detached portions of the *Teng-chen yin-chüeh* still survive in the canon. The auricular instructions from the biographies of Lord Mao and Lord Wang are found together with T'ao's annotations in the *Shang-ch'ing ming-t'ang yüan-chen ching-chüeh* 上清明堂元眞經訣 (TT 194, HY 424), and his reconstruction of the Shang-ch'ing pantheon, edited by Lü-ch'iu Fang-yüan 閭丘方遠 (ninth century), may be found under the title *Chen-ling wei-yeh t'u* 眞靈位業圖 (TT 73, HY 167).

The T'ang Taoist dispensations were also productive of scriptural exegesis. In 822, it was decreed that Taoist ordinations would be granted by the state to those who showed proficiency in the *Lao-tzu* and either the *Tu-jen ching* 度人經 (TT 1, HY 1, ch. 1) of the original Ling-pao corpus of Ko Ch'ao-fu or the *Huang-t'ing ching* of the Shang-ch'ing corpus. Several T'ang commentaries on these central scriptures are extant. The *Yüan-shih wu-liang tu-jen shang-p'in miao-ching ssu-chu* 元始無量度人上品妙經四注 (TT 38-39, HY 87), compiled in 1067 by Ch'en Ching-yüan 陳景元, preserves portions of the commentaries of Yen Tung 嚴東 (*fl.* 480) of the Northern Ch'i as well as those of Hsüeh Yu-hsi 薛幽棲 (*fl.* 750), Li Shao-wei 李少微, and Ch'eng Hsüan-ying 成玄英 (*fl.* 630) of the T'ang. These commentaries are based primarily on the oral instructions of the *T'ien-chen huang-jen* 天眞皇人 found in another of the original Ling-pao scriptures, the *Chu-t'ien nei-yin tzu-jan yü-tzu* 諸天內音自然玉字 (Inner Sounds of the Several Heavens in Self-generated Jade Graphs, TT 49, HY 97). The most influential commentary to the *Huang-t'ing ching*, both the inner and outer books, is that of Liang-ch'iu-tzu 梁丘子 (Pai Lu-chüng 白履忠, *fl.* 722) which may be found in *chüan* 55-60 of the *Hsiu-chen shih-shu* 修眞十書 (Ten Books for the Cultivation of Perfection, TT 122-131, HY 263). His commentary to the inner book also survives as a separate work (TT 190, HY 402). Part of an earlier commentary, attributed to Wu Ch'eng-tzu 務成子, is collected in the Sung *Yü-ch'i ch'i-chien** (TT 677-702, HY 1026, ch. 11-12), although only that portion through stanzas three of the inner scripture commentary is the work of Wu Ch'eng-tzu; the remainder is by Liang Ch'iu-tzu. These works are particularly valuable in explicating the numberous T'ang literary references to these scriptures.

The most important Taoist scholarly works for the modern researcher are the encyclopedic collections contained in the canon. The first comprehensive Taoist encyclopedia was the *Wu-shang pi-yao* 無上秘要 (Secret Essentials of the Most High, TT 768-

779, HY 1130), begun under imperial auspices in 574. This massive work was commissioned by Emperor Wu of the Chou 周武帝 as part of the Confucian and Taoist ideological synthesis which was to underlie his proposed reunification of the empire. The encyclopedia, now lacking over 30 of its original 100 *chüan*, was organized under 288 categories and encompassed all aspects of Taoism, from ritual procedure and implements to the palaces and heavens of the Perfected. The normative influence of such imperially sponsored collections of Taoist texts can best be seen in the fact that almost all of the scriptures cited in this text still exist as separate works in the canon (Lagerway, 1981).

A similar organizational principle was adopted by Wang Hsüan-ho 王懸河, writing in the first half of the seventh century, in his *San-tung chu-nang* 三洞珠囊 (Jewelled Satchel of the Three Caverns, TT 780-782, HY 1131). This ten-*chüan* work seems to have been intended as a manual of Taoist practice, for its forty-three sections include abundant scriptural citations on purgations and meditation as well as on heavens, hells, and celestial powers—the addressees of demonifuge spell and petition. Wang's *Shang-ch'ing tao-lei shih-hsiang* 上清道類事項 (Categorical Entries on Upper Clarity Taoism, TT 765, HY 1124) is even more specialized in subject matter. This work is a collection of scriptural references to both celestial and earthly observatories, pagodas, temples, and other religious structures. Particularly valuable are the portions of the work, drawn principally from the now lost *Tao-hsüeh chuan*, on historical Taoist edifices.

Finally, the extensive resources available for the study of the Taoist liturgical tradition deserve mention. In addition to the ritual sections of the works cited above, evidence of the earliest codification of Taoist ritual texts by Lu Hsiu-ching 陸修靜 (406-477) remains. Lu was responsible for collecting, in the earliest Taoist catalogue, the texts of the Ling-pao Revelations. In addition, he himself wrote scripts composed primarily of quotations and formulae drawn from the Ling-pao Scriptures, for several liturgies. The surviving copy of Lu's *Huang-lu chai* 黃籙齋 (Purgation of the Yellow Register), a rite for the salvation of the souls of the dead, is now collected in *Wu-shang huang-lu-chai li-ch'eng i* 無上黃籙齋立成儀 (Rites for the Accomplishment of the Most High Purgation of the Yellow Register, TT 278-290, HY 508) collected by Chiang Shu-yü 蔣叔輿 (1156-1217). This work also contains remnants of the work of the T'ang ritual masters Chang Wan-fu 張萬福 and Li Ching-ch'i 李景祈. Lu Hsiu-ching's *Wu-kan wen* 五感文 (Text on the Five [Heaven] Resonators, TT 1004, HY 1268), a text perhaps prepared for imperial perusal, provides a brief description of two Shang-ch'ing and nine Ling-pao purgations. Lu Hsiu-ching's works detail as well various aspects of ritual procedure and paraphernalia. His *Tung-hsüan ling-pao chai-shuo kuang-chu chieh-fa teng-chou yüan-i* 洞玄靈寶齋說光燭戒罰燈祝願儀 (A Description of the Ling-pao Purgations: Rites Concerning Shining Candles, Precepts, Fines, Lamps, Incantations, and Vows, TT 293, HY 524) provides a description of the lamps and censers used in Ling-pao ritual and details the duties of various ritual celebrants, while his *Chung-chien wen* 象簡文 (TT 191, HY 410) contains the earliest and most detailed account of the memorial tablets used in supplicatory rites and to seal celestial covenants. Another important work on the accoutrements used in Taoist ritual is found among the ritual texts of Chang Wan-fu 張萬福. This is the *San-tung fa-fu k'o-chieh wen* 三洞法服科戒文 (Text of Ordinances and Precepts Concerning the Garments of the Law of the Three Caverns, TT 563, HY 787), a text on the celestial origins of Taoist ritual garb, its symbolism, and the procedures associated with it. While Chang worked primarily in the Celestial Master tradition, his texts exemplify the T'ang codification of Taoist ritual which drew from all of the major pre-T'ang lineages.

Tu Kuang-t'ing stood in a unique position to sum up Taoist developments through the T'ang. Tu's two great ritual compendiums are a fifty-eight *chüan* collection of texts on the Purgation of the Yellow Register (TT 270-277, HY 507) and an eighty-seven *chüan* compilation of various rites to be conducted for the welfare of the state, including the Purgation of the Golden Register 金籙齋, a Ling-pao rite no longer found in separate form (TT 976-983, HY 1215). Numerous shorter works on Taoist rites attributed to Tu may also be found in the canon. Thanks to such scholarly efforts as Tu's, as much primary source material on early Taoism exists in datable collections as outside them.

EDITIONS:

Cheng-t'ung tao-tsang 正統道藏. 1976. Shanghai, 1924; rpt. Taipei. (Individual works may be located by reference to Weng Tu-chien 翁獨健, *Combined Indices to the Authors and Titles of Books in Two Collections of Taoist Literature*, Peking, 1975, Harvard-Yenching Institute Sinological Index Series, No. 25, rpt. Taipei, 1966.) The extant Taoist patrology, commissioned during the Ming and printed in 1444 or 1447. Also included in the modern printed edition is the Wan-li period supplement, originally printed in 1607.

Ōfuchi, Ninji 大淵忍爾. 1978. *Tonkō dōkyō modurokuhen* 敦煌道經目錄編. Tokyo. An inventory of the Taoist works from Tun-huang, including all textual variants.

———. 1980. *Tonkō dōkyō Zōrokuhen* 敦煌道經目錄編. Tokyo. Facsimile reproductions of the Taoist manuscripts from Tun-huang.

Tao-tsang chi-yao 道藏輯要. 1971. Ch'eng-tu, 1096; rpt. Taipei. Of the 187 rare editions collected in this work, 114 are not found in the *Cheng-t'ung tao-tsang*. These are listed in Weng's work above.

STUDIES:

Beck, B. J. Mansvelt. 1980. "The Date of the *Taiping jing*," *TP*, 66, 150-182.

Bokenkamp, Stephen R. 1983. "Sources of the Ling-pao Scriptures," in *Tantric and Taoist Studies in Honour of R. A. Stein; Mélanges chinois et bouddhiques*, Michel Strickmann, ed., Brussels, v. 2, pp. 435-487.

Ch'en, Kuo-fu 陳國符. 1963. *Tao-tsang yüan-liu k'ao* 道藏源流考. 2v. 2nd ed., Peking.

"Current Perspectives in the Study of Chinese Religions," 1978. *History of Religions*, 17, 3-4.

Dōkyō kenkyū 道教研究. *Etudes taoistes*. 1968, 1971. Yoshioka Yoshitoyo and Michel Soymie, eds. V. 3. Tokyo. V. 4. Tokyo.

Facets of Taoism. 1979. Holmes Welch and Anna Seidel, eds. New Haven.

Fukui, Kōjun 福井康順. 1957. *Dōkyō no kisoteki kenkyū* 道教の基礎的研究. Tokyo.

Fu, Ch'in-chia 傅勤家. 1957. *Chung-kuo tao-chiao-shih* 中國道教史. Shanghai.

Huang, Yung-wu 黃永武. 1980. "Tao-chia san-p'ien" 道家三篇, in *Chung-kuo shih-hsüeh, Ssu-hsiang p'ien* 中國詩學，思想篇. Taipei, pp. 163-201

Jao, Tsung-i 饒宗頤. 1956. *Lao-tzu hsiang-erh-chu chiao-chien* 老子想爾注校牋. Hong Kong.

Kroll, Paul W. 1981. "Notes on Three Taoist Figures of the T'ang Dynasty," *Society for the Study of Chinese Religions Bulletin*, 9, 19-41.

Lagerway, John. 1981. *Wu-shang pi-yao: Somme taoiste du Vie siécles*. Paris, 1981.

Maspero, Henri. 1971. *Le Taoisme et les religions chinoises*. Rpt. Paris.

Ōfuchi, Ninji. 1964. *Dōkyō shi no kenkyū* 道教史の研究. Okayama.

Robinet, Isabelle. 1976. "Randonnées extatiques des Taoistes dans les astres," *MS*, 32, 159-273.

———. 1981. "La revelation du shang-qing dans l'histoire du taoisme." Unpublished Ph.D. dissertation, University of Paris.

Schafer, Edward H. 1980. *Mao Shan in T'ang Times*. Society for the Study of Chinese Religions, Monograph No. 1.

———. 1977. *Pacing the Void: T'ang Approaches to the Stars*. Berkeley.

Schipper, Kristofer. 1969. *L'empereur Wou des Han dans la legende taoiste*. Paris, 1969.

———. 1975. *Concordance du Houang-T'ing King*. Paris.

———. 1982. *Le corps taoïste*. Paris.

Seidel, Anna. 1969. *La divinisation de Lao-tseu dans le taoïsme des Han*. Paris.

Sivin, Nathan. 1963. *Chinese Alchemy; Preliminary Studies.* Cambridge, Mass.

Strickmann, Michel. 1977. "The Mao Shan Revelations; Taoism and the Chinese Aristocracy," *TP*, 63, 1-64.

———. 1979. "On the Alchemy of T'ao Hung-ching," in *Facets of Taoism*, Holmes Welch and Anna Seidel, eds.

———. 1981. *Le taoïsme du Mao Chan: Chronique d'une revelation.* Paris.

"A Symposium on Taoism," 1969-1970, *History of Religions.* 9.

Wang, Ming 王明. 1960. *T'ai-p'ing ching ho-chiao* 太平經合校. Peking.

Yoshioka, Yoshitoyo 吉岡義豐. 1955. *Dōkyō kyōten shiron* 道教經典史論. Tokyo.

———. 1958, 1959, 1976. *Dōkyō to Bukkyō* 道教と祆教. 3v. Tokyo.

Zürcher, Erik. 1980. "Buddhist Influence on Early Taoism—A Survey of Scriptural Evidence," *IP*, 66, 84-137.

PART II. FIVE DYNASTIES TO THE MING

Judith Magee Boltz

A. Introduction

THE imprint made by Taoist religious traditions on Chinese literary history is easily comparable to the influence of the Judeo-Christian heritage on Western literature. Unfortunately, there has only recently been any sustained interest in pursuing the written tradition of China's higher indigenous religion. This is due in part to the fact that the *Tao-tsang*,* or Taoist Canon, was not made available in a distributable edition until the mid-1920s. Even so, native biases against Taoist tradition, not to mention a general reluctance to explore unfamiliar sacred texts, have made the study of not only the social history of Taoism but also its literary heritage slow to develop. In many ways it remains a virgin field, all the more so when compared to the history of scholarship on Chinese Buddhist literature. And yet it cannot be denied that the *Tao-tsang*, as well as extra-canonical collections of Taoist literature, offer invaluable source material for clarifying the creative resources of many Chinese literary traditions, from inspired verse to the stuff-material of the novelist.

By way of an introduction to the nature and diversity of canonic literature dating from the Five Dynasties to the Ming, a survey of some hundred titles is organized here under the following headings: (1) Revelation and Ritual, (2) Hagiography, (3) Topography and Historiography, (4) Literary and Dialogic Anthologies, and (5) Exegeses and Encyclopedic Compilations. The sources cited represent a variety of lineal and local traditions, the foundations of which left a lasting impression on Taoist revelatory history. Among the more conspicuous features found in many of these readings is the imprimatur of the Celestial Masters, a sure sign of their role throughout the history of canonic compilations. Only briefly during the Chin and Yüan did the Ch'üan-chen 全眞 brotherhood threaten that sacral autocracy, leaving in its wake an equally distinct mark on the makeup of the canon. Whether born of contemplative or demonifuge traditions, the literature of the *Tao-tsang* falls not on the periphery, but in the mainstream of Chinese literary history.

Thus far the best tool for immediate access to the *Tao-tsang* and the largest of extra-canonical compilations, the *Tao-tsang chi-yao* 道藏輯要, is the *Tao-tsang tzu-mu yin-te* 道藏子目引得(Combined Indices to the Authors and Titles of Books in Two Collections of Taoist Literature, Harvard-Yenching Institute Sinological Index Series, No. 25), edited by Weng Tu-chien 翁獨健. Besides assigning a sequential number to 1476 titles in the order they appear in the *Tao-tsang* (HY 1-1476), this reference also indicates provenance when known, the *Ch'ien-tzu wen* 千字文 code by which the collection was originally indexed, and the *Tao-tsang* fascicle number (TT 1-1120). Also included are title and author indices, as well as an index to biographical accounts in seventy-seven hagiographic sources. A more recent concordance to *Tao-tsang* titles (Schipper, 1975) gives a slightly revised numbering system which has been adopted by some European publications. Both Liu Ts'un-yan 柳存仁 at Canberra and the *Projet Tao-tsang* under the direction of Kristofer M. Schipper are independently preparing analytic catalogues to the *Tao-tsang*.

Until these more comprehensive catalogues become available, it behooves each reader to try to determine the provenance of any undocumented texts he consults. Prefaces and colophons are the most obvious aids to ascertaining the historical and social setting of any title, for a number of canonic texts have suffered centuries of editing, and such material may occupy a good portion of the introductory and closing texts as well as hide within the main corpus itself or even within ancillary materials. Not infrequently, inventories of sources for specific lineages are to be found embedded in scriptural codifications, thereby clarifying the origins of many otherwise undated and anonymous works. Equally discernible guides to historical placement are internal references to those patriarchs and Masters to whom transmission of distinct lineages is attributed. With such citations, the reader is cautioned to be aware of the attributions that are apparently called upon merely for the antiquity and legitimacy they lend a scriptural tradition. Fictive ascriptions, especially to patriarchs of the Celestial Master heritage, are common and can usually be recognized as such. More significant in terms of precise dating is the citation of contemporary or near contemporary transmitters to whom the author or compiler, in many cases anonymous or identified by sobriquet alone, may give credit with regard to his own edification and editorial role. Nor can the language of the text itself be overlooked, for it is here that some of the most valuable clues to provenance are to be found. Terminological preferences, especially in contemplative verses and exegeses, as well as datable deific titles and cosmological schemes, readily signify the historical settings of texts for which the origins might otherwise remain obscure (Boltz, 1984).

B. Revelation and Ritual

Imperial patronage of revelatory innovations has been the guiding force in the preservation of the written traditions of many diverse Taoist dispensations. Following in the footsteps of T'ai Wu-ti of Northern Wei and T'ang Hsüan-tsung were a series of monarchs from Sung on who also found advantages in viewing their regencies as testimony of a specific Taoist theocracy. The material and scriptural formulations led to what has been termed a Taoist renaissance (Strickmann, 1979). The interest Hui-tsung fostered in recording every manner of revelation shaped not only the composition of future canonic compilations, but also the direction of Chinese literary history. Renewed faith in divine intervention and demonifuge healing, such as that promoted daily throughout the countryside, inspired ever increasing numbers of prosodic and narrative works.

Hand in hand with the widespread revival of revelatory experience from the Sung period on was the codification of vast repertoires of ritual performance. These ritual codes went far beyond the rudimentary reenactment of the original revelation to encompass all variety of therapeutic programmes. The dramaturgical overtones of these rites recall nothing less than the propitiatory and apotropaic languages preserved in the *Shih-ching** and the *Ch'u-tz'u.** Building on centuries of penitential invocations addressed to the sacred realm, the ritual ministrant himself began to assume a new spiritual potency. The metamorphoses of deities within the sanctuary of their bodies that he and his antecedents had long achieved was carried a step further. Rather than be content with serving as a relatively static receptor of divinity, the adepts took on a more active role in orchestrating the therapeutic forces from above. In a manner reminiscent of their shamanic counterparts throughout Chinese religious history, the ministrants during this new age of ritual creation took on the full identity of their divine guardians. No longer was mere visualization (*ts'un*存) adequate for the purposes of these multifarious therapeutic rites. Instead, this new generation of adepts was instructed to personally "envision yourself as . . ." (*ts'un tzu-shen wei* 存自身爲 . . .) or "metamorphose yourself into . . ." (*pien wei* 變爲 . . .) the deity whose domain it was to convey the prescribed remedies. Thus transformed, the ministrant played the leading role in propitiatory sequences, summoning forth the essential sacred hosts to bring about the desired denouement. To that end, immense ritual compendia were compiled, with the precise specifications for every facet of ritual purifications, meditation chamber and altar settings, sacred dress and accouterments, and audio-visual aids, including the vitalizing application of incantations, talismans, and mudrā-like manipulations.

Chief purveyor of the Shen-hsiao scriptural lineage that defined Sung Hui-tsung's theocracy was Lin Ling-su 林靈素(1075-1119), whose homeland of Wenchow was the fountainhead of several innovative traditions of Taoist, Buddhist, and Manichaean origin. The *Kao-shang shen-hsiao tsung-shih shou-ching shih* 高上神霄宗師受經式 (Formulary for the Transmission of Scriptures According to the Patriarchs of the Exalted Divine Empyrean, TT 1005, HY 1272) outlines the history of the transmission of the Shen-hsiao scriptures from their mythic origins to Hui-tsung's reign. Drawing on the salvific dimensions of the Ling-pao heritage and the messianic expectations of Shang-ch'ing, the Shen-hsiao dispensation ascribed to Hui-tsung, as the Ch'ang-sheng ta-ti 長生大帝 (Grand Monarch of Long Life) incarnate, the responsibility for the universal salvation of his empire. The sixty-one titles listed as the original Shen-hsiao revelations correspond to the chapter headings of the 61-*ch. Ling-pao wu-liang tu-jen shang-p'in miao-ching* 靈寶無量度人上品妙經 (Wondrous Scripture of Supreme Rank on the Infinite Salvation of Ling-pao, TT 1-13, HY 1). Sixty of these chapters are ritual recastings of the first *chüan* of the *Tu-jen ching* 度人經(Scripture on Salvation) in light of the soteriological foundations of Shen-hsiao. The major beneficiary of Lin's scriptural legacy, Wang Wen-ch'ing 王

文卿(1093-1153), may have been responsible for the illustrated handbook, or *fu-t'u* 符圖(TT 67, HY 147) that supplements this corpus (Strickmann, 1978). Substantially more elaborate is the 72-ch. *Ling-pao wu-liang tu-jen shang-ching ta-fa* 靈寶無量度人上經大法 (Great Rites of the Supreme Scripture on the Infinite Salvation of Ling-pao, TT 85-99, HY 219), which depicts in great detail the sources for the sensory perception of sacred phenomena. Included is a rare recension of a meditation manual for the enactment of the *lien-tu* 鍊度 funereal rites as envisioned within the adept's corporeal chambers (Boltz, 1982). Central to a later redaction of Shen-hsiao ritual codes in *ch.* 198-206 of the late fourteenth-century *Tao-fa hui-yüan* 大法會元 (see below) is the "huo-ling" 火鈴(fiery tocsin) talisman. Transmitted from Lin Ling-su's second-generation disciple Ch'en Tao-i 陳道一 down to Liu Yü 劉玉(1257-1310), these codes include the only text directly attributed to Lin. Entitled "Chin-huo t'ien-ting shen-hsiao san-ch'i huo-ling ko" 金火天丁神霄三炁火鈴歌(Song of the Celestial Stalwart of the Golden Flames and the Fiery Tocsin from the Triple Emanations of the Divine Empyrean), Lin's visionary verse traces the origin of the flaming sacrament to mythic times.

The "huo-ling" was to figure prominently in a revitalization of the Shang-ch'ing revelations at Mao-shan, termed T'ung-ch'u ta-fa 童初大法(Great Rites of Youthful Incipience). Although the putative recipient is identified as Yang Hsi-chen 楊希眞(1101-1124), the transmission of the T'ung-ch'u rites in *ch.* 171-178 of the *Tao-fa hui-yüan* is dated by Chin Yün-chung 金允中(*fl.* 1224-1225) no earlier than two generations before his own initiation. Central to his codification is the evocation of the Celestial Master alongside the four demonifuge spirits encountered by Yang: (1) T'ien-p'eng 天蓬, (2) T'ien-yu 天猷, (3) I-sheng pao-te chen-chün 翊聖保德眞君 , initial guardian of the Sung, and (4) Chen-wu 眞武, the Perfected Militant.

Another major scriptural lineage promoted during Sung Hui-tsung's reign, the T'ien-hsin cheng-fa 天心正法(Corrective Rites of the Celestial Heart), claims as its spiritual font Mount Hua-kai 華蓋山 in central Kiangsi. Although the transmission of the T'ienhsin rites is dated to 994 when they were reportedly revealed to the first patriarch of the lineage, Jao Tung-t'ien 饒洞天 , the earliest received corpus was not prepared until 1116 by Master Yüan Miao-tsung 元妙宗 of Nan-yang 南陽(Honan). Responding to Huitsung's solicitation of editors for a reedition of the *Tao-tsang*, Yüan consolidated T'ienhsin and related codes into the 10-ch. *T'ai-shang chu-kuo chiu-min tsung-chen pi-yao* 太上助國救民總眞秘要 (Secret Essentials from the Aggregate Perfected of the Most High, for the Relief of the State and Delivery of the People, TT 986-87, HY 1217). The core of these iatro-talismanic rites is also found in Teng Yu-kung's 鄧有功(1210-1279) 7-ch. *Shang-ch'ing t'ien-hsin cheng-fa* 上清天心正法 (Corrective Rites of the Celestial Heart of Shang-ch'ing, TT 318-19, HY 566). At the base of T'ien-hsin rites are talismans calling forth the divine assistance of (1) San-kuang 三光, i.e., sun, moon, and stars; (2) Chen-wu 眞武; and (3) T'ien-kang 天剛(Ursa Major). The demonifuge rubric of T'ien-hsin that infused generations of ritual practice also left its mark on the history of the narrative, from Hung Mai's* *I-chien chih* to the *Shui-hu chuan.**

The syncretistic outlook in demonifuge ritual can perhaps be said to have reached its culmination with the Ch'ing-wei 清微 revelations. A Kwangsi native by the name of Tsu Shu 祖舒(*fl.* 889-904) is credited with achieving the Ch'ing-wei synthesis with a unification of the four major traditions of Shang-ch'ing, Ling-pao, Tao-te, and Cheng-i. As codified by a Chien-ning 建寧(Fukien) practitioner, Huang Shun-shen 黃舜申(1224-

c. 1286), these rites represented a merging of the therapeutic "Lei-t'ing" 雷霆 (Thunderclap) tradition with the maṇḍala teachings of Tantric Buddhism. The Ch'ing-wei ritual corpus that dominates the *Tao-fa hui-yüan* (*ch.* 1-55) is a fourteenth-century redaction achieved by the syncretist Chao I-chen 趙宜眞 (d. 1382).

The 268-*ch. Tao-fa hui-yüan* 道法會元 (TT 884-941, HY 1210) is the single largest canonic reservoir of the demonifuge rituals that were prevalent during the twelfth, thirteenth, and fourteenth centuries (van der Loon, 1979). Compiled sometime after 1356, this ritual compendium bears the imprimatur of several practitioners, notably the thirty-ninth Celestial Master Chang Ssu-ch'eng 張嗣成 (d. 1343), Chang Yü 張雨 (1283-*c.* 1356), and Chao I-chen. In addition to recording the practices of the lineages cited above, the *Tao-fa hui-yüan* preserves numerous Thunder Rites (*lei-fa* 雷法) associated with eminent Masters such as Pai Yü-ch'an 白玉蟾 (Ke Ch'ang-keng 葛長庚, *fl.* 1209-1224), Lei Shih-chung 雷時中 (1221-1295), and Mo Ch'i-yen 莫起炎 (1226-1293).

Of comparable bulk is the 320-*ch. Ling-pao ling-chiao chi-tu chin-shu* 靈寶領敎濟度金書 (Golden Writings on Salvation, Based on Instructions Received of the Ling-pao Tradition, TT 208-63, HY 466), a ritual collection compiled originally by Lin Wei-fu 林偉夫 (1239-1302) of Wenchow. The most comprehensive set of guidelines available for the wide variety of thirteenth-century ritual performance, this work enlarges upon the legacy of Ning Pen-li 寧本立 (1101-1181). Ning's practices, based in large part on the Shen-hsiao heritage, are given a full accounting in another ritual corpus edited by Wang Ch'i-chen 王契眞, the 66-*ch. Shang-ch'ing ling-pao ta-fa* 上清靈寶大法 (Great Rites of the Shang-ch'ing Ling-pao Tradition, TT 942-62, HY 1211). The T'ung-ch'u Master Chin Yün-chung 金允中 (*fl.* 1224) compiled a 44-*ch.* corpus of the same title (TT 963-72, HY 1212-13), documenting similar ritual activities originating from the T'ien-t'ai 天台 region of Chekiang. Another Wenchow Master, Chiang Shu-yü 蔣叔輿 (1156-1217), edited the ritual sequences of the Mount Lung-hu 龍虎山 (Kiangsi) Master Liu Yung-kuang 留用光 (1134-1206) in a 57-*ch.* work entitled *Wu-shang huang-lu ta-chai li-ch'eng i* 無上黃籙大齋玄成儀 (Protocols on the Establishment of the Great Fête of the Supreme Yellow Register, TT 278-290, HY 508).

C. Hagiography

Comparable in approach to biographies of the Confucianist and Buddhist traditions, Taoist hagiographies were compiled principally for commemorative and thus didactic purposes. These guides are basically composite accounts, organized according to a fairly standardized repository of formulaic passages. As in accounts of imperial births, among the *topoi* employed are divine conception and youthful precocity. Prose, often *p'ien-wen,** is the preferred mode of composition, although there are notable instances in which narrative and verse are combined in compact accounts comparable to standard epigraphic form. Just what influence these stylized hagiographies may have had on the genesis of the *chu-kung-tiao** and *pao-chüan* 寶卷 (precious scrolls) remains to be investigated.

In fleshing out the written core of oral tradition, hagiographers often relied upon epitaphs, eulogistic verse, and the imperial decrees bestowing honorary titles. Other than an occasional display of typically Confucianist virtues in the more syncretic texts, there is seldom any insight into the development of the saintlike personality. The emphasis falls instead on the sacred emissary's preordained role in mortal and immortal realms, be that chiefly revelatory, prophetic, intercessory, or salvatory. In that way, hagiographies serve equally well as a record of the society that played host to the many numinous manifestations of these transcendents.

A few hagiographies are comprehensive anthologies with no regional, lineal, or chronological restrictions, but a larger quantity are the products of specific scriptural traditions. The limitations are thus defined by the region and period in which a particular lineage or cult was active. Parallel to the early theogonies for individual Shang-ch'ing patriarchs are the occasional hagiographies that focus on one, or perhaps two, individuals alone, whether they be patriarchs of a local cult or tutelary spirits. From the Sung empire on, the state began to take a more intense interest in elevating local worthies of proven divinity to the ranks of the nationally venerated. By raising regional salvatory figures to the status of guarantors of imperial welfare, the state itself, often through the approbation of the Celestial Master hierarchy, promoted the manufacture of hagiographic literature.

By far the most comprehensive canonic hagiography is the 53-*ch. Li-shih chen-hsien t'i-tao t'ung-chien* 歷世眞仙體道通鑑 (Comprehensive Survey of Successive Generations of Perfected Transcendents and Those Who Embody the Tao, TT 139-48, HY 296) compiled by Chao Tao-i 趙道一 (*fl.* 1297-1307). Several other texts are attributed to Chao, but they appear to be the product of a later hagiography. Internal and external evidence seem to indicate that although the compilation was completed in the early decades of the Yüan dynasty, the sphere of influence within which it took shape was that of displaced Southern Sung notables. In gathering data from earlier, less than complete hagiographies, Chao views his task as the compilation of a comprehensive reference comparable to those sources available for the exemplars of Buddhist and Confucianist training. Over all other texts, he chooses as his authority on dating the *Hun-yüan shen-chi* 混元聖紀 (TT 551-53, HY 769) of Hsieh Shou-hao 謝守灝(1134-1212). Although he does not identify the sources, they range from the *Lieh-hsien chuan* to the 20-*ch. San-tung ch'un-hsien lu* 三洞群仙錄 (On the Concourse of Transcendents in the Three Caverns, TT 992-95, HY 1238), edited by the Cheng-i Master Ch'en Pao-kuang 陳葆光 in 1154, an encyclopedic compliation documenting transcendents from legendary to Sung times. Reflecting his own background at Mao-shan, Chang Yü favors the Shang-ch'ing lineage in his 5-*ch. Hsüan-p'in lu* 玄品錄(A Record of Arcane Ranks, TT 558-59, HY 780). The *Sou-shen chi* 搜神記 (In Search of the Sacred, TT 1105-1106, HY 1466) compiled in 1573 and printed with the 1607 imprimatur of the fiftieth Celestial Master Chang Kuo-hsiang 張國祥(d. 1611), offers a time capsule of the spirit world according to late Confucianist, Buddhist, Taoist, and folk traditions. Chang was also responsible for incorporating into the 1607 Canon a 4-*ch.* edition of the *Han T'ien-shih shih-chia* 漢天師世家 (A Genealogy of the Celestial Masters from the Han, TT 1066, HY 1451), tracing the Celestial Master lineage from its founder to the forty-ninth Master Chang Yung-hsü 張永緒(d. 1565). Insight into the Ch'ing-wei theogony according to Master Huang Shun-shen 黃舜申(1224-*c.* 1286) is provided by Ch'en Ts'ai 陳采 in his 1293 *Ch'ing-wei hsien-p'u* 清微仙譜 (An Inventory of Ch'ing-wei Transcendents, TT 75, HY 171), a source upon which many later codifiers of the tradition relied.

The northern Ch'üan-chen lineage is memorialized in the 5-*ch. Chin-lien cheng-tsung chi* 金蓮正宗記 (An Account of the True Lineage of the Golden Lotus, TT 75-76, HY

173), compiled in 1241 by an editor of the early Yüan Canon, Ch'in Chih-an 秦志安 (1191-1247). Endorsed by the thirty-ninth Celestial Master Chang Ssu-ch'eng, the *Chin-lien cheng-tsung hsien-yüan hsiang-chuan* 金蓮正宗仙源像傳 (An Illustrated Hagiography of the Transcendent Origins of the True Lineage of the Golden Lotus, TT 76, HY 174) is Liu Chih-hsüan 劉志玄 and Hsieh Hsi-ch'an's 謝西蟾 1326 version of the lives of the Five Patriarchs and Seven Perfected (Wu-tsu ch'i-chen 五祖七眞) of Ch'üan-chen (for a complete list see Boltz, 1985). A major archivist of the lineage, Li Tao-chien 李道謙 (1219-1296), compiled a chronology of the lives of the Ch'üan-chen Perfected, the *Ch'i-chen nien-p'u* 七眞年譜 (A Chronology of the Seven Perfected, TT 76, HY 175) and a hagiography of later affiliates, the 3-*ch. Chung-nan-shan tsu-t'ing hsien-chen nei-chuan* 終南山祖庭仙眞內傳 (A Private Hagiography of the Transcendent Perfected of the Ancestral Hall of Mount Chung-nan, TT 604, HY 954).

The divine manifestations of the Ch'üan-chen patriarch Lü Yen, a favorite subject of *tsa-chü** playwrights, are separately chronicled in Miao Shan-shih's 苗善時 (*fl.* 1324) 7-*ch. Ch'un-yang ti-chün shen-hua miao-t'ung chi* 純陽帝君神化妙通記 (An Account of the Wondrous Communications and Divine Transformations of the Sovereign Lord Ch'un-yang, TT 159, HY 305). This and similar exemplars of the subgenre of "transformation" (*hua* 化) hagiographies, such as the lost text of Lao-tzu's manifestations, the *Pa-shih-i hua t'u* 八十一化圖 (Illustrations of the Eighty-one Transformations), apparently figured in the heritage of the popular *pao-chüan*.

In the same vein is the 3-*ch. Hsi-shan Hsü Chen-chün pa-shih-wu hua lu* 西山許眞君八十五化錄 (A Record of the Eighty-five Transformations of the Perfected Lord Hsü of Mount Hsi, TT 200, HY 448) compiled by Shih Ch'en 施岑 (*fl.* 1224-50). At the center of this and an earlier composition, the *Hsiao-tao Wu Hsü erh chen-chün chuan* 孝道吳許二眞君傳 (A Hagiography of Wu and Hsü, the Two Perfected Lords of the Way of Filiality, TT 201, HY 449) is Hsü Sun 許遜 (239-292), around whom a local salvationist cult at Hsi-shan 西山 (Kiangsi) blossomed into a nationalistic movement known as Ching-ming Tao 淨明道 (Akizuki, 1978, 1981). Its prominence in the late thirteenth century led to the compilation of the *Hsü Chen-chün hsien-chuan* 許眞君仙傳 (A Hagiography of the Perfected Lord Hsü, TT 200, HY 447), the 2-*ch. Hsü T'ai-shih chen-chün t'u-chuan* 許太史眞君圖傳 (An Illustrated Hagiography of the Perfected Lord Hsü, the Grand Scribe, TT 197, HY 440), and the 6-*ch. Ching-ming chung-hsiao ch'üan-shu* 淨明忠孝全書 (A Comprehensive Source on the Ching-ming Tradition of Loyalty and Filiality, TT 757, HY 1102) edited by Huang Yüan-chi 黃元吉 (1270-1325), disciple of a major scriptural codifier, Liu Yü 劉玉 (1257-1310).

Also prominent in the lore of northern Kiangsi is a deity named Chiu-t'ien shih-che 九天使者 (Envoy of the Nine Celestial Realms) whose appearance before Hsüan-tsung in 731 led to the construction of a shrine at Mount Lu in propitiation of divine providence. At the heart of the 7-*ch. Lu-shan T'ai-p'ing hsing-kuo Kung Ts'ai-fang chen-chün shih-shih* 廬山太平興國宮採訪眞君事實 (A Verifiable Account of the Inquisitor, the Perfected Lord of the Palace of the Flourishing State of Grand Peace at Mount Lu, TT 1006-7, HY 1276) are Sung-dynasty chronologies of later manifestations, amplified by records of imperial homage down to 1306. Equally sustained were commemorations of three transcendent guardians sacred to Mount Hua-kai (central Kiangsi), Lord Fou-ch'iu 浮丘公 (*fl.* 592 B.C.) and two devotees of the third century, Wang Tao-hsiang 王道想 and Kuo Tao-i 郭道意. The *Hua-kai-shan Fou-ch'iu Wang Kuo san chen-chün shih-shih* 華蓋

山浮丘王郭三眞君事實 (A Verifiable Account of the Three Perfected Lords of Mount Hua-kai, Fou-ch'iu, Wang, and Kuo, 6-*ch.*, TT 556-57, HY 777), a composite work prepared by the forty-third Celestial Master Chang Yü-ch'u 張宇初(1361-1410), centers on the history of faith in these divine conservators, especially during the Sung when the T'ien-hsin revelations were discovered at the site.

For the first half of the Northern Sung empire, no sacred emissary surpassed the I-sheng pao-te chen-chün 翊聖保德傳 (Perfect Lord, Supporting Sage and Guarantor of Merit). The statesman Wang Ch'in-jo 王欽若(962-1025) compiled the *I-sheng pao-te chuan* 翊聖保德傳 (A Hagiography of the Supporting Sage, Guarantor of Merit, 3-*ch.*, TT 1006, HY 1275) in honor of this inaugural Sung guardian whose ascendence Wang promoted. A tutelary deity frequently invoked in later Sung rituals, Wen Ch'iung 溫瓊 of P'ing-yang 平陽(Chekiang), inspired Huang Kung-chin 黃公瑾 to compose the *Ti-ch'i shang-chiang Wen T'ai-pao chuan* 地祇上將溫太保傳 (A Hagiography of the Grand Guardian Wen, Supreme Commander of the Tutelary Deities, TT 557, HY 779) in 1274. Another target of eulogistic fervor throughout the Sung was the Cheng-i Master Yeh Fa-shan 葉法善(616-720 or 722?) of Kua-ts'ang 括蒼(Chekiang), whose teachings were assimilated in T'ien-hsin and other ritual codices. Based on early hagiographies and *ch'uan-ch'i*** accounts, Chang Tao-t'ung 張道統 compiled (*c.* 1241) the *T'ang Yeh Chen-jen chuan*唐葉眞人傳 (A Hagiography of Yeh the Perfected, of the T'ang, TT 557, HY 778) in verification of Yeh's therapeutic legacy.

Finally, three anonymously compiled works provide a collective encomium for the potent Hsüan-wu玄武(Dark Militant), or Chen-wu眞武(Perfected Militant), as the sacred guardian of the North was redesignated in 1012. Succeeding the *Hsüan-t'ien shang-ti ch'i-sheng lu* 玄天上帝啟聖錄 (An Account of Revelations to the Sages Made by the Supreme Sovereign of the Dark Celestial Realm, 8-*ch.*, TT 606-8, HY 957) of the eleventh century are two works attesting to the vitality of the deity in the ritual traditions of the Mongol and Ming empires, the *Hsüan-t'ien shang-ti ch'i-sheng ling-i lu* 靈異錄(On the Numinous Marvels and Revelations to the Sages of the Supreme Sovereign of the Dark Celestial Realm, TT 608, HY 959) and the *Ta Ming Hsüan-t'ien shang-ti jui-ying t'u-lu* 大明玄天上帝瑞應圖錄 (An Illustrated Account of the Auspicious Responses of the Supreme Sovereign of the Dark Celestial Realm During the Great Ming, TT 608, HY 958). The beliefs and practices at the base of this written tradition clearly stimulated a number of fictive writings, including the *Pei-yu chi Hsüan-ti ch'u-shen chuan* 北遊記玄帝出身傳 (An Account of Northern Travels, the Hagiography of the Incarnations of the Dark Sovereign) of the Fukien bookdealer Yü Hsiang-tou 余象斗(*fl. 1588-1609*).

D. Topography and Historiography

As with the hagiographic traditions, canonic topographies were generally designed as memorials to specific scriptural lineages or local ritual traditions. The focus falls almost inevitably on a mountain site renowned for its devotional sanctuaries. Whereas topographical writings were pursued primarily in the South, the Northern tradition (Ch'üan-chen) made up for its lack of local gazetteers by sponsoring epigraphic anthologies. Both endeavors, whether they entailed pilgrimages or arose from indigenous communities, sought to preserve for posterity a sense of the legacy of numinous phenomena to which a given terrain was beholden.

159

Among the more momentous of topographies is the *Mao-shan chih* 茅山志 (A Treatise on Mao-shan, 33-*ch.*, TT 153-158, HY 304), traditionally attributed to Liu Ta-pin 劉大彬 who was feted as the forty-fifth Shang-ch'ing patriarch in 1317. Based on a number of earlier studies, including perhaps that of Chang Yü, this monograph of the Shang-ch'ing *axis mundi* is the most comprehensive source on any regional lineage documented in the canon. The first nineteen chapters embrace everything from the genealogy of the brothers Mao after whom the range is named, the Shang-ch'ing revelations, and the history of imperial benefaction to the more usual hagiographic, geologic, botanical, and ecclesiological accounts. Large collections of epigraphy and literature complete the work.

Incorporated in the 1607 canonic supplement is a monograph devoted to the geographic and literary history of T'ai-shan 泰山, sacred peak of the East. Compiled in 1586 by Cha Chih-lung 查志隆, the 18-*ch. Tai-shih* 岱史 (A History of Tai, or T'ai-shan, TT 1092-96, HY 1460) is remarkable for its collection of Ming tributes to the mountain. The sacred peak of the West, Hua-shan, inspired a native son, Wang Ch'u-i 王處一, to compile the *Hsi-yüeh Hua-shan chih* 西嶽華山誌 (A Treatise on the Sacred Peak of the West, Mount Hua, TT 160, HY 307) *c.* 1183. Based in part on the *Hua-shan chi* 華山記 (An Account of Hua-shan) dating to the T'ang, the work chronicles the history of the region through the Northern Sung. The *Nan-yüeh tsung-sheng chi* 南嶽總勝集 (An Anthology on the Collective Highlights of the Sacred Peak of the South, TT 332, HY 606) of Ch'en T'ien-fu 陳因夫 offers a far more detailed ecclesiological survey than that found in the late T'ang gazetteer for Mount Heng 衡山, sacred peak of the South. In the *Ta-tsang ching* 大藏經 or *Tripitaka* (TT 2097) is a fuller edition of the text, printed intact with Ch'en's preface of 1163.

Five monographs preserve the sacred milieu of the mountains in Chekiang, the source of many ritual corpuses, including the Shen-hsiao revelations. An anonymous compilation dating to *c.* 1367, the *T'ien-t'ai-shan chih* 天台山志 (A Treatise on Mount T'ien-t'ai, TT 332, HY 603) draws on Hsü Ling-fu's 徐靈府 (*c.* 760-*c.* 841) *T'ien-t'ai-shan chi* 天台山記 (An Account of Mount T'ien-t'ai, T. 2096; ed. Hsü Cheng 徐徵, *fl.* 1236). The Ssu-ming Range, parallel to the T'ien-t'ai Ridge, is the subject of Tseng Chien's 曾堅 (*fl.* 1360-1361) *Ssu-ming tung-t'ien tan-shan t'u-yung chi* 四明洞天丹山圖詠集 (An Anthology of Illustrated Recitations on the Cinnabar Mountains and Grotto Heavens of the Ssu-ming Range, TT 332, HY 605). An outstanding corpus of literary tributes to Hsien-tu-shan (central Chekiang) is incorporated in the *Hsien-tu chih* 仙都志 (A Treatise on Mount Hsien-tu, TT 331, HY 602), compiled by Ch'en Hsing-ting 陳性定 and reedited by Wu Ming-i 吳明義 in 1348. Standing northwest of Mount Hsien-tu is Chin-hua-shan, or Ch'ih-sung-shan, to which Ni Shou-yüeh 倪守約 paid homage with his *Chin-hua Ch'ih-sung-shan chih* 金華赤松山志 (A Treatise on Mount Chin-hua Ch'ih-sung, TT 331, HY 601). Prepared *c.* 1265, the topography honors ten generations of local adepts, from the brothers Huang Ch'u-ch'i 黃 (黃初起) (b. 324) and Ch'u-p'ing 初平 (i.e., Ch'ih-sung-tzu 赤松子, b. 328) to Chu Chih-chang 朱知章 (*fl.* 1259-65). To the north outside Hangchow lies Ta-ti-shan 大滌山, host to patriarchs of both the Shang-ch'ing and Ling-pao traditions. A local Master Shen To-fu 沈多福 directed the preparation of two works on the legacy of spiritual rapture in the region, the 3-*ch. Ta-ti tung-t'ien t'u-chi* 大滌洞天圖記 (An Illustrated Account of the Grotto Heavens of Mount Ta-ti, TT 559, HY 781) edited by Teng Mu 鄧牧 (1247-1306) in 1305 and its companion volume, the extra-canonical *Tung-hsiao shih-chi* 洞霄

詩集(An Anthology of Verse from the Tung-hsiao Palace) organized by Meng Tsung-pao 孟宗寶 in 1302. The central point of interest at Mount Ta-ti is the Tung-hsiao Kung 洞霄宮, a shrine dating to 899 that remained for centuries a focus of imperial benefaction, especially after the Sung court relocated in Hangchow.

Two works are devoted to Wu-tang-shan 武當山 in northern Hupeh, the fountain-head of various Thunder Rites and martial codes. With an emphasis on the history of veneration for Hsüan-wu, the reigning deity of Mount Wu-tang, Liu Tao-ming 劉道明 completed the *Wu-tang fu-ti tsung-chen chi* 武當福地總眞集 (An Anthology on the Perfected Congregating in the Munificent Region of Mount Wu-tang, 3-*ch.*, TT 609, HY 960) in 1291. Earlier in the century Lo T'ing-chen 羅霆震 edited the *Wu-tang chi-sheng chi* 武當記聖集 (An Anthology on the Remarkable Sages of Mount Wu-tang, TT 609, HY 961), a collection of verse highlighting features of the Wu-tang landscape.

Unlike their Buddhist counterparts, historians of Taoist traditions were generally content to chronicle individual heritages and, with few exceptions, failed to create large-scale histories. Many transmitters of scriptural revelation independently recreated the historical setting against which a lineage was said to have been founded. And it was not unusual for these chroniclers to indulge in a bit of historical distortion if it served their purposes of claiming spiritual forefathers. As a less self-serving approach to historiography developed, the annalistic (*pien-nien* 編年) format began to attract a following. The unifying feature of these chronicles is an accounting of the providential meta-morphoses of the Lord Lao, a focus analogous to the centrality of divine birth and eternal manifestations in Buddhist historical narratives.

Following the rather limited annals of Tu Kuang-t'ing* there appeared a *Yu-lung chuan* 猶龍傳 (Like unto a Dragon, 6-*ch.*, TT 555, HY 773) authored by Chia Shan-hsiang 賈善翔 (*fl.* 1086). Titled for the epithet Confucius allegedly applied to Lao-tzu, the text includes cosmogonic and genealogical treatises in addition to a chronology of Lord Lao's manifestations from the founding of the Celestial Master tradition to Sung Chen-tsung's reign. Most attentively reported is the sacred aura surrounding the compiler's minster, the T'ai-ch'ing Kung 太清宮 at Po-chou 亳州(Anhui), the putative site of Lao-tzu's birth.

A latecomer to the cloisters of Lu-shan and Hsi-shan in Kiangsi, the classicist Hsieh Shou-hao 謝守灝(1134-1212) saw room for improvement in Chia's account and offered in its stead the extensively annotated 9-*ch.* *Hun-yüan sheng-chi* 混元聖紀(A Chronicle on the Sage of Vortical Primordiality, TT 551-53, HY 769). Drawing on his wide reading in everything from Buddhist cosmography to stone inscriptions, Hsieh chronicles the epiphanies of the Lord Lao down through Sung Hui-tsung's era. His text is the most frequently cited historical reference in many later canonic compilations. There are also two earlier redactions in print, the *T'ai-shang hun-yüan Lao-tzu shih-lüeh* 太上混元老子史略(An Historic Summary on Lao-tzu, Vortical Primordiality of the Most High, 3-*ch.*, TT 554, HY 772) and the *T'ai-shang Lao-chün nien-p'u yao-lüeh* 太上老君年譜要略 (A Concise Summary of the Chronicle of Lord Lao, the Most High, TT 554, HY 770). Hsieh's work was never superseded in canonical history.

E. Literary and Dialogic Anthologies

Preserved in both canonical and subsidiary collections are a wide variety of prose and verse compositions that are rarely extant in any other source. These works reveal a great deal about the development of many literary genres, not to mention something about the strata of society from which they arose. The subject matter, while diverse, is distinctly religious. All manner of prosodic forms came to accommodate everything from theoretical statements to communications among clergy and homiletic recitations to lay communities. Although this sacred literature was generally at home within the confines of established literary forms, it was no more restricted by those forms than were writings in which religious interests were less central. One area in which a number of adepts, from both Northern and Southern traditions, were most innovative was the employment of *tz'u** meters in the writing of sacred verse. Another popular instrument of didactic persuasion was the dialogic treatise (*yü-lu* 語錄), an idiom that could be as lyrical as any prosodic form. And as showcases of favored parables, such treatises gave rein to levels of narrative inventiveness that any professional storyteller would be proud to claim. Not surprisingly, those who empathized with Ch'an instruction, the Ch'üan-chen specialists, were the most regular patrons of the dialogic format. As bespeaks the milieu from which this syncretic tradition arose, the literary record for Ch'üan-chen happens to be, overall, the most complete.

As the transcendent purportedly responsible for the conversion of both the Ch'üan-chen founder Wang Che 王嚞(1112-1170) and the Nan-tsung 南宗(Southern School) patriarch Chang Po-tuan 張伯瑞(d. *c.* 1082), Lü Yen was credited with a number of writings that found their way into both Taoist and literary collections. The provenance of many prosodic compositions attributed to Lü in the *Tao-tsang chi-yao* and even the *Ch'üan T'ang shih** can be traced no earlier than the fourteenth-century anthology entitled *Ch'un-yang chen-jen hun-ch'eng chi* 純陽眞人渾成集 (A Comprehensive Anthology of the Perfected [Lü] Ch'un-yang, TT 727, HY 1048). According to a preface inscribed in 1311 by the cleric Ho Chih-yüan 何志淵, the 2-*ch.* text is based on the literary works of Lü salvaged from libraries in the Yung-le 永樂(Shensi) region, but internal evidence suggests that Ch'üan-chen masters had a hand in the actual writing. The subject matter, markedly similiar to that treated by Wang Che, is accommodated primarily by heptasyllabic *lü-shih*, although longer prosodic forms and *chüeh-chü* (see *shih*) are also well-represented. One verse ascribed to Lü of particular popularity is the epigrammatic *tz'u* written to the meter of "Ch'in-yüan ch'un" 沁園春(Springtime in the Ch'in Gardens). Transmitted in an annotated edition by the Nan-tsung exegete Yü Yen 俞琰(1258-1314), the *Lü Ch'un-yang chen-jen Ch'in-yüan ch'un tan-tz'u chu-chieh* 呂純陽眞人沁園春丹詞註解 (An Exegesis of the "Ch'in-yüan ch'un" *Tz'u* Lyrics of the Perfected Lü Ch'un-yang, TT 60, HY 136), the lyrics were widely imitated by Nan-tsung and Ch'üan-chen affiliates alike. By far the most comprehensive anthology dedicated to Lü Yen is the anonymously compiled 6-*ch. Lü-tsu chih* 呂祖志(A Treatise on the Patriarch Lü, TT 1112-13, HY 1473), a work in two parts printed in the late sixteenth century under Ch'üan-chen patronage. The "Shih-chi chih" 事蹟志 is a collection of hagiographic materials with narratives on Lü's manifestations dating as late as 1560. The second half of the corpus, the "I-wen chih"藝文志, records prosodic compositions attributed to Lü, including *ku-feng*古風(ancient airs), *lü-shih*, *tz'u*, and *ch'ü.*

Not surprisingly, the Ch'üan-chen lineage yielded quite a number of titles from the teachings of its founder Wang Che alone. The most extensive literary collection is the *Ch'ung-yang Ch'üan-chen chi* 重陽全眞集 (An Anthology of the Ch'üan-chen Tradition of [Wang] Ch'ung-yang, 13-*ch.*, TT 793-95, HY 1145), a text which has undergone many redactions since 1164 when Wang himself inscribed a preface. The somewhat disorganized anthology is principally arranged by verse form, with the heptasyllabic *lü-shih* outnumbering all other *shih* categories. Also of note are the "ts'ang-t'ou ch'ai-tzu" 藏頭拆字 verses, the potential wordplay of which Wang seems to have especially enjoyed. Prevailing over all, however, are some nine chapters of *tz'u* lyrics, the titles of which give ample testimony to Wang's broadly based alliance with Ch'an, Confucianist, and Taoist adherents.

Two texts record the prosodic exchanges between Wang and his first disciple Ma Yü 馬鈺 (1123-1183), the 3-*ch. Ch'ung-yang chiao-hua chi* 重陽教化集 (An Anthology on Instruction from Ch'ung-yang, TT 795-96, HY 1146) and the 2-*ch. Ch'ung-yang fen-li shih-hua chi* 重陽分梨十化集 (An Anthology Based on the Ten Transformations of the Pear Divided by Ch'ung-yang, TT 796, HY 1147). The title of the latter refers to the tradition that Wang ordered Ma and his wife Sun Pu-erh 孫不二 (1119-1183) to eat a pear, piece by piece, as he instructed them in the principles of ethical causality at Ning-hai 寧海 (Shantung). Dating from 1183, both collections were created as much to the memory of Ma as to Wang, with matching verses inscribed by the disciple entered for almost every *shih* or *tz'u* recorded for Wang.

Four other texts conserve the literary legacy of Ma Yü, the largest of which is the *Tung-hsüan chin-yü chi* 洞玄金玉集 (A Precious Anthology from the Tung-hsüan Tradition, 10-*ch.*, TT 789-90, HY 1141). The eleven categories according to which this anthology is organized fully demonstrate Ma's versatility as a poet. Although a quarter of the work is given over to heptasyllabic *chüeh-chü*, the author's preference for *tz'u* is unmistakable—*tz'u* fill four *chüan* here and the three other collections are devoted entirely to *tz'u*. Those within the 2-*ch. Chien-wu chi* 漸悟集 (An Anthology on Gradual Enlightenment, TT 786, HY 1134) were largely composed as homiletic presentations, several of which perhaps evoke in their repetitive style something of the gradual enlightenment epitomized in the title. Another corpus entitled *Tan-yang shen-kuang ts'an* 丹陽神光燦 (On the Lustre of the Hallowed Radiance of [Ma] Tan-yang, TT 791, HY 1142) offers a hundred commemorative verses written to the *tz'u* meter of "Man-t'ing fang" 滿庭芳. Lastly, the *Tzu-jan chi* 自然集 (An Anthology on Spontaneity, TT 787, HY 1136) presents some forty "Tao tz'u" 道詞, both *tz'u* and *san-chü* (see *ch'ü*), that further elucidate the principles Ma sought to convey through a language rich in symbolism. Two additional publications transcribe the sermons given by Ma at assemblies in the Lung-chou 隴州 (Shensi) region and in the area of his native Ning-hai, the *Tan-yang chen-jen chih-yen* 丹陽眞人直言 (Forthright Discourse from the Perfected Tan-yang, TT 989, HY 1224) and the *Tan-yang chen-jen yü-lu* 丹陽眞人語錄 (A Dialogic Treatise of the Perfected Tan-yang, TT 728, HY 1050).

All but ignored in the canon is Sun Pu-erh 孫不二 (1119-1183), the lone woman among the early, exceptional students initiated by Wang Che. Once she and her husband Ma Yü received instruction from Wang, they separated and pursued independent careers. Sun's legacy rests apparently in the environs of Lo-yang where she is reported to have attracted a large number of disciples. Although the hagiographic sources allude to her skill in the composition of *shih* and *tz'u*, and even include sample citations, there is no reference to the availability of any collections of her writings. Nonetheless, the *Tao-tsang chi-yao* carries the *Sun Pu-erh Yüan-chün fa-yü* 孫不二元君法語 (The Codified Sayings of the Primordial Goddess Sun Pu-erh), the textual history of which remains unclear. Composed of two sequences of *lü-shih* and *chüeh-chü*, the work gives instruction on the contemplative capacities of women.

Of all the early Ch'üan-chen Perfected, the exploits of Ch'iu Ch'u-chi 丘處機(1148-1227) are the most publicized. A native of Ch'i-hsia 棲霞(Shantung), Ch'iu sought instruction from Master Wang in 1167, shortly after Ma Yü first approached him. While ministering to communities in the region of his hometown, Ch'iu was invited in 1219 to be in attendance to both Sung Ning-tsung at Hangchow and Chinggis Khan. He finally cast his fortunes with the latter, who was at the time leading an expedition through Central Asia, and set out across North China under Mongol escort. Ch'iu's first audience with the Khan in the winter of 1222 is recorded in the *Hsüan-feng ch'ing-hui lu* 玄風慶會錄(A Record of a Felicitous Convocation with Regard to the Arcane Spirit of the Tao, TT 76, HY 176) compiled by Yeh-lü Ch'u-ts'ai 耶律楚材(1189-1243). Writings from his formative period are preserved in the 6-*ch. Ch'ang-ch'un-tzu P'an-hsi chi* 長春子磻溪集 (An Anthology of Ch'ang-ch'un-tzu's Writings from the P'an Tributary Region, TT 797, HY 1151). Titled for the P'an tributary of the Wei 渭 River (Shensi) beside which Ch'iu lodged in seclusion from 1174 to 1180, the received version of this text also incorporates works attesting to Ch'iu's role as ritual host on the Shantung peninsula as late as 1209. Weighted with heptasyllabic *lü-shih* and *tz'u*, the canonic edition reveals a remarkable consistency in prosodic preference with that established by Ch'iu's mentors. Most well-known among the miscellaneous verse forms included is a series of eight quatrains entitled "Ch'ing-t'ien ke" 青天歌(Songs of the Blue Skies), to which Wang Chieh 王玠(*fl.* 1310) committed extensive commentaries with his *Ch'ing-t'ien ke chu-shih* 註釋(An Exegesis of the "Songs of the Blue Skies," TT 60, HY 137).

Born of a prominent family in Ninghai two months before Ma Yü's birth, T'an Ch'u-tuan 譚處端(1123-1185) also sought out Master Wang in 1167. That we have any of his writings is due in part to the devotion of one of the younger initiates, Liu Ch'u-hsüan 劉處玄(1147-1203). Together with Ma Yü and Ch'iu Ch'u-chi, T'an and Liu make up the famed foursome who, after escorting their Master's remains to Chung-san Shan 終南山 in 1173, spread his teachings throughout the northern plains. Transmitted initially in 1187, the *T'an Hsien-sheng Shui-yün chi* 譚先生水雲集 (An Anthology of the Writings of Master T'an, TT 798, HY 1152) was put together by Liu after the blocks of the original manuscript were lost in floods the year before. The prosodic text in the canon today (two of three *chüan* are *tz'u*) is actually only a portion of the anthology Liu restored.

The literary legacy of Liu Ch'u-hsüan himself appears to have suffered from as much attrition as that of T'an. The son of a military family at Tung-lai 東萊, in the Ning-hai region, Liu did not encounter Wang until 1169 and was the last of the early quartet of disciples to realize his destiny. After leading a reclusive life in the Lo-yang region following the loss of his Master, Liu returned home to preside over local propitiatory ceremonies and, in his last years, ministered to Chin Chang-tsung at Yenching. His commentarial works as well as five literary collections cited in hagiographic sources have all vanished. The one anthology that survives, the *Hsien-le chi* 仙樂集(An Anthology on Transcendent Joy, 5-*ch.*, TT 785, HY 1133) is a mixture of essays on Ch'üan-chen tenets and more personal stanzaic statements on contemplative pursuits. Unlike his spiritual brothers, Liu chose to exploit the verse forms of shorter line length rather than oblige himself to fulfill the prosodic requirements of the heptasyllabic format. In addition to favoring synoptic songs of lines with three or four syllables, Liu inscribed over 300 *chüeh-chü*. With the exception of a few commemorative *tz'u*, he rarely seems to have been inclined toward occasional or epistolary verse. Further background on Liu's teachings is available in a dialogic treatise prepared by his disciples, the *Wu-wei ch'ing-ching ch'ang-sheng chen-jen chih-chen yü-lu* 無爲清靜長生眞人至眞語錄 (A Dialogic Treatise on Ultimate Perfection from the Perfected Wu-wei ch'ing-ching ch'ang-sheng, TT 728, HY 1051). According to a preface inscribed in 1202, the Master acquired such a following that his catecheses were often heard recited on the streets.

The remaining two ordained within the ranks of the Seven Perfected, Wang Ch'u-i 王處一(1142-1217) and Ho Ta-t'ung 郝大通(1140-1212), were contemporaries of Liu. Wang Che initiated them into the practices of Ch'üan-chen in 1168, after which he dispatched Ch'u-i to T'ieh-ch'a-shan 鐵查山 outside Wen-teng 文登(Shantung). From this hermitage he was often summoned on missions by Chin Shih-tsung and Chang-tsung, many of which are memorialized in the only extant anthology of his writings, the 4-*ch.* *Yün-kuang chi* 雲光集(An Anthology on Nebulous Radiance, TT 792, HY 1144). At home with *lü-shih* and *chüeh-chü*, as well as lyrical forms such as *sung* 頌, *ke* 歌, *yin* 吟, and *tz'u*, Wang often applied his skills in versification to addressing his fellow colleagues and the various parishes he served.

Ho Ta-t'ung also spent some time at Mount T'ieh-ch'a once he received instruction from Wang Che. After the Master's death Ho's ministry captivated vast congregations across the peninsula to Luan-ch'eng 灤城 on the coast where he was the beneficiary (through divine revelation) of sacred commentaries to the *I-ching*. Renowned thenceforth for his prognosticative talents, Ho returned home to Ning-hai in 1190 where he also attracted a large following. Among the more devout disciples was Fan Yüan-hsi 范圓曦 (1173-1249), who was responsible for reediting his Master's 4-*ch.* *T'ai-ku chi* 太古集(An Anthology on Grand Antiquity, TT 798, HY 1153). While Ho authored several works, including a study of the *Hṛdaya-sūtra*, this anthology is the only one remaining in print, albeit in an abridged redaction. Ho's own preface, inscribed in 1178, introduces a far more comprehensive collection, including dialogic exchanges, *shih*, *tz'u*, *ke*, and *fu*. The four *chüan* that survive comprise an 1178 exegesis entitled *Chou-i ts'an-t'ung ch'i chien-yao shih-i* 周易參同契簡要釋義 (A Concise Exegesis of the *Chou-i ts'an-t'ung ch'i*), a related series of conceptual diagrams with commentary, and a sequence of "Chin-tan shih" 金丹詩 (Golden Elixir Poems).

For several generations votaries of the Ch'üan-chen lineage expanded on the teachings of founder Wang and the Seven Perfected. The celebrated successor to Ch'iu Ch'u-chi, Yin Chih-p'ing 尹志平(1169-1251), was immortalized in two works, the 3-*ch.* *Pao-kuang chi* 葆光集(An Anthology on Concealed Radiance, TT 787, HY 1138) and the 4-*ch.* *Ch'ing-ho chen-jen pei-yu yü-lu* 清和眞人北遊語錄 (A Dialogic Treatise on the Northern Travels of the Perfected Ch'ing-ho, TT 1017, HY 1299). The literary anthology preserves foremost quantities of Yin's heptasyllabic *chüeh-chü* and *tz'u* lyrics, sufficient in themselves for reconstructing the Ch'üan-chen milieu at its height. Prefacing the *yü-lu* is a panegyric inscribed by Li Chih-ch'ang 李志常(1193-1256) two years after he inherited Yin's post as ranking Ch'üan-chen ecclesiastic in 1238. An important supplement to the anthology, this transcription records Yin's sermons in visits to monastic communities from Peking north in the latter half of 1233. In both extemporaneous remarks and in response to questions from the clergy Yin draws frequently upon the teachings of past Masters and also favors the narration of exempla.

Another native son of the Shantung peninsula, Yü Tao-hsien 于道顯 (1168-1232), journeyed to Lo-yang where he became a disciple of Liu Ch'u-hsüan. His career there, as well as at the T'ai-ch'ing Kung 太清宮 of Po-chou 亳州 c. 1224-1231, is commemorated in the *Li-p'eng lao-jen chi* 離峯老人集 (An Anthology of Old Man Li-p'eng, 2-*ch.*, TT 1001, HY 1254). In contrast to the literary legacy of his Master, the majority of Yü's verses are epistolary, written in heptasyllabic *lü-shih* or *chüeh-chü* meter.

One of the more masterly of later Ch'üan-chen adepts was Wang Chih-chin 王志瑾 (1178-1263). The son of wealthy landowners in Honan, he became a disciple of Ho Ta-t'ung after hearing him preach. In 1221 Wang was invited to take up residence at P'an-shan 盤山 (Hopeh), where he drew a large following and later received instruction from Ch'iu Ch'u-chi. Following Ch'iu's demise, Wang encouraged the southern migration of the Ch'üan-chen heritage by proselytizing along the coast and establishing several new temple complexes. An account of his activities, the *P'an-shan Ch'i-yün Wang Chen-jen yü-lu* 盤山棲雲王眞人語錄 (A Dialogic Treatise of the Perfected Wang Ch'i-yün of Mount P'an, TT 728, HY 1052), illustrates Wang's inductive approach. Although he recites numerous parables, Wang also seems to enjoy exploring the potential for sudden enlightenment through repartee, a technique in which his Ch'an contemporaries were expert.

Ancillary to Wang's treatise is the 8-*ch.* *Yün-shan chi* 雲山集 (The Cloudy Mountain Anthology, TT 783-84, HY 1132), an anthology of verse and prose composed by his disciple Chi I 姬翼 (1193-1268). Well-known within Confucianist circles, Chi was born of an aristocratic family of Kao-p'ing 高平 (Shansi) and educated according to the traditional standards preparatory to holding civil office. He turned to Ch'üan-chen pursuits upon hearing Wang Chih-chin's sermons in 1234. The northern circuit around P'an-shan where he settled and eventually served as ranking ministrant provided substantial inspiration for much of his writing. Among the more versatile spokesmen for the lineage, Chi displays his competence in various prosodic forms from *fu* to *tz'u* and in elegantly worded accounts of Ch'üan-chen temple sites and practices.

At the time Wang Chih-chin reportedly took the Ch'üan-chen mission southward into the environs of Nanking, the teachings of a contemporary of his were already established further south in Fukien. Pai Yü-ch'an of Min-ch'ing 閩清 is traditionally linked to what is called Nan-tsung, a rather amorphous lineage which is traced from Liu Ts'ao 劉操 (d. *c.* 1050) to Chang Po-tuan to Shih T'ai 石泰 (d. 1158) to Hsüeh Tzu-hsien 薛紫賢 (d. 1191) to Ch'en Nan 陳楠 (d. 1213), Pai's immediate mentor. By some accounts of the early fourteenth century Liu is credited with transmitting the teachings of the patriarchs Lü Yen and Chung-li Ch'üan to Wang Che in the north and Chang Po-tuan in the south. Such an interpretation was no doubt extremely useful to those textual codifiers who found some benefit to identifying a common origin for increasingly syncretic theses of divergent provenance. The formulation of the so-called *Wu-tsu* 五祖 (Five Patriarchs) of Nan-tsung listed above was itself probably no more than a late innovation on the model of the Ch'üan-chen hierarchy.

Until Pai Yü-ch'an emerged, the burden of the Nan-tsung heritage fell primarily on the shoulders of the T'ien-t'ai 天台 (Chekiang) native Chang Po-tuan. His assorted writings have long been regarded as treatises on laboratory alchemy (*wai-tan* 外丹) when in fact they fall more in the mainstream of physiological alchemy (*nei-tan* 內丹). Chief among transmitters of Chang's works is Weng Pao-kuang 翁葆光 (*fl.* 1173), who edited the infamous *Wu-chen p'ien* 悟眞篇 (Folios on Apprehending Perfection, TT 61-62, 65, HY 141, 145) and compiled the *Tzu-yang chen-jen wu-chen p'ien chih-chih hsiang-shuo san-ch'eng pi-yao* 紫陽眞人悟眞篇直指詳說三乘秘要 (On the Abstruse Points of the Three Vehicles Articulated with Forthrightness in the Folios on Apprehending Perfection of the Perfected Tzu-yang, TT 64, HT 143). The latter is a hagiographic account with full discussions of the *chin-tan* 金丹 (golden elixir) theories associated with Chang (Needham, 1976; Lu, 1973). Such theories built on the accomplishments of many practitioners active during the Five Dynasties, such as T'ao Chih 陶植, whose *Nei-tan fu* 內丹賦 (TT 121, HY 259) is among many related works cited in the anthology of 962 entitled *Ta huan-tan chao-chien* 大還丹照鑑 (A Reflective Survey of the Great Regenerative Enchymoma, TT 597, HY 925).

The versatile terminology of Chang's works was absorbed with little variation into the works of the putative successors to the Nan-tsung tradition. To Shih T'ai are ascribed a series of eighty-one pentasyllabic *chüeh-chü*, under the title *Huan-yüan p'ien* 還源篇 (Folios on Returning to the Source, TT 742, HY 1083). Similar formulaic verse is found in the writings of Shih's votary Hsüeh Tzu-hsien. A former Ch'an Master, Hsüeh composed, in addition to a commentary of Chang's *Wu-chen p'ien*, several series of *shih* and *tz'u* that were printed in the *Huan-tan fu-ming p'ien* 還丹復命篇 (Folios on the Restoration of Destiny by Means of the Regenerative Enchymoma, TT 742, HY 1080). The recipient of Hsüeh's legacy, Ch'en Nan 陳楠 of Hui-chou 惠州 (Kwangtung), was accomplished in both prose and poetry as witnessed by his *Ts'ui-hsü p'ien* 翠虛篇 (A Folio of the Writings of [Ch'en] Ts'ui-hsü, TT 742, HY 1082). In addition to a series of *chüeh-chü* entitled "Chin-tan shih-chüeh 金丹詩訣", many lengthier theoretical writings are included in narration of Ch'en's initiation of Pai Yü-ch'an at Lo-fou-shan 羅浮山 in 1212.

Although textual evidence is scant, Ch'en is also traditionally regarded as a student of the demonifuge techniques taught by a Thunder Master outside Ch'iung-chou 瓊州 on the island of Hainan. This seems to reflect more accurately on Pai's background, for several sources attest to the protégé's familiarity with the Thunder Rites of his age. His legacy in both the contemplative practices of *nei-tan* and in therapeutic ritual ministrations throughout the South is widely registered in compilations dating from the thirteenth century down to the last decade (Wang, 1976). Among the works paying tribute to Pai's role as heir to the Nan-tsung tradition is the *Hai-ch'iung ch'uan-tao chi* 海瓊傳道集 (An Anthology of [Pai] Hai-ch'iung's Transmission of the Tao, TT 1017, HY 1298) compiled by a disciple, Ch'en Shou-mo 陳守默. Pai's instructions are reminiscent of Ho Ta-t'ung's emphasis on the *Ts'an-t'ung ch'i*, the terminology of which Pai glosses according to alchemical codes. Another devotee, Liu Yüan-ch'ang 留元長, compiled the *Hai-ch'iung wen-tao chi* 海瓊問道集 (An Anthology of Hai-ch'iung's Inquiries on the Tao, TT 1016, HY 1297) in 1217, adding to Pai's contemplative verse his own theoretical abstracts. Both Liu and Ch'en are among those memorialized in the *Hai-ch'iung Pai Chen-jen yü-lu* 海瓊白眞人語錄 (A Dialogic Treatise of the Perfected Pai Hai-ch'iung, 4-*ch.*, TT 1016, HY 1296), a collection of writings compiled by several disciples. At the core of Pai's discourse is a syncretistic approach best exemplified in prosodic compositions such as the "Wan-fa kui-i ke" 萬法歸一歌 (Song on the Unity to which All Creeds Revert). Pai's reputation as a leading ministrant of Thunder Rites is most amply recorded in the *Tao-fa hui-yüan* and in three anthologies attributed to him in the thirteenth-century encyclopedic work entitled *Hsiu-chen shih-shu* 修眞十書: *Yü-lung chi* 玉隆集, *Shang-ch'ing chi* 上清集, and *Wu-i chi* 武夷集.

One claimant to Pai's schooling is Li Tao-ch'un 李道純(*fl.* 1290) whose ministry was centered along the waterways of east Chiang-nan. Aside from a number of exegetic works, two collections of his writings attest to Li's broad acquaintance with Taoist, Confucianist, and Buddhist Prajñāpāramitā traditions. The 6-*ch.* *Ch'ing-an Ying-ch'an-tzu yü-lu* 清庵瑩蟾子語錄 (A Dialogic Treatise of [Li] Ch'ing-an, Ying-ch'an-tzu, TT 729, HY 1053), edited in 1288, is Ch'ai Yüan-hao's 柴元皐 tribute to his encounter with the reclusive Li at Mao-shan. Comprising accounts collected from six disciples, the anthology illustrates the engaging manner in which Li held audience. In one episode recorded at Yangchow, the hierophant challenged his votaries to supply the closing line for his three lines of several heptasyllabic *chüeh-chü*, rewarding successful attempts with an advancement in rank. Another exchange on meditative practices edited by Ts'ai Chih-i 蔡志頤 is repeated in the editor's own anthology of Li's writings, the 6-*ch.* *Chung-ho chi* 中和集(An Anthology on Central Harmony, TT 118-19, HY 249). Central to the work are conceptual diagrams, accompanied by explications that seek in part to establish the common ground of three major concepts: *chin-tan* (golden elixir), *yüan-chiao* 圓覺(primal awakening) of Buddhism, and *t'ai-chi* 太極(grand ultimate) of Confucianism. The inherent unity of the three traditions represented is something Li pursues in everything from his theoretical essays to his *lü-shih* and *tz'u*.

Inheriting Li's scholastic tradition was Wang Chieh 王玠(*fl.* 1310) of Nan-ch'ang南昌(Kiangsi), the versatile compiler of a number of exegetic works, including that for Ch'iu Ch'u-chi's "Ch'ing-t'ien ke." In a 1392 preface to Wang's collected works, the 3-*ch.* *Huan-chen chi* 還眞集(TT 739, HY 1066), the forty-third Celestial Master Chang Yü-ch'u praises the text as a masterpiece on the principles of the regenerative enchymoma. Following a diagrammatic introduction to *chin-tan* is a series of essays and verse, including five "Pu-hsü tz'u" 步虛詞(Cantos on Pacing the Void) of customary visionary quality and a *tz'u* on the uniform principle of the three traditions (*san-chiao i-li* 三教一理).

Another heir to Li Tao-ch'un's propaedeutics, Miao Shan-shih 苗善時 of Chin-ling 金陵(Kiangsu), is memorialized in an account compiled in 1324 by his disciple Wang Chih-tao 王志道. With a title reminiscent of the condensed dialogic tradition of the Lin-chi 臨濟 brotherhood of Ch'an practice, the 2-*ch.* *Hsüan-chiao ta kung-an* 玄教大公案 (Great Case Studies of the Sublime Teachings, TT 734, HY 1057) presents Miao's own judgment on sixty-four citations, the main points of which are summarized in closing *sung*. Drawing on sources from the *Tao-te-ching* and *Tu-jen ching* to the sayings of Wang Che and Pai Yü-ch'an, Miao is a spokesman for the synthesis of variant traditions that was popularly termed Hsüan-men 玄門. This new wave of ecumenism gained prominence during the Yüan empire by attempting to reconcile all regional and partisan traditions.

Southwest down the Yangtze at Lu-ling 廬陵(Kiangsi) reigned another synthesizer of northern and southern traditions. The erudite commentator to the *Tu-jen ching*, *Ts'an-t'ung ch'i*, and *Wu-chen p'ien*, Ch'en Chih-hsü 陳致虛 (*fl.* 1329-36), wrote extensively on his training in the contemplative arts. The *Chin-tan ta-yao* 金丹大要(A Vast Summary on the Golden Elixir, 16-*ch.*, TT 736-38, HY 1059) he compiled was designed to be a complete guide to *chin-tan*, based on his assimilation and critical analysis of centuries of writing on the subject. Acknowledging his obligations to the heritage of Chang Po-tuan, Ch'en, at the same time, identified himself most directly with the Ch'üan-chen lineage. Although he pays due respect to the Confucianist tradition in his synthesis, it is clearly the Ch'an emphasis on intuitive recognition of one's Buddha-nature or *buddhatā* to which Ch'en most earnestly strives to equate the *chin-tan* experience. Among Ch'en's experiments in prosodic compositions is the "*Tao-te-ching* chuan-yü" 道德經轉語, a Ch'an-inspired series of heptasyllabic *chüeh-chü* that recasts each of the eighty-one passages of the classic as a *chin-tan* epigram.

Evidence for the revival of interest in Thunder Rites among late *chin-tan* practitioners is found in the writings of Wang Wei-i 王惟一 (*fl.* 1294-1304) of Sung-chiang 松江 (Kiangsu). A Confucianist scholar who gained his introduction into the contemplative procedures of *nei-tan* late in life, Wang in 1304 compiled the *Ming-tao p'ien* 明道篇 (A Folio on Illuminating the Tao, TT 133, HY 273) as a literary record of his discipline. Following a selection of *lü-shih*, *chüeh-chü*, and *tz'u* sequences is a theoretical essay espousing the superiority of Chang Po-tuan's heritage and the inherent conformity of Confucianism, Buddhism, and Taoism. An earlier work (compiled in 1294), the *Tao-fa hsin-chuan* 道法心傳 (Confidential Transmissions of Taoist Rites, TT 997, HY 1243), opens with over a hundred *chüeh-chü* that reveal Wang's assimilation of the conventions of Thunder Rites, to which are added essays clarifying his induction.

Foremost in initiating Wang to Thunder Rites was the renowned Master Mo Ch'i-yen, a native of Hu-chou 湖州 (Chekiang) who settled in Nan-feng 南豐 (Kiangsi). A rare example of Mo's verse is incorporated in the 9-*ch.* *Ming-ho yü-yin* 鳴鶴餘音 (Some Lingering Overtones of the Calling Crane, TT 744-45, HY 1092), primarily a reservoir of Ch'üan-chen literature compiled *c.* 1347 by P'eng Chih-chung 彭致中 of Mount Hsien-yu 仙游山 (Fukien). Chronicling the history of its compilation is a preface by Yü Chi 虞集 (1272-1348), to whom the anthology is also sometimes attributed. The original core of the work consists of a series of twenty lyrics to the tune of "Su-wu man" 蘇武慢 composed by a Reverend Master Feng 馮尊師 of Kuei-chi 會稽 (Chekiang), with matching verses by Yü. Additional *tz'u* lyrics fill all but the last *chüan*, which comprises a variety of prosodic and prose forms, from *fu* and *ke* to formal creeds entitled "Sheng-t'ang wen" 昇堂文. To Wu Ch'eng-en, the anthology offered substantial material for adaptation as prefatory and background material in the *Hsi-yu chi** (A. Yu, 1977).

One of the most advanced syntheses of the "san-chiao," the traditions of Buddhism, Taoism, and Confucianism, was accomplished by Chao I-chen 趙宜眞 (d. 1382), a descendant of the Sung imperial household who was instrumental in transmitting a large corpus of Ch'ing-wei ritual. Among his mentors were students of the *chin-tan* authority Chin Chih-yang 金志陽 (d. 1336), a native of Yung-chia 永嘉 (Chekiang) who settled at Lung-hu Shan after a quest both north and south for knowledgeable preceptors. Chao took refuge in the far West during the 1352 uprising and then after a brief session with the forty-second Celestial Master Chang Cheng-ch'ang 張正常 (1335-1378), finally settled in Yü-tu 鄂都 (Kiangsi). One of his many followers, Liu Yüan-jan 劉淵然, also of the southern Kan-chou 贛州 corridor, compiled the Master's teachings into a volume entitled *Yüan-yang-tzu fa-yü* 原陽子法語 (The Codified Sayings of Yüan-yang-tzu, TT 738, HY 1063). The 2-*ch.* text is a miscellaneous collection of prose and verse, many of which pay tribute to Chao's former Masters and sing the praises of *nei-tan*. Just as his cognizance of Buddhist sources is evident in this text, so do they also inform Chao's *Ling-pao kuei-k'ung chüeh* 靈寶歸空訣 (An Introduction to the Ling-pao Tradition of Returning to the Void, TT 319, HY 568), a series of annotated heptasyllabic *chüeh-chü* to which is appended a narrative on the therapeutic experiences of the Lin-chi Ch'an Master Tsung-ch'üan 宗泉 (1089-1163).

Chao is among those celebrated in the 12-*ch. Hsien-ch'üan chi* 峴泉集 (The Alpine Spring Anthology, TT 1018-21, HY 1300), one of the largest and most diverse literary collections in the Taoist Canon. This anthology of Chang Yü-ch'u's 張宇初 (1361-1410) writings includes everything from hagiographies, essays on eccesiological history and lineal transmissions, to five *chüan* of prosodic selections. The forty-third Celestial Master also prepared a volume of writings attributed to his forebear Chang Chi-hsien 張繼先 (1092-1126), the eminent thirtieth Celestial Master who served under Sung Hui-tsung. Compiled in 1395, the *San-shih tai T'ien-shih Hsü-ching chen-chün yü-lu* 三十代天師虛靜眞君語錄 (A Dialogic Treatise of the Perfected Lord Hsü-ching, the Celestial Master of the Thirtieth Generation, TT 996, HY 1239) consists of 1 *chüan* of prose writings and 6 *chüan* of verse. Most prevalent are heptasyllabic *lü-shih* and *tz'u*, largely epistolary or didactic compositions that reveal much about the company the Master kept. These writings invite comparison with those of the *Ming-chen p'o-wang chang-sung* 明眞破妄章頌 (Stanzaic Laudations on Exposing Falsehoods and Revealing Truths, TT 915, HY 977), a series of heptasyllabic quatrains also credited to Chang Chi-hsien.

F. Exegeses and Encyclopedic Compilations

Over the centuries a variety of instructional aids have been devised to introduce literate patrons to the tenets and practices of various Taoist traditions. Of particular vitality is the post-T'ang exegetic tradition, which in some ways rivals its ancestor, Han scholasticism. The sources of most appeal to commentators, at least in the history of canonic publication, are the *Huang-ti yin-fu ching* (TT 54-58, HY 108-127), the *Tao-te-ching* (TT 354-448, HY 676-725), the *Chuang-tzu* (TT 467-519, HY 734-44), and the *Chou-i ts'an-t'ung ch'i* (TT 621-29, HY 996-1005). Rather than reiterate the bibliographic history of the commentaries to these and comparably early sources (Balazs and Hervouet, 1978; Boltz, 1984), attention is directed here to two texts of the Ling-pao tradition that might easily be overlooked. Whether analyzing an edition of the more popular texts or a less well-known commentarial work, it is essential to clarify the specific contemplative or revelatory tradition from which a commentator takes his stance.

Although nothing as ambitious as the 60-*ch.* Shen-hsiao reinterpretations was ever again attempted, the *Tu-jen ching* was the only Ling-pao scripture made subject to almost perpetual scrutiny. Inspired by Ch'en Ching-yüan's 陳景元 (*fl.* 1067-1099) composite edition of commentaries dating from the fifth through the eighth centuries, Hsiao Ying-sou 蕭應叟 prepared the *Tu-jen shang-p'in miao-ching nei-i* 度人上品妙經內義 (A Commentary to the Wondrous Scripture of Supreme Rank on Salvation, 5-*ch.*, TT 43-44, HY 90) in 1226. In an interpretation based primarily on *chin-tan* theories, but drawing as well as Confucianist and Buddhist tenets, Hsiao reveals himself to be a partisan of the syncretic approach typical of his age. Of similar background is the undated *Tu-jen shang-p'in miao-ching chu* (A Commentary to the Wondrous Scripture of Supreme Rank on Salvation, TT 40-41, HY 88) in 3 *chüan*, attributed to a "Ch'ing-yüan chen-jen" 青元眞人 and edited by Kuo Kang-feng 郭岡鳳, a protégé of the Ching-ming 淨明 heritage of north Kiangsi. Closing the work are five narratives on the efficacy of chanting the *Tu-jen ching*, all of which are set in central Szechwan *c.* 1190-1204. Reminiscent of the *T'ai-shang kan-ying p'ien* 太上感應篇 (Folios on the Vibrant Responses of the Most High,

TT 834-39, HY 1159) annotated by the Szechwan native Li Ch'ang-ling 李昌齡(*fl.* 1233), these homiletic stories convey the sort of cure that can be expected through the recitation or copying of the scripture. Another *chin-tan* specialist from Kiangsi, one who is renowned for his edition of the *Ts'an-t'ung ch'i* (Needham, 1976), Ch'en Chih-hsü 陳致虛(*fl.* 1329-1336), completed the 3-*ch. Tu-jen shang-p'in miao-ching chu-chieh* 註解(An Exegesis on the Wondrous Scripture of Supreme Rank on Salvation, TT 45-46, HY 91) in 1336. An alleged recipient of Hsiao Ying-sou's secret codes on the regenerative enchymoma, Ch'en claims that his annotation arose from a collation of his commentaries to the *Tao-te-ching* and the *Vajracchedikā- sūtra*, as well as his definitive *Chin-tan ta-yao* 金丹大要. Also stationed in Kiangsi at about the same time, Hsüeh Chi-chao 薛季昭(*fl.* 1304-1316) transmitted a 3-*ch. Chu-chieh* 註解(TT 46, HY 92) which is centered on the "san-chiao" 三教 instruction purportedly revealed to him by the Thunder Master Lei Shih-chung. The Hun-yüan 混元 Thunder Rites to which Lei was heir likewise inspired the *Tu-jen shang-p'in miao-ching t'ung-i* 通義(A Comprehensive Interpretation of the Wondrous Scripture of Supreme Rank on Salvation, 4-*ch.*, TT 41-42, HY 89) of the forty-third Celestial Master Chang Yü-ch'u.

Almost equally appealing to scholars of the Ling-pao tradition is the *Sheng-shen ching* 生神經(Scripture on the Generation of Divine Spirits). The author of the widely acclaimed *Tao-te-ching chi-chieh* 道德經集解 in 4 *chüan* (Collected Annotations on the *Tao-te-ching*, TT 393-94, HY 705), Tung Ssu-ching 董思靖(*fl.* 1246-1252), also compiled the 4-*ch. Tung-hsüan ling-pao tzu-jan chiu-t'ien sheng-shen yü-chang ching chieh-i* 洞玄靈寶自然九天生神玉章經解義 (An Interpretation on the Tung-hsüan Ling-pao Scripture of the Jade Stanzas on the Spontaneous Generation of Divine Spirits within the Nine Celestial Realms, TT 186, HY 396). Affiliated with the T'ien-ch'ing Kuan 天慶觀 at Ch'ing-yüan 清源(Fukien), Tung reveals an expert command of the textual history of this revelation and pertinent Shang-ch'ing scriptures. Two other thirteenth-century analyses seek to identify the groundwork for *chin-tan* practices in the text, the *Chiu-t'ien sheng-shen yü-chang ching-chieh* 九天生神玉章經解 (An Analysis of the Scripture of Jade Stanzas on the Generation of Divine Spirits within the Nine Celestial Realms, 3-*ch.*, TT 187, HY 397) compiled in 1205 by Wang Hsi-ch'ao 王希巢 of Mien-chou 綿州(Szechwan) and the *Chiu-t'ien sheng-shen chang-ching chu* 章經注(A Commentary on the Stanzaic Scripture on the Generation of Divine Spirits within the Nine Celestial Realms, 3-*ch.*, TT 188, HY 398) attributed to a Hua Yang-fu 華陽復 presumably of Kiangsu.

Preserved in the collectanea or *lei shu** are many textual traditions that would no doubt otherwise remain obscure. As hosts to comprehensive bodies of sacred literature, these encyclopedic works are no less than time capsules of the social milieu from which they arose. Compilers of these sourcebooks were able to build on an established archival tradition, one that produced such works as the late sixth-century *Wu-shang pi-yao* and Wang Hsüan-ho's (*fl.* 883) *Shang-ch'ing tao-lei shih-hsiang* and *San-tung chu-nang*. The largest collectaneum printed in the Taoist Canon is the 122-*ch. Yün-chi ch'i-ch'ien,** compiled by Chang Chün-fang (*fl.* 1008-1025). An indispensable reference for textual critics, this work conserves a number of unique and variorum editions dating from the formative age of scriptural lineages to the early eleventh century (Yoshioka, 1955; Schipper, 1981-1982).

Two incomparable collections specializing in *nei-tan* literature appeared during the Southern Sung. First was the 42-*ch. Tao-shu* 道樞(Pivot of the Tao, TT 641-48, HY 1011), edited by Tseng Ts'ao曾慥(*c.* 1131-1193), a bibliophile who compiled the widely acclaimed 60-*ch.* lexicon of prose literature entitled *Lei-shuo*類說. The *Tao-shu* is organized in over 100 headings, under which are collected textual citations dating from the T'ang to the early twelfth century. Most predominant are sources central to the *chin-tan* tradition of the South, including a unique redaction of the *Ts'an-t'ung ch'i* and the writings of Liu Ts'ao劉操(*c.* 1050) and Chang Po-tuan. Many headings are also devoted to the dialogic tradition ascribed to the patriarchs Chung-li Ch'üan and Lü Yen, including the *Ling-pao pi-fa* 靈寶畢法 and a recension of Shih Chien-wu's 施肩吾(*fl.* 820) *Chung Lü ch'uan-tao chi* 鍾呂傳道集 (An Anthology on Chung [-li]'s Transmission of the Tao to Lü).

Shih's short treatise also makes up a heading in the *Hsiu-chen shih-shu* 修眞十書 (Ten Tracts on Cultivating Perfection, 60-*ch.*, TT 122-131, HY 263), the most comprehensive collection of Nan-tsung writings in the Taoist Canon. Four of the ten headings of the anonymously compiled collectaneum are dominated by the writings of Pai Yü-ch'an, one of which closes with a colophon inscribed by Liao Cheng 廖正 in 1244. The writings of Pai's mentor Ch'en Nan陳楠(d. 1213) are also included, followed by several early *nei-tan* treatises such as Ts'ui Hsi-fan's崔希範 (*fl.* 940) *Ju-yao ching* 入藥經(A Mirror to Penetrating Medications). One of the latest texts preserved is the *Chin-tan ta-ch'eng chi* 金丹大成集 (An Anthology on the Great Completion of the Golden Elixir) of Hsiao T'ing-chih 蕭廷芝(*fl.* 1260), a second-generation disciple of Pai.

A little recognized encyclopedic resource on the beliefs and practices of the Ming empire, the 8-*ch. T'ien-huang chih-tao t'ai-ch'ing yü-ts'e* 天皇至道太清玉冊 (The Jade Fascicles of T'ai-ch'ing on the Ultimate Tao of the Celestial August, TT 1109-11, HY 1472), was compiled by the playwright Chu Ch'üan* in 1444. Citing a variety of sources from the *Chen-kao* to Hsieh Shou-hao's *Hun-yüan sheng-chi*, Chu organized his text under nineteen headings. Among the topics covered are cosmology, origins of Taoism, bibliography, protocols and instructions for ritual performance, ranks of officialdom, and the various settings, accouterments, musical accompaniments, dress, offerings, and calendrical schedules for various rites. As a document assembled by a highborn observer of Taoist traditions in the early Ming, the *T'ai-ch'ing yü-ts'e* is unique.

BIBLIOGRAPHY:

Akizuki, Kan'ei 秋月觀映. 1978. *Chūgoku kinsei Dōkyō no keisei: Jōmeidō no kisoteki kenyū* 中國近世道教の形成：淨明道の基礎的研究 Tokyo. A monograph on the Ching-ming Tao, a nationalistic movement especially popular in the thirteenth and fourteenth centuries.

———. 1981. "Jōmeidō kenkyū ue no nisan no mondai" 淨明道研究上の二三の問題, *Tōhō shū-kyō*, 8 (October), 1-15.

Balazs, Etienne and Yves Hervouet, eds. 1978. *A Sung Bibliography.* Hong Kong. Includes several notices on exegetic texts in the *Tao-tsang*, contributed by Wong Shiu Hon.

Boltz, Judith M. 1982. "Opening the Gates of Purgatory: A Twelfth-century Taoist Meditation Technique for the Salvation of Lost Souls," in *Tantric and Taoist Studies in Honour of R. A. Stein*, Michel Strickmann, ed., *Mélanges chinois et bouddhiques*, 21, 488-510.

———. 1985. *A Survey of Taoist Literature, Tenth to Seventeenth Centuries.* Center for Chinese Studies, University of California, Berkeley.

Chang, Fu-jui 張馥蕊. 1976. *I-chien chih t'ung-chien* 夷堅志通檢. Taipei. An indispensable concordance to proper names in Hung Mai's* *I-chien chih*, many of which pertain to twelfth-century Taoist traditions.

Ch'en, Kuo-fu 陳國符. 1962. *Tao-tsang yüan-liu k'ao* 道藏源流. 2v. Peking. An essential reference to Taoist bibliographic traditions.

Fukui, Kōjun 福井康順, *et al.*, eds. 1981. *Dōkyō* 道教. 3v. Tokyo. A comprehensive survey of

Taoist studies, including essays on belles-lettres and hagiography.

Hawkes, David. 1981. "Quanzhen Plays and Quanzhen Masters," *BEFEO*, 69, 153-170.

Liu, Shih-p'ei 劉師培. 1936. *Tu Tao-tsang chi* 讀道藏記, in *Liu Shen-shu hsien-sheng i-shu* 劉申叔先生遺書. Ningwu (Shansi). v. 63. A collection of analytic notes on several canonic sources.

Liu, Ts'un-yan 柳存仁. 1967. "Yen-chiu Ming-tai Tao-chiao ssu-hsiang Chung Jih-wen shu-mu chü-yao" 研究明代道教思想中日文書目舉要, *Ch'ung-chi hsüeh-pao*, 6.2, 107-130. A bibliography of primary and secondary sources, with annotations on research problems of Ming and earlier periods.

———. 1970. "The Penetration of Taoism into the Ming Neo-Confucianist Elite," *TP*, 57, 31-102.

Liu, Ts'un-yan and Judith Berling. 1982. "The "Three Teachings" in the Mongol-Yüan Period," in *Yüan Thought: Chinese Thought and Religion*, Hok-lam Chan and W. T. deBary, eds., New York, pp. 479-512.

Loon, Piet van der. 1979. "A Taoist Collection of the Fourteenth Century," in *Studia Sino-Mongolica: Festscrift für Herbert Franke*, Wolfgang Bauer, ed., Wiesbaden, pp. 401-405. A study of the late fourteenth-century ritual corpus entitled *Tao-fa hui-yüan*.

Lu, Gwei-Djen. 1973. "The Inner Elixir (Nei Tan): Chinese Physiological Alchemy," in *Changing Perspectives in the History of Science: Essays in Honour of Joseph Needham*, Mikuláš Teich and Robert Young, eds., London, 1973, pp. 68-84.

Min, I-te 閔一得, ed. 1889. *Tao-tsang hsü-p'ien* 道藏續篇. Shanghai. An edition of some twenty works, many of which are annotated.

Miyakawa, Hisayuki 宮川尚志. 1975. "Sō no Kisō to Dōkyō" 宋の徽宗輿道教, *Tōkai Daigaku kiyō: Bungaku-bu*, 23, 1-10.

Needham, Joseph, ed. 1974, 1976, 1980, 198?. *Science and Civilisation in China*. V. 5. *Chemistry and Chemical Technology: Spagyrical Discovery and Invention*. Part II, with Lu Gwei-Djen: *Magisteries of Gold and Immortality*. Part III, with Ho Ping-yü and Lu Gwei-Djen: *Historical Survey, from Cinnabar Elixirs to Synthetic Insulin*. Part IV, with Ho Ping-yü, Lu Gwei-Djen, and Nathan Sivin: *Apparatus, Theories and Gifts* (with extensive bibliography of *Tao-tsang* texts). Part V: *Physiological Alchemy* (preliminaries in Lu, 1973). Cambridge.

Pai, Yün-chi 白雲霽. N.d. *Tao-tsang mu-lu hsiang-chu* 道藏目錄詳註. N.p. A reprint of the Wen-chien ke 文津閣 copy of the Ssu-k'u library edition is available in Ting, 1922 where the title page attributes it to Li Chieh 李杰, but the table of contents lists it as a work of Pai. Compiled in 1626, this is the earliest descriptive catalogue of the *Tao-tsang*.

P'eng, Wen-ch'in 彭文勤 and Ho Lung-hsiang 賀龍驤, eds. 1906. *Ch'ung-k'an Tao-tsang chi-yao* 重刊道藏輯要. 244v. Ch'eng-tu.

Sakai, Tadao 酒井忠夫. *Dōkyō kenkyū bunken mokuroku (Nihon)* 道教研究文獻目錄（日本）. Tokyo. Invaluable bibliography, organized by subject.

Saso, Michael, ed. 1975. *Chuang-Lin Hsü Tao-tsang* 莊林續道藏. 25v. Taipei. Facsimile editions of sacred texts transmitted from Lin Ju-mei 林汝梅 down to Chuang-Ch'en Teng-yün 莊陳登雲; with English summary.

———. 1978. *Dōkyō hiketsu shūsei* 道教秘訣集成. Tokyo. Additional facsimiles of scriptures Saso acquired in Taiwan; with English summary.

Sawada, Mizuho 澤田瑞穗. 1980. "Sōdai no shinju shinkō: *Iken Shi* no setsuwa o chūshin toshite" 宋代の神呪信仰—「夷堅志」の説話を中心として, *Tōhō shūkyō*, 56 (October), 1-30.

Schipper, Kristofer M. 1966. "Taiwan-chih Tao-chiao wen-hsien" 臺灣之道教文獻, *Taiwan wen-hsien*, 17.3, 173-192. Transcript of an oral address, with a listing of a manuscript texts Schipper acquired in Taiwan.

———. 1974. "The Written Memorial in Taoist Ceremonies," in *Religion and Ritual in Chinese Society*, Arthur P. Wolf, ed., Stanford, pp. 309-324.

———. 1975. *Le fen-teng: ritual taoiste*. Paris. Study and translation of a ritual text in the *Wu-shang huang-lu ta-chai li-ch'eng i*.

———. 1975a. *Concordance du Tao-tsang; titres des ouvrages*. Paris. Reprinted by Li Tien-k'uei 李殿魁 as *Cheng-t'ung Tao-tsang mu-lu so-yin* 正統道藏目錄索引. Taipei, 1977.

———. 1981, 1982. *Index du Yun-ji qi-qian*. 2v. Paris. Shen Tseng-chih 沈曾植 (1851-1922). 1962. *Hai-jih lou cha-ts'ung* 海日樓札叢. Peking. Ch. 6 is comprised of bibliographic notes on Taoist sources.

Sivin, Nathan. 1981. "Discovery of Spagyrical Invention," *HJAS*, 41.1 (June), 219-235. In review of Needham, 1976.

Strickmann, Michel. 1975. "Sōdai no raigi: Shinshō undō to Dōka nanshū ni tsuite no ryakusetsu" 宋代の雷儀：神霄運動と道家南宗についての略説. *Tōhō shūkyō*, 46, 15-28.

———. 1978. "The Longest Taoist Scripture," *History of Religions*, 17. 3-4 (February-May), 331-354.

———. 1979. "The Taoist Renaissance of the Twelfth Century," unpublished MS. of a presentation to the Third International Conference of Taoist Studies, Unterägeri, Switzerland, 3-9 September 1979.

———. 1980. "History, Anthropology, and Chinese Religion," *HJAS*, 40, 201-248. In review of Michael Saso, *The Teachings of Taoist Master Chuang*, New Haven, 1978.

Tao-tsang chü-yao 道藏擧要. N.d. 296v. Shanghai. A selection of some 175 titles from the *Tao-tsang* reprinted by Commercial Press.

Ting, Fu-pao 丁福保, ed. 1922. *Tao-tsang ching-hua lu* 道藏精華錄. Shanghai. Approximately 100 titles drawn from canonic and extra-canonic sources.

Tu, Chieh-hsiang 杜潔祥, ed. 1983. *Tao-chiao wen-hsien* 道教文獻. 20v. Taipei. This new collection of Taoist literature includes facsimile editions of rare hagiographic and topographic works.

Waley, Arthur. 1931. *Travels of an Alchemist*. London. A translation of Li Chih-ch'ang's

(1193-1256) *Ch'ang-ch'un chen-jen hsi-yu chi* on the life and travels of the Ch'üan-chen Master Ch'iu Ch'u-chi (1148-1227). Reviewed by P. Pelliot, *TP*, 28 (1931), 413-427.

Wang, Meng-yün 王夢雲 *et al.*, eds. 1976. *Sung Pai Chen-jen Yü-ch'an ch'üan-chi* 宋白眞人玉蟾全集. Taipei. Writings of Pai Yü-ch'an.

Weng, Tu-chien 翁獨健, ed. 1935. *Tao-tsang tzu-mu yin-te*. Peking, 1935. Harvard-Yenching Institute Sinological Index Series, No. 25. Indices to the *Tao-tsang* and *Tao-tsang chi-yao*.

Yen, I-p'ing 嚴一萍, ed. 1974. *Tao-chiao yen-chiu tzu-liao* 道教研究資料. 2v. Taipei, 1974. The hagiographic works in v. 1 include a reconstruction of Chia Shan-hsiang's (*fl.* 1086) *Kao-tao chuan*. Four texts from the eighteenth and nineteenth centuries on the Ch'üan-chen tradition comprise v. 2.

Yoshioka, Yoshitoyo 吉岡義豐. 1955. *Dōkyō kyōten shiron* 道教經典史論. Tokyo. Includes an index to 1403 titles cited in the *Yün-chi ch'i-ch'ien*.

Yu, Anthony C., tr. and ed. 1977. *The Journey to the West*. V. 1. Chicago. Yu's introduction (pp. 1-62) and commentary take into account Wu Ch'eng-en's (*c.* 1500-*c.* 1582) familiarity with Taoist literature and, in particular, alchemical terminology.

WOMEN'S LITERATURE

Sharon Shih-jiuan Hou

I. Introduction

IN the long history of classical literature women have for the most part played a small role. Except in a few isolated cases critics have not judged their work the equal of that of their far more numerous brothers. To a considerable extent, the general inferiority and mediocrity which characterizes women's literature when placed in the larger context of China's literary history may be attributed to the many and varied restrictions imposed on Chinese women.

In traditional China educational establishments, which were administered by the government and would lead to officialdom, were reserved exclusively for men. Family and clan were thus the only source of education for women. Practically, however, this source did not perform its educational function satisfactorily. For one thing, most Chinese—over ninety percent of the population—were peasants, artisans, or merchants and were illiterate. In the families of the educated elite, most girls did have some chance to acquire education. They received instruction in musical instruments, in chess, in calligraphy, and in painting. Not a few of these girls were, like their brothers, sent to clan schools or studied at home with their parents or private tutors. But such opportunities were accorded far less frequently to girls than to boys, for two reasons. First, for a girl the lure of wealth and fame for the family and the individual which usually accompanied success in the civil-service examinations and the resultant official career did not exist. Second, in Chinese society the first and foremost duty of a woman was to fulfill her prescribed functions in the family as wife, mother, and daughter-in-law. For centuries, the lives and education of virtually all Chinese women were wholly given over to the preparation for and actual undertaking of these prescribed roles in the families of their husbands.

The maidenhood of the daughters of official families consisted of an exclusively feminine training program carried out in strict seclusion. At the age of seven, the girl was separated from her brothers and male relatives. She lived in the inner apartments, kept company only by her nurse, maidservants, and female members of the family. At the age of ten, she began to receive instruction in various domestic arts; of supreme importance were sewing, weaving, embroidering, and supervising a household. Such education ended with her being married in her middle or late teens as arranged by her parents.

Marriage in China was not so much the alliance of two individuals as that of two families. The personal desires of the bride and groom were sometimes taken into account, but only insofar as these desires could be satisfied without disturbance of the concern and interest of the families. A bride was expected to fulfill three major responsibilites; to fall short in any one would be deemed as bringing disgrace on herself, her parents, and her clan. Her three obligations were performing domestic duties, attending to the needs and comfort of her husband and elders, and bearing and raising male descendants. It was in the fulfillment of this last obligation, bearing sons as a means to assure the continuity of the family line, that a woman's position and authority in the family largely hinged. If she did not have a natural son, she would adopt one from the clan or initiate and further the acquisition of concubines and be the mother of the children borne to them. Upon the death of her mother-in-law, the wife of the eldest son who had borne a male child succeeded as the matriarch of the household, assuming the authority and responsibility of the position. Throughout her lifetime a married woman was entirely confined within the sphere of her residence. Her experience of nature was limited to the gardens of the family premises. She might occasionally make a trip to a temple, a scenic spot, or a relative, but even then she rode only in a heavily curtained sedan-chair.

Ladies of the imperial harem, many of them well educated, were still more physically isolated and emotionally deprived. According to *Chou li* 周禮 (The Rites of the Kingdom of Chou), an emperor should have an empress, followed by three concubines of the first rank, nine of the second rank, twenty-seven of the third rank, and eighty-one of the fourth rank. In practice, the number of his consorts varied from several to over a hundred. In addition to these formal consorts, an emperor had at his disposal lower-ranking palace women, usually numbering in the thousands, such as attendants, musicians, and dancers, who either came from families of commoners or were the female relations forfeited by officials convicted of crimes. As long as they lived in the palace, many for their entire lifetimes, aside from eunuchs and little boys the only male imperial women were allowed to see was the emperor. Since one man could not satisfy several thousand women, many lived their lives without ever having been "favored" through a sexual relationship with the emperor.

The curtailment of the physical mobility and the intellectual and emotional development of Chinese upper-class women has been rightly attributed to a coupling of patriarchy with the dominance of Confucianism, which placed considerable emphasis on order and relations in society.

Perhaps the most distinctive feature of Chinese patriarchal society was the cult of ancestral worship performed by male members of the family and clan—a practice which began in childhood when on the holiday of *Ch'ing-ming* 清明 (Clear Brightness) boys were made to kneel or bow before ancestral graves while their sisters stood by and watched. Descent being traced through the male line, women were considered secondary in the continuity of the family, and their worth depended largely on the bearing of its heirs. Such social inequality was also manifested in legal and political formulations. Female violators of laws usually received heavier punishment than male counterparts. Moreover, women were rarely entitled to inheritance. Economically, a woman depended on her husband and, after his death, her sons. Participation in politics was rarely granted females, except for an empress assuming *de facto* power or a regency on the death of the emperor, if his successor was too young. Wu Tse-t'ien 武則天 (624-705), who seized power from the T'ang, was the only empress who ruled in her own right.

The inferior status of Chinese women in a social system of patriarchy was strengthened by the rise and eventual domination of Confucian philosophy, which advocated, among other things, male dominance and female compliance as the primary instruments of social stability. The cosmology of Confucianism originated from the *yin* 陰 and *yang* 陽 theory in the *I-ching* 易經 (The Book of Changes). This theory maintained that the cosmos was formed by the two elements *yin*, or the negative, and *yang*, or the positive, which in interaction and union underlie and determine all of the events and phenomena in the universe. *Yin*, the negative element, stands for darkness, the water, the moon, weakness, depth, and all things that are feminine; *yang*, the positive element, represents light, the mountains, the sun, strength, height, and all things that are masculine. These two elements are antithetical but not discordant and opposing forces. Rather, they reciprocate and complement each other to form an orderly and harmonious entirety. Neither element is superior, neither inferior; both are indispensable. In the human species, man constitutes the *yang* element, and woman the *yin* element. Within the particular sphere of family as the fundamental grouping in the human community, men are to take charge of affairs outside the house, and women those inside the house. More specifically, men are to assume the financial responsibility for the family, women to serve the daily needs of the husband and parents-in-law, raise the children, and take care of routine household tasks.

It would be unfair to assert that in intent and spirit Confucianism, especially in its early stages, attached importance in any significant degree to the difference in sex. Women were as respectable as men, provided their familial responsibilites were performed in accordance with social expectations. Nevertheless, in reality the feminine behavior formulated in the Confucian doctrine did impose strong restrictions on the thoughts and actions of women. In the course of history, except for occasional, brief periods when Taoism, with its absorption in spontaneity, or Buddhism, with its relative indifference to status, rose to prevalence, Confucianism held almost absolute sway over the minds of the Chinese. At various times there were a number of scholars who, in line with the Confucian view of education and self-cultivation as the civilizing force, endeavored to preach the feminine values defined in the Confucian ethics, illustrating them by examples or tenets. Among those scholars the most remarkable were the writers of basic textbooks for female education, *nü-hsüeh* 女學 or *nü-chiao* 女教 in traditional phraseology, and the philosophers of Neo-Confucianism from the Sung through the Ch'ing periods.

In content and format, writings for the education of women may be classified into two categories: biographies of women in history intended for emulation or as admonition and theoretical elucidation of feminine virtues with rules of conduct for everyday life. The first group of works was generally patterned on the *Lieh-nü chuan* 列女傳 (Biographies of Women), traditionally attributed to Liu Hsiang,* a Han-dynasty Confucian scholar. The second group of works had as their precedent the *Nü chieh* 女誡 (Commandments for Women) by Pan Chao 班昭 (d. A.D. 116), a woman moralist, historian, and creative writer.

Liu Hsiang's *Lieh-nü chuan*, which is based on the belief that a nation's prosperity or adversity was highly influenced by women and which was originally intended for the perusal of the emperor, recounted the lives and deeds of 125 women from legendary times to the Han period. Ranging from imperial consorts to peasant wives, these women were labeled either as paragons of one of the six womanly virtues or feminine incarnations of one deadly sin. The six virtues were: *mu-i* 母儀 (motherly correct deportment),

177

hsien-ming 賢明 (virtue and sagacity), *jen-chih* 仁智 (benignity and wisdom), *chen-shun* 貞順 (purity and obedience), *chieh-i* 節義 (chastity and righteousness), and *pien-t'ung* 辯通 (reasoning and understanding). The one sin was *nieh-pi* 孽嬖 (perniciousness and depravity). Each main section began with a short introduction. Each biography placed under it was completed by either a eulogy on the virtuous or a warning against the wicked. The book was widely circulated in its time and in succeeding generations. Texts and illustrations were frequently painted on household walls. *Lieh-nü chuan* became even more influential with the publication in the Ming dynasty of *Kuei fan* 閨範 (Standards within Women's Quarters) compiled by Lü K'un 呂坤 (1536-1618), a collection of biographies taken from the earlier work, but retold in a more comprehensive language. According to its compiler, the book intended to prepare a road of propriety which women might travel. He classified the biographies into three main categories—the way of maidens, the way of wives, and the way of mothers—and gave those biographies detailed annotations. In addition, Lü K'an supplied long quotations from classical works that dealt with the social relations of women.

Whereas each exemplary woman in *Lieh-nü chuan* was applauded for only one single virtue, Pan Chao's *Nü chieh* contained a system of moral principles and the practical application of these principles in accordance with a set of invented rules. *Nü chieh* thus constituted the first complete work of feminine ethics in the history of Chinese philosophy. Despite her own erudition in the classics, Pan Chao did not advocate identical education for men and women. Like men, women were born good but needed education in order that their nature would not deteriorate. The education intended for women should be one that could direct their thoughts and actions in personal behavior and family relationships. *Nü chieh*, the crystallization of this philosophy, comprised seven chapters: *Pei-jo* 卑弱 (Humility and Infirmity), *Fu fu* 夫婦 (Husband and Wife), *Ching shen* 敬慎 (Respect and Caution), *Fu hsing* 婦行 (Women's Behavior), *Chuan hsin* 專心 (Fixed Purpose in the Heart), *Ch'ü ts'ung* 曲從 (Bending the Will to Obedience), *Ho shu mei* 和叔妹 (Harmony with Husband's Younger Brothers and Sisters). In these seven chapters the author placed special emphasis on the cultivation, preservation, and exercise of womanly qualities, notably humility, resignation, subservience, self-abasement, and self-abnegation, advocating an unconditional obedience. In more practical terms, a woman must industriously occupy herself with domestic duties, constantly keep herself modest in manner and clean in appearance, and reverently deem her primary responsibility the perpetuation of ancestral worship in the home, i.e., the bearing of heirs for her family. Only then, the author stated, could the wife win the affection and respect of her husband and obtain harmony in the home. *Nü chieh*, like *Lieh-nü chuan*, became widely circulated after its publication and was unanimously regarded in succeeding generations as an indispensable text for the education of women, an influence that perhaps went far beyond what might have been foreseen by the author, whose short introduction to the book indicated that it was meant for her daughters. The influence of *Nü chieh* amply increased with the subsequent appearance of a number of works which promoted and developed the ideas it had set forth. Among them the most celebrated were *Nü Hsiao-ching* 女孝經 (Book of Filial Piety for Women) by the wife of Ch'en Miao 陳邈 (née Cheng 鄭) of the T'ang dynasty, *Nü Lun-yü* 女論語 (The Analects of Confucius for Women) by Sung Jo-hua 宋若華, a consort of Emperor Te-tsung (r. 779-805), *Nei hsün* 內訓 (Instructions of the Interior) by the empress née Hsü 徐 of Emperor Ch'eng-tsu (r. 1403-1424), *Hsin-fu p'u* 新婦譜 (*Instructions for the New Wife*) *by Lu Ch'i* 陸圻(*b. 1614*), *Nü hsüeh* 女學 by Lan Ting-yüan 藍鼎元 (1680-1733), and *Nü-fan chieh lu* 女範 捷錄 (A Concise Account of Basic Regulations for Women) by the mother of Wang Hsiang 王相(Ch'ing dynasty). Wang Hsiang collected *Nü chieh, Nü Lun-yü, Nei hsüan,* and *Nü-fan chieh lu* into *Nü Ssu-shu* 女四書 (The Four Books for Women), whose influence survived until the end of the imperial era.

In general, works for the education of women that were produced during the Ming and Ch'ing times embodied much sterner moralistic views of sexual relations than those of their predecessors. In large measure this attitude reflected the prevailing influence of Neo-Confucianism. With its profound concern for social order in accordance with traditionally defined roles, Neo-Confucianism greatly strengthened the classical discrimination between men and women and enlarged the gulf between the two sexes. To a considerable extent, Neo-Confucianism accounted for the reinforced convention that respectable women did not move about outside the house casually, and for the widespread and indelible social phenomenon of an intensified concern for the chastity of women. Widows, for instance, were prohibited from remarrying; this rule was applied even to young girls whose betrothed had died before marriage. Widows were expected to die rather than allow a violation of their chastity. Suicide by widows was, in fact, rationalized as part of *li-chiao* 禮教 (ethical propriety). Emphasis on female chastity took on added strength with the establishment of a system of court-sponsored rewards for chaste widows and their families. Chastity was, thus, sanctified by law.

This prudish Confucian morality was served by two non-Confucian customs: foot-binding, which was common in the upper classes from the Sung through the Ch'ing periods, and female illiteracy based on a concept embodied in the popular saying *Nü-tzu wu ts'ai pien-shih te* 女子無才便是德 (In a woman lack of talent is a virtue). Foot-binding can be traced to imperial palaces where in earlier times dancing girls would try to attract the attention of emperors by wrapping their feet in silk strips. In the Sung, this custom became popular among upper-class women. The technique was more constrictive: a female infant's feet were bound to produce arched, delicately pointed "golden lotuses," about half the normal size. The resultant tiny steps and swaying gaits made women attractively helpless. They also greatly impeded their independent movement in the outside world. Foot-binding heightened the physical bondage of women, and the concept of female illiteracy as a virtue, popular in the late Ming and early Ch'ing periods, severely hindered their intellectual development. This idea was based on the belief that literacy would adversely affect women's morality and, eventually, their well-being. What brought about such a notion was hard to explain. Remotely, it might have been related to the widely circulated story about Ts'ui Ying-ying 崔鶯鶯, a talented girl of the T'ang dynasty, who had an ill-fated premarital relationship with a young man. The tragic death of Hsiao Kuan-yin 蕭觀音 (1040-1075), Empress I-te 懿德 of Emperor Tao-tsung of the Liao (r. 1055-1100), on the charge of adultery with a court musician as evinced by a love poem written in her calligraphy might also have cautioned people against literacy. And the notion that talented women were always ill-fated was popular. The popular mind often associated literary training with depravity, for there were quite a few courtesans prolific in writing poems. In any case, through the concerted, though accidental, effort of Confucian morality and these two customs, women were kept shackled and ignorant, to attend with one single mind to their prescribed familial responsibilities, until they became for all practical purposes the mere servants of men, their sex objects, and reproducers of the human race.

Ironically, as modern scholarship has noted, the Chinese male-dominated social system, which deprived women of economic independence, and the conservative Confucian feminine ethics, which denied women education and social intercourse, worked, however indirectly and unintentionally, to foster an increased demand for prostitution, which can be traced to the Han dynasty when soldiers were provided with sleeping partners. In later periods, prostitutes had more functions to perform than gratification of sexual desires. In the Six Dynasties keeping cultivated women musicians and dancers in the household to entertain at banquets became a popular practice in wealthy families. Beginning with the T'ang, a class of official courtesans who served at public functions flourished; coming from the most expensive brothels, they usually were highly skilled in music, art, and literature. Prostitutes came from various sources; some were sold to brothels by their poverty-stricken parents or relatives or by kidnappers; others came from households of disgraced officals; still others were widows and divorcees of straitened means. From the T'ang onward, prostitution was also practiced by Taoist nuns, who traveled freely, took lovers at will, and acted as sexual teachers and initiators. Their temples became popular centers of social gatherings for the scholar-gentry class. Prostitutes and Taoist priestesses generally had more control over their lives and enjoyed larger economic freedom, social mobility, and access to literacy and artistry than their more correct but more confined sisters. Men, for their part, conspicuously welcomed the intellectual and social companionship of these relatively carefree and cultivated professional entertainers. Frequenting houses of prostitution was regarded as perfectly natural behavior for a man, especially if he was young and talented.

From the Sung onward, the oppressed status of women in society came to the attention of a group of scholars independent of, and often opposed to, the officially sanctioned Neo-Confucianism. With ever increasing intensity, old moralities concerning remarriage, suicide by widows, foot-binding, and concubinage were questioned. At the same time novel and revolutionary ideas on feminist issues, notably those of social and natural equalities between the two sexes, were introduced and promoted.

The first scholar who took note of the problem in question was Yüan Ts'ai 袁采 (chin-shih, 1163). In a sympathetic reflection on the general condition of women, he urged men to treat them with understanding and kindliness. In the Ming period, Kuei Yu-kuang* reasoned that since a young woman widowed during the period of betrothal had never actually been married, she should be encouraged to marry another man. Kuei's contemporary Li Chih* argued that intellectually women were as capable as men. Lü K'un, the author of *Kuei fan,* condemned widow-suicide, encouraged aged widows to support themselves, acknowledged women's rights to literacy, and portrayed marriage as a reciprocal relationship. Scholars of the Ch'ing times continued such attacks on the rigid and narrow-minded interpretation of Confucian propriety as applied in Neo-Confucianism to the conjugal loyalty of women, on the judgment of female virtue within the narrow confines of *li-chiao,* and on the physical and intellectual curbs imposed on women in general. Such a defense of the rights of women reached its culmination in Yü Cheng-hsieh's 俞正燮 (1775-1840) *K'uei-ssu lei-kao* 癸巳類稿. Yü questioned the validity of a distinction between men and women. He argued for the practice of conjugal loyalty by men, who, in his opinion, must not take concubines. He accused families of being so enslaved by old morality that they literally encouraged their widowed daughters to commit suicide. Yü also opposed foot-binding, arguing that its humble origin (among lower-class women dancers) lowered the position of all women who adopted the custom and that it weakened women and thereby destroyed the harmony and balance between the male and female components of the human race (*yin* and *yang*). These scholars of the Ming and Ch'ing times brought about an awareness of the injustices done to women and of the problem of sexual inequality in general. However, their ideas were basically conceived within the traditional framework defined in the early Confucian philosophy of womanhood. While they hoped for improvement of the condition of women, the social roles assigned women in Confucianism remained unchallenged. The opposition of those Ming and Ch'ing scholars to Sung Neo-Confucianism on the matter of feminine ethics could, thus, most properly be viewed as a return to the more liberal Han Confucianism. More vitally innovative thought on feminism had to come from a different source, from the fiction of three Ch'ing authors of fiction, P'u Sung-ling (see *Liao-chai chih-i*), Wu Ching-tzu (see *Ju-lin wai-shih*), and Li Ju-chen (see *Ching-hua yüan*), and in the efforts that the Ch'ing poets Yüan Mei* and Ch'en Wen-shu (see *Ching-hua yüan*) made in promoting the practice of writing poetry by upper-class women.

On such issues as widow-suicide, female chastity, monogamy, foot-binding, and concubinage, these five scholars basically shared the views of the Confucian conformists. Their vigorously liberal, fair-minded, and enlightened attitude toward women was rather more characteristically expressed through their according women a position of greater dignity and sexual equality than traditional thought would ever allow, and through their more positive recognition of women's native intelligence in scholarship and creative writing. In Pu Sung-ling's *Liao-chai chih-i* women were generally portrayed as strong-willed and were more active, intelligent, and courageous than men. Often they were the ones who determined the fate of their families. In Wu Ching-tzu's *Ju-lin wai-shih*, there were lower-class women who supported themselves and spoke up for their rights when harassed by domineering males. An exemplary marital relationship was depicted in the novel as one based on love, mutual respect, and a near equality between husband and wife. In Li Ju-chen's *Ching-hua yüan* imperial examinations were held for women. Li's radical feminist stand was revealed in the section on a certain Kingdom of Women (陳文述), where sexual roles were completely reversed. Yüan Mei had an even greater impact on the elevation of women's position in society. Yüan Mei personally tutored female members of his own family in versification, and he also recruited other women students, usually daughters of other prominent families, supervised the publication of many of the poems they wrote, and openly praised their works. Yüan Mei was succeeded by Ch'en Wen-shu, who encouraged many women to write poetry and sponsored the publication of their works. In great part because of the efforts of Yüan Mei and Ch'en Wen-shu, the study and composition of poetry became a popular pastime among upper-class women during the Ch'ing period. It was also in this period that the ability to write poetry was an expected part of a lady's dowry.

In a more subtle way, the defiant and revolutionary spirit of these five unorthodox scholars was revealed by their adoption of fiction as the mode of communication and their advocacy of female virtuosity in the art of poetry. For, while rarely overtly opposing literature, Confucian ethics harbored a disapproval of the power of the creative imagination, feeling that literary works could often lead both authors and readers astray. Insistent upon the dualism of the moral and animal nature within man, champions of Confucian ethics defended the principles of decorum and restraint. In contrast to the celebration in Taoism of the spontaneity of human nature was the Confucian argument for reason and moral judgment as correctives. Against the glorification of intuition and impulse, Confucian scholars preached the necessity of a discipline of conscience operating through vigorous self-examination. Accordingly, authors of the textbooks for female education promoted female literacy, but solely as a gateway to moral education. When literary works were recommended, it was for their informative and didactic content rather than their aesthetic value.

For centuries this view of literature was shared by most Chinese women writers. They regarded literature as an amusement or a diversion. Their works were usually circulated only among the members of their families. Some even burned their manuscripts. These actions have resulted in serious losses of literature by Chinese women.

II. A Historical Overview

There are few extant works from before the Han period that can be ascribed to women with certainty. The writings putatively attributed to women who lived before the Chou dynasty are almost certainly forged compositions from a later date. It is possible, but cannot be proved, that many of the folksongs collected in *Shih-ching** were composed by women. However, there are a handful of short verses from the Spring and Autumn and the Warring States periods which merit discussion.

These works were with but a few exceptions highly autobiographical. Subjects range from conjugal devotion, yearning for mates, and nostalgia for homeland to female chastity, filial piety, and womanly prudence, and further to the larger concerns of loyalty to the sovereign. The representative techniques of the great majority of these verses are reminiscent of *pi* , or the comparison mode, in the *Shih-ching.* Each of these works begins with a metaphor, characteristically an object or event drawn from the natural world, to parallel the human situation which follows. Lady Ho 何氏 (c. 300 B.C.), for instance, began her "Wu-ch'üeh ko" 烏鵲歌 (A Song of Magpies) with a pair of magpies soaring high at will, intending them to signify herself and her husband, a free and happily married couple. In a similar vein, the description of a tree flourishing on a secluded mountain at the opening of "Nü-chen-mu ko" 女貞木歌 (A Song of The Tree of Female Chastity) by a virgin from the state of Lu 魯 represents metaphorically her patriotic fervor and moral integrity otherwise unnoticed by the world.

The Han dynasty witnessed the emergence of manifold achievements in women's literature. Works of poetry were composed in the old-style four-word verse form, in the newly developed five-word verse form, and in *fu* or prose-poems. In addition, during the Latter Han period lived Pan Chao, the author of *Nü chieh*, whose versatility of knowledge and skill in historical, philosophical, and imaginative literature was not surpassed by any woman of letters in later ages.

The first well-known woman poet in Chinese history is Cho Wen-chün 卓文君 (*fl.* 150-115 B.C.), the wife of Ssu-ma Hsiang-ju,* one of the greatest *fu* writers in China. The beautiful daughter of a wealthy family in Szechwan, she was widowed at the age of seventeen and returned home to live with her parents, whereupon Ssu-ma Hsiang-ju, then a poor writer, fell in love with her. He wooed her with music at a banquet given by her father, and she eloped with him. Disowned and poverty-stricken, they opened a shop. This so humiliated her father that he gave them a large sum of money. Later, Ssu-ma Hsiang-ju, by then a leading poet for some years, thought of taking a concubine. Broken-hearted and in great rage, Cho Wen-chün composed "Pai-t'ou yin" 白頭吟 (A Song of White Hair), in sixteen five-word lines, declaring her determination to break off with her husband. On reading this poem, Ssu-ma Hsiang-ju was so moved that he returned to her. Although the story is probably fictitious, "Pai-t'ou yin" became in later literature a synonym for the grievance of a woman abandoned by a lover in favor of a younger rival.

Throughout Chinese history there has rarely been a dynasty which did not suffer from foreign border incursions or invasions. During the Han dynasty the most serious and persistent turmoils caused by foreign peoples came from Wu-sun 烏孫, a state west of the Han empire, and from the Huns in the north, and the adopted strategy was one of military operations in conjunction with diplomatic alliances by marriage. These alliances involved offering a Chinese "princess" (often merely a woman of the palace) in marriage to a foreign leader. It was against such a political background that two renowned lyrics were produced by Liu Hsi-chün 劉細君, a daughter of the royal house during the reign of Emperor Wu, and Wang Ch'iang 王嬙, better known as Wang Chao-chün 王昭君, a concubine of Emperor Yüan (r. 48-33 B.C.).

Liu Hsi-chün was married to the king of Wu-sun in an attempt to isolate the Huns by forming alliances with the other non-Chinese tribes. When her husband grew old, she was forced, in accordance with a local custom, to marry his grandson. Her poem, which consists of six eight-word lines, reveals her distress at residing in a foreign, uncivilized land and ends with a wish that she be transformed into a bird and fly home. More is known about Wang Chao-chün. At the age of seventeen, she was chosen for the harem of Emperor Yüan. Because she was too proud to bribe the court artisans who painted portraits of the palace ladies for the consideration of the emperor, her portrait was made unappealing and she consequently was never favored by an imperial visit. When the chieftain of the Huns proposed an alliance marriage, Wang Chao-chün, embittered, volunteered. The marriage was carried out, despite the emperor's regret upon discovering her beauty at a ceremony of farewell. She bore the foreign chieftain one son. After her husband died, his successor, Wang's son, again following local custom, intended to marry her. At the order of the Han emperor, she conceded, and had two daughters by her second husband. A different version of the story tells that she drowned herself on leaving China. Another version reports that she did not yield to the proposal of remarriage, but committed suicide. It is said that her tomb, covered with grasses, was the only verdant place in the wide stretch of barren land beyond the Great Wall. The poem attributed to her registers her unfulfilled yearning for home. Stylistically, it follows the tradition manifested in the *Shih-ching*, in that each line is composed of four words and the plight of the lyrical self is preceded by a metaphor, in the present case a displaced bird gradually pining away.

Pan Chao's father, Pan Piao 班彪 (A.D. 3-54), and brother Pan Ku* were both scholars and historians. Although Pan Chao's share in the compilation of *Han-shu* 漢書 (History of the Han) remains undetermined, it is certain that after Pan Ku died leaving the work unfinished, Pan Chao proceeded under imperial order to complete the eight tables (*piao*) and a treatise on astronomy (*T'ien-wen chih* 天文志). It is possible that she revised and reedited the work. She was summoned to court to teach the empress and other inmates of the harem. Many scholars and courtiers of her time were also her pupils, notably the scholar Ma Jung.* Aside from history, Pan Chao wrote *fu*, various types of court prose, and essays. Extant are merely two memorials and four *fu*.

One of these memorials was written in behalf of her brother Pan Ch'ao 班超 (32-102), a famous general, who on account of declining health had himself sent a memorial to the emperor asking to be relieved of his heavy responsibilities at the frontier. Pan Chao's memorial reiterates his plea. The presentation is in a remarkably straightforward and vigorous style, clear in exposition, logical in reasoning, and vivid in entreaty. On reading her memorial, the emperor ordered the immediate return of Pan Ch'ao.

Pan Chao's four *fu* are "Ta-ch'üeh fu" 大雀賦 (The Bird), "Ch'an fu" 蟬賦 (The Cicada), "Chen-lü fu" 針縷賦 (The Needle and Thread), and "Tung cheng fu" 東征賦 (Traveling Eastward). In subject matter and artistry of language, the least pleasing of the four is "Ta-ch'üeh fu," for the entire work is couched in a language of excessive formality. The work was composed by imperial mandate in praise of a bird from the Western Regions; it is laden with extravagant panegyric in honor of the throne. The "Ch'an fu" in its present form is but a fragment. The "Chen-lü fu" is fraught with the moral significance of Han Confucianism. Nevertheless, its literary value is noteworthy— the work is structured upon the composite metaphor of the needle and thread. The inflexible needle resembles moral strength and integrity; its tiny yet straight body bears analogy to moral subtlety and righteousness; the gradual piercing denotes the slow but unhindered influence of morality; the stringing into one of things originally far apart signifies the essential universality and unity of varied and diverse knowledge; and darning reflects the weaving of the moral character. In view of the role of the needle and the thread in everyday life, Pan Chao might have been seeking to glorify the humble instruments of women's needlework. It is, however, "Tung cheng fu" that has raised Pan Chao to a status of prominence in Chinese *fu* literature. A long essay preceded by a brief introduction, this *fu* poem records a succession of her intellectual and emotional reactions to the changing scenes and situations of a journey with her son Ku 穀 from the capital Lo-yang to Ch'en-liu 陳留 (southeast of modern K'ai-feng 開封 in Honan), where Ku was to assume the post of a district official. Her reactions reveal her great familiarity with the places she passed through, their people, and their historical heroes, all depicted in this piece. The work concludes with a moral exhortation, which reaffirms the value of such Confucian virtues as self-cultivation, acceptance of fate, reverence, prudence, diligence, humility, temperance, and freedom from desire. Placed in the larger context of travel literature, "Tung cheng fu" illustrates a rationalistic approach to scenery within the Chinese landscape tradition and a Confucian, utilitarian outlook on nature which was to emerge more fully developed in the second century.

According to tradition, during the final years of the Han dynasty there appeared the first great woman poet in Chinese history, Ts'ai Yen,* the daughter of Ts'ai Yung 蔡邕 (133-192), a celebrated writer and a learned scholar. In the early 190s, Ts'ai Yen, a widow, was abducted by the Huns. She became the wife of a Hunnish chieftain and bore him two sons. About 206 she was ransomed by Ts'ao Ts'ao 曹操 (155-220), a powerful warlord and a friend of her father's and brought back to China. Her two sons were left behind. Ts'ao Ts'ao later arranged for her to be married to one of his officials.

Ts'ai Yen attained distinction in literary history through three poems attributed to her, though their authorship is still sharply disputed. These three poems are entitled "Hu-chia shih-pa p'ai" 胡笳十八拍 (Eighteen Verses Sung to a Barbarian Reed Whistle) and "Pei-fen shih" 悲憤詩 (Poems [Two] of Lament and Resentment). "Hu-chia shih-pa p'ai" is a long poem of eighteen stanzas totaling over 150 lines varying in length from five to twelve words; its meter is predominantly that of the *Ch'u-tz'u* songs. The two poems which constitute the "Pei-fan shih" cycle are in over 100 five-word and 40 seven-word lines, respectively. The second poem is in a very regular meter of the *Ch'u-tzu*.

The three poems share autobiographical import with a nationwide political and social significance. Each chronicles the author's capture, life among the barbarians, separation from her children and return to China, a personal experience which took place against the backdrop of internal turmoil and barbarian invasion. The poems portray a woman torn between two conflicting roles, the cultural daughter of Han China and the natural mother of non-Chinese sons. In these poems, she expresses her wrath and anguish, crying out against the injustices of the cosmos. At the national level, her poems graphically describe a country seething with chaos and misery, where women were especially the victims of fear and violence. For centuries, these three poems have held a powerful appeal for the Chinese reader.

During the Western Chin, the only notable woman writer was Tso Fen 左芬 (fl. 275), the sister of Tso Ssu.* She took to scholarship as a youth, and attained a distinction equal to that of her brother. Inspired by her literary fame, Emperor Wu (r. 265-289) chose her for his harem. In the palace, she was highly respected for her virtue and talent and was often summoned by the emperor to compose on important occasions. Only a few of her writings—*fu*, prose pieces, and poems—have survived.

Literature by women in the Six Dynasties is best represented by *yüeh-fu*.* These songs deal exclusively with love, most of them linked to a background story. In language, they are characterized by a typically feminine, gentle, and sometimes plaintive tone.

These folksongs fall under one of three major categories: "Shen-hsien ko" 神絃歌 (Songs of Divine Strings); "Hsi-ch'ü ko" 西曲歌 (Songs of the Western Melody); "Wu-sheng ko-ch'ü" 吳聲歌曲 (Songs and Melodies of the Wu Dialect). As signified by the title, "Shen-hsien ko" includes popular songs used in sacrifices to divinities. These songs were orginally linked with legends, many of them now lost. Of "Hsi-ch'ü ko," the best known are two songs entitled "Mo-ch'ou lo" 莫愁樂 (The Joy of Mo-ch'ou). The authorship of these songs is controversial. One theory maintains that they were composed by a girl named Mo-ch'ou of Shih-ch'eng 石城 (modern Ching-ling 竟陵 in Hunan), who lived in the fifth and the sixth centuries. Another attributes the songs to later writers, arguing that the original is lost. Each song is composed of four five-word lines. They take the form of a dialogue between Mo-ch'ou and a man in which they express their longing for each other. "Wu-sheng ko-ch'u" are songs from the Wu region (modern Kiangsu and Chekiang), and among its varieties the most celebrated are "Tzu-yeh ko" 子夜歌 (The Songs of Tzu-yeh) and "Hua-shan chi" 華山畿 (On the Slope of Hua Mountain). "Tzu-yeh ko" is a group of forty-two extant songs attributed to a girl named Tzu-yeh, who lived in the third and fourth centuries. Whether or not she wrote these songs is an open question. It is possible, however, that she composed the original poem and melody, which afterwards became widely adopted and imitated. Records state that the melody, now lost, was extraordinarily sorrowful and anguished. The forty-two extant songs are all composed of four five-word lines. The style is colloquial and fluent, spontaneous in expressing emotions, and laden with puns. From the fourth to the ninth centuries the theme and the style of "Tzu-yeh ko" were widely emulated by both the common people and the educated elite. As a result, a number of variations which assume different titles were invented. "Hua-shan chi," another group of "Wu-sheng ko-ch'ü," consists of twenty-four extant songs headed by that attributed to an anonymous girl of the fifth century who lived at Hua Mountain. The style of this group of songs differs from that of "Tzu-yeh ko" in that they are in lines of uneven length and are burdened with an extravagant language. This language is, however, equally conversational and informal, and their utterance of love is as sincere and unrestrained.

Of equal prominence in literary merit and influence is an individual poem entitled "Hsi-ling ko" 西陵歌 (A Song of Hsi-ling Lake), attributed to Su Hsiao-hsiao 蘇小小, a leading courtesan of the Hangchow area, who lived in the late fifth century. Composed of four lines of five words each, the poem narrates in a simple but elegant manner how the girl and her lover bind their hearts in a love knot under cypress trees along the lake. For centuries this poem has seized the fancy and sympathy of the people, and has inspired the writing of numerous poems on Su, who also became one of the most frequently treated subjects in popular literary genres, especially the theater.

During the T'ang dynasty, political stability, economic affluence, imperial patronage, and the high esteem accorded poetic talents in public life and state examinations combined to bring about an unprecedented popularity in the composition of poetry. Moreover, the tremendous output of poetic works—preserved to this day are approximately 50,000 poems by some 2,300 poets—coincided with the attainment of artistic perfection in the modern-style poetry, which branched out into two forms, *lü-shih* 律詩 and *chüeh-chü* 絕句 (see *shih*).

Among these poets, there were a number of empresses, court ladies, wives of the gentry, courtesans, and Taoist nuns. Of most importance were Li Yeh 李冶 (eighth century), Hsüeh T'ao,* Yü Hsüan-chi,* and Lady Hua-jui 花蕊夫人 (tenth century).

Li Yeh, a Taoist nun, was noted for her beauty, wit, music, calligraphy, and poetry. She had a close relationship with many contemporary literati, notably Lu Yü 絕句 (d. 804), Chiao-jan,* and Liu Chang-ch'ing.* During the T'ien-pao (742-756) period, she was summoned to the court by Emperor Hsüan-tsung (r. 712-756) in admiration of her poetic talent. Nothing is known about the length or events of her life thereafter. A collection of Li Yeh's poems circulated until the Yüan period, but fewer than twenty pieces are extant, most of them composed in the modern style. The dominant mood is the sorrow of parting and separation. Other themes include the beauty of nature, the vivifying effects of music, and the transience of life.

Hsüeh T'ao was a native of Ch'ang-an. In her childhood her father took the family to Szechwan, where he had a government appointment. His death left the family in poverty, and Hsüeh T'ao soon took on financial responsibility by serving at banquets of public functions. She was renowned for her musical skills, quick wit, and poetic talent, the latter having won her the unofficial title of honor Hsüeh Chiao-shu 薛校書 (Hsüeh the Secretary). She was on intimate terms with a number of contemporary celebrities and poets, notably Ling-hu Ch'u 令狐楚 (766-837), Niu Seng-ju 牛僧孺 (779-847), P'ei Tu 裴度 (765-839), Yüan Chen,* Po Chü-i,* and Liu Yü-hsi.* Later in life, she took residence in Wan-hua hsi 浣花溪 (Washing Flower Creek), where she was wont to dress in Taoist attire and manufacture fine paper for poetry, which soon became widely known. She was over seventy when she died. A collection of Hsüeh T'ao's poems entitled *Hung-tu chi* 洪度集 (The Collection of Hung-tu) was in circulation for some time. Now extant are over one hundred poems, the great majority written in the modern style. A number of varied, if conventional, themes are treated, examples being friendship, lovesickness, the sorrows of parting and separation, the irretrievable passage of time, nostalgia for the past, and the vicissitudes of history. A group of *yung-wu* 詠物 (description of objects) poems is especially noteworthy, for some of the works in this category appear to be of biographical value. By definition *yung-wu* poetry refers to the kind of poetry which describes small objects from nature, such as flowers, birds, and insects. Because of its emphasis on the depiction of external scenes and absence of narrative elements, *yung-wu* poetry often admits of various interpretations. In the case of Hsüeh T'ao, some works appear to be predominantly interested in the physical features of the object being described, some appear to embody abstract ideas, such as lovesickness, moral integrity, exhortation against hedonism, and, most significant, some relate to the trade of courtesans. The last category occurs in her poems on flowers—their beauty, delicacy, and evanescence the obvious grounds of analogy. The overall tone of such poems is one of a sorrowful but resigned acceptance of fate. A more daring protest had to await Yü Hsüan-chi.

In traditional criticism Hsüeh T'ao and Yü Hsüan-chi are often called the two greatest women poets of the T'ang period. A native of Ch'ang-an, Yü Hsüan-chi became, probably in her teens, the concubine of an official. His wife was jealous, treated her cruelly, and finally drove her from the house. Thereafter Yü Hsüan-chi took to Taoism. She traveled widely, and had a number of close friends and lovers, the most notable being the poet Wen T'ing-yün.* She was executed about 870 after having been charged with murdering her maid.

Compared with that of Hsüeh T'ao, the poetry of Yü Hsüan-chi displays a wider range of mood which occasionally verges on a demand for political and social equality between the sexes. Besides commonly represented emotions such as friendship, the sorrows of parting and separation, boudoir laments, and cycles of history, she often depicts harmonious union with nature. More unconventional is a poem in which the poet clearly encourages a girl abandoned by her lover to find another man. Equally unorthodox is another poem in which the poet expresses regret that as a woman she is denied the opportunity of displaying her poetic talent in state examinations and the possibility of an official position which could result from success therein. These two poems embody the poet's aspirations to the wealth, fame, and sexual freedoms that were reserved for men. They may also be viewed as her implied protest against sexual inequality in society.

Lady Hua-jui, the most notable woman poet of the T'ang, was the wife of Meng Hsü 孟昶, the king of Szechwan during the Five Dynasties. Meng Hsü adored her and conferred on her the title "Hua-jui fu-jen," meaning "Lady of the Flower Pistil." Their kingdom later fell at the hands of Emperor T'ai-tsu (r. 960-975), the founder of the Sung dynasty. Meng Hsü died soon after his surrender. Lady Hua-jui was taken to the north by the emperor of Sung for his harem. Later she committed suicide at the emperor's order, or, according to a different story, was killed by T'ai-tsu's brother, the Emperor T'ai-tsung (r. 976-997).

Among women poets, Lady Hua-jui has a special place in that she lived in a transitional period when the *shih* verse moved from realism and didacticism to aestheticism and symbolism and when *tz'u** verse was still in a developmental stage. Lady Hua-jui composed in both forms. The *shih* attributed to her are a group of one hundred "kung-tz'u" 宮詞 (palace poems), a number of which are of disputed authorship, and an impromptu poem in response to Emperor T'ai-tsu's question of why her husband surrendered. In the *tz'u* genre only two pieces survive. One, attributed by some scholars to her husband Meng Hsü, is written to the tune "Yü-lou ch'un" 玉樓春 (Jade Tower Spring), and the other to the tune "Ch'ou nu-erh" 醜奴兒 (The Ugly Servant), of which only the first stanza was finished. Notwithstanding the uncertainty of authorship that envelops a great majority of her poetic works, general characteristics can still be discerned. In sentiment and diction, her poetry deviates considerably from the major trend of the late T'ang period. This is especially true of her *shih* verse.

With probably only one third of the corpus actually composed by Lady Hua-jui, the one hundred palace poems describe the scenery of the imperial harem and lives of its inmates. Composed in either five-word or seven-word *chüeh-chü*, in a language that is simple, fluent, elegant, and fresh, each poem constitutes a vignette of a moment of leisure or love in the lives of the palace women. Like many court poems written by her male contemporaries in the tradition of the Six Dynasties, her works are embellished with the fragrances and the colors of palace life. Yet, unlike some of those male poets, she does not appear to have engaged in a deliberate search for an abstruse diction. Nor do her poems seem to have been designed to arouse the erotic emotions, as were many of the court poems of her time, which dwelt on the seductive appeal of the female body. Rather, they strike an interest in the aesthetic pleasure derived either from her own experience or from that of other court ladies.

In sharp contrast to the court poems which attest the bliss of her days in Meng Hsü's harem, stands the seven-word *chüeh-chü* response to Emperor T'ai-tsu. In a brief but remarkably powerful statement, she accused the 140,000 troops of betrayal of her husband in laying down arms when faced with the Sung armies. Less can be said of her *tz'u* poetry. According to a story, "Yü-lou ch'un" was composed on a hot summer night when Lady Hua-jui and Meng Hsü rose from bed. Celebrating a blessed night in the privacy of a comfortably cool chamber, the poem exquisitely depicts the refreshing air, the fragrant breeze, the bright moon, the charming languor of the female persona, the stars crossing the Milky Way from time to time, and the moon, these last two being conventional symbols of love. The ending tempers the hitherto prevailing mood of bliss with a sense of grief in its apprehension of the passage of time.

In her efforts to compose *tz'u*, Lady Hua-jui was succeeded by a number of Sung women who lived in the two hundred years from the eleventh to the thirteenth centuries when the *tz'u* became the principal literary form. Among these later poets, the most celebrated were Li Ch'ing-chao,* universally esteemed as China's greatest woman poet, and Chu Shu-chen,* regarded as second only to Li Ch'ing-chao.

Li Ch'ing-chao's life spanned the turbulent years of transition from the Northern to the Southern Sung. She was the daughter of a wealthy scholar-official family in Shantung, and her early life was spent in an atmosphere of cultural refinement. Later she was married to a young scholar with whom she shared tastes in art and literature. The couple often had poetry contests with each other and with their literary friends.

They built up a vast collection of rare objets d'art, notably bronzes, rubbings from stone monuments, seals, paintings, and calligraphy. Their happiness lasted for several years, until the Jurchen invasion of Northern China in 1127. Thereupon Li and her husband fled south to the Yangtze region, leaving behind them most of their collection. The death of her husband two years later dealt Li Ch'ing-chao a blow from which she never recovered. For the remainder of her life, she lived alone, usually in flight, striving to save what was left of the collection.

Of Li Ch'ing-chao's *tz'u* poetry, very little—only some fifty poems—have survived, and some of these are of dubious authorship. These poems display two distinct moods: the joyful animation of a happily married young woman and the sorrow of a lonely and aging widow. Confining their examination of her work to a few pieces which have been considered genuine, modern scholars are of the opinion that the supremacy of Li Ch'ing-chao's *tz'u* art lies in her gift for depicting with all intimacy, delicacy, and immediacy the genuine feelings of a woman in response to the vicissitudes of life, an achievement hitherto excelled by no one, either male or female, who has dealt with this theme of the love-sick woman so common in Chinese poetry. Her daring experimentation with novel, usually difficult, prosodic devices is also praised. Literary critics beginning in her lifetime have ranked Li Ch'ing-chao among China's most eminent poets. The poem most often quoted was composed to the tune "Sheng-sheng man" 聲聲慢 (Every Sound, Lentemente), which is noted for its unique opening, with seven pairs of monosyllabic words creating a striking melodious effect when sung slowly to the music.

Although among women poets Chu Shu-chen is second only to Li Ch'ing-chao in prominence, almost nothing is known of her life. Her poems were first published in 1182 by Wei Chung-kung 魏仲恭, who claimed in his preface to the collection that he had obtained copies of her works from her friends, since after her death her parents had burned all her poems. Her father is supposed to have been an official in Chekiang, and she seems to have led an affluent and happy life as a young girl. A lifelong misery is thought to have begun with her marriage. Her husband, whose name is unknown, is said to have been either an uneducated merchant or a scholar-official and indifferent or even hostile to her poetic temperament and practice. Later in life, she appears to have been abandoned by her husband and thereafter to have taken at least one lover, from whom she was also separated. Many of these speculations about her life, even her approximate dates, are tentative and based on her own works. One theory claims she was the niece of Chu Hsi 朱熹 (1130-1200), which would place her in the Southern Sung. However, internal evidence from her poetry suggests she was a friend of Lady Wei 魏, wife of the statesman Tseng Pu 曾布 (1035-1107), and thus lived in the Northern Sung.

The extant poetry of Chu Shu-chen includes both *shih* and *tz'u*. Although there are poems on the cautionary implications of historical events and on the plight of peasants of her day, political or social poetry is rare. Aptly characterized by the expression *tuan ch'ang* 斷腸 (broken-hearted) which is also the title of her collected works, an overwhelming majority of her poems concern the loneliness, lovesickness, tearful self-pity, and ill health of the abandoned-woman persona who finds relief from her sorrows in wine. Critical reception of her works has been mixed. Her verse is said to have been very popular in the Sung and favorably received in succeeding generations. But some scholars condemn its obsession with the theme of boudoir laments and attribute its popularity to the vicarious pleasure readers sought in being privy to her adverse fortunes. Others attend to the genuineness of her emotions and her ability to embody such emotions in a language that is elegantly clear and simple, often conveying ideas which are refreshingly unconventional.

After the *tz'u* attained the height of its development, it became mellow and somber, lost its spontaneity, and gradually withered away. *San-ch'ü* poetry (see *ch'ü*), a variation of the *tz'u*, took its place. During the Yüan and the Ming periods, this new poetic form was enormously popular with all groups of writers, irrespective of sex, class, or profession. A number of women writers, including both wives of the scholar-gentry class and courtesans, experimented with the *san-ch'ü* melody and left abundant specimens of their work.

The subjects of these women writers extend little beyond the limited confines of the boudoir lament. This weakness is offset by a successful exploration of the innermost recesses of the female mind. In their works, the poets' sentiments and aspirations are carefully analyzed, tender situations are vividly portrayed, and much of their inward life is thus revealed. Among the *san-ch'ü* writers, Huang O 黄峨 (*fl.* 1535), the wife of Yang Shen,* a voluminous writer and learned scholar, is especially noted for her unbridled descriptions of love and sex (Jen, 1970).

At the end of the Ming period and throughout the entire Ch'ing dynasty, manifold achievements in women's literature can be seen in both the conventional elite forms and those which had a folk origin. These include the *shih, tz'u,* and *san-ch'ü,* drama of the literati, storytelling, the novel and the *t'an-tz'u** (A-ying, l937; Ch'en, 1974).

In view of her varied literary talent, Wang Tuan 汪端 (1793-1839) may be deemed as the most noteworthy woman of letters in the Ch'ing period. A poet, critic, novelist, editor, and publisher, Wang Tuan not only engaged herself in the two distinct enterprises of literary creation and critical scholarship, but employed both the literary and vernacular languages.

Her parents were both from well-known scholar-official families, and Wang Tuan reportedly began reading in infancy and composed poetry at the age of seven. After the death of her parents, she was cared for by her aunt Liang Te-sheng 梁德繩 (1711-1847), a poet and *t'an-tz'u* writer. When Wang Tuan married Ch'en P'ei-chih 陳裴之 (1794-1826), a poet-official and the son of Ch'en Wen-shu, the champion of women's education, she became not only his wife but also his collaborator in the writing of poetry, and her verse was greatly admired by her father-in-law. When Ch'en P'ei-chih died at Hankow (modern Hupei), their only son, overcome by the news, became seriously ill and thereafter was mentally deranged. To assuage her grief, Wang Tuan sought consolation in Taoism. She died at the age of forty-six.

The poems of Wang Tuan were collected and printed under the title *Tzu-jan-hao-hsüeh chai shih-chi* 自然好學齋詩集 (A Collection of Poems from the Studio Where One is Naturally Fond of Study). Also published was *Ming san-shih-chia shih-hsüan* 明三十家詩選 (Selected Poetry of Thirty Masters of the Ming), her anthology, in two series, of verses from thirty leading poets of the Ming period with a supplement containing selections from seventy minor poets of the same period. This anthology reveals her unusual literary taste and independence of judgment. She accorded Kao Ch'i* the highest status among poets of the Ming times, and in so doing she disagreed with such renowned critics as Ch'ien Ch'ien-i* and Shen Te-ch'ien.* Besides the study and writing of poetry, Wang Tuan was also interested in recreating history in the form of fiction. Her observations of the historical episodes during the Yüan and Ming periods were brought together in a work entitled *Yüan Ming i-shih* 元明佚史 (The Lost History of the Yüan and Ming). This work made her China's only vernacular-language woman novelist. But she later destroyed the manuscript. Her literary efforts extended to the editing and printing of the works of others, including those of her husband under the title *Ch'eng-huai-t'ang chi* 澄懷堂集 (A Collection from the Hall of Pure Embraces).

One of Wang Tuan's literary associates and a disciple of her father-in-law Ch'en Wen-shu, Wu Tsao 吳藻 (19th century), was a prolific writer of *tz'u* and *san-ch'ü*, and the producer of a drama entitled *Yin chiu tu "Sao"* 飲酒讀騷 (Drinking Wine and Studying the "Li sao"). A native of Jen-ho 仁和 (modern Chekiang), she was the daughter of a merchant and the wife of another, and was treated with slight sympathy and understanding by both. She displayed a literary predilection at an early age, and throughout her lifetime was a very popular song-writer. Later, she moved to a secluded place and took consolation in Buddhism, presumably for the remainder of her life. In her *tz'u* poetry she is generally considered to have emulated Li Ch'ing-chao, for it is characterized by an elegant and refreshing simplicity and naturalness rarely found in the works of her contemporaries. Of her play *Yin chiu tu "Sao"* little is known. From fragmentary sources it may be gleaned that the writer aspired for a life and career which might be comparable to that of Ch'ü Yüan.*

Another *tz'u* poet of even greater renown during the Ch'ing period is Ku T'ai-ch'ing,* who is often considered one of the two greatest *tz'u* poets of Manchu origin, the other being Na-lan Hsing-te.* As is often the case with women writers, obscurity and uncertainty envelops the dates of Ku's birth and death and her family background. She is thought to have been either of Chinese bannerman origin or a descendant of the great Manchu scholar-official O-er-t'ai 鄂爾泰 (1680-1745). Later, she became a favorite concubine of I-hui 奕繪 (1799-1838), a member of the royal family and a noted poet, calligrapher, and architect. The couple shared common interests in travel, art, and literature. When I-hui died and a son by an earlier marriage inherited his title and estate, Ku T'ai-ch'ing and her children were driven from the house, perhaps because of her reputed liaison with Kung Tzu-chen,* a famous scholar and poet. Thereafter she encountered considerable hardship and suffering in raising her children, and reportedly went blind in 1875.

Ku T'ai-ch'ing composed both *shih* and *tz'u*. Her prominence in the world of Ch'ing letters, however, rests primarily on her *tz'u*, collected under the title *Tung-hai yü ch'ang* 東海漁唱 (Songs of the Fisherman of Eastern Sea), which matches her husband's collection *Nan-ku ch'iao ch'ang* 南谷樵唱 (Songs of the Woodcutter of Southern Valley), also referred to as *Hsi-shan ch'iao ch'ang* 西山樵唱 (Songs of the Woodcutter of Western Hill). The great majority of Ku T'ai-ch'ing's *tz'u* describe an object or a piece of scenery in nature, entitle paintings, respond to the works by her husband, or celebrate social occasions. In style and technique, she is considered to have been strongly influenced by the two great masters of the *tz'u* in the Sung dynasty, Chou Pang-yen* and Chiang K'uei.* Many *tz'u* writers of her time took to flowery rhetoric and high-flown style, but Ku T'ai-ch'ing's language is plain and devoid of ornate embellishment, often verging on the colloquial. No individual lines are famous, but she is generally applauded for the atmosphere of sublimity which permeates her poetry when viewed as a whole. More specifically, her poems describing nature are marked by an exquisite picturesqueness and a rich association of ideas. She is also noted for her gifted manipulation of rhymes to achieve desired sound effects.

Besides poetry, women writers of the late Ming period and of the Ch'ing dynasty experimented with the art of drama amd wrote plays in either the *tsa-chü** or the *ch'uan-ch'i** types. The three most celebrated female dramatists were Yeh Hsiao-wan,* who wrote *Yüan-yang meng*, Liang I-su 梁夷素 (*fl.* 1644), who produced *Hsiang-ssu yen* 相思硯 (Inkstone of Lovesickness), and Wang Yün 王筠 (dates unknown), the author of *Fan-hua meng* 繁華夢 (Dream of Splendor and Prosperity). *Yüan-yang meng* was written to mourn the death of the author's two sisters. As indicated by the title, *Hsiang-ssu yen* is concerned with lovesickness; the play ends with the reunion of the two lovers. Wang Yün's *Fan-hua men* contains strong feminist thought—the author precedes the play with a *tz'u* poem in which she clearly expresses her regret that unlike men, she cannot have a good career of her own.

In folk literature, there were a number of *t'an-tz'u* produced by female writers. The three most celebrated *t'an-tz'u* works are *T'ien yü hua* 天雨花 by T'ao Chen-huai 陶貞懷 (*fl.* 1644), *Tsai sheng yüan* by Ch'en Tuan-sheng* (Ch'en, 1959), and *Pi sheng hua* 筆生花 by Ch'iu Hsin-ju 邱心如 (*c.* 1805-*c.* 1873). In both *Tsai sheng yüan* and *Pi sheng hua* the heroine in the guise of a male attains success in the civil-service examination and achieves great fame and wealth. These two stories may embody their authors' implied criticisms of sexual inequality. But a more advanced thought is expressed in T'ao Chen-huai's *T'ien yü hua*. In this story the author advocates monogamy for both sexes. This play is generally praised for its use of only one rhyme throughout.

III. Conclusion

Each of the women writers discussed in this essay has a place in Chinese literature. Viewed as a whole, literature by Chinese women displays four distinctive features, attributable to the authors' isolation from society beyond their immediate family circle and to their placing family responsibility before individual development. First, scholarly attainment, which demands time and persistence, plays less of a role in women's literature. Second, in the domain of creative writing, literary language was the medium more often than vernacular language. Third, works characterized by subjectivity and sensuality of expression outnumber those with a social import. Fourth, since the subject matter necessarily affects the choice of genre and style, it is in poetry, not fiction and drama, that women have shown their greatest achievements. Wang Tuan, for instance, was the only woman novelist, and there were no women *tsa-chü* dramatists until the end of the Ming period, though this literary form had already reached its height in the Yüan.

BIBLIOGRAPHY:

Ayscough, Florence. 1937. *Chinese Women Yesterday and Today.* Shanghai.

A-ying 阿英 (Ch'ien Hsing-ts'un 錢杏邨). 1937. *Tan-tz'u hsiao-shuo p'ing-k'ao* 彈詞小說評考 . Shanghai.

Chao, Shih-chieh 趙世傑 , ed. 1928. *Li-tai nü-tzu shih-chi* 歷代女子詩集 . Eight *chüan.* 4v. Shanghai.

———, ed. 1956. *Li-tai nü-tzu wen-chi* 歷代女子文集 . Twelve *chüan* in 1 v. Shanghai, 1922; rpt. Taipei.

Ch'en, Toyoko Yoshida. 1974. "Women in Confucian Society—A Study of Three *T'an-tz'u* Narratives." Unpublished Ph.D. dissertation, Columbia University.

Ch'en, Tung-yüan 陳東原 . 1967. *Chung-kuo fu-nü sheng-huo shih* 中國婦女生活史 . Shanghai, 1928, 1937; rpt. Taipei.

Ch'en, Wen-shu 陳文述 . 1883a. *Hsi-ling kuei yung* 西冷閨詠 , in *Wu-lin chang-ku ts'ung-pien* 武林掌故叢編 , Ting Ping 丁丙 , ed., v. 69-72. Chia-hui T'ang edition 嘉惠堂 . Sixteen *chüan.*

———. 1883b. *Lan-yin chi* 蘭因集 , in *Wu-lin chang-ku ts'ung-pien,* v. 60. Two *chüan.*

Ch'en, Yin-k'o 陳寅恪 . 1959. *Lun Tsai-sheng yüan* 論再生緣 . Hong Kong.

Cheng, Shou-lin. 1926. *Chinesische Frauengestalten.* Leipzig.

Ch'iu, Hsin-ju 邱心如 . 1971. *Pi sheng hua* 筆生花 , in *Chung-kuo t'ung-su chang-hui-hsiao-shuo ts'ung-k'an* 中國通俗章回小說叢刊 , v. 2. Taipei.

Chou, Shou-ch'ang 周壽昌 , ed. 1846 edition. *Kung-kuei wen-hsüan* 宮閨文選 . Twenty-six *chüan* in 10 v. Hsiao Peng-lai shan ts'ang-pan 小蓬萊山館藏板 .

Chung, Hui-ling 鍾慧玲 . 1981. "Ch'ing-tai nü-shih-jen yen-chiu" 清代女詩人研究 . Unpublished Ph.D. dissertation, National Cheng-chih University.

Cosman, Carol *et al.,* eds. 1978. *The Penguin Book of Women Poets.* Harmondsworth. Translations of five traditional poets.

Galik, Marián. 1979. "On the Literature Written by Chinese Women Prior to 1917," *AAS,* 15, 65-100.

Guisso, Richard W. and Stanley Johannesen, eds. 1981. *Women in China: Current Directions in Historical Scholarship.* New York.

Gulik, Robert Hans van. 1961. *Sexual Life in Ancient China; A Preliminary Survey of Chinese Sex and Society from ca. 1500 B.C. till 1644 A.D.* Leiden.

Hsieh, Chin-ch'ing 謝晉青 . 1925. *Shih-ching chih nü-hsing te yen-chiu* 詩經之女性研究 . Shanghai.

Hsieh, Wu-liang 謝无量 . 1927. *Chung-kuo fu-nü wen-hsüeh-shih* 中國婦女文學史 . Shanghai.

Hsiung, Te-chi 熊德基 . 1979. *T'ien yü hua* 天雨花 , in *Chung-hua wen shih lun-ts'ung* 中華文史論叢 , 4th ed., Chu Tung-jun 朱東潤 *et al.,* eds., pp. 295-328. Shanghai.

Hsü, Nai-ch'ang 徐乃昌 , comp. 1896. *Hsiao-t'an-luan-shih hui-k'e kuei-hsiu tz'u* 小檀欒室彙刻閨秀詞 .

Hsü, Shu-min 徐樹敏 and Ch'ien Yüeh 錢岳, eds. 1934. *Chung-hsiang tz'u* 衆香詞 . 6v. Shanghai.

Hu, Wen-k'ai 胡文楷 . 1957. *Li-tai fu-nü chu-tso k'ao* 歷代婦女著作考 . Shanghai.

Hui, Ch'ün 輝羣 . 1934. *Nü-hsing yü wen-hsüeh* 女性與文學 . Shanghai.

Jen, Chung-min 任中敏 , ed. 1970. *Yang Sheng-an fu-fu san-ch'ü* 楊升菴夫婦散曲 . Shanghai, 1934; rpt. Taipei.

Kuo, Mao-ch'ien 郭茂倩 . 1979. *Yüeh-fu shih-chi* 樂府詩集 . 4v. Peking.

Levy, Howard Seymour. 1966. *Chinese Footbinding: The History of a Curious Erotic Custom.* New York.

Li, Wei-p'ing 李偉萍 . 1981. "Nan-ch'ao wen-hsüeh chung te fu-nü hsing-hsiang" 南朝文學中的婦女形象 . Unpublished M.A. thesis, National Cheng-chih University.

Li, Yu-ning 李又寧 . 1981. "Historical Roots of Changes in Women's Status in Modern China," *St. John's Papers in Asian Studies,* 29.

——— and Chang Yü-fa 張玉法 , eds. 1981. *Chung-kuo fu-nü shih lun-wen-chi* 中國婦女史論文集 . Taipei.

Liang, I-chen 梁乙真 . 1958. *Ch'ing-tai fu-nü wen-hsüeh shih* 清代婦女文學史 . Taipei.

Lieh-nü-chuan chiao-chu 列女傳校註 . *SPPY.* Lin, Yutang. 1935. "Feminist Thought in Ancient China," *THM,* 1.2 (September), 127-150.

Liu, Ching-an 劉經菴 , ed. 1934. *Ko-yao yü fu-nü* 歌謠與婦女 . Shanghai.

Liu, Yün-fen 劉雲份 , ed. 1936. *Ming-yüan shih-hsüan ts'ui-lou chi* 名媛詩選翠樓集 . Shanghai.

Mei, Ida Lee. 1982. *Chinese Womanhood.* China Cultural Academy.

O'Hara, Albert Richard. 1945. *The Position of Woman in Early China According to* Lieh nu chuan. Washington, D.C.

Rexroth, Kenneth. 1972. Rexroth and Ling Chung, trans. and ed. *The Orchid Boat: Women Poets of China.* New York.

Ropp, Paul S. 1976. "The Seeds of Change: Reflections on the Condition of Women in the Early and Middle Ch'ing," *Signs,* 2.1 (Fall), 5-23.

Su, Chih-te 蘇之德 . 1963. *Chung-kuo fu-nü wen-hsüeh shih-hua* 中國婦女文學詩話 . Hong Kong.

Swann, Nancy Lee. 1932. *Pan Chao, Foremost Woman Scholar of China, First Century A.D.; Background, Ancestry, Life, and Writings of the Most Celebrated Chinese Woman of Letters.* New York.

T'ao, Chen-huai 陶貞懷. 1971. *Tien yü hua* 天雨, v. 1, in *Chung-kuo t'ung-su chang-hui-hsiao-shuo ts'ung-k'an.* Taipei.

T'an, Cheng-pi 譚正璧. 1982. *Chung kuo nü-hsing te wen-hsüeh sheng-huo* 中國女性的文學生活. Shanghai, 1931.

———. 1958. *Nü-hsing tz'u-hua* 女性詞話. Hong Kong.

Tseng, Chüeh-chih 曾覺之. 1931. "Fu-nü yü wen-hsüeh" 婦女與文學, *Fu-nü tsa-chih,* 17.7 (July), 15-23.

Wang, Ch'un-ts'ui 王春翠. 1931. "Chung-kuo fu-nü wen-hsüeh t'an p'ien" 中國婦女文學談片, *Fu-nü tsa-chih,* 17.7 (July), 45-53.

Wang, Fan-t'ing 王藩庭. 1968. *Chung-hua li-tai fu-nü.* 中華歷代婦女. Taipei.

Wang, Tuan 汪端 *Tzu-jan-hao-hsüeh-chai shih-ch'ao* 自然好學齋詩鈔, ten *chüan,* in *Ju-pu-chi-chai hui-ch'ao* 如不及齋彙鈔, v. 26-31, Ch'en K'un 陳坤, ed. Published in T'ung-chih (1862-1874) and Kuang-hsü (1875-1908) periods.

———. N.d. *Ming san-shih-chia shih-hsüan* 明三十家詩選. 2v.

Wu, Tsao 吳藻. *Hsiang-nan-hsüeh-pei tz'u* 香南雪北詞, one *chüan,* in *Ju-pu-chi-chai hui-ch'ao,* v. 33.

———. *Hua lien tz'u* 花簾詞, in one *chüan, Ju-pu-chi-chai hui-ch'ao,* v. 32.

Yeh, Te-chün 葉德均. 1979. "T'an-tz'u nü tso-chia hsiao-chi" 彈詞女作家小記, in Yeh's *Hsi-ch'ü hsiao-shuo ts'ung-k'ao* 戲曲小說叢考, Peking, v. 2, pp. 743-747.

Yen, Chi-hua 嚴紀華. 1981. "Ch'üan T'ang shih fu-nü shih-ko chih nei-jung fen-hsi" 全唐詩婦女詩歌之內容分析. Unpublished M.A. thesis, National Cheng-chih University.

Yüan, Mei 袁枚, ed. *Sui-yüan nü-ti-tzu shih* 隨園女弟子詩, in *Sui-yüan san shih chung* 隨園三十種, v. 68-69. Published in Chia-ch'ing (1796-1820) period.

PART II
ENTRIES

Bunkyō hifuron 文鏡秘府論 (Chinese: *Wen-ching mi-fu-lun*) is a unique collection of Chinese writings on poetics and prosody, most of which were lost in China after the T'ang dynasty. They owe their preservation to the monk Kūkai 空海 (774-835), founder of the Shingon sect of Buddhism in Japan, who collected some of the earliest discussions of the "four tones and eight faults" of Shen Yüeh* as well as several important works of literary criticism, chief among which is the *Shih-ko* of the T'ang poet Wang Ch'ang-ling.* It is hence an invaluable source for studying the development of Chinese *shih** poetry from the Six Dynasties to the mid-T'ang.

The last character of the title identifies it as belonging to that genre of Buddhist writing known as *sastra*, or scholastic commentary. The title also proclaims its function as both a "literary mirror" (文鏡) and a "treasury of marvels" (秘府)—that is, a guide to good writing and a thesaurus of literary expressions. It was intended to serve a range of audiences, from the Buddhist novice who needed to pronounce Chinese properly for the recitation of mantras and sutras to the courtier or diplomat whose social position required him to compose frequently in classical Chinese poetry and prose.

It was clearly designed to be a systematic and comprehensive introduction to Chinese literature, edited to omit the repetitions and contradictions in the Chinese authorities from which it was compiled. Its six chapter titles form a mandala of the literary universe: The "Heaven" chapter deals with tones and rhymes; "Earth" with models of different styles of writing; "East" and "West" with the problems of composing couplets and avoiding prosodic errors; "South" with literary theory; and "North" with lists of useful phrases and synonyms. Fourteen texts from which the *Bunkyō hifuron* was compiled have been identified, eleven of which were subsequently lost in China. Kūkai is thus responsible for only a very few sections of the work. His major role was to edit and re-arrange material and to provide suitable headings. While he occasionally inserted a Chinese text intact, he more frequently divided an original work into pieces and scattered them under a number of headings.

Kūkai, also known by his posthumous title of Kōbō Daishi, is Japan's best-known monk. While his principal accomplishment was the importation of Esoteric, or Shingon, Buddhism from China to Japan, he was also famous as a linguist, calligrapher, painter, and poet. His interests ranged from architecture to astronomy, and he served extensively at court. He is credited with the invention of the kana syllabary. He visited China from A.D. 804 to 806 and became the disciple and acknowledged heir of Hui-kuo, seventh patriarch of the Esoteric Sect. At the same time, he collected contemporary works on prosody and poetics, which on his return to Japan he gradually incorporated into the *Bunkyō hifuron*, completed in 819. Though exerting a strong influence on the Japanese literary criticism of the time, the *Bunkyō hifuron* gradually dropped into obscurity until its rediscovery at the beginning of this century by the Chinese bibliophile Yang Shou-ching. Since then it has been published in several editions and has been the subject of many textual studies, most notably those of Konishi Jinichi and Nakazawa Mareo.

EDITIONS:

Ikeda, Roshū 池田蘆洲, ed. *Nihon shiwa sōsho* 日本詩話叢書. 1922; rpt. Taipei, 1974. *Chüan* 7 contains the text of the *Bunkyō hifuron*.

Konishi, Jinichi 小西甚一, ed. *Bunkyō hifuron kō* 文鏡秘府論考. 3v. Tokyo, 1948-1953. V. 3 is a critical, annotated edition.

Chou, Wei-te 周維德, ed. *Wen-ching mi-fu-lun* 文鏡秘府論. Peking, 1975. Preface by Kuo Shao-yü.

STUDIES:

Bodman, "Poetics."

Cheng, A-ts'ai 鄭阿財. *K'ung-hai Wen-ching mi-fu-lun yen-chiu* 空海文鏡秘府論研究. M. A. thesis, Chung Kuo wen-hua hsüeh-yüan, Chung-kuo wen-hsüeh yen-chiu-so, Taipei, 1976.

Konishi, *Bunkyō*. V. 1 & 2 contain the results of Konishi's extensive research.

Nakazawa, Mareo 中沢希男. "Bunkyō hifuron kōkan ki" 文鏡秘府論校勘記, *Gunma daigaku kiyō*, 13.2, 14.1, 15 (1964-65); rpt. in *Chūgoku kankei ronsetsu shiryō* (the series devoted to Chinese literature, language, and art), v. 2 (July-December 1964), 149-180; and v. 6 (July-December 1966), 120-136.

—RB

Cha Shen-hsing 査慎行 (*tzu*, Hui-yü 晦餘; *hao*, Ch'u-pai 初白, T'a-shan 他山, Ch'a-t'ien 査田, and Chü-chou 橘州; 1650-1727), an official, scholar, poet, and playwright, was a native of Han-ning 漢寧 (modern Chekiang). His father, Cha Sung-chi 査崧繼 (1627-1678), and his mother, Chung Yün 鍾韞 (d. 1672), were both known for their literary skills, as were several other members of the influential Cha clan. When his quest for an official career was interrupted by the death of his father, Cha Shen-hsing was compelled by financial circumstances to take employment on the staff of a provincial governor. After a period of study with the famous scholar Huang Tsung-hsi 黃宗羲 (1610-1695), he became a private tutor to K'uei-hsü 揆敍 (*c.* 1674-1717) the younger brother of the poet Na-lan Hsing-te.* He next joined the scholarly commission engaged in the compilation of the *Ta-Ch'ing i-t'ung chih* 大清一通志 (Comprehensive Geography of the Empire). He passed the provincial examinations in 1693 but failed to secure the highest degree until a decade later. From that time until his retirement in 1713, he served in the Hanlin Academy and participated in the compilation of the standard phrase dictionary, *P'ei-wen yün-fu* 佩文韻府, and a companion anthology of poetry. His other scholarly accomplishments included work on local and provincial gazetteers, a commentary on the *I-ching*, an annotated edition of the poems of the famous Sung dynasty poet Su Shih,* the *Pu-chu Tung-p'o pien-nien-shih* 補註東坡編年詩, and various miscellaneous writings. Some time after retiring to his native place, Cha Shen-hsing and his brothers were arrested and imprisoned on the charge that one of them had impugned the imperial name. The real cause of their difficulties was more likely Cha Shen-hsing's relationship with K'uei-hsü, who as a high official had become entangled in the Yung-cheng succession affair. One of his brothers died in prison, and another was sent into exile; Cha was eventually permitted to return home, where he died soon after his return.

Except for one play (the *Yin-yang p'an* 陰陽判) and a substantial body of informal essays, poetry was the main outlet for Cha Shen-hsing's creative impulses. Considering the regularity with which he turned his thoughts and experiences into verse form, it was for him much more than a pleasant diversion. As a result, his total poetic corpus numbers about six thousand poems. Two hundred or so of these are *tz'u*,* and the remainder belong to one or another of the traditional *shih** forms. This prolific outpouring of verse, the careful attention he later gave to the organization of his works in proper chronological order with numerous sub-units, and the autobiographical nature of much of his verse suggest that he quite consciously used various poetic forms as a means of recording his life experiences, as a kind of diary. It has been stated that he consciously modeled his poetry on the works of Su Shih and Lu Yu,* which accounts for the objective, reportorial manner in which he depicts the world of his experience in all of its fullness. Cha Shen-hsing's nephew attributed to him a statement of poetic principles that placed primary emphasis on the ideals of profundity, vigor, sensibility, and simplicity of diction, all qualities detectable in his own poetry. Like the Sung dynasty poets he chose to emulate, he revealed in his best poems a complex vision and the discerning intellect of a sensitive observer of the human condition in its infinite variety and changing circumstances. The interior world of self is less his concern than the external world of man and nature. The poet Chao I* later said of his poetry that it possessed a clarity of language and manner which precluded heavy ornamentation. Although Cha Shen-hsing represents in his own unique way the continuing vitality of the classical tradition, like so many poets of the later dynasties he has been neglected by the modern scholar.

EDITIONS:
Ching-yeh-t'ang shih chi 敬業堂詩集. *SPPY.*
Ching-yeh-t'ang hsü-chi 敬業堂續集. *SPPY.*

198

STUDIES:

Chang, Wei-p'ing 張維屏. *Kuo-ch'ao shih-jen cheng-lüeh* 國朝詩人徵略, n.p., preface dated 1820, *ch.* 19, pp. 1a-7b; for a short biographical notice and critical comments on Cha's poetry.

Ch'en, Ching-chang 陳敬璋. *Cha T'a-shan Hsiensheng nien-p'u* 查他山先生年譜, in *Chia-yeh t'ang ts'ung-shu* 嘉業堂叢書. *SPPY.*

ECCP, pp. 21-22.

—WS

Chan-kuo ts'e 戰國策 (Intrigues of the Warring States or, according to some, Bamboo Records of the Warring States) is a collection of historical narratives, fictionalized stories, and persuasive speeches which portray the period of the Warring States (403-221 B.C.). The present text contains thirty-three sections organized around twelve states (Eastern Chou 東周, section 1; Western Chou 西周, section 2; Ch'in 秦, sections 3-7; Ch'i 齊, sections 8-13; Ch'u 楚, sections 14-17; Chao 趙, sections 18-21; Wei 魏, sections 22-25; Han 韓, sections 26-28; Yen 燕, sections 29-31; Sung 宋 and Wei 衛, section 32; and Chung-shan 中山, section 33), with the material concerning each state generally arranged in chronological order.

Chan-kuo ts'e was compiled by the Han bibliophile Liu Hsiang.* Liu explains in his preface that his basic source had fallen into disarray. He supplemented this source with material from a number of other texts. Thus, *Chan-kuo ts'e* as edited by Liu was composite work drawn from a variety of older texts. The theory, argued by Lo Ken-tse 羅根澤, that *Chan-kuo ts'e* was written by K'uai Tung 蒯通, a rhetorician of the Ch'u-Han 楚漢 transitional era (206-203 B.C.), is not supported by Liu's preface or by the content of the text itself.

During the Latter Han, the famous scholiast Kao Yu 高誘 (*fl.* A.D. 200) reorganized the text into twenty-one sections and appended a commentary. Later, the bibliographic section in the *Hsin T'ang-shu* 新唐書 listed a Kao Yu edition in thirty-two sections, apparently reshaped to comply more closely with the structure of Liu Hsiang's earlier edition.

In spite of Kao Yu's effort, *Chan-kuo ts'e* was generally neglected by textual schol-ars, and whole sections of the work were lost. Such neglect may have resulted from its reputation as a scurrilous work concerned more with *li* 利 (advantage) than proper Confucian virtues. Liu Hsiang himself expressed reservations about the content of his compilation, for it described an era when feudal rulers, "having rejected ritual and concession, esteemed conflict and contention, and, having cast aside humaneness and propriety, utilized artifice and deceit." By the Sung dynasty, one bibliography, *Ch'ung-wen tsung-mu* 崇文總目 (compiled between 1034 and 1038), notes that twelve chapters had been completely lost. Shortly thereafter, Tseng Kung,* an editor in the imperial library, skillfully reconstructed the text. Tseng justified this labor with the pious argument that one must understand evil doctrines to suppress them.

Approximately one hundred years after Tseng's effort, Yao Hung 姚宏 re-edited the text. Another, independent line of textual descent passes from Tseng to Pao Piao 鮑彪 (*fl.* 1140), who published an edition in 1147, one year after Yao's. Pao's edition was revised during the Yüan dynasty by Wu Shih-tao 吳師道 and is included in the *SPTK.* In spite of the noteworthy efforts of these editors, a sizeable amount of the original text has been lost. More than 120 *Chan-kuo ts'e* fragments quoted in other sources are not a part of the current text. Moreover, research suggests that certain portions of the text are structured in a way that does not reflect Liu's original work.

As mentioned above, Liu Hsiang compiled *Chan-kuo ts'e* from a variety of sources. In writing his history of the Warring States period, the great Han historian Ssu-ma Ch'ien* drew abundantly from the same sources Liu used. In fact, Cheng Liang-shu, the most knowledgeable modern-day expert on the history of the *Chan-kuo ts'e* text, calculates that forty-eight percent of Ssu-ma's material on the Warring States is paralleled by passages in *Chan-kuo ts'e*. Certain scholars have argued that later editors, such as Tseng Kung, may have reconstituted lost portions of *Chan-kuo ts'e* by copying from *Shih-chi* 史記. Although there may be a few interpolations of this type, comparative study indicates that the *Chan-kuo ts'e* version is usually terser than the parallel *Shih-chi* redaction, a feature which would argue for earlier authorship. Moreover, a silk manuscript discovered in 1973 at Ma-wang tui* contains passages parallel to *Chan-kuo ts'e*. A preliminary study by Yang K'uan 楊寬 suggests that the silk text is an earlier source for those materials Liu included in *Chan-kuo ts'e*, while the *Shih-chi* redaction is more distantly removed from the Ma-wang tui version.

Various portions of *Chan-kuo ts'e* recount historical episodes of the Warring States period in a relatively straightforward way. However, most of *Chan-kuo ts'e* serves an end other than historical record. Years ago Maspero noted that the work contained serious historical errors and suggested that it preserved fragments of a earlier "roman historique," perhaps the lost *Su-tzu* 蘇子 mentioned in the *Han-shu* bibliographic section. This argument is reiterated by Yang K'uan, who suggests that the silk Ma-wang tui manuscript may have come from the original *Su-tzu*. However, Liu Hsiang lists his sources, and *Su-tzu* is not among them.

The major portion of *Chan-kuo ts'e* contains examples of artful rhetoric. As such, it is generically related to the soberer collection of persuasive speeches found in *Kuo-yü** and the less artful but much more moralistic persuasions of *Yen-tzu ch'un-ch'iu* 晏子春秋. Thus, it reflects the culmination of a genre that developed from the intense political competition of the Eastern Chou. The ruthless machinations that so often accompanied the shifting enmities and alliances of this period increased cynicism, and *Chan-kuo ts'e* reflects a marriage of this emergent *realpolitik* with literary form that had once served moralistic ends.

Crump, whose two long studies and complete English translation are indispensable for the study of *Chan-kuo ts'e*, believes that many of the text's persuasions were developed as models to be studied by aspiring rhetoricians. Vasil'ev and Prusek disagree with Crump's conclusions and argue that even the more stylized persua-

sions are pieces of political propaganda rather than mere rhetorical exercises. Whatever their ultimate purpose, some of these passages are among the most skillfully written works of early Chinese literature, for even though *Chan-kuo ts'e* has often been suspect on moral grounds, its literary quality is attested by the large number of passages from it regularly included by Chinese editors in anthologies of ancient prose.

EDITIONS:

Chan-kuo ts'e chiao-chu 戰國策校注. *SPTK*. Indexes on p. 7.

Shan-ch'uan Yao-shih pen Chan-kuo ts'e 剡川姚氏本戰國策. Taipei, 1969. Best available edition.

Fidler, Sharon J., with J. I. Crump. *Index to the Chan-kuo Ts'e*. Ann Arbor, 1973.

Index du Tchan-kouo Ts'ö. Peking, 1948.

TRANSLATIONS:

Crump, J. I. *Chan-kuo Ts'e*. London, 1970.

Hübotter, F. *Aus den Plänen der kämpfenden Reiche nebst den entsprechenden Biographen des Sema Ts'ien*. Berlin, 1912.

STUDIES:

Chang, Hsin-ch'eng 張心澂. *Wei-shu t'ung-k'ao* 偽書通考. V. 1. 1939; rpt., Taipei, 1970, pp. 534-544.

Cheng, Liang-shu 鄭良樹. *Chan-kuo ts'e yen-chiu* 戰國策研究. Singapore, 1972.

Chung, Feng-nien 鍾鳳年. *Kuo ts'e k'an-yen* 國策勘研. *Yen-ching hsüeh-pao*, Monograph 11. Peking, 1936.

Crump, J. I. *Intrigues: Studies of the Chan-kuo Ts'e*. Ann Arbor, 1964.

———. "The *Chan-kuo Ts'e* and its Fiction," *TP*, 48.4-5 (1960), 305-375.

Lo, Ken-tse 羅根澤. "*Chan-kuo ts'e* tso yü K'uao T'ung k'ao" 戰國策作於剙通考, *Hsüeh-wen tsa-chih*, 1.1 (Nov. 1930), 2-7.

———. "Pieh-pen *Chan-kuo ts'e* ke p'ien te nien-tai he li-shih pei-ching" 別本戰國策各篇的年代和歷史背景, *Wen-wu*, 1974.4, 27-40.

Maspero, Henri. "Le Roman Historique dans la littérature Chinoise de l'Antiquité," in *Etudes Historiques*. Paris, 1967. V. 3, pp. 55-62.

Ma-wang-tui Han Mu po-shu cheng-li hsiao-tsu 馬王堆漢墓帛書整理小組. *Chan-kuo tsung-heng chia shu* 戰國縱橫家書. Peking, 1976.

Yang, K'uan 楊寬. "Ma-wang-tui Han mu ch'u-t'u po-shu Chan-kuo ts'e shih-wen" 馬王堆

漢墓出土帛書"戰國策"釋文, *Wen-wu*, 1975.4, 14-26.

Pokora, Timoteus. "Review of K. V. Vasil'ev, *Plany Srazajuscichsja cerstv*," *TP*, 55 (1968-69), 317-322.

Prusek, Jaroslav. "A New Exegesis of *Chan-kuo Ts'e*," *AO*, 34 (1966), 587-592.

Vasil'ev, K. V. *Plany Srazajuscichsja cerstv*. Moscow, 1968.

Watson, *Early*, pp. 74-91.

—SD

Ch'an yü-lu 禪語錄 (Dialogues of Ch'an Buddhists) are collections of sayings and anecdotes of an individual or group of Ch'an masters. They are productions of Ch'an Buddhism at a time when this school was popular in China. The Ch'an Buddhists claimed that their tradition had been transmitted outside the orthodox branches of Buddhism and that their teachings were not established in the Buddhist canons. The followers of the school distrusted the study of scriptures, and new ways and means of religious cultivation had to be found. Consequently, conversations and strange gestures and actions became the principal methods for the attainment of enlightenment. When this new religious experience proved to be successful, some disciples recorded the experiences for instructional purposes. As a result of these efforts, a good number of *yü-lu* accumulated. Although a recent Japanese collection (*Zen Nogoroku*) has claimed that a work attributed to Bodhidharma (*fl.* sixth century) was the earliest example of this literature, this seems questionable as the work is not written in the conversational style that, generally speaking, characterizes the *yü-lu*. Other Ch'an literature may not be regarded as *yü-lu* if it is not in conversational form.

Up to a century ago, all available *Ch'an yü-lu* were compilations done after the ninth century. The discovery of the Tun-huang manuscripts (*Tun-huang wen-hsüeh**) has enriched our knowledge of earlier compilations. The early *Ch'an yü-lu* were written in the eighth century. Most of these have been edited and some have been translated and studied by recent scholarship. The Tun-huang manuscripts, as well as other collections of *yü-lu*, may be class-

ified into three categories: (1) the sayings of an individual, (2) the sayings of a group of Ch'an masters, and (3) dialogical histories of various branches within Ch'an.

The sayings of a Ch'an master, especially one who founded a sect, are regarded as authoritative by his followers. Such collections are called *pieh-chi* 別集 (special collections) in the Buddhist catalogues. They make up the bulk of *Ch'an yü-lu* literature. Early accounts give more than a hundred works of the category in the *Taishō shinshū daizōkyō* 大正新修大藏經 and the *Hsü tsang-ching* 續藏經. Of these collections, the sayings of Shen-hui 神會 (670-762), dated 732, and the more authoritative and influential work, *Liu-tzu t'an-ching* 六祖壇經 (Platform Scripture of the Sixth Patriarch), attributed to Hui-neng 慧能 (d. 713), were both discovered at Tun-huang. Although they were not called *yü-lu*, dialogue forms the core of these two works. Others, such as the *P'ang chü-shih yü-lu* 龐居士語錄 (Recorded Sayings of Layman P'ang [i. e., P'ang Yün 龐蘊 (*fl.* 740-808)]), the *Lin-chi lu* 臨濟錄 (Recorded Sayings of Master Lin-chi [i. e., I-hsüan 義玄 (d. 866)]) and the *Tung-shan lu* 洞山錄 (Recorded Sayings of Master Tung-shan [i. e., Liang-chieh (807-869)]) are classics of *yü-lu* literature.

The collective sayings of groups of Ch'an monks are important scriptures in different Ch'an schools. Early works like the *Ssu-chia yü-lu* 四家語錄 (Recorded Sayings of the Old Worthies) are the best representatives of this category. The *Pi-yen lu* 碧巖錄 (The Blue Cliff Records) compiled by K'o-ch'in 克勤 (1064-1136) and the *Wu-men kuan* 無門關 (The Gateless Barrier) by Hui-k'ai 慧開 (1183-1260) are collections of *kung-an* 公案 (public cases) of the Ch'an tradition. These were authoritative textbooks in the schools, and there are more than twenty works of this category in various editions of the *Ta-tsang-ching*.

Like the collected sayings of an individual monk, the early compilations of Ch'an dialogical histories were also discovered at Tun-huang. The *Ch'uan-fa-pao chi* 傳法寶紀 compiled by Tu Fei 杜朏 in 713, the *Leng-chia shih-tzu chi* 楞伽師資記 by Ching-chüeh 淨覺 dated 716, and the *Li-tai fa-pao chi*

歷代法寶記 compiled in the eighth century are all important documents for the early history of the Ch'an movement; their discovery has changed our knowledge of early Ch'an Buddhism. Apart from these early compilations from Tun-huang, the *Tsu-t'ang chi* 祖堂集, compiled by monks Ching 靜 and Yün 筠, was also recovered from the Korean edition of the *Ta-tsang-ching*. This work, compiled in 952, records the dialogues of 256 Ch'an masters in 20 *chüan.* It is especially significant for Ch'an Buddhism in southeast China during the ninth and tenth centuries. A dialogical history of Ch'an Buddhism which has had a long-lasting influence is the *Ching-te Ch'uan-teng lu* 景德傳燈錄 (The Transmission of the Lamp) by Tao-yüan 道原 (1004). It is the authoritative and sectarian history of the Southern School of Ch'an, and has been highly respected by Ch'an Buddhists since its compilation. Because of its quality and authority, there are many supplements, the first compiled by Li Tsun-hsü 李遵勗 (d. 1038), with subsequent works by Wei-po 惟白 (*fl.* 1101), Cheng-shou 正受 (1146-1208), Wu-ming 悟明 (*fl.* 1183), and P'u-chi 普濟 (*fl.* 1252). These works constitute the orthodox history of Ch'an. The main difference between the dialogical histories of Ch'an Buddhism and other Buddhist historiography is that the Ch'an works give more attention to the experience of enlightenment than to historical facts, and are of a more dialogical nature than narrative. This dialogical quality, however, declined considerably in the works which were compiled to supplement Tao-yüan's original. Instead of stimulating conversations and vigorous encounters between Ch'an masters and their disciples, the supplements are often preoccupied with dry lineages and records of the worldly honors of the master.

The dialogical literature of Ch'an Buddhism contributed many new elements to Chinese literature in general. First, because Ch'an stressed "pointing directly to one's mind, and discovering the Buddha-nature thus attaining Buddhahood," relying on one's own experience and personal efforts became the center of religious life. The record of personal encounters makes the literature often autobiographical, full of life and deep in sentiment. This personal touch is the dominant quality of the literature. Second, as dialogues are the central technique for recording, the *yü-lu* literature retained the vernacular of the T'ang and Sung. Unlike early Confucian dialogues which underwent revision by literary transmitters, the *Ch'an yü-lu* faithfully record the living conversation of the masters. These vernaculars, forerunners of the vernacular literature of the Sung and Ming periods, are a treasure for linguistic researchers. Third, the Southern School of Ch'an advocated the doctrine of Sudden Enlightenment (*tun-wu* 頓悟), which requires personal effort for religious attainment: enlightenment does not come as the result of routine practices or the study of religious texts; instead, a sudden awareness may be triggered by a given situation or words. As a consequence of this tradition, the personal encounters recorded in the *yü-lu* literature are often dramatic and humorous with a high degree of unpredictability. Last, the Ch'an dialogues often quoted hymns to explain their doctrine. This form of hymn gradually developed into a purely poetic form in later collections of *kung-an* literature. Many poems in the *kung-an* cases are a fine blend of words and instructions for actions, written in a very concentrated style. This combination has been followed in Chinese vernacular stories. The Ch'an monks in medieval China, because of their religious vision, personal experiences, the scenic spots in which they lived, and their spiritual associations, were in a unique situation. Literature of this kind was much appreciated in China and in other neighboring East Asian countries during subsequent periods: The Neo-Confucianists and Japanese Zen monks often compiled the sayings and acts of their masters in the same form and called them by the same title, *yü-lu* or *goroku*.

EDITIONS:

Taishō shinshū daizōkyō 大正新修大藏經. Tokyo, 1924-1935. Nos. 1985-2007 in v. 47-48; 2075-2077 in v. 51; 2837-2838 in v. 85.

Ying-yen wan-tzu Hsü tsang-ching 影印卍字續藏經.
Taipei, 1968-1971. V. 110-127, 135-148.

Zen no goroku 禪の語録. S. Yanagita 柳田聖山 *et al.*, ed. and trans. 20v. Tokyo, 1969. Sino-Japanese bilingual texts; publication in progress.

TRANSLATIONS:

Chan, W. T. *The Platform Scripture.* New York, 1965.

Chang, Chung-yüan. *Original Teachings of Ch'an Buddhism Selected from the Transmission of the Lamp.* New York, 1969.

de Bary, William T., *et al. Sources of Chinese Tradition*, v. 1, New York, 1964, pp. 350-368.

Demiéville, P. *Entretiens de Lin-tsi.* Paris, 1972.

Gernet, J. *Entretiens du maître de Dhyana Chen-houei.* Hanoi, 1946.

Luk, Charles. *Ch'an and Zen Teaching.* 3v. London, 1960, 1971, 1973.

Ogata, S. *Zen-shu Mumonkuan: A Gateless Barrier to Zen Buddhism.* Kyoto, 1955.

Sasaki, R. F. *et al. The Recorded Sayings of Layman P'ang.* New York, 1971.

―――. *The Recorded Sayings of Ch'an Master Lin-chi.* Kyoto, 1975.

Senzaki, N., *et al. The Gateless Gate.* Los Angeles, 1934.

Shaw, R. D. M. *The Blue Cliff Records.* London, 1961.

Yampolsky, P. B. *The Platform Sutra of the Sixth Patriarch.* New York, 1967.

STUDIES:

Zeuschner, Robert B. "A Selected Bibliography on Ch'an Buddhism in China," *JCP,* 3 (1976), 299-311.

—YHJ

Chang Chi 張繼 (*tzu,* I-sun 懿孫, *fl.* mid-eighth century) was a poet of the T'ang dynasty. Little is known of his life, except for a few isolated details. He was a native of Hsiang-chou 襄陽 (modern Hsiang-yang 襄州, Hupei). He passed the *chin-shih* in 753, and thereafter was appointed to various posts in local and central government. He died, according to one account, in Hung-chou 洪州 (modern Nan-ch'ang 南昌, Kiangsi) where he had been in charge of finance and taxation.

Exclusive of about ten poems of dubious authorship, the extant poems of Chang Chi total around forty. Over half are accounts of feelings and thoughts inspired by places the poet visited, from a famous historic site or well-known scenic spot to a certain outpost or an unidentified path on an autumn day. In some cases the inspired feeling or thought is characteristically subjective and private—homesickness, nostalgia for younger days, or grief over old age. In others the inspired feelings and thoughts are more than personal. In these poems the poet expresses his concern for a larger group of people, or for humanity as a whole, and deals with such topics as the destruction of war, the irretrievable passage of time, and the preservation of moral integrity in the face of temptation. Other poems, apparently not inspired by the visiting of places, treat quite conventional subjects, notably friendship, separation, lovesickness, and retreat to a life of seclusion.

Neither traditional criticism nor modern scholarship has deemed Chang Chi a leading poet. He was not, for instance, included as one of the *Ta-li shih ts'ai-tzu* (Ten Talents of the Ta-li [Reign Period, 766-779], see Lu Lun). Yet for all his apparent mediocrity, a single short poem earned him a prominence far greater than that of any of the "Ten Geniuses"—"Feng-ch'iao yeh po" 楓橋夜泊 (A Night Mooring at Maple Bridge), a seven-character *chüeh-chü.* For centuries it has been among the most widely chanted T'ang poems, and its popularity has lasted to this day. It has also received much critical attention. Traditional discussions have centered on two areas: identification of the place-names in the poem and verification of the statement in the poem that bells were rung at midnight in T'ang temples. Modern study of the poem, on the other hand, is prompted by interest in the interaction of the real and imagined worlds and is based on a view of the poem as an artistic organism. Contempory interest concentrates on exegesis of the poem's intrinsic merits and attends to prosody, sound, parallelism, syntax, imagery, semantic features, mutual coordination of the constituent parts, and the overall structuring and organization.

EDITIONS:
Ch'üan T'ang shih, v. 4, pp. 2718-2725.

STUDIES:

Fu, *Shih-jen*, pp. 209-219: "Chang Chi k'ao" 考.

Fu, Shu-hsien 傅述先. "Tu 'Feng-ch'iao yeh po'" 讀楓橋夜泊, *Chung-wai wen-hsüeh*, 9.2 (July 1980), 110-115.

Kunst, Arthur E. "A Critical Analysis of Witter Bynner's 'A Night Mooring near Maple Bridge,'" *THHP*, 7.1 (August 1968), 114-142.

Liu, I-sheng 劉逸生. "Chang Chi: 'Feng-ch'iao yeh po'" 張繼: 楓橋夜泊, in his *T'ang-shih hsiao-cha* 唐詩小札. Rev. ed. Canton, 1978, pp. 181-183.

Nienhauser, William H., Jr. "Tied Up at Maple Bridge Once Again," *TkR*, 11.4 (Summer 1981), 421-429.

—SH

Chang Chi 張籍 (*tzu*, Wen-ch'ang 文昌, *c.* 776-*c.* 829) authored a corpus of *yüeh-fu*** poetry whose realistic descriptions of the economic ravages of warfare and administrative corruption on the populace underscored the political and social ills of his time. Both contemporary and later readers of Chang Chi praised his *yüeh-fu* poetry as an affirmation of the Confucian tradition of expressing social comment in verse.

Chang was a native of Wu-chiang 烏江 in Ho-chou 和州 (modern Anhwei). The lack of any information about his immediate family, except that a younger brother passed the *chin-shih* in 813, would suggest for him a more humble origin than was usual for most T'ang poets and may explain his sympathy for the sufferings of the T'ang lower classes. He seems to have spent the first thirty years of his life at home in Ho-chou. In 796, Meng Chiao, while on a journey to the Southeast, met him in Ho-chou, and the following year secured for him an appointment on the staff of Tung Chin 董晉 (724-799), military governor of the Hsün-wu 宣武 region, whose headquarters were at Pien-chou 汴州. Chang's colleagues there were Meng Chiao,* Li Ao,* and Han Yü,* under whose sponsorship he passed the provincial examinations in 798 and obtained the *chin-shih* the following year. After several years in mourning at Ho-chou and further service attached to southern military governors, he returned to Ch'ang-an in 806 as Great

Supplicator in the Court of Imperial Sacrifices, a low-ranking ceremonial post in which he remained for ten years. Frequent references to his failing eyesight and requests to friends to write letters for him suggest that during this period Chang's poor eyesight may have hampered his official career. He was obviously never totally blind, for in 816 Han Yü secured for him a teaching position in the Directorate of Education where he remained until 822 when he was made Vice Director of the Bureau of Waterways and Irrigation. He left this post in the summer of 824 to stay with Han Yü, who was then mortally ill, at the latter's villa south of Ch'ang-an. He returned to service in the autumn as Director of the Bureau of Receptions and was present at Han Yü's death in 824. Chang Chi's verse eulogy for Han Yü ("Chi T'ui-chih" 祭退之), his longest poem, is a moving tribute to their long friendship and an important source of information about Han Yü's last days. Chang came back to the Directorate of Education to serve as Director of Studies in 827. He associated and exchanged poems with other elder literati including Po Chü-i,* Liu Yü-hsi,* and P'ei Tu 裴度 (765-839). After a short trip home to Ho-chou in 828, he died in Ch'ang-an, probably in 829.

Chang Chi was among the first poets to recognize the merits of Tu Fu. He is even reputed to have burned a copy of a Tu Fu poem, mixed its ashes with oil, and ingested the mixture in order to absorb the spirit of Tu Fu's poetry. Chang Chi's own *yüeh-fu* poetry was a conscious continuation of the tradition of verse narratives, such as Tu Fu's "Shih-hao li" 石壕吏 (The Officer at Shih-hao), that depicted the sufferings of the populace during the An Lu-shan Rebellion. Po Chü-i acknowledged that Chang's poems in this tradition were the immediate inspiration for his own "New *Yüeh-fu*" poetry. In his poem "On Reading the Old-style *Yüeh-fu* of Chang Chi" 讀張籍古樂府, Po Chü-i wrote that Chang "was especially skilled at *yüeh-fu* poetry, in all the age few were his equal" 尤工樂府詩，舉代少其倫. He attributed this excellence to Chang's concious emulation of the Confucian principles of verse criticism as articulated in the traditional explication of the *Shih-ching*.* Although his government career was unsuccessful, Chang played an important role in the literary contacts with Han Yü's circle and with the group centering around Po Chü-i and Yüan Chen.* He was thus an important conduit for ideas between the two coteries, whose relations seem to have been strained by differing political viewpoints.

Chang's surviving corpus contains about four hundred poems, only seventy of which are in the *yüeh-fu* mode. Over twenty of these describe the hardship of incessant warfare on the peasantry. For example, the "Sai-shang Ch'ü" 塞上曲 (Song from the Frontier) concludes, "year after year, no rest from the wars;/the border people are all dead, and only the empty mountains remain" (年年征戰不得閒，邊人殺盡唯空山). Chang also portrays the effect on the poor of the taxes levied to support such wars. In the "Song of the Old Farmer" (野老歌), an old man's harvest is taken for taxes and then rots in the government granary. The old man and his son are forced to gather acorns to survive, "while a West River merchant, with a hundred chests of pearls, feeds meat to the dogs on his boat" (西江 買客珠百斛，船中養犬長食肉). This Confucian disgust with trade, further developed in Chang's satire "Chia-ko le" 買客樂 (The Merchant's Pleasures), and indignation over the economic exploitation of the peasantry is related to the conviction that such satires can serve as moral example to persuade the evil to mend their ways. Po Chü-i, in the same poem mentioned above, wrote that Chang's "Poem for Master Tung," a long encomium to the civil virtue of Tung Chin, "would admonish greedy and cruel officials" (讀君董公詩，可誨貪暴臣), presumably by acting as a positive example. On the other hand, "A Song of Sorrow" (傷歌行) describes in vivid detail the disgraced departure from Ch'ang-an in 809 of the Mayor Yang P'ing 楊憑 who had been convicted of corruption and exiled to the far South: "dressed in green robes, he rides an old horse; beyond the eastern gate there is no one to see him off" (身着青衫騎惡馬， 東門之外無送者). Officials of the lowest rank wore green robes. The poem provides a negative example to potential wrongdoers. Chang's satires in this mode are written in a simple and direct language that underlines the popular origins of the questions they discuss and that served as a base for the "New *Yüeh-fu*" poetry of Po Chü-i and Yüan Chen.

Chang Chi's reputation as a *yüeh-fu* poet, established by the praise of his contemporaries Han Yü and Po Chü-i, continued in later periods. Typical and most appropriate is the remark of the Sung critic Chang Chieh 張戒 (*fl.* 1135): "Chang's poetry is a on par with that of Po Chü-i and Yüan Chen. He was particularly good at expressing those concerns the people had in their hearts" (張司業詩與元白一律，專以道 得人心事為工).

Much of Chang Chi's writing has been lost. Although his works were first collected in the Southern T'ang and again in the Sung, neither edition survives. The modern corpus derives from an early sixteenth-century Ming edition that is textually unsatisfactory. Only two prose pieces remain, extant by virtue of their inclusion in the *Wen-yüan ying-hua*.* These are the famous letters criticizing Han Yü written at Pien-chou in 798. Chang also wrote a commentary to the *Analects*, the *Lun-yü chu-pien* 論語注辨, which has not survived.

EDITIONS:

Chang Ssu-yeh shih chi 張司業詩集, *8 chüan.* Ming *Cheng-te* 正德 (1506-1521) edition, reprinted in SPTK.

Ch'en, Yen-chieh 陳延傑, ed. *Chang Chi shih chu* 張籍詩注. Shanghai, 1938; rpt. Taipei, 1967. A pedestrian work, but the only modern edition.

Chang Chi shih chi. Peking, 1950. A modern, reset edition that mainly follows the SPTK text.

Hiraoka, Takeo 平岡武夫 and Maruyama, Shigeru 丸山茂. *Chō Seki kashi sakuin* 張籍歌詩索引. Tokyo, 1976. A complete concordance keyed to the 1959 Peking edition, a reprint of which is included.

Hsü, Ch'eng-yü 徐澄宇, ed. *Chang Wang yüeh-fu* 張王樂府. Shanghai, 1957.

STUDIES:

Akai, Masuhisa 赤井益久. "Chō Seki no kofū nijūnanashu" 張籍の古風二十七首. *Chūgoku kankei ronsetsu shiryō*, 21.2b (1979), 151-157.

Chang, Kuo-wei 張國偉. "Shih-lun Chang Chi shih te hsien-shih i-i" 試論張籍詩的現實意義, in *T'ang-shih yen-chiu*, pp. 237-246.

Chow, Chuen-tang. "Chang Chi the Poet." Unpublished Ph.D. dissertation, University of Washington, 1968.

Hua, Ch'en-chih 華忱之. "Lüeh-t'an Chang Chi chi ch'i yüeh-fu shih" 略談張籍及其樂府詩, in *Yüeh-fu shih yen-chiu lun-wen chi* 樂府詩研究論文集, v. 2, Peking, 1959, pp. 157-169.

Lo, Lien-t'ien 羅聯添. *"Chang Chi nien-p'u"* 張籍年譜, *Ta-lu tsa-chih*, 25.4 (Aug. 31, 1962), 14-19; 25.5 (Sept. 15, 1962), 15-22; 25.6 (Sept. 30, 1962), 20-29.

"Chang Chi chih chiao-yu chi ch'i tso-p'in hsi-nien" 張籍之交遊及其作品繫年. *Ta-lu tsa-chih*, 26.12 (June 30, 1963), 14-18.

"Chang Chi i-shih chi shih-hua" 張籍軼事及詩話. *Ta-lu tsa-chih*, 27.10 (Nov. 30, 1963), 13-16. Lo's articles organize most of the traditional source material on Chang Chi. They are basic research tools.

Waley, *Po Chü-i*, pp. 143-146.

—CH

Chang Chien 張堅 (*tzu*, Ch'i-yüan 齊元, *hao*, Sou-shih, 漱石, 1681-1771 or after) was a noted dramatist. Very little is known about his life. He came from Chiang-ning 江寧 in Kiangsu. He sat several times for the provincial examinations without any success. According to T'ang Ying's 唐英 preface to Chang's drama *Meng-chung yüan* 夢中緣 (Love in a Dream), he wrote "Chiang-nan i hsiu-ts'ai ko" 江南一秀才歌 (Song of a Chiang-nan First Degree Graduate) as a take off of his own failures, so the people of his time called him a "first degree graduate of Chiang-nan." The song is preserved as a supplement to the drama.

Chang Chien wrote four *ch'uan-chi** which were printed together under the title *Yü-yen T'ang ssu-chung ch'ü* 玉燕堂四種曲 (Four pieces from the Yü-yen Hall). The first and best of them is *Love in a Dream*, prefaced 1699 by the author, who was then only eighteen years old. In the preface to a later drama, Chang tells us that when very small he had gone in secret to see performances of *Hsi-hsiang chi** and *Pai-*

yüeh T'ing (see *Ssu-ta ch'uan-ch'i*) and, inspired by then, had composed some of the verses of *Love in a Dream*. "Fearing I would be reprimanded," he continues, "I hid them at the bottom of a trunk for over ten years, only then did I take them out to show others." The origins of his first work thus date very far back to his childhood.

The story of the drama concerns Chung Hsin 鍾心, a young scholar who sees a beautiful girl in a dream. She is the daughter of a retired Han-lin Academician, and she likewise sees Chung in a dream. They fall in love with and determine to locate each other. Many vicissitudes follow, including the inevitable, unjust imprisonment of the hero, humorous sections, the assumption of false names, women disguising themselves as men, etc. Finally Chung Hsin marries simultaneously not only the beloved of his dream but also a close and equally beautiful friend of hers.

Love in a Dream is long, with forty-six scenes in all. Yet the scenes could be split up and the drama was not performed as a totality. It appears to have commanded a following in its own time.

Among the other three of Chang's pieces only *Huai-sha chi* 懷沙記 (Record of the Huai-sha) has aroused any real interest. It deals with the career of the famous poet Ch'ü Yüan—*Huai-sha* is the name of the poem he wrote just before his suicide. This drama is thus much more serious than the comedy *Love in a Dream*: it is based upon historical fact, with the political events playing a major function as background. Aoki Masaru has criticized the piece severely on several grounds, including that the text follows the original *Ch'u-tz'u** too closely, and that Ch'ü Yüan himself appears too seldom on the stage—he plays a prominent part in only three of the sixteen scenes.

In his *Tz'u-yü ts'ung-hua* 詞餘叢話 (*chüan* 2) Yang En-shou 楊恩壽 (1834-after 1888) is rather critical of Chang Chien. He finds two of the four *ch'uan-ch'i*, *Mei-hua tsan* 梅花簪 (The Plum Blossom Hairpin) and *Yü-shih chui* 玉獅墜 (The Fall of the Jade Lion), as rather tasteless, and sees *Record of the Huai-sha* as lacking in invention. Yang sees fit to praise only *Love in a Dream*. Among its many virtues are its "excellent, fine, and delicate words." It is perhaps ironical that a dramatist who lived to be over ninety should have produced his best work at the age of eighteen!

EDITIONS:

Yü-yen T'ang ssu-chung ch'ü 玉燕堂四種曲. 1758. Contains the texts of all four *ch'uan-ch'i*.

STUDIES:

Aoki Masaru 青木正兒. Wang Kei-lu 王古魯, trans. *Chung-kuo chin-shih hsi-ch'ü shih* 中國近世戲曲史. Shanghai, 1936, pp. 400-404.

—CM

Chang Chiu-ling 張九齡 (*tzu*, Tzu-shou 子壽, 678-740) was the most important writer and statesman of the 730s, a decade in the prosperous and serene heyday of the great Emperor Hsüan-tsung 玄宗 (r. 712-756), that in many ways marked the apogee of T'ang culture. Born in Ch'ü-chiang 曲江 township on Shao-chou 韶州 (modern northern Kwangtung), Chang Chiu-ling was a native of the tropical south. The most conspicuous example of a southerner rising to fame and high influence in T'ang times, he was also partly responsible through his writings for the increasing acceptance and appreciation of the southern landscape in medieval Chinese literature.

It was through the examination system that Chang, an outsider of comparatively modest origins, made his entry into the privileged circles of T'ang officialdom and elite society, placing second in the *chin-shih* exam of 702 (the poet Shen Ch'üan-ch'i* was one of the examiners that year). Shortly thereafter, he made the acquaintance of Chang Yüeh,* who agreed to regard Chang Chiu-ling as a distant relative and in later years advanced the younger man's career when it was in his power to do so. In both 707 and 712 Chang sat for and passed special-decree examinations (the disquisitions he wrote for the latter test are still extant). His success in the 712 exam, of which he is recorded to have been the only successful candidate, led to a position as Reminder of the Left on the staff of the then Crown Prince Li Lung-chi 李隆基 (later Hsüan-tsung). In 716, as a result of disa-greements with higher officials, Chang resigned his position and returned to Shao-chou, where he remained for the next two years. During this time, he oversaw the construction of a new road through the daunting Ta-yü Pass 大庾嶺, just north of Shao-chou, which greatly facilitated trade and transportation between the North and Canton (and points southwest). Chang was recalled to court in 718. He received several promotions in the following years and in 723 was made Chang Yüeh's immediate subordinate in the Secretariat. In this year he was also granted ennoblement, as the Man of Ch'ü-chiang (曲江男). When Chang Yüeh suffered a temporary political setback in 727, Chang Chiu-ling was sent out to the provinces, holding office during the next years in Hung-chou 洪州 (Kiangsi) and then Kuei-chou 桂州 (Kwangtung). But he was back at court again in 731, following Chang Yüeh's death, and began to come to power in his own right. As the emperor reposed more and more confidence in him, Chang was rapidly promoted through a succession of important posts, attaining ministerial status and the control of the Secretariat in 734. Further ennoblement (as Patrician of Shih-hsing District [near Ch'ü-chiang] 曲江) and honors (e.g., receipt of the exalted title Auriporphyrian Great Official of Glorious Favor 金紫光祿大夫) were forthcoming. His regime became, in the eyes of later historians, the model of a "Confucian" ministership. But by the end of 736, Chang's administration was being challenged strongly by the aristocratic faction of Li Lin-fu 李林甫, and in May of 737 Chang was demoted to office in Ching-chou 荊州 (southern Hupei), the government falling into Li Lin-fu's dictatorial hands for fifteen years. Chang died on June 5, 740 in his native Ch'ü-chiang, where he had recently returned on leave from his post in Ching-chou.

More than 250 of Chang Chiu-ling's poems—all but a handful of which are in pentasyllabic meter—have been preserved. His style is fluid and, in general, descriptive. The greater part of Chang's verse is devoted to depictions of natural scenes, often in the south, and the traditional responses to the exotic landscape are sometimes, quite surprisingly, reversed. In several poems, for instance, the usually mournful cries of the gibbon in fact drive away the morose thoughts of the southern poet: for him they are welcome sounds of familiar companions. An especially large number of Chang's poems are "ascent" verses, depicting views from atop hills, storeyed buildings, city walls, and towers.

At his best, Chang has a flair for capturing precise visualizations—and vitalizations—of natural objects, particularly in parallel couplets with unexpected juxtapositions of elements in the landscape. He is often vivid and exciting (as, for example, in his several poems on the famous waterfall at Mount Lu), but he does at times lapse into a rather pallid manner—the other side of inspiration. A curious feature of Chang's diction is his common, though not invariable, substitution of either the colloquial *na* 那 or the archaic *hu* 胡 for the word *ho* 何 (how?). But Chang's poetic lexicon, while extensive, is not especially abstruse or allusive. Above all, he excels in compositions, such as his marvelous "Lichih fu" 荔枝賦 (Prose-poem on the Lichee), in which he celebrates the unappreciated (by northerners) glories of his native region and attempts to effect a reorientation of traditional geographic prejudice.

Over two hundred of Chang's prose pieces are also extant. Many of these are official documents drafted for Hsüan-tsung—policy statements, letters to rulers of foreign nations, and the like. Chang's style in these works—a number of which furnish very important material for the study of the political history of the time—is, of course, much more dense and academic than in his poetic works.

Just as Chang Yüeh had aided Chang Chiu-ling, so Chiu-ling was himself a notable patron of several younger poet-bureaucrats, such as Wang Wei* and Pao Jung 包融, and it was he who appointed Meng Hao-jan* in 737 to the only official post that poet ever held. His imposing influence on many of his contemporaries is nicely summed up in a military metaphor used by Hsüan-tsung, who on one occasion

pronounced Chang "the commander-in-chief of the literary fields."

Chang's tomb, situated at the foot of Mount Lo-yüan 羅源山, in the northwestern suburbs of the present-day city of Shao-kuan 韶關市, was excavated in 1960. The memorial inscription discovered there, along with the additional testimony of a eulogistic text preserved in the *Ch'üan T'ang wen*,* has enabled us to revise the date of birth of this great writer from the previously accepted year 673 to 678.

EDITIONS:
Chang Ch'ü-chiang chi 張曲江集. 12 *chüan. Kuang-tung ts'ung-shu* 廣東叢書. Shanghai, 1946. With annotations by Wen Ju-kua 溫汝适. Based on a lost Ch'ing (1743) edition.
Ch'ü-chiang Chang Hsien-sheng wen-chi 曲江張先生文集. 20 *chüan. SPTK.* (Also *Kuo-hsüeh chi-pen ts'ung-shu* edition, punctuated, under the title *Ch'ü-chiang chi* 曲江集). Based on a Ming edition, edited by Ch'iu Chün 丘濬 in 1473. The most reliable text.
Ch'ü-chiang chi 曲江集. 12 *chüan. SPPY.* Substantially the same as *Chang Ch'ü-chiang chi* above, but lacking annotation.

TRANSLATIONS:
Demiéville, *Anthologie*, pp. 208-209.

STUDIES:
Altier, Daniel P. "The *Kan-yü* of Chang Chiu-ling: Poems of Political Tragedy," *TkR*, 4.1 (April 1973), 63-73.
Herbert, P. A. "The Life and Works of Chang Chiu-ling." Unpublished Ph.D. dissertation, University of Cambridge, 1973.
———. *Under the Brilliant Emperor: Imperial Authority in T'ang China as Seen in the Writings of Chang Chiu-ling.* Canberra, 1978.
Ho, Ko-en 何格恩. "Chang Chiu-ling nien-p'u" 張九齡年譜, *Ling-nan hsüeh-pao*, 4 (1935), 1-21.
———. "Chang Chiu-ling chih cheng-chih sheng-hou" 張九齡之政治生活, *Ling-nan hsüeh-pao*, 4 (1935), 22-46.
———. "Ch'ü-chiang nien-p'u shih-i" 曲江年譜拾遺, *Ling-nan hsüeh-pao*, 6 (1937), 133-134.
Okazaki, Takashi 岡崎敬. "Tō Chō Kyūrei no funbo to sono boshimei" 唐張九齡の墳墓とその墓誌銘, *Shien*, 89 (1962), 45-83.
Schafer, *Vermilion Bird*, passim.
Wen, Ju-kua 溫汝适. "Ch'ü-chiang chi k'ao-cheng; Ch'ü-chiang nien-p'u" 曲江集考證; 曲江年譜, appended to *Chang Ch'ü-chiang chi*.

Yang, Ch'eng-tsu 楊承祖. *Chang Chiu-ling nien-p'u* 張九齡年譜. Taipei, 1964.

Yang, Hao 楊豪. "T'ang-tai Chang Chiu-ling mu fa-chüeh chien-pao" 唐代張九齡墓發掘簡報, *Wen-wu*, 1961.6, 45-51.

—PWK

Chang Cho 張鷟 (*tzu*, Wen-ch'eng 文成, *c.* 657-730) was a native of Lu-tse 陸澤 District of Shen-chou 深州 Prefecture (in southern modern Honan). A precocious child, he passed the *chin-shih* examination in 679. Thereupon he became the Defender of Ch'ang-an 長安 District. His writings were compared to "coins minted in bronze" (precious items), and he was known to his contemporaries as the "Bronze-coin Scholar." But he was notorious for his volatile disposition and loose conduct, which offended many people. The Grand Councilor Yao Ch'ung 姚崇 (651-721), in particular, had a grudge against him. About 720 he was demoted to the far South because of his criticism of the government. Later he returned to the capital, serving as the vice director of a bureau in the Ministry of Justice just before his death.

Chang wrote swiftly, had a genuine sense of humor, and gained widespread fame. Neighboring countries like Silla and Japan especially treasured his literary works. Their envoys often brought back Chang's writings from China, writings for which they had exchanged gold. His extant corpus includes *Ch'ao-yeh ch'ien-tsai* 朝野僉載 (Comprehensive Records of Affairs Within and Outside of the Court) and *Lung-chin feng-sui p'an* 龍筋鳳髓判 (Segregating Dragon Sinews and Phoenix Marrow).

Among Chang's extant works there is also a tale entitled "Yu-hsien k'u" 遊仙窟 (The Dwelling of Playful Goddesses). It was transmitted to Japan during the T'ang dynasty, but never recorded in Chinese sources. The edition transmitted to Japan contains an epigraph which reads: "Written by Chang Wen-ch'eng, Defender of Hsiang-lo 襄樂 District of Ning-chou 寧州 Prefecture [modern Kansu]." In *Kuei-lin feng-t'u chi* 桂林風土記 (Records of the Natural Scenery and Folk Traditions of Kuei-lin) written by Mo Hsiu-fu 莫休符 of the late T'ang, we have the following record:

"Chang Cho passed the civil-service examination at an early age, and he wrote with such spontaneity, . . . he was therefore conferred the title of Defender of Hsiang-lo District." From this it can be inferred that the work was written by Chang Cho in his youth. It was not until the late Ch'ing, when Yang Shou-ching 楊守敬 (1839-1915) wrote *Jih-pen fang-shu chih* 日本訪書志 (Records of a Search for Books in Japan) that the work was first recorded in China. "Yu-hsien k'u" was highly valued in Japan, where annotations were compiled for it quite early.

The story is narrated in the first person. The persona, Chang Wen-ch'eng, en route to Ho-yüan 河源 on an official mission seeks lodging one night in a large mansion. There he meets two women: Shih-niang 十娘, a young widow, and her sister-in-law, Wu-sao 五嫂. Wen-ch'eng and the two women then entertain themselves with banquets and all sorts of sumptuous entertainments in the mansion. They also compose poems and flirt with one another. Wen-ch'eng spends the night in Shih-niang's chamber and then departs. The story is very simple. It is written in parallel prose, interspersed with some T'ang colloquialisms. It can be regarded as an attempt to write erotic fiction in parallel prose (see *p'ien-wen*) during the early T'ang dynasty.

According to a legend which circulated in Japan, Chang Cho was handsome and licentious. He composed the "Yu-hsien k'u" to win Empress Wu Tse-t'ien's attention. But in the *T'ai-p'ing kuang-chi** (*chüan* 255, "Chang Cho") there is a satirical song written by Chang which criticizes Empress Wu, undermining the Japanese legend.

EDITIONS:

Yu-hsien k'u. Fang Shih-ming 方詩銘, coll. and comm. Shanghai, 1955.

———. Kawashima 川島 [Chang T'ing-ch'ien 章廷謙], ed. Preface by Lu Hsün dated 1929. N.p.

———, in *T'ang-jen hsiao-shuo*, pp. 19-36. Reliable edition.

TRANSLATIONS:

Levy, Howard S. *The Dwelling of Playful Goddesses.* 2v. Tokyo, 1965.

Yagisawa, Hajime 八木沢元. Yūsen kutsu kenkō 遊仙窟全講. Tokyo, 1967.

STUDIES:

Cheng, Hsi-ti 鄭西諦. "Kuan-yü *Yu-hsien k'u*," *Chung-kuo wen-hsüeh lun chi*, Taipei, 1970.

Egan, Ronald. "On the Origin of the Yu Hsien K'u Commentary," *HJAS*, 36 (1976), 135-146.

Utsunomiya, Mutsuo 宇都宮睦男. "Seigidō bunkobon *Yūsenkutsu* honbun to kunten," *Kobe kuntengo to kunten shiryo*, 53 (1973.8).

Wang, Chung-han. "The Authorship of the *Yu-shien k'u*," *HJAS*, 11 (1948), 153-162.

　　　　　　　　　　　　　　—CYi

Chang Feng-i 張鳳翼 (*tzu*, Po-ch'i 伯起, 1527-1613), a native of Ch'ang-chou 長洲 (modern Soochow), was an acknowledged calligrapher, dramatist, and poet. According to a local history, Chang did not speak a word until he was five years old. Then one day while watching his father sweeping the floor, he said to his mother, "Why don't you take over?" His precocity hence became very noticeable. He became a *chü-jen* at the age of thirty-seven, but in spite of four attempts failed to obtain a higher degree. Therefore, instead of spending his life serving the state, he devoted his time to literary activities, and he and his two younger brothers earned the sobriquet of the "Three Changs" of Soochow. He sold his calligraphy and literary works to earn a livelihood. It is said that for thirty years he posted the following notice on his front door: In this house there is a lack of paper and brush; applicants for one full page of calligraphy are required to pay one copper coin, for eight sentences, three-tenths [of a copper coin], and birthday poems or compositions, charges will be made accordingly."

He left the following works: *Ch'u-shih-t'ang chi* 處實堂集, *Hai-nei ming-chia kung-hua neng-shih* 海內名家工畫能事, *T'an-lu* 譚輅, and *Chao-ming hsüan-fu* 昭明選賦. The first of these works, which includes a sketch book, poems, and essays, was subsequently officially expunged.

Chang also wrote seven *ch'uan-ch'i** dramas: *Hung-fu chi* 紅拂記 (Red Duster), *Chu-fa chi* 祝髮記 (Hair Binding), *Kuan-yüan chi* 灌園記 (The Gardener), *Ch'ieh-fu chi* 竊符記

(Tally Stealing), *Hu-fu chi* 虎符記 (Tiger Tally), *Yen-i chi* 屍屚記 (The Upright Bar), and *P'ing-po chi* 平播記 (Level Sowing). The first six were published under the title, *Yang-ch'un liu-chi* 陽春六集. The last, written when Chang was an old man and at the request of Li Ying-hsiang 李應祥, is no longer extant.

Of the six extant dramas, five are complete. The one fragmentary text, *Yen-i chi*, is found in *Ch'ün-yin lei-hsüan* 群音類選 and *Yüeh-lu yin* 月露音.

The main plots of all his plays are derived from incidents associated with historical personalities. *Ch'ieh-fu chi* is based on military exploits of the states of Ch'in, Chao, and Wei of the Warring States period, and on an intrigue involving nobles of the Wei court. *Hu-fu chi*, which the *Ch'ü-hai tsung-mu t'i-yao* 曲海總目提要 mistakenly claims is anonymous, portrays the heroic acts of Hua Yün 花雲 in his loyal service to Chu Yüan-chang 朱元璋 in the early Ming dynasty. *Chu-fa chi*, written on the occasion of his mother's eightieth birthday (termed anonymous in *Ch'ü-hai tsung-mu t'i-yao*), is based on the filial acts of Hsü Hsiao-k'e 徐孝克 of the Sui dynasty. *Kuan-yüan chi* (termed anonymous in *Ch'ü-hai tsung-mu t'i-yao*) portrays the licentiousness in and the fall of the Ch'i court (during the Warring States period), the plight and romance of Fa-chang 法章, and the restoration of the state of Ch'i by T'ien Tan 田單. To this basic material, which is derived from the *Shih-chi*,* *Chan-kuo ts'e** and *T'ung-chien kang-mu* 通鑑綱目, Chang introduced two additional elements: Fa-chang's changing his name to Wang Li 王立 after he goes into exile, and T'ien Tan's marriage to Ch'ao-ying 朝英. *Hung-fu chi*, his first and still most popular drama, was written within a month after his marriage. Set in the transitional period between the Sui and the T'ang, *Hung-fu chi* is just as much a portrayal of the adventure and romance of Li Ching 李靖 and Hung-fu as of the separation and reunion of Hsü Te-yen 徐德言 and Princess Lo-ch'ang 樂昌. The plot is based on two T'ang tales, "Ch'iu-jan k'e-chuan" 虯髯客傳 by Tu Kuang-t'ing* and "Lo-ch'ang kung-chu" 樂昌公主 by Meng Ch'i 孟啓 (in *Pen-shih shih*).

Thematically, Chang's dramas stress the Confucian virtues of loyalty, filial piety, righteousness, and conjugal fidelity. His language is elegant, yet his use of rhyme leaves something to be desired. Further, his dramas generally have a large number of *dramatis personae*, loosening the plot structure and thus diminishing dramatic tension.

EDITIONS:

Chao Ming hsüan-fu 昭明選賦. N.p., 1850.

Ch'ieh-fu chi 竊符記, in *Ku-pen, san-chi.*

Chu-fa chi 祝髮記, *Hu-fu chi* 虎符記, *Hung-fu chi* 紅拂記, and *Kuan-yüan chi* 灌園記 in *Ku-pen, ch'u-chi.*

T'an-lu 譚輅. Shanghai, 1936.

STUDIES:

Aoki, *Gikyokushi;* ch. 9 contains biography and comments on *Hung-fu chi, Kuan-yüan chi,* and *Chu-fa chi.*

Chin, Meng-hua 金夢華. *Chi-ku-ko liu-shih-chung ch'ü hsü-lu* 汲古閣六十種曲敍錄. Taipei, 1969. Ch. 15 contains biography and studies on *Hung-fu chi;* ch. 46 contains studies on *Kuan-yüan chi.*

DMB, pp. 63-64.

Liu, Wen-liu 劉文六. *K'un-ch'ü yen-chiu* 崑曲研究. Taipei, 1969. Ch. 1 contains brief biography, a list of Chang's plays, and comments on the use of rhymes in *Hung-fu chi.*

—EY

Chang Heng 張衡 (*tzu,* P'ing-tzu 平子, 78-139) was an eminent author of *fu,** though he is better known as a great mathematician and astronomer. A native of Hsi-ao 西鄂 in the province of Nan-yang 南陽 (modern Honan), he was brought up in a family of reputation. His father, Chang K'an 張堪, had governed Shu Province 蜀郡 (modern Szechwan).

Chang Heng was a precocious youth and accordingly was sent to the capital, Lo-yang, to study at the National University. On his way to Lo-yang, he passed by Mount Li 驪山. Charmed by the hot springs there, he composed the "Wen-ch'üan fu" 溫泉賦 (Prose-poem on Hot Springs). He graduated from the university in due course, mastering the classics, but mathematics and astronomy were his forte. Around the turn of the first century he was recommended

for an official position in the capital, but instead he went back to Nan-yang and became the secretary to the provincial governor, Pao Te 鮑德. At that time, he was displeased with the wealthy upper classes who lived in excessive luxury. He wrote a lengthy piece modeled on Pan Ku's* "Liang-tu fu," called "Erh-ching fu" 二京賦 (Prose-poem on Two Capitals) that satirizes the extravagance of these people.

For nine years he served in Nan-yang until Pao Te was appointed Minister of Finance in Lo-yang. Chang Heng did not go with him but returned home and devoted his time to further study. During this time of seclusion, he wrote "Nan-tu fu" 南都賦 (The Southern Capital), depicting the topography, local products, scenic and historical spots, and social customs of the provincial captial, Nan-yang, which he knew so well. Because of his profound knowledge in astronomy and his technological ability in making heliometers, sky-charts, and seismographic apparatus capable of recording the direction of earthquakes, he was summoned to the capital and appointed the chief astronomer of the observatory in 116, an office he held for fourteen years, during which time he made a thorough study of uranology.

In 124 following Emperor An's 安帝 (r. 107-125) hunting in the suburbs of Lo-yang, Chang Heng composed "Yü-lieh fu" 羽獵賦 (The Plume) to commemorate the colossal spectacle of the imperial hunt. By that time, the composition of *fu* had been made a subject in the examinations, and a civil servant might get a promotion if he could compose effectively in the genre. Thus many wrote *fu,* but few really mastered the form. Chang Heng submitted a memorial to the throne cautioning the emperor to examine such works with care. Before long, he became a gentleman-in-attendance to the throne and gained the emperor's confidence. He was allowed to attend meetings in which important affairs of state were discussed. The eunuchs, however, viewed him as a potential enemy and slandered him. He found relief in composing the "Ssu-hsüan fu" 思玄賦 (Meditation on Mystery). It is a long poem, written on the pattern of Ch'ü Yüan's* "Li sao" 離騷 —its vast imaginative flight taking in the boundless space of Heaven and Earth.

In 136 he was appointed minister in the princedom of Ho-chien 河間 where a number of rich and powerful families were behaving lawlessly. On his arrival, Chang Heng acted with the utmost sagacity and daring and put the leading offenders in prison. Once the princedom was brought into good order, Chang Heng pleaded for leave to retire. His famous "Kuei-t'ien fu" 歸田賦 (Returning to the Fields) extols the bucolic life and pleasures of retirement. Unfortunately he died shortly after its composition (at the age of sixty-two), before he could return to his hometown.

Chang Heng is one of the most distinguished poets of the Latter Han period, and had great influence on the subsequent development of the *fu* genre. Chang was also a forerunner in the development of the seven-word poetic line. His "Ssu-ch'iu shih" 四愁詩 (Four-fold Sorrow), though written in the *sao* 騷 tradition, is a typical example of a successful poem in this new form. His "Ting-ch'ing fu" 定情賦 (Stabilizing the Passions) was written in a much simpler style than previous *fu*. It served as a model for Ts'ai Yung's* "Ching-ch'ing fu" 靜情賦 and several other pieces on this theme (see James R. Hightower's "Stabilizing the Passions"). His "Kuei-t'ien fu" was also imitated by later writers of *fu*.

EDITIONS:

"Chang Heng," in *Liu-ch'ao wen*, v. 1, "Ch'üan Hou-Han wen" 全後漢文, *ch*. 52-55, pp. 759-779.

Chang Ho-chien chi 張河間集, in *Pai san*, v. 2, pp. 139-201.

Chang P'ing-tzu chi 張平子集 in the *Han Wei Ming-wen sheng* 漢魏名文乘, Shen Ting-k'e 沈鼎科, Chang Yün-t'ai, 張運泰 and Yü Yüan-hsi 余元熹, commentators, 1642. In the Rare Book Collection of the Fung Ping Shan Library, University of Hong Kong.

TRANSLATIONS:

Demiéville, *Anthologie*, pp. 86-87.

Frankel, *Palace Lady*, pp. 183-185.

Hightower, James R. "Stabilizing the Passions" and "Returning to the Fields" in his "The

Fu of T'ao Ch'ien," in *Studies in Chinese Literature*, Cambridge, Mass., 1965, pp. 46-47 and pp. 90-92.

Hughes, "The Western Capital" ("Hsi-ching fu" 西京賦) and "The Eastern Capital" ("Tung-ching fu" 東京賦), in *Two Chinese Poets*, pp. 35-47 and pp. 60-81.

Knechtges, "Western Metropolis Rhapsody," "Eastern Metropolis Rhapsody," and "Southern Capital Rhapsody," in *Wen xuan*, pp. 181-242, 243-310, and 311-336 respectively.

Liu, Wu-chi 柳無忌. "Return to the Field" ("Kuei-t'ien fu" 歸田賦), in *An Introduction to Chinese Literature*, Bloomington, Ind., 1966, p. 54.

von Zach, "Erh-ching fu," *Anthologie*, v. 1, pp. 1-37; "Nan-tu fu," ibid., v. 1, pp. 38-44; "Ssu hsüan fu," ibid., v. 1, pp. 217-228.

Waley, *The Temple:* "The Skull" ("K'u-lou fu" 髑髏賦) and "Watching the Dance" ("Kuan-wu fu" 觀舞賦), pp. 81-86.

STUDIES:

Hughes. *Two Chinese Poets.*

Lai, Chia-tu 賴家度. *Chang Heng* 張衡. Shanghai, 1956; rpt. 1979.

Sun, Wen-ch'ing 孫文青. *Chang Heng nien-p'u* 張衡年譜. Shanghai, 1965.

Yang, Ch'ing-lung 楊清龍. "Chang Heng chu-tso hsi-nien k'ao" 張衡著作系年考. *Shu-mu chi-k'an*, 9.3 (Dec. 1975), 75-82.

—KH

Chang Hsieh 張協 (*tzu*, Ching-yang 景陽, *fl.* 295) was a native of An-p'ing 安平 (modern Kiangsi). His father, Chang Shou 張收, was magistrate of Shu Commandery 蜀郡 (modern Szechwan). As a youth, Chang Hsieh enjoyed a reputation equal to that of his brother, the distinguished Chin literatus Chang Tsai 張載 (*tzu*, Meng-yang 孟陽, *fl.* 285), in whose biography in the *Chin-shu* 晉書 (History of the Chin Dynasty) the scant records of Hsieh's career are included: Chang Hsieh was summoned into the bureaucracy and transferred to be Assistant in the Palace Library; he filled in as Intendant of Hua-yin 華陰 (modern Shensi); became Inner Gentlemen Retainer; and returned to the central government as Vice Director of the Secretariat. He was then transferred to be Chamberlain for the Capital of Ho-chien 河間 (modern Ho-chien

Hsien). His provincial administration seems to have been successful—the biographers claim he was frugal and honest.

By the turn of the fourth century, with the empire in great disorder and beset with banditry, Chang Hsieh abandoned public affairs and took to the countryside, where he pursued his own interests. At this time, he composed his extensive "Ch'i Ming" 七命 (Seven Mandates), the text of which swells his biography by some half dozen pages. The official record concludes with his summons to be Gentleman Attendant at the Palace Gate in 307. This he declined, pleading illness, and died at home.

Chang Hsieh's surviving works are not extensive: Thirteen pentasyllabic poems, including one "Yung shih" 詠史 (On History), one "Yu hsien" 遊仙 (Roving Immortal), one "Tsa-shih" 雜詩 (Miscellaneous Verse), and a set of ten tsa-shih 雜詩, two of which are contained in the Wen-hsüan* (see ch. 21 and 29); six fu* compositions, the long ch'i 七 (sevens) which appears in his biography and in the Wen-hsüan (ch. 35), and some ming 銘 (inscriptions).

The quality of this work was much appreciated, and Chang Hsieh is commonly discussed in Chinese literary history as one of the poets of the T'ai-k'ang 太康 era (280-289), together with his elder and younger brothers Chang Tsai and Chang K'ang 張亢 (fl. 307), the "two Lu" (Lu Chi* and his brother Lu Yün 陸雲 [262-303]), the "P'an pair" (P'an Yüeh* and his nephew P'an Ni*), and the "single Tso" (Tso Ssu*).

Chung Jung 鍾嶸 in his Shih-p'in* places Chang Hsieh in the first rank of poets. In his system of derivations, Chung sees Chang's work as originating in the poetry of Wang Ts'an* (whose poetic origins, according to Chung, stem from Li Ling 李陵 [d. 74 B.C.], another first-rank poet, and thence from the Ch'u-tz'u*). Chung particularly commended Chang for his skillful artistry in descriptive writing, and his properly regulated, literary style, for which he is one of the great poets of the ages.

Chang's style influenced both Hsieh Ling-yün* and Pao Chao,* and there are examples of deliberate imitation of Chang Hsieh's colorful style, the most famous of these being the imitation of his "K'u yü" 苦雨 (Bitter Rain) by Chiang Yen.* Chiang chose wisely—"Bitter Rain" is one of the masterpieces of early pentasyllabic poetry. Chiang Yen also borrowed ideas and diction from Chang Hsieh's poem "On History" in his imitation of Tso Ssu's "historical" verse. From Chiang Yen's particular fascination with Chang Hsieh's poetry arose a story recorded in the Shih-p'in, of a dream of Chiang Yen's in which Chang Hsieh came to him and took back a bolt of brocade (symbolic of literary skill) which he had given Chiang and thereafter Chiang's literary talents paled.

EDITIONS:
Chang Ching-yang chi 張景陽集, in Pai-san, v. 7, pp. 33-47.
Liu-ch'ao wen, v. 2, pp. 1951-1954. The prose.
Nan-pei-ch'ao shih, v. 1, pp. 522-525.

TRANSLATIONS:
Frodsham, Anthology, pp. 79-84.
von Zach, Anthologie, v. 1, pp. 316, 537-542; v. 2, pp. 628-639.

STUDIES:
Teng, Shih-liang 鄧仕樑. Liang-Chin shih-lun 兩晉詩論. Hong Kong, 1972, pp. 51-67.

—JM

Chang Hsien 張先 (tzu, Tzu-yeh 子野, 990-1078), an official and literatus of the early Northern Sung, is an important figure in the evolution of tz'u* poetry. A native of Wu-ch'eng 烏程 (modern Wu-hsing 吳興, Chekiang), Chang Hsien was born only three decades after the unification of China under the Sung. He passed the chin-shih examination in 1030, at age forty-one. Assigned to various posts in local governments, which took him as far as modern Szechwan in the southwest and Kansu in the west, he was serving in the capital when he left office. After ten years of retirement, he died in 1078. Throughout his lifetime he associated with some of the most celebrated literary figures of the time, Yen Shu,* Ou-yang Hsiu,* Sung Ch'i 宋祁 (998-1061), Su Shih,* Wang An-shih,* and Mei Yao-ch'en.* An active writer himself, he produced, aside from tz'u, both prose and *shih* poetry, in considerable amounts. But there remain only fragments of his prose scattered in works by others and ten *shih*, a genre in which Su Shih thought Chang best demonstrated his poetic craftsmanship. *Tz'u* poems thus constitute the bulk of Chang's extant works.

In both subject matter and style, Chang Hsien's *tz'u* poetry remains in the orthodox tradition, a tradition that was rooted in the late T'ang period and came to full growth during the Five Dynasties. Lovesickness, friendship, separation from loved ones, sex, the retreat of spring, and sentiments evoked by natural scenery dominate a significant portion of Chang Hsien's poems. These personal concerns and immediate aspects of life are generally couched in metaphorical language in the relatively short construction of the *hsiaoling* 小令 form of *tz'u*. Like his predecessors, Chang Hsien exhibits a genuine femininity in his art and perception of the world. His work is often a pictorial representation of a melancholy mood, a vignette laden with images drawn from the lighter, softer, and gentler aspects of nature—flowers, grass, willow branches and catkins, spring breezes, mists, clouds, and the moon—through which the poetic idea is not expressed outright, but sensed. However, examples of direct expressions also abound throughout his poems in which the tone of the lyrical self is relatively subdued. Moreover, they are often placed side by side with image-making elements. The juxtaposition of these two kinds of poetic language, one expressive and propositional, the other imagistic and suggestive, enables the two to complement and explain each other in transmitting an intended poetic message. By virtue of the expressive and propositional utterance, which informs, the poetic meaning is more readily grasped. On the whole, Chang Hsien's art and thought expressed in his *tz'u* poetry display an unmistakable kinship with many of his contemporaries, notably Yen Shu and Ou-yang Hsiu.

While Chang Hsien's lineage is undoubtedly in the orthodox tradition, his corpus reveals an innovative spirit, which has secured for him a position in the evolution of the *tz'u* genre. Now and then he went beyond the realm of personal concerns to depict the flourishing cities and their various activities, as well as people from the lower strata of society. In some other cases, he employed the poetic medium to fulfill a social function. The short prefaces he wrote for a number of his poems were also innovative. His language is often colloquial and effusive. But the most significant of Chang's innovations, and the one that has captured more critical attention than any other, is his experiment with the *man-tz'u* 慢詞 form, a construction of extended length evolving from *hsiao-ling*. He not only tried his hand with several existing *man-tz'u* tunes but composed several tunes himself.

These features which diverge from orthodox practice have caused Chang Hsien to be mentioned in the same breath with his contemporary, Liu Yung,* an influential innovator of *tz'u* poetry. While it is commonly agreed that Chang Hsien did not produce as many *man-tz'u* as Liu Yung and in general was far less influential than Liu in the development of the *tz'u* genre, critics have praised Chang for his refined taste and elegant style, apparently admiring his literary, sophisticated language and indirect, subtle modes of expression, areas in which they find Liu Yung wanting. Others focus their attention on the structure of Chang's *man-tz'u* and maintain that in general it suffers from a lack of sequential progression, continuous flow, and internal coherence. Again, comparisons with Liu Yung—strong in these respects—are common. Chang used *hsiao-ling* methods to compose *man-tz'u;* thus, his *man-tz'u* became an aggregate of imagistically elegant but syntactically isolated images, and the overall effect is one of fragmentation. Ch'en T'ing-cho 陳廷焯 (1853-1892) in his *Pai-yü-chai tz'u-hua* 白雨齋詞話 (published in 1894) observes that Chang Hsien's poetry served as a turning point in the history of *tz'u* and constituted a smooth transition from the orthodox tradition to the more radically changed style and form of the works of Liu Yung.

EDITIONS:

An lu chi 安陸集 . In appendix to *Fu ku p'ien* 復
古篇. By Chang Yu 張有 (b. 1054). Huai-nan
shu-chü 淮南書店 , 1882. Contains eight *shih*
poems.

Ch'üan Sung-tz'u 全宋詞. V. 1 of 5 volumes.
T'ang Kuei-chang 唐圭璋 ed., Peking, 1965,
pp. 57-87.

TRANSLATIONS:

Ayling, *Further Collection*, pp. 52-55.

STUDIES:

Chang. *Evolution*, pp. 15, 123, 153-157, 166,
169.

Hsia, Ch'eng-t'ao 夏承燾 . "Chang Tzu-yeh nien-
p'u" 張子野年譜 , in his *T'ang Sung tz'u-jen nien-
p'u* 唐宋詞人年譜 , Shanghai, 1979, pp. 169-
196.

Hsia, Ching-kuan 夏敬觀. "P'ing Chang Tzu-
yeh tz'u" 評張子野詞, passages cited in *T'ang
Sung ming-chia tz'u-hsüan* 唐宋名家詞選, Lung
Mu-hsün 龍沐勛 , ed., Shanghai, 1956, p. 57.

Murakami, Tetsumi 村上哲見. *Soshi kenkyu—To
Godai Hokuso hen* 宋詞研究─唐五代北宋篇.
Tokyo, 1976, pp. 194-214. Studies Chang
Hsien's life, his works in general, and the art-
istry of his *tz'u* poetry.

—SH

Chang Hua 張華 (*tzu*, Mao-hsien 茂先, 232-
300), a scholar-official of the Western Chin
dynasty, was born in Fang-ch'eng 方城 of
the Fan-yang 范陽 area (modern Ku-an 固
安 in Hopei). A prodigy, Chang was recognized in his youth and recommended to
Emperor Wen of Wei (Ts'ao P'i*). After
the establishment of the Chin dynasty, he
served as an advisor to the Chin founder,
Emperor Wu (r. 265-274), who greatly admired his scholarship and soon appointed
him Secretariat Director. Chang played a
major role in the conquest of the Kingdom
of Wu and was ennobled as a marquis. His
influence, which continued with the following emperor, was such that most of the
institutional system of the Chin dynasty was
designed by him. He eventually reached
the exalted position of Commander Unequalled in Honor. His high position invited
jealousy and his involvement in factional
politics led to disaster: he was executed by
an assistant of Ssu-ma Lun 司馬倫, Prince
of Chao, for refusing to take part in the
prince's usurpation.

Preoccupied with self-expression, Chang
Hua left only a small number of writings
of social significance. One example is the
poem "Li-shih" 勵志 (Self Encouragement), propounding a Confucian sense of
moral and spiritual self-improvement. His
"Chiao-liao fu" 鷦鷯賦 (Prose-poem on the
Tailor Bird), with obvious Taoist influence, argues that while the big and beautiful birds are being hunted or utilized, only
the inconspicuous tailor birds remain alive.
His critical attitude toward society is expressed in "Chuang-shih p'ien" 壯士篇 (On
Heroic Men), while the luxurious life of
the aristocracy is ridiculed in his "Yu-lieh
p'ien" 游獵篇 (On Hunting) and "Ch'ing-
po p'ien" 輕薄篇 (On Frivolity).

Chang Hua is best remembered for his
compilation *Po-wu chih* 博物志 (Account of
Wide-Ranging Matters) which, despite its
fictional quality and moderate size (in extant editions, ten *chüan*), provides excellent source materials to mythologists and
historians of science, geography, and society. Specialists in fiction find it important
as the earliest record of such key story-
cycles as sailing to the Milky Way and the
capture of Szechwan women by monkey
gods and as evidence of the development
of ancient stories like those of the Pu-chou
Mountain 不周山 and the deity K'ua-fu 夸
父. It influenced the *Sou-shen chi** among
other later fictional works.

EDITIONS:

Chang ssu-k'ung chi 張司空集 in *Ch'ien-k'un cheng-
chi chi* 乾坤正氣集 , Taipei, 1966, and in *Pai-
san*, v. 5, pp. 183-218.

Po-wu chih. Other than editions in various traditional *ts'ung-shu* collections, see Fan Ning
and T'ang Chiu-ch'ung below.

TRANSLATIONS:

Frodsham, *Anthology*, p. 72.

von Zach, *Anthologie*, v. 1, pp. 201-203, 227-279
and 532.

STUDIES:

Chang, Liang-fu 姜亮夫 . *Chang Hua nien-p'u*
張華年譜. Shanghai, 1957.

Fan, Ning 范寧 . *Po-wu chih chiao-cheng* 博物志
校正. Peking, 1980.

Nakajima, Chiaki 中島千秋 . "Chō Ka no *Shōryō
no fu* ni tsuite" 張華の鷦鷯の賦についへ , *Shinagaku kenkyū*, 32 (1967), 28-41.

Straughair, Anna. *Chang Hua: A Statesman-Poet of the Western Chin Dynasty.* Canberra, 1973.

T'ang, Chiu-ch'ung 唐久寵. *Po-wu chih chiao-shih* 博物志校釋. Taipei, 1980.

—WK and MSP

Chang Hui-yen 張惠言 (*tzu*, Kao-wen 皋文, 1761-1802) was a scholar of the Confucian classics and an author and critic of *tz'u* poetry. A native of Wu-chin 武進 (modern Kiangsu), he lost his father early and passed his childhood and teens in poverty. After several failures, he passed the *chin-shih* in 1799. He had been in office only three years when he died in 1802 at the age of forty-two.

Chang Hui-yen was a scholar of ancient philosophical texts and linguistics. He researched both the original texts of such classics (see *ching*) as the *I-ching*, the *I-li*, and the *Mo-tzu* and the commentaries and studied phonology utilizing the *Shuo-wen chien-tzu* 說文解字. Chang was especially noted for his work on the *I-ching*, having produced a bulky volume of collation and interpretation. While Chang's reading of the book generally follows the commentaries of Han scholars, he reserved his highest regard for Yü Fan 虞翻 (172-241) of the Latter Han and Three Kingdoms periods. To Yü Fan's particular school of thought Chang devoted much time and energy, seeking its order and logic, clarifying its guiding principle of discourse, resolving doubtful or puzzling points, and filling in missing parts. Chang's painstaking endeavors produced a total of six works that order, reinterpret, and expand the commentaries of Yü Fan.

Chang Hui-yen also tried his hand at both prose and *tz'u* poetry. His collected prose consists of prefaces and colophons to books, records of events, personal letters, articles written at partings, admonitions, biographies, epitaphs, sacrificial writings, and *fu.** Chang modeled his prose on that of Han Yü,* the T'ang proponent of the *Ku-wen yün-tung* (neoclassical movement in prose—see *ku-wen*); in *fu* he emulated Ssu-ma Hsiang-ju* and Yang Hsiung* of the Han dynasty. Generally speaking, Chang's prose is lucid, simple, and vigorous. This is mainly because he was considerably influenced by the contemporary writers of the T'ung-ch'eng p'ai,* with whom he was well acquainted, who advocated emulating the prose style of the *Tso-chuan** and *Shih-chi,** and that of the *T'ang Sung pa-ta-chia* (see Han Yü).

The *tz'u* poems of Chang Hui-yen, of which forty-six remain, express, in language that is elegant and refined, feelings and thoughts of the poet that arise from the more personal and immediate aspects of his life. Chang's expression is divested of erudition and pedantry and shows a high caliber of creativity.

It was, however, in poetic criticism that Chang Hui-yen exerted a far-reaching influence, as the founder of the Ch'ang-chou tz'u-p'ai,* the most prominent school of Chinese *tz'u* criticism. He and his brother Chang Ch'i 張琦 (1765-1833) compiled an anthology, entitled *Tz'u-hsüan* 詞選 (Selections of Tz'u), which consists of 116 poems from the late T'ang, Five Dynasties, Northern, and Southern Sung periods. In the preface they stated their anthology was a reaction against *tz'u* characterized by extravagant diction and lack of substance or by crudeness and vulgarity. Scholars agree that the Changs were referring especially to the poetry of the contemporary *tz'u* schools of Yang-hsien 陽羨, founded by Ch'en Wei-sung,* and Che-hsi 浙西, founded by Chu I-tsun.* In the opinion of the Chang brothers, *tz'u* poetry written since the end of the Yüan represented a degradation of the earlier tradition which they believed embodied the thoughts and feelings of frustrated officials, and thus originally possessed as great an intrinsic value and enjoyed as exalted a status as the *shih** and *fu** genres. The anthology was compiled to direct students of *tz'u* poetry back to this original elevation and dignity. Though the full development of the theories of the Ch'ang-chou tz'u-p'ai had to await Chou Chi,* the Changs' preface to the *Tz'u-hsüan* nevertheless established the school's basic approach for the school—namely, *tz'u* as allegory.

Scholars have proposed a possible connection between Chang Hui-yen's Confucian scholarship and his criticism. In advocating an allegorical reading of *tz'u*, Chang was likely following the Mao Commentary, which used *pi* 比 and *hsing* 興, the methods of comparison and allegory, to interpret the *Shih-ching*.* Moreover, as a specialist in the *I-ching*, a book relying on symbols to represent cosmic order, human history, and personal events, Chang Hui-yen would have been prepared to employ in his study of *tz'u* the methods used to unravel the highly laconic and cryptic *I-ching* text. Underlying both apparently unrelated disciplines is the impulse to seek in words a significance beneath the surface.

EDITIONS:

Chang, Hui-yen and Chang Ch'i 張琦. *Tz'u-hsüan hsü-tz'u-hsüan [chiao-tu]* 詞選續詞校讀. 2v. Taipei, 1961.

Ming-k'o wen-pien 茗柯文編. *SPPY.*

Chang Hui-yen I-hsüeh shih shu 張惠言易學十書. 2v. Taipei, 1970.

STUDIES:

Chao, Chia-ying Yeh. "The Ch'ang-chou School of *Tz'u* Criticism," in *Chinese Approaches*, pp. 151-188.

Ch'iu, Shih-yu 邱世友. "Chang Hui-yen lun tz'u te pi-hsing chi-t'o: Ch'ang-chou tz'u-p'ai te chi-t'o shuo chih-i" 張惠言論詞的比興寄託 常州詞派的寄託說之一, *Wen-hsüeh p'ing-lun*, 1980.3 (May 1980), 111-120.

Lien, E 廉鍔. "Chang Hui-yen lun tz'u," *Hsüeh-shu yen-chiu*, 1978.3 (September), 74.

Wu, Hung-i 吳宏一. *Ch'ang-chou-p'ai tz'u-hsüeh yen-chiu* 常州派詞學研究. Taipei, 1970.

—SH

Chang Jo-hsü 張若虛 (*c.* 660-*c.* 720) was a poet. Little is known about him today. He was a native of Yangchow (modern Kiangsu) and once occupied a minor military post in Yen-chou 兗州 (modern Shantung). His literary reputation was established in the capital during the first years of the eighth century in conjunction with a group of poets, all from the Lower Yangtze Basin, which included Ho Chih-chang,* Pao Jung 包融, and Wang Ch'i-jung 萬齊融.

It is no exaggeration to say that his "Ch'un-chiang hua-yüeh yeh" 春江花月夜 (The River by Night in Spring), one of only two extant poems, has made Chang a rep-

utation. It is one of the first successful poems of its type in the T'ang (old-style, seven syllables per line), one which initiated a stylistic break from Six Dynasties' verse. The title is a *yüeh-fu** title and was originally employed to depict aristocratic life at court. Chang Jo-hsü plays on this tradition, ironically depicting the sorrow of the common people.

The poem can be divided into quatrains—nine in all. Three lines of each quatrain use the same rhyme. There are three major parts to the work. The first describes the river and the neighboring forests under the moonlight and serves as a background for the next section. The second is a lament on the ephemeral nature of life. The third and final section describes the sorrow of travelers and the loved ones they have left at home. In both style and content the poem anticipates High T'ang poetry.

EDITIONS:

Ch'üan T'ang shih, v. 2, pp. 1183-1184.

TRANSLATIONS:

Demiéville, *Anthologie*, pp. 210-211.

Wu, John. "The River by Night in Spring," *THM*, 6.4 (1938), 358.

STUDIES:

Ch'ai, Fei-fan 柴非凡. "Lun Chang Jo-hsü 'Ch'un-chiang hua-yüeh yeh' " 論張若虛 春江 花月夜, *Wen-hsüeh p'ing-lun*, 2 (November 1975).

Cheng, Chi-hsien. *Analyse formelle de l'oeuvre poétique d'un auteur des Tang, Zhang Ruo-xu.* Paris, 1970. An extensive linguistic-literary analysis (and translation) of both of Cheng's extant poems.

Hu, Kuang-wei 胡光煒. "Chang Jo-hsü shih-chi k'ao lüeh" 張若虛事跡考略, *Wen-hsüeh lun-chi*, Shanghai, 1929.

Wen, I-to 聞一多. "Kung-t'i shih te tzu-shu" 宮體詩的自贖, in *Wen I-to ch'üan-chi*, v. 3, Shanghai, 1948, pp. 11-22.

—TS and PHC

Chang K'o-chiu 張可久 (*tzu*, Hsiao-shan 小山, 1270-1348) was long considered one of the most outstanding writers of *san-ch'ü* (see *ch'ü*). He and Ch'iao Chi-fu* were called the Li Po* and Tu Fu* of the *san-*

ch'ü. Chang was born in Ch'ing-yüan (modern Chekiang) and served as a minor official in Ningpo. But he was unsuccessful as an official and failed to attain his aspirations. He traveled much, mostly in Kiangnan, but also in other parts of southeast China. In his later years he lived in Hangchow, and many of his poems sing the praises of its West Lake.

Chang was a professional writer of *san-ch'ü.* He did not write plays. More than eight hundred of his *ch'ü** and nine song sequences are extant. His choice of material for this poetry, however, was narrow in scope. The majority of the poems are appreciations of natural beauty and sing the praises of a carefree life. He was famous even during his own lifetime, counting among his friends many officials and poets. Both *san-ch'ü* writers and later Ming and Ch'ing critics regarded him highly, because of the relaxed life reflected in his poetry, which catered to the tastes of literati, and because of his skill in incorporating the structures, phraseology, and rhythms of the *shih** and *tz'u** forms into *ch'ü* poetry. This integration resulted in a unique *san-ch'ü* style which the literati found both beautiful and natural. His poetry shows no signs of anger at the political corruption of the Yüan but reflects an attitude of finding happiness wherever possible. Some of his poems concern Taoist themes.

His style was similar to Ma Chih-yüan's,* though certainly it was not intended as imitation. It was considered clear and elegant, beautiful, but not to the point of fulsomeness. Chang devoted his life to the perfection of the *san-ch'ü* form. His poetry, as is characteristic of the *san-ch'ü* of this later period, lacks spontaneity in its use of language and depends more upon literary stylistics. An important achievement of his verse is its ability to incorporate clichés and famous verse phrases from earlier periods into completely new and refreshing combinations.

EDITIONS:

Chang Hsiao-shan hsiao-ling 張小山小令 , in *Yüeh-fu hsiao-ling* 樂府小令 , Yung-cheng (1723-1736) edition.

Yin-hung i so k'o ch'ü 飲虹簃所刻曲 . 2v. Lu Ch'ien 盧前 , ed. Taipei, 1961. Originally printed by editor, 1932. Also contains *Chang Hsiao-shan hsiao-ling.*

San-ch'ü ts'ung-k'an 散曲叢刊 . Jen Na 任訥 , ed. Taipei, 1964. Contains the complete collection *Hsiao-shan yüan-fu ch'ien-chi* 小山樂府前集 and the additional volumes *Hou-chi* 後集 , *Hsü-chi* 續集 , *Chü-chi* 劇集 , *Wai-chi* 外集 , *Pu-chi* 補集.

Yüan-jen hsiao-ling chi 元人小令集 . Ch'en Nai-ch'ien 陳乃乾 , ed. Peking, 1962. Considered one of the best of the modern anthologies; arranged according to verse form.

Ch'üan Yüan san-ch'ü 全元散曲 . 2v. Peking, 1964, 1981. Sui Shu-shin, ed. One of the best and most complete anthologies; arranged according to author; includes sources for each selection.

TRANSLATIONS:

Frankel, *Palace Lady,* pp. 96-98 and 174-76. Also contains analysis.

Sunflower, pp. 425-426.

Yang, *Fifty Songs,* pp. 52-53, 55-58.

STUDIES:

Schlepp, Wayne. *San-ch'ü. Its Technique and Imagery.* Madison, Wisconsin, 1970. This illuminating and instructive book on the *san-ch'ü* verse-form contains translations of several of Chang's poems, analyzed according to technique.

Wu, Shu-cheng Huang. "Chang K'o-ch'u, a Yüan *San-ch'ü* Poet." Unpublished Ph.D. dissertation, University of Washington, 1973.

—EB

Chang Ping-lin 章炳麟 (*tzu,* T'ai-yen 太炎 , 1868-1936) was a man of many parts: classical scholar, anti-Manchu revolutionary, leader of the Kuang-fuhui 光復會 (Restoration Society), editor of the newspaper *Su-pao* 蘇報 and later of the T'ung-menghui's *Min-pao* 民報 (People's Journal).

He was born and educated in Yü-hang 餘杭 (modern Chekiang) and learned to dislike the Manchus while still a youth. Although Chang later became a prominent and respected figure in the Chinese revolutionary movement, his most outstanding achievements were to be in the field of classical scholarship. During his years as a reformer and revolutionary he still maintained a deep interest in classical learning, and his early essays on Chinese philosophy and history bristle with allusions to the Manchu dynasty. In 1901 Chang published *Ch'iu-shu* 訄書 (Compelled Writings), a collection of these essays which in 1914 he revised, enlarged, and published under the title *Chien-lun* 檢論 (Revised Views). After arousing the Manchu authorities by cutting off his queue in public and assigning controversial essay topics in his classes in 1900 and 1901, Chang was forced to flee to Japan in 1902 for several months; he was in Tokyo again from 1906-1911. During his years of exile in Japan, while acting as editor of *Min-pao*, he continued his teaching and research in sinological studies. Over this period he published a number of major writings on ancient philosophers and the Chinese classics in the *Kuo-ts'ui hsüeh-pao* 國粹學報 (Journal of Classical Studies). His articles on anarchism in *Min-pao* are written in a crisp, incisive style, and his appreciation of anarchism as lying within the context of Lao-Chuang thought and Buddhism provides an insight into Chinese reception of Western political thought. He had a strong scholarly interest in Buddhism, concentrating on the *Abbedharma-kosa-sastra* 具舍維論 (Chü-she wei-lun). Under the tutelage of Yü Yüeh 俞樾 (1822-1907) Chang developed a great interest in the *Tso-chuan.** He was of the opinion that the *Tso-chuan* was superior to the two other commentaries on the *Ch'un-ch'iu*, the *Kung-yang chuan* 公羊傳 and the *Ku-liang chuan* 穀梁傳 (see *ching*).

Chang was an advocate of the *Ku-wen* 古文 (Old Text) School of classical learning (as opposed to contemporaries such as K'ang Yu-wei* who centered their studies of the *Ch'un-ch'iu* around the Kung-yang Commentary and the writings of the *Chin-wen* 今文 [New Text] School). Chang excelled in philology and linguistics. His major accomplishments in these spheres were his *Wen-shih* 文始 (Literature and History), on the origins of the Chinese script; *Hsin fang-yen* 新方言 (New Dialects), a geographical analysis of modern Chinese dialects; *Hsiao-hsüeh ta-wen* 小學答問 (Answers to Questions on Philology); and *Shuo-wen pu-shou chün-yü* 說文部首均語 (A Study of the Radicals in the *Shuo-wen*). Chang's *Kou-ku lun-heng* 國故論衡 (Discussions on Chinese Classics), perhaps his most well-known work, is an examination of philology's connection with literature and philosophy. Strangely, Chang chose to scoff at the study of oracle-bone inscriptions and the valuable contributions of his contemporaries in this field. In his self-imposed role as a defender of China's moral and cultural traditions he took a strong interest in the legal and ethical codes of the past.

Chang enjoyed an outstanding reputation as a representative and skilled stylist of the traditional *ku-wen** literature. His poetry was written mostly in a condensed, pentasyllabic style that bears a strong resemblance to poetry of the Wei-Chin period.

After the 1911 Revolution Chang attained the zenith of his intellectual influence as a scholar and literary stylist at National Peking University, where he had various friends and disciples within the faculty of literature. Chang saw the arrival of the vernacular literature movement headed by Hu Shih 胡適 (1891-1962) and Ch'en Tu-hsiu 陳獨秀 (1879-1942) as a threat to the literary traditions of China. In spite of his eloquent efforts to block this movement, Chang and the rest of the scholars of traditional literature failed to stem the rising tide of *pai-hua* 白話 (vernacular) literature. Chang's influence rapidly declined, and during the last years of his life his writings were increasingly looked on as literary anachronisms.

After 1918 Chang retired from political life and concentrated on teaching and classical scholarship. He served as editor-in-chief of the monthly magazine *Hua-kuo* 花國 (Flower Country) between 1923 and 1926, contributing many articles himself. In 1935 he set up his own private school in Soochow, where he continued his efforts to preserve China's tradition until his death in 1936.

EDITIONS:
Chang shih ts'ung-shu 章氏叢書. 24v. 1917-1919.
Chang T'ai-yen Hsien-sheng chia-shu 章太炎先生家書. Peking, 1962.
Kuo-hsü kai-lun 國學概論. Kowloon, 1965.

Ch'iu-shu 訊書 . Shanghai, 1958.

STUDIES:
BDRC, pp. 92-98.
Chang, Ping-lin. *T'ai-yen hsien-sheng tzu-ting nien-p'u* 太炎先生自訂年譜. Hong Kong, 1965.
Chang Ping-lin. Hsü Shou-chang 許壽裳, ed. Hong Kong, 1945.
Chang T'ai-yen te pai-hua-wen 章太炎的白話文 . Wu Ch'i-jen 吳齊仁, ed. Shanghai, 1925.
Shih, Meng 明萌 . "Lun Chang T'ai-yen te wen-hsüeh kuan" 論章太炎的文學觀, *Ku-tai wen-hsüeh li-lun yen-chiu,* 7 (November 1982), 217-229.
Tan, T'ao 但燾 . "Chang Hsien-sheng pieh-chuan" 章先生別傳 , *Kuo-shih-kuan kuan k'an,* 1 (December 1947), 98-99.
———. "Chang T'ai-yen Hsien-sheng hsüeh-an hsiao shih" 章太炎先生學案小識 , *Ta-lu tsa-chih,* 12.5 (March 1956), 1-6.
Yao, Yü-hsiang 姚漁湘 . "Kuan-yü Chang Ping-lin lüeh chuan" 關於章炳麟略傳 , *Ta-lu tsa-chih,* 12.8 (April 1956), 4, 29.

—RS

Chang Ta-fu 張大復 (*tzu*, Hsing-ch'i 星期 or Hsin-ch'i 心期 , dates unknown) was a prolific dramatist of the late Ming and early Ch'ing from Soochow. Very little indeed is known about his life. For a period at least he lived in the famous Han-shan Temple outside Soochow. For that reason and because many of his dramas are Buddhist in theme it seems likely that he was a Buddhist.

According to the contemporary scholar Chao Ching-shen, Chang Ta-fu wrote twenty-nine *ch'uan-ch'i** and six *tsa-chü*,* thirty-five dramas in all. He belonged to the Soochow group of dramatists (see Li Yü). Only a portion of Chang's work is still extant.

Chang's two best-known plays are the two *ch'uan-ch'i Ju-shih kuan* 如是觀 (A View of Justice and Evil) and *Tsui P'u-t'i* 醉菩提 (The Drunken Bodhi). The first of these deals with the the fall and execution of the wicked twelfth-century minister Ch'in Kuei 秦檜, who had sabotaged Yüeh Fei's attempts to recapture the North China Plain from the Jurchen and had Yüeh Fei executed. This great general's tragic death and Ch'in Kuei's perfidy were two of the more popular themes in vernacular literature,

and had been the subject of many dramas and short stories. Two scenes from this play are preserved in the sixth collection of the *Chui pai-ch'iu,** one being "Tz'u-tzu" 刺字 (Tattooing Characters), the scene in which Yüeh Fei's mother tattoos on his back the four characters *ching-chung pao-kuo* 精忠報國 (to serve the country with unreserved loyalty).

Tsui P'u-t'i deals with the Southern Sung Buddhist monk Chi-tien 濟顛 of Hangchow, an incarnate Bodhisattva who, though he flouts contemporary sensibility and Buddhist doctrine by eating meat and leading a generally unrestrained life on earth, also aids the poor and downtrodden. This legend was treated in some late Ming and early Ch'ing novels and, at the end of the Ch'ing, inspired the lengthy novel *Chi-kung Chuan*

EDITIONS:
Ku-pen hsi-ch'ü ts'ung-k'an san-chi 古本戲曲叢刊三集 . Shanghai, 1957. Contains eleven of Chang Ta-fu's dramas including *Ju-shih kuan* and *Tsui P'u-t'i.*

STUDIES:
Yüeh Fei ku-shih hsi-ch'ü shou-ch'ang chi 岳飛故事戲曲說唱集. Tu Ying-tao 杜穎陶, ed. Peking, 1957, pp. 219-313. Contains *Ju-shih kuan.*
Chao, Ching-shen 趙景深. *Ming Ch'ing ch'ü-t'an* 明清曲談 . Shanghai, 1959, pp. 181-187.
Fu, *Ch'ing tsa-chü,* p. 353.

—CM

Chang Tai 張岱 (*tzu*, Tsung-tzu 宗子 , Shih-kung 石公 ; *hao*, T'ao-an 陶庵 , 1599-1684?) was a romantic writer and historian of the late Ming period. Born into a prominent family in Shan-yin 山陰 (modern Shao-hsing 紹興, Chekiang) he lived in easy elegance and enjoyed every form of luxury until the Manchu conquest in 1644. Then forty-five, he was left without a country and reduced to squalid poverty. To hide his identity, he escaped into the mountains and frequently had to go without food.

Such a drastic change in his life, however, prompted him to produce two important works: *T'ao-an meng-i* 陶庵夢憶 (Recollections of T'ao-an's Past Dreams), a series of nostalgic sketches of the grand

and elegant life of the late Ming, and *Shih-kuei shu* 石匱書 (Book of the Stone Case), a history of the Ming dynasty. Chang set great store by this latter work, giving his wish to complete it as his only reason for not committing suicide after the Manchu conquest. Many scholars believe that this book later became an important source for Ku Ying-t'ai's 谷應泰 (*fl.* 1660) *Ming-shih chi-shih pen-mo* 明史紀事本末 (A History of the Ming Dynasty Arranged according to Events). It is *T'ao-an meng-i*, however, which earned him literary fame. Chang carried on the late-Ming prose style, which is marked by a disarming spontaneousness and refreshing unconventionality. But there is a nostalgic sadness always present in his writings which distinguishes Chang from other Ming romantic writers like Yan Hung-tao* and Hsü Wei.* Chang's other prose writings—prefaces, short biographies, and a few sketches—are collected in *Lang-huan wen-chi* 瑯嬛文集.

EDITIONS:

Lang-huan wen-chi. Shanghai, 1935.

Shih-kuei shu hou-chi 石匱書後集. 63 *chüan.* Shanghai, 1959.

T'ao-an meng-i, 8 *chüan,* in *Yüeh-ya t'ang ts'ung-shu* 粵雅堂叢書. Based on a woodblock-printed edition by Wang Wen-hao 王文浩, 1794. Rpt. Taipei, 1978.

STUDIES:

A-ying 阿英. "*Lang-huan wen-chi*" 瑯嬛文集, in his *Hai-shih chi* 海市集, Shanghai, 1936, pp. 155-169.

ECCP, pp. 53-54.

Fu, *Ch'ing tsa-chü,* p. 3.

—PTW

Chang Tsai 張載 (*tzu,* Meng-yang 孟陽, *c.* 289) and two younger brothers Hsieh 協 and K'ang 亢 were called the San-Chang 三張 (Three [Poets] named Chang). He was born in An-p'ing 安平 (Hopei), and led an official career culminating with the post of Vice Director of the Secretariat.

His extant oeuvre is extremely small. It consists of only five *fu,** one *lun* 論, one *sung* 頌 (discourse), three *ming* 銘 (inscriptions), and fourteen *shih** poems. His "Chien-ko ming" 劍閣銘 (Inscription for Chien-ko Mountain) in 184 characters is considered his most important work. It was written in 281 when the author was accompanying his father to Szechwan. "Chien-ko ming" describes the precipitousness of Chien-ko Mountain. In the text Chang Tsai warns the local military that someone could take advantage of it and start a rebellion.

In his poetry more attention is paid to formal aspects than to substance. Some of his poems are considered representative of the spirit of Wei-Chin literature, for example, "Ch'i-i-shih" 七哀詩 (The Seven Laments). Following the trend of the time, they depict history as permanent decline and life as interminable loneliness and sorrow. The following couplet is often cited: "Full of sorrow your feelings are easily hurt,/Whatever I see in this landscape only adds to my heart's pain." Here subject and object, landscape and emotion (*ching* 景 and *ch'ing* 情) form a unity. The idea that the outer world intensifies the melancholy of the interior world influenced the later literature of the Six Dynasties.

EDITIONS:

Chang Meng-yang chi 張孟陽集, in *Pai-san,* 3, pp. 2096-2109.

TRANSLATIONS:

von Zach, *Anthologie,* v. 1, pp. 365-369, 567f.

—WK

Chang Wen-t'ao 張問陶 (*tzu,* Chung-yeh 仲冶 and Lo-tsu 樂祖; *hao,* Ch'uan-shan 船山, Yao-an t'ui-shou 藥庵退守, Shu-shan lao-yuan 蜀山老猿, and Lao-ch'uan 老船; 1764-1814), an accomplished painter and calligrapher, a poet, and public official, was born in Lai-chou 萊州, Shantung, where his father, Ku-chien 顧鑑, was serving as a local magistrate. The family home was, however, situated in Sui-ning 遂寧, Szechwan, where the Changs had resided even before the days of Chang P'eng-ko 張鵬翮 (1649-1725), an eminent official and water-conservancy expert. After passing the *chin-shih* examination in 1790, Chang Wen-t'ao was assigned to the Han-lin Academy. Before his resignation from office in 1812 and his retirement to Wu-hsien, Kiangsu, he held a number of different offices in the central and provincial bureaucracy. He served on several different occasions as an examination official, was for a time a censor, in which capacity he acquired a reputation as a frank, outspoken critic of bureaucratic misconduct, and he was once a prefect in Shantung.

Chang Wen-t'ao was well known in his day as a painter and calligrapher. In the former regard, he has been compared to the eminent Ming-dynasty artist, poet, and dramatist Hsü Wei,* whose style has been described as uninhibited and turbulent. Chang's second wife, Lin P'ei-huan 林佩璟, was also skilled in the use of the brush. Because of the excellence of his calligraphy, Chang was one of twelve members of the Han-lin Academy chosen to decorate a hall in the imperial palace with examples of their calligraphic art.

Chang Wen-t'ao is probably best remembered today as a poet and most often for those poems which possess some special historical significance. The introduction to one of his poems, for instance, states that the final forty chapters of the novel *Hunglou meng** were authored by Kao E 高鶚 (fl. 1795), although that claim is frequently disputed by modern scholars of the novel. Of perhaps even greater historical interest are his poems inspired by the White Lotus Rebellion. That rebellion erupted in early 1796 and raged across west-central China for nearly a decade before it was finally suppressed. About one year after the outbreak of hostilities, Chang Wen-t'ao was granted leave to return to his native place in Sui-ning, which was then being threatened by White Lotus forces. On his journey he passed through the war zone, and his personal observations of the situation provided the basis for a number of poems on the subject. Among the most interesting of them is a cycle of eighteen poems which he set down upon reaching safety in the city of Pao-chi, Shansi, on his return trip to the capital. According to the scholar-poet Chang Wei-p'ing 張維屏 (1780-1859), who was not related to Chang Wen-t'ao, that cycle of poems was widely read and acclaimed by his contemporaries. These poems, as well as still others on the same general theme, gave voice to his loyalist sentiments, but even more important, they were the vehicle for a vigorously outspoken critique of the government's conduct of the suppression campaign. The military and civil officials charged with the task of restoring law and order were accused of blatant corruption, of inaction and dereliction of duty, and of general incompetence. That Chang Wen-t'ao chose to be so forthright in his denunciation of the government's mishandling of the situation at a time when the infamous Ho-shen 和珅 (1750-1799) still wielded power is a testimonial to the poet's courage.

As a poet, Chang Wen-t'ao reflects the richness and complexity of his world. In addition to the poems of social protest, there are those which record the typical social situation, or depict the physical world. While Chang Wen-t'ao could be soberly serious about the great events of the day and sensitive and compassionate about life around him, he was also capable of lighthearted humor and joy on the occasion of a family gathering in Sui-ning.

Chang Wen-t'ao seems to have conceived of the literary act in terms close to the ideas expressed by Yüan Mei* and other notable contemporaries. Generally speaking, he subscribed to the expressive ideal, believing that "a poem without a self is fit only to be discarded." He was critical of the imitative mode and opposed to the overuse of historical and literary allusions. Although not unmindful of the contributions of past masters to the form, he sought to escape the heavy hand of the past: "I will employ my own methods, stand alone, reject all labels." Although typically stated in only the most general of terms, this insistence on his independence as a poet implies a desire to break out of the established mold and discover a diction suitable to his own personality and the changing times. It was perhaps that desire which accounts for the vernacular manner of some of his poems, such as the delightful "A Poem on Returning Home." These admirable qualities notwithstanding, Chang Wen-t'ao, like most of his contemporaries with the possible exception of Yüan Mei, has been largely ignored by modern scholars.

EDITIONS:

Chang, Wen-t'ao. *Ch'uan-shan shih ts'ao* 船山詩草. 20 *chüan*. 1815.

Shih Yün-yü 石韞玉. *Ch'uan-shan shih-ts'ao hsuan* 選. 6 *chüan*. Soochow, 1818. Reprinted in the *Shih-li chü Huang-shih ts'ung-shu* 士禮居黃氏叢書; see the *Pai-pu ts'ung-shu chi-ch'eng* edition. Ku Han 顧翰 compiled a supplement (*pu-i* 補遺) in 6 *chüan* which was published in 1849.

STUDIES:

Chang, Wei-p'ing. *Kuo-ch'ao shih-jen cheng-lüeh* 國朝詩人徵略. N. p., preface dated 1820, *chüan* 51, 10a-16b.

Ch'ing-shih 清史, "Lieh chuan," 75/50a-b.

ECCP, pp. 59-60.

Lu, Cheng-kao 陸徵誥. "Chang Ch'uan-shan shih-chi" 張船山事蹟, *Chung-ho*, 3.

—WS

Chang Yüeh 張說 (*tzu*, Tao-chi 道濟 or Yüeh-chih 說之, posthumously Wen-chen 文貞, 667-731) was one of the most influential writers and statesmen of the first decades of the eighth century. Although his works are now somewhat eclipsed by those of the more famous poets of the succeeding generation (such as Wang Wei,* Li Po,* and Tu Fu*), he was in his day a greatly esteemed literary figure.

Chang came from a relatively undistinguished Lo-yang family (the family seat was traced to Fan-yang 范陽, near modern Peking). He entered court circles in 689, after placing second—out of a field of more than a thousand hopefuls—in a special examination decreed by Empress Wu (r. 690-705). He was an active figure at court during most of the years of that formidable lady's reign (enduring exile in Kwangtung for the final years of her sovereignty, 703-705, owing to his opposition of her persecution of the minister Wei Yüan-chung 魏元忠), as well as during the reign of Chung-tsung (705-710). But it was not until the accession of Jui-tsung (r. 684-690, restored 710-712) in 710 that he began to come to real prominence. During the first two years of this monarch's rule, Chang held several important positions and also was put in charge of compiling the "state history" (*kuo-shih* 國史), this latter being a charge that he was to maintain—even through periods of subsequent rustication, military service, and official demotion—till the end of his life. It was at this time also that Chang became a close friend and confidant of the crown prince, Li Lung-chi 李隆基. In 712 Chang was instrumental in convincing Jui-tsung of the wisdom of formally abdicating the throne in favor of his son (with whom he in fact shared authority till his own death a year later), and in 713 was perhaps the most trusted adviser of Li Lung-chi during that monarch's successful consolidation of his sole rule. Late in that year the emperor (Hsüan-tsung, r. 712-756) enfeoffed Chang in appreciation of his meritorious services. Chang also enjoyed a bureaucratic promotion to the prestigious post of Secretariat Director.

However, Chang was soon demoted to a series of provincial posts which took him successively to Hsiang-chou 相州 (Honan), Yüeh-chou 岳州 (Hunan), and Ching-chou 荆州 (Hupei), and then spent several years overseeing military operations on the northeast frontier. By 723 he was restored to his former position in the Secretariat and despite a two-year forced resignation lasting from 727 to 729, was thereafter continually in Hsüan-tsung's good graces, eventually rising to occupy the exalted office of Left Assistant Director of the Department of State Affairs (in functional terms, Secretary of State). During the last years of his life, no official was more highly honored than he. Upon his death—on February 9, 731, two days before the New Year—the sovereign declared three days of state mourning, and cancellation of the grand New Year's court levée, out of respect for the passing of his long-time minister.

As one might expect, in light of the career sketched above, many of Chang Yüeh's literary works were composed on "official" occasions—royal excursions, state banquets, and the like. Besides the obligatory pendant poems written "to accord with" (*ho* 和) those of a member of the imperial family or the monarch himself, Chang was often made responsible for turning out verses to be used at solemn ceremonies of state. In 725, for instance, he was commissioned to write new lyrics for the dignified *ya-yüeh* 雅樂 (classical music) performed at court and later that year, while supervising all aspects of the imperial progress to and encampment at Mount T'ai for the awesome *feng* 封 sacrifice, composed the works for the fourteen songs designed to bring down, welcome, entertain, and finally send off the divinity of T'aishan during the sacred rites on the holy peak.

But works such as these constitute only a part of the 350 poems by Chang that remain to us. Many of his best verses are found among the scores of poems written during his various assignments to the provinces. In most of these poems the literary refinement of the courtier is blended, with surprising suppleness, with the sounds and sights confronting the poet in these less aristocratic environments. While Chang's style is even here always controlled and elegant, it often admits an attractive emotional coloring absent in the courtly verses. This is especially so in the numerous verses written in Yüeh-chou. Although Chang's poems in general rarely sparkle with the unexpected, they warm one with the persistent pleasure of carefully considered diction and their mature, steady wordcraft. Chang's favored form was the pentasyllabic *lü-shih* (see *shih*), with more than a third (122) of his extant poems being in this form. Next on the scale of formal frequency are 108 ten-line poems in pentasyllabic meter, the majority of these being *p'ai-lü*.

In addition to his poems, over two hundred of Chang Yüeh's prose writings have been preserved. Most of these are official documents having little more than historical interest, but some—such as his preface to Shang-kuan Wan-erh's 上官婉兒 (664-710) collected poems, his memorial inscription for that same lady, and his account (with rhymed lauds) of nineteen auspicious phenomena encountered by Chung-tsung during various outings to Lu-chou 潞州 in the years 707-709—have great intrinsic interest.

Such was Chang's exceptional fame and standing during his lifetime that his conception was rumored to have been attended by uncanny circumstances: one T'ang source reports that he was conceived when his mother dreamed she saw a jade swallow cast itself into her bosom (the word for "swallow" is *yen* 燕, the name of the principality with which Chang was later to be enfeoffed). Another popular anecdote told of a magic pearl owned by Chang: it was phosphorescent, in hue a deep purplish-blue, and, when its owner held it in his mouth, had the virtue of calling up from the depths of his memory the details of any forgotten item he wished to recall. Regardless of the veracity of such tales, it is certain that a signal mark of imperial respect and honor was forthcoming from Hsüan-tsung following Chang's death, namely, the bestowal of a posthumous title—Wen-chen, meaning "Cultured (more narrowly, Literary) Probity."

EDITIONS:

Chang Yen-kung chi 張燕公集. *Kuo-hsüeh chi-pen ts'ung-shu.* 25 *chüan.* Typeset and punctuated reprint of edition copied into the *Ssu-k'u* collection, from the Ts'ung-shu lou 叢書樓 library of the famous bibliophiles Ma Yeh-kuan 馬曰琯 (1688-1755) and Ma Yüeh-lu 馬曰璐 (1697-1766); based on a Ming (1537) edition, but includes numerous supplemental additions. The best text.

Chang Yüeh-shih wen-chi 張說之文集. *SPTK.* 25 *chan.* Facsimile of Ming (1537) woodblock. The *chüan* placement of individual works differs from that of the above edition.

STUDIES:

Ch'en, Tsu-yen 陳祖言. "Chang Yüeh nien-p'u" 張說年譜. Unpublished M.A. thesis, Fudan University, 1983.

Kroll, Paul W. "The Dancing Horses of T'ang," *TP,* 67 (1981), 240-268.

———. "On the Date of Chang Yüeh's Death," *CLEAR,* 2 (1980), 264-265.

Ono, Jitsunosuke 大野實之助. "Tōdai shidan ni okeru Chō Etsu" 唐代詩壇における張說, Part I, *Chūgoku koten kenkyū,* 14 (1966), 109-130; Part II, *Chūgoku koten kenkyū,* 15 (1967), 119-144.

Yoshikawa, Kōjirō 吉川幸次郎. "Chō Etsu no denki to bungaku" 張說の傳記と文學, *Tōhō-*

gaku, 1 (1951), 54-75.

—PWK

Ch'ang Chien 常建 (*fl.* 749) grew up in Ch'ang-an, where he pursued his studies and passed the *chin-shih* examination in 727. He did not receive high office, and after serving in provincial posts he retired to the countryside. Little more is known about him, for he became isolated from public life.

Ch'ang Chien was thoroughly versed in the capital style of poetry, but he cut himself off from the social circles in Ch'ang-an and developed his own poetic style. Consequently he is noted for recluse poetry and frontier poetry, rather than for poems on court themes. Fewer than sixty of his poems survive (one *chüan*) but these show great variety and originality: one describes a primitive southern tribe and another treats his encounter with a dead man's corpse. "P'o-shan ssu hou ch'an-yüan" 破山寺後禪院 (The Meditation Court behind Broken-Mountain Temple) is a fine example of the pure, impersonal nature poetry at which Ch'ang Chien excelled.

EDITIONS:
Ch'üan T'ang shih, v. 2, pp. 1453-1464.

TRANSLATIONS:
Frankel, *Palace Lady*, pp. 115-116.
Sunflower, p. 101.

STUDIES:
Fu, *Shih-jen*, pp. 78-87: "Ch'ang Chien k'ao"

Harada, Ken'yū 原田憲雄. "Jō Ken shishū kō-chū" 常建詩集校注, *Jimbun ronsō*, 13 (1966), 1-38.
Owen, *High T'ang*, pp. 88-89.
Wu, Che-fu 吳哲夫. "Sung pan Ch'ang Chien shih-chi" 宋版常建詩集, *Ku-kung t'u-shu chi-k'an*, 1.2 (1970), 79-80.

—MW

Ch'ang-chou tz'u-p'ai 常州詞派 was a prominent school of *tz'u* criticism founded around the middle of the Ch'ing dynasty. It was a reaction against various practices of two contemporary *tz'u* schools, the Che-hsi 浙西 School and the Yang-hsien 陽羨 School. By the end of the eighteenth cen-

tury, poets of the Che-hsi School,* because of their excessive emphasis on stylistic elegance and refinement, gradually developed a tendency to write *tz'u* more or less empty of content. Meanwhile, writers of the Yang-hsien School, being overly committed to the principle of unrestrained expression, began to produce works which were stylistically unpolished. These developments signaled the urgent need for a new system of critical theories that would provide a balanced direction for *tz'u* writing.

The founder of the Ch'ang-chou School, Chang Hui-yen,* compiled his anthology, *Tz'u-hsüan* 詞選 (Selections of *Tz'u*), precisely with the hope of providing a remedy for the deficiencies of contemporary *tz'u*. He and his brother, Chang Ch'i 張琦 (1795-1833), proposed in their prefaces that allegory should be the basic principle of *tz'u* writing and that *tz'u*, like the classical *Shih-ching** and "Li sao" 離騷 (Encountering Sorrow), should be read as a form of allegorical literature, reflecting specific contemporary political events. Thus, even a purely descriptive *tz'u*-poem about a lonely woman, such as the "P'u-sa man" 菩薩蠻 by Wen T'ing-yün,* was assigned allegorical meaning to connect it with frustrated officials like Ch'ü Yüan.* Chang believed that only by focusing on allegory could *tz'u* poetry be respected again as a serious literary genre equal to *shih** and *fu*.* Chang thus advocated the traditional method of poetic interpretation employed by the Han Confucian scholars. Many scholar-poets from Chang's native Ch'ang-chou followed in his footsteps, taking this allegorical approach to *tz'u* reading and composition. The most notable among them were Tung Shih-hsi 董士錫 (Chang's nephew), Yün Ching 惲敬, Ch'ien Chi-Chung 錢季重, Ting Lu-heng 丁履恆, Lu Chi-lu 陸繼輅, Tso Fu 左輔, and Li Chao-lo 李兆洛. The publication of Chang Hui-yen's *Tz'u-hsüan* served as the first promulgation of the basic approach of the Ch'ang-chou School. The *Tz'u-hsüan* is a collection of 116 *tz'u* poems by 44 poets ranging from T'ang to Sung. In contrast with the *Tz'u-tsung* 詞綜 by Chu I-tsun,* the anthology included very few poems from the Southern Sung. This seems to suggest that while the Che-hsi School looked up to Southern Sung poets as models for emulation, the Ch'ang-chou School preferred the T'ang, Five Dynasties, and Northern Sung *tz'u* poets. However, the theoretical foundation of the Ch'ang-chou School was not fully developed until Chou Chi,* another native of Ch'ang-chou and student of Tung Shih-hsi, clearly articulated his theories in such works as the *Chieh-ts'un-chai lun tz'u tsa-chu* 介存齋論詞雜著 (Miscellaneous Essays on *Tz'u* from the Chieh-ts'un Studio) and *Sung ssu-chia tz'u-hsüan* 宋四家詞選 (Selected *Tz'u* from the Four Schools during the Sung).

Chou Chi was responsible for revising the basic theories of Chang Hui-yen and further consolidating the foundations of the Ch'ang-chou School. Knowing that Chang's allegorical reading of *tz'u* has inherent theoretical problems, Chou devised a theory of allegory which was convincing and practical: "Without the use of allegory a *tz'u* poet cannot enter the poetic world; yet if his allegory becomes too specific, he will not be able to escape from it" (夫詞非寄託不入，專寄託不出). This means that allegory is an important tool for *tz'u* beginners, but after long practice the poet need not confine himself to specific allegory to articulate his feelings.

Chou Chi was most concerned with the apprenticeship of *tz'u* poets. In his *Sung ssu-chia tz'u-hsüan*, he singled out four Sung poets as models for students of *tz'u*: Chou Pang-yen,* Hsin Ch'i-chi,* Wang I-sun 王沂孫 (1240-1290), and Wu Wen-ying.* His explanation was: "[One should] ask the way of Wang I-sun, learn the artistry of Wu Wen-ying and Hsin Ch'i-chi, and finally reach the sublime world of Chou Pang-yen" (問塗碧山，歷夢窗稼軒，以還清眞之渾化). Although Chou managed to present a coherent *tz'u* criticism by elevating these four poets, his views were clearly partisan. His bias against the Che-hsi poets made him exclude from his master list the two Southern Sung poets most honored by the Che-hsi School, namely Chiang K'uei* and Chang Yen 張炎 (1248-1320?).

The impact of the Ch'ang-chou School upon modern *tz'u* poetry was the greatest of all the schools. Many important works of *tz'u* criticism during the late Ch'ing were written under its influence. For example, T'an Hsien's 譚獻 (1830-1901) *Fu-t'ang tz'u-hua* 復堂詞話 (compiled by his students in 1900) echoes the definitive views of Chou Chi, while Ch'en T'ing-cho's 陳廷焯 (1853-1892) *P'ai-yü-chai tz'u-hua* 白雨齋詞話 (published in 1894) supports the allegorical heritage of Chang Hui-yen. These critics and poets in turn exercised their influence upon contemporary *tz'u* poets, making the Ch'ang-chou School among the most prominent schools of *tz'u* criticism in China.

Studies:

Aoki, *Shindai*, pp. 277-291.

Chang, Hui-yen and Chang Ch'i. "Prefaces" (1797 and 1830 to *Tz'u-hsüan hsü-tz'u-hsüan [chiao-tou]*) 詞選續詞選 (校讀). 2v. Taipei, 1961.

Chou, Chi. *Lun-tz'u tsa-chu* 論詞雜著, in *Tz'u-hsüeh yen-chiu* 詞學研究. Lo Fang-chou 羅芳洲, ed. Shanghai, 1947.

———, comp. "Preface" (1832) to *Sung ssu-chia tz'u-hsüan (chien-chu)* 宋四家詞選 (箋注). Annotated by K'uang Shih-yüan 鄺士元. Taipei, 1971.

K'uang, Shih-yüan 鄺士元 . "Ch'ang-chou tz'u-p'ai chia-fa k'ao" 常州詞派家法考. In appendix to *Sung ssu-chia tz'u-hsüan (chien-chu)* 宋四家詞選 [箋注]. Annotated by K'uang Shih-yüan. Taipei, 1971, pp. 397-415.

Nien, Shu 念迤 . "Shih t'an Chou Chi 'Chieh-ts'un-chai lun tz'u tsa Chu'" 試談周濟介存齋論詞雜著. *Wen-hsüeh i-ch'an tseng-k'an*, 9 (June 1962), 96-110.

Wang, Chung 汪中 . *Ch'ing-tz'u chin ch'üan* 清詞金荃. Taipei, 1965, pp. 79-105. A selection of works by the *tz'u* poets of the Ch'ang-chou School, with notes and commentaries.

Wu, *Ch'ang-chou.*

Yeh, "Ch'ang-chou."

—KISC

Ch'ang-lun 唱論 (Treatise on Singing) is a work on the art of singing *ch'ü.** The author's name is given as Chih-an from Yennan 燕南芝菴, obviously not his original name. From internal evidence it seems he was a dramatist or musician who lived just before the 1340s in the Yüan dynasty.

The *Ch'ang-lun* is a very short work, only four pages long in its modern edition and consisting of only thirty-one brief sections. In this small compass the work manages to comment upon famous ancient and contemporary musicians, singers, and composers. However, most of the work is concerned with the theory and practice of singing *ch'ü*, with a discussion of such matters as rhythm, singing of single syllables and musical phrases, differing qualities of singing voices, and pitfalls to be avoided by the singer.

Unfortunately, most of the author's discussion of vocal music is difficult to follow because of the brevity of each section and the general disorganization of the text. Perhaps even more serious is the author's penchant for using Yüan colloquial expressions and fourteenth-century singer's jargon that are practically incomprehensible to the modern reader, even one with a background in traditional Chinese music.

EDITIONS:

The text does not occur in any pre-modern independent edition and was first published as an appendix to the *Yang-ch'un pai-hsüeh* 陽春白雪. It was also found in T'ao Tsung-i's *Cho-keng-lu* and was printed in Tsang Mou-hsün's *Yüan-ch'ü-hsüan* (see *tsa-chü*). A complete textual history can be found in the first of the following entries.

Ch'ang-lun, in *Chung-kuo ku-tien hsi-ch'ü lun-chu chi-ch'eng*, v. 1, Peking, 1959, pp. 153-166.

Chou, I-pai 周貽白. *Hsi-ch'ü yen-ch'ang lun-chu chi-shih* 戲曲演唱論著輯釋. Peking 1962, pp. 1-67; complete annotated text with copious notes.

—JDS

Chao I 趙翼 (*tzu*, Yün-sung 雲崧 and Yü-sung 耘松; *hao*, Ou-pei 甌北; 1727-1814), historian, poet, and literary critic, was a native of Yang-hu 陽湖, Kiangsu. His father, Wei-k'uan 惟寬 (d. 1741), earned his livelihood as a private tutor in the homes of the wealthy. Chao I accompanied him from one teaching position to another and acquired a formal education by attending his classes. When his father died, Chao I, an excellent student but still an adolescent, had to shoulder the full burden of supporting the family. This was made possible when he was offered his father's former position. Chao I worked steadily in that profession until his early twenties, when he decided to seek other employment in Peking. After arriving in that city, he met many leading scholar-officials whom he seems to have impressed very favorably, including Liu T'ung-hsün 劉統勳 (1700-1773), who was at that time Minister of Works. Liu asked Chao I to assist him in the task of compiling the *Kung-shih* 宮史, a history of the imperial palaces. Thereafter, Chao I secured an appointment as a secretary in the Grand Secretariat, and still later a similar position with the Grand Council. When his patron, Liu T'ung-hsün, was despatched to the northwest to supervise the provisioning of Chinese armies then campaigning in distant Turkestan, Chao I was called upon to draft state papers relating to that military expedition.

Chao I passed the *chin-shih* examinations in 1761 with the rank of *optimus* (*chuang-yüan*), but because no one from the Northwest had received first-class honors in many years, the emperor put Chao I third on the list. Following a period of service as an examination official, Chao I was named to a succession of posts in the south, including a period of duty with a military headquarters staff stationed in Yunnan province to assist in the Burma campaign. Later, Chao I returned home because his mother was ill. With her illness and death and his observance of the traditional mourning period, it was seven years before he thought of returning to public life. He set out for Peking in 1780 to resume his official career, but he was struck down by an illness that left him partially paralyzed and forced him to return home. Thereafter, he accepted the position of director of the An-ting Academy in Yangchow. His tenure at that school was interrupted by a period of service with the military headquarters staff engaged in suppressing a rebellion in Taiwan. During his later years, he cultivated his literary and scholarly interests, and referred to himself somewhat whimsically during those years as "San-pan lao-jen" 三半老人 (The Oldster of Three Halves), meaning that he had lost half of his powers of speech, sight, and hearing.

Chao I was one of the foremost historians of his day, and his chief contribution to the study of the Chinese past is the much admired and often reprinted *Nien-erh shih cha-chi* 廿二史劄記 in thirty-six *chüan*, which was completed in 1796 and published three years later. This work represents a significant departure from the kind of historical and philological scholarship then in vogue. Instead, following a lengthy and careful study of the dynastic histories, Chao I turned his attention to the larger, more fundamental problems of historiographical method and social and institutional history in the series of essays which comprise the *Nien-erh shih cha-chi*. For instance, among the topics addressed in this work are those pertaining to the source materials used in the compilation of the dynastic histories, the standards followed in selecting biographical detail, the use of eunuchs in government administration in the various dynasties, and the role of the great clans in society and politics in the southern dynasties. Because of his attention to the broader issues of history, modern historians have praised his scholarship and linked his name with those of the other great historians of the eighteenth century, such as Wang Ming-sheng 王鳴盛 (1722-1798), Ch'ien Ta-hsien 錢大昕 (1728-1804), and Chang Hsüeh-ch'eng 章學誠 (1738-1801). In addition to his work in the fields of social and institutional history, Chao I also chronicled military affairs. The *Huang-ch'ao wu-kung chi-sheng* 皇朝武功紀盛, in four *chüan*, relates the story of major Ch'ing-dynasty military successes, a subject for which he was well prepared by virtue of his own experiences in military command structures.

Although still little known or appreciated in the West except as an historian, Chao I was one of the most popular poets of his day, his name often being linked with those of Yüan Mei* and Chiang Shih-ch'üan.* A serious and prolific practitioner of his art (his poems comprise fifty-three *chüan* in his collected works), he ranges over a wide field of topics, which he frequently invests with a light humor and wit. Critics of his own and later times have remarked upon his fresh, even startling imagery, his adroit manner in the use of classical allusions, and his sometimes rich, sometimes simple diction. He made no use of the song-lyric (*tz'u**) form but instead wrote exclusively in the standard *shih** patterns. He is especially noteworthy for his poems in the ancient style (*ku-t'i*). Given his lifelong study of history, it is not surprising that he is also highly regarded for his poems in the *yung-shih* 詠史 (contemplations of the past) manner.

The *Ou-pei shih-hua* 甌北詩話 is his major work in the field of literary criticism. In its present form, it consists of ten essays—on the poets Li Po,* Tu Fu,* Han Yü,* Po Chü-i,* Su Shih,* Lu Yu,* Yüan Hao-wen,* Kao Ch'i,* Wu Wei-yeh,* and Cha Shen-hsing*—plus three *chüan* of general critical and theoretical observations. An early reference to the work by Hung Liang-chi* suggests that in its original form the *Ou-pei shih-hua* contained only the essays on the first seven poets named above. If so, that may be taken as an indication of his preferences and also of a belief that the post-Sung era had also produced its own masters. That idea is made even more explicit in the following heptasyllabic quatrain: "The poetic works of Li Po and Tu Fu, handed down by a myriad voices,/In the present age no longer seem either fresh or new./From these hills and rivers in every age geniuses emerge,/Each to command the *Feng* and *Sao* for several centuries." Deeply conscious of the rich heritage of the past, he believed nonetheless that time and circumstances change and that one must make adjustments to historical change. His concept of the role and function of poetry differed rather little from that of his famous contemporary, Yüan Mei.* He was also, for instance, a strong proponent of the principle of *hsing-ch'ing* 性情 (individual nature and feelings), i.e., that one's own individual genius must be given free rein, unencumbered by ancient standards or conventions. This was, he believed, fundamental to the poetic act. He was also of the opinion that the poet should be broad of learning, rich in life's experiences, and possessed of a rich and active imagination. These qualities which he argued were found in all great literature are present in his own poems, and his poetry therefore merits more attention than it has received to date.

EDITIONS:

Chao, I. *Nien-erh shih cha-chi.* SPPY.

———. *Ou-pei ch'uan-chi.* Chan-i-t'ang k'an-pen 湛眙堂刊本, reprinted in 1877. This edition contains a *nien-p'u.*

———. *Ou-pei shih-hua.* Peking, l963.

TRANSLATIONS:

Demiéville, *Anthologie,* p. 543.

STUDIES:

Chang, Wei-p'ing 張維屏. *Kuo-ch'ao shih-jen cheng-lüeh* 國朝詩人徵略, *chüan* 38, 2b-7b, contains a brief biographical account of Chao I's life and some comments on his poetry.

ECCP, pp. 75-76.

Wu, *Ch'ing-tai.*

—WS

Chao Ping-wen 趙秉文 (*tzu,* Chou-ch'en 周臣, *hao,* Hsien-hsien 閒閒, 1159-1232) was an influential leader in the Chin literary world. A native of Tz'u-chou 磁州, Fu-yang 滏陽 (modern Hopei), Chao was reputedly a precocious youth; he passed the *chin-shih* in 1185 at the early age of twenty-six. He rose through the administration and in 1217 became Minister of Rites.

Chao's literary talents were manifold, encompassing those of poet, essayist, calligrapher, and critic. He mastered many poetic forms, including both old- and new-style verse. According to traditional critical views, his heptasyllabic poems are spontaneous and unrestrained and his regulated verse moves in an easy flow, imbued with a refined elegance. His short poems are indeed exquisite. His pentasyllabic poems in their directness and simplicity show the influence of T'ao Ch'ien.* Although Chao's poetry is said to have most closely followed that of Li Po* and Su Shih,* in his final years he composed in a style closer to that of the High T'ang.

In his essays, Chao expressed his ideas without restricting himself to rigid rules of composition. His analytical ability is noteworthy and was probably due to his solid background in classical learning. Chao's contributions to literary theory stem primarily from his theories of prose. He believed that content is essential to writing and that language is merely a tool for conveying meaning. In his mind, the ancient classics were outstanding chiefly because of their straightforward manner and lucid style, in which the right word was always chosen and ideas were expressed precisely and concisely. Chao believed that it was profitable for beginners to model themselves after these classical works, although he recognized the difficulty of this. Chao urged study of the *Tso-chuan,** the *Chuang-tzu,* and the *Shih-chi,** while to prepare for composing poetry one should study the *Shih-ching,** the *Ch'u-tz'u,** and the *Wen-hsüan.** But he also insisted that one create one's own individual style after a certain level of mastery of these classical styles was attained.

The essential point of writing, Chao felt, was to illuminate the Way of the Ruler and assist the people in cultivating themselves. Although his role as a literary critic is not well-known today, he commented on some of the better-known poets of the past. He felt that the works of the early poets were praiseworthy only in one or two aspects. The poetry of T'ao Ch'ien, Hsieh Ling-yün,* Wang Wei,* and Po Chü-i* was to be praised for its lighthearted simplicity, while that of Pao Chao,* Li Po, and Li Ho* is commendable for its lofty manner.

Chao's calligraphy is said to be his greatest artistic accomplishment, followed by his poetry and then his essays. It was in such great demand that he was forced to post a notice outside his office door stating that it was inappropriate for a high official, such as himself, to write inscriptions on personal fans.

Chao was a prolific writer, producing many works on a great variety of subjects, including history, politics, and philosophy. Unfortunately, only two of the more than twenty works in this vein are extant today: the *Fu-shui chi* 滏水集 (Collected Works of Fu River), a anthology of his poetry and essays, and the *Tao-te chen-ching chi-chieh* 道德眞經集解 (Collected Notes on the *Tao-*

229

te-ching), a collection of commentaries, by him and by others, on the Taoist classic.

Chao Ping-wen's knowledge of Taoism, Buddhism, and Confucianism was profound, and he wrote extensively on all three doctrines. He also composed numerous poems and epitaphs for his Buddhist and Taoist acquaintances. However, he deliberately excluded from the *Fu-shui chi* his writings on Buddhism and Taoism. One theory is that he brought these writings together in the *Hsien-hsien wai-chi* 閒閒外集 (A Separate Collection by Hsien-hsien); originally published by a Buddhist monk, it is no longer extant.

EDITIONS:

Hsien-hsien lao-jen Fu-shui wen-chi 閒閒老人滏水 文集 (*Fu-shui chi*). 20 *chüan*. This text is found in several editions; a punctuated version was published by Commercial Press, Shanghai, 1937. The *SPTK* edition is reliable and readily available.
Tao-te chen-ching chi-chieh, in *Tao-tsang*, 384-385.

TRANSLATIONS:

Bush, Susan. "Literati Culture under the Chin (1122-1234)," *Oriental Art*, 15 (1969), 107-109.

STUDIES:

Hsü, Wen-yü 許文玉. "Chin-yüan ti wen-yu" 金源的文囿, in *Chung-kuo wen-hsüeh yen-chiu* 中國文學研究. Cheng Chen-to 鄭振鐸, ed. Hong Kong, 1963, pp. 677-714.
Lin, Ming-te 林明德, "Chin-tai wen-hsüeh p'i-p'ing chia Chao Ping-wen" 金代文學批評家趙 秉文, *Yu-shih*, 46.5 (1977), 19-22.

—CTY

Che-hsi tz'u-p'ai 浙西詞派, one of the dominant schools of *tz'u** poetry in the early Ch'ing dynasty, was founded by Chu I-tsun* and continued by Li E 厲鶚 (1692-1752). "Che-hsi" (Western Chekiang) refers to the region from which all its members came. The school became popular following Kung Hsiang-lin's 龔翔麟 publication of the collection *Che-hsi liu-chia tz'u* 浙西 六家詞 (The *Tz'u* Poetry of Six Poets from Che-hsi), in which the works of Chu I-tsun, Kung Hsiang-lin 龔翔麟, Li Liang-nien 李 良年, Li Fu 李符, Shen Hao-jih 沈皞日, and Shen An-teng 沈岸登 were gathered.

Chu I-tsun and his followers reacted against the *tz'u* practices of the Ming dynasty, during which the form was regarded as a minor genre. Chu felt the *tz'u* poetry of the late Ming was hampered by the ornate language characteristic of the Five Dynasties (*Hua-chien chi*)* style, and by the "vulgar" (*su* 俗) diction associated with the anonymous Sung anthology *Ts'ao-t'ang shih-yü* 草堂詩餘. It was in this context that Chu and his friends advocated elegance" (*ya* 雅) in *tz'u* composition, finding their models in the the Southern Sung poets Chiang K'uei* and Chang Yen 張炎 (1248-c. 1320).

In modeling their *tz'u* after Chiang K'uei, these Che-hsi poets were in fact trying to set up the new poetic standards necessary for a *tz'u* revival. For decades during the Ming, *tz'u* was considered merely an entertainment form—the pure literati *tz'u* typical of the Southern Sung were almost forgotten. Thus, in the foreword to his anthology *Tz'u-tsung* 詞綜 Chu I-tsun lamented: "When people spoke of *tz'u*, they always mentioned those of the Northern Sung. But it was not until the Southern Sung that *tz'u* reached its most refined stage . . . and Chiang K'uei was the most distinguished poet. It is a pity that only two dozen poems have survived out of his 20-*chüan Pai-shih yüeh-fu* 白石樂府. . . ." The anthology *Tz'u-tsung* represents only one of Chu's many efforts at reviving interest in the long-forgotten Southern Sung *tz'u* works by making them available to the public. It was Chu who was responsible for the reappearance of Chou Mi's* 7-*chüan* anthology *Chüeh-miao hao-tz'u* 絕妙好詞.

The Che-hsi School was in opposition to another contemporary *tz'u* school called Yang-hsien tz'u-p'ai 陽羨詞派, which was led by Ch'en Wei-sung.* While the Che-hsi School looked up to the Southern Sung, the Yang-hsien poets followed such Sung poets as Su Shih* and Hsin Ch'i-chi.* Thus, the former valued the qualities of stylistic elegance and refinement in *tz'u*, while the latter focused upon the quality of unrestrained expression. Both schools were important and seemed to complement each other. However, the Che-hsi School eventually became the more influential of the two, partly because Chu's strict emphasis on adhering to the tonal schemes in *tz'u* was in keeping with the general spirit of textual studies advocated by Ch'ing scholars. The strict tonal patterns in *tz'u* continued to play an important role during the whole of the Ch'ing dynasty, and finally became the prime concern of *tz'u* composition in the works of Chu Tsu-mou 朱祖謀 (1859-1931).

Yet precisely because of their meticulous pursuit of fine images and metrical propriety, the followers of Chu I-tsun mostly tended toward vapid frivolity and superficial imitation. The only exception was Li E, who was able to create a style of his own, while continuing to conform to the original theory of the Che-hsi School. Moving one step beyond the basic tenet of "elegance" in *tz'u*, Li advocated that *tz'u* poetry be "pure and visionary" (*ch'ing k'ung* 清空). He explained that it was the "pure and visionary" quality of Chang Yen's *tz'u* that was responsible for his unusual success. Of course, Li was not without faults, and his *tz'u* poetry, like that of his fellow poets, sometimes suffered from ornate superficiality and empty diction.

STUDIES:

Aoki, *Shindai*, pp. 264-291.

Chang, Shao-chen 張少眞 "Ch'ing-tai Che-chiang tz'u-p'ai yen-chiu" 清代浙江詞派研究. Unpublished M.A. thesis, Tung-wu University, Taiwan, 1978.

Chu, I-tsun, ed. *Tz'u-tsung* 詞綜. Supplement by Wang Sen 汪森, 1691. Rpt. in 2v., Shanghai, 1978. Punctuated edition. Contains index to poems.

Ho, Hsü-hsien 何須顯. "Che-hsi Yang-hsien Ch'ang-chou san p'ai tz'u lüeh lun" 浙西陽羨 常州三派詞略論. *Ch'ang-liu yüeh-k'an*, 36.10 (1968), 11-13, and 11 (1968), 11-13.

Ho, Kuang-chung 賀光中. *Lun Ch'ing-tz'u* 論清詞. Singapore, 1956, pp. 6-10, 33-55, 69-81.

Wang, Chung 汪中. *Ch'ing-tz'u chin-ch'üan* 清詞金荃. Taipei, 1965, pp. 51-77. A selection of works by poets of the Che-hsi School, with notes on the poets and short comments on the poems.

—KIC

Ch'en Liang 陳亮 (*tzu*, T'ung-fu 同甫 and T'ung 同, *hao*, Lung-ch'uan Hsien-sheng 龍川先生, original *ming*, Ju-neng 汝能, 1143-1194) was a philosopher, a politician, and a poet. Born into a non-academic, rural family in Yung-k'ang 永康, Wu-chou 婺州 (modern Chekiang), he devoted his life to the political ideal of the restoration of Sung control in the northern part of China. In 1161 his skillfully written *Cho-ku lun* 酌古論 (An Evaluation of the Ancients) attracted the attention of Chou K'uei 周葵, prefect of Wu-chou, and he became Chou's secretary for some years. Thereafter his life can be described as a series of misfortunes and fruitless efforts to gain influence. As Chu-ko Liang 諸葛亮 (d. 234) tried to regain sway over northern China for his ruler, Ch'en sought to expel the Chin from the north. He even adopted Chu-ko's name, changing his *ming* to Liang in 1168. One year later, he presented his ideas in five famous memorials to the emperor, the "Chung-hsing wu-lun" 中興五論 (Five Essays on the Restoration). But they were ignored—the emperor himself never bothered to look at them.

After several unsuccessful attempts, Ch'en passed the *chin-shih* examination in 1193, one year before his death. As a result of misunderstandings and trumped-up charges he was imprisoned at least three times and was rescued only by the influence of his powerful friend, Hsin Ch'i-chi.* As a contemporary of the philosophers Chu Hsi 朱熹 (1130-1200), Yeh Shih 葉適 (1150-1223), and Lu Chiu-yüan 陸九淵 (1139-1193), Ch'en was well acquainted with the philosophical debates of *li-hsüeh* 理學, the rationalistic approach of Sung Neo-Confucianism. But he pleaded for the extreme utilitarian position against the more idealistic viewpoints of this school. Ch'en eventually (1184) fell out of favor with his former friend Chu Hsi, and he wrote a polemic essay against Chu in 1190. Some influence of Wang An-shih's* ideas are also to be found in Ch'en's thinking.

Ch'en never considered himself to be a poet, at least not as that term was understood by the literati of his own times. Nevertheless, besides letters, memorials, essays, prefaces, postfaces, and epitaphs, his corpus contains *shih** and *tz'u.** The latter have long been dismissed as "harsh." In fact, if Ch'en's sixty-four extant *tz'u* (some are probably spurious), transmitted under the title *Lung-ch'uan tz'u* 龍川詞, are compared with *tz'u* by Li Yü,* for example, a lack of literary refinement and allusiveness in Ch'en's corpus is apparent. He stated that his *tz'u* contained only "lamentations of the strife of day-to-day living." But his friends Hsin Ch'i-chi and Yeh Shih praised his work for its straightforwardness and courage. From a historical viewpoint, Ch'en's *tz'u* are to be classified as in the tradition of Su Shih* and Hsin Ch'i-chi. However, while Hsin's lyrics attain a heroic, sometimes tragic level, Ch'en's are mere complaints; while Hsin's often contain obscure historical allusions, Ch'en's words are frank and direct. His works are in the main utilitarian.

EDITIONS:

Ch'en Liang chi 陳亮集. 2v. Peking, 1974.

Ch'en Lung-chuan wen-chi . Taipei, 1956.

Lung-ch'uan tz'u 龍川詞. 1 *chüan*, in *Sung liu-shih ming-chia tz'u* 宋六十名家詞. SPPY.

Lung-ch'uan-tz'u chiao-ch'ien 龍川詞 敎淺. Hsia Ch'eng-tao 夏承燾, ed., Mou Chia-k'uan 牟家寬, comp. Peking, 1961.

Lung-ch'uan wen-chi 龍川文集. 30 *chüan*. SPPY.

STUDIES:

Ho, Ko-en 何格恩. "Ch'en Liang te p'ing-sheng" 陳亮的平生, *Ling-nan hsüeh-pao*, 2.2 (July 1931).

Yen, Hsü-hsin 顏虛心. "Sung Ch'en Lung-ch'uan Hsien-sheng liang nien-p'u" 宋陳龍川先生亮年譜, in Wang Yün-wu 王雲五, ed., *Hsin-pien Chung-kuo ming-jen nien-p'u chi-ch'eng, ti-chiu-chi* 新編中國名人年譜集成, 第九輯. Shanghai, 1940; rpt. Taipei, 1980.

Wilhelm, Hellmut. "The Heresies of Ch'eng Liang," *AS*, 11 (1957-58), 102-112.

—WSp

Ch'en Lin 陳琳 (*tzu*, K'ung-chang 孔璋, d. 217) was an official whose checkered career reflected the uncertainty of the closing years of the Latter Han. His literary reputation rests on the letters, proclamations, and official documents he wrote on behalf of his powerful patrons, who included Yüan Shao 袁紹 (d. 202) and Ts'ao

Ts'ao 曹操 (155-220). The elegance and rhythmical regularity of those writings foreshadow the heyday of *p'ien-wen** (parallel prose). It is said that Ts'ao Ts'ao, laid up one day with a high fever, felt suddenly restored to health after reading the works of Ch'en Lin. Chapter 44 of the *Wen-hsüan** preserves the text of two proclamations: in the first one, written at Yüan Shao's command, Ch'en belabors Ts'ao Ts'ao with relentless gusto; in the second, written later on behalf of Hsün Yü, Ts'ao Ts'ao's right-hand man, invective gives place to encomium.

As a poet, Ch'en Lin belonged to the so-called "Seven Masters of the Chien-an Era" (*Chien-an ch'i-tzu* 建安七子 —the group included Hsü Kan 徐幹 [170-217], Juan Yü,* K'ung Jung,* Liu Chen 劉楨 [d. 217], Wang Ts'an,* and Ying Yang 應瑒 [d. 236]). He has left some *fu*,* which seem to have been written on prescribed subjects or for the purpose of celebrating Yüan Shao's or Ts'ao Ts'ao's warlike feats. Those pieces, like the only three pentasyllabic *shih** by Ch'en that have survived, are of little interest. There remains one *yüeh-fu*,* unique of its kind, for which Ch'en Lin is still remembered today ("Yin ma Ch'ang-ch'eng k'u hsing" 飲馬長城窟行). This song in irregular lines takes the form of dialogues between three *personae:* the officer in charge of the building of the Great Wall, a private soldier engaged in the construction, and the soldier's wife, whom he urges to marry again as he has given up hope of ever returning home. This lament, which contemporary critics have praised for its realism and warm-hearted inspiration, plainly attests the influence of popular ballads on literary circles at the end of the Han period.

EDITIONS:

Ch'en Chi-shih chi 陳記室集, in *Pai-san*, v. 4, pp. 97-119.

Liu-ch'ao wen, v. 1, pp. 967-972. The prose and *fu*.

Nan-pei-ch'ao shih, v. 1, pp. 258-259. The verse.

TRANSLATIONS:

Hightower, J. R. "The *fu* of T'ao Ch'ien," *Studies in Chinese Literature*, J. L. Bishop, ed. Cambridge, Mass., 1965, pp. 178-179 ("Chih-yü fu" 止欲賦 [Putting a Stop to Desires]).

von Zach, *Anthologie*, v. 2, pp. 756-757, 811-825.

STUDIES:
Suzuki, *Kan Gi*, pp. 617-621.

—JPD

Ch'en Shih-tao 陳師道 (*tzu*, Lü-ch'ang 履常, also Wu-chi 無己, *hao*, Hou-shan 后山, 1052-1102) was known for both his prose and his poetry. He was listed by the Yüan critic Fang Hui as one of the orthodox models for regulated verse (*lü-shih*—see *shih*) and as one of the four poets whose style was especially exalted, the other three being T'ao Ch'ien,* Tu Fu,* and Ch'en's contemporary, Huang T'ing-chien.*

Ch'en was registered as a native of Hsü-chou 徐州 (modern Kiangsu). When he was a young man, he became a student of the prose master Tseng Kung,* who reportedly impressed on him the virtue of stylistic conciseness. A few years later, when he was given responsibility for editing court records, Tseng tried to recommend Ch'en for a position as his assistant, but the appointment was apparently opposed because Ch'en was a commoner who had not come up through the examination system. There are conflicting reports on the exact nature of the project and whether Ch'en was ever permitted to participate. Within a few months, however, Tseng died (in 1083).

The poems which Ch'en wrote in mourning for Tseng are justly famous for their intensity of feeling. Although he continued to think of himself as Tseng's student, in 1084 he met Huang T'ing-chien, burned the poems he had written up to that time, and began to study under Huang. So destitute was Ch'en at the time of his initial meeting with Huang that he had sent his wife and three sons to live with his father-in-law in Shu (modern Szechwan). The poems written in 1084 and in the next few years clearly show that, in theme and treatment, Ch'en was following Huang T'ing-chien's lead in learning from Tu Fu. But perhaps it was the similarity between his separation from his family and Tu's—

as much as Huang's influence—which led him to model his poetry after the T'ang master's. Ch'en's poverty stemmed in part from an aversion to public life during the period when the New Policies Faction (see Wang An-shih) was in power. But the political tides soon turned and 1086 found him in the capital with Huang, Su Shih,* whom he met at Hsü-chou in 1077, and other literary figures opposed to the New Policies. Even then, however, he seemed reluctant to seek an official position on terms that were not just to his liking. In 1087, Ch'ao Pu-chih 晁補之 (1053-1110), who had been a younger member of this circle for years, and Chang Lei 張耒 (1054-1114) recommended Ch'en for a post in the National University, but Ch'en declined. Although Chu Hsi 朱熹 (1130-1200) later claimed Ch'en, unlike Huang, was never frivolous in his poetry, Ch'en did write several jocular poems in this year, perhaps reflecting the fondness for wit and humor in this circle of poets.

In early 1087, Su Shih and Sun Chüeh 孫覺 (1028-90), noting the excellence of his writing and his equanimity in poverty, suggested that the state should make use of Ch'en. Their petition was successful and Ch'en was made an Instructor in his native Hsü-chou. In 1089, when Su Shih was on his way to become Administrator of Hangchow, Ch'en left Hsü-chou against the orders of his superior and accompanied Su for one leg of his journey. For this insubordination, Ch'en was dismissed. But he was soon reappointed and transferred to Ying-chou 潁州 (modern Anhwei), still as Instructor.

In 1094, the political winds shifted again, and Ch'en was relieved of his Instructorship. He was to go to P'eng-tse 彭澤 as Subprefect, but resigned when his mother died in 1095 (his father had died in 1076). In extreme poverty, he settled in a monastery in Hsü-chou. After the mourning period, he was unable to secure a post until 1100, when Emperor Hui-tsung ascended the throne. At this point, he was given another Instructorship, but before he reached the post, he was promoted to Proofreader in the Palace Library, probably on the recommendation of Tseng Pu 曾布 (1036-1107), his former teacher's younger brother. Ch'en died on January 12, 1102, after scarcely a year in office.

Ch'en had a reputation as a perfectionist. He did not compose easily, and when a line came to him, he would reportedly jump into bed and pull the covers over his head until he had worked out the whole poem. Children and dogs were herded away to the neighbors' so that nothing should disturb his concentration. He once said that poetry was more ruinous to one's life than drink, yet he maintained that all the spirit and energy of his life went into verse. The severe standards he set for himself supposedly explain why only 683 of his poems remain, not a large number for a major poet in that period.

Nevertheless, one occasionally finds in his collection a work that may not be a final version. There is one five-word regulated verse, "Teng Yen-tzu Lou" 登燕子樓 (Climbing Swallow Tower), in which the same word as the rhyme-word is used at the end of both the second and eighth lines. There are also several works which contain violations of the rules which govern tone sequences. Examples are "Pieh Fu-shan chü-shih" 別負山居士 (Saying Goodbye to the "Mountain-shouldering Retired Scholar") and "Hsüeh hou" 雪後 (After Snow). Disregard for the rules of regulated verse is also evident in several poems—in some every couplet is parallel; in others, the middle couplets are not parallel, as they normally should be. Ch'en Mo 陳模 (chin-shih, 1196) felt that Ch'en Shih-tao's fondness for ending a poem with a parallel couplet weakened the form.

Yet all of these "errors" and "non-poetic" touches, many of them obviously conscious, reflect common tendencies in Sung poetic practice. They can also be seen as aspects of Tu Fu's poetry which Ch'en adopted. From Tu he borrowed lines, diction, and configurations of ideas. Sometimes he expanded on Tu's lines (occasionally with disastrous results, as Wang Shih-chen [1526-1590]* pointed out), sometimes he shortened them, and sometimes he combined lines from different poems. From Tu he learned an "unorthodox" parallelism which he used to great advantage, the pairing of words of quite different semantic categories: nouns denoting actions are matched with nouns denoting objects, or colors with non-colors, etc. His five-word regulated verses, usually considered his finest poems, are also considered closest to those of Tu Fu, and superior even to those of his teacher, Huang T'ing-chien. In fact, according to some traditional critics, Ch'en was the bridge by which the novice poet might approach Tu Fu. Ch'en could not match Tu in breadth, of course, but he did write in a variety of modes with great skill and depth, and sometimes with elegance and subtlety.

He also excelled in prose: 140 pieces survive, some in parallel prose. Chu Hsi praised these writings, maintaining they were superior to the prose of Huang T'ing-chien. In the realm of the tz'u,* Ch'en claimed to be better than Huang or Ch'in Kuan 秦觀 (1049-1100), but only fifty of his lyrics survive. Despite some fine lines, they are not considered important in the history of the genre.

The Hou-shan shih-hua 后山詩話 (Poetry Talks of [Ch'en]Hou-shan), although attributed to Ch'en, contains at least some sections from another hand.

EDITIONS:

Ch'üan Sung tz'u 全宋詞, v. 1, pp. 584-92.
Hou-shan chi 后山集. SPPY.
Hou-shan shih chu 后山詩話. SPTK.
Hou-shan shih chu pu-chien 后山詩註補箋. Mao Kuang-sheng 毛廣生, ed. 1936. Rpt. Taiwan, 1967, 1980. Contains the same Southern Sung commentary as the above editions, with extensive additional material compiled by Mao; punctuated.

STUDIES:

Chang, Chien 張健. "Ch'en Shih-tao te wen-hsüeh p'i-p'ing yen-chiu" 陳師道的文學批評研究, Wen-hsüeh p'ing-lun, 1 (1975), 69-133.
———. "Lun Ch'en Shih-tao te wen-hsüeh tso-p'in" 論陳師道的文學作品, Chung-wai wen-hsüeh, 34 (September 1974), 10-23.
———. Sung Chin Ssu-chia wen-hsüeh p'i-p'ing yen-chiu 宋金四家文學批評研究. Taipei, 1975, pp. 218-311.

Ch'en, Hui-yüan 陳惠源. "Hou-shan shih yü Tu Fu" 后山詩與杜甫, *Hua-kuo*, 1 (July 1957), 66-73.

Cheng, Ch'ien 鄭騫. "Ch'en Hou-shan chuan" 陳後山傳, *Chung-hua wen-hua fu-hsing yüeh-k'an*, 9.12 (December 1976), 79-84.

———. "Ch'en Hou-shan nien-p'u, I" 陳後山年譜, *Yu-shih hsüeh-chih*, 16.2 (December 1980), 124-182.

———. "Ch'en Hou-shan nien-p'u, II," *Yu-shih hsüeh-chih*, 16.3 (June 1981), 94-149. This two-part chronological biography undoubtedly represents the most painstaking and thorough research on the life of Ch'en Shih-tao to date.

Chien, Chin-sung 簡錦松. "Lun Ch'en Shih-tao ch'i-chüeh" 論陳師道七絕, *Chung-wai wen-hsüeh*, 7.2 (July 1978), 68-98.

Huang T'ing-chien ho Chiang-hsi shih p'ao chüan 黃庭堅和江西詩派卷. Fu Hsüan-tsung 傅璇琮, ed. Peking, 1978, v. 2, pp. 471-591. A collection of comments on Ch'en and his works from Sung through Ch'ing times.

Pa, Hu-t'ien 巴壺天. "Ch'en Shih-tao," in *Chung-kuo wen-hsüeh lun-chi* 中國文學論集. Taipei, 1958, v. 2, pp. 647-656.

Yen, K'un-yang 顏崑陽. "Ts'ung Ch'en Hou-shan chih shih lun ch'i pei-chü hsing-ko" 從陳后山之詩論其悲劇性格, *Yu-shih*, 49.1 (January 1979), 54-58.

Yoshikawa, *Sung*, pp. 130-133.

—SHS

Ch'en To 陳鐸 (*tzu*, Ta-sheng 大聲, *hao*, Ch'iu-pi 秋碧, *fl.* 1506) was famous as a writer of *san-ch'ü* 散曲 (see *ch'ü*). He was born into a military family and lived in Chin-ling 金陵 (modern Nanking). He was Guard Commander, a hereditary post. Artistic pursuits were foremost in his mind—once during an interview with an official named Hsü on matters of security, he was asked if he was the famous lyricist Ch'en To. Upon acknowledgment and when pressed to sing, he took from his sleeve an ivory clapper and broke into song, shocking Hsü. Such incidents increased his artistic reputation but thwarted his official career. On another occasion when musicians from the music academy were ordered to play for him at a banquet, Ch'en made several remarks on the music to which they paid little attention. Finally, he took up a *p'i-p'a* and sang, to everyone's amazement. After that he was dubbed "Yüeh Wang" 樂王 (Prince of Music).

He is frequently linked with Hsü Lin 徐霖 (*tzu*, Tzu-jen 子仁), with whom he once collaborated on a set of *tour-de-force* pieces on the four seasons done at a banquet held in their honor. Ch'en's other talents included painting and writing *tz'u** and *shih.** Some criticize him for being derivative and rather shallow, but all recognize his fluent diction which perfectly fit the musical settings. A few of his pieces are considered unsurpassed even by Yüan lyricists. He was also known for his satirical wit, which is now enshrined in 136 short lyrics collected under the title *Hua-chi yü-yün* 滑稽餘韻. He left three collections of *san-ch'ü* (*Li-yün chi ao* 梨雲寄傲, *Yüeh-hsiang t'ing kao* 月香亭稿, and *Kung-yü man hsing* 公餘漫興), one of *shih* and *tz'u* (*Ts'ao-t'ang yü-i* 草堂餘意), and three plays (two *tsa-chü** and one *chuan-ch'i**).

EDITIONS:

Ch'en Ta-sheng yüeh-fu ch'üan-chi 樂府全集. *c.* 1610.

Ch'iu-pi yüeh-fu 秋碧樂府, and *Li-yün chi ao*, in *Yin-hung-i so k'o ch'ü* 飲虹簃所刻曲. Lu Ch'ien 盧前, ed. Taipei, 1961; the only readily available edition of these works, which contain about a third of Ch'en's extant *san-ch'ü*.

Ming-tai ko-ch'ü hsüan 明代歌曲選. Lu Kung 路工, ed. Shanghai, 1956, pp. 1-27; contains most of the songs in *Hua-chi yü-yün*. Many of Ch'en's *san-ch'ü* are included, some without attribution, in the following four collections: *Sheng-shih hsin-sheng* 盛世新聲, 1517; rpt. Peking, 1955; *Tz'u-lin chai yen* 詞林摘艶, Chang Lu 張祿 (*fl.* 1525), ed., rpt. Peking, 1955; *Nan-pei-kung tz'u chi* 南北宮詞記, Ch'en Suo-wen 陳所聞 (d. 1604), ed., Peking, 1959; *Wu sao ho-pien* 吳騷合編, Chang Ch'u-shu 張楚叔 (*fl.* 1637), ed., Shanghai, 1934. (See Chao Ching-shen, "Ming jen," below.)

STUDIES:

Chao, Ching-shen 趙景深. "Fang-chih chu-lu Ming Ch'ing ch'ü-chia k'ao leh" 方志著錄明清曲家考略, in *Ming Ch'ing ch'ü t'an* 明清曲談, Shanghai, 1957, p. 3.

———. "Ming jen san-ch'ü te chi-i" 明人散曲的輯逸, *Ibid.*, pp. 134-139; gives titles and locations of Ch'en's works that are scattered in the four collections listed above.

Cheng, Ch'ien 鄭騫. "Ch'en To (Ta-sheng) chi ch'i tz'u ch'ü" 陳鐸（大聲）及其詞曲, *Shu ho jen*, 118 (Sept. 16, 1969), 929-936.
DMB, pp. 184-185.

—WaS

Ch'en Tuan-sheng 陳端生 (1751-1796?), a native of Ch'ien-t'ang 錢塘 (modern Hangchow), was the granddaughter of the famous literatus Ch'en Chao-lun 陳兆崙 (1701-1771). She was given a good traditional education and developed a keen liking for literature. Both she and her younger sister, Ch'en Ch'ang-sheng 陳長生, were able poets. Little is known about her life. Her husband, a Mr. Fan 范 (possibly Fan Ch'iu-t'ang 范秋塘), had been indirectly involved in a case concerning the civil-service examinations, and had been banished to I-li 伊犁 in Sinkiang. Later he was pardoned, but before he could reach home, Ch'en Tuan-sheng had already died. Her poetry was collected under the title *Hui-ying-ko chi* 繪影閣集, but it has been lost. Among her other works, a *t'an-tz'u** entitled *Tsai-sheng yüan* 再生緣 (in seventeen *chüan*) is extant.

Ch'en began writing *Tsai-sheng yüan* in the winter of 1768 in Peking when she was eighteen. During this year she wrote the first eight *chüan*. The next eight were written between mid-1769 and early 1770 while she was in Teng-chou 登州, Shangtung. At that time her father, Ch'en Yü-tun (b. 1726) was the Vice Prefect there. Ch'en Tuan-sheng claims that during her first three years of work on the piece she worked day and night unceasingly. Later, her mother, Madam Wang 汪, died of an illness, and she had to return to Hangchow, putting aside the unfinished work for twelve years. During this long period of time, her mother and grandfather passed away, she was married, and her husband was banished. Not until 1784 did she continue with the seventeenth *chüan*, the last that she would write. The work was completed (*chüan* 18-20) later by another woman, Liang Te-sheng 梁德繩 (*tzu*, Ch'u-sheng 楚生, 1771-1847).

Tsai-sheng yüan tells the story of Meng Li-chün 孟麗君, who disguised herself as a male, attained the highest rank in the civil-service examination, became a prime minister, and was finally reunited with her fiancé, Huang-p'u Shao-hua 皇甫少華. In this voluminous work (some 600,000 characters) Ch'en voiced her dissatisfaction, through Meng Li-chün, with the unequal social status of the sexes and expressed her ideals. Ch'en Yin-k'o was probably the first to point out that Ch'en Tuan-sheng advocated freedom and independence for women, breaking with the traditional "Three Bonds" (obedience to the emperor, to one's father, and to one's husband). He also praised the work for its elegant language, its tightly and finely knit structure, and its clear lines of thought. The language is essentially poetic—the entire work can be read as an extended heptasyllabic regulated verse (*p'ai-lü* 排律). *Tsai-sheng yan* is considered the finest extant *t'an-tz'u*.

EDITIONS:

Hsiu-hsiang Tsai-sheng yüan ch'üan-chuan 繡像再生緣全傳. Shanghai, n.d.
Hui-t'u Tsai-sheng yüan 繪圖再生緣. Hu Hsieh-yin 胡協寅, collator. Shanghai, 1949.

STUDIES:

Ch'en, Yin-k'o. *Lun Tsai-sheng yüan* 論再生緣. Rpt. Hong Kong, 1970.
T'an, Cheng-pi 譚正璧. *Chung-kuo nü-hsing te wen-hsüeh sheng-huo* 中國女性的文學生活. Shanghai, 1931, pp. 411-423.
——— and T'an Hsün 譚尋. "*Tsai-sheng yüan*," in their *T'an-tz'u hsü-lu* 彈詞敍錄, Shanghai, 1981, pp. 154-156.
Yeh, Te-chün 葉德均. "*Tsai-sheng yüan* hsü-tso-che Hsü Tsung-yen Liang Te-sheng fu-fu nien-p'u" 再生緣續作者許宗彥梁德繩夫婦年譜, in Yeh's *Hsi-ch'ü hsiao-shuo ts'ung-k'ao* 戲曲小說叢考, Chao Ching-shen 趙景深, ed. Peking, 1979, v. 2, pp. 696-742.

—CYP

Ch'en Tzu-ang 陳子昂 (*tzu*, Po-yü 伯玉, 661-702), a native of Szechwan, was among the first poets in the T'ang dynasty to openly express discontent over the effeteness of contemporary poetry and to advocate a return to the seriousness of the Han-Wei Style.

Ch'en passed the civil-service examination held in Lo-yang in 684, after an unsuccessful attempt in 682. He assumed the post of Proofreader in the Palace Library, but his progress up the official ladder was slow. In 693 he became Reminder of the Right at the age of thirty-three. In 702, while in mourning for his father in Szechwan, persecution by the district magistrate, Tuan Chien 段簡, acting under instructions from Wu San-ssu 武三思 (d. 707), a cousin of Empress Wu (?627-705), resulted in his death. Ch'en had been a critic of Wu San-ssu's harsh governmental measures.

Ch'en Tzu-ang's extant literary views are contained in the introduction to his poem "Hsiu-chu p'ien" 修竹篇 (The Tall Bamboo). In it he criticizes the poetry of the Southern Dynasties for its obsession with formal beauty at the expense of profound feelings and advocates a return to more serious themes.

He was recognized for the remainder of the dynasty as an innovative poet who set an example for those poets of later ages concerned with social issues. Writers such as Li Po,* Tu Fu,* Han Yü,* Po Chü-i,* Liu Tsung-yüan,* and Yüan Chen* were admirers of Ch'en Tzu-ang.

Ch'en Tzu-ang's poetic reputation rests mainly on his cycle of thirty-eight poems entitled "Kan-yü" 感遇 (Stirred by My Experiences). This cycle was seen by Tu Fu as a paragon of "loyalty and righteousness," because many of the hidden accusations in the poems were directed at the usurper, Empress Wu. But the uncommon diction of these poems, probably deliberate to avoid political persecution, veiled the contents, so that by the close of the T'ang dynasty, readers no longer understood the allegorical flavor of these texts and appraised them in terms of the style in which they were written. Sung Ch'i 宋祁 (998-1061), who wrote Ch'en's biography in the *Hsin T'ang shu* 新唐書, mistook the "Kan-yü" for poetic exercises of Ch'en's early years. Some later critics even dismissed the poems as meaningless utterances clad in Taoist mysticism. It was not until the Ch'ing dynasty that Ch'en Hang 陳沆 (1785-1826) realized the allegorical qualities of the poems and attempted to decode the whole cycle in his *Shih pi-hsing chien* 詩比興箋 (Commentary on Selected Allegorical Poems).

EDITIONS:

Andō Shunroku 安東俊六. *Chin Shigō shi sakuin* 陳子昂詩索引. Nagoya, 1976.

Ch'en Po-yü wen-chi 陳伯玉文集. SPTK.

Ch'en Tzu-ang chi 陳子昂集. Peking, 1960. Contains a *nien-p'u*.

STUDIES:

Andō, Shunroku 安東俊六. "Chin Shigō no Kangōshi o sasaeru shisō ni tsuite" 陳子昂の感遇詩を支える思想について, *Chūgoku bungei zadankai nōto*, 16 (1967), 1-15.

———. "Chin Shigō no shiron to sakuhin" 陳子昂の詩論と作品, *Kyūshū Chūgoku gakkaihō*, 14 (1968), 47-62.

———. "Shotō bungakushi ni okeru Chin Shigō no ichizuke" 初唐文學史における陳子昂の位置づけ, *ibid.*, 15 (1969), 16-28.

Ch'en, Hang. "Ch'en Tzu-ang shih chien" 陳子昂詩箋, in *Shih pi-hsing chien*, Hong Kong, 1965, pp. 95-116.

Ho, Richard M. W. 何文滙. *Ch'en Tzu-ang Kan-yü shih-chien* 陳子昂感遇詩箋. Hong Kong, 1978. Appended is an article on Ch'en Tzu-ang's controversial memorials written by C. C. Chan

Liu, Mau-Tsai. "Der Dichter und Staatsman Ch'en Tzu-ang (661-702) und sein *jen-chi*-Konzept," *OE*, 24 (1977), 179-185.

Lo, Yung 羅庸. "Ch'en Tzu-ang nien-p'u" 陳子昂年譜, in *Ch'en Tzu-ang chi*, pp. 309-359.

Owen, "Ch'en Tzu-ang," in *Early T'ang*, pp. 151-223.

Suzuki, *Todai*, pp. 47-74.

Takagi, Masakazu 高木正一. "Chin Shigō to shi no kakushin" 陳子昂と詩の革新, in *Yoshikawa Hakushi taikyū kinen Chūgoku bungaku ronshu* 吉川博士退休記念中國文學論集, Tokyo, 1968, pp. 353-372.

—RH

Ch'en Tzu-lung 陳子龍 (*tzu*, Jen-chung 人中 or Wo-tzu 臥子, *hao*, I-fu 軼符 or Ta-tsun 大樽, 1608-1647) was a native of Hua-t'ing 華亭, Sung-chiang 松江 (modern Shanghai).

In his youth he founded the "Chi-she" 幾社 with Hsia Yün-i 夏允彝 and Hsü Fu-yüan 徐孚遠; the society insisted on moral behavior and encouraged criticism of the government. Ch'en placed great emphasis on practical learning, in which connection he compiled the *Huang-Ming ching-shih-wen pien* 皇明經世文編.

In 1634 he met Liu Ju-shih 柳如是, an unusual woman. Ch'en wrote the "Hsiang-o fu" 湘娥賦 to express his affection for her, and she responded with the "Nan Lo-shen fu" 男洛神賦, a vow, full of sorrowful expressions, describing her background and the ultimate goal of her life. The next year they began to live together. Most of the works in Ch'en's *P'ing-lu t'ang chi* 平露堂集 were written especially for Liu. Later they were forced to part because of opposition from Ch'en's family.

Passing the *chin-shih* examination in 1637, Ch'en was given a military post. After the Ch'ing forces crossed into Ming territory, he served the Southern Ming and presented a memorial suggesting a major expedition to recover the North. Two months after Nanking fell to the Ch'ing in 1644, Ch'en and his comrades in the Chi-she attempted to start a military campaign. It was quickly subdued and Ch'en had to flee for his life. But he secretly kept in contact with the Southern Ming, planning another rising. In 1647 Ch'en urged the Ch'ing Governor of Sung-chiang, Wu Sheng-chao 吳勝兆, to revolt, but there was a mutiny in Wu's regiment, and he was brought to Nanking and executed. Ch'en was also arrested, but en route to Nanking, when the boat was anchored by the K'ua-t'ang 跨塘 Bridge at Sung-chiang, he broke his bonds, jumped into the water, and put an end to his life.

His collected works, *Ch'en Chung-yü Kung ch'üan-chi* 陳忠裕公全集, are in thirty *chüan*: ten *chüan* of prose, seventeen of classical poetry, two of *fu*,* and one of *tz'u*.* He is the last important writer among the advocates of the ancient style who flourished from the mid-Ming onwards. His prose style followed that of the Wei-Chin Period. He was especially good at prose-poems. His poems bear witness to the great changes in the last years of the Ming and are full of the sorrows that were felt at the fall of the dynasty. Plaintive yet forceful and filled with an atmosphere of desolation, they are deeply touching works with splendid diction and sonorous tones. His works in hep-

tasyllabic regulated verse are stylistically the most original of his poetic corpus. A number of them were written in sets and expressed his concern over current politics—"Liao-shih tsa-shih" 遼事雜詩 (Miscellaneous Poems on Frontier Affairs [eight poems]) and "Tu-hsia tsa-kan" 都下雜感 (Miscellaneous Feelings at the Capital) are typical of these works.

EDITIONS:

Ch'en Chung-yü ch'üan-chi 陳忠裕全集. Wang Ch'ang 王昶, ed. N.p., with a postface dated 1869.

STUDIES:

Ch'en, Yin-k'o 陳寅恪. *Liu Ju-shih pieh-chuan* 柳如是別傳. Shanghai, 1980.

—YPC

Ch'en Wei-sung 陳維崧 (*tzu*, Ch'i-nien 其年, *hao*, Chia-ling 迦陵, 1626-1682) is generally regarded as one of the most influential *tz'u** writers of the early Ch'ing era.

Ch'en Wei-sung belonged to a family active in both literary and political circles. His grandfather, Yü-t'ing, was a censor and high-ranking official at the Ming court and a lecturer in the Tung-lin 東林 Academy. His father, Chen-hui, was an active member of the *fu-she* 復社 organization. In the struggle against the palace-eunuch clique, both Ch'en Yü-t'ing and Ch'en Chen-hui fell victims to political conflicts.

Ch'en Wei-sung obtained his first degree, *po-shih ti-tzu-yüan* 博士弟子員, at the age of sixteen, but was unsuccessful in the civil-service examinations afterwards. In his early thirties he began a period of protracted travel, seeking opportunities for employment. He traveled widely in Kiangsu, then north to Peking and west to Honan, where he finally took a minor official position.

Unlike some Ming loyalists who refused to participate, Ch'en Wei-sung took and passed the special *po-hsüeh hung-ju* 博學鴻儒 examination held under the auspices of the K'ang-hsi emperor in 1679. He was assigned the position of Corrector in the Han-lin Academy to work on the Ming-dynasty history-project. He led an active social life while in the capital, but the comfortable and carefree life that he longed for was never within his reach. Bad health, advancing age, and nostalgia cast a shadow over the last years of his life; he died at the age of fifty-six.

A prolific writer, Ch'en Wei-sung left behind a compendious heritage which was collected into six *chüan* of prose, ten of *fu*,* eight of *shih*,* and thirty of *tz'u*.* His approximately eight hundred *shih* poems have been widely praised for their deep thought and sincere emotion. They were said to have reached the standard of the High T'ang era. His *fu* were compared to those of the two masters, Hsü Ling and Yü Hsin,* and declared to be the best since the early seventh century. His robust style is often noted by critics. He found great satisfaction in the prose-essay form, and these efforts made him so popular as a writer that he received numerous requests for pieces, for which he was handsomely rewarded.

It was, however, in the realm of *tz'u* that Ch'en Wei-sung enjoyed the greatest success and influence. He undertook to establish a new theoretical ground for the *tz'u* form. In advocating allegorical and metaphorical meanings for the *tz'u*, he acknowledged its capacity to express serious emotional and intellectual concerns. He believed *tz'u* writers should take "Kuo-feng" 國風 of the *Shih-ching** and the "Li sao" 離騷 as models. In claiming these orthodox poetic forms as prototypes of the *tz'u*, his ideas were antecedents to both the *Chi-t'o shuo* 寄托說 (Theory of Poetic Suggestion) and the *Tsun-t'i shuo* 尊體說 (Theory of Revering the *Tz'u* Form) advocated by Chang Hui-yen,* leader of the *Ch'ang-chou tz'u-p'ai*.*

Ch'en Wei-sung is China's most prolific *tz'u* writer. His *tz'u* collection, *Hu-hai-lou tz'u-chi* 湖海樓詞集, contains 1,629 poems. While most *tz'u* writers of the Ming and Ch'ing dynasties used the short mode, Ch'en Wei-sung's *chefs d'oeuvre* are his verses in the long mode. He used 416 different tunes in his poems; approximately 100 verses were written to each of his two favorite tunes: *Man chiang hung* 滿江紅 and *Ho hsin lang* 賀新郎.

Ch'en Wei-sung's *tz'u* have been generally described as *hao-fang* 豪放 (heroic and unrestrained), after the fashion of Su Shih* and Hsin Ch'i-chi.* His *tz'u* have been criticized for being too straightforward and direct in expression and lacking in the suggestive power or meaning that goes beyond language, which the nature of the *tz'u* genre requires. On the other hand, he has been praised as having a surpassing sensitivity for the psychological states of grief and happiness, owing to his own natural tendencies and the career frustrations he experienced. The kaleidoscopic pattern and content, the vigorous style, the unrestrained spirit, and the dazzling power of his *tz'u* are also broadly recognized.

EDITIONS:
Ch'en Chia-ling shih wen tz'u ch'üan chi 陳迦陵 詩文詞全集. *SPTK.*
Hu-hai-lou tz'u-chi 湖海樓詞集. *SPPY.*
Wu-ssu tz'u 烏絲詞. Taipei, 1973.

TRANSLATIONS:
See Madeline Chu below.

STUDIES:
Chu, Madeline Men-li. "Ch'en Wei-sung, the *Tz'u* Poet." Unpublished Ph.D. dissertation, University of Arizona, 1978.

—MCh

Ch'en Yü-chiao陳與郊(*tzu*, Kuang-yeh 廣野, 1544-1611), a native of Hai-ning 海寧, was an acknowledged scholar and dramatist. Ch'en received an excellent education in early childhood, enabling him to become a *hsiu-ts'ai* at the age of fifteen. After becoming a *chü-jen* in 1567 and a *chin-shih* in 1574, he was appointed Prefect of Ho-chien fu 河間府 and transferred to Shun-te fu 順德府 in the same capital city the following year. He was summoned to Peking in 1582 to assume the position of Supervising Secretary of the Office of Scrutiny for Personnel. He became Minister of Personnel in 1588. In the years 1586 and 1589 he also served as an assistant examiner of the metropolitan examinations. In 1590 he was appointed Vice Minister of the Court of Imperial Sacrifices and Superintendent of the Translators Institute. Shortly after assuming office he resigned to attend his mother's eightieth birthday celebration but she died before his arrival. Two years later he was accused of having received a bribe while serving as examiner in the metropolitan examinations, and was consequently dismissed from office.

He retired to the family villa, named Yü-yüan 隅園, in the country and devoted his time to literary activities. In addition to being an editor and compiler on a number of works, he was also a rather prolific writer. The best known of his writings is the *Feng-ch'ang i-kao* 奉常俟稿 which consists of two main divisions: (1) compositions written for specific occasions such as birthdays, *tz'u*,* biographies, essays, and correspondence, and (2) his four *ch'uan-ch'i** dramas.

As a playwright Ch'en Yü-chiao was responsible for four *ch'uan-ch'i* and five *tsa-chü** dramas, of which only three remain. According to other sources, Ch'en wrote six *tsa-chü*, the last being *T'i-hung-yeh* 題紅葉 which, like his *Huai-yin-hou* 淮陰侯 and *Chung-shan lang* 中山狼, is no longer extant. His *ch'uan-ch'i* dramas are collectively entitled *Ling-ch'ih fu* 泠癡符 (The Selling of Talismans against Idiocy). *Ying-t'ao meng* 櫻桃夢 (The Dream of Ying-t'ao), based on the T'ang tale "Ying-t'ao ch'ing-i" 櫻桃青衣, portrays the illusory life of this world. *Pao-ling tao* 寶靈刀 (The Precious Sword) is a revision of *Pao-chien chi* 寶劍記 by Li K'ai-hsien* and portrays the adventures of Lin Ch'ung 林沖 as they are narrated in chapters 7-10 in *Shui-hu chuan.** To this basic plot Ch'en adds new elements: Lin's wife's renunciation of the world, his daughter's serving as a substitute at her mother's forced marriage, and the daughter's suicide. *Ch'i-lin jih* 麒麟罽, also known as *Ch'i-lin chui* 麒麟墜 (The Descending Unicorn), is based on the heroic acts of Han Shih-chung 韓世忠 and his wife Liang Hung-yü 梁紅玉 of Southern Sung, which had also inspired an earlier *ch'uan-ch'i*, *Shuang-lieh chi* 雙烈記 by Chang Su-wei 張四維. *Ying-wu chou* 鸚鵡洲 (Parrot Isle) portrays the romance between Yü-hsiao 玉簫, a courtesan, and Wei Kao 韋皐, a general. The plot of this play is traceable to a T'ang tale, "Yü-hsiao chuan" 玉簫傳, also the model for a *tsa-chü*, *Liang-shih yin-yüan* 兩世姻緣, and a *ch'uan-ch'i*, *Yü-huan chi* 玉環記. To this basic

plot, Ch'en added the story of Hsüeh T'ao.* With the exception of *Ying-wu chou*, all his other *ch'uan-chi* plays were written under the pen name Kao Man-ch'ing.

Ch'en also wrote the following *tsa-chü:* *Chao-chün ch'u sai* 昭君出塞 (Chao-chün Goes out of the Past—see Ma Chih-yüan), *Wen-chi ju sai* 文姬入塞 (Wen-chi Enters the Pass—see Ts'ai Yung), and *Yüan-shih i-ch'üan* 袁氏義犬 (The Faithful Dog of Yüan). The last portrays a faithful dog which avenges the murder of its master's young son. The play *Hu-lu hsien-sheng* 葫蘆先生, also known as *Mo-nai-ho k'u-tao chang-an chieh* 沒奈何哭倒長安街, by Wang Heng* is incorporated into Act I in this play. The plot is derived from a historical incident associated with Yüan Chieh 袁粲 of the Six Dynasties. While there is no question that Ch'en used this drama as a vehicle of topical political criticism, his actual targets are no longer clear. Some maintain that they were a few individuals who refused to help him when his son was in prison. Others speculate that his targets actually were the disgruntled students of Chang Chü-cheng, the prime minister, and his associates.

Ch'en Yü-chiao was further credited for compiling the *Ku-ming chia tsa-chü* 古名家雜劇, a collection of *tsa-chü* of the Yüan and Ming periods. Though parts of this work have been lost, it remains an important source of texts.

While his dramas as a whole receive favorable criticism, the *tsa-chü* out rank his *ch'uan-ch'i*.

EDITIONS:

Chao-chün ch'u sai 昭君出塞, *Wen-chi ju sai* 文姬入塞, *Yüan-chih i-ch'üan* 袁氏義犬 in *Sheng-ming*.

Feng-ch'ang i-kao 奉常俟稿. N.p., Ming edition. Contains biographies, essays, compositions, lyric poems, correspondence, and four *ch'uan-ch'i*.

Ku-ming-chia tsa-chü 古名家雜劇. N.p., Ming edition. Contains a collection of plays of the Yüan-Ming periods. Parts of this collection are no longer extant.

Ying-t'ao meng 櫻桃夢, *Ling-pao tao* 靈寶刀, *Ch'i-lin jih* 麒麟罽, and *Ying-wu chou* 鸚鵡洲 in *Ku-pen*, II.

STUDIES:

Aoki, *Gikyokushi;* Part III, ch. 9, sec. 4, contains biography, a list of Ch'en's extant plays, and comments on them.

DMB, pp. 188-192.

Fu, *Ch'uan-ch'i*. Contains a list of Ch'en's *ch'uan-ch'i* plays and information on extant editions.

———. *Tsa-chü*. Contains brief biography, a list of Ch'en's *tsa-chü*, and information on extant editions.

Li, Wei-chen 李維楨. "T'ao-ch'ang-ssu chao-ch'ing ch'en-kung mu-chih-ming" 太常寺少卿陳公墓誌銘, in *T'ai pi-shan-fang chi* 太泌山房集, *chüan* 78, n.p., Ming edition. Contains extensive biographical information.

Meng, Sen 孟森. "Hai-ning ch'en-chia" 海寧陳家, in *Kuo-li Pei-ching ta-hsüeh wu-shih chou-nien chi-nien lun-wen chi* 國立北京大學五十週年紀念論文集, Peking, 1948, p. 12. Contains extensive information on the Ch'en family.

Yagisawa, *Gekisakuka;* ch. 5 (pp. 269-362) contains information on Ch'en's family background, life, and literary achievements and comments on his extant plays.

—EY

Ch'en Yü-i 陳與義 (*tzu*, Ch'ü-fei 去非, *hao*, Chien-chai 簡齋, 1090-1139) is an excellent and at the same time neglected Sung *shih*** poet. The reason for this neglect appears to be historical rather than literary: the period in which he lived witnessed the fall of all North China to alien invaders and thus has often been characterized as a "dark era" of national humiliation which produced little outstanding poetry. Ironically, it was these very troubled times which inspired Ch'en Yü-i to compose some of the best *shih* poetry of the entire Sung era.

A native of Lo-yang, Ch'en came from an official family, which enjoyed both wealth and reputation. Little is known about his early years except that he was known in Lo-yang as the "poetry genius" (*shih-chün* 詩俊), and had established a reputation as a calligrapher and landscape painter.

After graduating from the National University in 1113, he was appointed to a succession of minor posts in what are now Hopei and Honan. Ch'en's earliest poetry (*chüan* 1-12 in his collected works) dates from this period, (1113-1125). These early works deal mainly with social themes (friendship, parting, echoing rhymes in other poet's works, etc.) and nature (travel poems, descriptions of scenic spots, quatrains for paintings, etc.), and express the dual qualities of quietude and contentment. It was also during this period that the poet met Ko Sheng-chung 葛勝仲 (1072-1144), an accomplished poet and man of fair reputation in the capital. Impressed with Ch'en Yü-i's poetic talents, Ko arranged to have a series of poems by Ch'en shown to Emperor Hui-tsung, himself a great connoisseur and composer of veres. The emperor summoned Ch'en to the capital at Kaifeng for an audience. Shortly thereafter, Ch'en was appointed to a new post in the capital. His future prospects looked bright.

During what may be termed the second period of his life, 1125-1131, two dramatic events took place. First, because of his "association" with a former grand councilor (a new regime had come to power in early 1125), the poet was banished to Ch'en-liu 陳留 just east of Kaifeng. Just one year later, in 1126, North China was attacked and shortly thereafter fell to the invading Chin armies. Ch'en immediately gathered his family together and fled southward. For the next five years he was literally on the run in Central and South China, and at one point was almost captured. It is important to note that his poetry underwent a significant change in subject matter, diction, and tone as a result of this situation: the lackluster verse of leisure and contentment found in his juvenilia now gave way to an emotionally charged poetry which expressed intense feelings of patriotic indignation, moral outrage, hope, and despair (*chüan* 12-29 in his works). This period not only marks the high point of his poetic activity, but also the emergence of his very best poetry.

The final period of his life (1131-1139) found Ch'en Yü-i back in government service, this time at the exiled Sung court based in Hangchow. Unfortunately, his return to official duty also marked the end of his activity as a poet, for two reasons. His administrative duties were very demanding, and his health was rapidly deteriorating, eventually forcing him to retire in April, 1138. "Mu-tan" 牡丹 (Peonies) was one of his very last poems (the I and Lo Rivers were near his home in Lo-yang):

> Ever since Tartar dust entered the China passes,
> Ten years, the road to the I and Lo is endless.
> On the banks of Green Mound Creek, an old and feeble traveler,
> Standing alone in the spring wind, gazing at peonies.

EDITIONS:

Tseng-Kuang chien-chu Chien-chai shih-chi 增廣箋註簡齋詩集. 30 *chüan*. Preface dated 1191. *SPTK; SPPY.*

Hsü-hsi Hsien-sheng p'ing-tien Chien-chai shih-chi 須溪先生評點簡齋詩集. 15 *chüan*. Includes seven poems not found in the *Tseng-kuang* edition and a valuable commentary by Liu Ch'en-weng,* who also was known as Mr. Hsü-hsi 須溪先生. Very rare; copies in the Seikadō Bunko and Kyōto Libraries.

Chiu-ch'ao-pen Chien-chai shih-chi 舊鈔本簡齋詩集. 15 *chüan*. Contains an important supplement collection (*wai-chi* 外集) to Ch'en's *Works* (64 poems in all) and three prose pieces not found in the *Tseng-kuang* and and Liu editions. Rare; copy in the National Central Library in Taipei.

Chien-chai chi 簡齋集, in *SKCS*. 16 *chüan*. Rpt. *TSCC*. Poems arranged according to poetic forms (*fen-t'i* 分體). Marred by errors.

Ch'en Chien-chai shih-chi ho-chiao hui-chu 陳簡齋詩集合校彙注. 30 *chüan*. Cheng Ch'ien 鄭騫, ed. Taipei, 1975. The most complete and best annotated edition. The poet's extant *tz'u* are appended, along with information related to Ch'en's life and poetry. An invaluable *nien-p'u* by Cheng is also included.

TRANSLATIONS:

Demiéville, *Anthologie*, pp. 360-361.
Sunflower, pp. 371-372.
Yoshikawa, *Sung*, pp. 139-143.

STUDIES:

Ch'en, Hsiao-ch'iang 陳曉薔. "Ch'en Chien-chao chi ch'i shih" 陳簡齋及其詩, *Yung-feng*, 4 (June 1958), 34-35.

Ch'en, Tsung-min 陳宗敏. "Chien shu chien-chai shih" 簡述簡齋詩, *Ta-lu tsa-chih*, 29.3 (August 15, 1964), 15-16.

Cheng, Ch'ien. "Ch'en Chien-chai chuan" 陳簡齋傳, *Yu-shih tsa-chih* 38.1 (July 1972), 17-22.

Hargett, James M. "The Life and Poetry of Ch'en Yü-i." Unpublished Ph.D. dissertation, Indiana University, 1982.

—JH

Cheng Chen 鄭珍 (*tzu*, Tzu-yin 子尹, *hao*, Tzu-weng 紫翁 and Wu-ch'ih tao-jen 五尺道人, 1806-1864), poet, scholar, and minor official, was a native of Tsun-i 遵義 (Kweichow). His father and grandfather were both medical practitioners, but Cheng Chen aspired to government service and social status. He was tutored in his youth by a maternal uncle, Li Hsün 黎恂 (1785-1863), whose daughter he later married. In 1825, he was named a Senior Licentiate by the noted scholar-official Ch'eng En-tsi 程恩澤 (1785-1837), after which Cheng Chen went to Hunan with Ch'eng as his personal secretary. Later, he was employed by Li Hsü in Yunnan when the latter held the post of Acting Magistrate. Cheng Chen became a *chü-jen* in 1837, but he later failed the *chin-shih* examination. In need of employment, he petitioned for an official appointment. As a result, he was made an Assistant Instructor. During the next decade, he served in that capacity in several cities in his native province. From his poetry it seems that he and his family enjoyed relatively few amenities of life. While Cheng was working in southern Kweichow, their situation became extremely precarious when the aboriginal Miao tribes rebelled against the government. Other dissident groups—local bandits, Muslim rebels, and the T'ai-p'ing army of Shih Ta-k'ai 石達開 (1821 or 1831-1863)—added to the growing disorder from which he and his family barely escaped with their lives. Cheng was recommended in 1863 for a District Magistracy, but he fell ill and died before he could assume his new duties.

Cheng Chen was a serious and able scholar of wide-ranging interests. With his friend and fellow poet Mo Yu-chih 莫友芝 (1811-1871), he compiled the local gazetteer *Tsun-i fu-chih* 遵義府志, a much admired work. He also wrote a study of sericulture, the *Shu-chien p'u* 樗繭譜, and compiled an anthology of poetry by his fellow townsmen, the *Po-ya* 播雅. As a classical scholar, he authored a number of different books, including studies of the *I-li* and the *Shuo-wen* 說文.

Cheng Chen has been ranked along with Chin Ho* and Huang Tsun-hsien* as one of the representative poets of his time. He belonged to a group of mid-Ch'ing poets who looked to the great T'ang and Sung poets, particularly Tu Fu,* Han Yü,* Su Shih,* and Huang T'ing-chien,* for inspiration. These men placed a high premium on the technical aspects of their craft and were closely allied in their conception of aesthetic values with Weng Fang-kang 翁方綱 (1733-1818). The latter was well known in his time as an exponent of the formal rules and conventions of *shih** poetry, and Cheng Chen manifested a similar concern without falling into imitation of ancient models or a mere mechanical manner. He was aware of that danger, and in a poem addressed to his students he stressed the importance of remaining independent of the past with respect to diction. Critics characterize the poetic styles of Cheng Chen and Mo Yu-chih as being "abstruse and profound," qualities reflecting their scholarly approach to the poetic act.

Cheng Chen was a fairly prolific poet—the *Ch'ao-ching-ch'ao chi* 巢經巢集 (Nesting in the Classics' Nest Collection) contains approximately eight hundred poems—but also a rather flexible one. While it is undoubtedly correct to call attention to the sometimes precise and even rigid formality of his poetic manner, many of his later poems, especially those deriving from the direct experience of war, are less concerned with formal conventional requirements, and more with content and feeling. As a result, his later verse is imbued with a sense of immediacy and observation of the human condition. Particularly noteworthy are the many poems he wrote to record his experiences as a minor government servant and a non-combatant in a time of momentous social disorder and rebellion. These poems, as well as those by Mo Yu-chih reflecting similar circumstances, are historically valuable as eyewitness testimony of the long, drawn-out conflict

that raged between the indigenous tribal minorities and the Han people then migrating into the Kweichow frontier region. In addition to their historical interest, some of these poems also serve to exemplify the greater attention devoted to the long narrative poem by Ch'ing poets. On several different occasions Cheng Chen turned to that form to relate in rich detail his flight from the depredations of rebel and bandit armies. The reportorial manner of these poems stands in clear contrast to the tone of other poems of Cheng's, often much shorter and only secondarily concerned with the narration of events, which gave voice to his criticism of the avarice, brutality, and inhumane behavior of public officials and rebels alike. As a social critic of his times, Cheng Chen invites comparison with other great poets of the past who wrote of social injustice. Cheng Chen was more than a master of the technical aspects of his craft; he was a compassionate observer and critic of his times.

EDITIONS:
Ch'ao-ching-ch'ao chi 巢經巢集. SPPY.

STUDIES:
Ch'ien, Ta-ch'eng 錢大成. "Cheng Tzu-yin shih lun-lüeh" 鄭子尹詩論略, *Kou-ch'uan yüeh-k'an*, 1.2 (April 1935).
DMB, pp. 107-108.

—ws

Cheng Hsieh 鄭燮 (*tzu*, K'o-jou 克柔, *hao*, Pan-ch'iao 板橋, 1693-1765) is one of the famous "Eight Eccentrics of Yang-chou," all of whom were painters in an "unorthodox" style, a style which exhibited more individualism than could be readily accepted in an age that worshiped tradition. While Cheng may not be the most notable painter of this eighteenth-century group, he certainly is the most successful poet and writer.

He was a native of Hsing-hua 興化 (modern Kiangsu), whose travels took him through several provinces in east and north China, including Hopei and the capital, Peking. His journeys gave him the chance to witness firsthand the extremes of abundance and scarcity, of wealth and poverty

243

that existed in eighteenth-century China. He passed the *chin-shih* examination in 1736 and served as magistrate in two counties of what is now Shantung Province from 1742 to 1753, retiring from official life at age sixty. After retirement he was forced to sell his writings and paintings to meet living expenses. Describing himself and his writings, he once wrote that he had done a bit of traveling around the country, a bit of studying, a bit of hobnobbing with brilliant and famous persons, had started out in dire poverty, later become rather wealthy, and still later become rather poor again: "Therefore, you'll find a taste of almost everything in my writings." Throughout his life he seems to have enjoyed spending time with Zen Buddhist masters and disciples, and this may help us to understand three characteristics revealed in his writing: an unrestrained spirit, a lofty disdain for material wealth, and an ever-present sympathy and respect for the poor and the powerless.

Poets of the Ch'ing period usually subscribed to a school of poetry and practiced writing verse in its particular style, such as that of the T'ang or of the Sung period. Wu Wei-yeh* and Wang Shih-chen* (1634-1711) followed the T'ang masters, for example, while Ch'ien Ch'ien-i* imitated the spirit of the great Sung poets. Cheng had little use for any imitative school, although he stated in an autobiographical essay that the verses of Tu Fu,* both regulated and old-style, were worth their weight in gold and that he had studied them all with care. His own poetry, however, belongs to the "inspirational" school, whose ideas were best formulated in the writings of Yüan Mei.* In Cheng's own words: "My poems and prose writings are all forms of self-expression, my own ideas. Their truths are always traceable to the ancients, but their style is always drawn from ordinary usage." In literature as in life he showed concern for the average man—hoping his writings would be comprehensible to all!

The independence of his thinking is well illustrated by his comment, in a letter to his cousin, on the traditional ranking of the main elements of society (scholar-gentry, peasant, artisan, and merchant): "In my opinion, the peasant is number one among mankind, while the scholar-gentry should fall at the bottom of the four classes ... without the peasant, the rest of the world would starve to death. ... The artisan manufactures tools that are useful; the merchant distributes products where they are needed; both perform a service to the people. Only the scholar-gentry constitutes a burden to the people, so is it any wonder that they should be placed at the bottom of the four classes? In fact, they are unworthy of the bottom, even if they should beg for it!"

Many of Cheng's best poems (about five hundred *shih** and more than seventy *tz'u**) are vivid, moving depictions of the "lower" orders of society: the common man in flight from a famine district, the fisherman, tavern keeper, mountain dweller, peasant, monk, poor scholar, and so on. Consistent with this is his well-known love for the lowly bamboo, a favorite subject for his paintings and the odes inscribed on them. His poems on the landscapes encountered in his travels reveal a mellow, almost mystical, identification with the beauties of the natural environment. This mellowness and his profound consciousness of history both serve to complement the impatience revealed in poems and other writings that treat the darker aspects of human society. His famous "Tao ch'ing" 道情 lyrics, ten "expressions of feeling" on subjects that range from praise for fishermen to reflections on the vanity of history, have been taught as songs to children in Chinese schools until recent times.

Cheng's sixteen letters written to his younger cousin Mo have been admired as models of stylistic clarity as well as for the honesty, sincerity, and wholesome family values revealed through them. In them Cheng touches on historical, philosophical, and literary themes and also reveals the day-to-day life of a poor provincial official.

His poetry, prose, calligraphy, and painting are fresh, free-spirited, and unencumbered by unnecessary conventions or allusions. He deserves more serious attention than he has received to date.

EDITIONS:

Cheng Pan-ch'iao chi 鄭板橋集. Peking, 1962.

Cheng Pan-ch'iao ch'üan-chi 鄭板橋全集. Hong Kong, 1975.

Hsiang-chu Cheng Pan-ch'iao ch'üan-chi 詳註鄭板橋全集. Shanghai, 1934. Annotated edition.

TRANSLATIONS:

Lin, Yutang, "Family Letters of a Chinese Poet," in *The Wisdom of China and India*, New York, 1942, pp. 1068-1082. Translations of eleven of the sixteen letters in Cheng's collection.

Sunflower, pp. 487-490.

STUDIES:

Diény, J. P. "Les Lettres familiales de Tcheng Pan-k'iao," in *Mélanges de l'Institut des Hautes Études Chinoises*, Paris, 1960, v. 2, pp. 15-67. The best study and translation of Cheng's "family letters."

DMB, p. 112.

Wang, Chien-sheng 王建生. *Cheng Pan-ch'iao yen-chiu* 鄭板橋研究. Taichung, 1976.

Wang, Huan 王幻. *Cheng Pan-ch'iao p'ing-chuan* 鄭板橋評傳. Taipei, 1968.

—JWW

Cheng Jo-yung 鄭若庸 (*tzu*, Chung-po 中伯 or Chung-po 仲伯, *hao*, Hsü-chou shan-jen 虛舟山人, *c.* 1480-*c.* 1565) was one of the earliest dramatists to be associated with the *K'un-ch'ü* 崑曲 or *Pien-ch'i p'ai* 駢綺派 (K'un-ch'ü or Euphuistic School—see *K'un-ch'ü*). Born in K'un-shan 崑山 (near modern Shanghai) he passed the *hsiu-ts'ai* examinations at age sixteen. But he abandoned an official career and secluded himself at Chih-hsing shan 支硎山 (southwest of modern Wu-hsien 吳縣 in Kiangsu), devoting all his energies to the study of classical literature. He soon became known for his *shih** poetry throughout the region. When his reputation reached Chu Hou-yü 朱厚煜 (d. 1560, Prince Chao-k'ang 趙康王), Chu summoned him to his residence in Honan where Cheng spent twenty-nine years compiling an encyclopedic collection of stories of the unusual, the *Lei chüan* 類雋 (30 *chüan*), and other no longer extant works. He was a court favorite and rejected offers from literary patrons in the capital to join them. The prince rewarded him with numerous palace women and female musicians. When his sponsor died in 1560, Cheng went to live in Ch'ing-yüan 清源 (modern northern Shensi), where he died shortly thereafter.

Yü-chüeh chi 玉玦記 (Broken Jade Ring) in thirty-six acts is his most famous (and only extant) work. Written in 1559 under the influence of Liang Ch'en-yü,* the story begins in the Southern Sung and tells of a certain Wang Shang 王商 from Shantung who is encouraged to go to the national literary examinations in Lin-an by his wife. She gives him a jade ring with a small segment missing to remind him to return home soon (the ring symbolizes their separation). He goes to the capital but fails in the examinations and is too ashamed to return home. He soon finds himself in the home of a courtesan named Li Chüan-nu. As Wang whiles away his days with his paramour at scenic spots such as West Lake, his wife is captured by invading Chin armies. Wang finally places his ring on the sword of a statue in the Kuei-ling 癸靈 Temple as a sign he intends to divorce his wife. But when his money is exhausted, the courtesan abandons him. While he returns to the temple to prepare himself for another attempt at the examinations, Li and her procuress rob and murder a rich customer. Wang's examination is the best and he becomes Metropolitan Governor. In the meantime, his wife has shaved her head and disfigured herself to thwart the intentions of her captors. Wang eventually hears the case against Li Chüan-nu and her procuress, sentencing them for their crime; he also interviews prisoners recently freed by the Chin armies and is thereby reunited with his wife. For her moral behavior, she is ennobled as the Lady of Hsing 邢國夫人.

Although the play was influenced by the T'ang *ch'uan-ch'i** tale "Li Wa chuan" 李娃傳, it is also based on the author's experience. As with many *ch'uan-ch'i** plays, the organization is unclear and confused by numerous and intricate subplots. Cheng's verse sections, while well written, are overburdened with allusions. Several critics have linked these characteristics to Cheng's work on the *Lei chüan*.

EDITIONS:

Yü-chüeh chi, in *Liu-chih*. Based on a Wan-li era (1573-1619) edition.

———, in *Ku-pen*, I, 51. Based on the Fu-ch'un T'ang edition.

———, a Ming, Wan-li edition printed by the Fu-ch'un T'ang 富春堂 in Nanking; now held by the Peking University Library. 4 *chüan*, with illustrations.

STUDIES:

Chao, Ching-shen 趙景深. "Cheng Jo-yung te *Yü-chüeh chi* 鄭若庸的玉玦記, in *Ming Ch'ing Ch'ü-t'an* 明清曲談, Shanghai, 1957, pp. 68-71. Stresses the important biographical sources in addition to providing a discussion of the play.

Fu, *Ch'uan-ch'i*, p. 31. *Major editions of the play.*

—WHN

Cheng Kuang-tsu 鄭光祖 (*tzu*, Te-hui 德輝, *c.* 1260 or earlier-*c.* 1320) was one of the greatest writers of Yüan *tsa-chü* drama. He came from Hsiang-ling 襄陵 in P'ing-yang 平陽 (modern Shansi). Well educated in the Confucian tradition, he gained only a minor post in the local government of Hangchow.

Such was the fame that his plays earned him throughout China, even in the imperial court, that any reference to "Venerable Mr. Cheng" would be recognized by members of the acting profession as meaning Cheng Kuang-tsu. When he died, numerous literati came to his funeral and wrote poems and prose pieces to honor his memory. Chung Ssu-ch'eng, his friend, judged him (in the *Lu kuei pu**) too fond of humor in his plays.

Eighteen plays are attributed to Cheng, of which eight are extant: *Chou-kung she-cheng* 周公攝政 (The Duke of Chou Acts as Regent), *Ch'ien-nü li-hun* 倩女離魂 (The Departed Soul of Ch'ien-nü), *Wang Ts'an teng-lou* 王粲登樓 (Wang Ts'an Ascends The Tower), *Han-lin feng-yüeh* 翰林風月 (A Han-lin Academician's Romance), *P'o lien-huan* 破連環 (Breaking Joined Rings), *San-chan Lü Pu* 三戰呂布 (Thrice Battling Lü Pu), *Lao-chün t'ang* 老君堂 (Old Master Temple), and *I-yin fu T'ang* 伊尹扶湯 (I-yin Assists T'ang). Some of the attributions are to plays written by others, which have the same title as those by Cheng. For instance, *I-yin fu T'ang* is probably an anonymous play of the Yüan-Ming interregnum, and *San-chan Lü Pu*

may be the work of Wu Han-ch'en 武漢臣 (thirteenth century). The attribution of *Lao-chün t'ang* to Cheng is also questionable.

In the stories of extant works and the titles of those lost, a fairly even balance between stern tales of war and government and plays of romantic love and poetry can be seen. The former include plays about male warriors, a doughty female general, a virtuous general who inspired discipline, a tyrannical minister, a man who became a minister in spite of his stiff pride, an empress's loyalty, and a ruler's great fondness for a loyal minister. Two plays were about loyal, selfless regents. Of the romantic plays, three centered on poetry or music and the palace, and two on the love of famous poets for singing-girls. Another concerned a tragedy in which ghosts of drowned lovers obtained revenge. Most famous in later ages have been *Han-lin feng-yüeh*, in which the witty manservant plays a vital matchmaking role, and *Ch'ien-nü li-hun*, a tangled tale of love. In the latter, scholar Wang Wen-chü 王文舉 departs to take the imperial examinations in the capital, and his beloved wife Chang Ch'ien-nü 張倩女 falls ill, missing him so much that her soul follows him to the capital. Wang's letter mentioning that "his wife" is with him, causes great consternation at home, until he eventually returns, and soul and body reunite. This play inspired others, principally the famous *Mu-tan t'ing* 牡丹亭 by T'ang Hsien-tsu.*

One song-suite (a boudoir plaint) and six other stanzas of Cheng's non-dramatic *ch'ü** poetry (on rustic reclusion, drinking, and forlorn love) survive.

EDITIONS:

Ch'ien-nü li-hun, in *Ku-pen*, IV. Mo-wang kuan 脈望館 ed.

———, in *Yüan-ch'ü hsüan.*

Chou-kung she-cheng, in *Ku-pen*, I. Original Yüan ed.

———, in Cheng Ch'ien 鄭騫, *Chiao-ting Yüan-k'an tsa-chü San-shih-chung* 校定元刊雜劇三十種, Taipei, 1962, pp. 349-362. Modern recension.

———, in *Yüan-ch'ü hsüan wai-pei.*

Han-lin feng-yüeh, in *Ku-pen*, IV. Mo-wang kuan ed.

———, in *Yüan-ch'ü hsüan*.

———, in *Hsin-chün ku-chin ming-chü* 新鐫古今名劇, in *Ku-pen*, IV.

I-yin fu T'ang, in *Ku-pen*, IV. Mo-wang kuan ed.

———, in *Yüan-ch'ü hsüan wai-pien*.

Lao-chün t'ang, in *Ku-pen*, IV. Mo-wang kuan ed.

———, in *Yüan-ch'ü hsüan wai-pien*.

P'o lien-huan, in *Ku-pen*, IV. Mo-wang kuan ed.

———, in *Yüan-ch'ü hsüan wai-pien*.

San-chan Lü Pu, in *Ku-pen*, IV. Mo-wang kuan ed.

———, in *Yüan-ch'ü hsüan wai-pien*.

Wang Ts'an teng-lou, in *Ku-pen*, IV. Mo-wang kuan ed.

———, in *Hsin-chün ku-chin ming-chü*, in *Ku-pen*, IV.

Fu Ch'eng-wang Chou-kung she-cheng 輔成王周公攝政, in Cheng Ch'ien 鄭騫, *Chiao-ting Yüan-k'ang tsa-chü san-shih chung* 校定元刊雜劇三十種, Taipei, 1962, pp. 349-364.

Tsui ssu-hsiang Wang Ts'an teng-lou 醉思鄉王粲登樓, *Li Ch'eng T'ang Yi-yin keng Hsin* 立成湯伊尹耕莘, *Chung-li Ch'un chih-yung ting Ch'i* 鍾離春智勇定齊, *Chou mei-hsiang p'ien Han-lin feng-yüeh* 㑳梅香騙翰林風月, *Mi Ch'ing-so Ch'ien-nü li-hun* 迷青瑣倩女離魂, *Hu-lao kuan san-chan Lü Pu* 虎牢關三戰呂布, and *Ch'eng Yao-chin fu-p'i Lao-chün t'ang* 程咬金斧劈老君堂, in *Mai-wang kuan ch'ao-chiao pen ku-chin tsa-chü* 脈望館鈔校本古今雜劇, nos. 33, 34, 35, 36, 37 & 165, *Ku-pen*, IV.

Ch'ien-nü li-hun, *Wang Ts'an teng-lou*, and *Han-lin feng yüeh*, in *Yüan-ch'ü hsüan* 元曲選, compiled by Tsang Mao-hsün 臧懋循 (d. 1621), Peking, 1955, pp. 705-719, 807-826, 1146-1171.

Wang Ts'an teng-lou in *Hsin-chüan ku-chin ming-chü Lei-chiang chi* 新鐫古今名劇酹江集, no. 6, in *Ku-pen*, IV.

Fu Ch'eng-wang Chou-kung she-cheng, Hu-lao kuan san-chan Lü Pu, Chung-li Ch'un chih-yung ting-ch'i, Li Ch'eng T'ang Yi-yin keng Hsin, and *Ch'eng Yao-chin fu-p'i Lao-chün t'ang*, in Sui Shu-sen 隋樹森, *Yüan-ch'ü hsüan wai-pien* 元曲選外編, pp. 458-544.

TRANSLATIONS:

Bazin, Antoine and Pierre Louis Bazin. *Tchao-mei-hiang, ou les intrigues d'une soubrette, co-médie in prose et en vers*. Paris, 1835.

Liu, Jung-en. *The Soul of Ch'ien-nü Leaves Her Body*, in *Six Yüan Plays*, Harmondsworth, England, 1972, pp. 83-113.

STUDIES:

Lo, Chin-t'ang 羅錦堂. *Hsien-ts'un Yüan-jen tsa-chü pen-shih k'ao* 現存元人雜劇本事考. Taipei, 1960, pp. 53-55, 253-260, 339.

T'an Cheng-pi 譚正璧. *Yüan-ch'ü liu ta-chia lüeh-chüan* 元曲六大家略傳. Shanghai, 1955, pp. 267-309.

Yen, Tun-i 嚴敦易. *Yüan-ch'ü chen-i* 元劇斟疑. Shanghai, 1960, pp. 14-21, 91-101, 177-182, 745-751.

—WD

Chi Yün 紀昀 (*tzu*, Hsiao-lan 曉嵐 and Ch'un-fan 春帆, *hao*, Shih-yün 石雲, 1724-1805) was one of the few scholar-officials in Chinese history who were equally successful in orthodox academic pursuits and in writing literature for the masses. Born to a family of local dignitaries in Hsien-hsien 獻縣, Chihli (modern Hopei Province), Chi Yün, through success in the examinations and performance in various positions related to education, was retained by the Ch'ien-lung Emperor (r. 1736-1795) in 1768 to serve in the capital. Later in the year, Chi was involved in a bribery case and was banished to Urumchi 烏魯木齊 (in modern Sinkiang Province). His optimistic attitude toward the exile and his dutiful approach to his obligations there facilitated his recall to normal service. Upon his return to the capital, he was restored to the rank of compiler in the Han-lin Academy. Thereafter, he had a smooth and exceptionally successful career, the preparation of the *Ssu-k'u ch'üan-shu* 四庫全書 (Complete Library of Four Branches of Books) being his greatest achievement.

The *Ssu-k'u ch'üan-shu* project, for all its merits, was part of an imperial attempt to weed out undesirable reading materials and to pacify the intellectuals by consuming energies which might otherwise have been applied for political ends. Most of the books destroyed or expurgated in the process were those considered either offensive to the governing regime or contradictory to orthodox scholarship. The lists of such censored works are formidably long and the *Ssu-k'u ch'üan-shu* itself, the main end product of the project, can be criticized on a number of counts. But on the whole, it has served scholarship well by preserving

247

a large number of works which otherwise would probably not have survived, by making it possible to reconstruct some 360 lost works from the citations in the *Yung-lo ta-tien* before that work itself suffered irreplaceable losses, by providing reasonably well edited copies of the works included, and by promoting the production of a whole range of very useful research aids (a tradition still current today). The project began with the recommendation of the Anhwei education commissioner Chu Yün 朱筠 (1729-1781) to reconstruct lost works from the *Yung-lo ta-tien*. In accepting the proposal, the Ch'ien-lung Emperor issued a decree in early 1772 to assemble in the capital rare books and manuscripts from all parts of the country (most eventually came from Kiangsu and Chekiang). These efforts were soon expanded and formalized to be the *Ssu-k'u ch'üan-shu* project. Chi Yün and Lu Hsi-hsiung 陸錫熊 (1734-1792) were appointed the chief editors. Although this unprecedented project was headed by sixteen directors and associate directors (mostly in name only) and served throughout its course by over four thousand assistants and copyists (including quite a few eminent scholars like Tai Chen 戴震 [1724-1777]), the project was largely designed and executed by Chi Yün and is justifiably identified with him.

The complexity of the work can be seen in the size of the final *Ssu-k'u ch'üan-shu* collection—3,460 works in 79,339 *chüan*—and in the fact that all together eight sets were copied for distribution to different locations for reasons of safety. Moreover, the sets were not exactly identical, because revisions and corrections were made in the later sets. Now only two more or less complete sets are extant. At the outset, even the emperor had little confidence that the project could be completed. Therefore, he ordered a smaller collection of 473 selected works to be made in two sets; known as the *Ssu-k'u ch'üan-shu hui-yao* 四庫全書薈要, only one set is extant today. Yet Chi Yün managed to complete the entire project in just twelve years.

Included in this corpus is the monumental collection of critical comments *Ssu-k'u ch'üan-shu tsung-mu t'i-yao* 四庫全書總目提要 (An Annotated Full List of the Complete Library of Four Branches of Books) in 200 *chüan*. With comments on 10,254 works (almost triple the number of books included in the *Ssu-k'u ch'üan-shu* itself) this serves as a handy review of most of the books available at that time. A significant proportion of these works are no longer extant, and these comments provide some useful information on those lost books. Although many scholars contributed materials, Chi Yün's revisions, judging by available data, were so extensive that it would only be fair to regard this indispensable reference work as basically a reflection of his scholarship. Comments and revisions made by later scholars like Shao I-ch'en 邵懿辰 (1810-1861), Hu Yü-chin 胡玉縉 (d. 1940), and Yü Chia-hsi 余嘉錫 (1883-1955) constitute a set of central references that every serious student of traditional China should have.

Aside from the *Ssu-k'u ch'üan-shu* project, Chi Yün indulged himself in writing fiction and proved a distinguished storyteller and charming stylist. In the decade from his mid-sixties to mid-seventies, Chi Yün brought out five collections of classical-language stories: *Luan-yang hsiao-hsia lu* 灤陽消夏錄 (Spending a Summer on the North Shore of River Luan), 1789, with 299 stories; *Ju-shih wo-wen* 如是我聞 (As the Way I heard Them), 1791, with 267 stories; *Huai-hsi tsa-chih* 槐西雜誌 (Miscellanies of the Huai-hsi Studio), 1792, with 295 stories; *Ku-wang t'ing-chih* 姑妄聽之 (Just Listen To Them), 1793, with 216 stories; and *Luan-yang hsü-lu* 灤陽續錄 (Again on the North Shore of River Luan), 1798, with 141 stories. Together the five collections are known as the *Yüeh-wei ts'ao-t'ang pi-chi* 閱微草堂筆記 (Jottings from the Thatched Abode of Close Observations), the second most important (after P'u Sung-ling's* *Liao-chai chih-i*) story collection of the Ch'ing period.

Both collections were widely imitated but they are as starkly different as their compilers, Chi Yün and P'u Sung-ling. Chi Yün was a member of high society, widely read, with regular contacts with the best scholars of the age, and with easy access to the emperor and other members of the ruling hierarchy. P'u Sung-ling was an impoverished village schoolmaster, with limited scholarly contacts and travel experience. All this is reflected in the differences in viewpoint, scope, and attitude between these two collections. In a sense Chi Yün, writing later, was also under the influence of P'u Sung-ling. But Chi Yün found P'u Sung-ling's mixing of the two different styles and traditions of *pi-chi** and *ch'uan-ch'i** in one collection unacceptable. Accordingly, he took examples from the Six Dynasties period as models in composing his own stories. Although such an approach would seem to be regressive, one may still argue that Chi Yün actually further advanced some of the causes advocated by P'u. *Liao-chai chih-i* is famous for its presentation of ghosts and spirits, mostly female, as virtuous, and human-like. In Chi Yün's stories, many of the ghosts and spirits are not only charming and human-like, they are also superior to humans morally and in many other ways.

Aside from the *Yüeh-wei ts'ao-t'ang pi-chi* and the works, associated with the *Ssu-k'u ch'üan-shu* project, Chi Yün produced little. His other works such as *Shih-t'ung hsüeh-fan* 史通削藩, a condensed version of Liu Chih-chi's 劉知幾 (661-721) *Shih-t'ung* 史通 (Comprehensive History), *Shen-shih ssu-sheng k'ao* 沈氏四聲考, a study on the phonetic theories of Shen Yüeh, and his comments on the *Wen-hsin tiao-lung*, are minor works from this master literatus.

EDITIONS:

Ssu-k'u ch'üan-shu. Since 1969, Taipei's Shang-wu yin shu kuan has been systematically reprinting in installment series the Wen-yüan ko 文淵閣 copy, which is the first of the eight sets made.

Ssu-k'u ch'üan-shu tsung-mu t'i-yao. 10v. Taipei, 1968. The most readily available edition of this superb reference tool—published by I-wen yin-shu kuan. It includes at the end the 1958 revised edition of Yü Chia-hsi's *Ssu-k'u t'i-yao pien-cheng* 四庫提要辨證, a monument of modern scholarship.

Yüeh-wei ts'ao-t'ang pi-chi. 2v. Shanghai, 1980. Collated and punctuated.

TRANSLATIONS:

Maeno, Naoki 前野直彬. *Etsubi sodo hikki* 閲微草堂筆記. Tokyo, 1971. Annotated Japanese translations of 268 selections. Part of Vol. 42 of Heibonsha's *Chūgoku koten bungaku taikei.*

STUDIES:

Ch'en, Yüan. *Ch'en Yüan hsüeh-shu lun-wen chi* 陳垣學術論文集, v. 2, Peking, 1982. A handy collection of nine articles on the *Ssu-k'u ch'üan-shu* project by the eminent historian Ch'en Yüan (1880-1971), who was among the first modern scholars to examine the collection firsthand.

Goodrich, Luther Carrington. *The Literary Inquisition of Ch'ien-lung.* New York, 1966. Reprint of the original 1935 edition, with a lengthy "Addenda and Corrigenda." Outdated but still useful for background information.

Hu, Yü-chin. *Ssu-k'u ch'üan-shu tsung-mu t'i-yao pu-cheng* 四庫全書總目提要補正. Compiled by Wang Hsin-fu 王欣夫. Shanghai, 1964.

Kuo, Po-kung 郭伯恭. *Ssu-k'u ch'üan-shu tsuan-hsiu k'ao* 四庫全書纂修考. Peiping, 1937. Still the best study of the *Ssu-k'u ch'üan-shu* project.

Lai, Fang-ling 賴芳玲. "Ch'ien-t'an Chi Yün te shih-wen kuan" 淺談紀昀的詩文觀, in *Chung-kuo ku-tien wen-hsüeh yen-chiu ts'ung-k'an: San-wen yü lun-p'ing chih pu* 中國古典文學研究叢刊散文與論評之部, Taipei, 1979, pp. 267-281.

———. *Yüeh-wei ts'ao-t'ang pi-chi chung te kuan-nien shih-chieh chi ch'i yüan-liu ying-hsiang* 閱微草堂筆記中的觀念世界及其源流影響. Taipei, 1976.

Lo, Chin-t'ang 盧錦堂 *Chi Yün sheng-p'ing chi ch'i Yüeh-wei ts'ao-t'ang pi-chi* 紀昀生平及其閱微草堂筆記. Taipei, 1974.

Shao, I-ch'en and Shao Chang 邵章. *Tseng-ting Ssu-k'u chien-ming mu-lu piao-chu* 增訂四庫簡明目錄標注, Shanghai, 1959. Chi Yün's *Ssu-k'u ch'üan-shu tsung-mu t'i-yao* should be used together with the works of Yü Chia-hsi (see Editions), Hu Yü-chin, and Shao I-ch'en as one coherent set.

—YWM

Ch'i-chi 齊己 (secular name Hu 胡, *fl.* 881), was a native of Ch'ang-sha 長沙. Orphaned at the age of seven, he found refuge in a Buddhist monastery at Mount Ta Kuei 大溈 in Hunan, where he was first employed as a cowherd. He was precocious, and it is said that he scratched verses on the backs of his cows with a bamboo stick. Eventually he was ordained as a monk and wandered far and wide, traveling on lakes and rivers and visiting sacred mountains and other holy places. His name is particularly associated with Heng Shan 衡山 in the south, and he styled himself "Sramana of Mount Heng." The scenery around Lake Tung-t'ing, especially views of its magic island, Chün Shan 君山, and that along the numinous reaches of the Hsiang River exalted and inspired him. He also spent several years in the vicinity of Ch'ang-an. But his career was centered in and around Chiang-ling 江陵, which early in the tenth century was the capital of a small kingdom called Nan-p'ing 南平 (sometimes known as Ching-nan 荊南) in a prosperous region commanding the river route where the Yangtze flows out of its gorges. Nan-p'ing was noted for its fine damasks, citrus fruits, medicinal herbs, and fish. It was fortunate enough to escape incorporation into the northern domains ruled by the ephemeral Five Dynasties. Its king, Kao Tsung-hui 高從誨 (r. 927-934), welcomed the poetic priest and gave him a position of authority in a monastery, the Lung-hsing ssu 龍興寺. He became the friend of some of the most eminent poets of the age, among them Ts'ao Sung 曹松, Fang Kan 方干, and Cheng Ku 鄭谷. Sun Kuang-hsien 孫光憲 (d. 968), an important official of Nan-p'ing, a notable poet, and author of *Pei-meng so-yen* 北夢瑣言, wrote a preface to Ch'i-chi's collected poems, a book named *Po lien chi* 白蓮集 (The White Lotus Collection). The preface is dated April 3, 938, and in it Sun reports that the talented monk was regarded by his contemporaries as one of the great Buddhist poets, conparable to Kuan-hsiu* and Chiao-jan.* Ch'i-chi's contemporary and fellow-believer Hsi-ch'an 棲蟾 described him as "The Literary Star That Lights Up the Sky of Ch'u." Besides his verses, Ch'i-chi wrote two critical typologies of early poetry, the *Hsüan chi fen pieh yao lan* 玄機分別要覽 and the *Shih-ko* 詩格 *(one chüan* each), neither of which appears to be extant.

The poems themselves are readily classified according to theme. Ch'i-chi wrote frequently about his own experience. He wrote about his close friends, most often Cheng Ku, to whom he addressed many verses in his lifetime and whose death he lamented. He wrote more than once about the great prelate Kuan-hsiu, who was in Nan-p'ing for a period before the height of his career in the court of the King of Shu. The poetry refers repeatedly to Buddhist monks, Taoist recluses, and ghosts and tells of visits to monasteries, highland retreats, sacred mountains, and the homes of deceased worthies. Ch'i-chi was haunted by Lake Tung-t'ing and the watershed of the Hsiang River to the point of obsession. He even took sympathetic note of the ancient deities who presided over these divine waterways. He wrote several poems on the dilapidated site of Chu kung 渚宮 (the Strand Palace), the old Ch'u palace overlooking the Yangtze. He was fond of drinking tea and often wrote about the pleasure it gave him. Nature was dear to him—but he had his preferences. Above all he loved old pines: the image of their gnarled and gnomish forms is constantly present in his verses. Wilting and fallen flowers were ever on his mind. His favorite flowers were the red rose and the white lotus. For him, the roses were not just symbols of transient earthly beauty, but also of blood (as he plainly says in one poem) and so of both life and death. The lotus, on the other hand, represented perfection and purity unknown to this world. Among animals, he gave special attention to flying creatures: butterflies, fireflies, crickets, and birds. Waterbirds in particular fascinated him: cranes, herons, wild geese, kingfishers, and gulls populate the poems. He shows his Buddhist concern for living things in a set of verses telling how he released a captive monkey and a number of caged birds, including a sacred crane. He was entranced by the evanescent forms of water and snow and the phantoms visible in reflections and shadows. He gives due attention to indications of holy power and sacred scenes, objects, and odors—as of sandalwood and incenses. Permeating everything is an atmosphere of transience and fragility, subtly conveyed: the setting sun, the tokens of autumn, the brevity of life. A characteristic poem, distinguished by strange internal sonorities, an untypical meter, and the sextuple presence of the graph for "sun/day" in the first two verses, may serve to illustrate his writing:

"Sun on sun—the sun goes up in the east":
Sun on sun—the sun sinks into the west.
Even though he may be a "Visitor of Divine Transcendence,"
Still, he will turn to rotten bones.
Drifting clouds are snuffed out—but born again;
Fragrant plants will die—then emerge again.
This I do not know: the men of a thousand ages, a myriad ages past,
Buried over there in the blue hills—what things are they now?

In this we see the constant themes of all-conquering time, the vain hopes of the Taoists (Visitors of Divine Transcendence), the resurrection or revitalization of some parts of nature, the unavoidable doom of men—and the question, "are the unnumbered dead alive in other forms, or escaped into nirvana?"

For all of his preoccupation with uncanny atmospheres and spectral apparitions, Ch'i-chi's writing has a quality of equanimity and resignation—of fortitude in tranquility. The stream of time flows by him, and he is fully conscious of mortality—indeed he sees fit to admonish his readers of the implications of this: the motif of *memento mori* is recurrent. But he retains his composure. Inevitably he is skeptical about the possibility of eternal life and the efficacy of theriacs and elixirs. He scorns the seemingly invincible optimism of the Taoists. At the same time, he regards them less as doctrinal enemies than as deluded friends. But once he went so far as to compose a poem which begins: "The Great Tao is a great laugh!"

EDITIONS:

Ch'üan T'ang shih, ch. 838-847, pp. 4855-4923.
Po lien chi 白蓮集. SPTK.

TRANSLATIONS:

Schafer, E. H. *The Divine Woman, Dragon Ladies and Rain Maidens in T'ang Literature.* Berkeley, Los Angeles, and London, 1973, pp. 84-85.

———. *Pacing the Void: T'ang Approaches to the Stars.* Berkeley, Los Angeles, and London, 1977, pp. 155-156.

—ES

Ch'i-lu teng 歧路燈 (A Lamp at the Fork), a novel of some 760,000 words in 108 chapters, was written by Li Hai-kuan 李海觀 (*tzu*, Lü-yüan 綠園, 1707-1790), an obscure Ch'ing official, whose other literary output was insignificant. The number of manuscript copies extant suggests that it was once quite popular, at least in Honan, the native province of the author and the setting of the book. It had, however, never been printed in full until 1980. Luan Hsing 欒星, the editor of the 1980 edition, has provided copious notes to the text. In the preface he includes his judgment that in artistic achievement the novel is on a par with the *Ju-lin wai-shih*,* though it falls short of the *Hung-lou meng.*.*

A *ch'i-lu* is a road that leads astray, probably to perdition; a *teng* is, of course, a lamp, one that will illuminate the peril. The substance of this novel is a squarely didactic tale. The hero, T'an Shao-wen 譚紹聞, is born as the only child to a Honan gentry-family. His father passes away before he reaches manhood, leaving T'an an estate of considerable value, an advantageous contract of marriage, and a will of eight words enjoining him to "study hard and keep to the company of virtuous people." Shao-wen, handsome and bright, shows great promise as a youth. His mother, however, is an illiterate woman of poor judgment who spoils him. Soon he deserts his study, associates with dissolute young men of similar backgrounds, and squanders his inheritance. But when he is quite far gone in ruination, he is stricken by remorse and mends his ways. In the end the family returns to prosperity.

While this summary may sound insipid, the novel is recommended by some merits. One of these is its use of vernacular in the great tradition of *Shui-hu chuan** and *Chin P'ing Mei.** The Honan dialect employed in it gives color to the narrative and vitality to the dialogues. Some of the Honan intellectuals—e.g., Feng Yu-lan 馮友蘭 (b. 1895) and his sister Feng Yüan-chün 馮沅君

([Feng Shu-lan 馮淑蘭] 1902-1975), who championed its first modern printing, the present editor, Luan Hsing, and the novelist Yao Hsüeh-yin 姚雪垠 (b. 1910), who provides a preface—must have felt the appeal quite strongly. Another strength of this novel lies in characterization, where Li Hai-kuan shows considerable talent. Like Wu Ching-tzu, the author of *Ju-lin wai-shih*, he possesses a sharp eye for idiosyncratic traits. Virtuous figures are oftentimes the bane of novelists, but here the several upright friends of the hero's father are presented with pleasing vividness: they are individuals who not only harangue Shao-wen, but also joke with one another, get tipsy, and have matrimonial troubles of their own. And the profligate Sheng Hsi-chiao is an achievement in portraiture not frequently met in traditional Chinese novels, even though in the end one may feel that his total reform at the end of the novel was not adequately prepared for. Several women in the book, such as the hero's gullible and headstrong mother and his histrionic second wife who keeps confusing the stage and the world, are drawn with a fine sense of humor.

However, much as they enhance its readability these saving graces cannot eradicate the basic dullness of the book, which stems ultimately from its superficiality. Its chief shortcoming is grave and obvious: the author simplifies and falsifies life. He offers to prepare young men for the battle of life with a straight tale of virtues rewarded and vices punished. At this juncture, one must disagree with Luan Hsing's judgment that this novel is artistically comparable to *Ju-lin wai-shih*. The latter is clearly superior, if for no other reason than that Wu Ching-tzu shows us how often the virtuous are lonely and discredited and that the one sure reward they can expect to enjoy is their own knowledge that they have tried their best. Li Lü-yüan renders a disservice to the Confucian tradition that he sets out to extol insofar as he heaps wealth and fame upon his hero and family, thereby laying it open to the charges of cupidity and hypocrisy so often leveled against it in the last century.

As a document of its times, *Ch'i-lu teng* is worth reading. It is a realistic depiction of its era.

EDITIONS:

Ch'i-lu teng. Luan Hsing, ed. 3v. Chengchow, 1980. The recommended text. Feng Yu-lan and Feng Yüan-chün only managed to bring out a one-volume modern edition for the first twenty-six chapters in 1927. Before this, the novel had circulated only in manuscripts.

STUDIES:

Ch'i-lu teng lun-ts'ung 歧路燈論叢. A new periodical exclusively for the studies of this novel. The first issue, dated August 1982, has twenty-four articles, most of which were first published in obscure places since the 1920s.

Feng, Yu-lan. "*Ch'i-lu teng* hsü" 歧路燈序, *Hsientai p'ing-lun* 現代評論, 135 (July 1927), 8-14. Also in *Ch'i-lu teng.* Feng Yu-lan and Feng Yüan-chün, ed. Peking, 1927, v. 1, pp. 1-15.

Tung, Tso-pin 董作賓. "Li Lü-yüan chuan-lüeh" 李綠園傳略, in *Ch'i-lu teng* (1927 edition), v. 1, pp. 1-10.

———. "*Ch'i-lu teng* tso-che Li Lü-yüan hsiensheng" 歧路燈作者李綠園先生, in Tung Tso-pin, *P'ing-lu wen-ts'un* 平廬文存, Taipei, 1963, v. 2, pp. 45-47. Also in *Tung Tso-pin hsiensheng ch'üan-chi* 董作賓先生全集, Taipei, 1977, v. 9, pp. 891-903.

—PS

Ch'i-wu Ch'ien 綦毋潛 (*tzu*, Hsiao-t'ung 孝通 or Chi-t'ung 季通, 692-*c.* 749), a native of Ching-nan 荊南 (modern Hupei), was one of the group of minor court poets during the K'ai-yüan period (713-741) of Emperor Hsüan-tsung. He passed the *chin-shih* examination in 726, and became part of the social network of capital poets which clustered around Wang Wei.

Ch'i-wu Ch'ien is noted for his sophisticated, graceful style. His poetry tends to be impersonal and finely crafted. His old-style poem entitled "Ch'un fan Jo-ya hsi" 春泛若耶溪 (Drifting on Jo-ya Stream in Spring) illustrates the relaxed quietude his work can express with a unified sequence of associated images.

Only twenty-six of Ch'i-wu Ch'ien's poems are still extant, and four of these are of dubious attribution. Most are pentasyllabic regulated verse about seeing off colleagues. The remainder take Taoist or Buddhist temples as their subject.

But Ch'i-wu Ch'ien is better known for poems written to him. Wang Wei's* "Sung Ch'i-wu Ch'ien lo-ti huan-hsiang" 送綦毋潛落第還鄉 (Seeing off Ch'i-wu Ch'ien Returning Home Having Failed in the Examinations), Li Ch'i's* "Chi Ch'i-wu San" 寄綦毋三 (Sent to Ch'i-wu Ch'ien), and Wang Wan's 王灣 (*fl.* 722) "K'u Ch'i-wu pu-ch'üeh shih" 哭綦毋補闕詩 (A Lament for Rectifier of Omissions Ch'i-wu) trace Ch'i-wu's career through its several successes and failures.

EDITIONS:

Ch'üan T'ang shih, v. 2, *ch.* 135, pp. 1368-1372.

TRANSLATIONS:

Bynner, *Jade Mountain*, p. 62.

STUDIES:

Owen, *High T'ang*, pp. 58-59.

—MW and SSK

Chia Chih 賈至 (*tzu*, either Yu-chi 幼幾 or Yu-lin 幼鄰, 718-772) has a place in literary history on the basis of his reputation as an author of rescripts, his reformist views on literary practice, and his verse. The son of a prominent literary official, he was a *ming ching* graduate (about 740). His early offices included a Junior Post in the Imperial Library and a Junior Officership in a county in modern Shantung. By the mid-750s, he was a Secretariat Drafter and he held this post again, following a period of political reverses and provincial service, after the accession of Emperor Tai-tsung in 763. His later posts included those of Vice Minister of Rites controlling doctoral examinations in the eastern capital, Vice Minister of War, and, from 770 until his death, Mayor of the capital.

The office of Secretariat Drafter in Charge of Rescripts, which Chia's father had also held, carried the duty of drafting rescripts in the name of the emperor, to provide, in the often cited phrase from the *Lun-yü*, "proper elegance and finish" (*jun se* 潤色) to the emperor's words. Rescript-writing had enormous prestige in the T'ang literary world, for it involved both recognition by the emperor himself of literary skill and a high level of political responsibility. Collections of rescripts by secretariat drafters and rescript-writers circulated widely in literary society and successful rescript-writers, like Chia's father and Chia himself, were often represented or mentioned in the literary subsection of the biographical section of the dynastic history. Chia Chih's documentary style was highly praised; moreover, of a group of scholars later recognized as forerunners of the *Ku-wen yün-tung* (Ancient-style Prose Movement—see *ku-wen*), Chia Chih was the only one who composed rescripts. He was also the only one to receive the coveted canonization of *Wen* 文 (Literary).

Chia had strong views on the literary climate of his day. After the An Lu-shan Rebellion he especially criticized the prestige that literary skill commanded in the *chin-shih* examination. When in 763 there were discussions of the content of the *chin-shih*, he condemned obsession with tonal patterning and euphuistic diction. Elsewhere he emphasized the preeminence of the Confucian canons as models for literary practice and the progressive decline in standards that he, like other reformist critics, held had taken place since the time of Confucius. Since Chia was a friend of one of the most influential of these critics, Tu-ku Chi,* he was later cited with Tu-ku as a forerunner of the much better known, more innovative, and more productive *ku-wen** writers of the next generation, Han Yü* and Liu Tsung-yüan.*

Chia Chih also wrote well-turned regulated verse (see *shih*). During a three-year period of exile at Yüeh-chou 岳州 on Lake Tung-t'ing, the indirect result of his membership, with Tu Fu* and others, in a losing faction at court, he compiled a small anthology, the *Pa-ling shih-chi* 巴陵詩集 (Pa-ling Anthology of Poetry), containing extant poems which express nostalgia for the life of the capital and interest in the company of fellow exiles, as well as impressions of the landscape and river journeys on the Yangtze. Li Po,* as well as Tu Fu and Tu-ku Chi, knew Chia during this period and praised his poetry. Earlier, Chia had composed verses with two other celebrated writers of the period, Wang Wei* and Ts'en Shen.*

Of Chia's original collection of thirty-five *chüan* only three *chüan* of prose, mainly rescripts, and one of verse are now extant, and these owe their survival in almost all cases to their inclusion in the main Sung literary and documentary anthologies. Chia was also a scholar of genealogy, but his work in this field has not survived.

EDITIONS:

Ch'üan T'ang shih, ch. 235, pp. 2591-2599. The poetry.

Ch'üan T'ang wen, ch. 366-368, pp. 4705-4732. The prose.

T'ang-wen shih-i, ch. 22, fol. 12.

STUDIES:

Fu, *Shih-jen*, pp. 171-191: "Chia Chih k'ao" 買至考.

—DLM

Chia I 賈誼 (200-168 B.C.) was a political thinker and poet whose productive years fell during the reign of Emperor Wen (r. 179-157 B.C.) of the Han dynasty. With the support of his patron Chia I was summoned by Emperor Wen and made an Erudite at about age twenty. He so outstripped his older colleagues in discussions of edicts and ordinances that within a year he had advanced to Grand Palace Grandee.

Chia believed that after twenty years of Han rule it was time for the dynasty to make certain changes. These proposed changes reflected the growing currency of the correlative thinking of *wu-hsing* theory in Han Confucianism and were quite similar to ideas successfully advocated a little later by Tung Chung-shu 董仲舒 (176-104 B.C.). The newly enthroned Emperor Wen declined to follow all of the suggestions made by Chia, but certain measures he had suggested were put into effect, and the emperor considered making Chia a high official. When this was opposed by powerful figures in the government, who disparaged Chia I as opportunistic, the emperor drew away from Chia, making him Grand Tutor to the King of Ch'ang-sha. About 175 B.C. Chia was summoned back to court and was soon made Grand Tutor to King Huai of

Liang, the youngest son of Emperor Wen. Several years later King Huai was killed in a riding accident and died without issue; Chia I himself died a year or so later in distress over his failure as a tutor.

As a poet Chia I is best remembered for two *fu*,* one written on the way to Ch'ang-sha, the other after his arrival there. The former is entitled "Tiao Ch'ü Yüan" (Condoling with Ch'ü Yüan). Ch'ang-sha was regarded as a miasmal region, and although recent archaeological finds suggest that the life of the nobility there was not so terribly deprived, Chia I did not expect to survive. Since, in addition, he was being exiled from the court by being sent there, it was natural that upon crossing the Hsiang River he should think of Ch'ü Yüan,* who tradition says drowned himself in the Mi-lo, a tributary of the Hsiang. Significantly, however, Chia's piece advocates withdrawal from the world instead of suicide as the means of dealing with unpropitious times and an unfortunate fate.

The other prose-poem for which Chia I is remembered is his "Fu-niao fu" 鵩鳥賦 (The Owl), which dates from 174 B.C. In this rhapsody an owl, traditionally a bird of evil omen, flies into the poet's room. More philosophical than most early *fu*, the piece uses the presence of the owl to speculate on the mutability of things, especially the transcience of success and the nature of life and death. Filled with Taoist ideas, the *fu* takes the stance that life is nothing to cling to and death nothing to fear.

Chia I's writings on government and political thought are contained in the work that has come down to us as the *Hsin shu* 新書 (New Writings). This title does not have to do with the contents of this book in particular, for it was a term applied by Liu Hsiang* to certain already collated books that he presented to the throne. It is something of an accident that it has been preserved as the title of Chia I's work in particular. One must note that some of the *Hsin shu* sections are also contained in *Han-shu* (see Pan Ku*), and that because there are often considerable differences in the versions, the authenticity of the *Hsin shu* has long been in question. Some have said it is entirely spurious, while others hold it to be genuine. It is probably composed of both spurious and authentic sections.

The content of Chia's political thought is eclectic, but may be called Confucian. Indeed, his writings were entered among those of the Confucian school in the bibliographical treatise of the *Han-shu*. In his philosophy there is a Mencian emphasis on the importance of the people.

EDITIONS:

Liu-ch'ao wen, v. 1, "Ch'üan Han wen" 全漢文, *ch.* 15-16, pp. 208-218.

Chia Ch'ang-sha chi 賈長沙集, *Pai-san*, v. 1, pp. 11-37.

TRANSLATIONS:

Hightower, James R. "Chia Yi's 'Owl Fu,'" *AM*, N.S., 8 (December 1959), 125-130.

Knechtges, David R. "Two Han Dynasty *Fu* on Ch'ü Yüan: Chia I's *Tiao Ch'ü Yüan* and Yang Hsiung's *Fan-sao*," *Parerga*, 1 (1968), 5-16.

Watson, *Rhyme-Prose*, pp. 25-28.

STUDIES:

Bönner, Theodor. "Übersetzung des zweiten Teiles der 24. Biographie Ssu-mà Ts'iens (Kià-i.) Mit Kommentar." Unpublished Ph.D. dissertation, Friedrich Wilhelms Unversity, Berlin, 1908.

Ch'i, Yü-chang 祈玉章. *Chia-tzu t'an-wei* 賈子探微. Taipei, 1969. Contains a bibliography (pp. 99-103).

Chia I chuan-chu 賈誼傳注. Shanghai, 1975.

Chiang, Jun-hsün 汪潤勳 et al. *Chia I yen-chiu* 賈誼研究. Hong Kong, 1958.

Hsiao, Kung-chuan. *A History of Chinese Political Thought*, V. 1: *From the Beginnings to the Sixth Century A.D.*, F. W. Mote, tr., Princeton, 1979, pp. 473-483.

Itō, Tomi 伊藤富雄. "Ka Gi no 'Fukucho no fu' no tachiba" 賈誼の鵩鳥の賦の立場, *Chūgoku bungaku hō*, 13 (October 1960), 1-24.

Kanaya, Osamu 金谷治. "Ka Gi no fu ni tsuite" 賈誼の賦について, *Chūgoku bungaku ho*, 8 (April 1958), 1-25.

Sites, Gordon M. "Chia I of Lo-yang (B.C. 201-168): The Political Thought of a Han Eclectic." Unpublished M.A. thesis, Indiana University, 1975.

Ts'ai, Shang-chih 蔡尚志. "Chia I yen-chiu" 賈誼研究. Unpublished M.A. thesis, Chengchih Ta-hsüeh 政治大學, 1977.

Wang, Chung 汪中 (1745-1794). "Chia I nien-piao" 賈誼年表, in Wang Chung, *Shu hsüeh* 述學, *SPTK*, 3.5b-8a.

—RJC

Chia-ku wen-tzu 甲骨文字, or *pu-tzu* 卜辭 (oracle-bone inscriptions), are the largest body of extant written materials from the late Shang dynasty. Writing was an important element of Shang culture, as several words in the Shang vocabulary reflect. For example, the oracle-bone graph for "book" portrays long, thin slips bound together with a cord, reminiscent of later books formed of bamboo slips fastened with leather thongs. Although no Shang books have been found, text written or incised on pottery, stone, bronze, and, most important, bones and shells have survived the millennia and have been recovered and deciphered in this century.

Shang oracle-bone inscriptions are texts incised or sometimes written with a brush on cattle scapula or turtle shells. With the exception of some record-keeping texts, oracle-bone inscriptions record divinations seeking either the meaning of past events or the course of future events. Some divinations about the past tried to interpret it: "The King dreamed of white cattle, shall there be a disaster?" (S450.3—S refers to the reference book by Shima Kunio cited in the bibliography below). Some sought the cause of problems: "Sick tooth, is Father I causing harm?" (S301.4). The bulk of the divinations attempted to pin down the future: "Shall it rain?" (S169.3), "Shall the western areas receive a harvest?" (S165.2), "Shall we kill ten Ch'iang persons in sacrifice to Ancestor I?" (S3.2), etc.

A full inscription (a rarity) has four parts: (1) the preface: "On Chia-shen [the shell] was cracked and K'o divined:"; (2) the charge: "The Wife Hao will give birth, shall it be a happy event?"; (3) the prognostication: "The King read the cracks saying, 'If the birthing is on Ting, it shall be a happy event. If the birthing is on Keng, it will be hugely auspicious!'"; and (4) the verification: "Three weeks and one day, Chia-yin, the birthing was not a happy event, it was a female" (S138.3). Some texts also include a postface giving the time or place of divination, but most divination inscriptions consist of just the preface and charge. In the first of the five oracle-bone periods, a positive version of the divination is frequently echoed on the other half of the scapula or plastron by a mirror-image negative: "The King shall make a city, shall Ti approve?" "The King shall not make a city, shall Ti approve?" (S43.2)

The oracle-bone texts are generally less than fifteen characters long. Only a very few exceed fifty characters, and texts of thirty characters are unusual. Although the oracle inscriptions were not composed with a literary intent, they often pulse with examples of Shang sensitivity and awareness of language, both in the manner in which characters were constructed and in the way in which they were used in writing. The character for "toothache" shows teeth with a worm in them, a deer in a pit represents "trap," and "kill in sacrifice" shows a person transfixed at the neck by a halberd. Words were used for more than one level of meaning: the king as well as the sun "goes forth" (S67-68), clouds "send down" rain and ancestors "send down" disasters (S178-4), "The King said, 'Yu!'" (S118.2). Some word usages reveal an awareness of metaphor: the image of a singing bird was used when the king divined about a ringing in his ears (S134.1), and in contrast to the plain "female" used when a girl's birth was noted, the use of "happy event" to refer to the birth of a boy speaks clearly of the values of the society as well as a basic skill with metaphor.

Phrases of considerable poetic power enliven the oracle texts, especially in the more spontaneous first period. The tip of a rainbow sips from the Yellow River rather than just touching it (S183.4). A feeling of stretching and experimenting with metaphor apparent in this text is reinforced by the arched, open mouthed serpentine form of the character for "rainbow"; "There is an eating of the moon" (S162.1) is indicative of Shang concern with natural phenomena and of their skilled use of implied simile.

Shang diviners possessed a well-developed ability to narrate a story within the particular constraints of the oracle inscriptions. If plot is understood as a sequence of events which can be followed presented within a definite timeframe, narrative skill is clearly present in the birthing text given above. It is also evident in the following text in which the king's prognostication that the coming week will have some form of disaster is verified as: "On Chia-wei the King chased rhinoceroses. A minor official drove the chariot. The horses hit a rock, overturning the King's chariot. Prince Yang also fell out" (S179.1). In addition to a sequence of events which the reader can easily follow, evidence of a subtle skill with words is shown in hinting at but avoiding direct reference to the king's human fallibility in falling out of the chariot by stating simply that the prince also fell out.

Further demonstrations of Shang facility with linear, historical time in telling of events are present in many other inscriptions. One of the longest oracle texts gives important historical information about interstate conflicts of the time and tells a story at the same time: "On Kuei-ssu [the bone] was cracked and K'o divined: 'Shall the week be without any disaster?' The King looked at the cracks and said, 'There shall be a disaster, there will be a coming of bad news.' Upon the fifth day, Ting-you, there indeed was a coming of bad news, from the west. Chih Hsia told us saying, 'The state of T'u surrounded our eastern area destroying two cities. The state of Kung also encroached on the fields of our western area'" (S307.3). The longest period of elapsed time in a single text is a fragmented illness divination which asks about the course of a person's disease and appears to end with the statement that the person died 170 days later (S13.3).

A problem arises when applying the criterion of meaning to these narratives. The intended audience for the inscriptions remains unclear, and it is uncertain whether the laborious task of recording the inscriptions was performed to keep records of certain divinations and their results, or as a further means of communicating with the oracular powers, or for some other purpose. However, the point of view adopted in Shang narration is clearly identifiable as an ancestor of the detached third-person reporter seen in parts of the *Shang-shu*. Texts report events in a detached manner: the prince also fell, the rainbow sipped from the river, areas were surrounded and cities destroyed. There is neither involvement nor comment on the inscriptions, but they are used to refer only to the king. First-person pronouns are not used to represent a narrative viewpoint. This is demonstrated in texts in which the narrative focuses on the king's actions: "The King twice said, 'Hai!' The King read the cracks and said, 'I shall have disaster. There will be a dream.' On the fifth day, Ting-you, the King hosted the Chung-ting sacrifice. [He] fell on the courtyard steps. In the tenth month" (S178.4). Though the style of interpretative comment on actions seen in a few parts of the *Tso-chuan** and other Chou narrative works was not yet developed, the detached third-person reports of the oracle inscriptions suggest the Shang origins of later Chinese narrative techniques.

Characterizations within any one inscription are flat and static. People appear and act without comment on their actions and without attention given to their thoughts or motivations. Only when several texts concerned with one personage are read as a body do a few individual features and some feeling of a specific human being emerge. The Wife Hao raised and commanded troops against Shang enemies, gave birth to children, went on missions for the king, etc. Wu-ting, king during the first period of the inscriptions, emerges as a person greatly worried about his health, proud of his hunting prowess, desirous of having sons, anxious to obtain help from the spirit-world, continually concerned with crops, enemies, and sacrifices. Detailed information about individuals in the oracle texts is rare. Most people are only a name, and, at that, often a name without an equivalent in modern characters.

The oracle-bone inscriptions were not written with a literary intent, and the greatest part of them contain no features which could claim kinship with literature. Nevertheless, they contain many examples of skilled use of language, and prototypes of some later Chinese literary techniques are scattered throughout them.

BIBLIOGRAPHY:

Ch'en, Meng-chia 陳夢家. *Yin-hsü pu-tz'u tsung-shu* 殷虛卜辭綜述. Peking, 1956. An encyclopedic study of the contents of the oracle bone inscriptions; though slightly dated, it is a useful source on many aspects of the subject.

Keightley, David N. *Sources of Shang History: The Oracle-Bone Inscriptions of Bronze Age China.* Berkeley, 1978. A thorough, English-language introduction to the oracle inscriptions as historical documents; it has a guide for reading original Shang texts.

Li, Hsiao-ting 李孝定. *Chia-ku wen-tzu chi-shih* 甲骨文學集釋. 8v. Nankang, 1965. A concordance of scholarly studies of individual Shang characters; it is helpful for studying specific Shang words.

Shima, Kunio 島邦男. *Inkyo bokuji sōrui* 殷墟卜辭綜類. Tokyo, 1967. A concordance containing most published oracle texts. Arranged under specific Shang characters, it is most helpful in seeing the range of usages of characters and as a handy source of inscriptions.

—SM

Chia Tao 賈島 (*tzu*, Lang-hsien 浪仙, 779-843) was among a group of poets that gathered around Han Yü* in the early ninth century, attracted by Han's advocacy of a literary "restoration of antiquity" (*fu-ku* 復古). Members of this circle, which included Meng Chiao,* Chang Chi,* and Chu Ch'ing-yü 朱慶餘 (b. 791), encouraged each other to experiment in a wide variety of poetic styles, all of which exhibited a self-conscious belief in the moral efficacy of literature and an affirmation of the poet's own role as a protector of traditional values. They sought to achieve poetic "sincerity" by broadening the range of diction, vocabulary, and themes allowable in a poem.

Knowledge about Chia Tao's early life is inexact. He was born in Fan-yang 范陽 (modern Cho County 涿縣 in Hopei, slightly north of Peking). Early in life, he entered a Buddhist order, presumably a Ch'an sect. He left his monastic order around 810 when he met Han Yü in Lo-yang and accompanied him to Ch'ang-an; he remained in Ch'ang-an for most of the latter period of his life.

In the capital Chia Tao successfully established a reputation as a poet but did not meet similar success in his attempt to embark on an official career. He repeatedly failed the *chin-shih* examinations and remained on the fringes of political life. In 837 he was sent to assume a minor post in Sui-chou 遂州 (modern Sui-ning County 遂寧縣 in Szechwan). In 840 he was transferred to P'u-chou 普州, north of Sui-ning, and in 843 was appointed Administrator of the Revenue Section for the same district. He died before he could assume the post. Throughout his life, he maintained close relationships with "poet-priests" (*shih-seng* 詩僧) and other Buddhist adepts and monks.

Chia Tao's poetry shows little stylistic development, and is written in one of two markedly different modes—the discursive or the lyric. His discursive poetry, mostly in old-style forms, praises Confucian virtues and complains about society's rejection of the honest man. Chia's lyric poetry, at which he particularly excelled, is mostly in the five-syllable regulated-verse form (see *shih*). These poems evoke a muted, though powerful, mood through skillfully balanced couplets and judicious use of the colloquial constructions that dominate his discursive poems. Although they may seem to lack overt intellectual content, diffuse Buddhist resonances may often be ascertained. The poem "Nan-chai" 南齋 (Southern Study) is a good example of this mode:

> Alone I lie in the southern study,
> My soul at ease; the scene is also bare.
> There is a mountain which comes onto my pillow,
> But no troubles get into my mind.
> The blinds roll up the moon that hits the bed;
> Screens block the wind from entering the room.
> I wait for spring—spring hasn't arrived yet—
> It ought to be east of the sea-gates.

Such artistic self-consciousness is evident in all his poetry.

He has also been credited with the authorship of a text entitled the *Erh-nan mi-chih* 二南密指, a primer of metaphor for apprentice poets. The body of this work defines certain common poetic images as metaphors for phases in the relationship between ruler and subject. However, the attribution to Chia Tao is uncertain.

Though Chia Tao professed the ideal of writing poems whose plainness reflected universal truths, traditionally his poetry is seen as limited in intellectual and emotional range and too dependent on literary artifice. His poetry was considered overly pessimistic; Su Shih* criticized both Chia Tao and Meng Chiao* in his "Chi Liu Tzu-yü wen" 祭柳子玉文, terming Chia "lean" (瘦) and Meng "cold" (寒), and these epithets have persisted. Chia Tao's attention to detail has been seen as evidence of a petty talent. However, others have praised Chia's technical artistry. Although his poems may lack intellectual depth, they show acute perception of the world and are exhaustive explorations of a particular realm of feeling.

EDITIONS:

Ch'en, Yen-chieh 陳延傑, annotator. *Chia Tao shih-chu* 賈島詩注. Shanghai, 1937.

Ch'ang-chiang chi 長江集. SPPY.

Mao, Chin 毛晉, comp. *T'ang-jen pa-chia-shih* 唐人八家詩. Shanghai, 1926.

TRANSLATIONS:

Demiéville, *Anthologie*, pp. 313-314.

Sunflower, pp. 226-227. Five poems. See also Witzling below.

STUDIES:

Arai, Ken 荒木健. "Ka Tō" 賈島, *Chūgoku bungaku hō*, 10 (1959), 52-95.

Chang, Yu-ming 張友明. *Ch'ang-chiang chi chiao-chu* 長江集校注. M.A. thesis, Kuo-li Shih-fan Ta-hsüeh, Taipei, 1969.

Li, Chia-yen 李嘉言. *Chia Tao nien-p'u* 賈島年譜. Rpt. Taipei, 1974.

Wen, I-to 聞一多. "Chia Tao," in his *T'ang-shih tsa-lun*, included in *Wen I-to ch'üan-chi* 聞一多全集, Shanghai, 1948, v. 3, *ping-chi* 丙集, pp. 37-43.

Witzling, Catherine. "The Poetry of Chia Tao: A Re-Examination of Critical Stereotypes." Unpublished Ph.D. dissertation, Stanford

University, 1980. Contains numerous translations.

—CW

Chiang Chieh 蔣捷 (*tzu*, Sheng-yü 勝欲, *hao*, Chu-shan 竹山, 1245-1310?) was a *tz'u* poet of the Southern Sung. A native of Yang-hsien 陽羨 (modern I-hsing 宜興 in Kiangsu), he obtained the *chin-shih* in 1275. After the fall of the Sung a few years later, he rejected office and took up a life in seclusion.

It is likely that the extant corpus of fewer than one hundred of Chiang Chieh poems constitutes only a small portion of his work. According to *Hao-an lun tz'u* 蒿菴論詞 by Feng Hsü 馮煦 (1843-1927), during the first half of the nineteenth century a group of poets who were emulating Chiang Chieh removed from his collection those poems which they considered badly written.

In addition to an outlook on life that is essentially Buddhist, Chiang Chieh's unflagging concern for the country and the people discloses a patriotic spirit that is genuinely Confucian. These feelings inevitably remind one of many *tz'u** poems by such poets as Yüeh Fei 岳飛 (1103-1141), Lu Yu,* Hsin Ch'i-chi,* and Ch'en Liang,* which, composed during the early years of the Southern Sung, are permeated with a strong sentiment of patriotism. Yet the unrestrained indignation against the foreign intruders and the heroic desire to regain their lost lands so characteristic of these earlier poets are absent in the patriotic poetry of Chiang Chieh. Doubtless partly because of fear of political harassment from the authorities, Chiang Chieh relies heavily on allusions, traditional symbols, and conventional tropes to express his emotions; in one case, he even conceals his emotions in an apparent description of a flower (to the tune "Chieh lien-huan" 解連環, entitled "*Yüeh-yüan mu tan*" 岳園牡丹 (On the Peonies of Yüeh Garden; in *Ch'üan Sung tz'u*, p. 3434).

Such a style, featuring a circuitous mode and a subdued tone, is not characteristic of Chiang's patriotic poetry alone. It also figures prominently in poems that record his personal concerns and accords with the poetry of the Southern Sung period in general, which prefers circumlocution to direct speech and reticence to effusiveness.

Nevertheless, Chiang Chieh's poetry remains distinct from the works of other major poets of the period, especially Shih Ta-tsu 史達祖 (active around the turn of the thirteenth century), Wu Wen-ying,* and Wang I-sun 王沂孫 (d. 1291). First of all, though Chiang Chieh has an unmistakable predilection for language that invites a reading beyond its literal denotation, his style is nonetheless limpid, compared to the abstruseness and obscurity that prevails in other poetry of the time. Metaphorical statements are often set in apposition to their tenors, and abstract discourse placed side by side with its imagistic counterpart, thereby enabling the two to explain, illuminate, and relate to each other in transmitting an intended poetic message. For instance, in the poem written to the tune "Hsiao ch'ung-shan" 小重山 (*Ch'üan Sung tz'u*, p. 3443), a pairing of bright colors with their symbolic idea of flourish and pomp (*fan-hua* 繁華) appears in the first stanza; in the second, which is written apparently in counterpoint to the first, pale and sombre colors are joined with an absence of all flourish and pomp. The vicissitudes of human fortune are thus captured in the larger metaphor of two radically different color systems set in contrast. Second, while other works of the Southern Sung period seem driven by a desire for intricacy of verbal structures and pursuit of nuance, Chiang Chieh's poetry seems spontaneous. Chiang's poetry employs non-allusive, simple literary language copiously. There are even a number of passages characterized by colloquialisms and a style bordering on prose. The third quality that sets Chiang Chieh's poetry apart from poems by other *tz'u* masters of the Southern Sung period is that while in perception, and description of the perception, the other poems of the period are sumptuously furnished with images and metaphors drawn from various realms of human experience and compressed into a single poem, Chiang Chieh's style is one of perceptual and technical economy. A number of poems in his corpus are formed mainly by reduplicated words and word-combinations.

At its best, Chiang Chieh's poetry is a happy medium between extremes. It is sophisticated, but not at the expense of naturalness. It is often simple, but never crude. It can not only be fully appreciated at first reading, but will also survive rereadings. Above all, the sense of unobstructed progression entailed in the reading of a simple and fine poetry like Chiang Chieh's assures an immediate recognition of its inherent rhythmic energy—an effect that is denied many poems by other *tz'u* masters of the Southern Sung period, because of their stylistic intricacy and subtlety.

EDITIONS:
Ch'üan Sung tz'u, v. 5, pp. 3432-3450.

TRANSLATIONS:
Ayling, *Collection*, pp. 187-189.

STUDIES:
Caudlin, *Herald*, pp. 97-99.

—SH

Chiang Ch'un-lin 蔣春霖 (*tzu*, Lu-t'an 鹿潭, 1818-1868) was a leading *tz'u* poet of the Ch'ing dynasty, known for his ability to express personal suffering within the larger context of political and social miseries. He was a native of Chiang-yin 江陰 (Kiangsu). He first worked as a salt administrator in the Huai River district but later lived on small printing jobs. Often in financial distress, he occasionally received help from Tu Wen-lan 杜文瀾 (1815-1881), a contemporary *tz'u* poet and critic. Chiang committed suicide by taking poison.

In his early years, Chiang was known for his *shih** poetry. But when he reached middle age, he burned most of his *shih* and devoted the rest of his life to composing *tz'u*. His choice was obviously the correct one. He later came to be recognized as one of the three greatest *tz'u* poets of the Ch'ing—the other two being Na-lan Hsing-te* and Hsiang Hung-tso.* Like Tu Fu's* *shih* poetry which is often regarded as "a history in *shih*" (*shih-shih* 詩史), Chiang's *tz'u* poetry is known as "a history in *tz'u*" (*tz'u-shih* 詞史). A great number of his *tz'u* depict the aftermath of civil wars of mid-nine-

teenth-century China or reflect the immediacy of other disastrous events, producing images that seem to become part of the larger political history of the period. Yet it is successful because it communicates a poetic world in which the enduring natural world stands in equilibrium with the intensity of human sadness. For instance, in lamenting the government's loss of the two cities Chenkiang and Yangchow to the T'ai-p'ing Army in 1853, Chiang wrote in his "T'a so hsing" 踏莎行: "All night the east wind whirls around the plains choked with weeds;/Pity the sorrow that wells over South and North of the River" (東風一夜轉平蕪／可憐愁滿江南北). Nature indeed became an objective correlative for his personal anguish. In a poem "Yü mei-jen" 虞美人, he sadly compares his ailing body to "a wasted *wu-t'ung* tree, whose every single branch, every single leaf lies in dread of the autumn wind" (病來身似瘦梧桐／覺道一葉怕秋風). This gloomy image seems particularly poignant when one realizes that the poem was written as the allied troops of Britain and France invaded Peking (1860).

Chiang lived in a dynasty during which most *tz'u* poets belonged to either the Che-hsi School* or the Ch'ang-chou School.* He, however, was free from these associations and constantly ranked himself alongside the Southern Sung poet Chiang K'uei.* Yet Chiang's greatness as a *tz'u* poet was defined rather by his strong individualized style, one which was shaped and refined by years of experience and exploration.

EDITIONS:
"Chiang Ch'un-lin Shui-yün-lou tz'u" 蔣春霖 水雲樓詞, in *Chin san-pai nien shih-erh chia tz'u-chi* 近三百年十二家詞輯, Hsia Ching-kuan 夏敬 觀, ed., Lu Chien 盧劍, collector, 1947. Rpt. Taipei, 1960.
Shui-yün-lou shih tz'u kao ho pen 水雲樓詩詞稿合 本, in *Chin-tai Chung-kuo shih-liao ts'ung-k'an* 近代中國史料叢刊, Taipei, 1969. 43 *chi*, v. 429-430.
Shui-yün-lou tz'u 水雲樓詞. Printed with *Na-lan tz'u* 納蘭詞, 1v. Taipei, 1966.
Hsü tz'u-hsüan 續選詞. Cheng Ch'ien 鄭騫, ed. Rpt. Taipei, 1973, pp. 91-102.

TRANSLATIONS:
Sunflower, pp. 499-500.

STUDIES:
Ho, Kuang-chung 賀光中. *Lun Ch'ing-tz'u* 論清
詞. Singapore, 1956, pp. 119-131.
Liu, Tsai-fu 劉載福. "Wan Ch'ing tz'u-jen
Chiang Lu-t'an" 晚清詞人蔣鹿潭, in his *Chung-
kuo li-tai ta tz'u-chia* 中國歷代大詞家, Tainan,
1976, pp. 218-227.

—KIC

Chiang-hsi shih-p'ai 江西詩派 (Kiangsi
School of Poetry) was a group of late
Northern and early Southern Sung dynasty poets, which formed around the great
master Huang T'ing-chien,* himself a native of Kiangsi. The term "Kiangsi School
of Poetry" was not used by Hung and his
immediate followers, but originated with
the poet and critic Lü Pen-chung 呂本中 (*fl.*
119), who wrote the *Chiang-hsi shih-she
tsung-p'ao t'u* 江西詩社宗派圖 (Diagram of the
Kiangsi Poetry Society's Ancestors and
Branches). According to the version recorded in the *T'iao-hsi yü-yin ts'ung-hua** by
Hu-tzu (*fl.* 1147), Lü's work listed twenty-
six authors as belonging to the Kiangsi
School.

In spite of the widespread use of the term
"Kiangsi School" from Southern Sung
times onward, many critics have expressed
doubts concerning the existence of a true
Kiangsi School of Poetry. Although a
number of the poets, including the "founder" Huang T'ing-chien, were from
Kiangsi, approximately half were not, including such important authors as Ch'en
Shih-tao* and Han Chü 韓駒 (d. 1135). The
Southern Sung poet and critic Yang Wan-
li* was already aware of this problem and
answered such objections by noting all the
authors had a similar spirit and, therefore,
their poems were native to Kiangsi.

A more serious problem is that not all
of the Kiangsi School's members considered Huang T'ing-chien their poetic master, some elevating Tu Fu,* Wei Ying-wu,*
or Su Shih* to that status. According to
Liu K'o-chuang,* Han Chü was quite displeased that he had been included in the
group, and we learn elsewhere that Han
claimed the ancients as his masters, not
Huang T'ing-chien.

Probably the most compelling objection
that can be made to the term "Kiangsi
School" is that there are considerable differences in style from one author to the
other, a problem which was already noted
by Yang Wan-li. Yang countered this argument by asserting that in spite of superficial disparities among the poets, their
verse is unified by the same "flavor" or
underlying spirit. The Ch'ing author
Chang T'ai-lai 張泰來 also recognized differing styles among the authors but claimed
they were various manifestations and
transformations of the same basic style. Not
all critics have been convinced by either
of these arguments.

In spite of doubts concerning the very
existence of this School, it must be conceded that there are striking similarities of
approach among most of the authors included in Lü Pen-chung's list and that the
writers are all indebted in varying degrees
to Huang T'ing-chien's poetic theory and
practice. Huang proposed that great poetry was the result of an exhaustive study
and imitation of the ancients, which would
eventually enable the aspiring poet to create his own individual style. Huang himself
applied the alchemical terms *tien-t'ieh
ch'eng-chin* 點鐵成金 (touch iron to trans-
form it into gold) and *tuo-t'ai huan-ku* 奪
胎換骨 (snatch the embryo and change the
bones) to describe the process by which a
poet gradually absorbs and then transforms his earlier poetic tradition.

In spite of the imitative aspects of the
Kiangsi School's literary theory and practice, a number of its poets including Ch'en
Shih-tao and Han Chü were deeply influenced by the Ch'an concept of sudden enlightenment. This may seem paradoxical
at first sight, but these authors obviously
saw a parallel between the Ch'an adept's
studying under various masters until he
obtained his own sudden enlightenment
and the similar process by which a poet
reaches poetic "enlightenment."

The Kiangsi School's literary theory and
practice have been of paramount importance in China ever since the Northern
Sung dynasty. Yen Yü 嚴羽 (*fl.* 1180-1235)
was strongly influenced by the Kiangsi

poets' literary theory in spite of his hostility to the authors' works. The three major poets of the early Southern Sung dynasty, Yang Wan-li, Lu Yu,* and Fan Ch'eng-ta,* all began by imitating poetry of the Kiangsi School, although they eventually rejected the school's labored style (Yang Wan-li burned all his earlier Kiangsi works). Attitudes toward the Kiangsi poets have subsequently varied greatly from critic to critic, some severely condemning the Kiangsi School's imitation of antiquity and others holding the school's approach to be the most valid path to original verse based firmly on a classical foundation.

EDITIONS:

Ch'ao, Ch'ung-chih 晁沖之. *Ch'ao Chü-tz'u hsien-sheng shih-chi* 晁具茨先生詩集. *Hai-shan hsien-kuan ts'ung-shu* 海山仙館叢書. 1846.

Han, Chü 韓駒. *Ling-yang chi* 陵陽集. *Chen-pen, II.* Taipei, 1972.

Huang, Ch'i-fang 黃啟方, ed. *Pei-Sung wen-hsüeh p'i-p'ing tzu-liao hui-pien* 北宋文學批評資料彙編. Taipei, 1978.

Huang T'ing-chien ho Chiang-hsi Shih-p'ai chüan 黃庭堅和江西詩派卷. Peking, 1978. A massive collection of critical materials from the Sung dynasty to Ch'ing times.

Hung, Ch'u 洪芻. *Lao-p'u chi* 老圃集. *Chen-pen, pieh-chi* 別集. Taipei, 1975.

Hung, P'eng 洪朋. *Hung kuei-fu chi* 洪龜父集. *Chen-pen, I.* Taipei, 1961-1963.

Hung, Yen 洪炎. *Hsi-tu chi* 西渡集. *Chen-pen, IX.* Taipei, 1979.

Hsieh, K'e 謝薖. *Hsieh Yu-p'an wen-chi* 謝幼槃文集. *Ts'ung-shu chi-ch'eng* 叢書集成. Shanghai, 1935.

Hsieh, I 謝逸. *Ch'i-t'ang chi* 溪堂集. *Chen-pen, pieh chi.* Taipei, 1972.

Jao, Chieh 饒節. *I-sung shih-chi* 倚松詩集. *Chen-pen, pieh-chi.* Taipei, 1975.

Li, P'ing 李彭. *Jih-she-yüan chi* 日涉園集. *Chen-pen, pieh-chi.* Taipei, 1975.

Lü, Pen-chung. *Tung-lai chih-chi* 東萊詩集. *SPTK.*

T'ung-meng shih-hsün 童蒙詩訓. Kuo, *Sung shih-hua.*

Wang, Chih-fang 王直方. *Wang Chih-fang shih-hua* 王直方詩話, in Kuo, *Sung shih-hua.*

STUDIES:

Bieg, Lutz. *Huang T'ing-chien (1045-1105), Leben und Dichtung.* Darmstadt, 1975.

Gōyama, Kiwamu 合山究. "Ryo Hon-chū no Kōsei shisha shūha zu ni tsuite" 呂本中の

江西詩社宗派圖について, *Kyūshū Chūgoku gak-kai hō*, 16 (1970), 32-48.

Li, Yüan-chen 李元貞. *Huang Shan-ku te shih yü shih-lun* 黃山谷的詩與詩論. Taipei, 1972.

Liu, Ta-chieh 劉大杰. "Huang T'ing-chien te shih-lun" 黃庭堅的詩論, *Wen-hsüeh p'ing-lun*, February 1964, 64-72.

Rickett, Adele. "Method and Intuition: The Poetic Theories of Huang T'ing-chien," in *Chinese Approaches*, pp. 97-119.

Yokoyama, Iseo 橫山伊勢雄. "Chin Shidō no shi to shiron" 陳師道の詩と詩論, *Kambun gakkai kaihō*, 26 (June 1967), 1-15.

———. "Kō Teiken shironkō" 黃庭堅詩論考, *Kokubungaku kambungaku ronsō*, 16 (March 1971), 91-130.

—JDS

Chiang K'uei 姜夔 (*tzu*, Yao-chang 堯章, *hao*, Po-shih tao-jen 白石道人, *c.* 1155-1221) was a major poet, musician, and critic of the Southern Sung period. He was born in Po-yang 鄱陽 (modern Kiangsi), but lived there only until he was about nine or ten years old when his scholar-official father, Chiang O 姜噩, moved the family to Han-yang 漢陽 (modern Hupei). Although his father died several years after the family moved to Han-yang, Chiang continued to stay in that region until the winter of 1186 when Hsiao Te-tsao 蕭德藻, a prominent poet and scholar-official of the time, took him to Hu-chou 湖州 (modern Wu-hsing 吳興 in Chek-iang). For the rest of his life Chiang lived in the lower Yangtze region and particularly in the urban surroundings of Hu-chou, Soochow, Hangchow, and Nanking, the richest cultural areas in the Southern Sung.

Despite his vast learning and varied talents, Chiang never succeeded in getting a place in the bureaucracy. In addition to the income from selling his calligraphy, he had to rely heavily on the patronage of eminent friends living in the cultural centers of the Yangtze delta area. He lived in an age when the life of the scholar-artist-recluse became popular among the educated elite.

Chiang had unusual competence as both a creative artist and a scholar. His original compositions, especially the seventeen *tz'u* songs and the "Yüeh chiu-ko" 越九歌 (Nine

Songs for Yüeh), and his notes on *tz'u* music have become invaluable for the study of Sung music.

Chiang's contribution as a critic lies chiefly in the *Shih-shuo* 詩說 (A Discourse on Poetry) and the *Hsü Shu-p'u* 續書譜 (A Sequel to the *Shu-p'u*), the more general and theoretical of his critical writings. The *Shih-shuo* consists of a long preface and thirty separate statements of varying lengths. It surpasses all previous treatises, known diversely as *shih-ke* 詩格, *shih-shih* 詩式, *shih-hua* 詩話, etc., as a serious, lucid, and relatively comprehensive treatment of the art of poetry writings. It is the most important Southern Sung treatise on poetry before the appearance of Yen Yü's *Ts'ang-lang shih-hua*** and Chang Yen's (1248-*c.* 1320) *Tz'u yüan*. Although the *Hsü Shu-p'u* is ostensibly a sequel to the *Shu-p'u*, written by Sun Kuo-t'ing 孫過庭 (*c.* 648-*c.* 703), it is a self-contained work in which Chiang offers a synthetic review of the art of calligraphy for aspiring artists. The *Hsü Shu-p'u* excels previous calligraphy of the written word as an objective entity and in its rigorous techniques of structural analysis. Both critical works demonstrate Chiang's emphasis on the pragmatic approach to the problem of composition. Moreover, they illustrate his more "academic" attitude in presenting a systematic and objective structure of discourses on the arts. In both aspects Chiang's critical writings exemplifies the new developments in late Sung criticism and aesthetics.

Although Chiang is best known to history as a great *tz'u** writer, his accomplishment in *shih** poetry must not be ignored. When Chiang was a young man, the influence of the Chiang-hsi (i.e., Kiangsi) School of poetry could still be felt. In the preface to his *Shih-chi* 詩集 (Collection of *Shih* Poetry), he said that for several years he modelled himself upon Huang T'ing-chien,* the founder of the Chiang-hsi School. Huang regarded imitation of previous masters and wide foraging for source materials in the writings of the past as the essential principles of composition. Huang's *shih* poetry is characterized by a vigorous energy, skillful use of allusions, and artistry in structure and expression. But Chiang soon reached an impasse in his emulation of Huang; he realized that imitation was stifling and turned his attention to originality and spontaneity. He looked to late T'ang poetry for an aesthetic model. But his early immersion in Huang's works also left a profound impression. The best of his *shih* poetry, the seven-character *lü-shih* and *chüeh-chü* (see *shih*), appears natural and unstilted, but upon closer scrutiny it reveals the poet's refinement, articulate energy, and craft in composition.

Tz'u poetry from the late T'ang to the Northern Sung consists of two distinct traditions: the "delicate restraint" (*wan-yüeh* 婉約) represented by Wen T'ing-yün,* Wei Chuang,* Liu Yung,* and Chou Pang-yen,* and the "heroic abandon" (*hao-fang* 豪放) represented by Su Shih.* In the former tradition, poets use the *tz'u* form to express their feelings and awareness, and strictly observing the intimate relation between music and poetry. Chiang is generally considered to belong to this "orthodox" tradition. As in the words of previous poets this tradition, the themes of love, loneliness, grief over separation, and mutability of life dominate Chiang's *tz'u* poetry. However, Chiang depicts these tender feelings with the vigor he learned from Huang T'ing-chien, creating a new style. Nearly half of his surviving *tz'u* contain prose prefaces, concise pieces of lyrical prose which can stand by themselves as artistic entities. Chiang uses the prefaces to describe the poetic situations which occasioned the powerful feelings presented in the songs. Thus each preface and song complement each other to form an integrated whole. About one third of his *tz'u* songs are cast in the mode of *yung-wu tz'u* 詠物詞 (songs on objects). These are not objective descriptions of objects but lyrical expressions of poet's feelings organized around small objects such as flowers, insects, or plants. His famous "An-hsiang" 暗香 and "Shu-ying" 疏影, two complementary songs on plum blossom, and "Ch'i-t'ien yüeh" 齊天樂 on a cricket are among the best of his *tz'u* poetry. The *yung-wu* songs are characterized by the frequent use of allusions, a dazzling sensory impact, and their abrupt transitions. A few reveal an "objective" structure in which the objects rather than the poet's lyrical self serve as the constitutive elements. This objective structure was further developed by Sung *tz'u* writers of the thirteenth century. Therefore, Chiang had a commanding influence on late Sung *tz'u* poetry.

During the great revival of *tz'u* poetry in the early Ch'ing period, Chiang's influence on the Che-hsi School* of poets represented by Chu I-tsun* was extremely great. The fact that there are more than thirty different editions of Chiang's collected *tz'u* from the Ch'ing dynasty, more than there are of the collected works of any other *tz'u* poet, attests to the popularity and achievement of Chiang K'uei.

EDITIONS:

Chiang Po-shih tz'u pien-nien chien-chiao 姜白石詞編年箋校. Hsia Ch'eng-t'ao 夏承燾, ed. Peking, 1961. This is the authoritative edition of Chiang's *tz'u* arranged chronologically. It contains Hsia's careful collation of all previous editions, some useful notes, an exhaustive collection of comments on Chiang's *tz'u* by previous scholars, a critical discussion of all available editions, and an extensive biographical study.

Chiang Po-shih shih-tz'u 姜白石詩詞. Tu Tzu-chuang 杜子庄, ed. Nanchang, 1981. Selections of the *tz'u* and *shih* with excellent commentary.

Hsü Shu-p'u. TSCC. Standard edition of this critical text on calligraphy.

Po-shih shih-tz'u chi 白石詩詞集. Hsia Ch'eng-t'ao 夏承燾, ed. Peking, 1959. An authoritative edition of Chiang's *shih* and *tz'u* poetry without commentary. Contains Hsia's article on Chiang's musical notation.

Po-shih tz'u chien-chiao chi yen-chiu 白石詞箋校與研究. Lai Ch'iao-pen 賴橋本, ed. Taipei, 1967. Contains a vast amount of useful materials on Chiang's *tz'u* poetry.

TRANSLATIONS:

Demiéville, *Anthologie*, pp. 374, 408-409.

Sunflower, pp. 401-405. See also Lin and Picken below.

STUDIES:

Jao, Tsung-i 饒宗頤 and Chao Tsun-yüeh 趙尊嶽. *Tz'u-hsüeh ts'ung-k'an* 詞學叢刊. Hong Kong, 1958.

Lin, Shuen-fu. *The Transformation of the Chinese Lyrical Tradition: Chiang K'uei and Southern Sung Tz'u Poetry*. Princeton, 1978.

———. "Chiang K'uei's Treatises on Poetry and Calligraphy," in *Theories of the Arts in China*, Susan Bush, ed., Princeton, 1983.

Pao, Ken-ti 包根弟. "Chiang Po-shih tz'u yen-chiu" 姜白石詞研究, *Fu-jen ta-hsüeh jen-wen hsüeh-pao*, 3 (1973), 675-728.

Pian, Rulan Chao. *Sonq Dynasty Musical Sources and Their Interpretation*. Cambridge, 1967.

Picken, Laurence E. R. "Chiang K'uei's Nine Songs for Yüeh," *Musical Quarterly*, 43 (1957), 201-219.

———. "Secular Chinese Songs of the Twelfth Century," *Studia Musicological Academiae Scientiarum Hungaricae*, 8 (1966), 125-172.

Yang, Yin-liu 楊蔭瀏 and Yin Fa-lu 陰法魯. *Sung Chiang Po-shih Ch'uang-tso ko-ch'ü yen-chiu* 宋姜白石創作歌曲研究. Peking, 1957.

—SL

Chiang Shih-ch'üan 蔣士銓 (*tzu*, Hsin-yü 心餘; *hao*, Ch'ing-jung 清容, 1725-1784) is considered the foremost dramatist of the long reign-period of the Ch'ien-lung Emperor (1736-1796) and one of the leading poets of the age. He was educated in the classics by his mother while the family led a rather spartan existence following Chiang's father to a series of minor government appointments. In 1745 the family returned to their home in Nanchang near Lake P'o-yang in Kiangsi. After a year of study Chiang Shih-ch'üan passed the district examinations. In 1747, at the age of twenty-three, he was successful in the provincial *chü-jen* examinations. However, Chiang's first attempt at the *chin-shih* examination the following year was unsuccessful. It was not until 1757 that Chiang finally passed the capital examinations and was assigned compilation tasks in the Han-lin Academy. In 1763, after serving approximately eight years as a minor official, he requested leave from his duties to care for his mother. He returned to government service in 1781 in another minor post, but partial paralysis soon forced his retirement to Nanchang, where he remained until his death in 1784.

It was shortly after Chiang's initial failure in the capital examinations and the death of his father one year later that his career as a dramatist began. Forced to find employment outside official circles, Chiang became an editor for a local history being compiled under the direction of Ku Hsi-ch'ang 顧錫邑, a local official in Nanchang. While in the employ of Ku in 1751, Chiang completed *I-p'ien shih* 一片石 (A Stone Chip), his first drama in four acts, and about the life of Lou Fei 婁妃, a concubine of the rebel Ming prince Chu Ch'en-hao 朱宸濠 (d. 1520). *I-p'ien shih* was the first of five plays he wrote while in Ku's service and one of two plays on Lou Fei. Before his success in the capital examinations, Chiang had earned recognition as a dramatist.

Chiang had attracted the attention of Yüan Mei* some years earlier, and although the two poets did not meet until 1764, they corresponded regularly, exchanging letters and poems. While in the capital Chang wrote one drama, *K'ung-ku hsiang* 空谷香 (A Fragrance in Empty Valley) which is based on the life of Yao Meng-lan 姚夢蘭, the concubine of Chiang's friend Ku Hsi-ch'ang. *Hsiang-tsu lou* 香祖樓 (Tower of Fragrant Ancestors), a piece composed twenty years later, is also about Yao's life.

Following his initial retirement from government service, Chiang moved to Nanking in 1764 and took up residence near Yüan Mei. For over a year Chiang and Yüan met frequently and discussed literary theory. Unlike his highly successful friend, however, Chiang was unable to support his family through his literary production and was forced to travel south to Chekiang where he began a career as an educator. For about nine years Chang directed private academies in Shaohsing, Hangchow, and Yangchow. During this period he wrote five plays, four of which are included in *Ts'ang-yüan chiu-chung ch'ü* 藏園九種曲, a collection of nine of Chiang's most popular plays. *Ssu-hsien ch'iu* 四弦秋 (Four-stringed Autumn), a four-act play dramatizing Po Chü-i's* "P'i-p'a hsing," was completed in 1772 and first performed in Yangchow the following summer. *Hsüeh-chung jen* 雪中人 (In a Snowstorm, 1773) dramatizes an alleged event in the life of Cha Chi-tso 查繼佐 (1601-1676), a scholar-

official who taught in private academies. In 1774 Chiang completed *Hsiang-tsu lou*, the second of two plays about Yao Meng-lan, and although both dramas appear in *Ts'ang-yüan chiu chung ch'ü*, the latter has enjoyed much greater acclaim. Chiang's most famous play, *Lin-ch'uan meng* 臨川夢 (Lin-ch'uan Dream), based on the life of T'ang Hsien-tsu* and his play *Mu-tan t'ing*, was also completed in 1774. T'ang's influence on Chiang can be seen throughout Chiang's dramatic works.

Following the death of his mother in 1775, Chiang observed the traditional mourning. During this nearly three-year period he wrote only *Ti-erh pei* 第二碑 (The Second Tablet), his second play about Lou Fei. Chiang returned to Peking in 1778 to await an appointment as censor but was temporarily made a compiler in the national historiographic bureau in 1781. At this time he completed *Tung-ch'ing shu* 冬青樹 (The Evergreen Tree), a drama in thirty-eight acts depicting the career of the Sung patriot Wen T'ien-hsiang. It is regarded as one of the most important and controversial of his plays, the debate concerning whether the play was written in praise of Wen's loyalty to the Sung or as veiled criticism of the reigning Manchu government.

Chiang Shih-ch'üan was a recognized master of the highly stylized *K'un-ch'ü** drama as well as the more traditional *tsa-chü*.* *Lin-ch'uan meng* is the most critically acclaimed of his *K'un-ch'ü*, while *Ssu-hsien ch'iu* is considered his best piece of writing. In his dramas Chiang adheres closely to the doctrines of T'ang Hsien-tsu and the Wu-chiang School. His dramas are remarkable for the purity and tenderness of their lyrics, a style concordant with his classical poetry. He wrote some two hundred *tz'u* and over twenty-three hundred *shih*, most in the new style (seven-character lines). His poetry was influenced by Yüan Mei.

Yüan, Chiang, and Chao I were known to their contemporaries as the "Three Masters of Chiang-tso." The three poets adhered to Yüan Hung-tao's theory of innate spiritual nature (*hsing-ch'ing* 性情) and emphasized internal inspiration and motivation in the creative processes. Through the proper expression of *hsing-ch'ing*, Chiang Shih-ch'üan believed that the poet's true inner nature would be revealed; without this innate subjective quality, one was doomed only to imitation.

In Chiang Shih-ch'üan's collected works is a cycle of thirty poems openly critical of many of China's leading poets. While Chiang taught that poetry should be progressive and devoid of imitation, in practice his own works fall largely within the realm of tradition and display a range of typical themes.

EDITIONS:

Chung-ya T'ang shih-chi 忠雅堂詩集. Canton, 1817.

Chung-ya T'ang wen-chi 忠雅堂文集. Canton, 1816.

Hung-hsüeh lou chiu-chung ch'ü 紅雪樓九種曲. Taipei, 1971; issued also under title *Chiang Shih-ch'üan chiu-chung ch'ü* 蔣士銓九種曲 or *Ts'ang-yüan chiu-chung ch'ü* 藏園九種曲.

STUDIES:

Chang, Ching 張敬. "Chiang Shih-ch'üan *Ts'ang-yüan chiu-chung ch'ü* hsi-lun" 蔣士銓藏園九種曲析論, *Shu-mu chi-k'an*, 9.1 (June 1975), 3-25.

Chao, Ts'eng-chiu 趙曾玖. "Chiang Ch'ing-jung te chiu-chung ch'ü" 蔣清容的九種曲, in *Wen-hsüeh nien pao: lun-wen fen-lei hui-pien* 文學年報: 論文分類彙編, v. 2, Hong Kong, 1969, pp. 303-310.

Chu, Hsiang 朱湘. "Chiang Shih-Ch'üan" 蔣士銓, in *Chung-kuo wen-hsüeh yen-chiu* 中國文學研究, Cheng Chen-to, ed., rpt. Hong Kong, 1963, pp. 467-488.

ECCP, pp. 141-142.

Fu, *Ch'ing tsa-chü*, pp. 154-158, 366-367.

Tseng, "Ch'ing-tai tsa-chü," pp. 154-157.

Wang, Wen-ju 王文儒. *Ch'ing shih p'ing-chu tu-pen* 清詩評註讀本. Shanghai, 1916. Contains annotated selections from Chiang's *Chung-ya T'ang shih-chi*.

—YPC

Chiang Tsung 江總 (*tzu*, Tsung-ch'ih 總持, 519-594) lived the span of the sixth century and rendered significant service to the three dynasties—Liang, Ch'en, and Sui—of this era. He was a scion of the main branch of the Chiang clan, associated with the K'ao-ch'eng 考城 area of Chi-yang 濟陽 District (modern Honan), which stemmed back ten generations to Chiang T'ung 江統 (d. 310). He was a brilliant youth and enhanced his native precociousness through diligent study. Orphaned at six, he inherited a large family library. At eighteen, he joined the entourage of Ho Ching-jung at the imperial court. There a verse he composed much impressed the emperor. Chiang Tsung was promoted and came to the notice of court literary eminences such as Chang Tsan 張纘, Wang Chün 王筠, and Liu Chih-lin 劉之遴.

Chiang Tsung was soon appointed to serve the crown prince, Hsiao Kang 蕭綱 (503-551). At the crown prince's salon in the Eastern Palace during the 530s and 540s, Chiang Tsung matured in the mainstream of Liang literary activity and participated in the evolution of *kung-t'i** composition. Indeed, after the fall of the Liang and the deaths of Hsiao Kang, Hsü Ch'ih 徐摛 (472-549), Yü Chien-wu 庾肩吾 (*fl.* 520), and others, he survived as one of the major exponents of the style during the second half of the sixth century.

Events might have developed differently. In 548 Chiang was selected to accompany Hsü Ling 徐陵 (507-582) on a mission to renew truce negotiations with Eastern Wei in the North. The threat of war with other Northern factions was intensifying, so he declined the commission, pleading illness. Hsü Ling never returned to the South, and in 549 the Southern capital at Chien-k'ang was sacked. With Emperor Wu murdered and his own patron Hsiao Kang a puppet ruler under a rebel Northern general, Chiang Tsung fled to Kuei-chi 會稽 (modern Kiangsu) in 550, taking refuge in the Buddhist Lung-hua Monastery there (the site of an old Chiang family residence). Here he composed his "Hsiu hsin fu" 修心賦 (Prose-poem on Cultivating the Mind), with a lengthy introduction narrating the circumstances of its composition. Later, he moved to Kuang-chou 廣州 and sought shelter with an uncle, a member of the ruling Hsiao clan, who controlled the area.

By 552, the Northern rebels had been defeated, and Hsiao Kang's seventh brother, Hsiao I 蕭繹, proclaimed himself emperor (Emperor Yüan of the Liang, r. 552-554). Hsiao I summoned Chiang to an appointment at the new capital of Chiang-ling. However, by 554 Chiang-ling had also been sacked by Northern Wei forces, and Chiang did not make the journey. For many years thereafter, he remained in the Ling-nan 嶺南 Mountains.

Finally, in 564 he joined the then eight-year-old Ch'en dynasty, summoned to office at the rebuilt capital at Chien-k'ang. He was drafted into the crown prince's service and again became an intimate of his patron. This favor continued upon the prince's accession to the throne (Ch'en Hou-chu, r. 583-588), and Chiang eventually became premier. But the habits of his youth at the Liang court seem to have cast a heavy shadow, and rather than attending assiduously to national affairs, he spent his time with the emperor in sport and banqueting. The dozen cronies he kept were known as the "Hsia-k'o" 狎客 (The Disrespectful). Critics were not tolerated.

The Ch'en fell in 589, but in the succeeding Sui dynasty Chiang Tsung was given an honorary title. In 594, while in Chiang-tu, he died, at the age of seventy-five.

Chiang's extant literary works typify refined late sixth-century palace-style composition. Like the Liang exponents and earlier Southern poets, he was attracted to the yüeh-fu* tradition, with its themes of parting, hardships of travel, "frontier" sentiments, or the softer, more romantic topics of plum-blossoms, snow, music, and so on. He also successfully addressed the fu* and various literary prose forms, and a considerable quantity of this work survives. His shih* poetry records palace banquets, parting feasts with colleagues, and leisured outings to idyllic scenic locations. His peregrinations among the southern hills are featured in a number of poems describing Buddhist mountain retreats and shrines.

The atmosphere of the salon pervades the poetry—in the elegant, courtly diction, in the finely contrived parallelisms, and in the indications of extempore literary games in the titles of his verses, such terms as ying-chao 應詔 (written to order) and fu te 賦得 (extemporized on a given theme). Chiang often employs the "palace plaint," which in the T'ang came to typify the treatment of courtesan themes and indeed "palace style" in general. He also begins the shift from the pentasyllabic to the septasyllabic line; the direct objectivity of earlier palace-style yung-wu "still-life" treatment also begins to give way to a certain abstraction. His poetry thus represents a pivot between late Six Dynasties and Early T'ang tastes.

EDITIONS:
Chiang Ling-chün chi 江令君集, in Pai-san, v. 13, pp. 3473-3517.
Chiang Tsung chi 江總集, in Liu-ch'ao wen, v. 4, "Ch'üan Sui wen" 全隋文, ch. 10-11, pp. 4068-4078.
Chiang Tsung, in Nan-Pei-ch'ao shih, v. 3, ch. 3, pp. 1677-1703.

TRANSLATIONS:
Demiéville, Anthologie, pp. 165-167.
Frodsham, Anthology, p. 184.

—JM

Chiang Yen 江淹 (tzu, Wen-t'ung 文通, 444-505) is remembered above other poets for his skill in capturing the diction and spirit of his models. Of special note are his fifteen verses in the style of Juan Chi.* Another celebrated set of thirty verses in pentameter form imitates poems by important writers of the Chien-an period (196-220, see Ch'en Lin) and by renowned literati of the Chin and Liu-Sung eras.

Particular features of Chiang's writing are his fascination with the fantastic, the brilliant glitter and color of his imagery, and his unique ability to depict heart-rending sentiment. Such features found a most suitable vehicle for expression in the fu* genre. For both the volume and quality of his compositions, Chiang is remembered as one of the greatest of fu writers. His "Pieh fu" 別賦 (Prose-poem on Parting) and "Hen fu" 恨賦 (Prose-poem on Resentment), both included in the Wen-hsüan,* are widely anthologized.

His official career spanned three of the six southern dynasties: the Liu-Sung, the Southern Ch'i, and the Liang. Through native intelligence and scholarly diligence he rose from provincial obscurity to positions at the imperial court and was eventually elevated to the peerage as Marquis of Li-ling 醴陵侯.

Actually, although his duties had for the most part been more literary than administrative, he exposed himself to personal danger by his fearless political criticism. On one occasion his pen saved him from prolonged imprisonment, and during his life he suffered only one period of rustication, and that was relatively congenial. Chiang himself claimed never to have attached himself to any particular faction, and he appears to have been an isolate—there are few references to him in the biographies of his contemporaries and scarce mention of him in their works.

EDITIONS:

Chiang Li-ling chi 江醴陵集, in Pai-san, v. 11, pp. 2777-2875.

Chiang Wen-t'ung chi 江文通集. SPPY.

Chiang Wen-t'ung chi. Collated appendix compiled by Yeh Shu-lien 葉樹廉 (Ch'ing). SPTK.

Chiang Yen chi 江淹集, Liu-ch'ao wen, v. 3, ch. 33-39, pp. 3140-3178. Punctuated.

"Ch'üan Liang Shih" 全梁文, ch. 5, in Nan-Pei-ch'ao shih, v. 2, pp. 1259-1288. Punctuated.

TRANSLATIONS:

Frankel, Palace Lady, 73-92.

Frodsham, Anthology, p. 174.

———, Murmuring, v. 1, pp. 94, 95.

Holzman, Poetry and Politics, p. 238.

Watson, Rhyme-Prose, pp. 96-101.

STUDIES:

Marney, John. Chiang Yen, Boston, 1981, pp. 444-505.

Mori, Hiroyuki 森博行. Kō En 'Zattai-shi sanjū su' ni tsuite" 江淹「雜體詩三十首」について Chūgoku bungaku hō, 27 (April 1977), 1-35.

Takahashi, Kazumi 高橋和己. "Kō En no Bungaku" 江淹の文學, in Yoshikawa hakase taikyū kinen Chūhoku bungaku ronsyū 吉川博士退休記念, 1968, pp. 253-270.

Toyofuku, Kenji 豊福健二. "Kō Gen no fū," 江淹の賦. Chūgoku chūsei bungaku kenkyū, 7 (August 1968), 55-63.

Wu, P'i-chi 吳丕績. Chiang Yen nien-p'u 江淹年譜. Shanghai, 1938.

—JM

Chiao-fang-chi 教坊記 (Record of the Court Entertainment Bureau) is a short work on the Chiao-fang (Court Entertainment Bureau) established by the T'ang Emperor Hsüan-tsung in 714. It was written by a certain Ts'ui Ling-ch'in 崔令欽 sometime after 762. All that is known of Ts'ui is that he was a minor court functionary and that he also wrote a one-volume annotation to Yü Hsin's* "Ai Chiang-nan fu." The Chiao-fang-chi was originally listed in the bibliography of the Hsin T'ang-shu under the category of musical works (yüeh-lei) in the Classics section (ching-pu). This classification was continued during the Yüan by the compilers of the Sung-shu, but Li Chih 李治 (1192-1279) argued with some indignation that it should not be classed along with works on "classical music" (ya-yüeh). Subsequent bibliographers have shifted it to the hsiao-shuo* category.

The work does indeed treat "vulgar music" (su-yüeh) and other entertainments offered to the T'ang court. The preface to the Record, restored to the text from the Ch'üan T'ang wen,* outlines the circumstances relating to the rather violent split between musical entertainers and classical musicians of the T'ai-ch'ang-ssu 太常寺, the office in charge of ritual music, and the subsequent formation of the Court Entertainment Bureau. This preface is one of twenty-eight separate entries on various aspects of life in the Bureau.

Nineteen of these entries are found in all three of the extant textual traditions, one dating from the Southern Sung, the others from the early and middle Ming (see Chung-kuo ku-tien hsi-ch'ü lun-chu chi-ch'eng edition, pp. 3-6). The other nine have been restored from various sources. Jen Pan-t'ang has grouped the anecdotes into six categories: 1. Ts'ui Ling-ch'in's preface; 2. institutions and human affairs in the Court Entertainment Bureau; 3. miscellaneous song titles; 4. Ta-ch'ü;* 5. sources of [five] song titles; 6. Ts'ui Ling-ch'in's postscript.

The second of these categories is the most important. In it one finds information on the location of the Bureau, the kinds of entertainments performed and clothing worn, anecdotes concerning the emperor or the imperial family, and short accounts of the most skilled actresses. The section on song titles lists the name of the most important songs, and the fifth section gives an account of how some of the titles and playlets came to be named or created. The postscript is a lament over the fall of Hsüan-tsung's court during the An Lu-shan Rebellion.

The work is a short but indispensable source of information not only on entertainments at the royal court of the High T'ang, but also, along with Tuan An-chieh's *Yüeh-fu tsa-lu,** on the foundation and development of musical entertainments and the Court Entertainment Bureau itself.

EDITIONS:

Chiao-fang-chi, 1 *chüan,* in *Chung-kuo ku-tien hsi-ch'ü lun-chu chi-ch'eng* 中國古典戲曲論著集成, v. 1. Peking, 1959. This is the variorum edition of the text, reconciling the three major textual traditions and appending a long list of collated variants between texts. It separates the nineteen shared entries and places the other nine in a supplement.

Chiao-fang-chi chien-ting 教坊記箋訂. Jen Pan-t'ang 任半塘, coll. and annot. 1v. Peking, 1962. A superbly annotated edition that gives complete information on all aspects of the text, drawing on T'ang as well as other contemporaneous texts. Important not only as an annotation of the text, but as a major work in the history of theater.

TRANSLATIONS:

Idema and West, "Preface to the *Record of the Court Entertainment Bureau,*" in *Chinese Theater,* pp. 96-98.

STUDIES:

Jen, *op. cit.*

Kishibe, Shigeo 岸邊成雄. *Tōdai ongakushi teki kenkyū: gakuseihen* 唐代音樂史的研究：樂制篇. Tokyo, 1960-61. Also as *T'ang-tai yin-yeh-shih te yen-chiu,* Liang Tsai-p'ing 梁在平, trans., 2v., Taipei, 1972. While not a study of the *Chiao-fang-chi* per se, it is an invaluable aid to an understanding of the *Record* and makes extensive use of it in discussions of the Court

Entertainment Bureau of the T'ang.

—SW

Chiao-Hung chi 嬌紅記 (Chiao-niang and Fei-hung) is a literati-style love story about seventeen thousand characters long, written in the Yüan period. Since the Ming, Sung Yüan 宋遠 (*fl.* 1280) has been accepted as its author, though some say that Yü Chi 虞集 (1272-1348) or Li Hsü 李詡 may have been the author. It is presumed that Sung Yüan (nom de plume, Mei-t'ung 梅洞) lived during the late Sung and early Yüan period in K'an-ch'uan 淦川 (Kiangsi); other than that, very little is known about his life.

The main theme of this romance is a tragic love affair between a learned young man, Shen Ch'un 申純, and his cousin Wang Chiao-niang 王嬌娘. The girl's parents oppose her love for the young scholar, and when Chiao-niang is forced to marry for her family's convenience she chooses to end her life by fasting. Shen Ch'un follows her in death. Their deaths arouse the sympathy of their families, and their burial mounds are placed side by side.

Chiao-Hung chi is noteworthy in two respects. Though technically influenced by *ch'uan-ch'i* (tale),* it is long for this genre, and it contains more than thirty-three *tz'u* lyrics. The title comes from the the names of Wang Chiao-niang and her mother's maid, Fei-hung 飛紅. This story was often dramatized in the Yüan and Ming periods, and most of these pieces were entitled *Chiao-Hung chi.* In order to distinguish the tale from the dramas, it is often called *Chiao-Hung chuan* 嬌紅傳.

Yüan editions are not extant; the oldest independent version is the *Shen-Wang ch'i-kou yung-lu* Chiao-Hung chi 申王奇遘擁爐 嬌紅記 (published in Fukien during the Wan-li era (1573-1619) by Mr. Cheng's Tsung-wen shu-t'ang 鄭氏宗文書堂, now owned by Itō Sōhei 伊藤漱平. Though it was recorded that many playwrights, including Wang Shih-fu (see *Hsi-hsiang chi*), dramatized this story, the only existing complete editions are the *Chin-t'ung Yü-nü Chiao-Hung chi* 金童玉女嬌紅記 which is a *tsa-chü** written by Liu Tui 劉兌 (*fl.* 1368-1398) in the early Ming and the *Chieh-i yüan-yang chung* Chiao-Hung chi 節義鴛鴦塚嬌紅記, a *nan-hsi** by Meng Ch'eng-shun 孟稱舜 (*fl.* 1629-1649) in the late Ming.

Chiao-Hung chi was popular among the young (alongside *Hsi-hsiang chi*) through the early Ch'ing; but after the appearance of the *Hung-lou meng*,* it fell into oblivion. Cheng Chen-to 鄭振鐸 rediscovered it and introduced it in the *Shih-chieh wen-k'u* 世界文庫, which has allowed this romance to regain some of its former acclaim.

EDITIONS:
"Chiao-Hung chi tsa-chü," in *Shih-chieh wen-k'u,* Cheng Chen-to, ed., v. 3, Shanghai, 1936, pp. 957-984.
Chiao-Hung chuan 嬌紅傳, *ibid.*, pp. 937-957.
Chiao-Hung chuan 嬌紅傳, in *Ming Ch'ing wen-yen hsiao-shuo hsüan* 明清文言小說選. Ch'ang-sha, 1981.
Liu, Tui 劉兌. *Chin-t'ung yü-nü* Chiao-Hung chi, in *Ku-pen*, I, photolithograph of the Ming edition. See Fu, *Ming-tai tsa-chü*, p. 9.
Meng, Ch'eng-shun 孟稱舜. "Chieh-i yüan-yang-chung *Chiao-Hung chi*," in *Ku-pen*, II, photolithograph of late Ming edition. See Fu, *Ming-tai tsa-chü*, p. 339.

TRANSLATIONS:
Itō, Sōhei. *Kyo-Ko-ki* 嬌紅記, in *Chūgoku koten bungaku taikei* 中國古典文學大系, 38 (1973).

STUDIES:
Chao, Ching-shen 趙景深. "*Chiao-Hung chi* yü *Chiao-Hung chuan*" 嬌紅記與嬌紅傳, in *Tu-ch'ü sui-pi* 讀曲隨筆, Shanghai, 1936, pp. 94-99.
Itō, Sōhei. "An Introduction to *Chiao-Hung chi* 嬌紅記," Appendix to the translation of *Chiao-Hung chi*, pp. 462-491.
———. "Formation of the *Chiao-Hung chi*: Its Change and Dissemination," *AA*, 32 (1977), 73-95.

—SI

Chiao-jan 皎然 (secular name, Hsieh Chou 謝晝, *tzu*, Ch'ing-chou 清晝, 730-799) dominated the literary scene on the lower Yangtze in the late eighth century with his versatility as a poet and his adeptness as a conversationalist equally well-read in Buddhist, Confucian, and Taoist thought. But he is best known for provocative literary criticism that reflects the High T'ang Style. A tenth-generation descendant of Hsieh

Ling-yün,* Chiao-jan resolved the traditional conflict between literature and Buddhist quietism by making poetry an intellectual instrument. Born and raised in Ch'ang-ch'eng 長城 (modern Chekiang) he took orders at Ling-yin Temple 靈隱寺 before the An Lu-shan Rebellion, was indoctrinated in *vinaya* teachings, traveled widely to study at monasteries throughout the country, and remained a Buddhist all his life.

His reputation as a poet probably first spread through poems for social entertainment that were composed by several hands and are considered the true beginnings of "linked verse." These were written between 773 and 776 in company with several prominent figures in Hu-chou, including Yen Chen-ch'ing 顏眞卿 (709-785), the noted calligrapher who was then Military Commissioner of the area. It was also in this period that Chiao-jan, Yen Chen-ch'ing, Lu Yü 陸羽, author of the *Ch'a-ching* 茶經 (Classic of Tea, 760), and other associates made a compilation of poetry extracts arranged by rhyme known as the *Yün-hai ching-yüan* 韻海鏡原 (360 *chüan*). In the 770s and early 780s he also exchanged verse with leading contemporary poets and served as a mentor for younger Buddhist poets such as Yüan-hao 元浩 and Ling-ch'e 靈澈 (746-816). Unfortunately, neither the *Yün-hai ching-yüan* nor any of Chiao-jan's apparently quite voluminous philosophical and anecdotal writing dating from this period survives.

In 785 Chiao-jan went into semi-retirement near the city of Wu-hsing 吳興. Immediately thereafter, he was engaged in the writing of his two major critical works, the *Shih-shih* 詩式 and *Shih-p'ing* 詩評, and literary figures continued to find their way to him. Wei Ying-wu wrote: "Vainly his literary fame spreads across the land,/ While his dharma mind remains at peace." It is likely that contact with the poet Meng Chiao* at this time resulted in the influence of Chiao-jan's theory of active reaction to the literary past upon the poetry and prose of the Ancient-style Prose Movement (see *ku-wen*) at the turn of the ninth century. In 793 Yü T'i 于頔 oversaw the compilation of Chiao-jan's complete works (in 10 *chüan*) at the behest of T'ang Emperor Te-tsung and submitted them for imperial preservation.

Although his reputation as a poet was founded largely upon work in regulated verse that grew out of the tradition of Wang Wei and *Ta-li shih tsai-tzu* (see Lu Lun), Chiao-jan was also respected for his old-style verse and literary ballads. His poems often develop the melancholic, *vanitas vanitatum* themes of a Zen Buddhist's perspective on life, unfolding images of tranquil beauty which are then rejected as earthly illusions. Esteem for Chiao-jan's poetry in his own time was considerable. His work was included in a contemporary anthology, the *Nan hsün chi* 南熏集, a collection of thirty poets of the Ta-li period (766-780) edited by Tou Ch'ang 竇常 in the 780s, and in several later T'ang anthologies. In 833 Liu Yü-hsi praised Chiao-jan as the only poet of the lower Yangtze in the late eighth century who truly had depth and range in all styles. Although later critics, most notably Yen Yü in his *Ts'ang-lang shih-hua*,* continued to rank him high among Buddhist poets of the T'ang, only one poem, "Hsün Lu Hung-chien pu yü" 尋陸鴻漸不遇 (Going to Visit Lu Yü but Not Finding Him at Home), remained a common anthology piece and was included in the *T'ang-shih san-pai-shou.**

Of more interest today than any of his other work, however, is the literary criticism of Chiao-jan's *Shih-shih* (5 *chüan*), *Shih-p'ing* (3 *chüan*), and *Shih-i* 詩式 (1 *chüan*). The former two works were probably substantially completed in 785. The *Shih-i* may be a simplification of the *Shih-p'ing* or, what seems more likely, is the series of critical essays Chiao-jan wrote in conjunction with the *Yün-hai ching-yüan* in the mid-770s. All three were well known by the early ninth century. Extracts from the *Shih-i* appear in the *Bunkyō hifuron*,* an anthology of criticism collected by the Japanese monk Kūkai. The five-*chüan* text of the *Shih-shih* in the *Shih-wan chüan lou ts'ung-shu* (1879) must be close to the original, but the numerous passages scattered there that begin with the words "P'ing yüeh" 評曰 probably

only partially represent the full original text of the *Shih-p'ing.*

The *Shih-shih* ranks verse selected from Han to T'ang dynasty poets in five levels of accomplishment according to the degree of mimetic immediacy and transparency of the verse. Chiao-jan follows the earlier critics Chung Jung (see *Shih-p'in*), Shen Yüeh,* Liu Hsieh (see *Wen-hsin tiao-lung*), and Wang Ch'ang-ling* in the quest for poetry that "fully expresses the poet's emotions through his description of scene" (窮情寫物) without the adulteration of allusions, archaisms, or any other literary or historical accoutrements. The progression from *chüan* 1 to *chüan* 5 is from immediacy and effectiveness to some rather dramatic examples of writing that are marred by literary fatuousness and lack of genuine feeling. The "Nineteen Words Concerning Style," introduced in *chüan* 1 and drawn upon for comments on selections in the first three *chüan*, influenced the terminology of later critics such as Ssu-k'ung T'u* and Yen Yü, but also occasionally led to castigation of Chiao-jan as a technical reductivist.

The *Shih-p'ing* consists of interpretive and theoretical expositions on style, literary history, and the nature of poetic creation. Not only in poetic images, but also in writing in general and in the material world we are always dealing, says Chiao-jan, merely with *traces*. What is beyond them or what they effect is more important. Great poetry therefore transcends the traces to lead to enlightenment, and when Chiao-jan talks of "the dharma of poetry" (詩道), he really means something that supersedes Buddhist, Taoist, and Confucian teachings. The poetry of the Chien-an poets, T'ao Ch'ien,* Shen Ch'üan-ch'i,* Sung Chih-wen, Meng Hao-jan,* Wang Wei,* and above all Hsieh Ling-yün* is immediate and reflects personal experience at a specific place and time. Contrary to contemporary opinion, Chiao-jan argues that a good poem does not reject embellishment, parallelism, or intellectual struggle (*k'u-ssu* 苦思), although the end product must *appear* effortless (*tzu-jan* 自然). It is typified by "lines in which the appearance of scenery conveys emotion'' (物色帶情句). Close to Wang Ch'ang-ling's arguments in his *Shih-ko* composed a decade or two earlier, Chiao-jan's literary theory remains the best abstract exposition of the High T'ang Style and was the first extensive statement of the juxtaposition of Zen Buddhism and the arts that became so important in later criticism.

The freshness of both the *Shih-p'ing* and the *Shih-i* arises from Chiao-jan's zest for radical inversions of commonly held opinions. Usually denigrated in the eighth century (and later), the poetry of the Ch'i and Liang dynasties should be recognized, he argues, as the source of much that comprises the High T'ang Style. Furthermore, radical "transformation that sustains continuity'' (*t'ung-pien* 通變) with earlier literature is superior to imitatively "returning to the past" (*fu-ku* 復古) precisely because it alone can breed freshness and immediacy. When Chiao-jan criticizes the use of colloquialisms and literary clichés, he is also attacking the Fu-ku School's infatuation with adaptations from the countryside vernacular in the literary ballad and with archaisms. Yet he simultaneously recognizes the potential for weakness in the new regulated verse, if overpowered by technical and rhetorical considerations. For Chiao-jan, great poets are "geniuses of change" (變之才).

EDITIONS:

Shih-i 詩議, in Konishi Jinichi 小西甚一, *Bunkyō hifuron kō* 文鏡祕府論考, v. 3, Tokyo, 1953. *Shih-i* selections in sections 121-124.

———, in *Bunkyō hifuron* 文鏡祕府論, Kūkai 空海, comp., Chou Wei-te 周維德, ed., Peking, 1975. *Shih-i* material runs from p. 141 ("Huo yüeh . . .") to p. 149; the most readily available text.

Shih-shih 詩式. In *Shih-wan chüan lou ts'ung-shu* 十萬卷樓叢書, Lu Hsin-yüan 陸心源 comp., 1979; rpt. in *PPTSCC*, Taipei, 1968. The only full, five-*chüan* text.

———, in *Li-tai shih-hua* 歷代詩話, Ho Wen-huan 何文煥, comp., 1770; rpt. Taipei, 1974. One *chüan;* the material only reflects the first half of *chüan* 1 of the *Shih-wan chüan lou* text.

———, Ch'ien Chung-lien 錢仲聯, comp. and annot., in *Chung-kuo li-tai wen-tun hsüan* 中國歷代文論選, Kuo Sho-yü 郭紹虞, ed., Peking, 1962. Selections from the first half of *chüan* 1 and the "Fu-ku t'ung-pien" section of *chüan* 5. Other unannotated selections, including material from the *Shih-hsüeh chih-nan* (see below), are appended. Ch'ien Chung-lien's commentary also appeared as an article in *I-lin ts'ung-lu* 藝林叢錄. 5th series. Hong Kong, 1964.

Wu-hsing Chou shang-jen chi 吳興晝上人集. Yü T'i 于頔, comp., 793. *SPTK.* 10 *chüan*. Photo-reprint of a handwritten Sung-dynasty text; complete poetry and prose, exclusive of critical writings.

TRANSLATIONS:

Bodman, Richard. "Poetics and Prosody in Early Medieval China: A Study and Translation of Kūkai's *Bunkyō hifuron*." Unpublished Ph.D. dissertation, Cornell University, 1978. Pp. 404-424 provide translation and notes for *Shih-i* material in sections 121-124 of Kūkai's collection.

Nielson, Thomas P. *The T'ang Poet-Monk Chiao-jan. Occasional Paper No. 3.* Tempe, Arizona, 1972. Includes translation of over thirty poems.

STUDIES:

Ch'en, Hsiao-ch'iang 陳曉薔. "Chiao-jan yü *Shih-shih*" 皎然與詩式, *Tung-hai hsüeh-pao*, 8 (1967), 113-125.

Ichihara, Kōkichi 市原享吉. "Chū Tō shoki ni okeru Kōsa no shisō ni tsuite" 中唐初期にお ける江左の詩僧について, *Tōhō gakuhō*, 28 (1958), 219-248.

Iriya, Yoshitaka 入矢義高, annot. "T'ang Hu-chou Chu-shan Chiao-jan ch'uan" 唐湖州杼 山皎然傳, in *Tōdai no shijin: Sono denki* 唐代 の詩人――その傳記, Ogawa Tamaki 小川環樹, ed., Tokyo, 1975, pp. 625-635. Text, translation, and notes for the Chiao-jan biography by Tsan-ning 贊寧 in the *Sung kao-seng ch'uan* 宋高僧傳 (988), which is also available in the *Taishō shinshū daizōkyō* 大正新修大藏經 (Tokyo, 1924-1932), 50, entry 2061, and is probably based on an epitaph written in 809 by Ling-ch'e and/or Fang Ch'uan-cheng 范傳正.

Konishi, Jinishi 小西甚一. *Bunkyō hifuron kō* 文 鏡祕府論考. I (Kyoto, 1948), pp. 52-55 and II (Tokyo, 1951), pp. 215-233 and 419-434.

Kuo, *P'i-p'ing shih*, pp. 130-132. Good, though polemical, summary of Chiao-jan's critical position.

Tang, Kok-seng (Teng Kuo-ch'eng) 鄧國成. "Chiao-jan te shih-p'ing chi ch'i shih-lun"

皎然的生平及其詩論. Unpublished M.A. thesis, Nanyang University (Singapore), 1979.
　　　　　　　　　　　　—CF

Chiao-se 脚色 (also written 角色) is the collective term for role categories in Chinese theater. Generally speaking, there are three major groups of categories—male roles, female roles, and painted-face roles. The specific terms and their meanings differ through time and between dramatic forms.

The earliest role categories are mentioned in reference to the *Ts'an-chün-hsi* 參軍戲 (Adjutant Play) popular during the T'ang period. These humorous skits were built around a two-man team of knave or rogue and the butt of his jokes, the adjutant. Although the scanty records contradict each other, the knave seems to have been called the *ts'ang-ku* 蒼鶻 (grey hawk), perhaps the forerunner of the later comic-cum-villain, or *ching* 淨, category. Chu Ch'üan,* however, traces the *ching* back to the adjutant role and the *mo* 末, or male lead, to the knave. In later, Sung-period "variety plays" (*tsa-chü**), the *mo-ni* 末泥 (stage director) and the *yin-hsi* 引戲 (play leader), who led on other actors for the farcical skit central to the play, were added. Chu Ch'üan sees the latter as the forerunner of the *tan* 旦 (leading female role). *Yüan-pen** farces included two major roles, the *fu-mo* 副末 (assistant male) and the *ching*, with the *mo-ni* serving to introduce the action.

The three major role categories first appeared together in the fully developed *tsa-chü* plays of the Yüan period. They were designated *mo, tan,* and *ching*. Most had subcategories that were constituted on the basis of either the role's function within the drama (subordinates) or the character of the role itself (serious, comic, conventional, etc.). Subcategories of *mo* were *cheng-mo* 正末 (the male lead); *fu-mo* 副末, *ch'ung-mo* 冲末, and *wai* 外 (the supporting roles); and *po-lao* 索老 (an elderly male). Female subcategories included *cheng-tan* 正旦 (the female lead); *wai-tan* 外旦 (extra female); *t'ieh-tan* 貼旦 (added female); *hua-tan* 花旦 (painted female) or *ch'a-tan* 搽旦 (an unconventional female); and *pu-erh* 卜兒 (an

old woman). The *ching* included several subcategories: *fu-ching* 副淨, *erh-ching* 二淨, and *t'ieh-ching* 貼淨, all of them painted roles that could portray either male or female characters. Yüan role categories distinguished the stage functions of the performers. There was only one singing role in a *tsa-chü* play. A male in the singing role was called the *cheng-mo;* a female, the *cheng-tan.* Consequently the types by these leading role categories may differ from play to play and occasionally even from act to act, from courtesan to queen and from emperor to lowly scout, depending upon which character held the singing role.

In the southern forms and in all other regional types of theater any role category might sing, either solo, in duets, or even in chorus. Simultaneously, the systems of role types diversified, although the tripartite division into males (now termed *sheng* instead of *mo*), females, and villain-comics was preserved. The *sheng* in southern forms were more limited to serious scholars and students than was the equivalent role, the *cheng-mo*, of Yüan *tsa-chü*, with subcategories reserved for dignified elders (*lao-sheng*), stewards (*mo* or *fu-mo*), romantic young men (*kuan-sheng* 官生), young military men (*chi-mao-sheng* 雞毛生 or *chih-wei-sheng* 雉尾生 —so called because of the long feathers worn in their headgear), and the like. *Tan* roles differed with social status and disposition of character portrayed: *tso-tan* 作旦 (active women), *tz'u-sha-tan* 刺殺旦 (assassin women), *kuei-men-tan* 閨門旦 (refined young ladies), *t'ieh-tan* 貼旦 (maidservants), and others.

Role categories in Peking opera are a further development of the southern traditions. Paralleling the division between *wen* 文 (civilian) and *wu* (military) plays are subcategories of role types. Among the *wen-sheng* (civilian literary figures) are *lao-sheng* 老生 (dignified elderly man, sometimes of low status), *hsü-sheng* 鬚生 (bearded statesmen, officials, and scholars), and *shan-tzu-sheng* 扇子生 (young scholars who sing in falsetto and carry a fan). *Wu-sheng* (military men) include *ch'ang-k'ao* 長靠 or *k'ao-pa* 靠把 (high-ranking and dignified generals) and *tuan-ta* 短打 (bandits, swordsmen, and the like). Female roles include the *ch'ing-i-tan* 青衣旦 (the middle-aged woman), *kuei-men tan* 閨門旦 (graceful and refined young ladies), *hua-tan* 花旦 (coquettes and singing girls), *ts'ai-tan* 彩旦 (schemers, match-makers, and the like), and *tao-ma-tan* 刀馬旦 (women who fight from horseback). *Ching* and *ch'ou* 丑 (clowns) are likewise divided between *wen* and *wu* characters.

The above lists are not exhaustive; they are meant to indicate the growing complexity of role categories within the Chinese theatrical tradition and the major groups into which they fall. In the later dramatic traditions role categories may dictate the manner of movement on stage (forceful vs. hesitant), the voice range (high, shifting falsetto, or low), the types of costume ("armor," patched robes, long gowns) and facial makeup, the props utilized (scepters of office, horse whips), and the style of speech (dignified "rounded pronunciation" or racy slang) as well as the more obvious range of theatrical function, social status, moral character, and temperament mentioned above. Role categories do not always indicate the performer's sex and could be played by actors of the opposite gender.

Despite the restrictions of the system, it provided a flexible method of training actors to master a set of symbolized and conventional gestures that could be adapted quickly to different characters in different dramas. It also trained the audience to be receptive to and appreciative of those conventions. At the same time, the system provided a set of norms against which to measure individual variations.

STUDIES:

Ch'i, Ju-shan 齊如山 (1876-1962). "Hsi-chü chiao-se ming-ts'e k'ao" 戲劇脚色名詞考, in *Ch'i Ju-shan ch'üan-chi* 齊如山全集, Taipei, 1964, v. 2, pp. 1-65 (separately paginated).

Crump, J. I. *Chinese Theater in the Days of Kubulai Khan.* Tucson, 1980, pp. 55-56, 188.

Dolby, William. *A History of Chinese Drama.* London, 1976, passim.

Idema and West, *Chinese Theater*, pp. 134-140.

Tseng, Yung-i 曾永義. "Yüan-jen tsa-chü pan-yen" 元人雜劇搬演, *Yu-shih hsüeh-pao*, 45.5 (1977), 21-33, esp. 23-25.

Wang, Kuo-wei 王國維 (1877-1927). "Ku-chü chiao-se" 古劇脚色, in *Sung Yüan hsi-ch'ü shih* 宋元戲曲史, Hong Kong, 1964, pp. 227-246.

—REH

Ch'iao Chi-fu 喬吉甫 (*ming* also but less reliably as Chi 吉, *tzu*, Meng-fu 夢符, *hao*, Sheng-ho weng 笙鶴翁 and Hsing-hsing-tao-jen 惺惺道人, *c.* 1280-1345) was a *tsa-chü** playwright and poet from T'ai-yüan 太原 (modern Shansi), who lived—either generally or later in his life—in Hangchow. Among his poems were a hundred *hsiao-ling* 小令, now lost, on the theme of the West Lake, to which eminent literati of the time payed tribute with their prefaces. Beside being a master literatus, for forty years he led an itinerant life in the entertainment world. Although it was his intention to publish his works, he died before he could do so.

Twelve plays have been attributed to Ch'iao, of which only three, *Yang-chou meng* 揚州夢 (Yangchow Dream), *Chin-ch'ien chi* 金錢記 (Golden Coins), and *Liang-shih yin-yüan* 兩世姻緣 (Marriage in Two Lives), have surviving versions. Some people, however, think that the extant *Chin-ch'ien chi* could belong to Shih Chün-pao 石君寶, a contemporary playwright. *Yang-chou meng* depicts the romance between the famous T'ang poet Tu Mu* and the singing-girl Chang Hao-hao 張好好. There is a subtle interweaving of dream and actual meetings between the two. The hero is a typical infatuated lover who yet, with the help of benign patronage, achieves a successful career. *Chin-ch'ien chi* has a similar hero and a similar plot. In *Liang-shih yin-yüan*, the impecunious scholar Wei Kao 韋皐 loves the courtesan Han Yü-hsiao 韓玉簫. When he goes to take the examinations, she pines to death. Grief-stricken, Wei, who has been made a Grand Marshal, meets a reincarnation of his beloved. There is bitter conflict between the girl's foster-father and Wei, however, including Wei's mounting a siege with his soldiers, before the lovers are miraculously reunited in a wedding.

In the late Yüan or early Ming three collections of Ch'iao's writings existed, entitled *T'ien-feng* 天風 (Heaven's Wind), *Huan-p'ei* 環佩 (Jade Waist-pendants), and

Fu-chang 撫掌 (Hand-claps). These titles are sometimes taken together as only two works. His *san-ch'ü* appeared in further collections: *Hsing-hsing-tao-jen yüeh-fu* 惺惺道人樂府, alternatively found as *Hsing-hsing-lao-jen yüeh-fu* 惺惺老人樂府.

Praised by Ming and later critics for the excellence of his dramatic poetry, Ch'iao has been even more admired for his *san-ch'ü* which were written in a colloquial and original style. As early as the time of Li K'ai-hsien,* his name was paired with Chang K'o-chiu's* for the quantity and quality of their *san-ch'ü*. Ch'iao's extant *san-ch'ü* (eleven *t'ao-shu* and around two hundred stanzas of *hsiao-ling*) outnumber those of any other early *san-ch'ü* poet except Chang. Chu Ch'üan* described his poetry as "a god-turtle drumming the waves" and "the God of the Sea straddling a god-turtle, spouting foam on the great ocean, and waves and billows surging and heaving, slicing through all the might of the currents."

From Ch'iao's *san-ch'ü* we learn of his life and feelings, and they reflect the unconventional, romantic nature of his existence. Many are addressed to singsong girls, some twenty of whom are named. He had a special relationship with Li Ch'u-i 李楚儀 from Yangchow, but their relationship was ended by a powerful mandarin. Ch'iao wrote and presented to her many poems in praise of her (including *shih** and possibly *tz'u**). She had two daughters, T'ung-t'ung 童童 and To-chiao 多嬌; T'ung-t'ung was an excellent *tsa-chü* actress.

EDITIONS:

Chin-ch'ien chi and *Liang-shih yin-yüan*, in *Ku-pen*, IV. The three extant plays are found in various editions in *KPHC*, IV and in *YCH*, pp. 14-31, 794-806, and 971-986.

Hsing-hsing lao-jen yüeh-fu. Li K'ai-hsien,* ed. Woodblock edition dated 1567.

Sui, Shu-sen 隋樹森. *Ch'üan Yüan san-ch'ü* 全元散曲. Peking, 1957, v. 1, pp. 573-647. His *san-ch'ü* lyrics.

T'ang, Kuei-chang 唐圭璋. *Ch'üan Chin Yüan tz'u* 全金元詞. Peking: 1979, p. 92. The *tz'u*.

TRANSLATIONS:

Link, Hans. *Die Geschichte von der Geld Münze*. Bochum, 1978.

STUDIES:

Fu, *Yüan*, pp. 236-241.

T'an, Cheng-pi 譚正璧. *Yüan-ch'ü liu ta-chia lüeh-chuan* 元曲六大家略傳. Shanghai, 1953, pp. 311-340.

—WD

Chien-teng hsin-hua 剪燈新話 (New Stories Written While Trimming the Wick) is a collection which represents the revived interest in *ch'uan-ch'i** fiction in the early Ming after a decline of this type of story in Sung and Yüan times. Its author, Ch'ü Yu 瞿佑 (1341-1427, *tzu*, Tsung-chi 宗吉, *hao*, Ts'un-chai 存齋), was an accomplished poet as well as a parallel-prose stylist who spent most of his life as a schoolteacher. Ch'ü was a productive writer, but most of his works have not survived. His other extant work of significance is the *Kuei-t'ien shih-hua* 歸田詩話 (Talks on Poetry Written in Retirement).

According to the information given in the authorial preface (dated 1378), *Chien-teng hsin-hua* was once much larger than it is today. The extant version containing twenty-two stories in four *chüan* represents only a small portion of the original work. As is typical of earlier *ch'uan-ch'i* stories, most of the pieces treat recent or contemporary events concerning romance, ghosts, and unusual encounters.

At least one of the stories, "Ch'iu-hsiang t'ing chi" 秋香亭記 (The Autumn-scent Pavilion), was regarded by Ch'ü's contemporaries as autobiographical. There are, however, arguments, both past and present, that Ch'ü could not have written or even compiled the work and that it is only a collection of stories drawn from different sources. The question warrants further investigation.

The popularity of the *Chien-teng hsin-hua* in Ming times can be attested to by the two imitation sequences prepared by other Ming writers: *Chien-teng yü-hua* 剪燈餘話 (More Stories Written While Trimming the Wick) by Li Chen 李禎 (1376-1452, *tzu*, Ch'ang-ch'i 昌祺, *hao*, Yün-p'i chu-shih 運甓居士), completed *c.* 1420, with twenty-two stories in five *chüan*, and *Mi-teng yin-hua* 覓燈因話 (Stories Written While Searching for a Lamp) by Shao Ching-chan 邵景詹,

completed in 1592, with eight stories in two *chüan*. Many stories in these three collections were used as sources by Ming playwrights and *hua-pen** writers, notably Ling Meng-ch'u.*

These collections declined into obscurity during the Ch'ing period partly because of the censorship caused by the suggestive amorous scenes. However, they became exceptionally influential in Korea and Japan, particularly *Chien-teng hsin-hua*. Imitations can be found in Kin Si-sup's 金時習 (1435-1493) *Kum-o sin-hua* 金鰲新話, Asai Ryōi's 淺井了意 (1612-1619) *Togibōko* 伽婢子 (1666), and Ueda Akinari's 上田秋成 (1734-1809) *Ugetsu Monogatari* 雨月物語 (1768).

EDITIONS:

Chou, I 周夷. *Chien-teng hsin-hua (wai erh-chung)* 剪燈新語（外二種）. Shanghai, 1957. This collated and profusely annotated volume of *Chien-teng hsin-hua, Chien-teng yü-hua*, and *Mi-teng yin-hua* is by far the best edition and it is easily available in the original edition and later reprints.

TRANSLATIONS:

Bauer, Wolfgang and Herbert Franke. *Die goldene Truhe.* Munich, 1959.

Levenson, Christopher. *The Golden Casket: Chinese Novelles of Two Millennia.* New York, 1964, pp. 214-301. English-language version of *Die goldene Truhe.*

Iitsuka, Akira 飯塚朗. *Sentō shinwa Sentō yowa* 剪燈新話 剪燈餘話. Tokyo, 1969. Complete, annotated Japanese translations of these two collections, along with the translations of two other works, from v. 39 of Heibonsha's *Chūgoku koten bungaku taikei.*

Kroll, Paul W. "The Golden Phoenix Hairpin," in *Traditional Chinese Stories*, Y. W. Ma and Joseph S. M. Lau, eds., New York, 1978, pp. 400-403. Translation of "Chin feng-ch'ai chi" 金鳳釵記.

STUDIES:

Chao, Ching-shen 趙景深. "*Chien-teng* erh-chung" 剪燈二種, *Wen-hsüeh*, 3.1 (July 1934), 389-394. Also in Chao Ching-shen, *Chung-kuo hsiao-shou ts'ung-k'ao* 中國小說叢考, Tainan, 1980, pp. 408-417.

"Ch'ü Yu," *DMB*, pp. 405-408.

Franke, Herbert. "Eine Novellensammlung der frühen Ming-Zeit: Das *Chien-teng hsin-hua* des Ch'ü Yu," *ZDMG*, 108.2 (1958), 338-383. Includes a German translation of the *Chien-teng hsin-hua.*

———. "Zur Novellistik der frühen Ming-Zeit: Das *Chien-teng yü-hua* des Li Ch'ang-ch'i," *ZDMG*, 109.2 (1959), 340-401. Includes a German translation of the *Chien-teng yü-hua.*

———. "Eine chinesische Novellensammlung des späten 16. Jahrhunderts: Das *Mi-teng yin-hua*," *ZDMG*, 110.2 (1960), 401-421.

Kuwa, Tokuji 久和得二. "*Sento shinwa to Tōyō kindai bungaku ni oyoboseru eikyō*" 剪燈新話と東卅東洋近代文學に及ぼせる影響, *Taihoku teikoku daigaku bunsiegakubu bungakuka kenkyū nempō*, 1 (May 1934), 1-134. A substantially detailed study of the impact of the *Chien-teng hsin-hua* in Japan.

"Li Chen," *DMB*, pp. 805-807.

Tai, Pu-fan 戴不凡. "*Chien-teng*" 剪燈. *Chung-yang jih-pao* (Shanghai) (*Su wen-hsüeh*, 86), 26 Oct. 1948. Also under title of "*Chien-teng hsin-hua* te tso-che" 剪燈新話的作者 in Tai Pu-fan, *Hsiao-shuo chien-wen lu* 小說見聞錄. Hangchow, 1980, pp. 240-241.

Wan, Hsin 溫辛 (Yeh Te-chün 葉德均). "Kuan-yü Li Chen te shih-liao" 關於李禎的史料. *Hsing-tao jih-pao* (*Su wen-hsüeh*, 13), 29 March 1941.

Wang, Shu-ch'eng 王淑琤. "*Chien-teng* san-chung k'ao-hsi" 剪燈三種考析. Unpublished Ph.D. dissertation, National Taiwan University, 1982.

—YWM

Ch'ien Ch'i 錢起 (*tzu*, Chung-wen 仲文, c. 722-c. 780) was the most celebrated figure in the group of poets known as the "Ta-li shih ts'ai-tzu" (see Lu Lun). He was a native of Wu-hsing 吳興 (modern Chekiang). Very little is known of his early years, since his fame and the vast majority of his works postdate the outbreak of the An Lu-shan Rebellion in 755. He passed the *chin-shih* examination in 750 or 751 and lived most of his adult life near Ch'ang-an, first as a minor official in Lan-t'ien 藍田, rising within the central bureaucracy to the post of Director of the Bureau of Evaluations. More than four hundred of his poems are extant.

Ch'ien was generally considered the poetic successor to Wang Wei.* His relationship with the older writer probably began during his tenure in Lan-t'ien, where Wang Wei's famous Wang River estate was situated. Ch'ien Ch'i's twenty-two poems on Lan-t'ien Creek, which explicitly imitate Wang Wei's "Wang River Sequence," are especially well-known. Although Ch'ien Ch'i was the most popular poet in capital society after Wang Wei's death, his reputation has not fared well. Indeed, his connection with Wang Wei may actually have worked against him in the eyes of later critics: many of Ch'ien's works invite comparison with Wang's, and as regards Buddhist themes, for instance, Ch'ien's works lack the profundity and intellect which animates Wang's poems.

Ch'ien was a poetic craftsman who continued to write in a style hearkening back to the court and the nature poetry of the High T'ang; the lack of distinguishing individual characteristics is probably what led to his lowered reputation. Thus, later critics often singled out couplets for admiration. but he was never regarded as a major poet. Nonetheless, his mastery at imagistic evocation of a scene, as in "Sheng shih: Hsiang-ling ku-se" 省試湘靈鼓瑟 (Examination Poem: Drum and Zither of the Hsiang River Spirits), one of the most famous examples of the examination poem genre, shows him to be a poet of formidable descriptive powers.

Ch'ien's name was often linked with that of Lang Shih-yüan 郎士元 (tzu, Chün-chou 君冑), especially as writers of occasional social poetry. In reading these works, one must remember that they were written for an audience that, despite greatly altered political conditions, retained tastes cultivated during the preceding reign of Emperor Hsüan-tsung. Ch'ien was above all fully conscious of his role as a master of the style of the occasional social poetry necessary for the preservation and continuation of the social and cultural life of his times. However, the pessimism and anxiety of the times is evident in some of his works, for instance, "Tung-ch'ing ch'u-hsien yü Hsüeh Yüan-wai Wang Pu-ch'üeh ming-t'ou Nan shan Fo ssu" 東城初陷與薛員外王補闕暝投南山佛寺 (Fleeing in the Night to a Buddhist Temple in the Southern Mountains with Auxiliary Secretary Hsüeh and Wang the Rectifier of Omissions when

the Eastern City Walls [of Ch'ang-an] Began to Fall [to the Tibetans]), written in 763 when Tibetan forces overran and sacked the capital.

EDITIONS:

Ch'ien K'ao-kung chi 錢考功集. SPTK. Contains misattributions, however, such as the series of quatrains "Chiang-hsing wu-t'i i-pai-shou" 江行無題一百首錢 (Traveling on the Yangtze: One Hundred Untitled Poems), which were actually written by his great-grandson Ch'ien Yü 錢珝.

TRANSLATIONS:

Bynner, Jade Mountain, translates three eremitic and occasional regulated verses.
Gundert, Lyrik, pp. 98-99.

STUDIES:

Fu, Shih-jen, "Ch'ien Ch'i k'ao" 錢起考, pp. 427-448.
Wu, Ch'i-ming 吳企明. "Ch'ien Ch'i Ch'ien Yü shih k'ao-pien" 錢起錢珝詩考辯, Wen-hsüeh p'ing-lun ts'ung-k'an, 13 (May 1982), 169-187.

—MW

Ch'ien Ch'ien-i 錢謙益 (tzu, Shou-chih 受之, hao, Mu-chai 牧齋, 1582-1664), was a native of Ch'ang-shu 常熟 (modern Kiangsu), the foremost poet and critic, and one of the most controversial scholar-officials, of the Ming-Ch'ing transitional period. He was in and out of office after passing the chin-shih examination with high honors in 1610. His first appointment was as a compiler in the Han-lin Academy, but soon he had to return to his native place to mourn his father's death. He resumed his post ten years later, and in 1621 was appointed provincial examiner in Chekiang (a position reserved only for distinguished scholars). Soon after, he was assigned to the compilation of the Veritable Records of Emperor Shen-tsung. However, he returned home in 1622 because of ill health. In 1624 he was recalled. In 1625 he supervised imperial instruction in the Han-lin Academy, until he was dismissed for his political affiliations with the Tung-lin Party. After the enthronement of the new emperor, Ch'ung-chen, in 1628, he held several positions, but his official career ended abruptly in a conflict between the Tung-lin

Party and the faction led by Wen T'i-jen 溫體仁 regarding the appointment of a grand secretary. In order to stop Ch'ien's candidacy (supported by the Tung-lin) the Wen faction accused Ch'ien of complicity in a bribery case in the provincial examination of 1621 (when he had been examiner). Ch'ien was dismissed; he remained in retirement in his hometown until 1644, except for a year spent in prison as a result of a trumped-up charge.

In spite of all this, Ch'ien's life had a brighter side. In the winter of 1640 a famous young courtesan-poetess, later known as Liu Ju-shih 柳如是, came to visit him at his Pan-yeh T'ang 半野堂 (Half-rustic Hall). They exchanged many verses, later collected in *Tung-shan ch'ou-ho chi* 東山酬合集 (Collection of Harmonized Verse from the Eastern Mountain). The following year when Ch'ien was already sixty years old and Liu only twenty-four, they married. In 1643 Ch'ien built a studio, the Chiang-yün Lou 絳雲樓 (Descending-clouds Tower), for her. It housed his great collections of rare books and art treasures, and they spent their leisure days there (unfortunately, in 1650 a fire destroyed the house and most of the collections).

Following the Manchu invasion of the North, Ch'ien was called in 1644 to serve in the exile court under Prince Fu at Nanking. When the city was besieged in the following year, Ch'ien and other high officials surrendered to the Manchus, instead of taking martyrdom as Liu Ju-shih had urged. In 1646 he was sent to Peking, offered a position there, and allowed to work on the compilation of the official history of the Ming dynasty as he requested. However, Ch'ien soon retired because of poor health. Over the next several years he returned to official life, but was arrested several times for alleged relations with Ming loyalists. He was saved only by huge ransom payments and probably through the intercession of some influential member of the new regime, such as Hung Ch'eng-ch'ou 洪承疇 or Ma Kuo-chu 馬國柱.

Ch'ien and Liu had probably been involved in the anti-Manchu campaigns. Two leaders of the Ming loyalist forces were Ch'ien's former students: Ch'ü Shih-ssu 瞿式耜 and Cheng Ch'eng-kung 鄭成功 (better known in the West as Koxinga). Ch'ien's poems modeled after Tu Fu's* "Ch'iu hsing" 秋興 (Autumn Meditations), collected in *T'ou-pi chi* 投筆集 (Abandoning the Brush Collection), reveal his longing for the victory of Cheng's troops. At any rate, he was a tragic figure; the Chinese condemned him for his surrender to the enemy, while the Manchus suspected him for his antagonistic attitude toward the new regime.

However, his contribution to our knowledge of Ming literary and intellectual history is not suspect. He compiled several large works, among them the *Lieh-ch'ao shih-chi* 列朝詩集 (Anthology of Ming Poetry), to which he appended about two thousand biographies, and a history of the Ming dynasty, and he edited a large collection of T'ang poetry which was a model for later anthologies. His writings from before the fall of the Ming were collected in *Mu-chai ch'u-hsüeh chi* 牧齋初學集 in 110 *chüan* (printed by Ch'ü Shih-ssu in 1643); his writings thereafter were collected in *Mu-chai yu-hsüeh chi* 牧齋有學集 in 50 *chüan* (printed in 1664). They are two most important sources of information on Chinese literary and intellectual circles during his lifetime.

EDITIONS:

Ch'ien Ch'ien-i T'ou-pi chi chiao-pen 錢謙益投筆集校本. P'an Ch'ung-kuei 潘重規, ed. Taipei, 1973.

Ch'ien tseng Mu-chai shih-chu 錢曾牧齋詩註. 5v. Chou Fa-kao 周法高, ed. Taipei, 1973.

Lieh-ch'ao shih-chi hsiao-chuan 列朝詩集小傳. Taipei, 1961.

Mu-chai ch'u-hsüeh chi 牧齋初學集, 110 *chüan*. SPTK. Reprint of a 1643 ed.

Mu-chai ch'e-tu 牧齋尺牘, in *Chiu chia shih wen chi* 九家詩文集, v. 5. Chou Fa-kao, ed. 3 *chüan*, Taipei, 1973.

Mu-chai wai-chi 牧齋外集, in *Chiu chia shih wen chi*, v. 6, 25 *chüan*.

Mu-chai yu-hsüeh chi 牧齋有學集. 50 *chüan*. SPTK. Rpt. of 1664 edition.

STUDIES:

Che, K. L. "Not Words But Feelings: Ch'ien Ch'ien-I (1582-1664) on Poetry," *TkR*, 6.1 (April 1975), 55-75.

Chen, Yin-ch'üeh 陳寅恪. *Liu Ju-chih pieh-chuan* 柳如是別傳. Rpt. Taipei, 1981.

Chou, Fa-kao. "Tu Ch'ien Mu-chai shao-hsiang ch'ü' 讀錢牧齋燒香曲, *Lien-ho shu-yüan hsüeh-pao*, 12.13 (February 1975), 11-19.

———. *Liu Ju-shih shih k'ao* 柳如是事考. Taipei, 1978.

Chow, Tse-tsung 周策縱. "Kuan-yü Ch'ien Ch'ien-i 'Mei-ts'un shih hsü' wen-t'i te chieh-lun" 關于錢謙益 '梅村詩序' 問題的結論, *Ta-lu tsa-chih*, 47.1 (July 1973), 45-46.

Chu, Tung-jun 朱東潤. "Shu Ch'ien Mu-chai chih wen-hsüeh p'i-p'ing" 述錢牧齋之文學批評, *Wu-han Ta-hsüeh wen che chi-k'an*, 2.2 (1932), 269-291.

ECCP, pp. 148-150.

Hsü, Hsü-tien 徐緖典. "Ch'ien Mu-chai chu-shu pei-chin k'ao" 錢牧齋著述被禁考, *Shih-hsüeh nien-pao*, 3.2 (December 1940), 101-109.

Ko, Wan-li 葛萬里. *Mu Weng Hsien-sheng nien-p'u* 牧翁先生年譜. Rpt. Taipei, 1971.

Li, Ping-kao 李丙鎬. "Ch'ien Ch'ien-i wen-hsüeh p'ing-lun yen-chiu" 錢謙益文學評論研究. M.A. thesis, National Taiwan University, 1981.

Yoshikawa, Kojirō 吉川幸次郎. "Bungaku hih-yōka to shite no Sen Keneiki" 文學批評家としての錢謙益, *Chūgoku bungaku hō*, 31 (April 1980), 64-89.

—MSH

Ch'ien Wei-yen 錢惟演 (*tzu*, Hsi-sheng 希聖, 977-1034), a high official of the Northern Sung, was a leading prose writer, poet, and erudite of the first three decades of the eleventh century. He was an important *p'ien-wen** prose stylist and one of the three leading composers of the ornate and allusive Hsi-k'un Style (see *Hsi-k'un ch'ou-ch'ang chi*).

Of royal birth, Ch'ien Wei-yen had the best of classical educations; his literary and political values were naturally conservative or traditional. He was the son of Ch'ien Ch'u 錢俶 (928-988), the last ruler of the Kingdom of Wu and Yüeh 吳越 (founded in 893), and came to the Sung capital in 978 when his father formally turned sovereignty of Wu and Yüeh over to the Sung.

Ch'ien Wei-yen's erudition was noted early in his life. After receiving many official titles as an infant and child, he passed the *chin-shih* examination at the age of twenty-two and was appointed to prestigious posts in the imperial library and ar-chives, where he was eventually put in charge of compiling the records of the Hsien-p'ing reign (994-1003). In 1005 he was included among scholars chosen to compile the encyclopedia *Ts'e-fu yüan-kuei* 冊府元龜, completed in 1013. During this period, poems which he had exchanged with other compilers, especially with Yang I, were published in the *Hsi-k'un ch'ou-ch'ang chi*.

Politically, Ch'ien associated himself with the clique headed by Wang Ch'in-jo 王欽若 (962-1025), chief editor of the *Ts'e-fu yüan-kuei* and a leading power-broker of the time. Ch'ien had important connections by marriage as well. His daughter's husband was the brother of Empress Liu 劉后 (969-1033), and his son was married to the daughter of the poet and *p'ien-wen* essayist Ting Wei 丁謂 (960-1040), a key associate of Wang Ch'in-jo. In 1020, this clique came to power partly through the help of Ch'ien, who was close to Emperor Chen-tsung (r. 998-1022). Ch'ien was instrumental in having the Grand Councilor, K'ou Chun 寇準 (961-1023), deposed. As a result, Ch'ien became Military Affairs Vice Commissioner.

Between 1023 and 1033, Ch'ien's attempts to rise further in the bureaucracy were stymied. His son-in-law, the Empress's brother, had died in 1021. And in 1022, when Emperor Chen-tsung died and his young son ascended to the throne under the regency of Empress Liu, Ch'ien's enemies at the court used a ban on nepotism to force Ch'ien into provincial posts in what is now Honan.

During this decade of exile he made three attempts to convince various factions in the capital to appoint him Grand Councilor. At last he succeeded, and served for four months until he was again demoted and returned to a post at Lo-yang where he died in 1034.

While serving in Lo-yang (1031-1034), Ch'ien lived in a grand style, opening his residence to the younger officials of the region, whom he brought together for literary and social conviviality. Included in this group were such important literary and political figures of the next generation as

Ou-yang Hsiu,* Mei Yao-ch'en,* and Yin Shu.*

Ch'ien Wei-yen did not leave a great number of literary works. His energies, according to contemporary accounts, were spent mostly as literary patron rather than practitioner. He was a bibliophile and possessed one of the largest personal libraries of the time. As he was brought up close to the court, it was natural that he should have mastered T'ang-style *p'ien-wen* prose, a highly prosodic and allusive form especially important in the conduct of imperial affairs. In the early eleventh century, Ch'ien, Yang I, and Liu Yün 劉筠 (974-1031), well known Hsi-k'un poets, were also the noted composers of T'ang-style prose in the writing of government documents. Concurrently *ku-wen** prose became the mode of composition for personal writings.

In addition to the *Ts'e-fu yüan-kuei* and the *Hsi-k'un ch'ou-ch'ang chi*, only several minor works of Ch'ien's survive, including a genealogy of his family, and descriptions of court life when he was a Han-lin Academician.

STUDIES:

Chaves, *Mei Yao-ch'en*, pp. 51-53, 64-77.
Morper, Cornelia. *Ch'ien Wei-yen (977-1034) und Feng Ching (1021-1094): als Prototypen eines ehrgeizigen, korrupten und eines bescheidenen, korrekten Ministers der Nördlichen Sung-Dynastie.* Bern, 1975.
SB, pp. 219-221.

—BL

Chih-kuai 志怪 (describing anomalies) is the generic name given collections of brief prose entries, primarily but not exclusively narrative in nature, that discuss out-of-the-ordinary people and events. Long treasured as a source of historical materials, early *chih-kuai* are also studied as an important stage in the development of the literary tale, since they demonstrate features of narrative technique and authorial sensibility that have drawn attention to them as the earliest examples of fiction in China.

Traditional bibliology associates *chih-kuai* with a complementary genre, *chih-jen* 志人

(describing men). In fact, biography is of central importance to the *chih-kuai*, which evolved primarily from earlier biographical narratives and only secondarily from annalistic records. In turn, the *chih-kuai* eventually evolved toward hagiography and more advanced literary biography. In particular, a consideration of the kinship of *chih-kuai* with the dynastic-history biographies illuminates characteristics of biography writing of the medieval period in both historical and fictional modes.

The original period of *chih-kuai* activity spanned the three and one-half centuries from the fall of the Han dynasty to the reunification of China under Sui Emperor Wen (589 A.D.). Within that long period, the formative stage of the genre occurred in the Eastern Chin dynasty, during which time a host of *chih-kuai* compilations were made. At least four of these were actually entitled *Chih-kuai*, a name which through a process of antonomasia became the recognized generic term by no later than the Ming. Collections of putative Eastern Chin origin include *Sou-shen chi** of Kan Pao, *Po-wu-chih* of Chang Hua,* *Chih-kuai* of Tsu T'ai-chih 祖台之, *Shih-i chi* 拾遺記 (Gathering Remaining Accounts) of Wang Chia 王嘉 (d. *c.* 324), *Shen-hsien chuan** of Ko Hung, and *Hsüan-chung chi* 玄中記 (Records from Within the Recondite) by Kuo P'u 郭璞 (276-324). Diverse as the genre became in later years, the definitive examples of the *chih-kuai* remained these Eastern Chin titles.

No examples of the early *chih-kuai* survive in original form—a fact illustrating the relative disesteem in which such materials were held by the Confucian guardians of the imperial archives. It was only with the proliferation of commercial publication in the Ming that the *chih-kuai* were redacted and published in sufficient volume to assure their survival and permit a useful degree of comparison between conflicting corrupt texts. Fortunately, from as early as the fourth century important *chih-kuai* were widely quoted in commentaries and *lei-shu*,* permitting Ming editors and subsequent scholars to make reasonably credible reconstructions of the fourth and fifth century collections.

The extant *chih-kuai* texts can be described as diverse in every sense. They include items ranging from brief notices of only a few words to lengthy and refined stories, in which a structured plot line is enriched by adept manipulation of the narrator's perspective and descriptive efforts are enhanced with poetic interludes. There are occasional discourses elaborating theories of physical transformation, explicating the meaning of portentous anomalies, or revealing esoteric knowledge of the world beyond daily life. The earliest collections were eclectic in both their sources and their interests. They embraced materials of popular origin that had generally not been considered fit for the dynastic histories. In preface after preface, *chih-kuai* compilers argued that such materials were worthy of preservation. Included are legends from local shrines about heroes and spirits, who brought everything from blessings and banes to an occasional practical joke. There were accounts of the strange inhabitants of remote lands surrounding China, some of whom could detach their heads at night and send them flying about the world. There were recollections of *fang-shih** conjurers, diviners, and healers, who circulated between the common people and officialdom, selling occult skills and touting marvelous tales. There were cautionary tales of fox and tortoise demons who assumed human form to seduce men and hortatory accounts of the filial and incorruptible reaping their rewards. There were sketchy biographies of the elusive immortals and faint adumbrations of their secrets. There were brief exposés of the emperors' private lives, records of cruel rulers and officials brought to judgment by heaven, and tragic stories of lovers and spouses crossed by their families or their fates.

In terms of formal qualities, antecedents of the *chih-kuai* are found in anecdotal philosophical texts, e.g., sections of the *Chuang-tzu* and the *Lieh-tzu;* treatises and biographies of the dynastic histories, e.g., Ssu-ma Ch'ien's "Feng-shan shu" 封禪書 (Treatise on the Feng and Shan Sacrifices) and "Ta-yüan chuan" 大宛傳 (Account of Fer-

ghana—recompiled from *Han-shu* 61) and Pan Ku's "Wu-hsing chih" 五行志 (Treatise on Five Phasis Omenology); and epigrammatic individual collections of stories that began in the Former Han and proliferated during the Latter Han, e.g., *Shuo-yüan* ascribed to Liu Hsiang* and Ying Shao's *Feng-su t'ung* 風俗通 (Penetrating Popular Ways). Given that the antecedents of *chih-kuai* are an integral and abundant part of the pre-Han and Han narrative canon, the emergence of *chih-kuai* as a genre of fiction is best described as a divergence of fictional and historical genres from a previously undifferentiated form of narrative prose.

The dynamics of this process of divergence make the study of *chih-kuai* germinal to understanding both early literary fiction and historiography. By the Eastern Chin, there was widespread sympathy for and interest in beliefs and practices that were either beyond the pale of classical learning as defined during the early Han or, worse yet, proscribed from the intellectual diet of the courtier-scholar. "Broad learning" (*po-hsüeh* 博學) was an accolade typically accorded the *chih-kuai* compiler, and it bespoke reading and research outside the Confucian canon. Literati with broad learning had knowledge that was not yet in the orthodox written record, but it was gradually being accepted and introduced for preservation and transmission. Kan Pao addressed the readers of his *chih-kuai* as *hao-shih-che* 好事者, meaning "the curious." The term is widely used in discussing unorthodox pursuits and suggests that the reading and writing of *chih-kuai* was motivated by personal interest and was not a part of the educational trappings useful to the literatus in his offical career. Later, Six Dynasties critics and theorists took note of a tide of interest in the recondite (*hsüan* 玄) and Huang-Lao Taoism that was particularly pronounced in the Eastern Chin, citing such figures as Kuo P'u, to whom are ascribed both recondite poetry and fiction. Powerful external factors converged to contribute to the broading of intellectual horizons: a revival of interest in Lao-tzu and Chuang-tzu and new developments in

Taoist thought; the large-scale introduction of Buddhist doctrine and lore; and the chronic political instability of the Six Dynasties which forced frequent relocation of the capitals with a consequent exposure of the literati to new locales and new cultural influences.

Riding the same currents of intellectual expansion were new attitiudes toward creative writing itself, both prose and poetry. Beginning in the Chien-an period, fascination with *belles lettres* was expressed in theories that spoke to the importance of individual and personal goals as well as the social and public ones that had previously been emphasized. It was a fascination with the literary in literature, the potentials of literary forms, and the affective and expressive potential of the literary spirit. The period was hospitable to experimentation with forms and explorations of new subjects. New prose formats, of a distinctly private nature, appeared and multiplied, including *chih-kuai, pieh-chuan* 別傳 (separate biographies), *chia-yü* 家語 (family lore), and individually collected materials that centered on a particular location, e.g., *Hsi-ching tsa-chi;** a type of character, e.g., *Lieh-nü chuan* 列女傳 (Biographies of Exemplary Women); or a system of thought or style of life, e.g., *Pao-p'u-tzu* (see Ko Hung).

In the evolution of narrative, fascination with the literary meant that aesthetic possibilities vied with standards of credibility and reliability in the selection of historical matter and the composing of historical accounts. Even in the collection of records for the imperial archives, the Eastern Chin was so tolerant of incredible materials that it was singled out for criticism by T'ang historiographer Liu Chih-chi,* who undertook China's first comprehensive and self-conscious look at its own historiographic tradition. Emperor Yüan, founder of the Eastern Chin, reestablished the Office of History and staffed it with *chu-tso lang* 著作郎 (squires for composition), selected for their literary skills. Among them was Kan Pao, who took the "historical leftovers" (*yü-shih* 餘史) and compiled them into the *Sou-shen chi.* There were others who indulged in *chih-kuai* compilation, and

at least one chapter of the *Shih-chi** ("Ta-yüan chuan" 大宛傳) was forged from other records and inserted in the history. One generation after the demise of the Eastern Chin, Fan Yeh 范曄 (398-445) compiled the *Hou Han-shu* 後漢書 (History of the Latter Han), which has broad areas of overlap with the *chih-kuai,* expecially in certain collective biographies and treatises. Fan Yeh had close personal associations with the Celestial Master K'ung Hsi-hsien 孔熙先, and he indulged his personal interest in the occult arts to such an extent that his narratives were criticized for being "irregular," or "out of line" (*pu-chin* 不經).

After Fan Yeh, dynastic histories moved steadily toward standards of plausibility that were normative by the time of the compilation of the *Hsin T'ang-shu* 新唐書 (New History of the T'ang) and endured until modern times. Concurrently, the *chih-kuai* and its descendants diverged to develop along a number of separate paths. In general, the eclecticism and naiveté of early works gave way to parochial interests and technical contrivance. The genre was put in the service of competing religious and philosophical traditions, with collections specializing in tales demonstrating the efficacy of one or another teaching. Notable examples of Buddhist miracle tales and the lives of sages include the *Hsüan-yen chi* 宣驗記 (Accounts Proclaiming Verifications), *Ming-hsiang chi* 冥祥記 (Accounts of Arcane Fortunes), and *Ching-i chi* 旌異記 (Accounts of Startling Oddities). From Buddhist and Taoist biographical *chih-kuai* emerged more advanced and sustained hagiography, e. g., Hui Chiao's *Kao-seng chuan** in the Tripitaka and the *Tsu-yang chen-jen nei-chuan* 紫陽眞人內傳 (Esoteric Biography of the Realized Person of Purple Solarity) in the *Tao-tsang.**

T'ang *ch'uan-ch'i** derived much in terms of themes and techniques from the *chih-kuai,* showing special favor to stories of crossed lovers, heroic individuals, supernatural encounters, unavenged ghosts, dreams and their interpretations, and utopian journeys. But the corpus of T'ang literary fiction is characterized by more complex articulation of story lines, finer use of descriptive poetic interludes, and more ornate and artful use of language—in short, a concentrated and conscious effort to improve the craft of fictional narrative. Apropos of these changes, during the T'ang the literary tale became known as the *ch'uan-ch'i*, a name which, compared to *chih-kuai*, stresses the marvelous and exotic rather than the anomalous and curious.

By the Sung dynasty, interest in the *chih-kuai* as an antique form surfaced; its simplicity and innocence were especially appreciated. The appearance of both official and private collections specializing in *chih-kuai* materials, e.g., the *T'ai-p'ing kuang-chi** and the *Kan-chu chi* 紺珠記 (Red Pearl Accounts), provided a handy source of examples for the Sung *chih-kuai* revivalists. Hsü Hsüan 徐玄 compiled the *Chi-shen lu* 稽神錄 (Records Examining Spirits), Wu Shu 吳淑 compiled the *Chiang-huai i-jen lu* 江淮異人錄 (Records of Exceptional Men around the Yangtze and Huai River Regions), Ch'en P'eng-nien 陳彭年 compiled the *Chih-i* 志異 (Recording Oddities), and Hung Mai* compiled his massive *I-chien chih* 夷堅志 (Accounts of I-chien). In the same spirit, *chih-kuai* were written in every succeeding dynasty, with only minor changes in style, content, or format. In the Yüan, the playwright Kuan Han-ch'ing* is credited with compiling the *Kuei Tung Hu* 鬼董狐 (The Tung Hu of Ghosts). In the Ming there were collections like Chü Yu's *Chien-teng hsin-hua*,* combining the collectanea format and thematic interests of the *chih-kuai* with the literary sophistication of the *ch'uan-ch'i*. The two most celebrated Ch'ing collections are P'u Sung-ling's *Liao-chai chih-i** and Chi Yün's* *Yüeh-wei ts'ao-t'ang pi-chi*. These last two writers brought to the *chih-kuai* refined talents and thorough familiarity with prevalent forms of fiction in the literary language, and they produced works of literary merit and enduring interest.

The early *chih-kuai* had a significant influence on not only its own direct descendants but later drama and fiction of every type. Early collections served as repositories of popular characters and plots, which through use and reuse achieved a sense of familiarity and ultimately a sense of historicity. The *chih-kuai* provided a legacy of character stereotypes, plot devices (e.g., demon impersonators, celestial intervention) and favorite props (e.g., magical mirrors, stones, gems, and swords). It can be argued that the *chih-kuai* established the degrees and kinds of supernaturalism and coincidence—in general, the canons of plausibility—that were tolerable in later literary fiction, and in so doing they defined the world in which later fiction functioned in its distinctive role as mock history.

TRANSLATIONS:

Bodde, Derk. "Some Chinese Tales of the Supernatural: Kan Pao and his *Sou-chen-chi*," *HJAS*, 6 (February 1942), 338-57.

———. "Again Some Chinese tales of the Supernatural," *JAOS*, 62.4 (1942), 305-308.

DeWoskin, Kenneth J. "In Search of the Supernatural: Selections from the *Sou-shen-chi*," *Renditions*, 7 (Spring 1977), 103-114.

Gjertson, Donald E. *Ghosts, Gods, and Retribution: Nine Buddhist Miracle Tales from Six Dynasties and Early T'ang China.* University of Massachusetts Asian Studies Committee Occasional Paper, 2 (1978).

Kao, Karl S. Y. *Classical Chinese Tales of the Supernatural and the Fantastic.* Bloomington, Indiana, 1985.

Traditional Chinese Stories, see finding list on page 597 for pre-T'ang titles.

Yang, Hsien-yi and Gladys Yang. *The Man Who Sold a Ghost.* Peking, 1958.

STUDIES:

DeWoskin, Kenneth J. "The Six Dynasties *Chih-kuai* and the Birth of Fiction," in *Chinese Narrative: Critical and Theoretical Essays*, Andrew H. Plaks, ed., Princeton, 1977, pp. 21-52.

Dien, Albert. "The *Yüan-hun chih* (Accounts of Ghosts with Grievances): A Sixth Century Collection of Stories," in *Wen-lin*, Chow Tse-tsung, ed., Madison, 1968, pp. 211-228.

Fan, Ning 范寧. "Lun Wei Chin chih-kuai hsiao-shuo te ch'uan-p'o ho chih-shih-fen-tzu ssu-hsiang te kuan-hsi" 論魏晉志怪小說的傳播和知識分子思想分化的關係, *Pei-ching Ta-hsüeh hsüeh-pao (Jen-wen k'o-hsüeh)*, 2 (May 1957), 75-88.

Fu, Hsi-hua 傅惜華. "Liu-ch'ao chih-kuai hsiao-shuo chih ts'un-i" 六朝志怪小說之存逸, *Han-hsüeh*, 1 (September 1944), 169-210.

Yen, Mao-yüan 嚴懋垣. "Wei Chin Nan-pei ch'ao chih-kuai hsiao-shuo shu-lu fu k'ao-cheng" 魏晉南北朝志怪小說書錄附考證 , *Wen-hsüeh nien-pao*, 6 (November 1940), 45-72.

—KD

Chih Yü 摯虞 (*tzu*, Chung-ch'ia 仲洽, d. 311) lived in the latter part of the Western Chin dynasty and died of starvation in Lo-yang in the year the city was invaded by the Hsiung-nu who in 304 had established the (Ch'eng) Han dynasty as a challenge to Chinese imperial rule.

Chih Yü came from an official family in the capital city of Ch'ang-an. He was a precocious youth, and his official career was successful and varied. Though we do not know his age at death, it seems likely he was quite old, for his first official position was that of Secretary to the Heir Apparent during the reign of Emperor Wu (265-289). During his life, he was most noted for his steady and rigid interpretation of the classics; this strong classical influence is very much evident in Chih's literary criticism and in the speeches and letters that, along with more literary compositions, make up a substantial part of his biography (*Chin-shu, ch.* 51). In one text Chih lectures the emperor on the proper responsibilities of the ruler when there are natural disasters. In another he argues for the absolute necessity of correcting the linear *ch'ih* 尺 measurement to match that used in antiquity, concluding "if not one basic point is amiss, then the myriad things will all be correct; yet if it is amiss, then all things will be counter to the correct."

Chih's biography credits him with several literary works; two of these, *fu* entitled "Ssu-yu fu" 思游賦 and a paean called "T'ai-k'ang sung" 太康頌, are recorded in the biography. Other pieces mentioned are an annotation of *San-fu chüeh-lu* 三輔決錄, his *Wen-chang chih* 文章志, and his anthology *Liu-pieh chi* 流別集. Besides these pieces Chih's collected works contain over sixty other compositions, ranging from *chen* 箴 (admonitions) to *shih*.* Chih Yü's now lost *Liu-pieh chi* anthology, more often called *Wen-chang liu-pieh chi* 文章流別集, was perhaps the first of its kind in the great tradition of anthology making in China. It certainly influenced the extant and famous anthology by Hsiao T'ung 蕭統, the *Wen-hsüan*,* compiled two centuries later.

Chih Yü's reputation rests largely on the extant "discussions" (*lun* 論) that originally accompanied his anthology. These "discussions" are critical comments on different aspects of literary theory, especially on questions of genre development; they are therefore comparable to much of Hsiao T'ung's famous preface. Although Chih does not mention nearly as many genres as Hsiao, his comments are much more detailed and developed; quite unlike much of Hsiao's work, which is often only a catalogue of genres, his discussions do not offer a general theory of literature. Some overriding considerations from his comments can, however, be extrapolated.

Chih Yü's critical method is basically that of a conservative idealist who is forever looking back to the "golden age" of Chou literature, specifically to the *Shih-ching.** Chih is different from Hsiao in that he does not believe in the progress of literature; for him all change is corruption. He builds most of his argument around the "six principles" (*liu i* 六義 or *liu shih* 六詩) of literature that were early associated with the *Shih-ching*. From these he offers the very conservative genre, the *sung* 頌 (paean), as the "finest pieces of poetry," and he likewise condemns the Han *fu** as a base corruption of the *fu* principle seen in the *Shih-ching*. In his remarks on the various genres, Chih also discusses specific poets and compositions, upon which he often heaps praise or blame. He offers several criteria for judging this literature, the most important of which is that poetry should "spring from emotion but end in righteousness." It was the failure of the Han *fu* to meet this criterion (because it took righteousness as "supplemental") that caused Chih Yü to dismiss it as viable literature. In the end the *Shih-ching* stands as the best of all literature; all poetry is derived from it and must be judged against it.

EDITIONS:
Chih T'ai-ch'ang i-shu 摯太常遺書, in *Kuan-chung ts'ung-shu* 關中叢書. Sian, 1934-36, 4th *chi.*

284

The collected works. His prose works (including *fu*) are also collected in *Liu-ch'ao wen*, v. 2, pp. 1896-1906.

Hsü, Wen-yü 許文雨, ed. *Wen-lun chiang-shu* 文論講疏. 1937; rpt. Taipei, 1973, pp. 67-84. This edition carries the text of *Wen-chang liu-pieh chi* with full annotation.

STUDIES:

Allen, Joseph Roe, III. "Chih Yü's Discussions of Different Types of Literature: A Translation and Brief Comment," *Parerga*, 3 (1976), 3-36.

—JA

Chin Ho 金和 (*tzu*, Kung-shu 弓叔, *hao*, Ya-p'ao 亞匏, 1819-1885) was one of the most original poets of mid-nineteenth-century China. Born in Ch'üan-chiao 全椒 (modern Anhwei), he came from an old Nanking family and resided in Nanking from his early childhood until 1853. Unfortunately, much of his early poetry has been lost, but the surviving verse already displays two of Chin Ho's later characteristics, his wit and his deep concern for political affairs. Such early poems as "Chu-yu P'u-yüan" 初遊樸園 (The First Time I Visited Simplicity Garden) and "Ch'ao yen" 嘲燕 (Making Fun of Swallows) were written under the carefree, prosperous condition of Chin's early life, but they both display a humor that Chin may owe to a study of Sung poetry.

Some of his first serious political poems are "Wei-ch'eng chi-shih liu-yung" 圍城紀事六詠 (Six Poems Recording the Siege of Nanking), written about the British invasion of the Yangtze Basin during the Opium War in 1842. Although they express Chin's loathing for the foreign aggressors, he is even more outraged at the collusion between some Chinese and the British and the general ineptness of the Ch'ing officials in dealing with the crisis. In the last two lines of one poem Chin writes: "Yesterday they also captured some poor skinny fellow:/ A chicken-stealing bandit for sure!" Such lines, in addition to showing the early development of Chin's satirical wit, demonstrate that he felt the bungling Ch'ing officials were not only incapable of repelling foreign aggressors, but only suc-cessful in bullying and oppressing the common people. Other early works such as his "Yin-tzu ch'ien" 印子錢 (Sealed Money) criticize the exploitation of the people through high interest loans and other questionable financial practices.

The most traumatic event in Chin's life was the occupation of Nanking by the T'ai-p'ing Rebels in 1853. Chin was disgusted by the cruelty and superstition of the T'ai-p'ing, and he attempted to plot together with the Ch'ing government forces still camped outside the city to raise a revolt against the rebels from inside. The Ch'ing commander did not attack on the day agreed upon, and although Chin Ho himself eventually escaped, many of his relatives and friends were executed when the plot was discovered.

The sufferings of Chin Ho during this period gave rise to some of his greatest poetry. His poem "Ch'u-wu-jih chi-shih" 初五日紀事 (A Record of What Happened on the Fifth) is a scathing satire on the ineptness and cowardliness of the Ch'ing forces. The general described in the poem calls off campaigns because of rain, windstorms, excessive heat, or moonlit nights which might allow the enemy to glimpse the imperial army. Chin concludes the poem by writing: "Our general's stratagems must be perfectly complete;/ The reason the bandits have not been destroyed lies with Heaven alone./ How can we find a blue sky, when it is neither cold nor hot,/ When the sun and moon don't come out and there's no wind or rain!" Another masterpiece of this period is Chin's "Ping wen" 兵問 (Questions to a Soldier) in which he depicts the utter degradation of the Chinese soldier and his effectiveness in oppressing the lower classes rather than fighting the enemy. However, Chin's most ambitious work from this time is probably his long cycle of poems "T'ung-ting-p'ien shih-san-jih" 痛定篇十三日, which describes the horrifying events that eventually led to the execution of his friends by the T'ai-p'ing Rebels.

After 1854 Chin Ho set out on a life of wandering, serving in low official positions and as a tutor in various families.

Throughout these years he continued to use his verse to describe his own personal experiences in a troubled society and to attack government abuses. Although he had already experimented with a more vernacular style, it was during these years that he perfected a new style of poetry based upon popular oral literature. One of the best examples is his "Lan-ling nü-erh hsing" 蘭陵女兒行 (Ballad of the Girl from Lan-ling), a long poem in which he employed popular meters to tell the story of a poor girl whom a powerful general attempted to force into marriage, but who escaped from his clutches by threatening to assassinate him.

Chin Ho was one of the most original authors of his time, and in many ways his poetry looked forward to the late Ch'ing poetic revolution of Huang Tsun-hsien* and others. His love for vernacular language, eccentric metric patterns, and long narrative verse must have had a strong influence on other late Ch'ing authors. His view of his poetry as a diary of his life bears a strong resemblance to Liang Ch'i-ch'ao's* theory of poetry as history, and his mordant wit and scathing satire are similar to the best of Huang Tsun-hsien's* political verse.

His works circulated widely in manuscript during his lifetime but were not printed until 1892, seven years after his death. The definitive edition was not printed until 1914. Because Chin Ho was so violently opposed to the T'ai-p'ing Rebels, his verse has been generally ignored since 1949.

EDITIONS:

Ch'iu-hui yin-kuan shih-ch'ao 秋蟪吟館詩鈔. 1914. The definitive edition.

Lai-yün-ko shih-kao 來雲閣詩稿. 1892.

Chin-tai shih-hsüan 近代詩選. Peking, 1963. Annotations for five poems.

STUDIES:

Ch'en, Tsung-shu 陳宗樞. "Ch'ing-tai te chi-luan shih-jen Chin Ho, fu nien-p'u" 清代的紀亂詩人金和附年譜, *Ling-tang*, 4 (July 1935), 55-74.

ECCP, pp. 163-164.

Ming-Ch'ing shih-wen yen-chiu-shih 明清詩文研究室. "Ch'ing-shih chi-shih shih-li: Chin Ho" 清詩紀事示例金和, *Ming-Ch'ing shih-wen yen-chiu ts'ung-k'an*, 1 (March 1982), 136-148.

—JDS

Chin-ku ch'i-kuan 今古奇觀 (Wonders of the Present and the Past), a Ming anthology of anthologies, selected its forty stories entirely from the five *hua-pen** collections of the *San-yen* (see Feng Meng-lung) and *Erh-p'o* (see Ling Meng-ch'u) series: *Ku-chin hsiao-shuo* (eight stories), *Ching-shih t'ung-yen* (ten), *Hsing-shih heng-yen* (eleven), *P'o-an ching-ch'i* (eight), and *Erh-k'o P'o-an ching-ch'i* (three). Since Ling Meng-ch'u's* *Erh-k'o P'o-an ching-ch'i*, the last of the five collections, was published in 1632, this date can be regarded as the *terminus post quem* of the *Chin-ku ch'i-kuan*. Its *terminus ante quem* could be as late as the last year of the Ming dynasty (1644). The compiler is merely known as Pao-weng Lao-jen 抱甕老人 (The Old Man Who Embraces an Earthen Jar) of Soochow; his identity has yet to be established.

Throughout the Ch'ing period, *Chin-ku ch'i-kuan* was virtually the only *hua-pen* collection in wide circulation. Thus it fulfilled the vital function of keeping *hua-pen* literature in vogue in an age dominated by classical-language stories. It was also through the prolific translation of the stories in the *Chin-ku ch'i-kuan* in the nineteenth and early twentieth centuries that *hua-pen* literature was introduced to Europe. Even in Japan, where quite a few unique copies of the *San-yen* and *Erh-p'o* collections have been preserved in several public and private libraries, the *Chin-ku ch'i-kuan* is still the representative of *hua-pen* literature for the general public. The best testimony of its popularity in modern Japan is the fact that the entire *Chin-ku ch'i-kuan* was included in Heibonsha's 平凡社 mammoth and authoritative *Chūgoku koten bungaku taikei* 中國古典文學大系 (Major Works of Traditional Chinese Literature) while only a few samples were selected from each of its parent collections. The influence of *Chin-ku ch'i-kuan* on Edo 江戸 (1615-1868) literature is also well established.

With its parent collections available in reliable reprints of excellent editions, *Chin-ku ch'i-kuan* may no longer be textually important. But this has not affected the circulation of the work. It has a special significance of its own. The book title indicates that the compiler had a strong preference for stories of contemporary or near contemporary settings. This is clearly unlike the dominating editorial policy of the parent collections, particularly that of the *San-yen* series, which placed considerable emphasis on the ancient origin of the stories and on past storytelling traditions. Consequently, *Chin-ku ch'i-kuan* not only offers us a chance to examine the editorial practices for fictional works and the prevailing literary taste of late Ming China, but also serves as a reliable reflection of the dominance of moral concerns, of the clashes between the individual and the society, of the popularization of Confucianism, and of socioeconomic problems of the period concerned.

EDITIONS:

Chin-ku ch'i-kuan. Shanghai, 1933.

Ku, Hsüeh-chieh 顧學頡, annotator. *Chin-ku ch'i-kuan.* Peking, 1957. The parent collections should also be consulted (see above), especially for the erotic passages which have generally been expunged from these modern editions.

TRANSLATIONS:

Chida, Kuichi 千田九一, Komada Shinji 駒田信二, and Tatema shōsuke 立間祥介. *Kinko kikan* 今古奇觀. Tokyo, 1970-73. 2v. Japanese translations of all forty stories, with excellent notes.

Howell, E. B. *Chin Ku Ch'i Kuan: The Inconstancy of Madam Chang and Other Stories from the Chinese.* London, 1924.

―――. *The Restitution of the Bride and Other Stories from the Chinese.* London, 1926. These two Howell volumes are among the better-known examples of the numerous early (before 1960) renderings of the *Chin-ku ch'i-kuan* stories into European languages.

Vel'gus, V. A. and I. E. Citproviv. *Udividtel'nye istorii nasego veremeni i drevonosti.* Moscow, 1962.

STUDIES:

Kern, Jean E. "The Individual and Society in the Chinese Colloquial Short Story: The *Chin-ku ch'i-kuan.*" Ph.D. dissertation, Indiana University, 1973.

Kuwayama, Ryūhei 桑山龍平 and Ōmura Umeo 木村梅雄. "*Kinko kikan* on kenkyū to shiryō" 今古奇觀の研究と資料, in *Chūgoku no hachi dai shōsetsu: Chūgoku kinsei shōsetsu no sekai* 中國の八大小說： 中國近世小說の世界. Osaka shiritsu daigaku Chūgoku bungaku kenkyūshitsu 大阪市立大學中國文學研究室, ed., Tokyo, 1965, pp. 412-427.

Niida, Noboru 仁井田陞. "*Kinko kikan* to Mindai no shakai" 今古奇觀と明代の社會, *Chūgoku koten bungaku zenshū geppō,* 1 (March 1958), 1-4. Also in Niida Noboru, *Chūgoku no dentō to kakumei* 中國の傳統と革命. Tokyo, 1974, v. 2, pp. 39-45.

Pelliot, Paul. "Le *Kin kou k'i kouan,*" *TP,* 24 (1926), 54-60.

Sun, K'ai-ti 孫楷第. "*Chin-ku ch'i-kuan* hsü" 今古奇觀序, in *Chin-ku ch'i-kuan,* Shanghai, 1933, v. 1, 1-42.

Shuang-i 雙翼 [Wu Yün-sheng 吳筠生]. *Chi-ku ch'i-kuan t'an-p'ien* 今古奇觀談片. Hong Kong, 1977.

Wang, Fu-ch'üan 汪馥泉. "*Chin-ku ch'i-kuan* chih chieh-p'ou" , *Wen-i yüeh-k'an,* 6.4 (October 1934), 1-10.

Yamaguchi, Ichirō 山口一郎. "*Kinko kikan* no jidai haikei" 今古奇觀の時代背景, in *Chūgoku no hachi dai shōsetsu,* pp. 384-392.

—YWM

Chin P'ing Mei 金瓶梅 (The Plum in the Golden Vase—the title literally consists of surnames of three of the major characters in the novel) is a very long, complex, and sophisticated novel, written anonymously in the late sixteenth century, and probably first published in 1617, or shortly thereafter. It is a landmark in the development of narrative art, not only from a specifically Chinese perspective, but in a world-historical context. With the possible exceptions of *The Tale of Genji* (1010) and *Don Quixote* (1615), neither of which it resembles, but with both of which it can bear comparison, there is no earlier work of prose fiction of equal sophistication in world literature. The only other work of Chinese fiction which can be said to equal or surpass it is the eighteenth-century novel *Hung-lou meng,** which is demonstrably in its debt.

Few other works of Chinese fiction have been subjected to such a bewildering variety of interpretations. In roughly chron-

287

ological order, it has been read as a *roman à clef*, a work of pornography, a Buddhist morality play, an exercise in naturalism, or a novel of manners. None of these readings, except the last, is very convincing, and the interpretation that is offered below is also controversial but is put forward in the conviction that it accounts for more of the features of the text than any of the others.

In its formal features the *Chin P'ing Mei* is a novel in one hundred chapters, of which all but chapters 53 to 57, which are by another hand or hands, can be demonstrated on the basis of internal evidence to be the work of a single author. Despite its reliance on a wide spectrum of earlier sources from both the classical and the vernacular literary traditions, in particular the earlier novel *Shui-hu chuan*,* these sources are integrated into the design of the overall structure in a way that sets the *Chin P'ing Mei* apart from its predecessors among the great Chinese novels. All of these are either the products of multiple authorship or represent the recasting of traditional materials, and all of them are episodic in structure, whereas the *Chin P'ing Mei*, despite its length, has a tightly controlled unitary plot. But the most pronounced feature that serves to set it apart from its predecessors is the degree of its figural density. It is replete with so many internal allusions, resonances, and patterns of incremental repetition or replication as to make it difficult to apprehend fully on the basis of a single reading.

The researches of Wu Han 吳晗 (1909-1969) and Patrick Hanan have established that the *Chin P'ing Mei* could probably not have been completed, in its present form, before 1582 and that a manuscript of the first part of the work was already in circulation, at least among the members of a small coterie, as early as 1596. The work in its entirety may not have been completed, however, until sometime after that date, possibly as late as 1606, the earliest date for which any reference to the existence of a complete manuscript is recorded. Further revisions could also have been made right up until 1617. Its composition,

therefore, took place during a span of years that falls entirely within the Wan-li period (1573-1620). These facts are significant for our understanding of the novel because, although the story is set in the final years of the Northern Sung, it is clear that the author was, in fact, describing the society of his own day.

The action of the novel takes place in the years 1112 through 1127 during the reign of Emperor Hui-tsung, and it describes the internal collapse of the Sung dynasty, culminating in the conquest of North China by the Jurchens in 1127. The collapse and demise of the empire is paralleled by the collapse and demise of the household of Hsi-men Ch'ing, the middle-class and provincial parvenu who is the protagonist of the novel. The following is a brief summary of the plot.

In the first twenty chapters the major characters are gradually assembled in Hsi-men Ch'ing's household, the setting for the main action of the novel, which takes place in the middle sixty chapters, during the first thirty of which Hsi-men Ch'ing enjoys a rapid rise in socio-economic status. In this segment of the novel his unremitting pursuit of his own gratification in the sexual, economic, and political spheres seems to be attended by every kind of success for which he seeks. His gross favoritism toward Li P'ing-erh, the widow of a sworn brother, whom he has taken into his own family as the last of his six wives, alienates the other members of his household, but he remains oblivious to his danger in the throes of an infatuation that gradually develops into a deep and genuine emotional attachment.

However, at exactly the mid-point of the novel, in chapters 49 and 50, he unwittingly sets the seal of destruction upon himself and everything that he holds dear through his acquisition of a potent aphrodisiac from a mysterious foreign monk, and his insistence on trying it upon his favorite wife while she is menstruating.

During the next thirty chapters Hsi-men Ch'ing's star appears to continue in the ascendant, but the seeds of self-destruction which he has planted in the first half of the book bear bitter fruit in the death of his son, followed by that of his favorite wife, and finally his own death (chapter 79), described in memorably gruesome detail, from an overdose of the aphrodisiac he had acquired at the mid-point of the novel.

In the last twenty chapters Hsi-men Ch'ing's household disintegrates as its members disperse to meet the individual fates which they have earned for themselves. In the last chapter, Hsi-men Ch'ing's only surviving heir, born to him by his neglected legitimate wife at the very moment of his own death, is inducted into a life of celibacy by a mysterious Buddhist monk who is, as it were, the mirror image of the monk who had appeared to Hsi-men Ch'ing in chapter 49. Thus, at the end of the novel, he has been replaced not by his own son but by his servant Tai-an, upon whom his widow has come to depend, and his family line, or dynasty, may be said to have come to its irrevocable end.

The author's concern with the creation of an intricate and symmetrical fictional structure is even greater than this brief outline would suggest. Not only is each of the hundred chapters composed of two or more episodes which serve to illuminate each other either by analogy or contrast, but the novel is built out of ten-chapter units which reveal a characteristic internal structure of their own. Each of these units tends to follow a particular thematic line through the early chapters, to be interrupted by the introduction of a significant twist or new development, usually in the seventh chapter, and to culminate in a climax of some kind in the ninth chapter. These repetitive configurations, recurring at ten-chapter intervals, have the effect of producing a subliminal wave-like pattern which underlies and reinforces the overall structure.

What kind of story is this that the author of the *Chin P'ing Mei* has taken such pains to tell? At first glance it appears to be a tale of what Hanan has called the "folly and consequences" type, fleshed out with an unprecedented amount of testamentary detail, and presented, for the most part, through the medium of a "formal realism"

that observes no reticences. This description is accurate enough, but it does not go far enough to account for the apparent inconsistencies in point of view, occasionally blatant violations of probability, and frequent and abrupt shifts in the level of diction from the convincing mimetic evocation of reality to passages of parody or burlesque. Nor does such a description tell very much about the probable intentions of the author or the value system by which he intends the actions of his characters to be judged.

The author of the first preface to the earliest edition notes that it was written by his friend Lan-ling Hsiao-hsiao Sheng 蘭陵笑笑生 (The Scoffing Scholar of Lan-ling), and that it was intended to be a serious moral critique of the age. Although nothing whatever is known about this mysterious figure, it is not improbable that his choice of this pseudonym was intended to invoke the figure of Hsün-tzu, the great Confucian philosopher of the third century B.C., who ended his career as the magistrate of Lan-ling, and who died and was buried there. If this hypothesis has any validity, it may provide a significant clue to the interpretation of the novel.

Hsün-tzu is most famous for his enunciation of the doctrine that, although everyone has the capacity for goodness, human nature is basically evil and, if allowed to find expression without the conscious molding and restraint of ritual, is certain to lead the individual disastrously astray. That the author of the *Chin P'ing Mei* endorsed this view should be apparent to even the most superficial reader, but he also made it quite explicit by quoting in four different places in his novel, including the first chapter, a line which reads, "In this world, only the heart of man is vile."

Hsün-tzu not only asserts that human nature is basically evil, but also reiterates the traditional Confucian view that the force of moral example moves downward from the apex of the social pyramid and that if the leaders of society do not exercise their moral responsibility to cultivate themselves and set a good example for their colleagues, subordinates, and family members, the inevitable result will be social disintegration. Though Hsün-tzu repeats these views on human nature and the force of moral example again and again, he offers no more in order to substantiate them than an already hackneyed set of allusions to the careers of the rulers of antiquity.

The author of the *Chin P'ing Mei* seems to have felt that Hsün-tzu's philosophy could be used to good purpose in diagnosing the ills of his own day. In so doing, however, he accepted the challenge of the philosopher to demonstrate the validity of his theory in terms of modern times and the human world. Innumerable clues, beginning with the prologue but also planted inconspicuously elsewhere in the narrative, indicate that Hsi-men Ch'ing, the bourgeois protagonist, is intended to function as a surrogate, not only for the feckless Emperor Hui-tsung of the world ostensibly depicted in the novel, but also for the Wan-li Emperor of the author's own time. His six wives are surrogates for the six evil ministers, who have been traditionally blamed for the fall of the Northern Sung dynasty. This particular emblematic correspondence is multivalent in its functions, however, for in popular Buddhism the term "six traitors" is also used as a metaphor for the six senses. Hsi-men Ch'ing's sycophants, servants, and employees, in their turn, act as surrogates for the eunuchs and lesser functionaries in the imperial administration. By deliberately restricting his focus to the events in a single middle-class household, but subtly suggesting to the reader that this microcosm stands in an analogical relationship to the society as a whole, the author was able to attack the abuses of the day with far greater candor and analytical rigor than would have been possible, or safe, if he had attacked the reigning monarch and the existing social and political structure directly.

The most controversial aspect of the *Chin P'ing Mei* is the explicit descriptions of sexual activity that have earned it the misleading reputation of a pornographic classic. It is probable that it was never the intent of the author to celebrate the pleasures of sex and that the particular sexual acts which are explicitly described are intended to express, in the most powerful metaphor available, the author's contempt for the sorts of persons who indulge in them. The spheres of sexual, economic, and socio-political aggrandizement are symbolically correlated in the novel in such a way that the calculated shock value of the sexual descriptions spills over into the other realms and colors the reader's response to them. It is an essential part of the author's rhetorical strategy to deliberately stimulate the latent sensuality of his readers by inducing them to empathize with the sensual experiences of his characters, only to shift abruptly from a realistic mode into one of mock-heroic or burlesque. The effect of this technique, which is used throughout the novel so repeatedly as to create a pattern, is to bring the reader up short and remind him that, to the extent that he has allowed himself to empathize with the events that he has just experienced vicariously, he has shown himself to be, at least potentially, capable of the same or similar acts. This technique is not, therefore, as some critics have alleged, evidence of the author's failure to maintain a consistent tone, but rather evidence of his constant endeavor to provoke the reader into self-examination by carefully modulated manipulations of his distance from the events described in the text. Far from wishing the reader to remain mesmerized by the mimetic evocation of reality, the author of the *Chin P'ing Mei* wants to make the reader periodically stop to evaluate not only the events and characters described in the text but himself and his own reactions to them.

If the above interpretation of the novel is valid, the moral value system by which the author intended the actions of the characters in his work to be judged was that of a conservative brand of orthodox Confucianism. In this case, rather than a manifestation of the syncretism, free thinking, and hedonism of the late Ming period, as some critics have suggested, the *Chin P'ing Mei* must be interpreted as a reaction against those very features of the intellectual life of the time.

Although the importance of the *Chin P'ing Mei* in the history of Chinese literature has long been acknowledged, the technical virtuosity of the author has not yet received adequate recognition. This is due in part to the relative unfamiliarity and controversial nature of the techniques he employed. His unprecedentedly complex use of a variety of earlier material, ranging from classical quotations and liturgical texts to the popular theater and song of his own day, on the one hand, and his explicit descriptions of sexual activity, on the other, have combined to inhibit anything approaching full critical assimilation of the nature of his achievement. This critical myopia has adversely affected the reception of the work in China and Japan as well as in the Western world and is due in part to the fact that the novel is usually read in bowdlerized editions or in translations that are incomplete or fail to do justice to significant features of the original text.

EDITIONS:

Chin P'ing Mei tz'u-hua 金瓶梅詞話. 5v. Tokyo, 1963. A facsimile edition of the earliest and most authentic version of the text. This edition has also been pirated in Taiwan.

Chin P'ing Mei tz'u-hua chu-shih 金瓶梅詞話注釋. 6v. Taipei, 1981. The first three volumes of this work comprise an unexpurgated modern typeset edition of the above text, without critical editing or apparatus. The last three volumes comprise a glossary, of only marginal value, by Wei Tzu-yün 魏子雲.

TRANSLATIONS:

Egerton, Clement. *The Golden Lotus*. London, 1939. A nearly complete and faithful translation of an inferior later recension of the text. In the first edition many passages of explicit sexual description were rendered in Latin. In the new edition of 1972 these passages have been translated into English. This is still the best available translation in any European language.

STUDIES:

Carlitz, Katherine. "The Role of Drama in the *Chin P'ing Mei:* The Relationship Between Fiction and Drama as a Guide to the Viewpoint of a Sixteenth Century Chinese Novel."

Unpublished Ph.D. dissertation, University of Chicago, 1978.

———. "Puns and Puzzles in the *Chin P'ing Mei*," *TP*, 67 (1981), 216-239.

Chu, Hsing 朱星. *Chin P'ing Mei k'ao-cheng* 小野忍. Tientsin, 1980.

Hanan, P. D. "A Landmark of the Chinese Novel," in *The Far East: China and Japan*, Douglas Grant and Miller Maclure, eds., Toronto, 1961, pp. 325-335.

———. "The Text of the *Chin P'ing Mei*," *AM, N.S.*, 9 (1962), 1-57.

———. "Sources of the *Chin P'ing Mei*," *AM, N.S.*, 10 (1963), 23-67.

Hsia, C. T. "*Chin P'ing Mei*," in his *The Classic Chinese Novel. A Critical Introduction*, New York, 1968, pp. 165-202.

Lévy, André. "About the Date of the First Printed Edition of the *Chin P'ing Mei*," *CLEAR*, 1 (1979), 43-47.

Ma Tai-lai 馬泰來 "Hsieh Chao-che te '*Chin P'ing Mei* pa'" 謝肇的〝金瓶梅跋〞, *Chung-hua wen-shih lun-ts'ung*, 1980.4, 299-305.

———. "Ma-ch'eng Liu-chia ho *Chin P'ing Mei*" 麻城劉家和〝金瓶梅〞, *Chung-hua wen-shih lun-ts'ung*, 1980.6, 111-120.

Martinson, Paul Varo. "*Pao* Order and Redemption: Perspectives on Chinese Religion and Society Based on a Study of the *Chin P'ing Mei*." Unpublished Ph.D. dissertation, University of Chicago, 1973.

Roy, David T. "Chang Chu-p'o's Commentary on the *Chin P'ing Mei*, in *Chinese Narrative: Critical and Theoretical Essays*, Andrew H. Plaks, ed. Princeton, 1977, pp. 115-123.

———. "A Confucian Interpretation of the *Chin P'ing Mei*," in *Proceedings of the International Conference on Sinology: Section on Literature*, Taipei, 1981, pp. 39-61.

Sun, Shu-yü 孫述宇. *Chin P'ing Mei te i-shu* 金瓶梅的藝術. Taipei, 1978.

Wei, Tzu-yün 魏子雲. *Chin P'ing Mei t'an-yüan* 金瓶梅探原. Taipei, 1979.

———. *Chin P'ing Mei te wen-shih yü yen-pien* 金瓶梅的問世與演變. Taipei, 1981.

Wu, Han 吳晗. "*Chin P'ing Mei* te chu-tso shih-tai chi ch'i she-hui pei-ching" 金瓶梅的著作時代及其社會背景, in his *Tu-shih cha-chi* 讀史劄記, Peking, 1957, pp. 1-38.

—DR

Chin Sheng-t'an 金聖嘆 (personal name, Jen-jui 人瑞, best known by his *tzu*, Sheng-t'an, 1610-1661) was a native of Wu-hsien (Soochow). The child of an impoverished scholar-gentry family, he studied for and obtained the *hsiu-ts'ai* degree. Possibly owing to his own rather individualistic personality, or the traumatic experience of the change of dynasty from Ming to Ch'ing in 1644, or both, he apparently did not go on to take more advanced examinations in order to qualify himself for an official career. As a result, he sometimes had to rely on the generosity of his friends for a living.

Chin started his formal education in a village school at the age of nine. He turned out to be a conscientious and inquisitive student. He enjoyed Confucian classics, but he seemed to be even more affected by such heterogeneous writings as the *Lotus Sutra* (*Saddharmapundariks*), Ch'ü Yüan's* "Li sao," Ssu-ma Ch'ien's* *Shih-chi*,* *Shui-hu chuan*,* and *Hsi-hsiang chi*,* which he poured over during his spare time. Eventually, he designated the "Li sao," *Shih-chi*, *Shui-hu chuan*, and *Hsi-hsiang chi*, together with *Chuang-tzu* (see *chu-tzu pai-chia*) and Tu Fu's* poetry, as the "Liu ts'ai-tzu shu" 六才子書 (Six Works of Genius).

Chin's enthusiasm for Buddhist writings and popular literature written in the vernacular language at such an early age is a good measure of his precociousness and intellectual independence. Indeed, he grew up to be a free and unconventional soul, seemingly more interested in pursuing his own likes and dislikes than observing social norms. An intimate glimpse of his personality is provided in the "Thirty-three Delights in Life" enumerated in his commentary on the *Hsi-hsiang chi.* Here we see vividly his enjoyment of things purely sensory, his love of personal freedom, and a certain tendency toward mischievousness.

Unfortunately, Chin was also vain and contentious by nature. And he was too much a Confucianist to completely withdraw from the mundane and troublesome world. To ridicule scholars renowned as public lecturers, for example, he would sometimes demonstrate his vast knowledge of books both orthodox and unorthodox by holding public forums himself, to the infinite delight and admiration of large crowds. He was greatly distressed by the chaos caused by the widespread ban-

ditry toward the end of the Ming dynasty, and in his commentary on the *Shui-hu chuan*, he was relentless in his attacks on the bandit-heroes as a group and on Sung Chiang, their leader, even though he showed sympathy to many bandit-heroes as individuals. He lost his life in an incident, known as "K'u-miao an" 哭廟案 (The Case of Lamenting in the Temple), that most tragically illustrates his inability to lead an exclusively quietist life. To protest the harsh magistrate of Chin's hometown of Soochow, a hundred or more local scholars seized the opportunity of the death of the Emperor Shun-chin in 1661 to air the people's grievances. Shaken by this unexpected turn of events, the local authorities arrested eighteen of the scholars, including Chin, and had them beheaded for treason.

Chin was a many-sided man. Some of his biographers, impressed by his elevation of popular fiction and drama to the realm of high literature and moved by his unjust death, have seized upon the eccentric aspects of his life and portrayed him as a thoroughgoing political rebel and social iconoclast. Others, unsympathetic with his attack on the bandit-heroes of *Shui-hu chuan*, have characterized him as a reactionary and an ultra-conservative. Neither view represents the full picture. There was a mixture of the iconoclast and the conservative in Chin, but the conservative was clearly dominant.

Though Chin was basically a Confucianist, he was also interested in Taoist and Buddhist teachings. He saw the basic duty of man in the sphere of social conduct—in cultivating oneself to be a useful member of society and a filial son. He was deeply concerned with a proper education for his son Yung 雍. Annotating Tu Fu's poetry in the last years of his life, he came to admire Tu Fu not only as a great poet, but also as a conscientious and loyal minister in the best tradition of Confucian statesmanship. And when in 1660, just one year before his tragic death, he heard news that the emperor had praised his commentary on classical prose, he was overwhelmed with joy. With tears in his eyes he kowtowed to the north and composed on the spot a series of eight poems to express his deep gratitude and his frustration at his inability to serve the emperor in any concrete way.

Chin was a prolific writer with diverse interests. But largely for financial reasons a good part of what he wrote probably never appeared in print and was therefore lost. Among his extant writings are a collection of more than 380 poems in manuscript form known as the *Ch'en-yin lou shih-hsüan* 沉吟樓詩選 (Selected Poems of the Tower of Intonation); various short pieces and treatises on Buddhism, Taoism, and the *I-ching;* as well as a number of commentaries on various forms of Chinese literature, including poetry, historical texts, literary essays, drama, and the novel. His best-known writings, however, remain his commentaries on the *Shui-hu chuan,* on the *Hsi-hsiang chi,* on about 600 regulated-verse poems by 145 T'ang poets, and on 187 poems of various forms by Tu Fu.

As a commentator, Chin laid major emphasis on technique. This followed from his conviction that any good literary composition must be the result of very careful planning and meticulous execution. The reader, he argued, must not be content with reading for mere entertainment or information: only by pondering the intricate devices which an author employs can he appreciate his true spirit. By concerning himself primarily with the art of composition and the artistic function of individual words or expressions, Chin also helped initiate a new criticism which stands in sharp contrast to the abstract talk and vague assertions of many other Chinese critics.

The second outstanding feature of Chin as a commentator is his inventive spirit, his strong desire to go beyond the obvious for a deeper and fuller understanding of the text. This accounts for much of the originality of his commentaries. Ironically, however, it also constitutes the source of his weakness. Not infrequently the urge to find deeper hidden meanings became an obsession to attract attention or merely differ from other commentators.

Chin's aesthetic judgments are often Taoist- and Buddhist-inspired, though his political and moral position is essentially Confucian. His style is highly personal, often witty or whimsical but rising at times to poetic heights.

In the cases of the *Shui-hu chuan* and *Hsi-hsiang chi,* Chin's activity as a critic was not confined to providing analyses and evaluations. Whenever he deemed it desirable, he altered a text, his discarding of the last 50 of the 120 chapters of the *Shui-hu chuan,* largely for political reasons, being the most notable example. Most of his deletions and revisions, however, were determined by aesthetic considerations. As a result, his versions of the novel and the play read better than their predecessors. Since he frequently reserved his most glowing praise for his own emendations, it is a good, cautionary maxim, to be suspicious about those passages he lauds loudest.

Chin was not the first critic in China to advocate literature written in the vernacular language; nor was he the first to provide commentaries on vernacular works. But his commentaries on the *Shui-hu chuan* and *Hsi-hsiang chi* became so famous that they were eagerly read by countless readers together with the works themselves. In fact, his editions of these two works became the most popular ones, completely overshadowing all others for more than two hundred years. It was largely through his fame and his efforts that the vernacular literature of China gradually acquired some prestige among the literati, until, after the turn of the present century, the best works written in this tradition were finally elevated to the rank of literary classics. Thus Chin played a crucial role in promoting the cause of vernacular literature in China. It was also here that Chin made his most significant contributions as a literary scholar.

EDITIONS:

Ch'en-yin lou shih-hsüan 沉吟樓詩選. Shanghai, 1979. A photographic reproduction of a manuscript version.

Hui-t'u Hsi-hsiang chi: *Ti-liu ts'ai-tzu shu* 繪圖 西廂記：第六才子書. 4v. Shanghai, 1918.

Kuan-hua T'ang ts'ai-tzu shu hui-kao 貫華堂才子書彙稿. 6v. Shanghai, 1915.

Kuan-hua T'ang yüan-pen Shui-hu chuan: Ti-wu ts'ai-tzu shu 貫華堂原本水滸傳：第五才子書. 24v. Shanghai, 1934. A photolithographic reproduction.

T'ang ts'ai-tzu shih (chia-chi) 唐才子詩 (甲集). Taipei, 1963.

T'ien-hsia ts'ai-tzu pi-tu shu 天下才子必讀書. 6v. Shanghai and Peking, n.d.

TRANSLATIONS:

Lin, Yutang 林語堂. *The Importance of Living.* New York, 1937, pp. 130-36, 334-38. Translations of Chin's "Thirty-three Happy Moments" and a piece on the art of travel.

———. *The Importance of Understanding.* Cleveland, 1960, pp. 75-82, 83-85. Translations of Chin's prefaces to the *Hsi-hsiang chi* and *Shui-hu chuan.*

STUDIES:

Chang, Kuo-kuang 張國光. *Shui-hu yü Chin Sheng-t'an yen-chiu* 水滸與金聖嘆研究. Cheng-chou, 1981.

Chao, Ming-cheng 趙明政. "Chin Sheng-t'an te hsiao-shuo li-lun" 金聖嘆的小說理論, *Wen-hsüeh p'ing-lun ts'ung-k'an*, 13 (May 1982), 84-103.

Ch'en, Teng-yan 陳登原. *Chin Sheng-t'an chuan* 金聖嘆傳. Shanghai, 1935.

Ch'en, Wan-i 陳萬益. *Chin Sheng-t'an te wen-hsüeh p'i-p'ing k'ao-shu* 金聖嘆的文學批評考述 (Kuo-li T'ai-wan Ta-hsüeh wen-shih ts'ung-k'an 台灣大學文史叢刊). Taipei, 1976.

Ho, Man-tzu 何滿子. *Lun Chin Sheng-t'an p'ing-kai Shui-hu chuan* 論金聖嘆評改水滸傳. Shanghai, 1954.

Liu, Ta-chieh 劉大杰, and Chang P'ei-heng 章培恆. "Chin Sheng-t'an te wen-hseh p'i-p'ing" 金聖嘆的文學批評 , *Chung-hua wen-shih lun-ts'ung*, 3 (May 1963), 145-162.

Wang, John C. Y. 王靖宇. *Chin Sheng-t'an.* New York, 1972.

Yü, Yüan 郁沅. "Chin Sheng-t'an Kuan-hua t'ang pen *Shui-hu chuan* k'ao-cheng" 金聖嘆貫華堂本水滸傳考證 . *Ku-tai wen-hsüeh li-lun yen-chiu*, 1 (December 1979), 387-402.

—JW

Chin-tai shih-ch'ao 近代詩鈔 (Jottings of Poetry from the Contemporary Age) is the most important anthology of poetry from the late Ch'ing dynasty. It was compiled by Ch'en Yen 陳衍 (*tzu*, Shu-i 叔伊, *hao*, Shih-i 石遺, 1857-1938), who was born in Min-hou 閩侯 (Fukien). Considered among the most influential poets and critics of late Ch'ing and early Republican times, Ch'en worked as an advisor to the late Ch'ing statesman Chang Chih-tung 張之洞 and also served in the central government. Later, he taught at the precursor to Peking University and finally at Hsia-men University in his native Fukien. He consistently opposed the late Ch'ing reform movement led by K'ang Yu-wei,* and after the establishment of the Republic, did not recognize the new government's legitimacy. In addition to the *Chin-tai shih-ch'ao*, he left a substantial collection of poetry, the *Shih-i-shih shih* 石遺室詩, plus a thick volume of literary criticism *Shih-i-shih shih-hua* 石遺室詩話 (Poetry Talks from Shih-i's [Ch'en Yen's] Lodge).

The *Chin-tai shih-ch'ao* is a massive anthology containing the works of 369 poets. Many of the more important authors are represented by a substantial body of verse. The *Chin-tai shih-ch'ao* is arranged in chronological order and is one of the major sources for nineteenth-century Chinese poetry, a period of intense literary creativity and diversity. Since the collected works of many of the authors included have never been printed, and since even those late-Ch'ing collected works printed in China are rarely available outside of the country, this anthology is frequently the only source for a number of important late-Ch'ing classical poets.

The making of anthologies is a notoriously difficult enterprise, and even the best intentioned anthologist often creates a work which represents his own personal literary views. Along with Ch'en San-li 陳三立 and Cheng Hsiao-hsü 鄭孝胥, Ch'en Yen was one of the major representatives of the late Ch'ing movement promoting and imitating Sung-dynasty poetry. Ch'en Yen seems to have been particularly influenced by Huang T'ing-chien.* Accordingly, the anti-traditionalist, innovative aspects of Sung poetry did not have so strong an impact on him as on some other late Ch'ing authors. Ch'en's own poetry easily rivals Huang T'ing-chien's in its love of learned allusion.

Poets sympathetic to his views on Sung poetry are well represented, and such authors as Ho Shao-chi 何紹基, Ch'en San-li, and Cheng Hsiao-hsü play an important role in the anthology. Ch'en's former patron Chang Chih-tung is also liberally represented. On the other hand, one of the greatest late Ch'ing poets, Huang Tsun-hsien,* is given only three pages, possibly because, as a major reformer and Westernizer, Huang was political anathema to Ch'en and his friends. However, in all fairness to Ch'en Yen, it should be noted that another major innovator, Chin Ho, who could hardly be construed as a supporter of the Sung revival, is represented by a generous twenty-four pages, including some of his most iconoclastic verse. Perhaps Chin's distance in time from Ch'en allowed greater impartiality.

In addition to the poems themselves, the *Chin-tai shih-ch'ao* contains valuable biographical and critical material preceding each poet's verse.

EDITIONS:

Chin-tai shih-ch'ao 近代詩鈔. Shanghai, 1923.
Shih-i-shih shih-hua 石遺室詩話. Shanghai, 1929.
Shih-i hsien-sheng shih-chi 石遺先生詩集, Taipei, 1964.

STUDIES:

Jung, T'ien-ch'i 容天圻. "Chi Ch'en Shih-i" 記陳石遺, in *Hua yü sui-pi* 畫餘隨筆, Taipei, 1970, pp. 216-18.

—JDS

Chin-wen 金文 (bronze inscriptions) refers to intaglio texts found on bronze implements cast during the late Shang, Chou, Ch'in, and early Western Han periods. Bronze inscriptions range in length from single clan marks on some late Shang pieces to texts nearly five hundred characters in length on pieces from the Chou period. Texts occur on swords, musical instruments, coins, seals, and other bronze objects. However, the inscriptions of greatest length, content, and literary importance are those on bronze sacrificial vessels cast to immortalize success and status.

Shang bronze vessels began to display inscriptions during the reigns of the last several Shang kings. The first inscriptions were clan signs of varying complexity. Although of some semiotic interest, they are completely without literary value. The first true bronze texts contain two or three characters which indicate the ancestor in whose memory the vessel was cast: "Ancestor Kuei," "Wife Hao," and so on. These texts were soon followed by those which name the ancestor or patron as well as the type of vessel: "Make Father Chi ting," "Make Lü Ting," etc. The vast majority are similarly simple, but a few are of much greater complexity. The longest known Shang text has forty-one characters. From the reign of the last Shang king, it tells of military merit rewarded and the commissioning of the vessel to commemorate it. Told from a detached, third-person perspective, the text shows skill in building narrative tension by delaying actual mention of merit until late in the text when it is introduced in a quotation from a feudal lord. This inscription is also important for the evidence it provides on the Shang genesis of several Chou Bronze textual usages.

The earliest identifiable Western Chou bronze is a *kuei* 簋 which bears an inscription stating that the vessel was commissioned eight days after the Chou victory over the Shang (*Wen-wu*, 1977.8, 1-12). The text is thirty-two characters long and was composed to record the contributions its patron made to the Chou victory. It is of literary importance in showing early use of phraseology which became formulaic in later inscriptions: "The King awarded metal to X," and "X used [the reward] to make this precious sacrificial vessel." It is also an excellent example of the general format of later texts of this type: time, action, and reward, followed by various clichés. Written with the desire to inform and impress the reader with a particular story, this bronze text is the earliest datable example of Western Chou literary effort.

The practice of composing commemorative texts for casting in bronze reached its zenith in the Western Chou. While many bronzes of the period contain no texts, and many others contain inscriptions which simply state that the vessel was made in the honor of a certain ancestor or by a particular person, others display texts hundreds of characters in length. These lengthy texts generally focus on the meritorious deeds of the patrons of the bronzes and the largesse of the Chou rulers. They often employ verbal formulas such as: "Dare to make known the King's magnificence," "Accomplished and old ancestors," and "May generations upon generations forever treasure and use this sacrificial vessel," as well as the two clichés mentioned in the preceding paragraph. The texts tend to state the date, discuss the deeds which merit rewarding, give an inventory of the acts of generosity of the ruler, and proclaim the desire of the patron of the bronze to make known the king's grandeur and have the vessel used by a myriad generations.

The *Shih-ch'iang P'an*史牆盤 provides a good example of a lengthy bronze inscription. With 284 characters, it has the longest Western Chou bronze text found since 1949 (*Wen-wu*, 1978:3, 21-34). It can be precisely dated to the reign of King Kung (946-935 B.C.), and it provides a firm reference point in a study of the evolution of bronze textual practices. It has the basic structural points discussed above, but it goes beyond simple clichés of language and story and shows a concern for literary style and organization.

The text divides itself by content and tone into two "chapters" of roughly equal length. The first begins with a discussion of the outstanding attributes and accomplishments of the six preceding kings. A verbal movement suggesting stately, royal progression is created through strings of sentences of an even number of syllables, most frequently four. Several sentences with an uneven number are balanced by another sentence of an equal number, further building an atmosphere of weighty, measured demeanor. Monotony is avoided by a controlled use of sentences of differing lengths. The overall tone is dignified and in keeping with the imperial subject matter.

There is an unmistakable interest in parallelism of content and structure through-out the entire composition. In this first section the names of five of the six kings are preceded by two adjectives, and the sixth name has two syllables of introduction before it. The accomplishments of the kings are listed in units of roughly equal length, and the efforts of King Wu in fighting barbarian tribes are given a balanced liveliness in two grammatically parallel structures of three syllables each.

There is a perceptible change of mood and pace when the present ruler is introduced. The subject matter changes from descriptions of past feats to expressions of the goodwill of the spirit world and hopes for the future. The change is signaled by a sentence of eight syllables followed by sentences with five and three syllable tempo previously established. There appears to have been an attempt to use rhyme in this first chapter, but the exact features of the rhyme scheme are obscure.

The second chapter represents a break in content and tone. The dignity of the ancestral heritage of the writer is underscored initially by the use of two four-syllable sentences, in telling of the experiences of the founder of the family at the court of the Chou conquerors. A less detached, third-person narrative stance is discernible in the use of the adverb "peacefully" to describe how the first ancestor was living at the time of the Shang defeat. Perhaps reflecting a reverberation of enduring suspicions caused by a shift of the loyalties of the ancestor from the Shang to the Chou, the adverb was probably chosen with great care. This text was composed by a court historian, a person presumably skilled with words. His use of language and structures similar to those found in the *Shih-ching* and the *Shu-ching* shows that he was versed in the major literature of his day.

A string of fourteen sentences of four syllables each, broken precisely in half by a six syllable sentence, is used to resume a stately and dignified rhythm in telling of the accomplishments of the writer's other ancestors. The text ends in a clatter of sentences of varying lengths of a list of empty, ritualistic expressions of filial sensitivities and hopes for various types of good fortune. The effect of these sentences is reinforced by the crowding together of the last twenty characters into a space no larger than that previously allotted to fifteen characters.

Recent discoveries are correcting earlier impressions that bronzes created after the Western Chou seldom if ever contain lengthy inscriptions. A set of sixty-four *chung* bells and accompanying materials from the state of Tseng yield texts with thousands of characters on musical laws and other subjects from 433 B.C. A *hu* 壺 and a *ting* 鼎 with texts of over 450 characters each outline the history of the ruling family of the state of Chung-shan 中山 down to *c.* 310 B.C., and skillfully tell a tale of pious, foreign adventures. However, Western Han bronze texts rarely do more than note the day and place of manufacture and give the capacity of the vessel.

Shang and Chou bronze texts were composed to tell a story from a particular point of view to a particular audience. While characterizations are often neglected, a sophisticated artistic ability is frequently revealed in the narrative techniques employed. By the middle of the Chou period narrative style had evolved from a completely detached, reportorial stance to the inclusion of unmistakable commentary. When these writing skills are considered in conjunction with the fact that many bronze vessels with lengthy texts were so poorly made as to be little more than a means to present the text to the reader, it becomes clear that bronze texts should be considered as works of literary art.

STUDIES:

Jung, Keng 容庚. *Chin-wen-pien, Hsü-pien* 金文編, 續編. Taipei, 1969. A compendium of individual bronze graphs. It gives brief comments on meanings and indicates textual sources of graphs.

Chou, Fa-kao 周法高, *et al. Chin-wen ku-lin* 金文詁林. Organized on the above (Jung Keng), it goes further and gives inscriptional contexts for individual graphs, also supplies extensive commentaries on meanings of graphs and includes texts from later finds.

Shirakawa, Shizuka 白川靜. "Seishū kōki no kimbun to shihen" 西周後期の金文と詩篇. *Ritsumeikan bungaku*, 6 (1967), 467-504.

—SM

Chinese as a Literary Language—Vietnam. For at least two millennia, Chinese has served as one of the methods of written communication in the area occupied by the modern state of Vietnam. The status of the Chinese language and the works produced therein as well as translations from it and its influence on Vietnamese will be summarized under three rubrics: (1) Chinese in Vietnam before the tenth century, (2) Chinese in independent Vietnam, and (3) Chinese impact on Vietnamese literature.

1. There is no evidence to date of the existence of any sort of writing in the area of the traditional Vietnamese homeland, the region roughly corresponding to modern northern Vietnam, until the arrival of the Chinese in the third century B.C. The Former Han offically annexed the area which was known to them variously as Chiao-chih (Giao-chi 交阯) or Chiao-chou (Giao-châu 交州); the T'ang employed the term An-nan 安南 (An-Nam) and with the establishment of a Chinese administration, particularly after A.D. 42, came all the apparatus of traditional Chinese culture with its peculiar literary emphasis as well as the wholesale immigration of ethnic Chinese. What language or languages were spoken by the autochthonous inhabitants is uncertain, but it is not unreasonable to suppose that an Austroasiatic ancestor of modern Vietnamese was in the ascendancy.

A number of the administrators appointed to govern Chiao-chih exercised great independence from central Chinese authority, but many, particularly Shih Hsieh (Sĩ Nhiếp 士燮, 137?-226), were credited with efforts to spread the knowledge and exercise of written Chinese. Native-born candidates for office, drawn from the Sino-Vietnamese population, were from time to time successful in the palace examinations and one, Chiang Kung-fu (Khương Công Phụ 姜公輔, d. *c.* 805), rose to be grand councilor under the T'ang. Apart from a single poem and an essay, both by Chiang, no evidence of literary output of the region has come down to us from this period. It is a surety, however, that the standard classics were being disseminated and that verse and prose of the sort found everywhere else in China were being composed here as well.

It should be added that Chiao-chih was the home of the famous third-century translator monk K'ang Seng-hui (Khang Tăng Hội 康僧會) and a foyer of early Buddhism, which doubtless arrived from South Asia in the wake of an already well-established commerce around the second century A.D. Works in Chinese of Buddhist inspiration trace their roots to this period as well, as the antiquity of Buddhist establishments in the region rivals that of China proper.

2. With the collapse of the T'ang, the Vietnamese, who had by now evolved a new separate cultural identity incorporating both indigenous and sinitic elements, successfully withdrew from Chinese hegemony and established themselves as an independent political entity. The literature which is known to have survived from this time is entirely in Chinese (which, when read with a Vietnamese pronunciation, is usually called Sino-Vietnamese) and consists, with rare exceptions, of poetry on Buddhist topics. The earliest extant expressions of Vietnamese nationalist sentiment, couched in highly Chinese terms, then began to appear in pieces such as the *Nim Quốc Sơn Hà* (*Nan-kuo shan-ho* 南國山河) of Lý Thường Kiệt (Li Ch'ang-chieh 李常傑, 1019-1105).

While most of the writers through the end of the Lý dynasty (Li 李, 1010-1225) were Buddhist monks and while the clergy had great influence at court during this period, Confucianism and the influence of the Chinese classics and Chinese secular literature in general via Confucian studies began a slow but steady ascent. The Văn Miếu (Wen-miao 文廟, Temple of Literature) was founded in 1070. In 1075, literary examinations for the mandarinate were instituted and in 1086 a Han-lâm (Han-lin 翰林) Academy was formed; but, acting rather as a brake on the wider spread of a knowledge of Chinese literature, access to these institutions was limited to the royal family and members of the aristocracy.

With the coming to power of the Trần dynasty (Ch'en 陳, 1225-1400), although Buddhist influences remained, literature composed in Chinese began more and more to also show the influence of more recent Chinese writing. Mạc Đĩnh Chi (Mo Ting-chih 莫挺之, d. 1346) was familiar with the T'ang poets, for example, and there is evidence of national self-awareness in the *fu* compositions of Trương Hán Siêu (Chang Han-ch'ao 張漢超, d. 1354) and the proclamations of Trần Quốc Tuấn (Ch'en Kuo-chün 陳國峻, 1213-1300). The extensive corpus of the Trần period in Chinese also includes the earliest extant historical and semi-historical writing from Vietnam which, especially in the case of officially commissioned works such as the *Đại Việt Sử Ký* (*Ta-Yüeh shih-chi* 大越史記), tends to rely heavily on the standard Chinese histories and summaries and on universal compendia such as the *Tzu-chih t'ung-chien* 資治通鑑.

The events which brought the Trần to a close had a particular bearing on the role of Sino-Vietnamese literature. The last prime minister, Hồ Quý Ly (Hu Chi-li 胡季犛, 1336?-1407?), instituted a number of reforms, especially after he usurped the throne in 1400, some of which aimed at lessening the sway of the Confucian literati. *Chữ nôm* (宁喃), a system for transcribing the Vietnamese vernacular, had by this time already been in existence for at least two hundred years; Hồ Quý Ly gave *chữ nôm* its first court sanction, at the expense of Sino-Vietnamese, for use in certain official ordinances. In 1407, the Ming invaded Vietnam in an effort to reincorporate the area in the Celestial Empire; to this end, they immediately proceeded with a heavy-handed program of re-sinicization that led to the burning of heterodox books, including any in *chữ nôm*, and all writings of a nationalist character. Vietnamese scholars have traditionally blamed the burning of the books for the paucity of non-Sino-Vietnamese works in the pre-Lê corpus.

The Vietnamese, under Lê Lợi (Li Li 黎利, c. 1385-1433), rid themselves of the Ming occupiers and while the newly established Lê dynasty (Li 黎, 1428-1788) witnessed a rebirth of vernacular writing, Sino-Vietnamese remained the preferred language of government and literature. Indeed, perhaps the most significant and certainly the most famous remaining Sino-Vietnamese work is the *Bình Ngô Đại Cáo* (*P'ing Wu ta-kao* 平吳大誥, 1428) of Nguyễn Trãi (Juan Chai 阮廌, 1380-1442), the proclamation announcing the victory over the Ming. And the preeminent place of Nguyễn Trãi in Sino-Vietnamese literature, dedicated nationalist though he was, attests to the continued importance of literary Chinese as a written language throughout this period.

Although the sixteenth to nineteenth centuries were in general troubled times for Vietnam, the rather conventional Sino-Vietnamese literature of the period seldom reflects this state of affairs. Royal governments continued to recruit mandarins through the literary-examination system and Sino-Vietnamese continued to be the language employed in nearly all formal communication, but there was little innovation in the creative sphere and, in all probability, Sino-Vietnamese literary output reached only a very limited audience inside the country and had little or no influence on the course of Chinese literature as a whole.

But if Sino-Vietnamese fiction and verse were highly derivative during this period, several books of significance were produced in the field of history. Ngô Sĩ Liên (Wu Shih-lien 吳士連, 15th century), recasting the *Đại Việt Sử Ký* gave us the *Đại Việt Sử Ký Toàn Thư* (*Ta-Yüeh shih-chi ch'üan-shu* 大越史記全書), a standard work on the history of pre-modern Vietnam which was, in turn, further extended in the mid-seventeenth century by Pham Cong Trứ (Fan Kung-chu 范公著, 1599-1675) *et al.* In the mid-nineteenth century there followed the *Khâm Định Việt Sử Thông Giám Cương Mục* (*Ch'in-ting Yüeh-shih t'ung-chien kang-mu* 欽定越史通鑑綱目), prepared under the direction of Pan Thanh Giản (Fan Ch'ing-chien 潘清簡, 1796-1867), essentially a correction and updating of the aforementioned work. Together, these two books serve as the backbone of our knowledge of traditional Vietnamese history to this day.

The prolific Lê Quý Đôn (Li Kuei-tun 黎貴惇, 1726-1784) was the bright spot in the generally drab, dully Confucian literary landscape of Vietnam in the eighteenth century. Reputed to have demonstrated his erudition in literary jousts while ambassador to the Ch'ing court, he can fairly be said to be the last of the great Sino-Vietnamese scholars, having left among other works the encyclopedic *Vân Đài Loại Ngữ* (*Yün-t'ai lei-yü* 芸臺類語) and the *Kiến Văn Tiểu Lục* (*Chien-wen hsiao-lu* 見聞小錄), as well as a history entitled *Đại Việt Thông Sử* (*Ta-Yüeh t'ung-shih* 大越通史).

While most traces of originality and innovation had long vanished from Sino-Vietnamese writing, all life was not yet extinguished. The brief populist Tây Sơn dynasty (Hsi-shan 西山, 1788-1802) had attempted to elevate the status of the demotic, but Chinese writing survived this onslaught and the Nguyễn dynasty (Juan 阮, 1802-1945) again used Sino-Vietnamese for record keeping and nearly all official intercourse. And when France annexed Vietnam late in the nineteenth century, major organized opposition to their presence was led by the literati, whose political writings were primarily in Sino-Vietnamese (whence, it may be supposed, their inefficacy). The official attitude of the French administration toward the teaching and propagation of Sino-Vietnamese wavered. Such debate as there was was brought to a head by French fears that revolutionary or, worse, pro-German propaganda was being brought in from or via China in the form of books in Chinese and a ban was imposed on their import beginning with the first World War. At the same time, the triennial literary examinations for entry into the mandarinate was suppressed and the death knell for Sino-Vietnamese writing began to toll. Today, knowledge of literary Chinese is no more widespread in Vietnam than is knowledge of Latin in the West and outside the steadily dwindling ethnic Chinese community, its daily use is now hardly more than decorative.

Chữ nôm, a transcription system for the Vietnamese language based on Chinese characters, was probably devised by Vietnamese Buddhists some time during the T'ang dynasty, but our earliest solid evidence for its employment does not come until the period of the first major independent Vietnamese dynasty, the Lý. To the extent that many aspects of Chinese culture had by this time been absorbed by Vietnamese culture, it is practically impossible to trace all the various Chinese elements which appear to have affected writing in Vietnamese. Nonetheless, three major areas of influence should be noted: translations from Chinese or Sino-Vietnamese, vocabulary borrowing in Vietnamese, and Chinese influence on creative writing in Vietnamese.

Translations of the standard Chinese classics seem to have existed for some time. Shih Hsieh was credited (apocryphally to be sure) with having made such translations as early as the second century, and Hồ Quý Ly at the beginning of the fifteenth century ordered translations to be made to facilitate the instruction of the people, clear evidence of the respect in which the Vietnamese elite held these works. Extant copies of the classics translated in *chữ nôm* are, however, extremely difficult to find, leading one to conclude that the content of the classics was still primarily acquired in Sino-Vietnamese after instruction in the latter was given via such *chữ nôm* primers as the so-called *Thousand Character Litany* or *Nhất Thiên Tự* (I ch'ien tzu 一千字, not to be confused with the well-known Chinese work of similar title). On the other hand, since the nineteenth century, when *quốc ngữ*, the romanized transcription of Vietnamese first introduced by Christian missionaries in the seventeenth century, started to replace *chữ nôm* as the preferred way of writing the vernacular, a considerable number of translations from the classics have appeared, beginning with the work of Trương Vĩnh Ký who published the first *quốc ngữ* translation of the

Tứ Thư (*Szu shu* 四書) in 1889. And the anti-French works in Chinese characters written by early Vietnamese nationalists, while inaccessible to the public in the original, eventually found their way into the language of the people, either in *quốc ngữ* translations or even in the form of songs. Today nearly all of the classics and many of the major works of Chinese literature are available in Vietnamese, as are translations of many pieces of Sino-Vietnamese literature.

Though Vietnamese appears to be an Austroasiatic language genetically related to Mon-Khmer, a substantial proportion of the available vocabulary (some estimates range as high as fifty percent) is borrowed directly from Chinese, and because of the phonological and morphological similarities between Vietnamese and Chinese, any Chinese word can be systematically integrated into Vietnamese, at least in theory. The process is still ongoing, though to a lesser extent than before, owing to renewed nationalist sentiment. A Chinese-based terminology is to be found throughout Vietnamese literature, particularly that portion produced by the old literati who were so steeped in sinitic culture as to have thought of much of it as a natural continuum of their own. This vocabulary exerted its subtle influence constantly, because of, among other things, the easy access it provided for literary allusion to Chinese works and the scope for refined and arcane bilingual word play it supplied.

While much of the vigor had disappeared from Sino-Vietnamese writing by the eighteenth century, the rapid growth of writing in *chữ nôm* allowed for the true expression of Vietnamese creativity. Nevertheless, the habits of centuries gone by were difficult to cast off, and though many of the great works of *chữ nôm* literature could only have been written by Vietnamese, the settings, as in the best known and most frequently quoted piece, the *Kim Vân Kiều* (*Chin Yün Ch'iao* 金雲翹), are often Chinese—mention is made of frost and snow and other phenomena unknown in Vietnam, and the language is replete with sinicisms. In some famous examples, there existed a Sino-Vietnamese version of the work which served as a skeleton upon which to sculpt the Vietnamese version; such was the case with both the *Kim Vân Kiều,* and that moving lament upon the continual civil strife in Vietnam, the *Chinh Phụ Ngâm (Cheng-fu yin* 征婦吟). With these examples as with many others, it is the vernacular version that is remembered while the original in Chinese characters is for all intents forgotten. In such cases, where Chinese influence is readily recognizable, the popularity of the work is largely due to the evocative beauty of the language and to dexterity in the juxtaposition of images, features directly linked to the realities of the Vietnamese, as opposed to the Chinese, language.

The role of literary Chinese in Vietnam might be likened to that of Latin in Europe. In each event, the language came as the tongue of the conqueror and stayed, long after the conqueror left, as the medium for administration and learned discourse. As new nations formed, they gradually shifted their writing to the vernacular, but by the time this later phenomenon occurred, the vernacular was heavily overlaid with borrowings from the classical. Images and themes drawn from the literature of the classical language were converted to the purposes of the new language and its literature, and thus the one was entwined with the other, only to be fully extricable in modern times, if at all.

EDITIONS:

Đào, Phương Bình *et al. Thơ Văn Lý-Trần.* V. I & III, Hanoi, 1977 and 1978. In Vietnamese with original texts in Chinese characters, this is the most complete anthology yet available of the early Sino-Vietnamese corpus.

DeFrancis, John. *Colonialism and Language Policy in Viet Nam.* The Hague, 1977. An excellent general survey of the roles various languages have played in Vietnamese history, including a clear account of the position of literary Chinese at various periods.

Đinh, Gia Khánh *et al. Hợp Tuyển Thơ Văn Việt-Nam.* V. 2 & 3, Hanoi, 1962 and 1963. Gives broader coverage to the later (post-14th c.) Sino-Vietnamese corpus than the work cited above, but lacks texts in characters.

Durand, Maurice. *Introduction à la littérature vietnamienne.* Paris, 1969. A general survey of Vietnamese literary history by one of the most respected scholars in the field, who died before his manuscript reached final form. Edited by Nguyễn Trần Huân.

Gaspardone, Emile. "Bibliographie annamite," *BEFEO,* 34 (1934), 1-173. The standard work on early Vietnamese bibliography; filled with highly detailed and useful notes. Based largely on the list of Phan Huy Chú 潘輝注 (1782-1840) to be found in his *Lịch triều hiến-chương loại chí* 歷朝憲章類誌.

———. "Les langues de l'annamite littéraire," *TP,* 39 (1950), 213-227. An analysis, with numerous illustrative examples, of the influence of classical Chinese on the Vietnamese literary idiom and their frequent intertwining in traditional poetry.

Huỳnh, Sanh Thông, trans. *The Tale of Kieu.* New York, 1977. The finest translation of the best known piece of traditional vernacular literature.

———, trans. and ed. *The Heritage of Vietnamese Poetry.* New Haven, 1979. Best introduction.

Lê, Thánh Khôi. *Le Viet-Nam, histoire et civilisation.* Paris, 1955. A useful reference tool for the non-specialist.

Nguyễn, Khắc Viên *et al. Anthologie de la littérature vietnamienne.* 2v. Hanoi, 1972-73. A standard anthology of traditional literature containing a broadly representative selection with background essays of a Marxist nature.

Nguyễn, Trãi 阮廌 (early 16th c.). *Ức Trai Tập* 抑齋集. 2v. Saigon, 1971-1972. An anthology (originally published *c.* 1865) of all known works in Sino-Vietnamese by Vietnam's greatest master of that idiom, reissued with both the original character text, a *quốc-ngữ* transliteration, and a vernacular Vietnamese translation (the rather rare *chữ-nôm* poems are not included).

O'Harrow, Stephen. "Nguyễn Trãi's *Bình Ngô Đại Cáo* 平吳大誥 of 1428: The Development of a Vietnamese National Identity," *Journal of Southeast Asian Studies,* X (1979), 159-174. Discusses the use by the Vietnamese of Chinese concepts, expressed via literary allusion in an important Sino-Vietnamese public document, to achieve Vietnamese ends.

———. "On the Origins of *chữ-nôm:* The Vietnamese Demotic Writing System," *Indo-Pacifica,* 1 (1981), 159-186. Discusses the reasons for, and venue of the origins of, the transcription system for the Vietnamese vernacular.

Trần, Văn Giáp *et al. Lược Truyện Các Tác Gia Việt-Nam.* v. 1 & 2, Hanoi, 1971 and 1972. The most complete general bibliography of Vietnamese literature currently available; no characters.

———. *Thơ Văn Yêu Nước, nửa sau thế kỷ* XIX (1858-1900). Hanoi, 1970. An anthology of the later nineteenth century Vietnamese corpus, including many works in Sino-Vietnamese with character texts.

Woodside, Alexander B. *Viet-Nam and the Chinese Model: A Comparative Study of Nguyen and Ch'ing Civil Government in the First Half of the Nineteenth Century.* Cambridge, Mass., 1971. Contains a useful discussion of the roles of Sino-Vietnamese and *chu-nom* in government and society.

—SOH

Chinese Literature in Japanese Translation

Chinese Literature in Japanese Translation can be said to have existed ever since Chinese literature first became known in Japan. Within the context of Japanese literary history, interpretation of Chinese literature is inseparable from the long history of *kanbungaku* 漢文學, the study of literature written in Chinese, whether by Chinese or Japanese, in China or in Japan, whether regarded as isolated bodies of literature or as the influence of the Chinese literary tradition on the Japanese.

The earliest mention of Chinese texts in Japanese records comes from the *Kojiki* 古事記 (712) which records the names of the *Lun-yü* 論語 and the *Ch'ien-tzu wen* 千字文, and it is generally assumed from this that many other Chinese texts were already known in Japan by the fifth century. This assumption is supported by the fact that other early texts such as the *Nihon Shoki* 日本書紀 (720) and the *Man'yōshū* 万葉集 (759) contain numerous citations from Chinese works.

Formal diplomatic missions between China and Japan began in 735 and were terminated in 894, but Japanese traveled to China as early as 552 and have collected literature there ever since. One early Heian-period catalogue, the *Nihonkou kenzai shomoku* 日本國見在書目 (*c.* 885) of Fujiwara Sukeyo 藤原佐世 records the presence in Japan of more than 17,000 *chüan* of Chinese works in 1500 divisions under some forty categories. Other sources reveal the existence of large numbers of non-classical works. Since the titles of the works known in Japan, which was at the eastern limit of Chinese culture, agree well with the titles of the works from about the same period found at the start of the twentieth century at Tun-huang, which was at the western limit, it seems likely that they are representative of what was then available in China itself.

It would seem that from early on the Japanese made their selections from the Chinese literature available to them without much regard for received Chinese critical opinion. Po Chü-i,* for instance, was enormously popular in Japan even in his own lifetime. While Po was practically canonized in the Japanese literary pantheon by the year 1000 under the auspices of his Japanese patron Fujiwara no Michinzane 藤原道實, poets like Tu Fu* and Han Yü* had to await Japanese interest in Sung reappraisals of these poets before their fame spread to Japan through the Zen monks of the fourteenth century and later.

From the tenth century on, the practice of reading Chinese works directly as Chinese gave way to reading them in an adaptation of Japanese for reading Chinese texts. This sort of reading, called *kundoku* 訓読, was the forerunner of today's *kaeriten* 返り点 reading marks and additional inflections, and was a development that paralleled the change in script from Chinese on the one hand, and 'Man'yōgana' 万葉仮名 on the other (i.e., Chinese characters used only to represent Japanese sounds), to *kana-majiri kanbun* 仮名交漢文 texts in which Chinese characters are used for their meaning but all inflections are represented by Japanese *kana*. From the tenth century onward the handling of Chinese texts became the prerogative of the great families such as the Sugawara, Ōe, etc. At the same time that the masculine court society adopted a severely "Chinese" style of letters for use in public affairs, the famous female writers of the Heian were reinterpreting Chinese literary influences through works like the *Genji Monogatari* 源氏物語 and *Makura no Sōshi* 枕草子 in a very elegant and thoroughly native Japanese. The same process can be seen operating in poetry in works like the *Wakan Roeishū* 和漢朗詠集 (1013) in which lines of Chinese poetry (overwhelmingly by the poet Po Chü-i) are set down next to poems written in Japanese.

In spite of the lack of formal embassies from Japan to China during the Sung period (there had been many during the T'ang) and in spite of official Sung interdiction on the export of nearly all books of Chinese origin, many contemporary and earlier Chinese works were brought to Japan privately by merchants and monks. An example is the *T'ai-p'ing yü-lan,** export of which was banned during the Sung but which managed nonetheless to find its way into the hands of Taira no Kiyomori 平清盛 in 1179. A century later several dozen sets of this work existed in Japan.

Japanese printed editions of Chinese works, known as *wakokubon* 和刻本, are known as early as the 1325 edition of the poetry of Han-shan.* The earliest of these sorts of works were printed from blocks carved by Chinese artisans. The earliest classical work still extant in *wakokubon* edition is the *Lun-yü* text and annotations known as the *Rongo shūkai* 論語集解 of 1364. Annotated texts printed in the late Kamakura and Muromachi periods under the auspices of the Zen Buddhist institutions are known as *gozanban* 五山版 and are important in the history of translation because they often provide detailed markings indicating the Japanese readings to be followed and are often extensively annotated according to their Japanese redactor's understanding of the text. A good example of this sort of work is the *Shiryū jikkai* 四流入海 (Four Streams into the Sea), a compilation of commentaries by four medieval Zen monks on the poetry of Su Shih.*

With the institutionalization in the Edo period (1615-1868) of Neo-Confucianism as the state creed came an unprecedented demand for Chinese literature of all varieties ranging from classical exegeses and encyclopedic compendia to vernacular fiction. During this period new methods of translating vernacular literature were adopted by important translators such as the famous Nagasaki interpreter and translator Okajima Kanzan 岡島冠山 (d. 1727). At its height between 1688 and 1703, the Nagasaki trade averaged seventy ships a year from China, a figure which rapidly dwindled along with the supply of Japan's chief export, copper. A century later only ten ships a year are recorded in the port. In 1699 these ships carried such works to Japan as the *Shih-san ching chu-shu* 十三經注疏 (Commentaries to the Thirteen Classics), the *Erh-shih-i shih* 二十一史 (The Twenty-one Histories), and the *Po-ch'uan hsüeh-hai* 百川學海 (Sea of Study in the One-hundred Streams)—in other words, the kinds of books a Chinese bureaucrat would find useful. Besides these sorts of works, however, there was a great interest in Chinese fiction in the vernacular as well as the classical languages, ostensibly for the furthering of the goals of Neo-Confucian policy.

By the Edo period there are three types of "translation" of Chinese works: the familiar *kundoku* renderings, a more extended translation known as *kunyaku* 訓訳, and the sort that accords with the modern notion of "translation" in the West, *iyaku* 意訳 or "translating the ideas" of the Chinese text. In a sense this type of translation occurred in Japan as early as the late Heian-period retellings of Chinese tales in such *setsuwa* 説話 collections as *Konjaku monogatari* 今昔物語 and *Kokin chomonjū* 古今著聞集.

The first "translations" in the modern sense of the word date from such works as Hayashi Razan's 林羅山 thirty-five translations of Chinese tales from *Hu-mei chü-t'an* 狐媚叢談 in his *Gobisho* 狐媚抄. In 1698 appeared the *Kaidan Zensho* 怪談全書 containing thirty-two tales from *Ch'ien-teng hsin-hua,** *Shuo-yüan* (see Liu Hsiang), *T'ai-p'ing kuang-chi,** and other sources. Other adaptations from this period include the tales in the *Otogibōko* 伽婢子 (Hand Puppets, 1666) by Asai Ryōi 浅井了意 (d. 1619), also inspired by the *Ch'ien-teng hsin-hua* of Ch'ü Yu. These translations from classical sources are paralleled by a number from vernacular sources. With the organization of a study group by the Edo thinker Ogyū Sorai 荻生徂徠 around Okarima Kanzan in the early eighteenth-century city of Edo (modern Tokyo), interest grew in the actual spoken language of Chinese and its literary products. During this period translations in the modern sense of the word, known as *tsūzokusho* 通俗書, first appeared. In 1692, for example, the *Tsūzoku Sangokushi*, a translation into *kanji* and *katakana* of the Chinese romance *San-kuo-chih yen-i*,* was published. This work was followed by the intermittent appearance between 1759 and 1790 of a Japanese translation of *Shui-hu chuan** entitled *Tsūzoku Suikoden* 通俗水滸傳. Works like these were made possible because of the labors of Okajima Kanzan and his group, who in 1727 had already published the first ten of one hundred chapters of a newly punctuated edition of *Shui-hu chuan.* Another ten chapters appeared in 1759, after Okajima's death. In similar fashion, a Japanese translation of *Hsi-yu chi*,* *Tsūzoku Saiyūki* 通俗西遊記, appeared in installments between 1758 and 1831. These were, strictly speaking, the first works intended as literal "translations" from Chinese, rather than as derivations, adaptations, or retellings. It might be noted that the modern term for "fiction," *shōsetsu* 小説, was used much earlier in Japan to indicate the sort of fiction that the Chinese themselves called *hsiao-shuo,* appearing as early as 1484 as a term of derision for another's opinion. By 1754, however, it had come to indicate a new category of book, at first fiction translated from the Chinese and later any work of fiction in general.

The recent history of Japanese translation of Chinese literature is particularly distinguished, known to a greater or lesser degree by all scholars of Chinese literature because of the gap it fills. While there is a certain amount of interpretative and especially textual literary scholarship in China, Hong Kong, and Taiwan, Chinese scholarship is too often bound by earlier traditions to be of much use to Western scholars, whose approaches to Chinese lit-

erature are most often radically different from those of the Chinese themselves. One may search in vain, for example, for a good annotated edition of a novel like *Hung-lou meng** which, like its Western counterpart, attempts to systematically define difficult or vernacular terms and to provide contexts for obscure names. Although the Chinese produce great numbers of inexpensive editions of literary works, they have rarely felt the need to interpret such works to themselves. The Japanese, however, have constantly been faced with the necessity of explicating Chinese literature, with the result that they have produced extremely able translations of the major works of Chinese literature, translations notable for their scholarly treatment of the texts as well as their appeal to a mass reading audience.

To highlight only some of the many modern series of translations of Chinese literature into Japanese, the 1922 *Kokuyakubun Taisei* 國訳文大成 in four categories (Tokyo: Kokumin Bunko Kankōkai), "Literature" and "Classics" each comprising twenty volumes, might be mentioned; the 1927 continuation *Zoku kokuyakubun taisei* 読國訳文大成 added another twenty volumes to each category. In more modern, or less traditional, format are the recent series published by the major publishing houses: the 1962 *Chūgoku koten bungaku zenshu* 中國古典文學全集 in thirty-three volumes by Heibonsha; Meiji Shoin's 1960 *Shinyaku kanbun taikei* 新訳漢文大系; Heibonsha's 1963 *Chūgoku gendai bungaku senshū* 中國現代文學選集 in twenty volumes; and Shūeisha's 1966 *Kanshi taikei* 漢詩大系 in twenty-four volumes. There are also individual studies of separate authors that contain complete translations of the works of major Chinese poets, philosophers, and the like, but these are far too numerous to list.

Following the introduction of Western culture into Japan, the field of "Chinese studies" (*kanbungaku* 漢文學), once of immediate and vital concern for Japanese culture, inevitably retreated into a different perspective. The modern practice of rendering Chinese works in Japanese translations just like any other foreign literature reflects the disappearance of a whole world of imtermediary culture surrounding the interpretation of China in Japan, only one of several paradoxes inherent in the question of the "translation of Chinese literature in Japan."

STUDIES:

Asō, Isoji 麻生磯次. *Edo bungaku to Shina bungaku* 江戸文學と支那文學. Tokyo, 1946.

Cheng, Ch'ing-mao 鄭清茂. *Chung-kuo wen-hsüeh tsai Jih-pen* 中國文學在日本. Taipei, 1968.

Ishizaki, Matazō 石崎又造. *Kinsei Nihon ni okeru Shina zokugo bungaku shi* 近世日本に於ける支那俗語文學史. Tokyo, 1940.

Keene, Donald. *World Within Walls: Japanese Literature of the Pre-Modern Era, 1600-1867.* New York, 1976.

Kojima, Noriyuki 小島憲文. *Jōdai Nihon bungaku to Chūgoku bungaku* 上代日本文學と中國文學. Tokyo, 1962.

Nakamura, Yukihiko 中村幸彦. "Wakokubon" 和刻本, in Mizuta Norihisa 水田紀久 and Rai Tsutomu 賴惟勤, eds., *Nihon kangaku* 日本漢學 (Chūgoku bunka sōsho, v. 9), Tokyo, 1968, pp. 260ff.

———. "Hon'yaku, Chūshaku, Hon'an" 翻譯, 注釋, 翻案, *ibid.*, pp. 272ff.

T'an, Ju-ch'ien 譚汝謙, ed. *Jih-pen i Chung-kuo chu tsung-ho shu-lu* 日本訳中國書綜合目錄. Hong Kong, 1981. With a long introduction.

Yen, Shao-t'ang 嚴紹璗. *Jih-pen te Chung-kuo hsüeh-chia* 日本的中國學家. Peking, 1980.

—DP

Chinese Literature in Korean Translation

Chinese Literature in Korean Translation began quite late. Because of geographical proximity, Chinese logographs and classics were introduced into the ancient Korean kingdoms sometime in or before the first century A.D. At least from the fourth century Koreans learned to use the Chinese writing system. In subsequent centuries, all official writings and much literature were written in Chinese and in Chinese literary forms. The Korean upper classes were therefore bilingual in a special sense of the term—they spoke Korean but wrote in Chinese.

Moreover, the civil-service examination required of every candidate a knowledge of Chinese verse and prose. From childhood each Korean aspirant for a public career was educated in and read more or less the same books, mostly books in Chinese. Because Chinese was the usual means of expression and communication of the Korean literati, they did not need translations. Translation activities began only after the invention of the Korean alphabet in 1443-1444, as an attempt to overcome a discrepancy between the spoken (Korean) and the written (Chinese) languages.

At first a number of Chinese Buddhist scriptures were translated—the *Lotus Sutra*, the *Diamond Sutra*, and the *Sukgavativyuha Sutra*. Major works of translation in the fifteenth century included those of the poetry of Tu Fu* (*Tusi ŏnhae* 杜詩諺解, 1481) and Huang T'ing-chien* (*Hwang San'gok chip* 黃山谷集, 1483). The beginning of the sixteenth century saw translations of language primers (*c.* 1520), such as the *Nogoltae ŏnhae* 老乞大諺解, the *Pak T'ongsa ŏnhae* 朴通事諺解, and the *No-Pak chimnam* 老朴輯覽. By the end of this century all the Chinese classics were available in translation (1590; rpt. 1612).

The number of extant stories and novels in Korean, especially a number of selections and adaptations from Chinese works, evince a continuous popularity of those works in traditional Korea. Translations of stories from the *T'ai-p'ing kuang-chi** (introduced into Korea after 1101), *Chien-teng hsin-hua,** and the *San-yen* (see Feng Menglung) collections (e.g., "The Oil Peddler Courts the Courtesan") were widely read by men and women. From the beginning of the seventeenth century the most popular classic Chinese novels were the *San-kuo-chih yen-i** and the *Shui-hu chuan,** which inspired undated translations and anonymous historical romances. Most of the latter share a common system of conventions and concern the exploits of Korean heroes, real or fictional, during the Japanese (1592-1599) and Manchu (1636-1637) invasions. The "Ch'ih-pi fu" 赤壁賦 (Song of the Red Cliff; *Chokpyok ka*), based on the accounts of the battle fought in 208, has been a favorite in the repertory of the *p'ansori*, a narrative verse performed by a single professional entertainer. Translations and adaptations that bear in their titles the word *yen-i* 演義 (romance) are many;

for example, the *Sun-P'ang yen-i*, the *T'ang-Ch'in yen-i*, the *Hsi-Han yen-i*, etc. Some thirty translations published from 1904 to 1968 indicate a countinued popularity of the "romance" in the present century.

The Naksonjae 樂善齋 (Royal Palace Library) in Seoul houses the single most valuable Korean collection of Chinese and Korean fiction, more than a hundred works in two thousand volumes of manuscripts. The research into these works began only in 1966-1967, but they encompass such titles as the *Chin-ku ch'i-kuan*,* *Shui-hu chuan*,* the *Hung-lou meng*,* *P'ing-shan leng-yen* 平山冷燕, *P'ing-yao chi* 平妖記, *Chung-lieh hsia-i chuan* 忠烈俠義傳 (1879), *Chung-lieh hsiao-wu-i* 忠烈小五義 (1890), and the like. Researches in the prose style and vocabulary may help date some of these translations, most of which seem to have been commissioned in the nineteenth century.

The most popular Yüan drama was the *Hsi-hsiang chi*.* There are also translations of individual poems and prose essays such as Ch'ü Yüan's* "Yü-fu" 漁父 (The Fisherman), T'ao Ch'ien's* "Kuei-ch'ü-lai tz'u" 歸去來辭 (The Return), Po Chü-i's* "Ch'ang-hen ko" 長恨歌 (Song of Everlasting Sorrow), and the anonymous ballad "K'ung-chüeh tung-nan fei" 孔崔東南飛 (Southeast Fly the Peacocks). Today, the works of major Chinese poets and classic novels exist in readable, accurate Korean translations.

TRANSLATIONS:

Kim, Jong-gil. "Korean Poems Written in Chinese," *Korea Journal*, 20.7 (July 1980), 29-30; 20.8 (August 1980), 53-54.

STUDIES:

Chong, Pyong-uk. *Naksonjae Mun'go-bon mong-nok mit haeje* 樂善齋文庫本目錄解題 (The Annotated Catalogue of the Naksonjae Library Collection). Seoul, 1969. 64 pp.

Kim, Hyon-ryong. *Han-Chung sosol sorhwa pigyo yon'gu: T'aep'yong kwanggi ui yonghyang ul chungsim uro* 韓中小說說話比較研究：太平廣記 의 影響 을 中心 으로(A Comparative Study of Chinese and Korean Stories and Novels: Especially on the Influence of the *T'ai-p'ing kuang-chi*). Seoul, 1976.

Skillend, W. E. *Kodae Sosol: A Survey of Korean Traditional Style Popular Novels*. London, 1968.

Yi, Kyong-son. *Samgukchi yonui ui pigyo mungak-chok yon'gu* 三國志演義의 (之)比較文學的研究(A Comparative Study of *The Romance of the Three Kingdoms*). Seoul, 1976.

—PHL

Chinese Literature in Manchu Translation is the basis of Manchu literature, which consists almost exclusively of translations from the Chinese. For this reason, and because Manchu was formerly considered a shortcut to the command of Chinese, whether Western scholars of Chinese need to study Manchu has always been a matter of contention. The eminent sinologist and translator Erwin von Zach (1872-1942), Ferdinand Lessing (1882-1961), and others have argued that Manchu translations are an important supplementary key to the understanding of Chinese traditional texts, since they were done by non-native speakers (who thus share the modern Western scholar's problem to a certain extent) with firsthand access to Chinese scholars. The Manchu translations usually provide the official interpretation of texts during the Ch'ing dynasty, and in this respect they are important material for the student of Chinese literature and the history of its reception and interpretation.

Though the Manchus were mainly interested in composing dictionaries and translating historical, administrative, philological, and strategic works from the Chinese, there are also quite a number of renderings of literary works, only some of which were printed.

Among poetical works there is the *Muk-den-i fu bithe* (*Yü-chih Sheng-ching fu* 御製盛京賦, 1743), the Ch'ien-lung Emperor's poem on Mukden. There is an edition of the poem (1748) in thirty-two different styles of seal script (discussed by Giovanni Stary): *Han-i araha Alin-i tokso de halhōn be jailaha gi bithe* (*Yü-chih Pi-shu shan-chuang chi* 御製避暑山莊記 [Thirty-six Views of the Summer Palace at Jehol, Accompanied by Poems by the K'ang-hsi Emperor], 4 *pen*, preface 1711; cf. W. Fuchs, "Neue Beiträge," *MS*, 7.1943, 18-19).

A nineteenth-century collection of well-known examples of four styles of poetry from the Sung, Ming, and Ch'ing dynasties is also important—the *Ubaliyambuha Uculen juru gisun irgebun fujurun* (*Fan-i tz'u lien shih fu* 翻譯詞聯詩賦, *Hymne tatare mantchou chanté à l'occasion de la conquête du Kin-tchoen* [Paris, 1972; the text of the eulogy is given in Manchu accompanied by a French translation by Father Amyot]). The original ms. seems to be lost. The collected works of the Ch'ien-lung Emperor, *Han-i araga yongkiyan mudan irgebun* (*Yü-chih ch'üan yün shih* 御製全韻詩), appeared in a bilingual—Manchu and Chinese—version (mss., Volkova, 134). The Chinese poems and couplets translated into Manchu by Jakdan 扎克丹 (Ms., Harvard-Yenching Library), entitled *Jabduha ucuri amtangga baita* (*Hsien-chung chia-ch'ü* 閒中佳趣), also deserve mention. There are also a number of poems and "mixed poems" (the lines of which are partly in Manchu and partly in Chinese) in a collection of popular Manchu texts which formerly belonged to E. Haenisch (Staatsbibliothek Preusischer Kulturbesitz, West-Berlin, call no. 34981: cf. Fuchs, *Chinesische und mandjurische Handschriften und seltene Drucke*, Wiesbaden, 1966, no. 243).

A popular ballad on crab eating which belongs to the *tzu-ti shu** genre and which also consists of "mixed lines," the *Katuri jetere juben-i bethe* (*P'ang-hsieh tuan-erh* 螃蟹段兒), was studied in detail by Hatano Tarō 波多野太郎 (*P'ang-hsieh tuan-erh yen-chiu* [Taipei, 1970]). The text had been edited earlier by Chin Chiu-ching 金九經 ("Manshūgo to kango o konyō shitaru kahon hitsubōkai", *Mammō*, 185 [Sept., 1935], 222-242). There are also some poems and songs published in Western anthologies of Manchu texts.

The *Nišan saman-i bithe* (Tale of the Nišan Shamaness) is an original Manchu text which gives important information on Manchu shamanism. It was first edited from the mss. by M. P. Volkova (Moscow, 1961) and then translated into several languages. There is also a Manchu version (with occasional Chinese characters) of the *Chin P'ing Mei,** the *Gin ping mei bithe*. The translation is traditionally ascribed to a brother of Emperor K'ang-hsi. According to Fuchs (1968), this is the highest achieve-ment of Manchu translation work, on account of its fluent and unpretentious style. There is a recent reprint (San Francisco: Chinese Materials Center, 1975). The rare 1650 ed. of the *San-kuo yen-i** is in Manchu only (*Ilangurun-i bithe*); a later, undated edition in Manchu and Chinese was reprinted in 1979 (San Francisco, Chinese Materials Center). Th. Pavie's nineteenth-century translation of the novel (*San-Koué-Tchy. Ilan koutroun-i pithé. Histoire des Trois Royaumes* [Paris, 1845-1851]) was made largely from the Manchu. Selections from the novel—the *Sam yok ch'ong hae* 三譯總解, 10 *chüan*, 1774, revised from a 1703 ed.—were also rendered into Manchu and Korean, with a *Hangul* transcription. A selection of 127 stories from P'u Sung-ling's* *Liao-chai chih-i* was translated by Jakdan (a reprint was published in 1975 by the Chinese Materials Center, San Francisco: *Manju nikan Liyoo jai j'i i bithe* [*Ho-pi Liao-chai chih-i* 合璧聊齋志異]). Other translations of fictional works include: *Si io gi bithe* (*Hsi-yu chi* 西遊記), mss. in Oslo and Leningrad (Volkova, 152-153); *Sui hō bithe* (*Shui-hu chuan* 水滸傳), mss. in Paris and Leningrad (Volkova, 149, 150); *Kin siyang ting-ni bithe* (*Chin-hsiang-t'ing* 錦香亭), mss. in Oslo (Sun, 142); *Zui pu ti-i bithe* (*Tsui p'u-t'i ch'üan-chuan* 醉菩提全傳), mss. in Manchester and Leningrad (Volkova, 171; Sun, 174); *Ciyoo Liyan cu-i bithe* (*Ch'iao lien chu* 巧連珠), mss. in Paris (Puyraimond/Simon, 130); *Geren gurun-i bithe* (*Lieh-kuo chih chuan* 列國志傳), mss. in Leningrad (Volkova, 141-143; Sun, 25); *Wargi Han gurun-i bithe* (*Hsi Han t'ung-su yen-i* 西漢通俗演義), mss. in Leningrad (Volkova, 146; Sun, 29); *Julergi Sung gurun-i bithe* (*Nan Sung chuan* 南宋傳), mss. in Leningrad (Volkova, 147; Sun, 48); *Amargi Sung gurun-i bithe* (*Pei Sung chih chuan t'ung-su yen-i* 北宋志傳通俗演義), mss. in East Berlin (Sun, 48); *Jeo gurun-i bithe* (*Tung Chou lieh-kuo chih* 東周列國志), mss. in Leningrad (Volkova, 148; Sun, 26); *Ing liye juwan-i bithe* (*Ying-lieh chuan* 英列傳), mss. in Leningrad (Volkova, 156; Sun, 57); *Hoo kiyo juwan-i bithe* (*Hao-ch'iu chuan* 好逑傳), mss. in Leningrad (Volkova, 158-160; Sun, 140); *Ioi giyoo li bithe* (*Yü Chiao Li* 玉嬌梨), mss. in Leningrad (Volkova, 161; Sun, 133); *Ping* *san leng yan-i bithe* (*P'ing-shan leng-yen*), mss. in Leningrad (Volkova, 162-163; Sun, 133); *Lin el boo* (*Lin Erh pao* 麟兒報), mss. in Leningrad (Volkova, 164-165; Sun, 135); *Seng hōwa meng-ni bithe* (*Sheng-hua meng* 生花夢), mss. in Leningrad (Volkova, 166-167; Sun, 144); *Fung hōwang c'i* (*Feng-huang ch'ih* 鳳凰池), mss. in Leningrad (Volkova, 169; Sun, 135); *Gin yun kiyoo-i bithe* (*Chin yün ch'iao chuan* 金雲翹傳), mss. in Leningrad (Volkova, 170; Sun, 134).

Other translations include various dramas including *Hsi-hsiang chi* and several anthologies of prose (see Gimm, 1968).

TRANSLATIONS:

Durrant, Stephen and M. Noval. *The Tale of the Nišan Shamaness.* London and Seattle, 1977.

Seuberlich, Wolfgang. "Nisan saman-i bithe," in *Fern stliche Kultur [Festschrift Wolf Haenisch]*, Marburg, 1975, pp. 197-249.

Stary, Giovanni. *Viaggio nell'Oltretomba.* Florence, 1977.

STUDIES:

Fuchs, W. *Beiträge zur mandjurischen Bibliographie und Literatur.* Tokyo, 1936.

———. "Die mandjurische Literatur," in *Handbuch der Orientalistik*, Part I, v. 5, Section 3, Leiden and Köln, 1968, pp. 1-7.

Grebenščikov, A. V. "Kratkij očerk obrazsov mańčzurskoj literatury," *Izvestija Vostocnogo Instituta*, 32 (1909), no. 2.

Gimm, Martin. *Die chinesische Anthologie Wen-hsüan.* Wiesbaden, 1968. Translation of *Wen siowan bithe.*

———. "Zur Kaiserlichen Ku-wen-Anthologie (Ku-wen yüan-chien) von 1685/6," *OE*, 15 (1968), 57-82.

Kanda, N. "Present State of Preservation of Manchu Literature," *MTB*, 26 (1968), 63-95.

Li, Te-ch'i 李德啓. *Man-wen shu-chi lien-ho mu-lu* 滿文書籍聯合目錄. Peking, 1933.

Ling, Johnson. *The Goldi Tribe on the Lower Sungri River.* Peking, 1934.

Ōta, Tatsuo 太田辰夫. *Manshū bungaku kō* 滿州文學考. Kobe, 1976.

Puyraimond, J. M., W. Simon, and M. R. Séguy. *Catalogue du fonds mandchou [de la Bibliothèque Nationale].* Paris, 1979.

Simon, W. and H. G. H. Nelson. *Manchu Books in London.* London, 1977.

Sinor, Denis. "Letteratura Mancese," in *Storia delle letterature d'Oriente*, Milano, 1969, pp. 383-411.

Sun, K'ai-ti 孫楷第. *Chung-kuo t'ung-su hsiao-shuo shu-mu* 中國通俗小說書目. Hong Kong, 1967.

Volkova, M. P. *Opisanie mańčzurskich rukopisej Instituta narodov Azii.* Leningrad, 1965.

Walravens, H. "Vorläufige Titelliste der Mandjurica in amerikanischen Sammlungen," *ZAS*, 10 (1976), 551-613.

—HW

Chinese Literature in Mongol Translation can be said to have begun with translations into Mongolian of texts dealing with statecraft, ethico-political literature, and Confucian classics during the Yüan dynasty. No poetry and no fiction were translated at this time. Apart from a few hitherto unidentified fragments, however, the only surviving Yüan translation into Mongolian is that of the *Hsiao-ching* 孝經 (Classic of Filial Piety), but it is possible that this bilingual xylograph print discovered in the 1930s may date from the early Ming. Although it does not seem that Chinese literary texts were translated under the Ming, bilingual texts were printed in China, such as the translators' handbook *Hua-i i-yü* 華夷譯語 of 1389 and a quadrilingual Buddhist text dated 1431.

The annexation of Mongolia in the second half of the seventeenth century revived cultural contacts between China and Mongolia. Many administrative documents were translated into Mongolian during the eighteenth century. Translation of Chinese literature in the strict sense became more frequent in the nineteenth and early twentieth centuries. A great many translations have survived in manuscipt, but the scholarly study of these texts, including the identification of the Chinese originals, has just begun. A fairly common characteristic is that the Mongolian versions take great liberties with the original. Many of them are adaptations rather than literal translations. The Chinese texts selected for translation were mostly vernacular novels and short stories. Historical romances with their tales of heroism and chivalry, such as the *San-kuo chih yen-i,** the *Shui-hu chuan,** and the *San-hsia wu-i*, became immensely popular in Mongolia through translation or adaptation. Among Chinese historical novels those dealing with

T'ang subjects enjoyed particular popularity. Other genres transmitted through translation were the collections of criminal cases solved by famous judges (*Pao kung-an* 包公案, *Shih kung-an* 施公案), and fantastic narratives like *Hsi-yu chi** or *Feng-shen yen-i*.* Sentimental or erotic novels, such as the *Hung-lou meng* (1819), the *Chin P'ing Mei*,* and *Erh-tu mei* 二度梅 (Twice Flowered Plum), were also translated, as were short stories in both the colloquial and the literary language, such as the *Chin-ku ch'i-kuan** and the *Liao-chai chih-i.** Most of the translators remain anonymous. It seems that they acted under the sponsorship of educated aristocrats influenced by Chinese ideals of literacy. The emergence of a purely Mongolian novel towards the end of the nineteenth century would not have been possible without the translations from Chinese, and many native productions show Chinese stylistic influences. Chinese theater troupes performing in border markets or at the the invitation of Mongol grandees, also informed Mongolian literature; their popular entertainments gave rise to a new kind of minstrel poetry among Mongol story-tellers and bards, one that combined Chinese and native motifs.

After the fall of the empire in 1911 Mongolia won a period of relative autonomy; translation activities continued and numerous Mongolian versions of Chinese fiction were printed. Following the establishment of the People's Republic of China in 1949 the Mongols in the Inner Mongolian Autonomous Region were allowed to retain their traditional script (in the Mongolian People's Republic officially replaced by a cyrillic alphabet since 1941). A stream of Mongolian translations from the Chinese, ranging from party documents, political literature, and journals like *Hung-ch'i* to Mao Tse-tung's poems, was produced in Inner Mongolia. Among recent publications after the elimination of the "Gang of Four" a complete translation of *Hung-lou meng* should be mentioned.

STUDIES:

Bawden, Charles R. "The First Systematic Translation of Hung Lou Meng: Qasbuu's Commented Mongolian Version," *ZAS*, 15 (1981), 241-306.

———. "Injansai's Novel *Nigen Dadqur Asar*," in *Studia Sino-Mongolica*, Wolfgang Bauer, ed., Wiesbaden, 1979, pp. 197-221. A study of Chinese influence on a late nineteenth-century Mongol novel.

Clunas, Craig A. "The Preface to Nigen Dadqur Asar and their Chinese Antecedents," *ZAS*, 14.1 (1980), 139-194.

Franke, Herbert. "Chinese Historiography under Mongol Rule," *Mongolian Studies*, 1 (1974), 15-26. On Yüan-dynasty translations.

Fuchs, Walter. "Analecta zur mongolischen Übersetzungsliteratur der Yüan-Zeit," *MS*, 9 (1946), 34-64. Thorough discussion of Yüan texts dealing with translation into Mongolian.

Haenisch, Erich. "Der chinesische Roman im mongolischen Schrifttum," *Ural-Altaische Jahrbücher*, 30 (1958), 74-92. Includes romanization and German translation from a Mongolian translation of *Fan-T'ang yen-i* 反唐演義.

Heissig, Walther. *Geschichte der mongolischen Literatur*. 2v. Wiesbaden, 1972. Authoritative study of Mongolian literature in the nineteenth and early twentieth centuries.

———. "Zwei Mutmaßlich mongolische Yüan-übersetzungen und ihr Nachdruck von 1431," *ZAS*, 10 (1976), 7-115.

Krueger, John R. "The Mongol bicig-ün qoriya," in *Collectanea Mongolica*, W. Heissig, ed., Wiesbaden, 1966, pp. 109-115. On a Mongol publishing house in Peking in the 1920s.

Laufer, Bertold. "Skizze der Mongolischen Literatur," *Keleti Szimle*, 8 (1907), 165-260. First treatment of the subject in a Western-European language.

Scholz, Alexander Georg. "Chinesische Stoffe und Motive in der populären mongolischen Literatur gegen Ende des 19. Jahrhunderts." Ph.D. dissertation, Bonn, 1975. A textual study of Mongolian versions of Chinese novels.

—HF

Ching 經 (classics) have exerted an enormous influence upon traditional China and its literature. For much of Chinese history, the Confucian classics formed a general course of study which both defined and united the Chinese scholar-bureaucracy.

The classics were usually memorized in youth and became a source of frequent reference and allusion as well as a model of literary elegance and style. Since they were regarded as rich repositories of those highly practical truths which the Chinese believed they perceived in history, study of them was a moral as well as an intellectual imperative.

Already in the *Lun-yü* 論語 (Analects—*c.* 400 B.C.), there is respect for certain older texts, specifically the *Shih* 詩 (i.e., *Shih-ching**), *Shu* 書 (i.e., *Shu-ching, Classic of Documents*), and perhaps also the *I* 易 (i.e., *I-ching, Classic of Changes*). Even the early Warring States non-Confucian text *Mo-tzu* 墨子 frequently quotes from the *Shih* and the *Shu* to lend authority to argument. The first evidence that a specific number of texts were associated with one another and incorporated into a "canon" appears in *Chuang-tzu* where the "Six Classics" are given as *Shih, Shu, I, Li* 禮 (Ritual), *Yüeh* 樂 (Music), and *Ch'un-ch'iu* 春秋 (Spring and Autumn Annals). From at least the time of the great Han historian Ssu-ma Ch'ien,* these texts had been granted peculiar status by reason of a tradition that they were either edited or composed by Confucius (551-479 B.C.) himself. There are reasons to doubt this tradition, but it was upheld by generations of Chinese literati.

With the noteworthy exception of the *I*, the classics were among the texts proscribed in 213 B.C. by the First Ch'in Emperor. This act, together with the destruction of Hsien-yang (in which the imperial library was found) in 207 B.C., interrupted the regular transmission of the classical texts. In fact, some have suggested that the *Yüeh-ching* 樂經 (Classic of Music) was lost in this period. During the early years of the Former Han dynasty, there was a concerted effort to reassemble and transmit the texts and teachings of the classics. The first stage in this process was brought to a conclusion with the standardization and formalization of the Confucian canon which occurred in 136 B.C. when Emperor Wu established *po-shih* 博士 (erudites) for five classics (the list given above excluding *Yüeh*). Emperor Wu not only legitimatized

a textual tradition which derived from *li-shu* 隸書 (clerical script) editions, but, in choosing erudites, he also gave imperial sanction to certain interpretations of the classics. Such involvement of Han Emperors in decisions regarding the composition of the classical corpus was one result of the Han elevation of Confucianism to the status of state religion.

Despite the establishment of the institution of erudites and an imperial academy in which official interpretations were taught and transmitted, intense controversy raged throughout the Han over the legitimacy of various texts and editions of the classics, leading on at least two occasions, in 51 B.C. and again in A.D. 79, to the convening of special imperial councils. The result of this controversy was a gradual increase in the number of *po-shih*. For example, during the reign of Emperor Hsüan (73-49 B.C.) there were twelve *po-shih*, and later fourteen. This did not reflect an increase in the number of classics, but a divergence in schools of interpretation—among the fourteen *po-shih* were represented four different schools for the interpretation of the *I*, three for the *Shih*, two for the *Li*, and two for the *Ch'un-ch'iu*. This picture was complicated still further when the great Han bibliophile Liu Hsin* began to promote several texts in the imperial library which had been written in the old pre-Ch'in script. Liu's texts came to be called the "new-script texts." The dispute between these two factions (new- and old-text) became much more than an academic rivalry over editions and interpretations; it involved important historical, political, and religious questions as well.

Through the course of Chinese history, the standard Confucian canon has been variously defined. It was common during the Han to refer to "five classics," but the term "seven classics," a collection which includes the *Lun-yü* and the *Hsiao-ching* 孝經 (Classic of Filial Piety), also appears in the Han. Throughout much of the T'ang dynasty, the civil-service examination required mastery of "nine classics"; three ritual texts, the *Chou li* 周禮 (Ritual of Chou), the *Li chi* 禮記 (Record of Ritual), and the

I li 儀禮 (Ceremony and Ritual); three commentaries to the *Ch'un-ch'iu*, the *Tso-chuan,** the *Kung-yang chuan* 公羊傳 (The Kung-yang Commentary), and the *Ku-liang chuan* 穀梁傳 (The Ku-liang Commentary); and the three texts, *I, Shih*, and *Shu*. In the Warring States text *Chuang-tzu* there is a reference to "twelve classics," and we can only guess what texts might have been included in this aggregate. Much later a Sung source testifies that during the T'ang there was a collection of twelve classics which included those texts named above as the "nine classics" plus the *Lun-yü*, the *Hsiao-ching*, and the *Erh-ya* 爾雅. In the Sung dynasty *Meng-tzu* 孟子 (Mencius) was added to the list, creating the present canon of "thirteen classics." Each of the texts in this last and largest collection of classics will be summarized briefly below.

The *I-ching* preserves an ancient system of divination which is based upon the sixty-four possible combinations of a broken line (the so-called "*yin* line") and an unbroken ling ("*yang* line") in six places. In the course of transmission, this divination manual acquired numerous layers of textual explanation and commentary, eventually becoming a compendium of the Chinese philosophy of transformation. Since the text is a storehouse of image and symbol from which Chinese literati frequently drew, a knowledge of basic *I ching* terminology is necessary to the understanding of many later literary references and allusions.

Plainly the text as we have it today is not the product of a single time but consists of materials produced over almost a millennium. According to the traditional "four-sage theory" of *I-ching* authorship, the hexagrams (the symbols which form the basic building block of the divination system) were fashioned by King Wen while he was imprisoned by the Shang (*c.* 1140 B.C.). These hexagrams were constructed by doubling the eight trigrams which had been invented long before by the mythical Emperor Fu Hsi (24th century B.C.). The next of the venerable four sages, the Duke of Chou (d. 1104 B.C.), supposedly added the earliest textual layer consisting of the hexagram judgement texts and the line texts. Confucius, who was very fond of the *I-ching*, added a series of commentaries known as "The Ten Wings." Although all of these attributions of authorship are questionable, the "four-sage theory" recognizes that the text today is the product of a long period of accretion.

Modern scholarship has reached no consensus on the age and source of the hexagram system itself, but there is reason to believe that it is related to the divination system so prevalent during the Shang dynasty. Although the earliest texts associated with the *I-ching* may not come from anyone so politically prominent as King Wen or the Duke of Chou, they are unquestionably very old and may date from the earliest years of the Western Chou. Iulian K. Shchutskii concludes that the basic text assumed its present shape sometime between the eighth and seventh centuries B.C. However, evidence indicates that the "Ten Wings," with the possible exception of a few sections, are not as early as their purported author, Confucius. Rather, they are products largely of the Warring States era with one "Wing," *tsa-kua* 雜卦 (miscellaneous notes on the hexagrams), almost surely coming from the Former Han dynasty.

The *Shu-ching* is a collection of historical documents which Confucius purportedly edited and prefaced. Most of the documents in this collection are pronouncements and thereby fall into the category of historical writing which Chinese scholars call *chi-yen* 記言 (recording words), a category standing in opposition to the historical style of the *Ch'un-ch'iu*, called *chi-shih* 記事 (recording events). There are two versions of the *Shu-ching*. The first version, which descends from the new-script tradition, consists of twenty-eight chapters and is generally considered authentic. The ancient-text version of the *Shu*, which is found in most Chinese collections and was translated into English by Legge, contains twenty-eight chapters of the new-text version along with twenty-two other chapters which are now known to be forgeries from the third or fourth century A.D. The doc-

311

uments from the authentic twenty-eight chapter text have to be dated individually, but some certainly come from the early Chou period and thereby represent, along with portions of the *I-ching* and the *Shih,* the earliest stratum of the Chinese language preserved outside of oracle bones and bronze inscriptions. Several of these documents articulate the doctrine of *t'ien-ming* 天命 (the mandate of heaven) and possibly were written to provide a philosophical justification for the Chou conquest of the Shang state.

The *Shih-ching* is an anthology of 305 poems which, according to the historian Ssu-ma Ch'ien, were chosen by Confucius from a larger body of three thousand poems, which the *Han-shu* (History of the Former Han—see Pan Ku) claims were originally gathered from among the people by the Chou court. A number of objections can be raised to the tradition of Confucius's editorial function, but it is clear from the *Lun-yü* (see 2:2 and 13:5) that a corpus of approximately three hundred poems was known to the Master and formed a part of his disciples' curriculum. Confucius even told his son, "If you do not study the *Shih,* you will have no basis for discussion" (16:13). Partially as a result of such traditions, the *Shih-ching* acquired great status and was frequently used in Chou and Han philosophical texts to support argumentation. One Han work, the *Han-shih wai-chuan* 韓詩外傳 (Han Ying's Illustrations of the Didactic Application of the Classic of Songs), even appears to be a handbook which was used as a guide to the technique of apt *Shih-ching* quotation. In the Han dynasty four different texts of the *Shih-ching* were extant, and *po-shih* were assigned for the preservation of each interpretation. Only the Mao version supported by Liu Hsin and the old-text scholars has been preserved in its entirety. This edition, which contains a commentary attributed to the Warring States scholar Mao Heng 毛亨, is noted for a highly didactic and political interpretation.

The content of the *Shih-ching* is highly diverse, ranging all the way from lofty religious liturgy and hymns in praise of dynastic heroes to simple folksongs. Of the four sections of the text, the *sung* 頌 (eulogies) are probably the oldest, dating in certain cases from the earliest years of the Chou dynasty. On the other hand, some of the pieces found in the *kuo feng* 國風 (airs of the states) section might be as late as the fifth century B.C.

The three major ritual texts—the *Chou li,* also known as the *Chou-kuan* 周官 (Institutes of Chou), the *Li chi,* and the *I li*—have a very complicated textual history which still leaves considerable room for additional research and clarification. Together, the ritual texts contain diverse material which touches upon the ideal structure of government, the highest state rituals, appropriate funeral, wedding, and banquet etiquette, proper interpersonal behavior within a hierarchical Confucian society, and many other topics.

The first of the three texts, the *Chou li,* purports to be a description of the early Chou bureaucracy. The great exegete Cheng Hsüan 鄭玄 (127-200) claimed that the *Chou li* was from the pen of the Duke of Chou. Others have suggested that it was a forgery by Liu Hsin. Both of these positions are in error. The *Chou li* was among the old-script texts recovered during the reign of Emperor Wu, and as such, it enjoyed the support of Liu Hsin and the old-text scholars. Ho Hsiu 何休 (129-182) correctly identified the *Chou li* as a product of the Warring States period. Placenames, terminology, and numerous ancient character forms, along with the general philosophical environment reflected by the text, all verify Ho's contention. Today the text is generally regarded as a somewhat utopian portrayal of the government of the early Chou period which was advanced during the chaotic Warring States period. However, it is possible that the *Chou li* does preserve some fragmentary information about the early Chou bureaucracy.

The *I li* provides a detailed description of a variety of ceremonies supposedly carried out during the Spring and Autumn period. It is to be identified with the text which Ssu-ma Ch'ien called the *Shih li* 士禮 (Ritual of the Scholar-Bureaucrats). This latter work is the only ritual text mentioned by Ssu-ma and was that most studied by Former Han *po-shih*. As such, it had considerable influence on both the Han perception of Chou ceremony and on Han institutions themselves. Although tradition asserts that this book "came forth from Confucius," quotations from the work do not appear in Chou literature before the *Hsün-tzu* 荀子 (240 B.C.), and then they are in somewhat different form from those in the current text. However, preliminary study of bamboo slips of this text unearthed in 1959 in Kansu Province has led contemporary Chinese scholars to the conclusion that it derives from as early as the first half of the Warring States period.

Two texts are now known by the name *Li chi*. According to early Chinese bibliographic literature (see especially the "Bibliographic Section" of the *Sui-shu*), a Han scholar of the first century B.C. by the name of Tai Te 戴德 made a collection of eighty-five sections from a much larger body of Confucian writings which were available in his time. Later a text compiled by a younger cousin of Tai Te's and called *Hsiao Tai Li chi* 小戴禮記 (Younger Tai's Record of Ritual) was included among the classics, but the writings which the younger Tai edited out of the larger eighty-five section text are extant and are called *Ta Tai Li chi* 大戴禮記 (Elder Tai's Record of Ritual). Both works contain useful information on ritual and the development of Confucian philosophy. Since the sources of these texts are apparently diverse, sections must be dated individually. It is now believed that they incorporate materials from the late Warring States period up to the early Former Han. Two of the chapters of the *Hsiao Tai Li chi*, the "Ta Hsüeh" 大學 (Universal Learning), and the "Chungyung" 中庸 (Doctrine of the Mean) were included with the *Lun-yü* and the *Meng-tzu* in the highly influential collection entitled *Ssu-shu* 四書 (Four Books) which was edited by the Neo-Confucian scholar Chu Hsi 朱熹 (A.D. 1130-1200).

The *Ch'un-ch'iu* is a chronicle of political events which occurred from 722 to 480 B.C. It was compiled in the state of Lu and reflects the political perception of its geographical locus. Chou texts mention other state chronicles, and it is likely that the compilation of such records was a regular feature of state governments during the Eastern Chou. Unfortunately the Ch'in book burning and subsequent political unrest exacted a heavy toll on such texts and only the *Ch'un-ch'iu* and portions of the Wei 魏 annals remain as examples of this genre. From at least the time of Mencius (372-289 B.C.), Confucius was considered the author of this classic. Mencius quotes the Master as saying, "Those who understand me will do so through *Ch'un-ch'iu;* those who condemn me will also do so because of *Ch'un-ch'iu*" (IIIB.9.). As a result of the importance which the Master supposedly attached to this work, a whole tradition of exegesis developed to explicate the profound but oblique meaning of this ostensibly straightforward annal. The praise-and-blame theory of *Ch'un-ch'iu* interpretation, according to which Confucius either condemned or approved through a highly subtle choice of words, was the result of this exegetical tradition. Two commentaries to the classic, the *Kung-yang chuan* and the *Ku-liang chuan*, are filled with praise-and-blame exegesis, and a third, the more famous and important *Tso-chuan*, also has certain passages which utilize such an interpretation to comment directly upon *Ch'un-ch'iu* entries. The research of George Kennedy has given serious reason to question the praise-and-blame interpretation of *Ch'un-ch'iu*, and it is likely that the text is little more than a simple chronicle of political events.

The three commentaries to the *Ch'un-ch'iu* mentioned above are also regarded as classics. The *Tso-chuan* is only peripherally related to specific *Ch'un-ch'iu* entries. It is possible that this classic was originally an independent history unrelated to *Ch'un-ch'iu* and was subsequently reorganized by an editor who put *Tso* passages under appropriate sections of *Ch'un-ch'iu* and added lines of direct commentary. Whatever the source of the present arrangement, Karlgren has proved that the bulk of the text is a genuine Warring States work. The *Tso-chuan* is one of the finest examples of the lapidary and restrained style of Chou narrative, and any study of the Chinese literary tradition must give serious consideration to this early and highly influential work.

The *Kung-yang chuan* and the *Ku-liang chuan* develop their praise-and-blame interpretation through a catechistic style which poses questions and then gives answers concerning the political and ethical meaning of *Ch'un-ch'iu* entries. The *Kung-yang chuan* is named after a Master Kung-yang, one of a number of *Ch'un-ch'iu* masters whose name has been preserved. The *Ku-liang chuan* is the product of another school which may have developed in conscious reaction to the Kung-yang masters. The *Kung-yang chuan* probably dates from the late Warring States or early Han, while the *Ku-liang chuan* is a work of the Former Han.

The *Lun-yü* is a collection of sayings attributed to Confucius or his immediate disciples along with numerous short dialogues and anecdotes. The text follows a very general topical arrangement, and its philosophical content is presented rather fragmentarily. Three texts of the *Lun-yü* were current in the Former Han, two new-script texts called after their places of origin, Lu and Ch'i, and an old-script text supposedly discovered in the wall of Confucius's home when it was torn down during the early years of the Emperor Wu. The text preserved today is basically the Lu version with some readings drawn from the other two versions by such early editors as Chang Yü 張禹 (*fl.* A.D. 25), Cheng Hsüan and Ho Yen 何晏 (190-249). Since the text calls not only Confucius *tzu* 子 (master), but also his disciples, it is believed to date, at the earliest, several decades after his death. The Ch'ing scholar Ts'ui Shu 崔述 (1740-1816) demonstrated that the last five chapters of the *Lun-yü* are of later authorship than the remainder of the text, and subsequent studies have questioned the uniformity of other sections as well. Most probably the text contains material assembled from various sources over the course of the fifth and early fourth centuries B.C.

The *Meng-tzu* was first numbered among the classics in the Sung dynasty. However, there was a tradition based upon Chao Ch'i's 趙岐 (d. A.D. 201) preface to his *Meng-tzu* commentary that an erudite was appointed for the work as early as the reign of the Emperor Wen of the Han (179-158 B.C.). This classic includes the discussions of Mencius, the second great Confucian sage, with feudal rulers and others. While several sections of the text, particularly VIIA and VIIB, are stylistically reminiscent of the *Lun-yü*, most of the book contains much more extended dialogues and explanations which allow a fuller development of Confucian ethical, political, and economic philosophy. The current text comes from the Han commentator Chao Ch'i who removed four chapters which he considered to be of little value. Some passages from those discarded chapters are quoted in other sources and have been assembled by Ma Kuo-han 馬國翰 (1794-1857).

The *Hsiao-ching* is a short text of approximately 1800 characters containing a discussion between Confucius and his disciple Tseng-tzu 曾子 on the Confucian principle of reverence for parents and, by extension, rulers. As a consequence of this subject matter, the book received a great deal of imperial patronage and has enjoyed a very lofty status for much of Chinese history. As early as the Han, it was referred to as a classic, and several Han sources mention it alongside the *Ch'un-ch'iu* as a work of Confucius. It was also included with the *Lun-yü* and the usual five classics in the Han category "seven classics." The transmission of the work is complex. Basically there are two texts. One is a new-text edition in eighteen chapters which was current in the early Han and became the basis both of Cheng Hsüan's edition and the edition subsequently prepared by Emperor Hsüan-tsung 玄宗 (r. 713-756). The other is an old-script text in twenty-two chapters which was supposedly found in the wall of Confucius's home along with other old-text works. The latter edition contains one chapter not found in the new-text version, with the remaining discrepancy in the number of chapters resulting from a slightly different arrangement of content. There is considerably more question about the authenticity of the old-text version than the new-text version. The latter is not as early as Confucius and Tseng-tzu, but there is evidence it was in existence by the time of the last years of the Chou dynasty. Several scholars have argued that the old-text version was written in the early Former Han and was based upon the already extant new-text version.

The *Erh-ya* is an ancient Chinese lexicographic work, apparently a collection of early glosses and explanation on words appearing in Chou texts. This classic has been variously ascribed to the Duke of Chou, Confucius, and Tzu-hsia 子夏, one of Confucius's disciples. However, from at least the time of Ou-yang Hsiu,* scholars have recognized it to be a collection from the Ch'in or early Han period. Whatever its precise time of authorship, and it may have assumed its present shape over a long period of time, it is a valuable source which must be tapped in the study of other classics as well as Chou texts in general.

The lexicon of this proto-dictionary is divided into nineteen categories. In each of these categories words are grouped together in synonym chains with the last word of the chain being the most standard equivalent. The semantic arrangement of lexicon which first appears in *Erh-ya* had great influence upon later Chinese lexicography and can be seen, in much more refined form, in Ch'ing polyglot dictionaries and traditional Chinese *lei-shu*.*

EDITIONS:

Shih-san ching chu-shu 十三經注疏. Juan Yüan . 8v. 1816; rpt. Taipei, 1973.
Shih-san ching so-yin 十三經索引. Compiled by Yeh Shao-chün 葉紹鈞. Shanghai, 1934. Concordances or indexes in the Harvard-Yenching Sinological Index Series are available for the following: *Chou li, Ch'un-ch'iu* (and commentaries), *Erh-ya, Hsiao-ching, I-ching, I li, Li chi, Lun-yü, Meng-tzu, Shih-ching,* and *Shu-ching.*

TRANSLATIONS:

GENERAL:
The Chinese Classics. James Legge, trans. 5v. 1893; rpt. Hong Kong, 1960. Includes the *Shu-ching,* the *Shih-ching,* the *Lun-yü,* the *Meng-tzu,* the *Ch'un-ch'iu* with the *Tso-chuan,* the "Ta hsüeh" and the "Chung yung."

I-CHING:
I Ging: Das Buch der Wandlungen. Richard Wilhelm, trans. Jena, 1924.
The I Ching or Book of Changes [Richard Wilhelm's translation rendered into English]. Cary F. Baynes, trans. New York, 1950.

SHU-CHING:
The Book of Documents. Bernhard Karlgren, trans., *BMFEA,* 22 (1950), 1-81.

SHIH-CHING:
The Book of Odes. Bernhard Karlgren, trans. Stockholm, 1950.
The Book of Songs. Arthur Waley, trans. London, 1937.

CHOU LI:
Le Tcheou-li ou Rites des Tcheou. 3v. Paris, 1851.

I LI:
I li. Seraphin Couvreur, trans. Sien Hsien, 1928.

LI CHI:
Li Gi, Das Buch der Sitte der ältern und jüngeren Dai. Richard Wilhelm, trans. Jena, 1930.

CH'UN-CH'IU:
Tch'ouen ts'iou et Tso-tchouan. Seraphin Seraphin Couvreur, trans. Paris, 1914.

HSIAO-CHING:
Hsiao King. James Legge, trans. *The Sacred Books of the East,* III. Oxford, 1879.
The Hsiao Ching. Mary Leloa Makra, trans. New York, 1961.

LUN-YÜ:
The Analects. D. C. Lau, trans. Harmondsworth, 1979.
The Analects of Confucius. Arthur Waley, trans. London, 1938.

MENG-TZU:
Mencius. D. C. Lau, trans. Harmondsworth, 1970.

STUDIES:
Ch'ü, Wan-li 屈萬里. *Ku-chi tao-tu* 古籍導讀. Taipei, 1964.
Creel, Herrlee G. "Appendix A: The Sources," in *The Origins of Statecraft,* Chicago, 1970, pp. 444-486.
Durrant, Stephen W. "On Translating *Lun Yü*," *CLEAR,* 3 (1981), 109-119.
Hightower, Robert James. *Han Shih Wai Chuan: Han Ying's Illustrations of the Didactic Application of the Classic of Songs.* Cambridge, Mass., 1952.

Karlgren, Bernhard. "On the Authenticity and Nature of the *Tso chuan*, *Götesborgs Högskolas Arsskrift*, 32 (1926.3), 1-65.

———. "The Early History of the *Chou Li* and *Tso Chuan* Texts," *BMFEA*, 3 (1931), 1-52.

Kennedy, George A. "Interpretation of the *Ch'un-Ch'iu*, *JAOS*, 62.1 (March 1942), 40-48.

Ku, Chieh-kang 顧頡剛 and Lo Ken-tse 羅根澤, ed. *Ku-shih pien* 古史辨. 6v. Rpt. Taipei, 1970. Articles on the classics scattered throughout these volumes are of great importance.

Ma, Tsung-huo 馬宗霍. *Chung-kuo ching-hsüeh shih* 中國經學史. 1937; rpt. Taipei, 1972.

P'i, Hsi-jui 皮錫瑞. *Ching-hsüeh li-shih* 經學歷史. With notes by Chou Yu-t'ung 周予同. 1927; rpt. [with notes] Hong Kong, 1961.

Pokora, Timoteus. "Pre-Han Literature," in *Essays on the Sources for Chinese History*, Donald D. Leslie, Colin Mackerras, and Wang Gungwu, eds., Columbia, South Carolina, 1973, pp. 23-35.

Shchutskii, Iulian K. *Researches on the I Ching*. William L. MacDonald, Tsuyoshi Hasegawa, with Hellmut Wilhelm, trans. Princeton, 1979.

Wang, C. H. *The Bell and the Drum*. Berkeley, 1974.

Wilhelm, Hellmut. *Heaven, Earth and Man in the Book of Changes*. Seattle, 1977.

—SD

Ching-chü 京劇 (Peking Opera) remains a popular music drama in Peking today and has become widely appreciated in other parts of China, being promoted by some as China's "national opera."

Peking opera does not have a very long history when compared to the classical *K'un-ch'ü*,* which was the form in which most late Ming and Ch'ing dynasty serious drama was written, or even to many regional operas (see *Ti-fang hsi*), but during its short lifetime (it achieved its present-day form around 1870) it has had a huge influence on Chinese theater.

By the end of the eighteenth century the long reign of *K'un-ch'ü* music in Chinese drama began to decline, and a large number of less refined but highly vigorous regional operas were beginning to compete with the older, classical drama. The Ch'ien-lung Emperor's (r. 1736-1796) travels in south China and his enjoyment of regional operas there seem to have played an important role in the eventual development of Peking opera. The first opera troupe from Anhwei was invited to Peking in 1790. By the second decade of the nineteenth century the Four Great Anhwei Troupes 四大徽班 had arrived in Peking, bringing with them the music of regional forms that would give rise to Peking opera. During the 1830s and 1840s the renowned Hupeh actor Wang Hung-kuei 王洪貴 combined the two basic musical components of Peking opera. Although the opera performed during this time could be considered an embryonic form of Peking opera, it was not until the rise of the famous *lao-sheng* 老生 (mature male role) actors in the 1850s and 1860s that Peking opera really assumed its mature form. The patronage of the Empress Dowager Tz'u-hsi during the final decades of the nineteenth century was also a major factor in its rise to preeminence.

As already mentioned, the music of Peking opera comes from two different sources, the *erh-huang ch'iang* 二黃腔, which may have originated in Kiangsi but came to Peking about 1790 via Anhwei, and the *hsi-p'i ch'iang* 西皮腔, which shows strong affinities to the music of *Ch'in-ch'iang* 秦腔, a *pang-tzu* 梆子, or clapper, opera from northeastern China, which came to Peking by way of Hupeh in the first decades of the nineteenth century. Since Peking opera combines both of the musical traditions, it is also called *p'i-huang chü* 皮黃劇.

The music of both *hsi-p'i* and *erh-huang* is totally different in its structure from the music of the *K'un-ch'ü*, since both operate on the *pan-ch'iang* 板腔 principle where one melody generates a score of melodies through a relatively complex process involving among other things tempo and rhythm changes.

There is also a good deal of improvisation as to how the melodies are actually realized by the performer. This form of music allows a much greater degree of freedom both to the singer and the libretto composer than the *ch'ü-p'ai* construction of the earlier *K'un-ch'ü* music, where the dramatist had to write his arias in strict conformance to the metric requirements of a preexisting set of melodies. Also, the *erh-huang* melodies were generally used for expressing more tragic emotions, while the *hsi-p'i* were usually happier. By using two types of melodies, the Peking opera could express the same range of emotions as in the earlier *K'un-ch'ü* without being limited by the *ch'ü-p'ai*.

In contrast to *K'un-ch'ü*, the music of Peking opera is dominated by percussion instruments such as drum, gongs, and clappers and wind instruments like the *suo-na*, and stringed intruments such as the *erh-hu*. Musical structure determined the poetic form of the arias. The author no longer had to follow restrictive meters, so he could write in a form that was closer to the rhythms in prosimetric literature. Most lines in Peking opera consist of either seven or ten syllables.

The musical and poetic freedom of the Peking opera ironically turned it into a performer's rather than a playwright's art. From its beginnings, Peking opera was dominated by great actors and singers rather than great dramatists. The freedom of the *pan-ch'iang* form allowed a wide diversity in singing styles and favored virtuosity, which was eagerly followed by the Peking theater audience. Among the best known twentieth-century actors is the famous Mei Lan-fang, who with the help of literary friends adopted scenes from earlier drama and narrative for his perfomance.

On the whole, writers for the Peking opera were extremely adaptive, and took stories from a wide variety of preexisting forms of vernacular literature. However, there were some authors who began interesting experiments with Peking opera at the end of the nineteenth century. Yü Chih 余治, a scholar from Wu-hsi (modern Kiangsu), wrote a collection of twenty-eight Peking opera texts, which were published in 1860. Unfortunately he adopted a rather heavy-handed didactic approach, and his works were rarely performed. Another, more significant author was Wang Shun 汪僢, usually known as Wang Hsiao-nung 汪笑儂 (1858-1918), who himself was an excellent amateur singer of *lao-sheng* roles.

His historical dramas are well crafted and were quite popular, but he also wrote a number of dramas in sympathy with the late-Ch'ing reform movement and gained a reputation as a "revolutionary" dramatist. Attempts to modernize Peking opera in the early twentieth century and in the 1960s have on the whole proved abortive. There is a rich collection of early Peking-opera texts in the Fu Ssu-nien 傅思年 Library at the Academia Sinica on Taiwan.

EDITIONS:

Chang, Po-chin 張伯瑾. *Kuo-chü ta-ch'eng* 國劇大成. Taipei, 1969.
Chiang, Tso-tung 姜作棟. *Hsiu-ting p'ing-chü hsüan* 修訂平劇選. Taipei, 1959.
Chung-kuo hsi-ch'ü yen-chiu-yüan 中國戲曲研究院 ed. *Ching-chü ts'ung-k'an* 京劇叢刊. 32v. Shanghai, 1953.
Hu, Chü-jen 胡菊人. *Hsi-k'ao ta-ch'an* 戲考大全. Taipei, 1974.
Pei-ching-shih hsi-ch'ü pien-tao wei-yüan hui 北京市戲曲編導委員會, ed. *Ching-chü hui-pien* 京劇彙編. Peking, 1957-1962.
Wang Hsiao-nung hsi-ch'ü chi 汪笑儂戲曲集. Peking, 1957.
Yü, Chih 余治. *Shu-chi-t'ang chin-yüeh* 庶幾堂今樂. Soochow, 1880.

TRANSLATIONS:

Chang, Tz'u-hsi 張次溪. *Ch'ing-tai Yen-tu li-yüan shih-liao* 清代燕都梨園史料. Taipei, 1964.
Ch'i, Ju-shan 齊如山. *Ch'i Ju-shan ch'üan-chi* 齊如山全集. Taipei, 1964.
Dolby, *History*, pp. 164-183.
Scott, A. C. *Traditional Chinese Plays*. 3v. Madison, 1967-75.

STUDIES:

Halson, Elizabeth. *Peking Opera: A Short Guide.* Oxford, 1966.
Hwang, Mei-shu. "A Brief Introduction to Peking Opera," *TkR*, 12.3 (Spring 1982), 315-329.
Li, Hung-ch'un 李洪春. Liu Sung-yen 劉松岩, ed. *Ching-chü ch'ang-t'an* 京劇長談. Peking, 1982.
Mackerras, C. P. *The Rise of the Peking Opera.* Oxford, 1972.
———. *The Chinese Theatre in Modern Times.* London, 1973.
Mei, Lan-fang 梅蘭芳. *Wu-t'ai sheng-huo ssu-shih-nien* 舞台生活四十年. Shanghai, 1953-54.
Scott, A. C. *The Classical Theatre of China.* London, 1957.

Schönfelder, Gerd. *Die Musik der Peking-Oper.* Leipzig, 1972.

Yang, Daniel S. P. *An Annotated Bibliography of Materials for the Study of the Peking Theater.* Madison, 1967.

—JDS

Ching-hua yüan 鏡花緣 (Romance of the Mirrored Flowers), a major work of Ch'ing fiction, was written by Li Ju-chen 李汝珍 (*tzu*, Sung-shih 松石, *c.* 1763-1830), a scholar from Ta-hsing 大興 in the Chih-li district (near Peking), whose widely diversified interests also found expression in three other works: *Yin-chien* 晉鑑 (System of Phonetics, 1805), a phonological treatise, *Shou-tzu pu* 受子譜 (Chess Handbook, 1817), a sophisticated chess manual, and *Kuang fang-yen* 廣方言 (Dictionary of Dialectology), an unfinished work in the tradition of the Han linguist Yang Hsiung.* It is only in *Ching-hua yüan*, however, that Li Ju-chen's encyclopedic knowledge is provided a theme and structure of appropriate scale.

This one-hundred-chapter vernacular novel is on the surface a simple story of a Taoist fairy's fall from grace and her subsequent trials in the mundane world to regain her immortality; on a deeper level the incorporation of various satirical and symbolic devices, as well as two leitmotivs—*ching-hua* 鏡花 (the flower in the mirror) and *shui-yüeh* 水月 (the moon in the water)—make it an allegory on the vicissitudes of human consciousness caught between appearance and reality, the temporal and the eternal. Further, though Li Ju-chen makes extensive use of Taoist and Buddhist lore, the metaphysics of the work as a whole are not imposed from external systems of belief, but from his own search for a unified sense of meaning in a society that denied him any worldly recognition (he failed to attain any examination degree higher than *hsiu-ts'ai*).

The storyline parallels the actions of immortals in Taoist paradise with a freely elaborated account of the Chou dynasty of Empress Wu (r. 690-705), who usurped power from the T'ang to become the only woman in Chinese history to found a dynasty. The relationship between the two planes—one mythical, the other quasi-historical—is left ambiguous, drawing metaphysical concern into the story, as the heroine, the Fairy of the Hundred Flowers (Pai-hua Hsien-tzu 百花仙子), is seen to forsake her duties in the regulation of nature and is banished to earth, gaining incarnation as the daughter of a T'ang loyalist scholar. Having lost all hope of any official position, the scholar takes leave of his family to embark on an overseas voyage to thirty-some strange lands, each of Swiftian satirical import, and en route undergoes a spiritual transformation in direct counterpoint to the fall of the Fairy. On searching for her vanished father, the Fairy incarnate is instructed to return to China, and take the imperial examinations of Wu's "woman's dynasty," after which they may be reunited. When she passes, a celebration ensues, allowing Li Ju-chen a twenty-five-chapter digression into his many interests in the arts and sciences, and the Fairy regains her divinity. The story ends with the moral forces of the T'ang loyalists making an allegorical assault on the Four Gates to Wu's stronghold, Wine, Wrath, Lust, and Wealth, and reinstating the T'ang emperor.

Much neglected by past critics, *Ching-hua yüan* has received acclaim from Marxist scholars in China for what they see as its satirical attacks on the social realities of traditional China and its postulation of a "woman's dynasty" advocating social reforms and female equality. Yet for all its sophistication—Li Ju-chen operates under the strikingly modern stance that the writer's own mental reality is the primary determinant of the novel's reality and thus its self-contained form—*Ching-hua yüan* ultimately falls back on the Confucian ideal for women, suggesting that it may be better seen as the grievances and spiritual struggles of an author unduly passed over by his times, yet unable to break free of their social influence.

EDITIONS:

Ching-hua yüan. 1828. Chieh-tzu yüan 芥子園 edition; original text preserved in Peking University Library.

———. 1832. Kwangtung edition; original text preserved in the British Museum Library.

318

———. Shanghai, 1932. Ya-tung tu-shu kuan edition.

———. 2v. Peking, 1955.

TRANSLATIONS:

Chang, H. C. 張心滄. *Allegory and Courtesy in Spenser: A Chinese View*. Edinburgh, 1955, pp. 39-71.

———. *Chinese Literature: Popular Fiction and Drama*. Edinburgh, 1973, pp. 405-466.

Engler, F. K. *Im Land der Frauen*. Zürich, 1970. Abbreviated German translation.

Lin, Tai-yi 林太乙. *Flowers in the Mirror*. Berkeley, 1965. An abridged translation.

Yang, Gladys. "A Journey into Strange Lands," *CL*, 1958.1, 76-122.

STUDIES:

Brandauer, Frederick P. "Women in the *Ching-hua yüan*: Emancipation Toward a Confucian Ideal," *JAS*, 36.4 (August 1977), 647-660.

Chang, *Allegory*. A comparative and critical study of *Ching-hua yüan* as an allegorical novel.

Eberhard, Wolfram. "Ideas About Social Reforms in the Novel *Ching-hua yüan*," in *Moral and Social Values of the Chinese*, Eberhard, ed., Taipei, 1971, pp. 413-421.

Evans, Nancy J. F. "Social Criticism in the Ch'ing: The Novel *Ching-hua yüan*," *Papers on China*, 23 (July 1970), 52-66.

Hsia, C. T. "The Scholar-Novelist and Chinese Culture: A Reappraisal of *Ching-hua yüan*," in *Chinese Narrative*, pp. 266-305.

Hu, Shih 胡適. "*Ching-hua yüan* te yin-lun" 鏡花緣的引論, in *Hu Shih wen-ts'un* 胡適文存. Shanghai, 1924, Series 2, v. 2, pp. 119-168.

Ōta, Tatsuo 太田辰夫. "*Kyōkaen kō*" 鏡花緣考, *Tōhōgaku*, 48 (July 1974), 57-69.

Wang, Pi-twan Huang. "Utopian Imagination in Traditional Chinese Fiction." Unpublished Ph.D. dissertation, University of Wisconsin, 1980. Discusses the novel as one of three major types of Chinese utopian works—the utopian satire.

Yüeh, Heng-chün 樂蘅軍. "P'eng-lai kuei-hsi: Lun *Ching-hua yüan* te shih-chieh kuan" 蓬萊詭戲：論鏡花緣的世界觀, *Hsien-tai wen-hsüeh*, 49 (February 1973), 92-105.

—HSK

Ching-pen t'ung-su hsiao-shuo 京本通俗小說 (Popular Stories from Capital Editions), first published by the bibliophile Miao Ch'üan-sun 繆荃孫 (1844-1919) in 1915, presumably on the basis of an incomplete Yüan manuscript, has long been regarded as the earliest extant collection of *hua-pen** stories of Sung dates. According to Miao, the manuscript consisted of nine stories, two of which he excluded because of obscenity and lack of textual integrity. In 1919 Yeh Te-hui 葉德輝 (1864-1927), another well-known bibliophile, claimed that he possessed a Sung edition of one of the rejected stories and published it independently.

Influential as this collection has been in shaping our understanding of the development of popular stories in the vernacular, it has had its share of critics. Cheng Chen-to 鄭振鐸 (1898-1958) questioned the possibility of having a collection of vernacular stories at such an early date and proposed to place it sometime before Feng Meng-lung's* (1574-1646) *San-yen* collections. Yeh Te-hui's claim, happily, has never been taken seriously; the story he published is none other than number 23 from the *Hsing-shih heng-yen* 醒世恆言 (Lasting Words to Awaken the World).

The following seven stories in the *Ching-pen t'ung-su hsiao-shuo* as brought forth by Miao Ch'üan-sun can be found under different titles in two of the *San-yen* collections, *Ching-shih t'ung-yen* 警世通言 (Comprehensive Words to Admonish the World) and *Hsing-shih heng-yen*: "Nien-yü Kuan-yin" 碾玉觀音 (Jade Avalokitesvara; *Ching-shih t'ung-yen* 8), "P'u-sa-man" 菩薩蠻 (Bodhisattva Barbarian; *T'ung-yen* 7), "Hsi-shan i-k'u kuei" 西山一窟鬼 (The West Hill Den of Ghosts; *T'ung-yen* 14), "Chih-ch'eng Chang Chu-kuan" 志誠張主管 (The Honest Clerk Chang; *T'ung-yen* 16), "Yao Hsiang-kung" 拗相公 (The Stubborn Prime Minister; *T'ung-yen* 4), "Ts'o-chan Ts'ui Ning" 錯斬崔寧 (The Erroneous Execution of Ts'ui Ning; *Hsing-shih heng-yen* 33), "Feng Yü-mei t'uan-yüan" 馮玉梅團圓 (The Reunion of Feng Yü-mei; *T'ung-yen* 12). The observation of this coincidence and other particularities of the collection led to stunning revelations in the 1960s and 1970s. It has been shown that editorial changes were made in the stories to lead readers to accept them as Sung writings, that some of the stories could not have been written in

Sung times, and that the texts used are inferior editions of the *Ching-shih t'ung-yen* and the *Hsing-shih heng-yen.* Under such circumstances, Miao Ch'üan-sun, who brought us this hitherto unknown work, has to remain under suspicion of attempting to perpetrate this forgery.

Ching-pen t'ung-su hsiao-shuo is thus a collection without textual and historical merit. Any study of the individual stories should be based on the versions in the Feng Meng-lung collections. But this is not to say that the *Ching-pen t'ung-su hsiao-shuo* as a collection is devoid of intrinsic value. Its popularity, though largely derived from the historical misunderstanding, cannot be divorced from the collective charm and power of these seven stories as representative of a distinguished type of literature. The editorial choice of selecting these seven stories from a total of eighty in the two collections of Feng Meng-lung, even in view of some apparent textual affinities, demonstrates a judicious critical insight.

EDITIONS:

Chin-nü Hai-ling-wang huang-yin 金虜海陵王荒淫. 1919. Facsimile ed.

Ching-pen t'ung-su hsiao-shuo, in *Yen-hua tung-t'ang hsiao-p'in* 煙畫東堂小品. 1915, facsimile ed.; Shanghai, 1954, punctuated ed.

Sung-jen hua-pen pa-chung 宋人話本八種. Shanghai, 1928. Punctuated ed. with preface by Hu Shih. The eighth story, "Ting-shan san-kuai" 定山三怪, is mentioned by Miao Ch'üan-sun but not included in his edition because the text is too fragmentary. For this story, the text in the *Ching-shih t'ung-yen* is used.

TRANSLATIONS:

Lévy, André with René Goldman. *L'antre aux fantômes des collines de l'Ouest: sept contes chinois anciens xxviie-xive siècle.* Paris, 1972.

Muramatsu, Ei 村松暎. *Kōshū kitan.* Tokyo, 1951.

Yang, Richard F. S. *Eight Colloquial Tales of the Sung.* Taipei, 1972. Contains the seven stories from Miao Ch'üan-sun's edition. Yang's translation is based on the 1928 edition.

Yoshikawa, Kōjirō 吉川幸次郎. *Seizan ikkutsuki* 西山一窟鬼. Tokyo, 1956.

STUDIES:

Cheng, Chen-to. "Ming-Ch'ing erh-tai te p'ing-hua chi" 明清二代的平話集, *Hsiao-shuo yüeh-*

pao, 22 (1931), 933-958, 1057-1084. Reprinted in Cheng, *Chung-kuo wen-hsüeh yen-chiu* 中國文學研究, Peking, 1957, v. 1, pp. 360-474.

Hu, Wan-ch'üan 胡萬川. "*Ching-pen t'ung-su hsiao-shuo* te hsin fa-hsien" 京本通俗小說的新發現, *Chung-hua wen-hua fu-hsing yüeh-k'an,* 10.10 (1977), 37-43.

Lévy, André. "Le problème de la date et de l'authenticité du recueil de contes anciens intitulé *King-pen t'ong-sou siao-chouo,*" in *Mélanges de sinologie offertes à Monsieur Paul Demiéville,* v. 2, Paris, 1974, pp. 187-196.

Ma, Yu-yüan 馬幼垣 and Ma T'ai-lai 馬泰來. "*Ching-pen t'ung-su hsiao-shuo* ko-pien te nien-tai chi ch'i chen-wei wen-t'i" 京本通俗小說各篇的年代及其眞僞問題, *THHP, N.S.,* 5 (1965), 14-32.

Nagasawa, Kikuya 長澤規矩也. "*Keihon tsūzoku shōsetsu* no shingi" 京本通俗小說の眞僞, Nagasawa, *Shoshigaku ronkō* 書誌學論考, Tokyo, 1937, pp. 147-158.

Prusek, Jaroslav. "Popular Novels in the Collection of Ch'ien Tseng," *AO,* 10 (1938), 281-294.

Su, Hsing 蘇興. "*Ching-pen t'ung-su hsiao-shuo* pien-wei" 京本通俗小說辨僞, *Wen-wu,* 1978.3, 71-74.

Yoshikawa, Kōjirō. " 'Shijō Chō shukan' hyō" 志誠張主管評, *Kokugo kokubun,* 11:2 (1941), 1-26. Reprinted in *Yoshikawa Kōjirō zenshū,* v. 13, Tokyo, 1969, pp. 525-548.

—YWM and TLM

Ch'ing-lou chi 青樓集 (Green Lofts Collection) is a short collection in one *chüan* of laconic biographical notices about sing-song girls who lived during the Yüan dynasty. It was written by a certain Hsia T'ing-shih 夏庭芝 (Po-ho 伯和, *c.* 1316-after 1368). He was a man of considerable means, who was befriended by some of the leading *tsa-chü** authors of the day. He also wrote *san-ch'ü* (see *ch'ü*) but none of these have been preserved.

In its seventy-odd items the *Ch'ing-lou chi* provides the names of more than 110 female entertainers and more than 30 male entertainers. Each item is headed by a courtesan's stage name. The information provided is summary in the extreme and often limited to the name of the form of entertainment in which the lady excelled. Mentioned are for instance: *tsa-chü,** *yüan-*

320

*pen,** songs, storytelling, *chu-kung-tiao,** and dance. In the case of *tsa-chü*, the specific role-types she favored may be mentioned. Sometimes information is provided on relatives. In a number of cases we are provided with an anecdote or two about association with leading officials or literati of the time. These anecdotes usually underline either the lady's wit or her virtue.

The text of the *Ch'ing-lou chi* has been transmitted in two slightly divergent recensions. The earliest recension, included in the Ming dynasty compilation *Shou-chi* 說集, may date from 1355. All other editions of the text derive from a slightly later recension that may date from 1360. The *Ch'ing-lou chi* itself has no great literary value but it is an extremely important document for Chinese theater history.

EDITIONS:

Hsia, T'ing-chih. *Ch'ing-lou chi*, in *Chung-kuo ku-tien hsi-ch'ü lun-chu chi-ch'eng* 中國古典戲曲論著集成, Chung-kuo hsi-ch'ü yen-chiu yüan 中國戲曲研究院, ed., v. 2, Peking, 1959, pp. 1-84.

TRANSLATIONS:

Idema and West, *Chinese Theater*, pp. 95-172, passim.

Waley, Arthur. "The Green Bower Collection", in his *The Secret History of the Mongols, And Other Pieces,* London, 1963, pp. 89-107. A selection of the more extended notices.

STUDIES:

Chou, Miao-chung 周妙中. "Ching-lou chi ho t'a te pan-pen" 青樓集和它的版本, in *Chung-kuo ku-tien wen-hsüeh yen-chiu lun-ts'ung* 中國古典文學研究論叢, v. 1, Ch'ang-ch'un, 1980, pp. 350-359.

—WI

Ch'ing-pai lei-ch'ao 清稗類鈔 (A Classified Collection of Ch'ing Fiction) was compiled by Hsü K'o 徐珂 (*tzu*, Chung-k'o 仲可, 1869-1928) and first published in 1916. Consisting of thousands of brief entries on countless topics, the *Ch'ing-pai lei-ch'ao* is a virtual encyclopedia of information on life in the Ch'ing period. Reminiscent of many *pi-chi** in its anecdotal style, Hsü K'o's work is in the tradition of the private history which includes not only the editor's per-

sonal observations, but also reports from his friends and acquaintances, popular stories, jokes, anecdotes, and gossip. Although reported as historical fact, and although many entries are indeed factual, it is often difficult to discern from fiction. If used as a historical source, the work must be read with caution, but it can be a useful source for students of the Ch'ing. At the very least it reveals what kinds of popular stories and information an observant scholar and voracious compiler could assemble in the late Ch'ing and early Republican period.

An indication of the range of stories and information in *Ch'ing-pai lei-ch'ao* may be seen from the following partial list of topics (there are ninety-two in all) in its table of contents: weather, geography, famous places, palaces, gardens, temples, palace life, foreign relations, ceremonial regulations, education, examinations, military campaigns, lawsuits, social control, etc.

On each of these topics there are twenty to three hundred separate entries. Most entries are short, but some run several pages.

In addition to *Ch'ing-pai lei-ch'ao*, Hsü K'o also left a variety of poetry and prose in two collections, *T'ien-su ko ts'ung-k'an* 天蘇閣叢刊, and *Hsin yüan ts'ung-k'o* 心園叢刊. He also edited two vernacular anthologies, the *Li-tai pai-hua shih-hsüan* 歷代白話詩選 (rpt. Taipei, 1966) and the *Li-tai nü-tzu pai-hua shih-hsüan* 歷代女子白話詩選 (Shanghai, 1922), the latter a collection of verse by women poets.

EDITIONS:

Ch'ing-pai lei-ch'ao 清稗類鈔. 48v. Shanghai, 1916; rpt. Taipei, 1966.

—PR

Ch'ing shih-hua 清詩話 (Poetry Talks of the Ch'ing Dynasty) is the most complete anthology of Ch'ing dynasty *shih-hua** compiled to date. It was edited by Ting Fu-pao 丁福保 on the same pattern as his *Li-tai shih-hua hsü-pien* 歷代詩話續編 (Continuation of Poetry Talks from Successive Ages), itself patterned upon Ho Wen-huan's 何文煥 *Li-tai shih-hua* 歷代詩話, which Ting reprinted.

Ting Fu-pao certainly performed an important service by making such a variety of texts readily available. But the haste with which the anthology was prepared and the desire to obtain as good a market as possible produced numerous shortcomings. First, Ting included certain rather insignificant works while leaving out a number of major ones. And some critics have argued that the selection of poetry talks is hardly representative of Ch'ing literary criticism: there are too many works on the technical aspects of writing poetry and too few theoretical essays. Ting's inclusion of the *Hui-ch'en shih-hua* 揮塵詩話, which is not even by a Ch'ing dynasty author, is also problematic. Finally, Ting was frequently careless in his selection of editions and in the collation of texts. Fortunately, Kuo Shao-yü eliminated many of these shortcomings in the modern, punctuated edition published by Chung-hua shu-chü in 1963.

Although Ting Fu-pao obviously felt that *shih-hua* are important to an understanding of Chinese literature, the preface to the anthology, written by his friend Yen Wei 嚴偉, displays a rather ambivalent attitude toward the genre. Yen argues that the flourishing of critical literature in the Ch'ing has harmed writers and that Ch'ing critics divided themselves into cliques, unfairly attacking both their contemporaries and those ancients who did not agree with their literary theories. Yen violently condemns Yüan Mei's* and Chao I's* critical works, praising Ting for having excluded them. Yen's preface also displays an inordinate concern for the technical aspects of poetry and a conservative outlook on literature, with which Ting Fu-pao was no doubt in sympathy. It is, however, difficult to determine Ting's exact feelings concerning the *shih-hua* he selected, since the comments he appended to each are brief and superficial.

Despite these shortcomings, the *Ch'ing shih-hua* is a valuable tool for studying certain aspects of Ch'ing criticism. The works included fall into three broad divisions: (1) those concerned with the technical problems of writing *shih* poetry, (2) works which involved the critical evaluation of poets, and (3) writings of a more theoretical nature. Of course, some pieces combine all three concerns. In the first category the most valuable are probably Wang Shih-chen's* (1634-1711) *Lü-shih ting-t'i* 律詩定體, which overturns certain mistaken notions about the tonal patterns of T'ang regulated verse held by Ming critics, and Chao Chih-hsin's 趙執信 *Sheng-tiao p'u* 聲調譜, which was the most systematic treatment of T'ang regulated-verse metrics up to its time—the result of a careful examination of thousands of T'ang poems.

The second type of "poetry talk" is represented by Sun T'ao's 孫濤 *Ch'üan T'ang shih-hua hsü-pien* 全唐詩話續編 which consists of historical and critical comments on a wide range of T'ang poets, by Chou Ch'un's 周春 *Liao shih-hua* 遼詩話 on poets of the generally neglected Liao dynasty, and by Fei Hsi-huang's 費錫璜 *Han-shih tsung-shou* 漢詩總說, a rambling discussion of Han-dynasty *shih* poetry.

The third type of work is represented by Wang Fu-chih's* *Chiang-chai shih-hua* 薑齋詩話, which emphasizes self-expression and attacks imitation, by Wang Shih-chen's *Jan-teng chi-wen* 然燈紀聞 and *Yü-yang shih-hua* 漁洋詩話, which contains material valuable for understanding Wang's theories of *shen-yün* 神韻 and *feng-chih* 風致, by Chao Chih-hsin's 趙執信 *T'an-lung lu,** which attacks Wang Shih-chen's *shen-yün* theory and stresses the importance of the presence of the individuality in his verse, by Shen Te-ch'ien's* *Shuo-shih sui-yü* 說詩晬語, the classic statement of his theory of *ke-tiao* 格調, and finally by Yeh Hsieh's* *Yüan-shih,* one of the most systematic and original works on literary theory from the Ch'ing dynasty.

EDITIONS:

Ch'ing shih-hua 清詩話. Shanghai, 1916.
Ch'ing shih-hua. Peking, 1963.

STUDIES:

Cheng, Ching-jo 鄭靜若. *Ch'ing-tai shih-hua hsü-lu* 清代詩話敍錄. Taipei, 1975.
Liu, Jo-yü 劉若愚. "Ch'ing-tai shih-shuo lun-yao" 清代詩說論要, in *Hsiang-kang Ta-hsüeh wu-shih chou-nien chi-nien lun-wen chi* 香港大學五十週

年紀念論文集, v. 1, Hong Kong, 1964, pp. 321-342.

—JDS

Ch'iu Yüan 邱園 (*tzu*, Yü-hsüeh 嶼雪, 1616-1689) was a dramatist and a painter of the early Ch'ing. A native of Ch'ang-shu 常熟 (modern Kiangsu), he lived the life of a recluse at Mount Wu-ch'iu 烏邱 and gave himself the literary names of Mr. Wu-ch'iu or the Man of Wu-ch'iu Mountain. He never participated in any official examination and did not serve in the government. In the late Ming, *K'un-ch'ü** flourished in the region of Soochow. Ch'iu Yüan was a member of a group of *K'un-ch'ü* dramatists headed by Li Yü* (*c.* 1591-*c.* 1671),* who were active at the beginning of the early Ch'ing.

Ch'iu wrote a total of eight *ch'uan-ch'i*,* of which only *Tang-jen pei* 黨人碑 (The Factionalist's Stele) and *Yü-p'ao en* 御袍恩 (Grace of the Imperial Robe, also entitled *Pai-fu tai* 百福帶 [Belt of a Hundred Good Fortunes]) are preserved in their entirety. Only one act ("Shan-t'ing" 山亭) of *Hu-nang tan* 虎囊彈 (Crossbow Pellets) is extant. The story of *Tang-jen pei* is woven around the proscription of the Yüan-yu Party by Grand Councilor Ts'ai Ching of the late Northern Sung. Ts'ai erected a stele condemning such conservative politicians and scholars as the famous Ssu-ma Kuang 司馬光 (1019-1086) and Su Shih.* In the play itself, Liu K'uei 劉逵 appeals to Emperor Hui-tsung to oppose the erection of the monument. Liu is thrown into prison and his son-in-law, Hsieh Ch'iung-hsien 謝瓊仙, is also persecuted. Hsieh damages the stele while drunk and is pursued by his tormentors. Liu, in the meanwhile, wins a pardon and gathers merit by suppressing the rebel T'ien Hu. He is finally reunited with his daughter and son-in-law. There is some evidence that Ch'iu was using his drama as contemporary political criticism and the play may refer to the factionalism that plagued the final decade of the Ming. In the late Ch'ing, Wang Hsiao-nung 汪笑儂, a famous Peking Opera actor, also arranged the drama for performance. In this case, the drama may have been performed to show some sympathy with the group of reformers who opposed the Dowager Tzu-hsi.

Yü-p'ao en, another play based on a Northern Sung political event, has not achieved the fame of *Tang-jen pei*. *Hu-nang tan* is about the *Shui-hu chuan** hero Lu Chih-shen 魯智深. He rescues Chin Ts'ui-lien 金翠蓮, whose husband, Chao Yüan-wai, is accused of carrying on secret relations with the bandits of Liang-shan. Chin appeals to Ch'ung Ching-lüeh 種經略 to release her husband. Ch'ung, however, has commanded that all who appealed an injustice to him first be hung on a post and shot a hundred times with crossbow pellets. Those who could endure such a test were the ones who had really suffered wrongs. Chin Ts'ui-lien offered to undergo this cruel test, and Ch'ung then heard her appeal. The extant act is based on the fourth chapter of the *Shui-hu chuan*, "Lu Chih-shen ta nao Wu-t'ai Shan" 魯智深大鬧五台山 (Lu Chih-shen Raises Hell at Wu-t'ai Shan) in which Lu got drunk and rampaged about the mountain. He was sent away from the mountain by his master. This act remains in the repertoires of *K'un-ch'ü*, Peking Opera, and *ti-fang hsi*.*

EDITIONS:

Tang-jen pei, in *Ku-pen*, III.

Yü-pao en, in *Ku-pen*, III.

"Shan-t'ing" (one act of *Hu-nang tan*), in the *Chi-ch'eng ch'ü-p'u* 集成曲譜, Wang Chi-lieh 王季烈, compiler.

Tang-jen pei (*Ching chü* version arranged by Wang Hsiao-nung), in *Wang Hsiao-nung hsi-ch'ü chi* 汪笑儂戲曲集, Peking, 1957.

TRANSLATIONS:

Deng, Shaoji. "Qui Yuan: 'The Drunken Monk' " (the scene 'Shan-men' 山門 from the *Hu-nang tan*), *CL*, December 1980, 86-95.

—BTW

Chou Chi 周濟 (*tzu*, Pao-hsü 保緒 and Chieh-ts'un 介存, *hao*, Chih-an 止庵, 1781-1839) was a leading master of the Ch'ang-chou* School of *tz'u** poetry and was particularly known for his criticism. After passing the *chin-shih* examination in 1805, he became Instructor in Huai-an Prefecture 淮安府. His interests ranged from poetry, classics, and painting to the martial arts. But in his old age Chou retired to the Ch'un-shui yüan 春水園 (Spring Water Garden) of Chin-ling 金陵 (modern Nanking) and devoted the rest of his life to writing. His works include *Shuo-wen tzu-hsi* 說文字系, *Yün-yüan* 韻原, *Chieh-ts'un-chai shih* 介存齋詩, *Tz'u-pien* 詞辨, *Sung ssu-chia tz'u-hsüan* 宋四家詞選, and his most celebrated work of *tz'u* criticism *Chieh-ts'un-chai lun-tz'u tsa-chu* 介存齋論詞雜著.

Chou Chi learned the technique of *tz'u* writing from Tung Shih-hsi 董士錫 (*fl.* 1811), the nephew of the founder of the Ch'ang-chou School, Chang Hui-yen.* In Chou's view, Tung was even greater than his predecessors: "Although Tung Shih-hsi looks up to the two Chang brothers [Chang Hui-yen and Chang Ch'i 張琦] as models, his works are actually superior to theirs" (Preface to *Tz'u-pien*). It was through Tung that Chou inherited the orthodox tradition of allegorical readings in *tz'u*. Realizing that Chou Chi's original theory of allegory entailed logical problems, Chou Chi revised and expanded the theory, in ways that were beneficial to the prestige of the School. He was particularly helpful in offering advice to apprentice writers: "The beginning stage of writing *tz'u* demands imagination and skill, and Wang I-sun 王沂孫 (d. 1291) can be said to be outstanding in both areas. ... The Southern Sung *tz'u* shows us the way. It provides a path, and so although it appears to be difficult, it is actually easy" (Preface to *Sung ssu-chia tz'u-hsüan*). Full of insights and common sense, Chou's theoretical work had a compelling influence upon the *tz'u* world through the remainder of the Ch'ing and into the twentieth century.

Chou Chi was particularly attentive to the rules of tonal patterns in *tz'u*. His discussions of rhythmic structures and prosodic principles were useful to later *tz'u* writers. In this aspect, Chou was greatly influenced by Wan Shu,* the author of the famous prosodic manual *Tz'u-lü* 詞律 (Prosody of Tz'u). And in turn Chou's interest in alliteration (*shuang-sheng* 雙聲) and rhyming compounds (*tieh-yün* 疊韻) inspired further discussions of these two poetic devices in *tz'u*.

EDITIONS:

"Chieh-ts'un-chai lun-tz'u tsa-chu" 介存齋論詞雜著, in T'ang, *Tz'u-hua*, V, pp. 1623-1635.

Sung ssu-chia tz'u-hsüan [chien-chu] 宋四家詞選箋注. K'uang Shih-yüan 鄺士元, annot. Taipei, 1971.

Wei-chün-chai tz'u 味雋齋詞, in *Ch'ing-tz'u pieh-chi pai san-shih-ssu chung* 清詞別集百三十四種. Taipei, 1976, v. 8.

STUDIES:

Ho, *Ch'ing tz'u*, pp. 97-110.

Nien, Shu 念述. "Shih t'an Chou Chi 'Chieh-ts'an-chai lun tz'u tsa-chu' " 試談周濟介存齋論詞雜著, *Wen-hsüeh i-ch'an tseng-k'an*, 9 (June 1962), 96-110.

Wang, Hsi-yüan 王熙元. *Li-tai tz'u-hua hsü-lu* 歷代詞話敍錄. Taipei, 1973, pp. 126-128.

Wu, *Ch'ang-chou*, pp. 52-86.

Yeh, "Ch'ang-chou."

—KIC

Chou Le-ch'ing 周樂清 (*tzu*, Wen-ch'üan 文泉, *hao*, Lien-ch'ing-tzu 鍊情子, *fl.* 1836) was a native of Hai-ning 海寧 (modern Chekiang). Because of hereditary privilege, Chou was given a minor official post in Tao-chou 道州 (modern Hunan)—the first of several provincial posts he held, some which are now parts of Szechwan and Shantung. He enjoyed friendships with many scholars in the areas he governed, especially in Hunan and Shantung.

In 1829 while en route to Peking to personally express his thanks for official appointment he wrote his masterpiece, *Pu-t'ien-shih ch'uan-ch'i* 補天石傳奇 (Dramas which Are Stones for Repairing Heaven) in eight *chüan*. The title alludes to the tradition that the goddess Nü-kua used smelted stones to repair a hole in the sky—but it had been proposed by Mao Sheng-shan 毛聲山 (see Mao Tsung-kang) in the preface he wrote for the *P'i-p'a chi* (see Kao Ming) as the name for a series of works which would reverse the unjust fates of certain well-known figures in Chinese history. Mao, however, never wrote the ten pieces he proposed. Chou selected eight stories which interested him.

In the first, *Yen Chin-t'ai* 宴金台 (The Feast at the Golden Terrace—in six acts), Chou alters events so that Prince Tan 丹 of Yen 燕 is able to overcome the state of Ch'in and prevent it from uniting China. In other plays Chu-ko Liang 諸葛亮 (181-234) unites China, Li Ling 李陵 crushes the Hsiung-nu, Wang Chao-chün 王昭君 returns to the Han palace, Ch'ü Yüan* is rescued from drowning and subsequently given an important position by the king of Ch'u, Yüeh Fei 岳飛 (1103-1141) defeats the enemy soundly, etc. Perhaps related to the general changes in dramatic taste of this period, Chou has shaped eight tragedies into comedies. The works are primarily of interest for the skillful manipulation of the familiar plots.

EDITIONS:

Pu-t'ien-shih ch'uan-ch'i. N.p., 1837.

Ching-yüan ts'ao-t'ang chi 靜遠草堂集. *Ping-ti hu-lu* 並蒂葫蘆. Chou Le-ch'ing, comp. Rpt. Yung-ho, Taiwan, 1974.

STUDIES:

Aoki, *Gikyokushi,* p. 426.

Fu, *Ch'ing tsa-chü,* pp. 283-287.

—XLW and WHN

Chou Mi 周密 (*tzu,* Kung-chin 公謹, *hao,* Ts'ao-ch'uang 草窗, Ssu-shui ch'ien-fu 四水潛夫, Pien-yang Lao-jen 弁陽老人, 1232-1299 or 1308) was a poet, chronicler, calligrapher, and lover of antiques. Descended from a clan of Chi-nan 濟南 (modern Shantung), his forefathers had followed Emperor Kao-tsung in his flight south and established a home in Pien-shan 弁山 (modern Wu-hsing 吳興, Chekiang). Chou was born in Fu-ch'un 富春 (Chekiang) but later lived in Kuei-hsin Street 癸辛街 in Hangchow.

His father, Chou Chin 周晉, had been a minor official and his mother was a poet. Thus Chou Mi grew up having been exposed to the regions where his father's appointments took the family, to the considerable family library (over 40,000 books and 1,500 rubbings of stone carvings and bronzes), and to his mother's literary tastes.

He held a minor post at I-wu 義烏 (Chekiang) as a youth (*c.* 1250) but does not seem to have served in office thereafter. In 1277 his home was destroyed by the Mongol invaders, and he moved to live with a relative in Hangchow. A staunch loyalist to the Sung, he spent his last years in retirement compiling various works intended to preserve Sung culture.

Chou's best known work is the *Wu-lin chiu-shih* 武林舊事 (Former Events in Hangchow, *c.* 1280—Wu-lin is an alternate name for Hangchow, derived from a neighboring mountain). The book is a highly detailed account of life in the capital during the Southern Sung dynasty. Although it contains a great deal of information about daily life, the emphasis is on the palace, its customs, rituals, and protocol. It also contains highly valuable information about theater, music and the entertainment arts of the late Sung, and it preserves the only known list of titles of dramas performed at the Sung court.

Together with the *Meng-liang lu* and the *Tu-ch'eng chi-sheng* (see *Tung-ching meng-hua lu*), the *Wu-lin chiu-shih* is the principal historical source for understanding the life of the Southern Sung capital. Some of it is duplicated in other works, but its value is enhanced by the fact that it preserves parts of other works now lost. Chapter seven, for example, on the imperial parents, contains parts of two other works on that subject: the *Te-shou kung ch'i-chü fa* 德壽宮起居法 and the *Feng-ch'en lu* 逢辰錄, which are both lost. Throughout the work, Chou intersperses poems in both the *shih** and the *tz'u** styles, many from his own hand. The subjects of the first nine chapters are: (1) court ceremonies and ritual; (2) review of the troops, archery ceremonies, the wedding of a princess, entrance into the civil service, ballet troupes, the animal sacrifices, and the daily life of the emperor; (3) a tour of West Lake (describes some forms of oral literature—such as storytelling, as well as puppet shows, which were performed during holiday celebrations at West Lake; (4) the Palace and the Imperial School of Music and Dance (1165-1189); (5) mountains and lakes in the surrounding countryside; (6) lives of the citizens of the capital; (7) the imperial parents; (8) imperial visitations to schools, the reception of ambassadors, the ceremonies of the imperial family; and (9) the visit of Kao-tsung to Chang Chün

The tenth and final chapter contains the only catalogue of dramas performed at the

Sung court. The list is not exhaustive, because no dramas performed in the theaters of the entertainment quarter are thought to be represented there. It is also possible that some titles of dramas dated from the Northern Sung are included.

Chou Mi also compiled several works chronicling the Southern Sung, including the miscellany of historical notes entitled *Ch'i-tung yeh-yü* 齊東野語 (Rustic Words of a Man from Eastern Ch'i, 1291—the title refers to the home area of Chou's clan in Shantung and is self-disparaging, alluding to *Mencius*). His *Chih-ya t'ang tsa-ch'ao* 志雅堂雜鈔 (Miscellaneous Documents From the Hall of Aiming for Elegance) is a collection of notes on paintings, curios, antiques, and sundry other topics.

A considerable body of *tz'u* and *shih* poetry also came from his pen (he and Chiang K'uei,* whom he admired, are considered the only *tz'u* poets of the Southern Sung who also produced *shih* of quality). In an era when the *tz'u* was in decline, he attempted to revive interest in the genre with a collection of *tz'u* by 132 authors entitled *Chüeh-miao hao-tz'u* 絕妙好詞 (Excellent Lyrics, *c.* 1290). His own *tz'u* style tended toward *yung-wu* 詠物 (descriptive of objects), although patriotism was also significant, especially in the later work. His early *tz'u*, collected in the *Ts'ao-ch'uang yün-yü* 草窗韻語 (Rhyming Words from the Grass Window, 1274—this also includes his early *shih*), were modeled on T'ang poets and consist primarily of verses exchanged with other poets and descriptions of famous places he visited. His later lyrics, found in the *P'in-chou yü-ti p'u* 蘋州漁笛譜 (Flute Music of the P'in-chou Fisherman, before 1279) reveals a more mature style influenced by Chiang K'uei and the eccentric Yang Tsuan 揚纘 (*tzu*, Ssu-weng 嗣翁). Chou's "Teng P'eng-lai ko yu-kan" 登蓬萊閣有感 (Thoughts on Climbing P'eng-lai Pavilion—written to the tune "I-e hung" 一萼紅) and "T'i Wu Meng-ch'uang *Shuang-hua sou* tz'u-chi" 題吳夢窗霜花腴詞集 (Introducing Wu "Dream-window's" [Wen-ying's] *Thin Blossoms in the Frost* Collection of Lyrics—written to the tune "Yü lou Ch'ih" 玉漏遲) are among his best lyrics,

both recalling nostalgically the fallen Sung dynasty. In structure his lyrics often resemble those of Wu Wen-ying*—the two poets are collectively known as "Erh-ch'uang" 二窗 (Two Windows) because of their similar *hao*. But Chou Mi is more often associated with Wang I-sun 王沂孫 (1240-1290) and Chang Yen 張炎 (b. 1248), both of whom he knew well, as the three best of the Sung loyalist poets.

His *shih* poetry resembles his *tz'u* in that his earliest writings in the genre were inspired by late T'ang verse (that of Li Ho* and Tu Mu* are usually cited) and limns delicate, *bonsai* landscapes (reflecting his *yung-wu* predilection). Much of his later corpus of *shih* is lost.

EDITIONS:

Ch'i-tung yeh-yü. (1) Taipei, 1969; (2) in *PPTSCC*, series 46: *Hsüeh-chin t'ao-yüan* 學津討原, *chüan* 200-206.

Chih-ya t'ang tsa-ch'ao. (1) Taipei, 1969; (2) in *PPTSCC*, series 55: *Te-yüeh-i ts'ung-shu Ch'üan Sung-tz'u,* v. 5, pp. 3264-3294.

Chüeh-miao hao-tz'u chien 絕妙好詞箋. Mai Ch'ao-shu 麥朝樞, ed. Wang Shu-ming 黃叔明, collator. Peking, 1956. Contains annotations by Cha Wei-jen 查爲仁 and Li E 厲鶚.

P'ing-chou yü-t'i p'u. Chih-pu-tsu chai ts'ung-shu.

Ts'ao-ch'uang yün-yü. Chih-pu-tsu chai ts'ung-shu.

Wu-lin chiu-shih. Chih-pu-tsu chai ts'ung-shu.

———, in *Tung-ching meng-hua lu* (*Wai ssu-chung*) 東京夢華錄, Peking, 1962, pp. 329-526.

TRANSLATIONS:

Jacques Gernet's *La Vie quotidienne en Chine à la veille de l'invasion Mongole, 1250-1276*, Paris, 1959, was based on the *Wu-lin chiu-shih*, although it is not properly a translation. An English translation by H. M. Wright, *Daily Life in China on the Eve of the Mongol Invasion, 1250-1276*, was published at Stanford in 1962.

STUDIES:

Feng, Yüan-chün 馮沅君. "Ts'ao-ch'uang nien-p'u ni-kao" 草窗年譜擬稿, *Pei-ching Ta-hsüeh Yen-chiu-so Kuo-hsüeh men yüeh-k'an*, 1.4 (January 1927).

Hsia, Ch'eng-t'ao 夏承燾. *Chou Ts'ao-ch'uang nien-p'u* 周草窗年譜, in *T'ang Sung tz'u-jen nien-p'u* 唐宋詞人年譜, Shanghai, 1955; rpt. Peking, 1961. Appends a study of his works.

SB, pp. 261-268.

Su, Wen-t'ing 蘇文婷. *Sung-tai i-min wen-hsüeh yen-chiu* 宋代遺民文學研究. Taipei, 1979, pp. 203-225. A thorough study of Chou Mi's life and works.

—DJ and WHN

Chou Pang-yen 周邦彥 (*tzu*, Mei-ch'eng 美成, *hao*, Ch'ing-chen 清眞, 1056-1121) was one of the most influential poets in the *tz'u** tradition. Wang Kuo-wei* said his position with regard to the Sung lyric was analogous to that of Tu Fu* in T'ang poetry. Another critic, Chu Wei-chih 朱維之, has written, "In the 'orthodox school of the lyric,' the style must be voluptuous, the lines finely crafted, and everything must harmonize with the music—this is what is meant by the "delicately restrained" (*wan-yüeh* 宛約) style. Liu Yung* began this school, Ch'in Kuan 秦觀 (1049-1100) and Ho Chu* established it, and Chou Pang-yen and Li Ch'ing-chao* brought it to culmination."

The course of Chou's official career is well known. The details of his personal life are more obscure, but he is the subject of several famous anecdotes portraying him as a romantic and an intimate of the most famous courtesans of the day.

His life seems to have been easier than that of many contemporary literati; he was apparently a supporter of the "New Policies" but not a principal in political infighting. In 1083, as a student in the National University, he presented to the throne a *fu** on the Sung capital, "Pien-tu fu" 汴都賦, in which he praised the New Policies. He was quickly raised to the office of Chief of Learning in the National University, where he remained for five years. From 1087 to 1092, Chou was outside the capital as an Instructor, as the "Old Policies Faction" held sway over the government. From 1093 to 1096, although the New Policies forces were regaining power, he did not return to the capital, but held the post of Administrator of Li-shui hsien 溧水縣. One lyric ("Man-t'ing fang" 滿庭芳) written there reveals his discomfort with the climate and nostalgia for the capital, and he may indeed have felt forgotten and oppressed in that out-of-the-way place. He had an interest in Taoism at this time:

Ch'iang Huan 强煥, who held office at Li-shui over eighty years later, reports seeing a pavilion and a hall to which Chou had given names from stories of "spirits and immortals." Ch'iang collected and published 182 lyrics by Chou, asserting that there was a connection between the popularity of his songs and the lingering good memories among the populace of his administration. Some of Chou's few surviving *shih** have Taoist themes; if they were written during his tenure in Li-shui, one wonders if the proximity of Mao-shan, center of a thriving Taoist tradition, influenced him.

In 1098, once again in the capital, Chou re-presented his "Pien-tu fu"; it was received by Emperor Che-tsung with even more enthusiasm than Emperor Shen-tsung had shown fifteen years earlier. From this time until 1118, Chou generally held office in the capital, with two brief tenures as Administrator in the provinces. In 1116, he was made Supervisor of the Imperial Music Bureau, an appropriate position for someone with his musical ability.

Chou had not been in the Ta-sheng fu very long before he was sent out again as an Administrator. Caught in the path of the Fang-la Rebellion in 1120, he fled to Hangchow. In the following year, soon after reaching Nanking and the imperial shrine there, of which he had been made Intendant, he died.

Chou Pang-yen was an essayist and poet as well as a lyricist, but most of his prose and *shih* have been lost. A printed edition of his works made at the beginning of the thirteenth century; it seems to have survived into the Ming, for it is cited by the *Yung-lo ta-tien.** The extant poems are, in the words of one modern researcher, "exhilarating and valiant," quite different from his lyrics.

The lyrics are, to quote James J. Y. Liu, "subtle and sophisticated but do not strike one with immediate force. The poetic worlds of his lyrics are translucent, if not opaque, rather than crystalline, and their verbal structures are like ornately carved ivory or jade. . . ." Chou's opacity is the result of several factors: frequent use of images of substitution and of transference; a tendency to requiring explication for the moderately educated reader, do have a distancing effect; and the absence of a definite persona speaking to a single specific theme—particularly in the longer lyrics. The situation or predicament of the speaker is often implied by the physical objects or phenomena around him/her, or it may be implied by the allusions used. Sometimes the train of thought shifts with the incorporation of a new allusion or a fresh association suggested by the scene. The result is not an unstable or bewildering pasticcio, but an engagement of one's senses, feelings, and imagination in a richly layered experience. In their "explications" of his lyrics, critics often fondly describe the links, contrasts, and leaps which occur as one progresses through them, much as a connoisseur mentally repeats the parses, turns, and invisible links when he "reads" a piece of calligraphy.

A few of Chou's lyrics are evidently allegorical, comprehensible only as they refer to Chou's political situation. However, it would be rash to impose such an interpretation on most of his lyrics, which treat the standard themes of love, longing, and ennui that come with the genre.

In comparison with Liu Yung, the great lyricist of the previous generation, Chou is clearly less direct. There is also an important difference in the two lyricists' musical sense. Whereas Liu may show a fairly wide variation in the number of syllables fitted to a given *tiao* 調 (tune) or adapt a given *tiao* to different musical modes, Chou standardizes the number of syllables and the mode to be used for each *tiao*. Chou composed new tunes and is often said to have had a genius for music, but it would seem that his talent or taste was for codifying and perfecting an existing heritage, rather than improvising new possibilities. The same tendency is apparent in his contemporary lyricists, as the genre matured. Because of the popularity of his lyrics throughout all levels of the literary audience, popular and elite, of the lyric tradition, Chou's metrical patterns became, and still are, the accepted models for the *tiao* which he used.

EDITIONS:

Ch'iang-ts'un ts'ung-shu 彊邨叢書. 40 *ts'e*. Chu Tsu-mo 朱祖謀, ed. Shanghai, 1922. Valuable variorum edition.

"Ch'ing-chen chi chiao-chi" 清眞集校輯. Chao Wan-li 趙萬里, comp. *Kuo-li Pei-p'ing t'u-shu kuan kuan-k'an*, 11.1 (February 1937), 47-64. Gives texts of nine prose works and twenty-eight *shih*, re-collected from various sources.

Chou Pang-yen tz'u-hsüan 周邦彥詞選. Liu Ssu-fen 劉斯奮, comp. Hong Kong, 1981.

Chou tz'u ting-lü 周調訂律. Yang I-lin 楊易霖. 1935; rpt. Hong Kong, 1963. Indicates the meter and prosody of the lyrics, and appends 451 Southern Sung lyrics written to "harmonize" with his.

Ch'üan Sung tz'u 全宋詞, v. 2, pp. 595-631.

P'ian-yü chi 片玉集. *SPPY*.

P'ian-yü tz'u chiao-chien 片玉詞校箋. Chang Hsi 張曦, comp. Taipei, 1972. Each lyric is followed by observations on the meter and the diction. Chang's own paraphrase and appreciation, and the comments of other critics, are often included.

TRANSLATIONS:

Demiéville, *Anthologie*, pp. 393-395.

Landau, Julie. "Nine *tz'u* by Chou Pang-yen," *Renditions*, 11 & 12 (Spring & Autumn 1979), 177-189.

Sunflower, pp. 361-364.

STUDIES:

Chang, Ling-hui 張玲蕙. "Chou Pang-yen: ch'i jen, ch'i tz'u" 周邦彥：其人其詞. *Che-chiang yüeh-k'an*, 5.8 (August 1973), 12-16. Includes a fairly clear textual history.

Hightower, James Robert. "The Songs of Chou Pang-yen," *HJAS*, 37 (1977), 233-272.

Liu, *Lyricists*, pp. 161-194. Contains translations.

Lo, K'ang-lieh 羅忼烈. "Chou Ch'ing-chen tz'u shih-ti k'ao-lüeh" 周清眞詞時地考略, in *Ta-kung pao tsai Hsiang-lang fu-k'an san-shih chou nien chi-chien wen-chi* 大公報在香港復刊三十周年紀念文集, Hong Kong, 1978, v. 2, pp. 883-935.

SB, pp. 268-270.

Wang, Kuo-wei 王國維. "Ch'ing-chen hsien-sheng i-shih" 清眞先生遺事, In Wang's *Wang Kuan-t'ang Hsien-sheng ch'üan-chi* 王觀堂先生全集, Taipei, 1968, v. 9, pp. 3641-3691. Wang's research is the basis for most modern scholarship on Chou's life.

—SHS

Chu Ch'üan 朱權 (*hao,* Ta-ming Ch'i-shih 大明奇士, Ch'ü-hsien 臞仙, Han-hsü-tzu 涵虛子, and Tan-ch'iu Hsien-sheng 丹邱先生, 1378-1448) wrote on a variety of subjects, but his place in the history of Chinese literature is almost completely determined by the value of his *T'ai-ho cheng-yin p'u* 太和正音譜 (A Formulary for the Correct Sounds of Great Harmony), the earliest preserved formulary of Northern *ch'ü.* Chu Ch'üan was the sixteenth son of Chu Yüan-chang 朱元璋 (1328-1398), the founder of the Ming dynasty. In 1391 Chu Ch'üan was enfeoffed as Prince of Ning 寧, and in 1393 he took up residence in his fief Ta-ning 大寧, an important garrison-town on the frontier. When Chu Ti became Emperor in 1402, Chu Ch'üan was reenfeoffed at Nan-ch'ang, after his requests for Hangchow and Soochow had been refused. His interests in literature were extremely wide-ranging, but his main contributions were in the field of drama. He was posthumously known as Ning Hsien-wang 寧獻王 (the Dedicated Prince of Ning). Traditional biographers credit him with having raised the cultural level of the backward Kiangsu region by his many scholary and literary undertakings.

The *T'ai-ho cheng-yin p'u* was completed (according to the preface) in 1398, but it has been argued (by Tseng Yung-i) that the present text is of a considerably later date. The work is divided into two *chüan.* The first provides miscellaneous information on *ch'ü** (both *san-ch'ü* and *tsa-chü*). It contains, among other things, a critical appreciation of Yüan and early Ming writers of *ch'ü,* in which Ma Chih-yüan* is given first place; a list of ten categories of subject matter of *tsa-chü;* a catalogue of Yüan and early Ming *tsa-chü;* comments on the art of singing mostly based on the *Ch'ang-lun;** a list of explanations of the names of role-types in *tsa-chü;* and a list of the *ch'ü* treated in the second *chüan.* Throughout this first *chüan,* a strong tendency to dissociate the writing of *ch'ü,* especially *tsa-chü,* from the acting profession is discernible.

The second *chüan* consists of a formulary treating 335 different *ch'ü,* grouped according to modes. For each *ch'ü* an ex-

ample is provided, making the *T'ai-ho cheng-yin p'u* also an important anthology of dramatic and non-dramatic *ch'ü.* For every *ch'ü* the required tone of each syllable and the places of the rhyme are indicated. This second *chüan* has served as the basis of later formularies of *ch'ü* compiled during the Ming and Ch'ing dynasties. The *T'ai-ho cheng-yin p'u* is an essential document for the study of Yüan and early Ming *ch'ü,* especially *tsa-chü,* even though its formulary does not fully reflect the considerable variations most *ch'ü* tunes allowed.

Chu Ch'üan also wrote a number of *tsa-chü.* Twelve titles are known, but only two of these plays have come down to us. His *Ch'ung-mo-tzu tu-pu Ta-lo-t'ien* 沖漠子獨步大羅天 (Master Boundless Mystery Ascends Alone to the Ta-lo Heaven) is an elaborate Taoist deliverance play, requiring a large cast and fanciful costumes. His *Cho Wen-chün ssu-pen Hsiang-ju* 卓文君私奔相如 (Cho Wen-chün Elopes with Hsiang-ju) is a version of the love-story of Ssu-ma Hsiang-ju* and the young widow Cho Wen-chün. Both plays are undistinguished as works of literature.

Chu Ch'üan is also sometimes identified as the author of the well-known Southern play *Ching-ch'ai chi* 荊釵記 (The Thorn Hairpin). This identification is, however, highly questionable.

EDITIONS:

Chu Ch'üan, comp. *T'ai-ho cheng-yin p'u,* in Chung Ssu-ch'eng 鍾嗣成, *Lu kuei pu (wai ssu-chung)* 錄鬼簿 (外四種), Shanghai, 1957, pp. 119-297.

———, in *Chung-kuo ku-tien hsi-ch'ü kun-chu chi-ch'eng* 中國古典戲曲論著集成, Chung-kuo hsi-ch'ü yen-chiu yüan 中國戲曲研究院 comp., v. 3, Peking, 1957, pp. 1-231.

Wang, Chi-lieh 王季烈, comp. *Ku-pen Yüan Ming tsa-chü* 孤本元明雜劇. 4v. Peking, 1957. Contains both plays.

STUDIES:

DMB, pp. 305-307.

Moule, A. C. "An Introduction to the *I T'u Chih,* or Pictures of Descriptions of Strange Nations in the Wade Collection at Cambridge," *TP,* 27 (1930), 179-188. Discusses a rare early fifteenth-century geographical work, *I-yü t'u-chih* 異域圖志, and its possible authorship by Chu Ch'üan.

Tseng, Yung-i 曾永義. "T'ai-ho cheng-yin p'u te tso-che wen-t'i" 太和正音譜作者問題, in *Shou hsi-ch'ü* 說戲曲, Taipei, 1976, pp. 75-98.

―――. "T'ai-ho cheng-yin p'u te ch'ü-lun" 太和正音譜的曲論, *ibid,.* pp. 99-109.

—WI

Chu Hao 朱㿾 (*tzu*, Su-Shen 素臣, *hao*, Sheng-an 笙庵, later known by his *tzu*, *fl.* 1644), a dramatist of the early Ch'ing, was a native of Wu-hsien 吳縣 (modern Kiangsu). Nothing is known of his life, except that he was a member of the Soochow School of dramatists (see Li Yü [*c.* 1591-*c.* 1671]). He wrote nineteen *ch'uan-ch'i,** collectively known as *Sheng-an ch'uan-ch'i* 笙庵傳奇, from which eight have been preserved in their entirety.

Chu's most successful work is the *Shih-wu kuan* 十五貫 (Fifteen Strings of Cash), derived from the *hua-pen** "Ts'o chan Ts'ui Ning" 錯斬崔寧. The story was adapted by Chu, who changed the time from Sung to mid-Ming, adding many new episodes. There are two major storylines, both on the theme of the falsely accused. The first relates how Hsiung Yu-hui 熊友蕙, a student, is involved in an apparent murder. He prepares some poisonous cakes intending to kill rats, but a rat takes some of the cakes into the chamber of Hou San-ku 侯三姑, a young neighbor woman. San-ku's husband eats the cake and is poisoned. The rat then takes fifteen strings of cash from the Hou home along with one of San-ku's earrings and returns to Hsiung's room. Hsiung Yu-hui, believing the earring is a gift from the heavens, exchanges it for rice. This is discovered by Hou Weng 侯翁, San-ku's father-in-law, who accuses Yu-hui of adultery with San-ku and of murdering her husband. The county official who hears the case sentences Yu-hui to death. This first half of the drama is composed of new incidents created by Chu.

The second half is about Hsiung Yu-lan 友蘭, Yu-hui's elder brother, who is away on business. It is largely based on the earlier *hua-pen*. A butcher named Yu Hu-lu 尤葫蘆 had borrowed fifteen strings of cash. He jokingly tells his foster-daughter, Su

Shu-chüan 蘇戌娟, that he has sold her for these fifteen strings. Frightened, Shu-chüan runs away at night. She forgets to close the main gate and a gambler, Lou A-shu 婁阿鼠, steals in, kills Yu Hu-lu, and takes the fifteen strings of cash. The next morning, neighbors find Yu dead and Shu-chüan gone. They assume Shu-chüan is the murderer and pursue her. Meanwhile, Shu-chüan meets Yu-lan on her way, and the two travel together. The neighbors catch up with them, search Yu-lan's luggage, and find the fifteen strings of cash given him. The neighbors assume that the two are lovers and had killed Yu Hu-lu and stolen his money. The two suspects are brought before the authorities and sentenced to death by the same county official who condemned Hsiung Yu-hui. The prefect of Soochow, K'uang Chung 況鐘 (historical figure, known as a good official), is scheduled to review all serious sentences. K'uang dreams of two bears (Hsiung literally means "bear"), each carrying a rat on its back. As the bears beg for their lives, he also hears four people complaining of injustice. K'uang then suspends the executions. He goes to the office of the governor and seeks a postponement for two months so that he might investigate the cases. The request is granted and K'uang uncovers the truth. Lou A-shu is caught and the innocent are set free.

The drama has retained its popularity in the *K'un-ch'ü* repertory. In 1956 it was revived by the Chekiang company albeit in a severely revised form.

Chu Tso-ch'ao 朱佐朝 (*tzu*, Liang-ch'ing 良卿, *fl.* 1644), a native of Wu-hsien 吳縣 (modern Kiangsu), was Chu Hao's brother and also a friend of Li Yü* (*c.* 1591-*c.* 1671). Thirteen of his dramas, written in the Soochow style, are extant.

Yü-chia le 漁家樂 (Joys of a Fisherman's Family) is the best known of Chu Tso-ch'ao's works. The main story is as follows. After the death of the Latter Han Emperor Ch'ung 冲帝 (r. 145) a general named Liang Chi 梁冀 (d. 159) wants to put Liu Tsuan 劉纘, the King of Po-hai 渤海, on the throne. He poisons the able ministers Li Ku 李固 (94-147) and Tu Ch'iao 杜喬, and

330

sends his troops to pursue and kill the King of Ch'ing-ho 清河, Liu Suan 劉蒜, who is the rightful successor to the throne. This part of the story is based on historical events; what follows is fictitious. The pursuing army shoots the wrong person, a fisherman named Wu. Liu Suan escapes in the fisherman's boat and is rescued by the fisherman's daughter, Fei-hsia 飛霞; they become husband and wife.

Some time later Liang Chi orders Ma Jung* to give him his daughter, Yao-ts'ao 瑤草, as a singing-girl. But Yao-ts'ao is already married to a poor literary man named Chien Jen-t'ung 簡人同. Fei-hsia, intending to take revenge for her father, volunteers to disguise herself as Yao-ts'ao. She is then taken into Liang's home by force, where she is able to kill Liang Chi with a magic pin. Finally, after Liu Suan ascends the throne, and Fei-hsia becomes queen, Chien Jen-t'ung and Ma Yao-ts'ao also gain wealth and dignity. The drama's structure is complex, but Fei-hsia's bravery and acumen are depicted vividly.

Of Chu's other dramas, *Chi-ch'ing t'u* 吉慶圖 (A Depiction of Auspicious and Joyous Affairs) and *Wan-hua lou* 萬花樓 (Myriad-Flowers Tower, no longer extant) were intended to attack Yen Sung 嚴嵩 (1480-1565), an oft-maligned minister of the early Ming, and were very popular in Chu's time.

EDITIONS:

Shih-wu kuan, Ku-pen, III.

Shih-wu kuan. An abridged version arranged by Huang Yüan 黃源 and Ch'en Ssu 陳思. Peking, 1956. All other extant dramas by both Chu brothers can be found in *Ku-pen*.

STUDIES:

Shih-wu kuan chuan-chi 十五貫專輯. Hangchow, 1956. A symposium of critical essays. Che-chiang-shen wen-hua-chü 浙江省文化局, comp.

—BTW

Chu I-tsun 朱彝尊 (*tzu*, Hsi-ch'ang 錫鬯, *hao*, Chu-ch'a 竹垞, 1629-1709) was a poet, essayist, and scholar of the early Ch'ing. He was born in Hsiu-shui 秀水 (Chekiang). His great-grandfather was a Grand Secretary in the Ming Court, but the family gradually became poor, and Chu suffered many hardships in his early years. In 1678 he

passed the special examination known as *po-hsüeh hung-tz'u* 博學宏詞, and the following year was appointed a Han-lin Academician and editor of the *Ming-shih*.

Chu was one of the most learned scholars and prolific authors of his time. He mastered all the major forms of prose, *shih*,* and *tz'u*.* In his prose, Chu emulated to Han Yü,* Ou-yang Hsiu,* and Tseng Kung.* In *shih* poetry he preferred the style of the T'ang to that of the Sung. He was considered the greatest *shih* poet in the South during his time (Wang Shih-chen* [1634-1711] was thought to be the North's best).

However, Chu is best remembered for his *tz'u* poetry and the role he played in the revival of *tz'u* writing in the early Ch'ing. In the preface to his *Tz'u-tsung* 詞綜, an anthology of *tz'u* poetry from the T'ang to the Yüan (in 18 *chüan*), he demonstrated his particular theory of *tz'u* poetry by promoting the reputation of such Southern Sung poets as Chiang K'uei* and Chang Yen.* His own *tz'u* poems, later collected, in *P'u-shu-t'ing chi* 曝書亭集, often recall the style of Southern Sung *tz'u*. He especially wished to emulate the *tz'u* poetry of Chang Yen. At a time when *tz'u* of the Southern Sung were simply forgotten, Chu I-tsun's theory and practice had a great impact upon contemporary poets, especially on those from his home region, Western Chekiang (i.e., Che-hsi). For this reason Chu was traditionally regarded as the founding father of the Che-hsi School of *tz'u* (Che-hsi tz'u-p'ai*). Later Ch'ing poets owed much to Chu's insistence on tonal rules and on the value of refined elegance in *tz'u*, qualities which were essential to the genre. However, he was criticized for confining himself to narrow imagistic worlds. Naturally the works of other writers of the Che-hsi School, who were not as talented and learned as he was, suffered from similar defects.

A prolific author, Chu I-tsun was also famous as a bibliophile. His *Ching-i k'ao* 經義考, a bibliography of the Classics, was compiled from works in his own collection and those of his friends. He was known to have collected 80,000 *chüan* in his private library, a portion of which later appeared in the *Ch'ien-ts'ai-t'ang shu-mu* 潛采堂書目. It was this ardent love for books that prompted Chu to search for the long-lost anthology *Chüeh-miao hao-tz'u* 絕妙好詞 by Chou Mi.* Legend has it that as soon as Chu found out that the only manuscript copy was preserved in the rare book room of the famous contemporary bibliophile Ch'ien Tsun-wang 錢遵王, he bribed Ch'ien's secretary to copy the entire manuscript. In any case, Chu I-tsun was responsible for the reprint of this *tz'u* collection. The reappearance of *Chüeh-miao hao-tz'u*, like the publication of Chu's *Tz'u-tsung*, had an immediate impact upon *tz'u* poets.

EDITIONS:

"Ching-chih-chü shih-hua" 靜志居詩話, 24 *chüan* (printed in 1819), in *Ming-shih tsung* 明詩綜, 2v., Taipei, 1962.

P'u-shu-t'ing chi 曝書亭集, 80 *chüan* (printed in 1714). *Kuo-hsüeh chi-pen ts'ung-shu* 國學基本叢書. Taipei, 1968. V. 313-314.

P'u-shu-t'ing tz'u san-chung 曝書亭詞三種. Taipei, 1978.

Tz'u-tsung 詞綜 (1678), with supplement by Wang Sen 汪森, 1691. 2v. Rpt. Shanghai, 1978. Punctuated edition, contains index to poems.

TRANSLATIONS:

Birch, *Anthology,* v. 2, pp. 139-142.
Sunflower, pp. 476-479.

STUDIES:

Chang, Shao-chen 張少眞. *Ch'ing-tai Che-chiang tz'u-p'ai yen-chiu* 清代浙江詞派研究. M.A. thesis, Tung-wu University, Taiwan, 1978, pp. 67-79.

ECCP, pp. 182-185.

Juan, Yüan 阮元 (1764-1849), ed. *Chu-ch'a hsiao-chih* 竹垞小志, 5 *chüan*, in *Pi-chi ssu-pien* 筆記四編, Taipei, 1971, v. 19.

Ho, *Ch'ing-tz'u,* pp. 43-55.

Yoshikawa, Kōjirō 吉川幸次郎. "Jutsu *Bakusho-tei* shi" 述曝書亭詞, *Shinagaku* 4.2 (1927), 148-157.

—KIC

Chu-kung-tiao 諸宮調 (all keys and modes) is the designation of a specific form of storytelling that flourished in the twelfth and thirteenth centuries. Like many other forms of traditional Chinese storytelling, the *chu-kung-tiao* belongs to a genre known as *shuo-ch'ang wen-hsüeh* (see essay on prosimetric literature). In the case of *chu-kung-tiao* the rhymed passages are written to *ch'ü** melodies. Melodies belonging to the same mode are arranged in suites. Within each suite a single rhyme is maintained regardless of the length of the suite. The different suites are connected by prose passages. As a rule, each suite belongs to a mode different from those of the suites preceding and following it. This musical characteristic of the quick succession of various modes gave rise to the (at first sight) peculiar name of the genre. The *ch'ü* of the *chu-kung-tiao* still consist of two stanzas like *tz'u*, but they allow some freedom in the use of padding words and can be organized into suites. Most of the suites in *chu-kung-tiao* are still very short and consist only of one *ch'ü* (in two stanzas!) and a three-line *wei* 尾 (coda). With the progression of time both the relative number of more complex suites and the length of the individual complex-suites increased.

The *chu-kung-tiao* originated in Southern Shansi near the end of the eleventh century. By the beginning of the twelfth century it had reached K'ai-feng, at that time the capital of the Sung empire. Its most famous performer there was K'ung San-chuan 孔三傳 (K'ung, The Learned), who hailed from Southern Shansi and well may have been responsible for bringing the form to the city. The genre was in vogue in North China during the Chin dynasty and it was still practiced during the second half of the thirteenth century. Apparently it fell into disuse during the fourteenth. Only a few texts in this genre have been preserved. The earliest example is the *Liu Chih-yüan chu-kung-tiao*, of which we have only parts. The only example extant in its entirety is the *Hsi-hsiang chi chu-kung-tiao,** written by Tung *Chieh-yüan* (Master Tung), who was active around 1200. The stylistic contrast between this work and the *Liu Chih-yüan chu-kung-tiao* is so great that it has been theorized that the earlier work was meant for roadside performance, whereas Tung wrote for the best houses of entertainment. Wang Po-ch'eng 王伯成, a dramatist of the second half of the thirteenth century, dealt with the famous romance of Emperor Hsüan-tsung and Yang Kuei-fei in his *T'ien-pao i-shih* 天寶遺事 *chu-kung-tiao,** of which only certain songs are preserved.

The titles of some lost *chu-kung-tiao* are also known. A very popular *chu-kung-tiao* must have been the one on the love-affair of the student Shuang Chien 雙漸 and the courtesan Su Hsiao-ch'ing 蘇小卿. It was originally composed in the middle of the twelfth century and rewritten in the early thirteenth. A suite of *ch'ü*, that may have been written as an introduction to this *chu-kung-tiao* by a certain Yang Li-chai 楊立齋, has come down to us. The *Wu-lin chiu-shih* by Chou Mi* mentions two further titles of *chu-kung-tiao*. The *Chang Hsieh chuang-yüan*, one of three early *hsi-wen* contained in one of the few preserved volumes of the *Yung-lo ta-tien* (see *Yung-lo ta-tien hsi-wen san-chung*), opens with a parody on a *chu-kung-tiao*.

Some scholars take the list in the introduction of the *Hsi-hsiang chi chu-kung-tiao* of items that will not be dealt with for a catalogue of *chu-kung-tiao* titles, but it is rather an enumeration of hackneyed subjects of storytelling in general and not confined to *chu-kung-tiao*. Research to date indicates that the *chu-kung-tiao* favored love over war, although battle scenes are treated with gusto. The language of the *chu-kung-tiao* songs ranges from the contemporary vernacular to a polished literary idiom. For its treatment of love and war the *chu-kung-tiao* exploited the conventional descriptions developed in *pien-wen** (see *Tun-huang wen-hsüeh*) and *tz'u*.* However, *chu-kung-tiao* authors often treated their subjects ironically, with the result that their works are very humorous.

In both the *Liu Chih-yüan chu-kung-tiao* and the *Hsi-hsiang chi chu-kung-tiao* the text is divided into *chüan*, each of which constituted that segment of the story that the artist performed on a single day. It has been argued that in each *chüan* at least one other moment of suspense (i.e., the *wa-t'an*) can be identified at which the performer might interrupt his, or more often her, performance in order to make the rounds of the audience for a collection. It would appear that this moment of suspense within one *chüan* coincides with the location of complex suites in each *chüan*. Also, the suspense at the *chüan*-ending is meant to outdo the one earlier in the same *chüan*. In this way the fixed placement of these moments of suspense in each *chüan* heavily influenced the narrative development of the story treated.

There are also a few contemporary documents concerning *chu-kung-tiao* performances. The high official Hu Chih-yü 胡祗遹 (1227-1293) provided a certain Miss Huang 黃 with a set of nine guidelines for "telling and singing," and chapter 51 of the novel *Shui-hu chuan** contains a description of a *chu-kung-tiao* performance in a public theater of a provincial town. The heroine in *Tzu-yün t'ing* 紫雲庭 (Purple Cloud Courtyard), a *tsa-chü* by the late thirteenth-century playwright Shih Chün-pao 石君寶, is also a *chu-kung-tiao* performer. but the play is unfortunately only preserved in a Yüan print and shows more concern for her private than her professional life.

An important factor in the disappearance of *chu-kung-tiao* must have been the rise of *tsa-chü* in the course of the thirteenth century. *Tsa-chü* employed *ch'ü* music just like the *chu-kung-tiao*. For its modal organization of melodies and the convention that only one actor or actress may sing throughout the play, *tsa-chü* may well be indebted to *chu-kung-tiao*. *Chu-kung-tiao* certainly played its role in molding the vernacular language of Northern China into the supple instrument for literary expression it was in the hands of the famous playwrights of the thirteenth century.

STUDIES:

Ch'en, Li Li. "The Relationship between Oral Presentation and the Literary Devices Used in *Liu Chih-yüan* and *Hsi-hsiang chu-kung-tiao*," *LEW*, 14 (1970), 519-528.

———. "Outer and Inner Forms of *Chu-kung-tiao*, With Reference to *Pien-wen*, *Tz'u* and Vernacular Fiction," *HJAS*, 32 (1972), 124-149.

———. "Some Background Information of the Development of *Chu-kung-tiao*," *HJAS*, 33 (1973), 224-237.

Cheng, Chen-to 鄭振鐸. "Sung Chin Yüan chu-kung-tiao k'ao" 宋金元諸宮調考, in his *Chung-kuo wen-hsüeh yen-chiu* 中國文學研究, v. 3, Peking, 1957, pp. 843-970.

Idema, W. L. "Performance and Construction of the *Chu-kung-tiao*," in *JOS*, 16 (1978), 63-78.

Idema and West, *Chinese Theater*, pp. 197-202.

Wang, T'ien-ch'eng 汪天成. "Sung Yüan chu-kung-tiao te chi-i" 宋元諸宮調的輯佚. *Chung-hua hsüeh-yüan*, 23 (September 1979), 127-186.

———. "Chu-kung-tiao te hsing-ch'i ho shuai-wei" 諸宮調的興起和衰微. *Chung-wai wen-hsüeh*, 10.4 (September 1981), 37-57.

West, *Vaudeville*, pp. 48-183. Chapters 2 and 3 and appendixes are devoted to various aspects of the *chu-kung-tiao*.

Wu, Tse-yü 吳則虞. "Shih-t'an chu-kung-tiao te chi-ko wen-t'i" 試談諸宮調的幾個問題, *Wen-hsüeh i-ch'an tseng-k'an*, 5 (December 1957), 278-296.

Yeh, Ch'ing-ping 葉慶炳. "Chu-kung-tiao te t'i-chih" 諸宮調的體製, *Hsüeh-shu chi-k'an*, 5.3 (March 1957), 26-45.

———. "Chu-kung-tiao cheng-kung tao-kung nan-lü-kung huang-chung-kung ting-lü" 諸宮調正宮道宮南呂宮黃鐘宮訂律, *Jen-wen hsüeh-pao*, 3 (December 1973), 189-224.

———. "Chu-kung-tiao kao-p'ing-tiao hsien-lü-tiao huang-chung-tiao pan-she-tiao shang-shiao-tiao yü-tiao ting-lü" 諸宮調高平調仙呂調黃鐘調般涉調商角羽調訂律, *Jen-wen hsüeh-pao*, 4 (May 1976), 215-260.

———. "Chu-kung-tiao yüeh-tiao ta-shih-tiao shuang-tiao hsiao-shih-tiao hsieh-chih-tiao shang-tiao chung-lü-tiao" 諸宮調越調大石調雙調小石調歇指調商調中呂調, *Jen-wen hsüeh-pao*, 4 (May 1975), 177-230.

Yoshikawa, Kōjirō 吉川幸次郎. "Shokyūchō sa-dan" 諸宮調瑣談, in *Yoshikawa Kōjirō zenshū* 全集, v. 14, Tokyo, 1970, pp. 565-583.

—WI

Chu Shu-chen 朱淑眞 was a Sung poet, calligrapher, and musician of the Ch'ien-t'ang 錢塘 (Hangchow) area. She is famous as the mistress of *kuei-yüan* 閨怨 (boudoir-plaint) poetry, employing the abandoned-woman persona and its stock of images—long used by male writers of such poetry—to describe her own frustrations as a neglected wife. The term *tuan-ch'ang* 斷腸 (heart-break) occurs in the title of her corpus, a key to the dominant mood of her extant poetry. Studies of Chu Shu-chen usually attempt to fill the many lacunae in her biography in order to understand the circumstances that drove her to write such poetry and thereby to style herself, "Yu-hsi chü-shih" 幽棲居士 (The Recluse of the Lonely Perch).

The most reliable evidence (from the preface by Wei Tuan-li 魏端禮 to the original Sung edition of her poetry, dated April 19, 1182) places her birth in the Northern Sung rather than the Southern. Wei mentions that her poetry was more popular than that of his own "near contemporary" Li Ch'ing-chao* (1084-c. 1155), implying that Chu Shu-chen lived earlier than Li.

Chu Shu-chen's relationship with her husband was paramount in her life. Wei Tuan-li notes that he was a rustic, uneducated man, but Chu's own poems describe her seeing him off to take the civil-service examination, his accepting an office, and his later traveling to Hupei, Hunan, and Kiangsi, where he evidently went to take up various official positions.

Whoever her husband was, he was absent for long periods of time. Much of Chu Shu-chen's boudoir-plaint verse was probably written during such periods of separation. Even when they were together, their relationship was not harmonious, as evinced by her poems. She most likely endured a husband indifferent or hostile to her literary ambitions, and could only find solace in poems such as the seven entitled, "Chou-hsing chi-shih" 舟行即事 (Events on a Boat Trip), describing a trip with her husband in which she poses five questions such as the following: "With whom on this river do I compose poetry?" Her most poignant expression of frustration is the poem "Tsu-tse" 自責 (Blaming Myself):

When a woman dabbles in literature, that's truly evil,
How can she "intone the moon" or "chant the wind"?
Wearing out the inkstone is not our business,
Let us rather be skilled at needlework and embroidery.

And when boredom comes without relief, "read"
    poetry,
See the poems speak of separation,
Accentuating emotions which turn melancholy.
Then one realizes how apt [for us] the saying,
    "better to be mad than bright."

Her strength as a writer of poetry lies in the simple, direct recounting of her unhappiness, expressed in a "fresh" and "pretty" (清新婉麗) style. These writings possess an attractive, melodic quality which was said to have appealed to people in Hangchow. The *Ssu-k'u ch'üan-shu tsung-mu t'i-yao* editors (see Chi Yün) saw shallowness in these compositions, however, because of their obsession with the boudoir-plaint theme, and they "blamed" the popularity of the poems on readers who sought vicarious pleasure in being privy to her private misfortunes.

It seems likely that she died in middle age since we know that her parents survived her and burned much of her poetry as an offering to her soul. In 1182, Wei Tuan-li collected what had survived of her writings from Soochow residents and published the first collection of her poetry. By 1203 Cheng Yüan-tso 鄭元佐 had compiled the interlinear commentary now found with all editions. Later editions of her *shih** poetry are based on a printed Yüan version, and her *tz'u** collection is based on fragments of a edition dated 1370 found by Mao Chin 毛晉 (1599-1659). They were first published together at the end of the nineteenth century.

EDITIONS:

Chu, Shu-chen 朱淑眞. *Chu Shu-chen tuan-ch'ang shih tz'u* 朱淑眞斷腸詩詞. Chu Wei-kung 朱惟公, ed. 1933; rpt. Hong kong, n.d.

TRANSLATIONS:

Rexroth, Kenneth. *One Hundred Poems from the Chinese*. New York, 1971, pp. 125-134.

———, and Ling Chung. *The Orchid Boat: Women Poets of China*. New York, 1973, pp. 45-48.

STUDIES:

K'uang, Chou-i 况周頤. "Colophon" to *Hui-feng tz'u-hua* 蕙風詞話. 1924; rpt. Taipei, 1962, *chüan* 4, pp. 9a-13b. The most detailed summary of the facts of her life.

K'ung, Fan-li 孔凡禮. "Chu Shu-chen i-shih chi-ts'un chi ch'i-t'a" 朱淑貞佚詩輯存及其他, *Wen-shih,* 12 (September 1981), 227-233.

—CBL

Chu Tun-ju 朱敦儒 (*tzu*, Hsi-chen 希眞, 1080/1-*c.* 1175) was a hermit poet and artist of the Southern Sung dynasty. Calling himself "Yen-ho lao-jen" 巖壑老人 (The Old Man of Cliffs and Valleys), he spent much of his life extolling communion with the natural world. One of his retreats was called Ta-kuan T'ang 達觀堂 (The Hall of Natural Communion). He is known today for a short, three-*chüan* anthology of *tz'u** poetry, *Ch'iao-ko* 樵歌 (The Songs of the Woodcutter).

Chu grew up in an official family but apparently never had the ambition to enter government service. He studied poetry with Ch'en Tung-yeh 陳東野 and developed a good reputation as a poet, Eventually, he was summoned to serve the Northern Sung court in 1126, its last year. He declined, however, and refused again to serve the exile government of Emperor Kao-tsung (r. 1127-1162) the following year. After 1127, Chu Tun-ju moved to the far south (Nan-hsiung Prefecture 南雄 in modern Kwangtung).

Chu Tun-ju eventually settled in Chao-ch'ing 肇慶 (west of Canton). In 1132, while war with the Chin was still raging, he was recommended to the emperor by local officials. This time, the court granted him an official rank and persuaded him to travel to its temporary capital, Hangchow. He was fifty-five years old and would serve the government, on and off, for the next twenty years. In 1135, he was granted a *chin-shih* degree without having to take the examination. He was also given an appointment in the Palace Library, and in 1137 he was made Vice Admininstrator of Hangchow. In 1139 he was made Librarian of the Palace Library and eventually Judicial Commissioner for the nearby province of Che-tung 浙東. About 1141 Chu was dismissed for having associated with the exiled Li Kuang 李光 (1078-1159). Later, in 1149, he was allowed to formally retire from public office.

Chu Tun-ju's retirement was short-lived, however, because he was summoned to court to teach poetry and to paint. He was induced to accept these posts by an offer of the honorary title of Vice Minister of the Court of State Ceremonial and because his son was held at court as an editor. Chu's apologists say that he returned to Hang-chow out of concern for his family's safety. As court artist he painted landscapes for the emperor, working side-by-side with Mi Yu-jen 米友仁 (1086-1165), son of the famous artist Mi Fei 米芾 (1052-1107).

In 1155 Chu was dismissed, and he spent the rest of his years in Chia-ho 嘉禾 (modern Chia-hsing 嘉興) northeast of Hang-chow, where he had maintained a residence since 1149, and where many students came to study poetry and Chu's eremitic lifestyle.

Chu Tun-ju's tz'u* poetry is praised by several contemporary critics, though they did not consider him to be one of the great writers of their day. An exception is the poet Wang Hsin 汪莘 (1155-1227) who said that Chu, along with Su Shih* and Lu Yu* were the great influences on his own tz'u writing. Wang characterized Chu's poetry as pure, refined, and otherworldly. He praised it for not exhibiting the licentious qualities typical of tz'u. Pursuing this idea, the twentieth-century scholar Hu Shih 胡適 likens Chu's tz'u to the shih* of T'ao Ch'ien.*

Until modern times, however, the Ch'iao-ko was largely ignored. Hung Sheng 黃昇 (d. after 1245) only included ten examples of Chu's poetry in his Chung-hsing i-lai chüeh-miao tz'u-hsüan 中興以來絕妙詞選. None of Chu's poems appeared in Chou Mi's* Chüeh-miao hao-tz'u 絕妙好詞 which included works by 132 Southern Sung tz'u writers, nor were any among those of sixty Sung tz'u poets in Mao Chin's 毛晉 (1599-1659) Sung liu-shih-i chia tz'u 宋六十一家詞 (though most extant copies of the Ch'iao-ko are based on a manuscript owned by Mao Chin). Even the Ssu-k'u ch'üan-shu tsung-mu t'i-yao (see Chi Yün) overlooked the Ch'iao-ko. Only after Juan Yüan 阮元 (1764-1849) included it in his 1822 supplement to the Ssu-k'u were old manuscript copies printed.

By 1900 several editions were available. Twentieth-century critics admire Chu's poetry because his diction resonates with vernacular expressions and because he does not adhere to the prosodic rules laid down in tz'u-p'u 詞譜.

EDITIONS:
Chu, Tun-ju 朱敦儒. Ch'iao-ko 樵歌. Based on Ssu-yin-chai tan-k'u edition; n.p.: Pei-hsin shu-chü 北新書局, 1926.

TRANSLATIONS:
Ayling, Further Collection, pp. 117-21.
Ch'u, Ta-kao. Chinese Lyrics. Cambridge, 1937, pp. 33-38.
Davis, Penguin, p. 44.
Sunflower, pp. 364-365.

STUDIES:
Chan, Hing-ho, "Ch'iao-ko," in A Sung Bibliography, pp. 467-468.
Hu, Shih 胡適. "Chu Tun-ju hsiao-chüan" 朱敦儒小傳, in Ch'iao-ko 樵歌, n.p., Pei-hsin shu-chü, 1926.
Jao, Tsung-i 饒宗頤. Tz'u-chi k'ao 詞籍考. Hong Kong, 1963, pp. 109-111.

—BL

Chu-tzu pai-chia 諸子百家 (The Various Masters and the Hundred Schools) traditionally refers to the philosophers and philosophies of the period extending from Confucius (551-479 B.C.) to the end of the Warring States period (221 B.C.). Although certain Han texts such as Huai-nan-tzu 淮南子 and even Lun-heng 論衡 are often included in collections of the texts on the Various Masters, this survey shall be confined to those works generally considered to be of Chou-dynasty (1122-221 B.C.) authorship.

Modern scholars have typically described the period of the Masters as "the golden age of Chinese philosophy." The traditional appraisal was less positive—the emergence of competing philosophies was viewed as a decline from a peaceful political and cultural unity that supposedly existed during the Western Chou (1122-771 B.C.). Chuang-tzu 莊子, for example, characterizes the rise of philosophical pluralism as follows:

Each man in the world does that which he desires, taking himself as the standard. How sad!

The hundred schools go forth, instead of turning back—fated never to join again! (ch. 33).

And this is not just nostalgic Taoist primitivism, for the "Bibliographic Essay" of the *Han-shu* (see Pan Ku) reads similarly:

The Various Masters . . . all arose when the doctrine of the kings had already weakened. The lords governed through strength; and the hereditary rulers differed in what they liked and disliked. Therefore, the theories of the nine schools arose like wasps (ch. 30).

Whether such pluralism is viewed positively or negatively, the variety of Chinese philosophy during the Warring States period equals that of Attic philosophy, which appeared on the other side of the world at approximately the same time. Scholars have offered several explanations for the sudden emergence and proliferation of Chinese philosophical discourse that occurred in the last centuries of the Chou dynasty. One factor mentioned by all is the decline of the centralized feudal order and the appearance of independent, competing states. The *Han shu* "I-wen chih" (Bibliographic Essay), for example, links each philosophical school with an earlier government office. That is, as centralized government collapsed, displaced officials, who had inherited the learning characteristic of a particular office, made this learning the basis of a philosophical school. Although such an explanation reflects the Chinese tendency to find institutional origins for all cultural manifestations, it probably does carry an important truth. Script usually emerges for very practical, or the bureaucratic, functions, and the early Chou court most likely held a near monopoly on literacy. However, with the collapse of centralized power, men of learning were free to travel and develop independent ideas which they could propagate to the competing feudal lords. In the words of Hsiao Kung-ch'üan, "All the old ceremonial behavior and customs that in the past had bound people together intellectually and spiritually lost their original significance" (*A History of Chinese Political Thought*).

Many of the most famous of the Chou philosophers were constantly on the move, seeking official support for their ideas among leaders who had lost faith in the old order. This climate encouraged intellectual freedom and also permitted considerable cross-fertilization between the various philosophies. Eventually the different schools found favor in particular states and each came to dominate a geographical region. Thus, Taoism took hold in the southern state of Ch'u, while Confucianism was centered in Lu and Tsou, Legalism in Ch'in and Chin, Mohism and Logicians in Sung, and the five-elements philosophy of Tsou Yen in Ch'i.

The texts of the Various Masters and Hundred Schools are typically studied from either a philosophical or a historical perspective, much less being said about their literary and rhetorical characteristics. Studied from the latter perspective, there is a gradual transformation and development in the expository style of Chou philosophical texts. Fu Ssu-nien has defined three stages in this transformation: "recording speech" (*chi-yen* 記言), "composing essays" (*chu-lun* 著論) and "forming books" (*ch'eng-shu* 成書). These stages overlap considerably, and the earliest of the three stages has a life of its own that continues even after "essays" and "books" appear. The following discussion is based on Fu Ssu-nien's three stages, adding some generalities about the stylistic features of each.

During the first stage, which Fu calls "recording speech," the brief dialogue and short quotation predominate. The clearest example of this stage is the *Lun-yü* 論語 (Analects), but the "Dialogue Chapters" of *Mo-tzu* 墨子 (chapters 46-49) and certain sections of *Meng-tzu* 孟子 (particularly chapters 7A and 7B can also be included. These texts rarely present a sustained argument. Rather, the style is dictated by an almost religious regard for the personality of the founder, disciples having dutifully recorded recollections and extant traditions of their master's words and behavior. Thus, *Lun-yü* preserves an oral tradition essentially as it stood two or three generations after Confucius' death, with certain portions added somewhat later. Again, the emphasis in this stage is not so much upon the argument and its logical presentation as upon the personality of a master and the authority inherent in his words and deeds.

Fu Ssu-nien refers to the second stage as "compiling essays." This stage begins with the *Mo-tzu* essays (chapters 7-39), a text which marks a major advance in the art of philosophical exposition. Although the emphasis is now upon the presentation of an argument, the break with earlier "recording speech" style is by no means complete. The first essays remain under the rhetorical influence of the dialogue. For example, in *Mo-tzu*, as in the later essays of *Hsün-tzu* 荀子 and *Han-fei-tzu* 韓非子, there is abundant use of hypophoric questions to guide the presentation of ideas. The questioning interlocutor of the dialogue has disappeared; now the early essayist interrogates himself:

> Who were those that loved others, brought profit to others, complied with the intentions of Heaven and obtained Heaven's rewards? We say, "Those like the earlier sage-kings of the three dynasties, Yao, Shun, Yü, T'ang, Wen, and Wu were thus." How did Yao, Shun, Yü, T'ang, Wen, and Wu pursue business? We say, "They pursued business in universality and did not pursue business in partiality" (*Mo-tzu*, ch. 27).
>
> When people pray for rain, it rains. Why? I say: There is no need to ask why (*Hsün-tzu*, ch. 17).

In addition, the early essays anticipate objections and provide refutation, again creating a hypothetical interlocutor. Finally, the authority of the master disappears slowly. In the *Mo-tzu* essays the argument is invariably clinched by a quotation from Mo Ti himself, for his authority remains the final proof.

Understanding the relationship between the rhetoric of stage one and stage two requires a consideration of the way in which these philosophical works were compiled. In both of the first two stages there is, as yet, no strong tradition of individual authorship. Most of these books emerged initially from the hands of unnamed editors. Thus, the writings of stage

one, though rather fragmented, have been edited into a general topical arrangement. The earliest essays of stage two appear to be an attempt by an editor to go one step further and forge fragments into a continuous, sustained argument. We would expect, therefore, to see the style of stage one mirrored quite clearly in at least the earliest examples of stage two. However, by the time of *Hsün-tzu* and *Han-fei-tzu*, when a tradition of individual authorship begins, the essays are less obviously the work of an editor patching much smaller fragments together.

In the third stage, "forming books," the text is no longer an anthology of miscellaneous recollections nor a collection of essays; it has an overall organizational scheme and was conceived from the outset as a book. The first clear example of this, and the only one that dates from the Chou, is *Lü-shih ch'un-ch'iu* 呂氏春秋 (The Spring and Autumn Annals of Mr. Lü). The organization of this text follows certain cosmological notions: three large sections corresponding to the triad of Heaven, Earth, and Man, twelve parts in the first of these sections, one for each month of the year, etc. But as might be expected from the first such attempt at general organization, the content of individual sections does not always correspond to the cosmological pattern reflected by the table of contents. In this third stage, there is a marked reduction in the type of repetition that characterizes earlier collections of essays. The very fact that a book had an overall, preconceived plan facilitated closer correlation between individual sections.

As noted above, each stage follows its own evolution after a new stage appears. The dialogue style of stage one, which appears in nascent form in *Lun-yü*, develops markedly in such texts as *Meng-tzu* and *Yen-tzu ch'un-ch'iu* 晏子春秋 (The Spring and Autumn Annals of Master Yen). In the case of *Lun-yü*, it is difficult to determine whether a particular dialogue is an actual recollection or a literary fabrication. By contrast, the dialogues of *Meng-tzu* and, even more obviously, those of *Yen-tzu ch'un-ch'iu*, are literary constructs. The interlocutor of the former is, with few exceptions, a wooden puppet who says and does precisely what is necessary to elicit the philosophical discourse of the master. In the latter, he is a chronic miscreant whose every word and deed provides an ideal teaching opportunity for Yen-tzu. As the dialogue form becomes more expansive and literary, the art of suasion is more obvious. For example, *Yen-tzu ch'un-ch'iu*, despite its heavy dose of moralizing, is at times stylistically reminiscent of that notoriously immoral *Chan-kuo ts'e*,* in that the emphasis now is not just upon the argument itself but also upon the cleverness of the presentation.

The two Chou-dynasty Taoist texts, *Tao-te-ching* 道德經 and *Chuang-tzu*, fit somewhat uncomfortably in the scheme elaborated above. The first of these is probably based upon a collection of apothegms that were edited not into a Mohist-style essay but into a highly rhythmic and frequently rhymed series of eighty-one short sections. D. C. Lau argues that "such passages must have been meant to be learned by rote with the meaning explained at length in an oral commentary" (*Lao-tzu: Tao-te-ching*). The latter text, *Chuang-tzu*, contains extended dialogues and lengthy anecdotes, almost a pure extension of the style of stage one. In only a few places, the first portion of the "T'ien-hsia" (chapter 33) being a prime example, does the exposition assume an essay format reminiscent of *Mo-tzu* or *Hsün-tzu*. However, the brilliant literary style of *Chuang-tzu*, particularly the early chapters (1-7), lifts it above easy categorization. The realism of such texts as *Meng-tzu* is shattered in *Chuang-tzu* by imagination. Animals speak, natural forces are personified, and dialogues which begin in soberness unexpectedly veer into humor, fantasy, and absurdity. Indeed, it is possible to see in *Chuang-tzu* one of the sources of Chinese fiction, particularly the stories of the supernatural (*chih-kuai**) that flourished during the Six Dynasties period.

Much greater attention needs to be paid to the development of Chou philosophical exposition and the way in which it influenced later Chinese prose. It is clear that by the Han dynasty a rich tradition had developed. Han works as diverse as Yang Hsiung's* *Fa-yen* 法言 and Wang Ch'ung's (27-91) *Lun-heng* find stylistic antecedents in the Chou texts.

The survey of major Chou philosophical texts presented below is by no means inclusive but focuses on what might be considered the major texts. Works of narrower interest (e.g., *Sun-tzu ping-fa* 孫子兵法), philosophical writings which are preserved only in fragments (e.g., *Shen-tzu* 慎子), genuine Chou materials embedded in post-Chou sources (parts of *Lieh-tzu* 列子 and *Kung-sun lung-tzu* 公孫龍子) and texts recently excavated from archaeological digs (e.g., *Ching-fa* 經法, *Tao-yüan* 道源, etc.) are not discussed.

Although the *Lun-yü* and the *Meng-tzu* are philosophical texts, they have typically been classified by traditional Chinese bibliographers in the category *ching** 經 (classics) rather than *tzu* 子 (masters or philosophers).

Mo-tzu supposedly reflects the teachings of the master Mo Ti 墨翟. The precise dates of this philosopher are a subject of considerable disagreement. Since many of Mo Ti's ideas are obviously a reaction against Confucius, and he is in turn roundly condemned by *Meng-tzu*, it might be safe to assume that Mo Ti was active in the late fifth century B.C.

The seventy-one chapters of *Mo-tzu* (eighteen now lost) fall neatly into five sections. The first section includes seven chapters which are very short statements of Mohist principles and can be called "Epitomes." Chapters 8 to 39, the second section, are the famous "Essays." These have a peculiar arrangement—each topic, with one exception, to be discussed below, is covered in three successive essays. There is not a continuous or correlated treatment of the subject from one chapter to another within each triad. Typically each of the three chapters contains material that is duplicated in the other two chapters. Yü Yüeh 俞樾 (1821-1907) has suggested that this unusual arrangement reflects the division of Mohism into three schools. Each school preserved its own account of the Master's lectures, and these variant accounts were eventually collected in a single text.

Chapters 40 to 45, the third section, are the famous "Logic Chapters." This portion of *Mo-tzu* was generally neglected by later scholars and fell into disarray. During the past two centuries scholars have attempted to reconstruct the text. All such attempts are problematic, but they do disclose some evidence of a sophisticated and complex logical system. It is presumed that the logic chapters are later than most of the essays and were produced by the so-called "Neo-Mohists," scholars who were embroiled in the controversies about logic which typified late Chou philosophy. The fourth section, chapters 6 to 49, might be called the "Dialogues." Stylistically reminiscent of the *Lun yü,* these chapters are made up of short anecdotes about Mo Ti and dialogues between him and his contemporaries. The final section, chapters 50 to 71, contains detailed information on defense strategy. The text of this section is also unusually corrupt, but it does preserve valuable details about materials used in the construction of city walls, military apparatus, etc.

Tao-te-ching (known originally as *Lao-tzu*) has been traditionally attributed to Lao Tan 老聃, an older contemporary of Confucius. Supposedly, as the aged Lao Tan traveled toward the west, Yin Hsi, a guardian of a pass, asked the learned philosopher to record his wisdom. Thus was written a book in two sections embodying Lao's ideas about Tao (the way) and Te (power), in somewhat more than 5,000 words (cf. *Shih-chi,** ch. 63). Few accept this romantic tale, and the dating of *Tao-te-ching* remains in dispute. Modern scholars conclude that the text is much later than the time of the legendary Lao Tan. Ku Chieh-kang, for example, argues that *Lao-tzu* is a collection of miscellaneous popular sayings brought together into a definite corpus during either the last years of the Chou dynasty or the early years of the Han (*Ku-shih pien* 古史辨, v. 4). D. C. Lau agrees, arguing that *Lao-tzu* surely postdates the other great Taoist text, *Chuang-tzu.* However, new evidence surfaced in 1973 when two manu-

scripts of *Lao-tzu,* both dating from the early years of the Han dynasty, were discovered at the archaeological dig at Mawang-tui.* Although these early manuscripts differ somewhat from contemporary versions of *Lao-tzu,* the most noteworthy distinction being the different order of the two major sections, they prove that the text was extant and well known by the early Han. Recent studies, which use these early manuscripts, date the compilation of *Lao-tzu* in the mid-fourth century B.C.

Whatever its date, this difficulty and enigmatic text has spawned numerous commentaries and translations. One can hardly avoid Lau's conclusion, mentioned earlier, that *Lao-tzu* was constructed so as to facilitate memorization and leaned heavily upon a tradition of oral exegesis for elucidation. It can now be shown, supporting Lau's thesis, that between the time of the Ch'ang-sha manuscripts and the edition prepared by the famous *Tao-te-ching* commentator Wang Pi 王弼 (226-249) numerous grammatical particles were deleted from the text, increasing both its poetic rhythms and its obscurity.

Although *Chuang-tzu* carries the name of the great Taoist philosopher Chuang Chou 莊周 (369-286 B.C.), it is neither the work of a single hand nor a single time. *Chuang-tzu* was re-edited several times between the Former Han, when it supposedly contained 52 chapters and more than 100,000 characters, and the time of Kuo Hsiang 郭象 (d. 312), to whom the present version in 33 chapters and approximately 65,000 characters is traced. The current text is divided into three sections, the "Inner Chapters" (1-7), the "Outer Chapters" (8-22), and the "Miscellaneous Chapters" (23-33). Such a division reflects a general principle of organization utilized by Han editors (cf., for example, *Yen-tzu ch'un-ch'iu* or *Huai-nan-tzu*), whereby that portion of the textual tradition judged most authentic is placed within the "Inner Chapters" while the less reliable traditions are relegated to "Outer" or "Miscellaneous" sections. Certainly the seven inner chapters of *Chuang-tzu* are not only the earliest layer of the text but also of the highest literary quality. The literary merit of the remaining sections varies considerably. Some have argued that the inner chapters are from the hand of Chuang Chou himself, while the remaining chapters stem from a variety of Taoist writers who lived during the latter years of the Warring States period and the early years of the Han. If this interpretation is correct, and at least the first assertion would be difficult to prove, Chuang Chou would be the first philosopher-author of ancient China, the earlier philosophical works having clearly been written by disciples rather than by the master himself. Whatever role Chuang Chou might have played in the authorship of certain chapters, the text in its entirety should be regarded as an anthology of early Taoist writings. Thus, no overall philosophical and literary unity can be expected.

Yen-tzu ch'un-ch'iu is a collection of remonstrances purportedly delivered by Yen Ying, prime minister of the state of Ch'i, to Duke Ching (r. 546-489 B.C.) and others. The existence of a rich lore centering upon Yen Ying is attested not just by *Yen-tzu ch'un-ch'iu*, but by stories in other Chou texts such as *Tso-chuan*.* Several collections of such lore were extant during the time of Liu Hsiang,* who then edited these materials into the present text in 8 sections and 215 chapters. Despite the fact that Liu removed many "duplicates," *Yen-tzu ch'un-ch'iu* still contains variant versions of several episodes. In addition, that many of the *Tso-chuan* passages concerning Yen Ying are also found in *Yen-tzu ch'un-ch'iu* has generally gone unappreciated. The consistently moralistic tone can become tedious, but there are sections that show a cleverness of argument the equal of the more admired suasive texts of late Chou China.

Considerable controversy attends the question of *Yen-tzu ch'un-ch'iu's* placement within the schools of Chou philosophy. The earliest bibliographies list the work as a Confucian text, but Liu Tsung-yüan* considered it a Mohist work, an opinion that has been followed by such famous bibliographers as Wang Ying-lin* and Chiao Hung

焦竑 (1541-1620). In fact, the text shows a certain philosophical eclecticism, leading some to conclude that it is a product of the time when school boundaries had not yet rigidified.

The vast collection known as *Kuan-tzu* 管子 is philosophically and stylistically heterogeneous. It is doubtful that any of the present text can be traced to Master Kuan (d. 645 B.C.), a famous prime minister who served Duke Huan of the state of Ch'i and enabled his lord to become hegemon of the other feudal rulers. A tradition associates *Kuan-tzu* with the famous Chi-hsia 稷下 Academy that thrived in the Ch'i capital of Lin-tzu. Assuredly many traditions about Kuan-tzu must have been preserved in Ch'i and gradually coalesced into texts under the aegis of the Chi-hsia Academicians. As is the case with many Chou texts, the present *Kuan-tzu* goes back to the editorial efforts of Liu Hsiang. In a preface Liu says that he collected several editions and collated them into 86 chapters, removing 474 duplicates. Unfortunately, 10 chapters are now missing, and several others have been interpolated from other sources.

Two major literary styles are found in *Kuan-tzu*. The first is a very sober, instructive essay (see, for example, I. 1, 2, 3, 4). These essays rarely contain the sort of illustrations and anecdotes that typify the essays of *Hsün-tzu* or *Han-fei-tzu*, nor do they display the dialogue-based, rhetorical technique of *Mo-tzu*. The second literary style is the dialogue, in almost all cases between Duke Huan and his brilliant minister Kuan Chung. Huan is portrayed neither as a chronic bungler, like the dukes of *Yen-tzu ch'un-ch'iu*, nor as the dull-witted feudal rulers of *Meng-tzu*. He is, on the contrary, an earnest seeker after wisdom. The relationship between Duke Huan and Kuan Chung refects the Confucian ideal—a ruler who humbly seeks the advise of a wise minister and the minister who dispenses such advice with courage and conviction.

Shang-chün shu 商君書 (The Book of Lord Shang) is attributed to the philosopher Shang Yang 商鞅 (d. 338 B.C.) whose Legalist ideas were implemented in the state of Ch'in and accounted in part for the phenomenal rise of Ch'in. Even though the text is probably an accurate reflection of Shang Yang's ideas, few scholars believe it comes directly from his hand. Duyvendak dates it from the 3rd century B.C.; it is very close in grammatical features to the other great Chou Legalist work *Han-fei-tzu*.

Of the twenty-nine chapters mentioned in the *Han-shu* "Bibliography," twenty-six remain. Except for the first chapter, which is also found almost verbatim in *Shih-chi* and contains a discussion between Duke Hsiao and Shang Yang, *The Book of Lord Shang* is comprised of topical essays. Unlike the other great Legalist work, *Han-fei-tzu*, these essays are rather wooden in style. The prose is dominated by the conditional construction, with sentence after sentence of the type "If A, then B." Watson's judgment is appropriate: "On the whole, *The Book of Lord Shang* is as grim as the doctrine it preaches, pounding over and over at the basic principles of its system, heavy and repetitious, though often capable of gripping the reader with a kind of horrid fascination" (*Early Chinese Literature*).

Hsün-tzu is attributed to the great Chou Confucian Hsün Ch'ing 荀卿 (*c*. 300-230 B.C.). Hsün-tzu's brand of Confucianism, which began from the premise that man's nature is evil, had profound impact through his students Han-fei-tzu and Li Ssu upon the development of Legalism and, consequently, upon early Han Confucianism as well. At the hands of the Sung Neo-Confucian Chu Hsi 朱熹 (1130-1200), the more optimistic branch of Confucianism taught by Meng-tzu was accepted as orthodox, and *Hsün-tzu* was largely neglected thereafter until the outburst of philological studies during the Ch'ing dynasty.

The first editor of *Hsün-tzu*, Liu Hsiang, declares that the text is written by Hsün Ch'ing himself. It is likely that many of the present 32 chapters do indeed descend from the master. Thus, he is the first philosopher whom can be confidently said to be an author himself. However, some chapters (8, 15, 16, 27-32) refer to Hsün Ch'ing as "master" (*tzu* 子) and may have been written by disciples. In fact, one portion of chapter 32 contains a criticism of Hsün Ch'ing and is possibly a later interpolation. Also, the famous *fu** of chapter 26, a piece which had great impact upon subsequent Chinese literature, may originally have been a part of another book by Hsün Ch'ing, entitled *Hsün Ch'ing fu*, which has now been lost. There are many passages in *Hsün-tzu* that are also found in the famous ritual texts *Ta Tai Li-chi* 大戴禮記 (Elder Tai's Record of Ritual) and *Hsiao Tai Li-chi* 小戴禮記 (Young Tai's Record of Ritual). It is believed that the *Hsün-tzu* versions of these parallels are the older and were borrowed by the *Li-chi* editors.

The topical essay takes a great step forward with *Hsün-tzu*. The literary quality of *Hsün-tzu* is somewhat uneven, but the best essays (e.g., 1, 17) are argued much more tightly than those of *Mo-tzu*. *Hsün-tzu* also lacks the rather tiresome repetition of many other Chou works and incorporates much livelier examples. Among Chou philosophical texts, *Hsün-tzu* perhaps stands second to *Chuang-tzu* in literary achievement. It is a work worthy of more detailed literary study than it has so far been accorded.

Han-fei-tzu is traditionally attributed to the great Legalist Han-fei-tzu (d. 233 B.C.), a prince of the Han state. According to Ssu-ma Ch'ien,* his works were introduced into Ch'in by his fellow student Li Ssu and were greatly admired by the king. From Ssu-ma's description it is apparent that Han-fei-tzu, like his master Hsün-tzu, committed his ideas to writing, and there is good reason to believe that many of the fifty-five chapters of *Han-fei-tzu* stem directly from Han-fei's hand. The authorship of several chapters, however, can be questioned. Chief among these is the famous first chapter, entitled "The First Interview with the King of Ch'in." This passage also appears in *Chan-kuo ts'e*,* where it is attributed to Chang I 張儀, an artful persuader who entered Ch'in almost a century before Han-fei-tzu. Anachronisms prove that the piece cannot have come from Chang I, but modern scholars have presented arguments that is also could not have been written by Han-fei.

In contrast to the rather dreary style of *The Book of Lord Shang*, *Han-fei-tzu* is a very lively text which is filled with artful rhetoric and clever anecdotes. Han-fei was very much a child of the Warring States period when skillful suasion was treasured. He wrote specifically on "Persuasion," beginning his discussion with the psychological observation that "the difficulties in the way of persuasion lie in my knowing the heart of the persuader in order thereby to fit my wording to it" (ch. 12). There seems to be a fundamental conflict between the harsh Legalism of this work and its buoyant, creative style of presentation.

Lü-shih ch'un-ch'iu, as noted above, is the first philosophical text with an overall structure that indicates it was planned from the outset as a unit. The book was commissioned by Lü Pu-wei 呂不韋 (d. 235 B.C.), a rich Ch'in merchant who served his state for several years as prime minister. Like several of his wealthy contemporaries, Lü assembled and supported large numbers of retainers. The scholars among these retainers were then put to work on the compilation of a text which was intended to "supplement the knowledge of the whole world's and all its myriad components' affairs, past and present" (*Shih-chi*, ch. 85). Although the book was produced in the state of Ch'in where Legalism predominated, it is clearly anti-Legalist in tone, advocating a kind of eclectic Taoism that revolves around a rather egocentric view of life.

The book has three sections, corresponding to the triad Heaven, Earth, and Man. The first contains twelve "chronicles" (*chi* 紀), the second eight "surveys" (*lan* 覽), and the last six "discourses" (*lun* 論). The individual sections often contain essays on a wide range of subjects. The book is both a forerunner of the Chinese *lei-shu** and of the topical essays of the dynastic histories (*shu* 書 in *Shih-chi* and *chih* 志 in later histories). Stylistically *Lü-shih ch'un-ch'iu* is noted for its clarity of expression. While it lacks the literary flourishes of *Chuang-tzu* or the rhetorical strength of *Hsün-tzu*, it is a highly readable compendium of late Chou thought.

BIBLIOGRAPHY

Listed below are just a few of the hundreds of sources dealing with Chou philosophical texts. For a fairly complete listing of Western-language works on the philosophical content of the works surveyed above, see Wing Tsit Chan, *An Outline and Annotated Bibliography of Chinese Philosophy*, New Haven, 1961.

EDITIONS:

The standard editions of the *SPTK* and the *SPPY* should be consulted. In addition, a useful edition is *Hsin-pien Chu-tzu chi-ch'eng* 新編諸子集成. 8v. Rpt. Taipei, 1972.

A Concordance to Chuang Tzu. Harvard-Yenching Institute Sinological Index Series, Supplement No. 20. Peking, 1947.

A Concordance to Han-fei Tzu. Taipei, 1975.

A Concordance to Hsün Tzu. Harvard-Yenching Institute Sinological Index Series, Supplement No. 22. Taipei, 1975.

A Concordance to Kuan-tzu. Compiled by Chuang Wei-ssu and Wallace Johnson. Taipei, 1970.

A Concordance to Mo Tzu. Harvard-Yenching Institute Sinological Index Series, Supplement 21. Peking, 1948.

Index du Liu Che Tch'ouen Ts'ieou. Index No. 2. Centre franco-chinois d'etudes sinologiques. Peking, 1943.

Konkordanz zum Lao-tzu. Compiled by the Fachschaft des Seminars für Ostasiatische Sprach- und Kulturwissenschaft der Universität München, Munich, 1968.

TRANSLATIONS:

MO-TZU:

Me Ti des Sozialethikers und seiner Schüler philosophische Werke. Alfred Forke, trans. Berlin, 1922.

Mo Ti. Gegen den Krieg und Solidarität und allgemeine Menschenliebe. Helwig Schmidt-Glintzer, trans. Düsseldorf, 1975.

The Ethical and Political Works of Motse. Y. P. Mei, trans. London, 1929.

LAO-TZU:

Lao Tzu: Tao Te Ching. D. C. Lau, trans. Harmondsworth, 1963.

Tao Te Ching. Ch'u Ta-kao, trans. 5th ed. London, 1959.

Tao te ching, the Book of the Way and its Virtue. J. J. L. Duyvendak, trans. London, 1954. See also the French translation by the same author: *Tao t king, le livre de la voie it de la vertu*. Paris, 1953.

Tao-te-king: das Buch des Alten vom Sinn und Leben. Richard Wilhelm, trans. Düsseldorf, 1957.

The Way and Its Power. Arthur Waley, trans. New York, 1934.

CHUANG-TZU:

Chuang tzu. Burton Watson, trans. New York, 1968.

Chuang Tzu: The Inner Chapters. A. C. Graham, trans. London, 1981.

Das Wahre Buch von südlichen Blütenland. Richard Wilhelm, trans. Jena, 1923.

L'oeuvre complète de Tchouang-tseu. Liou Kia-hway, trans. Paris, 1969.

KUAN-TZU:

Economic Dialogues in Ancient China: Selections from the Kuan-tzu. T'an Po-fu and Wen Kung-wen, trans. Carbondale, Illinois, 1954.

Kuan-tzu. A Repository of Early Chinese Thought. W. Allyn Rickett, trans. Hong Kong, 1965.

SHANG-CHÜN SHU:

The Book of Lord Shang. J. J. L. Duyvendak, trans. Chicago, 1928.

HSÜN TZU:

Basic Writings of Mo tzu, Hsün tzu, and Han-fei tzu. Burton Watson, trans. New York, 1967.

Hsün-tzu ins deutsche übertragen. Hermann Köster, trans. Kaldenkirchen, 1967.

HAN-FEI-TZU:

The Complete Works of Han Fei Tzu. W. K. Liao, trans. 2v. London, 1939-59.

LÜ-SHIH CH'UN-CH'IU:

Frühling und Herbst des Lü Bu We. Richard Wilhelm, trans. Jena, 1928.

STUDIES:

Chang, Hsin-ch'eng 張心澂. *Wei-shu t'ung-k'ao* 僞書通考. Shanghai, 1939; rpt. Taipei, 1970.

Forke, Alfred. "Yen Ying, Staatsman und Philosoph, und das Yen-tse Tch'un-ts'iu," in *AM*, (1923), 101-144.

Fung, Yu-lan. *A History of Chinese Philosophy.* V. 1. Derk Bodde, trans. Princeton, 1952.

Graham, A. C. *Chuang Tzu: Textual Notes to a Partial Translation.* London, 1982.

———. *Later Mohist Logic, Ethics and Science.* London, 1978.

Hendricks, Robert. "The Ma-wang-tui Manuscripts of the *Lao tzu* and the Problem of Dating the Text," *CC*, 20.2 (June 1979), 1-15.

Hsiao, Kung-ch'üan. *A History of Chinese Political Thought.* V. 1: "From The Beginning to the Sixth Century A.D." F. W. Mote, trans. Princeton, 1979.

Hsu, Cho-yün. *Ancient China in Transition.* Stanford, 1965.

Kaizuka, Shigeki 貝塚茂樹. *Shoshi hyakka* 諸子百家. Tokyo, 1962.

Karlgren, Bernhard. "The Authenticity of Ancient Chinese Texts," *BMFEA*, (1929), 165-183.

Ku-shih pien 古史辨. "Chu-tzu ts'ung-k'ao" 諸子叢考. Lo Ken-tse 羅根澤, ed. V. 4 (of 7).

Liang, Ch'i-ch'ao 梁啟超. *Chu-tzu k'ao-shih* 諸子考釋. Taipei, 1968.

Loewe, Michael. "Manuscripts Found Recently in China: A Preliminary Survey," *TP*, 63 (1977), 99-136.

Ma-wang-tui po-shu Lao-tzu shih-t'an 馬王堆帛書老子試探. Yen Ling-feng, ed. Taipei, 1976.

Maspero, Henri. *La Chine Antique.* Rev. ed. Paris, 1955. Trans. by Frank A. Kierman, Jr., as *China in Antiquity.* Boston, 1978.

Mei, Y. P. *Motse, The Neglected Rival of Confucius.* London, 1934.

Needham, Joseph. *Science and Civilisation in China.* V. 2. Cambridge, 1956.

Pokora, Timoteus, "Pre-Han Literature," in *Essays on the Sources for Chinese History*, Donald D. Leslie, Colin Mackerras, and Wang Gungwu, eds., Columbia, S.C., 1973, pp. 23-35.

Waley, Arthur. *Three Ways of Thought in Ancient China.* Garden City, 1956.

Walker, Richard. "Some Notes on the *Yen-tzu ch'un-ch'iu*," *JAOS*, 73 (1953), 156-163.

Wang, Chi-ssu 王季思. "Pai-chia tseng-ming ho Hsien-Ch'in chu-tzu te wen-hsüeh ch'eng-chiu" 百家爭鳴和先秦諸子的文學成就, in *Chung-hua hsüeh-shu lun-wen chi* 中華學術論文集, Chung-hua shu-chü 中華書局, ed. Peking, 1981, pp. 411-425.

Watson, Burton, *Early Chinese Literature.* New York, 1962.

—SD

Chu Yu-tun 朱有燉 (*hao*, Ch'üan-yang-tzu 全陽子, Lao-k'uang-sheng 老狂生, Chin-ch'ao Tao-jen 錦窠道人, and Ch'eng-chai 誠齋, 1379-1439) is the most important dramatist of the first half of the fifteenth century. He wrote thirty-one *tsa-chü** and they all have been preserved. Chu Yu-tun was a member of the Ming imperial family and the eldest son of Chu Su 朱橚 (1361-1425), the fifth son of the founder of the dynasty, Chu Yüan-chang 朱元漳 (1328-1398). He did not live a life of carefree luxury since he and his family were often implicated in royal intrigues for power. He is also known by his posthumous title as Chou Hsien-wang 周憲王 (the Exemplary Prince of Chou). Apart from his *tsa-chü*, he wrote *san-ch'ü* (a small collection entitled *Ch'eng-chai yüeh-fu* 誠齋樂府 [Popular Songs of Sincerity Studio] survives) and *shih** (of which very few remain). He was an expert calligrapher, too.

Chu Yu-tun had all of his plays printed during his lifetime. Collectively they are also known as *Ch'eng-chai yüeh-fu*. In contrast to the Yüan editions of *tsa-chü*, his editions contained nearly complete prose-dialogues. He also provided very detailed stage directions. For twenty-four of his thirty-one plays he wrote prefaces, and they are important documents in the history of dramatic criticism. Since most of his plays are dated, he is the first Chinese dramatist whose development can be traced over time in terms of developing themes.

Chu Yu-tun's many *tsa-chü* can be broadly divided into two groups. On the one hand, he wrote a great number of plays that were apparently meant to be performed in the royal palace at specific annual occasions. These "occasional plays" range from the *Hsien-kuan ch'ing-hui* 仙官慶會 (The Celebrational Gathering of Immortal Officials, 1433) which provides a scenario for the exorcistic *No* 儺 Ceremony of New Year's Eve, to a great number of deliverance plays intended to be performed at birthday parties. His earliest deliverance plays, like *Hsiao-t'ao hung* 小桃紅 (Little-Peach Red, 1408) and *Wu chen-ju* 悟眞如 (Realization of the Truth, 1422) have a Buddhist inspiration; his later deliverance plays, beginning with *P'an-t'ao hui* 蟠桃會 (The Peach Assembly) often feature the Eight Immortals and are a conscious attempt to reform the Taoist deliverance play by omitting scenes of violence. Beginning with *Mu-tan hsien* 牡丹仙 (Peony Immortals, 1430), Chu Yu-tun also wrote a number of *tsa-chü* to be performed at the periodic flower-viewing festivals for the peony, the winter plum, the crabapple, etc. His *Te tsou-yü* 得騶虞 (The Capture of the Tsou-yü, 1408) was written to celebrate the capture of a *tsou-yü*, a rare auspicuous animal, by his father in 1404; *Ling-chih ch'ing-shou* 靈芝慶壽 (Numinous Mushroom Celebrates Longevity, 1439) was written after the appearance of this miraculous fungus in the royal palace. All these "occasional plays" require large casts and elaborate costumes. They often depart from the musical conventions of *tsa-chü* by having two or more performers sing alternately or together. They also often contain other theatrical routines such as group dance. However attractive these plays may have been as pageantry, their literary value is usually slight. The plots are often nothing more than repetitive eulology. Still, a certain literary value cannot be denied in some of these works.

On the other hand, Chu Yu-tun wrote a number of important *tsa-chü* that are not tied to any specific occasion by subject matter and require only a small cast and simple costumes. As a rule they also strictly adhere to the musical conventions of the genre. These plays were apparently intended for performance both in the royal palace and in public theaters. The theme to which Chu Yu-tun often returned in these plays was loyalty, not as an imposed duty, but as a deliberate choice of the protagonist. Often the protagonist is a courtesan. In his early plays Chu looked to the past for perfect paragons of loyalty. *Ch'ing-shou T'ang* 慶朔堂 (The Ch'ing-shou Pavilion, 1406) is a tidy comedy that features the courtesan Chen Yüeh-o 甄月娥 and the famous statesman Fan Chung-yen.* *Ch'ü-chiang ch'ih* 范仲淹 (Serpentine Pond, 1409) is an elaborate melodramatic version of the story of Po Hsing-chien's* "Li Wa chuan." *I-yung tz'u chin* 義勇辭金 (The Righteous and Brave Refusal of Gold, 1416) is a history play on Kuan Yü, one of the heroes of the novel *San-kuo-chih yen-i.** In his loyalty plays of the early 1430s Chu Yu-tun was inspired by recent events. *T'ao-yüan ching* 桃源景 (Peach-spring Prospect, 1431), one of his finest plays, may be classified as a tragedy, since its heroine prefers to commit suicide rather than to be disloyal to her weak lover. However, *Fu-lo-ch'ang* 復落娼 (Becoming a Singsong Girl Again) of the same year is a farce about a courtesan who leaves every

345

husband as soon as he runs out of money, only to become in the end a singsong girl again.

Two other plays by Chu feature heroes best known from the novel *Shui-hu chuan.**Chang-i su ts'ai* 仗義疏財 (Spurning Riches out of Righteousness, 1433) has Li K'uei as its protagonist, and *Pao-tzu ho-shang* 豹子和尚 (The Leopard Monk, also 1433) concerns Lu Chih-shen. Both plays are skillful comedies. Chu Yu-tun also did some adaptations of earlier *tsa-chü*. In general, these plays of the second category have a carefully constructed plot and well-written dialogues, occasionally enlivened by the rather coarse humor. As a writer of lyrics he is best characterized as a virtuoso versifier who excels in vituperative arias.

Chu Yu-tun's plays have always been praised for their stageability. In the twentieth century the critical estimation of his work has been rather low. In the People's Republic of China he has been much criticized as a spokesman of feudal morality. His *Chang-i su-ts'ai* and *Pao-tzu ho-shang* have especially been attacked as vilifications of peasant rebellions.

EDITIONS:

Ch'eng-chai Yüeh-fu original woodblock editions of early fifteenth century. Two incomplete sets found in Peking Library contain between them all the plays. No complete modern edition of Chu Yu-tun's plays exists. The most important modern collections that include a number of his plays are the following:

Chou, I-pai 周貽白, ed. *Ming-jen tsa-chü hsüan* 明人雜劇選. Peking, 1958. Contains four plays by Chu.

Chu, Yu-tun. *Ch'eng-chai yüeh-fu,* in *Yin-hung-i-so k'e-ch'ü* 飲虹簃所刻曲, Lu Ch'ien 盧前, ed., Nanking, 1934; rpt. Taipei, 1961.

Fu, Hsi-hua 傅惜華 and Tu Ying-t'ao 杜穎陶, eds. *Shui-hu hsi-ch'ü chi ti-i-chi* 水滸戲曲集第一集. Shanghai, 1958. Contains *Chang-i su-ts'ai* and *Pao-tzu ho-shang.*

Wang, Chi-lieh 王季烈, ed. *Ku-pen Yüan Ming tsa-chü* 孤本元明雜劇. Peking, 1957. Contains five plays by Chu.

Wu, Mei 吳梅. *She-ma-t'a-shih ch'ü-ts'ung erh-chi* 奢摩他室曲叢二集. Shanghai, 1928. Contains four plays by Chu.

TRANSLATIONS:

Dolby, *History,* pp. 22-25. A translation of a *yüan-pen* (farce), included in Chu's play *Shen-hsien-hui* 神仙會 (A Meeting of Divine Immortals) of 1435.

STUDIES:

Ch'en, Wan-nai 陳萬鼐. "Shu Wen-shu p'u-sa hsiang shih-tzu tsa-chü" 述文殊菩薩降獅子雜劇, *Kuo-li Chung-yang t'u-shu-kuan kuan-k'an,* 2.2 (1968), 34-45.

Idema, W. L. "The Capture of the *Tsou-yü,*" in *Leyden Studies in Sinology,* W. L. Idema, ed., Leiden, 1981, pp. 57-74.

———. "Shih Chün-pao's and Chu Yu-tun's *Ch'ü-chuang-ch'ih:* The Variety of Mode within Form," *TP,* 66 (1980), 217-215.

Jen, Tsun-shih 任遵時. *Chou Hsien-wang yen-chiu* 周憲王研究. Taipei, 1974. A biographical study.

Na, Lien-chün 那廉君. "Ming Chou Hsien-wang chih tsa-chü" 明周憲王之雜劇, *Chü-hsüeh yüeh-k'an,* 3.11 (1934), 1-9 (no continuous pagination).

Tseng, Yung-i 曾永義. "Chou Hsien-wang chi ch'i Ch'eng-chai tsa-chü" 周憲王及其誠齋雜劇, *Ku-kung t'u-shu chi-k'an,* 2.2 (1971), 47-66, and 2.3 (1973), 39-58. The most comprehensive modern study of the plays.

Wu, Mei. "Ch'eng-chai yüeh-fu pa" 誠齋樂府, in Wu Mei, *She-ma-t'a-shih ch'-ts'ung erh-chi.* Shanghai, 1928.

Yagisawa, *Gekisakuka,* pp. 50-108. Mainly a biographical and bibliographical survey.

—WI

Ch'u Kuang-hsi 儲光羲 *(fl.* 742) was a poet from Kiangsu who spent his early life as a prominent figure in Ch'ang-an society. He knew and exchanged poems with Wang Wei,* Ts'ui Hao,* and others. He passed his *chin-shih* examination in 726 but returned to Kiangsu in 737 where he held minor positions. He was captured by the An Lu-shan rebels in 755-756 and forced to serve under them. After the restoration he was first imprisoned, then officially pardoned for his collaboration with the rebels but banished to the South where he died.

Though his court poetry is quite conventional, Ch'u Kuang-hsi's more relaxed old-style poetry in the style of T'ao Ch'ien* is outstanding. He wrote poems on farming which praise the joys of country life, sometimes containing a philosophical judgment opposing the constraints of court life. Some of his poems describe immortals, and Ch'u Kuang-hsi's "gift for vignette"—sketches of a significant human situation, mostly in extended old-style but also in the quatrain form—has also received praise.

Seventy *chüan* of Ch'u Kuang-hsi's poems were originally collected, but only four remain today.

EDITION:

Ch'u Kuang-hsi shih-chi 儲光義詩集. *Ssu-k'u ch'üan-shu chen-pen* 四庫全書珍本 ed. Taipei, 1978.

TRANSLATION:

Sunflower, pp. 99-100.

STUDIES:

Ch'en, T'ieh-min 陳鐵民. "Ch'u Kuang-hsi sheng-p'ing shih-chi k'ao-pien" 儲光義生平事迹考辨, *Wen-shih,* 12 (September 1981), 195-210.

Owen, *High T'ang,* pp. 63-70.

—MW

Ch'u-tz'u 楚辭 (Songs of Ch'u) is an anthology of poetry in the so-called *sao* 騷 mode, composed between the third century B.C. and the second century A.D. The work was compiled and provided with its first and most influential commentary by Wang I 王逸 (d. A.D. 158). The *Ch'u-tz'u* contains seventeen texts, the most important of which are:

1. "Li sao" 離騷 (Encountering Sorrow) is a narrative poem of 187 couplets, long by Chinese standards. Several eminent Western scholars have pronounced the "Li sao" a "confused" poem pervaded with "murky allegory." Traditional Chinese readers seem not to have encountered such difficulties with the poem, which narrates how the hero, slandered by political enemies and dismissed from court by his sovereign, undertakes a mystical journey through the sky in search of a virtuous lord, represented allegorically as a "fair one" (*mei-jen* 美人). The hero, in long dramatic monologues, laments the villainy of his opponents, the duplicity of his erstwhile allies, and the failings of his sovereign. After laying his plaint before the sage-king Shun, he attempts to engage several "matchmakers" in his search for the perfect "lady." When these go-betweens prove unsuitable or unreliable, he consults through divination two famous shaman oracles who advise him to pursue the "lady" on his own. Thus encouraged, the hero resumes his ethereal flight towards the K'un-lun Mountains:

> Yet when I had ascended to the shining light of Heaven
> Then suddenly could I see my old homeland below;
> And my charioteer in sorrow, my horses in grief
> Reared up and around and would not go on.

The poem concludes several lines later on a note of profound ambiguity, leaving the reader free to decide whether the hero will (1) return to his "homeland," (2) continue his mystical search for a more worthy sovereign, (3) retire to hermetic seclusion, or (4) commit suicide.

2. The "Chiu ko" 九歌 (Nine Songs) are adaptations by a literate author of popular verses from a shamanistic ritual, in which the shaman first purifies and adorns himself with flowers and perfumes, elicits an ecstatic trance through song and dance, undertakes a mystical journey through the sky in search of a deity of the opposite sex, unites sexually with the deity, and finally returns to earth. According to Wang I, the "Nine Songs" use these motifs to represent allegorically various aspects of the relationship between the sovereign (the deity) and his minister (the shaman).

3. The "T'ien-wen" 天問 (Heavenly Questions) is a long series of questions on early Chinese history and mythology. Its literary value is slight, for its terse, cryptic style and badly corrupt text render large sections barely intelligible. Wang I believed Ch'ü Yüan* wrote the "T'ien-wen" as descriptions for temple mural paintings in the ancestral temples of Ch'u. It is more likely they are remnants of riddles, which are known to have been an important literary genre in the late Warring States period.

4. The "Yüan-yu" 遠遊 (Far Journey) probably dates from the beginning of the

first century B.C. Like the "Li sao," it describes a celestial journey, but one in which the protagonist successfully attains his goal. Although the text borrows heavily from the "Li sao," it transforms the shamanistic motifs of the earlier poem into the mysticism of Han Taoism.

5. "Yü-fu" 漁父 (The Fisherman) is a verse dialogue between Ch'ü Yüan and a fisherman, in which the latter criticizes the former's resolution to leave office and commit suicide. The fisherman's concluding advice—"When the Ts'ang-lang's waters are clear, I can wash my hat-strings in them;/When the Ts'ang-lang's waters are muddy, I can wash my feet in them" (meaning the prudent official seeks office when times are favorable and retires when they are troubled)—became the classical formulation of the wise official's response to adversity.

6. The "Chiu pien" 九辯 (Nine Arguments), attributed to Sung Yü 宋玉, a shadowy third-century B.C. official of Ch'u, contain passages that constitute some of the best poetry in the anthology. The pensive descriptions of autumn with which the series begins became the *locus classicus* for later Chinese poetry of autumnal melancholy.

7. "Chao-hun" 招魂 (Summoning the Soul), the "Great Summons" ("Ta-chao" 大招), and "Summoning the Recluse" ("Chao yin-shih" 招隱士) are three separate yet thematically related texts, where it is possible once again to trace the evolution from shaman ritual to Confucian allegory. The first two poems seem to be transcriptions of shaman ritual healing prayers for a sick king. In the third, however, the genre has been adapted to "call back" the virtuous gentleman from reclusion.

The texts in the *Ch'u-tz'u* are written in one of two basic styles. The song style, typified by the "Nine Songs," consists of five stressed syllables per line with a sound carrier between the third and fourth syllable. David Hawkes schematizes a couplet in the song style thus:

tum tum tum hsi *tum tum/tum tum tum* hsi *tum tum*

The sound carrier, pronounced in modern Chinese *hsi* 兮, but probably sounding something like "ah" in pre-Ch'in times, is the most distinguishing stylistic feature of all *Ch'u-tz'u* verse. In the second or *sao* style, the *hsi* divides the first and second line of the couplet, and an unstressed grammatical particle acts as a caesura between the third and fourth syllables of each line:

tum tum tum tee tum tum hsi *tum tum tum tee tum tum*

This *sao* style takes its name from the "Li sao," the most prominent *Ch'u-tz'u* text to use this meter. The affinity of these two styles is apparent, with the song style probably being the older and more basic form. It is certain that these rhythms, both different from the four-character line of the *Shih-ching,** reflect a different musical background for the southern *Ch'u-tz'u*.

The unique rhythms of the *Ch'u-tz'u* are certainly related to the anthology's origins in the state of Ch'u and to that state's practice of institutionalized shamanism. Much of the vocabulary and imagery of the *Ch'u-tz'u* texts derives from shaman rituals, and there is much evidence to suggest that Ch'ü Yüan, the supposed author of the "Li sao" and other texts in the anthology, was a shaman in the service of the king of Ch'u. Nevertheless, in the commentary of Wang I, the shaman motifs are systematically allegorized to stand for Confucian values, and traditional readers understood the texts in this way.

As a verse repository of Confucian values, the *Ch'u-tz'u* stands second only to the *Shih-ching*, which, when read in traditional manner, represents the positive, optimistic side of official life: The virtuous sovereign listens to the thoughtful and carefully presented advice of his officials, and the country prospers. The *Ch'u-tz'u*, on the other hand, mainly by virtue of the preeminent position of the "Li sao," is the voice of the official out of office, whose access to his sovereign has been cut off by the slanders of "petty men." It is the dark side of official life, and although it remained always just outside the canon of orthodox Confucian studies, its powerful appeal as a source of personal solace and as a literary model for an official in southern exile kept the *Ch'u-tz'u* in the forefront of the Chinese literary consciousness.

EDITIONS:

Chu, Hsi 朱熹 (1130-1200). *Ch'u-tz'u chi-chu* 楚辭集注. Rpt. Taipei, 1967.

Takeji, Sadao 竹治貞夫. *Soji sakuin* 楚辭索引. First printed Tokushima, Japan, 1964. Rpt. with *SPPY* text, Taipei, 1972. A full concordance to the *Ch'u-tz'u*. Can be used with either the *SPTK* or the *SPPY* edition of the basic Wang I/Huang Hsing-tsu text.

Wang, Fu-chih 王夫之. *Ch'u-tz'u t'ung-shih* 楚辭通釋 First (?) edition 1709, rpt. Shanghai, 1959; Taipei, 1966.

Wang, I 王逸. *Ch'u-tz'u chang-ch'ü* 楚辭章句. With appended annotations by Huang Hsing-tsu 洪興祖 (1090-1155). The basic edition. *SPTK*. Ming copy of Sung edition. There are many reprints, for example, Taipei, 1967.

Yu, Kuo-en 游國恩. *Li sao tsuan i* 離騷纂義. Peking, 1980. The largest collection of commentary to date. This is the first volume in a projected multi-volume edition of the *Ch'u-tz'u*.

TRANSLATIONS:

Hawkes, *Ch'u Tz'u*. Complete, reliable translations.

STUDIES:

Chan, Ping-leung. "*Ch'u tz'u* and Shamanism in Ancient China," Unpublished Ph.D. dissertation, Ohio State University, 1972. A fine study of shamanism in Chou China and in the *Ch'u tz'u*.

———. "Recent *Ch'u-tz'u* Studies: A Review of Chinese Publications," *JCLTA*, 11.2 (May 1976), 140-145.

Chiang, Liang-fu 姜亮夫. *Ch'u-tz'u shu-mu wu-chung* 楚辭書目五種. Peking, 1961.

Chiang, T'ien-shu 蔣天樞. *Ch'u-tz'u lun-wen chi* 楚辭論文集. Sian, 1982.

Hawkes, "Quest." A major study of the shamanistic aspects of the "Nine Songs."

Hightower, James R. "Ch'ü Yüan Studies," in *Silver Jubilee*, pp. 192-223. A useful bibliographical study.

Huang, Chih-kao 黃志高. "Liu-shih nien lai chih *Ch'u-tz'u* hsüeh" 六十年來之楚辭學, *Kuo-li T'aiwan Shih-fan Ta-hsüeh Kuo-wen yen-chiu-so chi-k'an*, 22 (June 1978), 869-961.

Jao, Tsung-i 饒宗頤. *Ch'u-tz'u shu-lu* 楚辭書錄. Hong Kong, 1956. A useful bibliographic study.

Lin, Keng 林庚. "Ch'ü Yüan yü Sung Yü" 屈原與宋玉, in *Chung-hua hsüeh-shu lun-wen chi* 中華學術論文集, Chung-hua shu-chü 中華書局, ed., Peking, 1981, pp. 427-435.

Takeji, Sadao. *Soji kenkyū* 楚辭研究. Tokyo: 1978.

Tökei, F. *Naissance de l'élégie chinoise*. Paris, 1967. A Marxist study of the *Ch'u-tz'u*.

Waley, Arthur. *The Nine Songs. A Study of Shamanism in Ancient China*. London, 1955.

Walker, Galal LeRoy. "Toward a Formal History of the Chuci." Unpublished Ph.D. dissertation, Cornell University, 1982.

Waters, Geoffrey. "Three Elegies of Ch'u. An Introduction to the Traditional Interpretation of the *Ch'u tz'u*." Unpublished Ph.D. dissertation, Indiana University, 1981. A study of the first three of the "Nine Songs" with complete translation of all pre-Sung commentaries. Extremely useful for following the nuances of the traditional allegorical interpretations (to be published by the University of Wisconsin Press).

Wen, I-to 聞一多. *Wen I-to Ch'u-tz'u yen-chiu lun-chu shih chung* 聞一多楚辭研究論著十種. Hong Kong, n.d. A useful reprint of Wen I-to's major articles on the *Ch'u-tz'u*, also available in the first volume of his collected works, *Wen I-to ch'üan-chi* 聞一多全集, Shanghai, 1948.

—CH

Ch'ü 曲 (aria or lyric verse, earlier called *tz'u* 詞) has been used in China since ancient times to designate song, but in current usage the word specifically denotes *Yüan-ch'ü* 元曲, the large corpus of lyric and dramatic songs which ripened in the poetry and dramas of the Yüan and early Ming dynasties.

The *ch'ü* flourished in two separate traditions, the northern 北曲 and southern 南曲, each with separate musical conventions, but the appellation *ch'ü*, unless otherwise specified, normally refers to the large corpus of dramatic arias (*hsi-ch'ü* 戲曲) and lyric verse forms (*san-ch'ü* 散曲) composed in the northern style. Each *ch'ü* is written according to a different metrical pattern (the total repertoire is around 350) bearing the name of a musical air, and to one of various modes. In the Yüan, for example, there were the following modes: *hsien-lü kung* 仙呂宮, *huang-chung-kung* 黃鍾宮, *cheng-lü-kung* 正呂宮, *nan-lü-kung* 南呂宮,

shang-tiao 商調, *shuang-tiao* 雙調, *yüeh-tiao* 越調, and *ta-shih-tiao* 大石調.

The *ch'ü* is a branch of the long-short verse style (*ch'ang-tuan chü* 長短句) and a cousin of the *tz'u*.* Like the *tz'u*, it is a song form characterized by lines of unequal length and prescribed rhyme and tonal sequence. The composer is free to add any number of what are called padding words (*ch'en tzu* 襯字) to a line, and that permits considerable variation in the number of characters per line. The structure therefore is more complex than that of the *tz'u*.

In any phrase (*chü* 句) the words are normally of three types: padding words, base words (*cheng-tzu* 正字), and apostrophes. Apostrophes are exclamatory interjections; they are extra-metrical and therefore exempt from all rules of *ch'ü* prosody. Two types of padding words may be isolated: verse leader (found at the beginning of the line) and internal, which are scattered in the phrase among the base words. The base words are the vital segments of the phrase, because they embody the only clues to the metrical structure of the song, the music having been lost. Base word structure depends on seven primary phrase types and about twenty common mutation patterns.

The origins of the *ch'ü* lie in oral traditions of the Chin period such as *chu-kung-tiao*.* Many *ch'ü* titles were inherited from earlier literary traditions. Some were tunes of the T'ang or Five Dynasties, many were also well-known *tz'u* metrical formulas, and some came out of the *ta-ch'ü** entertainments of the Sung dynasty. Metrically few are related to their Yüan counterparts despite identical titles. The most conspicuous (metrical) ancestor of *Yüan-ch'ü* was the *chu-kung-tiao*. Some thirty to forty songs from that genre were appropriated by *Yüan-ch'ü* artists, and most of their metrical formulas were either borrowed or very closely imitated.

The bulk of these formulas emerged at a time when popular songs flourished and cultural influences from non-Han peoples were abundant. Jurchen music, songs, and dances were popular and the vocabulary of the Han dialects was fertilized by a con-

siderable number of Jurchen and Mongol words and expressions, many of them onomatopeic in nature. For Han languages, this was a critical period of change and adaptation: the *ju-sheng* 入聲 (entering tone) disappeared as a tonal class; old rhyme categories were no longer functional; the number of rhyme categories shrank; one could also rhyme across tone classes (see *Chung-yüan yin-yün*). The colloquial language enjoyed an elevated status in literature and literati freely wrote in the colloquial *ch'ü* form. These explosions of popular songs in the streets and taverns, among actors, entertainers and their patrons, occurred independently in various regional centers and eventually spread throughout Chinese urban society. Imitation and sharing in the formulation of the new genre was most likely a gradual and haphazard process, until finally *ch'ü* were composed simply by writing new lyrics to an established prosodic formula. Songs which had been vibrant turned into mere verse-formulas, each attached to a particular title, a process highly reminiscent of the development of the *tz'u*. Many formularies of *ch'ü*-style songs (*ch'ü-p'u* 曲譜, see *tsa-chü*) were created as repositories of tonal patterns and other metrical requirements, both to preserve the tunes and to function as guidebooks to poetic composition.

San-ch'ü is a general term for many varieties of lyric verse-forms. The simplest are single-stanza verses—*hsiao-ling* 小令, also called "leaves" (*yeh-erh* 葉兒). The *hsiao-ling* may be repeated by a reprise, labeled *yao-pien* 么篇 or *you* 又 (*ch'ien-ch'iang* 前腔 in the southern style), allowing the poet to extend the verse modestly, with a single repeat, or significantly with an unrestricted number of repeats. Other varieties of repeat forms are the "altered head" pattern (*yao-p'ien huan-t'ou* 么篇換頭), wherein the initial phrase is metrically different from the parent aria, and a "repeated head" form (*ch'ung-t'ou* 重頭) wherein the words in the initial phrase of the parent aria (sometimes the ultimate phrase) are retained in the repeat form. Some verses are pastiche forms. A *chi-ch'ü* 集曲 is a pastiche created by extracting phrases from two or more *hsiao-ling* in the same mode and fusing them to create a single aria. In the southern style, it is called *fan-tiao* 犯調—the initial and ultimate phrases remain intact, but the inner phrases are replaced by phrases from other arias. A final category of *hsiao-ling* are the binary, ternary, or quaternary clusters (*tai-kuo-ch'ü* 帶過曲), in which two, three, or four complete arias are bound together in a single unit.

In contrast to the above forms, which are either single-stanza forms or combined forms, is the suite style called *t'ao-shu* 套數. A suite is a string of single-stanza arias and cluster arias from the same mode, which rhyme and are arranged according to a favored sequence pattern characteristic of the mode. A suite has a fixed head-aria and a coda, which are the most predictable and constant elements. The head can consist of one or two arias in fixed sequence. The coda, or tail, can be a single-stanza form or a series of arias forming an ending sequence. The only variation in the suite is the mixed suite (*nan-pei ho-t'ao* 南北合套), in which arias in both the northern and southern style are alternated to insure that two arias in the same style are never juxtaposed.

The repertoires of the *hsiao-ling* and the suite style, although they share some arias, for the most part are quite distinct. The *hsiao-ling* style has the smaller repertoire. In the *Ch'üan Yüan san-ch'ü* 全元散曲 (Complete San-ch'ü of the Yüan) there are about 160 different formulas whereas about 246 are used in suite style. The *san-t'ao* 散套 (lyric suites) utilize a smaller portion of the repertoire than the *chü-t'ao* 劇套 (dramatic suites). Suite style is one of the more novel features of the *ch'ü* genre. It allows a poet to compose very long poems on a single theme and is ideal in *tsa-chü*, where each act is built on the structure of a single suite. In the drama, the *ch'ü* is an operatic aria, but lyric poetry (*san-ch'ü*) was also sung, in a manner referred to as "clear singing" (*ch'ing-ch'ang* 清唱), a style suitable in tea houses or in private-party settings. It was also referred to as "sold bench" style (*ling-pan teng* 冷板凳), meaning it was not de-

signed for the stage with orchestra accompaniment and the trappings of the theater, but to be sung with a flute or the *san-hsien* 三弦 and to the pulse of the clapper (*pan* 板).

The *hsi-ch'ü* 戲曲 are dramatic arias written for the stage. They function to enhance and prolong the dramatic moment rather than to advance the plot, which is developed in the dialogue. The aria is elaborative, descriptive, and highly emotive. Each *tsa-chü* consists of four suites; sometimes an additional *hsieh-tzu* 楔子 (short suite) is added. The suite structure (*t'ao-shih* 套式) is an accustomed sequence of arias tempered by considerable flexibility. The arrangement of single-stanza arias and cluster arias in a suite was influenced by tempo, pitch, and no doubt, unknown melodic and rhythmic factors. In any suite all arias adhere to a single rhyme scheme closed by a coda.

Some modes are strongly associated with a particular act. *Hsien-lü-kung*, for example, is always used in opening acts; *shuang-tiao* is strongly favored for final acts. Mode choice is less consistent in acts two and three, but act two is often in *nan-lü-kung*, and act three in *chung-lü-kung*.

EDITIONS:

Jen, Na 任納, ed. *San-ch'ü ts'ung-k'an* 散曲叢刊. 4v. Shanghai, 1931; rpt. Taipei, 1964. This work is a collection of all the most important anthologies of San-ch'ü made during the Ming and Ch'ing dynasties, as well as some important studies of the same material.

Sui, Shu-sen 隋樹森, compiler. *Ch'üan Yüan san-ch'ü* 全元散曲, 2v. Peking, 1964. The most comprehensive anthology devoted specifically to the lyric poetry of Yüan writers.

Yang, Chia-lo 楊家駱, compiler. *Ch'üan Yüan tsa-chü* 全元雜劇. 32v. Taipei, 1962. The most comprehensive anthology of Yüan dramas ever published; it contains photo-reprints of all the historical editions of Yüan dramas published between 1398 and 1633.

TRANSLATIONS:

Yang, Richard F. S., *et al. Fifty Songs from the Yüan.* London, 1967.
Sunflower, pp. 407-455.

STUDIES:

Cheng, Ch'ien 鄭騫. *Pei-ch'ü hsin pu* 北曲新譜. Taipei, 1973. The tune catalogue nearest to then contemporary standards. A carefully re-searched and well-documented study of northern-style *ch'ü* prosodic formulas, which attempts to resolve the many standing conflicts in formal analysis of Yüan prosody found in the old tune catalogues.

———. *Pei-ch'ü t'ao-shih hui-lu hsiang-chieh* 北曲套式彙錄詳解. Taipei, 1973. An analysis of the sequential structure of the suite form in lyric and verse forms (northern style).

Johnson, Dale R. *Yüan Music Dramas: Studies in Prosody and Structure and a Complete Catalogue of Northern Arias in the Dramatic Style.* Ann Arbor, 1980. The only tune catalogue in a language other than Chinese, and an analysis of the prosody of northern-style *ch'ü* forms.

Li, Tien-k'uei 李殿魁. *Yüan Ming san-ch'ü chih fen-hsi yü yen-chiu* 元明散曲之分析與研究. Taipei, 1965. A study of lyric verse forms in both the southern and northern styles.

Schlepp, Wayne. *San-ch'ü: Its Technique and Imagery.* Madison, Wisconsin, 1970.

—DJ

Ch'ü Yüan 屈原 (*tzu*, Ling-chün 靈均, 340?-278 B.C.) is the reputed author of the major poems in the *Ch'u-tz'u** anthology and one of the best-known names in traditional Chinese culture. Wang I 王逸 (d. A.D. 158), the compiler of the *Ch'u-tz'u*, attributes the authorship of the first seven works in the collection to Ch'ü Yüan: "Li sao" (Encountering Sorrow), the "Chiu ko" (Nine Songs), the "T'ien-wen" (Heavenly Questions), the "Chiu chang" (Nine Declarations), the "Yüan-yu" (Distant Journey), "Pu-chü" (Divination), and the "Yü-fu" (Fisherman). It is highly unlikely that Ch'ü Yüan, or any other single individual, actually composed all these texts.

The only source for the life of Ch'ü Yüan is the biography in the *Shih-chi** by Ssu-ma Ch'ien.* The main outlines of this biography are as follows: Ch'ü Yüan was a member of the royal house of Ch'u, who was in the service of King Huai (r. 328-299 B.C.). His talent drew the envy of another high-ranking retainer who tried to take credit for his work. When Ch'ü Yüan refused to allow this, the retainer slandered him to the king, claiming Ch'ü was vain and boastful. The king believed this slander and grew distant; Ch'ü Yüan com-posed the "Li sao" as a remonstrance and as evidence of his loyalty. But the king's greed and his inability to distinguish loyal from disloyal retainers drew him into disastrous foreign ventures. He died abroad, a captive of the foreign state of Ch'in. Ssu-ma Ch'ien comments, "This was the fatal result of being unable to judge peoples' characters." The king's eldest son inherited the throne but proved to be as deluded as his father, trusting in even worse advisors. When Ch'ü Yüan refused to discontinue his criticism, the new king banished him to the distant South. As a sign of protest, Ch'ü Yüan committed suicide by drowning himself in the Mi-lo River. A half century later, Ch'u was finally destroyed by Ch'in.

The key motifs in this biography are the integrity of Ch'ü Yüan, his talent, the slander by his opponents, the opacity of his sovereign, Ch'ü's refusal to discontinue criticism, his exile, and suicide. Wang I and later critics have read these motifs into the texts of the *Ch'u-tz'u* to such a degree that it is difficult to extricate fact from legend and imagination.

Nevertheless, there is no doubt that these motifs and the powerful literary impact of the "Li sao" combined to keep the Ch'ü Yüan legend alive in the minds of Chinese intellectuals, who so often found themselves faced with political difficulties similar to those the legendary Ch'ü Yüan had confronted. He had become already by Han times the exemplar of Confucian resistance to the often oppressive and arbitrary power of the state—a figure to identify with, to lament with, and, if need be, to die with.

STUDIES:

Hawkes, *Ch'u Tz'u.* Besides a complete translation, contains much of interest on Ch'ü Yüan.

Hightower, James R. "Ch'ü Yüan Studies," in *Silver Jubilee,* R pp. 192-223.

Schneider, Laurence A. *A Madman of Ch'u. The Chinese Myth of Loyalty and Dissent.* Berkeley, 1980. A fascinating study of Ch'ü Yüan in history and myth from ancient times to the present; has an excellent bibliography.

—CH

Chuan-tz'u 賺詞 was a musical form practiced in the entertainment quarters of Hangchow in Southern Sung. The formal structure of the suites was derived from the *ch'an-ling* 纏令 and *ch'an-ta* 纏達 of the Northern Sung. The *ch'an-ling* consists of one or more songs preceded by an introduction and concluded by a coda. The *ch'an-ta* was the same form, except that two songs repeated alternately after the introduction. These suites were different from previous suites of *tz'u* music, in that one could use different tunes of the same mode in a single suite. In early suites, the *tz'u* song was simply repeated with a variation in tempo (see *ta-ch'ü, ku-tzu-tz'u*).

A characteristic of *chuan-tz'u* is that the last air sung in the suite is one called "chuan" 賺. This air was created by the artist Chang Wu-niu 張五牛 in the Shaohsing 紹興 period (1131-1162), according to the *Meng-liang lu* (see *Tung-ching meng Hua lu*). Li Shuang-ya 李霜涯 was known as the most famous *chuan-tz'u* composer. *Chuan* suites were originally used for narrative performances, the subjects of which included love and war.

In Hangchow there also existed an amateur society of *chuan-tz'u* singers known as "The Cloud-stopping Society" 遏雲社. They developed a set of principles concerning the modes of performance of *chuan* singing known as "The Cloud-stopping Society's Rules of Thumb." The rules themselves, which can be found in the Yüandynasty popular encyclopedia, *Shih-lin kuang-chi* 事林廣記, are the only examples of the organization and arrangement of *chuan* music.

According to contemporary records, a *chuan* singer had to be well versed in the various vocal styles currently in use, such as the *ta-ch'ü** and other songs. The rules also stipulate precise articulation, correct vocal style, and a sonorous voice as prerequisites for a good singer.

EDITIONS:
Chen, Yüan-ching 陳元靚, comp. *Shih-lin kuang-chi.* Peking, 1963 (reprint of original woodblock ed. dated 1322).

STUDIES:
Feng, Yüan-chün 馮沅君. "Shuo chuan-tz'u" 說賺詞 and "Shuo *chuan-tz'u* pa" 說賺詞跋, in *Ku-chü shou-hui* 古劇說彙. Shanghai, 1947, pp. 117-156.
Josephs, H. K. "The Chanda: A Sung Dynasty Entertainment," *TP,* 62 (1976), 167-198.
West, *Vaudeville,* pp. 69-73.
Yang, Yin-liu 楊蔭瀏. *Chung-kuo ku-tai yin-yüeh shih-kao* 中國古代音樂史稿, v. 1, Peking, 1981, pp. 303-310, 326.

—CHu

Ch'uan-ch'i 傳奇 (romance) drama is the designation used for the corpus of several hundred "southern-style" plays of the Ming and Ch'ing periods. The term *ch'uan-ch'i,* "romance" (literally, "transmission of the remarkable"), was originally applied to certain short stories written in the classical language during the T'ang and Sung periods (see *ch'uan-ch'i* [tale]). The plots of numerous later *ch'uan-ch'i* plays were based on these early stories. Three anonymous "southern" plays preserved in the fifteenth-century encyclopedia *Yung-lo ta-tien* probably date from before the Yüan dynasty, whose leading playwrights favored the "northern-style" *tsa-chü** drama. *Ch'uan-ch'i* competed with *tsa-chü* for popularity in the early decades of the Ming dynasty and came to dominate the Chinese stage for fully two hundred years until the middle of the Ch'ing.

In comparison with *tsa-chü,* the music of *ch'uan-ch'i* seems to have been softer and more langorous, and the musical conventions are much less restrictive. All roletypes may sing, and there are arias for duet or trio singing and for chorus. Aria patterns may be repeated, often through three or four stanzas, and refrains are used. The song-set formed by a suite of arias within a scene is normally shorter than in the *tsachü,* and the variety of song-sets is greater. Musical modes may change in mid-scene, as may rhyme, and northern patterns may be used, either exclusively or in alternation with southern. Instruments used in *ch'uan-ch'i* were flute and samisen for accompaniment, drums and clappers for rhythm, and a variety of gongs and cymbals for entrances and exits, climactic moments, and martial effects.

The title of a *ch'uan-ch'i* play often indicates an object (jade hairpin, musical instrument, or the like) which plays an emblematic part in the action. There are usually between thirty and forty scenes, each with its own title, normally a bisyllabic verb-object phrase crystallizing the action. A single scene presents one, two, or a small group of characters in a specific location. Absence of sets makes possible radical shifts of locale from one scene to the next. It is rare for a scene to consist entirely of dialogue. Customarily, a single character will open the scene with an aria, which is followed by a recited entrance-verse and only then by a prose self-introduction. Scenes may be transitional (i.e., chiefly of narrative interest), comic, martial major or grand (numerous singers, and often set at court or in similar circumstances requiring elaborate costume). The first scene, often called *chia-men* 家門, is a prologue briefly outlining the action to follow. Scene two normally introduces the hero (*sheng* 生) and his circumstances, scene three the heroine (*tan* 旦) and her family (father, *wai* 外, and mother, *lao-tan* 老旦), often celebrating a birthday or festival with a garden feast. Other common role-types are *mo* 末 for older males, *t'ieh* 貼 for the maid-servant-confidante, *ching* 淨 for "heavy" characters (general, treacherous minister, heroine's boorish brother), and *ch'ou* 丑 for a wide variety of clownish, low-life characters. Stock comic characters bear considerable resemblance to those of the European tradition. They include the pedantic tutor and the venal, incompetent physician (these are usually *mo* roles), the *miles gloriosus*, and the amorous monk or nun. Role-types are distinguished in performance by makeup (the *ching* roles are especially elaborate) as well as by gait and costume. Since each major step in the action must be represented by a scene, and since plots bear a strong family resemblance, it follows that there will be stock scenes as well as stock characters. The hero's leave-taking of his mother or wife as he departs for the examinations in the capital provides a frequently encountered "major" scene, as do his observation of the landscape en route (transitional scene) and the examination scene itself (usually comic).

The first *ch'uan-ch'i* play to win national renown was Kao Ming's* *P'i-p'a-chi*, at the close of the Yüan period. *P'i-p'a-chi* treats domestic themes in a serious, even tragic manner: a scholar wins honors in the capital but permits his aged parents to die in a famine in their village. He is brought to realize and repent of this neglect by his devoted first wife, who seeks him out in the luxurious home made for him by his second wife, the Chief Minister's daughter. Numerous subsequent *ch'uan-ch'i* romances played variations on these themes. Of the four major plays of the early Ming period (see *Ssu-ta ch'uan-ch'i*), *Ching-ch'ai-chi* 荊釵記 copies the *P'i-p'a-chi* plot quite closely, and *Pai-t'u-chi* 白兔記, though its hero is the warrior-dynast Liu Chih-yan, has a heroine quite similar to the first wife in *P'i-p'a-chi*. *Pai-yeh-t'ing* 拜月亭 (also known as *Yu-kuei-chi* 幽閨記) and *Sha-kou-chi* 殺狗記 are the remaining two of these rather crude early plots (none of the four matches *P'i-p'a-chi* in quality); the stories of both are found also in Yüan *tsa-chü* versions.

From approximately 1550 to 1700 the writing of *ch'uan-ch'i* plays was a favorite occupation of leading men of letters, although plays were written also by the more humble managers of acting companies and by impecunious hacks. The reading of plays became a vogue, and fine illustrated editions were put out by the booksellers of Chiang-nan. *Huan-sha-chi* 浣紗記, by Liang Ch'en-yü,* was the first play to use the music of the K'un-shan Style, and set the vogue for *K'un-ch'ü*,* admired by connoisseurs to the present day. K'un-shan is near Soochow, the major center of drama (with Nanking) during the seventeenth and eighteenth centuries. *Huan-sha-chi* retells the well-known story of the rivalry between Wu and Yüeh in Warring States times, the seduction of the king of Wu by the beautiful Hsi Shih, and the sad fate of the loyal adviser and stern avenger Wu Tzu-hsü. The language of the play is free of the coarseness of the early *ch'uan-ch'i*, though at some sacrifice of naturalness (much of the dialogue is in parallel prose). Critics regard stilted dialogue as a major defect of *ch'uan-ch'i* plays, which frequently assign to servants dialogue rivaling that of their masters in elegance and erudition. But instances of the lively, realistic diction which is characteristic of the earlier theater may be found in plays of all periods. Another source of critical dissatisfaction is the "happy ending": the concluding scene often bears the title *t'uan-yüan* 團圓 or its equivalent. Some of the superior specimens of the genre, however, including *Huan-sha-chi* itself, end on a note of considerable ambiguity.

A pair of lovers is at the center of the plot of virtually every *ch'uan-ch'i* play, even when the major theme is recent politics, as in *Ming-feng-chi* 鳴鳳記 (which concerns the tyrannous excesses of the Grand Councilor Yen Sung), or a satire on place-seeking rogues built around a fable from Mencius (*Tung-kuo-chi* 東郭記), or a murder mystery (*Shih-wu-kuan* 十五貫). Leading Ming dramatists of the genre include Li K'ai-hsien,* author of *Pao-chien-chi* 寶劍記, on a *Shui-hu chuan** theme; T'ang Hsien-tsu,* whose "four dreams" include the masterpiece of the genre, *Mu-tan-t'ing* 牡丹亭; and Juan Ta-ch'eng,* whose *Yen-tzu-chien* 燕子箋 is a stylish treatment of the eternal triangle theme. In the early Ch'ing period Li Yü* (1611-1680) won popularity with plays like *Feng-cheng-wu* 風箏課; K'ung Shang-jen* movingly lamented the collapse of the Ming dynasty in his historical play *T'ao-hua-shan* 桃花扇; and Ch'en Hung 陳鴻 in his *Ch'ang-sheng-tien* 長生殿 presented the most fully developed treatment of the legendary love between Yang Kuei-fei and the T'ang Emperor Hsüan-tsung. Major contemporary works of criticism included *Nan-ts'u hsü-lu* 南詞敍錄, by Hsü Wei*; the *Ch'ü-p'u* 曲譜 of Lü T'ien-ch'eng 呂天成 (*c.* 1573-*c.* 1619); and *Hsien-ch'ing ou-chi* 閒情偶記, by Li Yü.

More successfully than any later form of Chinese theater, *ch'uan-ch'i* romances brought text, music, and stage technique into a harmonious balance. Many *ch'uan-ch'i* arias are comparable in lyric quality

with the best of Yüan *tsa-chü*, and far above *Ching-chü** (Peking Opera) standards. The rather stereotyped plots of the plays (which rely heavily on such devices as mistaken identities and reunions with long-lost relatives) proclaim moral values central to Chinese tradition: loyalty to prince or to parent, integrity between friends, faithfulness to one's origins. There is a strong strain of sympathy for women (cloistered maidens, neglected wives) and for the young, though parents (especially fathers) are seldom ridiculed or placed in the villain's role. This is reserved for the corrupt official, the tyrannous general, the boorish merchant, or the shrew.

Ch'uan-ch'i plays were performed both by professional companies and by household troupes, recruited from the ranks of servants and sometimes joined by amateurs of gentry status. The basic requirement, in addition to a small orchestra, was a red carpet, which might be laid in a garden pavilion or (at the village level) on a temporary stage erected by the gate of a temple. Complete performance of a *ch'uan-ch'i* play would usually need to be spread over two or three days, and by the Ch'ien-lung period was becoming a rarity. Single scenes, however, continue to be performed to the present day, and many plays of the Peking Opera stem from these "che-tzu hsi" 折子戲. The rise of Peking Opera in the late eighteenth century, followed by the havoc wrought in the homeland of "southern" drama by the T'ai-p'ing Rebellion in the mid-nineteenth century, ended the *ch'uan-ch'i*'s long occupation of the Chinese stage.

EDITIONS:
The most easily accessible major collection of *ch'uan-ch'i* texts is *Liu-shih chung ch'ü* 六十種曲, edited by Mao Chin 毛晉 (1599-1659) and first printed in the late years of the Ming dynasty. A modern reprint by K'ai-ming shu-tien, in six cases, was issued in 1935, and was the basis for 12-volume editions by Wen-hsüeh ku-chi k'an-hsing-she, Shanghai, 1955, and Chung-hua shu-chü, Taipei, 1958. With the exception of the *tsa-chü Hsi-hsiang-chi* 西廂記, listed as *Pei Hsi-hsiang* 北西廂, the contents represent *ch'uan-ch'i* plays from the late-Yüan to the late-Ming. They

355

include *P'i-p'a chi*, the "four great plays" of early Ming (*Yu-kuei-chi* or *Pai-yüeh-t'ing*, *Ching-ch'ai-chi*, *Pai-t'u-chi*, and *Sha-kou-chi*), *Huan-sha-chi* which is the earliest play in *K'un-ch'ü** style, the "four dreams" of T'ang Hsien-tsu (*Mu-tan-t'ing*, *Tzu-ch'ai-chi*, *Han-tan-chi* 邯鄲記, *Nan-k'e-chi*) and other celebrated plays. The texts used are not always the most authoritative, however, especially for the earliest plays.

Nine series of reproduced dramatic texts were projected in the nineteen-fifties under the general title *Ku-pen hsi-ch'ü ts'ung-k'an* 古本戲曲叢刊. The first, second and third series (Shanghai, Commerical Press, 1954 and 1955, and Wen-hsüeh ku-chi k'an-hsing-she, 1957, respectively) all comprise early editions of *ch'uan-ch'i* plays. The fourth series (Shanghai, Commercial Press, 1958) contains Yüan-Ming *tsa-chü*, the ninth series (Shanghai, Chung-hua shu-chü, 1964) contains Peking Opera texts. Series five through eight have not appeared.

Good modern editions of individual plays include a number made by Wang Chi-ssu 王季思 and the Chinese Department of Chung-shan University, 1959 onwards: *Ching-ch'ai-chi*, *Pai-t'u-chi*, *Sha-kou-chi*, *Ming-feng-chi* 鳴鳳記, *Tung-kuo-chi* 東郭記 and other Ming *ch'uan-ch'i*. An edition of *P'i-p'a-chi* annotated by Ch'ien Chi 錢箕 was published in 1960 by Chung-hua shu-chü, Shanghai. The most fully annotated edition of *Mu-tan-t'ing* is by Hsü Shuo-fang 徐朔方 and Yang Hsiao-mei 楊笑梅, published by Jen-min wen-hsüeh, 1963. The two most celebrated Ch'ing *ch'uan-ch'i* are Hung Sheng's* *Ch'ang-sheng-tien* 長生殿 (edition by Hsü Shuo-fang, Jen-min wen-hsüeh, 1958) and K'ung Shang-jen's *T'ao-hua-shan* (edition by Wang Chi-ssu, Jen-min wen-hsüeh, 1958).

For more information, see Fu Hsi-hua 傅惜華, *Ming-tai ch'uan-ch'i ch'üan mu* 明代傳奇全目, Peking, 1959.

ANTHOLOGIES:

Chao, Chin-shen 趙景深 and Hu Chi 胡忌, compilers. *Ming Ch'ing ch'uan-ch'i hsüan* 明清傳奇選. Peking, 1981.

TRANSLATIONS:

Birch, Cyril. *The Peony Pavilion.* Bloomington, 1980.

Chen, Shih-hsiang and Harold Acton. *The Peach Blossom Fan.* Berkeley, 1976.

Huang, Josephine Hung. *Ming Drama.* Taipei, 1966.

Mulligan, Jean. *The Lute.* New York, 1980.

Yang, Hsien-yi and Gladys Yang. *The Palace of Eternal Youth.* Peking, 1955.

—CB

Ch'uan-ch'i 傳奇 (tale) is a form of classical-language fiction which arose during the T'ang dynasty. The tales are short pieces of approximately 350 to 3500 characters, disciplined in both form and style. Their subject matter reflects a fundamental interest in human character: when something, possibly on the unusual side, happens to someone, how does he react? The term *ch'uan-ch'i* was first used by P'ei Hsing 裴鉶 (825-880) as a title for a collection of his short fiction. It came into use as a generic term during the Sung dynasty.

The *ch'uan-ch'i* form includes a stylized opening sentence that gives names, dates, and places. It commonly also makes use of an introduction and a closing frame that lie outside the main plot structure. The plot itself is often loosely constructed. Viewpoint, scene, or time may shift abruptly. For short pieces, the definition of relevant material is broad. The several incidents of a plot may receive approximately equal treatment with the effect that the tales are evenly and somewhat slowly paced.

The tales are characterized by a particular narrative method. The narrator views characters largely from the outside. He suggests their feelings or thoughts through the action, or more directly through the use of dialogue, but he rarely moves into their minds. The narrator confines his own ideas and judgments to the introduction or closing; it is unusual for him to intrude into the narrative itself. He makes little use of descriptions or summaries in which his interpretations would be evident. The viewpoint of the narrator moves very little from that of an objective observer and recorder.

This narrative method makes a strong implicit claim for the truthfulness of the tale. In many tales the narrator in his introduction or closing directly avows his tale's truthfulness, or, at the very least, the minimal hand he has had in shaping it. Documentary evidence may be included to bolster these claims. There is a strong expectation in all tales that they will contain reference to an apparently verifiable source.

The tales make use of a common, if ill-defined, narrative persona. His most important characteristics are his detachment and his self-conscious literary intent. The tone of the tales is frequently humorous. Even those most passionately meant are presented in a faintly detached manner. Themes are played with, references made to other literary traditions. The style is polished, with careful attention paid to formal conventions. The narrator clothes himself in the guise of a lower-level member of the official class. Literary, scholarly, and philosophical interests also touch the tales. Their sympathy lies with young and aspiring officials or with those who have withdrawn from the official life, not with successful, highly placed officials.

The range of both characters and plot patterns is relatively limited, so much so as to be one of the essential characteristics of the form. Characters are portrayed as variations within a category: young official, beautiful woman, eccentric old man, brash aristocrat. The common themes of Chinese narrative provide the content: loyalty, obligation, and friendship. There is a strong expectation of completeness in the plots, reflecting moral predilections. The good should triumph—lovers parted by cruel forces will be reunited, the minister wronged by slander is vindicated. Within these confines subtle variations are tried, and the tales often make their points by disappointing expectations.

The tales can be said to fall into two broad types, the polished anecdote and the tale proper. The polished anecdote is distinguished from the tale by its length (under 900 characters) and its one-incident plot, which very often has to do with an encounter with the supernatural. Patterns involving moral themes of wrongs made right do not appear in this group. The tale proper, then, consists of those pieces which are generally longer than 900 characters, frequently encompass more than one incident, and contain moral overtones.

The antecedents of T'ang ch'uan-ch'i lie primarily in the Six Dynasties chih-kuai.*

In range of subject matter, particularly, the two forms are similar, although the emphasis of ch'uan-ch'i is more on human motivations and on the exemplary side of human nature. More characters in ch'uan-ch'i fall into the lower official class, with less attention to eccentric or aristocratic types. The supernatural element appears frequently in both kinds of fiction. However, in ch'uan-ch'i the supernatural plays merely a supporting role. Its presence has become part of the conventions of the genre, the expectation of proof of its reality part of the conventional movement of the plots. In addition to being less central, the supernatural is less powerful, less arbitrary and arrogant, more benevolent and accessible in its relationship with humans. Thus in the liaison between human male and supernatural female, the female is likely to hide her divinity and approach the male in human shape. She is herself subject to human feelings. Likewise, the relationship is normally fulfilling in the T'ang tale, even if doomed to transience.

The form and style of all fictional narrative in T'ang and post-T'ang China bears a relationship to the writing of historical narrative, where the techniques for telling a story in writing were first developed. Thus the conventional opening sentences citing historical names, dates, and places in ch'uan-ch'i echo not simply orthodox historical literature, but other miscellaneous types of writing. Most of these forms also have in common the narrator who documents his material with verifiable sources and the basic method of terse narration, emphasizing action and using scenes built around and elaborated by segments of dialogue. However, ch'uan-ch'i draws more fully and consistently on historical biographies than did other fictional genres before it. The centrality of the themes of the motivations of character and the goodness of human nature and the strong expectation of narrative judgment suggest this debt.

Ch'uan-ch'i also draw from the realm of poetry. While the narrator of ch'uan-ch'i rarely moves very far from the position of objective observer, still he does move. He will sometimes follow one character's viewpoint closely. In T'ang *ch'uan-ch'i* the use of the first person makes its initial appearance in Chinese fiction. These points suggest a debt to the lyricism of poetry. T'ang love tales particularly draw on both contemporary and earlier love poetry in vocabulary and theme.

Thus *ch'uan-ch'i* are not a simple extension of the *chih-kuai* tradition or imitation historical biography, but a new genre. Their didacticism—a characteristic of both *chih-kuai* and historical biography—has been tempered by individual insight and personal feeling. Each tale is grounded in an individual author's perceptions about a specific circumstance. The tales have been written to be expressive, not broadly conformative. They are enlivened by wit and curiosity, intended to divert as much as to persuade. A new genre has been created which is more seriously literary than *chih-kuai* and more personally expressive.

The development of *ch'uan-ch'i* during the T'ang falls into two distinct periods dividing at about 830. The first period is characterized by experimentation. Early tales contain more variations in form and style than the later ones. Tales experiment with language ("Yu-hsien k'u"—see Chang Cho), their interrelationship with poetry ("Ch'ang-hen-ko chuan"—see Po Chü-i), narrative technique ("Huo Hsiao-yü chuan" 霍小玉傳), or plot structure ("San-meng chi"—see Po Hsing-chien). Their ties to other generic traditions are obvious and appear to be part of the experimentation, a desire to try something different to see whether it works. One experiment was in the use of the dramatized narrator drawn from *chih-kuai* and historical biography, which appears almost without exception in those tales known to be of an early date. His presence is important in these early works. The expectation for an appended judgment (echoing historical biography) is particularly strong. At the same time, there is a tendency for the explicit narrative judgment to conflict with the underlying thrust of a tale. On the average, the earlier tales are longer than later ones. Their plots are more static, with less forward drive.

They are more likely to take an atmosphere, a personality ("Jen-shih chuan" 任氏傳), or an idea as their central purpose. A number of the early tales are quite intensely personal ("Ying-ying chuan"—see Yüan Chen), unlike the later tales.

By the later period (after 830), the form of *ch'uan-ch'i* became standardized. There are fewer variations in length, and tales were generally shorter. More of the briefer, polished anecdotes were written. In general, the ties to traditions of poetry, history, and *chih-kuai* writing have become less obvious. These genres served their purpose in shaping *ch'uan-ch'i* but were by this time assimilated or abandoned. In consequence plot development took on added importance. Tales move more smoothly to their conclusion with less digressive material intervening to slow them down. There is much less use of a dramatized narrator. The same basic characteristics of narrative form, style, and judgment are employed but are made less explicit. The presentation of the narrator has been subtly adapted, and he has become more complex and worldly in his judgments. At the same time, the tales are less personal and intense. Thus the conflict found in the early tales between the traditional objective narrator and the personal intensity of the story has been resolved. There are now fewer disjunctions between the stated narrative judgment and the thrust of the tale.

The tales themselves suggest their relation to T'ang society. Like poems they were written to be shared with friends. Sometimes they appear to be later renditions of stories told in gatherings of officials, gatherings that were an important part of the life and unity of that class. Although the names of a few writers are reasonably well known—Yüan Chen,* Shen Chi-chi,* Li Kung-tso*—they are generally obscure men about whom little is known. A number were, as might be expected, lower-level officials, in some cases employed as historians. Moreover, the tales arose in importance at about the same time as the *ku-wen** movement. Their initial development is part of the flowering of prose writing in a direct, simple style which flourished in the period 780-820. The interest of Han Yü,* Tu Mu* and Liu Tsung-yüan* in *ch'uan-ch'i* suggests the involvement of scholars who advocated *ku-wen* in the development of this form.

T'ang *ch'uan-ch'i* had a lasting effect on the literature of later dynasties. Themes developed in *ch'uan-ch'i* became important sources for colloquial fiction, both short and long, and for drama; notably influential were "Ying-ying chuan," "Li Wa chuan" (see Po Hsing-chien), "Liu I" 柳毅, and "Chen-chung chi" (see Shen Chi-chi). Short, classical-language fiction also continued to be written in later dynasties, some of it titled *ch'uan-ch'i*. However, the form seems to have become less disciplined after the T'ang and was eclipsed by the rise of the colloquial story in the late Sung.

EDITIONS:

Chang, Yu-hao   . *T'ang Sung ch'uan-ch'i hsüan* 唐宋傳奇選. Peking, 1979.

Hsin-hsing shu-chü 新興書局, ed. *T'ai-p'ing kuang-chi*. 3v. 1753; rpt. Taipei, 1973. Source of most T'ang *ch'uan-ch'i*.

Li, Hua-ch'ing 李華卿, ed. *Sung-jen hsiao-shuo* 宋人小說. Shanghai, 1940.

Lu, Hsün 魯迅, ed. *T'ang Sung ch'uan-ch'i chi* 唐宋傳奇集. 1927; rpt. Hong Kong, 1959.

Wang, Meng-ou 王夢鷗, ed. *T'ang-jen hsiao-shuo yen-chiu* 唐人小說研究. 3v. Taipei, 1971-78.

Wang, Pi-chiang 汪辟疆, ed. *T'ang-jen hsiao-shuo* 唐人小說. 1936; various rpts. Best and most accessible edition of the better known *ch'uan-ch'i*.

TRANSLATIONS:

Chang, H. C. *Chinese Literature: Volume III: Tales of the Supernatural.* New York, 1983. Translations of *ch'uan-ch'i* from the T'ang, Sung and Ch'ing (P'u Sung-ling) eras.

Edwards, E. D. *Chinese Prose Literature.* 2v. London, 1938. Translates large portions of *T'ang-tai ts'ung-shu* 唐代叢書, with discussion.

Ma, Y. W. and Joseph S. M. Lau, eds. *Traditional Chinese Stories, Themes and Variations.* New York, 1978. Over a dozen *ch'uan-ch'i* renderings with excellent front and back matter.

Maeno, Naoaki 前野直彬. *Tōdai denkishū* 唐代傳奇集, v. 1. Tokyo, 1963.

STUDIES:

Adkins, Curtis P. "The Hero in T'ang *Ch'uan-ch'i* Tales," in *Chinese Fiction*, pp. 17-46.

———. "The Supernatural in T'ang *Ch'uan-ch'i* Tales: An Archetypal View." Unpublished Ph.D. dissertation, Ohio State University, 1976.

Chang, Ch'ang-kung 張長弓. *T'ang Sung ch'uan-ch'i tso-che chi ch'i shih-tai* 唐宋傳奇作者及其時代. Peking, 1951.

Chang, Han-liang. "Towards a Structural Generic Theory of T'ang *Ch'uan-ch'i*," in *Chinese-Western Comparative Literature: Theory and Strategy*, John L. Deeney, ed., Hong Kong, 1980, pp. 25-49.

Ch'en, Yin-k'o 陳寅恪. "Han Yü and the T'ang Novel," *HJAS*, 1 (1936), 39-43.

Chu, Hsiu-hsia 祝秀俠. *T'ang-tai ch'uan-ch'i yen-chiu* 唐代傳奇研究. Taipei, 1957.

Hung, Wen-chen 洪文珍. *T'ang ch'uan-ch'i yen-chiu* 唐傳奇研究. Taipei, 1973.

Kan, T. H. "The Rise of T'ang Ch'uan-ch'i and Its Narrative Art." Unpublished Ph.D. dissertation, Cornell University, 1979.

Knechtges, David. "Dream Adventure Stories in Europe and T'ang China." *TkR*, 4.2 (October 1973), 101-119.

Kondō, Haruo 近藤春雄. *Tōdai shōsetsu no kenkyū* 唐代小說の研究. Tokyo, 1978.

Li, Wen-pin 李文彬. "The Dusty Crown: An Intrinsic Study of the T'ang Ch'uan-ch'i." Unpublished M.A. thesis, National Taiwan University, 1972.

Li, Yao-chung, "Against Culture: Problematic Love in Early European and Chinese Narrative Fiction." Unpublished Ph.D. dissertation, Columbia University, 1980.

Liu, K'ai-jung 劉開榮. *T'ang-tai hsiao-shuo yen-chiu* 唐代小說研究.

Ma, Y. W. "Fact and Fantasy in T'ang Tales, *CLEAR*, 2.2 (July 1980), 167-181.

Nienhauser, William H., Jr. "A Structural Reading of the *chuan* in the *Wen-yüan ying-hua*," *JAS*, 36.3 (May 1977), 443-456.

———. "Some Preliminary Remarks on Fiction, the Classical Tradition and Society in Late Ninth-century China," in *Chinese Fiction*, pp. 1-16.

So, Francis. "The Romantic Structure: A Rhetorical Approach to *Ch'uan-chi* and Middle English Tales." Ph.D. dissertation, University of Washington, 1979.

Uchiyama, Chinari 內山知也. *Zui Tō shōsetsu kenkyū* 隋唐小說研究. Tokyo, 1977.

Wang, Meng-ou 王夢鷗. *T'ang-jen.* 4v. 1971-78. Along with a large number of excellent studies on individual stories and on several collections of stories, these four volumes pro-

359

vide us with superb collated versions of P'ei Hsing's *Ch'uan-ch'i*, Li Mei's 李玫 (*fl.* 827) *Tsüan-i chi* 纂異記, Ch'en Han's 陳翰 (*fl.* 874) *I-wen chi* 異聞集, and Meng Ch'i's 孟棨 (*fl.* 876) *Pen-shih shih* 本事詩.

Wong, Timothy C. "Self and Society in T'ang Dynasty Love Tales," *JAOS*, 99.1 (1979), 95-100.

—SY

Ch'üan Chin-shih 全金詩 (The Complete Chin Poetry), was compiled and edited by Kuo Yüan-yü 郭元釪 during the reign of Emperor K'ang-hsi (r. 1662-1722). It is based on the earlier *Chung-chou chi* 中州集 (A Collection of the Central Region) compiled by Yüan Hao-wen,* a well-known Chin literary figure. Kuo praised the selections in the *Chung-chou chi* but noted that the biographical sketches provided by Yüan Hao-wen sometimes contradicted contemporary sources and that the entries could be improved. Kuo combed through literary collections of Chin and Yüan writers, historical records, local gazetteers, and other materials, and expanded the original collection into the *Ch'üan Chin-shih*, which is also known as *Ch'üan Chin-shih tseng-pu Chung-chou chi* 全金詩增補中州集 (The Complete Chin Poetry—A Supplement to the *Chung-chou chi*).

In order to differentiate his later additions from the original materials in the *Chung-chou chi*, Kuo labeled information of primary importance (mostly biographical data about the poets) as *pu* 補 (supplements) and sources of secondary importance as *fu* 附 (appendices). While most of the supplements are taken from either Liu Chi's 劉祁 (1203-1250) *Kuei-ch'ien chih* 歸潛志 (Memoirs from Retirement), a Chin literatus' personal notes on Chin-dynasty affairs, or the official dynastic history, *Chin-shih* 金史 (The History of the Chin Dynasty), the appendices are quotations from more than one hundred different works.

After completing the *Ch'üan Chin-shih*, Kuo presented it to Emperor K'ang-hsi who, knowing that the official Chin history relied heavily on Yüan Hao-wen's *Chung-chou chi*, had himself felt that the gathering of more accounts about Chin poetry would correct the insufficiencies of the *Chin-shih*.

The emperor ordered Kuo to carry out more research and further expand the *Ch'üan Chin-shih*. The result is the present *Ch'üan Chin-shih*, known as the *Yü-ting* 御訂 (Imperial Edition), with a preface by the emperor dated 1711. While Yüan Hao-wen's *Chung-chou chi* in 10 *chüan* included 2,062 poems by 249 poets, the *Ch'üan Chin-shih* added 3,562 poems by 112 poets for a total of 5,624 poems by 361 poets. To see the usefulness of the expanded *Complete Chin Poetry*, compare the entries for Chao Ping-wen,* a prominent Chin literatus: Yüan included only 63 poems by Chao; Kuo added 535 more of Chao's poems to the *Ch'üan Chin-shih*.

Despite its comprehensiveness the *Ch'üan Chin-shih* suffers from an overall lack of quality; poems of different style and artistic standards are indiscriminately intermingled. Furthermore, in contrast to the *Chung-chou chi*, which has no particular subject categories of poets except in *chüan* nine and ten, all the poets in the *Ch'üan Chin-shih* are categorized into such groups as "Emperors," "Famous Writers," "Taoists and Buddhists" and "Unusual Personages." The largest group is "Miscellaneous Writers," which includes 235 poets. The smallest category, "Retired Virtuous People," has only one representative. The categorization seems unwieldy. Several categories, such as "Taoists and Buddhists" and "Banquet Poetry at the Hai-hui Temple 海會寺," are Kuo's later additions.

The *Ch'üan Chin-shih* calls itself "complete," and the section "Taoists and Buddhists" does include the Taoists Wang Chi 王嚞 (1113-1170) and T'an Ch'u-tuan 譚處端 (1123-1185). In fact, poems by Chin Taoists in the *Ch'üan Chin-shih* constitute a mere fraction of the large body of such works preserved in the *Tao-tsang*.* Nevertheless, the *Ch'üan Chin-shih* is still the most important extant collection and description of Chin poetry.

EDITIONS:

Kuo, Yüan-yü. *Ch'üan Chin-shih* (also known as *Yü-ting Ch'üan Chin-shih*). 2v. Photolithographic reprint of the 1711 edition, Taipei, 1968. This is the most readily available edition.

STUDIES:

Chan, Hok-lam. *The Historiography of the Chin Dynasty: Three Studies.* Wiesbaden, 1970, pp. 88-92.

—TCY

Ch'üan Han San-kuo Chin Nan-pei-ch'ao shih 全漢三國晉南北朝詩 (Complete Poetry of the Han, Three Kingdoms, Chin, and Northern and Southern Dynasties) is a comprehensive anthology of poetry composed during the period 206 B.C.- A.D. 618. It was compiled by the physician and polymath Ting Fu-pao 丁福保 (from Wu-hsi 無錫, Kiangsu, 1874-1952) and first published in 1916. Altogether it comprises 54 *chüan*, distributed as follows: Han 漢 (5), Three Kingdoms 三國 (6), Chin 晉 (8), Sung 宋 (5), Ch'i 齊 (4), Liang 梁 (14), Ch'en 陳 (4), Northern Wei 北魏 (1), Northern Ch'i 北齊(1), Northern Chou ⹀ (2), and Sui 隋(4). The inclusion of the poetry of the last dynasty suggests that the *Nan-pei-ch'ao* 南北朝 of the title was used somewhat loosely. No doubt Ting, like earlier anthologists, wished to bring his collection up to the point where the *Ch'üan T'ang shih** (Complete Poetry of the T'ang) begins. In each dynastic section the works of each author are grouped together, in chronological order, with certain exceptions: poems by emperors, if any, always come first, followed by the poems of princes, by temple odes, and by military songs. Poems by distinguished ladies are grouped together, as are poems by Buddhist monks and Taoist adepts. The dynastic sections usually end with anonymous poems and popular songs.

The compiler provided biographical notices for each author preceding his or her first poem. These are quite terse, serving to identify the poet and place him in a given reign or period. Sometimes individual poems or groups of poems are also preceded by explanatory material. Normally the sources of the poems are not given, though these can often be inferred from the numerous notes which address variant readings in both the titles and the poems themselves.

The extensive preface discusses many of the problems involved in assembling a complete anthology for a long period so distant in time, including poems lost or imperfectly preserved, wrong or disputed attributions, alternate titles and characters in text, and the like.

Finding a given poem is facilitated by the general table of contents of authors (*tsung-mu* 總目) and by the two indexes to the collection that have been separately published.

EDITIONS:

Ch'üan Han San-kuo Chin Nan-pei-ch'ao shih. Ting Fu-pao, comp. and ed. Wu-hsi, 1916; rpt. Taipei, 1961.

SOURCES:

Ch'ou-yin chü-shih tzu-ting nien-p'u 疇隱居士自訂年譜, in *Fo-hsüeh ta-tz'u-tien* 佛學大辭典, Ting Fu-pao, comp. and ed. Shanghai, 1929.

INDEXES:

Ch'üan Han San-kuo Chin Nan-pei-ch'ao shih tso-che yin-te 全漢三國晉南北朝詩作者引得. Harvard-Yenching Institute Sinological Index Series, No. 39. Peiping, 1941; rpt. Taipei, 1966.

Ch'üan Han San-kuo Chin Nan-pei-ch'ao shih p'ien-ming mu-lu 全漢三國晉南北朝詩篇名目錄. Mei-lan Marney, comp. Taipei, 1971.

—CSG

Ch'üan Shang-ku San-tai Ch'in Han San-kuo Liu-ch'ao wen 全上古三代秦漢三國六朝文 (Complete Prose from High Antiquity, the Three Dynasties, Ch'in, Han, Three Kingdoms, and the Six Dynasties) is a comprehensive anthology of prose literature of all periods before the T'ang dynasty compiled by Yen K'o-chün 嚴可均 (1762-1843), an outstanding philologist and classical scholar of Wu-ch'eng 烏程 (Chekiang). According to the compiler's preface, the work was begun in the fall of 1808. In that year the compilation of the *Ch'üan T'ang wen** was officially begun. Yen was not involved in this enterprise. Considering that pre-T'ang prose deserved to be collected in a similar manner, he undertook to do this as a private task. After nine years a rough draft of the anthology was complete; a further eighteen years were devoted to supplementing and correcting it. The preface makes clear the massive scope of the collection: the prose writings of 3,497 authors are included in the fifteen constituent collections (chi 集), comprising altogether 746 chüan 卷.

The work was not printed during the compiler's lifetime. This was finally accomplished by the Kuang-ya shu-chü 廣雅書局 during the period 1887-93. (This edition lacks the five chüan index of authors' names arranged according to rhyme that was promised by the original table of contents; hence it comprises only 741 chüan. This defect was remedied in 1931 when such an index, in five chüan, was separately published by Min Sun-shih 閔孫奭.)

As the title suggests, the arrangement is chronological, the first of the fifteen collections being entitled Ch'üan Shang-ku San-tai wen 全上古三代文 (Complete Prose of High Antiquity and the Three Dynasties) in sixteen chüan. In succeeding collections the dynastic principle governs regardless of the size of the corpus extant. Thus the Ch'üan Ch'in wen 全秦文 (Complete Prose of the Ch'in) comprises but a single chüan while the Ch'üan Han wen 全漢文 (Complete Prose of the [Former] Han) occupies sixty-three chüan. The fifth collection, Ch'üan San-kuo wen 全三國文 (Complete Prose of the Three Kingdoms) follows the formula laid down in the overall title of the anthology, but the so-called Six Dynasties (Liu-ch'ao 六朝) are actually dealt with differently. The prose literature of Wu 吳 becomes a subsection of the Ch'üan San-kuo wen while Western and Eastern Chin are gathered together into a single unit, Ch'üan Chin wen 全晉文 (Complete Prose of the Chin). This is followed by separate collections not only for Sung 宋, Ch'i 齊, Liang 梁, and Ch'en 陳, but also for the northern dynasties, Hou-Wei 後魏 (Later Wei), Pei-Ch'i 北齊 (Northern Ch'i), and Hou-Chou 後周 (Later Chou). So the Liu-ch'ao (Six Dynasties) of the general title is used rather imprecisely as a cover-name for the period between the Three Kingdoms and the reunification by the Sui 隋. This brings us to a more unexpected anomaly, namely that a Ch'üan Sui wen 全隋文 (Complete Prose of the Sui), not specified in the overall title, is indeed included, as implied by the compiler's pre-face. The anthology ends with a section entitled Hsien-T'ang wen 先唐文 (Pre-T'ang Prose) in one chüan, consisting in works by persons who were known to be of pre-T'ang date, but whose lifetimes could not be assigned to one of the dynastic categories.

Within the various dynastic collections the works of one author are grouped together regardless of form; this makes it fairly easy to locate a given work either through the table of contents (mu-lu 目錄), which introduces each such collection, or by means of one of the author indexes to the complete anthology. The authors are arranged in general in chronological sequence with certain exceptions: each collecton begins with the writings of emperors, followed by those of empresses, and the final chüan of each collection include the works of distinguished women, foreigners, anonymous writers and (especially for the period after the Three Kingdoms) Buddhist priests and Taoist adepts. Brief biographies of the authors were compiled by Chiang Jui 蔣瓛, a younger contemporary and fellow-townsman of Yen K'o-chün, and these precede the first work of a given author in all editions consulted.

An important feature of this anthology is the precision with which Yen K'o-chün specified his source for every work included. The title of the chüan (in the case of the dynastic histories) or its number (in the case of encyclopedias, anthologies, and similar works) is normally provided. Often two or more sources are named. In the cases of inscriptions lacunae are indicated by squares and appropriate notations. Fragments of otherwise lost works are often included. The fu* is considered a sub-category of wen 文 [although in the present work fu is deemed poetry—see fu and the essay on Poetry] and is therefore heavily represented. Surprising, however, is the occasional inclusion of songs, for example, the "Ch'iu-feng tz'u" 秋風辭 (Song of the Autumn Wing) by Emperor Wu of the Han. The early chüan of the first section undoubtedly include much material of doubtful authorship or date, for compositions ascribed to mythical or legendary figures such as T'ai-hao 太昊 and Shen-nung 神農. However, this great anthology is a model of painstaking literary scholarship, as may be seen, for example, in the learned prefatory remarks and the comprehensive list of sources appended to them. The degree of "completeness" promised by the title is awesome in itself, when one considers such things as the number of authors quoted, the meticulous searching out of fragmentary quotations, and the enormous range of literary and epigraphic sources used.

EDITIONS:

Ch'üan Shang-ku San-tai Ch'in Han San-kuo Liu-ch'ao wen. Yen K'o-chün, comp. and ed. Canton, 1887-93.

Ch'üan Shang-ku San-tai Ch'in Han San-kuo Liu-ch'ao wen. Yen K'o-chün, comp. and ed. An edition by Mr. Wang of Huang-kang 黃岡王氏. N.p., 1894. At least two copies of this exist: a facsimile copy to which ms. punctuation had been added (Shanghai, 1930) and an unpunctuated facsimile, Yang Chia-lo 楊家駱, ed., Taipei, 1963.

Ch'üan Shang-ku San-tai Ch'in Han San-kuo Liu-ch'ao wen tso-che so-yin 全上古三代秦漢三國六朝文作者索引. Peking, 1965.

Ch'üan Shang-ku San-tai Ch'in Han San-kuo Liu-ch'ao wen tso-che yin-te 全上古三代秦漢三國六朝文作者引得. Harvard-Yenching Institute Sinological Index Series, No. 8. Peking, 1932; rpt. Taipei, 1966.

STUDIES:

"Yen K'o-chün," in *ECCP*, pp. 910-912.

—CSG

Ch'üan Sung tz'u 全宋詞 is the most complete, authoritative, accurate, and reliable compendium of extant Sung *tz'u* available anywhere and is an indispensable reference tool for any student of the genre. The compiler and editor, T'ang Kuei-chang 唐圭璋, spent the years 1931-1937 preparing and editing the collection, which was published in 1940 More than 1200 writers were included. Brief biographies of each poet were provided (when information was available), and an author-index was appended. The collection totaled 300 *chüan* and was modeled after the *Ch'üan T'ang shih.** Works composed by emperors, ministers, and officials were given first, those by monks and women last. Despite the collection's obvious value to scholars, many critics and reviewers felt that the editor had not consulted and made full use of many relevant materials. This is true. The wartime situation in China prevented access to many collections and materials which T'ang might have used.

An opportunity to rectify this situation arose in the 1950s when the Chung-hua shu-chü suggested T'ang completely revise his 1940 edition. After two years' work, T'ang requested that the Classical Literature Section of the Chung-hua shu-chü re-edit his revised draft. The product of this collaboration was a totally revised edition of the *Ch'üan Sung tz'u* published in 1965.

The new version improved on the earlier edition in several ways. Works by T'ang, Five Dynasties, Chin, and Yüan writers included in the 1940 edition were deleted; practically all of the biographies were revised and rewritten, with birth, *chin-shih*, and death dates given when such information was available; the entire collection was rearranged so that authors and their works appear in chronological order; a complete bibliography of all editions and works cited is included; several new and very useful appendices were added, including a list of *tz'u* poems which hitherto had been attributed to the wrong author (corrections and sources are also provided), a useful listing of Sung *tz'u* poems which appear in Yüan and Ming fiction, and an extensive list of additions and corrections to the collection discovered by the editors after their revised draft went to press. As in the 1940 edition, an author index arranged by stroke number is also provided.

According to the editors of the 1965 edition (p. 5), their revised collection contains more than 19,900 *tz'u*, 1400 more poems than the earlier version. This represents the work of over 1300 writers, about 240 more than in the 1940 edition. Also appearing for the first time are more than 530 fragments of *tz'u* poems. Since the later editors were able to consult better editions and more reliable materials, the

1965 edition of the *Ch'üan Sung tz'u* is far superior to the earlier version and supersedes it in every respect.

EDITIONS:

Ch'üan Sung tz'u. T'ang Kuei-chang, comp. Changsha, 1940. 300 *chan.*

Ch'üan Sung tz'u. Peking, 1965. 5v. Completely revised. The most readily available and best edition; rpt. Taipei, 1970, 1976; Hong Kong, 1977.

STUDIES:

Sung-tz'u ssu-k'ao 宋詞四考. T'ang Kuei-chang, ed. Nanking, 1959. Useful essays dealing with editions, works of disputed authorship, and the dating of various authors.

—JH

Ch'üan T'ang shih 全唐詩 (Complete Poetry of the T'ang), the most comprehensive collection of T'ang-dynasty verse ever compiled, includes over 48,900 poems by more than 2,200 T'ang writers.

The compilation of the work was ordered by the K'ang-hsi Emperor (r. 1662-1723) in April of 1705. The work was put under the direction of the well-known official and scholar Ts'ao Yin 曹寅 (1658-1712). Collation, carving, and printing of this massive, imperially certified compendium took only two years; the preface to the collection, written by the monarch, is dated 17 May 1707. The surprising speed with which this enormous task of compilation was carried through was facilitated by the reliance of the editors on two previous and quite extensive collections of T'ang verse, which served as the primary—though not the only or, necessarily, the final—sources of the poems. These two works, referred to in Ts'ao Yin's progress reports to the emperor, in the sovereign's preface to the *Ch'üan T'ang shih*, and in the editors' "Fan-li" 凡例 (General Principles), were the *T'ang-yin t'ung-ch'ien* 唐音統籤 compiled by Hu Chen-heng 胡震亨 (1569-*c.* 1644) and a precursor text called *Ch'üan T'ang shih*, a copy of which was held in the imperial archives. The latter work has recently been identified conclusively as a huge but rarely seen collection of T'ang poetry originally compiled by the great scholar Ch'ien Ch'ien-i* and later aug-

mented by the renowned bibliophile Chi Chen-i 季振宜 (*chin-shih,* 1647). Ch'ien's name does not appear in any of the above-mentioned references to it, because his works were at that time under proscription by the Manchus. This text, which contains 42,931 poems by 1,895 T'ang authors, drew on nearly all the significant earlier anthologies and collections of T'ang verse, as well as on collections of individual writers. Each poet's works were also preceded in this text by an introductory biographical sketch of the author. Careful comparison and collation of the Ch'ien/Chi text with the *T'ang-yin t'ung-ch'ien* and with early (preferably Sung) editions of the works of individual poets formed the basis of the imperially sponsored *Ch'üan T'ang shih.*

One of the distinctive features of this work is the sequence in which authors appear in its pages. Following the lead of the Ch'ien/Chi text, the editors ignored the popular—but ultimately misleading—fourfold periodization of T'ang verse ("early" 初, "full" 盛, "middle" 中, "late" 晚) that had been *de rigueur* for most Ming and Ch'ing critics (and that had been used in the *T'ang-yin t'ung-ch'ien*). Instead, authors are presented in order of the year in which they passed the civil service examination. Where this date were unknown, or if a poet did not pass or did not take the exam, the year he entered official service was used as the deciding date. If this date too was unknown or inapplicable, then the year of death was used. If the year of death was uncertain also, then the poet's works were placed either immediately after or before those of another author to whom he had addressed poems or with whom he had composed "matching" verse. Otherwise his works were ranged alongside those of a poet with whom he had written on an identical, set theme on a formal occasion.

The *Ch'üan T'ang shih* comprises 900 *chüan.* The first nine *chüan* of the collection are devoted to poems attributed to the T'ang emperors, their consorts, princes and princesses of the blood, and the rulers of the succeeding Five Dynasties and their consorts. There follow seven chapters of ritual songs composed for use at the solemn imperial sacrifices, and thirteen chapters of *yüeh-fu** compositions, after which come the works organized according to the principles outlined in the preceding paragraph. They continue on through *chüan* 784. A chapter of anonymous works is next, then seven of *lien-chü* 聯句 (linked verses), and two of fragmentary verses by poets both known and unknown. There follow ten chapters (796-805) of poems by female writers, forty-six (806-851) by Buddhist monks, and eight (852-859) by Taoist adepts. The order here is suggestive of Ch'ing social attitudes. Chapters 860 through 881 include poems composed by transcendent beings (*hsien* 仙), both male and female, divinities, revenants, mountain imps, and talking animals; verses found inscribed on the bodies of fishes; verses conceived or overheard in dreams; poems of jest and ridicule; and mantic verses and ominous rhymes and ditties. Seven *chüan* (882-888) of addenda and twelve (889-900) of *tz'u** close the collection.

The biographical notes printed in the *Ch'üan T'ang shih* are most often based on those that had been included in the *T'ang-yin t'ung-ch'ien* and in the *T'ang-shih chi-shih,** rather than on the relatively more thorough notices in the Ch'ien/Chi compendium. It should be borne in mind that even the brief summaries of poets' lives furnished in the *Ch'üan T'ang shih* are sometimes untrustworthy. For example, the notice purporting to be about Hsüeh Yao 薛曜 (*fl.* 700) in fact describes the career of one Hsüeh Kuan 薛觀 (d. *c.* 672), thus perpetuating an error from the *T'ang-shih chi-shih.* The information given in these biographical extracts should always be checked against other sources.

Nor can the *Ch'üan T'ang shih* version of a poet's works always be considered the most reliable recension, from a text-critical standpoint. Where possible, one is well advised to consult other editions of the poet in question for variant readings that may not be indicated in this text: Excellent critical editions of some T'ang poets—such as Li Po,* Wang Wei,* Li Ho*—were produced by Ch'ing scholars active after the appearance of this collection. For the most part, though, this caveat applies only to the most famous or most prolific authors, whose works have been published over the centuries in different editions. For many other writers, indeed for the vast majority, the *Ch'üan T'ang shih* remains the best and sometimes the only source in which one may study their poems.

EDITIONS:

Ch'üan T'ang shih. Peking, 1960. Standard typeset edition; includes an author index; many reprints.

Wang, Ch'ung-min 王重民, *et al.,* eds. *Ch'üan T'ang shih wei-pien* 全唐詩外編. 2v. Peking, 1982.

STUDIES:

Ch'en, Hsiu-wu 陳修武. "*Ch'üan T'ang shih* te pien-chiao wen-t'i: Chien lun *Chüan T'ang shih* te chia-chih ho shih-yung" 全唐詩的編校問題 — 簡論全唐詩的價值和使用, *Shu-mu chi-k'an,* 9.1 (June 1975), 33-52.

Chou, Hsün-ch'u 周勛初. "Hsü *Ch'üan T'ang shih* ch'eng-shu ching-kuo" 敍全唐詩成書經過, *Wen shih,* 8 (March 1980), 185-196.

Liu, Chao-yu 劉兆祐. "Yü-ting *Ch'üan T'ang shih* yü Ch'ien Ch'ien-i, Chi Chen-i ti-chi *T'ang shih* kao-pen kuan-hsi t'an-wei" 御定全唐詩與錢謙益季振宜遞輯唐詩稿本關係探微, *Yu-shih hsüeh-chih,* 15 (1978), 101-136.

———. "Ch'ing Ch'ien Ch'ien-i, Chi Chen-i ti-chi *T'ang shih* kao-pen pa, chien lun *Yü-ting Ch'üan T'ang shih* chih ti-pen" 清錢謙益季振宜遞輯唐詩稿本跋, 兼論御定全唐詩之底本, *Tung-Wu wen-shih hsüeh-pao,* 3 (1978), 28-59.

Spence, Jonathan. *Ts'ao Yin and the K'ang-hsi Emperor: Bondservant and Master.* New Haven, 1966, pp. 157-165.

Wang, Ch'ung-min. "Pu *Ch'üan T'ang shih*" 補全唐詩, *Chung-hua wen-shih lun-ts'ung,* 3 (1963), 301-346.

Wu, Chien 吳 檢. "*Ch'üan T'ang shih* te pien-chi" 全唐詩的編集, *Yang-ch'eng wan-pao* 羊城晚報, February 8, 1961.

Yü, Ta-kang 俞大綱. "Chi *T'ang-yin t'ung-ch'ien*" 紀唐音統籤, *BIHP,* 7.3 (1937), 355-384.

—PWK

Ch'üan T'ang shih-hua 全唐詩話 (Complete Poetry Talks on the T'ang) is a collection of quotations and information concerning the lives and works of poets who lived during the T'ang dynasty. There is more than one edition, and the work has variously been divided into 2, 3, 5, 6, or 10 *chüan*, listing emperors, high ministers, and officials first, then monks, women, and anonymous authors. Although the types of information found in different entries varies greatly, usually included are biographical data such as the poet's personal (*tzu*) and style (*hao*) names, native place, official offices, travels, friendships, and family history, quotation from his works and critical remarks concerning his verse by other poets. Aside from the entry "Anonymous Poets," a total of 318 poets is represented in the collection.

The preface to the *Ch'üan T'ang shih-hua*, dated 14 October 1271, states that the collection was compiled in 1234. The signature *Sui-ch'u T'ang* 邃初堂 at the close of the preface has caused confusion regarding the true compiler of the collection. Since the Sung poet-official Yu Mao 尤袤 (1124-1193) owned a studio by that name and published a bibliography entitled *Sui-ch'u-t'ang shu-mu* 邃初堂書目, scholars and publishers, such as Mao Chin 毛晉 (1599-1659) in his well-known collectanea *Chin-tai pi-shu*, have traditionally regarded Yu Mao as the author of the collection. In the late Sung Chou Mi* was probably the first to correctly identify Chia Ssu-tao 賈似道 (1213-1275) as the actual compiler of the collection. Chou's identification went largely unnoticed until the *Ssu-k'u ch'üan-shu tsung-mu t'i-yao* (see Chi Yün) editors confirmed it.

The *Ssu-k'u* editors also correctly noted that the *Ch'üan T'ang shih-hua* is a derivative work based entirely upon Chi Yu-kung's 計有功 *T'ang-shih chi-shih*. The quotations and information selected by Chia Ssu-tao match corresponding entries in the *T'ang-shih chi-shih* verbatim and appear in almost exactly the same order. Despite its derivative nature, however, the *Ch'üan T'ang shih-hua* contains additional notes by Chia Ssu-tao who sometimes comments on poems cited (cf. entry on Ssu-k'ung T'u*), on variant names of poets (cf. entry on Chia Tao*), and on authorship of certain poems (cf. entry on Li Shang-yin*). Further, because Chia Ssu-tao selectively chose from the approximately 1150 poets represented in the *T'ang-shih chi-shih*, omitting Li Po,* Tu Fu,* Kao Shih,* Ts'en Shen,* and other poets considered famous today, his selection may shed light on late Sung attitudes towards T'ang poetry. Sun T'ao 孫濤 (*fl.* 1774) wrote a sequel to the collection entitled *Ch'üan T'ang shih-hua hsü-pien* 續編 in 2 *chüan*.

EDITIONS:

Ch'üan T'ang shih-hua. TSCC. Shanghai, 1935-1937. Rpt. of the *Chin-tai pi-shu* 津逮秘書 (1630-1642) text.

Ch'üan T'ang shih-hua, in *Index to the Ho Collection of Twenty-Eight Shih-hua (So-yin pen Ho-shih li-tai shih-hua* 索引本何氏歷代詩話), Helmut Martin, ed., Taipei, 1973, v. 1, pp. 27-155. Indexed and punctuated; the best edition available.

STUDIES:

Chou, Mi 周密. "Chia Liao K'an-shu" 賈廖刊書, in *K'uei-hsin tsa-shih (hou-chi)* 癸辛雜識 (後集). *Chin-tai pi-shu*, 29b-30a.

Kuo, Shao-yü 郭紹虞. *Sung shih-hua k'ao* 宋詩話考: Peking, 1979, pp. 121-125.

Kurata, Junosuke 倉田淳之助. "*Ch'üan T'ang shih-hua*," in Hervouet, *Sung*, pp. 447-448.

Peng, Yüan-jui 彭元瑞 *et al.*, comp. *T'ien-lu lin-lang shu-mu hou-pien* 天祿琳琅書目後編. Rpt., Taipei, 1968, v. 4, pp. 1452-1453.

—JH

Ch'üan T'ang wen 全唐文 (Complete Prose of the T'ang), the most comprehensive collection of T'ang prose works, contains more than 18,400 compositions from the hands of 3,042 named authors, plus anonymous writers, who were active during the T'ang era.

Conceived as a complement to the *Ch'üan T'ang shih,** which had been compiled a century earlier, the *Ch'üan T'ang wen* was commissioned by the Chia-ch'ing Emperor (r. 1796-1821) in 1808. Tung Kao 董誥 (1740-1818), a veteran official who had previously been assistant director of the enormous *Ssu-k'u ch'üan-shu* commission (see Chi Yün) and general director of the imperial printing establishment (the Wu-ying Tien 武英殿), was made the chief director of the project, and numerous scholars, such as Juan Yüan 阮元 (1764-1849) and Hsü Sung 徐松 (1781-1848), were part of the staff. The work took six years to complete (three times longer than the compilation of the *Ch'üan T'ang shih*), and the collection was presented to the sovereign in the spring of 1814. The basic sources were earlier anthologies such as the *Wen-yüan ying-hua** (two different versions of which were consulted), *T'ang wen-ts'ui,** and *Ku-wen yüan,** the official dynastic histories of T'ang, and separate (preferably Sung) edition of the works of individual writers. In addition, frequent mention is made in the "Fan-li" 凡例 (General Principles) of an "original text" (*yüan shu* 原書 —just as the *T'ang-yin t'ung-ch'ien* and the Ch'ien/Chi compendium of T'ang poetry had been for the *Ch'üan T'ang shih*), but there appears to be no information upon which to identify this work.

Despite the title, the *Ch'üan T'ang wen* does not contain all the extant prose works written under the T'ang. Works that the *Ssu-k'u* editors did not classify as *chi* 集 (belles-lettres), for instance, were systematically excluded; thus, writings primarily historical, pseudo-historical, anecdotal, or "fictional" are in most cases not to be found here. For T'ang writings of those sorts, one must normally consult the *T'ang-tai ts'ung-shu* 唐代叢書 and *T'ai-p'ing kuang-chi,** although the *Ch'üan T'ang wen* occasionally includes the prefaces or postfaces attached to such works. The coverage of Buddhist and Taoist writings is also not comprehensive, many works in these areas remaining accessible only in the Buddhist or Taoist canons. At the same time, however, the *Ch'üan T'ang wen* is the repository for *fu** which, although written in rhyme, were unaccountably excluded from the *Ch'üan T'ang shih;* their consequent inclusion here has unhappily contributed to the mistaken impression that T'ang *fu* are prose works. It should also be noted that official documents and memorial inscriptions of all kinds were copied into *Ch'üan T'ang wen* in great numbers.

The work comprises one thousand *chüan*. The first ninety-four are given over to works attributed to the emperors of T'ang and the following six to the imperial consorts and members of the royal family.

Chapters 101 through 127 contain the writings of the monarchs (and their consorts) of the successor Five Dynasties, while chapters 128 through 130 include those of the rulers of the so-called "Ten Kingdoms." *Chüan* 131 begins the presentation of the works of male, lay individuals, which continue through *chüan* 902. In ordering the sequence in which authors appear in these chapters, the organizational principles of the *Ch'üan T'ang shih* are employed. Under each writer, the works themselves are arranged according to genre—generally, *fu* come first, followed by official documents, eulogies, letters, random accounts and essays, and memorial inscriptions. Buddhist writers are represented in chapters 903 through 922 and Taoist authors in chapters 923 through 944. *Chüan* 945 is devoted to female writers (interestingly, they are placed after the religious figures, while the *Ch'üan T'ang shih* had placed them before). The works of named authors about whom nothing else is known are collected in chapters 946 through 959, and the writings of anonymous authors are transcribed in chapters 960 through 997. Some addenda are gathered in *chüan* 998, and the final two chapters offer the works of notable foreigners who were resident in the T'ang domains and learned to write in the Chinese language.

The *Ch'üan T'ang wen,* again following the example of the *Ch'üan T'ang shih,* includes brief biographical notices preceding the writings of individual authors. Indeed, this anthology occasionally errs not only in its biographical sketches, but also in its attribution of writings and in its transcription of the proper names of authors; there are also cases of its mistakenly melding several similarly named writers into a single entity as well as its wrongly creating two authorial identities where only one actually exists. Accordingly, the user should, whenever possible, check the identity and biographical details of authors (especially lesser-known authors) in other sources as well. It should further be kept in mind that, unlike the *Ch'üan T'ang shih,* the *Ch'üan T'ang wen* only rarely notes textual variants.

One of the many compilers on the staff of the project, Ch'en Hung-ch'ih, composed privately a companion volume to the *Ch'üan T'ang wen* called *Ch'üan T'ang wen chi-shih* 全唐文紀事 (Chronicle of Events for the Complete Prose of the T'ang). Never published during Ch'en Hung-ch'ih's lifetime, this work was first printed in 1873 (more than three decades after his death), when Ch'en Li 陳澧 (1810-1882), who had in his youth been a pupil of Ch'en Hung-ch'ih, acquired the manuscript from Hung-ch'ih's youngest son. The *Chi-shih* is a work in 122 *chüan*. Assembled in it are quotations from some 581 separate texts (the majority dating from the Sung period)—scrupulously cited by Ch'en—which provide information about the circumstances surrounding the composition of specific writings included in the *Ch'üan T'ang wen* or comments of a general nature relating to various types of T'ang prose. The usefulness of this work is unfortunately impaired by its arrangement. Instead of being organized around the T'ang authors themselves, the individual entries are disposed topically under eighty main heading such as "Loyalty and Devotion," "Renown and Acclaim," or "Empathetic Experiences." Considerable guesswork and page-flipping is often required to ascertain whether any information relevant to one's subject is contained therein. However, because of its compiler's extensive gleanings from sundry sources, the *Chi-shih* is often particularly valuable in affording important variora for many texts that appear in the *Ch'üan T'ang wen.*

EDITIONS:

Ch'üan T'ang wen. Canton, 1901, in 20 *t'ao.* Standard typeset edition published in Taipei, 1965; reprinted many times by various publishers.

Ch'üan T'ang wen chi-shih. 3v. Shanghai, 1959. Typeset.

STUDIES:

Fu, Hsüan-ts'ung 傅璇琮, Chang Ch'en-shih 張忱石, and Hsü I-min 許逸民. "T'an *Ch'üan T'ang wen* te hsiu-ting" 談全唐文的修訂, *Wen-hsüeh i-ch'an,* 1 (June 1980), 43-48.

—PWK

Chui pai-ch'iu 綴白裘 (Piecing Together a White Fur Coat) is an anthology comprising 487 scenes selected from more than 90 Yüan, Ming, and Ch'ing plays. It was begun by Wan-hua chu-jen 玩花主人 (original name unknown, a native of Wu-men 吳門, Kiangsu, *fl.* late sixteenth to early seventeenth century, author of *Chuang-kuo chi* 妝樓記 [In the Boudoir]) and continued by Ch'ien P'ei-ssu 錢沛思 (*tzu,* Te-ts'ang 德蒼, *fl.* 1763-1774). It was published in twelve series between 1764 and 1767 and then reissued collectively in 1767. Little is known of Ch'ien except that he was also from the region of K'un-shan 崑山, where *Kun-ch'iang* 崑腔 (i.e., *K'un-ch'ü**) plays originated. The majority of the plays (430 scenes) represented in this anthology are *K'un-ch'ü,* and 59 other scenes are from plays in various local styles, such as *Luan-t'an-ch'iang* 亂彈腔, *Kao-ch'iang* 高腔, and others.

The *Chui pai-ch'iu* was intended as a nontechnical guide for theatergoers but as the texts are primarily performing ones, their notations on stage conventions are usually more meticulous and detailed than in the original versions. It also preserves scenes from many lesser works and provides a good indicator of the range of the repertoire of early Ch'ing theatrical troupes.

This anthology is of particular importance to students of the history of Chinese stagecraft, but it is also an excellent selective anthology of the more enjoyable portions of Ming and Ch'ing plays of forbidding length.

EDITIONS:

Chui pai-ch'iu. 1764-1767. Chin-ch'ang Pao-jen T'ang 金閶寶仁堂 edition, reissued as a set (1767).

———. Wang Hsieh-ju 汪協如, collator and ed. Peking, 1955.

STUDIES:

Hu, Shih 胡適. "Preface," Wang Hsieh-ju, *op. cit.*

Cheng, Chen-to 鄭振鐸. "Chung-kuo hsi-ch'ü te hsüan-pen" 中國戲曲的選本, in Cheng Chen-to, ed., *Chung-kuo wen-hsüeh yen-chiu* 中國文學研究, Peking, 1957; rpt. Hong Kong, 1963, pp. 503-534.

———. "*Chui pai-ch'iu* so-yin" 綴白裘索引, in his *Chung-kuo wen-hsüeh yen-chiu*, Peking, 1957, pp. 818-816.

—JW

Chung Hsing 鍾惺 (*tzu*, Po-ching 伯敬, *hao*, T'ui-ku 退谷 and Wan-chih chü-shih 晚知居士, 1574-1624), was a poet, literary critic, anthologist, and founder of the Ching-ling School 竟陵 of poets that flourished in the late Ming period.

A native of Ching-ling 景陵 in Hukwang (modern Hupei), Chung Hsing was successful in the examinations only relatively late in life, passing the *chü-jen* examination in 1603 and the *chin-shih* in 1610. Thereafter he served in the central and provincial administrations in Peking (the Ministry of Works), Nanking (the Ministry of Rites), and Kweichow (where he managed the provincial examination of 1615). Chung traveled widely, freely recommending the worthies he encountered to his friends in high places.

Chung's literary theories are embodied in the prefaces to his anthologies and in his surviving letters. He clearly distinguishes himself from the Archaist School of Li P'an-lung,* then popular, that advocated imitation of the great poets of the T'ang. Instead, Chung Hsing emphasized that poets should take inspiration from the vital essence of earlier poetry, its *hsing-ling* 性靈, or "native sensibility." That is, Chung and his junior colleague, T'an Yüan-ch'un* praised originality over imitation, using the catchphrase *shen-yu ku-ch'iao* 深幽孤峭 (profundity and detachment). In contrast to the Kung-an School of Yüan Hung-tao* and his brothers, Chung and T'an espoused refined diction and original inspiration. Unfortunately, critics beginning with Ch'ien Ch'ien-i* were uniform in declaring Chung Hsing's own poetry less than successful in these areas. His followers have been criticized for obscurity, crudeness in diction, and pointless unconventionality. Furthermore, the Ching-ling School sought subjectivity and originality with far-from-objective eyes; the modern scholar Kuo Shao-yü laments that they fell victim to a logical trap of their own making, assuming that the standards for subjectivity and originality would remain standard through time. In fact, their theoretical approach came to appear arbitrary and fallacious as soon as literary tastes changed.

Chung Hsing wrote prolifically. While serving in Nanking, he published his *Shih-huai* 史懷 (Notes on the Histories) and soon afterward a commentary on the *Śūrangama sūtra* entitled *Leng-yen ju-shuo* 楞嚴如說. His major works are the anthologies *Ku-shih kuei* 古詩歸 (15 *chüan*) and *T'ang-shih kuei* 唐詩歸 (36 *chüan*) compiled together with T'an Yüan-ch'un between 1614 and 1617. Chung's own creative writing appeared in a block print edition of 1622, the *Yin-hsiu-hsüan chi* 隱秀軒集 (proscribed during the Ch'ien-lung reign but later reprinted). During the years 1616-1621, Chung edited collections of examination essays. This fact, coupled with his soaring reputation as the founder of a poetic school, seemingly prompted publishers to attribute a great variety of works to him. Among them are a book on letter writing (*Ju-mien t'an* 如面譚), several works on the Confucian classics (of which probably the 1620 edition of the *Shih-ching** with commentary is genuinely his), numerous anthologies, and a few historical studies, particularly the *Ming-chi pien-nien* 明紀編年. Chung's *Chung-p'ing Tso-chuan* 鍾評左傳 was published by Mao Chin's prestigious Chi-ku-ko 汲古閣 house that also published Ch'ien Ch'ien-i's notes on poets mentioned above. Editions of *Shui-ching chu,** *Yen-t'ieh lun* 鹽鐵論, *Shih-shuo hsin-yü,** and even *Wen-hsin tiao-lung** have been attributed to him.

Many books have been attributed to Chung's pen; a large portion of them are works of popular historical fiction. The Naikaku bunkō 內閣文庫 in Tokyo has copies of historical romances narrating events from highest antiquity through the Hsia— *An Chien yen-i ti-wang yü-shih Pan-ku chih T'ang Yü chuan* 按鑑演義帝王御世盤古至唐虞傳 (Chronicles of the Reigns of the Emperors Pan-ku to T'ang and Yü, Done in the Popular Style, Based on the [Comprehensive] *Mirror for Aid in Governing*) and *An Chien yen-i ti-wang yü-shih Yu Hsia chih-chuan* 按鑑演義帝王御世有夏誌傳 (Annals and Chronicles of the Reigns of the Emperors of the Hsia Dynasty, Done in the Popular Style, Based on the *Mirror*), both available on microfilm—that were published in Nanking. Either as "editor" or as commentator, Chung Hsing's name is also linked to fictionalized histories of the Shang, the Han, the Sui, a military romance concerning a T'ang hero, and the standard version of *Feng-shen yen-i.**

EDITIONS:

Chung Po-ching ho-chi 鍾伯敬合集, A Ying 阿英, ed., in *Chung-kuo wen-hsüeh chen-pen ts'ung-shu* 中國文學珍本叢書. First Collection, Chang Ching-lu 張靜廬, comp. Shanghai, 1936. First entitled *Yin-hsiu-hsüan chi.*

Shih-huai 史懷. 20 *chüan.* Changsha, 1939. *TSCC,* nos. 3560-63; *Hu-pei ts'ung-shu* 湖北叢書. Chao Shang-fu 趙尚輔, comp. Hupei: San-yü ts'ao-t'ang 三餘草堂, 1891.

Shih-ching 詩經. Chung Hsing, commentator. 3 *chüan. Ho-k'o Chou Ch'in ching-shu shih-chung* 合刻周秦經書十種. Lu Chih-i 盧之頤, comp. n.p., Hsi-hsiang shu-wu 溪香書屋, 1620.

STUDIES:

DMB, pp. 408-409.

Kuo, *P'i-p'ing shih,* v. 2, pp. 283-94. A survey of major tenets of the Chin-ling School.

Liu, *Buddhist and Taoist,* p. 104. A novel "edited" by Chung Hsing.

———, *London Libraries,* pp. 15, 30. Notes on novels attributed to Chung Hsing.

Sun, K'ai-ti 孫楷第. *Chung-kuo t'ung-su hsiao-shuo shu-mu* 中國通俗小說書目. Hong Kong, 1967, pp. 23, 24, 28, 44, 46. Novels attributed to Chung Hsing.

———. *Jih-pen Tung-ching so-chien Chung-kuo hsiao-shuo shu-mu* 日本東京所見中國小說書目. Hong Kong, 1967, p. 88. A novel attributed to Chung Hsing.

Yoshikawa, Kōjio 吉川幸次郎. *Gen min Shi Gaisetsu* 元明詩概說. Tokyo, 1964, pp. 230-234. Chin-ling School verse, with translations.

—REH

Chung-yüan yin-yün 中原音韻 (Central Plain Songs and Rhymes), written by Chou Te-ch'ing 周德清 (*c.* 1270-after 1324), is one of the most important books in the history both of Chinese poetry and prosody and also in the history of Chinese phonology and the phonetic development of the Chinese language. It furthermore affords a vivid glimpse of society under Mongol rule during the late thirteenth and early fourteenth centuries.

Chou's tour-de-force was produced in 1324. It consists principally of rhyme-tables, arranging some 5888 monosyllabic characters under nineteen rhyme categories, these nineteen further divided into pitch-tone sections, the distributions as below.

The work also contains a more specifically poetic and literary treatise, headed "Tso-tz'u shih-fa" 作詞十法 (Ten Regulations for Composing *Ch'ü*), divided as follows:

1. Understanding of Rhymes;
2. Phraseology;
3. Subjects;
4. Words;
5. Apportionment of Entering Tones into Level Tones;
6. Yin and Yang Level Tones;
7. Keypoint (*wu-t'ou* 務頭);
8. Parallelism;
9. Final Line;
10. Fixed Patterns (*ting-ke* 定格).

These cover such matters as pronunciations, archaic writings of characters, extra-metrical syllables (*ch'en-tzu* 襯字), the quality of language, and tonal patterns of meter. The Fixed Patterns are a number of songs and song-suites by various poets and are presented as models of *ch'ü** poetry and prosody.

Elsewhere, Chou provides a list of 335 titles of *ch'ü* tunes, arranged under their various mode categories. The prefaces and postfaces by Chou and others also contain much valuable information.

The intellectual motive for this work was to correct the abuses which Chou considered had marred much composition of songs in the *ch'ü* genre, a genre that originated in the region of Peking and used the northern language as its standard for rhyming. With the Mongol conquest of South China completed by 1280, southerners, among them Chou, came increasingly to adopt the genre. The southern elements which now appeared in *ch'ü* compositions were the prime object of Chou's corrections. He condemns the use of the rhymebook *Kuang-yün* 廣韻 (Expanded Rhymes), which had first appeared in 1008, and was reprinted during the period 1324-1328. *Kuang-yün* served as a "highbrow" or pedantically conservative and southern guide to rhyming, encouraging the intrusion of southern rhymes into *ch'ü* poetry.

That Chou's endeavours in this work were allied to problems of vaster immediate import is clear. He both supports and borrows strength from the movement to spread the northern language as the medium of government and official culture throughout China. Attacking adherents of *Kuang-yün*, for example, he quotes the following opinion with approval:

> They fail to bear in mind that the empire has now long been reunited, and that throughout the country the same pronunciation is in use. On a higher level—for the gentry in their discourses and ethical applications, in the language of translations from foreign languages into Chinese, and for education in the national studies, and, on the lower level—in the judicial courts, and in the government of the people, is it not indeed the pronunciation of the Central Plain which is used!

Yet, more personal reasons may also have encouraged Chou to publish this work. Sometime before 1324, probably in the fourteenth century, Yang Ch'ao-ying 楊朝英 (*c.* 1270-1352 or after) published an anthology of *ch'ü*, entitled *Yang-ch'un pai-hsüeh* 陽春白雪 (Sunny Spring and White Snow), which included none of Chou Te-ch'ing's *ch'ü*. Of the six songs that Chou scathingly analyzed in his *Chung-yüan yin-yün*, four were by Yang Ch'ao-ying and another was by Kuan Yün-shih,* the writer of the preface to Yang's anthology!

Phonologically, this work was remarkably bold in acknowledging the changes which had taken place in the northern Chinese language and in promoting its virtues so explicitly over long-dominant southern standards. In particular, Chou's recognitions that the northern tonal system was distinct from the southern and that the entering tone was no longer part of the standard northern language were vital pioneering contributions to scholarship.

EDITIONS:

Chou, Te-ch'ing. *Chung-yüan yin-yün* (with *Chung-chou yüeh-fu yin-yün lei-pien* 中州樂府音韻類編 appended). Peking, 1978.

Chung-yüan yin-yün, in *Chung-kuo ku-tien hsi-ch'ü lun-chu chi-ch'eng* 中國古典戲曲論著集成. Peking, 1959, pp. 267-285.

STUDIES:

Chao, Yin-t'ang 趙蔭堂. *Chung-yüan yin-yün yen-chiu* 中原音韻研究, Shanghai, 1936; revised edition Shanghai, 1956. The classical study.

Hattori, Shirō 服部四郎 and Tōdō Akiyasu 藤堂明保. *Chūgen on'in no kenkyū* 中原音韻の研究, Tokyo, 1958.

Ishiyama, Fukuji 石山福治. *Kōtei* Chūgen On'in 攷定中原音韻. Tokyo, 1925.

Stimson, Hugh M. "Phonology of the *Chung yüan yin-yün*," *THHP, N.S.*, 3 (1962), 114-159.

———. *The Jongyuan inyunn: A Guide to Old Mandarin Pronunciation*. New Haven, 1966.

Wang, Li 王力. *Chung-kuo yin-yün hsüeh* 中國音韻學, Shanghai, 1936; revised edition, as *Han-yü yin-yün hsüeh* 漢語音韻學, Peking, 1956.

Wang, Ching-ch'ang 汪經昌. *Chung-yüan yin-yün chiang-su* 中原音韻講疏. Taipei, 1962.

—WD

Fa-yüan chu-lin 法苑珠林 (A Grove of Pearls in the Dharma Garden) is the title of a Chinese encyclopedia of Buddhism compiled during the early decades of the T'ang dynasty by Tao-shih 道世 (*c.* 600-683), a prominent monk and the author or editor of numerous works concerned with Buddhism. A native and life-long resident of the T'ang capital of Ch'ang-an, Tao-shih was noted even as a youth for both his intelligence and piety—he left home to become a monk when only eleven. Both his teacher, Chih-shou 智首 (567-635), and especially one of his fellow students, Tao-hsüan 道宣 (596-667), are considered principal figures in the Chinese *lü* 律, or "discipline," school of Buddhism. Tao-shih lived for several years in the same monastery as Tao-hsüan, and his name has also been associated with the Discipline School.

The *Fa-yüan chu-lin* is one of two major works by Tao-shih to survive. According to a preface by Li Yen 李儼, it was completed in 668, though there is some evidence that it was in limited circulation earlier, perhaps in a preliminary draft. Divided topically into one hundred "units" (*p'ien* 篇) and subdivided into numerous "sections" (*pu* 部), the encyclopedia attempts to provide a comprehensive introduction to major aspects of Buddhist doctrine through explanations by the compiler and through quotations from translated Buddhist scriptures and non-canonical indigenous works. The first unit begins the encyclopedia with a description of the *kalpa*, or "eon," a term central to the Buddhist cosmological system, while the final unit is devoted to Buddhist bibliography; in between are units on such topics as "The Six Paths" (Unit 4), "Honoring Monks" (Unit 8), "Relics of the Buddha" (Unit 37), and "Retribution" (Unit 79).

Appended to many units or sections of the encyclopedia are what Tao-shih called *kan-ying yüan* 感應緣 (stories of response), intended to provide concrete illustration of how the Buddhist doctrine being explained in that particular section was manifested in everyday life. There are a total of ninety-four "stories of response" sections in the *Fa-yüan chu-lin*, which contain hundreds of anecdotes and tales from earlier works of philosophical, historical, biographical, geographical, and tale literature, all drawn from indigenous Chinese sources, both Buddhist and non-Buddhist. Within each section the stories and anecdotes are arranged chronologically according to when the events they relate occurred. Tao-shih added notes at the end of many items or groups of items that give the original sources. Although his annotation has suffered at the hands of copyists and editors across the centuries, it remains remarkably accurate. Comparison of his quotations with works which survive also shows him to have been quite faithful to the original texts, seldom significantly altering or abridging the passages he quoted. Among the more than seventy-five titles mentioned in the "stories of response" sections are more than two dozen collections of strange and miraculous tales that had been compiled during the Six Dynasties and Early T'ang periods. There are also several stories (of events that Tao-shih had witnessed personally or heard about from

participants) which are recorded by Tao-shih for the first time.

Although the *Fa-yüan chu-lin* was neither the first Chinese Buddhist work to make use of quotations from the translated Buddhist canon nor the first to include passages from non-canonical works to illustrate Buddhist concepts, its scope went far beyond any of its predecessors. The commonly used modern edition contains a total text of over one million characters. In addition to its obvious importance as a source on early Chinese Buddhism, the *Fa-yüan chu-lin* is also of great value to students of Chinese tale literature, because of its use of earlier collections of Chinese tales, many now lost.

EDITIONS:

Fa-yüan chu-lin, in *Taishō shinshū daizōkyō* 大正新脩大藏經. Tokyo, 1928; rpt. Tokyo, 1962. V. 53, no. 2122. A variorum edition based on the Korean edition of 1151, and collated against a Sung edition of 1239, a Yüan edition of 1290, a Ming edition of 1601, and an old Sung edition of 1104-1148 from the Library of the Japanese Imperial Household.

———. *SPTK*. Follows a Ming edition of 1591.

Paper, Jordan D. *An Index to Stories of the Supernatural in the Fa-yüan chu-lin*. Taipei, 1975.

STUDIES:

Kawaguchi, Gishō 川口義照. "*Hōon jurin* ni mirareru isson, besson kyō ni tsuite" 法苑珠林にみられる逸存, 別存經について, *Nanto bukkyō*, 37 (November 1976), 82-101.

———. "Kyōroku kenkyū yori mita *Hōon jurin* Dōsei ni tsuite" 經錄研究よりみた 法苑珠林 道世について, *Indogaku bukkyōgaku ken kyū*, 24.2 (1976), 794-797.

Satō, Kiyoji 佐藤喜代治. "*Hōon jurin* to kirokutai" 法苑珠林と記錄體, *Chūgoku kankei ronsetsu shiryō*, 21 (1979), 415-420.

—DG

Fan Ch'eng-ta 范成大 (*tzu*, Chih-neng 致能, *hao*, Shih-hu chü-shih 石湖居士, 1126-1191) is considered one of the four great masters of Southern Sung *shih** poetry, along with Yang Wan-li,* Lu Yu,* and Yu Mou 尤袤 (1127-1194) (whose works are largely lost). Fan was born in a moderately well-off family in P'ing-chiang-fu 平江府 (modern Soochow in Kiangsu). Because of the death of his parents Fan spent his youth in poverty and was not able to obtain the *chin-shih* degree until 1154. He served in a succession of local and central government posts over the years, the most exciting of which no doubt was his embassy to the Chin Tartars, who had occupied North China and were inveterate foes of the Sung. Although Fan was never in a position to influence central-government policy, he was fondly remembered for his compassionate administration and scrupulous honesty in local government.

Fan Ch'eng-ta is most famous for his verse written in the long tradition of *t'ien-yüan shih* 田園詩 (garden-and-field poetry), poetry expressing the harmony between man and the rural setting in which he lives. Fan's garden-and-field poetry differs from anything written before Southern Sung times, as is illustrated in his most famous sequence of rural poetry, sixty poems entitled "Ssu-shih t'ien-yüan tsa-hsing" 四時田園雜興 (Miscellaneous Emotions on the Four Seasons in the Fields and Gardens). Although T'ao Ch'ien* and many T'ang poets had celebrated the delights of rural life, no one had ever before created such a rich and diversified picture of Chinese peasant life; Fan's sequence of poems is a culmination of such divergent strands as the T'ang dynasty *Hsin Yüeh-fu* poetry of social criticism (see *yüeh-fu*) and the *chu-chih tz'u* 竹枝詞 (bamboo branch songs) written in imitation of Chinese rural folk poetry, along with the *t'ien-yüan shih* tradition initiated by T'ao Ch'ien.

However, Fan's poetic sequence is more than just a mixture of earlier traditions. Unlike the garden-and-field poetry of T'ao Ch'ien and many of the T'ang authors who wrote in this mode, Fan's verse is not primarily a vehicle for the poet to express the moral and ethical purity he has preserved by withdrawal to life of seclusion in rural surroundings. T'ao Ch'ien's poems are full of his subjective personal reactions to his surroundings, whereas Fan's sequence is an objective and highly realistic description of rural life with little obvious intrusion of the poet's personal emotions.

This sort of objective, detailed description of nature and rural life reminds one of Fan's contemporary and good friend Yang Wan-li, and it is likely the two poets influenced each other. In fact, their general poetic development was quite similar, as both writers started out imitating the Kiangsi School (see *Chiang-hsi shih-p'ai*) of poetry. That they both finally rejected the neo-classical artificiality of the Kiangsi poets suggests that the two authors had a similar spiritual and intellectual development, and although Fan Ch'eng-ta did not formulate his theory of literature as systematically as Yang Wan-li, he too was influenced by Ch'an Buddhist concepts of sudden enlightenment and superrational intuition. It is precisely this quality which separates Fan's rural poetry from that of earlier authors, for not only is his objective realism largely a result of ego-subduing meditation, but the sudden shifts and verbal surprises in Fan's poetry are inspired by the same Ch'an "shock techniques" employed by Yang Wan-li. Although in the particular sequence of poems just mentioned the Ch'an element is so thoroughly assimilated as to be invisible on the surface, there are many quite openly didactic Buddhist poems in Fan's complete works, indeed, rather more than in Yang Wan-li's collection.

Of course, Fan wrote in a large number of modes, and his rural verse of a more specifically political nature, attacking the oppression of the Sung peasantry, has been highly appreciated by Chinese Marxist critics. He also wrote a small quantity of "patriotic" verse, which is, however, somewhat more subdued than Lu Yu's works and more in line with Yang Wan-li's creations. Nonetheless, Marxist critics seem to have put too much emphasis on the "patriotic" aspects of Fan's poetry, as is probably even the case with Lu Yu himself.

EDITIONS:

Shih-hu chü-shih shih-chi 石湖居士詩集. *SPTK*.
Shih-hu chü-shih shih-chi. Shanghai, 1940.
Fan Shih-hu chi 范石湖集. Peking, 1974. Modern critical edition.
Chou, Ju-ch'ang 周汝昌. *Fan Ch'eng-ta shih-hsüan* 范成大詩選. Peking, 1959. Excellent, detailed commentary.

373

TRANSLATIONS:

Bullett, Gerald. *The Golden Years of Fan Ch'eng-ta.* Cambridge, 1946.

Demiéville, *Anthologie,* p. 362.

Sunflower, pp. 387-392.

STUDIES:

SB, pp. 308-309.

Yang Wan-li, Fan Ch'eng-ta chüan 楊萬里范成大卷. Peking, 1964. Collection of critical comments on Fan and Yang from Sung times to the present.

—JDS

Fan Chung-yen 范仲淹 (*tzu,* Hsi-wen 希文, 989-1052), author of the famous maxim, "First to worry about the world's troubles; last to enjoy the world's pleasures," was the leader of the first or "Minor Reform" of the Northern Sung dynasty, the founder of the Fan clan's charitable estate, and a leading essayist and poet of his day. His reform efforts were largely unsuccessful, but they set the stage for the later work of Ou-yang Hsiu* and Wang An-shih.* His prose essays and *shih** and *tz'u** poems, though few in number, are still highly regarded and frequently anthologized.

Fan's father died when he was very young and he followed his widowed mother, taking the surname of Chu when she remarried. He studied in a Buddhist temple in abject rural poverty. A number of patrons helped him through this difficult period and aided him in passing the *chin-shih* examination in 1015, after which he held minor posts in local administrations. In his teens he learned the true circumstances of his birth and petitioned successfully to return to the use of his father's surname. In 1024 he secured a palace appointment through the sponsorship of Yen Shu,* but Fan's idealistic Confucian reformism led to three demotions. Yet with each demotion, his prestige and following increased. When he was recalled and sent along with Han Ch'i to Shensi, the Hsi Hsia invaded Sung territory (1040). He re-established discipline and good administration in the military there, fought the Hsi Hsia to a stalemate, and negotiated a much desired peace, all of which made him very popular when his faction came to power

in 1043 and 1044. At that time, together with Han Ch'i, he submitted his famous "Ten-point Memorial" calling for various administrative reforms aimed at improving the performance and evaluation of the bureaucracy. But the reforms were rescinded within a year, Fan and his faction were disgraced, and the only lasting effect was a change toward more practical applications of imperial examination standards. The emperor admitted, however, that the administration was in need of reform and the stage was set for the more thorough-going improvement to come.

In literature, Fan is important as a transitional figure whose works began as imitations of late T'ang and Five Dynasties styles and went on to break new ground that led toward the mature prose and poetry of the Northern Sung style. He broke away early from the sentimental and ornate style of the Hsi-k'un School (see *Hsi-k'un ch'ou-ch'ang chi*) to produce a versatile poetry of genuine emotion. This verse may be characterized as at once profound and heroic, even tragic, as in his evocations of military life, and tenderly affectionate and finely wrought, as in his poems of separation. His most admired poems are his "short lyrics" (*hsiao-ling* 小令), in a style very close to that of the *Hua-chien-chi** writers of the late T'ang. In these pieces he exhibits both delicate sentiment and unrestrained vigor of expression. His prose is lucid, straightforward, functional, and realistic, moving toward the *ku-wen** style of Ou-yang Hsiu and his protégés.

His most lasting contribution to history was the corporate estate established in Soochow in 1050 and kept intact until 1760. Near the end of his life he went to Soochow, his father's birthplace, to claim his paternal lineage ties, but was given a cool reception by the clan elders. After he donated three-thousand *mou* of land to be set up in perpetuity as a "charitable estate" (*i-chuang* 義莊) for the benefit of all members of the clan and especially for those like himself who were less well off and had difficulty paying for their education, their response warmed considerably. His childhood experiences were the major motive behind his generosity, but the pressing necessity of Sung scholar-officials to establish family and regional roots after the decline of the T'ang aristocracy no doubt also played a role.

EDITIONS:

Fan Wen-cheng chi 范文正集. 10v. *SPTK*.

Fan Wen-cheng kung wen-chi 范文正公文集. 3v. Taipei, 1968.

TRANSLATIONS:

Demiéville, *Anthologie*, p. 379.

Yoshikawa, *Sung*, pp. 80-81.

STUDIES:

Burkis, P. "Fan Chung-yen's Versuch einer Reform des chinesischen Beamtenstaates in den Jahren 1043/44," *OE*, 3 (1956), 57-80 and 153-184.

Fischer, J. "Fan Chung-yen, das Lebensbild eines chinesischen Staatsmannes," *OE*, 2 (1955), 39-85 and 142-156.

SB, pp. 321-330.

Twitchett, Denis. "The Fan Clan's Charitable Estate," in David S. Nivison and Arthur F. Wright, eds., *Confucianism in Action*, Stanford, 1959, pp. 97-133.

—MSD

Fang Hsiao-ju 方孝孺 (*tzu*, Hsi-chih 希直 and Hsi-ku 希古, 1357-1402), was a major prose writer of his period. He was born in Hou-ch'eng li 侯城里, Ning-hai 寧海 (modern Chekiang), into a family which had produced scholars and officials during the Yüan dynasty. A child prodigy, he was known as "Little Han Yü" 小韓子. While on a visit to Nanking (the capital) in 1376, he met the great essayist Sung Lien,* who took him under his tutelage. He became Sung's leading disciple and honed his talents in expository prose in the *ku-wen** style through him. His teacher made of him a devout adept of the Ch'eng-Chu 程朱 School of Neo-Confucianism, the mainstay of his political thought. It was also with Sung that he collected the works of the Yüan *san-ch'ü* writer Chang K'o-chiu.*

His father died in prison (1376), convicted on a false charge. Fang had unsuccessfully requested to take his place. Little is known of his life thereafter until 1393 when he began to teach Confucian studies in Shensi. He acquired the favor of Prince Hsien of Shu 蜀獻王 and became titular mentor to his infant son. His fame as a thinker and essayist spread even to the emperor, who is said to have commented that it was "not yet time to put Hsiao-ju to use."

That time came in 1398 with the ascension to the throne of Emperor Hui, who employed Fang in several official capacities, mostly posts where his classical learning could be utilized. He discussed Confucian statecraft with the emperor at length, with an emphasis on the *Chou li* (see *ching*), upon which they based a series of reforms which were beginning to be implemented when the emperor's uncle, Chu Ti (later Ch'eng-tsu), rose in rebellion, finally taking Nanking in 1401. The would-be emperor was conciliatory towards Fang, whose integrity and learning he respected. He proposed that Fang draft the proclamation whereby he would assume power. Fang adamantly refused, branding him a usurper. Ch'eng-tsu's patience was eventually exhausted and he had Fang executed. His wife and four children committed suicide just before his execution. Nearly a thousand of his friends and relatives are said to have been killed as well, though the actual number may have been much smaller. His works were publicly burned, and anyone found to possess even a remnant of his writings was subject to death. He was exonerated by imperial order in 1584, and his tablet was placed in the Confucian Temple in 1863.

Fang's prose style was masterly and elegant, though he avoided the cadences and lengthy clauses favored by his contemporaries. His style has been dubbed *hao-fang* 豪放 (unbridled in vigor, virile), and he claimed that what he sought in writing was "to have spirit gather in the heart" 神會於心, an appeal to a quality beyond technique. He disapproved of the mere literariness in prose and saw it as a vehicle for the Way, after the fashion of the Ch'eng-Chu School. His life was dedicated to helping realize the "Kingly Way" (the Mencian *Wang tao* 王道), and he strove for a dignity of style to match that purpose. Yet his writings are not merely instruments of didacticism. His style is uncommonly clear, and his arguments are lucid and logical. He often employs contrasts. His essays touch upon a broad range of subjects (from literature to political theory, from orthodoxy to instructions for his family). Noteworthy among his pieces are "Shen-lü lun" 深慮論 (A Discussion of Profound Contemplation), in which he expounds the idea that no amount of forethought can insure success or avert calamity, unless self-cultivation and the promotion of virtue move Heaven to act in man's favor, and "Wen tui" 蚊對 (The Mosquitoes' Answer), in which he discusses the relativity of all occurrences and argues that man, too, preys on man, although most men, indignant over an insect bite, are blind to their own predatory tendencies. He also has a delightful piece called "Pi tui" 鼻對 (The Nose's Answer), in which his nose speaks to him and exhorts him to reform his ways. His writings are self-chastising and laden with moral undertones, yet the depth, wit, and grace of exposition render them endearing.

The *Hsün-chih Chai chi* 遜志齋集, his collected works (first published in 1463), was put together from writings preserved by one of his disciples. It first appeared under the title *Hou-ch'eng chi* 侯城集. His biography is found in the *Ming-shih* 明史 (*ch.* 141).

EDITIONS:

Hsün-chih Chai chi 遜志齋集. 24 + 1 *chüan. SPTK.*
The definitive edition based on a 1561 version, which in turn was based on a condensed version (1520) of the 40-*chüan* edition (1480). It includes 8 *chüan* of miscellaneous prose and 14 *chüan* of poetry. The appendix includes poems and letters to Fang by friends and disciples and posthumous tributes, as well as prefaces and colophons to several editions of his works.

Ming-tai wen-hsüeh p'i-p'ing tzu-liao hui-pien 明代文學批評資料彙編. 2v. Taipei, 1978, v. 1, pp. 200-233. Essays (28) dealing specifically with Fang's literary theory. An extensive and representative sampling of his writings on this subject.

TRANSLATIONS:
Margouliès, *Anthologie*, pp. 409, and 417.

STUDIES:
Ch'ien, Mu 錢穆. "Tu Ming-ch'u k'ai-kuo chu ch'en shih-wen chi" 讀明初開國諸臣詩文集, *Hsin-ya hsüeh-pao*, 6.2 (August 1964), 320-326.
Crawford, Robert B., Harry M. Lamley, and Albert B. Mann. "Fang Hsiao-ju in the Light of Early Ming Society," *MS*, 15 (1956), 303-327. Fang Hsiao-ju as a political thinker. Also includes short translations illustrative of his philosophy.
DMB, pp. 426-433. The most comprehensive study available in English; only touches upon his accomplishments as an essayist.
Epping-von Franz, Marilie. *Fang Xiao-ru (1357-1402), Ein Konfuzianer im Konflict.* Wiesbaden, 1983.
Fincher, John. "China as a Race, Culture, and Nation: Notes on Fang Hsiao-ju's Discussion of Dynastic Legitimacy," *Transition and Permanence: Chinese History and Culture*, David C. Buxbaum and Frederick W. Mote, eds., Hong Kong, 1972, pp. 59-67.
Margouliès, *Prose*, pp. 266-270, 278.
Shen, Kang-po 沈剛伯. "Fang Hsiao-ju te cheng-chih hsüeh-shuo" 方孝儒的政治學說, *Ta-lu tsa-chih*, 22.5 (March 1961), 1-6.

—PA

Fang Pao 方苞 (*tzu*, Feng-chiu 鳳九, *hao*, Ling-kao 靈皋 and Wang-hsi 望溪, 1668-1749), scholar-official, literary theorist, and celebrated essayist, was born in the Nanking area and spent much of his life in that city. But because the Fang ancestral home was located in T'ung-ch'eng 桐城 (modern Anhwei), it is with that city that he is traditionally identified. In his childhood, Fang Pao received a typical classical education. After passing the provincial examinations, he went to Peking and enrolled in the Imperial Academy. In 1699 he won highest honors in the *chü-jen* examinations. Seven years later he passed the *chin-shih* examination, but he was called home because his mother was ill and he was unable to participate in the palace examinations. Soon after that, his father died, and Fang took leave from government service to observe the traditional mourning period.

During the seventeenth and eighteenth centuries, there were frequent literary inquisitions, and Fang Pao had the misfortune to become involved in one of them. In 1711, he came under suspicion of having contributed a preface to the book *Nan-shan chi ou-ch'ao* 南山集偶鈔 by Tai Ming-shih 戴名世 (1653-1713), which contained a letter by Tai which allegedly employed the reign-title designations of one of the southern Ming courts instead of those of the reigning dynasty. Tai was accused of treason for this act and subsequently executed. Among others caught up in this incident, Fang Pao and the members of his family were arrested and sent as bondservants to the far north. Fang Pao alone was excused from servitude in exile. Instead, possibly because of the intercession of friends and his own reputation as a writer of note, the K'ang-hsi Emperor ordered him to serve in the Imperial Study. Thus, he became involved in the preparation of book manuscripts for publication, and he continued to work in an editorial capacity when later transferred to the Imperial Printing Office. When the Yung-cheng Emperor ascended the throne, he pardoned Fang Pao and his family. Thereafter, Fang was employed in several different positions in government, including that of Secretary in the Directorate of Education. During the early years of the Ch'ien-lung era, he again found employment in official compilation projects. He contributed to the selecting and editing of model *pa-ku** examination essays for an anthology, to a similar work containing commentaries on the ancient ritual texts, and to the preparation of standard editions of the *Shih-san ching* 十三經 (Thirteen Classics) and the *Erh-shih-i shih* 二十一史 (Twenty-one Dynastic Histories). He attained the rank of a Vice Minister of Rites before retiring from public service to return home.

Fang Pao was all his life an ardent student of the ancient Confucian classics and literary texts, but his interests were more literary and stylistic than historical or philological. Exegetical scholarship was then in vogue, but he chose instead to devote his energies to other matters. By virtue of his own example as a master of the essay form and his efforts to promote the cause in other ways, Fang Pao became known as an advocate of *ku-wen.** Toward that end,

he compiled an anthology of prose writings, the *Ku-wen yüeh-hsüan* 古文約選. Holding the view that the ancient Confucian texts represented a level of stylistic perfection not amenable to excerpting, he selected model essays that were mainly but not exclusively from the works of the Eight Masters of the T'ang and Sung: Han Yü,* Liu Tsung-yüan,* Ou-yang Hsiu,* Tseng Kung,* Wang An-shih,* and Su Hsün* and his illustrious sons, Su Shih* and Su Ch'e.* Instead of the rather more complex divisions of materials into genre categories found in other anthologies of this kind, Fang Pao chose a simple, chronological arrangement. Generally speaking, this collection was intended to serve the reader as a supplement to the Confucian canon, the *Shih-chi,** and other classical texts and also as a means of exemplifying the aesthetic and ethical principles he identified with that tradition.

The compilers of the *Ssu-k'u ch'üan-shu tsung-mu t'i-yao* (see Chi Yün) and modern scholars alike have traced the origins of the T'ung-ch'eng School,* which claimed Fang Pao, Liu Ta-k'uei 劉大櫆 (*c.* 1697-1779) and Yao Nai* as its founding fathers, to sixteenth- and early seventeenth-century predecessors. Among the more important figures cited in that context are Kuei Yu-kuang,* a famous teacher and essayist who practiced a rather plain but lucid style under the influence of the T'ang and Sung-dynasty masters; T'ang Hsün-chih,* also widely admired for his skills as a prose writer and as the compiler of the anthology *Hsing-ch'uan wen-pien* 荊川文篇, which was intended as a guide to good writing; Mao K'un 茅坤 (1512-1601), a celebrated master of archaic prose and the compiler of the *T'ang Sung pa-ta-chia wen-ch'ao* 唐宋八大家文鈔, an anthology in 144 *chüan* of the famous writers mentioned above; Hou Fang-yü 侯方域 (1618-1655), who sought to bring about a revival of the prose styles of Han Yü and Ou-yang Hsiu, and who singled out the principles of *ts'ai* 才 (talent) and *fa* 法 (method) as being fundamental to *ku-wen* prose; Wang Yüan 王琬 (1624-1691), one of the foremost essayists of the day and an advocate of *wen* 文 (belles-lettres) and *tao* 道 (the Way) as co-equal elements constituting the essence of the form; and Wei Hsi 魏禧 (1624-1681), who also looked back to the "Eight Masters" for guidance and inspiration. Wei Hsi also advanced the theory that *fa, i* 義 (rightness), *yung* 用 (utility), and the neo-Confucian concept of *li* 理 (principle) were the informing elements of a great prose style. Following in this tradition, Fang Pao raised the standard of *i-fa* (right method, or principle and method). He found sanction for these twin concepts in the *I-ching*, which he interpreted as representing an indissoluble but not necessarily inflexible relationship between content and form. He seems to have understood the *fa* as a variable function of *i*. Because of his concern for correct diction and his reverence for the ancient models, relatively little room was left for flexibility in expression. On the other hand, he, his predecessors, and his followers all tended to oppose the imitative manner and the subordination of content to form. These attitudes, as well as his awareness of changing social and historical circumstances, modified somewhat his adherence to ancient standards. Fang believed rather that ancient models were to serve as examples of general principles, not of invariable patterns. Although he was critical of the constrictions of the *pa-ku* form for these reasons, he nonetheless admitted it into his scheme of things on the basis of its utility in the civil-service examinations.

Fang Pao was in his own day highly respected as a skillful essayist, and later critics have echoed this praise. His style has been described as severe in manner and lacking in ornamentation. He did not favor the use of words not current, and there is a spare, lean quality in his writing. It is perhaps for that reason that he has been faulted for a lack of naturalness and ease. Apparently reacting on the candid evaluation a friend gave his verse, Fang Pao wrote little poetry. His main contribution to Chinese letters therefore rests on his advocacy of archaic prose and his prominent place in the emergence of the T'ung-ch'eng School which, in turn, held sway in the field of the prose essay for nearly two centuries.

EDITIONS:
Fang, Pao. *Wang-hsi Hsien-sheng ch'uan-chi* 望溪先生全集. *SPPY* and *SPTK* editions, which contain a chronological record of Fang's life by Su Tun-yüan 蘇惇元 (1801-1857).

STUDIES:
Aoki, *Shindai*, v. 1, pp. 518-526.
ECCP, pp. 235-237.
Pollard, David E. *A Chinese Look at Literature, The Literary Values of Chou Tso-jen in Relation to the Tradition*. Berkeley, 1973. See especially Appendix A on the T'ung-ch'eng School.
Wu, *Ch'ing-tai*, pp. 262-263.
Yeh, Lung 葉龍. *T'ung-ch'eng p'ai wen-hsüeh shih* 桐城派文學史, Hong Kong, 1975.
Yu, Hsin-hsiung 尤信雄. *T'ung-ch'eng wen-p'ai hsüeh-shu* 桐城文派學述. Taipei, 1975.

—ws

Fang-shih 方士 were mountebanks, magicians, doctors, and diviners who flourished from the late Chan-kuo period to the middle of the Six Dynasties. Their importance to literature is twofold, as authors or putative authors of many early fictional texts and as favored subjects of historical and quasi-historical biographies. *Fang-shih* were most commonly credited with the authorship of geographical tracts describing remote lands and famous immortals, texts that demonstrated the *po-hsüeh* 博學 (broad learning) of the *fang-shih*. These include Tung-fang Shuo's *Shih-chou chi** and Chang Hua's* *Po-wu chih*. Ssu-ma Ch'ien* wrote that the *fang-shih* came primarily from the Shantung areas of ancient Yen and Ch'i and were the intellectual descendants of the Yin-Yang philosopher Tsou Yen 鄒衍, but there is considerable uncertainty as to their origins.

The *fang-shih* reached the apotheosis of their political importance and cultural influence during the early Han, especially the reign of Emperor Wu. He was said to have favored *fang-shih* to such an extent that virtually anyone with a plausible "secret tradition" rushed to court to collect his reward. Emperor Wu was known to be a willing listener to a well-wrought tale of marvels and he in turn became the subject of important early fictional works (see *Han Wu-ti nei-chuan*). The repertory by which *fang-shih* won their patronage included not only storytelling, but glib dissertations on astrology, omenology, and esoteric philosophy and various performances of magical arts. The histories record many instances of a *fang-shih* challenge game, *she-fu* 射覆, where masters the likes of Tung-fang Shuo, Kuan Lu 管輅, and Kuo P'u 郭璞 (276-324) guessed the identity of hidden objects before gatherings of dinner guests or skeptical officials.

The *fang-shih* and their influence on early fiction represent a consolidation of several intellectual and popular traditions from the pre-Han period. Their divination practices can be traced back to late Shang-dynasty oracle-bone culture, Chou-dynasty milfoil-stalk procedures, and Chou astrological and calendric technology. The historical connection between divination practices, especially calendric and astrological types, and the chronicling of events is reflected in the conspicuous literacy of the *fang-shih* and their propensity for authoring biographical, geographical, and other narratives. Their medical practices combine elements of the Confucian medical tradition (*ju-i* 儒醫) and popular medical practices, derived in large part from shamanic ritual. Hence they practiced a range of therapies from acupuncture and pharmacology to incantation and talismanic exorcism. Their immortality practices encompass both alchemical (*wai-tan* 外丹) and hygienic (*nei-tan* 內丹) techniques adumbrated in the Taoist classics and elaborated in the emerging religious Taoist movements.

Biographies of *fang-shih* found in the *Shih-chi*,* *Han-shu* (see Pan Ku), *Hou Han-shu* 後漢書, *San-kuo chih* 三國志, and *Chin-shu* 晉書 contain some of the most vivid and imaginative writing in the early dynastic histories. The accounts were often criticized for their spurious contents by later historiographers and the *fang-shih* were generally relegated to positions of lesser importance in the histories by virtue of the popular origins of their practices and their low social position. Still, their increased presence at court and the inclusion of their biographies in the dynastic histories brought waves of new materials into the purview of court discourse and into the literary tradition, transplantation that resulted in the significant refinement and improved preservation of many narratives of a clearly fictional nature. There is evidence that the biographies of the *fang-shih* in the dynastic histories were based less on the imperial archives, which were typically consulted for officials' lives, and more on external sources, notably *pieh-chuan* 別傳 and *chih-kuai*,* two varieties of "unoffical histories." Though only small fragments of *pieh-chuan* can be reconstructed today, it is evident that they were written by family descendants or disciples, and as a result they emphasize somewhat uncritically the efficacy of the particular *fang-shih's* techniques and the importance of his influence. Some varieties of *fang-shih* tales were, accordingly, direct precedents for Six Dynasty miracle tales and Buddhist stories. *Fang-shih* were commonly described as possessing spirit books, of jade slips and gold thread bindings, in which the secrets of their traditions were recorded.

Chinese bibliographers working on the problems of generic classification identified *fang-shih* with *hsiao-shuo** in the earliest extant document, the "I-wen chih" 藝文志 from the *Han-shu*. This bibliography lists fifteen *hsiao-shuo*, and argues that nine are false attributions whereas the remaining six all belong to the era of Emperor Wu. A Six Dynasties commentator subsequently identified a *fang-shih* of Emperor Wu's court, Yü Ch'u 虞初, as the originator of *hsiao-shuo* (Commentary on Chang Heng's* "Hsi-ching fu" 西京賦 in the *Wen-hsüan**), though this cannot be corroborated.

TRANSLATIONS:

Watson, Burton. "The Biography of Tung-fang Shuo," in *Courtier and Commoner in Ancient China*, New York, 1974, pp. 79-106.
———. "Treatise on the Feng and Shan," in *Records of the Grand Historian of China*, New York, 1971, v. 2, pp. 13-69.
DeWoskin, Kenneth J. *Doctors, Diviners, and Magicians of Ancient China, Biographies of* Fang-shih. New York, 1982. Translations from the dynastic histories.

———. "Tales of the Supernatural: Translations from the *Sou-shen chi*," *Renditions*, 7 (Spring 1977), 103-114.

Straughair, Anna. *Chang Hua: A Statesman-Poet of the Western Chin Dynasty.* Canberra, 1973.

Van Zuyet, Ngo. *Divination, magie et politique dans la Chine ancienne; Essai suivi de la traduction des "Biographies des Magiciens" tirees de l'Histoire des Han posterieurs.* 1979, pp. 73-148.

STUDIES:

Ch'en, P'an 陳槃. "Chan-kuo, Ch'in, Han chien fang-shih k'ao-lun" 戰國秦漢間方士考論, *BIHP*, 17 (1948), 7-57.

Ch'en, Yin-ch'üeh 陳寅恪. "Tien-shih tao yü pin-hai ti-yü chih kuan-hsi" 天師道與濱海地域之關係, in *Ch'en Yin-ch'üeh Hsien-sheng ch'üan-chi* 陳寅恪先生全集, Taipei, 1977, v. 1, pp. 365-403.

DeWoskin, Kenneth J. "A Source Guide to the Lives and Techniques of Han and Six Dynasties *Fang-shih*," *Bulletin of The Society for the Study of Chinese Religions* (Fall 1981).

Ku, Chieh-kang 顧頡剛. *Ch'in Han te fang-shih yü ju-sheng* 秦漢的方士與儒生. Shanghai, 1962.

Needham, Joseph. *Science and Civilisation of China.* Cambridge, 1971, v. 2, pp. 172ff., 346-364.

Wang, Yao 王瑤. "Hsiao-shuo yü fang-shih" 小說與方士, in his *Chung-ku wen-hsüeh ssu-hsiang* 中古文學思想, Hong Kong, 1973, pp. 153-194.

—KD

Feng Meng-lung 馮夢龍 (*tzu*, Yu-lung 猶龍, Tzu-yu 子猶, Erh-yu 耳猶, *hao*, Lung-tzu Yu 龍子猶, pseudonyms Mo-han chai chu-jen 墨憨齋主人, Ku-ch'ü san-jen 顧曲散人, Chiang-nan Chan-chan wai-shih 江南詹詹外史, Mou-yüan yeh-shih 茂苑野史, Lü-t'ien kuan chu-jen 綠天館主人, Lung-hsi chü-shih 隴西居士, K'o-i chü-shih 可一居士, Yü-chang Wu-ai chü-shih 豫章無礙居士, Ch'i-le sheng 七樂生, P'ing-p'ing ko chu-jen 平平閣主人, and others—all crucial for identifying his numerous works, 1574-1646) was the personification of popular Chinese literature. As an ardent champion of popular literature in its numerous forms, he contributed more to its preservation, growth, and diversity than any individual in premodern China. He was a native of Ch'ang-chou 長洲 in the exceptionally prosperous Soochow Prefecture (modern Kiangsu), one of the main centers of publishing activities and humanities in Ming China. Since he also lived at a time when many major types of popular literature, developed since the Sung-Yüan times, had already reached maturity and when a sizable amount of this literature was still available, the task may have been easier for him. But his success was largely based on his appreciation of the value of the unrecognized low-brow literature of the masses, and his tireless devotion to collecting, editing, and publishing these materials and enriching them with his own creations. In the end, his fictional works alone are enough to earn him a permanent and unique position in China's literary history.

For a man with such a vocation and temperament, it is not surprising to learn that Feng Meng-lung fared poorly in civil service examinations, led a carefree but rather uneventful life (at least by worldly standards) of which not much is known, and only had the opportunity to serve as the head of a minor Fukien county, Shou-ning 壽寧, for a short four-year period (1634-1637) in his sixties. This brief service is however rather personally registered in his *Shou-ning tai-chih* 壽寧待志 (Provincial History of Shou-ning, 1637), which gives us some glimpses of his attitudes and actions. By the end of his term, the Ming government was already in miserable shape under the dual pressures of external invasion and internal unrest. Feng Meng-lung, patriotic and dedicated, participated in the reformist activities headed by the learned society Fu-she 復社 perhaps not much later than its founding in 1632 (there is still no concrete evidence on his membership, but he had at the very least communicated with its members and expressed similar political viewpoints). It is therefore natural to find him associating with the Southern Ming authorities in their hopeless but passionate resistance against the advancing Manchus. Feng Meng-lung died in distress in 1646 at the age of seventy-three. The speculation that he had escaped to Japan and died there can easily be dismissed.

As a writer and a patron of literature, Feng was exceptional in the quantity, quality, and range of his interests. His most distinguished contribution is to fiction in both the short story and the full-fledged novel. Without his involvement in *hua-pen** stories knowledge of *hua-pen* literature today would be radically different. Through the compilation of the *San-yen* 三言 collections, *Ku-chin hsiao-shuo* 古今小說 (Stories Old and New, *c.* 1620)—also known as *Yü-shih ming-yen* 喻世明言 (Illustrious Words to Instruct the World), *Ching-shih t'ung-yen* 警世通言 (Comprehensive Words to Admonish the World, 1624), and *Hsing-shih heng-yen* 醒世恒言 (Lasting Words to Awaken the World, 1627), Feng succeeded in making available to the general public a significant proportion of the *hua-pen* stories then extant, many of which had already become collector's items. Since only some thirty *hua-pen* stories from editions before Feng Meng-lung have passed down to modern times, the extent of the loss, had Feng spared his efforts at this critical moment, can be seen. But preservation was not Feng's only concern; from the few comparisons possible with earlier texts, the rather extensive modifications in Feng's versions can be detected. These may have resulted simply from a desire or sense of obligation to improve the quality of the pieces; however this makes it impossible for the literary historian to examine the stories in their original shape. Compounding the confusion caused by Feng's method of indiscriminately incorporating his own stories and those of his friends in the collections, the 120 stories in the *San-yen* series pose an exceedingly thorny problem of identification and dating. The general belief is that the percentage of earlier stories, a number of which can be dated back to Sung times, declines with each succeeding collection.

This concern of modern scholars should not be seen as a negative reflection of the care with which Feng Meng-lung carried out his task. Parallel to the *San-yen* collections, Feng brought out an anthology series of classical-language stories and anecdotes—*Ku-chin t'an-kai* 古今譚概 (Talks Old and New, 1620), *Chih-nang* 智囊 (The Wisdom Sack, 1626), *T'ai-p'ing kuang-chi ch'ao*

太平廣記鈔 (Selections from the Grand Gleanings of the T'ai-p'ing Period, 1626), *Ch'ing-shih* 情史 (History of Love, after 1628) or *Ch'ing-shih lei-lüeh* 情史類略 (A Classified Outline of the History of Love), and *Chih-nang pu* 智囊補 (Additions to the Wisdom Sack, 1634)—whose dates, coinciding roughly with those of the *San-yen* collections, suggest that they could have been compiled partly as aids for the preparation of the *San-yen*. A comparison of the two groups of works, which might reveal something of the creative processes of Feng Meng-lung, has yet to be done.

Feng's interest in anecdotes also resulted in the compilation of the *Hsiao-fu* 笑府 (Treasury of Jokes), which became a minor classic in Japan. Although no longer circulated in China in its original form, *Hsiao-fu* served as the basis of the Ch'ing collection *Hsiao-lin kuang-chi* 笑林廣記 (Forest of Jokes), a later version of which is still periodically reprinted in Hong Kong and Taiwan.

Feng Meng-lung's involvement with the novel is no less complex, though it was on a smaller scale, and revision appears to have been the main concern. *P'ing-yao chuan** is a well-known example in which Feng expanded the original twenty *chüan* to forty *chüan*. Another example is the *Hsin lieh-kuo chih* 新列國志 (A New History of the States, after 1627), which was based on the earlier *Lieh-kuo chih chuan* 列國志傳 (A Fictionalized History of the States) by Yü Shao-yü 余邵魚; Feng's *Hsin lieh-kuo chih*, in turn, was replaced by Ts'ai Yüan-fang's 蔡元放 (Ch'ing) modified *Tung-chou lieh-kuo chih* 東周列國志 (A History of the States of the Eastern Chou). A third novel attributed to him, also of historical context, is the *Huang-Ming ta-ju Wang Yang-ming Hsien-sheng ch'u-shen ching-luan lu* 皇明大儒王陽明先生出身靖亂錄 (The Debut of Wang Yang-ming of the Ming Dynasty and his Campaigns Against the Rebels), but the language is so different from that of the two novels just mentioned that a detailed examination is needed before its authorship can be ascertained.

The number of theatrical pieces credited to Feng Meng-lung is equally impressive; the general nature of his contribution here was also revision. The southern *ch'uan-ch'i** dramas associated with his name include *Shuang-hsiung chi* 雙雄記 (A Pair of Heroes), *Wan-shih tsu* 萬事足 (Perfect Satisfaction), *Hsin kuan-yüan* 新灌園 (The New Gardener), *Chiu-chia yung* 酒家傭 (Servant in the Tavern), *Nü chang-fu* 女丈夫 (The Heroine), *Liang-chiang chi* 量江記 (Measuring the River), *Ching-chung ch'i* 精忠旗 (Flag of Loyalty), *Meng-lei chi* 夢磊記 (Dream of Rocks), *Sa-hsüeh t'ang* 灑雪堂 (Hall of Sprinkled Snow), *Ch'u-chiang ch'ing* 楚江情 (Love Story by River Ch'u), *Feng-liu meng* 風流夢 (Romantic Dream), *Jen-shou kuan* 人獸關 (Men-Animal Pass), *Yung t'uan-yüan* 永團圓 (Eternal Union), *Sha-kou chi* 殺狗記 (Killing the Dog), *San pao-en* 三報恩 (Thrice Requiting Favors), *Han-tan chi* 邯鄲記 (Story of Han-tan), and others. The majority of these are revised versions of recently composed dramas. His efforts to revise the compositions of his contemporaries, particularly T'ang Hsien-tsu* and Li Yü (*c.* 1591-*c.* 1671),* have to do with his belonging to the Wu-chiang School 吳江派 of drama founded by his patron Shen Ching 沈璟 (1553-1610); this school was obsessed with prosodic regulations and perfection of music, whereas the Lin-ch'uan School 臨川派 headed by T'ang Hsien-tsu emphasized content and thought. To revise the dramas of the leaders of the rival group was to demonstrate the superiority of his own school. Ming playwrights took special interest in ranking their own peers; Feng Meng-lung was given an "A-minus" 上下品 rating by his contemporary Lü T'ien-ch'eng 呂天成 (1577?-1614?), who also belonged to the Wu-chiang School.

With such commitment to the theatre, Feng's equally outstanding contribution to *san-ch'ü* (see *ch'ü*) songs is not unexpected. There are three collections of *san-ch'ü* to his name: *Wan-chuan ko* 宛轉歌 (Songs of Charm and Harmony), which is only available in a modern reconstructed version, *Yü-t'ao chi* 鬱陶集 (The Anguish Collection), which is lost, and *T'ai-hsia hsin-tsou* 太霞新奏 (Celestial New Songs, 1627). His unfinished song manual *Mo-han chai hsin-ting tz'u-p'u* 墨憨齋新定詞譜 (Ink Crazy Studio's New

Song Manual) was later incorporated by his friend Shen Tzu-chin 沈自晉 (1583-1665) into his *Nan-tz'u hsin-p'u* 南詞新譜 (New Manual of Southern Songs).

Feng's interest in songs included the art of the folksong, as shown by his two famous collections *Shan-ko* 山歌 (Hill Songs; see *shan-ko*) and *Kua-chih erh* 掛枝兒 (Songs to the Tune Kua-chih erh). These carefully edited compilations are important in preserving the folksongs of the Ming period, particularly those of the Wu-dialect region. Feng's affection for the folk culture also prompted him to prepare guides like *Ma-tiao chiao-li* 馬吊脚例 (Rules of the Ma-tiao Games) and *P'ai-ching* 牌經 (Classic of Cards).

Feng Meng-lung was also an orthodox scholar and a noted historian. Specializing in the Confucian classic *Ch'un-ch'iu* (see *ching*), he authored at least three handbooks on the subject: *Ch'un-ch'iu chih-yüeh* 春秋指月 (Guide to the Spring and Autumn Annals, 1620), *Ch'un-ch'iu ting-chih ts'an-hsin* 春秋定旨參新 (New Lights on the Central Ideas of the Spring and Autumn Annals, *c.* 1623), and *Ch'un-ch'iu heng-k'u* 春秋衡庫 (A Spring and Autumn Annals Thesaurus, 1625). He also published a similar handbook for the Four Books, *Ssu-shu chih-yüeh* 四書指月 (Guide to the Four Books, 1630). His participation in the Southern Ming resistance activities motivated him to record contemporary events. His *Chung-hsing shih-lu* 中興實錄 *(Veritable Records of the National Restoration, 1644) was soon incorporated into his larger Chia-shen chi-shih* 甲申紀事 (Records of the Year Chia-shen, 1644), while *Chung-hsing shih-lu* itself was reissued in 1645 as *Chung-hsing wei-lüeh* 中興偉略 (Grand Designs of the National Restoration) with minor modifications.

It is only natural that many later works and compilations were attributed to him. The first category includes *Wu-ch'ao hsiao-shuo* 五朝小說 (Stories of Five Dynasties) and *Ku-chin lieh-nü yen-i* 古今列女演義 (Memorable Women of the Past and the Present). An example of the second category is the clumsy *San-chiao ou-nien* 三教偶拈 (Casual Selections from the Three Religions), which includes the Wang Yang-ming novel.

Fortunately, most of these forgeries are not difficult to detect.

Even ignoring the fabrications, the number of works Feng wrote or edited and the variety of disciplines he touched are incredible. Consequently, many modern scholars tend to praise Feng Meng-lung without reserve. There is, however, one area in which Feng did not excel—traditional style poetry. Feng did bring out a collection of his own poems, *Ch'i-lo chai kao* 七樂齋稿 (A Drafted Collection of the Seven-Happiness Studio), which survived into the early eighteenth century but may not be extant today. There is no indication that it could have been a thick volume, and judging from the mediocrity of his few available poems and the remarks of the Ch'ing scholar-critic Chu I-tsun,* Feng Meng-lung can be regarded as a poet only to the extent that there were few premodern intellectuals who could not compose a few lines when called upon to do so.

EDITIONS:

Original or early editions of Feng Meng-lung's numerous works can be found in several major sinological libraries. Here only good editions which are easily available are mentioned.

Ku-chin hsiao-shuo, Ching-shih t'ung-yen, Hsing-shih heng-yen. Taipei, 1958-59. Photographic reproductions of rare Ming copies preserved in Japan. No notes, and typographical errors of the originals uncorrected.

Ching-shih t'ung-yen. Yen Tun-i 嚴敦易, ed. Peking, 1956. Generally accurate, with copious notes, but some passages censored.

Hsin lieh-kuo chih. Hu Wan-ch'uan 胡萬川, ed. Taipei, 1981. Based on a Ming copy, with copious notes.

Hsing-shih heng-yen. Ku Hsüeh-chieh 顧學頡, ed. Peking, 1956. Same quality as *Ching-shih t'ung-yen* above.

Ku-chin hsiao-shuo. Hsü Cheng-yang 許政揚, ed. Peking, 1958. Same quality as *Ching-shih t'ung-yen* above.

Ku-chin t'an-kai. Peking, 1955. Photographic reproduction of a Ming copy.

Kua-chih erh. Kuan Te-tung 關德棟, ed. Peking, 1962.

Mo-han chai ting-pen ch'uan-ch'i 墨憨齋定本傳奇. Peking, 1960. Photographic combination of Ming and early Ch'ing editions. Includes most of the dramas related to Feng Meng-lung.

Shan-ko. Kuan Te-tung, ed. Peking, 1962.

Wan-chuan ko. Lu Ch'ien 盧前, ed. Changsha, 1941.

Wang Yang-ming ch'u-shen ching-luan lu. Taipei, 1968. Photographic reproduction of a Japanese edition.

TRANSLATIONS:

So many of the *San-yen* stories have been translated into English, French, German, and Japanese that the limited space here cannot do justice to them in a highly selected list. Readers are thus referred to the comprehensive list of English translations in Patrick Hanan, *The Chinese Vernacular Story*, Cambridge, Mass., 1981, pp. 245-248. For translations in other languages, see the multi-volume set prepared by André Lévy and others, *Inventaire analytique et critique du conte chinois en langue vulgaire*, Paris, 1978- .

STUDIES:

Ch'ien, Nan-yang 錢南揚. "Feng Meng-lung *Mo-han chai tz'u-p'u* chi-i" 馮夢龍墨憨齋詞譜輯佚. *Chung-hua wen-shih lun-ts'ung*, 2 (November 1962), 281-310.

DMB, pp. 450-453.

Fan, Yen-ch'iao 范煙橋. "Feng Meng-lung te *Ch'un-ch'iu heng-k'u* chi ch'i i-wen i-shih 馮夢龍的春秋衡庫及其遺文佚詩. *Chiang-hai hsüeh-k'an*, 1962.9 (September 1962), 38.

Hanan, Patrick. "The Authorship of Some *Ku-chin hsiao-shuo* Stories," *HJAS*, 29 (1969), 190-200.

———. *The Chinese Short Story: Studies in Dating, Authorship, and Composition*. Cambridge, Mass., 1973.

———. *The Chinese Vernacular Story*. Cambridge, Mass., 1981. Two chapters on Feng Meng-lung.

Harada, Suekiyo 原田季清. "*Jōshi ni tsuite*" 情史に就て, *Taidai bungaku*, 2.1 (March 1937), 53-60.

———. "*Zōkō Chinō hō* ni tsuite" 增廣智囊補に就て, *Taidai bungaku*, 2.3 (June 1937), 48-53.

———. *Wahon shōsetsu ron* 話本小說論. Taihoku, 1938.

Hu, Shih-ying 胡士瑩. *Hua-pen hsiao-shuo kai-lun* 話本小說概論. Peking, 1980.

Hu, Wan-ch'uan 胡萬川. *Feng Meng-lung sheng-p'ing chi ch'i tui hsiao-shuo chih kung-hsien* 馮夢龍生平及其對小說之貢獻. Taipei, 1973.

———. "Feng Meng-lung yü Fu-she jen-wu" 馮夢龍與復社人物, *Chung-kuo ku-tien hsiao-shuo yen-chiu chuan-chi*, 1 (August 1979), 123-136.

———. "Ts'ung *Chih-nang Chih-nang pu* k'an Feng Meng-lung" 從智囊智囊補看馮夢龍. *Chung-kuo ku-tien hsiao-shuo yen-chiu chuan-chi*, 1 (August 1979), 137-150.

Jung, Chao-tsu 容肇祖. "Ming Feng Meng-lung te sheng-p'ing chi ch'i chu-shu" 馮夢龍的生平及其著述. *Ling-nan hsüeh-pao*, 2.2 (July 1931), 61-91.

———. "Ming Feng Meng-lung te sheng-p'ing chi ch'i chu-shu hsü-k'ao" 續考. *Ling-nan hsüeh-pao*, 2.3 (June 1932), 95-124.

Miao, Yung-ho 繆詠禾. *Feng Meng-lung* 馮夢龍. Shanghai, 1979.

Mowry, Hua-yüan Li 李華元. *Chinese Love Stories from Ch'ing-shih*. Hamden, Conn., 1982. Discussion with translations.

Ogawa, *Sangen*. Offers summaries of all *hua-pen* in the *San-yen* (see Ling Meng-ch'u) and *Erh-p'ai* collections followed by a list of all identifications of sources by Chinese and Japanese scholars.

Ono, Shihei 小野四平. *Chūgoku kinsei ni okeru tampen hakuwa shōsetsu no kenkyū hyōronshū* 中國近世における短篇白話小說の研究評論集. Tokyo, 1978. Several substantial chapters on Feng Meng-lung.

T'an, *San-yen*. Provides the full text of the identified sources of each *hua-pen* in *San-yen* and *Erh-p'ai*.

Wang, Cheng-ho 汪正禾. "Feng Meng-lung shih-chi" 馮夢龍詩輯. *T'ien-ti*, 6 (March 1944), 40-41.

Yeh-ju 野孺. "Kuan-yü *San-yen* te tsuan-chi che" 關於三言的纂輯者, in *Ming Ch'ing hsiao-shuo yen-chiu lun-wen chi* 明清小說研究論文集. Peking, 1959, pp. 29-33.

———. "Kuan-yü Feng Meng-lung te shen-shih" 關於馮夢龍的身世, in *Ming Ch'ing hsiao-shuo yen-chiu lun-wen chi*, pp. 34-38. An amazing collection of biographical data.

—YWM

Feng-shen yen-i 封神演義 (Investiture of the Gods) is primarily a fantasy built on the framework of a historical romance. The novel in its present form is usually attributed to Hsü Chung-lin 許仲琳 (d. *c.* 1566). Supported only by a single, indirect bibliographical piece of evidence, the attribution has been rejected by Liu Ts'un-yan in favor of the Taoist priest Lu Hsi-hsing 陸西星 (*tzu*, Chang-keng 長庚, 1520-1601?). But as with most traditional vernacular novels, the "author" here is to be understood as a redactor who bases his work on existing texts and other materials. The more important sources for the *Feng-shen* story include the oral and written material contained in such works as *Wu-wang fa Chou p'ing-hua* 武王伐紂平話 (The *P'ing-hua* on King Wu's Campaign against Chou) and Chapter 1 of the *Lieh-kuo chih chuan* 列國志傳 (A Fictionalized History of the States), together with various Taoist and Buddhist legends.

The narrative elaborates on the historical campaign of King Wu of the Chou dynasty against King Chou's moral dissipation, particularly his indulgence in the beauty Tan-chi 妲己, his brutal treatment of loyal ministers and subjects, and his unsuccessful attempts to subdue the Chou state in a series of military expeditions. These events are followed by the gathering of the forces of Chou with those of other states and the siege of the Shang capital under the command of Chiang Tzu-ya 姜子牙. The story ends with King Chou taking his own life as the besieging armies close in on the royal palace. These human conflicts and especially the military encounters, are often conducted with the participation of the Taoist demiurges (some of them of a Buddhist origin) and their disciples, who take sides in the dynastic struggle and do battle with magic weapons and fanciful displays of wizardry. In fact the wars waged in the human world are conceived of as a part of the plan that is to lead to the "investiture of the gods," an event foreseen and agreed upon by the chiefs of the Taoist deities, who are divided into two sects called Ch'an-chiao 闡教 and Chieh-chiao 截教. Thus Chiang Tzu-ya, as the "protagonist" of the novel, is sent by the head of the Ch'an-chiao to conduct the campaign to overthrow the Shang, acting in accord with the divine course of events, or *t'ien-shu* 天數, while the "antagonist" Shen Kung-pao 申公豹, out of spite for Chiang, instigates the Chieh-chiao demiurges and their followers to oppose the campaign, in defiance of the divine plan. Yet ultimately Shen's interference is seen to fit the working of the plan in that it is precisely for the spirits of the warriors slain in the battles that the "investiture" is instituted.

The text makes use of a double principle of overall organization: a symmetrical arrangement of event-sequences is complemented by an order imposed by significant numbers. For instance the rebellious armies at Fort Meng-chin 孟津, before descending on the Shang capital, have a counterpart in Chiang Tzu-ya's positioning at Ch'i-shan 岐山 to meet the punitive armies sent by King Chou. Spatially, the eastward movement of the Chou troops toward Ch'ao-ko 朝哥 and their penetration of the resistance at the five passes mirrors Huang Fei-hu's 黃飛虎 earlier flight to join forces with King Wu in the west. Such spatial designs and parallelisms of events are supplemented by the numerical scheme implicitly tied in with the "divine plan" that seems to have a bearing upon the pattern of human affairs. King Wen's seven-year imprisonment is foreseen by himself as predestined, while the Chou camp at Ch'i-shan has to endure thirty-six sieges and attacks from the Shang forces before the Chou armies can march on to the east. Chiang Tzu-ya, in the course of his expedition, is foreordained to undergo "seven deaths and three catastrophes," just as King Wu must suffer a hundred-day confinement in one of the magic mazes set up by the Chieh-chiao Taoists.

Besides the frequent display of magic warfare that reveals a particular mode of fantasy in Chinese imagination, the novel also contains numerous wars of words, as each appeal to arms is preceded by a verbal debate. The arguments inevitably take the form of either the condemnation of, or justification for, the rebellion. Although they never vary in ideological content, the debates always differ slightly according to the situations and backgrounds of the individuals involved.

Cast as a military struggle between a liege house and a "vassal state," the narrative naturally points up the theme of rebellion with a bold questioning of the concept of allegiance dictated by the hierarchical structure of relationships. Indeed challenge to authority is manifested not only in the political struggle but in other fields of human relations: explicit treatments of the revolt of the son against the father, the disciple against the master, etc., all contribute to the same theme. Such unorthodox actions, however, are ultimately ascribed to the functioning of *t'ien-shu* 天數 (divine order of succession) in human history, and thus the contradiction between "loyalty" and "revolt" (as well as other conflicts) is resolved.

For all its imaginativeness and its lofty conception of action, *Feng-shen yen-i* seems to suffer from too much repetition. Unexpected elements are often introduced, apparently intentionally, to break up the routine, but these diversions fail to offset the monotony of the formulaic sequences.

EDITIONS:

Hsin-k'o Chung Po-chin Hsien-sheng p'i-p'ing Feng-shen yen-i 新刻鍾伯敬先生批評 封神演義, 100 chapters in 20 *chüan*. Published by Shu Tsai-yang 舒載陽 (Ming). In Naikaku Bunkō. At the beginning of *chüan* 2 of this edition is found the inscription "Chung-shan-i-sou Hsü Chung-lin pien-chi" 鍾山逸叟許仲琳編輯, which has been the basis for the attribution to Hsü.

Feng-shen yen-i, with alternative title *Feng-shen chuan* 封神傳 attached. 100 chapters in 8 *chüan*. Preface by Chou Chih-piao 周之標 (Ming). The same edition, with an additional title, *Shang Chou lieh-kuo ch'uan chuan* 商周列國全傳, published by Wei-wen t'ang 蔚文堂. Both in the collection of Peking University Library.

Ssu-hsüeh ts'ao-t'ang ting-cheng pen Feng-shen yen-i 四雪草堂訂正本封神演義. 100 chapters in 19 *chüan*. Preface by Ch'u Jen-huo 褚人穫 dated 1695. The woodblock edition on which most of the later lithographic editions are based.

Feng-shen yen-i, 100 chapters Peking, 1955, and subsequent reprints. The best modern critical edition.

Feng-shen yen-i. 2v. Canton, 1980.

TRANSLATION:

Grube, Wilhelm. *Feng-shen yen-i, Die Metamorphosen der Goetter: Historisch-mythologischer Roman aus dem chinesischen, übersetzung der Kapitel 1 bis 46.* Translation of Chapters 1-46 is followed by a synopsis of the rest of the text. Also includes information about editions and sources and critical commentaries.

STUDIES:

Liu, Ts'un-yan. *Buddhist and Taoist Influences on Chinese Novels. V. 1: The Authorship of the Feng-shen Yen-I.* Wiesbaden, 1962. Best study on

Koss, Nicholas. "The Relationship of *Hsi-yu chi* and *Feng-shen yen-i*," *TP*, 65 (1979), 143-165.

Porkert, Manfred. "Die zwiespaltige Rolle des Chiang Tzu-ya, der Zentralfigur im *Feng-shen yen-i*," *Sinologica*, 11 (1970), 135-144.

Shih, Shu-fang 施淑芳. *Feng-shen yen-i yen-chiu* 封神演義研究. Taipei, 1979.

Wei, Chü-hsien 衞聚賢. *Feng-shen pang ku-shih t'an-yüan* 封神榜故事探源, 2v. Hong Kong, 1960.

—KK

Feng Wei-min 馮惟敏 (*tzu*, Ju-hsing 汝行, *hao*, Hai-fu [or fou] shan-jen 海浮山人; 1511-1578?) was one of the best poets in the *ch'ü** form during the Ming dynasty. Indeed his work can be seen as the culmination of the *san-ch'ü* and *tsa-chü** traditions that had begun early in the thirteenth century.

During Feng's childhood his father served in a number of different places and as a growing boy he had an opportunity to see more of the country than did most young people of his period. He passed the local examination in 1537, but failed the *chin-shih* the next year, which he took along with his three brothers, two of whom passed. He then retired to a villa in his ancestral district, Lin-ch'ü 臨胸 in the Shantung hills, where he lived a life of leisure enlivened by occasional conflicts with rapacious local officials. In 1563 he finally returned to Peking and offered himself for service, holding several minor offices in various places during the ensuing ten years. He retired again in 1572 and spent the rest of his years in Lin-ch'ü. The year of his death is uncertain. The most likely date is 1578.

Feng's collected *tz'u** poetry is apparently no longer extant; two gazetteers that he edited or co-edited also seem to have disappeared. Although a few essays and *fu*,* as well as two overlapping collections of *shih** poetry totalling almost 250 pieces, have survived, Feng is known almost entirely for his *ch'ü* lyrics and for two plays.

These represent an important development in the history of the forms: they are among the most mature and accomplished works of their kind from the Ming period. *San-ch'ü* and *tsa-chü* had both suffered something of a decline after the founding of the Ming. It was only after 1500 that a few writers (some of them associated with the Archaist Movement typified by Li Meng-yang*), such as K'ang Hai,* Wang Chiu-ssu,* and Li K'ai-hsien,* attempted to preserve or even revive them. Their works were marked by a degree of formal innovation, but also by a change in thematic emphasis most noticeable in Feng's works. Where earlier plays and lyrics had often had a strong romantic element or an interest in ornate diction, Feng's works reflect an underlying commitment to Confucian values perhaps due to the influence of his father, a follower of Ch'en Hsien-chang 陳獻章 (1428-1500). The "Confucianization" of the *san-chü*, as it has been called, was reflected not simply in doctrinal content, but rather in a fundamentally serious, if often good-humored, concern with human and social well-being and in a broad range of themes and emotions. Thus Feng is to the *ch'ü* what Su Shih had been to the *tz'u*, but with one important difference; whereas Su had many followers, the *san-ch'ü* as an important literary tradition can be said to end with Feng. Of Feng's two plays, one is a partly autobiographical work about a man who succeeds in passing the *chin-shih* examination only in extreme old age, and the other concerns the return to lay life of Buddhist clergy.

Feng Wei-min had three brothers who lived to maturity and made contributions to literature. His older brothers, Wei-chien 惟健 (b. 1503) and Wei-ch'ung 惟重 (1504-1572) were both poets, and his younger brother Wei-na 惟訥 (?1512-1572) was both a poet and a scholar-editor. Wei-na's most important work was his *Ku-shih chi*,* a comprehensive collection of pre-T'ang verse in 156 *chüan*, completed by 1566, which led to the compilation of a series of similar works by others, including the *T'ang shih chi* 唐詩紀 of Wu Kuan 吳琯, an ancestor of the *Ch'üan T'ang shih*.*

EDITIONS:

Feng Hai-fu chi 馮海浮集, 1 *chüan*, in *Sheng-Ming pai-chia shih.*

Hai-fu shan-t'ang tz'u-kao 海浮山堂詞稿, 4 *chüan*, in *Feng shih chia-k'o.* The best text of Feng Wei-min's collected *san-ch'ü* and plays.

Ibid., in *San-ch'ü ts'ung-k'an.* The most accessible text; based on the preceding, but omits the plays, rearranges some of the material, and introduces a few misprints.

I-shih pu-fu lao 一世不伏老, in *Ku-pen hsi-ch'ü ts'ung-k'an ssu-chi,* v. 118.

Pu-fu lao, in *Sheng-Ming tsa-chü erh-chi.* Two accessible editions each of Feng's two plays. The first reproduces a manuscript text; the others are typeset. There are variations in the texts of both plays.

Shih-men chi 石門集, in *Feng shih wu hsien-sheng chi.* Two overlapping collections of Wei-min's *shih* and *fu.*

Seng-ni kung-fan ch'uan-ch'i 僧尼共反傳奇, in *Ku-pen hsi-ch'ü ts'ung-k'an ssu-chi,* v. 45.

Seng-ni kung-fan, in *Ku-pen Yüan-Ming tsa-chü.*

STUDIES:

Cheng Ch'ien 鄭騫. "Feng Wei-min chi ch'i chu-shu" 馮惟敏及其著述, in *Ching-wu ts'ung-pien* 景午叢編, Taipei, 1972, pp. 116-147. Revised version of an article originally published in 1940 in the *Yen-ching hsüeh-pao;* includes a detailed chronological biography and bibliographical notes on editions on Feng's works.

———. "Feng Wei-min yü san-ch'ü te chiang-lai" 馮惟敏與散曲的將來, *ibid.,* pp. 209-212. Reprinted from *Ch'ing-nien wen-hua,* 1946.

DMB, pp. 459-461.

Liang, I-chen 梁乙眞. "Ming san-ch'ü chia Feng Wei-min nien-piao" 明散曲家馮惟敏年表, *Ch'ing-nien chieh,* 8.1 (1935), 132-140.

—DB

Feng Yen-ssu 馮延巳 (also Yen-ssu 延嗣, *tzu,* Cheng-chung 正中, 903?-960), senior government official and song-lyric poet, was a native of Kuang-ling 廣陵 (modern Kiangsu). His father Ling-chün 令頵 (d. 926) held several different local offices, and finally that of a Secretary to the Ministry of Personnel. Feng Yen-ssu was in his early twenties when he was named to a post in the government of the Southern T'ang dynasty, thus beginning a long and eventful career that ultimately led to the office of Grand Councilor, a position which he held on at least three separate occasions, but only once for a period of more than several months. His career was attended by numerous ups and downs, resulting from the factional strife which plagued political life at that time. One modern scholar has also argued convincingly that political factionalism was a key factor in the rather unflattering portrait of Feng found in the standard histories, where he is described as being an arrogant, acerbic, and difficult man. The *Tiao-chi li-t'an* 釣磯立談, compiled by a participant in those partisan struggles, was widely used by such later historians as Ou-yang Hsiu,* Ssu-ma Kuang 司馬光 (1019-1086) and Lu Yu,* with the result that Feng may have been treated unfairly. After his death in 960, he was canonized with the title Chung-su 忠肅 (Loyal and Respectful).

Although much respected in his own time for his wide learning and his skill as a writer of prose, little of his prose writing has come down to us. In addition to a short fragment quoted in the *Nan-T'ang shu* 南唐書 by Ma Ling 馬令, only one commemorative essay from his hand has been preserved in the *Ch'üan T'ang wen.** By the same token, the *Ch'üan T'ang shih** contains only one sextasyllabic *shih* poem and a fugitive couplet.

Feng Yen-ssu's reputation as a man of letters therefore rests almost exclusively on his lyric (*tz'u**) verse. His poetry in that form was collected and published in 1058 by a grandson under the title *Yang-ch'un chi* 陽春集 (Warm Spring Collection), although there is some evidence that his lyric poetry may have circulated in his lifetime under the title *Hsiang-lien chi* 香奩集 (The Fragrant Trousseau Collection), also the name of Han Wo's* collection. The standard modern edition of his extant lyrics was later edited and supplemented by Wang P'eng-yün 王鵬運 (1849-1904), a gifted lyric poet in his own right. However, serious problems of attribution have existed since the *Yang-ch'un chi* came into being. Thirty-five of the 120-odd poems in that collection are also to be found in other early collections of lyric poetry, where they are attributed to such poets as

Wen T'ing-yün,* Wei Chuang,* Li Yü,* and Ou-yang Hsiu.* Efforts to sort out this confusion have not been altogether convincing, the arguments one way or another usually being based on personal impressions of individual stylistic characteristics. One modern writer has concluded that only 105 of the poems can be safely assigned to the hand of Feng Yen-ssu.

There is somewhat greater unanimity of opinion about the importance of Feng's contribution to the early development of the form and the excellence of his style. Like his predecessors and contemporaries, Feng Yen-ssu made exclusive use of the *hsiao-ling*, or short lyric patterns; however, within those constraints, he was more flexible than either Wen T'ing-yün or Wei Chuang, using more than thirty different patterns. Like them and the other *Hua-chien chi** poets, his thematic range was relatively narrow and limited mostly to bedroom topics and the evocation of personal grief and despair. Nonetheless, he is widely recognized as having had a strong influence on the lyric poets of Northern Sung times, such as Ou-yang Hsiu and Yen Shu.* In matters of style he reveals great depth of feeling, breadth of vision, beauty, and a concise manner. Other critics have stressed the individuality and objectivity of his better poems, as well as their vitality and impressive pictorial qualities. Kang-i Sun Chang, on the other hand, sees a difference between the use of implicit rhetoric in his poetry and that of Wen T'ing-yün, with both Feng Yen-ssu and Li Ching 李璟 (916-961) typically fusing "images of nature with subtle human feelings," and thereby making a significant contribution to the early development of lyric verse.

EDITIONS:
Ch'üan T'ang wen, v. 18, *chüan* 876, pp. 11557-11559. A lone essay written in 951.
Ch'üan T'ang shih, v. 11, *chüan* 738, pp. 8415-8416; one *shih* poem and a fragment.
Ch'üan T'ang Wu-tai tz'u hui-pien 全唐五代詞彙編. 2v. Taipei, 1967. Reprint of the Lin Ta-ch'un 林大椿 compilation *T'ang Wu-tai tz'u*. Contains 126 lyrics attributed to Feng Yen-ssu.
Wang, P'eng-yün, ed. *Yang-ch'un chi chi pu-i* 陽春集及補遺. *Ssu-yin Chai k'e tz'u* 四印齋刻詞

ed., on which most modern editions of Feng's poems are based.

TRANSLATIONS:
Sunflower, pp. 299-300.
Ayling, *Further Collection*, pp. 31-37.

STUDIES:
Bryant, Daniel. *Lyric Poets of the Southern T'ang: Li Yü and Feng Yen-ssu*. Vancouver, British Columbia, 1983.
Chang, *Evolution*, pp. 92-95.
Hsia, Ch'eng-t'ao 夏承燾. *T'ang Sung tz'u-jen nien-p'u* 唐宋詞人年譜. Shanghai, 1955; see pp. 35-71 for a chronological account of Feng's life and career.
Lin, Wen-pao 林文寶. *Feng Yen-ssu yen-chiu* 馮延巳研究, Taipei, 1974. The most extensive treatment of Feng and his poetry currently available.
Yeh, Chia-ying 葉嘉瑩. *Chia-ling t'an tz'u* 迦陵談詞. Taipei, 1970, see especially pp. 55-143.
—WS

Fu 賦 (prose-poetry) is a poetic genre both distinctive, because its modes of description and exposition are unique, and elastic, because it sometimes appears like verse and sometimes like prose. It cannot be adequately defined in purely formal terms because not all compositions designated as *fu* have the same characteristics. Therefore the word *fu* has been rendered into English by various expressions: "prose-poetry," "poetical description," "verse essay," "rhyme-prose," "rhapsody," "rhapsodic essay" and so forth. However, owing to a predominance of rhythmic and metrical elements in most *fu*, the genre is most strongly linked to poetry.

The *fu* derives from the rhymed riddles of Hsün Ch'ing 荀卿 (*c*. 300-230 B.C.), the florid debates and speeches of the diplomats and rhetoricians of the Warring States Period and, in particular, the "Li sao" 離騷 and *Ch'u-tz'u*.* In early Han times, there was no clear distinction made between the *fu* and the *sao*-poems, and the compositions of Ch'ü Yüan* and his followers are recorded in the *Han-shu* "I-wen chih" (Bibliographic Treatise) as *fu*.

The earliest specimen of *fu* whose authorship and date are certain is the "Fu niao fu" 鵩鳥賦 (Prose-poem on the Owl) by Chia I.* In many ways, it is closer to the poems of the *Ch'u-tz'u* than to the later *fu* and thus serves as a bridge between the two genres. Around the middle of the second century B.C., a group of poets, among whom Mei Sheng* was the best known, began to compose *fu* on various subjects at the court of Prince Hsiao of Liang 梁孝王 (*fl.* 178-144 B.C.). They broke ground with the new literary genre which became fully established when Ssu-ma Hsiang-ju's* descriptive *fu* on hunts, the "Tzu-hsü" 子虛賦 and "Shang-lin" 上林賦, appeared.

Ssu-ma Hsiang-ju was a prolific writer and his *fu* served as models for later imitations. His follower and admirer, Yang Hsiung,* composed on sacrificial ceremonies, the "Kan-ch'üan fu" 甘泉賦 (Prose-poem on Sweet Springs) and "Ho-tung fu" 河東賦, and on imperial hunts, the "Yü-lieh fu" 羽獵賦 (Prose-poem on the Plume Hunt) and "Ch'ang-yang fu" 長楊賦. Deriving inspiration from the works of his predecessors, Pan Ku* first wrote on the national capitals, the "Liang tu fu" 兩都賦 (Prose-poem on the Two Capitals). It covers a wide range of topics and also proved a source for imitations, notably by Chang Heng* and Tso Ssu.*

The descriptive Han *fu* tend to be lengthy and are frequently constructed in the form of a dialogue. They are characterized by the use of hyperbole, descriptive binomial compounds, and a number of "connectives" (*yü-shih* 於是, *yü-shih-fu* 於是夫, *ch'ieh-fu* 且夫, *jo-fu* 若夫, etc.) and "directives" (*ch'i tung* 其東, *ch'i nan* 其南, *ch'i shang* 其上, *ch'i hsia* 其下, etc.). Most were written by court poets who submitted these *fu* to the throne as a kind of offering, primarily for the purpose of giving pleasure to their royal patron through the richness and beauty of the language or the attractive scenes described. Indeed, the lengthy descriptive Han *fu* often contain an element of "feng-chien" 諷諫 (indirect admonition) as claimed by the poets. In the eyes of some critics, this claim is merely a conforming bow to the literary convention of the era, since Confucianism had become the orthodox creed of the state by Han times.

However, the *fu*-writers of the Han did not confine themselves to descriptions. They also utilized the prose-poem as a vehicle to proclaim their philosophy or to express their feelings and emotions. Among the best known of this type of *fu*, the so-called "*fu* of frustration," are Yang Hsiung's "Chu p'in fu" 逐貧賦 (Prose-poem on Driving Away Poverty), Pan Chieh-yü's 班婕妤 (*c.* 48 B.C.) "Tzu-tao fu" 自悼賦 (Prose-poem of Self-Commiseration), Chang Heng's "Ssu hsüan fu" 思玄賦 (Prose-poem Meditating on Mystery) and Ts'ai Yung's* "Chien-i fu" 檢逸賦 (Prose-poem on Curbing Excess).

The *fu* enjoyed its golden age in the Han period but later lost prestige, though it was still practiced by literati. Around the middle of the second century, the conflicts within the Han ruling class became acute and a succession of uprisings took place. The palaces, pleasure-gardens, and beautiful lodges, once subjects for *fu* compositions, were destroyed. Poets either sought consolation in Taoism or wrote on various minor subjects, with the detail of a delicate vignette. Thus in the hands of the writers of the Chien-an period (196-220), such as Ts'ao Chih,* Wang Ts'an,* Ch'en Lin,* and Ying Yang 應瑒 (d. 217), the nature of the *fu* changed drastically.

In the Six Dynasties, a growing aesthetic awareness of literature led to the distinction between *wen* 文 (belles-lettres) and *pi* 筆 (utilitarian prose). Emphasis was placed on linguistic, tonal, and formal structure. Literary theory and practice changed radically, in the course of which the *fu* developed a new style and adopted new themes. It was characterized by a tendency to four- and six-character parallel lines and antithetical binomes, and by special attention to euphony. The Six Dynasties' *fu* are comparatively short and predominantly descriptive. Their topics range widely from meteorological phenomena, natural scenery, plants, flowers, beasts, and birds to small insects and tiny artifacts. At the same time, the *fu* was also used to express personal philosophy, attitudes toward life, or emotional states. The best known examples are P'an Yüeh's* "Hsien-chü fu" 閒

居賦 (Prose-poem on the Idle Life), Lu Chi's* "Sui chih fu" 遂志賦 (Prose-poem on Fulfilling One's Ambition), T'ao Ch'ien's* "Hsien-ch'ing fu" 閑情賦 (Prose-poem on Stilling the Passions), and Chiang Yen's* "Pieh fu" 別賦 (Prose-poem on Parting). In the hands of Yü Hsin,* this type of *fu* reached its culmination. Combining the antithetical structure of parallel prose (*p'ien-wen**) and the prosody of the traditional *fu* he established an extremely artificial but delicate style, which, in spite of its rigid formalism and extensive allusions, served both lyrical and descriptive purposes. His "Ai Chiang-nan fu" 哀江南賦 (Lament for the South), a great moving poem about the fall of the Liang dynasty in which he himself appears as a major actor, has been acknowledged an incomparable masterpiece of Chinese literature.

During the T'ang period prose-poems developed into the *lü fu* 律賦 (regulated prose-poem), in which the author was compelled to write strictly parallel lines and to follow a prescribed rhyme pattern. The composition of *fu* became an academic exercise, as it had been made a requirement for the civil-service examination. A short quotation, usually from the Confucian Classics, would be given which had to be used as rhymes; the topic was also prescribed by the suggested meaning of the given lines. Under these strict rules, the composition was bound to be relatively short and mechanical. Of coures, there are some pieces, for example Li Po's* "Ta lïeh fu" 大獵賦 (Prose-poem on the Great Hunt) and Li Yü's (937-978)* "Liang tu fu" 兩都賦 (Prose-poem on the Two Capitals) entirely free from these fetters. They are lengthy, elaborate, and ornate, comparable to those of the Han times.

The *Ku-wen yün-tung* (Ancient-style Prose Movement—see *ku-wen*) in the mid-T'ang set a new course for the *fu*, which had by then become no more than systematic word play. Tu Mu* in his "Ah-fang kung fu," by increasing the prose element and deemphasizing rhyme, initiated a new style of *fu*, and in the hands of the great poets of the Sung dynasty, Ou-yang Hsiu* and Su Shih,* the transformation to the *wen-fu*

文賦 (prose prose-poem) was completed. This is characterized by loose structure, unpredictable rhyme, and a judicious use of parallelism.

After the Sung, the *fu* suffered a decline. At first it seemed moribund. Then in the Ming and Ch'ing periods, *pa-ku wen*,* a type of composition governed by strict rules which limited the length, fixed the number of paragraphs, and defined the technique of introduction and conclusion, was introduced to replace the *fu* as one of the main sections in the civil-service examination. Nevertheless, there are a number of *lü-fu* written by Ch'ing authors, but none has been incorporated in the *Yü-ting li-tai fu-hui* 御定歷代賦彙. Even the *Ch'ing-wen hui* 清文滙 includes only a few pieces. This suggests that the composition of *fu* was no longer important in the Ch'ing dynasty. In its place Ch'ing scholars turned to compilation, exegesis, and even rudimentary historical surveys of the *fu* genre.

EDITIONS:

Ch'i-shih-chia fu ch'ao 七十家賦鈔. Chang Hui-yen 張惠言 (1761-1802), compiler. Taipei, 1964. A collection of 206 *fu* by 70 poets, from Ch'ü Yüan to Yü Hsin, with some annotation and commentary.

Han Wei Liu-ch'ao fu hsüan 漢魏六朝賦選. Ch'ü Jui-yüan 瞿蛻園, ed. Shanghai, 1964. A selection of *fu* from Chia I to Yü Hsin with modern punctuation and annotation. Official biographies in dynastic histories are also important primary sources of *fu*.

Ku-wen yüan 古文苑, Anonymous, in *PPTSCC* 百部叢書集成, series 52: *Shou-shan ko ts'ung-shu* 守山閣叢書, v. 161-164, Taipei, 1968.

Wen-hsüan 文選. Hsiao T'ung 蕭統 (501-531), compiler. This anthology (*chüan* 1-19) contains numerous early *fu*. For information about editions, see the entry on *Wen-hsüan*.

Yü-ting li-tai fu-hui. Compiled under imperial auspices by Ch'en Yüan-lung 陳元龍 (1652-1736). Taipei, 1979. *Ssu-k'u ch'üan-shu chen-pen* 四庫全書珍本, series 9, v. 272-323.

TRANSLATIONS:

Hightower, James R. "The *Fu* of T'ao Ch'ien," *HJAS* 17 (1954), 169-230. A number of *fu* other than those of T'ao Ch'ien are also translated.

Knechtges, David R. *Wen xuan or Selections of Refined Literature. Volume 1: Rhapsodies on Me-*

tropolises and Capitals. Princeton, 1983. Carefully annotated translations of nine *fu.*

Margouliès, George. *Le "fou" dans le Wen-Siuan.* Paris, 1926.

von Zach, Erwin. *Die chinesische Anthologie.* 2v. Cambridge, Mass., 1958.

Waley, Arthur. *The Temple and Other Poems.* New York, 1926.

Watson, Burton. *Chinese Rhyme-Prose: Poems in the Fu Form from the Han and Six Dynasties Periods.* New York, 1971.

STUDIES:

Bischoff, Friedrich A. *Interpreting the Fu. A Study in Chinese Literary Rhetoric.* Wiesbaden, 1976.

Chang, Shou-p'ing 張壽平. "Liang Han tz'u-fu tsung-mu ti-yao k'ao-chih" 兩漢辭賦總目提要考識, *Kuo-li Chung-yang T'u-shu-kuan kuan-k'an,* (March, 1972), 1-29.

Ch'eng, Meng-t'ung 鄭孟彤. "Han-fu te ssu-hsiang yü i-shu" 漢賦的思想與藝術, *Wen-hsüeh i-ch'an tseng k'an,* 3 (1958), 59-80.

Chien, Chung-wu 簡宗梧. "Han fu wen-hsüeh ssu-hsiang yüan-liu" 漢賦文學思想源流, *Kuo-li Cheng-chih Ta-hsüeh hsüeh-pao,* 37-38 (December 1978), 49-73.

Chin, Chü-hsiang 金秬香. *Han-tai tz'u-fu chih fa-ta* 漢化辭賦之發達. Shanghai, 1934.

Chu, Chieh-ch'in 朱傑勤. "Han-fu yen-chiu" 漢賦研究, *Kuo-li Chung-shan Ta-hsüeh Wen-shih Yen-chiu-so yüeh-k'an* 3.1 (March 1934), 113-136.

Ho, Kenneth P. H. 何沛雄. "Tz'u-fu fen-lei lüeh-shuo" 辭賦分類略說, *The Youngsun* 人生雜誌, 32.9-10 (February 1968), 22-25.

———. *Six Critical Works on Fu* 賦話六種. Hong Kong, 1975; rev. ed. Hong Kong, 1982.

Knechtges, David R. *Two Studies on the Han Fu,* Parerga, 1, published by The Far Eastern and Russian Institute, University of Washington, Seattle, 1968.

———. "Yang Shyong, The *Fuh,* and Hann Rhetoric." Unpublished Ph.D. dissertation, University of Washington, 1968.

Lindberg, George D. "The Prose *fu* of the Sung Dynasty in Historical Perspective," *TkR,* 3.1 (April 1972), 279-293.

Nakajima, Chiaki 中島千秋. "Fu no seiritsu ni tsuite" 賦の成立について, *Tokyo Shinagaku hō,* 1 (1955), 165-275.

———. *Fu no seiritsu to tenkai* 賦の成立と展開. Matsuyama, 1963.

Suzuki, Torao 鈴木虎雄. *Fushi taiyo* 賦史大要. Tokyo, 1936.

T'ao, Ch'u-ying 陶秋英. *Han fu chih-shih te yen-chiu* 漢賦之史的研究. Shanghai, 1939.

Ts'ao, Tao-heng 曹道衡. "Shih-lun Han fu ho Wei-Chin Nan-pei-ch'ao te shu-ch'ing hsiao-fu" 試論漢賦和魏晉南北朝的抒情小賦, *Wen-hsüeh p'ing-lun ts'ung-k'an,* 3 (July 1979), 1-27.

Watson, *Chinese Rhyme-Prose.*

Wilhelm, Hellmut. "The Scholar's Frustration: Notes on a Type of *Fu,*" in J. K. Fairbank, ed., *Chinese Thought and Institutions,* Chicago, 1957, pp. 310-319 and 398-403.

—KH

Fu Hsüan 傅玄 (*tzu,* Hsiu-i 休奕, 217-278), although rarely referred to in traditional histories of Chinese thought, was the preeminent Confucian theorist of the Western Chin period. He was born into a Ni-yang 泥陽 (modern Shensi) family noted for its steadfastness in the orthordox virtues. A protégé of the reactionary Ssu-ma 司馬 clan, he held such offices as Grand Chamberlain, Palace Attendant (267), and Palace Aide to the Censor-in-chief (268) after the formation of the Chin dynasty. He probably would have achieved the highest civil office had he not several times been cashiered for intemperate behavior; he had a tendency to demonstrate moral outrage at inappropriate times. That he was merely dismissed rather than banished or executed indicates the high regard with which he was held by the rulers he served.

Fu Hsüan's extant literary remains include part of the collection of his philosphical writings, the *Fu-tzu* 傅子, memorials which are included in his biography (*Chin-shu* 晉書, ch. 47), poetry, and miscellaneous writings. The *Fu-tzu,* originally in several hundred *chüan* (its actual size and scope is uncertain), was lost after the Sung dynasty and not recovered until the compilation of the *Yung-lo ta-tien* 永樂大典. Modern scholars have since prepared expanded editions and compilations of Fu Hsüan's poetry.

In the *Fu-tzu* and the memorials, which are among the major extant documents on Wei-Chin economic and frontier policies, Fu Hsüan dealt with the major problems of his day from both theoretical and practical perspectives. In theory, Fu was Confucian and, foreshadowing the later Sung orientation, Mencian in tone. His approach to applying his theories, an approach typical of the late and post-Han periods, leans towards the Legalist position. His concrete proposals emphasize aspects of staffing the bureaucracy and economic concerns. Because of his criticism of individual wealth, his negative attitude towards merchants, and his emphasis on public over private values, he has even been considered a forerunner of communism by some modern Japanese scholars. More certain is his influence on Sung-dynasty literati; Ssu-ma Kuang 司馬光 (1019-1086), for example, quotes the *Fu-tzu* extensively in his *Tzu-chih t'ung-chien* 資治通鑑.

From a literary standpoint, Fu Hsüan's poetry is notable for its influence on later major poets. Ch'en Hang 陳沆 (1785-1826) in his *Shih pi hsing chien* 詩比興箋 wrote that Pao Chao* and Li Po* both were influenced by him. In the preface to his poem, "Sung po p'ien" 松柏篇, Pao Chao states that he wrote it in imitation of Fu Hsüan's "Kuei hao p'ien" 龜鶴篇 (not extant). Although Fu wrote in the variety of modes utilized in the third century, critics have been most appreciative of his *yüeh-fu*,* and have compared his best to those of Ssu-ma Hsiang-ju* and Mei Sheng.* In turn, Fu Hsüan's poems demonstrate influence from Ts'ao Chih* and others of the preceding generation.

Fu wrote on themes common to poets of his age and was rather eclectic in his prespectives, another characteristic of third-century intellectuals. His love poems tended to be moralistic, implicitly criticizing the romantic and unconventional tendencies of his time, yet he also wrote poems unusually sensitive to the plight of women. His historical pieces, which perhaps reflect his early employment in the writing of the *Wei-shu* 魏書 (eventually incorporated into the *San-kuo chih* 三國志), extoll heroes; but his poems criticizing the political and intellectual trends of his own day, referring to the Ts'ao Clan and the *hsüan-hsüeh* 玄學 theorists, tend to end on notes of despair. In this regard, his poems on the theme of change (*hua* 化) indicate that Fu Hsüan was a more complex figure than his philosoph-

ical writings imply, for in these poems he tended to utilize Taoist imagery. His poignant poems on the transitory nature of life, certainly written in his old age, are probably his finest.

EDITIONS:
Liu-ch'ao wen, v. 2, pp. 1714-1749.
Nan-pei-ch'ao shih, v. 1, pp. 387-406.
Kuan-ku T'ang so cho-shu 觀古堂所著書. Yeh Te-hui 葉德輝, ed. 1902.

TRANSLATIONS:
Frodsham, *Anthology*, pp. 251-252.
Gundert, *Lyrik*, p. 49.
Waley, *Translations*, pp. 71-73.

—JP

Fu-sheng liu-chi 浮生六記 (Six Chapters of a Floating Life) is unique in many ways. It records the lives of the author Shen Fu 沈復 (*tzu*, San-po 三白, 1762-after 1803) and his beloved wife Ch'en Yün 陳芸 (1763-1803), an extraordinary couple who were cultured but not bookish, playful but not compromising, and whose strong sense of individuality and need for privacy ran squarely against the familial and professional expectations of a society entrenched in Confucian behavioral standards. They were not, of course the only couple ever to encounter troubles of this kind, but their philosophy of life certainly aggravated the conflict and led to a vivid portrayal of tragedy unprecedented in Chinese literature.

Shen Fu's unpretentious style of narration also had no parallel in pre-modern China, where an open account of one's marital life was unthinkable. But *Fu-sheng liu-chi* is not an autobiography in the normal sense of the term. In the extant chapters (especially in certain significant portions), the center of attention is not Shen himself but his wife, although the narrative is consistently in the first person. Within a chapter, the presentation is largely chronological, but different aspects of an event are usually given in different chapters. The work is a thematically organized memoir, the only example of its kind in the traditional Chinese corpus.

It is through this unique thematic organization that the work acquires its force and persuasion. The accounts of brief joyful moments in the first two chapters do not reveal to the reader that Shen Fu and his wife were married for twenty-three years. The fourth chapter about Shen's travels around the country is of a rather different nature. With Shen Fu as the center of action, this chapter is little more than a recollection of unrelated trips. The third chapter, with its revelation of one tribulation after another, culminates with the bitter events leading to Ch'en Yün's death, the touching death scene itself, and the torturous episode in which he bids farewell to her spirit and reveals the real meaning of many of the events described earlier. If the presentation were strictly chronological, most of the seemingly pleasant moments, as fleeting and occasional as they are, would easily have been buried in the unceasing onslaught of various problems and conflicts. The concentration on happy times in the two opening chapters does not prepare the reader for the tremendous shock in chapter 3, and thus heightens the sense of tragedy of the final events.

Ironically, the artistic excellence of the *Fu-sheng liu-chi*, particularly the description of Ch'en Yün as a lovely, ideal companion, has caused it to be regularly classified as fiction. This is a misapprehension not only of the purpose and art of Shen Fu's work, but also of the nature of fiction itself.

Not much about the author, beyond what is given in the *Fu-sheng liu-chi*, is known. Indeed, other than this work, Shen Fu hardly achieved anything worth mentioning. With the exception of the scholar-official Shih Yün-yü,* almost none of his friends were memorable. But for the miraculous discovery in the mid-nineteenth century of a manuscript of the memoir, unpublished during Shen's lifetime, there would be no record of Shen and his wife at all. Only the first four chapters survived, fortunately including three of major literary value. All subsequent editions are derived from this manuscript.

Of the last two chapters only the titles remain. Chapter 5 would seem to concern Fu's trip to the Ryukyus after the death of his wife, and chapter 6 philosophical issues. A version including these two chapters appeared in 1935, and it has had a fairly wide circulation since. But these two chapters have long been recognized as fabrications. Recently, Cheng I-mei 鄭逸梅 (Cheng Chi-yün 鄭際雲), who in the early 1930s declined an offer to "compose" the two chapters, belatedly announced that these sections were either done or ordered by Wang Chün-ch'ing 王均卿 (Wang Wen-ju 王文濡), an editor of *ts'ung-shu* collections and popular reference works active in the late Ch'ing and early Republican eras. When the complete version was first published, Wang falsely claimed to have discovered them.

EDITIONS:
Fu-sheng liu-chi. Shanghai, 1935. A "complete" edition which is important not for including the spurious chapters, but for the various prefaces associated with the early editions as well as an informative preface by Chao T'iao-k'uang 趙苕狂, a well-known editor of traditional fiction in the 1930s, and, finally, for a helpful postscript by Chu Chien-mang 朱劍芒.
Fu-sheng liu-chi. Peking, 1980. Based on the 1923 P'u-she 樸社 edition prepared by Yü P'ing-po 俞平伯; Yü's preface and chronological summary are also included.

TRANSLATIONS:
Lin, Yutang 林語堂. *Six Chapters of a Floating Life.* Shanghai, 1935. Later available in many different editions, including bilingual ones, and in several of Lin Yutang's own anthologies.
Pratt, Leonard and Chiang Su-hui. *Shen Fu: Six Records of a Floating Life.* Harmondsworth, 1983.
Reclus, Jacques. *Récits d'une vie fugitive.* Paris, 1967. With a useful introduction by Paul Demiéville.
Ryckmans, Pierre. *Six récits au fil inconstant des jours.* Brussels, 1966.
Satō, Haruo 佐藤春夫, and Matsueda Shigeo 松枝茂夫. *Fushō rokki* 浮生六記. Tokyo, 1938.
All these translations render only the first four chapters.

STUDIES:
Ch'en, Yü-p'i 陳毓罴. "*Hung-lou meng* ho *Fu-sheng liu-chi*" 紅樓夢和浮生六記, *Hung-lou meng*

hsüeh-k'an, 1980, 4 (November 1980), 211-230.

Cheng, I-mei. *Fu-sheng liu-chi* te tsu-pen wen-t'i" 浮生六記的足本問題, *Tu-shu,* 1981.6 (June 1981), 155-157.

Cheng, K'ang-min 鄭康民. "*Fu-sheng liu-chi* chih-i" 浮生六記質疑, *Ta-lu tsa-chih,* 18.2 (January 1959), 20-26.

Doleželová-Velingerová, Milena and Lubomir Dolezel. "An Early Chinese Confessional Prose: Shen Fu's *Six Chapters of a Floating Life,*" *TP.* 58 (1972), 137-160.

Hu, Pu-kuei 胡不歸. "Shen Fu nien-p'u" 沈復年譜, *Sheng-liu,* 1.9 (May 1945), 19-21.

Liu, Fan 劉樊. "*Fu-sheng liu-chi* i-kao pien-wei" 浮生六記逸稿辨偽, *Kuo-wen chou-pao,* 14.6 (February 1937), 43-52.

"Shen Fu," in *ECCP,* pp. 641-642.

Wu, Fu-yüan 吳幅員. "Fu-sheng liu-chi 'Chung-shan chi-li' p'ien wei hou-jen wei-tso shuo" 浮生六記中山記歷篇爲後人偽作說, *Tung-fang tsa-chih,* N.S., 11.8 (February 1978), 67-78.

Yeh, Te-chün 葉德均. "Shen San-po yü Shih Cho-t'ang" 沈三白與石琢堂, *Ku-chin,* 39 (January 1944), 29-31.

—YWM

Han-shan 寒山 (Cold Mountain) is the name of a person the details of whose life and work remain unclear. First, there is no reliable material proving the existence of a person with this name; second, the stylistic similarity of the poetical works associated with this name is not unequivocal and does not allow the assumption that they were created by one man. It can only be said of the more than three hundred poems handed down that they were written in the T'ang dynasty. Probably several different compilations of poems have been edited together under the name of Han-shan.

The poems—mostly five-syllable eight-line verses in both the old- and regulated-verse forms—have quite different topics, which can usually be understood as containing a basic tension between idea and reality and between asceticism and secularization. Tightly woven with this tradition and with the spirit of the period, the poems reflect a view of life as unchangeable decline and the never-ending human sorrow at the transience of existence. This gives rise to two conflicting responses: on the one hand there is the traditional tendency toward *carpe diem* and the desire for longevity; on the other, the attempt to solve this contradiction by self-negation and retreat into the mountains, where enlightenment in the *Tao* and in Zen (*ch'an*) is sought. Nature plays here a double role: it appears as evil and dangerous—the mountains are unreachable; then it becomes the ideal place for insights into Zen, finally, in the new state of mind, *becoming* Zen. Thus, this opposition can also be discerned in the poetic description of nature. The view of nature as dangerous still implies a consciousness of the body that can be traced back to the hermit poetry (*chao-yin shih* 招隱詩) of the third and fourth century. But when enlightenment makes nature a home for the Zen Buddhist, the landscape is presented with an attitude, which although basically new, has predecessors in the Six Dynasties.

The Zen Buddhist impact on the Han-shan corpus is apparent in both its form and content. Poetry becomes a medium for propagating Zen and for attacking wrong attitudes towards life and learning. It often makes use of the spirit and technique of Buddhist didactic verse (*chi* 偈). Its admonitions are not meant only for the gentry and the Buddhists, but also for the common people. Thus, perhaps for the first time, poetry was aimed at educating the uneducated and the poor. At the same time, a new lyrical expression made its appearance in Chinese literature: simplicity and the advocacy of it brought the plain things of life into the foreground as the ultimate goals of existence. Things represented in colloquial and vulgar language are themselves—they do not have metaphoric or symbolic values. The basic dichotomy between idea and reality in the work of Han-shan, between his dedication to the world (which even finds its expression in love poems for young girls) and his new identity in Buddha, is partly mitigated by the fact that the person of Han-shan is always reflecting its own self. In this respect the outer world becomes the passage of his consciousness into Zen.

EDITIONS:

Han-shan-tzu shih-chi 寒山子詩集. *SPTK.*

Snyder, Gary. "Cold Mountain Poems," *Evergreen Review*, 2.6 (Autumn 1958), 69-80; reprinted in *Riprap & Cold Mountain Poems*, San Francisco, 1965; included in Cyril Birch, ed., *Anthology of Chinese Literature*, New York, 1965, pp. 194-202.

TRANSLATIONS:

Pimpaneau, Jacques. *Li Clodo du Dharma, 25 Poemes de Han-shan, Calligraphies de Li Kwok-wing.* Paris, 1975.

Schuhmacher, Stephan. *Han Shan. 150 Gedichte vom Kalten Berg.* Düsseldorf and Köln, 1974.

Waley, Arthur. "Twenty-seven Poems by Han-shan," *Encounter*, 3.3 (1954); 3-8.

Watson, Burton. *Cold Mountain. 100 Poems by the T'ang Poet Han-shan.* New York and London, 1962.

STUDIES:

Chao, Tzu-fan 趙滋蕃. *Han-shan te shih-tai ching-shen* 寒山的時代精神. Taipei, 1970.

Ch'en, Hui-chien 陳慧劍. *Han-shan-tzu yen-chiu* 寒山子研究. Taipei, 1974.

Ch'eng, Chao-hsiung 程兆熊. *Han-shan-tzu yü Han-shan-shih* 寒山子與寒山詩. Taipei, 1974.

Chung, Ling. "The Reception of Cold Mountain's Poetry in the Far East and the United States," in *China and the West: Comparative Literature Studies*, Hong Kong, 1980, 85-96.

Pulleyblank, E. G. "Linguistic Evidence for the Date of Han-shan," in *Studies in Chinese Poetry and Poetics*, Ronald Miao, ed., San Francisco 1978, pp. 763-795.

Wu, Ch'i-yü. "A Study of Han Shan," *TP*, 45 (1957), 392-450.

—WK

Han Wo 韓偓 (*tzu*, Chih-yao 致堯 or Chih-yüan 致元 or Chih-kuang 致光, 844-923) is traditionally remembered as a statesman and poet who remained loyal to the T'ang in its final decade. Han was born in the capital, Ch'ang-an. His father was related by marriage to Li Shang-yin,* and the elder poet cast an approving eye on the poetry of preadolescent Han Wo. Little is known of Han's life until he passed the *chin-shih* examination in 889, at the age of 46, and entered government service at court. His career coincides with the reign of Chao Tsung 昭宗 (r. 888-904), the last T'ang sovereign. Biographers dwell on how Han gained the emperor's favor by defending the sovereign's title and person from would-be usurpers, at great personal cost. Han was finally driven from court in 903 by Chu Ch'üan-chung 朱全忠, the first sovereign of Liang, and fled to the semi-autonomous state of Min 閩 on the southeast coast. Tradition has it that he spent the remaining fourteen years of his life in poverty, devoting his time to the study of Taoist alchemy.

The two historical stereotypes of Han Wo seen in biographies have greatly influenced critical perception of his poetry. He is usually cast as a lesser Tu Fu* or T'ao Ch'ien,* a tragic elder statesman lamenting political disaster, or seen as a youthful romantic rake, a protégé of Li Shang-yin. His extant work is now divided into two collections: the *Han Han-lin chi* 韓翰林集 (Collection of Academician Han) with 226 poems, and the *Hsiang lien chi* 香奩集 (Fragrant Trousseau) with 95 poems. The former collection is praised and accepted as the work of the loyal statesman; the latter is either faulted as "voluptuous, effeminate paint-and-skirts poetry," defended as allegorical criticism, or rejected as spurious. This latter opinion, alive since Sung times, has been laid to rest on internal evidence by modern scholars like Teng Chung-lung. It seems certain that despite a few forgeries, the majority of poems in both collections are Han Wo's. The compilation of the *Fragrant Trousseau*, and its preface, are probably from a later writer.

Despite critical ambivalence, Han Wo's poetry has always attracted a small but enthusiastic audience. Han is praised for his clear style and ability to convey events and emotions convincingly. Living at the end of a literary golden age, he managed to assimilate completely a variety of influences. His work contains fewer images and allusions than that of many T'ang poets. His relatively loose style, use of repetition and grammatical particles, and creative manipulation of standard tonal patterns bothers some critics and impresses others. The human emotional response to loss and change is one of his favorite themes.

Few of Han Wo's poems are well-known. One seven-syllable quatrain, "I liang" 已涼

(Already Cool) is included in the *T'ang-shih san-pai shou.** "An P'in" 安貧 (At Ease in Poverty) is also much admired and anthologized.

EDITIONS:

Han Han-lin chi 韓翰林集. Wu Ju-lun 吳汝綸 and Wu K'ai-sheng 吳闓生, eds. N.p., colophon dated 1922. The most comprehensive collection of Han Wo's writings, with occasional brief annotations.

T'ang liu ming-chia chi 唐六名家集. Shanghai, 1926 facsimile of *Wu-men han-sung t'ang* 吳門寒松堂 reproduction of *Chi-ku ko* edition of Mao Chin 毛晉 (1599-1659). Contains *Han nei-Han pieh chi* 韓內翰別集.

Wu T'ang-jen shih chi 五唐人詩集. Shanghai, 1926 facsimile of Mao Chin edition, as above. Contains *Hsiang lien chi.*

TRANSLATIONS:

Demiéville, *Anthologie*, p. 325.

Upton, Beth. "The Poetry of Han Wo." Unpublished Ph.D. dissertation, University of California, Berkeley, 1980. A study of Han's work and an in-depth translation of thirty-three poems.

STUDIES:

Hsü, Fu-kuan 徐復觀. "Han Wo shih yü *Hsiang-lien chi* lun k'ao" 韓偓詩與香奩集論考, in *Chung-kuo wen-hsüeh lun chi* 中國文學論集, Taichung, 1966, pp. 255-296.

Sun, K'o-k'uan 孫克寬. "Han Wo chien p'u ch'u-kao" 韓偓簡譜初稿, *T'u-shu-kuan hsüeh-pao*, 5 (1963), 119-136. Information collected from many sources. Sun attempts to date most of Han's poems.

———. "Han Wo shih chi ch'i sheng-p'ing" 韓偓詩及其生平, *Shih yü shih-jen* 詩與詩人. Taipei, 1965, pp. 49-64.

Teng, Chung-lung 鄧中龍. "Han Wo shih ch'ien-lun" 韓偓詩淺論, *Wen-hsüeh shih-chieh chi k'an*, 26 (Hong Kong, 1958), 48-52. A brief study remarkable for its focus on prosodic features of Han's poetry, rather than his life.

—BU

Han Wu-ti nei-chuan 漢武帝內傳 (Intimate Biography of Emperor Wu of the Han) or *Han Wu nei-chuan* 漢武內傳 is a Taoist mystery in the guise of a fictional romance, whose plot is an augmentation of the tradition of the visit of the mythical Hsi Wang Mu to Emperor Wu of the Han on the seventh day of the seventh month in 110 B.C. The significant part of the story is a series of revelations made by the goddess to the sovereign, in the form of a list of magical drugs and other esoteric texts, including a Taoist mandala showing the mountain residences of divine beings. Indeed, this role of custodian and revealer of arcana is typically given to Hsi Wang Mu in Six Dynasties literature. The scenario is essentially that of a typical Taoist ritual in the Mao Shan 茅山 (*Shang ch'ing* 上清) tradition. The major events are the announcement of the imminent arrival of the deity; purificatory and other preparatory rites, accompanied by musical performances and pyrotechnical displays; the ritual banquet, in the form of a hierogamy; finally, the departure of the goddess and her suite. An appended chronicle reveals that the sovereign was incapable of adhering to the precepts of the sacred literature, and so was denied the boon of immortality.

The book no longer exists in its entirety (early editions contained two or three *chüan*, today there is only one), but the most complete version is found in the *Tao-tsang.** In Sung times it became common to attribute it to Pan Ku,* but this was never taken very seriously. There seem to be some elements contributed by Ko Hung,* but the more immediate sources appear to have been a lost but often quoted biography of the Mao brothers, and the *Shih-chou chi** (erroneously attributed to Tung-fang Shuo 東方朔). Both of these works belong to the early Six Dynasties period, and the *Han Wu-ti nei-chuan* is accordingly a composition of the later part of that era; its author is unknown. The story was very popular in T'ang times, and many poets drew on incidents from the narrative, and exploited its rich, colorful and often mystical vocabulary. For instance, the avatars of the Jade Maidens who attend on the goddess in the T'ang romance *Yu-hsien k'u* (see Chang Cho) show the influence of this text; moreover, its plot and imagery both left their mark on various literary traditions about Yang Kuei-fei.

A related work is the *Han Wu ku-shih* 漢武故事 (Stories of Emperor Wu of the

Han). Originally in two *chüan*, the most complete extant version is that edited by Lu Hsün (see bibliography below). The work was noted already in the *Sui-shu* bibliography, as an anonymous compilation; later attributions to Pan Ku and others are spurious. Modern scholars feel, however, that the work known as *Han Wu ku-shih* today may not be that known to the authors of the *Sui-shu* bibliography. The work consists of distinct anecdotes concerning Emperor Wu, his family, and his courtiers. Taoist elements are not as prevalent as in *Han Wu-ti nei-chuan*.

EDITIONS:

Ch'ien, Hsi-tso 錢熙祚 (1801-1844). *Han Wu-ti nei-chuan. Shou-shan Ko ts'ung-shu* 守山閣叢書, 1844. A critical edition—reprinted in Schipper.

Han Wu ku-shih. TSCCCP ed.

———, in *Ku hsiao-shuo kou-ch'en* 古小說鈎沈 , Lu Hsün 魯迅, ed., in *Lu Hsün ch'üan-chi* 魯迅全集, Peking 1973, v. 8, pp. 449-471. The most complete edition; contains 53 sections.

———, in *Han-Wei Liu-ch'ao hsiao-shuo hsüan-chu* 漢魏六朝小說選集 , Hong Kong, 1977, pp. 2-24. Contains 21 sections; based on the *Ku hsiao-shuo kou-ch'en* ed.

TRANSLATIONS:

Schipper, K. M. *L'Empereur Wou des Han dans la légende taoiste; Han wou-ti nei-tchouan.* Paris, 1965.

"Histoire anecdotique et fabuleuse de l'Empereur Wou des Han," *Lectures chinoises,* 1 (1945), 28-91.

STUDIES:

Kominami, Ichiro 小南一郎. " 'Kan Butei naiden' no seiritsu (1)" 漢武帝內傳の成立 , *Tōhō gakuhō,* 48 (December 1975), 183-227.

Li, Feng-mao 李豐楙. "*Han Wu nei-chuan* te chuch'eng chi ch'i liu-ch'uan" 漢武內傳的著成及其流傳, *Yu-shih hsüeh-chih,* 17.2 (October 1982), 21-55.

Lü, Hsing-ch'ang 呂興昌. "P'ing *Han Wu nei-chuan*" 評漢武內傳, in *Chung-kuo ku-tien wen-hsüeh yen-chiu ts'ung-k'an—Hsiao-shuo chih pu (1)* 中國古典文學研究叢刊— 小說之部, K'o Ch'ing-ming 柯慶明 and Lin Ming-te 林明德, eds., Taipei, 1977, pp. 41-106.

—EHS and WHN

Han Yü 韓愈 (*tzu*, T'ui-chih 退之, 768-824) was a major figure in the history of Chinese literature, comparable in stature to Dante, Shakespeare, or Goethe in their respective literary traditions. He was among that small group of writers whose works not only became classics of the language—required reading for all those with claims to literacy in succeeding generations—but whose writings redefine and change the course of the tradition itself. Although Han Yü is best-known as a prose stylist—the master shaper of the so-called *ku-wen** style—he was a stylistic innovator in the many genres in which he wrote, including poetry. And he was a major influence on the literary and intellectual life of his time, an important spokesman for a rejuvenated traditionalism that later emerged as Sung Neo-Confucianism.

Han Yü was born into a family of scholars and minor officials in the area of modern Meng-hsien 孟縣 in Honan. He was orphaned at the age of two and raised in the family of his older brother Han Hui 韓會 (740-781), from whom he received his early education and his disdain for the current literary style descended from Six Dynasties *p'ien-wen.** The family endured southern exile in 777, and in the early 780s the provincial rebellions in the Northeast caused further dislocation. Han Yü seems to have spent these early years in the provinces studying. He came to Ch'ang-an in 786, and after four attempts passed the *chin-shih* examination in 792. He failed three times, however, to pass the "Erudite Literatus" examination, which would have meant an immediate appointment in the central government. In desperation, he accepted employment in 796 on the staff of Tung Chin 董晉 (724-799), the military governor at Pien-chou, and remained there until Tung's death in 799. These were important years for Han Yü's intellectual development, for in Pien-chou he formed lasting friendships with Li Ao,* Meng Chiao,* Chang Chi,* and a number of lesser figures who formed the nucleus of "Han Yü's disciples" (韓門弟子), a literary coterie that looked to Han Yü as their leader.

He eventually secured his first position in the central government in 802, as Eru-

397

dite in the Directorate of Education, an institution with which he maintained a sporadic lifelong association, eventually becoming Chancellor in 820. In 803 he refused to join the political faction formed by Wang Shu-wen 王叔文 (753-806) in support of the heir apparent, Li Sung 李誦 (761-806), and was exiled to Yang-shan 陽山 in the far South. When this faction, which included Liu Tsung-yüan* and Liu Yü-hsi,* was vanquished in 805, Han Yü's political fortunes also turned, and he was recalled to Ch'ang-an. His anticipation during the trip and the joy of reunion with literary friends in the capital, where the new government of Emperor Hsien-tsung (r. 805-820) was being formed, found expression in his works of the year 806, Han Yü's *annus mirabilis*. Two of his most important poems—the "Nan-shan shih" 南山詩 (Poem on the Southern Mountains) and the "Yüan-ho Sheng-te shih" 元和聖德詩 (Poem on the Sagacious Virtue of the Age of Primal Harmony), both extolling the virtue of the new emperor, date from this year. So probably does the "Ch'iu huai" 秋懷 (Autumn Sentiments), perhaps his most famous agenda for a revived Confucianism.

But factional jealousies made life difficult and thwarted his hopes for quick success in the new government, and he requested transfer to Lo-yang in 807, remaining there until 811, when he again returned to Ch'ang-an. Han Yü was an ardent royalist and supporter of the use of military power to extend central government control over the autonomous provinces of the Northeast. In this cause, he was a partisan of the great Grand Councilor P'ei Tu 裴度 (765-839), the architect of Emperor Hsien-tsung's eventual suppression of the separatist forces. Han Yü took part in the campaigns against the separatists in Huai-hsi province in 817 and recorded the events in his famous "P'ing Huai-hsi pei" 平淮西碑 (Inscription on the Pacification of Huai-hsi), a text that well demonstrates the intimate connection between his literary, philosophical, and political concerns.

In 819, perhaps lulled by the success of his patron P'ei Tu and misguided by ex-

cessive devotion to the emperor, he wrote the infamous "Lun Fo-ku piao" 論佛骨表 (Memorial on the Bone-Relic of the Buddha), in which he intimated that Hsien-tsung's participation in the veneration of a relic of the Buddha would shorten the sovereign's life. This was a severe act of *lèse majesté*, and only the intervention of Han Yü's powerful patrons saved him from the death penalty. He was exiled to Ch'ao-chou on the South China coast. He was back in the capital by 820, however, where he served in a series of upper echelon posts, including that of Mayor of Ch'ang-an, until his death in 824.

Han Yü's "ancient-style" prose was an attempt to replace the contemporary *p'ien-wen* with a less florid, looser style better suited to the needs of a more flexible, utilitarian prose. Han Yü's *ku-wen* was thus not an imitation of ancient prose, but rather a new style based on the ancient (pre-Ch'in and Han) ideals of clarity, conciseness, and utility. To this end, he incorporated elements of colloquial rhythm, diction, and syntax into both prose and poetry, while at the same time reaffirming the Confucian classics as the basis of education and good writing. His most successful *ku-wen* compositions fuse these classical ideals with contemporary realities, and the flexibility of their style furnished an example to later generations of how to relate the classical tradition to contemporary literary needs. Han Yü is appropriately the first of the *T'ang Sung pa-ta san-wen chia* 唐宋八大散文家 (Eight Great Prose Masters of the T'ang and Sung), which also included Liu Tsung-yüan, Ou-yang Hsiu,* Wang An-shih,* Su Hsün* and his sons Su Ch'e* and Su Shih,* and Tseng Kung.*

The style of Han Yü's poetry is governed by the same passion for clarity that pervades his prose. He strives always for an accuracy and clarity appropriate to the content of the poem and its social context. Thus some critics have labeled the intricate style of the "Southern Mountains" baroque. But this intricacy is not pursued for its own sake; rather the verbal complexity reinforces the actual terrain of the mountains themselves. The style becomes an accurate and appropriate reflection of the reality. On the other hand, Han Yü's poetic corpus contains a great number of seemingly casual, conversational poems whose style seems quite close to popular speech. Some critics have postulated that these two styles present a contradiction and constitute a conflict with Han Yü himself. Yet both styles are governed by the twin principles of accuracy and appropriateness. Han Yü articulated these principles several times in his letters, stating that "the language of composition should be in accord with reality" (其文章言語, 與事相侔) and that "to adhere to reality in forming expressions was precisely what the ancient authors did" (因事以陳辭, 古之作者正如是爾).

Han Yü's theory and practice of literary style is an extension of his drive to rejuvenate Confucianism as a viable intellectual concern. Intellectual life during the T'ang was largely dominated by the great monastic schools of Buddhist scholasticism. In the eighth century, the Ch'an school gained in popularity by virtue of its direct appeal to intuition and experience rather than looking to commentary and book learning as sources of wisdom. This movement rapidly gained ground after the An Lu-shan Rebellion of 755, and Han Yü was exposed to its influence from an early age. Although violently opposed to monasticism and monkish exploitation of a superstitious peasantry, his drive to rejuvenate Confucianism by encouraging personal master-disciple relationships and by establishing an orthodox line of transmission for Confucian teaching owes much to contemporary Ch'an practice.

Politically, Han Yü favored a strong central government. This explains the special affection he maintained for Emperor Hsien-tsung, known historically as the "restorer" of the T'ang's political fortunes. Han Yü deplored the political and cultural fragmentation that had been tolerated in order to hold together the multiracial and cosmopolitan T'ang state. He was not *per se* anti-Buddhist and xenophobic as much as he desired a central state that vigorously promoted a cultural orthodoxy that was to be identical to his own

rejuvenated Confucianism. When the emperor revealed himself to be more anxious to promote raw central power than to propagate cultural orthodoxy, Han Yü responded with the sense of outrage and betrayal that exudes from between the lines of the "Memorial on the Bone-Relic of the Buddha."

EDITIONS:

Ma, Ch'i-ch'ang 馬其昶, ed. *Han Ch'ang-li wen-chi chiao-chu* 韓昌黎文集校注. Rpt. Taipei, 1967. The best edition of Han Yü's prose.

Ch'ien, Chung-lien 錢仲聯. *Han Ch'ang-li shih hsi-nien chi-shih* 韓昌黎詩繫年集釋. Shanghai, 1957. A chronologically-arranged modern edition of the poetry with an excellent selection of commentary.

Chih-shui 止水, comp. *Han Yü shih-hsüan* 韓愈詩選. Hong Kong, 1980.

Hartman, Charles. "Preliminary Bibliographical Notes on the Sung Edition of Han Yü's *Collected Works*," in Nienhauser, *Critical Essays*, pp. 89-100. A study of the traditional editions and their relationship to each other.

Hanabusa, Hideki 花房英樹. *Kan Yu kashi sakuin* 韓愈歌詩索引. Kyoto, 1964. A useful concordance to Han Yü's poetry.

TRANSLATIONS:

Birch, *Anthology*, v. 1, 244-257, 262-264.

Demiéville, *Anthologie*, pp. 288-289.

Graham, *Late T'ang*, pp. 71-79.

Harada, Kenyū 原田憲雄. *Kan Yu* 韓愈. Tokyo, 1972. A selection of Han Yü's poetry with Japanese annotation and translation.

Margouliès, G. *Anthologie raisonnée de la littérature chinoise*. Paris, 1949. Contains numerous translations of Han Yü's best known prose pieces.

Shimizu, Shigeru 清水茂, *Kan Yu* 韓愈. Tokyo, 1959. A good small anthology of Han Yü's poetry with Japanese annotation and translation.

———. *Tōsō hakkabun* 唐宋八家文, Tokyo, 1966. Japanese translations with annotation and discussion of Han Yü's major prose texts.

Sunflower, pp. 165-190.

von Zach, *Han Yü*. A complete translation into German without commentary of Han Yü poetry.

STUDIES:

Chou, K'ang-hsieh 周康燮, comp. *Han Yü yen-chiu lun ts'ung* 韓愈研究論叢. Hong Kong,

1978. An extremely useful collection of major twentieth-century scholarship on Han Yü along with a reprinting of the traditional *nienp'u.* An essential book.

Ch'en, Yin-k'o. "Han Yü and the T'ang Novel," *HJAS,* 1 (1936), 39-43.

———. "Lun Han Yü" 論韓愈, *Li-shih yen-chiu,* 2 (1954), 105-114. Perhaps the most important single article on Han Yü.

Chi, Chen-huai 季鎮淮. "Han Yü te shih-lun ho shih-tso" 韓愈的詩論和詩作, in *Chung-hua hsüeh-shu lun-wen chi* 中華學術論文集, Chung-hua shu-chü 中華書局, ed., Peking, 1981, pp. 437-459.

Hartman, Charles. *Han Yü and the T'ang Search for Unity.* Princeton, 1985.

Lo, Lien-t'ien 羅聯添. *Han Yü yen-chiu* 韓愈研究. Taipei, 1977. Reprints all of Lo's studies on Han Yü's biography, contains a useful collection of traditional critical opinion on the prose and an excellent bibliography.

Ma, Y. W. "Prose Writings of Han Yü and *Ch'uan-ch'i* Literature," *JOS* 7 (1969), 195-223. Discusses the relationship of the *ku-wen* style to T'ang *ch'uan-ch'i* fiction.

Maeno, Naoaki 前野直彬. *Kan Go no shōgai* 韓愈の生涯. Tokyo, 1976. A full-length biography of Han Yü.

Mei, Diana Yu-shih Ch'en. "Han Yü as a *Ku-wen* Stylist," *THHP,* N.S., 7.1 (August 1968), 143-208.

Nienhauser, William H., Jr. "An Allegorical Reading of Han Yü's 'Mao-Ying Chuan' (Biography of Fur Point)," *OE,* 23.2 (December 1976), 153-174. Careful analysis of this important text, with full translation.

Owen, Stephen. *The Poetry of Han Yü and Meng Chiao.* New Haven, 1975. Also contains numerous translations.

Pollack, David. "Linked-verse Poetry in China: A Study of Associative Linking in 'Lien-chü' Poetry with Emphasis on the Poems of Han Yü and His Circle." Unpublished Ph.D. dissertation, University of California-Berkeley, 1976.

Pulleyblank, E. G. "Liu K'o, a Forgotten Rival of Han Yü," *AM,* 7 (1959), 145-160.

Schmidt, Jerry D. "Han Yü and His *Ku-shih* Poetry." Unpublished M.A. thesis. University of British Columbia, 1969.

Spring, "Tang *Guwen.*"

Sun, Ch'ang-wu 孫昌武. "Lun Han Yü te Ju-hsüeh yü wen-hsüeh" 論韓愈的儒學與文學, *Wen-hsüeh p'ing-lun ts'ung-k'an,* 13 (May 1982), 239-262.

Yoshikawa, Kōjirō 吉川幸次郎. "Kan Go bun" 韓愈文, in *Tōdai no shi to sambun* 唐代の詩と散文, Tokyo, 1967, pp. 53-122.

—CH

Hao-ch'iu chuan 好逑傳 (The Fortunate Union), also titled *Hsia-i feng-yüeh-chuan* 俠義風月傳 (A Tale of Chivalry and Love), is a seventeenth-century prose romance in eighteen chapters written by Ming-chiao-chung jen 名教中人 (Man of the Teaching of Names). Usually associated with the subgenre of *ts'ai-tzu chia-jen hsiao-shuo,** *Hao-ch'iu* is more of a deviant work because of its espousal of chivalry and Confucian courtship.

The romance succeeds largely because of entertaining characters and a compact plot. It is set in the late Ming. The narrative begins with the twenty-year-old hero, T'ieh Chung-yü 鐵中玉 (Jade Within Iron), traveling to see his parents in the capital. On the way he meets a young scholar who tries to commit suicide because his fiancee has been abducted by the lascivious Sha Li 沙利, Marquis of Ta-kuai. In Peking, T'ieh learns that his father, a censor, has been imprisoned for "falsely accusing" Sha Li of the same crime. T'ieh sympathizes with the scholar's plight and intercedes on behalf of him and his father. T'ieh, who has a robust physique in addition to his literary talents, forces his way into Sha's villa and rescues the girl and her parents. T'ieh becomes famous as a result of this chivalrous deed.

Attention shifts to the heroine, Shui Ping-hsin 水冰心 (Water Pure-Heart), who lives with her greedy, barely literate uncle, Shui Yün 水運, in Tsinan, Shantung. He is conspiring with Kuo Ch'i-tsu 過其祖 (Worse Than His Forebears or Disgrace to His Ancestors), the playboy son of the heir apparents's chief secretary, to marry Ping-hsin to Kuo and take control of the family property (Ping-hsin's father, an assistant secretary in the Board of War, has been exiled to the frontier for supporting the unlucky general, Hou Hsiao 侯孝). Ping-shin tricks Shui Yün by agreeing to the marriage, but writes her unattractive cousin Hsiang-ku's 香姑 astrological data on the marriage documents. When Kuo comes on the wedding day, Ping-hsin refuses to marry him on the grounds that Shui Yün intended to marry Hsiang-ku to Kuo all along. Ping-hsin proposes that her cousin be disguised as herself and substituted as Kuo's bride. The vivid description of their wedding night and Kuo's rage at discovering Hsiang-ku's identity provides a refreshing contrast to the work's didactic moralism.

Kuo and Shui Yün try to entrap Ping-hsin with several artifices but fail. Finally, they grab her when she comes out to receive her father's pardon, which they fabricated. On the road, she and Kuo's men encounter T'ieh, who has arrived on a "study tour" (yu-hsüeh 遊學). Hearing her cries of outrage T'ieh rescues her and is invited to stay as a guest of the magistrate. However, Kuo and Shui Yün slowly poison T'ieh's food and he falls ill. Ping-hsin gets wind of it and has him brought to her home and nursed back to health. The sentimental, moralistic conversations they have at this time betray their budding affection. The remaining half of the plot recounts how they preserve their honor in the face of slanderous comments by Kuo, Sha Li, and Shui Yün. Ping-hsin displays shrewdness and bravery in threatening to stab herself in front of the regional inspector whom Kuo has bribed to order her to marry him. While Ping-hsin is fending off repeated stratagems, T'ieh establishes himself by passing the examinations and acting as a guarantor for Hou Hsiao, who is almost executed. Hou, restored to his command on T'ieh's word, scores victories against the enemy, and he and Shui Chü-i propose that T'ieh marry Ping-hsin, but they refuse because it would be a crime against Ming-chiao 名教 (The Teaching of Names or Confucianism) while they were still being suspected of illicit sexual relations. The romance reaches a climax when the emperor and empress hear of the accusations against them and order Ping-hsin to undergo a physical examination to determine if she is a virgin. Proven chaste, she and T'ieh receive the emperor's marriage blessing, as the plot draws to a close amidst promotions and punishments.

Hao-ch'iu's similarity to Western comedy and its storehouse of Confucian customs explain its later popularity in the West and Japan. The romance is the first full-length work of Chinese fiction to be translated into a Western language. Takizawa Bakin adapted its plot for his unfinished historical romance, Kyōkaku den 俠客傳 (Tales of Chivalrous Men and Women). Because it possesses many qualities of good literature—individualized characters, a serious moral purpose, readable style, and an organized plot—Hao-ch'iu has endeared itself to generations of Chinese and foreign readers.

EDITIONS:

There are numerous editions: only the most reliable and most available are listed.

Ming-chiao-chung jen. Hao-ch'iu chuan. 4 chüan. Published by Tu-ch'u hsüan 獨處軒, 1683?. Earliest extant ed. and most reliable.

———. Hao-ch'iu chuan. Ch'eng Po-ch'üan 成柏泉, ed. Shanghai, 1956. Reliable, available.

———. T'ien tso chih ho 天作之合 or Hsia-i feng-yüeh chuan. Yeh Yen-min 葉蔭民 ed. with notes. Hong Kong 1959. Text differs slightly from Tu-ch'u hsüan ed.

TRANSLATIONS:

Percy, Thomas. Hau Kiou Choann or The Pleasing History. 4v. London, 1761.

Davis, John Francis. The Fortunate Union. 2v. London, 1829.

D'Arcy, Guillard. Hao-Khieou-Tchoan, ou la Femme Accomplie. Paris, 1842.

Kuhn, F. Eisherz und Edeljaspis; oder die Geschichte einer glücklichen Gattenwahl. Leipzig, 1926. 2nd ed. Wiesbaden, 1947.

—RCH

Ho Ching-ming 何景明 (tzu, Chung-mo 仲默, hao, Ta-fu Hsien-sheng 大復先生, 1483-1521) is generally considered one of the outstanding poets of the Ming dynasty. In particular, he was a leading figure in the fu-ku 復古 (archaist) movement of the mid-Ming, being counted a leader of the "Ch'ien Ch'i-tzu" (Early Seven Masters—see Li Meng-yang).

Ho distinguished himself at an early age, passing the chü-jen examination when he was fifteen and the chin-shih four years later. He spent most of the years 1502-1507 in the capital, Peking, where he held office and associated with some of the leading writers of the day, including Li Tung-yang* and Li Meng-yang.* His opposition to the powerful and corrupt eunuch Liu Chin 劉瑾 (d. 1510) eventually led him to retire from office, and he spent the years 1507-1511 at home studying and writing. He was restored to office in 1512, after the fall of Liu Chin, on the recommendation of Li Tung-yang. After several promotions, he was appointed an education official in Shensi in 1518 and remained there until failing health forced him to give up his post shortly before his death.

Apart from his poetry itself, the most important source of information about Ho's poetic ideals is a letter he wrote to Li Meng-yang in 1510 or 1511, after the latter had written to "correct" him for not following more closely the archaist program of self-conscious imitation of model writers of the past. The essential difference between the two men lay in their attitude toward the imitation of ancient literary forms. Li saw them as based on natural principles, and thus invariable by their very nature, while in Ho's view imitation was simply a valuable practice for the beginning poet, a "raft to be abandoned once the shore was reached." Ho's critical judgements on specific writers have proven controversial. Ch'ien Ch'ien-i* was offended by his claim that "the way of ancient poetry was lost with T'ao Ch'ien,*" and Suzuki Torao found it difficult to believe that his stated preference for early T'ang *yüeh-fu* poems over those of Tu Fu* was a considered opinion.

Poetry makes up the bulk of Ho Ching-ming's surviving work; his sixteen-hundred-odd poems occupy twenty-six *chüan* in the fullest editions, with the remaining twelve *chüan* containing his prose and *fu*.* Five-word regulated verse seems to have been his favorite poetic form. His poetry shows both an acute sensitivity to emotional tone and a fine grasp of structural detail. The latter characteristic in particular, according to Yokota Terutoshi, contrasts sharply with the rougher and less subtle style of Li Meng-yang. Aside from

the pieces concerning literature, the most interesting of his prose works are probably the two collections of essays on political and moral themes, the *Ho-tzu* 何子 (Master Ho) and the *Nei-p'ien* 內篇 (Inner Chapters), in which his insistence on strict standards and adherence to traditional values, consistent with his literary program, takes on a distinctly Legalist tinge (the first of the twelve essays in the *Ho-tzu* is titled "Yen chih" 嚴治 [On Strict Government]).

Although Ho's literary disagreement with Li Meng-yang led to a good deal of friction between their students and followers, the two men continued to be on good terms personally. Ho's opposition to imitation and his greatness as a poet earned him the praise of a number of important seventeenth-century critics, notably Ch'ien Ch'ien-i, who were opposed to the ideas of the Seven Masters generally. Indeed, until the twentieth century Ho's stature as a Ming poet was second only to that of Kao Ch'i.* In recent times, changing tastes and lack of interest in Ming *shih* poetry have led to a decline in his reputation, to the extent that a recent reprint project in Taiwan, intended to bring the works of all the Seven Masters into print, reproduced instead, under his name, the works of a different writer altogether (Ho Ch'iao-hsin 何喬新, 1427-1503) without the error being noticed.

EDITIONS:

Traditional editions are generally either in 26 *chüan*, containing the poetry only (as in the original edition published by Ho's associates shortly after his death) or in 38, including the prose works. The most accessible version of the 26 *chüan* collection is probably the *Ho Ta-fu shih-chi* 何大復詩集 included in the *Hung-Cheng ssu-chieh shih-chi* 弘正四傑詩集; for the 38 *chüan* collection, the *Ta-fu chi* 大復集 included in the *Ssu-k'u ch'üan-shu chen-pen*, seventh series. There are no modern editions.

TRANSLATIONS:
Bryant, "Selected Ming Poems," 85-91; for Ho Ching-ming's "Po Yün-yang chiang-t'ou wen-yüeh" 泊雲陽江頭問月, see p. 89.
Demiéville, *Anthologie*, pp. 476-478.
Yoshikawa, *Gen-Min*, pp. 184-189.

STUDIES:

Chu, Tung-jun 朱東潤. "Ho Ching-ming p'i-p'ing lun shu-p'ing" 何景明批評論述評, *Wu-han ta-hsüeh wen-che chi-k'an*, 1.3 (1930), 599-610; also in Chu's *Chung-kuo wen-hsüeh p'i-p'ing lun-chi* 中國文學批評論集. 1941; rpt. Hong Kong, 1962, pp. 65-75.

———. *Chung-kuo wen-hsüeh p'i-p'ing shih ta-kang* 中國文學批評史大綱. 1943?; rpt. Hong Kong, 1959, pp. 226-228.

DMB, pp. 510-513.

Iriya, Yoshitaka 入矢義高, *Mindai shibun* 明代詩文, Tokyo, 1978, pp. 48-67.

Liu, Hai-han 劉海涵. *Ho Ta-fu Hsien-sheng nien-p'u* 先生年譜, in *Lung-t'an ching-she ts'ung-k'o* 龍潭精舍叢刻 (1923). A Summary (14 pp.) chrono-biography, to which are appended three invaluable supplements, exhaustive compilations of biographical, bibliographical, and critical materials relative to Ho and his work.

Suzuki, Torao 鈴木虎雄. *Shina shironshi* 支那詩論史. Tokyo, 1927, pp. 156-164.

Yokota, Terutoshi 横田輝俊. "Ka Keimei no bungaku" 何景明の文學. *Hiroshima daigaku bungakubu kiyō*, 25 (1965), 246-261. Emphasizes stylistic analysis and comparison (based on both poetry and prose) of Ho with Li Meng-yang.

———, "Mindai bungakuron," 67-77, 81-82. The best discussion of the disagreements between Li Meng-yang and Ho Ching-ming.

—DB

Ho Chu 賀鑄 (*tzu*, Fang-hui 方回, 1052-1125) is best known as a *tz'u** poet. Nearly three hundred of his lyrics survive, and at least two or three are included in most anthologies of *tz'u*. Lesser known are his *shih*,* although almost six hundred are extant, most of them dated by the poet himself.

Ho Chu began his career in the military bureaucracy, though his duties were not always directly martial. In 1082-85, for example, he was in charge of a mint in Hsü-chou 徐州 which produced iron coins for the army's expenditures on the frontier with Hsi-Hsia. There he belonged to a "poetry society" which studied T'ang models and practiced versification.

Later, Ho Chu secured a transfer to the civil side of the bureaucracy, on the recommendation of Su Shih.* However, he did not ascend to a prominent position un-til the accession of Emperor Hui-tsung in 1101, and even then he remained outside the capital, in such places as Ssu-chou, Soo-chow, and Hangchow. So few of the *shih* he wrote after 1100 survive that it is impossible to follow his late life with any precision. He died on March 18, 1125 in Ch'ang-chou 常州.

He is described by contemporaries as extremely tall, with bristling eyebrows and an iron-colored face. In his youth he was a great drinker and took part in horse and dog racing. He was aggressive in debate and harsh with wrongdoers.

Yet this intense character also turned inward to intellectual and aesthetic pursuits of a different character. In his late years, he amassed a large library and collated tirelessly. He wrote tiny regular-script characters requiring great discipline and control, qualities which carried over into his poetry: critics praise him for the polish of his language, the "depth and density" of his lyrics, and place him in the company of such famous writers as Liu Yung,* Su Shih, Ch'in Kuan 秦觀 (1049-1100), and Chou Pang-yen.*

Ho Chu's corpus includes a variety of styles and themes, yet his lyrics are often characterized as *wan* 婉 (delicate) or *yen-yeh* 豔冶(voluptuous). Perhaps his most famous work is "Heng-t'ang lu" 橫塘路 (Heng-t'ang Road), written to the tune *Ch'ing-yü-an* 青玉案 (*Ch'üan Sung tz'u*, p. 513). It has a romantic, perhaps even "voluptuous" aspect, as the speaker focuses on a vision of a woman moving away from him across the waters, stirring up dust, like the river goddess in Ts'ao Chih's* "Lo Shen fu" (Goddess of the Lo). He imagines this woman spending her youth at "A moonlit bridge, blossomed court,/latticed window, vermilion door;/Only spring would know the place." Women who come and go like mysterious goddesses are common in Ho's lyrics, as are romantic encounters in luxurious settings. Significant as this is, there is more to his poetry, and to this poem, than the quest for love. The most famous lines in "Heng-t'ang Road" are the concluding ones: calling attention to his role as a fashioner of phrases, the speaker challenges himself to define his ennui and comes up with "One flat expanse of misty grass,/a whole city of wind-blown floss;/The rain that falls when plums are turning yellow." By shifting away from the specific cause of his feelings and the enclosed spaces he inhabits to this series of larger vistas, of natural images which tie his mood to the universal passing of time and the dreariness of the rainy season, the poet has made his experience deeper, more complex, and given it the rhythm of variation. As critics have recognized, there is strength within his "delicacy."

But there are also lyrics which fall into the "heroic" category, if one wished to follow the traditional division of *tz'u* into "delicate" and "heroic." A good example is "Liu-chou ko-t'ou" 六州歌頭 (Song of Six Prefectures, *Ch'üan Sung tz'u*, pp. 538-539), a tune whose music was said to be valiantly moving. The preponderance of rhyming three-character lines gives it a quick drumbeat rhythm, even today without the music. In his lyric, Ho Chu describes his youth as a time of frenetic carousing, high martial ambition, and comradeship, all replaced in old age by disillusionment, hopelessness, and solitude in an environment of national crisis and bureaucratic malaise. The combination of sadness and stalwartness, together with the strong rhythm of the short lines, makes this poem quite different from those whose theme is romantic love and, indeed, rather unique in the *tz'u* tradition.

In short, Ho Chu was a sensitive lyricist who excelled in many modes: allusive or plain, suggestive and delicate or unfettered and valiant. As the nineteenth-century critic Ch'en T'ing-cho 陳廷焯 wrote, his lyrics are extremely deep and dense, yet at the same time, "his brush-force flies and dances, working changes without end, impossible to name."

EDITIONS:

Ch'ing-hu i-lao shih-chi 慶湖遺老詩集. 11 *chüan*. Li Chih-ting 李之鼎, ed. 1916. In *Sung-jen chi*, 2nd. series 宋人集乙編. Li Chih-ting, comp.

Ch'üan Sung tz'u, v. 1, pp. 500-543.

Tung-shan tz'u chien-chu 東山詞箋注. Huang Ch'i-fang 黃啟方, ed. and comp. Taiwan, 1969.

TRANSLATIONS:

"Lyrics by Ho Chu," Stuart H. Sargent, trans., *Renditions*, 5 (Autumn 1975), 106-109.

STUDIES:

Sargent, Stuart H. "Experiential Patterns in the Lyrics of Ho Chu (1052-1125)." Unpublished Ph.D. dissertation, Stanford University, 1977.

—SHS

Ho Liang-chün 何良俊 (*tzu*, Yüan-lang 元朗, 1506-1573) was a noted scholar and drama lover from Sung-chiang 松江 (modern Kiangsu). In his career he was less successful than his younger brother Liang-fu 良傅 (1509-63) who passed the *chin-shih* examination in 1541, an honor Ho Liang-chün never reached. The only post Ho Liang-chün ever attained was a clerical position in the Nanking Han-lin Academy (1553-1558).

The Ho family possessed a library called the Ch'ing-sen ko 清森閣, which according to Ho Liang-chün, housed 40,000 books, one hundred famous paintings, and other artifacts including ancient libation cups and tripods. Unfortunately it was destroyed along with the rest of the family compound in 1555 during the pirate troubles.

Ho Liang-chün called his study the Ssu-yu Chai 四友齋 (The Four Friends Studio). The four included Chuang-tzu (see *Chu-tzu pai-chia*), Po Chü-i,* and himself. Ho's fantasy of friendship with such notable men of the past was matched in reality by his close relations with Wu Ch'eng-en (see *Hsi-yu chi*).

Ho's most important work was the *Ssu-yu Chai ts'ung-shuo* 四有齋叢說 (Collected Sayings from the Four Friends Studio) first printed in 1569. This book sets forward Ho's ideas on literature, music, and the classics and on various other subjects and contemporary incidents. It is a particularly important source on drama and a statement of his interest in the theater. He claims to have been a drama-lover since his youth. He kept private troupes and taught his house-boys to sing. He also employed the famous northern musician Tun Jen to teach his slave-girls to perform and sing *tsa-chü*,* at that time a declining art in Central China. They could, he states, remember more than fifty old dramas.

Ho's other works included the *Ho-shih yü-lin* 何氏語林 (Forest of Sayings by Master Ho) which deals with classical and historical studies. He also wrote some poetry. However, he is more noted as a commentator and patron of literature and drama than as a contributor.

EDITIONS:

Ssu-yu Chai ts'ung-shuo, in *Yüan Ming shih-liao pi-chi ts'ung-k'an chih-i* 元明史料筆記叢刊之一. Peking, 1959.

Ch'ü-lun 曲論, in *Hsi-ch'ü lun-chu*. v. 4, pp. 1-14. Taken from *chüan* 37 of the *Ssu-yu Chai ts'ung-shuo*.

STUDIES:

DMB, pp. 515-518.

—CM

Ho-sheng 合生 (impromptu verse) is a T'ang term first used to describe the song and dance entertainment—depicting the beauty, fame, and deeds of the princesses and imperial consorts—at the court of Emperor Chung-tsung (r. 705-710). This form of court performance later spread to urban centers. During the Sung period, it was one of the many types of entertainments that flourished in the capital cities. The nature of *ho-sheng* performance in Sung times seems to have undergone some change—the dance element was no longer mentioned, and the emphasis was on verbal skill. Kao Ch'eng's 高承 *Shih-wu chi-yüan* 事物紀源 identifies *ho-sheng* with "singing on a topic" (*ch'ang t'i-mu* 唱題目); Hung Mai* in his *I-chien chih* defines it as an impromptu composition on a given topic. This kind of composition may be *shih,** *tz'u,** or *ch'ü** verse. Its nature may be serious or comical; the latter kind is known as *ch'iao ho-sheng* 喬合生.

The three most outstanding characteristics of *ho-sheng*—singing on a topic, impromptu composition, and comical satire—can be seen in an anecdote recorded in another Sung account, Chang Chi-hsien's 張齊賢 (943-1014) *Lo-yang chin-sheng chiu-wen chi* 洛陽縉紳舊聞記. At a gathering in a Buddhist temple, a big spider suddenly drops down from the eaves. Using this as the topic, a woman singer who is good at *ho-sheng* immediately composes a poem:

> It stuffs itself until its belly bursts,
> Following its silken web, around the temple it goes.
> Stretching up a trap in the air,
> It lies in wait to devour the unaware.

Though this poem ostensibly describes the spider, it pokes fun at the fat-bellied monk at the same time. Rhyming and punning are the two essential features of this composition. The first, second, and fourth lines all rhyme. The term *hsün ssu* 尋絲 (following silken web) is a pun on *hsün ssu* 尋思 (to ponder), and thus the second line suggests the monk who paces around the temple trying to think of ways to trap people, perhaps for alms.

A similar kind of punning and improvisation is found in an earlier work, Chang Cho's* *Yu hsien-k'u*, in which the gentleman guest and the two hostesses take turns composing impromptu poems on a series of subjects. Fruit names are used for puns such as *ts'ao* 棗 (jujube)/*ts'ao* 早 (early), *fen-li* 分梨 (to divide the pear)/*fen-li* 分離 (separation), and *yu-hsing* 有杏 (have apricot)/*yu-hsing* 有幸 (fortunate). The practice of singing or chanting on a topic or a series of topics is continued into modern times in *hsiang sheng* 相聲, comic repartee in which one performer sings on a topic designated by his partner.

Some scholars see a relationship between *ho-sheng* and the drama. The *t'i-mu yüan-pen* 題目院本 drama of the Chin period may be similar to *ho-sheng*, since both share the characteristic of acting out or singing on a topic. Tunes bearing the titles of *ch'iao ho-sheng* and *ho-sheng* are still found in the Northern and Southern *ch'ü* repertory. Other scholars believe *ho-sheng* to function as a prologue to a narrative, much like the *ju-hua* or *te-sheng tou-hui* 得勝頭廻 of the *hua-pen* stories. If this were the case the verses describing the West Lake scenery in the beginning of a story such as "Hsi-hu san-ta chi" 西湖三塔記 (in *Liu-shih chia hsiao-shuo**) might be examples of *ho-sheng* functioning as prologue. However, this view could be erroneous, since no extant Sung

405

sources attribute such a function to *ho-sheng*.

Ho-sheng has also been considered one of the four major schools of professional storytelling in Sung times; evidence in support of this theory is still inconclusive.

TRANSLATION:
Idema and West, *Chinese Theater*, pp. 25-27.

STUDIES:
Hou, Pao-lin 侯寶林, *et al. Ch'ü-i kai-lun* 曲藝概論. Peking, 1980.
Jen, Pan-t'ang 任半塘 [Jen Na 任訥]. *T'ang hsi-lung* 唐戲弄. Peking, 1958.
Li, Hsiao-ts'ang 李嘯倉. "Ho-sheng k'ao" 合生考, in Li Hsiao-ts'ang, *Sung Yüan chi-i tsa-k'ao* 宋元技藝雜考, Shanghai, 1953, pp. 53-72.
Sun K'ai-ti 孫楷第. "Sung-ch'ao shuo-hua jen te chia-shu wen-t'i" 宋朝說話人的家數問題, in Sun K'ai-ti, *Su-chiang, shuo-hua yü pai-hua hsiao-shuo* 俗講、說話與白話小說, Peking, 1956, pp. 14-26.
Otagi, Matsuo 愛宕松男. "Gōshō to sangungi: Sanraku no shakai bungakushi no kōsatsu" 合生と參軍戲： 散樂の社會文化史の考察, *Bunka*, 30.3 (November 1966), 1-26; 31.1 (July 1967), 91-119.

—SLY

Hsi-ching tsa-chi 西京雜記 (Miscellanies of the Western Capital) is a collection of nearly 130 sections, most of which describe events and personages in Ch'ang-an during the Former Han dynasty. Although the work contains some historical and literary data not available elsewhere, its role in Chinese literary history is perhaps more distinguished by the attention it has received in a long series of bibliographic notes or by its influence on subsequent literature than by its own content.

The authorship has often been the subject of critical debate since early times. According to a spurious preface first circulated in the seventh century, the *Hsi-ching tsa-chi* derives from a "Han-shu" 漢書 (History of the Former Han) compiled by Liu Hsin.* This manuscript had been handed down over generations and came into the possession of Ko Hung's* family. Ko collated it with Pan Ku's* work of the same title, copying out discrepancies and items not included by Pan in a separate manu-

script. Later, the original Liu Hsin manuscript was lost in a fire. Ko edited his "miscellanies" and labeled it *Hsi-ching tsa-chi*. Actually, the work in its present form dates from around A.D. 500, possibly from the hand of Hsiao Pen 蕭賁 (*c.* 495-*c.* 552). Yet to speak of an "author" for this work is misleading, since much of it is copied from earlier sources.

The sections of the *Hsi-ching tsa-chi* exhibit a loose arrangement resembling a standard history: *chüan* 1-3 treat various subjects in chronological order from the early second century B.C. until the last years of the first; *chüan* 4 begins with events during the reigns of the last emperors of the Former Han, but "flashes back" to the mid-second century B.C.; *chüan* 5 again treats the early years of the dynasty; *chüan* 6 discusses tombs, with no particular time frame. In formal terms, too, the *Hsi-ching tsa-chi* shares features with standard dynastic histories—annalistic items, lists, tables, and memoirs are all included. The setting varies from Ch'ang-an to Ch'eng-tu, from the Liang court to Mou-ling 茂陵—the "Western Capital" of the title is a synecdoche for the Former Han empire.

The contents, however, are more varied than a dynastic history. Entire literary pieces (primarily *fu**), catalogues of imperial processions, legal dissertations, accounts of portents and privies, books and battles all appear. There is a strong emphasis on the unusual. Passages on the composition of *fu* (discussing the great master of this genre, Ssu-ma Hsiang-ju,* and his most noted "disciple," Yang Hsiung*) represent some of the earliest literary criticism on this genre.

Although some passages reflect a Taoist tone, there is no consistent underlying philosophy discernible. In a number of sections the extravagance and opulence of palace life are criticized. Some sections are in first-person (ostensibly Liu Hsin)—this device, which in combination with the forged preface, lends verisimilitude to the work, may have exerted an influence on similar efforts by T'ang authors of *ch'uan-ch'i.** Collected in a chaotic era when historical records and libraries were ill-kept and when the Former Han represented an ideal model of political and cultural stability, the *Hsi-ching tsa-chi* was probably intended to bring together all historical and literary notices available in the compiler's locale and era.

Over the centuries the *Hsi-ching tsa-chi* exerted a strong influence on *shih*,* *tz'u*,* and drama. It also served as a major source for *lei-shu** and has been cited by commentators, both Chinese and Western, from the seventh century through the twentieth.

EDITIONS:

Hsi-ching tsa-chi. SPTK. Copy of a Ming ed. (1552) printed by K'ung T'ien-yin 孔天胤 (*fl.* 1532-1552) based on a copy from the library of a Mr. Fu from Szechwan. Most reliable edition.

———. Lu Wen-ch'ao 盧文弨 (1717-1796) *et al.*, eds. *Pao-ching T'ang ts'ung-shu* 抱經堂叢書. Late 18th century. A collated edition containing a terse but useful commentary (there are no others).

TRANSLATIONS:

Heeren-Diekhoff, Elfie. *Das Hsi-ching tsa-chi, Vermischte Aufzeichungen über die Westliche Hauptstadt.* Weilheim (Oberbayern), 1981. A complete translation noting later citations or adaptions, previous translations, and possible sources for each passage. Brief critical introduction.

Nienhauser, William H., Jr. "An Interpretation of the Literary and Historical Aspects of the *Hsi-ching tsa-chi* (Miscellanies of the Western Capital)." Unpublished Ph.D. dissertation, Indiana University, 1972. Contains annotated translations of nearly forty sections.

STUDIES:

Chin, Chia-hsi 金嘉錫. "*Hsi-ching tsa-chi* chiao-cheng" 西京雜記斠正, *Wen-shih-che hsüeh-pao*, 17 (June 1968), 185-274.

Konan, Ichiro 小南一郎. "*Sai keizakki no den-shosha tachi*" 西京雜記の伝承者, *Nippon Chūgoku Gakkai hō*, 24 (1972), 135-152. Identifies oral traditions in this work.

Ku, T'ai-kuang 古苔光. "*Hsi-ching tsa-chi* te yen-chiu" 西京雜記的研究, *Tan-chiang hsüeh-pao*, 15 (September 1977).

———. "*Hsi-ching tsa-chi* tui hou-shih wen-hsüeh te ying-hsiang" 西京雜記對後世文學的影響, *Chung-wai wen-hsüeh*, 4.11 (April 1976), 102-118.

Nienhauser, William H., Jr. "An Interpretation" (see above). Critical study discussing textual history, editions, etc. Bibliography.

———. "Once Again, the Authorship of the *Hsi-ching tsa-chi* (Miscellanies of the Western Capital)," *JAOS*, 98 (1978), 219-236. Despite ignoring an important parallel passage in the *Shih-shuo hsin-yü*, the conclusion that the work was compiled *c.* 520 seems reliable.

—WHN

Hsi-hsiang chi 西廂記 (*The West Chamber Story*; also known by the alternate titles *Pei hsi-hsiang* 北西廂, *Wang hsi-hsiang* 王西廂, and *Ts'ui Ying-ying tai-yüeh Hsi hsiang-chi* 崔鶯鶯待月西廂記) has been praised by both traditional and modern critics not only as the masterpiece of the northern *tsa-chü** dramas, but of all Chinese drama. The story line may be summarized as follows: a young scholar of great literary promise, Chang Chün-jui 張君瑞 (Student Chang), while on his way from the capital to prepare for the examinations, stops off at a Buddhist monastery to visit an old friend who lives in the area. By coincidence, Widow Ts'ui, the wife of a deceased prime minister and a distant relative, is returning home with her two children to bury her husband. She has taken up temporary lodging in the monastery. Student Chang is immediately struck by the beauty of Mrs. Ts'ui's daughter, Ying-ying, and falls deeply in love with her. But she is already betrothed to another man (Cheng Heng). When a local military commander stages a revolt, Widow Ts'ui promises her daughter to anyone who can protect her and her daughter. Chang seizes the opportunity and has his friend, the powerful general Tu Chüeh, suppress the rebellion, thereby saving Ying-ying and her family from the bandits. But Mrs. Ts'ui reneges on her promise. Student Chang then tries to seduce the young girl, but she upbraids him for his lascivious designs. The dispirited Chang then falls ill, and eventually Ying-ying is brought by her maid servant Hung-niang 紅娘 to share his couch at night. When the affair is detected, Madam Ts'ui promises Ying-ying to Chang provided he succeeds in the state examinations. He departs, but is visited by Ying-ying's spirit in a dream; she pines away at the monastery, waiting for news of the examination results. When Chang succeeds and returns, he finds Cheng Heng, her original fiancé, at the monastery. Widow Ts'ui has again promised Ying-ying to Cheng Heng. Through the intervention of Tu Chüeh, the lovers are finally united in marriage.

The source of the *Hsi hsiang-chi* story is the T'ang dynasty tale "Ying-ying chuan" (see Yüan Chen). The immediate predecessor and main source for the Yüan play, however, is Tung Chieh-yüan's *Hsi-hsiang chi chu-kung-tiao.** Whereas Yüan Chen's story focuses on one central theme—Student Chang's seduction and later abandonment of Ying-ying—Tung Chien-yüan's *Medley* extensively elaborates on both plot and characterization. Furthermore to the delight of audiences and readers ever since, the *Hsi-hsiang chi* follows Tung's revision of the ending of the story: instead of rejecting Ying-ying, Chang marries her and they live happily ever after. The length (over five-thousand lines of verse) of the Tung Chien-yüan version may help to explain the unusual length of the Yüan play, actually a series of five plays (*pen* 本), each containing four acts (*che* 折).

Authorship of the Yüan *tsa-chü* version of the *Hsi-hsiang chi* is generally attributed to Wang Shih-fu 王實甫 (*ming*, Te-hsin 德信, *fl.* thirteenth century). Little is known about him. Entries in the extant versions of the *Lu-kuei pu,** mention only that he was a native of Ta-tu 大都 (near modern Peking), and that he composed a total of fourteen plays, three of which are extant. Several traditional scholars, most notably Chin Sheng-t'an,* held that the play was actually the collaborative work of Wang Shih-fu and Kuan Han-ch'ing.* Chin and other critics maintained that Wang Shih-fu wrote the first four plays and Kuan Han-ch'ing the final one. Modern critics such as Wang Chi-ssu 王季思 have convincingly argued against such a theory.

The plot construction, characterization, and superb poetry combine to make the *Hsi-hsiang chi* an outstanding work of dramatic literature. While the central conflict of pitting the natural inclinations of two young lovers against the forces of conventional morality (represented in the play by the stern mother) is a common theme in Yüan drama, Wang Shih-fu's tightly-knit plot skillfully blends moments of heightened tension, such as the scene where the monastery is surrounded by bandits attempting to kidnap Ying-ying, with moments of comic relief, such as the sacrificial scene in the temple when Ying-ying's extraordinary beauty totally disrupts what otherwise would have been a very solemn ceremony.

Student Chang and Ying-ying are both represented as emotional and sensual youngsters in the beginning of the play, and their interest as characters derives from the sometimes unpredictable way they diverge from the standard roles society assigned to young students and virtuous maidens. Even in light of literary expectations, Ying-ying is remarkably well-characterized as a young girl who fits neither the category of the virtuous maiden nor that of the licentious woman (one must remember that she is portrayed as the *hua-tan* character—the "painted woman"). The most memorable character in the play is Hung-niang, Ying-ying's handmaid. Developing remarkably throughout the play, she serves as the catalyst for the actions of the other characters. Though at first on the side of conventional morality (in Part I, Act II, for instance, she reprimands Chang for making "improper" inquiries about her mistress), she later becomes more sympathetic to the two when Mrs. Ts'ui withdraws her promise of Ying-ying's hand to Student Chang. Hardly the "stock" maid-character found in most Yüan dramas, Hung-niang ingeniously tells half-truths, persuades and manipulates Chang and Ying-ying into action, and even defies the authority of Mrs. Ts'ui, all for the purpose of uniting the lovers.

But the *sine qua non* of any successful Yüan playwright was skill at composing *ch'ü,** the dramatic lyrics. Wang Shih-fu was one of the most successful at this. Whether describing a natural scene to evoke a particular atmosphere or mood, or delineating human sentiments, he composes with great skill.

This play became the basis for innumerable later adaptations. The story reappeared in Southern *ch'uan-ch'i** plays, and in different forms of prosimetric literature during the Ming and Ch'ing.

EDITIONS:

Hsin-k'an ch'i-miao ch'üan-hsiang chu-shih Hsi-hsiang chi, (1498 ed. by the Yüeh Family 岳, Peking), in *Ku-pen*, I.

Hsi-hsiang chi. Wu Hsiao-ling 吳曉鈴, ed. and annot. Peking, 1954. Useful notes.

———. Wang Chi-ssu, ed. and annot. Shanghai, 1955; revised first edition, Shanghai, 1978. Extensive annotation.

Fu, *Tsa-chü*, pp. 52-63 has a complete list of editions.

TRANSLATIONS:

Hsiung, S[hih]. I. *The Romance of the Western Chamber (Hsi-hsiang chi); A Chinese Play Written in the Thirteenth Century.* New York, c. 1935; rpt., New York and London, 1968. Based on Chin Sheng-t'an edition. Many liberties taken with the text.

STUDIES:

Chang, Hsin-chang. "The West Chamber: The Theme of Love in Chinese Drama," *Annual of the China Society of Singapore*, 1957, 9-19.

Ch'en, Ch'ing-huang 陳慶煌. "*Hsi-hsiang chi* k'ao-shu (shang)" 西廂記考述 (上), *Chung-hua hsüeh-yüan*, 22 (March 1, 1979), 149-200.

Chiang, Hsing-yü 蔣興餘, ed. *Ming k'an-pen Hsi-hsiang chi yen-chiu* 明刊本西廂記研究. Peking, 1982. A collection of articles on various Ming editions, their editors, individual characteristics, and relationships.

Chou, Miao-chung 周妙中. "Hsi-hsiang chi tsa-chü tso-che chih-i" 西廂記雜劇作者質疑, *Wen-hsüeh i-ch'an tseng-k'an*, 5 (1957), 264-277.

Chou, T'ien 周天. *Hsi-hsiang chi fen-hsi* 西廂記分析. Shanghai, 1958.

Denda, Akira 傳田章, ed. *Minkan Gen zatsugeki Seishōki mokuroku* 明刊元雜劇西廂記目錄. Tokyo, 1970.

Fu, Hsi-hua 傅惜華. *Hsi-hsiang chi shuo-ch'ang chi* 西廂記說唱集. Shanghai, 1955.

Ho, Shang-hsien. "A Study of the *Western Chamber*: A Thirteenth Century Chinese Play." Unpublished Ph.D. dissertation, The University of Texas at Austin, 1976.

Huo, Sung-lin 霍松林. *Hsi-hsiang chi chien-shuo* 西廂記簡說. Peking, 1957.

Hsia, C. T. "A Critical Introduction [to the *Hsi-hsiang chi*]," in S. I. Hsiung, *op. cit.*, pp. xi-xxxii.

Tai, Pu-fan 戴不凡. *Lun Ts'ui Ying-ying.* Shanghai, 1963.

Tanaka, Kenji. "*Seishōki* banpon no kenkyū" 西廂記板本の研究, *Biburia*, 1 (January 1949), 107-148.

———. "*Seishōki* shohon no shipyōsei" 西廂記諸本の信憑性, *Nihon Chūgoku Gakkaihō*, 2 (1950), 89-104.

———. "Zatsugeki *Seishōki* ni okeru jinbutsu seikaku no kyōchō" 雜劇西廂記にあける人物性格の強調, *Tōhōgaku*, 22 (July 1961), 67-83.

Wang, Chi-ssu. *Ts'ung Ying-ying chuan tao Hsi-hsiang chi* 從鸎鸎傳到西廂記. Shanghai, 1955.

———. "*Hsi-hsiang chi* hsü-shuo" 西廂記敘說, in *Yüan Ming Ch'ing hsi-ch'ü yen-chiu lun-wen chi* 元明清戲曲研究論文集, Peking, 1957, pp. 152-170.

—JH

Hsi-hsiang-chi chu-kung-tiao 西廂記諸宮調, attributed to Tung Chieh-yüan 董解元 (Master Tung), is the only *chu-kung-tiao** surviving in its entirety. In the *Lu-kuei-pu*,* a Yüan roster of playwrights and lyric writers (preface 1330), Master Tung is said to have lived during the reign of the Chin Emperor Chang-tsung (1190-1208). Since in this roster Tung heads the list of notables and officials in the category "Famous Personages of an Earlier Generation Whose Lyrics Have Survived," he probably came from an elevated social class. Nothing else is known of him.

The plot of *Hsi-hsiang-chi chu-kung-tiao* loosely follows that of Yüan Chen's* *ch'uan-ch'i** "Ying-ying chuan," with the major difference that in the *chu-kung-tiao* the two protagonists, Ying-ying and Chang-sheng, manage to overcome all obstacles and marry each other at the end.

Hsi-hsiang-chi chu-kung-tiao consists of alternating verse sections (for singing) and prose passages (for narration). In all, there are 5263 lines of verse and 184—often lengthy—prose passages. There are three types of verse sections: a single poem set to a tune, a single poem and a coda, and a series of poems set to a suite of tunes terminated by a coda. In the second and third types, all tunes and the coda in a section belong to the same musical mode, and all rhyming lines share the same rhyme.

The work employs 15 musical modes comprising 126 different tunes, and the rhymes fall into 14 rhyme groups.

Compared with earlier *shih** and *tz'u,** the verses of *Hsi-hsiang-chi chu-kung-tiao* reveal new prosodic features. Chief among these are the use of *ch'en-tzu* 襯字 (added "outrides") which can extend a line to twice its prescribed length and a more varied rhythm within the lines (2/3 and 3/2 in five-character lines, 4/3 and 3/4 in seven-character lines, etc.). The verses also show a less stringent definition of rhyme: level- and oblique-tone words are no longer segregated into different rhyme groups; as long as they share the same final, they are used to rhyme with each other.

The prose passages in *Hsi-hsiang-chi chu-kung-tiao* for the most part are written in a terse and dignified *wen-yen* 文言 (classical language), and the verse sections in a lively, colorful northern vernacular, a vernacular which in terms of syntax and grammar, is a precursor of modern Mandarin.

Throughout the *chu-kung-tiao*, the only narrative voice interpreting events and evaluating characters is that of the omniscient singer-narrator. And the three modes of narrative conspicuous in early Chinese vernacular fiction—description, commentary, and presentation—are equally prominent in *Hsi-hsiang-chi chu-kung-tiao*.

EDITIONS:
Hsi-hsiang-chi chu-kung-tiao 西廂記諸宮調. Hou Tai-lin 侯岱麟, ed. Peking, 1955. A variorum edition.
Tung Chieh-yüan hsi-hsiang 董解元西廂. Shanghai, 1937. Reproduction of a Ming edition, edited and with marginal comments by T'ang Hsien-tsu.*
Tung Chieh-yüan Hsi-hsiang-chi 董解元西廂記. Ling Ching-yen 凌景埏, ed. Peking, 1962. With lexical notes.

TRANSLATIONS:
Ch'en, Li-li. *Master Tung's Western Chamber Romance.* Cambridge, England, 1976.

STUDIES:
Ch'en, Li-li. "The Relationship Between Oral Presentation and Literary Devices Used in

Liu Chih-yüan chu-kung-tiao and *Tung Hsi-hsiang chu-kung-tiao*," *LEW,* 14 (1970), 519-527.
Chu P'ing-ch'u 朱平楚, annot. and trans. *Hsi-hsiang chi chu-kung-tiao chu-shih* 西廂記諸宮調注釋. Lanchow, 1982. An annotated edition which provides a modern Chinese verse translation of the song-sections of the text.
Iida, Yoshirō 飯田吉郎. *Tō Saishō ibun hyō* 董西廂異文表. Tokyo, 1951.
———. *Tō Saishō goi intoku* 董西廂語彙引得. Tokyo, 1951.
Tanaka, Kenji 田中謙二. "*Tō Saishō* ni mieru zokugo no joji" 董西廂に見える俗語の助字, *Tōhō gakuhō,* 18 (1950), 55-77.
———, "Bungaku toshite no *Tō Saishō*" 文學としての董西廂, *Chūgoku bungaku hō,* 1 (1954), 93-112; 2 (1955), 75-100.

—LLC

Hsi K'ang 嵇康 (*tzu,* Shu-yeh 叔夜, 223-262) is in many ways a tragic figure. A man rich in talent—poetic, musical, philosophical—he died young as a result of political ties. He was from Chih 銍 county in the state of Ch'iao 譙 (modern Anhwei Province), then in the kingdom of Wei. Raised by his mother and older brothers, he was spoiled, a fact which he claimed greatly influenced his development—he grew up to love freedom and unrestraint and texts of *Lao* and *Chuang.*

About 245 he married a royal princess of the Ts'ao 曹 clan. In normal times this would have set his career for life. But in 249 the Ssu-ma 司馬 clan seized control of the government, and the Ts'ao family fortunes declined. Hsi K'ang refused to hold office under the Ssu-mas. He retired to his estate in Shan-yang where he reportedly headed a famous group of talkers and tipplers, the *Chu-lin ch'i-hsien* 竹林七賢 (Seven Worthies of the Bamboo Grove). In 262, involved in a spat between two brothers, he was arrested, maligned at court, and executed together with his friend Lü An 呂安.

Hsi K'ang was a man of strong emotions; frustrated and angry, morally indignant but frank and direct, he would not conceal his feelings. "Openness" (*kung* 公), in fact, is the hallmark of the moral theory expressed in his essay "Shih-ssu lun" 釋私論 (Dispelling Self-interest). His personality comes through admirably in his literary works, affecting both the content and style, but made him enemies as well, hence his early demise.

As a poet Hsi K'ang is overshadowed in the Wei by his contemporaries Juan Chi* and Ts'ao Chih.* His reputation is that of a writer of "philosophical verse," a fashion of the times, and is not totally undeserved. His "Liu-yen shih, shih shou" 六言詩十首 (Ten Poems in Six-word Verse), for example, are dry, insipid eulogia of recluses and heroes of the past and brief homilies on Taoist ideas. But these are the exceptions in his extant corpus of sixty poems. Most are artistic, technically well executed, and emotionally compelling. His best are the "Tseng hsiung hsiu-ts'ai ju-chün, shih-pa shou" 贈兄秀才入軍, 十八首 (Eighteen [or nineteen according to some editors] Poems Presented to My Brother the Hsiu-ts'ai as He Enters the Army). These pieces are all written in the archaic four-word verse which allows the writer to readily recognize allusions. Hsi K'ang expressed, often in hidden ways, his concern for the welfare of his brother as well as his own aspirations for freedom and (Taoist) immortality. The poems are filled with Ch'u-tz'u* imagery, and here as elsewhere Hsi K'ang more than once uses the Yüan-yu (Distant Journey) theme: the morally pure gentleman living in bad times, disgusted by what he sees (tristia), cuts all earthly ties, and ascends into the skies to frolic with the immortals (itineraria).

Hsi K'ang is well known as a debater and writer of the philosophical essay (lun 論); he was perhaps the best disputer in that age of ch'ing-t'an 清談 (pure talk). Of his essays, the most highly praised by contemporaries were his "Yang-sheng lun" 養生論 (Essay on Nourishing Life), and his "Sheng wu ai-lo lun" 聲無哀樂論 (Music Has in it Neither Grief nor Joy). His arguments are clear, well-reasoned, and easily understood, even by modern Westerners. For their intrinsic interest and attention to proper methods of disputation, the essays on residence and good fortune ("A Refutation of [Juan K'an's] Essay—Residence Has in it Neither Good Fortune nor Bad,"

and "An Answer to [Juan K'an's] Explanation to [My] Refutation of His Essay—Residence Has in it Neither Good Fortune nor Bad") are also deserving of mention. The Hsi K'ang chi contains thirteen essays, nine by Hsi K'ang and four by opponents in various debates.

Hsi K'ang has enjoyed a revival of interest in the mid-twentieth century. This is in part due to the interest taken in him by the great modern writer Lu Hsün 魯迅 (1881-1936), but also to sympathies with his anti-government stance, his escapist attitude, and the interest he and his friends had in narcotic and psychedelic drugs.

EDITIONS:
Hsi Chung-san chi 嵇中散集. SPPY; SPTK.
Hsi K'ang chi 嵇康集. Lu Hsün, ed., in Lu Hsün ch'üan-chi 魯迅全集. Shanghai, 1938; Peking, 1956; Hong Kong, 1962. Also in Lu Hsün san-shih nien chi 魯迅三十年集. Hong Kong, 1965; Hong Kong, 1971.
Hsi K'ang chi chiao-chu 嵇康集校注. Tai Ming-yang 戴明揚, ed. Peking, 1962. Best available edition. Thorough annotation. Notes all variant readings and discusses difficult passages. Appended essays on variety of issues.
Matsuura, Takashi 松浦崇. Kei Kō shū shi sakuin 嵇康集詩索引. Kyoto, 1975.

TRANSLATIONS:
Hightower, J. R. "Letter to Shan T'ao," in Anthology of Chinese Literature, Cyril Birch, ed. New York, 1965, pp. 162-166.
Henricks, Robert G. Philosophy and Argumentation in Third-Century China: The Essays of Hsi K'ang. Princeton, 1983.
Holzman, Donald. La vie et la pensée de Hsi K'ang. Leiden, 1957, pp. 83-130.
———. "La poésie de Ji Kang," JA, 268 (1980), 107-177; 323-378. Translation and explication of the entire poetic corpus.
Rushton, Peter. "An Interpretation of Hsi K'ang's Eighteen Poems Presented to Hsi Hsi on His Entry Into the Army," JAOS, 99.2 (April-June 1979), 175-190.
Swanson, Jerry. "A Third Century Taoist Treatise on the Nourishment of Life: Hsi K'ang and His Yang-sheng lun," in Studies in Philosophy and in the History of Science: Essays in Honor of Max Fisch. Lawrence, Kansas, 1970, pp. 139-158.
van Gulik, R. H. Hsi K'ang and His Poetical Essay on the Lute. Tokyo, 1941; rpt., 1968.

von Zach, *Anthologie,* v. I, pp. 250-258, 361-364, 388-389, 539-561, 783-789.

STUDIES:

Fukunaga, Mitsuji 福永光司. "Kei Kō ni okeru figa no nomdai: Kei Kō no seikatsu to shisō" 嵇康にあける自我の問題 (嵇康の生活 と思想). *Tōhō gakuhō,* 32 (1962), 92-119.

Funatsu, Tomihiko 船津富彦. "Kei Kō bungaku ni tōei seru shinsen" 嵇康文學に投影女子神仙, *Tōhō shūkyō,* 31 (1968), 44-67.

Henricks, Robert G. "Hsi K'ang and Argumentation in the Wei, and a Refutation of the Essay 'Residence Is Unrelated to Good and Bad, Fortune: Nourish Life," *Journal of Chinese Philosophy,* 8 (1981), 169-224. Also contains translations.

———. "Hsi K'ang (223-262): His Life, Literature, and Thought." Unpublished Ph.D. dissertation, University of Wisconsin, 1976.

Ho Ch'i-min 何啓民. *Chu-lin ch'i-hsien yen-chiu* 竹林七賢研究. Taipei, 1966, pp. 60-110.

Holzman, *La vie.*

Hou Wai-lu 侯外廬, et al. "Hsi K'ang ti hsin-sheng erh wu lun kuei-pien ssu-hsiang" 嵇康的心聲二物論詭辯思想, in *Chung-kuo ssu-hsiang t'ung-shih* 中國思想通史. Peking, 1950, v. 2, ch. 15, pp. 609-698.

Kōzen Hiroshi 興膳宏. "Kei Kō no hishō" 嵇康の飛翔, *Chūgoku bungaku hō,* 16 (1962), 1-28.

—RH

Hsi-k'un ch'ou-ch'ang chi 西崑酬唱集 (Anthology of Poems Exchanged in the Hsi-k'un Archives) is a collection of 250 *lü-shih* (regulated-verse poems—see *shih*) written by seventeen imperial archivists of the early eleventh century. From the title, critics derived the term *Hsi-k'un t'i* 西崑體 (*Hsi-k'un* style) to describe its poems, which are characterized by the use of ornate and allusive language with much parallelism. There is also heavy use of mythical allegory, in conscious imitation of the ninth-century Li Shang-yin* school of poetry. Not unexpectedly, the *Hsi-k'un* poets were also famous masters of the highly allusive and ornate *p'ien-wen** style of prose for which Li Shang-yin was also famous. Most critics view *Hsi-k'un* style as merely imitative of Li Shang-yin, serving only to mark its demise, as it gave way to newer styles of poetry and prose written by Ou-yang Hsiu* and Mei Yao-ch'en.*

The Hsi-k'un Archives were a legendary imperial book repository in the K'un-lun 崑崙 mountains, called Yü-shan ts'e-fu 玉山策府 (Jade Mountain Imperial Archives). The poems in this two-chapter anthology are classified according to sixty-nine themes arranged in a rough chronological order from 1005 to 1008 A.D. During these years at least six of the poets included in this collection worked in the imperial archives compiling the immense encyclopedia, *Ts'e-fu yüan-kuei* 册府元龜 (Tortoise Shells for Divining from the Imperial Archives)—hence the title.

The editor of the work was Yang I 楊億 (*tzu,* Ta-nien 大年, 974-1020/1), who wrote the preface and contributed seventy-four poems. His main collaborator was his close friend Liu Yün 劉筠 (971-1031) who also contributed seventy-four poems. The names Yang and Liu were frequently used by critics to describe their particular styles of prose and poetry. Ch'ien Wei-yen* was another important collaborator; fifty-five of his poems are included. The remaining fourteen poets were also mostly Yang's friends.

The *Hsi-k'un* collection was influential among Sung poets, especially through the middle of the eleventh century. Ou-yang Hsiu praised these poets as fine craftsmen, though he felt that their allusive writings were conducive to facile imitation. Only a few critics, however, such as Yu Mao 尤袤 (1124-1193) and Ch'iang Hsing-fu 強行父 (1019-1157), have found fine poems in the *Hsi-k'un* anthology. Most later critics, influenced by the eleventh century transformation away from allusive poetry, castigated the *Hsi-k'un* poets for corrupting literary values and the relationship of Confucian morality to literature. Shih Chieh 石介 (1005-1045), a *Hsi-k'un* contemporary, comdemned Yang I for his ornate and allusive writings, which he attributed to Yang's interest in Buddhism and Taoism. The success of poets who rejected *Hsi-k'un* style after the eleventh century overshadowed the fame of the collection, which was apparently not reprinted until the sixteenth century.

Though the school produced no following after the eleventh century, at least two important younger men carried on the tradition after Yang I's death: the erudite brothers, Sung Hsiang 宋庠 (996-1066) and Sung Ch'i 宋祁 (998-1061). Wang An-shih* was said to have used the style, and it was also used by the Emperor Hu I-tsung (r. 1100-1126). The style was said to be popular in the seventeenth and eighteenth centuries, a popularity which corresponded with the revival of *p'ien-wen* prose, and a revival of interest in the erudition of men such as Yang I. Ch'ing critics saw *Hsi-k'un* as a reaction to the strong influence of the Chiang-hsi Style (see *Chiang-hsi shih-p'ai*).

Yang I, editor of and contributor to the *Hsi-k'un ch'ou-ch'ang chi,* typified the traditional erudite scholar and possessed a profound knowledge and love of the history and institutions of the aristocratic Buddhist-dominated millennium then coming to a close. He perfected *p'ien-wen* prose style (used in government documents) and enjoyed composing the allegorical *Hsi-k'un* poetry to demonstrate his erudition.

Born in P'u-ch'eng 浦城 (Fukien), he was ten when recognized by the emperor as a prodigy. Following a special examination of his literary abilities, he was made an official in the Imperial Library. Seven years later (991) he passed the *chin-shih* 進士 examination and began to serve in various archival and library positions; in 1006 he became a Han-lin Academician.

Between 1012 and 1014 he left the court to see his ailing mother without the emperor's permission, and was consequently demoted for insubordination. Yang I returned to the capital in 1014, and by the time of his death (in December, 1020 or January, 1021) he had been reinstated as a Han-lin Academician. His demotion was not a true indication of the esteem in which he was held, and barely mars an otherwise long and successful bureaucratic career.

In addition to his poetry and prose, Yang I also demonstrated his erudition in several major compilations. When barely twenty he participated in the compilation of the *T'ai-tsung huang-ti shih-lu* 太宗皇帝實錄 (completed 998); he reportedly wrote fifty-six of the eighty chapters. His interest in Buddhism is shown by his role as a major compiler of the officially sponsored *Ching-te ch'uan-teng lu* 景德傳燈錄 (completed after 1008), to which he also wrote the preface. Between 1005 and 1013 he served as a chief editor of the *Ts'e-fu yüan-kuei.* Several of his fellow *Hsi-k'un* poets also participated in the project. Yang was responsible for writing and editing the prefaces to each of the thirty-one main sections.

In addition to the *Hsi-k'un* anthology, two collections of Yang I's personal writings survive. The *Wu-i hsin-chi* 武夷新集, in twenty *chüan,* is a collection of poems written during his first decade in the Imperial Library, (997-1007). There is also a four-*chüan* collection of his prose writings, the *Yang Wen-kung chi* 楊文公集.

EDITIONS:

Hsi-k'un ch'ou-ch'ang chi 西崑酬唱集. *Yüeh-ya-t'ang* 粵雅堂 edition, in *PPTSCC,* based on an edition of Mao Ch'i-ling 毛奇齡 (1623-1716), printed in 1708. Most other editions of the anthology are based on this edition.

Hsi-k'un ch'ou-ch'ang chi chu 西崑酬唱集注. Wang Chung-lo 王仲犖, comm. Peking, 1980. A copiously annotated and clearly punctuated edition based on the 1537 *Wan-chu T'ang* 玩珠堂 edition reprinted in *SPTK.* It includes the history of the collection, concise biographies of its major poets, and prefaces and colophons from other editions.

Yang, I. *Wu-i hsin-chi* 武夷新集, in *P'u-ch'eng i'-shu* 浦城遺書.

———. *Yang Wen-kung chi* 楊文公集, in *Liang Sung ming-hsien shao-chi* 兩宋名賢少集. *Ssu-k'u ch'üan-shu-chen-pen liu-chi.*

TRANSLATIONS:

Sunflower, pp. 309-310 (Yang I).

STUDIES:

Chaves, *Mei Yao-ch'en,* pp. 51-53, 64-77.

Yeh, Ch'ing-ping 葉慶炳. "*Hsi-k'un ch'ou-ch'ang chi tsa-k'ao*" 西崑酬唱集雜考, *Shu ho jen,* 195 (September 16, 1972).

Yoshikawa, *Sung,* pp. 49-52, 56-57.

—GL & CBL

Hsi-yu chi 西遊記 (The Journey to the West), attributed to the late Ming writer and official, Wu Ch'eng-en 吳承恩 (c. 1500-1582), is one of the most popular traditional

413

Chinese novels. Based loosely on the historical experience of the T'ang priest, Hsüan-tsang 玄奘 (596-664), who took seventeen years (the narrative claims fourteen years) to journey to India for Buddhist scriptures, the hundred-chapter narrative is an expansive tale combining religious allegory with romance, fantasy, humor, and satire.

For nearly a thousand years, the story of Hsüan-tsang has been told and elaborated in popular literary forms. Earliest among these are the *Ta T'ang San-tsang Fa-shih ch'ü-ching chi* 大唐三藏法師取經記 and the *Ta T'ang San-tsang ch'ü-ching shih-hua* 大唐三藏取經詩話, two virtually identical versions of the same story which date from the Southern Sung. One significant feature of these works (narrated in prose and punctuated with verse) is the appearance of a "monkey novice-monk" (猴行者), who becomes the companion and guardian of the historical pilgrim. This simian figure remains a permanent character in all known subsequent versions of the story, the notable ones of which include a twenty-four-act Yüan *tsa-chü** also titled *Hsi-yu chi*, and a mid-fifteenth-century Korean reader, the *Pak t'angsa onhae* 朴通事諺解.

The textual history of the *Hsi-yu chi* is complex and controversial. Scholarly opinions are divided on whether the earliest known preserved edition of 1592, published by Shih-te T'ang 世德堂 of Nanking, represents the closest approximation of the original or whether two shorter editions circulating in the late Ming period may have antedated the hundred-chapter version. More recent studies indicate that there are good reasons to postulate either an independent *Urtext* or the priority of the shorter version of the story titled the *T'ang San-tsang Hsi-yu shih-ni*[o] 唐三藏西遊釋尼 [厄]傳, compiled by the Canton book-dealer Chu Ting-ch'en 朱鼎臣. The Chu text features a lengthy rehearsal of the "Ch'en Kuang-jui 陳光蕊 story" which, echoing the *tsa-chü* account, tells of the disasters attending the birth and youth of Hsüan-tsang. This episode, absent from the 1592 edition and from several other editions immediately following, appears as Chapter 9 in an early Ch'ing abridged edition (*c.* 1662) and in all subsequent versions, abridged or unabridged.

Though reliant on a variety of antecedent themes and figures associated with the story of Hsüan-tsang's westward journey, the hundred-chapter novel is at once the culmination of a long tradition and an imaginative masterpiece that supercedes all previous versions. The modern edition may be outlined in five parts: (1) Chapters 1-7: the birth story of Sun Wu-k'ung 孫悟空 (Monkey), tracing his aquisition of magical power, his rebellion in Heaven, and his subjugation by Buddha beneath the Wu-hsing Shan 五行山 (Mountain of Five Phases); (2) Chapter 8: the Heavenly Council, in which Buddha sends the Bodhisattva Kuan-yin 觀音 to find a suitable scripture-pilgrim in China, and the introduction of all of Hsüan-tsang's future disciples, including Chu Pa-chieh 豬八戒, Sha Monk 沙和尚, and the dragon-horse; (3) Chapters 9-12: the background of Hsüan-tsang and his eventual commission by the T'ang Emperor T'ai-tsung to undertake the pilgrimage; (4) Chapters 13-97: the pilgrimage itself, elaborated as alternating capture and release of the pilgrims by a series of monsters, demons, animal spirits, and disguised deities, making up most of the eighty-one ordeals (*nan* 難) ordained for Hsüan-tsang; and (5) Chapters 98-100: the audience with Buddha, the return to China with the scriptures, and the final canonization of the five pilgrims.

Of the many characters that populate the narrative, the most engaging and memorable is Sun Wu-k'ung, the monkey of prodigious wit, intelligence, and magical prowess. Even before he became the chief disciple of Hsüan-tsang, Sun has already enjoyed extended exposure in the opening chapters. These episodes recounting his acquisition of magic, his quest for the title Great Sage, Equal to Heaven 齊天大聖, his disruption of the Immortal Peaches Festival in Heaven, his revolt against the Jade Emperor, and his subjugation by Buddha have been beloved by Chinese readers of all ages. Forming a virtually independent cycle of stories, they have been told and retold in a variety of popular media, including opera, puppet, and cinematic animation.

How a popular religious hero like Hsüan-tsang came to acquire a simian guardian is a question still eluding satisfactory scholarly explanation, though the association may be traced to the early Sung period. In antecedent vernacular stories and dramas, there are numerous examples of apes and ape-like figures, some even serving as attendants to clerics, but none can be considered the definitive ancestor of the *Hsi-yu chi* hero.

As the faithful and resourceful escort of Hsüan-tsang, Sun is directly or indirectly responsible for delivering his human master from all the ordeals encountered on the pilgrimage. Though given to occasional excesses and fits of mischief, Sun never swerves from fidelity to his master or dedication to seeking the scripture, earning for himself the title "Buddha Victorious in Strife" in his final apotheosis. In creating a character of courage, agility, generosity of spirit, and heroic energy, the author gives new meaning to the well-known metaphor, the Monkey of the Mind (*hsin-yüan* 心猿), a phrase popularized by both Buddhist and Taoist religious texts. To complete successfully his protracted, appallingly hazardous journey, Hsüan-tsang must simultaneously keep the ape firmly in control and use to the utmost its characterictic talents.In sharp contrast to Sun Wu-k'ung, and of almost equal fame and appeal, is the second disciple, Chu Pa-chieh. Originally a naval commander in the Taoist pantheon, he was banished to earth for getting drunk and insulting the beautiful Goddess of the Moon. A wrong turn on his way to incarnation transformed him into a a half-pig, half-human figure with the attendant flaws of sensuality, sloth, gluttony, and moronity befitting such an incongruous union. Portrayed with obvious care and affection by the author, Chu is one of the liveliest comic characters found in traditional Chinese literature. His acts and conversations are invariably reported with gusto, and add much vitality to the humor and satire. Though his hog-

gish appetite for food and sex more than once brings calamity to his companions, and though his occasional envious gestures and slanderous remarks directed toward Sun Wu-k'ung brought about dissension among the pilgrims, he is never evil or wicked nor is he ever allowed to appear as a true antagonist. Patently Hsüan-tsang's favorite, Chu embodies the failings and foibles of the human mortal, who nonetheless can redeem himself through meritorious striving and service.

Sha Wu-ching 沙悟淨 or Sha Monk, the third disciple, was a cannibalistic monster before he was converted by the Bodhisattva Kuan-yin. As Hsüan-tsang's disciple, this loyal and long-suffering priest of "gloomy complexion" is often slighted by readers, for he is neither as powerful and attractive as Sun Wu-k'ung, nor does he possess the irresistible charm of the idiotic Pa-chieh. The narrative, however, makes it quite clear that his participation, along with that of the white horse (who was originally a dragon prince), is crucial to the success of the pilgrimage.

Like his three disciples and his beast of burden, Hsüan-tsang is also given a divine pre-incarnate status as the Elder Gold Cicada (金蟬長老) before the Buddha Tathāgata. His punishment for dozing off during one of Buddha's lectures was again an exilic life on earth, where the endurance of many fated sufferings (eighty-one ordeals in all) from the moment of birth to the end of his journey would make him worthy of final reintroduction into the Buddhist assembly. His celestial origin notwithstanding, the fictive Hsüan-tsang hardly resembles the learned and eloquent heroic figure drawn in history and hagiography. As a fictional character Hsüan-tsang seems more like a timorous scholar of modest gifts than a priest, for his gentility and refinement, though endearing traits in themselves, are inadequate virtues for so rugged and dangerous a journey. In the course of the pilgrimage, it is his "active mind"—fear, suspicion, doubt, mistrust, misgiving, foolishness, attentiveness to slander and flattery, and even attachment to bodily wants and comforts—that lands him repeatedly in the lairs of demons. He is, therefore, not only utterly dependent on his disciples and, through them, on other higher deities for protection, but he must also rely on someone like Sun Wu-k'ung for periodic instruction on the need for detachment and the truth of no-mind.

The depiction of the five members of the pilgrimage makes it apparent that the author's deepest intention is not merely to dwell on their individual characters and accomplishments. They are meant to function as a united team. More than merely providing a mythic frame for the story, the pilgrims' common pedigree and collective fate in fact point up one central concern of the narrative, redemption through atoning merit.

Added to this principal theme is yet another dimension, elaborating the vicissitudes of the pilgrims' experience in terms of physiological alchemy. Though the modern scholar Hu Shih has charged that the novel has been ruined by centuries of "Taoists and Buddhists and their ridiculous nonsense," the traditional commentators and editors throughout the Ch'ing period to whom he refers have taken far more seriously the unique feature of this novel: namely, an unprecedented and massive appropriation of the concepts and terminologies taken from spagyrical literature. Through direct quotations from the *Tao-tsang** and allusions, an unbroken structure of allegorical meaning has been constructed. In every part of the novel there are extensive patterns of correspondence between the names of the pilgrims and the *Wu-hsing* 五行 (Five Phases), which are then further correlated with different physiological systems or functions. This complex system of correspondence not only enables the author to comment on the experience and action of the pilgrims, but also to endow specific landscapes with symbolic meaning as well. The object of physiological alchemy as written and practiced by the adepts in the cult of longevity in China is literally the prolongation of life. Since they believe that their techniques can prevail against the natural processes of mutual generation of the Five

Phases (*Wu-hsing hsiang-sheng* 五行相生), the journey of scripture-seeking is progressively developed to become a journey in alchemical self-cultivation as well.

Despite the intricate and insistent religious character of the narrative, its allegory is neither obtrusive nor jarring. What has first charmed and entertained centuries of general Chinese readers is the inventive genius of the storyteller and his enthralling use of language. The memorable elements are to be found, for example, in Sun Wu-k'ung's marvelous tricks and stunts, Pa-chieh's hilarious bouts of eating, the rousing battle scenes with fantastic instruments and feats of magic, and the compelling descriptions of both exotic landscapes and everyday life.

The novel is notable for its dialogues and speeches. Its author has managed to capture in engaging vividness the manners and idioms of the vernacular. With equal dexterity, he has penned some seven hundred poems of all varieties, from exquisite short lyrics of scenic description to the strongly rhythmic *p'ai-lü* (see *shih*) used for resounding autobiography and battle provocation, from enigmatic *tz'u** charged with Buddhist or alchemical mysteries to regulated verse ingeniously built on puns and the names of botanical or pharmaceutical substances.

In addition to enjoying its richly polysemous texture and its dazzling display of multiple rhetorical styles, readers of the novel have always taken to the novel's jocose but biting satire of traditional Chinese society. The hierarchies and policies of both the celestial and the nether worlds are exact counterparts to those of the human order. Loyalty to one's ruler and filiality to one's parents, two cardinal virtues of traditional Confucian culture, are praised as much as the Buddhist doctrine of mercy and the Taoist advocacy of simplicity. In a society where political motives and maneuvers pervade both home and office, where the administration of law is ineluctably tied to the motions of human sentiment, greed and graft can turn up everywhere. It is no surprise that the obstreperous Sun Wu-k'ung has elicited abid-

416

ing admiration not only for the great eleemosynary works he performs during a religious pilgrimage, but also for his heroic defiance of oppressive authority, winning recurrent praise from Marxist and non-Marxist critics alike and even a poetic tribute from Mao Tse-tung.

Considerable knowledge of this novel's putative author, Wu Ch'eng-en (*tzu*, Ju-chung 汝忠, *hao*, She-yang shan-jen 射陽山人), has been made available by modern scholarship. Wu passed the *hsiu-ts'ai* examination, but never succeeded in subsequent examinations. In 1544, however, he was chosen by the local authorities to be a *Kung-sheng* 貢生 (Tribute Student), which qualified him to reside in the city of Nanking as a scholar of the National University. Between 1546 and 1552, Wu lived in Peking where he was active in a small literary circle that included several noted writers of the time. Thereafter he undertook extensive travels, and for a brief period following 1566 he was given several minor posts in the provinces and the capital. In 1570 he returned to his native Huai-an 淮安 (modern Kiangsu); the *Hsi-yu chi* was allegedly a work of his final years. His collected works, the *She-yang Hsien-sheng ts'un-kao* 射陽先生存稿 (Extant Drafts of Mr. She-yang), published around 1590 in four *chüan*, showed him to be a lyric poet of no mean talent, and he was accordingly praised in the *Ming-shih tsung*.* He was known to have helped a friend, Ch'en Yao-wen 陳耀文, compile a poetic anthology, the *Hua-ts'ao ts'ui-pien* 花草粹篇, which took its selections from two famous *tz'u* anthologies to which Wu seems also to have contributed a preface. From extant writings it is evident that Wu had a predilection for "strange stories," tales of supernatural wonders, ghosts, and monsters. Attribution of the novel to him began in the Ch'ing period when scholars took note of entries in the local gazetteers which listed the *Hsi-yu chi* as one of Wu's works. Hu Shih reaffirmed this opinion, though it has been challenged subsequently. The most recent research on the Chinese mainland presents impressive evidence for considering the novel's *Sitz im Leben* to be most likely in the Huai-an region, even if no incontrovertible proof of Wu's authorship has yet been found.

EDITIONS:

K'o kuan-pan ch'üan-hsiang Hsi-yu chi 刻官板全像西遊記. Hua-yang tung-t'ien chu-jen 華陽洞天主人, collator and editor. Published by Shih-te T'ang 世德堂 of Chin-ling (Nanking). Earliest version 1592. 100 chapters.

Li Cho-wu Hsien-sheng p'i-p'ing Hsi-yu chi 李卓吾先生批評西遊記. Nanking: Ta-yeh T'ang 大業堂, early decades of the seventeenth century. 100 chapters. Commentary by Li Chih.* The one-hundred chapter version of the *Hsi-yu chi* is also available in a fairly large number of other Ming editions.

Hsi-yu chi. Peking, 1954. The standard modern edition, which though based mainly on the 1592 edition retains the Ch'en Kuang-jui chapters.

Hsi-yu chi shih-i 西遊記釋義. Taipei, 1976.

TRANSLATIONS:

Avenol, Louis. *Si yeou ki, ou le voyage en occident.* Paris, 1957.

Herzfeldt, J. *Die Pilgerfahrt nach dem Westen.* Rudolstadt, 1962.

Jenner, W. *The Journey to the West.* V. 1. Peking, 1983.

Ōta, Tatsuo 太田辰夫 and Torii Hisayasu 鳥居久靖. *Saiyūki.* 2v. Tokyo, 1971.

Rogačev, A. and V. Kolokolov. *Wu Ch'eng-en: Putešestvije na zapad.* 4v. Moscow, 1959.

Waley, Arthur. *Monkey, Folk Novel of China.* London, 1943.

Yu, Anthony C. 余國藩. *The Journey to the West.* 4v. Chicago, 1977-1983.

STUDIES:

Chang, Ching-erh 張靜二. "The Structure and Theme of the *Hsi-yu chi*," *TkR*, 11.2 (Winter 1980), 169-188.

Cheng, Chen-to 鄭振鐸. "*Hsi-yu chi* te yen-hua" 西遊記的演化, in *Chung-kuo wen-hsüeh yen-chiu* 中國文學研究, Peking, 1957, v. 1, pp. 263-299.

Chiang-su sheng she-hui k'o-hsüeh yüan wen-hsüeh yen-chiu-so 江蘇省社會科學院文學研究所, ed. *Hsi-yu chi yen-chiu* 西遊記研究. Shanghai, 1983. A symposium of the First Academic Conference on the *Hsi-yu chi.*

Dudbridge, Glen. "The Hundred-Chapter *Hsi-yu chi* and its Early Versions." *AM*, N.S., 14 (1969), 141-911.

417

———. *The Hsi-yu chi: A Study of Antecedents to the Sixteenth-Century Chinese Novel.* Cambridge, 1970.

Fu, Shu-hsien 傅述先. "*Hsi-yu chi* chung wu-sheng te kuan-hsi" 西遊記中五聖的關係, *Chung-hua wen hua fu-hsing yüeh-k'an*, 9.5 (May 1976), 10-17.

Hsia, *Novel*, pp. 115-164 and *passim*.

Hu, Shih 胡適. "*Hsi-yu chi* k'ao-cheng" 西遊記考證, in *Hu Shih Wen-ts'un* 胡適文存, Shanghai, 1924, Series 2, v. 4, pp. 51-118.

———. "Pa *Ssu-yu chi* pen te *Hsi-yu chi* chuan" 跋四遊記本的西遊記傳, in *Hu Shih lun-hsüeh chin-chu* 胡適論學近著, Shanghai, 1935, pp. 416-424.

Koss, Nicholas. "The Relationship of *Hsi-yu chi* and *Feng-shen yen-i*," *TP*, 65 (1979), 143-165.

———. "The *Xiyou ji* in its Formative Stages: The Late Ming Editions." Unpublished Ph.D. dissertation, Indiana University, 1981.

Liu, Hsiu-yeh 劉修業. *Ku-tien hsiao-shuo hsi-ch'ü ts'ung-k'ao* 古典小說戲曲叢考. Peking, 1958. Contains several important biographical studies.

Liu, Ts'un-yan 柳存仁. "*Ssu-yu chi* te Ming k'o pen 四遊記的明刻本." *Hsin-ya hsüeh-pao*, 5.2 (August 1963), 323-75.

———. "The Prototypes of *Monkey* (*Hsi-yu chi*)," *TP*, 51 (1964), 55-71.

———. "Wu Ch'eng-en 吳承恩: His Life and Career," *TP*, 53 (1967), 1-97.

Ōgawa, Tamaki 小川環樹. *Chūgoku shōsetsu-shi no kenkyū* 中國小說史の研究. Tokyo, 1968.

Ōta, Tatsuo. "A New Study on the Formation of the *Hsi-yu chi*," *AA*, 32 (1977), 96-113.

Su, Hsing 蘇興. "Chui-tsung *Hsi-yu chi* tso-che Wu Ch'eng-en nan-hsing k'ao-ch'a pao-kao" 追踪西遊記作者吳承恩南行考察報告, *Chi-lin shih-ta hsüeh-pao (Che-hsüeh she-hui k'o-hsüeh)*, 61 (1979), 78-92.

———. "Chui-fang Wu Ch'eng-en te tsung-chih" 追訪吳承恩的踪迹, *Sui-pi*, 3 (1979), 131-51.

Torii, Hisayasu. "*Saiyuki* kenkyū ronbun mo-kuroku" 西遊記研究論文目錄, *Tenri daigaku gakuhō*, 33 (1960), 143-54.

Tso-chia ch'u-pan she 作家出版社. *Hsi-yu chi yen-chiu lun-wen chi* 西遊記研究論文集. Peking, 1957.

Wang, Li-na 王麗娜. "*Hsi-yu chi* wai-wen i-pen kai-shu" 西遊記外文譯本概述. *Wen-hsien*, 4 (February 1981), 64-78.

"Wu Ch'eng-en," in *DMB*, pp. 1479-1483.

Wu, Kuang-chou 吳光舟. *Wu Ch'eng-en ho Hsi-yu chi* 吳承恩和西遊記. Shanghai, 1982.

Yu, Anthony C. "Narrative Structure and the Problem of Chapter Nine in the *Hsi-yu chi*," *JAS*, 34 (1975), 295-311.

—AY

Hsi-yu pu 西遊補 (Supplement to Journey to the West) is a short novel by the Ming scholar-poet Tung Yüeh 董說 (1620-1686). Tung was a precocious child and was said to have immersed himself in the Buddhist texts at a youthful age, even before he started the study of Confucian classics. Growing up to be an eccentric person, he attained literary fame early in his native region but failed to pass the civil-service examination. In 1656, after having burned most of his writings on three separate occasions, he shaved his head, became an itinerant monk, and started traveling in various areas of central China. But even as a wandering cleric, he continued to read and write widely on a great variety of subjects. His known writings, besides poetry, include textual studies, expositions of the *I-ching*, studies of the origin of the military ballad (see *yüeh-fu*) in the Han dynasty, records of his own dreams, and the novelette *Hsi-yu pu*.

Tung Yüeh wrote the *Hsi-yu pu* in 1640, just a few years before the downfall of the Ming. Divided into sixteen chapters, the novel adopts the characters and the fictional world of *Hsi-yu chi* and relates a Mackerel Spirit's 鯖魚精 attempt to capture Tripitaka by luring away his chief disciple Monkey into a series of illusory worlds. It constitutes an extra episode to be "inserted" into the *Hsi-yu chi* (i.e., the events supposedly occur after the episode of the Flaming Mountain concluded in chapter 61 of the parent novel). Though it uses the fictional reality conjured up in *Hsi-yu chi* as well as most of its narrative conventions, the new text significantly alters the traditional fantastic mode of the *Hsi-yu chi* with the inclusion of many preposterous happenings and dream-like occurrences. Seemingly incoherent in its sequence of events the text, upon a close reading, exhibits in fact a complexity of structure and multiplicity of significances that make it one of the few truly polysemous Chinese novels.

Monkey's delusion by the Mackerel begins at a roadside peony bush where he bickers over the redness of the flowers with Tripitaka. Then, annoyed by a group of women and children, he kills many of them while trying to chase them away. Following this, he is confronted with a long series of strange experiences. As he goes his way to beg alms, he catches sight of a city of New T'ang (新唐), and is informed that the Celestial Palace in Heaven has been stolen and he himself implicated as the chief engineer of the theft. In the New T'ang city he learns that its licentious emperor and his court council have decided to commission Tripitaka as a general. Afterwards he runs into a group of space-walkers (踏空兒) chiseling at the firmament (imagined to be solid) to dig a hole through it. Now venturing into a Green Green World (青青世界), he accidentally falls into a Tower of Myriad Mirrors (萬鏡樓). There, after witnessing a scene of civil-service candidates' reactions to the results of the examination reflected in one of the mirrors, he himself enters the World of the Ancient (古人世界) and the Future World (未來世界) by passing through a different mirror. Inside the former, he encounters, among others, the Hegemon of Ch'u, Hsiang Yü 項羽 (233-202 B.C.) and disguises himself as Beauty Yü, the Hegemon's consort. During his stay in the Future World, he is made a temporary Judge of the Dead in the netherworld to preside over the trial of Ch'in Kuei 秦檜 (1091-1155). Coming out of the Tower, he sees his master Tripitaka being entertained by the King Little Moon (小月王) with a lute-song recitation and sundry plays. After a brief visit with a hermit who tells his fortune, he returns to find his master married to a Lady Kingfisher Cord and made a general. Enlisted in Tripitaka's army, he is faced with an enemy commander by the name of Prince Paramita (蜜王) who claims to be his own son, born of Madame Rakshasa, the owner of the magic fan in Hsi-yu chi. During the melee that follows, Tripitaka and King Little Moon are cut down. As Monkey himself is about to join in the carnage, the Arya of Vacuity (虛空尊者) "awakened" him from

his hallucinatory experiences and sends him back to the peony grove, just in time to slay the Mackerel Spirit that has transformed itself into an acolyte and is about to harm his master.

The novel has been studied in detail recently by several critics for its multiple levels or dimensions of significance, including the satirical, mythological, religious and psychological. It contains elements of socio-political satire, for instance, in the scene of the civil-service candidates, the arraignment of Ch'in Kuei, and the allusions to other historical personages. The mythic dimension is manifested through the adventures in the perilous worlds of illusions, where the passage from the stage of desire, to the experiencing of illusions, to the final deliverance, or enlightenment, may be seen as corresponding to the pattern of the quest myth. The text can also be interpreted from a psychoanalytical perspective; its array of surrealistic images and events are suggestive of dream-experiences induced by Monkey's anxiety during his earlier encounter with Madame Rakshasa. As suggested by the prefatory "Answers to Questions Regarding Hsi-yu pu" (presumably written by the author himself) and by the framework of religious pilgrimage, the text also contains religious themes of the relationship of self and mind, the illusory nature of mental constructs, and the notion of nonduality reflecting the author's philosophical outlook and that of his times.

In addition, the text is a rare example of Chinese fiction that consciously explores the potentials of the linguistic properties of narrative and the narrative form itself in a self-reflective act of creation. The reflexive consciousness can be seen from the intertextual relationship established with the Hsi-yu chi on the one hand, and on the other, between the primary narrative and other embedded stories such as Hegemon Hsiang Yü's mythopoeic recounting of his past deeds and the lute-song of the "New Version of Journey to the West" recited by the blind musician that ends with mention of Monkey tarrying in the Tower of Myriad Mirrors, thereby pointing the musician's tale back to the first-level narrative. Adaptation and incorporation of a host of other literary genres (*p'ing-hua*,* *t'an-tz'u*,* epistle, proclamation, drama, etc.) also show the text's experimentation with the narrative form. On the linguistic and rhetorical levels, the text is not only permeated with symbolism (green and red colors symbolic of desires are prevalent), but also shows an abundance of word play and figuration. The punishments meted out to Ch'in Kuei, for instance, are mostly instances of literalizations of figures of speech while the characters of central thematic importance, such as King Little Moon (小月王) and the Mackerel Spirit (鯖魚精), are created by a linguistically informed imagination: the name of the former is derived from the components of the ideogram *ch'ing* 情 (desire/passion), while Mackerel, like the word for *green*, is a homophone of the same ideogram. Despite its brevity, the novel, through its exploration of the formal properties of narrative, represents an infusion of the fantastic mode in the Chinese tradition with a literary quality never before achieved.

EDITIONS:

Hsi-yu pu. Peking, 1955. Photoreprint of an early illustrated block print edition, with a preface by I-ju chü-shih 疑如居士 dated 1641. Includes at the beginning "*Hsi-yu pu* ta-wen" 答問 (Answers to Questions Regarding HYP), signed by Ching-hsiao-chai Chu-jen 靜嘯齋主人, and an appendix of Tung Yüeh's biography by Liu Fu 劉復.

———. Typeset edition. Hong Kong, 1958. Punctuated by Wang Yüan-fang 汪原放, with the preface by I-ju Chü-shih, "Ta-wen," and the biography included; in addition are included "Hsü [i.e. Tu] *Hsi-yu pu* tsa-chi 西遊補雜記" (Miscellaneous Notes from Reading HYP) by an anonymous author and a preface by T'ien-nu Shan-ch'iao 天目山樵. Canton, 1981. Punctuated by Yang Fu 羊阜. Includes the two prefaces, "Ta-wen" and "Tsa-chi."

TRANSLATION:

Lin, Shuen-fu and Larry Schulz. *The Tower of Myriad Mirrors: A Supplement of Journey to the West by Tung Yüeh (1620-1686)*. Berkeley, 1978.

STUDIES:

Brandauer, Frederick P. "The *Hsi-yu pu* and Its World as Satire," *JAOS*, 97.3 (1977), 305-22.

———. "The *Hsi-yu pu* as an Example of Myth-Making in Chinese Fiction," *TKR*, 6.1 (1975), 99-120.

———. *Tung Yüeh*. Boston, 1978.

Hegel, Robert E. "Monkey Meets Mackerel: A Study of the Chinese Novel *Hsi-yu pu*." Unpublished M.A. thesis, Columbia University, 1967.

Hsia, C. T. and T. A. Hsia. "New Perspectives on Two Ming Novels: *Hsi-yu chi* and *Hsi-yu pu*," *Wen-lin*, pp. 229-245.

Kao, Hsin-yung 高辛勇 [Karl]. "*Hsi-yu pu*" yü hsü-shu li-lun" 西遊補與敘述理論, *Chung-wai wen-hsüeh*, 12.8 (January 1984), 5-23. An English version of this piece is forthcoming in the long-awaited second volume of *Wen-lin*.

—KK

Hsi Yung-jen 嵇永仁 (*tzu*, Liu-shan 留山, *hao*, Pao-tu shan-hung 抱犢山農, 1637-1676) was a native of Wu-hsi (Kiangsu). Hsi was a man of many talents, known for his quick wit, his extraordinary singing voice, and his thorough knowledge of medicine and literature. In the early years of the K'ang-hsi Emperor's reign (1662-1722), Hsi served as advisor to the governor-general of Fukien. During the uprising of Keng Ching-chung 耿精忠 (d. 1682), the governor and Hsi were both captured, thrown in jail for three years, and then executed. Understandably, those three years were a time of fear, anger, agony, and despair in Hsi's life, and his dramatic works written during this period mirror this. Lacking paper and writing tools, Hsi burned woodsticks and used the charcoal to write on the walls of the prison cell and on anything else he could find. After his death, a jailer discovered an old book with poetry and prose written on the inside of the folded pages. Hsi's best works have come down to us through these sad relics.

Hsü Li-sao 續離騷 (Reencountering Sorrows—see *Ch'u-tz'u*) inherits its form from Hsü Wei's* *Ssu-sheng yüan*. Like its prototype, it is composed of four one-act plays. However, the total effect of the four pieces, each focusing on the expression of a single emotion, is of a thematically unified whole, which, in Hsi's own words, "continues where the 'Li sao' left off." Considering the circumstances, Hsi's identification with the poet-exile Ch'ü Yüan* hardly needs explication. However, *Reencountering Sorrows* is by no means an explosion of pent-up frustration. It distinguishes itself from other works on similar subjects through its poignant, dramatic irony and its powerful theatrical effect, all done with meticulous care and restraint. One of the plays, *Ch'e-tan ko* 扯淡歌 (An Insipid Song), employs a very effective chorus that reiterates and reenforces philosophical statements made by the protagonist, not unlike the chorus in Greek tragedy. Another play, *Ni-shen miao* 泥神廟 (Mud God Temple), has an ironic introduction which exemplifies Hsi's knack for dark comedy. This play deals with the familiar story of a scholar, who having failed the examination, shares his frustration with the deity Ch'u Pa-wang (the apotheosis of Hsiang Yü) in the latter's temple. Instead of the usual entrance of the unsuccessful candidate, the play opens with Ch'u Pa-wang, now the resident deity of the local temple, sending out his ghost-runners to check on sacrificial offerings presented to him by worshippers. The runners come back with the bad news that there are no offerings or worshippers to be found; instead, they report, they spotted a drunkard, an obviously useless pedant, "limping, faltering, staggering" towards the temple. Hardly a sympathetic note on which to begin a story of great empathy between the suffering living and the righteous dead.

Hsiao pu-tai 笑布袋 (Laughing at the Cloth Bag) another play in the group, belittles many prominent heroes and great men in Chinese history and pokes fun at all the vices and follies of the world, but the prevalent mood is one of nihilistic self-mockery. The only glimmer of hope Hsi displayed was in the last piece of the series, *Fen Ssu-ma* 慎司馬 (The Furious Ssu-ma), in which the playwright seems to indicate that, although this world is absurd and unjust, there may still be hope in the next. This hope of Hsi the political prisoner emerges again in his last work, a *ch'uan-ch'i** entitled *Shuang pao-ying* 雙報應 (Double Retribution). In this long play, Hsi's merits as dramatist are manifested. Two subplots intertwine and develop around a righteous and clever magistrate, who, with the help of a local deity, solves two cases which would otherwise have resulted in great injustice. The play has a tight structure and vivid characterization; it also demonstrates Hsi's attention to detail and his sense of the theatrical.

In contrast with the plays Hsi wrote in prison, an earlier *ch'uan-ch'i*, *Yang-chou meng* 揚州夢 (A Yangchow Dream), dealing with the escapades of the T'ang poet Tu Mu,* is light in tone and mood. Despite its beautiful lyrics and vivid stage realism, it lacks the depth and power of his later works.

EDITIONS:
Hsü Li-sao, in *Ch'ing-jen tsa-chü ch'u-chi* 清人雜
劇初集, v. 1, 1934.
Shuang pao-ying, in *She-mo-t'a-shih ch'ü-ts'ung* 奢
摩他室曲叢, Wu Mei 吳梅, ed., Shanghai, 1928,
v. 3 and 4.
Yang-chou meng, in *ibid.*

STUDIES:
Fu, *Ch'ing tsa-chü*, pp. 64-67.
Tseng, "Ch'ing-tai tsa-chü," pp. 138-141.

—CYC

Hsiang Hsiu 向秀 (c. 221-c. 300) was one of the *Chu-lin ch'i-tzu* 竹林七子 (Seven Sages of the Bamboo Grove). Two themes dominate the historical records about him, his intense friendship with Hsi K'ang,* about which he wrote his most famous surviving literary work, *Ssu-chiu fu* 思舊賦 (Prose-poem Meditating on Old [friends]), and his facility in explicating the *Chuang-tzu*. Reliable historical material on Hsiang Hsiu is scant. There is a brief biography in the *Chin-shu* 晉書 (History of the Chin), most of which is a fragment from Hsiu's *fu*. Additionally, there are several stories about him in the *Shih-shuo hsin-yü** and the *Hsiang Hsiu pen-chuan* 向秀本傳 (Basic Biography of Hsiang Hsiu) that are the basis of the traditional perception of his character. Finally, there are his *fu*, which is included in the *Wen-hsüan*,* and a few fragments from his commentary on *Chuang-tzu*.

Hsiu's friendship with Hsi K'ang is illustrated in the anecdote about Hsiang Hsiu pumping the bellows while Hsi K'ang forged metal. So engrossed were the two in their cooperative task that they paid no attention to visitors who came to meet them, even the worthiest gentlemen of the day. After Hsi K'ang's execution in 262, Hsiang Hsiu was rumored to be seeking retirement on Mount Chi, the traditional retreat of the sage who had become inconsolably disillusioned with a life of worldly concerns. According to the *Chin-shu*, he actually was given very prominent appointments, but he never assumed the duties of the offices.

Hsiu's commentary on the *Chuang-tzu* is lost. Traditionally it was linked in a number of anecdotes to the celebrated commentary by Kuo Hsiang 郭象 (d. 312). By some accounts, Hsiu's sons were too young at the time of his death to complete and organize his *Chuang-tzu* explications, so Kuo Hsiang did the work on their behalf, making many significant amplifications of Hsiu's original. By other accounts, Kuo Hsiang blithely plagiarized Hsiu's work, copying the entire text verbatim and circulating it as his own. The Hsiang-Kuo line of commentary found in the extant Kuo Hsiang version is consistent with themes in the Seven Sages lore. It emphasizes *tzu-jan* 自然 (nature) over Tao, being over non-being, the many over the one, and the immanence of principle in life rather than transcendence (as argued, for instance, by Wang Pi 王弼 [226-249]). There are a few fragments from Hsiu's original text quoted by other commentators in the fourth and seventh centuries, on the basis of which modern scholars have argued against the traditional allegation that Hsiang Hsiu was a source for Kuo.

EDITIONS:

Liu-ch'ao wen, v. 2, *ch.* 72, pp. 1876-1877.

TRANSLATIONS:

Bailey, Roger. "Hsiang Hsiu's '*Fu* on Remembering the Past,'" in *Kuei Hsing: A Repository of Asian Literature in Translation*, Liu Wu-chi, et al., eds., Bloomington and London, 1974.

Chan, Wing-tsit. *A Source Book in Chinese Philosophy*, Princeton, 1963, pp. 317, 326-335.

Holzman, Donald. "Les sept sages de la forêt des bambous et la société de leur temps," *TP*, 44 (1956), 317-346.

STUDIES:

Mather, *New Account*, pp. 40, 100-101, 109, 220, 371, 393, 525.

—KJD

Hsiang Hung-tso 項鴻祚 (*tzu*, Lien-sheng 蓮生, *hao*, I-yün Sheng 憶雲生, other name, T'ing-chi 廷紀, 1798-1835) was a leading *tz'u** poet during the early nineteenth century. He was regarded by the *tz'u* critic T'an Hsien 譚獻 (1830-1901) as one of the three greatest *tz'u* poets in the Ch'ing (with Na-lan Hsing-te* and Chiang Ch'un-lin*). Recent scholars such as Wu Mei 吳梅 and Ho Kuang-chung 賀光中 believed that T'an Hsien had overpraised Hsiang and that his poetry was rather limited in scope. However, it seems apparent that what T'an Hsien valued most in Hsiang was his independence from partisan views in an era characterized by factional debates and prejudiced judgment. A native of Chekiang, Hsiang was able to dissociate himself from the local influence of the Che-hsi School.* At the same time he was not swayed by the dominant poetic taste advocated by the Ch'ang-chou School* of *tz'u* poetry.

Hsiang was born with a tendency to melancholy, and his life was marked by prolonged depression and frequent illness. He died at thirty-eight, following a series of unsuccessful attempts at the *chin-shih* examinations (he was granted *chü-jen* in 1832). During his short life, Hsiang made the writing of poetry his ultimate goal, meticulously adhering to the metrical rules and musical aspects of the *tz'u*. So concerned was he with his own development as a *tz'u* poet that he carefully arranged his own manuscripts chronologically. The most famous extant collection of his *tz'u*, entitled "I-yün *tz'u*" 憶雲詞 consists of four sections, each representing a particular poetic style from a different period in his life.

Hsiang's painstaking self-discipline determined the models he sought for emulation. In his poems he often identified for the reader (or rather for himself) the au-

422

thors that he had chosen as models, using such sub-titles as "in imitation of Hou-chu 後主 [Li Yü*] of Southern T'ang." Generally speaking, most of his poems composed before 1829 followed the tradition of the Southern Sung poets. From 1830 on, in a drastic change, the Late T'ang and Five Dynasties poets, notably Li Yü, became his models. Hsiang's sudden shift in poetic style was probably due to the many misfortunes that he encountered after 1830—his house was burned and his mother drowned on their way to Peking. The recurrent images in his poems of fallen flowers, lonely swallows, crying birds, and floating weeds seem to foreshadow his grief-stricken final years.

EDITIONS:

Cheng, Ch'ien 鄭騫, ed. Hsü tz'u-hsüan 續詞選. Rpt. Taipei, 1973, pp. 86-91.

Ch'üan Ch'ing tz'u-ch'ao 全清詞鈔. Rpt. Taipei, 1975, v. 1. pp. 967-973.

I-yün tz'u (Chia i ping ting kao) 憶雲詞 (甲乙丙丁稿). Yü-yüan 榆園 edition. 4 chüan, 1893.

I-yün tz'u 憶雲詞, in Ch'ieh chung tz'u 篋中詞, T'an Hsien 譚獻, ed., chüan 4, 1882; rpt. in Li-tai shih-shih ch'ang-pien 歷代詩史長編, Taipei, 1971, no. 2, pp. 219-230.

STUDIES:

Ho, Kuang-chung 賀光中. Lun Ch'ing tz'u 論清詞. Rpt. in Li-tai shih-shih ch'ang-pien 歷代詩史長編, Taipei, 1971, no. 23, pp. 115-121.

Wang, I 王易. Tz'u-ch'ü shih 詞曲史. 1930; rpt. Taipei, 1971, pp. 477-479.

—KIC

Hsiao-shuo 小說 (generally translated "fiction") is a genre name that has a history extending back to the Former Han. A category for hsiao-shuo was included by Pan Ku* in the first dynastic history bibliography, the "I-wen chih" 藝文志 (Bibliographic Treatise) of the Han-shu. The hsiao-shuo group was the last of ten classes of philosophers. In the postscript to the philosophers' section, Pan Ku states that only nine of the ten were worth examining. He describes the hsiao-shuo as "street talk and alley gossip, made up by those who engage in conversations along the roads and walkways." At the same time, Pan Ku notes the association of hsiao-shuo with the respon-

sibilities of minor officials to collect intelligence about the people in their locales, and he quotes the well-known injunction credited to Confucius, "Though [petty talk is] a petty path, there is surely something to be seen in it. But if pursued too far, one could get bogged down; hence, the gentleman does not do so." The earliest literary definition of hsiao-shuo is credited to Huan T'an 桓譚 (c. 43 B.C.-A.D. 28) in his Hsin-lun 新論 (New Treatise, c. A.D. 2): "Hsiao-shuo writers gather together fragments and little sayings and collect stories they hear to make short books. For domestic affairs and the like, hsiao-shuo include words of some value."

The association with philosophers suggests that the earlier meaning was closer to a literal translation of the term's components, "petty talk" or "minor persuasions," than to our concept of fiction. This speculation is corroborated for the Han period by what is known from putative fragments of the texts and what can be inferred from the titles included in Pan Ku's generic list. The earliest hsiao-shuo on record, some fifteen works totalling 138 chapters, were entitled I Yin shuo 伊尹說 (The Sayings of I Yin), Huang-ti shuo 黄帝說 (The Sayings of the Yellow Sovereign), Sung-tzu 宋子 (Master Sung), Chou-k'ao 周考 (Studies of the Chou), and so forth. The similarity between the titles brings out two points: they were regarded as spurious, of questionable origin or marginal utility, and they did not have any obvious affinity with the major classical traditions nor with any of the more estimable schools of philosophy, though in style they were primarily discursive and resembled the writings of the philosophers.

Variety in the bibliographic listings of hsiao-shuo increased dramatically in subsequent bibliographies. None of the several bibliographies compiled between Pan Ku's and Wei Cheng's 魏徵 (580-643) bibliography in the Sui-shu are extant, but Wei Cheng's provides important clues to the evolution of genre theory during the Six Dynasties. His hsiao-shuo list included such works as the Wen-tui 文對 (Literary Dialogues), Hsiao-lin 笑林 (Forest of Laughs), and the *Tsa-yü* 雜語 (Miscellaneous Words). These were examples of a new group of Six Dynasties compilations that were, in comparison to other genres, more distinctly fictional than anything in Pan Ku's list. Wei Cheng also includes the *Yen Tan-tzu,** a sophisticated historical narrative that has been cited as a signal work in early fiction. However, the extant text cannot be documented prior to the Ming, and it is unlikely that it is the same work Wei Cheng had at hand.

In the interim between Pan Ku and Wei Cheng, Yin Yün 殷芸 (471-529), the official librarian of Emperor Wu of the Liang, was commissioned to compile a collection of materials which he named *Hsiao-shuo* 小說. Significant fragments are extant from this work, and in them we can see a gradual ascendance of narrative over discursive materials. In his comprehensive statement of historiography, the *Shih-t'ung*, Liu Chih-chi* argues that Yin Yün included narratives from *Sou-shen chi** and the *I-yüan* 異園 (Garden of Oddities), because the materials were notably "unhistorical" or "untraditional" (*pu-ching* 不經) in nature. Liu Chih-chi tries to sort good historical writing from bad, not historical writing from fictional. Accordingly, he does not recognize a *hsiao-shuo* genre. He succeeds, nonetheless, in assembling the first sustained critical treatment of narrative literature, and by circumscribing what he considered to be respectable historical writing, he called attention to the existence of narratives outside of it. It was not, however, until Ou-yang Hsiu's* bibliography in the *Hsin T'ang-shu*, compiled during the Sung, that the contents of the *hsiao-shuo* list became predominantly imaginative narratives of the sort we comfortably recognize as fiction. Also during the Sung, the *T'ai-p'ing kuang-chi** was commissioned expressly to collect *hsiao-shuo* materials. Its five hundred *chüan* compiled under imperial auspices show that fiction was considered collectable in its own right by the Sung.

The final significant official bibliographic undertaking in premodern China, the *Ssu-k'u ch'üan-shu* (see Chi Yün) did not expand the concept of the genre beyond the short literary pieces that had been included since the Sung. In fact, for its description of *hsiao-shuo*, the *Ssu-k'u* returns to quotations from Pan Ku and from Chang Heng's* *Hsi-ching fu*, in which *hsiao-shuo* were associated with the activities and stories of *fang-shih** in the court of Emperor Wu of the Han. The *Ssu-k'u* does suggest three "schools" of *hsiao-shuo* writers: those who narrate miscellaneous events, those who jot down oddities they have simply heard about, and those who collect and organize sundry conversations.

Even outside of official writings, there is little critical comment about early *hsiao-shuo* that addresses aesthetic issues or problems in the craft of writing them until the second millennium of *hsiao-shuo* activity. In the first millennium of their existence, *hsiao-shuo* were described primarily in terms derivative from the Pan Ku postscript. In their aggregate, Pan Ku's remarks dealt with the pedigree of the writings and their functionality. Prior to the T'ang, critical discussion of *hsiao-shuo* did not expand much beyond these concerns. However, critical discussion of music, poetry, and graphic arts developed dramatically between the Han and T'ang, and, from the late T'ang and early Sung those traditions began to have a significant impact on the perception and discussion of *hsiao-shuo*. The critical tradition reached a zenith in the late dynasties, when men like Hu Ying-lin* and Chin Sheng-t'an* earned reputations for their *hsiao-shuo* scholarship and admiration for their *hsiao-shuo* compilations. At its height, *hsiao-shuo* critical literature included bibliographic guides, textual analyses, and textual reconstructions, as well as manuals on both the craft of authorship and the craft of readership. It may be safely said, however, that serious interest in *hsiao-shuo* among the traditional literati was confined to relatively few individuals, virtually all of whom approached the materials apologetically. The name itself makes the humble origins of the genre apparent, and prevailing tastes dictated far greater interest in and esteem for poetic genres, genuine historical narrative, and highly crafted literary essays.

Modern scholars fixed different parameters for the *hsiao-shuo* genre than scholars in the native tradition. From early in the twentieth century, discussions of *hsiao-shuo* began to include works originally perceived as part of the historical canon and to exclude the discredited philosophical texts listed by Pan Ku. Among newly included materials were fictionalized records of events and elaborated biographies of popular figures, works that had traditionally been called *tsa-chuan* 雜傳 (miscellaneous transmissions), as well as pre-Han materials like *Chuang-tzu* (see *Chu-tzu pai-chia*) and the *Chan-kuo ts'e,* * works now identified as protofictional that contributed to the evolution of *hsiao-shuo* writing style and reader's tastes. Seeking a term appropriately translatable into the English "fiction," with its emphasis on vernacular literature and the rise of the novel, proponents of literary and linguistic reform in early Republican China swiftly brought vernacular novels into the center of *hsiao-shuo* critical discussion. Development in that direction continues in present scholarship.

The historical analysis that underlies modern *hsiao-shuo* scholarship defines a series of peaks in its development, with different subgenres representing the zenith of *hsiao-shuo* writing in different literary ages. The unadorned literary *chih-kuai* * was the flower of Six Dynasties *hsiao-shuo,* as the belletristic *ch'uan-ch'i* * was in the T'ang; the vernacular *hua-pen* * in the Sung, Yüan, and Ming; the vernacular romance *yen-i* 演義 (revelations of meaning) in the Yüan, Ming, and Ch'ing; and the serial novels of manners and customs in the Ming and Ch'ing. Within each subgenre one finds great variety, and the historically recognized ones were consistently revitalized in subsequent times by antiquarian-minded redactors, publishers, and imitators. All major subgenres of *hsiao-shuo* were written during the Ch'ing, with short-form types grouped under the rubric *pi-chi.* * One form of traditional *hsiao-shuo* scholarship was the meticulous modeling of a new work on an antique example, practiced, for example, by Chi Yün* and P'u Sung-ling (see *Liao-chai chih-i*). Some of the later *chih-kuai* and *ch'uan-ch'i* are of considerable literary merit, but they are generally not as highly regarded by contemporary historians of literature as the works written during the pioneering periods of the respective genres.

The contemporary sense of *hsiao-shuo* is generally compatible with the English term "fiction" (see essay on Fiction). Scholars of both traditional and modern *hsiao-shuo* observe the major formal division between short stories and novels. A major concern of pioneers in the study of *hsiao-shuo* was the peculiar nature of authorship in the Chinese narrative tradition. For many of the great monuments of *hsiao-shuo,* ascertaining who did what when in the writing poses great difficulties. Many *hsiao-shuo* were written anonymously. Many are collages of original writing and verbatim quotations from earlier works and other genres. Others passed through the hands of numerous writers and reached their present form in a process of gradual accretion. Still others appear to have derived from histories, possibly having been expanded along the way by storytellers. The problems in establishing authorship of traditional *hsiao-shuo* underscore two features of the genre. First, either authorship of *hsiao-shuo* was genuinely not something in which one could take pride, or, simply as a matter of firm convention, one wrote with a pseudonym and maintained anonymity. Second, popular works often circulated in a number of different versions, and critical discussion tried to determine which version was most engaging, rather than most authentic.

Scholars of long-form fiction have focused on a group of six novels, written during the Ming and Ch'ing, that are regarded as China's great classics, including *San-kuo-chih yen-i,* * *Shui-hu chuan,* * *Hsi-yu chi,* * *Chin P'ing Mei,* * *Ju-lin wai-shih,* * and *Hung-lou-meng.* * Many others, including the *Feng-shen yen-i,* * *Jou p'u-t'uan,* * and *Sui-T'ang yen-i* have been translated or studied extensively. Studies have been done of the historical evolution of themes, characters, and texts in both oral and written modes and have included interpretations of allegorical infrastructures and analysis of political, economic, social, and intellectual factors in the emergence of the novels.

Studies of the short story have focused primarily on the vernacular *hua-pen** of the Sung and Yüan and their relation to the mature popular tales of the Ming dynasty, such as those collected in three volumes (the *San-yen*) by Feng Meng-lung.* The major questions, particularly with the extensive collections of urban-based romantic tales, have been the historical evolution and dating of the texts, the interrelation of oral performance literature and written literature, and the social and moral context in which the tales were written and read. Short stories in the literary language, of both the *chih-kuai* and *ch'uan-ch'i* types, have been studied in relation to other genres of narrative and to the intellectual and social contexts in which they flourished.

TRANSLATIONS:

Bauer, *Golden Casket.*

Birch, Cyril, trans. *Stories from a Ming Collection.* New York, 1968.

Edwards, E. D. *Chinese Prose Literature of the T'ang Period, A.D. 618-906.* London, 1937-38; v. II: Fiction.

Traditional Chinese Stories.

STUDIES:

Cheng, Chen-to 鄭振鐸. *Chung-kuo su-wen-hsüeh shih* 中國俗文學史. Changsha, 1938; rev. ed., Peking, 1954.

Hanan, Patrick. *The Chinese Vernacular Story.* Cambridge, 1981.

Hsia, *Novel.*

Li, Tien-yi. *Chinese Fiction: A Bibliography of Books and Articles in Chinese and English.* New Haven, 1968.

Liu, James J. Y. *The Chinese Knight Errant.* Stanford, 1967.

Lu, Hsün. *A Brief History of Chinese Fiction.* Yang Hsien-yi and Gladys Yang, trans. Peking, 1959.

Maeno, Naoki. "The Origin of Fiction in China," *AA,* 16 (1969), 27-37.

Plaks, *Narrative.*

T'an, Cheng-pi 譚正璧. *Chung-kuo hsiao-shuo fa-ta shih* 中國小說發達史. Shanghai, 1935; rpt. Taipei, 1973.

Wilhelm, Hellmut. "Notes on Chou Fiction," in *Transition and Permanence, Chinese History and Culture,* David C. Buxbaum and Frederick W. Mote, eds. Hong Kong, 1972, pp. 251-268.

—KD

Hsiao Ying-shih 蕭穎士 (*tzu,* Mao-t'ing 茂挺, 717-758) enjoyed a considerable reputation in T'ang times for his learning, his success as a teacher of literature, his critical views, and, more controversial, his arrogant refusal to submit to factional enemies in power. He was a lifelong friend of Li Hua,* with whose name his is often joined as a forerunner of the *Ku-wen yün-tung* (see *ku-wen*).

Hsiao's official career was unsuccessful; though he was the highest *chin-shih* graduate of 735, he never went on to enjoy the long-term service in one of the academic institutions at Ch'ang-an that he seems to have hoped for, and he disdained lower prefectural or county posts and the routine administration they entailed. The need for a patron led him in 742 to write to the prominent official historian Wei Shu 韋述 (d. 757) one of the most extensive self-apologies to survive from the mid-eighth century. In this "Tseng Wei Ssu-yeh shu" 贈韋司業書 (Letter to Vice-president Wei) he described himself as a single-minded, isolated, and austere scholar, very different from the ambitious, opportunistic, and morally lax horde against whom he was forced to compete. He also questioned the validity of the examinations, in which he had been highly successful, as tests of a scholar's true abilities. Both these attitudes were to become established themes in later reformist critical writing. Other major events in his life, however, Hsiao described in *fu,** and his choice of this genre, for both narrative and analytical accounts of his own experience, belies the conventionally accepted view that by mid-T'ang times the *fu* was dead as a creative literary vehicle. He also wrote social verse and prefaces for collections of verse composed at feasts or on excursions. A collection written in Liang (modern Honan), the *Yu Liang hsin-chi* 遊梁新集 (New Collection of Travels in Liang) probably consisted of occasional verse of this kind.

Hsiao's main scholarly ambition was in the fields of history and genealogy. He was particularly interested in problems of dynastic legitimacy as they affected the line of succession (*cheng t'ung* 正統) from the Liang dynasty, from whose imperial house he was descended, to the T'ang. His highly moralistic attitude toward historical compilation was justified by appeal to the *Ch'un-ch'iu;* but he probably never completed the chronicle-style general history he planned. After the An Lu-shan Rebellion, his knowledge of history served him in the strategic advice he gave to officials in the (modern) Honan and Kiangsu areas.

Hsiao was particularly influential as a teacher and during the T'ien-pao period (742-755) helped a number of students who had left the metropolitan schools to prepare under him for the examinations. Like other reformist critics of his period, he emphasized the moral function of literature and condemned writing that showed mere technical virtuosity or powers of description. He also stressed, both explicitly and implicitly in his own sometimes densely allusive prose style, the primacy of Confucian canonical texts as models.

Hsiao's arrogance towards the dictatorial Grand Councilor of the T'ien-pao period, Li Lin-fu 李林甫 (d. 752), inspired one of his best known compositions, the "Fa ying-t'ao shu fu" 伐櫻桃樹賦 (Prose-poem on Felling a Cherry Tree), which was probably regarded with both awe and slight disapproval at the time. His controversial reputation prevented him from being allowed to accept an invitation to go to Japan as a teacher.

Most of Hsiao's writing was already lost by the end of the An Lu-shan Rebellion. That his friend Li Hua and some of his own former pupils promoted his reputation after his death, and that the great *ku-wen** writer Han Yü* knew his son, helped maintain his reputation in late T'ang times. What now survives of Hsiao's writing is preserved by virtue of its inclusion in early Sung anthologies.

EDITIONS:

Ch'üan T'ang shih, v. 3, *ch.* 154, pp. 1591-1598; and v. 12, *ch.* 882, pp. 9970-9971.

Ch'üan T'ang wen, v. 7, *ch.* 322-323, pp. 4123-4150.

Hsiao Mao-t'ing chi 蕭茂挺集, in Sheng Hsüan-huai 盛宣懷 (1844-1916), compiler, *Ch'ang-chou hsien-che i-shu* 常州先哲遺書, Section 1. Rpt. Taipei, 1971. Drawn from the *Wen-yüan ying-hua** and *T'ang wen ts'ui.**

STUDIES:

Hiraoka, Takeo 平岡武夫. "Shikan no ishiki to kotenshūgi no bungaku" 史官意識と古典主義の文學, in *Keisho no dentō* 經書の傳統, Tokyo, 1951, ch. 2, pp. 92-139.

McMullen, David. "Historical and Literary Theory in the Mid-Eighth Century," in *Perspectives,* pp. 307-342.

Owen, *High T'ang,* pp. 225-246.

P'an [Lü] Ch'i-ch'ang 潘 [呂] 棋昌. *Hsiao Ying-shih yen-chiu.* 蕭穎士研究. Taipei, 1983.

—DLM

Hsieh Hui-lien 謝惠連 (379-433) was a native of Yang-hsia 陽夏 (modern T'ai-k'ang 太康 in Honan). Not an important literary figure, he gained his literary reputation from his association with his cousin Hsieh Ling-yün,* and was called Hsiao Hsieh 小謝 (Little Hsieh) accordingly. It is said that Hsieh Ling-yün composed some of his best work when he was in the company of Hsieh Hui-lien.

The Hsieh was the mightiest and wealthiest clan of that time. Hsieh Hui-lien's official career, however, was unsuccessful because of his licentious character and involvement in several notorious love affairs. He composed more than ten pentasyllabic poems for Tu Te-ling 杜德靈, a provincial official and his lover, during the mourning period for his father. The circulation of these poems held back his advancement.

Hsieh Hui-lien's extant works stand completely in the literary fashion of his time. They are devoted to the description of natural phenomena and landscape excursions or to the expression of sorrow. His pentasyllabic verse imitates the style and the diction of the *yüeh-fu.** "Tao-i" 搗衣 (Washing Clothes with a Wooden Mallet) and "Ch'iu huai" 秋懷 (Autumn Meditations) are among his best. In addition, the "Hsüeh fu" 雪賦 (Prose-poem on Snow) which employed Ssu-ma Hsiang-ju* as a persona, is well known. He also composed linked verse (*lien-chu* 連珠) and various funerary genres, and can be numbered among those aristocratic nature poets who helped to further define the environment of Hsieh Ling-yün's poetry.

EDITIONS:

Hsieh Fa-ts'ao chi 謝法曹集. *Pai-san*, v. 9, pp. 2189-2204.

Liu-ch'ao wen, v. 3, pp. 2623-2624.

Nan-pei-ch'ao shih, v. 2, pp. 834-842.

TRANSLATIONS:

von Zach, *Anthologie*, v. 1, pp. 195, 336f., 429f., 545f.

STUDIES:

Owen, Stephen. "Hsieh Hui-lien's 'Snow Fu': A Structural Study," *JAOS*, 94 (1974), 14-23.
—WK and CPH

Hsieh Ling-yün 謝靈運 (385-443), also known as the Duke of K'ang-lo (康樂公), was the descendent of an illustrious and affluent northern émigré family of the Southern Dynasties. By universal acclaim he is considered be the foremost lyric poet of the Six Dynasties period. Though chiefly known as the "father of landscape poetry" (*shan-shui shih*)—an attribution not wholly appropriate, since he was by no means the first Chinese poet to make landscape a major vehicle to express his feelings—he was nevertheless one of the first to chisel and refine his verses with self-conscious craftsmanship. The skillful and subtle use of allusion, ambiguity, and parallelism make them hard reading, and earned him mild censure in his own day from critics like Chung Hung (see *Shih-p'in*), and nearly all later literary historians, for "facile extravagance" (*i-tang* 逸蕩) and "diffuseness" (*fan-wu* 繁蕪). But there is no denying the powerful impact on the imagination of the reader of his use of natural imagery as the poet moves from joyous discovery and exaltation, through quiet tranquility, to yearning and loneliness, and even to anguish and despair. He was a man of great sensitivity, given at times to violent passion, who at the age of thirty-three murdered one of his retainers with his own hands for having violated his favorite concubine.

From what must have been a very large corpus of poems (*shih**), fewer than one hundred have survived, over thirty of which have been preserved in the sixth-century anthology, *Wen-hsüan.** Most of these were composed between 422 and 432, during Hsieh's terms of office in Yung-chia 永嘉 (modern Chekiang) and Lin-ch'uan 臨川 (Kiangsi), including an interlude of enforced idleness on his ancestral estate in Shih-ning 始寧 (near modern Shaohsing, Chekiang). Fragments of several poetic essays, or prose-poems (*fu**), appear in the seventh-century compendium, *I-wen lei-chü* 藝文類聚. Two of considerable length are included in his official biography (*Sung-shu*, ch. 67). The first of these, "Chuang-cheng fu" 撰征賦 (A Record of the Expedition), details Liu Yü's 劉裕 (356-422) short-lived conquest of Ch'ang-an (416-418) before he mounted the Sung throne (420), an expedition in which Hsieh himself participated in a minor capacity. The second is the justly celebrated "Shan-chü fu" 山居賦 (Poetic Essay on Living in the Mountains), written between 424 and 426, describing his Shih-ning estate and his personal philosophy of reclusion.

The lyric poems fall naturally into three groups. The first comprises poems written during his brief tenure as governor of Yung-chia on the coast, where he had been exiled during 422 and 423 after his involvement in an abortive effort to help his friend and patron Liu I-chen 劉義眞, Prince of Lu-ling, succeed his father on the throne. In these poems, notably "Wan ch'u Hsi-she T'ang" 晚出西射堂 (Leaving West Archery Hall at Dusk) and "Teng Ch'ih-shang Lou" 登池上樓 (Climbing the Loft of the Pond), though resentment over the virtual end of his political ambitions is evident, his reaction to the natural surroundings he describes is, to use Francis Westbrook's terms, one of "discovery and revitalization."

The second group, dated between 423 and 430, were composed after his recall from Yung-chia, while he was convalescing from what appears to have been pulmonary tuberculosis on his Shih-ning estate. Here, in the company of like-minded Buddhist monks and laymen, he wrote some of his most successful nature poems, combining the aesthetic enjoyment of nature's splendor with a deeply religious quest for enlightenment. Typical of these are "Teng Shih-men tsui-kao ting" 登石門最高頂 (Climbing to the Highest Peak of Stone Gate Mountain) and "Shih-pi Ching-she huan hu-chung tso" 石壁精舍還湖中作 (Written on the Lake on the Way Back to Stone Cliff Retreat). It was in this period that he composed his "Pien-tsung lun" 辯宗論 (Discussion on Distinguishing What is Essential), written in dialogue form, in which he subtly and cogently argued for Chu Tao-sheng's 竺道生 (c. 306-434) then controversial theory of "instantaneous enlightenment" (tun-wu 頓悟). Tao-sheng had discovered this principle, along with the universal presence of the Buddha-nature (fo-hsing 佛性) in every creature, in the recently translated Mahāparinirvāna-sūtra, the "southern version" of which Hsieh himself was to help turn into smoother Chinese a few years later.

In this period Hsieh ran afoul of the local governor, Meng I 孟顗, who happened to have powerful connections in the capital. Hsieh's somewhat arrogant and dissolute way of life aggravated Meng. Moreover, Hsieh attempted to carry out large-scale land-reclamation projects, extending his already enormous estate into mountain areas which the grand warden deemed to be public land. In 431 Meng cited him for seditious activity and recommended execution. The emperor, unwilling to lose so talented a man, exiled him once again, to Lin-ch'uan (modern Kiangsi). The poems written in this period, "Ju Hua-tzu kang shih Ma-yüan ti-san ku" 入華子岡是麻源第三谷 (Entering Hua-tzu Ridge at the Third Valley of Mt. Ma-yüan), are characterized by an overwhelming disillusionment and bitterness.

Acting on reports of his "neglect of duty," his now numerous enemies at court soon arranged for his arrest, which with characteristic recklessness he resisted, resulting in a third and final banishment to the vicinity of modern Canton in the winter of 432-433. After about a year, again

on the flimsiest of evidence, he was summarily executed for plotting the restoration of the Chin dynasty. In his last poem he lamented:

> My sole regret is that my gentleman's resolve
> Has not found surcease in a mountain setting.

EDITIONS:

Nan-pei-ch'ao shih, Ch'üan Sung shih 全宋詩: *ch.* 3, v. 2, pp. 797-831.

Huang, Chieh 黃節. *Hsieh K'ang-lo shih-chu* 謝康樂詩注. Rpt. Taipei, 1967; original 1924.

TRANSLATIONS:

Chang, Hsin-chang. *Chinese Literature, v.2: Nature Poetry.* New York, 1977, pp. 39-55.

Demiéville, *Anthologie,* pp. 145-148.

Frodsham, *Anthology,* pp. 123-141.

Sunflower, pp. 58-66.

STUDIES:

Bezhin, Leonid Evgen'evich. *Se Lin-iun.* Moscow, 1980.

Demiéville, Paul. "Presentation d'un Poète," *TP,* 62 (1976), 241-261. Review article on Frodsham, *Murmuring Stream.*

———. "La vie et l'oeuvre de Sie Liang-yun," *Extrait de l'annuaire du Collège de France, 63e année (1962-1963) et 64e année (1963-1964),* pp. 325-331 and 349-360.

Frodsham, J. D. *The Murmuring Stream: The Life and Works of the Chinese Nature Poet Hsieh Ling-yün (385-433), Duke of K'ang-lo.* 2v. Kuala Lumpur, 1967.

———. "The Origins of Chinese Nature Poetry," *AM,* 8.1 (1960), 68-104.

Fukunaga, Mitsuji 福永光司. "Sha Rei-un no shisō" 謝靈運の思想, *Tōhō shūkyō,* 13-14 (1958), 25-48.

Ho, Li-ch'üan 郝立權. "Hsieh K'ang-lo nien-p'u" 謝康樂年譜, *Ch'i-ta chi-k'an,* 6 (1936), 39-59.

Kōzen, Hiroshi 興膳宏. *Sha Reiun shi sakuin* 謝靈運詩索引 (with "'Sankyo fu' goi sakuin" 山居賦語彙索引 and "Sha Reiun shūgaishi" 謝靈運集外詩 appended). Kyoto, 1981.

———. "Sōshō Sha Reiun denron o megutte" 宋書謝靈運傳論 をめくつて, *Tōhōgaku,* 59 (1980), 44-61.

Mather, Richard. "The Landscape Buddhism of the Fifth Century Poet Hsieh Ling-yün," *JAS,* 18 (1958-1959), 67-79.

Menśikov, L. N. "Les paraboles bouddhiques dans la littérature chinoise," *BEFEO,* 67 (1980), 303-336.

429

Obi, Kōichi 小尾郊一. *Chūgoku bungaku ni ara-wareta shizen to shizenkan* 中國文學に現われた自然と自然觀. Tokyo, 1962.

———. *Sha Reiun denron* 謝靈運傳論. Hiroshima, 1976.

Sheridan, Selinda Ann. "Vocabulary and Style in Six Dynasties Poetry: A Frequency Study of Hsieh Ling-yün and Hsieh T'iao." Unpublished Ph.D. dissertation, Cornell University, 1982.

Takaki, Masakazu 高木正一. "Sha Rei-un no shōgai" 謝靈運の生涯, *Ritsumeikan bungaku*, 174 (November, 1959) 32-48; 175 (December, 1959) 20-42.

———. "Sha Rei-un no shifū ni tsuite no ichi kōsatsu" 謝靈運の詩風についての一考察, *Ritsumeikan bungaku*, 180 (June, 1960), 75-107.

Westbrook, Francis A. "Landscape Description in the Lyric Poetry and 'Fuh on Dwelling in the Mountains' of Shieh Ling-yunn." Unpublished Ph.D. dissertation, Yale University, 1973.

———. "Landscape Transformation in the Poetry of Hsieh Ling-yün," *JAOS*, 100.3 (July-October 1980), 237-254.

Yeh, Ying 葉瑛, "Hsieh Ling-yün wen-hsüeh yü nien-p'u" 謝靈運文學與年譜, *Hsüeh-heng*, 33 (1924), 1-18.

—RBM

Hsieh T'iao 謝朓 (*tzu*, Hsüan-hui 玄暉, 464-499) is best known for the fresh originality of his landscape poems. For the first decade of his career he held a series of minor administrative positions in Chien-k'ang and was active in the circle of writers gathered at the Southern Ch'i court. In 491 he was sent out as Officer of Letters and Scholarship to one of the imperial princes but was soon recalled on the charge of exerting undue influence on him. He later directed the drafting of documents in the ministry of the regent Hsiao Luan, but after the latter's ruthless accession was sent out as Governor of Hsüan-ch'eng (modern Anhwei). In 498, he reported his father-in-law's intention to lead an army of rebellion against the throne. In the following year, after Hsiao Luan's death, Hsieh refused to join a plot to replace his heir. Fearing betrayal, the conspirators brought charges of sedition against him. He was sentenced to prison and died there.

Though by no means a prolific writer, his 160-odd poems span a rather wide range of forms and styles. Many of his early works were written for ceremonial occasions, or were otherwise intended for presentation to the throne. There are also a number of "poems on an object" (詠物詩) and lyrical *yüeh-fu** which demonstrate his facility in these popular genres. A few of these can be dated to the period of flourishing artistic and literary activity under the patronage of the Prince of Ching-ling. (Along with his mentor Shen Yüeh,* Hsieh is included among the writers known posthumously as the *Ching-ling pa-yu* 竟陵八友 (Eight Friends of [the Prince of] Chingling.) Other early works are from Hsieh's brief but productive service in the entourage of his brother, the Prince of Sui Commandery. Among works dedicated to the Prince of Sui, a charming set of short excursion poems bearing the *yüeh-fu* title "Ku ch'ui ch'ü" 鼓吹曲 (Songs of the Drum and Flute) illustrates the optimism of this period.

His later works reflect a growing ambivalence towards his status, as well as a general sense of frustration and anxiety. Indeed, this change may already be noted in the well-known poem written upon his recall to the capital in 493, "Chan shih hsia-tu yeh fa Hsin-lin chih ching-yi tseng Hsi-fu t'ung-liao" 暫使下都夜發新林至京邑贈西府同僚 (While Serving Temporarily in the Lower Capital, I Set Out by Night from Hsin-lin and on Reaching Jurisdiction of the Imperial City, Presented this Poem to My Colleagues in the Western Ministry). He also turned increasingly to more lengthy and expressive verse. Important from his later career are contemplative poems such as "Kuan chao yü" 觀朝雨 (Looking at the Morning Rain), in which a collage of simultaneous images serves as backdrop to the poet's introspective melancholy.

His landscape poetry is often linked with that of his kinsman and predecessor, Hsieh Ling-yün.* Although a number of poems from his tenure in Hsüan-ch'eng (495-497) adopt the explicitly "metaphysical" idiom of previous landscape poetry, as well as

Ling-yün's tone of chronicle-like realism, much of his mature work shows a clear departure from past tradition. First, he describes a more subtly dynamic form of nature, and one that is often humanized by the presence of man-made artifacts. His settings are typically expansive, with greater emphasis on the horizontal dimension than on the vertical. Due to the relatively simple diction of some of his landscape poems, the features of his scenes are more generalized, and his contrasts less pointedly drawn. Second, in earlier landscape poetry the repetition of a single syntactic pattern throughout the descriptive couplets gave a uniform solidity to the scene, but also reinforced the separation between the external world and the emotions of the *persona*. In Hsieh's poems, syntactic variation enlivens scene description and smoothes the change from description to emotional expression. The difference between his style and that of Hsieh Ling-yün is perhaps most obvious in works where his descriptive couplets actually embody subjective realities. For instance, in "Chih Hsüan-ch'eng chün ch'u Hsin-lin p'u Hsiang Pan-ch'iao" 之宣城郡出新林浦向板橋 (On the Way to Hsüan-ch'eng Commandery I Head toward Pontoon Bridge from Hsin-lin Ford) and "Hsin-t'ing chu pieh Fan [Yün] Ling-ling" 新亭渚別范 [雲] 零陵 (Farewell to Fan [Yün] of Ling-ling Commandery at the Island of the New Pavilion), the flow of a river is one of the terms in a comparison that expresses the poet's directional ambivalence. To some extent, his new treatment of the landscape may be understood as the application of techniques which were current in other poetic genres. Yet he was the only poet of his time to revitalize the landscape tradition and to signal, thereby, some of the concerns and methods of later nature poetry.

Traditional criticism favorably characterizes his style as spontaneous and rhythmically fluid. The sweeping drama of his opening couplets is also much admired. In this respect, however, most opinion agrees with the point first raised by his contemporary Chung Hung (see *Shih-p'in*) that their momentum is not always sustained. His ability to give new life to clichéd images is also sometimes cited, but his imagery is perhaps best known for the rich variety of ways in which it describes qualities of light.

His collected works originally filled five *chüan* each of poetry and prose. The latter were omitted from a printing of his works in the Southern Sung and are no longer extant.

EDITIONS:

Hsieh Hsüan-ch'eng chi 謝宣城集. *SPPY*. Reprint of the *Pai-ching lou* 拜經樓 edition, edited by Wu Chien 吳騫 of the late Ch'ing. The *Pai-ching lou* edition descends from the Southern Sung, *Chia-ting* era (1208-1224) reissue of Lou Shao's 樓炤 edition of the Shao-hsing era (1131-1163). It was Lou Shao's edition that first omitted Hsieh's prose writings. This edition is reliable, but the print is difficult to read.

Ho, Li-ch'üan 郝立權. *Hsieh Hsüan-ch'eng shih-chu* 謝宣城詩注. Peking, 1936. An attractive edition because of its large woodblock type. Rpt. Taipei, 1971.

Hsieh Hsüan-ch'eng chi chiao-chu 謝宣城集校注. Hung Shun-lung 洪順隆, ed. Taipei, 1969. Identifies discrepancies in various editions of Hsieh's poems, and is an invaluable aid to reading the flawed *SPTK*. Traditional commentary is included with Hung's own annotations.

Hsieh Hsüan-ch'eng shih-chi 謝宣城詩集. *SPTK*. A photolithographic reproduction of a Ming hand-copied text of Lou Shao's edition.

Shiomi, Kunihiko 塩見邦彦. *Sha Senjō shi ichi-ji sakuin* 謝宣城詩一字索引. Nagoya, 1975. A very useful index, with its own text.

Wu, Shu-tang 伍叔儻. "Hsieh T'iao nien-p'u" 謝朓年譜. *Hsiao-shuo yüeh-pao*, 17 (1926), 1-14. A well researched chronology of Hsieh's career and works.

TRANSLATIONS:
Demiéville, *Anthologie*, pp. 153-155.
Frodsham, *Anthology*, pp. 73-74.
Sunflower, pp. 159-165.

STUDIES:
Ami, Yūji 網祐次. *Chūgoku chūsei bungaku ken-kyū* 中國中世文學研究. Tokyo, 1960. Contains a detailed study of Hsieh's early poetry, with special focus on his "poems on an object" and their relationship to his landscape poetry.

Chennault, Cynthia L. "The Poetry of Hsieh T'iao." Unpublished Ph.D. dissertation, Stanford University, 1979.

Furuta, Keiichi 古田敬一. "Sha Chō no tsuiku hyōgen" 謝朓の對句表現, *Nihon Chūgoku Gakkai-hō*, 24 (1972), 99-113.

Hsieh Hsüan-ch'eng shih chu 謝宣城 詩注. Li Chih-fang 李直方, ed. Hong Kong, 1968. Includes traditional commentary, an essay on Hsieh's life and poetry, and a brief study of Li Po's regard for him.

Hung, Shun-lung. "Sha Chō no sakuin ni ara-wareta kikugan" 謝朓の作品に現れた危懼感, *Nihon Chūgoku Gakkai hō*, 26 (1974), 176-199.

Kōzen, Hiroshi 興善宏. "Sha Chō shi no jojō" 謝朓詩の抒情, *Tōhōgaku*, 39 (1970), 36-57.

Matsuura, Tomohisa 松甫友久. *Ri Haku Kenkyū: jojō no kōzō* 李白研究：抒情の構造. Tokyo, 1976. Contains an interesting comparison between Hsieh's images of light and those of Li Po.

Sheridan, Selinda Ann. "Vocabulary and Style in Six Dynasties Poetry: A Frequency Study of Hsieh Ling-yün and Hsieh T'iao." Unpublished Ph.D. dissertation, Cornell University, 1982.

—CLC

Hsin Ch'i-chi 辛棄疾 (*tzu*, Yu-an 幼安, *hao*, [Layman] Chia-hsüan 稼軒 [居士], 1140-1207) was born in Li-ch'eng 歷城 (Chi-nan 濟南, Shantung), then the center of armed opposition against the Chin 金 invaders, who in 1126 had captured the Northern Sung capital of Pien-liang 汴梁. In 1161, when Hsin was 21, he organized an uprising and joined forces with Keng Ching 耿京, the leader of a peasant revolt. Hsin's *Sung-shih* biography, which is not wholly reliable, gives a vivid account to his daring exploits in the struggle against the alien conquerors. The following year (1162) Hsin was sent to the southern capital at Lin-an 臨安 and in vain requested the government's support for the uprising. In 1165, he memorialized the throne and suggested that vigorous measures be taken to regain the lost territories in the north. In 1170 he approached the grand councilor with similar requests, but to no avail. From 1172-1181 he held various appointments as prefect, fiscal vice-commissioner, and military commissioner in various parts of the Yangtze Region. In 1181 he was forced to retire, and his retirement was broken only by a short-term appointment as pacification commissioner in Chekiang in 1203.

Hsin Ch'i-chi was the most prolific writer of *tz'u** in the entire Sung period. Six-hundred-twenty-six *tz'u*, written between 1168 and 1207, have been preserved. His remarkable versatility is shown by the fact that he used 101 different tunes, some of which are unique in the *tz'u* tradition. Of these, 46 are *hsiao-ling* 小令, 27 *chung-tiao* 中調, and 28 *ch'ang-tiao* 長調. Apart from *tz'u*, the extant writings of Hsin Ch'i-chi comprise some 120 *shih** poems and a few prose works, some considered spurious. The literary fame of Hsin Ch'i-chi rests entirely on his lyrical poetry.

Su Shih,* whom Hsin Ch'i-chi held in high regard, had broadened the range of styles of *tz'u* poetry and considerably narrowed the thematic difference between *shih* and *tz'u*. Aided by his poetic sensitivity, vivid imagination, superb command of the language, extensive learning, formidable memory, and mastery of the technicalities of *tz'u* composition, Hsin Ch'i-chi continued this trend and succeeded in revitalizing the *tz'u* genre. Many critics, past and present, have admired his ability to accommodate quotations of both prose and poetry from a great variety of sources within the strictly defined metrical framework of the *tz'u*.

Already in his lifetime Hsin Ch'i-chi was renowned for the "unbridled vigor" (*hao-fang chih ch'i* 浩放之氣) with which his and many of Su Shih's best *tz'u* are informed. Fan K'ai 范開, a student and friend of Hsin Ch'i-chi who edited the first known collection of the poet's works (*Chia-hsüan tz'u* 稼軒詞, 4 *chüan*, 1188-1203), stressed in his preface that his master did not consciously imitate Su Shih and that the affinity of their styles stems from their similar temperaments.

Hosts of admirers, and especially contemporary critics, have praised Hsin Ch'i-chi's patriotic poems. While patriotic fervor certainly inspired many of the poet's finest stanzas, his "poetic world" takes in a wide range of external scenes of the past and the present and moods ranging from the sensuousness of the *Hua-chien chi** poets, to the melancholy of Li Ch'ing-chao* and the pastoral serenity of T'ao Ch'ien,* whom Hsin Ch'i-chi greatly admired.

Whatever bitterness the poet may have felt over the lack of official recognition, it finds no expression in his *tz'u* poetry. Ironic self-awareness and caustic humor are his weapons in the struggle against his most relentless enemy, the wine-cup.

Hsin Ch'i-chi's circle of friends included many of the greatest thinkers, statesmen, and literary scholars of his time, including Chu Hsi 朱熹 (1130-1200) and his rival Lu Hsiang-shan 陸象山 (1139-1192), Ch'en Liang,* Hung Mai,* Fan Ch'eng-ta,* and Lu Yu.* Hsin Ch'i-chi's writings bear ample witness to the eclectic intellectual interests which characterized him and many of his contemporaries. Upholding the Confucian virtues of loyalty, integrity, and trustworthiness, he greatly inclined, especially during his forced retirement, to the Taoist view of life. The work of Chuang-tzu served him both as solace and as inspiration.

Many poets of later generations have tried to imitate Hsin Ch'i-chi without succeeding in capturing the naturalness and the spontaniety which informs his lyrical poetry.

EDITIONS:

Hsin, Ch'i-t'ai 辛啓泰, ed. *Chia-hsüan chi ch'ao ts'un* 稼軒集鈔存, 1811. A collection of prose works and *shih* poetry.

Teng, Kuang-ming 鄧廣銘. *Chia-hsüan shih-wen ch'ao ts'un* 稼軒詩文鈔存. Shanghai 1947. (An augmented edition of Hsin Ch'i-t'ai's work).

———. *Chia-hsüan tz'u pien-nien chien-chu* 稼軒詞編年箋注. Shanghai, 1957; revised and augmented editions: Shanghai, 1963; Hong Kong, 1974; Shanghai, 1978. The definitive critical edition of all known *tz'u* by Hsin Ch'i-chi, culled from all available sources. Contains bibliographical notes on the transmission of the major editions (*Chia-hsüan tz'u* 稼軒詞, 4 *chüan*: *Chia-hsüan ch'ang-tuan chü* 稼軒長短句, 12 *chüan*). An extensive account of the various editions is also found in Jao Tsung-I 饒宗頤, *Tz'u-chi k'ao* 詞籍考 (Examination of Documents Relating to *Tz'u*), Hong Kong, 1963, pp. 173-178.

Liu, Ssu-fen, comp. *Hsin Ch'i-chi tz'u-hsüan* 辛棄疾詞選. Hong Kong, 1981.

TRANSLATIONS:

Lo, Irving Yucheng. "Thirty Lyrics by Hsin Ch'i-chi, 'A Poet's Poet,'" *K'uei Hsing*, v. 1, Bloomington, 1974, pp. 21-66.

———. *Hsin Ch'i-chi*. New York, 1971. Includes a list of translations of Hsin Ch'i-chi's *tz'u*.

Malmquist, N. G. D. "On the Lyrical Poetry of Shin Chihjyi (Hsin Ch'i-chih) (1140-1207)," *BMFEA*, 46 (1974), 29-63. Attempts to analyze Hsin Ch'i-chi's *Ch'in-yüan-ch'un* 沁園春 poems on the basis of internal evidence; provides translations of Hsin Ch'i-chi's thirteen poems written to this tune.

STUDIES:

Ch'en, Shao-chi 陳紹箕, *Chia-hsüan tz'u-p'ing hui-shu* 稼軒詞評彙述, Taipei, 1973.

Cheng, Chien. "Su Tung-p'o and Hsin Chia-hsüan: A Comparison," *TkR*, 1.2 (October 1970), 45-57.

Chiang, Jun-hsün 江潤勳. *Tz'u-hsüeh p'ing-lun shih-kao* 詞學評論史稿. Hong Kong, 1966. Contains a short but important appreciation of Fan K'ai's preface to the first edition of Hsin Ch'i-chi's *tz'u*.

Chiang, Lin-chu 姜林洙. *Hsin Ch'i-chi chuan* 辛棄疾傳. Taipei, 1964.

Hsia, Ch'eng-t'ao 夏承燾. "Tu Hsin Ch'i-chi te tz'u" 讀辛棄疾的詞, *Shih-k'an*, 10 (1957), 99-108.

Li, Ch'ang-chih 李長之. "T'an Hsin tz'u" 談辛詞, *Yü-wen hsüeh-hsi*, 3 (1957), 3-6.

Teng, Kuang-ming. *Hsin Chia-hsüan nien-p'u* 辛稼軒年譜. Shanghai, 1979.

———. "Hsin Ch'i-chi and His Poetry," *Chinese Literature*, 1964.2, 73-78.

—GM

Hsü Ch'ao 許潮 (*tzu*, Shih-ch'uan 時泉, *fl.* 1600) is the author of thirteen *tsa-chü*,* eight of which are still extant. Hsü was born in Ching-chou 靖州 (modern Hunan); little is known of his life.

In keeping with then current custom, nearly all of Hsü's *tsa-chü* are based on well-known stories. The best of these are *Lan-t'ing hui* 蘭亭會 (The Gathering at the Orchid Pavilion), depicting the occasion at which Wang Hsi-chih wrote his noted preface, *Ch'ih-pi yu* 赤壁遊 (An Excursion to Red Cliff), *Hsieh feng-ch'ing* 寫風情 (A Record of Romantic Love), and *Wu-ling ch'un* 武陵春 (Spring in Wu-ling).

Lan-t'ing hui affords Hsü an opportunity to demonstrate his considerable poetic skills. The spoken part of this text is often criticized as too stilted and literary, although Hsü may have intentionally used such a style to illustrate the cultivation of the Lan-t'ing participants. *Ch'ih-pi yu* describes the night Su Shih,* Huang T'ing-chien,* and the Ch'an monk Fo-yin visit Red Cliff. Hsü Ch'ao has altered the story somewhat, by providing a fisherman of the traditional "gentleman-in-retirement" type. It is the fisherman who induces the three friends to go to Red Cliff for a night of conversation in exchange for the fish they want to buy from him. After a discussion of the general history of the battle which took place there, each person assumes the role of one of the actual participants in the engagement (Huang T'ing-chien becomes Ts'ao Ts'ao, etc.) to compose a poem. With moonset they depart and the play ends. The introduction of the fisherman makes the entire plot seem less contrived; despite criticism that the structure of Hsü's plays is faulty, this piece is well crafted.

Perhaps a better example of the problems Hsü sometimes encountered in plot construction would be *Hsieh feng-ch'ing*, based upon a rather insignificant historical incident. When the T'ang literatus Liu Yü-hsi stops off at Yangchou, the local magistrate plans to provide him with two courtesans as part of his hospitality. But the story line is neglected and the piece moves forward only by means of a series of humorous exchanges between the *ch'ou* 丑 (clown) and the *tan* 旦 (female lead) punctuated by her songs on various topics. The attention is directed thereby to the poetic quality of the songs.

The story of the *Wu-ling ch'un* is derived from T'ao Ch'ien's* "T'ao-hua-yüan chi," which describes a fisherman's adventure in a utopia inhabited by Taoist immortals. Here, too, the strength of the piece lies not in the plot, but in the songs and dialogues, which are written in a lofty and literary style. In a series of expressive lyr-ics, a group of Taoist immortals sing of their carefree way of life and reveal their elegant taste. In contrast are touching lyrics sung by two female immortals, expressing their longing for the love that they once had with two earthly men. After these songs have been sung, the drama comes to an abrupt end.

Of Hsü's *ch'uan-ch'i* plays, *T'ai-ho chi* 泰和記 (Great Peace) merits notice. In twenty-four acts, it develops six story-lines through all of the four seasons (i.e., twenty-four settings). Since the songs are relatively long, the play has been criticized as not easily performable (one critic suggests it would take twelve hours to perform completely). This piece has also been attributed to Yang Shen,* but structural similarities between it and Hsü Chao's *tsa-chü* have led scholars to conclude that the work is by Hsü.

Hsü seems to have emphasized the poetical aspects of his plays, rather than the musical or the dramatic, in an age when music and performance were beginning to gain predominance.

EDITIONS:
Sheng-ming tsa-chü 盛明雜劇 (Variety Plays of the Grand Ming Dynasty). Peking, 1958. *Chüan* 3-10 contain Hsü's eight extant *tsa-chü.*
Shan-shih-chi 山石集 (Mountain Rock Collection). Hsü's collected works.

STUDIES:
Aoki, *Gikyokushi*, pp. 241-242.
Fu, *Ming-tai tsa-chü*, pp. 160-165.

—WHN

Hsü Fu-tso 徐復祚 (*tzu*, Yang-ch'u 陽初, 1560-after 1630), also known as Tu Ju 篤儒, a native of Ch'ang-shu 常熟, is acknowledged as a dramatist, musician, and scholar. Hsü was born into a wealthy and cultivated family, which during his life was involved in fraud, murder, and lawsuits, exemplifying the degeneration of the rich and powerful families of late Ming. Hsü himself was involved in two lawsuits, one lasting for a decade. Perhaps for this reason he turned from government examinations and a career in officialdom, devoting his entire life to studies and literary activities, composing dramas and writing about social customs, religious practices, institutions, and Japanese piracy, as well as revealing the gruesome story of his family in essays and notes.

Hsü wrote four *ch'uan-ch'i** and two *tsa-chü:* Hung-li chi* 紅梨記 (Red Pear Blossom), *T'ou-so chi* 投梭記 (The Abandoned Shuttle), *Hsiao-kuang chi* 宵光記 (Night-glow) also known as *Hsiao-kuang chien* 宵光劍 (The Night-glowing Sword), *T'i-ch'iao chi* 題橋記 (Inscription on the Bridge), *I-wen ch'ien* 一文錢 (One Copper Coin), and *Wu-t'ung yü* 梧桐雨 (Rain on the Wu-t'ung Tree). *T'i-ch'iao chi* and *Wu-t'ung yü* (a *tsa-chü*) are no longer extant.

Hung-li chi, his first and best known play with eight pre-modern editions extant, is based on *Hung-li hua* 紅梨花 (Red Pear Blossom), a *tsa-chü* by Chang Shou-ch'ing 張壽卿. Set in the Sung period, it portrays the romance between Chao Ju-chou 趙汝州, a young scholar, and Hsieh Su-ch'iu 謝素秋, a beautiful and virtuous courtesan. Hsü, in this drama, pays particular attention to language and rhyme, reflecting the influence of the School of Poetic Meter (see Shen Ching) and the *Wen-tz'u p'ai* 文辭派 (School of Ornate Phraseology). *Hung-li chi*, embellished with flowery language and relatively free from rhyme violations, received both praise and criticism after its premiere. Hsü, for whatever reason, ceased writing drama for a time.

T'ou-so chi, the first drama to be written after Hsü resumed work, is traditionally thought to be anonymous. However, Hsü in his *Hua-tang-ko ts'ung-t'an* 花當閣叢談 (Collected Bibliographical Notes of Hua-t'ang Pavilion), claims authorship; the play is also attributed to him in the *Liu Nan sui-pi* 柳南隨筆 (Random Notes of Liu Nan) and the *Lu-i-shih ch'ü-hua* 菉猗室曲話 (Comments on Dramas from the Green Bamboo Studio). *T'ou-so chi*, while portraying the love, separation, and reunion of Hsieh Yu-yü 謝幼興 and Yüan P'iao-feng 元縹風, is generally considered to be a work of social criticism ridiculing a certain segment of upper-class society.

Hsiao-kuang chi, again traditionally considered an anonymous work of the Ch'ing, portrays sibling treachery, rivalry over wealth and property, and the altruism of

a Tartar slave. Hsü introduces in this work the Buddhist theme of of karma through the actions of the hero (the elder of two brothers) and his cohort (a Tartar slave who is also the younger brother).

The Buddhist philosophical frame of reference is evident in *I-wen ch'ien*, a *tsa-chü* in six acts. As the drama unfolds, the hero, Lu Chih 盧至, a fallen arhat in his previous existence, is portrayed as a miser who prefers starvation and tattered garments to dispensing a small sum from his vast holdings for food and clothing. Discovering that the four chief-beggars of his city leave nothing from their Hungry Ghost Festival dinner for him to pick up, he uses a copper coin which he accidently finds to purchase a few sesame seeds. He is plagued by the noises of a bird and a dog, and thinking that they are after his seeds, he runs up a mountain with seeds in hand, seeking refuge from his imagined enemies. There he meets Sovereign Sakra who has been sent by the Buddha to awaken him to the folly of possessing worldly goods. Having failed to persuade him, Sakra puts Lu to sleep and transforms himself into Lu's likeness. He then goes to Lu's home to dispense Lu's wealth to the poor. Ten days later Lu returns home to find his wealth gone; he receives a beating from his servants, who together with his wife are now convinced that he is an impostor. Even so, Lu fails to recognize the illusory nature of the world. It takes an act by the Buddha himself to awaken him.

In *Hung-li chi*, Hsü Fu-tso exalts wealth, honor, and achievement; in his later plays he becomes so critical of them that the pursuit of a moral or a spiritual life becomes the normative theme, distinguishing his earlier from his later works.

EDITIONS:

Chia-erh szu-yü 家兒私語, in *Ping-tzu ts'ung-pien* 丙子叢編, Chao I-shen 趙詒琛 and Wang Tai-lung 王大隆, n.p., 1939. Contains essays and stories about Hsü's family.

Ch'ü-lun 曲論, in *Hsi-ch'ü lun-chu*, v. 4, pp. 229-248.

Hsiao-kuang chi 宵光記, in *Ku-pen hsi-ch'ü ts'ung-k'an*, ser. 1. Shanghai, 1954. *Ch.* 1 is a reprint of the T'ang Chen-wu 唐振吾 edition, *ch.* 2 of the Yin-liu-chai 飲流齋 edition.

Hua-tang-ko ts'ung-k'an 花當閣叢刊 also known as the *Ts'un-lao wei-t'an* 村老委談 , 8 *ch.* In *Chieh-yüeh shan-fang hui-ch'ao* 借月山房彙鈔 , Chang Hai-p'eng 張海鵬 comp. Shanghai, 1920. Notes on Ming personalities, religious practices, institutions, dialects, and Japanese piracy.

Hung-li chi 紅梨記 and *T'ou-so chi* 投梭記 , in *Liu-shih,* of the Chi-ku-ko 汲古閣 edition.

I-wen-ch'ien 一文錢 in *Sheng Ming,* I.

Ming Ho Yüan-lang Hsü Yang-ch'u ch'ü-lun 明何元朗徐陽初曲論, in *Ku-hsüeh hui-k'an,* ser. 2 古學彙刊第二集 . Shanghai, 1912.

STUDIES:

Aoki, *Gikyokushi,* pp. 229-232.

Chin, Meng-hua 金夢華. *Chi-ku-ko liu-shih chung-ch'ü hsü-lu* 汲古閣六十種曲敍錄 . Taipei, 1969. *Ch.* 32 contains biographical information and a brief study on *T'ao-so chi,* ch. 35 a brief study on *Hung-li chi.*

DMB, pp. 580-582.

Fu, *Ch'uan-ch'i,* pp. 125-128.

———, *Ming tsa-chü,* pp. 135-136.

Yee, "Love." Chapters 2-4 contain comments on *Hung-li chi.*

—EY

Hsü Wei 徐渭 (*tzu,* Wen-ch'ang 文長, 1521-1593) was among the foremost *tsa-chü** dramatists of the sixteenth century. He was also a distinguished poet, essayist, calligrapher, and painter.

Hsü Wei came from Shao-hsing 紹興 (modern Chekiang), the son of an official, Hsü Ts'ung 徐鏓, and a concubine. He attempted a career in the bureaucracy, but the one promising period of his life ended in disaster. In his thirties he joined the staff of Hu Tsung-hsien 胡宗憲, governor of Chekiang, and became the latter's secretary. Hu commanded the armies defending the provinces of southeast China. Hsü Wei's service was of tremendous value because of "his knowledge of military and strategic skills" (*Ming-shih, chüan* 288) and the excellent memorials he wrote to the emperor in Hu's name.

In 1565 when Hu was dismissed and imprisoned, Hsü Wei, who had left him only three years earlier, feared implication and attempted suicide. Then in a fit of jealousy he killed his wife, for which he was thrown into jail for seven years. The sentence would have been heavier but for the intervention of an influential friend who secured his release and eventual pardon.

Hsü Wei spent the remainder of his life in retirement in Shao-hsing. During the whole of his life, including the years in prison, he continued literary activities of various kinds. A fairly prolific writer, he also compiled a few anthologies and edited and wrote commentaries on several authors of his own as well as earlier periods.

However, Hsü Wei's major contributions were his four *tsa-chü* dramas collectively entitled *Ssu-sheng yüan* 四聲猿 (The Four Shrieks of the Monkey). These are *K'uang ku-li Yü-yang san-nung* 狂鼓吏漁陽三弄 (The Mad Drummer Plays Thrice in Yü-yang), *Yü ch'an-shih Ts'ui-hsiang i-meng* 玉禪師翠鄉一夢 (A Dream of Ch'an Master Yü-t'ung and Liu Ts'ui), *Tz'u Mu-lan t'i-fu ts'ung-chun* 雌木蘭替父從軍 (The Heroine Mu-lan Joins the Army for her Father), and *Nü chuang-yüan tz'u-huang te-feng* 女狀元辭凰得鳳 (The Female Scholar Takes on a Man's Role).

The first play is a reenactment in the hellish court of King Yama of an incident involving Mi Heng, a defiant scholar of Ts'ao Ts'ao court. When Ts'ao Ts'ao tries to humiliate him by ordering him to become a drummer, Mi sheds his clothes, and, as he beats the drums, enumerates Ts'ao Ts'ao's crimes.

The second is about a monk called Yü-t'ung 玉通 and his dealings with a courtesan. This two-act *tsa-chü* tells how the chaste monk Yü T'ung is seduced by a courtesan. The monk is reborn as the courtesan Lu Ts'ui, and in turn is delivered by a former holy colleague. This story was also treated in other *tsa-chü* and in *hua-pen.**

The third play is an adaptation of the famous ballad of Mu-lan, a girl who disguises herself as a man to save her father and brother from conscription, then achieves military fame and high rank for her bravery. Huang Ch'ung-hu 黃崇胡, the "Female Scholar" of the fourth play, like Mu-lan, dresses as a man, but participates in the examinations. After she passes she becomes the object of the magistrate's passion.

Hsü Wei has departed in these dramas from the traditional structure of the *tsa-chü* which demanded that each piece contain four acts. *The Mad Drummer* has only one act, *The Female Scholar* five, and the others two each; moreover, *The Female Scholar* uses Southern tunes.

The contemporary scholar Chao Ching-shen 趙景深 draws attention to the creativity of Hsü's language, claiming it "is fresh and lively beyond expectations, fits the circumstances beautifully, and is rich in wit. Just as Hsü himself said, it can 'startle like cold water poured on the back.' "

Hsü's dramas show some sense of concern for suffering and for victims of authority. This is manifested most clearly in the attitude towards women. In both *Mulan* and *The Female Scholar* women are shown to be superior to men. They exhibit enthusiasm, courage, resourcefulness, unyielding determination, and confidence, and are successful in literature, administration, and war.

Hsü's *Nan-tz'u hsü-lu* 南詞敍錄 (On the Southern Drama), which appeared in 1559, is particularly important. It is the first serious study of the drama of South China and is an indispensable source. A manuscript copy of this work survives in the *Chiang-su Sheng-li Kuo-hsüeh T'u-shu-kuan.*

EDITIONS:
Hsü Wei chi 徐渭集. 4v. Peking, 1983.
Hsü Wen-ch'ang ch'u-chi 徐文長初集. 1590.
Hsü Wen-ch'ang ch'üan-chi 徐文長全集. 1614.
Hsü Wen-ch'ang chüeh-pien 徐文長闕編. 1590.
Hsü Wen-ch'ang ch'ang san-chi 徐文長三集. 1600.
Contains the earliest extant editions of *The Four Shrieks of the Monkey;* held in the Peking Library.
Ku-pen. Contains *The Four Shrieks* photolithographed from an edition of the Wan-li period (1571-1620).
Nan-tz'u hsü-lu 南詞敍錄, in *Hsi-ch'ü lun-chu,* v. 3, pp. 233-256.

TRANSLATIONS:
Faurot, Jeannette. "Four Cries of a Gibbon: A 'Tsa-chü' Cycle by the Ming Dramatist Hsü Wei (1521-1593)." Unpublished Ph.D. dissertation, University of California, Berkeley, 1972.

STUDIES:
Chao, Ching-shen 趙景深. *Hsi-ch'ü pi-t'an* 戲曲筆談, Peking, 1962, pp. 46-51.
DMB, pp. 609-612.
Liang, I-ch'eng 梁一成. *Hsü Wei Te wen-hsüeh yü i-shu* 徐渭的文學與藝術. Taipei, 1977.

—CM

Hsüan-ho i-shih 宣和遺事 (Past Events of the Hsüan-ho Period), by an anonymous author, is the longest single work of pro-Ming vernacular fiction extant. It recounts the saga of the decline and fall of the Northern Sung dynasty and centers on the life of Emperor Hui-tsung (r. 1101-1125). That this book contains an early, brief version of the story of Sung Chiang and his band, known to Chinese reading audiences through the novel *Shui-hu chuan,** probably accounts for its fame and even its continued existence.

Two different versions of the work—one in four parts and one in two—are extant. The four-part division seems to have been imposed upon an earlier two-part version. The first half begins with a summary of the rise and fall of the dynasties before Sung. The story proper begins with the reforms of Wang An-shih* in 1069, which the narrator identifies as the beginning of Sung decline. It proceeds to describe the lavishness and corruption of Hui-tsung's court, the gradual encroachment of the Jurchens, the gaiety and splendor of the capital, Pien-liang (modern Kaifeng), and the emperor's affair with the popular songstress, Li Shih-shih. It closes with a convergence of all the forces working to destroy the empire on the last night of the Lantern Festival in 1124. The second half narrates the fall of Pien-liang to the Jurchens, Hui-tsung's forced abdication and abduction along with his son, the new emperor Ch'in-tsung (r. 1126), to the wilderness of the northeast, their ignominious deaths, and the reestablishment of Sung rule in southern China by another of Hui-tsung's sons, Prince K'ang, who managed to flee the debacle and restore the Sung court in Hangchow.

Hsüan-ho i-shih was traditionally considered to have been written during the Southern Sung, since in some editions the title was given as *Ta-Sung Hsüan-ho i-shih*, and since the taboo on certain Sung imperial names is observed in the work (although not consistently). From internal evidence, Wang Chung-hsien proved conclusively that it is actually a product of the Yüan. It was probably not written much later than the turn of the fourteenth century. The bulk of the work is in the literary idiom, but some sections, such as the story of the emperor's affair and that of Sung Chiang's exploits, are written in a free vernacular. The narrator's comments are for the most part also in vernacular Chinese. Traditional commentators have viewed the work as a piece of biased, inaccurate history—mainly owing to its unflattering portrayal of Hui-tsung and its intimate account of his liaison with Li Shih-shih. From the notice of Hu Ying-lin,* it is evident that *Hsüan-ho i-shih* was a popular work in his own day. Notices by Ch'ing bibliophiles indicate that it had probably disappeared from general circulation before 1700. Wang Chung-hsien felt the entire book had been compiled from previous sources, although he was unable to prove this. However, most of the sections in literary Chinese can be found in Sung sources. Connections between this book and the storytelling traditions of historical narratives and of poems on historical themes have also been noted. In fact, lyrics by many popular poets of T'ang and Sung are included, such as Po Chü-i,* Li Ho,* and Hu Tseng 胡曾 (fl. 806).

Hsüan-ho i-shih shares some of the formal characteristics of the *p'ing-hua** narratives; nevertheless, in structure it is probably closer to the conventions of early Ming novels.

EDITIONS:

Hsin-k'an Ta-Sung Hsüan-ho i-shih 新刊大宋宣和遺事. Shanghai, 1954. The four-part version based on the Wang Lo-ch'uan (Ming) edition. Punctuated.

Hsin-pien Hsüan-ho i-shih 新編宣和遺事. 2 *chüan*. *SPPY*. The two-part version. Reprint of the *Shih-li-chü ts'ung-shu* 士禮居叢書 edition of 1819. Although unpunctuated it is the most reliable modern edition.

Several rare editions of either version can be found in the Chung-yang T'u-shu kuan (Taipei), Chung-yang yen-chiu yüan (Taipei), and Pei-ching T'u-shu kuan (Peking).

TRANSLATIONS:
Hennessey, William O. *Proclaiming Harmony*. Ann Arbor, 1981.

STUDIES:
Chang, Cheng-lang 張政烺. "Chiang-shih yü yung-shih shih" 講史與詠史詩, *CYYY*, 10 (May 1943), 601-646.

Wang, Chung-hsien 汪仲賢. "*Hsüan-ho i-shih* k'ao-cheng" 宣和遺事考證. *Hsiao-shuo yüeh-pao*, 17: Extra issue (June 1927), 1-10.

Hennessey, William O. "The Song Emperor Huizong in Popular History and Romance: The Early Chinese Vernacular Novel *Xuanhe yishi*." Unpublished Ph.D. dissertation, University of Michigan, 1980.

—WH

Hsüeh T'ao 薛濤 (*tzu*, Hung-tu 洪度, 768-831) was one of the two most distinguished women poets of the T'ang dynasty, the other being Yü Hsüan-chi.* She was born to an ordinary family in Ch'ang-an. Her father, Hsüeh Yün 薛鄖, was a minor government official who died in Szechwan, leaving his family stranded there with no means of support. Hsüeh T'ao, fourteen or fifteen at the time, was known for her talent in versification. To support herself and her widowed mother, she became a sing-song girl.

It is said that when Hsüeh T'ao was barely seven or eight, her father, to test her talent, asked her to finish a quatrain which he began with these lines: "In the garden an ancient *tung*-tree,/ With its trunk thrusting into the clouds." Without hesitation the child responded, "Its branches welcome birds which fly in from north or south;/ Its leaves bid adieu to winds that come and go." Although impressed with his daughter's precociousness, Hsüeh Yün was chagrined at the symbolic meaning of her imagery, which seemed to prognosticate her future as a courtesan.

When Hsüeh T'ao's literary fame spread throughout Ch'eng-tu, the capital of Szechwan, Wei Kao 韋皋, the provincial governor at the time, engaged her as an official performer to entertain honored guests at public functions. He also proposed recommending her to the throne for the honorable office of Female Editing Clerk. Although the plan was not carried out, the title was unofficially attached to her.

In this capacity, Hsüeh T'ao had occasion to meet many celebrities from Ch'ang-an. She was on intimate terms and exchanged poetry with no fewer than twenty eminent T'ang poets, among them, P'ei Tu 裴度 (765-839), Ling-hu Ch'u 令狐楚 (766-837), Liu Yü-hsi,* Po Chü-i,* and in particular Yüan Chen.* When Yüan Chen went to eastern Szechwan in 809 on an inspection tour as investigating censor, he expressed his desire to meet this renowned poetess. His host complied by sending Hsüeh T'ao to him, and a lasting, close relationship developed between them. After Yüan Chen returned to the capital, Hsüeh T'ao continued to send him poems written on colorful tablets with fir and flower patterns which she designed and manufactured herself.

In her lifetime, Hsüeh T'ao had a collection of over five hundred poems in circulation; only about ninety of them have survived. Most are love poems addressed to her male patrons in their absence, or occasional poems celebrating their brief unions. Her poems are noted for the rich, sensuous imagery and melodious rhythm, suitable for singing. Critics tend to dismiss Hsüeh T'ao's poetry as mere erotic and occasional verse of no significance. They overlook the subtle satire and hidden metaphors. Sadness pervades all her poems. Regardless of subject matter, her poetry reflects her own life and her melancholy.

After retiremant, Hsüeh T'ao moved to the outskirts of Ch'eng-tu. There she spent her remaining years composing poetry and practicing calligraphy. Aside from the information in her poems, little else is known about her life. The date given here for her death is the generally accepted one given by Wen I-to 聞一多 (1899-1946) in his *T'ang-shih tsa-lun* 唐詩雜論.

EDITIONS:
Ch'üan T'ang shih, v. 11, pp. 9035-9064 and 9804.

TRANSLATIONS:
Sunflower, pp. 190-191.
Orchid Boat, pp. 21-23.

STUDIES:
Chung-kuo fu-nü wen-hsüeh shih 中國婦女文學史. Hong Kong, n.d., pp. 205-214.
Karashima, Takeshi 辛島驍. *Gyo Genki* 魚玄機; *Setsu Tō* 薛濤. Tokyo, 1964. Contains translations.
Wimsatt, Genevieve B. *A Well of Fragrant Waters.* Boston, 1945.

—AJP

Hu Ying-lin 胡應麟 (*tzu*, Yüan-jui 元瑞 and Ming-jui 明瑞, 1551-1602) was the last of the major Ming literary archaists who advocated a return to antiquity (*fu-ku* 復古) and, especially, a strict adherence to High T'ang models in the writing of poetry. Born in Lan-ch'i 蘭谿 (Chekiang), he never managed to pass the *chin-shih* examination and spent most of his life in relative seclusion in his native home. Independent means allowed him to amass an enormous personal library, which he housed in his retreat, the Shao-shih shan-fang 少室山房, north of Lan-ch'i. His scholarly work on forgeries, the *Ssu-pu cheng-o* 四部正譌, and his research in history, Taoism, and Buddhism, as well as in various miscellaneous subjects including drama and fiction, attest to his extensive learning, scholarly industry, and methodic and inquisitive mind. His significance as a literary figure does not lie in his poetry (which, while extensive, seems rather conventional and hardly deserving the lavish praise accorded it by Wang Shih-chen [1526-1590],* his patron) but in the historical and critical work on the development of the poetic tradition in his *Shih-sou* 詩藪 (Thicket of Remarks on Poetry; 20 *chüan,* 1589).

The *Shih-sou* is divided into four major sections. The first, *nei-pien* (inner chapters), contains six *chüan,* each of which deals with one of the principal forms of *shih,* presented both in terms of their development—origin through maturity (or "final significant" form)—and in terms of what Hu considers to be their most salient formal and expressive features. These chapters are devoted almost exclusively to pre-Sung poetry, and the few concluding remarks made about Sung, Yüan, and Ming poets clearly indicate that Hu regards their accomplishments as derivative rather than original. Hu considers that all significant poetic development occurred during the T'ang and the pre-T'ang eras.

The *Wai-pien* (outer chapters), also in six *chüan*, are organized by historical periods: Chou-Han, Six Dynasties, T'ang (Part One), T'ang (Part Two), Sung, and Yüan. The materials presented here are more heterogeneous and include extensive analysis and evaluation of both general trends and individual poets, discussions of contemporary *shih-hua** and post-T'ang anthologies, quotations from and evaluations of later *shih-hua* which deal with earlier periods and figures, etc. Post-T'ang poets are given extensive and intensive critical treatment, yet the standards applied to them are never their own, but are drawn from the T'ang and the pre-T'ang eras—they are judged in terms of how well they follow the earlier masters. Hu admits that some of the Sung poets had great ability, but deplores their experimentation with unorthodox innovations—the expression of extreme individuality, a predilection to excessive ratiocination (*yung i* 用意), the abandonment of strict rules established by the T'ang masters of prosody, syntax, and diction (*shih-fa* 詩法)—for the sake of a more immediate and casual articulation of experience, something which in Hu's opinion resulted in crude and clumsy composition. By contrast, the Yüan poets may have been less talented, but in being so were forced to "keep to the rules." They brought poetry back to the correct and orthodox path. Hu seems to be the first critic to view Yüan poetry as a genuine renaissance of the T'ang style—a view that was later to obtain currency during the Ch'ing era.

The *Shih-sou's* third section—*tsa-pien* (miscellaneous chapters)—also contains six *chüan: P'ien-chang* 篇章 (Specific Literary Works) which deals with compositions in the *sao* form attributed to Ch'ü Yüan* and in the *fu** form of the Han through the Chin eras; *Tsai-chi* 雜籍 (Editions of Literary Works) which is a critical bibliography of poets beginning with Ch'ü Yüan and ending with the Five Dynasties (including both anthologies and individual collections); *San-kuo* (Three Kingdoms Era) which is a critical and bibiographical treatment of poets of that period; and three *chüan* of *Jun-yü* 閏餘 (Additional Materials) which deal critically with poets of the Five Dynasties, the Southern Sung, and the Chin.

The *Hsü-pien* (Supplementary Chapters), in two *chüan*, conclude the *Shih-sou* and are devoted to criticism of Ming poetry. Hu has elaborate praise for the poets of his own era and believes that they, especially the "Ch'ien-hou ch'i-tzu" (Former and Latter Seven Masters), have produced the best poetry since the T'ang; the minor renaissance initiated by the Yüan poets has, in his opinion, come to complete fruition with the grand renaissance of his own day.

The *Shih-sou* contains facts and opinions about nearly every significant aspect of the poetic tradition up to Hu's own era. Although he displays a strong archaist bias, he still manages to present materials and evaluations so extensively and in such detail that the work as a whole deserves the attention of every serious student of Chinese poetry.

Although less systematic and less voluminous, Hu Ying-lin's remarks on fiction, most of which can be found in his *Shao-shih shan-fang pi-ts'ung* 少室山房筆叢 (Notes from the Shao-shih shan-fang Studio), are by no means less significant. They range from insights on generic characteristics, such as his recognition of T'ang *ch'uan-ch'i* stories as a distinctive and distinguished type of writing, to observations of the current state of fiction, such as his notes on the growth of the *San-kuo chih yen-i** and the *Shui-hu chuan.**

EDITIONS:

Shih-sou 詩藪. Peking, 1958. Composite edition in modern punctuation, the best of all modern reprints.

Shao-shih shan-fang lei-kao 少室山房類稿. 120 *chüan. Ssu-k'u ch'üan-shu, Shao-shih shan-fang ssu-chi* 四集, and *Hsü Chin-hua ts'ung-shu* 續 金華叢書 editions. There are no modern editions or reprints, but the *pi-chi* portion of the collective work, *Shao-shih shan-fang pi-ts'ung*, is available in the Chung-hua shu-chü 1964 modern reprint.

TRANSLATIONS:

Yokota, Terutoshi 横田輝俊. *Shisō* 詩藪. Tokyo, 1975. Translation with copious annotation of one third of the text.

STUDIES:

Chan, Kwok Kou, Leonard 陳國球. "A Critical Study of Hu Ying-lin's Poetic Theories." Unpublished M.A. thesis, Hong Kong University, 1982.

DMB, pp. 645-647.

Lynn, Richard John. "Tradition and the Individual: Ming and Ch'ing Views of Yüan Poetry," *JOS*, 15 (1977), 1-19. A slightly different version of the same appears in *Studies in Chinese Poetry and Poetics*, Ronald C. Miao, ed. San Francisco, 1978, v. 1, pp. 321-375.

Wu, Han 吳晗. "Hu Ying-lin nien-p'u" 胡應麟年譜, *THHP*, 9.1 (January 1934), 183-252.

Yokota, Terutoshi. "Ko Ōrin no Shiron" 胡應麟の詩論. *Hiroshima Daigaku bungakubu kiyō*, 28.1 (December 1968), 305-323.

—RL and YWM

Hua-chien chi 花間集 (Among the Flowers Collection) is an anthology of five hundred poems, mainly concerning love and separation, in the *tz'u* form. It was compiled during the Later Shu dynasty (934-965) by a minor official named Chao Ch'ung-tso 趙崇祚 (*fl.* 934-965). There is a preface by Ou-yang Chiung* dated 940. The anthology is divided into ten *chüan*, each of which consists of fifty *tz'u* (but *chüan* 6 has fifty-one and *chüan* 9 has only forty-nine) written to seventy-five *tz'u tiao* 詞調 (tune-titles).

The *Hua-chien chi* is the first extant anthology devoted to *tz'u* composed by literati. A collection of thirty-three anonymous *tz'u* poems called the *Yün-yao chi* 雲謠集, probably compiled in the late T'ang and recovered from the Tun-huang manuscripts may have preceded it. Late T'ang *tz'u* are also represented in the *Ts'un-ch'ien chi*,* but evidence suggests that this collection was not compiled until the Sung. The poems in the *Hua-chien chi* date from the period 850-940. They were not the first *tz'u* by literati, for such poets as Po

Chü-i* and Liu Yü-hsi* had already experimented with the form, but in quantity and stylistic refinement the *tz'u* in the *Hua-chien chi* mark a departure from the popular songs from which they evolved.

The evidence of anonymous *ch'ü-tzu tz'u* 曲子詞 (*tz'u* song words) in the Tun-huang manuscripts indicates that the popular genre flourished as early as the eighth century. Based on popular music and Central Asian tunes, these *tz'u* undoubtedly influenced the literati, who in the middle of the ninth century began to use the form themselves. But because of the popular origins of the genre, members of the educated elite wrote *tz'u* for almost a century before their work was taken seriously enough to merit an anthology.

In the preface to the *Hua-chien chi*—the first piece of literary criticism of the *tz'u* form—Ou-yang Chiung uses allusive parallel prose to defend the ornate artifice of the style of the *tz'u* in the *Hua-chien chi*. He distinguishes them from Liang dynasty *Kung-t'i shih*,* which he regards as empty and decadent, and from common folk songs, which he regards as crude and vulgar. Thus, the *Hua-chien chi* poems are characterized by their beauty and refinement which surpasses previous love songs. However, Ou-yang Chiung acknowledges that this poetry was composed for aesthetic and emotional pleasure, which indicates a departure from the longstanding Confucian tradition of writing poetry for moral and didactic purposes. The love poems in the *Hua-chien chi* can generally not be read as political allegories.

Compared with the popular *tz'u* in the Tun-huang manuscripts, *Hua-chien chi* poetry is more refined in diction and more static in presentation. Whereas many of the folk songs narrate a series of events and use dramatic confrontations and dialogue, the *tz'u* of the literati tend to focus on a single moment in which a solitary figure reflects on his or her situation. A few of the *Hua-chien chi* poems describe a man's travels or idealize the carefree life of a fisherman; the majority concern women, often courtesans and singing girls from the entertainment quarters. Typically a lonely woman is presented in luxurious surroundings which ironically contrast with her emotional deprivation.

The characteristic *Hua-chien chi* imagery is highly conventional: the heartbroken woman keeps a cold bed beside a solitary lamp, a candle dripping tears of wax or a water clock relentlessly reminding her of the passage of time. Since her lover is absent, her mirror, cosmetics, elegant clothing, and embroidered covers are useless; in her grief she is separated by ornate screens and exquisite curtains from the outside world. The achievement of the best *Hua-chien chi* poems is the coherence and intensity of the melancholy mood evoked by this imagistic refinement. It remained for poets of the Southern T'ang dynasty such as Li Ching 李璟 (916-961) and Li Yü,* and those of the Northern Sung dynasty such as Liu Yung* and Su Shih,* to add a more personal lyric voice and to expand the themes and diction of the *tz'u* form.

The *Hua-chien chi* is a collection of *tz'u* poetry by eighteen authors, all of whom are identified by name and official title. Most were residents of Shu (modern Szechwan); a handful were refugees from Ch'ang-an after the fall of the T'ang capital in 906. Twelve of the eighteen poets were born in Shu. The splendid and luxurious Later Shu court, to which many were attached, represents a nostalgic afterglow of the lost T'ang court, and hence it is not surprising that these Shu poets continued the late T'ang *tz'u* style to perpetuate their cultural heritage. It is often said that the poems in the *Hua-chien chi* manifest an escapist attitude toward the political turmoil of the times; simultaneously, however, they promote the culture of the Shu region and its short-lived court.

The three best known poets in the *Hua-chien chi* flourished during the late T'ang period and were innovative models for the later Shu poets. The work of Wen T'ing-yün,* who established the literati *tz'u* style, is placed at the beginning of the anthology and is given the most emphasis with sixty-six examples. Wei Chuang follows, with forty-seven poems. The third important poet, Huang-fu Sung 皇甫松 (*fl.* 880), rep-

resented by eleven poems, is noted for the more popular quality of his *tz'u*. Wen T'ing-yün and Wei Chuang also experimented with the popular-song style, but in addition each mastered his own form of a more elegant style. Wen T'ing-yün dwells on delicately poised antitheses, such as nature vs. artifice, reality vs. dreams, exterior vs. interior, the present vs. the past. His solitary female figure is characteristically enclosed behind layers of veils, curtains, and mirrors in a self-reflective state of imagination and memory. Wei Chuang's style is more direct and active; his poems are more often written from the male point of view and may focus on the moment of separation rather than on a dreamy subjective state.

EDITIONS:

Chao, Ch'ung-tso, ed. *Hua-chien chi*. Peking, 1955. Photolithographic reprint of the edition by Ch'ao Ch'ien-chih 晁謙之; colophon dated 1148. Rpt. Taipei, 1961, under the title *Sung-pen Hua-chien chi* 宋本花間集 .

Hsiao, Chi-tsung 蕭繼宗 ed. *Hua-chien chi*. Taipei, 1977.

Hua, Lien-p'u 華連圃, ed. *Hua-chien chi chu* 花間集注. Shanghai, 1935.

Li, I-mang 李一氓, collator. *Hua-chien chi chiao* 花間集校. Taipei, 1971.

Li, Ping-jo 李冰若, ed. *Hua-chien chi p'ing-chu* 花間集評注. 1935. Rpt. Hong Kong, 1960.

TRANSLATIONS:

Baxter, Glen. "*Hua-chien chi*: Songs of Tenth Century China." Ph.D. dissertation, Harvard University, 1952.

Fusek, Lois. *Among the Flowers: The Hua-chien chi*. New York, 1982.

STUDIES:

Aoyama, Hiroshi 青山宏. *Kakanshū sakuin* 花間集索引(Concordance to *Hua-chien chi*). Tokyo, 1974. Aoyama is also the author of numerous articles on the *Hua-chien chi*.

Chang, K'ang-i, *The Evolution of Chinese Tz'u Poetry*. Princeton, 1980.

—MW

Hua-pen 話本 (vernacular short story) is a word taken from Sung or later colloquial language designating in modern usage the vernacular short story as a literary genre. However, in as recent a work as the 1979 edition of the *Tz'u-hai* 辭海, *hua-pen* is still

442

glossed (based on Lu Hsün's *Chung-kuo hsiao-shuo shih-lüeh* 中國小說史略, 1923), as a "prompt-book" used by professional storytellers during the Sung and Yüan periods. This usage, however, is obsolete. Two main kinds of *hua-pen* are to be distinguished, one linked with *hsiao-shuo** (meaning "short story"), the other with longer historical narratives, the so-called *p'ing-hua.** *Ni hua-pen* 擬話本 (imitation prompt-books) remains a term restricted to later short stories in the manner of earlier storytellers.

It cannot be demonstrated that *hua-pen* was ever used as a technical literary term before the early 1920s. In old colloquial language it could simply mean "story," synonymous with *hua*, as a glance into Lu Tan-an's 陸澹安 *Hsiao-shuo tz'u-yü hui-shih* 小說詞語滙釋 (Peking, 1964) would show. The "prompt-book" theory has been criticized from another angle, since professional storytellers are more likely to have relied on abstracts or notes in the classical language, of the sort included in *Tsui-weng t'an-lu* 醉翁談錄. It seems better to understand *pen* as "basis" in a general sense; that is to say the incidents likely to give rise to a story, and then the story itself, the written version more likely to be called *hua-wen.*

Such being the case, the opposition between "real" and "imitation" *hua-pen* loses pertinence as neither was intended for the professional storyteller. Still the term "imitation" might be reserved for the eighteenth-century revival of the genre modelled on older pieces.

The earliest occurrence of the word *hua-pen* appears in the *Tu-ch'eng chi-sheng* (see *Tung-ching meng Hua lu*) in connection with puppet and shadow plays. Whether the term is taken to mean narrative or synopsis, it does show that the same story-stuff was likely to be used by different genres. In order to understand the more restricted modern sense of *hua-pen*, it should be traced back to *hsiao-shuo* as a specific genre of storytelling. One cannot fail to notice that *hsiao-shuo* was the most common term used by editors or creators of so-called *hua-pen.* Tuan Ch'eng-shih 段成式 (?-863), as

early as 835, notes the existence of some sort of *hsiao-shuo* performers. One gets, however, fuller accounts of their oral art from descriptions of K'ai-feng in the twelfth century and Hangchow in the thirteenth. From these an increase in the artistic level and the popularity of *hsiao-shuo* can be determined, as well as a widening of the repertoire and a market perhaps already exploited by the printing of cheap, popular booklets. Those forms, whatever their differences had been in oral or in musical performance, were likely to be confused once they were recorded. A working definition of *hua-pen* may then be offered: an undivided piece of written, fictional narrative in a colloquial (or vulgarized) style. The only piece excepted by this definition would be "Yü kuan-yin" 玉觀音 (The Jade Bodhisattva) as rearranged in *Ching-pen t'ung-su hsiao-shuo,** but this collection has been shown to be a late forgery. It is true that about the middle of the seventeenth century a fashion arose for divided, longer short stories, collected in small numbers in single volumes. The well-known *Shih-erh lou* 十二樓 of Li Yü* (1611-1680) is an example of this vogue. But a glance through the standard anthology *Hua-pen hsüan* 話本選 (Peking, 1959; rpt. 1979) would confirm the fitness of the above definition for thirty-six out of thirty-eight pieces.

More important, this definition fits fully with *Chin-ku ch'i-kuan,** the classical anthology from around 1640 which is the consecration of this literary genre. As such it can be argued that the vogue of *hua-pen, sensu stricto,* is confined to the seventeenth century, less its first and last quarters.

Before the prestige given to the genre by Feng Meng-lung,* earlier collections were largely retrieved older popular pieces hardly edited. The earliest date of circulation of thin booklets containing a single story—printed or in manuscript—is but conjecture. None are extant. It is known that Hung P'ien 洪楩, a scion of Hung Mai,* was one of the first to take such an initiative, publishing sixty *hua-pen* in installments—the *Liu-shih chia hsiao-shuo** (mid-fourteenth century)—of which less than

443

half were rediscovered, some in Japan in the 1920s, others in China in the 1930s. This work took its alternate title—*Ch'ing-p'ing shan-t'ang hua-pen* 清平山堂話本 —from the hall in which Hung P'ien did his editing, the Ch'ing-p'ing shan-t'ang, probably referring to a hill near Hangchow. If Hung P'ien's venture was a commercial success, it would explain why, some decades later, a certain Hsiung Lung-feng 熊龍峯, probably from Fukien, published an unknown number of "hsiao-shuo," four of which are extant. To these should be added several pieces mentioned by Lu Kung 路工 as from the last years of Wan-li (*c.* 1619), and now published in Hu Shih-ying's 胡士瑩 *Hua-pen hsiao-shuo kai-lun* 話本小說概論 (Peking, 1980). Several of these *hua-pen* are also to be found, rearranged and with commentaries, in the prestigious *San-yen* 三言, the largest collection to date (see Feng Meng-lung).

Till Patrick Hanan applied more vigorous stylistic criteria, dating of older pieces, if not impressionistic, relied largely on external references, rash identification, or partial evidence, mostly geographical or chronological. It was wrongly assumed that the oldest *hua-pen* were mostly Sung, and they were considered sources for Yüan *tsa-chü*.* In his analysis of the dramatic structure of the short story, Wilt L. Idema pointed out that the reverse is probably true in many cases. Literary sources are tapped even less in earlier pieces (through the mid-fifteenth century), which number about thirty. They appear closer to oral performance and "urban folklore" in their oblique beginnings, the skill with which they maintain suspense, their harsh realism, and their drab subject-matter. A second group of roughly the same number of *hua-pen*, from a slightly later period, caters more to the taste of mercantile classes, a feature to be found as well in later *hua-pen*, though they are more often concerned with young literati.

The whole corpus, few from later than the seventeenth century, would include fewer than five hundred *hua-pen*, even if every written text were known. Their diversity defies description. Erotic themes became increasingly popular, as opposed to the supernatural and the satirical ones. For a long time the genre was little known. In China most collections other than the *Chin-ku ch'i-kuan*,* were lost or scarce, whereas in the West rough adaptations, presenting themselves as translations, have appeared regularly since the eighteenth century. A fairer appraisal is now possible through recent more accurate and complete translations of earlier pieces. For the period since the *Chin-ku ch'i-kuan* little has been done with the exception of the *Hsi-hu erh-chi* 西湖二集 (Second Collection of the West Lake), representative of the whole range of collections from the time of the fall of the Ming dynasty, and showing its political and social consequences. The standard features of the *hua-pen*, a narrative of some five to ten thousand characters with a certain admixture of verse and an introductory story or two, are often warped in these later productions. Verse tends to be sparingly used, introductory stories disappear, as in *Huan-hsi yüan-chia* (Pleasure and Grievance), the only later collection to have remained under different titles on the market, due no doubt to the steady appeal of its erotic and feminist themes.

Characteristics of these later productions, recently retrieved, are thinner volumes centered around a single theme or place. *Tsui-hsing shih* 醉醒石 (The Stone of Awakening), an early Ch'ing publication in fifteen chapters, is remarkable for its strong anti-gentry bias. *Tou-p'eng hsien-hua* 豆棚閒話 (Chats from under the Bean-stalks Awning, probably late seventeenth century), a kind of *Dodecameron*, offers a unique Chinese example of framed stories. Though none of these new experiments is a masterpiece, they deserve attention as records of over half a century during the transition from the Ming to Manchu rule. A mobile society in urbanized China was the setting for the vogue of the short story in the colloquial language. Its form and content bear witness to the times, and its legacy is a corpus of masterpieces of popular literature which have lost none of their vividness.

EDITIONS:
See entries for *Ching-pen t'ung-su hsiao-shuo*, Feng Meng-lung, Ling Meng-ch'u, and *Liu-shih-chia hsiao-shuo*.

TRANSLATIONS:
Bettin, L. and M. Liebermann. *Die Jadegöttin, zwölf Geschichten aus dem mittelalterlichen China.* Berlin, 1966.

Birch, Cyril. *Stories from a Ming Collection.* London, 1958.

Dolby, William. *The Perfect Lady by Mistake.* London, 1976.

Lévy, André. *L'amour de la renarde, marchands et lettrès de la vieille Chine, douze contes du XVIIe siècle.* Paris, 1970.

———. *L'antre aux fantômes des Collines de l'Ouest, sept contes chinois anciens, XIIe-XIVe siècles.* Paris, 1972.

———. *Sept victimes pour un oiseau.* Paris, 1981. *Traditional Chinese Stories.*

Scott, John. *The Lecherous Academician and Other Tales by Master Ling Mengchu.* London, 1973.

Yang, Hsien-yi and Gladys Yang. *The Courtesan's Jewel Box, Chinese Stories of the Xth-XVIIth Centuries.* Peking, 1957.

STUDIES:
Baus, Wolfgang. *Das P'ai-an ching-ji des Ling Meng-ch'u.* Bern, 1974.

Bishop, John L. *The Colloquial Short Story in China: A Study of the San-yen Collections.* Cambridge, Mass., 1956. The first book-length study of *hua-pen* other than Prusek's studies.

Ch'eng, I-chung 程毅中. *Sung Yüan hua-pen* 宋元話本. Peking, 1980.

Hanan, Patrick. "The Early Chinese Short Story: A Critical Theory in Outline," *HJAS*, 27 (1967), 168-207. A revolutionary approach using N. Frye's *Anatomy of Criticism* as a frame of reference.

———. *The Chinese Short Story: Studies in Dating, Authorship and Composition.* Cambridge, Mass., 1973. A landmark, with a valuable bibliography.

———. "The Nature of Ling Meng-ch'u's Fiction," in Plaks, *Narrative*, pp. 85-114. Draws attention to the satirical trend.

———. *The Chinese Vernacular Story.* Cambridge, Mass., 1981.

Hu, Shih-ying 胡士瑩. *Hua-pen hsiao-shuo kai-lun* 話本小說概論. 2v. Peking, 1980.

Idema, Wilt Lukas. *Chinese Vernacular Fiction: The Formative Period.* Leiden, 1974. Many new and stimulating views.

———. *Inventaire analytique et critique du conte chinois en langue vulgaire.* 3v. Paris, 1978, 1980, 1981.

Lévy, André. *Le conte en langue vulgaire du XVIIe siècle, vogue et déclin d'un genre narratif de la littérature chinoise.* Paris, 1981. Completed in 1972, a survey of the genre from its origins to the post-*San-yen* phase; fuller bibliography on French publications up to 1973.

Ma, Yau-woon. "The Knight-errant in *Hua-pen* Stories," *TP*, 61 (1975), 266-300. *Hua-pen* are also dealt with in Ma's recent "Kung-an Fiction," *TP*, 65 (1979), 200-259. A systematic survey.

Ono, Shihei 小野四平. *Chūgoku kinsei ni okeru tanpen hakuwashōsetsu no kenkyū* 中國近世にすける短篇白話小說の研究. Tokyo, 1978.

Průšek, Jaroslav. *Chinese History and Literature.* Prague, 1970. Collects the previous most important articles on *hua-pen*. Still extremely valuable, but no items from books like *Die Literatur des befreiten China und ihr Volkstraditionen* (Prague, 1955) or *The Origins and the Authors of the Hua-pen* (Prague, 1967).

Wang, Kuo-liang 王國良. "Chung-kuo ku-tien hsiao-shuo yen-chiu shu-mu: Hua pen hsiao-shuo" 中國古典小說研究書目— 話本小說, *Chung-kuo ku-tien hsiao-shuo*, 5 (1982), pp. 325-329.

Wivell, Charles. "Modes of Coherence in *The Second West Lake Collection*," *LEW*, 15 (1971), 392-409. One of the rare, valuable studies on the post-*San-yen Erh-p'ai* collections.

———. "The Term *Hua-pen*," in *Transition and Permanence*, pp. 295-306. An excellent statement of the problem, to be completed with Masuda Wataru 增田涉, "Wahon to iu koto ni tsuite—tsūsetsu (aruiwa teisetsu) e no gimon" 話本と言うことについて— 通說（ あるいは定說）への疑問, *Jinbun kenkyū*, 16.5 (1965), 456-467.

Yen, Alsace. "The Parry-Lord Theory Applied to Vernacular Chinese Stories," *JAOS*, 95 (1975), 403-416. A preliminary approach to the problem of orality.

—AL

Huang Ching-jen 黄景仁 (*tzu*, Chung-tse 仲則, 1749-1783), native of Wu-chin 武進 (Kiangsu), was a descendant of the famous Sung poet-calligrapher Huang T'ing-chien* and a leading poet of his time. In many ways, his life typified that of the star-crossed geniuses one so often encounters in the history of Chinese poetry. Although born to a family of distinguished lineage, he was struck by tragedy almost from the start of life. He lost both parents by the age of four and then his only brother while still in his teens. He was also plagued by frail health and seems to have suffered greatly from an acute awareness of the family's declining fortunes. Life for him was a continual battle, as his family became progressively poorer and he was forced to travel in search of patronage and employment, a search which eventually took him from his home region in the Yangtze Delta to Peking and then further north and inland. These travels won him an occasional emolument but no regular employment or steady income to meet the needs of a growing family, which by then included several children. To alleviate his financial problems, he tried repeatedly to enter the civil service, but was unable to pass the *chin-shih* examination (which he took eight times). The last few years of his life were particularly difficult as his health continued to deteriorate and he lived at the mercy of his creditors. In the spring of 1783, while en route from Peking to Sian in hopes of joining some friends there, he died at Yün-ch'eng 運城 (Shansi), at the age of thirty-four.

Despite a life of frustration and stark poverty, Huang Ching-jen did enjoy a sense of community with the literary circles of his time and was widely appreciated as a lyric poet, largely through the help of the poet-scholar Hung Liang-chi* and the patronage of Chu Yün 朱筠 (1729-1781) and Pi Yüan 畢沅 (1730-1797), two high officials known for their patronage of needy scholars. Huang was particularly indebted to Hung Liang-chi for a friendship which proved to be exemplary by any standard. It was Hung Liang-chi who introduced him to scholarly circles and who provided him with unfailing support whenever he found himself in a desperate situation. When Huang died a stranded traveler, Hung Liang-chi traveled to the Yün-ch'eng to look after the funeral arrangements, including transporting the coffin from Shansi to Wu-chin for burial. To Hung Liang-chi

should also go the credit for preserving most of Huang's literary works, which number about 2,000 poems. These fraternal bonds between the two poets were deeply admired by their readers. Their friendship also inspired a short story by the modern author Yü Ta-fu 郁達夫 (1896-1945), entitled "Ts'ai-shih chi" 采石磯 (Cliff of Many-colored Rocks), which was instrumental in generating a wave of enthusiasm for Huang Ching-jen during the 1920s and 1930s.

Huang Ching-jen's reputation as a *shih* poet rests largely upon three groups of works, all of which show him to be a true heir to the classical tradition. The first is a set of lively lyrics cast in the regulated-verse form which appears under the collective title "Ch'i huai" 綺懷 (Tender Thoughts) or "Kan chiu" 感舊 (Nostalgia). In mood and imagery, these poems subtly recall works in the same genre from the late T'ang, in particular the "Wu t'i" 無題 (Untitled) poems of Li Shang-yin* and some of the Yangchow *chüeh-chü* of Tu Mu.* The second group consists of a number of drinking songs which typically feature the free-flowing rhetoric of a lone drinker, a voice made famous by Li Po* many centuries earlier. Here, as in Li Po, the feigned nonchalance of the speaker frequently masks a profound despair over the way of the world and the human condition. The third and the finest group of Huang Ching-jen's works cannot be easily classified. They fall within the broad category of personal themes, ranging from the quiet reveries of a solitary traveler to graphic descriptions of an unsuccessful man living on the fringe of an affluent society, themes that are hauntingly reminiscent of the poems of Li Ho.* The best-known work from the latter category is a regulated-verse sequence entitled "Tu-men ch'iu-ssu" 都門秋思 (Autumn Thoughts at the Capital) in which the splendors of the imperial city are vividly contrasted with the abject existence of the failed literatus. Written at a time when the poetic scene was dominated by scholarly pedantry and such largely formalist concepts as *ko-tiao* 格調 (tone) and *chi-li* 肌理 (texture), these personal lyrics by

Huang Ching-jen are noteworthy for their expressive power and their truthful reflection of the ethos of the late Ch'ien-lung era.

Although recognized primarily as a *shih* poet, Huang Ching-jen was also accomplished in the *tz'u** form. He handled with equal competence both the compact *hsiao-ling* and the longer tunes. His *hsiao-ling* pieces are generally characterized by a colloquial charm which sets them apart from the contrived rhythms of the Che-hsi poets, who prevailed during most of the eighteenth century.

EDITIONS:

Liang-tang-hsüan ch'üan-chi 兩當軒全集. 6v. 1876.
Liang-tang-hsüan shih-tz'u ch'ao 兩當軒詩詞鈔. 4v. 1817.
Liang-tang-hsüan shih-tz'u ch'üan-chi 兩當軒詩詞全集. 2v. Taipei, 1970.

TRANSLATIONS:
Sunflower, pp. 491-492.

STUDIES:

Chang, I-p'ing 章衣萍. *Huang Chung-tse p'ing-chuan* 黃仲則評傳. Shanghai, 1931.
ECCP, pp. 337-338.
Huang, I-chih 黃逸之. *Huang Chung-tse nien-p'u* 黃仲則年譜. Shanghai, 1934.
Mao, Ch'ing-shan 毛慶善 and Chi Hsi-ch'ou 季錫疇. *Huang Chung-tse Hsien-sheng nien-p'u* 黃仲則先生年譜. Appended to the editions listed above.
Yü, Ta-fu 郁達夫. "Kuan-yü Huang Chung-tse 關於黃仲則," in Chin Min-t'ien 金民天, ed., *Huang Chung-tse shih-tz'u* 黃仲則詩詞, Shanghai, 1932; also included in *Ta-fu wen-i lun-wen chi* 達夫文藝論文集, Hong Kong, 1978, pp. 533-539.

—ssw

Huang T'ing-chien 黃庭堅 (*tzu*, Lu-chih 魯直, *hao*, Shan-ku 山谷 and Fu-weng 涪翁 among others, 1045-1105) was one of the most influential poets of the Northern Sung dynasty. He was ranked by his immediate followers as the most important of the five younger disciples of Su Shih* and as the father of the Kiangsi School (see *Chiang-hsi shih-p'ai*) of poetry. He is also considered one of the "Four Great Masters" of Sung calligraphy. Although severely denigrated by many later critics as

little more than cleverly elaborate imitation, Huang's verse has a very modernist appeal: he rejected the conventional poetic diction of his day and created an almost anti-poetic style that combined minute observation of everyday life with difficult, sometimes obscure, diction and allusion.

When Huang was in his teens, his father died, and he was educated in the vast library of his maternal uncle Li Ch'ang 李常. He passed the *chin-shih* examination in 1067 and was introduced to literary society by Su Shih in 1078. Huang had an insignificant official career. It was marred by two banishments due to his political association with the conservative faction led by Ssu-ma Kuang in opposition to the New Policies of Wang An-shih.* He cut short his official career to care for his ill mother during the last year of her life and for this exemplary conduct was made one of the famous twenty-four examples of filial piety. Although he had studied Buddhism, he was deemed a man of lofty moral character by the Neo-Confucianists of the Southern Sung, who regarded his poetry as an embodiment of this conduct and therefore as a part of their curriculum. He died in exile at I-chou 宜州 (modern Kwangsi), where he had been sent by the vindictive followers of Wang An-shih.

Huang's poetry, over 2,000 *shih* and 100 *tz'u*, is characterized by creative imitation and deliberate unconventionality. Borrowing concepts from Buddhism, Huang described his theory of creative imitation as *huan-ku* 換骨 (changing the bones) and *t'uo t'ai* 脫胎 (escaping the embryo): "the meaning (*i* 意) of poetry is infinite, but human talent is limited; even a T'ao Ch'ien* or a Tu Fu* could hardly manage to capture successfully the infinite by means of the limited. Not changing the meaning [of a former poem], but creating one's own diction—that is the method of *changing the bones*. To embrace the meaning and then give it [presumably, a new] shape and form—that is the method of *escaping the embryo*" (from *Yeh-lao chi-wen* 野老紀聞). Huang used both of these methods on the poetry of Tu Fu, his favorite, and on Li Po,* Han Yü,* and other poets of the

T'ang dynasty on the way to creating his own individualistic style (see also *Chiang-hsi shih-pai*).

Huang's deliberate unconventionality consisted in the creation of what was later called an *ao-t'i* 拗體 (unregulated style), a deliberate rejection of conventional diction and sentiment, and a passionate search for novelty and strangeness. Following Han Yü and others of the late T'ang, but making it a keynote of his prosody, Huang used both "unregulated sentences" (*ao-chü* 拗句 with 3/2 or 1/4 parsing instead of 2/3 for five-character lines, 3/4 or 2/5 instead of 4/3 caesura in seven-character lines) and "unregulated patterns" (*ao-lü* 拗律) in lines where "level" and "oblique" tones (*p'ing* 平 and *tse* 仄) are neither balanced nor properly antithetical. Eschewing the expression of lyrical emotion in poetry, Huang rejected the standard poetic diction of the past and used extreme care and deliberation in the choice of words and allusions.

In summation, he often employed unconventional and even anti-poetic metric structures, unusually difficult or obscure rhymes (called *hsien-yün* 險韻), and difficult-to-trace allusions. Many critics have claimed his poetry was created exclusively by a patchwork of strange characters, while others complained of a harsh or raw tone. Modern Japanese and European critics, however, admire Huang's difficult verse as an achievement of consummate artistry guided by a creative genius meditating on the deeper meanings of everyday human life and death.

EDITIONS:

Shan-ku ch'üan-chi 山谷全集. *SPPY.*

Huang Shan-ku shih chi-chu 黃山谷詩集注. Taipei, 1960. Best modern edition.

Yü-chang Huang hsien-sheng wen-chi 豫章黃先生文集. *SPTK.*

Huang T'ing-chien shih-hsüan 黃庭堅詩選. P'an Po-yang 潘伯鷹, ed. Peking, 1957 and Hong Kong, 1958.

Yü-chang Huang Hsien-sheng tz'u 豫章黃先生詞. Lung Yü-sheng 龍榆生, ed. Peking, 1957.

TRANSLATIONS:

Arai, Ken 荒井健. *Kō Teiken* 黃庭堅. Tokyo, 1963.

Kurata, Junnosuke 倉田淳之助, *Kō Sankoku* 黃山谷. Tokyo, 1967.

Sunflower, pp. 352-359.

Yoshikawa, *Sung,* pp. 122-130.

STUDIES:

Bieg, Lutz. *Huang Ting-chien (1045-1105), Leben und Dichtung.* Heidelberg, 1971.

Chang, Ping-ch'üan 張秉權, *Huang Shan-ku te chiao-yu chi tso-p'in* 黃山谷的交游及作品. Hong Kong, 1978.

Fu, Hsüan-ts'ung 傅璇琮. *Huang T'ing-chien ho Chiang-hsi shih-p'ai chüan* 黃庭堅和江西詩派卷. Peking, 1978.

Panish, Paul. "The Poetry of Huang T'ing-chien (1045-1105)." Unpublished Ph.D. dissertation, University of Calfornia, 1975.

Rickett, Adele Austin. "Method and Intuition: The Poetic Theories of Huang T'ing-chien," in *Chinese Approaches,* pp. 97-119.

Sargent, Stuart. "Can Latecomers Get There First? Sung Poets and T'ang Poetry," *CLEAR,* 4.2 (July 1982), 165-198.

SB, pp. 454-461.

Shan-ku Hsien-sheng nien p'u 山谷先生年譜. 30 *chüan.* Wu-ch'eng, 1914.

Workman, Michael E. "Huang T'ing-chien: His Ancestry and Family Background as Documented in His Writings and Other Sung Works." Unpublished Ph.D. dissertation, Indiana University, 1982.

—MSD

Huang Tsun-hsien 黃遵憲 (*tzu,* Kung-tu 公度, 1848-1905) is generally considered the foremost poet of the late Ch'ing dynasty *Shih-chieh ko-ming* 詩界革命 (Poetic Revolution). Huang was born to a Hakka family in Chia-ying chou 嘉應州 (modern Mei-hsien, Kwangtung), only two years before the outbreak of the T'ai-p'ing Rebellion. Although Huang's family was moderately wealthy and his father was serving as a local official, he suffered when his family was forced to flee remnants of T'ai-p'ing forces in 1865. His initial attempts to gain high position through the civil-service examinations were frustrated, but his traveling allowed him to experience Western culture on a visit to Hong Kong in 1870. He became even more interested in foreigners after a trip to Peking during the violent controversy there over the Margary Incident (1875). After passing the Peking provincial examination (1876) Huang was appointed to serve in the Chinese embassy in Tokyo, an event which altered the entire course of his political and literary life and eventually led him to believe that Meiji Japan's path of reform patterned on Western institutions was the only possible salvation for China. Subsequently Huang served as Chinese consul-general in San Francisco, secretary in the Chinese embassy in London, and consul-general at Singapore. Thanks to his travels, he was more familiar with Western ways than practically any other prominent late Ch'ing literary figure. Returning to China as the Sino-Japanese War broke out (1894), Huang became deeply involved with Liang Ch'i-ch'ao* and K'ang Yu-wei* in the late Ch'ing reform movement. During the abortive Hundred Days of Reform Huang was called to Peking to serve in the government, but illness forced him to delay his departure, and consequently he was not forced into exile or executed as the other major leaders were.

Huang Tsun-hsien was an amazingly precocious writer. His first surviving poems, written when he was only sixteen, are highly polished works which already contain his later literary theory in embryonic form. Although Huang was not a total iconoclast, he avoided all imitation and attempted to create a new realm of poetry. At twenty-one Huang had already written his famous couplet: "My hand writes what my mouth says;/How can antiquity inhibit me?" One of the basic tenets of Huang's literary theory was: "I write down what my ears and eyes experience"; i.e., he stressed the necessity for immediacy in poetry, for poetry to be a product of the poet's experience and a reflection of his own age. Critics such as Liang Ch'i-ch'ao likened Huang's verse to history in poetic form. Indeed, Huang's important role in the political events of nineteenth-century China and the striking vividness of his style made his poetry among the most valuable records of that age. Huang's political concerns also explain why he felt that poetry could be a force for altering political consciousness and regenerating Chinese society.

Huang's poetic practice was conservative by twentieth-century standards, but he made major innovations in Chinese poetic style. He certainly felt that the traditional *shih** form was capable of expressing the new ideas, but he frequently used eccentric verse forms and was noted for long narrative poems, which had been relatively rare until Ch'ing times. Of greater significance was Huang's readiness to inject colloquial expressions, foreign terms, and neologisms into classical-verse forms, and, long before Hu Shih and Ch'en Tu-hsiu, his advocacy of the abandonment of classical Chinese in favor of the vernacular (although he never put this into practice). However, probably the most startling innovation in Huang's poetry was his eagerness to introduce entirely new non-Chinese subject matter into his works, including the wonders of modern Western science and his observations of foreign society and culture.

Poems on his overseas experiences make up much of Huang's poetic corpus, works which range from pure observation to praise for the superior aspects of Western culture. But the collection also includes poems criticizing Western Christianity, imperialism, racism, and the shortcomings of bourgeois democracy. Another major portion of Huang's works describes the political debacle of late Ch'ing China and the attempts to arouse the Chinese people to resistance and reform. Closely connected to these creations is a large number of poems exposing and satirizing the dark side of nineteenth-century China, treating such problems as the low position of women in society, the poverty of the masses, the blind worship of tradition (including attacks on Confucianism), the moribund civil-service examination system, and the stultifying effects of imperial absolutism. In spite of Huang's great love for Chinese culture and his ardent nationalism, he consistently poked fun at Chinese ethnocentrism and advocated a future internationalism with all races living in harmony and mutual respect.

In addition to his main collection of poetry, Huang Tsun-hsien was famous for his

Jih-pen tsa-shih shih 日本雜事詩 (Poems About Miscellaneous Matters in Japan) and his prose *Jih-pen kuo-chih* 日本國志 (Treatises on Japan), in which he set up Meiji Japan as a model for Chinese emulation.

EDITIONS:

Jen-ching-lu shih-ts'ao 人境廬詩草 . Peking, 1930.

Jen-ching-lu shih-ts'ao chien-chu 人境廬詩草箋注. Shanghai, 1936. Detailed traditional commentary.

Jen-ching-lu shih-ts'ao chien-chu. Shanghai, 1957. Some new material added.

Jih-pen tsa-shih shih 日本雜事詩. Peking, 1879. Changsha, 1898. In this edition Huang incorporated numerous changes.

Jen-ching-lu chi-wai shih-chi 人境廬集外詩輯 . Peking, 1960.

Jih-pen kuo-chih 日本國志. Canton, 1890.

TRANSLATIONS:

Sunflower, pp. 500-505.

Shimada, Kumiko 島田久美子 , *Kō Junken* 黃遵憲. Tokyo, 1963.

Woon, Ramon L. Y. and Irving Y. Lo, "Poets and Poetry of China's Last Empire," *LEW,* 9 (1965) 331-361.

STUDIES:

Cheng, Tzu-yü 鄭子瑜. *Jen-ching-lu ts'ung-k'ao* 人境廬叢考 . Singapore, 1959.

Ch'ien, Chung-lien 錢仲聯. "Jen-ching-lu tsa-wen ch'ao" 人境廬雜文鈔 , *Wen-hsien,* March 1981, 62-78 and June 1981, 77-96.

ECCP, pp. 350-351.

Huang kung-tu Hsien-sheng chuan-kao 黃公度先生傳稿 . Hong Kong, 1972. Most extensive monograph on Huang to date.

Kamachi, Noriko. *Reform in China, Huang Tsun-hsien and the Japanese Model.* Cambridge, Mass., 1981.

Kuang-tung yü-wen hsüeh-hui chin-tai wen-hsüeh yen-chiu-hui 廣東語文學會近代文學研究會. *Huang Tsun-hsien yen-chiu* 黃遵憲研究. Mei-chou, 1982. An internal publication with papers read at a symposium on Huang Tsun-hsien held in Mei-chou 梅州 in 1982.

Mai, Jo-p'eng 麥若鵬 . *Huang Tsun-hsien chuan* 黃遵憲傳. Shanghai, 1957.

Schmidt, J. D. *Huang Tsun-hsien.* Boston: Twayne, 1982.

Wu, Chien-ch'ing 吳劍青. "Huang Tsun-hsien te shih-ko li-lun" 黃遵憲的詩歌理論 , *Huan-nan shih-yüan hsüeh-pao,* 3 (1980), 85-95.

Yang, T'ien-shih 楊天石 . *Huang Tsun-hsien.* Shanghai, 1979.

———. "Tu Huang Tsun-hsien chih Wang T'ao shou-cha" 讀黃遵憲致王韜手札 , *Shih-hsüeh chi-k'an,* 4 (1982), 32-38.

—JDS

Hung Liang-chi 洪亮吉 (*tzu,* Chün-chih 君直 and Chih-ts'un 稚存, *hao,* Pei-chiang 北江 and Keng-sheng 更生, 1746-1809), public official, scholar, poet, calligrapher, and literary critic, was a native of Yang-hu 陽湖 (Kiangsu). He twice changed his given name: from Lien 蓮 to Li-chi 禮吉 in 1772, and finally to Liang-chi in 1781. His father died when he was young, and, because of their poverty, his mother was compelled to return to her mother's home with her five children. Enjoying somewhat better circumstances, Hung Liang-chi and his brother were given typical schooling. Although he was ultimately to establish himself as one of the great scholars of his generation, he encountered numerous setbacks in the examination. He passed the *chü-jen* degree in 1780 after failing twice on previous attempts, and he was successful in the *chin-shih* examination in 1790, placing second on the list, after four successive failures. During the two decades preceding his ultimate success in the examinations, he served on the secretarial staffs of several prominent scholar-officials of the time. Both he and his friend Huang Ching-jen,* a leading contemporary, served under Chu Yün 朱筠 (1729-1781) when the latter was Education Commissioner in Anhwei. Following a period of similar employment with another official, Hung went to Peking where he was hired to assist the imperial commission then engaged in the compilation of the *Ssu-k'u ch'üan-shu* (see Chi Yün). In 1781 he was invited to join the staff of Pi Yüan 畢沅 (1730-1797), who was posted in Sian. As a result of his frequent travels and his service with these men, Hung made the acquaintance of many leading scholars, including Chang Hsüeh-ch'eng 章學誠 (1738-1801) and Wang Nien-sun 王念孫 (1744-1832), who undoubtedly stimulated his interests in scholarship.

When Hung Liang-chi finally obtained the highest examination degree, he was made a compiler in the Han-lin Academy. Thereafter, he served as Education Commissioner in Kweichow for a period of three years, after which he was assigned to the School for Imperial Princes in the capital. Following the death of the Ch'ien-lung Emperor, he addressed a letter to Yung-hsing 永瑆 (1752-1823), Prince Ch'eng, thus violating protocol. Moreover, he had spoken out too forthrightly about conditions in the empire and the person of the emperor. When Prince Ch'eng passed the letter on to the emperor, Hung was arrested and sentenced to decapitation. The emperor later commuted the sentence to banishment to Ili, Turkestan. Hung's stay in that distant city was unusually brief, however, for a serious drought in north China caused the emperor to issue a pardon allowing him to return home. For the next several years, he was employed as the director of the Yang-ch'uan 洋川 Academy in Ching-te, Anhwei.

Hung Liang-chi's career as a scholar was much more productive than his life as a civil servant. For instance, he made a distinguished contribution to regional history by assisting in the compilation of three local gazetteers during his Sian years. During the mid-1780s, he compiled a like number of local gazetteers for districts in Honan, and while director of Yang-ch'uan Academy, he compiled two more. He also authored the important geography of the empire entitled *Ch'ien-lung fu t'ing chou hsien chih* 乾隆府廳州縣志, as well as several works of historical geography. When he was an education commissioner in Kweichow, he wrote a study of its waterways, and as a result of his long trek to Ili on the western frontier, he compiled several works, including the travel diary, *I-li jih-chi* 伊犁日記. His interests as a *k'ao-cheng* 考證 scholar also embraced the classics and philosophy, and his complete works contain several studies of ancient texts, mostly of historical linguistics. As the century drew to a close and national social and economic problems became more apparent, Hung's attention shifted to current affairs, which he discussed in a series of essays. Several of these are of theoretical interest, for he called attention to the broad implications of the rapid population growth of the eighteenth century. The situation, he believed, was one of serious national concern, and he foresaw a widening gap between the productive capacity of the nation and its burgeoning population.

Hung Liang-chi was throughout his life a prolific writer, and his creative energies also found expression in poetic form. His complete works contain several large collections of verse which he carefully arranged and collated during his lifetime. Apparently quite conscious of how the future might judge his work, and always historical-minded, he dated most of his poems, and many have prefaces which carefully delineate the circumstances of their composition. His lifelong concern for the past is reflected in poems on historical sites and relics, for example the sixty-four poems on historical texts in the collection *Keng-sheng-chai shih-chi* 更生齋詩集. The thematic range of his verse is, of course, no less broad than his interests in formal scholarship, which makes his poems uniquely interesting as a literary record of his life and times. The overwhelming proportion of his poems are couched in the standard *shih** forms, but he chose on occasion to adopt the *tz'u** patterns, and these were gathered together in the collection *Keng-sheng-chai shih-yü* 更生齋詩餘.

Hung Liang-chi was also interested in poetic theory and practice, and his writings in that vein were collected in six *chuan* under the title *Pei-chiang shih-hua* 北江詩話. He had met Yüan Mei* early in his career and maintained close relations with him for many years. Not surprisingly, therefore, his own writings on poetry share with those of the older poet and theorist certain key concepts, such as the centrality of *hsing-ch'ing* 性情 (individual nature and feelings) to the poetic act. He also objected to excessive ornament, but he differed with Yüan Mei in stressing the importance of the historical factor in the achievements of past poets. Because he criticized Yüan Mei's own achievements as a poet after his death, later critics have faulted Hung for a lack of gratitude to his former friend and mentor.

EDITIONS:

Hung, Yung-ch'in 洪用勲, et al., eds. *Hung Pei-chiang Hsien-sheng i-chi* 洪北江先生遺集. 18v. Taipei, 1969. A photographic reprint of the 1877-79 edition.

Hung, Liang-chi. *Hung Pei-chiang shih-chi* 洪北江詩集. 66 *chüan*. SPTK.

———. *I-ming hui-shih* 彝銘會釋. Taipei, 1971. A study on bronzes not included in his collected works.

STUDIES:

Chang, Wei-p'ing 張維屏. *Kuo-ch'ao shih-jen cheng-lüeh* 國朝詩人徵略. N.p., preface dated 1820, *chüan* 51, fol. la-9b.

ECCP, pp. 373-375.

Jones, Susan Mann. "Hung Liang-chi (1746-1809): The Perception and Articulation of Political Problems in Late Eighteenth Century China." Unpublished Ph.D. dissertation, Stanford University, 1972.

———. "Scholasticism and Politics in Late Eighteenth Century China," *Ch'ing-shih wen-t'i*, 3.4 (December 1975), 28-49.

Lu, P'ei 呂培. *Hung Liang-chi nien-p'u* 洪亮吉年譜. Hong Kong, 1973. An emended and punctuated edition of this early work by one of Hung's disciples. A number of funerary inscriptions are also appended.

Ting, Yün-ch'in 丁蘊琴. "Hung Liang-chi p'ing-chuan" 洪亮吉評傳, *Tung-fang tsa-chih*, 41.20 (October 1945), 60-65.

Wu, *Ch'ing-tai*, pp. 245-248.

—WS

Hung-lou meng 紅樓夢 (The Dream of the Red Chamber), also known as *Shih-t'ou chi* 石頭記 (The Story of the Stone), is generally considered to be the greatest masterpiece of traditional Chinese fiction. Conceived and substantially completed by Ts'ao Hsüeh-ch'in,* it was first published in its 120-chapter form, with prefaces by Ch'eng Wei-yüan 程偉元 (c. 1742-c. 1818) and Kao E 高鶚 (c. 1740-c. 1815), in 1791, nearly thirty years after the author's death and probably more than fifty years after it had been begun. During the intervening period, unfinished manuscript transcriptions complete with commentary by a relative of Ts'ao writing under the pen-name Chih-yen Chai 脂硯齋 (Red Inkstone) were being circulated among the author's friends and the novel's growing circle of aficionados. Eventually such copies found their way onto the open market, where they sold for large sums. They all stopped short, however, at the eightieth chapter, leaving readers with scarcely a single strand in the complex plot resolved. Ch'eng and Kao claimed to have found a fragmentary original ending and to have edited it to produce a complete version. This claim of theirs has often been derided; they have been denounced as forgers and opportunists, who tacked their own "dog's fur" ending onto Ts'ao's "sable" masterpiece, in many ways going against the author's original intentions. The controversy over the authorship of the last forty chapters is one of many that still divide *Red*ologists, or *Stone*-scholars—*Hung-hsüeh chia* 紅學家 (*Red* Studies is a separate branch of scholarship comparable to Shakespeare Studies). Although no conclusive proof has yet been found to support either claim, most Chinese readers are familiar with the novel in its 120-chapter version.

If scholars cannot agree who wrote the last part of the novel, neither can they reach a consensus as to the novel's main theme. This is not just a question of difference in emphasis; what is in question is the very nature of the book. Is it primarily a novel of sentiment, a fiction treatise on love or a *Bildungsroman*, a record of Buddhist-Taoist disenchantment and enlightenment, or is it a novel of manners and social observation, chronicling in detail the decay of an aristocratic family and the roots of this decay in the social and historical contradictions of the late eighteenth century? Most critics agree that it is to a large extent autobiographical. The earliest interpretation saw the novel as a veiled attack on Manchu rule by a Han novelist; surely Ts'ao Hsüeh-ch'in had reason to write an attack of this sort. However, readers are unanimous in praising the genius with which the hundreds of characters are brought to life through physical and psychological observation and subtle differences in language.

The book begins with a prologue describing the origins of the attachment between the Divine Luminescent Stone-in-waiting 神瑛侍者 and the Crimson Pearl Flower 絳珠仙草. The first, endowed by the goddess Nü-wa with magical powers for the repair of the vault of heaven (though ultimately not used for this), is in fact the Stone of the book's alternative title. It is taken down into the world by an eccentric Buddhist monk and a Taoist priest, to live out a life as the young master of the wealthy Chia 賈 household, Pao-yü 寶玉, a strange child born with a jade in his mouth. The second, a delicate plant growing by the Magic River 靈河, attracts the roaming Stone, who conceives such a fancy for her that he takes to watering her every day with sweet dew, and thereby confers on her the gift of life. This fairy girl is born in the world as Lin Tai-yü 林黛玉, Pao-yü's frail and beautiful cousin, who after the death of her own mother comes to live with the Chia family; there her life is consumed in repaying the Stone for his kindness—her debt of tears. This level of mythical before-life existence, in terms of which the earthly destinies of the principal characters become intelligible, recurs again and again, and is one of the novel's main motifs. The otherworldly monk and priest often herald shifts between the mortal and divine levels; through dreams, characters make the journey from realm to realm.

The novel soon enters the mortal plane and establishes through several chapters filled with loving detail the ambience of the two huge and luxurious Chia family mansions, situated side by side in Two Dukes Street in the capital. This worldly structure is given its final touch in chapters 17 and 18 when Yüan-ch'un 元春, an imperial concubine and the eldest daughter of Chia Cheng 賈政, pays her family a ceremonial visit. In honor of the occasion, the family builds an elaborate landscape garden, linking together the two pleasure gardens of the adjoining mansions. This is Prospect Garden 大觀園. After the fleeting visitation is completed, it is Her Grace's wish that the girls of the family be allowed to occupy the garden. Each is given a little house of her own, and by a special dispensation Pao-yü is also allowed to join them. Ostensibly aloof from the physical and moral ugliness of the outside world, the garden provides an idyllic setting for the central section of the novel, chapters 23-80, where convivial picnics and poetry contests accompany the gradual movement of the young cousins through a charmed adolescence. It is only towards the end of this section that the outside decisively obtrudes, and the pressures and necessities of adult life begin to make themselves felt, leading to a concatenation of personal tragedies. Many have to do with the sexual desires—and responsibilities—of these pampered youths.

The growing love between Pao-yü and Tai-yü (the bond between Stone and Wood) from the start has been complicated by the presence of another girl-cousin, Hsüeh Pao-ch'ai 薛寶釵, who has a golden locket that corresponds in a mysterious way with Pao-yü's jade talisman (the bond of Gold and Jade). Pao-yü is also susceptible to her charms, which are quite different from Tai-yü's: her beauty is of the plumper sort; she is thoughtful, level-headed and mature, rather than slender, hyper-sensitive, and temperamental like Tai-yü. For many readers the triangular relationship between these cousins is the most absorbing theme of the book. It reaches its climax in chapters 97-98, when Pao-yü (now deranged after the loss of his jade) is tricked by his grandmother, mother, and sister-in-law into marrying Pao-ch'ai (he is led to believe that she is Tai-yü, whom he is by now determined to marry). While the ceremony is being performed, Tai-yü is dying a tragic and lonely death of consumption. The remaining chapters tell how after his marriage Pao-yü first fulfills his Confucian family obligations, then renounces the world and disappears from home to become a Buddhist monk.

If the filigree of these intense relationships provides the principal motif on the upper surface, the novel receives depth and structural support from the complex and powerfully depicted chronicle of the decline of the Chia family fortunes, the result of incessant abuse of power and dereliction of duty. This process reaches its climax with the traumatic governmental raid on both houses in chapter 105 and the subsequent imperial punishment of the worst offenders. This aspect of the novel is itself composed of many elements. Many characters and sub-plots contribute to its richness; the reader is presented with a totally convincing picture of a huge establishment packed with literally hundreds of individuals, who almost stand out from the page in three dimensions. This family universe is also connected at certain key points with the outside world, with Ch'ing society in the broader sense. Quite apart from the lords and ladies and young masters and mistresses (each of whom, whether the matriarch Grandmother Chia, the scheming manageress Wang Hsi-feng 王熙鳳, or the ill-fated young wife of Chia Jung 賈蓉, Ch'in K'o-ch'ing 秦可卿, seems to become an object of the reader's love or hate, friendship or enmity), there are servants of every rank. They include refined maids-in-waiting (whose personalities often serve as 'shadows' for their masters and mistresses), stewards, matrons, accountants, page-boys, cooks, tea-ladies, gardeners, cleaners. There are monks and nuns and their hangers-on; actors and actresses; officials, both upright and corrupt; members of the emperor's immediate entourage, princes, dukes, and a long procession of aristocrats; country bumpkins, estate managers, innkeepers, underworld characters, gamblers, pirates, prostitutes, kidnappers. Many of the sub-plots are substantial enough for novels in themselves.

The book is filled with detailed descriptions of clothes and customs, of buildings, gardens, plays, games, rules of etiquette, culinary delicacies, herbal prescriptions, fortune-telling, and liturgical rites. It is a mine of information on almost every aspect of traditional Chinese culture and social institutions. The novel is considered the purest repository of traditional Peking dialect. Furthermore, nearly every literary genre is represented in its pages. The *Hung-lou meng* is an encyclopedic novel, and yet its learning is worn lightly, never exhibited for its own sake, the details always convincingly presented as part of the characters' way of life.

The prominent lyrical and metaphysical themes (love, predestination and the "red dust" [i.e., the world in Buddhist perspective]) are balanced and supported by the elaborate presentation of a very material universe, the meticulous depiction of traditional Chinese culture during its last great flowering. And yet ultimately the very detail in which this reality is evoked serves only to underline the novels illusory, dreamlike nature, and to heighten the poignancy of the individual lives lived within it.

The novel's contrasting levels of "reality," whether the mythical world of goddesses, sylphs, and divine stones, or any of the social levels that appear in quotidian detail throughout its length, deliberately leave the reader confused over the author's or authors' vision and purpose. Ambiguity pervades every page, particularly through the narrative's elaborate structure (parallel events frequently take place on disparate social levels; servants reveal their master's traits), subtle plays on names and phrasing (for example, the numerous characters with shared elements in their names: *Pao*-ch'ai, *Pao*-yü, Tai-*yü*, Hung-*yü*, Miao-*yü*, etc.), and the absence of a reliable narrator (gossip between minor characters is a major source for information about the protagonists). Even the novel's multiple titles and several beginnings (all in chapter 1) increase the fascination *Hung-lou meng* has held for successive generations of readers.

Given the repeated references to the Buddhist sense of mortal life as suffering from which one should escape, many readers search the novel for religious and philosophical themes. Pao-yü remains very much immersed in the "red dust" of earthly attachments, particularly to Lin Tai-yü, until his sanity is nearly lost; only then, and through the initial assistance of Pao-ch'ai, does he manage to settle his social accounts and to break free, disappearing with the monk and priest on the path toward enlightenment. Other characters follow a similar route, particularly the pair of men who open and conclude the novel, Chia Yü-ts'un (whose name is a play on "gossip and hearsay") and Chen Shih-yin ("Real Facts Concealed" through homophones). While some readers claim that the perhaps greater bulk of social criticism in the novel constitutes the novelist's primary concern, clues supplied to the reader ("Truth becomes fiction when the fiction's true;/Real becomes not-real where the unreal's real") stress the unreliable nature of all realities narrated here and enhance the novel's legendary stature.

Hung-hsüeh has passed through several stages and has taken diverse directions. During the late Ch'ing period students of the novel often read it as the tale of a Manchu prince's illicit love affair; others saw it as an allegory for the problematic relations between Manchus and Chinese during that period of minority rule. The authorship was unknown during the Ch'ing, but later Hu Shih (1891-1962) identified autobiographical features in *Hung-lou meng* to usher in a new phase of Redology. Studies of texts and authorship flourished until the 1950s—and continue to do so outside the People's Republic—when Marxist critics condemned the individualism inherent in this approach and shifted attention to the novel's attack on the feudal social system and its ideology. The conscientious Paoch'ai thus represents the values of the Confucian elite—exemplified in its uglier side by Chia Cheng—while Pao-yü and Tai-yü represent a struggle for freedom from oppression. No one school of *Stone* scholars satisfactorily accounts for the novel's complex symbolism, although readers trained in Western literary criticism have made substantial contributions from this perspective. Surely the multiplicity of levels and realms of meaning can be identified as primary proof of the novel's greatness.

The *Hung-lou meng* has inspired numerous sequels, imitations, and adaptations in other literary and artistic forms. One of the most recent is a 1982 ballet on Tai-yü. International scholarly conferences have been held in Peking, Hong Kong, and Madison, Wisconsin. Exhibits of relevant materials and periodicals devoted to *Stone* studies have appeared in China and Hong Kong.

EDITIONS:

I. Available facsimiles of MS transcriptions
1. *Chia-hsü pen* 甲戌本 (original MS, 1754). Incomplete transcription once in the possession of Hu Shih. Published in Taipei (1961) under full title *Ch'ien-lung chia-shu Chih-yen chai ch'ung-ping Shih-t'ou chi* 乾隆甲戌脂硯齋重評石頭記. Subsequent reprints in both Taiwan and PRC.
2. *Chi-mao pen* 己卯本 (c. 1760). The transcription originally made for Prince I 怡親王. Edited by Feng Ch'i-jung 馮其庸 (Shanghai, 1981).
3. *Ch'üan ch'ao-pen* 全抄本. Full title, *Ch'ien-lung ch'ao-pen pai-nien hui Hung-lou meng kao* 乾隆抄本百廿回紅樓夢稿. A controversial 120-chapter manuscript, thought by some to be one of the transcriptions used by Kao E while editing his complete version (Peking, 1963).
4. *Keng-ch'en pen* 庚辰本 (c. 1761). Peking, 1955.
5. *Yu-cheng pen* 有正本. The first Chih-yen Chai edition to become popularly available. Published lithographically (Shanghai, first edition 1912).

II. EARLY PRINTED EDITIONS
1. *Ch'eng-Kao pen* 程高本. Two editions (at least), *chia* 甲 and *i* 乙, in movable type, followed each other in rapid succession in 1791-1792.
2. *Tao-kuang pen* 道光本. Popular designation for the common nineteenth edition with commentary by Wang Hsi-lien 王希廉, based on the Ch'eng-Kao *chia* edition. Later in the nineteenth century, commentaries by Yao Hsieh 姚燮 and Chang Hsin-chih 張新之 were added.

III. MODERN PRINTED EDITIONS
1. *Jen-min wen-hsüeh pen* A 人民文學本 A. First published in Peking, 1957, with notes by Ch'i-kung 啟功. Based on the second Ch'eng-Kao edition (*i-pen* 乙本). For twenty-five years the standard text.
2. *Pa-shih hui chiao-pen* 八十回校本. Edited by Yü P'ing-po 俞平伯. Peking, 1958. Based on *Yucheng pen* for first 80 chapters, on first Ch'eng-Kao edition (*chia-pen* 甲本) for last 40 chapters. Useful for the apparatus in volume 3, but now largely out of date.
3. *Jen-min wen-hsüeh pen* B 人民文學本 B. First published in Peking, 1982 (3v.), edited and annotated by a team under the general direction of Feng Ch'i-yung. First 80 chapters based on *Keng-ch'en*, last 40 based on first Ch'eng-Kao edition, *chia-pen*. Useful annotations.

TRANSLATIONS (IN CHRONOLOGICAL ORDER):

Dream of the Red Chamber. New York, 1958. C. C. Wang's second and enlarged version. Still worth reading if what you want is the love story without too many trimmings, but reduces the novel's grandeur.

Dream of the Red Chamber. New York, 1958. English version by Florence and Isabel McHugh of Franz Kuhn's German translation, *Der Traum der Roten Kammer.* Not recommended.

Kôrômu 紅樓夢. Itô Sôhei 伊藤漱平, trans., 3v. Tokyo, 1969.

A Dream of Red Mansions. 3v. Peking, 1978-1980. Yang Hsien-yi and Gladys Yang, trans. Complete and accurate, following *Jen-min* B.

Le Reve du Pavillon Rouge. Tche-houa Li, trans. Paris, 1967.

Son v krasnon tereme. V. A. Panasyuk. 2v. Moscow, 1958. Complete translation.

The Story of the Stone. 5v. Harmondsworth and Bloomington, 1973-1982. The first three volumes translated by David Hawkes, the last two by John Minford. A meticulous translation, mainly follows *Jen-min* A.

STUDIES:

Chao, Kang 趙岡 and Ch'en Chung-i 陳鍾毅. *Hung-lou meng hsin-t'an* 紅樓夢新探. Taipei, 1971. Many subsequent revised editions, with substantial changes.

Chen, Ch'ing-hao 陳慶浩. *Hsin-pien Shih-t'ou chi Chih-yen Chai p'ing-yü chi-chiao* 新編石頭記脂硯齋評語輯校. Rev. ed. Taipei, 1979. A systematic collection of Red Inkstone comments in the available transcriptions.

Chou, Ju-ch'ang 周汝昌. *Hung-lou meng hsin-cheng* 紅樓夢新證. Rev. ed. Peking, 1976.

Han, Chin-lien 韓進廉. *Hung-hsüeh shih-kao* 紅學史稿. Shih-chia-chuang, Hopei, 1981.

Hawkes, David. "The Translator, the Mirror and the Dream," *Renditions,* 13 (1980). See also his preface to the first three volumes of the Penguin (Hawkes and Minford) translation.

Hsia, C. T. *The Classic Chinese Novel.* New York, 1968. The chapter on *Hung-lou meng* is still the best short introductory essay available.

Hsiang-kang so-chien Hung-lou meng yen-chiu tzu-liao mu-lu 香港所見紅樓夢研究資料目錄. Hong Kong, 1972.

Hu, Shih 胡適. *"Hung-lou meng k'ao-cheng"* 紅樓夢考證. First published as preface to Ya-tung edition, 1927. Often reprinted, see *Hung-lou meng k'ao-cheng.* Taipei, 1961.

I-su 一粟 (Ch'ien Hsing-ts'un 錢杏邨), ed. *Hung-lou meng chüan* 紅樓夢卷. Peking, 1963.

———. *Hung-lou meng shu-lu* 紅樓夢書錄. Shanghai, 1958.

Li, Hsi-fan 李希凡 and Lan Ling 藍翎. *Hung-lou meng p'ing-lun chi* 紅樓夢評論集. Peking, 1957; 3rd rev. ed. Peking, 1973.

Lin, Yü-t'ang 林語堂. *P'ing-hsin lun Kao E* 平心論高鶚. Taipei, 1966; rpt. 1969.

Miller, Lucien. *Masks of Fiction in Dream of the Red Chamber.* Tucson, 1975. For a summary of textual studies, see Appendix B.

Na, Tsung Shun 那宗訓, ed. *Studies on Dream of the Red Chamber: A Selected and Classified Bibliography.* Hong Kong, 1979.

———. *Taiwan Studies on Dream of the Red Chamber.* Taipei, 1982.

P'an, Ch'ung-kuei. *Hung-hsüeh liu-shih nien* 紅學六十年. Taipei, 1974.

———. *Hung-lou meng hsin-pien* 紅樓夢新辨. Taipei, 1974.

Plaks, Andrew H. *Archetype and Allegory in the Dream of the Red Chamber.* New Jersey, 1976.

Wang, John C. H. "The Chih-yen chai Commentary and the *Dream of the Red Chamber,*" in *Chinese Approaches to Literature,* Adele Rickett, ed., Princeton, 1978, pp. 189-220.

Wang, Kuo-wei 王國維. *Hung-lou meng p'ing-lun* 紅樓夢評論, in I-su, ed., *Hung-lou meng chüan.* An inspired piece of criticism, written by the great early twentieth-century scholar who was also a follower of Schopenhauer.

Wu, Shih-ch'ang 吳世昌. *Hung-lou meng t'an-yüan wai-pien* 紅樓夢探源外編. Shanghai, 1980.

———. *On the Red Chamber Dream.* Oxford, 1961. The best introduction in English to the controversies of Redology, written by one of the greatest living Redologists.

Yü, P'ing-po 兪平伯. *Hung-lou meng pien* 紅樓夢辨. Shanghai, 1923.

———. *Hung-lou meng yen-chiu* 紅樓夢研究. Shanghai, 1952. This is a much revised version of Yü's pioneering work of the 1920s.

Yü, Ying-shih 余英時. *Hung-lou meng te liang-ko shih-chieh* 紅樓夢的兩個世界. Taipei, 1978.

PERIODICALS:

Hung-lou meng hsüeh-k'an 紅樓夢學刊. Tientsin, 1979- .

Hung-lou meng yen-chiu chuan-k'an 紅樓夢研究專刊. Hong Kong, 1967- .

Hung-lou meng yen-chiu chi-k'an 紅樓夢研究集刊. Shanghai, 1979- .

—JoM and REH

Hung Mai 洪邁 (*tzu*, Ching-lu 景廬, *hao*, Jung-chai 容齋, 1123-1202), famous together with his elder brothers Hung Kua 洪适 and Hung Tsun 洪遵, as one of the "Three Doctors Hung," was an extremely prolific essayist, storyteller, memorialist, and collector and critic of T'ang poetry; a friend, flatterer, and sometime critic of emperors; a historian of sorts, and an able provincial administrator who brought both material benefits and social security to the people under his care. The only blot on his reputation is his reputed penchant for concubines and courtesans, perhaps because of an unhappy married life. He lived to an advanced age and completed the bulk of his literary corpus during his last eleven years in retirement.

Born in P'o-yang 鄱陽 (modern Kiangsi), his early life was marred by the absence of his father, Hung Hao 洪皓 (1088-1155), who was sent as an envoy to the Chin in 1129, retained there for some years, and nearly executed several times for his loyalty to the Sung. Hung inherited his father's patriotic sentiments and he received the usual education of literati, developing an eclectic taste for the classics of Confucianism, Taoism, and Buddhism, as well as for history. He sharpened his prodigious memory by making three handwritten copies of Ssu-ma Kuang's 司馬光 (1019-1086) copious *Tzu-chih t'ung-chien* 資治通鑑. Passing the *chin-shih* examination in third place in 1145, he had an uneven official career, occupying a number of minor posts and being demoted once, until he went to the capital in 1158, served as a military advisor during a Sung victory at Ts'ai-shih, and was sent by Emperor Tao-tsung in 1162 as special envoy to the Chin to negotiate for the return of the body of Ch'in-tsung and the restoration of Sung territories. Involved in an altercation with the Chin emperor over the wording of his credentials, Hung refused to acknowledge Sung subordination to the Chin and was finally released after being imprisoned for several days without food. He was criticized, however, upon his return home for his failure to bring the negotiations to a successful conclusion.

After Hsiao-tsung became emperor in 1163, Hung held a number of minor posts during which time his memorials in parallel prose won the emperor's praise, and he was put in charge of expounding the *Shih-ching** to the emperor. Thus began a long friendship with Hsiao-tsung during which the emperor often presented him with specimens of his own poetry and calligraphy in the form of T'ang poems written on ornamental fans, and Hung in turn offered the emperor his vast collection of T'ang quatrains as well as good advice on running the empire. Coming into conflict with several court officials, Hung was retired briefly and then spent nearly fifteen years as a provincial administrator in parts of modern Kiangsi, Fukien, and Chekiang before he was recalled to the capital and reached his highest position as Han-lin Academician and Examination Director. His successes in the provinces included restoring military discipline, preventing the troops from making heavy exactions on the local population; constructing schools, bridges, and artificial lakes; famine and flood relief; and suppression of clan feuding and the practice of vendetta.

Hung Mai's literary works cover an extremely broad range including casual notebooks, official documents, his own verse, reports on local government, and tales of the supernatural. In this latter category Hung's *I-chien chih* 夷堅志 in 420 *chüan* (only a little over two-hundred *chüan* are extant) is the largest collection of stories after the *T'ai-p'ing kuang-chi.** Moreover, all of the nearly 2700 stories (original total) were written by Hung himself over the period 1161-1198. They deal with dreams, the human and supernatural worlds, origins of poems, etc.

Hung's *Jung-chai shih-hua* 容齋詩話 (Poetry Talks from the Tolerant Study) is also a remarkable work in that it contains primarily Hung's own comments on poetry rather than citing other authorities. The topics he addresses are diverse and still relevant today: Tu Fu's* poetic languages, and the influences of the *Ch'u-tz'u** and poetry of the T'ang on subsequent verse.

Hung also compiled a volume of colophons, a genre in vogue after Ou-yang

457

Hsiu* and Su Shih's* works in this area, entitled *Jung-chai t'i-pa* 容齋題跋 (Colophons from the Tolerant Study). It comments on poetic imitation (some comments identical to those in the *Jung-chai shih-hua*), linguistics, literature, and the classics.

Perhaps the best known work by Hung Mai is, however, his *Jung-chai sui-pi, wu-chi* 容齋隨筆五集 (Five Collections of Miscellaneous Notes from the Tolerant Study), a miscellany of 1217 useful, pithy essays on a host of subjects, classified under thirteen categories (women of the palace, civil and military functionaries, literature, language and orthography, etc.). In seventy-four *chüan*, the five collections were compiled over the last forty years of Hung's life.

Hung Mai was also an editor of note. His massive *Wan-shou T'ang-jen chüeh-chü* 萬首唐人絕句 (Ten Thousand Quatrains by Men of the T'ang) compiled during Hung's retirement in his home town during the 1180s (Hung was in his sixties at the time) was an influential collection (it also includes some pre- and post-T'ang works). It served as the "source" for Wang Shih-chen's* (1634-1711) *T'ang-jen wan-shou chüeh-chü hsüan.*

EDITIONS:

Chang, Fu-jui 張馥蕊, comp. *I-chien chih t'ung-chien* 夷堅志通檢 (Index du *Yi-kien tche*). Paris, 1976.

Harvard-Yenching Institute, comp. *Jung-chai sui-pi wu-chi tsung-ho yin-te* 容齋隨筆五集綜合引得. Rpt. Taipei, 1966.

I-chien chih 夷堅志. Original edition dated 1166; best edition is rpt. Shanghai, 1927; 216 *chüan*; rpt. Peking, 1960.

Jung-chai shih-hua. TSCC.

Wan-shou T'ang-jen chüeh-chü. Hung Mai, ed. 4v. Peking, 1955.

STUDIES:

Chang, Fu-jui. "Les themes dans le *Yi-kien-tche, Cina,* 8 (1964), 51-55.

———, "Le *Yi-kien-tche* et la société des Song," *JA,* 256 (1968), 55-93.

———. "L'influence du *Yi-kien Tche* sur les oeuvres literaires," in *Études d'histoire et de littérature offertes au Professeur Jaroslav Prusek,* Yves Hervouet, ed., Paris 1976, pp. 51-61.

———, [Tchang Fou-jouei]. "La vie et L'oeuvre de Hung Mai (1123-1202)." Unpublished Ph.D. dissertation, University of Paris VII, 1971.

Ch'ien, Ta-hsin 錢大昕. *Hung Wen-min kung nien-p'u* 洪文敏公年譜, in *Ssu Hung nien-p'u* 四洪年譜, Hung Ju-k'uei 洪汝奎, ed., n.p., 1909.

Eichhorn, W. "Zwei Episoden aus dem I-chien chih," *Sinologica,* 3 (1953), 89-96.

SB, pp. 469-478.

Wang, Te-i 王德毅. *Hung Jung-chai Hsien-sheng nien-p'u* 洪容齋先生年譜, in *Yu-shih hsüeh-pao,* 3.2 (April 1961), 1-63.

—MD & WHN

Hung Sheng 洪昇 (*tzu,* Fang-ssu 昉思, *hao,* Pai-hsi 稗畦, Pai-ts'un 稗村, Nan-p'ing Ch'iao-che 南屏樵者, 1645-1704) is one of the two most notable playwrights in the Ch'ing dynasty; he wrote in the style of *K'un-ch'ü.**

A native of Hangchow, Hung moved to Peking in 1666 to seek an advanced degree and an official career. In 1669 he was enrolled as a stipendiary student in the National University. His father was banished in 1672 for opposition to the Manchus. While he was living in Peking, Hung Sheng wrote and revised his representative work, the *Ch'ang-sheng tien* 長生殿 (The Palace of Eternal Youth), completed in 1688. The play, however, was condemned by the Manchu authorites for its allegedly seditious message, and Hung Sheng was expelled from the National University (1689). After his expulsion, he lived in retirement and poverty at West Lake in Hangchow until his death.

Although Hung Sheng is credited with twelve plays, most of them are now lost or in fragments; only the *Ch'ang-sheng tien* and *Ssu ch'an-chüan* 四嬋娟 (The Four Fair Ladies, *tsa-chü,** in four acts) are complete. He was also an accomplished poet, and two volumes of his poetry are extant.

The subject of the *Ch'ang-sheng tien,* in fifty scenes, is the well-known romance of Yang Kuei-fei and Emperor Ming-huang (r. 712-756) of the T'ang. Hung Sheng closely follows the historical incidents in the development of the story, but he uses his characters to comment on late-Ming society and politics.

The *Ch'ang-sheng tien* has been widely praised for the beauty of its poetry, and the perfect harmony of its musical compositions. The central theme is love. In an attempt to create a new order from the upheaval of the recent Ming-Ch'ing dynastic transition, Hung Sheng balances the traditional love for the state of the loyal subject with the new philosophy stressing the importance of personal love. He is strongly on the side of sentimentalism, and emphasizes love as the most essential element of life.

EDITIONS:

Ch'ang-sheng tien. Hsü shou-fang 徐朔方, ed. and annot. Peking, 1958; rpt. Taipei, 1975. The most reliable and the most readily available edition.
Pai-hsi chi, Pai-hsi hsü-chi 稗畦集，稗畦續集. Shanghai, 1957.
Ssu-ch'an ch'üan, in *Ch'ing-jen tsa-chü* 清人雜劇. Cheng Chen-to 鄭振鐸, ed. Rpt. Hong Kong, 1969.

TRANSLATIONS:

Yang, Hsien-yi and Gladys Yang. *The Palace of Eternal Youth.* Peking, 1955.

STUDIES:

Chang, Chun-shu and Hsueh-lun Chang. *Literature and Society in Early Ch'ing China.* Ann Arbor, Michigan, 1981. Chapter 2 studies Hung Sheng and his *Ch'ang-sheng tien;* it also summarizes much of Chinese and Japanese literature on Hung Sheng.
Chang, P'ei-heng 章培恆. *Hung Sheng nien-p'u* 洪昇年譜. Shanghai, 1979.
Ch'en, Wan-nai 陳萬鼐. *Hung Sheng yen-chiu* 洪昇研究. Taipei, 1970.
———. "Hung Pai-hsi hsien-sheng nien-p'u 洪稗畦先生年譜, *Yu-shih hseh-chih,* 7.2 (1968), 1-52; 3 (1968), 1-46.
ECCP, p. 375.
Fu, *Ch'ing tsa-chü,* pp. 78-79.
Huang, Ching-ch'in 黃敬欽. *Wu-t'ung yü yü Ch'ang-sheng tien pi-chiao yen-chiu* 梧桐雨與長生殿比較研究. Taipei, 1976.
Hung Sheng yü Ch'ang-sheng tien 洪昇與長生殿. Hong Kong, 1974.
Tseng, Yung-i 曾永義. *Ch'ang-sheng tien yen-chiu* 長生殿研究. Taipei, 1969.
———. "Hung Fang-ssu nien-p'u" 洪昉思年譜. *Chung-shan hsüeh-shu wen-hua chi-k'an,* 3 (1969), 825-941.

———. "Hung Sheng chi ch'i *Ch'ang-sheng tien*" 洪昇及其長生殿, in *Chung-kuo ku-tien hsi-chü lun-chi* 中國古典戲劇論集, Taipei, 1976, 245-277.

—CSC

Jen Fang 任昉 (*tzu,* Yen-sheng 彥昇, 460-508) was from Po-ch'ang 博昌 district of Yüeh-an 樂安, and claimed ancestry from the Han official Jen Ao 任敖 (second century B.C.). At fifteen he obtained employment as a recorder in the metropolitan area with a member of the Sung ruling clan, Liu Ping 劉秉. However, his manner seems to have given some offense in the Liu ménage, and shortly thereafter he was given the sinecure Audience Attendant, a sort of court usher. He gilded his reputation by sitting for the *hsiu-ts'ai* examination in Yen province and was promoted to be Erudite in the Court of Imperial Sacrifices and commissioned as adjutant.

He seems in no way to have been involved in the internecine intrigues among the Liu princes through which many of his colleagues met their fate, nor to have been affected by the overthrow of the Liu-Sung regime and the establishment of the Ch'i in 479. The only official record is that in 483 he was again at the capital, Chien-k'ang, as recorder to the powerful minister Wang Chien 王儉 (452-489). Jen's career prospered and he was appointed to the service of the Prince of Ching-ling, Hsiao Tzu-liang 蕭子良 (460-494), the great patron of letters.

The only shadow on Jen's career during these perilous decades was cast by a memorial he drafted on behalf of Emperor Ming of Ch'i (r. 494-498) during the latter's self-promotions leading to his usurpation of the throne. Emperor Ming deemed the text too abrasive, and as a result, Jen secured no preferment during his reign. But Shen Yüeh* lent him his support, and by the year 500, Jen had attained the office of vice director of the Secretariat.

In 501, Emperor Wu of Liang (r. 502-549) took Jen into his employ. In 507, Jen was commissioned as magistrate of Hsin-an 新安 (modern Honan) where he died after a year's service at the age of forty-eight. He was mourned by the emperor himself and given the posthumous rank of chamberlain for ceremonials.

During his lifetime he was admired for his literary abilities and worked as a hired pen for various princely courts. Under Emperor Wu of Liang, for example, the edicts of accession and other documents were mostly from his hand. He is said to have written in excess of a hundred thousand words. Although his poverty was a hallmark of his personal honesty, his household library contained over ten thousand *chüan*, including many rare texts. Indeed, the histories claim that after his death many of his books were borrowed to fill lacunae in the imperial holdings.

Jen was a gregarious man and in his later years endorsed many of the literati who would distinguish themselves during the Liang dynasty. Rare indeed is the Liang biography that does not include some admiring remark by Jen or Shen Yüeh, the "literary barons" of the time. At the height of his reputation, when he was Emperor Wu's palace aide to the censor-in-chief (502-507), he established the literary salon known as the Lan-t'ai chü 蘭臺聚 (Orchid-Terrace Association).

In an age when talent in lyrical poetry (*shih**) was paramount, the saying "Jen's prose (*pi* 筆) and Shen's poetry" was popular. Thus, while his prose is well-represented in the *Wen-hsüan,** his poetry is given no place in the *Yü-t'ai hsin-yung.** Fewer than two dozen of his verses and only one *fu** have been preserved, and these are mostly formal descriptions of banquets or presentation pieces. Nevertheless, while citing this neglect and suggesting that perhaps Jen had an unfavorable influence upon succeeding literati, Chung Hung's *Shih-p'in** awards Jen a secure position in the second category of poets—the equal of Shen Yüeh.

EDITIONS:

Jen Chung-ch'eng chi 任中丞集. *Pai-san*, v. 12, pp. 3047-3093.

Wen-chang yüan-ch'i 文章緣起. Ch'en, Mao-jen 陳懋仁, comm. *Wen-chang yüan-ch'i chu* 文章緣起註; Taipei, 1970; included in *Hsüeh-hai lei-pien* 學海類編, v. 138 (in *PPTSCC*, series 24), Taipei, 1967.

"Ch'üan Liang shih" 全梁詩, *ch.* 6: "Jen Fang" 任昉, *Nan-Pei-ch'ao shih*, v. 4, pp. 1300-1306.

Jen Fang chi 任昉集, in *Liu-ch'ao wen*, v. 3, *ch.* 41-44, pp. 3187-3206.

TRANSLATIONS:

von Zach, *Anthologie*, v. 1, pp. 372-373, 445, v. 2, pp. 648-650, 660-662, 702-715, 737-749, 764-767, 858-867, 1024-1036.

—JM

Jou p'u-t'uan 肉蒲團 (Prayer Mat of Flesh, also known as *Feng-liu ch'i-t'an* 風流奇談 [Marvellous Tales of the Romantic] and *Hsiu-hsiang Yeh-p'u yüan* 繡像耶蒲緣 [A Fable in Predestination—Illustrated Version]), is an erotic novel probably written by Li Yü* (1611-1680). According to the preface of an early Japanese edition (1705), it is the greatest erotic novel ever written. Its erotic nature notwithstanding, it deserves high praise as a novel. The storyteller's conventional mediation is discarded for an authorial stance allowing a refined interplay of irony between the characters, the plot, the readers and, less perceptibly, the author himself. The instructiveness of the conscious novelist may appear overindulgent, to paraphrase a remark of Liu T'ingchi 劉廷璣 at the beginning of the eighteenth century. As noted in the commentary to chapter 8, the story is clearly an allegory. On the other hand, the book does not pretend to hide its realistic, pornographic nature. The repetition which often becomes tedious in such works is carefully avoided. And the narrative is neatly woven towards a climax, the outcome of which is an apt, albeit artifical conclusion of the ironical Buddhist framework which follows the prologue (i.e., the first chapter). The structure of this rake's progress of a sort owes much to the drama.

The moralistic, Buddhist stance, which leads to self-emasculation, need not be taken seriously. Yet its assistance in denouncing the stingy Confucian puritanism it attacks, is certainly intended. However, this clashes with the prologue, where the author seems to express the view that sex is healthy, not at all devitalizing (as is the usual Chinese assertion) so long as it is "taken" as if it were a drug and not "consumed" as if it were an ordinary food. As a discriminating lover, the author is aware of the antinomies of conflicting claims between the sexes and within sexuality. His feminist stance, as in chapter 9, and his unusual interest in feminine sexuality, led Jeremy Ingalls to suggest the author was a woman.

The controversy about the authorship, initiated by James R. Hightower, should be resolved in favor of the traditional attribution to Li Yü* (1611-1680). The comments and contents of the novel fit his ideas well, approximate his taste in women, his craft of fiction, and his style and fluency in handling Chinese. The objection that such a mature book could not have been written at the young age of twenty-two does not stand up, since the presumed date of the preface (1633) is clearly given as 1693 in an older edition. Moreover, the said preface may not be the original one. The work could have been printed only after the death of Li Yü. For a long time its readership seems to have been restricted to a rather small circle of literate connoisseurs.

To compare *Jou p'u-t'uan* with the *Chin P'ing Mei** is rather irrelevant. Chapter 3 hints at an inspiration from medium-sized erotic novels fairly numerous in the late Ming period. Political undertones no doubt have been overstressed by the first translator, Franz Kuhn; still the role played by the masterthief who opposes officialdom and is raised to the level of a saintly monk cannot be overlooked.

EDITIONS:

Jou p'u-tu'an. Subtitle *Chüeh-hou ch'an* 覺後禪. 1693. Punctuated, four sections, each with 5 chapters. Woodblock printed.

———. "Translated" by Chūsuirō shujin 儔翠樓主人. Seishinkaku 青心閣 (Japan), 1705. Punctuated. Woodblock printed.

Hsiu-hsiang Yeh-p'u yüan. Kwangtung, 1894. With illustrations. Four sections, each with 4 chapters. Lithographically reproduced. No punctuation.

Feng-liu ch'i-t'an. N.p., n.d.; probably early Republican Period. Illustrated and punctuated; lithographically reproduced.

See also Martin's "Appendix D" (cited below) which discusses 19 editions and their inter-

relationships (recent facsimile versions of the 1705 edition have appeared in Hong Kong and Taiwan).

TRANSLATIONS:

Fushimi, Okitaka 伏見沖敬. *Niku futon* 肉蒲團. Tokyo, 1963.

Kuhn, Franz. *Jou Pu Tuan.* Zürich, 1959. A popular rendering which has been retranslated into English by Richard Martin (see below) and a number of other languages including Chinese (Hong Kong, 1968)!

Martin, Richard. *Jou Pu Tuan: The Prayer Mat of Flesh.* New York, 1963. From Kuhn's German rendering. Reprinted under the title *The Before Midnight Scholar,* London, 1965.

Pimpaneau, Jacques and Pierre Klossowski. *Jeou-P'ou-T'ouan, ou la chair comme tapis de prière, roman publié vers 1660 par le lettré Li-Yu.* Preface by René Etiemble. Paris, 1962. Though it omits the poems, this is the preferred translation, which best catches Li Yü's wry humor. Pimpaneau did the basic translation (based on the 1693 ed.) which was polished by Klossowski, a well known author with no knowledge of Chinese.

STUDIES:

Ao-ao 翱翱. "Kuan-yü *Jou p'u-t'uan*" 關於肉蒲團, *Ming-pao yüeh-k'an,* 79 (July 1972), 58-59.

Hightower, James R. "Franz Kuhn and his translation of *Jou p'u-t'uan,*" *OE,* 8 (1964), 252-257.

Huang, Chün-tung 黃俊東. "Feng-liu hsiao-shuo *Jou p'u-t'uan:* Ming-mo i-pu ch'i-t'e te se-ch'ing wen-hsüeh ming-chu" 風流小說肉蒲團 明末一部奇特的色情文學名著, *Wen-hsüeh pao,* 14 (September 1971), 27-29; 15 (October 1971), 28-31.

Ingalls, Jeremy. "Mr. Ch'ing-yin and the Chinese Erotic Novel," *YCGL,* 13 (1964), 60-63.

Martin, Helmut. Appendix D: "*Jou p'u-t'uan,* Textausgaben, Autorschaft, Datierung," in *Li Li-weng über das Theater,* Taipei, 1968, pp. 279-301. The most thorough investigation of these subjects.

—AL

Ju-lin wai-shih 儒林外史 (Unofficial History of the Literati) written in the mid-eighteenth century (first extant edition, 1803), occupies an important place among major Chinese novels as the first lengthy sustained piece of satire in the fictional mode.

The tradition of social concern it spawned was developed in the fiction of such turn-of-the-century authors as Li Pao-chia,* Wu Wo-yao,* and Liu E.* Under the political stresses of more recent times, this tradition took on great vitality and can be said to dominate the twentieth-century Chinese literary scene.

The morality which the *Ju-lin wai-shih* espouses, however, is neither modern nor political. The novel's satire is based on idealistic Confucianism, and the eremitic standards with which it measures Chinese society can be traced to the life and career of its author Wu Ching-tzu 吳敬梓 (1701-1754).

A member of an aristocratic Anhwei family with a long record of success in officialdom, Wu spent his youth preparing to compete in the civil-service examination and to enter the government bureaucracy. However, his initial taste of success in becoming a *sheng-yüan* in 1723 coincided with the death of his father, whom he worshiped. Weighed down by the responsibilities of managing the family estate and by the memory of having had to leave the side of a dying parent in order to compete for a conventional honor, he soon lost interest in career pursuits and began a life of dissipation in the pleasure districts of Nanking. In 1733, having squandered a large part of his inheritance and fast becoming the object of ridicule in his native town of Ch'üan-chiao 全椒, he decided to give up further aspiration for official position and move permanently to Nanking. There he led the life of a recluse, declining a final opportunity to enter officialdom by ignoring advice to take a special examination in 1736. He used up the last of his capital to finance a sacrificial ceremony for a Confucian sage and entered the destitution which plagued him for the rest of his days.

There is much evidence in Wu's extant poetry to indicate that he was not insensitive to criticism and that his decision to give up the conventional path to wealth and status was not made without some doubt and anguish. The *Ju-lin wai-shih*, which provides example after example of the moral and intellectual decay which

wealth and status bring, can therefore be seen as Wu's *Apologia pro Vita Sua*.

It is remarkable that Wu chose fiction as the vehicle for his essentially serious task. In his time fiction was associated with entertainment and was regarded as unworthy of thoughtful attention. On the other hand, there is an evident appropriateness in using fiction for satire, since it allowed Wu to present moral arguments with apparent casualness and indirection.

Because Wu's narrator adopts the objective pose and seldom interrupts to explain the point of the incidents he relates and because the particular conditions Wu criticizes have faded into history, the moral basis of the satire in the *Ju-lin wai-shih* has been greatly misunderstood. Nearly all critics appear to be aware of the work's satirical nature, but in recent times have tended to judge it according to principles of realism, in either the Marxist or nine-teenth-century European sense.

The *Ju-lin wai-shih* does show a finely textured depiction of detail as well as an acute awareness of the social conditions of its times. As satire, however, it is basically not intended to explore or reflect reality, but rather to persuade the reader to take a certain moral position. The account of the artist-hermit Wang Mien 王冕, in the opening chapter, and that of the four eccentrics, near the end, clearly argue for a life of uncompromising self-cultivation, possible only to those who are unencumbered by the competitive quest for riches and social position. Most of the rest of the work is taken up with a variety of characters who, in one way or another, fall short of Wu's moral standards and descend swiftly into inhumanity and ignorance.

The idealistic Confucian morality is matched by the terse and noncommittal manner in which it is expressed. The *Ju-lin wai-shih's* consistent method of presenting facts for the reader to decipher can be traced to the historiography of the *Ch'un-ch'iu* (see *ching*) attributed to Confucius himself. Such a method deviates from that employed in previous vernacular fiction and places a heavy demand on the reader, who is expected to have an alert and cultivated mind. With the *Ju-lin wai-shih*, Chinese fiction can be said to have moved from its folk origins a step closer to high-brow literature.

Still, the debt the work owes to the popular storyteller is undeniable. Like so many other works of fiction since the Ming, the *Ju-lin wai-shih* is written in free-flowing vernacular prose, and it bears the superficial trappings of entertainment narrative: a detached and omniscient narrator employing a variety of phrase-markers to signal bits of intrusive and formulaic commentary. The prose, moreover, is not always terse and elliptical but exhibits a paradoxical exhaustiveness in description as well as exuberance in speeches. It is therefore more accurate to characterize the *Ju-lin wai-shih* as a hybrid of the folk and belletristic traditions of Chinese literature.

Along with the celebrated *Hung-lou meng*,* the *Ju-lin wai-shih* marks the mid-eighteenth century as the time when the Chinese novel came into its own, even as the Chinese people remained totally isolated from the contemporary works of Defoe, Richardson, and Fielding which were shaping the directions of fiction in Enlightenment Europe.

EDITIONS:

Ju-lin wai-shih. Wo-hsien ts'ao-t'ang 臥閑草堂. 56 ch. Notes by an anonymous commentator; dated 1803. 4v. Rpt. Peking, 1975. Most authoritative text for scholarly purposes.

———. Tso-chia ch'u-pan she, ed. Peking, 1954. Faithful reproduction of the first 55 *chüan* of the Wo-hsien ed.; in modern type and punctuation; also explanatory notes. Available in several modern reprints.

———. Chang Hui-chien 張慧劍, ed. and annot. Peking, 1958. Modern edition in simplified characters; useful as reference.

TRANSLATIONS:

Tchang, Fou-jouei 張馥蕊. *Chronique indiscrète des mandarins.* Paris, 1976. Introduction by André Lévy.

Yang, Hsien-yi and Gladys Yang. *The Scholars.* Peking, 1957. Rpt. New York, 1972. Reset and reissued in Peking, 1973. A generally accurate and nearly complete translation (leaves out chapter 56 and various passages).

STUDIES:

Cheng, Ming-li 鄭明娳. *Ju-lin wai-shih yen-chiu* 儒林外史研究. Taipei, 1976. Valuable mostly for bibliography.

———. "Ju-lin wai-shih lun-chu mu-lu pu-p'ien 儒林外史論著目錄補編." *Shu-mu chi-k'an,* 11.1 (January 1977), 101-110. More bibliography.

Ho, Tse-han 何澤翰. *Ju-lin wai-shih jen-wu pen-shih k'ao-lüeh* 儒林外史人物本事考略. Shanghai, 1957. Indispensible work on the historical background of the novel.

Hsia, C. T. "The Scholars," *Novel,* pp. 203-244.

Hu, Shih 胡適. "Wu Ching-tzu nien-p'u 吳敬梓年譜," in *Hu Shih wen-ts'un* 胡適文存, Shanghai, 1924, Series 2, I, 1-50. Still the best source for facts on Wu's life.

Inada, Takashi. "*Jurin gaishi* no iwayuru kōtei-teki jimbutsu ni tsuite 儒林外史のいわゆる肯定的人物について." *Tōkyō Gakugei Daigaku kenkyū hōkoku,* 13.11 (1962), 21-29.

Kràl, Oldrich. "Several Artistic Methods in the Classic Chinese Novel *Ju-lin wai-shih,*" *AO,* 32 (January 1964), 16-43.

Lin, Shuen-fu 林順夫. "Ritual and Narrative Structure in *Ju-lin Wai-shih,*" in *Chinese Narrative,* pp. 244-265.

Ropp, Paul S. *Dissent in Early Modern China: "Ju-lin wai-shih" and Ch'ing Social Criticism.* Ann Arbor, 1981.

Tso-chia ch'u-pan she 作家出版社. *Ju-lin wai-shih yen-chiu lun-chi* 儒林外史研究論集. Peking, 1955. Most convenient source for expression of the Marxist view, by some of China's leading scholars.

Tsukamoto, Terukazu 塚本照和. *Nihon to Chūgoku ni okeru Jurin gaishi kenkyū yōran kō* 日本と中國における儒林外史研究要覽稿. Nara, 1971.

"Wu Ching-tzu," *ECCP,* pp. 866-867.

Wong, C. Timothy 黃宗泰. *Wu Ching-tzu.* Boston, 1978.

—TW

Juan Chi 阮籍 (*tzu,* Ssu-tsung 嗣宗, 210-263), son of Juan Yü* and a poet of the first rank, is popularly known as a drunkard and free-living Taoist, and a member of the Chu-lin ch'i-hsien 竹林七賢 (Seven Sages of the Bamboo Grove). His real importance in the Chinese poetic tradition rests on his eighty-two pentameter poems entitled "Yung-huai shih" 詠懷詩 (Poems from My Heart) which describe his anguish and fear and his desire to find constancy and purity in an inconstant and impure world.

The son of an intimate of the Ts'ao 曹 family, Juan Chi was himself an official of their dynasty (the Wei) from 239 and witnessed the gradual usurpation of power by the Ssu-ma 司馬 family, who set up their own Chin dynasty shortly after his death. Juan Chi himself served the Ssu-ma leaders and was thus at the center of poltical life although he never really took an active part in it. He must have realized very early that the Wei were doomed and that any political role he might play would help the Ssu-ma. The latter would consider, too, any lamenting of the passing of the Wei as seditious. Juan Chi's poetry therefore abounds in obscure satire and allegory, and some poems (e.g., nos. 56, 64, 66) are close to impenetrable. He is reduced to expressing, in the most "abstruse and distant" terms (as Ssu-ma Chao 昭 said of his conversation), the frustration and indignation of a courtier who finds it impossible to serve his lawful sovereign. This abstraction gives his verse a special quality which Juan Chi innovated; unable to find fulfillment in politics (the normal realm of action for a man of his class and times), he turned towards philosophy and religion, and in particular to Taoist mysticism, not, as previous poets had done, versifying Lao-tzu's and Chuang-tzu's doctrines mechanically, but debating with himself on philosophical and religious problems (poems 22, 41, 78), exploring, in a subjective, introverted way, themes unknown in earlier poetry.

There are also six *fu** by Juan Chi, three *lun* (essays), two letters, three set pieces (among which are a memorandum [*tsou-chi* 奏記] and a memorial [*chien* 牋], both included in *Wen-hsüan*), and a biography. His essays "Yüeh lun" 樂論 (On Music) and "T'ung I lun" 通易論 (Penetrating the *I-ching*) are Confucian in tone, the former being extremely conservative and traditional. The "Tung-p'ing fu" 東平賦 and "K'ang-fu fu" 亢父賦 are strange, misanthropic diatribes against these two localities (in modern Shantung); "Shou-yang shan" 首陽山 examines the problem of retreat from politics; "Chiu fu" 鳩賦 (Prose-poem on the Doves) and "Mi-hou fu" 獮猴賦 (Prose-poem on the Monkey) are sa-

tirical. "Ch'ing-ssu fu" 清思賦 (Prose-poem on Purifying the Thoughts) describes, in quasi-psychedelic language, a mystical encounter with a sexually-alluring, immortal woman. "Ta Chuang lun" 達莊論 (Essay on Understanding Chuang-tzu), while ostensibly a diatribe against a group of Confucianists, is actually an attempt to reanimate Confucianism with Taoist metaphysics. His longest prose work, "Ta-jen Hsien-sheng chuan" 大人先生傳 (Biography of Master Great Man), also his most influential, describes a figure inspired by Chuang-tzu who mocks vulgar Confucianists (whom he compares to a louse in a pair of drawers) and praises mystical freedom, ending in a *fu*-like evocation of a True Man (*chen-jen* 眞人).

Juan Chi has always been something of a poet's poet, his fame among the uninitiated being widely based on his "Taoist" eccentricities and on his drunkenness. But the great poets of China were not mistaken: their quotations of his poetry in their works and their allusions to him show that they understood his essential nobility, his purity and fidelity to Confucian principles when the times made political commitment impossible.

EDITIONS:

Juan Chi chi 阮籍集. Shanghai, 1978. Punctuated and with textual variants, based on the earliest edition (mid-sixteenth century). The order of the poems differs from that (based on the *Ku shih-chi**) in most later editions and used in the above article.

Huang, Chieh 黃節, ed. *Juan Pu-ping Yung-huai shih-chu* 阮步兵詠懷詩注 (preface dated 1926), Peking, 1957. The most useful commentary on the poetry alone.

Liu-ch'ao wen, v. 2, pp. 1303-1318.

TRANSLATIONS:

Frodsham, *Anthology*, pp. 53-67.

Gundert, *Lyrik*, pp. 47-48.

See also Holzman below.

STUDIES:

Holzman, Donald, *Poetry and Politics: The Life and Works of Juan Chi (210-263)*. Cambridge, 1976. Contains a complete translation of the poetry, *fu*, and most of the prose.

Matsumoto, Yukio 松本幸男. *Gen Seki no shōgai to Eikaishi* 阮籍の生涯と詠懷詩. Tokyo, 1977.

For the historical background, there is a complete translation of the eighty-two poems (with commentary) and a concordance.

Ch'iu, Chen-ching 邱鎮京. *Juan Chi Yung-huai shih yen-chiu* 阮籍詠懷詩研究. Yung-ho, Taiwan, 1980.

—DH

Juan Ta-ch'eng 阮大鋮 (*tzu,* Chi-chih 集之, *hao,* Yüan-hai 圓海, Shih-ch'ao 石巢, and Pai-tzu-shan Chiao 百子山樵, 1587-1646) was a notable dramatist and a poet.

A native of Huai-ning 懷寧 (Anhwei), Juan came from a line of prominent political figures. He passed the *chin-shih* examination in 1616, but chose to join Wei Chung-hsien 魏忠賢 (1568-1627) to advance his political career. Wei, one of the most powerful eunuchs in Chinese history, moved against his critics with savage ferocity. Among them were members of the Tung-lin 東林 politico-literary faction. When Wei finally fell, Juan was deprived of all titles, and had to live in retirement from 1629 to 1644. During these years he wrote several plays, including *Ch'un-teng mi* 春燈謎 (Spring Lantern Riddles); his aim was to rationalize his former connection with the eunuch faction. The attempt failed; Juan was denounced in a public statement signed by 140 prominent literati.

With the Manchu conquest of north China, Juan fled southward under the protection of his friend Ma Shih-ying 馬士英 (1591-1646). Together they headed the rump Ming government of Prince Fu in Nanking. Juan used this position to enrich himself and to take revenge on his enemies. Ultimately, he surrendered to the Manchus to punish further the Ming loyalists who had snubbed him. He was accidentally killed on a campaign with the Manchus. Hostile historians delight in noting that he died without male offspring.

A follower of T'ang Hsien-tsu's* Lin-ch'uan School, Juan concentrated on romanticism in his plays, many of which are now lost. According to Chang Tai,* Juan's private performances of his own plays were a great delight, with Juan striving to perfect every element of sight and sound with loving care. His political reputation adversely affected the reception given his writings.

Juan Ta-ch'eng's best known play is *Yen-tzu chien* 燕子箋 (The Swallow's Love Note), apparently written to celebrate the coronation of Prince Fu in 1645. In it, two young scholars, Huo and Hsien, arrive in the captial to take the examinations, taking lodging with a famous courtesan named Hsing-yün. Huo paints a portrait of himself with the prostitute, but the scroll-mounter confuses this with another order and delivers the painting to a high minister's daughter, Fei-yün. This sequestered maiden falls in love with the man in the painting and as she becomes more and more lovelorn, pours out her feelings in a note—conveniently carried to Huo by a swallow. He succumbs to longing for its author. The two men pass the examination, although Hsien resorts to cheating; civil war erupts, and the lovers become separated, taking false names for protection. Through a series of coincidences, Huo and Fei-yün are eventually wed, Hsien is discredited, and Hsing-yün becomes Huo's concubine to end the drama happily.

While this play and *Ch'un-teng mi* were performed into the twentieth century, Juan Ta-ch'eng is probably better known as a villain in K'ung Shang-jen's* play *T'ao-hua shan.* The character Juan tries to win a young hero over to his side in the late Ming political struggles. He even attempts to bribe the man's mistress. His gifts occasion (in scene 7) the lady's staunch declaration of her own political scruples. When repeatedly snubbed for his shady dealings, Juan has the young man imprisoned to prevent their reunion. His revenge is soon thwarted by political struggles at the fall of the Ming. Ultimately he falls, a victim of his own pettiness and greed.

EDITIONS:

Shih-ch'ao ch'uan-ch'i ssu-chung 石巢傳奇四種, rpt. in *Sung-fen-shih ts'ung-k'an erh-pien* 誦芬室叢刊二編. Tung K'ang 董康, ed. Wu-chin, 1919. In turn reproduced in *Ku-pen,* II. Includes the plays: *(Shih ts'o-jen) Ch'un-teng-mi* (十錯認) 春燈謎, 2 *chüan; (K'an hu-tieh) Shuang chin-pang* (勘蝴蝶) 雙金榜, 2 *chüan; (Ma-lang-hsia) Mou-ni-ho* (馬郎俠) 牟尼合, 2 *chüan; Yen-tzu*

465

chien, 2 *chüan*. The last has also appeared separately in various modern editions, the latest of which is *Yen-tzu ch'ien*, Hong Kong, 1965.

STUDIES:
Dolby, *History*, pp. 99, 102, 127.
ECCP, pp. 398-399.

—REH

Juan Yü 阮瑀 (*tzu*, Yüan-yü 元瑜, d. 212) was a native of Ch'en-liu 陳留 (modern Honan). This pupil of Ts'ai Yung* entered Ts'ao Ts'ao's service and was one of the poets patronized by the latter's two sons. Ever since Ts'ao P'i's* "Tien-lun lun-wen," he has been regarded as one of the Seven Masters of the Chien-an Era (see Ch'en Lin). It is said that in order to bring the reluctant Juan Yü over to his side, Ts'ao Ts'ao had to set fire to the mountain where the former was in hiding. This is mere legend, already challenged by P'ei Sung-chih 裴松之 (372-451) who quotes it in his commentary on the *San-kuo chih;* the story, however, derives some credibility from the nature of Juan Yü, who appears to have had little in common with the typical poet of his day.

In their capacity as secretaries to Ts'ao Ts'ao, Juan Yü and Ch'en Lin followed him on his campaigns and wrote most of his letters and proclamations. According to the "Tien-lüeh" 典略, quoted by P'ei Sung-chih, Juan Yü once composed on horseback the draft of a letter which Ts'ao Ts'ao, with his brush in his hand, passed unamended. Two letters written by Juan Yü on behalf of his general have survived.

Of the poet's work there remain only four *fu** and a dozen *shih*, several of which seem to be incomplete or apocryphal. His most famous poem, "Chia ch'u pei-kuo men" 駕出北郭門 (Driving My Chariot Out the Gate of the Northern Suburbs), draws its inspiration from popular ballads, like many other *yüeh-fu** of that period; it tells, in an unadorned and straightforward manner, the misfortunes of an orphan. Although some further pieces may be likened, because of their themes, to the works of his contemporaries (in the genre of the *fu:* the military campaign, the captive parrot; in that of the *shih:* separation, the ban-

quet, the death of the three gentlemen sacrificed over Mu-kung's grave), Juan Yü's favorite subjects appear to have been old age and death ("Ch'i-ai shih" 七哀詩 is a dead man's prosopopoeia), rather than the longings and disillusionments of youth. His style is characterized by an air of impassibility, as well as by a degree of rusticity and a conspicuous disdain of ornament. Lastly, the interest he takes in Taoism and the reclusive life (see in particular the poem entitled "Yin-shih" 隱士) sets him apart from his contemporaries, with their passion for action, and makes him a forerunner of the philosophical poets that flourished during the next period, especially his own son, the great poet Juan Chi.*

EDITIONS:
Juan Yüan-yu chi 阮元瑜集, in *Pai-san*, v. 1, pp. 151-162.
Liu-ch'ao wen, v. 1, pp. 973-974.
Nan-pei-ch'ao shih, v. 1, pp. 265-268.

TRANSLATIONS:
Frodsham, *Anthology*, p. 32.
Hightower, J. R. "The *Fu* of T'ao Ch'ien," in *Studies in Chinese Literature*, J. L. Bishop, ed., Cambridge, Mass., 1965, pp. 172-174 (*Chih-yü fu* [Putting a Stop to Desires]).
Liu, James J. Y. *The Chinese Knight-Errant.* Chicago, 1967, p. 77.
Miao, Ronald C. "The 'Ch'i ai shih' of the Late Han and Chin Periods" (I), *HJAS*, 33 (1973), p. 210.

STUDIES:
Suzuki, *Kan Gi*, pp. 467-471.
Shimosada, Masahiro 下定雅弘. "Gen U no go-gonshi ni tsuite" 阮瑀の五言詩について, *Chūgoku bungaku hō*, 24 (1974), 22-47.

—JPD

K'ang Hai 康海 (*tzu*, Te-han 德涵, *hao*, Tui-shan 對山, P'an-tung yü-fu 泮東漁夫, Hu-hsi shan-jen 湖西山人, 1475-1541), a native of Wu-kung 武功 (modern Shensi), was a versatile writer of poetry, essays, and drama from a family of officials. As a child K'ang was considered a prodigy; he reputedly so impressed his teacher with his writings that he predicted K'ang would attain the first rank in the capital examinations, which he did in 1502. He was appointed a compiler in the Han-lin Academy, but after one year retired to care for his parents. He remained in retirement until 1506 when he returned to the capital and obtained a post compiling historical records. The following year he lectured on the classics at the National University, and in 1508 he was appointed an examination official. During his years in the capital K'ang made a name for himself and attracted the attention of his superiors. His name became linked with those of six other young capital poets known collectively as the *Ch'ien-ch'i tzu* (Earlier Seven Masters—see Li Meng-yang).

Liu Chin 劉瑾 (d. 1510), a powerful court eunuch also from Shensi, was impressed by K'ang Hai and desired to attract the young man to his entourage, but K'ang resisted his advances. In 1506-1507 when Han Wen 韓文 (1441-1526) and other high officials attacked the power of the eunuch, K'ang Hai was drawn into the factional dispute through his friendship with Li Meng-yang.* It was Li who drafted the memorial accusing Liu of corrupting the emperor and leading him astray. When the attack against Liu failed, Li Meng-yang along with the others, was dismissed from office. He retired to his brother's farm in Kaifeng, but was arrested in the winter of 1508 and imprisoned in Peking for writing some poems critical of Liu Chin.

Li then begged K'ang Hai to appeal to Liu Chin on his behalf. K'ang interceded and Li was released. However, when Liu was arrested and executed in 1510, all those associated with him were dismissed. Since K'ang had been able to persuade Liu to pardon Li, he was charged with collaboration with Liu and dismissed from office. At the same time Li Meng-yang was praised for his opposition to Liu and recalled to office.

K'ang Hai spent the last thirty years of his life in retirement. Apparently he led the life of an eccentric hermit, cultivating the image of an unrestrained, dissolute drunkard. Together with his friend Wang Chiu-ssu, he passed the time drinking, composing songs, and playing the *p'i-p'a*. There are many stories which contribute to this image of K'ang.

During his years in retirement K'ang edited a local gazetteer and compiled a genealogy of his mother's family. In addition, he left a collection entitled *Tui-shan chi* 對山集 (Facing the Mountain Collection), but the prose and poetry therein have been judged mediocre. K'ang's literary reputation rests on his collection of *san-ch'ü* 散曲 (see *ch'ü*), *P'an-tung yüeh-fu* 泮東樂府 (in 2 chüan), and two *tsa-chü** attributed to him, *Chung-shan lang* 中山狼 (The Wolf of Chung-shan) and *Wang Lan-ch'ing* 王蘭卿.

Around the turn of the sixteenth century there was a reemergence of interest in the *san-ch'ü*. K'ang Hai and Wang Chiu-ssu are considered leaders of the *Hao-fang* 豪放 school, while Wang P'an 王磐 and Chen To** are representative of the *Ch'ing-li* 凊麗 school. Typically the song suites of the *Hao-fang* school are described as being direct, forceful, natural, and without artifice, in contrast to those of the *Ch'ing-li* school which are described as emphasizing beautiful, delicate diction, and restrained graceful lyrics. K'ang's own collection of *san-ch'ü* contains over two hundred individual songs (*hsiao-ling*) and some thirty longer suites (*t'ao-shu*). His *san-ch'ü* may be divided thematically into two major groups: poems of resentment or frustration, and poems on the pleasures of a life of leisure.

K'ang's best known work is his *tsa-chü* about the Mohist and the ungrateful wolf, *Tung-kuo Hsien-sheng wu-chiu chung-shan-lang* 東郭先生誤救中山狼 (Mr. Eastern-wall Mistakenly Rescues the Wolf from Central Mountain). This play has also been attributed to Li Meng-yang and to K'ang Hai's teacher, Ma Chung-hsi 馬中錫. Based on an early short story, the tightly constructed plot adheres closely to its model. In the first act Chao Chien-tzu 趙簡子, with his huntsmen, track and shoot the wolf. The wounded wolf meets the Mohist Tung-kuo Hsien-sheng, who after an initial fright, recalls the teachings of Mo-tzu (see *Chu-tzu pai-chia*) on universal love and agrees to aid the wolf by hiding him in his bag. Act two brings a confrontation between Chao and the Mohist, but the latter manages to prevent Chao from discovering the wolf. In act three the wolf, hungry after his efforts to evade the hunter, decides to eat the Mohist. Tung-kuo naturally objects. Finally they decide to ask the first three elderly "people" they encounter their opinions and to allow them to determine the issue. They first ask an apricot tree and then an old cow. Both agree with the wolf. In the final act they encounter "Old Mister Walking Stick" who tricks the wolf back into the bag and convinces the Mohist he should kill it. The plot aside, the play has been praised for both its powerful lyrics and clever dialogue.

K'ang Hai is also the author of *Wang Lan-ch'ing fu-hsin ming-chen lieh* 王蘭卿服信明貞烈 (Wang Lan-ch'ing, the Exemplary Chaste Widow, Keeps Faith in Her Heart). Although there is also controversy about the authorship of this work, Tseng Yung-i has pointed out that the fourth act includes a suite of songs in the *Nan-lü* 南呂 mode by K'ang's close friend Wang Chiu-ssu, strongly supporting the attribution to K'ang. The play tells the story of the prostitute Wang Lang-ch'ing who marries a commoner. Unfortunately, her young husband dies, leaving Wang and her mother-in-law to fend for themselves. Unable to repulse the advances of a wealthy suitor, the virtuous widow is driven to suicide. A friend of her husband, hearing of Wang Lan-ch'ing's great loyalty, organizes a sacrifice. K'ang used a suite by Wang Chiu-ssu as the elegy read at the sacrifice. During the ceremony the mourners suddenly see Wang Lan-ch'ing and her husband transformed into immortals and lifted to heaven on a cloud. This play is often compared to Chu Yu-tun's* several pieces about prostitutes, especially his *Hsiang-nang yüan*.

EDITIONS:

Chung-shan lang, in *Ku-pen*, II.
———, in Chou I-pai 周貽白, ed., *Ming-jen tsa-chü hsüan* 明人雜劇選, Peking, 1958; an annotated version.
P'an-tung Yüeh-fu, in *San-ch'ü ts'ung-k'an* 散曲叢刊, Wu Na, ed., Shanghai, 1930, v. 1, *ts'e* 8.
Tui-shan chi, in *Ssu-k'u ch'üan-shu*.
Wang Lan-ch'ing, in *Ku-pen*, II.

STUDIES:

Aoki, *Gikyokushi*, pp. 134-138.
Chao, Ching-shen 趙景深. "Tu K'ang Tui-shan wen-chi" 讀康對山文集, in Chao's *Ming Ch'ing ch'ü-t'an* 明清曲談, Shanghai, 1957, pp. 56-61.
DMB, pp. 692-694.
Fu, *Ming-jen tsa-chü*, pp. 83-84.
Liang, I-chen 梁乙眞, *Yüan Ming san-ch'ü hsiao shih* 元明散曲小史. N.p., 1934, pp. 267-277.
Lo, Chin-t'ang 羅錦堂. *Chung-kuo san-ch'ü shih* 中國散曲史. Taipei, 1957, v. 2, pp. 114-118.
Tseng, Yung-i 曾永義. *Ming tsa-chü kai-lun* 明雜劇概論. Taipei, 1978, pp. 197-210.
Yagisawa, *Gekisakuka*, pp. 109-171.

—HH and JTCS

K'ang Yu-wei 康有爲 (*tzu*, Kuang-hsia 廣廈, 1858-1927) was a major leader of the late-Ch'ing reform movement and one of the outstanding thinkers of late nineteenth-century China. Born in a wealthy family of literati in Nan-hai 南海 (Kwangtung), K'ang began his studies in earnest in 1876 under the philosopher Chu Tz'u-ch'i 朱次琦 (1807-1882). Throughout his life K'ang Yu-wei was deeply interested in the transcendent philosophies of Buddhism and Taoism, but under Chu he concentrated on the more practical concerns of such Ch'ing thinkers as Wei Yüan 魏源 (1794-1856) and Kung Tzu-chen,* and particularly the New Text School of classical scholarship (see *ching*). In his early twenties K'ang traveled to Hong Kong, and, deeply impressed by the Western way of life there, he began reading intensively on the West. From this time K'ang was constantly involved in promoting the reform of Chinese society and politics. From about 1888 until 1898 he wrote works urging reform, organized reformist societies, edited progressive journals, and sent numerous memorials to the Ch'ing court urging drastic changes for the sake of national survival.

Finally in 1898 he was summoned to court by Emperor Kuang-hsü and put in charge of reforming the empire, assisted by Liang Ch'i-ch'ao,* T'an Ssu-t'ung 譚嗣同 (1865-1898), and other notable progressives. However, this period of reforms (subsequently known as the "Hundred Days of Reforms") proved abortive because the

Empress Dowager Tz'u-hsi launched a coup against the reformers. K'ang escaped to Japan, but some of his colleagues were executed. While in Japan and during his extensive travels around the world, K'ang helped organize the Pao-huang hui 保皇會 (Emperor Protection Society) to force the Empress Dowager to restore Kuang-hsü to power. After the fall of the Ch'ing dynasty, K'ang returned to China but became increasingly out of touch with political realities and even supported an attempt to restore the imperial system. He died a bitter and disappointed man.

Although K'ang's renown as a political figure and philosopher have largely obscured his contributions to Chinese literature, he was certainly one of the finest poets of late-Ch'ing times. Liang Ch'i-ch'ao rightly considered him to be a major figure in the late Ch'ing *Shih-chieh ko-ming* 詩界革命 (Poetic Revolution). However, in a number of respects K'ang's poetry is rather distinct from that of most of the other reformers. K'ang identified himself closely with Tu Fu,* an affinity which K'ang's disciple Liang Ch'i-ch'ao noticed and to which K'ang himself frequently alluded. Early in his life K'ang resolved to attain sagehood, seeing himself as a savior of the Chinese people (if not mankind as a whole). Hence, he could easily identify with Tu Fu's noted humanity (仁) and Tu's desire to rescue his dynasty from political disintegration. Although other poets of the late-Ch'ing reform movement used poetry to promote for political and social change, none seems to have expressed his political views as passionately as K'ang. His view of himself as a sage help considerably to explain the intense emotions of his poems.

Another respect in which K'ang differed from such authors as Huang Tsun-hsien* was the great influence Taoism and particularly Buddhism had upon his world view. In a set of three poems written in 1909, when K'ang was in Penang, he expressed his view of literature: "In Indra's net of the *Avatamsaka*, it [poetry] is manifested layer by layer"; or "This matter [poetry] is vague, vast, profound, mysterious/It has moved men for a thousand ages and thus its miraculous sound is born." What K'ang seems to be saying is that the process of poetic creation is like Indra's jewel-net in which all being is reflected and re-reflected in an infinite progression, coming into being spontaneously and simultaneously as do the myriad phenomena of the world. Poetry is something beyond rational understanding ("vague, mysterious") and is the result of the resonance between man and the cosmos. Such a mystical view of poetry is directly at odds with that of late-Ch'ing reformers like Huang Tsun-hsien, who were willing to admit spontaneity and interaction with the universe into their view of literature, but would have violently disagreed with the more mystical implications of K'ang's theory. At first sight, K'ang's mystical conception of poetry may seem to contradict his view of the poet as Confucian sage, but the similarites between the Neo-Confucian (and particularly the New Text School) sage and the all-compassionate Bodhisattva show how blurred the lines between the two ideals can be. Many of these poems written during the Hundred Days are contained in the collection *Ming-i-ko shih-chi* 明夷閣詩集.

Although K'ang never totally abandoned his earlier esthetic views, his exile to Japan and subsequent travels had an enormous impact on his later verse. In one of the three critical poems just mentioned occur the following lines: "A new world, rare, miraculous; a marvelous realm arises./More and more I search Europe and Asia, creating new sounds." In such lines K'ang is clearly referring to the new realm of poetic creation opened up to him through his foreign experiences and reflected in works such as the two-hundred-line poem K'ang wrote about the Wailing Wall in Jerusalem. Yet even in that piece K'ang can hardly forget his vocation as a sage and savior, and the poem becomes a vehicle to express his deep sorrow over the fate of China, which seems to be destined for destruction similar to that of the Jewish state. As K'ang's alienation from the political situation in early Republican China grew, he withdrew into himself. In his late verse one senses both an increasing despair over the faltering republic and an attempt to seek transcendence in nature.

K'ang was an incredibly prolific writer; his poetry makes up only a small proportion of his surviving works. Although most of his writings are not strictly literary, the prose style that K'ang had developed by the time he wrote his greatest work of political philosophy, the *Ta-t'ung-shu* 大同書 (The Book of the One World), is in harmony with the grandeur of his scheme for a new utopian world order, and shows how the classical language could be a tool for communicating modern ideas.

EDITIONS:

K'ang Nan-hai wen-chi 康南海文集. Shanghai, 1914. *K'ang Nan-hai Hsien-sheng i-chu hui-k'an* 康南海先生遺著彙刊. Taipei, 1976. Valuable reprint of works difficult to obtain.

K'ang-Liang shih-ch'ao 康梁詩鈔. Shanghai, 1914.

[K'ang] Nan-hai Hsien-sheng shih-chi 南海先生詩集. Yokohama, 1911.

K'ang Nan-hai wen-ch'ao 康南海文鈔. Shanghai, 1914.

K'ang Nan-hai wen-chi hui-pien 康南海文集彙編. Shanghai, 1917.

K'ang Nan-hai Hsien-sheng shih-chi 康南海先生詩集. Shanghai, 1937.

K'ang Yu-wei shih-wen hsüan 康有為詩文選. Peking, 1958.

TRANSLATIONS:

Thompson, Laurence G. *The One-World Philosophy of K'ang Yu-wei.* London, 1958.

Wilhelm, Hellmut. "The Poems from the Hall of Obscured Brightness," in Jung-pang Lo, see below.

Woon, Ramon L. Y. and Irving Y. Lo, "Poets and Poetry of China's Last Empire," *LEW,* 9 (1965), 331-361.

STUDIES:

Hsiao, Kung-chuan. *A Modern China and a New World, K'ang Yu-wei, Reformer and Utopian.* Seattle, 1975.

Lo, Jung-pang. *K'ang Yu-wei, a Biography and a Symposium.* Tucson, 1967. Both Lo's and Hsiao's works contain extensive bibliographies.

—JDS

Kao Ch'i 高啟 (*tzu*, Chi-ti 季廸, *hao*, Ch'ing-ch'iu-tzu 青邱子, 1336-1374) is generally recognized as the greatest poet of the Ming dynasty. His short life, ended by a cruel execution on trumped-up charges by the first Ming emperor, is often seen as emblematic of the fate of letters under the Ming.

Kao was born and grew up during the last decades of the Yüan dynasty in Soochow, a city that had been a center of Chinese literary and artistic culture for centuries. He became known for his literary talent while still a young man, but was unable to begin a normal career in official service because of the unsettled nature of the times. After Chang Shih-ch'eng 張士誠 seized control of Soochow in 1356, many of Kao's friends became associated with his regime. It is very probable that Kao was also, but firm evidence for this is difficult to find, and indeed, may have been suppressed by Kao himself. Chang Shih-ch'eng's Soochow-based statelet was the last serious obstacle to the rise of Chu Yüan-chang, the first Ming emperor, and after its capture in 1366, Chang's subordinates, and the people of Soochow generally, were treated with considerable severity, suffering exile, heavy taxation, and in some cases execution. Having dissociated himself from Chang and gone into retirement early, Kao Ch'i escaped the worst of this retribution, but he evidently lived in considerable apprehension throughout this period. In 1369, he was summoned to the capital to serve on the editorial board compiling the *Yüan-shih* 元史, but he retired the following year and returned home. In 1374, while living in retirement, he was arrested and executed in the course of Chu Yüan-chang's first purges.

Although only seven years of his life were passed under Ming rule, Kao's position as the leading Ming poet is assured. Indeed, his early death cut short what otherwise might have been one of the dynasty's most brilliant literary careers, for he was an extraordinarily gifted writer. In spite of his gifts, some critics have suggested that he had not yet achieved a personal style by the time of his death, for his very facility, combined with the need to win a reputation at an early age (his family was not well off), encouraged him to concentrate much of his energy on writing self-consciously "literary" work, occasional poems, and pieces that demonstrated his remarkable ability to evoke poetic styles of earlier periods. In fact, he is one of the masters of the art of "imitating antiquity," so that he has been seen as a forerunner of the archaist movement that appeared around 1500. Unlike the archaists, however, he was eclectic in his choice of models, imitating styles from virtually every earlier period of Chinese literary history. Yoshikawa Kōjirō sees Kao as the high point in the long tradition of "citizen poets" from southeastern China, whose history went back at least to the Southern Sung period, but differing from his predecessors in that his poetry embodies a "soaring" inspiration of spirit unchartertistic of the "citizen poet" tradition in general.

Primarily a poet rather than an essayist or critic, Kao did express his ideas about poetic excellence in a preface that he contributed to the collected works of an acquaintance. In this he declared the three essential features of poetry to be *ko* 格 (form), *i* 意 (content), and *ch'ü* 趣 (interest). This relatively "non-partisan" poetics, together with his acceptance of poetry of all previous periods (and perhaps sympathy for his unhappy end), made him one of the few Ming poets on whose greatness most later critics could agree.

Kao Ch'i is often counted, together with three other poets, all his contemporaries and friends, as one of the *Wu-chung ssu-chieh* 吳中四傑 (Four Outstanding Men of Wu). The others were Chang Yü 張羽 (1333-1385), Hsü Pen 徐賁 (1335-1380), and Yang Chi 楊基 (1334-*c.* 1383). Like Kao Ch'i, these three men were renowned young poets in Soochow during the period of Chang Shih-ch'eng's regime, with which at least Yang Chi was associated. Although they eventually held office under the new dynasty, all three suffered because of Chu Yüan-chang's resentment and distrust of the Soochow literati, and only Hsü Pen seems to have died a natural death. Yang Chi died while serving a sentence at hard labor, and Chang Yü committed suicide

rather than face possible arrest. Their fate was symptomatic of the position of the educated elite during the early Ming. Perhaps because of this insecurity, the hundred years and more after their deaths was a period of unparalleled mediocrity in poetry that lasted until the appearance of Li Tung-yang* late in the fifteenth century.

EDITIONS:

Kao, Ch'i. *Kao T'ai-shih ta-ch'üan chi* 高太史大全集. SPTK. Reprint of a 1450 edition, with *tz'u** collection, *K'ou-hsüan chi* 扣舷集, and prose works, *Fu-tsao chi* 鳧藻集 appended. The best generally available edition.

———. *Ch'ing-ch'iu Kao Chi-ti Hsien-sheng shih-chi* 青邱高季廸先生詩集. SPPY. Typeset version of an edition with annotations of the poems by a Ch'ing scholar, Chin T'an 金檀, with *tz'u* and prose, as well as supplementary materials, appended; the most useful and readily available text.

Chang, Yü. *Ching-chü chi* 靜居集. 6 *chüan*. SPTK. A reprint of the earliest edition of Chang's poems.

———. *Chang Lai-i Hsien-sheng wen-chi* 張來儀先生文集. 1 chüan, plus supplement, in Hu Ssu-ching 胡思敬, ed., *Yü-chang ts'ung-shu*. Chang's collected prose; the same *ts'ung-shu** also includes a version of the *Ching-chü chi* in 4 *chüan* with a supplement and textual apparatus.

Hsü, Pen. *Pei-kuo chi* 北郭集. 10 *chüan*. SPTK. Reprint of the Fu 傅 edition published during the *Ch'eng-hua* period (1465-1488); the best text.

Ibid., in *Li-tai hua-chia shih-wen-chi*. Reprint of a manuscript edition; contents as in the preceding, but with a brief supplement; the most accessible edition.

Yang Chi. *Mei-an chi* 眉菴集. 12 *chüan*. SPTK. Reprint of the "Chang" 張 text, published during the *Ch'eng-hua* period.

Ibid., in *Ming-tai i-shu-chia chi hui-k'an, hsü-chi*. Reprint of the "Wang" 汪 text, with an appended collation record.

TRANSLATIONS:

Bryant, Daniel. "Selected Ming Poems," *Renditions*, 8 (Autumn 1977), 85-91; for Kao Ch'i's "Chih Tun An" 支遁菴, see p. 85.

Demiéville, *Anthologie*, pp. 462-465.

Sunflower, pp. 459-463 (Kao Ch'i only).

STUDIES:

DMB, pp. 696-699.

Fukumoto, Masakazu 福本雅一. "Minchō bun'enden, sono ichi: Gochū shiketsu" 明朝

文苑傳其一 吳中四傑, *Tezukayama Tanki Dai-gaku kenkyū nempō*, 26 (1978), 43-69. Mostly devoted to a translation, with copious annotation, of a contemporary biography of Kao Ch'i by Lü Mien 呂勉.

Iritani, Sensuke 入谷仙介. *Kō Kei* 高啟, *Chūgoku shijin senshū, nishū*, 10. Tokyo, 1962.

Kamachi, Kanichi 蒲池歡一. *Kō Seikyū* 高靑邱. 2v. Tokyo, 1966. These two volumes both include brief introductory discussions of Kao Ch'i.

Mote, F. W. *The Poet Kao Ch'i*. Princeton: Princeton University Press, 1962. The richest study in English of any Ming poet; masterful, but chiefly concerned with biography and historical background; many translations.

Weng, T'ung-wen 翁同文. "Yang Chi sheng-nien-k'ao chi ch'i shih-chung 'mu ju tou' wen-t'i'" 楊基生年考及其詩中，木入斗問題, *Nan-yang Ta-hsüeh hsüeh-pao*, 6 (1972), 162-170. Detailed study of Yang Chi's birthdate and related biographical questions.

Yokota, Terutoshi 橫田輝俊. "Mindai bungaku-uron no tenkai," pt. I 明代文學論の展開, *Hiroshima Daigaku bungakubu kiyō*, 37 (1977), 13-20.

Yoshikawa, Kōkirō 吉川幸次郎. *Gen-Minshi gaisetsu* 元明詩概說. Tokyo, 1963, pp. 129-139.

—DB

Kao Lien 高濂 (*tzu*, Shen-fu 深甫, *fl.* 1573-1581) is recognized within the dramatic tradition as an able poet who was a native of Ch'ien-t'ang 錢塘 (modern Hangchow). There is no extant record indicating his service in public affairs either in his native city or elsewhere.

His father's name was Ying-chü 應擧 (*tzu*, Yün-ch'ing 雲卿). Beyond this little is known of Kao. But judging from his extant works, Kao Lien's family must have been wealthy and cultured, for he seems to have had an excellent education. He was a bibliophile and, indeed, part of his collection has filtered down to posterity. But collecting books was obviously not his only interest. The content of his work *Tsun-sheng pa-chien* 遵生八牋 (Eight Discourses on Living), which covers a wide range of subjects including medicine, nutrition, esthetic criticism, antiques, and botany, reveals that he was a man with diverse interests, broadly knowledgeable with many talents.

As a dramatist, Kao Lien wrote only two *ch'uan-ch'i** plays: *Yü-tsan chi* 玉簪記 (The Jade Hairpin) and *Chieh-hsiao chi* 節孝記 (Fidelity and Filiality). The former is better known—scenes from it are still performed today.

Yü-tsan chi portrays the romance of P'an Pi-cheng 潘必正 and Ch'en Miao-ch'ang 陳妙常. The theme is conflict between society and an individual who flouts social convention; at the end love triumphs. This story can be traced to a literary tale, "Ch'en Miao-ch'ang," in *Ku-chin nü-shih* 古今女史 (Stories of Women Old and New), relating the frolic of Chang Yü-hu 張于湖 (a Sung-dynasty official) at Nü-chen kuan 女眞觀. A *tsa-chü,** *Chang Yü-hu wu-su nü-chen kuan* 張于湖誤宿女眞觀 (Chang Yü-hu Mistakenly Lodged at Nü-chen Convent) and a *hua-pen** story, *Chang Yü-hu su nü-chen kuan chi* 張于湖宿女眞觀記 (Chang Yü-hu Lodged at Nü-chen Convent), both of which influenced Kao Lien's work, also evolved from the same tale.

Yü-tsan chi's influence on subsequent works in drama and fiction is also considerable. For example, in addition to the Peking-opera version, "Ch'iu-chiang" 秋江 (Autumn River), which is based on a Szechwan opera, T'ao Chün-ch'i 陶居起, six regional plays listed in *Ching-chü chü-mu ch'u-t'an* 京劇劇目初探 (A Preliminary Index to Peking Operas), purportedly derived from *Yü-tsan chi*. Liu Yen-sheng 劉雁聲, in *Ching-chü ku-shih k'ao* 京劇故事考 (Peking Opera Stories), notes an additional regional play (Cantonese), which may also have been modeled on Kao's drama.

Moreover, two modern novels, *Ch'iu-chiang* (Autumn River) by Chang Hen-shui 張恨水, a romantic writer of the Mandarin Duck and Butterfly School, and *Yü-tsan chi* (1955) by Yü Jen 于人, are based on *Yü-tsan chi*.

Despite its poetic quality and literary legacy, *Yü-tsan chi* has drawn little favorable criticism from either traditional or modern critics. Lü T'ien-ch'eng 呂天成, the prolific Ming dramatist, relegated Kao Lien to a relatively mediocre rank (lower-middle group of authors) in his *Ch'ü p'in* 曲品 (An Evaluation of Arias). Contemporary critics are critical of Kao Lien's use of rhyme, his inability to create dramatic tension, and his neglect of the *ch'uan-ch'i* structure.

None of the critics have commented on the value of *Yü-tsan chi* as a piece of social criticism against the background of the rigidly Neo-Confucian Ming society. If Kao Lien's work were approached from this point of view, it would become distinguished as one of the first open literary presentations of sexual mores and related social problems in the Ming.

It calls for the liberation of women and advocates observance of the social and moral orders. Kao's use of drama as a vehicle of social criticism merits attention.

EDITIONS:

Chieh-hsiao chi, in *Ku-pen*, I, v. 110.
Tsun-sheng pa-chien. N.p., 1810.
Yü-tsan chi, in *Liu-shih.*

STUDIES:

Chin, *Chi-ku-ko;* ch. 14 contains biographical information and a study on *Yü-tsan chi.*

Huang, Shang 黃裳. "Hou chi" 后記 in *Yü-tsan chi* 玉簪記. Shanghai, 1956. Contains a critical essay on *Yü-tsan chi.*

Lo, Chin-t'ang 羅錦堂. "Nü-chen kuan yü Yü-tsan chi" 女眞觀與玉簪記, *Ta-lu tsa-chih* 46.6 (1974), 13-17. A brief study on the evolution of *Yü-tsan chi.*

Yee, Edmond. "Love Versus Neo-Confucian Orthodoxy: An Evolutionary and Critical Study of *Yü-tsan chi* by the Ming Dramatist Kao Lien." Unpublished Ph.D. dissertation, University of California, Berkeley, 1977.

—EY

Kao Ming 高明 (*tzu*, Tse-ch'eng 則誠, *c.* 1305-*c.* 1370) was born in Ju-an hsien 瑞安, Wen-chou 溫州 prefecture, the area associated with the birth of *Nan-hsi.** He passed the *chin-shih* examination in 1345 and held various official posts over the next ten years. With the uprising of Fang Kuo-chen 方國珍 (1348) in eastern Chekiang, Kao was made Assistant Commissioner-in-Chief charged with quelling the rebellion. Differences of opinion soon developed between him and his Mongol superiors. Disillusioned, he retired from public life. Soon afterward he was recruited again, serving first as prefectural judge and later assistant commissioner-in-chief for Fukien. He finally resigned around 1356, after declining an offer of a position from Fang (with whom the Mongols had made a settlement in 1352). He then retired to Li-she 櫟社 where he led the life of a recluse, immersing himself in drama and writing his famous *P'i-p'a chi.*

P'i-p'a chi 琵琶記 (The Lute) a *ch'uan-ch'i** in forty-two scenes, tells the story of Ts'ai Po-chieh 蔡伯喈 who, at the urging of his father, reluctantly leaves his old parents and new wife Chao Wu-niang to go to the capital for the examinations. There he wins first place, upon which Grand Councilor Niu pressures him to marry his daughter. Ts'ai accedes. Meanwhile, his parents die of starvation in the famine-stricken home; the son remains unaware of this tragedy while his own attempts to contact home are thwarted by a trickster. Having barely survived the famine herself, Wu-niang makes a meager living on her way to the capital in search of her husband by singing out her sad fate to the accompaniment of her lute. In the capital Ts'ai Po-chieh's new wife takes pity on her and arranges a reunion of the separated couple. Ts'ai relinquishes his post and eventually returns with both wives to his home to sacrifice at the tomb of his parents. The play ends with imperial honors for Ts'ai Po-chieh and his two wives.

Thematically, the work is noted for its depiction of the moral dilemma involved in the claims of filial piety. In earlier versions of the play written by others, Ts'ai Po-chieh is condemned for his lack of filial piety and compassion. Kao Ming rewrote the part so that Ts'ai may be viewed as "perfectly loyal and filial." If he errs, he does so under the highest moral authority of father and emperor.

Ming criticism of the *P'i-p'a chi* ranged from high praise of its moving power and linguistic excellence (Hsü Wei,* Wang Shih-chen* and others) to dissatisfaction with its literary diction and alleged lack of modal harmony (Ho Liang-chün,* Hsü Fu-tso*). Structurally, its alternating contrasting scenes (in mood and theme) and a sus-

473

tained use of imagery (food, music, the seasons) contribute to its unity. Yet the flaws in its plot are too obvious: Ts'ai Po-chieh's parents are strangely unaware of their son's success; he fails to recognize a fake letter supposedly in his father's handwriting, etc. Because of the playwright's announced intent of "not deliberately looking for harmony in keys and modes" (prologue) and their own ignorance of the existence of *hsi-wen* (see *nan-hsi*), Ming and Ch'ing critics (with the exception of Hsü Wei and Shen Ching*) tended to regard the *P'i-p'a chi* as the first example of (southern) drama to break loose from the northern *tsa-chü** tradition of strict modal harmony, which it was not. On the contrary, both in content (examination success leading to abandonment of wife) and in form (singing and musical conventions, *t'i-mu*, roles, lack of scene division) the Yüan edition of *P'i-p'a chi* is very much imbedded in the long established southern tradition of *hsi-wen*. What differentiates it markedly is its length, its imagery and elegant language, its dramaturgical sophistication, its sensitive exploration of theme, and, the Ming critics notwithstanding, its comparatively strict use of keys and modes.

Ch'ien Po-tsan 翦伯贊 places the date of composition between 1348 and 1368 (see his article in *P'i-p'a chi t'ao-lun chuan-k'an*). Yagisawa considers it to be after 1351. The *Jou-k'o chai chi* 柔克齋集 in twenty *chüan*, lost since the mid-Ming, is also attributed to Kao. There is no biography for Kao in the *Ming-shih*, which mentions him only in brief references (e.g., *chüan* 285).

EDITIONS:
P'i-p'a chi in *Liu-shih*.
———. Ch'en Mei-kung 陳眉公 (1558-1639), ed. Peking, 1954.
———. Ch'ien Nan-yang 錢南揚, ed. Shanghai, 1960. Contains excellent notes and a biography of the author. Based on a Yüan edition.

TRANSLATIONS:
Bazin, A. P. L. *Le Pi-pa-Ki ou L'Histoire du Luth*. Paris, 1841.
Hundhausen, Vincenz. *Die Laute von Gau Ming*. Leipzig, 1930.
Mulligan, Jean. *The Lute*. New York, 1980.

STUDIES:
Birch, Cyril. "Tragedy and Melodrama in Early *Ch'uan-ch'i* plays: 'Lute Song' and 'Thorn Hairpin' Compared," *BSOAS*, 36 (1973), 228-247.
Chang, Ti-hua 張棣華. *P'i-p'a chi k'ao-shu* 琵琶記考述. Taipei, 1966.
Chao, Ching-shen 趙景深. "Ts'ai Po-chieh P'i-p'a chi" in *Yüan-Ming nan-hsi k'ao-lüeh* 元明南戲考略, pp. 49-60. Peking, 1958.
DMB, pp. 699-701.
P'i-p'a chi t'ao-lun chuan-k'an 琵琶記討論專刊. Chü-pen yüeh-k'an she 劇本月刊社, ed. Peking, 1956.
Tai, Pu-fan 戴不凡. *Lun ku-tien ming chü P'i-p'a chi* 論古典名劇琵琶記. Peking, 1956.

—KCL

Kao-seng chuan 高僧傳 (Lives of Eminent Monks) is China's oldest surviving collection of Buddhist biography. Written by the monk Hui-chiao 慧皎 (497-554) and completed around 530, the work contains accounts of the careers of important figures in Chinese Buddhism from its introduction during the Han dynasty until the author's own time. Since he lived and worked under the Liang dynasty, Hui-chiao's collection is also known as the *Liang Kao-seng chuan*. A valuable source of information on numerous aspects of Chinese Buddhism during its formative period and a useful counterbalance to the mostly secular materials found in the dynastic histories, the *Kao-seng chuan* is also highly regarded as a model of Six Dynasties prose style. Hui-chiao was greatly indebted to an earlier work, Pao-ch'ang's 寶唱 *Ming-seng chuan* 明僧傳 (Lives of Famous Monks), which had appeared in 519, and he took that year as the cutoff date for material in his own collection. (Except for a list of its contents and several fragments, one or two of which appear to be complete biographies, the *Ming-seng chuan* is now lost). In a postface to his collection (in some editions, a preface), Hui-chiao also discussed a number of his other sources, which included earlier Buddhist compendia of biographical and bibliographical notices, historical accounts, monastic records, and tales of miracles and prodigies, as well as secular works. Since Hui-chiao and the authors of most of his sources were residents of South China—Hui-chiao spent most of his life in K'uai-chi 會稽 (modern Shao-hsing hsien 紹興縣 on the south shore of Hangchow Bay in Chekiang)—his work contains much more detail when treating monks who lived in South China. Its coverage of Buddhist activities in North China, especially after its occupation by non-Chinese tribespeople in the early fourth century, is understandably less complete.

The first thirteen of the *Kao-seng chuan's* fourteen chapters (*chüan*) contain 257 major biographies and an approximately equal number of lesser notices, divided into ten categories based on the principal religious orientation of the monk concerned. The fourteenth chapter is the postface, which discusses sources and provides a table of contents. Ten biographical categories have been translated (by Arthur Wright) as follows: translators (35 major biographies), exegetes (101), theurgists (20), meditators (12), disciplinarians (13), self-immolators (11), cantors (21), promoters of works of merit (14), hymnodists (11), and sermonists (10). In each category the biographies are arranged chronologically.

The *Kao-seng chuan* was followed by continuations in later dynasties, the first of which was Tao-hsüan's 道宣 (596-667) *Hsü Kao-seng chuan*). Tao-hsüan was an extremely active Buddhist scholar and a prolific author and editor, as well as the founder of the disciplinary school of Chinese Buddhism. His disciplinary school, which emphasized strict adherence to the *vinaya*, or monastic regulations, is sometimes also referred to as the Nan-shan school, after the Nan-shan 南山 (Southern Mountains) south of Ch'ang-an, the T'ang capital, where he lived and worked.

In the preface to his collection, Tao-hsüan stated that it contained 331 major biographies (variant reading 340), and that it was completed in 645. Since in its present state it contains more than 400 major biographies and a smaller number of lesser notices, as well as information that can be dated to as late as 665, it seems obvious that Tao-hsüan continued to add to his collection even after its initial "completion."

He began his coverage with the founding of the Liang dynasty in the early sixth century, and adopted, with some changes in category headings, the organizational pattern of Hui-chiao. Since he was a resident of North China and active under a reunited empire, Tao-hsüan was more able than Hui-chiao to provide geographically balanced coverage, and included biographies of noted monks from all principal areas of China. He seems, however, to have had a somewhat greater interest in the miraculous aspects of Buddhist piety than his predecessor, and his collection contains rather more descriptions of miraculous occurrences and supernatural interventions.

The second continuation of the *Kao-seng chuan* was Tsan-ning's 贊寧 (919-1002) *Sung Kao-seng chuan* 宋高僧傳 (Sung Dynasty Lives of Eminent Monks). Tsan-ning, a resident of the Northern Sung capital of K'ai-feng, continued the biographical coverage from the early T'ang up to 988, the year his collection was completed. His work follows Tao-hsüan's modifications of Hui-chiao's organization and contains 532 major biographies and a smaller number of lesser notices.

A third continuation of the *Kao-seng chuan* was completed in 1617 by a monk named Ju-hsing 如惺. His work, entitled *Ta-Ming Kao-seng chuan* 大明高僧傳 (Ming Dynasty Lives of Eminent Monks), includes biographies of monks who lived during the Southern Sung, Yüan, and early Ming dynasties. Much less comprehensive than the three earlier collections (it contains only 112 biographies), Ju-hsing's work has not generally been as highly esteemed by later scholars.

EDITIONS:

Hackmann, Heinrich. "Alphabetisches Verzeichnis zum Kao seng ch'uan [sic]," *AO*, 2 (1923). This index to Hui-chiao's collection contains occasional errors. Either of the two works listed below is to be preferred.

Kao-seng chuan, and sequels, in *Taishō shinshū daizōkyō* 大正新脩大藏經. Takakusu Junjirō 高楠順次郎 and Watanabe Kaigyoku 渡邊海旭, eds. Tokyo, 1927; rpt., 1960, v. 50, nos. 2059-2062, pp. 321-943. The editors followed a Korean text thought to date from the mid-twelfth century for the first three collections, and indicated in notes variant readings found in other major early editions. The fourth collection follows an edition published in 1651. Most other editions of the Chinese Tripitaka also contain at least the first two collections, and several independently published editions of the first three are also available. The *Taishō* editions are to be preferred, however, because of their copious indication of textual variants.

Makita, Tairyō 牧田諦亮 *et al.*, eds. *Chūgoku kōsōden sakuin* 中國高僧傳索引. 7v. Kyoto, 1972. Organized like the previous work, it contains separate indices to all four biographical collections.

Tsukamoto, Zenuyū 塚本善隆 *et al.*, eds. "Ryō kōsōden sakuin" 梁高僧傳索引, *Shina bukkyō shigaku*, 1.1 (1937) through 3.1 (1939). An index to all names of monks, laymen, monasteries, and books mentioned in Hui-chiao's collection. It is keyed to both the *Taishō* and an earlier Japanese edition.

Taishō shinshū daizōkyō sakuin 大正新修大藏經索引. v. 28, Shidenbu 史傳部, Tokyo, 1973.

Wright, Arthur F. "Biography and Hagiography: Hui-chiao's *Lives of Eminent Monks*," *Silver Jubilee Volume of the Zinbun-kagaku-kenkyūsyo*, Kyoto, 1954, pp. 383-432.

TRANSLATIONS:

Furuta, Kazuhiro 古田和弘. "*Kōsōden*—'Shin'i hen'" 高僧傳 — 神異篇, in *Bukkyō bungakushū* 佛教文學集, Iriya Yoshitaka 入矢義高, ed., Tokyo, 1975, v. 60. Translates into Japanese all twenty biographies in Hui-chiao's "Theurgists" category. Some helpful annotation.

Shih, Robert. *Biographies des Moines Eminents (Kao sheng tchouan) de Houei-kiao*. Louvain, 1968. Translates into French all thirty-five biographies in Hui-chiao's "Translators" category.

STUDIES:

Chang, Man-tao 張曼濤, ed. *Chung-kuo fo-chiao shih-hsüeh-shih lun-chi* 中國佛教史學史論集, in *Hsien-tai fo-chiao hsüeh-shu ts'ung-k'an* 現代佛教學術叢刊, v. 50, Taipei, 1978.

Ch'en, Yüan 陳垣. *Chung-kuo fo-chiao shih-chi kai-lun* 中國佛教史籍概論. Peking, 1955, pp. 20-43.

de Jong, J. W. "A Brief Survey of Chinese Buddhist Historiography," *Studies in Indo-Asian Art and Culture*, 1 (April 1972), 101-108.

Jan, Yün-hua, "Buddhist Historiography in Sung China," *ZDMG*, 114 (1964), 360-381.

Nogami, Shunjō 野上俊靜. *Zoku kōsōden shikō* 續高僧傳私考. Kyoto, 1959.

—DG and JYH

Kao Shih 高適 (*tzu*, Ta-fu 達夫, 716-765), a contemporary of Tu Fu* and Li Po,* was one of the major poets of the High T'ang. A native of Po-hai 渤海 (modern Hopei), Kao came from an impoverished official family. Biographical sources claim that as a youth Kao was forced to beg in the Sung region (modern Honan). After failing to find advancement in the capital, he set off around 737 for the northeastern frontier, probably in search of a military appointment. In 747 he was given the lowest position in the official hierarchy, and made District Defender of Feng-ch'iu 封丘. His fortunes began to rise when he attracted the notice of Ko-shu Han 哥舒翰, one of the most important generals of the day. Kao Shih accompanied him to Central Asia in 754. The following year when Ko-shu was decisively defeated by An Lu-shan's troops at T'ung Pass, which guarded the road to Ch'ang-an, Kao Shih presented a spirited defense of his superior before Emperor Hsüan-tsung. As a result he was promoted to Grand Master of Remonstrance. Kao's fortunes continued to rise in the court of Emperor Su-tsung. He vigorously opposed the policy of appointing imperial princes to key military commands and was vindicated when the Prince of Yung 永王 revolted. Appointed Regional Commander of Huai-nan, Kao was charged with helping to crush this rebellion (in which his acquaintance Li Po* was involved). Shortly after this, Kao found himself ousted from the court of the restored T'ang house, the result, according to the histories, of the enmity of the eunuch Li Fu-kuo 李輔國 (704-762). He was given an appointment in the crown prince's household in Lo-yang and then in 760 was appointed Prefect of P'eng-chou 彭州 (modern Szechwan). There he proved his considerable military skill by putting down two local rebellions and in recognition of his services was appointed Regional Commander of Chien-nan and Hsi-ch'uan. In 762 he tried to subdue a Tibetan rebellion, but failed this time and was recalled to Ch'ang-an. Despite this failure, Kao was enfeoffed and appointed Vice Minister of Justice and a Policy Adviser. He died shortly after. The *Chiu T'ang-shu* (*chüan* 111) observes that Kao was the only well-known poet in the T'ang who had an eminent political career.

Kao Shih's talent for military affairs and his dedication to public affairs are reflected in his works. Traditional critical comments describe his poetry as distinguished by *hsiung-i yü* 胸臆語 (mainly emotions); his works are at once *pei chuang* 悲壯 (robust and sad) and filled with *ch'i* 氣 (vigorous spirit) and strength of *feng ku* 風骨 (form and élan). The last three terms are all associated with Chien-an poetry and they suggest the poet's indebtedness to that tradition. The *Fu-ku* 復古 (Return to Antiquity) movement had taken Chien-an poetry as its model in its attempt to free poetry from the *k'ung-t'i** (courtly style) which had been dominant from the Six Dynasties to the early T'ang. The foremost poet of the early years of the T'ang identified with this movement is Ch'en Tzu-ang.* Kao Shih may be regarded as inheriting his legacy.

Kao Shih is now chiefly remembered by his masterpiece, the "Yen ko hsing" 燕歌行 (Song of Yen). On the basis of this one achievement, later critics have often designated him a *P'ien-sai t'i* 邊塞體 (frontier-style) poet, although only a portion of his 250 poems is on this subject. He is often paired with Ts'en Shen,* a contemporary who also wrote extensively of his experience on the frontier. Comparisons between the works of the two men have not been to Kao's advantage; the younger Ts'en was a greater master of the craft of poetry and his brilliant, often flamboyant style has instantaneous appeal. Kao, on the other hand, is the more serious and intellectual poet, and his works are less accessible. If he fails at times to emulate the stylistic refinements of the Six Dynasties and early T'ang, his response is always measured against the eternal values of the classical tradition.

EDITIONS:

Kao Ch'ang-shih shih chi 高常侍詩集. 8 *chüan*. The text is found in several editions, the most re-

liable and accessible being the *SPTK*, which is the reprint of a movable-type edition of the Ming (exact source unknown).

Kao Ch'ang-shih shih chiao-chu 高常侍詩校注. Juan T'ing-yü 阮廷瑜, comp. Taipei, 1965. Punctuated and annotated.

TRANSLATIONS:

Demiéville, *Anthologie,* pp. 257-258.

STUDIES:

Chan, Marie. *Kao Shih.* Boston, 1978.

Chou, Hsün-ch'u 周勛初. *Kao Shih nien-p'u* 高適年譜. Shanghai, 1980.

Fu, *Shih-jen,* pp. 142-170: "Kao Shih nien-p'u chung te chi-ko wen-t'i" 高適年譜中的幾個問題.

Juan, T'ing-yü. "Kao Ch'ang-shih Ts'en Chia-chou ch'i-jen yü shih chih p'ing-lun" 高常侍岑嘉州其人與詩之評論, *Ta-lu tsa-chih,* 37.10 (October 1968), 21-32.

Kamio, Ryūsuke 上尾龍介. "Kōteki no shifu" 高適の詩風, *Kyūshu Chūgoku gakkai hō,* (1965), 73-85.

Liu, K'ai-yang 劉開揚. "Lun Kao Shih te shih" 論高適的詩, in his "T'ang shih lun-wen chi" 唐詩論文集, Shanghai, 1979, pp. 52-67.

Owen, *High T'ang,* pp. 147-162.

Suzuki, Shūji 鈴木修次. "Kōteki to To Ho 高適と杜甫, *Kambun Kyōshitsu,* 85 (April 1968), 10-18, 86 (June 1968), 35-40.

———, *Todai,* pp. 349-392.

Wang, Ta-chin 王達津. "Shih-jen Kao Shih Sheng-p'ing hsi-shih" 詩人高適生平繫詩, *Wen-hsüeh i-ch'an tseng-k'an,* 8 (November 1961), 221-230.

Yang, Yin-shen 陽蔭深. *Kao Shih yü Ts'en Shen* 高適與岑參. Shanghai, 1936.

—MC

Kao Wen-hsiu 高文秀 (*fl.* 1270) was a prolific playwright of *tsa-chü.** He came from Tung-p'ing (modern Shantung) and at some time had served as an educational officer for the province. He must have passed his career as a dramatist mainly in Ta-tu (modern Peking), for there he made such a great reputation for himself that people nicknamed him "The Young (Kuan) Han-ch'ing" (*Hsiao Han-ch'ing* 小漢卿). He is said to have died early, but among the long-lived playwrights and poets of that time, "early" might mean forty or even fifty.

477

Thirty-four plays were attributed to Kao, thirty fairly reliably. Four of the total seem to be extant. The first, *Hsü Chia sui Fan Sui* 須賈譚范雎 (Hsü Chia Defames Fan Sui) relates how Fan Sui, Hsü Chia's retainer in the Warring States era, is slandered by his master, caned, and left to die in the privy. Sui is saved from death by a benefactor, changes his name, and flees to the state of Ch'in, where he rises to the position of minister. In this office, he later has the chance to wreak vengence on Hsü Chia, and indeed has him caned. However, he is prevented from killing his former master by his original benefactor, and the play ends with Hsü Chia's vow to bring the head of his own minister to Fan Sui.

The second play, *Hao-chiu Chao Yüan yü Shang-huang* 好酒趙元遇上皇 (The Drunkard Chao Yüan encounters the Emperor), relates how Chao Yüan loses his wife to a high official because of his drunkenness. The wife and her new husband plot to dispatch Chao to the Western Capital with an official message. Knowing that official rules call for the execution of a messenger who falls three days behind schedule, they expect him to get drunk and miss his deadline. Chao is held up because of a heavy snowfall and, knowing full well that he will not meet the deadline, starts drinking in a wine loft. There he saves from embarrassment the Sung emperor, T'ai-tsu, who has come to drink incognito. The Sung emperor questions Chao on the reasons for his sorrow and Chao tells all. The emperor then arranges for him to avoid execution and has him appointed Magistrate of Kaifeng, the capital. Chao then punishes his ex-wife and her husband for their conspiracy.

Hei-hsüan-feng shuang-hsien t'ou 黑旋風雙獻頭 (The Black Whirlwind Twice Presents Heads) is perhaps the best-known of Kao's plays. It shows the "villain" of the *Shui-hu* (see *Shui-hu chuan*) story, Li K'uei 李逵, at his worst. Setting off as a bodyguard, Li promises Sung Chiang that he will act mildly, but carries out a daring jail-rescue and cuts off the heads of two scoundrels. Violent and vengeful heroes seem to have been great favorites of Chinese audiences.

The final play of this quartet, *Liu Hsüan-te tu-fu Hsiang-yang hui* 劉玄德獨赴襄陽會 (Liu Hsüan-te Goes Alone to the Hsiang-yang Meeting), tells the story of Liu Pei's quick-witted escape from a scheme to kill him at a feast at Hsiang-yang. The plot is generally the same as that in chapters 34-36 of the *San-kuo chih yen-i*.*

Another play, *Pao Ch'eng-kung ching-fu Min-ch'ih hui* 保成公徑赴澠池會 (Protecting Duke Ch'eng Going to the Meeting at Min Pond), has also been attributed to Kao Wen-hsiu, although the attribution seems unsound. The plot centers around the prowess of Lin Hsiang-ju 藺相如 and his conflict with Lien Po 廉頗. Fragments of another play (*Yeh Lu Su* 謁魯肅 [Visiting Lu Su]) and some lyrics from non-dramatic *ch'ü** are also attributed to Kao; the attribution of the arias is questionable.

EDITIONS:

Chou Yü yeh Lu Su. Chao Ching-shen 趙景深. *Yüan-jen tsa-chü kou-ch'en* 元人雜劇鈎沈. Shanghai, 1959; pp. 19-22. Contains a fragment of the play.

Hao Chiu Chao Yüan yü shang huang, in *Yüan-ch'ü hsüan wai-pien*, Peking, 1959, pp. 129-183.

Hei-hsüan-feng shuang-hsien t'ou, in *Yüan-ch'ü hsüan*, pp. 681-704.

Hsin-k'an kuan-mu Hao-chiu Chao Yüan yü shang-huang . A Yüan woodblock in *Ku-pen*, IV.

———, in Cheng Ch'ien 鄭騫, *Chiao-ting Yüan-k'an tsa-chü san-shih-chung* 校定元刊雜劇三十種, Taipei, 1962, pp. 63-74.

Hsü Chia sui Fan Sui, in *Yüan-ch'ü hsüan*, pp. 1200-1220.

Liu Hsüan-te tu-fu Hsiang-yang hui, in *Yüan ch'ü hsüan wai-pien*, Peking, 1959, pp. 129-183.

[*KPHC*, IV contains all of the plays.]

STUDIES:

Lo, Chin-t'ang 羅錦堂. *Hsien-ts'un Yüan-jen tsa-chü pen-shih k'ao* 現存元人雜劇本事考, Taipei, 1960, 7-14, 121-126.

Yen, Tun-i 嚴敦易. "Lun Kao Wen-hsiu te *Shuang-hsien-kung*" 論高文秀的雙獻功, *Wen-hsüeh i-ch'an ts'eng-k'an*, 1 (1955), 236-244.

———. *Yüan-ch'ü chen-i* 元劇斟疑. Shanghai, 1960, pp. 36-48, 78-85, 131-134, 402-411, and 632-641.

—WD

Ko Ch'ao-fu 葛巢甫 (*fl.* 400), a native of Chü-jung 句容 (modern Kiangsu) and a grand-nephew of Ko Hung,* was the author of the Taoist Ling-pao ching 靈寶經 (Scriptures of the Numinous Gem). He completed these scriptures and transmitted them to his disciples Jen Yen-ch'ing 任延慶 and Hsü Ling-ch'i 徐靈期 during the Lung-an period of the Chin (397-402). Aside from these few facts, there is no biographical information concerning him.

On Ko Ch'ao-fu's compositions, however, the documentation is extensive. According to the earliest known Taoist catalog, compiled by Lu Hsiu-ching 陸修靜 (406-477) in 471, the Ling-pao scriptures originally totalled 29 titles in 35 or 36 *chüan*. Of these, 26 separate works (32 *chüan*) are still extant, preserved both in the *Tao-tsang** and in the Tun-huang manuscripts (see *Tun-huang wen-hsüeh*). There are also numerous citations of the scriptures in individual works, beginning with those of Lu Hsiu-ching, in Taoist encyclopedias such as the sixth-century *Wu-shang pi-yao* 无上祕要, and in various Buddhist polemical treatises such as Fa-lin's 法琳 *Pien-cheng lun* 辨正論 (626 A.D.).

The reason for our lack of information on the author of these extensive and important scriptures is simply that he never laid claim to having written them. The name of Ko Ch'ao-fu appears nowhere in the extant Ling-pao scriptures. Instead, Ko wrote that his scriptures were the result of a series of revelations bestowed by various Perfected 眞人 on his third-century ancestor Ko Hsüan 葛玄 (*tzu,* Hsiao-hsien 孝先, appellation, the Duke-transcendent Ko 葛仙公). Stimulated by slighting references to his ancestor in the works of Yang Hsi 楊羲 (b. 330), author of the Shang-ch'ing 上清 scriptures, Ko Ch'ao-fu has accorded Ko Hsüan a central position in his scriptures. Yang Hsi had learned from his celestial informants that Ko Hsüan was a mere Earth-bound Transcendent 地仙. Ko Ch'ao-fu asserted otherwise. The Ling-pao *Fa-lun tsui-fu* 法輪罪福 (Blame and Blessings of the Wheel of the Law; HY 346, 348, 455, and 347) portrays Ko Hsüan as studying under the highest Perfected and destined for the position of *San-t'ung Ta fa-shih* 三洞大法師 (Grand Master of the Law of the Three Caverns) in the unseen realms. Another of Ko Ch'ao-fu's scriptures, the *Chung-sheng nan* 衆聖難 (Trials of the Sages; HY 1107), shows the Duke-transcendent lecturing to a convocation of Earth-bound Transcendents on his pursuit of the benevolent doctrine of Ling-pao through various incarnations and recounts the vow that he took jointly with his disciples to be reborn as Taoists and to work for the salvation of all.

The Ling-pao scriptures were meant by their author to be a comprehensive compendium of the most sublime religious knowledge. Ko Ch'ao-fu had recourse to three bodies of religious literature in composing his scriptures: the Shang-ch'ing corpus of Yang Hsi, Buddhist scripture—particularly through the translations of Chih-ch'ien 支謙, and those scriptures of the southern T'ai-ch'ing 太清 tradition which informed Ko Hung's *Pao-p'u tzu*. Yet the Ling-pao scriptures, he claimed, represent an earlier and more pristine version of the themes and practices found in these other scriptures, for they originally sprang forth in the void and were the very words of the creator, flashing through the primordial murk in celestial script. This script, each graph a powerful talisman, is recorded in the *Wu-p'ien chen-wen* 五篇眞文 (Perfected Script in Five Fascicles; HY 22) and translated into the language of mortals in the *Yü-chüeh* 玉訣 (Jade Instructions; HY 352).

As a result of this synthesis of elements, the pantheon and cosmography of the Ling-pao scriptures are exceedingly complex. The texts describe a new and higher heaven, the Grand Veil Heaven 大羅天, which overtops the Three Heavens of Clarity 三清天 of the Shang-ch'ing scriptures and is presided over by a new supreme deity, the Primal Heavenly Worthy 元始天尊, whose name recalls one of the epithets of the Buddha. Under his sway come a multiplicity of heavens, powers and paradise-lands, including even the *ksetra* 刹 of the ten directions with their resident buddhas. The scriptures go on to recount the

479

earthly decay of this perfect order over four great kalpa-periods and to foretell the apocalypse of the final kalpa-period which prompted the revelations to Ko Hsüan. The scriptures of these revelations were to provide for the creation of a comprehensive community of believers, gentry and commoner, Buddhist and Taoist, whose goal, in imitation of the apotheosized Ko Hsüan, would be to spread the doctrine to rescue all humanity from the impending cataclysms.

In confronting the various evil influences attending the final age, the Taoist could arm himself through the recitation of a powerful mantra-like charm presented in the *Tu-jen ching* 度人經 (Book of Salvation; HY 1, *ch.* 1). This cantrip, again written in celestial script, is explained in the *Chu-t'ien nei-yin yü-tzu* 諸天內音玉字 (Inner Sounds of the Heavens in Jade Graphs; HY 97) to contain the secret names of the myriad spirits and demons, allowing the Taoist priest to avail himself of their protective powers. During the T'ang dynasty, the *Book of Salvation* was used together with the *Lao-tzu* as basic texts for the imperial Taoist initiation examinations.

While such individual practices were highly regarded, it was in the creation of rules, precepts and liturgies for the Taoist community that the Ling-pao scriptures made their strongest and most enduring impact. The soteric emphasis of the scriptures is particularly marked in such communal rites as the Most High Retreat of Ling-pao 靈寶无上齋 of the *Fu-chai wei-i chüeh* 敷齋威儀訣 (Instructions on the Performance of Retreats; HY 352) which was to be conducted for the "universal salvation of all men" 普度一切人. Ritual protection was extended as well to the "seven generations of ancestors" 七祖 in ceremonies such as that for the translation of souls from the purgatories into the celestial realms found in the *Ming-chen ko* 明眞科 (Ordinances of the Luminous Perfected; HY 1400). Such stately liturgies, including the recitation of verse, song, procession and public preaching, were highly popular and continue to be performed, little changed, in modern Taoist communities.

Specific rules for the Taoist church are delineated in the *T'ai-chi yin-chu pao-chüeh* 太極隱注寶訣 (Concealed Commentary and Treasured Instructions of the Grand Bourne; HY 425). This scripture contains ritual procedures for the copying, bestowal and recitation of scripture. It is here that perhaps the earliest delineation of what was to become the standard classificatory system of the Taoist canon is found, the *San-t'ung* 三洞 (see Taoist Literature essay). From this was derived the appellation *San-t'ung ti-tzu* 三洞弟子 (Disciple of the Three Caverns); that is, one who has been instructed in all three groups of scriptures. In addition, the *Shang-p'in ta-chieh wei-i* 上品大戒威儀 (Observances of the Major Precepts of the Upper Chapters; HY 177) outlines the practices appropriate to various grades of initiates.

That Ko Ch'ao-fu intended his scriptures to appeal not only to the literati but also to the masses is particularly evident in his *Chih-hui ting-chih t'ung-wei* 智慧定志通微 (Subtleties of the Affirmation of Wisdom; HY 325). In this text methods are expounded for the conversion and enlightenment of the illiterate and parables are recorded for use in public ritual. Didactic tales, some simply retellings of popular Buddhist *avadāna* stories, are to be found throughout the Ling-pao scriptures. In stories such as that recounting the former lives of two Perfected, a Taoist and a Buddhist, and that of the Heavenly Worthy descending as a beggar to expound precepts, the graphic depiction Ko Ch'ao-fu's hopes for the universal adoption of the Ling-pao faith can be seen.

EDITIONS:

Cheng-t'ung Tao-tsang 正統道藏. Rpt. Taipei, 1977. (Individual works are referenced by the number assigned them in Weng Tu-chien, *Combined Indices to the Authors and Titles of Books in Two Collections of Taoist Literature,* Harvard-Yenching Institute Sinological Index Series, No. 25, Rpt. Taipei, 1966—here abbreviated "HY".)

Ōfuchi Ninji 大淵忍爾. *Tonkō dōkyō mokurokuhen* 敦煌道經目錄編. Tokyo, 1978. This is a description and inventory of Taoist works from Tun-huang, including all textual variants.

Tonkō dōkyō zūrokuhen 敦煌道經圖錄編, Tokyo, 1980. Facsimile reproduction of Taoist scriptures from Tun-huang.

STUDIES:

Fukui, Kojun 福井康順. "Reihō-kyō no kenkyū 靈寶經の 研究," *Tōyō shisō no kenkyū*, Tokyo, 1955. ——

Kaltenmark, Max. "Ling-pao; note sur un terme du taoïsme religieux," *Mélanges publiés par Institut des Hautes Etudes Chinoises*, 2 (Paris, 1960), 559-588.

Ōfuchi Ninji. *Dōkyōshi no kenkyū* 道教史の研究. Okayama, 1964.
———. "On Ku Ling-pao ching," AA, 27 (1974), 33-56.

TRANSLATIONS:

Bokenkamp, Stephen R. "The 'Pacing the Void Stanzas' of the Ling-pao Scriptures," Unpublished M.A. thesis, University of California, Berkeley, 1981.

—SRB

Ko Hung 葛洪 (*tzu*, Chih-ch'uan 稚川, 283-343) is the author of the pseudonymous philosophical work, the *Pao-p'u-tzu* 抱朴子 (He Who Embraces Simplicity), and of an important contribution to the *chih-kuai** genre, the *Shen-hsien chuan.** Born to a prominent family of officials whose residence south of the Yangtze River dated from the Han-dynasty interregnum (*c.* A.D. 20), Ko Hung himself found no place in officialdom. Having served in a military capacity against the rebel Shih Ping 石冰 in 303-304, he went to Kuang-chou 廣州 in 306 as military aide to the newly appointed governor Chi Han 嵇含, but the death of his patron left Ko Hung again without employment. After the establishment of the exiled Chin court in Chien-yeh 建鄴 (modern Nanking), Ko, whether out of opposition to an administration swollen with northern emigrés or, as he himself claimed, convinced of the ephemerality of fame, repeatedly turned down the official positions offered to him in accordance with government policy designed to reconcile the southern gentry to the new order. Despite such refusals, in 330 Ko Hung was appointed Marquis of Kuan-chung 關中 by royal decree and given the revenue from two hundred households in his native Chü-jung 句容 (modern Kiangsu).

Frustrated in his pursuit of political position by the tenor of the times, Ko Hung embraced the role of literary recluse. He sought immortality both through study of the occult religious traditions of the South and through scholarly writing. Ko Hung's family had a tradition of preeminence in the arcane "Way of Transcendence" 仙道, and his first master, Cheng Yin 鄭隱 (Ssu-yüan) 思遠, had been the disciple of his granduncle Ko Hsüan 葛玄, a man reputed to have achieved the status of Transcendent. Ko also seems to have received religious texts and teachings from his father-in-law Pao Ching 鮑靚. These southern religious traditions were to become, within the century, the nucleus of the T'ai-ch'ing 太清 branch of Taoism. Although Ko himself showed no interest in "vulgar" organized religious movements, his writings played a formative role in the development not only of T'ai-ch'ing Taoism, but also of the Shang-ch'ing 上清 and Ling-pao 靈寶 sects, whose basic texts were produced in the milieu of his own kinsmen and descendents.

Ko Hung completed his *Pao-p'u-tzu* around 320. Written in the dialectical form commonly employed by such Han skeptics as Wang Ch'ung 王充 (A.D. 27-91), this work is an extended polemical defense of the conservative political, social, and religious Han scholarship which prevailed in southern China. The Outer Chapters 外篇, Ko's self-styled Confucianist writings, contain in elegant and fluid prose Ko's opinions on politics, society, customs, and morality. These essays are most interesting for the insights they provide into the intellectual and social life of the period and, in particular, the conflicts arising from the influx of northerners into the South after the fall of Lo-yang. The Inner Chapters 內篇 record Ko Hung's researches into the arts of transcendence. His essays here range over such topics as alchemy, meditation techniques, exorcism, sexual practices, herbalism, and talismanic charms—all presented with anecdotes and examples meant to convince the educated elite of his day that the state of transcendence was indeed obtainable. Connecting these two parts is

Ko's espousal, supported by classical precedent, of reclusive withdrawal from society when the times are not right for government service.

Because of his pivotal influence on the late fourth-century Taoist renaissance, it is not surprising that a number of later works in the Taoist canon are falsely attributed to Ko Hung. These are of three types. First, there are variant and sometimes expanded versions of essays in the *Pao-p'u-tzu*, such as the *Yang-sheng lun* 養生論 (HY 841) and the *Shen-hsien chin-chuo ching* 神仙金汋經 (HY 916). The second type may well have grown in similar fashion around a core drawn from the "310 *chüan*" of Ko Hung's miscellaneous writings. In this doubtful category we must place the *Ts'un-hou pei-chi fang* 肘後備急方 (HY 1295), a medical text listed in both Ko Hung's biography in the *Chin-shu* 晉書 and in the *Sui-shu* 隋書 bibliographic treatise. Third, and more demonstrably apocryphal, are those works in which Ko Hung's reputation is exploited to legitimize later alchemical and religious pursuits. Such works regularly provide detailed accounts of teachings Ko purportedly received from his master Cheng Yin (HY 938 and 949) or to divine revelations bestowed on him in the last years of his life (HY 166). This homage of imitation attests to the importance of Ko Hung's writings in the intellectual and religious currents of his age.

EDITIONS:

Pao-p'u-tzu. Cheng-t'ung Tao-tsang 正統道藏. Rpt. Taipei, 1977. Individual works are referenced by the number assigned them in Weng Tu-chien, *Combined Indices to the Authors and Titles of Books in Two Collections of Taoist Literature*, Harvard-Yenching Institute Sinological Index Series, No. 25, Rpt. Taipei, 1966. Here abbreviated "HY."

Pao-p'u-tzu. P'ing-chin-kuan ts'ung-shu 平津館叢書, edition of 1885. This is the collated edition of Sun Hsing-yen 孫星衍, based on the canonical edition and the Ming edition of Lu Shun-chih 盧舜治.

Pao-p'u-tzu nei-p'ien chiao-shih 抱朴子內篇校釋. Wang Ming 王明, ed. Peking, 1980. Prefaced by a brief study.

TRANSLATIONS:

Feifel, E. "Pao P'u-Tzu (Nei-p'ien)," *MS*, 6 (1941), 113ff. (*chüan* 1-3); 9 (1944), 1ff. (*chüan* 4); 11 (1946), 1ff. (*chüan* 11).

Honda, Wataru 本田濟. "*Hōhōshi*" 抱朴子, *Chūgoku koten bungaku taikei* 中國古典文學大系, 8, Tokyo, 1969, pp. 3-300. Annotated translation and study.

Liu, Li. *Légendes taoïstes du Chen-Sien-tchouan: traduction et étude annotées*. Ph.D. dissertation, University of Paris VII, 1978.

Sawada, Mizuho 沢田瑞穂. "*Shinsenden*" 神仙傳, *Chūgoku koten bungaku taikei*, 8, Tokyo, 1969, pp. 343-454. Translation and study.

Ware, James R. *Alchemy, Medicine, Religion in the China of A.D. 320: The Nei-p'ien of Ko Hung*. Cambridge, 1967. The only complete English translation of the *Nei-p'ien*, complete with footnotes and index, but lacking bibliography and reliability.

STUDIES:

Kaguraoka, Masatoshi 神樂岡昌俊. "*Hōhōshi* ni okeru initsu shisō" 抱朴子における隱逸思想, *Tōhō shūkyō*, 55 (1980), 51-69.

Lan, Hsiu-lung 藍秀隆. *Pao-p'u-tzu wai-p'ien chih yen-chiu* 抱朴子外篇之研究. Taipei, 1982.

Lin, Li-hsüeh 林麗雪. *Pao-p'u-tzu nei-wai-p'ien ssu-hsiang hsi-lun* 抱朴子內外篇思想析論. Taipei, 1980.

Miyazawa, Masayori 宮澤正順. "*Kakkō no rōshi hihan ni tsuite*" 葛洪の老子批判, *Tōhō shūkyō*, 56 (1980), 48-64.

Sivin, Nathan. "On the *Pao p'u tzu nei p'ien* and the Life of Ko Hung (283-343)," *Isis*, 60 (1969), 388-391.

—SRB

Ku-chi 滑稽 (modern *hua-chi*) and *hui-hsieh* 詼諧, both terms still much in use today, signify humor in traditional Chinese literature. Originally applied to both witty and glib speech, *ku-chi* literally means "a wine decanter pouring forth its contents ceaselessly." In the *Ch'u-tz'u** the phrase *t'u-t'i ku-chi* 突梯滑稽 (a slick and ingratiating manner) first appeared (it has since been used to describe broad comedy). Ssu-ma Ch'ien* included a chapter entitled "Ku-chi lieh-chuan" 滑稽列傳 (Biographies of the Jesters), in his *Shih-chi*,* celebrating three men of the Spring-and-Autumn and Warring-States periods—Ch'un-yü K'un 淳于髡, Jester Meng 優孟, and Jester Chan

優旃—whose amusing repartee produced salutary effects on their sovereigns. Pan Ku,* in his *Han-shu,* recorded the clever arguments of Tung-fang Shuo 東方朔, dubbed "the foremost of the *ku-chi* artists."

As recorded in the classics, humor in ancient China often had a didactic purpose, and its practice was not confined to the courtiers. The various schools of philosophers employed allegories, paradoxes, and satire to illustrate lofty truths. Confucius placed a high moral value on the *Shih-ching*＊ (Classic of Poetry) that he edited, which embodies folk "humor without hurting." Mencius' parable of the impatient farmer from Sung who pulled up the shoots "in order to help them grow" is a prototype of the latter-day moron and ethnic jokes. The Taoists have left epigrams such as this one from *Chuang-tzu:* "As long as sages are not dead, great robbers will continue to spread." A rich heritage of stories has been attributed, sometimes unreliably, to Lieh-tzu, Yin-tzu, Han-fei-tzu, *et al.* The old fool who would move mountains, the old man of the fort who lost his horse only to find that it was a blessing in disguise, the hawker of weapons who could not reconcile his toughest shield with his sharpest spear—these and other piquant commentaries on life have become idioms of timeless wisdom in the Chinese language.

In the *Wen-hsin tiao-lung*＊ Liu Hsieh devoted a chapter to humor, which he called "Hsieh yin" 諧隱 (Humor and Enigma). He regarded the two as essentially the same and cited with approval the examples of Ch'un-yü K'un, Sung Yü 宋玉, and the jesters Meng and Chan. Liu considered the artful parables with which they regaled their riddle-loving princes to be didactic and high principled. However, Liu warned against levity for its own sake, as represented by Tung-fang Shuo and later joksters of the Wei and Chin periods. He deprecated "thigh-slapping merriment" which served no practical purposes but "would have a damaging effect on moral living."

Ch'un-yü K'un's discourse on the five stages of drunkenness, designed to sober up King Wei of Ch'i, contrasts with the philosophies of some of the scholar-poets of the Wei-Chin era who indulged in drinking bouts and eccentric behavior to protect themselves against dangerous involvement in the degenerate politics of the time. Liu Ling 劉伶, one of the *Chu-lin ch'i-hsien* 竹林七賢 (Seven Sages of the Bamboo Grove) and a habitual drunkard, when mocked for disporting himself stark naked at home, retorted: "I regard heaven and earth as my shelter and my house as my clothing. So why do you gentlemen barge into my trousers?" As recorded in *Shih-shuo hsin-yü,*＊ this was an early example of the anecdotal strain in Chinese humorous literature.

The first collection of Chinese jokes, *Hsiao-lin* 笑林 (A Forest of Laughs) by Han-tan Ch'un 邯鄲淳, also appeared during the Wei period. This book is lost but some of its contents have been incorporated in later anthologies, such as *Ch'i-yen lu* 啟顏錄 (Breaking Into a Smile), attributed to Hou Po 侯白 of the Sui dynasty, *Hsiao-fu* 笑府 (Mansion of Laughter), compiled by Feng Meng-lung,* and a great number of joke books published in the Ch'ing. The corpus of the traditional "laugh-talk" is not a large one; stories were retold with variations and embellishments by successive generations of compilers. Many were stock situations: a grandfather chastises his grandson, causing the boy's father to administer vigorous self-punishment—"If you can beat my son, why can't I beat yours?"; an adulterous wife, surprised by the returning husband, quickly hides her lover, and when the husband demands to know what is in the sack, a small voice inside answers, "Rice!"

There are jests about physical deformities, corrupt officials, and lascivious priests, crooks and quacks of all professions, the miserly host and the greedy guest, the stupid son-in-law, etc. Some point up ethical values or make a clever play on words; just as many run to the crude and the scatological.

Under the moralistic governments of Confucian orthodoxy, humorous literature was frowned upon. But a tradition of storytelling in time evolved into dramas and fictions for popular entertainment. On the stage the *ch'ou* and *ching* roles (see *chiao-se*) represented venal officials, profligate rascals, and bumbling retainers, from the Yüan plays down to the later regional operas. Clever servants, like Crimson Maid (Hung-niang) in *Hsi-hsiang chi*,* and Spring Fragrance (Ch'un-hsiang) in *Mu-tan T'ing* (see T'ang Hsien-tsu), have won many chuckles and stolen scenes from their lovesick mistresses.

Ming stories and novels frequently contain passages of high humor. In *Hsi-yu chi*,* Monkey Sun, called "The Great Sage, Equal of Heaven," entertains the reader with his antics and superhuman prowess, but even his ability to turn six-thousand-mile somersaults cannot free him from the palm of Buddha. *Shui-hu chuan*,* a novel about heroic bandits of the Southern Sung, contains a rollicking drunken scene in which the "Tattooed Monk" wreaks havoc on the tranquil monastery where he is a reluctant inmate.

One of the outstanding works in Ch'ing fiction, *Ching-hua yüan*,* uses the Swiftian concept of a voyage to strange lands. These include the topsy-turvy Country of Gentlemen, where customers try to pay more while shopkeepers insist on selling for less, the Country of Women, the Black-Teeth Country, the Two-Faced Country, etc., all designed to reflect on the manners and mores of contemporary Chinese society. In contrast to satiric fantasies, the novel *Hung-lou meng** creates with surpassing artistry a real world with all its humor and pathos. The passages involving the distant country relation Liu Lao-lao 劉老老 (Granny Liu), come to pay her respects to the sophisticated ladies of the Jung-kuo Mansion, are cherished by each generation of new readers both for their comedy of human relationships and for the author's psychological insights. At this level, humor in traditional Chinese literature has moved beyond the realm of *ku-chi* and *hui-hsieh* into that of *yu-mo* 幽默, a neologism which has become firmly established in the Chinese vocabulary over the past fifty years and is akin in spirit to the English word *humor.*

EDITIONS:

Li, I-ting 李奕定. *Chung-kuo li-tai yü-yen hsüan-chi* 中國歷代寓言選集. Taipei, 1966. Selections, with emphasis on fables and allegories, from the early Chou philosophers to the Ch'ing.

Wang, Li-ch'i 王利器. *Li-tai hsiao-hua chi* 歷代笑話集, Shanghai, 1957; rpt. Peking, 1981. Selections from some seventy anthologies of jokes, dating from the Wei to the late Ch'ing.

TRANSLATIONS:

Kao, George. *Chinese Wit and Humor.* New York, 1946; rpt. New York, 1974. Selections in English translation arranged by genres and including a section on the modern "Humor of Protest."

Watson, Burton. "The Biography of Tung-fang Shuo" (translation of *Han shu,* chüan 65, "Tung-fang Shuo chuan"), in *Courtier and Commoner in Ancient China: Selections from the History of the Former Han,* New York, 1974, pp. 79-106.

Wells, Henry W. *Traditional Chinese Humor: A Study in Art and Literature.* Bloomington, 1971. A Westerner's appreciation of the Chinese sense of humor as expressed in the plastic arts and in literature.

STUDIES:

Giles, Herbert. "Wit and Humor," in *A History of Chinese Literature,* New York, 1901, pp. 430-436.

Hsia, C. T. "The Chinese Sense of Humor," *Renditions,* 9 (Spring 1978), 30-36.

Liu, Mau-tsai. "Prolegomena zum Wesen chinesischer Rätsel," *OE,* 26 (1979), 48-56.

Pokora, Timoteus. "Ironical Critics at Ancient Chinese Courts (*Shih chi,* 126)," *OE,* 20 (1973), 49-64.

Wang, Hsiao-i 王小逸, ed. *Yu-mo ku-wen hsüan* 幽默古文選. Hong Kong, 1977.

—GK

Ku-chin chu 古今註 is a small volume written by Ts'ui Pao 崔豹 (*tzu,* Cheng-hsiung 正熊 or Cheng-neng 正能, *fl.* 300). Ts'ui was an aide to the grand mentor in the court of Emperor Hui of the Chin dynasty (r. 290-306). One source identifies Ts'ui as a native of the northeastern area of Yen 燕 and perhaps the author of an edition of the *Lun-yü* (see *ching*). Other than this nothing is known of Ts'ui Pao.

The *Ku-chin chu* is a brief lexicon-encyclopedia composed of the author's notes on selected subjects, and a text entirely of anecdote, explanation, and lexical gloss. These are eight categories of information: carriages and clothes, cities and towns, music, birds and beasts, fish and insects, flora, miscellaneous notes, and questions and answers. A modern edition has collected ten more short entries from an early encyclopedia; these are largely anecdotes about several emperors of the Han.

There has been some concern over the authenticity of Ts'ui's text, but arguments offered by recent scholars seem to dispel those suspicions. The *Ssu-k'u ch'üan-shu ts'ung-mu t'i-yao* (see Chi Yün) editors originally suspected that the text, supposedly lost in the Sung dynasty, was reconstructed from a later expansion of Ts'ui's volume. These suspicions have been dismissed by Chang Yüan-chi 張元濟 (1866-c. 1960) and by other modern scholars. Thus, the three-*chüan* text now extant can be assumed to be authentic and to be the same one mentioned in the bibliographic treatise of the *Sui-shu*.

Ts'ui Pao's work is written in clean, precise prose. In all eight categories each of the separate entries, apparently in random order, begins a new column. The sections on carriages and clothes and on cities and towns are comprised mostly of the explication of terms and origins. The information in these two sections, especially that on clothes, is often legendary in nature. The sections on flora and fauna are composed of several different types of glosses and some explanatory notes. The glosses include apparent dialect and popular names for common terms (Ts'ui notes that dogs are also known as "yellow ears," and gives seven names for the firefly), while the notes sometimes reveal interesting popular beliefs (including why bats hang upside down). The miscellaneous notes are just that, and the question and answer section often deals with mysterious or confusing legendary material (it is explained, for example, why the cicada is also called "lady of Ch'i"). The questions are asked by three unidentifiable people, Niu Heng 牛亨,

Ch'eng Ya 程雅, and Sun Hsing-kung 孫興公.

The section most useful to the student of literature is, however, the one on music. In this section are anecdotes and background information concerning seventeen *yüeh-fu** poems. These passages often contain a line or two from the original composition, often all that remains of the poem. Three poems mentioned have become well-known *yüeh-fu* poems: "Mo-shang sang" 陌上桑, "P'ing ling tung" 平陵東, and "Shang liu t'ien" 上留田. In addition to these notes on specific poems, there are passages concerning two kinds of early music, *tuan-hsiao lao-ko* 短簫鐃歌 and *heng-ch'ui* 橫吹. The former is identified as a type of military music and the latter as a type of foreign (*hu* 胡) music. All these notes should be consulted when investigating early *yüeh-fu* poetry and music.

EDITIONS:
Ts'ui, Pao. *Ku-chin chu.* SPPY. Contains the prefaces in the SPTK along with one detailing the various textual problems.
———. *Ku-chin chu.* SPTK. Contains prefaces by Chang Yüan-chi and Li Tao 李燾 (1115-1184), 1220.
———. *Ku-chin chu, Chung-hua ku-chin chu, Su-shih yen-i* 古今註中華古今註蘇氏演義. Shanghai, 1956. This excellent edition also contains a four-corner index to entries, terms, names, etc. mentioned in the three texts collected.

—JA

Ku Fei-hsiung 顧非熊 (*tzu*, unknown, *fl.* 836) was a native of Soochow. Tuan Ch'eng-shih reports in his *Yu-yang tsa-tsu** that he was regarded as the reincarnation of another beloved son of Ku K'uang,* whose death his father lamented bitterly.

Ku Fei-hsiung is said to have displayed precocious literary gifts, but his attempts over many years to win certification as a *chin-shih* graduate proved fruitless until, in 845, Emperor Wu-tsung compelled the examiners to pass him. His official life was brief and has hardly been reported. He is reputed to have shared in some degree his father's wit and insolence, and this may explain his early departure to Mao Shan, where, as had his father, he spent what is known of the rest of his life. A poem by Wang Chien* on his departure from the capital is extant.

Only about seventy of Ku Fei-hsiung's poems survive. They are mainly about persons and events in his own life; many are addressed to Buddhist monks. The latter show appreciation of the devotion and fortitude of these men, but little concern with their beliefs. Sometimes a wry skepticism or even an occasional crankiness shows through. Like the poems of his father, his verse employs a rather plain diction. But unlike his father's, Ku's Mao Shan poems have little of the supernatural or religious in them. The writer honors the gentlemen-priests he met there, and he appreciates the advantages of the slow, peaceful rhythm of life on the mountain. But although he admits his failure in the world of practical affairs, he cannot shake off his bitterness. He may pose as a gentleman reconciled to exile in a well-pruned landscape, but even the sound of a spring dripping down the face of a cliff reminds him of the palace clepsydra and the splendid but ritualized life it governed. The attention to pines, wild deer, monkeys, unusual birds, and cold mountain water seems little more than the arranging of stage properties: his father's sense of the numinous in nature is absent. Surprisingly, the single piece of his imaginative prose to survive, the *Miao-nü chuan* 妙女傳, a popular tale of the supernatural in a Buddhist setting with some Taoist elements, displays a rather charming dreamlike atmosphere, quite unlike that of his more down-to-earth poems.

EDITIONS:

Kuo-tso-kung pu-i 國佐公補遺. 1v. Huang-ho Shan-chuang 黃鶴山莊, ed., 1839.

Miao-nü chuan 妙女傳. Changsha, 1939.

Ch'üan Tang shih, v. 8, *ch.* 509, pp. 5780-5793.

—ES

Ku K'uang 顧況 (*tzu*, Pu-weng 逋翁, *c.* 725-*c.* 814), a painter, poet, and calligrapher, was a native of Soochow. His ability attracted the attention of the powerful politicians Liu Hun 柳渾 (715-789) and espe-cially Li Pi 李泌 (722-789) when they were in the Wu Region in the late eighth century. Li Pi became his patron, possibly because, like himself, Ku K'uang was devoted to Taoist studies. The two courtiers obtained a position for the poet in the imperial library, where he stayed safe under Li Pi's shadow until the latter's death in 789. Then, exposed to the attacks of enemies he had made with his notoriously sarcastic wit, he was degraded to a minor post in Jao-chou 饒州, which he soon deserted to spend the rest of his life in retirement on Mao Shan 茅山, the sacred center of the dominant Taoist sect of T'ang times. (The T'ang chronicler Li Ch'o 李綽 avers that the popular view of Ku K'uang's "expulsion" is erroneous. Perhaps he was too "relaxed and uninhibited" for most courtiers, but he left Ch'ang-an voluntarily, rejecting preferment and patronage in favor of a contemplative life in religion). During his retirement he styled himself Hua-yang Chen I 華陽眞逸 —"Realized and Uncon-fined One of Hua-yang"— and lived out his peaceful days at Shih hei ch'ih 石黑池 (Stone Black Pool) (near the home of his fellow-poet Ch'in Hsi 秦系) overlooking an herb garden from a pine-shaded window.

It is difficult to find traces of Ku K'uang's alleged sarcasm in his poetry. His "old-style" compositions, much concerned with man's predicament, are often pathetic, occasionally tinged with irony. But his work as a whole is most characteristically engaged with supernatural themes and shows a sense of wonder at the mysterious forces working beyond the phenomenal world. The conventional figures who serve as foci for these musings include the star goddess known as *Chih nü* 織女 (Weaving Woman), the goddess of the Han River, and the familiar spirits of Lake Tung-t'ing. There are often glimpses of shamanistic rites or echoes of antiquity in the voice of the ghost-king of ancient Ch'u. More specifically Taoist are allusions to astral powers revealed through gemmy images of powerful entities behind the stars (the sun and moon are "jade discs"; the five planets are "pearls"). His most interesting poems were written in his congenial retreat at Mao

Shan. There his love of nature is finally fused with his otherworldly aspirations. The delights of a carefully selected or cultivated landscape are impregnated with both literary and religious attitudes. His ostensible themes range widely, from verses about trees, flowers, wild birds, and mountain scenery, in artfully arranged diction, to others addressed to priests or responding to musical performances. Looking out over the lush prospect of Willow Valley, he ponders the secrets of the *Huang-t'ing ching* 黃庭經 (Yellow Court Classic); he has intimations of immortality in the shadows of moonlit fanes which suggest the starry mansions of the gods; he is entranced by visions of holy but untouchable priestesses, and by the uncanny bugling of sacred cranes. One of his Taoist poems, "Pu-hsü tz'u" 步虛詞 (Canto on Pacing the Void), based on an old Mao Shan ritual, was written during his joyless residence in the capital; he composed it at the "T'ai-ch'ing kung" 太清宮 (Palace of Grand Clarity), a temple founded by Hsüan-tsung in honor of the "T'ai-shang Lao chün" 太上老君 (All-highest Lord Lao).

A small collection of Ku K'uang's prose survives. The most noteworthy are a number of *chi* 記 (records) which show a deep familiarity with nature, sometimes tinged with a haunting sense of divine presences. The unornamented but sensitive style recalls some of the compositions of Liu Tsung-yüan.*

Huang-fu Shih 皇甫湜, the ninth-century author of the preface to Ku K'uang's collected works, finds both poet and poetry well-suited to the rich and strange land of Wu, marked by the weird rocks of T'ai-hu, the fantastic calls of the cranes, and the great Buddhist establishments. "He gave warmth," wrote the critic, "to its freshness and glory in the making of his verses." Huang-fu even asserts that the poet's use of language was beyond the attainment of ordinary mortals—indeed, he finds him the only poet of his generation ranking with Li Po* and Tu Fu.*

EDITIONS:

Ku Hua-yang chi 顧華陽集. 3v. Huang-ho shan-chuang tsang pan 黃鶴山莊藏板, 1839.

Ch'üan T'ang shih, v. 4, *ch.* 264-267, pp. 2927-2972.

Ch'üan T'ang wen, v. 11, *ch.* 528-530, pp. 6797-6827.

TRANSLATIONS:

Sunflower, pp. 150-151.

Hsü, *Anthologie*, pp. 167-168.

Schafer, E. H. *Mao Shan in T'ang Times* (Society for the Study of Chinese Religions, Monograph No. 1). Boulder, Colorado, 1980, pp. 39-40, 43, 50.

STUDIES:

Fu, *Shih-jen*, pp.379-408: "Ku K'uang k'ao"

—ES

Ku-shih chi 古詩紀 (also called *Shih chi* 詩紀), an ambitious collection of all Chinese verse up to and including the Sui dynasty, is probably still the most complete work of its kind in existence. Its compiler, Feng Wei-ne 馮惟訥 (1512-1572), was a member of a prominent literary family from Shantung and was considered its best poet, albeit lacking in originality (see also Feng Wei-min). His teacher in canonical studies was Ou-yang Te 歐楊德 (1496-1554), a disciple of Wang Shou-jen. From 1540 to 1570 Feng Wei-ne pursued an exemplary official career which took him to posts in half a dozen provinces; he was given the title of Chief Minister of Imperial Entertainments upon retirement.

He began work on the *Ku-shih chi* in 1544 and completed it in 1557, drawing on a fairly large number of collections. These collections, which for the most part concentrated on Six Dynasties poetry, were conceived as selective anthologies, as encyclopedic reference works (in which the poetry was arranged according to its subject matter), or were very incomplete. Feng Wei-ne's work aims at a complete reprinting of all verse and songs, in chronological order from the earliest examples quoted in various pre-Ch'in canonical, historical, and philosophical texts (but excluding the poems in the *Shih-ching**) to poems by known authors down to the end of the Sui. There are short biographies of the poets and occasionally succinct textual notes. The book is thus divided into four parts: "Ku i-shih" 古逸詩 (Ancient Fragmentary Verse

古逸詩

487

in 10 *chüan,* probably inspired by the *Feng-ya i pien* 風雅逸編 of Yang Shen*); "Cheng chi" 正集 (Main Collection, in 130 *chüan* divided according to individual dynasties); "Wai chi" 外集 (Supplementary Collection, in 4 *chüan,* containing verse attributed to immortals and to ghosts); and a "Pieh chi" 別集 (Annex, 12 *chüan*) of literary criticism either contemporary with the verse included or concerning it. The first edition, by Chen Ching 正集, appeared in Shensi in 1560 and is very rare. There are three or four subsequent editions, all Ming, of which the most familiar was published by Wu Kuan 吳琯 in Nanking in 1586. The editors of the *Ssu-k'u ch'üan-shu* (see Chi Yün) prefer the Wu Kuan edition; Suzuki and Ikkai, the first edition.

A work of such enormous scope obviously could not be free of errors (especially of attribution) and omissions. And yet none of the many works designed to replace it rival its accuracy, convenience of arrangement, or completeness. The most serious omissions are those of *yao* 謠 (popular songs) and *yen* 諺 (sayings) that can now be found in the *Ku yao-yen* 古謠諺 in 100 *chüan* (preface dated 1860) of Tu Wen-lan 杜文瀾 (1815-1881). Corrections of the *Ku-shih chi* have been made by Feng Shu, Lu Ch'in-li, and others (see Bibliography below). The *Ch'üan Han San-kuo Chin Nan-pei-ch'ao shih** by Ting Fu-pao (Shanghai, 1916) claims to complete the *Ku-shih chi,* but it has actually only added about 160 items, and most of these are fragmentary single lines. All who have studied it agree that the *Ku-shih chi* is a monumental work, invaluable to anyone interested in the entire corpus of Chinese poetry from its origins to the end of the Sui. Some of its texts, such as the "Yung-huai shih" 詠懷詩 by Juan Chi,* are the oldest versions now in existence.

EDITIONS:

Ku-shih chi. Ssu-k'u ch'üan-shu chen-pen 四庫全書珍本. Based on the Wu Kuan edition of 1586.

STUDIES:

Feng, Shu 馮舒. *Shih-chi k'uang-miu* 詩紀匡謬 (preface dated 1634). *Chih-pu-tsu Chai ts'ung-shu* and *TSCC.*

Ssu-k'u ch'üan-shu k'ao-cheng 四庫全書考證 (1783), 92, pp. 3782-3786, in the *TSCC* edition.

Lu, Ch'in-li 逯欽立. "*Ku-shih chi* pu-cheng hsü-li" 古詩紀補正敍例, 12 (1947), 61-90.

Suzuki, Shūji 鈴木修次 and Ikkai Tomoyoshi 一海知義. "Fū Itotsu to sono *Shiki*" 馮惟訥とその詩紀, *Nihon Chūgoku gakkai hō*, 12 (1960), 70-91.

—DH

Ku-shih hsüan 古詩選 (also known as *Wu-ch'i-yen shih ch'ao* 五七言詩鈔) is a poetry anthology compiled in 1697 by Wang Shih-chen* (1634-1711), the eminent Ch'ing poet and literary critic. It is one of several anthologies compiled by Wang; the other major one being his *T'ang hsien san-mei chi* 唐賢三昧集. The *Ku-shih hsüan* appears near the end of a long line of anthologies in China. Often this anthologizing of the literary heritage has provided Chinese critics with the context for developing an understanding of genre theory. Wang's anthology is, however, limited to *shih** poetry, and thus avoids the basic question of how to categorize the diverse poetic types in classical Chinese literature. Wang needed only to decide what *shih* poetry was and then how to select and arrange it.

Wang Shih-chen was primarily concerned with collecting old-style poetry (*ku-shih* 古詩), but did include some new-style poetry (*hsin-t'i shih* 新體詩) in later chapters. The book is divided in half, with seventeen *chüan* devoted to pentasyllabic verse and fifteen to septasyllabic (with some authors, of course, appearing in both sections). The poems are arranged chronologically, except for the common practice of placing poems by emperors at the beginning of dynastic divisions. A group of *ku-ko* 古歌 (archaic songs), begins the septasyllabic section, but the rest of it traditionally dates no earlier than the Han dynasty. The pentasyllabic corpus includes pieces into the T'ang, although only five T'ang poets are represented: Ch'en Tzu-ang,* Chang Chiu-ling,* Li Po,* Wei Ying-wu,* and Liu Tsung-yüan* (the majority of the poems of these five poets are in "old style"). The septasyllabic section, however, includes poets up into the Yüan, with eleven from the T'ang, most notably Wang Wei,* Tu

Fu,* and Han Yü.* This may appear a slim representation of the great T'ang *shih* poetry, but Wang compiled other anthologies devoted to the verse of that era, such as the *T'ang hsien san-mei chi,* which includes work by forty-two poets.

The "archaic songs" that begin the septasyllabic poetry are *not* generally seven-syllable verse, but rather a mixture of different types of poetry, including four-syllable, six-syllable, and *sao* 騷 verse. This inclusion seems to be Wang's attempt to account for the development of *shih* poetry after the *Shih-ching**; Shen Te-ch'ien* did the same thing in his famous anthology *Ku-shih yüan** (1725). Wang also expands the definition of *shih* poetry to include *yüeh-fu,** which is found throughout the anthology. In a preface Wang names a few Han *yüeh-fu* poems and asks "How can these Music Bureau poems not be *shih* poetry?" Thus he collects pentasyllabic *yüeh-fu* poems, including the long narrative poem "K'ung-ch'üeh tung-nan fei" 孔雀東南飛, in the first section. *Yüeh-fu* poems that are not pentasyllabic are then included in the second section, whether they are seven-syllable or not (they usually are not).

The *Ku-shih hsüan* has two prefaces by Wang (one for each major division of the text), wherein he discusses *shih* poetry in general and his selection of poems and poets.

Wang's *Ku-shih hsüan* differs from his *T'ang hsien san-mei chi* in that it contains very little commentary. While *T'ang hsien* is full of comments and glosses, the *Ku-shih hsüan* contains only short prefaces to some of the "archaic songs" and occasional interlinear notes on variants. Neither actually represents the critic's own views, but are rather notes taken from the tradition. Thus, Wang's *Ku-shih hsüan* is a fairly orthodox, evenhanded collection of *shih* poetry up to the T'ang, with a smattering of later poems. As such it must have had substantial influence on Shen Te-ch'ien's later collection of pre-T'ang poems. While Wang had some strong critical views, they do not seem to have affected greatly his choice of poems for this anthology.

EDITIONS:

Ku-shih hsüan. SPPY.

Yü-yang shan-jen ku-shih hsüan 漁洋山人古詩選. Nanking, 1866.

Index to Pre-T'ang Poetry: A Combined Index to Ku-shih yüan *and* Ku-shih hsüan. Chinese Materials Center, Research Aids Series. Chikfong Lee, compilor. Taipei, 1982.

STUDIES:

Lun, Ming 倫明. "Yü-yang shan-jen chu shu-k'ao" 漁洋山人著書考, *Yen-ching hsüeh-pao,* 5 (1929), 913-964. See entries 50 and 51 for a short description of this text.

—JA

Ku-shih shih-chiu shou 古詩十九首 (Nineteen Old Poems) are traditionally considered the earliest extant examples of pentasyllabic verse, which became for several centuries the dominant form of Chinese poetry. As well as establishing the basic *shih* meter of five words per line, the "Nineteen Old Poems" also announced themes and techniques which were to reappear in Chinese poetry throughout the following centuries.

Since the Six Dynasties, questions concerning the dating and authorship of the "Nineteen Old Poems" have aroused considerable controversy. The title was first given to this group of anonymous poems when they were collected in the *Wen-hsüan** anthology by Hsiao T'ung in the sixth century. Eight of these poems also appeared in the *Yü-t'ai hsin-yung,** an anthology of love poetry compiled slightly later, though in the latter collection they were attributed to Mei Sheng.*

More recent critics also disagree about the origins of the "Nineteen Old Poems." Some maintain that they date from different periods; others claim they represent the work of one generation or even of a single poet. Those scholars who wish to prove (in accordance with the attribution to Mei Sheng) that some of the poems have come from the Former Han argue that the pentasyllabic meter and tight parallelism date back that far. But other critics point to evidence which shows origins in the Latter Han—the poems' use of certain taboo words and references to Lo-yang, the Latter Han capital. A number of readers have noted similarities between the anonymous "Nineteen Old Poems" and *shih* poetry by known authors of the Chien-an period at the end of the Han: both bodies of verse manifest a pessimism which may be a response to the social and political turmoil of the time; both use similar themes of separation from loved ones, long journeys, and alienation; and both employ pentasyllabic meter, similar rhyme schemes, reduplicated adjectives, and conventional images. For these reasons, Chien-an poets such as Ts'ao Chih* and Wang Ts'an* have been suggested as possible authors of the "Nineteen Old Poems."

It seems best to follow the middle road and assume that the attribution to Mei Sheng of the Former Han is too early, while that to Ts'ao Chih or the Chien-an period is too late. The "Nineteen Old Poems" probably represent all that remains of a large corpus of ancient-style poems in the five-word meter which flourished during the first and second centuries A.D. and were still in circulation in the Six Dynasties. The "Nineteen Old Poems" occupy a position between the popular *yüeh-fu** tradition and literati writings. They belong to a shared anonymous genre which reveals the transition from folk songs to self-conscious, elite, individual creations.

Like *yüeh-fu* songs, the "Nineteen Old Poems" tend to use conventional formulas, proverbs, and "tag" endings. Some appear fragmentary, with abrupt shifts in perspective and subject matter. Stock characters, dialogue, and apparent lower-class awe of wealth and power all indicate an indebtedness to the folk song. However, these popular elements have clearly been reworked, and many of the "Nineteen Old Poems" are remarkably unified in structure, with sophisticated thematic development and imagistic coherence. Often Chien-an and Wei poems imitate images, phrases, lines and topics of the "Nineteen Old Poems." Critics have postulated that the "Nineteen Old Poems" were composed by Latter Han literati who preferred anonymity because at the time the pentasyllabic *shih* genre was, though widely used, not yet fully accepted in elite circles.

The poems are characterized by two dominant perspectives: that of the lonely woman in her room longing for her far-away lover and that of the man who, forced to travel away from home, sees his life as a continual journey. Many of the poems emphasize the brevity of human life, the vanity of fame and fortune, and the inevitability of death. Some seek consolation in human community and available pleasures such as wine and music. But all are concerned with the universal human condition and are colored by an unrelenting melancholy.

The "Nineteen Old Poems" heavily influenced the style of pentasyllabic *shih* poetry for almost two millennia. These Han poems demonstrate the power of suggestiveness and understatement. The art of the evocative image is illustrated in opening lines such as "Green, green, the grass by the river bank,/Thick, thick, the willows in the garden" or "The clear moon shines brightly in the night,/ Crickets chirp by the eastern wall." The skillful use of open-ended closure is forceful in final lines such as "Gazing at each other, never able to speak" and in suggestive interrogatives like "Who knows when we will meet again?" The simplicity and directness of the "Nineteen Old Poems" contributes to their enduring appeal: the common experiences of ordinary people are concretely presented in images of the long road and flowing river, the shining moon and flying birds. Yet there is subtlety in the contrasts between the desolation of a lonely woman and the luxuriance of foliage or a pair of soaring cranes. Lines such as "Slender, slender, she lifts a pale hand" or "White poplars, how they whisper" contain a delicacy and poise which were widely imitated for hundreds of years. The "Nineteen Old Poems" not only mark the beginning of a poetic tradition, but also are treasured as some of China's most beautiful and immediately accessible literary works.

EDITIONS:
Ku-shih shih-chiu shou chi-shih 古詩十九首集釋. Sui Sen-shu 隋森樹, ed., Taipei, 1971. The most

comprehensive annotated edition of the poems with an anthology of commentary by various critics.

TRANSLATIONS:

Waley, Arthur. *170 Chinese Poems.* London, 1918, pp. 59-68.

———, *Chinese Poems,* pp. 50-57.

———, *Translations,* pp. 37-48.

Watson, *Lyricism,* pp. 15-32.

STUDIES:

Cheng, Wen 鄭文. "Lun *Ku-shih shih-chiu shou* 'Tung-ch'eng kao ch'ieh ch'ang' teng san-shou pu tso yü T'ai-ch'u cheng-li i-ch'ien" 論古詩十九首東城高且長等三首不作於太初正曆以前, *Kan-su Shih-ta hsüeh-pao* 甘肅師大學報 (chi-hsüeh she-hui k'o-hsüeh 哲學社會科學), 1979, 1 (February 1979), 64-72.

Diény, J. P. *Les Dix-Neuf Poèmes Anciens.* Paris, 1963.

Fang, Tsu-shen 方祖燊. "Han ku-shih shih-tai wen-t'i k'ao-pien" 漢古詩時代問題考辨, *Ta-lu tsa-chih,* 31.5 (September 1965), 13-16; 31.6 (September 1965), 30-35; 31.7 (October 1965), 31-35.

Kanno, Shōmei 簡野正明. "Kyū Yaku *Koshi jūkyū shu*" 舊譯古詩十九首, *Tenri Daigaku gakuhō,* 85 (1973), 65-89.

Kuang, Shih-yuan 鄺士元. "Ku-shih 'Ming-yüeh chiao yeh-kuang' ch'uang-tso nien-tai k'ao" 古詩明月皎夜光創作年代考, *Ta-lu tsa-chih,* 33.2 (July 1966), 17-19.

Sui, *Ku-shih.*

—MW

Ku-shih yüan 古詩源 (The Wellsprings of Verse, fourteen *chüan*) is an anthology of pre-T'ang *shih** poetry compiled in the early Ch'ing period by Shen Te-ch'ien.* In his preface, written in the summer of 1719, Shen explains that he traces the sources for the efflorescence of *shih* poetry during the T'ang. His aim was in part to show the evolutionary development of poetic sensibilities as expressed in *shih;* he likewise sought to demonstrate the excellence to be found in earlier verse. This latter aim seems to be a reaction against the Ming and Ch'ing fashion of imitating one or another group of T'ang poets while tending to ignore all others.

The earliest poems in the anthology are attributed to hoary antiquity; excluding *Shih-ching** and *Ch'u-tz'u,** Shen Te-ch'ien attempted an exhaustive collection of Chou and Han verse. To this end he used all the existing historical philosophical works of the pre-Chin period. Shen was much more selective in his choice of Six Dynasties verse. Since Kuo Mao-ch'ien's *Yüeh-fu shih-chi* collects all extant ballads and songs of the *yüeh-fu** tradition, and because the *Wen-hsüan** preserves much of the work of known Six Dynasties poets, Shen selected from these works what he considered the best. His work begins with songs from the time of the sage kings Yao and Shun (*c.* 2300 B.C. by tradition), the private songs of the Han emperors, verse attributed to Su Wu 蘇武 and Li Ling 李陵, many *yüeh-fu* ballads, and the "Ku-shih shih-chiu shou."* Among the Six Dynasties poets, Juan Chi,* T'ao Ch'ien,* Hsieh Ling-yün,* Pao Chao,* Hsieh T'iao,* and Yü Hsin* are particularly well represented.

Ku-shih yüan was compiled with the assistance of numerous literati from the Soochow area, including several of Shen's disciples. The collection was intended as a sequel to Shen's collection of T'ang verse, *T'ang-shih pieh-ts'ai chi* 唐詩別裁集 (1717, in 20 *chüan*), which he compiled with the assistance of Ch'en Shu-tzu 陳樹滋. A more fully annotated edition of the *Ku-shih-yüan,* giving additional biographical information concerning the poets represented, was produced in 1934 by Chu Nan-hui 朱南滙.

EDITIONS:

Shen, Te-ch'ien, ed. *Ku-shih-yüan.* 14 *chüan.* Hunan, 1891.

———, ed. *Ku-shih-yüan.* SPPY.

———, ed. *Ku-shih-yüan.* 2v. Changsha, 1939.

———, ed. *Ku-shih-yüan. Kuo-hsüeh chi-pen ts'ung-shu.* Taipei, 1956.

———, ed. *Ku-shih-yüan.* Peking, 1957.

———, comp. *Hsiang-chu Ku-shih-yüan* 詳註古詩源. Chu Nan-hui, ed. 1934; rpt. Taipei, 1963.

Index to Pre-T'ang Poetry: A Combined Index to Ku-shih yüan and Ku-shih hsüan. Chinese Materials Center, Research Aids Series. Chik-fong Lee, comp. Taipei, 1982.

TRANSLATIONS:

Uchida, Sennosuke 內田泉之助 and Hoshikawa Kiyotaka 星川清孝. *Koshigen* 古詩源. 2v. Tokyo, 1964-65. A complete translation.

—REH

Ku T'ai-ch'ing 顧太清 (*tzu*, Tzu-ch'un 子春, *hao*, Yüan-ch'a wai-chih 雲槎外史, and also known as T'ai-ch'ing ch'un 春 or Hsi-lin ch'un 西林春, 1799-*c.* 1875) was an outstanding woman poet of mid-Ch'ing times. There are several different versions of the dates of her birth and death and family background. According to some scholars she was of Chinese bannerman origin, but others contend that she was the great granddaughter of the Manchu scholar-official O-er-t'ai 鄂爾泰 (1680-1745). It is said that Ku T'ai-ch'ing was adopted out of a family surnamed Ku in the service of Yung-ch'i 永琪, the Prince Jung (1741-1766). Later, she was chosen as a concubine by I-hui 奕繪 (1799-1838), the grandson of Yung-ch'i. I-hui was well-known during his day as a poet, calligrapher, and architect. Ku T'ai-ch'ing, a beautiful, intelligent, and talented woman, was his favorite concubine, and the two of them shared common interests in travel, art, and literature. Although it is quite clear that theirs was a happy life together, rumors later circulated that she entered into a liaison with the famous scholar-poet Kung Tzu-chen,* and some writers have cited some of his poems as evidence of their relationship. Their reputed affair was fictionalized in the late Ch'ing novel *Nieh-hai hua* by Tseng P'u.*

When I-hui died, Ku T'ai-ch'ing's life of ease and cultured elegance came to an abrupt end. I-hui's son by an earlier marriage inherited his father's title and estate, and he forthwith expelled Ku and her seven children from his home, perhaps because of rumors about her and Kung Tzu-chen. Poverty-stricken and lonely, she encountered numerous difficulties in raising her children, and she reportedly went blind in 1875. The suffering she experienced in her later years can be detected in her poems, some of which contain strong Buddhist overtones.

Ku T'ai-ch'ing was skilled in the writing of *shih*-style verse, but she was even more important as a master of the *tz'u** form. One critic ranked her among the most accomplished Ch'ing-dynasty woman poets of Manchu origin and compared her skill to the early Ch'ing masters Na-lan Hsing-te* and Li E.* K'uang Chou-i 況周頤 (1859-1926), who sponsored the publication of her collected works, commented that she wrote in the Sung tradition, having read little *tz'u* poetry by post-Sung writers, that she was strongly influenced by Chou Pang-yen* and Chiang K'uei,* and that her best poems were simple and refreshing, devoid of ornament or naivete, and aptly phrased. K'uang stated that although her *tz'u* were less charming than Na-lan Hsing-te's, they surpass his in style and taste. He further observed that her works should be judged as a whole, not in part.

Ku T'ai-ch'ing's *tz'u* poems were collected under the title *Tung-hai yü ko* 東海漁歌 (Songs of the Fisherman of the Eastern Sea), thus matching her husband's collection, entitled *Nan-ku ch'iao ch'ang* 南谷樵唱 (Songs of the Woodcutter of Southern Valley). Although her extant verse was assembled and printed in two volumes in 1910 and again in 1914, it is not easily available. Perhaps as a result, her life and contributions to Ch'ing-dynasty letters have not received the scholarly attention they deserve.

EDITIONS:

T'ien-yu-ko chi 天游閣集. N.p., 1910 and 1914.
Tung-hai yü ko 東海漁歌. Part two of this collection can be found in *Tz'u-hsüeh chi-k'an* 詞學季刊, 1.2, 152-166. Hsu, Shih-ch'ang, ed., *Wan-ch'ing-i shih-hui* 晚晴簃詩匯, *chüan* 188, for selections of her *shih* poems.

TRANSLATIONS:
Sunflower, pp. 497-499.

STUDIES:

Man-shu Ch'i-kung 曼殊啟功. "Shu Ku T'ai-ch'ing shih" 書顧太清事, *Tz'u-hsüeh chi-k'an*, 1.4, 26.
Su, Hsüeh-lin 蘇雪林. "Ch'ing-tai nü tz'u-jen Ku T'ai-ch'ing" 清代女詞人顧太清, *Fu-nü tsa-chih*, 17.7 ( ).
———. "Ch'ing-tai nan-nü liang ta tz'u-jen lien-shih te yen-chiu" 清代男女兩大詞人 戀史的研究, *Wu-ta wen-che chi-k'an*, 1.3 (October 1930), 525-574, and 1.4 (January 1931), 715-745.

—PCL

Ku-tzu-tz'u 鼓子詞 (drum lyric) was a form of narrative performing art popular during the Sung dynasty. None of the surviving texts of *ku-tzu-tz'u* enlighten us about the use of the drum during performances, but references in Sung literature to related genres suggest that the drum was used much as in modern *ta-ku** or drum balladry, beating the rhythm during the sung portions and punctuating action. Both wind and string instruments were used to accompany a *ku-tzu-tz'u*, contrasting with the later *chu-kung-tiao** or medley, which used only string instruments.

The *ku-tzu-tz'u* are at least superficially similar to the T'ang-dynasty *pien-wen* (see *Tun-huang wen-hsüeh*) in that they consist of long prose sections interspersed with rhymed poetry. The prose sections usually end with a formula such as: "Now I trouble the singer to accompany us. First settle the tune. Now listen to my coarse lyrics." The sung poem which follows is always in the *tz'u** form, which reached its height during the Sung dynasty, although the meter of these poems is somewhat looser than normal *tz'u*. A typical performance would have required three participants, namely, the prose reciter, the singer, and one musician, although more musicians could easily have been added when available, much as in modern Chinese popular balladry. The *ku-tzu-tz'u*, however, were not, strictly speaking, popular literature, since it seems they were generally performed at banquets of Sung-dynasty scholar-officials, and the earliest text is written in a classical Chinese far from the spoken language.

The most extensive *ku-tzu-tz'u* surviving was composed by Chao Ling-chih 趙令畤, a Sung royal prince whose talents were highly regarded by his contemporary, Su Shih.* Chao's work is entitled *Yüan Wei-chih Ts'ui Ying-ying shang-tiao Tieh-lien-hua ku-tzu-tz'u* 元微之崔鶯鶯商調蝶戀花鼓子詞 (Drum Lyrics to the Tune of the "The Butterfly Dotes on Flowers" in the Shang Mode [on the Story of] Yüan Chen's "Tale of Ts'ui Ying-ying"); it is based on the extremely popular T'ang *ch'uan-chi** tale written by Yüan Chen.* According to Chao's own account, he composed his *ku-tzu-tz'u* so that the singsong girls of his time would be able to perform Yüan's story to

musical accompaniment. The prose sections of Chao's *ku-tzu-tz'u* are an almost verbatim repetition of the T'ang tale, abbreviated and abridged for ease of performance. All of the *tz'u* poems are in the same mode and tune, unlike the later *chu-kung-tiao* or medley, which employed many different tunes. The *tz'u* poems are not, strictly speaking, narrative verse and tend more to the lyrical, coming at dramatic points in the story. There are only twelve *tz'u* in the entire work, with the first poem summarizing the tale and the last one stating the author's reaction to its rather tragic denouement—in this, too, closely resembling modern Chinese balladry.

The other major *ku-tzu-tz'u* extant is the *Wan-ching yüan-yang hui* 刎頸鴛鴦會 (Love Birds to the Death), the earliest version of which survives in a collection of *hua-pen** short stories, *Ch'ing-p'ing shan-t'ang hua-pen* 清平山堂話本, printed in the Ming dynasty. Although this composition follows the pattern of Chao Ling-chih's work, consisting of prose narrative interspersed with *tz'u* poems and has been considered an authentic Sung work, recent scholarship has determined it to be a work of the early Ming. The ten poems were to be performed in the same mode as Chao's work, the *shang*, but to a different *tz'u* tune, in this case, *Ts'u hu-lu* 醋葫蘆 (Vinegar Gourd). However, the prose portions of this later work are very different from Chao's, because they are written in a lively colloquial language, indicating closer links to the popular tradition. *Love Birds to the Death* also centers on a tragic romance, the love affair of Chiang Shu-chen 蔣淑珍 with her neighbor Chu Ping-chung 朱秉中, which is terminated when Chiang's husband, Chang Erh-kuan 張二官, murders the lovers.

The small number of extant *ku-tzu-tz'u* makes it difficult to determine the genre's exact place in the history of Chinese literature. Although it is impossible to prove a direct connection with the T'ang dynasty *pien-wen*, it is not unlikely that the *ku-tzu-tz'u* is a distant descendant of this or related forms. One reason for the early demise of the *ku-tzu-tz'u* was undoubtedly its monotonous musical structure, in which one tune is repeated again and again. Even during the last century one can find numerous examples of simple one-tune rural operas or ballad types that gradually added other tunes or greatly modified their original tunes, so that the earlier, rather primitive forms were eventually transformed beyond recognition. The *chu-kung-tiao*, which first arose at the end of the Sung dynasty, admits a large number of tunes, and, hence, may very well be a direct lineal descendant of the *ku-tzu-tz'u* drum lyrics.

TEXTS:

Chao, Ching-shen 趙景深. *Ku-tz'u hsüan* 鼓詞選. Shanghai, 1957.

Chao, Ling-chih. *Hou-ch'ing lu* 侯鯖錄. *Chih-pu-tsu chai ts'ung-shu.*

Hung, Pien 洪楩. *Ch'ing-p'ing shan-t'ang hua-pen* 清平山堂話本. Peking, 1955. Facsimile reprint of the preserved fragments.

———. *Ch'ing-p'ing shan-t'ang hua-pen.* Collated by T'an Cheng-pi 譚正璧. Shanghai, 1957.

Liu, Yung-chi 劉永濟, comp. *Sung-tai ko-wu chü-ch'ü lu-yao* 宋代歌舞劇曲錄要. Shanghai, 1957.

TRANSLATIONS:

Lévy, André. "Un document unique sur un genre disparu de la littérature populaire, 'Le rendez-vous d'amour où les cous sont coupés,' " in his *Etudes sur le conte et le roman chinois*, Paris, 1971, pp. 187-210.

STUDIES:

Cheng, Chen-to 鄭振鐸. *Chung-kuo su-wen-hsüeh shih* 中國俗文學史. Peking, 1957.

Hsü, Fu-lin 徐傅霖, *et al. Chung-kuo su-wen-hsüeh lun-wen hui-pien* 中國俗文學論文彙編. Taipei, 1978.

Idema, W.L. "The *Wen-ching yüan-yang hui* and the *Chia-men* of Yüan-Ming *Ch'uan-chi*," *TP*, 67 (1981), 91-106.

—JDS

Ku-wen 古文 (ancient-style prose) is a polysemous term. Its first usage, in the sense of "ancient- or old-script texts," was in the Han dynasty (see *ching*), when it designated those classical texts which had survived the Ch'in proscriptions in opposition to the *chin-wen* 今文 (new-script texts) which had been lost in the Ch'in and then reconstructed and recorded from memory. During the Six Dynasties *ku-wen* signified "ancient texts," referring primarily to the Confucian Classics themselves, but gradually signifying an enlarged corpus of literary models dating from the Chou, Ch'in, and Han eras. In the T'ang, specifically in the late eighth and early ninth centuries, there was a redefinition of *ku-wen* as a type of prose intentionally modelled in style and content on these ancient texts—i.e., an "ancient-style prose." Subsequent eras use the term in anthologies of *ku-wen* to encompass all prose writings in which a straightforward, non-parallel style was employed to treat a single subject in an independent work or section of a work, provided this piece espoused a moral or philosophical message.

Although there is a certain degree of shared significance between these four meanings of *ku-wen*, the third and fourth are of the most concern to students of Chinese literature. Thus although later *ku-wen* anthologies include various passage from writings as early as those of the Chou dynasty and although some scholars point to Chia I* as the "founder" of the style, the Six Dynasties can justifiably be viewed as an era of *p'ien-wen*,* the euphuistic style of prose which became almost indistinguishable from the frivolous literary subjects of much of sixth-century literature. Not that this style was without its critics: Liu Hsieh (see *Wen-hsin tiao-lung*), Chung Jung (see *Shih-p'in*), Sun Cho 孫綽 (498-546), Li O 李諤 (*fl.* 600), and others assailed it. Indeed, although their influence was negligible, they are considered as the forerunners of the conscious effort to promote *ku-wen*, conceived and dubbed by modern scholars as the *Ku-wen yün-tung* 古文運動 (Ancient-style Prose Movement).

Beginning in the mid- to late-seventh century, and as a part of the weakening of the monopoly the old aristocracy had held on literature for several centuries, there was a reaction against Six Dynasties' thought in all forms (poetry, historiography, philosophy, and prose) which provided a basis for an increased role in literature by advocates of *ku-wen*. Ch'en Tzu-ang,* Yüan Chieh,* Tu-ku Chi,* Liang Su,* Hsiao Ying-shih,* Li Hua,* and Liu Mien 柳冕 (*fl.* 779-797) all promoted the idea of modelling prose on the classics. The basic reverence for the classics, the exhortation to view didacticism as the basic function of literature, and a return to a simpler, "classical" style is evident in their writings, especially those of Hsiao, Li, and Liu.

But like all reforms in language or script, the Ancient-style Prose Movement was directed toward a new audience, or at least attempting to arouse a new awareness in the old. And this audience, the local educated gentry, was only in its formative stages in the late eighth century.

It was not until the turn of the ninth century that significant literary changes—such as the *Hsin Yüeh-fu* Movement (see *yüeh-fu*), the *ch'uan-ch'i** tale, and the early *tz'u*—appeared. Several modern Chinese scholars have considered this era the dawn of a new age in literature. Moreover, these changes paralleled a social evolution. The An Lu-shan Rebellion had exacerbated the decline of the old aristocracy. The stage was thus set for a revolution in prose led by a group of "new men" from local elite families who were anxious to play a role in national politics. Onto it strode two of the greatest writers in the history of Chinese literature—Han Yü* and Liu Tsung-yüan.*

It is Han Yü who functioned as the fount from which all subsequent *ku-wen* writings, theoretical and practical, derive. Han attacked, as his predecessors had, *p'ien-wen* writings for their style, which demanded regular parallel lines and the expression of an idea in a couplet—something which directed the reader to the textures between lines, inhibited logical argument, and generally slowed the flow of the text. *P'ien-wen* was also inimical because of its long association with the trivial, exotic, often erotic subjects of late Six Dynasties' literature. To a certain extent literary development prepared the way for Han Yü. The formal features of *p'ien-wen* were mnemonically ideal at a time when nearly all literature was memorized. As the vast production of texts in the seventh and especially eighth century made such a task impossible, and no doubt as progress was made in adapting

from reading aloud to silent reading, longer, discursive lines began to appear (Han Yü has one line of over eighty characters).

In lieu of *p'ien-wen*, Han Yü promoted the study of the Confucian Classics, while establishing a style based on them in a corpus of prose writings he hoped would serve as the model for a "purer" literature of the future. He went beyond his eighth-century mentors to emphasize and adopt the literary attitudes, as well as the style, of the "Canon," and to reemphasize the Confucian nature of this corpus. Indeed, *Mencius*, which had been neglected before the T'ang, influenced his style and thought heavily. Han viewed the *Tao* 道 (Way) of government as inseparable from the *Tao* of literature. Thus he carefully selected for revival those genres which were suited to his goals: the *lun* 論 (dissertation), the *shu* 書 (personal letter), the *chuan* 傳 (biography), the various types of funerary inscriptions, the *hsü* 序 (preface), and the *shuo* 說 (discourse). He also recognized the importance of adapting style and diction to the form of the work. His best-known works include "Shih-shuo" 師說 (Discourse on Teaching), "Yüan Tao" 原道 (On the Origin of the Way), and "Liu Tzu-hou mu-chih-ming" 柳子厚墓誌銘 (Gravestone Inscription for Liu Tsung-yüan). Han also believed that deprivation or impoverishment (*ch'iung*   ), both literal and figurative, heightened a writer's skill (*kung*   ). Thus in Han Yü the Ancient-style Prose Movement took on an anti-establishment stance—*ch'iung* had not been related to literary motivation in the Six Dynasties—which it was to maintain with some consistency throughout its history.

Liu Tsung-yüan, a colleague of Han Yü, is the second great T'ang *ku-wen* stylist. More eclectic than Han, the influence of *Han-fei-tzu* (see *Chu-tzu pai-chia*) and Chia I can be seen in his works. In his youth Liu established a reputation as a rescript writer, composing government documents in *p'ien-wen*. Indeed, throughout his life some of his best works (especially his *fu* and *sao*) were in a style influenced by this early period. But through contact with late eighth-century *ku-wen* figures and Han Yü himself, Liu developed his own *ku-wen* during his long southern exile (806 until his death in 8l9). His best-known works are his *yu-chi*,* which depict the landscapes of the Hsiang River 湘 system (modern Hunan), his letters, and his allegorical writings such as "Pu-she-che shuo" (Discourse of the Snake-catcher). Liu believed that literature could illumine or clarify the Way (文以明道), a Way which he saw bifurcated in literature into historical and poetical writing.

Despite receiving a number of "students" during his sojourn in the South and keeping up a voluminous correspondence with other "disciples," Liu's influence on later T'ang writers is much less felt than that of Han Yü. Late T'ang *ku-wen* authors are seen as belonging to one of two schools traceable to Han and his immediate disciples: one which emphasized *Tao* (here referring to content, specifically the Confucian Way) at the expense of *wen* (here literary form or flourish). There was also a tendency among some of Han's followers (Fan Tsung-shih 樊宗師 [d. 821] is normally mentioned) to weight *ch'i* 奇 (the extraordinary) too heavily in their writing, resulting in obscure pieces. Other critics trace these two schools to Han and Liu themselves, arguing that Han led a conservative wing of the movement (later members are Li Ao,* Huang-fu Shih 皇甫湜 [*fl*. 810], and Sun Ch'iao 孫樵 [*fl*. 860-888]), while Liu guided the radical wing (which includes Shen Ya-chih,* Lo Yin,* P'i Jih-hsiu,* and Lu Kuei-meng* among its adherents). Li Ao,* in a draft biography of his father-in-law, Han Yü, asserts that most contemporary authors used Han's writings as the model in preparing for the examinations. Although most *ku-wen* writers of this era did look to Han as their master, Li Ao's assertion is questionable, since the style of the examinations and of court documents remained unaffected by *ku-wen* through the late T'ang. The great prose collections of the ninth and early tenth centuries belong to the court rescript writers such as Li Shang-yin* (over 350 pieces), Hsü Hsüan 徐鉉 (916-991, over 180 pieces), and Ch'ien

Yü 錢珝 (*chin-shih*, 880, 140 pieces). Collections of *ku-wen* writers are markedly smaller—P'i Jih-hsiu's is the largest (95 pieces), Lu Kuei-meng has but 55, and Sun Ch'iao's rather substantial reputation is built on a mere 32. *Ku-wen* remained a genre for outsiders, society's marginal men, who, though they had made inroads into national politics on occasion through the examinations, lacked the socio-economic base to sustain their influence. Many of the genres revived by *ku-wen* authors, such as the *shuo* 說 (discourse) and the *tui* 對 (response), show a similarity to the rhetoric of the Warring States persuaders. Like their predecessors, like Confucius himself, these late T'ang *ku-wen* authors sought positions at court or with a provincial satrap through their words. In this way their efforts paralleled the *Fu-ku* 復古 (Return to Antiquity) Movement in *shih** poetry and the *Hsin yüeh-fu*. But because the late T'ang courts, riddled by dissention and intrigue, were not able to seriously consider social or political reforms, this group of men actually lost influence at court throughout the last decades of the T'ang, the Five Dynasties, and the early Sung.

A parallel-prose style modelled on Li Shang-yin, known as *Hsi-k'un* (see *Hsi-k'ung ch'ou-ch'ang chi*), and promoted by members of the old elite dominated early eleventh-century prose. The great sequel to the *Wen-hsüan*,* the *Wen-yüan ying-hua*, completed in 987, is so much inclined towards parallel prose that a rival collection, the *T'ang-wen ts'ui*,* an anthology of *ku-wen* writings and *Hsin yüeh-fu*, was edited shortly thereafter (1011) to combat its influence.

Yet despite efforts by early Sung writers such as Liu K'ai 柳開 (947-1000) and Wang Yü-ch'eng,* *ku-wen* remained in the background.

At the same time a reaction against *Hsi-k'un* led by Shih Chieh 石介 (1005-1045) developed. Shih emphasized the utilitarian aspects of prose, borrowing some of Liu K'ai's ideas ("literature is intended to allow one to obtain the Way" [文以得道] and "literature is intended to allow one to practice the Way" [文以行道]). He attacked all belletristic writings and called for a *Pien-t'i* 變體 (Changed or Altered-body) style. His own work proved disjointed and obscure, but by providing an antithesis to *Hsi-k'un* it may have helped prepare the way for Ou-yang Hsiu's* second act of the Ancient-prose Style Movement.

This act is punctuated by the year 1059 when Ou-yang Hsiu, as chief examiner and literary arbiter of the era introduced *ku-wen* as the medium for the *chin-shih* examinations. This led to the acceptance of *ku-wen* at court (for a time) and the proliferation of the style as the major type of prose for non-official writings until the twentieth century. Ou-yang's success was due in part to the increased role of the local gentry in Sung court politics—*ku-wen* had continued to be popular in their circles. And the polarities of *Hsi-k'un* and *Pien-t'i* allowed Ou-yang to promote *ku-wen* as a middle course. But the seemingly effortless style Ou-yang Hsiu developed, a style which he employed equally in discursive and lyrical writings, was also a major factor. He also worked towards resolving the controversy over *Tao* and *wen* which had occupied late-T'ang authors, arguing against the utilitarianism of Liu K'ai and Shih Chieh and for a balance of the two (see his "Yü Yao Hsiu-ts'ai ti-i shu" 與姚孝才第一書 [First Letter to the Graduate Yao]). His major works include the famous "Tsui-wen-t'ing chi" 醉翁亭記 (Record of the Old Tippler's Pavilion), "P'eng-tang lun" 朋黨論 (Essay on Factions), "*Mei Sheng-yü shih-chi* hsü" 梅聖俞詩集序 (Preface to the *Collected Poetry of Mei Yao-chen**), "Ch'iu-sheng fu" 秋聲賦 (Prose-poem on Autumn Sounds), and the *Hsin T'ang-shu* 新唐書 (New T'ang History), in which he rewrote the *Chiu T'ang-shu* ostensibly in order to improve its style (he actually also altered the text considerably in favor of Neo-Confucian ideas). As the literary doyen of the mid-twelfth century, Ou-yang Hsiu helped establish Han Yü's reputation and effectively worked compromises between various *ku-wen* factions, fashioning an effective, yet highly literary style.

Although Ou-yang Hsiu was the most important *ku-wen* figure to his Northern Sung contemporaries and was instrumental in establishing Han Yü's corpus as a standard for the style, his successor as literary arbiter of the era, Su Shih,* has had a greater influence on writers of subsequent dynasties in terms of *ku-wen* theory. Su Shih took the ancient style a step further away from parallel prose toward a "natural" (*tzu-jan* 自然) prose style. The effect of his best-known pieces, such as the "Ch'ien" 前 and "Hou Chih-pi fu" 後赤壁賦 (Prose-poems on the Red Cliff, One and Two), is a style which seems less crafted and is more suited to discursive writings. Su himself drew an analogy between his writing and water flowing from a spring (see "Wen shuo" 文說 [On Prose]). Like Ou-yang Hsiu, Su Shih did not advocate either *wen* or *Tao*, but saw the two as inseparable. More in concert with Neo-Confucian philosophical ideas, he equated the *Tao* with *li* 理 (principle), to be found in each subject or work of art. He went further than Ou-yang in championing literature for its own sake. The process of writing, according to Su, consists in (1) learning about objects, (2) understanding their principle, and (3) subjectively comprehending them. This conceptualization, which Su called *i* 意, is primary to all writing. When combined with *fa* 法 (technique or style), a literary work is created. Since the aim of literature is to convey the author's conceptualization, clarity of style is vital. This tandem of *fa* and *i*, albeit not always in exactly these terms, continued to influence prose theory until modern times.

Su's prose corpus is extremely rich in both the number and the types of works. Aside from the standard, formal prose genres, he left many miscellaneous notes and incomplete pieces which were later collected as *pi-chi*,* in works such as the *Chih-lin* 志林 (A Forest of Records), works which in turn had considerable influence on the *hsiao-p'in wen* 小品文 (informal essays) of the late Ming and Ch'ing periods. Other well-known works by Su include "Jih yü" 日喻 (Allegory on the Sun), "Wu-ch'ang Chiu-ch'ü T'ing chi" 武昌九曲亭記 (A Record of the Nine-bends Pavilion at Wu-ch'ang), "Fang-ho T'ing chi" 放鶴亭記 (A

Record of Releasing-crane Pavilion), and numerous *lun* 論 (discursive essays).

The Southern Sung inherited the styles of Ou-yang Hsiu, followed primarily by Neo-Confucians such as Chu Hsi 朱熹 (1130-1200), and of Su Shih, to be seen in the *ts'e* 策 and *lun* of Hsin Ch'i-chi* and Ch'en Liang.* In North China which was under the rule of the Chin dynasty, Chao Ping-wen,* Liu Chung 劉中 (*tzu*, Cheng-fu 正夫), Wang Jo-hsü,* and Yüan Hao-wen* were noted *ku-wen* essayists.

The movement towards a style more comprehensible to a larger audience which had begun in the Sung dynasty continued in the Yüan—even court documents and the civil-service examination papers were affected. *Ku-wen* prose thus continued to flourish. Liu Yin 劉因 (*tzu*, Ching-hsiu 靜修, 1249-1293), Yao Sui 姚燧 (*tzu*, Mu-an 牧菴, 1238-1314), Yü Chi 虞集 (*tzu*, Tao-yüan 道園, 1272-1348), and Sun T'ien-chüeh (see *Kuo-ch'ao wen-lei*) are among the noted practitioners.

Although there were noted *ku-wen* writers such as Sung Lien,* Liu Chi,* and Fang Hsiao-ju* in the first decades of the Ming, the major developments in *ku-wen* during this dynasty involved the historical perception of *ku-wen* in the history of Chinese prose. Li Tung-yang* and the group associated with him advocated a *fu-ku* movement, but stressed the Han dynasty as the period in which prose (and *ku-wen*) reached its zenith. An opposition party, led by Kuei Yu-kuang* (who noted his support of *ku-wen*, but his disagreement with the definition of the term by Li), T'ang Shun-chih,* and Wang Shen-chung 王慎中 (1509-1559), argued against the slavish imitation of Li Tung-yang's group and the almost unintelligible prose it had produced. They also promoted T'ang and Sung *ku-wen* and were the first to assemble the major writers of these two dynasties under the heading *T'ang Sung pa-ta [san-wen] chia* (see Han Yü). Their spirit and theories influenced the Ching-ling p'ai 竟陵派 and the Kung-an p'ai (see Yüan Hung-tao), and led to a proliferation of *ku-wen* anthologies in the seventeenth and eighteenth centuries (see Bibliography below). Ming *ku-wen* writers were again primarily men with little court connection or influence in an era dominated by parallel-prose (*pa-ku wen**) in official circles.

During the Ch'ing the major *ku-wen* writers belonged to the T'ung-ch'eng p'ai.* This group, which traced its origins to Kuei Yu-kuang and T'ang Shun-chih and numbered Fang Pao,* Liu Ta-k'uei 劉大櫆 (1698-1779), and Yao Nai 姚鼐 (1732-1815) as its chief members, was based on the theory of the necessity for a unity between *i* 義 (rightness) and *fa* (method). This emphasis on a balance between substance (*i*, by which the Neo-Confucian *Tao* was meant) and form (*fa*) can be traced back to the two schools of Han Yü's followers and to Ou-yang Hsiu's efforts to effect a compromise between them. But in Yao Nai's writings the integration is elevated to a general literary theory which incorporates all literary genres. Yao also compiled an anthology, the *Ku-wen tz'u leitsuan*,* to illustrate the theories of the school. A rival school, the Yang-hu p'ai 陽湖派 (named after the district in modern Kiangsu from which its members came), was led by Yün Ching 惲敬 (1757-1817) and Chang Hui-yen.* They held similar ideas but, despite a general acknowledgment that Yün Ching's knowledge and style surpassed those of Yao Nai, had little historical significance. The T'ung-ch'eng p'ai, however, through its anthology and its disciples and admirers such as Tseng Kuofan,* greatly influenced modern conceptions and accounts of the development of traditional Chinese prose. The modern scholar Kao Pu-ying 高步瀛, for example, has been criticized for giving preference to *ku-wen* writers, specifically those admired by the T'ung-ch'eng p'ai, in his anthology *T'ang Sung wen chü-yao* 唐宋文舉要 (Essential T'ang and Sung Prose). The modern esteem for Ssu-ma Ch'ien* and the Eight Ancient-style Prose Masters of the T'ang and Sung to some extent derives from the predilections of this school, too. There is a certain irony therein, since these *ku-wen* authors to a man were much less successful in their own lifetimes than their parallel-prose, courtier counterparts.

ANTHOLOGIES:

Chin Yüan Ming pa-ta-chia wen-hsüan 金元明八大家文選 (A Selection of Prose from the Eight Masters of the Chin, Yüan and Ming Dynasties). Li Tsu-t'ao 李祖陶, ed. Includes works by Yüan Hao-wen,* Sung Lien,* T'ang Shun-chih,* Kuei Yu-kuang,* and others. N.p., 1868.

Chung-kuo li-tai san-wen hsüan 中國歷代散文選. Liu Fen-sui 劉盼遂 and Kuo Yü-heng 郭預衡, eds. 2v. Peking, 1980.

Ku-wen hsi-i 古文析義 (Explicating the Meaning of Ancient-style Texts). Lin Hsi-chung 林西仲, ed. Preface 1716, but first printed in 1680s. Emphasizes early prose (Han and pre-Han) and includes some poems. Poor commentary, but editor's note following each piece is of interest.

*Ku-wen kuan-chih.**

Ku-wen kuan-chien 古文關鑑 (A Key to Ancient-style Texts). Lü Tsu-ch'ien 呂祖謙 (1137-1181), ed. 2 *chüan*. First printed *c.* 1160-1180. *TSCC*. The earliest *ku-wen* anthology. Anticipates Mao K'un by including seven of the Eight Masters (Lü sees Han Yü, Liu Tsung-yüan, and Ou-yang Hsiu as the models, however). The "key" is a critical analysis of the rhetoric of each of these pieces.

Ku-wen p'ing-chu 古文評註 (Critical Notes on Ancient-style Texts). Kuo Kung 過珙, ed. Preface 1703; rpt. Taipei, 1975. Includes brief biographies; the traditional commentaries are followed by a more general (often moralistic) note by the editor. The coverage is a bit uneven: more than half the selections are from the Chou and Han and eleven selections of Su Hsün* are provided, about the same number as from all Ming writers.

*Ku-wen tz'u-lei-tsuan.**

*Ku-wen yüan.**

Ku-wen yüan-chien 古文淵鑑 (A Profound Mirror of Ancient-style Texts). Selected by Sheng-tsu Emperor. Hsü Ch'ien-hsüeh 徐乾學 (1631-1694), ed. Preface 1685. The emphasis is on official documents through the Sung.

Sung-wen chien 宋文鑑 (A Mirror of Sung Prose). Lü Tsu-ch'ien, ed. 150 *chüan*. Soochow: Chiang-su shu-chü 江蘇書局, 1886. Also *SKCS*. Works arranged according to sixty rubrics—includes some *p'ien-wen*. The three most represented authors are Su Shih (276 pieces), Wang An-shih (198), and Ou-yang Hsiu (166).

T'ang Sung wen chü-yao. Kao Pu-ying, ed. 3v. Peking, 1962. The best modern collection of T'ang and Sung *ku-wen* prose; also contains some *p'ien-wen* selections.

T'ang Sung pa-ta-chia wen-ch'ao 唐宋八大家文鈔 (A Collection of the Prose of the Eight Masters of the T'ang and Sung). Mao K'un 茅坤 (1512-1601), ed. 144 *chüan*. 1579.

T'ang Sung shih-ta-chia wen-chi 唐宋十大家文集. Chu Hsin 儲欣. Added Li Ao* and Sun Ch'iao 孫樵 (*fl.* 860-888) to the original eight masters.

*T'ang-wen ts'ui.**

Wen-chang kuei-fan 文章軌範 (Model Pieces of Prose). Hsieh Fang-te 謝枋得 (1226-1289), ed. *SKCS*. Also Osaka, 1794. Intended as a collection to further Confucian learning and as a corpus that would provide models for the writing of *ku-wen* prose, this anthology contains works from Han through Sung, but concentrates on the Eight Masters of T'ang and Sung. Very influential in Japan.

TRANSLATIONS:

Liu, Shih Shun. *Chinese Classical Prose, the Eight Masters of the T'ang Sung Period*. Hong Kong, 1979.

Margouliès, Georges. *Le kou-wen chinois*. Paris, 1926. Translations of *ku-wen* works from the *Kung-yang chuan* (see *Tso-chuan* and *ching*) through the Ming; Margouliès understands *ku-wen* similarly to Ch'ing anthologists as more comprehensive than just the prose of the Eight Masters. His long Introduction (pp. i-cxvi) is still useful.

———. *Anthologie raisonée de la littérature chinoise*. Paris, 1948. Contains prose and poetry, including a number of pieces by Han Yü and Liu Tsung-yüan.

Shimizu, Shigeru 清水茂. *Tō Sō hakkabun* 唐宋八家文. Tokyo, 1966.

STUDIES:

Bols, Peter K. "Culture and the Way in Eleventh Century China." Unpublished Ph.D. dissertation, Princeton, 1982.

Chang, Hsü 張須. "Sung Yüan Ming Ch'ing wen lun" 宋元明清文論, in Lo, *Lun-wen hsüan*, pp. 1327-1334.

Chen, Yu-shih. "T'ang-Sung Prose Masters: The Theory and Art of Ku-wen." Unpublished manuscript, 344 pp.

———. "Han Yü as a Ku-wen Stylist," *THHP*, 1 (1968), 143-207.

Ch'ien, Mu 錢穆. "Tsa-lun T'ang-tai ku-wen yün-tung" 雜論唐代古文運動, *Hsin-ya hsüeh-pao*, 3 (1957), 123-168.

———. "Chung-kuo san-wen" 中國散文, in *Chung-kuo wen-hsüeh yen-chiang chi* 中國文學演講集, Hong Kong, 1963, pp. 36-46.

Ch'ien, Tung-fu 錢多父. *T'ang Sung ku-wen yün-tung* 唐宋古文運動. Shanghai, 1962; rpts. 1979, 1982.

Chin, Chung-chü 金中樞. "Sung-tai ku-wen yün-tung chih fa-chan" 宋代古文運動之發展, *Hsin-ya hsüeh-pao*, 5.2 (August 1963), 79-146.

Chung-kuo ku-tien san-wen yen-chiu lun-wen chi 中國古典散文研究論文集. 2v. Peking, 1959.

Edwards, E. D. "A Classified Guide to the Thirteen Classes of Chinese Prose," *BSOAS*, 12 (1947-48), 770-788.

Hartman, Charles. "Historical and Literary Backgrounds," in Nienhauser, *Liu*, pp. 15-25.

Hightower, James R. "The Ku-wen Movement," in *Topics in Chinese Literature*, Cambridge, Massachusetts, 1952, pp. 72-75.

Kuo, Shao-yü 郭紹虞. *Chung-kuo wen-hsüeh p'i-p'ing shih* 中國文學批評史. Shanghai, 1934, pp. 174-302.

Liu, James T. C. "Master of Sung Literature," in *Ou-yang Hsiu, An Eleventh-century Neo-Confucianist*, Stanford, 1967, pp. 141-153.

Liu, Ta-chieh 劉大杰 and Ch'ien Chung 錢仲. "Chien-yen 前言, in *T'ang Sung wen chü-yao*, v. 1, pp. 1-7.

Lo, Lien-t'ien 羅聯添. "T'ang Sung ku-wen te fa-chan yü yen-pien" 唐宋古文的發展與演變, in *Chung-kuo wen-hsüeh te fa-chan kai-shu* 中國文學的發展概述, Taipei, 1982, pp. 121-194.

Locke, Marjorie A. "The Early Life of Ou-yang Hsiu and His Relation to the Rise of the *Ku-wen* Movement of the Sung Period." Unpublished Ph.D. dissertation, London University, 1951.

McMullen, David. "Historical and Literary Theory in the Mid-Eighth Century," in *Perspectives*, pp. 307-342.

———. "Yüan Chien and the Early *Ku-wen* Movement." Unpublished Ph.D. dissertation, Cambridge University, 1968.

Nienhauser, William H. Jr., "Some Preliminary Remarks on Fiction, the Classical Tradition and Society in Late Ninth-century China," in *Chinese Fiction*, pp. 1-16.

Obi, Koichi 小尾郊一. "Ryu Ben no bunron" 柳冕の文論, *Shinagaku kenkyū*, 27 (1962), 27-37. Discusses five letters on style.

Pulleyblank, E. G. "Liu K'o 劉軻, A Forgotten Rival of Han Yü," *AM*, 7 (1959), 145-160.

———. "Neo-Confucianism and Neo-Legalism in T'ang Intellectual Life, 755-806," in *The Confucian Persuasion*, Arthur F. Wright, ed., Stanford, 1960, pp. 77-114.

Sato, Ichiro 佐藤一郎. "Kobun" 古文, in *Chung-kuo wen-hsüeh kai-lun* 中國文學概論, Hung Shun-lung 洪順隆, tr., Taipei, 1980, pp. 162-182.

—WHN

Ku-wen kuan-chih 古文觀止 (The Finest of Ancient Prose) is an anthology of *ku-wen** (ancient-style prose) compiled by Wu Ch'u-ts'ai 吳楚材 and Wu Tiao-hou 吳調侯 and first published in 1695. The preface indicates that the work is intended for use by students and that beauty is the criterion by which sections have been selected. The title itself alludes to the *Tso-chuan** (Duke Hsiang, 29) where *Kuan-chih* 觀止, literally "the observation ceases," refers to the fact that the music and dance performed on that occasion was so outstanding as to make further performances unnecessary. Thus, we might translate the title somewhat loosely as "The Finest of Ancient Prose."

Ku-wen kuan-chih includes 220 selections, each edited and annotated by the compilers. Several peculiarities of the anthology should be noted. Although "ancient-style prose" is often thought to stand in contrast to "parallel prose" (*p'ien-wen**), the *Ku-wen kuan-chih* does contain several examples of the latter. In addition, there is a disproportionately large number of passages from the *Tso-chuan* (34), the *Chan-kuo ts'e** (14) and the *Shih-chi** (15), particularly in view of the fact that there are selections from neither the Chou philosophical texts nor the Pans' highly regarded *Han-shu* (see Pan Ku). Later scholars have also complained that the eight selections from the Six Dynasties are insufficient, that T'ang *ku-wen* writers other than Han Yü* (who is represented by twenty-four selections), and Liu Tsung-yüan (who has eleven selections), are generally overlooked, and that some selections from the Yüan dynasty, which is not represented at all in the anthology, should be added. These and several other "faults" have been corrected by Chao Ts'ung 趙聰 in a 1960 revision of *Ku-wen kuan-chih* entitled *Ku-wen kuan-chih hsin-pien* 古文觀止新編. This collection retains 134 selections from the earlier compilation supplemented by 106 others, making it slightly larger than the original collection.

Ku-wen kuan-chih has become an extremely popular anthology, and familiarity with its contents is presupposed of students interested in the Chinese prose tradition. Indeed, Chao Ts'ung compares the influence of this anthology with another famous collection, *T'ang-shih san-pai-shou.**

In addition to the Latin translation of one hundred of the 220 selections by Zottoli, Margouliès' numerous French translations, and the English language renditions by such scholars as Giles, Edwards, and Lin listed below, there is a manuscript Manchu translation of *Ku-wen kuan-chih* noted by Walter Fuchs in his *Chinesische und mandjurische Handschriften und seltene Drucke* (Wiesbaden, 1966), Nr. 223/4.

EDITIONS:

Chao, Ts'ung, ed. *Ku-wen kuan-chih hsin-pien.* 1960; rpt. Taipei, 1972.

Wu, Ch'u-ts'ai and Wu Tiao-hou, eds. *Ku-wen kuan-chih.* 1698; rpt. Shanghai, 1926.

TRANSLATIONS:

Edwards, E. D. *Chinese Prose Literature of the T'ang Period.* 2v. London, 1937-38.

Giles, H. A. *Gems of Chinese Literature.* Shanghai, 1922.

Lin, Shih-shun. *Chinese Classical Prose.* Hong Kong, 1979.

Margouliès, G. *Le kou-wen chinois.* Paris, 1926.

Zottoli, P. A. *Cursus Litteraturae Sinicae.* 4v. Shanghai, 1880.

—SD

Ku-wen-tz'u lei-ts'uan 古文辭類纂 (A Classified Compendium of Ancient-style Prose and Verse; in some early editions *chüan* 纂, closer to the intended meaning, is substituted for *ts'uan*—most modern editions use the latter) was compiled by Yao Nai 姚鼐 (*tzu*, Chi-ch'uan 姬傳, Hsi-pao 惜抱, and Meng-ku 夢穀, 1732-1815) in 1799. This influential anthology circulated in handwritten copies for nearly two decades before it was published under the auspices of K'ang Shao-yung 康紹鏞 (1770-1834), then the Governor-general of Kwangtung.

Yao Nai was born in T'ung-ch'eng 桐城 (Anhwei), and tutored in his youth by an uncle, Yao Fan 姚範 (*tzu*, Nan-ch'ing 南青,

hao, Chiang-wu 薑塢 and Chi-t'ung 己銅, 1702-1771). He later came under the tutelage of a famous fellow townsman, Liu Ta-k'uei 劉大櫆 (*tzu*, Ts'ai-fu 才甫, hao, Haifeng 海峯, 1698-1779). Like Fang Pao,* Liu Ta-k'uei and Yao Fan were avid proponents of *ku-wen,** or ancient-style prose, and they schooled Yao Nai in that tradition. After passing the *chin-shih* examination in 1763, Yao Nai was appointed to the Hanlin Academy. Terms of service with the Boards of War, Ceremonies, and Punishments followed. He was subsequently assigned to the commission engaged in the compilation of the *Ssu-k'u ch'üan-shu tsung-mu t'i-yao* (see Chi Yün). Yao Nai resigned from office in 1774 and devoted his energies over the next several decades to teaching in private academies in the lower Yangtze River Valley. Because of his reputation as a prose stylist and classicist, he attracted many students and inculcated in them the literary values and concepts he had inherited from his uncle and from Liu Ta-k'uei.

Through his energetic advocacy of ancient-style prose, the movement to restore it to widespread public acceptance made considerable headway during his lifetime and ultimately came to be known as the T'ung-ch'eng P'ai,* after the home of Fang Pao, Liu Ta-k'uei, and himself. By the midnineteenth century, this school was able to claim a large following of prominent officials and men of letters, such as Kuo Sung-tao 郭嵩燾 (1818-1891), Chang Yü-chao 張裕釗 (1823-1894), Hsüeh Fu-ch'eng 薛福成 (1838-1894), Wang K'ai-yün 王闓運 (1833-1916), Wu Ju-lun 吳汝綸 (1840-1903) Yen Fu,* and Lin Shu.* Because of shared commitments to prose and to the philosophical ideals of the Sung Neo-Confucianists, two other literary schools of the time are regarded as offshoots of the T'ung-ch'eng School: the Yang-hu School 陽湖派 of Yün Ching 惲敬 (1759-1817) and Chang Hui-yen,* and the Hsiang-hsiang School 湘鄉派 of Tseng Kuo-fan* and his numerous followers. Some scholars prefer to consider all three schools as a single entity, for their differences were not great. Tseng Kuo-fan did disagree with Yao Nai

501

on certain points of theory, but he acknowledged Yao's influence on his own development as a writer.

Philosophically, Yao Nai subscribed to the ethical ideals enunciated by Chu Hsi 朱熹 (1130-1200) and his predecessors, as Fang Pao and Liu Ta-k'uei had done before him. But unlike them, he also recognized the objectives and contributions to knowledge of the k'ao-cheng 攷證 (evidential research) scholars, although he failed to achieve any real distinction as a textual scholar. Nevertheless, a somewhat more sophisticated thinker than his mentors, he sought to provide a theoretical basis for the conflicting claims of ethical standards of behavior, for textual research of the kind represented by the Han School of learning, and for his primary area of interest and activity, literature. This is reflected in his adoption of the formula wen-tao ho-i 文道合一 (literature and the Way united in one), which provided metaphysical and ethical bases for the literary activities he espoused. With a similar objective in mind, he distinguished in the preface to the Ku-wen-tz'u lei-ts'uan eight principles of ancient-style prose: "In general, there are thirteen categories of literature, and what makes them literature are eight [principles], namely, shen 神 [spirit] and li 理 [principle—a primary Neo-Confucian metaphysical concept], ch'i 氣 [vital force] and wei 味 [flavor], ko 格 [form] and lü 律 [rules], and sheng 聲 [sounds] and se 色 [color]. Spirit, principle, vital force, and flavor constitute the essences of literature; form, rules, sounds, and color constitute the coarse [externals] of literature. However, if we discard the coarse, then wherein may the essences lodge?" Although he did not here or elsewhere precisely define terms, given his commitment to Neo-Confucian values, it is apparent that for him ancient-style prose and certain kinds of poetic expression possessed transcendent value, lending them in turn ethical meaning. Yao Nai's aesthetic theory of beauty, which was influenced by Liu Hsieh's observation (see Wen-hsin tiao-lung) that the vital force may be strong or weak, is similarly metaphysical. In Yao Nai's terms, there are two kinds of beauty: the yang 陽 (masculine) and yin 陰 (feminine). These polar concepts had, of course, been invested with new import by Chou Tun-i 周敦頤 (1017-1073) and his followers. Yao Nai's conception of ancient-style prose (and polite literature in general for that matter) was not exclusively metaphysical or aesthetic, for unlike the advocates of p'ien-wen* (parallel-prose) styles, he was fully aware of its practical applications. It was primarily on these grounds that he made a place in his hierarchy of literary values for the pa-ku wen* (eight-legged essay). Although he insisted on the superiority of the style of ancient-style prose and urged intensive study of the ancient models, the purpose of that study was to capture the inner animating qualities, the vital force and tone of the ancient masterworks. In that way, the aspiring writer could use such knowledge as a guide in his own writing. Yao Nai was careful, however, to distinguish between that act of personal discovery and the mechanical imitation of ancient models. The latter, he believed, led to narrowness of vision and expression and was to be avoided. Moreover, he was sensible to historical and linguistic change and what that entailed for the writer. The emotions of the individiual author were also recognized as an important element in the final act of creation. On at least one occasion Yao Nai expressed a belief in a kind of divine inspiration to account for the supreme moments in literature. His view of literature was thus a sophisticated and complex one.

Yao Nai's most lasting contribution to Chinese letters was the compilation ot the Ku-wen-tz'u lei-ts'uan, which he conceived as a guide to the great monuments of ancient-style prose and allied compositions in verse. Subscribing to the view earlier enunciated by Fang Pao that the Confucian Classics were of such superior quality as to defy partition, he regarded this anthology as no more than a supplement to such works as the Liu-ching (Six Classics), the Lun-yü, and the Meng-tzu. This did not mean, of course, that the works in the anthology could not also exemplifiy the principles named in his preface. Those selections were drawn from a large range of philosophical, historical, and literary works of the past, and these were in turn arranged under one or another of thirteen generic headings. For example, the first category, lun-pien 論辨 (discussions), contains Chia I's* "Kuo Ch'in lun" 過秦論 (The Faults of Ch'in), several essays by Han Yü,* including the classic "Yüan-tao" 原道 (On the Origin of the Way), and the essay "P'eng-tang lun" 朋黨論 (On Party Factionalism) by Ou-yang Hsiu,* among other works. The second category, hsü-pa 序跋 (prefaces and colophons), includes six selections from the Shih-chi* by Ssu-ma Ch'ien,* including the "Shih-erh chu-hou nien-piao hsü" 十二諸侯年表序 (Preface to the Annular Tables of the Twelve Nobles), and the essay "Chou-li i hsü" 周禮義序 (Preface to the Meaning of the Chou-li) by Wang An-shih.* The eighth section, pei-chih 碑誌 (memorial inscriptions), contains numerous examples of the form, with those of Han Yü, Ou-yang Hsiu, and Wang An-shih comprising a significant proportion of the total. The tenth category, chen-ming 箴銘 (admonitions), is represented by only a few examples, but one of these is the famous "Hsi-ming" 西銘 (The Western Inscription) by the eminent philosopher Chang Tsai 張載 (1020-1077). The penultimate section of the anthology, tz'u-fu 辭賦 (prose-poems), also contains numerous selections, including such popular literary masterpieces as the "Li sao" 離騷 (On Encountering Sorrow) by Ch'ü Yüan,* the two "summons" poems from the Ch'u-tz'u,* the "Tzu-hsü fu" 子虛賦 (Master Nil) by Ssu-ma Hsiang-ju,* and the "Kuei-ch'ü-lai tz'u" 歸去來辭 (On Returning Home) of T'ao Ch'ien.* The individual works and authors represented in the Ku-wen-tz'u lei-ts'uan span nearly two millennia, from the late Chou times down to Yao Nai's predecessors in the mid-Ch'ing. Just as they were in Fang Pao's anthology of ancient-style prose, the so-called "Eight Masters of the T'ang and Sung"—Han Yü, Liu Tsung-yuan,* Ou-yang Hsiu, Tseng Kung,* Wang An-shih, Su Hsün,* Su Shih,* and Su Ch'e*—are liberally represented in this anthology.

The phenomenal popularity of the Ku-wen-tz'u lei-ts'uan spawned a number of continuations and supplements by later anthologists. Among the most important are the Hsü Ku-wen-tz'u lei-ts'uan 續 (Continuation of The Classified Compendium of Ancient-style Prose and Verse) in twenty-eight chüan by Li Shu-ch'ang 黎庶昌 (1837-1897), a protégé of Tseng Kuo-fan and a distinguished diplomat. The arrangement of materials in this anthology follows the pattern established by its model, but it is rather broader and more liberal in its scope and coverage. It covers a larger span of time, containing excerpts from early- and mid-Chou works and selections from mid-nineteenth-century writers such as Cheng Chen* under whom Li Shu-ch'ang once studied. This anthology was completed in 1890 and published five years later. Wang Hsien-ch'ien 王先謙 (1842-1919) also compiled a continuation to the Ku-wen-tz'u lei-ts'uan. The coverage is comparable to the former work, but it is less admired. The Hsin Ku-wen-tz'u lei-ts'uan 新 (A New Classified Compendium of Ancient-style Prose and Verse), compiled by the modern scholar Chiang Jui-ts'ao 蔣瑞藻, is useful for its inclusion of representative selections from the writings of late nineteenth- and early twentieth-century members of the T'ung-ch'eng School, such as the indefatigable translator Liu Shu.* The existence of the Ku-wen-tz'u lei-ts'uan and its several continuations in modern annotated and punctuated editions testifies to its lasting value and the influence of Yao Nai and his imitators.

Yao Nai's collected works, the Hsi-pao hsüan ch'uan-chi 惜抱軒全集, contain, in addition to his scholarly writings, miscellaneous notes, letters, essays, and poetry. His essay style is notable for its simplicity and clarity of expression. These same qualities also characterize his better poems, such as those in the ancient-style pentasyllablic form, which are memorable for their unpretentious evocation of emotions prompted by a visit to an ancient historical site or a colorful landscape. In addition to his talents as an anthologist of singular importance, Yao Nai was also an accomplished calligrapher, a literary critic and theorist, an essayist, and a poet.

EDITIONS:

Yao, Nai. *Hsi-pao hsüan ch'uan-chi.* Sheng-hsin-ko k'an-pen 省心閣刊本, 1866.

———, ed. *Ku-wen-tz'u lei-ts'uan. SPPY.*

Li, Shu-ch'ang, ed. *Hsü Ku-wen-tz'u lei-ts'uan. SPPY.*

Wang, Hsien-ch'ien, ed. *Hsü Ku-wen-tz'u lei-ts'uan.* 2v. Taipei, 1967.

Chiang, Jui-ts'ao, ed. *Hsin Ku-wen-tz'u lei-ts'uan.* 3v. Taipei, 1967.

STUDIES:

Anhwei Jen-min ch'u-pan-she, ed. *T'ung-cheng p'ai yen-chiu lun-wen chi* 桐城派研究論文集. Anhwei, 1963.

Aoki, *Shindai,* pp. 518-526.

Pollard, David E. *A Chinese Look at Literature, the Literary Values of Chou Tso-jen in Relation to the Tradition.* Berkeley, 1973. See especially Appendix A on the T'ung-ch'eng School.

Wu, *Ch'ing-tai,* pp. 262-264.

Yeh, Lung 葉龍. *T'ung-ch'eng p'ai wen-hsüeh shih* 桐城派文學史. Hong Kong, 1975.

Yü, Hsin-hsiung 尤信雄. *T'ung-ch'eng wen-p'ai hsüeh-shu* 桐城文派學述. Taipei, 1975.

—WS

Ku-wen yüan 古文苑 (Garden of Ancient Literature) is a collection of more than 260 poems and essays from the Eastern Chou period to the Southern Ch'i dynasty. Tradition has it that it was compiled during the T'ang (the compiler is unknown) and was later discovered by Sun Chu 孫洙 (1032-1080) in a Buddhist monastery. The first edition, in nine *chüan,* was brought out by Han Yüan-chi 韓元吉 (1118-1187) in 1179. In 1232 Chang Ch'iao 章樵 (*chin-shih,* 1208) divided the work into twenty-one *chüan* and provided annotations, also adding texts from other sources. Thus the Han nine-*chüan* version is the older and presumably more reliable text.

Some of the texts in this collection seem to have been based upon Sung versions, others are taken from T'ang encyclopedias. A recent study (David R. Knechtges) suggests a possible adoption of most of the *Ku-wen yüan* from a work known as the *Tsa-wen chang* 雜文章 which Sun Chu found in the imperial library—it contained fifty-eight *fu** and *sung* by Sung Yü 宋玉 and others, approximating the fifty-seven *fu* in the Han version of the *Ku-wen yüan.*

Knechtges also notes that none of Yang Hsiung's* works in the *Ku-wen yüan* can be found in early versions and believes the compiler of the *Ku-wen yüan* may have had access to the collected works of Yang and other writers which were lost during the Sung. The *Ku-wen yüan* is also of significance since it includes materials (albeit possibly spurious) not found in the *Wen-hsüan.**

EDITIONS:

Ku-wen yüan. 9 *chüan.* Han Yüan-chiu, comp. *Tai-nan-ko ts'ung-shu* 岱南閣叢書 edition. Reprint of a Sung copy.

Ku-wen yüan. 21 *chüan.* Chang Ch'iao, compiler. *SPTK.* Reprint of a Sung copy.

STUDIES:

Ch'ien, Tseng 錢曾. "*Ku-wen yüan*" 古文苑, in his *Tu-shu min-ch'iu chi chiao-cheng* 讀書敏求記校證, Changchou, 1926, 4 (B):3a-4b.

Huang, P'ei-lieh 黃丕烈. "*Ku-wen yüan* ts'an-pen shih-chüan" 古文苑殘本四卷, in his *Jao-p'u ts'ang-shu t'i-chih* 蕘圃藏書題識 (1916 ed.), 10:5b-6b.

Knechtges, David R. "*Guu-wen yuann*" 古文苑, in "Yang Shyong, the *fuh,* and Han Rhetoric," Unpublished Ph.D. dissertation, University of Washington, 1968, pp. 19-21 and 43-44.

Ku, Kuang-ch'i 顧光圻. "Ch'ung-k'o Sung chiu-chüan-pen *Ku-wen yüan* hsü" 重刻宋九卷本古文序, *Ssu-shih chai chi,* 10:9ab.

———. "Yü Sun Yüan-ju kuan-ch'a lun chiu-chüan-pen *Ku-wen yüan* shu" 與孫淵如觀察論九卷本古文苑書, in his *Ssu-shih chai chi* 思適齋集(*Ch'un-hui T'ang ts'ung-shu* 春暉堂叢書 ed.) 6:11b-14a.

—SFL and WHN

Ku Yen-wu 顧炎武 (named Ch'iang 絳 before 1645, Yen-wu thereafter, *tzu,* Ning-jen 寧人, and known as T'ing-lin Hsien-sheng 亭林先生, 1613-1682), was the foremost exponent of the Ch'ing scholarship. Born in a renowned family in K'un-shan 崑山, he was strongly influenced in his childhood by his foster-mother's devotion to Neo-Confucian moral principles, and by his father's persistent interest in Neo-Confucian practical learning. He spent his youth preparing for the civil-service examinations, and was a member of the political-literary society, Fu-she 復社. About 1640, ashamed of his inability to prevent the degeneration of the Ming dynasty, he began to turn his attention to the kind of practical learning his grandfather had advocated and advised him to pursue.

Between 1640 and 1657, he witnessed the downfall of the Ming and the turmoil of the Ming loyalists' military resistance. His foster-mother stopped eating in order to perish with the Ming. Mourning her death may have prevented him from actively participating in action against the Manchus—two of his natural brothers and many of his friends died because of their anti-Manchu activities. Ku Yen-wu visited the Ming tombs in Nanking several times before he left his hometown for North China in 1657. Except for a brief return visit, he lived in the North until he died at Ch'ü-wo 曲沃 (modern Shansi). He was buried at K'un-shan.

After the Manchu conquest, Ku devoted his life to inquiries into ancient and recent history, the studies he believed would lead to enlightenment while still proving helpful to the world. Differing from the Wang Yang-ming School of Neo-Confucianism, which emphasized intuitive knowledge and claimed that "the mind is the divine principle" 心即理, Ku relied heavily on perceptive knowledge, with the Confucian Classics as his guideline. He claimed that "the study of classics is that of the divine principle" 經學即理學. But the development of this new trend in Neo-Confucianism after more than one hundred years of philosophical activities dominated by Wang's teaching was not initiated by Ku himself. His immediate predecessors included Ku Hsien-ch'eng 顧憲成 (1550-1612), the leader of the Tung-lin 東林 Movement, which was followed by the Fu-she, in which Ku took part. Among friends with similar views was Huang Tsung-hsi 黃宗羲 (1610-1695), another eminent early Ch'ing scholar. It was Ku, however, who made the ideas explicit and, most importantly, was able to produce many monumental works

which became paradigms for later generations. In his works, no direct discussion of *hsin* 心 (mind), *hsing* 性 (nature), or *Tao* 道 (the Way) was undertaken, since one would not find such discussions in the *Lun-yü* (see *ching*). Nevertheless, his philosophical concerns are discernible. His philological approaches to philosophical study, however, demanded so much time and energy that followers in later generations gradually turned away from the philosophical aspects, and shifted to pure philology—a trend which characterizes the scholarship of the later Ch'ing period.

Ku traveled unceasingly in the area from Shantung to Shensi, from Chekiang to the Great Wall. As a result of his travels, he wrote several massive geographical studies, including the *T'ien-hsia chün-kuo li-ping shu* 天下郡國利病書 and the *Chao-yü chin* 肇域志, emphasizing strategic and economic potentials of various areas. He routinely verified the first information he gathered against written sources. He used these written sources so extensively that his quotations from many Ming editions of gazetteers are still valuable.

His other major work includes the *Yin-hsüeh wu shu* 音學五書 (Five Writings on Phonetics) and the *Jih-chih lu* 日知錄. The former initiated the Ch'ing study of phonetics, and the latter is an anthology of his writings concerning Chinese culture and civilization. It contains Ku's comments on the classics, politics, economics, and literature. The broad interests and religious devotion to knowledge revealed in this voluminous, original, and carefully documented work made him the founding father of the *P'u-hsüeh* 樸學 (Practical Scholarship).

Before Ku, the study of Archaic Chinese had arrived at only a few tangible conclusions: that the rhyming system of the pre-T'ang writings was different from that of the *Kuang-yün* 廣韻 (demonstrated by Wu Yü 吳棫 of the Sung), and that the sounds changed from period to period, and from place to place (theorized by Ch'en Ti 陳第 [1541-1617]). Ku pushed one great step forward by applying a careful inductive method to the rhyming phenomena in the

505

classics, especially the *Shih-ching*.* The system he proposed was much more convincing than Wu's, and the phonological interpretation he derived from it constituted the basic framework for future studies on the finals of Archaic Chinese. His interest in epigraphy also led to the development of studies in Chinese etymology and accordingly to the discovery of the initial groups of Archaic Chinese.

Ku also achieved a certain reputation for his *shih** poetry, most of which was written to vent his strong feelings about the Ch'ing invaders (in contrast to the imitational or occasional verse then current). In poems such as "Ch'iu shan, ti-i" 秋山，第一 (Autumn Mountains, Number One), "T'ao-yeh ko" 桃葉歌 (Song of the Peach Leaves), and "Chin shan" 金山 (Golden Mountain), he revealed the cruelty of the Manchu troops, the suffering of the people, and his own patriotism. His diction is often reminiscent of Six Dynasty *yüeh-fu* verse.

In his essays Ku employed a simple, easy-to-understand style. Primarily devoted to politics or scholarship (see his influential "Yü yu-jen lun hsüeh-shu" 與友人論學書 [Discussing Scholarship with a Friend]), his "Yü jen shu shih-ch'i" 與人書十七 (Letters to a Certain Person, Number Seventeen) reveals some of his literary views—he opposed imitating the ancients—as does the "Wen-chang fan-chien" 文章繁簡 (Literature, Complex and Simple) section of his *Jih-chih lu.*

EDITIONS:

Jih-chih lu chi-shih 集釋. Originally printed by Huang Ju-ch'eng 黃汝成 (1799-1837) in 1834. *SPPY.*

Ku T'ing-lin shih-wen chi 顧亭林詩文集. Peking, 1959. Most accessible edition of Ku's poetry and prose.

T'ien-hsia chün-kuo li-ping shu. SPTK. Contains Ku's preface (1662) and a *nien-p'u* by Ch'ien Pang-yen 錢邦彥 (*fl.* 1908).

T'ing-lin Hsien-sheng i-shu hui-chi 亭林先生遺書彙輯. Also known as *Ku-shih ch'üan chi* 顧氏全集. Chu Chi-jung 朱記榮 (*fl.* 1882-1904), ed. 1888. Contains 23 works.

Yin-hsüeh wu-shu. Chengtu, 1933; rpt. Taipei, 1966. Five of Ku's most important works on phonetics.

Yüan ch'ao-pen Jih-chih lu 原抄本日知錄. Taipei, 1958. Preface by Hsü Wen-shan 徐文珊. Based on a manuscript purchased in Peking in 1935, one that was apparently not revised in order to avoid the Ch'ien-lung suppression.

TRANSLATIONS:

de Bary, William Theodore, *et al.*, comp. *Sources of Chinese Tradition.* New York, 1960, pp. 607-612.

Shimizu, Shigeru 清水茂. *Ko Enbu shu* 顧炎武集. Tokyo, 1974.

Wilhelm, Hellmut. "Die Mutter Gu T'ing-lins," *Sinica,* 6 (1931), 229-237. Contains a translation of Ku's epitaph for his mother.

STUDIES:

Ch'en, Yu-ch'in 陳友琴. "Lüeh lun Ku Yen-wu te shih" 略論顧炎武的詩, in *Ch'ang-tuan chi* 長短集, Hangchow, 1980, pp. 160-174.

Ch'ien, Mu 錢穆. "Ku T'ing-lin hsüeh-shu" 顧亭林學述, in *Ku-kung t'u-shu chi-k'an,* 11.2 (October 1973), 1-12.

ECCP, pp. 421-426.

Hagman, Jan. *Bibliographic Notes on Ku Yen-wu.* Stockholm, 1973.

Ho, I-k'un 何貽焜. "Ku T'ang-lin Hsien-sheng te wen-hsüeh kuan" 顧亭林先生的文學觀, *Shih-ta yüeh-k'an,* 18 (April 1935), 81-94.

Ho, Yü-sen 何佑森, "Ku T'ing-lin te ching-hsüeh-shu" 顧亭林的經學述, in *Ku-kung t'u-shu chi-k'an,* 16 (October 1967), 183-205.

Hsieh, Kuo-chen 謝國楨. *Ku T'ing-jen hsüeh-p'u* 顧寧人學譜. Shanghai, 1930; rpt, Shanghai, 1957. Huang Chieh 黃節 (1874-1935). *Ku T'ing-lin shih* 顧亭林詩. Peking, n.d.

Hummel, A. W. "Mss. of Ku Yen-wu (in the Library of Congress)," *Report of the Librarian of Congress,* Washington, 1937, pp. 170-174.

Liu, Tso-mei 柳作梅, "Ku T'ing-lin chih ch'u-yu so-yin" 顧亭林之出遊索隱, *Ta-lu tsa-chih,* 40.9 (May 1970), 1-11.

P'an, Chung-kuei 潘重規. *T'ing-lin shih k'ao-so* 亭林詩考索. Hong Kong, 1962.

Peterson, Willard J. "The Life of Ku Yen-wu," *HJAS,* 28 (1968), 114-156; 29 (1969), 201-247.

Rai, Tsutomu 賴惟勤, "Ko Enbu no *Shihon'on* ni tsuite" 顧炎武の詩本音について, *Ochanomizu Joshi Daigaku jimbun Kagaku kiyō,* 21.3 (March 1968), 107-143.

Shigezawa, Toshirō 重澤俊郎, "Ko Enbu no heika mondai" 顧炎武の評價問題, *Chūgoku bunka to shakai,* 12 (November 1963), 77-84.

Wang, Ch'i-chung 王氣中. "Ku Yen-wu te shih-ko yü san-wen" 顧炎武的詩歌與散文, *Nan-ching Ta-hsüeh hsüeh-pao*, 1963.3 & 4.

Yamai, Waku 山井湧, "Ko Enbu no Gakumon Kan" 顧炎武の學問觀 *Chūō Daigaku Bungakubu kiyō*, 35 (March 1964), 67-93.

—TFC

Kuan Han-ch'ing 關漢卿 (*hao*, I-sou-chai 已叟齋, *c.* 1240-*c.* 1320) was the most productive playwright of the traditional Chinese theater, with some sixty plays attributed to him. Despite his immense creative power and his fame as the father of traditional drama, only scanty and partly contradictory biographical data exist. He is listed first among the Yüan dramatists in the *Lu-kuei-pu** and was originally from Ta-tu (modern Peking). A contemporary of the famous playwright Pai P'u,* he probably lived during the years 1240-1320. Even his name is uncertain; only the surname Kuan is indisputable, and Han-ch'ing is most likely his style name (*tzu*).

Most of his sixty plays are no longer extant. Of the twenty-one plays now attributed to him, fifteen are complete, with dialogue and arias, three have complete texts for the arias with minimal dialogue and stage directions, and three exist only as fragments. The authorship of some plays, notably *Lu Chai-lang* 魯齋郎 (Lu Chai-lang), *P'ei Tu huan tai* 裴度還帶 (P'ei Tu Returns the Belt), *Tan-pien to shuo* 單鞭奪槊 (Robbing the Lance with a Single Whipstroke), and *Wu-hou yen* 五侯宴 (Banquet of the Five Marquises), is in dispute.

His plays have been transmitted in many editions; for some of his plays, single editions exist from the Yüan or Ming periods. Others have two, three, or even four separate editions from the years between Yüan and Ch'ing. All these editions differ. The older ones, such as the *Yüan-k'an pen* 元刊本 (see *tsa-chü*) are generally less polished, less elegant, and more colloquial than later editions that have passed through the hands of highly literate editors. In some cases, the arias hardly differ from colloquial speech.

The main characters of Kuan Han-ch'ing's plays are mostly female. This is not typical of *tsa-chü*.* Most of the women in his plays are virtuous and idealized. In *Tou O Yüan* 竇娥冤 (The Injustice to Tou O), his most famous play, a young widow is accused of murder when she obstinately refuses to marry a depraved vagrant who has poisoned his own father by mistake. To spare her mother-in-law from the pain of torture when she is accused of the murder, Tou O confesses and is executed. Her name is cleared by her father, who returns from the capital as a judicial intendant, and her ghost is released into the netherworld.

In *Hu-tieh meng* 蝴蝶夢 (The Butterfly Dream), Madam Wang is ready to sacrifice her own son for the sake of her two stepsons since only one person need be punished for the three sons' vengeance on their father's murderer. Thanks to the wisdom of the famous Judge Pao, however, her son is spared at the end of the play.

In another play, *Ch'en-mu chiao tzu* 陳母教子 (Mother Ch'en Instructs Her Sons), the widow of an official employs every possible means to teach proper moral behavior to her three sons. When a treasure is found in her garden, she insists that they bury it again. She rejects her third son when he alone fails to attain the highest degree in the examinations. When he finally wins the *chuang-yüan* degree, she beats him for having accepted presents from commoners. In the end, when Madam Ch'en is invited to the offices of a high official to be praised for having raised three "top degree" candidates, she uses her three sons and her stepson as sedan bearers to teach them humility.

The other female leads in Kuan Han-ch'ing's plays are notable for their resourcefulness, their intellectual powers, and their fearlessness. In *Chiu feng-ch'en* 救風塵 (The Rescue of a Courtesan), Chao P'an-erh, a prostitute, saves her friend from an unhappy marriage to a lascivious drunkard. In *Hsieh T'ien-hsiang* 謝天香, named after the heroine, the courtesan Hsieh demonstrates her profound literary knowledge and poetic facility when she changes the rhymes of a poem to avoid the taboo name of a prefect she encourages as a client. In the play *Wang-chiang t'ing* 望江亭 (The Pavilion above the River), the young widow and Taoist nun T'an Ch'i-erh marries again, but only to save her beloved husband from the schemes of a high official who lusts after her. In *Chin-hsien Ch'ih* 金線池 (The Golden Thread Pond), another courtesan, Tu Jui-niang, struggles with her procuress-mother for permission to marry a poor candidate under the patronage of the mighty prefect of Chi-nan.

With the exception of Chao P'an-erh, all of the courtesans and the widows of Kuan's plays marry candidates or high officials—unlikely in real life and only seldom seen in other literary genres. Kuan Han-ch'ing's female characters do not support the traditional Chinese image of women, bound by rituals designed by men, a mere maidservant from her childhood service to her father to her duty to her husband and her sons. Kuan's appreciation for women is seen in secondary characters as well. For instance, in the fragmentary play, *T'iao feng-yüan* 調風月 (Settling a Love Quarrel), Yen-yen, a maidservant has fallen in love with the intended husband of her mistress. Thanks to her resourcefulness she and her mistress come to share the same lover without violating any moral precepts.

In addition to these "social plays" with female leads, Kuan also wrote three (extant) history plays, two of them on the legend of the Three Kingdoms. *Tan-tao hui* 單刀會 (The Feast of the Single Sword) and the fragmentary *Hsi-Shu Meng* 西蜀夢 (Dream of Western Shu) are both *mo-pen* plays with male leads. The first concerns the exploits of the famed general Kuan Yü, then governing Ching-chou, the city which controls the Yangtze Valley, for his lord, Liu Pei, King of Shu, at the western end of the valley. Lu Su, minister to the rival eastern kingdom of Wu, invites Kuan Yü to a feast, intending to regain Ching-chou for his master, the King of Wu, by diplomacy or treachery. The play is notable for its psychological portrayal of a martial hero, Kuan Yü, who was then on the verge of deification in popular lore, and for its tragic note, since Kuan Yü is duped by Lu Su's plan and, at the height of his prowess, slain. In *Hsi-Shu meng*, Liu Pei, the king of Shu, is visited in a dream by his dead comrades Kuan Yü and Chang Fei. They have both been ambushed and slain and ask that he sprinkle the capital with the blood of their killers. Liu Pei impetuously begins a campaign to honor the dead souls of his comrades in arms and thereby loses his kingdom.

EDITIONS:

Chang, Yu-lan 張友鸞 and Ku Hsüeh-chieh 顧學頡. *Kuan Han-ch'ing tsa-chü hsüan* 關漢卿雜劇選. Peking, 1963. Contains four plays.

Fu, Ao 傅傲, ed. *Chung-kuo li-tai hsi-ch'ü hsüan* 中國歷代戲曲選. Hong Kong, 1962. Contains four plays.

Hu, Chi 胡忌, ed. *Ku-tai hsi-ch'ü hsüan chu* 古代戲曲選注. 3v. Shanghai, 1959. Contains four plays, one completely annotated.

Ku, Hsüeh-chieh 顧學頡. *Yüan-jen tsa-chü hsüan* 元人雜劇選. Peking, 1978. Contains two plays.

Kuan Han-ch'ing hsi-chü chi 關漢卿戲曲集. Peking, 1976. Provides textual notes for several plays.

Kuan Han-ch'ing hsi-ch'ü hsüan 關漢卿戲曲選. Peking, 1958. This collection with a preface by Cheng Chen-to contains eight well-annotated plays and several non-dramatic *ch'ü*-arias of Kuan Han-ch'ing.

Kuan Han-ch'ing Tsa-chü hsüan 關漢卿雜劇選. Hong Kong, 1961. Contains two plays.

Wu, Hsiao-ling 吳曉鈴, ed. *Kuan Han-ch'ing hsi-chü chi* 關漢卿戲劇集. Peking, 1958. This standard edition with more than 1000 pages contains minute textual comparisons of the Yüan and Ming editions of all plays and most of the non-dramatic *ch'ü*-arias attributed to Kuan Han-ch'ing. The different editions are compared word by word on the basis of the oldest editions such as *Yüan-k'an pen, Ku tsa-chü*, etc. In the appendix there is a copiously annotated list of all titles.

———, ed. *Ta hsi-chü-chia Kuan Han-ch'ing chieh-tso chi* 大戲劇家關漢卿傑作集. Peking, 1958. Contains six annotated plays with an alphabetically arranged glossary.

TRANSLATIONS:

Demiéville, *Anthologie*, pp. 437-439.

Shih, Chung-wen. *Injustice to Tou O*. Cambridge, 1972. The best translation of *Tou O Yüan*.

Yang, Hsien-i and Gladys Yang. *Selected Plays of Kuan Han-ch'ing*. Peking, 1958. Preface by Wang Chi-szu; eight translations of poor quality.

STUDIES:

Cheng, Ch'ien 鄭騫. "Kuan Han-ch'ing Tou O yüan i-pen pi-chiao" 關漢卿竇娥冤異本比較, *Ta-lu tsa-chih*, 29 (1954), 10. Textual study.

Dolby, Arthur W. "Kuan Han-ch'ing," *AM*, n.s., 16 (1971), 1-60. The best biographical study about Kuan Han-ch'ing, including annotated translations of some non-dramatic *ch'ü*-arias.

Hsieh, Chen-ooi Chin. "Evolution of the Theme of Tou O Yüan." Unpublished Ph.D. dissertation, Ohio State University, 1974.

Leung, Pui Kam 梁沛錦, ed. *Kuan Han-ch'ing yen-chiu lun-wen chi-ch'eng* 關漢卿研究論文集成. Hong Kong, 1969. Contains 39 articles about Kuan Han-ch'ing and his works, of which 24 already were published in the collection *Kuan Han-ch'ing yen-chiu lun-wen chi*, Shanghai, 1958.

Liu, Ching-chih 劉靖之. *Kuan Han-ch'ing San-kuo ku-shih tsa-chü yen-chiu* 關漢卿三國故事雜劇研究. Hong Kong, 1980. An excellent study about Kuan Han-ch'ing in general and the plays *Tan-tao hui* and *Hsi-Shu meng* in particular.

Seaton, Jerome P., Jr. "A Critical Study of Kuan Han-ch'ing. The Man and His Works." Unpublished Ph.D. dissertation, Indiana University, 1969. The only work in any Western language dedicated to Kuan Han-ch'ing's plays; contains interpretations of ten plays.

T'an, Cheng-pi 譚正璧. *Yüan-tai hsi-chü-chia Kuan Han-ch'ing* 元代戲劇家關漢卿. Shanghai, 1957.

Wu, Kuo-ch'in 吳國欽. *Chung-kuo hsi-ch'ü shih man-hua* 中國戲曲史漫話. Shanghai, 1980. Contains six articles about Kuan Han-ch'ing.

—CHP and WO

Kuan-hsiu 貫休 (secular surname, Chiang 姜; *tzu*, Te-yin 德陰, 832-912), was a native of Lan-ch'i 蘭溪 in Wu-chou 婺州 (modern Chekiang). Orphaned at an early age, he studied in a Buddhist monastery in his home town. He showed early promise as poet, painter, and calligrapher. For a while he joined the Buddhist community of Hung-chou 杭州 (modern Kiangsi); then, in the 890s, he returned to his homeland, now firmly under the control of Ch'ien Liu 錢鏐, future king of Wu-Yüeh.

During this period, when he was a resident of Hangchow, he painted the celebrated pictures of sixteen arhats. These are said to have been inspired by a dream (a poetic version of the affair was composed by Ou-yang Chiung,* later his colleague in Szechwan). Each shows an austere saint seated under an overhanging rock or in a stony niche. Critical opinion differs as to which of the paintings of arhats attributed to him are authentic; the set in the Imperial Household Collection in Tokyo is particularly well regarded.

Kuan's career as a court poet came to an end when he took offense at Ch'ien Liu's suggestion that he reword a laudatory poem to make it even more flattering. The poet—so the tale goes—made an impertinent reply, casting doubt on the prince's qualifications as a literary critic. Kuan-hsiu moved up the Yangtze to the domain of the warlord Ch'eng Jui 成汭, who was his patron for a brief period. Here he became the friend of the poet Wu Yung 吳融, with whom he could speak seriously about philosophic and literary matters. Ch'eng Jui's court proved no more satisfactory than that of Wu-Yüeh, and at the beginning of the ninth century Kuan continued westward into Szechwan, where he was given a suitably honorable welcome by Wang Chien 王建, founder of the new kingdom of Shu 蜀. In 907, already an ornament of the brilliant court at Ch'eng-tu and celebrated both as priest and prelate, he was invested with the title of *Ch'an-yüeh ta-shih* 禪月大師. There he ended his days full of years and glory.

Kuan-hsiu put together the first collection of his writings in 896, while he was still with Ch'eng Jui in Chiang-ling 江陵. It was titled *Hsi-yüeh chi* 西岳集, a name which reflects a period in the 850s when the poet resided at Hua Shan 華山. (Wu Yung wrote a prefatory essay for this collection in 899.) This was superseded by a new collection made posthumously by his disciple T'an-yü 曇域 —a version which now circulates as *Ch'an-yüeh chi* 禪月集 (Wu Yung's preface remains attached to some editions).

In the most characteristic of his confections, Kuan-hsiu reveals himself as a dreamer and visionary. Even his portrayals of the courts and gardens of this world are couched in the language of illusion and elegant hallucination. His symbols of immortality are largely drawn from the color spectrum and the many-faceted mineralogical world. An aristocratic pleasance is subtly transformed into a crystalline paradise, whose trees tinkle with leaves of gold and silver, through which shine gemmy fruits and jewelled flowers. Through all, a luminous atmosphere intimates the white light of eternity. Such visions characterize his courtly odes and lauds as much as his religious verses—chiefly occasional stanzas on Buddhist monasteries and Taoist ecclesiastics. Yet he was not an ecstatic poet like that dedicated star-traveller Wu Yün 吳筠. He saw religion as a civilizing agency; the life of this world was very much in his mind. He was, in fact, a syncretist, both in thought and in verse. He employed the imagery of Taoism, Buddhism, and "Confucianism" (that is, the secular idealism inherited from antiquity) interchangeably. His ideas on this theme are summarized in a poem entitled "Ta-hsing san chiao" 大興三教 (Greatly Exalted Are the Three Doctrines). Beyond this, he believed that the brilliant culture of Shu might, under his guidance, bring together men of all kinds and all traditions into a variegated but harmonious whole. Such utopian and apostolic beliefs are expressed, for instance, in another poem named "Shou tsai ssu i" 守在四夷 (Our Guard Lies with the Four Aliens), in which appears a typical transformational antithesis: "The incenses of Java seem to be snow; the horses of the Uighurs are like a forest"—that is, the northern wastes and the tropical jungles are identical when considered beyond phenomenal illusion.

In the estimation of literary persons of his era, Kuan-hsiu rated very highly. His name was linked with that of his Szechwanese contemporary, the poetical sramana Ch'i-chi.* His old friend Wu Yung thought him the only worthy successor to Li Po* and Po Chü-i.* The Buddhist hagiographer Tsan-ning 贊寧 held him to be the peer of Li Po and Li Ho.* After Sung times his reputation declined.

EDITIONS:
Ch'an yüeh chi 禪月集. *SPTK.*
Ch'üan T'ang shih, v. 12, *ch.* 826-837, pp. 9302-9440, and *ch.* 888, p. 10035.

TRANSLATIONS:
Schafer, E. H. "Mineral Imagery in the Paradise Poems of Kuan-hsiu," *AM*, 10 (1963), 73-102.

STUDIES:
Fan, Chih-min 范志民. *Kuan-hsiu*. Shanghai, 1981.
Kobayashi, Taichirō 小林太市郎. *Zengetsu daichi no shōhai to geijutsu* 禪月大師の生崖と藝術. Tokyo, 1947.
Lu, Chen 路振 (957-1014). *Chiu kuo chih* 九國志. *Shou shan ko ts'ung shu* 守山閣叢書.
Ou-yang, Chiung 歐陽炯. "Kuan-hsiu ying meng lo-han hua ko" 貫休應夢羅漢畫歌, *Ch'üan T'ang shih*, v. 11, *ch.* 761, pp. 8638-8639.
Schafer, E. H., "Mineral Imagery."
Tsan-ning 贊寧. "Sung kao-seng chuan" 宋高僧傳, *Tōkyō daizōkyō* 東京大藏經, v. 50, p. 897.
Wu, Chi-yu 吳其昱. "Le séjour de Kouan-hieou au Houa chan et le titre du recueil de ses poèmes: Si-yo tsi, "*Mélanges publiés par l'Institut des Hautes Études Chinoise*, 2 (1960), 159-178.
———. "Trois poèmes inédits de Kouan-hieou" *JA*, 247 (1959), 349-378.
Wu, Jen-ch'en 吳任臣. *Shih-kuo ch'un-ch'iu* 十國春秋 (ed. of 1793), *ch.* 47, pp. 1b-4b.
Wu, Yung 吳融. "Ch'an-yüeh chi hsü" 禪月集序, *Ch'üan T'ang wen*, v. 17, *ch.* 820, pp. 10892-10892.

—ES

Kuan Yün-shih 貫雲石 (*hao*, Suan-chai 酸齋, original Uighur name Hsiao-yün-shih hai-ya 小雲石海涯 [Sewinch Qaya], 1286-1324) is recognized as one of the great masters of the *san-ch'ü* 散曲 (lyric verse) of the Yüan and enjoyed in his own day an equal reputation as a writer of classical verse (*shih**) and prose. Both his father's and his mother's families were prominent in the non-Chinese elite ruling class of the Mongol period, and his own career began as a garrison commander and general in Yung-chou 永州 (Hunan), a post inherited from his illustrious grandfather Arigh Qaya, who subjugated central and south China during the Mongol conquest. After a brief military career, Kuan resigned and traveled to Peking to study Neo-Confucianism under Yao Sui (1308). A few years later he was appointed to the Han-lin Academy where he became a drafter of imperial edicts and state historiography. His pro-Chinese and pro-Confucian sympathies seem to have put him in danger, and this, together with his frustration at not seeing a large-scale reintroduction of traditional Confucian practices into government led him to resign (1317). He spent the rest of his life in retirement near Hang-chow.

Kuan's collected classical verse and prose were lost sometime in the late Ming or early Ch'ing, but enough of his verse is preserved in other sources to reveal its general characteristics. Highly allusive, often full of personal symbolism, prone to elaborate figures of speech, it is clearly cast in the late-T'ang style. Traditional critics have at times labeled it "demonic" and compared him to Li Ho.* However it is the *san-ch'ü* that really made Kuan's reputation and is why he is remembered today. Seventy-nine *hsiao-ling* (short songs) and nine *t'ao-shu* (song sets) can be attributed to him with reasonable assurance, one of the largest bodies of work in the genre to survive from the Yüan period. His lyrics seem to stand midway between an earlier stage characterized by raw exuberance and earthy sensuality and a later one marked by heightened refinement and self-conscious aestheticism; they often exhibit elements of both and the dialectic which results gives much vitality to their expression. The bulk of Kuan's lyrics dates from his years of retirement and expresses a number of interests: natural scenery of the West Lake and Ch'ien-t'ang River area, the joys and satisfactions of rustic life, dramatic portrayals of men and women from the pleasure quarters of the region, dramatic portrayals of neglected ladies (boudoir lyrics), and the celebration of wine, women, and song. More than half, short songs as well as song-sets, are dramatic rather than self-expressive; that is, the voices of the protagonists belong to personae not identifiable with the author himself. These, in effect, are mini-dramas which differ from the lyrics of *tsa-chü** only in that they are not integrated into a larger coherent structure. It is likely that *san-ch'ü* of this type were written for public performance.

Close to many important political, social, and intellectual trends, Kuan is a significant figure in general historical perspectives on the Yüan. Sources for his biography—supplemented with the historical perspectives provided by his creative writing—offer rich materials for the student of Yüan culture and society.

EDITIONS:
Ch'üan Yüan san-ch'ü 全元散曲. 2v. Peking, 1964, pp. 357-386.

TRANSLATIONS:
Lynn, Richard John. *Kuan Yün-shih.* Boston, 1980. Every extant piece of verse or lyric attributed to Kuan is translated here; an extensive biographical and critical study, this is the only book on Kuan in any language.
Sunflower, pp. 445-450.

STUDIES:
Lynn, *Kuan Yün-shih.*
Wang, Chung-lin 王忠林. "Kuan Yün-shih san-ch'ü hsi-p'ing" 貫雲石散曲析評, *Nan-yang Ta-hsüeh hsüeh-pao,* 7 (1973), 19-36.

—RL

Kuei Fu 桂馥 (*tzu,* Tung-hui 東卉 or 多卉, *hao,* Wei-ku 未谷, 1736-1805) was a native of Ch'ü-fu 曲阜 (modern Shantung). Although he was a well-known scholar of linguistics and literature, he did not pass the *chin-shih* examination until he was fifty-five. His official career was equally unimpressive. He served as the magistrate of Yung-p'ing 永平 in the isolated region of southern Yunnan, and died there. Perhaps his own career frustrations prompted Kuei to write a group of four plays about famous poets—the *Hou Ssu-sheng yüan* 後四聲猿 (Later Four Cries of the Gibbon). Like the *Ssu-sheng yüan* written by Hsü Wei,* it consists of four plays with independent plot-lines that nevertheless demonstrate a thematic unity; it also employs a mixture of southern and northern melodies.

Fang Yang-chih 放楊枝 (Letting Go of Yang-chih) expands the anecdote in which Po Chü-i,* in old age and ill health, decides against his own feelings to let go his favorite concubine, Yang-chih, and his favorite horse. Kuei Fu wrote the play as a reply to friends who advised him to acquire a concubine. He was at the time approaching seventy and rather content with his simple pleasures of drinking and reading poetry. The philosophical statement the author tried to make was one of "letting go," both in terms of physical and emotional attachment.

Yeh Fu-shuai 謁府帥 (An Audience Refused) is a play about the humiliation the poet Su Shih* suffered in the antechamber of his superior's office. Su, who had an independent temperament, was refused admission when he went to pay his regular, fortnightly visit to his superior, while other visitors were readily received. As he waited, he was even taunted by the doorman. Kuei Fu noted that when he first read of Su's embarrassment, he felt something choking him. Apparently something in the story brought the sense of humiliation home to the aged minor official in a backwood country and he decided to write a play about it.

T'i yüan-pi 題園壁 (A Message Written on the Wall) concerns Lu Yu's* reluctant divorce and his subsequent meeting with his former wife who was then remarried. Saddened by the meeting, Lu could only reveal his feelings by writing a poem on the wall of the garden he was visiting.

T'ou hun-chung 投溷中 (Thrown into the Privy) is a story of the jealous relative justly punished. Li Ho's* cousin was envious of his talent. After Li's death, the cousin managed to take possession of all of Li's writings and throw them into a privy. Kuei Fu showed such rage and indignation with this crime that he had the cousin punished in Hades, enduring all possible forms of torture.

These four plays are a moving testimony of the author's spontaneous sentiments. Some critics have pointed out that Kuei Fu had the talent of Li Ho, the reputation of Su Shih, and the advanced age of Po Chü-i at the time—thus he was really writing about himself. It is more certain, however, that the *Hou Ssu-sheng yüan* established Kuei's place in Ch'ing drama. He shared, with Yang Ch'ao-kuan (see *Yin-feng-ko tsa-chü*) the reputation of having achieved the utmost in one-act *tsa-chü* plays.

EDITIONS:

Cha-p'u 札樸. Changsha, 1883. 10 *chüan.*
Hou Ssu-sheng yüan, in Cheng Chen-to 鄭振鐸, ed., *Ch'ing-jen tsa-chü* 清人雜劇, v. 7.
Kuei-shih i-shu 桂氏遺書. 1841. 16 *chüan.*

—CYC

Kuei Yu-kuang 歸有光 (*tzu,* Hsi-fu 熙甫, K'ai-fu 開府, *hao,* Chen-ch'uan 震川, 1507-1571) was the second child and eldest son in a well-to-do family which had lived in K'un-shan 崑山 (modern Kiangsu) for ten generations. Though he began as a youth to study the classics and great works of history, developing an especial fondness for Ssu-ma Ch'ien,* he struggled in the examinations and had a rather nondescript career as an official.

In 1536, after several unsuccessful attempts in the examinations, he became a student at the National University in Nanking and in 1540 passed the *chü-jen* examination. He passed the *chin-shih* examination in 1565 when he was nearly sixty years old, serving subsequently in Ch'ang-hsing 長興 (modern Chekiang) as District Magistrate and in Shun-te fu 順德府 (Hopei), before he was summoned to the capital as a compiler of historical records. He died while serving in this capacity. He had six sons, the last born when Kuei was in his sixties, and several daughters. In his brief official career a number of cases testify to his humane and wise leadership.

His reputation grew from his work as a teacher based at An-t'ing chiang 安亭江 near Soochow. There he promulgated a more balanced view of literary history than was the current fashion under the aegis of Wang Shih-chen* (1526-1590) and the Hou ch'i-tzu (Later Seven Masters—see Li P'an-lung). By advocating the prose style of the T'ang and Sung masters—and of the classics and Ssu-ma Ch'ien—Kuei was seen by later critics (beginning with Wang Shih-chen) as a writer whose prose fell within the orthodox tradtion. His popularization of *ku-wen* * can be compared to that of Ou-yang Hsiu* in the Sung and prepared the way for more radical ideas than his own promulgated by the Kung-an p'ai (see Yüan Hung-tao) and others a generation after his death. As his style began to be more widely imitated, he carried on a verbal battle with Wang Shih-chen. Wang generously claimed in a eulogy that Kuei had not only created a style of his own, but was also the rightful descendent of Han Yü* and Ou-yang Hsiu. This praise from the literary arbiter of the time and Kuei's resultant popularity among subsequent literati such as Ai Nan-ying 艾南英 (1583-1646), Ch'ien Ch'ien-i,* and the T'ung-ch'eng p'ai* essayists secured him a place in the history of Chinese literature. Fame in his lifetime, however, was assured without Wang Shih-chen's assistance. By the 1540s Chen-ch'uan Hsien-sheng 震川先生 was said to have already had several thousand students.

But Wang's eulogy may go too far. Although Kuei's prose style does exhibit an affinity with the *ku-wen* of the T'ang and Sung masters, his subjects are more trivial and his tone more familiar. His masterpieces are informal essays which, despite their ability to recreate a scene or evoke a mood, seldom touch on themes of major philosophical or moral import, as the works of Han and Ou-yang did. His best-known work, "Hsiang chi hsüan-chih" 項脊軒志 (Record of the Studio of Nape and Spine) written while Kuei was still relatively young, depicts various encounters with members of his family in this passageway. Another touching vignette which was much praised is "Han-hua tsang-chi" 寒花葬記 (A Burial Note for Han-hua), a eulogy for his wife's maid. "Wu-shan t'u chi" 吳山圖記 (Note on a Landscape Painting of Mount Wu) is also frequently read. It describes a friend who had been given the painting by the people he ruled. "Chang Tzu-hsin chuan" 張自新傳 (Biography of Chang Tzu-hsin) again focuses on a single life, relating how Chang became a scholar despite great difficulties. Kuei laments Chang's fate—he remained undiscovered; whether Kuei was conscious of it or not, Chang's life reflects Kuei's own career. In a different tone, "*Shang-shu* pieh-chieh hsü" 尚書別解序 (Preface to an Unorthodox Exegesis on the *Book of Documents*) is a charming little piece introducing Kuei's commentary to the *Shang-shu;* it tells how he looked after his infant daughter as he wrote the exegesis. His "Hsien-p'i shih-lüeh" 先妣事略 (Brief Account of My Deceased Mother) is a poignant remembrance of the daily routine of the mother who died while he was still a child.

Kuei Yu-kuang's contemporaries had produced an almost incomprehensible style by attempting to imitate ancient syntax and vocabulary. Moreover, they violated the dicta of their own models with this slavish imitation—T'ang *ku-wen* writers had called for a return to a simple *wen-yen* 文言 style in lieu of the then fashionable *p'ien-wen.** This *wen-yen* was, however, a contemporary style (i.e., T'ang), with certain linguistic and stylistic elements borrowed from earlier models. These founders of *ku-wen* would have urged Ming writers to find a natural, contemporary (i.e., Ming) *wen-yen* in which to write and would have scoffed at the Archaists' attempt to reproduce Ch'in, Han, or even T'ang prose. Kuei understood this. "I am fond of the language of *ku-wen,* but I do not agree with that which my contemporaries have taken as *ku-wen*" ("Sung t'ung-nien Meng Yü-shih chih Ch'eng-tu hsü" [Preface to Seeing Fellow Graduate Meng Yü-shih off to Ch'eng-tu]). He advocated not only the study of ancient masters and the classics but also a naturalness (*tzu-jan* 自然) in style. He wanted to capture the spirit (*shen* 神) of the ancients. Kuei also mastered Han Yü's attention to detail and had the ability to bring to life the people he wrote about through a memorable moment. He depicts carefully, for example, how he tried to enter the kitchen and taste a dish his wife's maid was preparing and how she scolded him, providing an insight into the woman's character in ("Han-hua tsang-chi"). In this and other "close-ups" his work resembles that of Li Yü* (1611-1680).

Yet despite his successes in following the style and techniques of the T'ang and Sung masters, he eschewed their discursive genres for the more trivial birthday prefaces and funerary inscriptions. When he did write in genres used by them (*shuo* 說 or *chuan* 傳, for example) his work pales in

513

comparison. His 232 letters and nearly 800 prose writings, primarily dealing with local Soochow subjects or scenes, were nevertheless quite influential in the development of Ch'ing prose.

The empathy he gained for the common people during the many years he spent with his family makes his portrayal of them unique in the essay form. But he does not draw any larger conclusions from this experience. And prose, especially *ku-wen* prose, was a weighty medium. Thus Kuei has been criticized for using it for light subjects. Nevertheless he created a corpus of trivial literature which is often moving, and the influence of these writings on the tone and subjects of late Ming Kung-an writers was considerable. Although he may have been freer to attempt a reform in prose style because he had little official status to jeopardize, his notable successes with the *ku-wen* style merited the attention paid him by its subsequent advocates.

EDITIONS:

Chen-ch'uan chi 震川集. *SPTK.* Facsimile ed. of a K'ang-hsi (1660-1722) woodblock ed. There were two textual traditions—one version (known as the K'un-shan edition 崑山本) edited by his sons in 32 *ch.* (preface 1575) and one edited by his nephew (the Ch'ang-shu edition 常熟本, dated 1574), in 20 *ch.* His great-grandson Kuei Chuang 歸莊 (1613-1673) added unpublished pieces, collated the existing versions, and, with Ch'ien Ch'ien's* help, published the *Chen-ch'uan Hsien-sheng wen-chi* 震川先生文集 in 41 *ch.* (1667-1675).

Chen-ch'uan Hsien-sheng chi 震川先生集. Chou Pen-shun 周本淳, ed. 2v. Shanghai, 1981. Excellent, punctuated, critical edition.

Chen-ch'uan ta ch'üan-chi 震川大全集, *Pu-chi* 補集 (8 *ch.*), *Yü-chi* 餘集 (8 *ch.*), 1799. Most complete edition.

Kuei Chen-ch'uan chi 歸震川集. Lin Shu,* comp. and comm. Shanghai, 1924. Commentary on 83 pieces.

Kuei Yu-kuang wen 歸有光文. Shanghai, 1928. Hu Huai-ch'en 胡懷琛, comp. Selection, lightly annotated, of 30 prose pieces.

Kuei Chen-ch'uan Hsien-sheng wei k'o kao 歸震川先生未刻稿. 6 *ch.* Mss. (1580) now in National Central Library, Taipei.

Ming-tai wen-hsüeh p'i-p'ing tzu-liao hui-pien 明代文學批評資料彙編. Yeh Ch'ing-ping 葉慶炳 and Shao Hung 邵紅, eds. 2v. Taipei, 1979. Punctuated version of sixteen pieces, some excerpted only.

TRANSLATIONS:

"Essays," *Chinese Literature,* November 1962, 70-77.

STUDIES:

Chang, Ch'uan-yüan 張傳元 and Yü Mei-nien 余梅年. *Kuei Chen-ch'uan nien-p'u* 歸震川年譜. Shanghai, 1936.

Ch'ien, Chi-po 錢基博. *Ming-tai wen-hsüeh* 明代文學, Hong Kong, 1964, pp. 49-52 and 115-116. Comments on Kuei's *pa-ku wen.*

DMB, pp. 759-761.

Fan, Wen-fang 范文芳. "Kuei Yu-kuang wen hsi-p'ing" 歸有光文析評, *Hsin-chu Shih-chuan hsüeh-pao,* 6 (June 1980), 35-84.

Hsü, Shih-ying 許世瑛. "Kuei Yu-kuang" 歸有光, in *Chung-kuo wen-hsüeh shih lun-chi* 中國文學史論集, Taipei, 1958, pp. 859-869.

Kung, Tao-ming 龔道明. "Kuei Yu-kuang te wen-hsüeh kuan" 歸有光的文學觀, *Kuo-li Pien-i-kuan kuan-k'an,* 9.1 (June 1980), 135-147.

———. "Kuei Yu-kuang yen-chiu" 歸有光研究. M.A. thesis, National Taiwan University, 1979.

Kuo, Chung-ning 郭仲寧. *Kuei Chen-ch'uan san-wen shih-lun* 歸震川散文試論. Taipei, 1977.

Liang, Jung-jo 梁容若. "Kuei Yu-kuang p'ing-chuan" 歸有光評傳, *Shu han jen,* 125 (December 1969), 985-992.

———. "Kuei Yu-kuang te k'ao-yün yü wen-yün" 歸有光的考運與文運, *Wen-t'an,* 115 (January 1970), 20-22.

Margouliès, Georges. *La prose artistique chinois.* Paris, 1949, pp. 279-281.

Tseng, Li. "Kuei Yu-kuang and Early Ming Dynasty Essays," *CL,* November 1962, 78-83.

—WHN

K'un-ch'ü 崑曲 (also known as *K'un-chü* 昆劇 or *K'un-shan ch'iang* 崑山腔) is the predominant form of music used from the middle of the sixteenth century down to the nineteenth century for performing *ch'uan-ch'i* (romances).* There is still controversy about the origins of *K'un-ch'ü,* but all scholars agree that the sixteenth-century musician Wei Liang-fu 魏良輔 played an important role in its development. Wei was probably born in K'un-shan 崑山, near the major cultural center of Soochow (Kiangsu). Since he perfected the new style while living there, it eventually came to be called *K'un-ch'ü* or "songs of K'un." However, Wei Liang-fu was not a composer in the modern Western sense. The style of opera he created was a blending of the four major forms of southern music that go back to the Yüan, *I-yang ch'iang* 弋陽腔 (originally from Kiangsi and the ancestor of the later *Kao-ch'iang* 高腔 music spread throughout south and west China), *Yü-yao ch'iang* 餘姚腔 (from Chekiang), *Hai-yen ch'iang* 海塩腔 (northeast Chekiang), and *K'un-shan ch'iang* (native to K'un-shan), along with northern tunes (北曲) from Yüan drama. Wei chose the *K'un-shan ch'iang* as the basis for his new style, but greatly refined it, making it accessible to a much wider audience through a synthesis with all the forms just mentioned.

Wei was not the only person responsible for the new style. He received able assistance from his son-in-law Chang Yeh-t'ang 張野塘, who was familiar with northern music, as well as from a number of other musicians. When Wei's new musical style was adopted by the dramatist Liang Ch'en-yü,* *K'un-ch'ü* music became so popular that it eventually replaced all other styles in serious drama. Its dominance continued through the end of the eighteenth century. Little is known of how *K'un-ch'ü* music actually sounded in its early form, since the earliest scores were not printed until Ch'ing times.

The singer and all the other instruments are subordinated to and must follow the principal accompanying instrument, the *Ch'ü-ti* 曲笛, a long, horizontal bamboo flute with an additional hole covered with bamboo-membrane which imparts a pleasing low buzz. The *sheng* 笙 (bamboo wind organ) and the *hsiao* 簫 (vertical flute) are the other usual wind instruments. *K'un-ch'ü*, unlike many northern operas, banishes the shriller stringed instruments from the orchestra, and even the milder three-stringed fretless *san-hsien* 三弦, the *p'i-p'a* 琵琶, and *yüeh-ch'in* 月琴 play a minor role. Although gongs and cymbals can be used to punctuate the action, the normal percussion instruments are a small drum and a wooden clapper to beat time.

The music is based upon the *ch'ü-p'ai* 曲牌 principle; i.e., the poems are written to fit a large number of relatively fixed melodies (the same principle that had been used in Yüan drama and Ming southern drama). This means that the author is rather rigidly bound by the length of each musical phrase and must match the number of syllables per line with the pre-existing melody. As with other *ch'ü-p'ai* poetic forms, there are also constraints on the tones that can be used in any one syllable. However, it should be stressed that the *ch'ü-p'ai* formula is not quite as rigid as it might sound; the same *ch'ü-p'ai* may vary considerably in its musical realization from one occurrence to the next. No satisfactory study has been done so far on the exact relation between the music and the poetry, but it seems that a particular tune undergoes certain fairly predictable changes depending upon the various *ch'en-tzu* 襯字 (extra "padded" words) inserted but especially upon the liberty taken by the poet with the tonal patterns of the *ch'ü*. The art of fitting music to the poetry of a drama or *tu-ch'ü* 度曲 is quite complex, and since many of the late Ming and Ch'ing dramatists did not have sufficient musical backgrounds, they had to seek help from specialists in music. Today *K'un-ch'ü* operas are printed with the traditional Chinese *kung-ch'e* 工尺 (musical notation) written beside the words, indicating both the pitch and the duration of each note.

As mentioned above, the *K'un-ch'ü* is a compromise between northern and southern forms, with the balance in favor of the south. Hence, in any one opera one may find *ch'ü** of both northern and southern origin. These are of a different musical structure, since the southern tunes are based upon a pentatonic scale as opposed to the heptatonic scale used in northern tunes. Generally speaking, the southern *ch'ü* are used more for the contemplative and romantic passages, while the northern *ch'ü* are more in the heroic mode. Thus, by combining two types of music, the *K'un-ch'ü* is able to express a wider range of emotions than either the northern or southern style by itself.

Both the performance and appreciation of *K'un-ch'ü* opera are highly demanding, which may explain the decline of the form after the eighteenth century. The singer must sing for long stretches at a time, and the large-interval leaps in the *hsiao-sheng* 小生 (young-male role) in particular are especially taxing on the voice. The pronunciation of the *pai*, 白 or spoken parts, is governed by a complex set of conventions derived from the pronunciation of Northern Mandarin in the Yüan dynasty, preserving many distinctions lost in modern pronunciation. Every gesture, movement, and expression of the actor is choreographed to match the singing and dialogue perfectly.

Although *K'un-ch'ü* may be too refined for the average audience, it has left its mark on many of the three-hundred-odd forms of opera performed in modern China, including, of course, *Ching-chü** (Peking Opera).

EDITIONS:

Chiu-kung ta-ch'eng nan-pei-tz'u kung-p'u 九宮大成南北詞宮譜. Peking, 1746.

Wei, Liang-fu. *Ch'ü lü* 曲律, in *Hsi-ch'ü lun-chu*, v. 5, pp. 1-13.

TRANSLATIONS:

Scott, A. C. *Traditional Chinese Theater.* v. 2. Madison, 1967.

Yang, Hsien-yi and Gladys Yang. *Fifteen Strings of Cash.* Peking, 1957.

STUDIES:

Chao, Ching-shen 趙景深. "T'an K'un-chü" 談崑劇, in his *Hsi-ch'ü pi-t'an* 戲曲筆談, Shanghai, 1980, pp. 173-207.

Ch'en, Wan-nai 陳萬鼐. *Chung-kuo ku-chü yüeh-ch'ü chih yen-chiu* 中國古劇樂曲之研究. Taipei, 1974.

Hsia, Yeh 夏野. *Hsi-ch'ü yin-yüeh yen-chiu* 戲曲音樂研究. Shanghai, 1962.

Hung, Josephine. *Ming Drama.* Taipei, 1966.

Lu, E-t'ing 陸萼庭 and Chao Ching-shen. *K'un-chü yen-ch'u shih kao* 崑劇演出史稿. Shanghai, 1980.

Muramatsu, Kazuya 村松一彌. *Chūgoku no ongaku* 中國の音樂. Tokyo, 1965.

Su, Wen-liu 蘇文六. *K'un-ch'ü yen-chiu* 崑曲研究. Taipei, 1969.

Teng, Sui-ning 鄧綏寧. *Chung-kuo hsi-chü shih* 中國戲劇史. Taipei, 1956.

Tsiang, Un-kai. *K'ouen k'iu: le théâtre chinois ancien.* Paris, 1933.

Wang, Shou-t'ai 王守泰. *K'un-ch'ü ko-lü* 崑曲格律. Yang-chou, 1982.

Wong, Isabel K. F. "The Printed Collections of K'un Ch'ü Arias and Their Sources," *CHINOPERL,* 8 (1978), 100-129.

Yao Hsin-nung. "The Rise and Fall of K'un-ch'ü," *THM,* 2 (1936), 63-84.

Yang, Yin-liu 楊蔭瀏. *Chung-kuo yin-yüeh shih-kang* 中國音樂史綱. Shanghai, 1953.

—JDS

Kung-t'i shih 宮體詩 (palace-style poetry) is a formal term originated during the Liang dynasty and primarily associated with the style of composition developed by Hsiao Kang 蕭綱 (503-551, posthumously Emperor Chien-wen of Liang 梁簡文帝, r. 549-551) and members of his coterie. The *Pei-shih* 北史 biography of Yü Hsin* records that *Kung-t'i* style was also known by the names of its most famous exponents Hsü Ch'ih 徐摛 (472-551) and his son Hsü Ling (see *Yü-t'ai hsin-yung*) and Yü Chien-wu 庾肩吾 (*fl.* 520) and his son Yü Hsin as the "Hsü-Yü Style."

As the term signifies, palace-style composition was both a product and a reflection of palace life. Subject and diction were influenced by the "salon" environment of court literary entertainments, where verses were written individually, or with several poets acting in concert, on assigned themes. In this after-dinner milieu, the poet's social obligation was to demonstrate his wit and ready erudition.

Treatment of subjects became descriptive rather than contemplative. The word *yung* 詠 (composed on the subject of, singing of) in the title of such verse signified this, and the majority of Liang palace-style compositions fall within this category of *yung-wu* 詠物 (writing about things) verse. With little poetic inspiration, court literati exhausted the palace and its grounds as topics for poetic scrutiny, and then reduced their view to some frail novelty of observation—a moonbeam in a pool, a white plum-blossom on a snow-laden branch.

Objectivity further affected the form of palace-style verse. With only the scantiest content to convey, the poet was inhibited from any extended development of his theme, and under extempore conditions his verses inevitably became shorter. Typically, *yung-wu* verse consists of a quatrain of pentasyllabic lines, merely a series of images whose order is dictated by little more than parallel diction and obligatory rhyme.

The obsession with women and their affairs is perhaps the aspect of palace-style poetry most objectionable to later generations of critics influenced by Confucianism. Typically, women were objects either of admiration or of pity; in either view they were mere objects of *yung-wu* scrutiny. A new court favorite would attract the poet's fancy in the sway of her robes, the disarray of her coiffure, or the nuance of an eyebrow. Alternatively, the abandoned wife or once-favored now-neglected courtesan, aging alone in her ironically ornate chamber, provided the theme of tristesse upon which the poet could lavish mannered expressions of opulent grief.

The term palace-style poetry is sometimes used to identify all poetry written on court themes. In this sense the origins of the genre can be traced to the *Shih-ching*,* where court themes abound, and to the *Ch'u-tz'u** which continues and reinforces the concept of courtly love between a woman and her lord as allegorically representing the proper attitudes between a loyal minister and his gracious sovereign. Another major source of or influence on palace-style poetry was the songs indigenous to the southern Wu area, around the Lower Yangtze Valley, to which the Chinese nobility had emigrated during the invasion of North China in Chin times (*c.* 317). These *yüeh-fu*-type verses were known as *Wu-ko* 吳歌 (songs of Wu), *Tzu-yeh ko* 子夜歌 (Tzu-yeh songs) and *Hsi-ch'ü ko* 西曲歌 (Western songs). Sensuous, as befitted the warm climate and lush terrain in which they originated, these folk songs appealed to the Chinese emigré from the harsher North. He adopted their themes and refined their diction, allowing these songs to be absorbed into palace-style practice.

Critics of palace-style composition raised their voices in protest even as the style itself was emerging (cf. P'ei Tzu-yeh 裴子野 [469-530], "Tiao-ch'ung lun" 雕蟲論 [On Worm-Whittling]). Hsiao Kang too was conscious of the excessive concern of lesser palace-style practitioners with diction and detail rather than poetic compulsion and commissioned Hsü Ling to compile the *Yü-t'ai hsin-yung** "to elevate the genre." However, even before T'ang times it had become the tradition to condemn the style for its inherent immorality. It was thought to mock the deep-rooted concept of literature as a tool and to criticize government.

Nevertheless, palace-style composition exerted a powerful appeal, and it was dominant in the early T'ang. By the mid-T'ang, the resentments of the neglected palace courtesan had become the most commonly treated palace theme; this gave rise to a new term, *kung-yüan* 宮怨 (palace plaint).

EDITIONS:
Chien-chu Yü-t'ai hsin-yung 箋注玉台新詠 (New Songs of the Jade Terrace, with Annotations). Hsü Ling, comp. Wu Chao-i 吳兆宜 (*fl.* 1672), annot. Taipei, 1967.

TRANSLATIONS:
Frodsham, *Anthology*.
Marney, John. *Beyond the Mulberries: An Anthology of Poetry by Liang Chien-wen Ti.* San Francisco, 1982.

STUDIES:
Chou, Hsün-ch'u 周勛初. "Kuan-yü kung-t'i-shih te jo-kan wen-t'i" 關於宮體詩的若干問題, *Hsin Chien-she*, 2 (1965), 54-61.
Hu, Nien-i. "Lun Kung-t'i-shih te wen-t'i" 論宮體詩的問題, *Hsin-Chien-she*, 5-6 (1964), 167-173.
Lin, Wen-Yüeh 林文月. "Nan-ch'ao kung-t'i-shih yen-chiu" 南朝宮體詩研究, *Wen-shih-che hsüeh-pao*, 15 (1966), 407-458.
Marney, John. *Liang Chien-wen Ti.* Boston, 1976.
Miao, Ronald C. "Palace-Style-Poetry: The Courtly Treatment of Glamor and Love," in his *Studies in Chinese Poetry and Poetics,* San Francisco, 1978, v. 1, pp. 1-42.
Tabei, Fumio 田部井文雄. "Rikuchō kyūtai no shi ni tsuite" 六朝宮體の詩について. *Kanbun gakkai-hō*, 18 (1959), 6-11.

Wen, I-to 聞一多. "Kung-t'i-shih te tzu-shu" 宮體詩的自贖, in *T'ang-shih tsa-lun* 唐詩雜論, rpt. Peking, 1956, pp. 11-22.

Yeh, Jih-kuang 葉日光. "Kung-t'i shih hsing-ch'eng chih she-hui pei-ching" 宮體詩形成之社會背景, *Chung-hua Hsüeh-yüan*, 10 (1972), 111-178.

—JM

Kung Tzu-chen 龔自珍 (*tzu*, Se-jen 瑟人, *hao*, Ting-an 定盦, 1792-1841), native of Hang-chow, was a poet, a scholar, and one of the most influential figures in late Ch'ing thought. Born to a family with a long record of government service, he was exposed to politics early in life and repeatedly sought to play a useful role in the central government. Owing to poor penmanship, however, he was unable to advance in the bureaucracy despite his growing reputation as a scholar and political essayist. Although he did pass the *chin-shih* examination in 1829 (on the sixth try), his official career was limited to a series of minor secretarial jobs, mainly with the Grand Secretariat and the Board of Rites. In the summer of 1839, after more than twenty years of residency in the capital, he finally decided to end his office-seeking and left for his native region in the South. To record his moods at the time, he wrote during the subsequent months a large body of inter-echoing *chüeh-chü* (quatrains, see *shih*) under the collective title of *Chi-hai tsa-shih* 己亥雜詩 (Miscellaneous Poems of the Year Chi-hai). The quatrains—315 in all—won him wide and instant acclaim as a lyric poet. They have since been widely recognized as a unique performance in literary history. Two years after leaving the capital, the poet died in Tan-yang (Kiangsu) while serving as an instructor at a local college.

Kung Tzu-chen's failure in politics stood in sharp contrast to his literary and scholastic achievements, which are broad and varied. In addition to being a scholar of the classics, he was also adept in such diverse fields as epigraphy, geography, etymology, and the study of Buddhism. In all these scholarly pursuits, he had received a thorough early training under the tutelage of his maternal grandfather, the eminent etymologist and phonologist Tuan Yü-ts'ai 段玉裁 (1735-1815). Family tradition notwithstanding, he did not follow his grandfather's lead and concentrate on exegetical scholarship but chose to focus on the Confucian Classics, in particular on the moral and philosophical principles underlying the *Ch'un-ch'iu* (see *ching*). His interest in the *Ch'un-ch'iu* soon led him to the *Kung-yang chuan* and its modern exponents, the Ch'ang-chou hsüeh-p'ai 常州學派, a school of thought which advocated, among other things, practical scholarship and a thorough reorientation in the study of ancient classics. Of the key concepts embodied in the Kung-yang text, he was particularly drawn toward those of *pien* 變 (change/reform) and *chih* 治 (statecraft), both of which he found applicable to the needs of his own time. In a series of articles begun in 1815, he extended these two principles into scathing analyses of contemporary society and argued for immediate social and political reforms. The measures he proposed were broad, ranging from a complete overhaul of mid-Ch'ing bureaucracy to banning opium-smoking. These daring ideas, coupled with a forceful prose style, established Kung Tzu-chen as the most powerful and far-sighted thinker of his generation. Although Kung's proposals went largely unnoticed by the government in power at the time, they did catch the attention of many late Ch'ing reformers, including the statesman Li Hung-chang (1823-1901). Eventually these proposals inspired the Hundred Day Reforms of 1898 which rocked the Ch'ing establishment and ushered in a new era.

As a poet, Kung Tzu-chen is particularly renowned for his seven-character quatrains and ancient-style poems. He was equally accomplished in the *tz'u** form and left behind five *tz'u* collections covering his work of three decades. His *shih* works range broadly in tone and subject matter and fall into roughly three large categories. His protest poems and topical satires touch upon many contemporary social and political issues including inequitable taxation and such inhumane practices as foot-binding. These issue-oriented poems share a dense range of allegorical references and are generally couched in a caustic tone. His meditative poems record the heightened moments in the poet's religious and intellectual life, ranging from his early agony over career choices to his eventual embracement of the Buddhist philosophy of peace and compassion. Some of the later works from this group combine a reflective voice with persistent use of Ch'an language and metaphors, giving them a distinct ambience reminiscent of the quieter side of Sung poetry. Kung's short lyrics are vignettes from an emotional life of pain and tender memories, and are the most popular of his works. Some of the topics are fairly conventional; others, however, are rarely treated in classical Chinese poetry (i.e., childhood innocence or maternal love). Thematic diversity aside, one of the outstanding features of Kung Tzu-chen's work is his creative and integrative use of conventional symbols. Two of the images that recur frequently in his meditative and personal lyrics are the *hsiao* 簫 (flute) and the *chien* 劍 (sword). The flute is consistently associated with aesthetic sensitivity, and the sword with ambition or moral commitment. This diversity in subject and tone and innovative use of the poetic tradition have earned Kung Tzu-chen a secure position in the history of Ch'ing *shih;* they have also won him many admirers and imitators among the poets of the late Ch'ing and early Republic notably Huang Tsun-hsien* and Su Man-shu 蘇曼殊 (1884-1918).

EDITIONS:

Kung Ting-an ch'üan-chi 龔定盦全集. Shanghai, 1909 and 1915.

Kung Tzu-chen 'Chi-hai tsa-shih' chu 龔自珍己亥 雜詩注. Liu I-sheng 劉逸生, ed. and comm. Peking, 1980.

Kung Tzu-chen ch'üan-chi 龔自珍全集. 2v. Wang P'ei-cheng 王佩諍, ed. Shanghai, 1959.

Ting-an ch'üan-chi 定庵全集. *SPPY.*

TRANSLATIONS:

Yang, Hsien-yi and Gladys Yang, "Kung Tzu-chen: Poems," *CL,* 1966.4, 89-93.

Sunflower, pp. 493-497.

STUDIES:

Chu, Chieh-ch'in 朱傑勤. *Kung Ting-an yen-chiu* 龔定盦研究. Shanghai, 1940.

ECCP, pp. 431-434.

Liu, I-sheng. *Kung Tzu-chen shih-hsüan* 龔自珍 詩選. Hangchow, 1980.

Tanaka, Kenji 田中謙二. *Kyo Ji-chin* 龔自珍. Tokyo, 1962.

Wan, Tsun-i 萬尊嶷. *Kung Tzu-chen Chi-hai tsa-shih chu* 龔自珍己亥 雜詩注. 2v. Hong Kong, 1978.

Whitbeck, Judith. "Kung Tzu-chen and the Redirection of Literati Commitment in Early Nineteenth Century China," *Ch'ing-shih wen-t'i,* 4.10 (December 1983), 1-32.

Wong, Shirleen S. *Kung Tzu-chen.* Boston, 1975. Bibliography includes three *nien-p'u* and twenty-four miscellaneous essays and articles on Kung.

—SSW

K'ung Jung 孔融 (*tzu,* Wen-chü 文舉, 153-208), descendant of Confucius in the twentieth generation, was a statesman of the first rank renowned for his loyalty to the Han dynasty, a loyalty which cost him and his family their lives. Although some poetry is attributed to him, his prose and in particular his letters are the only authentic works of any importance as literature.

A precocious and courageous child with an outstanding gift for repartee that he would never lose, K'ung Jung began his career around 180. In 190 he became Administrator of Pei-hai 北海 (Shantung) where, thanks to his influence among the local gentry, he set up a Confucian colony, but was defeated by both the Yellow Turbans and Yüan T'an 袁譚. In 196 he became an official at the imperial court in Hsü 許 (Honan) where he was the most outspoken and respected of the emperor's Confucian advisers. He successfully opposed Ts'ao Ts'ao's* edict prohibiting wine and his clique's desire to reinstate corporal punishment. K'ung's haughtiness, banter, and firm and courageous opposition to Ts'ao Ts'ao's already obvious dynastic ambitions cost K'ung Jung his life; he was executed on charges of sedition in 208.

K'ung Jung's fame as a literary man probably stems from the fact that Ts'ao P'i* included him among the Seven Masters of the Chien-an Era. Ts'ao P'i praised his prose writings, and in particular his jests (*Tien-lun* 典論, "Lun-wen" 論文), and is said to have given rewards to anyone who presented K'ung Jung's works to the throne. Extant today are only seven poems and a larger number of prose pieces. Two of the latter are included in the *Wen-hsüan:** a memorial in chapter 37 and a letter in chapter 41. No traditional critic praised his poetry; Liu Hsieh (see *Wen-hsin tiao-lung*) mentions only his prose (not always with praise), and Chung Jung does not include him at all in the *Shih-p'in.** Of the seven remaining poems, only one appears in the *I-wen lei-chü* 藝文類聚, a more reliable collection than the *Ku-wen yüan,** in which the others appear for the first time. This poem is an enigma in tetrameters with double entendre throughout. On one level it is fairly coherent, preaching retreat when the times were not propitious. On another level, the lines describe how to "separate" (*li* 離) characters and then "unite" (*ho* 合) them to form new ones yielding a new meaning. The literary value of this extraordinary tour de force (called a *li-ho*) is probably slight, as with most other poems attributed to K'ung Jung. Exceptions are two *tsa-shih* 雜詩 (miscellaneous poems), one a moving *yüeh-fu**-like poem which describes the grief of a father who discovers his young son has died during his absence, and the other describing the poet's heroic ambitions and steadfast virtue. Two lines of this latter poem are repeatedly attributed to Li Ling 李陵 by Li Shan 李善 in his commentary to the *Wen-hsüan*. The pentameter "Lin-chung shih" 臨終詩 (Poem Written When About to Die) is made up of gnomic verses which the modern scholar Cheng Chen-to 鄭振鐸 praises as being close to the spoken language, and the three uninteresting hexameter poems are, strangely, in praise of Ts'ao Ts'ao (even the Sung-dynasty commentator of the *Ku-wen yüan*, Chang Ch'ao 章樵, thinks they are spurious). As far as can be ascertained today, K'ung Jung's strength was as a prose writer, and his two pieces preserved in the *Wen-hsüan*, as well as some of the fragmentary pieces found in the *Hou Han-shu* and elsewhere (collected in the *Ch'üan Hou Han-wen* 全後漢文, ch. 83), show a vigorous, erudite, but still straightforward style.

EDITIONS:

Sun, Chih-ch'eng 孫至誠. *K'ung Pei-hai chi p'ing-chü* 孔北海集評注. Shanghai, 1935. Contains a *nien-p'u*. Not seen.

"K'ung Shao-fu chi" 孔少府集, in *Pai-san*, v. 1, section 3, pp. 119-140.

TRANSLATIONS:

Demiéville, *Anthologie*, p. 88.

von Zach, *Anthologie*, v. 2, pp. 663-664, 769-770.

STUDIES:

Cheng, Chen-to 鄭振鐸. *Chung-kuo su-wen-hsüeh shih* 中國俗文學史. Shanghai, 1938; rpt. Peking, 1954, pp. 52-53.

Hsü, Ling 許齡. "K'ung Jung p'ing-chuan" 孔融評傳, in *Hsiang-kang Ta-hsüeh Chung-wen hsüeh-hui hui-k'an* 香港大學中文學會會刊, 1956, 19-35.

Suzuki, *Kan Gi*, pp. 467-471. Uncritically accepts all the remaining poems attributed to K'ung Jung as authentic.

Yü, Kuan-ying 余冠英. *Han Wei liu-ch'ao shih hsüan* 漢魏六朝詩選. Peking, 1958; rpt. 1979, pp. 14-16. Commentary on the two "miscellaneous poems."

—DH

K'ung Shang-jen 孔尚任 (*tzu*, P'in-chih 聘之, also Chi-chung 季重, *hao*, Tung-t'ang 東塘, also An-t'ang 岸堂, also Yün-t'ing shan-jen 云亭山人, 1648-1718) is considered one of the major playwrights of the K'ang-hsi era. His reputation is largely based on his authorship of China's greatest historical drama, *T'ao-hua shan* 桃花扇 (The Peach Blossom Fan, 1699). Born in Ch'ü-fu 曲阜 (modern Shantung) into the sixty-fourth generation of descent from Confucius, he spent the early years of his life engaged in the traditional studies of the literatus with particular emphasis on the ceremonies and music maintained by the K'ung clan in the Confucian Temple. As a scholar, he was an early exponent of *K'ao-cheng hsüeh* 考證學 (empirical studies), editing the *Ch'üeh-li hsin-chih* 闕里新志 (A New Gazetteer of Ch'ü-fu, 1683) and *K'ung-tzu shih-chia-p'u* 孔子世家譜 (A Genealogy of the K'ung Clan, 1684), as well as works on classical music. In 1684 he served as a lecturer to the K'ang-hsi Emperor, who visited Ch'ü-fu on his first southern tour; as a result, K'ung was appointed an erudite in the Directorate of Education. From 1685 to 1689 he served on a river-control project headquartered in Yangchow, where he was able to travel about visiting numerous historical sites and make the acquaintance of the leading survivors of the Ming. His poems and prose of this period were collected in *Hu-hai chi* 湖海集 (Poems from the Lakes and Seas, 1689). A large number of pieces are occasional, offering an excellent view of early Ch'ing literati society in the Kiangsu area. Among his best poems are those reflecting tragic or ironic emotions upon contemplating the past. Some mainland critics have regarded him as a "pragmatist" in his approach to poetry, but he himself wrote of his affinity for the "expressivist" position and advocated the cultivation of the poet's "hsing-ch'ing" 性情 (natural sensibility). Upon returning to Peking, he began a career in the Ministry of Revenue and turned to writing *ch'uan-ch'i** drama. His first play, *Hsiao-hu lei* 小忽雷 (Little Thunderclap, 1694) was based on a T'ang-dynasty instrument in his collection. K'ung researched its origins as an imperial treasure and created a story of the love affair between the literatus Liang Hou-pen and the palace courtesan Cheng Ying-ying, set during the reign of Wen-tsung (r. 827-841). In its extensive use of factual material, it went beyond most earlier attempts at historical drama while exercising freedom of imagination in recreating the political and literary life of the times. Another play, *Ta-hu lei* 大忽雷 (Big Thunderclap, n.d.), is based on the sister instrument which K'ung did not own. There are only two scenes; the T'ang poet Ch'en Tzu-ang purchases the instrument and then destroys it.

T'ao-hua shan 桃花扇 (The Peach Blossom Fan, 1699) is a music drama of forty-four scenes—forty regular scenes, an "interlude" following scene 20, a "prologue" preceding scene 21, plus a "prologue" at the beginning of the play and an "epilogue" at the end. The drama shows painstaking historical research. K'ung Shang-jen included both bibliographical notes and a chronology of the events of the Hung-kuang reign (1644-1645) of the Southern Ming, the historical background of the play. The time periods of all forty-four scenes are specified, and the characters are real persons who lived during that time.

The play, laid mainly in Nanking, includes the famous love story of Hou Fang-yü 侯方域 (1618-1655) and his mistress Li Hsiang-chün 李香君. Huo represents a group of honest and sincere intellectuals who wish to save their country from foreign invasion and internal disorder. Opposing them is a group of politicians, represented by Juan Ta-ch'eng 阮大鋮 (c. 1587-1646), who are less concerned about the fate of their country than about their own political power. The plot of the *T'ao-hua shan* develops through the political strife between these two groups, with the love story between Hou Fang-yü and Li Hsiang-chün as the connecting thread.

The drama emphasizes the principle of "praise and blame" that derives ultimately from the *Ch'un-ch'iu* (see *ching*), a chronology attributed to Confucius. According to K'ung Shang-jen, the network of obligations and relationships between men as social creatures is more important than individual rights, and he follows the Confucian conviction that an intellectual as an ethically developed person has an unavoidable responsibility to both society and the state. He thus holds that the fate of a dynasty is in the hands of the intellectual, and therefore Hou Fang-yü, through neglect of his obligations, is responsible for the fall of the Southern Ming. As a result of Hou's irresponsibility, the drama must end without the usual happy reunion of the *ch'uan-ch'i* opera; the lovers both convert to Taoism and retreat from the world. In addition to its superior historicity, critics have admired its complex plot structure, its innovative use of the *ch'uan-ch'i* form, and its fundamenatally tragic vision.

Shortly after the play's appearance, K'ung was obliged to retire from office. Though many scholars have assumed this was connected with the nationalist sentiments of his drama, it appears to have been a purely political event unrelated to his writing. The remainder of his life was mostly engaged in literary pursuits in Ch'ü-fu. He had previously published a second collection of poems from his Peking years, *An-t'ang kao* 岸堂稿 (Poems from the Waterside Studio, 1692), and a final collection *Ch'ang-liu chi* 長留集 (Poems from a Lingering Stay), containing the works of the last twenty years of his life, was completed around 1715.

EDITIONS:

Hsiao-hu lei, in Liu Shih-hang 劉世珩, ed. *Nuan-hung-shih hui-k'o ch'uan-chü* 暖紅室彙刻傳劇. Rpt. Shanghai, 1940.

Hu-hai chi. Shanghai, 1957.

K'ung Shang-jen shih-wen chi 孔尙任詩文集. Wang Wei-lin 汪蔚林, ed. Peking, 1962.

Ta-hu lei, ibid.

T'ao-hua shan. Wang Chi-ssu 王季思 and Su Huan-chung 蘇寰中, eds. Peking, 1961.

TRANSLATIONS:

Chang, H. C. *Chinese Literature: Popular Fiction and Drama.* Edinburgh, 1973, pp. 303-328. Translates two scenes.

Chen, Shih-hsiang, Harold Acton, and Cyril Birch. *The Peach Blossom Fan.* Berkeley, 1976. Complete translation, but with omissions.

Strassberg, Richard. "*The Peach Blossom Fan:* Personal Cultivation in a Chinese Drama." Unpublished Ph.D. dissertation, Princeton University, 1975. Includes good translation of five scenes.

———. "*The Peach Blossom Fan:* Scene 4," *Renditions,* 8 (1977), 115-122.

STUDIES:

Chang, Chun-shu and Hsueh-lun Chang. "K'ung Shang-Jen and His *T'ao-hua Shan:* A Dramatist's Reflections on the Ming-Ch'ing Dynastic Transition," *Journal of the Institute of Chinese Studies* (The Chinese University of Hong Kong), 9.2 (1978), 307-337.

Chao, Ching-shen 趙景深, *et al.* "Shih-shih ch'iu-shih te p'ing-chia K'ung Shang-jen yü *T'ao-hua shan*" 實事求是的評價孔尙任與桃花扇, *Wen-hsüeh p'ing-lun ts'ung-k'an,* 7 (October 1980), 1-21.

Ch'en, An-na 陳安娜. "*T'ao-hua shan* ch'uan-ch'i chih yen-chiu" 桃花扇傳奇之研究. *Ch'ü-hsüeh chi-k'an* (Taipei), 1964, 220-289. A technical examination of the dramatic art and musical composition of the *T'ao-hua shan.*

Ch'en, Wan-nai 陳萬鼐. *K'ung Shang-jen yen-chiu* 孔尙任研究. Taipei, 1971.

———. *K'ung Tung-t'ang Hsien-sheng nien-p'u* 孔東塘先生年譜, Taipei, 1973.

ECCP, pp. 434-435.

Keng, Hsiang-yüan 耿湘沅. *K'ung Shang-jen T'ao-hua shan k'ao-shu* 孔尙任桃花扇考述. Taipei, 1975. A detailed study of the literary art of the *T'ao-hua shan.*

K'ung Shang-jen yen-chiu tzu-liao hui-pien 孔尙任研究資料彙編. Hong Kong, 1974. A collection of articles and short essays.

Strassberg, Richard E. *The World of K'ung Shang-jen, A Man of Letters in Early Ch'ing China.* New York, 1983.

Struve, Lynn A. "History and *The Peach Blossom Fan,*" *CLEAR,* 2.1 (January 1980), 55-72.

———. "*The Peach Blossom Fan* as Historical Drama," *Renditions,* 8 (Autumn 1977), 99-114.

Tung, Pi 董弼. "Lun K'ung Shang-jen te shih ho shih-lun kuan-tien" 論孔尙任的詩和詩論觀點, in *Wen-hsüeh i-ch'an ts'eng-k'an,* 12 (1963), 143-153.

—RES, CSC and HLC

Kuo-ch'ao wen-lei 國朝文類 (Our National Dynasty's Literature Arranged by Genre) is an anthology of Yüan poetry and prose compiled by Su T'ien-chüeh 蘇天爵 (*tzu,* Po-hsiu 伯修, *hao,* Tzu-ch'i Hsien-sheng 滋溪先生, 1294-1352). Su was the son of Su Chih-tao 蘇志道 (1261-1320), who came from a family in Chen-ting 眞定 (Hopei). He had been a student of the Directorate of Education and passed the examinations first on the list. He served in various offices before he was transferred in 1324 to the Han-lin Academy. In addition he held various posts in the Censorate and served in a number of provincial and court positions in the 1340s before being promoted to Assistant Administrator in the Branch Secretariat of Chiang-che. He died while directing a campaign against sectarian rebel forces in 1352. Su's collected prose (*Tzu-ch'i wen-kao* 滋溪文稿, 30 *chüan*) is extant, but his poetry (7 *chüan*) seems to be lost, apart from the few poems collected in *Yüan-shih hsüan.** He also compiled the *Kuo-ch'ao ming-ch'en shih-lüeh* 國朝名臣事略 (15 *chüan*), a collection of biographies of forty-seven famous statesmen and generals of the early Yüan. The other works mentioned in his biographies do not seem to have survived.

The *Kuo-ch'ao wen-lei* was first printed in 1337 (the governmental authorization is dated January 8) by the Hsi-hu shu-yüan 西湖書院 (Western Lake Academy) in Hangchow after a joint request from Su's colleagues in the Han-lin Academy. This first edition was not free from omissions and misprints, and in 1341 a request was made to produce a revised version. This too was printed by the Hsi-hu shu-yüan, in 1342. This edition, of which a few copies are extant (National Palace Museum, Taipei; Seikadō Bunko, Tokyo, etc.) has been reproduced in facsimile in the *SPTK*. Apart from these two Yüan editions, a third edition in smaller characters was privately printed by the firm of Liu Chün-tso 劉君佐 in Chien-an 建安. No copies of this edition seem to have been preserved.

Under the Ming the work was reprinted at least twice, once in 1537 and once in the period 1620-1644. Copies are kept in Taipei, Tokyo, and the Library of Congress. The title of the Ming and Ch'ing editions was changed to *Yüan wen-lei* 元文類 (Yüan Literature Arranged by Genre). The work was copied into the Ssu-k'u imperial collection (see Chi Yün) under the Ch'ien-lung Emperor and again reprinted in 1889. All these early editions are block-prints.

The *Kuo-ch'ao wen-lei* contains seventy *chüan* and a table of contents of three *chüan*. The 1342 edition has an introduction which gives a detailed history of the printing and re-editing activities. There are two literary prefaces, one by Wang Li 王理, who was Investigating Censor in Chiang-nan, dated May 4, 1334, and one by Ch'en Lü 陳旅 (1287-1342), who was a teacher at the Directorate of Education, dated June 6, 1334. In these prefaces the anthology is described as modeled upon the *T'ang wen-ts'ui** and the Sung collection *Huang-ch'ao wen-chien* 皇朝文鑑 in order to show the flourishing of literature under the early Yüan emperors. The arrangement mostly follows that of the *Wen-hsüan*.* Chapter 1 has examples of *fu**; chapter 2, hymns for the state rituals. Chapters 3-8 have poetry in various meters. Chapters 9-17 are a selection of state documents such as edicts, memoranda, congratulatory addresses, etc. Of particular interest are the basic edicts from the formative stage of the Yüan state

under Khubilai. Chapters 17-18 contain admonitions, inscriptions, and eulogies. Chapters 19-26, inscriptions for tablets in temples, schools, and commemorative stelae. Chapters 27-31 have similar texts of a more private nature, such as essays on private buildings, academies, and memorial shrines. The section on prefaces (chapters 32-36) includes some to which the original texts have been lost. Chapter 37 is devoted to letters, chapters 38-39 include discourses (*shuo* 說) and colophons. Of great importance are chapters 49-42 where the introductory essays from the *Ching-shih ta-tien* 經世大典, a governmental handbook of the Yüan, are reproduced. Without these excerpts we would have no idea of the work's content because the greater part has been lost. Chapters 43-45 contain more miscellaneous writings, chapters 46-48 examination papers and ritual texts of several kinds. The remainder of the work (chapters 49-70) is a collection of selected exemplary anecdotes, tomb inscriptions, and biographies. It is an indispensable source for biographical research, particularly in cases where the author's works are lost or rare.

Practically all early and mid-Yüan authors of repute are represented in the anthology, such as Yüan Hao-wen,* Chao Meng-fu 趙孟頫 (1254-1322), and Yü Chi 虞集 (1272-1348). It is noteworthy that many authors are included who at the time of the compilation were still alive. Selection seems to have been based on writers' connections with the Han-lin Academy and its predecessors. The anthology is therefore a representative survey of the conventional poetic and prose genres, and excludes the Yüan innovations in vernacular poetry and fiction. It remains, however, an impressive source-book for the survival of traditional Confucian literary values into a period when the Chinese intellectuals had to struggle for self-preservation under an alien rule.

EDITIONS:

Kuo-ch'ao wen-lei. Rpt. of 1342 ed., *SPTK*. Best edition, many modern typeset reprints, e.g. Shanghai, 1937 and Taipei, 1962.

STUDIES:
Wu, K. T. "Chinese Printing under Four Alien Dynasties," *HJAS*, 13 (1950), 474, 489.

—HF

Kuo-yü 國語 is a work written by several persons in the Warring States period, compiled in the early Western Han, and passed down essentially unchanged since then. About 60,000 characters in length, it is divided into 21 chapters ostensibly concerned with selected elements of the histories of eight different states: Chou 周 (3 chapters), Lu 魯 (2), Ch'i 齊 (1), Chin 晉 (9), Cheng 鄭 (1), Ch'u 楚 (2), Wu 吳 (1), and Yüeh 越 (2). Chapters are chronologically subdivided into stories ranging from 35 to 1800 characters.

Orthodox Chinese scholarship attributes the work to Tso Ch'iu-ming 左丘明 and states that the *Kuo-yü* was written with materials left over from the *Tso chuan*.* Although repeated continually until this century, this attribution was questioned as early as the third century A.D. and denied in the eighth century. Modern studies of the grammar of the two works reveal enough differences to suggest that Tso Ch'iu-ming was not the author of both but enough similarities to indicate that both works were written in the same general period. A preponderance of detailed material on the state of Chin suggests that at least one of the authors may have had a special connection with that state.

Traditionally considered a history, though without the status of a classic or an officially sanctioned text, the *Kuo-yü* deals with events as early as the reign of King Mu of Chou (*c.* 1000-950 B.C.) and as late as 453 B.C. Most coverage is given to the period 770-464. The *Kuo-yü* presents many of the same stories found in the *Tso-chuan*, though they are frequently given in greater detail. Inclusions range from a thirty-seven-character anecdote in which Confucius praises a woman for knowing proper grieving rites to comments on the value of music and complex discussions of political strategies. Not intended as an exhaustive history of China, the *Kuo-yü* contains selected events chosen for their didactic value

and strict adherence to historical fact should not be expected.

Recent scholarship suggests that the *Kuo-yü* was written with specific goals in mind. One study of just the first three chapters interprets them as an exposition of philosophical principles. A second argues that the whole work is a piece of political propaganda written to demonstrate the value of political advisers and to illuminate the dire consequences to rulers of not following their advice. The author uses fictionalized speeches and dialogues attributed to historical figures as case examples. The majority of the examples are negative; that is, examples of the troubles which resulted when rulers did not seek or heed advice. Events are described only insofar as they help build the case for advisers. Historical facts which do not support the main thesis or help advance the story line are ignored. This understanding of the *Kuo-yü* is best demonstrated in the final three chapters. These chapters give three different views of the ultimate defeat of the state of Wu by that of Yüeh. There are some contradictions among the three, but the importance of advisers and advice is a constant.

Though dialogue and direct speech are essential elements of the style, it emphasizes eloquent rhetoric and speeches which are more prolix than analogous passages in the *Tso-chuan*. While there are passages of considerable beauty and evocative power, systematic use of parallelism and balancing of both characters and viewpoints often imparts a stiffness of diction which leads to boredom. There is no overall set of characters or events to give cohesion to the whole, and individual chapters are composed of discrete events which may or may not interconnect.

The impact the *Kuo-yü* has had on the Chinese imagination is undeniable. It has supplied metaphors, symbols, and a model of writing for generations, but the overlap of stories and characters with the *Tso-chuan* makes precise evaluation of its influence difficult.

In addition to the knowledge of life and events in the Eastern Chou that careful reading of the work imparts, it is, as an undisputed Eastern Chou literary document, an important early example of the compatibility of history and fiction in Chinese literature.

EDITIONS:

Kuo-yü 國語. *SPPY.*

Kuo-yü. SPTK.

Kuo-yü. 2v. Shang-hai Shih-fan Ta-hsüeh ku-chi cheng-li tsu 上海師範大學古籍整理組 , ed. Shanghai, 1978.

Kuo-yü hsüan 國語選. Fu, Keng-sheng 傅庚生, ed. Peking, 1958.

Kuo-yü Wei-shih chieh 國語韋氏解. Taipei, 1968. A photolithographic reprint of an 1800 facsimile of a 1033 edition.

TRANSLATIONS:

Hart, James. "The Philosophy of the Chou-yü." Unpublished Ph.D. dissertation, University of Washington, 1973. The first three chapters only.

Sargent, Howard W. "A Preliminary Study of the *Kuo yü.*" Ph.D. dissertation, University of Chicago, 1975. The last three chapters only.

STUDIES:

Bauer, Wolfgang. *Kuo-yü yin-te* 國語引得. 2v. Taipei, 1973.

Chang I-jen 張以仁. "*Kuo-yü* chi-cheng: chüan i" 國語集證卷一, *BIHP,* 44.1 (1972), 89-152; 44.2 (1972), 153-225.

Hart, James, "Philosophy."

Ch'un-ch'iu ching chuan yin-te 春秋經傳引得. Hung, William, ed. Peiping, 1937. v. 1, pp. lxxiv-lxxxvi. Primarily concerned with the interrelationship between the *Kuo-yü* and the *Tso-chuan.*

Sargent, Howard W., "Preliminary Study."

—SM

Lan Ts'ai-ho 藍采和 is the abridged version of the title of a Yüan comedy known fully as "Han Chung-li tu-t'o Lan ts'ai-ho" 漢鍾離度脫藍采和 (Chung-li of the Han Leads Lan Ts'ai-ho to Enlightenment). This anonymous work is one of a group of deliverance plays that focus on the enlightenmemt of a stubborn pupil by a Taoist master. This play is unique because Lan Ts'ai-ho is not only one of the famous Eight Immortals, but also a prominent actor and the stage manager of a flourishing urban theater troupe.

The character Lan Ts'ai-ho ultimately stems from a group of songs popular in the Nanking area during the Southern T'ang dynasty. These songs lamented the impermanence of human life and praised the pleasures of the hermit's existence. Three nonsense syllables, *lan-ts'ai-ho*, occurred regularly at the end of some lines. Also during the Southern T'ang, Lan Ts'ai-ho first makes his appearance in a human role, and a biography of him is found in the *Hsü hsien-chuan* 續仙傳, written by Shen Fen 沈分. During the late T'ang and the Northern Sung, Lan Ts'ai-ho became associated with several other Taoist adepts in a group known as the Eight Immortals, a filiation that enjoys immense popularity in folklore today. In his earliest characterization, Lan Ts'ai-ho is presented as a foot-stomping, singing beggar followed by a gaggle of children begging for coppers (this is also how he is presented *after* his enlightenment in the play). Current knowledge suggests that *Chung-li of the Han Leads Lan Ts'ai-ho to Enlightenment* is indeed the first work to represent the immortal as an actor.

Since it is a deliverance play, *Lan Ts'ai-ho* is dominated by the theme of enlightenment. In such plays a Taoist master, by hook or crook, makes an unwilling reluctant disciple aware of the transience of earthly splendors and leads him off to enlightenment. In such plays the future disciple is usually reluctant to acknowledge the truths presented him by his master and then undergoes a sudden and serious reversal of fortune. After being saved from any number of terrible fates, from torture, or even death, the disciple leaves his family to follow his master. In his further wanderings he will once again encounter his family but finally repudiates them and is brought to bliss at the Jasper Pool, where he lives for eternity in the abode of the Queen Mother of the West.

As a necessary element in such plays, the future immortals must put their utmost faith in their worldly existence: their worldview is completely *diesseitig.* The master's praises of immortality are met with derision, and the deluded pupil prefers his material wealth and happiness to the self-mortification and poverty of the master—who is usually disguised as a beggar or mendicant priest. In the case of *Lan Ts'ai-ho,* the still-to-be-enlightened immortal is cast as a brassy and self-confident stage manager and actor, whose fame has brought him status, wealth, and the friendship of high officials. He even boasts that he is a staunch Confucianist.

Since his earthly life is that of an actor, all the activity that precedes Lan Ts'ai-ho's enlightenment takes place within the theater. Although his characterization may be one-dimensional because of the conventions of the deliverance plays, a brief and vivid glimpse of life backstage is provided. Instead of the much more common viewpoint of a spectator or actress, the life of the troupe is seen through the eyes of its manager. The information in the initial portion of the drama on the organization of family troupes, on the preparation of a permanent commercial stage for public performance, on the relations between the actors and the public, on officialdom, and on playwrights is without parallel in Yüan drama. Towards the end, performances of a traveling troupe—the family without its star—as it wends its way through rural China are even shown.

This anomymous drama, which can be reliably dated to the late thirteenth or fourteenth century, has long been one of the major sources of information on early theater, and has been quoted extensively by scholars of theater in the Yüan.

EDITIONS:

Lan Ts'ai-ho, in the *Hsin-hsü Ku ming-chia tsa-chü* 新續古名家雜劇, *Ku-pen,* IV. The only known edition (1588).

———, in *Yüan-ch'ü hsüan wai-pien* 元曲選外編, Sui Shu-sen 隋樹森, ed., Taipei, 1959. Modern typeset and punctuated edition; a faithful transcription of the original text, except that extra stage directions have been added by the editor to clarify who is speaking and singing, thus bringing the text into line with modern editorial practice.

TRANSLATIONS:

Crump, J. I. *Chinese Theater in the Times of Kublai Khan.* Tucson, 1980, pp. 49-56. Partial translation of the first act.

Idema and West, *Chinese Theater,* pp. 299-349.

STUDIES:

Yen, Tun-i 嚴敦易, *Yüan-chü chen-i* 元劇斟疑. Peking, 1960, pp. 439-456.

—SW and WI

Lei-shu 類書 (classified book) is the name given a genre of collectanea of literary and non-literary materials compiled in pre-modern Chinese history. Commonly translated "encyclopedia," *lei-shu* is more accurately rendered "classified book," from the categories of topic, genre, or rhyme that were typically used to organize the contents. *Lei-shu* are properly regarded as encyclopedias in that they were intended to encompass and present synoptically the total of either existing knowledge or a specified field of knowledge. However, they did so in a characteristically Chinese way, by quoting existing texts and placing them in a synthetic rearrangement. *Lei-shu* contain little or no original writing, unlike our modern encyclopedias, a fact that suggests their compilation was motivated by a desire to preserve texts as well as to provide accessible surveys of knowledge. That *lei-shu* contain virtually no new material should not lead to an underestimation of their importance and influence. Many *lei-shu* in their time exerted great influence in shaping education, the intellectual climate, and literature by making available a particular selection of materials to a large number of readers from a vast canon of existing text not readily available to them. *Lei-shu* were the emperors' and officials' digests of important texts, the primers of early education, the handbooks of poets and playwrights, and the study guides of examination candidates.

As early as the Han dynasty, scholars expressed concern about the loss of important texts, a concern crystallized in stories about the inquisition and bibliocaust imputed to Ch'in Shih-huang-ti. At the same time, confusion and variation prevailed in those texts believed to have survived from the pre-Han period, and scholars presided over an ever accelerating growth of scholarly and belletristic writing. The situation prompted development of a bibliographic science with functional approaches to library organization and generic classification. The activities of Han bibliophiles ranged from the retrospective to the prospective, on one hand inventorying, correcting, and explicating classical writing, on the other tending to the practical organization and classification of books for current use and future preservation. In medieval China, the zeal for these activities was demonstrated not only in the compilation of lexicons and *lei-shu*, but in the related compilations of commentaries on historical works, such as P'ei Sung-chih's 裴松之 (372-451) commentary on the *San-kuo chih* 三國志, and on geographic works, such as Li Tao-yüan's commentary on the *Shui-ching* (see *Shui-ching chu*).

The beginnings of the *lei-shu* tradition are found in early lexical aids, for example the *Erh-ya* 爾雅 (2nd century B.C., see also *ching*). The *Erh-ya* explicated terms by organizing them, with brief glosses, into nineteen categories. Other early lexicons such as the *Shih-ming* 釋名 (Explication of Names), compiled by Liu Hsi 劉熙 in the second century A.D., quoted terms in their original contexts, taking sentences from the original documents and reorganizing them into groups of similar terms and phrases. In the early lexical tradition there is a preference for explication of terms by quoting them, *in situ*, and relying on comparison and contrast with other occurrences of the term or with similar terms. The earliest lexicons, which quoted rather than defined, were concordances rather than dictionaries. Their organization was based on the matter, not the medium, i.e., they were based on topics and categories rather than an ordering of the pronunciation or graphic features of the language. The *Shuo-wen chieh-tzu* 說文解字, the great etymological dictionary compiled by Hsü Shen 許慎 in the second century A.D., is the first example of a dictionary in the latter sense.

Other Han compilations that are formal antecedents of the *lei-shu* include numerous aphoristic philosophies written during the Former and the Latter Han. Important examples are Liu Hsiang's* *Shuo-yüan*,

Feng-su t'ung 風俗通 (Penetrating Popular Ways), and Pan Ku's* *Pai-hu t'ung-te-lun* 白虎通德論 (White Tiger Hall Discussions). These works discussed, *seriatim*, topics that commanded the interest of thinkers of the day. The particular articulation and ordering of topics in some larger collections directly influenced the organization of *lei-shu*.

The earliest known *lei-shu* was compiled during the Three Kingdoms, the *Huang-lan* 皇覽 (Emperor's Digest), ascribed to Wang Hsiang 王象, Liu Shao 劉邵, and others, for Emperor Wen of the Wei (Ts'ao P'i*). The text was said to have 120 *chüan*, divided into 40 sections. The title was echoed in many later compilations. From that point early in the third century, the *lei-shu* tradition was continuous throughout premodern times, culminating in the massive *Ku-chin t'u-shu chi-ch'eng* 古今圖書集成 (Completed Collection of Graphs and Writings of Ancient and Modern Times), completed in 1725 by Chiang T'ing-hsi 蔣廷錫 and a large imperially commissioned board of scholars. This final compilation boasted 10,000 *chüan* in 5020 volumes, with materials classified under 6109 headings.

Little is known of the *lei-shu* compiled during the early Six Dynasties. The earliest extant texts are fragments from the *Tiao-yü chi* 瑚玉集 (Carved Jade Collection), compiled by an unidentified author in 522, and the *Pien-chu* 編珠 (Stringed Pearls), compiled by Tu Kung-chan 杜公瞻 in the early seventh century. The former contains an assortment of narratives, the latter, materials for the writing of poetry and essays. The earliest extant and well-known *lei-shu* date from the Sui and T'ang dynasties, and include the *I-wen lei-chü* 藝文類聚 (A Categorized Collection of Literary Writing) compiled about 620 by Ou-yang Hsün 歐陽詢, the *Pei-t'ang shu-ch'ao* 北堂書鈔 (Scribed Texts from the Northern Hall), compiled about 630 by Yü Shih-nan 虞世南, and the *Ch'u-hsüeh chi* 初學記 (Records for Early Learning), compiled about 700, by Hsü Chien 徐堅.

By the seventh century two trends were apparent in *lei-shu* compilation, both of them in response to the growing volume of extant writing. The sheer size of the compilations was increasing, and they were demonstrating more strictly delineated areas of interest, no longer striving to be comprehensive. For example, the *Fa-yüan chu-lin** selects quotations from both Buddhist and non-Buddhist works that illustrate points of Buddhist doctrine. The *T'ung-tien* 通典 (Comprehensive Documents), compiled by Tu Yu 杜佑 (735-812) about 800, concentrates on texts of political and administrative importance. This trend toward specialization reached an important plateau of maturation in the four great collections of the Sung: *T'ai-p'ing-yü-lan*,* compiled in 983 and specializing in matters of historical, moral, and administrative import to the emperor; *T'ai-p'ing kuang-chi*,* compiled in 978 and specializing in fictional narratives; and the *Wen-yüan ying-hua*,* compiled in 985 and specializing in belles lettres—all three put together by Li Fang 李昉 (925-996) and others; and *Ts'e-fu yüan-kuei* 册府元龜 (Guiding Lights from the Imperial Book Treasury), compiled in 1013 by Wang Ch'in-jo 王欽若 (962-1025), and specializing in biographies of exemplary rulers and officials intended to serve as models for the present day.

During the Ming, *lei-shu* strove for a degree of reintegration, the primary example being the *Yung-lo ta-tien* 永樂大典 (Vast Documents of the Yung-lo Era) compiled during the first years of the fifteenth century by Hsieh Chin 解縉 (1369-1455) and a group of more than 3,000 others. This massive collection was in 22,877 *chüan*, filling over 11,000 volumes. The index along filled 60 *chüan*. Ironically (since much of the work has perished since the Ming) it was compiled primarily to preserve ancient texts. Another rather unique Ming compilation was the *San-ts'ai t'u-hui* 三才圖會 (Assembled Pictures of the Three Realms—i.e., Heaven, Earth and Man), compiled in 1607 by Wang Ch'i 王圻 (*fl.* 1565-1614). This collection brings together maps of areas, drawings of buildings, schemata of compounds and cities, sketches of items of everyday use, and portraits of important historical personages.

In terms of sheer size and scope, the official Ch'ing compilations eclipsed most *lei-shu* that had preceded them. In addition to the *Ku-chin t'u-shu chi-ch'eng* described above, there is the celebrated *P'ei-wen yün-fu* 佩文韻府, compiled in 1711 by Chang Yü-shu 張玉書 (1642-1711) and others, a vast compilation based on earlier rhyming dictionaries that assembled important quotations from poetic and non-poetic texts, organized according to their last characters, for the purpose of selecting words and phrases when composing poetry and identifying allusions when reading it.

Throughout the ages the exact schemes for dividing the contents of *lei-shu* differed considerably. In his preface to the *I-wen lei-chü*, Ou-yang Hsün criticized Six Dynasties *lei-shu* for concentrating exclusively on genre (i.e., formal considerations) or exclusively on topics (i.e., contextual considerations). The significant editorial advance of his own *lei-shu* was to divide entries first by topic, then to subdivide within a topic by genre. After Ou-yang Hsün, there are examples of collectanea organized according to either rhyme or genre, some of which certain scholars might not consider *lei-shu*. But the vast majority of subsequent compilations followed Ou-yang Hsün's approach. The premier examples of the genre divide their contents according to a list of substantive topics, which themselves are significant as a historically sanctioned, non-arbitrary, and prioritized order of intellectual concerns. These begin with "Heaven," "Earth," then proceed through geographical and geological features, to people, society, and material aspects of life, down to utensils, weapons, illnesses, and finally mourning apparatus. Similarly, the T'ang *lei-shu* generally proceed from heaven on down to barbarians and grasses. In the *T'ai-p'ing yü-lan*, the first major division is "Heaven," and the first entry is "Primal Pneuma." The last major division is the "Hundred Plants," and the last entry is *Ti-yü* 地榆 (Burnet Bloodwort). Fifteen centuries after the *Shih-ming*, the *Ku-chin t'u-shu chi-ch'eng* was divided into six major categories, "Celestial Matters," "Geography," "Human Relations," "Physical Sciences," "Literature," and "Polity." The subcategories began with "The Heavens" and concluded with "Industries and Manufactured Articles." The consistency of *lei-shu* organization demonstrates an impressive continuity in traditional bibliographic science, the importance attached to traditional formats and editorial procedures, and the intellectually substantive nature of the traditional priority of topics.

The durable *lei-shu* tradition is to be credited with the preservation of a vast amount of texts from pre-Ming China, especially of narrative materials written outside the purview of official historians, of poetic materials from the hands of lesser-known poets, discursive material regarded as somewhat unorthodox or of questionable reliability, and a range of other materials that would have been lost but for the efforts of text collectors. *Lei-shu* serve modern scholars in several important ways. First, as primary texts in traditional education and handbooks of writers and poets, they provide insight into the minds and the means of the traditional literati. Second, as well-organized repositories of voluminous textual materials, they are treasuries of reliable primary sources on every topic of expressed interest in premodern Chinese culture. Third, their early history was closely related to developments in literary theory, especially genre theory, and bibliographical science.

STUDIES:

Balazs, Etienne. "L'histoire comme guide de la pratique bureaucratique (les monographies, les encyclopédies, les recueils de statuts)," in *Historians of China and Japan*, W. G. Beasley and E. G. Pulleyblank, eds., London, 1961, pp. 78-94.

Bauer, Wolfgang. "The Encyclopaedia in China," *Cahiers d'histoire mondiale*, 9 (1966), 665-691.

Chang, Ti-hua 張滌華. *Lei-shu liu-pieh* 類書流別. Chungking, 1943.

Fang, Shih-to 方師鐸. *Ch'üan-t'ung wen-hsüeh yü lei-shu chih kuan-hsi* 傳統文學與類書之關係. Taichung, 1971.

Giles, Lionel. *An Alphabetical Index to the Chinese Encyclopaedia, Ch'in-ting ku-chin t'u-shu chi-ch'eng*. London, 1911. Esp. pp. ix-x.

———. "A Note on the *Yung-lo ta-tien*," *New China Review*, 2 (1920), 137-153.

Goodrich, L. C. "More on the *Yung-lo ta-tien*," *JHKBRAS*, 10 (1970), 17-23.

Haeger, John W. "The Significance of Confusion: The Origins of the *T'ai-p'ing yü-lan*," *JAOS*, 88 (1968), 401-410.

Liu, Yeh-ch'iu 劉葉秋. *Lei-shu chien-shuo* 類書簡說. Shanghai, 1980.

Nakatsuhama, Wataru 中津濱涉. *Geimon ruijū insho sakuin* 藝文類聚引書索引. Kyoto, 1974 (revised ed.).

Shu, Austin C. W. *Lei-shu: Old Chinese Reference Works and a Checklist of Titles Available in Taiwan*. Taipei, 1973.

Teng, Ssu-yü 鄧嗣禹. *Yen-ching ta-hsüeh t'u-shu kuan mu-lu ch'u-kao: Lei-shu chih pu* 燕京大學圖書館目錄初稿：類書之部. Peiping, 1935.

Yamada, Hideo 山田英雄. *Hokudō shoshō inshu sakuin* 北堂書鈔引書索引. Nagoya, 1974.

Yung-lo ta-tien. Rpt. Peking, 1959.

—KD

Li Ao 李翶 (*tzu*, Hsi-chih 習之, 774-836) was an official and literatus of the mid-T'ang period whose contribution toward an intellectual and practical synthesis of Buddhism and Confucianism laid a solid foundation for the Neo-Confucianism of the eleventh century. He associated for many years with Han Yü,* and his philosophical speculations had important implications for the theory of literary style.

Li Ao was born in Pien-chou 汴州 to a family of literati who traced its origins to Six Dynasties aristocracy. But Li Ao's immediate forebears held only minor posts. He was an only son. He arrived in the capital in 793 to sit for the *chin-shih* examination, for which he secured the support of Liang Su.* The latter died several months later, however, and Li Ao did not obtain the degree until 798. He met Han Yü in 796 in Pien-chou where Han was serving on the staff of the Military Commissioner. The pair associated there with Meng Chiao* and Chang Chi,* this quartet forming the initial nucleus of the "Han Yü circle." In 800 Li Ao married the daughter of Han Yü's cousin.

Li Ao served in over twenty different positions during the course of a long and stormy official career. His straightforward personality and outspoken directness made it impossible for him to remain in the capital. Apart from the years 817-818 when he served in the Directorate of Education, 823-825 when he was in the Ministry of Rites, 827-831 spent in the Censorate and then various ceremonial offices, and a brief tour as Vice-president of the Ministry of Justice in 834, Li Ao spent his life in the central and southern provinces. He died in 836 as Military Commissioner of Shannan East at Hsiang-chou 襄州 (modern Hupei).

Li Ao's three "Fu-hsing shu" 復性書 (Letters to Bring Back Nature) are the most important of his extant work; they articulate his thoughts on the problem of "human nature" (性). The first letter defines the perfection of "human nature" as the attainment of "sagehood" (聖人) through the stilling of the seven passions (情). The second outlines the proper methods used to cultivate and attain this goal. In the third letter Li Ao stresses the importance of this goal and affirms it as his own. The letters quote heavily from the *Chung-yung* 中庸 and from *Meng-tzu* (see *ching*) and did much to focus attention on these works as basic texts of Neo-Confucianism. Yet the main arguments of the letters, although expressed in Confucian terms, are Buddhist, specifically T'ien-t'ai and Ch'an, and there are textual affinities to the writings of Liang Su. Although his best-known Ch'an teacher was Yao-shan Wei-yen 藥山惟儼 (751-834), whom he met in Lang-chou 郎州 in 820, Li Ao had maintained extensive relations with other followers of the Ch'an patriarch Ma-tsu 馬祖 at least since 790.

It is more difficult to assess Li Ao's role as a man of letters. Although eighteen *chüan* of his writings survive, all his poetry is lost (except one quatrain transmitted in a Ch'an history), and many of the prose pieces are official and formal compositions included as models in ninth-century anthologies. Li Ao postulated a reciprocal connection between personal moral cultivation (仁義) and literary expression (文), whereby stylistic effectiveness was a result and a reflection of the author's moral cultivation. Such a theory has obvious Ch'an

affinities: the closer the adept comes to attaining this spiritual goal of enlightenment, the more natural (自然) become his behavior and expression. This critical stance was related to Liang Su's emphasis on *ch'i* 氣 (vitality) in literature and to Han Yü's dictum to "expunge clichés" (陳言務去) as artificial and unnatural.

It is difficult to judge the degree of agreement between Li Ao and Han Yü. A joint commentary by the two authors, the *Lun-yü pi-chieh* 論語筆解 (Penned Explanations of the Analects), in which the infusion of Ch'an concepts into the old Confucian text is readily apparent, suggests the agreement was considerable. It is probably the case that the dissimilar personalities of the two men caused them to emphasize different facets of their common goal to create a vibrant, contemporary Confucianism. Towards this goal, Li Ao's contributions were more philosophical, Han Yü's more literary.

EDITIONS:

Li Wen-kung chi 李文公集. 18 *chüan*. SPTK reprints Ming edition of 1475. There is no modern, punctuated edition.

STUDIES:

Barrett, Timothy Hugh. "Buddhism, Taoism and Confucianism in the Thought of Li Ao." Unpublished Ph.D. dissertation, Yale, 1978. Contains a complete, annotated translation of the "Fu-hsing shu" and an appendix on the bibliography of Li's *Collected Works*.

Lo, Lien-t'ien. "Li Ao yen-chiu" 李翱研究. *Kuo-li Pien-i-kuan kuan-k'an*, 2.3 (December 1973), 55-89. Contains information on family background, biography, and a chronological list of datable Li Ao writings.

Fukushima, Shunnō 福島俊翁. "Li Kō no gakuzen to 'Fukusei-sho'" 李翱の學禪と復性書, *Zengaku kenkyū*, 51 (February 1961), 32-44.

—CH

Li Ch'i 李頎, who passed the *chin-shih* examination in 725, was a member of the social network which included High T'ang capital poets such as Wang Wei* and Wang Ch'ang-ling.* However, he rarely wrote regulated verse in the conventional style of this group. Instead, Li Ch'i is noted for his poems in song style and heptasyllabic

530

old-style forms, and his work is dominated by the eremitic, supernatural, and hyperbolic. His eccentric approach suggests the influence of Li Po.*

When obliged to use verse to commemorate an occasion, Li Ch'i characteristically loosened the form—as in the banquet poem entitled "Ch'in ko" 琴歌 (Lute Song) which extends to ten lines its celebration of the musical performance at an evening banquet. When using the old-style form, Li Ch'i also included Taoist material: in "Sung Ch'en Chang-fu" 送陳章甫 (Farewell to Ch'en Chang-fu) for a friend who had just been dismissed from office, Li hyperbolically praises him for his erudition, loyalty to friends, and love of wine. Li Ch'i's work includes poems on music, border poems, and poems about eccentrics; 124 poems are extant.

EDITIONS:

Ch'üan T'ang shih, v. 2, ch. 132-134, pp. 1338-1367.

TRANSLATIONS:

Bynner, *Jade Mountain*, pp. 33-38. Includes seven of Li Ch'i's poems.
Gundert, *Lyrik*, p. 71.

STUDIES:

Owen, *High T'ang*, pp. 103-108.
Fu, *Shih-jen*, pp. 88-102: "Li Ch'i k'ao" 李頎考
—MW

Li Chiao 李嶠 (*tzu*, Chü-shan 巨山, 644-713) was an influential officer and a renowned man of letters during the reigns of Empress Wu (690-705) and Emperor Chung-tsung (705-710). He was a native of Tsan-huang 贊皇, Chao-chou 趙州 (modern Shansi), Li's family had been prominent in public life for generations. He was successful in the *chin-shih* examinations at an early age—his first post was a minor one in An-ting 安定 (modern Kansu). Li then proceeded to the capital where he held many important positions, enjoying Empress Wu's favor, though his arrogance caused him to be demoted on several occasions. Having been promoted to the rank of Grand Councilor at least four times in his life (698-700, 703, 704, 706-710), in 707 Li was given the title of Duke of Chao-

kuo; in 713, shortly before his death, he retired from the political world.

Li Chiao's poetry is characterized by the "Court Style" which had flourished in the Six Dynasties—many of his verses were also written at court. He is also well-known for his *yung-wu shih* 詠物詩, poems on objects, which deal with an encyclopedic spectrum of subjects, from the sun, various musical instruments, and household items to flora and fauna. Of the 209 poems attributed to him in the *Ch'üan T'ang shih** 120 are *yung-wu shih*. These 120 poems were collected independently and entitled *Li Chia Po-yung* 李嶠百詠 or *Li Chiao tsa-yung* 李嶠雜詠. This collection was brought to Japan during the Heian Period. There manuscript copies of the collection were made and preserved. Lost in China, they were reintroduced during the Ch'ing in a collection found in the *Itsu-zon sō-sho* 佚存叢書 edited by Hayashi Kō 林衡. Recently two short fragmental copies of this volume were found among the Tun-huang Manuscripts (Pelliot 3738 and Stein 555).

Li was also a well-known prose writer. His extant corpus of over 150 pieces suggest his connection with the court—most are *pan* 判 (judgments), a popular court genre of the era.

EDITIONS:

Ch'üan T'ang shih, v. 2, pp. 686-730.
Ch'üan T'ang wen, v. 5, pp. 3093-3192.
Li Chiao chi 李嶠集. *T'ang wu-shih-chia shih-chi* 唐五十家詩集 edition. Shanghai, 1981. A reprint of the Ming typeset edition.
Li Chiao tsa-yung 李嶠雜詠. *Itsu-zon sō-sho* edition (see above). Also found in the *Cheng-chüeh-lou ts'ung-k'o* 正覺樓叢刊 and the *I-hai chu-ch'ien* 藝海珠塵.
Li Chü-shan yung-wu-shih (Ri Kyozan eibutsu shi) 李巨山詠物詩. Japanese edition, 1761. This edition revised by Ishikawa Tei 石川貞 with his *kunten* readings is reprinted in *Wakokubon kanshi shūsei* 和刻本漢詩集成, v. 1, Tokyo, 1975.

TRANSLATIONS:

Owen, *Early T'ang*, pp. 119-121, 258-259, 266, 296, 298, 314-315.
Schafer, *Vermilion Bird*, p. 249.

531

STUDIES:

Kanda Kiichirō 神田喜一郎. "Ri Kyō hyaku-ei zakkō" 李嶠百詠雜考, Biburia(ビブリア) 1 (1949), 42-53.

———. "Tonkōbon Ri Kyō hyaku-ei ni tsuite" 敦煌本「李嶠百詠」について, Tōhōgakkai sō ritsu jū shū-nen kinen Tō hōgaku ronshū, Tokyo, 1962, pp. 63-70.

—TS

Li Chien 黎簡 (tzu, Chien-min 簡民, hao, Erh-ch'iao 二樵, 1747-1799) was highly respected by his contemporaries for his poetry, painting, and calligraphy. A native of Shun-te 順德 (Kwangtung), he was the son of a businessman. A self-educated man, Li was well-read in the classics and started to write poetry at the age of ten, maintaining a varied and prodigious output throughout his literary career. The bibliographer Li Wen-ts'ao 李文藻 (1730-1778) found him one of the greatest poets of Kwangtung, and Li T'iao-yüan* was so impressed with his "Ni Han Ch'ang-li shih-ting lien-chü" 擬韓昌黎石鼎聯句 (Imitation of Han Yü's Stone-tripod Linked Verse) that he appointed Li Chien to a minor official post, which, however, Li Chien had to decline because of ill health—most of his fifty-three years were spent in his sickbed. He is recognized, together with Chang Chin-fang 張錦芳, Huang Tan-shu 黃丹書, and Lü Chien 呂堅, as one of the "Ling-nan ssu-chia" 嶺南四家 (Four Ling-nan Masters) who rose to poetic prominence in the late eighteenth century.

His poems, which dealt with a wide range of subjects in traditional forms, embraced a spiritual connection to other eras. Ch'ing critics generally considered them a continuation of the "nature poetry" tradition of Hsieh Ling-yün,* yet Li differed from Hsieh in his discarding of stereotypes and metaphors for scenery. He was influenced by the strength of Han Yü's* work, by the tone of Li Ho,* by the sensuality of Li Shang-yin,* and by the spare style of Meng Chiao.*

A disciplined and diligent poet from the age of twenty-five, he wrote one volume of poetry a year until he was forty-nine. Then, on his fiftieth birthday, he published these twenty-five volumes, comprising altogether 1862 poems, in a monumental collection entitled Wu-pai-ssu-feng T'ang shih-ch'ao 五百四峯堂詩鈔 (Poetry Collection of Five-Hundred-and-Four-Summits Studio). Li was a devoted student of Taoism and Buddhism, and the latter part of this collection provides a conceptual framework for analyzing his struggles with, and eventual transcendence of, the problematic relationship between the self, poetry, and the world at large. Earlier poems such as "Tuan-liu" 斷柳 (The Broken Willow) and "Wang-shih" 往事 (Memories) treat the issues of emotions, sickness, and aging; and, though they express certain intellectual ambiguities which lie at the heart of his thinking, they remain nevertheless more sentimental and emotional. Later poems, such as "Wen-t'i" 聞笛 (Listening to the Flute) and "Ssu-keng" 四更 (The Fourth Watch) reflect upon non-action, transcendence, and inner tranquility.

During his lifetime, Li Chien also wrote tz'u* poems (collectively entitled Yao-yen-ko tz'u-ch'ao 藥烟閣詞鈔 [Tz'u Collection of Yao-yen-ko]), ch'ü* (Fu-yüng-t'ing yüeh-fu 芙蓉亭樂府 [Dramas of Fu-yüng T'ing]), a Chu Chuang 注莊 (Commentary on Chuang-tzu), and a work on prosody, the Yün-hsüeh 韻學 (Study of Rhymes).

In terms of the sheer volume of his literary work, the intrinsic beauty of his poetry, the depth of his commentary and thought, and the mastery of the classics he illustrates in his work, Li Chien, though little read today, should be ranked with other well-known Ch'ing literati.

STUDIES:

Ho, Hui-kao 何翽高. Ling-nan shih-ts'un 嶺南詩存. Shanghai, 1928. Contains critical analysis and comparison of the text of Li Chien's poetic work.

Hsien, Yü-ch'ing 冼玉清. "Hsiao-tzu k'uang-chien Li Erh-ch'iao" 小子狂簡黎二樵, I-lin ts'ung-lu, 3 (January 1962), 230-232.

I-ting 一丁. "Li Chien yü Fu-yung t'ing yüeh-fu" 黎簡與芙蓉亭樂府, I-lin ts'ung-lu, 3 (January 1962), 185-187.

Su, Wen-cho 蘇文擢. Li Chien hsien-sheng nien-p'u 黎簡先生年譜. Hong Kong, 1973.

Wang, Tsung-yen 汪宗衍. "Li Chien Fu-yung T'ing yüeh-fu" 黎簡芙蓉亭樂府, in Wang Tsung-yen, *Kuang-t'ung wen-wu ts'ung-t'an* 廣東文物 叢談. Hong Kong, 1974, pp. 123-125.

—HSK

Li Chih 李贄 (*tzu*, Hung-fu 宏父 and Szu-chai 思齋, *hao*, Cho-wu 卓吾 and Tu-wu 篤吾, also known as Wen-ling chü-shih 溫陵居士 or Pai-ch'üan chü-shih 白泉居士, 1527-1602) was born in Chin-chiang 晉江 near Ch'üan-chou 泉州 (Fukien). As Lin Tsai-chih 林載贄, his original name, he passed the *chü-jen* examination in 1552. He changed his name at the beginning of the reign of Emperor Mu-tsung in 1567 because of the taboo on the character *Tsai*, the new emperor's personal name. Li's ancestors were overseas tradesmen and some were Moslems. He held teaching posts in the northern and southern national universities. Finally he became prefect in Yao-an 姚安 (Yunnan) until 1580. He is famous for his benevolent and uncorrupted government. After his dismissal he retired to a small Buddhist monastery at Ma-ch'eng 麻城 near Huang-an 黃安 (Hupei), where he cut his hair and became a Buddhist novice. In 1602 he was accused of "renouncing the Way and instigating the people" and was arrested in Peking. His death in prison was officially declared a suicide.

Li Chih is one of the most outstanding antitraditional thinkers and Confucian heretics in Chinese intellectual history. As a disciple of Wang Ken's 王艮 (1483-1541) T'ai-chou school of philosophy 泰州學派, he rigorously attacked the Confucian scholar-officials for bigotry, for exploitation of the poor, and for falsifying history. His letters and essays on history and philosophy (especially Buddhism) and his poems are included in his *Fen-shu* 焚書 (A Book to Be Burnt), first published in 1590. His "Revaluation of History" is the *Ts'ang-shu* 藏書 (A Book to Be Hidden Away), which covers Chinese history up to the Yüan dynasty in the form of chronicles and biographies of some eight hundred historical figures. In the *Hsü Ts'ang-shu* 續藏書 (Continuation of *A Book to Be Hidden Away*) he expanded the records up to his own times. Li also wrote commentaries on the *I-ching, Lao-tzu, Chuang-tzu, Mo-tzu, Sun-tzu* (see *ching* and *chu-tzu pai-chia*), and on the philo-sophical works of Wang Shou-jen. His heretical works were so popular that they were proscribed by the Ming and Ch'ing governments. The *Ssu-shu p'ing* 四書評 (The Four Books with Critical Comments) and the *Shih-kang p'ing-yao* 史綱評要 (Critical Abstract of History) are attributed to Li, but the claim is disputed.

Li Chih was an enthusiastic promoter of popular literature. He edited and commented on numerous dramas including *P'i-p'a chi* (see Kao Ming) and *Hsi-hsiang chi,** and on works of fiction such as *Shih-shuo hsin-yü,** *San-kuo-chih yen-i,** and *Shui-hu chuan.** He considered the "standard literature" of the orthodox tradition as "non-literature," because it did not arise from the real nature of man, which he said was "the heart of a child" (*t'ung-hsin* 童心). Literature must reflect the true feelings and unspoiled thoughts of man, which would be lost if he indulged in writing "standard literature." In a letter to Teng Shih-yang 鄧石陽, Li wrote: "Only the words in daily use, only colloquial language and simple sentences are to be studied most carefully! This is the only important thing, but nevertheless the most difficult, too. And why? If you study the shallow words, you will find the real spirit of man, which is in harmony with nature." Hence Li highly respected works such as *Shui-hu chuan;* he commented on the 120-chapter version of the novel, and it is possible that he himself wrote some chapters of this edition, which was provided by the famous publisher Yüan Shu-tu 袁叔度 (*tzu*, Wu-yai 無涯) and first printed in 1614. In his preface to Yüan's edition of the *Shui-hu chuan*, Li called the novel an "eruption of equitable rancor," and praised the men gathered in the Liang-shan marshes as "heroes and examples of loyalty and justice." To Li Chih, the *Shui-hu chuan* was a specimen of literature "breaking from inside." As he explained to a friend, "Normally an author is writing from the outer world to the inner world, but in my way of writing, I have to break through from an inner world to the outer world." Li Chih's theory of literature is that the realities of life are by no means the art itself, but they are to be transformed into art. If an author neglects the realities of banal life, he will never be able to write real literature. This was the reason for his predilection for literature in the vernacular language.

Li Chih's thoughts played an important role during the May Fourth Movement of 1919, when his anti-Confucian writings were newly "discovered." During the Anti-Lin Piao, Anti-Confucius Campaign in the 1970s he was highly praised as a "Legalist Thinker," and some of his important writings were re-edited. His Buddhistic thinking and his writings on metaphysical problems, however, were neglected during these years.

EDITIONS:

Ch'u-t'an chi 初潭集 (First Collection of the Dragon-pool). 2v. Peking, 1974.

Fen-shu, Hsü Fen-shu 焚書 續焚書. Peking, 1975.

Hsü Ts'ang-shu 續藏書. Peking, 1959; rpt., 2v., 1974 with index of the biographies.

I-yin 易因, in *Wu-ch'iu-pei Chai* I-ching *chi-ch'eng,* and in *Hsü Tao-tsang* 續道藏.

Lao-tzu chieh 老子解, in *Wu-ch'iu-pei Chai Lao-tzu chi-ch'eng, Ch'u-pien.* Yen Ling-feng 嚴靈峯, ed. Taipei, 1971. Li Chih's *Mo-tzu p'i-hsüan* is included in *Wu-ch'iu-pei Chai Mo-tzu chi-ch'eng* by the same editor, and *Chuang-tzu chieh,* in *Wu-ch'iu-pei Chai Chuang-tzu chi-ch'eng.*

Li Cho-wu Hsien-sheng p'i-p'ing Yu-kuei chi 李卓吾先生批評幽閨記; *Li Cho-wu Hsien-sheng p'i-p'ing* Yü-ho chi 李卓吾先生批評玉合記; *Li Cho-wu Hsien-sheng p'i-p'ing* P'i-p'a chi 李卓吾先生批評琵琶記; *Ku-pen,* I, Shanghai, 1954.

Shih-kang p'ing-yao 史綱評要. 3v. Peking, 1974.

Ssu-shu p'ing. Shanghai, 1975. There is also a reprint of the first edition, probably late Wan-li (about 1615), by Ku-chi ch'u-pan-she (Shanghai) and San-lien shu-tien (Hong Kong Branch) in four *ts'e* (original size with multicolor printing), 1976.

Ts'ang-shu. 2v. Peking, 1959; rpt., 4v., with index of the biographies.

TRANSLATIONS:

Masui, Tsuneo 増井經夫. *Funsho. Mindai ittan no sho* 焚書。明代異端の書. Kyoto, 1969.

STUDIES:

Billeter, Jean-François. *Li Zhi. Philosophe maudit (1527-1602). Contribution à une sociologie du mandarinat chinois de la fin des Ming. La genèse et le développement de la pensée de Li Zhi jusqu'à*

la publication du Livre à brûler *(1590).* Geneva, 1979. Contains some translations.

———. "Li Chih (1527-1602): Additional Research Notes," *Chinese Studies in History,* 8.11 (Spring 1980), 81-84.

Chan, Hok-lam 陳學霖. *Li Chih (1527-1602) in Contemporary Chinese Historiography: New Light on His Life and Works.* New York, 1980.

Ch'en, Chin-ch'ao 陳錦釗. *Li Chih chih wen-lun* 李贄之文論. Taipei, 1974.

Cheng, Pei-kai. "Reality and Imagination: Li Chih and T'ang Hsien-tsu in Search of Authenticity." Unpublished Ph.D. dissertation, Yale University, 1980.

DMB, pp. 807-818.

Irwin, Richard G. *The Evolution of a Chinese Novel:* Shui-hu chuan. Cambridge, Mass., 1953, esp. pp. 75-82.

Min-tse 敏澤. "Li Chih te T'ung-hsin-shuo yü Shun-ch'i-hsing lun" 李贄的童心說 與 順其性 論, *Wen-i lun-ts'ung,* 9 (1979). 343-351.

Nan Shih 南石. "Chan-tou te wen-hsüeh ssu-hsiang-chia Li Chih" 戰鬥的文學 思想家李贄, *Wen-hsüeh p'ing-lun,* 1979.3 (June 1979), 88-97.

Spaar, Wilfried. *Die kritische Philosophie des Li Zhi (1527-1602) und ihre politische Rezeption in der Volksrepublik China.* Wiesbaden, 1984. Contains some translations.

Ts'ui Wen-yin 崔文印. "*Ssu-shu-p'ing* pu-shih Li Chih chu-tso te k'ao-cheng" 四書評 不是李贄 著作的考證, *Che-hsüeh yen-chiu,* 1980.4 (April 1980), 69-71.

—WSp

Li Ch'ing-chao 李清照 (*tzu,* I-an 易安, 1084-c. 1151) is China's greatest woman poet. Born in Li-ch'eng 歷城 (modern Chi-nan in Shantung), she came from a distinguished literary family. Her father, Li Ko-fei 李格非, was a noted prose writer and a member of Su Shih's* literary coterie; her mother, also a poet, was a granddaughter of the illustrious Grand Councilor Wang Kung-ch'en 王拱辰 (1012-1085). Nurtured in such a milieu and naturally gifted, she was recognized as a promising poet while still in her teens. At sixteen she wrote two verses in response to a poem written by her father's friend, Chang Wen-ch'ien 張文潛.

In 1101, Li Ch'ing-chao was married to Chao Ming-ch'eng 趙明誠 (1081-1129), a student at the Han-lin Academy and son of a powerful politician who opposed the conservative faction to which her own father belonged. Their union was happy, since they shared the same literary taste and a passion for painting and calligraphy. Having lived through the transition from the Northern Sung to the Southern, a period when China was torn by internal political strife and beset by foreign invasions, Li Ch'ing-chao endured personal tribulation. When her husband's official career was interrupted by the power struggle in the capital, the two lived in semi-retirement in Ch'ing-chou 青州 (Shantung), devoting themselves to research and art collecting. They also catalogued rubbings from ancient bronze vessels and stone monuments; the result of their collaboration, *Chin-shih lu* 金石錄 (A Catalogue of Bronze and Stone Inscriptions) in thirty *chüan* has unfortunately been lost. There remains only Li Ch'ing-chao's postscript, written after her husband's death.

Li Ch'ing-chao's personal tragedy coincided with the fall of the Northern Sung. In 1127, when the Jurchen sacked the capital Pien-liang (modern K'ai-feng), Li Ch'ing-chao was in Ch'ing-chou alone, her husband having gone to Nanking to attend his mother's funeral. When Ch'ing-chou was thrown into turmoil, Li Ch'ing-chao fled with only a few belongings. After months of arduous travels she was reunited with her husband, who had by then become the mayor of Nanking. But her peace and security were short-lived. In 1129 her husband died while en route to a new post, and after that Li Ch'ing-chao drifted from place to place. In 1131 she finally settled in Lin-an 臨安 (modern Hangchow). There she is said to have married a minor military official, Chang Juchou 張汝舟, divorcing him soon thereafter because of his malfeasance and his mistreatment of her. Not much is known about her life after that, except what can be inferred from a few somber poems making references to old age. She is mentioned in the *Sung-shih* 宋史 only in Li Ko-fei's biography, as his talented daughter known for her versification.

Despite the dearth of biographical data on Li Ch'ing-chao, her life can be recon-structed from her works, which demonstrate that she possessed great erudition and a versatile talent. Her early poetry, full of vitality and elegant diction, paints vignettes of her carefree days as a woman of high society who enjoyed the freedom to participate in drinking parties and poetry contests and who was fond of playing on the swing and of boating. But the poems written after her husband's death portray her as grief-stricken, "too lazy to comb her hair," mourning the loss of her homeland and her beloved, managing to "forget the past only when drunk."

Despite her meticulous observance of the metrical rules of the *tz'u*** genre, Li Ch'ing-chao was able to depict in everyday language and without affectation her true state of mind and the nuances of her feelings. Her sensitivity to music and cadence, her gift for fresh imagery, and her awareness of the sensuous beauty of nature give her *tz'u* an inimitable quality.

Unfortunately, the greater part of her works has been lost. The little that has survived is scattered in various collections. To date, five essays, eighteen *shih** poems, and seventy-eight *tz'u* have been attributed to her.

Li Ch'ing-chao's poetry has been called narrow in scope, because it deals mainly with her personal experiences. Such criticism overlooks the depth of her emotional intensity, which more than compensates for the lack of breadth in subject matter. Her impeccable craftsmanship and her liberating spirit place her among the best of *tz'u* masters.

EDITIONS:

Li Ch'ing-chao chi 李清照集. Shanghai, 1962.

Li Ch'ing-chao chi chiao-chu 李清照集校註. Wang Hsüeh-ch'u 王學初, ed. Peking, 1979.

Shu-yü chi 漱玉集. Kaoshiung, 1964.

TRANSLATIONS:

Birch, *Anthology*, v. 2, pp. 358-363.

Hsu, K. Y. "The Poems of Li Ch'ing-chao (1084-1141)," *PMLA*, 77 (1962), 521-528.

Liang, Paitchin. *Oeuvres poétiques complètes de Li Qingzhao*. Paris, 1977.

Rexroth, Kenneth and Ling Chung. *Li Ch'ing-chao; Complete Poems.* New York, 1979.

Sunflower, pp. 366-370.

STUDIES:

Chang, Shao-lin 張少林. *Li Ch'ing-chao*. Shanghai, 1931.

Chu, Ti 朱悌. *Li Ch'ing-chao yü Chu Shu-chen* 李清照與朱淑貞. Hong Kong, 1959.

Chiang, Shang-hsien 姜尚賢. *Li Ch'ing-chao tz'u hsin-shang* 李清照詞欣賞. Tainan, 1960.

Chung, Ling. "Li Ch'ing-chao: Another Side of her Complex Personality," *JCLTA*, 10.3 (October 1975), 126-136.

Ho, Kuang-yen 何廣棪. *Li Ch'ing-chao yen-chiu* 李清照研究. Taipei, 1977.

Hu, Pin-ching. *Li Ch'ing-chao*. New York, 1966.

SB, pp. 530-539.

She, Hsüeh-man 佘雪曼. *Nü tz'u-jen Li Ch'ing-chao* 女詞人李清照. Kowloon, 1955.

—AJP

Li Ho 李賀 (*tzu*, Ch'ang-chi 長吉, 791-817) was a tragic-romantic poet of the late T'ang. Born to a distant branch of the imperial clan, talented and with every prospect and desire for a prominent career, he achieved no material success in his short life. It is a truism that the poets of the T'ang did not measure their life's worth by their poetry, this was a matter for posterity. Rather it was high office in the government which counted as the essential measure of one's impact on the world. Li Ho's poetry reflects frustration and bitterness, offering sharp sarcasm, irony, and satire about political matters, and giving uncompromisingly precise details in erotic contexts. For the unusual richness of his diction, his simultaneous bluntness and allusiveness, and his courting of the macabre—the unlikely, unlucky image—he earned a reputation as a difficult poet to read and perhaps a dangerous one to befriend.

This characterization is drawn from the events of Li Ho's life and from the prefaces to his collected poems written by his near-contemporaries Tu Mu* and Li Shang-yin.* In his influential "Preface," Tu Mu argues, ostensibly, that Li Ho goes to excess in his diction and loses the sense of proportion between medium and message, and that he is in fact an eccentric poet whom the reader can choose not to understand. Li Shang-yin wrote a "Short Biography" in which he makes legend of the life, rendering both poet and poetry as fictional. The intent of both prefaces is to defuse the poetry, to present it as safe to enjoy and preserve. It is telling that some twenty years after Li Ho's death his life and work were still dealt with circumspectly.

In 809 Li Ho took the provincial examination in Lo-yang. (His father had died some years before, thus he was the hope of a family consisting of his mother, sister, and younger brother; it is not supposed that he ever married.) Two prominent albeit controversial figures, Han Yü* and Huang-fu Shih 皇甫湜 (*c.* 777-*c.* 830), were his sponsors. He easily passed and went on to Ch'ang-an to prepare for the *chin-shih* examination, but he was not allowed to take it. The complaint was that he would violate the taboo against using his father's name should he participate, since the *chin* was the same as that of his father's name, Chin-su 晉肅. The practice of the time was also to avoid homophones, and on this basis the charge stuck. It is not known who made the case against Li Ho or why.

In poems on his return to Ch'ang-ku 昌谷, the family home located in modern Honan, Li Ho contrasted the richness and fertility of place with the desolation of self. He had no choice but to go back to Ch'ang-an in 811 to take the placing examination: his father had reached the fifth rank, first class, and by heredity he was entitled to any position up to the eighth rank, third class. His "Jen-ho li tsa hsü Huang-fu Shih" 仁和里雜序皇甫湜 (Assorted Comments for Huang-fu Shih from the Jen-ho Quarter) expresses on various levels his feelings during this period. Between 811 and 814 he had the title Vice Director for Ceremonials; in effect, he was an usher.

The years in Ch'ang-an are undoubtedly the period of Li Ho's many portraits of the materially rich, emotionally difficult lives of courtesans. With extraordinary diction he captures the opulence of the high-class houses and the fragile, fugitive beauty of the women, often in ironic contrast to their commercial functions, as in his "Yeh-lai lo" 夜來樂 (Joys of the Night) and "Mei jen shu t'ou ko" 美人梳頭歌 (Song of a Beauty

Combing Her Hair). He continues the tradition of boudoir poetry, his work reminiscent of Li Po's poems on women.

His career stillborn, Li Ho grew increasingly conscious of his chronic illness and of the immediacy of death. This fueled his interest in the question of immortality, in images of death, and in the deceit of mythology. With a skeptical eye he measured immortality and found it an endless series of deaths. In his "Shen hsien" 神絃 (Spirit Strings) poems he witnesses shamanistic performances but places more magic in metaphor than in medium. Like many of his contemporaries he read the *Diamond Sutra*, yet the extent of Buddhist influence in his poetry remains uncertain. One instance might be found in his "Yao-hua yüeh" 瑤華樂 (Jasper Flower Music), a narrative poem on the legendary visit of King Mu to the Queen Mother of the West (Hsi Wang Mu), which is also a retelling of the tragic romance of Hsüan-tsung and Yang Kuei-fei. The last couplet bears a striking resemblance to descriptions of the annual ritual of bathing the Buddha. Evidently, religion offered him little solace, and mythology was itself a medium for allegory.

For all that distinguishes Li Ho from more conventional poets, he is a product of the innovators he follows. Unusual syntax, a penchant for dissimilar, discordant parallels, the delight in ambiguity, the freedom to fill his poems with intensity, all reflect the achievements of Tu Fu,* the forbidding imagery of Meng Chiao,* and the influence of Han Yü. But the romanticism, irony, bitter wit, delight in countering traditional expectations, all belong to the poet. He saw the world in colors, fragrances, sounds, textures, and he made no pretense of doing other than interpreting his experiences. His landscapes often project a state of mind, where reds or flowers weep, the mist has laughing eyes, and nature is measured in human terms. Repetition, onomatopoeia, alliteration, allusion—the most extensive borrowing from the *Ch'u-tz'u** since Hsieh Ling-yün*—and multiple levels of meaning in individual poems characterize Li Ho's poetry. And given his fondness for narratives, his best efforts tend to be old-style verse.

Li Ho spent his last years seeking a position outside the court, on the staff of a general. Unsuccessful, he returned home in 817 quite ill and died. His collected surviving poems total about 240; legend has it that a spiteful cousin got hold of the collection and threw a large part of it into a privy—such was Li Ho's luck in life and legend.

EDITIONS:

Li Ho ko-shih-pien 李賀歌詩篇. Taipei, 1971.
Li Ho shih hsüan 李賀詩選. Liu Ssu-han 劉思翰, comp. Hong Kong, 1980.
San-chia p'ing-chu Li Ch'ang-chi ko-shih 三家評注 李長吉歌詩. Peking, 1959. Includes the standard commentary by Wang Ch'i 王琦 (pub. 1760).

TRANSLATIONS:

Frodsham, J. D. *The Poems of Li Ho (791-817)*. Oxford, 1970.
Graham, *Late T'ang*, pp. 89-119.
Saitō, Shō 齋藤晌. *Ri Ga* 李賀. Tokyo, 1967.
Suzuki, Torao 鈴木虎雄. *Ri Chokichi kashishu* 李長吉歌詩集. 2v. Tokyo, 1961.
Sunflower, pp. 228-236.

STUDIES:

Fish, Michael B. "Mythological Themes in the Poetry of Li Ho 791-817." Unpublished Ph.D. dissertation, Indiana University, 1973.
———. "The Tu Mu and Li Shang-yin Prefaces to the Collected Poems of Li Ho," in *Chinese Poetry and Poetics*, v. 1, R. C. Miao, ed. San Francisco, 1978, pp. 231-286.
———. "Yang Kuei-fei as the Hsi Wang Mu: Secondary Narrative in Two T'ang Poems," *MS* 32 (1976), 337-354.
Harada, Kenyū 原田憲雄. *Ri Ga ronkō* 李賀論考. Kyoto, 1981.
Ri Ga kenkyū 李賀研究, 1-13 (1971-1975), Kyoto: Hokōsha 方向社. Mimeographed journal (sold by Hōyū shoten 朋友書店).
Robertson, Maureen. "Poetic Diction in the Works of Li Ho (891-917 [*sic*])." Unpublished Ph.D. dissertation, University of Washington, 1970.
Tu, Kuo-ch'ing. *Li Ho*. Boston, 1979.

—MF

Li Hua 李華 (*tzu*, Hsia-shu 遐叔, d. *c.* 769) was one of the most influential prose writers, critics, and literary patrons of the middle decades of the eighth century. His official career was crucially affected by the An Lu-shan Rebellion of 755. He had passed the *chin-shih* examination in 735, succeeded in a palace examination, and held high office. He was also connected with some of the leaders of intellectual opinion in Ch'ang-an in the 740s and early 750s and was by then considered an established literary figure. During the rebellion, however, he was captured and forced to collaborate. He presumably wrote edicts. After the recovery of the capital he retired to the southeast, declining summons and living in self-imposed exile until his death.

Like most mid-eighth century men of letters, Li composed in the euphuistic, ornamental, antithetical style (i.e., *p'ien-wen**), as well as in the free prose (i.e., *ku-wen**) that he is traditionally held to have advocated. Two of his early and best-known works demonstrate this. His "Han-yüan Tien fu" 含元殿賦 (Prose-poem on the Han-yüan Palace) was compared by his friend Hsiao Ying-shih* to two *fu** on palaces contained in the prestigious *Wen-hsüan.** It was, Hsiao said, not as good as one by Ho Yen 何晏 (d. 249), but better than that of Wang Yen-shou 王延壽 (*c.* 124-*c.* 148). Another of Li's well-known works "Tiao Ku chan-ch'ang wen" 弔古戰場文 (Dirge on an Ancient Battlefield) is also a highly rhetorical composition, using imagery from the period of Han frontier expansion and evoking the combination of romantic fascination and pity that literary men felt for those who died in battle on the northern and western borders.

Li's views on literary practice and theory were given mainly in prefaces to the collected works of friends. He held that literature was both the expression of an individual's moral life and a reflection of the moral and social climate of the age. He also emphasized that the Confucian canon embodied the highest standards of literary excellence, which contemporary literature failed to approach.

Despite his disgrace and departure from Ch'ang-an after the An Lu-shan Rebellion, Li maintained wide contacts with important figures of his day. He continued to write commemorative texts for Buddhist clergy, records for local institutions, epitaphs, sacrificial prayers, and occasional verse. He also composed essays, one of his most substantial being an analysis of history in terms of the traditional polarity of *wen* 文 (refinement) and *chih* 質 (austerity) that indicted his own time for its excess of *wen.* Another essay argued against the practice of divination using tortoise shells. A third commemorated three of his deceased friends, Hsiao Ying-shih, Liu Hsün 劉迅 (a son of the historian and critic Liu Chih-chi*), and Yüan Te-hsiu 元德秀 (696-754), a cousin and teacher of the prose writer Yüan Chieh.*

Most of Li Hua's early works were lost in the An Lu-shan Rebellion. A second collection was given a preface by Tu-ku Chi,* one of his most important followers in about 769, shortly before Li's death. Nearly all that is extant from this collection has been preserved by virtue of its inclusion in the general anthologies compiled in the early Sung.

Li's other followers include: Han Yün-ch'ing 韓雲卿, an uncle of the great prose writer Han Yü,* and Han Hui 韓會, Han Yü's elder brother; Ts'ui Yu-fu 崔祐甫 (721-780), a Grand Councilor and director of the dynastic history in the 770s; and Liang Su,* another literary figure, historian, and scholar who influenced Han Yü. The interest of these men, prepared as they were to overlook his crime of collaboration, helped ensure that his post-rebellion works were preserved and that his reputation for learning and literature remained high.

EDITIONS:
Ch'üan T'ang shih, v. 3, *ch.* 153, pp. 1585-1590.
Ch'üan T'ang wen, v. 7, *ch.* 314-321, pp. 4027-4122.

STUDIES:
Liu, San-fu 劉三富. "Ri Ka no shisō to bungaku 李華の思想と文學 " *Chūgoku bungaku ronshū*, 4 (1974), 62-71.
McMullen, "Literary Theory."
Owen, "*Fu-ku* Revival: Yüan Chieh, the *Ch'ieh chung-chi* and the Confucian Intellectuals," in *High Tang*, pp. 243-246.

—DLM

Li I 李益 (*tzu*, Chün-yü 君虞, 748-827), one of the leading poets of his day, belonged to the clan of Li K'uei 李揆, who attained the office of Grand Councilor during the reign of Emperor Su-tsung (r. 756-763). Li I, like his relative before him, may have resided in Honan province although the family home appears to have been in Lung-hsi 隴西 (modern Wu-wei District in Kansu). After passing the *chin-shih* examination at twenty, Li was posted to a district office. Frustrated in that menial position, he resigned to accept service on the secretarial staff of a military unit on the frontier. After nearly a decade of service in the northern marches, he was eventually recalled to the capital by Emperor Hsien-tsung (r. 806-820), and during his remaining years he occupied several middle- and high-level positions in the central government.

According to the official histories, Li I was known for his meanness of spirit and cruel treatment of the women in his life. These rather unattractive personality traits, whether real or not, gained even wider currency because of the well-known classical tale "Huo Hsiao-yü chuan" 霍小玉傳 (The Story of Huo Hsiao-yü) by Chiang Fang 蔣防 (*fl.* early ninth century), in which he is portrayed as a self-indulgent, unfeeling man who tyrannized his wives and concubines. Like many T'ang classical tales this story is an amalgam of fact and fiction. Li's suspicious and jealous tendencies were evidently so pronounced that insane jealousy came to be called "Li I's disease." By the end of the tale, the protagonist Li I is suffering from this disease—suggesting that the story may have been partly the result of speculation into the causes of the poet's affliction or that the tale influenced the historical accounts of Li I.

The narrative begins with Li I's search for a suitable match. A go-between introduces him to a prince's daughter, Huo Hsiao-yü, now living in Ch'ang-an in reduced circumstances—she has become a courtesan. Li I is charmed by her and pledges his eternal love. He is then appointed to an official post and leaves the capital, promising to send for her later. But before he can do so, his mother forces him to marry another woman. Meanwhile Hsiao-yü languishes, seeking in vain for in-formation about Li I. When Li returns to Ch'ang-an for his wedding, he attempts to avoid his former lover. But the author reunites the pair through a *deus ex machina*—a knight-errant appears to Hsiao-yü in a dream and then brings Li I to her. The knight-errant later appears before Li I and compels him to follow him to Hsiao-yü's home. There she reproaches Li I, swears to haunt him and his wives after her death, and dies. She apparently fulfills her oath: each of Li I's three marriages fail.

Chiang Fang may have been influenced by a similar story, Yüan Chen's "Ying-ying chuan" composed in 804—about four years before "Huo Hsiao-yü chuan." The two stories not only have similar plots, but even make use of similar poems. Like its predecessor, "Huo Hsiao-yü chuan" is a source of later drama: T'ang Hsien-tsu's* *Tzu-ch'ai chi.* The two stories, however, do have one major difference. Li I's counterpart in Yüan Chen's story, Chang, feels morally justified in deserting the courtesan who loves him and the narrator seems to agree with him. The narrator's praise of Chang seems inconsistent with the sympathetic portrayal of the courtesan, Ying-ying. This discrepency has stimulated some debate over whether Chang's justification is intended seriously or ironically. If "Huo Hsiao-yü chuan" was written as a commentary on "Ying-ying chuan," it woud seem that some T'ang readers took Chang's moralizing seriously. The end of Chiang Fang's tale can be interpreted as giving Chang, in the guise of Li I, his due.

Unlikable though he may have been as a person, the *Chiu T'ang-shu* 舊唐書 (Old T'ang History) states that he was skilled in song and poetry and that his poems were popular, some being set to music by members of the *Chiao-fang* for performance at court. Members of the upper class also had his poems inscribed on decorative panels for display in their homes. While still a relatively young man Li I was associated in the public mind with the "Ta-li shih ts'ai-tzu" (see Lu Lun). Still later, he was sometimes mentioned together with Li Ho,* although there is little resemblance between their poetic styles. That he was highly esteemed as a poet in his own day is revealed by the prominence accorded him in the *Yü-lan shih* 御覽詩, an anthology compiled under imperial auspices in the later eighth century by Ling-hu Ch'u 令狐楚 (766-837), in which his poems outnumber those of any other poet.

Li I is much admired for his mastery of the quatrain, which in diction and tone recalls the occasional social verse of the pre-T'ang era. He also excelled in *pien-sai shih* 邊塞詩 (frontier verse). Approximately one-third of his extant corpus of over 160 poems belongs to that category. After years of frontier duty when he was about forty years of age, he compiled a small collection of his poems under the title *Ts'ung-chün shih* 從軍詩 (Poems on Following the Army) and presented them to a certain Lu Ching-liang 盧景亮. The title of the collection is a variation on the well-known *yüeh-fu** song pattern, one that had previously been employed by such famous poets as Wang Ts'an* and Wang Ch'ang-ling* for their frontier poems. Steeped in that tradition, it is not surprising that Li I's frontier pieces follow well-established conventions in depicting the world of the northern border. That world is described as a cold and barren one, awesomely forbidding in its desolation, both physically and culturally repellant to the civilized people who live within the Great Wall. In poems of this type, Li typically evokes a brooding sense of death, desolation, and despair. Along the border life is difficult and death is common among those men who have been sent to defend China against invasion. The world of the northern frontier could however evoke other visions, and in some cases it is portrayed as serene. Bathed in moonlight, it possesses an ethereal beauty, with only the plaintive sounds of tribal pipes to remind the border guard of home and hearth. In still other poems in this mode, Li I occasionally sounds a heroic note. Examples of this type describe battles, or narrate the story of a young warrior of martial prowess, and in the process celebrate the ideals of personal honor and duty to country. Taken all together, Li I's *pien-sai* verse is richly diverse and representative of the best of that tradition.

EDITIONS:
Li Chün-yü shih-chi 李君虞詩集. *SPTK.*
Ch'üan T'ang shih, v. 5, *chüan* 282-283, pp. 3202-3231.
Ch'üan T'ang wen, v. 10, *chüan* 481, p. 6222.
"Huo Hsiao-yü chuan, in *T'ang-jen hsiao-shuo*, pp. 77-84. A reliable, punctuated text with useful background material.

TRANSLATIONS:
Bynner, *Jade Mountain*, pp. 87-88.
Wang, Chi-chen. "Huo Hsiaoyü," in *Traditional Chinese Tales*, New York, 1944, pp. 48-59.
Sunflower, p. 157.

STUDIES:
Wang, Meng-ou 王夢鷗. "Huo Hsiao-yü chuan chih tso-che chi ku-shih pei-ching" 霍小玉傳之作者及故事背景, *Shu-mu chi-k'an*, 7.1 (1972), 3-10.
T'ang shih-jen Li I sheng-p'ing chi ch'i tso-p'in 唐詩人李益生平及其作品. Taipei, 1973.
　　　　　　　　　　　　　　　　—WS and CY

Li K'ai-hsien 李開先 (*tzu*, Po-hua 伯華, *hao*, Chung-lu 中麓, 1502-1568) was one of the forerunners of the revival of interest in Yüan drama during the second half of the Ming dynasty, as well as a playwright in the southern *ch'uan-ch'i** style.

Born into a family of officials in Shantung, Li K'ai-hsien passed the *chin-shih* examination in 1529 and served as an official almost continuously until 1541, when he was forced to retire. He lived in considerable luxury on his estate for the rest of his life, collecting books, writing extensively, and maintaining a troupe of actors. From a literary standpoint, the most important event in his life was the few weeks he spent visiting the playwrights K'ang Hai* and Wang Chiu-ssu* in 1531, since it was probably their interest in drama and *san-ch'ü* 散曲 poetry (see *ch'ü*) that inspired Li's later contributions to this branch of literature.

Li's considerable wealth allowed him to amass a large collection of Yüan-dynasty *tsa-chü*,* a few of which he had printed under the title *Kai-ting Yüan hsien ch'uan-ch'i* 改定元賢傳奇 (Amended Versions of Plays by Worthies of the Yüan Dynasty). To judge by the title, he revised and rewrote the texts that he published, a practice typical of later Ming publishers of vernacular literature. His two surviving plays, the *Pao-chien chi* 寶劍記 (The Precious Sword), based on the Lin Ch'ung-Kao Ch'iu episode in the *Shui-hu chuan** cycle, and the *Tuan-fa chi* 斷髮記 (Cutting Off the Hair), are both *ch'uan-ch'i*, but follow the rhyming categories established for Yüan plays. Iwaki Hideo has suggested that this reflects Li's view of Yüan drama as a "model," analogous in some ways to that of T'ang poetry for the Archaist poets of Li's day.

Li also wrote *san-ch'ü* poetry, *yüan-pen*,* critical articles on painting and poetry, numerous *shih** poems, and prose works. His *shih* are conspicuous, as Yokota has pointed out, both for the number written to set rhyme words and for the predominance of bucolic subject matter, presumably reflecting Li's long period of enforced leisure in the country. Interestingly, this "playful" interest in composing to set rhymes also shows itself in Li's *san-ch'ü* and dramatic works. Indeed, the characterization of Li K'ai-hsien by modern Chinese critics as a "patriotic" and "popular" writer opposed to the formalism of the Archaists (see under Li Meng-yang) is superficial and one-sided. It is based on his use of the *Shui-hu* cycle of legends in *Pao-chien chi* and on certain of his works that refer to China's weakness in the face of pirate incursions. Li opposed the Archaists only in the later period of his life. As a younger man he was acquainted with Li Meng-yang,* for whom he always retained respect, and, as noted above, with K'ang Hai and Wang Chiu-ssu, all of whom are Archaists. Li's importance in Chinese literature lies mainly in the area of drama, in which he helped preserve the Yüan *tsa-chü* while contributing to the development of the southern *ch'uan-ch'i* that was to flower in the works of a succeeding generation of writers, such as Hsü Wei* and T'ang Hsien-tsu.*

EDITIONS:

Li K'ai-hsien chi 李開先集. Lu Kung 路工, ed. Peking, 1959. Includes all of Li's surviving works except for a few non-literary titles and the complete text of *Tuan-fa chi*, known only from a single copy in Japan.

TRANSLATIONS:

Acton, Harold. "Lin Ch'ung Yeh Pen," *THM*, 9.2 (1939), 180-188. Translation of one scene from the *Pao-chien chi*.

STUDIES:

Abe, Hirobumi 阿部泰記. "Gikyoku sakka Ri Kaisen no bungakukan: Nankyoku 'Hōshō-dai' o chūshin ni" 戯曲作家李開先の文学觀一南曲傍粧台を中心 に, *Kyūshu Daigaku Chūgoku bungakukai Chūgoku bungaku ronshū*, 5 (1976), 23-32.

Chung-hung 仲弘. "Tu *Lin Ch'ung pao-chien chi*" 讀林沖寶劍記, *Kuang-ming jih-pao*, March 18, 1956 (*Wen-hsüeh i-ch'an*, No. 96).

DMB, pp. 835-837.

Hsü, Fu-ming 徐扶明. "Li K'ai-hsien ho t'a te *Lin Ch'ung pao-chien chi* 和他的 林沖寶劍記," in *Yüan Ming Ch'ing hsi-ch'ü yen-chiu lun-wen chi, erh-chi* 元明清戯曲研究論文集, 二集, Peking, 1959, pp. 282-303. Previously published in *Wen-shih-che*, 1957.10, 35-43.

Hsü, Shuo-fang 徐朔方. "P'ing 'Li K'ai-hsien te sheng-p'ing chi ch'i chu-tso' " 評李開先的生平及其著作, *Wen-hsüeh i-ch'an tseng-k'an*, 9 (1962), 34-42.

Iwaki, Hideo 岩城秀夫. "Gekisakuka Ri Kaisen: sono koten sonchō no ishiki ni tsuite" 劇作家李開先——その古曲尊重の意識について, in *Iriya*, pp. 605-617.

Yagisawa, Hajime 八木澤元. "Ri Kaisen to sono gikyoku" とその戯曲李開先, *Nihon Chūhoku gakkaihō*, 8 (1956), 98-115. Reprinted in Yagisawa, *Gekisakuka*, pp. 172-268.

Yen, Tun-i 嚴敦易. "*Pao-chien chi* chung te Lin Ch'ung ku-shih" 寶劍記中的林沖故事, *Wen-hsüeh i-ch'an tseng-k'an*, 1 (1955), 245-252.

Yokota, Terutoshi 横田輝俊, "Ri Kaisen no shi ni tsuite," *Hiroshima daigaku bungakubu kiyō*, 22.3 (1963), 51-91.

—DB

Li Kung-tso 李公佐 (*tzu*, Chuan-meng 顓蒙, c. 770-c. 848), was one of the principal writers of literary-language tales (see *ch'uan-chi*) during the T'ang dynasty. His ancestral home was Lung-hsi 隴西 (modern Kansu), but he seems to have spent most of his long life in central and south China. There is also evidence that he was distant kin to the T'ang imperial family. He was a successful *chin-shih* examination candidate, probably in the mid-790s, and he subsequently held several rather low-ranking positions in various administrative offices in what are now the provinces of Kwangtung, Kiangsi, and Kiangsu. Many of his positions were under officials associated with the court faction of Li Te-yü 李德裕 (787-850), and in the early 840s he was clerk to Li Shen 李紳 (d. 846), then Military Commissioner of Huai-nan 淮南 (seat at modern Yangchow), who was one of Li Te-yü's principal supporters. When Emperor Hsüan-tsung assumed the throne in mid-846, Li Te-yü's faction fell from favor (a posthumous investigation of corruption involving Li Shen provided the final excuse for their dismissal), and in the sweep Li Kung-tso was also stripped of his official status. Wording in the memorial denouncing Li Shen and the others involved in the case is understood by some to indicate that Li Kung-tso was already dead when it was presented in 848.

Only four of Li Kung-tso's short stories survive, but they show his work to be remarkable for its variety. The longest, entitled "Nan-k'o T'ai-shou chuan" 南柯太守傳 (The Prefect of South Bough), is an expanded treatment of a theme seen in Shen Chi-chi's* earlier "Chen-chung chi" 枕中記 (The World Inside a Pillow), in that a man dreams a whole lifetime, complete with fame, fortune, and highly-placed marriage, in a brief, drunken nap. Like Shen's earlier work, Li's story carries a message concerning the ultimate vanity of striving for worldly fame and fortune; but unlike Shen, Li tied his story more closely to the real world, his dream world being identified with an ant colony located beneath the "south bough" of a nearby locust tree.

The second of Li's stories, "Hsieh Hsiao-o" 謝小娥 (the heroine's name), is one of the first treatments in Chinese literature of a crime and its solution. In the story a murderer is identified when riddles involving the characters of his name are solved. Although plays on the component parts of characters appear in works as early as the Tso-chuan,* this seems to be the first appearance of the device in a fictional setting. It is seen frequently is more modern fictional works.

Li's other two surviving stories are of lesser interest. "Lu-chiang Feng ao" 廬江馮媼 (Old Mrs. Feng from the Lu River), which tells of an encounter with a woman who turns out to have died the previous year, is quite similar in content and style to the strange tales collected and recorded earlier during the Six Dynasties period. "Ku Yüeh-tu ching" 古岳瀆經 (The Ancient Classic of Peaks and Rivers), records a story concerning a huge monkey-like river creature, and tells of Li Kung-tso later finding confirmation of the creature's existence in an ancient scripture which he discovered in a remote mountain grotto. The scripture appears to be completely fictional, most likely intended to bring to mind the Shan-hai ching,* an actual early book of fantastic geographical lore.

Li Kung-tso is known to have associated with other contemporary writers of literary language short stories, and his stories circulated widely already during the T'ang dynasty. "The Prefect of South Bough" and "Hsieh Hsiao-o" especially have become standard anthology selections.

EDITIONS:

Li, Fang, et al. T'ai-p'ing kuang-chi.* Peking, 1961, 343.2718-2719 [Feng ao], 467.3845-3846 [Yüeh-tu ching], 475.3910-3915 [Nan-k'o], 491.4030-4032 [Hsieh Hsiao-o].

Lu, Hsün 魯迅. T'ang Sung ch'uan-ch'i chi 唐宋傳奇集. Rpt. Hong Kong, 1967, pp. 75-90 [all four].

Wang, Meng-ou 王夢鷗. T'ang-jen hsiao-shuo yen-chiu erh-chi 唐人小說研究二集. Taipei, 1973, pp. 153-154 [Feng ao], 193-195 [Yüeh-tu ching], 201-208 [Nan-k'o], 226-229 [Hsieh Hsiao-o].

Wang, P'i-chiang 汪辟疆. T'ang-jen hsiao-shuo 唐人小說. Rpt. Shanghai, 1955.

TRANSLATIONS:

Edwards, Prose Literature, v. 2, pp. 150-154 [Hsieh Hsiao-o], 206-212 [Nan-k'o].

Wang, Elizabeth T. C. Ladies of the T'ang. Taipei, 1961, pp. 239-261 [Nan-k'o], 323-330 [Feng ao].

Wang, C. C. Traditional Chinese Tales. New York, pp. 87-92 [Hsieh Hsiao-o].

Yang, Dragon King's Daughter, pp. 44-56 [Nan-k'o].

Maeno, Naoake 前野直彬. *Tōdai denkishū* 唐代傳奇集. Tokyo, 1964, v. 1, pp. 120-149 [all four].

Uchida, Sennosuke 內田泉之助 and Inui Kazuo 乾一夫. *Tōdai denki* 唐代傳奇. Tokyo, 1971, pp. 211-251 [Nan-k'o and Hsieh Hsiao-o, in modern Japanese with Chinese text; extensive, useful annotation].

STUDIES:

Knechtges, David R. "Dream Adventure Stories in Europe and T'ang China," *TkR*, 4.2 (October 1973), 101-119.

Kondō, Haruo 近藤春雄. "Tōdai shōsetsu ni tsuite, Chinchūki, Nanka taishu den, Sha Shōga den" 唐人小説 について — 枕中記, 南柯太宋傳, 謝小娥傳, *Aichi kenritsu joshi daigaku kiyō*, 15 (1964), pp. 40-58.

Liu, K'ai-jung 劉開榮. *T'ang-tai hsiao-shuo yen-chiu* 唐代小説研究. Rev. Hong Kong, 1964, pp. 163-175.

Uchiyama, Chinari 內山知也. *Zui Tō shōsetsu kenkyū* 隋唐小説研究. Tokyo, 1977, pp. 377-411.

Wang, Meng-ou. *T'ang-jen hsiao-shuo yen-chiu erh-chi*, pp. 46-56.

—DG

Li Meng-yang 李夢陽 (*tzu*, Hsien-chi 獻吉, *hao*, K'ung-t'ung 空同, 1475-1529) was an important poet and literary theorist, leader of a group of *fu-ku* 復古 (recovery of antiquity) reformists, or Archaists, usually referred to as the Ming ch'i-tzu 明七子 (Seven Ming Masters) or the Ch'ien 前 ch'i-tzu (Earlier Seven Masters). Although recent research has cast a good deal of doubt on the existence of any clearly defined group of seven, Li was certainly the outstanding exponent of Archaist literary thought in his day, and the movement that he launched dominated the Chinese literary world for most of the sixteenth century before falling into disfavor under the attacks of "individualist" anti-Archaist schools.

Li Meng-yang was born of very humble stock, a family whose members had apparently been illiterate until the generation of his grandfather. In fact, it has been suggested (chiefly by Japanese scholars) that Li's lowly origins helped to condition his later political and literary career. The straightforward uprightness and adher-

ence to traditional values of the local "bravo" are reflected in his poetic style, which is direct and bold, in his literary theory, which stresses a return to "natural" forms, and in his activities as an official, characterized by repeated and fearless attacks on corrupt colleagues and superiors that more than once endangered his career and even his life.

In any event, Li Meng-yang succeeded in rising far above his origins, passing the *chin-shih* examination in 1493. Although he returned home to his native Shensi soon after to mourn his parents, he was back in Peking in 1498 and remained there in office until 1507, except for occasional missions to the provinces. While in the capital, he joined the literary circle around the grand secretary Li Tung-yang,* an important poet and critic in his own right who had supervised the examinations in which Li Meng-yang and his followers distinguished themselves. Among Li Meng-yang's close friends was Wang Yang-ming, who passed the *chin-shih* in 1499 and was later to become the most important and influential philosopher of the Ming dynasty. In 1507, Li was cashiered because of his opposition to the infamous eunuch Liu Chin. Although he was reinstated in 1511, he was dismissed from office again in 1514 and spent the rest of his life in retirement, except for a period of imprisonment during 1521 and 1522.

It was during Li Meng-yang's years in office in Peking, from 1498 to 1507, that the group of poets later known as the Earlier Seven Masters were associated with him. In addition to Li himself, they included two men who had passed the *chin-shih* examinatons in 1496, the playwright and poet Wang Chiu-ssu,* and a poet of considerable talent named Pien Kung 邊貢 (*tzu*, T'ing-shih 庭實, *hao*, Hua-ch'üan 華泉, 1476-1532); the playwright K'ang Hai,* who had taken top honors in the examinations of 1502; and two of his fellow successful examinees, Wang T'ing-hsiang 王廷相 (*tzu*, Tzu-heng 子衡, *hao*, Chün-ch'uan 浚川, 1474-1544), the only one of Li's close associates to enjoy a long and generally successful career in the civil service and also a philosopher who eventually took a line quite different from that of Wang Yang-ming, and a young man who was to prove the greatest poet of his generation and Li's only serious rival for the leadership of the Archaist movement, Ho Ching-ming.* With the arrival in Peking of a brilliant young poet from Soochow in the south (the rest of Li's circle were all northerners), Hsü Chen-ch'ing 徐禎卿 (1479-1511), who had already made a reputation as part of the circle around the artists T'ang Yin and Wen Cheng-ming, the group was complete. In fact, however, all seven were together in Peking only for a few months early in 1505, the year of Hsü's success in the *chin-shih* examination. In addition to the "members" of the Earlier Seven Masters, a considerable number of other writers were associated with Li Meng-yang or with his literary program.

Li was himself the disciple of two older writers, Li Tung-yang and Yang I-ch'ing 楊一淸 (1454-1530), who had led a successful movement to replace the currently dominant T'ai-ko t'i* 臺閣體 (Secretariat Style) with a style that allowed greater personal expression and, in particular, required a greater mastery of prosody and other aural effects in verse. Li Meng-yang went beyond this and called for the conscious imitation of model forms of antiquity, prose works from the Chin and Han dynasties, and High T'ang poetry. In his insistence upon imitation, Li differed from his mentor, Li Tung-yang, who had stressed the importance of technical command but disapproved of imitation as such. He also found himself soon in dispute with the most promising of his disciples, Ho Ching-ming, who believed that the imitation of ancient models was indeed excellent training for a poet just learning his craft, but that it could, and should, be given up once the ability to express a personal vision was developed. Li Meng-yang wrote to Ho urging him to abandon his position. Li's first letter has been lost, but Ho's reply is extant, as are two further replies to this by Li. The latter provides one of the best insights into Li's doctrines. Against Ho's assertion of the importance of individu-

ality, Li argued that being individualist in literary creation was like being a specialized artisan who could practice only one skill. The forms of the ancient masters were not restrictions, Li argued, but tools like the compass and square with which a skilled carpenter could make all sorts of windows and doors. The importance of the models lay not in their perfection per se, but rather in the innate natural principles of human existence and understanding that they perfectly embodied. By imitating their forms one would be brought to a state of enhanced understanding and sympathy with these principles, and it was this result that established the inherent importance of literature as an activity, quite apart from the particular propositional content of a specific poem or essay. In his use of poetry as a vehicle for self-understanding, as well as in the high seriousness with which he pursued his chosen vocation, Li showed himself to have concerns fundamentally similar to those of his friend Wang Yang-ming, who was also seeking an understanding of the self and the nature of its experience.

The literary disagreement between Li and Ho Ching-ming, though heatedly debated in their exchange of letters, does not seem to have affected the personal relationship between them. Indeed, Ho was the only friend to come to Li's rescue when, in the year after their exchange of letters, the latter came into conflict with Liu Chin. But the followers of the two men naturally tended to take sides, and Ho's rebuttal ironically furnished much of the ammunition used against the Archaists as a group by later generations of individualist critics.

In the twentieth century particularly, the Seven have been more criticized than read. The enormous effort required of the May Fourth generation to break free of the shackles of obsolete and oppressive traditions of every kind did not dispose them to look with sympathy upon an old school of poets that seemed to be insisting on the mechanical imitation of antique models. It has been left to foreign readers, particularly the Japanese, to begin to restore Li and his colleagues to the respectable place they merit in the history of Chinese poetics, though there are recent signs that Chinese critics, too, are beginning to take a more fair and understanding view of their movement.

EDITIONS:

Li, Meng-yang. *K'ung-t'ung Hsien-sheng chi* 空同先生集. 63 *chüan*. *Chia-ching* period (1522-1567); rpt. Taipei, 1976. The most accessible edition.

———. *K'ung-t'ung chi*. 66 *chüan*. *Ssu-k'u ch'üan-shu chen-pen*.

———. *K'ung-t'ung Hsien-sheng chi*. 66 *chüan* & appendices, published by Teng Yün-hsiao 鄧雲霄 in 1602. The fullest, if not the earliest, extant edition.

Pien, Kung. *Pien Hua-ch'üan chi* 邊華泉集. 8 *chüan*. Taipei, 1976. The most accessible text.

———. *Hua-ch'üan chi*. 14 *chüan*. *Ssu-k'u ch'üan-shu chen-pen*. A fuller text, especially as regards the prose works.

Wang, T'ing-hsiang. *Wang shih chia-ts'ang chi* 王氏家藏集. 65 *chüan*. Taipei, 1976. Reprint of an edition that incorporates several works by Wang, including the earliest editions of his collected poetry and prose; the best text and the only one readily available (see also entries for Ho Ching-ming, K'ang Hai, and Wang Chiu-ssu).

TRANSLATIONS:

Iritani, *Konsei*, pp. 208-212 (Li Meng-yang).

STUDIES:

Chien, Chin-sung 簡錦松. "Li-Ho shih-lun yen-chiu" 李何詩論研究, M.A. thesis, National Taiwan University, 1980. An excellent recent study that improves our understanding of a number of crucial points. Includes the best chronology of Ho Ching-ming and Li Meng-yang.

DMB, pp. 841-845.

Iriya, Yoshitaka 入矢義高. *Mindai shibun* 明代詩文. Tokyo, 1978, pp. 48-67.

Kou, *P'i-p'ing shih*, pp. 297-304.

Kung, "Ming-tai ch'i-tzu."

———, "Ming ch'i-tzu."

Ma, Mao-yüan 馬茂元. "Lüeh-t'an Ming ch'i-tzu te wen-hsüeh ssu-hsiang yü Li, Ho te lun-cheng" 略談明七子的文學思想與李, *Chiang-hai hsüeh-k'an*, 1962.1, 26-29.

Min, "Ming-tai." Li Meng-yang is discussed on pp. 66-77, Ho Ching-meng on pp. 77-82; the approach is negatively evaluative, but based on accurate reading and reasonably well-balanced.

Wang, Kuei-ling . "Ming-tai ch'ien-hou ch'i-tzu te fu-ku," *Wen-hsüeh tsa-chih*, 3.5, 6 (1958), 24-32, 20-29.

Yokota, Terutoshi 横田輝俊, "Mindai," 10-15.

———. "Mindai bungakuron no tenkai" 明代文人結社の研究, Pt. I. *Hiroshima Daigaku bungakubu kiyō*, 37 (1977). Probably the best and fullest treatment; Li Meng-yang is discussed on pp. 63-81, Wang T'ing-hsiang on pp. 82-84.

Yoshikawa, Kōjirō 吉川幸次郎. "Ri Bōyō no ichisokumen: 'Kobunji' no shominsei" 李夢陽の一側面——古文辭，の庶民性. *Ritsumeikan bungaku*, 180 (1960), 190-208. Keen insight into the possible relationship between Li Meng-yang's archaism and his social background.

———. *Gen-Min*, pp. 171-183.

—DB

Li P'an-lung 李攀龍 (*tzu*, Yü-lin 于鱗, *hao*, Ts'ang-ming 滄溟, 1514-1570) was the leader of a group of poets and critics active in the mid-sixteenth century known as the Hou ch'i-tzu 後七子 (Later Seven Masters). Although the members of the group differed to some extent in their ideals, they represented a self-conscious attempt to revive and continue the Archaist program of the Ch'ien ch'i-tzu 前七子 (Earlier Seven Masters) active several decades previously under the leadership of Li Meng-yang.*

Li P'an-lung passed the *chü-jen* examination in 1540 and the *chin-shih* in 1544. From 1544 to the mid 1550s he was in office in Peking and active in literary circles. He was discharged from government service in 1557, while holding a provincial post, and spent almost all his remaining years living in style in retirement in his native district, known for his incorruptibility and evident high regard for his own worth.

As a writer Li P'an-lung kept close to the stricter version of Archaism advanced by Li Meng-yang, insisting on the close imitation of selected literary models of the past. His prose writings are written in a somewhat crabbed and difficult style, full of patches of phraseology taken from Han and pre-Han texts. Although some of his verse is attractive, Li owes his place in Chinese literary history to his leadership of the Later Seven. The makeup of this

545

literary circle changed to a certain extent over the years, but the Seven are generally recognized to have included Hsieh Chen 謝榛 (*tzu*, Mao-ch'in 茂秦, *hao*, Ssu-ming 四溟, 1495-1575), Hsü Chung-hsing 徐中行 (*tzu*, Tzu-yü 子與, *hao*, Lung-wan 龍灣, T'ien-mu shan-jen 天目山人, 1517-1578), Liang Yu-yü 梁有譽 (*tzu*, Kung-shih 公實, *hao*, Lan-ting 蘭汀, *c.* 1520-1556), Tsung Ch'en 宗臣 (*tzu*, Tzu-hsiang 子相, *hao*, Fang-ch'eng shan-jen 方城山人, 1525-1560), and Wu Kuo-lun 吳國倫 (*tzu*, Ming-ch'ing 明卿, *hao*, Ch'uan-lou 川樓, 1529-1593), plus Li himself and the protean figure Wang Shih-chen* (1526-1590). All seven were from the South, unlike the Earlier Seven, all but one of whom had been northerners. Their literary program, however, was very similar to the former group, stressing the importance of taking selected masterpieces of the past as models for their own writing and rejecting the poetry of the Sung dynasty in particular. Interestingly, Li P'an-lung did not leave any substantial body of writing on literary theory or criticism. For explicit discussions of the ideals of the Later Seven, the writings of Wang Shih-chen and Hsieh Chen must be consulted.

The latter was, in fact, the original leader of the group. Considerably older than any of the others, he was actually only a little younger than some of the Earlier Seven. He also stands out from both groups in that he was the only member of either never to pass the *chin-shih* or hold office. It has even been suggested that snobbery played a part in his eventual expulsion from the Later Seven, although he is also said to have given offense to Li P'an-lung by his rudeness. In any event, his literary ideals were actually somewhat different from Li's, being closer to the individual and expressive emphasis represented in the Earlier Seven by Ho Ching-ming.* Even so, he was as uncompromising in his standards as any of the Archaists. In his critical work, the *Shih-chia chih-shuo*, he goes so far as to suggest "improvements" to some T'ang poems, something that even his fellow Archaist Wang Shih-chen could not approve. Hsieh may have supported himself by teaching poetry writing, and this sort of teaching of "commoners" may have had something to do with the enormous influence of the Archaists during the sixteenth century.

Aside from Li, Hsieh, and Wang Shih-chen (*chin-shih*, 1547), the other members of the Later Seven all passed the *chin-shih* in 1550 and held office in Peking for some years after. Thus they resembled the Earlier Seven in being essentially a group of promising young recent graduates in the capital, self-consciously articulating a literary program intended to raise standards of composition among their contemporaries. They also resembled the earlier group in facing a powerful political antagonist, in their case the minister Yen Sung, who was eventually responsible for having Wang Shih-chen's father executed. Except for Liang Yu-yü (who returned to his native Kwangtung only three years after passing the *chin-shih* and died not long after) and Hsieh Chen, the members were all reassigned to provincial posts during the years 1555-1557 and were never all together again, although they did occasionally meet in twos or threes in later years. After the death of Li P'an-lung, Wang Shih-chen became the leader; he was the center of a younger group as well (there is one inclusive listing that refers to no fewer than "Forty Masters"). Some of these men, like Wang himself, later moved closer to the individualist position that would become dominant around the end of the century.

If he was not a critic or theorist in his own writings, Li P'an-lung was an influential anthologist. He seems to have edited a collection of T'ang poems, drawn from Kao Ping's *T'ang-shih p'in-hui*, but this was not published during his lifetime. Three published anthologies apparently based upon it are better known, although their authenticity has been disputed. One of them, the *T'ang-shih hsüan* 唐詩選, became very influential in Japan and helped determine Japanese taste in T'ang poetry for many generations.

EDITIONS:

Li P'an-lung. *Ts'ang-ming Hsien-sheng chi* 滄溟先生集. 32 *chüan*. Taipei, 1976.

———. *Ts'ang-ming chi.* 31 *chüan. Ssu-k'u ch'üan-shu chen-pen.*

Hsieh, Chen. *Ssu-ming shan-jen ch'üan-chi* 四溟山人全集. 24 *chüan.* Rpt. Taipei, 1976. Consists of Hsieh's poems in 20 *chüan,* plus his critical work *Shih-chia chih-shuo* 詩家直說, in 4; the best available text.

———. *Ssu-ming chi.* 10 *chüan. Ssu-k'u ch'üan-shu chen-pen.* The poems only.

———. *Ssu-ming shih-hua.* 4 *chüan.* The same text as the *Shih-chia chih-shuo;* there are editions in the *Hai-shan hsien-kuan ts'ung-shu* (rpt. in *PPTSCC*) and the *Hsü li-tai shih-hua;* neither is a better text than the one in Hsieh's collected works (both are slightly incomplete), nor are they any longer more accessible than it.

Hsü, Chung-hsing. *T'ien-mu Hsien-sheng chi.* 20 *chüan.* Rpt. Taipei, 1976. A reprint of an early edition, perhaps the original; the only accessible text, and probably the best.

Liang, Yu-yü. *Lan-ting ts'un-kao* 蘭汀存稿. 9 *chüan.* Rpt., Taipei, 1976. Reprint of the best available edition, perhaps the original.

Tsung, Ch'en. *Tsung Tzu-hsiang Hsien-sheng chi.* 25 *chüan.* Not seen, apparently the fullest text.

———. *Tsung Tzu-hsiang chi.* 15 *chüan.* Rpt. Taipei, 1976, and *Ssu-k'u ch'üan-shu chen-pen.* Two accessible editions, the former more so and based on an earlier copy; contents the same.

Wu, Kuo-lun. *Tan-sui-tung kao* 甔甀洞藁. 54 *chüan.* Rpt. Taipei, 1976. Reprint of a Ming edition, perhaps the original. The *Tan-sui-tung hsü-kao* 甔甀洞續藁, 27 *chüan,* is not included in the reprint, but is available in a microfilm copy from the "Peiping Library Rare Books" collection.

TRANSLATIONS.

Bryant, "Selected Ming Poems"; for Li P'an-lung, see p. 90.

Davis, *Penguin,* p. 60.

Demiéville, *Anthologie,* pp. 484-485.

Iritani, Sensuke 入谷仙介, Fukumoto Masakazu 福本雅一, and Matsumura Takashi 松村昂. *Kinsei shishū* 近世詩集. Tokyo, 1971, pp. 229-239 (Hsieh Chen and Li P'an-lung).

STUDIES:

DMB, pp. 845-847.

Kung, "Ming ch'i-tzu."

———, "Ming-tai ch'i-tzu."

Kuo, *P'i-p'ing shih,* pp. 315-322.

Lynn, Richard John. "Orthodoxy and Enlightenment: Wang Shih-chen's Theory of Poetry and Its Antecedents," in *The Unfolding of Neo-Confucianism,* William Theodore deBary, *et al.,* eds., New York, 1975, pp. 233-234.

Maeno, Naoaki 前野直彬. "Ri Sōmei no buntai" 李滄溟の文體, *Tōhōgaku,* 4 (1952), 73-82.

———. "Mindai kobunjiha no bungakuron" 明代古文辭派の文學論, *Nippon Chūgoku Gakkaihō,* 16 (1964), 157-165.

Min, "Ming-tai"; the Later Seven and their followers are discussed on pp. 83-92.

Wong, Sui-Kit. "A Reading of the *Ssu-ming Shih-hua,*" *TkR,* 2.2/3.1 (1971-72), 237-249. The reading is brief and idiosyncratic.

Yamagishi, Tomoni 山岸共. "Tōshisen no jittai to gishosetsu hihan" 唐詩選の實態と僞書說批判, *Nippon Chūgoku gakkaihō,* 31 (1979), 197-210. A detailed study, replacing earlier attempts, of the nature and authorship of two poetry anthologies whose attribution to Li P'an-lung has been disputed.

Yokota, Terutoshi 横田輝俊. "Mindai bungakuron no tenkai, Pt. II" 明代文學論の展開. *Hiroshima Daigaku bungakubu kiyō,* 38 (1978), 75-135.

———, "Mindai," 15-20.

Yoshikawa, Kōjirō 吉川幸次郎. *Gen-Min shi gaisetsu* 元明詩概說. Tokyo, 1963, pp. 193-202 (Li P'an-lung).

—DB

Li Pao-chia 李寶嘉 (*tzu,* Po-yüan 伯元, *hao,* Nan-t'ing t'ing-chang 南亭亭長, 1867-1906), a prolific writer of the late-Ch'ing period, was born in Shantung, although his ancestral home was in Wu-chin 武進 (modern Ch'ang-chou 常州 in Kiangsu). He died in Shanghai at the early age of thirty-nine. As a multi-faceted littérateur, Li was a fiction writer, poet, essayist, ballad writer, seal carver, calligrapher, and the editor of several tabloids and a periodical on fiction. His works include several novels, including the well-known *Kuan-ch'ang hsien-hsing chi* 官場現形記 (The Bureaucracy Exposed), the *Wen-ming hsiao-shih* 文明小史 (A Brief History of Modern Times), and the *Hou ti-yü* 活地獄 (Living Hell). He also produced a ballad, *Keng-tzu kuo-pien t'an-tz'u* 庚子國變彈詞 (*T'an-tz'u,* on the Boxer Rebellion of 1900) and a collection of miscellaneous writings, *Nan-t'ing ssu-hua* 南亭四話 (Four Miscellanies from the Southern Pavilion). There are also a number of works of doubtful authorship attributed to him, such as the novels *Hai-t'ien hung-hsüeh chi* 海天鴻雪記 (Boundless Snow), *Fan-hua meng* 繁華夢 (Glittering Dreams), and *Chung-kuo hsien-tsai chi* 中國現在記 (Present-day China).

Li Pao-chia's life can be divided into three periods. He spent his childhood and early manhood (1867-1892) in Shantung. Then he moved with his parents back to their native district of Wu-chin. For the next five years he studied for the *hsiu-ts'ai* examination, which he passed. He was unsuccessful, however, in the *chü-jen* examination. At the age of thirty, Li Pao-chia left home, living his last ten years in Shanghai as a member of the new class of journalist-littérateurs.

Li began as the editor and principal writer of several Shanghai tabloids: *Chih-nan pao* 指南報 (The Guide), *Yu-hsi pao* 遊戲報 (Amusement News), and *Fan-hua pao* 繁華報 (sometimes also known as *Shih-chieh fan-hua pao* 世界繁華報 (The Glittering World). It was in the *Fan-hua pao* that Li's first major literary work, the *Keng-tzu kuo-pien t'an-tz'u*, was serialized. His *Kuan-ch'ang hsien-hsing chi* was serialized in the same newspaper in 1903. By this time Li Pao-chia was well known and he became the editor of the reputable *Hsiu-hsiang hsiao-shuo* 繡像小說 (Illustrated Fiction), published by the largest publisher at the time, the Commerical Press of Shanghai. From 1903 until his death, Li edited and contributed to this highly popular fortnightly.

Li Pao-chia's writings, characterized by some as satirical, vituperative, and exaggerated, were very popular at the time and suited the social and political climate of the late-Ch'ing era. Li's *Keng-tzu kuo-pien t'an-tz'u* recounts the events of the Boxer Rebellion from its origins to the disastrous conclusion in 1901. Written immediately after the incidents, Li wanted to keep the record straight and the memories alive as a historical lesson. *Kuan-ch'ang hsien-hsing chi*, a long novel in sixty chapters written over a five-year period (1901-1905), mercilessly exposes through a series of story-cycles the deceit, corruption, oppression, and exploitation rampant in government. *Wen-ming hsiao-shih* (1903), a shorter novel,

but also in sixty chapters, satirizes the pseudo-reformers who were not quite able to cope with the problems and complexities of modernization. *Huo ti-yü*, the last of Li's major works, which he left unfinished, gives a gruesome account of the malpractices of the penal and judicial systems.

Artistically uneven, Li's works served an important political and social function in a critical transitional period. These novels portrayed China in a serious state of disrepair and in need of drastic change. Although Li Pao-chia himself was a moderate reformer and did not believe in radical changes, his works, at least to later readers, indicated otherwise.

EDITIONS:

Huo ti-yü 活地獄. Shanghai, 1956.

Keng-tzu kuo-pien t'an-tz'u 庚子國變彈詞. Shanghai, 1935.

Kuan-ch'ang hsien-hsing chi 官場現形記. 2v. Peking, 1957.

Nan-t'ing ssu-hua 南亭四話. Taipei, 1971.

Wen-ming hsiao-shih 文明小史. Hong Kong, 1958.

TRANSLATIONS:

Lancashire, Douglas. "Modern Times," *Renditions*, 2 (Spring 1974), 126-164. A translation of the first five chapters of the *Wen-ming hsiao-shih*.

STUDIES:

Holoch, Donald. "A Novel of Setting: The Bureaucrats," in *The Chinese Novel at the Turn of the Century*, Milena Doleželová-Velingerová, ed., Toronto, 1980, pp. 76-115.

Lancashire, Douglas. *Li Po-yüan*. Boston, 1981.

Li, Mao-su 李茂肅. "Ts'ung *Huo ti-yü* k'an Li Po-yüan hou-ch'i tso-p'in te ch'ing-hsiang" 從活地獄看李伯元後期作品的傾向, *Kuang-ming jih-pao* (Wen-hsüeh i-ch'an, 545), 6 (March 1966).

Mugio, Tomie 麥生登美江. "Ri Hakugen no sōsaku ishiki" 李伯元の創作意識, *Shimmatsu shōsetsu kenkyū*, 1 (October 1977), 41-63.

Ruh, Christel. *Das Kuan-ch'ang hsien-hsing chi. Ein Beispiel für den politischen Roman der ausgehenden Ch'ing-Zeit (Versuch einer Analyse der Idee und Struktur der Kapitel 1-30 und 60 des Werkes)*. Bern and Frankfurt, 1974.

Wang, Chün-nien 王俊年. "Wan-Ch'ing she-hui te chao-yao ching: Ch'ung-tu chin-tai liang-pu ch'ien-tse hsiao-shuo" 晚清社會的照妖鏡:

重讀近代兩部譴責小說, *Tu-shu*, 1979 4 (July 1979), 40-45.

Wei, Shao-ch'ang 魏紹昌. *Li Po-yüan yen-chiu tzu-liao* 李伯元研究資料. Shanghai, 1980.

—PL

Li Po (or *Pai*) 李白 (*tzu*, T'ai-po太白 or T'ai-pai, 701-762) generally shares or competes with Tu Fu* for the honor of being the greatest of the T'ang poets. Li's birthplace is uncertain, perhaps in Central Asia, and a minor branch of Li Po studies centers on the irresolvable question of whether Li was of Turkic origin. Whatever his background, Li grew up in west China (modern Szechwan), and the conventions of the Szechwanese "type" exerted a strong influence on his self-image. The bravura of his poetic voice belonged to a long tradition of poets from the Szechwan region, from Ssu-ma Hsiang-ju* in the Western Han to Ch'en Tzu-ang* in the Early T'ang, and, after Li, to Su Shih* in the Northern Sung.

In the mid-720s Li Po traveled down through the Yangtze Valley, seeking the social connections necessary to gain public recognition. Through his acquaintance with Wu Yün 吳筠 (d. 778), a failed examination candidate turned wizard, Li was summoned to the court of Hsüan-tsung in 742 and given a post in the new Han-lin Academy (an appointment that lay outside the channels of usual bureaucratic advancement). While serving in court, Li Po traded on his reputation for drunken insouciance and became the subject of numerous anecdotes. However, the favor that he enjoyed rested on unstable ground, and in 744 he was expelled from court. Thereafter, Li wandered in the east and southeast, proclaiming himself an unappreciated man of genius who had been driven from court by powerful enemies. After the outbreak of the An Lu-shan Rebellion, he became implicated in the secondary revolt of the Prince of Yün. Whether Li's complicity was voluntary remains uncertain, but when the revolt was smashed, Li was arrested for treason. Eventually he was released and spent his last years wandering in the Yangtze Valley, vainly seeking patrons to restore him to favor with the central government.

Of the 1004 poems ascribed to Li in the *Ch'üan T'ang shih** (additional attributions in other sources bring the number to just over 1100), many are probably spurious. Li Po was an easy poet to imitate, and since most of his *yüeh-fu** and songs circulated orally, his name became a convenient one on which to hang poems of unknown authorship. Some studies have attempted to prove the spuriousness of certain attributions, but even so, Li's collected works in their present form may still include a great many false attributions.

Although Li Po's corpus contains about sixty pieces of prose and eight *fu*,* it is as a poet that Li is known. The first part of his poetic collection contains fifty-nine pentasyllabic "old-style" poems collectively entitled *Ku-feng* 古風 (Old Manner). They are written in the thematic and stylistic tradition of the poetry of the Chien-an and Wei eras, as it was understood in the T'ang. These works date from various periods of Li's life and include a number of concealed references to topical events. In the *Ku-feng* Li Po often adopts the voice of a Confucian moralist, a voice entirely proper for the style in which he was writing, but one opposed to his usual pose as inebriate eccentric.

After the *Ku-feng* in Li's collected works, there is a body of *yüeh-fu* and songs (*ko-hsing* 歌行). These two categories are only loosely differentiated, the former tending to adopt the personae of various *yüeh-fu* "types," the latter tending to be the poet speaking in his own voice. Li was best known to his contemporaries for these *yüeh-fu* and songs, and on them his later reputation was founded. "Shu-tao nan" 蜀道難 (Hard Roads to Shu), anthologized in Yin Fan's *Ho-yüeh Ying-ling chi* 河嶽英靈集 (753), is an excellent example of Li Po's *yüeh-fu* in the most extravagant manner. Using wildly irregular line lengths, Szechwanese exclamations, and long subordinate clauses normally excluded from both poetry and literary prose, Li hyperbolically described the difficulties of the mountain journey from Ch'ang-an to Ch'eng-tu. In reference to poems such as this, Li's contemporary Yin Fan described the poet's work as "strangeness on top of strangeness." Li Po's *yüeh-fu* and songs used folk motifs, fantastic journeys, mythic beings, and evocations of moments in history and legend to create a poetry of extreme and intense situations. Yet even in Li's wildest flights of fancy there is a strong undercurrent of irony, and his conscious excesses are such that the poet's stance is revealed as merely playful.

Occasional poems occupy the largest part of Li's collected works. A few of the more famous are merely occasional applications of the style of Li's *yüeh-fu* and songs, but most are formally more conventional. Li wrote such poems with great facility, and even though he frequently achieved a simple felicity beyond the reach of his more cautious contemporaries, his occasional works are often marred by carelessness. In general, Li Po lacked the carefully controlled craft that came so readily to his contemporaries, who were raised in the upper-class circles of the capital.

Following Li's occasional poems in the collected works, there is a small group of private poems containing many of Li's most famous pieces in even line lengths. Poems such as "Yüeh-hsia tu cho" (Drinking Alone by Moonlight) celebrate the self-image of drunken insouciance in which Li took pride. Readers of classical poetry have always valued a poem's ability to embody a strong and identifiable personality; in the case of Li Po, personality becomes the subject rather than the involuntary mode of the poem. Even Li's most speculative fantasy points more strongly to the poet's imaginative capacity than to the otherworldly objects of his vision.

Li Po's poetry caused something of a sensation in the 740s and early 750s, but his stature as a contemporary poet was probably lower than that of Wang Wei* or Wang Ch'ang-ling.* As is the case with Tu Fu, little attention was given to Li's work in the conservative atmosphere of the later part of the eighth century. The honor accorded Li by mid-T'ang poets such as

Han Yü* and Po Chü-i* first raised Li, along with Tu Fu, to preeminence among all the poets of the dynasty. Evaluation of the relative merits of Li Po and Tu Fu later became a minor critical genre, and while Tu Fu had perhaps the larger following, Li Po has had his partisans, from Ou-yang Hsiu* to the modern scholar Kuo Mo-jo.

Li Po was one of the first major figures in what was to become a cult of spontaneity in Chinese poetry. Li proclaimed, and others admired, his capacity to dash off poems in the heat of wine or inspiration. In the case of Li Po, the interest in rapid and spontaneous composition was linked to a belief in innate genius that found its purest expression when untainted by the reflective considerations of craft. Such a concept of individual and innate genius, inimical to plodding poetic craft, is a historical growth within civilization; and the development of such a concept of artistic genius in China owes much to Li Po, who so often made his own genius the true topic of his poetry.

Stylistic simplicity was a natural consequence of spontaneous composition (or of the desire to give the appearance of spontaneity). Not only is the diction and syntax of Li's poetry generally less bookish, but Li's poetry is noticably more straightforward than that of his contemporaries. Li Po often referred to persons and events of legend and history, but he did not use textual allusions with the same frequency or precision as his younger contemporary Tu Fu.

Li Po paid Taoist esoterica considerable attention, but this was perhaps less a satisfaction of genuine spiritual interests than appreciation of a source of delightful material for poetic fantasy. It is Li Po's capacity for fantasy which, more than any other quality, sets him apart from his contemporaries and won him the admiration of later generations. Most T'ang poets (with exceptions such as Li Po's spiritual descendent Li Ho) were most comfortable treating the world before their eyes; Li Po greets the immortals and watches their flights with greater ease and familiarity than when he bids farewell to a friend.

EDITIONS:

Kuo, Yün-p'eng 郭雲鵬, ed. *Fen-lei pu-chu Li T'ai-po shih* 分類補註李太白詩. *SPTK*. Kuo's commentary includes earliest efforts by the Yüan scholars Yang Ch'i-hsien 楊齊賢, and Hsiao Shih-yün 蕭士贇. This edition also includes Li Po's prose.

The most extensive commentary is that of Wang Ch'i 王琦 (1696-1774); it is the most frequently reprinted, under a number of titles. Wang draws from the commentaries of Yang and Hsiao as well as from notes by other scholars, but he also corrects them and adds his own commentary on Li Po's prose.

For a discussion of editions, see Hanabusa Hideki 花房英樹, *A Concordance to the Poems of Li Po*, Kyoto, 1957, pp. 6-30, and T'ang Ming-min 唐明敏, "Li Po chi ch'i shih chih pan-pen" 李白及其詩之版本, unpublished M.A. thesis, Kuo-li Cheng-chih ta-hsüeh, Taipei, 1975.

TRANSLATIONS:

Cooper, Arthur. *Li Po and Tu Fu.* Baltimore, 1973.

Demiéville, *Anthologie*, pp. 220-246.

Eide, Elling. *Poems by Li Po,* with a separate volume, *Translator's Note and Finding Lists.* Lexington, Kentucky, 1984. Elegant translations of fifty poems. A phonograph record of reconstructed T'ang music enclosed in the back cover.

Kubo, Tensui 久保天隨. *Ri Taihaku* 李太白. Tokyo, 1928. Complete Japanese translation.

Shigenyoshi, Obata. *Li Po, the Chinese Poet.* Tokyo, 1935.

Sunflower, pp. 101-114.

STUDIES:

These are more numerous than Li Po's poems: for a bibliography of articles see *Li Po yen-chiu lun-wen chi* 李白研究論文集, Peking, 1964, pp. 417-425; and *Chūgoku koten kenkyū*, 16 (1968), 78-84.

Chan, Ying 詹鍈. *Li Po shih-wen hsi-nien* 李白詩文繫年. Peking, 1958.

Ch'i, Wei-han 戚維翰. *Li Po yen-chiu* 李白研究. Taipei, 1975.

Eide, Elling O. "On Li Po," in *Perspectives on the T'ang*, Arthur Wright and Denis Twitchett, eds., New Haven, 1973, pp. 367-403.

Kuo, Mo-jo 郭沫若. *Li Po yü Tu Fu* 李白與杜甫. Peking, 1971.

Lin, Keng 林庚. *Shih-jen Li Po* 詩人李白. Shanghai, 1958.

Matsuura, Tomohisa 松浦友久. *Ri Haku kenkyū* 李白研究. Tokyo, 1976.

Moore, Paul Douglas. "Stories and Poems About the T'ang Poet Li Po." Unpublished Ph.D. dissertation, Georgetown University, 1982.

Ono, Jitsunosuke 大野實之助. *Ri Taihaku kenkyū* 李太白研究. Tokyo, 1959.

Waley, Arthur. *The Poetry and Career of Li Po.* London, 1950.

Wong, Siu-kit. *The Genius of Li Po.* Hong Kong, 1974.

—SO

Li Shang-yin 李商隱 (*tzu*, I-shan 義山, *hao*, Yü-hsi-sheng 玉溪生, also Fan-nan-sheng 樊南生, 813?-858) was born in Huo-chia 獲嘉 (modern Honan), where his father was then the magistrate. He grew up in Cheng-chou 鄭州 and Lo-yang after his father's death in 821, passed the *chin-shih* examination in 837, and subsequently held a number of junior posts both in the capital and in various prefectures. He never attained high rank and died without office in Cheng-chou.

Li Shang-yin's 598 extant poems can be divided into four groups. The first consists of ambiguous poems, either labeled "Wu t'i" 無題 (Without Title), or bearing titles that are simply the opening words. Apparently concerned with clandestine love, these poems are subjects of controversy. Some scholars interpret them as autobiographical poems about secret love affairs with court ladies and Taoist priestesses. It seems fruitless to read them as *poèmes à clef* and try to identify the supposed prototypes of the *dramatis personae;* instead, it is more rewarding to reconstruct, from the text of each poem, a dramatic context which allows a consistent reading, without identifying the speaker with the author. Seen in this light, these poems are effective explorations of various facets of love: desire, hope, joy, frustration, jealousy, tenderness, despair. They are unusual among Chinese poems for their intensity and complexity of emotion and their density and richness of language. Replete with sensuous imagery and recondite allusions, they are structurally tight and syntactically compact. Some of them, such as "Chin se"

錦瑟 (The Richly Painted Zither), his most famous poem, actually deal with more than love, using several levels of reality and fusing the past with the present, the real with the imaginary, and the historical with the mythical.

To the second group belong personal and social poems of a more conventional kind, including fond recollections of the poet's deceased wife, affectionate descriptions of his children, sad valedictions as well as playful jibes addressed to friends, and polite eulogies presented to patrons. They tend to be more straightforward in manner and simple in diction than the ambiguous poems, but they are by no means merely perfunctory. On the contrary, they are often fresh and limpid, treating conventional themes with new insight.

The third group comprises poems on historical or contemporary events. Sometimes he comments on history to draw a lesson for the present; at other times he openly voices his indignation against the abuses of power by court officials, eunuchs, and provincial warlords. Although his analysis of political and social conditions may not be original or even accurate, these are successful poems of protest. His sarcasm concerning high officials and even the emperor is biting and witty, and his use of historical analogies both ingenious and innovative.

To the last group may be assigned poems on objects (yung-wu shih 詠物詩), which also have been interpreted allegorically. In fact, the poems are heterogeneous in nature: some may contain specific references, others may be symbolic in a general way, still others may be jeux d'esprit or poetic conundrums. For instance, the willow (liu) may refer to a girl named Willow Branch (Liu-chih)—Li wrote a number of poems about her, with a preface explaining the circumstances in which he met her, but failed to have a love affair with her. Yet in other poems the willow may symbolize any beautiful woman, and in still others it may be a pun on the surname of one of Li's patrons, Liu Chung-ying 柳仲郢. Each poem in this category has to be treated on its own terms.

Li Shang-yin's poetry embodies passion, commitment, and conflict. It contains elements of Confucianism, Buddhism, and Taoism without reaching a complete synthesis of the three. There are signs of a conflict between Confucian puritanism and Buddhist asceticism, on the one hand, and sybaritic hedonism associated with the popular Taoist quest for the elixir of life, on the other. There is also a conflict between the Confucian ideal of public service and the wish to withdraw from society, prompted by both Buddhism and Taoism. These conflicts remain unresolved in Li's poetry, although towards the end of his life he embraced Buddhism and wrote a gatha on his deathbed.

In general, Li Shang-yin extended the scope of Chinese poetry by exploring spheres of experience previously untouched by poets, or by exploring familiar worlds with a new intensity and a self-awareness that often led to irony. It is perhaps this last quality, together with his striking use of language, that makes him particularly appealing to sophisticated modern readers. At the same time, his exploitation of the potentials of the Chinese language has exerted a profound influence on later poetry.

Apart from being a major poet, Li Shang-yin was also a master of p'ien-wen.* He made two collections of his works in this genre, although he apparently never compiled a collection of his poetry. His p'ien-wen pieces show some of the characteristics of his poetry: skillful use of allusions, exact parallelism, and elaborate phraseology. Less read than his poetry, they nonetheless remain superb specimens of this style.

EDITIONS:
Fan-nan wen-chi hsiang-chu 樊南文集詳注, Feng Hao, ed. 1765. SPPY.
Fan-nan wen-chi pu-pien 樊南文集補編, Ch'ien Chen-lun 錢振倫, ed., 1864. SPPY.
Li I-shan shih-chi 李義山詩集. Chu Ho-ling 朱鶴齡, ed., 1659. Rpt., 1870. Commentaries by Chu I-tsun,* Ho Cho 何焯, and Chi Yün,* with the words chi p'ing 輯評 added to the title. Valuable as a collection of traditional criticism of Li's poetry.

Li Shang-yin shih-hsüan 李商隱詩選. Anhwei Shih-fan Ta-hsüeh Chung-wen hsi 安徽師範大學中文系, ed. Peking, 1978. Selection of 104 poems, with notes and an introduction.

Li Shang-yin shih-hsüan 李商隱詩選. Ch'en Yung-cheng 陳永正, comp. Hong Kong, 1980.

Yü-hsi-sheng shih chien-chu 玉溪生詩箋註. Feng Hao 馮浩, ed. 1870. Rpt. *SPPY.* The standard edition.

TRANSLATIONS:

Liu, James J. Y. *The Poetry of Li Shang-yin.* Chicago, 1969.

Takahashi, Kazumi 高橋和巳. *Ri Shō-in* 李商隱. Tokyo, 1958.

von Zach, *Han Yü,* pp. 353-373.

STUDIES:

Chang, Shu-hsiang 張淑香. *Li I-shan shih hsi-lun* 李義山詩析論. Macao, n.d.

Chang, Ts'ai-t'ien 張采田. *Yü-hsi-sheng nien-p'u hui-chien* 玉溪生年譜會箋. Peking, 1917; rpt. Shanghai, 1963. Together with *Li I-shan shih pien-cheng* 李義山詩辨正.

Ku, I-chün 顧翊羣. *Li Shang-yin p'ing-lun* 李商隱評論. Taipei, 1958.

Liu, *ibid.*

Su, Hsüeh-lin 蘇雪林. *Li I-shan lüan-ai shih-chi k'ao* 李義山戀愛事跡考. Shanghai, 1927; rpt., Shanghai, 1948 as *Yü-hsi shih-mi* 玉溪詩謎.

Wu, Tiao-kung 吳調公. *Li Shang-yin yen-chiu* 李商隱研究. Shanghai, 1982.

Yang, Liu 楊柳. *Li Shang-yin p'ing-chuan* 李商隱評傳. Nanking, 1982.

—JL

Li T'iao-yüan 李調元 (*tzu*, Keng-t'ang 羹堂, *hao*, Yü-ts'un 雨村, T'ung-shan 童山, Ho-chou 鶴洲, Wan-chai 卍齋, Ch'un-weng 春翁, 1734-1803) was an official, a bibliophile, and a prolific scholar, compiler, and editor with wide-ranging interests. From Lo-chiang 羅江 (Szechwan), he passed the *chin-shih* examination in 1763, and served in a variety of official posts until his retirement in 1784. His official career included assignments in the Han-lin Academy and the Board of Civil Offices in Peking, a term as Education Commissioner in Kwangtung, and an appointment as a Circuit Intendant in Chihli.

Li T'iao-yüan is probably most notable for the range of his scholarly interests and his prolific writing, editing and compiling. During his official assignment in Kwang-

tung from 1777 to 1780, for example, he compiled a collection of works by local authors, *Yüeh-tung kuan-hai chi* 粵東觀海集 (10 *chüan*), a collection of local folksongs (*Yüeh-feng* 粵風, 4 *chüan*), a collection of notes on the examination system (*Chih-i k'e so-chi* 制義科瑣記, 5 *chüan*), and a collection of his own travel notes on Kwangtung (*Nan-Yüeh pi-chi* 南越筆記 16 *chüan*).

Of Li's literary writings, the most noteworthy are his collected essays (*T'ung-shan wen-chi* 童山文集, 20 *chüan*) and poetry (*T'ung-shan shih-chi* 童山詩集, 42 *chüan*), his selected writings (*T'ung-shan hsüan-chi* 童山選集, 12 *chüan*), short stories (*Wei-che ts'ung-t'an* 尾蔗叢談, 4 *chüan*), and notes on *fu,** *shih,** *tz'u,** *ch'ü,** and drama (see bibliography below). He also edited two major poetry collections: *Shu-ya* 蜀雅 (20 *chüan*), an anthology of Szechwan poets from the early- and mid-Ch'ing period, and *Ch'üan Wu-tai shih* 全五代詩 (100 *chüan*), an expansion of Wang Shih-chen's (1634-1711)* work of the same title.

Li T'iao-yüan also wrote a number of works of classical scholarship, and compiled several reference works on the pronunciation and meanings of rare and archaic characters and of classical phrases. He was particularly adept at this latter type of work, producing among other things an expanded version of Yang Shen's* *Ch'i-tzu yün* 奇字韻 under the title *Ch'i-tzu ming* 奇字名, a dictionary of obscure words; a separate work on archaic characters (*Tzu-lu* 字錄, 2 *chüan*); a list of characters with multiple sounds (*Hui-yin* 彙音, 2 *chüan*); a study of literary terms (*T'ung-ku* 通詁, 2 *chüan*); a collection of frequently-confused characters and meanings (*Liu-shu fen-hao* 六書分毫, 2 *chüan*); a collection of colloquial expressions found in literary works (*Fang-yen tsao* 方言藻, 2 *chüan*); and a reference work on sources of classical quotations (*T'o-yü hsin-shih* 唾餘新拾, 10 *chüan* with supplements).

Li T'iao-yüan was an avid book collector, and while working on the *Ssu-k'u ch'üan-shu* (see Chi Yün) compilation project, he had a number of rare works related to Szechwan province copied for his personal library. He was interested in history

553

and politics as well as language and literature, writing a local history of his native district (*Lo-chiang hsien-chih* 羅江縣志, 10 *chüan*), a work on official terminology (*Kuan-hua* 官話, 3 *chüan*), a series of notes on men who were famous through their success in the Ch'ing examination system (*Tan-mo lu* 淡墨錄, 16 *chüan*), and a set of notes on Szechwan (*Ching-wa tsa-chi* 井蛙雜記, 10 *chüan*). He admired the Ming scholar Yang Shen,* edited a number of Yang's writings, and included them in his own collected works.

EDITIONS:

Ching-wa tsa-chi. Taipei, 1969.
Chü-hua 劇話, in *Hsi-ch'ü lun-chu*, v. 8, pp. 31-72.
Chü-hua and *Ch'ü-hua* 曲話. Taipei, 1960.
Ch'üan Wu-tai shih. Taipei, 1972.
Fu-hua 賦話. Taipei, 1964 and 1971; also Hong Kong, 1976.
Tan-mo lu. Taipei, 1969.
T'ung-shan hsüan-chi, T'ung-shan shih-chi, and *T'ung-shan wen-chi,* in *Han-hai.* Taipei, *Hung-yeh shu-chü,* 1968. Facsimile reprint of the 1882 edition; also in *TSCC.*
Yü-ts'un ch'ü-hua 雨村曲話, in *Hsi-ch'ü lun-chu*, v. 8, pp. 1-29.
Yü-ts'un shih-hua. Taipei, 1971.

STUDIES:

ECCP, pp. 486-488.

—PR

Li Tung-yang 李東陽 (*tzu,* Pin-chih 賓之, *hao,* Hsi-ya 西涯, 1447-1516) was the most important poet and the most influential literary critic between the early Ming generation that included Kao Ch'i* and Liu Chi,* and that of the *Ch'ien ch'i-tzu* (Earlier Seven Masters—see Li Meng-yang) including Li Meng-yang and Ho Ching-ming.* The latter group was made up of writers who had been his followers or had entered government service under his sponsorship, and thus his influence on the course of literary history during the sixteenth century and thereafter was considerable.

Li began his career as a *Wunderkind,* presented in audience to the emperor at the age of three. At sixteen he passed the *chin-shih* examination and began an official career that lasted without interruption for

fifty years. For many years the leading figure in literary circles in the capital, he exerted a great influence on literary developments both through his own work and through the influence of his many disciples and followers. He was almost too successful, for the necessary compromises he made to retain influence at court—influence he seems to have wielded for the sake of public good rather than personal advantage—clouded his reputation among later commentators who could afford to be more exacting in their standards. His very success in attracting the most promising members of the younger generation of writers, including Li Meng-yang, Ho Ching-ming, and Yang Shen,* led to his literary reputation being eclipsed by theirs. Nevertheless, he is generally acknowledged to have been the most important Ming forerunner of the Archaist movement of the mid-Ming.

Li's position in literary history is thus a complex and interesting one. He shared some beliefs with the Archaists, such as the superiority of T'ang poetry over Sung. He pointed out (incorrectly) that it was only in the Sung that people began to theorize about poetry, and he himself valued the work of only one Sung critic, Yen Yü, whose *Ts'ang-lang shih-hua** was to become the favored text of the Archaists. Unlike the Archaists, however, Li was firmly opposed to the imitation of earlier poets or styles. He stressed naturalness instead, but a naturalness founded upon a firm control of poetic techniques, especially a mastery of prosody and rhythmic effects. It was his preference for natural expression over imitation that made him a favorite of Ch'ien Ch'ien-i,* who was a severe critic of the Archaists. In fact, Ch'ien included more poems by Li in his anthology, the *Lieh-ch'ao shih-chi,* than by any other poet except Kao Ch'i and Liu Chi.

In spite of his importance and the favor that his poetry found with early anthologists of Ming verse, Li is known today chiefly for his set of 101 "Ni-ku yüeh-fu" 擬古樂府 (Ballads in the Style of Antiquity), written in the manner of Han and early Six Dynasties *yüeh-fu* poetry. The form of these poems would seem to belie his expressed opposition to imitation, but it was presumably influential in forming the preference of such Archaists as Ho Ching-ming for pre-T'ang works as models for their old-style verse.

EDITIONS:

Huai-lu-t'ang kao 懷麓堂稿 (蕙). 100 *chüan*. The best edition is the original (1518). There is a reprint in the *Li-tai hua-chia shih-wen-chi* series.

[*Huai-]lu-t'ang shih-hua*. 1 *chüan*. *Chih-pu-tsu chai ts'ung-shu* (reprint in the *PPTSCC*) and *Hsü Li-tai shih-hua*. The latter is the most accessible edition; the *Pai-pu* reprint the best.

TRANSLATIONS:

Bryant, Daniel. "Selected Ming Poems," *Renditions*, 8 (Autumn 1977), 85-91; for Li Tung-yang, see p. 88.

Demiéville, *Anthologie*, pp. 471-472.

Iritani, Sensuke 入谷仙介, Fukumoto Masakazu 福本雅一, and Matesumura Takashi 松村昂. *Kinsei shishū* 近世詩集. Tokyo, 1971, pp. 180-194.

STUDIES:

ECCP, pp. 877-881.

Kuo, *P'i-p'ing shih*, pp. 289-295.

P'eng, Kuo-tung 彭國棟. "Chi Li Hsi-ya" 記李西涯, *I-wen chang-ku ts'ung-t'an* 藝文掌故叢談, Taipei, 1956, pp. 169-173. Chiefly composed of extracts from Ch'ing-dynasty poems and essays that touch on Li.

Yokota, "Mindai bungakuron," 57-62.

—DB

Li Yü 李煜 (*tzu*, Ch'ung-kuang 重光, 937-978), also known as *Nan-T'ang hou-chu* 南唐後主 (The Last Emperor of Southern T'ang), ascended the throne in 961 and was taken prisoner in 975 when the House of Sung conquered his kingdom. He is regarded as the first true master of *tz'u** poetry, which through him became the medium for self-expression among the literati. Because of its origin in the teahouse milieu, *tz'u* had previously been restricted to the topics of love between man and woman and of nature. It was often trivial. Li Yü, however, gradually opened the vista of the *tz'u* from women's apartments to larger concerns such as philosophical and political reflections on the downfall of the dynasty, the brevity of life, etc. Among his forty-five extant *tz'u* this transformation can be easily traced in three phases: (1) from his youth till the death of his first wife in 964 (songs 1-13); (2) from 965 until his captivity in 975 (songs 14-31); (3) the last three years of his life (songs 32-45). The songs of the first phase are devoted particularly to the unrestrained love-life at court. Famous are the two final lines of "I-hu chu" 一斛珠 (number 9) which describes one of Li Yü's favorites as she was "chewing pieces of red silk, /and spitting them at her lover with a smile." In the second phase loneliness and sorrow are common as in "Ch'ing-p'ing yüeh" 清平樂 (number 17): "The sorrow of separation is just like the spring grass, /The more you walk, the farther you go, the more it grows." Only the songs of the third phase, lamenting the downfall of his kingdom, develop a political tendency. They are filled with nostalgia.

Li Yü's earlier work is dominated by the descriptive and the narrative trends with a tendency toward creation of a plot—a *novum* for the *tz'u*—see, for instance, numbers 4 ("P'u-sa man" 菩薩蠻) and 9. The later work exhibits a dense, lyrical mood. The ever stronger autobiographical character of Li Yü's poetry leads to a change from a female persona to ego. The later author does not need persons or things to express himself, but puts his own *self* into the foreground. This kind of subjectivity was innovative in *tz'u*. It often approached sentimentality but was saved by turning Li Yü's personal suffering into a more universal set of emotions which could be shared by his audience.

In form, Li Yü introduced two-stanza composition and the long, flowing nine-character rhythm. The two-stanza composition treats two lyrical moments; the change from the first to the second stanza is often effected by a word like "suddenly" *i-tan* 一旦 (see, for example, number 32). The nine-character rhythm is used as an effective contrast to the three- or five-character line. The concentration on the suffering *ego* creates the emotional style typical of Li Yü. The domination of subjectivity centered on the past trans-

555

forms the outer world into the interior, and objects are personified, so that they exist not for themselves, but for the *ego*. This is most evident in Li Yü's handling of space and time, of the images of moon and blossoms. All are signs of the past, the unreachable, the lost. This irrecoverability finds its special expression in the frequent use in the forty-five *tz'u* of the negative modal verbs *mo* 莫 (four times), *hsiu* 休 (three times, both meaning "do not"), and the adverbs *k'ung* 空 ("forlornly," nine times) and *tzu* 自 ("as if reduced to itself," twice). Li Yu can find a home only in the world of dreams (see numbers 26, 27, 42, 45), which offer the only possibility of going back to the times gone by (number 42).

EDITIONS:

Li Ching, Li Yü tz'u 李璟李煜詞. Chan An-t'ai 詹安泰, ed. Peking, 1958.

Muramaki, Tetsumi 村上哲見, ed. *Ri Iku* 李煜. Tokyo, 1964.

Li Hou-chu tz'u 李後主詞. Tai Ching-su 戴景素, ed. Shanghai, 1927.

Wang, Tz'u-ts'ung 王次聰, coll. and comm. *Nan T'ang erh-chu tz'u chiao-chu* 南唐二主詞校注. Taipei, 1962.

TRANSLATIONS:

Hoffmann, Alfred. *Die Leider des Li Yü, 937-978, Herrschers der südlichen T'ang-Dynastie*. Cologne, 1950.

Liu, Yih-ling and Suhrawardy, Shahid. *Poems of Lee Hou-chu*. Bombay, 1948.

STUDIES:

Bryant, Daniel. *Lyric Poets of the Southern T'ang: Li Yü and Feng Yen-ssu*. Vancouver, British Columbia, 1983. Contains numerous translations.

Chang, *Evolution*, pp. 63-106.

Hoffmann, Alfred. *Die Lieder des Li Yü*. Cologne, 1950.

Yu, Kuo-en 游國恩, *et al. Li Yü tz'u t'ao-lun chi* 李煜詞討論集. Peking, 1957.

—WK

Li Yü 李玉 (*tzu*, Hsüan-yü 玄玉, *hao*, Su-men hsiao-lü 蘇門嘯侶, I-li-an chu-jen 一笠庵主人, *c.* 1591-*c.* 1671) is generally considered the foremost of the celebrated "Soochow playwrights" of the Ming-Ch'ing transition period.

A native of Wu-hsien 吳縣, Li Yü was attached in some capacity to the household of Shen Shih-hsing 申時行 (1535-1614) from Ch'ang-chou 常州 (northwest of Soochow), one of the powerful grand secretaries in the Ming court during the Wan-li era (1573-1620). Prosperous and influential, the Shen family kept the best theatrical troupes in the region. This rich theatrical environment partly explains Li Yü's extensive knowledge of tunes and musical techniques, as testified to by his work, *Pei-tz'u kuang-cheng chiu-kung p'u* 北詞廣正九宮譜 (Northern Lyrics Compendious Correction Tables), a comprehensive analysis of prosody in Yüan music dramas.

Known for his broad learning, Li Yü did not have a successful official career. After the collapse of the Ming in 1644, he discontinued his efforts in that direction and devoted himself completely to writing. A prolific playwright, he wrote at least twenty-nine plays, of which only thirteen are still extant. Of the lost plays, three were summarized in the *Ch'ü-hai tsung-mu t'i-yao* 曲海總目提要 (An Annotated Bibliography of Music Dramas). His four best-known plays in traditional times were *I-pang hsüeh* 一棒雪 (A Handful of Snow), *Jen-shou kuan* 人獸關 (Between Man and Animal), *Yung t'uan-yüan* 永團圓 (Forever Together), and *Chan hua-k'uei* 占花魁 (The Oil Peddler and the Queen of Flowers). All four plays emphasize political satire, moral preaching, or the exposure of the social and political evils of the day. In modern times, more scholarly attention was given to his post-1644 works, such as *Ch'ing-chung p'u* 清忠譜 (The Upright and Loyal) and *Wan-li yüan* 萬里緣 (The Journey of Ten Thousand Miles and Its Miracle), both of which are characterized by realism and heroism. It is notable that the basic setting of both plays is in Soochow, where Li Yü spent most of his life, and that most of the characters are heroes of Soochow folktales.

Li Yü, like many of his fellow Soochow dramatists, acquired a thorough knowledge of stagecraft and dramatic techniques through experience. As a result, his plays are more suitable for acting than those of many of his contemporaries. Aside from personal and didactic works, Li kept in mind the tastes and demands of the theatre-goers for whose pleasure his plays were composed. Consequently his plays encompass a broad spectrum of society.

EDITIONS:

Chan hua-k'uei, in *Ku-pen*, III.
Ch'i-lin ko 麒麟閣, in *Ku-pen*, III.
Ch'ien-chung lu 千鍾祿, in *Ku-pen*, III.
Ch'ing-chung p'u, in *Ku-pen*, III.
I-chung jen 意中人, in *Ku-pen*, III.
I-pang hsüeh, v. 40, in *Ku-pen*, III.
Jen-shou kuan, in *Ku-pen*, III.
Liang hsü-mei 兩鬚眉, in *Ku-pen*, III.
Mei-shan hsiu 眉山秀; v. 46, in *Ku-pen*, III.
Niu-t'ou shan 牛頭山; v. 43, in *Ku-pen*, III.
Pei-tz'u kuang-cheng chiu-kung p'u. Rpt. Peking, 1981.
T'ai-p'ing ch'ien 太平錢; v. 44-45, in *Ku-pen*, III.
Wan-li yüan, v. 50-53, in *Ku-pen*, III.
Yung tuan-yüan, v. 41, in *Ku-pen*, III.

STUDIES:

Chao, *Pi-t'an*, pp. 75-83. Comments on Li Yü's life and his representative plays, *Ch'ing-chung p'u* and *I-pang hsüeh*.

———. "Li Yü te *Chan hua-k'uei*" 李玉的占花魁, in *Ming-Ch'ing ch'ü-t'an* 明清曲談, pp. 188-191.

Chiao, Hsün 焦循. *Chü-shuo* 劇說, in *Hsi-ch'ü lun-chu*, v. 8, pp. 157-158.

—CSC and HKC

Li Yü 李漁 (*tzu*, Li-weng 笠翁, 1611-1680) was a playwright, theater critic, and writer of short stories and novels. Li came from a family of literary gentry. One of his close relatives was the famous landscape painter and poet Li Liu-fang 李流芳. His life was spent in the turmoil of the dynastic transition from Ming to Ch'ing: his youth coincides with the closing years of the Ming Empire, and the latter part of his life was marked by the disorders following its overthrow.

Born in 1611 in Ju-kao 如臯, Li spent his first years in Chekiang Province. About 1635 he passed the *hsiu-ts'ai* examination and attained a position in the lowest grade of the civil service. Although already acclaimed as a young literary genius, he remained unsuccessful in the provincial examinations. (It is, therefore, not coincidence that Li repeatedly expressed his opinions about the examination system, the inflexibility of which all too often denied success to those most talented.) He then lived for a decade on the family estate, which he was obliged to sell following the troubles of 1644. Until approximately 1658 he was a resident of Hangchow on the West Lake whence he acquired his literary name, Hu-shang li-weng 湖上笠翁 (The Old Man in Bamboo Rain Hat by the Lake), by which he is better known. He spent the following two decades in the Mustard Seed Garden (*Chieh-tzu yüan*) in Nanking, which he made well known as a publisher. His last years were spent living quietly near Hangchow.

Although Li was constantly in financial difficulties, he led a life of elegant luxury, with a household of up to fifty people, for as long as possible. He had good connections with various officials, some of them members of the Manchu court and sympathetic to the arts. But he also moved among an illustrious circle of Ming loyalists and literati such as Ch'ien Ch'ien-i.* From time to time high-ranking officials offered him their patronage. In the role of architect, he designed and laid out gardens for them. He bought and trained young girls and made them into actresses for his own theater company or passed them on to wealthy officials as concubines. He went on several wide-ranging tours with the company, which played dramas he composed himself. Many of his contemporaries resented his unrestrained behavior.

Li Yü took art as a substitute for a career in government. He saw himself as a "worthy stateman of the theater." His fiction he described as unorthodox history writing. His moods alternated between extreme self-deprecation, because he practiced such a "low art," and exaggerated self-confidence. Li's talent for survival in a heavily political world is also evident in the escapist elements of his literary work; he wrote unproblematical, light fiction in order to amuse. In his irresolute despair Li enjoyed transforming conventional morality into sardonic and subtle parody.

Li's extravagant way of life found literary reflection in the group of essays

Hsien-ch'ing ou-chi 閑情偶奇 (Sketches of Idle Pleasures). The fundamentally epicurean guideline in this book is *hsing-lo* (enjoy oneself). Thus he not only consciously pushed aside Confucian pedantry, but also rejected the simple Taoist life (the title of the complete works is *I-chia yen* 一家言 [My Own Teaching]). In addition to Li's dramaturgy, the *Sketches* contain a treatise on the education of women which expounds his views of the ideal woman. Li is against footbinding and argues for a literary education of women. In one part of the *Sketches*, he develops his ideas about architecture and landscape gardening and, giving advice on interior decoration, he writes about the design of numerous objects, from tables and chairs down to drinking vessels and small tools. Characteristically, this section had a great influence in Japan which was receptive to such aestheticism. A separate chapter is devoted to the pleasures of eating and drinking. A further chapter defines the comfortable life, leading to a section of how to maintain that comfort by properly using medicine to avoid disease.

Li Yü fame as a dramatist is based on the ten comedies, *Shih-chung ch'ü* 十種曲. The subjects of these plays are partly the same as those dealt with by the short stories. Li shows no hesitation about writing on controversial themes, including lesbianism. Each of these plays utilizes a material symbol as a unifying factor, and all are distinguished by their well-made plots, economical but effective dialogue, and lyrics written in a clear and lucid style. His treatise on the theater reflects his practical experience as a dramatist and an author of fiction. A formula which he suggested for the theater, and which he practiced successfully in his novels and short stories, was to demand *i-jen i-shih* 一人一事 (one principal character and one plot). Thus he opposed works of extreme length, such as overburdened novels and contemporary southern plays, because they demanded too much of their audiences. He also argued against a confused patchwork of secondary plots. Both his plays and his fiction are organized strictly according to these criteria.

Li Yü considered his treatise on the theater quite original, and indeed until 1900 the only other work comparable to it is *Li-yüan yüan* 梨園原 (The Origin of the Pear Garden), a late-Ch'ing handbook for actors which was circulated only in manuscript. Reacting against earlier *ch'ü-hua* 曲話 (see Wang Chi-te), he stressed dialogue, unity of structure, and stageability. His treatise contains some contradictions concerning the theater's ideological function. The tasks of entertaining and the presentation of emotion collide with conventional Confucian morality, which demands that a play should "admonish to do good and punish evil." Li suggested that the dramatist choose new, original subjects from the realms of the imagination rather than use well-known stories. Consequently he rejected, at least in his own creative writing, the use of historical topics. It was only during the Republican Period, when China increasingly compared itself with the West, that Li became China's most famous dramaturge.

In fiction Li favored the short story. His first collection of stories was *Wu-sheng hsi* 無聲戲 (Theater without Sound). Written around 1654, these works were completely forgotten in the eighteenth century and were superceded in popularity by his *Shih-erh lou* 十二樓 (Twelve Towers) which has some affinity with works like the Decameron. This is a collection of twelve stories artificially linked by the character *lou* 樓 (tower) in their titles. The stories are distinguished by their witty and personal style.

As a result of his fame numerous works were attributed to Li both while he lived and posthumously. Yet it seems justified to credit him with the authorship of the pornographic *Jou p'u-t'uan,** which, he pretended, had to be understood in terms of Buddhist purification. The earliest Chinese edition contains a forward from 1693. It survived the censor's effort only under the disguise of several other titles. That Li is the author of this well-structured novel was confirmed by his contemporaries. The soundest proof may be Li Yü's stylistic peculiarity of allowing the characters in his fiction to "come on stage" as if actors in a theater such as they do in *Jou p'u-t'uan.* A hundred years after his death Li's works were banned and destroyed in the Ch'ien-lung Emperor's literary inquisition. He was rediscovered only much later in the reorientation following the May Fourth Movement, in particular by Sun K'ai-ti 孫楷弟, who was fascinated by Li's contributions to the development and evolution of fiction. He was also promoted by Lin Yu-tang, whose *Importance of Living*, an influential book in the West, owes much to Li Yü's "art of living."

EDITIONS:

Ch'en, To 陳多. *Li Li-weng ch'ü-hua* 李笠翁曲話. Changsha, 1980.
Hsien-ch'ing ou-chi, in *Hsi-ch'ü lun-chu*, v. 7, pp. 1-114.
Li Yü ch'üan-chi 李漁全集. Ma Han-mao 馬漢茂 (Helmut Martin), ed. 15v. Taipei, 1970. Includes collected writings *I-chia yen*, the plays *Shih-chung ch'ü*, the short-story collections *Wu-sheng-hsi* and *Shih-erh lou*, and pertinent articles by Sun K'ai-ti on *Wu-sheng hsi*.

TRANSLATIONS:

Klossowski, Pierre [J. Pimpaneau]. *Jeou-P'ou-T'ouan, ou la chair comme tapis de prière*. Paris, 1962. The only reliable translation.
Kuhn, Franz. *Jou Pu Tuan*. Zürich, 1959. (Retranslated by Richard Martin from the German, New York, 1963).
Mao, Nathan. *Li Yü's Twelve Towers*. Hong Kong, 1975. A free translation.
See also Chen, *Li Li-weng*, pp. 307-325, listing 170 items; N. Mao, *Li Yü*, pp. 156-158; and Helmut Martin, *Li Yü*, which contains a comprehensive bibliography.

STUDIES:

ECCP, pp. 495-497.
Martin, *Li Yü*. (Includes translation of *ch'ü-hua* 曲話, history of drama criticism, biography of Li).
Mao, Nathan K. and Liu Ts'un-yan. *Li Yü*. Boston, 1977.
Huang, Li-chen 黃麗貞. *Li Yü yen-chiu* 李漁研究. Taipei 1974.
Matsuda, Shizue. "Li Yü: His Life and Moral Philosophy as Reflected in his Fiction." Unpublished Ph.D. dissertation, Columbia University, 1978.

—HM

Liang Ch'en-yü 梁辰魚 (*tzu*, Po-lung 伯龍, *c.* 1520-*c.* 1593) came from K'un-shan 崑山 and was one of the first practitioners of the aristocratic drama style called *K'un-ch'ü*.* Very little is known about his career. He enjoyed no success in the examinations and never entered the bureaucracy. Throughout his life he wandered through the Lower Yangtze Valley. He had a certain reputation among the literati and enjoyed the company of theater people.

Shortly before 1522 Liang wrote the first major *K'un-ch'ü, Huan-sha chi* 浣紗記 (Washing the Silken Gauze). The drama is set in the sixth century B.C., when Wu and Yüeh were at war. Fan Li, a minister of Yüeh, enlists the beautiful Hsi Shih (whom he meets as she washes silk) to bring about the downfall of the King of Wu through sexual excess. After the success of her mission, Hsi Shih is reunited with Fan Li, and they leave Yüeh to live happily ever after. The story derives basically from the *Wu-Yüeh ch'un-ch'iu*.*

Huan-sha chi is a lengthy work of forty-five scenes. It is complicated in plot and structure, with twelve major characters. Liang was an expert musician and blended both northern and southern music into the work.

It has been suggested that Liang's motive for writing this play can be found in the prologue, where the author gives vent* to his disappointment and frustrations in his search for office and hints that writing is a compensation for this failure.

The drama was immensely popular in its own time and remained so into the Ch'ing. It is said to have been so well adapted to the music of the *K'un-ch'ü* that, alone among the early items of its genre, actors were unable to adapt it to any other theater styles. It firmly established the *K'un-ch'ü* as an important style.

In addition to his famous *K'un-ch'ü*, Liang wrote two *tsa-chü*.* One of them, the *Hung-hsien Nü yeh-ch'ieh huang-chin ho* 紅線女夜竊黃金盒 (The Red-Thread Maid Steals the Golden Box by Night), is based on a T'ang classical tale and is still extant. Liang also established a modest reputation as a poet.

EDITIONS:

Hung-hsien Nü yeh-ch'ien hung-chiu-ho, in *Sheng Ming*, and in *Ku-pen*, IV. See also Fu, *Ming-tai tsa-chü*, pp. 107-108.

Huan-sha chi. This compilation includes *Huan-sha chi;* the most recent editions of this play were published in Shanghai, 1955.

TRANSLATION:

" 'Secret Liaison with Chancellor Bo Po' Act VII from the *Chuangqi* Play *Washing Silk* by Liang Chenyu," in William Dolby, trans., *Eight Chinese Plays from the Thirteenth Century to the Present*. New York, 1978, pp. 84-92.

STUDIES:

Birch, Cyril. "The Dramatic Potential of *Xi Shi: Huanshaji* and *Jiaopaji* Compared," *CHINO-PERL*, 10 (1981), 129-140.

DMB, pp. 893-894.

—CM and SW

Liang Ch'i-ch'ao 梁啓超 (*tzu*, Chou-ju 卓如, *hao*, Jen-kung 任公, also called the Master of the Ice Drinking Studio 飲冰室主人, 1873-1929) is renowned as one of the most important political and intellectual figures of late Ch'ing and early Republican China. Liang Ch'i-ch'ao, born in Hsin-hui 新會 (Kwangtung), was a student of K'ang Yu-wei* and, like K'ang, became one of the major activists in the nineteenth-century reform movement. He cooperated with his mentor in attempting to unify Chinese intellectuals behind K'ang's petitions to the central government calling for reform, and he was a major leader in the Ch'iang-hsüeh hui 強學會 (Self-Strengthening Society) in both Peking and Shanghai. Then he worked together with Huang Tsun-hsien* to edit the *Shih-wu pao* 時務報 (Journal of Contemporary Affairs), one of the most influential nineteenth-century reform periodicals. Later he was also involved with Huang and other leading reformers in the Hunan reform movement, which was the precursor to the ill-fated Hundred Days of Reform, upon the collapse of which Liang was forced to flee to Japan. There he organized the Pao-huang hui 保皇會 (Emperor Protection Society) in opposition to the Empress Dowager. During his long exile he edited a number of political and literary journals and wrote innumerable works introducing Western culture and political ideals to China. Upon the overthrow of the Ch'ing dynasty, Liang returned to China, where he was bitterly criticized by the Nationalists for his relations with Yüan Shih-k'ai 袁世凱 (1859-1916) and the warlord Tuan Ch'i-jui 段祺瑞 (1865-1936). During the May Fourth Movement, Liang frequently sided with more conservative elements. His final years were spent in scholarly pursuits.

Liang Ch'i-ch'ao's importance as a political figure and propagandist for Western culture has largely obscured his contributions to late Ch'ing literature. Yet it is difficult to separate Liang the literati from Liang the polemicist. Nonetheless, he was an excellent poet in the classical language, and it is to be regretted that few of the poems he wrote before his exile have survived. He was one of the major theorists of the late Ch'ing poetic revolution, and his verse from the first years of his exile exhibits innovation and freshness in subject matter. Such works as "Lei An hsing" 雷庵行 (Ballad of Thunder Monastery) display a quite eccentric form at variance with most traditional poetry. Much of the poetry from this period is permeated by a moving expression of Liang's efforts to arouse his fellow countrymen and save the Ch'ing dynasty. There are also many poems describing his reactions to his foreign travels, which rank with some of Huang Tsun-hsien's* best works in this vein. However, as Liang became older and increasingly isolated from the Chinese political mainstream, the earlier innovative spirit gradually disappeared and was replaced by gloom and despair. Although his *shih** poetry does not exhibit the richness of Huang Tsun-hsien or the intense feeling of K'ang Yu-wei, he made a notable contribution to late nineteenth-century poetry.

Liang Ch'i-ch'ao was one of the most prolific prose writers of his age, and although most of his prose would hardly pass as *belles lettres*, he strongly influenced the development of Chinese prose style. Earlier Ch'ing prose was unsuitable for expressing modern ideas. By coining many new terms, simplifying syntax, and generally avoiding older rhetorical devices, Liang created a classical-prose style that was as practical for modern expository writing as the vernacular itself. Although he was hostile to the May Fourth Movement, the new kind of vernacular expository prose that was created then would have been inconceivable without the preparatory work of Liang and his fellow reformers.

Liang Ch'i-ch'ao is also beginning to be recognized as a major contributor to forms of Chinese literature other than *shih* poetry and the essay. Although his *K'un-ch'ü* drama *Hsin Lo-ma* 新羅馬 (New Rome) cannot rank with the greatest Ch'ing plays, it makes fascinating reading, and shows how a traditional form could be used effectively to tell the story of Italian independence, with obvious implications for Chinese patriots. Although Liang wrote no major fiction, he edited the highly influential *Hsiao-shuo pao* 小說報 (Fiction Journal), which was part of a burgeoning in fiction during the late nineteenth and early twentieth centuries in China. In spite of Liang's condemning some aspects of traditional Chinese fiction in his critical essays, he was instrumental in raising the esteem for certain traditional novels. Even more significant was his new realistic attitude and his systematic formulation of a theory for a new fiction designed to educate the Chinese people and rouse them to modernization and resistance against foreign imperialism.

Finally, Liang exerted a major influence on late Ch'ing literary theory through his *Yin-ping shih shih-hua* 飲冰室詩話 (Poetry Talks of the Ice Drinking Studio). The main purpose of this work was to promote the late Ch'ing Poetic Revolution, and most of the major authors of the movement find favorable comment in the book. In addition, certain generally neglected earlier Ch'ing poets are given due attention. Throughout the entire work Liang never strays very far from his overriding concern for literature in the cause of national regeneration, and although he constantly stresses the need for innovation, he also concentrates on the poet as patriot and historian to his age. Liang was one of the first Chinese critics to praise Western literature and hold it up as a model for emulation, even though he knew it only in Chinese translation.

EDITIONS:

A-ying 阿英 [Ch'ien Hsing-ts'an 錢杏邨]. *Wan-ch'ing wen-hsüeh ts'ung-ch'ao: Ch'uan-ch'i tsa-chü chüan* 晚清文學叢鈔傳奇雜劇卷. Peking, 1962.

Liang Jen-kung shih shou-chi 梁任公詩手蹟. Shanghai, 1957.

Yin-ping-shih ho-chi 飲冰室合集. Peking, 1936.

Yin-ping-shih wen-chi 飲冰室文集. Shanghai, 1926.

TRANSLATIONS:

Dolby, *History*, pp. 198-201. A translation of the "wedge" of the *Hsin Lo-ma*.

Hsü, Immanuel C. Y. *Intellectual Trends in the Ch'ing Period*. Cambridge, 1959. An annotated translation of Liang's *Ch'ing-tai hsüeh-shu kai-lun* 清代學術概論.

STUDIES:

BDRC, pp. 346-351.

Chang, Hao 張灝. *Liang Ch'i-ch'ao and Intellectual Transition in China*. Cambridge, Massachusetts, 1971.

Chu, Mei-shu 朱眉叔. "Liang Ch'i-ch'ao yü hsiao-shuo chieh ko-ming" 梁啓超與小說界革命. *Wen-hsüeh i-ch'an tseng-k'an*, 9 (June 1962), 111-129.

Hsia, C. T. "Yen Fu and Liang Ch'i-ch'ao as Advocates of New Fiction," *JOS*, 14.2 (July 1976), 133-149; included in *Chinese Approaches*, pp. 221-257.

Levenson, Joseph R. *Liang Ch'i-ch'ao and the Mind of Modern China*. Berkeley, 1967.

Martin, Helmut. "A Transitional Concept of Chinese Literature 1897-1917: Liang Ch'i-ch'ao on Poetry-reform, Historical Drama and the Political Novel," *OE*, 20 (1973), 175-217.

Masuda, Wataru 增田涉. Ryō keichō ni tsuite: Bungakushi teki ni mite" 梁啓超について：文學史的に見て, *Jimbun kenkyū*, 6.6 (June 1955), 49-66.

Nakamura, Tadayuki 中村忠行. "Chūgoku bungei ni oyoboseru Nihon bungei no eikyō: Ryō Keichō no yakugyō to sono eikyō" 中國文藝に及ぼせる日本文藝の影響：梁啓超の譯業とその影響, *Taidai bungaku*, 7.4 (Dec. 1942), 24-53; 7.6 (April 1943), 72-94; 8.2 (Aug. 1843), 12-78; 8.4 (June 1944), 27-85; 8.5 (Nov. 1944), 42-111.

—JDS

561

Liang Su 梁肅 (*tzu*, Chiang-chih 敬之 and K'uan-chung 寬中, 753-793) was an important figure in intellectual and literary circles during the last quarter of the eighth century. He was a key transition figure linking the pre-An Lu-shan generation of scholars such as Hsiao Ying-shih* and Li Hua* with Han Yü* and Liu Tsung-yüan* in the Yüan-ho period (806-820). He is representative of that generation of thinkers who first began to contemplate the possibility of the Buddhist-Confucian synthesis that later developed into Neo-Confucianism.

Liang was descended from an aristocratic family of the Six Dynasties period originally based in An-ting 安定 (modern P'ing-liang 平涼 in Kansu). Early in the T'ang, the family still produced officials for the central government, but several generations before Liang Su, his immediate ancestors had moved to Honan where they occupied only local posts. Liang was born in Han-kuan 函關 (modern Hsin-an 新安 in Honan). In 761 the family fled to the Ch'ang-chou 常州 area in the Southeast to avoid the military aftermath of the An Lu-shan Rebellion in Honan. In 770, at age seventeen, Liang became acquainted with Li Hua and Tu-ku Chi,* both established literary leaders of the time, who praised his early writings. He departed the next year for the T'ien-t'ai 天台 Mountains where he probably began his lifelong study of the T'ien-t'ai School of Buddhism with the master Chan-jan 湛然 (711-782), under whom this school enjoyed a revival in the late eighth century. In 774, Tu-ku Chi was appointed Prefect of Ch'ang-chou, and Liang returned there to study formally with him. When Tu-ku died in 777, Liang edited his works in twenty *chüan* and added a postface.

In 780, by virtue of his outstanding literary ability, Liang was summoned to Ch'ang-an to serve as Reader-in-waiting in the Eastern Palace. His literary prestige and influence were now at their peak, as an unusually high percentage of the candidates he supported for the *chin-shih* examinations was successful. He supervised the 792 *chin-shih* examinations which grad-

uated Han Yü and a slate of other literary and political leaders of the early ninth century. Liang Su died in Ch'ang-an in 793.

In his Confucian studies, Liang Su was an adherent of the "new school" of textual commentary associated with Tan Chu 啖助 (725-770), which advocated increased attention to the "general meaning" (大義) of the Confucian classics rather than to textual detail. This "general meaning," of course, was found to be relevant to contemporary social and political issues. Thus these scholars advocated "reverence for the classics" not as objects of adoration but as texts profound with meaning for their own age.

His *Shan-ting chih-kuan*, an abridgment of *Mo-ho chih-kuan* 摩訶止觀 (The Great Concentration and Insight), written by Chih-i 智顗 (539-597), the founder of the T'ien-tai School, reaffirmed the school's basic eclectic and syncretistic tendencies, which made it possible for thinkers to interpret certain passages in Confucian texts as rudimentary expositions of Buddhist metaphysical principles, thus laying the ground for Neo-Confucian philosophy.

In the literary domain, Liang Su inherited from Hsiao Ying-shih and Li Hua an impatience with *p'ien-wen** as a vehicle for the kind of literary discourse they envisioned as necessary for their time: a literature that recaptured the fundamental Confucian link between literary and moral-political activity. Liang Su wrote, for instance, "the *tao* of literature is closely connected with the *tao* of good government." Although Hsiao and Li articulated the philosophical desirability, even necessity, of such a union, they were unable to develop a style that was appropriate to their vision and continued to write in *p'ien-wen*.

Liang Su carried the realization of a *ku-wen** style a step forward by postulating the concept of *ch'i* 氣 (spirit or vitality) as an intermediate stage between a piece of writing's *tao* 道 (moral power) and its *tz'u* 辭 (diction). *Ch'i* had been used earlier in Six Dynasties' criticism to designate an author's inherent mode or style of writing. Liang Su's use of the term, however, seems to derive from *Mencius*, where *ch'i* means something like "moral character." Thus, for Liang Su, the moral power of a piece of writing is tied to the moral character of its author, and this quality in turn affects the diction and style of a piece (道能兼氣, 氣能兼辭). In modern terms, this means that a text's power to influence its readership is a function of the author's rhetorical skills, which themselves are a product of his own self-cultivation, both as a writer and as a member of society.

Although Liang Su was active as a teacher in Ch'ang-an during the last several years of his life, it is unlikely he had any meaningful, direct contact with either Han Yü or Liu Tsung-yüan. Rather his ideas on scholarship and literature were probably already part of the general anti-establishment literary world in which the famous *ku-wen** authors matured.

EDITIONS:

Ch'üan T'ang wen, v. 11, *ch.* 517-522, pp. 6655-6730.

STUDIES:

Kanda, Kiichirō 神田喜一郎. "Ryō Shuku nempu" 梁肅年譜, in *Tōhō gakkai sōritsu 25 shūnen kinen Tōhōgaku ronshū* 東方學會創立二十五周年紀念東方學論集, Tokyo, 1972, pp. 259-274.

—CH

Liao-chai chih-i 聊齋志異 (Strange Stories from the Leisure Studio) is a collection of classical-language stories whose author, P'u Sung-ling 蒲松齡 (*tzu,* Liu-hsien 留仙, *hao,* Liu-ch'üan 柳泉; 1640-1715), has been acknowledged as the most outstanding story writer of the early Ch'ing period. P'u was a frustrated man of letters from Tzu-ch'uan 淄川 (modern Shantung). He failed the provincial examination repeatedly, never achieving a distinction higher than *hsiu-ts'ai.* He became a personal secretary to an official and later a tutor for a local-gentry family. Throughout, P'u maintained close contact with the common people, from whom he solicited stories and anecdotes of strange events; these he later embellished stylishly. P'u completed the bulk of the *Liao-chai chih-i* in 1679, revealing his creative intent as well his methods of collection in a preface. Later he added more

entries to the original manuscript, some as late as in 1707. Though the work was not printed and published until 1766, fifty years after his death, handwritten copies of the manuscript had been widely circulated among friends and associates. Since 1766 the *Liao-chai chih-i* has undergone numerous editions and printings with many commentaries and annotations.

P'u claimed that the collection was modeled after Kan Pao's *Sou-shen chi.** In fact, P'u rearranged and elaborated some of Kan Pao's entries as well as many other writings from later periods; some entries were provided by his friends and associates. P'u himself also wrote many of these marvelous stories, and his reliance on contemporary records has been well established.

The narrative style of his stories follows, but also expands upon, the *pi-chi.** Only a small percentage are plot-centered stories. A number of the pieces are parodies of biographical writings like those found in Ssu-ma Ch'ien's *Shih-chi** and T'ang *ch'uan-ch'i.** This enabled P'u to employ Ssu-ma's "commentary" structure freely to convey his personal views. One other unique feature in the collection is P'u's technique of using dialogues and speeches for characterization. This technique had not been successfully developed in classical-language stories before P'u's.

Liao-chai chih-i is known for its numerous stories about ghosts and fox-spirits, but it also contains a great variety of other beings, both immortal and mortal: hornets, crows, frogs, fish, mice, pigeons, peonies, chrysanthemums, tigers, and wolves, to name but a few. These beings, like the ghosts and fox-spirits, are often transformed into human form and interact with men and women. There are a few horror stories, but most of the spirits in mortal disguise are examples of an ideal human existence: the males are wise and loyal, the females beautiful and sensuous.

The collection is especially famous for the depiction of such female ghosts and fox-spirits. Though unbound by the moral restrictions of mortals they remain faithful to their mortal lovers. Among a variety of other characters, the most innovative are the frustrated scholars who attempt to pass the provincial examinations, and the women who pursue security and satisfaction in their relationships. Besides the theme of a mortal-spirit romance, P'u also dealt seriously with social issues, such as the rigors of the civil-service examination system, the tyranny of the wealthy, and the corruption among officials.

The *Liao-chai chih-i* has always been popular. The term *Liao-chai* has become synonymous with stories of the fantastic. However, the collection was not seriously studied until the 1950s, when it was suggested, with obvious political overtones, that many of the stories demonstrate a subtle sense of nationalism and anti-Manchu sentiment. Recently a journal has been devoted to the study of P'u Sung-ling and his magnum opus: *P'u Sung-ling yen-chiu chi-k'an* 蒲松齡研究集刊 (August 1980-).

The modern scholar Hu Shih has argued that P'u Sung-ling wrote the early Ch'ing novel *Hsing-shih yin-yüan chuan* 醒世姻緣傳 (Marriage to Awaken the World). The argument is strained and Hu seems to have been the sole supporter of this theory. However, P'u was indeed a versatile writer. The diversity of his many works is impressive, ranging from *shih*,* *tz'u*,* folk songs, and prose essays to medical guides and agricultural treatises.

EDITIONS:

Liao-chai chih-i hui-chiao hui-chu hui-p'ing pen 聊齋志異會校會注會評本. Chang Yu-ho 張友鶴, ed. Peking, 1962. Rpt. with a new preface; Shanghai, 1978. The most comprehensive edition available today; includes all the commentaries and annotations by previous *Liao-chai* readers and publishers, from Wang Shih-chen (1634-1711)* to Tan Ming-lun 但明倫 (*fl.* 1842). This 12-*chüan* edition consists of 491 entries, 60 more than the 16-*chüan* editions popular since 1766, but the attribution of some stories has been questioned.

Liao-chai chih-i. Taipei, 1956. A facsimile reproduction of the 1766 Ch'ing-k'o-t'ing 青柯亭 edition, the first printed edition of the collection with 431 entries in 16 *chüan*. Most of the later editions are based on this work.

———. 5v. Peking, 1955. A facsimile reproduction of the original, incomplete, handwritten

manuscript. Later reprinted in Taiwan in 1972 under the title *Liao-chai chih-i shou-kao pen* 聊齋志異手稿本.

Liao-chai chih-i. 4v. Chi-nan, 1982. A facsimile reproduction of the handwritten manuscript in twenty-four *chüan*.

P'u Sung-ling chi 蒲松齡集. 2v. Lu Ta-fang 路大荒, comp. Peking, 1962. A gold mine for the study of P'u Sung-ling. Includes a detailed *nien-p'u*.

TRANSLATIONS:

Giles, Herbert A. *Strange Stories from a Chinese Studio*. London, 1880.

Hervouet, Yves, *et al. Countes extraordinaire du Pavillon du Loisir*. Paris, 1969.

Masuda, Wataru 增田涉, *et al. Ryōsai shii*. Tokyo, 1970-71.

Shibata, Tenma 柴田天馬. *Kanyaku Ryō-sai shii* 完訳聊齋志異. Tokyo, 1969.

STUDIES:

Chang, Chun-shu 張春樹 and Hsüeh-lun [Lo] Chang 駱雪倫. "The World of P'u Sung-ling's *Liao-chai chih-i*: Literature and the Intelligentsia During the Ming-Ch'ing Dynastic Transition," *JICS*, 6.2 (December 1973), 401-423.

Fu, *Ch'ing tsa-chü*, pp. 68-69.

Fujita, Yūken 藤田祐賢. "*Ryōsai shii* no kenkyū to shiryō" 聊齋志異の研究と資料, in *Chūgoku no hachidai shōsetsu* 中國の八大小說, Tokyo, 1965, pp. 466-476.

Ho, Man-tzu 何滿子. *P'u Sung-ling yü Liao-chai chih-i* 蒲松齡與聊齋志異. Shanghai, 1955.

Hom, Marlon Kau. "Characterization in *Liao-chai chih-i*," *THHP*, 12 (1979), 229-279.

———. "The Continuation of Tradition: A Study of *Liaozhai zhiyi* by Pu Songling (1640-1715)." Unpublished Ph.D. dissertation, University of Washington, 1979.

Keio Gijuku Daigaku Chūgoku Bungaku Kenkyūshitsu 慶應義塾大學中國文學研究室. "Keio Gijuku Daigaku shozō *Ryōsai* dandei shiryō mokuroku" 慶應義塾大學所藏聊齋關係資料目錄, *Geibun kenkyū*, 4 (February 1955), 127-144.

Liu, Chieh-p'ing 劉階平. *P'u Liu-hsien chuan* 蒲留仙傳. Taipei, 1970.

Muhleman, James V. "P'u Sung-ling and the *Liao-chai chih-yi*: Themes and Art of the Literary Tale." Unpublished Ph.D. dissertation, Indiana University, 1978.

"P'u Sung-ling," in *ECCP*, pp. 628-630.

Prusek, Jaroslav. "*Liao-chai chih-i* by P'u Sung-ling: An Inquiry into the Circumstances under Which the Collection Arose," in Jaroslav Prusek, *Chinese History and Literature, Collection of Studies*, Prague, 1970, pp. 92-108.

———. "P'u Sung-ling and His Works," in *Chinese History and Literature*, pp. 109-138.

Tung, Wan-hua 董挽華. *Ts'ung* Liao-chai chih-i *te jen-wu k'an Ch'ing-t'ai te k'o-chü chih-tu ho sung-yü chih-tu* 從聊齋志異看清代的科舉制度 和 訟獄 制度. Taipei, 1976.

Yang, Jen-k'ai 楊仁愷. *Liao-chai chih-i yüan yen-chiu* 聊齋志異原稿研究. Shenyang, 1958.

—MH

Liao-shih chi-shih 遼詩紀事 (Recorded Occasions in Liao Poetry) is one of the three works dealing with the factual genesis of poems compiled by Ch'en Yen 陳衍 (*tzu*, Shih-i 石遺, 1856-1937), himself a poet and a professor at Peking University. The two others are *Chin-shih chi-shih* 金詩紀事 (Recorded Occasions in Chin Poetry) and *Yüan-shih chi-shih* 元詩紀事 (Recorded Occasions in Yüan Poetry). Ch'en compiled these three books in an effort to continue the tradition of *chi-shih* 紀事 (recorded occasions in poetry).

The principle of these three works was to gather poems which were related to contemporary events or which had historical value. In Ch'en's opinion, although the Liao, Chin, and Yüan were all dynasties founded by non-Chinese invaders, their histories nonetheless were considered as legitimate as those of the indigenous T'ang, Sung, and Ming (the *Ming-shih chi-shih** had already been compiled). Therefore, his major motive in collecting facts on Liao, Chin, and Yüan poetry was to insure the perpetuation of the legitimate tradition of the poetry of these dynasties.

The *Liao-shih chi-shih* incorporates some eighty poems by more than sixty poets, including several anonymous writers. In addition to various orthodox forms of poems, such as heptasyllabic and pentasyllabic old-style, regulated verse, and quatrains, the collection includes nursery rhymes, proverbs, incantations, and several types of popular songs. The poets range from Khitan emperors to the Korean Koryŏ king, from scholar-officials to Buddhist monks. The poet best represented, with fourteen poems in all, is Empress I-te 懿德 (also known as Hsüan-i 宣懿), the wife of Emperor Tao-tsung (r. 1055-1100), who was granted the right to commit suicide by the emperor for her alleged affair with a court musician. Most of the poets in this collection are represented only by a single selection, making it extremely difficult to judge their true literary value.

Ch'en Yen supplied biographical information, anecdotes, historical facts, and popular legends for most of the selections, citing some sixty sources. The two most extensively quoted works are the official history of the Liao (the *Liao-shih*) and Wang Ting's 王鼎 (d. 1106) *Fen-chiao lu* 焚椒錄 (Records on Burning the Pepper Chamber), a detailed account of Empress I-te's love affair and mandated suicide. In Ch'en Yen's opinion, the *Fen-chiao lu* is an even better historical source than the *Liao-shih* itself.

While weaving history and poetry together, Ch'en Yen also corrected a number of mistakes found in other works. For example, Ch'en pointed out that five of Emperor Hsing-tsung's (r. 1031-1054) poems were mistakenly attributed to Emperor Sheng-tsung (r. 983-1030) by Wang Jen-chün 王仁俊 (1866-1913) in the *Liao-wen ts'ui* 遼文萃 (An Anthology of Liao Writings). He also noted that Miao Ch'üan-sun 繆荃孫 (1844-1919), in the *Liao-wen ts'un* 遼文存 (Repository of Liao Writings), failed to identify the authors of several poems. In his preface to the *Liao-shih chi-shih*, Ch'en expressed the hope that his book would help prevent readers of the various Liao literary collections from repeating past compilers' mistakes.

The first important study on Liao poetry was Chou Ch'un's 周春 (1728-1815) *Liao shih-hua* 遼詩話 (Talks on Liao Poetry, preface 1795), in which some fifty Liao poets were discussed, some without any of their poetry included. In 1934, Wu Mei 吳梅 (1883-1939) published his *Liao Chin Yüan wen-hsüeh shih* 遼金元文學史 (A History of Liao, Chin, and Yüan Literature), in which the section on Liao poetry relied heavily on the *Liao shih-hua*. Since the preface to the *Liao-shih chi-shih* was dated 1936, Ch'en had probably consulted both Chou's and

Wu's works, although he made no mention of Wu. He may have already finished the *Liao-shih chi-shih* before the *Liao Chin Yüan wen-hsüeh shih* was published. Ch'en's work has more historical value than that of Wu and Chou, for while all three works cite historical facts, only Ch'en gives sources.

Readers who hope to find some examples of poetic masterpieces here will likely be disappointed. Not only are there a small number of selections, but the quality is less than might be expected. It is obvious that Ch'en Yen's pretext for choosing these particular poems was to mark significant historical events.

EDITIONS:

Chin-shih chi-shih. Chen Yen, comp. Original typeset edition; Shanghai, 1936.

Liao-shih chi-shih. Ch'en Yen, comp. Shanghai, 1936; rpt. Taipei, 1971. The most readily available edition.

Yüan-shih chi-shih. Ch'en Yen, comp. Shanghai, 1921; rpt. Taipei, 1968 (in *Basic Sinological Series*).

Yüan-shih chi-shih chu-che yin-te 著者引得 (Index to Authors in Recorded Occasions in Yüan Poetry). Harvard-Yenching Institute Sinological Index Series, 20. Rpt. Taipei, 1966.

—TY and HF

Lieh-hsien chuan 列仙傳 (Biographies of Immortals) is a collection of seventy brief hagiographies of Taoist adepts who supposedly achieved the goal of immortality. The work has traditionally been ascribed to the Han polymath Liu Hsiang,* but the *Han-shu* "Bibliographic Treatise" does not list this text among Liu's work. It is known, however, that the great Chin dynasty Taoist Ko Hung* accepted the tradition of Liu's authorship and also that a book by the name of *Lieh-hsien chuan* is cited in Wang I's 王逸 (*c.* A.D. 89-*c.* 158) commentary on the *Ch'u-tz'u.** Thus, the authorship of the work is attested within two hundred years of Liu's death. However, several anachronisms which appear in the text and have been noted by the editor of *Ssu-k'u ch'üan-shu tsung-mu* (see Chi Yün) and more recently by Max Kaltenmark argue against Liu's authorship of the present text.

Whether the book is by Liu Hsiang or more properly assigned to the Latter Han, it remains the earliest extant collection of Taoist hagiography and inspires later Taoist collections such as *Shen-hsien chuan,** *Hsü hsien chuan* 續仙傳, and Wang Shih-chen's* (1526-1590) *Lieh-hsien ch'üan-chuan* 列仙全傳, the latter describing the lives of 640 Taoist immortals. The *Lieh-hsien chuan* biographies are much shorter than those of later collections, the longest about 220 characters and the average approximately 100 characters. Consequently, the typical biography only lists the Taoist skills acquired by the adept and describes a single important event from his life, often a dramatic departure from the "dusty" world. Among the traditional Taoist skills mentioned in the text, those which Maspero labels "dietetic" and "alchemical" predominate, with occasional allusions also to yogic and sexual practices.

The literary significance of *Lieh-hsien chuan* is twofold. First, it is one of the earliest collections of "exemplary lives" among the sizable body of Chinese biographical literature. Such hagiography was to become an important part of Chinese religious literature, seen among the Buddhists, for example, in a source such as *Kao-seng chuan.** Second, as a result of its fantastic content, *Lieh-hsien chuan* is sometimes seen as a forerunner of the *chih-kuai** tradition that flowered during the Six Dynasties.

The best current edition of *Lieh-hsien chuan,* found in the *Tao-tsang,** appends a short eight-line, four-character *tsan* (eulogy) to the end of each of the seventy biographies. From the *Sui-shu* we know that two sets of *tsan* were written, one by the noted poet Sun Ch'o 孫綽 (314-371) and the other by the little-known figure Kuo Yüan-tsu 郭元祖. From the descriptions of the two sets in the bibliographic literature, the current *tsan* apparently are the set authored by Kuo.

EDITIONS:

Lieh-hsien chuan in *Cheng-t'ung Tao-tsang* 正統道藏, v. 128.

TRANSLATIONS:

Kaltenmark, Max. *Le Lie-sien Tchouan.* Peking, 1953.

STUDIES:

Durrant, Stephen. "The Theme of Family Conflict in Early Taoist Biography," *Selected Papers in Asian Studies* [Western Conference of the Association of Asian Studies], 2 (1977), 2-8.

—SD

Lin Hung 林鴻 (*tzu,* Tzu-yü 子羽, *c.* 1340-*c.* 1400) was a *shih** poet whose particular importance in the history of Chinese literature is due to his role in promoting the primacy of T'ang-dynasty verse as a standard of excellence, a standard taken up and developed by the Archaist movements led by Li Meng-yang* and Li P'an-lung* later in the dynasty.

Lin Hung went to Nanking about 1370 where his poetic gifts made a great impression. But he failed in the civil-service examinations and returned home. Later, he was briefly in office in the capital but lived most of his life in retirement in his native Fukien. There, he became the acknowledged leader of a group of poets known as the *Min-chung shih ts'ai-tzu* 閩中十才子 (Ten Talents of Fukien). Most members of the group, which probably formed in the 1380s and must have disbanded by 1394, were only minor poets, but one of them, Kao Ping 高棅 (later, Kao T'ing-li 廷禮, *tzu,* Yen-hui 彥恢, *hao,* Man-shih 漫士, 1350-1423) compiled a large and very influential anthology of T'ang poetry, the *T'ang-shih p'in-hui* 唐詩品彙 (T'ang Poems Graded and Collected), based on Liu Hung's critical opinions. Indeed, the little that we know of Lin's ideas comes from citations in the preface to Kao's anthology.

One of these ideas concerned the division of T'ang poetry into four stylistic periods, Early 初, High 盛, Middle 中, and Late 晚—periods that have remained commonplaces of Chinese literary history ever since. Three points should be noted concerning this periodization. First, the periods are stylistically determined, rather than being strictly chronological. Second, they were not entirely original with Lin and Kao

Ping—the Southern Sung critic Yen Yü had referred to elements of a similar periodization in his *Ts'ang-lang shih-hua,** and an analogous scheme had been used in a Yüan-dynasty anthology, the *T'ang yin* 唐音 (1344) of Yang Shih-hung 楊士弘. Third, and related to the preceding, the periods were evaluative rather than simply descriptive, for they carried with them Yen Yü's conclusion that High T'ang was the acme of *shih* poetry. This made Early T'ang potentially worthwhile, as a forerunner of High T'ang, but it cast Middle and Late T'ang poetry into disfavor. Developed to an extreme by some later Archaist critics, this judgment of post-High T'ang poetry took the form of an assumption that no verse written later than the Ta-li period (766-780) was worth reading.

The *T'ang-shih p'in-hui* is a large work, including almost six thousand poems by over six hundred poets, plus a supplement added later. Its presentation to the court earned Kao Ping, who had held no office previously, an appointment to the Han-lin Academy, perhaps because its inclusiveness and systematizing impulse were in tune with the spirit of such court-sponsored enterprises of the early Ming as the *Yung-lo ta-tien* encyclopedia. The poems are first divided by form (e.g., pentasyllabic regulated verse). Within each form, poets are classified under nine heads, from *cheng-shih* 正始 (orthodox beginnings) and *cheng-tsung* 正宗 (orthodox ancestors) to *yü-hsiang* 餘響 (remnant echoes) and *p'ang-liu* 旁流 (side currents). Poets are separately classified for each form, but in general the first group corresponds to Early T'ang, the next four to High T'ang, the next two to Middle T'ang, *yü-hsiang* to Late T'ang, and *p'ang-liu* to undated poets. Kao's table of contents is interspersed with extensive passages explaining the categories and his reasons for the placement of poets in them.

As a "demonstration" of Yen Yü's literary ideals, the *T'ang-shih p'in-hui* played a large role in conditioning the eventual rise of Archaism as a self-conscious literary movement. As poets, Lin Hung and Kao Ping were both much less influential. Lin's collected works form a quite slim volume, which includes no prose, while Kao's two collections, though extant, are very rare, and only a selection of his poetry is generally available.

EDITIONS:

Lin, Hung. *Ming-sheng chi* 鳴盛集. 4 *chüan.* Printed several times during the Ming dynasty; the only readily accessible edition is in the *Ssu-k'u ch'üan-shu chen-pen.*

———. *Lin Shan-pu chi* 林膳部集. 5 *chüan,* in *Min-chung shih-tzu shih* 閩中十子詩, rpt. *Ssu-k'u ch'üan-shu chen-pen.* An abridged version of the preceding, though in more *chüan;* contained in an anthology (30 *chüan*) of poems by members of Lin Hung's circle.

Kao, Ping, comp. *T'ang-shih p'in-hui.* 90 *chüan. T'ang-shih shih-i* 拾遺. 10 *chüan.* Numerous Ming editions; the reprint in the *Ssu-k'u ch'üan-shu chen-pen* and that issued by Ku-chi ch'u-pan-she (Shanghai, 1982) are the most accessible texts.

———. *Kao Man-shih hsiao-t'ai chi* 嘯臺集. 20 *chüan.*

———. *Kao Man-shih mu-t'ien ch'ing-ch'i chi* 木天清氣集. 14 *chüan.* Not seen; two collections of Kao's work, possibly entirely distinct. A copy of the first is said to be in the National Central Library, Taipei; the second in the Seikadō Bunko, Tokyo.

———. *Kao Tai-chao chi* 高待詔集. 5 *chüan,* in *Min-chung shih-tzu shih.* The only readily accessible selection of Kao's poetry.

STUDIES:

Chu, Tung-jun 朱東潤. *Chung-kuo wen-hsüeh p'i-p'ing shih ta-kang* 中國文學批評史大綱. 1941; rpt. Hong Kong, 1962, pp. 218-224.

DMB, pp. 922-924.

Yokota, "Mindai," 84-89.

———, "Mindai bungakuron," 49-53.

—DB

Lin Shu 林紓 (original *ming,* Ch'un-yü 群玉; *tzu,* Ch'in-nan 琴南; *hao,* Wei-lu 畏廬 and Leng-hung-sheng 冷紅生, 1852-1924), translator, poet, novelist, playwright, and painter, was born in Min-hsien 閩縣, Fukien. The Lin family was poor, and during his early childhood his mother and sister earned a bare subsistence income for the family from their needlework. Although Lin Shu was a bright and eager learner, his formal education was delayed until the age of ten, when an uncle provided the necessary funds. The family situation soon improved, however, for shortly thereafter his father found a position on the secretarial staff of an official stationed in Taiwan. With his father's help, Lin Shu acquired inexpensive copies of classical books, for which he already had a passion. He was an avid student, and during the next decade he read widely in the classics, history, and literature. Two years after his father's death in 1870, circumstances forced him to seek employment as a teacher in the local school. Before long, however, he contracted tuberculosis and did not recover for nearly seven years. When his health improved, he began the long process of seeking official-degree status. He passed the *chü-jen* examination in 1882, but during the next fifteen years he was repeatedly thwarted in his attempts to pass the *chin-shih* examination. His frustration at being denied an official career was compounded by the loss of his mother, then his wife, a son, and a daughter in the short space of several years. These crushing events led to a period of erratic personal behavior, but new interests and his responsibilities as a teacher restored a measure of stability to his life. After several decades of teaching in local public and private schools, he joined the faculty of the National University in Peking, eventually rising to a College Deanship before changing social events forced him from the staff. During the final years of his life, he eked out a living from the sale of his paintings and the publishing rights to his books.

Lin Shu's contributions to modern Chinese arts and letters assumed many forms, but he is best remembered today for his unique gifts as a translator of Western fiction and drama. Although seemingly ill-equipped for such a task because he knew no foreign languages, he nonetheless overcame that difficulty with the assistance of friends who were not similarly handicapped. After the loss of his mother, wife, and two children, a young friend, hoping to rescue him from his depression, suggested that they jointly undertake the task of producing a Chinese version of *La Dame aux camélias* by Dumas *fils.* The young man translated the novel into the spoken vernacular, and Lin Shu quickly turned the oral version into a rich and fluid classical idiom. This was the method he employed in all of his subsequent translations. The result was a free rather than a precise, literal rendition, but one which frequently captured the spirit of the original. The Dumas novel proved a resounding success and launched Lin Shu and a succession of different collaborators on an unusually remarkable career. During the next two decades, perhaps 180 translations flowed from his pen. There is considerable discrepancy between the number cited by different scholars, because some of his translations did not reach printed form. In any case, the number that reached the Chinese reading public was large, and the impact of his efforts on an audience eager to learn of Western literature and ideas was clearly enormous. Such famous novelists and writers as Lao She 老舍 (1899-1966) and Kuo Mo-jo 郭沫若 (1892-1978) have testified to the influence Lin Shu's translations had on their own development as writers.

The books Lin Shu and his collaborators selected for translation were mainly drawn from the writings of English, American, and Western European authors and included some of the great masterworks of western literature: Aesop's *Fables;* Homer's *Iliad* and *Odyssey;* Lamb's *Tales from Shakespeare;* prose versions of several plays by William Shakespeare, such as *Julius Caesar, Henry IV,* and *Henry VI;* the novels *Oliver Twist, David Copperfield,* and *Nicholas Nickleby,* among others, by Charles Dickens; Goldsmith's *The Vicar of Wakefield; The Talisman* and *The Betrothed* by Sir Walter Scott; *Robinson Crusoe* by Defoe; selections from the writings of Balzac, Hugo, and Montesquieu; *Don Quixote* by Cervantes; *Ghosts* by Ibsen; and *Tales of a Traveller* and *Alhambra* by Washington Irving. English-language versions of Leo Tolstoy were used to translate such works as *The Death of Ivan Ilyich* and *The Kreutzer Sonata* into Chinese. Lin Shu was a man of pronounced romantic sensibilities, and he was therefore much taken by the combination of sentimental-ity, social consciousness, and moral fervor in the novels of Charles Dickens. For somewhat different reasons, he was also attracted to the novels of the ultra-romanticist H. Rider Haggard and rendered twenty-five of his novels into Chinese, which is also indicative of the temper of the times and the limitations of the translation method he was compelled to employ. Although Lin Shu's translations would ultimately be supplanted by new versions couched in modern idiom, as were those of his friend Yen Fu* who translated such scientific and sociological classics as Thomas H. Huxley's *Evolution and Ethics,* Adam Smith's *Wealth of Nations,* and Montesquieu's *Esprit des Lois,* Lin's contribution to his times was an epochal one.

Lin Shu authored eight novels and several collections of short fiction, and while few if any of these works are much read or appreciated today for their intrinsic literary qualities, they have been shown by Cheng Chen-to 鄭振鐸 (1898-1958) and subsequent modern literary historians to be of historical importance. The literary and social significance Lin Shu assigned to prose fiction was untraditional, and his assertion that the novels of Dickens were equal in value to the monumental history of Ssu-ma Ch'ien* was a startlingly radical departure from the norm. No less important to the emergence of the modern Chinese novel was the example of such novels as *Ching-hua pi-hsüeh lu* 京華碧血錄, *Chin-ling ch'iu* 金陵秋, and *Kuan-ch'ang hsin hsien-hsing chi* 官場新現形記 in abandoning traditional narrative structures for new ones. Moreover, his use of the fictional form to depict historical and contemporary political and social movements, such as the Boxer Affair, foreshadowed in some degree the social concern of the writer in later years.

Some of these same qualities are discoverable in his poetry: the use of the classical idiom and the expression of ideas progressive in the context of the times. There is little by way of structural innovation (he preferred the regular heptasyllabic line), but his poetry still merits more attention than it has so far received. His use of that form to express his ideas on a wide range of social issues, such as lower taxation and other measures designed to relieve the troubles of the common man, the abolition of footbinding, and the education of women, for instance, is of historical interest. Those and similar ideas were voiced in a cycle of poems entitled "Min-chung hsin yüeh-fu" 閩中新樂府. Being a painter of some skill and reputation, he also wrote many poems as inscriptions for his paintings.

EDITIONS:

Lin, Shu. *Wei-lu wen-chi* 畏廬文集. Shanghai, 1910.
———. *Wei-lu hsü-chi* 續集. Shanghai, 1916.
———. *Wei-lu man-lu* 漫錄. 4v. Shanghai, 1922.
———. *Wei-lu so-chi* 瑣記. Shanghai, 1922.
———. *Wei-lu shih-ts'un* 詩存. 2v. Shanghai, 1923.
———. *Wei-lu san chi* 三集. Shanghai, 1924.
———. *Lin i hsiao-shuo ts'ung-shu* 林譯小說叢書. 97v. Shanghai, 1914.

STUDIES:

BDRC, pp. 382-386.
Cheng, Chen-to. "Lin Ch'in-nan Hsien-sheng" 林琴南先生, in *Chung-kuo wen-hsüeh yen-chiu*, Peking, 1957, v. 3, pp. 1214-1227.
Ch'ien, Chung-shu 錢鍾書, *et al.. Lin Shu te fan-i* 林紓的翻譯. Peking, 1981.
Chu, Hsi-chou 朱羲冑. *Lin Ch'in-nan Hsien-sheng hsüeh-hsing p'u-chi ssu chung* 林琴南先生學行譜記四種. Rpt. Taipei, 1961.
Han, Kuang 寒光. *Lin Ch'in-nan.* Shanghai, 1935.
Lee, Leo Ou-fan. *The Romantic Generation of Modern Chinese Writers.* Cambridge, Mass., 1973. Especially pp. 41-57, for an extremely informative analysis of his life and works.

—ws

Ling Meng-ch'u 凌濛初 (*tzu*, Hsüan-fang 玄房, *hao*, Ch'u-ch'eng 初成 and Chi-k'ung kuan chu-jen 即空觀主人, 1580-1644), like Feng Meng-lung,* is best remembered for his contribution to *hua-pen** stories. Although Ling was less versatile than Feng, his influence, like Feng's, was by no means limited to the short story. Ling came from a prestigious family in Wu-ch'eng 烏程, Hu-chou 湖州 Prefecture (modern Chekiang), that had produced generations of outstanding scholar-officials. He was the

fourth son of Ling Ti-chih 凌迪知 (*tzu*, Chih-che 稚哲, *chin-shih*, 1556), seven of whose books are listed in the *Ssu-k'u ch'üan-shu tsung-mu t'i-yao* (see Chi Yün)—Ling Meng-ch'u also had seven titles in this supreme bibliography.

Against such a background, the official career of Ling Meng-ch'u was a disappointment. Like Feng Meng-lung, he did not get a significant appointment until late in life (1634) when he became the assistant magistrate of Shanghai at the age of fifty-five. He stayed there for eight years, taking charge of coastal defense and other duties. In his next post as the Assistant Prefect of Hsü-chou 徐州 (near Nanking), he had some success in river control and in handling the local bandits. When a branch of Li Tzu-ch'eng's 李自成 (1605?-1645) rebels overran Hsü-chou in February 1644, he chose to die in its defense.

Ling Meng-ch'u's late entrance to officialdom made it possible for him to concentrate on writing and publishing during the better part of his productive years. In his mid-twenties, Ling was a protégé of the eminent writer Feng Meng-chen 馮夢禎 (1546-1605, no kin to Feng Meng-lung) and later brought to completion their cooperative work *Tung-p'o ch'an-hsi lu* 東坡禪喜錄 (Tung-p'o on Zen Buddhism, 1621). During the three decades from 1606 to his Shanghai appointment, Ling Meng-ch'u, using Nanking as his base, engaged in compiling, commenting, editing, and writing. Besides his short-story collections and theatrical pieces, he brought out *Hou Han-shu tsuan* 後漢書纂 (Edited History of the Latter Han, 1606), *Kuo-men chi* 國門集 (The Capital Collection), *Kuo-men i-chi* 乙集 (The Second Capital Collection), *Ho-p'ing shih-hsüan* 合評詩選 (Poems from the Select Literature with Commentaries), *T'ao-Wei ho-chi* 陶韋合集 (Combined Collections of T'ao Ch'ien and Wei Ying-wu), *K'ung-men liang ti-tzu yen-shih i* 孔門兩弟子言詩翼 (Two Disciples of Confucius on the Book of Songs), and *Sheng-men ch'uan-Shih ti-chung* 聖門傳詩嫡冢 (The Orthodox Tradition of the Book of Songs). Although a number of his other works might not have survived, some works associated with his name could have been wrongly attributed to him.

Despite his productivity, Ling Meng-ch'u's position in literary history largely rests on his work in the short story. His two story collections, *P'o-an ching-ch'i* 拍案驚奇 (Striking the Table in Amazement at the Wonders, 1628) and *Erh-k'o P'o-an ching-ch'i* 二刻 (The Second Collection of Striking the Table in Amazement at the Wonders, 1632), though clearly under the influence of Feng Meng-lung (there is still no evidence of their direct contact), might be argued to be far more innovative and influential than Feng's because they initiated a trend rather than, as in Feng's collections, concluding a tradition. The seventy-eight stories in these two collections (nominally eighty stories, but one is a theatrical piece and another the second version of a story) are not a mixture of stories from many different sources and times. They were all written by Ling Meng-ch'u himself, partly because the available old stories had already been more or less exhausted by Feng Meng-lung's endeavors. This explains the unity in Ling's collection of style, theme, viewpoint, and technique. This development gave a new life to the otherwise stagnant *hua-pen* tradition and resulted in a round of collections by individual writers. Some better-known examples of these collections are *Shih-erh lou* (by Li Yü, 1611-1680*), *Hsi-hu erh-chi* 西湖二集 (Second West Lake Collection, by Chou Ch'ing-yüan 周清原), *Hsi-hu chia-hua* 西湖佳話 (Memorable Stories of the West Lake), *Chao-shih pei* 照世杯 (The Cup That Reflects the World), *Tou-p'eng hsien-hua* 豆棚閑話 (Casual Talks Under the Bean Arbor), *Tsui-hsing shih* 醉醒石 (The Sobering Stone), and *Yü-mu hsing-hsin pien* 娛目醒心編 (Stories That Please the Eyes and Enlighten the Heart).

Ling Meng-ch'u was also an important critic of drama and a fine playwright. His views on *ch'uan-ch'i** are found in his *T'an-ch'ü tsa-cha* 譚曲雜劄 (Notes on Plays), which is appended to his anthology *Nan-yin san-lai* 南音三籟 (Three Kinds of Southern Sound). In this short treatise he stresses plain language. None of his three *ch'uan-ch'i* survived. However, three of his eight *tsa-chü* have come down to us. His *Sung*

Kung-ming nao yüan-hsiao 公明鬧元宵 (Sung Kung-ming Throws the Lantern Festival Night into an Uproar) deals with a well-known *Shui-hu chuan** episode: Sung Chiang's journey to Kaifeng and visit to its famous courtesan Li Shih-shih 李師師. It also deals with her love for Chou Pang-yen.* This play, in nine acts, combines the tunes and conventions of Northern and Southern drama; its modes alternate between "light and graceful" and "loud and roistering."

Three other *tsa-chü** by Ling Meng-ch'u, of which two have been preserved, are based on the "Ch'iu-jan k'o ch'uan" by Tu Kuang-t'ing,* which some decades earlier had been adapted for the stage as *ch'uan-ch'i* by Chang Feng-i* under the title *Hung-fu chi*. Ling Meng-ch'u's two plays are regular four-act *tsa-chü*. In *Ch'iu-jan weng* 虬髯翁 (The Curly-bearded Fellow), the singing role is assigned to the title-hero; in *Mang tse-p'ei* 莽擇配 (The Impetuous Choice of a Mate), it is assigned to Hung-fu. Authors of *tsa-chü* often wrote plays on subjects that had already been dealt with by earlier playwrights in the genre; changing the focus of observation by assigning the one singing role to a different character was a common technique. But cases of repeated treatment of the same materials by the same playwright are rare.

Ling Meng-ch'u's edition of both *Hsi-hsiang chi** and *P'i-p'a chi* (see Kao Ming) are outstanding for their quality; his edition of *Hsi-hsiang chi* has often served as the base of modern annotated editions.

One reason why Ling Meng-ch'u published so much was that he was a professional publisher himself, and a remarkable one at that. By the time of his generation, the Ling family had been in the publishing business for quite a few generations and they conducted the business in both co-operation and competition with the Min family of the same town. There also seem to have been frequent intermarriages between the two families. During the Wan-li years, Min Ch'i-chi 閔齊伋 (*tzu*, Yü-wu 遇五, 1575-after 1656) invented multi-color printing, and the Ling family, particularly Ling Meng-ch'u and his uncle Ling Chih-lung 凌稚隆, joined in the venture. With this as their specialty, many of the books published by these two families during the Wan-li period and after were naturally done in multi-colors (from the basic black-and-red two-color printing to five-color printing of red, blue, black, yellow, and purple). Therefore, if an early and apparently complete edition of one of Ling Meng-ch'u's works is in regular black-and-white printing, one should question whether it is the original edition published by the author himself. Until a multi-colored edition of the *Erh-k'o P'o-an ching-ch'i* is found, the possibility that Ling Meng-ch'u might have written forty stories for this second collection of the *Erh-p'o* series should not be ruled out.

EDITIONS:

Early or original editions of Ling Meng-ch'u's works as well as copies of the books he published can be found as rare items in several sinological libraries. Here references are only given to commendable and easily available editions, usually based on rare copies.

Ch'iu-jan weng, in *Sheng-Ming tsa-ch'ü erh-chi* 盛明雜劇二集, Shen T'ai 沈泰 (Ming), ed.

Ch'u-k'o P'o-an ching-ch'i 初刻. Wang Ku-lu 王古魯, ed. Shanghai, 1957. Generally accurate, with copious notes, but also with passages censored. Lacking Chapters 37, 39, and 40; last four chapters missing in all other modern typeset editions.

Erh-k'o P'o-an ching-ch'i. Wang Ku-lu, ed. Shanghai, 1957. Same quality as the other collection edited by Wang.

Erh-k'o P'o-an ching-ch'i. Li T'ien-i 李田意 ed. Taipei, 1960. With all forty chapters and authorial remarks, but no modern critical apparatus.

Mang tse-p'ai, in *Ming-jen tsa-ch'ü hsüan* 明人雜劇選, Chou I-pai 周貽白, ed., Peking, 1958, pp. 269-295.

Nan-yin san-lai. Shanghai, 1963. Photographical reproduction of Ming and early Ch'ing editions.

P'o-an ching-ch'i. Li T'ien-i, ed. Hong Kong, 1967. Same quality as the other collection edited by Li.

Sung Kung-ming nao yüan-hsiao. As Chapter 40 of the *Erh-k'o P'o-an ching-ch'i*.

T'an-ch'ü tsa-cha, in *Hsi-ch'ü lun-chu*, v. 4, pp. 249-261.

TRANSLATIONS:

Of Ling Meng-ch'u's works, only stories from the *Erh-p'o* collections have been translated, but there are so many translations into English, French, German, and Japanese that they cannot be listed here. Readers are referred to the comprehensive list of English translations in Patrick Hanan, *The Chinese Vernacular Story*, Cambridge, Mass., 1981, pp. 245-248. For translations in other languages, see the multi-volume set prepared by André Lévy and others, *Inventaire analytique et critique de conte chinois en langue vulgaire*, Paris, 1978- .

STUDIES:

Araki, Takeshi 荒木猛. "Ryō Mōsho no kakei to sono shōgai" 凌濛初の家系とその生涯, *Bunka*, 44.1.2 (September 1980), 16-30.

Chao, Ching-shen 趙景深, *Ch'ü-lun ch'u-t'an* 曲論初探. Shanghai, 1980, pp. 38-41.

Chou, Yüeh-jan 周越然. "Shu-t'an: T'ao-yin shu" 書談：套印書, *Hsiao-shuo yüeh-pao*, 22.7 (July 1931), 983-987.

DMB, pp. 930-931.

Hanan, *Vernacular Story*, pp. 140-164, 231-236.

Ogawa, *Sangen*. Offers summaries of all *hua-pen* in the *San-yen* and *Erh-p'ai* collections followed by a list of all identifications of sources by Chinese and Japanese scholars.

T'an, *San-yen*. Provides the full text of the identified sources of each *hua-pen* in *San-yen* and *Erh-p'ai* (see Feng Meng-lung).

T'ao, Hsiang 陶湘. "Ming Wu-hsing Min-pan shu-mu" 明吳興閔板書目, *Ch'ing-ho*, 5.13 (May 1937), 1-10.

Yeh, Te-chün 葉德均. "Ling Meng-ch'u shih-chi hsi-nien" 凌濛初事跡繫年, in Yeh Te-chün, *Hsi-ch'ü hsiao-shuo ts'ung-k'ao* 戲曲小說叢考, Chao Ching-shen, ed., Peking, 1979, v. 2, pp. 577-590.

———. "Shu Cheng Lung-ts'ai chuan Ling Meng-ch'u mu-chih-ming hou" 書鄭龍采撰凌濛初墓誌銘後, *Ta-kung pao* (Tientsin) (*Wen-shih chou-k'an* 文史週刊, 12), 1 January 1947. Also in *Ta-kung pao* (Shanghai) (*Wen-shih chou-k'an*, 12), 8 January 1947.

—YWM and WI

Liu Chang-ch'ing 劉長卿 (*tzu*, Wen-fang 文房, *hao*, Sui-chou 隨州, *c.* 710-after 787) was one of the more important poets of his day and is the most representative poet of the period immediately following that of the major High T'ang figures Wang Wei,* Li Po,* and Tu Fu.*

His birthdate is unknown. It can be inferred that he was born around 710, since he passed the *chin-shih* in 733, and had he done so before his mid-twenties he would probably have been described somewhere as precocious. He appears to have had an undistinguished career in the capital until shortly before the outbreak of the An Lushan Rebellion in 755. A low-ranking, provincial official when the rebellion began, it is possible he fled his post to avoid capture or death. In any event, he spent the rest of his long life in central China, holding positions in the newly organized Salt Administration. His checkered career—he was imprisoned or banished and subsequently restored to office several times—during this latter period seems to reflect the changing fortunes of his sponsors in the central government, rather than any particular merit or demerit of his own. He was generally in comfortable economic circumstances, for he owned a number of rural estates in various parts of the country. By 780 he had been appointed to his most important official post, prefect of Suichou 隨州 (modern northern Hupei). He had evidently retired from this post by the last datable occurrence in his life, but it is not known where or when he died.

Over five hundred of Liu's poems are extant. Many of them are occasional pieces of no great literary interest, but they also include a number of fine landscape poems in a style that owes much to both T'ao Ch'ien* and Wang Wei.* Although he is not included amoung the "Ta-li shih-ts'ai-tzu" (see Lu Lun), a grouping of typical—and generally mediocre—younger contemporaries, his style has much in common with theirs in its concentration on bucolic subjects and a cultivated casualness of manner. Only a decade younger than Wang Wei and Li Po, he clearly belongs to a very different generation. That difference was compounded by his long life and his obscurity as a younger man. Indeed, he scarcely emerged as a poet at all until after the An Lu-shan Rebellion, and most of his extant poems were probably written after the deaths of all the major High T'ang poets except Tu Fu. The persistence of the

High T'ang landscape manner in his work is perhaps due to his prolonged absence from the capital and his lack of involvement with advanced literary circles in the provinces. He is often grouped with Wei Ying-wu,* but it is not certain that the two men were acquainted.

EDITIONS:
Liu Sui-chou chi 劉隨州集. 10+1 *chüan*. SPTK. The former is the best edition, the latter the most readily accessible.

TRANSLATIONS:
Gundert, *Lyrik*, p. 98.
Owen, *High T'ang*, pp. 258-261.
Sunflower, pp. 116-117.

STUDIES:
Ch'en, Hsiao-ch'iang 陳曉薔. "Liu Chang-ch'ing sheng-p'ing shih-chi ch'u-k'ao" 生平事跡初考, *Ta-lu tsa-chih*, 29.3-5 (1964), 81-84, 129-134, 170-175. Thorough study of Liu's biography with a collection of comments by traditional critics appended.
Fu, *Shih-jen*, pp. 238-268: "Liu Ch'ang-ch'ing shih-chi k'ao-pien"
Konami, Ichirō 小南一郎. "Ryū Chōkei" 劉長卿, in Ogawa, *Tōdai*, pp. 266-270. A heavily annotated translation of the biography of Liu in the *T'ang ts'ai-tzu chuan*.
Takahashi, Yoshiyuki 高橋良行. "Ryū Chōkei shū tembon kō" 劉長卿集傳本考, *Chūgoku bungaku kenkyū* (Waseda Daigaku), 3 (1978), 52-71. A thorough study of the textual history of Liu's works.
Tu, Shui-feng 杜水封. "Sui-chou ch'i-lü shang-hsi" 隨州七律賞析, *Hsüeh-shu lun-wen chi-k'an*, 3 (1976), 97-134. Discussion of thirty of Liu's heptasyllabic regulated verse poems, preceded by a detailed gathering of biographical and critical materials.

—DB

Liu Ch'en-weng 劉辰翁 (*tzu*, Hui-meng 會孟, *hao*, Hsü-hsi 須溪, 1232-1297) was a writer and critic of the Southern Sung. He passed the *chin-shih* in 1262, though only at the third level because his criticism of the current state of affairs during an audience with the emperor offended the Grand Councilor, Chia Ssu-tao 賈似道 (1213-1275). Thereafter, he held government posts at various times, resigned once from office to be a teacher in the Lien-hsi

濂溪 Academy (modern Kiangsi), and declined several recommendations to office. After the fall of the Sung, he lived out his life in seclusion.

Traditionally, Liu Ch'en-weng has not been considered a major author or literary critic. There is evidence, however, that he was a voluminous writer who had an aptitude for a variety of literary genres and areas of study. Liu Ch'en-weng's writings were already rare in the Ming dynasty. Nevertheless, despite its incompleteness, the present collection of Liu's works is amazingly bulky, including both creative writings and critical commentaries.

Liu's prose writings span the gamut of traditional genres. The style is unusual, for his language diverges from the ordinary, often to the point of obscurity. Liu Ch'en-weng also wrote *shih** and *tz'u** poetry. His *shih* poems, numbering less than thirty, reflect in both their language and in their descriptions the sufferings of the people during war time, the irretrievable passage of time, and a strong sense of history. In this sense it is reminiscent of the works of Tu Fu.* His *tz'u* poems number over three hundred. Although many of them reflect the more personal, immediate aspects of the poet's life, a significant portion of this corpus displays the poet's allegiance to, and concern for, the nation. His style is vigorous and unrestrained, and was regarded by traditional critics as close to that of Su Shih* and Hsin Ch'i-chi.*

Liu Ch'en-weng was also a book collector, collator, annotator. He worked on philosophical and historical texts and belles lettres, especially T'ang and Sung *shih* poetry and Sung *tz'u* poetry. As a critic Liu preferred novelty in style combined with profundity in meaning. He was especially intrigued with poetic language that embodies more than is signified by the literal, surface value. His high regard for Li Ho,* for instance, was based on Li's practice of representing emotions and thoughts in unconventional language. This unorthodoxy of Li's style, according to Liu Ch'en-weng, afforded Li a distinctive position among Chinese poets. Liu Ch'en-weng's highest admiration, however, was reserved for Tu

Fu, whose major strength, so Liu held, was his ability to choose from the many alternatives the one word that yielded the greatest multiplicity of meaning.

EDITIONS:

Hsü-hsi chi 須溪集. *Ssu-k'u ch'üan-shu chen-pen ssu-chi*. Reprint of the hand-copied edition of Wen-yüan-ko 文淵閣. 10 *chüan*. Taipei, 1973.

Ch'üan Sung tz'u, v. 5, pp. 3186-3254.

STUDIES:

Hsü-hsi-tz'u yen-chiu chi chien-chu 須溪詞研究及箋注. Huang Hsiao-hsien 黃孝先, annot. N.p., preface dated 1973.

—SH

Liu Chi 劉基 (*tzu*, Po-wen 伯溫, *hao*, Yü-li tzu 郁離子, 1311-1375), from Ch'ing-t'ien 青田 (modern Chekiang) was born into a family noted for military (in the Sung) and scholarly achievements. Liu's father and grandfather were both pedants. Liu Chi was an excellent student with a good memory whose interests were shaped under his grandfather's influence. Thus Liu avidly studied, besides the *Ch'un-ch'iu* (see *ching*), military tactics, astronomy, mathematics, and the natural sciences. At age fifteen (1316) he passed the prefectural examination and became a *chü-jen*. A local scholar, Cheng Fu-ch'u 鄭復初 (*chin-shih*, 1318), introduced Liu to Neo-Confucianism. In 1333 he passed the *chin-shih* examination.

For the next decade he served in minor provincial posts. From 1343 on he traveled through Kiangsu and Chekiang—this was also a period of great literary activity for Liu. In 1352 he joined in the defense of the Chekiang coastal region and in 1357 enjoyed a successful tenure as advisor to a Mongol general.

Liu Chi was, however, generally very critical of Mongol rule, giving vent to these feelings in a collection of essays entitled *Yü-li tzu* 郁離子 (Master of Refined Enlightenment). The work is in eighteen sections, each with a separate title, and these sections all contain a number of essays on the section topic (a total of over 180 essays, ranging from a few dozen words to over one thousand). Each essay treats a single event and espouses one principle or idea.

For example, under the first section, "Ch'ien-li ma" 千里馬 (Thousand-*li* Horses), there are various essays on perceptions of value. Some begin, in a traditional manner, with the phrase "The Master of Refined Enlightenment in discussing such-and-such a topic said, "..." followed by an exemplum or anecdote. Other pieces begin with a question put to the Master by an adversarius. Still others contain no mention of the Master at all (cf. under "Thousand-*li* Horses" the essay on the musical-instrument craftsman Chih-ch'iao 之僑 whose *ch'in* 琴 goes unheeded until he ornaments it and buries it so that it is thought to be an "ancient" piece). The creation of or use of fictional characters as adversaria for the Master is common throughout. Chü-kung 狙公, the monkey trainer from the well-known anecdote (recorded in the *Chuang-tzu* and the *Lieh-tzu*) in which he tricks his wards by verbal artifice, appears in the *Yü-li tzu* as a tyrant whose charges eventually revolt against his harsh treatment. The use of allegory seen here is common in other essays and again suggests influence from the *Chuang-tzu* and the *ku-wen** tradition of such argumentation as intiated by Han Yü* and Liu Tsung-yüan.*

Another originally separate collection is Liu's *Ch'un-ch'iu ming-ching* 春秋明經 (Clarification of the Classic *Spring and Autumn Annals*) in two *chüan* and forty-one sections. In a style which has been compared to that of *Kuo-yü*,* Liu explicates selected passages from the *Ch'un-ch'iu*, most on misrule.

Among his other prose works (over 260 pieces) are 8 *fu** and 15 *sao* (see *Ch'u-tzu*). His "T'ung T'ien-t'ai fu" 通天臺賦 (Prose-poem on the Terrace of Communication with Heaven), on a terrace built by Emperor Wu of the Han in 109 B.C., assumes the style of Ssu-ma Hsiang-ju,* who, had he not died in 117 B.C., would likely have written on the subject himself. The piece was written when Liu was barely twenty (1333), an age at which such imitational works were considered a normal part of a student's preparation for the examinations. This piece transcends, however, the norm. Liu's clever use of a Han subject treated in the style of the Han master reveals both his literary talent and his identification with antiquity. "Shu-chih fu" 述志賦 (Prose-poem Explaining my Aspirations) is modeled on the "Li sao" (see *Ch'u-tz'u*), and "Tiao Chu-ko Wu-hou fu" 弔諸葛武侯賦 (Prose-poem on the Military Marquis Chu-ko Liang) eulogizes one of Liu Chi's models. These models—Chu-ko Liang 諸葛亮 (181-234), Ch'ü Yüan,* and Yüeh Fei 岳飛 (1103-1141)—indicate Liu's ambivalence toward the alien Mongol regime he first served and may help explain his eventual decision to serve a second dynasty, the Ming, by suggesting his uneasiness in his role with the first.

Liu's other prose works reflect a strong *ku-wen* influence in genre selection (*shuo* 說, *chi* 記, *wen-ta yü* 問答語, etc.), content, and tone (often ironic). He is considered a stylist of the first order and his name is often paired with that of Sung Lien.*

Liu's passion for antiquity—which may also stem from his distaste for Mongol contemporaneity—is also evident in his verse. He has 265 ancient-style *yüeh-fu** poems, 54 *ko-hsing* 歌行 (songs), 22 four-word poems modeled on the *Shih-ching*,* nearly 600 *lü-shih* (see *shih*), and over 230 *tz'u*.* The *yüeh-fu*, though on traditional themes such as "Wang Chao-chün" 王昭君 or "Shao-nien hsing" 少年行 are unique in that they include philosophical twists to the conventional subjects. "Shao-nien hsing," for example, begins with the traditional account of a prodigal son enjoying the pleasure districts of the capital. The entire last half of the poem is devoted to an account of the now aging "youth": his home town has completely changed when he returns from years of revelry in the capital; his friends and neighbors are gone; he finds himself too old to re-apply himself to study, too weak to begin farming—he can only lean on a wall and listen to the sounds of the loom at a neighbor's (reminding him he hasn't married). The poem closes with the persona in tears over a man who has become "like a tumbleweed," with no roots. "Pei-feng hsing" 北風行 (Song of the Northern Winds), a seven-word *chüeh-chü*

575

(see *shih*) written in the "border convention," contrasts the harsh life of the common soldiers to that of their general, who sits in furs drinking warmed wine and enjoying the falling snow from his window.

Liu often emphasizes the didactic role of literature in his prefaces to others' collected works (see "*Chao-hsüan Shang-jen shih-chi* hsü" 照玄上人詩集序) and practiced it in his own work as well, many poems depicting the plight of the common people.

His "Erh-kuei" 二鬼 (Two Ghosts) is a long poem (more than 1200 characters) set in mythical antiquity. Two ghosts, Chiehlin 結麟 and Chüeh-i 爵儀 restore the universe to order, paying especial attention to the life of the masses. They do so against the will of T'ien-ti 天帝. The poem has been understood as an allegory of Liu Chi and Sung Lien's political efforts under the first emperor of the Ming.

Although the breadth and style of Liu's literary corpus mark him as one of the few writers after the eleventh century to approach the excellence of the T'ang and Sung literary giants, he is perhaps best known in his popular image as Liu Po-wen, prognosticator par excellence and hero of various tales and stories (see Hok-lam Chan, especially chapter 4).

EDITIONS:

Ch'eng-i Po wen-chi 誠意伯文集. Taipei, 1968.

Ch'eng-i Po Liu Hsien-sheng wen-chi 誠意伯劉先生文集. 1470. Best edition.

T'ai-shih Ch'eng-i Po Liu Wen-ch'eng Kung chi 太師誠意伯劉文成公文集. *SPTK*. Reproduces a 1572 edition. The *Yü-li tzu* in the *Hsüeh-chin t'ao-yüan* 學津討原 is based on the *SPTK*, but has been carefully collated with other editions.

Yü-li tzu 郁離子. Shanghai, 1981. A punctuated edition based on the 1470 edition, but collated with the *Hsüeh-chin t'ao-yüan* and other editions.

TRANSLATIONS:

Chan, Hok-lam William. "Liu Chi (1311-1375): The Dual Image of a Chinese Imperial Advisor." Unpublished Ph.D. dissertation. Princeton University, 1967. Partial translation of "Shu-chih fu" on pp. 66-67.

Demiéville, *Anthologie*, p. 470.

Margouliès, *Kou-wen*, pp. 320-321. Translation of "Ssu-ma Chi-chu lun-pu" 司馬季主論卜.

"Selected Fables from 'Yu Li Zi,'" *CL*, October 1983, 81-91.

STUDIES:

Chan, "The Dual Image."

Ch'ien, Mu 錢穆. "Tu Ming-ch'u k'ai-kuo chu-ch'en shih-wen chi" 讀明初開國諸臣詩文集, *Hsin-ya hsüeh-pao*, 6.2 (August 1964), 243-326.

Fukumoto, Masaichi 福本雅一. "Ryu Ki shi josetsu" 劉基詩序說, *Chūgoku bungaku hō*, 18 (1963), 91-107.

Kao, Hai-fu 高海夫. "T'an Liu Chi te 'Yü-li tzu' 談劉基的〃郁離子〃, *Wen-hsüeh i-ch'an tseng-k'an*, 10 (July 1962), 73-79.

Liu, Te-yü 劉德隅. *Ming Liu Po-wen-kung sheng-p'ing shih-chi shih-i* 明劉伯溫公生平事蹟拾遺. Taipei, 1976.

Ming, 932-938.

Wang, Hsin-i 王雿一. *Liu Po-wen nien-p'u* 劉伯溫年譜. Shanghai, 1935. Gives detailed account of Liu Chi including family background and early life. Is often uncritical and sometimes in error on chronology.

—WHN

Liu Chih-chi 劉知幾 (*tzu*, Tzu-hsüan 子玄, 661-721), *chin-shih*, *c.* 680, primarily known as a critic of historical writing, was a scholar-official whose service in the metropolitan academic institutions of the T'ang spanned the period from 699 until he was banished from the capital in the year of his death. He compiled or took part in the compilation of at least twelve works, was briefly a rescript writer, and participated in scholarly debates on Confucian canonical texts, on their commentaries, and on state ritual prescriptions. He also wrote verse. His highest post was that of Secretary of the Left of the Crown Prince's Household and he was posthumously canonized *Wen* 文 (Literary).

Liu Chih-chi's *Shih-t'ung* 史通 (Generalities on History), the work that has given him his reputation, was completed in 710. Attempting to do for the discipline of history what Liu Hsieh's *Wen-hsin tiao-lung** did for that of belles lettres, it critically surveyed all aspects of historical scholarship from its origins in Confucian canonical texts to the compilations by the early T'ang official historians who were Liu's

576

immediate precedessors in the history office. Comprising thirty-six "inner sections" and thirteen "outer sections," it opens with a description of six schools of history writing in antiquity, and then focuses on two of them, *pien-nien* 編年 (chronicle) and *chi-chuan* 紀傳 (composite), as the models followed in later times. Then it reviews in detail the constituent parts of the composite model, principally the *pen-chi* 本紀 (basic annals), *lieh-chuan* 列傳 (biographies), and *shu-chih* 書志 (treatises). After this come a number of sections on technical matters, such as the appropriate span of a history, terms by which figures in it should be referred to, titles, and commentaries. A group of sections is concerned with style, narrative imitation, the technique, the problems of imitation, the desirability of concise diction, and the need for moral objectivity. The "outer" portion of the work opens with an account of the history office, first founded as a separate institution by the T'ang itself in 629, and of its precursors, reviews the sequence of "orthodox" (*cheng* 正) histories produced for successive dynasties, and goes on to collect Liu's criticisms of Confucian canonical historical texts, the *Shu-ching* and the *Ch'un-ch'iu* (see *ching*), and to plead the special value as history of the *Tso-chuan*.* Further sections gather Liu's miscellaneous judgments and his criticisms of the "Wu-hsing chih" 五行志 (Monograph on the Five Phases) in the *Han-shu*, a piece that he considered undisciplined and unreliable. Liu's letter of 708 to Hsiao Chih-chung 蕭至忠, director of the dynastic history, attempting to resign from the history office, is appended as a final section.

The *Shih-t'ung* is a work of wide erudition and brave critical insight, for Liu draws from, or refers to, nearly three hundred works and cites an even larger number of authors. Despite a highly moralistic perspective, it conveys a sense of romantic enthusiasm for history-writing and for the role of the individual historian. Liu's independent imagination also led him to believe that classical antiquity, despite differences in dress, speech, and mores, was not radically different from his own time

and was by no means as utopian as convention accepted it to be. His belief in the function of history as a register of change led him to suggest, from within the discipline of history as T'ang scholars understood it in its broadest sense, new topics for treatises in composite-form histories. Yet for all his strikingly organic understanding of the past, he believed that the compilation of histories was a discipline governed by strict formal rules and capable of great precision and consistency, and he never broke free of the classificatory, schematic approach to learning that characterized official scholarship in T'ang times.

Liu's sense of compartmentalization led him to demarcate history from literary composition or belles lettres, and the importance of the *Shih-t'ung* to the literary historian, an incidental result of Liu's main purpose, derives from the concern he expressed in it for the concise in narrative style and diction. Probably no other writer of the medieval period stated so clearly what he considered desirable in narrative prose.

Running through Liu's critique of style is a demand that only the essential be included. He seems to have been exhilarated by brevity and condemned any hint of wordiness. Conjunctions, interjections, and other particles were to be considered carefully. Parenthetical or editorial remarks were to be included only if they contributed substantially to the sense. "The laconic writer is already comprehensive with a single expression; the prolix talent can shine only with the aid of several sentences." Liu identified four basic narrative techniques: describing a man's qualities directly; letting his actions speak for themselves; letting the facts be known through direct speech; and expounding them in supplementary essays or assessments.

If his comments were restricted to narrative in official histories, it was precisely this category of writing, commanding great prestige in the medieval scholarly world, that set the tone for other narrative genres—the countless biographies, epitaphs, and reports of conduct, and beyond them the less formal sources, collections of vignettes and anecdotes, and even *ch'uan-ch'i** (tales).

EDITIONS:

Gagnon, G. Avec la collaboration de E. Gagnon, *Concordance combinée du Shitong et du Shitong Xiaofan*. 2v. Paris, 1977.
Shih-t'ung 史通 and *Shih-t'ung cha-chi* 史通札記. Sun Yü-hsin 孫毓修, ed. Rpt. of 1602 edition, *SPTK*.
Shih-t'ung chien-chi 史通箋記. Ch'eng Ch'ien-fan 程千帆, comm. Peking, 1980.
Shih-t'ung t'ung-shih 史通通釋. Edited with commentary by P'u Ch'i-lung 浦起龍, ed. and comm. Revised by P'u Hsi-ling 浦錫齡, 1893, *SPPY*.

TRANSLATIONS:

Masui, Tsuneo 増井經夫. *Shitsū: Tōdai no rekishikan* 史通唐代の歴史觀. Tokyo, 1966. With introduction and index.
Sargent, Stuart H. " 'Understanding History: The Narration of Events,' by Liu Chih-chi (661-721)," in *The Translation of Things Past: Chinese History and Historiography*, George Kao, ed., Hong Kong, 1982.

STUDIES:

Fu, Chen-lun 傅振倫. *Liu Chih-chi nien-p'u* 劉知幾年譜. 3rd ed. Peking, 1963.
Hsü, Kuan-san 許冠三. *Liu Chih-chi te shih-lu shih-hsüeh* 劉知幾的實錄史學. Hong Kong, 1982.
Hung, William. "A Bibliographical Controversy at the T'ang Court A.D. 719," 20 (1957), 74-134.
———. "A T'ang Historiographer's Letter of Resignation," *HJAS*, 29 (1969), 5-52.
Koh, Byongik. "Zur Werttheorie in der chinesische Historiographie auf Grund des Shiht'ung des Liu Chih-chi (661-721)," *OE*, 4 (1957), 5-51, 125-181.
Masui, Tsuneo. "Liu Chih-chi and the *Shih t'ung*," *Memoirs of the Research Department of the Tōyō Bunkō*, 34 (1978), 113-162. Contains a list of editions, textual history, and a useful bibliography.
Pulleyblank, E. G. "Chinese Historical Criticism: Liu Chih-chi and Ssu-ma Kuang," in W. G. Beasley and E. G. Pulleyblank, eds., *Historians of China and Japan*, London, 1961, pp. 135-166.
Quirin, Michael. "Beiträge zur Erforschung von Liu Zhiji's *Shi Tong*." Unpublished M.A. thesis, Rheinischen Friedrich-Wilhelms-Universität, Bonn, 1980.

—DLM

Liu Chih-yüan chu-kung-tiao 劉知遠諸宮調 ("All Keys and Notes" about Liu Chih-yüan), by an unknown author, is one of three extant texts of *chu-kung-tiao,** a genre of narrative ballad which flourished in the twelfth and thirteenth centuries. It is written in alternating sections of verse and prose, the brief prose-linking passages recapitulated and amplified in verse-interludes sung to a muscial accompaniment. The prevalent rhymed passages are assembled into song suites, each in a musical mode different from the preceding one. The name of the genre ("all keys and notes") derives from this distinctive feature. The choice of musical suites following a fixed sequence of modes is the strongest link between *chu-kung-tiao* and the later fully staged operatic dramas of the Yüan and Ming dynasties, but *chu-kung-tiao* is performed by a single entertainer.

The surviving text of the *Liu Chih-yüan chu-kung-tiao* is a woodblock print dating from the time when this particular ballad was actually performed. The small sized print, with many characters in their simplified popular form, comes from a workshop in what today would be Shansi, presumably the place of origin of the *chu-kung-tiao* genre. It was discovered at the site of the ancient city of Karakhoto by the Kozlov expedition (1907-8). The text, comprising forty-two folios, is incomplete. Of a total of twelve chapters there remain only the first (with one page missing), the second, the beginning of the third, a major part of the eleventh (except its beginning), and all of the last.

The hero of the narrative is Liu Chih-yüan, a successful military commander of Sha-t'o (Turkish) origin, who founded the short-lived Han regnum during the Five Dynasties period in 947 and died a little less than a year later. The *chu-kung-tiao*, however, ignores the historical personage and limits the story strictly to the early years of the emperor-to-be. The first three chapters describe the bitter lot of the Liu family and Liu Chih-yüan himself: his father, a soldier, was killed in battle; his widowed mother fled famine with her two little sons and later remarried. After falling out with his half-brothers, Liu Chih-yüan left home and wandered penniless, until he was hired as a farmhand by a village elder. Li San-niang 李三娘, the daughter of the village elder, is overwhelmed by the youth's good looks, and impressed by the auspicious signs of his great future; she visits him in the middle of the night, offering the frightened hero half of her precious hairpin as a token of betrothal. The father gives his consent to their marriage, because he too saw signs which augured well for the future emperor. However, Li San-niang's two brothers, village bullies, oppose the match and try to kill Liu. At every attempt, however, Heaven intervenes and saves the hero. Unable to bear their insults and threats, Liu Chih-yüan takes tearful leave of his wife (who is by now three months pregnant) and enters the army at T'ai-yüan. A military dignitary, seeing both the new recruit's awesome strength and auspicious signs about his head, arranges Liu Chih-yüan's second marriage, to his daughter. Meanwhile Li San-niang is forced by her brothers to do lowly menial work, because she refuses to remarry. In due time she bears a healthy son.

In chapters eleven and twelve we read of the happy reunion of Liu Chih-yüan and Li San-niang after a long separation. During the thirteen-year interval, Liu Chih-yüan has risen to a high position as military governor of the area of modern Shansi. His son, taken as a newborn baby to T'ai-yüan, was brought up by Liu Chih-yüan's new wife as her own child. On a hunting party, the boy meets accidentally with his mother, who does not recognize him and tells him her sad life story. Moved by his son's plea to search for the poor woman's lost husband, Liu Chih-yüan decides to rescue his still much abused wife and rewards her faithfulness with splendor and wealth. From now on, Liu Chih-yüan will live in perfect harmony with his two beloved wives and son. The two mean brothers are chided, but spared. The ballad ends with the gathering of the whole Liu family whose numerous members had been scattered all over the country.

Liu Chih-yüan's official biography, included in the *Han-shu,* is focused primarily on his successful career as a skillful general and governor. As a storyteller theme, the story of Liu Chih-yüan appeared in popular chronicles called *p'ing-hua** which retained the historical framework, but enriched it with legends.

The *Liu Chih-yüan chu-kung-tiao* shares basic structural features with the *Tung Hsi-hsiang chi chu-kung-tiao* 董西廂記諸宮調 (Master Tung's Western Chamber Romance), the only complete text in this genre. Master Tung's sophisticated love story appeals to a highly literate group. In comparison, *Liu Chih-yüan* appears less advanced in narrative techniques and musical composition. It also lacks the subtle poetic characterization used in describing Master Tung's lovers. Yet the artistic achievement of *Liu Chih-yüan* resides in different qualities: a thrilling plot, hyperbolic description of characters harking back to the myths and legends, rumbustious humor, and a racy, rustic vernacular permeated with popular proverbs. It is highly probable that *Liu Chih-yüan* is the only genuine "marketplace and street" *chu-kung-tiao* in existence.

EDITIONS:

Cheng, Chen-to 鄭振鐸, ed. *Liu Chih-yüan chuan (chu-kung-tiao)* 劉知遠傳 (諸宮調), in *Shih-chieh wen-k'u,* 2 (1935), 483-508. Contains several wrong characters which do not correspond to the original and alter the meaning of the text.

Chin-pen chu-kung-tiao Liu Chih-yüan 金本諸公調 劉知遠. Peking, 1937. A photolithographic reprint after photographs taken by Kano Naoki 狩野直喜 in 1928 in Leningrad and later stored at Tōhoku University. Unreliable, because of rather substantial differences with the original print, probably due to corrections in the negatives. Cheng Chen-to based his edition on Kano Naoki's photographs.

Liu Chih-yüan chu-kung-tiao 劉知遠諸宮調. An original woodblock print which dates from the twelfth or thirteenth century and comes from a workshop of P'ing-yang 平陽 in Shansi.

After its discovery by the Kozlov expedition in 1907-8, the print remained in the Leningrad Oriental Institute until April 1958 when the Soviet government made a gift of this priceless volume to the People's Republic of China. It is now in Peking National Library. The print is a fragment, with the cover missing. The actual title is only alluded to in the epilogue.

Liu Chih-yüan chu-kung-tiao 劉知遠諸宮調. Peking, 1958. A photolithographic reprint of the original woodblock print with a postface by Cheng Chen-to giving details of the discovery of the text, its contents, and form.

Uchida, Michio 內田道夫, ed. "Kōchū Ryu Chien shokyūchō" 校注劉知遠諸宮調, in *Tōhoku daigaku bungakubu kenkyū nempō*, 14 (1963), 240-323. A critical edition with excellent annotations in Japanese. It is both reliable and accessible.

TRANSLATIONS:

Dolezelova-Velingerova, Milena and James I. Crump Jr. *Ballad of the Hidden Dragon (Liu Chih-yüan chu-kung-tiao)*. London, 1971.

STUDIES:

Aoki, Masaru 靑木正兒. "Ryū chien shokyūcho kō" 劉知遠諸宮調考, *Shinagaku*, 6 (1932), 195-230. Chinese translation by Tao Chen 悼眞 in *Ta-lu tsa-chih*, 1.3 (1932), 51-65 and by Ho Ch'ang-ch'ün 賀昌群 in *Kuo-li Pei-p'ing t'u-shu-kuan-k'an*, 6.4 (1932), 3-20. First extensive study of the text.

Chang, Hsing-i 張星逸. "Kuan-yü Chin k'o *Liu Chih-yüan chu-kung-tiao* te chiao-chu" 關於金刻劉知遠諸宮調 的校注, *Chiang-hai hsüeh-k'an*, 1964.1, 59-65.

———. "Pu Kuan-yü Chin k'o *Liu Chih-yüan chu-kung-tiao* te chiao-chu" 補關於金刻劉知遠諸宮調的校注, *Chung-kuo yü-wen*, 1965.5, 389-393.

Chao, Wan-li 趙萬里. Ch'ung-kao te yu-i: chi Su-lien cheng-fu tseng-sung te *Liu Chih-yüan chu-kung-tiao* ho *Liao-chai t'u shuo*," 崇高的友誼: 記蘇聯政府贈途的劉知遠諸宮調和聊齋圖說, *Wen-wu ts'an-k'ao tzu-liao*, 7 (1958), 15-16, 22. Technical description of the original woodblock print and location of its origin.

Ch'en, Chih-wen 陳治文. "*Liu Chih-yüan chu-kung-tiao* chiao-tu" 劉知遠諸宮調校讀, *Chung-kuo yü-wen*, 1966.3, 219-222. Interpretation of individual morphemes, punctuation, and the identification of graphs.

Ch'en, Li-li. "The Relationship between Oral Presentation and the Literary Devices used in *Liu Chih-yüan* and *Hsi-hsiang chu-kung-tiao*," *LEW*, 14.4 (1970), 519-127.

Chiang, Li-hung 蔣禮鴻. "Tu *Liu Chih-yüan chu-kung-tiao*" 讀劉知遠諸宮調, *Chung-kuo yü-wen*, 1965.6, 480-482. Author's divergent or supplementary opinions to the studies by Chang Hsing-i, Uchida Michio, and Liu Chien.

Doleželová-Velingerová, Milena. "Introduction" to *Ballad of the Hidden Dragon (Liu Chih-yüan chu-kung-tiao)*. London, 1971, pp. 1-28. Literary analysis of *Liu Chih-yüan chu-kung-tiao*.

Hanan, Patrick. "Some Remarks on Stylistic Comparison (*ad* Lili Ch'en)," *LEW*, 14 (1970), 529-534.

Liu, Chien 劉堅. "Kuan-yü *Liu Chih-yüan chu-kung-tiao* ts'an-chüan tz'u-yü te chiao-shih" 關於劉知遠諸宮調殘卷詞語的校釋, *Chung-kuo yü-wen*, 1964.3, 231-235, 237. Notes on punctuation, pronunciation, graphs, and rearrangement of characters in syntactical units.

Pelliot, Paul. "Les documents chinois trouvés par la mission Kozlov à Khara-khoto," *JA*, Onzième Série, 3 (1914), 503-518, esp. 510-511. Pelliot was the first to examine the text in 1910 in the Asiatic Museum in St. Petersburg. He mistakenly identifies it as "une pièce de théatre à rirs chantés."

Velingerová, Milena, "The Editions of the Liu Chih-yüan chu-kung-tiao," *AO*, 28 (1960), 282-289.

West, *Vaudeville*, pp. 108-125.

—MD

Liu E 劉鶚 (*tzu*, Tieh-yün 鐵雲, *hao*, Hung-tu pai-lien sheng 洪都百鍊生, 1857-1909), a native of Tan-t'u 丹徒 (modern Kiangsu), was the second and youngest son of a minor scholar-official Liu Ch'eng-chung 劉成忠 (*chin-shih*, 1852). At once novelist, poet, philologist, musician, medical practitioner, entrepreneur, and mathematician, Liu E, with his devotion to both the continuity of traditional culture and the introduction of Western knowledge, was as controversial and bewildering as he was learned and fascinating. Although disillusioned with the political system and set early against a conventional official career, he succeeded in earning the friendship and confidence of key officials like Wu Ta-ch'eng 吳大澂 (1835-1902), Chang Yao 張曜 (1832-1891), and Fu-jun 福潤 (d. 1902), serving under them either in formal or advisory positions. But because of ill fortune, his own temperament and indiscretion, and the persistent misunderstanding he managed to create in his various endeavors, he seldom stayed long in one position or even in one profession, and most of his numerous enterprises, particularly those involving foreign interests, were short-lived and frequently made him the object of libelous attacks. The accumulated hostility and the defamation of his name were such that he eventually fell victim to spurious charges and was banished to Sinkiang in 1908. He died there a year later.

Liu E is best remembered for his 20-chapter novel *Lao-ts'an yu-chi* 老殘遊記 (The Travels of Lao-ts'an), the first thirteen chapters of which were serialized in the well-known periodical *Hsiu-hsiang hsiao-shuo* 繡像小說 (Illustrated Fiction) in 1903 and 1904. Completed later in the *T'ien-chin jih-jih hsin-wen* 天津日日新聞 (Tientsin Daily News), this novel, vigorously promoted by Hu Shih 胡適 (1891-1962) and other champions of vernacular literature in the 1920s and repeatedly chosen for secondary-school language courses since then, has become a major work of the late Ch'ing period and one of the few novels consistently popular.

Through the travels of Lao-ts'an, an itinerant medical practitioner who is well received in official circles, *Lao-ts'an yu-chi* exposes the ills of China, relates the evils of the brazenly bad officials as well as those of officals presumed to be conscientious and incorruptible, and tells captivating, though episodic, stories with highly memorable scenes in exceptionally vivid and well-polished language. One such passage is the charming account of the performance of two singing girls in chapter 2. The lyrical elements of the novel and its psychological description have also been critically acclaimed.

Though the novel is not autobiographical, Liu E incorporated so such of his own experience in it that Lao-ts'an is clearly the personification of the author himself. Many of Liu's friends and enemies can be found in the characters of the novel, too. For instance, the benevolent Governor Chuang

莊宮保 in the early chapters stands for Liu's patron Chang Yao, and the two arch examples of maladministration of justice, Yü-hsien 玉賢 and Kang-pi 剛弼, represent the Manchu officials Yü-hsien 毓賢 (d. 1901) and Kang-i 剛毅 (d. 1900), both of whom were deeply involved in the Boxer Rebellion of 1898-1900.

Liu E was a follower of a pseudo-religious branch of philosophy known as the T'ai-ku School 太谷學派, which blended Buddhist and Taoist elements into Confucianism. The mysterious and esoteric encounters in chapters 8-11, which also divide the novel into two thematically different parts, are seemingly unrelated to the main line of narrative and are difficult to understand. These chapters have thus been abridged in some editions. But an analysis of them from the perspective of the teachings of the T'ai-ku School is crucial to the understanding of Liu E's principle of moderation and his criticism of both the Boxers and the future revolutionaries, and to comprehending the severe, and often malicious, attacks directed at Liu E and the *Lao-ts'an yu-chi* in China in the 1950s and 1960s.

A sequel of at least nine chapters, generally known as the *Lao-ts'an yu-chi erh-chi* 老殘遊記二集 (Sequel to the Travels of Lao-ts'an), was serialized in the *T'ien-chin jih-jih hsin-wen* in 1907. The first six chapters tell a rather different story of how the newly acquired concubine of Lao-ts'an, on the home with her husband, becomes a nun at T'ai-shan 泰山, after engaging with the young but highly cultured nun I-yün 逸雲 there. The next three chapters are about Lao-ts'an's dream-trip to the underground court of King Yama 閻羅王. There is also a fragmanted supplement known as the *Lao-ts'an yu-chi wai-pien* 老殘遊記外編 (Supplement to the Travels of Lao-ts'an); its authenticity has yet to be verified. The last twenty chapters of a 40-chapter version circulated in the early Republican era have long been recognized as a forgery.

Besides fiction, Liu E exerted considerable influence in the studies of Chinese characters and Shang culture. He was the first to recognize the significance of oracle-bone inscriptions and was their earliest serious collector. His *T'ieh-yün tsang-kuei* 鐵雲藏龜 (Tortoise Shells Collected by T'ieh-yün, 1903) was the original book on other private and public collections.

Other books by Liu E include *Chih-ho wu-shuo* 治河五說 (Five Essays on Yellow River Conservancy), 1892, with two appendixes; *Li-tai Huang-ho pien-ch'ien t'u-k'ao* 歷代黃河變遷圖考 (Maps and Studies on the Historical Changes of the Yellow River), 1893; *T'ieh-yün tsang-t'ao* 鐵雲藏陶 (Earthware Inscriptions Collected by T'ieh-yün), 1904; and *T'ieh-yün tsang feng-ni* 鐵雲藏封泥 (Mud Seals Collected by T'ieh-yün), 1904. He also published two works on mathematics and left several manuscripts on diverse subjects. In 1980, an annotated collection of Liu E's poems, under the title of *T'ieh-yün shih-ts'un* 鐵雲詩存 (Extant Poems of T'ieh-yün), was published by his grandson Liu Hui-sun 劉蕙孫 (Liu Hou-tsu 劉厚滋) in Tsinan 濟南, the location of some of the major episodes in the *Lao-ts'an yu-chi*.

EDITIONS:

Ch'en, Hsiang-ho 陳翔鶴 and Tai Hung-sen 戴鴻森, eds. *Lao-ts'an yu-chi* 老殘遊記 Peking, 1957. Collected and annotated version.

Lao-ts'an yu-chi 老殘遊記. Taipei, 1976. It includes authorial notes for the first eleven chapters, the surviving chapters of the sequel, and the fragmented supplement, and is recommended for its convenient availability, although all these materials, along with the appended studies, are reprinted from other sources.

Yen, Wei-ch'ing 嚴薇青. *Lao-ts'an yu-chi*. Tsinan, 1981. The best annotated text.

TRANSLATIONS:

Cheng, Tcheng 盛成. *L'odyssee de Lao Ts'an.* Paris, 1964.

Liu, Yutang 林語堂. "A Nun of Taishan," in Liu Yutang, *Widow, Nun and Courtesan,* New York, 1950, pp. 115-180. First published in 1936, this is an English translation of chapters 1-6 of the sequel.

Shadick, Harold. *The Travels of Lao Ts'an.* Ithaca, 1952. Replaces earlier English translations of the novel. With a helpful introduction.

STUDIES:

Chiang, I-hsüeh 蔣逸雪. *Liu E nien-p'u* 劉鶚年譜. Tsinan, 1980.

Ch'ien, C. S 錢鍾書. "A Note to the Second Chapter of *Mr. Decadent,*" *Philoblon,* 2.3 (September 1948), 8-14.

Hsia, C. T. 夏志清. "*The Travels of Lao Ts'an:* An Exploration of Its Arts and Meaning," *THHP, NS,* 7.2 (August 1969), 40-68.

Hu, Shih. "*Lao-ts'an yu-chi* hsü" 老殘遊記序, in *Lao-ts'an yu-chi,* Shanghai, 1925, pp. 1-39. The first major study on the novel.

Kung, P'eng-ch'eng 龔鵬程. "Ts'ung meng-huan yü shen-hua k'an *Lao-ts'an yu-chi* te nei-tsai ching-shen" 從夢幻與神話看老殘遊記的內在精神, *Yu-shih yüeh-k'an,* 48.5 (November 1978), 36-40.

Li, Ou-fan 李歐梵. "Hsin-lu li-ch'eng shang te san-pen shu" 心路歷程上的三本書, in Li Ou-fan, *Hsi-ch'ao te pi-an* 西潮的彼岸, Taipei, 1975, pp. 141-160.

Liu, Ta-shen 劉大坤. "Kuan-yü *Lao-ts'an yu-chi*" 關於老殘遊記, *Yü-chou feng i-k'an,* 20 (January 1940), 18-21; 21 (February 1940), 103-106; 22 (March 1940), 198-201; 23 (April 1940), 262-266; 24 (May 1940), 340-343. Revised version in *Lao-ts'an yu-chi tzu-liao* (see below), pp. 54-104. One of the most informative studies on Liu E, by his fourth son; revised version with large number of notes prepared by Liu Hou-tse 劉厚澤, the author's second son.

Ma, T'ai-lai 馬泰來. "*Ch'ing shih-lu* chung te Liu E" 清實錄中的劉鶚, *Ch'ing-mo hsiao-shuo yen-chiu* (Chinese edition of *Shimmatsu shōsetsu kenkyū*), 1983, 25-29.

Ma, Yu-yüan 馬幼垣. "Ch'ing-chi T'ai-ku hsüeh-p'ai shih-shih shu-yao" 清季太谷學派史事述要, *Ta-lu tsa-chih,* 28.10 (May 1964), 13-18.

———. "Tu Liu-chu *Lao-ts'an yu-chi* erh-pien ts'un-i' " 讀劉著老殘遊記二編存疑, *Chung-yang jih-pao* (Taipei), 20-22 June 1981.

Shimmatsu shōsetsu kenkyūkai 清末小說研究會. "Ryū Tetsuun kenkyū shiryō mokuroku" 劉鐵雲研究資料目錄, *Shimmatsu shōsetsu kenkyū,* 1 (October 1977), 87-111.

Sargent, Stuart H. "Lao-ts'an and Fictive Thinking," *JCLTA,* 12.3 (October 1977), 214-220.

Tarumoto, Teruo 樽本照雄. "*RōSan yūki gaihen* wa gisaku ka" 老殘遊記外編 は偽作か, *IA,* 3 (December 1975), 1-13.

———. "Rōzan yūki shiron" 老殘遊記試論. *Shimmatsu shōsetsu kenkyū,* 1 (October 1977), 27-40.

Wei, Shao-ch'ang 魏紹昌. *Lao-ts'an yu-chi tzu-liao* 老殘遊記資料. Peking, 1962. The most important source book.

Yen, Wei-ch'ing. "Liu E ho T'ai-ku hsüeh-p'ai" 老殘遊記和太谷學派. *Liu-ch'üan*, 1980.2 (October 1980), 134-138.

—YWM

Liu Hsiang 劉向 (original *ming*, Keng-sheng 更生, *tzu*, Tzu-cheng 子政, *c.* 79-*c.* 6 B.C.) is known primarily as a bibliographer, a compiler of anecdotal literature, and, to a lesser extent, as a poet and author of prosodic lamentations.

Liu was of noble birth—his family was descended from the younger brother of the founder of the Han dynasty—and at the age of twelve he was named a page. He distinguished himself by submitting his first *fu** at the age of nineteen (in 60 B.C.) to the Emperor Hsüan (The *Han-shu* "I-wen chih" lists a thirty-three-fascicle collection of the *fu* of Liu Hsiang). But Liu's young career ended in disaster. He had earlier obtained through his father a copy of the *Hung-pao yüan mi-shu* 鴻寶苑秘書 (Secret Documents of the Garden of Extensive Treasures) by Liu An, the unfortunate King of Huai-nan whose patronage had produced the *Huai-nan-tzu* (see *Chu-tzu pai-chia*). *The Secret Documents of the Extensive Treasures*—said to have been kept "within a pillow" to indicate that the work was a rare treasure not intended for wide circulation—included magical recipes for forcing ghosts to make gold. In 56 B.C., Liu Hsiang, who throughout his career would show great interest in things supernatural, presented the book to the emperor promising that gold could be obtained by following its techniques. After vast but vain expenditures, the recipes proved to be ineffective and young Liu was cast in jail. He avoided the death penalty only after his elder brother, Liu An-min 劉安民, purchased a pardon by turning over to the state half of the households of his fief.

In 55 B.C., Liu Hsiang was readmitted to court life and given a scholarly post as reader of the *Ku-liang* interpretation of the *Ch'un-ch'iu* (see *ching*). In this capacity he participated in the Shih-ch'ü Pavilion debates (convened in 51 B.C. on the 500th anniversary of Confucius's birth). The debates were devoted to establishing the proper interpretation of the rituals recorded in the "Five Canons." Being favored by the great scholar, Hsiao Wang-chih 蕭望之, Liu was named to an even higher government position in 48 B.C., the first year of Emperor Yüan's reign. Liu submitted numerous, extremely learned remonstrances—models of how the ancient canonical texts were cited to serve Han-dynasty political purposes—cautioning the new ruler to take personal interest in statecraft. He held a clandestine meeting with Hsiao Wang-chih and others to debate how to curb the powers of the emperor's maternal relatives, but news leaked, Liu was again imprisoned and Hsiao stripped of office. It appeared that they might regain favor, because of their abilities to interpret unfavorable portents which worried the emperor, but the eunuchs Hung Kung 弘恭 and Shih Hsien 石顯 conspired to keep Liu in jail and to drive Hsiao to suicide in 47 B.C.

Liu remained without court position for the next fifteen years, a period which marked the consolidation of power in the hands of the maternal relatives, the eunuchs, and their followers. At one point, in 40 B.C., Liu's friends Chou K'an 周堪 and Chang Meng 張猛 gained favor when the emperor was made fearful by an eclipse. But Shih Hsien hounded Chou K'an to death and conspired to have the emperor order Chang Meng's suicide. Liu composed four lamentations, now lost, in mourning for his friends.

Liu's fortunes changed for the better in 32 B.C. with the ascension of Emperor Ch'eng and the demise of Shih Hsien. He was accepted back at court and to mark the occasion changed his given name from Keng-sheng to Hsiang. In 26 B.C., an imperial rescript was issued ordering the search for rare books throughout the realm. The rescript also commanded that extant works be collated on the basis of the discovered manuscripts and fair copies be deposited in the imperial library. Liu Hsiang, newly named Collator of Secret

Documents within the Palace, was charged with collating canonical, philosophical, and poetical texts. In editing the texts Liu employed a technique known as "hostile comparison" (ch'ou chiao 讐校), a method for establishing proper textual readings which can be traced to the debates held by the various sects of the early Mohist school to establish an orthodox version of their canon. The technique involved having a person offer textual emendations to a problematic passage for contextual reasons and then have such suggestions challenged by another scholar who acted "as if he were his enemy."

Upon completing these editorial tasks and copying each work onto carefully prepared bamboo strips, Liu Hsiang composed a lu 錄 (account) of each book which included notes on its authorship, sometimes drawn from early biographical accounts, the significance of the work's contents, and notes on what editorial tasks were required to establish a proper text, including identification of all manuscript sources. These accounts were presented, along with the books themselves, to the emperor. Later, the accounts were collected together and transmitted, apart from the books, as the Pieh lu 別錄 (Detached Accounts). Liu Hsin,* Liu Hsiang's son, abridged the Pieh lu and, adding notes and changes of his own, composed the Ch'i lüeh 七略 (Seven Epitomes), a version of which survives as the Han shu "I-wen chih" (Bibliographic Treatise).

Liu wrote, also in 26 B.C., his now lost commentary to the passages on the "Five Activities" in the Hung Fan chapter of the Shang-shu. In 16 B.C., he compiled the Lieh-nü chuan 列女傳 in which he set forth the traditions surrounding illustrious women. (The similarly titled Lieh-hsien chuan* is not one of Liu Hsiang's compilations.) He then collected and edited a number of moral tales and political persuasions which he issued as the Shuo-yüan 說苑 and the Hsin-hsü 新序. At their best both works show an admirable conciseness of style, clarity of narrative, and, occasionally, lively dialogue. This style was influential on ku-wen* writers, especially Li Ao* and Tseng Kung.*

Perhaps Liu's most famous collection is the Chan-kuo ts'e,* a collection of clever political anecdotes set in the various courts of the Warring States period and designed to show the skills and subtleties of the rhetoric of early political intriguers. It is uncertain how much of these three collections Liu actually composed. Certainly his editorial skills contributed to their literary interest. Liu died in 8 or perhaps 6 B.C.

EDITIONS:

Chang, Kuo-ch'üan 張國銓. Hsin-hsü chiao-chu fu i-wen chiao-chi 新序校注附佚文校輯. 2v. Ch'eng-tu, 1944.

Hsin-hsü. SPTK.

Index du Sin siu/Hsin-hsü t'ung-chien 新序通檢. Peking, 1946; rpt. Taipei, 1968.

Lieh-nü chuan. Liang Tuan 梁端 (d. 1825), ed. Shanghai, 1900.

Liu, Wen-tien 劉文典. Shuo-yüan chiao-pu 說苑斠補. Kunming, 1959.

Pieh-lu. Reconstructed in Hung I-hsüan 洪頤煊, Wen-ching T'ang ts'ung-shu 文經堂叢書 and in T'ao Hsün-hsüan 陶滬宣, Chi-shan kuan chi-pu shu 稷山館輯補書.

Shuo-yüan. SPTK.

Shuo-yüan Hsin-hsü chiao-p'ing 說苑新序校評. Chu Chün-sheng 朱駿聲 (1788-1858), ed. Ling-nan Ta-hsüeh ts'ung-shu.

Shuo-yüan yin-te 說苑引得. Peking, 1931. Based on the SPTK.

STUDIES:

Chao, Chung-i 趙仲邑. "Hsin-hsü shih-lun" 新序試論, Chung-shan Ta-hseh hsüeh-pao, She-hui k'o-hsüeh pao, 1957.3, 170-183.

Ch'ien, Mu 錢穆. "Liu Hsiang/Hsin fu-tzu nien-p'u" 劉向歆父子年譜, Yen-ching hsüeh-pao, 7 (1930), 1189-1318.

Haenisch, Erich. Mencius und Liu Hsiang, zwei Vorkämpfer für Moral und Charakter. Leipzig, 1942.

Hsü, Su-fei 許素菲. Liu Hsiang Hsin-hsü yen-chiu 劉向新序研究. Taipei, 1980.

van der Loon, Piet. "The Transmission of the Kuan Tzu," TP, 41 (1951), 357-393.

Wong, Timothy C. "Notes on the Textual History of the Lao Ts'an yu-chi," TP, 69 (1983), 23-32.

—JR

Liu Hsiao-cho 劉孝綽 (original name Jan 冉, tzu, Hsiao-cho 孝綽, 481-539) was a distant scion of the ruling clan of the Liu-

Sung dynasty. His father, Liu Hui 劉繪, who held significant offices in the Sung and Ch'i regimes, and other forebears, were all associated with P'eng-ch'eng 彭城 District (modern Kiangsu). Histories emphasize Liu Hsiao-cho's precociousness—his father used to have him draft imperial edicts.

Liu Hsiao-cho began his official career at the beginning of the Liang dynasty. In this respect, he enjoyed the best of these uncertain times, and he lived his adult life amid the flourishing and peaceful courts of the first decades of the sixth century. His literary skills were much in demand, and he was appointed to various provincial and metropolitan posts, in the employ of the princely courts and imperial government.

His literary reputation also prospered. However, it seems that he presumed too heavily upon his abilities, that he was an abrasive braggart, contentious and disparaging. He particularly demeaned the writing of his erstwhile friend Tao Hsia 到洽 (477-527) at court banquets. Tao's retaliation, typically in literary form, resulted in Liu Hsiao-cho's dismissal from office. In another dispute, Tao Hsia's brother, Tao Kai 到溉 (478-549), actually brawled with Liu Hsiao-cho. Despite this, Emperor Wu continued to invite Liu to court banquets.

Liu Hsiao-cho was introduced very early into the cliquish court-salon society of his day. His father had gained entrée into a coterie attended by the most famous literary barons of the day—Shen Yüeh,* Jen Fang,* and Fan Yün—and Liu Hsiao-cho had attracted notice there as a boy. Jen Fang particularly admired him and admitted him into his exclusive Lan-t'ai chü 蘭臺聚 (Orchid Terrace Association). Here, the diction and phraseology of his poetry was most admired by the hou-chin 後進 (arrivistes, brought to high office under Emperor Wu), and the whole generation highly valued his style. It was said that if Liu completed a piece in the morning, by evening it was universally known.

He became increasingly attracted to the salon of Crown Prince Chao-ming at the East Palace. There the Cheng-t'i p'ai 正體派 (Orthodox School) was formed, to which

the generation of scholars endorsed by the leaders of the Orchid Terrace Association gravitated. Liu Hsiao-cho, Yin Yün,* Lu Ch'ui 陸倕 (470-526), Wang Chün 王筠 (481-549), and Tao Hsia were all entertained there. The Crown Prince especially favored Liu and Wang. Ho Sun 何遜 (d. c. 527) is often in later criticism linked with Liu, too.

Liu Hsiao-cho was also in the service of the Prince of Hsiang-tung 湘東王, Hsiao I 蕭繹 (508-554), in whose salon he became familiar with the Ku-t'i p'ai 古體派 (Ancient-forms School), led by P'ei Tzu-yeh 裴子野 (469-530). After the death of Crown Prince Chao-ming in 531, he fell under the pervading influence of the kung-t'i* (palace-style) vogue which prevailed as the literary taste of the succeeding century.

Liu Hsiao-cho is said to have written several hundreds of thousands of words, which were still extant in T'ang times. Thirteen of his five dozen extant poems found a place in the Yü-t'ai hsin-yung.*

He appears as the salon-man par excellence of the first half of the sixth century, active and skilled in the literary fashions and vogues of his day. He thus represents in his poetry the transition from the emphasis on historical reference and allusion in the verse of Jen Fang and his Orchid Terrace Association, through the several schools seeking more natural, yet dignified, forms and diction, to the captivating "new forms" and "free art" of the palace-style vogue.

EDITIONS:
Liu Mi-shu chi 劉秘書集. Pai-san, v. 12, pp. 3181-3205.
Liu Hsiao-cho. Nan-Pei-ch'ao shih, "Ch'üan Liang shih" 全梁詩, v. 3, pp. 1440-1459.
Liu Hsiao-cho chi 劉孝綽集. Liu-ch'ao wen, "Ch'üan Liang wen," v. 4, ch. 60, pp. 3310-3313.

—JM

Liu Hsin 劉歆 (tzu, Tzu-chün 子駿, since 6 B.C., Liu Hsiu 劉秀, tzu, Ying-shu 穎叔, c. 50 B.C.-A.D. 23) was a Confucian scholar, a politician, an astrologist, and a bibliographer. He matured in the scholarly milieu of the palace collection where his father, Liu Hsiang,* worked, helping with the collation work. Early in his career he and Wang Mang 王莽 (45 B.C.-A.D. 23) served as Gentlemen Attendants of the Palace Gate. During the last decade of the millennium Liu Hsin vigorously supported the establishment of chairs for several of the classics, including the *Tso-chuan*,* which he championed over the other commentaries to the *Ch'un-ch'iu* (see *ching*), in their *ku-wen** (old text) versions. Because of opposition to this and to other policies of his, Liu Hsin left court in 6 B.C. to become Governor of Ho-nei 河內. When Wang Mang took the reins of government a few years later he recalled Liu Hsin who then served in a series of high positions. In A.D. 5 he participated in a congress of scholars where he proposed his theories regarding the relation of pitch-pipes to the calendars—work which led to a reformed calendar and to a new date for the Chou conquest. Upon Wang Mang's enthronement in 9 A.D. Liu Hsin was made *Kuo-shih* 國師 (National Teacher). Later, in the last years of the Hsin dynasty, Wang came to distrust Liu Hsin and had his three sons put to death. In retaliation Liu plotted against Wang Mang, but the plans were discovered and Liu took his own life.

Liu Hsin's theories on the role of portents (under the rubric of *wu-hsing*) are preserved in the "Wu-hsing chih" 五行志 (Treatise on the Five Agents) in the *Han-shu* (see Pan Ku). These portents, taken not only from the Han era, but from the *Ch'un-ch'iu* and the *Tso-chuan*, were interpreted by Liu Hsin for use in contemporary Han politics. These ties led to claims that these works had been interpolated or even falsified by Liu Hsin himself. A carefully documented attack of Liu's supposed forgery had to await K'ang Yu-wei's* work in the late nineteenth century, however. Today K'ang's work is seen to have been biased in order to support the *Chin-wen* 今文 (New Text) School, and it is generally conceded that no one man—not even Liu Hsin—could have perpetrated such a massive forgery.

Liu Hsin's literary legacy is notably slight—three *fu*,* a few court documents, and one letter. Aside from some study aids for young scholars (now lost), his main contribution to literature was the completion of the bibliographic catalogue *Ch'i lüeh* 七略 (Seven Epitomies) which Liu's father had begun. This work described 38 types of works by 596 authors in 13,269 *chüan*. Although it no longer exists as such, it formed the basis of the bibliographic "I-wen chih" chapter in the *Han-shu*.

EDITIONS:
"Ch'i-lüeh" 七略 , in *Chi-shan-kuan chi-pu shu* 稷山館輯補書, T'ao Chün-hsüan 陶濬宣 (Ch'ing dynasty), ed.
———. *Yü-han shan-fang chi i-shu* 玉山房集遺書. Ma Kuo-han 馬國翰, ed. N.p., 1853.
Liu-ch'ao wen, v. 1, *ch.* 40, pp. 345-353.

STUDIES:
Bielenstein, Hans. "The Restoration of the Han Dynasty, Vol. IV, The Government," *BMEFA*, 51 (1979), 1-300.
Ch'ien, Mu 錢穆. "Liu Hsiang Hsin fu-tzu nien-p'u" 劉向歆父子年譜, *Yen-ching hsüeh-pao*, 7 (1930), 1189-1318.
Eberhard, Wolfram. "Der Beginn der Dschou-Zeit: ein Beitrag zur Geistesgeschichte der Han-Zeit," *Sinica*, 8 (1933), 182-188.
———. "The Political Function of Astronomy in Han China," in *Chinese Thought and Institutions*, John K. Fairbank, ed., Chicago, 1967, pp. 33-70.
Eitel, E. J. "A Translation of Liu Hsin's Biography," *China Review*, 15 (1886), 90-95.
Hughes, E. R. "Concerning the Importance and Reliability of the I wen chih," *Melanges chinois et bouddhiques*, 6 (1938-1939), 173-182.
K'ang, Yu-wei. *Hsin-hsüeh wei-ching k'ao* 新學僞經考. Peking, 1931.
Schneider, L. A. *Ku Chieh-kang and China's New History.* Berkeley, 1971.
Tjan, Tjoe Som. *Po Hu T'ung, the Comprehensive Discussions in the White Tiger Hall.* V.1. Leiden, 1949.

—TP

Liu K'o-chuang 劉克莊 (*tzu*, Ch'ien-fu 潛夫, *hao*, Hou-ts'un 後村, 1187-1269) is probably best known for his association with the so-called Chiang-hu shih-p'ai 江湖詩派 (Rivers and Lakes Poetry School) and as one of the leading literary critics of the late Southern Sung. A native of P'u-t'ien 莆田 (modern Fukien), he was the most prolific writer of the thirteenth century. Liu's extant works, which total 196 *chüan*, include several thousand *shih** poems, sizeable collections of *tz'u** and *shih-hua*,* and a large body of prose writings including memorials to the throne, scholarly explications on classical texts such as the *Lun-yü* and *Chou li*, prefaces and colophons to the poetry collections of many different writers, and funerary stelae inscriptions. In addition to his literary activities, Liu K'o-chuang was also quite active in politics, especially during the reign of Emperor Li-tsung (r. 1224-1264). At one time he was even the hated opponent of the powerful Prime Minister Shih Mi-yüan 史彌遠 (d. 1233). On the other hand, two important statesmen of the period, Chen Te-hsiu 眞德秀 (1178-1235) and Cheng Ch'ing-chih 鄭清之 (1176-1251), treated him with great favor, enabling Liu to eventually rise to the post of Academician of the Dragon Illustrations Gallery. Liu K'o-chuang has been much criticized by some historians for his close association with Chia Ssu-tao 賈似道 (1213-1275), a politician who was subsequently held by many to have been responsible for the fall of the Sung to the Mongols. This may be one reason why there is no official biography for Liu. In his later years, Liu retired to the countryside, where he lived in poverty until his death.

The *shih* poetry of Liu K'o-chuang reveals a substantial range of styles. As a young man, he actively wrote in the style of the Four Lings of Yung-chia 永嘉四靈, who in turn attempted to emulate the intimate landscape verse of the late T'ang poet Chia Tao.* Later, he became associated with the Rivers and Lakes Poets and, like them, composed an eremitic style of poetry describing the sights and events encountered in everyday life. Although proclaimed by many to be the "leader" of the Chiang-hu School, none of Liu's poems are in the extant editions of the *Chiang-hu shih-chi* 江湖詩集 (The Rivers and Lakes Poetry Collection). This is because a group of poems by Liu entitled *Nan-yüeh kao* 南嶽稿 (The Southern Marchmount Drafts), which originally had been in the *Chiang-hu shih-chi*, were later purged from that anthology.

Supposedly, one of the poems by Liu criticized the prime minister Shih Mi-yüan. After his retirement, Liu wrote verses expressing concern over Sino-Mongol relations, as well as works dealing with the routines of farm life. Practically all of his surviving poetry is written either in regulated verse or the quatrain form. In general, he preferred to model his poems after late T'ang poets, especially Chia Tao, and expressed great distaste for what he viewed as the contrived and artificial practices of Huang T'ing-chien* and his followers (i.e., the Chiang-hsi shih-p'ai*).

In addition to his importance as a *shih* poet, Liu also holds a prominent position among lyricists of the Southern Sung. His collection of *tz'u*, entitled *Hou-ts'un ch'ang-tuan-chü* 後村長短句 (also known by as *Hou-ts'un pieh-tiao* 別調), is characterized by heroic themes and a free-flowing style. In this respect, he seems to have been particularly influenced by Hsin Ch'i-chi* and Lu Yu.*

The major repository of Liu K'o-chuang's critical remarks on poetry is his *Hou-ts'un shih-hua* 後村詩話 (Back Village's Poetry Talks). Actually this work is comprised of four separate collections (*chi* 集) of criticism written at different times. It is not organized into a coherent whole; rather, it is made up of random comments and observations dealing almost exclusively with T'ang and Sung poetry. Although Liu rejected the Ch'an-poetry analogy of his contemporary Yen Yü (see *Ts'ang-lang shih-hua*), he agreed with Yen that T'ang verse offered the supreme examples for emulation by later poets (it should be pointed out that whereas Yen Yü favored the verse of the High T'ang period, Liu K'o-chuang was more inclined towards late T'ang models). And like Yen Yü, Liu rejected much of Sung poetry because of its expository and prose-like qualities. Aside from his "poetry talks," Liu offers many critical observations of T'ang and Sung poetry in the numerous prefaces he wrote for collections of other poets.

Although a few influential critics such as Fang Hui 方回 (1227-1306) later demeaned Liu's *shih* poetry, these criticisms seem to be based more on Liu's political activities than on his literary accomplishments. Despite his association with Chia Ssu-tao, Liu K'o-chuang remains one of the leading figures in late Sung literature, both as a poet and as a critic.

EDITIONS:

Hou-ts'un chi 後村集. *Ssu-k'u ch'üan-shu*. 50 *chüan*.

Hou-ts'un Hsien-sheng ta ch'uan-chi 後村先生大全集. *SPTK*. 196 *chüan*. Photocopy of a handwritten edition from the library of the Ch'ing bibliophile Ku Yüan 顧沅; the most complete edition of Liu K'o-chuang's works.

Hou-ts'un shih-hua 後村詩話. *Shih-yüan ts'ung-shu* 適園叢書. This is the best edition of Liu's "poetry talks." It has fewer errors than the *SPTK* edition and also includes collations by Chang Chüan-heng 張鈞衡 (*chü-jen*, 1894).

TRANSLATIONS:

Yoshikawa, *Introduction*, pp. 179-181.

STUDIES:

Chan, Hing-ho 陳慶浩. "Hou-ts'un Hsien-sheng ta ch'uan-chi," in Hervouet, *Sung*, pp. 428-430.

Chang, Chien 張健. "Hou-ts'un Hsien-sheng ta ch'uan-chi," in *Nan-Sung wen-hsüeh p'i-p'ing tzu-liao hui-pien* 南宋文學批評資料彙編, Taipei, 1978, pp. 456-503. A collection of 222 quotations culled dealing with literary history and literary criticism.

Ch'ien, *Sung-shih*, pp. 278-284. Includes an excellent introduction to Liu's verse and commentary on seven poems.

Fang, Hui 方回. *Ying-k'uei lü-sui* 瀛奎律髓. *Ssu-k'u ch'üan-shu* ed. In *chüan* 20 of his anthology, Fang discusses Liu K'o-chuang's famous "Lo mei" 落梅 poem, which supposedly was a veiled criticism of Shih Mi-yüan.

Kuo, Shao-yü 郭紹虞. "Hou-ts'un ch'ang-tuan-chü," in Hervouet, *Sung*, p. 472.

Sun, K'o-k'uan 孫克寬. "Wan Sung shih-jen Liu K'o-chuan pu-chuan" 晚宋詩人劉克莊補傳, *Tung-hai hsüeh-pao*, 3.1 (June 1961), 73-88. The best biography of Liu available.

———. "Liu Hou-ts'un shih-hsüeh p'ing-shu" 劉後村詩學評述, *Tung-hai hsüeh-pao*, 7.1 (June 1965), 27-40. A thorough treatment of Liu's theories of poetry and his relation to the Chiang-hu School.

—JH

Liu-shih chia hsiao-shuo 六十家小說 (Sixty Stories), generally known as *Ch'ing-p'ing-shan T'ang hua-pen* 清平山堂話本 (Vernacular Short Stories from the Clear and Peaceful Studio), is the collective title for six *hua-pen** collections of ten stories each that were published by the Ming scholar-official Hung Pien 洪楩 in the years 1541-1551. It is the earliest major *hua-pen** collection for which there are extant original texts, since the so-called Sung collection *Ching-pen t'ung-su hsiao-shuo* is a forgery. Hung Pien, who saw his role primarily as that of publisher, did not take it upon himself to make serious editorial changes. These stories of various compositional dates and sources, therefore, are much closer to the stage of professional storytelling than the stories in the later *San-yen* collections published by Feng Meng-lung,* who made many changes in the stories he selected for inclusion.

So far only twenty-nine of the stories have been discovered; even the titles of all sixty stories are not known. When these stories were first discovered in Japan and in China and subsequently reprinted in photographic editions in 1929 and 1934, the original collective title and the individual titles of the six collections were still unknown. The title *Ch'ing-p'ing-shan T'ang hua-pen* (from the name of Hung Pien's studio) was made up for the reprinted collections, and this title has been widely used since then. In 1941 Tai Wang-shu 戴望舒 (1905-1950) discovered the titles of the six constituent collections: *Yü-ch'uang chi* 雨窗集 (The Rainy Window Collection), *Ch'ang-teng chi* 長燈集 (The Eternal Lamp Collection), *Sui-hang chi* 隨航集 (The Sailing Along Collection), *I-chen chi* 欹枕集 (Leaning on the Pillow Collection), *Chieh-hsien chi* 解閑集 (The Idleness-Dispelling Collection), and *Hsing-meng chi* 醒夢集 (Awakening from the Dream Collection). Later Sun K'ai-ti 孫楷第 (b. 1898) noticed the collective title *Liu-shih chia hsiao-shuo* in T'ien Ju-ch'eng's 田汝成 (*chin-shih*, 1526) *Hsi-hu yu-lan chih* 西湖遊覽志 (Guide to the West Lake). With these facts known, there is no reason why the original collective title should not be used, though the substitute title will remain in library records.

Variant versions of eleven of the twenty-nine extant stories exist: one in a collection brought out by the publisher Hsiung Lung-feng 熊龍峯 (*fl.* 1592), seven in Feng Meng-lung's *Ku-chin hsiao-shuo,* and three in his *Ching-shih t'ung-yen.* This provides a rare opportunity to investigate the extent of alteration early *hua-pen* stories might have gone through before appearing in the versions known to us in later collections. An investigation of this process is an investigation of the growth of *hua-pen* literature itself. Besides their historical and textual importance, those *Liu-shih chia hsiao-shuo* stories with variant versions in other sources offer excellent chances for thematic studies. The story "Ch'en Hsün-chien Mei-ling shih-ch'i chi" 陳巡檢梅嶺失妻記 (Captain Ch'en Loses His Wife at the Mei Mountain), about the kidnapping of an army captain's wife by an ape, is a case in point. It links thematically and contextually with a large number of stories and dramas of different times and generic types to form a complex story-cycle.

Many of the stories which cannot be found elsewhere are both fascinating as imaginary literature and revealing as socio-historical documents. These include "Yang Wen lan-lu hu chuan" 楊溫攔路虎傳 (Yang Wen, The Road-Blocking Tiger) and "K'uai-tsui Li Ts'ui-lien chi" 快嘴李翠蓮記 (The Loose-Tongued Li Ts'ui-lien). Although quite a few variant versions from later sources of *Liu-shih chia hsiao-shuo* stories are available in English translations, only these two stories have been rendered directly from Hung Pien's versions; they are happy choices indeed.

TRANSLATIONS:

Chang, H. C. 張心滄. "The Shrew," in H. C. Chang, *Chinese Literature: Popular Fiction and Drama,* Edinburgh, 1973, pp. 23-55. Translation of "K'uai-tsui Li Ts'ui-lien chi" with a critical introduction.

Li, Peter 李培德. "Yang Wen, The Road-Blocking Tiger," in *Traditional Chinese Stories,* pp. 85-96.

STUDIES:

A-ying 阿英 (Ch'ien Hsing-ts'un 錢杏邨). "Chi Chia-ching pen 'Fei-ts'ui hsien' chi 'Mei Hsing cheng-ch'un': Hsin fa-hsien te *Ch'ing-p'ing-shan T'ang hua-pen* erh-chung" 記嘉靖本翡翠軒及梅杏爭春：新發現的清平山堂話本二種, in A-

ying, *Hsiao-shuo hsien-t'an* 小說閒談, Shanghai, 1958, pp. 24-28. Only reference to the two outstanding stories not included in any modern editions of the collection.

Hanan, *Vernacular Story,* pp. 54-59.

Hu, Hsing-chih 胡行之. "Lüeh-t'an Ch'ing-p'ing-shan T'ang hua-pen ho t'a-te chiao-chu" 略談清平山堂話本和它的校注, *Kuang-ming jih-pao* (*Wen-hsüeh i-ch'an,* 211), 1 June 1958.

Idema, Wilt Lukas. *Chinese Vernacular Fiction: The Formative Period.* Leiden, 1974, pp. 12-30.

Ma, Lien 馬廉. "Ch'ing-p'ing-shan T'ang hua-pen yü *Yü-ch'uang I-chen chi*" 清平山堂話本與雨窗欹枕集. *Ta-kung pao* (Tientsin) (*T'u-shu fu-k'an,* 22), 14 April 1934. Also in *Pei-p'ing t'u-shu kuan kuan-k'an,* 8.2 (April 1934), 33-48.

Sun, K'ai-ti. *Chung-kuo t'ung-su hsiao-shuo shu-mu* 中國通俗小說書目. Rev. ed. Peking, 1957, pp. 89-91.

Tai, Wang-shu. "Hou-lu so-chi: (2) Ch'ing-p'ing-shan T'ang so-k'an hua-pen" 螻盧瑣記：(2) 清平山堂所刊話本, *Hsing-tao jih-pao* (*Su wen-hsüeh,* 10), 8 March 1941. Also under title of "Pa *Yü-ch'uang I-chen chi* 跋雨窗欹枕集 in Tai Wang-shu, *Hsiao-shuo hsi-ch'ü lun-chi* 小說戲曲論集, Wu Hsiao-ling 吳曉鈴, ed., Peking, 1958, p. 58.

Wang, Yüeh-shan 王岳山. "Ch'ing-p'ing-shan T'ang hua-pen yü *San-yen* hsiang-t'ung p'ien-chang te p'i-chiao" 清平山堂話本與三言相同篇章的比較, *Nan-yang ta-hsüeh Chung-kuo yü-wen hsüeh-hui nien-k'an,* 8 (August 1976), 32-47.

—YWM

Liu Tsung-yüan 柳宗元 (*tzu,* Tzu-hou 子厚, also known as Liu Liu-chou 柳柳州, 773-819) is traditionally recognized as a master essayist of the *Ku-wen yün-tung* 古文運動 (Ancient-style Prose Movement—see *ku-wen*) and one of the more eclectic minds of his era. He was born and raised in the T'ang capital, Ch'ang-an. After a meteoric rise in the civil government under the aegis of Wang Shu-wen 王叔文 (753-806) and his faction, he fell into disgrace after Emperor Shun-tsung (r. 805) was forced to abdicate because of severe illness. Assigned to a minor post in Yung-chou 永州 (modern Ling-ling 零陵 hsien in Hunan) in 805, he was recalled to the capital a decade later only to be reassigned immediately as prefect in the aboriginal region of Liu-chou

柳州 (modern Kwangsi), where he died in 819.

His earliest writings (before his exile to Yung-chou) are primarily bureaucratic, but they served to mark him as a stylist of documentary prose and to win him a reputation among his colleagues in the capital. Many of these colleagues joined him in promoting the studies of a type of "Neo-Legalism" based on the iconoclastic *Ch'un-ch'iu* (see *ching*) scholarship of Lu Ch'un 陸淳 (d. 806.) This group may also have provided Liu's first contacts with members of the Ancient-style Prose Movement. The influence of these studies can be seen in Liu's numerous textual studies such as his attacks on the authenticity of *K'ang-ts'ang-tzu* 亢倉子 or *Ho-kuan-tzu* 鶡冠子, and his determination that the *Lun-yü* (see *ching*) was compiled by disciples of Tseng-tzu 曾子. A similar approach can be seen in the *Fei* Kuo-yü 非國語 (Contra *Conversations of the States*), an attack on the superstitions and unfounded traditions of this early "history." Indeed, Liu himself claims he considered literature only a means to forward his career during this period.

It was not until he was exiled that literature began to dominate his life. While still en route to Yung-chou, Liu began to adopt the literary garb of a neglected or banished official in "Tiao Ch'ü Yüan wen" 弔屈原文 (A Lament for Ch'ü Yüan) written in T'an-chou 潭州 (modern Hunan). While in Yung-chou he perfected the euphuistic style of prose in numerous *fu*,* *sao* 騷, and landscape essays. The latter corpus, most notably the "Yung-chou pa-chi" 永州八記 (Eight Records [of Excursions] in Yung-chou) established the *yu-chi** as a subgenre and gained Liu a position as a major stylist in Chinese literary history. His interest in the didactic functions of literature grew during this exile as can be seen in various letters on the subject. Although many of his works in this vein are tied to his personal political misfortunes, general allegories such as "Pu-she-che shuo" 捕蛇者說 (Discourse of a Snake-catcher), which tells of a man who prefers snaring poisonous snakes and presenting their venom to court to paying taxes (so onerous were the taxes!),

or "Kuo T'o-t'o chuan" 郭橐駝傳 (Humpback Kuo the Gardener), which suggests that the effective, albeit passive, techniques of this old gardener might serve as a model for high-ranking politicians in their treatment of the common people, are masterpieces of this form. In these allegorical writings, and in the numerous fabulistic works such as "Niu fu 牛賦 (Prose-poem on the Ox), "Lin-chiang chih mi" 臨江之麋 (Deer of Lin-chiang), or "Fu-pan chuan" 蝜蝂傳 (Account of the Dung Beetles), a strong Taoist influence, especially from Chuang-tzu (see *Chu-tzu pai-chia*), can be seen. On the basis of this exile corpus Liu Tsung-yüan was later included, along with Han Yü,* as one of two T'ang-dynasty members of the Eight Great Prose Masters of the T'ang and Sung (see Han Yü).

His poetry (only 180 some pieces) is considered to have been influenced by earlier "nature poets": Hsieh Ling-yün,* Wang Wei,* Meng Hao-jan,* and Wei Ying-wu.* Although clearly a Mid-T'ang poet, Liu's verse is atavistic, resembling that of the High T'ang—little influence of early ninth-century poetic movements such as Han Yü's "prosification" of poetry, the *Hsin Yüeh-fu* 新樂府 (New Music-Bureau Verse), or the proto-*tz'u*,* can be seen in his verse. *Yüeh-fu* titles such as "Ku-tung men hsing" 古東門行 or "Hsing-lu nan" 行路難 become allusive and allegorical in Liu's hands. Nature and historical themes were his primary concerns. Though he is accorded the status of a minor poet, his "Chiang-hsüeh" 江雪 (River Snow) is a poem known to every literate Chinese. Another well-known piece, "Hsi-chü" 溪居 (Dwelling Brookside), which extols the free and easy way of living Liu enjoyed in exile, might be read ironically in view of the countless poems and letters surrounding it in the text, poems and letters which lament life in the provinces, which appeal to friends for assistance in having him reassigned to the capital, or which call for the release from exile of some other members of their faction. Some of these appeals were also allegorical, ostensibly describing a bird or an animal—"Fang che-ku tz'u" 放鷓鴣詞

(Release the Chukar) is typical. Finally, some Buddhist verse such as "Ch'en i Ch'ao Shih yüan tu Ch'an ching" 晨詣超師院讀禪經 (Paying an Early Morning Visit to Priest Ch'ao's Monastery to Study the Ch'an Sutras) indicates Liu found solace at times during his long banishment.

Although his Buddhist and even Taoist leanings are sometimes stressed, Liu Tsung-yüan approached both religions in the spirit of a Confucian. That is to say, he was a precursor of the Neo-Confucians of the early Sung who were also not averse to Taoist or Buddhist notions. In works such as his "T'ien shuo" 天說 (Discourse on Heaven), in which he argued his views of heaven for Liu Yü-hsi,* or the "Hsiao shih-ch'eng shan chi" 小石城山記 (Record of [an Excursion to] the Mountain of Little Stone City-walls), in which he speculates on the existence of a "creator," Liu shows himself more concerned with developing a valid philosophy, than in adhering to any particular established school.

Long considered a "materialist" by Marxist historians of philosophy in the People's Republic, he was promoted as a Legalist and a central figure in the Anti-Lin Piao Anti-Confucius Campaign of 1973-74. Those accounts of the Ancient-style Prose Movement aver that Liu was the leader of important, Legalist-influenced "reform wing" (including Liu Yü-hsi, Tu Mu,* et al.), while relegating Han Yü and his conservative Confucian wing to a role of secondary importance. In recent, post-1976 scholarship, however, a return to a more balanced view of Liu and Han is apparent.

EDITIONS:

Ku-hsün Liu Hsien-sheng wen-chi 詁訓柳先生文集. *Ssu-k'u ch'üan-shu chen-pen* ed. Descends from corpus as put together by Liu's literary executor, Liu Yü-hsi—most complete traditional edition.

Liu Ho-tung chi 柳河東集. 2v. Shanghai, 1961; rev. rpt., 1974. Includes Liu's official biography; based on Sung *Ho-tung Hsien-sheng chi* 河東先生集 printed by Shih-ts'ai T'ang 世綵堂. Punctuated in traditional fashion; reliable and easily available.

Liu Tsung-yüan chi 柳宗元集. Wu Wen-chih 吳文治, ed. 4v. Peking, 1979. An excellent crit-

ical edition which combines the traditional commentaries with extensive textual notes. Contains a preface and two appendixes—a list of all traditional commentators and a colophon which discusses editions. Replaces *Liu Ho-tung chi* as basic edition.

Ryū Sōgen kashi sakuin 柳宗元歌詩索引. Maekawa Sachio 前川幸雄, comp. Kyoto, 1980.

Tseng-kuang chu-shih yin-pien T'ang Liu Hsien-sheng chi 增廣注釋音辯唐柳先生集. *SPTK*. An important early edition based upon three earlier Sung commentaries; noted for its glosses of difficult words.

TRANSLATIONS:

Chang, H.C. "Liu Tsung-yüan (773-819), in *Chinese Literature 2, Nature Poetry*, New York, 1977, pp. 93-124. Poetry and prose. Free, uneven translation.

Kakei, Fumio 筧文生. *Kan Go, Ryū Sōgen* 韓愈柳宗元. Tokyo, 1973.

Liu, Shih Shun. "Liu Tsung-yüan (773-819)," in *Chinese Classical Prose, The Eight Masters of the T'ang-Sung Period*, Hong Kong, 1979, pp. 98-131. Relatively free versions.

STUDIES:

Chang, Shih-chao 章士釗. *Liu-wen chih-yao* 柳文指要. 3v. Peking, 1971.

Ch'ien, Mu 錢穆. *Tu Liu Ho-tung chi* 讀柳河東集. Hong Kong, 1969.

Crump, James I., Jr. "Lyō Dzūng-ywán," *JAOS*, 67 (1947), 161-171.

Gentzler, J.M. "A Literary Biography of Liu Tsung-yüan." Unpublished Ph.D. dissertation, Columbia University, 1966. An excellent study containing over thirty translations (all but one in prose).

Hartman, Charles. "*Alieniloquium:* Liu Tsung-yüan's Other Voice," *CLEAR*, 4.1 (January 1982), 23-73.

Lamont, H. G. "An Early Ninth Century Debate on Heaven, Part I," *AM*, NS, 18 (1973), 181-206, "Part II," *AM*, NS, 19 (1974), 37-85.

Lo, Lien-t'ien 羅聯添, ed. *Liu Tsung-yüan shih-chi hsi-nien chi tzu-liao lei-pien* 柳宗元事蹟繫年暨資料類編. Taipei, 1981. A collection of previous comments of Liu's genealogy, life, prose writings and editions of his collected works.

Nienhauser, William H., Jr., et al. *Liu Tsung-yüan*. New York, 1973. Also contains translations of fables (Lloyd Neighbors), poetry (Jan B. Walls), and prose (Nienhauser).

Spring, Madeline Kay. "A Stylistic Study of Tang *Guwen*: The Rhetoric of Han Yu and

591

Liu Zongyuan." Unpublished Ph.D. dissertation, University of Washington, 1983.

Sun, Ch'ang-wu 孫昌武. *Liu Tsung-yüan chuan lun* 柳宗元傳論. Peking, 1982. The best available biographical account.

Wu, Wen-chih. *Liu Tsung-yüan chüan* 柳宗元卷. 2v. Peking, 1964. Collection of traditional comments on Liu and his works.

—WHN

Liu Yü-hsi 劉禹錫 (*tzu*, Meng-te 夢得, 772-842) was born into a family of minor officials in P'eng-ch'eng 彭城 (modern Hsü-chou 徐州, Kiangsu) that had a long tradition of Confucian scholarship. After passing the *chin-shih* in 793 Liu spent a short time under Tu Yu's 杜預 (735-812) tutelage at court, where he held the position of Censor. On account of his participation in the Legalist-reform faction led by Wang Shu-wen which sought to restrain the power of the eunuchs, local army commanders, and aristocratic families, he was sent into the provinces as Prefect of Lang-chou 郎州 (modern Ch'ang-te 常德, Hunan) in 805 and spent the next decade there among minorities. Liu was called back to court in 815, but because of his satirical poem "Hsi-tseng k'an-hua chu chün-tzu" 戲贈看花諸君子 (For Presentation to Flower-Viewing Noblemen) he was banished for another ten years to Lien-chou 連州 (modern Lien-hsien 連縣, Kwangtung). Since in his later years he filled the position of Adviser to the Heir Apparent, his collected works bears the name *Liu Pin-k'o wen-chi* 劉賓客文集.

Liu Yü-hsi, who was a close friend of Liu Tsung-yüan* and Po Chü-i,* is important both as a poet and as an essayist. His most famous essay is his philosophical dissertation, "T'ien-lun" 天論 (On Heaven), which discusses the relationship between heaven (natural forces) and man. This text, which belongs to the tradition of Hsün-tzu, develops a materialistic and dialectical conception of nature, and was written in opposition to the idealistic theory of Han Yü.* In contradiction to Han Yü who regarded heaven as an animated being punishing or rewarding man for his deeds, Liu maintained that "heaven and man can defeat each other" (天與人交相勝).

Though as a poet Liu Yü-hsi is regarded as an equal of Liu Tsung-yüan and Han Yü, neither his poetry nor his essays have received much attention. Only four of his poems are included in the *T'ang-shih san-pai-shou.** In his poetry, most of which was written after 805, new topics and stylistic innovations are noteworthy. Liu shares with his contemporaries reflections on the transitoriness of man, for instance, in the poem "Shih-t'ou ch'eng" 石頭城 (The Stone Wall City), on history as steady decline, in "Yang-liu-chih tz'u" 楊柳枝詞 (Willow Branch Songs), and on loneliness, in the poem "Kuei-yüan tz'u" 閨怨詞 (A Boudoir Plaint).

In his nature and love poetry, besides traditional aspects, there are also fresh ideas. For example, in the poem "Shih tao-huan ko" 視刀環謌 (Song of Looking at a Dagger), Liu considers the limitations of language ("Often I despise the limitations of language,/It cannot express the depth of the inner heart" 常恨語言淺，不如人意深).

But Liu's most essential contributions to Chinese poetry are his political poems and his poems written under the influence of non-Chinese folk literature. The political poems, which are directed against autonomous tendencies among the local military commanders, the growing influence of the eunuchs at court, and the old aristocracy, set forth a view of history as a process leading to something new. Most obviously this view finds its expression in the poem "Chü-wen yao" 聚蚊謠 (Mosquitoes), which attacks the greedy for power who, like mosquitoes, do mischief in the darkness and leave with the dawn. In his poem "Hsi-sai-shan huai-ku" 西塞山懷古 (Longing for the Past at Western Pass Mountain), Liu writes against the movement for autonomy by certain military commanders. Giving the example of the Kingdom of Wu and its capital, Chin-ling, which was conquered by Wang Chün in 230, he relates that after the unification of China nothing was left of the autonomous kingdoms but ruins blown by the autumn wind. Here history is not transfigured as often happens in *huai-ku* poetry, but understood in the sense of *Historia docet.*

The best examples of Liu's political poems are two poems on visits to the Hsüan-tu Temple 玄都觀 in Ch'ang-an, written in 816 and 828. Each poem caused the banishment of the poet. The first poem, "For Presentation to Flower-Viewing Gentlemen" describes the peach trees which were planted by a Taoist priest in the Hsüan-tu Temple after Liu's first banishment (805), which are now being enjoyed by those in power. The second poem, "Tsai yu Hsüan-tu Kuan" 再遊玄都觀 (Visiting Hsüan-tu Temple Again), reports the decay of the temple and its garden: moss and wild cabbage have replaced the peach trees. The poem concludes in a self-confident manner with a hint at the return of the author.

The banishments into aboriginal regions allowed Liu contact with non-Chinese folk literature. Like Ch'ü Yüan,* Liu felt himself bound to write new words to the shaman ritual texts to make them more suitable for Confucian sacrificial ceremonies. Still extant are the "Chu-chih-tz'u" 竹枝詞 (Bamboo Branch Songs), and the "Willow Branch Songs" which portend a future for folk songs in the development of Chinese literature: "Play no more tunes, sir, of bygone dynasties/But hear the new Willow Ballads."

EDITIONS:

Liu Meng-te wen-chi 劉夢得文集. *SPTK.*
Liu Pin-k'o wen-chi 劉賓客文集. *SPPY.*
Liu Yü-hsi chi 劉禹錫集. Chu Ch'eng 朱澂, ed. Shanghai, 1975. A modern typeset edition based on the *Liu Pin-k'o wen-chi* in the *Chieh-i-lu sheng-yü ts'ung-shu* 結一廬賸餘叢書.
Liu Pin-k'o chia-hua lu 劉賓客嘉話錄. *TTTS.*

TRANSLATIONS:

Bynner, *Jade Mountain*, pp. 100-101.
CL, 1975.6, 87-93.
Gundert, *Lyrik*, pp. 118-119.
Demiéville, *Anthologie*, p. 311.
Frankel, *Palace Lady*, pp. 97-98.
Sunflower, pp. 196-201.
Waley, *Po Chü-i*, p. 168.

STUDIES:

Kemura, Sanshigo 木村三四吾. "Sōhan Ryū Mu-toku bunshū kaidai" 宋版劉夢得文集解題, *Tenri biburia*, 4 (1955), 36-37.

Lo, Lien-t'ien 羅聯添, "Liu Pin-k'o chia-hua lu chiao-pu chi k'ao-cheng" 劉賓客嘉話錄校補及考證 (1 & 2), *Yu-shih hsüeh-chih*, 2.1 (January 1963), 1-39, 2.2 (April 1963), 1-50.
———. "Liu Meng-te nien-p'u" 劉夢得年譜, *Wen-shih-che hsüeh-pao*, 8 (1958), 181-295.
Ogawa, Shōichi 小川昭一. "Ryū Ushaku ni tsuite" 劉禹錫について, *Tōyō bunka fukukan*, 10 (April 1965), 34-45.
Pien, Hsiao-hsüan 卞孝萱 and Wu Ju-yü 吳汝煜. *Liu Yü-hsi* 劉禹錫. Shanghai, 1980.
———. *Liu Yü-hsi nien-p'u* 劉夢得年譜. Peking, 1963.
———. *Liu Yü-hsi shih-wen hsüan chu* 劉禹錫詩文選注. Ch'ang-sha, 1978.
T'ang, Lan 唐蘭. "Liu Pin-k'o chia-hua lu te chiao-chi yü pien-wei" 劉賓客嘉話錄的校輯與辨偽, *Wen-shih*, 4 (1965), 75-106.
Wu, Ch'i-min 吳其敏. "Ch'u tu Liu Pin-k'o wen-chi" 初讀劉賓客文集, in *Wen-shih cha-chi* 文史剳記, Hong Kong, 1976, pp. 4-7.
Yang, Ch'iu-sheng 楊秋生. "Liu Yü-hsi chi ch'i shih yen-chiu" 劉禹錫及其詩研究. M.A. thesis, Kao-hsiung shih-fan hsüeh-yüan kuo-wen yen-chiu-so 高雄師範學院國文研究所, 1981.

—WK

Liu Yung 柳永 (*tzu*, Ch'i-ch'ing 耆卿, other names, San-pien 三變 and T'un-t'ien 屯田, 987-1053) was a renowned poet and musician, skilled in *tz'u** versification. He was a native of Ch'ung-an 崇安 (modern Fukien), but spent much of his youth wandering from one place to another. Not until he was forty-seven years old did he pass the *chin-shih* examination and assume an administrative post as Agricultural Supervisor in Chekiang.

Frustrated by his frequent failures in the civil-service examinations, the young Liu Yung spent much of his time in the entertainment quarters of Pien-ching 汴京 (Kaifeng), the capital of the Northern Sung. As a *tz'u* poet who created new songs for the city courtesans, he became immensely popular in those quarters. A story has it that there was a custom among courtesans to visit Liu Yung's tomb annually. Clearly no other Chinese poet was as admired and celebrated by the singsong girls.

Unlike Yen Shu* and Ou-yang Hsiu,* his two contemporaries, who wrote mainly in the traditional *hsiao-ling* 小令 form, Liu Yung composed mostly the so-called *man-*

tz'u 慢詞, a new form that was originally borrowed from the popular *yün-yao* 雲謠 tradition. It was in Liu Yung's hand that *man-tz'u* gradually formed its generic conventions and ultimately became a major *tz'u* form. Many of his *man-tz'u* poems depict the contemporary life in such flourishing cities as Hangchow, Soochow, and Pien-ching. The immediate success of these poems lies partly in the fact that the sheer length of the *man-tz'u* structure seemed to be ideally suited for elaborated and particularized description. The shortened *hsiao-ling* form could not have supported the same effect. By adopting the long form, Liu Yung was able to express a variety of ideas in an otherwise limited poetic genre. The *man-tz'u* form was thus most suitable to his temperament and purposes.

Liu Yung's free use of colloquial language and other devices of popular songs made him at once a controversial figure in the poetic tradition and a pioneer of *tz'u* style. This explains why traditional critics often had reservations in their praise for Liu Yung. A critical note by the woman poet Li Ch'ing-chao* represents the traditional assessment: "Liu Yung transformed old music into new. He published *Yüeh-chang chi* 樂章集, which won great acclaim everywhere. Although the musical tones of his *tz'u* are harmonious, the language is vulgar."

However, Liu Yung did not write all his poems in the popular style. In fact, one of his poetic merits lies in his ability to maintain a proper balance between the colloquial and the literary language. Two well-known poems, "Yü-lin ling" 雨霖鈴 and "Pasheng kan-chou" 八聲甘州, are good examples of such artistic blending. On the one hand, his literary expressions capture the static and sublime qualities of natural imagery; on the other, his colloquial diction tends to generate a delightful sense of the expressiveness of common speech. This particular achievement of Liu Yung has not been sufficiently recognized by traditional critics.

EDITIONS:

Ch'ien, *Sung-shih*, pp. 33-35.
Chu, Tsu-mou 朱祖謀 (1857-1931), comp. *Sung-tz'u san-pai-chou chien-chu* 宋詞三百首箋注. An-

notated by T'ang Kuei-chang 唐圭璋. Hong Kong, 1961, pp. 26-36.
Ch'üan Sung tz'u, v. 1, pp. 13-57.
Liu, Yung 柳永. *Yüeh-chang chi* 樂章集. Cheng Wen-cho 鄭文焯 (1956-1918), annot. Taipei, 1973.

TRANSLATIONS:

Ayling, *Collection*, pp. 107-109.
Leung, Winnie Lai-fong, trans. "Thirteen *Tz'u* by Liu Yung," *Renditions*, 11/12 (Spring/Autumn 1979), 62-82.
Liu, James J. Y. *Major Lyricists of the Northern Sung*. Princeton, 1974, pp. 54-99.
Sunflower, pp. 320-324.

STUDIES:

Chan, An-t'ai 詹安泰. "T'an Liu Yung ti Yü-lin ling" 談柳永的雨霖鈴, *Yü-wen hsüeh-hsi*, 67 (1957), 1-4.
Chang, *Evolution*, pp. 107-157. Includes translations.
Cheng, Ch'ien. "Liu Yung and Su Shih in the Evolution of *Tz'u* Poetry," Ying-hsiung Chou, trans., *Renditions*, 11/12 (Spring/Autumn 1979), 143-156.
Hightower, James R. "The Songwriter Liu Yung: Part I," *HJAS*, 41.2 (December 1981), 323-376; "Part II," *HJAS*, 42.1 (1982), 5-66.
Ke, Kuo-liang 蓋國梁. "Lun Liu Yung tz'u" 論柳永詞, *Wen-hsüeh p'ing-lun ts'ung-k'an*, 13 (May 1983), 406-418.
Leung, Winnie Lai-fong. "Liu Yung and His *Tz'u*." Unpublished M.A. thesis. University of British Columbia, 1976.
Liu, *Lyricists*, pp. 53-99. Includes translations.
Liu, James J. Y. "The Lyrics of Liu Yung," *TkR*, 1.2 (October 1970), 1-44.
Murakami, Tetsumi 村上哲見. "Ryū Kikyō shi no keitai jō no tokushoku ni tsuite" 柳耆卿詞 の形態上の 特色について, *Tōhōgaku*, 43 (1972), 61-76.
T'ang, Kui-chang 唐圭璋 and Chin Ch'i-hua 金啓華. "Lun Liu Yung te *tz'u*" 論柳永的詞, in *T'ang Sung ts'u yen-chiu lun-wen chi* 唐宋詞研究論文集, Peking, 1969, pp. 70-79.
Yuh, Liou-yi. "Liu Yung, Su Shih and Some Aspects of the Development of early *Tz'u* Poetry." Unpublished Ph.D. dissertation, University of Washington, 1972.

—KIC

Lo Kuan-chung 羅貫中 is a name that can be said to symbolize traditional Chinese popular literature itself. It is a name which has been associated with at least six major novels and three *tsa-chü** dramas. Yet hardly anything is known about Lo's life and even less about his career as a writer. His names, dates, place of origin, and activities are all uncertain. His personal name has been variably given as Pen 本, Kuan 貫, and Tao-pen 道本, his *tzu* as Kuan-chung, and his *hao* as Ming-ch'ing 名卿. Both T'ai-yüan and Hangchow have been mentioned as his place of origin; one source states he was born in T'aiyüan and settled down in Hangchow. He has been regarded as a subject of the Sung, as a Yüan writer living into the Ming period, and as someone who flourished mainly in Ming times. To this evasive figure history has credited the beginning of the practice of writing full-fledged novels in China and the authorship of quite a few of the most important works in this genre.

There is only one nearly contemporary reference to Lo Kuan-chung and it reveals very little about him. In the short biography of him in the early Ming work *Lu-kuei pu hsü-pien* 錄鬼簿續編 (The Second Registry of the Ghosts), we are told that Lo Kuan-chung, *hao*, Hu-hai san-jen 湖海散人, was a native of T'aiyüan and was a noted playwright of a reserved personality, that he and the author of the registry, who was at least twenty years his junior, met in 1364 (three years before the end of the Yüan) for the last time, and that he produced three dramas—*Sung T'ai-tsu lung-hu feng-yün hui* 宋太祖龍虎風雲會 (The Wind-Cloud Meeting of the Sung Founder [extant]), *Chung-cheng hsiao-tzu lien-huan chien* 忠正孝子連環諫 (The Repeated Admonition of a Upright Devoted Son [lost]), and *San p'ing-chang ssu-k'u fei-hu tzu* 三平章死哭蜚虎子 (lost). No other sources can be taken seriously, and even this fairly reliable report has given rise to much speculation. Some modern scholars have erroneously attributed this registry to Chia Chung-ming 賈仲明 (1343-after 1422) and, using the known minimum age difference between Lo and the author of the registry and the date of their last meeting, have tried to deduce, among other things, probable dates for Lo. Unfortunately, Chia Chung-ming could not have authored the registry.

The associations between Lo Kuan-chung and such novels as *Sui T'ang liang-ch'ao chih-chuan* 隋唐兩朝志傳 (Romance of the Sui and T'ang Dynasties), *Ta-T'ang Ch'in-wang tz'u-hua* (see *tz'u-hua* [doggerel story]), *Ts'an-T'ang Wu-tai shih yen-i* 殘唐五代史演義 (Romance of the Late T'ang and the Five Dynasties), and the 20-*chüan* version of the *P'ing-yao chuan** are only shakily established, depending on evidence no stronger than traditional attribution, attribution which is notoriously unreliable when it comes to famous names like Li Chih,* Chin Sheng-t'an,* Feng Meng-lung,* Chung Hsing 鍾惺 (1574-1624), and Lo Kuan-chung himself. Such attributions should be taken as clues to possible authorship, rather than proofs. The making of most of these novels involved processes like professional storytelling, communal transmission, cyclical evolution, and radical editorial modification, which tend to dilute (if not hide or even erase) individual identities and to enhance shared features. It is thus not surprising that even the discovery of certain thematic and contextual similarities in these works is of little use in resolving the authorship of these novels.

Though widely accepted, the claim that Lo Kuan-chung was the author of the *San-kuo chih yen-i** is equally unfounded. If there was such a sizable and impressive work to his credit, why should his friend choose to mention only three dramas, which from the only surviving piece do not seem to merit much notice. Playwrights were not rare in Yüan and early Ming times. Three dramas did not constitute a memorable record. Should Lo Kuan-chung have been a productive novelist, responsible for either the *San-kuo chih yen-i* or the *Shui-hu chuan** (if not both), it is inconceivable that his friend would have been silent about this. Given the absence of information and the fact that the earliest extant edition of the *San-kuo chih yen-i* was published more than one hundred years after the possible span of Lo Kuan-chung's life, even the argument that all extant editions list him as the author does not carry much weight. The case of the *Shui-hu chuan* is similar. The evolutionary histories of the *San-kuo chih* *yen-i* and the *Shui-hu chuan* have yet to be systematically studied. Very little is known about the differences between the various simpler texts and the fuller text of these two novels, about the differences between the texts of the same categories, or about the meaning of the differences. It is simply premature to take any individual as mainly or wholly responsible for either of these novels. Even though it may eventually be possible to show that Lo Kuan-chung was responsible for either one or both of these works, it will require much more research before the text or series of texts he concerned himself with are identified. In the meantime, there is nothing to lose in considering Lo Kuan-chung merely as a minor playwright with three dramas to his name.

STUDIES:

Cheng, Chen-to 鄭振鐸. "Lo Kuan-chung" 羅貫中, *Ch'ing-nien chieh*, 1.1 (April 1931), 135-153.

DMB, v. 1, pp. 978-980.

Feng, Ch'i-yung 馮其庸. "Lun Lo Kuan-chung te shih-tai" 論羅貫中的時代, *Chiang-hai hsüeh-k'an*, 1963.7 (July 1963), 53-58.

Hsieh, Wu-liang 謝无量. *Lo Kuan-chung yü Ma Chih-yüan* 羅貫中與馬致遠. Shanghai, 1930.

Li, Hsiu-sheng 李修生. "Lun Lo Kuan-chung" 論羅貫中, *Shan-hsi shih-yüan hsüeh-pao* (*She-hui k'o-hsüeh*), 1981.1, 59-64.

Liu, Ts'un-jen 柳存仁. "Lo Kuan-chung chiang-shih hsiao-shuo chih chen-wei hsing-chih" 羅貫中講史小說的眞偽性質, *Hsiang-kang Chung-wen ta-hsüeh Chung-kuo wen-hua yen-chiu so hsüeh-pao*, 8.1 (December 1976), 169-234.

—YWM

Lo Pin-wang 駱賓王 (before 640-684) was a master of Six-Dynasties-style *p'ien-wen*** prose and an important early reformer of Ch'i-Liang-style 齊梁體 court poetry. He, Lu Chao-lin,* Wang Po,* and Yang Chiung* were called *Ch'u T'ang ssu-chieh* (The Four Eminences of the Early T'ang).

Lo Pin-wang, unlike the other three "Eminences," did not attempt to seek a simplicity in his poetic diction, but rather carried over to his poetry all the complex prosodic rules and allusive language of his *p'ien-wen*. He attempted to divorce himself from the superficial sentiments found in Ch'i-Liang-style poetry and to enter the world of deep emotional expression without forgoing his desire to display his erudition.

Lo Pin-wang's family was from I-wu 義烏 (modern Chekiang), but he was raised mostly in North China (modern Shantung), where his father was an official. Sometime during the 650s he was recommended to the court as a companion for Prince Tao, Li Yüan-ch'ing 李元慶 (636-664), and probably served the prince until the latter's death in 664.

Between 665 and 670, Lo drafted documents in Ch'ang-an. However, in 670 he was banished to the remote post of An-hsi hsi-chen 安西西鎮 (modern Turfan—Sinkiang), and later traveled with the imperial army to Yao-chou 姚州 (modern Yao-an 姚安) in another remote district (modern Yünnan). During these years Lo wrote many detailed and emotional descriptions of these desolate regions and of his exile.

By 674 Lo's political fortunes had improved and he was made a secretary at Wu-kung 武功, not far from Ch'ang-an; in 677 or 678 he was made a secretary in Ch'ang-an itself. Concurrently he was also made a censor, but he was soon thrown in jail for criticizing the growing power of Empress Wu. In 679 he was released during an amnesty and appointed a magistrate at Lin-hai 臨海 (modern Chekiang). Finding himself at odds with Empress Wu (she had deposed the new emperor), he resigned and joined the rebellion of Hsü Ching-yeh 徐敬業 (who had once used the imperial surname Li 李) at Yangchow. Lo Pin-wang's contribution to the rebels' cause was a dispatch (see below) addressed to Empress Wu explaining their motives. In 684 the rebellion was crushed and Lo is presumed to have been one of thousands who perished. In the sixteenth century Lo's grave was rediscovered and he became the object of veneration by late Ming scholars. One of these men successfully petitioned the emperor to grant Lo the posthumous title Wen-chung 文忠 (Literate and Loyal).

Lo is best known for his old-style poetry—it makes up the bulk of his extant verse corpus. During his lifetime his "Ti ching p'ien" 帝京篇 (Poem on the Imperial

Capital), written in five-syllable lines, was well received, although later critics tend to agree that his "Ch'ou hsi p'ien" 疇昔篇 (Poem on Former Times), a very long autobiographical poem (over 1300 characters) written in both five- and seven-syllable lines, far surpasses it. In fact this poem is an example of early narrative poetry and as such occupies an important place in Chinese literary history. Another of Lo's well-known poems is "Tsai yü yung ch'an" 在獄詠蟬 (In Prison Chanting about Cicadas), a five-syllable poem in regulated verse written in 678. This piece was anthologized by many popular collections of T'ang poetry, such as the *T'ang-shih san-pai shou** and has also been frequently translated into English (see bibliography below).

In the realm of prose, his essay "Wei Hsü Ching-yeh t'ao Wu Chao hsi" 爲徐敬業 討武曌檄 (A Dispatch on Behalf of Hsü Ching-yeh Condemning [Empress] Wu Chao) is an excellent example of parallel prose and one of the representative pieces of this genre from the early T'ang period. It is likely that Lo's training and expertise in writing parallel prose influenced his later poetry, often resulting in a highly ornamental and somewhat artificial effect. Whereas his adept skill at couching literary allusions in elaborate language is quite appropriate in his prose, the same is not always applicable to his verse. Nonetheless it is significant that he attempted to expand the acceptable limits of poetry by using this format to express his personal experiences and sentiments. In this way Lo provided a precedent for later T'ang poets who further developed the use of poetry for self-expression.

Lo's writings were probably proscribed during Empress Wu's reign (690-705). Subsequently Emperor Chung-tsung issued an appeal for publication of whatever survived. The task fell to Ch'ih Yün-ch'ing 郗雲卿 whose preface still appears with some editions. The anthology appeared in ten *chüan* and may be substantially the same collection we have today. During the Ming, several fairly complete annotated editions of Lo's works were published in four *chüan*, including that of Yen Wen-hsüan 劉開揚 in

1615; they were based largely on writings copied from general anthologies of T'ang writers.

EDITIONS:
Lo, Pin-wang. *Lo Ch'eng chi* 駱丞集. 1615. 4 *chüan*. In *Ssu-k'u ch'uan-shu chen-pen*, Series 4. Taipei, 1974. Annotated by Yen Wen-hsüan.
———. *Lo Lin-hai chi chien chu* 駱臨海集箋注. 10 *chüan*. 1853; rpt. Peking, 1961. Modern, punctuated edition with text annotated by Ch'en Hsi-chin; includes extensive biographical materials.
———. *Lo Pin-wang wen-chi* 駱賓王文集. 10 *chüan*. SPTK. Photocopy of a Ming reprint of a Yüan edition.

TRANSLATIONS:
Bynner, *Jade Mountain*, p. 102.
Frankel, *Flowering Plum*, p. 91.
Lee, Orient. "A Poem on the Cicada Written in Prison," *Chinese Culture*, 5.3, p. 44.
Owen, "Deadwood," pp. 163-165.
———, *Early*, pp. 111-115, 138-150.
von Zach, *Han Yü*, p. 312.

STUDIES:
Ch'en, Hsi-chin 陳熙晉. "Hsü-pu *T'ang-shu* Lo Pin-wang shih-yü chüan'續補唐書駱賓王侍御傳, in *Lo Lin-hai chi chien chu*, pp. 387-394.
Furukawa, Sueyoshi 古川末喜. "Sho-Tō yonketsu no bungaku shisō" 初唐四傑の文學思想, *Chūgoku bungaku ronshū*, 8 (1979), 1-27.
Liu, K'ai-yang 劉開揚. "*Lun Ch'u-T'ang ssu-chieh chi ch'i shih*" 論初唐四傑及其詩, in *T'ang shih lun-wen chi* 唐詩論文集, Shanghai, 1961, pp. 1-28.
Liu, Wei-ch'ung 劉維崇. *Lo Pin-wang p'ing-chuan* 駱賓王評傳. Taipei, 1978.
Owen, *Early T'ang*, pp. 1-14.
Takagi, Masakuzu 高木正一. "Raku Hinnō no denki to bungaku" 駱賓王の傳記と文學, *Ritsumeikan bungaku*, 245 (1965), 95-117.
                                   —BL and MS

Lo-yang ch'ieh-lan chi 洛陽伽藍記 (Record of the Monasteries of Lo-yang) by Yang Hsüan-chih 楊衒之 or 陽衒之 is a description of Lo-yang, the Northern Wei capital that was founded in 493 and compulsorily evacuated in 534. This memoir, probably written within three years of the author's passing through the deserted ruins of the great capital he had known in both prosperity and decline as a court official, brings Lo-yang to life with vivid descriptions of places, events, and people. It is the earliest substantial prose account of the Chinese city to survive. Its language is clear and expressive, avoiding the gratuitous ornateness and obscurity of some other writing of this period.

The work consists of an introduction and five chapters, one for the inner city and one each for the suburbs to the east, south, west, and north. Although each chapter is in form a series of articles on the principal Buddhist monasteries and convents, much of the information given concerns secular events, buildings, and personalities. Yang celebrates the aristocratic Han-Chinese culture of the city, a culture whose values were under threat in the Eastern Wei state at the time he wrote. Yang has been classified as both a Buddhist apologist—as such he has an entry in the *Hsü Kao-seng chuan* (see *Kao-seng chuan*)—and an opponent of the religion as in *Kuang-hung ming chi* 廣弘明集. His book gives the impression that he was not really either. He may have been inclined to philosophical Taoism, and his book devotes more attention to the fine buildings and great public rituals of Lo-yang's monasteries and convents than to questions of doctrine.

Lo-yang ch'ieh-lan chi was originally divided between main entries written in full-sized script and longer descriptions and anecdotes in smaller, double-column writing within the columns of the main text: the *tzu-chu* 子注 format. This distinction was lost before the earliest surviving editions were produced, and attempts by some later editors to restore it are speculative.

The book's interest today lies in its wealth of factual information on a great and short-lived city—from ruins to a population of over half a million and back to ruins again in forty-one years—presented in a readable and rather informal style. Yang had access to official and private archives and may also have witnessed some of the events he describes. He ranges from palace coups and wars and rebellions to market gossip and ghost stories. The book has in it elements of private history, of *pi-chi** notebooks, of urban history (such as

the lost accounts of earlier Lo-yang), and of an anthology of the city's best writing, including an extensive digest of several accounts of the journey through Central Asia to Udyana and Gandara (in modern Pakistan) by the diplomat Sung Yün 宋雲 and his monkish companions between 518 and 522. It also gives useful descriptions of the greatest of the city's many monasteries and convents and supplements the records of the Northern Wei capital's prosperity and collapse available in the standard dynastic histories.

EDITIONS:

Lo-yang ch'ieh-lan chi chiao-shih 洛陽伽藍記校釋. Chou Tsu-mo 周祖謨, ed. Peking, 1956; rpt. Peking, 1963. A reliable modern edition.

Lo-yang chieh-lan chi chiao-chu 洛陽伽藍記校注. Fan Hsiang-yung 范祥雍, ed. Shanghai, 1958. A useful modern edition.

TRANSLATIONS:

Jenner, W. J. F. *Memories of Loyang: Yang Hsüan-shih and the Lost Capital, 493-534*. Oxford, 1981. A full English translation.

STUDIES:

Hatanaka, Jōen 畑中淨園. "*Rakuyō garanki no sho hampon to sono keito*" 洛陽伽藍記の諸版本とその系統, *Ōtani gakuhō*, 30.4 (1951), 39-55.

—WJ

Lo Yin 羅隱 (original name Heng 橫, *tzu*, Chao-chien 昭諫, 833-909) was a native of Yü-hang 餘杭 (some say of Hsin-ch'eng 新城) in Hangchow. He and his kinsmen Lo Ch'iu 羅虬 and Lo Yeh 羅鄴, also talented writers, were collectively styled "The Three Los" (三羅). Yin aspired to a career in government but failed the metropolitan examinations six times, despite the support of important persons, notably the minister Cheng Tien 鄭畋. Unfortunately his censorious character, which often showed itself in a mocking and sarcastic manner, alienated other highly placed men whose favor was necessary for preferment. Despite his ugly visage, which is said to have spoiled a promising alliance with Cheng Tien's daughter, a physiognomist prophesied that he would ultimately find success in the Wu 吳 area. Bitter because of his failure at court, he left Ch'ang-an in 880. It appears that another factor in this decision was the chaos attendant upon the military successes of the revolutionist Huang Ch'ao 黃巢, who occupied the capital and, on 6 January 881, inaugurated the reign "Binding [authority] of Metal" (Chin t'ung 金統) over the new nation of Ch'i 齊. Yin appears to have found peace and profit in his pleasant old homeland, fortunate in its wealth of such resources as cinnabar, ginger, clams, and silk. He spent the rest of his life as the loyal servant of Ch'ien Liu 錢鏐, prince of the semi-independent state of Wu-Yüeh 吳越 during the waning years of the T'ang.

Lo Yin was a prolific writer, but the greater part of his production is now lost. What survives of his prose is scattered through a number of short texts, some of them, for example the Ch'an shu 讒書 (Defamatory Writings), mixed with pieces of poetry. In that collection the author offers revisions of Confucian notions about antiquity and novel opinions about society and history. Elsewhere are his reflections on kingship, duty, and public morality (Liang t'ung shu 兩同書). He also wrote wonder tales and stories of adventure. Examples are preserved in Kuang-ling yao luan chih 廣陵妖亂志. Some official correspondence, prefaces to literary works, descriptions of town and country, and a fair number of reflective essays on many subjects—matters of belief and tradition preponderate—usually infused with a moral tone, also survive.

The themes of Lo Yin's poems fall into readily definable groups. One is made up of verses about the capital city, especially the Ch'ü chiang 曲江 (Serpentine River), the pleasure park of the aristocracy; others focus on Lo-yang, Hunan, the Yangtze River, and, above all, the Wu area, including Hangchow, Chiang-tu 江都 (Yangchow), and Ku-su 姑蘇 (Soochow). His poems on the former homes and the tombs of eminent men form another category. There are references to his correspondence with such distinguished contemporaries as Kuan-hsiu* and Lu Kuei-meng.* Many of his poems tell of religious events and festivals and visits to temples and monasteries. He sometimes displays a longing for the world above, as when he wistfully addresses a Taoist priest: "I wish to visit you, Prior Born, to ask about the scriptures and the oral arcana. In this world it is hard to gain anything which does not spring from yourself." He also wrote of such popular celebrations as Ch'i hsi 七夕 (Seventh Evening) and Ch'ing-ming 清明 (Clear and Bright) and about the goddess of the Hsiang River (Hsiang Fei 湘妃). There are a great many poems about the natural world, including peonies, chrysanthemums, swallows, goshawks, snow fireflies, the moon, bees, wildflowers, and the blooms of the peach, the apricot, and the paulownia. Characteristically he showed a strong preference for wilted flowers, red leaves, and other aspects of autumn, along with ghosts, dust, and other tokens of the transience and decay that eat away at the living world. But he found many other subjects suitable to his pen, among them incense, embroidery, music, pictures, and even horoscope astrology. In all of these topics he found occasion for a cultural analogy or moral allegory—usually a pessimistic one. A caged parrot leads him to comment that plain speech tends to stand in the way of advancement in the world of men, as he knew well from his own experience. Many of his poems are undisguised attacks on public practice; one such is his treatment of "Snow," in which he finds the supposedly auspicious character of a heavy snowfall a sorry mockery: the poor folk of Ch'ang-an are freezing to death. Although he has a reputation as a writer on historical themes (yung shih 詠史), he shows his contempt for cherished views of historical process; an example is his poem about the beauty Hsi Shih, in which he attacks the traditional notion that a kingdom can be subverted by the gift of an enchanting woman to its ruler. "If Hsi Shih knew how to subvert the Kingdom of Wu, who then was it that brought about the downfall of the Kingdom of Yüeh?" Here, in effect, he was refuting the "great man" theory of history.

In addition to these lyric effusions, Lo Yin wrote a number of fu,* of which five survive. They treat the subjects of spider webs, drifting snow, screens, markets, and the labyrinthine palace of Emperor Yang of the Sui. Like his *shih*,* these also contain strong allegorical elements.

Traditional accounts of Lo Yin and his writing say little more than that he was a "satirist." But he was much more than that. He was an honest man with a well-developed sense of ethics, and capable of making penetrating insights through shallow conventions. His style favored parable more than true satire.

EDITIONS:

Ch'an shu 讒書 . *Shao-wu Hsü shih ts'ung-shu* 邵武徐氏叢書 , 1886.

Chia-i chi 甲乙集 . *SPTK*.

Ch'üan T'ang shih, v. 10, *ch*. 655-665, pp. 7531-7624.

Ch'üan T'ang wen, v. 19, *ch*. 894-897, pp. 11769-11819.

Liang t'ung shu 兩同書 , in Yang Chia-lo 楊家駱 ed., *Sui T'ang tzu-shu shih chung* 隋唐子書十種 , v. 2, Taipei, 1962; also included in *PPTSCC*, series 18: *Pao-yen t'ang mi-chi* 寶顏堂秘笈 , v. 146.

Ling-pi-tzu 靈璧子 , in *Chu-tzu hui han* 諸子彙函 , from Chü-ying T'ang ts'ang-pan 聚英堂藏板 , *c.* 1660.

Shih-chia-tzu nien-shih 拾甲子年事 , in *Chiu hsiao-shuo* 舊小說 , Shanghai, 1921, v. 2, pp. 155-156.

Shuo Shih lieh shih 說石烈士 in *Chiu hsiao-shuo*, pp. 156-157.

TRANSLATIONS:

Kroll, Paul. "The Egret in Medieval Chinese Literature," *CLEAR*, 1.2 (July 1979), 186.

Nienhauser, William H., Jr. *Sunflower*, pp. 266-267.

Yang, Xianyi, trans. "Selections from 'Slanderous Writings,' " *Chinese Literature*, February 1982, 119-122.

STUDIES:

Deng, Kueiying, trans. by Yang Xianyi. "The Late Tang Writer Luo Yin," *Chinese Literature*, February 1982, 113-118.

Wang, Te-chen 汪德振 . *Lo Yin nien-p'u* 羅隱年譜 . Shanghai, 1937.

—ES

Lu Chao-lin 盧照鄰 (*tzu*, Sheng-chih 昇之, *c.* 634-c. 684) is traditionally regarded as one

of the *Ch'u T'ang ssu-chieh* (Four Eminences of the Early T'ang—see Yang Chiung). These writers, however, did not constitute a real coterie; the social contacts between the four were rare and fleeting, and indeed Lu Chao-lin and Lo Pin-wang* were nearly a generation older than Wang Po* and Yang Chiung.* It is better to examine each of these authors individually, rather than regard them as representatives of a homogeneous seventh-century "school" or "period-style."

Lu Chao-lin was a native of Fan-yang 范陽 (near modern Peking). In his youth he studied under the famous classical scholars Ts'ao Hsien 曹憲 and Wang I-fang 王義方 and was early given a position in the private archive of Li Yüan-yü 李元裕, Prince of Teng, seventeenth son of the founding emperor of the T'ang. A fine scholar, Lu was said to have exhausted the resources of the prince's extensive library; this erudition is evident in the many uncommon allusions employed in his poems. It is not certain how long Lu remained in the entourage of Li Yüan-yü (who died in 665), but he appears to have been at court through at least 666, when he was a member of the party accompanying the third T'ang emperor—Kao Tsung (r. 649-683)—on the latter's pilgrimage to Mount T'ai for the sacred *feng-shan* rites. Shortly thereafter Lu was posted to Hsin-tu 新都 in the province of Shu (near modern Ch'eng-tu, Szechwan), as a district Defender. During the last four of the five years he spent in Shu, he suffered from what seems to have been progressive rheumatoid arthritis, a debilitating disease that eventually left him lame of foot and palsied in one hand. This physical disability led to his resignation from official service. For some time around the year 673 he became an avid disciple of the great physician and alchemist Sun Ssu-miao 孫思邈, both at the latter's retreat on Mount T'ai-po 太白山 and his official lodgings in Ch'ang-an. It was at this time that Lu took for himself the sobriquet "Master of Shrouded Sorrow" (Yu-yu Tzu 幽憂子) and seems to have begun the experiments with drugs to abate his disease that were to be an important part of his remaining years. Later he shifted his residence to the Tung lung-men shan 東龍門山 near Lo-yang and then finally to Mount Chü-tz'u 具茨山 (in modern Yü 禹 county, Honan). When his chronic physical agony became unbearable, he drowned himself in the river Ying 潁. While we can firmly date several of the events of Lu's life and some of his poems, the dates of his birth and death are uncertain. When on internal evidence and statements in his works are correlated with known social and political incidents, a span of 634-684 seems the most reliable supposition. But, in any case, the commonly accepted dates of 641-680, based on Lu's laconic "official" biography in the *Chiu T'ang-shu* 舊唐書, cannot be upheld: Lu was definitely nearer to fifty years old than forty when he died, and he probably just outlived Kao-tsung.

Although only about one hundred of his compositions remain, Lu's *shih** and *fu** show him to have been an exceptionally gifted writer, with a total command of the classical literary heritage and tradition. While he was a practiced hand at composing courtly poems and was one of the earliest T'ang authors to write "frontier" verse, his real achievements lie in other areas. His three most famous works are the philosophical "Ping li-shu fu" 病梨樹賦 (Prose-poem on the Diseased Pear Tree), the nostalgically colorful "Ch'ang-an ku-i" 長安古意 (Olden Reflections of Ch'ang-an), and the allegorical poem set to the old *yüeh-fu* title "Hsing-lu nan" 行路難 (Hardships of the Road). The latter two works (both *shih*) are written in the heptasyllabic meter—an old song-style form—that was beginning to find favor during the second half of the seventh century in *shih* poems of a decidedly narrative bent; Lu was one of the first writers to master the form for use in long poems (the first of these two works comprises sixty-eight lines, the second forty). The great majority of his *shih*, however, are written in the prevalent pentasyllabic meter.

Lu's most memorable works were composed during roughly the final fifteen years of his life, beginning from the time of his residence in Shu. Many of these poems are allegories of solitary birds or blighted trees, containing harsh and cutting images played off against a general tone of melancholy and frustration. During his last years he created two lengthy and remarkable works in the *sao* style, "Wu pei" 五悲 (Five Griefs) and "Shih-chi wen" 釋疾文 (Text to Dispel Illness), which are artfully contrived and often painful meditations on fate, flux, and existence, composed in varying prosodic schemes borrowed from different sections of the *Ch'u-tz'u** (particularly those of the "Li sao," as well as the "Chiu ko," and "Chiu chang" sections).

Among his prose writings, perhaps the most interesting are his entreating letter to several courtiers in Lo-yang, requesting high-quality cinnabar granules for use in his medicinal concoctions, and his fictional "Tui Shu fu-lao wen" 對蜀父老問 (Response to the Question of a Fatherly Elder of Shu) in which he seeks to explain why he is not ashamed that he holds an influential position at court.

EDITIONS:

Yu-yu-tzu chi 幽憂子集. *SPTK*. A late Ming edition; typeset and punctuated version of this text, collated with the texts printed in *Ch'üan T'ang shih* and *Ch'üan T'ang wen*, and the selections included in *Wen-yüan ying-hua* and *Yüeh-fu shih-chi*, is contained in *Lu Chao-lin chi, Yang Chiung chi* 盧照鄰集，楊炯集, Hsü Ming-hsia 徐明霞, ed., Peking, 1980. No annotated version of Lu's works exists.

TRANSLATIONS:

Frankel, *Palace Lady*, pp. 130-143.
Owen, "Deadwood," 160-162. ("Ping li-shu fu" [Prose-poem on a Sick Pear Tree]).

STUDIES:

Furukawa, Sueyoshi 古川末喜. "Sho-Tō yon-ketsu no bungaku shisō" 初唐四傑の文學思想, *Chūgoku bungaku ronshū*, 8 (1979), 1-27.
Takagi, Masakazu 高木正一. "Ryo Shōrin no denki to bungaku" 盧照鄰の傳記と文學, *Ritsumeikan bungaku*, 196 (October 1961), 777-809.
Wen, I-to 聞一多. "Ssu chieh" 四傑, in Wen, *T'ang-shih tsa-lun* 唐詩雜論, in *Wen I-to ch'uan-chi*, Peking, 1948, v. 1, pp. 23-29.

—PWK

Lu Chi 陸機 (*tzu*, Shih-heng 士衡, 261-303), famous in his own time as a statesman, general, and author, ended his life far from home, a defeated general executed on a false charge of treason, whose prolific literary output was soon to be condemned as imitative and ornate. His reputation rests on a single short work of literary criticism, the *Wen fu* 文賦 (Prose-poem on Literature).

The size of Lu Chi's surviving corpus marks him as one of the most prolific authors of his day. The *Lu Shih-heng chi* 陸士衡集, originally in fourteen *chüan*, still contains ten *chüan* and over one hundred individual pieces, of which the most famous is his *Wen fu,* written when he was about forty.

The *Wen fu* concerns itself with the process of writing, from the search that precedes inspiration to the transforming effect on the reader that follows putting down the pen. In between, the writer's task is to harmonize his inner world of thoughts and feelings with the outer world of things and to find words (*wen* 文) to match his perception of meaning (*i* 意) or truth (*li* 理). Lu's choice of terms reflects the debate among Neo-Taoist philosophers on whether "words can exhaust meaning"; the writer's task is difficult, he concludes, precisely because they do not. His discussion of matching internal states of feeling (*ch'ing* 情), meaning, or truth with the outer world (*wu* 物) may also prefigure subsequent critical discussions of the importance of harmonizing scene (*ching* 景) with feeling (*ch'ing* 情). The protagonist of the *Wen fu,* like the shaman-hero of the "Yüan yu" 遠遊 in the *Ch'u-tz'u** or the emperor of Ssu-ma Hsiang-ju's* "Ta-jen fu" 大人賦 undertakes a cosmic journey or hunt for the right expressions. His flight of fancy—the act of writing—comprises three stages. First he gathers fuel: He "rinses his mouth with the essence of the Six Arts" and hunts down "submerged words" and "flying beauties." Next he compresses his far-flung material in his mind, achieving a concentrated view of the world and his work: "He sees past and present in a moment; he touches the four seas in the twinkling of an eye" (1.16);

"he traps Heaven and Earth in the cage of form; he crushes the myriad objects against the tip of his brush" (1.24). Finally, the completed work flows from his pen with the force of a rushing wind to carry out literature's task of mortal transformation: "A laughing wind will fly and whirl upward . . ." (1.35); "It travels over endless miles, removing all obstructions on the way . . . It propagates good ethos, never to perish" (1.126-129). The process of writing is like a ramjet engine, repeatedly going trough the cycle of intake, compression, and explosion described above and sending a shock-wave to the world below. Writing is internal combustion.

The *Wen fu* is the first systematic treatment of literary criticism in Chinese and one of only a very few to be cast in literary form. It pays attention to the definition of genres in more detail than does Ts'ao P'i's* *Tien-lun lun-wen* 典論論文 and to the description and solution of faults, in which it foreshadows T'ang manuals of composition. Unlike many of its successors, it is unconcerned with questions of literary history, the relative ranking of poets, or the appreciation of famous lines. The text of the *Wen fu* may be found in *ch.* 17 of the *Wen-hsüan.**

EDITIONS:

Gotō, Akimasa 後藤秋正. *Riku Ki shi sakuin* 陸機詩索引. Tokyo, 1976.

Ho, Li-ch'uan 郝立權 ed. *Lu Shih-heng shih-chu* 陸士衡詩註. Chinan, 1932; rpt. Peking, n.d.

Lu Shih-heng chi 陸士衡集, *SPPY.*

Lu Shih-heng wen-chi 陸士衡文集, *SPTK.*

TRANSLATIONS:

Ch'en, Shih-hsiang. "Essay on Literature," in Birch, *Anthology,* v. 1, pp. 204-214.

Demiéville, *Anthologie,* pp. 133-134.

Fang, Achilles. "Rhymeprose on Literature: the *Wen Fu* of Lu Chi A.D. 261-303," *HJAS,* 14 (1951), 527-566. The preferred translation; introduction, interlinear Chinese text, and notes.

Frodsham, J. D. *An Anthology of Chinese Verse.* Oxford, 1967, pp. 89-91.

Hughes, Ernest Richard. *The Art of Letters: Lu Chi's "Wen fu," 302 A.D., A Translation and Comparative Study.* New York, 1951. With a forenote by I. A. Richards. Serious problems of translation and interpretation.

Kōzen, Hiroshi 興膳宏. *Han Gaku, Riku Ki* 潘岳陸機. Tokyo, 1973.

STUDIES:

Chou, Ju-chang. "An Introduction to Lu Chi's *Wen fu*," *Studia Serica*, 9.1 (1948), 42-65.

Liu, Wei-ch'ing 廖蔚卿. "Lun Lu Chi te shih" 論陸機的詩, in *Chung-kuo ku-tien wen-hsüeh yen-chiu ts'ung-k'an: Shih-ko chih-pu, (1)* 中國古典文學研究叢刊詩歌之部, K'o Ch'ing-ming 柯慶明, ed. Taipei, 1978, pp. 71-105.

Wang, Meng-ou 王夢鷗. "Lu Chi *Wen-fu* so tai-piao te wen-hsüeh kuan-nien" 陸機文賦所代表的文學觀念, *Chung-wai wen-hsüeh*, 8.2 (July 1979), 4-14.

—RB

Lu Chih 陸贄 (*tzu*, Ching-yü 敬輿, 754-805) was one of the most influential inner-court politicians of his time and master of a polemical *p'ien-wen** prose-style which anticipated the *ssu-liu* 四六 *p'ien-wen* of the eleventh century. His extant prose works are official documents written over a fifteen-year period (779-794) during which he served as a key adviser to Emperor Te-tsung (r. 779-805).

Lu was born into one of the four leading southern clans. His immediate family came from Chia-hsing 嘉興 (modern Chekiang). At the age of nineteen, he placed sixth (out of thirty-four) in the *chin-shih* examination and began a meteoric climb to the center of political power. Having spent the intervening six years in provincial posts, he was called to Ch'ang-an in 779 to serve as a censor. Emperor Te-tsung, impressed with Lu's judgment and prose style, had Lu made a Han-lin Academician the next year. In this capacity, Lu Chih developed an extremely close relationship with Te-tsung through a position that was outside the normal bureaucratic chain.

Te-tsung had come to the throne with the intention of wresting control of the nation from rebellious northeastern military leaders who then ruled large parts of the empire with virtual independence. The emperor's actions provoked a series of rebellions in the early 780s. One rebel group forced him to flee to Feng-t'ien 奉天, where he became most dependent on the advice and support of Lu Chih and a few other officials who accompanied him there. Many of Lu's extant memorials date from 783 and 784 and seem to have been influential in determining the direction of imperial policy. The rest were written from 792 through 794 when he was a Grand Councilor, attempting to convince the emperor to carry out reforms of the national economy and to restrain his own avarice.

During most of his fifteen years of service, Lu Chih enjoyed the emperor's companionship and protection. However, after the recovery of the capital in 784 and especially after Lu Chih became Grand Councilor (and was no longer an imperial adviser), his remonstrations of imperial actions led to strained relations with Te-tsung. Lu's vitriolic attack on another adviser, P'ei Yen-ling 裴延齡 (738-796), finally provoked the emperor to demote Lu. But for the intervention of Lu Chih's influential friends, including the heir apparent, he would have been executed. In 795 he was exiled to a post at Chung-chou 忠州 (modern Chung-hsien 忠縣, Szechwan). Ten years later, in 805, both the emperor and Lu Chih died. By the end of the year, Lu Chih was granted the posthumous title *Hsüan* 宣 (Proclaimer).

Lu's writings have been traditionally cited as examples of straightforward, loyal remonstrations of one's monarch. Indeed, his memorials, especially those of 783 and 784, are unusually frank. At least three times during the bureaucrat-dominated eleventh and twelfth centuries, copies of Lu Chih's memorials were presented to Sung emperors as polite reminders that officials be allowed to speak their minds on public issues.

Lu Chih's *p'ien-wen* style was different from the style of the Six Dynasties which had continued to influence prose through the early eighth century. To a certain extent Lu's style was an outgrowth of the changes brought about by Chang Yüeh* and Su T'ing* during the early eighth century. It was used to compose official rather than personal prose pieces and contained fewer historical allusions than the older style, but it adhered more strictly to the *p'ien-wen* format of parallel four- and six-syllable lines. Lu Chih's prose diction is unique. The polemical qualities of his writing, using a relatively uncomplicated vocabulary to appeal directly to the emperor's reasoning powers and emotions, like a modern political speech, are also noteworthy.

Lu Chih's prose seems to have survived nearly intact since first published, but little of his poetry is extant. Modern editions of his prose writings can be traced to at least three different Sung textual traditions, all including the same writings. According to the *Hsin T'ang-shu*, his prose was originally published in two works, a twelve-*chüan* collection of memorials, both official (*chung-shu tsou-i* 中書奏議) and private (*tsou-ts'ao* 奏草), and a ten-*chüan* anthology of edicts (*chih-kao* 制誥) he wrote on the emperor's behalf. An extant preface to the latter collection by his follower Ch'üan Te-yü 權德輿 (759-818) says that the memorials were published in fourteen *chüan*. However, all extant editions of his prose include the same eighty-three edicts and fifty-six memorials.

EDITIONS:

Lu, Chih. *P'ing-chu Lu Hsüan-kung chi* 評註陸宣公集. 15 *chüan*. Taipei, 1970. Original title: *Chu Lu Hsüan-kung tsou-i* 註陸宣公奏議. Chronologically the second of three textual traditions; includes Lang Yeh's 1191 memorial and annotations. A photocopy of Liu T'ieh-leng's 劉鐵冷 1925 collation of a 1354 edition with other versions, including one with punctuation.

―――. *T'ang Lu Hsüan-kung chi* 唐陸宣公集. 22 *chüan*. SPTK. The oldest text tradition; includes Su Shih's* memorial of 1193. No annotations. Reprint of Sung edition.

―――. *T'ang Lu Hsüan-kung han-yüan chi chu* 唐陸宣公翰苑集注. 24 *chüan*. Taipei, 1964. Based on a sixteenth-century edition, includes Hsiao Sui's 蕭燧 memorial (1186) and annotations by Chang P'ei-fang 張佩芳. This is the only modern annotated edition with both the edicts and the memorials.

STUDIES:

Twitchett, Denis. "Lu Chih (754-805): Imperial Adviser and Court Official," in Arthur F. Wright, ed., *Confucian Personalities*, Stanford, 1962, pp. 84-122.

Yen, I-p'ing 嚴一萍. *Lu Hsüan-kung nien-p'u* 陸宣公年譜. Taipei, 1975.

—BL

Lu Kuei-meng 陸龜蒙 (*tzu*, Lu-wang 魯望, d. *c.* 881), was a native of Wu-chün 吳都, Soochow. Although he was a precocious student of the classics and reputed to be an authority on the *Ch'un-ch'iu*, he was, with good reason, treated by the *Hsin T'ang-shu* as a Taoist: his biography is in the section called "Yin i" 隱逸 (Hidden and Uninhibited), along with those of the learned physicians Sun Ssu-miao 孫思 and Meng Shen 孟詵, the ecstatic poet Wu Yün 吳筠, and P'an Shih-cheng 潘師正 and Ssu-ma Ch'eng-chen,* the eleventh and twelfth Mao-shan Patriarchs respectively. Most of Lu's life was spent in the village of Fu-li 甫里, near Sung-chiang 松江 in the Wu region, hence his byname Fu-li Hsien-sheng 甫里先生 (he was also sometimes styled T'ien-sui-tzu 天隨子 and Chiang-hu san-jen 江湖散人). In this pleasant land adjacent to the Grand Lake and Mao-shan he wrote prolifically, much of the time in the company of his poetic friend P'i Jih-hsiu* and the scholarly Taoist Chang Pen 張賁 (*tzu*, Jun-ch'ing 潤卿), both of whom are frequently addressed in the titles of his poems.

Lu Kuei-meng is reported to have been a brooding, melancholy person, who suffered much from illness and poverty. But this official characterization seems inadequate: he was fond of good company and laughter, by no means a despondent hypochondriac, and it is difficult to understand how a pauper could have amassed a fine library of more than ten thousand scrolls. In fact, he led the life he chose to lead, away from the turmoil of urban and political life and the winds of fashion. His library contained many fine manuscripts, and he was himself a conscientious editor, collator, and restorer, who did not hesitate to repair the rare books he borrowed from his friends. The notion that he suffered from poverty seems to be based on the observation that he loved the land and was constantly to be seen laboring in his extensive fields—where he also owned a large house—like any ordinary peasant. Having abandoned wine-bibbing to become a tea fancier, he made tea one of his favorite crops. He did not like to travel about on horseback, preferring to go everywhere in his watery realm by boat, carrying his own bedding, desk, bundles of books, angling gear, and tea stove. In short, he played the role of a sophisticate who enjoyed wearing the mask of Yao or Shun—supermen who chose or were obliged to strip themselves of worldly pleasures and ambitions.

The subjects of his poems are often trees, flowers, birds, insects, clouds—all manner of natural things—with which he felt an intimacy that he enjoyed with few men. He frequently wrote of landscapes in the Wu area, especially temple precincts, haunted grottoes, holy mountains, and numinous springs, and also of the seasons and such daily activities as walking, sitting, sleeping, and eating. He particularly liked to write of rural technologies in which he could claim mastery: he left a sequence of twenty poems on the art of fishing, including vignettes of weirs, moles, traps, boats, reels, and the like; a set of ten on wood-cutting and wood-gathering; another set of ten on wine and winemaking; and still another ten on tea, all written in a knowledgeable, affable, good-humored tone. He also produced many verses on his experiences in the company of boon-companions—eating, drinking, talking, and writing: to them and to such admirable producers as farmers and fishermen, he presented a face different from that which he showed to the rest of the world.

Many of his poems tell of the tropical south—although there is no record that he ever visited the region. A poem addressed to an acquaintance in Hainan, referring to sorcery and pearl-fishing, suggests a probable source for his exotic imagery, which includes dragon-haunted Hanoi, the non-Chinese aborigines of Canton, and local taxes paid in cowrie shells there.

His familiarity with nature extended to the supernal world. Such preoccupations were related to his familiarity with Taoist rites, especially those at Mao-shan, and his close acquaintanceship with priests and adepts. He is confident of the divinity of nature and familiar with the rites due the moon and the Northern Dipper. Among the pleasures of visits to Mao-shan he enumerates the opportunities to take rubbings from ancient incised texts, to find and collate old manuscripts, to participate in alchemical demonstrations, to search for invigorating herbs and sacred mushrooms, and to explore mysterious grottoes in the company of learned ecclesiastics.

Lu Kuei-meng has also left us many skillful and imaginative *fu,** on themes such as moss, lice, and mythical animals, not to mention "living in obscurity."

A small number of prose writings show similar preoccupations. Two pieces have been regularly anthologized: "Hsiao-ming lu" 小名錄 (Register of Little Names), about the juvenile names of persons of antiquity (it survives only in part), and "Chin-ch'ün chi" 錦裙記 (Record of a Damask Apron).

There is also a short but witty autobiography, composed as if about a stranger of unknown antecedents. This alter-ego is described as "rustic and uninhibited . . . fond of reading the writings of the incomparable men of antiquity." So Lu Kuei-meng liked to represent himself—but his writings are far from being rustic and uninhibited. Their well-flavored language is as carefully contrived as was the man himself.

EDITIONS:

Chin-ch'ün chi 金裙記, in *TTTS*. 1 *chüan*.

Ch'üan T'ang shih, v. 9, ch. 617-630, pp. 7108-7233.

Ch'üan T'ang wen, v. 17, ch. 800-801, pp. 10585-10618.

Hsiao-ming lu 小名錄, in *TSCC*. 2 *chüan*.

Lei-ssu ching 耒耜經, in *TSCC*. 1 *chüan*.

Li-tse ts'ung-shu 笠澤叢書. Shanghai, 1914. 4 *chüan*.

Sung-ling chi 松陵集. Reprint of Sung ed. in *Chi ku ko* 汲古閣. 10 *chüan*.

T'ang Fu-li Hsien-cheng wen-chi 唐甫里先生文集. *SPTK*. 20 *chüan*.

Yü-chü yung 漁具詠, in *Shuo-fu* 說郛 (Wan-wei shan-t'ang 宛委山堂 ed.).

TRANSLATIONS:

Edwards, E. D. "The Embroidered Skirt," in *Chinese Prose Literature*, v. 2, pp. 311-313.

Davis, *Penguin*, p. 30.

Nienhauser, William H., Jr. *P'i Jih-hsiu*. Boston, 1979, pp. 70-71, 89-90, 106-107 and 112. Several *shih* and one *fu*.

Schafer, *Golden Peaches*, p. 67.

———. *Mao Shan in T'ang Times* (Society for the Study of Chinese Religions, Monograph No. 1), University of Colorado, 1980, pp. 31-32, 37-38, 41.

STUDIES:

Maegawa, Yokio 前川幸雄. "*Shōryōshū* sho shū shi no kenkyū (1)" 松陵集所收詩の研究, *Fukui kōhyō kōtō semmon gakkō kenkyū kiyō* (*Jimbun shakai kagaku*), 11 (1978), 1-29.

Nienhauser, *P'i Jih-hsiu*.

—ES

Lu kuei pu 錄鬼簿 (A Register of Ghosts) compiled by Chung Ssu-ch'eng 鍾嗣城 (*tzu*, Chi-hsien 繼先, *hao*, Ch'ou-chai 醜齋, *c.* 1279-1360) is a major source of information on the Yüan dramatists. First completed in 1330 (the date of the preface), the original *Lu kuei pu* contains brief biographical notes on 152 songwriters and playwrights of the Chin-Yüan era, with elegiac verses for nineteen of them. The entries are divided into seven sections and arranged in roughly chronological order. The first two sections deal with *ch'ü** writers; the next five are devoted to dramatists. Each entry begins with the author's name, followed by his style name and native place. His official positions and other facts about his life and works are also briefly given. For the playwrights, a list of plays attributed to each is included in the biography, with a total of some four hundred titles listed. The 111 dramatists in the *Register* belong to roughly two periods: those who lived before Chung's time and those contemporary with him.

Chung's purpose in compiling the *Register*, as can be seen from his preface, was to honor the great talents so that they will be remembered as "the ghosts who never die." A playwright himself, he was knowledgeable about his subject. Because he was a contemporary of some of the playwrights he wrote about and because the *Register* was written only some sixty years after the most flourishing period of Yüan drama, his information is particularly valuable.

The Ming enlarged version (preface dated 1422) is by Chia Chung-ming 賈仲明 (*hao*, Yün-shui san-jen 雲水散人, *c.* 1343-*c.* 1422), also a playwright. Chia combined the original seven sections into three and added elegiac verses for twenty-eight playwrights. Chia's version also varies slightly from Chung's original in the order of the authors listed and in the information given about their lives.

A sequel, the *Lu kuei pu hsü-pien* 錄鬼簿續編 (A Supplement to *Lu kuei pu*), is also attributed to Chia Chung-ming. Following the same format as the original *Register*, the *Supplement* extends the list to include seventy-one more song writers and playwrights from the late Yüan and early Ming periods. A list of seventy-eight plays by anonymous authors is appended.

Lu kuei pu, together with its enlarged version and supplement, covers the early Yüan through early Ming—a period known as the golden age of *tsa-chü** drama. Given the paucity of information on Yüan dramatists in the official histories, these works, brief as they are, are indispensable in the study of these dramatists and their works.

EDITIONS:

Lu kuei pu chiao-chu 錄鬼簿校注. Wang Kuo-wei 王國維, ed. and annot., in *Wang Chung-chüeh kung i-shu* 王忠慤公遺書, Shanghai, 1930; *Hai-ming Wang Ching-an Hsien-sheng i-shu* 海寧王靜安先生遺書, Changsha, 1940; and *Wang Kuo-wei hsi-ch'ü lun-wen chi* 王國維戲曲論文集, Peking, 1957.

Lu kuei pu hsing chiao-chu 錄鬼簿新校注. Ma Lien 馬廉, ed. and annot. Peking, 1957. Based on an early manuscript.

Lu kuei pu (Wai ssu-chung) 錄鬼簿外四種. Shanghai, 1957 and 1980.

Lu kuei pu, in *Hsi-ch'ü lun-chu*, v. 2. A comprehensive modern variorum edition, using Ts'ao Lien-t'ing's 曹楝亭 1706 edition as the basic text. Contains copious notes.

STUDIES:

Sun, K'ai-ti 孫楷第. "Shih *Lu kuei pu* so-wei tz'u-pen" 釋錄鬼簿所謂次本, in his *Ts'ang-chou chi* 滄州集, Peking, 1965, pp. 399-405.

—SLY

Lu Lun 盧綸 (*tzu*, Yün-yen 允言, 737?-798?) is known as a leading member of the group of poets known as the *Ta-li shih ts'ai-tzu* 大曆十才子 (Ten Talents of the Ta-li Era [766–779]; the grouping included a dozen or so poets at various times including Ch'ien Ch'i* and Li I*). A native of P'u-chou 蒲州 (modern Yung-chi hsien in Shansi), he sat repeatedly for the *chin-shih* examination but never passed it. Consequently, he was dependent on his literary talents to obtain employment.

His first important patron was the Grand Councilor Yüan Tsai, under whose sponsorship he rose to the post of Investigating Censor, only to lose it during Yüan's precipitous downfall in 777. Fortunately, Emperor Te-tsung, an admirer of his poetry, recalled him to Ch'ang-an in 780. He was still in the capital during its occupation by the rebel Chu Tz'u in 783. Freed in 784 by Hun Chen (736–799), the Military Commissioner of Ho-chung 河中, he joined the latter's staff and probably died in that position.

Lu Lun's poetry reveals a variety of thematic material—a reflection of his broad experiences and extensive travels. His "Wan-tz'u O-chou" 晚次鄂州 (Mooring at Night in O-chou) is an early example of his imagistic powers, written while in the South during the An Lu-shan Rebellion. The six quatrains comprising "Ho Chang P'u-yeh sai-hsia ch'ü 和張僕射塞下曲 (Frontier Songs: Matching Rhymes with Assistant Executive Secretary Chang), a product of his years in Hun Chen's camp, are some of the best-known examples of "frontier poetry."

However, like the work of the other "Ten Talents," his consists mainly of social poetry and occasional verse written in the favored form for such verses: pentasyllabic regulated verse. Indeed, it is such verses with which the group is traditionally identified.

The name of the group itself refers to a number of poets who resided in the capital and enjoyed great popularity among the social elite about 770, a time of stability at court brought about by the autocratic Yüan Tsai, Grand Councilor from 762 to 777. The roster of the "Ten Talents," however, began changing during the Northern Sung as poets whose works had been lost in transmission came to be replaced by others. The original "Ten Talents," based on near contemporary sources, were Lu Lun, Han Hung 韓翃, Ch'ien Ch'i,* Miao Fa 苗發, Hsia-hou Shen 夏侯審, Chi Chung-fu 吉中孚 (for the last three, only one or two poems are still extant), Ts'ui T'ung 崔峒, as well as the following three poets who are discussed below: Ssu-k'ung Shu, Lu Tuan, and Keng Wei. Ssu-k'ung Shu 司空曙 (*tzu*, Wen-ming 文明, also Wen-ch'u 文初, d. *c.* 790) was one of the better poets of the group, whose verses are known for their impersonal, objective descriptive passages and their imagistic power. Coming from a relatively poor family, he spent the years of the An Lu-shan Rebellion in the South, served for a long period in the capital in the post of Imperial Remonstrant of the Left, suffered banishment to Ch'ang-lin 長林 (near modern Ching-men hsien in Hupei), and late in life served under Wei Kao, Military Commissioner of Chien-nan 劍南 (central and western Szechwan). His regulated verses, mostly pentasyllabic, are especially noted for the precise yet natural use of antithesis, as in the well-known "Tsei p'ing-hou sung jen pei-kuei" 賊平後送人北歸 (Sending off Someone Returning North after the Rebels Were Subdued). He was a cousin of Lu Lun.

Li Tuan 李端 (*tzu*, Cheng-chi 正己, d. *c.* 787) is reputed to have studied poetry with the poet-monk Chiao-jan,* but this is yet to be proved. A native of Chao-chou 趙州 (modern Chao hsien in Hopei), he was an Editor in the Palace Library and probably died while holding a minor post in Hang-chow (modern Chekiang). His poetry has been compared to, but ranked below, that of Ssu-k'ung Shu, because of his less skillful use of antithesis. He also wrote in the heptasyllabic meter with some success, both in occasional verses and in songs and ballads. He was a nephew of Li Chia-yu 李嘉祐, celebrated poet of the same period who is sometimes counted as one of the "Ten Talents" by later writers.

Keng Wei 耿湋 (*tzu*, Hung-yüan 洪源?) was stylistically the least ornate writer of the group. He held a long tenure as an Imperial Remonstrant alongside Ssu-k'ung Shu. His poetry also concentrates on personal themes, but often lacks detachment, making him less of a "nature poet" than his colleague. He also wrote many heptasyllabic verses with realistic, descriptive passages reflecting the social disturbances of the latter half of the eighth century, such as "Lu-p'ang lao-jen" 路傍老人 (The Old Man by the Roadside). These pieces, along with his "frontier poetry," were often set in desolate landscapes which accord with the generally melancholy mood of most of his works.

While critics often mention a *Ta-li t'i* 大曆體 (Ta-li style), there is no evidence to show that the "talents" ever consciously espoused any literary ideals or that they even considered themselves a literary clique. This term, however, has become a stylistic designation referring, at its best, to the polished (if undistinguished) pentasyllabic verses of the "talents" and, at its worst, to wholly derivative mediocre poetry lacking in moral and ethical concerns.

Besides revealing contemporary poetic tastes, modern literary historians tend to view the role of the "Ten Talents" as helping to set the background for the reactions that gave rise to the various styles of the Mid-T'ang or as "transitional poets" between the High and Mid-T'ang.

EDITIONS:

Han Hung shih-chi chiao-chu 韓翃詩集校注. Ch'en Wang-ho 陳王和, ed. Taipei, 1973. Contains the photolithographic reprint of the text of Han Hung's poems in the *Ch'üan T'ang shih* (1707 edition), which is used as the basic text for collation; with extensive annotation. For the other "Ten Talents," individual collections are poorly edited and often incomplete; use *Ch'üan T'ang shih.*

TRANSLATIONS:

Sunflower, p. 157.

Translations of the anthology *T'ang-shih san-pai shou** have poems by Lu Lun, Ssu-k'ung Shu, Ch'ien Ch'i Han Hung, and Li Tuan.

STUDIES:

Fu, *Shih-jen.* Collection of articles, over half of which are devoted to the "Talents"; see especially "Lu Lun k'ao" 考, pp. 469-492.

Ogawa, Shōichi 小川昭一. "Taireki no shijin" 大曆の詩人, *Shibun,* 24 (1959), 22-33.

Owen, *High T'ang,* pp. 253-280.

—OL

Lu Ts'ai 陸采 (original name, Cho 灼, *tzu,* Tzu-hsüan 子玄, *hao,* T'ien-ch'ih 天池, also called Ch'ing-ch'ih-sou 清癡叟, "Pure Old Fool," 1497-1537) was born in Ch'ang-chou 長洲 (modern Wu-hsien 吳縣, Kiangsu) and became an important figure in the then burgeoning dramatic activity of that region. Rejecting formal studies, he spent his time with actors learning dramatic techniques, perfecting his songs, and generally carousing. In all, five *ch'uan-ch'i** are attributed to him, three of which are still extant.

At age nineteen he wrote the *Ming-chu chi* 明珠記 (Bright Pearls, also called *Wang Hsien-k'o Wu-shuang ch'uan-ch'i* 王仙客無雙傳奇 [Wang Hsien-k'o and (Liu) Wu-shuang]). Lu actually revised a draft his brother, Lu Ts'an 陸粲 (*chin-shih,* mid-sixteenth century), had written, relying on his acquaintance with local *ch'ü* music-masters to standardize the prosody and tunes. He also composed *Huai-hsiang chi* 懷香記 (Longing for Fragrance) and *Nan Hsi-hsiang (A Southern West Chamber).* A renowned traveler, Lu visited T'ai-shan and other famous mountains and journeyed through South China.

Lu's masterpiece is *Ming-chu chi.* The story involves the vicissitudes of a betrothed couple, Wang Hsien-k'o and Liu Wu-shuang, living in the mid-T'ang era. Wang lives with Liu's family (her father, Liu Chen 劉震, is his uncle) after his father dies. During a revolt Wang is asked to take the family's belongings and flee Ch'ang-an—Liu Chen and the family members will follow. Liu Chen gives Wang one of a set of "bright pearls" as a keepsake and symbol of his betrothal to Wu-shuang—she has the other. Before the Lius can follow Wang out of the city, they are captured by rebels. Liu Chen is imprisoned and his wife and daughter taken into the palace. After a series of rather complex transferrals, Wu-shuang is being moved back into the harem of the newly enthroned emperor when Wang chances upon her. He sends a maid servant into her quarters with a gift of tea and his pearl. Soon thereafter a Taoist adept from Mao-shan provides a potion which makes Wu-shuang appear lifeless for three days. When her body is moved out of the palace, Wang's associates collect it. She revives and the reunited couple head for Chengtu, where they have relatives. En route they collide with a boat and rescue its passengers, including Wu-shuang's father who has just been granted his freedom. With their fortuitous reunion, the play ends.

The larger structure of the play is praised by most critics, and rightly so, since the dramatic tension is effectively built and the plot, though complex, remains dynamic. But Lu has been criticized for following his sources too assiduously. Others feel that on a lower level the sequence of spoken and sung sections is often jumbled. On the songs themselves, the verdict is mixed. Lu trained his own actors; thus the final version as performed in Lu's day was the result of the collaborative efforts of Wu ch'ü-masters, the Lu brothers, and actors hand-picked and trained by Lu Ts'ai. Although there is no record of its popularity in comparison with similar efforts of the time, *Ming-chu chi* must have been rather successful in performances. Nevertheless, it was revised at least twice (by Liang Ch'en-yü* and Li Yü* [1611-1680]—Li didn't like the idea of Wang's male servant presenting the tea and pearl and gave the task to Wu-shuang's former maid).

Records tell us that *Huai-hsiang chi*, which dealt with the secret affair between Han Shou 韓壽 and Chia Ch'ung's 賈充 daughter, was not popular. The other extant piece, *Nan Hsi-hsiang*, was written because Lu was not content with Li Jih-hua's 李日華 version. Critical judgment generally accords Li's version the better verdict.

Lu also wrote a *Yeh-ch'eng-k'o lun* 冶城客論 (in two *chüan*) about fox-fairies and other strange events.

EDITIONS:

Huai-hsiang chi ting-pen 定本, in *Ku-pen*, I, 58. Based on the Chi-ku ko edition.
Liu-huan Hsi-hsiang chi 六幻西廂記 (Western Chamber of Six Illusions). 2 *chüan*. One of

two remaining copies is in the Peking Library.

Ming-chu chi. A Ming Wan-li Edition in the possession of Kanda Kiichirō 神由喜一郎 in Japan. 2 *chüan*.

———. A multi-colored (red and black *t'ao-pen* 套本) edition collated and carved by Min Ch'i-chi 閔齊伋 of Wu-hsing 吳興 during the late Ming. 4 *chüan*. Appends *Wang Wu-shuang chuan* 王無雙傳 in 2 *chüan*. Now in the Naikaku bunkō.

Ming-chi chi ting-pen 定本, in *Liu-shih*, III. Based on the Chi-ku-ko edition.

——, in *Ku-pen*, I, 57. Photolithically reproduced from the Chi-ku ko edition.

Nan Hsi-hsiang. A Wan-li Edition printed by Chou Chü-i 周居易. 2 *chüan*. In Fu Hsi-hua's personal collection.

———, in *Ku-pen*, I, 56. Based on Chou Chü-i's collated version; with a preface by Lu Ts'ai.

Nuan-hung shih Hui-k'o ch'uan-chü "Hsi-hsiang fu-lu shih-san chung" 暖紅室彙刻傳劇 西廂附錄十三種. Kuei-ch'ih 貴池, 1912. Reprinted by Liu Shih-heng 劉世珩 with a postface by Liu. Based on a late Ming edition.

STUDIES:
Aoki, *Gikyokushi*, pp. 158-161.
Chu, Shang-wen 朱尚文. "Lu Ts'ai," in *Ming-tai chü-ch'ü shih* 明代曲劇史, Taipei, 1959, pp. 89-93.
Fu, *Ch'uan-ch'i*, pp. 36-38.
　　　　　　　　　　　　　　　—WHN

Lu Yu 陸游 (*tzu*, Wu-kuan 務觀, *hao*, Fang-weng 放翁, 1125-1210) was the most prolific lyric poet of the Southern Sung dynasty. His powerfully individual personality and his romantically intransigent irredentism, expressed in some ten thousand *shih** poems spanning sixty-five years of mature creativity, have made him popular through more than seven hundred years of Chinese history. Twentieth-century readers and critics have tended to emphasize the nationalistic, pro-Sung anti-Chin aspects of his verse and have dubbed him the "patriotic poet." Marxist critics have praised him for his social awareness, sympathy for the common people, and sharp criticism of the policies of an effete and parasitic Sung bureaucracy. He had many other wide-ranging interests, however, and recent Western studies have shown his life and work to be far more complex and sophisticated than the single epithet "patriotic poet" would imply.

A refugee for the first nine years of his life and educated first by his father, Lu Tsai 陸宰, who had the utmost contempt for Grand Councilor Ch'in Kuei and his policy of peace with the Chin, Lu Yu was romantically pro-war all of his life, supported the efforts of defeated generals like Chang Chün and even usurpers like Han T'o-chou, and attacked the peace policies of Sung emperors in hundreds of poems. His "patriotism" was a traditional loyalty to the Chinese empire, and he looked forward to the reestablishment of the glory that was Han and the grandeur that was T'ang, to the day when the Chinese emperors and Chinese cultural values would once more hold sway over their rightful territory and regain their rightful destiny. Despite his concern for the lot of the Chinese peasantry, he had little knowledge of their conditions under the Chin, and he was in no sense anti-monarchical or in favor of radical social change. In his later years, the ratio of "patriotic" verse to other more personal themes declines sharply and even what remains is more in the nature of wistful dreams of reconquest rather than stirring calls to arms.

Lu Yu learned how to write poetry and how to play the role of a poet by appropriating almost the entire Chinese poetic tradition and blending it with his own experiences to create a powerful personal statement. From the Chiang-hsi shih-p'ai* he learned the seriousness of poetic technique, from the Shih-ching* the use of poetry as social comment, from the Ch'u-tz'u* the lyrical expression of genuine emotions, and from Ch'ü Yüan,* Tu Fu* (his favorite), Li Po,* and T'ao Ch'ien,* poetry as self-dramatization, philosophy, and transcendent consolation. He was a serious student of the Confucian Classics, an ardent practitioner of Taoist meditation and alchemy, and a frequent reader of the I-ching (see ching) and the Chuang-tzu (see Chu-tzu pai-chia—there are more allusions to the Chuang-tzu than to any other work), his erudition was rescued from bookishness by

his great love for the Chinese countryside and his identification with the simple though difficult life of the rural people, as well as, perhaps, his great capacity for strong drink. The physical presence of nature—the Chinese landscape—is never far from his poetic expression.

The major themes of his poetry are Taoism and the quest for transcendence, with patriotic verse ranking a distant second, followed by nature poetry of both landscape (shan-shui) and pastoral (t'ien-yuan) modes, poems written while or after drinking wine, and poetic expressions of dream experiences. His entire life and thought is presented in his verse as the working out of a creative tension between the culturally conditioned and contradictory demands of Confucian loyalty (patriotism) and public service and Taoistic individualism, universalism, and religious passion. As he grew older, especially during twenty years of rural retirement after age sixty-four, he grew increasingly concerned with the expression of spiritual values; but the tension with immediate temporal concerns never ended, his transcendence was never complete, and even near death he wrote poems of Taoist resignation and return to Nature, and patriotic laments at never seeing the lost territories reconquered.

Lu Yu's travel diary, Ju-Shu chi 入蜀記 (Record of a Journey to Shu), describes his long journey from Shan-yin 山陰 (modern Shao-hsing, Chekiang) to K'uei-chou 夔州 (modern Feng-chieh Hsien, Szechwan) from July to December in 1170. Lu Yu wrote about the condition and outstanding features of the places he visited; about the special characteristics of the people he visited; and about the organizations and problems of the local authorities which hosted him. The diary thus provides valuable information on the political and military structure, economic development, population growth and urban change, social customs, religious life, communication and transportation networks, popular festivals, and general living conditions of twelfth-century Southern Sung China. Written in elaborate and elegant prose, with allusions to the classics, to the histories, and to other literary works, the *Ju-Shu chi* itself has literary value. It is the longest and most comprehensive Chinese diary written before the seventeenth century.

EDITIONS:

Ch'ien, *Sung-shih*, pp. 192-215. Excellent comments.

Huang, Yi-chih 黃逸之, ed. *Lu Yu shih* 陸游詩. Taipei, 1970.

Lu Fang-weng ch'üan-chi 陸放翁全集. 6v. SPPY. Rpt. in 2v., Taipei, 1973. Punctuated with continuous pagination. Contains the *Ju-Shu chi*.

Lu Fang-weng shih-tz'u-hsüan 陸放翁詩詞選. Chi Feng 疾風, ed. Hangchow, 1957. Most balanced PRC selection and commentary.

Lu Yu chi 陸游集. 5v. Peking, 1976. Contains *Ju-Shu chi* (v. 5, pp. 2406-2459).

Lu Yu shih-hsüan 陸游詩選. Yu Kuo-en 游國恩 and Li I 李易, eds. Peking, 1957.

Ogawa, Tamaki 小川環樹. *Riku Yū* 陸游. Tokyo, 1974.

TRANSLATIONS:

Chang, Chun-shu and Joan Symthe. *South China in the Twelfth Century: A Translation of Lu Yu's Travel Diaries, A.D. July 3rd–December 6th, 1170.* Hong Kong, 1980. A complete, annotated translation.

Sunflower, pp. 377-392.

Watson, Burton. *The Old Man Who Does As He Pleases: Selections from the Poetry and Prose of Lu Yu.* New York, 1973. Pp. 69-121 contain excerpts from the *Ju-Shu chi*.

Yoshikawa, *Introduction*, pp. 145-159.

STUDIES:

Chai, Chan-na 翟瞻納. *Fang-weng tz'u yen-chiu* 放翁詞研究. Taipei, 1972.

Chang, Chun-shu. "Notes on the Composition, Transmission, and Editions of the *Ju-Shu chi*," *BIHP*, 48.3 (1977), 481-499.

Chu, Tung-jen 朱東潤, *Lu Yu chuan* 陸游傳. Shanghai, 1960.

———. *Lu Yu yen-chiu* 陸游研究. Shanghai, 1961.

Duke, Michael S. *Lu You.* Boston, 1977.

Ho, Peng Yoke. *Lu Yu, The Poet Alchemist.* Canberra, 1972.

K'ung, Fan-li 孔凡禮 and Ch'i Chih-p'ing 齊治平, eds. *Lu Yu chüan* 陸游卷. Shanghai, 1962.

Liu, Wei-ch'ung 劉維崇. *Lu Yu p'ing-chuan* 陸游評傳. Taipei, 1966.

Lu Yu tso-p'in p'ing-shu hui-pien 陸游作品評述彙編. Taipei, 1970.

Lu Yu yen-chiu hui-pien 陸游研究彙編. Hong Kong, 1975.

Yü, Pei-shan 于北山, ed. *Lu Yu nien-p'u* 陸游年譜. Shanghai, 1961.

—MSD and CSC

Ma Chih-yüan 馬致遠 (*hao*, Tung-li 東籬, *c.* 1260-1325) was perhaps the most outstanding of the *san-ch'ü* (see *ch'ü*) playwrights. As is the case with most Yüan dramatists, little is known about his life except that he was a native of Ta-tu 大都 (modern Peking) and that he once served in the Kiangsi provincial government. There is a brief entry for him in *Lu kuei pu*,* and his *ch'ü** songs also provide some information about his life and character. In his youth, he was very much disposed toward an official career. Disillusioned by his failure to achieve fame and fortune, he found peace in nature and poetry in his later life.

Among his seven extant plays, *Han-kung ch'iu* 漢宮秋 (Autumn in the Han Palace) is generally considered his best work. Drawing his sources from both the historical and fictional accounts of the Han court lady Wang Chao-chün, who married a Tartar chieftain as a part of China's *ho-ch'in* 和親 (marriage between a Chinese "princess" and a foreign prince) diplomacy, Ma nevertheless gave the leading role to the emperor—a kind but ineffectual ruler who is torn between duty and love. This play is justly famous for its use of autumnal imagery to depict the emperor's sorrow.

In Ma's other plays, Taoism is the dominant theme. These plays celebrate the carefree life of the Taoist Immortals or the Taoist recluses. He has often been criticized by modern scholars for his failure to reflect social reality, and for the escapist sentiment found in his plays. However, viewed against the background of Yüan religion and intellectual climate, his Taoist plays are a faithful reflection of their time, showing the popularity of religious Taoism, especially the Ch'üan-chen Taoism 全真教, and the prevailing tendency among the intellectuals to lead a reclusive life. Since traditional criticism put great emphasis on poetry, Ma Chih-yüan received lavish praise for the poetic quality of his plays. In modern times, he has not fared as well. Critics in the People's Republic praise his technical skill but reject his ideology. Generally speaking, his plays contain good poetry but often lack dramatic action.

While his plays draw mixed reviews, his *san-ch'ü* songs have received unanimous critical acclaim. Among the extant 104 *hsiao-ling* 小令 (short lyrics) and 17 *t'ao-shu* 套數 (song sequences), the short lyric "Ch'iu ssu" 秋思 (Autumn Thoughts) is the best known. It is much admired for its economy—a pervading sense of desolation and sadness is conveyed by a series of natural images. The song sequence "Yeh hsing ch'uan" 夜行船 (Sailing at Night) is another representative work; it combines his lyricism with his pessimistic view of life, a view shared by many intellectuals of his time.

Ma Chih-yüan's place in *ch'ü* poetry has often been compared to that of Su Shih* in *tz'u.* Like Su, he greatly widened the range of subject matter of his chosen genre. He also mastered different modes of expression to suit his subjects. His contribution was important in making *ch'ü* a major form of Chinese poetry.

EDITIONS:

Yüan-ch'ü hsüan 元曲選. Tsang Mao-hsün 臧懋循, ed. 4v. 1616; rpt. Peking, 1958. Contains Ma's seven extant plays.

Ch'üan Yüan tsa-chü ch'u pien 全元雜劇初編. Yang Chia-lo 楊家駱 ed. Taipei, n.d.

San-ch'ü: Tung-li yüeh-fu 東籬樂府. Jen Na 任訥, ed. Not easily available.

Ch'üan Yüan san-ch'ü 全元散曲. Sui Shu-sen 隋樹森, ed. 2v. Peking, 1964. Contains all of Ma's extant songs.

TRANSLATIONS:

Keene, Donald. "Autumn in the Palace of Han," in Birch, *Anthology,* pp. 422-448.

Liu, Jung-en. "Autumn in the Han Palace," in his *Six Yüan Plays,* Harmondsworth, 1972, pp. 189-224.

Yen Yüan-shu. "Yellow Millet Dream: A Translation," *TkR,* 6.1 (1975), 205-239.

Yü, Shiao-ling. "Tears on the Blue Gown," *Renditions,* 10 (Autumn 1978), pp. 131-154.

Sunflower, pp. 420-425.

STUDIES:

Chang, I 張逸. "Ma Chih-yüan te sheng-p'ing chi ch'i chu-tso"馬致遠的生平及其著作, *Hsüeh-shu chi-k'an,* 6.3 (1958), 134-154.

Ch'en, An-na 陳安娜. "Ma Chih-yüan yen-chiu" 馬致遠研究 in *Kuo-li Tai-wan Shih-fan Ta-hsüeh Kuo-wen Yen-chiu So chi-k'an,* 13 (1969), 913-992.

Hsü, So-fang 徐朔方. "Ma Chih-yuan te tsa-chü" 馬致遠的雜劇. in *Yüan Ming Ch'ing hsi-ch'ü yen-chiu lun-wen chi* 元明清戲曲研究論文集, Peking, 1959, v. 1, pp. 104-114.

Jackson, Barbara Kwan. "The Yüan Dynasty Playwright Ma Chih-yüan and His Dramatic Works." Unpublished Ph.D. dissertation, University of Arizona, 1983.

Shen, Yao 沈堯. "Ma Chih-yüan tsa-chü te ssu-hsiang ch'ing hsiang yü i-shu te-se" 馬致遠雜劇的思想傾向與藝術特色, *Hsi-ch'ü yen-chiu* 戲曲研究, 1 (1980), 232-244.

Sui, Shu-sen 隋樹森. "Ma Chih-yüan te 'T'ien-ching-sha' hsiao-ling ho 'Yeh-hsing-ch'uan' t'ao-shu," 馬致遠的天淨沙小令和夜行船套數, *Yü-wen hsüeh-hsi,* 7 (1975), 12-14.

T'an, Cheng-pi 譚正璧. *Yüan-ch'ü liu ta-chia lüeh-chuan* 元曲六大家略傳. Shanghai, 1955, pp. 221-266.

Wang, Chi-ssu 王季思. "Ma Chih-yüan te 'Ch'iu ssu' ho Kuan Han-ch'ing te *Tou O yüan,*" 馬致遠的秋思和關漢卿的竇娥寃, *Yü-wen hsüeh-hsi,* 11 (1975), 24-26.

Yen, Yüan-shu. "Yellow Millet Dream: A Study of Its Artistry," *TkR,* 6 (1975), 241-249.

—SLY

Ma Jung 馬融 (*tzu,* Chi-ch'ang 季長, 79-166) a scholar-official and exegete, was scion of one of the Latter Han's most powerful clans. He is best known for bringing to fruition the growing interest in writing commentaries to the *ku-wen* 古文 (ancient-text) versions of the Confucian Classics. These versions eventually supplanted the *chin-wen* 今文 (modern-text) tradition of the Former Han dynasty.

Ma Jung's exegetical writing also marked the fullest development of Latter Han erudition. Over the previous two centuries exegetes had broadened their studies from just one Confucian classic to several, and then all major and minor works of the canon. By Ma's time some commentators began to focus attention on Taoist works and poetry as well. Ma Jung, moreover, would draw upon any one of these texts to study any other; for example, he cited Taoist texts to explicate the most orthodox of Confucian writings. Unlike his predecessors, he also drew upon contemporary historical writings, "modern-text" classics and works of divination (ch'an-wei shu 讖緯書) in his exegeses. In his breadth of textual and philosophical interests Ma Jung anticipated his student Cheng Hsüan 鄭玄 (127-200) and a tradition of erudition which culminated in the work of the Han-hsüeh p'ai 漢學派 (School of Han Learning) of the Ch'ing dynasty.

Ma Jung's family was very influential at the Lo-yang court during the first century A.D., because Ma's great-uncle, Ma Yüan 馬援 (14 B.C.-A.D. 49), had been instrumental in helping Emperor Kuang-wu (r. 25-57) restore the Han dynasty. The clan maintained its power through a daughter who was empress to Emperor Ming (r. 57-75) and stepmother to Emperor Chang (r. 76-88). After her death in the year 79, other clans came to dominate the court and emperor.

From at least the age of twelve, Ma Jung was exposed to the work of the leading ancient-text scholars who worked at the Tung-kuan 東觀 Library in the capital. He may also have been predisposed to follow their work, since two of these scholars, Tu Lin 杜林 and Chia K'uei 賈逵 (30-101), were from the Ma family's home-district, Mao-ling 茂陵 (modern Hsing-p'ing 興平, Shensi) in Fu-feng Commandery 扶風. Furthermore, while the youthful Ma Jung was serving as Secretary of the Heir Apparent with some responsibilities in the Tung-kuan Library, Hsü Shen 許慎 (30-124) was working on his dictionary Shuo-wen chieh-tzu 說文解字 and Pan Chao 班昭 (c. 45-c. 115) was finishing the Han-shu (see Pan Ku).

Ma probably did not have any direct contact with these scholars when he first came to the court. Eventually, however, he probably did meet Chia K'uei 賈逵 (30-101), and later followed that scholar's choice of ancient-text classics. In 110 he and Hsü Shen were colleagues in the Tung-kuan Library. Hsü wrote commentaries to the Taoist classics and probably inspired Ma

to do the same. In 106 Ma and one of his brothers studied with Pan Chao, and Ma later used Han-shu materials in his commentaries.

By his own account, Ma worked in an official capacity in the Tung-kuan Library from 106 to 115. Between 116 and 121, Ma retired to his home after he had angered a powerful clan by writing a prose piece critical of Emperor An (r. 106-125), who had been dominated by clan members. The piece, entitled "Kuang-ch'eng sung" 廣成頌 (Hymn on Kuang-ch'eng Park), is written in the form of matching couplets, a style later called p'ien-wen,* and makes up nearly two-thirds of Ma's biography in the Hou Han-shu.

After 121 Ma Jung served in an advisory post with the Prince of Ho-chien 河間王, son of Emperor An. In 125 Ma resigned and for the next eight years served in a government bureau in his native region. In 133 Ma Jung was recommended to serve in an advisory position at the court. From 138 to 144 he also served as Governor of Wu-tu Commandery 武都郡 (near modern Wu-tu, Kansu). During these years he was instrumental in pacifying the Ch'iang tribes of that region, and found the time to complete many of his important commentaries, including those to the I-ching, Shih-ching,* Shang-shu, Li-chi, and Chou-kuan 周官.

Between 144 and 159 Ma seems either to have been a close follower of Liang Chi 梁冀 (d. 159), or to have at least tried not to run afoul of Liang, who dominated the court through his sister the empress dowager. Historians have been critical of Ma for supporting Liang, in particular for writing a letter of accusation against Liang's enemy Li Ku 李固 (who later died in prison) during the succession struggles of 145-147.

Between 148 and 151, Ma was Governor of the Southern Commandery (Nan chün 南郡, a large area including modern Wuhan 武漢, Hupei). His activities during his last years at court are unclear. He was briefly exiled for corruption in 151. In 153 he wrote another hymn to criticize an emperor dominated by a rival clan. By 159, at the age of eighty, Ma had returned to Mao-ling where, during his last years, he taught a great number of students including Cheng Hsüan.

Ma's commentaries on the ancient-text Confucian canon primarily followed the ideas of Chia K'uei. In particular, he followed Chia's studies of Mao's *Shih-ching*, the *Chou li*, and the ancient-text *Shang-shu* with those of his own. Ma Jung is credited with piecing together the present text of the *Li-chi* from ancient- and modern-text schools, and he followed a Former Han tradition of commenting upon an ancient-text *I-ching*. He did not however, work on the important *Tso-chuan* commentary to the *Ch'un-ch'iu*. His biographers say that he felt he could not in this one instance improve upon the work of Chia K'uei. Cheng Hsüan followed Ma with his own commentaries on all of the above works. In addition to these Confucian works, Ma also wrote commentaries to the *Tao-te-ching*, the *Huai-nan-tzu* and the "Li sao."

No complete text of any of Ma's commentaries survived the Six Dynasties period. In the eighteenth and nineteenth centuries the extant fragments were collected and published; they include parts of his commentaries to the *I-ching*, *Shang-shu*, *Shih-ching*, *Li-chi*, and *Lun-yü*. Anthologies of his personal writings were also made during the Ch'ing era.

EDITIONS:
Liu-ch'ao wen, v. 1, *ch.* 18, pp. 565-571. Most complete collection of Ma's poetry and prose.
Ma, Kuo-han 馬國翰, ed. *Yü-han shan-fang chi i-shu* 玉函山房輯佚書. Taipei, 1967 (photolithographic reprint of the 1871 edition of the Huang-hua-kuan shu-chü 皇華館書局 in Tsinan), v. 1, pp. 97-108, 375-400, 525-526; v. 2, pp. 738-743, 807-817, 880-882, 1239-1242; v. 3, pp. 1618-1629. Includes fragments of eight of Ma's commentaries.

TRANSLATIONS:
Künstler, Mieczyslaw Jerzy. *Ma Jong vie et oeuvre.* Warsaw, 1969, pp. 66-211. Annotated translation of "Kuang-ch'eng sung."

STUDIES:
Künstler, *Ma Jong.*
Li, Wei-hsiung 李威熊. "Ma Jung chih ching-hsüeh" 馬融之經學. Unpublished M.A. thesis,

Kuo-li Cheng-chih Ta-hsüeh Kuo-wen-hsüeh Yen-chiu-so, 1975. Detailed discussion of Ma's commentaries; includes a *nien-p'u.*

—BL

Ma-wang tui 馬王堆 is the name of the site in south-central China (Changsha, Hunan) where three tombs of early Han date were excavated in 1972-1974, tombs which proved very rich in archaeological remains. While great interest has been shown in the well-preserved corpse of a woman, and in the beautifully painted funerary banner contained in tomb No. 1, the greatest excitement has been generated by the discovery of a large store of texts—texts written on silk—found in tomb No. 3, a tomb that can safely be dated to 168 B.C.

The texts are written on eleven scrolls, and there are estimated to be around 120,000 characters in all. Although the scrolls were contained in a lacquer box, deterioration has naturally set in and lacunae abound. Nevertheless, the texts are generally quite readable. There are texts on medical theories and practices, on astronomy and astrology, and on political thought, to mention but a few of the topics. Some are texts already known, here appearing in slightly different form; others are long-lost texts, previously known only by name or description; others still are completely new to scholarship.

An inventory of the texts presented at the "Ma-wang tui Workshop" in Berkeley (June, 1979) by Li Hsüeh-ch'in 李學勤 of the Institute of History, Chinese Academy of Social Sciences, reveals a corpus of fifty-one items, which can be grouped into fourteen categories, as follows:

1. Two copies (A & B) of the *Lao-tzu*, here untitled except for the notation "Tao" 道 at the end of section one and "Te" 德 at the end of section two. (Almost all of the texts are untitled in the original, but a name has been assigned to each by the mainland scholars working on them. It is those assigned names that are given below, unless otherwise noted.)

2. Four texts appended to the end of *Lao-tzu* Text A, texts called *Wu-hsing* 五行 (The Five Virtues), *Chiu-chu* 九主 (The Nine Kinds of Rulers), *Ming-chün* 明君 (The Wise

Lord), and *Te-sheng* 德聖 (Virtue and Sagacity) in the 1980 edition of *Ma-wang tui Han-mu po-shu* 馬王堆漢墓帛書, v. 1 (but labeled differently elsewhere). The first deals with five Confucian virtues (*jen* 仁, *chih* 智, *i* 義, *li* 禮, *sheng* 聖)—not with the "five elements" as one might suspect; the second is a conversation between T'ang 湯 and I Yin 伊尹 on the nature of the "model ruler" (法君); the third is a treatise supporting aggressive warfare; and the fourth is, as its title says, on "virtue" and "sagacity."

3. Four texts on statecraft prefaced to the *Lao-tzu* Text B. These are *Ching-fa* 經法, *Shih-liu ching* 十六經 (The Classic in Sixteen Parts), *Ch'eng* 稱 (Weighing, or Balancing), and *Tao-yüan* 道原 (Tao, the Source)—titles in the original.

4. Two collections of historical anecdotes, one in the manner of the *Tso-chuan*,* the other similar to the *Chan-kuo ts'e*,* with which it shares eleven of its twenty-seven items. The former has sixteen "chapters" (*chang* 章) and is being called *Ch'un-ch'iu shih-yü* 春秋世語 (Tales of the World of the Spring and Autumn Period); the latter is called *Chan-kuo ts'e* or *Chan-kuo tsung-heng-chia shu* 戰國縱橫家書 (On the Political Strategists of the Warring States Period).

5. A copy of the *I-ching* with six commentaries (?) appended: (1) *Erh-san-tzu wen* 二三子問 (Question of the Disciples), Part A; (2) *Erh-san-tzu wen*, Part B; (3) *Yao* 要 (title in the original); (4) *Mou Ho* 繆和 (title in the original); (5) *Chao Li* 昭力 (title in the original); and (6) the *Hsi-tz'u* 繫辭 (title in the original). The copy of the *I-ching* itself has the basic text for each of the sixty-four hexagrams, but does not have the *t'uan* 象, *hsiang* 象, or *wen-yen* 文言 commentaries.

6. Fourteen texts on medical matters, dealing with such topics as: conduits of the circulatory system, fatal signs exhibited by the conduits, remedies for diseases, childbirth, nourishing life, diet, and secret prescriptions.

7. Two texts on astronomy/astrology, one called *Wu-hsing chan* 五星占 (Prognostications Related to the Five Planets) and the other, *T'ien-wen ch'i hsiang chan* 天文氣象占 (Prognostications Related to Astronomical and Meteorological Phenomena).

The latter is an illustrated scroll with captions and covers four kinds of phenomena—clouds, *ch'i*, stars, and comets.

8. A text telling how to determine certain qualities in horses on the basis of physical appearance—*Hsiang-ma ching* 相馬經.

9. Five texts discussing good and bad fortune in terms of Yin-Yang and the Five Elements. The first three relate to warfare and are called *Hsing-te* 刑德, Texts A, B, C. The other two pertain to everyday matters and are called *Chuan-shu yin-yang wu-hsing* 篆書陰陽五行 (Ying-yang and the Five Elements—the Seal Script) and *Li-shu yin-yang wu-hsing* 隸書陰陽五行 (Yin-yang and the Five Elements—in Clerical Script).

10. The *Mu-jen chan* 木人占 (Divination Using a Wooden Image).

11. Some talismans (?)—*Fu-lu* 符籙.

12. Four diagrams (*t'u* 圖): one illustrating the "Nine Kinds of Rulers" (九主); one showing mourning garments (喪服); one being pictures of gods (?) (神圖); and one illustrating therapeutic calisthenics (導引).

13. Two maps (also *t'u* 圖): one showing troop deployment in the Han kingdom of Chang-sha, the other topographical in nature, showing eight prefectures in Chang-sha.

14. Two plans (also *t'u* 圖): one is described as a plan for building a miniature city, the other is a plan of a large tomb and shrine in the Changsha area.

Plans have been announced for publication of the entire corpus. There will be six volumes, each giving facsimiles of the originals and modern character transcriptions. Volume I, which has already appeared, comprises the two copies of the *Lao-tzu* and their eight appended texts; volume II, also out, has the *Ch'un-ch'iu shih-yü* and the *Chan-kuo ts'e*. Volume III will have the *I-ching* and the texts appended thereto; volume IV, the medical treatises; volume V, the texts relating to the history of science (astronomy/astrology, maps and plans, the *Hsiang-ma ching*); and volume VI, the texts on divination and good and bad fortune. Transcriptions of most of the texts, the *I-ching* materials being a major exception, have already appeared in issues of *Wen-wu*.

Almost all of the texts have been described and discussed in a preliminary way, and the significance of the texts on astronomy/astrology and medicine for the history of science in China has been clearly recognized. But without question, the greatest interest raised by the texts thus far concerns the possibility that in the materials appended to text B of the *Lao-tzu* we have texts illustrating the brand of thought known as Huang-Lao, a philosophy popular in the early years of the Han. Relevant is T'ang Lan's 唐蘭 identification of the four texts with the *Huang-ti ssu-ching* 黃帝四經 (The Four Classics of the Yellow Emperor) mentioned in the "I-wen chih" of the *Han-shu* (see Pan Ku), an identification based in part on the fact that the *Shih-liu ching* records conversations between Huang-ti and various ministers on matters of political concern. If these are Huang-Lao texts then Huang-Lao had nothing at all to do with the health and immortality cult, as has commonly been supposed. Rather, it appears to have been a kind of political thought characterized by attention to *fa* 法 (laws or models) and *li* 理 (principles), which follow naturally from the Tao and must be perceived by a selfless ruler and followed without interference. Mainland scholars see Huang-Lao as a branch of Legalism, but Western scholars (Jan Yün-hua, Tu Wei-ming) tend to disagree.

Work has also been done on the two copies of the *Lao-tzu*. The two texts are not entirely the same, but they tend to agree where they disagree with other versions of the text. In both, parts I (chapters 1-37) and II (chapters 38-81) of the text are reversed, a fact which has occasioned much speculation. Moreover, some differences occur in the sequence of chapters: in the Ma-wang tui texts, what is traditionally chapter 24 comes between 21 and 22, 41 comes after 39, and 80 and 81 come between 66 and 67. There are, however, no chapter names or numbers in these texts, and punctuation separating chapters is only found in part II of text A. In general the content of the texts is the same as previously known. There are word, phrase, and line additions and omissions. These improve the quality of the text but seem not to affect the thought. There are also numerous character variants, many of which are *chia-chieh* 假借 (loan characters). The heavy use of *chia-chieh*, the omission and addition of radicals to characters, and the use of different graphs for the same word—features found in all of the Ma-wang tui texts—testify to a lack of language standardization.

Ma-wang tui studies are in their infancy, and questions fundamental in nature remain to be answered: Why were these texts placed in this tomb in the first place? Do the language, ideas, and topics of these texts represent something unique of the culture of Ch'u? Nonetheless, the significance of the Ma-wang tui texts as a source for the study of early Han thought, medical theories and practices, ideas on astrology, etc., is undeniable. Ma-wang tui is a major find, comparable to Tun-huang.

EDITIONS:

Ch'ang-sha Ma-wang tui shan-hao Han mu po-shu 長沙馬王堆二號漢墓帛書. Shanghai, 1974. Transcriptions and facsimiles of the *Lao-tzu* texts and the eight texts appended thereto.

Chan-kuo tsung-heng-chia shu 戰國縱橫家書. Peking, 1976. Transcriptions in inexpensive paperback.

Hsi, Tse-tsung 席澤宗, ed. *Chung-kuo T'ien-wen-hsüeh shih wen-chi* 中國天文學史文集. Peking, 1978. Contains a transcription of the *Wu-hsing chan*.

Ma-wang tui Han mu po-shu 馬王堆漢墓帛書, I. Peking, 1974. Elaborately produced in traditional Chinese style—eight sewn *ts'e* in a latched, cloth-covered box. Has facsimiles and transcriptions of *Lao-tzu* A and B plus the eight appended texts. Transcriptions in simplified characters. Very expensive.

———, I. Peking, 1980. Volume I in a large format, done in regular, modern binding. Has facsimiles and transcriptions of *Lao-tzu* A and B plus eight appended texts. Good quality and price is reasonable. Transcriptions are in standard characters. Some errors in the transcription.

———, II. Peking, 1979. Facsimiles and transcriptions of the *Chan-kuo ts'e* and *Ch'un-ch'iu shih-yü*, produced in the same fashion as the 1974 volume I.

Ma-wang tui Han mu po-shu Lao-tzu. Peking, 1976. Transcription in inexpensive paperback.

Wen-wu 文物. Transcriptions of various texts can be found in the following issues: 1974.10, 1974.11, 1975.4, 1975.6, 1975.9, 1977.1, and 1977.8.

Wu-shih-erh ping-fang 五十二病方. Peking, 1979. Transcription plus analysis in inexpensive paperback.

STUDIES:

Harper, Donald. "The Wu Shih Erh Ping Fang: Translation and Prolegomena." Unpublished Ph.D. dissertation, University of California, Berkeley, 1982.

Henricks, Robert G. "Examining the Ma-wang tui Silk Texts of the *Lao-tzu*," *TP*, 65 (1979), 166-199.

Jan, Yün-hua 冉雲華. "Tao, Principle, and Law: The Three Key Concepts in the Yellow Emperor Taoism," *JCP*, 7 (1980), 205-228.

Kanaya, Osamu 金谷治. "Hakusho *Rōshi* ni tsuite: Soo shiryōsei no shohoteki gimmi" 帛書老子について：その資料性の初歩的吟味, in *Chūgoku tetsugakushi no tembō to mosaku* 中國哲學史の展望と摸索, Tokyo, 1976, pp. 177-198.

Kao, Hen 高亨, and Ch'ih Hsi-chao 池曦朝. "Shih t'an Ma-wang tui Han mu chung ti po-shu *Lao-tzu*" 試談馬王堆漢墓中的帛書老子, *Wen-wu*, 1974.11, 1-7.

Lau, D. C., tr. *Tao Te Ching.* Hong Kong, 1982. This re-issue of Lau's translation of the *Lao-tzu*, first published by Penguin in 1963, includes a new translation, with accompanying Chinese text, which is based on a conflation of Ma-wang-tui texts A and B.

Loewe, Michael. *Ways to Paradise: The Chinese Quest for Immortality.* London, 1979. Discussion of the funerary banner found in tomb No. 1.

T'ang, Lan 唐蘭. "*Huang-ti ssu-ching* ch'u-t'an" 黃帝四經初探, *Wen-wu*, 1974.10, 48-52.

"Tso-t'an Changsha Ma-wang tui Han mu po-shu" 座談長沙馬王堆漢墓帛書, *Wen-wu*, 1974.9, 45-57. An initial discussion of the texts by various mainland scholars.

Tu, Wei-ming 杜維明. "The 'Thought of Huang-Lao'; A Reflection on the Lao Tzu and Huang Ti Texts in the Silk Manuscripts of Ma-Wang Tui," *JAS,* 39.1 (November 1979), 95-110.

Wen-wu. Studies (descriptive and interpretive) of the various texts appear in the following

issues: 1974.7, 1974.9, 1974.10, 1974.11, 1975.2, 1975.3, 1975.4, 1975.6, 1975.7, 1975.8, 1975.9, 1976.3, 1976.4, 1977.1, 1977.8, 1977.10, and 1978.2

Yen, Ling-feng 嚴靈峰. *Ma-wang tui po-shu Lao-tzu shih-t'an* 馬王堆帛書老子試探. Taipei, 1976.

—RH

Mao Tsung-kang 毛宗崗 (*tzu,* Hsü-shih 序始, *hao,* Chieh-an 孑菴, *fl.* 1660) was a native of Ch'ang-chou 長洲 (modern Wu-hsien 吳縣, Kiangsu). From the scanty biographical information that is available, it is known that he collaborated with his father, Mao Lun 毛綸 (*tzu,* Te-yin 德音 or, in his late years, Sheng-shan 聲山), in revising the *San-kuo chih yen-i** and the *P'i-p'a chi* (see Kao Ming), and in writing critical commentary for both works, and that he once studied with Ch'u Jen-huo 褚人穫, who is well known for having revised the *Sui T'ang yen-i.** Mao Lun went blind in middle age, and in revising the *San-kuo,* depended on his son to write down his ideas. Since Mao Tsung-kang was responsible for the final edtiorial work, it is reasonable to assume that he played a more significant role in the whole task. Thus in the following discussion, reference will be made to him only.

Mao Tsung-kang was an admirer of Chin Sheng-t'an,* who revised and wrote critical comments for two major works, the novel *Shui-hu chuan** and the drama *Hsi-hsiang chi.** Mao did the same for the *San-kuo* (which he calls the first *ts'ai-tzu shu* 才子書 [book by a genius]) and the *P'i-p'a* (which he calls the seventh). Like Chin's *Shui-hu,** Mao's *San-kuo* replaced all older versions and became the standard edition. Mao falsely claimed that he had obtained a certain old edition, and called the then prevalent editions "vulgar." He referred to his revised version of the *San-kuo** as the *Sheng-t'an wai-shu* 聖歎外書 (An Unauthenticated Work by Chin Sheng-t'an). It contains a preface dated 1664 and attributed to Chin Sheng-t'an, which is probably a forgery by Mao himself.

Mao's version of the *San-kuo* was completed in the early years of the reign of the Emperor K'ang-hsi (1662-1722). Compared with Chin's revision of the *Shui-hu,* Mao's work on the *San-kuo* is of a much smaller scale. The six major concerns of his revision are stated in his prefatory notes.

1. Revising history as presented in the story-lines of the novel. In this Mao is guided by two principles: first, to make the stories closer to genuine history, and second, to uphold Shu 蜀 as the orthodox state during the San-kuo Era and thereby condemn Wei 魏. In chapter 80 (chapter numbers refer to the 120-chapter editions), concerning Ts'ao P'i's* usurpation, the older editions describe Empress Ts'ao as on the side of her brother, Ts'ao P'i, while in Mao's edition she is said to be on the side of the Han Emperor and to condemn her brother's action. This is an example of alteration. An addition can be found in chapter 84, where Madame Sun's 孫 suicide has no basis in extant historical records. An example of deletion can be found in chapter 103. There the claim that Chu-ko Liang 諸葛亮 in trying to burn out Ssu-ma I 司馬懿 also had hoped to kill Wei Yen 魏延 has been deleted.

2. The addition of interesting episodes. In chapter 107, for example, Mao has included an episode about Teng Ai's 鄧艾 being ridiculed for his stuttering.

3. The deletion or addition of poems or pieces of prose. All the poems attributed to Chou Ching-hsüan 周靜軒, for example, are deleted. Poems by celebrated poets of the T'ang and Sung are added.

4. The addition of works of prose. Works of prose from the San-kuo period, such as K'ung Jung's* memorial recommending Mi Heng* and Ch'en Lin's* proclamation against Ts'ao Ts'ao, are also added.

5. Rearrangement of the text. Mao discards the 240-chapter division in favor of the 120-chapter scheme, and recasts the title for each chapter in a parallel couplet.

6. The deletion of superfluous phrases and the general refinement and tightening of the style.

Besides revising the text, Mao disposed of the critical remarks in the vulgar editions that had been attributed to Li Chih,* and replaced them with his own. Mao's method of criticism is very similar to Chin Sheng-t'an's on the *Shui-hu chuan.* His main

concerns are to comment on the personalities of the characters and to remark upon the artistry of writing at critical points of interest. As Chin expresses his ill feeling towards Sung Chiang 宋江 on occasion, Mao calumniates Ts'ao Ts'ao often. His literary analysis is largely based on the principles of *pa-ku wen.**

Li Yü* (1611-1680) was dissatisfied with Mao's *San-kuo* revisions and produced another version that is more faithful to the original. But Li's version never attained the wide popularity that Mao's enjoys.

EDITIONS:

San-kuo [chih] yen-i 三國演義. 2v. Peking, 1953; 1v. edition, 1955. In the 1953 edition, most of the poems that the Mao version has inherited from the earlier versions are expunged; in the 1955 edition, however, they are restored. Mao's critical comments are not included in these editions.

Tsu-pen San-kuo yen-i 足本三國演義. Taipei, 1958.

STUDIES:

Arai, Mizuo 荒井瑞雄. "Mō Seisan ni tsuite" 毛聲山に就いて, *Kangakkai zasshi,* 8.1 (1940), 79-91.

Cheng, Chen-to 鄭振鐸. "*San-kuo chih yen-i* te yen-hua" 三國志演義的演化, in his *Chung-kuo wen-hsüeh yen-chiu,* Peking, 1957, pp. 166-239.

Ogawa, Tanaki 小川環樹. "Sankoku engi no Mō Seisan hihyō hon to Ri Ryūō hon" 三國演義の毛聲山批評本と李笠翁本, *Kanda [Kiichirō] hakushi kanreki kinen shoshigaku ronshū* 神田─喜一郎─博士還曆記念書誌學論集. Tokyo, 1957. Also included in Ogawa's *Chūgoku shōsetsu shi no kenkyū* 中國小説史の研究, Tokyo, 1968, pp. 153-161.

Yü, P'ing-po 俞平伯. "*San-kuo chih yen-i* yü Mao-shih fu-tzu" 與毛氏父子, in his *Tsa-pan chi* 雜拌几, v. 2, Shanghai, 1933, pp. 123-126.

—SSK

Mei Sheng 枚乘 (also read Mei Ch'eng, *tzu,* Shu 叔, d. 141 B.C.) was born in Huai-yin 淮陰 (modern Kiangsu). He served briefly at the court of Liu P'i 劉濞, the Prince of Wu 吳王, but left Liu P'i's service when he failed to dissuade him from his plans to revolt. The memorials Mei wrote in his attempts to persuade Liu P'i not to revolt clearly display Mei's remarkable abilities as a rhetorician. After leaving Liu P'i's service, Mei went to Liang 梁, arriving there around 157 B.C. According to his *Han-shu* biography (*ch.* 51), Mei was the best of the many poets attracted to the court of Prince Hsiao of Liang 梁孝王. This court was perhaps the literary center of Han China in this period, since Emperor Ching (r. 156-141 B.C.) had declared a dislike for the then popular *tz'u-fu* 辭賦 style of poetry. When Emperor Wu (r. 140-87 B. C.) ascended the throne he summoned Mei to court, but Mei died on the way.

The "I-wen chih" 藝文志 (Treatise on Literature) in the *Han-shu* credits Mei with authoring nine *fu*.* Of these, three pieces are extant: "Ch'i fa" 七發 (The Seven Stimuli), "Liang wang T'u-yüan fu" 梁王兔園賦 (The Rabbit Garden of the Prince of Liang), and "Wang-yu Kuan liu fu" 忘憂館柳賦 (The Willows of the Lodge for Forgetting Troubles). The latter two pieces are of doubtful authenticity. Thus, Mei Ch'eng's fame as a poet rests on the merits of "The Seven Stimuli" alone.

"The Seven Stimuli" represents a significant advance in the development of the *fu*. Not only is the piece strikingly long, four to five times the length of Chia I's* "Fu-niao fu," but it uses a rhetorical technique known in Chinese as *feng* 諷 (criticism by indirection), vividly describing a long list of excesses to display their harmful effects. Some scholars argue that this technique from the time of its inception was simply an excuse for the poet to display his virtuosity, and there is little doubt that it certainly degenerated into that in later works. In either case, Mei Ch'eng's "The Seven Stimuli" was widely emulated by later writers in the *fu* genre.

EDITIONS:

Han-shu 漢書. Hong Kong, 1970. *Ch.* 51, pp. 2359-2365, contains Mei's biography and several memorials.

I-wen lei-chü 藝文類聚. Peking, 1965. Contains the two extant *fu* of doubtful authenticity— "Liang-wang T'u-yüan fu" (65.1162) and the "Wang-yu kuan liu fu" (65.1162).

TRANSLATIONS:

Frankel, *Palace Lady*, pp. 186-211 ("Ch'i-fa").
Gundert, *Lyrik*, p. 42.

Knechtges, David R. and Jerry Swanson. "Seven Stimuli for the Prince: the Ch'i-fa of Mei Ch'eng," *MS*, 29 (1970-71), 99-116.

Scott, John. *Love and Protest: Chinese Poems from the Sixth Century B. C. to the Seventeenth Century A. D.* New York, 1972, pp. 37-48 ("Ch'i fa").

von Zach, *Anthologie*, v. 2, pp. 607-617 ("Ch'i fa"); pp. 729-734 (memorials).

STUDIES:

Knechtges, *The Han Rhapsody*, pp. 30-34.

—JLo

Mei Ting-tso 梅鼎祚 (*tzu*, Yü-chin 禹金, 1549-1615) is known as a scholar, poet, and dramatist. His family was originally from Hsüan-ch'eng 宣城, but he was born in Peking where his father, Mei Shou-te 梅守德, was an official. When Mei was nine years old, his father resigned as Left Administration Vice Commissioner of Yunnan to return home and devote himself to studies. Under his father's influence Mei soon became a serious student of literature. When he was ten years old, both his elder brothers died on the same day. His father, deeply grieved, attributed the death of his sons to their over-concentration on their studies, and for the next three years Mei Ting-tso was excused from attending school. It was at his mother's insistence that he resumed schooling at the age of thirteen. Three years later his precociousness caught the attention of Lo Ju-fang 羅汝芳 (1515-1588), an authority on Wang Yang-ming 王陽明 (1472-1529). Lo wanted Mei to study with him, but the young man's seeming distaste for classical studies coupled with his interest in literature soon caused Lo to abandon the pursuit. This perhaps explains why Mei gave up the pursuit of higher tests soon after he successfully passed the district examination.

In 1590, already well known as a dramatist and poet, Mei was selected to be an Envoy. When he arrived in Peking in 1591, Grand Secretary Shen Shih-hsing together with his colleagues Wang Hsi-chüeh and Hsü Kuo offered him a position in the Hanlin Academy. Mei turned it down, preferring retirement and studies. The year 1591 marked the turning point in his life. From then until his death in 1615, Mei devoted his full attention to collecting books, compilation, and writing.

His early work includes poetry, prose, and drama. Mei's literary works, except for the three dramas, were collected by his friend T'ang Pin-yin 湯賓尹 (*chin-shih*, 1595) and published in 1623, eight years after his death. This collection, *Lu-ch'iu shih-shih chi* 鹿裘石室集 (Collected Works from Deerpelt Stone Studio), in sixteen volumes contains twenty-six *chüan* of poetry, twenty-five of prose, and fifteen of correspondence. Mei also made many compilations, ranging from ancient prose to lighter genres, such as the *Ch'ing-ni lien-hua chi* 青泥蓮花記 (Lotus Flowers on Pure Soil), a collection of biographical anecdotes of courtesans known for certain virtues.

As a playwright Mei is recognized as a representative of the P'ien-ch'i p'ai 駢綺派 (School of Euphuism). Far from being a prolific dramatist, he composed only three dramas, two *ch'uan-ch'i*,* *Yü-ho chi* 玉合記 (The Jade Box) and *Ch'ang-ming lü* 長命縷 (The Thread of Longevity), and a *tsa-chü*,* *K'un-lun-nu chien-hsia ch'eng-hsien* 崑崙奴劍俠成仙 (How the Bravo, K'un-lun Slave, Becomes an Immortal).

Yü-ho chi was written in 1583 when Mei was thirty-five years old. His best-known work, it is based on a story about Han Hung 韓翃 recorded in the *Pen-shih shih* 本事詩 (The Original Incidents of Poems) by Meng Ch'i 孟啟 (*fl.* 841-886) and the "Chang-tai liu chuan" 章臺柳傳 (Account of the Willow of the Ornamented Terrace) by Hsü Yao-tso 許堯佐. The story features a double plot; a tale of romance and separation between Han Hung and Madam Liu 柳氏 and a story of Li Wang-sun 李王孫 and Ch'ing-o's 輕娥 renunciation of the world. This play shows the results of the process of classicization of theatrical prose which began in the Yüan and reached its pinnacle in the Ming—most of the characters, including some minor ones from the lower classes, speak in the classical language, which makes their speeches rather unnatural.

Mei in his later years was not very satisfied with *Yü-ho chi.* Perhaps for this reason, he wrote *Ch'ang-ming lü,* completing it in 1614 when he was sixty-six years old.

This drama is derived from the tale "Fu-ch'i fu-chiu-yüan" 夫妻復舊約 (The Conjugal Reunion) by Wang Ming-ch'ing 王明清 of the Sung dynasty. In this play Mei attempted to rectify what he considered to be the shortcomings of *Yü-ho chi* in the areas of music, rhyme scheme, and language.

Kun-lun nu chien-hsia ch'eng-hsien (better known as *K'un-lun nu*), written in 1584 when he was thirty-six years old, is based on the T'ang story "K'un-lun nu." It portrays the romance of Ts'ui Ch'ien-niu 崔千牛 and Hung-hsiao 紅綃 and the heroic feats of the "slave."

EDITIONS:

Ch'ang-ming lü, in *Ku-pen,* I.
K'un-lun nu chien-hsia ch'eng-hsien, in *Sheng-Ming.*
Lu-ch'iu shih-shih chi. 16v. N.p., 1623. Housed in the Naikaku Bunkō.
Yü-ho chi, in *Liu-shih.*

STUDIES:

Aoki, *Gikyokushi.* Ch. 9 contains biographical information on Mei and comments on *Yü-ho chi* and *K'un-lun nu.*
Chin, *Chi-ku-ko.* Ch. 28 contains information on Mei and *Yü-ho chi.*
DMB, 1057-1059.
Yagisawa, *Gekisakuka,* pp. 363-418. Contains information on Mei's family background, life, literary achievements and comments on his three dramas.
Yee, "Love." Chapters 2-4 contain comments on *Yü-ho chi.*

—EY

Mei Yao-ch'en 梅堯臣 (*tzu,* Sheng-yü 聖俞, *hao,* Wan-ling Hsien-sheng 宛陵先生, 1002-1060) is said to have initiated the "new realism" in Sung literature, together with his friend Ou-yang Hsiu.* He came from a minor-official family which settled in Hsüan-ch'eng 宣城, ancient Wan-ling 宛陵 (modern Anhwei). Only his father's brother, Mei Hsüan 梅詢 (962-1041), had been able to get a high position in the civil service. Mei Yao-ch'en was early (1014) committed to the charge of his uncle for his education. Mei failed in all attempts to pass the *chin-shih* examination until 1051, and his official career was characterized by patronage and minor posts, forcing him to alternate between the capital and the provinces. The highest position he ever obtained was that of a lecturer in the National University.

His poetic corpus of 2800 poems, edited in 60 *chüan* by Ou-yang Hsiu, is extant, but of his other writings, only a commentary to the *Sun-tzu* remains. A historical work on the T'ang (*T'ang tsai-chi* 唐載記) and a commentary to the *Shih-ching** have been lost.

His literary career started about 1031 in Lo-yang, where Mei met members of the literary circle headed by Ou-yang Hsiu. His oeuvre can be more or less divided into two parts: work written in his early phase of social criticism and that characterized by a *p'ing-tan* 平淡 (even and bland) style. This style was in contrast to the superficial, bombastic, and often obscure style of the Late T'ang and Hsi-k'un schools and was the beginning of a new realism which typifies Sung literature.

The ideological basis of the sociocritical poems is a Neo-Confucianism aimed at reforms in the civil service, the army and in the countryside. Because of Mei's engagement in Neo-Confucianism, man, rather than nature, was at the center of his literary creativity. Examples of this kind of poetry are "T'ao-che" 陶者 (The Potter, 1036), which expresses in two paratactical images the differences between the the gentry and the common people, rich and poor, luxury and labor, "Keng-niu" 耕牛 (The Farm Ox, 1057), in which the ox symbolizes the farmer and his difficulties, "Chü-wen" 聚蚊 (Swarming Mosquitoes, 1034), in which the corrupt civil service is compared to blood-sucking mosquitoes, and, finally, "Hsiao-ts'un" 小村 (A Little Village, 1048), which describes the distress of farmers faced with military conscription.

The means of social criticism was the old-style verse (see *ku-shih* under *shih*), which is especially suited for the new realistic style of Mei, because it permits more emphasis on narrative. The topics Mei chose emphasized the aesthetics of the ugly and the trivial. For the first time in Chinese literature an entire poem described an ugly stone, an earthworm, a maggot, a rat, or

a louse. In these works Mei often makes use of the colloquial. He often moves from the object to philosophical reflection. Faced with an ugly stone ("Yung . . . ch'ou shih" 詠 . . . 醜石 [On . . . an Ugly Stone], 1059) or earthworms ("Ch'iu-yin" 蚯蚓 [Earthworm], 1045), the poet emphasizes the relativity of aesthetic perception. The most famous example of this kind is the poem on the river-pig ("K'o yü shih ho-t'un yü" 客語食河豚魚 [On Hearing Some Travelers Speak of Eating River-pig Fish], 1037), which resulted in the nickname "River-pig Mei." The poem notes the savoriness of the river-pig, but also points to a danger: if not prepared properly, the dish can become a deadly poison. The poem concludes philosophically that the good and the bad condition each other.

These poems, which belong to the late phase of Mei's writings, are characterized by detailed observation and description. In them experience is the starting point for literary creativity. Thus personal matters are also often made into the topic of a poem. The pain of the poet after the death of his first wife (1044) in the cycle "Tao-wang" 悼亡 (Mourning for my Wife), or the dimming of his sight "Mu-hun" 目昏 (My Eyes Go Dim, 1049), or his children, or even trivial things such as the first white hair in his beard are depicted.

The ability to notice and describe the most simple and unimportant things of everyday life allows things to be themselves. In this is to be found a new view of the real, a new aesthetic standpoint expressed in the stark *p'ing-tan* style. *P'ing-tan* meant for Mei the harmony of the poet with things and the realistic description which results from this harmony. The emotional tranquility based on overcoming sorrow which typified much of previous literature led to an increased emphasis on things in Mei's verse and provided a basis for subsequent realistic Sung verse.

EDITIONS:
Wan-ling chi 宛陵集. *SPTK*.
Wan-ling Hsien-sheng wen-chi 宛陵先生文集. Rpt.
   Shanghai, 1940.

TRANSLATIONS:
Chaves, *Mei Yao-ch'en, passim.*
Leimbigler, Peter. *Mei Yao-ch'en (1002-1060). Versuch einer literarischen und politischen Deutung.* Wiesbaden, 1970, *passim.*
Sunflower, pp. 311-320.

STUDIES:
Chaves, *Mei Yao-ch'en.*
Hsia, Ching-kuan 夏敬觀. *Mei Yao-ch'en shih* 梅堯臣詩. Shanghai, 1940.
Huo, Sung-lin 霍松林. *Mei Yao-ch'eng shih-ko t'i-ts'ai* 梅堯臣詩歌題材. Peking, 1962.
Leimbigler, *Mei Yao-ch'en.*
SB, pp. 761-770.
Yokohama, Iseo 横山伊勢雄. "Bai Gyōshin no shiron" 梅堯臣 の 詩論, *Kambun gakkai kaihō,* 24 (1965).
Yoshikawa, *Sung,* pp. 72-78.

—WK

Meng Chiao 孟郊 (*tzu,* Tung-yeh 東野, 751-814) was the eldest and most difficult of the *fu-ku* writers who gathered around Han Yü* at the turn of the ninth century. Meng was from Hu-chou 湖州 (modern Wu-hsing in Chekiang), and during his younger years he seems to have had contact with the Chiao-jan* Circle, then active in the region. However, it was not until 791, when Meng went to the capital to take the examination and met the young Han Yü, that he began to write poetry in the harsh, idiosyncratic style for which he was later famous.

Meng Chiao twice failed the examination for the *chin-shih,* in 792 and 793, and those failures occasioned angry, disillusioned lyrics that were to win Meng the shocked contempt of many later readers. In 796 Meng took the examination for the third time and passed, but lacking the necessary support from powerful patrons in the government, he did not receive a position until 800, and then it was the lowest provincial post in the official hierarchy. By 806 Meng had given up official life and settled in Lo-yang, where he spent the rest of his life.

With the exception of two letters and one brief encomium, Meng Chiao's extant work consists of just over five hundred poems, almost all pentasyllabic old-style verse. As Meng himself so proudly claimed,

his style was out of harmony with the gracious occasional poetry of his contemporaries. In Meng's own occasional poetry, even when he aspired to simple graciousness, there is almost always some jarring note: whether he erred in excessive directness or in excessive obliquity, he always erred. His *yüeh-fu** and non-occasional poems are often straightforward and consciously rough, sometimes developing complex conceits, but usually avoiding the polish and ornament of contemporary poetics. Meng Chiao conceived of his work as being in the "ancient style," and ethical messages, associated with the mid-T'ang revival of Confucian values, occur throughout his poetry. Yet even in his ethics there is discord, and such poems often possess a shrill stridency that undermines and complicates the magisterial calm of the would-be didactic poet.

Meng Chiao's most interesting and difficult works are his remarkable poem-sequences: among these are the fifteen "Ch'iu huai" 秋懷 (Autumn Meditations), the ten poems of "Shih tsung" 石淙 (Stone Run), the nine poems of "Han hsi" 寒溪 (Cold Creek), the twelve "Tiao Yüan Lu-shan" 弔元魯山 (Elegies for Yüan), ten "Hsia ai" 杏殤 (Laments of the Gorges), nine poems on "Hsing shang" 峽哀 (The Death of Apricots), and ten "Tiao Lu Yin" 弔盧殷 (Elegies for Lu Yin). These sequences contain some of the most difficult and disturbing poetry of the T'ang, at times verging on madness. "The Death of Apricots," for example, explores the correspondences and reciprocal relations between the early death of Meng's infant sons and the destruction of blossoms in a late-spring frost. The theme might have been a merely convenient analogy for another poet; in Meng Chiao the correspondences provoke the suspicion of an invisible and malicious order governing the world's operations. "Cold Creek" and "Laments of the Gorges" likewise concern encounters with cosmic malice embodied in landscapes. Through such poems many later readers came to hate the poetry of Meng Chiao, but comments preserved in *shih-hua** often attest to the disturbing power of Meng Chiao's best work.

Meng Chiao's linked-verses, written always with Han Yü and sometimes including several other participants, show Meng in a different light. Speculative buffoonery, erudite word games, and stylistic *tours de force* make such poems a delight to read. "Ch'eng-nan lien-chü" 城南聯句 (South of the City), written on an excursion south of Ch'ang-an, remains the greatest linked-verse in the language.

For two centuries after his death, Meng Chiao's reputation remained very high. However, a pair of famous poems by Su Shih,* "Tu Meng Chiao shih" 讀孟郊詩 (On Reading Meng Chiao's Poetry), attacked Meng with a directness that only the brash Su Shih would dare. The second of these poems begins baldly: "I detest the poems of Meng Chiao" (an outrageous inversion of a conventional opening of panegyric, "I love . . .") and continues with a memorable parody of Meng's easily parodied style. The careful reader of Su Shih will note, however, that Su borrowed extensively from the poet whose work he so abhorred. Between this attack and the growing literary-historical orthodoxy that freely damned the whole mid-T'ang style, Meng was placed back among the second rank of T'ang poets, and his work continues to be generally unpopular.

EDITIONS:

Meng Tung-yeh shih-chu 孟東野詩注. Ch'en Yen-chieh 陳延傑, ed. and comm. Shanghai, 1939. Ch'en used a poor text, but his annotations are valuable.

Meng Tung-yeh shih-chi 孟東野詩集. Hua Ch'en-chih 華忱之, ed. Peking, 1959. The best critical edition, with introduction and chronology.

TRANSLATIONS:

Graham, *Late T'ang*, pp. 57-69.
Sunflower, pp. 157-164.

STUDIES:

Lin, Tuan-ch'ang 林端常. *Meng Tung-yeh yen-chiu* 孟東野研究. Nanking, 1974.
Owen, *Meng Chiao*. Also contains numerous translations.

—SO

Meng Hao-jan 孟浩然 (689-740) ranks among the most renowned poets who lived during the reign of Emperor Hsüan-tsung (712-756), an age blessed with a host of gifted writers whose works constitute one of the chief treasures of Chinese literature. Meng was a decade or more older than most of the other famous poets—Li Po,* Wang Wei,* Tu Fu*—who were active during this period. He may thus be regarded, along with Chang Chiu-ling,* as a senior representative of the so-called High T'ang poets.

Meng's tie to his natal place, Hsiang-yang 襄陽 (in modern north-central Hupei) was exceptionally strong, and he seems to have spent all but eight or ten years of his life there. Hsiang-yang's historical heritage—especially as the home of many of the most famous recluses of the late Han and early Three Kingdoms (such as Chu-ko Liang 諸葛亮 [181-234], P'ang T'ung 龐統 [179-214], Hsü Shu 徐庶 [*fl.* 220], Ssu-ma Hui 司馬徽 [*fl.* 200], and P'ang Te-kung 龐德公 [*fl.* 200])—was both rich and illustrious. Abundant references to the local lore, legends, and history of the area are found in Meng's numerous poems on the lovely hills and streams of Hsiang-yang. Two sites may be noted as being of especial importance to him. The first is his family seat, a place called "The Garden South of the Branch (of the Han River)" or simply "South Garden," located near Phoenix Mountain (Feng-huang shan), about three miles south of the city. This site is also often referred to in Meng's poems as "South Mountain." It is this spot—not the Chung-nan Mountains south of Ch'ang-an, as commonly asserted—that is the locus of his well-known poem "Sui-mu kuei Nan-shan 歲暮歸南山 (Returning to South Mountain on the Eve of the Year). The other place with which Meng was most closely associated is Lu-men shan (Deer Gate Mountain), ten miles southeast of Hsiang-yang. Although the evidence is scanty, it appears that at some time Meng briefly established a hermitage for himself on the slopes of this mountain, in conscious imitation of P'ang Te-kung who secluded himself there five centuries earlier. Meng celebrated his habitation on Deer Gate Mountain and his self-identification with P'ang Te-kung in the famous poem "Yeh kuei Lu-men ko" 夜歸鹿門歌 (A Song on Returning at Night to Deer Gate). Later writers invariably link Meng's name with this mountain, although his period of residence there was short.

In contrast to most writers of his day, Meng Hao-jan did not enjoy a career in government service. In 728, at the relatively advanced age of thirty-nine, he sat for—and failed—the *chin-shih* examination. However, a year-long stay in Ch'ang-an at this time, as well as earlier and later visits to Lo-yang, put him on familiar terms with several of his more successful contemporaries. In the autumn of 737 the influential statesman and writer Chang Chiu-ling, who had recently been ousted from his high position at court and rusticated to central China, appointed Meng as his assistant, thus allowing Meng for the first and only time in his life to don the garb of a T'ang official (his rank was but one step from the bottom of the thirty-rung bureaucratic ladder). But any exhilaration Meng may have felt over this was fleeting, for he resigned this post less than a year later. Two years afterward he died, at home in Hsiang-yang.

It has long been a cliché of traditional criticism to pair Meng Hao-jan and Wang Wei* as the two exemplars of a "school" of T'ang "nature poetry." But this facile and reductive characterization, based primarily on a dozen or so "anthology pieces," does justice to neither poet. In Meng's case, an examination of his entire *oeuvre* reveals him to be a poet of more parts than is customarily acknowledged. Many of his verses, for example, display elegantly allusive turns of phrase that remind one strongly of the work of Six Dynasties poets or exhibit his scholarly command of pre-T'ang literature and history.

Comparing his so-called "nature poems" with those of Wang Wei, reveals striking differences in the diction, tone, and viewpoint of the two writers. Meng's depictions of natural scenes are usually precise and individualized, with most attention given to foreground objects—in contrast to Wang Wei, whose landscapes are more generalized and non-specific, focusing often on large, background images. This difference is reflected in the range of vocabulary employed in each poet's work: the various kinds of flora, fauna, and topographic features presented by Meng—and the detail with which he describes them—far exceed what one finds in Wang Wei's verses. A notable human presence, or at least the unmistakable persona of the poet, is another feature common to Meng Hao-jan's landscapes. He is a warm poet, who does not often lose himself totally in his scenes. Meng is, however, an extremely moody and erratic poet, whose peaks of verbal excellence are sometimes commeasured by vales of unremarkable platitudes. In this regard, he is perhaps the least consistent of the major poets of the period.

EDITIONS:

Kroll, Paul W. and Joyce Wong Kroll. *A Concordance to the Poems of Meng Hao-jan.* San Francisco, 1982. Keyed to the *SPTK* text.

Meng Hao-jan chi 孟浩然集. *SPTK.* The standard text of the poems; copy of a Ming woodblock edition.

Meng Hao-jan chi. SPPY.

Meng Hao-jan chi chien-chu 孟浩然集箋注. Yu Hsin-li 游信利, annotator. Taipei, 1968. The most thorough and best annotated edition, based on the *SPTK.* However, frequent typographical errors require one always to check these versions against the *SPTK* text.

TRANSLATIONS:

Chang, Hsin-chang. "Meng Hao-jan," in his *Chinese Literature, Volume 2: Nature Poetry,* New York, 1977, pp. 81-96.

Demiéville, *Anthologie,* pp. 213-215.

Owen, *High T'ang,* pp. 71-88. Critical translations.

Sunflower, pp. 92-96.

STUDIES:

Bryant, Daniel. "The High T'ang Poet Meng Hao-jan: Studies in Biography and Textual History." Unpublished Ph.D. dissertation, University of British Columbia, 1977.

Ch'en, I-hsin 陳貽焮. "Meng Hao-jan shih-chi k'ao-pien" 孟浩然事跡考辨, *Wen-shih,* 4 (Peking, 1965), 41-74.

———. "T'an Meng Hao-jan te yin-i" 談孟浩然 的隱逸, *T'ang-shih yen-chiu,* pp. 46-52.

Frankel, Hans H. *Biographies of Meng Hao-jan.* Berkeley, 1952.

Kroll, Paul W. *Meng Hao-jan.* Boston, 1981. Contains numerous translations.

———. "The Quatrains of Meng Hao-jan," *MS,* 31 (1974-75), 344-374. Contains translations.

———. "Wang Shih-yüan's Preface to the Poems of Meng Hao-jan," *MS,* 34 (1979-80), 349-369.

Liu, K'ai-yang 劉開揚. "Lun Meng Hao-jan ho t'a-te shih" 論孟浩然和他的詩, in *T'ang-shih,* pp. 29-41.

Rust, Ambros. *Meng Hao-jan (671-740), Sein Leben und religioses Denken nach seinen Gedichten.* Ingenbohl, 1960.

Suzuki, Shūji 鈴木修次. *Tōdai shijin ron* 唐代詩人論, Tokyo, 1973, v. l, pp. 75-137.

Taniguchi, Akio 谷口明夫. "Mo Kōnen jiseki kō: jōkyō ōshi o megutte" 孟浩然事跡考：上京應試をあぐって, *Chūgoku chūsei bungaku kenkyū,* 11 (1976), 48-65.

—PWK

Mi Heng 禰衡 (*tzu,* Cheng-p'ing 正平, 173-198)

was an eccentric, unpredictable, and sometimes arrogant young genius who lived at the end of the Han dynasty. Most of his works were already lost by the time of the compilation of the *Hou Han-shu* in the early fifth century, and only a small amount survives today.

The end of the Han was a turbulent time. Following a course of action favored by many men of letters, in 194 or 195 Mi Heng vacated the North to take refuge in Ching-chou 荊州 under Liu Piao 劉表 (144-208), a noted patron of scholars. In 196 the literarily distinguished Chien-an period (196-220) was inaugurated when Ts'ao Ts'ao 曹操 (155-220) took the last Han emperor under his protection and installed him in a new capital at Hsü 許 (modern Hsü-ch'ang hsien in Honan). In that same year Mi Heng proceeded to the Hsü area. He seems to have been quite particular about his acquaintances there, for it is said that he carried his calling card tucked away for so long without using it that the characters on it gradually became obliterated. In fact, he admired only K'ung Jung* and Yang Hsiu 楊脩 (175-219), both of whom were later put to death by Ts'ao Ts'ao. Although he was two decades older than Mi Heng, K'ung Jung was greatly impressed by the younger man and used his own access to Ts'ao Ts'ao to praise Mi's talents on many occasions. He even wrote a "Chien Mi Heng piao" 薦禰衡表 (Memorial Recommending Mi Heng) which survives today.

Being recommended to Ts'ao Ts'ao was an unfortunate event for Mi Heng. As long as he remained in relative obscurity his *outré* behavior was harmless enough, but once he came into direct contact with the powerful, his eccentricity became dangerously offensive. When, intrigued by K'ung Jung's frequent praise, Ts'ao Ts'ao expressed a desire to meet Mi Heng, Mi was not only unwilling to go, he also spoke recklessly. Although Ts'ao Ts'ao might have had Mi killed, he was unwilling to bear the onus attendant upon that act. His decision to humiliate Mi instead provides the most famous story about Mi Heng. Ts'ao made Mi Heng one of the drummers at a great feast. Before entering each drummer was to change into a new uniform, but when Mi's turn came, he went straight in, gave a rousing performance, and stopped in front of Ts'ao Ts'ao. When Ts'ao Ts'ao chastised him for not changing clothes, Mi Heng stripped naked on the spot, slowly donned the new outfit, and then stirringly drummed his way out. Ts'ao Ts'ao had to admit that it was he himself who had been humiliated. After this performance K'ung Jung tried to effect a reconciliation, but while Ts'ao Ts'ao was willing, Mi Heng once more behaved outrageously. Ts'ao Ts'ao then determined to have the intractable Mi escorted back to Liu Piao.

Once more in Ching-chou Mi Heng was treated with considerable respect by Liu and the literati there, even becoming an arbiter in matters of writing and discussion. But after a time he reverted to his old ways and was intolerably insulting to Liu Piao. Liu followed the example set by Ts'ao Ts'ao and in turn shunted Mi Heng off on Hung Tsu 黃祖 (d. 208), the short-tempered Governor of Chiang-hsia 江夏 Commandery. Though Huang treated Mi Heng well, and the two men got along well at first, before long Mi spoke insolently to Huang at a feast. When Huang scolded

625

him, Mi talked back. Huang Tsu originally intended only to have Mi Heng beaten, but Mi cursed him so vilely that Huang ordered him killed. Mi Heng might have lived even then had luck been on his side. He had become friends with Huang Tsu's son Huang I 黃射, and the latter attempted to intercede with his father but was too late.

The most important extant work by Mi Heng is the rhapsody "Ying-wu fu" 鸚鵡賦 (The Parrot). It is ostensibly a representative example of the subgenre of the rhapsody known as *yung-wu fu* 詠物賦 (rhapsodies on objects), but is actually a frustration *fu*.* Mi's piece came to be written when a guest at a feast given by Huang I presented his host with a parrot. Huang thereupon requested that Mi pen a rhapsody on the bird for the delectation of the guests. The first third of the rhapsody is, as one might expect of a *yung-wu* piece, a treatment of the background and rare properties of the parrot. It is in the remaining sixty-odd lines that the poet departs from the expected, for in these lines he expresses the parrot's misery over its fate and captive state. It is clear that the main thrust of Mi's rhapsody lies in its departure from innocuous convention in favor of personal allegory.

EDITIONS:

Liu-ch'ao wen, v. 1, "Ch'üan Hou-Han wen" 全後漢文, *ch.* 87, pp. 942-943.

TRANSLATIONS:

Graham, William T., Jr. "Mi Heng's 'Rhapsody on a Parrot'," *HJAS,* 39 (1979), 39-54.

STUDIES:

Li, Pao-chün 李寶均. *Ts'ao shih fu-tzu ho Chien-an wen-hsüeh* 曹氏父子和建安文學, Peking, 1962, pp. 69-71.

— RJC

Min-ko 民歌 (folksongs) are any anonymous songs which circulate among the common people. They also go by a plethora of other names (*min-yao* 謠, *li-ko* 俚歌, *li-yao* 謠, *li-ch'ü* 曲 and *su-ko* 俗歌, *su-yao* 謠, *su-ch'ü* 曲), a good indication of their broad distribution. There are numerous specialized categories of folksongs, among them *lien-ko* 戀歌 (love songs), *nung-ko* 農歌 (farm-ing songs), *yang-ko* 秧歌 (planting songs, also an early type of variety play), *mu-ko* 牧歌 (shepherds' songs), *ch'uan-ko* 船歌 (boatmen's songs), *ch'iao-ko* 樵歌 (woodcutters' songs), *ts'ai-ch'a-ko* 採茶歌 (teapickers' songs, also the name of a tune in northern dramas), *ts'ui-mien-ko* 催眠歌 (lullabies), and so on. Other kinds of folksongs include *k'u-ch'i-tz'u* 哭泣詞 (lays expressing the sorrows of peasant women), *chiao-hua ch'iang* 叫化腔 (beggars' laments), *wan-ko* 挽歌 (funeral dirges), and *feng-yao* 風謠 (ditties revealing local custom). As is obvious from the names of these categories, folksongs usually describe the daily life and concerns of the common people. Such songs are frequently referred to collectively as *ko-yao* 歌謠. If a distinction is to be drawn between *ko* and *yao*, the former may be said—in accordance with an old commentary to the *Shih-ching**—to have fixed rhythms and tunes, while the latter are more freely intoned. There is also an old tradition, dating back to the first Chinese dictionary (*Erh-ya*—see *ching*) that *yao* means "an unaccompanied song" (*t'u-ko* 徒歌).

Orthodox poets usually scorned the vulgarity of the folksong, even though the folksong's unorthodox diction, form, and choice of subject matter frequently inspired the revitalization of poetic tradition. Many collections of Chinese poetry, beginning with the *Shih-ching* itself, contain material that is attributed to folk origins. However, folksongs were frequently modified as they were recorded, and the task of distinguishing between authentic folksongs and their imitations or adaptations is an arduous one, which is further complicated by the realization that poems composed to popular tunes could enter the folk repertoire. However, even if folksongs were modified as they were written down, structural features, vernacular diction, and ribald themes still hint at folk origins. Thus, one of the most popular collections of folk songs, Feng Meng-lung's* *Shan-ko,** attests to its folk origins and inspirations by its extensive use of Wu dialect and the erotic and humorous overtones of many of the songs.

The study of folklore in early twentieth-century China actually began with an emphasis on the collection of folksongs. Avid folklorists published songs they collected in the field in the *Ko-yao chou-k'an* 歌謠週刊 (Folksong Weekly). In accordance with the European definition of folksong, most folklorists took care to record only songs that circulated in the repertoire. Thus they did not adhere to fixed texts, and individual songs were often represented by many versions. Their goals were to provide material for the study of local customs and dialects and to provide inspiration and direction for a new poetry that would reflect the longings of the people in a way that classical poetry no longer could.

Unfortunately, the folksong collectors did not transcribe the music that went with the songs. They did not provide much information about the contexts in which the songs were sung, nor did they engage in extensive study of their collections. This was to be deferred until a comprehensive body of songs from every area of China could be assembled. Nevertheless, the songs collected do provide some basis for generalization about the nature of Chinese folksongs.

One of the most striking characteristics of Chinese folksongs is the wide regional variation. This variation is evident both in the proliferation of sub-genres and in the differences between versions of single songs collected from different parts of China. Tung Tso-pin applies the Finnish method to variations of a single song in a monograph entitled *K'an-chien t'a* 看見她 (I Saw Her). In the song "I Saw Her," a young boy describes how he leaves his parents' home, arrives at the home of his future in-laws, is entertained by the in-laws, manages to catch a glimpse of his future bride, and returns home to tell his mother that he must marry her. Tung Tso-pin analyzes similarities and differences among the many recorded versions of this song and concludes that the geographical distribution of this song has followed major waterways and that two major types of the song are discernible, one found along the Yellow River and one in areas along the Yangtze.

Themes of folksongs vary widely. Songs of erotic love are common in the corpus of folksongs, as are songs sung to and by children. "I Saw Her" was sung to young boys by their mothers. There are work songs, songs about events in the distant or recent past, and admonitory songs. Some songs are serious and didactic in tone, while others are humorous or satiric.

The meters of folksongs also vary in accordance with the tunes to which they are sung. Although the lines of most songs contain three or seven syllables, in some songs the lines can have four or five syllables each or can vary in length. Most songs contain rhymes, but rhyming patterns also vary.

Songs may be sung by individuals with or without group participation. The Hakka engage in singing duels with two sides alternating lines. Singers in these duels improvise to a great degree and continue until one singer can no longer provide lines and concedes defeat.

The language of folksongs is repetitious and formulaic. Words, phrases, and entire sentences may be repeated within one song or may appear in many different songs. It is usually (but not always) the opening lines that are migratory.

Folksongs are sung in dialect. This means that fieldworkers must often struggle to transcribe dialect words not found in Mandarin. It often proves impossible for fieldworkers to capture all of the rhymes and puns of folksongs.

Collectors in the early twentieth century remarked that with the advent of widespread literacy, young people no longer learned the art of singing folksongs. They feared that as the generation they used as informants died out, genuine folksongs would become extinct. Although literate young people may learn to sing versions of folksongs recorded in texts or may even compose songs to folk tunes, they lack the versatility and the inclusive repertoire of active bearers of oral tradition. This makes the collections compiled in the early twentieth century, however incomplete, all the more valuable.

EDITIONS:

Chu, Chieh-fan 朱介凡. *Chung-kuo ko-yao lun* 中國歌謠論. Taipei, 1974.

Chu, Tzu-ch'ing 朱自清. *Chung-kuo ko yao* 中國歌謠. Peking, 1957; rpt. Taipei, 1961.

Eberhard, Wolfram. "Pounding Songs from Peking" [Revised and translated version of "Pekinger Stampflieder," *Zeitschrift für Ethnologie*, 67 (1936), 232-248], in Eberhard, *Studies in Chinese Folklore and Related Essays*, Bloomington, 1970, pp. 147-172.

———. *Taiwanese Ballads: A Catalogue*. Taipei, 1972.

Hu, Huai-ch'en 胡懷琛. *Chung-kuo min-ko yen-chiu* 中國民歌研究. Shanghai, 1925.

Ko-yao chou-k'an (Folksongs Weekly of National Peking University), 1932-1937. Facsimile reproduction Taipei, 1970.

Lou, Tzu-k'uang 婁子匡 and Chu Chieh-fan 朱介凡. *Wu-shih-nien lai te Chung-kuo su-wen-hsüeh* 五十年來的中國俗文學. Taipei, 1963.

Tung, Tso-pin 董作賓. *K'an-chien t'a*. Peking, 1924; Taipei, 1970.

Vitale, Guido Amedeo, *barone. Chinese Folklore: Pekinese Rhymes, First Collected and Edited with Notes and Translation by Baron Guido Vitale*. Peking, 1896.

—VM and MWe

Ming-pao chi 冥報記 (Records of Miraculous Retribution) is a collection of Buddhist miracle tales compiled by T'ang Lin 唐臨 (c. 600-c. 659), a powerful government official from an established North Chinese family who was also a devout lay Buddhist. With the exception of a few memorials produced as part of his official duties, the *Ming-pao chi* is his only known work. Completed between 653 and 655, it was widely quoted in Buddhist literature of the mid- and late-T'ang, but was lost in China by the end of the Sung dynasty and has survived only through manuscripts preserved in Japan. It contains fifty-three (in one manuscript, fifty-seven) accounts of Buddhist miracles and prodigies, all intended to illustrate the concept of karmic retribution, and is one of the principal examples of the Chinese Buddhist tradition of writing and collecting miracle tales. The earliest known collection of such tales was compiled in South China near the end of the fourth century, and although similar tale collections have continued to be compiled until modern times, the genre seems to have already passed the peak of its vitality by the end of the T'ang dynasty.

The miracle tales can be understood as a Buddhist adapation to didactic ends of the previously existing, indigenous Chinese *chih-kuai.** In their use of tale literature as a didactic tool, the Chinese Buddhists had ample precedent in the Indian Buddhist *avadāna* tales, several collections of which had already been translated into Chinese by the late fourth century. But while the *avadāna* tales illustrated concepts of the earlier Theravāda Buddhism, the miracle tales were indebted for their religious inspiration to the then developing Mahāyāna concepts of faith and piety. Although the miracle tales were a significant step in the development of the narrative techniques that were drawn upon by the writers of the later *ch'uan-ch'i** tales, they were not considered fiction by their compilers. Presented as straightforward accounts of actual events, they were intended to illustrate through concrete examples the operation in daily life of the basic tenets of Mahāyāna doctrine. Along with descriptions of the efficacy of invocations to the bodhisattva Avalokitesvara and the merit accrued through the copying or recitation of sutras, there is also a large amount of popular Buddhist cosmological lore. There are, for example, many tales about journeys to the netherworld which give detailed accounts of both its physical appearance and bureaucratic structure. There are descriptions of the tortures of the hells and the pleasures of the heavens and stories of persons being reborn as animals or ghosts. The tales vary in length from fewer than one hundred characters to more than fifteen hundred. Because they were considered factual, the tales were often used as source material by later Chinese Buddhist historians and biographers.

By modern times all the early collections of miracle tales had, like the *Ming-pao chi*, been lost in China. Many are known only through tales quoted in later anthologies and encyclopedias; other have been preserved in Japan. In addition to the *Ming-pao chi*, early collections which have survived in Japan include:

1. *Kuan-shih-yin ying-yen chi* 光世音應驗記 (Records of Miracles Concerning Avalok-

itesvara) recorded by Fu Liang 傅亮 (374-426) based on what he remembered of an earlier collection by Hsieh Fu 謝敷, which had been destroyed during a rebellion in 399. The seven tales that Fu Liang recalled are the earliest known Chinese Buddhist miracle tales, and all tell of people being saved from distress by invoking the bodhisattva Avalokitesvara.

2. *Hsü Kuan-shih-yin ying-yen chi* 續光世音應驗記 (Supplement to Records of Miracles Concerning Avalokitesvara) by Chang Yen 張演 (active mid-fifth century) adds ten tales to Fu Liang's collection.

3. *Hsi Kuan-shih-yin ying-yen chi* 繫光世音應驗記 (More Records of Miracles Concerning Avalokitesvara) by Lu Kao 陸杲 (459-532) adds sixty-nine more tales to the two previous works. Lu's preface is dated 501.

4. *Chin-kang po-je ching chi-yen chi* 金剛般若經集驗記 (Collected Records of Diamond Wisdom Sutra Miracles) by Meng Hsien-chung 孟獻忠 (active early eighth century) contains approximately seventy tales. Most of them had never before been recorded, but several were drawn from three earlier collections: fourteen from Hsiao Yü's 蕭瑀 (575-648) *Chin-kang po-je ching ling-yen chi* 金剛般若經靈驗記 (Records of Diamond Wisdom Sutra Miracles), a collection otherwise completely lost; one from T'ang Lin's *Ming-pao chi* (the only tale in the fifty-three tale manuscript that deals with the *Diamond Wisdom Sutra*); and ten from Lang Yü-ling's 郎餘令 (active mid-seventh century) *Ming-pao shih-i* 冥報拾遺 (Addenda to Miraculous Retribution), a continuation of the *Ming-pao chi* completed in 663. All of the tales in Meng's collection, as its title indicates, tell of miracles in which the *Diamond Wisdom Sutra* played a central role. His preface is dated 718.

Collections which have been lost, but from which significant numbers of tales have survived through quotation in later works include:

1. *Hsüan-yen chi* 宣驗記 (Records of Revealed Miracles) is attributed to Liu I-ch'ing (see *Shih-shuo hsin-yü*). Thirty-five have been located in various collectanea.

2. *Ming-hsiang chi* 冥祥記 (Records of Miraculous Omens) by Wang Yen 王琰 (active

late fifth and early sixth centuries) was completed in the late fifth century. The 131 tales that seem accurately attributed to the *Ming-hsiang chi* make it the largest and one of the most interesting of the early Chinese Buddhist miracle tale collections.

3. *Ching-i chi* 旌異記 (Records of Unusual Manifestations) by Hou Po 侯白 was compiled at the command of Emperor Wen of Sui (r. 581-604). Only ten quoted tales have been located.

The collections mentioned above are those which were devoted solely to Buddhist miracle tales. Similar tales are also found in other, more heterogeneous, collections which were not specifically Buddhist.

EDITIONS:

Chin-kang po-jo ching chi-yen chi, in *Dai-Nihon zoku zōkyō* 大日本續藏經. Kyoto, 1905-1912, part 1, section 2b, case 22, v. 1.

Ching-i chi, in Lu Hsün 魯迅, *Ku hsiao-shuo kou-ch'en* 古小說鈎沈; in *Lu Hsün ch'üan-chi* 魯迅全集, Peking, 1973, v. 8, pp. 505-509.

Hsüan-yen chi, in *ibid.*, pp. 547-559.

Kuan-shih-yin ying-yen chi (and its two supplements), in Makita Tairyō 牧田諦亮, *Rikuchō koitsu Kanzeon-ōkenki no kenkyū* 六朝古逸觀世音應驗記の研究. Kyoto, 1970, part 1.

Ming-hsiang chi, in Lu Hsün, *Ku hsiao-shuo kou-ch'en*, pp. 561-648.

Ming-pao chi, in (1) *Taishō shinshū daizōkyō* 大正新脩大藏經, rpt. Tokyo, 1973, v. 51; and in (2) Uchida Michio 內田道夫, *Kōhon Meihōki* 校本冥報記, Sendai, 1955.

TRANSLATIONS:

Andō, Tomonobu 安藤智信. "*Meishōki*" 冥報記, in Iriya Yoshitaka 入矢義高, ed., *Bukkyō bungakushū* 佛教文學集, Tokyo, 1975, pp. 295-382. A complete translation into modern Japanese of Lu Hsün's 131-tale recension of the *Ming-hsiang chi* with helpful annotation.

Gjertson, Donald E. "Ghosts, Gods, and Retribution: Nine Buddhist Miracle Tales from Six Dynasties and Early T'ang China," *University of Massachusetts Asian Studies Occasional Papers Series*, 2 (1978). Includes tales from the *Kuang-shih-yin ying-yen chi, Ming-hsiang chi, Ching-i chi*, and *Ming-pao chi*.

———. "A Study and Translation of the *Ming-pao chi*: A T'ang Dynasty Collection of Buddhist Tales." Unpublished Ph.D. dissertation, Stanford University, 1975. A complete translation with notes.

STUDIES:

Gjertson, "A Study and Translation."

Lin, Ch'en 林辰 (Wang Shih-nung 王詩農). "Lu Hsün *Ku hsiao-shuo kou-ch'en* te nien-tai chi so-shou ke-shu tso-che" 魯迅古小說鉤沈的輯錄年代及所收各書作者, *Wen-hsüeh i-ch'an hsüan-chi*, 3 (May 1960), 385-407.

Shimura, Ryōji 志村良治. "*Meihōki* no denpon ni tsuite" 冥報記 の傳本 について, *Bunka*, 19.1 (January 1955), 53-69.

Shōji, Kakuichi 莊司格一. "*Meishōki* ni tsuite" 冥祥記 について, *Shūkan Tōyōgaku*, 22 (November 1969), 41-65.

Ts'en, Chung-mien 岑仲勉. "T'ang Lin *Ming-pao chi* chih fu-yüan" 唐臨冥報記之復原, *BIHP*, 17 (April 1948), 177-194.

Tsukamoto, Zenryū 塚本善隆. "Koitsu rikuchō *Kanzeon ōkenki* no shutsugen" 古逸六朝觀世音應驗記 の出現, in *[Kyōto daigaku jimbun kagaku kenkyūjo] Sōritsu nijūgo shūnen kinen ronbunshū* [京都大學人文科學研究所] 創立廿五周年記念論文集, Kyoto, 1954, pp. 234-250.

Uchida, Michio. "*Meihōki* no seikaku ni tsuite" 冥報記 の性格について, *Bunka*, 19.1 (January 1955), 1-23.

Uchiyama, Chinari 內山知也. *Zui-Tō shōsetsu kenkyū* 隋唐小說研究. Tokyo, 1977. Contains sections on both the *Ching-i chi* and the *Ming-pao chi*.

—DG

Ming-shih chi-shih 明詩紀事

Ming-shih chi-shih 明詩紀事 (Recorded Occasions in Ming Poetry), compiled by Ch'en T'ien 陳田 (*fl.* 1883-1911), is a voluminous collection of Ming-dynasty *shih*** poetry and appended critical comments, even more compendious than Chu I-tsun's *Ming-shih tsung*,* though not complete in its published form.

The entire work consists of 199 *chüan*, subdivided as follows: Ming emperors and members of the imperial house (*chüan* 1-2), followed by poets active during the Hung-wu period (1368-1398), including such figures as Kao Ch'i,* Liu Chi,* and Lin Hung* (32 *chüan*); poets of the first half of the fifteenth century (22 *chüan*); poets of the second half of the century, including Li Tung-yang* (12 *chüan*); poets of the period around the turn of the sixteenth century, including Li Meng-yang,* Ho Ching-ming,* other members of their Archaist movement (18 *chüan*); poets of the first half of the century, particularly those who were independent of the Archaists, such as Yang Shen* and Li K'ai-hsien* (22 *chüan*); poets of the second half of the century, both those who associated with the "Later Seven Masters" group, such as Li P'an-lung,* Wang Shih-chen* (1526-1590), Hu Ying-lin,* and others, such as Hsü Wei* (21 *chüan*); poets active during the Wan-li period (1573-1620), including T'ang Hsien-tsu,* Yüan Hung-tao,* and Chung Hsing* (33 *chüan*); poets active during the last reigns of the Ming, to 1644, and those who remained loyal to the fallen dynasty even after the Manchu conquest, such as Ku Yen-wu* (39 *chüan*).

The published sections include the work of about four thousand poets, the great majority of whom are represented by only one or two poems. The table of contents lists two additional sections, the *jen-* 壬 and *kuei-* 癸 *ch'ien*, each in 11-19 *chüan*, that were to appear subsequently, but these were never printed, and it is not known if they were completed in manuscript or, if so, whether the manuscript is extant. They presumably were to include classes of poets, most importantly Buddhist monks and women, not found in the other sections.

Each section of the *Ming-shih chi-shih* has a short preface, which outlines the development of *shih* poetry during the period it covers, generally including brief comments on some of the most important poets of the time. Taken together, these prefaces form a concise history of the Ming *shih*, perhaps the first to be attempted without a serious bias in attitude toward the various contending poetic schools of the dynasty. It should be noted, however, that Ch'en's selection does not necessarily follow the evaluations in the prefaces. For example, Li Meng-yang and Ho Ching-ming, acclaimed in the preface to the *ting-ch'ien*, are represented by only ten and five poems respectively, while other poets not even mentioned in the prefaces may have up to fifty or so poems included. Each poet has at least a brief biographical entry, together with a collection of critical comments drawn from a variety of sources.

EDITIONS:

Ming-shih chi-shih. Original woodblock edition in installments, 1897-1911, in the author's studio, Ting-shih chai 聽詩齋.

———. 6v. Taipei, 1971. Reprint of the typeset edition previously issued in the *Wan-yu wen-k'u* and *Kuo-hsüeh chi-pen ts'ung-shu;* the most accessible text.

Pa-shih-chiu chung Ming-tai chuan-chi tsung-ho yin-te 八十九種明代傳記綜合引得. William Hung *et al.*, eds. Harvard-Yenching Sinological Index Series, 24. Rpt. Taipei, 1966. Indexes the names of authors, referring to the original edition, in the *Ming-shih chi-shih.*

—DB

Ming-shih tsung 明詩綜, compiled by Chu I-tsun,* is one of the major anthologies of Ming-dynasty *shih** poetry, being fuller than Shen Te-ch'ien's* *Ming shih pieh-tsai-chi* 明詩別載集 and more accessible than the *Lieh-ch'ao shih-chi* 列朝詩集 of Ch'ien Ch'ien-i.* After the latter was prohibited during the Ch'ien-lung period, the *Ming-shih tsung* became the standard comprehensive selection of Ming verse, a position it still retains.

Chu I-tsun completed the compilation of the *Ming-shih tsung* in 1705, near the end of his life and after the enormous labor of preparing his bibliography of classical studies, the *Ching-i k'ao* 經義考. There had been earlier attempts at anthologies of Ming *shih,* going back at least to the huge *Sheng-Ming pai-chia shih* 盛明百家詩 compiled by Yü Hsien 俞憲 (prefaces dated 1570). But this collection did not, of course, cover the entire dynasty (which lasted until 1644) and the same was true of other somewhat later compilations such as the selection from Yü Hsien's work by Chu Chih-fan 朱之蕃, the *Ming pai-chia shih-hsüan* 選(1616), Li T'eng-p'eng's 李騰鵬 *Huang Ming shih-t'ung* 皇明詩統 (1591), and the published parts of the monumental *Shih-ts'ang li-tai shih-hsüan* 石倉歷代詩選 (1632) of Ts'ao Hsüeh-ch'üan 曹學佺. There were also two much more selective anthologies that appeared just at the end of the Ming, the remarkably well-balanced *Ming-shih hsüan-tsui* 明詩選最 (*c.* 1640) of Hua Shu 華淑 (reprinted as *Ming-jen hsüan Ming-shih* 明人選明詩) and Ch'en Tzu-lung's* *Huang Ming shih-hsüan* 皇明詩選, heavily biased in favor of the Archaist schools led by Li Meng-yang* and Li P'an-lung.* Finally, there was Ch'ien's *Lieh-ch'ao shih-chi* (1649), which was both comprehensive and the work of a dominant literary figure of his age.

That Ch'ien's anthology was eventually supplanted by the *Ming-shih tsung* was due in part to events beyond either compiler's control—Ch'ien posthumously became a *persona non grata* during the literary inquisition of the Ch'ien-lung period, and the republication of his work was forbidden—but it does appear that Chu I-tsun consciously set out to provide a "corrective" to what he saw as the defects of the earlier work, its anti-Archaist bias and its sometimes idiosyncratic method of selection. As a result, the two books complement each other in many ways. Where Ch'ien included many poems, sometimes several hundred, by each poet, but a smaller number of poets, Chu's anthology is broader in its coverage, but shallower in selection, consisting of works by over three thousand poets, the great majority of whom are represented by only one or two poems each. The selection of poems is greatly increased in value by an extensive collection of earlier critical comments on each poet, with Chu's own remarks appended in many cases. Useful as this supplementary material is, it must be handled with considerable care, for the sources are identified only by the surname and *tzu* of the original writer, and comparison of Chu's versions with the originals (where these can be identified) often reveals errors in transcription as well as silent revision and abridgment. All the same, Chu was able to correct some errors made by Ch'ien Ch'ien-i, whose opinions are not often explicitly cited, although they are occasionally found in somewhat disguised form. While Chu's selection is more balanced than Ch'ien's it is not immune to charges of bias itself, most notably in the inclusion of fifty-eight poems (only four other poets have more) by Chu Kuo-tso 朱國祚 (*chin-shih,* 1583), whose claim to such poetic importance, not recognized elsewhere, apparently lay chiefly in his having been Chu I-tsun's great-grandfather! These defects notwithstanding, the *Ming shih tsung* remains the most comprehensive and accessible anthology of Ming *shih* poetry.

EDITIONS:

Ming-shih tsung. 100 *chüan.* 2v. Rpt. Taipei, 1970. The only readily available edition; the woodblock text used for this reprint is not identified; there are signs of slight deletions, perhaps the results of the Literary Inquisition.

Jung, Keng 容庚. "Lun *Lieh-ch'ao shih-chi* yü *Ming-shih tsung,*" *Ling-nan hsüeh-pao,* ll.1 (1950), 135-166. An excellent and very detailed discussion of both anthologies.

—DB

Ming-wen heng 明文衡, compiled by Ch'eng Min-cheng 程敏政 (1445-1499), was the earliest important anthology of Ming-dynasty prose writings. Ch'eng, a *chin-shih* of 1466 and a member of the Han-lin Academy, wrote or compiled a number of works. The *Ming-wen heng* was intended as a selection of the best prose from the beginning of the dynasty down to the late fifteenth century. Since it covers a period neglected by most anthologies and literary historians and includes pieces by many writers whose work is otherwise difficult or impossible to consult, it is a valuable source, especially for the period after the first generation of Ming writers, such as Kao Ch'i.*

The contents of the *Ming-wen heng* are subdivided according to almost forty literary genres, including *fu** and *yüeh-fu,** but not other poetry, and arranged according to a roughly chronological sequence. Ch'eng's comprehensiveness and relative independence are shown by his inclusion of writings by Fang Hsiao-ju,* executed in 1402 after his defiant refusal to accept the successful usurpation of the throne by Emperor Chu. Ch'eng did, however, recognize Fang's ambiguous status by listing his works under his *tzu* rather than his formal name. A few works, by a variety of authors, listed in the table of contents are lacking in the text, for reasons that are unclear.

Since the *Ming-wen heng* covers only the first half of the Ming, there was a need for a more comprehensive anthology covering the entire dynasty. This need was answered by the great seventeenth-century scholar Huang Tsung-hsi* (1610-1695), who compiled the *Ming-wen hai* 海 during the period 1668 to 1693. Huang originally prepared a shorter collection, the *Ming-wen an* 案, but later expanded it to more than twice its original size on the basis of his reading in as many as two thousand Ming *wen-chi.*

EDITIONS:

Ch'eng, Min-cheng. *Ming-wen heng.* 100 *chüan.* Rpt. Taipei, 1962. The best and most accessible text; to the original 98 *chüan,* it adds 2 *chüan* of supplementary material, consisting of some of the works listed in the original table of contents but missing from the text. The same text is reprinted in the *SPTK.*

Huang Tsung-hsi. *Ming-wen hai.* 482 *chüan.* Rpt. *Ssu-k'u ch'üan-shu chen-pen,* Seventh Series. A good text, and the only one readily accessible.

—DB

Mu T'ien-tzu chuan 穆天子傳 (An Account [of the Travels] of Emperor Mu) is an anonymous historical romance in six *chüan* describing the journeys of the Chou-dynasty Emperor Mu (r. 1023-983 B.C.). The work was probably written during the first years of the fourth century B.C. but was lost until a copy was discovered in a tomb in 279 A.D. along with numerous other ancient works (a find comparable to the Ma-wang tui* cache).

Along with the *Shan-hai ching** the *Mu T'ien-tzu chuan* is often noted as an important precursor of Chinese fiction. However, the influence of the two works is very dissimilar. The laconic, enigmatic depictions of various mythical figures in the *Shan-hai ching* often served as the source for later, more elaborate fictional depictions—but the work itself contains no extended narratives or "fiction" as such. The *Mu T'ien-tzu chuan,* on the other hand, is a relatively unified piece which could be considered historical fiction. Moreover, it is the earliest extant work which treats a human, rather than mythical, protagonist. Its influence on later literature is twofold:

(1) the theme of a ruler meeting the goddess Hsi-wang-mu 西王母 was much imitated (most obviously in the several works on Emperor Wu of the Han meeting her—see *Han Wu-ti nei-chuan*); (2) the journey structure influenced early fictional works, other travel accounts, the quest type of *fu*,* and even *chang-hui hsiao-shuo* (see essay on Fiction). Rémi Mathieu in a recent study (p. 203) has also traced the work's role in subsequent Buddhist literature.

The first five chapters describe Emperor Mu's Western exodus. The original story-complex involved his journeys to the four corners of the empire, but most of the text of his other three expeditions has been lost. The final chapter describes the illness, death, and burial of a woman whom the emperor knew well, the lady Sheng Chi 盛姬. The first three chapters are most likely close to the original version of the text. The fourth seems to have been an early interpolation (before the text's burial). The fifth was probably composed shortly after the work was discovered in the third century A.D. The final chapter was also appended about this time, probably by the first editor and commentator, Kuo P'u 郭璞 (276-324), and is a reconstruction from other ancillary sources related to Emperor Mu's voyages to the East.

From a literary perspective, the most significant passages are those in which the Emperor meets Hsi-wang-mu at Yao-ch'ih 瑤池. Their exchange of promises and poems is a favorite motif of later authors. Hsi-wang-mu's acceptance of vassal status during this meeting supports those critics who have argued that the work has an underlying political significance—expressing in the time of disorder the wish for a reunification of the nation under a benevolent ruler such as Emperor Mu (further support for this thesis can be seen in certain variants found in the *SPTK* edition). Mathieu, however, believes the work originates in the oral tradition and that the current text is a stylized, court version of actual contacts between the Chou and the non-Chinese peoples of the Northwest. The emperor's *pa-chün* 八駿 (eight bayards) are also a popular subject of later poets and painters.

Following Kuo P'u's numerous other critics have worked on the text, most attempting to identify its geography. From their comments it seems that the current text (less than seven thousand Chinese characters) is about one-fourth shorter than that extant in Sung times.

EDITIONS:

Mu T'ien-tzu chuan. Kuo P'u, comm. Hung I-hsüan 洪頤煊 (1765-1837), coll. *SPPY*. A good version, but Hung did not have access to all early editions.

———. Kuo P'u, comm. Fan Ch'in 范欽 (1506-1585), ed. *SPTK*. Photolithographic reprint of the T'ien-i-ko 天一閣 edition.

Mu T'ien-tzu chuan hsi-cheng chiang-shu 穆天子傳西征講疏. Ku Shih 顧實, ed. Shanghai, 1934. Punctuated. Reproduces all principal commentaries. Best edition.

Mu T'ien-tzu chuan hsin-chu 穆天子傳新注.

TRANSLATIONS:

Cheng, Te-k'un. "The Travels of Emperor Mu," *JNCBRAS*, 64 (1933), 124-142 and 65 (1934), 128-149.

Eitel, E. J. "Mu-t'ien-tzu chuan," *China Review*, 17 (1888), 223-240, 247-258.

Mathieu, Rémi. *Le Mu tianzi zhuan, traduction annotée, étude critique.* Paris, 1978.

STUDIES:

Ch'ang, Cheng 常征. "*Mu T'ien-tzu chuan* shih wei-shu ma?" 穆天子傳是偽書嗎?, *Ho-pei Ta-hsüeh hsüeh-pao*, 1980.2, 30-53. Useful bibliography. Concludes that the work is not a forgery.

Hulsewé, A. F. P. "Texts in Tombs," *AS*, 18-19 (1965), 79-89.

Liang, Tzu-han 梁子涵. "*Mu T'ien-tzu chuan* tsa-k'ao" 穆天子傳雜考, *Kuo-li Chung-yang t'u-shu-kuan kuan-k'an*, 3.3-4 (October 1970), 56-67.

Mathieu, *Le Mu Tianzi zhuan* (see above).

Mitarai, Masaru 御手洗勝. "*Boku Tenshi den* seiritsu no haikei" 穆天子傳成立の背景, *Tōhōgaku*, 26 (1962), 17-30.

Pelliot, Paul. "L'Etude du *Mou t'ien tseu tchouan*," *TP*, 21 (1922), 98-102.

Tkei, F. "A Propos du genre du *Mou t'ien-tseu tchouan*," *AOr*, 9 (1958), 45-49.

Wei, T'ing-sheng 衛挺生. *Mu T'ien-tzu chuan chin-k'ao* 穆天子傳今考. 3v. Taipei, 1970. Incorporates material from Wei's earlier articles. Good bibliography. V. 1-2 most useful to literary study.

—WHN

Na-lan Hsing-te 納蘭性德 (original *ming*, Ch'eng-te 成德; *tzu*, Jung-jo 容若; *hao*, Leng-chia shan-jen 楞伽山人; 1655-1685) is widely acclaimed as a master of *tz'u** verse. He was born and raised in Peking; a member of the influential Yehe Nara 葉赫納蘭 clan, he enjoyed the very best that society had to offer. According to Manchu banner-records, his family traced its ancestry back to Turmed Mongol chieftains. His father Mingju 明珠 (1635-1708) rose to high office during the early years of the K'ang-hsi era and for a time wielded great power and influence at court. His mother was a daughter of Ajige 阿濟格 (1605-1651), Prince Ying 英, the twelfth son of the famous Manchu leader Nurhachi 努爾哈赤 (1559-1626). As a wealthy and politically powerful member of the conquest elite, Mingju occupied a great estate in the capital, where he profited enormously from the lucrative salt trade and cultivated his expensive tastes for ancient art treasures. Because of his wealth and cultured tastes, he arranged to have his sons tutored in traditional Chinese arts and letters by leading scholars of the time.

Na-lan Hsing-te had an active and enquiring mind, was studious by nature, and took an early interest in the literary arts. Excelling in his studies, he passed quickly up the civil-service-examination ladder, passing the *chü-jen* examination in 1673 and the *chin-shih* several years later, following his recovery from a bout of illness.

Because his family belonged to the Manchu Plain Yellow Banner, one of three from which the personnel of the imperial bodyguard was chosen, Na-lan Hsing-te was made a junior officer in that elite organization after passing the *chin-shih* examination. In that capacity, he was frequently required to accompany the K'ang-hsi Emperor on periodic excursions. In 1682, he accompanied an expedition to Albazin in the Amur region to investigate Russian incursions. Two years later, he was a member of the imperial retinue on the first of six grand tours K'ang-hsi made of the Yangtze River Valley.

When not in attendance at court, Na-lan Hsing-te enjoyed an active social and intellectual life. The private study in the Lu-shui 淥水 Pavilion on his father's estate was a welcome refuge from the cares of the courtier's life. There he indulged his scholarly interests and hosted gatherings of some of the leading literary figures of the day, such as Ch'en Wei-sung,* Chu I-tsun,* and Yen Sheng-sun 嚴繩孫 (1623-1702). It is clear from the testimony of friends and his own writings that he much preferred a life of scholarly retirement to the formality and decorum of the court or the rough-and-tumble world of national politics where his father was active. In 1684, he wrote to the leader of the Lan-hu she 蘭湖社 (Orchid Lake School) of Kwangtung poets, Liang P'ei-lan 梁佩蘭 (1632-1708), inviting him to come to Peking and participate in the compilation of an anthology of Northern and Southern Sung *tz'u*. However, the next summer, following a gathering of literary friends at his garden studio, Na-lan caught a chill. Though the emperor ordered that he be kept informed of his condition and sent his personal physicians to attend the young poet, he died seven days later, thus ending a promising political and literary career. His death was mourned by many prominent men of letters, for he had been a generous patron and friend, who had won affection by gaining the release from exile of the poet Wu Chao-ch'ien 吳兆騫 (1631-1684).

Na-lan Hsing-te's *tz'u* verse was published in 1678 or possibly earlier in two collections: the *Ts'e-mao tz'u* 側帽詞 (The Cocked Hat Song-lyrics), and the *Yin-shui tz'u* 飲水詞 (Drinking Water Song-lyrics). The latter collection was compiled by Na-lan's poet-friend Ku Chen-kuan 顧貞觀 (b. 1637) and the poet-official Wu Ch'i 吳綺 (1619-1694) and printed in 1678. As a result, he was immediately hailed as an accomplished writer at a time when the *tz'u* form was enjoying a remarkable revival. His contemporary Ch'en Wei-sung labeled him a successor to Li Yü (937-978).* His reputation has, if anything, grown with the years, and the modern critic Wang Kuo-wei* praised him lavishly: "Na-lan Jung-jo observed things with a natural vision and

634

described emotions in the patterns of natural speech . . . , and thus is his poetry genuine and incisive. Since Northern Sung times there has been only one such person like this." More recently, scholars have quite correctly called attention to the persistent note of melancholy that marks his *tz'u*, suggesting that it sprang either from the untimely death of his wife or an unfortunate love affair. Whatever the cause of his sadness and despair, which may have been nourished by his Buddhist leanings, this feeling of melancholy runs as a leitmotiv throughout his verse. It is voiced most strongly in the moving threnodies written in memory of his wife, but it also lingers in rather unexpected places. Some of his most frequently translated and anthologized poems derive from visits to the cold, wind-swept northern steppes, his ancestral homeland. These poems, however, do not evoke the spirit of a nomadic warrior returning to his native heath, but instead that of the cultured gentleman longing to return to the peaceful serenity of home and garden. His vision of the stark landscapes of the frontier region is therefore typically Chinese in its abhorrence of the unsettled, uncultured world beyond the Great Wall.

As a *tz'u* poet, Na-lan Hsing-te tended to identify with the early masters of the form. This is reflected in his preference for the *hsiao-ling* patterns, although he also made effective use of the longer *ch'ang-tiao* modes. By the same token, his *tz'u* poems are strongly lyrical in character. External scene and event serve mainly to illuminate and define the inner state of consciousness and emotion of the poet. This feature and their plain diction remind the reader of those poems which are assigned to the last period of Li Yü's life.

Na-lan Hsing-te's poems were collected and edited for publication by his friend and mentor Hsü Ch'ien-hsüeh 徐乾學 (1631-1694), a much respected scholar and official of the time. The *T'ung-chih-t'ang chi* 通志堂集 contains, in addition to his *tz'u* poetry, five *fu,** somewhat more than three hundred *shih** poems, and a number of prose prefaces which he wrote for the famous collectanea of classical scholarship of previous dynasties, the *T'ung-chih-t'ang ching-chieh* 經解, which seems to have been compiled under his personal sponsorship and the editorial supervision of Hsü Ch'ien-hsüeh. His collected works also include a number of casual prose recordings of his impressions as a student and general reader, all gathered under the title *Lu-shui T'ang tsa-chih* 渌水堂雜識 (Miscellaneous Records of Pure-Water Pavilion).

When writing *shih*, Na-lan Hsing-te favored the compact heptasyllabic quatrain—approximately half of his *shih* are in that form. Some are command verse, as would be expected of a member of the court. Among those which served less formal occasions, whether quatrains or in some other form, such as the pentasyllabic ancient-style poem which he also favored, there is perhaps more diversity of theme than is the case with his *tz'u*, but in diction, general tone, and spirit they often echo the qualities typical of the *tz'u*. There is, therefore, a fairly high degree of consistency in his poetry, whatever genre he elected to use at a given moment.

Na-lan Hsing-te occupies a prominent place in Chinese letters of the seventeenth century, and his personal contribution to the revival of the *tz'u* tradition at that time is one measure of his importance.

EDITIONS:

T'ung-chih-t'ang chi. 2v. Shanghai, 1979.
Li, Hsü 李勖, ed. *Yin-shui tz'u chien* 飲水詞箋. Taipei, 1959. In addition to the *tz'u* with annotations, this volume contains biographical and critical materials.

TRANSLATIONS:

Ayling, *Collection*, pp. 205-209. See also *Further Collection*, pp. 193-195.
Birch, *Anthology*, v. 2, pp. 143-149.
Demiéville, *Anthologie*, pp. 547-549.
Soong, Stephen C. *Song Without Music: Chinese Tz'u Poetry.* Hong Kong, 1980, pp. 252-264.
Sunflower, pp. 482-486.

STUDIES:

Su, Hsüeh-lin 蘇雪林. "Ch'ing-tai nan-nü ta tz'u-jen lien-shih ti yen-chiu" 清代男女大詞人戀史的研究, *Wu-ta wen-che chi-k'an*, 1.3 (October 1930), 525-564; 1.4 (January 1931), 715-745.

Yin-shui tz'u-chi. Hong Kong, 1963. With an introduction by Hu Yün-i 胡雲翼.

—ws

Nan-hsi 南戲, generally refers to pre-Ming Southern drama which began as regional entertainment some time in the twelfth century in the Yung-chia 永嘉 area of Southeast China (modern Wen-chou 溫州, Chekiang)—hence, its early name *Yung-chia tsa-chü* 永嘉雜劇, or *Wen-chou tsa-chü* 溫州雜劇. The term *nan-hsi* is sometimes used loosely in the broad sense of "the Southern style of drama," especially when the time reference is extended beyond the early Ming to include *ch'uan-ch'i,** the later sophisticated variety of Southern drama. Synonymous with the narrower meaning of *nan-hsi* is the earlier term *hsi-wen* 戲文, misinterpreted by Wang Kuo-wei* as a separate entity and precursor of *nan-hsi.* *Hsi-wen,* or *nan-hsi,* was also referred to as *ch'uan-ch'i* in the Sung and the Yüan. Two more labels, *nan-tz'u* 南詞 and *nan-ch'ü* 南曲, with all their multiplicity of meanings, have been used by traditional Chinese scholars to denote Southern drama as a whole, of which *nan-hsi* (in its narrower sense) is of course a part. *Nan-hsi* probably began as a marriage of local folk songs and ballads "of the alleys" with the Northern Sung tradition of *tsa-chü* "variety shows." As the genre evolved it borrowed its musical structure from a variety of sources.

Exactly when *nan-hsi* came into full being is a matter of controversy. Some scholars accept Chu Yün-ming's 祝允明 (1461-1527) statement that it arose between 1119 and 1127; others tend to follow Hsü Wei* in placing its emergence around 1190-1194. According to Hsü, the first two notable Southern plays were *Chao Chen-nü* 趙貞女 and *Wang K'uei* 王魁. Both are now lost; both allegedly depicted the scholar-official class in a rather poor light (in each the hero's infidelity leads to his wife's death). In the first work the male lead, Ts'ai Yung 蔡邕, after success in the examination deserts his wife, Chao Chen-nü, in favor of the daughter of a grand councilor. He is eventually struck down by lightning as a sign of divine retribution.

The plot of the second play is quite similar. Wang K'uei meets the courtesan Kuei-ying 桂英 at a time when the aspiring scholar is down on his luck. Kuei-ying sees much promise in Wang and helps him become successful in the examinations. As soon as he passes the examinations, Wang forget his oath and marries a wealthy woman proposed by his father. Eventually Kuei-ying commits suicide. Her ghost comes to haunt Wang and he dies, it is implied, from this haunting.

Another lost play, *Wang Huan* 王煥, was based on a contemporary political scandal and was banned by the authorities. *Nan-hsi* continued to flourish as a regional form throughout the Sung and Yüan. In the 1360s it was firmly established on the literary scene due to the quality of Kao Ming's* *P'i-p'a chi,* whose elegant language and dramaturgical sophistication ushered in new standards of Southern drama—indeed, a new genre, the *ch'uan-ch'i.*

About 170 titles of Yüan and early Ming *nan-hsi* are now known. Of these some 20 are extant plays, while excerpts from about 120 titles are preserved in varions *ch'ü* formularies. Recent studies of the fifteenth-century (?) *Feng-yüeh chin-nang* 風月錦囊 anthology (preserved only in the Escorial in Spain) have uncovered some works and titles hitherto unnoticed by scholars. Perhaps the best known complete *nan-hsi* are *Chang Hsieh chuang-yüan* 張協狀元, *Huan-men tzu-ti ts'o li shen* 宦門子弟錯立身, and *Hsiao Sun-t'u* 小孫屠, contained in *chüan* 13991 of the now mostly lost Ming collectanea *Yung-lo ta-tien*

The roles in *nan-hsi* (mainly *sheng* 生, *tan* 旦, *wai* 外, *ch'ou* 丑, *ching* 淨, *mo* 末) are not as many, nor as well-defined, as those in Yüan *tsa-chü** or in *ch'uan-ch'i* (see *chiao-se*). *Nan-hsi* are introduced by the *mo* 末 (a male supporting role comparable to the *fu-mo* 副 of Yüan *tsa-chü*) who provides a short summary of the plot in one or two poems. This introduction later developed into the *chia-men* 家門 of *ch'uan-ch'i.* In most plays, following the *mo's* exit the *sheng* (male lead) enters and his presence signifies the beginning of drama proper. As in Northern drama, spoken passages and arias alternate, and even the language of the songs tends to be very colloquial.

Other *nan-hsi* features inherited by the *ch'uan-ch'i* are the roles all being entitled to sing and the practice of sharing an aria or suite by two or more singers. The musical conventions of the drama were apparently less strict than in the case of Ming *ch'uan-ch'i*. The themes are taken from popular tales or history; many titles are similar to those of Yüan *tsa-chü* or *ch'uan-ch'i*. For example, the so-called *Ssu-ta ch'uan-ch'i,** *Ching-ch'ai chi*, *Pai-t'u chi*, *Pai-yüeh t'ing*, and *Sha-kou chi*, all have predecessors in earlier *nan-hsi* or Yüan *tsa-chü* with slightly different titles.

Being the work of amateur writers (including those belonging to *shu-hui**) and written for the entertainment of a popular audience, the language of pre-Ming *nan-hsi* was generally earthy and sometimes vulgar. The only notable early critic of *nan-hsi* was Hsü Wei, who saw in the very earthiness of language a naturalness that was a refreshing contrast to the linguistic artificiality plaguing the *ch'uan-ch'i* of his own day. Indeed, he catalogued the *nan-hsi* that he knew of and collected information about them in the *Nan-tz'u hsü lu* 南詞敘錄. As a result of the general ignorance of *nan-hsi*, prejudice and confusion characterized Ming and Ch'ing views of Southern drama: it was generally thought that Southern drama was a product evolved from Yüan *tsa-chü*. Not until the 1930s, after the discovery in London (1920) of the lost *chüan* of the *Yung-lo ta-tien*, did modern scholars begin a systematic study of *nan-hsi*. Some scholars indeed believe that early *nan-hsi* in Wen-chou might well have been the earliest form of Chinese drama.

STUDIES:

Chao, Ching-shen 趙景深. *Sung-Yüan hsi-wen pen-shih* 宋元戲文本事. Shanghai, 1934.

———. *Yüan-Ming nan-hsi k'ao lüeh* 元明南戲考略. Peking, 1958.

———. "Ming Ch'eng-jua pen nan-hsi 'Pai-t'u chi' te hsin fa-hsien" 明成化本南戲 '白兔記' 的新發現, *Wen-wu*, 1 (1973), 44-47.

———. Li P'ing 李平, and Chiang Chü-jung 江巨榮. "Chung-kuo hsi-chü hsing-ch'eng te shih-tai wen-t'i" 中國戲劇形成的時代問題, in

Ku-tien wen-hsüeh lun ts'ung 古典文學論叢, Chang Chih-che 張志哲, ed., Shanghai, 1980, pp. 119-137.

Ch'ien, Nan-yang 錢南揚. "Sung-Yüan nan-hsi k'ao" 宋元南戲考, *Yenching Journal of Chinese Studies*, 7 (1930), 1381-1409.

———. "Chang Hsieh hsi-wen chung te liang chuang chung-yao ts'ai-liao" 張協戲文中的兩椿重要材料, *Quarterly Journal of Liberal Arts* (Wuhan University), 2 (1931), 137-144.

———. *Sung-Yüan nan-hsi pai-i lu* 宋元南戲百一錄. Peiping, 1934.

———. "Sung-Chin-Yüan hsi-chü pan-yen k'ao" 宋金元戲劇搬演考, *Yenching Journal of Chinese Studies*, 20 (1936), 177-194.

———. *Sung-Yüan hsi-wen chi-i* 宋元戲文輯佚. Shanghai, 1956.

———. *Hsi-wen kai-lun* 戲文概論. Peking, 1981.

Hsü, Wei 徐渭. *Nan-tz'u hsü lu* 南詞敘錄, in *Chung-kuo ku-tien hsi-ch'ü lun-chu chi-ch'eng* 中國古典戲曲論著集成. Peking, 1959.

Hu, Hsüeh-kang 胡雪岡 and Hsü Shun-p'ing 徐順平. "T'an tsao-ch'i nan-hsi te chi-ke wen-t'i" 談早期南戲的幾個問題, *Hsi-chü i-shu* 戲劇藝術, 2 (1980), 87-99.

Leung, Kai-cheong. "Hsü Wei as Dramatic Critic: An Annotated Translation of the *Nan-tz'u hsü lu*." Unpublished Ph.D. dissertation, University of California, Berkeley, 1974.

Liu, James J. Y. "The *Feng-yüeh chin-nang*: A Ming Collection of Yüan and Ming Plays and Lyrics Preserved in the Royal Library of San Lorenzo, Escorial, Spain," *Journal of Oriental Studies*, 4 (1957-58), 79-107.

Lo, Chin-t'ang 羅錦堂. *Chin-t'ang lun ch'ü* 錦堂論曲. Taipei, 1977.

Lu, K'an-ju 陸侃如 and Feng Yüan-chün 馮沅君. *Nan-hsi shih-i* 南戲拾遺. Peiping, 1936.

Yeh, Te-chün 葉德均. "Ming-tai nan-hsi wu ta ch'iang-tiao chi ch'i chih-liu" 明代南戲五大腔調及其流, in his *Hsi-ch'ü hsiao-shuo ts'ung-k'ao* 戲曲小說叢考, Peking, 1979, pp. 1-67.

Zbikowski, Tadeusz. *Early Nan-hsi Plays of the Southern Sung Period.* Warsaw, 1974. The only work available in English, but not reliable.

—KCL and JDS

Nan-pei-kung tz'u-chi 南北宮詞紀 (Compilation of Song Verses in Northern and Southern Styles), compiled by Ch'en So-wen 陳所聞 (*tzu*, Chin-ch'ing 藎卿, *fl.* 1596), is one of the important anthologies of *san-ch'ü* 散曲 assembled and published during the Wan-li era (1573-1620) of the Ming

637

dynasty. The original edition was published in two parts, the first entitled *Hsin-chien ku-chin ta-ya Nan-kung tz'u-chi* 新鐫古今大雅南北宮詞紀 (The Grand, Elegant, Newly Printed Compilation of Song Verses Old and New in the Southern Style) and the second, *Pei-kung tz'u-chi* 北宮詞紀 (Compilation of Song Verses in the Northern Style). Each part contains six sections and has a separately dated preface: the former is dated 1605 and the latter, 1604. The northern style dominated *ch'ü** writing during Yüan times, a fact borne out by the large number of Yüan poets (126) represented in the *Pei-kung tz'u-chi*, compared to the mere two in the *Nan-kung tz'u-chi*. Southern style *ch'ü* became more popular during the Ming dynasty, and the figures for Ming poets writing in the two styles are more balanced: eighty poets are represented in the northern style and seventy-four in the southern style. The contents are organized according to general themes such as "Chu ho" 祝賀 (In Congratulations).

EDITIONS:

Nan-pei-kung tz'u-chi. Shanghai, 1959. The work was reprinted in 1959 under the editorship of Chao Ching-shen 趙景深. Chao based his edition on the text in the Shanghai Library, all of which were printed after the Wan-li period and were in poor condition; at that time no copies of the Wan-li original were known. With the aid of a dozen other *san-ch'ü* anthologies, he was able to reconstruct missing, imperfectly printed, and fragmented pages. Shortly after publication, however, two parts of the original edition came to light—one entered the Peking Library collection after the death of the scholar Cheng Chen-to 鄭振鐸, and another was owned by Wu Hsiao-ling 吳曉鈴. Using the Peking Library edition, Sui Shu-san 隋樹森 collaborated with Wu Hsiao-ling in the 1961 (Shanghai) publication of the *Nan-pei-kung tz'u-chi chiao-pu* 南北宮詞紀校補 (The Revised Supplement to the Compilation Song Verses in the Northern and Southern Style), a one-volume work, to which Wu appended a supplemental anthology entitled *Pei-Kung tz'u-chi wai-chi* 北宮詞紀外集 (A Supplemental Anthology of Regulations for Song Verses in the Northern Style). The supplemental anthology contains poetry in the northern style by Yüan and Ming poets that was not a part of the original work. Of particular interest in this anthology and the Supplemental Anthology are the sections on humor, satire and jest, a category not well-defined in the genres earlier then the *san-ch'ü*. The edition is bound in traditional Chinese style and printed on paper of excellent quality, and the printing is extremely beautiful.

—DJ

Ou-yang Chiung 歐陽炯 (*tzu*, unknown, 896-971) was a native of Hua-yang 華陽 in I-chou 益州 (Szechwan). The most productive part of his career was spent in Szechwan as an ornament of the courts of Earlier and Later Shu 蜀 in the tenth century. He also served the Late T'ang and, at the end of his career, the new rulers of Sung. He was distinguished as a Han-lin Academician by Meng Ch'ang 孟昶 of Later Shu, and was raised to Privy Councillor by the same king in 961. When, in 965, his master was obliged to bow to the might of Sung, he accompanied him into honorable captivity. After the final consolidation of the Sung empire with the fall of Canton in 971, T'ao Tsung proposed to send him thither to make sacrifices, but he avoided the commission on the pretext of illness. The irritated sovereign terminated his court appointments. Ou-yang Chiung died later in the same year, at the age of seventy-five.

The poet was reputed to have a candid and unreserved nature; he was a skilled flautist, and often did command performances for the founder of Sung. His reputation in early Sung times was more as a successful administrator than as a writer—indeed his official biography makes rather light of his achievements in the literary arts.

Few of his poems in the *shih** form survive; most notable among them are two ekphrases—that is, odes on works of plastic art. Both describe his reactions to Buddhist paintings, of which the more significant is a characterization of the celebrated arhat monochromes painted by his distinguished fellow-courtier in Szechwan, the great prelate Kuan-hsiu.* But Ou-yang Chiung's chief legacy is the extant body of his compositions in the *tz'u** forms. This small corpus contains, along with a few others, nine poems in the *Ch'un-kuang hao* 春光好 form, four each in the *P'u-sa man* 菩薩蠻 form and in the *Mu-lan hua* 木蘭花 form, and eight in the *Nan-hsiang tzu* 南鄉子 form. The last of these may be taken as examples of his best and most original art. Together with the compositions of Li Hsün 李珣 in the same mode they injected new and vitalizing flavor into Chinese literature—the exoticism of the partially assimilated tropical south. For the first time such images as palm-leaf mats, cardamom flowers, laughing wenches clad in dawn-pink dresses and golden earrings, in an atmosphere of unconventional witchery, adapted to a pattern familiar in other *tz'u* scenarios—hope, uneasy transition, initiation, and the expectation of bliss—become a part of the literary heritage of China.

Beyond this, there is a debt to Ou-yang Chiung for the preface of the first anthology of *tz'u*, the *Hua-chien chi*,* whose lucky survival is the foundation of all of our knowledge of a unique and brilliant epoch in Chinese literature.

EDITIONS:

Chao, Ch'ung-tso 趙崇祚. *Sung Shao-hsing pen Hua-chien chi fu chiao-chu* 宋紹興本花間集附校注. Taipei, 1974.

Ch'üan T'ang shih, v. 11, *ch.* 761, pp. 8638-8640.

Ch'üan T'ang wen, v. 18, *ch.* 891, pp. 11739-11740.

TRANSLATIONS:

Chen, Shih-chuan. *Chinese Lyrics from the Eighth to the Twelfth Centuries*. Taipei, 1969, pp. 26-28.

Hsü, *Anthologie*, p. 193.

Schafer, E. H. "The Capeline Cantos," *AS*, 32 (1978), 54-55.

———, *Vermilion Bird*, pp. 84, 85, 260.

—ES

Ou-yang Hsiu 歐陽修 (*tzu*, Yung-shu 永叔, 1007-1072), advocate of a free style of prose (see *ku-wen*), historian, epigraphist, statesman, and leading personality of his time, was brought up after the early death of his father in an isolated area of what is now Hupei. Studying mostly by himself, he came across the almost forgotten writings of Han Yü,* whose ideologically moti-

vated dislike of the embellished style of prose (*p'ien-wen**) and Confucian ardor left a deep impression on Ou-yang Hsiu.

Having passed the *chin-shih* examination in 1030, he started a long and highly successful career as a minor official in Lo-yang, leaving him many leisure hours for contacts with eminent scholars like the essayist Yin Shu* and the famous poet Mei Yao-ch'en.* His lifelong engagement in politics and administration, his vital and open personality, and his firm Confucian convictions lend his writings a striking diversity, ranging from love poems through monographs on the cultivation of peonies to official documents.

In his politico-philosophical dissertations, such as "Pen lun" 本論 (On Fundamentals) and treatises on the classics, such as "Ch'un-ch'iu" 春秋論 (On the *Spring and Autumn Annals*), Ou-yang Hsiu presents himself as a pragmatic rationalist and exegetical fundamentalist, both attitudes unfavorable for any metaphysical reevaluation of established Confucian values. His most provocative thesis—set up in "P'eng-tang lun" 朋黨論 (On Factions)—that forming a political faction is not improper, was more an ad hoc political measure than a philosophical position.

His main works as historian (he wrote or edited much of the *Hsin T'ang-shu* 新唐書 [New T'ang History] and compiled single-handedly the *Hsin Wu-tai-shih* 新五代史 [New History of the Five Dynasties]) suffer from an overdidactic and overinterpretative approach, as well as from stylistic rigorism, which resulted in an arbitrary selection of facts and events presented, and in the summarizing and shortening of official documents, written in an embellished style which he disliked. His greatest contribution to historiography, however, was the *Chi-ku-lu pa-wei* 集古錄跋尾 (Postscripts to Collected Ancient Inscriptions), containing historically relevant commentaries on almost four hundred inscriptions from the beginning of the Chou down to the Five Dynasties. This product of a hobby established epigraphy as a prime tool in historical research.

Ou-yang Hsiu must also be regarded as a pioneer in the field of poetics. His "Liu-

639

i shih-hua" 六一詩話 (Talks on Poetry of Mr. One-six [Hsiu's pen name]) is a loosely arranged *causerie* on poets and poetry, through which he created a new literary genre. To write *shih-hua* in the manner of epigraphical studies immediately became a fashionable pastime among Sung scholars.

The more belletristic of Ou-yang Hsiu's writings are his poems, *fu,* * and prose pieces. Though his poems in the *lü-shih* (see *shih*) and *tz'u* * forms differ by their naturalness and readability from the more manneristic pieces of the then popular Hsi-k'un* and Hua-chien Schools (see *Hua-chien chi*), they don't reveal distinctly new or individual traits. This is also true of his numerous erotic *tz'u*, for love at this time still belonged to the common themes of this young lyrical genre. Highly remarkable, however, are some of his prose writings and several of the less stringently controlled *fu* and old-style poems (see *shih*), which traditionally allow a wider range of content. Here we find a new, almost scientific interest in the manifold things and matters of the phenomenal world, combined with a subtle humor and a tranquil, sometimes stoical serenity. This is displayed with a marked tendency to avoid ornate language and stylistic monotony. Thus many of the old-style poems—especially those written in his later years—contain interspersed irregular lines. Some of the *fu*—for example, the famous "Ch'iu-sheng fu" 秋聲賦 (The Sounds of Autumn)—contain prose passages as well as numerous changes of meter and rhyme which are similar to the original *fu* form. On the other hand, his prose essays, such as the "Ts'ui-weng-t'ing chi" 醉翁亭記 (The Pavilion of the Old Drunkard), make occasional use of parallelism, the main characteristic of *p'ien-wen*, as a deliberate stylistic device.

Aside from a genuine appreciation of the literary merits of his writings, Ou-yang Hsiu's lasting renown as one of China's outstanding prose masters was built also on the *Zeitgeist*, and on his own political influence and personal courage which enabled him to promote *ku-wen** as the dominant prose style. Next to his prose, he is esteemed for his poetry—his fame as thinker and historian is overshadowed by personalities such as Chu Hsi 朱熹 (1130-1200) and Ssu-ma Kuang 司馬光 (1019-1086).

EDITIONS:

Liu-i shih-hua 六一詩話, in *Li-tai shih-hua* 歷代詩話, Ho Wen-huan 何文煥, comp. Taipei, 1956, v. 1, pp. 156-162.

Liu-i chü-shih shih-hua 六一居士詩話, in *PPTSCC*, series 2: *Pai-ch'uan hsüeh-hai* 百川學海, v. 97.

Liu-i tz'u 六一詞, [bound with *Erh-yen tz'u* 二晏詞], ed. Yang Chia-lo 楊家駱. Taipei, 1962.

Ou-yang Hsiu ch'üan-chi 歐陽修全集. 2v. Taipei, 1961; *Chung-kuo hsüeh-shu ming-chu* edition. Like the *SPPY* and *SPTK* editions, based upon the *Wen-chung chi* 文忠集 edited by Chou Pi-ta (1126-1204). It includes a *nien-p'u* and a supplement with funeral odes, epitaphs, etc. on Ou-yang Hsiu. This edition has modern punctuation and lists variants; it is reliable and readily available.

Ou-yang Wen-chung-kung wen-chi 歐陽文忠公文集. *SPTK*. This unpunctuated edition, gives more variants than the two mentioned above.

Shih, P'ei-i 施培毅, comp. *Ou-yang Hsiu shih-hsüan* 歐陽修詩選. Ho-fei, 1982.

Ts'ai, Mao-hsiung 蔡茂雄, coll. and comm. *Liu-i tz'u chiao-chu* 六一詞校注. Taipei, 1969.

Tu, Wei-mo 杜維沫 and Ch'en Hsin 陳新, comps. *Ou-yang Hsiu wen hsüan* 歐陽修文選. Peking, 1982. Contains about 60 pieces.

TRANSLATIONS:

Ayling, *Collection*, pp. 93-105.

Demiéville, *Anthologie*, pp. 340-341, 382-383.

Egan, Ronald C. *The Literary Works of Ou-yang Hsiu (1007-72)*. Cambridge, England, 1984.

Liu, *Lyricists*, pp. 33-52.

Olbricht, P. "Elf Gedichte von Ou-yang Hsiu," in *Studia Sino-Altaica—Festschrift E. Haenisch*, Wiesbaden, 1961, pp. 93-105.

Sunflower, pp. 325-332.

STUDIES:

Chang, Chien 張健. *Ou-yang Hsiu chih shih-wen chi wen-hsüeh p'ing-lun* 歐陽修之詩文及文學評論. Taipei, 1973.

Chaves, *Mei Yao-ch'en*, pp. 9-11, 25-26, 70-71, 74ff., 76-79, 81ff., 98-100, 109ff. Gives much information about Ou-yang Hsiu's views on poetry and poets.

Chen, Y. S., "The Literary Theory and Practice of Ou-yang Hsiu," in *Chinese Approaches*, pp. 67-96. Includes a translation and psychological interpretation of the "Ts'ui-weng-t'ing chi" and several poems.

Egan, *The Literary Works.*

Huang, Kung-chu 黃公渚. *Ou-yang Hsiu tz'u-hsüan i* 歐陽修詞選譯. Peking, 1958.

Kung-an 躬庵. "Ou-yang Hsiu Chi ch'i tz'u" 歐陽修及其詞, *Wen-shih-che*, 1958.1 (January 1958), 6-12.

Lapina, Z. G. "Recherches Epigraphiques de Ou-yang Hsiu," *Etudes Song / Song Studies*, Ser. II, 1980, pp. 99-111.

Li, Ch'i 李栖. *Ou-yang Hsiu tz'u yen-chiu chi ch'i chiao chu* 歐陽修詞研究其及校注. Taipei, 1982.

Liu, J. T. C. *Ou-yang Hsiu: An Eleventh-century Neo-Confucianist.* Stanford, 1967. An abridged English version of the following.

Liu, Tzu-chien 劉子健. *Ou-yang Hsiu te chih-hsüeh yü ts'ung-cheng* 歐陽修的治學與從政. Hong Kong, 1963.

P'ei, P'u-hsien 裴普賢. *Ou-yang Hsiu Shih pen-i yen-chiu* 歐陽修詩本義研究. Taipei, 1981.

SB, pp. 808-816.

Tanaka, Kenji 田中謙二. "O Yōshū no chi ni tsuite" 歐陽修の詞について, *Tōhōgaku*, 7 (1953), 50-62.

Ts'ai, Shih-ming 蔡世明. *Ou-yang Hsiu te sheng-p'ing yü hsüeh-shu* 歐陽修的生平與學術. Taipei, 1980.

Wals, Karl. "Biographie des Ou-Yang Hsiu." Unpublished Ph.D. dissertation, Rheinischen Friedrich-Wilhelms University, Bonn, 1983.

—RVF

Pa-ku wen 八股文 (eight-legged essay or composition in eight limbs) is a generic term for a certain type of classical-prose essay which became the prescribed form of composition for the civil-service examinations during the Ming and Ch'ing periods. *Pa-ku wen* refers to the primary feature of this essay form: its division into a fixed number of rhetorical units constructed on the principle of strict parallelism, although the precise structure required was subject to considerable variation. Since the exegetical and compositional skills demanded for this exercise constituted the core of the education of virtually all literati in Ming and Ch'ing China, the impact of this essay form across a wide range of late imperial cultural activities is predictably great.

The *pa-ku* essay consisted of an exposition, in the prescribed form, of the meaning of the examination-topic set for a given examination. The examination-topic was normally a quotation no more than several words in length drawn from the Five Classics, or more often, the Four Books of the Confucian canon (hence the alternate designation *Ssu-shu wen* 四書文 [Four Books Essay]). In an essay of from three-hundred to six-hundred words (the length variously stipulated at different times), the candidate was expected to demonstrate his recognition of the passage cited, his ability to recall the original context of the passage, his familiarity with the relevant orthodox commentaries, and his ability to elaborate upon the full meaning of the text in question—in addition to his mastery of the form itself. In general, the essay set a premium on lucid, forceful prose, but in time, especially during the Ch'ing, the use of rhetorical flourishes was also prescribed, including such things as the employment of metrical patterns.

Descriptions of the structure of the *pa-ku* essay vary according to different observers. Generally speaking, this structure is conceived as a methodical treatment of the examination topic through a carefully phased set of parallel arguments. In its paradigmatic form, the essay begins with an introductory statement consisting of two parallel sentences (known as the *p'o-t'i* 破題 [breaking open the topic]), in which the candidate was expected to indicate immediately his full grasp of the original context while avoiding any direct citation of the adjacent text. In the second section (known as *ch'eng-t'i* 承題 [carrying forward the topic]) the writer would elaborate on his opening statement to a length of from three to as many as five of seven sentences, leading up to a clear definition of the intention of the sage-author of the classical passage. In both of these initial sections, the candidate was enjoined to speak in the voice of the original sage (*tai sheng-hsien li-yen* 代聖賢立言), a rhetorical posture supported by the mandatory use of classical exclamatory particles to evoke the sage's unalloyed earnestness. At this point, the candidate would turn to his own voice to restate the basic meaning of the topic-citation in a transitional section called *ch'i-chiang* 起講 (opening statement). In some but not all cases, this unit would conclude with an additional transitional section called *ling-t'i* 領題 (taking up the topic), in which the words of the examination-topic themselves are brought back into focus.

The following four sections constitute the body of the essay, made up of a series of double-units composed in strict parallel construction. The first of these double-units, the *ch'i-ku* 起股 (opening limb) presents the first main exposition of the candidate's interpretation of the meaning of the passage. This is followed by the *hsü-ku* 虛股 (empty limb), a brief relaxation of the rhetorical momentum of the essay which provides a summation of the state of the argument, before plunging into the *chung-ku* 中股 (central limb) which presents the fullest exposition of the ideas of the piece. After this comes the *hou-ku* 後股 (last limb), which functions to tie the loose ends of the writer's arguments in the body of the essay, followed by a formal conclusion section known as the *ta-chieh* 大結.

Most scholars explain the meaning of the term *pa-ku* as a reference not to the eight sections outlined above, but to the eight parallel parts ("limbs") of the four double-units of the body of the essay (sometimes termed *pi* 比, as distinguished from *ku*). On the other hand, in view of the fact that it was quite common for the structure of the *pa-ku* essay to consist of either less or more than eight such units (or, four double-units), it is preferable to understand the term as a loose designation for this type of examination essay.

The specific structure of the *pa-ku* essay form is considered by most scholars to have consolidated during the Ch'eng-hua era (1465-1488) of the Ming, particularly at the examination of the year 1487. Of course, the use of an exegetical examination on the Confucian classics as the major medium for the state examinations can be traced at least as far back as the T'ang, and by the Sung the specific use of an essay on an examination-topic drawn from the classics was institutionalized in the so-called *ching-i* 經義 essays (a term which remained in usage to refer to the *pa-ku* in later periods). This practice was continued under the Yüan, at which time the examination-topic came to be limited primarily to the Four Books based on Chu Hsi's commentary, and the institution was reaffirmed at the time of the founding of the Ming. In view of this continuous development, some scholars point to particular extant essays by such figures as Wang An-shih* and Chang T'ing-chien 張庭堅 of the Sung and Huang Tzu-ch'eng 黃子澄 (1350-1402) of the early Ming as incipient examples of *pa-ku wen*. But it was only in 1487 and thereafter that a format such as that outlined above became prescribed as the exclusive form for the examination essay. This does not mean, however, that the form of the *pa-ku* remained static after that point. In addition to the margin of variation noted above for individual essays, literary historians have attempted to trace certain phases of development in *pa-ku* styles in general, trends which appear to roughly parallel the corresponding periods and movements in classical prose style during the Ming and Ch'ing.

The importance of the *pa-ku wen* in the development of late-imperial literary culture cannot be overestimated. By the late Ming and early Ch'ing, the composition of *pa-ku* essays was regarded not only as a necessary formal exercise, but as a major genre of literary prose in its own right (in this latter sense, it was often referred to as *shih-wen* 時文 [contemporary prose] or *shih-i* 時藝 [contemporary literary-art]). At this time, the practice of publishing collections of successful examination essays for the benefit of up-and-coming candidates was extended to include the compilation of anthologies of outstanding essays as examples of a serious literary form. Numerous contemporary critics, among them Li Chih* and Li Yü,* pointed with varying degrees of enthusiasm to the *pa-ku* as perhaps the major form of Ming literary expression. Given the central role of the *pa-ku* in the process of acquiring literacy, it is not surprising that its influence is observable in a number of areas of literature. In addition to the symbiosis that developed between the *pa-ku* (*shih-wen*) and more conventional forms of classical prose art (*ku-wen**), the structural principles of *pa-ku* composition can also be traced in colloquial narrative, and even in the area of poetry, as demonstrated by the use of technical terms of *pa-ku* analysis in the relation drawn between *pa-ku wen* and dramatic art, with respect to the use of metrics noted above, as well as to the development of a type of dramatic voice within the essays. The privileged position of the *pa-ku* made it subject to widespread abuse and debasement, but in its best examples it represented some of the resources of classical Chinese prose as a vehicle of serious intellectual discourse.

EDITIONS:

Chih-i t'i-yao 制藝體要. Ch'en Chao-lun 陳兆崙, ed. Preface 1877. Collection of Ch'ing *pa-ku wen* with critical annotation.

Ch'in-ting Ssu-shu-wen 欽定四書文. Fang Pao 方苞, ed. *Ssu-k'u ch'üan-shu chen-pen* 四庫全書珍本, Series 9, v. 325-340. Taipei, 1979. Fullest extant collection of major *pa-ku* essays of Ch'ing period.

Ming Wen-hai 明文海. Huang Tsung-hsi 黃宗羲, ed. *Ssu-k'u ch'üan-shu chen-pen*, Series 7, v. 313-388. Taipei, 1977. *Ch.* 307-313 devoted to selections of *pa-ku wen*.

STUDIES:

Chou, Tso-jen 周作人. *Chung-kuo chin-tai wen-hsüeh shih-hua* 中國近代文學史話. Hong Kong, 1955. See esp. ch. 3, "Ch'ing-tai wen-hsüeh te fan-tung" 清代文學的反動, and the Appendix, "Lun pa-ku wen" 論八股文. Transcriptions of lectures including rare open-minded evaluation of significance of *pa-ku*.

Liang, Jung-jo 梁容若. "T'an *pa-ku wen*" 談八股文, in *Kuo-yü yü kuo-wen* 國語與國文, Taipei, 1961, pp. 57-62.

Lu, Ch'ien 盧前. *Pa-ku hsiao-shih* 八股小史. Shanghai, 1937.

Shang, Yen-liu 商衍鎏. *Ch'ing-tai k'e-chü k'ao-shih shu-lu* 清代科舉考試述錄. Peking, 1958, pp. 227-287. Thorough treatment of subject by authority on imperial examination system.

Sung, P'ei-wei 宋佩韋. *Ming wen-hsüeh-shih* 明文學史. Shanghai, 1934, pp. 204-245. Most comprehensive treatment of *pa-ku wen* as literary form.

Tseng, Po-hua 曾伯華. *Pa-ku wen yen-chiu* 八股文研究. Taipei, 1970. Popular, but useful review of the subject.

Tu, Ching-i. "The Chinese Examination Essay: Some Literary Considerations," *MS*, 3.1 (1975), 393-406. Good review of *pa-ku* in English.

Yokota, Terutoshi 横田輝俊. "Yakōbun ni tsuite" 八股文 について, *Bungaku* (Hiroshima University Studies, Literature Department), 24.3 (March 1965), 144-160.

—AP

Pai P'u 白樸 (*tzu*, Jen-fu 仁甫, *hao*, Lan-ku 蘭谷, 1227-1306) is regarded as one of the four great masters of the *tsa-chü** which flourished in China during the thirteenth and fourteenth centuries. He wrote at least fifteen dramas but only two of them, *Wu-t'ung yü* 梧桐雨 (Rain on the Phoenix Tree) and *Ch'iang-t'ou ma-shang* 牆頭馬上 (On Horseback at the Garden Wall), are complete and of unquestioned authenticity. Another complete play, *Tung-ch'iang chi* 東牆記 (Tale of the East Wall), and fragments of several other plays survive, but there is considerable doubt whether they are indeed by Pai P'u. A collection of his *tz'u** entitled *T'ien-lai chi* 天籟集 (Collection of Natural Sounds) and a number of *san-ch'ü* (see *ch'ü*) are also extant.

Born in 1226 near the end of the Chin dynasty, Pai P'u was taught by his father, Pai Hua 白華, a former high official of the Chin dynasty, and by a famous literary figure of the time and friend of the family, Yüan Hao-wen.* Although Pai P'u prepared to take the literary examinations during his youth, sometime later, probably in the 1250s, he became disenchanted with the world and began to devote his life to self-cultivation, scholarship, and the literary arts. He is known to have twice refused recommendations for official posts under the Mongol Yüan dynasty and appears to have spent most of his adult life traveling about China. During his travels he met with other literati, wrote poetry and songs, and may even have served as secretary to some of the prominent northern officials residing in the south. Although there is no mention in the prefaces to his lyric poems as to his also writing dramas, the *Rain on the Phoenix Tree* can be dated to after 1261 because of the use of an anachronistic term in Act II. The time of his death is unknown but he most likely lived into his eighties.

Pai P'u's lyric poems were soon praised by critics as being "derived from a great inner integrity" and "subtle and genial," but owing to the scarcity of editions they were never anthologized in the standard collections.

Pai P'u's fame rests principally upon his acknowledged masterpiece drama, *Rain on the Phoenix Tree*. It is a poignant tale set in the T'ang dynasty which depicts the great love of Emperor Hsüan-tsung for his beautiful concubine Yang Kuei-fei 楊玉環, her subsequent death at the hands of rebellious imperial troops (who blamed her and her family for the misfortunes that had befallen the dynasty), and the laments and pinings of the emperor for her after her death.

Despite a general lack of action and a seemingly interminable amount of lamentation by the emperor, the high literary qualities of this play's well-crafted *tz'u*-like *ch'ü* and the many onomatopoetic *tours-de-force* in it have delighted generations of readers.

On Horseback at the Garden Wall, also set in the T'ang dynasty, is a rather improbable tale in the *ts'ai-tzu chia-jen* "handsome-young-man-meets-beautiful-young-maiden" school of popular motifs. While on a trip to Lo-yang the hero falls in love with, seduces, and then elopes with, a young girl. He takes her to his family residence in Ch'ang-an. Unknown to the young man's family she is installed in their back garden where she lives for some seven years, gives birth to two children, and is then discovered one day by the young man's father. After pressuring the young man to give her a bill of divorce, the father casts the young woman out and sends his son off to take the imperial examinations. The son, of course, passes with honors and is sent to Lo-yang as an official where he attempts to look up the mother of his children, now heiress to her deceased parents' estates. At first she refuses to take him back but when the young man's father comes in with her children claiming that many years ago he had intended to wed his son to the daughter of her father, she relents and all live happily ever after.

Although the plot is hackneyed and improbable, Pai P'u has skillfully interwoven songs and dialogue to create an artful characterization of the hero, the heroine, and the hero's father. The song arias here have a natural charm and spontaneity not found in the arias from the *Rain on the Phoenix Tree*.

EDITIONS:

Chao, Ching-shen 趙景深. *Yüan-jen tsa-chü kou-ch'en* 元雜劇鉤沈. Shanghai, 1959. Fragments of lost plays.

Ku, Chao-ts'ang 顧肇倉. *Yüan-jen tsa-chü hsüan* 元人雜劇選. Peking, 1978. Annotated *Wu-t'ung yü*, pp. 77-113.

Sui, Shu-sen. 隋樹森. *Ch'üan Yüan san-ch'ü* 全元散曲. Shanghai, 1964. 2v. Pai P'u's song medleys, v. 1, pp. 192-207.

Sui, Shu-sen. *Yüan-ch'ü hsüan wai-pien* 元曲選外編. Peking, 1959. 3v. Edition of *Tung-ch'iang chi*, v. 1, pp. 202-218.

T'ang, Kuei-chang 唐圭璋. *Ch'üan Chin Yüan tz'u* 全金元詞. Peking, 1979. 2v. Pai P'u's lyric poems, v. 2, pp. 624-647.

Yüan-ch'ü hsüan. Unannotated texts of *Wu-t'ung yü* and *Ch'iang-t'ou ma-shang*, pp. 332-364.

TRANSLATIONS:

Cavanaugh, Jerome. "The Dramatic Works of the Yüan Dynasty Playwright Pai P'u." Unpublished Ph.D. dissertation, Stanford University, 1975. Annotated translations of the *Wu-t'ung yü* and *Ch'iang-t'ou ma-shang*.

Demiéville, *Anthologie*, pp. 445-446.

Matsuda, Shizue. "Rain on the Wu-t'ung Tree," *Renditions*, 3 (Autumn 1974), 53-61.

Yang, Richard F. S. *Fifty Songs from the Yüan.* London, 1967. Translation of several of Pai P'u's song medleys.

Yang, Richard F. S. *Four Plays of the Yüan Drama.* Taipei, 1972. Translation of the *Wu-t'ung yü*.

STUDIES:

Cavanaugh, "Dramatic Works." Research into Pai P'u's life and his extant and "lost" plays.

Ch'en, Chien 陳健. "Lüeh-lun *Wu-t'ung yü* tsa-chü" 略論梧桐雨雜劇, "Wen-hsüeh i-ch'an" no. 93, in *Kuang-ming jih-pao* (February 26, 1956).

Cheng, Ch'ien 鄭騫. "Pai Jen-fu nien-p'u" 白仁甫年譜, *Ching-wu ts'ung-pien* 景午叢編. Taipei, 1972, 2v., v. 2, pp. 90-146.

———. "Pai Jen-fu chiao-yu sheng-tsu k'ao" 白仁甫交遊生卒考, *ibid.*, v. 2, pp. 147-167.

(Shan-hsi Shih-fan Hsüeh-yüan) Chung-wen-hsi San-nien-chi Ku-tien Wen-hsüeh Yen-chiu-tsu (山西師範學苑) 中文系三年級古典文學研究組. "Pai P'u ho t'a-te tsa-chü" 白樸和他的雜劇, *Shan-hsi Shih-fan Hsüeh-yüan hsüeh-pao*, 1959.3 (March 1959), 53-62.

Hsü, Ling-yün 徐凌雲. "Yüan ch'ü-chia Pai P'u chi ch'i chü-tso" 元曲家白樸及其劇作, *Nan-k'ai Ta-hsüeh jen-wen k'o-hsüeh chiao-hsüeh yü yen-chiu hui-k'an*, 1957.1 (January 1957), 51-66.

Sung, Yin-ku 宋蔭谷. "Lun tsa-chü *Wu-t'ung yü*" 論雜劇梧桐雨, *Tung-pei Jen-min Ta-hsüeh jen-wen k'o-hsüeh hsüeh-pao*, 1957.2/3 (October 1957), 81-96.

Yao, Shu-i ㄠ書儀. "Pai P'u yen-chiu" 白樸研究. Peking, 1981. Unpublished thesis from the *Chung-kuo K'o-hsüeh-yüan Wen-hsüeh-hsi Yüan-Ming-Ch'ing Wen-hsüeh Chuan-yeh-pan*.

Yeh, Te-chün 葉德均. "Pai P'u nien-p'u" 白樸年譜, in his *Hsi-ch'ü hsiao-shuo ts'ung-k'ao* 戲曲小說叢考, Peking, 1979, pp. 342-370.

Yü, K'o-p'ing 于克平. " 'Tung-ch'ang chi' yü 'Hsi-hsiang chi' " 東牆記與西廂記, in *Wen-yüan tsung-heng t'an* 文苑縱橫談, 4 (Chi-nan, 1982), 93-109.

—JC

Pan Ku 班固 (*tzu*, Meng-chien 孟堅, 32-92) was not only a grand historian of the Latter Han dynasty but also a noted writer of *fu*.* A native of An-ling 安陵 in the district of Fu-feng 扶風 (modern Hsing-p'ing 興平 in Shensi), at the age of nine he was writing literary compositions and chanting poems and *fu*. As he matured, he made an exhaustive study of the classics and various schools of philosophy, becoming a man of great erudition. When his father Pan Piao 班彪 (3-54) died, Pan Ku composed the "Yu-t'ung fu" 幽通賦, his most important early work, to express his grief.

His father had been compiling a history of the Former Han dynasty. Pan Ku committed himself to completing the project. Unfortunately he was accused of writing a private history of the nation—a punishable offense—and was thrown into prison. When the matter was clarified, his work obtained the emperor's approval and he was put in charge of the Lan-t'ai Archives 蘭臺令史 and given access to the palace archives. Before long, he was promoted to Gentleman (*lang* 郎) under imperial auspices and with the assistance of his sister, Pan Chao 班昭 (*c.* 48-*c.* 112), he completed the *Han-shu* 漢書 (History of the Former Han dynasty).

This work—100 *chüan* covering the period 206 B.C. to A.D. 23—became the model for most subsequent dynastic histories. Pan's earliest historical work had been a continuation of the *Shih-chi** entitled *Hou chuan* 後傳 (The Later Tradition/Account). It was this work that led to his imprisonment. Once given imperial sponsorship he expanded the scope to include the entire Former Han era. For the early years he used the *Shih-chi* texts, for the following period various sequels and records. He revised the organization of the *Shih-chi* by eliminating the *shih-chia* 世家 (hereditary houses), since he felt the *pen-chi* 本紀 (basic [imperial] annals) were more appropriate for a centralized monarchy (much of the *shih-chia* material went into his *lieh-chuan* 列傳) and by changing the *shu* 書 into *chih* 志 (treatises). He also added new subjects to the *chih*—law, geography, and, most significantly for the student of literature, bibliography ("I-wen chih" 藝文志), this last named treatise heavily indebted to Liu Hsin.* The work remained incomplete at Pan Ku's death and was finished by his sister, Pan Chao, and her staff. In the majority of the *Han-shu* Pan Ku's efforts were editorial, but in the eulogies he appended to each *chüan* (included—the *Wen-hsüan**) he reveals himself to be an excellent stylist. The *Han-shu* is also important in the transmission of Han literary works, many existing in their earliest rendition in its pages. Moreover, the parts of the *Han-shu* seem to have served as a "source" for editors of the *Shih-chi* over the centuries who used *Han-shu* texts to replace or supplement lost sections of their work.

Pan Ku is also known for his purely literary corpus. After his promotion, he found easier access to the throne. At that time, there was a long period of peace and the government undertook to beautify the capital, Lo-yang, refurbishing old palaces, building new ones, deepening the moats, and raising the height of the city walls. There were a number of old men of the former capital, Ch'ang-an, who resented this development and pleaded with the emperor to return to Ch'ang-an. Following the models of earlier poets like Ssu-ma Hsiang-ju* and Yang Hsiung,* Pan Ku composed the "Liang-tu fu" 兩都賦 (Prose-poem on Two Capitals) in opposition to these men. Pan argued the merits of the present regime and the importance of keeping it distinct from its predecessor.

When Emperor Chang (r. 76-88), who had a liking for literature, succeeded to the throne, Pan Ku received more favor. He was frequently admitted to the imperial library and often accompanied the emperor on his hunts or travels. However, in spite of his profound scholarship and literary attainments, he received no promotion for many years. In frustration, he composed the "Ta pin hsi" 答賓戲 (Reply to a Guest's Mockery) to console himself.

In 89 when General Tou Hsien 寶憲 (d. 92) led a successful expedition against the Hsiung-nu, Pan Ku was on his staff. On Tou Hsien's return, he pressed his victories too hard in attempting to gain favor; as a result jealousies against him were fostered. Accused of improprieties, he was removed and Pan Ku was also involved in the case. Before the matter could be investigated, Pan died in prison.

Pan Ku was the first poet to write an elaborate *fu* on the national capitals. His "Liang-tu fu" is in the form of a dialogue between two *dramatis personae*, the Western Capital Guest 西都賓客 and the Eastern Capital Host 東都主人. It covers a wide range of topics, including the topography of the cities, the imperial demesne, royal palaces, public buildings, scenic spots, local products, customs of the inhabitants, different kinds of ceremony, spectacles of imperial hunts, and the achievements of the government. The panorama of the cities presented may be considered a supplement to the accounts given in the standard histories. Moreover, Pan Ku's critical statements on *fu* in the preface to his "Two Capitals" and in the "I-wen chih" of the *Han-shu* are important works to the understanding of the Han *fu*. He maintained that the *fu* derived from the poetry (*shih**)

of ancient times and that court poets composed *fu* either to convey the feelings of the masses to the government, thus exercising a reprimand, or to broadcast the virtues of the emperor, thereupon giving full expression to the ideals of loyalty and filial piety.

Only six of Pan Ku's *fu* are extant and four of these are fragmentary. His "Two Capitals," which is preserved in the *Wen-hsüan*,* has been widely read and greatly admired by scholars from generation to generation.

EDITIONS:

Han-shu. Po-na 百衲 edition. *SPPY.* Yen Shih-ku 顏師古 (581-645), comm.

———. 10v. Peking, 1959. Punctuated, critical edition.

Han-shu chi pu-chu tsung-ho yin-te 漢書及補注總合引得. Cambridge, Mass., 1936.

Liu-ch'ao wen, v. 1, "Ch'üan Hou-Han wen" 全後漢文, ch. 24-26, pp. 602-616.

Pan Lan-tai chi 班蘭臺集, in *Pai-san*, v. 2, pp. 83-119.

Wang, Hsien-ch'ien 王先謙, comm. *Han-shu pu-chu* 漢書補注. Changsha, 1900; rpt. Shanghai, 1959.

TRANSLATIONS:

Dubs, Homer H. *The History of the Former Han Dynasty by Pan Ku.* 3v. Baltimore, 1938, 1944, 1955. Translations of ch. 1-12, 99, and parts of 24A-B.

Hughes, "Liang-tu fu," in *Two Chinese Poets*, pp. 25-59.

Knechtges, David R. "Two Capitals Rhapsody," in *Wen Xuan, or Selections of Refined Literature, Volume I: Rhapsodies on Metropolises and Capitals*, Princeton, 1982, pp. 93-180.

Margouliès, G. "Liang-tu fu," in *Le 'fou' dans le Wen-siuan*, Paris, 1926, pp. 31-74.

von Zach, "Yu-t'ung fu" 幽通賦, in *Anthologie*, v. 1, pp. 211-216.

Watson, Burton. *Courtier and Commoner in Ancient China. Selections from the History of the Former Han by Pan Ku.* New York and London, 1974.

———. "Preface to the Fu on the Two Capitals" 兩都賦序, *Rhyme-prose*, pp. 111-112.

See also Timoteus Pokora, "Pan Ku and Recent Translations from *Han-shu*," *JAOS*, 98 (1978), 451-460.

STUDIES:

Bodde, Derk. "Types of Chinese Categorical Thinking," *JAOS*, 59 (1939), 200-219. Deals with the table of men of modern and ancient times in the *Han-shu*.

Ho, P. H. (Kenneth) 何沛雄. "A Study of the *Fu* on Hunts and on Capitals in the Han Dynasties (206 B.C.-220 A.D.)." Unpublished Ph.D. dissertation, Oxford University, 1968.

———. "Pan Ku 'Liang-tu fu' yü Han-tai Ch'ang-an" 班固兩都賦與漢代長安, *The Continent*, 34.7 (April 1967), 11-19.

Hughes, *Two Chinese Poets*. Provides a translation of the "Liang-tu fu" and a critique of it.

Husewé, A. F. P. "Notes on the Historiography of the Han Period," in *Historians of China and Japan*, W. G. Beasley and E. G. Pulleyblank, eds., London, 1961, pp. 30-43.

Kao, Pu-ying 高步瀛. "Pan Ku 'Liang-tu fu' i-shu" 班固兩都賦義疏, in *Wen-hsüan li chü i-shu* 文選李注義疏, rpt. Taipei, 1966, v. 1, pp. 1-92.

Lo, Tchen-ying. *Les formes et les méthodes historique en Chine; Une famille d'historiens en Chine et son oeuvre*. Paris, 1931.

Swann, Nancy L. *Pan Chao, Foremost Woman Scholar of China*. New York, 1932.

van der Sprenkel, O. B. *Pan Piao, Pan Ku, and the Han History*. Canberra, 1964.

Vernon, Charles. " 'Keito fu' no taiwa bubun" 京都賦の對話部份, *Chūgoku chūsei bungaku kenkyū* 中國中世文學研究, 12 (September 1977), 1-14.

—KH and TP

P'an Ni 潘尼 (*tzu*, Cheng-shu 正叔, d. *c*. 310) was the grandson of P'an Hsü 潘勗, an officer of the Han dynasty. His father, P'an Man 潘滿, also held office, and was known for his scholarship. P'an Ni gained a reputation early, enhanced by his relationship to P'an Yüeh,* his paternal uncle.

According to the meager biographical information, P'an first joined the local bureaucracy but resigned to care for his aging father. Then, during the 280s he passed the *hsiu-ts'ai* 秀才 examinations, and was made Erudite in the Court of Imperial Sacrifices, a title by which he was often identified, and commissioned an Adjutant. In 291 he was appointed to the service of the Crown Prince in metropolitan Lo-yang. He held several other positions in the central government until he pleaded illness and took leave to avoid a tyrannical favorite of Ssu-ma Lun 司馬倫 who usurped the throne in 300. When he heard that the Prince of Ch'i 齊王 (Ssu-ma Chiung) had risen against Lun, he made his way to Hsü-ch'ang 許昌 (modern Honan), where Chiung employed him as a strategist and secretary. After Lun was defeated and executed, P'an was enfeoffed as Duke of An-ch'ang 安昌公, and served successively in several posts. Sometime after 307, when it became obvious that Lo-yang would soon be embroiled in yet another armed struggle for power, P'an took his family and made his way east to Ch'eng-kao 成皋 (modern Honan), intending to return to his native district, Jung-yang Chung-mou 滎陽中牟 (also in Honan). En route he encountered bandits and could go no further. He sickened and died; he was just over sixty years old.

About two dozen *shih*,* nearly twenty *fu** and *sung* 頌 compositions, and several other prose works survive. P'an's poetry consists of two sets of ten and a set of six verses and other single presentation verses in tetrasyllabic lines; congratulatory verses written to imperial order; poems addressed to colleagues and friends; and verses describing outings in the metropolitan district. Subjects for his *fu* include "bitter rain," "fishing," "fire," "the fan," "pomegranates," "mulberry trees," "lotus," and other "still life" topics.

Two of P'an's poems were chosen for inclusion in the sixth century *Wen-hsüan*.* Consciously ornate phraseology, stylized form, and clichés, noticed already by Chung Tung in his *Shih-p'in** are common in P'an's verse. P'an Ni thus emerges as a noted writer of the late third century who exemplified the literary style and interests of his day.

EDITIONS:

"Ch'üan Chin shih" 全晉詩, *ch*. 4, in *Nan-Pei-ch'ao shih*, v. 1, pp. 502-510.

"Ch'üan Chin wen" 全晉文, in *Liu-ch'ao wen*, v. 2, *ch*. 94-95, pp. 1999-2005.

P'an T'ai-ch'ang chi, 潘太常集, in *Pai-san*, v. 6, pp. 107-128.

TRANSLATIONS:

von Zach, *Anthologie*, v. 1, pp. 404-407, 449-450.

STUDIES:

Teng, Shih-liang 鄧仕樑. *Liang Chin shih lun* 兩晉詩論. Hong Kong, 1972, pp. 91, 103-104.

—JM

P'an Yüeh 潘岳 (*tzu*, An-jen 安仁, 247-300) and Lu Chi* were the foremost poets of their time, and P'an's physical beauty is legendary. He was born in Chung-mou 中牟 in the Ying-yang Commandery 滎陽郡 to a family of moderate wealth—both his father and grandfather had held office. Known throughout his district as a youth of talent, he first attracted wide attention, and reportedly jealousy and resentment, with his "Chi t'ien fu" 籍田賦 (Prose-poem on the Imperial Groundbreaking) in praise of Emperor Wu of the Chin. His first office was under General-in-chief Chia Ch'ung 賈充, father of Emperor Hui's consort. After a succession of other posts, he resigned in 278, the year in which he wrote his famous "Ch'iu-hsing fu" 秋興賦 (Prose-poem on Autumn Meditations), which describes his dissatisfaction with official life. His retirement ended in 285, when he became Magistrate of Ho-yang 河陽; various provincial and court positions followed. In 290 he became Yang Chün's 楊駿 Recorder. When Yang was assassinated in 291, P'an was reduced to the status of commoner. The next year, however, he was called again to serve as Magistrate of Ch'ang-an. Soon after, P'an entered Chia Mi's 賈謐 famous literary salon; he became the foremost, and reportedly the most sycophantic, of the group known as the "twenty-four friends of Chia Mi," which included nearly every well-known literary figure of the time. Another string of positions followed, before P'an was finally implicated in an attempt to set up Chia Mi in place of the crown prince. This last of several dangerous alliances proved fatal—P'an was executed in 300.

P'an is famous as a writer of *fu**; his best known include the "Ch'iu-hsing fu," the "Hsien-chü fu" 閒居賦 (Prose-poem on the Idle Life), which has a very frank autobiographical preface, and the "Hsi-cheng fu" 西征賦 (Prose-poem on the Western Journey), which describes his trip from Lo-yang to Ch'ang-an to assume the position of magistrate. This work creates a mosaic of descriptions of his own career with the physical landscape—a region pregnant with historical associations—en route. Though somewhat experimental in language and style, his *fu* are typical of the descriptive *fu* of the time.

The prevailing mood in P'an's work is grief. His *lei* 誄 (eulogies) are among the best known of that genre; and at least half of P'an's approximately twenty surviving poems, written in both four- and five-word lines, are dominated by grief or bereavement. His is a personal grief, differing from the all-encompassing sorrow characterizing poets such as Juan Chi.* The three "Tiao wang shih" 悼亡詩 (Poems on His Dead Wife) are typical of this mode and are P'an's most famous works. They incorporate a colloquial language similar to some *yüeh-fu** and are marked by finely crafted use of alliteration, parallelism, *enjambement,* and rhyme. P'an achieves in these poems an emotional immediacy often lacking in eulogistic verse; these poems remained models for verse on a departed wife. His poetic departures from this mode, as in the scenic descriptions of the "Chin-ku chi tso shih" 金谷集作詩 (Poems from the Chin-ku Assembly) and his praise poems, are markedly less successful. He is generally criticized, along with other poets of his generation, for superficiality and empty artifice.

EDITIONS:

The majority of P'an's work seems to have disappeared at a fairly late date. What remains is collected in *Pai-san*, v. 6, pp. 25-72.

TRANSLATIONS:

Chalmers, J. "The Foo on Pheasant Shooting," *China Review*, 1 (1872/3), 322-324.

Frodsham, *Anthology*, pp. 86-87.

Kōzen, Hiroshi 興膳宏. *Han Gaku, Riku Ki* 潘岳陸機. Tokyo, 1974.

Watson, *Rhyme-Prose*, pp. 64-71.

von Zach, *Anthologie*, v. 1, pp. 98-103, 136-158, 193-195, 229-233, 239-244 [*fu*].

STUDIES:

Fu, Hsüan-tsung 傅璇琮. "P'an Yüeh hsi-nien k'ao-cheng" 潘岳繫年考證, *Wen-shih*, 14 (July 1982), 237-257.

Ho, Yung 何融. "P'an Yüeh nien-p'u" 潘岳年譜, in *Chih-yung ts'ung-k'an* 知用叢刊, 2nd collection.

Takahashi, Kazumi 高橋和己. "Han Gaku ron" 潘岳論, *Chūgoku bungaku hō*, 7 (October 1957), 14-91.

—CC

Pao Chao 鮑照 (*tzu*, Ming-yüan 明遠, *c.* 414-466) is the most important *yüeh-fu** poet of the Six Dynasties and one of the most famous masters of *yüeh-fu* in the whole of Chinese literary history. He was a native of Tung-hai 東海 (modern Ch'ang-shu in Kiangsu). Born into a poor gentry family, he did not have access to a successful official career. Liu I-ch'ing 劉義慶 (the Prince of Lin-ch'uan, 403-444), author of the *Shih-shuo hsin-yü** and patron of many literati, admired Pao Chao's literary talents, and appointed him Attendant Gentleman (*c.* 439). Later, he was granted the same position under another prince and also became a Magistrate. During the reign of Emperor Hsiao-wu (454-464) of the Sung dynasty, he was for a short time Secretariat Drafter and Master of Literary Arts. In the last years of his life, he held a military position in the service of the Prince of Lin-hai, who was still a child. During a revolt in which his patron was involved, Pao Chao was killed by mutinous soldiers.

About two decades after his death, his literary works were collected by Yü Yen 虞炎. In addition to *shih** poetry Pao Chao also wrote *fu*,* *sung* (hymns), and *ming* (inscriptions). In his famous "Wu ch'eng fu" 蕪城賦 (The Ruined City), he meditates on the culture and history of the five-hundred-year-old city Kuang-ling, in ruins after the Kuang-ling revolt of 459. The preface to the hymn "Ho ch'ing sung" 河清頌 (The Purity of the Yellow River), a panegyric on the prosperous reign of Emperor Wen (424-454), testifies to his high literary talents. Four chapters of *shih* poetry contain forty-four *yüeh-fu* ballads and eighty-eight poems. Six poems by his younger sister, Pao Ling-hui 鮑令暉 have also been added. He excelled in *yüeh-fu* ballads of the five- and seven-word lines. Most famous is "Ni hsing lu nan" 擬行路難 (In Imitation of "The Weary Road"), which often has been im-

itated. Favorite themes in his poetry include history and contemporary history, official career and military service, the melancholy of love, friendship, fauna, and nature.

Despite some colloquial elements in his *yüeh-fu* ballads, Pao Chao's language is considered complicated. His style is characterized by the use of evocative images arousing associations, metaphors, and similes. Some of his nature poems have been interpreted allegorically as referring to topical events. Pao Chao's works were favorably received by the T'ang poets. He influenced Li Po* and Tu Fu,* who once compared Li Po's verse to Pao Chao's. Pao Chao has gained a high reputation among literary critics. Hsieh Ling-yün,* Pao Chao, and Yen Yen-chih* are traditionally considered the three outstanding poets of the Yüan-chia period (424-454).

EDITIONS:

Pao-shih chi 鮑氏集. Mao Fu-chi 毛斧季, ed. *SPTK*.

Pao Ts'an-chün chi chu 鮑參軍集注. Ch'ien Chung-lien 錢仲聯, ed. Shanghai, 1958. The best critical edition, including extensive commentary, biographical sources, and opinions of literary critics.

Pao Ts'an-chün shih chu 鮑參軍詩注. Huang Chieh 黃節, ed. Peking, 1957. Reliable edition of his *yüeh-fu* ballads and poems.

TRANSLATIONS:

Frodsham, *Anthology*, pp. 142-156.

Sunflower, pp. 66-68.

Watson, *Rhyme-Prose*, pp. 92-95.

STUDIES:

Chang, Chih-yüeh 張志岳. "Pao Chao chi ch'i shih hsin-t'an" 鮑照及其詩新探, *Wen-hsüeh p'ing-lun*, 1979.1, 58-65.

Ch'en, I-hsin 陳貽焮. "Pao Chao ho t'a te tso-p'in" 鮑照和他的作品, *Wen-hsüeh i-ch'an tseng-k'an*, 3 (1957), 182-190.

Frodsham, J. D., "The Nature Poetry of Pao Chao," *Orient/West*, 8/6 (1964), 85-93.

Fujii, Mamoru 藤井守. "Hōshō no gakufu" 鮑照の樂府, *Chūgoku chūsei bungaku kenkyū*, 1965.10.

———. "Hōshō no 'Gikōrōnan jūhasshu ni tsuite" 鮑照の擬行路難十八首について, *Shina gaku kenkyū*, 36, 25-36.

———. "Hōshō no fu" 鮑照の賦 *Hiroshima Daigaku Bungakubū ki yō* 34, 230-244.

Kotzenberg, H. *Der Dichter Pao Chao (†466). Untersuchungen zu Leben und Werk.* Ph.D. dissertation, Bonn, 1971.

Lin, Wen-yüeh 林文月. "Pao Chao yü Hsieh Ling-yün te shan-shui shih" 鮑照與謝靈運的山水詩, *Wen-hsüeh p'ing-lun*, 2 (1980), 1-21.

Lü, Cheng-hui 呂正惠. "Pao Chao shih hsiao lun" 鮑照詩小論, *Wen-hsüeh p'ing-lun*, 6 (1980), 119-134.

Nakamori, Kenji 中森健二. "Hōshō no bungaku" 鮑照の文學, *Ritsumei bungaku*, 364, 365, 366 (1975), 119-164.

Ts'eng, Chün-i 曾君一. "Pao Chao yen-chiu" 鮑照研究, *Ssu-ch'uan Ta-hsüeh hsüeh-pao*, 1957.4, 1-25.

—HK

Pei-li chih 北里志 (Record of the Northern Sectors) is a brief description of the *geisha* section of Ch'ang-an written by Sun Ch'i 孫棨 (*tzu*, Wen-wei 文威, *fl.* 880), a petty official in the T'ang government. Sun describes the northern sectors of Ch'ang-an, also known as the P'ing-k'ang 平康 Quarter, and the world of entertainers and prostitutes who resided there. The style is anecdotal. In the introduction he describes the stratified nature of the *geisha's* world, the high- and lower-class women; he also briefly depicts their surroundings, social structure, and social origins. Many houses were customarily run, for example, by adoptive mothers (*chia mu* 假母), themselves often retired *geishas*. He tells how assignations were made and what areas the *geishas* visited outside of their own quarter. This introductory description is followed by a series of profiles of several women. They were talented and often well trained in music or literature (hence the term *chinü* 妓女 is best rendered *geisha*).

The value of this brief text lies in several areas. From a sociological point of view it provides a picture of the daily life and society of the entertainers of T'ang Ch'ang-an. Sun's portrayal of the women, their relationship with their clients or lovers, with their adoptive mothers, and with one another provides a rare glimpse of a little-documented world. His references to the scholar-officials who frequented the quarters are also unusual. The profiles of the women are crafted biographical vignettes,

in the convention of the abandoned beauty. In fact, the *Pei-li chih* has been traditionally viewed as a work of fiction.

In describing the training and talents of the women, Sun Ch'i cites some of the poetry they composed. They wrote *shih** similar to that of their scholar-clients. Thus the *Pei-li chih* is one of the handful of texts that describe musical and literary entertainments outside the court. Other works that provide similarly unofficial views of T'ang entertainment and art outside of the palace are Ts'ai Ling-ch'in's *Chiao-fang chi*,* the *Yüeh-fu tsa-lu** by Tuan An-chieh, and the *T'ang ch'üeh shih* 唐闕史 by Kao Yen-hsiu 高彥休. These works describe performances of *tz'u** poetry, comic dialogues, farces, and primitive military and comic skits laced with singing and dancing.

EDITIONS:

Pei-li chih. T'ang-tai ts'ung-shu ed. Rpt. of a Ch'ing edition.

Ts'ui, Ling-chin. *Chiao-fang chi (wai er chung)* 教坊記(外二種). Shanghai, 1957. Contains the *Chiao fang chi*, the *Pei-li chih*, and the *Ch'ing-lou chi.**

TRANSLATIONS:

des Rotours, Robert. *Courtisans Chinois à la fin des T'ang, entre circa 789 et le 8 janvier 881; Pei-li tche (Anecdotes du quartier du Nord) par Souen K'i.* Paris, 1968.

Levy, Howard. "The Gay Quarters of Ch'ang-an," *Orient / West*, 7.10 (1962), 121-128; 8.6 (1963), 115-122; 11.1 (1964), 103-110.

—VC

Pi-chi 筆記 (note-form literature) is distinguished by two basic characteristics: brevity and casualness. Since these characteristics cannot be measured in exact terms, there are no hard-and-fast rules for defining *pi-chi* literature; nor is it possible to make clear distinctions between *pi-chi* and similar terms like *sui-pi* 隨筆, *cha-chi* 札記, *pi-t'an* 筆談, *ts'ung-t'an* 叢談, and *ts'ung-cha* 叢札, although some broad differences may be detected. *Cha-chi*, for example, may suggest closer thematic relationships among the entries in the work.

Given their brevity and casualness, *pi-chi* entries seldom exist individually but are generally grouped together in book form with sectional divisions, which are not necessarily governed by themes or subject matters. Cursory as they are, there is no limitation to the coverage of *pi-chi* entries. This working definition helps to identify the *pi-chi* tradition as one extending from the Six Dynasties to the present. The monumental *Kuan-chui pien* 管錐編 (The Pipe and Awl Collection, 1979) by the eminent modern scholar Ch'ien Chung-shu 錢鍾書 (b. 1910) bears testimony to the timelessness of the *pi-chi* form. This long tradition may even reach back to the Han dynasty, but works customarily ascribed to this period exist either only in isolated fragments or in versions that should better be regarded as Six Dynasties' products.

Despite their catholic nature, which makes them stores of primary data for the historian and the literary historian, *pi-chi* collections can be divided into three main categories: fictional, historical, and philological. This categorization is based mainly on proportion, because entries of all these descriptions can be found in most of the *pi-chi* collections. The *Sou-shen chi,** the *Shih-shuo hsin-yü,** and the *Yu-yang tsa-tsu** are examples of the fictional group, while Li Chao's 李肇 *T'ang kuo-shih pu* 唐國史補 (Supplement to the History of the T'ang), Shen Te-fu's 沈德符 (1578-1642) *Wan-li yeh-huo pien* 萬曆野獲編 (Private Gleanings of the Wan-li Reign), and Wang Shih-chen's 王士禎 (1634-1711) *Ch'ih-pei ou-t'an* 池北偶談 (Casual Talks by the North Side of the Pond) represent the historical group, and Wang Ying-lin's* *K'un-hsüeh chi-wen,* Ku Yen-wu's* *Jih-chih lu,* and Ch'ien Ta-hsin's 錢大昕 (1728-1804) *Shih-chia Chai yang-hsin lu* 十駕齋養新錄 (Nourishing the New in the Ten-Horse Studio) stand for the philological group.

Given the length of the tradition and the scope of its coverage, the number of *pi-chi* collections could easily be considered tens of thousands—the number varies according to how *pi-chi* is defined. This sheer bulk poses two problems to the user: (1) availability, and (2) the absence of a reliable way to predict the contents. However, most of the *pi-chi* works have been included in *ts'ung-shu** and can be easily located

through standard tools like the *Chung-kuo ts'ung-shu tsung-lu.* But the fact that a *pi-chi* volume can treat almost anything can be discouraging, particularly to those who have been spoiled by the convenience of modern sinological indexes and expect handy information literally at their fingertips.

While we should be thankful for having indexes to major *pi-chi* collections like Su E's 蘇鶚 (*fl.* 890) *Su-shih yen-i* 蘇氏演義 (Explanations of Mr. Su), Hung Mai's* *Jung-chai sui-pi* and *I-chien chih,* and T'ao Tsung-i's* *Cho-keng lu,* comprehensive attempts like Saeki Tomi's 佐伯富 *Chūgoku zuihitsu sakuin* 中國隨筆索引 (1954) and *Chūgoku zuihitsu zatcho sakuin* 中國隨筆雜著索引 (1960), altogether indexing a little more than two hundred works, might have carried the idea too far. Ungrateful as it may sound, such honest attempts may be rather misleading. Unlike the indexing of classical canons and historical works and their commentaries, the mere registering of names and terms in *pi-chi* collections may not be able to adequately convey the import of the entries, and readers tend to overlook books which have been indexed. Such comprehensive indexes, no matter how much warning the compilers provide in the front matter, tend to promote the idea that a significant proportion of the genre has been covered, whereas the coverage is actually extremely selective.

The nature of *pi-chi* collections does not normally render them as sources for quick reference. There is no surer way to fully utilize *pi-chi* collections, including those with individual indexes, than to read through them entry by entry, book by book. The variety and richness of the materials will almost always guarantee handsome rewards. If guides are needed in selecting the collections for closer reading, mechanical indexes are far less helpful than critical biobibliographical comments, such as those provided in the indispensable *Ssu-k'u ch'üan-shu tsung-mu t'i-yao,* and in the works of Chang Shun-hui 張舜徽 (whose detailed analytical study of one hundred Ch'ing *pi-chi* collections has yet to appear in print) and Hsieh Kuo-chen 謝國楨 (1901-1982).

Since 1973 Taipei's Hsin-hsing shu-chü 新興書局 has published over thirty series of *pi-chi* under the collective title of *Pi-chi hsiao-shuo ta-kuan* 筆記小說大觀 (A Parade of Note-form Fiction). With thousands of titles, this is the largest and most convenient "collection" of *pi-chi* works, but it has to be used cautiously. The title is definitely misleading; many of the works included in the later series are not normally categorized as *pi-chi* fiction, and quite a few of them (like collections of government archives, synopses of drama, and works of philosophers) cannot be regarded as *pi-chi* even in the broadest sense of the term. The choice of editions is also largely uncritical; the readers should consult more reliable editions when it comes to citing passages.

STUDIES:

Chang, Shun-hui. "*Ch'ing-jen pi-chi t'iao-pien* hsü-mu" 清人筆記條辨敍目, *Wen-shih-che*, 1979.4, 45-48.

Chou, Li-an 周黎庵 (Chou Shao 周邵). "T'an Ch'ing-jen pi-chi" 談清人筆記, in Chou Li-an, *Wu-kou chi* 吳鉤集, Shanghai, 1940, pp. 94-101.

Hervouet, Yves, ed. *A Sung Bibliography*. Hong Kong, 1978. Includes biobibliographical comments of different lengths and quality on major Sung *pi-chi* collections.

Hsieh, Kuo-chen. *Ming Ch'ing pi-chi t'an-ts'ung* 明清筆記談叢. Peking, 1964; rpt. Shanghai, 1982.

I-shih 一士 (Hsü Jen-chin 徐仁錦). "Chin-tai pi-chi kuo-yen lu" 近代筆記過眼錄. *Chung-ho yüeh-k'an*, 2.7 (July 1941), 57-66; 2.8 (August 1941), 77-86; 2.9 (September 1941), 75-87; 2.10 (October 1941), 60-71; 2.11 (November 1941), 79-88; 2.12 (December 1941), 88-99; 3.1 (January 1942), 99-111; 3.3 (March 1942), 89-93; 3.4 (April 1942), 92-99; 3.5 (May 1942), 77-87; 3.10 (October 1942), 88-94; 4.1 (January 1943), 95-103; 4.5 (March 1943), 64-70; 4.11-12 (December 1943), 16-22; 5.4 (April 1944), 54-57. Comments on many late Ch'ing and early Republican *pi-chi* collections, many of which are not registered in the *Chung-kuo ts'ung-shu tsung-lu*.

Liu, Yao-lin 劉耀林. *Ming Ch'ing pi-chi ku-shih hsüan i* 明清筆記故事選. Shanghai, 1978.

McMullen, D. L. *Concordances and Indexes to Chinese Texts*. San Francisco, 1975. Most of the indexes to *pi-chi* collections published before the mid-1970s are listed in this handy reference tool.

Pi-chi hsiao-shuo ta-kuan ts'ung-k'an so-yin 筆記小說大觀叢書索引. Hsin-hsing shu-chü 新興書局, ed. Taipei, 1981.

Yeh, Yün-chün 葉雲君 (Yeh Te-chün 葉德均). "Kuan-yü pi-chi" 關於筆記, *Ku-chin*, 29 (August 1943), 28-30; 30 (September 1943), 28-30.

—YWM

Pi-chi man-chih 碧雞漫志 (Random Notes from Pi-chi) in five *chüan* was written by Wang Cho 王灼 (*tzu*, Hui-shu 晦叔, *hao*, I-t'ang 頤堂, *fl.* 1145). Wang Cho's native place was Hsiao-hsi 小溪 in Sui-ning 遂寧 County (modern T'ung-nan 潼南). He held no important official posts, although he was a government adviser at one time. He spent his later years in seclusion, absorbed in the study of Buddhism and Taoism. During the winter of 1145, the year he began to write his "Random Notes," he was living at the Miao-sheng Compound 妙勝院 in the Pi-chi District 碧雞坊 in the southwestern section of Ch'eng-tu.

Wang's book is about music and poetry, subjects on which he was an authority. In chapter one, he briefly traces the history of song forms (*ko* 歌 and *ch'ü* 曲) from early times down to the T'ang dynasty, touching on the origins, the preservation, and the decline of ancient songs during the Han, Tsin, and T'ang dynasties. He also speaks of the relationship between T'ang-dynasty *chüeh-chü* (see *shih*) and song forms and lists some *chüeh-chü* forms that were more commonly associated with songs: *Chu chih* 竹枝, *Lang-t'ao sha* 浪淘沙, *P'ao-ch'iu-le* 拋球樂, and *Yang-liu chih* 楊柳枝. His comments elucidate the popular practice of singing poetry to instrumental accompaniment in taverns and at parties and he names many poets, singsong girls, and entertainers who were famous in their day for these practices. Wang writes about the process of matching texts and melodies, begging the question of which came first. In summary, he notes that all lyrics were acknowledged as poems but that any of them could be sung to instrumental accompaniment and that performing poems as songs, or the deliberate composing of new lyrics to popular melodies in the public domain, was not done according to rigid rules but happened spontaneously as fitted the occasion.

Wang praises songs which flow naturally, independent of prosodic restrictions, and he concludes that ancient songs are generally superior to contemporary works. Notable among his many anecdotes is the story of Huang Fan-ch'o 黃幡綽 who, when requested by Emperor Hsüan-tsung to write a book on meter, simply drew an ear on a piece of paper and submitted it, with the explanation: "Meter is rooted in the ear." He further illustrates his ideas of naturalness by citing the reactions of an infant to music: a child opening and closing its fist in time to a song it heard while sucking at its mother's breast, keeping perfect time with the music.

Some have accused Wang of poor organization because his history of song forms includes a list of names of accomplished male and female singers who were active between the period of the Warring States and the end of the T'ang dynasty. But since his text is peppered with song titles and snippets of information about the practice of singing poetry in brothels and tea houses and at private social gatherings, this information fits comfortably into the surrounding text.

The entire section in part one on *chung-sheng* 中聲 and *cheng-sheng* 正聲 as applied to musical performances is not a rare insight into the aesthetic subtleties of sound production on a musical instrument, but rather a philosophical flight of fantasy into the realm of musical sounds and their moral implications, a tendency that has been present in Chinese treatises on music since the most ancient times, and one difficult to anchor to reality.

Chapter two is a literary critique of the *tz'u** and its practitioners. The account rambles from topic to topic, touching on particular poets or poems, often divulging stories behind the poems, drawing subtle references to people, events and their interrelationships, and revealing much about the world of art and letters. In one illustration, Wang quotes a verse inspired by the gift of a handkerchief from an attendant, surnamed Hui, whom a poet met while drinking with a wealthy gentleman at a restaurant. The poet vowed to meet the attendant "when next the peonies bloomed." Inspired by this incident the poet wrote a verse in which he concealed the attendant's name (Hui 惠, meaning "favors"), referring to a next meeting when the peonies bloom, with the closing line: "I fear only that should the peonies learn of our intent, they will delay their blooming."

In another example, he mentions a line of verse he saw on a fan, which was ingeniously devised by conflating the titles of the three songs *Yü hu-tieh* (Jade Butterfly), *Tieh lien hua* (The Butterfly Loves Blossoms), and *Hua-hsin tung* (The Heart of the Blossom Stirs): 玉蝴蝶戀花心動 "The love of flowers stirs the jade butterfly's heart."

In his assessment of Sung-dynasty *tz'u*, Wang never hesitates to reveal his personal poetic tastes. He finds most of it inferior to poems written during the Five Dynasties, and he is antagonistic toward poets who overemphasize style or the technicalities of prosodic descriptions. Wang reveals a highly sensitive and sophisticated understanding of poetry. He argues that the requirements of form should not act as an impediment to the content of a verse. He greatly admired the poetry of Su Shih,* to whom he refers frequently. Su, he finds, was not enamored of prosodic rules. He could compose a lyric on the spur of the moment, which illuminated a higher level of creativity by "giving new eyes and ears to the world, and serving as an inspiration for others to follow." For some poets he has little praise. Liu Yung's* verses are described as "wild-fox slobber," and Wang bemoans the fact that the young poets of his day took Liu Ch'i-ch'ing 劉耆卿 and Ts'ao Yüan-ch'ung 曹元寵 as their models, neither of whom can favorably compare to a Su Shih. He goes out of his way to mention two poets who were not members of the literati class: Chang Shan-jen 張山人, and K'ung San-ch'uan 孔三傳, revealing, perhaps, the catholicity of his tastes and his willingness to consider, without prejudice, the works of persons of humble origin.

Chapters three, four, and five constitute a detailed history of twenty-nine song forms, some of which emerged as popular *tz'u* and *ch'ü** forms in the Sung and Yüan periods. Wang traces the evolution of these song forms over a period of time. He is interested in their origins, the meanings and derivations of their titles, why some are known by more than one title, the modes to which they belong, how the prosodic features of a song became frozen into a model formula for other poets to imitate, and how variants on a formula were formed.

EDITIONS:

Pi-chi man-chih, Chih-pu-tsu chai ts'ung-shu ed.
———, in *Chung-kuo ku-tien hsi-ch'ü lun-chu chi-ch'eng* 中國古典戲曲論著集成, Peking, 1959, v. 1, pp. 93-152.

STUDIES:

Chou, Hsiao-lien 周曉蓮. "Pi-chi man-chih yen-chiu" 碧雞漫志研究. M.A. thesis, Chung-kuo Wen-hua Hsüeh-yüan 中國文化學院, Taipei, 1978.

—DJ

P'i Jih-hsiu 皮日休 (*tzu*, Hsi-mei 襲美, *c.* 834-*c.* 883) is known for his poetry, which portrayed the social injustices of his era, for his advocacy of Mencius and Han Yü,* and for his literary association with an insular Soochow coterie centered about Lu Kuei-meng.* By virtue of the breadth of his literary interests and the variety of his work, P'i Jih-hsiu's reputation since his death has been mercurial, closely tied to the transmission of the several collections of his works. P'i's *Wen-sou* 文藪 (866), which contains primarily prose (the influence from *ku-wen** is prominent) along with a few "socially conscious" verses, seems to have been much more widely circulated than the three hundred or more euphuistic poems still extant (included in the *Sung-ling chi* 松陵集) which he wrote with Lu Kuei-meng in a single year (*c.* 870). Although his work is well represented in several Sung anthologies including the *T'ang-wen ts'ui,** the better-known poems (all didactic) were not in concert with the tastes of the compiler

of the *T'ang-shih san-pai-shou.** Thus P'i is known to the modern reader primarily through his series of ten poems called "Cheng yüeh-fu" 正樂府 (Orthodox Music-bureau Ballads), through Lu Hsün's praise of his essays, and through his reassessment in China since 1949.

Born into a local gentry family based in Hsiang-chou 襄州 (Hsiang-yang, Hupei—one of the major preoccupations of PRC critics has been his possible peasant lineage, a claim which seems specious), P'i retired at an early age to the hermitage on Lu-men shan 鹿門山 (Deer-gate Mountain) nearby to prepare for the literary examinations. Although he certainly studied the classics, he seems to have had a special predilection for the *Ch'u-tz'u,** for the poetry of Po Chü-i,* and for the prose of Han Yü.* He traveled widely in his late teens, perhaps seeking a patron. Provincial life kept him in close touch with the people and much of his early verse reflects their concerns and hardships:

> Deep into autumn the acorns ripen,
> Scattering as they fall into the hillside scrub.
> Hunched over, a hoary-haired crone
> Gathers them, treading the morning frost.
> (From "Hsiang-wen t'an" 橡媼嘆 [Lament of an Old Acorn-gatherer])

During this year he also composed the *Lu-men yin-shu* 鹿門隱書 (Writings of a Recluse at Deer-gate, or Elliptical Writings from Deer-gate), a collection of sixty pasquinades in which the government and society of the times comes under sharp attack, often in comparison to some model from antiquity:

> In ancient times a worthy man was employed for the benefit of the state;
> Today he is employed for the benefit of a single family (section 56).
> In ancient times drunken rages were caused by wine;
> Today they are caused by the state of mankind (section 57).

Although the style and ideas of this ana were not destined to mark P'i as a major writer or thinker, the commitment to improving the lot of his fellow man is impressive for someone barely twenty. He wrote numerous other prose works including ten imitations of Han Yü's *yüan* 原 ("On the Origin of . . .") and four *fu.** Although his work was obviously influenced by Mencius and Han Yü, his style never attains their clarity or force.

Yet another side of P'i's personality can be seen in his early writings. They reveal a haughty, often self-indulgent man. Apparently conscious of this, P'i once compared himself to the notoriously impudent Mi Heng,* who had run afoul of Ts'ao Ts'ao.

Having been in the capital off and on since 864, P'i passed the *chin-shih* examination in 867. He seems to have never been comfortable in the capital city, which was indeed not the mecca for young graduates it had been several generations earlier. Unable to find either patron or position—the two went hand in hand in the late T'ang—he went to Soochow and attached himself to the coterie of the prefect, Ts'ui P'u. In a matter of months he and Lu Kuei-meng, a scion of a prominent local clan, had become fast friends. In the next year P'i was to write over three hundred poems, many in concert with Lu. Taking advantage of a virtual sinecure, he frequented the homes of several literati with large personal libraries, reading widely in many fields including local Soochow history. In the security of his new home and the lushness of the environs of the Great Lake his literary and personal styles quickly changed. The didacticism and prose of the once pragmatic young graduate gave way to the ornamental, occasional poem of the aesthete:

> Thick like an orangutan's blood smeared on a
> white cloth,
> Light as the swallows intending to fly to the empyrean—
> What a pity this delicate beauty can scarcely stand
> the sun:
> It throws its rays upon the deep reds, creating
> lighter hues.
> ("Ch'ung-t'i ch'iang-wei" 重題薔薇 [Again
> on the Rose]).

From man's sufferings which had been so evident in his travels his eye had turned to the natural beauty and past greatness of Soochow. He had withdrawn from the everyday world.

P'i's theoretical transformation paralleled this development. He abandoned didacticism for a kind of formalism, advancing the theory that poetry had evolved from the prosodically simple old-style to the complex regulated verse (see *shih*). The next form to dominate, he maintained, would be the *tsa-t'i shih* 雜體詩 (verse of miscellaneous forms). By this he meant the literary exercises including *hui-wen* 回文 (palindromes) or *tsa-sheng yün* 雜聲韻 (alliterative verse).

Leaving Soochow after a sojourn of just over a year, P'i traveled back to the capital and served in the government there, attaining the rank of Erudite of the National University. His family may have stayed in the South. And as he returned there in 880 with an appointment to a post in Ch'ang-chou 長州 he encountered Huang Ch'ao 黃巢 and his rebel horde returning from Canton. Apparently swept up by the possibility of replacing a corrupt regime, P'i joined the rebels and upon their arrival in Ch'ang-an was made a Han-lin Academician in the Ta-Ch'i 大齊 dynasty. It soon became apparent that Huang Ch'ao was not receptive to advice from his courtiers; many of them were persecuted for admonishing him. Although there are several accounts of P'i's death (this is the other major concern of modern critics, but none of the theories has solid textual support), it seems most likely that P'i offended Huang Ch'ao and was put to death by the rebel leader.

P'i Jih-hsiu's poetic legacy represents the two major tendencies of the late T'ang (didactic and baroque) and perhaps illustrates by its inadequacies some of the reasons for the prominent place of the new lyrics (*tz'u**) on the literary stage of the Five Dynasties and Sung. The inner drive which seems to have steered P'i through his capricious career—from avid reformer, to recluse-poet, to rebel—in addition to the large and varied corpus he has left, make him one of the most fascinating minor literary figures of the late T'ang. But his adherence to ancient-style prose, his advocacy of *Men-*

cius, his interest in philosophy, and his lowly social origins tie him more closely to the intellectual milieu of the early Sung.

EDITIONS:

Ch'üan T'ang shih, v. 9, *ch.* 608-616, pp. 7012-7107.

Ch'üan T'ang Wen, v. 17, *ch.* 796-799, pp. 10523-10584.

Hsiang Chen-hsiang 項貞詳, ed. (Ming dynasty). *Hsiang-shih P'ing-sheng hsin-k'o P'i Hsi-mei shih* 項氏瓶笙樹新刻皮襲美詩, in the Rare Book Collection of the Peking Library.

P'i-tzu wen-sou 皮子文藪 (Literary Marsh of Master P'i). Peking, 1959; rpt. Shanghai, 1982. Punctuated and collated edition. Contains 36 old-style poems and all but 7 of P'i prose pieces—i.e., his creative production prior to 867.

———. *SPTK.* Photolithic reprint of a Ming edition then in the possession of Mr. Yüan 袁 of Hsiang-t'an 湘潭, probably first printed during the Hung-chih era (1488-1506).

Sung-ling chi 松陵集 (Pine Kroll Anthology). *Hupei Hsien-cheng i-shu* 湖北先正遺書 ed.

TRANSLATIONS:

Nienhauser, William H., Jr. *P'i Jih-hsiu.* Boston, 1979. Nearly 40 poems and 13 prose pieces are rendered—see pp. 151-152 ("Finding List of Translations").

Schafer, Edward H. *Golden Peaches of Samarkand.* Berkeley, 1963, pp. 99, 123 and 129. Three poems.

Sunflower, pp. 259-266.

STUDIES:

Chou, Lien-k'uan 周連寬. "P'i Jih-hsiu te sheng p'ing chi ch'i tso-p'in" 皮日休的生平及其作品, *Ling-nan hsüeh-pao,* 12.1 (June 1952), pp. 113-144. Good introduction to P'i Jih-hsiu.

Hsiao, Ti-fei 蕭滌非. "Ch'ien-yen" 前言, in *P'i-tzu Wen-sou,* Peking, 1959, pp. 1-21.

Masuda, Kiyohide 增田清秀. "Hi Jitsukyu no 'Seigakufu' to jiji hihan" 皮日休の正樂府と批判, in *Gakufu no rekishiteki kenkyū* 樂府歷史的研究, Tokyo, 1975, pp. 407-430.

Miao, Yüeh 繆鉞. "P'i Jih-hsiu ti shih-chi ssu-hsiang chi ch'i tso-p'in" 皮日休的思想及其作品, in *T'ang-shih yen-chiu lun-wen chi* 唐詩研究論文集, Peking, 1959, pp. 371-389.

Nakajima, Chōbun 中島長文. "Hi Jitsukyū" 皮日休, in *Tōdai no shijin—sono denki* 唐代の詩人一その傳記, Ogawa Tamaki 小川環樹, ed., Tokyo, 1975, pp. 581-589. Contains a carefully annotated version of the notice on P'i in *T'ang*

ts'ai-tzu chuan,* a translation thereof, and a useful bibliography.

Nienhauser, *P'i Jih-hsiu.*

Yao, Yao 姚垚. "P'i Jih-hsiu, Lu Kuei-meng ch'ang-ho shih yen-chiu" 皮日休陸龜蒙唱和詩研究. Unpublished M.A. thesis, National Taiwan University, 1980.

—WHN

P'ien-wen 駢文 or *p'ien-t'i wen* 駢體文 (parallel prose) is a Ch'ing denotation of an ancient technique employed in the writing of extra-poetic literary genres. Its most salient features are a preponderance of couplets in which metrical identity (most often four or six graphs) and syntactical parallelism occur between corresponding lines. Thus, in terms of form, it shows many of the same prosodic qualities of Chinese poetry (other qualities are described below). *P'ien-wen* also has extraliterary connotations as the style of writing favored by the literati of the late Han through early T'ang eras.

In both senses, parallel prose figured prominently in the rhetoric of philosophic, literary, and political debate of the late T'ang through the Ch'ing. Critics attacked the artificiality of its prosodic features and language, sometimes denouncing its values and the accomplishments of its authors. These critics favored the use of another kind of prose known as *ku-wen.** Ch'ing critics called the latter *san-wen* 散文 (prose composition, using random-length lines), a more accurate description of the chief attributes of the style and one which neatly expresses its opposition to the primary features of *p'ien-wen.*

At least forty-two genres were at some time or another said to be suited to the employment of *p'ien-wen* style. In attempting to demarcate parallel prose genres and those which were not, anthologists and critics of pre-T'ang times believed that each style of writing (such as *p'ien-wen*) was infused with formal attributes which clearly delineated for the writer the nature of the subject matter (historical facts, feelings, emotions) he would he permitted to describe. As for the genres themselves (letters, memorials, prefaces, etc.), while they obviously denoted a function, they were also believed to be vehicles for a similarly limited range of subjects.

The work of these early critics and anthologists (not to mention that of the writers) was to match a style and its limited subject range with the genre which was a fit vehicle for the range of subjects. Because *p'ien-wen* first appeared in the *fu** genre, and since it was similar to the *shih** style of writing, early critics identified it with the articulation of a writer's emotions and ideas, which was the generally accepted function of the *fu* genre and the subject matter of the poetic style. *P'ien-wen* was therefore deemed to be only fit for employment in other genres which were vehicles for emotions and ideas.

During the T'ang, parallel prose was gradually divorced from its early "poetic" *functions* (not *forms*) and was replaced in the expression of emotions and ideas by the "non-poetic" *ku-wen*. Consequently, *ku-wen* and *p'ien-wen* anthologies of the Ming and Ch'ing years include many of the same prose genres.

In its forms, parallel prose is not limited merely to the composition of metrically parallel lines and couplets. A second important aspect is a preponderance of grammatical and lexical pairing of one or more graphs of the first couplet with the corresponding graphs of its successor.

Examples of this, and of further attributes, may be seen in the first lines of a parallel prose piece by Yü Hsin,* "Wei Liang Shang-huang Hou shih-tzu yü fu shu" 爲梁上黃侯世子與婦書 (A Letter Written on Behalf of the Son of the Marquis Shang-huang of Liang, Addressed to his Wife):

昔仙人導引，尙刻三秋；
神女將疏，猶期九日

In former times, though immortals learned breathing techniques,
It still took them three autumns to do so, and
Though the invisible spirit-woman's presence was disclosed by her man,
She still agreed to come to him on the ninth each year.

A word-for-word rendering of lines one-three and two-four demonstrates their grammatical and lexical parallelness: (1) "immortal-man-induce-stretch"/ (3) "spirit-woman-do-tell," and (2) "yet-limit-three-autumns"/ (4) "still-period-ninth-day." The parallelism of lines one and three is largely synonymic, while the second graphs in each are antonymic. Lines two and four are synonymic.

A third characteristic of parallel prose is the possible matching of lines or of couplets to exploit the euphonic or antiphonic qualities of corresponding tonal schemes, also characteristic of Chinese poetry. Lines one and two are tonally antiphonous (*p'ing-p'ing-tse-tse / tse-tse-p'ing-p'ing*), while lines one and four are tonally euphonous (*p'ing-p'ing-tse-tse* in each line).

There are other significant qualities of *p'ien-wen*, those which are also key markers of shifts in the ideas or arguments of the writers. One of these is the frequent change of meter between couplets, which contain usually lines of four and six graphs. Couplets often scan as four-four (as in the above example), six-six, or four-six and six-four (lines of three, five, six and seven graphs each are not uncommon, however). Other markers are the extra-metrical graphs found at the beginning of a couplet (graphs extrinsic to any parallelism), such as the word *hsi* 昔 (former times) in the above example. Another marker, not found in the Yü Hsin piece, is the use of end rhyme. Usually the second line of each couplet within each section rhymes with every other second line, and a shift to another rhyme scheme is often a further indication of a shift in argument.

A final characteristic of parallel prose is an abundance of tropes. There are several in this piece. No understanding of *p'ien-wen* would be possible without penetrating the complexity of its figurative language, a natural outgrowth of the brevity of the style and of the freedom provided within its prosodic strictures to explore the graphic, tonal, metrical, and semantic qualities of the language. *Ku-wen* proponents often criticized *p'ien-wen* style for an excessive use of such figurative language.

The foregoing description of *p'ien-wen* is but a summary of a style which was first demonstrated in the *fu* genre during the Han dynasty and which gradually came to be used in the writing of other genres deemed suitable vehicles for expressing emotion and ideas. Though Han prose in genres other than the *fu* actually exhibited a high incidence of the qualities of *p'ien-wen*, it was not "self-consciously" a parallel-prose style.

This would only occur during the Six Dynasties when *p'ien-wen* prosodic features were described, prized, deliberately used, and codified in prose composition.

The key critical arbiters of this period were the Ch'i and Liang rulers, their families, and their entourages. They were most suited to this task since they spent much of their time gathering in literary societies, steeping themselves in previous literary works, delving into obscure meanings of words, and delighting in the brocades of rhyme, tonal patterns, and metrical schemes. So closely did they come to identify their own unique literary traditions with *p'ien-wen* style that they often referred to it as *chin-t'i* 近體 (contemporary style), in opposition to all prose (with or without elements of parallelism) written before their era.

The most important views on *p'ien-wen* style are found in Liu Hsieh's *Wen-hsin tiao-lung*,* Hsiao I's 蕭繹 (508-554) *Chin-lou-tzu* 金樓子, and in the preface to the *Wen-hsüan** by Hsiao T'ung. Liu Hsieh said that the identifying factor was the presence of rhyme. Hsiao I and Hsiao T'ung claimed highly embellished language (parallelism, rhyme, tonal patterns, and tropes) used in the expression of deep-seated feelings identified *p'ien-wen* with belles lettres. The idea of these embellishments is carried in the common graph used by these scholars to describe *p'ien-wen*, *li* 麗, meaning both "parallelism (pairs)" and "literary embellishments."

The best known practitioners of *p'ien-wen* were contemporaries of the Hsiao and Liu literati, Yü Hsin* and Hsü Ling (507-583). The work of both epitomized the finest qualities of Six Dynasties' *p'ien-wen*, expressing their innermost thoughts, and varying the prosodic structure in a broad range of personal and public belletristic genres.

The role of *p'ien-wen* as a belletristic style gradually faded after the Six Dynasties, largely because in the T'ang it was appropriated for use in the newly devised system of civil-service examinations and in court and government documents. Thus, while mastery of parallel prose was incumbent upon all aspirants to high office, it was used only for composing the minor belletristic genres used for official purposes and for the *fu*. Genres such as the *chao* 詔 (proclamation) *chih* 制 (edict) and *kao* 誥 (patent) received more attention from literary figures thereafter than did the personal genres such as letters, prefaces, and obituaries, which had earlier been considered *p'ien-wen* genres. Furthermore, T'ang examiners imposed tight rhythmic and metric schemes on examination *p'ien-wen*, which gradually came to apply to *p'ien-wen* court writing in general. Without the old freedom to vary prosodic features, and with a more restrictive range of vehicles of expression, parallel prose naturally lost its appeal as a means of expressing a writer's most personal thoughts.

P'ien-wen gradually exploited its examination role to wed itself to a new kind of subject matter, the display of historical and literary erudition, a possible response to the requirements of the special, advanced examination known as the *hung-tz'u* 宏詞 (resonant prose), which unlike the regular civil-service test, granted an immediate and lofty post to literati who passed it. Throughout much of subsequent history, the masters of *p'ien-wen* style were usually also among the most learned of classicists and historians.

In spite of the evolution of a new, "T'ang-style *p'ien-wen*," some writers in the early T'ang still wrote in the Six Dynasties' fashion, employing the style in a variety of genres. Wang P'o* in particular deserves note.

The apotheosis of the T'ang parallel-prose style can be found in the prose of Li Shang-yin,* whose anthology, *Fan-nan chia-chi i-chi* 樊南甲集乙集, was taken as the model of parallel-prose writing for the subsequent century and a half, in particular influencing early Sung writers such as Yang I (see *Hsi-k'un ch'ou-ch'ang chi*).

The evolution of the new *ku-wen* prose style from the eighth through the eleventh centuries had a profound impact on *p'ien-wen*. Though T'ang-style parallel prose was required form for the examination of Sung times, some writers of the Northern Sung began to modify its strict metrical formula by blending in the irregular-length lines and looser metrical formulae and rhyme schemes of *ku-wen*. This amalgamated style came to be known as *ssu-liu t'i* 四六體 (four-six style). The name came from its tendency to adhere to the four-six meter common under the Six Dynasties and mandated by the T'ang. However, the four-six scheme was more of an artifice in *ssu-liu* style, because a single "sentence" of prose, using the vocabulary and syntax of *ku-wen* was composed to run on through several couplets, with the traditional four or six graphs being allotted to each of the couplet's two "lines."

This new style of parallel prose, like that of the T'ang, was used to display erudition. However, it exploited a wider range of genres, adding especially those of historical criticism and political persuasion, important functions in the new bureaucratic regimes which dominated the late T'ang and Sung governments. In this sense, *ssu-liu* had been employed at an early time by Lu Chih,* and was later mastered by the Northern Sung scholar-officials Ou-yang Hsiu* and Su Shih.*

During the Southern Sung, the *ssu-liu* style was used to display erudition in the most difficult of all Chinese examinations, the special *po-hsüeh hung-tz'u* 博學宏詞 (polymaths and resonant prose), and, by government determination, became the medium of twelve prose genres. Many famous writers and politicians of Southern Sung were known as *ssu-liu* masters, including Chou Pi-ta 周必大 (1126-1204), Hung Mai,* Lu Yu,* and Yang Wan-li.* And, from this period also are the earliest extant guides to parallel-prose style, including Wang Ying-lin's* *Tz'u-hsüeh chih-nan* 辭學指南 (Guide to Rhetoric).

Parallel prose also exerted some influence on the official writings of the Yüan and Ming governments. However, when the examination system was first reintroduced in 1313, there was little emphasis on the expression of erudition or elegance, the bastions of *p'ien-wen* style. Consequently, there was little impetus for most scholars to continue mastering this style. The new format reflected the Neo-Confucian philosophy of the Sung, requiring knowledge of only the *Ssu-shu* and the classics with Neo-Confucian commentaries (see *ching*). It also wedded this format to *ku-wen* style, or at least to a simpler, less learned parallel prose.

P'ien-wen was thus without the official sanction it had earlier enjoyed and it did not regain such sanction until the Ch'ing dynasty. However, after 1488 it was the stipulated form of the new *pa-ku-wen** required in the civil-service examination. This new type of essay emphasized the careful development of an argument and reasoning and paid little attention to style. Talented prose writers of Ming ignored *p'ien-wen* styles; *ku-wen* was the accepted means of composing belletristic prose, the debate centering around which sort of *ku-wen* was to be employed.

During the Ch'ing, *p'ien-wen* style was consciously revived in private and public writings by many of the erudite scholars associated with the Han-hsüeh p'ai 漢學派. The revival was partly a reaction to the Ming "Archaists" (*Fu-ku p'ai* 復古派) who saw *ku-wen* as the style of antiquity. The revival was aided in no small measure by the official policies of the Ch'ing government which saw in the movement a way to win the loyalty of the influential scholars of the South who comprised much of the Han-hsüeh p'ai. Part of the Ch'ing effort materialized in the revival of the Sung *po-hsüeh hung-tz'u* examination in 1679 and 1736.

The *p'ien-wen* writers of the Ch'ing made few innovations in parallel-prose style. They did, however, revive scholarly interest in, and respect for, *p'ien-wen*, which had been held in disrepute under the Ming. Most *p'ien-wen* anthologies and style guides are a product of their activities. Three of the most noted of these scholars are Mao Ch'i-ling 毛奇齡 (1623-1716), Ch'en Wei-sung,* and Juan Yüan 阮元 (1764-1849). In spite of their influence, most prose, including official documents, continued down to the present century to be written in the *ku-wen* style.

ANTHOLOGIES:

Ch'ing-ch'ao p'ien-t'i cheng-tsung (p'ing-pen) 清朝駢體正宗 (評本). Tseng Yü 曾燠, ed. Taipei, 1961. A Ch'ing collection of Ch'ing *p'ien-wen*, punctuated, with some marginal notes.

Hsü Ku-wen yüan 續古文苑. Sun Hsing-yen 孫星衍, ed. A Ch'ing supplement to the *Ku-wen yüan**; pieces from Han through Yüan with some annotation.

Li-tai p'ien-wen hsüan 歷代駢文選. Chang Jen-ch'ing 張仁青, ed. Taipei, 1965. A modern work of Han through Ch'ing pieces; punctuated, with much annotation.

Liu-ch'ao wen-hsieh (chien-chu) 六朝文絜 (箋注). Hsü Lien 許槤, ed., Li Ching-kao 黎經誥, comm. Taipei, 1964. A late Ch'ing anthology to which Li Ching-kao added his annotations in 1889. The latter are not found in the standard *SPPY* edition of this work.

Nan-pei ch'ao wen-ch'ao 南北朝文鈔. P'eng Chao-sun 彭兆蓀, ed. *Yüan-ya t'ang ts'ung-shu* 粵雅堂叢書. A Ch'ing anthology of one hundred pieces, none by Yü Hsin or Hsü Ling.

Pa-chia ssu-liu (wen-chu) 八家四六 (文註). Wu Tzu 吳鼐, ed. Hsü Chen-kan 許貞幹, comm. Shanghai, 1884. A Ch'ing collection of eight of the most respected *p'ien-wen* scholars and writers of the dynasty; with extensive commentaries. See also *Ch'üan Shang-ku San-tai Ch'in Han Liu-ch'ao wen, Ku wen yüan, Kuo-ch'ao wen-lei Wen hsüan,* and *Wen-yüan ying-hua.*

P'ing-hsüan Ssu-liu fa-hai 評選四六法海. Chiang Shih-ch'üan 蔣士銓, ed. Shanghai, 1871. This is a Ch'ing selection of pieces from the *Ssu-liu fa-hai,* punctuated with annotation.

Ssu-liu fa-hai 四六法海. Wang Chih-chien 王志堅, ed. Taipei, 1976. A Ming collection of pieces from Han through Yüan; primarily official documents; some annotation.

Sung ssu-liu hsüan 宋四六選. P'eng Yüan-jui 彭元瑞, ed. Taipei, 1966. A Ch'ing collection of mostly court materials; punctuated, no annotation.

STUDIES:

Chang, Jen-ch'ing 張仁青. *Chung-kuo p'ien-wen fa-chan shih* 中國駢文發展史. Taipei, 1970.

Ch'en, Yao-nan 陳耀南. *Ch'ing-tai p'ien-wen t'ung-i* 清代駢文通義. Taipei, 1977. Covers material found in Hsieh (below) with a longer list of Ch'ing *p'ien-wen* masters.

Chiang, Chü-sung 江菊松. *Sung ssu-liu wen yen-chiu* 宋四六文研究. Taipei, 1977.

Edwards, "A Classified Guide."

Egan, Ronald C., "Prose Style of Fan Yeh," *HJAS,* 39 (1979), 339-401.

Graham, William T., Jr. *"The Lament for the South," Yü Hsin's "Ai Chiang-nan Fu."* Cambridge, 1980.

Hightower, James R. "Some Characteristics of Parallel Prose," in Soren Egerod and Else Glahn, eds., *Studia Serica Bernhard Karlgren Dedicata,* Copenhagen, 1959, pp. 60-91. Important description of various facets of *p'ien-wen.*

———. "The *Wen-hsüan* and Genre Theory," *HJAS,* 20 (1957), 512-534.

Hsieh, Hung-hsüan 謝鴻軒. *P'ien-wen heng-lun* 駢文衡論. Taipei, 1973. The most complete study of *p'ien-wen*'s history. Includes sections on the Yüan and the Ming, not found elsewhere.

Liu, Lin-sheng 劉麟生. *Chung-kuo p'ien-wen shih* 中國駢文史. Shanghai, 1937. A short general history emphasizing work of the Six Dynasties through the Sung.

Marney, John. *Liang Chien Wen-ti.* Boston, 1976. Study of the literary circles of the Liang dynasty.

Tökei, Ferenc. *Genre Theory in China in the Third through Sixth Centuries.* Budapest, 1971.

Ts'ao, Tao-heng 曹道衡. "Kuan-yü Wei-Chin Nan-pei-ch'ao te p'ien-wen ho san-wen" 關於魏晉南北朝的駢文和散文, *Wen-hsüeh p'ing-lun ts'ung-k'an,* 7 (October 1980), 238-268.

—BL

P'ing-hua 平話 (plain narrative, or commenting narrative) is the general designation for a group of vernacular narrative texts dealing with an extended period of history rather than with the adventures of single individual. The texts can be considered the forerunners of the full-fledged vernacular novel as preserved in printed versions from the sixteenth century onwards. Some *p'ing-hua* texts (but not all) carry the words *p'ing-hua* in their titles.

The Ming encyclopedia *Yung-lo ta-tien* (see *lei-shu*) originally also contained a section entitled *p'ing-hua*, so the term was used as a generic designation as early as the fifteenth century. In their present form, practically all preserved *p'ing-hua* texts date from the Yüan dynasty.

The earliest known example of *p'ing-hua* is the *Ta-T'ang San-tsang ch'ü-ching shih-hua* 大唐三藏取經詩話 (The Story with Poems of How Tripitaka of the Great T'ang Fetched Sutras). This text has been preserved in two incomplete editions that may even date from the last years of the Southern Sung dynasty. It tells the story of Tripitaka's journey to the Far West in order to obtain the true sutras; the theme was developed in the novel *Hsi-yu chi.* * This work is exceptional in having the text divided into chapters, each concluded by a poem or poems presented by the characters in the story. Fragments of a later and fuller *p'ing-hua* version of the same story have also been preserved.

The most important *p'ing-hua* are the *Wu-tai shih p'ing-hua* 五代史平話 (The *P'ing-hua* of the History of the Five Dynasties) and those in the collective set "Ch'üan-hsiang p'ing-hua wu-chung" 全相平話五種 (Five Completely Illustrated *P'ing-hua*): *Wu-wang fa-Chou p'ing-hua* 武王伐紂平話 (The *P'ing-hua* on How King Wu Chastised Chou), *Ch'i-kuo ch'un-ch'iu p'ing-hua* 七國春秋平話 (The *P'ing-hua* on the Events of the Seven States), *Ch'in ping liu-kuo p'ing-hua* 秦併六國平話 (The *P'ing-hua* on the Annexation of the Six States by Ch'in), *Ch'ien Han-shu p'ing-hua* 前漢書平話 (The *P'ing-hua* on the History of the Former Han dynasty), and the *San-kuo chih p'ing-hua* 三國志平話 (The *P'ing-hua* on the History of the Three Kingdoms Period). The collective title is the modern designation; these *p'ing-hua* were all printed in or around the Chih-chih 至治 period (1321-1323) in Chien-an 建安 (modern Fukien). To judge from the titles of some of these works, the set originally must have contained at least two more texts. In terms of textual features all the works of this set belong to a similar edition. In this edition, the upper one-third of each page is occupied by an illustration while the text occupies the lower part. Irrespective of length, each *p'ing-hua* of the set is divided into three *chüan*. One of them, the *Wu-wang fa-Chou p'ing-hua*, was by the late sixteenth century rewritten into the novel *Feng-shen yen-i.* * The longest of the set is the *San-kuo chih p'ing-hua*, which deals with the civil wars at the end of the Han dynasty that lead to a tripartition of the realm. A copy of a later and inferior edition of this *p'ing-hua* entitled *San-fen shih-lüeh* 三分事略 (A Summary Account of the Tripartition) is also extant. This story was later developed into the novel *San-kuo chih yen-i.* * The *Wu-tai shih p'ing-hua* consists of five *p'ing-hua* (two of which are only partially preserved), devoted to the Five Dynasties that ruled Northern China from 907 to 960. The *Wu-tai shih p'ing-hua* may be slightly later than the "Ch'üan-hsiang p'ing-hua wu-chung". Each of the five parts of the text is divided into two *chüan*: the first one relating the career of the founder of the dynasty, the second one detailing the decline and fall of the dynasty.

Other *p'ing-hua* are the *Hsüan-ho i-shih** and the *Hsüan Jen-kuei cheng Liao-shih lüeh* 薛仁貴征遼事略 (A Summary Account of Hsüeh Jen-kuei's Subjugation of Liao). The latter has been preserved in the *Yung-lo ta-tien* (outside the lost *p'ing-hua* section!). It deals with the campaign of the early T'ang dynasty against kingdoms in present-day southern Manchuria and northern Korea. The text shows a great similarity to one of the recently discovered fifteenth-century *tz'u-hua.* *

The language of the *p'ing-hua* is best characterized as simple classical Chinese with many vernacular elements. The printed versions contain many incorrect and vulgar characters. Evidently the texts were not meant for a highly literate public. But it also appears unlikely that the *p'ing-hua* were intended as prompt-books for professional storytellers, as sometimes has been assumed, even though some of them, especially the *San-kuo chih p'ing-hua* and the *Wu-tai shih p'ing-hua*, deal with subjects that already for centuries had been a favorite with them. In their present form, the *p'ing-hua* were clearly meant for reading. They were evidently composed on the basis of a wide variety of sources, ranging from the canonical tradition to no longer extant vernacular works similar to *tz'u-hua*. Popular with the anonymous *p'ing-hua* authors were the *yung-shih shih* 詠史詩 (poems on historical themes) by the minor late T'ang poet Hu Tseng 胡曾, which at that time also circulated as primary-school textbooks. *P'ing-hua* may best be considered as popular history books, partly reflecting a view of the past that had developed, in contrast to the official historiography, in legend and anecdote and been further fashioned by puppeteers, actors, and storytellers. Of course, *p'ing-hua* may also have been among the storytellers' sources.

The *p'ing-hua* narrate stories that later were developed into full-fledged vernacular novels. As a rule there is no direct textual link between a particular *p'ing-hua* and the novel on the same theme. However, in some cases, especially in the historical novels compiled by Hsiung Ta-mu 熊大木 in the mid-sixteenth century, long passages from *p'ing-hua* were incorporated into these later works. These adaptations show that some features of the so-called storytellers' manner were consciously imposed on traditional Chinese vernacular fiction at a rather late date, rather than being a relic carried over from its earliest beginnings.

EDITIONS:

The five works included in the "Ch'üan-hsiang p'ing-hua wu-chung" have long been obtainable in several photographic reproductions. They are also easily available in the modern editions published by Ku-tien wen-hsüeh ch'u-pan she (Shanghai) in 1955.

A photographic reproduction of the *San-fen shih-lüeh* was published in 1980 by Tenri University, the owner of the unique copy.

Hsüeh Jen-kuei cheng-Liao shih-lüeh is included in two reprinted sets of the *Yung-lo ta-tien*, and there is a modern edition prepared by Chao Wan-li 趙萬里 and published by Ku-tien wen-hsüeh ch'u-pan she in 1957.

TRANSLATIONS:

Liu, Ts'un-yan 柳存仁. *Buddhist and Taoist Influences on Chinese Novels. V. I: The Authorship of the Fen Shen Yen I.* Wiesbaden, 1962. Con-

tains (pp. 6-75) a translation of the *Wu-wang fa-Chou p'ing-hua*.

STUDIES:

Hsi-ti 西諦 (Cheng Chen-to 鄭振鐸). "Lun Yüan-k'an ch'üan-hsiang p'ing-hua wu-chung" 論 元刊全相平話五種, *Pei-tou*, 1.1 (September 1931), 95-106.

Crump, James I. Jr. "*P'ing-hua* and the Early History of the *San-kuo Chih*," *JAOS*, 71 (1951), 249-255.

———. "Some Problems in the Language of the *Shin-bian Wuu-day shyy Pyng-huah*." Unpublished Ph.D. dissertation, Yale University, 1950.

Dudbridge, Glen. *The Hsi-yu-chi: A Study of the Antecedents of the Sixteenth Century Chinese Novel.* Cambridge, England, 1970. Discussion (pp. 25-45) of the *Ta-T'ang San-tsang ch'ü-ching shih-hua*.

Idema, W. L. "Some Remarks and Speculations Concerning *P'ing-hua*," *TP*, 60 (1974), 121-172. Also in W. L. Idema, *Chinese Vernacular Fiction*, Leiden, 1974, pp. 69-120.

Lo, C. T 羅錦堂. "Clues Leading to the Discovery of *Hsi Yu Chi P'ing-hua*," *JOS*, 7 (1969).

Lo, Tsung-t'ao 羅宗濤. "Yüan Chien-an Yü-shih hsin-k'an wu chung p'ing-hua shih-t'an" 元建安虞氏新刊五種平話試探, in *Ch'ü Wan-li Hsien-sheng ch'i-chih jung-ch'ing lun-wen chi* 屈萬里先生七秩榮慶論文集, Taipei, 1978, pp. 389-405.

Shōji, Kakuichi 莊司格一. "Heiwa ni okeru gohō" 平話における語法, *Shūkan Tōyōgaku*, 11 (May 1964), 46-58.

Tai, Pu-fan 戴不凡. "Wu-tai shih p'ing-hua te pu-fen ch'üeh-wen" 五代史平話的部份闕文, in Tai Pu-fan, *Hsiao-shuo chien-wen lu* 小說見聞錄, Hangchow, 1980, pp. 68-89.

—WI

P'ing-yao chuan 平妖傳 is an early novel of intrinsic as well as historical value. It exists in two markedly different forms: the original work of twenty chapters, entitled *San Sui p'ing-yao chuan* 三遂平妖傳 (The Tale of How the Three Sui Quelled the Demons' Revolt), and a forty-chapter revision and expansion of it by Feng Meng-lung.* In all likelihood, the original work was composed after the first few decades of the Ming dynasty. On this ground alone, the early editions' attribution of the authorship to Lo Kuan-chung* cannot be seriously entertained. Feng's expansion was first published in 1620 and then republished a decade later. While the 1620 edition claims to be the authentic original, the second freely acknowledges Feng's responsibility.

Like the other early novels, the *P'ing-yao chuan* had its historical nucleus, in this case the short-lived rebellion of Wang Tse 王則 in 1047. By the Yüan dynasty at the very latest, the subject of Wang's rebellion had entered the storytellers' repertoire. The novel is far more concerned with witches, wizards, and magic than with history. Indeed, its account of the rebellion, itself full of magic and counter-magic, takes up little more than the last third of the book. Its first twelve chapters deal with the comic exploits of witches and wizards. The comedy is of a mildly subversive kind, which may be labeled the comedy of mischief, in which the institutions of family and state are successively disrupted. Although apparently naive, it is actually a work of considerable art.

The elements of several identifiable stories have been worked into the novel. In fact, its opening has been described as made out of other fiction. Yet, although some names have been carried over from other works, no appreciable amount of text has been borrowed, and it remains a question as to whether the material was acquired in oral or written form.

The *P'ing-yao chuan* and the *Shui-hu chuan,** both of which are concerned with historical rebellions, are the earliest novels that are written mainly in the vernacular. The *P'ing-yao chuan* also has certain other features, notably its rather abrupt beginning, which set it apart from the *Shui-hu chuan* and the other novels.

Opinions differ on the merits of the expanded version. Some critics hold that Feng's sophisticated satire tends to obscure the artfully naive humor of the original work.

EDITIONS:

San Sui p'ing-yao chuan. 4 *chüan* and 20 chapters. Late sixteenth-century edition, copies of which are preserved in Peking University Library and Tenri Library. A reproduction of

the Tenri copy (for which a number of new blocks were made in the Ch'ing dynasty), is included as Vol. 12 of the Chinese series of the *Tenri toshokan zempon sōsho* 天理圖書館善本叢書, 1981.

Pei-Sung San-Sui p'ing-yao chuan 北宋三遂平妖傳. 40 chapters. Revised and expanded by Feng Meng-lung. Both first and second editions are preserved in the Naikaku bunkō. A typeset, 40-chapter edition, entitled *P'ing-yao chuan*, was published in Peking in 1956 and later reprinted. It was based on Ch'ing editions derived from Feng's.

TRANSLATION:

Ōta, Tatsuo 太田辰夫. *Heiyōden* 平妖傳. Tokyo, 1967. A translation of the 40-chapter version.

STUDIES:

Ch'u, Yü 楚茹. "*P'ing-yao chuan* yü p'ing-yao" 平妖傳與平妖, *Yu-shih wen-i* 幼獅文藝, 45.5 (May 1977), 186-193.

Hanan, Patrick. "The Composition of the *P'ing-yao chuan*," *HJAS*, 31 (1971), 201-219. On the date and composition of the 20-chapter version.

Ōta, Tatsuko. "Kaisetsu" 解說, in *Heiyōden*, Ōta Tatsuo, tr., ch. 5, pp. 405-413. This backmatter to the Japanese translation of the novel contains a comparison of the two versions.

Yokoyama, Hiroshi 横山弘. "Kaisetsu," in *Hoku-Sō San-Sui heiyōden* 北宋三遂平妖傳, included in the *Tenri toshokan zempon sōsho*, pp. 29-44. This back-matter to the reproduction of the 40-chapter version describes the characteristics of the 20-chapter version.

—PH

Po Chü-i 白居易 (*tzu*, Lo-t'ien 樂天, *hao*, Hsiang-shan 香山, 772-846) was one of the most popular of T'ang poets. He was born in Hsin-chen 新鄭 (modern Honan) to an impoverished, scholarly family originally from T'ai-yüan 太原 (Shansi). Before his birth, the family had lived in Hsia-kuei 下邽, on the south bank of the Wei River, not far from Ch'ang-an, the T'ang capital. When Po Chü-i was about ten, his father took the family to P'eng-ch'eng 彭城 (modern Hsü-chou, Kiangsu) where he served as a magistrate. Po Chü-i, however, was sent to live with some relatives in Hsia-kuei, possibly for the purpose of education. A precocious child, he could read before he was two and knew the rules of prosody when he was seven; nevertheless, he did not pass the *chin-shih* examination until 800, when he was twenty-seven. In 802 he passed the *pa-ts'ui* 拔萃, a selective placement examination. Among the eight successful candidates was Yüan Chen,* who became his lifelong friend, whose name became linked with his because of their many joint literary ventures, and who was appointed, along with Po, a government collator following the examination. During their tenure as collators, Po Chü-i and Yüan Chen prepared themselves for the ultimate palace examination. They cloistered themselves for six months, studying, discussing current events, and trying to find solutions to problems concerning the affairs of the state in anticipation of the possible examination questions. Seventy-five essays which resulted from their studies are preserved in Po Chü-i's collected works under the title "Ts'e-lin" 策林 (Forest of Plans). Although the questions they had anticipated were not asked, they both passed with flying colors.

In their lifetimes, Po Chü-i's literary reputation paralleled that of Yüan Chen, but outdistanced that of his friend after their deaths. His political career, however, never reached the heights attained by Yüan Chen, although neither realized his youthful dreams of effecting social reform. The nearest Po Chü-i ever came to the emperor was when he was a member of the Han-lin Academy and served concurrently as Reminder of the Left (807-815). Because of his outspoken criticism of governmental policies and his remonstrances against injustice, especially that done to Yüan Chen (who was banished in 809), Po was exiled from Ch'ang-an in 815. Although he held several desirable positions afterwards—Prefect of Hangchow (822-825) and Prefect of Soochow (825-827)—he was never in a position to exercise his influence in the central government. Disappointed in politics in later years, Po Chü-i turned to Buddhism for consolation. After retiring from an honorary post as Junior Mentor of the Heir Apparent, he remained in Loyang until his death at the age of seventy-four.

A prolific writer, Po Chü-i wrote more than 2,800 poems, taking pains to preserve his works for posterity, which may account for his lasting fame. When he was banished to Chiang-ling 江陵 in 815 he sent fifteen *chüan* of his writings, classified under different categories, to Yüan Chen. In 824 and 825, Yüan Chen edited and compiled Po's collected works, *Po-shih Ch'ang-ch'ing chi* 白氏長慶集. In his introduction to this volume, dated the twelfth month of the fourth year of the Ch'ang-ch'ing period (January 825), Yüan Chen gives a full account of Po's life, the popularity of Po's poetry, and its international reputation (Po's verse was especially prized in Japan— see below). He speaks of their joint endeavor in promoting the new *yüeh-fu* style and the long poems in regulated verse (*p'ai-lü*—see *shih*) with hundreds of rhymes which were devised by the two friends and known to posterity as *Yüan-ho shih* 元和詩 (after the reign period, 806-820, during which much of this verse was written) or *Yüan-Po t'i* 元白體. Two years before he died, Po Chü-i added twenty-five more *chüan* to this collection, for a total of seventy-five *chüan*. He then made five copies and housed them in different locales to insure their preservation.

Of his own poems Po Chü-i most treasured the *feng-yü shih* 諷諭詩 (satirical and allegorical poems) and the new *yüeh-fu* poems, such as "Hsin-feng che-pi weng" 新豐折臂翁 (An Old Man with a Broken Arm), an attack on militarism, "Mai-t'an weng" 賣炭翁 (The Charcoal Vendor), a plaint against official harassment, and "Shang-yang pai-fa jen" 上陽白髮人 (The White-haired Person of Shang-yang Palace), a lament on the fate of palace ladies. For posterity, however, the most popular of his poems are his romantic ballads: "Ch'ang-hen ko" 長恨歌 (Song of Everlasting Sorrow), which narrates the love story of the Emperor Ming-huang and his consort Yang Kuei-fei, and "P'i-p'a hsing" 琵琶行 (Song of the P'i-p'a), which describes the music and the sad life of a female entertainer, whom the poet encountered during his exile in Chiang-ling.

Po Chü-i's greatest literary contribution was to popularize literature and make it readily accessible to the masses. In order to have his poetry understood by people of all social strata, Po strove for clarity and simplicity of language and beauty and harmony in rhythm. Because of these characteristics, his poems were widely read and admired by people from all walks of life. They were recited by school urchins and peasant women, sung by courtesans and palace ladies, and written on the walls of temples and hotels. Copies of his poems were sold in marketplaces and housed in the Imperial Secretariat of Japan. Most of the poems quoted in the *Tales of Genji* are those by Po Chü-i and his friends. Even today, Po Chü-i's poetry is better known internationally than that of his contemporaries. And he is honored in the People's Republic of China because of his influence on the development of realism and utilitarian literature.

Po Chü-i's "Ch'ang-hen ko" provides a good example of how the developments of poetry and fiction in T'ang times were mutually influenced. After the Song had been completed, Ch'en Hung 陳鴻 (*chin-shih*, 805), a close friend of Po, read it and wrote a *ch'uan-ch'i* tale based on it. The combined influence of the tale and the poem has been enormous, especially in the field of drama, and the Yang Kuei-fei theme has become a major tradition in Chinese popular literature.

EDITIONS:

Po Chü-i chi 白居易集. 4v. Ku Hsüeh-chieh 顧學頡, collator. Peking, 1979.

Po Hsiang-shan chi 白香山集. 2v. Taipei, 1960.

Po Hsiang-shan shih-chi 白香山詩集. SPPY.

Po-shih Ch'ang-ch'ing chi 白氏長慶集. SPTK edition.

TRANSLATIONS:

Demiéville, *Anthologie*, pp. 290-308, 329.

Levy, Howard S., *et al. Translations from Po Chü-i's Collected Works*. 4v. New York, 1971-75.

Sunflower, pp. 201-211.

Waley, *Translations*, pp. 126-273.

Wang, Elizabeth Te-chen 王德箴. "Story of Everlasting Sorrow," in Elizabeth Te-chen Wang, *Ladies of the T'ang*, Taipei, 1961, pp. 107-132. English translation of "Ch'ang-hen ko chuan."

von Zach, *Han Yü*, pp. 318-347.

STUDIES:

Ch'iu, Hsieh-yu 邱燮友. *Po Chü-i* 白居易. Taipei, 1978.

Chu, Chin-ch'eng 朱金城. *Po Chü-i nien-p'u* 白居易年譜. Shanghai, 1982.

Feifel, Eugene. "Biography of Po Chü-i" 白居易: Annotated translation from *Chüan* 166 of the *Chiu T'ang-shu* 舊唐書," *MS*, 17 (1958), 255-311.

Hanabusa, Hideki. 花房英樹. *Haku Kyoi kekyū* 白居易研究. Kyoto, 1971.

———. *Hakushi monjū no hihanteki kenkyū* 白氏文集の批評的研究. Kyoto, 1974.

Hiraoka, Takeo 平岡武夫. *Haku Kyoi*. Tokyo, 1977.

———. "Hakushi bunshū no sōritsu" 白氏文集の成立, in *Tōhō gakkai sōritsu 15 shūnen kinen tōhōgaku ronshū* 東方學會成立十五週年記念東方學論集, Tokyo, 1962, pp. 260-275.

Ku, Hsüeh-chieh. "Po Chü-i shih-hsi chia-tsu k'ao" 白居易世系家族考, *Wen-hsüeh p'ing-lun ts'ung-k'an*, 13 (May 1982), 131-168.

Lin, Wen-yüeh 林文月. " 'Ch'ang-hen ko' tui 'Ch'ang-hen ko chuan' yü *Yüan-shih wu-yü* ('t'ung-hu') te ying-hsiang" 長恨歌對長恨歌傳與源氏物語（桐壺）的影響, in *Chung-kuo ku-tien wen-hsüeh yen-chiu ts'ung-k'an: Hsiao-shuo chih-pu (1)* 中國古典文學研究叢刊：小說之部, Taipei, 1977, pp. 191-216.

Tanaka, Katusmi 田中克己. *Haku Rakuten* 白樂天. Toyko, 1964.

Waley, Arthur. *Life and Times of Po Chü-i*. London, 1945.

Wang, Meng-ou 王夢鷗. *T'ang-jen hsiao-shuo yen-chiu ssu-chi* 唐人小說研究四集. Taipei, 1978, pp. 213-238. Clarifies much of the controversy concerning Ch'en Hung and his authorship of "Ch'ang-hen ko chuan" and other writings.

Wang, Shih-i 王拾遺. *Po Chü-i yen-chiu* 白居易研究. Shanghai, 1954.

Yü, P'ing-po 俞平伯. " 'Ch'ang-hen ko' chi 'Ch'ang-hen ko chuan' te chih-i" 長恨歌及長恨歌傳的質疑, *Hsiao-shuo yüeh-pao*, 20.2 (February 1929), 357-361.

　　　　　　　　　　　　　　　　—AJP and YWM

Po Hsing-chien 白行簡 (*tzu*, Chih-t'ui 知退, 775-826), was the younger brother of Po Chü-i.* He passed the *chin-shih* examination in 807, held a number of provincial posts, and late in life (beginning in 820) served as Censor in the Chancellery and then Director of the Bureau of Receptions.

He was a talented writer, whose collected corpus amounted to twenty *chüan*, most of it, unfortunately, now lost. His poetic style has been compared to that of his elder and better-known brother, with whom he lived until 814. Among his extant works the *ch'uan-ch'i** tale "Li Wa chuan" 李娃傳 is the most famous.

This tale celebrates Miss Li, a courtesan of Ch'ang-an in the T'ien-pao period (742-755), who becomes the lover of a young man of good family who has come to Ch'ang-an to study for the examinations. After a year the young man's money is exhausted, and Miss Li and her "mother" desert him. Bewildered and despairing, he falls into disgrace. Eventually, in rags and ill, begging from house to house in the snow, he meets Miss Li again. She realizes that because of her he has been cast out by his family and has not fulfilled his earlier great promise as a scholar. To make amends she buys her freedom, takes him into her house, and nurses him back to health. Then she encourages and supports him while he studies. After passing a special examination with highest honors, Po is appointed to a military post in the Ch'eng-tu area. As a result, he is reconciled with his family and finally marries Miss Li.

An important theme in this tale is alienation and reconciliation. The young lovers are, of course, parted and reunited during the course of the plot. However, more significant is the young man's having been separated from everything of value in his life—family, friends, career, social standing—as a result of his initial affair with Miss Li. His father, for example, beats him almost to death when he finds the young man in disgrace. Miss Li's sacrifice and the young man's struggle to regain his scholarship are the means to his reconciliation with his family and society.

The tale is unusual among T'ang *ch'uan-chi* for the detail used to describe the young man's feelings and experiences. It also includes a number of scenes of life of the lower classes in Ch'ang-an. This emphasis is particularly striking since it does not contribute directly to the stated theme of the tale. However, it is important in supporting the theme of alienation and reconciliation. The extremity of the young man's distress makes clear the degree of his alienation and is furthermore a kind of penance for his earlier transgressions. It is interesting that it is the lower classes in this tale who treat the young man with warmth and kindness in contrast to the unsympathetic, if theoretically justifiable, coldness of his father. Altogether, the tale portrays lower-class life in Ch'ang-an with uncommon sympathy.

The tale is more typical in its portrayal of the young man as essentially passive. He survives severe difficulties but as the recipient of a great deal of care from others. Complementing this is the expected presentation of Miss Li as a woman of strength and imagination.

The tale appears in *T'ai-ping kuang-chi*, *chüan* 484, which attributes it to the T'ang collection *I-wen chi* 異聞集. However, it seems also to have circulated separately and was well known. At least two later dramas were based on it.

Po was also the author of "San-meng chi" 三夢記 (Three Dreams), in which he claims there are three kinds of extraordinary dreams: (1) someone dreams of something and another person encounters it; (2) a person does something and someone dreams of it; and (3) two persons dream the same dream. In three short stories reminiscent of *chih-kuai** fiction he strives to provide actual examples of such dream types. Only seven of his *shih* poems are extant along with nineteen *fu*, the genre which first gained him a reputation in the early ninth century. Among this later corpus is the "Ta-le fu" 大樂賦 (Prose-poem on the Greatest Pleasure), a text discovered at Tun-huang (Pelliot 2539) (see *Tun-huang wen-hsüeh*) which depicts various historical and practical aspects of traditional sexual life.

EDITIONS:
Ch'üan T'ang shih, v. 7, pp. 5304-5306.
Ch'üan T'ang wen, v. 15, pp. 8985-8998.
Lu Hsün 魯迅. *T'ang Sung ch'uan-ch'i chi* 唐宋傳奇集. Hong Kong, 1967.

Wang Kuo-yüan 汪國垣, ed. *T'ang-jen hsiao-shuo* 唐人小說. Hong Kong, 1966, pp. 100-112. The *ch'uan-ch'i* tales.

TRANSLATIONS:
Bauer, *Golden Casket*, pp. 118-136.
Birch, *Anthology*, v. 1, pp. 300-312.
Idema, W. L. *Het hoogste genot [Ta-le fu]. Cahiers van De Lantaarn, No. 19.* Leiden, 1983.
Traditional Chinese Stories, pp. 163-171.

STUDIES:
Dudbridge, Glen. *The Tale of Li Wa, Study and Critical Edition of a Chinese Story from the Ninth Century.* London, 1983.
Tai, Wang-shu 戴望舒. "Tu Li Wa chuan" 讀李娃傳, in his *Hsiao-shuo hsi-chü lun-chi* 小說戲曲論集, Peking, 1958, pp. 7-26.
Uchiyama, Chinari 內山知也. "Haku Kōkan to 'Ri Ai den'" 白行簡と李娃傳, *Daitō bunka daigaku kiyō*, 10 (March 1972), 169-197.
Van Gulik, Robert H. *Sexual Life in Ancient China.* Leiden, 1974. A summary (partly in Latin) and discussion of the "Ta-le fu" is found on pp. 203-208.
Wang, Meng-ou 王夢鷗. " 'Li Wa chuan' hsieh-ch'eng nien-tai te shang-ch'üeh" 李娃傳寫成年代的商榷, *CWWH*, 1.4 (September 1972), 32-39.

—SY, CYi, and WHN

San-hsia wu-i 三俠五義 (Three Heroes and Five Gallants), the late nineteenth-century novel attributed to the storyteller Shih Yü-k'un 石玉崑 (*fl.* 1870), is a quasi-historical novel of adventure, crime detection, and political intrigues, features that place it in the category of *kung-an* 公案 (crime-case) fiction. With a plot revolving around the famed Northern official Pao Cheng 包拯 (999-1062), *San-hsia wu-i* represents the final stage in the development of the Lord Pao 包公 figure, one of the best-known "incorruptible officials" (*ch'ing-kuan* 清官) in Chinese popular literature.

Not long after his death, Pao-kung began appearing in Sung anecdotal writings of judicial wisdom. Pao figured in a large number of Yüan *tsa-chü** involving the courtroom. He can be found in several Ming *hua-pen** stories and the novel *P'ing-yao chuan,** and he is the central figure in a collection of one hundred short stories entitled *Lung-t'u kung-an* 龍圖公案 (The Crime Cases of the Lord of the Dragon Pattern). In this collection, dating at least as early as the end of the sixteenth century, Pao is a man of supernatural powers. Finally, in the Ch'ing dynasty, he appeared frequently in a great range of popular literary genres (*pao-chüan* 寶卷 [precious scrolls], *tzu-ti shu,** *t'an-tz'u,** etc.) and in two major novels, *Wan-hua lou* 萬花樓 (The Mansion of Myriad Flowers) by Li Yü-t'ang 李雨堂 (dates uncertain) and *San-hsia wu-i.*

The structure of *San-hsia wu-i* is binary. Two distinct but intimately related storylines run through the novel: the courtroom cases of Lord Pao and the adventures of the heroes and gallants. Pao himself plays a major role only in the first third of the novel, which consists of criminal episodes he personally solves. The first of the heroes and gallants are introduced in chapter 3, and they gradually gain importance through the course of the narrative. Furthermore, by chapter 37, a substitute for Pao is introduced in the figure of Yen Cha-san 顏查散, and he essentially replaces Pao, in all his functions, after that point. Although the novel is episodic and consequently somewhat loosely structured, these two major storylines are cleverly interwoven by the storyteller to create a moving narrative about the struggle between good and evil on the local, as well as the national, level. Pao and the heroes capture petty thieves and murderers, and at the same time, they quell an incipient rebellion by the Prince of Hsiang-yang against the benevolent Sung emperor, Jen-tsung, Pao's supporter.

Although the language of *San-hsia wu-i* is semi-classical, the narrative abounds in the sort of lively and colorful colloquial descriptions used by traditional storytellers. Without exception, the characters are drawn with consummate skill; from the heroes and gallants to Lord Pao, his wife, and his servant, Pao-hsing, all are depicted as realistic and convincing men and women. The narrator has made each hero or gallant a totally unique individual. All work together in this compelling story of the search for justice during a period of political upheaval, a period that closely resembles the chaotic conditions existing in China during the storyteller's lifetime.

San-hsia wu-i is derived from oral literature. It originated in an oral story-cycle made popular in the middle of the nineteenth century by the famous storyteller Shih Yü-k'un, about whom we know very little. Shih was born in Tientsin but earned his fame as a storyteller in Peking, where he told narratives of the "unofficial" or "spurious" history type (*yeh-shih* 野史). His most famous narrative was known as the *Lung-t'u kung-an* (not to be confused with the Ming collection of short stories mentioned above). Shih Yü-k'un was the founder of a school of storytelling, Shih-p'ai shu 石派書, which belonged to the *ta-ku** tradition. At the Academia Sinica in Taiwan there are extant manuscript versions (*ch'ang-pen* 唱本) of *Lung-t'u kung-an*, which bear characteristics peculiar to oral or orally dictated literature. Aside from several song-book versions of *Lung-t'u kung-an*, the first prose version of the story cycle, traditionally considered to have been written down by someone who heard Shih's oral version, is also at Academia Sinica. The prose version, in 120 chapters, is entitled *Lung-t'u erh-lu* 龍圖耳錄 (The Aural Record of the Lord of the Dragon Pattern). It lacks, however, the sung sections of the *Lung-t'u kung-an*. This prose version first became *Chung-lieh hsia-i chuan* 忠烈俠義傳 (A Tale of Loyal Heroes and Gallants), a 120-chapter version printed in 1879, with three prefaces, one by Wen-chu chu-jen 問竹主人 (Master of Questioning Bamboo), the supposed reviser of *Lung-t'u erh-lu*. *Chung-lieh hsia-i chuan* was then revised again by Wen-chu chu-jen and republished in 1879 under the title *San-hsia wu-i*.

This latter version was again revised and retitled *Ch'i-hsia wu-i* 七俠五義 (Seven Heroes and Five Gallants) in 1889 by the classicist Yü Yueh 俞樾 (1821-1907). There are three major differences between *Ch'i-hsia wu-i* and the earlier three versions: in *Ch'i-hsia wu-i* the language is more terse and literary, the entire first episode concerning the palace intrigue of substituting a cat for the crown prince is omitted, and the number of heroes in the title is changed from three to seven in recognition of the importance of four other protagonists.

Finally, in 1956, *San-hsia wu-i* was reprinted in China with some minor revisions by Chao Ching-shen 趙景深 (b. 1902) that were based on ideological concerns.

EDITIONS:
Ch'i-hsia wu-i. Revised by Yü Ch'ü-yüan 俞曲園 (Ch'ing). Hong Kong, 1961, and other recent rpts.
Chung-lieh hsia-i chuan. Now rare.
San-hsia wu-i. Revised by Chao Ching-shen 趙景深. Shanghai, 1956, and other recent rpts.

TRANSLATIONS:
Blader, Susan. "The Pig-head Purchase," *Renditions*, forthcoming.

STUDIES:
Blader, Susan. "A Critical Study of *San-hsia wu-yi* and Its Relationship to the 'Lung-t'u kung-an' Song-book." Ph.D. dissertation, University of Pennsylvania, 1977.
———. "*San-hsia wu-yi* and Its Link to Oral Literature." *Chinoperl*, 8 (1978), 9-38.
———. "'Yan Chasan Thrice Tested': Printed Novel to Oral Tale," *CHINOPERL*, 12 (1983), 84-111.
Hu, Shih 胡適. "*San-hsia wu-i* hsü" 三俠五義序, in Hu Shih, *Hu Shih wen-ts'un*, Third Series, Shanghai, 1930, pp. 661-705.
Li, Chia-jui 李家瑞. "Ts'ung Shih Yü-k'un ti *Lung-t'u kung-an* shuo tao *San-hsia wu-i*" 從石玉崑的龍圖公案說到三俠五義, *Wen-hsüeh chi-k'an*, 2 (April 1934), 393-397.
Liu, Shih-te 劉世德 and Teng Shao-chi 鄧紹基. "Ch'ing-tai kung-an hsiao-shuo te ssu-hsiang ch'ing hsiang" 清代公案小說的思想傾向, *Wen-hsüeh p'ing-lun*, 1964.2 (April 1964), 41-60.
Ma, Y. W. "The Textual Tradition of Ming *Kung-an* Fiction: A Study of the *Lung-t'u kung-an*," *HJAS*, 35 (1975), 190-220.
———. "*Kung-an* Fiction: A Historical and Critical Introduction," *TP*, 65 (1979), 200-259.
—SB

San-kuo-chih yen-i 三國志演義 (Romance of the Three Kingdoms), about the spectacular events within and among the three kingdoms of Wei, Shu, and Wu in the third century, is one of the earliest classic Chinese novels. It is traditionally attributed to Lo Kuan-chung.* The earliest extant edition, however, is dated 1522, or at the earliest, 1494. Editors of modern reprints of this edition believe it to be a work from the Yüan period, basing their argument mainly on the usage of Yüan place-names in interlinear commentaries to this edition.

Related to the problem of the dating of the novel is the hypothesis that the work developed from the *San-kuo-chih p'ing-hua* 三國志平話 (see also *p'ing-hua*) through an intermediary *tz'u-hua** (doggerel story) stage. However, there is no evidence that a *San-kuo-chih tz'u-hua* ever existed. Admittedly, much ground has been broken in research on oral forms of the Sung and Yüan periods. But since the novel is based on historical figures, and since historiography represents a major and vital component of Chinese narrative, the novel must be set in this written tradition that precedes Sung-Yüan oral forms. Thus, rather than searching for the origins of the novel in the *San-kuo-chih p'ing-hua*, scholars should compare the novel and the appropriate section in Chu Hsi's 朱熹 (1130-1200) *Tzu-chih t'ung-chien kang-mu* 資治通鑑綱目 (Summary of the Comprehensive Mirror for Aid in Government). Considerable similarities in form and content can be found. Comparing, for example, the episode titles in the novel with the *kang* 綱 (topic entries) in the *Tzu-chih t'ung-chien kang-mu* or comparing their sequences of events will bear out this claim. There is, nevertheless, a crucial difference in intent between historiographical writings on the Three Kingdoms period and treatment of the same period in the novel form. While the *Tzu-chih t'ung-chien kang-mu* is written in the tradition of the so-called *Ch'un-ch'iu pi-fa* 春秋筆法 (Rhetoric of the *Spring and Autumn Annals*) and attempts to praise and censure through a precise choice of vocabulary, the novelist shows figures in comparable situations in all three kingdoms and leaves the moral conclusions to be drawn by the reader.

In comparing the novel with essays on the San-kuo period by traditional literati such as Su Hsün,* Su Shih,* Li Chih,* Chung Hsing,* or Wang Fu-chih,* the contrast between historiography and the novel becomes all the more evident. On the issue of *i* 義 (righteousness), for example, the *shih-lun* 史論 (essays on history) written by these figures judge San-kuo characters according to their adherence to, or deviation from, this standard. In the novel, the issue of *i* also often appears, on an average of almost every fifth page in a modern reprint. The difference, however, is that the novelist is not interested in judging a character against an absolute righteousness. Rather, he is concerned with a controlled exploration of the various meanings of righteousness. This can be substantiated by an analysis of the patterns formed by different compounds of the word *i*, such as *ta-i* 大義 (major righteousness), *chung-i* 忠義 (loyalty and righteousness), *hsiao-i* 小義 (minor righteousness), etc., that appear in the novel. In this sense, then, the term *yen-i* 演義, traditionally used in the titles of texts to mean "an explication of meaning," might be interpreted differently in the title of the novel to mean a playing out of the various implications of moral principle.

Many editions of the novel appeared in the sixteenth and seventeenth centuries. The second earliest extant edition, with a preface dated 1549, is kept in the Biblioteca Real de San Lorenzo del Escorial, Madrid, Spain. Liu Ts'un-yan argues that editions of the novel using the term *chih-chuan* 志傳 (records and biographies) in the title are an earlier form of the novel than the 1522 edition, although the evidence he presents is questionable. There is generally not much difference between the various Ming editions other than variations in the arrangement of *chüan* 卷 (section) and *hui* 回 (chapters) and the integration of *hui*—the textual variants are minor, except that some editions include the story of Kuan So 關索, the fictional third son of Kuan Yü 關羽. (A *tz'u-hua* text on Hua Kuan So 花關索 dated 1478, which fleshes out the skeletal biography of Kuan So in the novel, has recently been discovered.) Some Ming editions, beginning as early as the 1549 edition, include poems by Chou Li 周禮 (*tzu*, Ching-hsüan 靜軒), a historian of the late fifteenth century. On the whole, however, these differences are negligible, especially in comparison with the changes Mao Lun and his son Mao Tsung-kang* made in the novel during the early Ch'ing period.

The Maos tightened and refined the language throughout the novel. They abbreviated some official documents mainly because of verbose language, and added others for the sake of documentary realism. They shortened, omitted, or replaced poems and added anecdotes. Heroes from the Shu Kingdom are cast in a more favorable light than those from Wei or Wu, although the distinction is never black and white. The major value of the Mao edition, however, is in the commentaries, which were completed in 1679. Showing critical insight into both the textural and structural aspects of the novel, the value of this commentary is comparable to Chin Sheng-t'an's* commentary on *Shui-hu chuan** which was completed in 1641. Other commentaries to *San-kuo chih yen-i* include ones attributed to Li Chih, Chung Hsing, and Li Yü* (1611-1680), but it was the Mao edition that came to dominate the Ch'ing market, as can be seen in the number of extant Ch'ing reprints in major collections.

The popularity of the novel and its impact on folk culture can be seen in the extent, in both chronological and geographical terms, to which San-kuo episodes have been adapted in the theater and performing arts in their numerous forms and genres and in the way San-kuo heroes have been symbolized (i.e., Chu-ko Liang [181-234] as the idealization of wisdom, Hua T'o 華佗 [c. 141-203] as the perfection of professional skills, Ts'ao Ts'ao 曹操 [155-220] as the personification of Machiavellianism, and Chou Yü 周瑜 [175-210] as the symbol of the unfortunate talent) and deified (i.e., Lord Kuan [Kuan Yü] as the god of war). The glorification of traditional behavorial standards (i.e., friendship, brotherhood, and loyalty) in the narratives of the novel and its later adaptions has had immense effects on secret societies and clan organizations still common today. Although not as popular as the *Hung-lou meng** in modern times, the *San-kuo chih yen-i* is, with the possible exception of the *Shui-hu chuan*,* the most influential novel produced in traditional China.

EDITIONS:

Nikoku Eiyūfu 二刻英雄譜. Kyoto, 1980. Facsimile reprint of *ch'ung-chen* edition.
San-kuo-chih t'ung-su yen-i 三國志通俗演義. 8v. Peking, 1975. Facsimile reprint of 1522 edition.
San-kuo-chih t'ung-su yen-i 三國志通俗演義. Shanghai, 1980. Modern reprint of 1522 edition.
San-kuo-chih yen-i 三國志演義. Hong Kong, 1973. Modern reprint of Mao edition with commentary.
San-kuo yen-i 三國演義. Peking, 1972. Reprint of Mao edition without commentary; most commonly read edition today.

TRANSLATIONS:

Brewitt-Taylor, C. H. *Romance of the Three Kingdoms.* 2v. Shanghai, 1925. Reprint with an introduction by Roy Andrew Miller, Rutland, 1959.
Ogawa, Tamaki 小川環樹, and Kaneda Junichirō 金田純一郎. *Sangokushi* 三國志. Tokyo, 1961.
Roberts, Moss. *Three Kingdoms.* New York, 1976. Translation of excerpts.

STUDIES:

Chang, Cheng-liang 張政烺. "Chiang-shih yü yung-shih-shih" 講史與詠史詩, *BIHP*, 10 (1948), 601-645.
Liu, Ts'un-jen [yen] 柳存仁. "Lo Kuan-chung chiang-shih hsiao-shuo chih chen-wei hsing-chih" 羅貫中講史小說之眞僞性質, in *Ho-feng T'ang tu-shu-chi* 和風堂讀書記. Hong Kong, 1977, pp. 235-300.
Lo, Andrew H. "Structure and Meaning in *Ying-hsiung p'u*—An Interpretive Study of the *San-kuo* and *Shui-hu* Narratives in the Context of Chinese Historiography." Unpublished Ph.D. dissertation, Princeton University, 1981.
Ogawa, Tamaki. "*Sangoku engi no Moseisan hihyobon to Ri Ryūōbon*" 三國演義の毛聲山批評本と李笠翁本, in Ogawa Tamaki, *Chūgoku shosetsushi no kenkyū* 中國小說史の研究, Tokyo, 1968, pp. 153-161.
———. "*Sangokushi engi no motozuita rekishisho ni tsuite*, 三國志演義のもとついた歴史書について, in *Tōyō no bunka to shakai*, 2 (March 1952), 15-21.

Onoe, Kaneyoshi 尾上兼英. "Seika setsushō shiwa shiron (1) Ka-kan Saku den o megutte" 成化說唱詞話試論㈠ 花關索傳をあぐ, *Tōyō bunka*, 58 (March 1978), 127-142.

Riftin, B. L. *Istoricheskaiia epopeia i fol'klornaia traditsiia v Kitae*. Moscow, 1970.

Sun, K'ai-ti 孫楷第. "*San-kuo-chih p'ing-hua* yü *San-kuo-chih-chuan t'ung-su yen-i*" 三國志平話與三國志傳通俗演義, in Sun K'ai-ti, *Ts'ang-chou chi* 滄州集, Peking, 1965, pp. 109-120.

Tso-chia ch'u-pan she 作家出版社. *San-kuo yen-i yen-chiu lun-wen chi* 三國演義研究論文集. Peking, 1957.

—ALo

Shan-hai ching 山海經 (The Classic of Mountains and Seas) is a fantastic geography of ancient China and surrounding lands. Liu Hsin, the Han editor of this text, ascribed it to the thearch Yü 禹 (23rd century B.C.), mythological regulator of the great Chinese flood, and his assistant I 益. Supposedly, Yü traveled the world during his heroic labors and learned much about the mountains, seas, inhabitants, and gods of his own and other lands. Yü's travelogue was written down by his assistant in thirty-four sections, which were edited millennia later by Liu Hsin* into the present eighteen-section classic.

From at least the time of Yen Chih-t'ui* this account of authorship has been rejected, but considerable controversy still surrounds the dating of the text. Assuredly, the present work consists of several textual layers. One study of considerable influence has ascribed the earliest of these layers to the Eastern Chou. However, a more meticulous and persuasive study by the modern scholar Yüan K'o 袁珂 has assigned the earliest textual layer, "Ta-huang ching" 大荒經 (The Classic of the Great Wild) in four sections and "Hai-nei ching" 海內經 (The Classic of the Area within the Seas), section eighteen in modern editions, to the middle years of the Warring States period (*c.* 320 B.C.) and the latest layer, "Hai-wai ching" 海外經 (The Classic of the Area beyond the Seas) in four sections and "Hai-nei ching" (the same title as above, but a different portion of the text) which comprises sections ten to thirteen in modern editions, to the earliest years of the Han dynasty. At any rate, the existence of a work by the name "*Shan-hai ching*" is first attested in Ssu-ma Ch'ien's* *Shih-chi.**

After Liu Hsin edited the text, it was transmitted in several different versions. The one in eighteen sections (the only version currently available) is that most frequently referred to, but an edition in thirteen sections is mentioned in the *Han-shu*, and one in twenty-three sections is attested in the *Sui-shu*. Most authorities agree that these editions differed only in arrangement and not in content. The earliest commentary on the text was prepared by the great Chin scholar Kuo P'u 郭璞 (276-324). No further commentaries appeared until the work of Wang Ch'ung-ch'ing 王崇慶 (*c.* 1525), which added little to Kuo P'u's study. The most important works on the text were completed by Pi Yüan 畢沅 (1730-1797), who perhaps gave too much space to highly problematic identifications of placenames, and Hao I-hsing 郝懿行 (1757-1825), whose *Shan-hai ching chien-shu* 山海經箋疏 (A Commentary on the *Classic of Mountains and Seas*) remains a fundamental source for scholarship on this book.

In the traditional Chinese bibliographical literature, the *Shan-hai ching* is variously categorized as a work of geomancy (*hsing-fa* 形法), geography (*ti-li* 地理), and fiction (*hsiao-shuo**). However the book is classified, its chief value exists in its preservation of much ancient Chinese myth and folklore. Such material is organized according to a geographical scheme that gives the precise spatial location of the various fantasies it describes. Hawkes perceives in this work some "ritual-religious intent" and several Chinese scholars, Lu Hsün the most prominent, have linked *Shan-hai ching* to the early Chinese shamanic tradition. *Shan-hai ching* has been commonly assigned to the Ch'u literary realm and compared to the rather mysterious poetic work "T'ien-wen" 天問 (see *Ch'u-tz'u*). Recently, Yüan K'o has added some lexical evidence to other arguments that *Shan-hai ching* in fact was produced in the southern Chinese region of Ch'u.

Shan-hai ching is of considerable literary significance. It is described by Hu Ying-lin* as "the ancestor of ancient and modern works that discuss the strange." As such, it has been listed as a forerunner of the traditional Chinese *chih-kuai.** The narrative sections of the work are extremely brief and somewhat disjointed, but they contain valuable fragments of early Chinese mythology of such important figures as Hsi-wang-mu 西王母, who appears not as a beautiful immortal of Taoist texts, but as a manlike creature with a leopard tail, tiger teeth, and dishevelled hair, Nü Wa 女媧, a creatrix whose bowels are transformed into ten gods, Kun 鯀, the rebellious official who was executed only to come alive again and give birth to the great Yü, Ch'ang-hsi 常羲, the imperial wife whose duty is to bathe the twelve moons, and many others.

The faithful descriptions of *Shan-hai ching* and the illustrations that once accompanied the text inspired a number of later Chinese writers. Perhaps chief among these works is the cycle of thirteen poems written by T'ao Ch'ien* entitled "Tu *Shan-hai ching*" 讀山海經 (On Reading the *Classic of Mountains and Seas*).

EDITIONS:

Shan-hai ching. SPTK. Reprint of a Ming edition.
Shan-hai ching chiao-chu 山海經校注. Yüan K'o, ed. Shanghai, 1980. This annotated version is the most important text.
Shan-hai ching chien-shu. Hao I-hsing, ed. Rpt. Taipei, 1970.
Shan-hai ching t'ung-chien 山海經通檢. Peiping, 1948. Nieh, Ch'ung-ch'i 聶崇岐 and Hung Yeh 洪業, comps. A useful concordance.

TRANSLATIONS:

de Rosny, Leon. *Chan hai king: antique géographie chinoise.* Paris, 1891.
Mänchen-Helfen, Otto. "The Later Books of the *Shan-Hai-King*," *AM*, 1 (1924), 550-586.
Mathieu, Rémi. *Étude sur la mythologie et l'ethnologie de la Chine ancienne, Traduction annoteé du* Shanhai jing. 2v. Paris, 1983.

STUDIES:

Chang, Hsin-ch'eng 張心澂. *Wei-shu t'ung-kao* 偽書通考. Rev. ed. Shanghai, 1957, pp. 688-703.
Cheng, Te-k'un 鄭德坤. "*Shan-hai ching* chi ch'i shen-hua" 山海經及其神話, *Shih-hsüeh nien-pao,* 1.4 (June 1932), 127-151.

de Harlez, C. "Le *Tcheou-li* et le *Shan-Hai-King*," *TP*, 5.1 (March 1894), 11-42; 5.2 (May 1894), 107-122.
Hawkes, "Quest."
Hightower, James R. *The Poetry of T'ao Ch'ien.* Oxford, 1970, pp. 229-248.
Ho, Kuan-chou 何觀洲. "*Shan-hai ching* tsai k'o-hsüeh shang chih pi-pan chi tso-che chih shih-tai kao" 山海經在科學上之批判及作者之時代考, *Yen-ching hsüeh-pao,* 7 (June 1930), 1347-1375.
Schiffler, John W. "Chinese Folk Medicine: A Study of the *Shan-hai ching*," *Asian Folklore Studies,* 39 (1980), 41-83. With an excellent bibliography of both primary and secondary sources.
Tu, Erh-wei 杜而未. Shan-hai ching *shen-hua hsi-t'ung* 山海經神話系統. Taipei, 1960.
Wei, T'ing-sheng 衞挺生 and Hsü Sheng-mu 徐聖謨. *Shan-ching ti-li t'u-k'ao* 山經地理圖考. Taipei, 1974.
Yüan, K'o. "Lüeh-lun *Shan-hai ching* te shen-hua" 略論山海經的神話. *Chung-hua wen-shih lun-ts'ung,* 1979.2, 59-74.
———. "*Shan-hai ching* hsieh-tso te shih ti chi p'ien-mu k'ao" 山海經寫作的時地及篇目考. *Chung-hua wen-shih lun-ts'ung,* 1978.7, 147-172.

—SD

Shan-ko 山歌 (rustic songs) is a name applied to a variety of popular songs composed and sung by boatmen, farmers, herdsboys, woodcutters, and the like in South China. They are simple tunes, usually of four lines of expandable rhymed verse, and deal almost exclusively with love and romance. The best known of these songs come from the Wu-dialect areas (Chekiang and Kiangsu) as well as the Hakka-dialect areas (Kwangtung, Kwangsi, and Fukien). In the north songs of this type are known by the names of *hsin-t'ien yu* 信天游, *hua-erh* 花兒 and *p'a-shan tiao* 爬山調.

The most famous collection of these rustic songs was compiled by Feng Meng-lung* near the end of the Ming dynasty and entitled (*T'ung-ch'ih erh-nung*) *Shan-ko* 〔童痴二弄〕山歌. The first nine *chüan* of the ten-*chüan* work are all in Feng's native Wu dialect; those in the tenth *chüan* are in Mandarin. The songs are frankly pornographic, over one third of them directly or indirectly discussing sexual intercourse. They abound in word plays, puns, and double entendres

672

and have been widely known in China since their rediscovery in the 1930s.

It is impossible at this late date to determine the amount of "editing" given these songs by Feng but certainly some were written by himself and his literati friends. Those which may have been originally written by unlettered persons were certainly improved by altering the smoothness of the wording, rhymes, etc.

EDITIONS:

Feng, Meng-lung 馮夢龍. *Shan-ko* 山歌. Shanghai, 1935. Prefaces and colophons by famous literary researchers of the 1930s; marginal notes on Wu-dialect expressions. Best reading edition.

Shan-ko. Peking, 1962. A typeset edition of the original late Ming edition. With explanatory preface.

Mo-han-chai, Chu-jen 墨憨齋主人 (Feng Meng-lung). *Huang-shan-mi* 黃山謎. Shanghai, 1935. Contains four song collections by Feng Meng-lung; *Shan-ko, Huang-ying-erh* 黃鶯兒, *Kua-chih-erh* 掛枝兒, and *Chia-chu-t'ao* 夾竹桃.

TRANSLATIONS:

Töpelmann, Cornelia. *Shan-ko von Feng Meng-lung: Eine Volksliedersammlung aus der Ming-Zeit.* München, 1973. A study and translation of the *Shan-ko.*

—JC

Shao Ts'an 邵璨 (*tzu,* Wen-ming 文明, *fl.* mid-fifteenth century), was the author of the *ch'uan-ch'i** drama *Hsiang-nang chi* 香囊記 (The Perfume-pouch, also entitled *Tzu hsiang-nang* 紫香囊 [The Purple Perfume-pouch]). According to Hsü Wei's* *Nan-tz'u hsü-lu* 南詞敘錄, the *Hsiang-nang chi* was written by an old *sheng-yüan* 生員 (graduate) known as Shao Wen-ming, who was a native of I-hsing 宜興 (east of modern Nanking). In Chiao Chou's 焦周 *Shuo k'u* 說楛, the author of the drama is referred to as Shao Hung-chih 宏治 (which is probably his *hao*) and is said to be a native of Ching-hsi 荊溪 (I-hsing and Ching-hsi are adjacent districts in Kiangsu). The Counsellor surnamed Shao 邵 of Ch'ang-chou 常州 mentioned in Lü T'ien-ch'eng's 呂天成 (b. 1580) *Ch'ü-p'in* 曲品 (An Evaluation of Arias) is probably another person. Apart from the scanty information in the *I-hsing hsien-chih*

宜興 縣志 (Local Gazetteer of I-hsing), almost no record of Shao Ts'an's life can be found. In the gazetteer a contemporary of Shao Ts'an named Shao Kuei 邵珪 (*tzu,* Wen-ching 文敬) is mentioned; both the name and *tzu* seem to suggest he was a brother or cousin. If so, from what is known, Shao Ts'an came from a quite well-to-do family. This may explain why he could have the leisure and means to amuse himself with drama. Besides the *Hsiang-nang chi,* he also wrote a collection of poems entitled *Le-shan chi* 樂善集 (Pleased to Do Good Collection), which apparently was never published.

In the *Hsiang-nang chi* Shao states that he was following the example of Ch'iu Chün's 邱濬 *Wu-lun ch'üan-pei chung-hsiao chi* 五倫全備忠孝記 (Story of Loyalty and Filial Obedience, Containing Full Illustration of the Five Moral Obligations), which, as its title suggests, is a drama that aims at expounding moral principles. In this respect the two dramas share a common aim. The *Hsiang-nang chi* tells a story set at the end of the Northern Sung dynasty. A young man named Chang Chiu-ch'eng 張九成, who had infuriated the prime minister by criticizing the latter's misgovernment, was sent to guard the border against northern invaders. He was captured by the enemy and detained for more than ten years. During this period the dynasty completed its southward exodus. In the chaos the remaining members of Chang's family—his mother, his younger brother, and his wife—lost touch with one other. Finally Chiu-ch'eng managed to escape, and the family was fortunate enough to reunite. The purple perfume-pouch referred to in the title was the means of recognition leading to reunion.

The plot of the drama contains obvious borrowings from Kao Ming's *P'i-p'a chi** and Shih Hui's *Pai-yüeh t'ing* (see *Ssu-ta ch'uan-ch'i*). In addition, it contains episodes about Sung Chiang 宋江, the hero of the *Shui-hu chuan,** and the bibulous Lü Tung-pin 呂洞賓 of popular lore; there is no apparent reason for the inclusion of these episodes. The plot is chaotic; structurally, the drama is a failure.

A drama entitled *Wu-lun chuan tzu hsiang-nang* 伍倫傳紫香囊 (Story of the Purple Perfume-pouch Illustrating the Five Moral Obligations) can be found in a collection known as *Feng-yüeh chin-nang* 風月錦囊 (Embroidered Pouch Containing Stories of Romantic Affairs) that has been discovered at Escorial, Spain. This work was probably the rudimentary source for Shao's *Hsiang-nang chi*. In comparison with Shao's drama, this work is less refined and badly structured. It is likely that Shao simply reorganized the plot and refined the language. But in this attempt, Shao went to extremes. The songs are laden with flowery expressions and parallel phrases. The dialogues, too, are written in parallel style, and in them Shao shows off his knowledge of the classics.

Hsü Wei (in *Nan-tz'u hsü-lu*) blames Shao for introducing poetic diction and parallelism into drama, and accuses him of initiating the trend of drama writing that lays its emphasis on language. Hsü Fu-tso* in *Ch'ü-lun* 曲論 (On the Aria) also condemns Shao's dramatic diction as too far removed from usual language and as too gaudy. On the other hand, Lü T'ien-ch'eng, who favored the use of florid language in drama, has a high regard for Shao's *Hsiang-nang chi*.

EDITIONS:

Hsiang-nang chi. (1) Chin, *Chi-ku-ko*. (2) *Ku-pen*, I; a photolithographic reprint of the Chi-chih-chai 繼志齋 edition printed in the Wan-li period.

STUDIES:

Aoki, *Gikyokushi*, pp. 100-102.

DMB, pp. 1168-1169.

Lo, Chin-t'ang 羅錦堂. "*Wu-lun ch'üan-pei* yü *Tzu hsiang-nang* te kuan-hsi" 伍倫全備與紫香囊的關係, in his *Chin-t'ang lun ch'ü* 錦堂論曲, Taipei, 1977, pp. 338-348.

—SSK

Shen Chi-chi 沈既濟 (*c.* 740-*c.* 800) is known principally for his authorship of two perennially popular literary-language short stories, "Jen-shih chuan" 任氏傳 (Miss Jen) and "Chen-chung chi" 枕中記 (The World Inside a Pillow). He was a member of the Shen family of Wu-hsing 吳興 (modern Chekiang), which also produced the famous Six Dynasties historian, poet, and literary theorist Shen Yüeh,* and another writer of literary-language short stories, Shen Ya-chih 沈亞之 (*c.* 770-*c.* 830). Shen Chi-chi's grandfather had been an official at court and later served as a provincial official in what is now Fukien, while his father had held a comparatively low official position in Chekiang. All that is known of his early years is that his son, Shen Ch'uan-shih 沈傳師 was born in 769 (d. 827), and that he resided in Chung-ling 鐘陵 (modern Nan-ch'ang 南昌 in Kiangsi) during the mid-770s, before traveling to Ch'ang-an in 778 to take a position in the Court of Imperial Sacrifices.

A new emperor, Te-tsung, ascended the throne in the summer of 779 and, in an attempt at political and fiscal reform, made Yang Yen 楊炎 (727-781), a financial expert, his chief minister. Yang Yen had heard of Shen Chi-chi's skill at historical writing and had him appointed to a position in the Chancellery and concurrently made an editor in the History Office, where he was in charge of the compilation of the records concerning the emperor's daily actions. Although Yang Yen and his party introduced a number of important reforms, they also made many enemies very rapidly and soon fell from power. Yang Yen was demoted, exiled, and sentenced to death in mid-781, and Shen Chi-chi was at the same time transferred to a minor position at Ch'u-chou 處州 (modern Chekiang). He seems to have been pardoned as part of the general amnesty of 785, for he returned to the capital to serve as a Vice-director in the Ministry of Personnel before his death. The two short stories and seven brief pieces of official prose are all that have survived of Shen's writings.

Shen was one of the first writers of literary-language tales to combine the interest in supernatural events that colored the earlier strange accounts of the Six Dynasties period with a more elaborate plotting, characterization, and incidental detail that helped to raise the T'ang short tales to new levels of literary art. The plots of both of Shen's surviving tales were drawn from Six

Dynasties sources. "Miss Jen" is based on an earlier tale which tells of a beautiful young woman who, after having lived with a young man for quite some time, was killed by hunting dogs and shown to have been a fox spirit in human form. Shen elaborated this simple plot into a story of considerable length, providing his characters with well-rounded personalities and motivation for their acts and enlivening his narration with scenes of excitement, vigorous action, and suspense. That he endowed his fox spirit, Miss Jen, with qualities more admirable then those seen in her human acquaintances is thought to be an ironic comment by Shen on contemporary society.

In a sense, Shen's second tale, "The World Inside a Pillow," also deals with irony, in this instance the irony implicit in the human condition. Again taking its basic plot from an earlier work, it tells of a man who dreams an entire lifetime while napping with his head on a porcelain pillow. The man gains a highly-placed marriage, imperial favor, and powerful position—marked realistically with occasional setbacks—and sons who go on to successful careers and provide him with numerous grandchildren. The man awakens, however, to find that this entire lifetime had taken place in the time needed to cook a bowl of gruel. The story is usually interpreted in light of contemporary Buddhist and Taoist ideas concerning the illusory nature of life and the vanity of striving after worldly gain. Some also see connections between the tale's message and the major setback experienced by the author in his own career. Other tales expanding the same theme appeared not long after Shen's death (see Li Kung-tso), and his own tale has been used as the basis for dramatic works in both China and Japan.

EDITIONS:

"Chen-chung chi." *T'ai-p'ing kuang-chi,* * ch. 82.

———. *T'ang-jen hsiao-shuo,* pp. 37-42.

———. *T'ang-jen hsiao-shuo yen-chiu erh-chi* 唐人小說研究二集. Wang Meng-ou 王夢鷗, comp. Taipei, 1973, pp. 196-200.

———. *Wen-yüan ying-hua,* * ch. 883.

"Jen-shih chuan." *T'ai-p'ing kuang-chi,* ch. 452.

———. *T'ang-jen hsiao-shuo,* pp. 43-48.

———. *T'ang-jen hsiao-shuo yen-chiu erh-chi,* pp. 186-192.

TRANSLATIONS:

Nienhauser, William H., Jr. "Miss Jen," in *Traditional Chinese Stories,* pp. 339-345.

———. "The World Inside a Pillow," *Traditional Chinese Stories,* pp. 435-438.

Tsai, Fredrick C. "Miss Jen," *Renditions,* 8 (Autumn 1977), 52-58.

Wang, C. C. *Traditional Chinese Tales,* New York, 1944, pp. 20-34 (both).

Wang, Elizabeth T. C. *Ladies of the T'ang* (Taipei: Heritage Press, 1961), pp. 203-223 (both).

STUDIES:

Knechtges, David R. "Dream Adventure Stories in Europe and T'ang China," *TkR,* 4.2 (October 1973), 101-119.

Kondō, Haruo 近藤春雄. "Tōdai shōsetsu ni tsuite, Tōjō rōfu den, Jinshi den, Ri Shōbu den" 唐代小說について東城老父傳任氏傳李章武傳, *Aichi Kenritsu Daigaku bungakubu ronshū (gogaku, bungaku),* 18 (1967), 63-81.

———. "Tōdai shōsetsu ni tsuite, Chinchūki, Nanka taishu den, Sha Shōga den" 唐代小說について、枕中記, 南柯太守傳, 謝小娥傳, *Aichi Kenritsu Joshi Daigaku kiyō,* 15 (1964), 40-58.

Liu, K'ai-jung 劉開榮. *T'ang-tai hsiao-shuo yen-chiu* 唐代小說研究. Hong Kong, 1964, revision of 1947 edition, pp. 163-175.

Uchiyama, Chinari 內山知也. *Zui Tō shōsetsu kenkyū* 隋唐小說研究, Tokyo, 1977, pp. 326-349.

Wang, Meng-ou. *T'ang-jen hsiao-shuo yen-chiu erh-chi,* pp. 37-46.

—DG

Shen Ching 沈璟 (*tzu,* Po-ying 伯英, Tan-ho 聃和, *hao,* Ning-an 寧菴, 1553-1610), a native of Wu-chiang 吳江, is traditionally recognized as the master of the *Ko-lü p'ai* 格律派 (School of Poetic Meter) and a prolific Ming dramatist. The strong emphasis on meter and rhyme and the careful selection of words of this school is reflected in Shen's own statements: "It is better to have harmonious meter, though the lyrics may not be artistic. When the songs are read they may not make any sense; yet when they are sung, they begin to rhyme. In the composition of songs this is craftsmanship."

Shen came from a wealthy family which provided him with a good education; he

675

acquired a reputation as a precocious child. Receiving the *chin-shih* degree in 1574, he was assigned to the Ministry of War. After a brief stay, he resigned for personal reasons. Recalled in 1579 as a Secretary in the Ministry of Rites, Shen rapidly received a succession of various assignments in the civil government. In 1586 however, he was punished and demoted because of his objections to Cheng Kuei-fei's elevation to imperial consort. Three years later Shen was indicted by Kao Kuei 高桂 (*chin-shih*, 1577) for showing favoritism to four candidates in a provincial examination. Though a subsequent investigation cleared Shen of any wrongdoing, he found official life untenable and resigned, devoting the rest of his life to studies and writing.

Shen Ching was obsessed with using drama as a vehicle for spreading "morality" and for promoting "natural color (本色)." His first concern is quite evident in his play *Shih-hsiao chi* 十孝記 (The Ten Filial Sons), which portrays worthies from different dynasties, while his attempt to promote natural color is demonstrated in his esteem for, and incorporation of, the dramatic texts of the Sung and Yüan periods into his own works.

He wrote a total of seventeen dramas, collectively known by the title *Shu-yü-t'ang shih-ch'i chung* 屬玉堂十七種 (Seventeen Plays of Shu-yü-t'ang), but not all are extant. Two of his plays (*Shih-hsiao chi* and *Po-hsiao chi* 博笑記), each having several unrelated tales, are far closer in form to the *tsa-chü** than the *ch'uan-ch'i.** *I-hsia chi* 義俠記 (The Altruistic Knight-errant), considered his best-known work, is based on Wu Sung's 武松 exploits, as they are narrated in chapters 22-30 of the novel *Shui-hu chuan.** To this narrative, Shen added the episode of Wu Sung's marriage to Lady Chia making the story conform to the thematic requirements of the *ch'uan-ch'i* genre.

Shen Ching also rewrote two of T'ang Hsien-tsu's* dramas, *Mu-tan t'ing* and *Tzu-ch'ai chi* to improve their rhymes and to make them more suitable for singing in the Wu dialect. Though neither of the Shen texts are extant, his attempt drew a sharp rejoinder from T'ang: "How can he know

the purpose of the songs? As long as I can express my thoughts to the fullest, I don't care if I crack the throat of every actor under heaven." Shen was also credited with the annotating and editing of *P'i-p'a chi* by Kao Ming.* This work is likewise lost.

Shen Ching's literary talents were not limited only to composing plays; his writings include *san-ch'ü* (see *ch'ü*), literary theory, lyrical poems, transpositions of northern lyrics into southern tunes, and compilations. Unfortunately most of his works are no longer extant. His *Nan-kung shih-san-tiao ch'ü-p'u* 南宮十三調曲譜 (22 *ch.*) was based on *Chiu-pien nan-chiu-kung-p'u* 舊編南九宮譜, compiled by Chiang Hsiao 蔣孝. Shen greatly revised and enlarged it. This work is now considered one of the basic sources for the study of southern *ch'ü*.

EDITIONS:

I-hsia chi 義俠記, in *Liu-shih*.
Ku-pen, I and III contain the following dramas: I-hsia chi 義俠記, *T'ao-fu chi* 桃符記, *Mai-chien chi* 埋劍記, *Shuang-yü chi* 雙魚記, *Po-hsiao chi* 博笑記, *Chui-ch'ai chi*, and *Hung-ch'ü chi* 紅蕖記.
Nan chiu-kung shih-san tiao ch'ü-p'u 南九宮十三調曲譜 (22 *ch*). Peking, 1921. This edition is a lithoprint based on *Nan chiu-kung-p'u* compiled by Chiang Hsiao.

STUDIES:

Aoki, *Giyokushi*, pp. 183-189 contains biographical information, a list of his plays and brief comments on *I-hsia chi;* Part IV, ch. 16 is a comprehensive study of Shen's *Nan-chiu-kung shih-san tiao ch'ü-p'u* and Chiang Hsiao's *Chiu-kung* and his *Shih-san tiao*.
Chang, Ching 張敬. *Ming Ch'ing ch'uan-ch'i tao-lun* 明清傳奇導論. Taipei, 1961. Part II, ch. 2, sec. 2 gives a brief study of Shen Ching and T'ang Hsien-tsu.
Chao, Ching-shen 趙景琛. "Ming-tai te hsi-ch'ü ho san-ch'ü, 8: Shen Ching" 明代的戲曲和散曲沈璟, in *Hsi-ch'ü pi-t'an* 戲曲筆談, Shanghai, 1962, pp. 73-75. Gives brief biographical information and comments on Shen's writings.
———. "Shen Ching ch'uan-ch'i chi-i" 沈璟傳奇輯逸, in Chao's *Ming Ch'ing ch'ü t'an* 明清曲談, Shanghai, 1957, pp. 90-95.
Chin, Meng-hua 金夢華. *Chi-ku-ko liu-shih-chung ch'ü hsü-lu* 汲古閣六十種曲敍錄. Taipei, 1969. Ch. 50 contains biographical information and a brief study on *I-hsia chi*.

676

DMB, pp. 1172-1173.

Fu, *Ming-tai ch'uan-ch'i*, pp. 70-81 contains a list of Shen's *ch'uan-ch'i* plays and information on extant editions.

Hsü, Fu-ming 徐扶明. "Kuan-yü Shen Ching chi ch'i chü-tso-ti p'ing-chia" 關於沈璟及其劇作的評價, *Wen-hsüeh i-ch'an tseng-k'an*, 7 (1959), 244-257.

—EY

Shen Ch'üan-ch'i 沈佺期 (*tzu*, Yün-ch'ing 雲卿, *c.* 650-713) and **Sung Chih-wen** 宋之問 (*tzu*, Yen ch'ing 延清, d. 712) were two poets whose names are usually paired, and whose works are traditionally taken as the epitome of the poetry that marked the transition from the Early to the High T'ang.

Both men passed the *chin-shih* examinations in 675 and were associated with the government of Empress Wu, specifically with the literary salon of her favorite Chang I-chih 張易之 (d. 705). They were both exiled to the provinces when this government fell in 705. A general amnesty returned them to the capital soon afterwards, but Sung Chih-wen apparently could not refrain from involvement in the politics of the imperial succession. When the ascension to the throne of Hsüan-tsung (r. 712-755) returned firm control of the state once again into the hands of the Li family, Sung Chih-wen was ordered to commit suicide.

Both men were schooled in the late seventh-century traditions of court poetry, a tradition where wit and decorum were paramount. Many poems in their corpuses were *ying-chih shih* 應制詩 (poems composed according to command) for formal state occasions. It was in this atmosphere that the tonal requirements for *lü-shih* 律詩 (regulated verse—see *shih*) assumed their final shape, and the works of Shen and Sung probably represent the earliest major body of Chinese verse to contain sizable amounts of standard *lü-shih* forms.

At the same time as they were perfecting the formal aspects of *lü-shih*, Shen and Sung both expanded the parameters of the subject matter for *lü-shih* by making more personal the stereotyped guises of seventh-century court verse. They achieved this goal by integrating the subject matters traditional to other verse genres into the *lü-shih*. Shen Ch'üan-ch'i, for example, wrote fine poetry in the *yüeh-fu** style. "Tu pu-chien" 獨不見 (Alone and Seeing Not), one of his two poems included in the *T'ang-shih san-pai-shou*,* employs the *yüeh-fu* motif of the solitary wife's lament for her husband away on the king's business, yet the form is close to a standard seven-character *lü-shih*, complete with parallelism and tonal euphony. Through the use of the *yüeh-fu* mode, Shen Ch'üan-ch'i was able to modify the rhetorical excesses of the court style and thereby provide a working prototype of the developed *lü-shih* of the next generation. Sung Chih-wen achieved similar results through his revival of the old "Ch'u Songs," a precursor of the *yüeh-fu*, that had been popular in the Han dynasty.

EDITIONS:

Shen Chan-shih chi 沈詹事集. 7 *chüan;* preface by Wang T'ing-hsiang 王廷相 dated 1518. The only separate edition of Shen's work.

Sung Chih-wen chi 宋之問集. 2 *chüan*. SPTK. Rpt. of a Ming edition, probably of the Chia-ching (1522-1566) period.

STUDIES AND TRANSLATIONS:

Liu, K'ai-yang 劉開揚. "Kuan-yü Shen Ch'üan-ch'i, Sung Chih-wen te shu-p'ing" 關於沈佺期宋之問的述評, *She-hui k'o-hsüeh yen-chiu*, 1981.4.

Owen, *T'ang*, pp. 339-380.

—CH

Shen-hsien chuan 神仙傳 (Biographies of Divine Immortals) is a collection of the biographies of eighty-four Taoist immortals. The text has traditionally been ascribed to Ko Hung,* a Taoist scholar most famous for his encyclopedic *Pao-p'u tzu* 抱朴子 (The Master Who Embraces Simplicity). Most of the biographies are extracted from various earlier works, so Ko is really much more an editor than an author of *Shen-hsien chuan*. The current text appears with an introduction in which Ko explains that he compiled the text in answer to a disciple's inquiry as to whether there actually were immortals. The existence of the text and its association with the famous Ko Hung is attested by the Former Sung scholar P'ei Sung-chih 裴松之

(372-451), who doubts the veracity of the biographies but does cite them as the work of Ko Hung. The editors of *Ssu-k'u ch'üan-shu tsung-mu** also accept the tradition of Ko's editorship and strongly recommend the edition which they have included in their collection, arguing that the often used *Han Wei ts'ung-shu* 漢魏叢書 edition, which contains ninety-two biographies, has been copied from *T'ai-p'ing kuang-chi** rather than directly from an earlier *Shen-hsien chuan* edition.

Shen-hsien chuan continues the tradition of Taoist hagiography that began with the Han collection *Lieh-hsien chuan.** Ko, however, criticizes the earlier work for its extreme simplicity and brevity. Indeed, Ko's biographies are much more detailed than those of *Lieh-hsien chuan,* in which the longest biographies are rarely more than two thousand words. This allows for a much more satisfying portrayal of the immortals' personalities and activities.

The biographies found in this collection are a valuable, although largely untapped, source for the study of both Six Dynasties Taoism and Chinese hagiographic literature. Although the text was compiled for a didactic purpose—that is, to prove the existence of immortals—its lively and entertaining narratives place it squarely within the *chih-kuai** tradition that flourished during the Six Dynasties period. It is noteworthy in this regard that Kan Pao, author of the famous *chih-kuai* collection *Sou-shen chi,** was a close associate of Ko Hung.

According to the biographies found in *Shen-hsien chuan,* acquisition of immortality was no easy task. Taoists who strove for such a goal had to obtain esoteric alchemical and dietetic knowledge at the hands of a worthy and skilled master, and these masters were difficult both to find and to please. The pursuit of a suitable master and the harrowing and sometimes degrading tests that aspirants had to pass in order to gain knowledge of Taoist secrets constitute one of the more interesting and delightful themes of *Shen-hsien chuan.*

Although a number of these biographies have been translated by Giles, Wilhelm, and others, there is as yet no complete translation in any Western language of this important text.

EDITIONS:
Shen-hsien chuan. Han Wei ts'ung-shu.
———. *Lung-wei mi-shu* 龍威祕書.
———. *Shuo k'u.*

TRANSLATIONS:
Giles, Lionel. *A Gallery of Chinese Immortals.* London, 1948.
Wilhelm, Richard. *Chinesische Märchen.* Dusseldorf, 1952.

STUDIES:
Durrant, Stephen. "The Taoist Apotheosis of Mo Ti," *JAOS,* 97 (1977), 549-546.
———. "The Theme of Family Conflict in Early Taoist Biography," *Selected Papers in Asian Studies (Western Conference of the Association for Asian Studies, Albuquerque, New Mexico, 1977),* v. 2, pp. 2-8.

—SD

Shen Te-ch'ien 沈德潛 (*tzu,* Ch'üeh-shih 確士, *hao,* Kuei-yü 歸愚. 1673-1769) was a poet, anthologist, official, and literary critic. He was born into a scholarly family in Ch'ang-chou 常州 (Kiangsu). His poetic talent was recognized at the age of six; nonetheless the path to officialdom was extremely difficult—he finally obtained the *chin-shih* degree at the age of sixty-seven, after almost fifty attempts. His reputation as a poet and critic had been established much earlier, however, and when he passed the examinations, the Ch'ien-lung emperor took him into his inner circle of literary friends and wrote prefaces for two of Shen's works, the *Kuei-yü shih-wen ch'ao* 歸愚詩文鈔 (1767), a collection of his own poetry and essays, and the *Kuo-ch'ao* 國朝 (1759), a collection of early Ch'ing poetry. From 1742 to 1749 he held various posts in the capital and was honored in his retirement by imperial audiences and visits. He died at ninety-seven and was canonized as Wen-k'o 文慤. Nine years later, however, he was stripped of all honors for having written a short work on Hsü Shu-k'uei 徐述夔 (*fl.* 1740), the author of allegedly slanderous poems.

In his formative years, he was probably much influenced by two contemporary masters: his teacher, the renowned poet Yeh Hsieh,* and the poet and critic, Wang Shih-chen* (1634-1711). From the former, he gained an appreciation of the great poets of the past, and from Wang Shih-chen, he learned the *shen-yün* 神韻 theory of poetry—a theory concerned with the subjective-intuitive expression of external reality.

Shen Te-ch'ien's theory of poetic form and metrics, *ko-tiao* 格調, emphasizes three fundamental concepts. First, in direct contrast with Yüan Mei's* theory of *hsing-ling* 性靈 (natural sensibility), he advocates a poetic that is morally didactic and classically refined. Second, the meter should be modelled after great poems of the past. Third, poetic form should achieve an effortless artistic quality, leaving no traces of effort.

Shen Te-ch'ien's major creative works are collected in *Kuei-yü shih-wen ch'ao*. His notes on literary theories and criticism are gathered in *Shuo-shih tsui-yü* 說詩晬語 (Commentary on Poetry, 1731). Under the auspices of the imperial court, his lasting contribution lies in his compilation and editing of anthologies such as the *Ku-shih-yüan** and the *Kuo-ch'ao*.

EDITIONS:

Ch'ing-shih pieh-ts'ai chi 清詩別裁集. Shen Te-ch'ien, ed. Peking, 1975.

Kuo-ch'ao wen lu 國朝文錄. Li Tsu-t'ao 李祖陶, ed. Shanghai, 1846.

Shen Kuei-yü shih-wen ch'üan-chi 沈歸愚詩文全集. Peking, 1975.

STUDIES:

Aoki, *Shindai*, in *Aoki Masaru zenshū*, v. 1, pp. 473-481. An informative analysis of Shen's *k'o-tiao* theory.

ECCP, pp. 645-646.

Kuo, Shao-yü 郭紹虞. *Chung-kuo shih te shen-yün, ko-tiao chi hsing-ling shuo* 中國詩的神韻，格調及性靈說. Rpt. Taipei, 1975, pp. 16-19, 23-43, and 92-101. A discussion of *shen-yün*, *ko-tiao*, and *hsing-ling*.

So, Man-jock 蘇文擢. *Shuo-shih tsui-yü ch'üan-p'ing* 說詩晬語詮評. Hong Kong, 1978. A lengthy and detailed commentary, supplemented by three official autobiographies of the poet himself.

Wu, *Ch'ing-tai*, pp. 211-219. A definitive critique and interpretation of the theory, char-acteristics, and development of Shen's poetry.

—HSK

Shen Tzu-cheng 沈自徵 (*tzu*, Chün-yung 君庸, 1591-1641) was one of the most acclaimed *tsa-chü* writers of the late Ming. A native of Wu-chiang 吳江, Kiangsu, Shen was the nephew of Shen Ching,* leader of the Wu-chiang School of Ming *ch'uan-ch'i.** Even as a child he showed unusual promise and self-confidence, which soon turned into eccentricity and arrogance. Shen ostensibly scorned wealth and position. Legend has it that when his father bestowed on him a small parcel of family land, Shen only laughed and asked, "What is a man to do with fifty *mu* of land?" He sold the land, spending the proceeds on feasts and charity. Later, after his decade-long stay in the capital as a military adviser brought him fame and wealth, he returned to his hometown to build an estate, but he eventually donated everything to a Buddhist temple. In 1640, Shen was recommended for an official post, but he declined, claiming that he could no longer subject himself to the bondage of officialdom after so many years of freedom.

Shen was a spontaneous writer. He was known for having never written drafts in prose or poetry. Nor did he keep copies of his works or collect them into anthologies. He wrote three one-act *tsa-chü** plays, which have fortunately been preserved for posterity. These plays give ample proof of his dramatic talent, but at the same time they betray the author's preoccupation with the frustration of the unrecognized and unappreciated genius. *Pa-t'ing ch'iu* 霸亭秋 (Autumn in the Pavilion of Ch'u Pa-wang) deals with the frustration of a talented student, Tu Mo, who has failed the examinations. On his journey home, Tu lodges in the Temple of Ch'u Pa-wang and expresses his grievances in front of the image of the great warrior turned deity. The play centers around the comparison of Ch'u Pa-wang's humiliation as a defeated head of state with Tu's as an unsuccessful candidate in the examinations. The climax of the play is reached when the clay image of Ch'u Pa-wang, moved by the student's misfortune and reminded of his own defeat, sheds tears.

Pien ko-chi 鞭歌妓 (Whipping the Singsong Girls) treats the story of Chang Chien, a poverty-stricken yet proud young scholar, who encounters the Minister of Rites one day and impresses the latter so much that the minister bestows on him, besides much gold and silk, two singsong girls from his own retinue. The girls, however, are disdainful of Chang's humble appearance. They refuse his orders to perform, and verbally insult him. Enraged, Chang lashes out at them, threatens them with his sword, and orders them whipped. Much of the drama stems from the power of the language Chang employs to express his righteous wrath.

Tsan-hua chi 簪花髻 (The Coiffure with Flowers) is a story about the eccentric poet Yang Shen.* During his exile in Yunnan, Yang would become drunk and then scribble his poetry on the robes of singsong girls. His verse was so much in demand that the singsong girls would put on special robes of white silk for him to write on. One spring day Yang did his hair in two topknots which he adorned with red flowers, then borrowed a robe of brocade from a girl, and ventured out for a stroll. Public opinion held he was mad.

Shen's three plays focus on human emotions: frustration, anger, and the desire to be different. As one-act plays they are dramatically effective not on account of any structural merit, but because of their powerful lyrics and monologues.

EDITIONS:

Pien-ko-chi, in *Ku-pen*, IV.

Shen, T'ai 沈泰, ed. *Sheng-Ming tsa-chü san-shih chung*. 3v. Shanghai, 1925. Contains *Pa-ting ch'iu*, *Pien-ko-chi*, and *Tsan-hua chi*.

—CYC

Shen Yüeh 沈約 (*tzu*, Hsiu-wen 休文, 441-513) is probably best known as the originator of the first deliberately applied rules of tonal euphony in the history of Chinese prosody, though many have disputed this self-made claim. The *Yung-ming t'i* 永明體 (Yung-ming Style) of the late fifth century was associated with him and with other gifted poets like Hsieh T'iao* and Wang Jung 王融 (468-494) who gathered in the Hsi-ti 西邸 (Western Villa) of the Prince of Ching-ling 竟陵王. Their work was both admired by contemporaries for its graceful elegance and criticized for the insincerity and sensuality of its love songs, sometimes referred to as *Kung-t'i shih.** Above all it was condemned for its crippling strictures—the so-called *pa-ping* 八病 (eight defects) of tone, rhyme, and alliteration. The contemporary critic Chung Hung in the preface to his *Shih-p'in,** where he assigns Shen Yüeh to the second class of poets, is especially scornful of imposing such artificial restraints, and, like Emperor Wu of the Liang (r. 502-549), claimed not to understand what was meant by the *ssu-sheng* 四聲 (four tones): *p'ing* 平 (level), *shang* 上 (rising) *ch'ü* 去 (departing), and *ju* 入 (entering). Shen Yüeh himself, though somewhat inconsistent in observing his own rules, produced some of the most painstakingly crafted poems to appear since those of Hsieh Ling-yün,* whose work he admired and imitated, the most conspicuous example being the long autobiographical poetic essay "Chiao-chü fu" 郊居賦 (On Living in the Suburbs), which was modeled on Hsieh's "Shan-chü fu" 山居賦 (On Living in the Mountains). Like Hsieh, Shen was also a "landscape poet" in the sense that he had a strong kindred feeling for mountains and streams, birds and animals—even plants and insects—which he described in his poems with the keen observation and tender affection of a true nature lover. He cherished a lifelong dream, nourished by his Taoist religious heritage, of transcending the "dusty world" of political intrigue to live in the mountains as a recluse. For a few months in 494, fleeing from a purge of his political faction at the Ch'i court in Chien-k'ang (modern Nanking), he obtained an appointment as Governor of Tung-yang 東陽 (in Chekiang), where he hoped to fulfill this dream. But his Confucian conscience could never resist the call to public service, and only nine months after leaving the capital he was back at court where he was showered with ever higher titles. In 498, he made a pilgrimage to a Taoist temple in the T'ien-t'ai Mountains (also in Chekiang) on the eve of the bloody interregnum of the Marquis of Tung-hun, Hsiao Pao-chüan 蕭寶卷 (r. 499-501). Taoism was not, however, the only influence in his life that created a tension with his ever-increasing political engagement. Through the influence of the devout Ch'i royal family he embraced the Buddhist religion, which enhanced his innate love for all living creatures and for the untrammeled space of the mountain wilds which were the favored sites for Buddhist monasteries and Taoist temples alike. In the later years of his life he wrote many Buddhist tracts, now preserved in the seventh-century anthology *Kuang Hung-ming chi* 廣弘明集 (Expanded Collection on Propagating the Light), dealing with the survival of the "soul" (*shen* 神), with "ultimate compassion" (*chiu-ching tz'u-pei* 究竟慈悲), and with vegetarianism.

But quite apart from his prosodic innovations, his mildly sensual love poems, his exuberant nature poems, and uplifting Buddhist apologues, Shen's reputation as a writer rests on his part in editing the official *Sung-shu* 宋書 (History of the Sung), a task he began in the spring of 487 and completed less than a year later, building on the work of several predecessors in the historian's office. It was a delicate assignment and Shen's political acumen may be judged from the fact that he held major offices through three successive dynasties, beginning with the Sung itself. He completed the *Sung-shu* during the declining years of the succeeding dynasty, the Ch'i, and was well aware that much of what he would say in defense of the founders of Ch'i would be considered unfair to the last rulers of Sung whom they had ruthlessly displaced, just as he would be deemed disloyal to the following dynasty, which, even as he wrote, was threatening to displace the obviously incompetent holders of the Ch'i mandate. Caught in this dilemma, he could not escape the obloquy of later historiographers, but he managed to rescue his reputation through certain unique features of the history. There is an unusually large proportion of literary biographies, including that of the poet Hsieh Ling-yün mentioned earlier, with its famous postface in which Shen's poetic theories are adumbrated, and the *Yüeh-chih* 樂志 (Monograph on Music, *chüan* 20-23), which remains one of our best sources for the texts of the ritual songs and ballads known as *yüeh-fu** from the Han through the Sung.

Shen Yüeh was born into a southern military family whose ancestors had migrated from North China to the area of T'ai-hu 太湖 (modern Chekiang) some time in the first century A.D. Since his great-grandfather had served under the Taoist rebel-leader Sun En 孫恩 in 399 and his own father had been executed for suspected implication in a political coup in 453 when Shen was only twelve, Shen Yüeh was unusually careful all his life to prove his loyalty to the ruling houses of the Southern Dynasties he served. So successful was he in concealing his real sentiments that after his death in 513 the last emperor he served, Emperor Wu of Liang, bestowed on him the posthumous title *Yin-hou* 隱侯 (Elusive Marquis). Though some of his religious statements, notably his "Ch'an-hui wen" 懺悔文 (Remorse and Repentance) [in *Kuang Hung-ming chi*, 28], are startling in their frankness and unreserved honesty, the reader of his darkly veiled poems is often forced to agree with Emperor Wu's characterization.

EDITIONS:

Ch'üan Liang shih 全梁詩, ch. 4, in *Nan-pei-ch'ao shih*, v. 2, pp. 1207-1257.

Ch'üan Liang wen 全梁文, v. 3, ch. 25, pp. 3097-3139.

Shen Yin-hou chi 沈隱侯集, in *Pai-san*, v. 11, pp. 2877-3004.

TRANSLATIONS:

Demiéville, *Anthologie*, p.158.

Frodsham, *Anthology*, pp. 171-172.

Sunflower, pp. 69-73.

von Zach, *Anthologie*, v. 1, pp. 304-305, 310, 349-351, 470-471, 558-562; v. 2, pp. 749-752, 936-939, 1011-1024.

STUDIES:

Bodman, *Poetics*, pp. 116-150.

Brooks, E. Bruce. "A Geometry of the *Shr Pin*," in *Wen-lin*, pp. 121-150. Deals somewhat with Shen Yüeh's prosodic theories.

Mather, Richard B. "Shen Yüeh's Poems of Reclusion," *CLEAR*, 5.1 (January 1983), forthcoming.

Suzuki, Torao 鈴木虎雄. "Shin Kyūbun nenpo" 沈休文年譜, in *Kanō kyōju kanreki kinen shinagaku ronsō* 狩野教授還暦記念支那學 論叢, Tokyo, 1928, pp. 567-617.

Yoshikawa, Tadao 吉川忠雄. "Shin Yaku no denki to sono seikatsu" 沈約の傳記とその生活, *Tōkai daigaku kiyō, bungakubu,* 11 (1968), 30-45.

———. "Shin Yaku no shisō—rikuchō-teki shōkon" 沈約の思想 — 六朝的傷痕, in *Chūgoku chūseishi kenkyū* 中國中世史研究, Tokyo, 1970, pp. 246-271.

—RM

Shih 詩 (poetry or classical poetry) is perhaps the most general term in Chinese for "poetry." As such, it is loosely applied to a variety of specific verse forms, which, although unrelated either historically or generically, were all thought of as *shih*.

I. INTRODUCTION

These forms were (1) the odes of the *Shih-ching*,* (2) the *yüeh-fu** and the *ku-t'i shih* 古體詩 (old-style poetry) of the Han and after, and (3) the *lü-shih* 律詩 (regulated verse)—also known as *chin-t'i shih* 近體詩 (modern-style poetry)—of the T'ang and after. The *sao* 騒 ("elegiac" poetry) of the *Ch'u-tz'u** is often included in the *shih* tradition, although the *sao* form is usually called *tz'u* rather than *shih*. The term *shih* is never used to refer to verse in the *fu** (prose-poetry), *tz'u** (lyrics), or *ch'ü** (aria) forms.

The odes of the *Shih-ching* are a distillation of many ancient verse traditions, both oral and written. Yet the common verse stanza of four syllables per line, four lines per stanza, seems the most basic underlying pattern and was related to Chou dynasty music and dance. It is highly likely that the *Shih-ching* was compiled when this music was still a living tradition, and so there was no need for formal rules of versification. The resulting rhythmic flexibility of the *Shih-ching* corpus tempted later Chinese scholars to see in it the origins of all later Chinese verse forms. For example, because lines with five and seven syllables do occur in the *Shih-ching*, some scholars believed old-style poetry must have derived from these lines. Although such beliefs were ahistorical, they did serve to reinforce the importance of the *Shih-ching* as the beginning of the Chinese poetic tradition.

Old-style poetry arose during the Han dynasty, probably as a result of Chinese contact with Central Asian music encountered during the military expansion of the second century B.C. The oldest form contained five syllables per line. The number of lines was optional, although poems longer than thirty lines are unusual. Later, a seven-syllable line was also employed. Rhyming was usually by couplets, every other line ending in a rhyme which the poet was free to maintain or to change throughout the course of the poem. There were no rules regarding the placement of tones throughout the line, other than general requirements of euphony. This old-style poetic form afforded the author an easy and natural medium, especially for longer, narrative poems, which tended throughout Chinese history to be written in this form.

II. REGULATED VERSE

The T'ang dynasty witnessed the appearance of a new poetic genre known as "regulated" (modern-style verse). Knowledge of this form was a prerequisite both for the imperial examinations and for membership in upper-class society. Anyone with an education was expected to compose regulated verse on virtually every social occasion, from greeting and leave-taking to poetry contests and outings. As a brief form, it was best suited to lyrical expression, and so left narration to old-style poetry. Regulated verse was largely occasional verse, composed and chanted on the spot and later circulated in manuscript or even scribbled on the walls of teahouses. In a few cases poets achieved national fame by having verses for a particular occasion transformed into popular songs by courtesans and entertainers. Though the *tz'u* began to compete with it in popularity by the very end of the T'ang, *lü-shih* (regulated verse) continued to be popular in the subsequent Sung dynasty, and the ability to write it remained one of the distinguishing marks of the man of letters.

The brevity of most regulated verse made it particularly suitable as a vehicle for describing a natural scene and a state of mind, while at the same time requiring the poet to use all the resources of language and rhetoric—including unusual syntax and deliberate ambiguity—to pack within its brief space "a meaning beyond words." While the contemporary reader had to be alert for allusion and symbolism, the modern translator must struggle with a language that consistently avoids grammatical particles and the first person pronoun and fails to indicate number and tense.

Regulated verse (lü-shih) is both a general term covering several specific varieties of T'ang poetry, all of which employ tonal prosody, as well as a specific term for one particular variety. The poems below represent the two most common forms of regulated verse and display the standard Chinese method of obliquely portraying human feelings through the description of a natural scene.

Seven-syllable lü-shih: Tu Fu,* "Teng kao" 登高 (Climbing to a Height)

> The wind is rushed, the sky high, the call of gibbons keen;
> The islet fresh, the sand white, and bird flight circling.
> Boundless the shedding trees and bleak the leaves that fall,
> Never ending the Long River rolling on and on.
> Ten thousand li of sad autumn: always a traveler;
> A hundred years of many ills: alone I climb the tower.
> Hardship and sharp regret have so frosted my temples
> That I've even had to give up my cup of homemade wine.

Five-syllable chüeh-chü 絕句: Liu Tsung-yüan,* "Chiang hsüeh" 江雪 (River Snow)

> Over a thousand mountains, birds have ceased to fly,
> On ten thousand paths man's tracks have been wiped out.
> In a lone boat, in grass cape and hat, an old man
> Fishes alone the cold river snow.

The reader of Chinese poetry in translation can normally recognize these two major forms of regulated verse by the number of lines. The first, lü-shih, always has eight lines, while chüeh-chü has four. In addition, lü-shih always employs "parallel couplets" in lines 3-4 and 5-6, and often in lines 1-2 also, as in Tu Fu's poem above. A third and relatively less frequently form of regulated verse is the p'ai-lü 排律 created by repeating the quatrain as often as desired, though normally in multiples of twenty lines. It requires the use of parallel couplets throughout, except in the last couplet.

In a parallel couplet, the words in the first line match their partners in the second line syntactically, while frequently contrasting with them in meaning. Tu Fu's lines 1-2, for example, may be analyzed as follows:

風急	/	天高	//	猿嘯哀	
1 WIND SWIFT	/	SKY HIGH	//	GIBBON-CRY	SAD
noun stative		noun stative		noun-phrase	stative
verb		verb			verb

渚清	/	沙白	//	鳥飛廻	
2 ISLET CLEAR	/	SAND WHITE	//	BIRD-FLIGHT CIRCLING	

Each line is composed of three sentences in the form: noun + stative verb, where the first two sentences are separated by a phrase boundary (/) and the last two by the caesura (//). In addition, the nouns of the first line ("wind" "sky" "gibbon-cry") all relate to height and contribute to describe the high cliffs above the Yangtze inhabited by gibbons. In contrast, the nouns of the second line ("islet" "sand" "bird-flight") emphasize lowness and describe the base of the gorge. Similarly, the stative verbs of line 1 ("swift" "high" "sad") all share a certain intensity, while their counterparts in line 2 ("clear" "white" "circling") emphasize static qualities.

A second structural characteristic of many lü-shih and chüeh-chü may also be seen in these examples: the division of the poem into two sections, the first of which describes the scene, the second of which expresses the poet's feelings in that scene. While the two sections thus contrast, they also complement each other, for the description of the scene should itself suggest the emotions of the second section. In Tu Fu's poems above, the poet's restlessness is suggested in advance by the birds' purposeless, circling flight; his resentment of his old age and of time passing is already present in the suggestion that the leaves which keep on falling cannot stop the Long River from flowing.

The contrast between scene and feeling is further emphasized by the use in the two parts of two different kinds of syntax, which Mei Tsu-lin and Kao Yu-kung have dubbed "imagistic" and "propositional" language. "Imagistic" language, characteristic of the first couplet of a poem, packs lines with one or more noun images or intransitive sentences; hence it reads slowly. "Propositional" language, characteristic of a poem's last couplet, stretches out a single sentence or thought to fill both lines; thus it reads quickly. Common grammatical patterns are questions, questions and answers, hypotheses in the form "if . . . then," or statements of the form "x thus y." While the former appeals to the senses, the latter invokes the reasoning intellect.

III. PROSODY

The scansion of regulated verse (and indeed of most Chinese poetry) differs greatly from that of classical poetry in the West, largely because the virtual absence of polysyllabic words in classical Chinese as well as the lack of a clear-cut distinction between long and short syllables have never suited the scansion of lines in terms of "feet." While lines of classical Western poetry are normally divided into a standard number of "feet" made up of a varying number of long and short syllables, *lü-shih* are divided into lines of a fixed length— either all 5- or all 7-syllables—each syllable of which is usually a separate word. Variety in rhythm is achieved not by alternating different kinds of "feet" but rather by alternating syllables in different *tones*. The pattern of this alternation is called tonal prosody. In its final form in the T'ang, tonal prosody required the contrast of tones within the line and between the two lines of a couplet, and the mirror-sym-

metry of the two couplets of a quatrain and the two quatrains of a complete poems.

Not until the latter part of the fifth century did Chinese scholars in the south, influenced by contact with Indian priests versed in Sanskrit and techniques of chanting, realize that their own language was tonal. They soon discovered that the four tones of Ancient Chinese—*p'ing* 平 (level), *shang* 上 (rising), *ch'ü* 去 (departing), and *ju* 入 (entering)—could be regrouped into two: the level tone, comprising about half of all the syllables, and the *tse* 仄 (deflected) tones (rising, departing, and entering), comprising the other half. Scholars such as Shen Yüeh experimented with alternating level and deflected tones in poetry, much as Buddhist hymns based their meter on the alternation of long and short syllables.

Chinese scholars have traditionally taught the tonal prosody of regulated verse by simply listing the possible patterns of alternating level and deflected syllables for each variety of verse. As Downer and Graham have shown, it is possible to derive a more general pattern from these traditional ones, by identifying separate patterns of alternation for the even-numbered syllables and for the odd-numbered syllables. In what follows, the general pattern of tonal prosody for regulated verse will be described in terms of 7-syllable *lü-shih*, from which pattern all other varieties may be derived. Even-numbered syllables (i.e., Nos. 2, 4, 6) are represented by A's and B's, where A and B stand for opposing values of level and deflected; odd-numbered syllables (i.e., Nos. 1, 3, 5, 7) are signified by x's, y's, and hyphens (-), where x and y stand for opposing values of level and deflected, and hyphens represent syllables that can vary freely.

Within a line, the pattern of syllables is determined by the principle of contrast, such that the even-numbered syllables alternate in the pattern A B A and the odd-numbered syllables in the pattern - - x y. Hence the general pattern for a line of verse is

$$- A - B x A y$$

where syllables 1 and 3 are not specified in tone.

The pattern of a couplet is also governed by the principle of contrast; the second line of a couplet is generated by matching each specified tone in the first line with its tonal opposite, i.e.:

1 - A - B x A y
2 - B - A y B x

Beyond the level of the couplet, the patterning of the odd-numbered syllables does not grow more complex; instead, the same pattern is repeated from couplet to couplet. But in terms of the even-numbered syllables, the second couplet of a quatrain is generated from the first by the principle of mirror-symmetry. Imagine a horizontal axis dividing the quatrain between lines 2 and 3—it can then be seen that the first couplet is rotated, or folded over onto the second couplet, so that line 1 matches line 4, and line 2 matches line 3:

```
        1 A B A
        2 B A B
                    →axis
        3 B A B
        4 A B A
```

Finally, the principle of mirror-symmetry also operates to generates the second quatrain of a *lü-shih* by folding the first quatrain over an axis between lines 4 and 5. In the final result we see mirror symmetry on two levels, between the two quatrains and between the two couplets of each quatrain:

TABLE 1: MIRROR-SYMMETRY

Mirroring of quatrains		Mirroring of couplets	
1	A B A	1	A B A
2	B A B	2	B A B
		[minor axis]	
3	B A B	3	B A B
4	A B A	4	A B A
		[MAJOR AXIS]	
5	A B A	5	A B A
6	B A B	6	B A B
		[minor axis]	
7	B A B	7	B A B
8	A B A	8	A B A

The pattern of even syllables outlined here for the complete *lü-shih* has a distinct shape, with a definite beginning, middle and end. T'ang critics speak of a poem's "head," "belly," and "tail," where the

"head" and "tail" are the first and last couplets and the "belly" the two middle couplets on either side of the axis. The poem may be thought of as a living creature with its tail in its mouth, for the tonal pattern comes full circle and ends as it began. Each of these parts and the concept of circularity as well take on significance in the thematic development of the complete poem. The principle of contrast, moreover, operates in the selection of words in parallel couplets.

The patterns for both the even and the odd-numbered syllables combine to create the general pattern for 7-syllable *lü-shih*:

TABLE 2: GENERAL PATTERN FOR REGULATED VERSE

syllable number

	1)	2)	3)	4)	5)	6)	7)
1	-	A	-	B	x	A	y
2	-	B	-	A	y	B	x
3	-	B	-	A	x	B	y
4	-	A	-	B	y	A	x
5	-	A	-	B	x	A	y
6	-	B	-	A	y	B	x
7	-	B	-	A	x	B	y
8	-	A	-	B	y	A	x

(Taken from Downer and Graham, 1963)

All varieties of regulated verse allow the first line to enter the rhyme scheme, in which case lines 1-2 above would read:

- A - B y A x
- B - A y B x

The pattern for 5-syllable regulated verse can be derived by omitting columns 1) and 2) above. The *chüeh-chü* pattern, in either 5- or 7-syllable varieties, may be taken from lines 1-4 above, while the *p'ai-lü* pattern—in 5-syllable lines only—results from multiplying the pattern of lines 1-4 as often as desired.

The final syllables of each line are governed by stricter conventions than just the alternation of level and deflected tones required in the above chart. First, the final syllables of even-numbered lines must not only rhyme, but the rhyming syllables must also be in the same one of the four tones; that is, they should be all level, all rising, all departing, or all entering. Second, the last syllables of a non-rhyming line should

685

never be in the same tone (of the four tones) as the rhyme. Lastly, the final syllable of consecutive non-rhyming lines—i.e., the final syllables of line 1 and line 3, or of line 3 and line 5, or of line 5 and line 7—should never be in the same one of the four tones. While *lü-shih* almost always rhyme in the level tone, *chüeh-chü* may rhyme in either level or deflected tones. In a *chüeh-chü* rhyming in a deflected tone, the first line normally enters the rhyme scheme.

Problems arise when the modern Western student attempts to determine whether a particular poem is or is not a *lü-shih*, because (1) many anthologies—particularly those compiled before the Sung—fail to group *lü-shih* together or identify them as such; (2) a knowledge of tones in modern Mandarin cannot be used to guess either the T'ang tones or the level-deflected distinction; and (3) T'ang poets thought not in terms of charts such as the one above when composing verse, but rather in terms of a series of tonal combinations to avoid, some of which they observed more strictly than others.

The greatest difficulty is the second, arising from the poor correspondence between the tones of modern Mandarin and those of T'ang Chinese. Of all modern dialects, Mandarin is probably the furthest removed from the ancient pronunciation. Syllables that were level tone in the T'ang are now distributed between Mandarin tone 1 and tone 2. T'ang rising tones normally become Mandarin tone 3, and departing tones normally become tone 4, but there are many cases of cross-over. None of the above changes would be serious, however, if it were not for the fact that T'ang entering tone syllables have been distributed randomly amongst all four tones of Mandarin. Hence there is no way of knowing *a priori* whether a Mandarin 1st or 2nd tone syllable corresponds to a T'ang level tone or to an entering tone. If the student knows a dialect such as Cantonese which has preserved the entering tone category, he can check to see if the syllable in question ends with a -p, -t, or -k. Otherwise, his only recourse is to look up the word in question in a handbook or dictionary of ancient Chinese pronunciation such as those by Chou Fa-kao, Shen Chien-shih, or Ting Sheng-shu.

The formula given above is cumbersome to check and if applied strictly could result in rejecting some poems that are in fact considered *lü-shih* even though they may occasionally violate prohibitions such as those against the last two even syllables or the last two odd syllables of a line being in the same tone. Downer and Graham's chart is derived from detailed tonal patterns prescribed for students by Ch'ing scholars; in their own time T'ang poets had no such detailed rules to work from, and we must assume that a fair amount of experimentation was still going on. While the rule of tonal contrast within the line is occasionally violated, however, the contrast of tones between lines in the second-syllable column is never violated, and hence the simplest rule of thumb for recognizing a *lü-shih* is to see whether these syllables follow the pattern ABBAABBA, i.e.,

```
1 - A - - - - -
2 - B - - - - -
3 - B - - - - -
4 - A - - - - -
5 - A - - - - -
6 - B - - - - -
7 - B - - - - -
8 - A - - - - -
```

This rule is supported by a statement from the poet Yüan Ching 元兢 (*c.* 661 A.D.) preserved in the *Wen-ching mi-fu-lun.**

IV. *CHÜEH-CHÜ*

Chüeh-chü, the other verse form in the modern style, is a five- or seven-character quatrain which, like the *lü-shih*, must observe rigid rules governing tonal pattern and rhyme scheme, the only difference being that in a *chüeh-chü* verbal parallelism is not absolutely required as it is in the *lü-shih*. The regulated five-character *chüeh-chü* did not come into full maturity until the second half of the seventh century: the seven-character quatrain, until the beginning of the eighth century, the seven-character quatrain, although some earlier prototypes can be found. From the middle decades of the eighth century onward, *chüeh-chü* began to be written on a large scale and the form was soon distinguished as a lyric vehicle of extraordinary range and capability, a verse form particularly suited to encapsulating a lyric moment or driving home a pointed argument or witty idea. Many T'ang poets were renowned for their achievements in this verse form, notably Wang Wei,* Li Po,* Wang Ch'ang-ling,* Tu Mu,* and Li Shang-yin.* After the T'ang period, *chüeh-chü* continued to be written by poets of all inclinations. The popularity of the verse form has led to the compilation of several anthologies of *chüeh-chü* beginning with the massive *Wan-shou T'ang-jen chüeh-chü* 萬首唐人絕句 (Ten Thousand Quatrains from the T'ang) by Hung Mai.*

Critics over the centuries have disputed the origin and history of the *chüeh-chü* form. Traditional opinion generally divides into two views. The first view, expounded by Hsü Shih-tseng 徐師曾 (1517-1580) and Shih Pu-hua 施補華 (1835-1890), among others, equates *chüeh-chü* with the term *chieh-chü* 截句 (cut-off lines) and regards the modern-style *chüeh-chü* as essentially a shortened form of *lü-shih*, four lines "cut off" from the eight-line *lü-shih*. Observations cited as evidence are: (1) Since the *lü-shih* consists of two nonparallel couplets and two parallel middle couplets, the verse form lends itself to four possible permutations in the case of truncation (namely, two nonparallel couplets, two parallel couplets, a nonparallel couplet followed by a parallel couplet, and a parallel couplet followed by a nonparallel couplet), all of which can be found in the *chüeh-chü*. (2) In some collected works of T'ang authors, *chüeh-chü* are grouped under the rubric of *lü-shih* rather than being treated as an independent form.

The second view, whose chief proponents include Hu Ying-lin (1551-1602) and Wang Fu-chih (1619-1692), rejects the notion that *chüeh-chü* evolved out of the *lü-shih* and proceeds to trace the origin of the form to the short old-style poetry of Han-Wei times and the four-line folk songs of the Six Dynasties period. This view is supported by the fact that the term *chüeh-chü* and its variants *tuan-chü* 短句 and *tuan-chü* 斷句 existed long before the codification of *lü-shih* rules. *Chüeh-chü*, for instance, appear in the sixth-century anthology *Yü-t'ai hsin-yung.** Futhermore, some poets of Ch'i-Liang times already wrote quatrains whose rhythmic regularity virtually qualifies them as modern-style *chüeh-chü*. Modern scholars on the subject (Hung Wei-fa and Lo Ken-tse, for example) tend to take a more synthetic view and regard the emergence of the modern-style *chüeh-chü* as the outcome of a combination of literary and historical factors, among which were the availability of the quatrain form in pre-T'ang folk songs, the influx of a new type of music during the Sui-T'ang period, and the corresponding changes in the *chüeh-chü* prosody to accommodate the changes in the musical setting with which it was originally associated. The final word on the issue perhaps should go to Wang Li, who has properly distinguished between *cheh-ch* proper and what he calls *ku chüeh-chü* 古絕句 (old *chüeh-chü*). The term *chüeh-chü*, he maintains, should be reserved for those five- or seven-character quatrains which adhere to the phonic rules of the modern style; the non-conforming quatrains should all be relegated to the category of *ku-feng* 古風 or "ancient manner."

The regulated *chüeh-chü* is unquestionably one of the most exacting forms in Chinese poetry, the composition of which calls for exceptional poetic skills. A *chüeh-chü* poet not only has to work within the strictures imposed by the prosodic requirements of the modern style, he is also forced by the form's brevity to pack the maximum amount of meaning into a space of twenty or twenty-eight characters. Since Sung times, a great deal of critical reflection has centered around the question of what constitutes the most effective way to compose a *chüeh-chü*. As a result, several broad principles were formulated in conjunction with both the writing and the evaluation of *chüeh-chü*. The first consensus is that a good *chüeh-chü* should have the fluidity and coherence of a compact essay and should move effortlessly from a crisp introduction (*ch'i* 起) to a swift reinforcement of the theme (*ch'eng* 承) and then to a "turn" or transition (*chuan* 轉) which is capable of sweeping what went before into a climactic conclusion (*ho* 合). Of the four lines in a *chüeh-chü*, the third line is the most crucial because it nearly always coincides with the "turn" and is therefore the most instrumental in thrusting forward the thought of the poem. The second consensus is that a *chüeh-chü* should at all times observe the principle of verbal economy, saying the most in the least obtrusive manner. Whenever possible, a *chüeh-chü* should avoid direct assertions and build its effect on the subtle manipulation of tone and imagery. Instead of clarity, it should strive for nuance (*yü-yin* 餘音), implicit meaning (*yen-wai chih-i* 言外之意), and the art of suggestion (*han-hsü* 含蓄). There are many other principles governing the choice of diction and imagery and the structuring of a *chüeh-chü*, all of which are geared toward enabling the short *chüeh-chü* to register its impact with the greatest force and precision.

Chüeh-chü is generally considered the ideal form for expressing a fleeting mood or capturing the essence of a landscape scene. This is particularly true with the quatrains of the High T'ang, where a profusion of nature imagery and landscape motifs has given rise to the oft-quoted dictum that an effective *chüeh-chü* is one which has attained the state of "fusion of mood and scene" (*ch'ing-ching chiao-yung* 情景交融). The mood pieces, however, represent only one end of the *chüeh-chü* spectrum. Since the ninth century, a variety of subjects and modes have found their way into the *chüeh-chü* form, ranging from the elegiac *huai-ku* 懷古 to the taut and frequently satiric *yung-shih* 詠史. The *Yung-shih chüeh-chü* (quatrains on history and historical events) in particular has remained a subgenre of great vitality throughout the centuries. Another important category is the cerebral, at times highly allusive, *lun-shih* 論詩 *chüeh-chü* (quatrain on poets and poetry), first attempted by Tu Fu in his "Hsi-wei liu chüeh-chü" 戲爲六絕句 and popularized into a permanent subgenre by the thirteenth-century poet Yüan Hao-wen.*

STUDIES:

Bodman, Richard Wainwright. "Poetics and Prosody in Early Mediaeval China: A Study and Translation of Kūkai's *Bunkyō hifuron.*" Unpublished Ph.D. dissertation, Cornell University, 1978. See Chap. 2, "The Development of Regulated Verse and the Evidence of the *Bunkyō hifuron.*"

Brooks, E. Bruce. "Journey Toward the West: An Asian Prosodic Embassy in the Year 1972," *HJAS*, 35 (1975), 221-274.

Chen, Matthew Y. "Metrical Structure: Evidence from Chinese Poetry," *Linguistic Inquiry*, 10 (1979), 371-420.

———. "The Primacy of Rhythm in Verse: A Linguistics Perspective," *JCL*, 8.1 (January 1980), 15-41.

Chou, Fa-kao 周法高, *et al.*, eds. *Han-tzu ku-chin yin-hui* 漢字古今音彙: *A Pronouncing Dictionary of Chinese Characters in Archaic and Ancient Chinese, Mandarin, and Cantonese.* Hong Kong, 1974. A standard handbook for determining the ancient pronounciation and tone of a given character.

Chow, Tse-tsung. "The Early History of the Chinese Word *Shih* (Poetry)," in *Wen-lin*, pp. 151-209.

Chu, Jen-sheng 朱任生. *Shih-lun fen-lei tsuan-yao* 詩論分類纂要. Taipei, 1971, pp. 217-230. A collection of *shih-hua* excerpts on the *chüeh-chü.*

Downer, G. B. and A. C. Graham. "Tone Patterns in Chinese Poetry," *BSOAS*, 26 (1963), 145-148.

Fu, Shou-sun 富壽蓀, comp. "T'ang-jen chüeh-chü chi-p'ing" 唐人絕句輯評, in Liu Pai-shan 劉拜山 and Fu Shou-sun, eds., *T'ang-jen chüeh-chü p'ing-chu* 唐人絕句評注, Hong Kong, 1980, pp. 288-367.

Guillén, Claudio. "Some Observations on Parallel Poetic Forms," *TkR*, 2.3 & 3.1 (October 1971 and April 1972), 395-415.

Hightower, *Topics*, pp. 69-71.

Hirano, Hikojirō 平野彥次郎. "Zekku ni tsuite" 絕句について, in *Tōshisen kenkyū* 唐詩選研究, Tokyo, 1974, pp. 56-77.

Jakobson, Roman. "The Modular Design of Chinese Regulated Verse," in Jean Pouillon and Pierre Maranda, eds., *Echanges et communications: mélanges offerts à Claude Lévi-Strauss à l'occasion de son 60ème anniversaire*, The Hague, 1970, pp. 597-605.

Kao, Yu-kung and Mei Tsu-lin. "Ending Lines in Wang Shih-chen's 'ch'i-chüeh': Convention and Creativity in the Ch'ing," in Christian F. Murck, ed., *Artists and Traditions,* Princeton, 1976, pp. 131-144.

———. "Syntax, Diction and Imagery in T'ang Poetry," *HJAS,* 31 (1971), 51-135.

Lin, James Kuo-chiang. "Versification of *Chin t'i shih.*" Unpublished Ph.D. dissertation, Georgetown University, 1981.

Liu, James J. Y. *Art of Chinese Poetry.* Chicago, 1962.

Lo, Ken-tse 羅根澤. "Chüeh-chü san-yüan" 絕句三源, in *Chung-kuo ku-tien wen-hsüeh lun-chi* 中國古典文學論集, Peking, 1955, pp. 28-53.

Lu, Chih-wei 陸志韋. "Shih lun Tu Fu lü-shih te ko-lü" 試論杜甫律詩的格律, *Wen-hsüeh p'ing-lun,* 4 (1962), 13-35.

Ripley, Stephen Allan. "A Statistical Study of Tone Patterns in T'ang Regulated Verse." Unpublished Ph.D. dissertation, University of Toronto, 1979.

Shen, Chien-shih 沈兼士, ed. *Kuang-yün sheng-hsi* 廣韻聲系. Shanghai, 1945.

Sun, K'ai-ti 孫楷第. "Chüeh-chü shih tsen-yang ch'i-lai-te" 絕句是怎樣起來的, *Hsüeh-yüan* 學原, 1.4 (1947), 83-88.

Suzuki, Torao 鈴木虎雄. "Zekku sogen" 絕句遡源, in *Shina bungaku kenkyū* 支那文學研究, Kyoto, 1925, pp. 157-172.

Takagi, Masakazu 高木正一 and Cheng Ch'ing-mau 鄭清茂, trans. "Liu-ch'ao lü-shih chih hsing-ch'eng" 六朝律詩之形成, *Ta-lu tsa-chih,* 13.9 (1956), 17-18, 13-20, 24-32.

Ting, Sheng-shu 丁聲樹. *Ku-chin tzu-yin tui-chao shou-ts'e* 古今字音對照手冊. Hong Kong, 1966.

Wang, Li 王力. *Han-yü shih-lü hsüeh* 漢語詩律學. Shanghai, 1962. The basic treatise on Chinese versification.

Yang, Ch'un-ch'iu 羊春秋, *et al. Li-tai lun-shih chüeh-chü hsüan* 歷代論詩絕句選. Changsha, 1981.

Yip, Moira. "The Metrical Structure of Regulated Verse," *JCL,* 8.1 (January 1980), 107-125.

—RB and SSW

Shih-chi 史記 (Records of the Grand Historian), is a comprehensive history of China, which covers the 2500-year period from the reign of the mythical Yellow Emperor (traditionally, 2697-2599 B.C.) to the reign of Emperor Wu of the Han (140-87 B.C.). The *Shih-chi* is the first of the vast collection of historical texts known as *Erh-shih-wu shih* 二十五史 (The Twenty-five Histories). Although the general structure of the *Shih-chi,* as well as certain portions of the text itself, may have been the work of Ssu-ma T'an 司馬談, Grand Astrologer of the Han court during the early years of Emperor Wu's reign, credit for the completed work is usually given to T'an's son Ssu-ma Ch'ien.*

The organization of the *Shih-chi,* which became the model for later Chinese dynastic histories, is distinct from that of the early historical writings of the West. The latter recount history in a continuous, sweeping narrative, perhaps influenced structurally by the Western epic, but the *Shih-chi* is broken into smaller, overlapping units. Jaroslav Prusek's important study of this subject describes this Western narrative style as *unterbrochener Fluss* (uninterrupted flow) and contrasts it with the Chinese penchant for *Treppenabsatz* (segmented progress). As the following description of the structure of the *Shih-chi* shows, it is one of the clearest examples of Chinese "segmented progress."

The *Shih chi*'s 130 chapters are grouped into 5 sections. These are, in order of occurrence: "Pen-chi" 本紀 (Basic Annals), 12 chapters; "Piao" 表 (Tables), 10 chapters; "Shu" 書 (Treatises), 8 chapters; "Shih-chia" 世家 (Hereditary Households), 30 chapters; and "Lieh-chuan" 列傳 (Memoirs), 70 chapters. The first of these sections, "Basic Annals," chronicles the major events involving the emperor and his ruling bureaucracy. The section begins with the "Basic Annals of the Five Emperors," an account of the mythical sage-rulers of antiquity, and continues with one chapter per dynasty until the record reaches the Han dynasty, after which each chapter covers the reign of a single emperor. As this structure implies, the detail increases as the chronology draws nearer to Ssu-ma's lifetime. Thus, the "Basic Annals of Yin" is little more than a list of emperors, with very little historical information presented, whereas the "Basic Annals of Kao-tsu," which concerns the career of the founder of the Han dynasty, contains prolonged narrative sequences which dramatically recreate certain critical episodes in Kao-tsu's life. The antecedent for the "Basic Annals" section of the *Shih-chi* is probably the Confucian classic the *Ch'un-ch'iu* (see *ching*), a text which Ssu-ma Ch'ien esteemed highly. However, while the great classic lists major historical events in the tersest chronicle form, the *Shih-chi* periodically interrupts the simple list of historical events with long and sometimes complex narratives.

The "Tables" section arranges chronologically the sequence of rulers, feudal lords, famous ministers, generals, and other noteworthies. It is useful both for its clear presentation of temporal relationships and for its proposed solutions to various problems of chronology. Edouard Chavannes suggests that the idea for a section of this type originated with Ssu-ma Ch'ien himself, but because so many early Chinese texts have perished, this assertion is difficult to prove. In the hands of Pan Ku,* the author of the second of the official "Twenty-five Histories," the "Tables" became an instrument not just to show temporal relationships but also to rank the moral worthiness of important persons.

The eight "Treatises" are topical discussions of a select number of institutions or practices that are particularly relevant to an understanding of ancient Chinese history. These include studies of ritual, music, the calendar, and the *feng* 封 and *shan* 禪 sacrifices. The idea for the "Treatises" might have derived from the topical essays of the philosophers and, still more directly, from the discussions of *Lü-shih ch'un-ch'iu* (see *chu-tzu pai-chia*). Nevertheless, their valuable detail marks them as an important addition to the traditional Chinese historical text. Although "treatises" continued to be a part of official histories, with a tendency as time went by towards a proliferation of topics (the *Ming-shih* has thirteen subjects), the *Shih-chi* name for this section, *shu*, was replaced by the name *chih* 志.

The section entitled "Hereditary Households" is unique to the *Shih-chi* and was apparently included by Ssu-ma Ch'ien to deal with an important fact of Eastern Chou politics: the feudal lords typically exercised greater power than the titular Chou sovereign. Ssu-ma also includes in this section the hereditary households of eminent Han families, even though they exercised much less independence than their Chou predecessors. This section chronicles major events in much the same way as the "Basic Annals," but here the feudal lineages, rather than the imperial line, occupy the narrative focus. Since "Hereditary Households" implies, by its very existence, a diffusion of sovereignty beyond the imperial line, it was not a part of later official histories.

The "Memoirs" is by far the largest section of the *Shih-chi* and, in terms of literary influence, the most important. The Chinese title *lieh-chuan* is often translated as "biographies," but the section contains not just accounts of individuals but also of groups such as the Hsiung-nu and the southwestern barbarians. Even where the focus is upon individuals, there is a tendency for two or more persons with perceived affinities to be placed in a single chapter. For example, Lao-tzu and Han-fei-tzu are discussed in the same chapter, indicating Ssu-ma Ch'ien's belief that Han-fei's legalism derived from Lao-tzu's Taoism.

Within the structure of the *Shih-chi* presented here, certain historically important persons are treated rather unusually. The two most discussed of these anomalies are the inclusion of Hsiang Yü, one of the rebels who brought the downfall of Ch'in and tried unsuccessfully to found a new dynasty, in "Basic Annals," and the treatment of Confucius "Hereditary Households" rather than in "Memoirs" with Lao-tzu, Mencius and other prominent Chou philosophers. Ssu-ma's treatment of Hsiang Yü presumably acknowledges the fact that the rebel, though never recognized throughout the realm as emperor, was for several years the most powerful man in China. The placement of Confucius among the "Hereditary Households" possibly derives from the belief, reported by Ssu-ma, that Confucius was the rightful heir to the throne of Sung and also from Ssu-ma's desire to honor the Master by setting him apart from other Chou philosophers.

The *Shih-chi* is not a continuous narrative, but a series of reports that supplement one another and are best studied through a system of cross-reference rather than by reading the chapters in sequence. For example, in the "Basic Annals of the First Ch'in Emperor" a reference to the Prime Minister Lü Pu-wei 呂不韋 is not followed by a long digression telling about this important historical figure; instead, such information is supplied in the "Memoirs" chapter dealing specifically with Lü (ch. 85). Or, to give a further example, a reference to a musical performance in one of the "Memoirs" may be given full context only by cross-reference to the "Treatise on Music" (ch. 24). The arrangement of the *Shih-chi* may not facilitate rapid comprehension of the full "story of history," in the manner of Herodotus or Thucydides, but it greatly facilitates the isolation and ready comprehension of a particular subject or an individual life.

Like all good historians, Ssu-ma Ch'ien drew upon earlier sources. Indeed, his extreme dependence upon previous works gives support to his description of himself as a "transmitter" and not a "creator," a description, incidentally, which is itself drawn almost verbatim from Confucius. For example, one scholar has estimated that fully half of Ssu-ma's material for the Warring States period (403-222) derives from the sources which Liu Hsiang* later collected in *Chan-kuo ts'e*.* Thus one recent article, which praises Ssu-ma Ch'ien's "brilliant use of language," cites example after example which Ssu-ma has demonstrably borrowed from elsewhere. Tracing the sources of the *Shih-chi* is a difficult task, because some of them, the *Ch'u Han ch'un-ch'iu* 楚漢春秋 being one of the most important, have perished, and because Ssu-ma rarely states the origin of passages cited in his history. Ssu-ma must not be judged too harshly on this account. As Chavannes notes: "A historical text [in China] is always considered as belonging to the public domain. One regards it as the strictest honesty to copy without changing anything, and one need not even give the source of the extract." Ssu-ma does, however, alter the language, and in a few places he introduces small changes to give the episode a slightly different interpretation. Nevertheless, any study of the narrative style of Ssu-ma Ch'ien the man, as opposed to that of the *Shih-chi* the text, must begin with the almost impossible task of defining precisely which portions of the *Shih-chi* were done by Ssu-ma Ch'ien.

While the authenticity of most of the present *Shih-chi* is accepted without question, there are some problems. In his *Han-shu* biography of Ssu-ma Ch'ien, Pan Ku notes that ten of the 130 chapters of *Shih-chi* had been lost (chs. 11, 12, 17, 23, 24, 25, 60, 98, 127 and 128), and some scholars argue that the texts of these chapters, as they appear today, are not the originals. Ch'u Shao-sun 褚少孫 (*c.* 30 B.C.) is often said to have forged the present version of these chapters by reference to other sources. In some cases there is even the suspicion that portions of today's text have been back-copied from the *Han-shu*. However, the noted Japanese *Shih-chi* specialist Kametarō Takigawa argues that Pan Ku's observation is incorrect; the disputed chapters, he asserts, do stem from the hand of Ssu-ma Ch'ien. It is unlikely that this problem will ever be satisfactorily resolved, but there is no doubt that the present text contains a number of minor interpolations. The most obvious of these might be the anachronistic reference to Yang Hsiung* in the "Memoirs of Ssu-ma Hsiang-ju" (ch. 117) and a quotation from Ch'u Shao-sun that appears in ch. 127.

As noted above, the *Shih-chi* had a profound impact upon the style and structure of much later Chinese historical writing, one that has extended to the popular Chinese genre of "historical fiction." Indeed, in the Chinese tradition the boundary between "history" and "fiction" is even less clear than it is in the West, and this ambiguity derives, in some measure, from the influence of the stylistic devices of the *Shih-chi*. The latter, for example, makes frequent use of dialogue and, at times, even monologue to both advance the plot and portray character, even though much of this speech could not have been overheard by the recorder. The tendency away from the strictly mimetic and towards the symbolic portrayal of character is another "fictional element" that has impact upon later Chinese narrative, particularly that of such historical romances as the *San-kuo chih yen-i** and the *Shui-hu chuan.** A few of these categories of characters might be the wise minister, the decadent king, the man who recognizes virtue in others, and the *femme fatale.* As with most "symbolic" characterization, as soon as a character is placed in a category, he acquires all the features of his category—his individuality dissolves into the symbol.

EDITIONS:

Shih-chi 史記. 10v. Peking, 1959.

Shih-chi i-pai-san-shih chüan 史記一百三十卷 1747; rpt. Taipei, 1968.

Takigawa, Kametarō 瀧川龜太郎. *Shiki kaichū kō-shō* 史記會注考證. Tokyo, 1934.

TRANSLATIONS:

Although there is no comprehensive Western-language translation, most of the *Shih-chi* has been translated in one source or another (there is a useful list of translations, complete up to 1969, in *Les Mémoires Historiques,* v. 6, pp. 123-146—see below).

Bodde, Derk. *Statesman, Patriot, and General in Ancient China.* New Haven, Connecticut, 1940.

Chavannes, Edouard. *Les Mémoires historiques de Se-ma Ts'ien.* 6v. Paris, 1895-1905 and 1969 (v. 6).

Kierman, F. A. *Ssu-ma Ch'ien's Historiographical Attitude as Reflected in Four Late Warring States Biographies.* Wiesbaden, 1962.

Watson, Burton. *Records of the Grand Historian.* Hong Kong, 1971.

Yang, Hsien-yi and Gladys Yang. *Records of the Historian.* Hong Kong, 1974.

STUDIES:

The body of scholarship on the *Shih-chi* is immense. Only a few Chinese sources can be listed below. For further references, see the *Shih-chi yen-chiu te tzu-liao lun-wen so-yin,* which is cited below.

Allen, Joseph Roe. "An Introductory Study of Narrative Structure in the *Shi ji,*" *CLEAR,* 3.1 (January 1981), 31-66.

Chin, Te-chien 金德建. *Ssu-ma Ch'ien so-chien shu k'ao* 司馬遷所見書考. Shanghai, 1963.

Chung, Hua 鍾華. *Shih-chi jen-ming so-yin* 史記人名索引. Peking, 1977.

Hervouet, Yves. "La valeur relative des textes du *Che ki* et du *Han chou,*" in *Mélanges de sinologie offerts à Monsieur Paul Demiéville, II.* Paris, 1974, pp. 55-76.

Kroll, Jurij L. "Ssu-ma Ch'ien's Literary Theory and Practice," *Altorientalische Forschungen,* 4 (1976), 313-325.

Li, Chang-chih 李長之. *Ssu-ma Ch'ien chih jen-ko yü feng-ko* 司馬遷之人格與風格. Rpt. Taipei, 1961.

Pokora, Timoteus. "The First Interpolation in the *Shih chi,*" *AO,* 29 (1961), 311-315.

Prusek, Jaroslav. "History and Epics in China and the West," in Prusek's *Chinese History and Literature,* Prague, 1971, pp. 17-34.

Shih-chi yen-chiu te tzu-liao ho lun-wen so-yin 史記研究的資料和論文索引. Peking, 1957.

Ssu-ma Ch'ien yü Shih-chi 司馬遷與史記. Shanghai, 1958.

Watson, Burton. *Ssu-ma Ch'ien: Grand Historian of China.* New York, 1958.

—SD

Shih-ching 詩經 (Classic of Poetry) is one of the six classics of the Confucian school and the fountainhead of Chinese literature. It is an anthology of 305 poems edited by Confucius (551-479 B.C.), as the traditional belief has it, on the basis of about three thousand compositions collected for the education of his disciples. The Confucian emphasis on the *Shih-ching* was so strong that the Master and his disciples were criticized by other philosophers of their time, notably the Mohists. The book, nevertheless, remained a classic and required reading for the literati for more than two thousand years; not until the turn of the twentieth century did it cease to be read as scripture and begin to be appreciated as a collection of poetic compositions.

The poems of *Shih-ching* may be dated from the twelfth century to the seventh century B.C. External and internal evidence attests that the earliest pieces of the corpus are the Chou hymns 周頌 (Nos. 266-296). But many of their stylistic qualities underwent modification until the time of Confucius, when these hymns, together with later poems (including the so-called

Shang hymns 商頌 which were composed in the state of Sung long after the fall of the Shang dynasty), assumed their final shape. The book in its definitive form was officially banned in the third century B.C., along with the other Confucian Classics, but the text survived orally and in hidden manuscripts so that it was possible to restore the collection under imperial sanction during the Han dynasty. Four separate versions were reconstructed. Of the four, the text preserved by a certain Master Mao 毛公 and commented on by some of the most thoughtful scholars in Chinese history, has survived almost intact to the present day, while those of the other three schools exist only in fragments.

The *Shih-ching* is divided into four sections, namely *kuo-feng* 國風 (songs), *hsiao-ya* 小雅 (elegantiae), *ta-ya* 大雅 (odes), and *sung* 頌 (hymns). The *kuo-feng* section (Nos. 1-160) comprises fifteen groups of songs with salient folk features, from fifteen geographical areas, each labeled with a proper name (e.g., *Cheng feng* 鄭風). The first two groups of the section, however, are called *nan* 南 instead of *feng*, and their superiority over the others is so implied. The *hsiao-ya* section (Nos. 161-234) includes some poems which overlap with the *kuo-feng* in folk attributes and others which constitute celebrations composed for banquets and feasts. The *ta-ya* section (Nos. 235-265) contains poems of greater scope, more grandiloquent in style and more sublime in theme than the *hsiao-ya*. Scattered in the section are some important pieces, which together can be seen as an epic of early Chou history. This section also contains hyperbolic odes extolling heroism. Finally, the *sung* section (Nos. 266-305) is divided into the Chou hymns, Lu hymns (魯頌, Nos. 297-300), and Shang hymns (Nos. 301-305). Most of these are formal, ritual hymns that praise the ancestors envisioned in the rites.

The subject matters of *Shih-ching* poetry vary greatly from one section to another. Love, war, agriculture, sacrifice, and dynastic legends are among the most prominent themes. While in the presentation of themes the tone may be positive and eu-

logistic or licentious and censuring (hence the notion of "decorous" 正 and "deviated" 變 poetry devised by later exegetes), Confucius argued that a single judgment may describe all the poems: "Having no depraved thoughts" (思無邪).

The style of *Shih-ching* poetry is, in general, straightforward and natural, typical of ancient literature in terms of the immediacy of imagery and pervasive musical quality. The modes of expression, however, are by no means simple: the poems are rich in metaphors and similes, both indirect (*hsing* 興) and direct (*pi* 比) as well as narrative displays (*fu* 賦). An unmistakable formulaic language, furthermore, characterizes the style of *Shih-ching* poetry and reveals that the majority of the poems were composed spontaneously before specific audiences. It indicates, too, that the poetic tradition before Confucius was primarily oral.

EDITIONS:

Ch'en Huan 陳奐. *Shih Mao-shih-chuan shu* 詩毛氏傳疏. Rpt. Taipei, 1968. A restoration of Han scholarship executed through meticulous philology, typical of the great eighteenth-century exegesis.

Chu, Hsi 朱熹. *Shih chi-chuan* 詩集傳. Rpt. Taipei, 1967. Representative of Sung scholarship.

K'ung, Ying-ta 孔穎達. *Mao-shih cheng-i* 毛詩正義. *Shih-san-ching chu-shu* 十三經注疏. Rpt. Taipei, 1963. A T'ang variorum edition based on Cheng Hsüan's 鄭玄 commentaries on the Mao text.

Mao-shih yin-te 毛詩引得. Peiping, 1934.

TRANSLATIONS:

Akatsuka, Tadashi 赤塚忠. *Shikei* 詩經. 2v. Tokyo, 1977.

Couvreur, S. J. *Cheu-king; Texte chinois avec une double traduction en Francais et en Latin.* Hokien, 1892. Rigorously follows Chu Hsi's interpretation.

Legge, James. *The Chinese Classics*. V. 3. Rpt. Hong Kong, 1960.

Karlgren, Bernhard. *The Book of Odes*. Stockholm, 1950.

Pound, Ezra. *The Confucian Odes: The Classic Anthology Defined by Confucius*. Cambridge, Mass., 1954.

Waley, Arthur. *The Book of Songs*. New York, 1937.

STUDIES:

Chen, Shih-hsiang. "The *Shih Ching:* Its Generic Significance in Chinese Literary History and Poetics," *BIHP*, 39 (1969), 371-413.

Granet, Marcel. *Festivals and Songs of Ancient China.* E. D. Edwards, tr. London, 1932.

Hightower, James R. *Han shih wai chuan: Han Ying's Illustrations of the Didactic Application of the Classic of Songs.* Cambridge, Mass., 1952.

McNaughton, William. "The Composite Image: *Shy Jing* Poetics," *JAOS*, 83 (1963), 92-103.

Suzuki, Shūji 鈴木修次. *Chūgoku kodai bungaku ron* 中國古代文學論. Tokyo, 1977.

Wang, C. H. *The Bell and the Drum: Shih Ching as Formulaic Poetry in an Oral Tradition.* Berkeley, 1974.

———. "The Countenance of the Chou: *Shih Ching* 266-296," *JICS*, 7 (1974), 425-449.

Yu, Pauline R. "Allegory, Allegoresis, and the *Classic of Poetry,*" *HJAS*, 43.2 (December 1983), 373-412.

　　　　　　　　　　　　　　　—CHW

Shih-chou chi 十洲記 (Record of Ten Islands) or *Hai-nei shih-chou chi* 海內十洲記 (Record of Ten Islands in the Sea) is a fourth or fifth century A.D. work in one *chüan* falsely attributed to Tung-fang Shuo 東方朔 (154-93 B.C.). In the *chih-kuai** genre, it presents itself as the record of a monologue delivered by Tung-fang Shuo to Emperor Wu of the Han. Included are descriptions of fantastic plants and animals, herbs and elixirs of immortality, objects with magical properties, ascendents (*hsien* 仙), and Taoists to be found on each of the ten islands (*chou* 洲) of the sea: Tsu-chou 祖, Ying-chou 瀛, Hsüan-chou 玄, Yen-chou 炎, Ch'ang-chou 長, Yüan-chou 元, Liu-chou 流, Sheng-chou 生, Feng-lin-chou 鳳麟, and Chü-k'u-chou 聚窟. The sections on the last two islands differ noticeably from the previous eight: they are much longer, and include several extended narratives in which Emperor Wu figures as a principal. Entries on four other islands, K'un-lun 崑崙, Fang-chang 方丈, Fu-sang 扶桑, and P'eng-ch'iu 蓬丘, appended to the end of the text may be a later, though still Six Dynasties, accretion to the text.

Dating and authorship are somewhat problematical. It was not included in the *Han-shu* "I-wen chih" (see Liu Hsin and Pan Ku). It is listed in the "Ching-chi chih" of the *Sui-shu* among geographical works and in the *T'ang-shu* as a piece of *shen-hsien hsiao-shuo* 神仙小說. Quotations from it can be found in several Six Dynasties and T'ang poems about ascendents. The *Ssu-k'u ch'üan-shu tsung-mu t'i-yao* (see Chi Yün) editors argue that it postdates the *Shen-hsien chuan** and the *Han-wu-ti nei-chuan,** and place it in the latter part of the Six Dynasties. The historical Tung-fang Shuo was a debater, adviser, and trickster in the court of Emperor Wu of the Han. The emperor's fascination with *fang-shih** and his quest for immortality helped give rise to legends of Tung-fang Shuo's supernatural powers and knowledge of strange lands. Since Tung-fang is the narrator of the *Shih-chou chi* it was natural that he be credited with the authorship of the work.

This book is written in the simple *wen-yen* style favored by historical texts, and avoids classical allusions. Structurally it is a series of anecdotes and descriptive items arranged within a geographical framework. Although the entire work is cast as a conversation, the passages on individual islands focus on physical action or description, not dialogue. The content is folkloristic and exhibits interest in the fantastic. It is very similar in this respect to the *Shen-i-ching* 神異經 of approximately the same date, which is also attributed to Tung-fang Shuo and arranged geographically.

What sets this work apart is its use of the narrative persona Tung-fang Shuo. The use of such a figure implies a greater self-consciousness on the part of the author and a greater awareness of the ironic, of the potential for manipulating point-of-view and audience expectation. The use of a historical figure combined with mention of actual historical incidents accords verisimilitude to otherwise implausible assertions. The tone adopted by the Tung-fang Shuo persona is that of the traditional Chinese historian; his account opens with the disclaimer that, while he has traveled to the ends of the earth, his knowledge is still incomplete and fragmentary, and can only be evaluated on that basis. It is likely that the work was attributed to Tung-fang Shuo to lend it a long history and thus a legitimacy.

EDITIONS:

Shih-chou chi. Han-Wei ts'ung-shu ed. An unpunctuated blockprint edition edited by Ch'eng Jung 程榮 in 1791 based on a Ming edition. The most frequently used edition of the text.

—JEC

Shih-hua 詩話 (talks on poetry) is a form of literary criticism that consists of a critic's comments on various aspects of Chinese poetry. A comment may contain the original thoughts of the writer himself, or quotations from other critics, which are then criticized by the writer. It may be as short as one or two lines or as long as a page or more, but each is a unit in itself. There may be a relationship between a unit and one which follows or precedes it, for several comments about one poet are usually grouped together, but no sustained argument or development of ideas carries from one page to the next. There is also in some works a rough chronological arrangement with comments about early history and poets preceding those on the contemporary scene. Some collections of *shih-hua* are a few pages long; others, like Yüan Mei's* *Sui-yüan shih-hua,* may run to 800 pages or more.

One definition of *shih-hua* which points up the diversity of content is that of Hsü I 許顗 (*fl.* 1111), who stated in the opening lines of his *Yen-chou shih-hua* 彥周詩話 (Hsü Yen-chou's Talks on Poetry), "*Shih-hua* distinguish ways of expression, fill in gaps in information about many points ancient and modern, record examples of superlative virtue, make note of extraordinary things, and correct misrepresentations and errors." A less serious view is given by Ou-yang Hsiu,* whose *Liu-i shih-hua* 六一詩話 (Liu-i's Talks on Poetry) is considered the first example of this literary form: "When he retired to Ju-yin I made this collection as an aid to light conversation." Ssu-ma Kuang 司馬光 (1019-1086) continued the pattern set out by Ou-yang Hsiu with a work which he called *Hsü shih-hua* 續詩話

(Supplemental Talks on Poetry). Both works are very short, fourteen and eleven pages respectively, and they appear to be little more than random jottings.

Shih-hua, as they developed in the Sung dynasty, derived their form and scope from earlier types of literary criticism in China. The many comments that are devoted to an evaluation of poets in terse patterns such as "I would rank A's poetry above B's but below C's" are reminiscent of Chung Jung's *Shih-p'in,** a classic in the categorization of poets. Short comments on rhyme, figures of speech, and other techniques of prosody find their prototype in the craft books of the T'ang dynasty that became popular as tools for young scholars faced with the increasing emphasis on poetic skills in the official examinations. The monk Chiao-jan's* *Shih-shih* 詩式 (Models of Poetry) is one of the few books of this type to have been preserved. Other comments show a close relationship to the T'ang-dynasty *pen-shih* 本事 (background stories). These were compilations of anecdotes about poets, scholars, entertainers, courtesans, even emperors, which explained how they came to write certain poems or how certain poems came to be written about them. The best-known of these still extant is Meng Chi's 孟棨 *Pen-shih shih* 本事詩 (The Original Incidents of Poems).

Less formal than the *pen-shih* are the *pi-chi,** jotted down in the margins of books or on odd pieces of paper over an extended period of time and finally compiled into book form. Such notes range from simple anecdotes remembered from a drinking party to profound statements on any aspect of nature or society written in the quiet of one's study. The difference between *pi-chi* and *shih-hua* is simply one of scope, the latter being restricted to the field of poetry. Similiar to the *pi-chi* are the *yü-lu* 語錄 (lecture notes) compiled by disciples from the lectures given by their masters. Note-taking was a common practice among Buddhist disciples in the T'ang dynasty, and in the Sung dynasty, Neo-Confucian students compiled books of notes transcribed from the lectures of noted Confucian scholars. In the field of literature, *shih-hua* also included direct quotations from conversations with leading literary figures. In the West, Coleridge's *Table Talks*, a compilation put together by Coleridge's nephew of succinct remarks made by the poet at informal gatherings, comes closest to this Chinese literary form.

Although many poets and critics used other vehicles, such as letters to friends, colophons, prefaces, family instructions, essays, and poetry itself, the *shih-hua* continued to stand from the Northern Sung on as the accepted form for presenting one's views on poets and poetry. Ho Wen-huan 何文煥 (late 18th c.) gathered together twenty-seven extant *shih-hua* from the T'ang through the Ming dynasties into a collection entitled *Li-tai shih-hua* 歷代詩話 (Talks on Poetry Chronologically Arranged) (prefaced 1770), and appended his own *Li-tai shih-hua k'ao-so* 歷代詩話考索. Included as his first entries are Chung Jung's *Shih-p'in*, the monk Chiao-jan's *Shih-shih*, and Ssu-k'ung T'u's* *Erh-shih-ssu shih-p'in*. An index to the collection was compiled by Helmut Martin and published in 1973 with a punctuated edition of the text. Ting Fu-pao 丁福保 (1874-1952) compiled a supplement entitled *Li-tai shih-hua hsü-pien* 續編 (1916), containing twenty-eight works from the T'ang through the Ming, starting with Meng Ch'i's *Pen-shih shih*. In 1927 he published the *Ch'ing shih-hua* 清詩話, a compilation of forty-two Ch'ing dynasty works. An exhaustive title index of the *shih-hua* contained in these collections as well as in a number of other *ts'ung-shu** forms part of the *Chung-kuo ts'ung-shu tsung-lu* 中國叢書綜錄 (Comprehensive Record of Chinese Collections; 3v., Beijing, 1959-1962). Kuo Shao-yü 郭紹虞 reconstructed thirty-two *shih-hua*, parts of which had been preserved in other works, to produce the *Sung shih-hua chi-i* 宋詩話輯佚 (Fragments of Sung Criticism of Poetry; Peiping, 1937). Lo Ken-tse 羅根澤 in his *Chung-kuo wen-hsüeh p'i-ping shih* 中國文學批評史 (History of Chinese Literary Criticism), has compiled a chart of extant and lost *shih-hua* of the Sung dynasty (v. 3., pp. 223-241) as well as a short description of twenty-one *shih-hua* that exist in fragments in other works,

sixteen of which are included in Kuo's *Fragments*. More recently, two collections of *shih-hua* have been published in Taiwan: *Ku-chin shih-hua ts'ung-pien* 古今詩話叢編 (Taipei, 1971), containing thirty-three titles from the T'ang through the Ch'ing; and *Ku-chin shih-hua hsü-pien* 續編 (Taipei, 1973), thirty-five titles from the Sung through the Ch'ing, plus one in Japanese.

EDITIONS:

Martin, Helmut, comp. *So-yin-pen Ho shih Li-tai shih-hua* 索引本何氏歷代詩話 (Index to the Ho Collection of Twenty-eight *Shih-hua* with a Punctuated Edition of the Ho Collection). 2v. Taipei, 1973.

Ting, Fu-pao 丁福保, ed., *Hsü li-tai shih-hua* 續歷代詩話. Taipei, 1974.

TRANSLATIONS:

Debon, Günther. *Ts'ang-lang's Gespräche über die Dichtung*. Wiesbaden, 1962.

STUDIES:

Fisk, Craig. "Chu-kuan yü p'i-ping li-lun: chien t'an Chung-kuo shih-hua" 主觀與批評理論一兼談中國詩話, *Chung-wai wen-hsüeh*, 6.11 (1978), 46-78.

Funatsu, Tomihiko 船津富彥. *Chūgoku shiwa no kenkyū* 中國詩話の研究. Tokyo, 1977.

Kuo, Shao-yü. *Sung shih-hua k'ao* 宋詩話考. Rpt. Peking, 1979.

Levy, Howard S. "The Original Incidents of Poems," *Sinologica*, 10 (1969), 1-54.

Wong, W. L. "Chinese Impressionistic Criticism: A Study of the Poetry-talk (*Shih-hua tz'u-hua*) Tradition." Unpublished Ph.D. dissertation, Ohio State University, 1976.

———. "Selections of Lines in Chinese Poetry-Talk Criticism—With a Comparison between the Selected Couplets and Matthew Arnold's 'Touchstones,' " in *China and the West*, pp. 33-44.

Wu, Hung-i 吳宏一. *Ching-tai shih-hsüeh ch'u-t'an* 清代詩學初探. Taipei, 1977. A useful list of 346 Ch'ing dynasty *shih-hua*.   —AR

Shih-jen yü-hsieh 詩人玉屑 (Jade Splinter of the Poets), compiled by the Sung scholar Wei Ch'ing-chih 魏慶之 and introduced by a foreword of Huang Sheng 黃昇 (dated 1244), is considered by modern critics to be the most intriguing and representative selection of literary criticism of the Sung dynasty. Gunther Debon calls the work "the most noble source for the classical period," Yoshikawa Kōjirō describes its contents as "the best of the *shih-hua** genre."

Very little is known about Wei Ch'ing-chih (*tzu*, Ch'un-fu 醇甫, *hao*, Chü-chuang 菊莊). The *Ssu-k'u ch'uan-shu* (see Chi Yün) editors quote from the foreword where he is described as someone who "in spite of his great talent despised an official career, but only cared for his chrysanthemums" so that he belonged to the *Chiang-hu p'ai* 江湖派 (School of the Rivers and the Lakes) of the declining Southern Sung. They see the *Shih-jen yü-hsieh* as the counterpart of Hu Tzu's 胡仔 *T'iao-hsi yü-yin ts'ung-hua** dated earlier and therefore mainly containing criticism of the Northern Sung. The two collections also differ in their structure: Hu Tzu sticks to a very strict chronological order and lists the snippets under the respective author, whereas Wei Ch'ing-chih divides his work into two parts, the one supplying general headings of literary phenomena and thereby establishing a catalogue of terms of literary criticism (*chüan* 1-12), the other following the more conventional order of times and poets chosen already by his forerunner Hu Tzu (*chüan* 13-20).

The title of the collection already hints at the variety of literary and philosophical schools represented. Jade splinters are a medicine frequently mentioned in Taoist alchemy which grants immortality. The comparison between the use of criticism and the use of medicine is repeatedly drawn in Huang Sheng's foreword. Taoist concepts influence literary terms like *tuo-t'ai huan-ku* 奪胎換骨 (appropriating the embryo and changing the bones) or *tien-t'ieh ch'eng-chin* 點鐵成金 (the transformation of iron into gold). A complete sequence of Taoist dicta on poetry, Chiang K'uei's 姜夔 *Pai-shih shih-shuo* 白石詩說 (in *Li-tai shih-hua*, also given as *Pai-shih tao-jen shih-shou* 白石道人詩說), is quoted in the first *chüan* of the work.

Not less important are the influences of Buddhist concepts and Confucian ideology. Yen Yü's *Ts'ang-lang shih-hua*,* which propagates the distrust of language as an appropriate medium of poetry, aiming at the enlightenment of the individual, is given in full length in the introductory two *chüan*. Confucian submissiveness can be seen in attacks on social criticism when gentleness is called for. Among these different viewpoints the compiler Wei Ch'ing-chih seems to remain undecided; he often quotes several contradictory opinions without trying to settle the issue by adding his own judgment.

The texts compiled by Wei Ch'ing-chih are not limited to the *shih-hua* genre. The works cover the whole range from Chung Jung's *Shih-p'in** and Shang-kuan I's 上官儀 (d. 664) rules of parallelism to passages from T'ang poems, tomb inscriptions, and biographies up to the bulk of quotations from the *shih-hua* of numerous Sung contemporaries. Thus the *Jade Splinters of the Poets* represents seven centuries of Chinese literary criticism, from the late Six Dynasties to the end of the Southern Sung.

Although unsystematic and sometimes repetitive the arrangement of the entries selected seems to follow a didactic concept. After two introductory *chüan* (the headings of which are taken from the *Ts'ang-lang shih-hua*) there are two *chüan* quoting exemplary verse samples from the T'ang and Sung period. *Chüan* 5 sums up some pithy formulas for writing poetry, *chüan* 6 and 7 concentrate on the dualism of meaning and form (with remarkable examples for the *yung-shih* 用事, the use of quotations and allusions). *Chüan* 8 centers on the weight of literary tradition and the right way of dealing with it, *chüan* 9 treats rhetorical devices like metaphor and allegory, *chüan* 10 lists several qualities of poetry like *han-hsü* 含蓄 (suggestiveness) or *ch'i-li* 綺麗 (extravagance), and *chüan* 11 deals with poetic flaws (*shih-ping* 詩病 and *ai-li* 礙理 [absurdities]). Headings like *ch'u-hsüeh hsi-ching* 初學蹊徑 make it clear that the book was meant to introduce novices to the realm of poetry—although the claim may be found often in the *Jade Splinters* that there is no way of *learning* how to write perfect and "enlightened" poems.

The *Jade Splinters of the Poets* is a practical work of reference for the important terms and concepts of Sung literary criticism. Most of the sources of the quotations are given at the end of each entry, so that their reliability and correctness can be verified.

All extant versions of the *Jade Splinters* are based on the Sung edition and count 20 *chüan*. The most reliable text is a Japanese version dated 1639. After collating these editions and adding pages lost in the Chinese versions, Wang Kuo-wei established a text of 21 *chüan* generally accepted today.

EDITIONS:

Shih-jen yü-hsieh 詩人玉屑. 2v. Shanghai, 1958; 2nd ed., 1978. Reliable and readily available. A Taipei reprint (4th ed. 1975) is based on this edition and only slightly differs in the pagination. Another Taiwan reprint (藝文 in the series 四庫善本叢書) follows the Ming edition of 1527.

TRANSLATIONS:

Klöpsch, Volker. *Die Jadesplitter der Dichter, Die Welt der Dichtung in der Sicht eines Klassikers der chinesischen Literaturkritik.* Bochum, 1983. A complete translation with an introduction, notes, bibliography, and glossary with Chinese characters.

STUDIES:

Chang, Chien 張健. *Sung Chin ssu-chia wen-hsüeh p'i-p'ing yen-chiu* 宋金四家文學批評研究. Taipei, 1975.

Chaves, Jonathan. "Ko Li-fang's Subtle Critiques on Poetry," *BSYS,* 14 (1978), 39-49. Discusses three sections included in the *Jade Splinters.*

Ch'en, Yu-jui 陳幼睿. "Sung shih-hua hsü-lu" 宋詩話敍錄, *Kuo-wen yen-chiu suo chi-k'an,* 5 (1961), 357-404.

Debon, Günther. *Ts'ang-lang's Gespräche über die Dichtung. Ein Beitrag zur chinesischen Poetik.* Wiesbaden, 1962.

Fisk, Craig William. "Formal Themes in Medieval Chinese and Modern Western Literary History: Mimesis, Intertextuality, Figurativeness, and Foregrounding." Unpublished Ph.D. dissertation, University of Wisconsin, 1976.

Okamoto, Fujiaki 岡本不二明. "Shū hyōgen no chikaku gengo teki kentō" 隱秀表現の知覺言語的檢討, *Chūgoku bungakuhō,* 28 (1977), 71-111.

—VK

Shih Jun-chang 施閏章 (*tzu,* Shang-pai 尚白 and Ch'i-yün 屺雲; *hao,* Yü-shan 愚山, Chü-chai 矩齋, Huo-chai 蠖齋; 1619-1683), a native of Hsüan-ch'eng (Anhwei), was orphaned when young and raised by an uncle. Following the completion of his schooling, he passed up through the examination system, receiving the *chin-shih* in 1649. During the next eighteen years he held a variety of positions in the capital and the provinces. He was active in sponsoring the establishment of local private academies. Retiring in 1667, he worked at home as a scholar and poet until nominated to participate in the *po-hsüeh hung-tz'u* of 1679. After passing that examination, he was posted to the Han-lin Academy and also made a member of the editorial board charged with the compilation of the history of the Ming dynasty.

He was acclaimed by his contemporaries as one of the leading poets of the day. His name was linked with that of Sung Wan.* Ch'ien Ch'ien-i* stated that his poetry was as "resonant as golden bells, comparable to the beauty of jade chimes." Wang Shih-chen* also spoke highly of his literary talents, noting in particular his mastery of pentasyllabic verse. Although he drew inspiration from the High T'ang poets Tu Fu,* Wang Wei,* and Meng Hao-jan,* he was successful in avoiding a narrowly imitative manner. A prolific and rather versatile poet thoroughly dedicated to his craft, he favored a spare, economical style. This manner is exemplified, for instance, in his verse dating from a period of public service in Kiangsi, where he gained a reputation as a just official. The land was relatively infertile and the inhabitants were beset by the depredations of local bandits, and Shih's poems depict the suffering of the people in direct and moving terms. Although the standard literary histories readily acknowledge his importance to seventeenth-century literary developments, his life and works have been largely ignored by the modern scholars.

EDITIONS:

Hsüeh-yü-t'ang wen-chi 學餘堂文集, in *Ssu-k'u ch'üan-shu chen-pen.*

Huo-chai shih-hua 蠖齋詩話, in *Ch'ing shih-hua* 清詩話, Shanghai, 1978, pp. 375-411.

STUDIES:

Aoki, *Shindai*, pp. 415-417.
ECCP, p. 651.

　　　　　　　　　　　　　　—ws

Shih Nai-an 施耐庵 has long been associated with the making of the *Shui-hu chuan.** This traditional attribution is at the very least inconsistent. If the authorship is not credited solely to either Shih Nai-an or Lo Kuan-chung,* then it is described as a joint or successive venture, with Lo Kuan-chung regarded either as an editor or as responsible for the later parts of the novel. None of this is supported by evidence stronger than perfunctory and unverifiable remarks in the extant Ming editions of the novel or casual and contradictory comments found in mid- or late-Ming sources. Although modern *Shui-hu* scholarship hardly supports the involvement of Shih Nai-an in the creation of the novel, the attribution not only persists in modern times but has developed into elaborate fabrications.

Ming sources place Shih Nai-an as a Yüan writer from Ch'ien-t'ang 錢塘 (modern Hangchow), but reveal little more about him. Even if this scanty information is correct, there is still a considerable gap between the assumed dates of the author and the earliest records about him. Chin Sheng-t'an's truncated version of the *Shui-hu*, which appeared toward the end of the Ming period, carries a preface that is supposed to have been written by Shih Nai-an. Both this preface and Chin's claim of having based his version on an old text have been recognized as spurious. Thus as late as the mid-seventeenth century, nothing substantial was known about Shih Nai-an.

The modern scholar Wu Mei 吳梅 (1884-1939) advanced the theory that Shih Nai-an was the Yüan playwright Shih Hui 施惠. Although this was mere speculation, the idea seems to have gained a currency in the late Ch'ing. In the absence of evidence, this theory has been ignored in modern times. Another, more captivating, set of data was in circulation no later than the mid-nineteenth century and eventually grew to be a part of the accepted Shih Nai-an lore. There is supposed to have been a tomb inscription dated 1453 for Shih Nai-an's son Shih Jang 施讓 (*tzu*, I-ch'ien 以謙, 1373-1421); the text is available in a Shih clan genealogy (1854), and it provides a whole set of detailed data. According to this, Shih Nai-an, a native of the Hsiang-hua 興化 district of Yangchow, was a Yüan *chin-shih* of 1331. Going into retirement after the establishment of the Ming government, he wrote the *Shui-hu chuan.* This inscription also tells us the dates of birth and death of Shih Jang's wife and his concubine, the names and *tzu* of each of Jang's seven sons (and limns their careers), as well as the names of his three daughters and their husbands.

Other recent sources provide other details. Shih Nai-an's given name is identified as either Erh 耳 or Tzu-an 子安, and he is said to have lived from 1296 to 1370. He served as the magistrate of Ch'ien-t'ang for two years. The names of his two wives and those of his nine grandsons are also provided. The most surprising turn of events is that Shih Nai-an was recommended to the late Yüan revolutionary Chang Shih-ch'eng 張士誠 (1321-1367), who humbly visited Shih to ask for his service but was bluntly rejected. For fear of Chang's retaliation, Shih moved to Huai-an 淮安. Besides *Shui-hu chuan*, which is said to have had the lackluster original title of *Chiang-hu hao-k'o chuan* 江湖豪客傳 (Heroes from All Over the Country), other novels such as *San-kuo-chih yen-i,** *Sui T'ang chih chuan* 隋唐志傳 and *P'ing-yao chuan** are also attributed to Shih. Shih was also supposed to have sought the help of several assistants, one of them being none other than Lo Kuan-chung.

There are so many errors, contradictions, and impossibilities in such accounts that they could easily be dismissed as pure fantasy. Yet the legend, because of its fascinating details, attained wide circulation in the early days of the Republic, particularly in Hsing-hua, the alleged hometown of Shih Nai-an. In the early 1950s, the Chinese authorities took considerable interest in the legend and attempted to substantiate it with extensive fieldwork and interviews—obtaining information from the direct descendants of Shih Nai-an! The result of all this was the routine listing of Shih Nai-an as the author of the *Shui-hu chuan* in both its numerous editions and library catalogues, as well as the perpetuation of the legend in some of the most authoritative reference works like the *Ming Biographical Dictionary* and the 1979 revised edition of the *Tz'u-hai* 辭海 (Sea of Terms).

The generation of this legend and its warm acceptance have much to do with the common belief that a novel can only be produced by an individual or by a team of writers. That a novel of composite authorship can evolve over a long period of time without definite planning at the outset has not been understood. It is generally impossible, if not meaningless, to attempt to identify any individual as responsible for novels of this nature, and many of China's early novels belong to this category.

Unless concrete evidence of the existence of Shih Nai-an is found, there is no need to associate his name with the *Shui-hu chuan.*

STUDIES:

DMB, pp. 1204-1205.

Ho, Hsin 何心 (Lu Yen-wen 陸衍文). *Shui-hu yen-chiu* 水滸研究. Rev. ed. Shanghai, 1957, pp. 14-21.

Hsieh, Hsing-yao 謝興堯. "*Shui-hu* tso-che k'ao" 水滸作者考, *Ku-chin,* 23 (June 1943), 15-18; 24 (June 1943), 18-23.

Ma, T'i-chi 馬蹄疾 (Ch'en Tsung-t'ang 陳宗棠). *Shui-hu tzu-liao hui-pien* 水滸資料彙編. Rev. ed. Peking, 1980, pp. 491-497.

Ting, Cheng-hua 丁正華 and Su Ts'ung-lin 蘇從麟. "Shih Nai-an sheng-p'ing tiao-ch'a pao-kao" 施耐庵生平調查報告, *Wen-i pao,* 21 (November 1952), 37-45.

—YWM

Shih P'an 史槃 (also 史磐, *tzu,* Shu-k'ao 叔考, sometimes K'ao-shu 考叔, 1531-1630) is known primarily for his *ch'uan-ch'i** plays. Little is known of his life, except that he lived to be nearly one hundred years old. A native of Kuei-chi 會稽 (modern Chekiang), he was a good friend of the play-wright Wang Chi-te.* Shih P'an studied with the great calligrapher, painter, and dramatist Hsü Wei,* who was said to be unable to distinguish his own calligraphy from that of Shih P'an. In addition to writing plays, Shih P'an was known to be an accomplished actor.

Thirteen *ch'uan-ch'i* plays, three *tsa-chü,** and a collection of *san-ch'ü* (see *ch'ü*) are attributed to Shih P'an. All have been lost except for three *ch'uan-ch'i: Chien-ch'ai chi* 鶼釵記 (The Paired-Phoenix Hairpin), *Ying-t'ao chi* 櫻桃記 (The Oath at the Cherry Tree), and *T'u-jung chi* (Spitting Velvet Threads, also called *T'u-hung chi* 唾紅記). These plays are quite humorous, often relying for their comic effect on cases of mistaken identity which are resolved only in the final scenes of the plays. Each plot centers around a young couple whose desire to marry is repeatedly thwarted by each new and unexpected development. Each intricate, multi-leveled plot is woven around a single element which eventually serves to resolve the confusions and unite the couple. Though at times the plots may seem repetitive or unnecessarily complicated, through his skillful variations on this central element, Shih P'an maintains a lively pace throughout each work.

The influence of Hsü Wei is seen in Shih P'an's independence of style. Shih does not belong to any of the three great dramatic "schools" of the late Ming. Though he had contact through Wang Chi-te* with the Wu-chiang 吳江 School, in his own writing he balanced the meticulous prosodic concerns of that group with simplicity and sensitivity toward the popular origins of dramatic lyrics. At times he is too direct, but at his best, his unaffected style is refreshingly sincere.

EDITIONS:

Hsin-k'o ch'u-hsing tien-pan ying-t'ao chi 新刻出相點板櫻桃記 , in *Ku-pen*, II. Based on a Ming edition in the collection of the Pei-ching t'u-shu kuan 北京圖書館.

Hsin-k'o Sung Ching chien-ch'ai chi 新刻宋璟鶼釵記, in *Ku-pen,* III. Based on a Ming edition printed by Yang Chü-ts'ai 楊居宷 found in the collection of Wu Hsing-hsü 吳興徐. A Ch'ing copy is also preserved in the Chung-kuo hsi-ch'ü yen-chiu yüan 中國戲曲研究院.

T'u-jung chi 吐絨記 , in *Ku-pen*, III. Based on a mss. copy from 1855 found in the Peiching t'u-shu kuan.

STUDIES:

Ch'i, Piao-chia 祁彪佳. *Yüan-shan T'ang Ming ch'ü-p'in chiao-lu* 遠山堂明劇品校錄 . Shanghai, 1955. Lists each of Shih P'an's plays (even those lost), adding a brief summary and a few critical comments.

—DW

Shih-p'in 詩品 (An Evaluation of Poetry), composed between 513 and 517, is the earliest work devoted exclusively to the appreciation of lyric poetry. Its enduring importance stems from the fact that it summarized many new ideas on the nature of the lyric that dominated later aesthetics. These include the notions that the best poetry "expresses states of mind" (*yin-yung ch'ing-hsing* 吟詠情性), accomplishing this by means of an artful reflection of personal mood in a sympathetic landscape while avoiding the adulterating complications of allusions and metrics. The *Shih-p'in* also is important as an evaluation of the early history of the lyric that largely has remained consistent with the judgments of subsequent scholars even into the modern period. Its view of the work of the heroic Chien-an generation of Ts'ao Chih,* Wang Ts'an,* and others as a standard for purely expressive poetry, after which all else was a decline, was codified by T'ang writers and has never been seriously questioned.

Chung Jung 鍾嶸 (also pronounced Chung Hung, *tzu*, Chung-wei 仲偉, *c.* 465-518), author of the *Shih-p'in*, was a native of Ch'ang-she 長社 in Ying-ch'uan 潁川 (modern Honan). Little information exists about his life aside from brief biographical notices in the dynastic histories (*Liang-shu*, *ch.* 49, and *Nan-shih*, *ch.* 72). After serving in a number of official posts, Chung Jung was made Secretary to Yüan Chien 元簡, Prince of Heng-yang, in his later years and in that capacity was able to occupy himself primarily with literature. He was not a poet—a point occasionally used to take issue with his views as a critic.

Referred to as *Shih-p'ing* 詩評 (A Criticism of Poetry) by the earliest sources, the title *Shih-p'in* is a corruption arising from Chung Jung's use of the term *p'in* in the preface. The *Erh-shih-ssu shih-p'in* by Ssu-k'ung T'u* was probably only of secondary importance in bringing about the gradual adoption of the title *Shih-p'in*. In the Sung authors still commonly referred to the work by its original title.

The *Shih-p'in* almost certainly accompanied a soon-lost anthology, as was also the case with earlier criticism by Chih Yü,* Li Ch'ung 李充, and Hsieh Ling-yün.* Chung Jung wrote in explicit reaction to the shortcomings of earlier works of this type. The *Shih-p'in* was intended to put forward a coherent theory of poetry as an independent field of study and to take clear positions on the evaluation of individuals in the scheme of literary history. Both were points Chung Jung found lacking in his predecessors.

The *Shih-p'in* comments on 122 poets from the third to the sixth centuries who wrote in the new, pentasyllabic verse and covers all the major figures in its history. Like Liu Hsieh in the *Wen-hsin tiao-lung*,* Chung Jung believes that the older, four-syllable line that traced its ancestry to the *Shih-ching** was best suited to a poetry of simplicity, moralizing, and a classical or archaic air. By contrast, the new five-syllable line more readily lent itself to personal expression. But whereas the *Wen-hsin tiao-lung* discusses every accepted genre of literary writing, it is the view of the *Shih-p'in* that pentasyllabic verse combines the strengths of all genres in one form.

The poets in the *Shih-p'in* are assigned to one of three ranks according to their quality and presented in chronological order within each of these sections: eleven poets are rated superior, thirty-nine good, and seventy-two fair to weak. Later critics have occasionally quarreled with Chung Jung's rankings. Frequently their doubts have focused on the placement of Lu Chi* and Hsieh Ling-yün in the top rank, T'ao Ch'ien* in the middle rank, and Ts'ao Ts'ao 曹操 (155-220) in the lower rank. The first rank includes the anonymous *Ku-shih shih-chiu shou*,* Li Ling 李陵 (d. 74 B.C.), Pan Chi 班姬 (*c.* 48-*c.* 6 B.C.) (both of the

701

Han dynasty), Ts'ao Chih,* Liu Chen 劉楨 (d. 217), Wang Ts'an,* Juan Chi,* Lu Chi, P'an Yüeh,* Chang Hsieh,* Tso Ssu,* and Hsieh Ling-yün. Clearly it is not a group unified by any school or tradition. Rather, Chung Jung's first rank includes poets he considers to have expressed genuine feeling with clarity and force, the middle rank those who used language to striking effect, and the lower rank those who achieved nothing truly outstanding in either regard. Among the poets of the first rank, Ts'ao Chih and Hsieh Ling-yün are preeminent in Chung Jung's conception of the lyric.

The preface to the *Shih-p'in,* which may be an amalgam of prefaces to the three sections, develops Chung Jung's aesthetic and historical views. What he looks for in a poem is a balanced mixture of figurative evocation (*hsing pi* 興比) and description (*fu* 賦). If there is too much of the former, the poem is overburdened by an effort to be meaningful; if too much of the latter, by superficiality. The *hsüan-hsüeh* metaphysical discourse in philosophy of the fourth and fifth centuries, which he feels was often responsible for bad poetry, provided a new conceptual framework for dealing with the relation between the physical and the transcendental worlds. Critics such as Chung Jung and his contemporary Liu Hsieh used this new way of thinking to formulate an aesthetics of subtlety and transcendence that was well suited to the lyric poem. The *Shih-p'in* is especially concerned with the poet's ability to produce the kind of "artful verisimilitude" (*ch'iao ssu* 巧似) that at once captures the essence of an object or scene and conveys a sympathetic reflection of the poet's mood. The fascination with this technique is also apparent in the *Wen-hsin tiao-lung,** especially the *Wu se* 物色 chapter. But Chung Jung, like Liu Hsieh, also feels that much current poetry puts too much emphasis on striking description (*ching ts'e* 警策) for its own sake.

Although the *Shih-p'in* supports the idea that literature is a field of study unto itself, it does not divorce poetry from life. Good poetry is an expression of life, not of art. In fact, the whole of the *Shih-p'in* could be viewed as an expression of the Confucian dictum that "poetry can be used to join with the rest of society in harmony, or to express dissatisfaction." A poem is, for Chung Jung, an instrument of personal reflection and expression vis-à-vis society and the natural world. The *Shih-p'in* represents a catalogue of the ways in which that personal instrument can manifest itself artfully. When Chung Jung rejects Shen Yüeh's* new theory of tonal metrics or the preciosity of literary allusions, he is rejecting what he views as debilitating constraints upon the spontaneity of this personal instrument. A poem should be spontaneous, understated, clear, resonant, striking in its effectiveness, and the generalized expression of one person's experience at one point in space and time.

The *Shih-p'in* describes several major episodes in the history of the lyric. The great formative period is represented by the poets of the Chien-an period (196-220), especially Ts'ao Chih and Wang Ts'an. The next is the T'ai-k'ang period (280-289), which saw a literary revival in the poetry of Chang Hsieh, P'an Yüeh, Lu Chi, and Tso Ssu. The Yung-chia period (307-312) witnessed a decline of the Chien-an tradition in poetry by Sun Cho 孫綽 (314-371), Hsü Hsün 許詢, and others who "sounded like philosophical discourse." The Yüan-chia period (424-453), says Chung Jung, still showed traces of philosophy in the guise of poetry but featured powerful poets such as Hsieh Ling-yün, Yen Yen-chih,* and Pao Chao* who could overcome that limitation.

There is also an overriding historical continuity implied by the *Shih-p'in* in that it ascribes to 37 of its 122 poets stylistic derivations that lead back ultimately to either the *Shih-ching* or the *Ch'u-tz'u.** This aspect of the *Shih-p'in* has often provoked argument on the part of its later readers. In particular, the treatment of T'ao Ch'ien, whose hermetic poetry Chung Jung says is reminiscent of the work of Ying Ch'ü 應璩 (190-252), dismayed many T'ang and post-T'ang critics. In later centuries Ying Ch'ü, who along with Hsi K'ang* is stylistically related to Ts'ao P'i,* was held in fairly low regard, while T'ao Ch'ien became the touchstone for naturalness and simplicity. In the early sixth century, however, the three styles that were popular were those of Hsieh Ling-yün, Ying Ch'ü, and Pao Chao, according to the "Essay on Literature" in the *Nan Ch'i-shu*. One should also view what Chung Jung means by relating T'ao Ch'ien to Ying Ch'ü in the light of what he says in his comments on the latter: He excelled in the use of archaic language (*ku yü* 古語) to express righteous indignation reminiscent of the "Kuo feng" 國風 (Airs of the States) poems of the *Shih-ching*. T'ao Ch'ien likewise is praised for his use of *ku yü*, though also granted a position as the archetypal hermit poet who clearly is imbued with more grace in his language than a mere rustic. It is difficult to evaluate the relative merits of T'ao Ch'ien and Ying Ch'ü today, because very little of Ying Ch'ü's work survives, but it is apparent that the context in which they were judged by the *Shih-p'in* was different from that which existed for later critics.

The problem for critics such as Chiao-jan,* Yeh Meng-te 葉夢得 (1077-1148), Hsieh Chen 謝榛 (1495-1575), Wang Shih-chen* (1634-1711), and Shen Te-ch'ien* was that it was impossible to conceive of a T'ao Ch'ien who had imitated the style of a poet who himself had merely imitated an older style and was, in their view, patently a much lesser poet. But aside from the disparity between Chung Jung's evaluation of T'ao Ch'ien and that of later critics, it is important to bear in mind that the *Shih-p'in* does not really suggest that any of these thirty-seven poets were imitating earlier writers, as had been claimed by later critics. The idea of *yüan ch'u* 源出 (derivation) is only applied in the *Shih-p'in* to the tone and style (*t'i* 體) of these poets. It does not imply imitation, but only that the work of one poet is a kind of logical extension of the work of another.

This is an example of why the *Shih-p'in* is of great interest to modern readers. In no more than about five thousand words it offers an often provocative overview of the initial critical reception of many poets in the first major period of the Chinese lyric, states a theory of the lyric that was

to be repeated by critics of High T'ang poetry such as Wang Ch'ang-ling* and Chiao-jan and also provides some idea of the work of many authors whose poems have survived only in small numbers or not at all.

Although there is little information about the immediate reception of the work in Chung Jung's time, direct or indirect reference to the *Shih-p'in* is evident in most poetry criticism from the early T'ang onwards. In it we have the first clear formulation of an aesthetics for the new poetry of the third to sixth centuries that had incorporated the themes of the ballad, the introspection of metaphysical philosophy, and the intoxication with landscape of the Han-dynasty *fu** to create a pentasyllabic lyric that became the greatest poetry of the Chinese tradition.

EDITIONS:

Chung Jung Shih-p'in chi-chiao 鍾嶸詩品集校. Chang Hing-ho (Ch'en Ch'ing-hao) 陳慶浩, ed. Paris and Hong Kong, 1978. Introduction, concordance, bibliography, and edited text based on the Ku text of 1517. Divides the preface into the presumed original three parts at the heads of each of the three *chüan*.

Shih-p'in chu 詩品注. Ch'en Yen-chieh 陳延傑, ed. Peking, 1958. Originally written in 1925 and first published in 1927, this edition has been reprinted numerous times. Based on the text of the *Li-tai shih-hua*, it provides annotation on the sources of citations in the *Shih-p'in*, as well as an appendix containing all the poems to which the *Shih-p'in* makes reference.

TRANSLATIONS:

Takagi, Masakazu 高木正一. *Shō Kō Shi-hin* 鍾嶸詩品. Tokyo, 1978.

STUDIES:

Brooks, E. Bruce. "A Geometry of the She Pin," in *Wen-lin*, pp. 121-150.

Fu, Keng-sheng 傅庚生. "*Shih-p'in* t'an-so" 詩品探索, *Kuo-wen yüeh-k'an*, 82 (1949), 7-19.

Hayashida, Shinnosuke 林田慎之助. "Shō Kō no bungaku ruron" 鍾嶸の文學理論, *Chūgoku bungaku ronshū*, 7 (1978), 1-16.

Liao, Wei-ch'ing 廖蔚卿. "Chung Jung *Shih-p'in* hsi-lun" 鍾嶸詩品析論, in *Wen-hsüeh p'ing-lun* 文學評論, Taipei, v. 1, pp. 1-68; v. 2, pp. 163-239. See also "*Shih-p'in* hsi-lun" 詩品析論

in Liao's *Liu-ch'ao wen-lun* 六朝文論, Taipei, 1978, pp. 211-369.

Satake, Yasuko 佐竹保子. "Shō Kō *Shi-hin* no senpyō ni naizai suru bungakuteki dachi kijun" 鍾嶸詩品の選評に內在する文學的價值基準, *Shūkan tōyōgaku* 40 (1978), 41-55.

Takagi, Masakazu 高木正一. *Shō Kō Shi-hin* 鍾嶸詩品. Tokyo. 1978.

Wang, Ch'ung 王忠. "Chung Jung p'in shih ti piao-chun chih-tu" 鍾嶸品詩的標準尺度, in *Chung-kuo wen-hsüeh p'i-p'ing chia yü wen-hsüeh p'i-p'ing*, Taipei, 1971, v. 1, pp. 1-13.

Wang, Kuei-ling 王貴苓. "T'ao shih yüan-ch'u Ying Ch'ü shuo t'an-ting" 陶詩源出應璩說探訂, *Wen-hsüeh tsa-chih*, 2.6 (1957), 39-47.

Wang, Yün-hsi 王運熙. "Chung Jung *Shih-p'in* T'ao shih yüan ch'u Ying Ch'ü chieh" 鍾嶸詩品陶詩源出應璩解, *Wen-hsüeh p'ing-lun*, 5 (1980), 135-138.

Wilhelm, Hellmut. "A Note on Chung Hung and his Shih-pin," in *Wen-lin*, pp. 111-120.

Yeh, Chia-ying 葉嘉瑩. "Chung Jung *Shih-p'in* p'ing shih chih li-lun piao-chun chi ch'i shih-chien" 鍾鍾嶸詩品評詩之理論標準及其實踐, in Yeh's *Chung-kuo ku-tien shih-ko p'ing lun chi* 中國古典詩歌評論集, Hong Kong, 1977, pp. 1-30.

Yeh, Chia-ying and Jan W. Walls. "Theory, Standards, and Practise of Criticizing Poetry in Chung Hung's *Shih P'in*," in Miao, *Studies*, v. 1, pp. 43-80.

Yüan, Hsing-p'ei 袁行霈. "Wei Chin hsüan-hsüeh chung te yen i chih pien yü Chung-kuo ku-tai wen-i li-lun" 魏晉玄學中的言意辨與中國古代文藝理論, in *Ku-tai wen-hsüeh li-lun yen-chiu ts'ung-kan* 古代文學理論研究叢刊, v. 1, Shanghai, 1979, pp. 125-147.

—CF

Shih-shuo hsin-yü 世說新語 (New Account of Tales of the World), compiled under the aegis of the Liu-Sung prince Liu I-ch'ing 劉義慶 (403-444) about the year 430, is an anthology of anecdotes, noteworthy conversations or remarks, and brief characterizations of historical persons who lived in the period between the declining years of the Latter Han and the founding of the Liu-Sung state (roughly A.D. 150-420). Most of the one thousand or more entries are set in the Eastern Chin, either in the court at Chien-k'ang 建康 (modern Nanking) or the hilly region to the southeast (modern Chekiang).

There are thirty-six chapters (*p'ien* 篇). It begins with a somewhat sober depiction of civic and personal virtues, continues through a series of special topics like recluses, outstanding women, technicians, artists, and eccentrics, and ends with a colorful catalogue of human folly and vice which is by far the most interesting part. Though most of the over six hundred figures involved in the anecdotes are known from other contemporary historical sources, the wit and mordancy of some of the dialogue, as well as the refinement of the literary style, suggest a certain degree of fictionalization.

Identification of the sources for most of the subjects recounted is made easier by the extensive commentary of the Liang scholar and bibliophile, Liu Chün 劉峻 (*tzu*, Hsiao-piao 孝標, 462-521), which cites relevant passages—passages which were often drastically abridged by eleventh-century editors—from over four hundred works (unofficial histories and biographies, family registers, local gazetteers, etc.) from the Latter Han through Liu Chün's own times. Since most of these works are now lost, the quotations from them in Liu's and other similar commentaries such as P'ei Sung-chih's 裴松之 (372-451) commentary on the *San-kuo chih* 三國志 (History of the Three Kingdoms) provide valuable supplementary material and occasional corrections to the idiosyncratic accounts in the *Shih-shuo hsin-yü*.

Although the subject matter is narrowly selective, dealing as it does with the gilded lives and values of the ruling elite in a highly stratified "aristocratic" society during a period of political disunion, the characters described in the anecdotes do maintain a certain psychological and artistic consistency, and some details of both official and family life of the times are revealed with vivid clarity. The work therefore has significance for social and cultural historians as well as serving as a link in the chain of development for narrative literature (*hsiao-shuo**), where it is classified in traditional Chinese bibliographies.

One of the most interesting sources for the study of "Gentry Buddhism" in the

Southern Dynasties is chapter 4, "Wen-hsüeh p'ien" 文學篇 (Letters and Scholarship), in which several well-educated and urbane Buddhist monks from prominent families, together with their high-born lay supporters, meet for learned debates, for *ch'ing-t'an* 清談 (pure conversation), and for expositions of Buddhist sutras. The second half of this chapter and its accompanying commentary also yield some fragments of lost poems by contemporary writers, thus supplementing our scanty knowledge of the literature of this very creative period.

For the historical sociologist, chapter 19, "Hsien-yüan p'ien" 賢媛篇 (Worthy Beauties), which deals with outstanding women, offers a wealth of information on the status of women in gentry society as well as insight into the sexual attitudes of the time. Not least, the work is laced with a delightful brand of humor which appeals across cultural lines.

EDITIONS:

Hung, Yeh 洪業. *Shih-shuo hsin-yü yin-te fu Liu-chu yin-shu yin-te* 世說新語引得附劉注引書引得. Peking, 1933.

Shih-shuo hsin-yü. SPTK. Reproduces the eighteenth-century woodblock edition of Shen Yen 沈巖; the edition used in the Harvard-Yenching Institute Sinological Index Series by Hung Yeh.

Shih-shuo hsin-yü. 2v. Peking, 1956. Reproduction of a thirteenth-century edition by Wang Tsao 王藻 now in a Japanese collection. It includes genealogical tables of major families mentioned in the text (*Jen-ming p'u* 人名譜) and a collation of all variant readings in later editions (*Chiao-k'an chi* 校勘記) by Wang Li-ch'i 王利器.

Shih-shuo hsin-yü chiao-chien 校箋. Yang Yung 楊勇, ed. Hong Kong, 1969. Incorporates all of Wang Li-ch'i's collations plus Yang's own notes.

Takahashi, Kiyoshi 高橋清. *Sesetsu Shingo sakuin* 世說新語索引. Hiroshima, 1959.

T'ang-hsieh pen Shih-shuo hsin-shu ts'an-chüan 唐寫本世說新書殘卷. Photolithographic facsimile in traditional binding published by Lo Chen-yü 羅振玉 in Shanghai, 1916. Also a half-tone facsimile in western binding (*Tō-shōhon Sesetsu shinsho* 唐鈔本世說新書), No. 176 in the series *Shoseki meihin sōkan* 書跡名品叢刊, Tokyo, 1972, and a reduced facsimile attached to the Peking edition listed above. Includes the text and (unabridged) commentary of chapters 10-13, dating probably from the eighth century and brought to Japan sometime in the ninth.

TRANSLATIONS:

Belpaire, Bruno. *Anthologie chinoise des 5e et 6e siècles: le Che-chouo-sin-yu par Lieou (Tsuen) Hiao-piao.* Paris, 1974.

Mather, Richard B. *Shih-shuo hsin-yü: A New Account of Tales of the World.* Minneapolis, 1976.

Mekada, Makoto 目加田誠. *Sesetsu shingo.* 3v. Tokyo, 1975-78.

STUDIES:

Chan, Hsiu-hui 詹秀惠. *Shih-shuo hsin-yü yü-fa t'an-chiu* 世說新語語法探究. Taipei, 1972.

Chou, I-liang 周一良. "*Shih-shuo hsin-yü cha-chi*" 世說新語札記, in Chou I-liang, *Wei-Chin nan-pei-ch'ao lun-chi* 魏晉南北朝論集, Peking, 1963, pp. 397-401.

Eichhorn, Werner. "Zur chinesischen Kulturgeschichte des 3. und 4. Jahrhunderts," *ZDMG,* 19 (1937), 451-483.

Kawakatsu, Yoshio 川勝義雄. "*Sesetsu shingo no hensan o megutte*" 世說新語の編纂をめぐって. *Tōhō gakuhō,* 41 (March 1970), 217-234.

Utsunomiya, Seikichi 宇都宮清吉. "*Sesetsu shingo no jidai*" 世說新語時代, *Tōhō gakuhō,* 10.2 (1939), 199-255. Revised version in Utsunomiya Kiyoyuoshi, *Kandai shakai keizaishi kenkyū* 漢代社會經濟史研究, Tokyo, 1955, pp. 473-521.

Yang, V. T. "About *Shih-shuo hsin-yü*," *JOS,* 2.2 (June 1955), 309-315.

Yoshikawa, Kōjirō 吉川幸次郎. "The Style of the *Shih-shuo hsin-yü*," Glen Baxter, trans., *HJAS,* 18 (1955), 124-141.

—RM

Shih Ta-tsu 史達祖 (*tzu,* Pang-ch'ing 邦卿, *hao,* Mei-hsi 梅溪, *c.* 1200) was a *tz'u** poet of the Southern Sung. A native of Pien 汴 (modern Kaifeng), he served Han T'o-chou 韓侂冑, a powerful courtier early in the reign of Emperor Ning-tsung (r. 1195-1224). Shih was entrusted with the official records and the composition of legal documents on behalf of the minister himself. Following Han's murder by political opponents, Shih Ta-tsu was branded on the face and banished. He died in exile.

The poetry of Shih Ta-tsu reflects the personal, immediate aspects of his life. His verse can be divided into three categories. The first is concerned with the poet's mental reflections on daily life, his yearning for loved ones, or reactions to travel. The second category includes works describing an object, such as a flute, natural scenery, local flora or fauna, or even the weather. Poetry of this kind, generally designated as *yung-wu shih* 詠物詩 (poetry on objects), occupies a significant portion of the corpus. There are also a number of poems—the third category—in his corpus which are not provided with titles. They too embody the poet's personal, rather than public concerns. Their themes are lovesickness, homesickness, nostalgia, and concern for the approach of old age and death.

These sentiments and sensibilities are represented by a language that is elegant and sophisticated in itself, but defies easy comprehension. It demands, rather, to be read in terms of the emotions and ideas which it seeks to embody. The periphrastic, roundabout expression of Shih's poetry is partly the result of literary tradition and partly attributable to his attempts to endow nature with his own feelings and thoughts.

Two main sources of the first mode of circumlocution are traditional symbols and allusions to the works of earlier poets. Among the symbols that frequently appear in Shih's poetry are willow trees and grass, which stand for parting; the spring season, which suggests amorous thoughts; mating birds, notably the swallow and the mandarin duck, which symbolize marital bliss; orioles and wild geese, representing message-carriers between separated lovers. There are also cases where Shih Ta-tsu adapts the lines of earlier poets to his own poetic purposes. In fact, Shih relies heavily on allusions to prior literature to secure for his poetry emotional congruity and semantic continuity. A simple example occurs in the poem written to the tune "San-shu mei" 三姝媚 (Three Charming Ladies, *Ch'üan Sung tz'u*, p. 2330). In the second stanza of this poem, the poet employs *t'ung-t'o* 銅駝 (bronze camel) to trigger, among other things, the association of "T'ung-t'o pei" 銅駝悲 (The Grief of Bronze Camel)

by the late T'ang poet Li Ho,* a poem concerning the retreat of spring and man's steady march toward his inevitable end. As a result, the image of bronze camel in Shih's poem at once conveys the meaning of temporal flux that is embedded in the immediate context and heralds the emergence of fallen flowers, a traditional symbol of the fragility of life, in the later portion of the text. In the same vein, with perhaps more subtlety, the smooth progression from the penultimate strophe to the ending lines in "Wan-nien huan" 萬年歡 (Joy for Ten Thousand Years, *Ch'üan Sung tz'u*, p. 2328) is partly achieved by the allusion to a *yüeh-fu** poem by Li Po,* entitled "Yü-chieh yüan" 玉階怨 (The Lament of Jade Steps). In Li's poem, a lovesick woman stands on the steps outside her boudoir, waiting in vain for her lover; when her silk stockings are finally wet with dew, she retreats to her room and, through the window curtains, gazes wistfully at the moon, traditionally a symbol of union. Through the allusion to this T'ang poem, the steps and silk stockings which appear in the penultimate strophe of Shih Ta-tsu's text conjure up the image of a woman neglected by her lover, whereas the presence in its ending lines of dew and the moon suggests paradoxically the absence of this woman whom the man is now thinking of with yearning. Failure to recognize the allusion to Li Po's poem would thus preclude a full appreciation of the internal coherence, and emotional significance, of these two strophes.

The second source of circumlocution in Shih's poetry is the endowment of natural scenery with the poet's own feeling and thought. Generally speaking, the natural objects in Shih's poetry function in two ways. First, they form the poetic setting and create an atmospshere that befits the poetic emotion being described. Second, they assume the appearance of a human female, and thereby evoke the image of a woman. An example of this is "Apricot flowers display their unadorned faces" (杏開素面: in "Tung-feng ti-i chih" 東風第一枝 [First Branch in the East Wind], *Ch'üan Sung tz'u*, p. 2327). Shih Ta-tsu's personification is not noteworthy in itself. Yet, particular instances found in his poetry of natural objects being endowed with life nevertheless reveal a vivacious imagination which fosters a close union of man and nature. For instance, the moon is able to appear from behind the clouds only after the clouds have been persuaded by the West Wind to make way: "The West Wind comes to persuade the chilly clouds to depart" (西風來勸涼雲去: in "Ch'i t'ien yüeh" 齊天樂 [Music Fills the Sky], *Ch'üan Sung tz'u*, p. 2342). The leaves and the blossoms display their spring beauty in full only after rains urge them to do so: "Encouraging the green by rewards and urging the red to make haste—Not until the fall of fertilizing rains, do they start to display spring beauty" (獎綠催紅, 仰一番膏雨, 始張春色; in "Chin-chan-tzu" 金盞子 [Golden Cup], *Ch'üan Sung tz'u*, p. 2329). This simultaneous projection into and identification with nature is confirmed by the poet's own words: "Gazing on the tired willow trees and sorrowful lotus flowers/ I am moved together with them by the autumn scenery" (望倦柳愁荷, 共感秋色; in "Ch'iu chi" 秋霽 [Autumn Rains Have Stopped], *Ch'üan Sung tz'u*, p. 2343).

In Shih's *yung-wu* poetry, the object being described is much less an object in nature that can be easily identified; it is rather an embodiment of the viewer's own highly idiosyncratic observation of the world around him. For example, in the poem written to the tune "Shuang shuang yen" 雙雙燕 (Swallows in Pairs), entitled "On Swallows" 詠燕 (*Ch'üan Sung tz'u*, p. 2326), acclaimed by critics as one of the most skillful of all *yung-wu* poems, the implicit viewer describes two swallows flying and sleeping side by side; this happy pair forms a sharp contrast with a lonely woman, who emerges at the end of the poem thinking of her faraway lover. In representing the pair of swallows, Shih Ta-tsu is concerned not so much with the appearance of the objects *per se,* as with the intellectual and emotional significances that he discerns in the objects. It must be noted, however, that "Shuang shuang yen" is easier to understand than other works of Shih's *yung-wu*

poetry, for the descripion of the birds in this poem is closer to our ordinary knowledge of them as they exist in nature. Most of Shih's *yung-wu* poems, however, are laden with traditional symbols and allusions to prior literary works. As a result, the objects being described are difficult to identify without knowledge of these symbols and allusions. In either case, the focus of Shih Ta-tsu's creative attention in his *yung-wu* poetry is not on the static phenomena or material conditions of the external world. Rather, it is the transmutation and metamorphosis of this world that matters.

EDITIONS:
Ch'üan Sung tz'u, v. 4. pp. 2325-2347.

TRANSLATIONS:
Ayling, *Further Collection,* pp. 176-177.

STUDIES:
Lin, *Transformation,* pp. 10, 36, 60, 183f.
Mo, Ming-li 莫明麗. "Lun Shih Mei-hsi tz'u" 論史梅溪詞, *Hsin-ya Shu-yüan Chung-kuo wen-hsüeh-hsi nien-k'an,* 7 (September 1969), 77-79.

—SH

Shih Yün-yü 石韞玉 (*tzu,* Chih-ju 執如, *hao,* Cho-t'ang 琢堂, Hua-yün-an Chu-jen 花韻庵主人, also known as Tu-hsüeh Lao-jen 獨學老人, 1756-1837), a native of Wu-hsien 吳縣 (modern Kiangsu), was a dramatist of the mid-Ch'ing. In 1785, he passed the *chin-shih* examination and became a Han-lin Academician. Thereafter, he held a number of provincial posts in Fukien, Hunan, and Szechwan, culminating in the post of Surveillance Commissioner of Shantung. Then he was again assigned a post in the Han-lin Academy, but before long resigned on the grounds of poor health. He spent his last twenty or so years as a lecturer at Tzu-yang 紫陽 College in Soochow. While in Soochow he participated in the compilation of a local gazetteer. His collected works of verse and prose include the *Tu-hsüeh-lu kao* 獨學廬稿, the *Wan-hsiang-lou chi* 晚香樓集, and the *Hua-yün-an shih-yü* 花韻庵詩餘.

Ch'en K'ang-ch'i 陳康祺, in his *Lang-ch'ien chi-wen* 郎潛紀聞, claims that Shih was a strict moralist. Whenever he came across writings he deemed immoral, he would make every effort to burn all the copies he could locate. Despite this ultra-conservative moral outlook, he held a liberal view toward drama. He wrote and sponsored the publication of dramas. Shen Ch'i-feng's 沈起鳳 (b. 1741) *Shen-shih ssu-chung* 沈氏四種 was edited and published by Shih and contains Shih's preface and epigraph.

Shih's *Hua-chien chiu tsou* 花間九奏 is a collection of nine one-act *tsa-chü**: *Fu Sheng shou ching* 伏生授經 (Fu Sheng Transmits the Classics), *Lo Fu ts'ai sang* 羅敷采桑 (Lo Fu Picks the Mulberries), *T'ao-yeh tu chiang* 桃葉渡江 (T'ao-yeh [concubine of Wang Hsien-chih 王獻之 (344-386)] Crosses the River), *T'ao-yüan yü-fu* 桃源漁父 (The Fisherman's Adventure in the Peach-blossom Fount), *Mei-fei tso fu* 梅妃作賦 (Mei-fei [concubine of the T'ang Emperor Hsüan-tsung] Sings of Her Loneliness), *Le-t'ien k'ai ko* 樂天開閣 (Le-t'ien [Po Chü-i*] Has the Women Go to Their Marriages), *Chia Tao chi shih* 賈島祭詩 (Chia Tao's Poetical Offerings), *Ch'in-ts'ao ts'an ch'an* 琴操參禪 (The Singsong Girl Ch'in-ts'ao Understands the Zen) and *Tui-shan chiu yu* 對山救友 (Tui-shan [K'ang Hai*] Strives to Save His Friend). All are set to Southern-style music, with the exception of *Ch'in-ts'ao ts'an ch'an,* which uses a mixture of Northern and Southern songs. The stories of these dramas are either based on well-known literary works (for instance, the story of *Lo Fu ts'ai sang* is based on the *yüeh-fu** poem "Mo-shang sang" 陌上桑, and the *T'ao-yüan yü-fu* on T'ao Ch'ien's* "Tao-hua-yüan chi" 桃花源記), or on the anecdotes of prominent literary figures or scholars (for instance, as is clear from their titles, the *Chia Tao chi shih* is about the T'ang poet Chia Tao* and the *Fu Sheng shou ching* tells of the Han scholar Fu Sheng). The stories are presented in a straightforward manner—Shih cares little to add subleties to the plots. By the mid-Ch'ing, this kind of short *tsa-chü* in one act had developed into such a state that the works were no longer intended for the stage, but only to be read. Shih's works can be considered typical examples of this trend. Furthermore, Shih

Yün-yü used these works as a platform to preach his moral views. Thus a song sung by the female lead in *Lo Fu ts'ai sang* is essentially a sermon on chastity.

The *Hua-chien chiu tsou* has received little attention from modern scholars; the few who have remarked on these works have found little to praise. They especially criticize them for lack of dramatic interest and the dullness of their design and Shih for his lack of originality in the treatment of the plots and his use of rhyme words in his own dialect.

EDITIONS:

Hua-chien chiu tsou, in *Ch'ing-jen tsa-chü ch'u-chi* 清人雜劇初集, Cheng Chen-to 鄭振鐸, comp., n.p., 1931.

STUDIES:

Cheng, Chen-to. "Ch'ing-jen tsa-chü ch'u-chi hsü" 序, in *Ch'ing-jen tsa-chü ch'u-chi* (see above); also included in *Chung-kuo wen-hsüeh yen-chiu* 中國文學研究, Peking, 1957, v. 2, pp. 795-808.

ECCP, pp. 658-659.

Fu, *Ch'ing tsa-chü*, pp. 203-207.

Tseng, "Ch'ing-tai tsa-chü," pp. 190-191.

—SSK

Shu-hui 書會 (writing clubs) were associations organized by authors of various forms of vernacular literature. The limited information on these organizations has been collected several times, and scattered references lead to the conclusion that members of such groups wrote riddles (*mi-yü* 謎語), songs, *tsa-chü,** and *nan-hsi.** Sometimes the members of such clubs performed their own plays, and a considerable rivalry existed between such organizations.

The earliest meaning of the term *shu-hui* appears to have been simply "school." A letter from Chu Hsi 朱熹 (1130-1200) used it in this sense, and the memoir on the Southern Sung capital, *Tu-ch'eng chi-sheng* (see *Tung-ching meng Hua lu*), makes similar use of the term. To judge by these early references and by the term itself, the first *shu-hui* were probably schools where students prepared themselves for the state examinations by practicing essays. From such a basis they developed into literary salons interested in writing the newly popular vernacular literature of the Sung period.

Most early references to writing clubs as organizations of authors refer primarily to the central part of China. The *Wu-lin chiu-shih* (see Chou Mi), a record of city life in Hangchow in the late Southern Sung, contains several lists of such persons as poets, painters, and chess players who were on call for imperial amusement. Under the heading "Writing Clubs" are six names; as some of them are clearly stage names, it seems likely that professional entertainers in Hangchow in the thirteenth century were active members of writing clubs.

One of the three southern plays preserved in the *Yung-lo ta-tien, Hsiao Sun T'u* (see *Yung-lo ta-tien hsi-wen san-chung*), was supposedly written by "a writing club from Hangchow." Since the *Lu kuei pu** attributes authorship to a certain medical man from Hangchow, Hsiao Te-hsiang, it can be assumed that he was a member of this club. Chia Chung-ming, author of the *Hsü Lu kuei pu*, actually states that Hsiao "displayed his mighty talents in the Wu-lin [i.e., Hangchow] Writing Club," but he may simply be considering the same evidence used above. Another of the three plays, *Chang Hsieh chuang-yüan* (see *Yung-lo ta-tien hsi-wen san-chung*) was also, according to the introductory scene, written by members of the *Chiu-shan Shu-hui* 九山書會 (Nine Mountains Writing Club). The club was located in Wenchow, a city that contemporary sources cite as the cradle of southern drama (*nan-hsi**). According to this introductory scene, the members of the club performed the play themselves, in competition with an earlier performance. The recently discovered fifteenth-century printed edition of the southern play *Pai-t'u-chi* (see *Ssu-ta ch'uan-ch'i*) was, according to its introductory scene, written by "the poets of the Yung-chia [i.e., Wenchow] Writing Club" (*Yung-chia shui-hui ts'ai-jen*).

As organizations of amateur-actors, the writing clubs had a forerunner in *Fei-lü she* 緋綠社 (The Scarlet and Green Association) in Hangchow. This was but one of Hangchow's many associations and brotherhoods. Some of the associations specialized in a certain form of entertainment; the Scarlet and Green Association performed skits and plays. Most of them were connected with a specific temple and were responsible for the organization of periodic festivals held there. Such temple festivals often included various theatrical entertainments. The members of such associations did not limit themselves to organization but also took an active part in the activities.

The Scarlet and Green Association was no exception. The *Tu-ch'eng chi-sheng* lists the name of the organization as *Fei-lü ch'ing-yüeh she* 緋綠清樂社 (The Scarlet and Green Association of Pure Music) and says that it was composed of "wealthy and noble people" and was "unsurpassed in smartness." According to the *Wu-lin chiu-shih*, the association participated with its plays in the celebration of the birthday of the deity, Prince Chang, on the eighth day of the second month of each year, along with comparable groups.

The reputation of the Scarlet and Green Association must have been quite widespread, for the members of the Nine Mountains Writing Club compared themselves to them, boasting of the similarity. The boast can be found in two passages in the introductory scene to *Chang-Hsieh chuang-yüan*, in which the members of the Nine Mountains Writing Club introduce themselves and alternately address the public and their rival clubs. In these passages, undoubtedly the richest source for understanding the composition, activities, and self-conception of a writing club, they state their desire "to dominate the festivities in Eastern Ou," indicating that perhaps the occasion was a temple festival in the region of Wenchow.

In North China writing clubs appear to make their debut at a somewhat later date. The *Ts'o-li shen* (mid-thirteenth century, see *Yung-lo ta-tien san-chung*) is the earliest text to refer to a "writing club of the Imperial Capital." Writing clubs in the north would naturally have concentrated on *tsa-chü*, and so it is that the lead actor of the Yüan play *Lan Ts'ai-ho**—an actor and

709

troupe manager—assures a visitor that the comedies that he will enumerate have been recently composed by the poets' writing club. None of the other North China references are earlier than the beginning of the fifteenth century. Chu Yu-tun* mentions their existence a number of times in his plays and Chia Chung-ming, in his postface to the *Lu kuei pu*, says that Chung Ssuch'eng listed "the poets from Yen and Chao who were of the writing clubs of the Imperial Capital and the lords and gentlemen of the four quarters. . . ."

It has long been a tradition that Kuan Han-ch'ing,* the first of the playwrights Chung listed, himself performed in plays (see the preface to *Yüan-ch'ü hsüan* 元曲選). It is conceivable, of course, that such men also performed, but there is no material to suggest that the writing club members of North China ever performed their plays together. As far as *tsa-chü* is concerned, the various references to writing clubs stress the social distance between the acting profession and the "gentlemen poets of the writing club." One puzzling exception is the statement by Chia Chung-ming about the collaboration of Li Shih-yung, Ma Chih-yüan,* and the two actors Hua Lilang and Hung-tzu Li Erh, on the comedy *Huang-liang meng* 黃粱夢 (Yellow Millet Dream) in which the expression *Yüan-chen shu-hui* 元貞書會 heads the first line of the song to the tune *Ling-po-hsien*. In this position, it may be conceived of as an adjective to the first name only (Li Shih-yung), or to all four, meaning they were members of a writing club. But, since *Yüan-chen* is also the name of a reign period (1295-1296), it might simply be a sentence adjunct.

After the first half of the fifteenth century, there are no further references to writing clubs in any part of China.

SOURCES:

Chang Hsieh chuang-yüan 張協壯元 (Anon.), in *Yung-lo ta-tien hsi-wen san-chung* 永樂大典戲文三種, Ch'ien Nan-yang 錢南揚, ed., Peking, 1980, pp. 1-2.

Chia, Chung-ming 賈仲名. *Hsü Lu kuei pu* 續錄鬼簿, in *ibid.*, pp. 42, 90.

Chou, Mi 周密. *Wu-lin chiu-shih* 武林舊事, in *ibid.*, pp. 377, 454.

Chung, Ssu-ch'eng 鍾嗣成. *Lu kuei pu*, in *Lu kuei pu; wai ssu-chung* 錄鬼簿外四種, Peking, 1959, p. 5.

Kuan-yüan nai-te-weng 灌園耐得翁 (Pseud.). *Tu-ch'eng chi-sheng*, in *Tung-ching meng Hua lu; wai ssu-chung* 東京夢華錄；外四種, Peking, 1653, p. 101.

STUDIES:

Ch'en, Ju-heng 陳汝衡. *Shuo-shu shih-hua* 說書詩話. Peking, 1958, pp. 89-92.

Dolby, Michael. "Kuan Han-ch'ing," *AM*, 16 (1971), 39-40.

Feng, Yüan-chün 馮沅君. *Ku-chü shuo-hui* 古劇說彙. Peking, 1956, pp. 15-22, 57-58.

Idema and West, *Chinese Theater*, pp. 128-136.

Ogawa, Tamaki 小川環樹. *Chūgoku Shōsetsu no kenkyū* 中國小說の研究. Tokyo, 1970.

Prusek, Jaroslav. *The Origins and Authors of Huapen.* Prague, 1967, pp. 52-63.

Sun, K'ai-ti 孫楷第. *Yeh-shih-yüan ku-chin tsa-chü k'ao* 也是園古今雜劇考. Peking, 1953, pp. 349-355.

—SW

Shui-ching chu 水經注 (A Commentary to the Classic of Waterways) by Li Tao-yüan 酈道元 (d. 527) is the major work of geographical writing from the Six Dynasties. Its forty chapters trace the various river courses of China, providing a wealth of anecdotal and historical material concerning cities and areas through which the rivers pass. As the title indicates, it is actually a commentary on a Three Kingdoms work not independently extant that is known as the *Shui-ching*. Kuo P'u 郭璞 (276-324) is also credited with having composed a commentary to the *Shui-ching*, but it has not survived. Li Tao-yüan's work is much longer and broader in scope than the original *Shui-ching*, which simply indicated the physical courses of the waterways.

Between the T'ang and Sung dynasties five chapters of the *Shui-ching chu* were lost, then reconstructed by an unknown hand. The earliest extant edition is found in chapters 11,127 through 11,141 of the *Yung-lo ta-tien*, although fragments of a late Sung woodblock edition circulated in the Ch'ing and were seen by the *Ssu-k'u ch'üanshu tsung-mu t'i-yao* (see Chi Yün) editors.

Many of the most eminent scholars of the Ming and Ch'ing labored to restore the text, focusing particularly on demarcation between the text and the commentary. Among these scholars the names of Tai Chen 戴震 (1724-1777), Chao I-ch'ing 趙一清 (c. 1710-c. 1764), Yang Shou-ching 楊守敬 (1839-1915), and Wang Kuo-wei* are prominent.

Little is known about Li Tao-yüan. Biographical entries in the dynastic histories are scanty and repetitive. Li held several minor government posts, and was noted for his harsh administration. He was said to be widely read, particularly in "strange writings." He was the author of commentaries on the *Pen-chih* 本志, in thirteen *chüan*, and annotations to the *Ch'i-lüeh* 七聘, neither of which has survived.

The *Shui-ching chu* is unique among Chinese works of literature and history. It is cast as a work of geography, but its true aim is much grander. It was meant as nothing less than a historical portrait of China, drawn from the literary and historical sources at Li's disposal. While Li was quite familiar with the tradition of geographical writing which had preceded him, and shared some of its concerns, his techniques, the bulk of his source materials, and the information he presents are those of the historian rather than the geographer. His choice of a work like the *Shui-ching* as a framework for his vast text was based on two factors: the central importance in Chinese history of water and waterways and the recognition that the political unity of China had ceased to exist during the era of the Six Dynasties. Li Tao-yüan's work is the only geographical text of the period to go beyond simple political geography or to operate in a context larger than a single region or area.

This then is the broad strategy of the text. Specific information included centers on the historical significance of the cities and districts through which the rivers pass. Li cites liberally from all the standard historical and philosophical texts, as well as great numbers of local gazetteers and biographies, and a few *chih-kuai** texts in his quest for information. Occasionally notes on unusual flora, fauna or geological formations are included, as well as the location of shrines, spots of particular spiritual efficacy, or areas of great beauty. On a few occasions the author offers personal observation and reflection on places he has himself visited. In this sense it had considerable influence on later landscape writings (see *yu-chi*).

Although the *Shui-ching chu* has been vilified over the centuries for its dependence on *chih-kuai* and other irregular, disreputable texts, examination of the sources cited by Li Tao-yüan reveals the importance of such works to be quite minor. Standard works outnumber borderline ones by an overwhelming margin. Futhermore, Li was quite selective in his use of *chih-kuai* materials. He has chosen some of the least colorful stories, and further abbreviated them by eliminating all but the essential details. There are many potentially relevant extant works which are never noted, including the various mythological-geographical texts on the correspondence of the topography of the earth and the configurations of the heavens.

Viewed as historiography, the *Shui-ching chu* is also interesting. It embodies, although it does not state, many of the principles of critical historiography set forth by Liu Chih-chi* in the *Shih-t'ung*. Li attempts to evaluate his source materials, actually choosing among them when they conflict, in a notable advance over Six Dynasties historiography.

Most of the recent scholarship on the *Shui-ching chu* has continued to deal with questions of text reconstruction, the accuracy of its geographical information, or its potential usefulness for archeological exploration. The literary and historiographic aspects of the work have been largely ignored.

EDITIONS:

Shui-ching chu 水經注. Taipei, 1974. This new reprint is based on Tai Yün's corrected edition (1774), based on the *Yung-lo-ta-tien* edition to which he had access as an editor in the *Ssu-k'u*. Modern punctuation.

Shui-ching chu shih 水經注釋. Chao I-ch'ing, ed. Taipei, 1970. This is a photo-offset repro-

711

duction of the 1794 woodblock edition with Chao I-ch'ing's annotations.

Yang Hsiung ho-hsüan Shui-ching-chu shu 楊熊合撰水經注疏. 20v. Taipei, 1971. This photo-offset of a handwritten text incorporates all the annotations and corrections found in the editions edited by Yang Shou-ching and Hsiung Hui-chen 熊會貞 (1859-1936).

TRANSLATIONS:

Iriya Yoshikata 入矢義高 *et al. Chūgoku koten bungaku taikei* 中國古典文學大系. V. 21. To-kyo, 1974. Includes a translation of chapters 1-5, and 15-19, as well as a brief introduction to the text. There are copious notes identi-fying persons, book titles, and variant sources, although difficult passages are occasionally rephrased rather than explicated.

STUDIES:

Ch'in, Ping-lang 勤炳琅. "*Shui-ching chu* yin-shu-k'ao" 水經注引書考, *Shih-ta Kuo-wen Yen-chiu-suo chi-k'an*, 16 (1972), 377-580.

Hu, Shih. "A Note on Ch'uan Tsu-wang, Chao I-ch'ing and Tai Chen: Study of independent Convergence in Research as illustrated in their works on the *Shui-ching chu*," in *ECCP*, pp. 970-982.

Min, Nan-ts'ai 閩南蔡. "*Shui-ching chu* chih yen-chiu" 水經注之研究, *Kuo-hsüeh hui-p'ien*, 2.3 (1924), 1-7. A discussion of the history of the text and scholarship on it.

Mori, Shikazō 森鹿三. *Tōyōgaku kenkyū* 東洋學研究: *Rekishi chirihen* 歷史地理篇. Kyoto, 1971. Contains various articles on the *Shui-ching chu*, its source materials, and the development of Chinese historical geography.

Yang, Shou-ching. *Shui-ching chu t'u* 水經注圖. Taipei, 1967. Photo-offset of Yang's series of maps of China and the Western Regions, in two colors, showing his reconstruction of the information presented in the *Shui-ching chu* contrasted with the geographical under-standing current in the Ch'ing dynasty.

—JCC

Shui-hu chuan 水滸傳 (Water Margin), a novel, in its most complete form tells of the growth of the Shantung bandit group headed by Sung Chiang 宋江, its honorable surrender to the government, the subse-quent campaigns against the Liao King-dom and other rebellious groups, and its fatal but successful final mission. There is a considerable amount of evidence, though mostly fragmentary, on the historicity of Sung Chiang and his major partners, and such evidence generally tallies with the time frame of the novel, i.e., the Hsüan-ho pe-riod (1119-1125) of the last but one of the Northern Sung emperors, Hui-tsung. From this historical core (whether it is substan-tial enough to be a core is still debatable) to the advent of the earliest known edi-tions in the early sixteenth century, the development of the work can be plotted only in rather vague and broad terms. There are isolated records of the different stages of the development, such as the cryptic remarks of the painter Kung K'ai 龔開 (1222-after 1304), the several related episodes in the *Hsüan-ho i-shih*,* and the repeated use of the *Shui-hu* themes in a fairly large number of Yüan dramas. The ample differences among these sources could be explained as various stages of the development, but since each differs from the novel's present shape, the evolutionary process of the novel's development is still largely unknown. Such problems as the un-certainty of the sources and compositional date of the *Hsüan-ho i-shih*, and the au-thenticity and dating of many of the Yüan dramas concerned further complicate the situation.

It can be argued that the novel evolved from the historical events that inspired it through professional storytelling, differ-ent phases of creating, editing, expanding, and revising, and possibly even the com-bination of several originally unrelated traditions. This accounts for the numerous contextual inconsistencies and factual er-rors throughout the novel. The evidence excludes the possibility of a single author or even several working in different pe-riods. The two traditional attributions of the novel, to Shih Nai-an* and to Lo Kuan-chung,* cannot be taken seriously.

Scholars are on only slightly firmer ground since the discovery of the earliest known editions, which survive in frag-ments. The basic problem is that there are radical differences among the editions from the early sixteenth century down to the mid-seventeenth century when the evolu-tionary process concluded. The full-size

Shui-hu has six main sections: (1) from the escape of the devil spirits to the grand assembly of 108 heroes at the Liang-shan-po 梁山泊 stronghold, (2) events leading to the honorable surrender, (3) the expedition against the Liao Kingdom, (4) campaign against T'ien Hu 田虎, (5) campaign against Wang Ch'ing 王慶, and (6) campaign against Fang La 方臘 and the end of the group. Not all editions contain all six sections, and this is related to the problem of elaboration.

Shui-hu has two major groups of texts: one uses approximately two to three times more words to describe an otherwise identical episode, thereby resulting in a simpler-text series (*chien-pen* 簡本) and a fuller-text series (*fan-pen* 繁本), with a number of different versions in each series. A typical fuller-text version has sections (1), (2), (3), and (6), while its simpler-text counterpart has all six sections. There is also a compromised version in which the two sections that can only be found in the simpler texts, (4) and (5), have been revised and combined with the other four sections from the fuller-text series to form the most complete version in 120 chapters.

The result of all this is two distinctively different groups of texts, though even texts belonging to the same group exhibit ample differences. That *Shui-hu chuan* (disregarding the truncated seventy-one chapter version of Chin Sheng-t'an*) can be found in versions of 100, 109, 110, 115, 120, and 124 chapters, and in versions with only *chüan* divisions (25 and 30 *chüan*) easily makes it the most complicated Chinese novel with regard to textual diversity. This situation has resulted in a heated controversy concerning its growth: are simpler texts abridged versions of fuller texts, or are fuller texts expanded versions of simpler texts, or are there other possibilities? Other novels of an evolutionary nature, such as *San-kuo-chih yen-i** and *Hsi-yu chi,** present similar problems, but their textual differences are far less complicated.

This textual diversity, and the resultant scholarly controversy, is a result of the highly episodic structure of the *Shui-hu chuan* in terms of both individual events and major sections. The repeated use of certain themes and even minor motifs also heightens the independence of the various narrative units. This kind of structural independence is especially evident after the grand assembly of the 108 heroes. The most obvious problem is the absence of casualties among the original 108 heroes during the numerous battles in the campaigns against the Liao, T'ien Hu, and Wang Ch'ing (all those sacrificed are latecomers and defected former enemies), vis-à-vis the defeat or deaths of most of them, including heroes highly enhanced as super fighters in the early chapters (such as Wu Sung 武松, Ch'in Ming 秦明, and Yang Chih 楊志), in the last campaign against Fang La, a historical rebellious leader (the others are all fictitious). This contrast is at best absurd. Those who promote the fuller texts as earlier than the simpler texts capitalize on this in their attempt to show that the superfluous sections are late additions (those who are destined to die in the Fang La campaign cannot be killed in earlier episodes which were composed later), thereby identifying the simpler texts as mere abridgments of the fuller texts. In these arguments they forget that the anti-Liao campaign, which is of the same status as the T'ien Hu and Wang Ch'ing sections, is as much an integral part of the fuller-text system as of the simpler-text system, and that because an edition has one part of late origin does not mean that the entire work is necessarily of late origin. Questions like this, so inseparable from the study of the novel, can only be answered when the major versions of both the fuller and simpler text series have been carefully studied and compared.

All these textual problems and their implications do not concern the general reader, for whom the standard text is Chin Sheng-t'an's* seventy-one-chapter version, which stops abruptly right after the grand assembly. As a matter of fact, most of the Ming and Ch'ing editions, which are normally not available in later reprints, are even beyond the reach of the specialists. This is particularly true for the simpler texts. Here the study of the *Shui-hu chuan* is at a marked disadvantage in comparison with that of the *Hung-lou meng*,* the other novel with serious textual problems, in that most of the key *Hung-lou meng* texts are in Peking and many of them are available in photographic reproductions, while only a few early *Shui-hu* texts have ever been reproduced, and the majority of the rare copies are scattered in China, Japan, and Western Europe. This explains why even for changes which took place after the discovery of the earliest editions, knowledge is still very limited. Only after the appearance of the compromised 120-chapter version, did the basic bibliographical data become more reliable, but by then the development of the novel had been completed.

This ignorance of the background of the novel, and the disastrous association it has had with modern politics (see below), result in a broad spectrum of ideas concerning the nature of the novel, its value, and the characterization of its major figures, particularly Sung Chiang. In the foreseeable future, there is little hope of reaching disinterested and generally accepted conclusions.

In premodern times, *Shui-hu* was considered a book of sedition, a textbook for banditry, and it was occasionally banned (though usually perfunctorily). Indeed many late Ming raiders and bandits fashioned sobriquets after the nicknames of the *Shui-hu* heroes. Modern rightist politicians and their intellectual supporters, after their humiliating failure in 1949, have also seen much similarity between the rise of the Chinese Communists and the activities of the Sung Chiang group as described in the novel. This helps explain the lack of scholarly and public interest in the novel in Taiwan up to the mid-1970s, when the novel was cast in a negative light in mainland China.

The similarities between the rise of the Communists and the events in the novel had not of course been overlooked by the ruling hierarchy and the intellectuals in China since 1949. They regarded the novel as a glorification of peasant revolution and thought Sung Chiang a fine example of revolutionary leadership (with a not too subtle reflection on Mao Tse-tung). This was the norm for almost three decades until the autumn of 1975, when Mao himself suddenly launched a fierce nationwide campaign against the novel and against Sung Chiang. The novel was now recommended only for its value as a negative lesson of the tragedy in store for those who betray the revolutionary cause; Sung Chiang was labeled a wicked traitor who blindly serves the emperor to the extent of sacrificing his devoted brothers and the honorable cause which brought them together. The 120-chapter version replaced the seventy-one chapter version as the one for mass consumption, for only in the "complete" edition can one find the episodes of Sung Chiang's arm-twisting the brothers to surrender and the government's repeated exploitation of the group in fights against other rebel groups. History, fiction, and present-day political dogma became hopelessly mixed in the discussion. The return of pragmatic leadership in 1978 restored the reputation of the novel and of Sung Chiang, but the events after the grand assembly are still basically considered negative. Communist ideology would probably never find it possible to approve one bandit group wiping out other bandit groups on government orders.

Sweeping generalization has been perhaps the norm in evaluating the novel and its major characters, and in analyzing the world and its time as reflected in the work. Many of these claims are erroneous: (1) Nearly every member of the group of 108 is an easily identifiable individual. (To the general reader perhaps no more than thirty or forty of them are memorable.) (2) The novel, with its events explicitly and inexplicitly linked, succeeds in producing a narrative coherent in presentation and captivating in atmosphere. (Any such statement has to exclude the events after the grand assembly, even though some of these events are indistinguishable from the earlier events as far as the evolutionary history is concerned.) (3) Oppression by corrupt officials and the appeal of brotherhood bring the members together. (This is to forget that so many of them truly are professional bandits and, more disastrously, that many of them are forced or tricked into joining.) (4) Life in the Liang-shan-po stronghold is almost utopian. (This ignores the factional tension, political maneuvers, and high-handed actions too commonly found in their daily life.) (5) The novel is a faithful representation of life in Sung-Yüan times. (No extant editions or their archetypes can be dated earlier than the early sixteenth century.)

It is perhaps premature to make generalizations of any kind. Thorough studies of the various texts—particularly the almost totally neglected simpler texts—and of how the novel reached its final shape, have to be pursued first. At present most critics of the *Shui-hu chuan* are not even careful in choosing their working texts.

As with other major Chinese novels, the *Shui-hu* has played a role in drama and in the various branches of the performing arts. This role has been tripartite: Yüan dramas that appeared before the earliest known editions of the novel (still not fully studied, these could in part explain the early growth of the tradition), Ming dramas that may represent a parallel and/or mutually affected development, and a large number of theatrical pieces in the major forms, regional dramas, and different kinds of performing arts that elaborate on well-known episodes of the novel, usually those before the grand assembly.

Shui-hu chuan has three major sequels, all different from one another in approach, theme, and context. Ch'en Ch'en's 陳忱 (1613-after 1663) 40-chapter *Shui-hu hou-chuan* 水滸後傳 (Continuation of Water Margin) picks up after Sung Chiang's death and successfully carries on the narrative line of the original novel in its rebellious spirit and style. It is an admirable novel in its own right. Yü Wan-ch'un's 余萬春 (1794-1849) *Tang-k'ou chih* 蕩寇志 (Quell the Bandits), in seventy chapters, starts from the end of the Chin Sheng-t'an version and is in stark contrast to the original novel in that Sung Chiang and his brothers are viewed strictly as bandits and accordingly are brutally demolished by a group of

"real" heroes. Not surprisingly, it has been severely condemned in China since the early 1950s. *Hou Shui-hu chuan* 後水滸傳 (Sequel to Water Margin), in forty-five chapters, by the anonymous Ch'ing writer Ch'ing-lien shih chu-jen 清蓮室主人, continues the narration after the death of Sung Chiang with a strange twist. The early Southern Sung rebel Yang Yao 楊么 (*c.* 1115-1135) is described as the reincarnation of Sung Chiang. There is also a non-sequel, the 49-chapter *Cheng ssu-k'ou* 征四寇 (Campaigns Against the Four Bandit Groups), which is actually the second half of the 115-chapter simpler-text version issued as a separate book.

EDITIONS:

As explained above, many Ming and early Ch'ing versions exist only in unique copies which are not accessible even to the specialist. While *Shui-hu chuan* can easily be found in countless modern editions, usable editions are few. Here only three easily available ones are listed.

Cheng, Chen-to 鄭振鐸, ed. *Shui-hu ch'üan-chuan* 水滸全傳. Shanghai, 1961. This 120-chapter variorum edition, edited by Cheng Chen-to and others, is the best and most complete modern typeset edition, although the number of texts used is inadequate and the textual methods employed faulty. Available in many reprints.

Ming Jung-yü t'ang k'o Shui-hu chuan 明容與堂刻水滸傳. Shanghai, 1975. This softbound photographic reprint is also available in several expensive editions with traditional Chinese binding. 100-chapter fuller-text edition.

Ti-wu ts'ai-tzu shu Shih Nai-an Shui-hu chuan 第五才子書施耐庵水滸傳. Peking, 1975. A handy softbound photographic reproduction of the 1641 Chin Sheng-t'an 71-chapter version. There is also a 1970 Taipei hardbound edition.

The three major sequels are now available in good modern typeset editions.

Hou Shui-hu chuan. Shenyang, 1981. Based on the only known copy.

Shui-hu hou-chuan. Shanghai, 1956.

Tang-k'ou chih. Peking, 1981. The first modern reprint in China in more than three decades.

TRANSLATIONS:

Dars, Jacques. *Au bord de l'eau (Shui-hu-zhuan).* 2v. Paris, 1978.

Komada, Shinji 駒田信二. *Suikoden*. Tokyo, 1967-68. Annotated Japanese translation of the 120-chapter version.

Shapiro, Sidney. *Outlaws of the Marsh*. Peking and Bloomington, 1981. Complete translation of the first seventy chapters, slightly abridged translation for the last thirty chapters (based on a 100-chapter fuller-text version). Effectively supersedes earlier English translations like Pearl S. Buck, *All Men Are Brothers* (New York, 1933), and J. H. Jackson, *Water Margin* (Shanghai, 1937).

STUDIES:

Chang, Kuo-kuang 張國光. *Shui-hu yü Chin Sheng-t'an yen-chiu* 水滸與金聖嘆研究. Cheng-chou, 1981.

Cheng, Chen-to. "*Shui-hu chuan* te yen-hua" 水滸傳的演化. *Hsiao-shuo yüeh-pao*, 20.9 (September 1929), 1399-1426. Also in Cheng Chen-to, *Chung-kuo wen-hsüeh yen-chiu* 中國文學研究(Peking, 1957), v. 1, pp. 101-157.

Ho, Hsin 何心 [Lu Tan-an 陸澹安]. *Shui-hu yen-chiu* 水滸研究. Rev. ed. Shanghai, 1957. The revised edition is substantitally different from the original 1954 edition.

Hsia, C. T. *The Classic Chinese Novel: A Critical Introduction*. New York, 1968, pp. 75-114, 337-346.

Irwin, Richard. *The Evolution of a Chinese Novel: Shui-hu chuan*. Cambridge, Mass., 1953.

Nieh, Kan-nü 聶紺弩. "Lun *Shui-hu* te fan-pen yü chien-pen" 論水滸的繁本與簡本. In Nieh Kan-nu, *Chung-kuo ku-tien hsiao-shuo lun-chi* 中國古典小說論集, Shanghai, 1981, pp. 140-204.

Plaks, Andrew H. "*Shui-hu chuan* and the Sixteenth-century Novel Form: An Interpretative Analysis," *CLEAR*, 2.1 (January 1980), 3-53.

Sun, Shu-yü 孫述宇. *Shui-hu chuan* te *lai-li hsin-t'ai yü i-shu* 水滸傳的來歷心態與藝術. Taipei, 1981.

Tso-chia ch'u-pan-she 作家出版社, ed. *Shui-hu yen-chiu lun-wen chi* 水滸研究論文集. Peking, 1957.

Widmer, Ellen Bradford. "The *Shui-hu hou-chuan* in the Context of Seventeenth Century Chinese Fiction Criticism." Unpublished Ph. D. dissertation, Harvard University, 1981.

Yen, Tun-i 嚴敦易. *Shui-hu chuan* te *yen-pien* 水滸傳的演變. Peking, 1957.

—YWM & TLMa

Sou-shen chi 搜神記 (In Search of the Supernatural) is the most highly regarded example of *chih-kuai*.* The work was first mentioned in the biography of Kan Pao 干寶傳(*fl.* 320) in the *Chin-shu* 晉書 (History of the Chin Dynasty), which recounts two peculiar experiences in the life of Kan Pao, who is credited with the authorship of the *Sou-shen chi*. Upon his father's death, Kan Pao's vindictive mother sealed his father's favorite concubine in the father's tomb. The mother died ten years later, and when the tomb was opened for the interment of her corpse, the concubine's body was found undecayed. It was carried back to the house where the concubine came back to life. In a similar story, Kan Pao's elder brother stopped breathing for several days, then revived, making an extensive report on the activities of ghosts and spirits. The biography argues that the *Sou-shen chi* resulted from Kan Pao's search for similar occurrences in his own time and amongst the historical records of earlier times. Because of these stories and because of Kan Pao's appointment as the official court compiler under Emperor Yüan of the Chin, later historians and bibliophiles referred to the *Sou-shen chi* as *yü-shih* 餘史 (leftover history).

Kan Pao's preface to the *Sou-shen chi* is also quoted in the biography. It has generally been regarded by scholars as the most reliable remnant of the original work. In it, Kan Pao defends the importance of committing historical information to writing; defends the recording of accounts that are, on the surface, incomplete or at variance with other accounts; and, finally, defends the recording of events that pertain to the "spirit world," which he states unequivocally is not a "falsehood."

Taken together with the stories of the resurrections in Kan Pao's family, the preface seems to argue that the *Sou-shen chi* was intended to be a historical collection. It makes reference, however, to the particular enjoyment that the *hao-shih che* 好事者 (cognoscenti) take in reading such materials, and the preface ends with a more than the usually modest disclaimer of the importance of the collection as an historical source. If viewed in the context of the philosophical and historiographic skepticism of the late Han and early Six Dynasties and the increased interest in literature per se, the *Sou-shen chi*, appears to be an ironic and largely decorative statement on history writing placed before a collection of materials that were recognized value of the materials and the compelling need to preserve them were echoed in the prefaces other *chih-kuai*, such as the *Tung-ming chi* 洞冥記. In this regard, the *Sou-shen chi* preface and the claims for the work made in the *Chin-shu* constitute a preamble to the tradition of literary fiction in early China.

There are several extant texts entitled *Sou-shen chi*. These divide into four families, no one of which is accepted today as Kan Pao's original. A twenty-chapter version and an eight-chapter version can be traced back to Ming dynasty collectanea. A related but briefer text was discovered among the manuscripts at Tun-huang, and six chapters of distinct materials are included under the title in *Tao-tsang* (TT 1476). Until the compilation of the bibliographical reference *Ssu-k'u ch'üan-shu tsung-mu t'i-yao* (see Chi Yün), the twenty-chapter version and the eight-chapter version were considered credible redactions of the original work. Recently in examining the eight-chapter version, scholars have noted evidence of Buddhist influence, the presence of T'ang and Sung dynasty place names, official titles, and colloquialisms, and a generally higher level of narrative sophistication than can be attributed to the early Six Dynasties. Although there is a close kinship between the twenty-chapter version and the eight-chapter version, the latter is consistently more developed in a literary sense. At the same time that doubts have been substantiated vis-à-vis the eight-chapter version, much of the twenty-chapter text has been corroborated by quotations attributed to the *Sou-shen chi* or to Kan Pao in *lei-shu** and in commentaries from the Six Dynasties and Han. As a result, the twenty-chapter version is now widely accepted as the best representation of Kan Pao's original work.

A related title, the *Sou-shen hou-chi* 搜神後記 (Sequel to In Search of the Supernatural), was often mentioned by early bibliographers in conjunction with the *Sou-shen chi*. The sequel, often attributed to T'ao Ch'ien, but almost certainly not by his hand, presently exists only in a text that largely duplicates the twenty-chapter *Sou-shen chi*. More related titles are found in the bibliographies, *Sou-shen lun* 搜神錄, and *Hsü Sou-shen chi* 續搜神記, to name but two, but none is extant, and it is virtually impossible to determine which was a variant title, which was a variant text, and which was a generic descriptor. Scholars have argued that what might have at one time existed as a series of distinct works are now melded into the extant twenty-chapter text. Virtually this entire text is found in quotations in T'ang and Sung sources, with attributions to various originals. This suggests that what we currently have is a redaction that dates from the Ming and that no text was transmitted intact from the Six Dynasties.

The oldest manuscript edition of the *Sou-shen chi* is in the *Pi-ts'e hui-han* 祕册彙函 (A Collection of Rare Texts), compiled during the Ming by Hu Chen-heng 胡震亨 (1569-1645). It includes 464 items, divided into roughly topical chapters and ranging in length from a few characters to several hundred. The contents are nearly all narratives, with the exception of a few essays on technical matters. Topics range from deities, immortals, Taoist adepts, divination, medicine, dreams, filial behavior, strange marriages, and criminal spirits to explanations of omens that foretold new dynasties.

The style of the writing is terse, almost austere. It has qualities of documentary prose, a reflection of its common ancestry with historical writing. Biographical structure is the most prevalent, and later writers derived from the *Sou-shen chi* and its contemporaneous *chih-kuai* fiction a format easily adapted to Buddhist and Taoist hagiography.

Most of the stories of immortals and adepts are also found in early collections of immortals' biographies, such as *Shen-hsien chuan* 神仙傳 (Biographies of Spirit Immortals). Other portions duplicate materials in the dynastic histories and their commentaries or other *chih-kuai*. It is impossible,

717

however, to ascertain which are the earlier texts or whether these different versions were separately derived from a common source.

The transmission of the text apparently was interrupted during the Sung, but its influence on many forms of literary fiction and drama was continuous. Specific *Sou-shen chi* stories and characters (the magical reward of the self-sacrificing son Tung Yung 董永, the infallible swordsman Kan-chiang Mo-yeh) were expanded in later fiction and drama. The work also enriched the stock of plot elements and devices with tales of violations of graves, visits from mysterious adepts or spirits, natural and supernatural transformations, dreams and their import, and mental and physical contests between humans and spirits.

EDITIONS:

Sou-shen chi. P'i-ts'e hui-han. A 1603 edition.
Sou-shen chi chiao-chu 搜神記校注. Taipei, 1974.
Wang, Shao-ying 汪紹楹, ed. *Sou-shen chi.* Peking, 1979.
———, ed. *Sou-shen hou-chi.* Peking, 1981.

TRANSLATIONS:

DeWoskin, Kenneth J. "*In Search of the Supernatural:* Translations from the *Sou-shen chi,*" *Renditions,* 7 (Summer 1977), 103-114.
Bodde, Derk. "Some Chinese Tales of the Supernatural: Kan Pao and his *Sou-shen chi,*" *HJAS,* 6 (1942), 338-357.
———. "Again Some Chinese Tales of the Supernatural," *JAOS,* 62 (1942), 305-308.
Takeda, Akira 竹田晃. *Sōshin ki* 搜神記. Tokyo, 1964.
Yang, Hsien-yi 楊憲益 and Gladys Yang. *The Man Who Sold a Ghost: Chinese Tales of the 3rd and 6th Centuries.* Peking, 1958, pp. 11-54.

STUDIES:

DeWoskin, Kenneth J. "The *Sou-shen chi* and the *Chih-kuai* Tradition: A Bibliographic and Generic Study." Unpublished Ph.D. dissertation, Columbia University, 1974.
Fan, Ning 范寧. "Kuan-yü *Sou-shen chi*" 關於搜神記, *Wen-hsüeh p'ing-lun* (Peking), 1 (February 1964), 86-92.
Maeno, Naoaki 前野直彬. "The Origins of Fiction in China," *AA,* 16 (1969), 27-37.
Toyoda, Minoru 豐田穰. "*Sōshin ki* 搜神記, *Sōshin kōki genryū ko*" 搜神後記源流考, *Tōhō gakuhō,*

12.3 (November 1941), 43-66.

—KD

Ssu-k'ung T'u 司空圖 (*tzu*, Piao-sheng 表聖, *hao*, Chih-fei-tzu 知非子 and Nai-ju chü-shih 耐辱居士, 837-908), one of the major poets of the late T'ang period, owes his place in literary history to the "Erh-shih-ssu shih-p'in" 二十四詩品 (The Twenty-four Moods of Poetry), commonly considered to be one of the most important works of T'ang literary criticism.

Reliable biographical data on Ssu-k'ung T'u are sparse. He was probably born in Ssu-shui 泗水 (modern Anhwei), although some sources give Yü-hsiang 虞鄉 (modern Shansi) as his birthplace. His family had a long tradition of government service. His father, Ssu-k'ung Yü 司空輿, held an important post as a Salt Commissioner. Ssu-k'ung T'u passed the *chin-shih* examination in 869. When the Chief Examiner Wang Ning 王凝 was accused of favoritism and banished, Ssu-k'ung T'u followed him. A short official career from 878 to 880 culminated in a position as Minister of Rites. It was interrupted by the siege and capture of Ch'ang-an by Huang Ch'ao's 黃巢 rebels. Later attempts to resume his career were thwarted by social and political instability.

Ssu-k'ung T'u retired to his estate in Wang-kuan ku 王官谷 (Imperial Official's Valley) in the Chung-t'iao Mountains. In the preface to his collected works he justified his retirement by emphasizing the impossibility of realizing his social and political ambitions. He turned to Buddhism and Taoism and when summoned to court a few years later was reluctant to resume office. Many anecdotes grew around the person of Ssu-k'ung T'u. For example, it is said that when he heard that the last T'ang emperor had been murdered and the throne usurped, he stopped eating and died.

Although Ssu-k'ung T'u gathered around him a varied group of intellectuals (scholar-officials, Taoists, and Buddhist monks), he did not belong to any of the poetic groups of the time and had no connections with contemporaries such as P'i Jih-hsiu* or Lu Kuei-meng.* His poetry does not appear in the anthologies of his time. His life and the attitudes expressed in his poetry place Ssu-k'ung in the tradition of T'ao Ch'ien,* Wang Wei,* and Wei Ying-wu.* Most of the nearly four hundred extant poems are in the *chüeh-chü* (see *shih*) form. Isolation and loneliness are central themes symbolized in the recurrent image of the lonely firefly.

"Erh-shih-ssu shih-p'in," a series of twenty-four poems, is in the tradition of poems about poetry. This kind of criticism—unlike Chung Hung's earlier prose work also called *Shih-p'in**—tries to embody its principles in the verse of the critical text itself. Ssu-k'ung T'u does not give a classification and evaluation of poets, nor does he try to construct any artistic kinship between them. He need not give any names. More than any other work of Chinese literary criticism the "Erh-shih-ssu shih-p'in" 二十四詩品 (Twenty-four Moods of Poetry) tries to penetrate into the realm of poetry itself. But a certain vagueness results from the lack of concrete examples and from this intuitive method.

The structure and the form of the twenty-four poems is remarkably simple: twelve ancient-style four-syllable verses make up one poem; each poem has one rhyme occurring at the end of the even-numbered lines. The twenty-four pieces describe literary "qualities," "modes," and "moods" (*p'in*) in a highly artistic language.

The language chosen by Ssu-k'ung T'u is highly suggestive, betraying strong Buddhist and Taoist influences. Such influences are even more distinct in letters like "Yü Li Sheng lun-shih shu" 與李生論詩書 (Letter to Mr. Li on Poetry) or "Yü Chi-p'u shu" 與極浦書 (Letter to Chi-p'u), in which he describes his concepts of "a meaning beyond flavor" (*wei-wai chih chih* 味外之旨) and "an image beyond the image" (*hsiang-wai chih hsiang* 象外之象).

Ssu-k'ung T'u's literary criticism influenced later critics such as Mei Yao-ch'en,* Yen Yü (see *Ts'ang-lang shih-hua*), and Wang Shih-chen* (1634-1711).

EDITIONS:

Ssu-k'ung Piao-sheng wen-chi 司空表聖文集 and *Ssu-k'ung Piao-sheng shih-chi* 司空表聖詩集. SPTK.

Tsu, Pao-ch'üan 祖保泉. *Ssu-k'ung T'u Shih-p'in chieh-shuo* 司空圖詩品解說. Hofei, 1964; rpt. Hong Kong, 1966 (as *Ssu-k'ung T'u Shih-p'in chu-shih chi i-wen* 司空圖詩品注釋及譯文).

Kuo, Shao-yü 郭紹虞, ed. *Chung-kuo li-tai wen-lun hsüan* 中國歷代文論選. Shanghai, 1962, v. 1, pp. 478-488. Annotated pieces of literary criticism.

TRANSLATIONS

Yang, Hsien-yi and Gladys Yang. "The Twenty-four Modes of Poetry," *Chinese Literature*, 1963.7, 65-77.

STUDIES:

Alexeev, V. M. *Kitajkaja poema o poete. Stancy Sykun Tu.* Petersburg, 1916. The standard work on Ssu-k'ung T'u.

Funazu, Tomihiko 船津富彦. "Shikū To no 'san kan no gai' ni tsuite" 司空圖の酸鹹之外につい て, *Tōkyō shinagakuhō*, 5 (1959), 62-76.

Lo, Lien-t'ien 羅聯添. "T'ang Ssu-k'ung T'u shih-chi hsi-nien" 唐司空圖事蹟繫年, *Ta-lu tsa-chih*, 1969.11, 14-31.

Robertson, Maureen A. "To Convey What is Precious: Ssu-k'ung T'u's Poetics and the *Erh-shih-ssu Shih P'in*," in *Transition and Permanence: Chinese History and Culture*, David C. Buxbaum and Frederick W. Mote, eds., Hong Kong, 1972, pp. 323-357.

Tu, Ch'eng-hsiang 杜呈祥. "Ssu-k'ung T'u" 司空圖, in *Chung-kuo wen-hsüeh-shih lun-wen chi* 中國文學史論文集, Chang Ch'i-yün 張其昀, ed., v. 2, Taipei, 1959, pp. 467-483.

Wong, Yoon Wah. *Ssu-k'ung T'u: A Poet-Critic of the T'ang.* Hong Kong, 1976. A carefully written, brief (68 pp.) biography with further bibliographical reference; see also the author's unpublished Ph.D. dissertation "Ssu-k'ung T'u: The Man and His Theory of Poetry," University of Wisconsin, Madison, 1972.

Yu, Pauline. "Ssu-k'ung T'u's 'Shih-p'in': Poetic Theory in Poetic Form," in *Studies in Chinese Poetry and Poetics*, Ronald C. Miao, ed., San Francisco, 1978, v. 1, pp. 81-103.

—VK

Ssu-ma Ch'eng-chen 司馬承禎 (*tzu*, Tzu-wei 子微, 647-735), the twelfth patriarch of the Shang-ch'ing 上清 (Upper Empyrean) school of Taoism, was one of the most eminent religious figures of the T'ang dynasty and an important member of the literary world during Emperor Hsüan-tsung's reign (712-756). A grandson of Ssu-ma I-hsüan 司馬裔玄, a former local official in Chin-chou 晉州 (modern Shansi), Ch'eng-chen was said to be from Wen-hsien 溫縣 (modern Honan). As a young man he served as a functionary for a time, then began religious studies with P'an Shih-cheng 潘師正 at the sacred mountain Sung-shan. He was so proficient a student that he was eventually chosen as P'an's successor. Later (precisely when is not known), he left Sung-shan, traveled to many sacred sites, and finally settled at T'ien-t'ai-shan 天台山 (in Chekiang).

Ssu-ma Ch'eng-cheng was summoned to court from T'ien-t'ai by each of the successive rulers, Wu Tse-t'ien, Jui-tsung, and Hsüan-tsung. His relationship with the latter was especially close. In 721 he ordained Hsüan-tsung as an official Taoist. The two worthies collaborated on an edition of *Lao-tzu* with a fixed length of 5380 graphs, penned in three different styles by Ssu-ma. A few years later, when Ssu-ma's new abode at Wang-wu-shan 王屋山 was completed, Hsüan-tsung personally wrote the name *Yang-t'ai kuan* 陽臺觀 (Belvedere of the Solar Terrace) on a horizontal plaque and sent it to him with three hundred bolts of silk.

Ssu-ma spent the remainder of his days at Wang-wu-shan. His biographies state that he died in 727 at the age of 89. Other, earlier sources claim he died in 735.

Ssu-ma's many extant works (several have been lost) show him to have been a man of great versatility. They include poetry and meditation manuals. One of the more interesting texts is the "Shang-ch'ing han-hsiang chien-chien t'u" 上清含象劍鑑圖, an illustrated description of swords and mirrors, important liturgical implements. Ssu-ma was also a skilled painter and calligrapher.

As important as the texts written by him are the lives he touched and impressed with his piety. Some evidence of this may be found in T'ang literature. The *Ch'üan T'ang shih** preserves two poems written to him by Hsüan-tsung, as well as a number of verses in his honor by noted T'ang poets—Sung Chih-wen (see Shen Ch'üan-ch'i), Li Chiao,* and Chang Chiu-ling.* Ssu-ma also met Li Po,* who recorded their meeting in the allegorical and rather satirical "Ta p'eng fu" 大鵬賦 (Prose-poem of the Great Roc). The poet-official Ch'en Tzu-ang* also wrote of an encounter with him.

The life of Ssu-ma Ch'eng-chen contains some contradictions. A Mao-shan patriarch who rarely resided at Mao-shan, he was a hermit who hobnobbed with poets and princes. Yet he always retained an aura of holiness and commanded respect. As was said of him, "His body is like a cold pine, his heart like a bright mirror."

EDITIONS:

Cheng-t'ung Tao-tsang 正統道藏. Rpt. Taipei, 1976. (To locate specific works consult Weng Tu-chien, *Combined Indices to the Authors and Titles of Books in Two Collections of Taoist Literature.* Rpt. Taipei, 1966.)

Kroll, Paul W. "Ssu-ma Ch'eng-chen in T'ang Verse," *BSSCR*, 6 (Fall 1978), 16-30.

—DN

Ssu-ma Ch'ien 司馬遷 (*c.* 145-*c.* 85 B.C.), the great Han historian, had an enormous impact on Chinese culture. His monumental *Shih-chi** (Records of the Grand Historian) was the first comprehensive history of China and established, in broad outline, the structure of most subsequent Chinese historical writing. The literary style and narrative technique of Ssu-ma Ch'ien's *Shih-chi* had a profound impact upon later Chinese fiction, particularly the historical romance, as well as upon historical writing, the line between these two genres being even less clear in China than in the West.

Almost all that can be known of Ssu-ma Ch'ien's life is autobiographical and comes from two documents: the postface to the *Shih-chi* and a long letter written in either 93 or 91 B.C. to Jen An 任安, a friend who was in prison. These documents leave numerous gaps, for they focus almost exclusively upon two critical episodes in his life. In addition, they raise problems of interpretation. For example, to what extent is Ssu-ma Ch'ien's self-portrayal shaped by those same rather romantic patterns that he perceived in the lives of such admired, tragic figures as Ch'ü Yüan* and Confucius?

Even the year of Ssu-ma Ch'ien's birth is a subject of dispute. Most experts argue that he was born in 145 B.C., but a minority opinion, argued most persuasively by Li Chang-chih 李長之, holds for 135 B.C. The controversy revolves around two sources which are in direct conflict, Ssu-ma Chen's 司馬貞 (fl. 720) Shih-chi so-yin 史記索隱 and Chang Shou-chieh's 張守節 (fl. 736) Shih-chi cheng-i 史記正義. However, it is certain that almost all of Ssu-ma's life was spent under the energetic but problem-filled reign of Emperor Wu (r. 140-87 B.C.).

Ssu-ma Ch'ien says that he was born at Lung-men 龍門 (Dragon Gate), a mountain on the east bank of the Yellow River near modern Han-ch'eng 韓城 in Shensi Province. Just eighty-five miles from the Han capital of Ch'ang-an 長安, Lung-men was in the loess region where Chinese civilization had emerged. In fact, Lung-men itself, according to tradition, had been bored out by the thearch Yü during his suppression of the great Chinese flood.

Ssu-ma Ch'ien, true to his profession of historian, was intent upon locating himself in the flow of history. He looked to both the past, where precedents for his own behavior and sentiments can be found, and the future, when his own place in history would be granted and his actions vindicated. Thus, he began his autobiography by tracing his descent through an illustrious family which "for generations had charge of the historical records of Chou." The Ssu-ma family's involvement in record keeping, which Ch'ien says was interrupted during the mid-Chou, was renewed when Emperor Wu appointed Ch'ien's father, Ssu-ma T'an, Grand Astrologer (T'ai-shih 太史), a mid-level administrative position overseeing not only the notation and interpretation of astronomical phenomena, but also the recording of the emperor's daily activities. T'an's appointment took his family from their native home near Han-ch'eng, where Ch'ien had "plowed and pastured on the sunny side of the hills along the river," to the capital which was, at least during the time of Emperor Wu, one of the most cosmopolitan cities in the world.

By the age of ten, Ssu-ma Ch'ien could "recite the old texts," and, living in Ch'ang-an, he studied under such brilliant contemporaries as the Ch'un-ch'iu master Tung Chung-shu.* In addition to his studies, Ssu-ma Ch'ien traveled extensively in his youth. It has been said that he was one of the best-traveled men of his age, and references to information gleaned from these journeys are frequent in Shih-chi, for however bookish Ssu-ma Ch'ien might have been, he did not overlook the oral tradition.

At the age of twenty, he entered government service in the rather low position of Gentleman of the Interior. These "gentlemen" attended to and protected the emperor both in the palace and on the road. In this capacity, Ssu-ma accompanied the peripatetic Emperor Wu on numerous inspection tours. Upon his return from an official trip in 110 B.C., there occurred the first of the two events that form the center of his autobiographical writing. His father, disappointed that he had been left out of the royal entourage's journey to Mt. T'ai to perform the most august imperial sacrifices, fell gravely ill. Ssu-ma T'an previously had used his official access to the imperial library to begin a personal task—the compilation of a comprehensive history of China. The extent to which the endeavor had been completed is not known, but from his death-bed, T'an enjoined his son to complete the work.

Three years later (105 B.C.), when his period of filial mourning was over, Ch'ien succeeded his father in the position of Grand Astrologer, thereby gaining full access to "the various historical records and books of the stone rooms and metal caskets." For the next few years, Ssu-ma was engaged in both his official duties and the continuation of the history begun by his father. During this time, it is likely that he also participated in the revision of the calendar which took place in 104 B.C., a calendar which was to remain in official use for the next two thousand years.

Ssu-ma Ch'ien still was not finished with his history in 99 B.C., when the second critical episode of his life occurred. Li Ling 李陵, a military man who was known and admired by Ssu-ma Ch'ien, had led a force of five thousand men deep into Hsiung-nu territory. Poorly supplied and badly outnumbered, Li Ling was defeated and captured. With the exception of Ssu-ma Ch'ien, who continued to speak out in support of the general, all Emperor Wu's high officials turned against Li Ling. The Emperor, enraged that Li Ling had allowed himmself to be captured alive, cast the general's defender, Ssu-ma Ch'ien, into prison. Shortly thereafter, Ssu-ma was found guilty of "defaming the emperor," a crime carrying the sentence of death. Such a sentence could be commuted upon payment of a large sum of money, but Ssu-ma's family was poor and no friends came to his aid. It was fully expected that a man of noble character caught in such an unfortunate situation would commit suicide, but Ssu-ma agreed to undergo the humiliation of castration in place of either suicide or execution. Several years later, Ssu-ma wrote to Jen An concerning this episode. In a deeply moving text which might be described as a "confession," Ssu-ma explained his choice:

> . . . the reason I bear these insults and continue to live, hidden in filth without taking my leave, is that I grieve that I have things in my heart which I have not been able to express fully, and I am shamed that I might die and my writings not be known to later generations.

Ssu-ma Ch'ien was caught between the filial demand of his father's charge to complete the *Shih-chi,* with the attendant hope of eventual fame and vindication, and the preservation of his own self-esteem. He chose the former, completed the *Shih-chi* and won the praise of later generations, but his letter clearly indicates that the price was considerable self-loathing:

> Although a hundred generations pass, my defilement will only increase! Thus, in a single day,

my bowels are wrenched nine times. When I am at home, I am befuddled and confused. When I go out, I do not know where I am going. Whenever I think of this shame, the sweat always pours from my back and soaks my robe. I am now no more than a servant in the women's quarters.

The date and precise circumstances of Ssu-ma Ch'ien's death are also disputed. One theory places his death in either 86 or 85 B.C., another in 78 B.C., and there are suggestions that he may have died during a second period of imprisonment.

Although the authenticity of certain portions of the *Shih-chi* is questioned, there is little doubt that most of the 130-chapter text of over half-a-million characters stems from the eminent Han historian. In addition to the *Shih-chi,* the *Han-shu* 漢書 bibliographic section ascribes eight *fu** to Ssu-ma Ch'ien. Only one of these remains, preserved in the T'ang encyclopedia *I-wen lei-chü* 藝文類聚, and though some have doubted its authenticity, a recent study by Chao Hsing-chih 趙省之 supports the traditional ascription. The *fu,* modeled upon an earlier work by Tung Chung-shu, contains themes which appear both in Ssu-ma Ch'ien's autobiographical and historical writings (e.g. "Alas for the gentleman born out of his time," "To die nameless was the ancient's shame," etc.). Certain portions of this *fu* support the old argument that Ssu-ma Ch'ien was a Taoist. However, such a claim must be seriously qualified. First of all, Ssu-ma T'an's famous essay on the six schools, which his son includes in the postface to the *Shih-chi* and which has become the most often cited evidence of Ssu-ma Ch'ien's Taoist affinities, is an endorsement of the eclectic form of Taoism reflected by such texts as the "T'ien-hsia" 天下 chapter of the *Chuang-tzu* and the *Huai-nan tzu;* it is assuredly not to be confused with either the contemplative *wu-wei* Taoism of the earlier chapters of *Chuang-tzu* or the Taoism of immortality which appeared during the Han. Moreover, the moral perspective of much of the *Shih-chi* is decidedly Confucian. To Ssu-ma Ch'ien Confucius was the great sage, and he is esteemed by being placed among the *Shih-chia* 世家 (Hereditary Households) while such Taoists as Lao-tzu and Chuang-tzu are treated in the biography section.

Li Chang-chih, the most original biographer of Ssu-ma Ch'ien, sees a certain conflict between the great historian's "romantic" and "classical" inclinations. This interpretation is useful in understanding the complex author of *Shih-chi*. For example, one occasionally can perceive tension between the sympathies of the narrative and the author's more detached moral judgments, the latter often appearing as the final words of the chapter, prefaced by "The Grand Astrologer says . . ." (*T'ai shih kung yüeh* 太史公曰). This conflict becomes common in later Chinese narrative, appearing not only in historical texts but also in such literary works as the short stories of P'u Sung-ling (see *Liao-chai chih-i*) and the detached, moralistic, and apparently obligatory authorial judgments in Chinese erotic literature such as *Jou p'u-t'uan*.*

STUDIES:

Chavannes, Édouard. "Introduction," *Les mémoires historiques de Se-ma Ts'ien*. Rpt. Paris, 1967, v. 1, pp. viii-ccnvii.

Ch'eng, Ho-sheng 鄭鶴聲. *Ssu-ma Ch'ien nien-p'u* 司馬遷年譜. Shanghai, 1956.

Dzo, Ching-chuan. *Sseu-ma Ts'ien et l'historiographie chinoise* (Préface R. Etiemble). Paris, 1978.

Hu, P'ei-wei 胡佩韋. *Ssu-ma Ch'ien ho Shih-chi* 司馬遷和史記. Peking, 1962.

Kierman, Frank. *Ssu-ma Ch'ien's Historiographical Attitude as Reflected in Four Late Warring States Biographies*. Wiesbaden, 1962.

Krol', Yu. L. *Syma Tsyan'—istorik*. Moskva, 1970.

Li, Chang-chih 李長之. *Ssu-ma Ch'ien chih jen-ke ho feng-ke* 司馬遷之人格和風格. Shanghai, 1949.

Ma, K'ai-hsüan 馬凱旋. *Ssu-ma Ch'ien* 司馬遷. Hsing-chou, 1962.

Pokora, Timoteus. "Review of Burton Watson, *Ssu-ma Ch'ien Grand Historian of China*," *TP*, 50 (1963), 294-322. Contains good bibliography (pp. 303-305).

Shih-chi yen-chiu te tzu-liao ho lun-wen so-yin 史記研究的資料和論文索引, edited by Chung-kuo K'o-hsüeh yüan Li-shih Yen-chiu so, ti i, erh so 中國科學院歷史研究所, 第一, 二所. Peking, 1958.

Ssu-ma Ch'ien 司馬遷. Ch'en Fan 陳凡, ed. Shanghai, 1975.

Ssu-ma Ch'ien yü Shih-chi 司馬遷與史記. Wen-shih-che tsa-chih Pien-chi Wei-yüan hui 文史哲雜誌編輯委員會, ed. Peking, 1957.

Takeda, Taijun 武田泰淳. *Shiki no sekai* 史記の世界. Tokyo, 1975.

Watson, Burton. *Ssu-ma Ch'ien Grand Historian of China*. New York, 1958.

—SD

Ssu-ma Hsiang-ju 司馬相如 (*tzu*, Ch'ang-ch'ing 長卿, 179-117 B.C.) is the best-known and most celebrated *fu** writer in the history of Chinese literature. He brought this genre to its highest level of development in the Han dynasty, and his *fu* were regarded as models for many later imitations.

He was a native of Ch'eng-tu 成都, the provincial capital of Shu 蜀 (modern Szechwan). As a youth, he had great admiration for Lin Hsiang-ju 藺相如, a famous statesman of the Warring States period and accordingly named himself Hsiang-ju. He served Emperor Ching (r. 156-141 B.C.) for a time and then journeyed to Liang 梁, where he was well received by distinguished poets such as Mei Sheng,* Tsou Yang 鄒陽 (206-129 B.C.) and Chuang Chi 莊忌 (*fl.* 154 B.C.), all patronized by Prince Hsiao of Liang 梁孝王 (*fl.* 178-144 B.C.). Ssu-ma Hsiang-ju's talent for writing *fu* began to develop under the influence of these Liang poets, who had broken new ground for the genre. In particular, he was stimulated by Mei Sheng, the doyen of contemporary *fu*-writers, whose "Ch'i fa" 七發 (Seven Stimuli) and "T'u Yüan fu" 兔園賦 (The T'u Park) were the forerunners of his descriptive *fu* on hunts.

During his stay in Liang, he wrote the "Tzu-hsü fu" 子虛賦 in the form of a debate between two envoys from Ch'u 楚 and Ch'i 齊, in which they describe the hunts and hunting preserves of their sovereigns. This *fu* came to the attention of Emperor Wu (r. 140-87 B.C.) who read it with much delight. Thereupon, Ssu-ma Hsiang-ju was summoned to the capital, Ch'ang-an, and was ordered to compose a similar *fu* on the imperial hunts. He re-worked his earlier composition and added a third member to the debate, who overwhelmed both the envoys by telling them of the unsurpassed magnificence of the imperial hunts and the wonders of the emperor's way of life. This last section of the *fu* is considered a separate piece and referred to as the "Shang-lin fu" 上林賦 —the whole composition is entitled "T'ien-tzu yu-lieh fu" 天子游獵賦. It is a long poem, elaborately constructed with a skillful plot, rich in vocabulary, vivid in description, and stately in movement. When he presented this *fu* to the throne, Emperor Wu was exceedingly pleased and appointed him a Gentleman at court. Afterwards, he often accompanied the emperor on hunting parties. Later, he submitted the "Ai Ch'in Erh-shih fu" 哀秦二世賦 (Lamenting the Second Ch'in Emperor) and "Ta jen fu" 大人賦 (The Mighty One) to the throne. Because of failing health, Ssu-ma Hsiang-ju retired from his post at court to Mou-ling 茂陵, where he was later laid to rest.

According to the "I-wen chih" in the *Han-shu* (see Pan Ku), Ssu-ma Hsiang-ju wrote a total of twenty-nine *fu*, but of these only the four mentioned above are considered genuine. The other two surviving pieces, "Mei-jen fu" 美人賦 (The Beautiful Person) and "Ch'ang-men fu" 長門賦 (The Tall-gate Palace) are of questionable authenticity.

Ssu-ma Hsiang-ju's *fu* bear the unmistakable stamp of his original genius as a poet. He was so complete a master of words and rhetorical devices that the reader is captivated by the color and cadence of his poems. Yang Hsiung* declared that his *fu* were *shen-hua* 神化, i.e. not of this world. Wang Shih-chen* (1526-1590) praised his superb creative vitality that exhibited beautiful language and lofty vision. Arthur Waley maintained that "his glittering torrent of words has never since poured from the pen of any writer in the world and beside him Euphues seems timid and Apuleius cold" (*The Temple*, pp. 43-44).

Ssu-ma Hsiang-ju had his own theory on *fu* composition:

> Form and substance should be given to the *fu* by the interlacing of strands of the weaving of colors in a rich brocade; just as in music, skillful organization of tones imparts to the *fu* its pleasing rhythm. These are the external traces of the *fu*,

but the mind of a *fu* writer encompasses the whole universe, and holds in its view everything from human beings to the inanimate world. This embracing vision comes from within and cannot be transmitted.

EDITIONS:

Liu-ch'ao wen, v. 1, "Ch'üan Han wen" 全漢文, ch. 21, pp. 241-248.

Ssu-ma wen-yüan chi 司馬文園集, in *Pai-san*, v. 1, pp. 39-62.

Ssu-ma Ch'ang-ch'ing chi 司馬長卿集, in Ting Fu-pao 丁福保, ed., *Han Wei Liu-ch'ao ming chia chi* 漢魏六朝名家集. Shanghai, 1911.

Ssu-ma Ch'ang-ching chi 司馬長卿集, in *Liang Han Wei Chin shih-i-chia wen-chi* 兩漢魏晉十一家文集. Taipei, 1973. A reprint of Wang Shih-hsien's 汪士賢 (1572-1619?) revised edition of the Ming period.

TRANSLATIONS:

van Gulik, Robert. "Mei jen fu," in *Sexual Life in Ancient China*, Leiden, 1961, pp. 68-69.

Hervouet, Yves. "Tzu-hsü fu," "Shang-lin fu," "Ai Ch'in Erh-shih fu," and "Ta-jen fu," *Le Chapitre 117 du Che ki: Biographie de Sseu-ma Siang-jou*. Paris, 1972, 11-142, pp. 181-184, and 186-203.

Margouliés, George. "Mei Jen Fu," in *Anthologie raisonnée de la littérature chinoise*, Paris, 1948, pp. 324-326.

Scott, John. "Mei jen fu," in *Love and Protest*, New York, 1972, pp. 49-51.

von Zach, E. "Tzu-Hsü fu," *Anthologie*, v. 1, pp. 103-107; "Ch'ang-men fu," *Anthologie*, v. 1, pp. 233-236.

Waley, Arthur. "Tzu-hsü fu" [introduction only], in *The Temple*, pp. 41-43.

Watson, "Tzu-hsü fu," "Shang-lin fu," *Rhyme-Prose*, pp. 30-37 and 37-51; "Ai Ch'in Erh-shih fu," *Records*, v. 2, pp. 331-332; "Ta-jen fu," *Records*, v. 2, pp. 332-335.

STUDIES:

Chien, Chung-wu 簡宗梧. "Tzu-hsü Shang-lin Fu yen-chiu" 子虛上林賦研究, *Chung-hua hsüeh-yüan*, 19 (March 1977), 11-35.

Gaspardone, Emile. "Les deux premiers *fou* de Sseu-ma Siang-you," *JA*, 246 (1958), 447-452.

Hervouet, Yves. *Un Poète de cours sous les Han: Sseu-ma Siang-jou*. Paris, 1964.

Ho, P. H. Kenneth 何沛雄. "The relationship between Mei Sheng's 'Chi-fa' and Ssu-ma Hsiang-ju's 'Tzu-hsü fu and Shang-lin fu'" 枚乘七發與司馬相如子虛上林賦的關係, *The Youngsun*, 32.12 (April 1968) 24-28.

Knechtges, David R., "Ssu-ma Hsiang-ju and His Contemporaries," *Han Rhapsody*, pp. 28-40.

———. "Ssu-ma Hsiang-ju's 'Tall Gate Palace Rhapsody,'" *HJAS*, 41.1 (June 1981), 47-64. Contains a carefully annotated translation.

Liu, K'ai-yang 劉開陽. "Lun Ssu-ma Hsiang-ju *fu* chih pen-yüan ho te-tien" 論司馬相如賦的本原和特點, *Wen-hsüeh i-ch'an tseng k'an,* 10 (1962), 41-51.

Mao, I-po 毛一波. "Wen wei shih-chü te Ssu-ma Hsiang-ju" 文爲世矩的司馬相如, *Ssu-ch'uan wen-hsien,* 157 (December 1957), 65-71.

Nakashima, Chiaki 中島千秋. "Shikyo Jōrin no fu no genryū" 子虛上林賦の源流, *Tōhōgaku,* 17 (November 1958), 13-26.

T'ien, Ch'ien-chün 田倩君. "Ssu-ma Hsiang-ju chi ch'i fu" 司馬相如及其賦, *Ta-lu tsa-chih,* 15.4 (August 1957), 115-120; 15.5 (September 1957), 154-157; 15.7 (October 1957), 230-237.

Yoshikawa, Kōjirō 吉川幸次郎. "Shiba Shōjo ni tsuite" 司馬相如について, *Shosetsu,* 5 (1950), 46-84.

—HI

Ssu-ta ch'uan-ch'i 四大傳奇 (Four Great Southern Plays) is the collective designation of a group of four moralistic melodramas that, together with Kao Ming's* *P'i-p'a chi,* were among the most widely performed plays in the early *ch'uan-ch'i** repertoire. They are also referred to as "Ching Liu Pai Sha" 荊劉拜殺, an anagrammatic conflation using one word from each of the four titles. They are generally assumed to date from the late Yüan or early Ming dynasties, but are with one exception preserved only in heavily adapted editions of the late sixteenth and early seventeenth centuries. These editions may be divided into two groups: more refined, literary ones, probably meant for reading, and crude and popular ones, probably reflecting stage practice. Late Ming critics often deprecated these plays for their simplicity of language, or even vulgarity.

The *Ching-ch'ai chi* 荊釵記 (The Thorn Hairpin) shows in many details of its plot a striking similarity to *P'i-p'a chi.* It apparently was written to provide even more immaculate paragons of virtue than Kao Ming's Ts'ai Yung and Chao Wu-niang. In *Ching-ch'ai chi* the poor young student Wang Shih-p'eng 王十朋 leaves for the capital to take part in the examinations shortly after his marriage to Ch'ien Yü-lien 錢玉蓮, who had preferred him to his rich friend Sun Ju-ch'üan 孫如權. After Wang's success in the examinations, the chancellor wants him to marry his daughter and, when Wang refuses, has him appointed to an outlying district. Wang's letter to his family, informing them of this state of affairs, is intercepted by Sun and replaced by one in which Wang divorces his wife. When her mother-in-law urges her to marry Sun, Ch'ien Yü-lien attempts to commit suicide by jumping into a river, but she is saved from drowning by the official Ch'ien Tsai-ho 錢載和, who is en route to his post. A servant sent out by Ch'ien Tsai-ho to inquire about Wang erroneously reports him deceased. Eventually the couple is reunited when both, each believing the partner dead, perform sacrifices to the wandering ghost in a temple in Soochow. The play derives its name from the thorn hairpin that is Wang's only betrothal gift and that in the end, when he cannot believe that Ch'ien Yü-lien is still alive, proves her to be his wife. Early sources ascribe the play to K'o Tan-ch'iu 柯丹丘, about whom nothing else is known. Wang Kuo-wei's attribution to Chu Ch'üan* is not generally accepted.

The plot of *Pai-yüeh t'ing* 拜月亭 (Moon Prayer Pavilion, also known as *Yu-kuei chi* 幽閨記 [Women's Quarters]) is extremely complicated. The play is set during the final decades of the Chin dynasty, which saw many Mongol incursions. In the capital Chung-tu 中都 (modern Peking), the young student Chiang Shih-lung 蔣世隆 becomes the sworn brother of T'o-man Hsing-fu 陀滿興福, the son of a patriotic Chin chancellor. After the fall of the capital, Chiang Shih-lung flees the invaders together with his sister Chiang Jui-lien 蔣瑞蓮. They are separated in the melée, and when he searches for her, shouting her name, he comes across Wang Jui-lan 王瑞蘭, the daughter of the minister of war (who is on a mission to the Mongols), who has become separated fom her mother. Chiang Shih-lung and Wang Jui-lan continue southward together and soon become man and wife. They are forcibly separated by Minister Wang, who, returning from his mission, meets the couple at an inn. Later he also finds his wife, who has adopted Chiang Jui-lien as a daughter. When, in the new capital (Kaifeng), Chiang Jui-lien overhears Wang Jui-lan praying at night to the moon, she discovers Jui-lan is in love with her brother. Eventually Wang Jui-lan is reunited with Chiang Shih-lung, after he has passed the metropolitan examinations with highest honors, while Chiang Jui-lien is married to T'o-man Hsing-fu, who is the top graduate in the military examinations.

Some sixteenth-century sources ascribe *Pai-yüeh t'ing* to a certain Shih Hui 施惠, who in one seventeenth-century source is called a physician from Wu-men 吳門 (Soochow). He has also been identified with a Hangchow merchant of that name, mentioned in the *Lu kuei pu.** The story of *Pai-yüeh t'ing* had also been adapted as a *tsa-chü** of the same title by Kuan Han-ch'ing*; this *tsa-chü* has been preserved only in a Yüan edition.

If *Pai-yüeh t'ing*, in contrast to *Ching-ch'ai chi*, stressed romantic love, *Pai-t'u chi* 白兔記 (The White Hare) dramatizes another tale of wifely devotion. This *ch'uan-ch'i* tells the story of Liu Chih-yüan 劉智遠 and Li San-niang 李三娘, which also had been adapted as a *chu-kung-tiao** (see *Liu Chih-yüan chu-kung-tiao*) and a *tsa-chü* (now lost) and treated in *p'ing-hua.** The historical Liu Chih-yüan was a soldier who rose from the ranks to become the founder of the short-lived Later Han dynasty (947-950) in Northern China. *Pai-t'u chi* recounts how the young and destitute Liu Chih-yüan is hired as a farmhand by the village squire Li, who later, aware of Liu Chih-yüan's future greatness, marries his daughter Li San-niang to him. After the death of squire Li, his son and his wife make life miserable for their brother-in-law, who finds a miraculous suit of armor and decides to leave his pregnant wife to join the army. In the provincial capital the governor also soon realizes Liu Chih-yüan's promise and forces him to marry his daughter. Meanwhile, in the village Li San-niang is treated as a slave and has to give birth to her child without any help. She has the baby boy delivered to his father, whereupon he is brought up by Liu Chih-yüan's second wife without knowing that she is not his real mother.

Sixteen years later, when Liu Chih-yüan himself has become governor, his son, while hunting, is led by a miraculous white hare to a village where a woman at the well-side recounts to him her life of misery and woe because of her fidelity to the husband who left her many years ago. The boy, puzzled by the correspondence in names, reports this meeting to his father, who realizes the woman must have been Li San-niang. To test her fidelity, he presents himself to her next day in the guise of a poor common soldier. When eventually Liu Chih-yüan is reunited with Li San-niang, his second wife willingly cedes her preeminent position in the household, as in *P'i-p'a chi*. According to the *chia-men* or opening scene of the recently discovered edition of *Pai-t'u chi* from the Ch'eng-hua period (1465-1488), the play was written by members of the *Yung-chia shu-hui* (see *shu-hui*). The various late Ming editions show remarkable divergencies.

The last play, *Sha-kou chi* 殺狗記 (Killing a Dog), tells the tale of two brothers, Sun Hua 孫華 and Sun Jung 孫榮. Under the spell of two ne'er-do-wells, Sun Hua, despite the pleadings of his wife Yang Yüeh-chen 楊月貞, drives his younger brother from the house and keeps their rich inheritance to himself. To effect a reconciliation, Yang Yüeh-chen buys a big dog, kills it, and places the corpse, dressed as a man, in front of the backgate of the house. When her husband returns from a drinking party that night, he stumbles over it and, believing it to be a human corpse, is afraid he will be accused of murder. When he looks for help to carry the corpse away and bury it someplace, the idlers turn him a deaf ear—only Sun Hua is willing to risk his life. In this way family concord is reestablished by Yang Yüeh-chen's wifely wisdom.

Sha-kou chi is often attributed to a certain Hsü Chen 徐畖, who lived in the early years of the Ming dynasty. It has also been argued that the play is by Hsiao Te-hsiang 蕭德祥, a Hangchow medical man of the early fourteenth century, who appears in *Lu kuei pu* and may also be the author of *Hsiao Sun t'u* (see *Yung-lo ta-tien hsi-wen san-chung*). Some scholars take Hsiao Te-hsiang to be the writer of a *tsa-chü* on the same subject, *Sha-kou ch'üan-fu* 殺狗勸夫 (Admonishing One's Husband by Killing a Dog), which is more generally believed to be an anonymous work.

EDITIONS:
Ku-pen, I.
Liu-shih.
Ming Ch'eng-hua shuo-ch'ang tz'u-hua ts'ung-k'an 明成化說唱詞話 叢刊. Shanghai, 1973. Also contains a photographic reprint of the Ch'eng-hua edition of the *Hsin-pien Liu Chih-yüan huan-hsiang Pai-t'u-chi* 新編劉知遠幻 想白 兔記.

STUDIES:
Birch, Cyril. "Tragedy and Melodrama in Early *Ch'uan-ch'i* Plays: 'Lute Song' and 'Thorn Hairpin' Compared," in *BSOAS*, 36 (1973), 228-247.
Chao, Ching-shen 趙景深. "Ming Ch'eng-hua pen nan-hsi Pai-t'u-chi te fa-hsien" 明成化本 南戲白兔記的發現, *Wen-wu*, 1973.1, 44-47.
Ch'ien, Nan-yang 錢南揚. *Hsi-wen kai-lun* 戲文 概論. Shanghai, 1981.
Chu, Tzu-li 朱自力. *Pai-yüeh-t'ing k'ao-shu* 拜月 亭考述. Taipei, 1969.
Liu, Hsiao-p'eng 劉效鵬. "Yung-lo ta-tien san-pen hsi-wen yü wu-ta nan-hsi te chieh-kou pi-chiao" 永樂大典三本戲文與五大南戲的結構比 較, *Wen-hsüeh p'ing-lun* (Taipei), 3 (1976), 63-134.

—IT and WI

Su Ch'e 蘇轍 (*tzu*, Tzu-yu 子由, 1039-1112) was the second son of Su Hsün* and the younger brother of Su Shih.* Although his achievements are overshadowed by theirs, he was a conscientious scholar and official as well as a consumate prose essayist, considered one of the "Eight Great Prose Masters of the T'ang and Sung" (see Han Yü). His works are one of the best contemporary sources for the study of the effects of Wang An-shih's New Policies, to which Su was basically opposed.

Su's official career was determined by the political factionalism of his day. Although he passed the famous *chin-shih* examination of 1057, administrated by Ou-yang Hsiu,* with high marks and was successful in another special examination a few years later, his opposition to Wang An-shih* and his outspoken criticism of the emperor caused him to be given only minor provincial posts before 1086, when the Conservatives came to power. In the provinces, he continued to write polemical reports and essays in opposition to the New Policies. From 1086 to 1093, he held a number of important appointments in Kai-feng as a member of the *Shu-tang* 蜀黨 (Szechwan faction) then favored by the Empress Dowager Hsüan-jen who was acting Regent. During this time, he impeached one of Wang's supporters, wrote many essays on politics and adminstration, and negotiated a peace treaty with the Hsi-Hsia kingdom. He was also honored as a Han-lin Academician. When the latter-day followers of Wang An-shih came to power again under Emperor Che-tsung in 1193, his official career was basically ended. He was demoted and sent into exile for several years. Although he was allowed to return to court in 1101 when Hui-tsung took the throne, he was once more demoted by the vindictive Ts'ai Ching. At this point, he went into seclusion, retired one year later, and spent the last years of his life in study and writing.

Su's voluminous works include scholarly commentaries on the *Shih-ching*,* the *Ch'un-ch'iu* (see *ching*—it was the favorite classic of the conservative faction), and the *Lao-tzu* (in keeping with the eclectic interests of the Su family). He also wrote a study of ancient history called the *Ku-shih* 古史. *Luan-ch'eng chi* 欒城集 in 96 *chüan*, is a large collection of Su's essays, memorials, letters, and other miscellaneous writings, which Su himself edited.

EDITIONS:
Ch'un-ch'iu chi-chieh 春秋集解. 2v. Taipei, 1967.
Ku-shih. 3v. Taipei, 1976.
Lao-tzu chieh 老子解. 2v. Taipei, 1965.
Luan-ch'eng chi. 20v. *SPTK;* and 18v. *SPPY*.
Luan-ch'eng ying-chao chi 欒城應詔集. 2v. *SPTK*.

Lung-ch'uan lüeh-chih, pieh-chih 龍川略志, 別志. Shanghai, 1920.

San Su wen-hsüan 三蘇文選. Yeh Yü-lin 葉玉麟, ed. Hong Kong, 1966.

San Su wen-hsüan p'ing-chieh 三蘇文選評解. Ch'en Hsiung-hsün 陳雄勳, ed. Taipei, 1967.

STUDIES:

Lin, Yutang. *The Gay Genius.* New York, 1948.

SB, pp. 882-885.

Sun, Ju-t'ing. *Su Ying-pin nien-piao* 蘇穎濱年表, in *Yung-lo ta-tien* 永樂大典, v. 2399.

—MSD

Su Hsün 蘇洵 (*tzu,* Ming-yün 明允, *hao,* Lao-ch'üan Hsien-sheng 老泉先生, 1009-1066) was the father of Su Shih* and Su Ch'e* and, from Ming times on, has been ranked with his illustrious sons as one of the "Eight Great Prose Masters of the T'ang and Sung" (see Han Yü). He was primarily a political essayist and his chief works consist of a number of penetrating essays on various themes in Chinese politics, history, and government, which taken as a whole offer an unorthodox critique of Confucian social ideology. He was lionized by Ou-yang Hsiu* and other high officials of the Chia-yu period (1056-1063), who praised his works as models for the new prose style they advocated as the basis for reforming Confucian literature, scholarship, and the examination system. Subsequently, Su's rhetorical style continued to receive high praise in standard anthologies, but his political ideas were passed over for having gone beyond the bounds of the orthodox post-Sung Neo-Confucian consensus.

Su's life and career revolved around his wife, his sons, and his studies, in that order, and he was often held up as a model to encourage late starters on the road to fame through scholarship. Coming from an obscure provincial family in southwestern Szechwan, and armed with an impressive though improbable genealogy stressing social virtue over class distinction, Su married an able and industrious woman of the wealthy Ch'eng 程 clan, and she supported him by running a clothing store during his early wanderings and his later studies. It was only after Su Shih was born in 1037, that Su Hsün, then nearing thirty, finally began to study for the official examinations. He failed twice, in 1038 and 1047, and never again dared to face the examiners; but this shock inspired him, according to a famous letter he wrote to Ou-yang Hsiu in 1056, to seclude himself for eight years to study the works of Confucius, Mencius, Han Yü,* and all of the "sages and worthies" of Chinese history until he reached a sort of "sudden illumination," after which he feverishly wrote down his thoughts in the essays that established his fame. His reputation was confirmed in 1057 when his essays were advertised by Ou-yang Hsiu and others as the equal of the works of Ssu-ma Ch'ien,* Chia I,* and other famous writers, while Su Shih was placing second and Su Ch'e near the top in the renowned *chin-shih* examination—in which *ku-wen** essays received preference—of the same year.

Su's most original writing is contained in the essays entitled "Liu ching lun" 六經論 (On the Six Classics) in which he presented a realistic view of the Confucian sages' manipulative strategies (similar to the *Tsung-heng* 縱橫 school of the Warring States) to employ certain texts they held up (particularly the religious symbolism of the *I-ching* [see *ching*] and the classics of music and poetry) to restrain human nature in society. He also argues that poetry, as a kind of catharsis, permits one to express anger or desire without falling into improper conduct. In further essays on contemporary politics, Su extended this novel thesis to a discussion of the dialectical relationship between imperial authority and social customs (including the historical development of social institutions) that concluded with the adumbration of a concept of historical contingency aimed at reducing the scope of imperial power and increasing the role of men of ability in the government of the state. He found his available models for such men in the intimate advisers and heroic talents of the Warring States and Early Han periods, men whose natural abilities (*T'ien-ts'ai,* "Heaven-sent talents," as opposed to Confucian virtues or literary talents, i.e., book learning) were recognized by connoisseurs of men, who gave them their opportunity to serve—see his "Yang Ts'ai" (On Nurturing Talent). In literature as well, Su took the diplomatic polemics of Su Ch'in and Chang I in the *Chan-kuo ts'e** as his models for a rhetoric of contingent political action rather than the orthodox transmission of a predetermined morally correct *Tao,* or Confucian Way. In all of his works, including a corpus of unskillful but bravura verse, the workings of a powerful and honest mind seeking answers to important questions and untrammeled by any fixed ideological shackles can be sensed.

EDITIONS:

Chia-yu chi 嘉祐集. 2v. *SPTK.* Reset and punctuated, Taipei, 1968.

San Su Wen-hsüan chiao-chien-p'ing 三蘇文選校箋評. Ch'en Hsiung-hsün 陳雄勳, ed. Taipei, 1969.

Su Lao-ch'üan chi 蘇老泉集. N.p., 1825.

Su Lao-ch'üan Hsien-sheng ch'uan-chi 蘇老泉先生全集. Shao Jen-hung 邵仁泓 ed., 1698.

TRANSLATIONS:

Margouliès, Georges. "Dissertation sur Kouan Tchong" (管仲論) and "Dissertation sur les Six Royaumes" (六國論), *Le Kou-wen chinois,* Paris, 1925, pp. 264-266 and 267-240.

STUDIES:

Chang, P'u-min 張樸民. "Huai-ts'ai pu-yü te Su Lao-ch'uan" 懷才不遇的蘇老泉, in *T'ang Sung pa-ta-chia p'ing-chuan* 唐宋八大家評傳, Taipei, 1978, pp. 95-108.

Hatch, George C. "The Thought of Su Hsün: An Essay in the Social Meaning of Intellectual Pluralism in Northern Sung." Unpublished Ph.D. dissertation, University of Washington, 1972.

K'ang, I-yung 康義勇, ed. "Su Hsün" 蘇洵, in *T'ang Sung San-wen hsüan-chu* 唐宋散文選註, Kaohsiung, 1981, pp. 270-285.

San Su nien-p'u hui-cheng 三蘇年譜彙證. I Su-min 易蘇民, ed. Taipei, 1969.

SB, pp. 885-900.

—MSD

Su Shih 蘇軾 (*tzu,* Tzu-chan 子瞻, *hao,* Tung-p'o 東坡, 1037-1101) was born in Mei-shan 眉山 (Szechwan) to a family of scholarly distinction. The so-called "Three Sus" were Su Shih, his father Su Hsün,* and his younger brother Su Ch'e*—all three were among the Eight Great Prose Masters of T'ang and Sung (see Han Yü). The two Su brothers earned their *chin-shih* degrees in 1057, and it was in that year that the chief examiner Ou-yang Hsiu* came to notice the talents of Su Shih.

Su Shih was one of the few Chinese literati to have mastered virtually all literary and artistic forms—*shih** poetry, *tz'u** poetry, *fu,** prose essays, calligraphy, and painting. His *shih,* especially the seven-character old-style poetry, was known for its spontaneity. About 2400 *shih* poems by Su are extant today, most of them explicit descriptions of the poet's actual experiences. He produced only 350 *tz'u* poems, but they played a vital role in widening the poetic scope of this genre. In the hands of Su, *tz'u* poetry became a major literary genre through which a poet could express the full range of his feelings and ideas. Su is famous not only for his many stylistic innovations in *tz'u,* but also as the founder of the school of *hao-fang* 豪放 (heroic abandon).

The tendency to be unrestrained characterizes Su's style. The art of writing prose, according to him, was no more than letting words flow where they should flow and stop where they should stop. Su often compared the art of painting to that of poetry, saying that both should, like streaming water, run spontaneously. This emphasis on the expressive function of art, however, is complemented by the impression of objectification so prevalent in Su's works. Such is exactly what good art should be: at once a spontaneous expression of feelings and an objective rendering of them.

Su's literary experiences were enriched by his many political setbacks. His famous series of political writings criticizing the emperor and the reformist Grand Councilor Wang An-shih* resulted in repeated demotions to insignificant provincial posts and exile to such remote places as Hainan Island. All his life he moved from place to place, from post to post. Thus, the theme of separation stands out powerfully in his poetry.

Despite these sad experiences, Su manifested in his literature a transcendental outlook that rose above momentary human sorrow. His philosophical affirmation of the meaning of human existence was best expressed by the two prose-poems entitled "Ch'ih-pi fu" 赤壁賦 (The Red Cliff). Su's genuine interest in life made it possible for him to be optimistic even in difficult times. For example, during his exile in Huang-chou 黃州 (1080-1083), he contented himself with the lonely life of farming and compared himself to T'ao Ch'ien.* Life in Huang-chou was so valuable to him that he began to call himself Tung-p'o (Eastern Slope) after the name of his farm. In his old age Su wrote 120 *shih* poems following T'ao Ch'ien's rhyme schemes; they are epitomes of his transcendental spirit.

EDITIONS:

Ch'en, Erh-tung 陳邇冬, ed. *Su Tung-p'o shih tz'u hsüan* 蘇東坡詩詞選. Peking, 1979.

Ch'ien, Chung-shu 錢鍾書, ed. *Sung-shih hsüan-chu* 宋詩選註, 1958; rpt. Peking, 1979, pp. 75-86.

Ch'üan Sung-tz'u, v. 1, pp. 277-337.

Feng, Ying-liu 馮應榴, ed. and annot. *Su Shih shih-chi* 蘇軾詩集. 8v. Peking, 1981.

Lung, Mu-hsün 龍沐勛, ed. *Tung-p'o yüeh-fu chien* 東坡樂府箋. Shanghai, 1958.

Su Tung-p'o chi 蘇東坡集. *Kuo-hsüeh chi-pen ts'ung-shu* edition. Shanghai, 1933; rpt. Peking, 1958; rpt. Taipei, 1969.

Su Tung-p'o ch'üan-chi 蘇東坡全集. 2v. Taipei, 1974.

Ts'ao, Shu-ming 曹樹銘, ed. *Tung-p'o tz'u* 東坡詞. Hong Kong, 1968.

TRANSLATIONS

Ayling, *Collection*, pp. 111-123.
———, *Further Collection*, pp. 65-89.
Demiéville, *Anthologie*, pp. 346-352, 385-386.
Liu, *Classical Prose*, pp. 225-285.
Liu, *Lyricists*, pp. 121-160.
Watson, Burton, trans. *Su Tung-p'o: Selections from a Sung Dynasty Poet*. New York, 1965.

STUDIES:

Bush, Susan. *The Chinese Literati on Painting: Su Shih (1037-1101) to Tung Ch'i-ch'ang (1555-1636)*, Cambridge, 1971, pp. 29-43.

Chang, *Evolution*, pp. 158-206. Includes translations.

Chen, Diane Yu-shih. "Change and Contribution in Su Shih's Theory of Literature: A Note on His 'Ch'ih-pi-fu'," *MS*, 31 (1974-75), 375-392.

Cheng, Chien. "Su Tung-p'o and Hsin Chia-hsuan: A Comparison," *TkR*, 1.2 (October 1970), 45-57.

Cheng, Ch'ien. "Liu Yung and Su Shih in the Evolution of *Tz'u* Poetry," Ying-hsiu Chou trans., *Renditions*, 11/12 (Spring/Autumn 1979), 143-156.

Ginsberg, Stanley M. "Alienation and Reconciliation of a Chinese Poet: The Huangzhou Exile of Su Shih." Unpublished Ph.D. dissertation, University of Wisconsin, 1974.

Holzman, Donald. "Une Fête Chez Su Shih à Huang Chou en 1082," *Etudes Song In Memoriam E. Balazs*, Paris, 1980, pp. 121-137 Includes translations into French.

Lin, Yutang. *The Gay Genius*. New York, 1947. Includes translations.

Liu, *Lyricists*, pp. 121-160. Includes translations.

SB, pp. 900-968.

Yu, Hsin-li 游信利. *Su Tung-p'o te wen-hsüeh li-lun* 蘇東坡的文學理論. Taipei, 1981.

—KIC

Su Shun-ch'in 蘇舜欽 (*tzu*, Tzu-mei 子美, 1008-1048) was, along with Ou-yang Hsiu* and Mei Yao-ch'en,* one of the major early Northern Sung *shih** poets. His ancestors came from modern Chung-chiang County in Szechwan, but he was born in the Northern Sung capital Kaifeng. Su received his *chin-shih* degree when he was twenty-six years old and then served in a succession of fairly minor local- and central-government posts. Throughout these years he was in sympathy with the reformist policies of Fan Chung-yen,* and eventually the more conservative elements in court managed to have him stripped of his titles, after which he retired to live in Soochow. He was later reinstated to a local post but soon died at the age of only forty (Ou-yang Hsiu passed away at sixty-five and Mei Yao-ch'en at fifty-eight).

Su Shun-ch'in's major contribution to Chinese letters lay in his participation in the establishment of a new style of poetry, which represented a major break with previous verse and was the foundation upon which later Sung poets built. During the early Sung dynasty, the *Hsi-k'un t'i* (see *Hsi-k'un ch'ou-ch'ang chi*) was popular. Hsi-k'un poets found their major inspiration in the highly allusive and ornate poetry of the late T'ang poet Li Shang-yin,* but their performance was not up to that of their inimitable master. In fact, earlier Northern Sung authors such as Wang Yü-ch'eng* and Lin Pu 林逋 (967-1028) had already written in a style quite different from the Hsi-k'un poets, but it was not until Su Shun-ch'in's time that a definite break with the older tradition was made. Su and Mei discarded Li Shang-yin as their master and began developing their own style, one deeply indebted to the T'ang poets Tu Fu* and particularly Han Yü.* Ou-yang Hsiu also made important contributions to this new direction in Chinese verse, and his high position in court enabled him to serve as a patron to Su and Mei in the same way that he was able to promote the revival of the dormant *ku-wen** prose style.

Discussions of Su Shun-ch'in's contribution to the new Sung style inevitably center around a comparison of his achievements with those of Mei Yao-ch'en. Their patron Ou-yang Hsiu was the first critic to point out the differences, using such terms as *hao* 豪 (heroic) or *k'uang* 狂 (wild) to describe Su in contrast to *tan* 淡 (bland) or *ch'ing* 清 (pure) for Mei. Such a distinction is generally valid, and many critics have ascribed Su's more emotional and unrestrained style to his largely unsuccessful political career and his resentment toward the conservative powers in government.

Certainly Su Shun-ch'in shows an even greater tendency than either Ou-yang or Mei to use poetry as a vehicle for social protest, as in his "Ch'eng-nan kan-huai ch'eng Yung-shu" 城南感懷呈永叔 (Opening my Heart to Ou-yang Hsiu South of the City) or "Wu Yüeh ta-han" 吳越大旱 (The Great Drought in Wu and Yüeh), where he shows his strong compassion for the plight of the masses. There is also an important body of his poetry which attacks the Sung government's ineptitude in handling the Hsi-hsia threat from the northwest, and other poems which look forward to the great "patriotic verse" of such Southern Sung writers as Lu Yu.*

However, there is another side to Su Shun-ch'in's work, and here he is much closer to Mei Yao-ch'en. One of his most delightful poems is "Ch'eng-nan kuei-chih ta feng-hsüeh" 城南歸值大風雪 (Encountering a Blizzard While Returning Home from South of the City), in which he depicts how his face seems to be adorned by jade pendants (snow), and how the flush of youth seems to be restored to his skin (by the cold). The unorthodox poetic form, the freshness of imagery, the realistic description, and the gentle bantering tone of the work were all qualitites esteemed by late Sung authors. Although much of Su Shun-ch'in's verse is imbued by a more "heroic" or even tragic spirit than Mei's, Su also wrote a large number of poems describing the tranquil beauties of nature in that concrete, realistic style (so different from most T'ang nature poetry) which was to become the hallmark of Sung-dynasty literature.

In addition to his poetry, Su Shun-ch'in also left a modest body of prose writings. Although many of them are in the newly revived *ku-wen* style, they have not found the audience or acclaim enjoyed by Ou-yang Hsiu's prose works.

EDITIONS:

Su Hsüeh-shih chi 蘇學士集. *SPPY.*
Su Hsüeh-shih chi. SPTK.
Su Hsüeh-shih wen-chi 蘇學士文集. Shanghai, 1922.
Su Shun-ch'in chi 蘇舜欽集. Shanghai, 1961.

TRANSLATIONS:
Sunflower, pp. 332-333

STUDIES:
Chaves, *Mei Yao-ch'en,* pp. 26-28 and *passim.*
Huo, Sung-lin 霍松林. "Lun Su Shun-ch'in te wen-hsüeh chuang-tso" 論蘇舜欽的文學創作, *Wen-hsüeh i-ch'an tseng k'an,* 12 (February 1963), 101-115.
Hu, Yün-i 胡雲翼. *Sung-shih yen-chiu* 宋詩研究. Shanghai, 1933.
Yoshikawa, *Sung,* pp. 79-80.

—JDS

Su T'ing 蘇頲 (*tzu,* T'ing-shuo 廷碩, enfeoffed as the Duke of Hsü, Hsü-kuo kung 許國公, 670-727) was a high official and literary arbiter at the courts of emperors

Chung-tsung (r. 705-710) and Hsüan-tsung (r. 712-756). Together with Chang Yüeh* he was among the earliest of *p'ien-wen** prose writers to devote his energies to writing official, imperial documents. The writings of both men are said to have begun the trend towards the limitation of *p'ien-wen* style to bureaucratic writings, and they set the standard of prose writing in their time. Their names, since at least the eleventh century, have been linked together in the accolade, *Yen-Hsü ta-shou-pi* 燕許大手筆 (The Great Penmen, Dukes Yen and Hsü).

Su T'ing was from Wu-kung 武功, just west of the capital. His father, Su Kuei 蘇瓌 (639-710), was a noted scholar-official who had passed the special degree examination, the *Yu-su k'o* 幽素科 in 666 along with Wang Po.* The elder Su held high offices under Empress Wu (r. 684-705) and served as a Grand Councilor under Chung-tsung. Su T'ing passed the *chin-shih* examination in 690, and served as an Assistant Prefect in Wu-ch'eng 烏程 (modern Wu-hsing 吳興, Chekiang). In 696 he passed the special-degree examination *Hsien-liang fang-cheng* 賢良方正 and was eventually promoted to the post of Investigating Censor.

With the accession of Chung-tsung (705), and with Su Kuei's appointment as Grand Councilor, Su T'ing was promoted to Reviewing Policy Adviser and Academician in the Institute for the Cultivation of Literature, the institute which served as a reservoir of literary talent for Chung-tsung's entourage. Su participated, with other leading poets of the day, in the excursions organized by Chung-tsung, on which he would elicit cycles of poems from his courtiers. Many of the poems from these occasions are still extant. Su also became an important drafter of imperial edicts at this time.

When his father died in 710, Su T'ing was offered higher posts but declined to serve, probably to mourn his father's death. Su T'ing was back at the court following Hsüan-tsung's accession and in 713 was given the high post of Vice Minister of Works. In early 714, he was further promoted to the office of Executive of the Secretariat and also made Participant in the Drafting of Proclamations. Together with Li I 李乂 (649-716), Su was in charge of drafting all official edicts from 713 through 716. In the latter year, he was named Grand Councilor, and with Sung Ching 宋璟 (663-737), controlled these offices until both were demoted in 720. Su T'ing's demotion was to the office of Minister of Rites, a position he held until his death in 727. In 720 he was also sent to Szechwan as an inspecting official at I-chou 益州 (modern Ch'eng-tu 成都) and is credited with preventing an alliance of the Man people with the Tibetans. According to one account, he also interviewed the young Li Po* at this time and likened his poetry to that of Ssu-ma Hsiang-ju.*

By 724, Su T'ing was back at the court where he, Chang Yüeh, and Chang Chiu-ling* were leading court poets and edict writers for Hsüan-tsung. After his death, Su T'ing was granted the posthumous name Wen-hsin

Although prominent in his own day, very little was said about Su T'ing's writings subsequently. However, much of his work was, and is, extant. In the literary history of the years 705 to 730, he is overshadowed by many political peers, Sung Chih-wen (see Shen Ch'üan-ch'i), Li Chiao,* Chang Yüeh, and Chang Chiu-ling, among others. Most of his extant 102 poems date from Chung-tsung's reign. They were set to rhymes determined by the emperor and, generally speaking, are "court-poetry" written "at imperial command" (*ying-chih shih* 應制詩).

Almost all of Su T'ing's 290 extant prose pieces are edicts he wrote on the emperor's behalf. This figure alone assures Su T'ing's place in the history of Chinese prose. During the early eighth century there was an enhanced imperial interest in acquiring skilled prose writers for civil servants, and in promoting these men to top offices. Whereas prior to this time *p'ien-wen* prose writers (from Wang Po back to Hsü Ling—see *Yü-t'ai hsin-yung*) used the style primarily to write for themselves or for friends, subsequently their energies were devoted to writing for the emperor or for other civil servants. For a time, this had the effect of broadening the applications of *p'ien-wen* from purely literary to utilitarian purposes. Imperial interest in prose led to new norms and standardizations (promoted in some examinations), and eventually divorced the *p'ien-wen* style from belles lettres altogether, since it was seen as an "official" style.

Thus, Su T'ing is one of the earliest *p'ien-wen* writers after the Six Dynasties to have made a reputation solely for his official edicts, anticipating later masters such as Lu Chih,* Ch'üan Te-yü 權德輿 (759-818) and Li Te-yü 李德裕 (787-850).

In terms of style, Su T'ing's *p'ien-wen* followed most of the prosodic features of earlier, belletristic *p'ien-wen*. Because of its official applications, however, there was a tendency to limit the breadth of vocabulary, and allusive passages were held within the bounds of history and politics.

EDITIONS:

Ch'üan T'ang shih, v. 2, *ch.* 73-74, pp. 795-815, and v. 12, *ch.* 869 and 882, pp. 9851, 9967-9968.

Ch'üan T'ang wen, v. 6, *ch.* 250-258, pp. 3195-3314.

Su T'ing shih-chi 蘇頲詩集. Found only in T'ang poetry collectanea of the sixteenth and seventeenth centuries—no modern editions.

TRANSLATIONS:

Owen, *Early T'ang*, pp. 259, 282.

STUDIES:

Chang, Jen-ch'ing 張仁青. *Chung-kuo p'ien-wen fa-chan shih* 中國駢文發展史. Taipei, 1970, pp. 469-473.

—BL

Sui T'ang yen-i 隋唐演義 (Romance of the Sui and the T'ang) is a historical novel composed by Ch'u Jen-huo 褚人穫 (*c.* 1630-*c.* 1705) around 1675. One hundred chapters in length, the text narrates events of the Sui period and part of the T'ang, roughly the two centuries from 570 to 770.

The first half of the work concentrates alternately on the moral decadence of Emperor Yang of the Sui 隋煬帝 (r. 605-617), through whose sensuality and dereliction of duty his state falls, and the unrest and

suffering in the countryside that promote the rise of banditry and rebellion. The character receiving the most attention in the latter context is Ch'in Shu-pao 秦叔寶. Confronted frequently by difficult moral choices, Ch'in ultimately joins forces with Li Shih-min 李世民 (r. 627-649), the martial son of the first ruler of the emerging T'ang state. After a center section that relates various battlefield love affairs, the narrative proceeds rapidly through the sequence of early T'ang emperors from T'ai-tsu (r. 618-626) to Hsüan-tsung 玄宗 (r. 712-756, better known as Ming-huang). The reign of the latter constitutes the last quarter of the novel; he, like his regal predecessors, takes the throne with dedication to duty but falls prey to the pleasures of the flesh, thus putting his throne at risk. Ming-huang's well-known love affair with Yang Kuei-fei 楊貴妃 is recorded in detail. However, their liaison is shown to parallel that of the Emperor Yang and his favorite Chu Kuei-erh 朱貴兒; the novelist presents the former couple as reincarnations of the latter as a means to tie the work together.

Sui T'ang yen-i is a remarkable divergence from the ever-popular *San-kuo-chih yen-i** in structural terms. That is, instead of the rise and fall of states, this novel demonstrates how the personal morality of prominent persons produces a series of rise-fall cycles in society. Determinism appears here only to the extent that human transgression never goes unpunished. Emperor Yang, for example, could choose self-abnegation and thus strengthen his state. He steadfastly refuses to mend his ways and falls to assassins as a consequence.

Ch'u Jen-huo was a native of Ch'ang-chou 長洲 (in the Soochow district); men of his family were highly educated and may well have harbored Ming loyalist sentiments long into the Ch'ing period. Ch'u's courtesy names, Chia-hsüan 稼軒 and Hsüeh-chia 學稼, apparently refer to the Sung loyalist Hsin Ch'i-chi.* Many of Ch'u Jen-huo's extant writings were printed by his own publishing house, the Ssu-hsüeh Ts'ao-t'ang 四雪草堂 in Soochow. He published what was to become the standard edition of *Feng-shen yen-i** in the same year (1695) as *Sui T'ang yen-i*. His friends included the Han-lin Academician Chang Ch'ao, the dramatist Hung Sheng,* and the fiction critic Mao Tsung-kang.*

Sui-t'ang yen-i is not, strictly speaking, original; Ch'u Jen-huo copied or edited the bulk of his novel from earlier fiction. His sources included *ch'uan-ch'i** tales, *hua-pen** stories, historical anecdotes, and novels. Among the latter are *Hsi-yu chi,** *Sui T'ang liang-ch'ao chih-chuan* 隋唐兩朝志傳 (Chronicles of Two Courts, Sui and T'ang, anon., c. 1550; extant ed. 1619), *Sui Yang-ti yen-shih* 隋煬帝豔史 (The Merry Adventures of Emperor Yang of the Sui, anon., 1631), and *Sui shih i-wen* 隋史遺文 (Forgotten Tales of The Sui, by Yüan Yü-ling 袁于令 [1592-1674], 1633). From the first of these, Ch'u took little, and he condensed portions of the second to form several middle chapters. But a large section of the third and the bulk of the last are grafted into his narrative, usually with only minor modifications. The significance of the borrowed material is altered by its new function in *Sui T'ang yen-i;* throughout, Ch'u Jen-huo maintains a balance between borrowed elements contrasting violence, moral uprightness, political significance, and the like.

Sui shih i-wen was Ch'u Jen-huo's major source. Although artistically superior to Ch'u's work, this novel disappeared after its first edition, perhaps simply because Ch'u had incorporated its finest sections into his own novel. These deal for the most part with Ch'in Shu-pao, a young man of great physical strength who matures, after a long sequence of embarrassments and hard knocks, into an able but otherwise uninteresting military commander in the service of the T'ang founder. His creator, Yüan Yü-ling, used the realistic emotional and moral development of this character as a framework around which to build his outspoken attacks on the abuses of power and privilege in his day. Brigandage and its causes attract his particular ire, as it did that of Chin Sheng-t'an* in the latter's version of *Shui-hu chuan*. In addition to its realism and political and social seriousness,

Sui shih i-wen is to be praised for stylistic virtuosity. Yüan Yü-ling is here particularly successful in creating lively minor characters whose speech reflects the slangy colloquial of late Ming.

Yüan Yü-ling is better known as a playwright and poet than as a novelist, although he compiled two other historical novels in addition to *Sui shih i-wen*. The son of a distinguished family of Soochow literati, Yüan was also renowned for his rather bohemian behavior. Detractors called him physically and morally repulsive, identifying him as the man who surrendered Soochow to the Manchu invaders. The latter allegation is false; Yüan was in Peking during the conquest, and although he took a provincial position in the new Ch'ing government, he was soon cashiered for peculation.

As a poet and dramatist, Yüan's name is often linked with that of his friend Feng Meng-lung.* Both strove for a high degree of literary polish in poetry and perfection in both prosody and musical structure in theatrical pieces. Yüan dramatized one of Feng's short stories (*Chen-chu chi* 珍珠記 [The Pearl Shirt Story], employing the *Ku-chin hsiao-shuo* version); his best-known play was *Hsi-lou chi* 西樓記 (The Western Mansion) in the *ch'uan-ch'i** format.

EDITIONS:

Sui-shih i-wen. Ho Li-ku 何理谷 [Robert E. Hegel], ed. Taipei, 1975. Includes several useful studies by C. T. Hsia and others.

Sui T'ang yen-i. 2v. Shanghai, 1956. One of several good modern reprints of the novel.

Ssu-hsüeh Ts'ao-t'ang ch'ung-pien t'ung-su Sui T'ang yen-i 四雪草堂重編通俗隋唐演義. 20 *chüan*. Soochow, 1695. Still accessible.

STUDIES:

Ch'en Wan-i 陳萬益. "Chu-men yü ts'ao-mang: Lun *Sui T'ang yen-i* li te Ch'in Ch'iung" 朱門與草莽：論隋唐演義裡的秦瓊, *Hsien-tai wen-hsüeh*, 45 (December 1971), 149-164.

Feng, Ch'eng-chi 馮承基. "Lun *Sui T'ang yen-i* ching-ts'ai chih ch'u yin-chi chang-hui hsiao-shuo te hsüan-lu wen-t'i" 論隋唐演義精采之處因及章回小說的選錄問題. *Hsien-tai wen-hsüeh*, 33 (December 1967), 8-28.

Harada, Suekiyo 原田季清. "Zui Tō kōbō haishi kō" 隋唐興亡稗史考, *Ritsumeikan daigaku ronsō*, 15 (August 1943), 22-31.

Hegel, Robert E. "Maturation and Conflicting Values: Two Novelists' Portraits of The Chinese Hero Ch'in Shu-pao," in *Chinese Fiction*, pp. 115-150.

———. "*Sui T'ang yen-i* and The Aesthetics of the Seventeenth-Century Suchou Elite," in *Chinese Narrative*, pp. 124-159.

———. *The Novel in Seventeenth-Century China*. New York, 1981. Studies of six novels of the period, including *Sui T'ang yen-i* and *Sui-shih i-wen*.

Hsia, Chi-an 夏濟安. "I-tse ku-shih, liang-chung hsieh-fa" 一則故事，兩種寫法, *Wen-hsüeh tsa-chih* (Taipei), 5.5 (January 1959), 16-23.

—REH

Sung Lien 宋濂 (*tzu*, Ching-lien 景濂, 1310-1381), prose writer and poet, was a literary and political adviser to the Ming-dynasty founder and one of the principal figures in the Yüan-dynasty Chin-hua 金華 school of Neo-Confucianism. He was a strong advocate of the *ku-wen** prose style and a precursor of the Archaist movement of later Ming prose theorists.

Born in Chin-hua County 金華縣, Wu-chou Route 婺州路 (modern Chekiang), he joined his native region's renowned academies as a youth, studying with such leading literary figures as Liu Kuan 柳貫 (1270-1342), Huang Chin 黃溍 (1277-1357), and Ou-yang Hsüan 歐陽玄 (1283-1357). His most important teacher was probably Wu Lai 吳萊 (1296-1340), who lived in P'u-chiang County 浦江縣 (also in Wu-chou Route). Wu was known for his unusually eclectic philosophical interests (Buddhism and Taoism as well as Confucianism) and catholic tastes in literature, and Sung Lien may well owe his later studies of Buddhist and Taoist texts to Wu Lai's example. After Wu's death, Sung succeeded to the directorship of a private family-school Wu had headed. He thereupon transferred his legal residence from Chin-hua to P'u-chiang.

From the time he became director of this school at the age of thirty until he first served the rebel Ming government at the age of fifty, Sung Lien lived as a semi-reclusive man of letters. His fame as a writer of prose and poetry attracted the attention of most of his literary contemporaries, including those who were in the active service of the Yüan government. He wrote commemorative pieces for many of these people and through some of them obtained an appointment to the Yüan Han-lin Academy in 1349, though he never assumed the duties of this office. Eventually, Sung Lien moved his home to Ch'ing-lo Mountain 青蘿山 on the eastern border of P'u-chiang County, where he wrote and published anthologies of his prose and poetry as well as commentaries on the classics. By the end of the Yüan, Sung was one of the best known and most widely read of Chinese poets and essayists.

When the forces of the future Ming emperor, Chu Yüan-chang 朱元璋 (1328-1398), conquered the Chin-hua region in 1359, Sung was summoned to serve the aspirant dynasty and to lend his literary renown to the rebel cause. At first he was appointed a director of the Chin-hua Confucian Academy, but in 1360 he was summoned to Nanking to serve as an adviser to Chu and to provide his court with a mantle of Confucian learning and respectability. Sung also served as court diarist, and while in temporary retirement during the period 1365-1368, he composed many official statements for Chu Yüan-chang.

With the official proclamation of the Ming dynasty in 1368, Sung returned to Nanking and was directed to be one of the chief compilers of the official history of the Yüan, the *Yüan-shih* 元史. He finished most of his assignment in six months; materials acquired with the conquest of Peking were added and the completed work was eventually submitted to the emperor in 1370. Because of the haste with which most of it was compiled, the history has many weaknesses and is generally considered to be the poorest done on any dynasty.

For the next seven years, Sung served in various offices in the Han-lin Academy and was the emperor's close adviser on matters of history and classical studies. During this period he directed numerous compilation commissions, including one to compile a daily record of early Ming history, and others to record the policy decisions of those times. Sung also served as

735

tutor to the heir apparent, Chu Piao 朱標 (1355-1392), a post he had held since 1360. In 1377, Sung was allowed to resign. Subsequently, his residence in P'u-chiang became the object of official and unofficial pilgrimages from Nanking, and his activities were the subject of concern on the part of the emperor.

In 1379 Sung was caught up in the treason case of Hu Wei-yung 胡惟庸 (d. 1380). Many of his family members were executed for their involvement, but Sung himself escaped the ensuing slaughter through the intercession of Chu Piao and the empress, and his death sentence was commuted. However, in 1381 he died while on his way to exile in Szechwan (whether of natural causes or by suicide is not clear). In 1514, the Ming dynasty granted him the posthumous title of Wen-hsien 文憲.

As a Chin-hua erudite, Sung Lien could trace his roots to Lü Tsu-ch'ien (1137-1181), the friend of Chu Hsi. These antecedents were significant in the fourteenth century because they implied that men such as Sung Lien maintained a broad range of interests in all strands of Confucian, Neo-Confucian, and non-Confucian ideas. This was in contrast to the circumscription of erudition symbolized in the canonization of Chu Hsi's interpretations of the Confucian Classics, and by their use as the sole means of answering questions on the crucial civil-service examination under the Yüan.

Chin-hua erudites also promoted an interest in *ku-wen* prose style, though Sung Lien's ideas on prose were less concerned with the stylistic aspects of *ku-wen* (irregular lines and the absence of parallel expressions) than with the function of the style, allowing the writer to clearly and straightforwardly articulate his ideas. He spoke of the principles by which a writer conceived and then gave birth to the ideas which were later put into writing. Sung believed that in order to understand these principles, a writer had to examine their functions in the creation of ancient literature. Thus, *fu-ku* (recovery of ancient writings) was a study of the ideas and not of the forms used by ancient writers.

Sung Lien also wrote *p'ien-wen** prose, but the bulk of his private and official writings were in *ku-wen* style. In his critical writings on poetry, he was less in the mainstream of later Ming admiration of the T'ang poets, preferring to dwell upon the traditional notions of the didactic qualities of the poetry of the *Shih-ching.**

In addition to producing the *Yüan-shih*, Sung Lien also edited a phonetic dictionary, *Hung-wu cheng-yün* 洪武正韻. A more important effort was his own collection of biographies of the famous writers and scholars of his native region, entitled *P'u-yang jen-wu chi*

Sung's writings were printed and circulated during his lifetime and were known in Japan, Korea, and Vietnam. Extant editions are reprints of sixteenth-century texts, the most complete being the *Sung Hsüeh-shih ch'üan chi* 浦陽人物記 of 1551 included in the *Ssu-k'u ch'üan-shu* (see Chi Yün). This edition is surpassed in comprehensiveness by another of 1810 (see below).

EDITIONS:

Sung, Lien 宋濂. *Sung Wen-hsien Kung chi* 宋文憲公集. SPPY. Reprint of 1810 edition, most comprehensive of Sung Lien anthologies.

STUDIES:

Ch'ien, Mu 錢穆. "Tu Ming-ch'u k'ai-kuo chu-ch'en shih wen chi" 讀明初開國諸臣詩文集, *Hsin-ya hsüeh-pao*, 6.2 (1964), 245-267.

DMB, pp. 1225-1231.

Hsiao, Chi-tsung 蕭繼宗. "Sung Lien," in Chang Ch'i-yün 張其昀 *et al.*, *Chung-kuo wen-hsüeh-shih lun-chi* 中國文學史論集, Taipei, 1958, v. 3, pp. 835-844.

Kuo, *P'i-p'ing shih*, v. 2, pp. 142-151, 161-164.
—BL

Sung-shih ch'ao 宋詩鈔 (Jottings from Sung Dynasty Poetry) was a highly influential anthology of Sung-dynasty poetry compiled in the Ch'ing. The original preface to the work is dated 1671 and is written by Wu Chih-chen 吳之振, who was himself the author of a collection of poems entitled *Huang-yeh ts'un-chuang shih-chi* 黃葉村莊詩集. However, Wu Tzu-mu 吳自牧 and the famous anti-Manchu writer Lü Liu-liang 呂留良 (1629-1683) are mentioned in the preface and also played an important role in the anthology's compilation. The rather puzzling lack of a preface by such a famous scholar as Lü may be a result of the general proscription placed on his work by Ch'ing authorities from the time his posthumous trial was concluded in 1733, after which his writings were sedulously ferreted out and burned by the Ch'ing government.

The *Sung-shih ch'ao* is the most complete anthology of Sung-dynasty *shih** poetry to date. It begins with the works of the early Northern Sung poet Wang Yü-ch'eng* and ends with such famous figures as Wen T'ien-hsiang 文天祥 (1236-1282). Over a hundred poets are included and the great length of the anthology allows for a wide presentation of each writer. The book's principal significance today is that it preserves much poetry by minor Sung authors, some of whose works are difficult to obtain.

The presently available texts of the *Sung-shih ch'ao* are not the same which left its original redactor's hands, since the work has undergone subsequent revisions. Originally the editors selected poems from one hundred prominent Sung-dynasty authors, but some relatively major writers such as Yen Yü (see *Ts'ang-lang shih-hua*), Hsieh Fang-te 謝枋得 (1226-1289), and Cheng Ssu-hsiao 鄭思肖 were left out, so the eighteenth-century scholar Ts'ao T'ing-tung 曹庭棟 added selections from these authors along with thirteen others to make a total of one hundred and sixteen. Also, when Lü Liu-liang's works were subsequently proscribed, publishers who printed the *Sung-shih ch'ao* cautiously eliminated words and poems that might be offensive to the Manchu authorities, a difficult task given the large amount of "patriotic" poetry written by such Southern Sung authors as Lu Yu* urging resistance to the Chin Tartars, whom the Manchus considered their ancestors. Finally, Wu Chih-chen seems to have compiled much of the anthology in great haste without consulting the best editions, so that further revisions were made in the nineteenth century when these textual inaccuracies became apparent.

As a whole, the anthology is a representative sampling of Sung-dynasty poetry, but

the editors display their prejudice toward early Northern Sung verse by totally omitting the Hsi-k'un 西崑 School and starting with Wang Yü-ch'eng. From their point of view the decision to omit these earlier authors was justifiable, since their writings lie outside what was considered the "Sung Style." In spite of some of the anthology's shortcomings, its importance to Ch'ing-dynasty literature cannot be overstressed. Throughout the Yüan and particularly the Ming dynasty, Sung poetry was generally despised, while poets lauded the High T'ang poets, especially Li Po* and Tu Fu,* as models for imitation. In spite of the rising spirit of innovation and protest in the sixteenth and early seventeenth centuries, Sung poetry does not seem to have to have grown much in popularity, and it was not until the late seventeenth and eighteenth centuries that there was a revival, of which the *Sung-shih ch'ao* was both a product and a catalyst.

The preface to the anthology is a highly significant document in the evolution of Ch'ing literary criticism and poetic style. In this work Wu Chih-chen bemoans the exaltation of T'ang poetry and the disdain for Sung poetry, which he says date back to the sixteenth century, but which actually began much earlier. On the relationship between T'ang and Sung verse, he states: "The poetry of Sung was transformed out of T'ang poetry, achieving its own self-realization, entirely eliminating the superficiality, and retaining the true spirit." He blames the low esteem for Sung poetry on earlier Ming anthologies of it, which purposely selected poems similar to T'ang verse and, hence, unrepresentative of the Sung style. Wu also approvingly quotes an earlier opinion on Sung poetry: "[It] chooses its subject matter widely, and its ideas are new, not plagiarizing even one word from earlier authors." In such statements the chief significance of Sung poetry for many eighteenth and nineteenth century authors is evident: it was a weapon against conservative and imitative tendencies in the Ch'ing poetic tradition. Many of the most innovative eighteenth- and nineteenth-century authors were deeply indebted to Sung poetry, and even Yüan Mei's* students noted the resemblance between his work and that of Yang Wan-li,* an author liberally represented in the *Sung-shih ch'ao*.

EDITIONS:

Sung-shih ch'ao. Shanghai, 1935.

Sung-shih ch'ao. Ssu-k'u ch'üan-shu chen-pen 四庫全書珍本. Taipei, 1979.

STUDIES:

Yuasa, Yukihiko 湯淺幸孫. "*Sō shi shō* no senja tachi hito ni yotte shi o sonsu" 宋詩鈔の選者たち人によって史を存す, *Chūgoku bungaku hō*, 20 (1965), 68-92.

—JDS

Sung-shih chi-shih 宋詩紀事 (Recorded Occasions in Sung Poetry), jointly compiled and edited by Li E 厲鶚 (*tzu*, T'ai-hung 太鴻, *hao*, Fan-hsieh 樊榭, 1692-1752) and Ma Yüeh-kuan 馬曰琯 (*tzu*, Ch'iu-yü 秋玉, *hao*, Hsieh-ku 嶰谷, 1688-1755). This is one of the largest compendia of Sung *shih** poetry ever assembled and an indispensable source to any serious student of the genre. Following the organizational format employed by the *T'ang-shih chi-shih*,* selections from the poetic works of Sung emperors and empresses are presented first (*chüan* 1). The main body of the anthology comprises *chüan* 2 through 81, which list poems by authors in approximate chronological order; works by writers whose dates could not be ascertained are found in *chüan* 82 and 83. Following are individual *chüan* dealing with such diverse categories as "[Poems from] the Palace Apartments," "Imperial Household," "Women," "Eunuchs," "Taoists," "Buddhists," and "Tributary States." The remaining four *chüan* (96-100) of the anthology are devoted to further categories such as "courtesans," "planchette (trace) productions," "spirits and specters," and "popular ditties." Each group of poems is preceded by a short biographical note on the author when such information was available. According to the preface (dated 1746), the poetic works of no fewer than 3,812 different authors are represented in the anthology.

The primary importance of the *Sung-shih chi-shih* is twofold: first, some (but not all) of the selections and fragments included by the compilers are culled from sources other than the standard collections; and second, the "notes" which sometimes accompany the biographical introductions or the individual poems often provide valuable background information regarding the poet's life, later critical opinions concerning his poetry, or relevant anecdotes from historical or geographical works, *pi-chi*,* epigraphic handbooks, etc. At times Li E or Ma Yüeh-kuan add their own "notes" to clarify points of possible confusion or else to provide the reader with additional background information.

An important supplement to this collection, in one hundred *chüan*, was published in 1893 by Lu Hsin-yüan 陸心源 (1834-1894), entitled *Sung-shih chi-shih pu-i* 補遺 (A Supplement to Recorded Occasions in Sung Poetry). Along with his *Supplement*, which includes poems and fragments by about three hundred poets not found in the *Sung-shih chi-shih*, Lu Hsin-yüan also published *Sung-shih chi-shih hsiao-chuan pu-cheng* 小傳補正 (Additions and Corrections to the Brief Biographies in Recorded Occasions in Sung Poetry) in four separate *chüan*. Scholars consulting either the *Sung-shih chi-shih* or the *Supplement* are urged to make use of the *Sung-shih chi-shih chu-che yin-te* 著者引得 (Index to Authors in Recorded Occasions in Sung Poetry), an invaluable index to the more than 6800 individual poets listed in both collections.

EDITIONS:

Sung-shih chi-shih. Original woodblock edition of 1746 (11th year of the Ch'ien-lung reign). Modern typeset reprints are found in the *Wan-yu wen-k'u* and *Basic Sinological Series* (*Kuo-hsüeh chi-pen ts'ung-shu*; 14v. Taipei, 1968).

Sung-shih chi-shih chu-che yin-te. William Hung *et al.*, eds. Harvard-Yenching Institute Sinological Index Series, 19. Rpt. Taipei, 1966.

Sung-shih chi-shih pu-i. Original woodblock edition of 1893; rpt., 8v., Taipei, 1971.

—JH and HF

Sung Wan 宋琬 (*tzu*, Yü-shan 玉叔, *hao*, Li-shang 荔裳 and Man-shan jen 漫山人, 1614-

1673), a well-known poet and calligrapher in his day, was a native of Lai-yang 萊陽 (Shantung). He obtained the *chin-shih* degree (1647) as his father and elder brother had done before him and was subsequently named to a position on the Board of Revenue. Thereafter he held a succession of positions at the district and provincial levels in the modern provinces of Anhwei, Kansu, Chihli, and Chekiang. Falsely implicated in a local rebellion in his native district by a fellow clansman, Sung Wan was arrested in 1661 and imprisoned for three years. Not until several years after he had been cleared of all charges, however, was he recalled to public service and named the Surveillance Commissioner of Szechwan. Shortly after being summoned to Peking for an interview with the emperor, he fell ill and died in that city.

Wang Shih-chen* (1634-1711), a leading poet-critic of the time, spoke highly of his poetry, and was perhaps responsible for linking Sung's name with the poet Shih Jun-chang* in the popular phrase "Sung of the North and Shih of the South." Other critics have commented on the vigorous northern manner of his verse, the excellence of his poems in the heptasyllabic old style and regulated verse, and the general tone of realism that is characteristic of his best poems. Modern scholars have assigned him to the T'ang and the Sung schools of poetry alike, thus reflecting considerable difference of opinion concerning the main stylistic features of his poetry (as well as the limited usefulness of such classifications). It is reasonable to regard him as a poet who responded to a wide range of classical literary infuences and who chose to explore different genres and styles at different times in his life. This innovative approach is evident in his experiments in the seldom-used sexasyllabic quatrain. His poems can be serious and contemplative at one moment, gently humorous at another, even those written when he was incarcerated. The thematic range and changing moods of his poetry are attractive qualities, but it is his warmth and depth of human feeling, his unruffled manner and temperate outlook, that are perhaps his most distinctive features as a poet.

Although chiefly remembered (but little studied) as a poet, Sung Wan was also regarded as an accomplished calligrapher in his day. He was the chief compiler of the gazetteer for Yung-p'ing County 永平 (Chihli) and the author of one play.

EDITIONS:
An-ya-t'ang shih-chi 安雅堂詩集 and *An-ya T'ang wei-k'o-kao* 安雅堂未刻稿 . SPPY.

STUDIES:
ECCP, p. 690.
Fu, *Ch'ing tsa-chü*, pp. 39-40.
Schultz, William. "Sung Wan and the Narrative Poem," *JCLTA*, 14.2 (May 1979), 9-26.
Tseng, "Ch'ing-tai tsa-chü," pp. 137-138.

—WS

Ta-ch'ü 大曲 is an ancient form of entertainment, the musical composition of which dates back to the Han, belonging then to the *hsiang-ho ko* 相和歌 (matching songs). By Wei-Chin times it had undergone substantial development. According to the "Yüeh-chih" 樂志 in the *Sung-shu* (see Shen Yüeh), among the music compositions in the three *ch'ing-shang* 清商 modes (i.e., the *ch'ing* 清 mode, the *p'ing* 平 mode, and the *se* 瑟 mode) prevalent in the Han-Wei times, there were sixteen *ta-ch'ü*, of which *Tung-men hsing* 東門行, *Che yang-liu hsing* 折楊柳行, *Mo-shang sang* 陌上桑, *Yen-ko hsing* 艷歌行, and *Pai-t'ou yin* 白頭吟, were most widely sung. Their influence continued even after the Six Dynasties. This kind of *ta-ch'ü* had music and words interwined in its structural scheme. Its main body was divided into a number of sections, called *chieh* 解. Besides having the *chieh*, a *ta-ch'ü* may also have *yen* 艷, *ch'ü* 趨, and *luan* 亂 sections. Kuo Mao-ch'ien 郭茂倩 (twelfth century), in his *Yüeh-fu shih-chi* 樂府詩集 notes: "*Yen* is used before the *ch'ü* 曲, while *ch'ü* 趨 and *luan* are after the *ch'ü* 曲." *Luan* as a structural coda, or envoi, had been extensively used in the *Ch'u-tz'u.** And in general the *ta-ch'ü* of Han-Wei times absorbed the structural elements of various musical compositions from the Warring States era.

After the Six Dynasties, the music of China proper was much influenced by that of the western border regions and Central Asia. *Yen-yüeh* 燕樂 (feast music) developed and became popular in the Sui and T'ang. There were marked changes in the *ta-ch'ü* during this time, both in its formal structure and in its mode of performance. The *yen-yüeh ta-ch'ü* reached its zenith in the T'ang and gradually declined during the Sung. According to the various contemporary sources on the *ta-ch'ü*, the structure of *yen-yüeh ta-ch'ü* can be summarized by the following table:

A. san-hsü 散序:
   1) san-hsü
   2) sa
B. chung-hsü 中序:
   1) p'ai-pien
   2) tien
   3) cheng-tien
C. p'o 破:
   1) ju-p'o
   2) hsü-ts'ui
   3) kun-pien
   4) shih-ts'ui
   5) kun-pien
   6) hsieh-p'ai
   7) sha-kun

(B.3 together with C.1-7 are known as *ch'ü-p'o* 曲破)

A *ta-ch'ü* consists of three main sections: *san-hsü*, *chung-hsü*, and *p'o*. The *san-hsü* is an instrumental piece with no words. It is followed by the *chung-hsü*, in slow tempo, with both music and words. Then comes the *p'o*, with music and words and dances, in accelerating tempo. Each main section consists of a number of smaller sections. Each of these smaller sections is called a *pien* 遍. *San-hsü* and *p'ai-pien* usually use several *pien* in succession. *Ta-ch'ü* was also known as *ta-pien* 大遍 in the Sung dynasty.

Ta-ch'ü as a whole consists of music, song, and dance. It contains both sound and action. Every *ta-ch'ü* is different in content, with numerous performers in different costumes of various colors. Well known *ta-ch'ü* of the T'ang, such as *Ni-ch'ang* 霓裳, *Lü yao* 綠腰, *Liang-chou* 涼州, and *Che chih* 柘枝, not only were applauded by the people of that time, but also had great influence on the later development of music and dance. Some of these *ta-ch'ü* even spread to Korea and Japan.

After the Northern Sung, *ta-ch'ü*, except for those that had been preserved in their entirety in the *Chiao-fang* 教坊 (Entertainment Bureau) established by the royal court, were abridged in their performance. There were two ways of abriging a *ta-ch'ü*: one was to use the last section of a *ta-pien*, the *p'o*, as the main body, to arrive at an abridged version called *ch'ü-p'o* 曲破; another was to pick out one of the *pien* from a *ta-pien* and tailor it to suit one's purpose; this was called *chai-pien* 摘遍. Some tunes used in Sung *tz'u** are *chai-pien* of *ta-ch'ü*, such as *Po mei chai-pien* 薄媚摘遍, *Fan ch'ing po chai-pien* 泛清波摘遍, *Shui tiao ko-t'ou* 水調歌頭, *Ch'i t'ien le* 齊天樂, and *Ni-ch'ang chung-hsü ti-i* 霓裳中序第一. *Ch'ü-p'o* and *chai-pien* have left their traces and influence in Sung and Yüan drama and in the art of storytelling by song.

In modern folk music, such as the *ku-yüeh* 鼓樂 of Sian 西安 and the temple music at Wu-t'ai Shan 五台山, remnants of T'ang-Sung *ta-ch'ü* can still be found. Exactly how these melodies are related to *ta-ch'ü*, however, has yet to be studied.

There is no extant record of the scores and librettos of *ta-ch'ü*. Fragmentary remains of librettos, such as the *Tao-kung po-mei* 道宮薄媚 written by Tung Ying 董穎 of the Sung, a *ta-ch'ü* singing the story of Hsi Shih 西施, can be found in a number of books, including Shen Yüeh's* *Sung-shu*, Kuo Mao-ch'ien's *Yüeh-fu shih-chi*, and Tseng Tsao's 曾慥 (*fl.* 1131-1163) *Yüeh-fu ya-tz'u* 樂府雅詞. Records of *ta-ch'ü* titles and records about such items as the form, the performance, and the costumes of *ta-ch'ü*, though fragmentary and scattered, are quite substantial.

SOURCES:

Kuo, Mao-ch'ien. *Yüeh-fu shih-chi.* 4v. Peking, 1979, pp. 377-638 ("hsiang-ho ko-tz'u" 相和歌辭).

STUDIES:

Ch'en, Chung-fan 陳中凡. "Ts'ung Sui-T'ang ta-ch'ü shih-t'an tang-shih ko-wu-hsi te hsing-ch'eng" 從隋唐大曲試探當時歌舞戲的形成, *Nan-ching ta-hsüeh hsüeh-pao*, 31.3 (1964).

Hsü, Chia-jui 徐嘉瑞. *Chin-ku wen-hsüeh kai-lun* 近古文學概論. Shanghai, 1936, pp. 141-183, citing Liu Yao-min 劉堯民, *Ta-ch'ü k'ao* 大曲考.

Jen, Pan-t'ang 任半塘. *Chiao-fang chi chien ting* 教坊記箋訂. Peking, 1962.

Liu, Yung-chi 劉永濟. *Sung-tai ko-wu chü ch'ü lu-yao* 宋代歌舞劇曲錄要. Shanghai, 1957.

Lu, K'an-ju 陸侃如. *Yüeh-fu ku tz'u k'ao* 樂府古辭考. Shanghai, 1926.

Mei, Ying-yün 梅應運. "Tz'u-tiao yü T'ang-Sung ta-chü kuan-hsi" 詞調與唐宋大曲關係, *Ta-lu tsa-chih*, 14 (1957), 1.24-28, 2.18-26, 3.19-36.

Ou-yang, Yü-ch'ien 歐陽予倩, ed. *T'ang-tai wu-tao* 唐代舞蹈. Shanghai, 1980.

Wang, Kuo-wei 王國維. "T'ang-Sung ta-ch'ü k'ao" 唐宋大曲考, in *Wang Kuo-wei hsi-ch'ü lun-wen chi* 王國維戲曲論文集, Peking, 1959, pp. 149-197.

Yang, Yin-liu 楊蔭瀏. *Chung-kuo ku-tai yin-yüeh shih kao* 中國古代音樂史稿. V. 1. Peking, 1981.

Yin, Fa-lu 陰法魯. "T'ang-Sung ta-ch'ü chih lai-yüan chi ch'i tsu-chih" 唐宋大曲之來源及其組織, in *Pei-ching Ta-hsüeh wu-shih chou-nien chi-nien lun-wen chi: wen-hsüeh-yüan ti-shih chung* 北京大學五十年紀念論文集：文學院第十種, Peking, 1948.

—HC

Ta-ku 大鼓 (drum ballad) has been one of the most popular forms of performing-arts literature in northern China from the late Ch'ing period down to the present. Since the drum ballad was originally a product of rural China and only began being performed in cities during the nineteenth century, its early history is obscure. It is impossible to trace many of the forms of *ta-ku* now popular in China to before the last century. However, *ta-ku* is a descendant of much earlier popular Chinese literature, the earliest texts of which are found in the T'ang-dynasty *pien-wen* (see *Tun-huang wen-hsüeh*). In the Southern Sung a poem by Lu Yu* refers to a form of storytelling which sounds remarkably like modern *ta-ku*, and although none of the genres presently heard have such a long history, they are the result of centuries of gradual evolution.

The social milieu in which *ta-ku* was and is performed vary widely. Probably most of the forms originated in the countryside, but after they became popular in big cities they underwent great transformations. Generally speaking, the urban teahouse audiences appreciated the lyrical side of drum ballads more than the narrative element, and one has only to compare the highly lyrical pieces performed by a contemporary *Hsi-ho ta-ku* 西河大鼓 artist like Ma Tseng-fen 馬增芬 (b. 1921) with narrative works performed in rural areas to appreciate this difference. In addition to demanding more emphasis on the sung, poetic portions, the urban audience also expected a higher standard of music (such famous Peking drum-ballad 京韻大鼓 performers as Liu Pao-ch'üan 劉寶全 received Peking opera training) and a greater refinement in the poetic texts.

Although there are wide variations from type to type, *ta-ku* are generally performed in the following manner. The artist holds some sort of clapper device made from wood, metal, or bamboo in his left hand, while his right hand grasps the drumstick, which is used to beat on a large, flat drum roughly thirty centimeters in diameter. The performer is not responsible for any other musical instruments, and he is always accompanied by at least one other person, who usually plays the three-string *san-hsien* 三弦, an unfretted banjo-like instrument. It is quite common, however, for other instruments such as the *ssu-hu* 四胡 (four-stringed fiddle) to be added, and in recent decades the accompaniment has become increasingly complex. The drum and clapper mentioned are not necessarily in continuous use throughout a performance but punctuate the action and are commonly played during breaks in the singing and during instrumental interludes.

In addition to singing the text, the artist must perform the story, and the clapper in his left hand along with the drumstick in the right hand are used in the same effective way that a Chinese storyteller employs his fan. The combination of singing, facial expressions, and gestures into one artistic whole closely resembles Chinese drama, and a skilled *ta-ku* performer can keep an audience spellbound for hours. However, it must be stressed that unlike the southern Chinese form of *t'an-tz'u,* the performer does not attempt to imitate the voices and mannerisms of his male and female characters; he sings in his normal voice throughout. Also, rural *ta-ku* frequently include long prose sections that advance the action of the story, but these are largely eliminated in urban-teahouse or stage performances.

The musical structure of *ta-ku* is intimately related to the more literary elements, so that it is necessary to understand the music to appreciate the texts themselves. The basic music of *ta-ku* is based upon the *pan-ch'iang* 板腔 principle also found in Peking Opera and other Ch'ing-dynasty regional operas, which is to say that a few basic melodies generate variations or even new melodies which may not seem apparently related to their original tunes. This is quite a different principle from the *ch'ü-p'ai* 曲牌 form used in older popular balladry like the Sung-dynasty *chu-kung-tiao*,* where the words were written to match pre-existing tunes with strict limitations on meter. Of course, *ta-ku* also admits *chü-p'ai*, but they make up a small proportion of the actual music.

The *pan-ch'iang* musical form affects the poetic structure of the *ta-ku*, because the poetic line need not be limited by the number of syllables dictated by the particular fixed melody, as it is in *chü-p'ai*. The basic line of *ta-ku* is heptasyllabic, but decasyllabic lines are almost equally common, with wide variations in line length. Rhyme is invariably used but according to vernacular rhyme-schemes. The texts are frequently of a high literary quality, because although most of the performers were from low social origins and were often illiterate, *ta-ku* texts performed in the cities were commonly composed by literati for their favorite performers. As with the earlier *tzu-ti shu*,* most of the stories were taken from popular novels and dramas, although more contemporary material satirizing current events or lamenting the sad fate of the performer is also found. Since some of the female performers were involved in prostitution, and urban performances were given in teahouses before male audiences, it is not surprising to find a certain number of mildly off-color pieces.

Practically every area of North China developed its own form of *ta-ku* during late Ch'ing times, and new *ta-ku* types have continued to be created in the twentieth century. Following is a brief account of some of the more popular and highly developed forms. *Ching-yün ta-ku* 京韻大鼓 (Peking drum song) developed in late Ch'ing times from *tzu-ti shu* and rural Hopeh *ta-ku* and reached its height with the great performer Liu Pao-ch'üan. It is performed with a hard wood clapper and the usual drum, accompanied by *san-hsien* and *ssu-hu*. Peking drum song performers tend to favor stories from the *San-kuo-chih yen-i** and *Shui-hu chuan.** Because of its popularity in a great cultural center like Peking, it is not surprising that the literary value of Peking drum ballads is often quite high. Another form that evolved in Peking and has a longer history than Peking drum songs is *mei-hua ta-ku* 梅花大鼓 (apricot blossom drum songs), which probably originated with the Manchus. The music is soft and melodious compared to the more vigorous Peking drum songs, and most of the performers in recent decades have been women. The stories are usually based on the eighteenth-century novel *Hung-lou meng.** From a historical standpoint, *li-hua ta-ku* 梨花大鼓 (or plum blossom drum songs—probably a miswriting of 犁鏵大鼓 or "plowshare" drum songs, so called from the resemblance of the clappers to plowshares) is central to many of the other forms of *ta-ku* spread throughout North and East China. It originated in rural Shantung, growing out of local folk songs, but became so popular by late Ch'ing times that it spawned a large number of regional descendants. The clapper used consists of two pieces of metal shaped roughly like quarter moons and identical to those used in Shantung *K'uai-shu* 山東快書 (Shantung storytelling). Although the texts of *Li-hua ta-ku* are not as polished as in some of the Peking forms, they still can be very satisfying aesthetically; witness the enthusiastic description in chapter 2 of the late Ch'ing novel *Lao-ts'an yu-chi.** Two forms that probably grew from *Li-hua ta-ku* are *Hsi-ho ta-ku* from the rural region to the southwest of Tientsin in Hopeh and *Lao-t'ing ta-ku* 樂亭大鼓 from Lao-t'ing County in Hopeh, also a famous center for puppet theater. Although both these forms have fused with local traditions, they use the same kind of metal clapper and have much in common regarding performing traditions and texts.

There are many other forms of popular literature which resemble *ta-ku* but cannot be classified with it because of their *ch'ü-p'ai* musical and poetic structure, among them the highly refined *pa-chiao-ku* 八角鼓, or "tambourine songs" (also called *tan-hsien* 單弦), popular in Peking, *Ho-nan ch'ü-tzu* 河南曲子, a genre with a long history from Honan, and *ch'ing-yin* 清音, which originated in Szechwan. All told, there are over a hundred varieties of such performing arts still surviving in North China.

The largest collection of old *ta-ku* texts is in the Fu Ssu-nien 傅斯年 Library of the Academia Sinica on Taiwan. There are also numerous texts available for twentieth-century recordings done in China, but, particularly since 1949, older texts have been greatly revised.

CATALOGUES:

Chao, Ching-shen 趙景深. *Ku-tz'u hsüan* 鼓詞選. Peking, 1960

Hua, Kuang-sheng 華廣生. *Pai-hsüeh i-yin* 白雪遺音. Shanghai, 1959.

Liu, Fu 劉復 and Li Chia-jui 李家瑞. *Chung-kuo su-ch'ü tsung-mu-kao* 中國俗曲總目稿. Peking, 1932.

TRANSLATIONS:

Pimpaneau, Jacques. *Chanteurs, conteurs, bateleurs, littérature orale et spectacles populaires en Chine*. Paris, 1977.

Wimsatt, Genevieve and Geoffrey Chan. *The Lady of the Long Wall: A Ku-shih or Drum Song of China*. New York, 1934.

STUDIES:

Chang, Ch'ang-kung 張長弓. *Ku-tzu-ch'ü yen* 鼓子曲言. Taipei, 1966.

Chang, Ts'ui-feng 章翠鳳. *My Life As a Drum Singer* (as told to Liu Fang), trans. by Rulan Chao Pian. Cambridge, Mass., 1972. Privately printed.

———. *Ta-ku sheng-ya te hui-i* 大鼓生涯的回憶. Taipei, 1967. Fascinating autobiography of a *ta-ku* performer with appendix containing texts.

Chu, Chieh-fan 朱介凡. *Wu-shih nien lai te Chung-kuo su-wen-hsüeh* 五十年來的中國俗文學. Taipei, 1963.

Fu, Hsi-hua 傅惜華. *Ch'ü-i lun-ts'ung* 曲藝論叢. Shanghai, 1954.

Hai, Ch'en 海晨. *Ho-nan ta-tiao ch'ü-tzu chi* 河南大調曲子集. Wuhan, 1957.

Hrdlicka, Zdenek. "Old Chinese Ballads to the Accompaniment of the Big Drum," *AO*, 25 (1957), 83-145.

Hsüeh-chiang 雪江. *Hsi-ho ta-ku* 西河大鼓. Shanghai, 1954.

Li, Chia-jui 李家瑞 . *Pei-p'ing su-ch'ü lüeh* 北平俗曲略. Peking, 1932.

Liang, Tsai-ping. "Chinese Drum Music," *West and East*, 6.1 (January 1961), 5-8.

Sawada, Mizuho 澤田瑞穗. "Daikosho shiroku" 大鼓書私錄, *Tenri daigaku gakuhō*, 34 (March 1961), 40-59; 36 (December 1961), 109-124; 37 (March 1962), 127-141.

Sha-tzu 沙子. *Ssu-ch'uan ch'ing-yin* 四川清音. Chungking, 1957.

Stevens, Catherine. "Peking Drumsinging." Unpublished Ph.D. dissertation, Harvard University, 1973.

Yü, Hui-yung 于會泳. *Shan-tung ta-ku* 山東大鼓. Peking, 1957.

—JDS

T'ai-ko t'i 臺閣體 (cabinet style) is the name given to the styles dominant during much of the fifteenth century in both poetry and prose. They are associated chiefly with men who held high office for extended periods and whose values, in politics and literature alike, emphasized stability and consistency. Rejected at last by the generation that came to maturity at the end of the century, *t'ai-ko t'i* has remained synonymous with literary dullness ever since.

The *t'ai-ko t'i* is associated in particular with the "Three Yangs," Yang Yü 楊寓 (*tzu*, by which he is generally known, Shih-ch'i 士奇, *hao*, Tung-li 東里, 1365-1444), Yang Jung 楊榮 (or Tzu-jung 子榮, *tzu*, Mien-jen 勉仁, 1371-1440), and Yang P'u 楊溥 (*tzu*, Hung-chi 弘濟, 1372-1446). These men rose to prominence early in the century and held office at court under four successive emperors. Their continuing prestige lent influence to their literary tastes, even though literature was not their most important field of activity (even this lack of strong interest in literary questions was influential). In prose they favored the style of Ou-yang Hsiu* for its clarity and balance. Their taste in poetry likewise favoured simplicity and moral rectitude rather than "new-fangled cleverness," and they quoted Chu Hsi's opinions on poetry with approval. The more important cabinet-style poets, aside from the Three Yangs, were Wang Chih 王直 (*tzu*, I-an 抑菴, 1379-1462), Chin Shan 金善 (known by his *tzu*, Yu-tzu 幼孜, 1368-1431), and Tseng Ch'i 曾棨 (*tzu*, Tzu-ch'i 子啟, *hao*, Hsi-shu 西墅, 1372-1432), all well-known officials in the capital.

At present, the fifteenth century is the least studied period in the history of Chinese literature. It is thus possible that future research will alter our picture of the *t'ai-ko t'i*, perhaps finding greater diversity among the host of writers presently associated with it, or reducing its apparent dominance by comparison with writers not so associated, such as the philosophers Hsüeh Hsüan 薛瑄 (1389-1464) and Ch'en Hsien-chang 陳獻章 (1428-1500), the short-story writer Li Chen 李禎 (or Li Ch'ang-chi 李昌祺, 1376-1452), the calligrapher Wu K'uan 吳寬 (1436-1504), and the painter Shen Chou 沈周 (1427-1509).

EDITIONS:

Yang, Shih-ch'i. *Tung-li chi* 東里集. Rpt. in *Chen-pen*, seventh series.

Yang, Jung. *Yang Wen-min chi* 楊文敏集. Rpt. in *Chen-pen*, fourth series.

Chin, Yu-tzu. *Chin Wen-ching chi* 金文靖集. Rpt. in *Chen-pen*, second series.

Three of the most accessible personal collections of *t'ai-ko* writers.

STUDIES:

Li, Yüeh-kang 李曰剛. "Sheng-Ming shih t'ai-ko t'i yü chu pieh-t'i chih liu-pien" 盛明詩臺閣體與諸體之流變, *Chung-kuo shih chi-k'an*, v. 4 (1976), 46-93. The most recent and detailed survey of the period, but still sketchy and derivative.

Yokota, Terutoshi 横田輝俊. "Mindai bungaku-uron no tenkai" 明代文學論の展開, Pt.1, *Hiroshima Daigaku Bungakubu kiyō 37-tokushūgo*, (1977), 53-56. Concise account of the literary ideals of Yang Shih-ch'i and Yang Jung.

—DB

T'ai-p'ing kuang-chi 太平廣記 (Extensive Gleanings of the Reign of Great Tranquility) is one of three huge *lei-shu** compendia compiled during the T'ai-p'ing reign (976-983) by imperial order under the nominal supervision of Li Fang 李昉 (*tzu*, Ming-yüan 明遠, 925-996). The other two works are the *T'ai-p'ing yü-lan** and the *Wen-yüan ying-hua.** The trio are sometimes included with the *Ts'e-fu yüan-kuei* 册府元龜 (Outstanding Models from the Storehouse of Literature) edited by Wang Ch'in-jo 王欽若 during the early eleventh century as the "Sung ssu ta-shu" 宋四大書 (Four Great Books of the Sung).

These works were compiled as a part of the ritual of establishing a dynasty's legitimacy (cf. the historical work at the beginning of the T'ang or the various early Ch'ing scholarly projects, for example). They seem also to have originated in the Sung founder's shift of emphasis from the martial (*wu* 武) to the cultural (*wen* 文).

The compilation work on the *T'ai-p'ing kuang-chi* began in March 977 and was finished within eighteen months—a much shorter period than it took to complete the *Wen-yüan ying-hua* (over four years) or *T'ai-p'ing yü-lan* (over six). It was printed in 981.

Li Fang, since he had numerous other offical duties and may not even have been in the capital during all of this period, was only a figurehead. Of the other compilers listed in his memorial to the throne several were scholars, but it is likely that Hsü Hsüan 徐鉉 (*tzu*, Ting-ch'en 鼎臣, 916-991), a scholar who participated in many editorial projects, was a major figure in the project. His career developed under the aegis of Li Fang and one of the other principal scholars involved in the work was Wu Shu 吳淑 (*tzu*, Cheng-i 正義, 947-1002), Hsü's son-in-law. Wu himself compiled an encyclopedia in the form of a prose-poem, the *Shih-lei fu* 事類賦 (100 *chüan*). Hsü was moreover interested in *hsiao-shuo** and published several collections of supernatural accounts.

Work on the *T'ai-p'ing kuang-chi* was yoked to that on the *T'ai-p'ing yü-lan*. Source materials which were considered informal (*yeh-shih* 野史 [unoffical histories], ch'uan-ch'i [tales],* and hsiao-shuo are normally cited) were collected in the *T'ai-p'ing kuang-chi* under one of 92 classifications and 150 sub-classifications (the formal material went into the *T'ai-p'ing yü-lan*). Thus the work begins with passages on Lao-tzu 老子 (under Shen-hsien 神仙) and moves in the *lei-shu* tradition through accounts of menageries and mirabilia to the final sections on foreigners (*Man-i* 蠻夷) and miscellaneous topics (*Tsa-lu* 雜錄). As in the case of its sister work the *T'ai-p'ing yü-lan*, earlier *lei-shu* or encyclopedias, rather than the original texts, were often used as source material. As a result of this practice, the speed with which the compilation was completed, and the probable lack of organization (Li Fang's participation was only nominal, and several scholars were transferred off the project midway through) in the work itself, the *T'ai-p'ing kuang-chi* should only be consulted with care.

Nevertheless, its importance as a compendium of early fiction rivals that of the *Wen-hsüan** in the field of belles lettres. It is by far the most important source of early fiction available today. About one-third of the 475 sources are from the T'ang, the remainder predate the T'ang; over half of these works have been lost.

Despite its unrivaled position in the study of Chinese fiction today, and the extensive influence stories in the collection had on genres such as *hua-pen,** *tsa-chü,** and *chu-kung-tiao** over the centuries, the work was not widely available until it was printed in two editions during the Chia-ching reign period (1522-1566) of the Ming. The collection is widely valued as a source for numerous non-literary disciplines as well.

EDITIONS:

T'ai-p'ing kuang-chi. 10v. Peking, 1961. A critical edition based on that printed by T'an K'ai 談愷 (*tzu*, Wen-jui 文瑞, *chin-shih*, 1526) during the Chia-ching reign period (1522-1566).

T'ai-p'ing kuang-chi hsüan 太平廣記選. Wang Ju-t'ao 王汝濤, *et al.*, eds. 2v. and 1v. supplement. Chi-nan, 1980, 1981, and 1982. Simplified-character version rearranged under sources (first 2v.) with annotation and illustrations; supplementary volume arranged by title of each entry (e.g., Mao Yen-shou 毛延壽).

T'ai-p'ing kuang-chi jen-ming shu-ming so-yin 太平廣記人名書名索引. Chou Tz'u-ch'i 周次吉, comp. Taipei, 1973.

T'ai-p'ing kuang-chi p'ien-mu chi yin-shu yin-te 太平廣記篇目及引書引得. Teng Ssu-yü 鄧嗣禹, ed., Peiping, 1934; rpt. Taipei, 1966.

TRANSLATIONS:

Although there is no complete translation of this collection, numerous excerpts have been rendered—see Studies.

STUDIES:

Dars, Jacques. "Quelques aspects du fantastique dan la littérature chinoise des Tang et des Song; Les histories de démons et de fantômes du *Tai-ping Guang-ji.*" Unpublished Ph.D. dissertation, Paris, 1965.

Haeger, John W. "Li Fang," in *SB*, v. 2, pp. 552-555.

Kuo, Po-kung 郭伯恭. *Sung ssu ta-shu k'ao* 宋四大書考. Shanghai, 1940.

Ts'ai, Kuo-liang 蔡國梁. "*T'ai-p'ing kuang-chi* sui-cha" 太平廣記隨札, *Wen-i lun-tsung*, 7 (1979), 455-481.

Wilhelm, Hellmut. "Hsü Hsüan," in *SB*, v. 1, pp. 424-427.

Yeh, Ch'ing-ping 葉慶炳. "Yu kuan *T'ai-p'ing kuang-chi* te chi-ko wen-t'i" 有關太平廣記的幾個問題, in *Chung-kuo ku-tien wen-hsüeh yen-chiu ts'ung-k'an—hsiao-shuo chih pu (2)* 中國古典小說研究叢刊 — 小說之部, K'o Ch'ing-ming 柯慶明 and Lin Ming-te 林明德, eds., Taipei, 1977, pp. 11-44. Discusses reasons for compilation, editions, and shortcomings, giving extensive examples and corrections of errors.

—WHN

T'ai-p'ing yü-lan 太平御覽 (Imperial Digest of the T'ai-p'ing Reign Period) is one of the four major early Sung-dynasty encyclopedias (see *lei-shu*). It was compiled in one thousand *chüan* by a team of sixteen scholars headed by Li Fang 李昉 in response to an imperial mandate dated 977. Completed in 982, it took the emperor an entire year to read it (at the rate of three *chüan* a day). For this reason the original title, *T'ai-p'ing tsung-lei* 太平總類 (A General Classification Book of the T'ai-p'ing Reign Period) was changed to the present one. Among the compilers, Wu Shu 吳淑 (947-1002), Lü Wen-chung 呂文中, T'ang Yüeh 湯悅, and Wang K'o-chen 王克貞 were most responsible for the final result.

In its present form the compilation consists of excerpts from about two thousand books and pamphlets, most no longer extant, and a large number of individual pieces. Nearly seventeen hundred of these works are listed in a bibliography at the beginning of the work. It is descended from the *Huang Lan* (see *lei-shu*) and the *Hsiu-wen tien yü-lan* 修文殿御覽 (Imperial Digest of the Hall for Cultivating Literary Skill—early sixth century). A comparison with the latter shows the *T'ai-p'ing yü-lan* to have been based on it in part. The compilation of the *T'ai-p'ing yü-lan* was linked to that of the *T'ai-p'ing kuang-chi**—both works were compiled concurrently by the same editorial group. Material considered acceptable according to the standards of history was included in the *T'ai-p'ing yü-lan;* the rest went into the *T'ai-p'ing kuang-chi.*

The vast collection of excerpts cited in the *T'ai-p'ing yü-lan* are divided into fifty five categories—from "Heaven" (天) to "Flowers" (花)—each of which is further subdivided. There are five thousand sub-topics. Some of them seem redundant and others are reduplicative.

Moreover, the citations are unevenly distributed—some categories contain one hundred *chüan*, some only two. Under each subdivision (such as *mei* [plum]) are listed a number of citations from traditional works arranged in the following order: (1) dictionary glosses for the work; (2) excerpts from the classics which contain the work; (3) excerpts from the *wei-shu* 緯書 (Han-dynasty complements to the Classics); (4) excerpts from historical works; (5) excerpts from the philosophers (*chu-tzu pai-chia**); and (6) excerpts from belles lettres. Sources are provided and the citations are arranged chronologically.

Because of the scope of the work, the nature of its compilation, and the speed with which it was prepared, citations in the *T'ai-p'ing yü-lan* cannot serve as substitutes for the original text. There are numerous scribal errors, many inherited from earlier encyclopedias which were regularly consulted by the *T'ai-p'ing yü-lan* editorial staff (in lieu of consulting the original texts). Other infelicities—the name of an author

or a work appearing in two or more versions—are also attributable to the method of compilation.

Despite these shortcomings, the *T'ai-p'ing yü-lan* is valuable for two reasons: (1) it provides early, though not always reliable, texts which can be used in textual criticism, and (2) it preserved parts of many books which are otherwise lost.

EDITIONS:

T'ai-p'ing yü-lan. 4v. Rpt. Shanghai, 1960. Combines texts from the Sung-dynasty Shu edition (蜀本) with other Sung editions held in Japanese libraries. Best edition.

———. 7v. Taipei, 1968. Readily available.

———. *SPTK.* Also based on Sung edition.

T'ai-p'ing yü-lan so-yin 太平御覽索引. Ch'ien Ya-hsin 錢亞新, ed. Shanghai, 1934. Based on the ed. published by Pao Ch'ung-ch'eng 鮑崇城 (*fl.* 1818). Main-topic heading must be consulted in order to find subtopic.

T'ai-p'ing yü-lan yin-te 太平御覽引得. Hung Yeh 洪業, ed. Peking, 1935. In two sections, one listing all sub-topics and the other all book titles cited.

STUDIES:

Haeger, John W. "The Significance of Confusion: The Origins of the *T'ai-p'ing yü-lan,*" *JAOS*, 88 (1968), 401-410.

Huang, Ta-shou 黃大受. *T'ai-p'ing yü-lan k'ao-i wen* 太平御覽考乙文.

Kuo, Po-kung 郭伯恭. *Sung ssu ta-shu k'ao* 宋四大書考. Changsha, 1940.

See also front matter in Ch'ien Ya-hsin and Hung Yeh above.

—PLC

T'an-lung lu 談龍錄 is a short critical work comprising thirty-seven entries of reflections on poetry. Though brief the work became influential almost upon its publication in the eighteenth century and has remained an important piece of literary criticism. The author, Chao Chih-hsin 趙執信 (1662-1744), was alone in his opposition to the poetics of Wang Shih-chen* (1634-1711), which then enjoyed universal acclaim. The difference in their poetical concepts is clearly set out in the first entry of the work. Wang regards poetry as a *shen lung* 神龍 (mystical dragon) concealed in the clouds, occasionally showing a scale or a claw, but never baring itself in its entirety. Total exposure, Wang argues, should be tolerated only in the humbler arts of painting and sculpture. Chao accepts the analogy of the "mystical dragon" and emphasizes its liveliness. But he believes that the "mystical dragon" should be represented whole. He argues that the indication of no more than a scale or a claw is inadequate, since this represents the imperfect grasp of the contemplator or poet's subjective self. What Chao objects to is Wang's mystification of poetry. The corrective is a return to traditional views of poetry. These include the belief that poetry must have its "propriety," with the poet writing about real experience, using a language that is demonstrably appropriate (entry 6). Another way of saying the same thing is that in poetry, the human presence must be strong (entry 9), and the poetic voice must be highly individual (entries 11 and 34). To write this poetry of more solid substance, the poet must constantly seek to understand life more accurately (entry 16) and be familiar with a great range of earlier poetry, instead of restricting himself to one or two chosen masters as Wang encouraged (entries 17 to 22).

EDITIONS:

T'an-lung lu. Ch'en Erh-tung 陳邇冬, ed. (in same volume as *Shih-chou shih-hua* 石洲詩話, pp. 3-19). Peking, 1981.

T'an-lung lu (preface 1709) in *Ch'ing shih-hua* 清詩話. Peking, 1981. Most accessible.

STUDIES:

Li, Ch'ih-wen 李赤文. " 'Chao Chih-hsin wei-k'an shih-kao' pien-wei" 趙執信未刊詩稿辯偽, *Shan-tung wen-hsüeh*, 1963.1

—SKW

T'an-tz'u 彈詞 (plucking rhymes), used broadly, refers to the commonest form of popular balladry spread throughout South China. The origin of the term is problematical, but one reasonable explanation is that *t'an* meant "to play an instrument" while *tz'u* meant "to sing," hence, *t'an-tz'u* was a form of singing accompanied by instrumental music.

T'an-tz'u is possibly a direct descendant of the Sung-dynasty *t'ao-chen* 淘眞, which,

according to what we know of the genre in Ming times, was probably a kind of heptasyllabic, rhymed storytelling performed by blind women accompanying themselves on the lute-like *p'i-p'a.* It was not until the last century of the Ming dynasty that modern *t'an-tz'u* grew up in the great commercial cities of South China, and one of the first references to the form is made by the Ming scholar T'ien Ju-ch'eng 田汝成 (*chin-shih*, 1526). However, the form must have existed before that time—Chinese intellectuals were usually slow to acknowledge the existence of popular forms of literature.

By early Ch'ing times *t'an-tz'u* had already become immensely popular, particularly with the women in large southern cities, and the stories concentrated on the theme of romantic love. Some of these early texts reached enormous lengths; the *T'ien-yü hua* 天雨花 (Heaven Rains Flowers), of the nineteenth-century female writer T'ao Chen-huai 陶貞懷, stretches to thirty *chüan* and must have taken months to perform. Late Ming and early Ch'ing *t'an-tz'u* were also closely related to the *pao-chüan* 寶卷 (precious scrolls), which promulgated popular Buddhism and various folk religions.

In a narrower sense, the term *t'an-tz'u* is used to refer specifically to *Su-chou t'an-tz'u*, the highly refined form that *t'an-tz'u* took in Soochow, the great commercial and cultural center of the Yangtze delta region in the late Ming. The early history of the form is quite obscure, but according to one authority, one of the earlier schools of *Su-chou t'an-tz'u*, the Ch'en-tiao 陳調, was created by Ch'en Yü-ch'ien 陳遇乾, who lived in the mid-eighteenth century. However, the oldest school still performed is the Yü-tiao 俞調, which was originated by Yü Hsiu-shan 俞秀山, who flourished in the early nineteenth century. Thus, throughout the latter half of the Ch'ing dynasty, *Su-chou t'an-tz'u* has certain similarities with all Chinese balladry, but it is actually quite different from the *ta-ku** popular in North China. The simplest form of performance, or *tan-tang* 單檔, consists of one artist who both sings and plays the three-stringed banjo-like *san-hsien* 三弦. Unlike the *ta-ku* performer, his only prop is a storyteller's fan; i.e., he does not employ clappers or drums as in the north. Even more distinct from *ta-ku* is the performer's adoption of the voice and expressions proper to all of his characters, ranging from old males 老生 to young heroines 旦. The ease with which a skilled performer slips from one role to another is amazing to witness. More complex performances also exist, and it is quite common to add a *p'i-p'a* player (then called a *shuang-tang* 雙檔), who enriches the musical texture of the singer's *tan-hsien* and may himself take on acting roles. In the twentieth century more instruments have been added, and the instrumentalists may all be given an opportunity to sing, so that the performance begins to approach opera.

The music of the *Su-chou t'an-tz'u* is not patterned after the *ch'ü-p'ai* structure of *K'un-ch'ü** opera and some earlier forms of balladry such as the Sung dynasty *chu-kung-tiao,* and yet it is not quite the same as the purely *pan-ch'iang* music used in northern *ta-ku.* Each performer usually sings according to the *tiao,* or "tune," of the school to which he belongs or which he has himself developed. However, these *tiao* are not as rigid as the earlier *ch'ü-p'ai* and undergo considerable modification according to the mood and rhythm of the individual lines. The *kuo-men* 過門, transitional instrumental passages between sung portions, consist of fragments from the basic "tune." In a way then, the music of *t'an-tz'u* could be seen as midway between *ch'ü-p'ai* music and *ta-ku pan-ch'iang* music.

The musical form determines the poetic form of the sung portions, for they need not be composed according to the relatively rigid formulae of *ch'ü-p'ai* music. The basic line is heptasyllabic, although decasyllabic lines of three and seven or three, three, and four syllables are quite common. The rhymes are almost invariably in the level tones 平聲, and this feature, added to a preference for the rhymes *t'ung, chung* 銅鐘 and *chiang, yang* 江洋, accounts for the smooth, rather feminine sound of much *Su-chou t'an-tz'u* poetry. As with *ta-ku* in the

north, literati frequently composed poems for performers, so many works have considerable literary merit, particularly the *k'ai-p'ien* 開篇, or opening pieces.

The mellifluousness of the genre is also partly due to the Soochow dialect, which sounds musical even in normal speech. The *t'an-tz'u* are not entirely in pure colloquial Soochow dialect; as with many southern ballad forms, elaborate linguistic conventions have developed. The speech of upper-class characters follows the syntax and vocabulary of Mandarin, as befitting people of the official class. Although the basic phonology is still that of colloquial Soochow dialect, the sound of many syllables is changed to coincide with the rhyming schemes of the Chung-chou System, based on northern Mandarin in the Yüan dynasty. Lower-class characters speak in a lively colloquial Soochow dialect, and there are even conventions for representing the pronunciation of rustic characters, utilizing rural accents of the countryside around Soochow.

The repertoire of *Su-chou t'an-tz'u* is immense, although performers tend to favor romances of the talented young scholar and beautiful woman variety, which borrow their plots from classical drama, vernacular novels, and local traditions. However, there is also a sprinkling of heroic stories, and some of the works based upon folk and local traditions are quite humorous. Although the sections written in pure Soochow dialect are difficult for a Mandarin speaker to read, many of the texts display a high poetic talent and fertility of imagination.

As mentioned earlier, various kinds of *t'an-tz'u* are performed all over South China, and although the Soochow variety is one of the most highly developed, others have created a rich popular dialect literature. Fukien is just as rich in *t'an-tz'u* as Kiangsu, and in northern Fukien the major form is *Fu-chou p'ing-hua* 福州評話 (Foochow storytelling). A large number of texts in this genre survive from the end of the nineteenth and beginning of the twentieth century. It was immensely popular in Foochow, frequently being performed at weddings and festivals when a family could not afford a Foochow opera troupe. Often performances were not accompanied by any musical instruments, the storyteller punctuating the rhythm by striking a bell-like object with a jade ring on his finger. In addition to the *t'an-tz'u* tunes, tunes from the Foochow opera were used.

In southern Fukien and in Taiwan is found the *ch'üan-shih ko* 勸世歌 (exhortatory song), also known as *ch'i-shih tiao* 乞食調 (beggar's melody), since it was frequently recited by itinerant beggars. In these performances no special props are used; the accompaniment was a *yüeh-ch'in* 月琴. The lyrics are in the Min-nan dialect, and there is a wide range of stories with emphasis upon deserted women or love romances, but some of the stories are also very humorous. The music and poetry of this genre has had an enormous influence on *ko-tsai hsi* 歌仔戲, the most popular regional opera in Taiwan.

Finally, Kwangtung Province is extremely rich in *t'an-tz'u* forms, such as *nan-yin* 南音, *mu-yü shu* 木魚書, and *lung-chou* 龍舟, to mention a few in the dialect of Canton alone. *Nan-yin* were sung by blind artists who accompanied themselves on the zither-like *cheng* 箏. There is a huge printed literature of *nan-yin* dating from the nineteenth century into the early twentieth century, with many works of literary value.

The Fu Ssu-nien Library of the Academia Sinica in Taiwan contains a large collection of old *t'an-tz'u* texts. The recordings issued in China during the twentieth century are another valuable source for texts, although many older works have been revised since 1949.

CATALOGUES:

Chao, Ching-shen 趙景深. *T'an-tz'u hsüan* 彈詞選. Shanghai, 1937. The introduction of this anthology has a very helpful *t'an-tz'u* list.
Hu, Shih-ying 胡士瑩. *T'an-tz'u pao-chüan shu-mu* 彈詞寶卷書目. Shanghai, 1957.
Liu, Fu 劉復 and Li Chia-jui 李家瑞. *Chung-kuo su-ch'ü tsung-mu-kao* 中國俗曲總目稿. Peiping, 1932.

TRANSLATIONS:

Pimpaneau, Jacques. *Chanteurs, conteurs, bateleurs, littérature orale et spectacles populaires en Chine.* Paris, 1977.

STUDIES:

A-ying 阿英 (Ch'ien Hsing-ts'un 錢杏邨). *T'an-tz'u hsiao-shuo p'ing-k'ao* 彈詞小說評考. Shanghai, 1937.
Chao, Ching-shen 趙景深. *T'an-tz'u k'ao-cheng* 彈詞考證. Shanghai, 1937.
Cheng, *Su-wen-hsüeh.*
Fu, Hsi-hua 傅惜華. *Ch'ü-i lun-ts'ung* 曲藝叢論. Shanghai, 1954.
Hatano, Tarō 波多野太郎. *Chūgoku Bungakushi kenkyū* 中國文學史研究. Tokyo, 1974. Pp. 423-549 introduce *t'an-tz'u* and other popular genres.
Li, Chia-jui 李家瑞. "Shuo t'an-tz'u" 說彈詞. *BIHP*, 6.1 (March 1936), 103-120. Also in *Li Chia-jui Hsien-sheng t'ung-su wen-hsüeh lun-wen chi* 李家瑞先生通俗文學論文集, Wang Ch'iu-kuei 王秋桂, ed., Taipei, 1982, pp. 73-101.
Liang, P'ei-chih 梁培熾. *Hsiang-kang Ta-hsüeh so-ts'ang mu-yü shu hsü-lu yü yen-chiu* 香港大學所藏木魚書敍錄與研究. Hong Kong, 1978.
T'an, Cheng-pi 譚正璧 and T'an Hsün 譚尋. *T'an-tz'u hsü-lu* 彈詞敍錄. Shanghai, 1981. Contains summaries of two hundred *t'an-tz'u,* in each case accompanied by bibliographical information and other relevant materials.
Yeh, Te-chün 葉得均. *Sung Yüan Ming chiang-ch'ang wen-hsüeh* 宋元明講唱文學. Shanghai, 1953.

—JDS

T'an Yüan-ch'un 譚元春 (*tzu*, Yu-hsia 友夏, c. 1585-1637), a native of Ching-ling 景陵 (modern Hupei), was a literary critic and poet in the late Ming. A senior poet from his hometown, Chung Hsing,* appreciated his early verse and later joined him in editing two anthologies: the *Ku-shih kuei* 古詩歸 (Return to [the Original Spirit of] Ancient Poetry) and the *T'ang-shih kuei* 唐詩歸 (Return to [the Original Spirit of] T'ang Poetry). These two anthologies with their commentaries and analysis were widely read by contemporary students of poetry and gained immediate fame for the compilers. Later, T'an and Chung were regarded as founders of the Ching-ling 竟陵 School, derived from the name of their native place.

Although he enjoyed early fame in literary circles, T'an was not successful in the civil-service examinations. Only in 1627, when he was forty-two years old, did he pass with highest honors the provincial *chü-*

jen examination. Thereafter, he repeatedly failed in the *chin-shih* examinations; he died in 1637 on his way to Peking for yet another attempt.

T'an and Chung Hsing had probably been influenced intially by Yüan Hung-tao,* the central figure of the Kung-an School, who advocated originality and spontaneity in poetry. Chung had been a member of the Yüan brothers' circle in Peking as early as 1610, and T'an was a close friend of Yüan's eldest son, Yüan P'eng-nien 袁彭年 (b. 1586). In his preface to the second volume of Yüan Hung-tao's collected works, T'an claimed he read Yüan's writings during his early travels among the mountains and lakes in Hunan. He commended Yüan as a great genius who was original, confident, and capable of self-criticism. T'an shared with Yüan a disdain for the imitationists.

T'an was probably more eclectic than Yüan, since he still felt the necessity of learning from the ancient models, as his work on the two anthologies, shows. Furthermore, T'an stressed *shen-yu* 深幽 (profundity) and *ku-ch'iao* 孤峭 (detachment) in the art of poetry. His poems were criticized as obscure and difficult. In the early Ch'ing, Ch'ien Ch'ien-i* regarded him as a *shih-yao* 詩妖 (devil of poetry), and Chu I-tsun* held him responsible for the "fall of poetry," an assessment surely influenced by the concurrent demise of the Ming.

EDITIONS:

Hsin-k'o T'an Yu-hsia ho-chi 新刻譚友夏合集. Chang Tse 張澤, ed. 23 *chüan*. Soochow, 1633. Rpt. as *T'an Yu-hsia ho-chi*, Taipei, 1976.

Ku-shih kuei 古詩歸. The 1617 edition can be found in The National Central Library in Taipei, and the 1641 edition in National Palace Museum in Taipei.

T'ang-shih kuei 唐詩歸. 36 *chüan*, printed by Chün-shan T'ang 君山堂, during the period 1628-1644. At the Academia Sinica in Taipei.

STUDIES:

Ch'en, Wan-i 陳萬益. "Ching-ling-p'ai te wen-hsüeh ssu-hsiang" 竟陵派的文學思想, in *Ta-ti wen-hsüeh* 大地文學, v. 1, Taipei, 1978, pp. 274-337.

DMB, pp. 1246-1248.

Iriya, Yoshitaka 入矢義高, "Kōan kara Kyōryō e: En Shōshū o chūshin toshite" 公安 から 竟陵 へ: 袁小修 を中心 として, "*Tōhō gakuhō*, 25 (1954), 305-330.

Shao, Hung 邵紅. "Ching-ling-p'ai wen-hsüeh li-lun te yen-chiu" 竟陵派文學理論的研究, in *Wen shih che hsüeh-pao*, 24 (February 1975), 195-244.

—MSH

T'ang chih-yen 唐摭言 (Picked-up Words of T'ang) is a mid-tenth-century collection of anecdotes about T'ang literati, with special emphasis on incidents relating to the civil-service examinations. The author of the book, Wang Ting-pao 王定保 (870-after 954), took his *chin-shih* degree in 900. After the final dissolution of the T'ang dynasty seven years later, Wang fled to South China where he served in the government of the state of Southern Han (907-971). Son-in-law to the important writer and official Wu Jung 吳融 (d. *c.* 903), he was of the same sept as Wang P'u 王溥 (922-982), a younger kinsman who compiled in 961 the conclusive editions of the *T'ang hui-yao* 唐會要 and *Wu-tai hui-yao* 五代會要, two invaluable collections of documents. Although the date of Wang Ting-pao's death is not known, a reference in the *T'ang chih-yen* indicates that he did not complete his great work till 954, when he was well into his ninth decade.

The anecdotes in the *T'ang chih-yen* are grouped under 103 disparate topic headings, such as "Court Audiences," "Bosom Friends," "Dreams," and "Dwelling in Reclusion After Passing the Examinations," in fifteen *chüan*. Concluding many of the sections is a *lun* 論 (appraisal), offering Wang Ting-pao's own reflections (usually moralistic) on the preceding stories and accounts.

The *T'ang chih-yen* provides detailed information on the official examination system, particularly the various presentations, banquets, and other formal occasions that a prospective or successful degree-holder normally participated in during his heady months at the capital. Examples are the festive day-long gatherings of successful candidates held in the lovely serpentine park in the southeast corner of Ch'ang-an, and the ceremonial inscribing of the names of the fortunate scholars at the Tzu-en Ssu 慈恩寺 (Monastery of Compassionate Grace), a well-favored Buddhist establishment at the capital (both customs arose in the Shen-lung period [705-707]). While some of these entries, such as those giving the enrollment figures of the capital colleges, are rather dry, many are quite lively narrations centered on individuals, and thus add to our historical picture of certain T'ang literati.

Indeed, the *T'ang chih-yen's* importance to students of medieval literature rests as much on the particularized incidents not included in "official" biographies, as on its depiction of examination customs and formalities. While the first three *chüan* are devoted exclusively to examination-related topics, the remaining twelve constitute a miscellany of sundry tales, varying in their validity, regarding famous writers of the T'ang. Here are found the earliest accounts of Meng Hao-jan's* disastrous (and surely apocryphal) recitation of verse before Emperor Hsüan-tsung, of palace ladies dousing a drunken Li Po* with ice-water to sober him enough to compose on command before this same monarch, of Chang Chi's* (c. 766-c. 829) criticism of his mentor Han Yü's* fondness for gambling, of Li Ao's* rudeness toward a powerful Taoist adept (which had the ultimate effect of rendering all of Li's sons unsuccessful and unaccomplished), and a host of other anecdotes about diverse figures of the literary world. Some entries are no more than a column or two in length, others stretch on for pages. Heavy use is made of conversation and monologue; in addition, numerous poems and letters are quoted. This was later utilized extensively by Chi Yu-kung when he compiled his well known *T'ang-shih chi-shih.**

Although Wang Ting-pao's book touches on persons and events from all periods of the T'ang dynasty, the majority of the chapters focus on the ninth century, especially the last half. Wang declared that he had first-hand knowledge of many of the stories he reports from these years and that many others he records were passed on to him by those involved—men like Wang Huan 王渙 (821-910), Lu I 陸扆 (847-905), and his father-in-law, Wu Jung. Hence, this book is of especial historical value for students of late T'ang literature.

EDITIONS:

T'ang chih-yen, in *Ya-yü T'ang ts'ung-shu* 雅雨堂叢書. 1756.

T'ang chih-yen, in *Hsüeh-chin t'ao-yüan* 學津討源, 7th series. 1805.

T'ang chih-yen, in *T'ang-tai ts'ung-shu* 唐代叢書. 1806.

T'ang chih-yen. Shanghai, 1978. Typeset, punctuated. Based on the *Ya-yü T'ang* edition, but including a collation table of variants from the *Hsüeh-chin t'ao-yüan* text.

—PWK

T'ang Hsien-tsu 湯顯祖 (*tzu*, I-jen 義仍, *hao*, Jo-shih 若士, 1550-1617) was the most talented playwright of the Ming dynasty and of the late Ming drama that identified itself by T'ang's birthplace in Kiangsi. T'ang and his followers prized literary quality over strict musical form, whereas his opponents, those of the Wu-chiang School 吳江派, led by Shen Ching,* criticized him bitterly for his disregard of order and restraint and discredited his plays as "irregular" in terms of musical convention. While T'ang Hsien-tsu's intricate and subtle literary style inspired contemporary imitation by such well-known dramatists as Wu Ping,* Meng Ch'eng-shun 孟稱舜 (*fl.* 1644), and Juan Ta-ch'eng,* some later historians have held that his special attention to the literary, rather than the theatrical, aspect of drama contributed to the eventual decline of the vitality of Ming *ch'uan-ch'i** plays.

T'ang received his *chin-shih* degree at the age of thirty-four and held a post as secretary of the Ministry of Rites in Nanking until his frank criticism affronted the throne, and he was banished to Kwangtung Province. Later he was reinstated and appointed District Magistrate (in Chekiang). A man of principle, T'ang refused to flatter officials in power; he shunned Chang Chu-cheng and Wang Shih-chen* (1526-1590), and consequently never gained political power.

In the twenty years after his retirement from office in 1598, he wrote some of his best plays. His studio, Yu-ming T'ang 玉茗堂, was always crowded with men of learning and littered with literary and historical texts. Because of his meager means, it was also in the midst of chicken coops and pigpens, yet the old man was oblivious to it all. He went on singing, reciting poetry, and writing plays, all the time growing more mellow and more philosophical. When asked why he decided against giving lectures in the academies, T'ang replied that while other scholars might lecture on certain doctrines, he would only talk about emotion and feeling. It is little wonder that his dramatic works mirror his faith in emotion as a higher guide than reason. They also probe deeply into human life and its philosophical foundations.

T'ang left five *ch'uan-ch'i*. His first work, *Tzu-hsiao chi* 紫簫記 (The Purple Flute) was derived from "Huo Hsiao-yü chuan," a famous T'ang-dynasty story (see *ch'uan-ch'i* tale) about Li I and Huo Hsiao-yü. Now generally regarded as the weakest of all his dramatic works, the play was, nevertheless, immensely popular. According to T'ang, as soon as one piece of the play's lyrics was composed, it was snatched up by accomplished performers and played to audiences of up to ten thousand people. *Tzu-ch'ai chi* 紫釵記 (The Purple Hairpin) is a recasting of *The Purple Flute*. The basic story remains the same—the love between Huo Hsiao-yü and Li I. But the second play is much more elaborate, and T'ang's alteration of the plot reveals his preoccupation with love and his sympathy toward Li I, one of the most famous betrayers of love in Chinese literature. In T'ang's version he becomes a victim of circumstances, not nearly as unfeeling and power-craving as in the original tale.

Mu-tan T'ing 牡丹亭 (The Peony Pavilion), also known more fully as *Mu-tan T'ing huan-hun-chi* 還魂記 or simply as *Huan-hun chi* (The Return of the Soul), is his masterpiece. The story is taken from an obscure *hua-pen,** entitled *Tu Li-niang mu-se huan-hun* 新城. The action of the play is as follows: Tu Li-niang is the daughter of Tu

Pao, Prefect of Nan-an in Southern Sung times. Her father's social aspirations have delayed her betrothal, but a young scholar named Liu has dreamed of her and subsequently adopted the name Meng-mei, "Dream of Apricot." Her readings with her tutor, Ch'en, in the *Shih-ching** awake springtime longings in her heart, and during a garden stroll with her maid, Ch'un-hsiang, she dreams that Liu makes love to her by a pavilion set among peonies. On waking she revisits the garden and yearns for Liu. Fearful of dying, she expresses her wish to be buried beneath a flowering apricot tree (*mei*). She paints a self-portrait and asks that after her death it be buried close by the peony pavilion. She dies, and her father leaves to become Military Commissioner at Yangchow. Tutor Ch'en and a Taoist nun named Shih are charged with the maintenance of Li-niang's shrine. Liu Meng-mei, journeying to the capital at Lin-an for the examinations, falls sick and recuperates in the garden of Tu Pao's former residence. He finds Li-niang's buried self-portrait and worships it under the impression that it is an image of Kuan-yin, the goddess of mercy. Meanwhile, Li-niang's spirit has received permission from Judge Hu, in the netherworld, to return to her mortal body. Summoned by a mass said by the nun Shih, Li-niang returns in spirit form and gives herself to Liu Meng-mei. She reveals her identity and secures Liu's aid in the disinterment of her corpse.

Restored to her body and the world of light, Li-niang marries Liu and accompanies him to Lin-an. The examinations over, she sends him in search of her father, who is besieged in Huai-an by the rebel army of Li Ch'uan. The latter tricks Tu Pao into believing that his wife and the maid Ch'uan-hsiang have been killed, but Li is in turn tricked by Tu Pao into surrendering. Liu Meng-mei reaches Tu Pao only to be accused of desecrating Li-niang's grave. Tu Pao flogs Liu Meng-mei but is interrupted by the announcement of Liu's nomination as Top Graduate. Li-niang, her mother, and Ch'un-hsiang, now reunited, present themselves before Tu Pao, who had believed all three dead. Only in the imperial audience chamber is he brought at last to recognize their miraculous escapes from death and to accept Liu Meng-mei as his son-in-law.

In extended sequences of arias, principally sung by Li-niang herself, the author stresses the claims of *ch'ing* 情 (feelings) against those of *li* 理 (reason). Central to this theme is the power of love, which has caused Li-niang's death (from pining) and brought her back to life (through Liu Meng-mei's devotion). In strong contrast with Liu's loving support stands the cold rationalism which prevents Li-niang's father, Tu Pao, from accepting the miracle of his daughter's return from the grave. The argument reflects the influence on T'ang Hsien-tsu of the philosophical schools of Wang Yang-ming and Wang Ken with their insistence on the cultivation of the spontaneous feelings of the heart. T'ang's fable is primarily a tale of the power of passion. The most memorable and best-loved passages of the entire play are those depicting Li-niang as a cloistered maiden yearning for love. Scene 10, "Ching-meng" 驚夢 (The Interrupted Dream); scene 12, "Hsün-meng" 尋夢 (Pursuing the Dream); scene 14, "Hsieh-chen" 寫眞 (The Portrait); scene 28, "Yu-kou" 幽媾 (Union in the Shades), and others create the most moving image of a lovelorn girl ever presented on the Chinese stage. They are still staples of *K'un-ch'ü** performance. Only Ts'ui Ying-ying of *Hsi-hsiang chi** comes close to rivaling Tu Li-niang as a romantic heroine.

T'ang Hsien-tsu enriches the lyric quality of his arias with many symbols, both from the common stock (particularly moon and star images) and others especially appropriate to this play (e.g., the peony as symbol of the "late-blooming" maiden). He makes erudite allusions to a wide range of early anecdotes of portraits coming to life, ghostly returns, and so on and borrows frequently from the diction of Yüan plays on similar themes, especially *Hsi-hsiang chi* and *Ch'ien-nü li-hun* 倩女離魂 (Ch'ien-nü's Spirit Journey). T'ang's love of wordplay leads him into exuberant displays, as when in scene 17 he has the Taoist nun deliber-

ately misapply quotations of half the text of the *Ch'ien-tzu wen* 千字文 (Thousand-character Text), or when in scene 23 he puns on the names of thirty-eight flowers. T'ang also excels in naturalistic dialogue, which he uses to create a whole gallery of comic minor characters. Li-niang is assisted by the comic "rotten pedant," Tutor Ch'en, and by the bawdy nun Shih, as well as by her pert maidservant Ch'un-hsiang, whose teasing of Ch'en in scene 7, "Kuei-shu" 閨塾 (The Schoolroom) is one of the most frequently staged of all *K'un-ch'ü* scenes. The hen-pecked rebel chieftain Li Ch'uan, the satirically drawn infernal bureaucrat Judge Hu, and a drunken barbarian prince who babbles in nonsense syllables are all considerably superior to the comic stock characters of *ch'uan-ch'i*.

The last plays of T'ang Hsien-tsu are testimonies of his changing outlook. They transcend the individual and achieve universality through philosophical contemplation. *Han-tan chi* 邯鄲記 (Record of Han-tan) took its material from the T'ang-dynasty tale, *Chen-chung chi* (see Li Kung-tso). *Nan-k'o chi* 南柯記 (Record of Southern Bough)—(see *ch'uan-ch'i* [tale])—was derived from its namesake, another T'ang story. It deals with a discharged officer who experiences a rise and fall of fortune in a dreamland called "Huai-an." When he wakes up, he discovers that the Kingdom of Huai-an is a world that a swarm of ants built under the root of a locust tree in his own backyard. He sees that human life, with all its institutionalized values, is as trivial as the existence of an ant. This realization leads to his achievement of instant Buddhahood. *The Purple Hairpin, The Peony Pavilion, Record of Han-tan*, and *Record of Southern Bough* are collectively known as the *Lin-ch'uan ssu-meng* (Four Dreams of T'ang Lin-ch'uan—after T'ang's hometown).

EDITIONS:
Yu-ming-t'ang ch'uan-chi 玉茗堂全集. 1612 edition. 40 *chüan*.
Yu-ming-t'ang ssu-meng ch'u 玉茗堂之夢曲. Early Ch'ing dynasty edition. 8 *chüan*.
Mu-tan T'ing huan-hun-chi 牡丹亭還魂記. Ming Wan-li edition. 2 *chüan*.

T'ang Hsien-tsu chi 湯顯祖集. 4v. Hsü Shuo-fang and Ch'ien Nan-yang, ed. Peking, 1962.

T'ang Hsien-tsu shih-wen chi 湯顯祖戲曲集. 2v. Hsü Shuo-fang 徐朔方, coll. and comm. Shanghai, 1982.

TRANSLATIONS:

Birch, Cyril. *The Peony Pavilion.* Bloomington, Ind., 1980.

Hundhausen, Vincenz. *Die Ruckehr der Seele. Ein romantisches Drama, in deutscher Sprache.* Zurich und Leipzig, 1937.

STUDIES:

Birch, Cyril. "The Architecture of the Peony Pavilion," *TkR,* 10.3 (Spring/Summer 1980), 609-640.

———. "Some Concerns and Methods of the Ming *ch'uan-ch'i* Drama," in *Literary Genres,* pp. 220-258.

Chao, Ching-shen 趙景深. "Tu T'ang Hsien-tsu" 讀湯顯祖, in Chao's *Ming Ch'ing ch'ü t'an"* 明清曲談, *Shanghai, 1957, pp. 82-85.*

Ch'en, Chung-fan 陳中凡. *"T'ang Hsien-tsu Mu-tan-t'ing* chien-lun" 湯顯祖 牡丹亭 簡論, *Wen-hsüeh p'ing-lun,* 4 (1962), 56-70.

Cheng, Pei-kai. "Reality and Imagination: Li Chih and T'ang Hsien-tsu in Search of Authenticity." Unpublished Ph.D. dissertation, Yale University, 1980.

ECCP, pp. 708-709.

Hsia, C. T. "Time and the Human Condition in the Plays of T'ang Hsien-tsu," in *Self and Society,* pp. 249-290.

Iwaki, Hideo 岩城秀夫. *Chūgoku gikyoku engeki kenkyū* 中國戲曲演劇研究, Tokyo, 1973, pp. 5-416.

P'an, Ch'ün-ying 潘群英. *T'ang Hsien-tsu Mu-tan-t'ing k'ao-shu* 湯顯祖 牡丹亭 考述. Taipei, 1969.

Yagisawa, *Gekisakuka,* pp. 419-525.

—CB and CYC

T'ang-shih chi-shih 唐詩紀事 (Recorded Occasions in T'ang Poetry) is basically an anthology of T'ang poems, compiled by the Southern Sung scholar Chi Yu-kung 計有功 (*chin-shih,* 1121). However, what distinguishes this collection from other early anthologies is the inclusion of a wealth of anecdotes about the composition of many of the poems. Although this format had been used in two T'ang-dynasty works known to Chi (the *Pen-shih shih* 本事詩 of Meng Ch'i 孟棨 and the *Yün-hsi yu-i* 雲溪友議 of Fan Shu 范攄; these two brief works are still extant in the *T'ang-tai ts'ung-shu*), Chi was the first to employ this method on a large scale and to arrange such a collection systematically around the individual poets, instead of randomly or by topic.

The *T'ang-shih chi-shih* comprises eighty-one *chüan.* The poets are arranged in roughly chronological fashion. The T'ang monarchs, however, all appear in the first two *chüan,* while Buddhist poets and women writers appear in the final chapters. Over eleven hundred poets are quoted and commented upon at varying length, with from two to twenty-six poets in a single chapter. Brief biographical sketches were supplied by Chi Yu-kung for most of the authors; in many cases these were copied into the *Ch'üan T'ang shih** some six centuries later. Owing to the compiler's extensive cullings from all manner of T'ang texts, many poems and a large amount of anecdotal information from works now lost have been preserved in this anthology. Much of this material—for instance, the conflicting opinions voiced in several texts current in Chi's day about the background of Li Po's* famous poem "Shu-tao nan" 蜀道難 (The Way to Shu is Hard)—is of especial value to literary historians. Chi's own reason, as stated in his preface, for including the short biographies and copious anecdotes, was that this knowledge would allow one to "read the poem and recognize the person" 讀其詩, 知其人 —a phrase that found its way into the terminology of Chinese literary criticism.

The *T'ang-shih chi-shih* itself was the model for the various *chi-shih* poetry volumes of later dynasties (see *Liao-shih chi-shih, Ming-shih chi-shih,* and *Sung-shih chi-shih*).

EDITIONS:

T'ang-shih chi-shih. 1234 edition from Wang Hsi 王禧.

T'ang-shih chi-shih. 1545 edition from Hung P'ien 洪楩; reprinted in *SPTK.* Based on Wang Hsi's text.

T'ang-shih chi-shih. 1545 edition from Chang Tzu-li 張子立; rpt. from Chi-ku ko 汲古閣 of Mao Chin 毛晉 (1599-1659). Based on Wang's text.

T'ang-shih chi-shih. Hong Kong, 1972. 2v. Typeset and punctuated edition; based on Hung

P'ien's text, with textual notes and thorough collation of other editions; includes a four-corner index to poets in this work. The best text.

T'ang-shih chi-shih chu-che yin-te 著者引得 (Index to the Authors in the T'ang Shih chi-shih). Peking, 1934; rpt. Taipei, 1966. Harvard-Yenching Institute Sinological Index Series, No. 18. An index keyed to the *SPTK* text.

—PWK

T'ang-shih san-pai-shou 唐詩三百首 (Three Hundred Poems of the T'ang dynasty, henceforth *San-pai-shou*) was compiled by Heng-t'ang T'ui-shih 蘅塘退士 (The Recluse of Heng-t'ang) and published in either 1763 or 1764. Recent scholarship has firmly established that Heng-t'ang T'ui-shih is one of the literary names of Sun Chu 孫洙 (*tzu*, Lin-hsi 臨西 or Ling-hsi 苓西, *hao*, Heng-t'ang 蘅塘 [Heng-t'ang] and T'ui-shih 退士, 1711-1778), a scholar-official from Wu-hsi 無錫 (Kiangsu). Sun Chu's talented second wife Hsü Lan-ying 徐蘭英 also participated in the compilation of the anthology.

Among some 130 anthologies of T'ang poetry compiled since the eighth century, the *San-pai-shou* is today the most popular and widely read. During the two centuries since its original publication, it has been the Chinese child's first introduction to his poetic tradition and has been enjoyed by countless adult readers as well.

The exact number of poems selected by Sun Chu is not known, since the original edition is no longer extant. The book has been reprinted numerous times with additional commentaries and extra selections of poems by later scholars. Examination of the early editions leads to the surmise that the original number of poems was probably 310. Sun Chu himself says in his preface that he has selected 300 pieces because he wanted to put to the test the saying, "Having mastered three-hundred T'ang poems, one will learn how to compose poetry." But Sun Chu might have been inspired also by the idea of the *shih san-pai* 詩三百 (three hundred songs) of the *Shih-ching** which contains 305 songs.

The *San-pai-shou* has been enormously successful because it can be enjoyed by both refined and uncultured readers. Sun Chu states in his preface that he chose the T'ang poems that enjoyed the greatest popularity over the centuries. Furthermore, in his attempt to prepare a text for young children, Sun Chu specifically selected those masterpieces that were easy to understand and memorize.

Yet, despite its popular nature, the *San-pai-shou* reflects a high editorial standard. Although Sun Chu must have consulted many previous anthologies of T'ang poetry, his selection is believed to be based on the excellent anthology *T'ang-shih pieh-ts'ai-chi* 唐詩別裁集, edited by Shen Te-ch'ien* with the assistance of Ch'en Shu-tzu 陳樹滋 and first published in 1717. An expanded edition with 1,928 poems was published in 1763.

Of the 313 poems in one popular edition of the *San-pai-shou*, 240 or so can be found in the *Pieh-ts'ai chi*. Shen Te-ch'ien divided his selections into *ku-shih* 古詩, *lü-shih* 律詩, *ch'ang-lü* 長律 (extended regulated verse), and *chüeh-chü* 絕句 (see *shih*) categories. Each of these is further subdivided into pentasyllabic and septasyllabic sections. Sun Chu followed this general organization except that he left out *ch'ang-lü* and provided a separate category for *yüeh-fu** poems which were classified by Shen Te-ch'ien under either *ku-shih* or *chüeh-chü*. As in *Pieh-ts'ai chi*, Tu Fu is represented in the *San-pai-shou* with the largest number of poems (about 36) and Li Po within the second largest number (about 29).

Shen Te-ch'ien was a didactic critic and believed poetry should conform to Confucian ideals. His theory of poetry, therefore, emphasizes moderation, sincerity, simplicity, and refinement of expression. Several of Sun Chu's brief comments found in early editions of the *San-pai-shou* illustrate his adherence to Shen Te-ch'ien's views as the guiding principle in his selection of poems. However, Sun Chu's originality and the critical and aesthetic contexts in which the *San-pai-shou* was put together should not be ignored. In addition to Shen Te-ch'ien's theory, the influence of Wang Shih-chen* (1634-1711), who valued the quintessential *shen-yün* 神韻

(spirit-resonance) in poetry, can also be seen. The ideas of the talented Yüan Mei* who emphasized a poet's *hsing-ling* 性靈 (native sensibility) were already very popular in Sun Chu's lifetime. This collection reflects the editor's attempt to synthesize the theories of these three poet-critics.

Among T'ang poets, Wang Wei* was esteemed most highly by Wang Shih-chen and his followers. He is represented in the *San-pai-shou* with 29 poems, and so as a poet of the same stature as Li Po.* This contrasts sharply with the situation in the *Pieh-ts'ai chi* in which Tu Fu is represented with 254 poems, Li Po with 139, and Wang Wei with only 88. Moreover, some critical terms that often appear in Wang Shih-chen's writings—terms like *shen-hui* 神會 (communion with the spirit), *shen-wei* 神味 (spiritual flavor), and *san-mei* 三昧 (*samadhi*)—are also used in Sun Chu's brief comments in early editions of the *San-pai-shou*.

Although Yüan Mei never compiled an anthology of T'ang poetry, his *Sui-yüan shih-hua* 隨園詩話 values highly the poetry of the mid- and late-T'ang periods. His critical position differs, therefore, from that of Shen Te-ch'ien who viewed the High T'ang as an age of unsurpassable greatness and from that of Wang Shih-chen who saw Wang Wei and Meng Hao-jan* as ideal models. Nearly half of the *chin-t'i* 近體 or "recent style" poems are by mid- and late-T'ang writers. Yüan Mei also takes a more liberal attitude toward the ornate love poems (*yen-t'i shih* 艷體詩) by late-T'ang poets such as Li Shang-yin,* Wen T'ing-yün,* and Han Wo* because they are good expressions of the poets' "native sensibilites." Shen Te-ch'ien finds the ornate love poems objectionable by Confucian ethical standards. There is not even a single *wu-t'i shih* 無題詩 (poem without a title) by Li Shang-yin in the *Pieh-ts'ai chi*. The inclusion of Li Shang-yin's *wu-t'i shih* and some love poems by Wen T'ing-yün and Han Wo indicates the influence of Yüan Mei's ideas on Sun Chu. In terms of editorial criteria, the *San-pai-shou* seems to have relied on a broader critical perspective than its model.

EDITIONS:

T'ang-shih san-pai-shou chi-shih 唐詩三百首集釋. Yüan-hu san-jen 鴛湖散人, ed. Taipei, 1977.

T'ang-shih san-pai-shou chu-shu 注疏. Chang Hsieh 章燮, ed. Sao-yeh shan-fang 掃葉山房, 1913. Reprint of Chang Hsieh's 1834 edition, further edited by Sun Hsiao-ken 孫孝根. Contains some original comments by Sun Chu.

T'ang-shih san-pai-shou hsiang-chu 詳注. Yü Shou-chen 喻守眞, ed. Hong Kong, 1965. Contains useful annotation for the modern reader.

T'ang-shih san-pai-shou hsin-chu 新注. Chin Hsing-yao 金性堯, ed. Shanghai, 1980. Contains useful commentary for the modern reader.

T'ang-shih san-pai-shou pu-chu 補注. Chen Wan-chün 陳婉俊, ed. 1844. Useful commentary.

TRANSLATIONS:

Bynner, *Jade Mountain*. Among available translations, this may be the best, though still very unsatisfactory.

Mekada, Makoto 目加田誠. *Tō shi sambyaku shu* 唐詩三百首. 3v. Tokyo, 1972-74.

STUDIES:

Ch'en, Yu-ch'in 陳友琴. "Lüeh-t'an *T'ang-shih san-pai-shou* te lan-pen chi ch'i-t'a" 略談唐詩三百首的藍本及其他, in *Wen-ku chi* 溫故集, Peking, 1959.

Chu, Tzu-ch'ing 朱自清. "*T'ang-shih san-pai-shou* chih-tao ta-kai" 唐詩三百首指導大概, in *Lüeh-tu chih-tao chü-yü* 略讀指要舉隅, Shanghai, 1943.

P'eng, Kuo-tung 彭國棟. *T'ang-shih san-pai-shou shih-hua hui-pien* 唐詩三百首詩話薈編. 2v. Taipei, 1963 (3rd edition). (A scholarly exchange on this work and its author can be found in a series of articles published in the *Kuang-ming jih-pao* and other journals in the late 1950s—see *Chung-kuo ku-tien wen-hsüeh yen-chiu lun-wen so-yin* 中國古典文學研究論文索引 [Hong Kong, 1980], pp. 102-103).

—SL

T'ang Shun-chih 唐順之 (*tzu*, Ying-te 應德, *hao*, Ching-ch'uan 荊川, I-hsiu 義修, 1507-1560) has long been recognized as a major essayist and literary theorist of the Ming dynasty. He was born to a family of scholar-officials in Wu-chin 武進 (modern Kiangsu) and, having passed the *chin-shih* examination in 1529, was first appointed to the Han-lin Academy and then transferred to the Ministry of War. In 1533 he was transferred back to the Han-lin as a compiler. Because of both his repeated requests for leave of absence on account of illness and his criticism of the Emperor's failure to maintain the tradition of daily audiences, he was dismissed from governmental service in 1541.

Four years later, he was recalled to serve in the Nanking office of the Ministry of War. Largely due to his association with such prominent political figures as Chao Wen-hua 趙文華 (d. 1557), Hu Tsung-hsien 胡宗憲 (1511-1565), and Yen Sung 嚴嵩 (1480-1565), T'ang's official career in his later years was very successful. After several appointments in the military campaigns against the pirates on the offshore islands along Kiangsu and Chekiang provinces, he rose to be Governor of Feng-yang 鳳陽 in 1560. Later in the same year he died on a journey to the south. Some seventy years after his death he was honored with the title Hsiang-wen 襄文.

T'ang was a man of broad learning, versed in subjects ranging from astronomy and geography to divination and mathematics. His literary career also underwent several changes. First, he followed the trend of his time, represented by scholars like Li Tung-yang* who maintained that prose writing had been brought to perfection in the Ch'in and Han and poetry in the T'ang. Consequently, he tended to imitate the Ch'in-Han writers. At the age of forty, however, he experienced a "turning point" while in exile at I-hsing 宜興. Discarding the practice of imitating the writings of the Ch'in and Han, he took the master essayists of the T'ang and Sung as models, particularly Ou-yang Hsiu* and Tseng Kung,* and endeavored to make his own expression more natural and fluent. Along with Wang Shen-chung 王慎中 (1509-1559), Mao K'un 茅坤 (1512-1601), and Kuei Yu-kuang,* T'ang has been credited with the revival of the tradition of T'ang-Sung prose style and the rejuvenation of Ming literature. The anthology he compiled, known as the *Ching-ch'uan wen-pien* 荊川文編, is of importance in two respects. First, it embodied T'ang's principles about the writing of prose. Second, through the

exclusive selection of the writings of Han Yü,* Liu Tsung-yüan,* Ou-yang Hsiu, Su Hsün,* Su Shih,,* Su Ch'e,* Tseng Kung, and Wang An-shih,* for the T'ang-Sung period, T'ang was originally responsible for coining the term "T'ang Sung pa-ta chia" 唐宋八大散文家 (Eight Great [Prose] Masters of the T'ang and Sung).

In his own writing, T'ang strove to achieve a natural and harmonious blending of ideas and language, without leaving any traces of the labor and effort of creation. In other words, he aimed at literature in which the method lies in having no visible method. The best of his writings are biographies, inscriptions, and epitaphs.

In literary theory, like his predecessor Sung Lien,* T'ang stressed the importance of *fa* 法 (method). In his words, the method of the prose literature before the Han lies in the absence of methods and, therefore, is "esoteric and cannot be espied"; the method of the prose literature of the T'ang and Sung lie in having methods and, therefore, is "rigid and must not be broken." It is T'ang's conclusion that literature must have methods which appear and develop naturally and cannot be changed. Furthermore, it is the presence of methods which separates the prose of the T'ang and Sung from that of the Ch'in and Han. Although both the Ch'in-Han and T'ang-Sung schools in the Ming era advocated imitation of the ancients, because of their different interpretation of *fa*, their accomplishments also show a marked difference. A piece of literary writing, in T'ang's opinion, is a coherent and congruous unity. It cannot exist without the four elements of *t'i* 體 (form), *chih* 志 (idea), *ch'i* 氣 (vitality), and *yün* 韻 (resonance or personal tone).

After T'ang was forty, under the influence of the left wing of the Wang Yang-ming School and especially of Wang Chi's 王畿 (1498-1583) doctrine of "four non-beings," his literary theory showed significant change. The most important thing in literature, T'ang argued, was *pen-se* 本色 (true or original visage). The concept of *pen-se* implies sincerity and truthfulness. A successful piece of composition must have true feelings and original ideas as its substance or content. Thus, sincerity and truthfulness become the criteria for literary creation and evaluation. It is in the concept of *pen-se* that T'ang distinguished himself from other prose writers and literary theorists of his time. While many of his contemporaries still sought artistry in language, T'ang turned his attention to the problem of content.

The Ancient-style Prose Movement (see *ku-wen*) of the T'ang and Sung period was twofold in nature: on the one hand, it was concerned with the form or style of prose, and, on the other, with the revival of Confucianist ideas. The latter concern finally resulted in the emergence of Neo-Confucianism. By the Ming period, most of the literary schools focused only on the formal aspects, totally neglecting the importance of the philosophical basis, originality, and the content of literature. In demanding attention for the latter, as well as for natural or spontaneous ways of expression, T'ang's concept of *pen-se* established a new trend in prose writing, which dominated the remainder of the Ming and early Ch'ing periods and anticipated many of the ideas later developed by the Kung-an (see Yüan Hung-tao) and Ching-ling (see T'an Yüan-ch'un) schools.

EDITIONS:

Ching-ch'uan Hsien-sheng wen-chi 荊川先生文集. SPTK.

T'ang Ching-ch'uan Hsien-sheng wen-chi 唐荊川先生文集, in *Ch'ang-chou hsien-che i-shu* 常州先哲遺書, compiled by Sheng Hsüan-huai 盛宣懷, rpt. Taipei, 1971.

TRANSLATIONS:

Tu, Ching-I, "A Letter to Mao K'un (Lu-men) by T'ang Shun-chih," *Renditions*, forthcoming.

STUDIES:

Ch'ien, Chi-po 錢基博. *Ming-tai wen-hsüeh* 明代文學, Changsha, 1939, pp. 43-48, 113-115.

Chu, Tung-jun 朱東潤. *Chung-kuo wen-hsüeh p'i-p'ing shih ta-kang* 中國文學批評史大綱. Kweilin, 1944, pp. 243-248.

DMB, pp. 1252-1256.

—CIT

T'ang ts'ai-tzu chuan 唐才子傳 (Biographies of T'ang Geniuses), ten *chüan*, by the Yüan scholar Hsin Wen-fang 辛文房 (*tzu*, Liang-shih 良史, *fl.* 1300) is a piece of historiographical scholarship as well as an indispensable source for the study of T'ang poetry. Included in the 278 biographies is information on 398 T'ang and Five Dynasties poets. Only one hundred of these poets can be found in the dynastic histories.

Little is known about Hsin Wen-fang, except that he was a Central Asian serving in a minor position in the Yüan government. His introduction was dated 1304, giving some idea of when he lived. The importance of the *T'ang ts'ai-tzu chuan* has much to do with his being an established poet (whose *P'ei-sha shih-chi* 披沙詩集 [Spreading Out the Sand Collection of Poems] unfortunately may not have survived), for the *T'ang ts'ai-tzu chuan* is much more than a first-rate, historical study of the poets. It offers penetrating observations of the changing trends of T'ang poetry and critical evaluations of the art of the poets. Considering the quality of the poems rather than the existing ranking of the poets, he included a large number of minor figures, particularly those from the second half of the T'ang. This does not mean that the book is without its share of hearsay and error; most of this fortunately has been identified.

The usefulness of the *T'ang ts'ai-tzu chuan* has recently been enhanced by the exhaustive research of Nunome Chōfu 布目潮渢, who, with Nakamura Takashi 中村喬, brought out in a massive volume a collated text with ample notes, a Japanese translation, a host of helpful appendixes, and a list of the source materials probably used by Hsin Wen-fang.

Later biographical works similar to the *T'ang ts'ai-tzu chuan* include Ch'ien Ch'ien-i's* *Lieh-ch'ao shih-chi hsiao-chuan* 列朝詩集小傳 (1649), Wang Chieh-hsi's 王介錫 (*chin-shih*, 1649) *Ming ts'ai-tzu chuan* 明才子傳, and Chang Wei-p'ing's 張維屏 (1780-1859) *Kuo-ch'ao shih-jen cheng-lüeh* 國朝詩人徵略 (1830-1842).

EDITIONS:

Tō saishi den 唐才子傳. Tokyo, 1972. The 10-*chüan* complete editions have survived only in Japan; this one has been photographically reproduced from a manuscript in the Nai-kaku bunkō 內閣文庫. Since the late Ch'ing, 10-*chüan* editions have also been available in several *ts'ung-shu* collections.

T'ang ts'ai-tzu chuan. Peking, 1965. Punctuated and collated; for general reference: users should be alerted to errors noted in article by Kuo Chün-man (see below).

Tō saishi den no kenkyū 唐才子傳研究. Nunome Chōfu and Nakamura Takashi, comps. and trans. Osaka, 1972. The ultimate edition, for its accuracy and its rich collection of reference materials.

TRANSLATIONS:

Nunome, Chōfu and Nakamura Takashi. *Tō saishi den no kenkyū.* Osaka, 1972.

Ogawa, Tamaki 小川環樹. *Tōdai no shijin: Sono denki* 唐代の詩人：その傳記. Tokyo, 1975. Has many translations from the *T'ang ts'ai-tzu chuan.*

STUDIES:

Ch'en, Chan 陳鱣. "*T'ang ts'ai-tzu chuan* chien-tuan chi" 唐才子傳簡端記, *Pei-p'ing Pei-hai T'u-shu kuan yüeh-k'an,* 2.1 (January 1929), 33-46.

Ch'en, Yin-k'o 陳寅恪. "Shu *T'ang ts'ai-tzu chuan* K'ang Ch'ia chuan hou" 書唐才子傳康洽傳後, in *Chou Shu-t'ao Hsien-sheng liu-shih sheng-jih chi-nien lun-wen chi* 周叔弢先生六十生日紀念論文集, Tientsin, 1950, pp. 259-262.

Ch'en, Yüan 陳垣. *Western and Central Asians in China Under the Mongols.* Ch'ien Hsing-hai 錢星海 and L. Carrington Goodrich, trans. Los Angeles, 1966, pp. 138-140.

Kuo, Chün-man. "Hsin-pan *T'ang ts'ai-tzu chuan* chiao-tu chi" 新版唐才子傳校讀記, "Wen-hsüeh i-ch'an," 175 in *Kuang-ming jih-pao,* September 22, 1957.

Nunome, *Kenkyū.*

—YWM

T'ang-wen ts'ui 唐文粹 is one of the earliest collections of T'ang prose and poetry. Edited by Yao Hsüan 姚鉉 (*tzu,* Pao-chih 寶之, 968-1020), from Ho-fei 合肥 (modern Kiangsu), it was completed in 1011 and first printed in 1039. This 100-*chüan* anthology and the much larger *Wen-yüan ying-hua** are the basic repositories of T'ang writings. Since many of the individual *wen-chi* 文集 (collected works) of the T'ang have been lost, their value has long been recognized.

Indeed, the *T'ang-wen ts'ui* was compiled in reaction to the *Wen-yüan ying-hua,* which, as an intended sequel to the *Wen-hsüan,** deemphasized *ku-wen** writings. The *T'ang-wen ts'ui,* however, includes only the *ku-t'i* 古體 (old-style) forms of prose and poetry—parallel prose and poems in the *chin-t'i* (new style) are excluded, thus reflecting the influence of *ku-wen.*

The first 18 *chüan* contain *shih** and *fu.** Following 2 *chüan* of *sung* 頌 and *tsan* 贊, the remaining 80 *chüan* are all *san-wen* 散文 (free prose—see Prose essay), setting the tone for subsequent, essay-dominated anthologies. *Chüan* 43-49 contain most of the important T'ang *ku-wen* pieces.

A sequel, *T'ang-wen ts'ui pu-i* 唐文粹補遺, in 26 *chüan,* was compiled by Kuo Lin 郭麐 (*tzu,* Hsiang-po 祥伯) from Wu-chiang 吳江 (modern Kiangsu) during the Ch'ing dynasty.

EDITIONS:

T'ang-wen ts'ui. SPTK. Photolithic reproduction of a Ming edition with appended textual notes.

———. *Kuo-hs eh chi-pen ts'ung-shu.* Modern typeset edition based on an 1893 edition.

———. *Yü-yüan ts'ung-k'o* 楡園叢刻. 1893. Collated edition; best edition.

STUDIES:

Ch'ien, Mu 錢穆. "Tu Yao Hsüan *T'ang-wen ts'ui*" 讀姚鉉唐文粹, *Hsin-ya hsüeh-pao,* 3.2 (1958), 45-51.

—SFL and WHN

T'ang Yin 唐寅 (*tzu,* Po-hu 伯虎, *hao,* Tzu-wei 子畏, Liu-ju chü-shih 六如居士, 1470-1524) is best known as a painter, a calligrapher, and a romantic figure in popular literature. As a poet, he was famous in his own time as one of the *Wu-chung ssu-tzu* 吳中四子 (Four Gentlemen of Wu [Soo-chow])—the other three, all poet-painters, are Chu Yün-ming 祝允明 (1461-1527), Wen Cheng-ming 文徵明 (1470-1559), and Hsü Chen-ch'ing 徐禎卿 (1479-1511).

T'ang had a brilliant but erratic youth capped by winning first place in the provincial examination of 1498, having finally resolved to settle down to his studies after the deaths of both parents, a sister, and his wife within a two-year period (1493-1494). Following the metropolitan examination held in Peking in 1499, however, he was jailed for suspicion of being involved in a cheating scandal, thus ending one of the most promising official careers of his day. He returned in disgrace to Soochow and, needing a way to earn a living, soon began to study painting under the famous Chou Ch'en 周臣 (c. 1450-c. 1535). T'ang quickly became famous as a painter; an unlikely legend states that his commissioned works were so greatly in demand he paid Chou to help him.

In 1614 T'ang was invited by Chu Ch'en-hao 朱宸濠, Prince of Ning 寧 (d. 1521) to join his staff. Upon discovering that Chu was planning to rebel, T'ang managed to leave his employment by feigning madness. After his return to Soochow, T'ang is reported to have led a riotous life, and to have finally expired of "overindulgence" in wine and women. This interesting life stimulated the proliferation of scandalous stories about T'ang that provide a picture of him as a madcap rake; fact and fiction have blurred to the point that it is difficult to distinguish between the two. An example is the substitution of T'ang's name for that of the hero of a Yüan play in the Ming short story "San-hsiao yin-yüan" 三笑因緣 (Romance of the Three Smiles).

Although some of his earlier poetry pokes fun at both Taoists and Buddhists, in his later years T'ang found consolation of a sort in Buddhism, adopting a phrase from the Diamond Sutra, liu-ju 六如 (six likenesses) as his sobriquet. It seems probable that this was later than the motto carved on one of his seals, "Foremost Rake South of the Yangtze River." Even in his poems on Buddhist themes, however, it is clear that Neo-Confucian metaphysics plays at least as important a role as Buddhism.

T'ang's collected works were compiled in 1534 in the one-chüan T'ang Po-hu ch'üan-chi 唐伯虎全集, additional material being added in the later editions of 1592, 1607, 1614 and 1801. It would appear, however, from a letter T'ang wrote late in life that the greater part of his work was early lost to posterity, for besides mentioning an anthology of his works in eight chüan, T'ang-shih wen-hsüan 唐氏文選, T'ang refers to a number of other works on various subjects not extant. Besides T'ang's collected writings in four chüan, the only work extant attributed to T'ang is the Hua p'u 畫譜 (Painting Manual) in three chüan. But this attribution is widely held to be spurious.

That T'ang wrote works on a broad range of interests suggests the necessity of drastically revising received opinion about him, for these very mainstream-literati interests accord well with the broad range of painting styles and themes in works generally acknowledged to be from T'ang's own hand. The early failure of his official career, his class background and lack of gentry means, and the fictions that he may have helped to foster concerning his "libertine" lifestyle combined with the often mundane realism of some of his painting and poetry (not typical of literati) all caused writers until recently to classify T'ang as a "professional" rather than a wen-jen—that is, someone who worked in the style of those who painted at others' beck and call for a living, rather than as a refined pastime suitable to cultivated "gentlemen." While T'ang never produced anything so startling in its realism as his teacher Chou Ch'en's famous painting of twenty-four Liu-min 流民 (Vagrants), his ten "P'in-shih yin" 貧士吟 (Poems of an Impoverished Gentleman) are unusual for their time and employ a realism rich in everyday detail.

Besides this series, two other groups stand out in T'ang's poetry: first are the tz'u,* ch'ü,* and tsa-chü* works that range from the faintly to the graphically erotic (if we accept a series of six tz'u not included in his present collection but attributed to T'ang by the critic Wang Shih-chen* [1526-1590]); and secondly, the group of shih* poems that weave variations, almost metaphysical in their complexity, on the theme of the poet, wine, moon, and blossoms, poems that would appear to reflect the sort of Buddhist speculation that T'ang is said to have adopted in later life.

EDITIONS:

T'ang Po-hu Hsien-sheng ch'üan-chi 唐伯虎先生全集. 2v. Taipei, 1970. Reproduction of the best extant edition of 1614 compiled by Ho Ta-ch'eng. There are also various later editions in modern reprints.

TRANSLATIONS:

Davis, *Penguin*, p. 58.

Lai, T. C. *T'ang Yin, Poet-painter.* Hong Kong, 1969. Unreliable.

Sunflower, pp. 466-67.

STUDIES:

Chiang, Chao-shen 江兆申. "Liu-ju chü-shih chih shen-shih" 六如居士之身世, *Ku-kung chi-k'an*, 2.4 (April 1968), 15-32.

———. "Liu-ju chü-shih chih shih-yu yü tsao-yü" 六如居士之師友與遭遇, *Ku-kung chi-k'an*, 3.1 (July 1968), 33-60.

———. "Liu-ju chü-shih chih yu-tsung yü shih-wen" 六如居士之遊蹤與詩文, *Ku-kung chi-k'an*, 3.2 (October 1968), 31-71.

———. "Liu-ju chü-shih chih shu-hua yü nien-p'u" 六如居士之書畫與年譜, *Ku-kung chi-k'an*, 3.3 (January 1969), 35-79.

Sirén, Osvald. *Chinese Painting: Leading Masters and Principles.* London, 1956-58, v. 4, pp. 193-205.

Tseng, Yu-ho 曾幼荷. "Notes on T'ang Yin," *Oriental Art*, 2.3 (Autumn 1956), 103-108.

Wilson, Marc, and Kwan S. Wong. *Friends of Wen Cheng-ming: A View from the Crawford Collection.* New York, 1975, pp. 54-75.

Yang, Ching-an 楊靜盦. *T'ang Yin nien-p'u* 唐寅年譜. Shanghai, 1947. Best chronology available.

—DP

T'ang yin t'ung-ch'ien 唐音通籤, compiled by Hu Chen-heng 胡震亨 (*tzu*, Hsiao-yüan 孝轅, *hao*, Tun-sou 遯叟, 1569-1644/45), is (or was) an enormous compendium of T'ang poetry and related material. Still not printed in its entirety, it served as one of the two main sources for the imperially compiled *Ch'üan T'ang shih.** One section, the *T'ang yin kuei-ch'ien* 癸籤, consisting of a classified collection of critical materials on T'ang verse, was printed separately in 1718 and is an important reference in its own right.

Hu Chen-heng never succeeded in passing the *chin-shih* examination and served only occasionally and briefly in office. Most of his life was spent in his native district (Hai-yen 海鹽, Chekiang), where he was known as a scholar and book collector. He was responsible for a number of scholarly works, but the *T'ang yin t'ung-ch'ien* is certainly the largest and most important among them. It consists of ten divisions, designated according to the "Heavenly Stems" (*chia-ch'ien* 甲籤, *i-ch'ien* 乙籤, etc.), with contents as follows: poems by members of the T'ang imperial house (7 *chüan*), Early T'ang poets (79 *chüan*), High T'ang poets (125 *chüan*), Middle T'ang poets (341 *chüan*), poets of the Late T'ang and the Five Dynasties (201 + 64 *chüan*), a supplement containing works from all periods by poets having only a few extant poems or scattered lines (54 *chüan*), poems by Buddhist and Taoist clerics, women, and non-Chinese (39 + 6 + 9 + 1 *chüan*), poems in miscellaneous forms, such as *yüeh-fu, tz'u*, rhymed jokes, insults, and the like, as well as liturgical verse from Taoist and Buddhist sources (66 *chüan* in all), poems attributed to ghosts and other supernatural manifestations, reported from dreams, etc. (8 *chüan*), and critical comments on T'ang poetry (33 *chüan*).

The manuscript of the *T'ang yin t'ung-ch'ien* eventually found its way into the Ch'ing palace library and was heavily drawn upon by the compilers of the *Ch'üan T'ang shih*. Indeed, the editors of the *Ssu-k'u ch'üan-shu* (see Chi Yün) gave it as the main source. But the editorial preface to the *Ch'üan T'ang shih* makes it clear that another work, a "complete T'ang poems in the Palace Library" was used as well. Recent scholarship has identified the latter as a compilation begun by Ch'ien Ch'ien-i* and completed by Chi Chen-i 季振宜 (*chin-shih*, 1647), presently in the collection of the National Central Library in Taipei. Ch'ien's involvement in this project presumably explains why the *Ssu-k'u* editors did not mention it, since all works by Ch'ien had been prohibited by the time the *Ssu-k'u* was compiled. Careful comparison of the *Ch'üan T'ang shih* with Ch'ien's and Chi's work shows that in fact the latter seems to have been the chief source for much of the former. In general, it appears

761

that the compilers of the *Ch'üan T'ang shih* drew their texts for the works of the more important poets from Ch'ien and Chi, while relying on the *T'ang yin t'ung-ch'ien* for biographical introductions, minor poets, and miscellaneous works. Unfortunately, they omitted most of the citation references found in their sources and also left out some material (liturgical poetry and criticism) found in the *T'ang yin t'ung-ch'ien*. Ch'ien and Chi, in turn, had based their compilation on a variety of Sung and Yüan editions, supplemented by an earlier large-scale Ming compendium of T'ang verse, the *T'ang shih chi* 唐詩紀 (preface dated 1585) of Wu Kuan 吳琯.

Because only portions of the *T'ang yin t'ung-ch'ien* were known to have been printed and the location of the manuscript was not generally known, it was widely assumed to have been lost. But in the 1930s Yü Ta-kang was able to inspect a composite copy (put together by a townsman of Hu Chen-heng), in the palace museum in Peking. This was found to include printed versions of various sections, filled out with a manuscript transcription of the rest of the entire work. The present location of this copy is uncertain and only portions of the printed section are recorded as extant in Taiwan.

EDITIONS:

T'ang yin kuei-ch'ien. Rpt. Taipei, 1970. Reprint of a recent Chinese typeset edition, the most accessible text.

STUDIES:

Liu, Chao-yu 劉兆祐. "Yü-ting Ch'üan T'ang shih yü Ch'ien Chien-i Chi Chen-i ti-chi T'ang shih kao-pen kuan-hsi t'an-wei" 御定全唐詩與錢謙益季振宜遞輯唐詩稿本關係探微, *Yu-shih hsüeh-chih*, 15 (1978), 101-136.

———. "Ch'ing Ch'ien Ch'ien-i Chi Chen-i ti-chi T'ang shih kao-pen pa: chien lun *Yü-ting Ch'üan T'ang shih* chih ti-pen" 清錢謙益季振宜遞輯唐詩稿本跋 兼論 唐詩之底本, *Tung-wu wen-shih hsüeh-pao*, 3 (1978), 28-59. The latter is a rearranged and revised version of the former.

Yü, Ta-kang 俞大綱. "Chi *T'ang yin t'ung-ch'ien*" 記唐音通籤, *BIHP*, 7.3 (1937), 355-384.

—DB

T'ang Ying 唐英 (*tzu*, Chün-kung 俊公, *hao*, Wo-chi lao-jen 蝸寄老人, 1682-*c.* 1755) was a writer and dramatist of the mid-Ch'ing period from Shen-yang. T'ang was a native Chinese and member of the Plain White Banner who served from boyhood in the court of Emperor K'ang-hsi. After a period of servitude, T'ang was appointed, at thirty-five, an inspector of the imperial porcelain works at Ching-te-chen in Kiangsi. He served there from 1724 to 1749 and was concurrently Superintendent of Customs at Huai-an (1736-1738) and at Kiukiang (1739-1756?). In 1750 he was sent briefly to Canton to supervise customs there but returned in 1752 to his post in Kiukiang. He was very fond of porcelain and produced works of such fine quality that they were called "T'ang's porcelains."

His literary collection is named *T'ao-jen-hsin yü* 陶人心語 (Words from the Heart of a Porcelain Maker) and contains many pieces about the manufacture of porcelain. He was primarily known in literary circles, however, as a dramatist, and he left behind a collection of seventeen works known as *Ku-pai-t'ang ch'uan-ch'i* 枯柏堂傳奇 (Dramas from the Hall of the Withered Cypress). There is a preface by Tung Jung,* a fellow dramatist; T'ang wrote critical notes for one of Tung's plays, *Chih-k'an chi* 芝龕記 (The Record of the Fungus Shrine). In a preface that T'ang Ying wrote for yet another dramatist in 1750, he remarked that he had written more than ten dramas, but modern research attributes at least seventeen to his name.

Six of the pieces, which T'ang himself designates as *ch'uan-ch'i*,* are in fact four-act plays; six are *tsa-chü*,* style dramas of one act; two are *tsa-chü* in two acts; and the remainder are all *ch'uan-ch'i* of standard length. His one-act *tsa-chü* are: *Chia-sao* 笳騷 (Vexation of the Flute), with a preface dated 1742; *Yung-chung-jen* 傭中人 (The Worker), with a preface written by Tung Jung dated 1753; *Nü t'an-tz'u* 女彈詞 (The Female Ballad Singer), with a preface by Tung Jung written in 1754; *Ch'ing-chung-p'u cheng-an* 清忠譜正案 (The True Case of the Register of the Pure and Loyal), with an epigraph by Tung Jung dated 1754;

Ying-hsiung pao 英雄報 (Hero's Revenge); and *Shih-tzu p'o* 十字坡 (Shih-tzu Slope).

The Register of the Pure and Loyal is a dramatization of the revenge Chou Shun-ch'ang 周順昌 (1584-1626) wreaked on Wei Chung-hsien 魏忠賢 (1568-1627). Chou, one of the five Tung-lin loyalists, was incarcerated by Wei, the notorious eunuch, and later died under torture in prison. In the play, Chou is reincarnated by Shang-ti (The Divine Ruler) as the City-moat God of Soochow; Wei Chung-hsien and his faction are brought by a celestial spirit before the City-moat God for punishment. Despite their clever lies, they are punished. The play is heavily satirical. Politics also figure in another of these plays, *The Worker*. During the transfer of power to the Manchus in 1644, a purveyor of vegetables and hot water sees the coffin of the last Ming emperor on the road. After weeping bitterly and offering sacrifice, he kills himself by dashing his head against the coffin. The political satire is clear here; T'ang is criticizing the civil and military officials of the Ming court who surrendered to the Manchus, leaving loyalty and righteousness to the commoners. *Shih-tsu Slope* is, of course, based on chapter 27 of the *Shui-hu chuan*,* in which Wu Sung flees from his captors and escapes to Liang-shan Marshes, following an encounter at an inn that specializes in human-meat dumplings.

The two-act *tsa-chü* are: *Yü-hsi meng* 虞兮夢 (A Dream of Lady Yü) and *Ch'ang-sheng tien pu-ch'üeh* 長生殿補闕 (A Supplement to The Palace of Long Life). The *Dream of Lady Yü* is actually two independent scenes that take place in a temple in Wu-chiang dedicated to Hsiang Yü, who lost the empire to the first emperor of Han. Yü was the name of the consort who perished with him. In the first act the commoners of the ford at Wu-chiang, where Hsiang Yü met his end, beseech the spirit for a bountiful harvest; in the second, a young scholar named Wang Na 王訥 weeps in front of Hsiang Yü's portrait, bewailing his lack of success. This scene has much in common with the "crying in the temple" plays of Shen Tzu-cheng,* Chang Tao 張韜, and Hsi Yung-jen.* The supplement to

the *Palace of Long Life* should rightly be called a "mini-*ch'uan-ch'i*," since it supplements this famous drama by Hung Sheng.*

The *ch'uan-ch'i* are: *Lu-hua hsü* 蘆花絮 (Reed Flower Floss); *San-yüan pao* 三元報 (Recompense via the Three Great Principles), both in four acts; *Chuan-t'ien hsin* 轉天心 (A Heart to Turn Heaven) in thirty-eight acts (preface dated 1748); *Shuang-ting an* 雙釘案 (The Case of the Doubled Nails), in twenty-six acts; *Ch'iao-huan chi* 巧換記 (The Clever Switch); *T'ien-yüan chai* 天緣債 (A Debt of Heavenly Affinity); *Liang-shang yen* 梁上眼 (An Eye on the Beam); *Mei-lung chen* 梅龍鎮 (Plum-dragon Town); and *Mien-kang hsiao* 麵缸笑 (The Dough Vat Bursts into Laughter). Several of these works, including *Mei-lung chen*, *Mien-kang hsiao*, and *Shuang-ting an*, were very popular in the repertoire of regional drama and were probably adopted into the classical repertoire of *K'un-ch'ü** dramas by T'ang.

EDITIONS:

The seventeen dramas are found in original editions published by the Ku-pai T'ang between 1740 and 1755. According to Tseng Yung-i (see below), there is also an edition of the *Ku-pai-t'ang ch'uan-ch'i*, consisting of six dramas, *Chung-chung-p'u cheng-an*, *Shih-tzu-p'o*, *Yung-chung-jen*, *Yü-hsi-meng*, *Chang-sheng-tien pu-ch'üeh*, and *Lu-hua-hsü* (published in 1754), circulating in Taiwan, probably at the Fu Ssu-nien library at Academia Sinica.

T'ao-jen-hsin yü. Ku Chen-tsang 雇震滄, comp. Ch'ien-lung ed.

STUDIES:

Fu, *Ch'ing tsa-chü*, pp. 113-117.

Li, Hsiu-sheng 李修生. "T'ang Ying chi ch'i chü-tso" 唐英及其劇作, *Wen-hsüeh i-ch'an tseng-k'an*, 12 (1963), 39-47.

Tseng, "Ch'ing-tai tsa-chü," pp. 161-163.

—XLW and SHW

Tao-tsang 道藏 (Taoist Canon) is the most comprehensive collectaneum of Taoist literature, comparable to the *Ta-tsang ching* 大藏經 (see the Buddhist Literature essay) of the Buddhist tradition. The edition used today is based on the *Cheng-t'ung Tao-tsang* printed in 1444-1445, together with the Wan-li supplement of 1607. It wasn't until 1926 that the entire corpus was made

763

available by means of a photolithographic reproduction. The research evident in Maspero's *Le Taoïsme* and cognate works might never have been undertaken, had this reprint not appeared. The field of Taoist studies would, in fact, not be what it is today were it not for the foresight of President Hsü Shih-ch'ang 徐世昌 (1855-1939; in office 1918-1922) and several of his colleagues, including the former Minister of Education and renowned bibliophile Fu Tseng-hsiang 傅增湘 (1872-1950). After publishing a handful of canonic sources from his own library in 1918 under the title *Tao-tsang pen wu-tzu* 道藏本五子, Fu proposed that the Commercial Press of Shanghai make a reproduction of the woodblock concertina edition housed in the Pai-yün Kuan 白雲觀 of Peking. It was primarily due to the financial backing of Hsü that this was accomplished under the guidance of Chang Yüan-chi 張元濟 (1866-1959), the Han-fen-lou 涵芬樓 Archivist of Commercial Press. Because of the rarity of the 1926 edition, I-wen Publishers in Taipei sponsored a reprinting in 1962 with the support of several National Taiwan University professors, including the specialist in early Taoist bibliography, Yen Ling-feng 嚴靈峯. This edition preserves the 1923 prefatory remarks signed by Fu, Chang, and a host of reformists including K'ang Yu-wei* and Liang Ch'i-ch'ao.* A very great debt is owed these early patrons of the textual history of Taoism. What they achieved is apparently now irreplicable for, as Sawada Mizuho 澤田瑞穂 reports (*Tōhō shūkyō*, 57 [May 1981]), the Pai-yün Kuan edition has since been dispersed to Peking University Library and other unnamed institutions. The whereabouts of the copy kept at the sister abbey in Shanghai as late as the 1940s is even more of a mystery. The only other early woodblock printings known of the *Cheng-t'ung Canon* are fragmentary copies of the sixteenth century within the holdings of the Bibliothèque Nationale of Paris and the Imperial Library of Tokyo.

The history of early canonic compilation upon which the present edition is founded is repeated in a number of English, French, Chinese, and Japanese sources. Early in the fifth century the tripartite classificatory system (*San-tung* 三洞 [The Three Caverns]) under which the received texts are ordered was determined according to a ranking of revelatory traditions: (1) the *Tung-chen* 洞眞 dominated by the Shang-ch'ing 上清 revelations, (2) the *Tung-hsüan* 洞玄 dominated by the Ling-pao 靈寶 revelations, and (3) the *Tung-shen* 洞神 dominated by the San-huang 三皇 revelations. Each of the *San-tung* headings is subdivided into twelve categories of writings: (1) scriptural sources, (2) sacred talismans, (3) exegeses, (4) revelatory diagrams, (5) historical and genealogical writings, (6) precepts and prohibitions, (7) ritual, (8) prescriptive codes, (9) special techniques, i.e., alchemical, geomantic, numerological, etc., (10) hagiographic accounts, (11) declamations and liturgy, and (12) sacred transmissions, i.e., reports and petitions to celestial authorities. About 300 to 350 titles are retained for each of the *San-tung*, with the heaviest concentration generally in the scriptural and exegetic categories and secondarily in the prescriptive codes of the *Tung-chen* and *Tung-shen* divisions and ritual settings in the Ling-pao division. Ōfuchi Ninji proposes that a sixth-century reformation rectified obvious lacunae with the addition of four supplements (*ssu-fu* 四輔): (1) *T'ai-hsüan* 太玄, (2) *T'ai-p'ing* 太平, (3) *T'ai-ch'ing* 太清, and (4) *Cheng-i* 正一, to which the *Tao-te-ching*, *T'ai-p'ing ching*, *T'ai-ch'ing* alchemical works, and Celestial Master sources are central, respectively. Throughout ten centuries of canonic compilation, these seven divisions (the Three Caverns and the Four Supplements) have apparently remained constant, even amidst various reshufflings of texts, multiple accretions, and irrecoverable losses.

A number of catalogues of Taoist writing were completed by imperial order, starting with Lu Hsiu-ching's 陸修靜 (406-477) *San-tung ching-shu mu-lu* 三洞經書目錄 presented in 471. At the behest of Emperor Hsüan-tsung of the T'ang, a collection of several hundred texts was compiled and the *San-tung ch'iung-kang* 三洞瓊綱 that resulted was the first canon transcribed for circulation (*c.* 748). The blocks of that compilation as well as another prepared under the aegis of Emperor Hsi-tsung (r. 873-888) were lost in the An Lu-shan and Huang Ch'ao uprisings. Emperor T'ai-tsung of the Sung initiated efforts to re-establish an imperial library of Taoist writings, and in 1008 Emperor Chen-tsung put Wang Ch'in-jo 王欽若 (962-1025) in charge of preparing a catalogue. Eleven years later, after recovering sources from a number of widely dispersed canonic editions, Wang's successor Chang Chün-fang (see *Yün-chi ch'i-ch'ien*) presented the *Ta Sung t'ien-kung pao-tsang* 大宋天宮寶藏, the first definitive edition of that which came to be called the *Tao-tsang*. Under Emperor Hui-tsung, a nationwide search for sacred texts culminated in the first printed *Canon*, the *Cheng-ho wan-shou Tao-tsang* 正和萬壽道藏 of 1116-1117. What blocks survived after the desecrations of war served as the core from which the *Ta Chin Hsüan-tu pao-tsang* 大金玄都寶藏 was printed under the auspices of the Chin court in 1191.

Most of the blocks of the Jurchen *Canon* were later lost in a fire that consumed the T'ien-ch'ang Kuan 天長觀, the shrine antecedent to the present Pai-yün Kuan. Using an extant copy of the *Canon*, the Ch'üan-chen affiliate Sung Te-fang 宋德方 (1183-1247) headed a massive editorial project to recompile the *Hsüan-tu pao-tsang*, a feat completed in 1244. Severe losses to this, the largest *Taoist Canon* ever compiled, were suffered in the book burnings ordered during the latter half of the thirteenth century following a series of debates between Buddhist and Taoist leaders. Just how much was irretrievably lost can be discerned by comparing the contents of the Ming *Canon* with the *Tao-tsang ch'üeh-ching mu-lu* 道藏闕經目錄 (2 *ch.*, TT 1056, HY 1419), a catalogue of lost texts compiled in 1275. Under mandate of Emperor Ch'eng-tsu of the Ming, the forty-third Celestial Master, Chang Yü-ch'u 張宇初 (1361-1410), initially supervised the compiling of what became the *Cheng-t'ung Tao-tsang* of 1444-1445. His descendant, the fiftieth Master Chang Kuo-hsiang 張國祥 (d. 1611), was placed in charge of compiling the Wan-li *Hsü Tao-tsang* in 1607.

The present catalogues for the *Tao-tsang*, from Pai Yün-chi's 白雲霽 *Tao-tsang mu-lu hsiang-chu* 目錄詳註 to the 1935 *Harvard-Yenching Index* of Weng Tu-chien (see Taoist Literature essay), will soon be surpassed by Liu Ts'un-yan's annotated *mu-lu* of two-million Chinese characters and by a descriptive and analytic catalogue of the *Canon* promised by a European consortium organized in 1977 to work on the "Project *Tao-tsang*" under the direction of K. M. Schipper at the École Pratique des Hautes Études in Paris. Schipper has already supervised the preparation of a concordance to the titles in the *Canon* (1975), a reprint of which is now widely available as an index to the 1977 printing of the *Tao-tsang* issued by I-wen Publishers. By reading six titles as three and listing fourteen additional titles separately, Schipper has expanded the total number of titles in the *Harvard-Yenching Index* from 1476 to 1487. This revised numbering system is now generally adopted in Paris publications with the abbreviation TT for *Tao-tsang*, a prefix that is traditionally reserved for the fascicle number (s) of a text. The discrepancies in the numbering systems of the two indices are charted in Judith M. Boltz's "A Survey of Taoist Literature: Tenth–Seventeenth Centuries" (forthcoming in the China Research Monograph series, Institute of East Asian Studies, University of California, Berkeley).

EDITIONS:

Cheng-t'ung Tao-tsang 正統道藏. 1120v. Shanghai, 1923-1926; rpt. Taipei, 1962; 1977 reduced-size printing in 60v. includes a reprint of Schipper's 1975 *Concordance* reprinted by Li Tien-k'uei 李殿魁, *Cheng-t'ung Tao-tsang mu-lu so-yin* 目錄索引. Fragmentary editions printed in 1598 are preserved in the Bibliothèque Nationale of Paris and the Imperial Library of Tokyo. Samples of early manuscript editions are available in the National Central Library of Taipei.

STUDIES:

Barrett, T. H. "Introduction" to Henri Maspero, *Taoism and Chinese Religion*, Frank A. Kierman, Jr., tr., Amherst, Mass., 1981, pp. vii-xxiii. A detailed bibliographic survey of

Maspero's legacy, Japanese studies, and a history of the *Canon*.

Ch'en, Kuo-fu 陳國符. *Tao-tsang yüan-liu k'ao* 道藏源流考. 2v. Peking 1962. An enlarged edition of the 1949 text. See "Li-tai Tao shu-mu chi *Tao-tsang* chih tsuan-hsiu yü lou-pan" 歷代道書目及道藏之纂修與鏤板, pp. 105-231.

Fukui, Kōjun 福井康順. *Dōkyō no kisoteki kenkyū* 道教の基礎的研究. Tokyo, 1957. See "Dōkyō kyōten no shosō" 道教經典の諸相, pp. 133-214.

Gauchet, L. "Contributions à l'étude du Taoïsme," *Bulletin de l'Université l'Aurore*, ser. 3, no. 9 (1948), 1-38.

Kubo, Noritada 窪德忠. *Dōkyō to Chūgoku shakai* 道教と中國社會. Tokyo, 1948. See "Dōzō" 道藏, pp. 126-145.

Liu, Ts'un-yan. "The Compilation and Historical Value of the *Tao-tsang*," in *Essays on the Sources for Chinese History*, Donald D. Leslie *et al.*, eds., Columbia, S. C., 1973, pp. 104-119.

Needham, Joseph, ed., with the collaboration of Ho Ping-yü and Lu Gwei-djen. *Science and Civilisation in China*, v. 5, pt. 3. Cambridge, 1974. See "Alchemy in the Taoist Patrology (*Tao Tsang*)," pp. 113-117.

Ōfuchi, Ninji 大淵忍爾. *Dōkyō-shi no kenkyū* 道教史の研究. Okayama, 1964. See "Dōkyō kyōten-shi no kenkyū" 道教經典史の研究, pp. 215-434.

———. "The Formation of the Taoist Canon," in *Facets of Taoism: Essays in Chinese Religion*, Holmes H. Welch and Anna Seidel, eds., New Haven, 1979, pp. 253-267. A study of the *San-tung* and *Ssu-fu*.

Pai, Yün-chi 白雲霽. *Tao-tsang mu-lu hsiang chu* 道藏目錄詳註. N.p., T'ui-keng T'ang 退耕堂, n.d.; the Wen-chien Ko 文建閣 copy of the *Ssu-k'u ch'üan-shu* edition is reprinted in Ting Fu-pao 丁福保, ed., *Tao-tsang ching-hua lu* 道藏精華錄, Shanghai, 1922; while in the latter edition Pai Yün-chi is cited as the compiler in the table of contents, the name Li Chieh 李杰 actually appears on the title page itself.

Schipper, K. M. *Concordance du Tao-tsang; Titres des ouvrages*. Paris, 1975.

Weng, Tu-chien 翁獨健, ed. *Tao-tsang tzu-mu yin-te* 道藏子目引得 (Combined Indexes to the Authors and Titles of Books in Two Collections of Taoist Literature). Peking, 1935. Harvard-Yenching Institute Sinological Index Series, no. 25.

Wieger, L. *Taoïsme*, v. 1. Hsien-hsien, Ho-chien fu (Chihli), 1911. Reviewed by P. Pelliot, *JA*, 20 (1912), 141-156, and by E. Chavannes, *TP*, 12 (1911), 749-753.

Yoshioka, Yoshitoyo 吉岡義豐. *Dōkyō kyōten shi-ron* 道教經典史論. Tokyo, 1955. See "Dōzō hensan-shi" 道藏編纂史, pp. 1-180, with closing summary chart.

—JB

T'ao Ch'ien

T'ao Ch'ien 陶潛 (original name, Yüan-ming 淵明, *tzu*, Yüan-liang 元亮, 365-427) is generally considered one of the two or three greatest pre-T'ang poets. He was a native of Ch'ai-sang 柴桑 (modern Chiu-chiang 九江 in Kiangsi). The T'ao family belonged to the Hsi 溪 minority. T'ao Ch'ien's great-grandfather was the illustrious statesman and general T'ao K'an 陶侃 (259-334); his maternal grandfather, Meng Chia 孟嘉 (*fl.* 330), was a close associate of Huan Wen 桓溫 (312-373), possibly the most powerful person in China at the time. Yet despite these illustrious beginnings, the fortunes of the T'ao house declined rapidly, and T'ao Ch'ien was born into a poor family—even his father's name is unrecorded.

T'ao was a very complicated person. He manifested early an ambivalence that plagued him half his life. On the one hand, he maintained he was ill-fitted to the common world and did not want to be involved in human affairs. He enjoyed the simple life, the freedom to roam the hills and mountains and to chat leisurely with others of like mind. According to his friends, he kept mostly to himself and had a distaste for social rules. On the other hand, by his own admission, he had a "fierce ambition not bounded by the four seas, [an ambition] to spread [his] wings and soar afar." He considered it almost an obligation to accomplish great things, and he viewed as shameful his failure to do so:

> The teaching that the late master left behind,
> Have I forgotten it?
> "If a man is still unknown at forty,
> He is not someone you should respect."
> Grease my famous chariot!
> Whip up my famous steed!
> Although a thousand miles is a long way,
> Dare I not reach my destination?
> from "Jung mu" 榮木 (Trees in Bloom)

The quotation from Confucius in this poem points to the likelihood that T'ao's ambition was a result of his Confucian upbringing. Pressure to live up to his illustrious family name may also have been a factor. The conflict between these two selves lasted a long time. Although he cried, "mountains and lakes have long been beckoning,/Why am I still hesitating," again and again he "cast away [his] staff and readied [himself] for the . . . journey,/ bidding temporary farewell to fields and gardens."

After briefly serving in the local government as a Libationer when he was about thirty, he resigned from the post, finding it intolerable. Soon after, he accepted a post that took him away from his family for a long time. The nature of the job is unclear, except that he reported to work at Chiang-ling 江陵, which was within Ching-chou 荆州. It is possible that he served in some capacity under the then Grand Warden of Ching-chou, Huan Hsüan 桓玄 (368-404). This service was interrupted by the death of his mother. During the mourning period, Huan Hsüan rebelled and ascended the throne, but was quickly overthrown and decapitated—all in less than two years. What calamity would have befallen T'ao Ch'ien had he not been home in mourning can only be surmised.

T'ao's ambition soon got the upper hand again. He accepted a post as adjutant to a general, perhaps Liu Yü 劉裕 (356-422), who later became the first emperor of Sung. For reasons unknown, the position did not work out, and the next year he had another title. By the end of the same year, he became magistrate of P'eng-tse 彭澤, a small town thirty miles from his home. Yet eighty-some days later he resigned. Two explanations for this rapid resignation have been given.

One anecdote appears in all his biographies. It seems a censor was sent by the provincial government to his district, and T'ao was advised to receive him in the accepted protocol. T'ao refused and uttered the now famous line: "How could I bend my waist to this village buffoon for five pecks of rice!" He returned the official seal and left the job. However, in his famous *fu* "Kuei-ch'ü-lai tz'u" 歸去來辭 (The Return) T'ao gave a different reason for his resignation. He stated that he discovered he liked to be himself: he had held office merely for economic reasons, which he considered enslaving himself to his mouth and stomach. He was ashamed to have compromised his principles.

More likely it was his sister's death (which heightened his awareness of the brevity of life and impressed on him the folly of enslaving himself with an official career) that led to this decision—immediately after his resignation he went to her funeral. In "The Return" he wrote: "Alas, how much time does one have in this world and in this human form? Why not let one follow the dictate of his heart? Where do we want to go with all this commotion and agitation. . . . I would just ride with the course of change until the ultimate end. Rejoicing in what Heaven imparts to me—what is there to doubt?" This then seems to be the reason for his retirement. He had finally resolved the lifelong struggle in favor of his heart. He never again entered government service, living in retirement for the next twenty-two years, until his death in 427. He tried to support himself and his family by farming, but was not successful. Yet despite several opportunities to re-enter officialdom, he was steadfast in his resolution. He died poor, but apparently content.

He reflected on his life in his "Tzu chi wen" 自祭文 (Eulogy for Myself):

> My rice bin and wine gourd have often been empty. I have worn thin clothing in winter. Yet I have gone happily to draw water from the spring and have sung with a load of firewood on my back. In my humble thatched hut, I performed my chores day and night. As spring and autumn alternated, I busied myself in the fields. I sowed, I plowed. Things grew and multiplied. I pleased myself with the seven-string zither. In winter I soaked in the sun, and in summer I bathed in the springs. I have had little rest from my work, yet my mind has always been at leisure. I enjoyed Heaven's gifts and accepted my lot, until I lived out my years.

Nowhere in the works that describe his decision to retire and his life in reclusion is there either the bitterness at being unjustifiably neglected or the resentment at having lived in inopportune times that can be found in the works of many Chinese recluses. Instead, T'ao's works express the joy of one who has found himself and followed the true dictate of his heart.

And it is more through his verse than his life that T'ao lives on today. His popularity has remained high throughout the centuries and his influence on such literary giants as Tu Fu* and Su Shih* often noted. Many of the over 120 pieces in his extant corpus could be considered philosophical. One of his best-known works of this sort was a trio of poems entitled "Hsing, ying, shen" 形影神 (Substance, Shadow, Spirit). He is also noted for having established a type of landscape poetry known as *t'ien-yüan* 田園 (fields and gardens), a pastoral foil to the wilder scenes of the *shan-shui* 山水 (mountains and rivers) tradition. Drinking was another subject T'ao particularly favored—his series of twenty verses on "Yin chiu" 飲酒 (Drinking Wine) contain some of his best-known lines and works. For T'ao drinking releases the true self from all worldly worries and social inhibition: "I try a cup and all my concerns become remote./Another cup, suddenly I forget even Heaven./But is Heaven really far from this state after all?/Nothing is better than to trust one's true self" [from "Lien-yü tu-yin" 連雨獨飲 (Drinking Alone in the Rainy Season)]. Farming is another favorite topic. T'ao made it a symbol of the ideal life of simplicity, self-sufficiency, and self-reliance, as in his description of the life of farmers in antiquity: "They were proud and self-sufficient,/and they embraced simplicity and the true" [the opening lines to "Ch'üan nung" 勸農 (An Exhortation to Farmers)].

His love of simplicity is matched by the diction of his verse. T'ao opted for simple language and straightforwardness that speak from his heart directly to the reader, scorning the more ornate language and the obliqueness favored by many of his contemporaries, notably Hsieh Ling-yün.* Many think his diction is too simple and crude, but it perfectly matches his philosophy. It is his insight into the joys of reclusion, his integrity, and the contagious joy expressed in his poetic works that have endeared him to generations of Chinese readers.

Aside from his *fu*, T'ao is also known for two prose works, "T'ao-hua yüan chi" 桃花源記 (A Record of Peach-blossom Spring) and the "Wu-liu Hsien-sheng chuan" 五柳先生傳 (Biography of Mr. Five Willows), a wry autobiography. Both works exerted some influence on the *ch'uan-ch'i* tale and other fiction of the T'ang.

EDITIONS:

Horie, Tadamichi 崛江忠道. *Tō Emmei shibun sōgō sakuin* 陶淵明詩文綜合索引. Kyoto, 1976. An excellent concordance.

Li, Kung-huan 李公煥. *Chien-chu T'ao Yüan-ming chi* 箋註陶淵明集. *SPTK*.

Lu, Ch'in-li 逯欽立. *T'ao Yüan-ming chi* 陶淵明集. Peking, 1979. Good commentary with very useful appendices.

T'ao, Shu 陶澍. *Ching-chieh hsien-sheng chi* 靖節先生集. *SPPY*. Contains a generous assortment of prefaces from editions no longer extant and extensive commentaries.

Yang, Yung 楊勇. *T'ao Yüan-ming chi chiao-chien* 陶淵明集校箋. Hong Kong, 1971. A useful collection of commentaries. Yang's own comments are often interesting; a detailed chronology of T'ao is appended.

TRANSLATIONS:

Acker, William. *T'ao The Hermit: Sixty Poems by T'ao Ch'ien.* London, 1952. Translations are generally good.

Chang, Hsin-chang. "T'ao Yüan-ming," in his *Chinese Literature*, Volume 2: *Nature Poetry*, New York, 1977, pp. 21-38.

Davis, A. R. *T'ao Yüan-ming.* 2v. Cambridge, England, 1984.

Frodsham, *Anthology*, pp. 113-122.

Hightower, James Robert. *The Poetry of T'ao Ch'ien.* Oxford, 1970. Translations of all T'ao's poems and some of his compositions in other genres, with good notes.

STUDIES:

Hashikawa, Tokio 橋川時雄. *Tō Shū han bon gen-ryū ko* 陶集版本源流考. Peking, 1931. An exhaustive guide to the textual history of T'ao Ch'ien's collected works; still unsurpassed.

Hightower, James R. "Allusion in the Poetry of T'ao Ch'ien," *HJAS*, 31 (1971), 5-27.

Muda, Tetsuji 牟田哲二. *Tō Emmei den* 陶淵明傳.
Tokyo, 1977.

Okamura, Shigeru 岡村繁. *Tō Emmei* 陶淵明.
Tokyo, 1974.

T'ao Yüan-ming shih-wen hui-p'ing 陶淵明詩文彙
評. Peking, 1961. The arrangement is chronological.

T'ao Yüan-ming yen-chiu tzu-liao hui-pien 陶淵
明研究資料彙編. Shanghai, 1962. A complementary volume to that immediately above;
collects notes and articles on T'ao Yüan-ming.
These two books were published together as
T'ao Yüan-ming chüan 陶淵明卷, Peking, 1965.

T'ao Yüan-ming yen-chiu 陶淵明研究. 2v. Taipei,
1977. The first volume is identical to the *Hui-
pien;* the second contains new material by
contemporary scholars.

Ōyane, Bunjiro 大矢根文次郎. *Tō Emmei kenkyū*
陶淵明研究 Tokyo, 1967. A traditional view.
—MC

T'ao Tsung-i 陶宗儀 (*tzu*, Chiu-cheng 九成,
hao, Nan-ts'un 南村, 1316-1403), a native
of Huang-yen 黃巖, T'ai-chou 台州 Prefecture (modern Chekiang), was well-known
for the scope of his interests and the depth
of his learning. His hermitic lifestyle and
his unorthodox philosophy of life made
him an unlikely candidate for a official career. For a Chinese intellectual living under the Mongol rule, this is not an unexpected course of action, and given the
treacherous political climate of the early
Ming period, his repeated refusal to accept
offers of positions was apparently a wise
decision. As a result T'ao was able to devote most of his long life to study and to
writing.

One major work by T'ao Tsung-i is the
ts'ung-shu* collection *Shuo-fu* 說郛 (The Environs of Fiction), presumably in 100 *chüan*
in its original form. Inspired by, if not patterned after, Tseng Ts'ao's 曾慥 (*fl.* 1131)
Lei-shuo 類說 (Categorized Fiction), *Shuo-fu*
was compiled on the basis of selected and
abridged passages from perhaps as many
as one thousand sources—classics, history,
fiction, and miscellaneous writings. The
size of the work and T'ao's lack of finances
kept the compilation from print during his
lifetime. This together with the random
organization of the work rapidly led to textual loss. The *Shuo-fu* was already complete

when Yu Wen-po 郁文博 (*chin-shih*, 1454)
printed it along with a number of manuscripts; to make up the figure of 100 *chüan*,
he had to add some one-hundred-fifty titles mainly from the *ts'ung-shu* collection
Pai-ch'uan hsüeh-hai 百川學海 (A Sea of
Knowledge Formed by Hundreds of
Streams). It is thus not surprising that down
to the late 1920s all known copies of the
Shuo-fu are manuscripts, among which serious discrepancies exist in both form (organization and titles of works included) and
content. The 69-*chüan* manuscript in the
University of Hong Kong, traceable to
Shen Han 沈瀚 (*chin-shih*, 1535), is believed
to be a reasonably close representation of
T'ao Tsung-i's original compilation. This
book has attracted much scholarly attention, because many of the works included
therein have long been lost. Even though
the *Shuo-fu* consists of abstracts from the
works it cites, they provide at least a
glimpse of those works. But there is also
the possibility that T'ao had no access to
many of these works and offered only versions reconstructed from *lei-shu** materials.

The 120-*chüan Shuo-fu* is the work of late
Ming publishers. There are also several
continuations to the *Shuo-fu.*

Tao's other major work is the 30-*chüan
Cho-keng lu* 輟耕錄 (Records Complied after
Retiring from the Farm), prepared about
1366. Although based on a large number
of sources, it is significantly different from
Shuo-fu in that the majority of the passages
represent T'ao Tsung-i's own life experience and his scholarly pursuits. Its casual
and haphazard nature identifies it as belonging to the *pi-chi** genre. As such, it is
a work that reflects T'ao the man and the
scholar. Immense attention has been given
to it throughout the ages, and modern
scholars still turn to it as a valuable source
of information for Yüan history and popular literature.

T'ao Tsung-i was as profilic as he was
erudite. At least the following works deserve mention. *Shu-shih hui-yao* 書史會要 (Essentials of the History of Calligraphy), in
9 *chüan* (plus a lengthy supplement),
chronicles the famous calligraphers

throughout the ages with increasing details for the more recent periods (listing almost three-hundred Yüan calligraphers). It pays great attention to bibliographical sources, and to the principles of calligraphy. His collection of poems, *Nan-ts'un shih-chi* 南村詩集 (Collection of Poems from Southern Village), was not published until the late Ming period and cannot be complete. His *Ku-k'e ts'ung-ch'ao* 古刻叢鈔 (An Assembly of Old Inscriptions) is a collection of the texts of seventy-four rare inscriptions dating from the Han through the Sung periods; the manuscript copy in T'ao's own calligraphy was acquired by the modern scholar and calligrapher Yeh Kung-chao 葉恭綽 (1881-1968). Tao's *Ts'ao-mang ssu-ch'eng* 草莽私乘 (A Private History of Common Heroes) contains biographies written by Yüan writers of twenty exemplary figures, from national heroes to local personages, of the late Sung and Yüan periods.

EDITIONS:

Cho-keng lu. TSCC edition, based on Mao Chin's 毛晉 (1599-1659) version.
Index du Tcho Keng lou 輟耕錄通檢. Rpt. Taipei, 1966.
Shuo-fu. Chang Tsung-hsiang 張宗祥 , ed. Shanghai, 1927. Based on six manuscripts—the best generally available edition.

STUDIES:

Ch'ang, Pi-te 昌彼得. *Shuo-fu k'ao* 說郛考. Taipei, 1979. Detailed textual and bibliographical studies of the works, both lost and extant, included in the *Shuo-fu.*
Ch'en, Hsien-hsing 陳先行. "Shuo-fu tsai k'ao-cheng" 說郛再考證, *Chung-hua wen-shih lun-ts'ung*, 3 (August 1982), 257-265.
Ching, P'ei-yuan 景培元. "*Shuo-fu* pan-pen k'ao" 說郛版本考, *Chung-Fa Han-hsüeh Yen-chiu-so T'u-shu kuan kuan-k'ao*, 1 (March 1945), 19-126.
DMB, pp. 1268-1272.
Jao, Tsong-yi 饒宗頤. "Un inedit du *Chouo-fou*: Le manuscrit de Chan Han de la periode Kia-tsing (1522-1566)," in *Melanges de Sinologie offerts a Monsieur Paul Demieville*, Paris, 1966, v. 1, pp. 87-104.
Kurata, Junnosuke 倉田淳之助. "*Setsufu* hanpon shosetsu to shiken" 說郛版本諸說と私見, *Tōhō gakuhō* (Kyoto), 25 (November 1954), 287-304.

Mote, Frederick W. "Notes on the Life of T'ao Tsung-i," in *Silver Jubilee Volume of the Zinbun-Kagaku Kenkyusyo*, Kyoto, 1954, pp. 279-293.
———. "T'ao Tsung-i and His *Cho Keng Lu.*" Unpublished Ph.D. dissertation, University of Washington (Seattle), 1954.
Pelliot, Paul. "Quelques remarques sur le Chouo-fu," *TP*, 23 (1924), 163-220.
Watanabe, Kozo 渡邊幸三. "Setsufu Ku" 說郛考, *Tōhō gakuhō* (Kyoto), 9 (October l938), 218-260.

—YWM

Ti-fang hsi 地方戲 (regional drama) is probably the most elemental form of theater in China. It stemmed from strong ethnic or regional groups and played an important part in the rituals of those groups, especially those dedicated to local or cultural deities. *Ti-fang hsi* were performed to celebrate the birthday of a deity, in the forecourt of his deity's temple or as part of exorcistic rituals to suppress wandering spirits and orphan souls. This second kind of performance was held every three to ten years in the public square, where all images of village deities were displayed. Such dramas were considered indispensable in appeasing the various deities invited to ceremony. Members of local ethnic groups were eager to maintain such theatrical performances for fear that they would be punished by their gods if they neglected to stage dramas. Religious motivation provided the basis, therefore, for the widespread development of local theater in China. Evidence suggests that these dramas developed during the early Sung period, some two hundred years before the advent of Yüan *tsa-chü.**

Ti-fang hsi were also staged in ancestral halls. Distinct from those kinds mentioned above, which were primarily developed through ethnic or regional bonds, this latter type of drama was clan-centered. It was held during clan festivals such as birthdays or festivals for orphan souls within the clan, and was usually sponsored by a consanguineous group. From the time that regional drama began in the early Sung until the mid-Ming, the gentry controlled both consanguineous and territorial groups, for they had control both over the clan and over the local village community. Therefore, dramas with a strong conservative bent, such as the so-called *Ssu-ta ch'uan-chi*,* were preferred. But after the mid-Ming, the preferences of the landlords were superseded by those of the new audience made up primarily of peasants and merchants. Dissatisfied with the more didactic and conservative dramas, they enjoyed types of plays that had long been suppressed by local authority—including those openly licentious or implying rebellion. As the landlords' power declined during the latter half of the Ming, and riots broke out in many districts, the subject matter of the popular village or market drama came more and more to accentuate love and rebellion. Such dramas as *Hsi-hsiang chi*,* *Yü-tsan chi* 玉簪記 (The Jade Hairpin), and plays like *Hsüeh Jen-kuei chuan* 薛仁貴傳 (The Story of Hsüeh Jen-kuei), or those on the *Shui-hu chuan** bandits flourished on village and market stages.

The older and more conservative dramas still under the control of the gentry, primarily those performed in the ancestral halls and for clan rituals, still retained their old flavor. Therefore, by late Ming, there were two distinct classes of regional drama—one performed within the clan community and another, more vulgar form, performed on the local public stage. From late Ming to Ch'ing, these two forms vied for audiences, and the latter finally won out.

As important as their development in the rural countryside were the intrusions of the vulgar plays onto the urban stage. Carried there by emigrant groups of peasants or merchants or summoned by the rich who wanted to hear songs in their native tongue, they were performed at local guild festivals or banquets of regional groups.

K'un-ch'ü,* a local form from the Wu Region, developed into the standard operatic form of late Ming and early Ch'ing. Peking Opera was formed in a similar manner when Soochow opera was brought to Peking by bureaucrats from the South.

Similarly, in the guildhalls and regional clubs, troupes from Hui-chou 徽州 performed before the merchants of Hsin-an

新安, drama companies from Shansi and Shensi were summoned by merchants from their respective homelands, and troupes from Honan and Hopei delighted the emigrant craftsmen and impoverished laborers of their native places as they sojourned in the capital. Thus Peking became the confluence of several local traditions, and in the two hundred years after the founding of the Ch'ing, these traditions fused into the form commonly known as *Ching-hsi* 京戲 or *Ching-chü** (Peking Opera).

The last century or so has belonged to Peking Opera, and this form, although much refined by the cultural influence of the capital, still retains much rich regional color. Modern regional drama continues to be an active art form in every district throughout China and remains a major force in the theater of modern times.

EDITIONS:

Ching-chü ts'ung-kan 京劇叢刊 (Series of Peking Opera). Peking, Shanghai, 1953-1958.

Chung-kuo ti-fang hsi-ch'ü chi-ch'eng 中國地方戲曲集成 (Collective Series of Chinese Regional Dramas): Pei-ching, Shang-hai, Shan-tung Province, Nei-meng-k'u, An-hui, Che-chiang, Shan-hsi, Hu-pei, Liao-ning, Chi-lin, Hei-lung-chiang, Kuang-tung, Chian-hsi, He-pei. Chung-kuo hsi-chü-chia hsieh-hui. Beijing, 1958-1963.

STUDIES:

Chao, Ching-shen 趙景深. "T'an Su-chü" 談蘇劇, in *Hsi-ch'ü pi-t'an* 戲曲筆談. Peking, 1962, pp. 208-213.

———. "T'an Shao-chü" 談紹劇, in Chao, *Hsi-ch'ü*, pp. 214-223.

———. "T'an Wu-chü" 談婺劇, in Chao, *Hsi-ch'ü*, pp. 224-229.

Chou, I-pai 周貽白. "T'an Han-chü" 談漢劇, in *Chung-kuo hsi-ch'ü lun-chi* 中國戲曲論集. Peking, 1958, pp. 326-144.

———. "Min-chü" 閩劇 in Chou, *Chung-kuo hsi-ch'ü,*, pp. 360-375.

———. "Hsiang-chü man-t'an" 湘劇漫談, in Chou, *Chung-kuo hsi-ch'ü*, pp. 249-325.

———. "T'an Ch'u-chü" 談楚劇, in *Chung-kuo hsi-ch'ü*, pp. 345-359.

Huang, Chih-kang 黃芝岡. "Lun Ch'ang-sha Hsiang-chü liu-pien" 論長沙湘劇流變, "*Chung-kuo hsi-ch'ü yen-chiu tzu-liao ch'u-chi*, pp. 48-108.

Kalvedova, Dona. "The Baroque Spirit of the Chinese Traditional Stage," *LEW*, 14 (1970), 511-518.

———. "The Original Structure of the Szechwan Theatre," *AO*, 34 (1966), 505-523.

van der Loon, Piet. "Les origines rituelles du theatre chinois," *JA*, 265 (1977), 141-168.

MacKerras, Colin. *The Chinese Theatre in Modern Times: From 1840 to the Present Day.* London, 1975.

———. "The Growth of Chinese Regional Drama in the Ming and Ch'ing," *JOS*, 9 (1971), 58-91.

Mai, Hsiao-hsia 麥嘯霞. "Kuang-tung hsi-chü shih-lüeh" 廣東戲劇史略, in *Kuang-tung wen-wu* 廣東文物, v. 3, Hong Kong, 1944, pp. 791-835.

Ou-yang, Yü-ch'ien 歐陽予倩. "Shih-t'an Ao-chü" 試談粵劇, in *Chung-kuo hsi-ch'ü yen-chiu tzu-liao ch'u-chi* 中國戲曲研究資料初輯, Peking, 1957, pp. 109-157.

Tanaka, Issei 田仲一成. "A study of *P'i-p'a-chi* in Hui-chou Drama—Formation of Local Plays in Ming and Ch'ing Eras and Hsin-an Merchants," *AA*, 32 (1977), 34-72.

———. "Jūgo-roku seiki o chūshan to suru Kōnan chihō-geki no kenshitsu in tsuite" 十五、六世紀を中心とする江南地方劇の變質について (#1-5), *Tōyō bunka kenkyūjo kiyo*, 60 (1973), 113-175; 63 (1974), 1-40; 65 (1975), 113-182; 71 (1977), 1-166; and 72 (1977), 129-440.

———. "Shindai chihō-geki shiryōshū" 清代地方劇資料集. v. 1, "Kahoku-hen" 華北編, and v. 2, "Kachū-hen 華中編. Tokyo, 1968.

Ti-fang hsi-ch'ü hsüan-pien 地方戲曲選編. 3v. Peking, 1980.

—IT

T'iao-hsi yü-yin ts'ung-hua

T'iao-hsi yü-yin ts'ung-hua 苕溪漁隱叢話 (A T'iao-hsi Hermit Fisherman's Anthology of Poetry Criticism), first edition in sixty *chüan* dated 1148 and second edition in forty *chüan* dated 1167, is an anthology of poetry criticism by late eleventh and twelfth century writers. This eclectic and extensive collection covers literary history, poetics, and individual poets from the *Shih-ching** through the early twelfth century. The compiler, Hu Tzu 胡仔 (*tzu*, Yüan-jen 元任), was a native of Chi-hsi 績溪 in Hui-chou 徽州 (modern Anhwei). After serving in several official posts, he took up residence in the famous literary center of Wu-hsing 吳興 (modern Chekiang) on the T'iao-hsi River. Here he spent his leisure time fishing, reading, and collecting poetry criticism—hence the title.

Hu Tzu organized his critical selections in the chronological order of the poets they discussed. He chose this form in reaction to the *Shih-hua tsung-kuei* 詩話總龜, which was compiled by Juan Yüeh 阮閱 in 1123, and was organized by common poetic topics, such as chrysanthemums, plum blossoms, winter, or sorrow. Juan Yüeh's work was meant primarily for poets; Hu Tzu's for readers. The form and the assumptions about audience made by Hu Tzu in the *T'iao-hsi yü-yin ts'ung-hua* were adopted within a few years by two important collections of criticism on T'ang dynasty poetry: Chi Yu-kung's *T'ang-shih chi-shih** and Yu Mao's 尤茅 *Ch'üan T'ang shih-hua* 全唐詩話. Hu Tzu frequently appends his own insights and commentaries to the passages he gathered from other critics. These were later apparently also available as an independent book which circulated as widely as the *T'iao-hsi yü-yin ts'ung-hua*, which in Hu Tzu's time already enjoyed a broad audience as a printed book.

The *T'iao-hsi* devotes nearly half its space to seven major poets: Su Shih,* Tu Fu,* Huang T'ing-chien,* Wang An-shih,* Han Yü,* Ou-yang Hsiu,* and T'ao Ch'ien* (in order of the number of *chüan* given to each). Su Shih, to whom fourteen *chüan* are devoted, is also repeatedly cited as a critic elsewhere in the book. But it is Tu Fu, whose reputation had only been established in the preceding century, who actually dominates the perspective of the *T'iao-hsi*. Passages on other poets frequently refer to his poems for comparison, and Hu Tzu says, "In compiling the *T'iao-hsi*, I considered Tu Fu the consummate poet."

Since the dogmatism of competing literary schools limits the range of much critical writing from this period, the eclecticism of the *T'iao-hsi* is refreshing. A good example of Hu Tzu's style as a compiler is the first *chüan* on T'ao Ch'ien, which opens with a passage from Su Shih's preface to a poem based on T'ao's "Peach Blossom

Spring" in reaction to poems on the same subject by the T'ang poets Wang Wei,* Liu Yü-hsi,* and Han Yü, who had all misread the original "Peach Blossom Spring" as a fantasy. Furthermore, Wang An-shih's "Ballad of Peach Blossom Spring" concurs with Su Shih's reading of T'ao Ch'ien. The *topos* is political: "Fathers and sons respect each other there,/ But there are no rulers and no subjects. . . . Paradise, once lost, cannot be regained,/ And those who rule by force perish overnight." Hu Tzu's anthology abounds in such *conflits des intérêts.*

The *T'iao-hsi yü-yin ts'ung-hua*, because it does not avoid such differences of interpretation, has much material for the study of literature from the third through the early twelfth century. The late Sung critic Fang Hui 方回 once said, "The serious study of poetics began with the *T'iao-hsi.*"

EDITION:

Hu, Tzu 胡仔. *T'iao-hsi yü-yin ts'ung-hua* 苕溪漁隱叢話. Liao Te-ming 廖德明, ed. 2v. Hong Kong, 1976.

STUDY:

Kuo, Shao-yü 郭紹虞. *Sung shih-hua k'ao* 宋詩話考, Peking, 1979, pp. 81-83. A revised and expanded publication of Kuo Shao-yü's work that originally appeared in *Yen-ching hsüeh-pao,* 21 (1937) and 26 (1939).

—CF

T'ien-pao i-shih chu-kung-tiao 天寶遺事諸宮調 (An All Keys and Modes on the Events of T'ien-pao Years) is one of three extant narrative ballads of the Chin and Yüan dynasties (the other two are *Liu Chih-yüan chu-kung-tiao** and *Hsi-hsiang-chi chu-kung-tiao**). The theme of the ballad is the love story of Emperor Hsüan-tsung of the T'ang and Yang Kuei-fei. The work is attributed to Wang Po-ch'eng 王伯成 (late 13th century) and currently exists only as scattered arias in one late fourteenth-century and several sixteenth-, seventeenth- and eighteenth-century music formularies.

The musical structure of the ballad is heavily influenced by drama, and the songs which are attributed to the ballad are akin to the long suites (*t'ao-shu*) we associate with *tsa-chü* rather than the shorter one- or two-verse song-sets of the other *chu-kung-tiao.**

Whereas only about half of the song titles found in the other *chu-kung-tiao* are shared in common with *tsa-chü* drama, all of the tunes of *T'ien-pao i-shih* are found among the song titles of drama. The suites found in *T'ien-pao i-shih* are all modes found in the *ch'ü** music of Yüan drama.

There have been several attempts to reconstruct the story of the ballad by collecting and arranging the arias found scattered throughout the formularies. This process is aided by three prologues (*yin-tzu* 引子) to the work, all of which summarize the action of the story. None of these attempts are entirely reliable. First, Ming compilers of the music formularies were notoriously careless both in the titling and authorial attribution of suites. Secondly, since *T'ien-pao i-shih* clearly uses full-length arias that are in every respect similar to *tsa-chü*, it is conceivable that suites from lost dramas about Yang Kuei-fei and Hsüan-tsung have been attributed to Wang Po-ch'eng. There are four lost dramas on the theme of this imperial love story, and all of them treat the years before the tragedy of Yang's death. Yen Tun-i 嚴敦易 has argued that at least one of the arias attributed to Wang Po-ch'eng is the first act of Pai P'u's* lost drama *Hsing yüeh-kung* 幸月宮, which he believes was the first of a pair of dramas written about the love story, the second being the justly famous *Wu-t'ung yü.*

The *T'ien-pao i-shih* appears to be based on Po Chü-i's* "Ch'ang-hen-ko" and on Le Shih's 樂史 "T'ai-chen wai-chuan" 太眞外傳 (An Unofficial Biography of the Perfectly True) and shows a story development similar to that of *Ch'ang-sheng tien* 長生殿 (The Palace of Long Life), a *ch'uan-ch'i** by Hung Sheng* of the Ming.

In its use of a complex musical structure *T'ien-pao i-shih* is the most developed of the three extant "all keys and modes," and its structure and dense language indicate that perhaps it was conceived as a literary rather than performing work.

EDITIONS:

Arias are found primarily in the following sources:

773

Chou, Hsiang-yü 周祥鈺. *Chui-kung ta-ch'eng nan-pei tz'u* 九宮大成南北調 (preface dated 1746).

Chu, Ch'üan 朱權. *T'ai-ho cheng-yin p'u* 太和正音譜 (preface 1398), in *Chung-kuo ku-tien hsi-ch'ü lun-chu chi-ch'eng* 中國古典戲曲論著集成, v. 3, Peking, 1959.

Kuo, Hsün 郭勳. *Yung-hsi yüeh-fu* 雍熙樂府 (preface 1566). *SPTK.*

Li, Yü 李玉. *Pei-tz'u Kuang-cheng p'u* 北詞廣正譜 (c. 1644).

The following are reconstructions:

Chao, Ching-shen 趙景深. "*T'ien-pao i-shih* chu-kung-tiao chi-i" 天寶遺事諸宮調輯逸, *Hsüeh-shu chi-k'an*, 3 (1940), 125-155.

Cheng, Chen-to 鄭振鐸. "*Sung Chin Yüan* chu-kung-tiao k'ao" 宋金元諸宮調考, in *Chung-kuo wen-hsüeh yen-chiu* 中國文學研究, Peking, 1957, pp. 931-940.

Endō Jitsuō 遠藤實夫. *Chōkonka kenkyū* 長恨歌研究, Tokyo, 1935, pp. 84-90.

STUDIES:

Cheng Chen-to, "Chu-kung-tiao k'ao."

Feng, Yüan-chün 馮沅君. "*T'ien-pao i-shih* chi-pen t'i-chi" 天寶遺事輯本題記, in *Ku-chü shuo-hui* 古劇說彙, Peking, 1956, pp. 230-308.

West, *Vaudeville*, pp. 100-107.

—SW

Tsa-chü 雜劇 is a term that has many meanings, most of them tied to specific, or generic, dramatic forms that evolved from the term's first use, in the late T'ang (c. 780), to its last use in the Ch'ing period. The confusion of terminology persisted through the ages, but the earliest meaning of the term was "variety show," and it was interchangeable with another term, *tsa-hsi* 雜戲. During the subsequent Sung period, the two terms, *tsa-chü* and *tsa-hsi* were synonymous when used generally to denote that variety performance that was featured both at court and at the urban commercial theater.

On the other hand, it could also refer specifically to a form of proto-drama that used a troupe of actors who specialized in farce skits. According to the *Tu-ch'eng chi-sheng* (see *Tung-ching meng Hua lu*), the specific *tsa-chü* was a four-part performance with by a musical prelude and a postlude:

> In the *tsa-chü*, the male lead [*mo-ni* 末泥] was the leader, and in each instance, four or five persons would constitute one performance. First they would perform one common, well-known story— it was named the *yen-tuan* 艷段. Then the main portion of the *tsa-chü* [*cheng tsa-chü* 正雜劇] is performed, and together they are called the "two pieces." The male lead role does the directing, the play leader [*yin-hsi* 引戲] issues orders, the second comic role [*fu-ching-se* 副淨色] acts stupid, and the second male role [*fu-mo-se* 副末色] makes jokes [about the second comic]. Sometimes one person dressed as an official [*chuan-ku* 裝孤] is added. The one who plays the musical prelude and the postlude is called the bandleader [*pa-se* 巴色]. Generally, they take old stories and contemporary affairs and treat them in a comic vein. Basically, it is done to warn by example, or sometimes to hide indirect criticism and remonstrance. Therefore, when they reveal it little by little, they are called "faultless insects."

Another Sung text, the *Meng-liang lu* (see *Tung-ching meng Hua lu*), copies this passage, expanding it with the following statement:

> Generally, the whole thing is a story, and the emphasis is on the comic; singing, reciting, and dialogue constitute the whole . . . . Generally, if there was remonstrance, or if a remonstrating official had something he wanted to explain, and the emperor would not accede to it, these performers would clothe it in a story, hide the intent and remonstrate, but there would be no anger on the emperor's face. There were also parodies of country bumpkins, which were also known as *tsa-pan* 雜扮 . . . . It was the dispersal section of the *tsa-chü*. Formerly, in the Northern Sung, rustic hicks from the villages never got to town very often, so they composed these pieces. Mostly, [the actors] costumed themselves as old village bumpkins from Shantung or Hopeh to provide some pretext for humor.

Thus the shape of the Sung *tsa-chü* (as a specific performance) was in four parts: (1) *Yen-tuan:* a beginning section, usually performed by a single actor, often the *fu-ching*, and usually composed of jokes, japes, and crude doggerel. If performed at court, this often took the form of an encomium to the emperor. (2) *Cheng tsa-chü:* this was generally a full-fledged performance, usually farcical, involving the whole troupe. It could be either musical or comical (see below). (3) *San-tuan:* a postlude, usually celebratory, musical, or dance, or as mentioned above, parodies of country bumpkins.

Three important pieces of information come from this source: first is the constituent of role-types, which figure so prominently in the development of Chinese theater (see Drama essay and *chiao-se*). The role types of Sung-dynasty *tsa-chü* provided the basic form from which all other role types developed. Second, the four-part structure of the variety performance led to the four-act structure of Yüan *tsa-chü*. And third, already in this primitive drama is found a feature of all later forms: the ability to isolate and perform alone any of its segments.

There is extant a list of some 280 titles of *tsa-chü*, found in Chou Mi's* *Wu-lin chiu-shih*, a late Southern Sung work. From an examination of this list, and another list in the late Yüan period (see *Yüan-pen*), it can be seen that Sung and Chin variety shows were composed of five major categories of entertainments. First were the satiric skits. This form is represented mainly by the specific *tsa-chü* just described. The main feature of such plays were the knave-and-butt routine, in which the *fu-mo* and *fu-ching* engage in a scenario that ends with the knave driving the butt from the stage with a leather slapstick. Second were music and dance performances. Many of these extant titles of Sung *tsa-chü* have tune titles attached to them, indicating they were meant to be sung, or performed to music. Third, puppet plays are much in evidence. Fourth are the random acts that have been performed since antiquity, and which continue today. These include juggling acrobatics, weapon play, and other assorted kinetic performances. Fifth and finally, since the *nan-hsi** is also called *Wen-chou tsa-chü*, it must be assumed that these Southern Plays also constituted part of the performance, especially in the Southern Sung.

During the Chin period the variety show was also known as *yüan-pen*, a term that is a contraction of *hang-yüan chih pen* 行院之本 and means literally "scripts from the entertainer's guild." By the end of the Chin, the term *tsa-chü* had undergone a great change. Since the terms *yüan-pen* and *tsa-chü* were then interchangeable terms for the variety show, *tsa-chü* gradually came to

refer only to the main portion, the troupe act of the variety performance. As T'ao Tsung-i pointed out, it was during the early Yüan that *yüan-pen* and *tsa-chü* came to mean two different things (see *Yüan-pen*), that is, *tsa-chü* came to refer to northern-music drama, which grew as an amalgam of the farce play (or main variety performance) and the All Keys and Modes (see *chu-kung-tiao*). So, in the Yüan period, *yüan-pen* appears to have been retained to mean the variety performance, and *tsa-chü* came to mean the four-act music drama now referred to as Yüan *tsa-chü*.

The numerous musical and dramatic conventions of this new four-act poetic music-drama give it great formal and generic interest. It consisted of four (rarely, five) acts with the option of a moveable demi-act, called a "wedge," and in some earlier examples, an epilogue (*san-ch'ang*). Each act was actually a set (*lien-t'ao* 聯套) of arias all written to the same mode (*Kung-tiao* 宮調), with their accompanying dialogue and stage business. There was only one singing role in a given act and the star of the troupe sang all such roles in all acts, even when that called for a female role in one act and a male role in another. *Dramatis personae* were role-typed, just as in the variety performances of the Sung. The male singing role was called the *cheng-mo*, the female singing role was called the *cheng-tan* (the role was derived from the *yin-hsi*), the secondary male role (non-singing) was called the *wai*, the comic-cum-villain roles were designated as *ching*, and on occasion there was added a venal official (*ku*), the clown (*ch'ou*), and the wicked woman (*ch'a-tan*), as well as a limited number of other role types. Most of these designations come from earlier performances.

The poetic value of these dramas is considerable, and in fact, in the opinion of modern scholars, is the one factor that assured their entry into the preserve of the classical canon. What has special attraction to the Chinese are the fresh and spontaneous lyrics of the plays. The form created and introduced into Chinese literature a new language (see *ch'ü*): there were padding words, echoics, slang, aphorisms, language from the histories, from the classics, and from the streets mixed together in prose, a compressed colloquial lyric poetry, and even legal injunctions—writs of divorce, etc. The language was so well controlled that it could be "simple without leading to vulgarity" and "elegant without leading to the weak and flowery." It is, in fact, the quality of the language alone that puts Yüan *tsa-chü* into the same class as the other great literary traditions of China.

The content and theme of the Yüan dramas were fairly typical of Chinese drama as a whole (see Drama essay). Since most of the topics came from a well of traditional tales and from storyteller accounts of history, they were well known, and in the corpus of Yüan plays are many plays devoted to the theme of justice and retribution—not personal retribution, but that levied by the judicial system, by ghosts and spirits in a bureaucratic underworld, and by bands of roving bandits—the Chinese equivalent of Robin Hood stories in the West (see *Shui-hu chuan**). One does not find in Yüan drama specific allegory, that is, the literary retribution that later playwrights often satirically visited upon their contemporaries through characters in their plays. In the Yüan theater, the resentment and sense of injustice is often more generalized, and probably is attributable to the injustices that the Chinese suffered under Mongol rule. Another feature that makes Yüan theater distinct from its descendants is the number of plays that show the scholar in conflict with the merchant over the love of a singsong girl. In these plays, some of the disenchantment of the scholar is felt, whose position of social authority (normally pursued through the examination system) had been usurped by the merchant, whose wealth could now bring him the benefits normally reserved for the scholar-official.

In terms of staging, the Yüan *tsa-chü* was severely handicapped by its formal structure. Its presentation of plot was fairly cut-and-dried: the first act introduced the story, the second and third acts carried the development of the story to its high point in the third act, and the fourth act restored social, judicial, or comic harmony. The first part of the first act was usually fluff; it was the place where the story was mechanically introduced, where characters introduced themselves through a standard four-line doggerel verse and a bit of formalized personal history. The third act was generally the point at which the dramatic climax was reached. The fourth act was much shorter than the other three and resolved in the most manipulative and economical way possible the interpersonal or social conflict.

Plot was also hampered by the use of a single singer. The literary powers of the playwright were generally focused on the arias this character sang; other characters who were important to the development of the story were often given short shrift. Other times, characters were given songs to sing that were useless to the development of plot, story, or characterization and were there simply to fill out the prescribed aria patterns. (Moreover, it must have been quite monotonous to listen to four long arias in the northern mode, sung by one person.) These factors contribute to the haphazard plot development and inattention to historical or factual accuracy (and even to common sense) which was a major characteristic of Yüan *tsa-chü*.

The major writers of *tsa-chü* in the Yüan were Kuan Han-ch'ing,* Wang Shih-fu (see *Hsi-hsiang chi*), Pai P'u,* Ma Chih-yüan,* Cheng Kuang-tsu,* Kao Wen-hsiu,* and Ch'iao Chi-fu.*

It should be mentioned that during the Yüan period, *tsa-chü* was also used as a generic term (since it was the most representative form) to designate "northern drama" as contrasted with *nan-hsi*,* which was used generically to designate forms of southern drama.

A major change took place in *tsa-chü* drama with the advent of the Ming dynasty. It was at this time that it developed into a literati art, and the authorship and thematic content of *tsa-chü* both changed radically, as did the musical structure. If one looks at the question of authorship, both in terms of status and of geographical distribution, there was a quintessential change. Of the 108 known authors of Yüan drama 34 came from Hopeh, 11 from Shansi, 8 from Shantung, 1 from Anhui, 21 from Chekiang, 9 from Kiangsu, and 1 from Kiangsi. The other 18 authors have no registery listed. The distribution of writers in the Ming period is far wider. There were 125 writers of Ming tsa-chü, 83 of whom have a registery listed: 38 come from Chekiang, 24 from Kiangsu, 9 from Anhui (including 3 from the royal house and 2 foreigners: a Mongol and a Uighur), 6 from Shantung, 2 each from Hopeh and Shensi, and 1 each from Kiangsi, Szechwan, Fukien, and Hunan.

In terms of status, Ming playwrights were much higher in the bureaucratic service and social status than their Yüan counterparts. As Yoshikawa Kōjirō has shown, the majority of Yüan playwrights were educated, but were unemployed (or underemployed) in traditional pursuits. If any held bureaucratic posts, they were primarily scribes or clerks in local government offices. In the Ming, however, not only did the ranks of playwrights include members of the royal family (see Chu Yu-tun and Chu Ch'üan), but there were at least 28 others who held high bureaucratic posts (see, for instance, Wang Chiu-ssu, K'ang Hai, and Li K'ai-hsien), and there are, in addition to these 28, at least 13 others who had taken their chin-shih examinations. Nowhere is this rise of the status of drama so well attested as in Chu Ch'üan's* remark that "the true tsa-chü is written by great Confucians" and that professional theater people were the "real amateurs" (see Idema and West, 1982, pp. 129-130 for a discussion of this passage).

Another major difference between the Yüan and Ming playwrights is that, while Yüan writers did not write any other forms of drama, at least 31 Ming authors also wrote ch'uan-ch'i.* This accounts partially for the fact that Yüan dramatists were more prolific in the tsa-chü form. Of the 700 known Yüan plays, only 167 are extant, but of the lesser number of Ming plays—approximately 500—there are over 300 extant. The higher survival rate of Ming manuscripts also reflects the influence of the self-conscious bibliographical and textual tradition of the scholar.

Other consequences derived from this elevation of drama to legitimate art. One was that the thematic categories began to shrink. With the advent of the Ming many laws were promulgated to ensure that only plays that spread religious, moral, and ethical values would be performed. There were other, more subtle, changes. No longer were the heroes of the bandit plays Chinese men of the greenwood, ready to challenge authority, exterminate evil, or redress grievances for the common folk. They became instead, in the plays of Chu Yu-tun,* for instance, models of compliant virtue, men who realized their mistaken course and returned to the ethical fold. (Of course, it would hardly behoove a member of the royal house to preach antiauthoritarian behavior, especially in the days of the Yung-lo usurpation.) More and more, traditional values like chastity and filiality came to be stressed. Singsong girls, for instance, often showed no desire to quit their professions in Yüan plays, but in the Ming, in the hands of such writers as K'ang Hai* and Chu Yu-tun, they all became paragons of chastity. Many of the Ming plays were performed at court, and a large number of the extant tsa-chü, both Yüan and Ming, exist only as "court" texts—that is, as texts of plays performed before the imperial family. One can imagine the limitations that might place on dramatists' choice of material.

By the beginning of the fifteenth century, southern singing styles began to influence the tsa-chü form. Of course, in southern drama, any number of players could sing. In the early Ming (fifteenth century), perhaps eighty percent of the plays abided by the strict formal regulations of Yüan tsa-chü, restricting themselves to fleshing out the acts from four to five, and to using the method of singing of southern drama—that is, either parcelling out singing roles to any major character, or singing in unison. By the mid-Ming, however, only sixty percent of the dramas written during that period still adhered to the original stipulations of the

Yüan form. By then, the signs of radical transformations were present. For instance, more than one modal suite could be used within an act, songs from different modes were used within the same act—not arranged according to prescribed sequence—and southern songs and music (which had earlier been used only for comic relief) now appeared as part of the main arias. An introduction, similar to the *chiamen* of *ch'uan-ch'i*, which gives a brief introduction to the play that follows, began to appear, and finally, strings of plays began to be put together to form cycles. By the seventeenth century, only ten percent of the *tsa-chü* written still used the original conventions. The form had been so corrupted that it actually utilized *ch'uan-ch'i* stage conventions and southern songs to the exclusion of northern modal music.

The major writers of the Ming period were Chu Yu-tun, Chu Ch'üan, K'ang Hai, Wang Chiu-ssu,* Feng Wei-min,* Hsü Wei,* Wang Heng,* Yeh Hsien-tsu,* and Ling Meng-ch'u.*

As might be expected, the term *tsa-chü* underwent several transformations during this period. It was still used to refer generically to northern music, and was now coupled with *ch'uan-ch'i*, the general referent for southern drama. With the rise of southern influence, the dramas written to southern music were called *nan tsa-chü*, or "southern tsa-chü."

Toward the end of the Ming, many one-act *tsa-chü* plays were written, and to complicate matters further, these were also called *tuan-chü* 短劇, or "short plays," to differentiate them from the other *tsa-chü* plays, which then could run to as many as eleven acts. The trend continued and by the interregnum between the Ming and the Ch'ing, *tsa-chü* and *ch'uan-ch'i* as terms of designation changed again, this time to mean short plays and long plays, respectively.

By the Ch'ing period, the *tsa-chü* had undergone another transformation, and now referred to a short one- or two-act play. Cheng Chen-to (1934; preface) has divided the history of Ch'ing *tsa-chü* into four different periods: 1644-1722, 1723-1795, 1796-1861, and 1862-1908. The writers of the first period, for the most part, carried to the fullest the predilections of the Ming writers. They developed *tsa-chü*, as they called it, to a highly refined literary form that was meant primarily for the desk-top, not for the stage. By now the *tsa-chü* had been transformed from a folk art, looked down upon because of its vulgar nature, to a highly refined classical form that was so well accepted that even the great Confucian scholars, such as Shih Yün-yü,* Wang Fu-chih,* and Liang Ch'i-ch'ao* actually wrote drama.

The writers of the earliest period, among whom such scholars as Wu Wei-yeh,* Hsü Shih-ch'i 徐石麒 (*fl.* 1644), Hsi Yung-jen,* and Hung Sheng* stand to the fore, set the tone for the rest of the dynasty, making every possible attempt to remove drama from the sordid theater world. The second stage of development is represented by such playwrights as Yang Ch'ao-kuan, Chiang Shih-ch'üan,* and Kuei Fu.* Cheng Chen-to calls this the period of "greatest flourishing," but a more recent opinion by Tseng Yung-i (1975, p. 120) claims that, except for the thirty-two plays by Yang Ch'ao-kuan (known as the *Yin-feng-ko tsa-chü*), none of the other writers can match the creativity and power of the earliest Ch'ing playwrights. In the later periods, from 1796 to 1908, the *tsa-chü* went into a state of decline, although such writers as Chou Yüeh-ch'ing,* and Shih Yün-yü tried new experiments. Chou Yüeh-ch'ing,* for instance, wrote a series of "what-if" plays, in which the historical circumstances surrounding a particularly odious or sad event were reversed; Yueh Fei, for instance, defeats the Jurchen and returns in glory to the Sung court instead of being executed at the command of the evil Ch'in K'uei. There was even a series of eighteen short plays that were strung together as an autobiography (the *Hsieh-hsin tsa-chu* 寫心雜劇 by Hsü Hsi 徐爔).

As one would expect, there are significant differences in the themes of Ch'ing *tsa-chü*, owing primarily to the fact that they were pure literary plays. The three major characteristics, as far as theme is con-

cerned, are: first, many plays enlist historical incidents in which to cloak criticism
about the fall of the Ming to the Manchus;
second, there are a great number of plays
about women, primarily extolling them for
their talent, their virtue, or their chastity;
and third, there are very few plays on the
topic of love between the sexes. Another
major characteristic is that many of the
dramas borrow stories found in literature—either the classical tale, or even contemporary sources such as the *Liao-chai
chih-i** of P'u Sung-ling or the *Hung-lou
meng** of Ts'ao Hsüeh-ch'in.*

The term *tsa-chü*, then, begins by first
denoting a variety performance then, during the Sung, a simple one-scene farce skit.
By the Yüan it means a four-act music-
drama with a highly conventional and stipulated form. The term is used generically
during the Yüan and the Ming to identify
northern drama. By the Ming, however, it
has lost the stipulated format and begins
to include elements of southern drama in
both its stagecraft and its music. The so-
called "southern *tsa-chü*" indeed incorporates southern music into its acts, and in
reality becomes a short drama (usually four
or five acts, but sometimes expandable to
eleven) in the *ch'uan-ch'i* mode. Thus, the
term finally comes to denote short plays,
whatever their formal structure, and
ch'uan-ch'i is then reserved for longer plays.
During the Ch'ing the *tsa-chü* becomes primarily a short one- or two-act play, returning in a roundabout fashion to its original length.

EDITIONS:

Because of the popular nature of *tsa-chü* during
the early Yüan period, the history of texts is
quite important. There are seven major collections of Yüan texts, all of which can be found
in *Ku-pen,* IV. Understanding their textual history, however, is an important first step to understanding their literary quality. Of the seven
collections of Yüan dramas, only one is au-
thentically Yüan. The rest have been preserved
in various editions by scholars of the Ming and
have often undergone extensive editing at the
hand of the literary collector.

Edition A: This is a set of thirty plays from the
   commercial book wards of Peking and Hang-

chow, published sometime during the fourteenth century. All of these plays have only
minimal stage directions and the very tersest
of dialogue, often no more than prompt lines
for the arias. The originals, which passed
through the hands of various book collectors
as curiosity pieces, are often badly printed.
Photolithographic reproductions of the original editions can be found in *Ku-pen* IV, and
two modern editions, both of which are collated, punctuated, and annotated versions:

Cheng, Ch'ien 鄭騫. *Chiao-ting Yüan-k'an tsa-chü
   san-shih-chung* 校訂元刊雜劇三十種, Taipei,
   1962.

Hsü, Ch'in-chun 徐沁君. *Hsin-chiao Yüan-k'an tsa-
   chü san-shih-chung* 新校元刊雜劇三十種, 2v. Peking, 1981. A superior collation and annotation.

Edition B: The *Ku-ming-chia tsa-chü* 古名家雜劇
   edition, published serially between 1573 and
   1620, is attributed to Wang Chi-te.* The collection contains 60 plays, 44 by Yüan writers,
   and 16 by Ming writers. The work is sloppily
   edited, containing many errors and mistaken
   characters. The texts are primarily badly-cut
   commercial editions. Although the seals on
   the original works indicate the hand of Wang
   Chi-te, when compared with Wang's other
   editions (see Edition E, below), they are far
   inferior. Fifty-five of the plays are also found
   in Edition D. The worth of the edition is that
   it contains some plays that have not undergone extensive editing.

Edition C: *Tsa-chü hsüan* 雜劇選, probably
   printed in 1598, is the earliest Ming printed
   edition. Contains 30 plays, 29 of which are
   Yüan editions. The language of the dramas
   seems archaic, and much closer to that of
   Yüan editions than to the more refined language of the Ming recensions. The major
   value of this work is that the language of the
   texts is superior to later recensions.

Edition D: The so-called *Mai-wang kuan* 脈望館
   edition, edited by Chao Ch'i-mei 趙琦美 (1563-
   1624). These are mostly manuscript copies,
   originally more than 300 in number, of which
   only 242 are extant. Of these approximately
   105 are Yüan, and 135 are Ming *tsa-chü* (2
   plays are repeated in different editions). Seventy of them are wood-block commercial editions, copied from editions B and C. The
   other 172 are all hand-copied manuscripts,
   most from the Ming imperial archives (*nei-fu
   pen* 內府本). The work is poorly collated but

contains many plays that are unavailable elsewhere. Moreover, since not much was done in the way of annotating the text, it still preserves, in some cases, the original Yüan dialogue. The text was discovered in the war years of the 1930s and part of the contents were published by Commercial Press as:

Wang, Chi-lieh 王季烈. *Ku-pen Yüan Ming tsa-chü* 古本元明雜劇. Shanghai, 1938.

Edition E: *Ku tsa-chü* 古雜劇, published by Wang Chi-te sometime between 1615 and 1622. More commonly known as the *Ku-ch'u chai* 雇曲齋 edition. This is an excellently cut woodblock that repeats, word for word, twenty of the plays found in Edition B and C, but is far easier to read.

Edition F: *Yüan-ch'ü hsüan* 元曲選, edited by Tsang Mou-hsün in 1615 and 1616. This work, originally known as *Yüan-jen pai-chung ch'ü* 元人百種曲, contains one hundred Yüan dramas and is the most commonly used edition of Yüan plays. The work was originally printed in a very handsome edition, which may have accounted for its popularity. Tsang made many changes in the original plays, subtracting or adding arias at will, often changing the focus of the original play, and destroying the quality of the originals. Modern editions include:

Yüan-ch'ü hsüan. Shanghai, 1936. A typeset, punctuated version, the errors of which were mainly corrected in a revised version published in Peking, 1958 in 4v.

Edition G: *Ku-chin ming-chü ho-hsüan* 古今名劇合選 edited by Meng Ch'eng-shun,* printed in 1633. Contains sixty *tsa-chü,* twenty by Ming writers and forty by Yüan writers. This work is later than Edition F, and is a collection of carefully collated dramas, including marginalia by the editor. Since Meng was a dramatist himself, he made very judicious decisions about choosing which texts to collate, and has produced a volume of plays for reading that are far superior to those in Tsang Mou-hsün's edition.

Cheng Ch'ien (1969) has compared all seven editions and makes the following five points: (1) The Yüan edition is the only reliable representation of what a Yüan play was like; but its lack of dialogue makes it difficult (and sometimes impossible) to tell what is happening in the story. (2) In general, all the Ming editions are the same as far as the presentation of the plot. Where the Ming editions are simplified or inconsistent, the *Yüan-ch'ü hsüan* has taken great liberties to make the story complete. Meng Ch'eng-hsün, in Edition G, has often combined the dialogue of the *Yüan-ch'ü hsüan* with the older arias, producing for all intents and purposes the best reading text. (3) The dialogue is altered significantly only in the *Yüan-ch'ü hsüan,* which brings the plays' spoken passages into line with mid-Ming language. Therefore, the older editions incline towards archaic simplicity, while the last two editions reflect a more refined language. (4) The arias of all the Ming recensions are essentially the same, again with the exception of Edition F, which has altered the poetry significantly, often fleshing out the fourth act to parity with the other three in length. (5) The arias of the Yüan edition (A) differ from those of the Ming editions, which in turn differ from those of the *Yüan-ch'ü-hsüan* version.

Other collections of Yüan plays:

Sui, Shu-sen 隋樹森, *Yüan-ch'ü hsüan wai-pien* 元曲選外編 (Shanghai, 1959), a collection of sixty-two authenticated Yüan plays not found in *Yüan-ch'ü hsüan.*

Yang, Chia-lo 楊家駱. *Ch'üan Yüan tsa-chü* 全元雜劇. 4v. Taipei, 1962, 1963. The first two volumes collect the extant plays of the authors mentioned in the first and last volumes of the *Lu-kuei-pu,* * and the other two volumes, other plays that are by Ming authors. Generally, this work has been superseded by *Ku-pen.*

Ku, Chao-ts'ang 顧肇倉. *Yüan-jen tsa-chü hsüan* 元人雜劇選. Peking, 1956. Contains excellent annotations of fifteen Yüan plays.

Aoki, Masaru, Yoshikawa Kōjirō, Tanaka Kenji, and Iriya Yoshitaka, eds. *Genkyokusen shaku* 元曲選釋. V. 1-2; Kyoto, 1951, 1952. V. 3-4, Kyoto, 1977. Contains excellent notes to twelve plays.

The history of editions after the early Ming is much less complicated, since drama began to be written by the literati. Most of these editions will be found in *Ku-pen* (I, IV, IX), in G, and in other collections.

Shen, T'ai 沈泰 (*c.* 1600), ed. *Sheng Ming tsa-chü* 盛明雜劇. 2v. Woodblock edition, dated 1908, 1915. Contains sixty plays by the best of the Ming writers.

Chou, I-pai 周貽白. *Ming-jen tsa-chü hsüan* 明人雜劇選. Peking, 1958. A collection of punctuated and annotated plays.

Cheng, Chen-tuo 鄭振鐸. *Ch'ing-jen tsa-chü* 清人雜劇. V. 1-2, Shanghai, 1931, 1934. Contains eighty of the more than 240 texts in Cheng Chen-tuo's collection. The best collection of Ch'ing plays.

TRANSLATIONS:

The translations listed here are those that include more than two plays by separate authors. For individual authors and works, see the specific entries.

Bazin, Antoine Pierre Louise. *Théâtre chinois, ou Choix de pièces de théâtre composées sous les empereurs mongols.* Paris, 1838. Translations of four Yüan plays.

———. *Li Siécle des Youên.* Paris, 1850. Summaries of a number of plays.

Chinesische Drama der Yüan-Dynastie, Zehn nachgelassene Übersetzungen von Alfred Forke. Martin Gimm, ed. Wiesbaden, 1978.

Crump, James I., Jr. *Chinese Theater in the Days of Kubulai Khan.* Tucson, 1980.

Idema and West, *Chinese Theater.*

Ikeda, Taigo 池田大伍. *Genkyoku go-shu* 元曲五種. Tokyo, 1975. With annotations by Tanaka Kenji 田中謙二.

Iriya, Yoshitaka 入矢義高 and Tanaka Kenji. *Genkyoku senshaku* 元曲選釋. V. 7-12. Kyoto, 1976-77.

Li, Tche-houa 李治華. *Le signe de patience, et autres pièces bu théâtre des Yuan.* Paris, 1963. Three plays.

Liu, Jung-en. *Six Yüan Plays.* Harmondsworth, 1972.

Rudelsberger, Hans. *Altchinesische Liebes-Komödien.* 1923. Free renderings of five Yüan plays.

Yang, Hsien-yi and Gladys Yang. *Selected Plays of Kuan Han-ch'ing.* Peking, 1958. Translations of eight plays.

Yang, Richard Fu-sen. *Four Plays of the Yüan Drama.* Taipei, 1972.

STUDIES:

A, Ying 阿英. "Yüan-jen tsa-chü shih" 元人雜劇史, *Chü-pen*, 4 (1954) 12-128; 6 (1954), 123-133; 7 (1954), 156-165; 8 (1954), 140-152; 9 (1954), 146-161; and 10 (1954), 119-128.

Aoki, Masaru. *Yüan-jen tsa-chü hsü-shuo* 元人雜劇序說. Sui Shu-sen, trans. Shanghai, 1941; revised Hong Kong, 1959.

Chang, Hsiang 張相. *Shih tz'u ch'ü yü tz'u-hui shih* 詩詞曲語辭彙釋. Shanghai, 1953.

Chao, Ching-shen 趙景深. *Yüan-jen tsa-chü kou-shen* 元人雜劇鈎深. Peking, 1959.

Ch'en, Shou-yi. "The Chinese Orphan: A Yüan Play. Its Influences on European Drama of

the Eighteenth Century," *T'ien-hsia Monthly,* 3 (1936) 89-115.

Cheng, Chen-to. *Chung-kuo wen-hsüeh yen-chiu* 中國文學研究. Peking, 1957. Contains important articles on Yüan drama.

Cheng, Ch'ien. *Pei-ch'ü hsin-p'u* 北曲新譜. Taipei, 1973.

———. *Pei-ch'ü t'ao-shih hui-lu hsiang-chieh* 北曲套式彙錄詳解. Taipei, 1973.

Cheng, Ch'ien. *Ching-wu ts'ung-pien* 景午叢編. 2v. Taipei, 1972. Twenty-four articles on *tsa-chü* by the elder statesman of Chinese drama in Taiwan.

———. "Tsang Mou-hsün kai-ting Yüan tsa-chü p'ing-i" 臧懋循改訂元雜劇評議, *Wen-shih-che hsüeh-pao*, 10 (1961), 1-13.

———. "Yüan Ming ch'ao-k'o Yüan-jen tsa-chü chiu-chung t'i-yao" 元明抄刻元人雜劇九種提要, *THHP*, n.s., 7 (1969), 145-155.

Cheung, Ping Cheung. "Melodrama and Tragedy in Yüan *Tsa-chü.*" Unpublished Ph.D. dissertation, University of Washington, 1980.

Ch'ien, Chung-shu. "Tragedy in Old Chinese Drama," *T'ien-hsia Monthly* 1 (1935), 37-46.

Ch'ien, Nan-yang 錢南揚. "Sung Chin Yüan hsi-chü pan-yen k'ao" 宋金元戲曲搬演考, *Yen-ching hsüeh-pao*, 20 (1936), 177-194.

Chu, Chü-i 朱居易. *Yüan-ch'ü su-yü fang-yen li-shih* 元曲俗語方言例釋. Shanghai, 1956.

Chūgoku koten gikyoku goshaku sakuin 中國古典戲曲語釋索引. Osaka, 1970. An indispensable guide to the annotations and notes to all extant modern annotated editions of drama.

Crump, James I., Jr. "The Elements of Yüan Opera," *JAS*, 17 (1958), 417-434.

———. "The Conventions and Craft of Yüan Drama," *JAOS*, 91 (1971), 14-29.

———. *Chinese Theater in the Days of Kubulai Khan.* Tucson, 1980.

Demiéville, Paul. "Archaismes de prononciation en chinois vulgaire," *TP*, 45 (1951), 1-59.

Dew, James. "The Verb Phrase Construction in the Dialogue of Yüan *Tsai jiuh*: A Description of the Arrangements of Verbal Elements in an Early Modern Form of Colloquial Chinese." Unpublished Ph.D. dissertation, University of Michigan, 1965.

Feng, Yüan-chün 馮沅君. *Ku-chü shou-hui* 古劇說彙. Peking, 1956. Important discussions on staging of drama.

Forke, A. "Die Chinesische Umgangssprache im XIII Jahrhundert," in *Actes du Douzième Congrès International des Orientalistes*, v. 2, Rome, 1899, pp. 49-67.

Fu, Hsi-hua 傅惜華. *Yüan-tai tsa-chü ch'üan-mü* 元代雜劇全目. Peking, 1957.

———. *Ming-tai tsa-chü ch'üan-mü.* Peking, 1958.

———. *Ch'ing-tai tsa-chü Ch'üan-mü.* Peking, 1981.

Fu, Ta-hsing 傅大興 *Yüan tsa-chü k'ao.* Taipei, 1960.

Hawkes, David. "Some Reflections on Yüan *tsa-chü,*" *AM,* 16 (1971), 69-81.

Hayden, George. "The Courtroom Plays of the Yüan and Early Ming Periods," *HJAS,* 34 (1974), 168-207.

———. "The Legend of Judge Pao: From the Beginning through the Yüan Drama," in *Studia Asiatica,* San Francisco, 1975, pp. 339-355.

———. *Crime and Punishment in Medieval Chinese Drama: Three Judge Pao Plays.* Cambridge, 1978.

Ho, Ch'ang-ch'ün 賀昌群. *Yüan-ch'ü kai-lun* 元曲概論 Shanghai, 1930.

Hsü Chia-jui 徐嘉瑞. *Chin Yüan hsi-ch'ü fang-yen k'ao* 金元戲曲方言考. Shanghai, 1948; revised 1956.

Hsü, Fu-ming 徐扶明. *Yüan-tai tsa-chü i-shu* 元代雜劇藝術. Shanghai, 1981.

Hsü, Tiao-fu 徐調孚. *Hsien-ts'un Yüan-jen tsa-chü shu-lu* 現存元人雜劇書錄, Shanghai, 1955.

Hu, Chi 胡忌. *Sung Chin tsa-chü k'ao* 宋金雜劇考. Peking, 1957. A superb study of the farce plays and proto-dramatic skits of the Sung and Chin period.

Hu, Chu-an 胡竹安. "Sung Yüan pai-hua tso-p'in chung te yü-ch'i chu-tz'u" 宋元白話作品中的語氣助詞, in *Chung-kuo yü-wen,* 72 (1958), 270-294.

Hu, William and James I. Crump, Jr. "A Bibliography for Yüan Opera," in *Occasional Papers in Chinese Studies,* v. 1 (Ann Arbor, 1962), 1-32.

Huang, Ching-ch'in 黃敬欽. *Yüan-chü p'ing-lun* 元劇評論. Taipei, 1979.

Huang, Li-chen 黃麗貞. *Chin Yüan pei-ch'ü yü-hui chih yen-chiu* 金元北曲語彙之研究. Taipei, 1968.

Idema and West. *Chinese Theater.* A study of plays and other forms of literature that deal with drama and dramaturgy.

Iriya, Yoshitaka. "Genkyoku joji zakkō" 元曲助字雜考, *Tōhōkakuhō* (Kyoto), 1 (1943), 70-97.

Iwaki, Hideo 岩城秀夫. "*Genkan kokon zatsugeki sanjusshu no ryūden*" 元刊古今雜劇三十種の流傳, *Chūgoku bungakuhō,* 14 (1961) 67-89.

Johnson, Dale. "One Aspect of Form in the Arias of Yüan Opera," *Michigan Papers in Chinese Studies,* 2 (1968), 47-98.

———. "The Prosody of Yüan Drama," *TP,* 61 (1970), 96-146.

———. *Yüan Music Dramas: Studies in Prosody and Structure and a Complete Catalogue of Northern Arias in the Dramatic Style.* Ann Arbor, 1980.

Ku, Hsüeh-chieh 顧學頡. *Yüan Ming tsa-chü.* Shanghai, 1979.

Liu, James J. Y. "Elizabethan and Yüan: A Brief Comparison of Some Conventions of Poetic Drama," *Occasional Papers of the China Society,* London, 1955, pp. 1-12.

Lo, Ch'ang-p'ei 羅常培. "Chiu chü chung-te chi-ko yin-yün wen-t'i" 舊劇中的幾個音韻問題, *Tung-fang tsa-chih,* 1 (1936), 393-410.

Lo, Chin-t'ang 羅錦堂. *Hsien-ts'un Yüan-jen tsa-chü pen-shih-k'ao* 現存元人雜劇本事考. Taipei, 1960.

Nozaki, Shunpei 野崎駿平. "Gen no zatsugeki ni arawareta riji ni tsuite" 元の雜劇に現われた「罵詞」について, *Chūgoku gogaku,* 58 (1957), 3-12.

Perng, Ching-hsi. *Double Jeopardy: A Critique of Seven Yüan Courtroom Dramas.* Ann Arbor, 1978.

Shih, Chung-wen. *The Golden Age of Chinese Drama: Yüan tsa-chü.* Princeton, 1976.

Sun, K'ai-ti 孫楷第. *Yeh-shih-yüan ku-chin tsa-chü k'ao* 也是園古今雜劇考. Shanghai, 1953. A study of the plays of Edition D.

Takahashi, Moritaka 高橋盛孝. "Genkyoku ni arawareta kogo to shiji" 元曲に現われた胡語と視字, *Chūgoku gogaku,* 112 (1961), 1-2.

T'an, Cheng-pi 譚正璧. *Hua-pen yü ku-chü* 話本與古劇. Shanghai, 1956.

———. *Yüan-ch'ü-chia k'ao-lüeh* 元曲家考略. Shanghai, 1953.

———. *Yüan-ch'ü liu-ta-chia lüeh-chuan* 元曲六大家略傳. Shanghai, 1957.

Tanaka, Kenji. *Genkyoku tekisuto no kenkyū* 元曲テキストの研究. (*Mombusho kagaku kenkyūhi Kenkyūhōkoku-shūroku* 文都省科學研究費研究報告集錄.) Kyoto, 1951.

———. "Genjin no ren'aigeki ni okeru futatsu no nagare" 元人の戀愛劇に於けるふたつの流れ. *Tōkō,* 3 (1948), 34-42.

———. "Gen satsugeki no daizai" 元雜劇題材, *Tōhōgakuhō* (Kyoto), 13 (1943), 128-158.

Ts'ai, Mei-piao 蔡美彪. "Yüan-tai tsa-chü chung-te jo-kan i-yü" 元代雜劇中的若干譯語, *Chung-kuo yü-wen,* 55 (1957), 34-36.

Tseng, Yung-i 曾永義. "Ch'ing-tai tsa-chü kai-lun" 清人雜劇概論, in *Chung-kuo ku-tien hsi-ch'ü lun-chi,* Taipei, 1976, pp. 215-243.

———. *Ming-tai tsa-chü kai-lun* 明代雜劇概論. Taipei, 1978. Superb introduction to Ming plays.

———. "Yu kuan Yüan tsa-chü te san-ke wen-t'i" 有關元雜劇的三個問題, in *Chung-kuo ku-tien hsi-chü lun-chi* 中國古典戲劇論集. Taipei, 1975, pp. 49-106.

———. "Yüan Ming tsa-chü te pi-chiao" 元明雜劇的比較, in *ibid.*, pp. 107-116.

———. "Ch'ing-tai tsa-ch'ü kai-lun" 清代雜劇概論, in *ibid.*, pp. 117-244.

Wang, Chi-ssu 王季思. "Yüan-ch'ü chung hsieh-yin shuang-kuan yü" 元曲中諧音雙關語, in *Kuo-wen yüeh-k'an*, 67 (1948), 15-19.

Wang, Chung-lin 王忠林 and Ying Yu-kang 應裕康. *Yüan-ch'ü liu-ta-chia* 元曲六大家. Taipei, 1977.

Wang, Kuo-wei 王國維. *Wang Kuo-wei hsi-ch'ü lun-wen-chi* 王國維戲曲論文集. Peking, 1957. Includes *Sung Yüan hsi-ch'ü shih* (1915), the first history of Chinese theater during the Sung and Yüan periods.

Yagisawa, *Gekisakuka.*

Yen, Tun-i 嚴敦易. *Yüan chü chen-i* 元劇斟疑. Peking, 1960.

Yoshikawa, Kōjirō 吉川幸次郎. *Gen zatsugeki kenkyū* 元雜劇研究. Tokyo, 1948. Translated into Chinese by Cheng Ch'ing-mao 鄭清茂 under the same title, Taipei, 1954.

—SW

Ts'ai-tzu chia-jen hsiao-shuo 才子佳人小說 (scholar and the beauty novels) is a group of approximately fifty medium-length popular narratives, all of which center upon the relationship between a scholar and a beauty, at the turn of the eighteenth century (*c.* 1650-1730). Comic works primarily concerned with love, courtship, ceremony, intrigue, and adventure, they have been held in low esteem by modern critics. However, although they are part of the many short and novel-length works that comprise the large second rank below the level of the six fictional masterpieces, *San-kuo-chih yen-i,** Shui-hu chuan,** Chin P'ing Mei,** Hsi-yu chi,** Hung-lou meng,** and Ju-lin wai-shih,** several deserve mention. The origin of these novels can be traced, at least in part, to earlier *hua-pen** stories of comparable themes. The lack of variety in theme and plot, and overproduction in a relatively short period of time, contributed to their decline.

Remarks on this corpus will be based mainly on eight representative works: *Yü Chiao Li,** Hao-ch'iu chuan,** P'ing Shan Leng Yen* 平山冷燕, *Liang chiao-hun* 兩交婚 (The Double Marriage—a sequel to *P'ing Shan Leng Yen*), *Jen-chien lo* 人間樂 (The World Rejoices), *Hua-t'u yüan* 畫圖緣 (Romance of the Paintings), *Hsing Ming-hua* 醒名花 (Awakening Under the Peonies), and *Wu-feng yin* 五鳳吟 (Song of the Five Phoenixes). Their authors are known only by their pseudonyms. Sources containing thorough listings of these novels are noted at the end of this entry.

Ts'ai-tzu chia-jen novels are a recognizable category because they share many similarities of structure, plot, characterization, style, themes, authorship, and audience. They are arranged in chapters and vary from twelve to twenty-six chapters in length. Plots are in accord with western comic structure—meeting (courtship ensues), separation (barriers to love), and reunion (marriage). Since their compass is narrower, the plots are frequently well integrated and nonepisodic compared to plots of other vernacular novels. These novels are also complex and sometimes "overplotted," full of the tricks, mistaken identities, and disguises that are earmarks of romantic comedy. The hero often takes more than one beauty for a wife. Double weddings occur (i.e., two couples), both expanding the plot and creating a greater feeling of harmony. Journeys, chivalric adventures, and even military campaigns are common, but these elements are balanced roughly equally with domestic scenes from the life of the scholar-official class, such as audiences at court, poetry and drinking contests, the official examinations, judicial proceedings, and the like.

Yü Chiao Li, whose title is composed of parts of the heroine's names, is representative in its stereotyped characters, in its complex comic plot, and in the popularity of its themes—love, courtship, manners, poetry, an official career, and fate. In contrast, novels like *Hao-ch'iu chuan* and *Hsing Ming-hua* employ elements of knight-errant fiction and the military romance, forming hybrid and in some ways deviant works. The hero of *Hao-ch'iu chuan*, T'ieh Chung-yü 鐵中玉, is depicted as a chivalrous scholar; his martial talents receive more attention than his literary abilities, especially since he overcomes his adversaries in several vivid and humorous fight scenes. The first half of *Hsing Ming-hua* follows the typical plot: The hero comes upon a beautiful garden, exchanges love poems with the beauty through her maid, is kidnapped by her jealous brother, and later is rescued by a bandit leader. The second half narrates how the hero, his friends, and the bandit accumulate merit by defeating rebels in the lake region of the mid-Yangtze River. In *Hua-t'u yüan*, the hero, Hua T'ien-ho 花天荷, pursues a military career in helping to suppress bandits in the Liang-Kwang region of the south. On his way to the region, Hua visits Mount T'ien-t'ai, where an old Taoist bestows on him two maps, one of the bandits' lairs and one of a garden where he will meet the beauty he will marry. Such Taoist and chivalric elements doubtless were meant to cater to popular tastes.

The characters are primarily drawn from the scholar-official class and its hangers-on. The majority are either stereotypes or typical characters endowed with a few individual traits. Su Yu-po of *Yü Chiao Li* is a typical scholar: young, handsome, orphaned, talented, but not a knight errant or military man. His first love, Po Hung-yü, typifies the beauty: a more gifted poet, virtuous, shy, and not particularly clever. Her cousin, Lu Meng-li, is further individualized by her boldness in arranging her own marriage to Su. Disguising herself as a boy, she gets Su to agree to marry her nonexistent "younger sister." Chü Chang-chu 居掌珠 of *Jen-chien lo* is another typical beauty who becomes more individualized by impersonating a scholar. She has no wish to return to womankind until she is married.

Hua T'ien-ho and T'ieh Chung-yü are individualized heroes infused with military prowess, physical strength, and chivalric spirit, in addition to their poetic talents. Hua is portrayed in psychological detail as he visualizes his ideal beauty in terms of his close friend's qualities and constantly doubts that the friend can keep his promise of finding a beauty for him. While T'ieh

is presented as larger than life—an idealistic, "high-mimetic" character (to use Northrop Frye's term)—there is a combination of chivalry, maturity, Confucian morality, loyalty, and simplicity in his personality that causes him to transcend the typical. Of the heroines, Shui Ping-hsin and Hsing Ming-hua of *Hao-ch'iu chuan* are the most individualized beauties. Ping-hsin's altruism, cleverness, chastity, and bravery make her one of the most lovable heroines in traditional fiction. Her adroitness at foiling the numerous schemes of the villains and her moral purity constitute a large measure of *Hao-ch'iu chuan*'s appeal. She has remained popular into modern times in the Kwangtung folk drama *Shui Ping-hsin san-ch'i Kuo Ch'i-tsu* 水冰心三氣過其祖 (Shui Ping-hsin Thrice Infuriates Kuo Ch'i-tsu). Hsing Ming-hua is a virtuous beauty beset by obnoxious suitors and an untrustworthy brother. But she is distinguished more for her philosophical insight than her moral purity. In the end she plays a trick on the scholar-hero Chan I-wang 湛翌王, making him wake up from drunkenness under the peonies and realize the vanity of wealth and rank.

Whether depicted as types or more individualized characters, the protagonists tend to be epicenes. Typical scholars like P'ing Ju-heng 平如衡 and Yen Po-han 燕白頷 of *P'ing Shan Leng Yen*, whose title is also composed from the names of the key figures, are more effeminate than manly; and T'ieh Chung-yü has a feminine face (hence his nickname T'ieh Mei-jen 鐵美人 or "Iron Beauty"). The villains are mostly stereotypes descended from the villains and clowns of Yüan drama. They range from comic impostor-poets and ignorant relatives to wicked eunuchs and powerful noblemen. A more individualized villain is Shui Yün of *Hao-ch'iu chuan*, Ping-hsin's greedy uncle. He has a sense of right and wrong, but his desire for material gain causes him to betray his niece. Later he is humiliated by Ping-hsin and repents. Minor characters in the works include maids, parents, magistrates, military offices, the emperor, astrologers, fortune-tellers, and occasionally a Taoist wizard.

Like most traditional fiction, the style of *ts'ai-tzu chia-jen* novels is a mixture of the rhetoric of the storyteller-narrator and elements of the historiographical tradition, with the addition of liberal amounts of poetry. Storyteller formulas are prevalent at the beginning and end of chapters; also common are significant plot changes in the middle of a chapter and the practice of ending a chapter on a note of suspense in the middle of an episode. The influence of historical writing is felt in genealogies, in the specific historical setting that frequently contains the plot, and the use of local legends and beliefs and journeys to historical sites. There are few passages of extended narrative description and most of the action is conveyed by dialogue and dramatic narration. While the narrative is in the vernacular, the characters speak a combination of the vernacular and literary languages called *kuan-hua* 官話 (official talk), which probably mirrors with some accuracy the speech of the scholar-official class. Dialogues and speeches are often adorned with allusions, references either to the Confucian classics or to famous poets and beauties of the past. The authors sometimes try to overwhelm readers with their erudition, but occasional errors betray this pretense. This is further confirmed in the generally undistinguished poetry. The authors compose in all the major forms—*shih,** tz'u,* fu,* ch'ü,** and *lien-chü* 聯句— mostly with unhappy results. One exception is the poetry of *Hsing Ming-hua*, which far surpasses that of the other representative works.

The popular themes of love, genius, beauty, morality, Providence, and an official career are paramount in *ts'ai-tzu chia-jen* romances. Beauty and talent may be indispensable for a proper match, but beauty is not just a physical attractiveness: It is a blend of inner virtue and a pleasing outward appearance conveyed by the word *mei* 美. Many of the romances are didactic in their espousal of Neo-Confucian morality and propriety, especially *Hao-ch'iu chuan*, which is one of the most ideologically pure Confucian narratives. Others like *Hsing Ming-hua* and *Wu-feng yin* take on a suggestive hue. Providence (*yüan* 緣) or Heaven's will (*t'ien-i* 天意) guides the scholar and beauty together, while it also accounts for the many unexpected meetings, coincidences, and twists in the plot. Ironically, many of the scholars in the works doubt the advantages of the examination system and have to be convinced by their fiancées and families to take the examinations. This perhaps points to the authors' own dissatisfaction with the examinations. Most importantly, the authors transformed the romantic tradition of *ch'ing* 情 (passion) and, one might say, made it antiromantic, substituting for it genius, wit, virtue, sentimentalism, and chivalry. In earlier works of the genre like *Yü Chiao Li, Hua-t'u yüan,* and *Hao-ch'ui chuan* these substitutions were fresh and entertaining for a time, but soon the genre declined into the mechanical and dull volumes criticized by Ts'ao Hsüeh-ch'in* in the *Hung-lou meng*.

The authors, most of whom are unfortunately known only by their pseudonyms, were probably commercial writers—some conceivably having failed the examinations—active in the lower Yangtze area. Their identities were privy to a small circle of writer-friends but unknown to the public. One personality, however, emerges as a major figure since he is linked with fifteen novels in the capacity of author, editor, or writer of a preface: T'ien-hua ts'ang chu-jen 天花藏主人 (Master of the Heavenly Flower Studio), who states in a preface dated 1658 to a combined edition of *Yü Chiao Li* and *P'ing Shang Leng Yen* that he failed the examinations and wrote out of wish fulfillment. A staunch moral conservative, he appears to be on a personal crusade to root out pornography and restore the "true spirit" of Confucian romance. Other authors are far less distinct. The early Ch'ing scholars Chang Yün 張匀 (*fl.* 1660), his son Chang Shao 張劭 (*fl.* 1680), and Hsü Chen 徐震 (*fl.* 1720) have been identified as authors, but Hsü is the only one to whom authorship definitely can be assigned.

Given their emphasis on upper-class life and broad comic appeal, it can be concluded that these novels were read by elite and popular audiences alike, including women. The same work often was printed in editions of varying quality, from handsome large-sized, illustrated volumes to little "sleeve volumes" (hsiu-pen 袖本). Moreover, the reluctance of the heroine of *Jen-chien lo* to give up her male identity links the works to the *t'an-tz'u** genre of the Ch'ing, which was intended mainly for a female readership.

Developing out of, and in reaction to, the previous *ts'ai-tzu chia-jen* romantic tradition that stressed passion, these novels left a significant legacy. *Hung-lou meng*, written partly out of dissatisfaction with them, is in a sense a tragic *ts'ai-tzu chia-jen* novel, although it is admittedly much more as well. Wen-k'ang's *Erh-nü ying-hsiung chuan* exhibits a debt to *Hao-ch'iu chuan*. Takizawa Bakin 瀧澤馬琴 (1767-1848) adapted *Hao-ch'iu chuan's* plot in their unfinished historical novel *Kyōkaku den* 俠客傳 (Tales of Chivalrous Men and Women). Several of these novels were translated into Western languages in the eighteenth and nineteenth centuries to meet the growing European demand for translations from Chinese literature.

EDITIONS:

Only a few of these novels are obtainable in modern editions. For information on the old editions, some of which in unique copies, see Sun K'ai-ti, *Chung-kuo t'ung-su hsiao-shuo shu-mu* 中國通俗小說書目, rev. ed., Peking, 1957, pp. 133-150; Sun K'ai-ti, *Jih-pen Tung-ching so-chien Chung-kuo hsiao-chuo shu-mu* 日本東京所見中國小說書目, rev. ed., Peking, 1958, pp. 64-67, 187-190; Liu Ts'un-yan 柳存仁, *Chinese Popular Fiction in Two London Libraries*, Hong Kong, 1967, pp. 118-122, 313-320.

TRANSLATIONS:

Fresnel, F. "Hoa thou youan (*Hua-t'u yüan*) ou le livre mysterieux," *JA*, 1 (1822), 202-225.

———. "Scenes chinoises, extraits du *Hoa thou youan*," *JA*, 3 (1823), 129-153.

Julien, Stanislas. *P'ing-chan-ling-yen: Les deux jeunes filles lettrées.* 2v. Paris, 1826. 2nd ed. Paris, 1860.

STUDIES:

Crawford, William Bruce. "Beyond the Garden Wall: A Critical Study of Three 'Ts'ai-tzu chia-jen' Novels." Unpublished Ph.D. dissertation, Indiana University, 1972.

Hessney, Richard C. "Beautiful, Talented, and Brave: Seventeenth-Century Chinese Scholar-Beauty Romances." Unpublished Ph.D. dissertation, Columbia University, 1979.

Kuo, Ch'ang-ho 郭昌鶴. "Chia-jen ts'ai-tzu hsiao-chou yen-chiu, (shang)" 佳人才子小說研究 (上) *Wen-hsüeh chi-k'an*, 1 (January 1934), 194-215; 2 (April 1934), 303-323.

Tai, Pu-fan 戴不凡. "T'ien-hua ts'ang chu-jen chi Chia-hsing Hsü Chen" 天花藏主人即嘉興徐震, in Tai Pu-fan, *Hsiao-shuo chien-wen lu* 小說見聞錄, Hangchow, 1980, pp. 230-235.

—RCH

Ts'ai Yen 蔡琰 (*tzu*, Wen-chi 文姬, b. *c.* 178), daughter of Ts'ai Yung,* had an unusual life, which was often treated in literature, music, and art. She was born in or before 178 and was married at the age of fifteen to a literatus of the Wei 衛 family whose *tzu* was Chung-tao 仲道. Soon after his early death, in or about 192, she was abducted by non-Chinese troops and eventually fell into the hands of the Southern Hsiung-nu. There she was married to a Hsiung-nu leader and bore him two children. She lived among the Hsiung-nu for twelve years (probably in the Fen 汾 River valley in southern Shansi) until about 206, when she was ransomed and brought back to Han territory at the behest of Ts'ao Ts'ao,* who then arranged her marriage to Tung Ssu 董祀, one of his provincial administrators. Nothing is known about the length or events of her life thereafter.

Her *Hou-Han shu* biography presents her as a highly educated lady, skilled in literature and music, but there is no hard evidence for this. No prose writings by her are extant or even mentioned. Three remarkable poems are attributed to her, each one relating her capture, her life among the barbarians, her separation from her children, and her return to Han China. Poem One is in 108 five-syllable lines. Poem Two consists of 38 seven-syllable lines in a very regular meter derived from the "Chiu-ko" of the *Ch'u tz'u*,* with *hsi* 兮 as the fourth syllable of every line. Both are titled "Pei-fen shih" 悲憤詩 (Poems of Lament and Resentment) and are included, ostensibly as her own work, in her biography in the *Hou-Han shu* (compiled between 424 and 445). Poem Three, "Hu-chia shih-pa p'ai" 胡笳十八拍 (Barbarian Reed-Whistle Song in Eighteen Stanzas), totals 159 lines varying in length from 5 to 14 syllables, predominantly in the meter of the *Ch'u tz'u* songs, with *hsi* in the middle of most lines. Poem Three first appeared in the *Yüeh-fu shih chi* 樂府詩集 (late eleventh century), which gives Ts'ai Yen as the author.

The authenticity of all three poems has been debated since the eleventh century. Although scholarly opinion is still sharply divided on each poem, there is strong evidence that none of the three poems is by her. They were written by three different authors, each probably responding to a tradition that she had composed a song in eighteen sections. They are instances of the literary phenomenon of dealing with historic (sometimes contemporary) individuals in the first-person form, a phenomenon that seems to have originated in the third century. Poems One and Two must date from the third, the fourth, or the early fifth century; Poem Three may be as late as the eighth century.

Consideration of the poems' literary merits should be separated from the problem of authorship. Most Chinese critics have thought highly of Poems One and Three, and less favorably of Poem Two, though it too has its champions.

The stirring events of Ts'ai Yen's real and imagined life have inspired many poets (beginning in her lifetime, but especially during the T'ang and thereafter), musicians (commencing perhaps in the third century), playwrights (from Ming to the present), and painters (starting under the Sung) to elaborate her legend.

EDITIONS:

Han Wei Liu-ch'ao wen-hsüeh tso-p'in hsüan tu 漢魏六朝文學作品選讀. Hong Kong, 1961, pp. 110-123. Text of all three poems with full modern commentary.
Hou-Han shu 後漢書 (History of the Latter Han). Peking, 1965, *ch.* 84, pp. 2801-2803. Critical, punctuated text of Poems One and Two in their earliest version.

Wei Chin Nan-pei ch'ao wen-hsüeh shih ts'an-k'ao tzu-liao 魏晉南北朝文學史參考資料, Peking, 1962, pp. 161-173. Punctuated text of Poem One with good modern commentary; punctuated text of Poems Two and Three; supplementary materials.
Yüeh-fu shih chi. Peking, 1979, *ch.* 59, pp. 860-865. Critical, punctuated text of Poem Three in its earliest version.

TRANSLATIONS:

Alley, Rewi. *The Eighteen Laments.* Peking, 1963. Free rendition of Poem Three.
Frodsham, *Anthology*, pp. 9-13; Poem One.
Sunflower, pp. 36-39.

STUDIES:

Frankel, Hans H. "Ts'ai Yen and the Poems Attributed to Her," *CLEAR*, forthcoming. Includes translation of all three poems, a discussion, and bibliography.
Kuo, Mo-jo 郭沫若 (1892-1978) *et al. Hu-chia shih-pa p'ai t'ao-lun chi* 胡笳十八拍討論集. Peking, 1959. Articles (29) by scholars (21), primarily on Poem Three. Text of all three poems.

—HHF

Ts'ai Yung 蔡邕 (*tzu*, Po-chieh 伯喈, 133-192) was a preeminent figure in the literary and court life of the final days of the Latter Han. His importance in literary history lies in his status as one of China's greatest masters of *p'ien-wen** (parallel prose) and in his strong influence on his contemporaries and on literati of succeeding generations. He was born into a wealthy and powerful family in Yü hsien 圉縣 in Ch'en-liu Commandery 陳留郡, which with neighboring Ju-nan 汝南 and Ying-ch'uan 潁川 was a center for the leading intellectuals of the time, as well as home to many scholars of the "Ch'ing-liu" 清流 (Purist) movement who suffered under the Proscribed Factions.

Major early influences on his life were his teacher Hu Kuang 胡廣, who held positions under Emperor Huan, and Chu Mu 朱穆; both were leading intellectual figures. His compositions, mainly *pei* 碑 and *ming* 銘 (funerary stone-inscriptions), began to appear in his early twenties and established his reputation. In 159, after the rise of a eunuch faction to power, Ts'ai was summoned to serve at court. Before arriving, however, he returned to Ch'en-liu on a pretext, and remained in reclusion for twelve years. Two of his most famous works, the "Shu hsing fu" 述行賦 (Prose-poem on a Journey), and the "Shih hui" 釋誨 (Teachings), a reflection on the nature of recluse life, date from this period.

In 172, after a decisive defeat of the "purist" faction with whom Ts'ai had maintained sympathy but a cautious distance, he accepted a court appointment. He served for nine years, ending as Court Gentleman for Consultation. During this period, he was at the center of court-literati activity. His main accomplishments include participation in the inscribing of the classics on stone, participation in the compilation of the "Tung Kuan Hou Han Chi" 東觀後漢記 (Tung Kuan Annals of the Latter Han), and many works in parallel prose. Following his opposition to certain self-aggrandizing policies of the eunuchs, he was punished and banished, and spent the next twelve years in exile, a period of diminished literary output.

Tung Cho's 董卓 ascension to power occasioned his second official career. At Tung's court, Ts'ai rose through a dizzying succession of offices, becoming Inner Gentleman of the Left in 190. He was the most prominent literatus at court, and it was during this period that he had contact with and influence on Wang Ts'an,* K'ung Jung,* Yang Hsiu 楊修 (175-219), and other literary figures generally associated with the following generation. The overthrow of Tung Cho resulted in Ts'ai's death in prison in 192.

The overwhelming majority of Ts'ai's surviving work is in four- or six-character-line parallel-prose, chiefly *pei* and *ming*, forms which had begun to enjoy a great vogue in the Latter Han. His best-known pieces in this genre include his inscriptions for Kuo Yu-tao 郭有道, Ch'en T'ai-ch'iu 陳太丘, Yang Tz'u 楊賜, and Hu Kuang. Ts'ai continued, but also refined and polished, a tradition in prose writing characterized by elaborate stylization and dense and elegant language that goes back

through Ma Jung* and Chang Heng* to Ts'ui Yin and Pan Ku.* Important refinements were Ts'ai's sophisticated and conscientious parallelism and his complex use of allusion. Much of his parallel-prose is equal in style to that of the Ch'i and Liang dynasties. He is often mentioned in conjunction with Chang Heng as the foremost Han prose stylist. Only a few poems survive, some of doubtful authenticity, and though few of his *fu* are extant, they are known to have been very influential in subject and style. Ts'ai bridged two distinct periods in literary history, carrying on the traditions of Han court literature and serving as a model and source of inspiration to *Chien-an* 建安 writers.

EDITIONS:

Ts'ai Chung-lang chi 蔡中郎集. SPPY. Somewhat corrupt, but the most reliable text. No modern editions.

STUDIES:

Okamura, Chigeru 岡村繁. "Sai Yū o meguru Go Kan makki no bungaku no sūsei" 蔡邕をめぐる 後漢末期の文學の趨勢, *Nihon Chūgoku Gakkai hō*, 28 (1976), 61-78.

Niwa, Takeo 丹羽兌子. "Sai Yu ten oboegaki" 蔡邕傳 おぼえがき, *Nagoya Daigaku Bungakubu kenkyū ronshū* 名古屋大學文學部研究論集, 56, *Shigaku* 史學, 19 (1972), 95-110.

Suzuki, *Kan Gi*, pp. 463-466.

—CC

Ts'ang-lang shih-hua 滄浪詩話 (Poetry Talks by [the Escapist of] the Ts'ang-lang River) is not only the most important work of poetic criticism of the Sung period in terms of theory, but also one of the most influential poetics to ever appear in China.

Little is known about the author, Yen Yü 嚴羽 (*tzu*, I-ching 儀卿 or Tan-ch'iu 丹邱, *hao*, Ts'ang-lang pu-k'o 滄浪逋客, *fl.* 1200). He was a native of Shao-wu 邵武 (modern Fukien). He and his brothers Jen 仁 and Shen 參 were known as "The Three Yen." Perhaps the most prominent poet in touch with him was Tai Fu-ku 戴復古 (*fl.* 1198), a leading member of the *Chiang-hu p'ai* 江湖派. Yen Yü left a collection of poems in two *chüan*, the *Ts'ang-lang yin* 吟 or *Ts'ang-lang chi* 集, and some remarks on poems by Li Po. But he is almost exclusively known as author of the *Ts'ang-lang shih hua*, which originally served as an introduction to his own poems.

Primarily a man of letters, Yen Yü did not close his mind to the Ch'an-Buddhist spirit of his age. It is precisely in the fusion of Ch'an and poetry that one of the two significant features of his treatise lies; the second was his promotion of the "High T'ang" era (713-765) as the golden age of poetry. Yen Yü thus opposes the stylistic trend of his century, which bore the stamp of the Kiangsi School and its spiritual leader Huang T'ing-chien.*

The *Ts'ang-lang shih-hua* consists of five chapters. In the first, "Shih-pien" 詩辯 (On Classifying Poetry), poetry is divided into "orthodox" and "heterodox," the orthodox being defined as an emotional yet calm poetry, the beauty of which lies beyond words, and the heterodox as an intellectual-reflective, poetry like that of Su Shih* and Huang T'ing-chien. The second chapter, "Shih-t'i" 詩體 (Styles [or Forms] of Poetry), covers period and personal styles and the most important forms of poems and verses. Here the way is paved for the later division of T'ang poetry into four periods, the "Early" 初 (618-712), the "High" 盛 (713-765), the "Middle" 中 (766-835), and the "Late" 晚 (836-906). The brief third chapter is concerned with "Shih-fa" 詩法 (Rules for Writing Poetry). It begins with a list of *wu-su* 吾俗 (five vulgarities), which have often been cited since. According to it, the poet should eschew vulgar style, vulgar thoughts, vulgar verses, vulgar words, and vulgar rhymes. The fourth chapter, "Shih-ping" 詩評 (Criticism of Poetry), illuminates the spirit of individual poets and periods. The unattainable greatness of Li Po and Tu Fu is stressed once more. The "Shih-cheng" 詩證 (Textual Criticism) of the fifth chapter rounds off the work.

When a passage from the *Ts'ang-lang shih-hua* is quoted, it is nearly always from the first chapter with its Buddhist allusions. Two points must be distinguished in Yen Yü's use of Ch'an: the transference of Ch'an Buddhist terms and metaphors to poetry and his requirement of "enlightenment" (*wu* 悟, *miao* 妙, Japanese, *satori*) as a sine qua non for poetry. By this Yen Yü advocated that the poet himself should be enlightened. Huang T'ing-chien nota bene had, in his forty-ninth year, experienced mystical enlightenment.

Fundamentally, the union of poetry and Ch'an was not new; it was also stressed within the Kiangsi School. When Yen Yü uses the image of the zither with which "at a single touch three strings vibrate," and when he says "the words have an end, but the thought is not exhausted," he is quoting Huang T'ing-chien and Su Shih.

The *Ts'ang-lang shih-hua* has had to submit to considerable criticism. Some censure Yen Yü's lack of familiarity with Buddhist terminology, while others point out that poetry is not to be compared to a doctrine "beyond text and characters." A further contradiction lies in the peculiar prominence given to Li Po and Tu Fu, whose work does not display those features of "enlightened" poetry. An author such as Wang Wei on the other hand, who was not only associated with Buddhism but whose verses are in accordance with Yen Yü's conceptions, is not mentioned in the fundamental part of the poetic—to say nothing of the poet-monks of the T'ang period.

Nevertheless Yen Yü had a greater effect on the poetological debates of subsequent centuries than any other theorist. The Ming, as an epoch of literary reminiscence, was particularly responsive to his classicism. He influenced not only the Early Seven Masters (see Li Meng-yang) in their emulation of the High T'ang, but also the Later Seven Masters (see Li P'an-lung) with their *Ko-tiao shuo* 格調說 (Resonance of Spirituality Theory) of Wang Shih-chen* (1634-1711).

The five chapters of the poetic are incorporated in the *Shih-jen yü-hsieh** by Wei Ch'ing-chih: chapter 1 and 3 in *chüan* 1, chapter 4 and 2 in *chüan* 2, chapter 5 in *chüan* 11.

EDITIONS:

Ts'ang-lang shih-hua chien-chu 滄浪詩話箋注. Hu Ts'ai-fu 胡才甫, comm. Shanghai, 1937.

Ts'ang-lang shih-hua chiao-shih 校釋. Kuo Shao-yü 郭紹虞, comm. Peking, 1961. The best annotated edition; makes use of the version in the *Shih-jen yü-hsieh*.

TRANSLATIONS:

Debon, Günther. *Ts'ang-lang's Gespräche über die Dichtung, Ein Beitrag zur chinesischen Poetik.* Wiesbaden, 1962.

STUDIES:

Chu, Tung-jun 朱東潤. "*Ts'ang-lang shih-hua* ts'an-cheng" 參證 *Kuo-li Wu-Han ta-hsüeh wen-che chi-k'an*, 2.4 (1933), 693-716.

Kunisaki, Mokutarō 國崎望久太郎. "*Sōrō shiwa* no kinsei karon e no tōei" 滄浪詩話の近世歌論への投影, *Ritsumeikan bungaku*, 180 (1960), 521-535.

Yip, Wai-lim. "Yen Yü and the Poetic Theories in the Sung Dynasty," *TkR*, 1.2 (October 1970), 183-200.

—GD

Ts'ao Chih 曹植 (*tzu*, Tzu-chien 子建, posthumously called Ch'en Ssu Wang 陳思王, 192-232), Ts'ao Ts'ao's* third son by his consort née Pien 卞, was an imaginative, influential poet. He never held office, but was enfeoffed ten times in eight different places. The family elders and the court restricted his freedom, and most of his adult life kept him away from the capital and his family. He was gregarious and fond of acting, singing, and talking, but politically naive. A court clique tried to influence Ts'ao Ts'ao to make Chih his heir, but in 217 Ts'ao Ts'ao chose Ts'ao P'i, his first son by Lady Pien. Before and after becoming emperor (220), P'i was jealous and understandably suspicious of his talented, popular brother Chih and kept him isolated. The same policy continued under P'i's son and successor, Ts'ao Jui (Emperor Ming, r. 226-239).

The number, generaic classification, and authenticity of Ts'ao Chih's extant works are problematical. In Ting Yen's edition, there are 54 *fu*,* 54 *shih*,* 67 *yüeh-fu*,* and 158 other works. A few are almost certainly spurious, and many are suspect, but most are probably authentic, constituting the largest individual literary collection surviving from this period.

Ts'ao Chih was not a profound thinker. He was educated in the tradition of conservative Han Confucianism, and attracted by philosophical Taoism and neo-Taoism. There is no evidence of acquaintance with Buddhism. The Buddhist claims that he composed *fan-pai* 梵唄, a type of Buddhist chant, were disproved by K. P. K. Whitaker [*BSOAS*, 20 (1957), 585-597].

Much of his prose and some of his poems reiterate complaints about restrictions and isolation, appeals for military or civil employment, and eulogies of the Wei dynasty. But when read closely and critically, these writings illuminate the daily life, thoughts, aspirations, and frustrations of the elite during the transition from Han to Wei.

His longest and most famous *fu*, "Lo-shen fu" 洛神賦 (The Goddess of the Lo River), was inspired by local legends of the Lo River nymph and by two *fu* attributed to Sung Yü ("Kao-t'ang fu" and "Shen-nü fu"), not, as has often been asserted, by an infatuation with his brother P'i's late consort, née Chen 甄.

He stood out in the literary circle assembled by Ts'ao Ts'ao and Ts'ao P'i, and in the literary movement which began during (and was named after) the Chien-an 建安 era (196-220). Even more than other poets of the group, he brought the anonymous *yüeh-fu*-ballad tradition into the literary mainstream by blending it with elements from the *Shih-ching*,* the *Ch'u-tz'u*, Han *fu*, and the *shih* of the Han literati. He perfected the five-syllable line. As a result it became the predominant meter of *yüeh-fu* and personal *shih* for many generations. What puts him above his contemporaries and imitators is his rich imagination. He excels in creating idealized figures and scenes of knights-errant, warriors, hunters, dandies, beautiful women, deserted wives, banquets and entertainment in noble society, encounters with *hsien-jen* 仙人, and fantastic travels. His reputation as a great poet has remained virtually undiminished, though the reasons for praising him vary considerably.

EDITIONS:

Diény, Jean-Pierre, *et al.* Ts'ao Chih wen-chi t'ung-chien 曹植文集通檢. *Concordance des oeuvres complétes de Cao Zhi.* Paris, 1977. Full concordance, based on Ting Yen's text as corrected in Peking 1957 edition, which is included in this volume, with additional corrections and textual variants.

Ts'ao chi ch'üan p'ing 曹集銓評. Ting Yen 丁晏 (1794-1875), ed. Preface dated 1865. Rpt. with a few revisions, Peking, 1957. Best edition of complete works. Based on Wan-li (1573-1620) edition by Ch'eng 程, noting variants in Chang P'u's 張溥 (1602-1641) *Han Wei liu-ch'ao po-san (ming) chia chi* 漢魏六朝百三 (名) 家集, in the *Wen hsüan*, in five T'ang and Sung encyclopedias, and in thirteen other texts. Works contained neither in Ch'eng's nor in Chang's edition were collected by Ting Yen from eight sources and appended to *Ts'ao chi ch'üan p'ing* as "Ts'ao chi i-wen" 曹集逸 文.

Ts'ao Tzu-chien chi 曹子建集. *SPTK*. Ming, movable-type edition. Good, readily available, complete edition of bare text.

Ts'ao Tzu-chien shih chu 曹子建詩注. Huang Chieh 黃節 (1873-1935), ed. Preface dated 1928. Shanghai, 1930. Typeset rpt., traditional punctuation added, Peking, 1957. Good critical, annotated edition of 36 *shih* and 41 *yüeh-fu*, omitting others as spurious.

(Ts'eng ping t'ang) Ts'ao Tzu-chien shih chien (層 冰堂) 曹子建詩箋. Ku Chih 古直 (b. 1887), ed., preface dated 1935. Unpunctuated rpt. Taipei, 1966. Arranges 34 *shih* and 44 *yüeh-fu* in what he believes to be chronological order. Commentary, of uneven quality, cites and goes beyond Huang Chieh's, identifies many allusions. Chronological arrangement is not reliable, but has been accepted by Yü Kuan-ying and others.

San Ts'ao shih hsüan 三曹詩選. Yü Kuan-ying 余冠英, ed. Peking, 1956. Excellent introductory essay; section on Ts'ao Chih has text and well-informed, readable commentary for 51 poems. Rev. ed., Peking, 1979 adds two more poems.

TRANSLATIONS:

Demiéville, *Anthologie*, pp. 118-122.
Frodsham, *Anthology*, pp. 35-50.
Itō, Masafumi 伊藤正文. *Sō Shoku* 曹植. Tokyo, 1958. Forty-five poems.
Kent, George W. *Worlds of Dust and Jade, 47 Poems and Ballads of the Third Century Chinese Poet Ts'ao Chih.* New York, 1969.
Sunflower, pp. 46-49. Five poems.
Watson, *Rhyme-Prose*, pp. 55-60.

STUDIES:

Cutter, Robert Joe. "Cao Zhi (192-232) and His Poetry." Unpublished Ph.D. dissertation, University of Washington, 1983.
Diény, Jean-Pierre. "Les sept tristesses (*Qi ai*). A propos des deux versions d'un 'poème à chanter' de Cao Zhi," *TP*, 65 (1979), 51-65.
Frankel, Hans H. "Fifteen Poems by Ts'ao Chih: An Attempt at a New Approach," *JAOS*, 84 (1964), 1-14.
———. "The Problem of Authenticity in the Works of Ts'ao Chih," in *Essays in Commemoration of the Golden Jubilee of the Fung Ping Shan Library (1932-1982).* Hong Kong, 1982, pp. 183-201.
Hsü, Kung-ch'ih 徐公持. "Ts'ao Chih shih-ko te hsieh-tso nien-tai wen-t'i" 曹植詩歌的寫作年 代問題, *Wen-shih*, 6 (June 1979), 147-160.
———. "Ts'ao Chih sheng-p'ing pa-k'ao" 曹植 生平八考, *Wen-shih*, 10 (October 1980), 199-219.
Liu, Wei-ch'ung 劉維崇. *Ts'ao Chih p'ing chuan* 曹植評傳. Taipei, 1977. Very informative.
Suzuki, *Kan Gi*, pp. 635-667.

—HHF

Ts'ao Hsüeh-ch'in 曹雪芹 (formal name, Ts'ao Chan 曹霑, *tzu*, Ch'in-pu 芹圃, *hao*, Ch'in-ch'i chü-shih 芹溪居士, Meng-Juan 夢阮, 1715-1763; some studies suggest *c.* 1724-1764) is considered China's greatest novelist, although his sole major work *Hung-lou meng** was not finished by him, and little is known about his life.

Ts'ao's ancestors were famous generals and officials. One of the earlier known of these, Ts'ao Yün 曹芸, was a military officer during the Five Dynasties. Yün's son, Ts'ao Pin 曹彬 (931-999), was a great general and minister of the early Sung dynasty. One of Pin's granddaughters became a queen. Ts'ao Hsüeh-ch'in's fifth-generation ancestor, Ts'ao Pao 曹寶 (also named Ts'ao Hsi-yüan 曹錫遠 or Ts'ao Shih-hsüan 曹世 選), served in the Ming dynasty as an officer in Shenyang 沈陽 and moved his family from Kiangsi in China proper to Manchuria, then a part of Ming territory. There, Ts'ao Hsüeh-ch'in's great-great-grandfather, Ts'ao Chen-yen 曹振彥, may have been captured by the Manchu rulers, probably about 1630; he was made a bondservant in a military force called the Plain

White Banner, after serving under General T'ung Yang-hsing 佟養性 for a short period. T'ung's grand-niece later gave birth to a boy who became the K'ang-hsi emperor. The Plain White Banner, one of the most prestigious of the "Three Upper Banners" of the Manchu "Eight Banners," was commanded by the powerful noble Dorgon and was instrumental in the sacking of the Ming capital, Peking, in 1644. After Dorgon's death in 1650, the Plain White Banner was put under the direct command of the mother of the First Manchu emperor, Shun-chih. It was she who held the real power in the court until her death in 1688. The bondservants of the banner were later made part of the Imperial Household, and thus some of them enjoyed the confidence of the emperors.

During the early years of the Ch'ing, when the Manchu emperors needed to consolidate their control of the Chinese empire, particularly in the lower Yangtze valley, they acted to secure the rich resources of that region, to watch and pacify the Han Chinese, and to report on local officials. To do this they often appointed bondservants of the Imperial Household to serve as Commissioners for Imperial Textile Supplies and Salt Inspectors in Nanking, Soochow, and Hangchow, all prominent cultural and commercial centers of this area. Although the formal status of such a commissioner was still that of the emperor's slave, in actuality, with two or three thousand employees under his command, handling a yearly revenue of thousands of silver taels, and sending confidential reports directly to the emperor, he became a very rich and powerful person.

Ts'ao Hsüeh-ch'in's great-grandfather, Ts'ao Hsi 曹璽, who had served in the palace guard of the Shun-chih emperor, was appointed Commissioner for Imperial Textile Supplies for Nanking in 1663. He stayed in that position for twenty-one years, until his death. His wife, née Sun (1632-1706), served as the K'ang-hsi emperor's nanny, and thus Hsi's son, Ts'ao Yin,* grandfather of the novelist, may have been the future emperor's childhood compan-

ion. After his father's death, Ts'ao Yin became the assistant supervisor in the Nanking Textile Administration, and in 1690 he was appointed textile commissioner for Soochow. Two years later, he served concurrently as textile commissioner in Nanking. In 1693, his Soochow appointment was transferred to his wife's elder brother, Li Hsü 李煦 (1655-1729), and Yin continued in the Nanking position till he died. Meanwhile, from 1704 on, commissioners Ts'ao Yin and Li Hsü served in turn as Salt Inspectors in Yangchow; this duty actually covered a large region of four rich provinces. Ts'ao Yin was a talented and learned man, a well-recognized poet and playwright, skillful also in archery and horsemanship. A bibliophile and patron of the arts, he enjoyed close friendships with many prominent poets, writers, and scholars. Although he died before Ts'ao Hsüeh-ch'in was born, to a certain degree his lifestyle may have influenced his grandson.

In his four tours to the South in 1699, 1703, and 1707, the K'ang-hsi emperor was hosted by Ts'ao Yin. Yin's two daughters married Manchu princes by the emperor's order. The expenses of these relations with the imperial court, along with the standard of living which they imposed upon the Ts'ao household, left Yin deeply in debt. After Ts'ao Yin's death, the emperor appointed Yin's only son, Ts'ao Yung 曹顒, to succeed him as Textile Commissioner in Nanking. But three years later Ts'ao Yung died without a son to succeed him, and so the emperor, out of concern for the family's welfare, ordered Ts'ao Yin's wife, Old Lady Li, to adopt one of Ts'ao Yin's nephews, Ts'ao Fu 曹頫, as a posthumous son so that he would inherit Ts'ao Yung's position. Old Lady Li seems to be the model for Grandmother Chia in the *Hung-lou meng.*

There are two theories regarding the identity of Ts'ao Hsüeh-ch'in's father. In a memorial to the throne dated April 10, 1715, Ts'ao Fu said that Ts'ao Yung's wife had been pregnant for seven months. Later it was found in a Ts'ao clan genealogical record that Ts'ao Yung had a son named Ts'ao T'ien-yu 曹天佑. It seems likely that this posthumous son of Ts'ao Yung was the novelist Ts'ao Hsüeh-ch'in, since many early writings testify that Hsüeh-ch'in was Ts'ao Yin's only grandson, and Hsüeh-ch'in's formal name, Chan (Favor Received), is similar in meaning to the name T'ien-yu (Heaven Helped). If this is the case, Ts'ao Hsüeh-ch'in spent more than eleven years of his youth living in luxury, which experience helped him later to describe the extravagant life so vividly in his novel. Another theory suggests that Ts'ao Hsüeh-ch'in was Ts'ao Fu's son. At any rate, in January 1728, Ts'ao Fu was dismissed from his post and his estate confiscated. This happened in a changed political situation: after the K'ang-hsi emperor's death in 1722, his ruthless son, later the Yung-cheng emperor, seized the throne in a power struggle with his brothers. He purged his brothers and their allies, with whom the Ts'ao family was suspected to have associated.

Estate confiscation during the Yung-cheng period was a terrifying event. In addition to having one's property seized, one's family and servants were usually given away as slaves. But Ts'ao Fu and a small number of members of the family were allowed to move to Peking and to live in a few of the clan's houses there. This was probably through the aid of relatives and friends who included the emperor's favored brother, Prince Yin-hsiang, whose descendants were later found to have preserved copies of Ts'ao's novel, and Prince Fu-p'eng, who was the son of Ts'ao Yin's daughter, and who still had the emperor's favor at the time.

Nevertheless, such a change of fortune must have been a great shock to young Ts'ao Hsüeh-ch'in, and the ensuing six years must have been difficult. The family's life in Peking may have improved somewhat in the four or five years following 1734, when the Yung-cheng regime became less strict, and after his death in 1735, as the new Ch'ien-lung emperor showed great favor to Prince Fu-p'eng. However, conceivably the Ts'ao family had to live at the mercy of such relatives. Then, in 1739 a new political purge took place,

disgracing most of Ts'ao's relatives. Thus he had possibly reached the end of privileged life at about the age of twenty-four.

It may have been around this time that Ts'ao Hsüeh-ch'in started to work on the novel, spending the ten years, roughly from 1740 to 1750, writing most of it, and revising it five times. Around this period he also worked for some time in the Imperial Clan's School for the children of the nobility and bannermen, probably as a clerk. The dates he worked at the school are not known for certain, but he could not have left there before 1748, the year his last prominent relative, his cousin Prince Fu-p'eng, died. At the school, Ts'ao became good friends with two Manchu students of the imperial family, the brothers Tun-min 敦敏 (1729-c. 1796) and Tun-ch'eng 敦誠 (1734-1791). Their poems to and about Ts'ao later were to provide most of the first-hand information we have about Ts'ao's life and personality.

After leaving his post at the school, Ts'ao moved from place to place in the capital, hardly receiving enough help from the rich and prosperous to continue. Utterly frustrated, he settled in the countryside west of Peking, probably somewhere near a Plain White Banner camp below Hsiang Hill. He supported himself in part by selling his own paintings. It is also possible that he received some income from people who had copied for private sale part of the unfinished draft of his novel. At some time Ts'ao may have taken and passed the lower-rank civil-service examinations, or perhaps he inherited local official status; he may have served in the local government in Nanking in 1759. It is even possible that some imperial official asked him to serve as a painter in the court. It is definite that he had no interest in serving the government.

As a novelist and poet, Ts'ao was admired and encouraged by only a handful of relatives and friends. An uncle, a cousin, and the brothers Tun-min and Tun-ch'eng, were among the few. He had one other good friend, Chang I-ch'üan 張宜泉, a school teacher whose ancestors had also been purged for unknown reasons. Chang's poems are yet another valuable source of information about Ts'ao's life.

Ts'ao's financial situation must have been very distressing to him and his family. He was a great drinker, and the money from the sale of his paintings was probably not enough to pay his wine-shop debts, while his whole family often could only afford to eat porridge. Their living quarters were also quite poor and rustic.

Little is known about his marital life. His first wife must have died before him. The death of his infant son in the fall of 1762 saddened him so deeply that he fell sick and died on the eve of the Lunar New Year, February 12, 1763. He was survived by his second wife, whom he had married not long before.

Ts'ao Hsüeh-ch'in was a versatile and widely learned person. Besides fiction, poetry, and painting, he was knowledgeable in both theater and music; he was an impressive singer and lute player. He might have also taken to acting in opera as a hobby. A lusty drinker and attractive conversationalist, as well as a great admirer of women, Ts'ao, whose unconventional thinking and behavior were influenced by Chuang-tzu and the Neo-Taoists of the Wei-Chin period, and perhaps also by Buddhism, became well known by many only long after his death.

STUDIES:

Chao, Kang 趙岡 and Ch'en Chung-i 陳鍾毅. *Hung-lou meng hsin-t'an* 紅樓夢新探. Hong Kong, 1970.

———. *Hung-lou meng lun-chi* 紅樓夢論集. Taipei, 1975.

———. *Hua-hsiang t'ung-ch'ou tu Hung-lou* 花香銅臭讀紅樓. Taipei, 1975.

Chou, Ju-ch'ang 周汝昌. *Ts'ao Hsüeh-ch'in hsiao-chuan* 曹雪芹小傳. Tientsin, 1980.

———. *Hung-lou meng hsin-cheng* 紅樓夢新證. Revised and enlarged edition. 2v. Peking, 1967.

Chow, Tse-tsung 周策縱. "Yü-hsi, hun-yin, *Hung-lou meng*—Ts'ao Hsüeh-ch'in chia-shih cheng-chih kuan-hsi so-yüan" 玉璽婚姻紅樓夢 — 曹雪芹家世政治關係溯源, *Lien-ho yüeh-k'an*, 17 (December 1982), 18 (January 1983).

Feng, Ch'i-yung 馮其庸. *Ts'ao Hsüeh-ch'in chia-shih hsin-k'ao* 曹雪芹家世新考. Peking, 1981.

Hawkes, David. "Introduction" to *The Story of the Stone*. V. 1: *The Golden Days*. London, 1973, pp. 15-46.

Hu, Shih 胡適, et al. *Hung lou-meng k'ao-cheng* 紅樓夢考證. Shanghai, 1922; rev. ed. Taipei, 1961.

I-su 一粟 (Chou Shou-liang 周紹良 and Chu Nan-hsien 朱南銑). *Hung-lou meng chüan* 紅樓夢卷. Peking, 1963.

Lu-kung po-wu-yüan 故宮博物院. *Kuan-yü chiang-ning chi-tsao Ts'ao chia tang-an shih-liao* 關於江寧織造曹家檔案史科. Peking, 1975.

P'an, Chung-kuei 潘重規. *Hung-lou meng hsin-chieh* 紅樓夢新解. Singapore, 1959; 2nd ed. Taipei, 1973.

Shen-yang shih-fan hsüeh-yüan 瀋陽師範學院. *Ts'ao Hsüeh-ch'in chia-shih tsu-liao* 曹雪芹家世資料. Shenyang, 1979.

Spence, Jonathan D. *Ts'ao Yin and the K'ang-hsi Emperor: Bondservant and Master*. New Haven, 1966.

Wu, En-yü 吳恩裕. *Yu-kuan Ts'ao Hsüeh-ch'in shih-chung* 有關曹雪芹十種. Peking, 1963.

———. *Ts'ao Hsüeh-ch'in ti ku-shih* 曹雪芹的故事. Peking, 1964.

———. *K'ao pai hsiao-chi* 考稗小記. Hong Kong, 1979.

———. *Ts'ao Hsüeh-ch'in i-chu ch'ien-t'an* 曹雪芹佚著淺探. Tientsin, 1979.

———. *Ts'ao Hsüeh-ch'in ts'ung-k'ao* 曹雪芹叢考. Shanghai, 1980.

Wu, Shih-ch'ang 吳世昌. *On the Red Chamber Dream*. Oxford, 1961.

—TTC

Ts'ao P'i 曹丕 (*tzu*, Tzu-huan 子桓, 187-226) was a poet and critic, the second son of Ts'ao Ts'ao and elder brother of Ts'ao Chih. Ts'ao P'i came to the throne in 220 and ruled as Emperor Wen of the Wei dynasty 魏文帝. He was the first emperor who was also a successful man of letters. His surviving forty five-syllable poems, in addition to about thirty *fu*,* are certainly only a fraction of his poetic work. Slightly later sources mention that he wrote over a hundred poems in a vernacular style as artless as daily conversation. His "Yen ko hsing" 燕歌行 is believed to be the first seven-syllable poem by a known author. The poem, rhymed in every line, is of considerable interest for the early history of the form.

Perhaps better known are some of his prose writings. His two letters to a friend named Wu Chih 吳質 have a lyrical quality in their depiction of nostalgic memories of friendships and happy gatherings.

Ts'ao P'i apparently held the conviction that an author should produce a book of his own ideas. His own effort, the *Tien lun* 典論, is no longer extant. However, the chapter on literature, called "Lun wen" 論文 (Essay on Literature), survives, thanks to Hsiao T'ung, who included it in his *Wen-hsüan.* In its complete form, this text firmly establishes Ts'ao P'i as one of the most important figures in the history of Chinese literary criticism. Contrary to previous views that treated literature as didactic and political, Ts'ao P'i asserted that literature was valuable in its own right. He also put forward a concept of genres. He listed the requirements of each genre according to its function and evaluated each writer of his time in terms of merits and shortcomings.

EDITION:

Wei Wen-ti shih chu 魏文帝詩注. Huang Chieh 黃節, annot. Peking, 1958.

TRANSLATIONS:

Demiéville, *Anthologie*, pp. 115-117.

STUDIES:

Debon, Günther. "Der Jadering des Chung Yu (*Wen-hsüan*, 42.4)," *Münchener Ostasiatische Studien*, 25 (1979), 307-314.

Fusek, Lois Mckim. "The Poetry of Ts'ao P'i (187-226)." Unpublished Ph.D. dissertation, Yale University, 1975.

Holzman, Donald. "Literary Criticism in China in the Early Third Century A.D.," *AS*, 28 (1974), 111-149.

Lin, Wen-yüeh 林文月. "Ts'ao P'i yü Ts'ao Chih" 曹丕與曹植, *Wen-hsüeh tsa-chih*, 1.6 (1957), 30-36.

Ping, Ch'en 炳宸. "Ts'ao P'i te wen-hsüeh li-lun" 曹丕的文學理論, in *Wen-hsüeh i-ch'an hsüan-chi* 文學遺產選集, v. 3, Peking, 1960, pp. 128-134.

Schulte, Wilfred. "Ts'ao P'i (187-226), Leben und Dichtungen." Unpublished Ph.D. dissertation, University of Bonn, 1973.

Suzuki, *Kan Gi*, pp. 566-588.

—SLD

Ts'ao-t'ang shih-yü 草堂詩餘 is an anthology of *tz'u** compiled about 1195. It includes over three hundred lyrics, most written by Sung, a few by T'ang and Five Dynasties authors. As one of the earliest collections of lyric poetry, it ranked with the *Hua-chien chi** as a model for later generations. It is, however, traditionally criticized for its inclusion of some less refined pieces.

There is some doubt about the compiler of the anthology. The *Chih-chai shu-lu chieh-t'i* 直齋書錄解題 by Ch'ao Kung-wu 晁公武 (d. 1171) lists this work as having been compiled by an anonymous "bookseller." But on the title page of the 1351 edition (one of the earliest extant editions), the compiler's name is given as Ho Shih-hsin 何士信. This edition, however, may not represent the original work. Its full title, *Tseng-hsiu chien-chu miao-hsüan ch'ün-ying ts'ao-t'ang shih-yü* 增修箋註妙選群英草堂詩餘, suggests that by the mid-fourteenth century the original anthology had already been "expanded" (*tseng-hsiu*) by later hands. And there is no indication in this edition of the exact role played by Ho in the compilation. We have no idea whether he was the first compiler or an editor responsible for the expanded edition. Nor do we know exactly when he lived. The textual history of the work is somewhat complicated. The Sung print has been lost. The earliest extant texts are the 1351 edition mentioned above and a manuscript copy based on a 1343 edition. Both are now preserved in the library of the National Palace Museum in Taipei. For scholarly purposes it is essential to realize that there are two textual traditions. The 1343 and 1351 editions, as well as some early Ming editions, classify their selections topically (under such traditional headings as *ch'un-ching* 春景, *hsia-ching* 夏景, *t'ien-wen* 天文, etc.). In 1550, Ku Ts'ung-ching 顧從敬 brought out an entirely new edition called *Lei-pien ts'ao-t'ang shih-yü* 類編草堂詩餘. He reclassified the selections according to their meters (*hsiao-ling* 小令, *chung-tiao* 中調, and *ch'ang-tiao* 長調). His edition gained immediate popularity and became the base text of many later editions from 1550 onward. Thus the two textual traditions are distinguished by their different schemes of classification. We shall refer to them as A and B editions respectively.

From the mid-sixteenth century through the nineteenth century, the earlier A Editions were all but forgotten. As a result, in the late eighteenth century, when the *Ssu-k'u ch'üan-shu tsung-mu* (see Chi Yün) was compiled, its editors erred in saying that the classification of lyrics by meter began with this anthology, an error still found in modern publications. The editors reached this conclusion simply on the basis of the Ku Edition alone. They did not see any of the A Editions, which began to re-emerge only in 1915 with a reprint of the 1382 edition. Modern texts, it should be noted, may be either A or B editions.

EDITIONS:

Tseng-hsiu chien-chu miao-hsuan ch'üan-ying ts'ao-t'ang shih-yü 增修箋註妙選群英草堂詩餘. (A) In *Ying-k'an Sung Chin Yüan Ming pen tz'u* 景刊宋金元明本詞, 1915; rpt. Shanghai, 1961. Reprint of a 1382 edition. Includes annotations and comments. One of the best editions. (B) *SPTK*. Photocopy of an A Edition published in the Chia-ching Period. Reliable and readily available.

Ts'ao-t'ang shih-yü 草堂詩餘. Shanghai, 1958. Modern punctuated text based on the 1382 edition. Unfortunately, all the original comments and annotations have been deleted.

Lei-pien ts'ao-t'ang shih-yü 類編草堂詩餘. *SPPY*. Modern text based on a B Edition.

STUDIES:

Li, Ting-fang 李鼎芳, "*Ts'ao-t'ang shih-yü* chih-lueh" 草堂詩餘志略, in *Ho-pei Ta-hsüeh hsüeh-pao*, 1981.2, 39-42. A good, general study.

—SFL

Ts'ao Yin 曹寅 (*tzu*, Tzu-ch'ing 子清, *hao*, Lien-t'ing 楝亭, Li-hsien 荔軒, and others, 1658-1712) played an important mediating role between the Chinese and the Manchu worlds in the years shortly after the founding of the Ch'ing dynasty. As a hereditary bondservant (*pao-i*) of a Chinese family in Shenyang 沈陽 that had been enrolled first in a Chinese banner then shifted to the Manchu Plain White Banner, Ts'ao Yin followed in the footsteps of his father Ts'ao Hsi 曹璽 and made a career as Com-

missioner for Imperial Textile Supplies (*chih-tsao* 織造), serving first in Soochow from 1690 to 1693 and then in Nanking from 1693 to 1712. He also served as Commissioner of the Liang-huai Salt Monopoly for four years between 1704 and 1710. Both these posts were financially delicate ones, requiring a shrewd knowledge of local economic conditions, since the surplus income gleaned from these activities was passed back to the Imperial Household (*Wei-wu fu* 內務府) and became a part of the emperor's privy exchequer. Ts'ao Yin may have owed these appointments to the fact that his mother, née Sun 孫, had once been wet-nurse to the Chun-chih emperor's son, who ascended the throne in 1661 as the K'ang-hsi emperor; in any case, both appointments enabled him to amass a very considerable private fortune, as well as to satisfy the emperor's requirements.

Ts'ao Yin was a widely cultured and gregarious man. From the colophons to some of his poems and from the inscriptions to the collections of album leaves and poems that he collected, under the name of his studio, as the *Lien-t'ing t'u* 楝亭圖, we can see how wide a range of contacts he had with talented local Chinese scholars, such as Yu T'ung,* Shih Jun-chang,* Ku Ching-hsing 顧景星 (1621-1687), Chu I-tsun,* Yeh Hsieh,* and the brilliant young Manchu writer of Chinese *tz'u* poems, Na-lan Hsing-te.* At the same time he was a collector of Sung and rare editions (some of which he published under the titles *Lien-t'ing shih-erh chung* 楝亭十二種 and *Lien-t'ing wu chung* 楝亭五種), a dramatist (he is now widely believed to have been the author of *Hu-k'ou yü-sheng* 虎口餘生 [Escape from the Tiger]) and an able poet, who collected fourteen *chüan* of his *shih** and *tz'u** poems under the title *Lien-t'ing chi* 楝亭集.

Ts'ao Yin shared the K'ang-hsi emperor's love of archery, riding, and rare Western objects, and he hosted the emperor at his Nanking home on four of K'ang-hsi's southern tours, in 1699, 1730, 1705, and 1707. These magnificent occasions gave Ts'ao Yin further opportunity to meet with famous local scholars as well as senior members of the bureaucracy in the Kiangnan Region. He was also on familiar terms with many of the wealthiest salt merchants. The K'ang-hsi emperor used Ts'ao Yin (along with Ts'ao's cousin Li Hsü 李煦, the textile commissioner of Soochow) to provide him with confidential information on political matters in central China and as a source for accurate data on rice prices and rainfall levels. Ts'ao was also given special assignments, such as checking out trade conditions among the Chinese merchants in Nagasaki. (These initially informal arrangements were later institutionalized in the Ch'ing palace-memorial system.)

In the cultural realm, the K'ang-hsi emperor gave Ts'ao Yin a number of extremely important assignments. Among these were the block-carving and printing of the great rhyming dictionary, the *P'ei-wen yün-fu* 佩文韻府, and the enormous collection (in 900 *chüan*) of the complete poetry of the T'ang dynasty, the *Ch'üan T'ang shih*.*

Perhaps partly because of the heavy expenses involved in entertaining the emperor and directing these huge publication projects, Ts'ao Yin began to fall heavily into debt near the end of his life. After his death in 1712, however, the K'ang-hsi emperor continued to show the family favor, by canceling many of the debts and appointing Ts'ao Yin's young and inexperienced son Ts'ao Yung 曹顒 to the textile commissioner's post his father had held. After Ts'ao Yung's sudden death in 1715, K'ang-hsi appointed Ts'ao Yung's cousin Ts'ao Fu 曹頫 to the same post. But Ts'ao Fu was not successful at the job and was dismissed in 1728 by orders of the Yung-cheng emperor. Many of the family possessions and estates in Nanking were confiscated at this time, and the remnants of the family moved to Peking.

Ever since the pioneering work of Hu Shih 胡適 and Yü P'ing-po 俞平伯 in the 1920s, it has been known that Ts'ao Yin was an ancestor of Ts'ao Hsüeh-ch'in,* the author of the *Hung-lou meng*.* Though the precise relationship is still not certain, it seems probable that Ts'ao Yin was great-uncle to Ts'ao Hsüeh-ch'in, who was the son of Ts'ao Yin's nephew (and posthumous adopted son) Ts'ao Fu. The famous commentator on the novel Chih-yen-chai 脂硯齋 (Red Inkstone) was probably Ts'ao Yin's grandson (Ts'ao Yung's son, Ts'ao T'ien-yu 曹天祐).

The known historical details of Ts'ao Yin's life form a fascinating backdrop to any analysis of the *Hung-lou meng*. The powerful Jung-kuo and Ning-kuo houses in the novel may well be echoes of Ts'ao Yin's Nanking household; the imperial consort Yüan-ch'un's 元春 visit to the Chia 賈 family in their Ta-kuan Yüan 大觀園 (Grand View Garden) may well echo K'ang-hsi's southern tour visits to the Ts'aos; and the sudden disastrous fall of the Chia family at the novel's end seems to follow rather faithfully what is known of the dismissal of Ts'ao Fu in 1728 on the orders of the Yung-cheng emperor. The Western objects and curios that litter the Chia house seem very similar to the kinds of objects that Ts'ao Yin was fond of collecting. Since the Ta-kuan Yüan was in great part an imaginative and allegorical construct, one can hardly accept Yüan Mei's* later claim that his "Sui-yüan" 隨園 *was* the Ta-kuan Yüan; yet Yüan bought the property for the Sui-yüan from Ts'ao Fu's successor as textile commissioner in Nanking, and this same property had probably once belonged to Ts'ao Yin.

EDITIONS:
Ku-kung wen-hsien, 2.1 (December 1970), 128-194; 2.2 (March 1971), 59-77, facsimile memorials by Ts'ao Yin (107 items), Ts'ao Yung (9 items) and Ts'ao Fu (26 items).
Lien-t'ing chi 楝亭集. Shanghai, 1978.
Lien-t'ing ch'üan-chi 楝亭全集. Taipei, 1976.
Lien-t'ing shih-erh chung 楝亭十二種 and *Lien-t'ing wu chung* 楝亭五種. Shanghai, 1921.

TRANSLATIONS:
See selected memorials and poems in Spence, *Ts'ao Yin*, below.

STUDIES:
Chao, Kang 趙岡, and Ch'en Chung-i 陳鍾毅. *Hung-lou-meng yen-chiu hsin-pien* 紅樓夢研究新編. Taipei, 1975.
Chou, Ju-ch'ang 周汝昌. *Hung-lou-meng hsin cheng* 紅樓夢新證. 2v. Peking, 1976.

Feng, Ch'i-yung 馮其庸. *Ts'ao Hsüeh-ch'in chia-shih hsin-k'ao* 曹雪芹家世新考. Shanghai, 1980.

Kuan-yü Chiang-ning chih-tsao Ts'ao-chia tang-an shih-liao 關於江寧織造曹家檔案史料. Peking, 1975.

Spence, Jonathan D. *Ts'ao Yin and the K'ang-hsi Emperor: Bondservant and Master.* New Haven, 1966.

Sun, E-tu Zen 孫任以都. "Sericulture and Silk Textile Production in Ch'ing China," in *Economic Organization in Chinese Society*, W. E. Willmett, ed., 1972, pp. 79-108. Basic material on the *chih-tsao* establishments.

Sung, Ch'i 宋淇. "Tu Ts'ao Yin *Lien-t'eng chi hou*" 讀曹寅棟亭集後, *Ming-pao yüeh-k'an*, 167 (November 1979), 53-56.

Torbert, Preston. *The Ch'ing Imperial Household Department: A Study of its Organization and Principal Functions, 1662-1796.* Cambridge, Mass., 1977. Basic material on the *pao-i* system.

Wu, Silas H. L. 吳秀良. *Communication and Imperial Control in China: Evolution of the Palace Memorial System, 1693-1735.* Cambridge, Mass., 1970.

—JS

Ts'en Shen 岑參 (*tzu*, unknown 715-770) was a major poet in the High T'ang era. A member of the Ts'en clan of Nanyang 南陽 and orphaned at an early age, he spent his youth in the Sung Mountains 嵩山 near Lo-yang. He passed the *chin-shih* in 744 and was appointed to a minor post in the office of the crown prince's bodyguard. After languishing in that position for four years, he found a patron in the powerful general Kao Hsien-chih 高仙芝. He accompanied Kao to Kucha in Central Asia in 749, returning to Ch'ang-an in 751 after Kao's disastrous defeat in the Battle of Talas. In 752 Ts'en joined Kao Shih,* Tu Fu,* Ch'u Kuang-hsi,* and Hsüeh Chü 薛據 in a visit to the Temple of Compassionate Mercy in the capital, where the group composed the later much anthologized poems celebrating the pagoda of the famous temple. In 754 Ts'en returned to Central Asia, where he served General Feng Ch'ang-ch'ing 封常清. The eight years between 749 and 757 in Central Asia were perhaps Ts'en's most creative period. He returned to China after the An Lu-shan Rebellion had erupted, arriving in 757 at Emperor Su-tsung's temporary court in Feng-hsiang, where, on the recommendation of his friend Tu Fu, he was appointed Rectifier of Omissions of the Right. When the court returned to Ch'ang-an, Ts'en suffered the same fate as Tu Fu: he was dismissed from court and sent to Kuo-chou 虢州 (modern Honan). He was recalled to the capital in 762 where he held a series of posts; he also accompanied the future Emperor Te-tsung on a campaign against Shih Chao-i. In 765 he became Prefect of Chia-chou 嘉州 (modern Szechwan). A local rebellion delayed his departure until 766, when he accompanied Tu Hung-chien's 杜鴻漸 campaign to put down the insurgence. By 767 he was able to take his post at Chia-chou. In the summer of 768 he headed homeward again, but his route was cut off by yet another local rebellion. He died in Ch'eng-tu in 770.

Ts'en Shen is now chiefly remembered for the "frontier" poetry he composed during his two sojourns in Central Asia. His achievement in this subgenre may be viewed both as a departure from and as the culmination of a tradition. Writing after the great frontier songs such as Kao Shih's "Yen-ko hsing" 燕歌行 (Song of Yen), Wang Han's 王翰 (*fl.* 713) "Liang-chou tz'u" 涼州詞 (Lyrics of Liang-chou) and Wang Ch'ang-ling's* exquisite quatrains, Ts'en's most memorable poems may be considered the apogee of a vigorous tradition. On the other hand, his personal knowledge of a region that hitherto had been only the stuff of poetic convention allowed him to extend the tradition. Recent studies have shown that Ts'en's knowledge of the geography of Central Asia far exceeded that of the other poets who wrote on the frontier; poems on such topics as the hot volcanic lakes explore subjects previously unknown in Chinese poetry.

Yet this identification of Ts'en Shen with the poetry of the frontier and martial exploits is a late critical emphasis that may be misleading. Only a small portion of Ts'en's more than four hundred poems has the frontier as its subject, and these were written during only eight years of the poet's life. Contemporary scholars pay little attention to the nature and eremitic works of the poet's early years or the artistically mature pieces written after 757. A more balanced critical perspective, perhaps, is to consider Ts'en Shen as a master of the craft of poetry, a stylist who creates daring, original, and ingenious effects with the most ordinary of themes. As testament to Ts'en's craftsmanship, traditional critics cite couplets that are among the most felicitous in T'ang poetry. They also observe, however, that Ts'en's mastery of his poetic art is not matched by the strength of his emotion. Ts'en's works are a triumph of art over feeling; in them technical cunning and brilliant ornamentation mask and relieve basically pedestrian sentiments.

EDITIONS:

Chang, Hui 張輝. Ts'en Shen pien-sai shih hsüan 岑參邊塞詩選. Peking, 1981. Contains over 70 poems, with lengthy annotations.

Ch'en, T'ieh-min 陳鐵民 and Hou Chung-i 侯忠義. Ts'en Shen chi chiao-chu 岑參集校注. Shanghai, 1981.

Ch'üan T'ang shih, v. 3, ch. 198-201, pp. 2023-2107.

Juan, T'ing-yü 阮廷瑜. Ts'en Chia-chou chi chiao-chu岑嘉州詩校注. Taipei, 1980.

Shimmen, Keiko 新冤惠子. Shin Shin kashi sakuin 岑參歌詩索引. Hiroshima, 1978.

Ts'en Chia-chou shih 岑嘉州詩. SPTK.

TRANSLATIONS:

Sunflower, pp. 143-149.

STUDIES:

Chan, Marie. "The Frontier Poems of Ts'en Shen," JAOS, 97.4 (1979), 420-437.

Li Chia-yen 李嘉言. "Ts'en shih hsi-nien" 岑詩系年, Wen-hsüeh i-ch'an tseng-k'an, 3 (1956), pp. 119-154.

Liu, K'ai-yang 劉開揚. "Lüeh-t'an Ts'en Shen ho t'a te shih"略談岑參和他的詩, in his T'ang shih lun-wen chi 唐詩論文集, Shanghai, 1979, pp. 68-82.

Nankano, Miyoko 中野美伐子. "Shih Shin no saigai shi" 岑參の塞外詩, Nihon Chūgoku Gakkai-hō, 12 (1960), 38-54.

Owen, High T'ang, pp. 169-182. Contains translations.

Shih, Mo-ch'ing 史墨卿. Ts'en Shen yen-chiu. Taipei, 1966.

Sugaya, Shōgo 菅谷省吾. "Shih Shin no koshi ni tsuite" 岑參 の 古詩 について, Shinagaku kenkyū, 24-25 (1960), pp. 152-162.

Sun, Shu-shan 孫述山. Sheng T'ang pien-sai shih-jen Ts'en Shen chih yen-chiu 盛唐邊塞詩人岑參之研究, M.A. thesis, Fujen University, Taiwan, 1971.

Suzuki, Todai, pp. 393-451.

Waley, Arthur. "A Chinese Poet in Central Asia," in The Secret History of the Mogols, London, 1963, pp. 30-46. On Ts'en Shen's life and verse; contains translations of seven poems.

—MC

Tseng Kung 曾鞏 (tzu, Tzu-ku 子固, also known as Nan-feng Hsien-sheng 南豐先生 [Gentleman from Nan-feng], 1019-1083) was an official, a scholar, and an author from Nan-feng 南豐 (modern Kiangsi). As a youth Tseng demonstrated a skill in composing prose which attracted the notice of Ou-yang Hsiu.* A correspondence between Ou-yang, already known throughout the nation, and the youthful Tseng began during the 1040s; Tseng also exchanged letters with Wang An-shih* and was instrumental in introducing these two important literary figures to one another.

In 1047 Ou-yang Hsiu asked Tseng to write an antithesis to his famous "Tsui-weng T'ing chi" 醉翁亭記 (The Drunken Old Man's Pavilion) which Tseng entitled "Hsing-hsin T'ing chi" 醒心亭記 (Pavilion of a Sober Mind). That same year his father died and Tseng went into mourning. During this period he composed one of his best-known works, "Mo-ch'ih chi" 墨池記 (Record of Inky Pond), an informal essay on the pond in which Wang Hsi-chih 王羲之 (307-365) is said to have washed his writing brushes when practicing calligraphy causing the waters there to turn inky black.

It was another decade before Tseng passed the chin-shih examination in the famed competition of 1057 which Ou-yang Hsiu administered. Ou-yang used this opportunity to include several questions in the controversial area of statecraft and expected responses to be written in ku-wen.* Although there was an outcry by numerous candidates who were unsuccessful, the literary world (including many of these protesters) was eventually convinced by the outstanding careers of the candidates who passed—which besides Tseng Kung in-

799

cluded Su Shih* and Su Ch'e*—and gradually accepted *ku-wen* as the style of most prose writing for nearly a millennium.

The examination also marked a beginning for Tseng Kung—in 1059 he took his first official position in T'ai-p'ing chou太平州 (modern Anhwei). Shortly thereafter he was recalled to the capital where he served as a professor in the National University (1063-1065). During this period Tseng edited and wrote prefaces to many classical works including the *Hsin-hsü* 新序, the *Lieh-nü chuan* 烈女傳, the *Shuo-yüan* 說苑, the *Chan-kuo ts'e*,* and several poetic corpuses including that of Li Po.* In 1069 he was sent to Hangchow and served in the provinces until 1080, distinguishing himself especially in Yüeh-chou 越州 (Chekiang), where his efforts in flood relief are noted, and in Ch'i-chou 齊州 (Shantung), where he reduced the power of the local satrap, placating the populace and as a result almost eliminating banditry in the area. He also attracted numerous students during his service at nearly a dozen provincial cities and towns during this period. In 1080 he returned to the capital to take a position in the history office. In the early 1080s he was a popular figure at court, eventually receiving the appointment of Secretariat Drafter in 1082. The following year he died in Chiang-ning 江寧 (modern Nanking) where he had gone to mourn his mother.

Tseng Kung is known as one of the "T'ang Sung pa-ta (san-wen) chia" 唐宋八大 (散文) 家 (Eight Great [Prose] Writers of the T'ang and Sung—see also Han Yü) and as Ou-yang Hsiu's major disciple. His poetry (197 old-style and 213 modern-style pieces) is generally considered undistinguished. A ditty of his day ran: "There are three things people regret: first, that shads have many bones, second, that peonies have no fragrance, and third, that Tseng Kung cannot compose verse." However, although in comparison to other members of the group of eight—such as Han Yü, Liu Tsung-yüan,* Ou-yang Hsiu, and Su Shih—Tseng's poetry pales, it is not without merit. One poem in particular, "Shang yüan" 上元 (The Fifteenth of the First Lu-

nar Month), a theme of several of Tseng's poems, is often included in anthologies. It is moreover important to note that Han, Liu, Ou-yang, and Su are all literary giants. None of the other four members of the eight can measure up on a purely literary scale—they were all included for various nonliterary reasons. Tseng Kung is one of the eight because of his close relationship to Ou-yang Hsiu and the role he played in the examination of 1057, because of the esteem Chu Hsi 朱熹 (1130-1200) paid his staunch Confucianist stance, and because of his editorial work.

Aside from "Mo-ch'ih chi," his letters to Wang An-shih and Ou-yang Hsiu, and the "Hsing-hsin T'ing chi," his works have been little read. Many of his other writings (verse and prose) are occasional, a good number commissioned by wealthy families to commemorate a lost loved one or a new edifice (the defense for such writings he provides in one of his letters to Ou-yang Hsiu may be in part a self-defense, although it is ostensibly written to reassure the master who had written an epitaph for Tseng's grandfather). There are also many edicts, rescripts, and memorials he drafted while at court in the fifty *chüan* which remain today (the corpus was originally in one hundred *chüan*).

As a strict Confucian, Tseng Kung saw little difference between style and subject—he admired solely those predecessors who wrote on orthodox subjects. His views of literary history can be inferred in part from his preface to the poetic collections of Wang Tzu-chih 王子直 (*fl.* 520), Li Po, and Pao Jung 鮑溶 (*fl.* 820). Chu Hsi saw Tseng's style as *yen* 嚴 (strict—it was no accident that Ou-yang Hsiu asked Tseng to write the "Hsing-hsin T'ing chi"!). Tseng modeled his writing on the classics. Yet this limpid, simple style has drawn criticism, since it tended to become trite and clichéd. Critical opinion has praised its elegance and classical nature but lamented its lack of literary embellishment. There are hints that Tseng may have been aware of his shortcomings—his claim, for example, that only works in a strong style such as that of Ou-yang Hsiu would be transnitted (in his "Shang Ou-yang Hsüeh-shih i-i shu" 上歐陽學士第一書) or his emphasis on the importance of study (rather than talent) in the "Mo-ch'ih chi." Yet it is his concern with content that recommends him to the modern reader over numerous stylists of the intervening centuries.

EDITIONS:

Nan-feng Hsien-sheng Yüan-feng lei-kao 元豐類稿 南豐先生 , 50 *ch.* Appendix, 1 *ch. SPTK.* Photolithic reprint of a Yüan edition, edited by Chao Ju-li 趙汝礪 (1042-1095) and again *c.* 1205 by unknown hands.

Yüan-feng lei-kao pu 元豐類補稿 . 2 *ch.* Collected by Lu Hsin-yüan 陸心源 (1834-1894) in *Ch'ien-yüan tsung-chi* 潛園總集 , *Ch'üan-shu chiao-pu* 群書校補 , *ch.* 73-74.

Selected prose, poetry, and letters are also available in various anthologies (usually of the "Eight Great Prose Writers of the T'ang and Sung").

TRANSLATIONS:

Liu, *Classical Prose*, pp. 308-343.

Margouliès, *Kou-wen*, pp. 302-305.

STUDIES:

Ami, Yūji 網祐次 . "Sō Kyō" no bunshō" 曾鞏 の文章 , *Jōnan kangaku*, 12 (October 1970), 52-66.

Chu, Feng-ch'i 朱鳳起 , ed. *Tseng Kung wen* 曾鞏 文 . Shanghai, 1928. Thirty-one texts annotated, with a preface.

Wu, Che-fu 吳哲夫 . "Yüan-pan *Yüan-feng lei-kao*" 元版元豐類稿 , *T'u-shu chi-k'an*, I, 17 (1970), 52-54.

Wu, T'ien-sheng 吳天聲 . "Tseng Kung" 曾鞏 , in *Chung-kuo wen-hsüeh-shih lun-chi* 中國文學 史論集 , Taipei, 1958, pp. 551-562.

Yang, Hsi-min 楊希閔 , ed. "Tseng Wen-ting Kung wei Kung" 曾文定公諱鞏 , in *Shih-wu-chia nien-p'u* 十五家年譜 , Taipei, 1966. Separate pagination.

—WHN

Tseng Kuo-fan 曾國藩 (*tzu,* Po-han 伯涵, *hao,* Ti-sheng 滌生, 1811-1872) was a poet, an essayist, a literary theorist, and an anthologist active during the mid-nineteenth century. As a leading figure in the suppression of the Taiping Rebellion (1850-1864) and the subsequent T'ung-chih Restoration (1862-1874), he achieved a widespread reputation as a military and political leader, a reputation which has overshadowed his literary achievements.

Born and raised in Hsiang-hsiang 湘鄉 (modern Hunan), his early education was dominated by his preparation for examinations. Having become a *hsiu-ts'ai* in 1833 and a *chin-shih* in 1838, he began nine years of service in the Han-lin Academy. In 1847, he began to rise in the metropolitan bureaucracy when he was appointed Subchancellor of the Grand Secretariat. For five years thereafter he served, at different times, as Vice-Minister of five of the six ministries in Peking. Between 1853 and 1864, he fought the Taiping rebels, first in central China and then in the lower Yangtze regions. After the Taiping Rebellion had been suppressed, he served as Governor-general of Chihli, and then of Liang-kiang, before his death in Nanking in 1872.

After becoming a member of the Han-lin Academy and thus freeing himself from examination preparations, he began to devote himself to scholarship, especially in literature and philosophy. He had the good fortune to study Neo-Confucianism under T'ang Chien 唐鑑 (1778-1861) and the Manchu statesman Wo-jen 倭仁 (d. 1871). He also studied literature under Mei Tseng-liang 梅曾亮 (1786-1856), a disciple of Yao Nai (see *Ku-wen tz'u lei-tsuan*), who had been an important figure in the T'ung-ch'eng P'ai.* After leaving Peking in 1852 and becoming involved in various military and political campaigns in the provinces, he continued to spend much of his time on his literary activities. For a period of nearly twenty years, he gathered around himself a group of *mu-yu* 幕友 (private secretaries), composed of over eighty talented writers, scholars, and administrators. Among them, Wu Min-shu 吳敏樹 (1805-1873), Wu Chia-ping 吳嘉賓 (1803-1864), Chang Yü-chao 張裕釗 (1823-1894), Hsüeh Fu-ch'eng 薛福成 (1838-1894), and Li Shu-ch'ang 黎庶昌 (1837-1897) were all noted writers of the *ku-wen** prose.

As a poet, he is generally considered to have been influenced by the Sung masters, especially Huang T'ing-chien,* even though he himself admired other great poets of the past, including T'ao Ch'ien,* Tu Fu,* Li Po,* and Su Shih.* He is also considered an important pioneer figure of a movement of late Ch'ing poetry which advocated the imitation not only of the T'ang poetic style, but also those of the Sung and Ming, a movement which became widespread during the T'ung-chih (1862-1874) and Kuang-hsü (1875-1908) reigns and thus came to be known as the *T'ung-Kuang t'i* 同光體 (Poetic Style of the T'ung-chih and Kuang-hsü Reigns). His views on poetry are the best illustrated in the anthology of poetry he edited, *Shih-pa-chia shih-ch'ao* 十八家詩鈔 (Anthology of Eighteen Poets' Poetry), which included representative works written by eighteen poets from the Wei dynasty to the Sung.

As a writer of the *ku-wen* prose, he was no mere follower of the T'ung-ch'eng School. Although he confessed that he had initially learned prose-writing from reading the works of the T'ung-ch'eng master Yao Nai, he did much to revitalize this school. By Tseng's time, the T'ung-ch'eng School had been under attack by critics for having produced essays with little substantial content and a lack of solid study as a foundation. Writers of the T'ung-ch'eng School, these critics maintained, had only paid lip service to their emphasis on *i-li* 義理 (Neo-Confucian principles) as the content of their essays. Tseng, who himself agreed with these criticisms, advocated that ideas of *ching-shih* (statecraft) replace the *i-li* and thereby provided that T'ung-ch'eng School with a concrete method for dealing with the problem of content. In so doing, Tseng essentially expanded the concept of prose literature to include topics such as politics and economics which had previously been ignored. He also believed the Confucian classics to be the basic sources for all subsequent Chinese prose literature, a view significantly different from that held by earlier T'ung-ch'eng masters.

To illustrate his views on the art of prose composition, Tseng edited an anthology, entitled *Ching-shih pai-chia tsa-ch'ao* 經史百家雜鈔, which consisted of selections from the Confucian classics and various histories. He classified these selections, on the basis of form, into eleven classes, a slight deviation from the method of Yao's anthology, the *Ku-wen tz'u lei-tsuan*, which utilized a system of thirteen classes. A more important difference between Tseng's anthology and that of Yao Nai is that Tseng viewed all the Confucian classics as literature, and each of his eleven classes of selections thus begins with a selection from the classics. He also placed greater emphasis on historical writings. The title of his anthology, which carries the literal translation "Selections from One Hundred Writers of the Classics and History," makes obvious his attempt to expand the boundaries of Chinese prose. His other views on literature, and particularly on prose, are to be found in his *Ming-yüan-t'ang lun-wen* 鳴原堂論文 (Theories on Prose-writing from the Ming-yüan Studio), his diaries, and his correspondence with his associates and family members.

Tseng was also a noted writer of parallel couplets; most worthy of note are those written as eulogies for his friends and associates. During his military campaigns against the Taiping Rebellion, he also wrote a small number of exhortatory songs to be sung by his troops or by civilians under his jurisdiction. In so doing he created a genre later imitated by some early twentieth-century warlords, most notably by Feng Yü-hsiang 馮玉祥 (1882-1948).

Tseng had acquired a thorough knowledge of the classics from his experience in the examination system and his years in Peking, and he later gained broad experience in the political military world. In his literary efforts he essentially synthesized all these experiences and thereby significantly expanded the scope of Chinese literature, especially that of prose. He revitalized the T'ung-ch'eng School, a school characterized by clear and straightforward prose. These qualities of clarity and simplicity were acknowledged as valuable even by writers of vernacular literature of the May Fourth Era. Although not among the most talented authors of the Ch'ing dynasty, Tseng certainly stands out as one of the most innovative figures of the mid-nineteenth century.

EDITIONS:

Tseng Wen-cheng kung ch'üan-chi 曾文正公全集. 171v. Ch'uan-chung shu-chü 傳忠書局 edition.

Tseng Wen-cheng-kung shih-chi wen-chih 曾文正公詩集文集. 6v. *SPTK.*

STUDIES:

Chiang, Hsing-teh 蔣星德. *Tseng Kuo-fan chih sheng-p'ing yü shih-yeh* 曾國藩之生平與事業. Shanghai, 1935.

Ho, I-k'un 何貽焜. *Tseng Kuo-fan p'ing chuan* 曾國藩評傳. Taipei, 1957.

Kondō, Hideki 近藤秀樹. *Sō Koku-han* 曾國藩. Tokyo, 1966.

Sakurai, Nobuyoshi 櫻井信義. *Sō Koku-han* 曾國藩. Tokyo, 1943.

—AH

Tseng P'u 曾樸 (*tzu,* Meng-p'u 孟樸: *hao,* Tung-ya ping-fu 東亞病夫, 1872-1935) is best known as the author of the late Ch'ing novel of social criticism *Nieh-hai hua* 孽海花 (A Flower in an Ocean of Sin). Although trained in the Confucian classics to become a scholar-official in the imperial bureaucracy, Tseng P'u, like many other late Ch'ing figures, was never to fulfill his family's dream. Due to the changing social conditions of the time, he was to pursue a career in literature instead. Tseng P'u was a transitional figure whose literary career spanned two eras—the late Ch'ing imperial period and the early Republican period, and he made contributions in both.

He was born in the scenic city of Ch'ang-shu 常熟, Kiangsu, northwest of Shanghai. The Tsengs were a wealthy landowning family, and Tseng P'u was raised in the shelter of the family compound. During his early manhood from 1889 to 1895, he was engrossed in classical scholarship and spent much time in Peking with the eminent men of his day such as Weng T'ung-ho 翁同龢 (1829-1904) Wang Ming-luan 汪鳴鑾 (1839-1907), and Hung Chün 洪鈞 (1839-1893). In 1895 his studies culminated in a work of historical scholarship: *Pu Hou-Han shu i-wen chih ping k'ao* 補後漢書藝文志並考 (A Supplementary Historical Bibliography of the Later Han Dynasty with Critical Notes), which contributes to the ongoing effort of supplementing the bibliographical information in the various dynastic histories.

That same year Tseng P'u became uneasy with his classical scholarship. China's defeat in the Sino-Japanese War of 1894-1895 convinced him to enroll in the French curriculum of the T'ung-wen kuan 同文館 (College of Foreign Languages) in Peking to learn about the West. Thus he abandoned the traditional path of the literati. After mastering the language, Tseng P'u read much French literature and philosophy under the guidance of his friend and tutor Ch'en Chi-t'ung 陳季同, once the military attaché in France. In 1904 Tseng P'u became an active participant in the literary scene when he became involved in, and then completed, the writing of the *Nieh-hai hua* which had been begun by Chin Sung-ts'en 金松岑.

The work (in twenty chapters in the first edition [1905]) was based on Ts'eng's many years of experience in Peking. It is a panoramic novel which depicts primarily the degeneration of the high-level scholars and statesmen of late Ch'ing society—their passions, indulgences, and vices—before the backdrop of the intellectual trends and aspirations of the time. The novel is heavily burdened with traditional literary and cultural paraphernalia but shows some influence of Western literature. It caused quite a sensation at the time of its publication, particularly because so many of the characters and events depicted therein are thinly veiled representations of real persons and deeds. The portrayal of the famous socialite Sai Chin-hua 賽金花 was especially sensational. During this period, Tseng P'u also helped found the Hsiao-shuo lin she 小說林社 (Forest of Fiction Company), which specialized in the publication of works of fiction and issued a literary monthly (which ran from 1907 to 1908) by the same name.

From 1908 to 1926 Tseng P'u withdrew from the literary scene and became active in Kiangsu provincial politics. While so engaged he maintained touch with literature by translating several plays, a novel by Victor Hugo, and other shorter works into Chinese.

From 1927 to 1931 he was active again in literature and founded the magazine

Chen Mei Shan 眞美善 (Truth, Beauty, and Goodness) with his son Tseng Hsü-pai 曾虛白 as well as a publishing company by the same name. He also wrote an autobiographical novel in the confessional mode, *Lu Nan-tzu: Lien* 魯男子：戀(The Real Man: Love) which tells of his childhood and youth and of his romance with his cousin. This was the final stage in Tseng P'u's transformation from a traditional literati to a modern writer.

Corresponding to the changing literary and social climate, Tseng P'u produced a work of classical scholarship, a traditional novel of social criticism, and a modern confessional novel. He died quietly at his home in Ch'ang-shu, after several years of poor health, at the age of sixty-three.

The popularity of the *Nieh-hai hua* is attested to not only by its constant circulation, but by such sequels as Lu Shih-e's 陸士諤 *Hsin Nieh-hai hua* 新孽海花 (1910) and Chang Jo-ku's 張若谷 (1866-1941) *Hsü Nieh-hai hua* 續孽海花.

EDITIONS:

Nieh-hai hua 孽海花. 2v. Shanghai, 1905. 20 chapters.

———. 2v. Revised edition. 30 chapters. Rpt. Taipei, 1966.

———. Peking, 1962. Expanded and revised edition. 35 chapters.

Lu Nan-tzu: Lien. 2v. Rpt. Taipei, 1966.

Pu Hou-Han shu i-wen chih ping k'ao. in *Erh-shih-wu shih pu-pien* 二十五史補編. Shanghai, 1936.

STUDIES:

Ch'en, Tse-kuang 陳則光. "Cheng-ch'üeh ku-chi *Nieh-hai hua* tsai Chung-kuo chin-tai wen-hsüeh shih shang te ti-wei" 正確估計孽海花在中國近代文學史上的地位. *Chung-shan ta-hsüeh hsüeh-pao (She-hui k'o-hsüeh),* 1956, 3 (June 1956), 39-48.

Li, Peter 李培德. *Tseng P'u.* Boston, 1980.

Lin, Jui-ming 林瑞明. "*Nieh-hai hua* yü wan-Ch'ing hsin-chiu chiao-t'i te shih-tai" 孽海花與晚清新舊交替的世代. *Chung-kuo ku-tien hsiao-shuo yen-chiu chuan-chi,* 1 (August 1979), 215-254.

Liu, Ts'un-yan. "Introduction: 'Middlebrow' in Perspective," in *Middlebrow,* pp. 1-40.

McAleavy, Henry. "Tseng P'u and the *Nieh-hai hua,*" *St. Anthony Papers* 5.7 (1960), 88-137.

Torii, Hisayasu 鳥居久靖. "*Getsukaika* no hampon" 孽海花の版本, *Tenri daigaku gakuhō,* 39 (December 1962), 68-84.

Wei, Shao-ch'ang 魏紹昌. *Nieh-hai hua tzu-liao* 孽海花資料. Shanghai, 1962. A useful collection of source materials on the author and his novel.

—PI

Tso-chuan 左傳 (Tso Documentary) is not only the earliest comprehensive historical account of the major political, social, and military events of the Spring and Autumn Period, but also the first sustained narrative work in Chinese literature, noted for its dramatic power and realistic details. Its designation, together with the *Kung-yang chuan* 公羊傳 and *Ku-liang chuan* 穀梁傳, at the turn of the Christian era as one of the three commentaries on the *Ch'un-ch'iu* 春秋 (Spring and Autumn Annals), one of the five Confucian Classics allegedly compiled by Confucius himself, further established it as an integral part of the Confucian canon. As such, countless students of Chinese history, literature, and philosophy since the Han have gone to it for information and insight. In terms of its intrinsic value as a genuine historical and literary text as well as its tremendous influence on later readers and writers, the *Tso-chuan* has to be ranked as one of the most important works in traditional China.

Yet, in spite of the central position the *Tso-chuan* occupies in the Chinese world of letters, nothing is known about its alleged author Mr. Tso. Various attempts have been made to identify him, but they remain speculations. The text was most probably compiled and edited by one person from existing materials (for it was apparently the custom for each state during the Spring and Autumn period to keep a chronicle for itself) during the early part of the Warring States period. In the process of being put together, however, it is possible that there was significant influence from an oral tradition.

The narratives in the *Tso-chuan,* as they exist today, are arranged in correspondence to the entries in the *Ch'un-ch'iu* and are therefore based on the chronology of the dukes of the state of Lu. As such, they serve to provide a detailed background for events merely chronicled in the *Ch'un-ch'iu.* In its original state, however, the *Tso-chuan* may have existed in the same format as the *Kuo-yü.** That is, narratives arranged according to the various feudal states to which they refer and within each state arranged chronologically. Some scholars believe the person responsible for the cutting up of the *Tso-chuan* to fit its parts to the entries in the *Ch'un-ch'iu* was Liu Hsin,* who had such a high opinion of the *Tso-chuan* that he wanted to make it part of the Confucian canon. He may have also added to the original text the many short passages of exegesis on the entries in the *Ch'un-ch'iu* to make it appear more like the *Kung-yang* and the *Ku-liang* commentaries. If so, it would explain the curious discrepancies between the *Tso-chuan* and the *Ch'un-ch'iu*: not only do some entries of each not have corresponding passages of elaboration in the other, but there is sometimes even conflict in the accounts of the two.

The relationship between the *Tso-chuan* and the *Kuo-yü* is another question that has attracted scholarly attention. They not only cover the same historical period and therefore very often the same persons and events, but they also contain passages that are strikingly similar even in phraseology. Even more intriguing, if an event is recounted in great detail in one, it will usually appear in a summary form in the other. For this and other reasons, some scholars, notably K'ang Yu-wei,* maintained that the *Tso-chuan* and the *Kuo-yü* were originally the same work. When Liu Hsin took parts of it and made them into a commentary on the *Ch'un-ch'iu*, what was left fell under the title of *Kuo-yü.* More careful comparison of the two texts in terms of both content and language, however, has shown this view false. The apparent similarities of the two works may have been the result of use of the same source materials. Another possibility is that one author may have had a copy of the other's work during his own compilation.

Although the *Tso-chuan* may not have been intended as a commentary on the *Ch'un-ch'iu*, the basic philosophy underlying the whole work is unmistakably Confucian. The recurrent theme is that just as the evil, the stupid, and the haughty will usually bring disaster upon themselves, the good, the wise, and the humble tend to meet their just rewards. The Confucian principle singled out for emphasis is *li* 禮 (rites, ceremonies, or propriety depending on the specific context). *Li* governs every action, including war. While those who observe *li* may not always triumph, ill consequences follow if it is transgressed. To the author of the *Tso-chuan* history was more than just a listing of a succession of events. Among other things, it meant connecting the various isolated events recorded to achieve meaning out of an otherwise confusing and incoherent past. History, in other words, was nothing if it didn't have lessons to teach.

To characterize the content of the *Tso-chuan* this way, however, is not to turn it into a Confucian handbook for moral instruction. Its author was too good a historian to allow himself to become a moralist or an allegorist. The pattern of virtue triumphant and evil punished found in the book is not so neat that there are no exceptions. While most of the intriguers and murderers come to bad ends, the book is also full of examples of innocent people persecuted and killed senselessly. Moreover, there is too much sordid detail for the book to become a straightforward morality play. In fact, it is precisely for the relentlessly realistic portrayal of a turbulent era marked by violence, political strife, intrigues, and moral laxity that the book is treasured as a literary masterpiece.

Tso-chuan is distinguished by its laconic style, its ability to narrate a complicated event in an orderly, economical, and lively manner, and its vivid recounting of several major battles. The narrative as a whole exhibits several characteristics that were to become hallmarks of Chinese narrative in general: the dominance of the third-person point of view, the frequent use of dreams and flashbacks in plot structuring, and the distinctive preference for direct speech and action in the portrayal of characters (as against psychological penetrations into their minds).

EDITIONS:

Ch'un-ch'iu ching chuan yin-te 春秋經傳引得. Peiping, 1937, v. 1.

TRANSLATIONS:

Legge, James. *The Ch'un Ts'ew, with the Tso chuen.* Rpt. Taipei, 1972.

STUDIES:

Ch'ü, Wan-li 屈萬里. "*Tso-chuan,*" in Ch'ü Wan-li, *Ku-chi tao-tu* 古籍導讀. Taipei, 1964, pp. 183-195.

Egan, Ronald. "Narrative in the *Tso-chuan,*" *HJAS,* 37 (1977), 323-352.

Hung, William. "Preface to the *Ch'un-ch'iu ching chuan yin-te,*" v. 1, pp. i-cvi.

Karlgren, Bernard. *On the Authenticity and Nature of the* Tso Chuan. 1926; rpt. Taipei, 1968.

Wang, John C. Y. "Early Chinese Narrative: The *Tso-chuan* as Example," in *Chinese Narrative,* pp. 3-20.

Watson, *Early,* pp. 40-66.

—JoW

Tso Ssu 左思 (*tzu,* T'ai-ch'ung 太沖, *c.* 253-*c.* 307) was born into a lowly family in the state of Ch'i 齊 in Lin-tzu 臨淄 Prefecture. His father had a minor office, and in the class-conscious age in which he lived, where powerful families dominated life at court, Tso's humble origins were an almost certain barrier to a career. His short official biography in the *Chin-shu* gives little information. The picture that emerges from official and unofficial accounts is that of a homely, socially awkward, and solitary man, unsuccessful in his official ambition and slow, methodical, and sparse in literary output. Today fewer than twenty of his works survive, and even the *Sui-shu* bibliography lists his output at only two *chüan.*

His younger sister Tso Fen 左芬, an accomplished poet herself, became a concubine of Emperor Wu of the Chin in 272, and it was probably this event that occasioned Tso's move to the capital. His "San tu fu" 三都賦 (Prose-poem on the Three Capitals) attracted wide attention. Several major contemporary literati wrote prefaces or annotations to the work, which also elicited the admiration of Chang Hua* and Lu Chi.* These *fu* are largely in the tradition of Pan Ku* and Chang Heng.* Tso states in his preface a commitment to realism and factual exhaustiveness, qualities for which these works are famous— they have stood as models for the subgenre of *fu,* in conjunction with his sister's position at court, that won him office and entry into Chia Mi's 賈謐 famous literary-salon, known as the "twenty-four friends of Chia Mi." He was, however, almost certainly not an important member of this group. He probably served during this time as Assistant in the Palace Library.

His celebrated "Yung shih shih" 詠史詩 (Poems on History) belong to a subgenre dating back at least as far as Pan Ku, with notable contributions by Juan Yü,* Chang Hsieh,* Wang Ts'an,* and Ts'ao Chih.* Many poems of this kind use meditations on historical subjects as a means of self-expression, and Tso's eight poems are some of the finest specimens in this mode. All of his subjects have backgrounds similar to Tso's own: the poet's ambition, frustration, and resignation are reflected in his treatment of historical figures. These poems greatly influenced later writers in this subgenre, including T'ao Ch'ien,* Pao Chao,* and Li Po.* His two "Chao yin shih" 招隱詩 (Summoning the Recluse) treat different aspects of reclusive life. The first and best known contains attitudes of natural self-containment that figured importantly in later nature poetry. "Chiao nü shih" 嬌女詩 (Poem on My Beloved Daughter) is one of the first of a subgenre of poetry on a poet's children, a corpus notable for playful and comic elements.

Although he is often grouped with the so-called T'ai-k'ang Poets (named after the reign period, 280-289), Tso's poetry stands apart from that of his contemporaries like Lu Chi or P'an Yüeh,* showing little of their emphasis on embellishment and intricate verbal refinement. Tso's poetry is profoundly personal, solidly in the *yung huai* 詠懷 tradition, and while his avoidance of artifice may have denied him contemporary acclaim, it added to his enduring reputation.

EDITIONS:

Since his works are so few, most major studies include texts of nearly all his poetry. Ten annotated poems are included in the *Wei Chin Nan-pei ch'ao wen-hsüeh-shih ts'an-k'ao tzu-liao* 魏晉南北朝文學史參考資料, Peking 1961.

Nan-pei-ch'ao shih v. 1, pp. 510-516.

Liu-ch'ao wen, v. 2, *ch.* 74, pp. 1882-1890.

TRANSLATIONS:

Demiéville, *Anthologie*, pp. 131-132.

Frodsham, *Anthology*, pp. 94-97.

von Zach, *Anthologie*, v. 1, pp. 44-92.

STUDIES:

Hayashida, Shinnosuke 林田愼之助. "Sa Shi no bungaku" 左思の文學, in *Chūgoku bungaku ronshū—Mekada Makoto hakushi koki kinen* 中國文學論集——目加田誠博士古稀紀念, Tokyo, 1974, pp. 143-169.

Kōzen, Hiroshi 興膳宏. "Sa Shi to eishi shi" 左思と詠史詩, *Chūgoku bungaku hō*, 21 (1966), 1-56.

Liu, Wen-chung 劉文忠. "Tso Ssu ho t'a-te *Yung-shih* shih" 左思和他的詠史詩, *Wen-hsüeh p'ing-lun ts'ung-k'an*, 7 (October 1980), 139-152.

Yeh, Jih-kuang 葉日光. *Tso Ssu sheng-p'ing chi ch'i shih chih hsi-lun* 左思生平及其詩之析論. Taipei, 1969.

—CC

Tsui-weng t'an-lu 醉翁談錄 (Talks of the Old Drunkard) has been billed as a genuine example of the source books used by professional storytellers in Sung China ever since its discovery in Japan and its subsequent photographic reproduction in 1940. Such an interpretation has yet to be substantiated. Internal evidence suggests that the only surviving copy might have come from the Yüan period, but we know next to nothing about the compiler Lo Yeh 羅燁 and the role he played in preparing the work, except for the meager information that he was a native of Lu-ling 盧陵 (Chi-an 吉安 in present Kiangsi).

Divided into ten sections, each further divided into two chapters and labeled in a repetitive fashion, the *Tsui-weng t'an-lu* is clumsily organized. Except for the introductory chapter, "She-keng hsü-yin" 舌耕敘引 (An Introduction to the Industry of the Tongue), each chapter has either one or two thematic groupings of stories. The first chapter, though distinct from the others, is the most important; in its second half, "Hsiao-shuo k'ai-pi" 小說開闢 (The Cradle of Fiction), professional storytelling is divided into eight schools, each with sample titles to illustrate the type of stories narrated. These eight schools are "Ling-kuai" 靈怪 (miraculous and ghost stories), "Yen-fen" 煙粉 (love stories), "Ch'uan-ch'i" 傳奇 (stories of the unusual), "Kung-an" 公案 (crime stories), "P'u-tao" 朴刀 (stories of sword dueling), "Kan-pang" 捍棒 (stories of dueling with staves), "Yao-shu" 妖術 (stories of witchcraft), and "Shen-hsien" 神仙 (stories of gods and immortals). Altogether 107 sample titles are given. Some of these titles are well-known story-cycles, but some are extremely obscure.

Because other references to early professional storytelling are sketchy, the information concerning the eight schools of storytellers and the stories they narrated is understandably of great interest to students of *hua-pen** literature. It shows, among other things, a professional storytelling far more advanced than that seen in another earlier group of sources (e.g., *Tu-ch'eng chi-sheng*—see *Tung-ching meng Hua lu*). According to the latter, professional storytelling had only reached the moderate level of four schools not too long before the end of the Southern Sung period. This suggests that the *Tsui-weng t'an-lu* is a later work; it may well be a Yüan compilation.

Serious students have frequently been concerned with determining the exact contents of the stories listed in the introductory chapter. Such knowledge could clarify to a considerable extent the nature of early professional storytelling activities, the way in which these activities were conducted, and the range and context of the stories popular with the audience. Regrettably, much of what has been done remains speculative.

The composition of the *Tsui-weng t'an-lu* (as seen in the unique copy now housed in the library of the Tenri University 天理大學) is a major difficulty. The introductory chapter and the rest of the book are largely unrelated. The main text carries eighty stories, some of which are actually parts of one story which has been arbitrarily divided and given an individual title. These stories are as diverse in form as they are in content, and a number of them can be found in such sources as *T'ai-p'ing kuang-chi,** *Lü-ch'uang hsin-hua* 綠窗新話, *Pei-li chih,** and *Pen-shih shih.** Given the fact that the first chapter introduces the work, one may expect the introduction and the main text to be mutually related and that the stories in the main text would illustrate the terse information given in the introduction. This is not so. Connections between the titles listed in the first chapter and the stories given in the main text are minimal, suggesting that the introduction and the main text might have come from different sources. Although the textual integrity of the only surviving copy lessens such a possibility and it is possible that some of the stories mentioned in the introduction might have existed only in an oral form, the extreme differences between the introduction and the main text still have to be explained. Pending such an explanation, the *Tsui-weng t'an-lu,* particularly the main text, can be used only with reservation as testimony of early professional storytelling activities.

There is at least one work of the same title, the *Tsui-weng t'an-lu* by Chin Ying-chih 金盈之 (*fl.* 1126) of the early Southern Sung dynasty. Except for three pieces in common, the two books are completely different. Even the commonality of the three stories can be explained: they might have been derived from the same origin.

EDITIONS:

The 1940 Bunkyūdō 文求堂 photographic reproduction is indispensible if one has to examine the textual features of the only surviving copy. Otherwise the Shanghai, 1957 punctuated edition, with ample collation notes, should be recommended.

TRANSLATIONS:

Foccardi, Gabriele. *The Tale of an Old Drunkard.* Wiesbaden, 1981.

Prusek, Jaroslav. *The Origin and the Authors of the Hua-pen.* Prague, 1967, pp. 64-75. An annotated English translation of the second half of the introductory chapter.

STUDIES:

Ch'eng, I-chung 程毅中. *Sung Yüan hua-pen* 宋元話本. Peking, 1980, pp. 14-16, 58-63.

Chien, Mou-sen 簡茂森. "*Tsui-weng t'an-lu* hsiao-shuo li-lun ch'u-t'an" 醉翁談錄小說理論初探, *Ku-tien wen-hsüeh lun-ts'ung* (Tsinan), 1 (August 1980), 319-338.

Inada, Osamu 稻田尹. "*Suiō danroku to Taihei kōki*" 醉翁談錄と太平廣記, in *Kanada hakushi kanreki kinen shoshigaku ronshū* 神田博士還暦紀念書誌學論集, Kyoto, 1957, pp. 517-529.

Lévy, André. "*Hsin-pien Tsui-weng t'an-lu*" 新編醉翁談錄, in *A Sung Bibliography,* Yves Hervouet, ed., Hong Kong, 1978, pp. 481-482.

Ning, Ting-i 寧定一. "*Ts'ung Tsui-weng t'an-lu* t'an shu-hua i-shu" 從醉翁談錄談說話藝術, *Nan-k'ai ta-hsüeh hsüeh-pao (Che-hsüeh she-hui k'o-hsüeh),* 4-5 (August 1978), 134-141.

Prusek, Jaroslav. *The Origin and the Authors of the Hua-pen.* Prague, 1967, pp. 64-77.

T'an, Cheng-pi 譚正璧. "Sung Yüan hua-pen ts'un-i tsung-k'ao" 宋元話本存佚綜考, in T'an Cheng-pi, *Hua-pen yü ku-chü* 話本與古劇, Shanghai, 1957, pp. 2-12.

———. "*Tsui-weng t'an-lu* so-lu Sung-jen hua-pen ming-mu k'ao" 醉翁談錄所錄宋人話本名目考, in *ibid.,* pp. 13-37.

Uemura, Kōji 上村幸次. "*Suiō danroku o tsūjite mita Sōdai no setsuwa ni tsuite*" 醉翁談錄を通じて見た宋代の說話について, *Yamaguchi Daigaku bungaku zasshi.* 4.2 (November 1953), 48-58.

—YWM

Ts'ui Hao 崔顥 (d. 754), received his *chin-shih* degree in 723 after joining Wang Wei* and others in the prestigious literary salon of Li Fan 李範, the Prince of Ch'i 岐王. Here he perfected the early T'ang court-poetic style of regulated verse. But although Ts'ui Hao continued his friendship with Wang Wei, he broke away from this decorous style. He served under Chang Chiu-ling,* but earned a reputation largely for wild and reckless behavior and for multiple marriages.

Ts'ui Hao generally avoided both courtly and eremitic themes in his verse. He composed poems in the *yüeh-fu** and heptasyllabic song forms; even his regulated verse frequently violated rules for parallelism. He is well known for his quatrains, such as the folksong imitation, "Ch'ang-kan hsing" 長干行 (Song of Ch'ang-kan). His eight-line

poem "Huang-ho Lou" 黄鶴樓 (Yellow
Crane Tower) is one of the most famous
of the High T'ang period. Li Po,* who
admired Ts'ui Hao for his free spirit and
his unrestrained style, conferred the greatest honor on him by deriving the ending
for his "Teng Chin-ling Feng-huang T'ai"
登金陵鳳凰臺 (Climbing Phoenix Terrace at
Chin-ling) from Ts'ui's closure to "Yellow
Crane Tower."

EDITIONS:
Ch'üan T'ang shih, ch. 130, v. 2, pp. 1321-1330.

TRANSLATIONS:
Bynner, *Jade Mountain,* pp. 142-143.
Owen, *High T'ang,* pp. 60-63.

STUDIES:
Ch'en, Yu-ch'in 陳友琴. "Kuan-yü Ts'ui Hao te
   Huang-ho lou shih" 關於崔顥的黃鶴樓詩,
   Kuang-ming jih-pao, May 12, 1958; included
   in Ch'en's *Wen-ku chi* 溫故集, Peking, 1959,
   pp. 172-176.
Fu, *Shih-jen,* pp. 66-77: "Ts'ui Hao k'ao" 崔顥考
Fu, Tseng-hsiang 傅增湘. "Ts'ui Hao shih-chi
   pa" 崔顥詩集跋, *Pei-p'ing t'u-shu-kuan kuan-
   k'an,* 6.2 (April 1932).
Owen, *High T'ang,* pp. 60-63.

—MW

Tsun-ch'ien chi 尊前集 is an anthology of
early *tz'u** compiled by an unknown hand
around the mid-eleventh century. Its importance is twofold. First, it is the earliest—and in some cases the only—source for
many of the almost three hundred poems
that it contains, roughly one fifth of the
surviving pre-Sung *tz'u.* Second, it is the
most catholic of the few sources for early
tz'u; the *Yang-ch'un chi* 陽春集 and *Nan-T'ang
erh-chu tz'u* 南唐二主詞 are limited to one or
two poets each (Feng Yen-ssu* and Li Yü*),
the *Hua-chien chi** to a single school, and
the manuscripts from Tun-huang to an
anonymous, popular tradition.

   In view of its importance, it is fortunate
that scholarship of the past few decades
has been able to resolve most of the questions—some of them of long standing—
concerning its nature and reliability. It does
seem possible now to say with some assurance that the *Tsun-ch'ien chi* is a genuine
Sung collection of, for the most part, genuine eighth-, ninth-, and tenth-century
poems and that it was compiled as a supplement to the *Hua-chien chi.*

   The poems in the *Tsun-ch'ien chi* are not
explicitly divided into groups, except that
those attributed to each individual poet occur together in most cases. Some editions
do present the text in two *chüan* rather
than one, but this does not correspond to
a natural division of the contents. However, it is possible to discern the following
four sections: (1) poems by T'ang emperors and "Prince Li" (i.e., Li Yü)—twelve
poems by four poets; (2) poems by other
T'ang and Southern T'ang writers, including Feng Yen-ssu—131 poems by thirteen poets; (3) poems by writers of the
"Hua-chien" school—120 poems by twelve
poets; (4) miscellaneous poems, including
more by Li Yü and Feng Yen-ssu, as well
as by two additional *Hua-chien* poets not
represented in the preceding section—
twenty-six poems by nine poets.

   That the *Hua-chien* poets in section three
appear in the same sequence as in the *Hua-
chien chi* and with almost no duplication of
poems suggests that the present work was
consciously intended as a supplement (it
has been suggested that the few duplicated
poems were copied from the *Tsun-ch'ien chi*
later in order to make up for omissions in
the *Hua-chien chi*). The miscellaneous character of the last group of poems suggests
that it may be a supplement added after
compilation of the rest of the text. We do
not know when this took place, but it was
presumably earlier than the Ming dynasty,
because all extant texts include this section, and all can be traced back to Ming
sources.

   Although some attributions of individual poems to particular poets have been
questioned, the only really important case
of demonstrable misattribution concerns a
group of *tz'u* assigned to Li Po.* The authenticity of these poems has often been
questioned, since they considerably antedate any other lyrics to the same melodies,
and a good deal of misapplied ingenuity
has gone into attempts to prove their authenticity by showing that the melodies had
been introduced into China by Li Po's time,

even if no other extant lyrics were written to them then. However this may be, study of the rhyming categories of the disputed poems (excluding three short ones to the melody "Ch'ing-p'ing tiao") shows them to be virtually textbook examples of all the features that distinguish early Northern Sung *tz'u* rhyming, with which they agree, from that of earlier periods. They are thus roughly contemporary with the latest poems in the anthology, and certainly not by Li Po.

EDITIONS:

Wu, No 吳訥 (1372-1457). *T'ang-Sung ming-hsien pai-chia tz'u* 唐宋名賢百家詞. Printed in 1940 on the basis of Wu's manuscript.

Mao, Chin 毛晉. *Tz'u-yüan ying-hua* 詞苑英華. Published at Mao's Chi-ku Ko 汲古閣, based on the edition of Ku Wu-fang 顧梧芳, whose Preface was dated 1582.

Chu, Tsu-mo 朱祖謀. *Chiang-ts'un ts'ung-shu* 彊村叢書. Based on a Ming manuscript with emendations from Mao Chin's edition.

Wang, Kuo-wei 王國維. Manuscript copy presently in the collection of the Tōyō Bunko, Tokyo. First *chüan* copied from a copy of Ku Wu-fang's edition, second *chüan* from Mao Chin's.

STUDIES:

Ch'i, Huai-mei 祁懷美. "*Hua-chien chi* chih yen-chiu" 之研究, *T'ai-wan Sheng-li Shih-fan Ta-hsüeh yen-chiu chi-k'an*, 4 (1960), especially pp. 13-14.

Enoki, Kazuo 榎一雄. "Ō Kokui shushō shukō shikyokusho nijūgoshu—Tōyō Bunko shozō no tokushuhon (sono san)" 王國維手鈔手校詞曲書 二十五種——東洋文庫所藏 の 特殊本 (その三), *Tōyō Bunko shohō*, 8 (1976), 1-25, esp. 17.

Juan, T'ing-cho 阮廷焯. "Chi-ku Ko pen *Tsun-ch'ien chi* pa" 汲古閣本 尊前集跋, *Ta-lu tsa-chih*, 40 (1970), 376.

Li, Hsin-lung 李信隆. "*Tsun-ch'ien chi* yen-chiu," in *Ch'ing-chu Lin Ching-yi hsien-sheng liu-shih-chih tan-ch'en lun-wen-chi* (Taipei, 1969), pp. 2261-2388.

Mao, Kuang-sheng 冒廣生. "*Tsun-ch'ien chi* chiao-chi" 校記, *T'ung-sheng yüeh-k'an*, 2.6 (1942): 73-80; 2.9, 82-94.

Shizukuishi, Kōichi 雫石皓一. "*Sonzenshū* zakkō" 尊前集雜考, *Kangakkai zasshi*, 9 (1941), 97-106. The best study of the nature and Sung origin of the text; remarkable resourcefulness in gathering and evaluating evidence; subsequent studies by Chinese scholars have unfortunately ignored this work; consultation of it would have saved them some duplication of effort and much error.

Wang, Chao-yung 汪兆鏞, "Chi-ku Ko pen *Tsun-ch'ien chi* shu-hou" 書後, *Tz'u-hsüeh chi-k'an*, 3.2 (1936), 161-162.

—DB

Ts'ung-shu 叢書 (collectanea) are one of the most important resources scholars of Chinese civilization have at their disposal. The term *ts'ung-shu* refers to those compilations which gather together and print or reprint a number of independent works. While they vary significantly in size, content, and sophistication, all *ts'ung-shu* are intended to serve two primary and complementary purposes: to preserve works that are rare or that the compilers have determined are in some way important and to facilitate the wider circulation and greater availability of the works included. The great bibliographic scholar Miao Ch'üan-sun 繆荃孫 (1844-1919) once wrote in *Shu-mu ta-wen* 書目答問, the student guide he composed on behalf of Chang Chih-tung 張之洞 (1837-1909), that "if one wants to read a lot of old books, one has to buy *ts'ung-shu*."

Some would see the underlying origins of *ts'ung-shu* in such ensembles as the ten "wings" of the *I-ching* and the stone classics of Eastern Han and later times. Possibly early formations of Buddhist and Taoist canons provided an example to early *ts'ung-shu* compilers. Ironically, the first use of *ts'ung-shu* in a title seems to be Lu Kuei-meng's* *Li-tse ts'ung-shu* 笠澤, a work which is not a collectanea. The earliest extant collectanea is, rather, the *Ju-hsüeh ching wu* 儒學警海 (1201), a *ts'ung-shu* compiled by Yü Ting-sun 俞鼎孫 and Yü Ching 俞經 and containing seven works in forty *chüan*. It was lost as a set until the end of the nineteenth century, when an incomplete Ming edition came to light. This was collated with other sources to make a complete edition which was published in the early 1920s and which has been included in the *Pai-pu ts'ung-shu chi-ch'eng* 百部叢書集成. The next oldest *ts'ung-shu* is the Sung collectanea *Po-*

ch'uan hsüeh-hai 百川學海 (1273) compiled by Tso Kuei 左圭.

It has been stated that to be a *ts'ung-shu* a compilation ought to reprint fully, even down to prefaces and colophons, the works selected for inclusion. This has been the view of many bibliographic scholars, including Miao Ch'üan-sun and Arthur Hummel, and it is the reason why such early works as *Kan-chu chi* 紺珠集 by Chu Sheng-fei 朱勝非 (1082-1144) and Tseng Tsao's 曾慥 (*fl.* 1131-1163) *Lei shuo* 類說 are not considered *ts'ung-shu*. This strict bibliographic definition is not always easy to apply. The *Shuo-fu* (see T'ao Tsung-i) is a case in point, for there have been differing opinions on the relationship of *Shuo-fu* to *ts'ung-shu*. It may be that the *Shuo-fu* is destined to be considered a *ts'ung-shu* after all, for two versions of it are catalogued in the *Chung-kuo ts'ung-shu tsung-lu* 中國叢書綜錄, the best *ts'ung-shu* catalogue.

In Ming times the publication of *ts'ung-shu* grew, a development that continued into the Ch'ing and Republican periods. They are still produced, moreover, with the result that there are about 2800 *ts'ung-shu* in existence today. Already in the Ming most *ts'ung-shu* types are represented. One of the largest categories of *ts'ung-shu* is made up of those *ts'ung-shu* not limited in terms of topic or authorship. Mao Chin's 毛晉 (1599-1659) *Chin-tai mi-shu* 津逮秘書, for instance, contains about 145 titles on a wide range of subjects. It was published in fifteen parts from 1630 to *c.* 1645. Hu Wen-huan's 胡文煥 *Ko-chih ts'ung-shu* 格致, which exists in a 1603 edition, is another comprehensive collectanea. Also from the Ming is Ch'eng Jung's 程榮 *Han Wei ts'ung-shu* 漢魏, which prints thirty-eight works which are or purport to be by writers from the Chou to the Six Dynasties periods. But besides such general collectanea, Ming compilers also published various kinds of more specialized *ts'ung-shu*. *Erh-shih tzu* 二十子 contains twenty philosophical works, mostly items traditionally assigned to the Chou and Han periods. Unfortunately, the Ming dynasty was a period in which editors and publishers often took a very haphazard and cavalier attitude toward titles, number of *chüan*, and accuracy.

It is with the Ch'ing that *ts'ung-shu* publication really came into its own. Of course, as in the Ming, many *ts'ung-shu* of a general or miscellaneous nature exist from the Ch'ing period also. One such is Chang Hai-p'eng's 張海鵬 (1755-1816) *Hsüeh-chin t'ao-yüan* 學津討原, which includes over 170 items in 20 parts and is based partly on items in Mao Chin's *Chih-pu-tsu chai ts'ung-shu* 知不足齋, a very fine collectanea in 30 parts and 220 works. *Chih-pu-tsu chai ts'ung-shu* focuses on rare works from Pao's huge library, and this points up the way Ch'ing *ts'ung-shu* reflect the intellectual concerns of the age. The Ch'ing was a time of great contributions to scholarship and much attention to texts. One way in which the preoccupation with texts manifested itself was in the printing of reproductions of old editions. In this regard may be mentioned Huang P'i-lieh's 黃丕烈 (1763-1825) *Shih-li chü ts'ung-shu* 士禮居, a work of exceedingly high craftsmanship, and Li Shu-ch'ang's 黎庶昌 (1837-1897) *Ku-i ts'ung-shu* 古逸. Li's collectanea was printed in Tokyo during the period 1882-1884 and contains over twenty-five items. It was mainly compiled by Yang Shou-ching 楊守敬 (1839-1915). The collation work on Huang's *ts'ung-shu* was largely done by Ku Kuang-ch'i 顧廣圻 (1776-1835). Ku was only one of a number of outstanding Ch'ing-dynasty collators. *Ts'ung-shu* which reflect this trend in Ch'ing scholarly activities include the famous textual critic Lu Wen-ch'ao's 盧文弨 (1717-1796) *Pao-ching t'ang ts'ung-shu* 抱經堂 and Pi Yüan's 畢沅 (1730-1797) *Ching-hsün t'ang ts'ung-shu* 經訓, each of which mainly contains works written or collated by the compiler. Another collectanea of this sort is Sun Hsing-yen's 孫星衍 (1753-1818) *Tai-nan ko ts'ung-shu* 岱南閣, which is made up largely of works collated by Sun. Here and in his *P'ing-chin kuan ts'ung-shu* 平津館 Sun seems to have been assisted by Ku Kuang-ch'i and Yen K'o-chün 嚴可均 (1762-1843).

A somewhat related form of textual scholarship is the collecting of fragmentary lost texts practiced by a number of Ch'ing scholars. These endeavors are represented by Ma Kuo-han's 馬國翰 (1794-

1857) *Yü-han shan-fang chi-i-shu* 玉函山房輯佚書 and Huang Shih's 黃奭 *Han-hsüeh t'ang ts'ung-shu* 漢學堂. The latter, while less comprehensive, still collects the fragmentary remains of eighty-five works on the Classics, fifty-six on the apocrypha, and seventy-four on history and philosophy. All of these Ch'ing collectanea reflect the concrete and philological approach which characterizes much Ch'ing scholarship. Nowhere is this approach more apparent than in researches on the Classics. Two large and famous collectanea gather such Classical scholarship. Juan Yüan's 嚴焦 (1764-1849) *Huang Ch'ing ching-chieh* 皇清經解 includes studies of the Classics by 180 Ch'ing scholars. First printed in 1829, the work was begun in 1825 under the editorship of Yen Chieh 阮元 (1763-1843). Wang Hsien-ch'ien's 王先謙 (1842-1918) *Huang Ch'ing ching-chieh hsü-pien* 續編 contains 209 titles. A forerunner of these *ts'ung-shu* on the Classics was done under the auspices of the young poet Nara Singde (Nan-lan Hsing-te*). It is *T'ung-chih t'ang ching-chieh* 通志堂, perhaps actually compiled by Hsü Ch'ien-hsüeh 徐乾學 (1631-1694), a collection of about 138 works on the Classics, mostly by Sung and Yüan authors.

Ch'ing *ts'ung-shu* fall into several other categories, depending on the foci of the compilers. There are many *ts'ung-shu* which print the works of members of a particular family or individual. One example of the latter is *Ch'uan-shan i-shu* 船山遺書, edited by Tsou Han-hsun 鄒漢勛 (1805-1854), which prints fifty-five works by Wang Fu-chih.* There are also *ts'ung-shu* which include authors who are connected with a particular geographical area. Wang Hao's 王灝 (1823-1888) *Chi-fu ts'ung-shu* 畿輔, which collects works by natives of the metropolitan district, is an example of this type, as is *Ling-nan i-shu* 嶺南, by Wu Ch'ung-yao 伍崇曜 (1810-1863) and Wu Yüan-wei 伍元薇, which contains works by fifty-five writers of Ming and Ch'ing times and six works by earlier ones. Wu Ch'ung-yao, incidentally, was also responsible for the general collectanea *Yüeh-ya t'ang ts'ung-shu* 粤雅堂, which was printed over a thirty-year

period and included almost two hundred works by writers from T'ang to Ch'ing. It was actually edited by Tan Ying 譚瑩 (1800-1871). The last two types of specialized *ts'ung-shu* that will be mentioned here are those that collect works on history and geography. An example of the former is the anonymous *Shih-hsüeh ts'ung-shu* 史學, compiled just at the end of the nineteenth century. It is made up entirely of works on history by scholars who lived during the Ch'ing. From the beginning of the twentieth century comes *Che-chiang tu-shu-kuan ts'ung-shu* 浙江圖書館, compiled by Ting Ch'ien 丁謙. It was published in 1915 and contains a broad range of works on foreign areas and peoples throughout Chinese history.

Although there have been many *ts'ung-shu* on special subjects compiled since the end of the Ch'ing, undoubtedly the two most famous and most frequently consulted modern *ts'ung-shu* are *Ssu-pu ts'ung-k'an* 四部叢刊 and *Ssu-pu pei-yao* 四部備要. These are both collectanea of a general nature. *Ssu-pu ts'ung-k'an* and its supplement were originally printed by Commercial Press in Shanghai between 1919 and 1936. It photolithographically reproduces several hundred original old editions in their entirety. *Ssu-pu pei-yao* includes about 350 works. It was first printed in moveable type by Chung-hua shu-chü in Shanghai in the years 1927-1936. Despite the inevitable errors that creep into re-set editions, *Ssu-pu pei-yao* is often both convenient and sufficiently reliable, *pace* Yang Chia-lo's 楊家駱 statement that it is good for beginners.

Finally, notice should be taken of two related collections which both bring together about a hundred *ts'ung-shu*. The first is entitled *Ts'ung-shu chi-ch'eng* 叢書集成. It is typeset and was first published by Commercial Press in Shanghai 1935-1939. This *ts'ung-shu* collection was not finished. The second is *Pai-pu ts'ung-shu chi-ch'eng*. A photo reproduction of selected editions of titles from *Ts'ung-shu chi-ch'eng*, it was published by I-wen yin-shu kuan 藝文印書館 of Taiwan beginning in 1967, and has been completed. Each contains about four thousand individual works.

Chung-kuo ts'ung-shu tsung-lu, the union catalogue compiled by the Shanghai Library and published by Chung-hua shu-chü in the period 1959-1962, far surpasses any other *ts'ung-shu* catalogue or index. For others that may be useful, however, see the sources cited under bibiography below.

CATALOGUES AND INDEXES:

Shanghai t'u-shu-kuan 上海圖書館, comp. *Chung-kuo ts'ung-shu tsung-lu* 中國叢書綜錄. 3v. Shanghai, 1959-1962.

Lo, Karl. *A Guide to the* Ssu pu ts'ung k'an. Lawrence: University of Kansas, 1965.

STUDIES:

Hsieh, Kuo-chen 謝國楨. Ts'ung-shu k'an-k'o yüan-liu k'ao" 叢書刊刻源流考, in Hsieh Kuo-chen, *Ming Ch'ing pi-chi t'an-tsung* 明清筆記談叢, rpt. Shanghai, 1962, pp. 202-241.

Hummel, Arthur, ed. *Eminent Chinese of the Ch'ing Period (1644-1912).* Washington, 1943.

———. "Ts'ung Shu," *JAOS,* 51 (1931), 40-46.

Liu, Ts'un-yan. "The Compilation and Historical Value of the Tao-tsang," in *Essays on the Sources for Chinese History,* Donald D. Leslie *et al.,* eds., Columbia, South Carolina, 1975, pp. 104-119.

Ninji, Ōfuchi. "The Formation of the Taoist Canon," in *Facets of Taoism: Essays in Chinese Religion,* Holmes Welch and Anna Seidal, eds., New Haven and London, 1979, pp. 253-267.

Report of the Librarian of Congress (1923), 174-179.

Report of the Librarian of Congress (1930), 342-345.

Teng, Ssu-yü and Knight Biggerstaff, comps. *An Annotated Bibliography of Selected Chinese Reference Works.* Cambridge, Mass., 1971 (third edition), pp. 66-68.

Tsien, Tsuen-hsuin and James K. M. Cheng, comps. *China: An Annotated Bibliography of Bibliographies.* Boston, 1978, pp. 151-156.

Wang, Mien 王緜, comp. *Shu-mu ta-wen pu-cheng suo-yin* 書目答問補正索引. Hong Kong: Ch'ung-chi shu-tien, 1969, pp. 107, 205-214.

Wang, Pi-chiang 汪辟疆 (Wang Kuo-yüan 汪國垣). "Ts'ung-shu chih yüan-liu lei-pieh suo-yin fa" 叢書之源流類別索引法, in Wang Pi-chiang, *Mu-lu-hsüeh yen-chiu* 目錄學研究, rpt., Shanghai: Commercial Press, 1956, pp. 95-125.

Wilkinson, Endymion. *The History of Imperial China: A Research Guide.* Cambridge, Mass., 1974, pp. 23-25.

Wolff, Ernst and Maureen Corcoran. *Chinese Studies: A Bibliographic Manual.* San Francisco, 1981, pp. 77-80.

Yang, Chia-lo 楊家駱 *et al.,* comps. *Ts'ung-shu ta tz'u-tien* 叢書大辭典. Taipei, 1967, v. 1, pp. 1-5.

—RJC

Tu Fu 杜甫 (*tzu,* Tzu-mei 子美, 712-770) was one of the great geniuses of world literature. As a poet he drove himself to develop every potentiality, strenuously harmonizing some tendencies that we might regard as contrary—bookish allusiveness, for example, and creative spontaneity:

> Reading, I've tattered ten thousand scrolls,
> Setting brush to paper, I was like a god—

or beauty of versification and earnestness of appeal to social conscience:

> Though by nature rustic, I craved a lovely line,
> With words I'd stir mankind, or I'd die yet never sleep.

Tu Fu's enormous range of talents was equaled by the range of men and matters, exalted and humble, that woke his curiosity and his human sympathy—hence his modern fame as a literary "realist" and as a "people's poet."

But his great powers of admiration and compassion hardly won a response in his own time:

> All my hundred years a song of sorrow
> Never meeting any who'd "know my tune."

(For these passages of self-assessment, see *A Concordance to the Poetry of Tu Fu,* v. 2, pp. 1, 409, and 395.)

Like other synthesists, Tu Fu made a too-ambiguous exemplar for any particular school of art or thought to champion immediately. Although he claimed early renown as a prodigy of letters and mingled with the writers of his time, he led no coterie—indeed his ambitions, however delusive they may have been, lay in the realm of real and not literary politics. Tu Fu's works were scattered, and many of them probably lost, after his death in provincial obscurity, during a time of warlordism and foreign invasions following the An Lu-shan

Rebellion. No poem by him appears in known anthologies earlier than the *Yu-hsüan chi* 又玄集 (dated 900). While now generally considered the greatest of Chinese poets, Tu Fu was not established as preeminent until the eleventh century. Part of Tu Fu's fascination has always been the drama of his neglect and rediscovery. In literary sinology the millennial effort to reassemble, date, and interpret Tu Fu's surviving works has been a labor of ingenuity and controversy rivaled only—and distantly—by the scholarship of the *Hung-lou meng.**

Tu Fu belonged—but during much of his life in the status of a poor relation—to the aristocracy, the old ruling class of the Six Dynasties, which had temporarily recouped its political power during his years of maturity, although in the long term it was yielding place to the new gentry of scholar-bureaucrats, more dependent for entry to office upon the examination system. The distaff side of Tu Fu's immediate family is an illustration of the networks of marriage alliance formed among northwestern aristocratic clans in the poet's day.

Tu Fu always referred to himself as a man of Ching-chao 京兆 (the prefecture including Ch'ang-an); of Tu-ling 杜陵, a place in the south of Ching-chao associated with Tu clans; or of Shao-ling 少陵, in Tu-ling. His ancestors served the southern courts through most of the Six Dynasties. Tu Fu's places of birth and education are unknown (the standard histories associate him with Hsiang-yang [modern Hupeh], probably an error due to the prominence of the Tu clan of that place). The family seems to have owned property at Tu-ling—in the neighborhood were many of their graveyard poplars (*Concordance*, p. 171)—and also at Yen-shih, burial-place of the great scholar-general Tu Yü, near the secondary capital, Lo-yang.

Tu Fu's many occasional poems, restored where possible to their original sequence, permit us to reconstruct much of the poet's detailed self-portrayal during and after the An Lu-shan Rebellion.

There is no comparable testimony regarding his earlier years. By his forties Tu Fu claimed to have written over 1,000 pieces, yet only 5-15 percent of them survive. Perhaps none of his poems antedates 735. It nevertheless seems clear that Tu Fu was groomed from an early age for the examination career—like that of his grandfather, Tu Shen-yen,* a *chin-shih* of 670—which could lead relatively quickly to literary and advisory posts in the capital, rather than for a more pedestrian career of provincial administration such as his father had entered, probably by hereditary privilege. The pattern thus set was to endure for life. When not living in retirement or engaged upon his restless travels, Tu Fu sought government employment only by examination or by submission of writings. His routine provincial appointments were limited to a minor police position, which he declined, and one in provincial education, which he quickly resigned. Unfortunately Tu Fu was no better suited to the advisory-admonitory posts he sought than to the ordinary administrative posts he avoided. His employment as Reminder under Emperor Su-tsung led within days to his arrest and trial for outspokenness (his message of thanks for pardon remained obdurately outspoken).

Tu Fu's adult life may be envisaged as a triptych, each panel representing a period with a different geographical center. The first period (*c.* 731-745), in the East and Southeast, was largely given over to his wanderings as a young bachelor devoted (by his account) to furs and silks, archery, falconry, and revelry. After travels down the coast as far as Chekiang, he journeyed to Ch'ang-an to take part in the *chin-shih* examination of 736. Despite his favorable position as an entrant of the capital prefecture, Tu Fu failed, for unknown reasons. Thereafter he traveled in the Northeast, perhaps at that time becoming family-head following his father's death. At Ch'en-liu 陳留 (modern Kaifeng) in 744 and the next year at Lu-chün 魯郡 south of T'ai-shan occurred the only actual meetings between the famous literary friends Tu Fu and Li Po.* What reality may have underlain the odd coupling of Li Po, the elder, Taoist "immortal of poetry" (*shih-hsien* 詩仙) and Tu Fu, the younger, Confucian "sage of poetry" (*shih-sheng* 詩聖) is hard to judge. The ascription of intimate friendship to pairs of persons named Li and Tu is formulaic, with a number of instances ascending to Latter Han times (Li Ku 李固 and Tu Ch'iao 杜喬, both d. 147). Tu Fu's friendship for the romantic older celebrity has been termed one-sided, yet Tu Fu himself claimed Li Po had shown a liking for him (*Concordance*, pp. 79, 339).

Tu Fu's poetry of the first period already exhibits some of the peculiarities of the later work. An example is the perhaps earliest poem in Tu Fu's corpus, "Yeh yen Tso-shih chuang" 夜宴左氏莊 (Evening Banquet at the Tso Village), *Concordance*, p. 278). Tu Fu's indifference to the decorum of subgenres and their themes—perhaps the reason for his slow acceptance in the literary world—is already evident in this poem, which is simultaneously a poem of meeting on the Double Third and of parting on a journey. Also evidenced here, and related to his characteristic hyperbole, is Tu Fu's penchant for contrasts of sublime magnitude (here between a rustic grange and the Milky Way) compressed into a single couplet or line: "Spring stars wreathe a thatched hall." Tu Fu's balanced concern for the book and the sword makes its appearance, as does his celebrated arrogance—here the hint (conveyed in a double allusion) that the poet, in his twenty-fourth year, has completed a literary conquest of the Wu Region comparable to the military conquest of Wu by Fan Li 范蠡 in the time of Confucius.

Tu Fu's second period (745-759) belonged to the capital region. Now fatherless and (from a late but uncertain date) himself a husband and father, he spent the first ten of these years in a frustrating search for the financial security of government employment. Unfortunately Emperor Hsüan-tsung (r. 712-756), preoccupied with Taoism, Tantrism, and Yang Kuei-fei, had in old age left practical affairs in the hands of despotic ministers. From 744 his Grand Councilor, Li Lin-fu, had engaged in vendettas against potential ri-

vals. On arriving in the capital Tu Fu had come under the politically harmless patronage of the Prince of Ju-yang 汝陽, a favorite nephew of the emperor. But he also maintained multiple connections to the entourage of the heir apparent, hated and feared by Li Lin-fu, including Fang Kuan 房琯, Li Shih-chih 李適之, and Tu Fu's early mentor Li Yung 李邕. All three fell in the purges of 746-747. Tu Fu's family tie to Li Lin-fu may possibly have protected the poet from harm, but it could hardly obtain him advancement. With all other entrants (including Yüan Chieh*) Tu Fu failed a special examination to discover neglected talent (747). Three times in the ensuing years he approached the emperor directly with virtuosic works of the *fu* genre, accompanied by pleas for favor. On one occasion (751) he actually won Hsüan-tsung's attention with three *fu* on major rites. A special examination was set for him, which he passed, being then enrolled among those awaiting office; yet two years went by without further result. During this time Tu Fu seems to have played the role of small gentleman-farmer and village-elder in Tu-ling. Owing to a local famine in 754 he removed his family to Feng-hsien 奉先 (modern P'u-ch'eng). In 755 he objected to the offer of a somewhat demeaning post and received instead a sinecure in the heir apparent's household. The appointment ironically became a dead letter, owing to the outbreak of the An Lu-shan Rebellion.

Returning to Feng-hsien, Tu Fu found that his infant son had died, he believed of starvation. In the face of the rebellion Tu Fu conveyed his family, under conditions of great hardship, to a more remote retreat (Fu-chou 鄜州) in northern Shensi. Meanwhile the rebels seized Ch'ang-an and Lo-yang and Hsüan-tsung fled to Szechwan, then abdicated. En route he had been forced to execute Yang Kuei-fei. Leaving his family, Tu Fu apparently sought to join the former heir apparent, now ruling from exile in the far Northwest as Emperor Su-tsung, but was captured by rebels. After a year's detention in Ch'ang-an he escaped to Su-tsung's court and received the ceremonial office of Reminder. He erred by taking literally the formal designation of this post, coming too vehemently to the defense of his friend Fang Kuan. He was arrested but pardoned. After revisiting his family he probably joined Su-tsung's triumphal entry into liberated Ch'ang-an, where he continued to serve as Reminder, until in 758 with the rest of the Fang Kuan group he suffered a mild degree of banishment.

In Tu Fu's poetry of this second period the syncretism of poetic subgenres, seen already earlier, became a syncretism of poetry with *fu* and prose: words and themes previously confined to *fu*, to prose, or even to common speech, are now admitted to poetry (*shih**). From the viewpoint of traditional decorum this can be rephrased negatively: Tu Fu, having violated accepted boundaries of poetic subgenres, now violated those of poetry as such. One result is that his *shih* addressed the homely and traditionally "unpoetic" details of everyday private life. It also addressed the equally "unpoetic" details of public life, political, military, or economic—beginning with his "Ping-chü hsing" 兵車行 (Ballad of the Army Carts) of 750 (*Concordance*, pp. 9-10), a *yüeh-fu* ballad belonging to the *fu-ku* 復古 revival of poetry as remonstrance. This poem, rather than expressing a generalized sympathy for soldiers and their families or a generalized antimilitarism, presents an ethical judgment of specific events (the Tibetan campaigns of 747-750), probably reflecting the views of General Wang Chung-ssu 王忠嗣, another person in the ambiance of the heir-apparent, and placing blame squarely on Hsüan-tsung. Tu Fu's style in such poems embodies an additional syncretism too: namely, of *fu-ku* seriousness with a minute concreteness derived from the synecdochic circumlocutions of court poetry, as it had been written, for example, by his grandfather, Tu Shen-yen. (On Tu Fu's then-unfashionable taste for court poetry, balanced against his contrary taste for the plain style, see his six *chüeh-chü*, "Hsi-wei" 戲爲 [Done in Jest] [*Concordance* pp. 37-39]). Finally, Tu Fu's crowning syncretism of this period, first fully evident in "Tzu ching

fu Feng-hsien yung-huai wu-po tzu" 自京赴奉先縣詠懷五百字 (Five Hundred Words Expressing My Feelings on a Journey from the Capital to Feng-hsien) (*Condordance*, pp. 37-39) is that of the public combined with the private "realism" or unpoeticism, an interweaving of national and personal joys and sorrows. It is harmony that the poet—now in his own estimation aged—himself beautifully characterizes in "Tui hsüeh" 對雪 (Facing the Snow) (*Concordance*, p. 295):

> Weeping in wartime, many new ghosts,
> Sadly changing, a lone old man.

Tu Fu's third period (759-770) belonged to the West and South: modern Kansu, Szechwan, and Hunan. Quitting his employment at Hua-chou 華州 and with the eastward route to Lo-yang closed by the rebel Shih Ssu-ming, Tu Fu headed west to Ch'in-chou 秦州 (modern T'ien-shui) and then T'ung-ku 同谷 (modern Ch'eng-hsien) in Kansu; in the winter of the same year (759), joining a considerable flow of southbound refugee intelligentsia, he moved to Ch'eng-tu. From this time the ailing Tu Fu and his small family were permanent charges upon their friends, relatives, and admirers. They moved repeatedly, no doubt as the available local literary commissions and charity were exhausted or, sometimes, to avoid rebellions or outbreaks of banditry. Nonetheless a certain serenity came as Tu Fu no longer needed to contemplate so seriously the duty of public service or excuse himself from it on the pretext (unconvincing, at least in later life) of practicing Taoist arts. Now he had the more natural excuse of physical illness—lung trouble (asthma?) and chronic cough from 754 onward, summer malarial fevers from 757, then rheumatism, headaches, deafness in one ear. An almost idyllic retreat in 760-762 was his "thatched hut" near Ch'eng-tu, where an old friend and patron, Yen Wu 嚴武, soon became Military Commissioner, while Kao Shih,* Fang Kuan, and a cousin numbered among the magistrates of nearby prefectures. In 764-765 he served as a military adviser under Yen, which post he soon resigned because of illness. Yen's death in 765 lessened the attraction of Ch'eng-tu, and Tu Fu now traveled down the Yangtze, staying two years in K'uei-chou 夔州 (modern Fengchieh, Szechwan), where he found a generous patron in the local prefect. The poet's last three years were spent largely in boat-travel, thoughts of return to Ch'ang-an being thwarted by Tibetan invasions. In 769 he journeyed southward across Lake Tung-t'ing and up the Hsiang River. In 770 he returned to T'an-chou 潭州 (modern Changsha), where he died.

Tu Fu's poems of the third period are by far his most numerous. With characteristic tenacity, though ill and isolated from literary centers, he undertook works of ever greater technical difficulty and perfection. In its time Tu Shen-yen's *p'ai-lü* 排律 or extended *lü-shih* (see *shih*) of forty couplets had been unprecedented; his grandson now produced a tour-de-force of one hundred couplets (*Concordance*, pp. 436-442). Artistically more significant are his carefully unified *lü-shih* series such as "Ch'iu hsing" 秋興 (Autumn Sentiments) (*Concordance*, pp. 467-469). In this and others of his masterpieces written in K'uei-chou, the playful representationalism of his earlier "thatched hut" poems is countered by a somber richness of symbolism scarcely rivaled in Chinese poetry. Despite their classical precision of versification these works share the free idiosyncratic inwardness of the greatest artistic masters (such as Michelangelo or Beethoven) in their late periods. Especially noteworthy is Tu Fu's syntax, which becomes at once more tortuous and more ambiguous; realism becomes surrealism as line after line invites construal in a variety of complementary ways. This ambiguity in the "Autumn Sentiments" reinforces Tu Fu's ability to fuse the sorrow of his own personal situation with passionate concern for the larger agony of his country. In these poems the poet's own age and approaching death parallel his vision of the decimated population and ruined country. The series is without doubt Tu Fu's crowning masterpiece and among the greatest poems in the Chinese language.

EDITIONS:

Ch'ien, Ch'ien-i 錢謙益 (1582-1664), comm. *Tu-shih ch'ien-chu* 杜詩箋注. Taipei, 1974.

Ch'iu, Chao-ao 仇兆鰲 (1638-1713 or after), comm. *Tu shih hsiang chu* 杜詩詳註. 5v. Peking, 1979.

Hung, William. *A Concordance to the Poetry of Tu Fu.* Harvard-Yenching Institute Sinological Index Series, Supplement, no. 14. 3v. Peiping, 1940.

P'u, Ch'i-lung 浦起龍 (b. 1679), comm. *Tu Tu hsin-chieh* 讀杜心解. 3v. Peking, 1961.

Tu Kung-pu chi 杜工部集. 2v. 20 *chüan.* Taipei, 1967. A photolithographic reprint of Wang Chu's 王洙 edition, with a preface by Wang dated 1039.

Ts'ao-t'ang shih chien 草堂詩箋 [caption title: *Tu Kung-pu Ts'ao-t'ang shih chien* 杜工部草堂詩箋]. 2v. 40 *chüan* plus *Wai-chi* 外集 1 *chüan,* with *Tu Kung-pu Ts'ao-t'ang shih-hua* 杜工部草堂詩話 2 *chüan* appended. Taipei, 1971. A photolithographic reprint of the edition edited by Lu Yin 魯訔 (1100-1176), with the commentary by Ts'ai Meng-pi 蔡夢弼 (*fl.* 1247); one contains a preface by Lu (dated 1153) and one by Ts'ai (dated 1204) respectively.

Yang, Lun 楊倫 (1747-1803), comm. *Tu-shih ching-ch'üan* 杜詩鏡銓. 2v. Shanghai, 1962.

TRANSLATIONS:

Demiéville, *Anthologie,* pp. 260-273.

Graham, A. C. "Late Poems of Tu Fu (712-70)," in *Late T'ang,* pp. 39-56.

Hawkes, David. *A Little Primer of Tu Fu.* London, 1967.

Hung, William. *Tu Fu: China's Greatest Poet.* Cambridge, Mass., 1952.

Yoshikawa, Kōjirō 吉川幸次郎. *To Ho shi chu* 杜甫詩注 , v. 1-5. Tokyo, 1977-1983.

Zach, Erwin von. *Tu Fu's Gedichte.* 2v. Cambridge, Mass., 1952.

STUDIES:

Ch'en, Yao-chi 陳瑤璣. *Tu-shih t'e-chih yüan-yüan k'ao* 杜詩特質淵源考. Taipei, 1978.

Chien, Ming-yung 簡明勇. *Tu Fu Ch'i-lü yen-chiu yü chien-chu* 杜甫七律研究與箋註. Taipei, 1973.

Davis, A. R. "The Poetry of Tu Fu (712-770)," *Journal of the Australasian Universities Language and Literature Association,* 22 (November 1964), 208-220.

———. *Tu Fu.* New York, 1971.

Feng, Chih 馮至. *Tu Fu chuan* 杜甫傳. Peking, 1952.

Fisk, Craig. "On the Dialectics of the Strange and Sublime in the Historical Reception of

817

Tu Fu," in *Proceedings of the Ninth Congress of the International Comparative Literature Association*, Innsbruck, 1980, v. 2, pp. 75-82.

———, ed. *Tu Fu shih-hsüan* 杜甫詩選. Hong Kong. 1961.

Hsiao, Ti-fei 蕭滌非. *Tu Fu* 杜甫. Hong Kong, 1963.

———. *Tu Fu shih hsüan chu* 杜甫詩選注. Peking, 1979.

———. *Tu Fu yen-chiu* 杜甫研究. 2v. Chi-nan, 1956-1957.

Hu, Ch'uan-an 胡傳安. *Shih-sheng Tu Fu tui hou-shih shih-jen te ying-hsiang* 詩聖杜甫對後世詩人的影響. Taipei, 1975.

Hua, Wen-hsüan 華文軒, comp. *Tu Fu chüan* 杜甫卷, *shang-p'ien* 上編. 3v. Peking, 1964.

Huang, Ch'i-yüan 黃啟原. *Tu Fu shih hsü-tzu yen-chiu* 杜甫詩虛字研究. Taipei, 1977.

Hung, William. Review of A. R. Davis, *Tu Fu*, *HJAS*, 32 (1972), 265-284.

Jao, Tsung-i 饒宗頤. "Lun Tu Fu K'uei-chou shih" 論杜甫夔州詩, *Chūgoku bungaku hō*, 17 (1962), 104-118.

Kurokawa, Yōichi 黑川洋一. *To Ho* 杜甫. Tokyo, 1973.

———. *To Ho no kenkyū* 杜甫の研究. Tokyo, 1977.

Li, Tao-hsien 李道顯. *Tu Fu shih-shih yen-chiu* 杜甫詩史研究. Taipei, 1973

Liu, Chung-ho 劉中和. *Tu shih yen-chiu* 杜詩研究. Taipei, 1968.

Ma, T'ung-yen 駧儼 and Chiang Ping-hsin 姜炳炘. "Tu shih pan-pen mu-lu" 杜詩版本目錄, in *Tu Fu yen-chiu lun-wen chi* 杜甫研究論文集, v. 3, Peking, 1963, pp. 350-394.

Mei, Tsu-lin and Yu-kung Kao. "Tu Fu's 'Autumn Meditations': An Exercise in Linguistic Criticism," *HJAS*, 28 (1968), 44-80.

Owen, Stephen. "Tu Fu," in *High T'ang*, pp. 183-224.

Shu Ying 叔英. "Tu Fu shih-chi te chi-chung chiao-tsao k'o-pen" 杜甫詩集的幾種較早刻本, *Tu Fu yen-chiu lun-wen chi*, v. 3, Peking, 1963, pp. 346-349.

Suzuki, Toraō 鈴木虎雄. *To shih* 杜詩. Tokyo, 1963.

Ts'ao, Shu-ming 曹樹銘. *Tu-chi ts'ung-chiao* 杜集叢校. Hong Kong, 1978.

Tu Fu yen-chiu lun-wen chi 杜甫研究論文集. 3v. Peking, 1962 (v. 1), 1963 (v. 2 & 3).

Tu Fu yen-chiu tzu-liao hui-p'ien 杜甫研究資料彙編. Taipei, 1973.

Wan, Man 萬曼. "Tu chi shu-lu" 杜集敘錄, in *Tu Fu yen-chiu lun-wen chi*, v. 3, Peking, 1963, pp. 311-345.

Yeh, Chia-ying 葉嘉瑩. *Tu Fu Ch'iu-hsing pa-shou chi-shuo* 杜甫秋興八首集說. Taipei, 1966.

Yoshikawa, Kōjirō. *To shi kōgi* 杜詩講義. Tokyo, 1963.

—DL

Tu Hsün-ho 杜荀鶴 (*tzu*, Yen-chih 彥之, *hao*, Chiu-hua-shan jen 九華山人, 846-907), a poet-official who was also skilled in music, was born in Ch'ih-chou 池洲 (modern Anhwei). Several Southern Sung accounts claim his father was Tu Mu.* They related that during Tu Mu's service in Ch'ih-chou one of his concubines became pregnant. Tu Mu's wife, out of jealousy, forced the woman out of the household to be married to a local, Tu Yün 杜筠. In any case, Tu Hsün-ho seems to have grown up in a family of rather limited means.

His adult life encompassed the gradual collapse of the T'ang dynasty, from the army revolt of 868, through the devastating Huang Ch'ao Rebellion of the late 880s and early 880s, to the chaos of the final quarter century of the T'ang house.

Much of Tu's youth and manhood was spent living and studying at Chiu-hua shan 九華山 (Nine-flowers Mountain), about twenty miles southeast of the Yangtze River and Ch'ih-chou. This region served as a refuge for scholars. Tu studied and wrote verse with other literati there—Ku Yün 顧雲 (*tzu*, Ch'ui-hsiang 垂象; *chin-shih*, 874; d. *c.* 895), Yin Wen-kuei 殷文圭 (*tzu*, Kuei-lang 桂郎), Chang Ch'iao 張喬 (*chin-shih*, 860-873), all three natives of Ch'ih-chou, and Li Chao-hsiang 李昭象 (*tzu*, Hua-wen 化文), a Buddhist whose father had served in Ch'ih-chou. He also exchanged poems with Lo Yin,* who visited Nine-flowers Mountain. Although the group was considered eremitic, most of these men, including Tu, sought a patron through their writings. This goal was perhaps the reason for the extensive travels in the Yangtze and southeastern littoral regions which are documented in Tu's verse. And eventually Tu and Yin Wen-kuei became retainers of T'ien Chün 田頵 (d. 903), a general in the Huai-nan region, probably shortly after Tu's success (he had made numerous earlier attempts), at age forty-five in the *chin-shih* examinations of 891. Following T'ien's defeat in 903, Tu entered the service of Chu Wen 朱溫 (852-912), a former lieutenant of Huang Ch'ao turned warlord. Under Chu's aegis, Tu rose to a high office in the Han-lin Academy (903). Chu was the virtual ruler during the last decade of the T'ang; he had the penultimate emperor executed and kept a tight rein on his successor. Because of Tu's service to Chu, some T'ang loyalists reputedly plotted to murder Tu. Before this plan could be carried out, and in the year 907 in which his patron chose to formally overthrow the T'ang, Tu Hsün-ho fell ill and died.

All of Tu's surviving poetry—about three hundred *shih** in the modern style—antedate his success in the examinations. He collected this corpus himself under the title *T'ang-feng chi* 唐風集 —*feng* referring both to the style (the "T'ang style") and to the content ("criticism of the T'ang") of his verse. This is a poetry of lament: the two primary subjects are the common people, who suffered in the disorders which plagued these years, and Tu himself, who had been unsuccessful in passing the examinations and in finding a patron. It is also an unusual corpus in that the medium for socially critical poetry was normally old-style verse.

The general pattern of a large corpus of socially conscious verse before beginning an official career, followed by virtual silence thereafter (none of Tu Hsün-ho's writings after 891 are extant), can be seen in the lives of several of Tu's contemporaries (P'i Jih-hsiu,* for example). This pattern fits the times. Scholar-officials hoped to serve the state—poetry was the means to achieve that goal during the T'ang. The didactic verse written by many late T'ang poets was intended more to garner a position or a patron, than it was to establish a poetic reputation. The social fabric had been shaken by rebellion so that it was significantly easier for a relatively unknown literatus to rise quickly through the ranks in the late ninth century than ever before under the T'ang. Thus these "poets" threw themselves into their work and literature was neglected. Moreover, given the mercurial temperaments and sanguinary reputations of many of the patrons they found, it was perhaps prudent not to compose anything so open to varied interpretation as a traditional poem.

Tu's literary career may also serve to illustrate the regional tendency of late T'ang poetry, which centered more and more on a local literary group or patron. Analogous to Stephen Owen's concept of a "capital poetry" during the mid-eighth century, the late ninth was one of a "provincial verse."

Tu's best-known poems are "Tsai ching Hu-ch'eng hsien" 再經胡城縣 (On Again Passing through Hu-ch'eng County-seat), which illustrates his social concern, and "Lü-kuan yü-yü" 旅館遇雨 (Encountering Rain at an Inn), "Ch'un kung-yüan" 春宮怨 (A Palace-lady's Lament in Springtime), and "Ma-shang hsing" 馬上行 (Traveling on Horseback), which bemoan his personal lot. The last mentioned is also an example of Tu's use of a more vernacular style, an attribute which has invited comparison with Lo Yin's works.

Several of Tu Hsün-ho's works appeared already in T'ang anthologies and Hung Mai* writes that his poetry was popular during the Sung. A single poem, "Ch'un kung-yüan," appeared in the *T'ang-shih san-pai shou.** Although he was neglected thereafter, recent PRC critics have shown a renewed interest in his socially relevant verse.

EDITIONS:

Ch'üan T'ang shih, pp. 7925-7984.

Nieh I-chung shih, Tu Hsün-ho shih 聶夷中詩, 杜荀鶴詩. Chung-hua shu-chü Shang-hai pien-chi-so 中華書局上海編輯所, ed. Shanghai, 1959.

T'ang-feng chi, in *Ssu-k'u ch'üan-shu.*

Tu Hsün-ho wen-chi 杜荀鶴文集 . Shanghai, 1980. Photolithic reprint of a Sung edition.

TRANSLATIONS:

Bynner, *Jade Mountain*, p. 143.

Li, Teresa, "A Nocturne," *THM*, 8 (1940), p. 75.

Watson, *Lyricism*, pp. 83-84 and 122.

STUDIES:

Hsiao, Wen-yüan 肖文苑. "Tu Hsün-ho te sheng-ho tao-lu chi ch'uang-tso" 杜荀鶴的生活道路及創作, *Pei-ching Shih-ta hsüeh-pao*, 1979.3.

Hsü, Hsiao-hsing 徐曉星. "Wan-T'ang shih-jen Tu Hsün-ho" 晚唐詩人杜荀鶴, Wen-hsüeh i-ch'an tseng-k'an, 2 (1956), 141-156.

Kamio, Ryūsuke 上尾龍介. "Tō Junkaku no shi—sono shakaisei ni tsuite" 杜荀鶴の詩—その社會性 について, Nihon Chūgoku gakkaihō, 20 (1968.10).

—WHN

Tu Jen-chieh 杜仁傑 (original name Chih-yüan 之元, tzu, Chung-liang 仲梁 or Shan-fu 善夫, hao, Chih-hsüan 止軒) was a native of Ch'ang-ch'ing 長清 County (Shantung). The dates of his life are not clear. He was already active as a writer shortly after 1221 and was recommended by Yüan Hao-wen* to Yeh-lü Ch'u-ts'ai in 1233. In the Chih-yüan period of the Yüan (1264-1294) he was summoned by Emperor Shih-tsu (Qub-ilai) to serve as Han-lin Academician, but declined. It seems that he spent most of his life in retirement in the mountains of Ling-yen 靈巖 and Wu-feng 五峰, southeast of his native town of Ch'ang-ch'ing. Under Emperor Wu-tsung (r. 1307-1311) Tu Jen-chieh was posthumously awarded the rank of Grand Master Admonisher and Recip-ient of Edicts. He was also canonized as Wen-mu 文穆. This was due primarily to the initiative and influence of his son, Tu Yüan-su 杜元素, who had reached the po-sition of Surveillance Commissioner of Min-hai 閩海 Circuit in Fukien.

Tu was on familiar terms with many of the leading literati of the late Chin period, such as Yüan Hao-wen, who held Tu's po-etry in high regard. The greater part of Tu's productions seems, however, to be lost. A selection of his poems is collected under the title Shan-fu hsien-sheng chi 善夫先生集. Tu has also written several tomb inscriptions for Taoists of the Ch'üan-chen sect which have survived in the Taoist Canon. Only a few of Tu's san-ch'ü (see ch'ü) have been preserved. Prominent among these is the san-ch'ü suite "Chuang-chia pu-shih kou-lan" 莊家不識勾闌 (The Country Bumpkin Knows Nothing of the Theater). This text is not only a delightful farce written in colloquial language, but an important source on theatrical perfor-mances in the early thirteenth century, be-cause it describes the first three parts of a show, i.e., the prelude of instrumental mu-sic played by a female troupe, the clown's skit, and the final dramatic performance.

EDITIONS:

Shan-fu hsien-sheng chi, in Yüan-shih hsüan, san-chi chia-chi 元詩選三集甲集. Hsiu-yeh ts'ao-t'ang 秀野草堂, ed., 1694-1720, 1 ch. (poems).

Ch'ao-yeh hsin-sheng t'ai-p'ing yüeh-fu 朝野新聲太平樂府. Taipei, 1968, ch. 9, pp. 1-3 (Chuang-chia pu-shih kou-lan).

Kan shui hsien-yüan lu 甘水仙源錄 in Tao-tsang, ch. 5, pp. 6b-8b; ch. 8, pp. 13b-17a (tomb in-scriptions).

TRANSLATIONS:

Crump, James I., Jr. "Yüan-pen, Yüan Drama's Rowdy Ancestor," LEW, 14 (1970), 481-483.

Hawkes, David. "Reflections on Yüan tsa-chü," AM, 16 (1970), 75-77.

West, Vaudeville, pp. 11-15.

STUDIES:

Crump, op. cit.

Hawkes, op. cit.

Ogawa, Yōichi 小川陽一. "To Zenbu saku sank-yoku 'Chuang-chia pu-shih kou-lan' 杜善夫作散曲 莊家不識勾闌," Shūkan tōyōgaku, 18 (1967), 78-86.

Wang, Te-i 王德毅 et al. Yüan-jen chuan-chi tzu-liao so yin 元人傳記資料索引. Taipei, 1980, p. 566 (lists practically all references to Tu Jen-chieh in Chinese works).

West, Vaudeville.

—HF

Tu-ku Chi 獨孤及 (tz'u, Chih-chih 至之, 725-777) is known mainly as a literary critic, an advocate of free prose, and an early, though indirect, influence on the great free-prose writer Han Yü.* He came from an aristocratic Turkic clan that married into the imperial families of both the Sui and the T'ang. After being successful in a Taoist-decree examination of 754, he served just before the An Lu-shan Rebel-lion as Junior Officer of Hua-yin 華陰, not far east of Ch'ang-an. After the rebellion and a period of service in the southeast, his most important posts were under Tai-tsung as Commissioner of the Left, Erudite in the Court of Imperial Sacrifices, and Vice Director of the Headquarter Bureau. Two provincial prefectships, those of Hao-chou 濠州 and Shu-chou 舒州 (both modern

Anhwei), followed. His final posting, to the prefectship of the strategically important prefecture of Ch'ang-chou 常州 in modern Kiangsu, was particularly sought by administrators because of its prestige. After his death he received the canonization of Hsien 憲 "exemplary."

Tu-ku's views on literature were close to those of Chia Chih,* Li Hua,* and Hsiao Ying-shih,* with whom he was acquainted. He emphasized the primacy of the Confucian canon and the moral function of writing, condemned ornamental or euphuistic style, and endorsed the traditional Confucian theory of poetic composition which saw it as the patterned expression of feelings from within. Despite his purism, he recognized, as did most of his contemporaries, merit in some of the developments in tonality that had taken place in verse writing earlier in the eighth century.

Much of Tu-ku's prose writing was occasioned by his official career. Two early works, the "Hsien-chang ming" 仙掌銘 (Inscription for the Immortal's Handprint) and "Ku Han-ku kuan ming" 古函谷關銘 (Inscription for the Ancient Han-ku Pass) prove that he could use the high-flown and hyperbolic style that was valued for such monumental pieces. After the rebellion, as an erudite in the Court of Imperial Sacrifices, he composed examples of one of the minor but much respected genres of T'ang bureaucratic writing, the *shih i* 諡議 (discussion of canonization), in which he argued the appropriateness or otherwise of canonization titles proposed for recently deceased officials. He also wrote a large number of epitaphs (both for members of his own family and for others), sacrificial prayers, inscriptions for institutions, texts for monasteries, and occasional verse.

Among Tu-ku's admirers were Ts'ui Yu-fu 崔祐甫 (721-780), Chief Minister and director of the dynastic history at the start of Te-tsung's reign and Ch'üan Te-yü 權德興 (759-818), an influential, eclectic intellectual of the reigns of Te-tsung and Hsien-tsung. But Tu-ku's most important close pupil was Liang Su,* whom he taught

when he was prefect of Ch'ang-chou and who edited his literary collection. Liang Su in turn influenced the great Han Yü. Han himself was said to have been influenced by Tu-ku, whom he cannot have known personally. One of Tu-ku Chi's sons, Tu-ku Yü 獨孤郁 (778-816), however, was a long-term friend of Han Yü.

Extant editions of Tu-ku Chi's literary collection, the *P'i-ling chi* 毗陵集, which consists of seventeen *chüan* of prose and three of verse, derive from a manuscript copy made in the imperial library by Wu K'uan 吳寬 (1436-1504). Much of his writing was also contained in the major early Sung anthologies.

EDITIONS:
P'i-ling chi. Preface 1791. *SPTK.* Tu-ku's verse may also be consulted in *Ch'üan T'ang shih,* v. 4, pp. 2760-2779; his prose in *Ch'üan T'ang wen, chüan* 384-393.

STUDIES:
Lo, Lien-t'ien 羅聯添. "Tu-ku Chi k'ao-cheng" 獨孤集考證, *Ta-lu tsa chih,* 48.3 (March 15, 1974), 117-138.

—DLM

Tu Kuang-t'ing 杜光庭 (*tzu,* Pin-sheng 賓聖, *hao,* Tung-yin tzu 東瀛子, 850-933), was a native of Kua-ts'ang 括蒼 (or Chin-yün 縉雲) in Ch'u-chou 處州 (in modern Chekiang). After failing an examination in the classics he went to Mount T'ien-t'ai 天台, where he prepared himself for the Taoist priesthood. He was invited to join the court of Emperor Hsi-tsung 僖宗 (r. 874-888) and followed that sovereign into exile in Ch'eng-tu in 881, during the insurrection of Huang Ch'ao 黃巢 (d. 884). He returned to the capital with him in 885. Hsi-tsung died in 888. Meanwhile his captain Wang Chien 王建 (847-918) was bringing Szechwan under his personal control. He was supreme there by 891 and later created a kingdom (known to posterity as the Former Shu 蜀) out of the province. Tu Kuang-t'ing was affably received at this splendid new court and was awarded high authority and magnificent titles, including the Taoist one of (*Kuang-ch'eng hsien-sheng* 廣成先生) "Prior Born of Broad Achievement." He was appointed tutor to the heir

821

to the throne. Later, after further honors under the second ruler of Shu, Wang Yen 王衍 (r. 919-925), who conferred on him the title "Heavenly Master who Transmits the Truth" (Ch'uan-chen t'ien-shih 傳眞天師), he resigned his posts and retired to Ch'ing-ch'eng Mountain 青城山, the summit of the Ming-shan 岷山 complex, which had been held in high regard by Taoists since the time of the first Celestial Masters of Later Han times.

A considerable number of Tu Kuang-t'ing's prose writings survive. Three of these deserve special mention because of their length and the importance of their contents. One is Yung-ch'eng chi-hsien lu 墉城集仙錄 (Register of the Transcendents Gathered at Yung-ch'eng), devoted to the careers, both mortal and immortal, of Taoist women and goddesses. These are both edifying examples of devotion, piety, and miracles, and also—differently considered—specimens of the typical wonder tale of the late T'ang, saturated with mystery, exoticism, and the evidence of unseen worlds. In short, this is hagiography assimilated to the literary short story: its author clearly intended his readers to take his histories seriously as representations of religious truths. (The version of this collection preserved in the early Sung Taoist anthology, Yün-chi ch'i-ch'ien,* which appears to be close to Tu Kuang-t'ing's original, omits a number of exalted beings of the pantheon of Highest Clarity [shang ch'ing 上清] who appear in full panoply in the Ming version of the Tao-tsang;* on the other hand, a number of the ladies in the former gallery are conspicuously absent from the latter.)

Another major contribution by Tu Kuang-t'ing to the history of medieval religion is his Tung-t'ien fu-ti yüeh-tu ming-shan chi 洞天福地嶽瀆名山記, a spiritual baedeker for the subterranean worlds styled "grotto heavens" (tung t'ien), hidden in the lowest roots of China's sacred mountains and equipped with their own skies, planets, sun, and moon. An elegant preface to this work describes also the cities of the sky, the high counterparts of those dreamlike underworlds, whose palaces and basilicas were shaped from coagulated clouds and frozen mists. There is also his Li-tai ch'ung-tao chi 歷代崇道記, a historical account of the honors conferred on the Taoist religion and its adherents by the royal court from the earliest times down to the tenth century. This reverent relation of benefactions, promotions, preferments, architectural endowments, celebrations, and honors is particularly rich in information about the rulers of the T'ang, above all Emperor Hsüan-tsung.

Prominent among the many shorter prose compositions of Tu Kuang-t'ing is a considerable number of highly formalized texts outlining the procedures of Taoist rituals. These fall chiefly into two groups: chai tz'u 齋詞 (texts for purgations) and chiao tz'u 醮詞 (texts for cosmodramas). The former category of scenario refers to rites conducted in special theaters on holy occasions. The second group outlines the plots and purposes of triumphal proceedings which often marked the climax of preparatory days of purgation.

Many other prose writings survive, some of them concerned with court business, some related to religious affairs. Virtually all are in some measure concerned with cosmic or metaphysical matters. To judge from such compositions as these, Tu Kuang-t'ing appears as a conservative thinker, an adherent of fashionable orthodoxy, which implies that, like his associate Kuan-hsiu,* he was a religious syncretist.

The rather small corpus of his extant poems, however, gives a different view of his creative talents. Almost all of them have a purely Taoist content, but they are by no means merely reverent and ceremonial. Their themes range from allusions to holy grottoes and sacred mountains, through holy men, perennial cranes, and spectral apes, to the divine spectacles presented by radiant clouds and blazing stars. Like other Taoist writers he lets his fancy roam throughout space in faery fantasies: He harnesses the moon toad, he actualizes divine birds in his personal microcosm, he finds infinity in the inner space of his mind. His writing, always competent, in such instances seems inspired.

To those outside the Taoist circle, Tu Kuang-t'ing is best remembered as the author of a remarkable T'ang story "Ch'iu-jan k'o chuan" 虬髯客傳 (The Curly-bearded Stranger). Set at the end of the Sui dynasty, the story purports to be a reconstruction of some of the events behind the rise of Li Shih-min 李世民 (599-649), who later became the T'ang emperor T'ai-tsung (r. 626-649). The narrative follows the travels of Li Ching (571-649)—later a military officer under Li Shih-min—after eloping with a maid in the household of the Sui minister Yang Su 楊素 (d. 606). The minister declines Li Ching's offer to counsel him, but the maid Hung-fu 紅拂 recognizes Li's merit and decides to run away to him. The love affair is not allowed to develop much further. On their way eastward Li Ching and Hung-fu meet a curly-bearded stranger. The stranger asks Li Ching whether he knows of any men of worth. Li Ching responds that he knows of only one man—Li Shih-min—worthy of becoming emperor and later arranges a meeting between him and the stranger. At the meeting the stranger immediately recognizes that Li Shih-min is destined to become emperor and gives up his own ambition of ruling China. He bequeaths his considerable fortune to Li Ching and Hung-fu and disappears, eventually becoming a ruler in another land.

At one level of interpretation the story illustrates the importance of the custom of *pao* 報 (reciprocation)—the stranger repays Li Ching and Hung-fu for the favors they have done. But the story's explicit didactic purpose is to illustrate the futility of rebellion, of striving against the will of Heaven. This aim is only at the expense of historical fact: Li Shih-min won the throne after killing his older brother, the crown prince. The story's idealization of Li Shih-min's rise to power accords with the political mood toward the end of the T'ang. To those living in the time of fragmentation, Li Shih-min's prosperous reign seemed a golden age. "Ch'iu-jan k'o chuan" has been interpreted as an expression of this late T'ang nostalgia—as a political protest expressing the hope that a

true emperor would appear to restore order. This interpretation, however, is difficult to fit to Tu's political ideas, though in some poems he does lament a lack of social order.

The story's textual history indicates that there may have been some uncertainty about its intended meaning—perhaps on the author's own part. The story is extant in two basic versions. What is considered the earlier text appears in Tu Kuang-t'ing's *Shen-hsien kan-yü chuan* 神仙感遇傳 (Encounters with Divine Transcendents), under the title "Ch'iu-hsü k'o" 虬鬚客 (The Curly-whiskered Stranger). In this version the political allegory seems to be emphasized: The curly-bearded stranger is mentioned at the beginning as the narrative's focus, and Li Ching's elopement with Hung-fu is only briefly sketched. In the later text, included in the *T'ai-p'ing kuang-chi* 太平廣記 (T'ai-p'ing Miscellany) and believed by some to contain Tu Kuang-t'ing's own revisions, the emphasis changes. The stranger is not introduced until about one-fourth through the story, and the romance between Hung-fu and Li Ching is described in greater detail. More stress is placed on Hung-fu's courage as manifested by her escape from Yang Su's household and by her equanimity in dealing with a stranger who lies down beside her without warning to watch her comb her hair. Li Ching's characterization changes too: A colorless character to begin with, he recedes further into the background, serving as a foil to both Hung-fu and the stranger and as a plot device for bringing together various characters.

Whoever revised the story seems to have realized that the relationships established in the first half—Hung-fu's interaction with Li Ching and the stranger—would overshadow the political lesson drawn in the second. To compensate for this, passages stressing the story's political import were added—for example, an insertion that reads: "A subject who foolishly thinks of rebellion is a mantis trying to stop a rolling wheel with its arms." Nevertheless it is the trio of Li Ching, Hung-fu, and the stranger—later referred to as "the three well-traveled gallants" (*feng-ch'en san-hsia* 風塵三俠)—that inspired later writers. The characters served as subjects of Ming drama: for example, Ling Meng-ch'u's* *Ch'iu-jan weng* and Chang Feng-i's *Hung-fu chi*.

EDITIONS:

Cheng-t'ung Tao tsang 正統道藏. Rpt. Taipei, 1976. (Individual works may be located by reference to Weng Tu-chien, *Combined Indices to the Authors and Titles of Books in Two Collections of Taoist Literature* [Harvard-Yenching Institute Sinological Index Series, No. 25], rpt. Taipei, 1966. For instance, No. 599 is *Tung-t'ien fu-ti yüeh-tu ming-shan chi*, and No. 782 is *Yung-ch'eng chi-hsien-lu*.)

"Ch'iu-jan k'o chuan," in *T'ai-p'ing kuang-chi*, *ch.* 193. Reliable text of the later version.

———, in *T'ang-jen hsiao-shuo*, pp. 178-184. A reliable, punctuated text of the later version, appended with useful background material, including a punctuated text of the early version.

———, *T'ang Sung ch'uan-ch'i hsüan* 唐宋傳奇選, Shih Yen 師言, ed., Peking, 1963, pp. 124-130. A heavily annotated text.

Ch'üan T'ang shih, v. 12, *ch.* 854, pp. 9663-9669. *Ch'üan T'ang wen*, v. 19, *ch.* 929-944, pp. 12213-12394.

Yung-ch'eng chi-hsien-lu (different version of *Yün-chi ch'i-ch'ien*,* *ch.* 114-116).

TRANSLATIONS:

Birch, Cyril. "The Curly-bearded Hero," in *Anthology of Chinese Literature*, v. 1, New York, 1965, pp. 314-322.

Chai, Ch'u, and Winberg Chai. "The Curly-Bearded Guest," in *A Treasury of Chinese Literature*, New York, 1965, pp. 117-124.

Chavannes, Edouard. *Li Jet des Dragons* (*Mémoires concernant l'Asie Orientale*, 3 [1919]), pp. 172-214 (translation of *T'ai-shang ling pao-yü kuei-ming chen-ta chai yen kung-i* 太上靈寶玉匱明眞大齋言功儀 [Weng Tu-chien, No. 521]).

———. "Les lieux célestes profondes" (translation of *Tung-t'ien fu-ti yüeh-tu ming-shan chi*), *Ibid.*, pp. 131-168.

Schafer, E. H. "Three Divine Women of South China," *CLEAR*, 1 (1979), 31-42.

STUDIES:

Chavannes, Edouard. "Biographie de Tou Kouang-t'ing," *Le Jet des Dragons*, p. 130.

Imaeta, Jirō 今枝二郎, "To Kōtei shōkō" 杜光庭小考, in *Yoshioka hakase kanreki kinen dōkyō*

kenkyū ronshū—dōkyō no shisō to bunka— 吉岡博士還暦記念道教研究論集 — 道教の思想と文化—, Tokyo, 1977, pp. 523-532.

Jao, Tsung-i 饒宗頤. "Ch'iu-jan k'o chuan k'ao" 虯髯客傳考, *Ta-lu tsa-chih*, 18.1 (1959), 1-4.

Liu, James J. Y. *The Chinese Knight-Errant*. Chicago, 1967, pp. 87-88.

Liu, K'ai-jung 劉開榮. *T'ang-tai hsiao-shuo yen-chiu* 唐代小說研究, rev. ed. Hong Kong, 1964, pp. 187-215.

Wu, Jen-ch'en 吳任臣. *Shih-kuo ch'un-ch'iu* 十國春秋 (1793 ed.), *ch.* 47, pp. 5b-8a.

Yeh, Ch'ing-ping 葉慶炳. "Ch'iu-jan k'o chuan te hsieh-tso chi-ch'iao" 虯髯客傳的寫作技巧, *Wen-hsüeh tsa-chih*, 7.2 (1959), 9-16.

—ES and CY

Tu Mu 杜牧 (*tzu*, Mu-chih 牧之, 803-852) is a late T'ang poet-essayist traditionally known for his lyrical, romantic quatrains and for similar qualities attributed to his life. The romantic image is due largely to the "Yang-chou meng chi" 揚州夢記 (Record of a Yang-chou Dream), an embellished summation of anecdotes and legends compiled shortly after Tu Mu's death by Yü Yeh 于鄴 (*fl.* 867). Until recent years, his many lengthy narrative poems were neglected for the popular quatrains, but it is primarily in the longer poems, as in his letters and essays, that Confucian issues are raised and that he invariably provides testimony on the politics of his age.

Born in Ch'ang-an at the home of his grandfather, Tu Yu 杜佑 (735-812), Tu Mu spent his childhood amid the culture and opulence of a Grand Councilor's estate. However, the family's fortunes dwindled rapidly after the death of Tu Yu, and Tu Mu's father died some years later, so that Tu Mu could describe his youth as a time when servants deserted the household and the family survived only by selling off property. It is implied that because of the domestic imperatives, he did not begin to study the classics until he was twenty, but he must have learned fast, for he was writing letters to high officials and *fu** (prose-poems) at twenty-three, and he passed the *chin-shih* at twenty-five.

The "Ah-fang kung fu" 阿房宮賦 (Prose-poem on the Ah-fang Palace), composed in 825, supposedly presaged his success in he *chin-shih* examination. Ostensibly it is a critique of the excesses of Ch'in-shih Huang-ti, but its Confucian judgments are really aimed at the brief reign of Emperor Ching-tsung (825-827). The *fu* is his earliest poetic effort; it is considered stylistically original and a precursor of the *wen-fu* 文賦 of the Sung dynasty. His first datable poem was written in 827, the same year he passed the examination, and it, too, is a lengthy, moralistic self-advertisement entitled "Kan huai shih" 感懷詩 (Deep-seated Feelings); the title and format have been used by many poets.

His career began well enough: from 828 to 833 he was an assistant to the imperial son-in-law, Shen Ch'uan-shih 沈傳師 (769-827) and then moved to the staff of Niu Seng-ju 牛僧孺 (d. 847) in Yang-chou. He returned to Ch'ang-an early in 835 as an Investigating Censor and by mid-year had himself transferred to Lo-yang, where he marked time for two years before retiring to care for his younger brother, Tu I 杜顗 (806-851), who was going blind. Various minor positions in Ch'ang-an between 838 and 842 ended with a series of prefectships in the southeast, which he considered a six-year exile. Tu Mu returned to Ch'ang-an to a post too lowly to support his and his brother's families, and after much lobbying he was made Prefect of Hu-chou in 850. His brother died in 851; Tu Mu then returned to the capital.

The expression of frustration is constant in Tu Mu's writings, and it raises the question of who or what kept him from high office. Thanks to Tu Yu, the Tu family had good connections with both sides in the Niu-Li factional dispute; Tu Mu eventually worked for both. His relations with Niu were particularly warm, and he seemed to have had an almost continuous correspondence with Li Te-yü 李德裕 (787-850). Evidence from his poetry suggests that 835 actually was the turning point in his career, when he joined those opposed to the appointments of Cheng Chu 鄭注 and Li Hsün 李訓 as Grand Councilors. The episode took the life of one good friend and affected several careers; Tu Mu found it the better part of valor to lie low in Lo-yang. Openly

in his "Li Kan" 李甘, more obscurely in "Hsi shih Wen Huang-ti, san-shih-erh yün" 昔事文皇帝三十二韻 (Formerly in the Service of Emperor Wen, thirty-two rhymes), and in several poems on the family estate at the Vermilion Slope 朱坡 (in the Southern Mountains), he describes the events of this year, argues his somewhat shameful innocence, grieves over friends, and generally mourns the impact on his career. The Sweet Dew Incident, an abortive attempt to assassinate powerful eunuchs which ended in a massacre of officials, occurred at the end of the year and seems not to have had the same relevance for Tu Mu as the earlier conflict.

Throughout his life Tu Mu wrote letters to those in high places, telling them what was wrong with policy and military strategy and what was right about his own credentials for advancement. A prime example is his "Tsui yen" 罪言 (Guilty/Inappropriate Words) of 834; the title refers to his presumption in criticizing policy from his lowly position, but he does so anyway, offering an inventory of Confucian ideals. His claim to being a military strategist was belatedly lent credence by his widely accepted commentary to the *Sun-tzu* 孫子 (Art of War), completed sometime before 849. He wrote Li Te-yu frequently in the 840s, when Li was Grand Councilor, to offer strategies, and once his ideas were followed (with positive results). The single-mindedness of such pieces, pedantic, formal, and lyrical by turns, reflects Tu Mu's public concern and ambition. They remind the reader of the link between *ku-wen** prose and Confucian ideals, but Tu Mu's style is really best described as eclectic.

The lament of the scholar-official is summarized in his "Chiu-jih Ch'i-shan teng kao" 九日齊山登高 (Climbing High on Mt. Ch'i on the Double Ninth). In it he makes use of the "climbing to high places" motif not to display his worth but to wax philosophical and allusive on the transitory nature of political life. He often is autobiographical, as in "Ta-yü hsing" 大雨行 (Ballad of Heavy Rain), and in "Chang Hao-hao shih" 張好好詩, where he poignantly tells the story of the singsong girl, of the happy times at their first meeting, and of their consequent fates as barmaid and refugee. His many poems on partings, with travel itself as metaphor, digress to the vicissitudes of (his) public life.

Tu Mu's quatrains tend to be more subdued than his longer poems, although internal rhyme, alliteration, repetition, and allusion still are abundant. The total effect remains one of smoothness and understatement, with most allusions evident and historical, and but a few altogether obscure. He favors the Later Han dynasty as the source for parallels with the late T'ang. Irony is an often used vehicle of expression, as in his "Ch'ih pi" 赤壁 (Red Cliff) and "Po Ch'in-huai" 泊秦淮 (Mooring on the Ch'in-huai River). His romantic-erotic quatrains also provided material for the stories in the "Yang-chou meng chi." Reference is commonly made to his "Ts'eng pieh" 贈別 (Offered at Parting) which described a thirteen-year-old beauty; "Ch'ien huai" 遣懷 (Chasing Cares Away), which mentions a ten-year Yang-chou dream; and "T'an hua" 歎花 (Sighing Over Flowers), which tells of his coming too late to find a flower/woman, it/she having already gone to fruit.

His lifelong search for high office ended in 852 when he was made a Secretariat Drafter; he died a few months later. That a great number of his poems (524) remain is in part the result of his careful editing, particularly of his earlier poems. It is difficult to say who the ultimate influences were for his poetry; early models and his respect for masters like Tu Fu,* Li Po,* Han Yü,* and Liu Tsung-yüan* do not fully explain his style, but anticipate his acquaintance with allegory.

EDITIONS:

Fan-ch'uan shih-chi chu 樊川詩集注. *SPPY*. Includes the standard commentary by Feng Chi-wu 馮集梧.

Fan-ch'uan shih-chi chu 樊川詩集注. Peking, 1962. Modern typeset reprint of annotated edition of Tu's poetic works.

Fan-ch'uan wen-chi 樊川文集. *SPTK*. pp. 121-140.

Tu Mu shih-hsüan 杜牧詩選. Chou Hsi-fu 周錫馥, ed. Hong Kong, 1980.

Tu Mu shih-hsüan. Miao Yüeh 繆鉞, comp. Peking, 1957.

Tu Mu shih-wen hsüan-chu 杜牧詩文選註. Chu Pi-lien 朱碧蓮 and Wang Shu-chün 王淑均, eds. Shanghai, 1982.

TRANSLATIONS:

Demiéville, *Anthologie*, pp. 315-316.

Graham, *Late T'ang*, pp. 121-140.

Kubin, Wolfgang. *Das lyrische Werk des Tu Mu (803-852)*. Wiesbaden, 1976.

Sawatorao, Ichino 市野澤寅雄. *To Boku* 杜牧. Tokyo, 1965.

STUDIES:

Arai, Ken 荒井健. *To Boku*. Tokyo, 1974.

Fish, Michael B. "The Tu Mu and Li Shang-yin Prefaces to the Collected Poems of Li Ho," in *Chinese Poetry and Poetics, Vol. 1*, by R. C. Miao, ed., San Francisco, 1978, pp. 231-286.

———. "Tu Mu's Poems on the Vermilion Slope: Laments on a Meager Career," *OE*, 25.2 (1978), 190-205.

Kubin, *op. cit.*

Kung, Wen-kai. "The Prosody and Poetic Diction of Tu Mu's Poetry," *THHP*, 12 (1979), 281-307.

———. "Tu Mu: The Poet." Unpublished Ph.D. dissertation, University of Washington, 1976.

Miao, Yüeh. *Tu Mu chuan* 杜牧傳. Peking, 1977.

———. *Tu Mu nien-p'u* 杜牧年譜. Peking, 1980.

T'an, Li Tsung-mu 譚黎宗慕. *Tu Mu yen-chiu tzu-liao hui-pien* 杜牧研究資料彙編. Taipei, 1972.

—MF

Tu Shen-yen 杜審言 (*tzu*, Pi-chien 必簡, d. c. 705), was a native of Hsiang-yang 襄陽 in Hsiang-chou 襄州 (modern Hupei). After earning the *chin-shih* 進士 distinction he went on to an erratic career in the central administration at Lo-yang. The Empress Wu was delighted with his writing and gave him an honorable position at the palace— in effect, as a court poet. In 705, just before the death of Wu Chao 武曌, he was exiled to Feng-chou 峯州 (up the Red River from Hanoi), accused of complicity in a political conspiracy. His compulsory residence was a precarious frontier outpost, whose garrison was responsible for the good behavior of the Ts'uan barbarians, a Tibeto-Burman people, centered in what is now Yunnan. This fortified settlement, aside from its strategic value, benefited the distant aristocracy by annual tribute of areca nuts, cardamoms, iridescent kingfisher feathers, and rhinoceros horn. He was soon recalled, assigned honorable service in the education of the heir apparent, and given an appointment in the court literary academy. He died in his sixties and was awarded posthumous honors at the insistence of the poet Li Chiao* and others.

This biographical sketch is a stereotype of the official record of the career of any gifted writer cast in the role of a minor court functionary in the seventh century. It helps us little, if at all, in understanding what was good about his writing. The small fraction of the ten *chüan* of verse that are said to have circulated after his death provides a rather flimsy basis for evaluation. His contemporaries, we are told, recognized his talents, especially his skill in contriving five-syllable verses, and he numbered excellent writers among his intimates—notably the poets Li Chiao, Ts'ui Yung 崔融 (653-706), and Su Wei-tao 蘇味道 (648-705). Perhaps these associations count for more than his reported boast that his literary craft was superior to that of Ch'ü Yüan* and Sung Yü 宋玉 (c. 290 B.C.-c. 223 B.C.), and that his calligraphy exceeded that of Wang Hsi-chih 王羲之 (321-379).

Most of his surviving poems are expressions of his courtly responsibilites, specifically compositions—command performances—contrived for grand occasions at royal request (*ying chih* 應制). Often these were composed at parties for ambassadors and newly appointed provincial magistrates about to leave the capital; some were occasioned by garden parties, picnics, moon-watching meets, and "Seventh Eve" celebrations. Two are in honor of the great public festivals called *Ta p'u* 大酺 (Great Bacchanals), for which free wine was provided to the whole citizenry. Astrological allusions are not uncommon in Tu's verses, and these, understandably, favor starry omens of prosperity and stability for the realm. A few stanzas are more personal and reveal his affection for his friends. For instance, there are two addressed to Ts'ui Yung, and another to Su Wei-tao. All of these poems show a good inventiveness—often cooled by the formality of the occasion.

The poems written in exile, however miserable Tu Shen-yen may have been, benefit from the absence of such restraints. Although Tu Shen-yen's period of banishment is given only perfunctory treatment in his official biographies, that episode looms large in what remains of his poetry. The verses written at that time show, as do the comparable ones of Shen Ch'uan-ch'i (see Sung Chih-wen) and Sung Chihwen,* the beginning of a new awareness of the deep south during the second half of the seventh century. They display a sense of personal tragedy, but also point the way to the full-blown exoticism of the eighth century and the true assimilation of the ninth and tenth centuries. In short, they lack entirely the exuberance of the tropical verses of men like Li Hsün 李珣 (*fl.* 896) and Ou-yang Chiung.* Tu Shen-yen expresses amazement at the lack of true seasonal divisions and at the disorderly wildness of the countryside—which for him was ameliorated in some measure by the glorious and even violent colors of both the mineral substrate and the organic life. But unlike Liu Tsung-yüan,* he lacked a truly flexible and adaptable spirit. He always yearned for his northern homeland, with its familiar garden birds and flowers and the company of sophisticated men.

It is possible to detect magical images in many of his poems, but hard to make an overall estimate of his writing that would justify—or confute—the high reputation he earned. This is the inevitable result of the scantiness of the extant relics of his writing.

EDITIONS:
Ch'üan T'ang shih, v. 2, *ch.* 62, pp. 731-740.

TRANSLATIONS:
Bynner, *Jade Mountain*, p. 146.
Owen, *Early T'ang*, pp. 327-337.
Schafer, *Vermilion Bird*, pp. 126, 258.

STUDIES:
Fu, *Shih-jen*, pp. 21-36: "Tu Shen-yen k'ao" 考
Owen, *Early T'ang*, pp. 325-338.

—ES

T'u Lung 屠隆 (*tzu*, Chang-ch'ing 長卿 or Wei-chen 緯眞, *hao*, Ch'ih-shui 赤水 or in his late years, Hung-pao Chü-shih 鴻苞居士, with various fancy names such as Yu-ch'üan Shan-jen 由拳山人, I-na Tao-jen 一衲道人, P'eng-lai Hsien-k'o 蓬萊仙客, and So-lo Chu-jen 娑羅主人, 1542-1605), was a native of Yin-hsien 鄞縣 (modern Ningpo, Chekiang). In 1577, he attained the *chin-shih* degree and became the Magistrate of the district of Ying-shang 潁上 (modern Anhwei). In 1578, he was transferred to Ch'ing-p'u 青浦 (east of Soochow), where he made friends with the eminent literary men of the region, such as Shen Ming-ch'en 沈明臣 and Feng Meng-chen 馮夢禎. They enjoyed one another's company drinking wine and composing poems. At the same time T'u managed to direct public affairs very well. In 1582, he was promoted to the position of secretary in the Ministry of Rites. Before long, he became a close friend of Sung Shih-en 宋世恩, the Marquis of Hsining 西寧. Yü Hsien-ch'ing 俞顯卿, a secretary in the Ministry of Justice, who held a personal grudge against T'u, accused him of improper relations with Sung Shih-en's wife. T'u lost his post, and from then on could barely eke out a living by selling his writing for money. He abandoned himself to the carefree enjoyment of wine and poetry and led the life of a Taoist immortal, among the mountains and rivers.

T'u Lung was a prolific writer. His collected works of verse and prose include the *Yu-ch'üan chi* 由拳集, the *Ch'i-chen-kuan chi* 棲眞館集, the *Pai-yü chi* 白榆集, and the *Hung-pao chi* 鴻苞集. He wrote three *ch'uan-ch'i** dramas, *T'an-hua chi* 曇花記 (The Night-blooming Cereus), *Ts'ai-hao chi* 綵毫記 (The Colorful Brush), and *Hsiu-wen chi* 修文記 (Finely Crafted Writings), which are collectively known as the *Feng-i-ko yüeh-fu* 鳳儀閣樂府 (Muscial Dramas of the Mansion of Phoenix Pomp). His other miscellaneous works include the *Ts'ai-chen chi* 采眞集, the *Nan-yu chi* 南遊記, the *Heng-t'ang chi* 橫塘集, the *Chiang-hsüeh-lou chi* 絳雪樓集, the *Ming-liao-tzu chi-yu* 冥寥子記遊, the *So-lo-kuan ch'ing-yen* 娑羅館清言, and the *So-lo-kuan i-kao* 娑羅館逸稿. Other works that have been attributed to him are the *Huang-cheng k'ao* 荒政考 and the *K'ao-p'an yü-shih* 考槃餘事. All are extant.

T'u wrote with great spontaneity; there are anecdotes that describe the swiftness and ease with which he wrote verse. While this may have been a blessing, perhaps because of this, his works contain little of enduring interest. However, his writings are not without their peculiar attractions. Wang Shih-chen* (1526-1590) says that his poetry is strangely beautiful, with a leisurely loftiness.

T'u was not only a writer of *ch'uan-ch'i* plays but also an accomplished performer. We are informed that whenever he went to the theater, he mingled with the actors and joined in the performance. On one occasion, he demonstrated his virtuosity on the drum.

T'u's dramas are as spontaneous as his verse and prose but are crudely structured. The *T'an-hua chi* is a long piece about Mu Ch'ing-t'ai 木淸泰 of the T'ang. Mu had won military merit and had been awarded the title Prince of Hsing-ting 興定. A Buddhist monk and a Taoist priest persuade him to embark on a journey seeking the Way, on which he passes through various kinds of temptation before finally attaining enlightenment. This drama, written in T'u's late years, bears witness to his inclination toward Taoist speculation. The drama contains too many episodes. Lü T'ien-ch'eng's 呂天成 *Ch'ü-p'in* 曲品, while praising the drama for the fluency and beauty of its diction, points out the structural defects. The *T'an-hua chi* has another peculiarity (noted by Tsang Chin-shu 臧晉叔 in his preface to the *Yüan ch'ü hsüan* 元曲選): on occasion not a single song can be found within an act. The drama attempts to present more of the story than the genre can accommodate. The result is an overdependence on dialogue, a paucity of songs, and a badly marred play. T'u's other two dramas are the *Ts'ai-hao chi*, which relates the events surrounding Li Po's sojourn at Emperor Hsüan-tsung's 玄宗 court (T'u probably intends here to compare himself to Li Po) and the *Hsiu-wen chi*, which focuses on the T'ang poet Li Ho.*

T'u's dramas represent the culmination of a trend to lay emphasis on flowery diction, which had its origin in Shao Ts'an's 邵璨 *Hsiang-nang chi* 香囊記. Hsü Lin 徐麟, in his preface to Hung Sheng's 洪昇 *Ch'ang-sheng tien* 長生殿, remarks of Tu's *Ts'ai-hao chi* that its diction is laden with "emeralds and gold, and that not a single phrase in simple and plain language can be found in the entire work."

EDITIONS:

Hsiu-wen chi. (1) *Ch'uan-ch'i san-chung* 傳奇三種. Shanghai, 1932; a photolithographic reprint of the Wan-li 萬歷 edition. (2) *Ku-pen*, I, no. 73; a photolithographic reprint of the Wan-li edition.

T'an-hua chi. (1) Mao Chin, *hai chi* 亥集. (2) *Ku-pen*, I, no. 72; a photolithographic reprint of the T'ien-hui lou 天繪樓 edition printed during the Wan-li period.

Ts'ao-hao chi. (1) Mao Chin, *ch'en chi* 辰集. (2) *Ku-pen*, I, no. 71; a photolithographic reprint of Mao Chin's edition.

STUDIES:

Aoki, *Gikyokushi*, pp. 177-182.
Araki, Kengo 荒木見悟. "To Ryō to Kan Shidō" 屠隆と管志道, *Nihon Chūgoku Gakkai-hō*, 28 (1976), 187-199.
Chao, Ching-shen 趙景深. "T'u Lung te ch'uan-ch'i" 屠隆的傳奇, in his *Hsiao-shuo hsi-ch'ü hsin-k'ao* 小說戲曲新考, Shanghai, 1939, pp. 199-208.

—SSK

Tun-huang wen-hsüeh 敦煌文學 is a general term used to refer to manuscripts discovered at Tun-huang (modern Kansu) early in this century by the Taoist caretaker of the Mo-kao k'u 莫高窟 (None Higher Caves, also called Caves of the Thousand Buddhas). Tun-huang lies near the western extremity of the Great Wall and, during the T'ang and Five Dynasties periods, was situated at the confluence of Chinese civilization with Tibetan, Uighur, Sogdian, Khotanese, and other strongly Buddhicized cultures. This mixing of cultures is reflected in the languages of the manuscripts that were sealed up in a side-room of cave sixteen sometime around the year 1035. Successive expeditions from various nations visited Tun-huang and recovered an enormous number of manuscripts. In chronological order, these were led by Au-

rel Stein (England and India), Paul Pelliot (France), representatives of the Ch'ing government, Ōtani Kōzui (Japan), and Sergei F. Oldenburg (Russia). Some manuscripts also found their way to collections in the United States, Denmark, Taiwan, and elsewhere. Altogether, the Chinese manuscripts alone total over 30,000 and constitute a rich resource for the study of Chinese society, history, thought, religion, language, and literature. Fortunately, nearly all of this material has now been made available to scholars, either in the form of microfilm copies or as photographic reproductions and published texts.

Although the bulk of the Chinese materials are copies of canonical Buddhist texts written for members of the religious establishment, there are also a significant number of writings intended for laymen. These are particularly important for students of popular literature, for among them are the earliest examples of extended prosimetrical (chantefable) narrative and the forerunners of *tz'u*,* all of which are unprecedentedly written in a colloquial language.

Perhaps the single most noteworthy genre to emerge from the study of the Tun-huang manuscripts has been *pien-wen* 變文. This designation may be rendered in English as "transformation text" and is intimately related to pictures that were known as *pien-hsiang* 變相 (transformation tableaux). Indeed, it may be demonstrated that *pien-wen* was a type of storytelling with pictures and that its origins can be traced through Central Asia to India.

The subjects of *pien-wen* may be either secular or religious. There are *pien-wen* about the Han generals Wang Ling 王陵 and Li Ling 李陵, about the Han heroine Wang Chao-chün 王昭君, and about the local Tun-huang heroes, Chang I-ch'ao 張義潮 and Chang Huai-shen 張淮深. Among the most celebrated religious stories are the *Ta Mu-ch'ien-lien ming-chien chiu mu pien-wen* 大目乾連冥間救母變文, which tells of Mahāmaudgalyāyana's search for his mother in hell, and the *Hsiang mo pien-wen* 降魔變文, which describes Śāriputra's exciting magic contest with the six heretics. There is also among the Tun-huang manuscripts a uniquely precious illustrated scroll (P4524) which closely matches the *pien-wen* version of the latter story. All of the above-mentioned stories are genuine *pien-wen* written in the prosimetric form and characterized by a distinctive formula ("the place [where] X [happens]; how does it go?) that occurs just before the verse portions.

One of the most intriguing problems about *pien-wen* is how they came to be written down and by whom. Clearly they have an intimate connection to an eighth- and ninth-century storytelling tradition known as *chuan-pien* 轉變 (turning transformation [scrolls]). The best information now available indicates that the performers of these transformations were professional entertainers and that individuals who became enamored of their performances transcribed them as *pien-wen* so that they might have a more permanent record. The copyists of the extant manuscripts were mostly lay students studying a largely secular curriculum in schools attached to Buddhist monasteries.

Other types of popular narrative were also discovered at Tun-huang. Some, like the stories of Wu Tzu-hsü 伍子胥 and Meng Chiang-nü 孟姜女, both legendary figures from pre-Han times, resemble *pien-wen* in certain respects, but seem less likely to have been the immediate products of an oral tradition. Others, such as the story of Chi Pu's 季布 cursing the Han king in front of his assembled troops and Tung Yung's 董永 reward for filial devotion, consist entirely of heptasyllabic verse. Still others, including the accounts of the youthful Shun's 舜 extreme filial piety and Ch'iu Hu's 秋胡 disloyalty to his wife, are, except for an occasional quoted poem, composed exclusively of prose.

Apart from *pien-wen*, genres of popular literature that are identified by specific designations in the titles of recovered Tun-huang manuscripts include *fu*,* *lun* 論 (discussion), *tsan* 讚 (eulogy), *ya-tso wen* 押座文 (seat-settling text or introit), *yüan-ch'i* 緣起 (legend, Sanskrit *pratītyasamutpāda*), and *chiang-ching wen* 講經文 (sutra lectures).

Chiang-ching wen were part of religious services for laymen known as *su-chiang* 俗講. In contrast to *pien-wen*, they were delivered by ordained Buddhist monks, were systematic expositions of sūtras, and were marked by a recurring formula containing the word *ch'ang* 唱 functioning in the optative or imperative mood. The best-known and lengthiest *chiang-ching wen* is the group of texts dealing with the *Vimalakīrti-nir-deśa-sūtra* 維摩詰所說經.

The Tun-huang manuscripts have also yielded various types of verse, including poems and ballads in the *shih** form, and most notably the words of popular songs of the period. These songs are referred to interchangeably in the manuscripts as *ch'ü*,* *tz'u*,* and *ch'ü-tzu tz'u* 曲子詞 (lyrics of songs). Virtually every verse is identified by a tune title, which indicates musical origins, although the music has been lost.

These songs provide valuable evidence of the early stages of the development of the *tz'u* form, showing that the genre had widespread circulation among a popular audience during the eighth century and perhaps even before. Although most of the songs are anonymous, some are closely related to *tz'u* poems written by members of the literate elite; two are attributable to Emperor Chao-tsung (r. 888-904), one to Wen T'ing-yün,* and two more to Ou-yang Chiung.* Many of the Tun-huang *ch'ü-tzu tz'u* arise out of the dynamic interaction between popular and elite cultures at the end of the T'ang dynasty.

Nevertheless, the majority of the *tz'u* songs bear characteristics of folk songs, including colloquialisms, dialogue, formulaic phrases, sequential narrative, direct expression of emotion, and abrupt, fragmented structure. Moreover, unlike early literati *tz'u*, which are devoted to the theme of unrequited love, the Tun-huang poems exhibit a wide variety of subject matter, including songs of soldiers, recluses, students, and traveling merchants, as well as many Buddhist songs.

Jen Erh-pei's edition divides the *tz'u* into three categories: a handful of *ta-ch'ü*,* suites of songs and dances with instrumental interludes; eighteen *ting-ko lien-chang* 定格聯章 (song sequences in fixed form), cycles of from 5 to 134 stanzas linked to form a set or series of songs on a fixed chronological topic such as the five watches of the night, the one hundred years of an individual's life, or the twelve months of the year, mostly on Buddhist themes such as "The Twelve Hours of Meditation"; about two hundred *p'u-t'ung tsa-ch'ü* 普通雜曲 (miscellaneous common songs), independent stanzas, mostly on secular themes. The majority of these latter, isolated, secular lyrics treat the theme of love and exerted significant influence on late T'ang literati *tz'u* such as those collected in the *Hua-chien chi.**

The discovery of the Tun-huang manuscripts has provided scholars with an incomparable fund of primary materials for the study of the popular literature of the T'ang and Five Dynasties periods. At the same time, these materials have also had far-reaching significance for the study of Chinese popular literature in general. Because of them, many questions relating to the origins of lyric meters, extended narrative, episodic construction, dramatic plot, prosimetric form, and written colloquial language have been enunciated and partially answered.

EDITIONS:

Chou, Shao-liang 周紹良. *Tun-huang pien-wen hui-lu* 敦煌變文彙錄. Shanghai, 1955.

Jen, Erh-pei 任二北. *Tun-huang ch'ü chiao-lu* 敦煌曲校錄. Shanghai, 1955.

Shang-wu yin-shu-kuan 商務印書館, ed. *Tun-huang i-shu tsung-mu so-yin* 敦煌遺書總目索引. Peking, 1983.

Wang, Chung-min 王重民. *Tun-huang ch'ü-tzu-tz'u chi* 敦煌曲子詞集. Rev. ed. Shanghai, 1956.

———, et al. *Tun-huang pien-wen chi* 敦煌變文集. Peking, 1957.

CATALOGUES:

Bibliothèque Nationale, Départment des Manuscrits. *Catalogue des Manuscrits Chinois de Touen-houang*, I. Paris, 1970.

Giles, Lionel. *Descriptive Catalogue of the Chinese Manuscripts from Tunhuang in the British Museum.* London, 1957.

Kanaoka, Shōkō. *Tonkō shutsudo kanbun bungaku bunken bunrui mokuroku fu kaisetsu* 敦煌出土漢文學文獻分類目錄附解說. Tokyo, 1971.

TRANSLATIONS:

Chen, Tsu-lung. "Note on Wang Fu's 'Ch'a Chiu Lun' 茶酒論," *Sinologica*, 11 (1961), 271-287.

Eoyang, Eugene. "The Great Maudgalyayana Rescues his Mother from Hell," in Ma and Lau, *Traditional Chinese Stories*, pp. 443-455.

Iriya, Yoshitaka 入矢義高. *Bukkyō bungaku shū* 佛教文學集. Tokyo, 1975.

Jao, Tsong-yi, and Paul Demiéville. *Airs de Touen-houang: Touen-houang k'iu. Textes a chanter des VIIIe-Xe siècles.* Paris, 1971.

Waley, Arthur. *Ballads and Stories from Tunhuang: An Anthology.* New York, 1960.

STUDIES:

Chang, Kang-i Sun. *The Evolution of Chinese Tz'u Poetry: From Late T'ang to Northern Sung.* Princeton: Princeton University Press, 1980.

Chen, Shih-chuan. "Dates of Some of the Tunhuang Lyrics," *JAOS*, 88 (1968), 261-270.

———. "The Rise of the *Tz'u*, Reconsidered," *JAOS*, 90 (1970), 232-242.

Cheung, Samuel Hung-nin. "The Use of Verse in the Dun-huang bian-wen," *JCL*, 8.1 (January 1980), 149-162.

Chiang, Li-hung 蔣禮鴻. *Tun-huang pien-wen tzu-i t'ung-shih* 敦煌變文字義通釋. Rev. and enlarged ed. Peking, 1962.

Demiéville, Paul. *Récents travaux sur Touen-Houang, apercu bibliographique et notes critiques.* Leiden, 1970.

Eoyang, Eugene C. "The Historical Context for the Tun-huang pien-wen," *LEW*, 15.3 (1971), 339-357.

———. "Word of Mouth: Oral Storytelling in the *Pien-wen*." Unpublished Ph.D. dissertation, Indiana University, 1971.

Fujieda, Akira. "The Tun-huang Manuscripts," in *Essays on the Sources for Chinese History*, Donald Leslie, Colin Mackerras, and Wang Gungwu, eds. Columbia, South Carolina, 1973, pp. 120-128.

———. "The Tunhuang Manuscripts—A General Description," parts 1 and 2, *Zinbun*, 9 (1966), 1-32, and 10 (1969), 17-39.

Giles, Lionel. *Six Centuries at Tunhuang, A Short Account of the Stein Collection of Chinese Mss. in the British Museum.* London, 1944.

Jen, Erh-pei. *Tun-huang ch'ü ch'u-t'an* 敦煌曲初探. Shanghai, 1954.

Johnson, David. "The Wu Tzu-hsü *Pien-wen* and its Sources: Part I," *HJAS*, 40 (1980), 93-156; "Part II," *HJAS*, 40 (1980), 465-505.

Kanaoka, Shōkō 金岡照光. *Tonkō no bungaku* 敦煌の文學. Tokyo, 1971.

Kanda, Kiichirō 神田喜一郎. *Tonkō gaku gojūnen* 敦煌學五十年. Tokyo, 1960.

Kōza Tonkō 講座敦煌. Tokyo, 1980-1982. A series of lectures by eminent Japanese scholars in 13 vols.

Lin, Mei-i 林玫儀. "Lun Tun-huang ch'ü te she-hui hsing" 論敦煌曲的社會性, *Wen-hsüeh p'ing-lun*, 2 (1976), 107-144.

Ma, Shih-ch'ang 馬世長. "Kuan-yü Tun-huang ts'ang-ching tung te chi-ko wen-t'i" 關于敦煌藏經洞的幾個問題, *Wen-wu*, 1978.12, 21-33.

Mair, Victor. "Lay Students and the Making of Vernacular Narrative: An Inventory of Tun-huang Manuscripts," *CHINOPERL*, 10 (1981), 5-96.

Men'shikov, Lev Nikolaevich, *et al. Opisanie Kitaiskikh Rukopisei*, 2v. Moscow, 1963-1967.

Strassberg, Richard E. "Buddhist Storytelling Texts from Tunhuang," *CHINOPERL*, 8 (1978), 39-991.

—VHM and MWe

Tung-ching meng Hua lu 東京夢華錄 (The Eastern Capital: A Dream of Splendors Past), written by Meng Yüan-lao 孟元老 (*fl.* 1110-1160) in 1147, is a reminiscence of the Eastern Capital of the Sung dynasty (then known as Pien-liang 汴梁, modern Kaifeng). The text relates life during the last years of the reign of Emperor Hui-tsung (1119-1126), when the material and cultural life of the citizens there was at its height. Over the years, this work has been used extensively in academic discussions of the literature, art, architecture, history, and economics of the Northern Sung.

The journal is divided, in its modern edition, into ten chapters (*chüan*). Chapter arrangement has little to do with theme, and the work itself is composed of two major sections: the first is a synchronic description of everyday life in the capital, and the second is a chronological treatment of the major festivals and rituals of the civil year, beginning with New Year's Day and ending with New Year's Eve.

The first section begins with a description of the physical layout of the city, starting with the walls and gates, rivers and canals, palace grounds, and the various civil and military offices that lie within the For-bidden City (chapter 1). It then moves on to describe major streets, various official bureaus of the central imperial and city governments, and the wards of the city itself. It treats tea districts, markets, wine lofts, and their assorted fare site by site, hinting indirectly at the localized nature of commerce and industrial activity in the city (chapter 2). The next section includes descriptions of wards set aside for trade and bartering as well as discussion of the major religious temples, shops, hired labor, food transport, fire prevention, money and script, and early morning markets (chapter 3).

The vehicles of the concubines and empresses, the imperial guard, and the more mundane activites of the city—butchering, wine provendering, restaurants (including names and locations of famous inns), and fish-mongering are covered in the fourth chapter. The final chapter of the first section lingers over local customs, entertainments and performing skills of the capital "pleasure precincts," marriage and betrothal customs, and pregnancy and childbirth practices.

The next portion of the work is a chronological list of the major festivals and rituals that occur from the lunar New Year until the end of the twelfth civil month. Chapter 6 describes the customs and rites of the first sixteen days of the New Year, the most important of Chinese festivals. This touches not only on the role of these festivals in the life of the common citizen, but also relates an account of the imperial feast for foreign envoys, and describes the imperial visits to local temples where elaborate feasts were spread for civil officers.

Chapter 7 details the emperor's visit to the Garden of Jasper Trees and the Reservoir of Metal Luster to view the naval and cavalry exercises and entertainments that were put on annually in the third month. These performances were open to the public, and the citizens sallied through the parklands and bowers of the Garden and Reservoir. Here they gambled, ambled, fished, and viewed the theater. This chapter also relates the customs of the Clear and Bright Festival and other spring revels, including gathering herbs in the parks that lay outside the city itself.

The next section (chapter 8) covers the festivals of the fourth through the ninth lunar months, giving detailed accounts of the entertainments, foodstuffs, clothing, and customs associated with each. Chapter 9 is mainly given over to a long and elaborate description of the ceremony of the Emperor's birthday, complete with a menu and theatrical bill. The final chapter relates the customs of the winter festivals of the twelfth month, including the Great Exorcism rite at court and lesser but equally important exorcism rituals in the houses of commoners. The parade of war chariots and elephants through the streets of the capital, the imperial review of the Palace Guard, the ceremony of pardoning criminals, and a description of the suburban sacrifice to Heaven, the most important of all court rituals, fill out the final parts of the text.

This brief thematic description fails to do justice to the complexity of the material presented in this rather short work. It is notable as the progenitor of later works on Chinese capitals and cities, and for its use of a rough-hewn style that mixes poorly written (by literati standards) classical Chinese with street-slang and occasional vernacular passages. It remains the most important source for early theater and narrative, and also provides a rich and varied picture of the life of a Sung urbanite.

Meng-liang lu 夢梁錄 (Record of the Millet Dream) by Wu Tzu-mu 吳自枚 (*fl.* 1300) is a work in 20 *chüan* often compared to the *Tung-ching meng Hua lu*. Little is known of the compiler, a native of Ch'ien-t'ang (near Lin-an). This work also records the customs, products, architecture, etc., of a capital city, in this case Lin-an 臨安 (modern Hangchow), the capital of the Southern Sung. Also included is a section on storytelling that is an important source for the history of fiction.

Tu-ch'eng chi-sheng 都城紀勝 (A Record of the Splendors of the Capital City), compiled by Kuan-yüan Nai-te-weng 管園乃德翁 (The Patient Gaffer who Waters His Garden—other than this sobriquet it is only known that his surname was Chao), was written in conscious imitation of the *Tung-ching meng Hua lu*. It depicts Lin-an, its shops, guilds, markets, parks, inns, and entertainers in fourteen sections. It is valued as a literary source on the development of prosimetric literature.

Two other works on Lin-an which are often associated with the *Tung-ching meng Hua lu* (included with it in one of the modern editions [Shanghai, 1956], for example) are the *Hsi-hu Lao-jen fan-sheng-lu* 西湖老人繁盛錄 (The Old Man of West Lake's Record of the Multitudinous Splendors) by Hsi-hu Lao-jen (The Old Man of West Lake, pseud.), marked by regional and colloquial language of *c.* 1250 and the *Wu-lin chiu-shih* (see Chou Mi).

EDITIONS:

Tung-ching meng Hua lu. Seikaido edition 靜嘉堂. The early extant edition, cut during the Yüan, and not printed until the early Ming (it is printed on waste paper from the Ming National University [*Kuo-tzu-chien*]). This edition carries a colophon by a certain Chao Shih-hsia, who published the work in 1187. Other editions from the Ming and Ch'ing dynasties are primarily recuttings of this Ur-text. For a general discussion see Balazs and Nakazawa below.

Tung-ching meng Hua lu chu 東京夢華錄注. Teng Chih-ch'eng 鄧之誠, comm. Peking, 1957. This is the most useful text.

Tung-ching meng Hua lu; Wai ssu-chung 東京夢華錄外四種. Shanghai, 1956. It was revised first in 1957, then in 1963, when several errors that were due to poor collating were corrected (without, however, mentioning them in the preface). Huang, P'ei-lieh's 黃丕烈 (1763-1825) colophons to the various editions that passed through his hands are appended (pp. 63-64, 67-69).

TRANSLATIONS:

While there are no complete translations, the following works contain partial renderings:

Idema and West. *Chinese Theater*, pp. 1-100 and passim.

Muramatsu, Kazuya 村松一彌, in *Kiroku bungakushū* 記錄文學集. *Chūgoku koten bungahu taikei* 中國古典文學大系, v. 56. Tokyo, 1970, pp. 18-45.

Whitfield, Roderick, "Chang Tse-tuan's *Ch'ing-ming shang-ho t'u*." Unpublished Ph.D. dissertation, Princeton University, 1965.

STUDIES:

Iriya, Yoshitaka 入矢高義. "*Tōkei mukaroku no bunshō*" 東京夢華錄の文章, *Tōhōgakuhō*, 20 (1951), 135-152.

Kan, Han-ch'üan 甘漢銓. "*Tung-ching meng Hua lu* chung te yin-shih wen-t'i chi ch'i tz'u-hui" 東京夢華錄中的飲食問題及其詞彙. Unpublished M.A. thesis, Tunghai University, Taichung, 1976.

K'ung, Hsien-i 孔憲易. "Meng Yuan-lao ch'i jen" 孟元老其人, *Li-shih yen-chiu*, 4 (1980), 143-148.

———. "Tu *Tung-ching meng Hua lu chu* hsiao-i" 讀東京夢華錄注小議, *Hsüeh-lin man-t'an*, 4 (Peking, 1981), 119-123.

Nakazawa, Kikuya 長澤規矩也. "Tōkei mukaroku shō honkō" 東京夢華錄諸本考, *Shōshigaki*, 17.1 (1941), 1-6.

Sung Bibliography, pp. 150-152. Gives good citations of editions.

Umeharu, Kaoru 栂原郁. *Tōka makaraku Muryōroku nado goi sakuin* 東京夢華錄夢梁錄等語彙索引. Kyoto, 1979.

—sw

Tung Chung-shu 董仲舒 (*c*. 179-*c*. 104 B.C.) was a native of Kuang-chuan 廣川 (modern Hopei). His achievement in officialdom was not as great as his enormous fame would suggest. His most noteworthy official accomplishment was apparently the presentation of the three memorials to Emperor Wu. These pieces discussed the mutual activation of Heaven and man and the political utilization of such a principle, advocating the establishment of Confucianism as the official ideology. But these petitions did not earn him an important official position. He served as prime minister in two princedoms, then spent ten years teaching the *Kung-yang chuan* (see *ching*), finally retiring in 121 B.C. Thereafter he devoted himself entirely to studying and writing. But whenever the court had important decisions to make, officials would be sent to ask for advice from him. Some of these responses have been collected by Chang T'ang 張湯 (d. 115 B.C.) as the *Ch'un-ch'iu chüeh-yü* 春秋決獄 (Deciding Court Cases According to the *Spring and Autumn Annals*). Tung also continued to petition the court: just before his death he presented a memorial to Emperor Wu objecting to the state monopolies of salt and iron. The response he earned is reflected in the story that once when Emperor Wu rode past Tung's tomb (in the western suburb of Ch'ang-an), he dismounted and saluted Tung. The tomb thus came to be known as Hsia-ma ling 下馬陵 (Dismounting-the-Horse Tumulus).

Tung is chiefly remembered as a Confucian scholar, the supreme exponent of the New Text exegetic school of the Classics (in particular, of the *Ch'un-ch'iu*—see *ching*). It is generally believed that a history of literature can dispense with his name. To be sure, Tung was neither a belletrist nor a literary theorist. Among his extant works only the "Shih pu-yü fu" 士不遇賦 (Prose-poem on Neglected Men of Worth) can be regarded as a piece of literary writing and its authenticity is questionable. The bulk of his surviving corpus, collected in the *Ch'un-ch'iu fan-lu* 春秋繁露 (Luxuriant Dew of the Spring and Autumn Annals), consists of eighty-two essays essentially philosophical in character and political in intention. Since, in the Han dynasty, literature was considered to have important political functions, it follows that Tung's political philosophy had significant implications for Han and subsequent theories of literature.

In explicating the mutual interactions between Heaven and man in terms of *yin-yang* and the five agents, and in speaking of portents and the like, Tung's philosophy seems to lie outside the orthodox tradition of Confucianism. But Chu Hsi 朱熹 (1130-1200), the most orthodox of the Neo-Confucianists, claimed: "Among the Han scholars only Tung Chung-shu was pure; his learning was strictly orthodox . . ." (*Chu-tzu yü-lei* 朱子語類, *ch*. 137). Tung's philosophical doctrines can thus be said to embody the cardinal concepts of the orthodox Confucian theory of literature.

Tung Chung-shu was instrumental in making Confucianism the official ideology, and in so doing he also rendered the Confucian theory of literature the official doctrine. The classical expression of this theory can be found on the "Mao *Shih* hsü" 毛詩序 (Preface to the Mao Version of the *Shih-ching**), for which Tung Ching-shu's philosophy provided an elaborate metaphysical foundation.

Tung also elaborated the Confucian doctrine of *cheng-ming* 正名 (rectification of names). He held the view that there should be an exact correspondence between rectified language and reality, and he worked out this correspondence in the minutest detail—even down to the level of morphophonemics. For example, in a discussion of human nature (in "Shen-ch'a ming-hao" 深察名號 [The Profound Examination of Names and Appellations], chapter 35 of *Ch'un-ch'iu fan-lu*), he puts forward the premise that "nature" means what is inborn, and he develops this premise simply by taking the word *sheng* 生 (what is inborn) as a gloss for *hsing* 性 (nature). The concepts embodied in our language are thus expressive of some essential principles of reality, which in turn are the expressions of the Will of Heaven. Linguistic concepts as such are not merely arbitrary differentiations within a closed conventional system, as a de Saussurean structuralist would assert. Instead, those concepts—or rather, the principles that they represent—exist independently of the consciousness and will of the language users. Those ideas are revealed when, upon "profound examination," they are perceived "clearly and distinctly." According to Tung, however, common people are simply blind to them. It is only the sage who can perceive them and have a true understanding of the world (or the Will of Heaven). But in speaking of the Will of Heaven Tung's philosophy is not essentially theological in character despite claims of many scholars in Mainland China. Tung's teleological interpretation of nature culminates in the notion that nothing other than the existence of man *as a moral agent* can be regarded as having "worth" in which the supposed purposiveness of the universe must finally reside. In Tung's speculative image man stands between Heaven above and Earth below, and his supreme goodness consists in his actively participating in the perpetual creative transformation of Heaven and Earth. And though the common people are unable to perceive the "ideas," they are not incapable of becoming good: they can be led to become so, through education. (Tung's concept of human nature is subtle: he agreed with Mencius' doctrine that human nature is good, but maintained that the incipient substance of goodness in human nature—reminiscent of Mencius' *Ssu-tuan* 四端 [Four Beginnings]—is brought to fruition through education. It is the duty of the sage to educate the common people.)

Since only the sage has the ability to perceive the "ideas" clearly and distinctly, in the use of language ordinary people should look to the sage for guidance. And since linguistic concepts express essential truths about the world, the sage is very careful in instituting the correct use of language; the exemplary case is Confucius's rectification of names. Furthermore, the results of such rectification and institutionalization are to be embodied in some paradigmatic generic types, namely, the Classics, of which the *Ch'un-ch'iu* (traditionally attributed to Confucius) is the supreme exemplar. Fundamentally, the use of language is aimed at achieving a correct understanding of the Way—that is, to apprehend the place of man between Heaven and Earth and thus to participate in the creative transformation of the world, so as to attain the highest goodness. Therefore, the use of language should always have as its major premise the illumination of the Way. These three cardinal concepts of the orthodox Confucian theory of literature: *ming-tao* 明道 (to illuminate the Way), *cheng-sheng* 徵聖 (to look to the sage for guidance), and *tsung-ching* 宗經 (to orginate from the Classics), were later to find expression in the literary theory of Yang Hsiung,* in the *Wen-hsin tiao-lung** (where these notions are expounded systematically in the first three chapters), in *ku-wen** theories, and in Tseng Kuo-fan's* attempt to trace the origins of the major literary genres to the Classics in his *Ching-shih pai-chia tsa-ch'ao* 經史百家雜鈔 .

As noted above, Tung Chung-shu's philosophy provided a metaphysical basis for the Han Confucianists' contention of the educational and the political functions of literature as expressed in the "Mao *Shih* hsü." In according man an important position and in assigning a significant role to the creative agency of man, Tung's philosophy also provided a metaphysical foundation for the view that literature is a monumental enterprise, having the power to "activate Heaven and Earth, and move the spirits" ("Mao *Shih* hsü").

It also has significant implications for the technical details of literary composition. In the "Shen-ch'a ming-hao," for instance, he refers to an example expounded in the *Kung-yang chuan* 公羊傳 (see *ching*) to illustrate that in writing, it is of the utmost importance to arrange the words in the right order. In the *Ch'un-chiu* it is recorded that in the sixteenth year of Duke Hsi (642 B.C.) five meteorites fell in the state of Sung and six fishhawks flew backward over the Sung capital. In describing the event of falling meteorites the number "five" is mentioned last whereas in the case of flying fishhawks the number "six" is mentioned first. The *Kung-yang Commentary* gives a detailed explanation for the word orders in both cases in terms of the natural sequence of observation and perception. This understanding will help in appreciating the spirit underlying the composition of the *fu*,* the most popular literary genre in Tung's time. When *fu* writers are engaged in what seems a luxuriant display of words, they are not merely concerned with the manipulation of language as such, but consider the language to be reflecting reality in every minute detail. Furthermore, as Pan Ku* points out in the preface to his "Liang-tu fu" 兩都賦, *fu* descended from ancient poetry and, like poetry, it has important educational and political functions. Based upon the metaphysical foundation provided by a philosophy like Tung Chung-shu's, the *fu* writers asserted that *fu*, like poetry, could "activate Heaven and Earth, and move the spirits."

EDITIONS:

Ch'un-ch'iu chüeh-yü 春秋決獄. *PPTSCC*, series 38a: *Ching-tien chi-lin* 經典集林, v. 2. Taipei, 1968.

Ch'un-ch'iu fan-lu. SPPY.

―――. SPTK.

―――. *Chen-pen, pieh-chi* 別輯 (Taipei, 1975), v. 46-47. *Ch'un-ch'iu fan-lu chu* 注. Ling Shu 凌曙 (1775-1829), comm., in *Huang-Ch'ing ching-chieh hsü-pien* 皇清經解續編, ch. 865-881, rpt. Taipei, 1962.

Ch'un-ch'iu fan-lu i-cheng 義證. Su Yü 蘇興, comm. Taipei, 1975. Facsimile reproduction of the 1910 ed. *Liu-ch'ao wen,* pp. 250-258.

Tung-tzu wen-chi 董子文集. *PPTSCC. Chi-fu ts'ung-shu* 畿輔叢書, v. 5. Taipei, 1966.

TRANSLATIONS:

Only a small portion of Tung Chung-shu's writings is available in translation. Partial translations of the *Ch'ung-ch'iu fan-lu* are in:

Chan, Wing-tsit. *A Source Book in Chinese Philosophy.* Princeton, 1963, pp. 271-288.

Hughes, E. R. *Chinese Philosophy in Classical Times,* London, 1954, pp. 293-308.

Sources of Chinese Tradition. William T. de Bary, *et al.,* New York, 1960, pp. 174-183 and 218-220. For translations of the *Ch'un-ch'iu fan-lu* in other languages and for translations of Tung's other writings, see the "Appendix" (pp. 267-268) in Pokora's study below.

STUDIES:

Chou, Fu-ch'eng 周輔成. *Lun Tung Chung-shu ssu-hsiang* 論董仲舒思想. Shanghai, 1962.

Ch'un-ch'iu fan-lu t'ung-chien 春秋繁露通檢 (Index du Tch'ouen ts'ieou fan lou). Chung-Fa Han-hsüeh yen-chiu-so 中法漢學研究所 (Centre franco-chinois d'études sinologiques), ed. Peking, 1944; rpt. Taipei, 1968.

Davidson, Steven Craig. "Tung Chung-shu and the Origins of Imperial Confucianism." Unpublished Ph.D dissertation, University of Wisconsin-Madison, 1982.

Fung, Yu-lan. "Tung Chung-shu and the New Text School," in Fung's *History of Chinese Philosophy,* trans. Derk Bodde, Princeton, 1953, v. 2, pp. 7-87.

Malmqvist, Göran. *Han Phonology and Textual Criticism.* Canberra, 1963.

Pokara, Timoteus. "Notes on New Studies on Tung Ching-shu," *ArO,* 33 (1965), 256-271. Review of Chou's study above, with rich bibliography.

Yao, Shan-yu. "The Cosmological and Anthropological Philosophy of Tung Chung-shu," *JNCBRAS,* 73 (1948), 40-68.

―TP and SSK

Tung Jung 董榕 (*tzu*, Heng-yen 恆岩, *hao*, Fan-lu chü-shih 繁露居土, 1711-1760) was a native of Feng-jun 豐潤 (Hopei). He obtained a *kung-shih* degree around 1735 and served with distinction as prefect in several posts in south-central China. Among his friends were the dramatists Chiang Shih-ch'üan* and T'ang Ying,* both of whom penned comments to his *ch'uan-ch'i* play, *Chih-k'an chi* 芝龕記 (The Fungus Shrine). He ended his life by suicide when his mother died.

Chih-k'an chi is in six chapters and sixty acts. It is based on the story of two female generals of the late Ming, Ch'in Yü-liang 秦良玉 and Shen Yün-ying 沈雲英. Ch'in Yü-liang received the same training, both literary and unliterary, as her brothers, and she eventually married Ma Ch'ien-ch'eng 馬千乘, a native chieftain of Szechuan who held a hereditary rank as Military Governor. Ma was falsely accused of treason by court eunuchs and thrown in prison, where he died. Ch'in Yü-liang took up his post and won high merit in the last years of the Ming. She became a high military officer and worked together with another female general of Tao-chou 道州, Shen Yün-ying. Shen's father was the commander of Tao-chou, where he was killed by peasant rebels. Yün-ying then took up arms against the rebels. She defeated them and recovered her father's corpse. Because of her merit, she was awarded the position of general.

The fifty-fifth act, "K'an szu" 龕祀, is the climax of the drama. It tells of Ch'in Liang-yü's visit to Shen Yün-ying at Tao-chou. When they met at a local temple a divine fungus (*ling-chih* 靈芝) sprouted in a grove of bamboo. The generals gathered some of the plant and made two niches, side by side. Into these niches they put the tablets of members of their families who had died in the chaos of the time. This incident supplies the drama its title. The play has been criticized for its random and episodic nature.

EDITIONS:

Two editions of *Chih k'an-chu* are extant: a woodblock edition (1757) and a recut (1889) of the same edition. There is a preface to the 1257 edition by Chiang Shih-ch'üan, dated 1752, and an epigraph by Po Ch'ao 柏超, also dated 1752.

STUDIES:

Aoki, *Gikyokushi*, Chapter 11, section 2.

Yang, En-shou 楊恩壽. *Tz'u-yü ts'ung-hua* 詞餘叢話. *PPTSCC.*

—XLW

T'ung-ch'eng p'ai 桐城派 (T'ung-ch'eng School) derived its name from the hometown of the three leading essayists of the school, Fang Pao,* Liu Ta-k'uei 劉大櫆 (1698-1780), and Yao Nai (see *Ku-wen-tz'u lei-tsuan*)—T'ung-ch'eng (Anhwei). Of the three, Fang Pao has been regarded as the pioneer and Yao Nai the founder of the school, with Liu Ta-k'uei as a transitional figure.

Fang Pao distinguished himself early in life as a prose writer and as a scholar. He ranked first in the provincial (Kiangnan) *chü-jen* examination in 1699 and became a *chin-shih* in 1706. In 1711, however, because of his involvement in a serious case of literary inquisition regarding the writings of Tai Ming-shih 戴名世 (1653-1713), a renowned scholar also from T'ung-ch'eng, he was first imprisoned and then sentenced to serve as a nominal slave to bannermen in Peking until an imperial pardon in 1723. Afterwards, he was appointed to a variety of central government posts rising eventually to the position of Vice Minister of Rites in 1738. But throughout his bureaucratic career his actual work was almost entirely scholarly in nature. He was in charge of several imperial editorial projects including an anthology of *pa-ku wen** examination essays and a compilation of the commentaries to the *San Li* 三禮 (Three Ritual Works—see *ching*). As a classical scholar he has been particularly known for his view that the *Chou li* 周禮 is actually a later forgery—a view that exerted a considerable influence on the Modern Text Classical School of the late Ch'ing period. As a precursor of the T'ung-ch'eng School, however, Fang's most important contributions were the development of a literary theory known as *I-fa* 義法 and the compilation of an anthology of writings exemplifying it.

I-fa is a term traceable to Ssu-ma Ch'ien.* It refers to both the substance (*i*) and the form (*fa*) of literary art. In Fang's view no prose was worthy of the name of *ku-wen** if it did not successfully bring substance and form into a harmonious union. The substance is the Confucian *Tao* 道 (or Way) as transmitted through the Ch'eng-Chu 程朱 School of Neo-Confucianism; the form is essentially exemplified in the styles of such classical writers as Ssu-ma Ch'ien,* the works of the eight writers who are collectively known as the *T'ang Sung pa-ta chia* (see Han Yü), and Kuei Yu-kuang.* By identifying *i* with *Tao*, however, Fang did not mean that the substance of prose must be moral and didactic in nature. Rather the ideas and feelings a writer expresses in his work, whatever its subject matter, must not go contrary to the Confucian (and Neo-Confucian) moral principles. Substance and form are ultimately inseparable and, ideally, they ought to grow together in an organic relationship. In this way he went beyond the orthodox Neo-Confucian view of the function of literature. Literature is not merely a vehicle of the Way; in its highest form it is the Way.

Fang provided classic examples of *ku-wen* prose for students to follow in *Ku-wen yüeh-hsüan* 古文約選 (A Concise Anthology of Ancient-style Prose, 1733). His selections range from early historical writings to the masterpieces of T'ang and Sung prose. In his preface to the anthology and elsewhere he stated that a student might readily discover for himself what the *I-fa* really consists of by studying these examples. This anthology exerted a considerable influence on the subsequent development of the T'ung-ch'eng School.

Liu Ta-k'uei failed twice in the provincial examination and therefore remained a private scholar throughout his life. In 1726 he visited Fang Pao (in Peking), and Fang immediately recognized his unusual talent as a prose writer. It was through Fang Pao's unreserved praise that he became nationally famous. In addition to his achievement in prose writing, he also made theoretical contributions to the T'ung-ch'eng School. In his well-known work on

literary criticism, *Lun-wen ou-chi* 論文偶記 (Casual Notes on Literature), he distinguishes three dual components of literature, namely, *shen* 神 (spirit) and *ch'i* 氣 (vital force), *yin* 音 (intonation) and *chieh* 節 (rhythm), and *tzu* 字 (diction) and *chü* 句 (syntax). According to his analysis, spirit and vital force are the finest essences of literature, intonation and rhythm coarser elements, and diction and syntax the coarsest. However, he stresses that the study of literature must begin with the coarsest and end with the finest. In other words, only after diction and syntax are mastered can intonation and rhythm be grasped, and only when intonation and rhythm are grasped can a clear view of spirit and vital force be developed. It is interesting to note that Liu's literary theory moved in the direction of the theory of classical studies espoused by the *K'ao-cheng p'ai* 考證派 (School of Evidential Investigation) of his day. According to this school, philology must first be studied in order to understand a text, and only a full and sound understanding of a text can lead to a correct interpretation of the ideas of the sages. Liu accepted Fang Pao's theory in terms of *I-fa*, but his own emphasis was clearly placed more on *fa* than on *i*. His fundamental contribution to the T'ung-ch'eng School lay in the technical aspects of literary theory.

To Yao Nai, the last of the three giants, the T'ung-ch'eng School actually owed its *raison d'etre*. Had it not been for his influence, the whole group of prose writers from T'ung-ch'eng might never have been referred to as a school. In his youth Yao Nai studied under Liu Ta-k'uei and his learned uncle Yao Fan 姚範 (1702-1771), also regarded as a forerunner of the school. He became a *chü-jen* in 1750 and a *chin-shih* in 1763. After a decade in government service, he decided to devote his whole life to teaching and scholarship. During the next forty years (1776-1815) he headed various academies in Yangchow, Anking, and Nanking and therefore gathered many talented students who later promoted the principles of *ku-wen* prose-writing of the school. Among his leading disciples were Kuan T'ung 管同 (1780-1831), Mei Tseng-liang 梅曾亮 (1786-1856), and Fang Tung-shu 方東樹 (1772-1851).

While taking his *chin-shih* examinations in Peking in the mid-1750s, Yao Nai associated with prominent *k'ao-cheng* scholars such as Ch'ien Ta-hsin 錢大昕 (1728-1804) and Tai Chen 戴震 (1724-1777) and became fascinated with the new evidential scholarship. In 1755 he even formally requested that Tai Chen accept him as a student, a request which the latter politely declined. This interest in *k'ao-cheng* scholarship remained with him the rest of his life. It was he who publicized Tai Chen's three-way division of Confucian scholarship into philosophy (*i-li* 義理), philology (*k'ao-cheng*) and literature (*wen-chang* 文章). As a matter of fact, he reinterpreted Fang Pao's *I-fa* theory in the light of this new intellectual development. Instead of going into classical philology, however, he applied the *k'ao-cheng* method to the study of literary history. The result was his influential anthology, entitled *Ku-wen-tz'u lei-tsuan** in 75 *chüan* (1779). He distinguished in prose literature thirteen different forms and traced the evolution of each of them in the literary tradition. This historical approach is clearly in line with the evidential study of classical texts as carried out by Tai Chen and other classicists of his day.

In literary theory Yao Nai broadened the scope of Fang Pao's *I-fa* to its greatest extent. For Fang *I-fa* referred primarily to prose-writing; Yao Nai applied it to the entire realm of literary art including poetry. In a sense he may be said to have raised the idea of unity between *wen* and *Tao* to its theoretical level. Thus, just as the *Tao* consists of nothing but the *yin* and the *yang*, literature is also the manifestation of these two opposing (as well as complementary) forces. He therefore sees two contrasting types of beauty in literature: the masculinity of the *yang* and the femininity of the *yin*. The closest Western paired concepts are probably "the sublime" and "the graceful" or Hazlitt's masculine and effeminate styles. According to Yao, however, neither type can be found in its pure form. An actual work of literary art is always a mixture with an inclination either toward masculinity or toward femininity.

Yao Nai also developed Liu Ta-k'uei's technical theory of literature. In the preface to his *Ku-wen-tz'u lei-tsuan*, he identifies eight basic elements in literature: spirit, principles, vital force, flavor, formal style, rules, sound, and color. The former four are the essences of literature; the latter four are the coarse elements. But like Liu, he also holds the view that the coarse elements form a concrete base on which the spiritual essence of literature stands.

From the middle of the nineteenth to the early part of the twentieth century, the T'ung-ch'eng School dominated the Chinese literary world owing, to a large extent, to the popular influence of Tseng Kuo-fan,* who was a great admirer of Yao Nai. Since the T'ung-ch'eng style of prose-writing is essentially characterized by the elegance and the purity of its language, it served its purpose well as a vehicle for the expression of traditional ideas, feelings, and things. But its emphasis on elegance and purity inevitably restricts its usefulness as a medium for things new and modern. Both Liang Ch'i-ch'ao* and Chang Ping-lin* expressed their profound dissatisfaction with the T'ung-ch'eng prose style, and Yen Fu's* failure to use it as an effective vehicle for translation was emphatically pointed out by Hu Shih 胡適 as evidence that the classical prose was already a dead language by the end of the nineteenth century. During the May Fourth Movement, the T'ung-ch'eng School came under fierce attack. The radical iconoclast Ch'ien Hsüan-t'ung 錢玄同 (1887-1939) even dubbed it *T'ung-ch'eng miu-chung* 桐城謬種 (the bad seed of T'ung-ch'eng). At any rate, by the 1920s, the glory of the school had definitely faded.

EDITIONS:

Fang, Pao. *Fang Wang-hsi Hsien-sheng ch'üan-chi* 方望溪先生全集. *SPTK*.

Yao, Nai. *Hsi-pao Hsien ch'üan-chi*.

Liu, Ta-k'uei. *Lun-wen ou-chi* 論文偶記. Peking, 1959.

STUDIES:

Hu, Shih 胡適. "Wu-shih nien lai Chung-kuo chih wen-hsüeh," 五十年來中國之文學, in *Hu Shih wen-ts'un* 胡適文存, Second Series, Taipei, 1971, pp. 184-187.

Kuo, *P'i-p'ing shih*, pp. 627-676.

Liu, *Chinese Theories*, pp. 45-46 and 95-97.

T'ung-ch'eng p'ai yen-chiu lun-wen chi 桐城派研究論文集. An-hui Jen-min ch'u-pan she 安徽人民出版社 , ed. Hofei, 1963. A collection of articles dealing with various aspects of the T'ung-ch'eng School.

Yeh, Lung 葉龍, *T'ung-ch'eng P'ai wen-hsüeh shih*, 桐城派文學史. Hong Kong, 1975.

—YSY

T'ung-Kuang T'i 同光體 (T'ung-Kuang Style), a distinctive poetic style, flourished during the T'ung-chih 同治 (1862-1874) and Kuang-hsü 光緒 (1875-1908) periods of the Ch'ing dynasty. According to Ch'en Yen (1856-1937), a major poet of this style, this designation was first used by him in Peking around 1886 during a jocular conversation with another major figure in this style, Cheng Hsiao-hsü 鄭孝胥 (1860-1938). Poets who adhered to this style formed a school and maintained that the poetic styles of both the T'ang and Sung dynasties, rather than that of the T'ang alone, should serve as models for poetry. In particular, they praised certain poets who lived during the *san-yüan* 三元 (three-yüans), that is, the three reign periods of K'ai-yüan 開元 (713-741) and Yüan-ho 元和 (806-820) of the T'ang and Yüan-yu 元祐 (1086-1093) of the Sung. The poets who elicited this praise included Tu Fu* of the K'ai-yüan, Han Yü* of the Yüan-ho, and Huang T'ing-chien* of the Yüan-yu.

It has generally been recognized that the T'ung-Kuang Style emerged as a result of efforts by earlier poets, such as Tseng Kuo-fan,* Ho Shao-chi 何紹基 (1799-1873), Cheng Chen 鄭珍 (1806-1864), Wei Yüan 魏源 (1794-1856), and Mo Yu-chih 莫友芝 (1811-1871), to revive the Sung poetic style. Those participating in this revival of Sung style, sometimes called the *Sung-shih yün-tung* 宋詩運動 (Sung Poetry Movement), regarded Huang T'ing-chien as a major master and believed that his work exhibited significant connections with the works of the T'ang masters. This revival stood as a reaction against at least two schools of the earlier Ch'ing. The first of these, the "Shen-yün" 神韻, founded by Wang Shih-chen* (1634-1711), advocated the achievement of an intuitive apprehension of reality, intuitive artistry, and personal tone. The second, the "Hsing-ling" 性靈, represented by Yüan Mei,* gave the highest praise to the revelation of the poet's "native sensibility" and intended that poetry should serve as an expression of "personal nature" or of emotion. During this earlier Sung revival, China encountered severe internal and external crises, and poets such as Tseng Kuo-fan, Ho Shao-chi, and others came to believe that poetry should reflect the socio-political condition of the time. Modern critics have thus viewed the proponents of the Sung revival as overly intellectual or scholarly poets, as contrasted with the supposedly "pure poets" of the Shen-yün and Hsin-ling schools.

Poets who adhered to the T'ung-Kuang Style followed the beliefs of this earlier revival. However, despite their proclaimed desire to foster the imitation of both the T'ang and Sung styles, they chose to imitate only the Sung masters. Their work has generally been criticized as being archaic and overly formal in style, obscure in diction, and hence difficult to chant.

Most of the major T'ung-Kuang poets, including Ch'en Yen, Cheng Hsiao-hsü, Shen Tseng-chih 沈曾植 (1850-1922), and Ch'en San-li 陳三立 (1852-1937), survived until the 1920s and 1930s and thus experienced the 1911 revolution. They continued, even after the revolution, to believe in the imperial system and frequently expressed their loyalty to the fallen Ch'ing. Holding extremely conservative political views, they were attacked both by the revolutionary and the vernacular poets. Despite any possible artistic or political shortcomings of the T'ung-Kuang School, it exerted much influence, as it represented one of the dominating forces in Chinese poetry for at least three decades before the emergence of modern vernacular poetry in the 1920s.

EDITIONS:

Ch'en San-li's *San-yüan ching she shih chi* 散原
精舍詩集, Ch'en Yen's (ed.) *Chin-tai-shih-chao*
近代詩鈔, Cheng Hsiao-hsü's *Chin-tai-shih-chao*,
and Shen Tseng-chih's *Hai-jih-lou shih* 海日樓詩
are the representative works of this style; they
are available in a wide range of *ts'ung-shu* collections and modern reprints.

STUDIES:

Ch'en, Yen. *Shih-i-shih shih-hua* 石遺室詩話.
    Available in different editions.
Kuo, *Pi-ping shih*, pp. 345-353.
Kurata, Sadayoshi 倉田貞美. *Chūgoku kindai shi
    no kenkyū* 中國近代詩 の 研究. Tokyo, 1969.
Wang, I-t'ang 王揖堂. *Chin-ch'uan-shih-lou shih-
    hua* 今傳是樓詩話. Tientsin, 1933.

—AH

T'ung-su lei-shu 通俗類書, although part of
the *lei-shu** category, have been slighted
by both traditional and modern scholarship, and information on them is at best
perfunctory and sketchy. In the past they
served a clientele substantially different
from that catered to by the orthodox *lei-
shu;* their academic significance in modern
times is also accordingly different. The
golden period of the orthodox *lei-shu* was
during the T'ang and Sung, although a
few important collections like the *Yung-lo
ta-tien* (see *lei-shu*) were produced later. The
golden age of the *t'ung-su lei-shu*, however,
was the Ming period. Like their orthodox
counterparts, *t'ung-su lei-shu* are thematically organized selections of passages from
various sources. But they were intended
for mass consumption, and are less rigid
in form, less didactic in tone, and more
attentive to daily necessities. They were
more casually prepared and less lavishly
manufactured but contain numerous illustrations.

T'ung-su lei-shu* can be divided into seven
major groups: encyclopedic references,
examination guides, manuals of social
writing, handbooks of poetic quotations
and vocabulary, records of surnames and
names, collections of anecdotes and stories, and beginner texts. Orthodox *lei-shu*
could be similarly classified, because the
major distinction between the two is the
intended readership, rather than the nature and the function.

As reference works, orthodox *lei-shu*
have not been popular among *ts'ung-shu**
compilers. This accounts for their general
unavailability, particularly those that have
not been reprinted in modern times. *T'ung-
su lei-shu* are even rarer and are often accessible only to a fortunate few. In addition, casual publications without much attention given to copyright and related
matters, some *t'ung-su lei-shu* have a mind-
boggling range of versions: the researcher
may have to acquire them all to ensure a
full grasp of the material. One example is
Ch'en Yüan-ching's 陳元倩 *Shih-lin kuang-
chi* 事林廣記 (Grand Gleanings of Miscellaneous Matters), which represents the early
encyclopedic *t'ung-su lei-shu* of the Yüan
period; it has versions of 12, 20, 29, 35,
50, and 94 *chüan*, mostly in unique copies.
No orthodox *lei-shu* would impose a textual problem of this magnitude.

But those who manage to overcome this
difficulty will be richly rewarded. Neither
the *lei-shu* nor the *t'ung-su lei-shu* perform
the same functions they were intended to
perform in the past. *Lei-shu* are mainly used
for textual comparison and for reconstruction of lost texts; thus those produced after
the mid-Ming period, an era from which
more extensive and more reliable sources
are easily available, are of less value. The
most useful of the *t'ung-su lei-shu* are those
produced in the Ming period. A mass medium, they registered, frequently in both
words and pictures, various aspects of the
popular culture not normally recorded in
the literature of high culture. Thus they
are potentially important to the anthro-
pologist, the historian of science, the
scholar of material culture, the linguist, and
the historian of religions, although such
potentials have been only slightly recognized.

To the student of classical Chinese literature, they are of special value for studies of fiction and, to a smaller extent, of
drama. One case in point is *hua-pen** studies, where no research is complete without
reference to the versions in such *t'ung-su
lei-shu* as *Kuo-se t'ien-hsiang* 國色天香 (Celestial Beauties), *Wan-chih ch'ing-lin* 萬錦情林
(Myriad Brocades of the Sentimental For-

est), *Hsiu-ku ch'un-jung* 繡谷春容 (Spring in the Multi-colored Valley), and the three different versions of the *Yen-chü pi-chi* 燕居筆記 (Leisure Life Notes). Except for *Kuo-se t'ien-hsiang*, these works are only available in exceptionally rare, if not unique, copies, and less than a handful of scholars have been able to use them adequately.

There is only one handy collection of *t'ung-su lei-shu*, the *Wakokuhon ruisho shūsei* 和刻本類書集成 prepared by the well-known sinologist Nagasawa Kikuya 長澤規矩也 (1902-1980) in 1976. It includes twenty-one relatively rare *t'ung-su lei-shu* in Japanese printings.

STUDIES:

Otsuka, Hidetaka 大塚秀高. "Wahon to tsū ruisho: Sōdai shosetsu wahon e no apurōchi" 話本 と 通俗類書：宋代小說話本 へのアプローチ, *Nihon Chūgoku Gakkai hō*, 28 (October 1976), 141-156.

Sakai, Takeo 酒井忠夫. "Mindai no nichiyō ruisho to shomin kyōiku" 明代の日用類書と庶民教育, in *Chūgoku kinsei kyōikushi kenkyū: Sono bunkyō seisaku to shomin kyōiku* 中國近世教育史研究：是の文教政策と庶民教育, Hayashi Tomoharu 林友春, ed., Tokyo, 1958, pp. 25-154. Contains the most detailed bibliographical information, though still far from being complete, on *t'ung-su lei-shu*.

Sun, K'ai-ti 孫楷第. *Jih-pen Tung-ching so-chien Chung-kuo hsiao-shuo shu-mu* 日本東京所見中國小說書目. Rev. ed., Peking, 1958, pp. 127-140.

—YWM

Tzu-chuan 自傳 or *tzu-hsü* 自敍 (autobiography) was first treated as a separate genre in Chinese literature by the Confucian scholar Liu Chih-chi* in the *hsü-chuan* 敍傳 section of his *Shih-t'ung*. Liu traced the beginning of this genre to Ch'ü Yüan's* long narrative poem "Li sao," which began by giving the names of the poet's ancestors. The principal aim of autobiography, Liu stated, was "to celebrate one's name and make known one's parents." The Han philosopher Wang Ch'ung 王充 (A.D. 27-91) was thus criticized for including disparaging remarks about his ancestors in the autobiographical postface to his *Lun-heng* 論衡. Anecdotes without any redeeming moral value, such as those in the poet Ssu-

ma Hsiang-ju's* account of his own life, were also deemed out of place in an autobiographical writing.

The best-known of the early autobiographical *chuan* 傳 are probably those of Ssu-ma Ch'ien* and T'ao Ch'ien,* representing the two principal traditions in the style and content of these accounts. T'ao Ch'ien's "Wu-liu Hsien-sheng chuan" 五柳先生傳 (Account of Mr. Five Willows) was actually a very brief parody of the official biographies, or *lieh-chuan* 列傳. These usually included the incidents from his life chosen to illustrate his filial piety and high moral conduct. Ssu-ma Ch'ien's postface to his *Shih-chi** was the first autobiographical account in this form. Such accounts, often appended to larger philosophical or historical works, were written with the idea of telling the reader something about the author, how he came by his views, and why he wrote the book. The emphasis was more on the author's intellectual growth than on the intimate details of his life. Later *tzu-chuan* 自傳, written independently of any work, became more literary and subjective, influenced no doubt by T'ao Ch'ien's short account of his simple life in retirement. Besides being eulogies to an eremitic existence, most of these self-accounts reflect a primary concern with a dominant theme in Chinese philosophy: man in society, how he conducts himself and how he is viewed by others. Actual portrayal of personality is generally served by a list of attributes which include ingrained qualities of character as well as physical characteristics or defects, such as pockmarks, weak eyesight, or stuttering. Personality is hidden behind rather formalized descriptions of stereotyped roles and behavior patterns.

T'ao Ch'ien's "Wu-liu Hsien-sheng chuan," a short piece of no more than a few hundred characters, was the progenitor for the recluse type of self-portrait eulogizing the joys of a life in retirement. Its use of the term *chuan* in the title placed it in the tradition of the biographical *lieh-chuan*, yet the author used a whimsical nickname. The usual detailed list of alternative names, the record of ancestors, their official titles, and the author's place of birth are omitted, suggesting a dissociation from family and society as well as from history and tradition. Many of the patterns of motifs occurring in later self-portraits follow this model, beginning with the adoption of a humorous name, such as "Mr. Drunk" or the "Clear and Fresh Hermit."

After T'ao, this basic form, which is a characterization of a man through a description of his manner of life rather than his accomplishments, was used by a dozen or more writers. Po Chü-i's* "Tsui-yin Hsien-sheng chuan" 醉吟先生傳 (An Account of Mr. Drunk) and Lu Kuei-meng's* "Fu-li Hsien-sheng chuan" 甫里先生傳 (An Account of Mr. Fu-li), both very similar in spirit to T'ao Ch'ien's "Wu-liu," are more detailed, more intimate, and give a fuller portrait of the author. Such accounts usually have little chronological narration of the author's life or even of episodes in the life and are often no more than sketchy portraits consisting of descriptions of daily activities, personal inclinations, habits and predilections, sometimes even presenting a special philosophical outlook.

Though these early autobiographies were traditionally given over to descriptions of the delights of retirement and a rejection of officialdom, many were written as a kind of apologia or self-justification. Liu Yü-hsi's* autobiography relating incidents in his political career is such an account. Others are very individualistic, auch as the autobiography of Lu Yü 陸羽 (d. 805), the author of the Ch'a-ching 茶經; the "Ch'ang-le lao tzu-hsü" 長樂老自敍 (Autobiography of Old Eternally Happy) of Feng Tao 馮道 (882-954); and the autobiographical postface of the Sung poetess Li Ch'ing-chao* appended to her husband's Chin-shih lu.

In the sixteenth century two unusually long autobiographies by Hu Ying-lin* and Wen Yüan-fa 文元發 (b. 1528) appeared. These accounts retain the basic form of official biographical writings, but also contain retrospective analysis and a quest for some sense of unity in the life story. Incidents are not merely listed objectively; rather the reflective presence of the au-

thor, despite the use of the third person, is evident. The lengthy, chronological account of Wen Yüan-fa, grandson of the scholar Wen Cheng-ming, entitled "Ch'ing-liang chü-shih tzu-hsü" 清凉居士自敍 (The Self-account of the Clear and Free Hermit), is probably the most integrated and complex portrait of an individual in the genre. The author seeks some continuity and meaning in the narration of his life and gives subjective reflections on events. He seems to be trying to explain himself to himself, rather than to the world at large. A gradual realization of the limits put on him by the realities of his fate (he continually fails the imperial examination) and his coming to terms with this give a unity to the work.

A greater number of autobiographies were written in the Ch'ing period. Many of these were by men who for one reason or another never became officials, such as Ch'en Tsu-fan 陳祖范 (1675-1753), or who chose an early retirement, such as Ying Hui-ch'ien 應撝謙 (1615-1683). They are relaxed in tone and more subjective and realistic in their treatment of life's experiences than previous essays.

Though the terms hsü and chuan seem to be used interchangeably in these essays, it is possible that as more writers began describing very personal experiences, as well as the trivia of daily life, family affairs, and the struggle to earn a living, they preferred to call them hsü. This was a more loosely defined form and was not, like chuan, associated with the idea of transmitting a moral principle.

By Ch'ing times the weight of this tradition in autobiography, i.e., its association with the style of life described in T'ao's "Wu-liu," may have made it inadequate for giving expression to the new views of the self and its relation to society. The form did not seem to lend any organizational unity to the realistic, introspective work of Shen Fu in his Fu-sheng liu-chi* (Six Chapters of a Floating Life), a work of the early eighteenth century. Some scholars consider this to be the first Chinese autobiography in the Western mold, revealing a new interest in subjective description and a skillful handling of daily life. This is an account of the author's early adult years and his relations with his wife and her family. It delves into the inner world of his emotional experience, giving an account of both the pleasant and the unpleasant aspects of his life. The work of Shen Fu indicates that China had become ripe for the appearance of a new kind of autobiography, the essential ingredients of which are a realistic, perhaps more tragic, view of life, attention to inner emotional states, and a sense of unity in one's experience. In this case, this unity came from the author's recollections, which gave the material form from within rather than from without, as was the case in the protypical *lieh-chuan* by Ssu-ma Ch'ien. In these earlier models moral comments were placed at the end, separated from the narrative itself, as was true in many of the *tzu-chuan*, where a short, final comment (*tsan* 贊)in a poetic mode summarized the theme of the essay.

That a work like Shen Fu's *Fu-sheng liu-chi* should appear when it did says much about the changes in the social and intellectual milieu of the period. It may be that the changes in the lives of the writers themselves necessitated the creation of a new form to portray these life stories. The early Ch'ing dynasty was a time when the literate class was broadened and large families were breaking up, all of which meant greater freedom for the individual. These factors probably contributed in part to the optimistic outlook and greater interest in the details of the author's immediate existence which can be found in the autobiographies of this period. While the later *chuan* and *hsü* contained hints of the changes in the old themes of achieving the scholar-statesman ideal and cultivating oneself in solitude, they never probed deeply enough to create any new conception of a life history. Shen Fu's work remained a unique example, and autobiography for the most part never grew out of its rather narrow mold to become more than a minor genre in traditional China.

EDITIONS:

Kuo, Teng-feng 郭登峰 , ed. *Li-tai tzu-hsü-chuan wen-ch'ao* 歷代自敍傳文鈔 . Taipei, 1965.

STUDIES:

Bauer, Wolfgang. "Icherleben und Autobiographie im älteren China," *Heidelberger Jahrbücher*, 8 (1964), 12-40.

Dolezelová-Velingerová, M., and L. Dolazel, "An Early Chinese Confessional Prose: Shen Fu's *Six Chapters of a Floating Life*," TP, 58 (1972), 137-160.

Hervouet, Yves, "L'autobiographie dans la Chine traditionnelle," in *Etudes d'histoire et de littérature chinoise offertes au Professeur Jaroslav Prusek*, Paris, 1976, pp. 107-141.

Wang, Gung-wu 王廣武 . "Feng Tao: An Essay on Confucian Loyalty," *Confucian Personalities*, pp. 123-145, 346-351.

Wu, Pei-yi 吳百益 . "The Spiritual Autobiography of Te-ch'ing," in *The Unfolding of Neo-Confucianism*, W. T. de Bary, ed., New York, 1975, pp. 67-92.

—JK

Tzu-ti shu 子弟書 was one of the most popular forms of performing art in the city of Peking during the Ch'ing dynasty. *Tzu-ti shu* received its name from the fact that it originated among the *Pa-ch'i tzu-ti* 八旗子弟 (Young Men of the Eight Banners), i.e., the Manchu Bannermen residing in Peking. To what extent the form continued older traditions of performing arts or was influenced by Manchu forms is still unknown. *Tzu-ti shu* reached the height of its popularity between 1735 and 1850, after which it rapidly declined in favor. At present no one in China seems to be able to perform the genre, although performers may have survived into this century.

Unlike many other types of performing arts, *tzu-ti shu* consisted solely of poetry without long stretches of prose alternating with rhymed passages. The basic poetic line was heptasyllabic, but there was a wide variation in the number of syllables per line. Many of the *tzu-ti shu* are quite long and would have taken several days to perform. Knowledge of the actual mode of performance and the music utilized is conjectural and based on somewhat vague contemporary descriptions, although modern performances of *ta-ku** probably incorporate elements of *tzu-ti shu*, since it seems to have exerted a strong influence on the later forms.

According to contemporary accounts the music of *tzu-ti shu* was divided into two types: *Tung-tiao* 東調 (East City Tunes) and *Hsi-tiao* 西調 (West City Tunes), named after the parts of Peking in which they were first popular. The eastern variety was supposedly similar to the music of *kao-ch'iang* 高腔 opera, sad and heroic in its sound, while the western style was compared to *K'un-ch'ü** opera, softer and more melodious, especially suited to love stories. However, such a description is impressionistic and, musically speaking, probably inaccurate, because both *kao-ch'iang* and *K'un-ch'ü* operas are organized on the *ch'ü-p'ai* 曲牌 system of set tunes, whereas *tzu-ti shu* was certainly performed with *pan-ch'iang* 板腔 style music (as were later *ta-ku* and Peking opera [see *Ching-chü*]).

Over four hundred compositions in the *tzu-ti shu* style survive, and the greatest collection of these materials can be found in the Fu Ssu-nien Library of the Academia Sinica (Taipei). Although many of these works are anonymous or are signed with pennames, enough of them can be assigned authors so that a general idea of the more outstanding performers and writers can be obtained. One of the earliest authors whose works have survived is Lo Sung-ch'uang 羅松窗, who was active during the Ch'ien-lung period (1736-1796). Three of his works are known: *Yu-yüan hsün-meng* 遊園尋夢 (Searching for a Dream while Strolling in the Garden), based upon the Ming dramatist T'ang Hsien-tsu's famous work *Mu-tan t'ing*, *Hung-fu ssu-pen* 紅拂私奔 (The Elopement of Hung-fu), taken from the Ming drama *Hung-fu chi* by Chang Feng-i, and *Ts'ui-p'ing shan* 翠屏山 (Green-screen Mountain), deriving from the anonymous Ming drama, *Yü-ni ho* 淤泥河 (Mud Sediment River). Obviously, it was common for *tzu-ti shu* composers to borrow their stories from well-known novels or classical dramas. In fact, Lo Sung-ch'uang followed his originals quite closely, even paraphrasing whole sections.

The author with the largest number of surviving *tzu-ti shu* to his credit is Han Hsiao-ch'uang 韓小窗, who is generally re-garded as the best writer of the genre. There is controversy concerning his dates, but it seems reasonable to suppose that he died sometime before the last quarter of the nineteenth century. There are at least nineteen works which can be ascribed to him, and like those of Lo Sung-ch'uang, all are based upon vernacular novels and dramas popular at the time. Nevertheless, Han Hsiao-ch'uang did not follow his original sources as closely as Lo, and he was able to expand greatly upon minor incidents in the originals and create *tzu-ti shu* which are vastly superior to the source texts. Han possessed a great talent for both narrative and description, and his works are the most moving and artistically wrought poems of the entire tradition. In general, Lo Sung-ch'uang is judged the major representative of the western school, because his works concentrated on the theme of talented young scholars and beautiful women, with highly sensitive descriptions of romantic love, while Han Hsiao-ch'uang is considered the master in the eastern tradition, most of his stories centering on the heroic themes of faithful officials, filial sons, and chaste women, often with tragic overtones.

One other author, Ho-lü shih 鶴侶氏 (*fl.* during the first half of the nineteenth century), wrote at least sixteen *tzu-ti shu*, six based upon earlier dramas or novels and ten created in response to contemporary events, an innovation in this genre. These ten original works are full of social criticism, but generally speaking Ho-lü shih's works do not reach the artistic excellence present in the works of Lo Sung-ch'uang and Han Hsiao-ch'uang.

Tzu-ti shu lives on in an altered form today, because many of the stories, and in some cases whole sections of scripts, were adopted by popular performers of *ta-ku* and other genres as these became popular in Peking during the second half of the nineteenth century.

EDITIONS AND CATALOGUES:

Fu, Hsi-hua 傅惜華. *Pei-ching ch'uan-t'ung ch'ü-i tsung-lu* 北京傳統曲藝總錄 Peking, 1962.

———. *Tzu-ti shu tsung-mu* 子弟書總目. Shanghai, 1957.

Hatano, Tarō 波多野太郎. "Shiteisho shū" 子弟書集, *Yokohama Shiritsu Daigaku kiyō (Jimbun kagaku)*, 6 (1975).

Liu, Fu 劉復, and Li Chia-jui 李家瑞. *Chung-kuo su-ch'ü tsung-mu kao* 中國俗曲總目稿. Peiping, 1932.

STUDIES:

Chao, Ching-shen 趙景深. "*Tzu-ti shu ts'ung-ch'ao hsü*"子弟書叢鈔序, *Wen-shih-che*, 1979.6 (December), 58-59.

Ch'en, Chin-chao 陳錦釗. *Tzu-ti shu chih t'i-ts'ai lai-yüan chi-ch'i tsung-ho yen-chiu* 子弟書之題材來源及其綜合研究. Ph.D. dissertation, Cheng-chih ta-hsüeh 政治大學, 1977. The best work on this topic.

———. "Tzu-ti shu chih tso-chia chi ch'i tso-p'in" 子弟書之作家及其作品, *Shu-mu chi-k'an* 書目季刊, 12.1-2 (September 1978), 21-56.

Hatano, Tarō. *P'ang-hsieh tuan-erh yen-chiu* 螃蟹段兒研究 (Studies in a Song Book, *Pang xie duan er*). Taipei, 1970 (Asian Folklore and Social Life Monographs, No. 9). This book contains the author's articles from *Yokohama Shiritsu Daigaku kiyō*, 164 and 178, as well as facsimiles of the text, transcriptions, comments, and a translation into Japanese.

———. "Shiteisho kenkyū" 子弟書研究. *Yokohama Shiritsu Daigaku kiyō*, Series A-38, 164 (1967).

Hu, Kuang-p'ing 胡光平. "Han Hsiao-ch'uang sheng-p'ing chi ch'i tso-p'in k'ao-ch'a chi" 韓小窗生平及其作品考查記, *Wen-hsüeh i-ch'an tseng-k'an*, 12 (February 1963), 90-100.

Kao, Chi-an 高季安. "Tzu-ti shu yüan-liu" 子弟書源流, *Wen-hsüeh i-ch'an tseng-k'an*, 1 (September 1955), 337-341.

Sawada, Mizuho 澤田瑞穗. "Shiteisho issekiwa" 子弟書一夕話, *Tenri Daigaku gakuhō*, 33 (December 1960), 18-39.

—JDS

Tz'u 詞 (lyric or "song-words"), one of the major poetic genres in China, was originally a song text set to existing musical tunes. It emerged in the T'ang dynasty in response to the popularity of foreign musical tunes newly imported from Central Asia. At first, *tz'u* replaced the old *yüeh-fu** ballads and thus came to be regarded as a continuation of *yüeh-fu*. Yet the ancient musical notations have been lost, and it is no longer possible to know how *tz'u* mel-odies differed from *yüeh-fu* music. It is certain, however, that *tz'u* finally formed a special tradition of composition: titles of *yüeh-fu* poems do not refer to fixed metric patterns, yet *tz'u* titles always point to particular *tz'u-p'ai* 詞牌 (tune patterns) for which the poems are composed. These *tz'u-p'ai*, totaling about 825 if the numerous variant forms are excluded, came to be viewed as definite verse patterns. Even today, poets still write to these tune patterns without knowing the original melodies. This unique practice of *tz'u* composition is called *t'ien-tz'u* 填詞 (filling in words).

Tz'u poetry is characterized often by lines of unequal length, in sharp contrast to *lü-shih* 律詩 (regulated verse) in strictly five-character or seven-character lines. Long before the T'ang poets of *lü-shih* began to view *tz'u* as a serious poetic genre, *tz'u* already flourished as a "popular" song-form. The Tun-huang songs, which have given so many clues to T'ang and Five Dynasties popular culture, attest to this fact. The early "popular" *tz'u* songs were vital to the development of *tz'u* poetry; many devices formerly restricted to the "popular" song style later became important ingredients in the "literati" *tz'u*. The evolution of the *tz'u* genre was a history of the intermingling of the "literati" style and the "popular" style. Wen T'ing-yün* (c. 812-870) was the first prolific *tz'u* poet in China, but before him such authors as Po Chü-i* and Liu Yü-hsi* had already experimented with occasional *tz'u*. These early writers composed *tz'u* primarily to meet the needs of the singing girls in the entertainment quarters. Yangchow, Soochow, and Hangchow were among the cities known for this newly emerging T'ang song culture. When Ou-yang Chiung,* the compiler of the first *tz'u* anthology *Hua-chien chi,** said that the "literati" *tz'u* were written for the "Southern singing girls," he was no doubt referring to the growing demand for *tz'u* in the entertainment quarters of the Lower Yangtze Region.

As with other literary genres, the cumulative efforts of numerous poets throughout the centuries contributed to the evolution of *tz'u*. Some focused more on stylistic changes and some on the innovations of formal structure. Some were revolutionary and introduced new blood into the tz'u. Others were conservative and stayed within the orthodox tradition. Interruption and continuation are both necessary for the growth of a literary form, though a drastic change of direction often sheds greater insight into the process of its evolution. Yet considering the overall development of the tz'u genre, the importance that the Chinese poets ascribed to the notion of tradition and continuity is striking: tz'u poets over the centuries continued to emulate a few set stylistic models and often acknowledged proudly that they were the followers of certain schools.

The late T'ang poet Wen T'ing-yün has been traditionally regarded as the pioneer poet of the form. His poetic style of refined subtlety became typical of the early tz'u, as may be seen from his works in the Hua-chien chi. The only poet among the Hua-chien Circle to break away from the overwhelming influence of Wen T'ing-yün was Wei Chuang.* Wei's tz'u style was deliberately more direct, and thus represented a style contrary to Wen's. A few decades later the last monarch of the Southern T'ang, Li Yü* (937-978), went a step further and synthesized these two stylistic modes.

Tz'u, however, are generally associated with the Sung dynasty, for the genre reached the height of its literary status during this period. At the beginning of the Sung, Liu Yung* changed the direction of tz'u poetry by boldly mixing the "popular" song style with the literati style in such a mannner that it was difficult for critics to place his work in a particular stylistic category. Before his time, tz'u poems were written only in the shorter form called hsiao-ling 小令. Liu Yung first introduced the longer man-tz'u 慢詞 form from the "popular" song tradition and transformed it into a vehicle that allowed for more complex lyrical expression.

During the early Sung, perhaps only Su Shih's* achievement in extending the poetic scope of tz'u paralleled Liu Yung's formal contributions. In his hands, tz'u became a poetic genre through which, as one Ch'ing critic put it, "there was no idea which could not be expressed." Under Su's influence tz'u began to free itself from music and became primarily a literary creation. For this and other reasons, Su Shih has been traditionally regarded as the founder of the School of Hao-fang 豪放 (Heroic Abandon). Tz'u criticism henceforth classified poets into either the Hao-fang School or the School of Wan-yüeh 婉約 (Delicate Restraint). For example, the Northern Sung poets Yeh Meng-te 葉夢得 (1077-1148) and Ch'ao Pu-chih 晁補之 (1053-1110) were assigned to the former school, while Ch'in Kuan 秦觀 (1049-1100), Yen Shu,* Yen Chi-tao,* Chou Pang-yen,* and Li Ch'ing-chao* belonged to the latter. During the Southern Sung, Hsin Ch'i-chi,* Ch'en Liang,* and Yüan Hao-wen* were considered to be Hao-fang poets, but Chiang K'uei* and his followers were all Wan-yüeh poets.

Once the formal aspects of tz'u, in both hsiao-ling and man-tz'u, were fully developed, poets began to explore new metaphorical complexities that tended toward symbolism. The development of yung-wu tz'u 詠物詞 in the Southern Sung best demonstrates this point. In yung-wu tz'u poetry the poetic self appears to be almost absent—personal feelings are expressed through such external objects as plums and fallen leaves. The works of Chiang K'uei, Wu Wen-ying,* Chang Yen 張炎 (1248-1320), Wang I-sun 王沂孫 (1240-1290), and Chou Mi* were representative of this new poetic mode. Later this imagistic symbolism came to be known as the "Southern Sung style," as distinguished from the more explicit and direct tz'u of the Northern Sung.

During the Yüan and the Ming the tz'u form underwent an artistic eclipse. The Ming loyalist Ch'en Tzu-lung 陳子龍 (1608-1647) who wrote in the refined style of Chiang K'uei was the only distinguished tz'u poet of this period. But in the beginning of the Ch'ing dynasty tz'u again became a major poetic genre. This renaissance of tz'u was due largely to the efforts of Chu I-tsun* and other scholar poets in the Che-hsi School. In an attempt to elevate the status of *tz'u* poetry, Chu I-tsun set out to advocate the importance of elegance in *tz'u* writing and modeled his own work after the ornate and polished style of the Southern Sung. Around the middle of the Ch'ing dynasty a new school of *tz'u* called the Ch'ang-chou tz'u-p'ai* emerged as a reaction against the Che-hsi School; it celebrated instead the poetry of the T'ang, the Five Dynasties, and the Northern Sung. In the meantime, other minor schools arose, all searching particular stylistic modes as their models for emulation.

The constant competition among various *tz'u* schools in the Ch'ing eventually made *tz'u* poetry a subject of serious scholarly pursuit and theoretical debate—a development unprecedented in the history of *tz'u*. Aside from a few individualistic poets like Na-lan Hsing-te,* Hsiang Hung-Tso 項鴻祚 (1798-1835), and Chiang Ch'un-lin,* *tz'u* poets in the Ch'ing were primarily scholars. This new tendency was most evident toward the end of the dynasty. For example, poets in the famous *tz'u* club *Hsüan-nan tz'u-she* 宣南詞社 devoted their lives to the compilation and editing of *tz'u* anthologies. The *Sung Yüan san-shih-i chia tz'u* 宋元三十一家詞 by Wang P'eng-yün 王鵬運 (1849-1904) and *Ch'iang-ts'un ts'ung-shu* 彊村叢書 by Chu Tsu-mou 朱祖謀 (1859-1931) were only two among the numerous collections of *tz'u* made at this time. In addition, the number of critical works on *tz'u* was impressive—chief among them, the *Hui-feng tz'u-hua* 蕙風詞話 of K'uang Chou-i 況周頤 (1859-1926) and the *Jen-chien tz'u-hua* 人間詞話 of Wang Kuo-wei.*

Wang Kuo-wei is considered the greatest modern *tz'u* poet by virtue of his philosophical insight and psychological depth. The combination of meticulous scholarship in classical literature and genuine appreciation of Western philosophy made him a rare poet. He represented the transition from the traditional to the modern and served as the model for future *tz'u* writing. Yet in the last several decades no *tz'u* poet has come forward to rival Wang. The late Chairman Mao Tse-tung 毛澤東 (1893-1976) was perhaps one of the few poets in the twentieth century who successfully produced a *tz'u* poetry of original vigor.

EDITIONS:

Cheng, Ch'ien 鄭騫, ed. *Hsü Tz'u hsüan* 續詞選. Rpt. Taipei, 1973.

———, ed. *Tz'u hsüan* 詞選. 1954; rpt. Taipei, 1973.

Chiang, Shang-hsien 姜尚賢. *T'ang Sung ming-chia tz'u hsin-hsüan* 唐宋名家詞新選. Tainan, 1963.

Ch'ing-tz'u pieh-chi pai-san-shih chung 清詞別集百三十種 (Rpt. of *Ch'ing ming-chia tz'u* 清名家詞). Taipei, 1976.

Jen, Erh-pei 任二北. *Tun-huang ch'ü chiao-lu* 敦煌曲校錄. Shanghai, 1955.

Kuo, Mao-ch'ien 郭茂倩, ed. *Yüeh-fu shih-chi* 樂府詩集. 4v. Peking, 1979, *chüan* 80-82.

Lin, Ta-ch'un 林大椿, ed. *T'ang Wu-tai tz'u* 唐五代詞. Peking, 1956.

T'ang, Kuei-chang 唐圭璋, ed. *Ch'üan Chin Yüan tz'u* 全金元詞. 2v. Peking, 1976.

———, ed. *Ch'üan Sung tz'u* 全宋詞. 5v. Peking, 1965.

TRANSLATIONS:

Ayling, Alan, and Duncan Mackintosh. *A Collection of Chinese Lyrics.* London, 1965.

———. *A Further Collection of Chinese Lyrics.* London, 1969.

Lau, D. C. *Selected Chinese Lyrics.* Hong Kong, 1981.

Soong, Stephen C., ed. *Song Without Music: Chinese Tz'u Poetry.* Hong Kong, 1980. Includes criticism.

STUDIES:

Baxter, Glen W. "Metrical Origin of the *Tz'u*," in *Studies in Chinese Literature,* John L. Bishop, ed., Cambridge, Mass., 1966, pp. 186-225.

———. *Index to the Imperial Register of the Tz'u Prosody, Ch'in-ting tz'u-p'u.* Cambridge, Mass., 1956.

Chang, Kang-i Sun. *The Evolution of Chinese Tz'u Poetry: from Late T'ang to Northern Sung.* Princeton, 1980. Includes translations.

Chow, Tse-tsung. "On the Term *Tz'u* as a Poetic Genre," in (as "Foreword") *A Bibliography of Criticism on T'ang and Sung Tz'u,* by Stanley M. Ginsberg, Wisconsin China Series (Madison), 3 (1975), pp. i-iv.

Hoffman, Alfred. *Die Lieder des Li Yü, 937-978, Herrschers der Südlichen T'ang-Dynastie als Ein-*

848

führung in die Kunst der Chinesischen Lieddichtung. Köln, 1950. A classic study—the glossary of terms and symbols (pp. 237-251) is still unparalleled.

ao, Tsung-i 饒宗頤. *Tz'u chi k'ao* 詞籍考. V. 1. Hong Kong, 1963.

en, Erh-pei 任二北. *Tun-huang ch'ü ch'u-t'an* 敦煌曲初探. Shanghai, 1954.

en, Pan-t'ang 任半塘. *T'ang sheng-shih* 唐聲詩. 2v. Shanghai, 1982.

iu, James J. Y. *Major Lyricists of the Northern Sung: A.D. 960-1126.* Princeton, 1974. Includes translations of 28 poems.

in, Shuen-fu. *The Transformation of the Chinese Lyrical Tradition: Chiang K'uei and Southern Sung Tz'u Poetry.* Princeton, 1978. Along with studies by Kang-i Sun Chang and J. Y. Liu provides a history of the *tz'u* through Sung times.

Murakami, Tetsumi 村上哲見. *Sōshi kenkyū* 宋詞研究. Tokyo, 1976.

Yeh, Chia-ying 葉嘉瑩. *Chia-ling lun tz'u ts'ung-kao* 迦陵論詞叢稿. Shanghai, 1980. Includes material already published in *Chia-ling t'an tz'u* 迦陵談詞, Taipei, 1970.

—KIC

Tz'u-hua 詞話 (doggerel story) is a term that has been used to designate three distinct types of literature. In chronological sequence it has been used as (1) a generic name for collections of critical notes on the genre of poetry known as *tz'u;* * (2) one of several generic names for a variety of prosimetric narrative in which the story is told in alternating passages of verse and prose, sometimes translated as chantefable; and (3) a loosely used designation for any work of vernacular fiction which contains examples of verse, whether this poetry is used for narrative purposes or not.

The first of these usages is self-explanatory and completely unrelated to the other two (see *tz'u-hua* [talks on lyrics]). It can be regarded as a subcategory of the voluminous genre of collections of critical notes on poetry designated by the term *shih-hua.* *

The third of these usages appears to have come into being only in the second half of the sixteenth century. It may have been a result of the mistaken assumption that the word *tz'u* in the expression *tz'u-hua* denotes the poetic genre of that name and

that the term *tz'u-hua* must therefore refer to works of fiction which contain examples of this type of poetry. In fact the word *tz'u* in the expression *tz'u-hua* is a general term for doggerel verse employed for narrative or descriptive purposes. As such it does not denote any particular prosodic form, although most of the verse in works that are genuine *tz'u-hua* is either heptasyllabic or decasyllabic. Seventeenth century writers sometimes used the term *tz'u-hua* as a generic name for the vernacular short story, but the only major work that has been so designated in this loose usage is the late sixteenth-century novel *Chin P'ing Mei tz'u-hua* (see *Chin P'ing Mei*) which includes a great deal of verse in every prosodic form but, unlike genuine *tz'u-hua*, does not employ it for narrative purposes.

It is the second usage that is the most important here. In this sense the term *tz'u-hua* can be understood to mean "doggerel story" and was used from the thirteenth to the sixteenth century to designate narratives told either entirely in doggerel verse or, more commonly, in alternating passages of verse and prose.

The earliest extant examples of this genre are thirteen works printed in Peking in the 1470s that were discovered in a tomb near Shanghai in 1967 and were republished in a facsimile edition by the Shanghai Museum in 1973. Seven of these works, either on their title pages or internally, refer to themselves as *tz'u-hua*, although other terms such as *tz'u* 詞, *tz'u-chuan* 詞傳, and *tz'u-wen* 詞文 are also employed. One of these works is entirely in heptasyllabic verse, but the rest consist of alternating passages of heptasyllabic verse and prose, both of which are employed for narrative purposes, although verse tends to play the predominant role. Examples of other verse forms used for non-narrative purposes, such as comment or description, also occur, but none of these works contains a single example of *tz'u* or *ch'ü** written to a preexisting tune and intended to be sung. This is significant because, as noted above, the word *tz'u* in this usage of the term *tz'u-hua* has sometimes been misunderstood to refer to the poetic genre of that name.

Thematically, this body of thirteen works can be subdivided into a number of categories. Three of them are examples of historical fiction dealing with the exploits of Kuan So 關索, the putative second son of Kuan Yü 關羽 (160-219), Hsüeh Jen-kuei 薛仁貴 (614-683), and Shih Ching-t'ang 石敬瑭 (892-942), heroes who were active in periods that have always been favored by writers of Chinese fiction and drama; eight of them are early examples of court-case fiction dealing with the exploits of Pao Cheng, the legendary archetype of the incorruptible magistrate; and two are examples of didactic and cautionary tales. Although these works eventually went out of circulation in their chantefable form, by the end of the sixteenth century the story of Kuan So and several of those about Pao Cheng had undergone the process of genre translation and were incorporated in summary prose form in certain editions of the *San-kuo-chih yen-i** and the *Pai-chia kung-an* 百家公案, an early collection of prose court-case fiction. Thus they are important in the history of Chinese literature for both their form and their content.

In form, the bulk of all these works consists of metrically regular lines of heptasyllabic verse with the caesura after the fourth syllable and mandatory rhyme at the end of the couplet. With but a single exception all of them employ the same rhyme throughout the work, although this rhyming category is much more broadly defined than is the case in most classical poetry. The passages of narrative prose which are distributed fairly evenly throughout all but one of these works are relatively short and are written in a style that is closer to the literary language than to the vernacular.

The language in which these works are written is formulaic. This is true at every linguistic level, from the basic lexicon, through the three and four syllable components of the heptasyllabic line, the couplet, the larger blocks of verse on stock motifs, and right up to the level of narrative segmentation and the configurational patterns of the works considered as a whole. It is clear that the authors were not highly educated and that they were not concerned to make their works congruent

with the ascertainable facts of history, geography, or the elite cultural tradition. Although their formal characteristics may reflect to some extent the prevailing norms of contemporary oral performance, these works are best understood as examples of *written*, rather than *oral*, formulaic literature, produced for a semiliterate reading audience by professional purveyors of written popular literature who did not strive for originality of expression.

There are striking resemblances between the formal characteristics of these works and those of some of the *pien-wen* manuscripts, dating from the tenth century, that were discovered at Tun-huang. One of the latter, in fact, resembles the fifteenth-century *tz'u-hua* so closely as to be virtually indistinguishable from them. It is entitled *Chi Pu ma-chen tz'u-wen* 季布罵陣詞文 (*Tz'u-wen* on Chi Pu Shouting Abuses at the Battlefront), thus designating itself by one of the same terms that is used to designate the fifteenth-century works. It is written entirely in regular heptasyllabic verse, employs the same rhyme throughout, and even uses the same rhyme category as all but one of the Ming *tz'u-hua*. There is therefore good reason to believe that the *tz'u-hua* form can be traced back at least as far as the tenth century, although no intervening specimens are extant. The connection between the Ming *tz'u-hua* and the various chantefable forms that proliferated during the following three centuries is unmistakable. There can be little doubt that the forms of chantefable literature that came to be known in the Ch'ing dynasty as *ku-tz'u*,* *t'an-tz'u*,* and so forth, represent the further development, under different names, of the same genre that was known between the thirteenth and sixteenth centuries as *tz'u-hua*.

It has been suggested that the prototypes of the famous novels *San-kuo-chih yen-i*, *Shui-hu chuan*,* and *Hsi-yu chi** may have been in the *tz'u-hua* form, but this theory remains unsubstantiated. There are, however, two major works dating from the Ming period that share some of the formal characteristics described above and that are described as *tz'u-hua* in their titles. These are the *Li-tai shih-lüeh shih-tuan chin tz'u-hua* 歷代史略十段錦詞話 (Ten *Tz'u-hua* Stories on the History of the Various Dynasties), attributed to Yang Shen,* one of the most famous men of letters of the mid-Ming period, and the *Ta-T'ang Ch'in-wang tz'u-hua* 大唐秦王詞話 (*Tz'u-hua* on the Prince of Ch'in of the Great T'ang), by an otherwise unknown figure named Chu Sheng-lin 諸聖鄰, which was published in the early decades of the seventeenth century.

The first of these is not a work of fiction but an epitome of Chinese history from the creation of the world through the Yüan dynasty written almost entirely in decasyllabic lines, but with *tz'u* and *shih** poems and brief passages of prose at the beginning, and couplets of heptasyllabic verse and a *tz'u* at the end, of each section. Later, expanded versions of this work are respectively known as *Nien-i shih t'an-tz'u* 廿一史彈詞, (*T'an-tz'u* on the Twenty-one Histories) or *Nien-wu shih t'an-tz'u* 廿五史彈詞 (*T'an-tz'u* on the Twenty-five Histories).

The *Ta-T'ang Ch'in-wang tz'u-hua* is in sixty-four chapters, each introduced by a number of *shih* or *tz'u* poems; the text of each chapter is largely in prose, but contains many extended passages of both heptasyllabic and decasyllabic narrative verse. This work is one of the many vernacular accounts of the founding of the T'ang dynasty and narrates the career of Li Shih-min 李世民 (599-649), the *de facto* founder of the dynasty and its second emperor, from the moment he forces his father Li Yüan 李淵 (566-635) to revolt against the Sui dynasty until his own accession to the throne. In the struggle against the rival rebels against the Sui, the T'ang emerges victorious and in extended wars Li Shih-min gathers around him a band of dedicated followers, like Ch'in Shu-pao and Yü-ch'i Kung 尉遲恭. Li Shih-min's very success makes his elder brothers jealous and suspicious. They try to do away with him, whereupon Li Shih-min, with the aid of his generals, kills his brothers. His father then abdicates, and Li Shih-min assumes the crown. The *Ta-T'ang Ch'in-wang tz'u-hua* shows how Li Shih-min's *te* 德 (imperial virtue) constrains him to violate both filial

piety and brotherly devotion and tells the slow development and the sudden and dramatic climax of this conflict with true epic grandeur.

Although the second of these books may have incorporated some material from earlier versions in the popular tradition, both of these works appear to have been written by members of the educated elite who were consciously imitating certain formal features of the *tz'u-hua* genre.

By the end of the seventh century, except in the first of the meanings defined above, the term *tz'u-hua* had become obsolete.

EDITIONS:

Chu, Sheng-lin. *Ta-T'ang Ch'in-wang tz'u-hua.* Peking, 1956. A facsimile edition of late Ming woodblock edition.

Ming Ch'eng-hua shuo-ch'ang tz'u-hua ts'ung-k'an 明成化說唱詞話叢刊. 12 *ts'e.* Shanghai, 1973. A luxuriously produced facsimile edition in traditional Chinese format.

TRANSLATIONS:

Oman, Gail. "Hua Guan Suo zhuan." Listed below. An annotated translation of a long *tz'u-hua* published in 1478.

STUDIES:

Chao, Ching-shen 趙景深. "T'an Ming Ch'eng-hua k'an-pen shuo-ch'ang tz'u-hua" 談明成化刊本說唱詞話, *Wen-wu,* 11 (1972), 19-22.

Hanan, Patrick. "*Judge Bao's Hundred Cases* Reconstructed," *HJAS,* 40.2 (December 1980), 301-323.

Hu, Shih-ying 胡士瑩. *Hua-pen hsiao-shuo kai-lun* 話本小說概論. 2v. Peking, 1980.

Oman, Gail. "A Study of *Hua Guan Suo zhuan:* A Prosimetric Narrative Printed in 1478." Unpublished Ph.D. dissertation, University of Chicago, 1982.

Onoe, Kanehide 尾上兼英. "Seika sessho shiwa shiron (1): *Ka Kan Saku den o megutte*" 成化說唱詞話試論(1)：花關索傳 を めぐつて , *Tōyō bunka,* 58 (March 1978), 127-142.

Roy, David T. "The Fifteenth-Century *Shuo-ch'ang Tz'u-hua* as Examples of Written Formulaic Composition," *CHINOPERL,* 10 (1981), 97-128.

Sawada, Mizuho 澤田穗瑞. "Shitei Jinsō yūdō kun: Mindai sessho shiwa no kaijō kanyōgo ni tsute" 四帝仁宗有道君：明代說唱詞話の 開

851

場慣用語について, *Chūgoku bungaku kenkyū*, 4 (December 1978), 46-65.

T'an, Cheng-pi 譚正璧, and T'an Hsün 譚尋. "Ming Ch'eng-hua k'an-pen shuo-ch'ang tz'u-hua shu-k'ao" 明成化刊本說唱詞話述考, *Wen-hsien*, 1980.3 (October 1980), 63-77, and 1980.4 (February 1981), 44-63.

Wang, Kuang-cheng 汪廣正. "Chi wen-hsüeh hsi-ch'ü ho pan-hua shih shang te i-tz'u chung-yao fa-hsien" 記文學戲曲和版畫史上的一次重要發現, *Wen-wu*, 1973.11 (November 1973), 46-57.

—DR

Tz'u-hua 詞話 (talks on lyrics) is a form of literary criticism that consists of a critic's comments on various aspects of Chinese *tz'u** poetry and poets. It is similar to the *shih-hua** in form and scope, but as the term indicates, it deals primarily with the form, content, and historical background of *tz'u* with only occasional references to *shih* for comparison.

As the writing of *tz'u* grew in popularity in the Sung dynasty, it was only natural that books and essays about *tz'u* prosody, particularly tonal patterns, should burgeon. At the same time, the *tz'u-hua* form was used by poets and critics to comment on many other aspects of *tz'u*. Wang Cho's preface (1149) to his *Pi-chi man-chih*, one of the earliest *tz'u-hua*, has a more organized form than many of the later *tz'u-hua*, but it is representative of their subject matter. Its five *chüan* include comments on concepts of the ancients about poetry and song, discussion of various poets from the T'ang to the Sung dynasties, discussion of particular songs, anecdotes from history books about poetry and music in the court, and discussion of various *tz'u* patterns.

Wang Kuo-wei's* *Jen-chien tz'u-hua*, compiled some 760 years after the *Pi-chi man-chih*, is a small book in two *chüan* that shows the persistence of the tradition among Chinese critics. Rather than write full-length books on his theories of poetry, Wang was content to let terse comments on poems, lines of poems, evaluations of poets, and prosodic techniques and general remarks on the periodization of Chinese poetry convey his ideas.

EDITIONS:

T'ang, Kuei-chang 唐圭璋. *Tz'u-hua ts'ung-pien* 詞話叢編. 6v. 1934; rpt. Taipei, 1967. Includes 60 titles, 7 dating from the Sung, 2 from the Yüan, 4 from the Ming, 41 from the Ch'ing, and 6 Republican-period works.

TRANSLATIONS:

Rickett, Adele Austin. *Wang Kuo-wei's Jen-chien tz'u-hua, a Study in Chinese Literary Criticism*. Hong Kong, 1977.

STUDIES:

Lin, Mei-i 林玫儀. "Tz'u-hua ch'i-chung k'ao-i" 詞話七種考佚, in *T'ai Ching-nung Hsien-sheng pa-shih shou-ch'ing lun-wen chi* 臺靜農先生八十壽慶論文集, Taipei, 1981, pp. 729-742.

Wang, Hsi-yüan 王熙元. *Li-tai tz'u-hua hsü-lu* 歷代詞話敍錄. Taipei, 1973. An annotated, nearly exhaustive bibliography of 82 *tz'u-hua*.

—AR

Wan-ch'ing-i shih-hui 晚晴簃詩滙 (Poetry Collected at the Wan-ch'ing Studio) is the largest and most widely known anthology now extant of Ch'ing-dynasty verse. During his tenure as President of the Republic, the statesman-scholar Hsü Shih-ch'ang 徐世昌 (c. 1855-1939) and a number of literary associates formed a poetry club named after his studio. They compiled this anthology under Hsü's general editorial supervision, and it was published in 1929 with prefatory remarks by Hsü.

Hsü Shih-ch'ang and his circle of friends shared a conservative outlook in literary and other matters, which is reflected in the anthology. It was compiled along traditional lines and was in part modeled after the *Ming-shih tsung*.*

In addition to 240 poems by the Ch'ing emperors, the *Wan-ch'ing-i shih-hui* contains 27,420 poems selected from the individual collections of 6,159 poets who were alive when the dynasty was founded in the middle of the seventeenth century or were born before it collapsed early in this century. The main body of the text is divided into 200 *chüan*, which are subdivided into the following sections: *chüan* 1-4, the Ch'ing emperors; 5-10, members of the nobility; 11-182, officials and commoners; 183-192, women poets (of good family!); 193-194, Taoist priests; 195-198,

Buddhist monks; 199, Buddhist and Taoist nuns; and *chüan* 200, poets of the "dependent states" of Korea, Annam, Vietnam, and the Liu-ch'iu (Ryuku) Islands. In addition to prefatory materials, the contents of the collection are listed first by the names of all poets represented in the collection according to their *chüan* location and secondly by the total number of poems to be found in each *chüan*. In the main body of the text, selections from the individual poets follow a rather loose chronological arrangement. In each *chüan*, degree holders' selections precede those of non-degree holders. The poems chosen to represent Na-lan Hsing-te,* for instance, appear before those of his father Mingju. Short biographical notices, including data on secondary names, place of birth, date of highest examination degree, and offices held, are provided for each poet. When known, the title of the poet's collected works is also specified. Critical remarks from various *shih-hua** are quoted after the biographical data when available, although there was no attempt to be exhaustive in this respect. The poems selected for each poet are reproduced without annotation or commentary.

There is some correlation between the literary standing of the individual poets and the number of poems chosen to represent them in this anthology, but this general principle was not consistently applied. Although some importance was attached to comprehensiveness of coverage by the compilers, nonliterary considerations sometimes prevailed, as in the case of the decision to devote four *chüan* to the poetry of Ch'ing emperors. This situation is also apparent in the relative space alloted other poets. Yüan Mei,* for instance, perhaps the major poet of the entire Ch'ing, is made to share a *chüan* with the poet-anthologist Shen Te-ch'ien,* while the prominent official Chang Chih-tung 張之洞 (1837-1909) is represented by an entire *chüan*. Most scholars would argue that the latter figure was a mediocre poet. There are other disparities of this kind, but otherwise the *Wan-ch'ing-i shih-hui* possesses the advantages of uniform format and general convenience.

Because the collected works of many Ch'ing-dynasty poets are not readily accessible, this latter consideration is an important one. However, the principles which guided the compilers in their work should be kept in mind when using the anthology.

EDITIONS:
Wan-ch'ing-i shih-hui. Hsü Shih-ch'ang, ed. 8v. Taipei, 1961. The title on the spine is *Ch'ing shih-hui* 清詩匯.

—WS

Wan Shu 萬樹 (*tzu*, Hua-nung 花農, Hung-yu 紅友, *hao*, Shan-weng 山翁, *c.* 1625-1688) was a famous *tz'u** and *ch'ü** writer. A native of I-hsing 宜興 (modern Kiangsu), he was heavily influenced in terms of style by his uncle, Wu Ping,* a late Ming dramatist. Wan also was a close friend of Ch'en Wei-sung,* the eminent *tz'u* poet from his native village. In 1674 he left his hometown to live in Wu-hsi 無錫, there to study *tz'u* composition with his friend Hou Wen-ts'an 侯文燦. In 1682, a governor serving in the South, Wu Hsing-tso 吳興祚, asked Wan to serve as his private secretary. He soon proved a valued and trusted functionary, in charge of documents.

Wan used his spare time to compose dramas, which were performed by Wu's private acting troupe. In 1686, Wu financed the printing of Wan's *ch'uan-ch'i** *Yung shuang-yen san-chung* 擁雙豔三種 (Three Versions of Embracing a Pair of Beauties), and in 1687, he also published Wan's great work on *tz'u* prosody, the *Tz'u-lü* 詞律. Wan died in 1688 en route to his native home. Wan's *Tz'u-lü* attempted to recover the correct prosodical and metrical structure on some 660 *tz'u-p'ai* (see *tz'u*) which had become lost in the years between the Sung and Ch'ing. The work in 20 *chüan* became the standard novel book of *tz'u* writers.

Of the dramas composed by Wan, only three are extant. They are *Feng-liu pang* 風流棒 (The Romantic Rake), *K'ung ch'ing-shih* 空青石 (Empty Azurite), and *Nien-pa fan* 廿八翻 (Twenty-eight Reversals). These dramas all tell of a talented youth falling in love with one beautiful woman and then another. They all end happily and are therefore collectively called *Yung shuang-yen san-chung*. The plays employ a good deal of irony and reversed situations, playing on the disparity between actuality and appearance. For instance, a good official would be accused of a crime, while a sinful man would achieve merit, or an apparently good man would turn out to be evil, while an apparently evil man would actually be good. This technique, which can be traced to the judgment-reversal plays of the Yüan *tsa-chü*, is the main feature of *Twenty-eight Reversals*. All Wan's other works are lost. His collected *tz'u* poems, called *Hsiang tan tz'u* 香膽詞, can be found in the anthology *Ch'ing ming-chia tz'u* 清名家詞. The *hui-wen tz'u* 回文詞 (palindrome lyrics), which he wrote in his youth and titled *Hsüan-chi sui-chin* 璇璣碎錦, are partially preserved in the *Chao-tai tsung-shu* 昭代叢書 compiled by Yang Fu-chi 楊復吉.

EDITIONS:

Hsing-tan-tz'u, in *Ch'ing ming-chia tz'u*.

Hsüan-chi sui-chin, in *Chao-tai ts'ung-shu*.

Tz'u-lü (with the *Tz'u-lü shih-i* 詞律拾遺 by Hsü Pen-li 徐本立 and Tu Wen-lan 杜文蘭 appended). 4v. Peking, 1958.

Yung shuang-yen san-chung. Originally printed in 1686; not easily available, no reprint.

STUDIES:

Fu, *Ch'ing tsa-chü*, pp. 84-86.

—BTW and XL

Wang An-shih 王安石 (*tzu*, Chieh-fu 介甫, *hao*, Pan-shan 半山, 1021-1086) is remembered as the promoter of the controversial *Hsin-fa* 新法 (New Regulatory System) of the Northern Sung period, as one of the *T'ang Sung pa-ta chia* (see Han Yü), and as an outstanding writer of regulated *shih** verse. His promotion of the New Regulatory System (also known as the New Policies) seems to have been motivated by an aspiration to rectify popular customs, whose deterioration he believed responsible for the problems faced by the state. To create conditions that would result in a wealthy and strong empire, he promulgated a series of radical reforms in the military, public service, agricultural economy, trade and commerce, governmental finance, public works, and education. The swift and allegedly imperfect implementation of these reform measures created powerful opposition and generated a debate on Wang An-shih that has continued into this century. Even his harshest political critics, however, agree that he was a master of poetry and prose composition.

Wang's literary views were on the whole similar to those of Ou-yang Hsiu,* who, as the arbiter of literary style and merit during his day, praised Wang's talent early in his career. In Wang's view, literature should be functional, and the function of literature was first to work for the improvement of society. The relation of literary embellishment to social function, then, is comparable to the artistic designs on the surface of a vessel. Beautification of a useful substance is desirable, but the process of beautification should not hamper or obscure the original function. It comes as no surprise, therefore, that Wang's prose writings, which include letters, memorials to the throne, funerary inscriptions, discussions of historical figures and literary works, and records of social activities, are regarded as models of tight structure, succinctness, and logical clarity in free-flowing, simple language. In his prose, Wang is remembered more for his powers of reasoning than for appealing style. His most famous political treatises are the "Wan yen shu" 萬言書 (Myriad Word Memorial, Submitted to Emperor Jen-tsung), the "Yen shih shu" 言事書 (Memorial on Current Events, Submitted to Emperor Jen Tsung), and "Ta Ssu-ma chien-i shu" 答司馬諫義書 (Letter in Response to Grand Master of Remonstrance Ssu-ma Kuang). His views on literature, particularly on the subordination of style to substance and function, are clearly expressed in "Shang jen shu" 上人書 (A Letter to a Certain Person).

Wang's achievements in poetry are as great as his accomplishments in prose, although few would rank him as one of the eight greatest poets of the T'ang and Sung periods. His poems number more than 1,500. Most are *shih*, but there are a few *tz'u** lyrics as well. During the early years of the Sung period, the Hsi-k'un Style (see

Hsi-k'un ch'ou-ch'ang chi) of poetry, with its emphasis on diction and clever technique, generated a countermovement whose adherents emphasized naturalness, clarity, and readability. Wang An-shih, with his utilitarian views of literature, was understandably attracted to this countermovement. Perhaps it was a desire to avoid the stylistic demands of regulated verse that directed his early efforts toward the less rigorously structured old-style verse. In his younger, more robust years, he wrote many old-style poems that today would be called poems of social protest. The more famous are "Chien ping" 兼並 (Land Grabbing), "Shou yen" 收鹽 (Confiscating Salt), and "Hopei min" 河北民 (The Hopei Folk). His efforts at old-style verse also include many Buddhistic poems, the most famous of which are a set of twenty in the style of Han-shan.*

But the poems written in later life are best remembered, and the most successful of these were in the regulated eight-line (*lü-shih*) or quatrain (*chüeh-chü*) form (see *shih*). Stylistically, they have been compared to the great works of Tu Fu,* for Wang has added the suasive force of rhetorical structure to his sincerity and his identification with the vicissitudes of the natural and human worlds. Even though composed in the complex and highly structured regulated verse form, the effortless simplicity of these works link them to his prose style and to his earlier old-style poems.

EDITIONS:

Lin-ch'uan chi 臨川集. SPPY.

Lin-ch'uan Hsien-sheng wen-chi 臨川先生文集. SPTK.

Wang Ching-kung shih chu 王荊公詩注. Li Pi 李壁, ed. Taipei, 1976. Ssu-k'u ch'üan-shu chen-pen, series 6, v. 249-252.

Wang Wen-kung wen chi 王文公文集. Peking, 1974.

TRANSLATIONS:

Gundert, *Lyrik*, p. 131.

Liu, *Classical Prose*, pp. 345-359. Translations of four essays, with Chinese texts.

Sunflower, pp. 333-339.

Williamson, H. R. *Wang An Shih*. 2v. London, 1937, v. 1, pp. 48-84, and v. 2, pp. 319-390. Translations of several famous essays.

STUDIES:

Higashi, Ichio 東一夫. *Ō Anseki* 王安石. Tokyo, 1975.

K'o, Ch'ang-i 柯昌頤, ed. *Wang An-shih p'ing-chuan* 王安石評傳. Shanghai, 1934.

Liang, Ch'i-ch'ao 梁啓超. *Wang Ching-kung* 王荊公. Shanghai, 1936. Rpt. Taipei, 1956.

Liu, James T. C. *Reform in Sung China: Wang An-shih (1021-1086) and his New Policies.* Cambridge, 1959.

Meskill, John Thomas. *Wang An-shih, Practical Reformer?* Boston, 1963.

SB, pp. 1097-1104.

Teng, Kuang-ming 鄧廣銘. *Wang An-shih* 王安石. Peking, 1975.

Ts'ai, Shang-hsiang 蔡上翔. *Wang Ching-kung nien-p'u k'ao-lue* 王荊公年譜考略. Shanghai, 1973.

Williamson, *Wang An Shih*. A thorough study of the life, times and writings of Wang An-shih. Williamson is generally very sympathetic to Wang.

—JWW

Wang Ch'ang-ling 王昌齡 (*tzu*, Shao-po 少伯, *c.* 690-*c.* 756), one of the pre-eminent literary figures of the first half of the eighth century, is best known today for his mastery of seven-syllable *chüeh-chu* (see *shih*), for his poems of parting and for his poems recounting the hardships of the soldier on the frontier and the laments of the lonely soldier's wife or neglected palace lady. His newly rediscovered critical works, moreover, reveal him as perhaps unique in Chinese literary history as a poet able to explain both the aesthetics and the techniques of poetry in relatively simple language and with an abundance of useful examples.

Born in Ch'ang-an about 690, Wang passed the *chin-shih* (727) and *po-hsüeh hung-tz'u* (734?) examinations late in life but never held an important post. He served in the Secretariat under Chang Chiu-ling* and as a county official in Ssu-shui 汜水 (modern Honan). After a brief banishment to Kwangtung in 738 following the fall of Chang Chiu-ling, Wang returned to serve in the administration of Chiang-ning 江寧 County (modern Nanking). He thus acquired his subsequent cognomen of "Wang Chiang-ning." He was killed during the An

855

Lu-shan Rebellion about 756. His friends include the best-known poets of the day as well as many Buddhist and Taoist priests. He is credited with an anthology in five *chüan* (lost), with a work on *yüeh-fu** poetry entitled the *Yüeh-fu ku-chin t'i-chieh* 樂府古今題解 in three *chüan* (also lost), and with a work of criticism in one *chüan* entitled the *Shih-ko* 詩格 (recovered).

The peak of Wang's fame as a poet came in the last two decades of his life and is marked by his inclusion in two anthologies: the mid-century *Kuo-hsiu chi* 國秀集 and the *Ho-yüeh ying-ling chi* 河嶽英靈集 of about 753. In the latter, editor Yin Fan 殷璠 gives him more space than even Wang Wei,* Li Po,* or Meng Hao-jan,* praises him for continuing the "forceful style" (*feng-ku* 風骨) of Ts'ao Chih,* Liu Chen 劉楨 (d. 217), Lu Chi,* and Hsieh Ling-yün,* and selects for praise examples of his lines that "startle the ear and surprise the eye." Among his best-known poems are his "Farewell to Hsin-chien at Hibiscus Tower" and his "Autumn in the Palace of Eternal Faith," both seven-syllable *chüeh-chü*, and two ancient-style poems in five-syllable meter entitled "Above the Pass" and "Below the Pass." Many of his best poems, including his frontier poems, are written to traditional *yüeh-fu* titles and thus can neither be dated nor used as evidence for his biography.

Wang's major critical work, the *Shih-ko*, is innovative in its style, philosophy, and attention to technique. Its informal organization, semi-vernacular language, and abundance of examples set it apart from the highly difficult and literary criticism of the preceding Six Dynasties and set the stage for Sung *shih-hua.** His work is more concerned with the psychology of composition and with the poem as a fusion of the author's mind with the world than it is with questions of defining genres or ranking poets. For him poetry "concentrates the sea of heaven in the inch-space of the heart"; he prefers the short poem which crystallizes a mood through the poet's observation of nature and which acts as a catalyst for the reader's continuing pleasure. He is new in adopting a critical

vocabulary with borrowings from Buddhism. He uses the metaphor of the mind as a mirror, traces the history of "northern" and "southern" schools of poetry, and defines poetic worlds (*ching* 景). For Wang, a poem is a living creature, with a "head," "belly," and "tail," each part of which requires a certain kind of couplet and use of language so that the whole will work together. In reviewing examples of fine couplets and fine lines he seems to be aware of the central importance of verbs in creating the "world" of a poem. The *Shih-ko*, long-lost in China, has fortunately been preserved by quotation in the *Bunkyō hifuron** of the Japanese monk Kūkai.

Since their loss in the late T'ang, Wang's complete works have never been recollected. Though a relatively complete collection of 190 poems has been collated and annotated by Li Kuo-sheng, his prose works and criticism must be sought elsewhere. The *Ch'üan T'ang wen* (ch. 331) preserves six prose pieces, while the *Wen-yüan ying-hua** contains an examination *fu.** The *Shih-ko* may be found in the "Earth" and "South" chapters of Kūkai's work in the sections entitled "Shih-ch'i shih" (sections 33-40 in Konishi's ed.) and "Lun wen i" (112-120)—see *Bunkyō Hifuron.*

EDITIONS:
Li, Kuo-sheng 李國勝, ed. *Wang Ch'ang-ling shih chiao-chu* 王昌齡詩校注. Taipei, 1973.
See also above and under *Bunkyō hifuron.*

TRANSLATIONS:
Demiéville, *Anthologie*, pp. 218-219.
Gundert, *Lyrik*, p. 85.
Sunflower, p. 100.
See also Bodman, Owen, and Yoshikawa below.

STUDIES:
Bodman, Richard W. "Poetics and Prosody in Early Mediaeval China." Unpublished Ph.D. dissertation, Cornell University, 1978. See especially Chapter 1, "The Poetics of Wang Ch'ang-ling" pp. 22-98 and translations from his criticism, pp. 363-403.
Fu, *Shih-jen*, pp. 103-141: "Wang Ch'ang-ling shih-chi k'ao lüeh" 王昌齡事迹考略. A critical attempt to reconstruct Wang's biography.
Lee, Joseph J. *Wang Ch'ang-ling.* Boston, 1982.

Liu, K'ai-yang 劉開揚. "Lun Wang Ch'ang-ling te shih-ko ch'uang-tso" 論王昌齡的詩歌創作, in his *T'ang shih lun-wen-chi* 唐詩論文集, Hong Kong, 1963, pp. 38-51. Uses Wang's own critical terms to discuss his poetic achievements.

Owen, *High T'ang*, pp. 91-108.

Suzuki, *Todai*, pp. 139-182.

T'an, Yu-hsüeh 譚優學. "Wang Ch'ang-ling hsing-nien k'ao" 王昌齡行年考, *Wen-hsüeh i-ch'an tseng-k'an*, 12 (February 1963), 174-192. An ambitious attempt at a *nien-p'u*.

Yoshikawa, Kōjirō 吉川幸次郎. "Ō Shōrei shi" 王昌齡詩, in *Yoshikawa Kōjirō zenshū* 全集, v. 11, Tokyo, 1968-1970, pp. 189-221. Written in 1948, it discusses several of Wang's most famous seven-syllable *chüeh-chü*.

—RB

Wang Chi 王績 (*tzu*, Wu-kung 無功, *hao*, Tung-kao-tzu 東皋子, 585-644) was a poet who eschewed the embellished and oblique style of his time. Instead he opted for simplicity and directness in the fashion of T'ao Ch'ien,* whom, together with Juan Chi,* he admired greatly. The following four-line poem, "T'i chiu-tien pi" 題酒店壁 (Written on the Wall of a Wineshop), is typical of his style:

Only last night the bottle was emptied,
Immediately this morning a new jug was opened.
After finishing dreaming in another dream,
I, again, return to the wine shop.

Although his eight-line poems do not always conform to the regulated-verse style, they anticipate this later poetic form.

Wang Chi was a native of Lung-men 龍門 in Chiang-chou 絳州 (Shansi). His brother Wang T'ung 王通 was a famous and well-respected scholar in the Sui dynasty. Another brother, Wang Ning 王凝, was appointed to work on the compilation of the dynastic history of the Sui, but died before the work was completed.

Unlike his brothers, Wang Chi did not attain contemporary success. His life closely paralleled that of T'ao Ch'ien. He was well known for his eccentricity and his capacity for wine. He held several insignificant posts under the Sui before retiring to his farm during the chaos at the end of the dynasty. There he heard of a recluse named Chung-chang Tzu-kuang 仲長子光 who lived alone and had supported himself by his own labor for thirty years. Wang Chi was greatly impressed by Chung-chang's way of life and moved his entire family closer to the hermit. However, Wang became an official again when he took a minor post in the early T'ang period. Later he asked to be transferred to the Imperial Music Office because he discovered that the director there brewed a good wine. After the death of the director, Wang resigned from the post. There is no record that he ever took a government position again. This episode is similar to the story that Juan Chi requested a military appointment because three hundred jugs of good wine were stored in the cellar of the headquarters or to that which maintains T'ao Ch'ien applied for a position because the government land there would provide enough crops for him to make wine. These resemblances suggest that historical motifs may have shaped the extant account of Wang's life.

Wang also composed several prose works, including "Wu-tou Hsien-sheng chuan" 五斗先生傳 (The Biography of Mr. Five Dippers), an autobiographical sketch, modeled on T'ao Ch'ien's "Wu-liu Hsien-sheng chuan" 五柳先生傳 (The Biography of Mr. Five Willows). The title alludes to the fact that Wang could remain sober even after drinking five large dippers of wine. He also wrote his own obituary, as T'ao Ch'ien did. It was in this work, however, that he revealed a bitterness and arrogance not found in the writings of the other Six Dynasty tippler-hermits:

This man Wang Chi had father and mother but no friends. He called himself "Wu-kung" [no merits]. People asked him the meaning [of this appellation], but he simply sat there with outstretched legs not caring to answer, [because he believed] he had the Way, even though he had no achievement in his time. ... He had great talents but occupied low positions. ...

This attitude was perhaps one of the reasons why Wang did not enjoy as great a reputation as, for example, T'ao Ch'ien. Nevertheless, the naturalness and simplicity of his work, at a time when an over-decorative style was the vogue, lends it a historical importance.

EDITIONS:

Tung-kao Hsien-sheng chi. SPPY.

Tung-kao-tzu chi. SPTK.

Wang, Kuo-an 王國安, comm. *Wang Chi shih chu* 王績詩注. Shanghai, 1981.

STUDIES:

Ono, Jitsunosuke 大野實之助. "Ō Seki to sono shifū" 王績とその詩風, *Chūgoku koten kenkyū*, 18 (1971), 64-92.

Owen, *Early T'ang*, pp. 60-71. This is the only extended study of Wang Chi, the man and his works, in English.

Takagi, Masakazu 高木正一. "Ō Seki no denki to bungaku" 王績の傳記と文學, *Ritsumeikan bungaku*, 124 (1955), 40-70.

Yeh, Ch'ing-ping 葉慶炳. "Wang Chi yen-chiu" 王績研究, *Fu-jen Ta-hsüeh jen-wen hsüeh-pao*, 1 (1970), 167-189.

Yu, Hsin-li 游信利. "Wang Chi i-nien lu" 王績疑年錄, *Chung-hua hsüeh-yüan*, 8 (1971), 149-185.

—MC

Wang Chi-te 王驥德 (*tzu*, Po-liang 伯良, d. c. 1623), a native of Kuei-chi 會稽 (modern Chekiang), is recognized within the dramatic tradition as one of the two leading authorities on rules for composing songs. He was also a prolific dramatist. His *Ch'ü-lü* 曲律 (On Rules of Songs) and the *Ch'ü-p'in* 曲品 (An Evaluation of Songs) by Lü T'ien-ch'eng 呂天成 (b. 1580) are said to be "the two jewels on the rules of songs." As a dramatist he nominally belonged to the Ko-lü p'ai 格律派 (School of Poetic Meter), but the influence he derived from Shen Ching,* the recognized master/founder of this school, does not seem to go beyond the matter of rules in dramatic composition.

He left the following works: *Fang-chu-kuan yüeh-fu* 方諸館樂府, a collection of *san-ch'ü* (see *ch'ü*); *Nan-tz'u cheng-yün* 南詞正韻 (True Rhymes for Southern Lyrics); and *Ch'ü-lü*, also known as *Fang-chu-kuan ch'ü-lü*. The last consists of seventeen chapters in four *chüan* and, since the Ming period, has been one of the primary sources for the study of musical prosody and lyrics.

Wang is known to have written two *ch'uan-ch'i** plays, *T'i-hung chi* 題紅記 (Writ-ten on Red Leaves) and *Shuang-huan chi* 雙環記 (The Double Rings), and Fu Hsi-hua 傅惜華 attributes four other plays to him. He also wrote five *tsa-chü**: *Nan wang-hou* 男王后 (The Male Queen), *Chin-wu chao-hun* 金屋招魂 (Summons of the Soul from the Golden House), *Ch'i-kuan chiu-yu* 棄官救友 (Abandoning an Official Post and Rescuing a Friend), *Liang-tan shuang-juan* 兩旦雙鬟 (Two Actresses and their Maids), and *Ch'ien-nü li-hun* 倩女離魂 (The Soul Left Ch'ien-nü). Of all these works, only *T'i-hung chi*, *Nan wang-hou*, and a few songs from *Shuang-huan chi* found in *Ch'ün-yin lei-hsüan* 群音類選 are extant.

Wang was also credited with annotating *Hsi-hsiang chi** and *P'i-p'a chi* (see Kao Ming) and with contributing a scene to *Chui-ch'ai chi* 墜釵記 (The Fallen Hairpin). His annotated texts of the first two plays are no longer extant, however.

T'i-hung chi was written when Wang was a young man and is a revised version of *Hung-yeh chi* 紅葉記 (Red Leaves, no longer extant), a play by his grandfather. It is based on the romantic tale of Yü Yu 于祐 and Madame Han 韓 of the T'ang dynasty. This tale has four versions, some with other couples as the leads, all of which center on the romantic theme of composing poems on red leaves and the subsequent meeting of the writers, who fall in love and eventually become united in marriage. The version that first appeared during the Sung dynasty and on which the drama is based is perhaps the best known. The play itself, embellished with elegant poetry, reflects more the influence of the *Wen-tz'u p'ai* 文辭派 (School of Ornate Phraseology) than that of the School of Poetic Meter.

Nan wang-hou, inspired by the *Nü chuang-yüan* 女狀元 (A Female Top-graduate) of Hsü Wei,* portrays the triangular love affair centering on the character Ch'en Tzu-kao 陳子高, who agrees to be installed as a queen in order to save his life, but ultimately wins the forgiveness of the king and the heart of the king's sister. The fantastic nature of the plot is beyond question, a fact which Wang himself acknowledged in this play. Aside from the plot, it is a good example of the *tsa-chü* in this period and illustrates the process of generic transition of form, language, music, and singing roles from the *tsa-chü* of the Yüan to that of the Ming. This process is clearly seen in the language of the spoken parts and the singing roles, which are far closer to the prevailing practice in southern plays, though its form, music and the language of the songs continue to resemble the *tsa-chü* of Yüan.

His dramas as a whole received favorable comments from traditional critics.

EDITIONS:

Ch'ü-lü. Shanghai, 1932.

Fang-chu-kuan yüeh-fu 方諸館樂府. Changsha, 1941.

Nan wang-hou, in *Sheng-Ming.*

T'i-hung chi, in *Ku-pen,* II.

STUDIES:

Aoki, *Gikyokushi,* Part III, ch. 9, sec. 2 contains a brief biography, a list of some of his plays, and comments on *Nan wang-hou* and *T'i-hung chi.*

Chou, I-pai 周貽白. *Hsi-ch'ü yen-ch'ang lun-chu chi-shih* 戲曲演唱論著 輯釋. Peking, 1962, pp. 67-111.

Fu, *Ch'uan-ch'i,* pp. 164-167.

———. *Ming tsa-chü,* pp. 115-118.

Lo, Chin-t'ang 羅錦堂. *Ming-tai-chü tso-chia k'ao-lüeh* 明代劇作家考略. Hong Kong, 1966. Contains biography and list of his works.

Lo, K'ang-lieh 羅忼烈. "Ch'ü-chin shu-cheng" 曲禁疏證, in *Tz'u-ch'ü-lun k'ao* 詞曲論稿, Hong Kong, 1977, pp. 303-405.

Tseng, *Ming tsa-chü,* pp. 285-290.

Wang, Ku-lu 王古魯. *Ming-tai Hui-tiao hsi-ch'ü san-ch'u chi-i* 明代徽調戲曲散齣輯佚. Shanghai, 1956. Contains excerpts from *T'i-hung chi* and information on its evolution.

—EY

Wang Chien 王建 (*tzu,* Chung-ch'u 仲初, *c.* 751-*c.* 830) was a minor mid-T'ang poet best known for his *kung-t'i shih** (palace-style) and new *yüeh-fu* (see *yüeh-fu*) poems. He was a native of Ying-ch'uan 潁川 (modern Honan); the exact date of his birth is unknown. After passing the *chin-shih* examination in 775, Wang was appointed to serve as Defender of Wei-nan District 渭南縣 (modern Shansi). Thereafter he held various provincial posts—later in his life Wang returned to Hsien-yang 咸陽 (modern Shansi), where he reportedly lived as a recluse.

Throughout his long career Wang was friendly with a number of well-known poets and writers, such as Han Yü* and Chang Chi* (*c.* 766-*c.* 829). He and Chang often exchanged poems and have come to be grouped together by literary critics interested in the "new *yüeh-fu*" poetry that gained popularity during the early ninth century. These works are characterized by the belief that poetry should serve as a vehicle for the expression of moral values. Although major literary figures such as Po Chü-i* and Yüan Chen* were more instrumental in applying these principles to this subgenre, Wang Chien, Chang Chi, and other less known figures also played significant roles in the movement. Wang is, however, perhaps better known for his palace-style poems (there are one hundred), which were quite popular among his contemporaries and have been frequently included in collections of T'ang poetry. Apparently a relative of his named Wang Shou-ch'eng 王守澄, who served as a eunuch in the court of Emperor Te-tsung (r. 806-820), told him of events that occurred there, providing him with much of the material upon which these poems were based. Many of Wang's poems, such as his well-known "Hsin chia niang tz'u" 新嫁娘詞 (Words of a Newlywed Bride), a five-syllable *chüeh-chu,* employ a female persona and carry an indirect criticism against the unfair treatment suffered by many women at this time.

EDITIONS:

Chang Wang yüeh-fu 張王樂府. Hsü Ch'eng-yü 徐澄宇, ed. Shanghai, 1957.

Wang Chien shih-chi 王建詩集. Peking, 1959.

TRANSLATIONS:

Bynner, *Jade Mountain,* p. 184.

Frankel, *Palace Lady,* p. 153.

Sunflower, pp. 191-195.

Schafer, *Golden Peaches,* pp. 160, 162, 205-206.

Waley, *Chinese Poems,* p. 119.

———, *Translations,* pp. 314-315.

Watson, *Lyricism,* pp. 119-120.

Yang, Hsien-yi and Gladys Yang. "T'ang Dynasty 'Yüeh-fu' Songs—Chang Chieh [sic] and

Wang Chien," *Chinese Literature*, 1965.1, 77-84.

STUDIES:

Miyazaki, Ichisada 宮崎市定. "Ō Ken no shi sairon" 王建の詩再論, *Tōyōshi kenkyū*, 18.3 (December 1959), 26.

Nagata, Natsuki 長田夏樹. "Hakuwa shijin Ō Ken to sono jidai: Tō, Godai kōshō bungaku hattatsushi no ichisokumen toshite" 白話詩人王建とその 時代 — 唐五代講唱文學發達史の 一 側 面 として, *Kōbe gaidai ronsō*, 7.1-3 (June 1956), 141-165.

———. "Ō Ken shiden keinen hikki" 王建詩傳 繫年筆記, *Kōbe gaidai ronsō*, 12.3 (August 1961), 35-52. Pien, Hsiao-hsüan 卞孝萱. "Kuan-yü Wang Chien te chi-ko wen-t'i" 關 於王建的幾個問題, in *T'ang shih yen-chiu lun-wen chi* 唐詩研究論文集, Ch'en I-hsin 陳貽焮, ed., Hong Kong, 1970, v. 2, pp. 193-205.

Tung, Chiung 東裊. *T'ang Wang Chien kung-tz'u i-pai shou* 唐王建宮詞一百首. Kyōto, 1953 [reviewed in *HJAS*, 14 (1955), 491].

—MSp

Wang Chih-huan 王之渙 (*tzu*, Chi-ling 季陵, 688-742) was an accomplished writer of *chüeh-chü* (quatrains—see *shih*). A native of Ping-chou 幷州 (modern Shansi), he held a series of minor posts. It would appear that he did not seek political advancement in life. Although only six of his poems are extant, he made a reputation writing songs of the frontier. A well-known anecdote suggests his contemporary reputation. While he was drinking in a wine shop with Kao Shih* and Wang Ch'ang-ling,* singing girls sang verses by the latter two bards, who then jocularly boasted to Wang Chih-huan of their prominence. Wang entreated them to wait to see what the most beautiful of the girls sang, and, of course, it turned out to be one of his songs.

Despite an extremely small extant corpus, two are well known. The most famous is "Teng Kuan-ch'üeh lou" 登鸛雀樓 (Ascending the Tower of the Hooded Crane) which has been included in numerous anthologies. Although the form is strictly regular (a five-syllable *chüeh-chü* with no violations in pattern), the poem is of interest because of its philosophic tone:

The bright sun rests on the mountain, is one,

The Yellow River flows into the sea.
If you want to see a full thousand miles,
Climb one more story of this tower.
(Owen, *High T'ang*)

The second well-known piece, a seven-syllable quatrain, is "Liang-chou tz'u" 涼州詞 (Song of Liang-chou), a piece depicting the isolation of the northwestern frontier. According to Yang Shen* the poem is an allegory which suggests that imperial favor and concern stopped, like the spring winds, somewhat short of the area. It is also said that this was the poem sung by the courtesan in the gathering with Wang Ch'ang-ling and Kao Shih described above.

These two poems have attracted great attention from PRC scholars since the late 1950s (over fifty articles have been written on them).

EDITIONS:
Ch'üan T'ang shih, v. 4, pp. 2849-2850.

TRANSLATIONS:
Owen, *High T'ang*, pp. 247-248.

STUDIES:
Fu, *Shih-jen:* "Chin-neng so tso Wang Chih-huan mu-chih-ming" 靳能所作王之渙墓誌銘, pp. 56-65.

I-shan 宜珊. "Wang, Ts'en, Kao te pien-sai shih" 王岑高的邊塞詩, *Chin-jih Chung-kuo*, 57 (January 1976).

Ma, Mao-yüan 馬茂元. "Wang Chih-huan sheng-p'ing k'ao-lüeh" 王之渙 生平考略, *Chung-hua wen-shih lun-ts'ung* 中華文史論叢, 4 (1979).

—TS and PHC

Wang Chiu-ssu 王九思 (*tzu*, Ching-fu 敬夫, *hao*, Mei-p'o 渼陂 or Tzu-ke shan-jen 紫閣山人, 1468-1551) was a native of Hu-hsien 鄠 (modern Shansi). He was the eldest son of a family of some repute; his father had served for many years and in many places as an educational official. Wang was noted as a handsome and precocious child; he sat for, and passed, the provincial degree in 1489 and became a *chin-shih* in 1496. When he passed one of his examinations, he composed a poem in the style of Li Tung-yang* and was subsequently acknowledged to be one of his devotees. Under Li's tutelage, Wang rose quickly in the bureaucracy. Later, however, when

K'ang Hai* and Li Meng-yang* came to the capital and advocated a return to "ancient-prose style," Wang Chiu-ssu changed his allegiance from Li Tung-yang to K'ang Hai and Li Meng-yang. This action led Li Tung-yang to trump up charges that Wang was part of the faction of Liu Ch'in 劉瑾, a court eunuch. When Li Tung-yang succeeded in removing Liu Ch'in from office and having him executed, he subsequently stripped Wang Chiu-ssu of his position in the Han-lin Academy, claiming that the geographical tie between Liu and Wang (they were both from the same province) was an indication of factionalism. Wang was demoted to be a Vice-magistrate of Shou-chou 壽州 (modern Anhwei); later, like his lifelong friend and fellow dramatist, K'ang Hai, he was cashiered for good.

He and K'ang Hai returned to their home village, where they spent their time in song and drink and learned to become accomplished musicians. Wang became a poet of some renown; about 360 pieces are included in his *Pi-shan yüeh-fu* 碧山樂府 (Popular Song from the Azure Mountain). These poems are appended to his collected works, *Mei-p'o-chi* 湄陂集, which went through several editions in the Ming period. He also edited a gazetteer of his local district, the *Ch'ung-hsiu Hu-hsien chih* 重修鄠縣志.

His fame, however, rests primarily on his skill as a dramatist. He has two extant works, the *Chung-shan lang yüan-pen* 中山狼院本 (The Wolf of Chung-shan: A Short Drama), and *Tu Tzu-mei ku-chiu yu-ch'un* 杜子美沽酒遊春 (Tu Fu Sells Wine and Roams in the Spring).

The first drama is based on a *ch'uan-ch'i** tale entitled *Chung-shan lang-chuan* 中山狼傳 (The Wolf of Chung-shan) and on a longer drama of the same name by K'ang Hai. This one-act piece tells the story of a clever wolf who convinces a Mohist scholar to hide him from a band of pursuing hunters. The scholar does so, tying the animal up and hiding him in his bookbag. When the wolf is set free, it reflects that it should eat the scholar in order to stay its hunger. The scholar convinces the wolf to consult "three wise old creatures." The wolf asks an apri-

cot and then a bullock; both say the scholar should be eaten. The third old one of whom the question is asked turns out to be the earth-spirit of Chung-shan, who tricks the wolf back into the scholar's bookbag, thus saving the Mohist.

Tu Tzu-mei ku-chiu yu-ch'un recounts a tale in which Tu Fu,* the great T'ang poet, runs a wine shop. The first two acts of the drama are given over to Tu Fu reviling Li Lin-fu and Yang Kuo-chung, both evil T'ang ministers. The second two acts, in contrast to the opprobrium against the two ministers, recount the pleasures Tu Fu and Ts'en Shen* had as they roamed in the countryside. This particular play is clearly political satire directed against Li Tung-yang (i.e., Li Lin-fu) and Yang T'ing-ho (Yang Kuo-chung). The pleasures of Tu Fu and Ts'en Ts'an are also those of Wang and K'ang Hai in retirement. Political satire is also evident in the *Chung-shan-lang yüan-pen*.

While Wang Chiu-ssu's plays have drawn much attention through the years for their vehement satire, they have fared less well as literary and musical works. Li K'ai-hsien,* for instance, was critical of the liberties that Wang took with poetic meter and musical form. Other critics, such as Wang Chi-te,* found Wang's poetry to be the equal of the Yüan dramatists.

EDITIONS:
Mei-p'o ch'üan-chi 湄陂全集 (1640 edition), includes *Mei-p'o chi* (16 *chüan*), *Mei-p'o hsü-chi* (3 *chüan*) and *Pi-shan yüeh-fu* (8 *chüan*). This work also contains both plays.
Sheng Ming, II contains both plays.
Chou, I-pai 周貽白. *Ming-jen tsa-chü hsüan* 明人雜劇選, Peking, 1958, pp. 261-268. An annotated version of *Chung-shan lang.*

TRANSLATIONS:
Crump, J. I. "Wang Chiu-ssu: The Wolf of Chung-shan," *Renditions,* 7 (1977), 29-38.
Dolby, William. *Eight Chinese Plays.* London, 1978, pp. 93-102.

STUDIES:
Cheng, Ch'ien 鄭騫. "Pa *Pi-shan yüeh-fu,*" in *Ts'ung shih tao ch'ü* 從詩到曲, Taipei, 1971, pp. 217-219. A textual study of the *Pi-shan yüeh-fu,* originally written in 1941-1943.

———. "*Pi-shan yüeh-fu* shou-lü chü-li," in *ibid*, pp. 213-216, originally written in 1944.

DMB, pp. 1366-1367.

Fu, *Ming tsa-chü*, pp. 85-86.

Idema, W. L. "*Yüan-pen* as a Minor Form of Dramatic Literature in the Fifteenth and Sixteenth Centuries," *CLEAR*, 6.1 (January 1984). Discusses *Chung-shan lang yüan-pen*.

Li, K'ai-hsien. "Mei-p'o Wang Chieh-t'ao chuan" 渼陂王檢討傳, in *Li K'ai-hsien chi*, Lu Kung 路功, ed., Peking, 1959.

Tseng, Yung-i 曾永義. *Ming tsa-chü kai-lun* 明雜劇概論. Taipei, 1976, pp. 210-217.

—sw

Wang *Fan-chih* 王梵志 is the name associated with a sizable corpus of T'ang vernacular poetry, the vast majority of which exists only in manuscript copies found at Tun-huang in the early part of this century. *Fan-chih* is not a given name, but a title, a Chinese equivalent of Sanskrit *brahmacarin*, which designates a lay Buddhist zealot (thus Demiéville's translation "Wang le Zélateur)."

A paragraph in the *T'ai-p'ing kuang-chi** records that Wang *Fan-chih* was born from a tumescence on a crab-apple tree in the garden of one Wang Te-tsu 王德祖, a Sui dynasty resident of Honan. The myth of magical birth is probably a folk etymology to explain *Fan-chih* and testifies to the popularity of the poems in the latter half of the T'ang. The language of the poems is the vernacular of the eighth century. The earliest references to Wang *Fan-chih* also suggest that the poems began to be popular in Buddhist educational circles in this period. The *Li-tai fa-pao chih* 歷代法寶記, a history of the Ch'an sect completed about 780, quotes a poem by Wang *Fan-chih* and explains that such verses were often used for instructional purposes in Buddhist institutions. The late ninth-century *Yün-hsi yu-i* 雲谿友議 has a similar remark and quotes nineteen poems. This practice is perhaps confirmed by the fact that several Tun-huang manuscripts containing "Wang *Fan-chih* poems" are obviously schoolboy calligraphy exercises (notably P2842). Finally, the *Shih-shih* 詩式 manuscripts divide into two distinct collections of verse, each attributed to Wang *Fan-chih*, yet different in form, content, and tone. A single *chüan* collection of ninety-two pentasyllabic *chüeh-chü* was obviously the most common of the two, being represented by five complete (P2718, P3558, P3656, P3716, and S3393) and six fragmentary manuscripts. The quatrains in this "Ninety-two Poem Collection" are all didactic and gnomic, emphasizing such basic moral virtues as filial piety, social manners, fiscal responsibility, and abstinence from alcohol. A few of the later poems stress Buddhist piety. The first quatrain in this collection reads:

> Brothers should live in harmony,
> cousins shouldn't mistreat each other.
> Put all valuables in a common chest,
> don't hoard up possessions in your own room.

And the last reads:

> Renounce evil deeds,
> don't resist good ones.
> The wise who seek the Good Law
> will surely behold the *Tathagata*.

Such verses were probably composed by Buddhist monks to instruct the lay children in their schools and are of little intrinsic literary interest.

Quite otherwise is the much longer and varied collection in three *chüan*. Although no single copy of the entire "Three *Chüan* Collection" survives, most of its contents can be reconstructed from seven manuscripts; S778 and S5796 (*chüan* 1); P3211, S5441, and S5641 (*chüan* 2), and P2914 and P3833 (*chüan* 3). The poems are preceded by a preface, unfortunately undated and anonymous, which states that the collection contains "over three hundred poems." Together with the ninety-two quatrains in the single *chüan* collection, this figure brings the number of poems attributed to Wang *Fan-chih* to about four hundred. The poems in the "Three *Chüan* Collection" are marked by melancholy meditations on the vanity of human life and on the impermanence and nonreality of worldly existence. There is an almost macabre fascination with death, evident from the first poem in the collection:

> I watch from afar the world's people—
> villages and peaceful towns.

When a family has a death in the house,
the whole town comes to weep.
With open mouths they bewail the corpse,
not understanding that bodies go fast.
Actually we're ghosts of the long sleep,
come for a time to stand on the earth.
It's almost like babies' diapers—
at once dry then wet in turn.
The first to die is buried deep,
the later ones are thrown in on top.

Other poems maintain the conciseness of the quatrains in the "Ninety-two Poem Collection," but also possess psychological sophistication and artistic impact absent from the didactic poems:

I saw the man die,
and my gut was hot like fire;
not that I pitied the man,
I was afraid I'd be next.

The poems in both collections are written without allusions in a vigorous, colloquial language that intensifies the immediacy and simplicity of the content.

Both Demiéville and Iriya Yoshitaka have suggested that Wang *Fan-chih*—"Wang le Zélateur"—may never have existed as a historical person and that the poems now attributed to him were collected together by virtue of their common didactic origin and colloquial language. Both scholars see in this process a parallel to that which shaped the present Hanshan* collection, which linguistic evidence has demonstrated comprises poems whose dates of composition span at least a century. In the case of Wang *Fan-chih* it seems probable that the "Ninety-two Poem Collection" arose in this way. The texts in the "Three *Chüan* Collection," on the other hand, reveal a dynamic yet basically cohesive personality which suggests they are more likely to be the work of a single hand.

The value of both collections for the history of Chinese poetry is considerable: they provide as close a glimpse as we are likely to obtain of T'ang dynasty popular poetry, and thus constitute an important measure against which to judge the "orality" of traditionally transmitted T'ang poetry. In the same vein, a detailed study of the colloquialisms in the Wang *Fan-chih* corpus will probably suggest that the normative language of T'ang poetry contains more colloquial elements than has hitherto been suspected. Finally, these fragmentary Wang *Fan-chih* texts provide a vivid picture of the didactic use of poetry at lower, nonliterate and semiliterate levels of T'ang society. This picture suggests that this ubiquity of poetry provided an important background for the creation of the enduring poetic masterpieces of the period.

EDITIONS:

Demiéville, Paul. *L'oeuvre de Wang le Zélateur (Wang Fan-tche). Poèmes populaires des T'ang, VIII-IX siècle.* Paris, 1982. The definitive work on Wang *Fan-chih*.
Wang Fan-chih shih chioo-chi 王梵志詩校輯. Chang Hsi-hou 張錫厚, coll. and ed. Peking, 1983.

STUDIES:

Chang, Hsi-hou. "Kuan-yü Tun-huang hsieh-pen Wang Fan-chih shih cheng-li te jo-kan wen-t'i" 關於敦煌寫本王梵志 詩整理的若干問題, *Wen-shih*, 15 (September 1982), 185-202.
Demiéville, Paul. *Annuaire du Collége de France*, 1957, pp. 253-357; 1958, pp. 386-391; 1959, pp. 436-439. Short, work-in-progress notes on Demiéville's reading of the Wang *Fan-chih* corpus. Superseded by his 1982 book, but still useful.
———. "Le Tch'an et la poésie chinoise," *Hermès* 7 (1970), 123-136.
Iriya Yoshitaka 入矢義高. "Ō Bonshi ni tsuite" 王梵志について, *Chūgoku bungakuhō*, 3 (1955), 50-60; 4 (1956), 19-56.

—CH

Wang Fu-chih 王夫之 (*tzu*, Erh-nung 而農, *hao*, Chiang-chai 薑齋, Ch'uan-shan 船山, I-hu Tao-jen 一瓠道人, Hsi-t'ang 夕堂, 1619-1692) came from Heng-yang 衡陽 (modern Hunan) and is primarily known for his studies in philosophy and the classics.

From youth on, under the influence of his elder brother Wang Chieh-chih 王介之 (1607-1686), he began preparing for the examinations. In 1642 he passed the *chü-jen*, but the Manchu takeover caused him to return to studying the classics. After a brief stint as a follower of the Ming refugee prince in the south, he retired to Heng-yang in 1651, declining all contacts with the new dynasty and devoting himself to scholarship.

Aside from his classical and philosophical studies, Wang was also a literary critic. There were two ways in which a critic in traditional China could publish his literary opinions—literary tracts or anthologies. Wang Fu-chih adopted both manners of expression. His three judicious anthologies—*Ku-shih p'ing-hsüan* 古詩評選, *T'ang-shih p'ing-hsüan* 唐詩評選, and *Ming-shih p'ing-hsüan* 明詩評選 —deserve a closer scrutiny than they have received. But the central work in Wang's critical thinking is the *Chiang-chai shih-hua* 薑齋詩話.

The *Chiang-chai shih-hua* is made up of entries transcribed from three of Wang's other works. It has widely been supposed that the present title was a late coinage, probably invented by Ting Fu-pao 丁福保, the twentieth-century editor of the *Ch'ing shih-hua* 清詩話 (Poetry Talks from the Ch'ing Dynasty). The latest edition of the *Chiang-chai shih-hua* dispels that supposition, pointing out that this title was used in the earliest editions of Wang's corpus.

The *Chiang-chai shih-hua* has many of the characteristics, and weaknesses, of the conventional *shih-hua*.* It consists of disparate entries of limited length which are not always sensibly arranged into a whole. Important ideas and insights are juxtaposed with trivial assertions of personal preference. Some points are repeated in much the same form in several places, and others are fragmented. Poems and the critical opinions of other critics are often quoted or referred to without any indication of source or location at all.

But behind the apparent casualness and disorder is a vigorous mind, doing battle with some of the most taxing problems in literary criticism. The central idea of Wang's poetics is that poetry is a totally independent human activity which serves the needs of man's moral and spiritual growth and enables him to be more fully integrated with the universe. Poetry is not to be confused with scholarship, not even the scholarship surrounding the Confucian Classics. This insistence on the independence of poetry would have been useful in any critic; coming from Wang, whose mastery of both history and the classics was not surpassed by many, it must be regarded as an accurate and objective recognition of the essential character of poetry.

Being independent of other areas of knowledge and thoroughly human, poetry is not to be reduced to any man-made law or rule (*fa* 法), any contrived or mechanical regularity. Wang repeatedly condemns *fa* in general and, in particular, considers it misguided to seek to set up standards for poetry. In the same spirit, Wang reprobates the formation of "schools" in which general similarity usurps individual style.

The inner movements of a poem should be governed by the intention or will (*i* 意) of the poet. When they are so governed, the poem has its own momentum (*shih* 勢) and develops in its own ineluctable terms. A poem that comes into existence through intention and momentum has a life and wholeness of its own. The organic whole is like a live snake, which cannot possibly be made up of a number of shorter worms linked together.

This does not mean, however, that the poet is a "creator" of his poems in the European sense. The Coleridgean poet with an imagination that "shapes," as the Christian God shaped the world into existence, does not feature in Wang's criticism. It is true that Wang encourages his poet to contemplate the world around him, in terms of minute details and in terms of large, abstract principles. It is also true that he sees poetry as an embodiment of things. But this acknowledgement of a bond in poetry between World and Poet, Poet and Language, Language and Reader occupies only a small area of Wang's critical awareness. And it is an area dominated by the Confucian ideal of man as conscious or self-conscious being.

Far more characteristic of Wang's poetics is the poet who is conscious without being at all self-conscious. This poet is free from the obsessions and merely private feelings of his individual being. He is fully and harmoniously attuned to the universe and knows the peace and tranquillity that poetry permits. Unlike Tu Fu,* he does not fret—because he does not assert himself.

It is in this view of poetry that the concepts of emotion (*ch'ing* 情) and scene (*ching* 景) become so important. In the vocabulary of other Chinese critics, *ch'ing* and *ching* are largely technical notions. Wang gives them new definition and they come to concern the nature and value of poetry, as well as something of the process of its making. They are no more than critical labels, often used for the sake of convenience. Lines of poetry to which we apply one of the labels are not necessarily devoid of the substance of the other label. Borrowing from Confucian thinking, Wang explains that "names" 名 do not always tally with "realities" 實. If so, things that we distinguish in name may not be distinguishable in reality. In reality, "emotion" and "scene" are indistinguishable—contrary to what most critics say. This has two levels of significance. On the literary level, Wang helps us to understand the nature of poetic language, that metaphor and meaning are not artificially yoked together but integrated. On the moral level, he reminds us that in poetry, Man and Universe become intimately engaged, and the engagement is beneficial to man.

Wang's criticism is not confined to the poet's point of view. He also comments on the reading of poetry. In this connection, he quotes from the seventeenth book of the *Lun-yü* where Confucius says, "An apt quotation from the *Odes* may serve to stimulate the imagination, to show one's breeding, to smooth over difficulties in a group and to give expression to complaints" (D.C. Lau's translation). Commentators tend to be interested in the operative verbs in this passage (*hsing* 興, *kuan* 觀, *ch'ün* 群 and *yüan* 怨). Wang, however, draws our attention to the auxiliary *k'o-i* 可以 (Lau's "may"). He enlarges the auxiliary into something of a full verb meaning "can do" and argues that *k'o-i* is the key word in the pronouncement. If a poem has a single meaning intended by its poet, he continues, it should not stop each reader from reading the poem in his own way and according to his own emotional response. This may seem like a willful distortion of Confucius' sense and an encouragement to read inaccurately and

subjectively; nonetheless, it *is* consonant with Wang's critical beliefs. For ultimately what really matters is not the poem; it is the amelioration of personality, that of the reader and that of the poet.

EDITIONS:

Chiang-chai shih-hua, in Ting Fu-pao, comp., *Ch'ing shih-hua*, Shanghai, 1978, v. 1, pp. 3-22.

Chiang-chai shih-hua, collated and punctuated by I-chih 夷之, bound together with Hsieh Chen's 謝榛 *Ssu-ming shih-hua* 四冥詩話. Peking, 1961.

STUDIES:

Ch'en, Yu-ch'in 陳友琴. "Kuan-yü Wang Ch'uan-shan te shih-lun" 關於王船山的詩論, in *Wang Ch'uan-shan hsüeh-shu t'ao-lun chi* 王船山學術討論集, Peking, 1965, pp. 466-488.

ECCP, pp. 817-819.

Fu, *Ch'ing tsa-chü*, p. 52.

Kuo, Ho-ming 郭鶴鳴, "Wang Ch'uan-shan shih-lun t'an-wei" 王船山詩論探微, *Kuo-li T'ai-wan Shih-fan Ta-hsüeh Kuo-wen Yen-chiu-so chi-k'an*, 23 (1979), 855-957.

Shou-ch'un 壽春. "Kuan-yü Wang Ch'uan-shan shih-lun chung te i-hsieh wen-t'i" 關于王船山詩論中的一些問題. *Kuang-ming jih-pao*, March 7, 1965, *Wen-hsüeh i-ch'an*, 501.

Tseng, "Ch'ing-tai tsa-chü," pp. 127-129.

—SKW

Wang Heng 王衡 (*tzu*, Ch'en-yü 辰玉, 1561-1609), a native of T'ai-ts'ang 太倉 (modern Kiangsu), was a scholar, calligrapher, and dramatist. His father, Wang Hsi-chüeh 王錫爵 (1534-1611), was a high official and a scholar with an impeccable record of public service. His family was one of the two illustrious and prominent Wang families in T'ai-ts'ang—the other being that of Wang Shih-chen* (1526-1590). Born into such a family Wang Heng received an excellent education at an early age. He became a *chü-jen* in 1588. He headed the list, and some critics accused his father, who was then a Grand Secretary, along with other officials whose sons were also high on the list, of nepotism. A second examination was given to Wang, who proved his ability. He never, however, took another examination as long as his father was a Grand Secretary. After he received the *chin-shih* degree in 1601, ranking second among the participants, he was made a Han-lin compiler, and was subsequently assigned to a post in Chiang-nan 江南. Due to ill health, he asked to retire; his request was eventually granted. He died in 1609.

He left the following works: *Kou-shan chi* 緱山集, *Chi-yu kao* 紀遊稿, *Kuei-t'ien tz'u* 歸田詞, and *Ming-hsin pao-chien* 明心寶鑑. The last, collated by him, consists of a collection of wise sayings offering moral advice on practical living.

As a dramatist he was also responsible for a number of *tsa-chü.** The exact total is a matter of dispute, some scholars maintaining that he wrote four, others five. The argument has to do with two titles: *Mo-nai-ho k'u-tao chang-an chieh* 沒奈何哭倒長安街真 ("Can't Be Helped" Cried in the Streets of Ch'ang-an) and *Chen k'uei-lei* 眞傀儡 (The Real Puppet). The first is recorded in *Chung-ting ch'ü-hai-mu* 重訂曲海目, *Chin-yüeh k'ao-cheng* 今樂考證, and *Ch'ü-lü* 曲錄, under two titles: *Mo-nai-ho* and *Ku-tao chang-an chieh*, giving the impression that there are two different plays. It appears that the authors of these works erred in breaking down the title. The extant text of the play is found under the title *Hu-lu Hsien-sheng* 葫蘆先生 (Mr. Bottle-gourd) in the first act of *Yüan-shih i-ch'üan* 袁氏義犬 by Ch'en Yü-chiao,* which corresponds to the text of a Ming edition of Wang's play housed in the Naikaku Bunkō.

The second, *Chen k'uei-lei*, is attributed to an anonymous author in the *Sheng-Ming tsa-chü* 盛明雜劇, but the author of *Ch'ü-hai t'i-yao* 曲海提要 states: "[The author's] name cannot be traced. But some said it was composed by Wang Heng."

It may therefore be reasonable to attribute the following dramas to Wang Heng: *Wang-mo-lu p'o-sui yu-lun-p'ao* 王摩詰拍碎鬱輪袍 (How Wang-mo-lu Broke the Robe of the Wheel of Sorrow), also known as *Yü-lun-p'ao; Mo-nai-ho k'u-tao chang-an chieh; Tsai-sheng yüan* 再生緣 (Twice Destined in Marriage); and *P'ei-chan ho-ho* 裴湛和合 (The Grand Harmony), no longer extant. The first, set in the T'ang period, portrays the poet-painter Wang Wei's* attempts in the examination—an impostor, Wang T'ui 王推, pretends to be Wang Wei

in his effort to win favor from the princess. The impostor's impropriety is finally discovered and honor is restored to Wang Wei, who at this point renounces worldly glory and returns to his native place. At the end of the drama, it is revealed that Wang Wei is a reincarnation of a Buddha. Though *Yü-lun-p'ao* distorts the life of Wang Wei, the work is believed to be autobiographical, protesting Wang Heng's mistreatment in 1588.

In Wang's dramas there is a strong thematic dependence on Buddhism as a philosophical frame of reference for the actions of the *dramatis personae*. This is even true in *Tsai-sheng yüan*, a romantic play, in which the theme of reincarnation is prominent.

EDITIONS:

Kou-shan chi 緱山集, also known as *Wang Kou-shan Hsing-sheng chi* 王緱山先生集. Taipei, 1970. Contains poems, lyric poems, essays, memorials, eulogies, correspondence, biographies, etc., in 27 *chüan*.

Ming hsin pao-chien 明心寶鑑, in *Kinsei Bungaku Shiryō ruijū* 近世文學資料類從, Tokyo, 1972. Contains a collection of wise sayings, offering advice on practical and moral living.

Mo-nai-ho k'u-tao chang-an chieh 沒奈何哭倒長安街, *Tsai-sheng yüan* 再生緣, and *Wang-mo-ku p'o-sui yü-lun-p'ao* 王摩詰拍碎鬱輪袍 in Shen T'ai 沈泰, ed., *Sheng-Ming tsa-chü ch'u-chi* 盛明雜劇初集, n.p., 1918. The text of the first play is in the first act of *Yüan-shih i-ch'uan* by Ch'en Yü-chiao, which is also in the *Sheng-Ming*.

STUDIES:

Aoki, *Gikyokushi*, pp. 239-240. Contains a brief biography, an incomplete list of his plays, and comments on two of them.

Fu, *Ming tsa-chü*, pp. 113-115.

Liu, Wen-liu 劉文六. *K'un-ch'ü yen-chiu* 崑曲研究. Taipei, 1969.

Lo, Chin-t'ang 羅錦堂. *Ming-tai-chü tso-chia k'ao-lüeh* 明代劇作家考略. Hong Kong, 1966. Contains biography and a list of his plays.

Tseng, Yung-i 曾永義. *Ming tsa-chü kai-lun* 明雜劇概論. Taipei, 1976, pp. 318-328.

Wang, Shih-chen 王士禎. *Hsiang-tsu pi-chi* 香祖筆記. Shanghai, 1938. *Chüan* 12 lists two of his plays and a single comment referring to critics' opinions on the plays.

—EY

Wang Jo-hsü 王若虛 (*tzu*, Ts'ung-chih 從之, 1174-1243) is considered the leading classicist and most learned scholar of the short-lived Chin dynasty (1115-1234), a kingdom founded in North China by the Tungusic Jurchen people. He was a prolific writer and critic and author of two literary collections. One, called the *Yung-fu chi* 慵夫集 (Collection of the Indolent One) is no longer extant; it was lost within a hundred years after Wang's death. The other is the *Hu-nan i-lao chi* 滹南遺老集 (Collection of the Remanent Elder from South of the Hu [River]); it consists of forty-five chapters of critical writings ranging from classics to poetry, including some prose essays on a miscellany of topics which can be broken into roughly four categories: (1) criticism of the classics, (2) historical works, (3) poetry and prose, and (4) selections of Wang's own belletristic writings. His criticism of classical commentaries focuses on the forced interpretations of the Han Scholiasts and the overwrought extrapolations of the same canonical works by Sung Neo-Confucianists; that is, he constantly takes the Han scholars to task for being too literalist with the text and the Sung commentators for being too imaginative in creating abstractions that range far beyond the basic meaning of the work.

His historical criticism seems imbalanced. He is often overly meticulous in his comments on Ssu-ma Ch'ien* and Sung Ch'i 宋祁 (998-1061). Ssu-ma Ch'ien, in particular, is criticized in eleven lengthy chapters for what Wang considered his trite, contradictory, and repetitive style. The preponderance of historical criticism is a reflection of contemporary issues and the debate of that time between Wang Jo-hsü and other members of the history office over the correct format and style of the veritable records (*shih-lu*) that they were compiling. While the criticism of the *Shih-chi* 史記 is excessive in many places, it has been lauded for its accurate analysis of Ssu-ma Ch'ien's shortcomings as a historian and prose stylist.

Wang's "discriminations" of prose are balanced between an evaluative discussion of writers, weighing their relative worth, and a kind of textual analysis that focuses on the metaphorical usage of language and the appropriate usage of classical particles—singling out infelicitous use of key particles in the prose works of even major writers.

Of particular interest to the student of literature are Wang's *shih-hua*,* in which he evaluates major poets from the late T'ang through the Northern Sung. The work praises the poetry of Tu Fu,* Po Chü-i,* and Su Shih* and criticizes the poetics of Huang T'ing-chien* and the Kiangsi *shih-p'ai*.* Wang wrote this work during a period of intense debate over poetic models, which is recounted in the *Kuei-ch'ien-chih* 歸潛志, a private history written by a minor literary figure of the Chin. It was then commonly accepted that Huang T'ing-chien and the Kiangsi School were the rightful heirs to the mantle of Tu Fu, already considered the greatest of T'ang poets. This was a position that Wang attacked with zeal, supporting Su Shih as the prime antithesis to the meticulous and technical style of Huang and the Kiangsi School. Wang's strong advocacy of Su Shih arose not only because of Su's free and unfettered style, but also because Su considered poetry a spontaneous expression of moral awareness. The emphasis on technique mitigated the expression of true (and, to Wang, ethical) feeling. In his predilection for the style of Su Shih, Wang's name is inextricably linked with two other Chin writers, Chao Ping-wen* and Yüan Hao-wen,* as the leading triumvirate of contemporary scholars and writers. Because of their contemporary influence—Chao as the leading patron of Chin letters, Yüan as the major lyrical poet, and Wang as the major classicist and critic—historical retrospect has naturally focused on the values these writers shared, namely their advocacy of Su Shih. This has sometimes resulted in a more homogenized view of Chin poetics and an unjustifiably high estimation of Wang's criticism. As noted previously, the strident tone of Wang's criticism of Huang T'ing-chien is understandable only if it is put into the context of equally cogent but diametrically opposed arguments by his contemporaries. Thus, his polemical advocacy of Tu Fu, Po Chü-i, and Su Shih is probably more than personal preference and represents his attempt to refute current assessments of Huang T'ing-chien.

There is a consistent tone and unity to Wang's critical writings, no matter what the subject. His emphasis on spontaneity of expression, on the appropriateness of language to subject, and on the flexible but structured criticism of literature in general mark both his literary and classical criticism and show that he conceived of his critical writings as an organic system of interpretation.

In general, Wang's extant prose pieces and poetry follow the dicta of his critical works—they are unadorned, straightforward, generally unimaginative pieces. They are also a major source for the study of literary history in the Chin dynasty. His critical writings, however, are more significant.

EDITIONS:

Hunan i-lao chi 湋南遺老集 . 45 *chüan.* This text is found in several editions, the two most important of which are the edition of Wu Ch'ung-hsi 吳重熹 , originally printed in 1886 from a manuscript copy compiled during the Yüan, combined in 1909 with eight other Chin-dynasty collections, and published as *Shan-tung Hai-feng Wu Shih-lien-an hui-k'o chiu Chin-jen chi* 山東海豐吳石蓮盦彙刻九金人集 , and the *Ts'ung-shu chi-ch'eng* 叢書集成 (1935), a typeset, punctuated recension of the Chi-fu ts'ung-shu 畿輔叢書 edition by Wang Hao 王灝 (1828-1888).

STUDIES:

Chang, Chien 長健 . *Sung Chin ssu-chia wen-hsüeh p'i-p'ing* 宋金四家文學批評 . Taipei, 1975, pp. 315-404.

Hsü, Wen-yü 許文玉 . "Chin Yüan te wen-yu" 金元的文囿 , in *Chung-kuo wen-hsüeh yen-chiu* 中國文學研究 , Peking, 1954, pp. 336-347.

—sw

Wang K'ai-yün 王闓運 (*tzu,* Jen-ch'iu 壬秋 or Jen-fu 壬父, *hao,* Hsiang-ch'i 湘綺, 1832-1916) was a native of Hsiang-t'an 湘潭 (Hunan). When he was only eighteen, he founded Ch'eng-nan College in Changsha 長沙 and had a number of disciples. In 1852 he became a *chü-jen,* but his later attempts at obtaining the *chin-shih* degree all failed. He worked for a time as a private tutor at the home of the Grand Secretary Su Shun 肅順. After Su Shun was killed, Wang went to serve Tseng Kuo-fan,* then commander of the Hsiang 湘 Corps. But when Tseng later rose to high position he refused to give Wang any post. From then on Wang gave up all thoughts of getting an official position. He lectured at a number of colleges, including Tsun-ching 尊經 College in Ch'eng-tu 成都, Chiao-ching 校經 College in Changsha, Ch'uan-shan 船山 College in Heng-chou 衡州, and the Nan-ch'ang 南昌 Senior School. His students called him Master Hsiang-ch'i, for he had once named his dwelling the Hsiang-ch'i House. In 1906 he was given the position of Examining Editor in the Han-lin Academy. After the Republic was founded, he retained his queue, and looked upon himself as a survivor of the former dynasty. Yüan Shih-k'ai once employed him as the Head of the Bureau of National History, but he held the post for only a short time and then returned to his home village. He died in 1916.

In verse and prose, he advocated imitation of the styles of the Han-Wei and the Six Dynasties eras. His ideas on literature can be found in "Hsiang-ch'i lou lun-wen" 湘綺樓論文 (in *Kuo-ts'ui hsüeh-pao* 國粹學報, 22) and in "Hsiang-ch'i lou lun shih-wen t'i fa" 論詩文體法 (in *Kuo-ts'ui hsüeh-pao,* 38). Although Wang lived in a time of political instability, his writings rarely reflect the turmoils of his time. He differs from the antiquarianism of the Ming (see Li Tung-yang and Li Meng-yang) only in his broadening the models for imitation to include Six Dynasties works. His own best work, such as "Ch'iu-hsing tz'u hsü" 秋醒詞序 (A Preface to the *Lyrics of Autumn-awakes*), "Tao Kuang-chou yü fu shu" 到廣州與婦書 (A Letter to My Wife on Arriving at Canton), and the heptasyllabic old-style poem "Yüan-ming yüan tz'u" 圓明園詞 (Verse on the Yüan-ming Garden), reflects the Six Dynasties' style in its richness of diction. Some critics, however, attack his predilection for the past.

Wang abandoned himself to carefree behavior, especially in his late years. This is clearly reflected in his *Hsiang-ch'i lou Diary.*

His collected works, *Wang Hsiang-ch'i Hsien-sheng ch'üan-chi* 王湘綺先生全集, include eight *chüan* of prose, fourteeen *chüan* of *shih*,* three *chüan* of miscellaneous writings, and one *chüan* of *tz'u.**

EDITIONS:

Wang Hsiang-ch'i Hsien-sheng ch'üan-chi 王湘綺 先生全集. Changsha, 1923.

STUDIES:

BDRC, v. 3, pp. 384-385.

Wang, Tai-kung 王代功. *Hsiang-ch'i Fu-chün nien-p'u* 湘綺府君年譜 . Taipei, 1970.

Wu, Wan-ku 吳萬谷. "Wang K'ai-yün," in *Chung-kuo wen-hsüeh-shih lun-chi* 中國文學史 論集, Taipei, 1958, v. 4, pp. 1183-1204.

—YPC

Wang Kuo-wei 王國維 (1877-1927), scholar, poet, and teacher, was born in Haining 海寧 (modern Chekiang) to an old family rich in the patriot-scholar-official tradition. Like many of his contemporaries, however, when he failed to pass the official examinations, he turned his back on the traditional path of officialdom. In 1898 he moved to Shanghai, where he studied mathematics, science, philosophy, Japanese, and English. It was at this time that he formed an intimate and lasting relationship with Lo Chen-yü 羅振玉 (1866-1940), who became well known as an archaeologist, bibliophile, and ultra-conservative royalist.

After a brief period of study in Japan in 1901, Wang returned to China where for the next few years he worked as editor or teacher while pursuing in his spare time the study of Western philosophy and the writing of Chinese poetry. Unlike many of the intellectuals of that time who were concentrating on the study of Western political systems, economics, and science, Wang turned to the philosophers in an attempt to discover universal, timeless truth. His political conservatism was already apparent in his critical attitude toward K'ang Yu-wei,* T'an Ssu-t'ung 譚嗣同 (1865-1898), and other reformers whom he attacked for being interested in Western

philosophy only as a political tool. Having studied several general works, he concentrated on Kant, Schopenhauer, and Nietzsche, wrote several essays in which he analyzed their ideas, and translated some portions of their work into Chinese. In his "*Hung-lou meng* p'ing-lun" 紅樓夢評論 (Critical Essay on the *Dream of the Red Chamber,* 1904), he attempted what no Chinese had tried before, the application of Schopenhauer's ideas on "the will" to an analysis of Chinese literature. Western ideas on the beautiful, the sublime, and the concept of genius also permeated his writing at that time.

In 1907, about the time when Wang moved from Soochow to Peking to work in the Ministry of Education and to serve as an editor in the Ministry Library, he took stock of his intellectual progress and decided that his "emotions were too strong and reasoning capacity too weak to be a philosopher." He had also, even at the time of writing the "*Hung-lou meng* p'ing-lun," begun to have some doubts about Schopenhauer's powers as a philosopher to solve the problems of universal salvation. He accordingly turned from Western philosophy to concentrate on Chinese literature, particularly poetry, in the hope of finding "direct comfort." During the next few years his scholarly efforts were directed toward collating, editing, and commenting on Chinese literary works, while he continued to write poetry, particularly *tz'u.** One of his most important works of literary criticism was the *Jen-chien tz'u-hua* 人間詞話 (Talks on *Tz'u* in the Human World), which contains the essence of his literary theory.

In developing his theories, although Wang Kuo-wei retained traces of Western philosophical views, he turned primarily to traditional Chinese literature for inspiration. Unhappy with the didactic Confucian, praise-and-blame approach which he saw as always tied to political needs of a particular time, he sought an approach that could express the universal truth to be found in the creation of all things. The intuitive attitudes found in Taoism and Ch'an Buddhism as applied to literature by

Yen Yü (see *Ts'ang-lang shih-hua*), Wang Fu-chih,* and Wang Shih-chen* (1634-1711) gave him the basis for the concept of *ching-chieh* 境界, a state of reality delineated by a boundary that assures the uniqueness of the object it describes. In a way, he anticipated the New Critics of the West by saying that a poem "has its *ching-chieh*," not tied to any age or place, an expression of an emotion or description of a scene that is genuine, spontaneous, inherently simple. This same emphasis on genuineness is expressed in the term *pu-ko* 不隔 (not obstructed by a veil), which he used to indicate that the poet should describe his object in such a way that the reader can experience the "thingness" of that object directly with no obstruction.

Wang's search for fidelity in description led him, in the years he devoted to literature, gradually into the field of Chinese drama, an area that in the past had not been considered worthy of a scholar's attention. Between 1908 and 1912 he wrote several works on the origins of drama, and actors' roles, the history of Sung and Yüan drama, and several catalogues of plays, prompt books, and tune patterns. However, with the completion of the *Sung-Yüan hsi-ch'ü k'ao* 宋元戲曲考 (Examination of Sung and Yüan Drama), his attention to literary history and criticism came to an end. When the revolution of 1911 took place Wang decided to take his family and follow Lo Chen-yü to Japan, where he remained until 1916. Supported by Lo, he came more and more under his patron's influence and was persuaded to give up his studies of drama and poetry for the more acceptable fields of classics, history, and etymology. He made extensive use of Lo's large library and collection of oracle bones for his research and also took advantage of the large private libraries of Chinese books in Japan to collate and edit editions of the classics and histories.

In 1916 Wang returned with his family to Shanghai, where he taught in a university founded by the wealthy Jewish merchant, Silas Aaron Hardoon (1847-1931). With the publication of his work based on the oracle-bone inscriptions his reputation increased and he began to enjoy great popularity as a leading scholar with advanced views on methodology. In inverse proportion to his progressive views in scholarship, however, was the conservatism of his political views. In 1923 he moved to Peking to become a tutor to Henry P'u-yi, the deposed Manchu emperor who had been allowed to maintain court in the Forbidden City. This position was terminated the following year when P'u-yi was forced to move to the Japanese Legation in Tientsin. Wang remained in Peking and in 1925 accepted a professorship at Tsinghua University. It was in these years that he produced a study of Mongol history.

A highly respected scholar in several fields, much loved by his students, and affiliated with a prestigious university that provided him with optimum conditions for continued research, Wang seemed to enjoy a position that many would covet. Yet on June 2, 1927, he left his office, rode over to the Summer Palace a mile or so away, walked to the lake, and drowned himself. Whether his action was a political one motivated by his fear that Nationalist troops who were advancing rapidly northward would execute him for his connection with P'u-yi or whether it was due to family tensions, particularly between himself and Lo Chen-yü, brought on by economic pressures, has never been made clear. There are some who feel that these external factors may have contributed to his decision, but that it was the contradictions in his own temperament that made the suicide inevitable.

Some scholars have characterized Wang primarily as a historian whose research, based on his etymological studies of the oracle bones, helped to clarify much of the hitherto unsubstantiated material on China's ancient society as recorded in the early histories. His work on the Mongols also represented a contribution to Yüan-dynasty history. Others have stressed his contribution to historical linguistics by citing his painstaking work in identifying oracle-bone characters. Bibliophiles have looked on his absorbing interest in collating, editing, and restoring manuscripts and rare editions as his greatest contribution to Chinese scholarship. And finally, scholars of literature see his own poetry and his works of literary criticism in poetry, drama, and fiction as representative of the traditional Chinese approach to literature and at the same time of a modern, Western approach that characterizes him as an innovator. His lifelong dedication to scholarship encompasses all these fields and, considered together, his works accord him a high place in the scholarly world of the twentieth century.

EDITIONS:

Hai-ning Wang Ching-an Hsien-sheng i-shu 海寧王靜安先生遺書. Chao Wan-li 趙萬里, ed. Changsha, 1940.

Hai-ning Wang Chung-ch'üeh kung i-shu 海寧王忠愨公遺書. Lo Chen-yü 羅振玉, ed. Privately printed, 1927-1928.

Wang Kuan-t'ang Hsien-sheng ch'üan-chi 王觀堂先生全集. 16v. Taipei, 1968.

TRANSLATIONS:

Rickett, Adele Austin. *Wang Kuo-wei's Jen-chien tz'u-hua, A Study in Chinese Literary Criticism.* Hong Kong, 1977.

Tu, Ching-i. *Poetic Remarks in the Human World, Jen Chien Tz'u Hua.* Taipei, 1970.

STUDIES:

BDRC, v. 3, pp. 388-391.

Chao, Yeh Chia-ying. "Practice and Principle in Wang Kuo-wei's Criticism," *TkR,* 2.1 (April 1971), 117-127.

Ch'en, Yüan-hui 陳元暉. *Wang Kuo-wei yü Shu-pen-hua che-hsüeh* 王國維與叔本華哲學. Peking, 1981.

Chow, Tse-tsung 周策縱. *Lun Wang Kuo-wei jen-chien tz'u* 論王國維人間詞. Hong Kong, 1972.

Huang, Wei-liang 黃維樑. "Wang Kuo-wei *Jen-chien tz'u-hua* hsin-lun" 王國維人間詞話新論, in his *Chung-kuo shih-hsüeh tsung-heng lun* 中國詩學縱橫論, Taipei, 1977, 27-118.

Kogelschatz, Hermann. *Wang Kuo-wei und Schopenhauer, ein philosophisches Ereignis in der neueren Geistesgeschichte Chinas.* Munich, 1984.

Smythe, E. Joan. "The Early Thought of Wang Kuo-wei: An Analysis of His Essays on German Voluntaristic Philosophy (1903-1907)," *Papers on China,* East Asian Research Center, Harvard University, 18 (December 1964).

Tu, Ching-i. "Conservatism in a Constructive Form: The Case of Wang Kuo-wei (1877-1927)," *MS,* 28 (1969), 188-214.

———. "Some Aspects of *Jen-Chien Tz'u-hua,*" *JAOS* 93.3 (July/September 1973), 306-316.

Wang Kuo-wei chuan-chi tzu-liao 王國維傳記資料 9v. Taipei, 1979-1981.

Wang, Te-i. *Wang Kuo-wei nien-p'u* 王國維年譜. Taipei, 1967.

Wang, Wen-sheng 王文生. "Wang Kuo-wei te wen-hsüeh ssu-hsiang ch'u-t'an" 王國維的文學思想初探, *Ku-tai wen-hsüeh li-lun yen-chiu,* 7 (November 1982), 230-248.

Yeh, Chia-ying 葉嘉瑩. "Ts'ung hsing-ko yü shih-tai lun Wang Kuo-wei chih-hsüeh t'u-ching chih chuan-pien" 從性格與時代論王國維治學途徑之轉變, *Journal of the Chinese University of Hong Kong,* 1 (1973), 59-96.

———. "Jen-chien tz'u-hua chung p'i-p'ing chih li-lun yü shih-chien" 人間詞話中批評之理論與實踐, *Wen-hsüeh p'ing-lun,* 1 (1975), 199-291.

———. *Wang Kuo-wei chi ch'i wen-hsüeh p'i-p'ing* 王國維及其文學批評. Hong Kong, 1980.

—AR

Wang Pao 王褒 (*tzu,* Tzu-yüan 子淵, first century B.C.) was a man of letters who served in the court of Emperor Hsüan of the Han dynasty (r. 73-49 B.C.). A native of I-chou 益州 (modern Szechwan), Wang Pao achieved his prominence as a writer by three panegyrics which he wrote at the behest of the governor of the region, Wang Hsiang 王襄, to celebrate the virtues and political achievements of the emperor and his ministers. Wang Hsiang had these three works set to music and performed, which greatly pleased the emperor when he saw them. As an exegesis to the three works, Wang Pao wrote another panegyric. Because of this set of four works, Wang Hsiang recommended Wang Pao to the emperor, who summoned him to the capital for an audience. Still another composition in praise of the government won for Wang Pao further favor from the emperor. He was kept at court, a constant companion of the emperor on hunting expeditions, and composed laudatory works on the lodges and palaces they visited. In the course of time he was awarded the honorary appointment of Grand Master of Remonstrance. On one occasion, he was sent to entertain the Heir Apparent, who fell ill. In the latter's palace he recited his own writings and those of other people, returning to his own residence only when the prince was fully recovered. The Heir Apparent regarded his writings with considerable favor. He especially liked "Tung-hsiao sung" 洞簫頌 (The Flute) and "Kan-ch'üan" 甘泉 (Sweet Springs) and had the ladies and attendants of his harem recite them. Wang Pao died on his way home to I-chou, where he had been sent to bring back to the capital a golden horse and a green cock which were reported to have appeared in the area.

Like many literary men of his time, Wang Pao owed much of his success not only to his talent per se, but to his ability to incorporate flatteries into his verses. Most of his extant works are political eulogies. Even though "Chiu huai" 九懷 (The Nine Regrets), which was modeled on Ch'ü Yüan's* "Chiu ko" 九歌 (The Nine Songs) and was later included in the Ch'u-tz'u,* was critical of the government as was prescribed for a work written in the style of the sao 騷 songs, it contains elements of the supernatural which suited the taste of the emperor.

Among his works, "Tung-hsiao sung" deserves praise for its literary value. The piece assumes a profound significance in the development of yung-wu 詠物 (describing objects) literature. Before Wang Pao, such works either had just begun to take shape or had been essentially devoted to serious discussion and argument which scarcely pertained to the given object. Through laborious description, however, of the quality, appearance, sound, and function of the flute, Wang Pao brought the literary form to maturity. Aside from its significance for the genre, the work displays a skill in the use of language. It is laden with ornate expressions, balanced sentences, and striking figures of speech. Critics claim it anticipated the p'ien-wen* style which flourished in the Six Dynasties.

Not all of Wang Pao's extant works are as sophisticated in language and formal in subject. "T'ung yüeh" 僮約 (The Slave's Contract), which was written when Wang Pao still resided in I-chou, is a listing of a great variety of duties to be performed by a headstrong and unruly slave whom Wang Pao pretended to want to buy. Not only does it reveal the humorous and more private side of Wang Pao, it also reflects the vernacular language of the people who inhabited the upper Yangtze region in his time.

EDITIONS:
Wang Chien-i chi 王諫議集, Pai-san, pp. 171-191.

TRANSLATIONS:
Hawkes, David. "Chiu Huai" (The Nine Regrets), in Ch'u Tz'u, pp. 141-149.

STUDIES:
Chien, Tsung-wu 簡宗梧. "Wang Pao tz'u fu yung-yün k'ao" 王襃辭賦用韻考, Chung-hua hsüeh-yüan, 17 (March 1976), 203-226.
Hsieh, Fu-ya 謝扶雅 "Liang-ch'ien-nien-ch'ien Shu-chung san-ta fu-chia" 兩千年前蜀中三大賦家, in Nan-hua-hsiao-chu shan-fang wen-chi 南華小住山房文集, Hong Kong, 1971, v. 2, pp. 834-838.
Mao, I-po 毛一波. "Kuang-ch'ien ch'i-hou te Wang Pao" 光前啓後的王襃, Ssu-ch'uan wen-hsien, 159 (June 1976), 56-59.
Ts'ai, Hsiung-hsiang 蔡雄祥. "Wang Pao chi ch'i tso-p'in" 王襃及其作品, Hsüeh ts'ui, 19.6 (December 1977), 14-18.

—SH

Wang Po 王勃 (or Wang P'o, tzu, Tzu-an 子安, 649-676) was a master of Six-Dynasties-style p'ien-wen* prose and an important early reformer of Ch'i-Liang-style 齊梁體 court poetry. Though there is little evidence of close association between him, Lo Pin-wang,* Lu Chao-lin,* and Yang Chiung,* they were all included in the literary grouping Ch'u-T'ang ssu-chieh 初唐四傑 (Four Eminences of the Early T'ang), because they (especially Wang and Lo) have been traditionally considered among the best p'ien-wen prose writers of the 660s through 680s.

The Six-Dynasties-style p'ien-wen written by the Four Eminences used parallelism between lines and couplets, end rhyme, and a high incidence of historical allusions; the style was applied to all forms of prose writing. In the late seventh century, p'ien-wen prose had not been limited to the writing of government documents and civil-service examination essays (as would be the case thereafter). The Four Eminences were perhaps the last generation of scholars to successfully use the style in purely literary endeavors. Wang Po's best-known prose pieces, for example, are prefaces to poems.

Though their prose styles were similar, each of these men had a different approach to the reform of court poetry (see *kung-t'i shih*), that style best exemplified in the works of their predecessor, Shang-kuan I 上官儀 (d. 664). Generally speaking, they brought personal feelings into the court-style verse, experimented with stylistic changes, and used new (or revived old) themes such as descriptions of frontier garrisons and poems of farewell. Nonetheless, their writings were still within the accepted context of court poetry and contrasted sharply with those of the late seventh-century poet Ch'en Tzu-ang,* who reformed poetry by dropping the court style altogether. The Four Eminences anticipated the gradual change in themes and style made by the late seventh-century court poets Sung Chih-wen (see Shen Ch'üan-ch'i), Shen Ch'üan-ch'i,* and Tu Shen-yen.* The formalization of these changes became the style since known as "regulated verse" (see *shih*), a style most closely associated with the great eighth-century poets.

Wang Po was probably born in Lung-men 龍門 (modern Ho-chin 河津, Shansi) into a family which had produced at least two previous generations of imperial civil servants. His biographers describe him as a child prodigy who, at the age of ten or eleven, wrote a critique of a *Han-shu* (see Pan Ku) commentary and was presented to the emperor along with Yang Chiung and several other talented sons of officials. Shortly afterwards, Wang was attached to the household of the even younger Prince P'ei (Li Hsien 李賢, 655-686) as a Reader-in-waiting.

While with the boy prince, Wang also studied medicine with Ts'ao Yüan 曹元 and began to write prose pieces that attracted the attention of his seniors. One, written at the age of fourteen, was a letter to the Grand Councilor, Liu Hsiang-tao 劉祥道 (596-666). Some biographers claim that he wrote his best-known piece, "T'eng-wang-ko hsü" 滕王閣序 (A Preface to the Poem "Pavilion of Prince T'eng") at this time, though others say it was written a decade later. In 666, he was invited to take the *Yu-su k'o* 幽素科 examination and thereby officially entered the civil service. In 667 or 668, Wang's appointment in the prince's household was terminated because he had written a composition which lampooned cock fighting, a sport enjoyed by the prince and his brothers.

Unable to obtain another post, Wang Po took himself to Szechwan in 669. During the next three years he traveled widely in that region, writing prose and poetic descriptions of his experiences and observations. He also visited Lu Chao-lin and the two "Eminences" exchanged poems. By 672, Wang Po had returned to Ch'ang-an and sought a post in an area known for its medicinal herbs, Kuo-chou 虢州 (near modern Ling-pao hsien 靈寶縣, Honan). In 674, he murdered a slave whom he had first attempted to harbor. Wang was sentenced to death, then released following a general amnesty in late 674. The next year he set out to join his father in Chiao-chih 交阯 (modern Vietnam near Hanoi). The elder Wang had been exiled there as a magistrate following his son's arrest. Wang wrote many descriptions of his travels to Vietnam, including one in which he mentions leaving Canton in December 675, presumably to go by boat to Chiao-chih. Wang's biographers say he drowned within a month, during his passage to Vietnam. Yang Chiung, in a preface to Wang's works, says that Wang died about eight months later in 676 at the age of twenty-seven and makes no mention of drowning. Presumably Wang either died in Chiao-chih or on his way back.

Although his *p'ien-wen* prose is nearly like that of the other three "Eminences," Wang Po attempted to avoid using a superabundance of allusive expressions in developing a lively, extemporaneous style. In his poetry, he was famous as a master of the parallel couplet, which critics say seemed less contrived than those written by his contemporaries. It was then usual in court-style poetry to express a moral or a summary in the last line, but Wang eschewed the practice, leaving the last line open-ended and demanding that the reader find his own conclusion.

Most of Wang Po's thematic innovations were made while away from court and the influence of court-style poetry. The poems he wrote in Szechwan or during travels to other parts of the country deal with thoughts of exile and include descriptions of a less-than-benign natural world, subjects foreign to the "court" tradition. At court, however, Wang Po and the other three Eminences wrote the sort of court poetry considered most characteristic of the seventh century. Wang's tentative steps toward another kind of verse were little appreciated by later generations who had access to works of the great eighth-century poets. Only Tu Fu* admired Wang Po, but he, ironically, appreciated Wang for his genius as a court poet.

The original edition of Wang Po's anthology is lost, though most of what it contained appears to be extant today; it appeared shortly after his death and included Yang Chiung's preface. Several complete texts were reported to have existed between the eighth and thirteenth centuries, but none of these is extant. An edition of his poetry and *fu*,* published in 1007, seems to have survived until the sixteenth century and served as the basis of a reprinted edition in 1552 (original copies still extant). Chang Hsieh 張燮 (1574-1640) garnered many pieces of Wang's prose writings from the *Wen-yüan ying-hua** and, using the 1552 edition of poetry and *fu*, edited a relatively complete collection of Wang's writings (1640).

In 1781, Hsiang Chia-ta 項家達 filled in some lacunae in the prose sections of Chang's edition and published a more complete anthology of Wang's prose (together with prose writings of the other Eminences) in a work entitled *Ch'u-T'ang ssu-chieh chi* 初唐四傑集.

EDITIONS:

Wang, Po. *T'ang Wang Tzu-an chi chu* 唐王子安集注 (title also listed as *Wang Po ch'uan-chi chien-chu* 王勃全集箋注). Wu-hsien, 1883. Text

annotated by Chiang Ch'ing-i; most complete, and only annotated, edition.

———. *Wang Tzu-an chi* (1640). *SPTK*. Edition compiled by Chang Hsieh; no annotations; more readily available than Chiang Ch'ing-i's edition.

———. *Wang Tzu-an i-wen* 王子安佚文, in *Yung-feng hsiang-jen tsa-chu hsü-p'ien* 永豐鄉人雜著續編, n.p., 1918. Reprinted in *Lo Hsüeh-t'ang Hsien-sheng ch'uan-chi ch'u-p'ien* 羅雪堂先生全集初編, Taipei, 1968. Largest collection of writings not found in other editions; compiled by Lo Chen-yü 羅振玉.

TRANSLATIONS:

Bynner, *Jade Mountain*, p. 152.

STUDIES:

Furukawa, Sueyoshi 古川末喜. "Sho-Tō yonketsu no bungaku shisō" 初唐四傑 の 文學思想, *Chūgoku bungaku ronshū*, 8 (1979), 1-27.

Liu, K'ai-yang 劉開揚. "Lun Ch'u-T'ang ssu-chieh chi ch'i shih" 論初唐四傑及其詩, in *T'ang shih lun-wen chi* 唐詩論文集, Shanghai, 1961, pp. 1-28.

Owen, *Early T'ang*, pp. 123-137.

Suzuki, Torao 鈴木虎雄. "Ō Botsu nempu" 王勃年譜, *Tōhō gakuhō*, 14.3 (1944), 1-14.

T'ien, Tsung-yao 田宗堯. "Wang Po nien-p'u" 王勃年譜, in *Ta-lu tsa-chih*, 30.12 (June 1965), 379-389.

—BL

Wang Shih-chen 王世貞 (*tzu*, Hüan-mei 元美, *hao*, Feng-chou 鳳洲, Yen-chou shan-jen 弇州山人, 1526-1590) was the dominant figure in Chinese literature during much of the late sixteenth century. Originally a member of the Archaist "Later Seven Masters" group led by Li P'an-lung,* he moved toward a more eclectic approach to literature in his later years.

Wang Shih-chen was born into a distinguished family. His immediate ancestors were important officials, and their ancestry went back to the Wang clan of Lang-ya, prominent during the Six Dynasties. Wang demonstrated his own qualities by passing the *chin-shih* examination in 1547 and holding office in the capital from 1548 to 1556. He abandoned a provincial post in 1559 to return to the capital in a fruitless attempt to obtain clemency for his father, who was executed the following year.

Wang's opposition to Yen Sung, the Grand Secretary responsible for the execution, and later to Chang Chü-cheng, seriously damaged his prospects for a successful official career, and he was out of office for most of the rest of his life.

Wang's promise as a poet had been recognized by Li P'an-lung and others soon after his arrival in Peking, and he quickly became the most important member of Li's literary circle other than Li himself. He wrote his major critical work, the *I-yüan chih yen* 藝苑 (compiled 1558-1565, with a supplement added in 1572) with Li's collaboration and brought to his association with the Archaists the prestige of the South, the acknowledged center of artistic and literary culture.

In spite of the collaboration with Li P'an-lung, the *I-yüan chih yen* is essentially Wang's work. Its ideals are less strictly Archaist than those of Li, whom it mildly criticizes in a few passages. After Li's death in 1570 Wang Shih-chen inherited the leadership of the Archaists, but within a few years he himself began to move away from their doctrines. From the mid-1570s he showed an increased eclecticism in his style of writing and his taste in poetry. Even such writers as Po Chü-i,* Su Shih,* and Lu Yu,* generally looked down upon by the Archaists, were accepted and enjoyed by Wang, and he showed a new interest in Buddhism and Taoism. In part, as Matsushita Tadashi has suggested, this more tolerant attitude may have been the result of personal trials such as serious illness and the death of his father. His southern background may also have been significant. Archaism had begun in the North, led by Li Meng-yang* and Ho Ching-ming.* In adopting some of its ideals as his own, Wang combined them with somewhat broader, if still very high, standards acquired during his youthful association with the circle around Wen Cheng-ming. Some of his own followers, such as T'u Lung,* continued this trend, approaching the more individualist positions of such slightly later writers as Yüan Hung-tao and his brothers.

Wang's domination of the literary world was due not only to his eclectic ideals, but also to his productivity—his belletristic writings alone amount to more than three hundred *chüan*. He published his collected works, the *Yen-chou shan-jen ssu-pu kao* 四部稿, in his fiftieth year (1575); a subsequent posthumous collection, the *Hsü* 續 - *kao*, appeared during the last years of the Ming. In addition, he published a separate collection of historical writings, the *Yen-shan-t'ang pieh-chi* 弇山堂別集, near the end of his life, and compiled a number of other scholarly works of various kinds. Material important as a supplement to the *I-yüan chih yen* is found in another posthumous collection, the *Yen-chou shan-jen tu-shu hou* 讀書後. Perhaps because of the eclecticism of his later years, as well as his astonishing fecundity, Wang Shih-chen's name is associated with several vernacular works whose actual authorship is uncertain, such as the novel *Chin P'ing Mei** and the historical play *Ming-feng chi* 鳴鳳記.

EDITIONS:
Ch'ü tsao 曲藻, in *Hsi-ch'ü lun-chu*, v. 4, pp. 15-42.
Yen-chou shan-jen ssu-pu kao. 174 *chüan*. Rpt. Taipei, 1976. Reprint of the original edition, the best text.
Yen-chou shan-jen hsü-kao. 207 *chüan*. Rpt. *Ming-jen wen-chi ts'ung-k'an*, No. 22, Taipei, n.d. Reprint of a Ch'ung-chen (1628-1644) period text, probably the original edition; the best and most accessible text.
Yen-shan-t'ang pieh-chi 弇山堂別集. 100 *chüan*. Rpt. *Chung-kuo shih-hsüeh ts'ung-shu*, No. 16, Taipei, 1965.
Yen-chou shan-jen tu-shu hou. 8 *chüan*. Rpt. *Ssu-k'u ch'üan-shu chen-pen*. Wang's uncollected later critiques and colophons.
I-yüan chih yen. 8+4 *chüan*. *Li-tai shih-hua hsü-pien*. The most accessible text; the best is included in the *Ssu-pu kao*, see above.

TRANSLATIONS:
Iritani, Sensuke 入谷仙介, Fukumoto Masakazu 福本雅一, and Matsumura Takashi 松村昂, *Konsei shishū* 近世詩集. Tokyo, 1971, pp. 239-250.

STUDIES:
Cheng, Liang-shu 鄭良樹. "Wang Shih-chen 'tuan-ch'ang shuo' pien-wei" 短長說辨偽, *Ta-lu tsa-chih*, 49 (1974), 163-169. Detailed argument against the authenticity of a sup-

posedly pre-Ch'in historical work found in the *Ssu-pu kao.*

Chiang, Kung-t'ao 姜公韜. *Wang Yen-chou te sheng-p'ing yü chu-shu* 王弁州的生平與著述, *Wen-shih ts'ung-k'an,* No. 39, Taipei (National Taiwan University), 1974.

DMB, pp. 1399-1405.

Huang, Ju-wen 黃汝文. "Yen-chou Hsien-sheng wen-hsüeh nien-piao" 先生文學年表, *Wen-hsüeh nien-pao,* 4 (1938), 189-226. The fullest biographical treatment, includes summary tables of contents of the *Ssu-pu kao* and *Hsü-kao.*

Krafft, Barbara. "Wang Shih-chen (1526-1590): Abriss seines Lebens," *OE,* 5 (1958), 169-201. The only extended discussion in a Western language; Wang's biography and its sources.

Kung, "Ming ch'i-tzu."

Kung, "Ming-tai ch'i-tzu."

Liang, Jung-jo 梁容若. "Wang Shih-chen p'ing-chuan" 王世貞評傳, in *Tso-chia yü tso-p'in,* T'ai-chung, 1971, pp. 67-86.

Ma, Mao-yüan 馬茂元. "Wang Shih-chen te *I-yüan chih-yen:* Tu-shu cha-chi chih i" 王世貞的藝苑卮言讀書札記之一, *Hsüeh-shu yüeh-k'an,* 1962.3, 35-37.

Matsushita, Tadashi 松下忠. "Ō Seitei no ko-bunjisetsu yori no dakka ni tsuite" 王世貞の古文辭說よりの脫化について, *Chūgoku bunga-kuhō,* 5 (1956), 70-85. The best discussion of the evolution of Wang's literary ideals.

Pao, Tsun-p'eng 包遵彭. "Wang Shih-chen chi ch'i shih-hsüeh"王世貞及其史學, *Hsin shih-tai,* 5.8 (1965), 27-31; rpt. *Shih-yüan,* 7 (1966), 3-6.

Yokota, Terutoshi 横田輝俊. "Mindai bungak-uron no tenkai, Pt. 2" 明代文學論の展開, *Hi-roshima Daigaku bungakubu kiyō,* 38 (1978), 75-135, esp. 80-88.

Yoshikawa, Kōjirō 吉川幸次郎. *Gen-Min shi gais-etsu* 元明詩概說, Tokyo, 1963, pp. 202-219.

—DB

Wang Shih-chen 王士禎 (*tzu,* Tzu-chen and I-shang 貽上, 1634-1711) was a major poet and critic of the seventeenth century. He was a prolific writer, editor, and anthologist, and his works probably constitute the most influential body of writings of his time. He was a native of Hsin-ch'eng (Shantung), and his family had been prominent in Ming officialdom during the sixteenth century. He himself had a long and illustrious career, rising to Censor-in-Chief and Minister of Justice. Official duties carried him to all parts of the empire, and his travels provided him with opportunities to write nature poetry. A sense of the immediacy of nature is readily apparent in his poetry, much of which is written in the "serene and placid" Wang Wei* style; this sets him quite apart from the countless "studio" poets of the later imperial era whose landscape poetry is too often derived from literary models. Wang, however, was a genuine virtuoso in practically all styles—from Wang Wei landscapes to the complex and emotionally charged verbal expressions of Tu Fu's* later writings.

Wang the critic and theorist is as interesting as Wang the poet. His writings attempt to realize his own theory of poetry in concrete examples. For him, the highest and finest achievement in poetry was to imbue it with the quality or dimension of *shen-yün* 神韻. *Shen* (spirit/spiritual) refers to both perfect, spontaneous, intuitive (spiritual) control over the poetic medium and perfect, intuitive, "enlightened" (spiritual) apprehension of reality. *Yün,* which means the tone, mood, or atmosphere with which the poem is charged, refers to the inner psychological and spiritual realities which characterize the individual poet. Poetry is a fusion of the poet's apprehension of objective reality with the subjective mood or feeling which that reality engenders in him. Wang had a rich knowledge of and appreciation for the critical tradition up to his own day, and his own theory of poetry is in many ways a synthesis of what he considered the best in that tradition. The late T'ang critic Ssu-k'ung T'u* and the Sung critic Yen Yü (see *Ts'ang-lang shih-hua*) seem to have exerted the most influence on him. He was also influenced by the Archaist critics (see Li Meng-yang and Li P'an-lung) of the Ming era, especially Hsieh Chen 謝榛 (1495-1575), the author of the *Ssu-ming shih-hua* 四溟詩話, and Hu Ying-lin,* both of whom attempted to raise the Archaist Movement out of sterile imitation to a higher plane of self-realization and spiritual insight with tradition as inspiration and guide. Wang's view of poetry reflects these interests as well, and the dialectic in his writings—creative and critical—between the tradition and the self is one of the principal dimensions of their interest and appeal.

EDITIONS:

Tai-ching T'ang shih-hua 帶經堂詩話. 1760; several reprints.

Yü-yang shan-jen ching-hua lu hsün-tsuan 漁洋山人精華錄訓纂. 12 *chüan*. SPPY. Annotations by Hui Tung 惠棟 (1697-1758).

Wang Shih-chen shih 王士禎詩. Hu Ch'ü-fei 胡去非, ed. and ann. Shanghai, 1932. Also contained in *Wan-yu wen-k'u* 萬有文庫 .

TRANSLATIONS:

Hashimoto, Jun 橋本循. *Ō Gyōyō*. Tokyo, 1965.

Lynn, Richard John. "Tradition and Synthesis: Wang Shih-chen as Poet and Critic." Unpublished Ph.D. dissertation, Stanford University, 1971.

Sunflower, pp. 479-482.

Takahashi, Kazumi 高橋和己. *Ō Shinshi* 王士禎. Tokyo, 1962.

STUDIES:

Aoki, *Shindai*, pp. 64-92.

Chu, Tung-jun 朱東潤. "Wang Shih-chen shih-lun shu-lüeh" 王士禎詩論述略, *Wen-che chi-k'an*, 1934, 453-476.

ECCP, pp. 831-833.

Kuo, *P'i-p'ing shih*, pp. 968-990.

Lynn, *op. cit.*

———. "Orthodoxy and Enlightenment: Wang Shih-chen's Theory of Poetry and Its Antecedents," in W. T. de Bary, ed., *The Unfolding of Neo-Confucianism*, New York, 1975, pp. 217-269.

—RL

Wang T'ao 王韜 (1828-1897) was a traditional literatus from the Soochow area and a gifted writer involved in academic activities in both the East and the West. He was born and raised in Fu-li 甫里, a small village in Kiangsu. Educated in the Confucian Classics and traditional literature, he obtained his first degree (*hsiu-ts'ai* 秀才) at the age of seventeen. In February 1848, he met the British missionary-scholar Walter H. Medhurst (1796-1856), who procured for him in the summer of 1849 a post in the Mission Press (*Mai-hai shu-yüan* 墨海書院), then under Medhurst's direction. For the next thirteen years Wang T'ao worked with the British missionaries at Shanghai.

Many Chinese scholars believed that Wang took the civil-service examination given by the Taiping rebels in Nanking and passed as the top graduate. In 1862 representatives of the Ch'ing government at Shanghai indicted him for collusion with the rebels. His life was saved by the intervention of the British missionary William Muirhead (1822-1900) and the Acting British Consul, Medhurst. Despite pressure from the Ch'ing government for his extradition, including a request from Prince Kung 恭親王 (I-hsin 亦訢 , 1833-1898), the British sent Wang to Hong Kong, where he lived as an exile for twenty-three years.

In Hong Kong Wang T'ao began his academic association with James Legge (1814-1897), the distinguished missionary-sinologist, whom he assisted for eleven years in translating the Chinese Classics. During this time he prepared several collections of glosses and commentaries on the canon. In concert with Legge's larger perspective, he did not adhere to any of the traditional schools. The result is a corpus which conflates the conclusions of various scholars who had interpreted the classics from different approaches. Wang T'ao's sound judgment and extensive bibliographical knowledge stood him in good stead in this task. Unfortunately, of all these exegetic collections only the manuscripts of Wang's *Mao-shih chi-shih* 毛詩集釋, *Li-chi chi-shih* 禮記集釋, and *Chou-i chi-shih* 周易集釋 are extant, preserved in the New York Public Library.

Wang was then invited (in 1867) by Legge to visit the United Kingdom. He spent over two years in the British Isles and Europe, gave a lecture at Oxford University, and paid a call on the French sinologist Stanislas Julien (1799-1873) in Paris. In 1879 he was invited to visit Japan where his writings were well known—he was enthusiastically received. These trips abroad influenced him greatly and he was won over to the side of Western culture. From this time on his writings reveal a bicultural quality.

In his later years Wang T'ao enjoyed considerable prestige among his contemporaries; Li Hung-chang 李鴻章 (1823-1901), Kung Ch'ao-yüan 龔照瑗 (d. 1897), Wu T'ing-fang 伍廷芳 (1848-1922), Huang Tsun-hsien,* Jung Hung 容閎 (1848-1912), and Cheng Kuan-ying 鄭觀應 (1841-1923) can be numbered among his acquaintances. Even Sun Yat-sen (1866-1925), the youngest member of this coterie, sought Wang's advice on current affairs.

Aside from his work on the classics, Wang T'ao was also known for his poetry. He wrote only seven-syllabic regulated verse (see *shih*) and a small number of *p'ai-lü* 排律 (see *shih*). His poems draw on his thought and his life as the main sources. Many of them are occasional verses, written in response to colleagues or contemporary events. In communicating with his friends, he revealed his feelings; even his verse on nature, such as blushing flowers, has implied human analogues. He preserved his writings in a conscious attempt to memorialize the joy of union and the agony of separation from his youth through his old age. For this reason, they tend to build up a rather coherent picture of his life. Yet his poetry lacks the ability to move readers through the presentation of perception of an experience or emotion new to them.

His *pi-chi*,* essays, and prose constitute a sizable portion of his corpus. They are interesting because they often focus on foreign cultures or the "unusual deeds" of Westerners. Their significance has diminished in the course of time, but Wang T'ao revived a somewhat clichéd style and genre through this introduction of fresh elements. His ingenuity is seen much more in his prose. As a pioneer journalist in China, he developed a vigorous style of prose suitable for the ideas and concepts of modern Western thought. His editorials are especially noteworthy. Until his death in 1897 at Shanghai, he was recognized as a leading figure among men of letters and a founder of journalistic literature.

EDITIONS:

Fu-sang yu-chi 扶桑遊記, in Wang Hsi-ch'i 王錫祺, *Hsiao-fang-hu chai yü-ti ts'ung-ch'ao* 小方壺齋輿地叢鈔 (hereafter *Hsiao-fang-hu*), series 10. Shanghai, 1890-1891. A brief journal of a trip to Japan.

Hai-tsou yeh-yu lu 海陬冶遊錄, in *Yen-shih ts'ung-ch'ao* 艷史叢鈔, Wang T'ao, ed. Hong Kong, 1878. Describes dancing, singing, and the love affairs of contemporary youth.

Heng-hua-kuan shih-lu 蘅華館詩錄. Hong Kong, 1880; 2nd ed., Shanghai, 1890. Contains the poetic corpus—627 pieces.

Heng-hua-kuan tsa-chi 蘅華館雜記. 6 *ts'e*. A collection of diaries and miscellaneous jottings, it exists only in manuscript (in the library of Academia Sinica in Taipei).

Hua-kuo chu-t'an 花國劇談, in *Yen-shih ts'ung-ch'ao*. Anecdotes of courtesans.

Man-yu sui-lu 漫遊隨錄, in *Hsiao-fang-hu*, series 11. A collection of random notes of travels, it contains important information about Wang T'ao's life.

Sung-pin so-hua 淞濱瑣話. Shanghai, with a preface of 1887. Supernatural tales of ghosts, spirits, and marvels.

Sung-yin man-lu 淞隱漫錄. Shanghai, 1884. Supernatural tales and stories concerning Westerners.

T'ao-yüan ch'ih-tu 弢園尺牘. Shanghai, 1883. Wang's letters.

T'ao-yüan ch'ih-tu hsü-ch'ao 弢園尺牘續鈔. Shanghai, 1889. A supplementary collection of letters; an important source for the development of his thought.

T'ao-yüan wen-lu wai-pien 弢園文錄外編. Hong Kong, 1883. A collection of editorials and essays.

Tung-k'u lan-yen 遯窟讕言. Shanghai, 1875. Anecdotes about the Taiping Rebellion.

Weng-yu yü-t'an 甕牖餘談. Shanghai, 1875. Entries concerning foreigners and their cultures.

Yao-t'ai hsiao-lu 瑤台小錄, in *Ch'ing-tai Yen-tu li-yüan shih-liao* 清代燕都梨園史料, Chang Tz'u-hsi 張次溪, ed., Peiping, 1934. A brief account of boy-actors well known in Wang T'ao's time.

Ying-juan tsa-chih 瀛壖雜志, in *Hsiao-fang-hu*, series 9. Shanghai, 1890-1891. Presents aspects of life in contemporary Shanghai.

STUDIES:

Cohen, Paul A. *Between Tradition and Modernity: Wang T'ao and Reform in Late Ch'ing China.* Cambridge, Mass., 1974.

ECCP, pp. 836-839.

Hsieh, Wu-liang 謝无量. "Wang T'ao: Ch'ing-mo pien-fa-lun chih shou-ch'uang-che chi Chung-kuo pao-tao wen-hsüeh chih hsien-ch'ü-che" 王韜 — 清末變法論之首創者及中國報導文學之先驅者, Chiao-hsüeh yü yen-chiu 教學與研究, March 1958.

Lee, Chi-fang. "Wang T'ao and His Literary Writings," TkR, 9.3 (Spring 1981), 267-285.

———. "Wang T'ao (1828-1897): His Life, Thought, Scholarship, and Literary Achievement." Unpublished Ph.D. dissertation, University of Wisconsin-Madison, 1973.

McAleavy, Henry. Wang T'ao (1828-?1890): The Life and Writing of a Displaced Person. London, 1953.

—CFL

Wang Ts'an 王粲 (tzu, Chung-hsüan 仲宣, 177-217) is commonly regarded as the most brilliant of the Seven Masters of the Chien-an Era (see Ch'en Lin) who enjoyed the Ts'ao family's patronage. He was born of a great Shantung family; both his great-grandfather and grandfather had been ministers of the first rank, and his father had taken part beside General Ho Chin 何進 in the aristocracy's fight against the palace eunuchs. His talents promptly secured him the protection of Ts'ai Yung.* But he was driven away from Lo-yang to Ch'ang-an by the civil war and was later a neglected refugee at the court of Liu Piao. It was not until he attached himself to Ts'ao Ts'ao in 208 that he was elevated to office and official titles (including that of Shih-chung 侍中 [Palace Attendant], under which he was to be known to posterity).

Wang Ts'an's extant work is fairly extensive, and more conspicuous for originality than that of many of his contemporaries. A widely read scholar, he was endowed with an exceptionally good memory and a talent for fluency in writing. For elegance of style, his work compares with Ts'ao P'i,* the patron of the literary circle, and like his friend Ts'ao Chih,* he was especially adept at combining the richness of literary tradition with the spontaneity of popular poetry. In this respect he is typical of his generation.

Ts'ao P'i described him as an expert in the fu,* which held sway in the age of the Han, and Wang's own corpus reveals a re-markable evolution: his fu become shorter, and in the description of natural scenery as in the expression of personal feelings, they take a more direct, less pedantic turn. Several of Wang Ts'an's fu must have been written on set themes for poetical contests. The best known of them, the "Teng-lou fu" 登樓賦 (Prose-poem on Climbing to the Loft) fuses together, in one remarkable synthesis, traditional themes and the poet's private experiences and yearnings.

Among his poems—some twenty-six pieces in all—the yüeh-fu* are of small consequence. Unlike the Ts'aos, Wang Ts'an left a few ceremonial hymns which show the influence of the ya and sung of the Shih ching.* The same distinction and elegance characterize the four-word poems addressed to his friends.

His most deservedly famous compositions, however, are written in five-word lines, as was then the fashion: the five pieces in the "Ts'ung-chün shih" 從軍詩 (Poems on Following the Army) and the three in the "Ch'i-ai shih" 七哀詩 (Seven Lamentations Poems), group of poems. The dating of the first group has been controverted; perhaps because he was more keenly sensitive than most to the evils of his day, Wang Ts'an wrote here of war, exile, vagrancy, and destitution; but contrary to the view taken by Li Shan 李善 (c. 630-689) in his commentary, the five pieces do not seem to refer to a single military expedition. The poems in this first group are somewhat marred by the author's flattery of Ts'ao Ts'ao, the victorious general. Their merits—an unaffected manner, a sincerity of feeling, and a realism that tends to free descriptive passages from traditional symbolism—also characterize the "Ch'i-ai shih" pieces, especially the opening one: as a picture of the ravages of war, it owes much to the models provided by the Ch'u-tz'u* and ancient philosophy, but the pathetic figure of the mother made to part with her child must have its source elsewhere—either in actual experience or in the subgenre of the mournful folk-ballad.

Like Wang Ts'an, Ying Yang 應瑒 (tzu, Te-lien 德璉, d. 217) entered Ts'ao Ts'ao's service, joined the Chien-an circle, and died in 217. He was the son of Ying Shao 劭, the famous scholar and author of the *Feng-su t'ung* 風俗通, *Han-kuan i* 漢官儀, and a commentary on the *Han-shu*. Of Ying Yang's work only about ten *fu* and six poems, five of them in five-word lines, survive. All of these are reminiscent of the themes dear to the Ts'ao brothers, with whom Ying Yang was intimate. His younger brother, Ying Ch'ü 璩 (190-252), was also an accomplished poet.

EDITIONS:

Liu-ch'ao wen, v. 1, *ch.* 90-91, pp. 958-966.
Nan-pei-ch'ao shih, v. 1, *Ch'üan San-kuo shih* 全三國詩, *ch.* 3, pp. 249-258.
Wang Shih-chung chi 王侍中集, *Pai-san*, v. 4, pp. 121-149.
Ying Te-lien chi 應德璉集, in *Pai-san*, v. 4, pp. 175-185.

TRANSLATIONS:

Frankel, *Palace Lady,* pp. 28-29.
Frodsham, *Anthology,* p. 26.
Hightower, J. R. "The *Fu* of T'ao Ch'ien," *HJAS*, 17 (1954), 169-230. Pp. 174-177 (Wang Ts'an's "Hsien-hsieh fu" 閑邪賦, Ying Yang's "Cheng-ch'ing fu" 正情賦).
Miao, Ronald C., "The 'Ch'i-ai shih' of the Late Han and Chin Periods (I)," *HJAS*, 33 (1973), 207.
Watson, *Lyricism*, pp. 35-37.
———, *Rhyme-Prose*, pp. 52-54.

STUDIES:

Itō, Masafumi 伊藤正文. "Ō San Shi ronkō" 王粲詩論考, *Chūgoku bungakuhō*, 20 (1965), 28-67.
Miao, R. C. "A Critical Study of the Life and Poetry of Wang Chung-hsüan." Unpublished Ph.D. dissertation, University of California, Berkeley, 1969. Contains lengthy chapters on Wang's *shih* and *fu*.
———. *Early Medieval Chinese Poetry, the Life and Verse of Wang Ts'an (A.D. 177-217).* Wiesbaden, 1982. A revised, better organized version of the dissertation which nevertheless omits some interesting details of the original.
Shimosada, Masahiro 下定雅弘. "Ō San shi ni tsuite" 王粲詩について, *Chūgoku bungaku hō*, 29 (1978), 46-81.
Suzuki, *Kan Gi*, pp. 607-616.

—JPD

Wang Wei 王維 (*tzu*, Mo-chieh 摩詰, 701-761) is one of the major poets of the T'ang dynasty, acclaimed in particular for his limpid depictions of nature. Born in the district of Ch'i 祁 (modern Shansi), he distinguished himself as poet, painter, and musician at an early age and passed the most literary of the imperial civil-service examinations in 721. From his subsequent appointment as Assistant Director of the Imperial Music Office, he enjoyed a slow but steady rise through government ranks which took him through various offices in the court at Ch'ang-an and several provinces to his highest position, Right Assistant Director of the Department of State Affairs, attained in 759. This career was interrupted only three times: by an unknown infraction committed at his first post, which led to a brief but virtual exile as an official in modern Shantung, by the death of his mother around 750, and by the An Lu-shan Rebellion of 755-757, during which he was captured and forced to serve under the puppet government. Only the intercession of his powerful younger brother led to his pardon after the return of the imperial family to the capital.

Of his relatively small poetic corpus—about four hundred poems in all—those for which Wang Wei is best known present scenes from various retreats enjoyed at different periods throughout his life. Perhaps the most famous of these were written at his country home on the Wang River in Lan-t'ien, south of Ch'ang-an, especially the quatrains of his "Wang Ch'uan chi" 輞川集 (Wang River Collection), which describe twenty different spots on his estate. (He is also said to have painted a long continuous scroll of the same scenes, but this work is no longer extant, although there are numerous imitations by later artists.) Equally well known are the quatrains written in response to each of Wang Wei's by his friend P'ei Ti 裴廸 (b. 716), a minor poet who eventually attained the post of Prefect of Shu-chou (modern Szechwan) after the An Lu-shan Rebellion. Wang Wei spent much of his leisure time with P'ei Ti, and his corpus contains several other poems written to or about his friend; his

"Shan chung yü P'ei Hsiu-ts'ai Ti shu" 山中與裴秀才廸書 (Letter from the Mountains to Candidate P'ei Ti) is his most famous prose evocation of the pleasures of life in retreat.

Wang Wei's appreciation of nature was no doubt fostered by his involvement with Buddhism. He studied for ten years with the Ch'an master Tao-kuang. After his wife's death around 730 he remained celibate and later converted part of his Lan-t'ien estate into a monastery. He wrote stele-inscriptions for both Tao-kuang and the Ch'an patriarch Hui-neng, as well as more general essays in praise of Buddhism and Amida, the Buddha of the Western Paradise. Particularly illuminating is his choice of cognomen (tzu), for, together with his given name, it forms the Chinese transliteration of the name of Vimalakirti (Wei-mo-chieh), the contemporary of Sakyamuni Buddha who was said to have spoken a sutra affirming the layman's practice of the religion. Indeed, Wang Wei's commitment to Buddhism is evident not so much in explicit doctrinal argument or vocabulary—of which there is little—as in the attitudes implicit in his poetry. For example, his contemplative, dispassionate observations of the sensory world affirm its beauty at the same time that they put its ultimate reality into question, by emphasizing its vagueness, relativity, and "emptiness," as well as problems of perception in general. In addition, the simple, natural diction and syntax of much of his poetry suggests an effortlessness analogous to that moment of enlightenment which masks the care taken to achieve it. This subtle or "bland" aspect of his style led to his later elevation as the "father" of the Southern School of literati (as opposed to professional) painters. For all Wang Wei's religious devotion, he never abandoned the engagement with the bureaucratic world expected of any good Confucian. Several of his works are court compositions, and, indeed, his very style is heavily indebted to the conventions of court-poetry established during the seventh century. Some modern biographers have seen nothing but contradiction in his ties to both court and country, secular activity and religious retreat. In fact, such dual allegiances were not so much the exception as the rule at the time. The primary thrust of Wang Wei's poetry—on this question as elsewhere—is one of compromise and balance between potentially opposing forces or issues. Just as his landscape scenes evince a harmony of self and world or even the submergence of man in nature, so his work and life as a whole display a tendency toward integration rather than conflict.

EDITIONS:

Lei-chien Wang Yu-ch'eng ch'üan-chi 類箋王右丞全集 . Ku Ch'i-ching 顧起經 , ed. 2v. 1557; rpt. Peking, 1957, Taipei, 1970.

Ō I shi sakuin 王維詩索引. Kyoto, 1952.

Tsukuru, Haruo 都留春雄 et al. Ō I shi sakuin 王維詩索引. 1952; rpt. Nagoya, 1971.

Wang Wei shih-chi 王維詩集 . Ku Ch'i-ching, ed. Photo-reproduction of 1590 ed. Kyoto, 1975.

Wang Wei shih-hsüan 王維詩選 . Fu Tung-hua 傅東華 , ed. 1933; rpt. Hong Kong, 1973.

Wang Yu-ch'eng chi chien-chu 王右丞集箋註 . Chao Tien-ch'eng 趙殿成 , ed. Introduction by Wang Yün-hsi 王運熙 . 2v. Peking, 1961. Punctuated edition of the Ch'ing-dynasty complete works, below; most easily accessible.

Wang Yu-ch'eng chi chu 王右丞集注 . Chao Tien-ch'eng, ed. 2v. 1736. SPPY.

TRANSLATIONS:

Chang, Hsin-chang. "Wang Wei," in his Chinese Literature, Volume 2: Nature Poetry, New York, 1977, pp. 58-79.

Chang, Yin-nan and Lewis C. Walmsley. Poems by Wang Wei. Rutland, Vt., 1958.

Ch'en, Jerome and Michael Bullock. Poems of Solitude, London, 1960, pp. 47-79.

Demiéville, Anthologie, pp. 247-254.

Harada, Ken'yū 原田憲雄 . Ō I 王維 . Tokyo, 1967.

Kobayashi, Taiichirō 小林大市郎 and Harada Ken'yu. Ō I 王維. Tokyo, 1964.

Robinson, G. W. Poems of Wang Wei. Baltimore, 1973.

Tsukuru, Haruo. Ō I 王維 . Tokyo, 1958.

Yip, Wai-lim. Hiding the Universe: Poems by Wang Wei. New York, 1972.

Yu, Pauline. The Poetry of Wang Wei: New Translations and Commentary. Bloomington, 1980.

———. "Wang Wei: Seven Poems," The Denver Quarterly, 12.2 (Summer 1977), 353-355.

STUDIES:

Ch'en, T'ieh-min 陳鐵民. "Wang Wei nien p'u" 王維年譜, *Wen-shih*, 16 (November 1982), 203-227.

Chou, Shan. "Beginning with Images in the Nature Poetry of Wang Wei," *HJAS*, 42.1 (June 1982), 117-137.

Chuang, Shen 莊申. *Wang Wei yen-chiu* 王維研究. V. 1. Hong Kong, 1971.

Feinerman, James Vincent. "The Poetry of Wang Wei." Unpublished Ph.D. dissertation, Yale University, 1979.

Gong, Shu. "The Function of Space and Time as Compositional Elements in Wang Wei's Poetry: A Study of Five Poems," *LEW*, 16.4 (April 1975), 1168-1193.

Iritani, Sensuke 入谷仙介. *Ō I kenkyū* 王維研究. Tokyo, 1976.

Juhl, R. A. "Patterns of Assonance and Vowel Melody in Wang Wei's Yüeh-fu Poems," *JCLTA*, 12.2 (May 1977) 95-110.

Liou, Kin-ling. *Wang Wei le poète*. Paris, 1941.

Liu, Wei-ch'ung 劉維崇. *Wang Wei p'ing-chuan* 王維評傳. Taipei, 1972.

Luk, Thomas Yuntong. "A Cinematic Interpretation of Wang Wei's Nature Poetry," *NAAB*, 1 (1978), 151-161.

———. "A Study of the Nature Poetry of Wang Wei in the Perspective of Comparative Literature." Unpublished Ph.D. dissertation, University of Michigan, 1976.

———. "Wang Wei's Perception of Space and His Attitude Towards Mountains," *TkR*, 8.1 (April 1977), 89-110.

Wagner, Marsha L. "The Art of Wang Wei's Poetry." Unpublished Ph.D. dissertation, University of California at Berkeley, 1975.

———. "From Image to Metaphor: Wang Wei's Use of Light and Color," *JCLTA*, 2 (May 1977), 111-117.

———. *Wang Wei*. Boston, 1982.

Walmsley, Lewis C. and Dorothy B. *Wang Wei the Painter-Poet*. Rutland, Vt., 1968. Biography.

Wen-hsüeh i-ch'an tseng-k'an, 13 (1963), 147-184. Four articles on Wang Wei.

Yu, Pauline. "Wang Wei: Recent Studies and Translations," *CLEAR*, 1.2 (July 1979), 219-240. Review article.

———. "Wang Wei's Journeys in Ignorance," *TkR*, 8.1 (April 1977), 73-87.

—PY

Wang Ying-lin 王應麟 (*tzu*, Po-hou 伯厚, 1223-1296) is recognized as one of the most erudite scholars in the history of Chinese letters. He was a compiler of encyclopedic works that served as tools of instruction for China's scholar-bureaucracy and a man who played a key role in the reconstruction of nearly lost texts and commentaries. Wang was a descendant of northerners who had settled in the southern city of Ming-chou 明州 (modern Ningpo) after the Chin conquest of Northern Sung in 1127. His father, Wang Hui 王撝 (1184-1253), educated him in the conservative tradition of such men as Lü Tsu-ch'ien 呂祖謙 (1137-1181)—men whose scholarly endeavors were imbued with an awareness that the Southern Sung marked the final disintegration of China's Han-through-T'ang "aristocratic" cultural patrimony. Wang Ying-lin's own scholarship was an implicit refutation of the emerging Neo-Confucian "order," which sought to denigrate much of the political, intellectual, scholarly, and literary accomplishments of the patrimonial age.

Between 1246 and 1275, Wang served as a drafter of imperial edicts and a leading imperial adviser on literary, historical, and ceremonial matters. In 1275, he was made Minister of Rites, but resigned from the government the same year, when the Sung court decided to negotiate surrender terms with the Mongols. He spent his last twenty years in seclusion at Ming-chou, teaching and preparing his writings for publication.

During his lifetime, Wang Ying-lin produced twenty-nine compilations. Sixteen are now extant and three survive in fragments. The best known is the encyclopedia, *Yü hai* 玉海 (A Sea of Jades), which is still found in all major Chinese collections. It is a compendium of twenty-one classifications of knowledge, including entries from classics, histories, scientific writings, and literature. It notes all sources of information so that many texts, otherwise lost after the Sung, are carefully preserved and described in this compilation.

Wang Ying-lin began to collect materials for the encyclopedia as early as his eighteenth year (1241) when he needed a personal study aid to prepare for the Erudite Literatus examination, which required memorization of vast quantities of old texts. It was a quintessential expression of conservative values at which only forty men in the Sung ever succeeded. Wang Ying-lin finished the *Yü hai* in 1252 and passed the examination in 1256. He had hoped that the *Yü hai* would help other Sung scholars prepare for the examination by providing them with requisite knowledge, but the *Yü hai* was only readied for publication after the fall of the Sung forty years after Wang's death, in 1337. Furthermore, except for unsuccessful revivals in 1679 and 1736, this examination was never again held.

The *K'un-hsüeh chi-wen* 困學紀聞 (Record of Observances from Arduous Studies) contains most of Wang Ying-lin's original thinking and observations on the whole corpus of Chinese classics, history, philosophy, and literature. It was the key product of his twenty-year retirement and is important because it studies pre-Sung classical texts and commentaries as well as those of the Sung Neo-Confucians. It measures the accuracy of both against the scale of Wang's own erudition and does not hesitate to cite weaknesses in Neo-Confucian scholarship, even though the latter was gaining contemporary favor. Ch'ing-dynasty scholars, highly critical of Sung Neo-Confucianism, admired the work and also praised its preservation of fragments of pre-Sung texts not otherwise available.

Wang's other scholarly endeavors included the reconstruction of fragmented texts of several important classical works, chief among these was the *Shih k'ao* 詩考 (A Study of the *Shih-ching*), which he finished in 1264. It is a partial reconstruction of the fragmented Han, Lü, and Ch'i commentaries to the *Shih-ching*.*

In his study of history, Wang was primarily interested in the *Tzu-chih t'ung-chien* 資治通鑑 (Comprehensive Mirror and Aid to Government) of Ssu-ma Kuang 司馬光 (1019-1086). Four of Wang's twenty-nine compilations treat this subject.

Wang Ying-lin made several important contributions to the genre of *hsiao-hsüeh* 小學 (elementary studies), works which evolved from the pedagogical methodol-ogy practiced at his school for the children of Ming-chou's leading families. Such writings were designed to teach young children the accouterments of their civilization through the memorization and recitation of rhyming lines of three, four, and seven words. They are still useful indexes to Sung knowledge. The numerological encyclopedia, *Hsiao-hsüeh kan-chu* 小學紺珠 (Purple Pearls of Elementary Studies), for example, taught Chinese children to recite from memory the numerically prefixed motifs of Chinese history, literature, and philosophy.

Although Wang Ying-lin did not live to see many of his works published, his disciples and descendants succeeded at the task during the Yüan dynasty. During the Ch'ing, Wang's belief that China's pre-Sung past had to be studied without prejudice to philosophical content won many adherents; scholars of the *Han-hsüeh p'ai* 漢學派 (School of Han Learning), such as Ku Yen-wu* and Hu Wei 胡渭 (1633-1714), were especially dedicated to this principle.

EDITIONS:

Hsiao-hsüeh kan-chu 小學紺珠. Taipei, 1966.

Shen-ning Hsien-sheng wen-ch'ao chih-yü pien 深寧先生文鈔摭餘編. 1828. A Ch'ing collection of further (cf. *Ssu-ming wen-hsien chi*) fragmentary remains of Wang's prose anthologies. Appended to the *Weng-chu k'un-hsüeh chi-wen*.

Shih k'ao 詩考. Taipei, 1966.

Ssu-ming wen-hsien chi 四明文獻集. c. 1370. An early Ming collection of the fragmentary remains of Wang's literary anthologies; appended to the *Weng-chu k'un-hsüeh chi-wen*.

Weng-chu k'un-hsüeh chi-wen 翁注困學紀聞. Taipei, 1963. A punctuated edition of the *k'un-hsüeh chi-wen* text and its major Ch'ing commentaries; addenda include anthologies of Wang's literary fragments and three *nien-p'u*, all photo-reprinted from the *Ssu-ming ts'ung-shu* 四明叢書, collection one, 1932-1948.

Yü hai 玉海. Che-chiang shu-chü, 1883. The most recent, and most carefully emended, edition; 14 of Wang's 16 extant works are also appended to this and all previous *Yü hai* editions—only the *K'un-hsüeh chi-wen* has (since 1327) been published as a separate work.

———. Ch'ing-yüan Confucian School, 1340; rpt. Taipei, 1967. Copy of the original *Yü hai* edition published during the Yüan.

STUDIES:

Fish, Michael B. "Bibliographical Notes on the *San Tzu Ching* and Related Texts." Unpublished M.A. thesis, Indiana University, 1968. A study of the attribution to Wang Ying-lin of a well-known children's primer.

Hsü, Kuang-ming 許光明. *Wang Ying-lin yen-chiu* 王應麟研究. Taipei, 1975. A summary of traditional biographical and bibliographical sources.

Langley, C. Bradford. "Wang Ying-lin (1223-1296), a Study in the Political and Intellectual History of the Demise of Song." Unpublished Ph.D. dissertation, Indiana University, 1980.

Lü, Mei-ch'üeh 呂美雀. "Wang Ying-lin chu-shu k'ao" 王應麟著述考. Unpublished M.A. thesis, National Taiwan University, 1972. A detailed summary of bibliographical descriptions of Wang Ying-lin's compilations.

SB, pp. 1167-1176.

—BL

Wang Yü-ch'eng 王禹偁 (*tzu*, Yüan-chih 元之, 954-1001) was born into an obscure family in Chü-yeh 鉅野 County (modern Shantung). Through the patronage of a local official Wang Yü-ch'eng was able to gain entry into the bureaucracy of the early Northern Sung. In 982 he passed the *chin-shih* examinations and began an official career which alternated between positions of prestige and responsibility at the capital and lowly provincial posts. At the capital he was entrusted with the drafting of government documents, policy criticism, and the editing of Emperor T'ai-tsung's (r. 976-992) *shih-lu;* in the provinces, he became famous as a participant in poetry exchanges (*ch'ang-ho* 唱和 verse) and other types of social verse.

The most striking feature of the verse and prose writings that Wang included in his collection, which he compiled, edited, and prefaced himself in the year 1000, is the prominence of a theoretical bias. His theory, however, is not narrowly restricted to technique, but is based on a broad, Confucian concept of the purpose of literature. As Wang Yü-ch'eng explains in the preface and in his letters, literature is a vehicle for personal expression, which essentially means personal expression of public values. These values must be expressed in literature when the individual is unable to establish them in praxis. This is the rationale for the seemingly self-effacing title of his collection: *Hsiao-ch'u chi* 小畜集 (The Collection of Lesser Cultivation).

These values also permeate most of Wang's writing, both poetry and prose, though their function in each form of writing varies. In prose they are occasionally the main subject of an entire piece, but much more frequently they are the basis for a wide variety of arguments. His most belletristic treatment of these values may be seen in his prose pieces included in the great anthology of "ancient-style" prose models, the *Ku-wen kuan-chih.** They give his prose an air of Confucian seriousness that has led critics to link him with Liu K'ai 柳開 and other early Northern Sung advocates of an "ancient-prose" style.

In his old-style poetry these values remain explicit, but as theme rather than topic. In these poems men of the past, historical sites, and landscapes are often the vehicles for ethical lessons. Among these poems are the encomia of "Chen-niang mu" 吳王墓 (The Grave of a Virtuous Woman) and "Wu Wang mu" 貞娘墓 (The Grave of the King of Wu) as well as didacticism ("Kan-lan" 橄欖 [The Olive]). Here too are Wang's most concerted efforts to capture the moral seriousness of Tu Fu's* "Pa-ai shih" 八哀詩 (Eight Laments) in his own "Wu-ai shih" 五哀詩 (Five Laments). His language captures the formal style in which Tu Fu praised great men of the immediate past, but lacks the master's sense of significant detail and telling gesture.

In his modern-style poetry, however, the presence of these principles is overshadowed by the circumstantial experiences of the life related in the poems themselves. Indeed, the corpus of modern-style verse in the *Hsiao-ch'u chi* constitutes a poetic autobiography chronicling the events and responses which reveal the poet's inner nature. Here values and principles are embodied by the autobiographical self and revealed through them. They are the themes, not merely of individual poems, but of a life.

Stylistically, Wang Yü-ch'eng's poetry covers a wide range, moving from the extremely formal to the near colloquial. At times his poems reveal the craft of a master poet who is capable of writing the kind of "startling lines" much admired in the late T'ang, while at other times his poetry shows a clumsiness that had never been attractive. His work is filled with verbal echos of famous T'ang poems, but the strength and clarity of those echos varies. In some cases the relationship between Wang Yü-ch'eng's borrowed line and the source is irrelevant, or nearly so, within the context of the poem. In other cases, as in the later poems which frequently echo Tu Fu, the relationship is important because it contributes to Wang Yü-ch'eng's autobiographical image of himself as poet. Nevertheless, there are equally frequent echos of other famous T'ang poets like Wang Wei,* Li Po, the Ta-li poets (see Lu Lun), and Li Shang-yin.* Because of this range and variation, it is probably wrong to see him as a practitioner of a single style modeled on Po Chü-i, although he does occasionally promote this view himself. It is perhaps his very diversity which prevented him from developing an individual stylistic signature and, consequently, forces him to be seen as the best of a group of minor poets in the early Northern Sung.

Po Chü-i compiled his own collection, but he did not make it a vehicle for autobiography and moral, Confucian principles; Po Chü-i may have written didactic poetry, but that kind of poetry only represented part of his collection; Po Chü-i may have organized part of his collection around certain themes, but they were broad categories of modal expression, not Confucian moral principles; and Po Chü-i may have said that all of his life was to be found in his writings, but he did not edit and organize his writings to illustrate his life. Wang Yü-ch'eng did all of these things. Ultimately, his self-consciousness about the act of writing and his need to justify the compilation of his own writings have left a collection which obscures some of his real diversity, but allows the great Ch'ing anthologists of Sung poetry to call him "the father of Sung poetry."

EDITIONS:

Hsiao-ch'u chi 小畜集. *SPTK.*

Hsiao-ch'u chi 小畜集. *Kuo-hsüeh chi-pen ts'ung-shu* 國學基本叢書. Adds punctuation to *SPTK* ed.

Wang, Yü-ch'eng. *Wu-tai-shih ch'üeh-wen* 五代史闕文, in *Ssu-k'u ch'üan-shu chen-pen* 四庫全書珍本, Series 7, v. 70-75, Taipei, 1977.

TRANSLATIONS:

Gundert, *Lyrik*, p. 127.

Walls, Jan W. "Wang Yü-ch'eng's Prose Essay 'The Bamboo Pavilion Tower,'" in *K'uei Hsing: A Repository of Asian Literature in Translation*, Liu Wu-chi, *et al.*, eds., Bloomington and London, 1974.

STUDIES:

Huang, Ch'i-fang 黃啟方. "Wang Yü-ch'eng shih-wen hsi-nien"王禹偁詩文繫年, *Shu-mu chi-k'an*, 11.4 (March 1978), 41-78.

———. *Wang Yü-ch'eng yen-chiu* 王禹偁研究. Taipei, 1979.

Liang, Tung-shu 梁東淑. *Wang Yü-ch'eng chi ch'i-shih* 王禹偁及其詩. Unpublished M.A. thesis, National Taiwan University, 1973.

Iritani, Sensuke 入谷仙介. *Sōshi zen* 宋詩選, Tokyo, 1969, pp. 1-28.

—MRS

Wei Chuang 韋莊 (*tzu*, Tuan-chi 端己, *c.* 836-910), high government official, poet, and anthologist, was a native of Tu-ling, a district in the Ch'ang-an metropolitan area, and a member of a once powerful and prominent clan, which counted Wei Chien-su 韋見素 (687-762), who attained the position of Grand Councilor late in life, among its members. By Wei Chuang's time his immediate family had apparently fallen on hard times. Although he was orphaned when quite young, he managed to obtain an education and prepare himself for the civil-service examinations. Little is known about his activities until he went to Ch'ang-an in 881 to take the *chin-shih* examinations shortly before the city was captured and plundered by the rebel armies of Huang Ch'ao 黃巢 (d. 884). His moving depiction of those momentous events in the famous narrative poem "Ch'in-fu yin" 秦婦吟 (The Lament of the Lady of Ch'in) brought him fame and attention. But the chaotic events of the time forced him into a long period of wandering in the south and east, and it was more than a decade later (894) before he was able to compete successfully for the highest examination degree. Although nearly sixty years of age, he was given an appointment as a minor official in the capital and three years later posted to what is now Szechwan to the staff of a senior official. There he met and became an adviser to Wang Chien 王建 (847-918). When the T'ang collapsed in 907, Wang Chien proclaimed the founding of the Ch'ien Shu 前蜀 (Former Shu) dynasty in his own name and called upon Wei Chuang to join the new regime. As a result, Wei Chuang played a key role in the formation of the government and followed the T'ang model in defining the institutions for the Former Shu. Until his death three years later, he held a succession of high offices, culminating in that of Grand Councilor. He is said to have been responsible for drafting many of the official documents of state. Because of the Former Shu's relative stability in politically troubled times, Wang Chien was successful in attracting to his regime many of the leading literary figures of the day.

After taking up permanent residence in the city of Ch'eng-tu, Wei Chuang purchased and restored the Huan-hua hsi ts'ao-t'ang 浣花溪草堂, the former home of Tu Fu.* Thus, when his younger brother Ai compiled and edited his poems for publication in 903, the collection was given the title Huan-hua chi 浣花集 (The Flower-loving Collection). In a poem probably written rather late in life, Wei Chuang stated, perhaps somewhat hyperbolically, that he had written "a thousand songs and poems." The modern edition of his collected works is much smaller. It contains about three hundred shih* poems and does not include "The Lament of the Lady of Ch'in" poem, which was apparently deleted from the collection at his express wish, nor his tz'u poems. Fortunately, several manuscript versions of the former poem were recovered early in this century from the cave-temples of Tun-huang. Most of his extant tz'u have been preserved in the Hua-chien chi.*

"The Lament of the Lady of Ch'in," one of Wei Chuang's best loved works then and now, is a unique example of a genre only occasionally practiced in pre-modern times—namely, the long narrative poem. It is remarkable for its sheer length (238 lines in the heptasyllabic mode), its rather realistic depiction of the capture and brutal sack of Ch'ang-an by the rebel armies of Huang Ch'ao, and its dramatic power and intensity. Few writers of the past cared, or perhaps dared, to express their feelings about contemporary political events so openly. But in this instance Wei Chuang chose to do so with clarity and detail, perhaps best exemplified by the famous couplet "The Inner Treasury consumed in ashes of embroidery and brocade,/Along imperial avenues nowhere to walk but on the bones of high officials."

Compared with the "Lament" poem and his tz'u verse, Wei Chuang's shih-style poems have been little studied except for several well-known anthology pieces (two poems appear in the T'ang-shih san-pai-shou*). When notice is taken of his shih poetry, they are usually cited as evidence of his travels and personal experiences or of his class attitudes. It can be said, however, that Wei had a strong preference for the longer line-length (approximately three-fourths of the collection is in the heptasyllabic form), and regulated-verse patterns in the pentasyllabic and heptasyllabic line lengths predominate. His concerns as a shih poet are more often personal than public, although echoes of the turbulent times so dramatically described in the "Lament" poem are occasionally heard. A muted pathos informs his verse on such time-tested themes as separation and parting or contemplations of the past, and these are expressed in a diction less given to artifice than was characteristic of the times.

As a contributor to the then emerging literati tz'u tradition, Wei Chuang stood between the generation of Wen T'ing-yün* and that of Feng Yen-ssu* and Li Yü* (937-978). These four men are often considered as the four early masters of the form, and comparisons of their respective styles have proven to be particularly illuminating. Generally speaking, traditional criticism usually regarded Wen T'ing-yün and Wei

Chuang as differing little in matters of style, but modern analytical methods have enabled scholars to uncover important distinctions between these two men. Both poets share a similar thematic range—namely, the so-called "bedroom topos" and the personal plaint. And both poets also wrote exclusively in the *hsiao-ling*, or short lyric patterns. But in other respects, as Kang-i Sun Chang in particular has demonstrated, their styles are fundamentally different. Wei Chuang characteristically employs a rhetoric of explicit meaning, by which means he speaks directly to the listener/reader, carefully maintaining a sequential narrative progression, both within and between the stanzas. He adopts a language logically consistent with his chosen stance as the explicit narrator, one which retains elements of colloquialism and is hypotactically expressive. Thus, Wei Chuang is closer stylistically to the popular Tun-huang *tz'u* than is Wen T'ing-yun or his imitators among the *Hua-chien* Poets. It is also closer to the style of the post-*Hua-chien* poets of the mid-tenth century who were to carry the form to new heights.

During his later years Wei Chuang compiled a large anthology of T'ang-dynasty verse, the *Yu-hsüan chi* 又玄集 (Restoring the Mystery Collection), which contains selections from the verse of 150 poets of the era. The title chosen for this work suggests that Wei Chuang regarded it as a kind of continuation to the *Chi-hsüan chi* 極玄集 (The Supreme Mystery Collection), a much smaller compilation by Yao Ho 姚合 (*fl.* 831).

EDITIONS:

Chao, Ch'ung-tso 趙崇祚 , ed. *Hua-chien chi* 花間集 . SPPY.

Chiang, Ts'ung-p'ing 江聰平 . *Wei Tuan-chi shih chiao-chu* 韋端己詩校注 . Taipei, 1969.

Ch'üan T'ang Wu-tai tz'u hui-pien 全唐五代詞彙編 . 2v. Taipei, 1967. Rpt. of the Lin Ta-ch'un 林大椿 compilation *T'ang Wu-tai tz'u*. Contains 54 *tz'u* attributed to Wei Chuang.

Huan-hua chi 浣花集 . SPTK.

Tang-jen hsüan T'ang-shih 唐人選唐詩 . Shanghai, 1958. (*Yu-hsüan chi*, pp. 348-442).

TRANSLATIONS:

Demiéville, *Anthologie*, pp. 324, 331-332.

Soong, Stephen C. *Song Without Music: Chinese Tz'u Poetry*. Hong Kong, 1980, pp. 45-56.

Sunflower, pp. 267-284.

Wixted, John Timothy. *The Song-Poetry of Wei Chuang (836-910)*. Tempe, Arizona, 1979. Translations of 48 *tz'u* with an introduction.

STUDIES:

Chang, *Evolution*, especially pp. 33-62.

Diény, J. P. "Review of J. T. Wixted's *The Song-Poetry of Wei Chuang*," TP, 67 (1981), 111-116.

Hsia, Ch'eng-t'ao 夏承燾 . *T'ang Sung tz'u-jen nien-p'u* 唐宋詞人年譜 , Shanghai, 1955, pp. 1-33. A chronological account of Wei Chuang's life.

Tang, Raymond Nai-wen. "The Poetry of Wei Chuang (836-910)." Unpublished Ph.D. dissertation, Stanford University, 1982.

—ws

Wei Ying-wu 韋應物· (737-*c.* 792) was a T'ang poet whose verses are best known for their tranquil settings and clear diction. A native of Ch'ang-an, he was born into an illustrious clan and served in his youth as an imperial guard in the retinue of Emperor Hsüan-tsung. He never obtained or even sat for any degree, but he did hold, intermittently, a number of posts in the capital and in Lo-yang before being appointed in 783 to the first of three prefectships in the south. He probably died shortly after resigning the third prefectship, that of Soochow (modern Kiangsu), in 790.

His poetry (the only other extant works being a single *fu** and two funerary inscriptions) is often associated with that of the earlier "nature poets," due to the great number of pieces that treat nature and personal themes, often in the High T'ang style of Wang Wei* and Meng Hao-jan.* Examples are "Ch'u-chou Hsi-chien" 滁州西澗 (West Stream at Ch'u-chou) and "Ch'iu-yeh chi Ch'iu Yüan-wai" 秋夜寄丘員外 (Sent to Secretary Ch'iu [Tan 丹] on an Autumn Night). At the same time, he was also an admirer of Hsieh Ling-yün*: such pieces as "T'ing-ying ch'ü" 聽鶯曲 (Song: Listening to the Orioles) contain descriptive passages in the "mountains and waters" tradition of landscape poetry.

But the poet most commonly linked with him is the putative originator of "fields and gardens" poetry, T'ao Ch'ien,* not only because of shared Taoist leanings, but also from the meditative tone and relaxed diction that Wei adopted from him, especially in his pentasyllabic verses. Wei was also adept at writing old-style verse and composed many pieces in imitation of earlier poetry, such as the "Ni-ku" 擬古 (Imitations of Old [Poetry]), inspired mainly by the "Ku-shih shih-chiu shou."* As such, he became a recognized master of pentasyllabic ancient-style verse, with the direct, unmannered, and yet dignified style especially apparent in pieces treating complex personal themes, such as "Sung Yang-shih nü" 送楊氏女 (Sending my Daughter Off [Upon Her Marriage] to the Yang Family) or the set of poems mourning the death of his wife. The discursive tone and the clarity of diction no doubt account for his popularity with many Sung-dynasty poets, including Mei Yao-ch'en* and Su Shih.* In his own lifetime, however, he was not especially renowned, perhaps precisely because of the qualities which set him apart from contemporary tastes as exemplified by the clever, if unexceptional, verses of the Ta-li shih ts'ai-tzu (see Lu Lun).

While he derived much of his personal style from earlier poetry, he was not blind to contemporary events and developments. Many pieces, including his ko-hsing 歌行 (songs and ballads), realistically depict the economic and social disorder following the An Lu-shan Rebellion; they also reveal his own complex responses: outrage at military abuses, sympathy for the victims, and nostalgia for the cultural and material wealth of his courtier days. Of interest are his "T'iao-hsiao ling" 調笑令 (Song of Flirtatious Laughter), several lyrics set to contemporary music which are regarded both as yüeh-fu* poems and as early examples of the tz'u* lyric.

EDITIONS:

Nielson, Thomas Peter. A Concordance to the Poems of Wei Ying-wu. San Francisco, 1975.

Keyed to SPPY edition of Wei Su-chou chi. Includes biographical study.

Wei Su-chou chi 韋蘇州集. SPPY is the most reliable edition, but lacks the eight poems in the shih-i 拾遺 (omissions) section of other editions. Wan-yu wen-k'u 萬有文庫 is complete and punctuated, has marginal notes and criticisms, but is not as good a text.

Wei Chiang-chou chi 韋江州集. SPTK. Not as carefully edited as Wei Su-chou chi, but has appendix with all prefaces, colophons, and biographies from previous editions.

TRANSLATIONS:

Bynner, Jade Mountain, pp. 206-212.
Demiéville, Anthologie, pp. 278-284.
Sunflower, pp. 153-154.

STUDIES:

Fu, Shih-jen, pp. 269-325: "Wei Ying-wu hsi-nien k'ao-cheng" 系年考證; pp. 532-534: appendix on extant prose works.

Fukazawa, Kazuyuki 深澤一幸. "I Ōbutsu no kakō" 韋應物の歌行, Chūkgoku bungakuhō, 24 (1974), 48-74.

Hsia, Chi-an 夏濟安, "Wei Ying-wu," in Chung-kuo wen-hsüeh-shih lun-chi 中國文學史論集, v. 1, Taipei, 1958, pp. 331-337.

Lo, Lien-t'ien 羅聯添. "Wei Ying-wu shih-chi hsi-nien" 事蹟繫年, Yu-shih hsüeh-chih, 8.1 (1969), p. 72.

Nielson, Thomas Peter. "The T'ang Poet Wei Ying-wu and his Poetry." Unpublished Ph.D. dissertation. University of Washington, 1969.

Wan, Man 萬曼. "Wei Ying-wu chuan" , Kuo-wen yüeh-k'an, 60 (1958), 23-32; 61 (1958), 23-28.

Yoshikawa, Kōjirō 吉川幸次郎. "I Ōbutsu no shi" 韋應物の詩, in Chūgoku shishi 中國詩史, Tokyo, 1967, pp. 80-84.

—OL

Wen-chang pien-t'i 文章辦體 (Distinguishing the Forms of Literature) is a huge anthology of poems and prose writings from the earliest times down to the Ming. Edited by Wu No 吳訥 (1372-1457), it consists of the basic fifty chüan called nei-chi 內集 (inner collection), and the supplementary five chüan called wai-chi 外集 (outer collection). All the selections are grouped under their respective t'i 體 (form or genre), such as tsou-shu 奏疏 (memorials) and lun-chien 論諫 (admonitions). Fifty-four types of poetry and prose are included. In format as well as in its principle of selection, it was modeled after the *Wen-chang cheng-tsung* 文章正宗, edited by Chen Te-hsiu 眞德秀 (1178-1235).

Wu No has written a brief preface (*hsü-shou* 序説) to each section of the anthology, in which he discusses the meaning and historical evolution of each form of writing. These prefaces, taken together, constitute a kind of literary theory. Not only do they demonstrate a standard of judgment, but they also evaluate the meaning of each type of writing in the entire history of Chinese literature. For these reasons, modern scholars generally consider them to be the most important part of the anthology. It should be noted, however, that Wu No's definition of each form of writing is by no means authoritative. Moreover, in assigning a particular piece of writing to a particular form, his judgment is sometimes questionable. Nonetheless, it is one of the best-known anthologies compiled in the Ming period. A similar work is the *Wen-t'i ming-pien.**

EDITIONS:

Wen-chang pien-t'i. 1555 blockprint ed. Available at National Central Library, Taipei and Gest Oriental Library, Princeton University. No later reprint.

Wen-chang pien-t'i hsü-shuo 序說. Peking, 1962. Includes only the prefaces. Printed together with the *Wen-t'i ming-pien hsü-shuo.*

STUDIES:

Ssu-k'u ch'üan-shu tsung-mu t'i-yao (Ta-tung ed.), 192.39ab. Still the best description of this work; no other significant study by modern scholars.

—SFL

Wen-hsin tiao-lung 文心雕龍 (The Literary Mind and the Carving of Dragons) by Liu Hsieh 劉勰 (*c.* 465-*c.* 520) was the first book-length study in the Chinese language to address itself to some of the main problems that arise in the study of literature. Literary opinions had been expressed since Confucius in the sixth century B.C., and before, and some of those opinions are as sound as anything we find in the *Wen-hsin tiao-lung.* But none of the earlier work had been presented in a single treatise devoted exclusively to literary considerations. The *Wen-hsin tiao-lung* is the first *book* of literary criticism in the Chinese language.

The work was not always well known; only in the eighteenth century did it come to be regarded as a critical work of great importance and authority. In recent decades, its significance has been exaggerated. A balanced view would be to see it as a conveniently concentrated single work, the first of its kind, whose value lies in its preservation of earlier critical thinking as much as in the development of new ideas.

The *Wen-hsin tiao-lung* contains approximately 37,000 characters. It is divided into ten *chüan*, each consisting of five chapters carrying a descriptive title. The organization of the work is logical, and it is possible to describe its main contents in the order in which they occur. (Some scholars believe that the systematic organization was in imitation of the Buddhist classics with which the author was familiar.)

In the first five chapters, the author presents the theoretical—or, more precisely, doctrinal—foundation of the *Wen-hsin tiao-lung.* All literature, he states, must have its basis in the Confucian Classics and the wisdom therein. Liu Hsieh argues that as literature exists with heaven and earth, the writer ought to seek to understand heaven and earth, and its *Tao*, and that *Tao* could best be comprehended through the classics. Of the first five chapters, the third most readily provides an example of Liu's thinking and its texture.

Chapters 6-25 constitute the second section. They treat the genres of writing known in Liu's time. The genres are divided into the two large categories then current: *wen* 文 and *pi* 筆. The distinctions between the two are a matter of great complexity. The most widely accepted view suggests that *wen* is writing with *yün* 韵, and *pi* is writing without *yün.* "Yün" usually means "rhyme," but should be understood somewhat more broadly here. Thus we might think of *wen* as *embellished* writing, and *pi* as writing which is *unadorned*, normally intended for practical purposes. The embellished genres are dissected in chapters 6-15, the unadorned ones in chapters

16-25. Liu traces the origin and development of each genre, comments on its name, enumerates some examples, and discusses its general characteristics.

The third section of the *Wen-hsin tiao-lung* consists of chapters 26-49. Here Liu is no longer concerned with literature as artifacts, but with its making, what in the West would be called the "creative process" but should *not* be here since "creative process" implies an analogy which does not apply in the Chinese case. Liu goes through what he believes is at work in the *writing* process, and the *planning* process that occurs earlier, and the *preparing* process which is all the time during a writer's life. The writer should be well-educated; for Liu this means familiarity with book-knowledge, together with an awareness of nature. When one is about to write, one should try and respond to nature, for poetry is essentially a product of the meeting of individual sensitivity with the subtleties of nature. This is essentially a psychological account of the process. Separately Liu Hsieh also considers the most important stylistic or rhetorical skills that could be used in writing, which is the second main area of interest in this section. There is also a third—literary criticism itself. In chapter 48, Liu discusses first the qualities he expects to discover in a critic, and then the "six considerations" (*liu kuan* 六觀) whereby the critic could proceed in the practice of criticism.

The fourth and final section of the *Wen-hsin tiao-lung* is a single chapter, the fiftieth. As in several other early Chinese works, this chapter serves most of the purposes of the modern introduction. One of the more interesting points that Liu makes here concerns the reasons why he undertook to write the *Wen-hsin tiao-lung*. All the Confucian Classics had been furnished with excellent commentaries and Liu was debarred from making further contributions. That being the case, he turned to an explication of criticism, arguing that it too was a worthy endeavor.

EDITIONS:

Fan, Wen-lan 范文瀾, comm. *Wen-hsin tiao-lung.* 2v. Peking, 1978.

Wang, Li-ch'i 王利器. *Wen-hsin tiao-lung hsin-shu fu t'ung-chien* 文心雕龍新書附通檢. Taipei, 1968.

Yang, Ming-chao 楊明照, coll. and comm. *Wen-hsin tiao-lung chiao-chu.* Shanghai, 1958. Contains the commentaries of Hung Shu-lin 黃叔琳 (1672-1756) and Li Hsiang 李詳 (1859-1931).

TRANSLATIONS:

Shih, Vincent Yu-chung. *The Literary Mind and the Carving of Dragons: A Study of Thought and Pattern in Chinese Literature.* New York, 1959.

Toda, Kōgyō 戸田浩曉. *Bunshin chōryū* 文心雕龍. 2v. Tokyo, 1977-1978.

STUDIES:

Chi, Ch'iu-lang. "Liu Hsieh as a Classicist and His Concepts of Tradition and Change," *TkR*, 4.1 (April 1973), 89-108.

Gibbs, Donald Arthur. "Literary Theory in the *Wen-hsin tiao-lung.*" Unpublished Ph.D. dissertation, University of Washington, 1970.

———. "Liu Hsieh, Author of the *Wen-hsin tiao-lung, MS,* 29 (1970-1971), 117-142.

Hayashida, Shinnosuke 林田愼之助. "Bunshin chōryū bungaku genriron no sho mondai: Ryū Kyō ni okeru bi no rinen o megutte" 劉勰における美の理念をめぐつて:文心雕龍文學原理論の諸問題, *Nippon Chūgoku gakkaihō,* 19 (1967), 131-143.

Huang, K'an 黃侃. *Wen-hsin tiao-lung cha-chi* 文心雕龍札記. Shanghai, 1962.

Jao, Tsung-i 饒宗頤, *et al.,* comms. "*Wen-hsin tiao-lung* chi-shih kao" 文心雕龍集釋稿, *Hsiang-kang Ta-hsüeh Chung-wen hsüeh-hui nien-k'an,* 1962, 35-80.

"*Wen-hsin tiao-lung* t'an-yüan" 文心雕龍探原, *Hsiang-kang Ta-hsüeh Chung-wen hsüeh-hui nien-k'an,* 1962, 1-12.

Kōzen, Hiroshi 興膳宏. "Bunshin chōryū to shihin no bungakukan no tairitsu" 文心雕龍と詩品の文學觀の對立, in *Yoshikawa hakushi taikyū kenen Chūgoku bungaku ronshū* 吉川博士退休紀念中國文學論集, Tokyo, 1968, pp. 271-288.

Kuo, Chin-hsi 郭晉稀. *Wen-hsin tiao-lung i-chu shih-pa p'ien* 文心雕龍譯註十八篇. Hong Kong, 1964.

Kuo, Yü-heng 郭預衡. "*Wen-hsin tiao-lung* p'ing-lun tso-chia te chi-ko t'e-tien" 雕龍評論作家的幾個特點, *Wen-hsüeh p'ing-lun,* 1963.1 (February 1963), 28-45.

Liu, Yung-chi 劉永濟. *Wen-hsin tiao-lung chiao-shih* 文心雕龍校釋. Shanghai, 1962.

Lu, K'an-ju 陸侃如 and Mou Shih-chin 牟世金. *Liu Hsieh ho Wen-hsin tiao-lung* 劉勰和文心雕龍. Shanghai, 1978.

Shao, Paul Yong-shing. "Liu Hsieh as Literary Theorist, Critic and Rhetorician." Unpublished Ph.D. dissertation, Stanford University, 1981.

Shiba, Rokurō 斯波六郎. *Bunshin chōryū Hanchū hosei* 雕龍范注補正. Hiroshima, 1952.

Shih, Vincent Y. C. "Liu Hsieh's Conception of Organic Unity," *TkR*, 4.2 (October 1973), 1-10.

Wang, Keng-sheng 王更生. *Wen-hsin tiao-lung yen-chiu* 文心雕龍研究. Taipei, 1976.

Wang, Shu-min 王叔岷. *Wen-hsin tiao-lung chui-pu* 文心雕龍綴補. Taipei, 1975.

Wang, Yüan-hua 王元化. *Wen-hsin tiao-lung ch'uang-tao lun* 文心雕龍創作論. Shanghai, 1979.

—SKW

Wen-hsüan 文選 (Anthology of Literature) is the most influential of all medieval anthologies of verse and prose. It was compiled to provide an anthology of traditional prose and verse in opposition to current literary fashion as expressed in the contemporary collection, *Yü-t'ai hsin-yung.** Its sixty *chüan* contain thirty-eight genres and more than 700 pieces written by 129 authors from the period of the Han through the Liang dynasties. The work itself and its generic division provided models for subsequent anthologies such as the *Wen-yüan ying-hua** and the *Ku-wen-tz'u lei-tsuan.**

The earliest known anthology of literature is the *Shan-wen* 善文, compiled by Tu Yü 杜預 (222-284). After the *Wen-hsüan* had become popular, the *Shan-wen* sank into oblivion and was lost. In the Sui and T'ang dynasties, the *Wen-hsüan* was included in the syllabus of the official examination, and became the candidate's basic reader for learning the art of writing. Li Shan 李善 (*c.* 630-689) wrote a commentary for the collection, giving detailed notes on the numerous allusions. Another commentary was provided by the *Wu-ch'en* 五臣 (Five Officials) of the early T'ang. Their work has generally been considered inferior to that of Li Shan, with whose exegesis theirs is often combined under the rubric *Liu-ch'en chu* 六臣經 (Commentary of the Six Officials). From the T'ang to the Ch'ing, the study of the *Wen-hsüan* came into prominence, and was considered a field of learning—"*Wen-hsüan* Studies." A maxim current in the Sung dynasty says, "When your *Wen-hsüan* falls to pieces, you are halfway to becoming a *hsiu-tsai* 秀才." From the time of the May Fourth on, the advocates of literary reforms slighted the parallel style of writing, labeling those who wrote in such a style as "monsters of *Wen-hsüan* studies." But traditionally the *Wen-hsüan* occupied an important position in the history of Chinese literature.

The *Wen-hsüan* was compiled by Hsiao T'ung 蕭統 (501-531), Crown Prince Chao-ming 昭明 of the Liang dynasty. The prince was fond of literature, and loved those who were learned. The collaborators he gathered around himself were called the "Ten Scholars of the East Palace," of which Liu Hsiao-ch'o 劉孝綽 (481-539), Wang Yün 王筠 (481-549), and Lu Ch'ui 陸錘 (470-526) were the leaders. The prince died in 531. Lu Ch'ui had died five years earlier (526); the *Wen-hsüan* contains Lu Ch'ui's works but not those of Liu and Wang, i.e. the work must have been completed between the years 526 and 531.

In his preface to the *Wen-hsüan,* Hsiao T'ung says that the criterion for selection is whether or not a work has beautiful diction. According to the principle underlying the scheme of the book, the classics, the histories, and the philosophers were to be excluded. However, the *tsan* 贊 and *lun* 論 portions of the histories, if they were well written, would be included. On the other hand, official documents such as memorials and presentations to the emperor form a substantial part of the book— a single writer like Jen Fang* is represented by ten works in these genres. From this viewpoint, it is apparent that Hsiao did not altogether neglect literary works of a practical nature.

The *Wen-hsüan* generic classification has been criticized for being too diffuse and fragmentary. If the genre theory of the *Wen-hsüan* is compared with that of the *Wen-hsin tiao-lung,** certain points in common become apparent. The *Wen-hsin tiao-lung* preceded the *Wen-hsüan;* it is probable that the compilers of the latter made use of the former. But many of the genres established by the *Wen-hsüan* are actually subgenres or so similar to other categories they are redundant. In this respect the *Wen-hsin tiao-lung* is more precise.

EDITIONS:

Printed editions of the *Wen-hsüan* exist from the Sung on. There are a large number of editions, which can be traced to four different lines:
1. Editions without commentary. In this category belong the original edition of Hsiao T'ung, in 30 *chüan,* and a fragment of a Six Dynasties manuscript copy (discovered in Tun-huang) which are now in the Bibliothèque Nationale.
2. Editions with Li Shan's commentary, in 60 *chüan.* Fragments (containing the *Hsi-ching fu* 西京賦) of a T'ang manuscript copy (680) are extant. In 1011, the National University first put this edition into print (a fragmentary copy of this is now in the possession of the Peking Library). The edition printed by Yu Mao 尤袤 in 1181 is the most important.
3. Editions with the "commentaries of the five officials," in 30 *chüan.* In the 730s Lü Yen-tso 呂延祚 gathered together the commentaries by Lü Yen-chi 呂延濟, Liu Liang 劉良, Chang Hsien 張銑, Lü Hsiang 呂向, and Li Chou-han 李周翰. This collection is known as the "commentaries of the five officials." A T'ang manuscript copy is now in Japan (in possession of Tenri 天理 University; it has been photolithographically reprinted as one of the items of the rare book collection of the University). The National Central Library of Taiwan possesses an edition printed by Ch'en Pa-lang 陳八郎 of Chien-yang 建陽 (1144).
4. Editions with the "commentaries of the six ministers." This combines Li Shan's commentary with those of the five ministers. Three Sung editions are available. The first is the Kan-chou 贛州 edition, with Li Shan's commentary preceding those of the five ministers. The *SPTK* edition is a reprint of this. The second is the Ming-chou 明州 edition printed in 1158, with the commentaries of the five ministers preceding that of Li Shan. It has been included in the series of rare book reprints of the Ashikaga 足利 College of Japan (printed by the Kyūko 汲古 College). The third is the edition printed by P'ei Chai 裴宅 of Kuang-tu 廣都 in 1106. There is a Taiwan reprint.

There is also an edition with collected commentaries (120 *chüan*) now in Japan. The compiler of the collected commentaries is not known, but the Li Shan commentary in this edition is more detailed than that in the Sung editions. There is a photolithographic reprint by Kyoto University.

TRANSLATIONS:

Knechtges, David R. *Wen Xuan, or Selections of Refined Literature: Volume 1: Rhapsodies on Metropolises and Capitals.* Princeton, 1982. Contains an excellent bibliography.

Margouliès, Georges. *Le "Fou" dans le Wen siuan: étude et textes.* Paris, 1926.

Obi, Kōichi 小尾郊一 and Hanabusa Hideki 花房英樹. *Monzen* 文選. 7v. Tokyo, 1974-1976.

von Zach, *Anthologie.*

STUDIES:

Ch'eng, I-chung 程毅中 and Pai Hua-wen 白化文. "Lüeh t'an Li Shan chu *Wen-hsüan* te Yu K'o pen" 略談李善注文選的尤刻本, *Wen-wu,* 1976.11, 77-81.

Ch'i, I-shou 齊益壽. "*Wen-hsin tiao-lung* yü *Wen-hsüan* tsai hsüan-wen ting-p'ien chi p'ing-wen piao-chun shang te pi-chiao" 文心雕龍與文選在選文定篇及評文標準上的比較, in *Ku-tien wen-hsüeh* 古典文學, v. 3, Taipei, 1981.

Ch'iu, Hsieh-yu 邱燮友. "Hsüan-hsüeh k'ao" 選學考, *T'ai-wan Sheng-li Shih-fan Ta-hsüeh Kuo-wen Yen-chiu-so chi-k'an,* 3 (1959), 329-396. Annotated list of 141 Chinese works on the *Wen-hsüan.*

Chu, Lien-hsien 祝廉先. "*Wen-hsüan* Liu-ch'en chu ting-o" 文選六臣注訂譌, *Wen-shih,* 1 (October 1962), 177-217.

Furuta, Keiichi 古田敬一. "Monzen hensan no nin to ji" 文選編纂の人と時, in *Obi hakushi taikyu kinen Chūgoku bungaku ronshū* 小尾博士退休紀念中國文學論集, Tokyo, 1976, pp. 363-378.

Gimm, Martin. *Die chinesische Anthologie Wen-hsüan; In mandjurischer Teilübersetzung einer Leningrader und einer Kölner Handschrift.* Wiesbaden, 1968.

Hightower, James R. "The *Wen-hsüan* and Genre Theory," *HJAS,* 20 (1957), 512-533.

Jao, Tsung-i 饒宗頤. "Tun-huang pen *Wen-hsüan* chiao-cheng" (1 and 2) 敦煌本文選斠證, *Hsin-ya hsüeh-pao,* 3.1 (1957), 333-403, and 3.2 (1958), 305-328.

Kao, Pu-ying 高步瀛. "*Wen-hsüan* Li chu i shu" 文選李注義疏, in *Hsüan hsüeh ts'ung-shu* 選學叢書, Taipei, 1966.

Lin, Ts'ung-ming 林聰明. *Chao-ming Wen-hsüan k'ao lüeh* 昭明文選考略. Taipei, 1974.

Lo, Hung-k'ai 駱鴻凱. *Wen-hsüan hsüeh* 文學選. Taipei, 1963.

Schmitt, Gerhard. "Aufschlüsse über das Wenxuan in seiner frühesten Fassung durch ein Manuskript aus der Tang-Zeit," in *Mitteilungen des Instituts für Orientforschung der Deutschen Akademie der Wissenschaften su Berlin*, 14.3 (1968), 481-488.

Shiba, Rokurō 斯波六郎. "Monzen shohon no kenkyū" 文選諸本の研究, in *Monzen sakuin* 文選索引, v. 1, 1957.

—TIJ

Wen-kuan tz'u-lin 文館詞林 (Forest of Writings from the Hall of Literature) was originally a huge collection in one thousand *chüan* compiled under imperial auspices by the Grand Councilor Hsü Ching-tsung 許敬' (592-672) in 658. However, most of it seems to have been lost as early as the Southern Sung period. During the next few centuries, this work was virtually forgotten. In the late eighteenth century, surviving manuscripts were discovered in Japan. So far about 27 *chüan* (some fragmentary) are known and are published in various editions.

Judging from its surviving portion, this work seems to have included both private writings and official documents, such as imperial edicts, from the early Han through the early T'ang. Even though less than one-tenth of it has survived, the importance of the extant portion need hardly be stressed. Many poems and documents, long presumed to be lost, appear here for the first time. Many are not found in the two earlier "complete" collections: the *Han Wei Liu-ch'ao pai-san ming-chia chi* 漢魏六朝百三名家集 compiled by Chang P'u 張溥 (1602-1641) and the *Ch'üan Shang-ku San-tai Ch'in Han San-kuo Liu-ch'ao wen.**

The work is one of a series of similar anthologies going back to the Northern Ch'i era. Its purpose, similar to these precursors, was to define a corpus of traditional genres and works—the selection of genres herein seems to fall between that of the earlier *Wen-hsüan** and its Sung-dynasty sequel, the *Wen-yüan ying-hua.**

EDITIONS:

Wen-kuan tz'u-lin. Yang Pao-ch'u 楊葆初, ed. 1893. Includes 6 *chüan*.

———, in *I-ts'un ts'ung-shu* 佚存叢書 (1800), contains 4 *chüan;* in *Ku-i ts'ung-shu* 古佚叢書 (1884), contains 14 *chüan*. These two (in all, 18 *chüan*) are incorporated into *PPTSCC*, series 75, v. 50-57.

———, in *Shih-yüan ts'ung-shih* 適園叢書. 1914. Contains 23 *chüan* including several earlier published versions.

See also *Bunkan shirin* below.

STUDIES:

Meng, Shen 孟森. "Wen-kuan tz'u-lin chiao-chi" 文館詞林校記, *Pei-p'ing T'u-shu-kuan kuan-k'an*, 7.1 (February 1933), 81-102.

Bunkan shirin 文館詞林. Abe Ryūichi 阿部隆一, ed. Tokyo, 1969. Facsimile reprint of an *MSS.* copy dated 823. Includes a lengthy study by Abe.

—SFL

Wen-t'i ming-pien 文體明辨 (Clearly Distinguishing Literary Forms) is modeled after the *Wen-chang pien-t'i,** and the two anthologies of poems and prose writings are frequently mentioned together. Edited by Hsü Shih-tseng 徐師曾 (*chin-shih*, 1553), the *Wen-t'i ming-pien* consists of 84 *chüan*. Its scope is even larger than that of the *Wen-chang pien-t'i*—it includes 127 forms of prose and poetry (the *Pien-t'i* has only 54).

Again, as in the case of its predecessor, the most important parts of this anthology are the 127 brief prefaces to each section of the work. Hsü Shih-tseng's discussion of the various types of writings is well-informed and in many respects fuller than that of Wu No. However, not all forms of writings are well represented—the selection of poetry is especially weak. Nevertheless, of the many such anthologies compiled during the Ming period, these two works are among the best. While both have not been reprinted in modern times, their prefaces have been collected and printed together in a handy volume (see below). The admirably concise definitions given in these prefaces could well serve as a dictionary of classical literary terms.

EDITIONS:

Wen-t'i ming-pien. Woodblock-print ed. of 1530, available at Gest Oriental Library, Princeton University. No other reprint.

———. Woodblock-print ed. of 1663, *Wen-t'i ming-pien hsü-shuo* 序說. Peking, 1962. Includes only the prefaces. Printed together with the *Wen-chang pien-t'i hsü-shuo.*

STUDIES:

Ssu-k'u ch'üan-shu tsung-mu t'i-yao (Ta-tung ed.), 192.36ab. Still the best comment. No other significant study by modern scholars.

—SFL

Wen T'ing-yün 溫庭筠, sometimes T'ing-yun 廷筠 or T'ing-yün 庭雲, original *ming*, Ch'i 岐 (*tzu*, Fei-ch'ing 飛卿; *c.* 812-870), a versatile and innovative poet and writer, was a native of T'ai-yüan, Shansi, and a lineal descendant of Wen Yen-po 溫彥博, who held various high offices, including that of President of the Imperial Secretariat, during the reign of Emperor T'ai-tsung (r. 627-650). The older brother of Wen Yen-po, Wen Ta-ya 溫大雅, was the author of the well-known *Ta-T'ang ch'uang-yeh ch'i-chü chu* 大唐創業起居注 (Record of Activity and Repose of the Founding of the Great T'ang) and also influential at the T'ang court. Wen T'ing-yün's grandfather and father both had modestly successful official careers. Because of numerous references in his poetry to the lower Yangtze Valley Region, it is thought that Wen T'ing-yün may have spent his youth there. He traveled widely in the area in his later years.

When Wen T'ing-yün arrived in Ch'ang-an in his early twenties to participate in the *chin-shih* examinations, he was already regarded as a promising literary talent and a skilled performer on the flute and various stringed instruments. Frequent mention is also made in the historical sources of his practiced skill in the examination-style *fu.** Two of his compositions in that genre are contained in the *Ch'üan T'ang wen,** both elegant displays of word magic. Nonetheless, he failed to pass the examinations, apparently disqualified on one occasion for assisting eight fellow candidates with their papers. Although it seems that he never received the coveted *chin-shih* degree, he was appointed to a minor provincial post on the basis of personal connections. Some sources also indicate that

he was ultimately made a tutor in the Imperial Academy because of his friendship with the powerful official Ling-hu T'ao 令狐綯 (*c.* 802-879). His failure to distinguish himself in the examinations or later in public service may have resulted from his personal habits and mannerisms, for the historical sources describe him as an arrogant non-conformist, a decadent ne'er-do-well, and an habitué of the gay quarters. He apparently formed a temporary liaison with the famous woman poet Yü Hsuan-chi*—their relationship was later fictionalized by Japanese novelist Mori Ogai (1862-1922). Wen T'ing-yün's familiarity with the world of popular entertainment had other important consequences, for it was in that environment that the new musical and *tz'u* patterns were then much in vogue. Inspiration gained in that milieu, along with his own talents as a musician, explain why he was the first literati poet to seriously explore the potentials of the *tz'u* form as a medium of polite verse.

Although other writers before him, such as Li Po,* Liu Yü-hsi,* and Po Chü-i,* had rather infrequently experimented with *tz'u* verse-patterns, their efforts actually differed little in either form or content from the traditional *shih** modes. Wen T'ing-yün, however, elected to follow a bolder course in distinguishing between *shih* and *tz'u* and in making extensive use of the latter. As a result, two collections of his *tz'u* poems were in circulation during his lifetime: the *Wo-lan chi* 握蘭集 (Plucking the Orchid Collection) in three *chüan* and the *Chin-ch'üan chi* 金荃集 (The Golden Fish-trap Collection) in ten *chüan.* Both of these works were subsequently lost, but seventy of his *tz'u* survive, most of which have been preserved in the *Hua-chien chi,** the famous ninth-century anthology. Because of Wen T'ing-yün's vital contribution to the development of the *tz'u* as a new literati verse-form and his pervasive influence on many of the other authors represented in his anthology, he was accorded him more space than any other figure.

Critical reaction to Wen T'ing-yün's *tz'u* has varied enormously over the centuries. Some critics have found them morally objectionable because of their exotic and sensuous imagery and their bedchamber topos. On the other hand, there are those who admired their obvious aesthetic qualities. The influential critic Chang Hui-yen,* for instance, defined the stylistic qualities of Wen's *tz'u* as being "profound, beautiful, broad, and concise." Although Wang Kuo-wei* rejected those labels, he nevertheless acknowledged the general excellence of Wen T'ing-yün's diction and observed that the line "A pair of partridges on a golden screen" exemplifies his personal style. More recently, specialists writing on the early history of the form and its major practitioners have sought to go beyond the traditional impressionistic generalities to discover the underlying elements of form and style. Cheng Ch'ien 鄭騫, for instance, found the characteristic point-of-view of his poems to be an objective one, and Chia-ying Yeh Chao 葉嘉瑩 has called attention to the pictorial quality of his *tz'u*. Kang-i Sun Chang has carried the analysis a long step forward by exploring the key component elements of his "rhetoric of implicit meaning." In this way, she has drawn attention to the important differences between the single- and two-stanza *hsiao-ling* (short lyric) poems. The former tend to be explicit in manner, linguistically hypotactic, and normally concerned with the depiction of a young woman and her lover. The latter, on the other hand, are more complex, where meaning is usually implied rather than stated. The persona in these poems is typically the neglected woman, who seems to be immobilized by her loneliness. She is seen to be languishing in bed, sitting before her mirror, or leaning disconsolately against a balustrade. Her inner feelings are suggested metaphorically by the physical environment which she inhabits, an opulent world of crystal curtains, incense burners, figured embroideries, and the like. These and other objects, animate and inanimate, personify her emotions and are dynamic in contrast to her own languid, unmoving state. These visual, aural, and olfactory images invest the scene with color and movement and meaning, but seem to

lack order. In these ways, Wen T'ing-yün's song-lyrics represent a sharp break with earlier examples of the form, whether popular *tz'u* from Tun-huang with their vernacular language, their open and direct manner, and their greater variety of subject matter, or the relatively unimaginative *tz'u* of his predecessors. Thus, it is to Wen T'ing-yün's credit that the *tz'u* form achieved a new stature and also began to move in new directions.

As a poet of ancient- and modern-style *shih* verse forms, Wen T'ing-yün was linked in his own day with his contemporaries Li Shang-yin* and Tuan Ch'eng-shih 段成式 (d. 863) although the only real connection between these men seems to have been the marriage of Wen's daughter to Tuan's son. Their differences as individuals and men of letters are greater than their similarities. It is more useful to compare Wen's *tz'u* with his poems written to the traditional forms. Generally speaking, his *shih* poems reveal a greater range of diction, mood, and theme than is the case with his *tz'u*. Among his three hundred-odd extant *shih*, there is a slight preference for the longer heptasyllabic line than the pentasyllabic; nonetheless, at one time or another he adopted all of the major forms. Variety of form is matched by diversity of language and style. For instance, "Su Wu miao" 蘇武廟 (The Temple of Su Wu, one of four poems included in the anthology *T'ang-shih san-pai-shou**) is classical in its restraint and concision, while some poems in the ancient-style mode are unburdened by allusion and open and direct in manner. Similarly, many of his regulated-verse poems depict in approving terms the simple, bucolic existence of the rustic farmer or fisherman, and the untrammeled happiness of reclusion in nature. Still other poems belong to the *yung-shih* 詠史 (on history) subgenre; among these are celebrations of the grandeur and affluence of former political leaders which are notable for their absence of critical comment. These and other themes lend his *shih* a degree of richness and diversity generally lacking in his *tz'u*.

In addition to the *fu*, *tz'u*, and *shih* already mentioned, a number of letters from

895

his hand are to be found in the *Ch'üan T'ang wen.** Other prose writings on a variety of subjects are also preserved in various collectanea.

EDITIONS:

Chao, Ch'ung-tso 趙崇祚, ed. *Hua-chien chi. SPPY.*

Ch'üan T'ang Wen, v. 16, *chüan* 786, pp. 10377-10387, contains his *fu* and correspondence.

Ch'üan T'ang Wu-tai tz'u hui-pien 全唐五代詞彙編. 2v. Taipei, 1967. Reprint of the Lin Ta-ch'un 林大椿 compilation *T'ang Wu-tai tz'u*—contains 70 of Wen's *tz'u.*

Iwama, Keiji 岩間啟二. *On Teiin kashi sakuin* 溫庭筠歌詩索引. Kyoto, 1977.

Wen Fei-ch'ing chi chien-chu 溫飛卿集箋注. Annotated by Tseng I 曾益 with supplementary notes by Ku Yü-hsien 顧予咸 and Ku Ssu-li 顧嗣立, Taipei, 1959.

Wen Fei-ch'ing shih chi 溫飛卿詩集. Taipei, 1967. A photolithographic reprint of the edition with Tseng I's annotation and Ku Yü-hsien's supplementary notes, with a postface by Ku Ssu-li dated 1696.

TRANSLATIONS:

Chaves, Jonathan. "The *Tz'u* Poetry of Wen T'ing-yün." Unpublished M.A. thesis, Columbia University, n.d. Includes translations of all 70 extant *tz'u.*

Demiéville, *Anthologie*, pp. 321-322, 330.

Sunflower, pp. 244-254.

STUDIES:

Chang, Kang-i Sun. *The Evolution of Chinese Tz'u Poetry, from Late T'ang to Northern Sung.* Princeton, 1980, pp. 33-62. A superb study.

Cheng, Ch'ien 鄭騫. *Ts'ung shih tao ch'ü* 從詩到曲. Taipei, 1961.

———. "Wen T'ing-yün, Wei Chuang yü tz'u te ch'uang shih" 溫庭筠韋莊與詞的創始, in *Ching-wu ts'ung-pien* 景午叢編, v. 1, Taipei, 1972, pp. 103-109.

Fang, Yü 方瑜. *Chung-wan T'ang San-chia shih-hsi lun* 中晚唐三家詩析論 [Analytic Studies of the Poetry of Li Ho, Li Shang-yin, and Wen T'ing-yün]. Taipei, 1975.

Hsia, Ch'eng-t'ao 夏承燾. *T'ang Sung tz'u-jen nien-p'u* 唐宋詞人年譜. Shanghai, 1955, pp. 383-434. A chronological account of Wen's life and career.

Lu, I. *Wen Fei-ch'ing und seine literarische Umwelt.* Würzburg, 1939.

Murakami, Tetsukmi 村上哲見. "On Hikyō no bungaku" 溫飛卿の文學, *Chūgoku bungakuhō*, 5 (1956), 19-40.

Yeh, Chia-ying 葉嘉瑩. "Wen T'ing-yün tz'u kai-shuo" 溫庭筠詞概說, in *Chia-ling t'an-tz'u* 迦陵談詞, Taipei, 1970, pp. 13-54.

—WS

Wen tse 文則 (Principles of Writing) by Ch'en K'uei 陳騤 (1128-1203) is regarded as the first study concentrated on rhetoric in China. Prefaced in 1170, the treatise consists of ten sections with a total of sixty-two items. Drawing examples mainly from the classics, the author discusses such rhetorical devices as gradation, parallelism, repetition, quotation, irony, borrowing, and metaphor. In section three, ten categories of metaphor are differentiated, including *chih-yü* 直喻 (equivalent to *ming-yü* 明喻 or simile) and *yin-yü* 隱喻 (metaphor). Like Aristotle, Ch'en emphasizes the importance of this verbal technique. Though subject to criticism, Ch'en's treatment of metaphor is perhaps the most comprehensive and meticulous in traditional Chinese criticism.

Apart from studying specific literary devices, Ch'en claims spontaneity, simplicity, and ulteriority as virtues to be sought in composition. By ulteriority Ch'en means the selection of significant fact (s) to connote a certain idea; for example, the fact that "neither a single horse nor chariot returned" suggests a severe defeat. Ch'en also compares the different styles of the classics and the possible influences one part of the canon had on another.

Unlike many of the *shih-hua** and *tz'u-hua** of Ch'en's times, in which biographical anecdotes abound, the *Wen tse* limits itself to the art of writing. The order of the book suggests a logic, although the structure could be improved. The *Wen tse* is by no means the first work concerning rhetoric; the fifth-century *Wen-hsin tiao-lung,** for example, devoted several chapters to antithesis, metaphor, and other techniques. The *Wen tse* is, however, the first work entirely devoted to this area.

EDITIONS:

Wen tse, Wen-chang ching-i 文則、文章精義. Liu Ming-hui 劉明暉, ed. Hong Kong, 1977.

STUDIES:

T'an, Ch'üan-chi 譚全基. *Wen tse yen-chiu* 文則研究. Hong Kong, 1978.

—WLW

Wen-yüan ying-hua 文苑英華 (Finest Flowers of the Preserve of Letters) is one of the three great compendia of writings whose compilation was ordered by the Sung Emperor T'ai-tsung (r. 976-998). The *Wen-yüan ying-hua* was the last of this trio of anthologies to be conceived and completed. Its creation was ordered in 982, a year after the completion of the *T'ai-p'ing kuang-chi** and just before the presentation to the throne of the *T'ai-p'ing yü-lan.** The commission charged with undertaking the task included Li Fang 李昉 (925-996), who had superintended the compilation of the *Yü-lan,* along with numerous other scholars who had likewise worked on that earlier project. In 987, the *Wen-yüan ying-hua* attained its finished form and was submitted to the emperor. But in 1007 and again in 1009, at the demand of the succeeding monarch Chen-tsung (r. 998-1023), certain revisions and additions were made. The work was reprinted with some further emendations, at the beginning of the thirteenth century. The text as we have it today, however, is founded on a Ming reprinting done in 1567. Only 140 chapters of the Sung edition (*ch.* 201-210, 231-240, 251-260, 291-300, 601-700) have been preserved; these are included—in place of their Ming counterparts—in modern versions of the work. Prior to 1567 the *Wen-yüan ying-hua* was not widely circulated, suffering during the first centuries of its existence the same general neglect that befell the *Yü-lan* and *Kuang-chi* in those years.

The *Ying-hua* is, in both title and contents, a true florilegium. Comprising 1,000 *chüan,* it was conceived as a gigantic successor to the influential sixth-century anthology of refined literature, the *Wen-hsüan.** Chronologically, the contents of the *Ying-hua* cover the period from the early sixth century (including a few items that also appear in the *Wen-hsüan*) to the early tenth. But, since more than nine-tenths of the material is in fact drawn from the T'ang era, there is good reason to consider the work predominantly an anthology of T'ang literature. Roughly 20,000 individual compositions are contained in the work, representing nearly 2,200 writers. Works in all forms and styles, both poetry and prose, are included in this massive colleciton. Like the *Wen-hsüan,* the *Ying-hua* divides the writings contained within it into 38 separate categories. However, while the number of generic divisions thus remains the same, the designations of the categories themselves differ between the two anthologies. The *Ying-hua* regularly subdivides its general categories into numerous smaller sections, based primarily on theme or subject (e.g., the large category of *shih** poetry is divided into more than 150 topical subsections) and organized chronologically by author. This feature of the anthology makes it particularly useful if one wishes to gain an overview of late Six Dynasties and T'ang works on a particular topic.

The contents of the *Wen-yüan ying-hua* are arranged as follows: 1. *Fu** (*ch.* 1-150); 2. *Shih** (*ch.* 151-330); 3. *Ko-hsing* 歌行 (Songs and Sequences, *ch.* 331-350); 4. *Tsa-wen* 雜文 (Mixed Texts, *ch.* 351-379); 5. *Chung-shu chih-chao* 中書制誥 ([Imperial] Announcements and Orders from the [Bureau of] Penetralian Writs, *ch.* 380-419); 6. *Han-lin chih-chao* 翰林制誥 ([Imperial] Announcements and Orders from the Forest of Quills [Academy], *ch.* 420-472); 7. *Ts'e-wen* 策文 (Dissertation Questions [for the civil-service exams], *ch.* 473-476); 8. *Ts'e* 策 (Dissertations [from the civil-service exams], *ch.* 477-502); 9. *P'an* 判 (Judgments, *ch.* 503-552); Piao 表 (Manifestos, *ch.* 553-626); 11. *Chien* 牋 (Reports, *ch.* 627); 12. *Chuang* 狀 (Representations, *ch.* 628-644); 13. *Hsi* 檄 (Incitements, *ch.* 645-646); 14. *Lou-pu* 露布 (Public Notifications, *ch.* 647-648); 15. *T'an-wen* 彈文 (Texts of Impeachment, *ch.* 649); 16. *I-wen* 移文 (Despatches, *ch.* 650); 17. *Ch'i* 啓 (Disclosures, *ch.* 651-666); 18. *Shu* 疏 (Letters/Writs, *ch.* 667-693); 19. *Shu* 書 (Petitions, *ch.* 694-698); 20. *Hsü* 序 (Prefaces, *ch.* 699-738); 21. *Lun* 論 (Discourses, *ch.* 739-760); 22. *I* 議 (Deliberations, *ch.* 761-770); 23. *Lien-chu* 連珠 (Linked Pearls, *ch.* 771); 24. *Yü-tui* 喻對

(Parables and Parallels, *ch.* 771); 25. *Sung* 頌 (Lauds, *ch.* 772-779); 26. *Tsan* 讚 (Appraisals, *ch.* 780-784); 27. *Ming* 銘 (Inscriptions, *ch.* 785-790); 28. *Chen* 箴 (Remonstrations, *ch.* 791); 29. *Chuan* 傳 (Biographies/Traditions, *ch.* 792-796); 30. *Chi* 記 (Records, *ch.* 797-834); 31. *Shih-ai ts'e-wen* 謚哀冊文 (Tabulate Texts of Lament and Posthumous Titles, *ch.* 835-839); 32. *Shih-i* 謚議 (Deliberations on Posthumous Titles, *ch.* 840-841); 33. *Lei* 誄 (Eulogies, *ch.* 842-843); 34. *Pei* 碑 (Incriptions, *ch.* 844-934); 35. *Chih* 誌 (Commemorations, *ch.* 935-969); 36. *Mu-piao* 墓表 (Epitaphs, *ch.* 970); 37. *Hsing-chuang* 行狀 (Accounts of Career, *ch.* 971-977); 38. *Chi-wen* 祭文 (Texts for Oblation, *ch.* 987-1000). The extensive scope and coverage of the *Ying-hua* renders it a most important reference for the study of virtually all branches of polite letters during the T'ang dynasty. Indeed, the Ch'ing scholars who compiled the *Ch'üan T'ang shih** and *Ch'üan T'ang wen** made abundant use of the work. Modern scholars continue to find it an extremely valuable text against which to collate other editions of individual writings. Nevertheless, the text does contain numerous errors and must be consulted with some caution.

EDITIONS:

Wen-yüan ying-hua. 1,000 *chüan.* Sung edition no longer extant, except for fragments. Ming edition of 1567, reprinted during Wan-li period (1573-1620), is the basis of modern editions. Standard text is the Peking, 1966 edition, a photoligthographic production which includes the 140 remaining chapters from the Sung text, as well as the ten-*chüan Wen-yüan ying-hua pien-cheng* 文苑英華辨證 of P'eng Shu-hsia 彭叔夏 (preface 1204), the one-*chüan Wen-yüan ying-hua pien-cheng shih-i* 文苑英華辨證拾遺 of Lao Ko 勞格 (late 18th century), and an author index. This text has been reprinted several times in Taiwan.

STUDIES:

Hanabusa, Hideki 花房英樹. "Bun'en eika no hensan" 文苑英華の篇纂, *Tōhōgakuhō,* 19 (1950), 116-135.

Lo, Chen-yü 羅振玉 and Sung Ch'ien 宋槧. "Wen-yüan ying-hua ts'an-pen chiao-chi" 文苑英華殘本校記, *Pei-hai T'u-shu-kuan yüeh-k'an,* 2

(1929), 367-383.

—PW

Wu Chi 吳激 (*tzu,* Yen-kao 彥高, *hao,* Tung-shan 東山, d. 1142) and **Ts'ai Sung-nien** 蔡松年 (*tzu,* Po-chien 伯堅, *hao,* Hsiao-hsien lao-jen 蕭閒老人, 1107-1159) were two of the most famous *tz'u* poets during the early years of the Jurchen Chin dynasty (1115-1234). Their *tz'u* were collectively known as the "Wu-Ts'ai Style."

Wu Chi, a native of Chien-chou 建州 (modern Fukien), was the son of a Sung dynasty minister and son-in-law of the well-known painter Mi Fu 米芾 (also known as Mi Fei, 1051-1107). An acknowledged master of both poetry and prose, excelling especially in *tz'u** poetry, he was also an accomplished artist whose calligraphy and paintings reflect the influence of his father-in-law. When Wu was despatched a Northern Sung envoy to the Chin court in 1126, his literary fame compelled the Chin to retain him as a resident scholar in the Han-lin Academy. In 1136, Wu represented the Chin ruler to the Korean Koryo court in conveying birthday congratulations to their king. Six years later, in 1142, he was appointed by the Chin government as Prefect of Shen-chou 深州 (in modern Hopei), but he died after only three days at his new post.

His longing for his native southern homeland translated into powerful elegiac poetry. Although it is recorded that Wu Chi left a collection of his writings in ten *chüan* entitled *Tung-shan chi* 東山集 (Collected Works of East Mountain, i.e., Wu Chi) and a one-*chüan* volume of *tz'u* poetry entitled *Tung-shan yüeh-fu* 東山樂府 (Songs of East Mountain), neither are extant. The *Tung-shan yüeh-fu* available today is a reconstruction of the lost volume of extracts collected from various other works. Some of Wu's poems are also included in Yüan Hao-wen's* *Chung-chou chi* 中州集 (An Anthology of the Central Land), a collection of Chin poetry. Yüan praised Wu as the greatest *tz'u* poet of the Chin.

Ts'ai Sung-nien, like Wu Chi, originally was a Sung subject and a native of Hangchow, but grew up in Pien-ching 汴京 (Kaifeng, in Honan), the Northern Sung capital. After the defeat of the Northern Sung by the Chin, Ts'ai was recruited by the Chin government where he worked his way from Staff Supervisor of the Chen-ting Prefecture 眞定府 (in Hopei) to Grand Councilor of the Right.

Ts'ai's poetry and essays are celebrated for their lucidity and elegance, and he was especially adept at *tz'u* poetry. His style shows the freedom of Su Shih* and the refinement of Ch'in Kuan 秦觀 (1049-1100). Although Ts'ai appeared to be a very successful scholar, his *tz'u* poetry revealed that he always longed for a carefree Taoist lifestyle. It is said that from boyhood he had a strong desire for a forest retreat where he could escape worldly affairs. Indeed, a very strong Taoist flavor can be detected in his *Ming-hsiu chi* 明秀集 (Collected Works of the Bright and Beautiful), a collection of *tz'u* originally in six *chüan* (three *chüan* remain). Yüan Hao-wen held Ts'ai in high regard and considered some of his *tz'u* among the finest of the Chin corpus.

Both Wu Chi and Ts'ai Sung-nien were accomplished *tz'u* poets and occupy a position of importance in Chin literature. However, because both were Sung subjects before they became trained in the Sung literary tradition, they may best be viewed as pioneers who laid the cornerstone of Chin poetry.

EDITIONS:

Wu, Chi. *Tung-shan yüeh-fu,* in Chao Wan-li 趙萬里, ed., *Chiao-chi Sung-Chin-yüan-jen tz'u* 校輯宋金元人詞. Shanghai, 1931.

Ts'ai, Sung-nien. *Ming-hsiu chi,* in Wu Ch'ung-hsi 吳重熹, ed., *Chiu Chin-jen chi* 九金人集. Taipei, 1967.

T'ang, Kuei-chang 唐圭璋. *Ch'üan Chin Yüan tz'u* 全金元詞. 2v. Peking, 1979, v. 1, pp. 4-6 (Wu Chi's *tz'u*), and pp. 6-26 (Ts'ai Sung-nien's *tz'u*).

STUDIES:

Chang, Tzu-liang 張子良. "Chin 'Wu-ts'ai' *tz'u* shu" 金吳蔡詞述, *Kuo-wen hsüeh-pao,* 1 (1972), 159-164.

—TCY

Wu Chia-chi 吳嘉紀 (*tzu,* Pin-hsien 賓賢, *hao,* Yeh-jen 野人, 1618-1684), poet, was a na-

tive of An-feng-ch'ang 安豐場, T'ai-chou 泰州 Prefecture (modern Kiangsu). The Wu family had resided in that coastal area since late Yüan times, where its members derived a living from the salt trade and agriculture. In the late Ming, Wu's grandfather Wu Feng-i 吳鳳儀 achieved local prominence as a disciple of his fellow townsman, Wang Ken 王艮 (1483-1541), the famous philosopher-teacher and founder of the so-called T'ai-chou School of Neo-Confucianism. Wu Chia-chi, the fifth son of Wu I-fu 吳一輔, about whom little is known, was tutored in the Confucian Classics in his youth by one of his grandfather's students, Liu Kuo-chu 劉國柱. Wu ultimately passed the district civil-service examinations with distinction. For reasons which are not entirely clear, however, he did not participate in the provincial examinations, but returned to his native place where he went into retirement. Throughout the remainder of his life, he eked out a bare existence from a few acres of land and devoted himself to the perfection of his chosen craft, poetry.

The poverty which he and his immediate family seem to have calmly endured and his own self-imposed isolation are mentioned frequently in contemporary and later sources. But his own collected poems testify that he was not a recluse who shunned contact with his fellowman. Judging from the large number of exchange and parting poems he wrote, he enjoyed the frequent companionship of a wide circle of friends among the local elite. Among his closest associates were Wang Chi 汪楫 (1639-1699), a scholar, bibliophile, and official, Sun Chih-wei 孫枝蔚 (1620-1687), a poet of some standing and perhaps his closest friend, and Chou Liang-kung 周亮工 (1612-1672), a scholar-official from Nanking who served briefly in the Huai River area as a salt controller and to whom Wu addressed numerous poems. Most likely, it was Chou who was responsible for bringing Wu's name to the attention of the influential literatus Wang Shih-chen* (1634-1711), who later wrote approvingly of the simplicity and purity of his verse, and compared him to the T'ang dynasty poets Meng

899

Chiao* and Chia Tao.* In 1662, Chou Liang-kung compiled a selection of Wu's poems for publication, which Wang Shih-chen favored with an introduction. Other literary notables of the day, including the sometime Buddhist monk and poet Ch'ü Ta-chun 屈大均 (1630-1696) and the scholar-playwright K'ung Shang-jen,* also commented favorably on his literary accomplishments.

Following his death from consumption in 1684, a new edition of his poetry was compiled and published under the title *Lou-hsüan chi* 陋軒集 (The Humble Studio Collection), the name he had given his residence. This collection was later supplemented and reissued on several different occasions, serving to keep his reputation alive as an early Ch'ing-dynasty master of classical verse. He was also liberally represented in the late seventeenth-century anthology of Ming loyalist poets, the *Ming i-min shih* 明遺民詩, with sixty-three poems. Perhaps unaware of that collection, P'an Te-yü 潘德與 (1785-1839), poet-critic and minor official, observed that as a true successor of the famous poets T'ao Ch'ien* and Tu Fu* Wu was inadequately represented in the *Ming shih-tsung** (five poems) and *Kuo-ch'ao shih pieh-ts'ai chi* 國朝詩別裁集 (nineteen poems) anthologies.

Although his collected poems are now generally available in several different formats, Wu Chia-chi has yet to be studied in systematic fashion. Those poems which describe the life and suffering of the lower classes, and the realistic manner in which Wu depicts their experiences with marauding bandits and conquering armies, with frequent flooding and drought, have received praise from contemporary critics, but the rest of his verse remains to be studied. It seems apparent that the simple, limpid style which he perfected is not as derivative as is sometimes implied by the frequent comparison of it to that of earlier poets, such as those already noted and the Chin-dynasty poet Yüan Hao-wen.* Nor does it invite comparison with the sometimes rigidly classical and allusive manner typical of his age. At their best, his poems vividly and realistically portray the humble and often harrowing circumstances of his place and time. The cycle of ten poems entitled "T'i-chüeh shih" 隄決詩 (Poems on the Rupture of the Dikes), for instance, describe in striking detail the personal experiences of the poet and his family when they are marooned by a devastating flood. Few poets of his era so fully or compassionately recorded the joys and sorrows of village life in a traditionally depressed economic area as did Wu Chia-chi.

EDITIONS:

Lou-hsüan shih chi 陋軒詩集. Taipei, 1966. A reprint of the 1840 Hsia 夏 edition in twelve *chüan*, with a supplement in two *chüan;* an introduction by Shen Yün-lung 沈雲龍 surveys earlier editions.

Yang, Chi-ch'ing 楊積慶, comp. *Wu Chia-chi shih chien-chiao* 吳嘉紀詩箋校. Shanghai, 1980. A modern, punctuated and liberally annotated edition of about 1,000 *shih* also containing useful appendixes such as a *nien-p'u* and comments by critics on his verse, but marred by the compiler's decision to excise a number of poems "feudal" in outlook.

—WS

Wu Ping 吳炳 (*tzu*, Shih-ch'ü 石渠, *hao*, Ts'an-hua Chu-jen 粲花主人, d. 1646) was the author of *ch'uan-ch'i** plays in the Ming dynasty. His *Ts'an-hua Chai Wu-chung ch'ü* 粲花齋五種曲 (Five Plays of the Ts'an-hua Villa) are well-structured, rich in incident and character, and full of theatrical vitality. Wu's success did not come from talent alone, however, for his drama was steeped in the Ming *ch'uan-ch'i* traditions. He not only was regarded as the most celebrated follower of the Lin-ch'uan School led by T'ang Hsien-tsu,* but also benefited from consultations with Yeh Hsien-tsu* of the Wu-chiang School. As a result, his works inherited the best of the two worlds, demonstrating a fusion of literary excellence and musical discipline. Wu received his *chin-shih* degree in 1619, and was serving in one of a series of high official posts to which he had been appointed when he was captured by the Manchus in the mid-1640s. A loyalist, he refused to serve the Ch'ing and starved to death.

Ch'ing-yu chi 情郵記 (The Courier Station) is considered by some as the best of the

Ts'an-hua plays. In it a poverty-stricken young student writes a poem on the wall of a courier station. The poem, on different occasions, inspires the poetic response of two beautiful and talented women. When the student passes by the courier station again and sees the new poems, he sets out to find the women. The plot is complicated, with many political and domestic intrigues. But the ending is not altogether surprising: the student achieves overnight prominence through the examinations, and becomes happily united with both women, who turn out to be a lady and her maid forced by circumstances to disguise their identity.

The play *Hua-chung jen* 畫中人 (The Lady in the Painting) tells how an artist paints a portrait of his imagined ideal beauty and by his sincerity induces the spirit of a beautiful maiden to leave her body and take substance from the painting. She descends from the scroll and joins the artist in conjugal bliss. Eventually the artist chances to pass by the temple in which her body is resting and is able to resuscitate her. The play incorporates an episode parallel to the story of *Mu-tan T'ing* (see T'ang Hsien-tsu) betraying Wu Ping's indebtedness to T'ang Hsien-tsu, yet it stands as excellent drama in its own right.

Hsi-yüan chi 西園記 (The Western Garden) is strictly Wu's own creation. Its involved plot weaves the highly dramatic (and fashionable) formula of mistaken identity into the fabric of a love relation between man and fey. Wu won considerable critical acclaim for the skill with which he handled the development of the dramatic action, as well as his comic vision, which was not diminished by his elegant lyrics.

Liao-tu keng 療妬羹 (The Medicine to Cure Jealousy) derives its main plot from the contemporary legend of Hsiao-ch'ing, a woman of utmost beauty and literary talent. The story is set in two households, each with a barren wife who seeks to remedy the situation by procuring a concubine for her husband. The wife of the Ch'u household gets Hsiao-ch'ing for her husband but is driven to murderous actions by her own jealousy. The magnanimous

lady of the Yang household, in contrast, tries everything she can to make a match between Hsiao-ch'ing and her husband. The story ends happily: Master Yang gets Hsiao-ch'ing as concubine, Lady Yang is rewarded by heaven with a son of her own, and Lady Ch'u is cured of her jealousy.

Lü Mu-tan 綠牡丹 (The Green Peony) is a brilliant comedy of errors that ruthlessly ridicules the pseudo-intellectuals of the day, reportedly with topical references. Two wealthy but barely literate students try to bluff their way into favorable marriages by asking a talented friend to compose poetry and essays for them. But their schemes are foiled by the shrewd and observant girls whom they woo, who manage to choose better husbands for themselves. The delight of the play comes from the two comics, who are immensely funny.

EDITIONS:

Lü Mu-tan, in Wu Mei 吳梅, ed., *She-mo-ta-shih Ch'ü-ts'ung* 奢摩他室曲叢, Shanghai, 1928, v. 19.

Hua-chung jen, ibid., v. 20.

Liao-tu keng, ibid., v. 21.

Hsi-yüan chi, ibid., v. 22.

Ch'ing-yu chi, ibid., v. 23 and 24.

STUDIES:

Wei, Ming 衛明. "Wu Ping te *Ch'ing-yu chi*" 吳炳的情郵記, in *Hsin-min wan-pao* 新民晚報, February 22, 1963.

—CYC

Wu Wei-yeh 吳偉業 (*tzu*, Chün-kung 駿公, *hao*, Mei-ts'un 梅村, 1609-1672) was among the foremost poets of the seventeenth century. A native of T'ai-ts'ang 太倉 (Kiangsu, near modern Shanghai), Wu became a member of the Late Ming political-literary organization known as the Fu-she 復社 and passed the *chin-shih* examination in 1631. He served the Ming during the fierce party strife of its last decade, his fortunes rising and sinking with those of the Fu-she group. When the capital fell and the emperor committed suicide in 1644, Wu determined to take his own life but was prevented from doing so by his family. Had he succeeded, his poetry would be little remembered, for his greatness as a poet rests on work based upon his experiences

901

and reflections about the collapse of the Ming and the Ch'ing conquest. In 1645 he went to serve briefly in the court of the Prince of Fu, but was soon driven out by the intense party strife. Soon afterwards, fleeing with his family from the victorious Ch'ing army, Wu witnessed the conquest of his native region.

Although Wu was resolved to spend the rest of his days as a private citizen, in 1653 he was compelled to take office under the Ch'ing—not without ample poetic comment on his humiliation at being forced to serve under two dynasties: "I am indeed like the dogs and chickens of the former Prince of Huai; but I did not follow my lord to heaven; I fell back down into the world of men." In 1656, he resigned his office to mourn his mother, and in 1661 became implicated in the famous Chiang-nan tax case, for which he was deprived of his official rank. He spent the last decade of his life living as a private citizen in his native region.

Despite Wu's having taken office under the Ch'ing and his many moving poems on the fall of the Ming, Wu's poetry was spared the literary inquisition of the eighteenth century; the Ch'ien-lung Emperor's particular fondness for Wu's poetry was probably a significant factor in saving his work from condemnation. Indeed, throughout the Ch'ing, Wu Wei-yeh was perhaps the most honored poet of recent times. In his *Ou-pei shih-hua* 甌北詩話, Chao I* devoted an entire chapter to Wu, beginning: "After Kao Ch'i* there is no one worth considering in the Ming—until Wu and his contemporary Ch'ien Ch'ien-i.*" No fewer than three annotated editions of Wu's poetry were made during the Ch'ing, and the nineteenth-century poet Kung Tzu-chen* first learned poetry listening to his mother reciting the works of Wu Wei-yeh.

Although Wu wrote with genius on the common poetic occasions of a world at peace, he was, first of all, the poet of the fall of the Ming. His long heptasyllabic poems and ballads on this theme are among his most famous works. The "Yüan-yüan ch'ü" 圓圓曲 (The Song of Yüan-yüan) is an elaboration of the popular legend that

the Ming general Wu San-kuei went over to the Manchus on learning that his favorite concubine Ch'en Yüan-yüan had been seized by the rebel Li Tzu-ch'eng. "Fan-ch'ing Hu" 攀清湖 (Fan-ch'ing Lake), echoing Tu Fu's* "P'eng-ya hsing" 彭衙行 (Journey to P'eng-ya), recalls Wu's flight with his family during the invasion of his native region. "Kuo Nan-hsiang Yüan sou huo fu pa-shih yün" 過南廂園叟感賦八十韻 (Eighty Rhymes on Meeting an Old Man in the Garden of the Southern Chamber [of the National Academy in Nanking]), written in 1653 when taking office under the Ch'ing, is another lovely elegy on the desolation caused by dynastic upheaval: "He pointed to a tangle of weeds and brush: 'And here was the Southern Chamber.'" Not only did Wu write directly of contemporary events, he also used the venerable device of alluding to present history by reference to the past: in this mode are many of the eighteen versions of the old ballad "Hsing-lu nan" 行路難 (Hard Travels).

Wu Wei-yeh was not a sharp partisan in the disputes about poetic theory that raged through the late Ming and early Ch'ing. He was, however, by disposition a follower of the T'ang. His heptasyllabaic regulated verses in particular recall the work of Tu Fu. He did not imitate Tu Fu so much as assimilate Tu Fu's voice. He spoke the poetic language created by Tu Fu to perfection and, like him, was a highly allusive poet. The result is that in Wu's regulated verse, as in Tu Fu's, we find a rare fusion of intense sentiment and masterfully controlled craft.

Wu Wei-yeh's extant corpus of poetry includes almost 1,100 *shih* and 98 *tz'u*. He also wrote 35 *chüan* of prose works, including a large number of prefaces that contain much valuable information on his views about literature. His *shih-hua*,* the *Mei-t'un shih-hua* 梅村詩話, consists primarily of biographical notices on contemporary poets.

EDITIONS:
Mei-ts'un chia-tsang-kao 梅村家藏藁. 1911. Rpt. *SPTK.*
Wu-shih chi-lan 吳詩集覽. 1775. Rpt. *SPPY.*

TRANSLATIONS:
Sunflower, pp. 473-475.
Fukumoto Masakazu 福本雅一. *Go Igyō* 吳偉業.
Tokyo, 1962. With good introduction.

STUDIES:
Cheng, Ch'ien-fan 程千帆. "Shu Wu Mei-ts'un
'Yüan-yüan ch'ü' hou" 書吳梅村圓圓曲後, in
Cheng Ch'ien-fan and Shen Tsu-fen 沈祖棻,
eds., *Ku-tien shih-ko lun-ts'ung* 古典詩歌論叢,
Shanghai, 1954, pp. 250-253.
Chou, Fa-kao 周法高. "Wu Mei-ts'un shih hsiao
chien" 吳梅村詩小箋, in his *Chung-kuo yü-wen
lun-ts'ung* 中國語文論叢, Taipei, 1963, pp. 198-
229.
———. "Wu Mei-ts'un shih ts'ung-k'ao" 叢考,
JICS, 6.1 (December 1973), 245-317.
ECCP, pp. 882-883.
Fu, *Ch'ing tsa-chü*, pp. 29-32.
Tseng, "Ch'ing-tai tsa-chü," pp. 124-127.
　　　　　　　　　　　　　　　　—SO

Wu Wen-ying 吳文英 (*tzu*, Chüan-t'e 君特,
hao, Meng-ch'uang 夢窗 and Chüeh-weng
覺翁, *c.* 1200-*c.* 1260) was a *tz'u** poet of
the Southern Sung. Most of the scanty biographical information on Wu is speculation. The date of his birth is not recorded,
but it was very likely between 1195 and
1201. The absence of a biography in both
official history and local gazetteers suggests, further, that he did not take the civil-
service examination or did not pass it and
hence never held office. There is evidence
in his poetry that he worked for some time
in the Grain Transport Office, once served
as a private secretary to a high-ranking official named Wu Ch'ien 吳潛, and, in later
years, was a protégé of Prince Jung 榮王,
the brother of Emperor Li-tsung (r. 1225-
1264) and the father of Emperor Tu-tsung
(r. 1265-1274). He was a native of Ssu-ming
四明 (modern Yin-hsien 鄞縣, Chekiang) but
seems not to have lived there for any significant length of time. Most of his life was
spent in the Soochow area or in Hangchow, the capital city. The date of his death
is an open question. The more convincing
theory claims he died in late 1260.

Wu Wen-ying lived in a time when the
Sung was moving toward its ultimate collapse at the hands of the Mongols. During
this era, the nation was beset by corrupt
government, the strains of fending off incessant invasions from the north, and a resultant series of economic crises. Against
this background, there have been two opposed readings of Wu Wen-ying's poetry.
According to the first, neither the foreign
threats nor the internal problems captured
the creative attention of the poet. Of the
approximately three hundred and fifty extant poems (which ranks him the second
most prolific *tz'u* poet of the Sung—only
Hsin Ch'i-chi* wrote more), nearly all embody Wu's personal concerns. He was pre-
possessed especially with former love affairs, notably with his two concubines, one
of whom he kept in Soochow, the other in
Hangchow. His yearning for them finds
expression not only in untitled poems, but
in poems which, as indicated by their titles,
were generated by a festival day, an incident in daily life, or an object in nature,
often a flower. Another reading detects in
Wu's poetry a genuine concern for his
country and people. The coexistence of
these two opposed readings may be traced
partly to Wu's style: the intricacy and subtlety of his language lends itself to different interpretations.

The artistry and craftsmanship of Wu
Wen-ying is reflected in four pieces of advice that the poet himself gave concerning
the composition of *tz'u* as recorded by Shen
I-fu 沈義父 (*fl.* 1247), a friend, in the *Yüeh-
fu chih-mi* 樂府指迷: "The musical pitch must
attain to harmony; failure to do so would
result in a *shih** poem that is of irregular
line-length. The words that are written
down must be elegant; a practice to the
contrary would produce a song close to a
ch'an-ling in style. Words chosen must not
state too explicitly; overexpressiveness
would mean being straightforward, bluntly
abrupt, and devoid of profound, long-lasting aftereffects. In setting forth a meaning, one must refrain from making high-
sounding statements; he would otherwise
produce wildness and eccentricity, while
losing the gentle and agreeably insinuative
effect."

The passage proposes four literary tenets for *tz'u* composition: the first concerns
musical and prosodic aspects; the following three the semantic aspect. Each tenet

presents a lyric quality which Wu holds dear and which in combination would form the ideal of *tz'u* poetry he has in mind. These qualities are musical and prosodic nicety, elegant language, an oblique mode of expression, and a subdued manner of setting forth meanings. In Wu's advocation of these qualities, as in his disparagement of *ch'an-ling* 纏令 (a folk art combining dance and music) as vulgar, one senses a strong tone of elitism. He believed *tz'u* poetry to be an essence that is to be embodied in certain particular elements and is to be composed of these elements and of nothing else.

In these beliefs, Wu Wen-ying is carrying on a tradition prominent in the Southern Sung. This tradition is noted especially for delicacy of feeling and technical virtuosity: refined sentiments and sensibilities are revealed circuitously through matters drawn from literary heritage. This accounts for the intricacy of verbal structures and the stylistic subtlety that feature prominently in poems of this particular tradition.

Even compared with many of the poets that belong to the same tradition, such as Chiang K'uei,* Shih Ta-tsu,* Chou Mi,* and Chang Yen 張炎 (1248-1320), Wu Wen-ying seems to have more often adopted periphrastic devices to express his emotional and aesthetic experiences, and to have more often preferred to use allusions. This stylistic idiosyncrasy has earned him criticism from two poles. He has been accused of obscurity, triviality, and incoherence by, most notably, Chang Yen and many modern scholars including Wang Kuo-wei,* Hu Shih 胡適 (1891-1962), and Liu Ta-chieh 劉大杰 (1904-1978). Chang Yen in his *Tz'u yüan* 詞源 compared Wu's poetry to "a fabulous building that dazzles the eyes, but when taken apart, the pieces do not fit," 七寶樓台眩人眼目，拆碎下來不成片段. Wang Kuo-wei maintained that Wu Wen-ying's preference for allusions and oblique, periphrastic language was caused by his limited talent and produced a poetry that is shallow and mediocre. Hu Shih and Hu Yün-i regarded Wu's poetry as merely a heap of conventional expressions and

stock images not tied together by any genuine poetic feeling or unifying emotional current. Essentially of the same opinion, Liu Ta-chieh further charged Wu's poetry with embodying no greater concern than the personal life of the poet himself. There are, on the other hand, not a few critics who have expressed an unqualified admiration for the vigor of Wu's imagination, for the sophistication of his poetic craftsmanship, and for the acumen of his perception of life and the world. Among the second group of critics, the most notable are those who belonged to the *Ch'ang-chou tz'u-p'ai.** This school advocated the idea that a profound work of poetry is one that embodies allegorical meanings and encompasses a deeper vision of life and reality than is represented by the surface value of the work. These virtues were discovered in the poems of Wu Wen-ying, who was thus proclaimed by Chou Chi,* the leader of the school, as among the four greatest *tz'u* masters of the Sung, the other three being Chou Pang-yen,* Hsin Ch'i-chi, and Wang I-sun 王沂孫 (1240-1290). Wu Wen-ying's poetry has exerted a considerable influence on both the critical theories and the creative writings of this particular school.

EDITIONS:
Ch'üan Sung tz'u, v. 4, pp. 1873-2942.

TRANSLATIONS:
Ayling, *Collection,* p. 183.

STUDIES:
Chao, Chia-ying Yeh. "The Ch'ang-chou School of *Tz'u* Criticism," in *Chinese Approaches,* pp. 151-188.

———. "Wu Wen-ying's *Tz'u:* A Modern View," *HJAS,* 29 (1969), 53-92.

Ch'en, Hsün 陳洵. "Sung Wu Wen-ying Meng-ch'uang tz'u" 宋吳文英夢窗詞, in *Hai-hsiao shuo tz'u* 海綃說詞 v. 12 of *Tz'u-hua ts'ung-pien* 詞話叢編, T'ang Kuei-chang, ed., Taipei, 1967, pp. 4407-4437.

Ch'en, Lien-chen 陳廉貞. "Tu Wu Meng-ch'uang tz'u: I-wei pei wu-chieh te tz'u-jen" 讀吳夢窗詞：一位被誤解的詞人, in *Wen-hsüeh i-ch'an hsüan-chi* 文學遺產選集, 3 (1960), pp. 289-297.

Chih-yüan 芝園. " 'Chin-lü ch'ü' chung te shih
yü jen" 金縷曲中的時與人, *I-lin ts'ung-lu*, 6
(1966), 175-179.

———. "T'an Wu Wen-ying 'Ho hsin-lang' "
談吳文英賀新郎, *I-lin ts'ung-lu*, 6 (1966), 166-
169.

Chou, Chi 周濟. *Chieh-ts'un-chai lun-tz'u tsa-chu*
介存齋論詞雜著, v. 5 of *Tz'u-hua ts'ung-pien*,
T'ang Kuei-chang, ed., Taipei, 1967, pp.
1623-1629.

———, comp. "Preface" (1832) to *Sung ssu-chia
tz'u-hsüan [chien-chu]* 宋四家詞選箋注. K'uang
Shih-yüan 鄺士元, annot. Taipei, 1971.

Hsia, Ch'eng-t'ao 夏承燾. "Wu Meng-ch'uang
hsi-nien" 吳夢窗繫年, in his *T'ang Sung tz'u-
jen nien-p'u* 唐宋詞人年譜, Shanghai, 1955, pp.
455-483.

———. "Meng-ch'uang wan-nien yü Chia Ssu-
tao chüeh-chiao pien" 夢窗晚年與賈似道絕交
辨, in his *Tz'u-jen nien-p'u*, pp. 484-486.

Hsia, Shu-mei 夏書枚. "Wu Meng-ch'uang" 吳
夢窗, *Wen-hsüeh shih-chieh chi-k'an*, 35 (September 1962), 52-61.

Hsia-an 暇庵. "T'an Wu Meng-ch'uang 'Chin-
lü ko' " 談吳夢窗金縷歌, *I-lin ts'ung-lu*, 6
(1966), 172-175.

Hsin-yüan 新園. "Yeh t'an Wu Wen-ying 'Ho
hsin-lang' " 也談吳文英賀新郎, *I-lin ts'ung-lu*,
6 (1966), 169-172.

Yang, T'ieh-fu 楊鐵夫. "Wu Meng-ch'uang shih-
chi k'ao" 吳夢窗事蹟考, in *Meng-ch'uang-tz'u
ch'üan-chi chien-shih* 夢窗詞全集箋釋, Yang
T'ieh-fu, annot., Hong Kong, 1973, pp. 359-
378.

Yen, T'ien-yu 顏天佑. *Nan-Sung Chiang-Wu tz'u-
p'ai chih yen-chiu* 南宋姜吳詞派之研究. N.p.,
preface dated 1974.

—SH

Wu Wo-yao 吳沃堯 (*tzu*, Chien-jen 趼人,
1866-1910) was well known at the turn of
the twentieth century as a bohemian writer
of fiction in Shanghai. He originated from
the small town Fo-shan in Nan-hai County
west of Canton, and thus used Wo-fo shan-
jen 我佛山人 (Buddhist Hermit from Fos-
han) as one of his pseudonyms. He admired his great-grandfather, Wu Jung-
kuang 吳榮光 (1773-1843), a compiler in the
Han-lin Academy and a censor, who was
also a prolific writer and a connoisseur. Although the family had become wealthy
handling salt, his grandfather and father
both died when Wu was still young.

About twenty years old and without
means when he arrived in Shanghai, Wu
was influenced by the aspiring author and
later colleague, Li Pao-chia,* and became
a journalist. In 1898 he launched his own
satirical journal, *Ts'ai-feng pao* 采風報
(Gathering What's In the Wind). At about
the same time (1902) in Yokohama Liang
Ch'i-ch'ao* started China's first specialized journal of fiction, the *Hsin hsiao-shuo*
新小說 (New Fiction). It is said that Wu visited Japan; he soon (1903-1905) began to
publish several novels, as well as his
thoughts on the changing role and new
scope of fiction, in this magazine. In 1905
Wu left the Hankou-based *Ch'u-pao* 楚報
(Central China Post), which was run by
Americans, in protest against the exclusion policy directed against Chinese cool-
ies in the United States. A gifted orator,
he returned to Shanghai and agitated for
a boycott of American goods. Wu also began to collaborate with Li Pao-chia, who
edited the influential *Hsiu-hsiang hsiao-shuo*
繡像小說 (Illustrated Fiction). In it Wu published his *Hsia-p'ien ch'i-wen* 瞎騙奇聞 (Fantastic Tales of a Blind Man) and continued
Li's *Huo ti-yü* 活地獄 (Living Hell), a cruel
account of the judicial system. Returning
to Shanghai, Wu spent three very productive years (1906-1908) as editor in chief of
Yüeh-yüeh hsiao-shuo 月月小說 (Monthly Fiction), which the censors closed down in
1908. During the last two years of his life
the author worked quietly as the principal
of a primary school for Cantonese children
in Shanghai. He died in poverty.

Among the Shanghai literary coterie Wu
was considered a talented *ts'ai-tzu* 才子 with
broad interests and a love for exciting plots,
a man who would not rigidly attach himself
to any literary or political school for long.
As a journalist Wu was notorious for his
hasty writing, pressured always by an acute
need for money. Foreign literary models
influenced his writings only indirectly via
the vast translation activities of the time,
since he mastered no foreign language. He
hated all Neo-Confucianists, from "the
swindler Chu Hsi" to his followers in the
Ming and Ch'ing dynasties. His own philosophy advanced little beyond giving neg-

ative examples; he had little to say of consequence concerning how the new nation which he aspired for was to be built.

His novels which continue to be well known are the panoramic chef d'oeuvre *Erh-shih-nien mu-tu chih kuai hsien-chuang* 二十年目睹之怪現狀 (Strange Events Seen in the Past Twenty Years), the detective novel *Chiu-ming ch'i-yüan* 九命奇冤 (The Strange Case of Ninefold Murder), the historical *T'ung shih* 痛史 (Annals of Sorrow), and the sentimental *Hen hai* 恨海 (Sea of Woe). His short stories such as those in *Chien-jen shih-san chung* 趼人十三種 (Wu Wo-yao's Thirteen Stories; 1910) are seldom read nowadays.

Strange Events was published from 1905 to 1910 in four parts and 108 *chüan*. It covers the years 1882-1902, from the Franco-Chinese and Japanese-Chinese wars until the aftermath of the Boxer Uprising. The hero is a man who comes to Shanghai, where an older colleague from schooldays (first an official and later a businessman) employs him as a collaborator. Wu convincingly shows how the attitudes of the young protagonist change from naive credulity to bitter knowledge as he observes the decay of all human values around him. This young man provides the author with a focus as the narrator of anecdotes and nonaction discourse; his business trips around the country establish the loose structure in which the hundred-odd miscellaneous stories are embedded. This episodic composition develops both the weakness and richness of *Ju-lin wai-shih.** Wu Wo-yao's "patriotic, anti-feudal, and anti-imperialistic" novel uses first person narration, influenced by foreign literature as well as by the indigenous autobiographical tradition. The novel uses satire and a strong anti-Manchu tone to characterize Chinese officialdom and the business world with its imitation Westerners, the "talents of the foreign arena" (*Yang-ch'ang ts'ai-tzu* 洋場才子), concluding that "in the world of bureaucracy all men are robbers and all women prostitutes." The author is so successful in treating the "foreign theme" that Chinese literary historians have complained about Wu's foreigners who are portrayed as more civilized than the Chinese. The twenty-chapter *Tsui-chin she-hui wo-ch'uo shih* 最近社會齷齪史 (Biased History of Society Today, 1910), is a little-known sequel.

Some of Wu's writings do not attempt to give such a general picture of society, but concentrate on special aspects. *Fa-ts'ai mi-chüeh* 發財秘訣 (The Secret of How to Become Rich) in eight *chüan* (also known by its alternative title, *Unofficial History of Yellow Slaves*) treats the loss of Hong Kong in 1841 and sarcastically portrays Cantonese compradors and their shady dealings with foreigners. One of them does not conceal his conviction that it might be "better to be a dog than a Chinese." The fight against superstition, traditional religions, and popular beliefs was one of the favorite themes of the didactically inclined late Ch'ing novel. Wu repeatedly touches upon this theme, as in *Ninefold Murder*. The *Hsia-p'ien ch'i-wen* (1902) presents such a moralistic story about a greedy, blind fortune-teller who is eventually slain by one of his victims.

Wu never fulfilled his dream of complementing satire with portraits of positive heroes as "guides" for the reader. The episodic *Hu-t'u shih-chieh* 糊塗世界 (A World of Stupidity; 12 *chüan*, 1906) was, however, written in this vein. It describes the failure of an uprising and portrays, not very convincingly, the tragic figure of an "ideal hero." The "replica-novel" *Hsin Shih-t'ou chi* 新石頭記 (New *Story of the Stone*) transfers a mature Chia Pao-yü from the *Hung-lou meng** into Wu's time, depicting him in conflict with the authorities during the Boxer Uprising. Females, the perplexed reader learns, are banned from this "educational novel" in 40 chapters. Wu Wo-yao's skeptical views on a revolutionary scenario for China's future and on the revolutionaries around Sun Yat-sen are offered in *Shang-hai yu-ts'an chi* 上海遊驂記 (Journey to Shanghai), a story in 10 *chüan* published in 1907. Wu's plot is based on the P'ing-hsiang Revolt (萍鄉) of 1906, caused, the author explains, by the degeneration of the Ch'ing military and the Manchu bureaucracy.

In his theoretical statements Wu repeatedly expounded the educational values of fictionalized history for China, adapting the traditional *yen-i* 演義 forms and the classical novel in general. His *Annals of Sorrow* in 27 *chüan* (1902) was a well-received, patriotic account of the fall of the Sung dynasty to the Mongols during the thirteenth century. The impatient Wen T'ien-hsiang 文天祥 is the central hero. The work has been called the best Chinese historical novel of the early twentieth century. The author certainly never dealt with the historical dimension academically; following traditional historiographical conventions this novel was really a thinly veiled attack on contemporary Manchu-ruled China, ridiculing even the Empress-Dowager Tz'u-hsi and Emperor Kuang-hsü. His *Liang-chin yen-i* 兩晉演義 (A Popular History of the Two Chin Dynasties, 24 *chüan*, 1906-1908) did not appeal to the reader, though it was a well-conceived and well-documented continuation of the *San-kuo* (Three-Kingdoms) cycle, possibly because his earlier, allegorical work in this genre (*Annals of Sorrow*) had been too far-fetched. Wu discontinued the 1907 *Yün-nan yeh-sheng* 雲南野乘 (An Unofficial History of Yunnan) after 2 *chüan*, probably because he sensed that a history of China's noble pacification of the Southwest could not be combined convincingly with his intended attacks on the French for their role in Yunnan and on foreign imperialism in Taiwan, Hong Kong, and Chiao-chou.

Wu's fiction shows a marked development from satiric patriotism to romantic sentimentalism, exemplifying at the same time a gradual degeneration of late Ch'ing urban fiction from social didacticism (such as Liang Ch'i-ch'ao had envisaged) to plain entertainment. Many of Wu's later novels and stories should, in fact, be considered as immediate precursors of the wave of so-called Mandarin Duck/Butterfly-love stories (*Yüan-yang hu-tieh* 鴛鴦蝴蝶) which was to be attacked later by the foreign-oriented, young, elite writers of the May Fourth Era.

One aspect of this process was Wu's inclination toward detective stories and thrilling plots. In 1906 in *Monthly Fiction* he published a collection *Tao-chen-t'an* 盗偵探 (Mysteries) in 24 *chüan*, and in the same year *Chung-kuo chen-t'an san-shih-ssu an* 中國偵探三十四案 (Thirty-four Chinese Detective Stories). His novel *Chiu-ming ch'i-yüan* in 36 *chüan* is based on an earlier novel by a certain An He 安和 and on other popular sources about a family feud in Kwangtung which ended in arson and murder. Wu Wo-yao draws on the *kung-an* tradition (see Fiction essay) as well as Western influences such as translations of Sherlock Holmes stories. Through flashbacks and time inversion the author creates an exciting atmosphere of suspense, which is impaired by too many innuendos in the second half of the book. This case, which occurred in 1738, was remolded by Wu to destroy the image of the Golden (Manchu) Age during the middle years of the Ch'ing by depicting corruption in officialdom from the top to the bottom.

Among Wu's sentimental or psychological fiction (*hsieh-ch'ing* 寫情) the novelette *Hen hai* (10 *chüan*, 1906) is notable. It has a symmetrical plot and a unitary (not episodic) structure, combatting with allusions the conceptual world of the classic *Hung-lou meng*: the story shows how the uncertain times during the Boxer Uprising brought about the degeneration of character of two young couples. An intelligent young man ends up as a thief and opium addict in Shanghai's underworld, while his fiancée, devastated by her lover's downfall, enters a nunnery. The second heroine of this flamboyant drama is eventually discovered by her fiancée in a Shanghai brothel. Two other novels in this genre were the adaption *Tien-shu ch'i-t'an* 電術奇談 (A Fantastic Tale about Electricity, 24 *chüan*, 1903-1905) of a Japanese story by Kikuchi Yūhō 菊池幽芳 and *Chieh-yü-hui* 劫餘灰 (Ashes, 16 *chüan*, 1907-1908). *A Fantastic Tale* is the only story which Wu placed entirely outside China. It relates the triangular love story of an Indian woman in England and France, ending with a miraculous "electrical" reshaping of her crippled lover. *Ashes* might be described as an idyllic reunion of two lovers from the countryside after two decades of separation—the hero had been sold abroad as a coolie.

EDITIONS:

Most of Wu Wo-yao's novels were serialized in journals (such as *Hsin hsiao-shuo*) before appearing in book form (see A Ying, *Wan-ch'ing hsiao-shuo shih* and *Wan-Ch'ing hsi-ch'ü hsiao-shuo mu* below).

Chiu-ming ch'i-yüan. Shanghai, 1956.

Erh-shih-nien mu-tu chih kuai hsien-chuang. Peking, 1959. Annotated with a portrait of the author.

Hen hai. Peking, 1955.

Kao, Po-yü 高伯雨. *Tu hsiao-shuo cha-chi Shui-hu chuan ho Erh-shih-nien mu-tu chih kuai hsien-chuang so-yin* 水滸傳和二十年目睹 讀小說箚記 之怪現狀索引. Hong Kong, 1957.

T'ung-shih. Shanghai, 1956.

TRANSLATIONS:

Liu, Shih-shun. *Vignettes from the Late Ch'ing: Bizarre Happenings Eye-witnessed over Two Decades.* Hong Kong, 1975. An abridged translation of 44 chapters (of 108) of *Erh-shih nien mu-tu chih kuai hsien-chuang.*

van Gulik, Robert. *The Chinese Bell Murders.* London, 1958. The second half of the novel is a free adaption of the *Chiu-ming ch'i-yüan.*

STUDIES:

A, Ying 阿英. "Kuan-yü *Erh-shih-nien mu-tu chih kuai hsien-chuang*," in *A Ying wen-chi* 阿英文集, Hong Kong, 1979, v. 2, pp. 673-680.

———. *Wan-Ch'ing hsi-ch'ü hsiao-shuo mu* 晚清 戲曲小說目. Shanghai, 1954. Contains bibliographical details.

———. *Wan-ch'ing wen-i pao-k'an shu-lüeh* 晚清 文藝報刊述略. Shanghai, 1958. Gives information on Wu's editorial activities.

———. *Wan-Ch'ing hsiao-shuo shih* 晚清小說史. Shanghai, 1937; revised Shanghai, 1955. The Japanese translation under the same title by Iizuka Akira 飯塚朗 and Nakano Miyoko 中野美代子 (Tokyo, 1979) as v. 349 of the Heibonsha *Tōyō-bunko* series is most convenient, with an index and annotations.

ECCP, pp. 873-874.

Egan, Michael. "Characterization in *Sea of Woe*," in *The Chinese Novel at the Turn of the Century*, Milena Doleželová-Velingerová, ed., Toronto, 1981, pp. 165-176.

Fong, Gilbert Chee Fun. "Time in 'Nine Murders': Western Influence and Domestic Tradition," *The Chinese Novel at the Turn of the Century*, Milena Doleželová-Velingerová, ed., Toronto, 1981, pp. 116-128.

Hsiu-hsiang hsiao-shuo. 8v. Rpt. Shanghai, 1980.

Kōsaka, Jun'ichi 香坂順一. "*Kyumei kien no seiritsu*" 九命奇冤の成立, *Nihon Chūhoku gakkaihō*, 15 (1963), 179-196.

Lau, Michael Wai-mai. "Wu Wo-yao (1866-1910): A Writer of Fiction of the Late Ch'ing Period." Unpublished Ph.D. dissertation, Harvard University, 1969.

Lin, Jui-ming 林瑞明. *Wan-ch'ing ch'ien-tse hsiao-shuo te li-shih i-i* 晚清譴責小說的歷史意義. Taipei, 1980.

Link, Perry. *Mandarin Ducks and Butterflies, Popular Fiction in Early Twentieth-Century Chinese Cities.* Berkeley, 1981.

Liu, Ts'un-yan. "Introduction: 'Middlebrow' in Perspective," in *Middlebrow*, pp. 1-40.

Lu, Hsün 魯迅. *Hsiao-shuo chiu-wen-ch'ao* 小說 舊聞鈔, in *Lu Hsün ch'üan-chi* 魯迅全集, n.p., 1938, v. 10, pp. 148-151.

Miyata, Ichiro 官田一郎. *Nijūnen mokuto no kaigenjō goi sakuin* 二十年目睹之怪現狀語彙索引. Nagoya, 1978.

Nakashima, Riro 中島利郎. "Go Genjin denraku kō" 吳研人傳略稿, *Shinmatsu Shōsetsu kenkyū* 清末小說研究, 1 (1977), 64-80.

Wang, Chün-nien 王俊年. "Tsen-yang k'an-tai *Erh-shih-nien mu-tu chih kuai hsien-chuang*" 怎 樣看待二十年目睹之怪現狀, *Kuang-ming jih-pao*, April 18, 1965.

Wu, Hsiao-ju. "Tu *Erh-shih-nien mu-tu chih kuai hsien-chuang* tsa-chi" 讀 二十年目睹之怪現狀 雜 記, in *Chung-kuo ku-tien hsiao-shuo p'ing-lun chi* 中國古典小說評論集, Peking, 1957.

—HM

Wu-Yüeh ch'un-ch'iu 吳越春秋 (Spring and Autumn Annals of Wu and Yüeh) is a highly fictionalized account in 10 *chüan* of the history of the states of Wu and Yüeh. It was compiled in the Latter Han dynasty by Chao Yeh 趙曄 (*tzu*, Ch'ang-chün 長君, *fl.* 40 A.D.). The first five *chüan* are devoted to: (1) the history of Wu's ruling house from its legendary beginnings as descendants of Hou Chi 后稷 (*c.* 2255-2205 B.C.) to the reign of Shou Meng 壽夢 (r. 585-561 B.C.); (2) Shou Meng's attempts to have his youngest son, Chi Ch'a 季札, whom he recognized as a worthy (*hsien* 賢), succeed to the throne, and Chi Ch'a's repeated refusal to accept after the fashion of the founder of Wu, T'ai-po 吳太伯; (3) the escape of Wu Tzu-hsü 伍子胥 (d. 486 B.C.) from Ch'u 楚, his arrival in Wu, and the assassination of King Liao 僚王 (r. 526-515 B.C.) by Kung-tzu Kuang 公子光, who ascended the throne as King Ho-lü 闔閭王 (r. 514-496 B.C.); (4) an account of the rise of such strategists as Sun Wu 孫武 (best known as the author of the *Sun-tzu ping-fa* 孫子兵法 [Art of War]), Wu Ch'i 吳起, and Wu Tzu-hsü culminating in the defeat of Ch'u by the heir apparent Fu-ch'ai 夫差 (r. 495-477 B.C.) in 504 B.C.; (5) the fall of Wu Tzu-hsü from Fu-ch'ai's favor due to the slanderous intrigues of Po Pi 伯嚭 and the subsequent destruction of the state of Wu at the hands of the King of Yüeh, Kou-chien 勾踐 (r. 496-*c.* 475 B.C.), who allowed Fu-ch'ai to commit suicide and had Po Pi executed.

The remaining five *chüan* present a parallel account of the history of the state of Yüeh. The subjects treated in these five *chüan* are: (6) the founding of Yüeh by Wu Yü 無余, who was sent to Yüeh by the Hsia ruler Shao K'ang 少康 (r. 2079-2057 B.C.) to insure the continuation of sacrifices to Yü 禹 (r. 2205-2197); (7) the humiliation of Kou-chien after his defeat by Fu-ch'ai at Fu-chiao 夫椒 in 494 B.C.; (8) the strategies used by Kou-chien to strengthen Yüeh morally, militarily, and economically while simultaneously weakening Wu in those same areas; (9) a detailed account of the strategies suggested by Chi Yen 計硯 for the ultimate defeat of Fu-ch'ai, King of Wu, and a description of their implementation (this chapter contains the stories of the discovery and training of the two famous beauties Hsi Shih and Cheng Tan 鄭旦 who are sent to Wu to debauch Fu-ch'ai; further, a woman whose superhuman abilities with the sword and halberd were gained by magical means without the aid of teachers, and an archer of similar skill are recruited); (10) the climax of the entire work, the final defeat of Fu-ch'ai of Wu in 478 B.C.

The last five *chüan*, which are more favorably disposed to Yüeh than the first five were to Wu, are written in a livelier, less annalistic style than the others. Nonetheless, the *Wu-Yüeh ch'un-ch'iu* is not regarded as highly as the *Yüeh chüeh-shu** in matters of style or literary quality.

EDITIONS:
Wu-yüeh ch'un-ch'iu. SPPY. Best readily available edition.
———. *SPTK.* Worst of the readily available editions.
———. Taipei, 1959. Has Hsü T'ien-yu's 徐天祐 (*fl.* 1265) preface and notes, and an additional addendum (*pu-chu* 補註) by him. Also has an explanatory introduction written in 1501 by Ch'ien Fu-yü 錢福興. Available and useful.
———. *TSCCCP.* Shanghai, 1935. No introduction, no colophon, but notes are identical to both *SPPY* and *SPTK.* Divided in 6 *chüan*, but is the same as the 10-*chüan* editions. Claims a commentary by the Ming-dynasty scholar Wu Kuan 吳珀, but is no different than editions which do not mention him.

STUDIES:
Ku, Kuan-kuang 顧觀光 (1799-1862). *Wu Yüeh ch'un-ch'iu chiao-k'an chi* 校勘記, in *Wu-ling shan-jen i-shu* 武陵山人遺書, fifth *ts'e* 冊. Very useful studies of the third through the tenth *chüan* of the text plus a collection of lost fragments (*i-wen* 逸文).

TRANSLATION:
Eichhorn, Werner. *Heldensagen aus dem Untern Yangtse-tal (Wu-Yüeh ch'un-ch'iu).* Wiesbaden, 1969.

—JLo

Yang Chiung 楊炯 (*tzu*, unknown; 650-*c.* 694) was a poet, scholar, and sometime official of the late seventh century. He came to court a prodigy, passing in 659 the *Shen-t'ung* 神童 (Examination for Divine Lads) in which youthful candidates of nine years or under were tested in their knowledge of the *Lun-yü*, the *Hsiao-ching* (see *ching*), and one other classic text of their own choosing. Following his success in this examination, Yang was given a place in the Hung-wen kuan 弘文舘 (College for the Enhancement of Letters) at the capital, where he was fortunate to pass his adolescence and early manhood. His life seems to have been a privileged and pleasant one until the year 685, when he was rusticated to Tzu-chou 梓州 (near modern San-t'ai 三台 district in Szechwan) as a judicial administrator in punishment for his family relationship to a paternal uncle who had been involved in an abortive rebellion the year before. By 690 he had been recalled to the capital and given a teaching post in the palace school. But late in 693 he was again sent to the provinces, this time to Ying-ch'uan 盈川 (near modern Chü 衢 district in western Chekiang) as Director (the district's chief civil official). He died there, sometime during the next year or two; the precise date of his death is uncertain.

Yang Chiung is today the least widely read of the quartet of writers known collectively as the *Ch'u-T'ang ssu-chieh* 初唐四傑 (Four Distinguished Ones of the Early T'ang), the other three being Wang Po,* Lu Chao-lin,* and Lo Pin-wang.* He is best remembered—if at all—for his preface to the works of Wang Po. This relative disregard is due in part to the fact that only thirty-four of Yang's *shih* poems have been preserved. All but four of these are pentametric *lü-shih* or *p'ai-lü* (see *shih*), and most are exercises on standard themes, occasionally with striking effects. However, Yang's true skill as a writer is best exhibited in the eight *fu** of his that remain to us. These compositions—undeservedly neglected today—are rich confections of scholarly lore and effusive wordplay; here one sees the lavish talent that won Yang the respect of his contemporaries and prompted Chang Yüeh,* the literary arbiter of the succeeding generation, to compare his works to "the gushing waters of a precipitate stream—pouring down, never drying up." Among Yang's *fu*, especially notable are those on "Hun-t'ien fu" 渾天賦 (The Enveloping Sky) and on "Lao-jen hsing fu" 老人星賦 (The Old Man Star; i.e., the exceptionally bright and auspicious star known to us as Canopus), both of which contain much fascinating information about T'ang astral beliefs. Equally interesting is the *fu* on the grand Buddhist Ullambana festival ("Yü-lan-p'en fu" 盂蘭盆賦) held under Empress Wu's direction in Lo-yang in 692. A large quantity of Yang's prose writings, mostly memorial inscriptions, has also been preserved.

EDITIONS:

Yang Ying-ch'uan chi 楊盈川集. 10 *chüan*. SPTK. This is a Ming edition, from the Wan-li period (1573-1620), compiled by T'ung P'ei 童珮. A typeset and punctuated revision of this text, collated with the versions appearing in *Ch'üan T'ang shih* and *Ch'üan T'ang wen*, and early anthologies such as *T'ang-wen ts'ui** and *Wen-yüan ying-hua*,* is included in *Lu Chao-lin chi, Yang Chiung chi* 盧照鄰集, 楊炯集, Hsü Ming-hsia 徐明霞, ed., Peking, 1980.

STUDIES:

Fu, *Shih-jen*, pp. 1-20: "Yang Chiung k'ao" 楊炯考.
Furukawa, Sueyoshi 古川末喜. "Shō Tō yonketsu no bungaku shisō" 初唐四傑の文學思想, *Chūgoku bungaku ronshū*, 8 (1979), 1-27.
Yang, Ch'eng-tsu 楊承祖. "Yang Chiung nien-p'u" 楊炯年譜, *JOS*, 13 (1975), 57-72.

—PWK

Yang-chou hua-fang lu 揚州畫舫錄 (A Record of the Painted Boats at Yang-chou) is an extremely important source book for the history of drama in Yangchow during the second half of the eighteenth century. It is in the tradition of works such as the *Tung-ching meng Hua lu** and the *Wu-lin chiu-shih* (see Chou Mi).

The author, Li Tou 李斗, dated his preface January 1796. Other prefaces include one by Yüan Mei,* dated January 16, 1794, and Juan Yuan 阮元 (1764-1849) dated 1797, the year in which the book was apparently first published.

Li Tou was unsuccessful in his official career but was evidently acquainted with distinguished contemporaries. He was born and lived most of his life in Yangchow; however, he traveled frequently. Li was a dramatist and poet, but the work for which he is known is the *Yang-chou hua-fang lu*, written from the author's personal experience over a thirty-year period in Yangchow, at that time an extremely important economic and cultural center.

All but two of the eighteen chapters of the *Yang-chou hua-fang lu* concern districts of the city. The subjects covered include the demarcation of areas within the city, technology, commerce, gardens, ancient monuments, and customs. There are notes and biographies on many literary figures, such as Ch'ien Ta-hsin 錢大昕 (1728-1804), Yüan Mei, and Mei Wen-ting 梅文鼎 (1633-1721); the entire fifth *chüan* is devoted to drama. This chapter lists over one thousand items subject to censorship by the Ch'ien-lung Emperor, gives biographies of dramatists and actors, and discusses well-known patrons of the theater. As such it is an invaluable source for the variety and development of various forms of regional theater. In the ninth *chüan* there is a lengthy discussion of the brothels which gives the work its name (painted boats, i.e., pleasure boats) and includes accounts of famous courtesan-actresses who contributed so much to theater.

EDITIONS:

Li, Tou. *Yang-chou hua-fang lu.* Peking, 1960, in the series *Ch'ing-tai shih-liao pi-chi ts'ung-k'an* 清代史料筆記叢刊.

STUDIES:

Hsieh, Kuo-chen 謝國楨. *Ming Ch'ing pi-chi t'an-ts'ung* 明清筆記談叢, Peking, 1960, pp. 142-145.

Mackerras, Colin. "The Theater in Yang-chou in the Late Eighteenth Century," *Papers on Far Eastern History*, 1 (1970), 1-30.

Scott, A. C. *Traditional Chinese Plays.* V. 2. Madison, Wisconsin, 1969.

—CM

Yang Hsien-chih 楊顯之 (*hao*, Pu-ting 補丁, *fl.* 1246) was a native of Ta-tu 大都 (modern Peking). He was nicknamed Yang Pu-ting 楊補丁 by his contemporaries. Eight *tsa-chü** dramas have been attributed to him, but only two are extant: the *Lin-chiang i hsiao-hsiang yeh-yü* 臨江驛蕭湘夜雨 (A Rainy Night at the Lin-chiang Station by the Hsiao and Hsiang Rivers) and the *Cheng K'ung-mu feng-hsüeh K'u-han T'ing* 鄭孔目風雪酷寒亭 (Secretary Cheng, Braving Wind and Snow, at the Pavilion of Bitter Cold).

Yang was a close friend of Kuan Han-ch'ing,* and often discussed the art of drama with him. Thus it is natural that Yang's works are written in a plain and straightforward style similar to Kuan's. Yang's dramatic diction is somewhat more elegant but not so forceful as Kuan's. The *T'ai-ho cheng-yin p'u* 太和正音譜, compiled by Chu Ch'üan,* comments that Yang's dra-

matic style can be compared to moonlight over a jade terrace.

Both of Yang's extant works are considered masterpieces; their structure especially deserves praise. The *Lin-chiang i hsiao-hsiang yeh-yü* tells of Chang Ts'ui-luan 張翠鸞, who lost touch with her father, Chang T'ien-chüeh 張天覺, as they were traveling. Ts'ui-luan was saved by a fisherman and married his nephew, Ts'ui T'ung 崔通. Later, Ts'ui went to the capital to sit for the civil examination. He passed, and married the daughter of an examination official. When Ts'ui-luan found him, he refused to recognize her as his wife and told his new wife that Ts'ui-luan was a former maid-servant of his. Then he accused Ts'ui-luan of theft and sent her into exile, intending to have her murdered en route. But on her way Ts'ui-luan met her father. With his help, she was able to regain her status as Ts'ui's wife. The drama has a compact structure, and both the songs and dialogues are masterly. Chang Ts'ui-luan's grief is depicted with great subtlety. The scenes of Chang's traveling in the rain and of her crying in the night are especially touching. This drama is marred only by its somewhat cumbrous ending. The *Cheng K'ung-mu feng-hsüeh K'u-han T'ing* tells of Cheng Sung 鄭嵩 who keeps a singing-girl as a mistress. His wife cannot bear this and dies. Later, Cheng, on learning that the singing-girl had relations with another man, kills her. Cheng is then sent into exile. The guard who is to accompany him is the man who had seduced the girl. However, Cheng is rescued en route by a man whose life he had saved before. This story was popular and allusions to it in the works of other Yüan dramatists were common (Shih Chün-pao's 石君寶 *Ch'ü-chiang ch'ih* 曲江池 [The Serpentine Pool], Ch'in Chien-fu's 秦簡夫 *Tung-t'ang lao* 東堂老 [Old Man from the Eastern Hall], and the anonymous *Huo-lang tan* 貨郎旦 [The Pedlar, Female-lead Version]). But the structure of this drama is unwieldy here and there. Nevertheless Yang seems to have been successful in designing a plot that sustains the interest of the audience to the very end.

There appear to have been two versions of *K'u-han T'ing:* one in which the *tan* 旦

role is prominent and another in which the *mo* 末 role dominates (see *chiao-se*). In the version that is now extant, Cheng Sung's wife dies in the first act, leaving the *mo* role of Cheng Sung prominent. The T'ien-i-ko 天一閣 manuscript copy of the *Lu kuei pu** lists a *K'u-han T'ing* by Hua Li-lang 花李郎. Thus it may be that of the *tan* and *mo* versions mentioned above, one is by Yang and one is by Hua. Some scholars, Yen Tun-i 嚴敦易 for one, have compared the full titles of the two versions listed respectively under the names of Yang and Hua in the T'ien-i-ko copy of the *Lu kuei pu* with the content of the extant work. They conclude that the extant *mo* version was written by Hua. But since the evidence is not completely persuasive, the question remains open.

EDITIONS:

Lin-chiang i hsiao-hsiang yeh-yü. (1) Tsang Chin-shu 臧晉叔, comp. *Yüan-ch'ü hsüan* 元曲選, *I chi* 乙集. Shanghai, 1918 (photolithographic reprint of the 1616 Tiao-ch'ung-kuan 雕蟲館 edition). (2) *Yüan-ch'ü ta-kuan* 元曲大觀. Shanghai, 1928. (3) Lu Ch'ien 盧前, comp. *Yüan-jen tsa-chü ch'üan-chi* 元人雜劇全集, v. 6. Shanghai, 1935-1936.

Cheng K'ung-mu feng-hsüeh K'u-han T'ing. (1) *Yüan Ming tsa-chü* 元明雜劇 (the same edition as the one in *Ku ming-chia tsa-chü* 古名家雜劇, *Hsin chi* 信集, ch. 3, *Ku-pen hsi-chü ts'ung-k'an*, series 4, Shanghai, 1958), Nanking, 1929. (2) *Yüan-ch'ü hsüan, Chi chi* 己集. (3) *Yüan-jen tsa-chü ch'üan-chi*, v. 6.

TRANSLATIONS:

Crump, J. I. "Yang Hsien-chih: Rain on the Hsiao-hsiang," *Renditions*, 4 (Spring 1975), 49-70.

STUDIES:

Yen, Tun-i. "K'u-han T'ing," in his *Yüan-chü chen-i* 元劇斟疑, Shanghai, 1962, pp. 220-229.

—SSK

Yang Hsiung 揚雄 (*tzu*, Tzu-yün 子雲, 53 B.C.-A.D. 18) was an important philosopher and leading *fu**-writer of his day, whose works continued to be admired in later ages. He was born in Ch'eng-tu 成都, the provincial capital of Shu 蜀 (modern Szechwan), which produced a number of scholars and poets during the Han. He stuttered, but was well-versed in literary composition. He greatly admired Ch'ü Yüan* and culled vocabulary and phrases from the "Li sao" 離騷 (Encountering Sorrow) to compose the "Fan 'Li sao' " 反離騷 (Contra Sao) to mourn him.

He had a predilection for *fu* and became an ardent imitator of Ssu-ma Hsiang-ju's* style. Because of his success in writing *fu* in this style, he was summoned to the imperial capital, Ch'ang-an, and appointed Expectant Official (his duties were to compose poems, *fu* and other literary works for the emperor) at the Ch'eng-ming Court 承明庭. During the reign of Emperor Ch'eng (r. 32-7 B.C.) Yang was asked to accompany the imperial party to the sacrificial ceremonies and imperial hunts. Subsequently, he submitted four *fu* to the throne: the "Kan-ch'üan fu" 甘泉賦 (Sweet Spring) and the "Ho-tung fu" 河東賦 (Ho-tung) described the stately sacrificial ceremonies to Heaven at Kan-ch'üan and to Earth at Fen-yin 汾陰; "Yü-lieh fu" 羽獵賦 (The Plume) or "Chiao-lieh fu" 校獵賦 (The Barricade) and the "Ch'ang-yang fu" 長楊賦 (Ch'ang-yang) pictured the colossal imperial hunts at Shang-lin Park 上林苑 and at Ch'ang-yang. As a court poet, he had to praise the emperor's virtue and the grandeur of the spectacles he was privileged to attend, but he was also appalled by the wasteful extravagance of these activities. So in addition to his panegyrics, he reminded his sovereign that such indulgences were unseemly by adding to his *fu* subtle moral reprimands known as *feng chien* 諷諫 (indirect admonitions). However, he found that the sovereign was impervious to such didacticism, and Yang eventually repudiated the *fu* genre. Later, in his *Fa yen* 法言 (Model Sayings) he condemned the *fu* as "the worm-and-seal-carving of children," advocating guidelines for the genre such as those followed by authors of *shih.**

Among the twelve *fu* attributed to Yang Hsiung in the "I-wen chih" 藝文志 of the *Han-shu* (see Pan Ku), only those mentioned above are extant in their original and complete form; others are lost, extant in fragments, or are of questionable authenticity. His "Chieh ch'ao" 解嘲 (Dissolving Ridicule), belonging to the subclass of *fu* of frustration, is widely read because it represents a more forthright, personal expression than any of Yang's other verse.

In the histories of Chinese literature, Yang's achievement in the *fu** is well recognized. Tu Fu* singled out Yang's *fu* as a model he hoped to emulate. However, some modern Chinese scholars under the influence of May Fourth tendencies, derogate his *fu* as lifeless, clichéd and obscured by their rich and exuberant verbiage. Yang Hsiung's artistry is, however, best displayed in his rhetorical skill, particularly in his use of the techniques of indirect criticism.

EDITIONS:

Liu-ch'ao wen, v. 1, "Ch'üan Han wen," *ch.* 51-54, pp. 402-422.

Pai-san, v. 2, pp. 1-38.

Yang Tzu-yüan chi 揚侍郎集, in *Han Wei Liu-ch'ao ming-chia chi* 漢魏六朝名家集, Ting Fu-pao 丁福保, ed., Shanghai, 1911.

———, in *Liang Han Wei Chin shih-i-chia wen-chi* 兩漢魏晉十一家文集, Taipei, 1973. A reprint of Wang Shih-hsien's 汪士賢 (1573-c. 1619) revised edition.

See also Chapter I, "Sources," in David R. Knechtges, "Yang Shyong, the *Fuh,* and Hann Rhetoric" (see below).

TRANSLATIONS:

Belpaire, Bruno. *Le catechisme philosophique de Yang-Hiong-ts'e* [translation of *Fa yen*]. Brussels, 1960.

Knechtges, David R. "Sweet Spring," "Ho-tung," "Barricade Hunt," "Ch'ang-yang," "Dissolving Ridicule," and "Expelling Poverty," in his *The Han Rhapsody,* pp. 45-51, 58-61, 63-73, 80-85, 97-103, and 104-107.

———. *The Han shu Biography of Yang Xiong (53 B.C.-A.D. 18).* Occasional Paper No. 14, Center for Asian Studies, Arizona State University, May 1981.

Kopetsky, Elma E. "Two *fu* on Sacrifices by Yang Hsiung, *The Fu on K'an-ch'ung* and *The Fu on Ho-tung,*" *JOS,* 10 (1972), 104-14.

Waley, Arthur. "Driving Away Poverty," *The Temple,* pp. 76-80.

von Zach, E. "Sweet Spring," in *Anthologie,* v. 1, pp. 93-98; "The Plume," v. 1, pp. 117-125; "Ch'ang-yang," v. 1, pp. 122-131; "Dissolving Ridicule," v. 2, pp. 834-840.

———. "Yang Hsiung's *Fayen:* Wörter strenger Ermahnung," *Sinologische Beiträge,* 4 (1939), 1-74.

STUDIES:

Doeringer, F. M. "Yang Hsiung and his Formulation of a Classicism." Unpublished Ph.D. dissertation, Columbia University, 1971.

Forke, Alfred. "Der Philosoph Yang Hsiung," *Sinica,* 7 (1932), 169-178.

Knechtges, David R. *The Han Rhapsody, A Study of the Fu of Yang Hsiung.* Cambridge, 1976.

———. "Yang Shyong, the *Fuh,* and Hann Rhetoric." Unpublished Ph.D. dissertation, University of Washington, 1968.

T'ang, Lan 唐蘭. "Yang Hsiung tsou 'Kan-ch'üan,' 'Ho-tung,' 'Yü-lieh,' 'Ch'ang-yang,' ssu fu te nien-tai" 揚雄奏甘泉河東羽獵長揚四賦的年代, *Hsüeh yüan,* 2.8 (1949), 8.

T'ang, Ping-cheng 湯炳正. "Yang Tzu-yüan nien-p'u" 揚子雲年譜, *Lun hsüeh,* (April 1937), 25-44; (June 1937), 59-83.

Ting, Chieh-min 丁介民. *Yang Hsiung nien-p'u* 揚雄年譜. Taipei, 1975.

—KH

Yang Shen 楊愼 (*tzu,* Yung-hsiu 用修, *hao,* Sheng-an 升菴, 1488-1559) was perhaps the most important *shih** poet of the sixteenth century not affiliated with any Archaist or Anti-archaist literary movement. He was certainly one of the most prolific and many-sided scholars of the Ming dynasty.

Son of a Grand Secretary (Yang T'ing-ho 楊廷和, 1459-1529) and member of a prosperous Szechwan family, Yang combined the advantages of birth and training with inborn literary and intellectual gifts. After taking the highest place in the *chin-shih* examination of 1511, he held office until 1517 and again between 1520 and 1524. In the latter year, however, he joined many other scholars at court in protesting the intention of the young emperor, Shih-tsung (1507-1567; r. 1521-1567), to offer imperial sacrifices to his father, who had not occupied the throne (Shih-tsung had been chosen by the court from a collateral line, after Wu-tsung died without issue) in what became known as the Great Ritual Controversy. Some of the participants in the protest lost their lives as a consequence; Yang was severely flogged and banished to Yunnan, one of the most remote parts of the empire. This proved to be the end of his promising career as an official. Although he enjoyed a good deal of freedom and comfort in his place of exile, and even returned to visit his native Szechwan, he was never recalled to court, and the unrelenting Shih-tsung even refused him permission to retire to private life when he reached the customary age of 65.

As cruel a blow to his prospects for an official career as banishment was, it proved to be the occasion for one of the most extraordinary scholarly careers in Chinese history. Far from the distractions of Peking's social and political life, without any official duties to speak of, and wealthy enough to amass an enviable library, Yang plunged into research and writing in a wide variety of fields, including literature, the fine arts, historical phonology, and the history and customs of Yunnan, his place of exile. Later scholars, in some cases motivated by disapproval of Yang's free-and-easy style of life, have proved him wrong in points of detail, but his writings remain a much-used source, especially for the study of Yunnan in early times. Unfortunately a good deal of confusion surrounds Yang's *oeuvre*. Some material appears under more than one title, and the authorship of some items is disputed. Some of the responsibility lies with well-meaning friends and relatives who printed Yang's works after his death, with more enthusiasm than care. But Yang himself contributed to the confusion by his attempts to pass work of his own off as fragments of lost writings of antiquity.

While a young man in Peking, Yang Shen had naturally been active as a poet. He was a follower of Li Tung-yang,* formed a poetry society with several friends, and also associated with Li Meng-yang* and Ho Ching-ming,* the most important members of the Archaist Movement then beginning to dominate the literary scene. Whatever his literary affiliations during this early period, Yang took an independent stance after his exile, and rejected the Archaists' doctrine that High T'ang was the acme of *shih* poetry. His preference was for

Six Dynasties poetry on the one hand, and for some later T'ang poetry on the other. His most vehement criticism was reserved for Chu Hsi and other Sung dynasty Neo-Confucianists and literary critics, excepting only Yen Yü, author of the *Ts'ang-lang shih-hua.** His comments on poetry are found in his *Sheng-an shih-hua* 升菴詩話, one of the most extensive examples of the *shih-hua** genre from the Ming. It is a difficult text to evaluate, for several reasons. Different editions of it are somewhat different in their arrangement, some comments are taken without acknowledgment from the work of earlier writers, and Yang doesn't always reveal the basis for his judgments. It appears that Yang's taste in poetry ran to the "sensuously beautiful" (*yen* 艷) both in Six Dynasties and late T'ang.

Yang's second wife (his first died early), Huang O 黃峨 (*ming* sometimes given as 峨, *tzu*, Hsiu-mei 秀眉, 1498-1569), like Yang, was the child of a prominent official and a native of Szechwan. She was married to Yang in 1519, while he was still considered to have a brilliant future. After his disgrace and banishment in 1524, she returned to his family home in Szechwan, where she spent the rest of her life (except for short trips and a brief period with Yang in Yunnan, 1526-1529), managing his property and keeping him supplied with funds. After his death, she brought his remains home and assumed responsibility for the care of two sons borne to him by concubines that he had taken in Yunnan.

Huang was herself well educated and a gifted poet, especially in the *san-ch'ü* 散曲 form (see *ch'ü*). Most of her *shih* poetry has been lost (and what remains is not of great interest), but a collection of her *ch'ü*, together with Yang's, has been published. The striking thing about her poems is that they frankly portray her passion and longing for, and some resentment of, Yang after he took his concubines, while the woman who wrote them fulfilled all the requirements of Confucian propriety in her wise and far-sighted management of her husband's family property throughout the long years of his exile.

EDITIONS:

Sheng-an wen-chi 升菴文集. 81 *chüan* (1582; rpt. 1795); *Sheng-an i-chi* 遺集, 26 *chüan* (1606; rpt. 1844); *Sheng-an wai-chi* 外集, 100 *chüan* (1616; rpt. 1795, 1844). Three successive collections of Yang Shen's works, including not only his poems and essays, but also various other writings. A collective edition in 240 *chüan*, *Sheng-an ho-chi* 合集, was published in 1882. The *Wen-chi*, under the title *Sheng-an ch'üan-chi* 全集 was reprinted in a typeset edition in the *Wan-yu wen-k'u*, and the original edition of the *Wai-chi* reproduced by the T'ai-wan hsüeh-sheng shu-chü in 1971; 192 *chüan* of miscellaneous writings are included in the *Han-hai* 函海, Li T'iao-yüan, ed., rpt. in *PPTSCC*.

Sheng-an shih-hua, in Ting Fu-pao's *Hsü Li-tai shih-hua*. The fullest and most accessible text put together after collation of all the important earlier editions. Ting's rearrangement of the entries, however, is inconvenient to use and obscures the coherence of Yang's views. The best traditional edition is that in the *Han-hai*.

Tz'u p'in 辭品 (*Tz'u-hua ts'ung-pien* ed.).

Yang Shen fu-fu san-ch'ü 夫婦散曲. Shanghai, 1929.

Yang Shen fu-fu yüeh-fu 樂府. Shanghai, 1940.

TRANSLATIONS:

Demiéville, *Anthologie*, pp. 482-483.

STUDIES:

DMB, pp. 1531-1535.

Liang, Jung-jo 梁容若. "Huang Hsiu-mei he t'a te san-ch'ü" 和他的散曲, *Ch'un wen-hsüeh*, 14.40 (1970), 26-39.

———. "Yang Shen sheng-p'ing yü chu-tso" 生平與著作, in *Tso-chia yü tso-p'in*, Taichung, 1971, pp. 1-25. A useful introduction, the notes on the texts of some of Yang's more important works being particularly helpful.

Lu, Ch'ien 盧前. "Hsin-tu Yang shih ch'ü-lun" 新都楊氏曲論, *Wen-shih tsa-chih*, 3.5/6 (1944), 74-84.

Tung-ni 多尼. "Wen-hsüeh-chia Yang Sheng-an" 文學家楊升菴, *Ts'ao-ti*, 1957.7, 53-58.

Yokota, Terutoshi 横田輝俊. "Yō Shin no shi-ron" 楊愼の詩論, *Hiroshima Daigaku Bunga-kubu kiyō*, 20 (1962), 207-222.

—DB

Yang Wan-li 楊萬里 (*tzu*, T'ing-hsiu 廷秀, *hao*, Ch'eng-chai 誠齋, 1127-1206) is one of the four great poets of the early Southern Sung dynasty (with Lu Yu,* Fan Ch'eng-ta,* and Yu Mou 尤袤—a poet most of whose works have been lost). He was born in Chi-shui 吉水 County (Kiangsi) and did not obtain his *chin-shih* degree until 1154. Subsequently he served in a number of minor local- and central-government positions. But the most important event during these years was his poetic "sudden enlightenment" in 1178, while he was serving as Prefect of Ch'ang-chou. Shortly afterward, Yang was appointed to Kwangtung, where he successfully put down a local rebellion, and, as a result, was returned to the capital. However, after clashes with the emperor, he was finally forced out of the central government. In 1192 he resigned from a local post in protest against new Sung monetary and fiscal policies. Throughout his entire career he was generally on the side of officials who favored an aggressive policy against the Chin Tartars.

According to one of Yang's prefaces, he first imitated the masters of the Kiangsi School of poetry (see *Chiang-hsi shih-p'ai*), then the pentasyllabic regulated verse of Ch'en Shih-tao* (strictly speaking, also a Kiangsi poet), then the heptasyllabic *chüeh-chü* (see *shih*) of Wang An-shih,* and finally the *chüeh-chü* of the late T'ang poets. After this long stage of imitation, Yang made a breakthrough in 1178, experiencing a Ch'an-like enlightenment which enabled him to discard his former masters and create a style fully his own. Since Yang burned his juvenilia, it is impossible to follow his earliest development as a poet. But it is true that many of the poems in his earliest extant poetry collection show a debt to such Kiangsi masters as Huang T'ing-chien.* However, even before his enlightenment there are numerous poems that do not imitate any of these masters and clearly adumbrate his subsequent style.

Yang Wan-li's literary theory represents the culmination of the Ch'an-inspired aesthetics that had already been developing in Northern Sung times. Yang Wan-li considered the process by which a poet acquires his own style to be akin to that by which a Ch'an adept obtains sudden enlightenment; i.e., both must undergo a rigorous period of study under a series of masters, whom they must eventually transcend before they can achieve their final awakening. Such a view of literature meant that Yang Wan-li was not totally opposed to imitation during the initial stages of a poet's career. But after the poet's enlightenment, he must reject his masters and strike out in new directions—a view strongly at odds with the more imitative, "neo-classical" literary theories common among some of Yang's contemporaries.

Yang's Ch'an-inspired literary theory also had other implications for his poetic ideals. As the Ch'an master believed that after enlightenment the student could act in a totally spontaneous manner, so Yang felt that the enlightened poet could write almost effortlessly. Such poetry would be completely natural. Hence, Yang had no great love for the artificiality of the Kiangsi School.

Later critics adopted one of the major technical terms used by Yang Wan-li himself to describe his style—*huo-fa* 活法 (live method). The term seems to be of Ch'an origin but was used by contemporary Neo-Confucians. It could best be described as a non-dualistic theory of literature designed to prevent stale imitation. Although neither Yang himself nor any of his contemporaries have provided a definition of the term, Yang's "live method" seems to include a number of literary devices. First, it incorporates an iconoclasm, as the author overturns his masters in order to avoid imitation. Second, it invokes a widespread use of paradox and illusionistic imagery, both of which constantly startle the reader from his normal thought patterns. Closely connected to these devices is a love of abrupt shifts, which create a sensation of "sudden enlightenment" in the poetry. Finally, it is distinguished by humor and the intrusion of vernacular language—devices imparting liveliness to poetry. All of these characteristics are common in Yang's verse.

The range of Yang Wan-li's work is wide; he treats practically every theme touched upon by other Southern Sung poets as well as some that he was the first to write about, such as the house fly. Nature provides much of Yang's poetic material, with the mountain landscape frequently symbolizing absolute truth and the experience of enlightenment. One of the most delightful aspects of his verse is the large number of poems on plants and animals. Yet he did not totally ignore the world of man. Like other Sung authors, Yang valued the socially and politically critical capabilities of verse although this type of poetry is fairly rare in his collection. Commoner is poetry which attempts to give a realistic view of Chinese peasant life, which, unlike many T'ang authors, Yang rarely idealizes. Finally, like other Sung writers, Yang often expresses an alienation from society, the vulgar nature of which interferes with his strivings for spiritual transcendence. It is precisely this transcendent spirit, present in so much of Yang Wan-li's poetry, which makes his work a source of delight.

EDITIONS:

Ch'eng-chai chi 誠齋集. Shanghai, 1936.

Ch'eng-chai shih-chi 誠齋詩集. Taipei, 1970. *SPPY* ed.

Chou, Ju-ch'ang 周汝昌. *Yang Wan-li hsüan-chi* 楊萬里選集. Peking, 1964; rpt. Shanghai, 1979. Detailed annotation and excellent introductory essay.

TRANSLATIONS:

Chaves, Jonathan. *Heaven My Blanket, Earth My Pillow.* New York, 1975.

Sunflower, pp. 372-377.

STUDIES:

Chang, Chien 張健. "Yang Wan-li wen-hsüeh li-lun yen-chiu" 楊萬里文學理論研究, *Kuo-li pien-i-kuan kuan-k'an*, 9.1 (1980), 67-95.

Hu, Ming-t'ing 胡明珽. *Yang Wan-li shih p'ing-shu* 楊萬里詩評述. Taipei, 1976.

SB, pp. 1238-1246.

Schmidt, J. D. *Yang Wan-li.* Boston, 1976.

Yang Wan-li Fan Ch'eng-ta chüan 楊萬里范成大卷. Chan-chih 湛之, comp. Peking, 1965. Exhaustive collection of critical comments on Yang from Sung to modern times.

—JDS

Yang Wei-chen 楊維楨 (*tzu*, Lien-fu 廉夫, *hao*, T'ieh-ya 鐵崖, 1296-1370) was to his contemporaries the foremost figure in classical poetry during the transition period between the Yüan and the Ming. Yang passed the *chin-shih* examination in 1327 and held a number of minor official posts during the Yüan. Yang Wei-chen's personality seems to have joined the eccentric *bon vivant* to outspoken morality: that combination did not augur well for an official career, and Yang never rose to a public post commensurate with his literary fame. Several times in the 1330s and 1340s he withdrew from office to travel in the Lower Yangtze Region, write poems, and enjoy himself.

When the series of rebellions that eventually led to the downfall of the Yüan broke out in this area, Yang fled to the mountains around Hangchow, refusing an invitation to serve in the government of the rebel Chang Shih-ch'eng. After the founding of the Ming, Yang Wei-chen also spurned repeated invitations to serve in the Ming government (although he did help out in an imperial compilation project). Yang's unwillingness to serve two dynasties was a moral position of convenience: his fame in the mid-fourteenth century was such that he led a better (and safer) life as a private citizen, teaching, writing poetry, and enjoying the hedonistic pursuits for which the Lower Yangtze Region was famous.

Although much of Yang Wei-chen's literary output is supposed to have been lost, much survives, scattered in a confusing variety of editions. Most of Yang's prose is preserved in the *Tung-wei-tzu chi* 東維子集, in thirty *chüan* plus one *chüan* of addenda. The *Tung-wei-tzu chi* contains only one and a half *chüan* of poetry (plus some poems in the addenda). That these are almost the only surviving occasional poems by Yang is a good indication of how much has been lost. An unusually large proportion, twenty-one *chüan*, of the *Tung-wei-tzu chi* consists of prefaces and records (*chi* 記); the predominance of these "private" prose genres attests to the belletristic direction of Yang's talents (although he did have a

considerable reputation as a *Ch'un-ch'iu* scholar and historian).

The most famous of Yang's poetry collections is the *T'ieh-ya ku yüeh-fu* 鐵崖古樂府 (later published with a commentary by the Ch'ing scholar Lou Pu-ch'an 樓卜瀍). This work consists of 416 *yüeh-fu** on gods, figures from legend and history, and set *yüeh-fu* situations. These are sensual, often wildly imaginative songs that belong more in the tradition of Li Ho* and Wen T'ing-yün* than in that of the original *yüeh-fu*. Many of the *T'ieh-ya ku yüeh-fu* have prefaces that cite the original text of a legend or story; the poem then gives an imaginative evocation of some crucial moment or main event of the story. This poetic mode, though its origins lie firmly in the ninth century, in many ways parallels the contemporary interest in drama, which also focuses on intensely lyric moments set in a narrative frame.

Yang Wei-chen's interest in history found poetic expression in another collection, the "Yung-shih shih" 詠史詩 (Poems on History—also with a commentary by Lou Pu-ch'an). The practice of composing a complete collection of *ying-shih shih* originated, like Yang's *yüeh-fu* style, in the ninth century. The mode of presentation of these poems is similar to that of the *T'ieh-ya ku yüeh-fu*: prefaces often frame expression of some significant moment in history, usually containing an element of ethical evaluation.

Most of the remainder of Yang Wei-chen's poetic oeuvre are in two overlapping collections: the six *chüan* of *T'ieh-ya hsien-sheng fu-ku shih* 鐵崖先生復古詩, with introductory notes by Chang Wan 章琬 and critical comments by Huang Chin 黃溍; and the eight *chüan* of Lou Pu-ch'an's *T'ieh-ya i-p'ien* 鐵崖逸編. The latter has a commentary by Lou, and where the two collections overlap, Lou retains Cheng Wan's introductory notes. The *T'ieh-ya hsien-sheng fu-ku shih* contains a number of short series: "lute songs," palace poems, poems on immortals, the "Yung-nü shih" 詠女史 (Poems on Famous Women), and two series recreating the style of the gently erotic *Hsiang-lien chi* 香奩集 from the late ninth or early tenth centuries. The *T'ieh-ya i-p'ien* contains many of the same series as well as a few occasional poems and a number of poems on paintings.

In his extant poetry Yang Wei-chen demonstrated a remarkably consistent fascination with the various poetic styles popular at the very end of the T'ang, a period whose poetry was usually condemned as decadent. Yang was himself denounced as a decadent writer; yet by unconscious affinity or conscious choice, Yang Wei-chen, the historian and *Ch'un-ch'iu* scholar, made an implicit comment on his own age through his T'ang models.

EDITIONS:

Tung-wei-tzu wen-chi 東維子文集. *SPTK.*

T'ieh-ya Hsien-sheng ku-yüeh-fu 鐵崖先生古樂府 (with *T'ieh-ya hsien-sheng fu-ku shih-chi* 鐵崖先生復古詩集). *SPTK.*

T'ieh-ya san-chung 鐵崖三種 (incorporating the three works with commentary by Lou P'u-ch'an: *T'ieh-ya yüeh-fu chu* 鐵崖樂府注, *T'ieh-ya yung-shih chu* 鐵崖詠史注, and *T'ieh-ya i-p'ien chu* 鐵崖逸編注). 1910.

STUDIES:

DMB, pp. 1547-1553.

Maeno, Naoaki 前野直彬. "Min shichishi no sensei—Yō Itei bungakukan ni tsuite" 明七子の先聲 — 楊維楨文學觀 について, *Chūgoku bungakuhō*, 5 (1956), 41-69.

—so

Yeh Chih-fei 葉稚斐 (named Shih-chang 時章, better known by his *tzu*, Chih-fei, *fl. c.* 1650) was a native of Wu-hsien 吳縣 (modern Kiangsu) and one of the Soochow dramatists of the early Ch'ing. Among this group of *ch'uan-ch'i** writers were the eminent dramatist Li Yü,* and such men as Chu Tso-ch'ao,* Chu Shu-ch'en,* Ch'iu Yüan,* Pi Wei 畢魏, and Chang T'a-fu.* Yeh, Pi Wei, and Chu Su-ch'en are known to have assisted Li Yü in editing Li's celebrated work the *Ch'ing-chung p'u* 清忠譜 (A Register of Loyalty and Integrity). Yeh wrote eight *ch'uan-chi* dramas, two of which are extant: *Hu-p'o-shih* 琥珀匙 (The Mandolin) and *Ying-hsiung kai* 英雄慨 (Heroic Resolution). Kao I's 高奕 *Hsin ch'uan-ch'i p'in* 新傳奇品 (which contains lists of works by twenty-seven dramatists of the late Ming

and the early Ch'ing with brief comments on their dramatic styles) compares the vigor of Yeh's dramatic style to that energetic piece of drum music the *Yü-yang ts'an-chua* 漁陽參撾. Wang Chung-shao's 王鍾珝 *Chiu-pien tsan-yü* 酒邊贊語 (Talks from a Jade Wine Ladle at a Banquet—a collection of notes, some of which address drama), quoting phrases from the *Hu-p'o-shih*, notes that Yeh's dramatic diction is straightforward and severe.

The *Hu-p'o-shih* tells of the story of Hsü Hsün 胥塤 and T'ao Fo-nu 桃佛奴. Just as Hsü and T'ao are about to marry, T'ao's father is put into jail because he once traded with the robber Chin Jan 金髯. In the course of trying to find money to redeem her father, T'ao is cheated and sold into a brothel. But she steadfastly refuses to become a prostitute, and compiles a book, *K'u chieh chuan* 苦節傳 (Steadfast Chastity), to show her determination; a blind man named Chia 賈 helps her distribute the book. When Chin Jan learns of T'ao's situation, he comes to her rescue, and T'ao and Hsü are finally reunited. The *hu-p'o-shih*, which is variously called *hun-pu-ssu* 渾不似, *huo-pu-ssu* 火不思, or *chin-kang t'ui* 金剛腿, is a musical instrument similar to the *p'i-p'a* 琵琶. The drama was so entitled because T'ao's skill at playing this instrument enchants Hsü. In the repertoire of *Ch'uan* 川 regional drama, there is a *Fu-nu chuan* 芙奴傳 (also known as *K'u chieh chuan* 苦節傳) which is based on this drama.

According to the *Chien-weng hsien-hua* 繭甕閒話 (Casual Talks from the Cocoon-jar, a collection of notes—the passage in question has been cited in Chiao Hsün's *Chü-shuo*), Yeh's *Hu-p'o-shih* was modeled upon the story of Wang Ts'ui-ch'iao 王翠翹 of the mid-Ming. But in fact parallels between the two stories can hardly be drawn. The essence of the story of Ts'ui-ch'iao is that she betrayed Hsü Hai 徐海, who then was put to death. If T'ao Fo-nu corresponds to Wang Ts'ui-ch'iao and Chin Jan to Hsü Hai, then the two stories clearly move in opposite directions. Also, according to the *Chien-weng hsien-hua*, the *Hu-p'o-shih* contains phrases that explicitly insult the government and praise outlaws, and because of this Yeh was thrown into jail and nearly put to death. In the extant edition of the drama, the two phrases cited as examples in the *Hsien-hua* cannot be found. Probably they have been deleted to avoid government persecution. However, less explicit phrases that produce the same effect can still be found. It is reasonable to suppose that in writing this drama Yeh was alluding to some specific events of his time. This is all the more probable if we consider the fact that the drama was written at a time not remote from the fall of the Ming dynasty.

The *Ying-hsiung kai* relates the story of the late T'ang-dynasty rebel Huang Ch'ao 黃巢 reset in the Five Dynasties. In it Huang Ch'ao fails in an uprising and then wanders away following a monk. Thus Yeh in this piece does not choose to praise rebellion as he had elsewhere. In the older repertoire of *ching-chü** a work entitled *Ts'ang-mei ssu* 藏梅 (The Plum-hoarding Monastery) is based on an act taken from the *Ying-hsiung kai*.

Yeh was not unlike the Yüan dramatists who wrote about the deeds of the robber-heroes of the Liang-shan p'o 梁山泊; grieving over the fall of the Ming, he gave vent to his feelings in his dramas.

EDITIONS:

Hu-p'o shih. Ku-pen, III.

Ying-hsiung kai. (1) *Ku-pen*, III. (2) *Pai-chung ch'uan-ch'i* 百種傳奇. [This collection contains the hand-written copies of about a hundred works of *ch'uan-ch'i* and *tsa-chü*, copied by a man surnamed Chang 張 of Soochow, from copies that he had borrowed from Hsü Chih-heng 許之衡. For more information about this collection, see Cheng Chen-to 鄭振鐸, "Ch'ao-pen pai-chung ch'uan-ch'i te fa-hsien" 鈔本百種傳奇的發現, in his *Chung-kuo wen-hsüeh yen-chiu* 中國文學研究, Peking, 1957, pp. 617-621.]

STUDIES:

Chou, I-pai 周貽白. "Ch'ing-tai ch'u-nien te K'un-shan ch'iang" 清代初年的昆山腔, in his *Chung-kuo hsi-ch'ü fa-chan shih kang-yao* 中國戲曲發展史綱要, Shanghai, 1979, pp. 345-354.

—SSK

Yeh Hsiao-wan 葉小紈 (*tzu*, Hui-ch'ou 蕙綢, 1613-1660), a native of Wu-hsien 吳縣

(Kiangsu), was a poet and dramatist of the late Ming. She was the second daughter of Yeh Shao-yüan 葉紹袁 (*tzu*, Chung-shao 仲韶, 1589-1648). Both her elder sister Wan-wan 紈紈 (*tzu*, Chao-ch'i 昭齊) and her younger sister Hsiao-luan 小鸞 (*tzu*, Ch'iung-chang 瓊章) were noted for their literary talents, but both died young. Hsiao-wan's only drama, the *Yüan-yang meng* 鴛鴦夢 (Dream of Mandarin Ducks), was written to mourn their early deaths. Hsiao-wan was related to Shen Tzu-cheng,* the eminent dramatist of the late Ming, and Shen Ching,* the founder of the Wu-chiang 吳江 School of drama writing. Hsiao-wan's mother, Shen I-hsiu 沈宜修 (*tzu*, Wan-chün 宛君, 1590-1635), was a sister of Shen Tzu-cheng and a niece of Shen Ching, and Shen Ching was also the grandfather of Hsiao-wan's husband. With such a background, it is not surprising that Hsiao-wan should have chosen to express her grief over the deaths of her sisters in the form of drama.

Both Wan-wan and Hsiao-luan died in 1632; one edition of the *Yüan-yang meng* (a copy has been preserved in Japan) contains a preface by Shen Tzu-cheng dated 1636. Thus the drama must have been written between 1632 and 1636. It is a short piece in four scenes describing Hui Pai-fang's 蕙百芳 sorrow at the deaths of his two sworn brothers. The plot is very simple. The text is largely composed of expressive lyrics and the spoken part is insignificant. Northern-style songs are employed throughout. In his preface to the *Yüan-yang meng*, Shen Tzu-cheng remarks that the euphony of the songs can be compared to that of Chu Yu-tun's,* and that songs of such beauty can even rival the works of such Yüan songwriters as Kuan Yün-shih* and Ch'iao Chi-fu.*

Yeh Hsiao-wan was also a poet of considerable talent. She wrote a large number of classical poems (*shih**), discarding many in her late years. The remainder, no more than one-twentieth of the original corpus, was put into a collection entitled *Ts'un yü ts'ao* 存餘草 (Remaining Grasses); but even it is no longer extant. Some fifty poems from this collection, however, have been preserved in the *I-ch'i chi* 已畦集 of Yeh

Hsieh,* Hsiao-wan's younger brother. They are either occasional poems written in memory of or in response to her relatives or lyrical poems about her life. Her other extant poems (about forty; all of them are elegies for the deceased members of the Yeh family) can be found in the *Wu-meng-t'ang chi* 午夢堂集 (Collection of the Daydream Hall, first published in 1636), a collection of verse and prose by members of the Yeh family.

EDITIONS:

Yeh, Shao-yüan, comp. *Wu-meng-t'ang ch'üan-chi* 午夢堂全集. Shanghai, 1936. *Chung-kuo wen-hsüeh chen-pen ts'ung-shu* 中國文學珍本叢書, series 1, no. 49. A photolithographic reprint of the edition in the collection of the Pei-yeh shang-fang 貝葉山房 in Shanghai. When the *Wu-meng-t'ang chi* was first published in 1636, the *Yüan-yang meng* was not included. The drama is included, however, in nearly all the subsequent editions of this collection.

STUDIES:

Fu, *Ch'ing tsa-chü*, pp. 35-36.
T'an, Cheng-pi 譚正璧. *Chung-kuo nü-hsing te wen-hsüeh sheng-huo* 中國女性的文學生活, Shanghai, 1931, pp. 337-343.
Yagisawa, *Gekisakuka*, pp. 577-652. An expanded version of the article listed below.
———. "Mindai joryū gekisakuka Yō Shōgan ni tsuite" 明代女流劇作家葉小紈について, *Tō-hōgaku*, 5 (1952), 85-98.

—SSK

Yeh Hsieh 葉燮 (1627-1703) was a literary critic, author and scientist. His main critical treatise, the *Yüan shih* 原詩 (Origins of Poetry), is of a quality and historical importance that invite comparison with Liu Hsieh's *Wen-hsin tiao-lung,** conventionally regarded as the finest critical writing in the Chinese language.

Yeh Hsieh's collected prose, his verse, the *Yüan shih,* and an astronomical study are briefly described in the *Ssu-k'u ch'üan-shu tsung-mu* (see Chi Yün)—all rather unenthusiastically. Critics have generally accorded the *Yüan shih* a place subordinate to the theorizings of such Ch'ing critics as Wang Shih-chen* (1634-1711) and Yüan Mei.* But there has been recent and significant change in the evaluation of Yeh Hsieh and his poetics. The higher estimation now accorded the *Yüan shih* is just, although the heavy-handed emphasis on Yeh's supposed Materialism hinder a proper appreciation of Yeh's achievement.

From the eleventh century on, with the emergence of the *shih-hua** as a form for the expression and retention of critical opinions, Chinese literary criticism became increasingly occasional, casual, subjective, and disjointed. While the *Yüan shih* is generally regarded as a work in the *shih-hua* tradition (its inclusion in the *Ch'ing shih-hua* 清詩話 attests to the view), it really was a conscious break from that tradition. The work is not a collection of idle jottings, but organized work with a strong philosophical foundation which considers the central issues that arise in the reading and writing of poetry and in the practice of literary criticism. With most poet-critics of China it is safe to concentrate on their poetry and by and large ignore their criticism. In the case of Yeh Hsieh, the poetry and the rest of his prose writings are of limited interest. Like Liu Hsieh before him in China and Aristotle in Greece, Yeh deserves to be remembered because he wrote a profound critical work.

The *Yüan shih* is made up of four parts (in four *chüan*). Part one begins with a brief history of Chinese poetry from its first beginnings to Yeh's day. From the historical account, Yeh moves on to the first general question he raises and seeks to answer—whether the writing of poetry can be taught and learned. The question gives Yeh the opportunity to separate poetry into poetry understood in terms of prosody and poetry based on *personality*. The argument is traditional, but Yeh succeeds in using it to provide for poetry a *moral* basis and a justification. The next general issue that Yeh examines is the concept of *fa* 法 (law) in poetry. On this issue, Yeh comes very close to isolating *imposed* rules from *observed* law; the distinction is comparable to that between "law" as understood in civil jurisdiction and "law" as understood in the modern natural sciences; and the critical concept that this leads to is that poetry must be understood as an *autonomy*. He then moves to the most important and original theoretical discussion in the *Yüan shih*. Poetry, according to Yeh, is like all the rest of human experience, conceivable on three distinct levels; that of *li* 理 (possibility) that of *shih* 事 (fact), and that of *ch'ing* 情 (reality—the English translations take into account Yeh's own explanations of the terms). The *Possibility* of a thing's happening is understood in the most general and abstract of terms. The *Fact* of its happening is less general, but still abstract. The *Reality* of its happening is specific and concrete. Yeh uses the first two of these terms in their accepted senses, but he restores to the word *ch'ing* its early, pre-Ch'in meaning, with the emphasis not on "feeling," but on the "real," the "actual." His illustrations (trees, flowers, etc.) demonstrate that the world is perceived and understood with varying degrees of particularity. Poetry differs from all other types of writing in that it represents the minutest, the clearest, and the most accurate observation of life; therein lies the peculiarity of the language of poetry. Yeh's speculations on this subject give one of the most satisfactory views of poetry and the poet in the entire range of Chinese critical thinking. Many of the recurrent critical problems are solved—the question, for instance, of why poetic language must be permitted to be "strange," to differ from the norms of daily discourse, or of why poetry, which insists on the sharpest and most precise visions of life with its multifarious details, should be regarded as a basis for moral judgments.

Part two of the *Yüan shih* opens with a scheme intended to match the theory of Possibility, Fact, and Reality. Just as the poet's world can be seen in those three terms, so the poet himself can be viewed in terms of four personal qualities, *ts'ai* 才 (talent), *tan* 膽 (courage), *shih* 識 (knowledge), and *li* 力 (energy). This is a less effective scheme. Still, it should be noted that Yeh considers knowledge the most important of the four. A collection of Yeh's practical criticism follows. The exceedingly detailed analysis of four lines of Tu Fu's poetry, concentrating on the ambiguity of a key word in each case, provides the most convincing examination of the functioning of poetic language in traditional Chinese criticism.

Part three consists of further observations on the personality and emotions of the poet as a foundation for poetry. This is essentially meta-criticism. He considers the natures and implications of a number of critical notions and labels that are commonplace in Chinese literary criticism. He urges more caution in responses to poetry and in the critical language employed to discuss it. At the end of this part, Yeh attempts to explain the decline of poetry.

Part four does not measure up to the preceding parts. Yeh's attempt to write an organized treatise relapses into the common failings of the conventional *shih-hua*: brief, itemized entries on periods and individual poets recorded impressionistically in a chronological order. The *Yüan shih* concludes with the injunction that modern literati should be aware of the ancient masters, but not cowed by them.

EDITIONS:

Yeh, Hsieh. *Yüan shih.* Peking, 1979.

———, in Ting Fu-pao 丁福保, comp., *Ch'ing shih-hua*, Shanghai, 1978, v. 2, pp. 561-612.

STUDIES:

Ch'en, Hui-feng 陳惠豐. *Yeh Hsieh shih-lun yen-chiu* 葉燮詩論研究. Taipei, 1977.

Jen, Chung-chieh 任中杰. "Yeh Hsieh lun hsing-hsiang ssu-wei" 葉燮論形象思維, *Pei-fang lun-ts'ung*, 1979.4 (July 1979), 58-64.

—SKW

Yeh Hsien-tsu 葉憲祖 (*tzu*, Mei-tu 美度 and Hsiang-yu 相攸, *hao*, Liu-t'ung 六桐, T'ung-pai 桐柏, Hu-yüan chü-shih 槲園居士, and Tzu-chin Tao-jen 紫金道人 1566-1641), was a prolific dramatist of the Wu-chiang 吳江 School and an official during the late Ming.

A native of Yü-yao 餘姚 (Chekiang), Yeh came from a family of officials. He earned the *chü-jen* degree in 1594, but it was another twenty-five years (1619) before he received the *chin-shih*. Because of his connection with opponents of the influential eunuch Wei Chung-hsien 魏忠賢 (1568-1627)—his eldest daughter had married the philosopher Huang Tsung-hsi 黄宗羲 (1610-1695)—his official career proceeded slowly until 1626; then his overt disgust with the eunuch's faction brought his dismissal. After Wei died, Yeh earned a sequence of provincial posts until his retirement at age seventy.

Yeh Hsien-tsu was a follower of Shen Ching's* Wu-chiang School of drama, which placed most emphasis on technical perfection in musical terms. Among his disciples and close friends was the dramatist and novelist Yüan Yü-ling (see *Sui T'ang yen-i*); the famous playwright Wu Ping* also sought his advice. His best-known plays are in the *ch'uan-chi** form, *Luan-pi chi* 鸞鎞記 (The Barb of Love) and *Chin-so chi* 金鎖記 (The Golden Lock). The latter is attributed both to Yeh and to Yüan Yü-ling; presumably the two collaborated on it.

Luan-pi chi narrates the romantic attachment between the T'ang poet Wen T'ing-yün* and the courtesan-Taoist nun Yü Hsüan-chi.* The play is structured around the complications of their affair as it is interwoven with that of another couple. It is known also for its attacks on corruption in government. *Chin-so chi* is an adaptation of one of the more famous *tsa-chü** plays by Kuan Han-ch'ing,* *Tou O yüan* 竇娥冤. Seven scenes are extant; like the earlier play, they narrate the plight of a guileless young woman who finds herself wrongly accused of murder. In contrast to Kuan's original, this version ends happily: on the execution ground Tou O appeals to the elements to testify to her innocence. When snow falls even though the time is midsummer, the magistrate releases her to be reunited with her father. (In the original, her father vindicates her posthumously.)

In addition to his *ch'uan-ch'i*, Yeh composed twenty-four *tsa-chü* plays (eleven are extant). They include romantic, historical, and philosopical themes. Among the more outstanding is *I-shui han* 易水寒 (Everlasting Fame), which narrates the attempt by Ching K'o 荊軻 to assassinate the King of Ch'in in 227 B.C. In an epitaph, Huang Tsung-hsi praises Yeh for his skill in writing dramatic verse and for his success with the *tsa-chü* form.

EDITIONS:

Chin-so chi, in *Ku-pen,* III.
Ch'ing-chin-yüan fu-ts'ao 青錦園賦草, in *Li-chao-l ts'ung-shu* 黎照盧叢書; Lin Chi-hsü 林集康 comp., 1 *ch.,* rpt. n.p., 1935.
Han-i chi 寒衣記, in *Yüan Ming tsa-chü.*
I-shui han, Sheng-Ming tsa-chü, v. 2, *ch.* 11.
Kuang-lien chu 廣連珠, in *Li-chao-lu ts'ung-shu, ch.*
Luan-pi chi, in *Liu-shih,* v. 6.
Ma-tso chi 罵座記, in *Yüan Ming tsa-chü.*
Pei-mang shuo-fa 北邙說法, *Sheng-Ming,* v. 1, *c* 15 (*tsa-chü*).
Ssu-yen chi 四艷記, in *Ku-pen,* II. Includes th following four *tsa-chü,* also in *Sheng-Ming,* 2, *ch.* 12-14: *Yao-t'ao-wan shan* 夭桃紈扇; *P lien hsiu-fu* 碧蓮繡符; *Tan-kuei tien-ho* 丹桂鈿合 *Su-mei yü-ch'an* 素梅玉蟾.
T'uan-hua feng 團花鳳, *Sheng-Ming,* v. 1, *ch.* 1 (*tsa-chü*).

STUDIES:

DMB, pp. 1570-1571.
Dolby, *History,* p. 100.
Fu, *Ch'uan-ch'i,* p. 116.
———, *Ming tsa-chü,* pp. 138-148. Bibliograph ical references for Yeh's twenty-four plays i this form.
Huang, Wen-yang 黄文暘 (b. 1736). *Ch'ü-ha tsung-mu t'i-yao* 曲海總目提要; Kowloon, 1967 pp. 623-625, 860-861.
Hung, *Ming,* pp. 198-199.
Tseng, *Ming tsa-chü,* pp. 304-317.

—RE

Yen Chi-tao 晏幾道 (*tzu,* Shu-yüan 叔原 1030 or 1041?-1106 or 1119?), was a con temporary of Liu Yung* and Su Shih,* bu he was only minimally influenced by thei poetic innovations. Stylistically he is close to poets of the generation before him, such as his father Yen Shu* and Ou-yang Hsiu.* Yen Chi-tao claims distinction as the las master of the *Hua-chien chi** and Souther T'ang style of *tz'u** poetry.

Little is known of Yen Chi-tao's life; the primary source of biographical informa tion is the collection of all 258 of his extan *hsiao-ling tz'u,* entitled *Hsiao-shan tz'u* 小山詞 (Lyrics of the Little Mountain), with pre liminary comments by the author and preface by his friend Huang T'ing-chien.* As the youngest son of Yen Shu, Yen Chi tao grew up sheltered in an opulent aris tocratic household, but after his father's death he lost paternal protection and the desire to advance his official career. Unable or unwilling to provide adequately for himself and his family, Yen soon squandered his inheritance and spent his later years drifting from one minor post in Honan to another. He attained some notoriety for his aloof unconventionality, his haughty attachment to an aristocratic way of life even in the face of poverty, as well as his poetic virtuosity.

In the preface to *Hsiao-shan tz'u* Huang T'ing-chien praises Yen for his eccentricity and compares his decline from prosperity to misery with the unhappy fate of Li Yü.* Yen Chi-tao's own introduction recalls youthful memories of visits to the households of literati, where men would drink wine and compose *tz'u* for singing girls to perform. These girls are the explicit subjects of Yen's retrospection. His mature poetry captures the elegance and poise of the refined, aristocratic setting, yet the tone is characterized by a profound melancholy and nostalgia. Present sadness is typically contrasted with past splendor, intensified by a conviction gained from personal experience. Memories which might offer consolation prove to be as fleeting as dreams; yet the absent-minded speaker of the poems flees the present in drinking and retrospection. The result is a complex layering of insubstantiality.

It is characteristic of a poetry of decadence and nostalgia to focus on striking and complex imagery. This is illustrated by a double conceit in the second stanza of Yen Chi-tao's poem to the tune "Tieh-lien hua" 蝶戀花 (Butterflies Lingering over Flowers), which begins "Upon sobering I do not recall leaving the western pavilion":

> On my robe, stains of wine; words in my poem:
> Drop by drop, line by line, all express sad and lonely feelings.
> The red candle pities itself for having no future purpose:
> In vain it sheds tears for me in the cold night.

The distraught poet associates the pattern of distinct isolated droplets of spilled wine with lines of words formed by spots of ink

on the page; the drops of melted wax dripping from the candle, which suggest his own human tears, complete the set of four fluids spilled in vain and increasingly intensify the feelings of desolation, futility, and despair.

In an *oeuvre* which represents the culmination of the *Hua-chien chi* and Southern T'ang style, Yen Chi-tao uses conventional images in personal and emotionally charged contexts. Reiterating his intense loneliness and yearning for the women of his youth, he presents a compelling poetry of painful isolation and poignant nostalgia.

Yen Chi-tao's six extant *shih** are recorded in the *Sung-shih chi-shih.**

EDITIONS:
Hsiao-shan tz'u chien 小山詞箋. Wang Huan-yu 王煥猷, ed. Shanghai, 1947.
Erh Yen tz'u hsüan-chu 二晏詞選注. Hsia Ching-kuan 夏敬觀, ed. Taipei, 1965.

TRANSLATIONS:
Sunflower, pp. 339-342.
Frankel, *Palace Lady*, pp. 44-45.

STUDIES:
Lin, Ming-te 林明德. *Yen Chi-tao chi ch'i tz'u* 晏幾道及其詞. Taipei, 1975. A study of Yen Chi-tao's life and works (pp. 1-94), the text of the *Hsiao-shan tz'u* (pp. 98-162), and bibliography (pp. 163-165).
Wan, Min-hao 宛敏灝. *Erh Yen chi ch'i tz'u* 二晏及其詞. Shanghai, 1934. Praises Yen Chi-tao and disparages Yen Shu.

—MW

Yen Chih-t'ui 顏之推 (*tzu*, Chieh 介, 531-*c.* 590), probably best known as the author of the *Yen-shih chia-hsün* 顏氏家訓 (Family Instructions of Mr. Yen), was descended from a family of high status which originated in Lang-yeh 琅邪 (near modern Lin-i 臨沂, Shantung). It was one of a number of emigré families which came south in the early part of the fourth century, and from which officials of the Eastern Chin and its southern-dynasty successors were drawn, because their literary talents and prestigious status added luster to the courts at which they served. These officials, however, wielded little power. Among Yen's ancestors was Yen Yen-chih.* Yen fol-

923

lowed his father in serving at the Liang princely court of Hsiao 蕭繹 (508-554). He took part in the battles against the rebel Hou Ching 侯景, who seized the capital at Nanking in 549 and attempted to usurp the throne. After Hou's defeat in 552, Yen, who had been captured and narrowly escaped death, returned to serve Hsiao I, now Emperor Yüan at Chiang-ling 江陵, where he took part in a project to put in order the imperial library. The collection was largely burned in 554 when Chiang-ling was captured by the Western Wei armies; the emperor was killed, and Yen soon (556) managed to escape to Northern Ch'i, hoping thereby to find his way to the surviving Liang state at Nanking. Finding this impossible, Yen took service in the Northern Ch'i court, rising to a relatively high position. Again, in 577, his career was disrupted when Northern Ch'i was conquered by the Northern Chou (formerly Western Wei), and Yen was taken back to Ch'ang-an. His talents do not seem to have been utilized—there is mention of great poverty at this period—until the Sui was established in 581. Yen's name then occurs as a collaborator on the rhyme dictionary *Ch'ieh-yün* 切韻 (preface dated 600); he took part in the compilation of a new *Wei-shu*, and in various learned discussions at court concerning music, inscriptions, and the calendar. He seems to have died some time after 590.

Yen's writings include historical and lexicographical works, of which only fragments remain, and poetry, the most important work being the autobiographical "Kuan wo sheng fu" 觀我生賦 (Prose-poem Viewing My Life), included in his biography in *Pei Ch'i-shu* 北齊書 (History of the Northern Ch'i Dynasty). There is a Ming recension of his collection of short stories entitled *Huan-yüan chi* 還冤記 (originally *Yüan-hun chih* 冤魂志) which has the theme of vengeful ghosts, probably compiled with the purpose of discouraging the murder of innocent persons, rather than to propagate Buddhist beliefs, as is sometimes claimed.

The best known of Yen's works is the *Yen-shih chia-hsün*, belonging to the genre of advice to one's children. But this book is also an especially rich source of information on the society and thought of his time. It is divided into twenty sections, each of which deals with a topic such as the education of children, supervision of the family, personal conduct, literature, care for one's health, and a defense of Buddhism. The format is a general statement followed by relevant citations from the classics and a few anecdotes, often from personal experience, which bear out the validity of the advice. Yen was addressing members of an elite who had easier access to official position because of nepotistic connections—he urged them to be educated and responsible, since reliance on family connections was too uncertain in times of disorder. The ideal he set forth was popular with the literati office-seekers of later ages who found office exactly through the education he advocated. From this work Yen can be seen to have been a person of meticulous scholarship, possessing high standards of integrity and a strong sense of responsibility toward his family and society, with a disdain for mere show and easy compromise. The edifying and moralizing comments were presented in a clear style and an interesting manner, affording the work a continuous popularity.

Yen's statements on literature emphasized control and clarity as opposed to spontaneity and purely literary considerations; some critics identify Yen as one of the earliest proponents of the *ku-wen** style. He has been also considered representative of the realism and moralism associated with the North, as against the southern tendency toward aesthetic considerations, but he certainly displays evidence of sensitivity to excellence in poetry, condemning only what he considers to be artificial and exaggerated.

Yen's descendants include his grandson Yen Shih-ku 顏師古 (581-645), the famous commentator on the *Han-shu* (see Pan Ku), and the more distant Yen Chen-ch'ing 顏眞卿 (709-785), the famous scholar and calligrapher of the T'ang, whose family stele, housed in the Pei-lin 碑林 in modern Sian, is an important source of information for the life of Yen Chih-t'ui.

EDITIONS:

Chou, Fa-kao 周法高, ed. *Yen-shih chia-hsün hui-chu* 顏氏家訓彙注. Taipei, 1960.

TRANSLATIONS:

Teng, Ssu-yü. *Family Instructions for the Yen Clan.* Leiden, 1968.

STUDIES:

Dien, Albert E. "Yen Chih-t'ui (531-591+): A Buddho-Confucian," in *Confucian Personalities*, pp. 43-64.

———. *Pei Ch'i shu 45: Biography of Yen Chih-t'ui.* Frankfurt, 1976.

———. "The *Yüan-hun chih* (Accounts of Ghosts with Grievances): A Sixth-Century Collection of Stories," in *Wen-lin*, pp. 211-228.

Hayashida, Shinnosuke 林田愼之助. "Gen Shisui no seikatsu to bungakukan" 顏之推の生活と文學觀, *Nihon Chūgoku Gakkaihō*, 14 (1962), 107-124.

Katsumura, Tetsuya 勝村哲邊. "Ganshi kakun kishin-hen to Enkon-shi o megutte" 顏氏家訓心篇と冤魂志をめぐつて, *Tōyōshi kenkyū*, 26 (1968), 350-362.

Kōzen, Hiroshi 興膳宏. "Gan Shisui no bungakuron" 顏之推の文學論, *Kaga Hakushi taikan kinen Chūgoku bunshitetsu ronshū* 加賀博士退官紀念中國文史哲論集, 1979.

Miao, Yüeh 繆鉞. "Yen Chih-t'ui nien-p'u 顏之推年譜," *Chen-li*, 1 (1944), 411-422.

Satō, Ichiro 佐藤一郎. "Gan Shisui den kenkyū" 顏之推傳研究, *Hokkaidō Daigaku Bungakubu kiyō*, 18.2 (1970), 1-23.

Utsunomiya, Kiyoyoshi 宇都宮清吉. "Gan Shisui no takuchidusu" 顏之推のタクチクス, in *Tamura hakushi shōju Tōyōshi ronsō* 田村博士頌壽東洋史論叢, Kyoto, 1968, pp. 71-88.

———. "Ganshi kakun kishin-hen oboegaki" 顏氏家訓婦心篇覺書, *Nagoya Daigaku Bungakubu kenkyū ronshū*, 44 (1967), 27-33.

———. "*Honku-Sei-sho* bun'en-den chū Gan Shisui-den no issetsu ni tsuite" 北齊書文苑傳中顏之推の一節について, *Nagoya daigaku bungakubu kenkyū ronshū*, 41 (1966), 47-63.

———. "Kanchū seikatsu o okuru Gan Shisui" 關中生活を送る顏之推, *Tōyōshi kenkyū*, 25 (1967), 509-519.

Yoshikawa, Tadao 吉川忠夫. "Gan Shisui shō-ron" 顏之推小論, *Tōyōshi kenkyū*, 20 (1962), 353-381.

—AED

Yen Fu 嚴復 (original *ming*, T'i-ch'ien 體乾, *tzu*, Yu-ling 又陵 and Tsung-kuang 宗光, *hao*,

Chi-tao 幾道, Yü-yeh lao-jen 癒壄老人, T'ien-yen che-hsüeh-chia 天演哲學家, etc., 1854-1921), translator extraordinary, educator, publicist, and poet, was born in Hou-kuan 候官 County, Foochow Prefecture (modern Fukien). In late T'ang times, the Yen family migrated to the small village of Yang-ch'i hsiang 陽屹鄉 (modern Fukien). Much later, Yen Fu's grandfather, Huan-jan 煥然, became a *chü-jen* in 1810 and served for a time as an education official. His father, Chen-hsien 振先, made his living as a practitioner of traditional medicine, but he apparently had other hopes for his son (his eldest son had died some years before), for he hired a live-in tutor, Huang Shao-yen 黃少巖, to instruct Yen Fu in the Confucian Classics and the rigorous examination-style essay. A stern disciplinarian, Huang introduced his young charge to the scholarship of the Sung and Han schools of learning, as well as the standard-school texts. Huang's death, followed shortly by that of Yen Fu's father, brought an abrupt end to Yen's education and a severe decline in the family's circumstances. His preparations for the civil-service examination degrees thus ended, a new and rather unexpected opportunity to continue his studies nevertheless soon presented itself.

Tso Tsung-t'ang 左宗棠 (1812-1885), shortly before his transfer to the north-west as Governor-general of Shensi and Kansu provinces, had recommended to the court that a modern shipyard and a naval academy be established in Foochow, and that Shen Pao-chen 沈葆楨 (1820-1879), like Yen Fu a native of Hou-kuan County, be entrusted with that responsibility. Under Shen's able leadership, both facilities were soon in operation. In 1867 Yen Fu passed the entrance examinations to the new naval academy, where he specialized in navigation. Thus began a five-year course of instruction in the English language, mathematics, modern sciences, and naval science. Throughout his years as a cadet, Yen Fu continued to study the Confucian Classics and the *pa-ku wen** essay style. He graduated in 1871 at the head of his class; there followed several years of training at sea and a period of detached duty on the personal staff of Shen Pao-chen, then the minister of naval affairs. In 1877, Yen Fu was one of twelve graduates of the Naval Academy selected for advanced professional training in Europe. He spent nearly two years at the Greenwich Naval College in England, where he received advanced instruction in mathematics, chemistry, physics, and naval science. In his free time, he schooled himself in English politics and social philosophy, seeking to discover the foundations of Western wealth and power. After his return to China, he taught for a time at his alma mater, and was then appointed dean of the newly founded Pei-yang Naval Academy in Tientsin. In 1889, he was named vice-chancellor of that institution, and one year later promoted to chancellor.

What must be regarded as a remarkably rapid advancement in his chosen profession apparently failed nonetheless to satisfy his yearning for a voice in the conduct of national affairs. Because a foreign-style education was still viewed with deep suspicion, he sought to remedy the situation by acquiring the traditional credentials for high office in the governmental bureaucracy; namely, the examination degrees. In 1885, Yen Fu purchased the *chien-jen* degree, which qualified him to participate in the *chü-jen* examinations. However, he failed to pass, and he fared no better on three subsequent attempts. Thus frustrated, he next turned his attention to writing and translation, which soon brought him the public visibility and influence he so much desired. During the mid- and late-1890s, he wrote a series of essays arguing the need for national reforms of a political, social and educational nature. These essays were initially published in Tientsin newspapers, and later in the influential *Shih-wu pao*. In 1898, his famous "Shang-huang-ti wan-yen shu" 上皇帝萬言書 (Ten Thousand Word Memorial) was published in the *Kuo-wen pao*. As a result, he was ordered to appear at court for an audience with the Kuang-hsü Emperor to discuss his recommendations. This was shortly before the Empress Dowager Tz'u-hsi 慈禧

(1835-1908) and her radically conservative allies terminated the so-called Hundred Days Reform Movement by a *coup d'etat.* Apparently forewarned, Yen Fu prudently withdrew to Tientsin, avoiding involvement in the swift retribution visited upon those officials who had been most intimately connected with the reform program.

Before these momentous events, Yen Fu had already begun a task which would claim much of his attention over the next decade, and as a result, firmly establish him as one of the two greatest translators of that era, the other being Lin Shu.* The task of translation was one for which he was eminently qualified by virtue of his solid command of English and his wide-ranging reading in modern Western philosophy and the social sciences. Heretofore, most translations of Western works belonged to the fields of science and technology. But with the upsurge of interest among young intellectuals in reform measures, what he was to accomplish in this realm would have a major impact on the minds of his own and later generations of readers anxious to learn about foreign social and political institutions and ideas. In 1897, his translation of and commentary on the first two chapters of Thomas Huxley's *Evolution and Ethics and Other Essays* appeared in the newspaper *Kuo-wen pao*, and the next year in book form. Wu Ju-lun 吳汝綸 (1840-1903), a reform-minded official and educator and a leading proponent of T'ung-ch'eng style classical prose (see *T'ung-ch'eng p'ai*), provided an introduction for this epochal work. Over the next ten years, there followed in quick order complete or partial translations with commentaries of Adam Smith's *An Enquiry into the Nature and Causes of the Wealth of Nations,* John Stuart Mill's *On Liberty,* Herbert Spencer's *Study of Sociology,* Edward Jenks's *A History of Politics,* Charles Louis Montesquieu's *De l'Esprit des Lois,* John Stuart Mill's *System of Logic,* and William S. Jevons's *Primer of Logic.* Yen Fu had concluded that the West's technological superiority was more a symptom than a cause of its sudden rise to prominence. As the titles of the books he selected for translation clearly suggest, he had come to believe that the exaltation of human physical, moral, and intellectual energies, the placement of heavy stress on the importance of the individual, constituted the wellspring of Western dynamism and success in modernization. These were values, he believed, that the Chinese would do well to emulate if they were to resist foreign aggression and ultimately claim their rightful place in the world. These ideas found an enthusiastic and appreciative audience among the younger generation, and his translations exerted a profound impact on the minds of many who were to become the future political and intellectual leaders of China. That his translations were couched in the laconic and difficult classical language would later prove to be a serious obstacle to their continuing popularity. Nevertheless, readers of his own day could appreciate his skillful use of the *ku-wen** idiom. As a translator, Yen Fu also made a lasting contribution to the language in the form of neologisms he coined to express foreign terms and concepts. Moreover, his experiences as a serious translator led to the development of a theory of translation. In his view, superior translation required that the translator achieve three goals: *hsin* 信 (fidelity to the original work), *ta* 達 (precision and intelligibility of language), and *ya* 雅 (elegance of style). This formulation of the problems and ideals of translation is still regarded as insightful and worthy of emulation.

Yen Fu's activities as a translator by no means occupied all of his energies during these years. After leaving the navy and resigning the chancellorship of the Peiyang Naval Academy in 1900, he took on a number of new responsibilities, including those of a member of the board of directors of the Kaiping Mining Company, the direction of a translation bureau at the Imperial University in Peking, then headed by Wu Ju-lun, and a role in promoting the study of logic. Still later, he accepted the position of principal of Fu-tan Academy in Shanghai, membership on an advisory council for political affairs in the imperial government (he had been named a *chin-shih* in 1909, thus providing him with the degree status he had so long desired), the chancellorship of Peking University during the early Republican era, and (still later) the role of an advisor on legal and foreign affairs to Yüan Shih-k'ai 袁世凱 (1859-1916). His failure to publicly oppose the latter's imperial ambitions in 1916 seriously impaired his standing among young intellectuals. At the same time, it signaled changes in his thinking that began with the collapse of the dynasty in 1911 and the outbreak of World War I a few years later. The latter event tended to undercut his commitment to a pro-Western liberal outlook, and thereafter he became increasingly conservative in his views, so that later he would lend his support to those seeking to establish Confucianism as a state religion, and oppose the vernacularization and westernization movements.

In 1916, somewhat embittered, Yen Fu retired from public life to devote his remaining years to antiquarian interests. His classical scholarship had already assumed tangible form in 1903 with the publication of his commentaries on the Wang Pi 王弼 (226-249) text of the *Tao-te-ching* (see *ching*): the *Yen-shih p'ing-tien Lao-tzu* 嚴氏評點老子. A similar study of another Taoist classic was completed and published during his years of retirement—the *Chuang-tzu p'ing-tien* 莊子評點 exemplified in part the degree to which the ancient past had become for him a sanctuary from the disappointing realities of contemporary life.

Yen Fu's skill as a poet in the classical manner is often noted but seldom explained in critical terms. He was not a prolific poet by normal standards, but small though his poetic corpus may be, it deserves more attention than it has yet received. His collected poems, the *Yü-yeh-t'ang shih-chi* 癒壄堂詩集, has until recently been difficult to obtain; however, selections from his *shih** poems have been reprinted from time to time along with his selected essays. Some of these poems are densely textured and verbally rich, while others are rather straightforward in manner and diction, as is the case with those poems more overtly autobiographical in nature. Yen Fu also cultivated the *tz'u** form, although only sparingly, if the few examples reproduced in *Yen Chi-tao Hsien-sheng i-chu* 嚴幾道先生遺著 are taken as representative of his total efforts in that direction. The product of fugitive moods, the *tz'u* poems are intrinsically less interesting than his other verse.

EDITIONS:

Chou, Chen-fu 周振甫, ed. *Yen Fu shih wen hsüan* 嚴復詩文選. Peking, 1957. Annotated selections of his essays and poems.

Nan-ching Ta-hsüeh Li-shih Hsi 南京大學歷史系, comp. *Yen Fu shih wen hsüan-chu* 選注. Kiangsu, 1975. Annotated selections of his essays and poems.

Nan-yang Hsüeh-hui yen-chiu 南洋學會研究, comp. *Yen Chi-tao Hsien-sheng i-chu* 嚴幾道先生遺著. Singapore, 1959. Includes some of his essays and *tz'u* poems.

Shen, Yün-lung 沈雲龍, ed. *Hou-kuan Yen-shih ts'ung-k'e* 侯官嚴氏叢刻. Taipei, n.d. Reprint of his early essays and the *nien-p'u* by Wang Ch'ü-ch'ang listed below.

———. *Yen Chi-tao shih wen ch'ao* 詩文鈔. Taipei, n.d. Reprint of selected essays and poems.

Yü-yeh-t'ang shih-chi 癒壄堂詩集. Rpt. Taipei, 1980.

STUDIES:

BDRC, v. 4, pp. 41-47.

Chou, Chen-fu. *Yen Fu ssu-hsiang shu-p'ing* 嚴復思想述評. Shanghai, 1940.

ECCP, p. 643.

Hsia, C. T. "Yen Fu and Liang Ch'i-ch'ao as Advocates of New Fiction," in *Chinese Approaches*, pp. 221-257.

Liu, Fu-pen 劉富本. *Yen Fu te fu-ch'iang ssu-hsiang* 嚴復的富強思想. Taipei, 1977. Especially pp. 98-100 for a full listing of Yen Fu's translations and scholarly works, and pp. 101-108 for a bibliography of secondary sources.

Schwartz, Benjamin. *In Search of Wealth and Power, Yen Fu and the West.* Cambridge, Mass., 1964. An excellent and insightful study.

Wang, Ch'ü-ch'ang 王蘧常. *Yen Chi-tao nien-p'u* 嚴幾道年譜. Shanghai, 1936.

Wang, Shih 王栻. *Yen Fu chuang* 嚴復傳. Shanghai, 1957.

—ws

Yen-shan wai-shih 燕山外史 (The Tale of a Yen-shan Scholar) is a short novel in *p'ien-wen** (parallel prose) by Ch'en Chiu 陳球 (*tzu*, Yün-chai 蘊齋, *fl.* 1808). It is an interesting attempt to adapt the euphuistic-prose style to narrative and recalls the example set earlier by Chang Tsu's* *Yu hsien-k'u* (although Ch'en probably never knew of the existence of the T'ang work). As such, the text is often looked upon as an instance of the brief resurgence of parallel prose in the Ch'ing dynasty, but it also merits consideration merely as a narrative.

The work does not tell an original story; it re-presents in parallel prose the story told in the Ming writer Feng Meng-chen's 馮夢楨 (1546-1605) tale "Tou-sheng chuan" 竇生傳, a work of the *ts'ai-tzu chia-jen** type written in classical Chinese. Relating primarily the love affair and marriage of Tou Sheng-tsu 竇繩祖 and Li Ai-ku 李愛姑, it also contains, in addition to the essential ingredients of the "scholar and beauty" story, many other motifs taken from other related genres. Its plot follows the conventional pattern closely: an initial meeting is succeeded by a separation (in this case caused by a family-arranged marriage forced on the hero by his father). Finally there is a reunion after certain complications have been resolved. In the "complication" and "resolution" portions of the text are incorporated the motifs and narrative situations that seem to reflect the influence of earlier and contemporary fiction and drama. Before the reunion can be achieved, for example, the heroine is made to suffer many trials and hardships, such as a period in a brothel, subjection to malicious treatment by the hero's jealous, wicked wife, and refuge in a nunnery. Some episodes concerning a friend of the hero's are suggestive of the knight-errantry motif, and at the end of the story the topos of Taoist enlightenment is introduced to top off the happy ending. This source story is thus a variation on an established form by accretion of extra elements and represents the evolution of a narrative form in a cumulative mode.

By retelling such an accretive story, *Yen-shan wai-shih* has directed its narrative energy to a different process than that normally required of a narrative (such as selection, invention, and arrangement of events). The creative imagination is shown mainly in the derivation that elaborates the given story by means of a new form of expression. The elaboration operations most frequently employed in the text can be summarized as of three types: that of concretization (i.e., dramatization of an abstract or general term in the source text), that of "filling out" of details (i.e., making explicit the information implied in the original), and finally, that of supplementation of extra information neither implied nor inferrable from the original. Generally these operations have the effect of creating new thematic emphases and narrative foci in the derivative text. Parallelism, even on the sentence level, also has a tendency to put the narrated events into a paired relationship, thus making each event a part of a situation rather than allowing it to be perceived as a unique happening.

Utilization of a ready-made story implies a literary principle on which parallel prose itself is based. By transforming the source material into a new form of expression with new import, *Yen-shan wai-shih* is using an existing system of signification for the purpose of its own system of meaning, while the use of allusions and literary phrases in *p'ien-wen* is similarly an adaptation of old elements into a new context. This re-working and transformation of elements from the past tradition, as well as the re-channeling of the creative energy, embodies a fundamental nature of the literary activity, as literature seems to evolve through reinterpretation and transformation of the more constant of the elements in its own tradition.

Yen-shan wai-shih is often criticized for being inept as a piece of literary work, but the criticism fails to take into consideration its synthesizing nature and its peculiar form of creativity. Insipid to the modern taste, the work nevertheless sheds light on an integrating tendency of the literary development (cf. drama in the Chinese tradition) and may be profitably studied from that perspective.

EDITIONS:
Yen-shan wai-shih. 2 *chüan.* Ōhashi Atsushi 大橋穆, annot. Tokyo, 1878; rpt. Tokyo, *c.* 1907-1911; both in Naikaku Bunkō.
Yen-shan wai-shih. 2 *chüan.* Shanghai, 1938. With a preface by Wu Chan-ch'eng 吳展成 (1811). The edition contains the text of "Tou-sheng chuan" and annotations indicating the locus classicus of most allusions; it is more easily available in later reprints.

—KK

Yen Shu 晏殊 (*tzu*, T'ung-shu 同叔, 991-1055), was the elder of the "Two Yens" of Northern Sung *tz'u** poetry. Together with his son, Yen Chi-tao,* and his fellow scholar-official, Ou-yang Hsiu,* Yen Shu carried on the late T'ang *Hua-chien chi** and Five Dynasties style. His verse is often said to be particularly influenced by the elegant *tz'u* poetry of Feng Yen-ssu,* a Grand Councilor of the Southern T'ang state.

Yen Shu was born in Lin-ch'uan 臨川 (modern Kiangsi), which had been part of the Southern T'ang kingdom. He was a prodigy, at the age of fourteen earning the *chin-shih* degree and receiving his first official position. Though he came from a relatively poor family, Yen Shu was well educated, and became a successful Confucian scholar-official. Many anecdotes recorded in the *Sung-shih* 宋史 (History of the Sung Dynasty) attest to his talent and tact as a diplomatic statesman. His moderation and sense of justice enabled him to advance quickly, and when he was appointed Grand Councilor at the age of forty-four, he became one of the few southerners to achieve high rank in the Northern Sung court. Dismissed at age fifty-four for offenses which remain unclear, Yen Shu spent the last ten years of his life traveling and serving in provincial positions.

Yen Shu's poetry consistently reflects elite literati taste. His home became a literary salon, in which scholar-officials mingled with singing girls; their poetry expressd their sophisticated aristocratic lifestyle of leisure and luxury. It was traditionally believed that Yen Shu's elegant style of writing *tz'u* in the shorter *hsiao-ling* form had flourished before Liu Yung's*

development of the more colloquial *tz'u* in the longer *man-tz'u* form, but recent scholarship has revealed that the two schools coexisted at the same time. Yen Shu represented the affluent conservative literati who resisted Liu Yung's* innovations in the popular style.

Yen Shu's 137 *tz'u* poems in his collection *Chu-yü tz'u* 珠玉詞 (Pearls and Jade) primarily use the two-stanza form and employ many of the tunes used in the Southern T'ang. They are noteworthy for their emotional restraint and subtlety. Exquisite imagery and delicate suggestivity create a graceful effect. Aristocratic decorum is balanced by personal equanimity in a setting of self-conscious luxury and good taste. Though there are few obligatory court poems, most of the *tz'u* in *Pearls and Jade* are on love. In some Yen Shu's work is gracefully fluent, musical, and slightly colloquial, not burdened by allusions or intensity. The mood is often tinged with melancholy, but tempered by a balanced sense of resignation and even philosophical understanding.

An illustration of Yen Shu's acceptance of both the beauty of the moment and the sorrow of its inevitable passing is the second stanza of his *tz'u* to the tune "*Huan-hsi sha*" 浣溪沙 (Sands of the Washing Stream):

> Mountains and rivers as far as I can see;
> In vain I recall what is beyond them.
> Amidst the fallen flowers in wind and rain
> One grieves even more for spring.
> The best thing is to love the one who's here before my eyes.

This verse is more than a sequence of conventional images for the end of spring and longing for a distant lover: in each line there is a delicately suggested tension between the immediate and the remote, the present and the past; the pattern of these contrasts reinforces the idea that, ironically, one longs most for the lost lover or season when it is most unattainable.

Yen Shu rose to prominence under the peaceful reigns of Emperors Chen-tsung (998-1022) and Jen-tsung (1023-1063), but his luxurious lifestyle and the untroubled era do not sufficiently account for the elegant refinement and smooth delicacy of his verse. The combination of his nostalgic interest in the traditional *Hua-chien chi*-Southern T'ang style and his thoughtful and diplomatic temperament also contributes to the balanced poise and gracefulness of his poetic work.

EDITIONS:
Chu-yü tz'u chiao-ting chien-chi 珠玉詞校訂箋注. Chang Shao-to 張紹鐸, ed. Rpt. n.p., 1971.
Erh Yen tz'u hsüan-chu 二晏詞選注. Hsia Ching-kuan 夏敬觀, ed. Taipei, 1965.
Yen Yüan-hsien i-wen 晏元獻遺文, in *Sung erh-shih chia chi* 宋二十家集, v. 17.

TRANSLATIONS:
Sunflower, pp. 310-311.
Liu, *Lyricists*, pp. 17-34.

STUDIES:
Wan, Min-hao 宛敏顥. *Erh Yen chi ch'i tz'u* 二晏及其詞. Shanghai, 1934. Praises Yen Chi-tao and disparages Yen Shu.
Yeh, Chia-ying 葉嘉瑩. "An Appreciation of the *Tz'u* of Yen Shu" 大晏詞的欣賞, James R. Hightower, trans., *Renditions*, 11/12 (Spring/Autumn 1979), 83-99. Reacting against Wan Min-hao, praises Yen Shu as a mature, intellectual poet.

—MW

Yen Tan-tzu 燕丹子 or *Yen T'ai-tzu Tan* 燕太子丹 (Prince Tan of Yen), in three *chüan* and of unknown authorship, has long been considered a rare piece of fiction handed down to us from as early as the second century B.C. Concerning the adventures of the well-known political assassin Ching K'o 荆軻 and particularly his attempt on the life of the King of Ch'in 秦王政 (r. 246-210 B.C.), this account is closely parallel to the biography of Ching K'o in Ssu-ma Ch'ien's* *Shih-chi*.* What makes it significantly different and gives it a distinctively fictional character are the abundance of fantastic and supernatural elements, the extremity of exaggeration, and the absurdity with which Prince Tan, Ching K'o's patron, bends to take his revenge on the King of Ch'in for personal abuse. Ching K'o's eccentric behavior and his demand of lavish, and largely unreasonable, hospitality from the prince also mark him not as an itinerant knight-errant eager to right wrongs, but as one relentlessly seeking a high price for his service. As seen in the *Yen Tan-tzu*, Ching K'o's is an expensive "hired gun" and an incompetent one at that.

Yen Tan-tzu has a problematic textual history. First registered in the dynastic history *Sui-shu* and later quoted by Li Shan in annotating the *Wen-hsüan*,* by Chang Shou-i 張守義 (T'ang) in commentating the *Shih-chi*, and in the T'ang encyclopedia *Pei-t'ang shu-ch'ao* 北堂書鈔 (Excerpts from Books in the Northern Hall), this work must have been composed before the T'ang period. However, it had become fairly rare by the Ming. The Ch'ing scholar Sun Hsing-yen 孫星 (1753-1818) resurrected it from the *Yung-lo ta-tien* (see *lei-shu*) and restored the text on the basis of various previous quotations. All modern editions of the work are based on Sun's version, in which serious textual problems still exist, particularly toward the end.

This textual situation complicates dating. Those who believed that the work could be pre-Han and might have served as the basis of the Ching K'o biography in the *Shih-chi* include such eminent figures as Sung Lien,* Sun Hsing-yen, Chou Chung-fu 周中孚 (1768-1831), T'an Hsien 譚獻 (1830-1901), and Lu Hsün 魯迅 (Chou Shu-jen 周樹人, 1881-1936). In view of the stylistic sophistication of the work, however, it is unlikely that it indeed dates from such antiquity. More conservative views were expressed by Li Tz'u-ming 李慈銘 (1830-1894), Hu Yü-chin 胡玉縉 (d. 1940), and Yü Chia-hsi 余嘉錫 (1883-1955), who considered it a work composed before the Southern Dynasties (prior to 420). Some scholars simply declare it a forgery without providing evidence, while the authoritative *Ssu-k'u ch'üan-shu tsung-mu t'i-yao* (see Chi Yün) regards it a mere patchwork. The first modern scholar to make an extensive study of the work was Lo Ken-tse 羅根澤 (1900-1960). The overwhelming evidence he presented in a 1929 study should at least underscore the doubts about the origin and antiquity of the work. Kuo Wei-hsin 郭維新

reexamined the issue (1947) and confirmed Lo's finding that the *Yen Tan-tzu* was composed during the Southern Ch'i dynasty. Unfortunately these studies have not received the attention they deserve and *Yen Tan-tzu* has repeatedly been referred to in later studies and translations as a unique example of pre-Han fiction.

Despite a compositional date much later than previously assumed, *Yen Tan-tzu*, with its stylistic strength and expression of the Chinese concept of reciprocation, still stands as fine example of early (Six Dynasties) fiction.

EDITIONS:

Yen Tan-tzu, in *P'ing-chin kuan ts'ung-shu* 平津館叢書, Sun Hsing-yen, ed., *PPTSCC*. Recommended text.

TRANSLATIONS:

Franke, Herbert. *Prinz Tan von Yen: Eine chinesische Novelle aus der Chan-kuo-Zeit.* Zurich, 1969.

Rushton, Peter. "Prince Tan of Yen," in *Traditional Chinese Stories*, pp. 43-49.

STUDIES:

Franke, Herbert. "Die Geschichte des Prinzen Tan von Yen," *ZDMG*, 107.2 (1957), 412-425.

Lo, Ken-tse. "Yen Tan-tzu chen-wei nien-tai k'ao" 燕丹子眞偽年代考, *Chung-shan Ta-hsüeh Yü-yen Li-shih-hsüeh Yen-chiu-so chou-k'an*, 78 (April 1929), 23-31. Also under title of "Yen Tan-tzu chen-wei nien-tai chih chiu-shuo yü hsin-k'ao" 燕丹子眞偽年代之舊說與新考 in Lo Ken-tse, *Chu-tzu k'ao-so* 諸子考索, Peking, 1958, pp. 416-421.

Kuo, Wei-hsin. "*Yen Tan-tzu* k'ao-lüeh" 燕丹子考略, *Hsüeh-i*, 17.11 (November 1947), 14-20.

—YWM

Yen Yen-chih 顏延之 (*tzu*, Yen-nien 延年, 384-456) was ranked together with Hsieh Ling-yün* by early literary critics as one of the two greatest poets of the Yüan-chia period (424-453). Yen as also an essayist of some distinction and served as an official in a period of considerable chaos.

Yen was born near present-day Nanking where he pursued an official career, though his family hailed from Lin-i 臨沂 (modern Shantung). Orphaned in early youth, he took to books with a great voracity and soon achieved distinction through his own writing. The destitution of his early years taught him to be frugal and practical, yet led him to take an almost unnatural (for his own day and society) pride in his own achievements. At thirty he remained unmarried. He had, at the time, a chance to enter officialdom, but refused to exercise the option—a rejection of nepotism rarely found in the annals of Chinese intellectual history.

During a military campaign launched against the north by Liu Yü 劉裕, Emperor Wu of the Sung (r. 420-422), Yen composed, near the overgrown ruins of the former imperial palace at Lo-yang, two verses in the vein of Shelley's "Ozymandias," which won him great acclaim. By his late thirties, the emperor had already bestowed upon him the title of Secretary of the Heir Apparent. Subsequent to this he held, at various times throughout the reigns of four Liu Sung emperors, several coveted bureaucratic appointments.

Yen was eventually implicated, along with Hsieh Ling-yün, in an abortive attempt to support the Prince of Lu-ling 盧陵王 for succession to the throne (422). He was banished to a post as Governor of Yung-chia 永嘉, where he composed the brooding verses "Wu-chün yung" 五君詠 (In Praise of Five of the Seven Sages of the Bamboo Grove), which placed him in further danger and distinction. Several of the concluding couplets from these poems were intended as a mirror of his own misfortunes, seen through the fates of past worthies:

> Egrets' plumage at times can ruffle,
> But your dragon-like nature bent to no man.
>   [In Praise of Hsi K'ang]
> He spoke naught of worldly affairs,
> Yet would weep at the end of a road.
>   [In Praise of Juan Chi]
> Repeated recommendations never resulted in office,
> But one wave dispatched you to far-off exile.
>   [In Praise of Juan Hsien]
> Talent concealed in the depths of daily drinking,
> Who can discern your true reasons for dissipation?
>   [In Praise of Liu Ling]

Since he clearly identified with the figures praised, the poems infuriated Yen's enemies, but he was shielded from their wrath by Emperor Wen.

After biding his time in exile, Yen was eventually restored to favor and lived until his seventy-third year. Upon his death he was granted the posthumous title of *Hsien* 憲 (Exemplary).

Pao Chao* once told Yen: "Hsieh Ling-yün's verse in pentasyllabics is natural in its beauty—like a lotus in its early stages poking its head up above the water. Yours is a verse of well-arranged fineries, with more decorative embroidery than can meet the eye." History has dealt even more harshly with Yen's ornate and formalistic style, his emphasis on technique at the expense of mood. Although his reputation has since suffered because of his florid style, it should be remembered that when the ancients wrote poetry, they hoped to induce the reader to contemplate the meaning of a line on several levels. In this, Yen is certainly no failure. It is a pity that only twenty-four of his poems are now extant. His works were originally compiled into a volume entitled *Yen Kuang-lu chi* 顏光祿集 (Works of Yen, Grand Master of the Palace). He and Shen Yüeh* were among the earliest annotators of Juan Chi's* "Yung-huai shih."

EDITIONS:
Nan-Pei-ch'ao shih, "Ch'üan Sung shih" 全宋詩, v. 2, *ch.* 2, pp. 777-789. Contains twenty-four poems by Yen.
Chu, Tung-jun 朱東潤. *Chung-kuo li-tai wen-hsüeh tso-p'in hsüan* 中國歷代文學作品選. 4v. Shanghai, n.d. Contains (v. 1, pp. 344-348) Yen's poems in honor of five of the Seven Sages of the Bamboo Grove; texts are based on an early woodblock edition of the *Wen-hsüan**; heavy annotation.

TRANSLATIONS:
Frodsham, *Anthology*, pp. 157-158.

—JK

Yin-feng-ko tsa-chü 吟風閣雜劇 (Variety Plays of the Poetry-chanting Tower) is a collection of thirty-two one-act plays by Yang Ch'ao-kuan 楊潮觀 (*tzu*, Hung-tu 宏度, *hao*, Li-hu 笠湖, 1712-1791). Yang was a native

of Wu-hsi 無錫 (Kiangsu) and, from childhood on, a close friend of the poet Yüan
Mei.* His literary talent was recognized
early, but after taking the *chü-jen* degree
he entered into an official career that was
to last until his retirement at age seventy.
He spent most of his later years serving as
magistrate of various counties in Szechwan. "Yin-feng ko" was a tower he built
in Ch'iung-chou 邛州, Szechwan, on the
supposed site of the abode of Cho Wen-
chün 卓文君, Ssu-ma Hsiang-ju's* wife.
Yang came at the end of a long line of late
Ming and early Ch'ing writers who excelled in the short play form, including Hsü
Wei,* Yu T'ung,* Hsi Yung-jen,* and Kuei
Fu.* According to most critics, Yang was
the greatest artist in this genre.

As is often the case with short plays from
this period, many were not suited for performance. But they are tightly structured
and always eminently readable for their
brisk, lively, and often humorous dialogue.
Though the plots of these plays are based
mostly on anecdotes of well-known historical figures, Yang's imaginative handling
of these old materials gives them a delightful freshness and a new dimension.

Traditionally, his best piece of work is
considered to be "K'ou-lai kung ssu-ch'in
pa-yen" 寇萊公思親罷晏 (Remembering His
Mother, Lord K'ou-lai Calls off the Banquet), a moving play which celebrates filial
piety and the virtue of frugality. According to Chiao Hsün's 焦循 (1763-1820) *Chü-
shuo* 劇說 (Notes on Plays—a collection of
notes on music and drama), the scholar-
statesman Juan Yüan 阮元 (1764-1849)
while Governor of Chekiang, saw this play
and was so moved that he also called off a
scheduled banquet. Another play in the
collection, "Han-tan chün ts'o-chia ts'ai-
jen" 邯鄲郡錯嫁才人 (A Mismarriage in Han-
tan) is noteworthy for its powerful pathos
created by a juxtaposition of dream and
reality. This work is all the more remarkable for its unusual brevity—it is only two
and a half printed pages long.

To most modern critics, however, comedy rather than tragedy is Yang's forte.
His humor is never facetious or coarse—
all his plays have a guiding moral purpose

set forth in a prefatory remark. Yang had
the talent of making morality entertaining
without trivializing it. In his best comedies,
the comic elements often depend on the
moral lesson for their effect. This can be
most clearly seen in "Chi Ch'ang-ju chiao-
chao fa-ts'ang" 汲長濡矯詔發倉 (Chi Ch'ang-
ju Opens the Granaries by Forging an Imperial Edict). Among his successful comedies are "T'ou-t'ao chuo-chu Tung-fang
Shuo" 偷桃捉住東方朔 (Tung-fang Shuo
Caught Stealing Peaches), "Huang-shih P'o
shou-chi t'ao-kuan" 黃石婆授計逃關 (Stealing through the Mountain Pass by
Grandma Huang-shih's Strategy), and
"Hsi-sai shan yü-weng feng-pai" 西塞漁翁
封拜 (The Old Fisherman of West-border
Mountain Accepts an Honorary Title).

Unique in this collection is a play which
addresses the question of the compatibility
of Confucianism, Taoism, and Buddhism:
"Han Wen-kung hsüeh-yung Lan-kuan"
韓文公雪擁藍關 (Han Wen-kung at a Snow-
bound Lan-kuan). In this play, Han Yü,*
a disgraced Confucian official, and Han
Hsiang-tzu, a Taoist immortal, argue their
beliefs with equal eloquence and cogency.
In the end neither convinces the other.
The transcendental view of religion, an
implicit theme of the play, is by no means
original, but it is treated with a degree of
sophistication rarely encountered in literary works.

EDITIONS:

Yin-feng ko tsa-chü. Ch'ia-hao ch'u 恰好處 ed.,
1764.
——. Wu-wai shan-fang 屋外山房 ed. 1820.
——. Liu-i shu-chü 六藝書局 ed., Shanghai,
1913, based on Hsieh-yün lou 寫韻樓 hand-
copied version.
——. Hu Shih-ying 胡士瑩 collated and annotated edition, Shanghai, 1963; the most
useful modern edition, but it contains only
thirty of the plays.

STUDIES:

Chou, Miao-chung 周妙中. "Yang Ch'ao-kuan
ho t'a te *Yin-feng ko*"楊潮觀和他的吟風閣, *Wen-
hsüeh i-ch'an tseng-k'an*, 9 (June 1962), 43-61.
Chu, Hsiang 朱湘. "Yin-feng ko," in *Chung-kuo
wen-hsüeh yen-chiu* 中國文學研究, Cheng Chen-
to, ed., rpt. Hong Kong, 1969, pp. 478-480.
Fu, *Ch'ing tsa-chü*, pp. 118-149.

Tseng, "Ch'ing-tai tsa-chü," pp. 164-187.

—JW and PTH

Yin K'eng 陰鏗 (*tz'u*, Tzu-chien 子堅, *fl.* mid-sixth century) was a leading poet in a period which saw a flourishing of literary activity amidst civil disorder and dynastic change. Very little is known of his life except that he was born in Wu-wei 武威 (modern Kansu), served in various capacities under both the Liang and the Ch'en dynasties, and rose eventually to a position as prefect. A short biography in the *Nan-shih* 南史 (History of the Southern Dynasties) notes he was well-read in the histories and adept at pentasyllabic verse. He is said to have left behind three collections of literary writings, of which only thirty-five poems remain.

Yin K'eng wrote in a period which is known as the age of *kung-t'i shih** (palace-style poetry), and his surviving works clearly reflect the force of this tradition. About one third of his extant works belongs to the categories of *ying-chih* 應制 (poems written on imperial command), *yung-wu* 詠物 (poems on objects), and *kuei-yüan* 閨怨 (poems on boudoir sorrow), all of which were standard in mid-sixth century *kung-t'i shih*. His work often exhibits considerable originality, especially in the *yung-wu* genre. Unlike most *yung-wu* poetry from the period, Yin K'eng's "poems on objects" tend to deal with reminders of the seasons and are charged with a strong undercurrent of feeling, showing a sensibility which transcends the limitations of the palace style.

What distinguishes Yin K'eng are his landscape and many travel poems which are structured around the mode of *huai-ku* 懷古 (meditation on things past). Neither verse-type was his invention, but he brought to both an emotional realism and an attention to descriptive detail rarely seen in works by his predecessors or contemporaries. His *huai-ku* poems were among the earliest efforts in pre-T'ang poetry to blend the *ubi sunt* motif with descriptions of actual landscape, a procedure which helped to define the *huai-ku* mode as an independent subgenre in classical Chinese

poetry. In addition, Yin K'eng is also remembered for playing a key role in the development of *chin-t'i* 近體 (modern style) poetry during the sixth century. While none of his extant poems qualifies as "modern style" in the strict sense, some bear sufficient resemblance to the latter in their relative brevity, their tonal and rhythmic harmony, and their ample use of parallel structures.

As a key figure in the development of the *chin-t'i* verse, Yin K'eng was well appreciated by traditional critics and Tu Fu,* who ranked him as one of the most accomplished poets from the Six Dynasties.

EDITIONS:

Ch'üan Ch'en shih 全陳詩, in *Nan-pei-ch'ao shih*, v. 3, pp. 1622-1630.
Yin Ch'ang-shih shih-chi 陰常侍詩集, in *Erh-yu-t'ang ts'ung-shu* 二酉堂叢書 [also known as *Chang-shih ts'ung-shu* 張氏叢書], v. 11, Chang Chu 張澍, comp., 1821.
———. *TSCCCP*, v. 2219.

TRANSLATIONS:

Demiéville, *Anthologie*, p. 164.
Frodsham, *Anthology*, pp. 179-181.

—SSW

Yin Shu 尹洙 (*tzu*, Shih-lu 師魯, 1001-1047), scholar and military adviser, was a key transmitter of the *ku-wen** prose movement begun in the ninth century by Han Yü.* He is said to have inspired Ou-yang Hsiu* to employ *ku-wen* instead of *p'ien-wen** in prose writing. Yin was from Ho-nan 河南 (modern Lo-yang), a major cultural center, and is often referred to as "Ho-nan Hsien-sheng" 河南先生 (Mr. Ho-nan).

Born into a family of officials, he passed the *chin-shih* 進士 examination in 1024 and served the first six years of his career in minor provincial posts mostly close to his native city. In 1030 he was allowed to take a special qualifying examination and, as a result, was promoted to the office of Prefect in I-yang 伊揚 County south of Lo-yang.

This post proved important for it enabled him to associate with other talented, young officials, and to enjoy with them the patronage of the administrator of the greater Lo-yang area, Ch'ien Wei-yen,* an influential scholar, poet and politician. Among the men Yin met at this time were Ou-yang Hsiu and the poet Mei Yao-ch'en.*

In 1034, through the recommendation of his immediate superior, Yin Shu began a two-year tour of duty in the capital, Kai-feng, where he wrote several of his best-known military policy statements (in *ku-wen* style) including "Shu Yen" 紋燕 (Discussing the Yen Area) and "Hsi shu" 息戍 (On Stopping Frontier Defense). Yin Shu's close association with the reformist political figures Fan Chung-yen,* Han Ch'i 韓琦 (1008-1075), and Fu Pi 富弼 (1004-1083) also dates from this time. Because Fan Chung-yen attacked members of the imperial government (1036), he and his supporters, including Yin Shu, were banished from the capital.

Yin Shu's fortunes improved in 1038 when he (along with most of Fan's clique) was recalled to help the government put down the rebellion of the Hsi-hsia leader Chao Yüan-hao 趙元昊 (1003-1048). Yin Shu, Han Ch'i, and Fan Chung-yen served at the war front in what is now Kansu, where Yin wrote many well-received discussions on tactics and on war strategy (again, in *ku-wen*). This earned him a promotion (1043) to Director of Administration for the Ching and Yüan 涇原 Routes and to Prefect of Wei-chou 渭州 (modern P'ing-liang 平凉). His career was probably furthered when Fan Chung-yen began his short-lived program to reform the central government and civil service in 1043 and 1044. But, when Fan and his supporters were demoted (1044), Yin Shu was impeached by a rival and removed from his post.

The following year a zealous censor uncovered some financial irregularities in Yin Shu's administration of Wei-chou, and Yin was reduced to the post of Supervisor of Liquor Taxes at Chün-chou 均州 (Hupei). His health began to fail, and in 1047, while visiting nearby Nan-yang 南陽 (modern Teng-hsien 鄧縣) to seek medical help through Fan Chung-yen, he died. Ten years afterwards, Ou-yang Hsiu petitioned the emperor to exonerate Yin and to give him a posthumous promotion. Both measures were carried out.

In Yin Shu's day, *p'ien-wen* was still required form on the civil-service examinations and in government documents. There were only a few Sung heirs to the ninth-century *ku-wen* movement: Liu K'ai 柳開 (947-1000), Mu Hsiu 穆修 (979-1032), and Cheng T'iao 鄭條 (*chin-shih*, 1030) are most often mentioned. None of these men seems to have been considered as important as Yin, whose role in fostering *ku-wen* was argued by some very influential contemporaries. Fan Chung-yen maintained that Yin Shu was the true founder of the Sung-dynasty *ku-wen* movement (though Yin may have learned of Han Yü's *ku-wen* writings through Mu Hsiu and Cheng T'iao, with whom he is said to have associated). Ou-yang Hsiu, who had admired *ku-wen* style as a youth, said he only began to practice this kind of writing after seeing a piece written by Yin Shu when both were visiting their patron Ch'ien Wei-yen. After 1057, Ou-yang Hsiu went on to establish *ku-wen* as the dominant prose style when he required it on the civil-service examination for that year.

Ou-yang Hsiu described Yin Shu's style as terse and straightforward like the *Ch'un-ch'iu* (see *ching*). In fact, Yin wrote a history of the Five Dynasties period in the manner of the *Ch'un-ch'iu* (entitled *Wu-tai ch'un-ch'iu* 五代春秋). Yin's importance as a *ku-wen* stylist, however, was not recognized after Ou-yang Hsiu's time, perhaps because his style was too much like that of the *Ch'un-ch'iu*, too terse, too limited to policy statements—without the depth and breadth of applications developed by the great eleventh-century *ku-wen* masters such as Ou-yang Hsiu himself. Yin was overshadowed by men who would be counted among the *T'ang Sung pa-ta san-wen chia* (see Han Yü). None of his writings appear in the important eighteenth century *ku-wen* anthology, *Ku-wen tz'u lei-tsuan,** either. His extant writings consist mostly of letters and policy statements written between 1034 and 1044.

EDITIONS:
Yin, Shu. *Ho-nan Hsien-sheng wen-chi* 河南先生文集. *SPTK*. Preface by Fan Chung-yen; *chüan* 28 includes descriptions of his life and works.

STUDIES:

Liu, James T. C. *Ou-yang Hsiu: An Eleventh-Century Neo-Confucianist*, Stanford, 1967, pp. 26-27, 106-107, 141-154, 170-171.

SB, pp. 1255-1257.

T'ang Sung wen chü-yao 唐宋文舉要. Kao Pu-ying 高步瀛, ed., Peking, 1963, v. 2, pp. 659-665. Extensively annotated text of tomb inscription by Ou-yang Hsiu.

—BL

Yin Yün 殷芸 (*tzu*, Kuan-su 灌蔬, 471-529), of Ch'en-ch'ün 陳郡 (in modern Honan), was one of the scholars in Hsiao T'ung's (see *Wen-hsüan*) famous literary entourage. He studied diligently and had the reputation of an encyclopedic reader. Sometime between 514 and 516 Emperor Wu of the Liang dynasty (r. 502-549) assigned Yin Yün to compile a collection of anecdotes left out in the standard histories. This collection is called the *Hsiao-shuo* 小說, but is generally known as *Yin Yün hsiao-shuo* to avoid confusion with the generic term *hsiao-shuo*.* It is also known as the *Liang Wu hsiao-shuo* 梁武小說, because of its imperial sponsorship, and the *Shang Yün hsiao-shuo* 商芸小說 in the Sung dynasty when "yin" was a taboo work for the imperial Chao family.

The *Hsiao-shuo*, recorded in the bibliographic treatise of the *Sui-shu*, as of ten *chüan*, is now lost. Fortunately, both Ch'ao Tsai-chih's 晁載之 (twelfth century) *Hsü T'an chu* 續談助 and T'ao Tsung-i's* *Shuo-fu* have quoted it extensively, apparently in the original sequence. Aided by quotations from other sources, Lu Hsün 魯迅 (Chou Shu-jen 周樹人, 1881-1936), Yü Chia-hsi 余嘉錫 (1883-1955) and T'ang Lan 唐蘭 (1900-1979) all attempted to reconstruct the original text. Both Yü and T'ang consulted Lu Hsün's compilation, but worked independently. With 154 items, Yü's compilation has three additional items and is slightly better annotated.

With the exception of the first *chüan* which is devoted to the rulers from the Ch'in to the Liu Sung dynasties, the other nine *chüan* are arranged chronologically from the Chou to the Ch'i. It is not an original work, but rather a selection of choice anecdotes from various sources. In fact, a special feature of the *Hsiao-shuo* is Yin Yün's indication of his individual sources—many writers, especially those of tales, copied from one another without acknowledgment. Consequently, *Hsiao-shuo* is useful for collating and reconstructing the various works from which it was derived. Of these sources, the *Shih-shuo hsin-yü*,* with twenty-two items, appears to have been the most important. *Yü lin* 語林, *Hsi-ching tsa-chi*,* and *I yüan* 異苑 come next, with nine, eight and seven items respectively. These figures underline the two main concerns of the collection: legends about famous people and supernatural stories. It also shows that the term *hsiao-shuo* had a more restricted meaning in the Six Dynasties than its present usage as a generic term for fiction.

A poem and an incomplete letter by Yin Yün have survived. It is also likely that Yin Yün took part in the compilation of the *Wen-hsüan*.*

EDITIONS:

"Hsiao-shuo," Lu Hsün, ed., in *Ku hsiao-shuo kuo-ch'en* 古小說鉤沈, in *Lu Hsün Ch'üan-chi*, Shanghai, 1938, v. 8, pp. 203-234. This compilation is superseded by the following two.

T'ang, Lan. "Chi Yin Yün *Hsiao-shuo* ping pa" 輯殷芸小說并跋, in *Chou Shu-t'ao Hsien-sheng liu-shih sheng-jih chi-nien lun-wen chi* 周叔發先生六十生日紀念論文集, Tientsin, 1950; rpt. Hong Kong, 1967, pp. 191-229.

Yü, Chia-hsi. "Yin Yün *Hsiao-shuo* chi-cheng" 殷芸小說輯證, in *Yü Chia-hsi lun-hsüeh tsa-chu* 余嘉錫論學雜著, Peking, 1963, v. 2, pp. 280-324.

Liu-ch'ao wen, "Ch'üan Liang wen" 全梁文, v. 4, *ch.* 54, pp. 3269-3270.

Nan-pei ch'ao shih, "Ch'üan Liang shih" 全梁詩, v. 3, *ch.* 12, p. 1513.

STUDIES:

Tominaga, Kazunori 富永一登. "Rikuchō shōsetsu kō—In Gei *Shōsetsu* o chūshin to shite" 六朝小說考 —殷芸小說 を中心として, *Chūkoku chūsei bungoku kenkyū*, 11 (1976), 38-47. Based on Lu Hsün's compilations.

—TLM

Yu-chi wen-hsüeh 遊記文學 (travel-record literature) is an important body of prose writings which has flourished in China ever since the Sung dynasty. The term itself is a modern one and includes works which exhibit the following characteristics. First, they contain a first-hand account of an excursion of some kind, be it to an adjoining county, a distant province, or even a foreign land. Second, they are often written in diary form, with individual entries chronologically arranged. Third, they contain facts, usually of a geographical or historical nature. A travel record might describe, for instance, the topographical features of a particular area and the historical sites witnessed there, the tumulus of a historical figure, a famous temple, the remains of an ancient palace, etc. At times, social and political observations are recorded as well. A fourth and final characteristic is the presence of the subjective opinions and interpretations of the author. In addition to a description of geography, this genre also affords the display of the activities of the human imagination.

Although the origins of this genre can be traced to the accounts of Chang Ch'ien's 張騫 (second century B.C.) travels to the "Western Regions" found in his biographies in the *Shih-chi* and the *Han-shu*, and to some of the landscape descriptions and geographical commentaries of Hsieh Ling-yün,* Wu Chün 吳均 (469-520), Li Tao-yüan (see *Shui-ching chu*), Tsu Hung-hsün 祖鴻勳 (d. *c.* 550), and others, "travel records" as defined did not emerge as an independent prose genre until the T'ang period, when influential writers such as Yüan Chieh* and Liu Tsung-yüan* began composing accounts of specific locales, employing both "objective-descriptive" and "subjective-personal" modes of language. The latter's "Yung-chou pa-chi" 永州八記 (Eight Records of Yung Prefecture) are seminal in this respect. From the title of the first of Liu Tsung-yüan's "Eight Records" comes the title, *yu-chi* 遊記 (travel records), often used for this corpus in traditional times. The T'ang period also witnessed the appearance of the first travel diary of the type that was to proliferate later: Li Ao's* *Lai-nan lu* 來南錄 (A Register of Coming to the South), which chronicles a journey from Lo-yang to

Kwangtung undertaken in 809. It was not until the Sung period, however, that the travelogue became a popular literary genre. One of the first major literary figures to try his hand at the form was Ou-yang Hsiu,* who kept a diary of a diplomatic embassy to the Liao empire in the 1050s entitled *Yü-i chih* 于役志 (A Chronicle of Being in Service).

Although several reasons probably account for the popularity of composing travel accounts during the Sung, three immediately come to mind. First, communication and transportation were more advanced and convenient than they had ever been before, offering greater opportunity for travel. Second, as has been pointed out by other scholars, Sung poets were much more inclined than their predecessors to record the sights, events, and experiences encountered in everyday life. This same tendency is also evident in the travelogues of the Sung (needless to say, the travel diary was an ideal vehicle to record such experiences). And finally, since the total number of officials who served in the Sung civil bureaucracy far exceeded that of any previous era, and since the great majority of these officials held a variety of different bureaucratic posts during their careers, it is hardly surprising that many of them would keep journals describing their experiences while "on the road."

In general, the large corpus of extant travelogues dating from the Sung can be roughly classified into three categories. The first are records of excursions to specific locales, such as a particular mountain, monastery, or river. Wang An-shih* and Su Shih* are probably the best-known composers of such accounts. Most often these essays are relatively short, running from 200 to 600 characters, and are usually entitled "*Yu* such-and-such-a-place *chi*" (A Record of a Trip to Such-and-Such-a-Place). The second category includes travelogues which record the sights and experiences witnessed during an extended excursion from one place to another. These accounts were usually written by officials on their way to a new bureaucratic post. The length of such works is generally much greater than those described in the first category above. These are perhaps the best-known of all Sung travelogues, and would include such works as Lu Yu's* *Ju-Shu chi*, which describes a trip from Chekiang to Szechwan made in 1170, and two diaries by Fan Ch'eng-ta,* the *Wu-ch'uan lu* 吳船錄 (A Register of a Wu Boat) and the *Ts'an-luan lu* 驂鸞錄 (A Register of Riding a Simurgh), the former being an account of a journey from Szechwan to Soochow in 1177, and the latter describing an excursion from Wu-chün 吳郡 (modern Kiangsu) to Kweilin 桂林 (modern Kwangsi) undertaken in 1172-1173. It was probably these works, along with the *Lan-p'ei lu* (see below), which more than any other helped to establish the prototypes for the hundreds of travel accounts written in later periods. The third and final category would include works which might be called "diplomatic travelogues." Mention was made earlier of the diary Ou-yang Hsiu kept during his mission to the Liao empire in the 1050s. Later, both before and after the Chin (or Kin) conquest of North China (1127), diplomatic envoys were often shuttled back and forth between the Sung and Chin capitals. Several of these emissaries kept records of their experiences, both in poetry and in the travel-diary form. A list of the best-known and most important of these "diplomatic travelogues" would probably include Lou Yüeh's 樓鑰 (1137-1213) *Pei-hsing jih-lu* 北行日錄 (A Daily Register of a Northbound Excursion) of 1169-1170, Fan Ch'eng-ta's *Lan-p'ei lu* 攬轡錄 (A Register of Grasping the Carriage Reins) of 1170, Chou Hui's 周煇 (or 煇, 1126-after 1198) *Pei-yüan lu* 北轅錄 (A Register of Northbound Thills) of 1177, and Ch'eng Cho's 程卓 (1153-1223) *Shih-Chin lu* 使金錄 (A Register of An Embassy to the Chin) of 1211-1212. The lines of demarcation between the categories described above are far from being fixed and rigid; at times one category may overlap with another.

In the Ming and Ch'ing eras, the travelogue became one of the most widely practiced forms of literary expression. Practically every major literary figure in these periods, including Yüan Hung-tao,* Ch'ien Ch'ien-i,* Chu I-tsun,* and Yüan Mei,* has left travel diaries to posterity. The best-known and most prolific composer of travel journals in traditional China, Hsü Hung-tsu 徐宏祖 (1586-1641; also known as Hsü Hsia-k'o 徐霞客), was a product of this period. Hsü's numerous excursions to various parts of China spanned more than thirty years, and his extant journals describing these trips contain, according to some estimates, more than 400,000 characters. Certainly no other explorer-geographer-litterateur in traditional China has received more critical attention and praise than Hsü Hsia-k'o.

Until very recently, China's rich heritage of "travel record literature" had gone almost completely unnoticed by historians, literary critics, and Sinologists, both in China and in the West. The appearance of several articles, translations, and monographs dealing with *yu-chi wen-hsüeh* in recent years, however, indicates that there has been a slight reversal of this earlier trend. The genre remains an important one, not only because of its admirable literary qualities, but also because the travelogues of traditional China are valuable repositories of geographical, historical, and other types of information which are not generally found in the more standard source works.

ANTHOLOGIES:
Yeh, Yu-ming 葉幼明 and Pei Yüan-ch'en 貝遠辰. *Li-tai yu-chi hsüan* 歷代游記選. Changsha, 1980. The best *yu-chi* anthology available.

TRANSLATIONS:
Chang, Chun-shu and Joan Smythe, trans. *South China in the Twelfth Century, A Translation of Lu Yu's Travel Diaries, July 3-December 6, 1170.* Hong Kong, 1981. A complete translation, with copious notes, of Lu Yu's *Ju-Shu chi*.
Chavannes, Édouard. "Voyageurs chinois chez les Khitan et les Joutchen," *JA*, 9th Series, 9 (May-June 1897), 377-442; 11 (May-June 1898), 361-439.
———. "Pei Yuan Lou, Récit D'un Voyage Dans Le Nord," *TP*, 5.2 (1904), 163-192. A complete and annotated translation of Chou Hui's *Pei-yüan lu*.
Li, Chi. "Hsü Hsia-k'o's Huang-shan Travel Diaries," in *Two Studies*, pp. 1-23.

Walls, Jan W. "Wang An-shih's 'Record of an Excursion to Mount Pao-ch'an': A Translation and Annotation," in *Critical Essays,* pp. 159-165.

Watson, *The Old Man,* pp. 69-121. Contains excerpts from Lu Yu's *Ju-shu chi.*

Weulersse, Delphine. "Journal de voyage d'un letter chinois en 1177, *Wu ch'uan Lu* de Fan Cheng-Da," Unpublished Ph.D. dissertation, Paris, 1967. A complete and annotated translation of Fan Ch'eng-ta's *Wu-ch'uan lu.*

STUDIES:

Boulton, Nancy E. "Early Chinese Buddhist Travel Records as a Literary Genre." Unpublished Ph.D. dissertation, Georgetown University, 1982.

Chang, Chun-shu. "Hsü Hsia-k'o (1586-1641)," in *Two Studies in Chinese Literature,* Chang Chun-shu et al., eds., Ann Arbor, 1968, pp. 24-39.

———. "An Annotated Bibliography of Hsü Hsia-k'o," in *Two Studies,* pp. 40-46.

Chen, Cheng-siang 陳正祥. *Wu-ch'uan lu te chu-shih* 吳船錄的注釋. Hong Kong, 1976.

Ch'eng, Kuang-yü 程光裕. "Shih-hu chi-hsing san-lu k'ao-lüeh" 石湖紀行三錄考略, in *Sung-shih yen-chiu chi* 宋史研究集, No. 11, Taipei, 1979, pp. 505-512.

Chiang, Shao-yüan 江紹源. *Chung-kuo ku-tai lü-hsing chih yen-chiu ti-i fen-ts'e, Ts'e-chung ch'i fa-shu te ho tsung-chiao te fang-mien* 中國古代旅行之研究第一分冊, 側重其法術的和宗教的方面 Shanghai, 1935.

Chu, Wen 朱雯 and Juan Chi-ming 阮无名. *Sung Yüan Ming jih-chi hsüan* 宋元明日記選. Hong Kong, 1957. Includes selections from 15 travel diaries, all of which are punctuated. No annotation.

Franke, Herbert. "A Sung Embassy Diary of 1211-1212: The *Shih-Chin lu* of Ch'eng Cho," *BEFEO,* 69 (1981), 171-207.

Ho, P'ei-hsiung 何沛雄. *Liu Tsung-yüan Yung-chou pa-chi* 柳宗元永州八記. Hong Kong, 1974.

Hsü, Lien 許槤 and Li Ching-kao 黎經誥. *Liu-ch'ao wen chieh chien-chu* 六朝文絜箋注. Peking, 1962. Pages 99-135 of this anthology contain several of China's earliest known prose landscape descriptions, all of which are written in the *shu* 書 (letter) form.

Ku, Chieh-kang 顧頡剛 *et al.,* eds. *Chung-kuo ti-li ming-chu hsüan-tu* 中國地理名著選讀. Peking, 1962.

Li, Chi. *The Travel Diaries of Hsü Hsia-k'o.* Hong Kong, 1974.

Mirsky, Jeannette, ed. *The Great Chinese Travelers.* Chicago, 1964.

Murayama, Yoshihiro 村山吉廣. "Ri Kō no 'Rainan roku' ni tsuite" 李翺 の 來南錄 について, *Chūgoku koten kenkyū,* 18 (1971), 43-63.

Nienhauser, *Liu Tsung-yüan,* pp. 66-79, treats Liu's "Eight Records."

Sun, Chi-shu 孫季叔, ed. *Chung-kuo yu-chi hsüan* 中國遊記選. Shanghai, 1936.

Syrokomla-Stefanowska, A. D. "Fan Ch'eng-ta's Wu-boat Journey of 1177," *JOSA,* 10.1-2 (June 1975), 65-80.

Ting, Wen-chiang 丁文江 (or V. K. Ting). "On Hsü Hsia-k'o (1586-1641), Explorer and Geographer," *The New China Review,* 3.5 (October 1921), 225-337. The only in-depth study of Hsü in English.

Wang, Hsüan-ch'eng 王軒成. *Chung-kuo ku-tai t'an-hsien-chia yü lü-hsing chia* 中國古代探險家與旅行家. Hong Kong, 1962.

—JH

Yu T'ung 尤侗 (*tzu,* Chan-sheng 展成, *hao,* Hui-an 悔菴, 1618-1704), a native of Ch'ang-chou 長州 (modern Kiangsu), was a poet, calligrapher, essayist, and dramatist. Yu was equally well-known for his scholarship and for his creative talents. His writings were appreciated by the K'ang-hsi Emperor and one of his plays, *Tu "Li sao"* 讀離騷 (Reading "Encountering Sorrow") was even performed in the palace. Although such distinction brought him renown and assured him a place among the men of letters of the time, he had misfortune in the examinations. Success in officialdom did not come until he was over 60, when he was appointed in the Han-lin Academy to assist in the compilation of the official history of the Ming dynasty.

Many of Yu's dramatic works reflect his career frustrations. *Chün-tien lo* 鈞天樂 (The Pleasures of Heaven), a *ch'uan-ch'i** play, deals with the familiar theme of the talented scholar who fails to succeed in examinations. But instead of following the "k'u-miao" 哭廟 (weeping at the temple) tradition, a deity lends a sympathetic ear to a scholar's account of his misfortune. Yu has his politically thwarted scholars rewarded in heaven, where they are compensated for positions they failed to obtain on earth. In that wonderful world beyond, all wrongs are redressed.

The most celebrated of Yu's five *tsa-chü** plays, *Tu "Li-sao"* is a brilliant dramatic arrangement of material from the *Ch'u-tz'u*.* In this play Yu's elegant poetry and the myth, heroism, and romance of his subject matter are enhanced by his sense of the theatrical *tz'u*. The stage effect of the drum-dance of the shaman, the dance of the gods, and the ritualistic dragon-boating are brilliant dramatic interludes.

Yu's other *tsa-chü* plays include *Tiao P'i-p'a* 弔琵琶 (Pitying the P'i-p'a), a version of the story of Wang Chao-chün, *T'ao-hua yüan* 桃花源 (The Peach-blossom Fount), which treats T'ao Ch'ien's retirement, *Hei-pai wei* 黑白衞 (Guardians of the Black Horse and the White Horse), which retells the T'ang story of the magical Nieh Yin-niang 聶隱娘, and *Ch'ing-p'ing tiao* 清平調 (Peaceful Tunes), in which Yu alters history and makes the T'ang poets Li Po,* Tu Fu,* and Meng Hao-jan* successful in the examinations.

Yu tended to employ a great number of allusions in his plays; he also introduced unexpected turns in familiar stories. As a result, some critics have complained about his plays being burdened with learning and his own idiocyncrasies. Nevertheless, few have found fault with his craftsmanship in plot construction, his attention to stage effect, his elegant lyrics, and his beautiful melodies.

EDITIONS:
Hsi-t'ang ch'üan-chi 西堂全集. Published during the K'ang-hsi reign. 18v.
Hsi-t'ang yü-chi 西堂餘集. 1694. 36v.
Yu Hsi-t'ang tsa-tsu 尤西堂雜組. Shanghai, 1935. 2v.
Tu "Li sao," in *Ch'ing-jen tsa-chü* 清人雜劇, Cheng Chen-to 鄭振鐸, ed., Ch'u-chi 初集, 1934, v. 3.
Tiao P'i-p'a, in *Ch'ing-jen tsa-chü*, v. 3.
Hei-pai wei, in *Ch'ing-jen tsa-chü*, v. 4.
Ch'ing-p'ing tiao, Ch'ing-jen tsa-chü, v. 4.

STUDIES:
ECCP, pp. 935-936.
Fu, *Ch'ing tsa-chü*, pp. 48-51.
Tseng, "Ch'ing-tai tsa-chü," pp. 133-137.

—CYC

Yu-yang tsa-tsu 酉陽雜組 (Assorted Notes from Yu-yang), in thirty *chüan* (including the continuation), is the work of Tuan Ch'eng-shih 段成式 (*tzu*, K'o-ku 柯古, *c.* 800-863), bibliophile, word-fancier, and collector of curiosa. He was born a little before 800 and spent most of his life along the Yangtze, from Yangchow to Ch'eng-tu. His father, the sometime great minister Tuan Wen-ch'ang 段文昌 (772-835), obtained a position for him in the royal library. This job was ideally suited to his personality and interests, and as a collator in the archives he learned many well-buried secrets which he later incorporated in the book. Subsequently, when he was able to live the pleasant life of a private gentleman, he spent most of his time in his well-stocked household library, becoming particularly conversant with Buddhist literature.

It is easy to regard him as but a collector of marvels, but what is merely strange today was to his contemporaries informative about the wonders of the world. In any case, he collected data on every subject, especially information that was outside the realm of common knowledge—such as the use of wooden traps to catch elephants in some foreign land, knowledge that he picked up from a Cantonese physician who had it from a foreign ship captain. Indeed, he sought new knowledge far outside the walls of his library and was noted for his rather scandalous consorting with vagabonds, maid-servants, and foreigners, and even counted "Romans" (Anatolians? Syrians?) and Indians among his informants. Much of the data he collected in this way was linguistic, and it would not be an exaggeration to characterize him as a pioneering field linguist. He also reported on foreign scripts and book-styles; he knew imported incenses and perfumes, such as gum guggul, ambergris, and balm of Gilead—as well as their commercial names in exotic languages—and the names and characteristics of foreign medicinal herbs and garden flowers. He collected reports on the unseen or supernal worlds from persons who claimed expert knowledge of such places; for instance, he recorded a detailed description of the jewelled surface of the moon, transmitted by a mysterious visitor to the earth. But he was no mere recorder: he often voices his own doubts about the reliability of reports he has received and sometimes goes to considerable pains to check their accuracy with supposed witnesses. For this and other reasons the *Yu-yang tsa-tsu* is no mere mindless collectanea—it has very much the personal stamp of its author, an open-minded booklover not bound by books.

Tuan Ch'eng-shih's literary reputation is based mainly on the tales of wonder he has preserved or rewritten, but, judging from his few extant poems, he was also a fine poet. He was a good friend of Wen T'ing-yün,* and moved easily through the belletristic circles of his generation. He died at his home in Hsiang-yang on the Han River in 863.

The contents of the present versions of *Yu-yang tsa-tsu*—it has had a complex textual history, and there is considerable variation among modern editions—include, in addition to brief notes, reports, and anecdotes, a number of detailed studies which deserve to be called "short monographs." Among these is his valuable description of the great Buddhist monasteries of Ch'ang-an. He wrote this account, which includes data on their valuable holdings in art, and their beautiful gardens, in 843, two years before they were ravaged in the great persecution of Wu-tsung. The attempts of Sung scholars to reconstruct the map of T'ang Ch'ang-an rely heavily on the information he supplies about the streets and buildings of the metropolis which vanished forever in 904.

In his youth Tuan Ch'eng-shih was an ardent falconer. He drew on his imtimate knowledge of the art to compose the specialized account of T'ang hawking practice which now survives in *Yu-yang tsa-tsu*. This is particularly valuable for its classification of the varietal names of Chinese goshawks and the listing of technical terms then applied to the paraphernalia of the sport, which turn up from time to time in T'ang poetry.

An important collection of tales of daring and wonderful exploits, the *Chien-hsia chuan* 劍俠傳 (Traditions of Swords and Chivalry), sometimes attributed to Tuan is

now regarded as the work of his contemporary P'ei Hsing 裴鉶. It contains such familiar imaginative works as "K'un-lun nu" 崑崙奴 and "Nieh Yin-niang" 聶隱娘 .

EDITIONS:
Fang, Nan-sheng 方南生, ed. *Yu-yang tsa-tsu*. Peking, 1981. An excellent collated edition which replaces *TSCC* and other common editions. With several useful appendixes, including a collection of traditional prefaces and postscripts, a collection of traditional bibliographical information, and a chronological biography prepared by Fang Nan-sheng himself.

TRANSLATIONS:
Belpaire, Bruno. *T'ang kien wen tse (Florilège de littérature des T'ang)*, Paris, 1959, pp. 225-245. Translation of a catalogue of miracles attributable to the Diamond Sutra.
Imamura, Yoshio 今村與志雄. *Yūyō zasso* 酉陽雜俎. Tokyo, 1980. The only complete translation in any language.
Schafer, Edward H. "Falconry in T'ang Times," *TP*, 46 (1959), 293-338.
Soper, A. C. "A Vacation Glimpse of the T'ang Temples of Ch'ang-an, The Ssu-t'a chi by Tuan Ch'eng-shih," *Artibus Asiae*, 23 (1960), 15-40.

STUDIES:
Imahori, Seiji 今堀誠二. "Yūyō zasso shōkō" 酉陽雜俎小考, *Shigaku kenkyū*, 12.4 (January 1942), 52-90. Only substantial modern study of the book.
Schafer, Edward H. "Notes on Tuan Ch'eng-shih and his Writings," *AS*, 16 (1963), 14-34.
—ES

Yü Chiao Li 玉嬌梨, also entitled *Ti-san ts'ai-tzu shu* 第三才子書 (Third Book of Genius) or *Shuang-mei ch'i-yüan* 雙美奇緣 (The Unusual Marriage of a Pair of Beauties), is a twenty-chapter novel of the late Ming and/for early Ch'ing. One of the best known and most representative of the *ts'ai-tzu chia-jen hsiao-shuo*,* it is of uncertain authorship, having been ascribed variously to Chang Yün 張勻 (*fl.* 1660), his son Chang Shao 張劭 (*fl.* 1680), and the pseudonymous authors I-ti san-jen 荑荻散人 (Recluse of the Reeds) and T'ien-hua-tsang chu-jen (see *ts'ai-tzu chia-jen hsiao-shuo*). The work was published at least as early as the Shun-chih period (1644-1661) of the Ch'ing dynasty.

The plot of *Yü Chiao Li,* whose title is composed of characters from the heroines' names, is set in the mid-Ming following the execution of the eunuch Wang Chen 王振 in 1449. Po Hsüan 白玄, chief minister of the Court of Imperial Sactifices, seeks a talented husband for his beautiful daughter Hung-yü 紅玉. A venal censor, Yang T'ing-shao 楊廷詔, wants to marry his son to Hung-yü, but Po Hsüan rejects him because the son failed to recognize a quotation from the *Shih-ching.** In revenge, Yang arranges to have Po banished. Hung-yü lives with her father's friend Wu Kuei 吳珪 and his unattractive daughter Wu-yen 無豔 (Without Voluptuousness); she adopts the name Wu-chiao 無嬌 (Without Loveliness) to match that of her new "sister." One day Wu Kuei visits a temple in Nanking and notices a poem by the hero Su Yu-po 蘇友白 written on a wall. Wu investigates Su's background and decides he is a fitting match for Hung-yü. However, Su, approached by a go-between with Wu's marriage offer, wants to first steal a peek at his bride and mistakenly spies on Wu-yen. Su refuses Wu's offer, Wu has him dimissed from the provincial academy, and Su takes a journey north to seek a true beauty. On the way he helps a man rescue his wife from kidnappers, as had been foretold by a fortune-teller who also predicted his marital destiny. Su also meets the impostor-poet Chang Kuei-ju 張軌如, a candidate for the post of Hung-yü's brother's tutor. Chang steals some of Su's poetry and passes it off to Hung-yü as its own. Chang's scheme is exposed with the help of the maid Yen-su 嫣素.

Su travels on to the capital and meets an old friend Su Yu-te 蘇友德 (no relation), who tries unsuccessfully to impersonate Yu-po to Po Hsüan in hopes of marrying Hung-yü. On the journey he also meets the second heroine, Lu Meng-li 盧夢梨, disguised as a boy. She adroitly gets Su to agree to make her non-existent "younger sister" his second wife after Hung-yü. In the capital, Su learns that he has been reappointed as a student in the provincial academy. He passes the *chin-shih* examination and is awarded a magistrate's post in Hangchow.

Stopping to see Lu Meng-li on his way to assume his post, Su discovers that she has departed. It turns out that Meng-li and Hung-yü are cousins, and Meng-li's mother decides to visit her brother, Po Hsüan, in Nanking. The reunited cousins, realizing they are both interested in Su, agree to share him as a husband. Meanwhile, Su meets Po Hsüan, both under assumed identities, at the Cave of Yü the Great. Po is impressed with Su's looks and poetic talent, and asks him to come to Nanking and marry his daughter. In despair of ever marrying Hung-yü, Su consents. The mistaken identities are cleared up on Su's arrival and the plot closes with a colorful account of his wedding to Hung-yü and Meng-li.

The characters are mostly stereotypes. The work's appeal lies in its complex, comic plot and in the popularity of its themes—love, courtship, manners, poetry, an official career, and fate. It was early translated into French and, along with *Hao-ch'iu chuan,** helped meet a growing demand in Europe for translations of Chinese fiction.

EDITIONS:

There are numerous editions; only the most reliable and available are listed. I-ch'iu san-jen 羨秋散人 (probably a mistake for I-ti san-jen 羨荻散人, Recluse of the Reeds), ed. *Hsin-chüan p'i-p'ing hsiu-hsiang Yü Chiao Li* 新鐫批評繡像玉嬌梨. Preface by T'ien-hua-tsang chu-jen 天花藏主人, n.p., n.d. (preserved in the Harvard-Yenching Library, Cambridge, Massachusetts). Perhaps the earliest extant edition.

Shuang-mei ch'i-yüan 雙美奇緣 *(Yü Chiao Li).* Shanghai, 1923 (?).

TRANSLATIONS:

Abel-Rémusat, Jean Pierre. *Iu-kiao-li, ou les deux Cousines.* 4v. Paris, 1826.

Julien, Stanislas. *Les deux cousines.* 2v. Paris, 1842. 2nd ed. Paris, 1964.

STUDIES:

P'i, Shu-t'ang 畢樹棠. "Ta Liu Wu-chi shu: Lun *Yü Chiao Li*" 答柳無忌書: 論玉嬌李, *Ch'ing-hua chou-k'an,* 32.3 (November 1929), 59-61.

—RCH

Yü Hsin 庾信 (*tzu,* Tzu-shan 子山, also known as Yü K'ai-fu 庾開府 or Yü the Commander Unequalled in Honor, 513-581) was born in the year of the death of Shen Yüeh* and died in the year of the founding of the Sui dynasty. His poetry marked a culmination of the richly innovative Six Dynasties and served as a harbinger for the flowering of verse under the T'ang. In his lifetime he was the preeminent literary figure of China, north and south. The record of him consists of his collected works in 16 *chüan*, edited by the Ch'ing scholar Ni Fan 倪璠 (*chü-jen*, 1705) and containing a laudatory preface by his sponsor and friend in the north, Yü-wen Yü 宇文逌 (d. 580), and of the biographies of him and his contemporaries in various dynastic histories.

Yü Hsin was long associated in literary circles with Hsü Ling in the same way as their fathers had been; their collective literary style came to be known as Hsü-Yü Style 徐庚體. All four of these men had free access to the Eastern Palace (in Chien-k'ang, capital of the Liang dynasty) of the Crown Prince, and Hsin's two uncles were tutors to Hsiao T'ung, compiler of the *Wen-hsüan** anthology. According to an amusing anecdote in the *Nan-shih*, which, if nothing else, demonstrates that he was a man of passion and temper, Yü Hsin had a homosexual relationship with a grandnephew of Emperor Yüan of the Liang.

Yü's life in the capital is described as carefree and happy; the elegant and literate society of the capital fostered a literature that grew more and more effete, making up in literary precocity what it lacked in emotional or intellectual substance. Word games and palindromes were much in vogue; this *kung-t'i** (palace style) of literature was a sort of Chinese Gongorism at which Yü Hsin was extraordinarily gifted.

After Hou Ching rebelled in 554, Yü Hsin was sent on an ambassadorial mission to Ch'ang-an, capital of the Western Wei (later the Northern Chou), where he was detained in comfortable exile for the rest of his days.

Despite the prestige and honor he enjoyed in the north, Yü suffered acutely from homesickness for his beloved southland. This pining produced a unique work,

the "Ai Chiang-nan fu" 哀江南賦 (Lament for the South), a flowing history in *fu**-form of the Liang dynasty and its fall. It is characterized by extreme emotionalism coupled with the strictest stylistic formalism. This extraordinary balance in Yü's later works between substance and form earned him the admiration of Tu Fu* and others.

The dichotomy in Yü's oeuvre and life—a "southern" period of gaiety and frivolity and a "northern" period of sadness and melancholy—is, insofar as it is possible to date individual poems, a genuine one. Many of Yü Hsin's northern pieces are studies in despair, self-doubt, and self-pity.

While he was perfectly capable of pouring out endless lines of parallel verse, his genius lies perhaps in his uncanny knack for breaking that parallelism and preventing it from seeming tedious or monotonous. This rigorous formal freshness, together with a sensitivity and depth of feeling, has earned a secure place in Chinese literary history for Yü Hsin.

EDITIONS:

Yü Hsin shih fu hsüan 庚信詩賦選. Tan Cheng-pi 譚正璧 and Chi Fu-hua 紀馥華, eds. Shanghai, 1958. Punctuated and richly annotated texts of 10 *fu* and many *shih* and *yüeh-fu*, with introduction.

Yü Tzu-shan chi chu 庚子山集注. *SPPY*. Contains Ni Fan's commentary, a *nien-p'u*, T'eng Wang-yü's introduction, the *Pei shih* 北史 biography, etc.

TRANSLATIONS:

Demiéville, *Anthologie*, pp. 172-173.

Frodsham, *Anthology*, pp. 188-197.

Owen, "Deadwood," pp. 157-160 ("K'u-shu fu" 枯樹賦 [Prose-poem on the Barren Tree]).

Watson, *Fu*, pp. 102-109. Contains a translation of the "Small Garden" *fu*.

STUDIES:

Bear, Peter Michael. "The Lyric Poetry of Yü Hsin." Unpublished Ph.D. dissertation, Yale University, 1968. Excellent critical studies of numerous *shih*.

Chang, Chiang 章江. *Wei Chin Nan-pei ch'ao wen-hsüeh chia* 魏晉南北朝文學家. Taipei, 1971. Section on Yü Hsin, pp. 306-316.

Graham, William T., Jr. *'The Lament for the South': Yü Hsin's 'Ai Chiang-nan fu'.* Cambridge, 1980.

———. "Yü Hsin and 'The Lament for the South,' " *HJAS*, 36 (1976), 82-113.

Graham, William T., Jr. and James R. Hightower. "Yü Hsin's 'Songs of Sorrow,' " *HJAS*, 43.1 (June 1983), 5-55.

Liu, K'ai-yang 劉開揚. "Lun Yü Hsin chi ch'i shih fu" 論庾信及其詩賦, *Wen-hsüeh i-ch'an tseng-kan*, 5 (1959), 58-79.

Obi, Kōichi 小尾交一. "Yu Shin no hito to bungaku" 庾信の人と文學, *Hiroshima Daigaku Bungakubu kiyō*, 23 (1964), 97-137.

Owen, "Deadwood," esp. pp. 170-171.

—RIN

Yü Hsüan-chi 魚玄機 (*tzu*, Yu-wei 幼微, *c.* 844-868) is one of the best-known women poets of the T'ang period (see also Hsüeh T'ao). Chinese women have written good poetry during every period of literary history from the *Shih-ching** down to modern times. Anthologies of poems from any given period usually contain, at the back of the collection, a small number of works by women, ghosts, clergymen, and others whose efforts might provide amusement, if not enlightenment, following the more serious writings that form the bulk of the collection proper.

Most women poets are remembered primarily as someone's wife or concubine, or as a courtesan or a nun, although there are notable exceptions such as Li Ch'ing-chao.* Yü Hsüan-chi is known to have been a talented courtesan, the concubine of a government official, and a Taoist nun who entertained gentlemen in her quarters at the Convent of Gathered Blessings in Ch'ang-an, the T'ang capital. Her fifty extant poems give ample evidence of her activities in each of the three roles and ways of life. The earliest biographical account states that she was executed in the year 868 (at the age of twenty-four) for the murder of her maid, whom she suspected of carrying on with one of her gentleman callers. The account of this murder, which appears in the *San-shui hsiao-tu* 三水小牘 (A Little Tablet from Three Rivers) of Huang-fu Mei 皇甫枚 (*fl.* 880), is told in such dramatic detail that its historical accuracy becomes suspect. The many activities of her short life are richly reflected in her extant poems. The topics touched upon include the joys of banqueting, love poems to her absent husband, poem-letters to friends, elegies, travel poems, poems on historical sites, introspective poems, poems to fellow Taoists and fellow courtesans, allegorical poems reflecting the courtesan's trade, and several boudoir laments. Another feature of Yü Hsüan-chi's collected poems which makes her stand out among other Chinese women poets is the relative variety of verse types and line lengths employed. Her collection includes verses of four, eight, twelve and twenty-four lines, written not only in the standard five- and seven-character lines, but in the rare six-character line as well. This is noteworthy, since most female poets excelled in a single verse form and only on certain themes.

EDITIONS:

T'ang nü-lang Yü Hsüan-chi shih 唐女郎魚玄機詩. *SPPY.*

TRANSLATIONS:

Sunflower, pp. 286-288.

STUDIES:

Karashima, Takeshi 辛島驍. *Gyo Genki-Setsu Tō* 魚玄機 薛濤. Tokyo, 1964.

Walls, Jan W., "The Poetry of Yü Hsüan-chi: A Translation, Annotation, Commentary and Critique." Unpublished Ph.D. dissertation, Indiana University, 1972. Contains translations.

Wimsatt, Genevieve B. *Selling Wilted Peonies.* New York, 1936. Contains translations.

Yokoyama, Eisan 横山永三. "Gyo Genki ni tsuite" 魚玄機 について. *Chūgokukei ronsetsu shiryō*, 10 (July-December 1968), 218-225.

—JWW

Yü-t'ai hsin-yung 玉臺新詠 (New Songs from a Jade Terrace) is an anthology of love poems compiled *c.* 545 A.D. by the court poet Hsü Ling (see below). It comprises 656 poems in 10 *chüan* dating from the late third century B.C. to the mid-sixth century A.D. It is traditionally held that Hsiao Kang 蕭綱 (503-551), crown prince of the Liang dynasty, commissioned this work in order to elevate and preserve the modern sub-genre of love poetry which had become fashionable at his court. This sub-genre is variously called *kung-t'i shih** (palace-style poetry, referring in part to the Eastern Palace, official residence of the Crown Prince), or *Yung-ming t'i* 永明體 (the style of the *Yung-ming* era [483-494 in the Ch'i dynasty]), or "*Hsü-Yü-t'i*" 徐庾體 (the style of Hsü Ling and Yü Hsin*). The variety of these names indicates the confusion among traditional sources concerning the origin of the new poetic style. It is probably safe to conclude that palace-style poetry originated with poets of the Ch'i such as Shen Yüeh,* was developed by court poets of the Liang such as Hsü Ch'ih 徐摛 (472-549) and Yü Chien-wu 庾肩吾 (*c.* 487-551), was patronized and made fashionable by Hsiao Kang, and immortalized by Hsü Ling and Yü Hsin.

The *Jade Terrace* is a monument to contemporary literature and a repository of palace-style poetry. Of its 656 poems and 105 identifiable poets 502 and 74 respectively are from the Southern Dynasties. The poets best represented are Hsiao Kang (76 poems), Hsiao Yen 蕭衍 (464-549) (41), Shen Yüeh (30), Wu Chün 吳均 (469-520) (26), Wang Seng-ju 王僧孺 (465-522) (19), Pao Chao* (17), Ho Sun 何遜 (d. 527) (16), and Hsieh T'iao* (16). Two major tendencies are evident in Hsü Ling's method of selection: a deference to the Liang royal house (*chüan* 7 is by members of the ruling Hsiao family), and a preference for practitioners of palace-style poetry.

This sub-genre is governed by numerous conventions. The setting is a palace boudoir, luxurious and erotic; the persona is a palace lady deserted by her lover; the emotional tenor is melancholy pathos; the expression of love is decorous, graceful, and courtly, avoiding explicit sexuality. The style derives its name in part from this palatial, courtly ambience.

The title of the anthology is a complex pun: *yü-t'ai* may refer to the erotic mountain haunt of a goddess, to the prison of a legendary princess in antiquity, or to a mirrorstand in the contemporary noblewoman's boudoir; "hsin" indicates the modern emphasis of the anthology, while "yung" is a general term for emotional lyricism.

The organizational principle is basically chronological: *chüan* 1-6 span *c.* 130 A.D.-*c.* 525 A.D.; *ch.* 7 interrupts this time sequence with the royal Liang Poets *c.* 485-*c.* 545; *ch.* 8 continues the sequence of non-royal poets from 525-545; *ch.* 9 and 10 each recommence the chronological sequence (the former opening with the late third century B.C.) with different poetic forms.

In terms of meter the anthology is fairly homogeneous, representing pentasyllabic *shih** (*ch.* 1-8, and 10), varying in length from 355 to 2 lines. *Ch.* 9 has irregular meters. *Ch.* 10 has only five-word quatrains. Of these meters the pentasyllabic quatrain is the most frequent (157 poems), followed by the pentasyllabic eight-line poem (129).

Various forms are represented: Han *yüeh-fu,** Han *ku-shih* 古詩 (old-style poems), *t'ung-yao-ko* 童謠歌 (children's rhymes), *ko* 歌 (songs), *ch'ü* 曲, old *chüeh-chü* 絕句, *yung-wu* 詠物 (poems on a given object), *chin-tai Wu ko* 近代吳歌 (modern songs from south of the Yangtze), *yen-ko hsing* 豔歌行 (folk lovesongs, anon. or imitations by named poets), and *chin-tai Hsi-ch'ü ko* 西曲歌 (modern folk songs from the West [Hupei and Honan]), besides *shih*, or lyrics, of different lengths.

Two novel features of Southern Dynasties love poetry are its dedicatory and occasional elements. It was the fashion, especially in the late Liang, to be assigned a topic for composition at a formal banquet (Fu 賦 . . . *te* 得); it was also the custom to dedicate verse to one's superior, sometimes harmonizing with his choice of rhymes (*feng* 奉, or *feng-ho* 和). The phrases *ying chiao* 應敎 or *ying ling* 令 in poem titles indicate a royal commission.

Viewed against the background of Southern Dynasties literary theory and practice, this anthology marks a new departure. Previously the concept of literature was didactic; It was considered a means of ameliorating human nature and of advancing the progress of civilization. In his preface to the *Jade Terrace*, Hsü Ling avoids this functional approach, preferring the belletristic view: he opines that his selection will entertain his readers.

Hsü Ling (*tzu*, Hsiao-mu 孝穆, 507-583) was a native of T'an 郯, Tunghai 東海 (mod-

945

ern Shantung). The post of his father, Hsü Ch'ih, as Junior Mentor to the Crown Prince Hsiao Kang, gave Ling early entrée to court life where he enjoyed royal patronage in his twin careers of the civil service and literature. He outlived eleven Liang and Ch'en emperors. His official biography lists numerous posts, ranging from imperial tutor to ambassador. He was commissioned to draft the Liang abdication document which inaugurated the Ch'en dynasty, and later served the Ch'en. A trusted, urbane official, he managed to pursue a distinguished career for over fifty years in the most unpromising circumstances.

EDITIONS:

Chao, Chün 趙均. *Yü-t'ai hsin-yung.* Peking, 1955. 1633 reissue of Ch'en Yü-fu's 陳玉父 1215 Sung edition. The earliest extant complete edition. The control text. It contains 656 poems.

Chi, Jung-shu 紀容舒, ed. *Yü-t'ai hsin-yung k'ao-i* 考異 (Critical Text of). 1752; rpt. Shanghai, 1937.

Lo, Chen-yü 羅振玉, ed. *Ming-sha shih shih ku-chi ts'ung ts'an* 鳴沙石室古籍叢殘. Fasc. 1-6. Shenyang, 1917. A collection of ancient texts from Tun-huang which contains a fragment of the T'ang edition of the *Jade Terrace*, 12 poems from *ch.* 2.

Obi, Kōichi 小尾郊一 and Takashi Sadao 高志貞夫, eds. *Gyokudai shin'ei sakuin* 索引. Tokyo, 1976.

Wu, Chao-i 吳兆宜, ed. *Hsü Hsiao-mu chi* 徐孝穆集 (Hsü Ling's opus). Basic Sinological Series, 1939. Collated from *I-wen lei-chü* (see *lei-shu*) and *Wen-yüan ying-hua* and other texts, it comprises, in 6 *chuan*, 39 poems, 85 prose pieces (including the *Yü-t'ai* preface), and 1 prose-poem. Annotated, punctuated edition, also including his official biography by Yao Ch'a 姚察 and Yao Ssu-lien 姚思廉 (T'ang dynasty).

———. ed. *Yü-t'ai hsin-yung chien-chu* 箋註 (Annotated Text of). 1675, revised in 1774 by Ch'eng Yen 程琰, *SPPY*. Wu adds 179 more poems to the 656 of the control text, but these are readily discounted, appearing as they do at the end of each volume.

Wu-hsi Sun-shih Wu-yün chi kuan pen 無錫孫氏五雲溪館本. *SPTK*.

TRANSLATIONS:

Birrell, A. *New Songs from a Jade Terrace.* Leiden and London, 1982. Complete translation of the *Yü-t'ai hsin-yung* with a long introduction a compendium of notes alphabetically arranged, and brief biographies of the poets.

Suzuki, Torao 鈴木虎雄. *Gyokudai shin'ei shu* 玉臺新詠集. Tokyo, 1953-1956, rev. ed. 1970 Translations into *kambun* with free paraphrase into modern Japanese; textual variants, notes, biographical data, and discussion of poetic forms and titles.

Uchida, Sennosuke 內田泉之助. *Gyokudai shin'ei.* Tokyo, 1974-1975. Similar to Suzuki, but presentation improved. Includes Western dates, fuller citations, (rudimentary) indices and an annotated translation of the preface

STUDIES:

Birrell, Anne M. "Erotic Decor: A Study of Love Imagery in the Sixth Century A.D. Anthology *Yü-t'ai hsin-yung.*" Ph.D. dissertation Columbia University, 1978.

—AB

Yü-yen 寓言 (literally "lodged words") is the Chinese expression now usually linked with the Western concept of allegory. But the correspondence is far from exact. *Yü-yen*, in addition to "allegory," also designates a genre of Chinese didactic fables, which probably do not qualify as allegory in a Western sense. On the other hand, there is an important tradition of poetic exegesis in China that is definitely kindred with the Western practice of allegoresis, yet not directly related to *yü-yen*.

Yü means "to lodge" and is usually glossed by *chi* 寄, both characters having the meaning in common "to lodge or dwell temporarily." *Yen*, however, is ambiguous and can refer either to the "words" of the text or to the "message" that has been supposedly lodged in them. Accordingly, Liu Hsieh (see *Wen-hsin tiao-lung*) avoids the term *yü-yen*, preferring the much clearer *yü-i* 寓意 "to lodge a meaning." Fundamental to traditional Chinese conceptions of *yü-yen*, however, is the bifurcation of the text into *yen* 言 (words) and *i* 意 (meaning), and these seem roughly synonymous with the Western concepts of "vehicle" and "tenor." Thus in the West one speaks of "saying one thing to mean another," while

946

in China one speaks of "the words being here, but the meaning being there" 言在此而意在彼.

The term *yü-yen* derives from the title of the twenty-seventh chapter of *Chuang-tzu*, which begins *yü-yen shih chiu* 寓言十九. This phrase is usually interpreted to mean that ninety percent of the material in *Chuang-tzu* is to be read as *yü-yen*. Indeed, this mode was especially popular among the "hundred philosophers" of the Warring States period (403-221 B.C.), who used it to articulate their philosophical, religious, and political positions. Other Chinese terms relating to techniques of allegory include *yü* 喻 "a figure or metaphor," *pi* 比 "comparison/metaphor," *hsing* 興 sometimes meaning "allegory," and *to-wu* 託物 "to make use of an object [as an allegory]."

Basic to allegory, Chinese and Western, is the concept of concealment: the author may not wish to, or may not be able to, or may not dare to, express himself directly. The reasons may be threefold: (1) for didactic purposes, he may wish his readers to "struggle" to obtain his meaning. So St. Augustine observed that "although we learn things which are said clearly and openly in other places, when these things are dug out of secret places, they are renewed in our comprehension, and being renewed become more attractive." Basic to this is the notion that a figurative presentation is more aesthetically pleasing, thus more easily remembered, than a literal presentation of the same material. (2) Social convention may prohibit the author from directly presenting politically or culturally sensitive material. (3) Fear of legal or political reprisals may force the author to adopt figurative expression for his own safety. Allegory in the "hundred philosophers," Buddhist religious allegory, and the allegorical readings of some Chinese novels fall in the first category. Court presentation of "criticism" (*feng* 諷) directed at the ruler, such as the Han-dynasty *fu*,* belong to the second category. Into the third category fall many of the greatest masterpieces of Chinese literature, especially poetry: Ch'ü Yüan,* Juan Chi,* Ch'en Tzu-ang,* Liu Tsung-yüan,* Su Shih*—to name only a few—have sizable amounts of allegorical verse written under the direct threat, or reality, of political persecution.

Allegory in China, if not *yü-yen*, originates in the *Shih-ching*.* Although this anthology's earliest commentaries, which date from the Former Han period, explicate much of the text as specific political allegory, there is seldom independent historical confirmation for these readings. In one case, however—*Shih-ching*, Ode 155, "Ch'ih-hsiao" 鴟鴞 (The Owl)—the allegorical explication of the traditional commentaries is confirmed by a passge in the "Ch'in t'eng" 金縢 (The Metal-bound Coffer) chapter of the *Shu-ching*. This fact makes it possible to date allegory as a technique of composition to perhaps the seventh or eighth century B.C.

The popularity of allegorical and figurative modes throughout the long course of Chinese history is intimately linked to the supremacy of the Confucian political system. A prime responsibility of the conscientious Confucian official was to comment openly on public affairs, yet to do so without offending his sovereign and, if possible, without damage to his own career. Allegorical discourse thus afforded both a moral refuge and the closest thing to legal protection from the autocratic power of the state. The great progenitor of this tradition of allegorical protest was, of course, Ch'ü Yüan. The *Ch'u-tz'u*,* together with the *Shih-ching*, had already become by late Han times, the basic repositories of allegorical figures for use in political verse.

Prominent in both anthologies is the use of plants and animals as figures for human moral qualities. For example, in the *Ch'u-tz'u* literature, epidendrums and orchids stand for the moral degradation of the corrupt. Birds with solitary habits—the egret, the crane, the hawk—stand for the man of unique virtue; birds that travel in flocks—geese, swans—stand for the ranks of routine officials. Handbooks, such as the T'ang-dynasty *Erh-nan mi-chih* 二南密旨 (The Profound Senses of Poetry) which contains lists of these correspondences, suggest that such figures evolved quite early into a universally understood code language for use in political poetry.

Another allegorical technique, akin to typology in the Western tradition, is "using the past to criticize the present" (以古諷今). For example, it became a convention, attested in a Tu Fu* poem as early as 752, to criticize the T'ang emperor Hsüan-tsung (r. 713-756) for his liaison with the courtesan Yang Kuei-fei by writing about the legendary visits of King Mu of Chou to the Queen Mother of the West. Such typological figures became a standard feature of Chinese political discourse. The best-known example of this practice in recent times was the 1961 play *Hai Jui pa kuan* 海瑞罷官 (The Dismissal of Hai Jui) by the historian Wu Han 吳晗, in which the virtuous Ming official Hai Jui is a type for Mao Tse-tung. It should also be mentioned that this practice of "using the past to criticize the present" was never limited to "imaginative" literature, but was, and still is, often used in Chinese scholarship as well, a good example being Kuo Mo-jo's 郭沫若 work *Li Po yü Tu Fu* 李白與杜甫, where T'ang-dynasty poems are studied and interpreted so as to provide criticisim on twentieth-century events.

The Chinese translations of Sanskrit Buddhist anagogic and pedagogic literature, such as the *avadana* and *jataka*, enlarged the native Chinese tradition of religious allegory during the Six Dynasties. The *jataka* in particular, tales in which the Buddha draws explicit analogies between happenings in his former incarnations and events in his present life, are by definition typological. In the T'ang, more sinicized versions of Buddhism, such as Ch'an, gave rise to a genre of "nature" poetry in which elements of the traditional Chinese landscape—moon, water, mountains, clouds—acquired significance as symbols for spiritual states. Such poetry found its classical expression in Wang Wei* and Han-shan.* Most T'ang poets tried their hand at such meditative verse; Liu Tsung-yüan was among the best.

The grand conceptions of at least two major Chinese novels—*Hung-lou meng** and *Hsi-yu chi**—are also governed by structures that can profitably be viewed as allegorical. However, the exact relationship between the allegorical mode in Chinese fiction as opposed to its older, more traditional use in lyric verse has yet to be explained in detail. There is also a strong tradition of allegorical expression in the Chinese visual arts, especially painting, which parallels and supplements literary allegory in many ways. For example, the metaphor that to govern the empire is like herding horses—the capable monarch is a judge of men as the skilled groom is a judge of horses—with its *locus classicus* in *Chuang-tzu*, is ubiquitous as background for T'ang "horse" poems, and inspired the famous "horse" paintings of Chao Meng-fu.

STUDIES:

Fish, Michael B. "Yang Kuei-fei as the Hsi Wang Mu: Secondary Narrative in Two T'ang Poems," *MS*, 32 (1976), 337-354.

Hartman, Charles. "*Alieniloguium*: Liu Tsung-yüan's Other Voice," *CLEAR*, 4.1 (July 1981), 23-73.

Li, Chu-tsing. "The Freer 'Sheep and Goat' and Chao Meng-fu's Horse Paintings," *AA*, 30 (1968), 279-364.

Nienhauser, William H., Jr. "An Allegorical Reading of Han Yü's 'Mao Ying chuan' (Biography of Fur Point)," *OE*, 23.2 (1976), 153-174.

———. "Diction, Dictionaries, and the Translation of Classical Chinese Poetry," *TP*, 64 (1974), 1-63).

Plaks, Andrew. *Archetype and Allegory in the Dream of the Red Chamber.* Princeton, 1976.

———. "Allegory in *Hsi-yu chi* and *Hung-lou meng*," in *Chinese Narrative*, pp. 163-202.

Pusey, James R. *Wu Han: Attacking the Present Through the Past.* Cambridge, Mass., 1969.

Silbergeld, Jerome. "The Political Landscapes of Kung Hsien, in Painting and Poetry," *Journal of the Institute of Chinese Studies of the Chinese University of Hong Kong*, 8.2 (December 1976) 561-573.

Tuan, Hsing-min 段醒民. *Liu Tzu-hou yü-yen wen-hsüeh t'an-wei* 柳子厚寓言文學探微 Taipei 1978.

Wang, Huan-piao 王煥鑣. *Hsien-Ch'in yü-yen yen chiu* 先秦寓言研究. Peking, 1959.

Weggel, Oskar. "Klassenkampf unter einer Glocke von Symbolismus und esoterischer

Kommunikation," *China aktuell* (April 1974), 173-174.

Yu, Anthony C. "Introduction," in *The Journey to the West*, v. 1 Chicago, 1976, pp. 1-62.

—CH

Yüan Chen 元稹 (*tzu*, Wei-chih 微之, 779-831) was one of the most celebrated poets and statesmen of the mid-T'ang period. He was a complex person with a complicated family background. According to the T'ang dynastic histories, Yüan Chen was a native of Lo-yang and a tenth-generation descendant of the royal house of Toba-Wei, which ruled northern China during the fifth and sixth centuries. One of its rulers, Emperor Hsiao-wen (r. 471-495), adopted the Chinese surname Yüan after he moved the capital from Ping-ch'eng (modern Ta-t'ung, in Shansi) to Lo-yang. After the unification of China, the offspring of the Toba house chose to remain in Lo-yang; they were generally referred to as "Lo-yang-jen" 洛陽人 (natives of Lo-yang). Yüan Chen, however, was born in Ch'ang-an, where his father held a minor post on the Board of Justice. When Yüan Chen was seven years old his father died and the family was left destitute. He passed the examinations under the *ming-ching* 明經 (clarification of the classics) category in 793, but it was not until after he passed the *pa-ts'ui* 拔萃 (highly selective) examination in 803 that he received an appointment, along with Po Chü-i,* his lifelong friend, as collator in the imperial library. Between 803 and 806 Yüan Chen and Po Chü-i prepared themselves for the ultimate palace examination to be monitored by the emperor. They anticipated all possible questions concerning current national affairs and attempted their solutions. Having personally experienced poverty in his youth and witnessed the sufferings of common people caused by official corruption and wars, Yüan Chen and his friend were intent on changing the status quo. Upon passing the examination with the highest score, Yüan Chen was the first to be appointed Reminder of the Left. Taking advantage of the proximity to the emperor, Yüan Chen offered a ten-point proposal, suggesting political reform, beginning with the court. For this presumption he was banished from the capital. By coincidence, his mother died at about this time, and Yüan Chen retired to observe the period of mourning. In 809 he was appointed a censor to inspect eastern Szechwan. There he exposed local government corruption, making enemies in high places. Once more he was banished, this time for ten years. His talent was finally recognized and he was made a Secretariat Director in 822, only to be removed from office in less than four months, because of factional struggles. Although he held, until his death, several high offices in the province, he was unable to carve out the political reforms he had envisioned.

Yüan Chen was more successful in bringing about literary reform. When he was a member of the Han-lin Academy in charge of drafting imperial rescripts, he was responsible for changes in the documentary language, stressing a classical simplicity.

Although generally attributed to Po Chü-i, it was in reality Yüan Chen and Li Shen 李紳 (780-846) who initiated the new *yüeh-fu** movement. As early as 809, Yüan Chen wrote twelve *yüeh-fu* with new titles to harmonize the twenty by his friend, Li Shen, and sent them to Po Chü-i, who then composed fifty of his own. It was their conscious effort to liberate poetry from the rigid rules of prosody practiced by most T'ang poets. It is true that the *yüeh-fu* form had been revived by earlier poets, such as Li Po* and Tu Fu,* but Yüan Chen and his friends went beyond the structural freedom of meter and rhyme advocated by others and stressed simplicity of language and seriousness of purpose. They firmly believed that poetry could effect social and political changes.

One of the most exemplary of Yüan Chen's political poems is "Lien-ch'ang kung tz'u" 連昌宮詞 (Lien-ch'ang Palace), a new *yüeh-fu* in ninety seven-character lines. It voices an anti-military attitude and questions the government's responsibility for causing war. The criticism is typically veiled in the recent past, the time of the An Lushan Rebellion (755-763). It was said that

Yüan Chen's poems were the stepping stones for him to climb to the lofty height of Secretariat Director, for the new emperor, Mu-tsung (r. 821-825), sought him out from relative obscurity after reading this poem.

During his long exiles and less strenuous appointments at outlying districts, Yüan Chen had ample time for literary pursuits. He exchanged poems constantly with his friends; special messengers were assigned to deliver the poems Yüan and Po wrote to each other when they were governors of neighboring provinces. In 823, Yüan Chen completed his own collected works in one hundred *chüan* and titled it *Yüan-shih Ch'ang-ch'ing chi* 元氏長慶集. Then he edited Po Chü-i's collected works in fifty *chüan* and gave it a similar title: *Po-shih Ch'ang-ch'ing chi* 白氏長慶集.

There is also a *ch'uan-chi** tale known as "Hui-chen chi" 會眞集 (A Tale of an Encounter with an Immortal) or "Ying-ying chuan" 鶯鶯傳 (The Story of Ying-ying) written by Yüan Chen, which had a great influence on subsequent literature. It concerns the love affair between a young scholar Chang 張 and an enigmatic maiden Ts'ui Ying-ying 崔鶯鶯 while both were staying temporarily in a monastery. As perhaps the finest example of *ch'uan-ch'i* fiction, this story was later modified and expanded into a *chu-kung-tiao** by Tung Chieh-yüan in the thirteenth century (see *Hsi-hsiang chi chu-kung-tiao*). Eventually, this latter version evolved into the famous Yüan-dynasty drama *Hsi-hsiang chi.** Because of the sustained popularity of the original story and of the two subsequent versions, it is no exaggeration to say that "Ying-ying" was the single best-known love story in traditional China.

Scholars who have studied this story, however, have tended to take the historical/biographical approach rather than to assess the reasons for its undeniable appeal. In the usual case, they either assume (as does Ch'en Yin-k'o), or attempt to show (as does Hightower), that the hero Chang and the putative author Yüan Chen are essentially one and the same. For this reason, the fictiveness of the tale is played down in favor of history or biography as necessary guides to its understanding. Discussion tends to dwell on why Chang does not simply arrange to marry Ying-ying, or why he so casually leaves her. In either case, the rationale provided in the tale itself seems to be less than convincing.

Such an apparent shortcoming, however, has clearly not detracted from the story's manifest ability to capture and sustain a reader's interest, and the reasons for this are more crucial than historical or biographical circumstance. The story does not really concern itself with the rounded portrayal of Chang; nor is it actually a self-confession on the part of the author. Rather, as either of its titles suggests, it is essentially a portrait of its fascinating heroine Ying-ying. How this portrait is presented constitutes the basis of its meaning and artistic merit.

The reader first meets Ying-ying through Chang's startled eyes, as she comes out with great reluctance to greet him. The narrator notes her everyday dress, her lack of makeup, her look of resentment, and her utter refusal to be drawn into conversation. It is this very negative manner that marks her as uncommon and brings about an overwhelmingly positive response in Chang (and, through him, in the reader). He finds her to be uniquely captivating and radiantly beautiful, and he falls madly in love.

This kind of ironic reversal characterizes the entire portrayal of the heroine and, in large measure, accounts for the enduring hold the story has over the imagination. She sends Chang a verse which appears to be a coy invitation, but she rebuffs him with cold formality when he arrives. Then, without explanation, she goes to him herself, blushing and leaning weakly on her maid's arm. Even as Chang rejoices in the initial fulfillment of their love, she says nothing. When Chang first leaves her, she makes no open objection, though the narrator is careful to note that her usually impassive face shows traces of pain. There is also mention of her literary and musical skills, along with her stubborn refusal to display them to others. When she realizes that Chang is overhearing her as she plays the zither alone at night, she abruptly stops.

Internal irony is therefore the most prominent feature of Ying-ying's character. Moreover, because irony permeates the way the character is described, the reader becomes thoroughly stimulated and is drawn into active participation. When the narrator says that Ying-ying is silent during stressful situations, the reader is conditioned to formulate on his own a greater depth of feeling than direct telling could possibly convey.

Because of this, the tale is charged with emotional tension in spite of its terse and understated classical prose. Toward the end of the story, Ying-ying attempts to express her grief directly by agreeing to play her zither as a parting gift for her lover. As she proceeds, however, she finds her feelings too intense for her music to express and so she stops and runs to her mother's quarters in tears. The incident itself is related in a line and a half of text; like her music, it breaks off because what is left unsaid is, in context, more profound and meaningful.

Like other fine works of literature in the classical mode, "The Story of Ying-ying" challenges the critic to take the reader into careful consideration, for it is the reader who must fill in with his imagination the empty spaces that are an integral part of the total text. Much as Yüan Chen would have liked to be remembered for his poems of social protest, it is this story along with his romantic poems—especially his elegies—which ensure his reputation.

EDITIONS:

"Ying-ying chuan," in *T'ai-p'ing kuang-chi, ch.* 488.

———. in *T'ang-jen hsiao-shuo yen-chiu erh-chi* 唐人小說研究二集, Wang Meng-ou 王夢鷗, ed., Taipei, 1973, pp. 255-262.

Yüan Chen chi 元稹集. Chi Ch'in 冀勤, ed. V. 1 of 2. Peking, 1982.

Yüan Chen shih-hsüan 元稹詩選. Shanghai, 1957.

Yüan-shih Ch'ang-ch'ing chi. SPPY.

TRANSLATIONS:

Hightower, James Robert. "The Story of Ying-ying," in *Traditional Chinese Stories*, pp. 139-145.

Sunflower, pp. 216-226.

STUDIES:

Chang, Ta-jen 張達人. *T'ang Yüan Wei-chih Hsien-sheng Chen nien-p'u* 唐元微之先生稹年譜. Taipei, 1980.

Ch'en, Yin-k'o 陳寅恪. "Tu Ying-ying chuan" 讀鶯鶯傳, *BIHP*, 10.2 (1942), 189-195. Argues that Ying-ying is patterned after a courtesan with whom Yüan Chen was once involved.

———. *Yüan Po shih chien-cheng kao* 元白詩箋證稿. Shanghai, 1978.

Hanabusa, Hideki 花房英樹. *Gen Shin sakuhin shiryō* 元稹作品資料. Kyoto, 1958.

———. *Gen Shin nenpu kō* 元稹年譜考. Kyoto, 1962.

——— and Maegawa Yukio 前川幸雄. *Gen Shin kenkyū* 元稹研究. Tokyo, 1977. Includes a genealogy, a chronological biography, textual criticisms and works, a linguistic analysis of Yüan's poetry, and a concordance.

Hightower, James Robert. "Yüan Chen and 'The Story of Ying-ying,' " *HJAS*, 33 (1973), 93-103.

Hsia, C. T. "A Critical Introduction" to *The Romance of the Western Chamber*, S. I. Hsiung, trans., rpt. New York, 1968, pp. xi-xxxii. Discussion of differences between the story, the *chu-kung tiao*, and the Yüan play.

Liu, Wei-chung 劉維崇. *Yüan Chen p'ing-chuan* 元稹評傳. Taipei, 1977.

Palandri, Angela Jung. *Yüan Chen.* Boston, 1977.

Pien, Hsiao-hsüan 卞孝宣. *Yüan Chen nien-p'u* 元稹年譜. Shantung, 1980.

Wang, Chi-ssu 王季思. *Ts'ung "Ying-ying chuan" tao "Hsi-hsiang chi"* 從鶯鶯傳到西廂記. Shanghai, 1955.

Wong, Timothy C. "Self and Society in Tang Dynasty Love Tales," *JAOS*, 99 (1979), 95-100.

—AJP and TW

Yüan Chieh 元結 (*tzu*, Tz'u-shan 次山, 719-772) was among the most innovative writers of the mid-eighth century. Like others of his generation, he also had emphatic views on the literary practice of his day. His literary career divides into three main stages. Common to all three was a sense of indignation, a directness of style, and an occasional eccentricity. The first period extended from his youth in Honan to the outbreak of the An Lu-shan Rebellion in 755. Over this period his writing was colored by his failure to obtain official status and by his reaction to the corrupt political world in Ch'ang-an dominated by the autocratic Li Lin-fu 李林甫 (d. 752). He wrote brief autobiographical vignettes, satirical anecdotes, Taoistically inspired condemnations of decadent metropolitan life, and a few *yüeh-fu** style verses describing popular suffering. In his essay "Kai lun" 丐論 (On Begging), he told how friendship with a beggar in Ch'ang-an led him to conclude that mendicancy was preferable to the corruption of official life; it is one of his best prose sketches.

The second period spans the rebellion itself and his early official career, which was late in starting and interrupted by a spell of retirement. During this period, old-style verse, sometimes eremitic in its setting, alternates with official writing.

The third period covers the years when he was twice appointed Prefect of Tao-chou 道州 (modern Hunan) and finally of Jung-chou 容州 (modern Kwangsi). At Tao-chou the local Chinese population had suffered badly from incursions by the non-Chinese tribes to the south and were further oppressed by rapacious tax collectors sent by the central government. Two old-style poems of this period describe how he mediated this situation: "Ch'ung-ling hsing" 舂陵行 (Ballad of Ch'ung-ling) and "Tsei t'ui shih kuan-li" 賊退示官吏 (Shown to my Staff on the Withdrawal of the Insurgents) have traditionally been considered his best verse. Over the same period he also wrote in a much more tranquil mode in both prose and verse about the landscape in and around Tao-chou and about the pleasures of drinking and making excursions in it.

Like Hsiao Ying-shih* and Li Hua,* with whom he was connected through their admiration for his cousin and teacher Yüan Te-hsiu 元德秀 (696-754), Yüan Chieh condemned literary practice for failing to fulfil its responsibility to explicitly promote moral standards. In a preface to the *Ch'ieh-chung chi* 篋中集 (Anthology from a Literary Box), a collection of verse by friends on the periphery of official life, and in an introduction to his own collection he emphasized that literature must not be merely euphuistic or descriptive. It must not be obsessed by technical rules of tonality or antithesis and should return to the standard exemplified by the Confucian Canon. If Yüan overemphasized this message, his directness, his occasional humor, and his ability to innovate rescue his writing from unrelieved moralizing.

Yüan Chieh was connected throughout his life with the famous calligrapher, lexicographer, and loyalist, Yen Chen-ch'ing 顏眞卿 (709-784). After Yüan's death Yen himself composed and wrote out the text for a commemorative stele which still exists. Tu Fu* knew Yüan and enthusiastically commended his Tao-chou verses. Han Yü* and other literary figures of the early ninth century also praised him. His links with these men, combined with his record for courage as Prefect of Tao-chou, kept his standing high in T'ang times.

Some of the works in the three collections Yüan compiled in his own lifetime did not survive the disapproval of Sung scholars. But in the Ming his writings were collected and republished. In recent years, his humanitarian attitudes have again found favor, and his collected works have been collated and republished.

EDITIONS:

Ch'üan T'ang shih, v. 4, *ch.* 240-241, pp. 2690-2717; v. 12, *ch.* 890, pp. 10052-10053.

Ch'üan T'ang wen, v. 7, *ch.* 380-383, pp. 4877-4930.

Yüan Tz'u-shan chi 元次山集. Sun Wang 孫望, ed. Peking, 1960.

Yüan's literary collection is also contained in the *SPTK*.

TRANSLATIONS:

Nienhauser, William H., Jr. " 'Twelve Poems Propagating the Music Bureau Ballad': A Series of *Yüeh-fu* by Yüan Chieh," in *Critical Essays*, pp. 135-146.

Owen, *High T'ang*, pp. 228-237.

Sunflower, pp. 149-150.

STUDIES:

Ichikawa, Momoko 市川桃子 "Gen Ketsu shakai shi kō" 元結社會詩考, *Chūtetsubun Gakkai hō*, 2 (1976), 88-108.

———. "Gen Ketsu 'Shunryō kō' kō" 元結春陵行考, *Tōhōgaku*, 60 (July 1980), 45-61.

Itō, Masafumi 伊藤正文. "To Ho to Gen Ketsu: *Kūchū shū* no shijintachi" 杜甫の元結篋中集の詩人たち, *Chūgoku bungakuhō*, 17 (1962), 123-147.

Kawakita, Yasuhiko 川北泰彦. "Gen Ketsu ni okeru bungakuteki kiseki" 元結における文學的軌跡, in *Mekada Makoto hakushi koki kinen Chūgoku bungaku ronshū* 目加田誠博士古稀記念中國文學論集, Toyko, 1974, pp. 255-275.

Lung, Kung 龍龔. "Shih-jen Yüan Chieh" 詩人元結, in *Wen-hsüeh i-ch'an tseng-k'an*, 2 (1956), pp. 128-140.

McMullen, "Literary Theory."

———. "Yüan Chieh and the Early *Ku-wen* Movement." Unpublished Ph.D. dissertation, Cambridge University, 1968.

Nienhauser, "Twelve Poems."

Owen, *High T'ang*, pp. 225-238.

Sun, Wang 孫望, *Yüan Tz'u-shan nien-p'u* 元次山年譜. Shanghai, 1957.

———. "*Ch'ieh-chung chi* tso-che shih-chi" 篋中集作者事輯, *Chin-ling hsüeh-pao*, 8.1-2 (1930), 37-66.

Yang, Ch'eng-tsu 楊承祖. "Yüan Chieh nien-p'u" 元結年譜, *Tan-chiang hsüeh-pao*, 5 (1963), 25-69.

———. "Yüan Chieh nien-p'u pien-cheng" 元結年譜辨正, *Tan-chiang hsüeh-pao*, 5 (1966), pp. 277-292.

—DLM

Yüan Hao-wen 元好問 (*tzu*, Yü-chih 裕之, *hao*, I-shan 遺山, 1190-1257), one of the greatest of Chinese poets, was the outstanding literary figure of the Chin dynasty. A descendant of the T'ang poet Yüan Chieh,* he was born in Hsin-chou 忻州 (in Shansi) and raised by his paternal uncle, who held a series of provincial posts. Initially unsuccessful in passing the imperial examinations, Yüan spent most of his twenties in Honan, eventually passing the examination in 1221 under the aegis of the Chief Examiner Chao Ping-wen.* He eventually served for a short time as the magistrate at two posts in Honan before temporarily leaving official life. He was later called to the capital Kaifeng, where he became a major official at the disintegrating Chin court over the two-year period before the city's fall to the Mongols in 1233. His action in helping to draft an inscription praising Ts'ui Li 崔立, the tyrant who took over the capital immediately before its demise, has been the source of both partisan criticism and defense of the poet over the centuries. When Kaifeng fell, Yüan wrote a famous letter to the Mongol official Yeh-lü Ch'u-ts'ai 耶律楚材 asking that fifty-four outstanding cultural figures of the Chin be spared. He was himself interned by the Mongols in Shantung for two years, during which time he started the compilation of a collection of extant Chin-dynasty poetry, the *Chung-chou chi* 中州集 (Anthology of the Central Land). Upon his release, he was free to pursue this and another self-appointed task, that of preserving the records of the Chin dynasty and drafting its history. He received the patronage of certain powerful local officials of the Yüan but refused to serve the new dynasty. Making his base mostly at the family site of Tu-shu shan 讀書山 (Book-reading Mountain) near Hsin-chou and at Lu-ch'üan 鹿泉 (Deer Spring) in Huo-lu Prefecture (modern Hopei), Yüan constructed a "Yeh-shih T'ing" 野史亭 (Unofficial History Pavilion) at each of the sites and made frequent trips throughout North China during his final score of years to gather materials for his history. His work formed a major source for the *Chin-shih* 金史 (History of the Chin Dynasty), which was compiled in the decades immediately after his death.

Yüan is most famous for his poems lamenting the demise of the Chin and for his series of poems on poetry. In these, as well as in most of the rest of his poetic corpus (totaling 1,366 *shih** poems), he balances directness and indirectness of statement, allusiveness and originality in diction, and intensity of feeling and restraint in expression. The central characteristic of his poetry is its dignity and gravity, in which regard he was said to have been perhaps the foremost poet since Tu Fu.*

Yüan's poems narrating historical events, specifically those surrounding the fall of the Chin, present descriptions of events in highly selected fashion, written in allusive and carefully controlled language that heightens the effect of the poet's anguish over the fall of the dynasty. The allusiveness and compression of statement in these poems are of the highest technical order, and intensity of communicated statement is effected through surface restraint of emotion. The most famous examples are the three-poem series "Ch'i-yang" 岐陽 (Ch'i-yang), the five-poem series "Jen-ch'en shih-erh-yüeh ch'e-chia tung-shou-hou chi-shih" 壬辰十二月車駕東狩後即事 (An Account of What Happened in January 1233, After the Imperial Carriage Went on Tour to the East), and the fifteen-poem series "Hsü hsiao-niang ko" 續小娘歌 (Maidens' Songs, Another Series). Yüan's critical views are expressed in three series of poems on poetry, the most famous being "Lun-shih san-shih-shou" 論詩三十首 (Thirty Poems on Poetry), and in selected prose prefaces and essays. His stated critical aim is to order the poetic tradition by distinguishing between its "pure" and "impure" elements. The critical theory implied in his poems, and made more explicit in some of his prose writings, is not original, whereas the specific cast of his applied criticism often is. Yüan emphasizes sincerity (the Shih-ching*), naturalness (T'ao Ch'ien*), and strength of expression in writing (the Chien-an Poets). He decries poetry that is self-consciously novel (Lu T'ung 盧仝) or belabored (Ch'en Shih-tao*), weak in expression (Ch'in Kuan*), or captive to rules of versification (the Chiang-hsi poets). He argues that poetry should be the sincere expression of directly experienced feeling, decorously expressed; poetry must also be well-written. He has great praise for Tu Fu and (with some ambivalence) for Su Shih.* He is said by some to show partiality to poets who reflect the heroic strengths he associates with North China. His critical comments, so well-turned and memorably expressed, became the model for a later series of poems on poetry, most notably that by Wang Shih-chen* (1634-1711).

Yüan also wrote a wide variety of traditional *shih* poems on other themes, which are generally of outstanding quality. Moreover, he is characterized as an innovator in the *tz'u** genre, especially in the use of new themes.

EDITIONS:

Yüan I-shan shih-chi chien-chu 元遺山詩集箋注. Mai Ch'ao-shu 麥朝樞, ed. Peking, 1958; rpt. Taipei, 1978. The best edition for Yüan's poetry; punctuated. Includes the commentary of Shih Kuo-ch'i 施國祁 (1822), Yüan's only extended commentator, who is strong on historical sources. Shih incorporated most of the textual emendations suggested by Cha Shen-hsing 查慎行 (1650-1727).

I-shan Hsien-sheng wen-chi 遺山先生文集, in *Wan-yu wen-k'u* 萬有文庫. The only punctuated edition of Yüan's prose writings, best checked for misprints against the *SPTK*.

I-shan Hsien-sheng wen-chi 遺山先生文集. SPTK. The best edition of Yüan's prose, based on the 1498 edition of the author's complete works, which in turn was apparently based on the earliest edition of his writing (*c.* 1298), now no longer extant.

I-shan yüeh-fu 遺山樂府, in *Sung Chin Yüan Ming pen tz'u ssu-shih chung* 宋金元明本詞四十種. Shuang-chao Lou 雙照樓 , 1911-1917. An edition of Yüan's *tz'u* which are not included in the works listed above.

TRANSLATIONS:

Demiéville, *Anthologie*, pp. 413-416.

Li, Kuan-li 李冠禮. *Shih-jen Yüan I-shan yen-chiu* 詩人元遺山研究. Taipei, 1975. Apparently draws on Suzuki (see below) for his translations; also includes a study of the poet.

Sunflower, pp. 405-408.

Suzuki Shūji 鈴木修次. *Gen Kōmon* 元好問. Tokyo, 1965. An excellent study of the poet, with an extensive selection of translated and annotated poems.

Wixted, John Timothy. "A Finding List for Chinese, Japanese, and Western-Language Annotation and Translation of Yüan Hao-wen's Poetry," *Bulletin of Sung-Yüan Studies*, 17 (1981), 140-185. Lists all translations of Yüan's poetry, including partial ones, as well as any studies that treat his work; also lists all *nien-p'u* for the author.

STUDIES:

Chan, Hok-lam. "Yüan Hao-wen and His *Chung-chou chi*," in *The Historiography of the Chin Dynasty: Three Studies*, Wiesbaden, 1970, pp. 67-119.

Hsü, K'un 續琨. *Yüan I-shan yen-chiu* 元遺山研究. Taipei, 1974.

Wang, Li-ch'ing 王禮卿 . *I-shan lun-shih ch'üan-cheng* 遺山論詩詮證 . Taipei, 1976.

West, Stephen. "Shih Kuo-ch'i's Commentary on the Poetry of Yüan Hao-wen," *THHP*, 10.2 (July 1974), 142-169.

Wixted, John Timothy. *Poems on Poetry: Literary Criticism by Yüan Hao-wen (1190-1257)*. Wiesbaden, 1982.

Yoshikawa, Kōjirō 吉川幸次郎. "Gen Kōmon" 元好問, in *Gen-Minshi gaisetsu* 元明詩概說, Tokyo, 1963, pp. 29-49.

—JTW

Yüan Hung-tao 袁宏道 (*tzu*, Chung-lang 中郎, 1568-1610) was a poet and critic who campaigned against the antiquarian, imitationist tendency of the late Ming. He and his two brothers, Yüan Tsung-tao 宗道 (*tzu*, Po-hsiu 伯修, 1560-1624) and Yüan Chung-tao 中道 (*tzu*, Hsiao-hsiu 小修, *hao*, Shang-sheng chü-shih 上生居士, 1570-1624) were known as the "three Yüan brothers from Kung-an" 公安三袁, a name derived from their native place in modern Hunan. They formed a literary club known as the *P'u-t'ao she* 蒲桃社 (Grape Society) in Peking which they used as a forum for literary reform.

Yüan Hung-tao was educated in the Confucian tradition. Upon passing the *chin-shih* examination at the age of twenty-four, he was made magistrate of Wu County (Soochow). A year later, however, he resigned out of boredom and took an extensive trip through the south. The natural beauty there inspired his poetic sensibility. The publication of his earlier poems and prose, the *Chin-fan chi* 錦帆集 (Embroidered Sail Collection), and that of his work written during this period of travel, the *Chieh-t'o chi* 解脫集 (Collection of One Released), established his reputation. His work was greatly appreciated by Li Chih,* Tung Ch'i-ch'ang 董其昌 (1555-1636), and T'ang Hsien-tsu.* His travelogues were also acclaimed and had definite influence on Chang Tai* and Hsü Hsia-k'e (see *yu-chi wen-hsueh*), the great geographer-traveler.

In numerous letters and essays Hung-tao argued for originality and spontaneity in poetry and urged the recognition of vernacular novels such as the *Shui-hu chuan** and *Chin P'ing Mei** and of folksong—neither had been recognized by most contemporary critics. His literary views (as well as those of his brothers) were best summarized by his elder brother Yüan Tsung-tao in his "Lun-wen" 論文 (Essay on Literature), in which he stressed the linguistic changes in language and the importance of clarity and sincerity in literary expressions. The brothers' influence—their writings, along with those of some of their literary associates came to be identified as a school known as the Kung-an p'ai 公安派—expanded as a new generation of poets and writers, among them Chung Hsing* and Ch'ien Ch'ien-i,* flocked to them a decade later.

After his elder brother's death in 1600, Yüan Hung-tao became a recluse for six years, residing on a small islet in the middle of Willow Lake in Kung-an. There he practiced Zen and wrote most of his metaphysical poems during this time of political turmoil and repression. His works during this period were collected in *Hsiao-pi-t'ang chi* 瀟碧堂集 (Jade Green Bamboo Hall Collection). Not until 1606, when the political conditions had improved, did he go back to office. In a memorial to the throne, he campaigned for rehabilitation of exiled officials. However, frustration again brought him back to seclusion, and shortly afterward he died prematurely at the age of forty-two.

As a poet and critic, Yüan Hung-tao was unique. He found his spiritual roots in ancient Ch'u culture as exemplified by Ch'ü Yüan* and the Madman of Ch'u 楚狂 who sang in protest; he appreciated the eccentric poets of the Bamboo Grove; he admired Su Shih* for his wit and Po Chü-i* for his realism; and he experimented with *yüeh-fu** poems in the living language, demanding that poetry be an expression of its own time. His uncompromising stand on individuality inspired later generations to a new consciousness of "self" which characterized the spirit of some of the most independent writers in recent centuries. The modern scholar Chou Tso-jen 周作人 proclaimed Yüan Hung-tao and his brothers the distant forerunners of the May Fourth vernacular literary revolution of the modern era.

Both his elder and younger brothers were famous in their own rights. Yüan

Tsung-tao won first place in the National Examination at the age of twenty-six. In the last three years of his short life, he served as a tutor to the eldest prince (later the heir apparent). A collection of his works was entitled the *Po-Su-chai lei-chi* 白蘇齋類集 (Classified Collection from the Study [which Exalts] Po and Su), reflecting his admiration of Po Chü-i and Su Shih. Yüan Chung-tao also passed the *chin-shih* examinations, though belatedly—he was forty-six years old (1616). He was a prolific writer with a journalistic mind. His diary, entitled *Yu-chü fei-lu* 遊居林錄 (Notes Taken while Traveling and Resting), contains many anecdotes about his brothers as well as his contemporaries; it also collects comments on works of art by his artist friends. Various anthologies of his works were published under the title of his studio, K'o-hsüeh Chai 珂雪齋 (Jade Snow Studio).

EDITIONS:

Yüan Chung-lang ch'üan-chi 袁中郎全集. Shanghai, 1936. The most accessible edition available—reprinted many times in Taiwan and Hong Kong.

———. Liu Ta-chieh 劉大杰, ed. Shanghai, 1934-1935.

———. 40 *chüan*. Chung Hsing 鍾惺, ed. 1629. Reprinted in a limited number of copies, Taipei, 1976.

Yüan Chung-lang Hsien-sheng ch'üan-chi. 24 *chüan*. Li-yün-kuan 黎雲館 ed., P'ei-yüan shu-wu, 1829.

Yüan Hung-tao chi chien-chiao 袁宏道集箋校. Ch'ien Po-ch'eng 錢伯城, comm. Shanghai, 1981.

TRANSLATIONS:

Chaves, Jonathan. *Pilgrim of the Clouds: Poems and Essays by Yüan Hung-tao and His Brothers.* New York, 1978.

Iriya, Yoshitaka 入矢義高. *En Kōdō* [Yüan Hung-tao]. Tokyo, 1963.

Lévy, André. "Un document sur la querelle des ancien et des modernes more Sinico," *TP*, 54 (1968), 252-274.

Lin, Yutang. "Be Yourself," in *The Chinese Theory of Art*, New York, 1967, pp. 124-126.

———. "The Vase Flowers," in *The Importance of Living*, New York, 1938, pp. 310-316.

———. "On Zest of Life," in *The Importance of Understanding*, New York, 1960, pp. 112-113.

———. "A Cock-fight in Old China," in *A Nun of Taishan and Other Translations*, Shanghai, 1936, pp. 263-267.

STUDIES:

Chou, Chih-p'ing 周質平. "P'ing Kung-an p'ai chih shih-lun" 評公安派之詩論, *Chung-wai wen-hsüeh*, 12.10 (March 1984), 70-94.

———. "Yüan Hung-tao (1568-1610) and Trends of Self-expression in Late Ming Literature." Unpublished Ph.D. dissertation, Indiana University, 1982.

DMB, pp. 1635-1638.

Hung, Ming-shui. "Yüan Hung-tao and the Late Ming Literary Movement." Unpublished Ph.D. dissertation, University of Wisconsin (Madison), 1974.

———. *Yüan Hung-tao.* Boston, 1982.

Matsushita, Tadashi 松下忠. *Edo jidai no shifū shiron* 江戸時代の詩風詩論. Tokyo, 1969. Contains many previously published articles on Yüan Hung-tao.

Vallette-Hemery, Martine. *Yuan Hongdao, théorie et pratique litteraires.* Paris, 1982.

Yang, Te-pen 楊德本. *Yüan Chung-lang chih wen-hsüeh ssu-hsiang* 袁中郎之文學思想. Taipei, 1976.

Yokota, Terutoshi 横田輝俊. "Kōanha no bungakuron" 公安派的文學論, *Hiroshima Daiguku bungakubu kiyō*, 26 (1967), 157-179.

—MSH

Yüan Mei 袁枚 (*tzu*, Tzu-ts'ai 子才, *hao*, Chien-chai 簡齋, Ts'un-chai 存齋, and Sui-yüan 隨園, 1716-1798) was one of the most interesting and prolific eighteenth-century poets and essayists. Born in the Hangchow area to a cultured family that had not attained high office, Yüan Mei proved extremely successful in the state examination system—passing the *chin-shih* examination in 1739, while still only twenty-three, he was at once appointed to the Han-lin Academy, with the special assignment of studying the Manchu language. However, he proved totally incapable of learning Manchu and after failing the Manchu exams received appointment as a provincial magistrate. Between 1742 and 1748 he served with considerable success as the magistrate of four separate counties in Kiangsu, but in 1748, shortly after being appointed to administer part of the city of Nanking, he resigned from official life and devoted the rest of his life to writing poetry, studying, and teaching.

Yüan Mei's range of interests was remarkable, representing well the levels of high culture that were attained in the mid-Ch'ing period, under the Ch'ien-lung Emperor. His many poems, written in unusually clear and elegant language, celebrate the conventional joys of friendship and scholarship, yet are also of surprising frankness autobiographically, especially with respect to his reactions to old age and its attendant physical pains and psychological depressions. Yüan had a serious interest in cooking and wrote several essays analyzing food and its enjoyment, which in some ways closely follow contemporary intellectual expositions of the need for form, order, and clarity in the cultural world. Yüan was especially critical of Li Yü* (1611-1680), whose overprecious writings on food, despite their fame, seemed to Yüan to defy the major tenets of sophisticated judgment. In education, he paid particular attention to teaching young women pupils and was for a time the informal "director" of a school for young women poets, whose work he also published. Though several of these women pupils, such as Hsi P'ei-lan 席佩蘭, were indeed accomplished writers and there is no evidence of specific impropriety on Yüan's part, he was censured by many contemporaries, among them the philosopher and historian Chang Hsüeh-ch'eng 章學誠 (1738-1801), for the way he encouraged this mingling of the sexes.

Yüan had a deep and abiding interest in ghost stories, like P'u Sung-ling (see *Liao-chai chih-i*) before him, and he collected and re-rendered a considerable number: since Yüan used simpler language than P'u, his collections, such as *Tzu pu-yü* 子不語 (What the Master [Confucius] Would Not Discuss), are more accessible to the general reader. Always an avid fan of the theater, Yüan presided over a troupe of actors and also went on extended travels with some of the most handsome male stars of his company, whom he apostrophized in letters and poems.

Another interesting side of Yüan's character lies in his continued close connections with a number of influential Manchu figures. Perhaps the most important of these was O-erh-t'ai 鄂爾泰 (1680-1745), the powerful chief minister under both the Yung-cheng and Ch'ien-lung emperors, who got to know Yüan when he was a precocious young scholar in the Han-lin Academy; others were Te-p'ei 德沛, the Grand Councilor Yin-chi-shan 尹繼善, and the formidable Manchu general Fu-k'ang-an 福康安.

Yüan Mei's garden home, which he named the Sui yüan 隨園 in punning reference to its previous owner Sui-ho-te 隋赫德, once textile commissioner of Nanking, had also probably belonged to Ts'ao Yin,* and in later years Yüan argued that this garden was the origin of the famous garden known as the Ta-kuan yüan, which played such a crucial role in Ts'ao Hsüeh-ch'in's* novel the *Hung-lou meng.* Under the gregarious ownership of Yüan Mei the garden remained a meeting place for scholars throughout the latter half of the eighteenth century and helped establish his fame as a leading literary figure of his time, despite his obvious lack of that higher seriousness which some have seen as essential to true quality in a literatus.

Yüan Mei is best known as a literary critic, for his advocacy of *hsing-ling* 性靈 (spirit and mind) in poetry, and especially for the *Sui-yüan shih-hua* 隨園詩話 (Poetry Talks from the Sui Garden), a work he had printed himself twice in the early 1790s. This *shih-hua** goes beyond the usual citation of anecdotes and bon mots to include Yüan's own views of literature. He rejected all imitation of past masters, arguing instead for an emphasis on the poet's own sentiments and for a perfection of poetic technique. This work had widespread influence, rivaled perhaps only by Yen Yü's *Ts'ang-lang shih-hua.**

One hundred and fifty years after his death, Yüan Mei was fortunate to find in the English scholar Arthur Waley an outstanding sympathetic biographer, even though some may feel that Yüan, as drawn by Waley, has an eerie resemblance to some of the figures within Waley's own Bloomsbury Circle. Yüan's amusing perceptions of his own worth have recently been illuminated by the translation of a long letter he sent to his portraitist, Lo P'ing 羅聘, a painter who shared Yüan's passion for ghost stories. In this letter Yüan stated that he had examined the painting with the greatest care and had concluded that it did not look like either his present self or those of his past and future incarnations; he had therefore decided to let Lo P'ing keep it in his own home, where Yüan was sure it would "be honored and treasured forever." This gracious rejection has been seen as typical of Yüan's finesse in handling difficult situations.

Two of Yüan's sisters had some renown as poets, though his own children were not well known; one of his grandsons, Yüan Tsu-te 袁祖悳 (1811-1853), became a magistrate in Shanghai and was killed there by Taiping rebels.

EDITIONS:

Hsiao-ts'ang shan-fang shih-wen chi 小倉山房詩文集. 18v. Shanghai, 1936.
Sui-yüan ch'üan-chi 隨園全集. 2v. Taipei, 1960.
Sui-yüan nü-ti-tzu shih-hsüan 隨園女弟子詩選. Chu T'ai-man 朱太忙, ed. *ch.* 1934. Draws together the best works of Yüan Mei's women pupils.
Sui-yüan san-shih-pa chung 隨園三十八種. 40v. 1892.
Sui-yüan shih-hua 隨園詩話. 2v. Peking, 1960. A punctuated edition.

TRANSLATIONS:

See James Cahill, Jonathan Spence, and Arthur Waley below.

STUDIES:

Belpaire, Bruno. *L'Épistolier Yuen Mei (1715-1797), Deuxième série de la lettre 75 à la lettre 149*. 2v. Bruxelles, 1976; Wetteren, Belgique, 1977.
Cahill, James. "A Rejected Portrait by Lo P'ing: Pictorial Footnote to Waley's *Yüan Mei*," *AM*, n.s., 7 (1959), 32-39.
ECCP, pp. 955-957.
Kuo, Mo-jo 郭沫若. *Tu Sui-yüan shih-hua cha-chi* 讀隨園詩話札記. Peking, 1962.
Spence, Jonathan. "Ch'ing," in *Food in Chinese Culture*, K. C. Chang, ed., New Haven, 1977, pp. 259-294.
Waley, Arthur. *Yüan Mei, Eighteenth Century Chinese Poet*. London, 1956.

Yang, Hung-lieh 楊鴻烈. *Yüan Mei p'ing-chuan* 袁枚評傳. Shanghai, 1935.
*Yüan Tzu-ts'ai yen-chiu tzu-liao hui-pien*袁子才研究資料彙編. 2v. Hong Kong, 1974. Draws together many recent critical and biographical essays.

—JS

Yüan-pen 院本, like *tsa-chü*,* is a term that has a long and complex history. It was first roughly synonymous with *tsa-chü* as it was used in the Northern Sung period, as a general term for variety show and as a specific term for a four-act performance that included farce skits, individual performances, music, and dance. According to traditional theories of the term's etymology, it was a contraction of *hang-yüan chih pen* 行院之本, which means literally "scripts from the entertainer's quarters." The earliest statement about the actual performance is found in an early Ming work by T'ao Tsung-i,* the *Cho-keng lu*, which attempted a definition it claims was found in an earlier source. This description, partially translated here, heads a list of 690 *yüan-pen* titles, broken into fourteen categories, that T'ao included in his work:

> T'ang had its *ch'uan-ch'i* (literary tales),* Sung had its *hsi-ch'ü* 戲曲 (*nan-hsi*?), its *ch'ang-hun* 唱諢 (bawdy singing?), and its prosimetric stories (*tz'u-shuo*, see essay on Popular Literature); the Chin dynasty had its *yüan-pen*, its *tsa-chü*, and its *chu-kung-tiao*.* In our dynasty [the Yüan], *yüan-pen* and *tsa-chü* first separated to become two [different genres]. In *yüan-pen* there are five people. . . .
> There is also the *yen-tuan* 炎段 (艷段), which also means *yüan-pen* but differs by being simpler. It takes its meaning from [the character *yen* 炎], which means a fire flickering—that is, it is both easy to make brighter or to extinguish. In [this part of the performance] the second clown has random words, recitation, chanting, tumbling, and acting things out. . . .

The split between genres that T'ao Tsung-i is referring to here is between the farce skit (specific *yüan-pen*) and *tsa-chü* as Northern Drama, a split that is already anticipated in the list of extant titles, some of which are clearly early forms of Northern drama. The *yüan-pen* that T'ao describes uses the same five role-types (see *chiao-se*) as the Sung dynasty *tsa-chü*, and it is safe to assume that the term *yüan-pen*, at this time, was simply a Northern synonym for *tsa-chü*. (For a discussion of the fourteen categories of *yüan-pen*, see Hu Chi, 1957, pp. 171-258; West, 1977, pp. 1-45; and Tanaka, 1968, *passim*.)

By the time Northern drama under the title *tsa-chü* had come to dominate the Chinese stage, the term *yüan-pen* was used to refer to a farce skit that was performed before the main four-act drama; it was usually a slapstick farce in which the dual roles of the *fu-mo* and *fu-ching* were featured in a kind of straight-man and comic, or knave-and-butt, routine. There is one extant poetic cycle, written by Tu Shan-fu 杜善夫 (*fl.* 1230), that describes such a skit (it has been translated in Hawkes, 1972; Crump, 1970; West, 1977; and West and Idema, 1982).

After the Ming, however, the term *yüan-pen* was used in a much broader sense. It referred, first, to the comic scenes based on the old farces that were interspersed within the text of a drama to provide moments of relief from an otherwise straight performance. One of the most famous of these skits, *Shuang tou-i* 雙鬥醫 (Two Physicians Raise Cain) has been translated for the Western reader and provides a good example for the kind of slapstick that went on on the Yüan and Ming stage (see West, 1977, pp. 33-43; and Dolby, 1978, pp. 21-29).

By the Ming, however, the usage of the term was not quite so circumscribed. For instance, two of Hsü Wei's* "Four Cries of the Gibbon" were titled as *yüan-pen*, as was Wang Chiu-ssu's* story of the "Chung-shan lang" (Wolf of Chung-shan). There are even records of puppet plays and long Ming *ch'uan-ch'i* being called *yüan-pen*. This practice was especially prevalent in the late Ming and early Ch'ing period, when, for instance, Mao Ch'i-ling* called Hung Sheng's* *Ch'ang-sheng tien* a *yüan-pen*.

In general, however, after the rise of Northern drama, the main roles of which were the singing leads, the *cheng-mo* and *cheng-tan*, the term *yüan-pen* was used primarily to denote a farce interlude, the main roles of which were the knave and the butt.

By late Ming it had expanded to include short one-act plays (such as "The Wolf of Chung-shan") and also came to refer to long dramas in the *ch'uan-ch'i* style. As is the case with most dramatic terminology, its use is dictated by the context of the work in which it appears and, to some extent, by region.

EDITIONS:

There are no editions of *yüan-pen* per se. Residuals and farce skits from Ming texts can be found in Hu Chi (see below).

TRANSLATIONS:

Crump, James I. "The Conventions and Craft of Yüan Drama," *JAOS*, 91.1 (1971), 14-29.

Crump, James I. and Stephen West, "Two Physicians Raise Cain," in West, *Vaudeville*, pp. 33-43; reprinted with corrections in Crump, *Chinese Theater in the Days of Kublai Khan*, Tucson, 1980, pp. 152-167.

Dolby, William. "Battling Doctors," in *Eight Chinese Plays*, London, 1978, pp. 21-29.

STUDIES:

Crump, James I. "Yüan-pen, Yüan Drama's Rowdy Ancestor," *LEW*, 14 (1970), 473-490.

Hawkes, David. "Reflections on Some Yüan *tsa-chü*," *AM*, 16 (1971), 69-81.

Hu, Chi 胡忌. *Sung Chin tsa-chü k'ao* 宋金雜戲考. Shanghai, 1957. Compendious work on early theater; storehouse of texts and annotations; a virtually indispensable work for the study of early drama.

Tanaka, Kenji 田中謙二. "Genpon kō" 院本考, *Nihon Chūgoku Gakkaihō*, 20 (1968), 169-191.

West, *Vaudeville*, pp. 1-47.

—SW

Yüan-shih hsüan 元詩選 (Selection of Yüan Poems) was compiled by Ku Ssu-li 顧嗣立 (*tzu*, Hsia-chün 俠君, 1665-1722), who came from a family in Ch'ang-chou 長洲 near Canton. After having passed the *chin-shih* examination in 1682 he served for some time in metropolitan offices, but retired on grounds of ill health and lived the rest of his life in Soochow. Ku was a book-collector and a poet in his own right. He also seems to have been a great drinker, which earned him the nickname of "Chiu-ti" 酒帝 (Wine Emperor). His works include, in addition to the *Yüan-shih hsüan*, two collections of his own poetry and commentaries on the poems of Han Yü* and Wen T'ing-yün.* Ku also enjoyed a reputation as a calligrapher.

The *Yüan-shih hsüan* is an anthology of Yüan poems (*shih**) published in three installments from 1694 to 1722. The work has altogether 111 *chüan*. It is by no means a complete collection of Yüan poems, covering three hundred poets from whose works a small selection of representative poems is reprinted. The subchapters for each author have the same title as the original collections from which the selection has been made, and each is preceded by a short biography of that author. The work begins with a chapter containing the few poems written by, or attributed to, Yüan emperors. A supplement to the *Yüan-shih hsüan* based on materials collected by Ku Ssu-li in his lifetime was printed by Hsi-shih-ch'en 席世臣 in 1798 and titled *Yüan-shih kuei-chi shih-chi* 元詩癸集十集; this continuation, which includes selections from another hundred Yüan authors, is not subdivided into chapters.

The *Yüan-shih hsüan* has limited value for our knowledge of major poets of the Yüan; their works have in the main been transmitted in their entirety and are easily accessible in either modern editions or reprints. The collection includes, however, many minor poets whose poems are difficult to find elsewhere.

EDITIONS:

Yüan-shih hsüan. Original woodblock edition published in Ku Ssu-li's studio, Hsiu-yeh ts'ao-t'ang 秀野草堂, 1694-1722; rpt. 2v. Taipei, 1962.

STUDIES:

Langlois, J. D., "Chinese Culturalism and the Yüan Anthology," *HJAS*, 40 (1980), 355-398, esp. 374-398.

—HF

Yüeh-chüeh shu 越絕書 (The Book of the Culmination of Yüeh) is probably a Latter Han dynasty production. The work has been attributed to such diverse figures as Tuan Mu-tz'u 端木賜 (*tzu*, Tzu-kung 子貢, *c.* 520-456 B.C.) and Wu Tzu-hsü 伍子胥 (d. 485 B.C.). A more likely candidate for the author of the work is Yüan K'ang 袁康 (*fl.*

40 A.D.). Most scholars consider the work to have been seriously corrupted in transmission. All extant editions have fifteen *chüan*, but texts with as many as twenty *chüan* are listed in various bibliographic works. Nor do the *chüan* titles always give an accurate indication of the contents of the *chüan*. For example, the first *chüan* entitled, "Yüeh-chüeh wai-chuan pen-shih" 越絕外傳本事, may well be an introduction to the text. It treats such matters as the meaning of the title of the work.

In spite of such problems, the work is a valuable source for the tales which emerged concerning such figures as Wu Tzu-hsü, King Fu-ch'ai of Wu 吳王夫差 (r. 495-477 B.C.), King Kou Chien of Yüeh 越王勾踐 (r. 496-*c.* 475 B.C.), and the legendary beauties Hsi Shih 西施 and Cheng Tan 鄭旦. The work also contains a treatment of the geography of the area of the states of Wu and Yüeh. Though very similar in content to the *Wu-Yüeh ch'un-ch'iu,** the treatment of the major figures in both works is much livelier. And the accounts of the strategies used by both these states in their continual struggles with each other are more detailed.

Although these two works treat much the same material, and in much the same manner—highly fictionalized historical accounts—the *Yüeh-chüeh shu* is clearly superior to the *Wu-Yüeh ch'un-ch'iu* in style and technique.

EDITIONS:

Ching Yüeh-chüeh shu chiao-chu kao-pen 景越絕書校注稿本. T'ieh Ju-i 鐵培名, ed. Taipei, 1959. Same as Chang Tzung-hsiang's edition except that it excludes Yü Yüeh's *ch'a-chi*.

Yüeh-chüeh shu 張宗祥. Chang Tsung-hsiang 越絕書, ed. Shanghai, 1956. Best available edition. Thoroughly annotated and includes Yü Yüeh's 俞越 "reader's notes" (*ch'a-chi* 札記) and Ch'ien P'ei-ming's 鐵如意 addendum. Handwritten copy sometimes difficult to decipher.

———. *SPPY*. No notes, no addenda.

———. *SPTK*. No notes, no addenda.

STUDIES:

Schüssler, Alex. "Das *Yüeh-chüeh shu* als hanzeitliche Quelle zur Geschichte der *Chan-kuo-ts'e*." Unpublished Ph.D. dissertation, University of Munich, 1966.

—JLo

Yüeh-fu 樂府 originally referred to the Music Bureau founded in 117 B.C. during the reign of Emperor Wu of the Han and abolished by Emperor Ai in 6 B.C. when its entertainment function was terminated and its sacrificial, military, and protocol functions were taken over by other bureaus. Its sizable staff—829 at the time it was abolished—was charged with collecting folksongs, creating sacrificial music, and performing rites. *Yüeh-fu* or *yüeh-fu shih* 樂府詩 (music-bureau poems) also designated works related to these activities; namely, poems commissioned for ritual purposes, poems selected to be set to music, or simply anonymous folksongs collected by the bureau from provincial regions as a way of gauging the common people's reactions to the central government. In time, the term *yüeh-fu* was extended to include songs by the common people as well as works by men of letters which drew on the titles, tunes, and narrative motifs of the original folk ballads. These latter sometimes included literary pieces that showed compassion for the common people.

The *Yüeh-fu shih-chi** compiled by Kuo Mao-ch'ien 郭茂倩 in the twelfth century classifies *yüeh-fu* poetry into twelve categories. Based on the works of his predecessors from Emperor Ming of the Latter Han onward, Kuo's classification leaves something to be desired because it is based on the songs' musical settings, which have long since been lost. However, a historical survey of *yüeh-fu* poetry and its writers can be made from this anthology, which is the most comprehensive *yüeh-fu* collection of all time.

Though the earliest *yüeh-fu* poems were alleged to have been composed in the mythical times of Yao 堯, the Han dynasty saw the appearance of the first significant groups of *yüeh-fu* poems. Aside from commissioned sacrificial music and aristocratic songs, there remain today some thirty Han folksongs belonging to the musical categories of *Hsiang-ho ko-tz'u* 相和歌辭 and *Tsa-ch'ü* 雜曲. These are mainly narrative poems about the lives of the common people. The language is generally simple and unadorned, the plots often straightforward and uncomplicated. The reader sees the essential details presented in the simplest language in a highly dramatic format. "Ping-ling tung" 平陵東 is typical of the narrative *yüeh-fu* poems of the period. A servant's dramatic account of this master's abduction, the narrative begins *in media res*, after the master has been taken away. This incomplete story-line corresponds to the irregular meter of the piece. The twelve lines vary from three to seven characters. Yet the structure is not loose, for the different forms of repetition help the poem achieve unity.

The second major corpus of folk *yüeh-fu* ballads dates from the fourth to the sixth centuries. The corpus includes *Wu-sheng ko* 吳聲歌 and *Hsi-ch'ü ko* 西曲歌 as well as four other groups of lesser importance. These songs, totaling about five hundred, come from the metropolitan and commercial centers along the Yangtze River around modern Nanking and Hupei. Unlike their counterparts in Han, they are mainly lyrical songs that express the personal sentiments of the common people. The speakers in the forty-two *Tzu-yeh ko* 子夜歌 songs in the *Wu-sheng ko* category, for example, are occupied with love and often do not hesitate to express it in suggestive terms. These lyric songs are much more unified than the *yüeh-fu* ballads of Han. Most assume a five-character-line quatrain form, and claims have been made that they were the prototypes of the five-character *chüeh-chü*, 絕句 (see *shih*) of subsequent periods. As for style, the corpus is known for its skillful manipulation of language, especially its numerous use of puns. The word for "lotus roots" (*ou* 藕), for instance, plays on the word for "spouse" (*ou* 偶). The device makes it possible to talk about the external world while making references to one's own human relationships.

While *yüeh-fu* were originally created by the folk as a way of voicing their feelings, scholar-poets also contributed to the corpus. In the Han, aside from the folk pieces already mentioned, there are three groups of aristocratic songs directly related to the Music Bureau. "An-shih fang-chung ko" 安世房中歌, a suite of seventeen hymns composed by Lady T'ang-shan 唐山夫人 around 206 B.C., glorify Confucian values, particularly filial piety. They were supposedly performed in the ancestral temples and in the banquet halls.

In the nineteen "Chiao-ssu ko" 郊祀歌, both authorship and subject are more varied. They were written by, among others, Ssu-ma Hsiang-ju,* Tsou Tzu 鄒子, Li Yen-nien 李延年 (c. 140 B.C.-c. 87 B.C.), and presumably Emperor Wu himself. Though created primarily for religious purposes—specifically for suburban sacrifices to Heaven, Earth, and the Grand Unity, for which the Music Bureau was initially founded—they actually deal with various auspicious events in Emperor Wu's reign. They celebrate the acquisition of such marvelous creatures as a white unicorn, wild red geese, and the so-called "T'ien-ma" 天馬 (Heavenly Horses), fantastic beings thought to have great bearing on the well-being of the nation. Like "An-shih fang-chung ko," these nineteen hymns abound in seven-character lines typical of poetic works from the southern land of Ch'u 楚.

The third important corpus of Han aristocratic songs, "Ku-ch'ui jao-ko" 鼓吹鐃歌, were said to have been military marches of Central Asian flavor. In actuality, the subject matter of these poems is quite varied. There are official odes, battle hymns, and love poems. Some of these texts are, moreover, not yet deciphered, because the words are intermingled with the transcribed musical notations.

The "literary yüeh-fu" are the works of scholar-poets who presumably tried to approximate yüeh-fu in terms of their musicality, simplicity, and, perhaps to a lesser extent, their humanitarian concern for the common people. The pattern of imitation varies from age to age. In the Latter Han dynasty, the themes in the imitations seldom deviate from the original, and the titles normally correspond to the contents of the poems. "Yin ma Ch'ang-ch'eng k'u" 飲馬長城窟 (Watering Horses at Water Holes at the Great Wall) by Ts'ai Yung* is, for instance, about the homesickness of a conscripted laborer at the Great Wall. Writers of this period include Fu I 傅毅 (c. 47-c. 92), Chang Heng,* Hsin Yen-nien 辛延年, Sung Tzu-hou 宋子侯, Fan Ch'in 繁欽 (d. 218), Chu-ko Liang 諸葛亮 (181-234), and Ts'ai Yung.*

In the Wei dynasty, and especially at the hands of the Ts'ao family, literary yüeh-fu underwent radical changes. The tune titles were borrowed rather indiscriminately, and poets were free to express individual feelings regardless of the original models. "Hsieh lu hsing" 薤露行 by Ts'ao Chih,* for instance, has nothing to do with the elegiac feelings of the original, but rather, describes the poet's frustration in his official career. In this period, there is actually more creativity than pure imitation in literary yüeh-fu, with the exception perhaps of full-length narrative poems which continued to be expressions of the experiences of the common people written by literati. Poets like Wang Ts'an,* Juan Yü,* Ch'en Lin,* and Tso Yen-nien devoted themselves to describing the plight of the common people. Like their Han predecessors, they made extensive use of dialogue and maintained a certain objectivity with their use of dramatic structures.

The narrative tradition continued into the Chin, with Fu Hsüan, Shih Ch'ung 石崇 (249-300), Lu Chi,* and Chang Hua* telling stories of the ancient days in a language which is fairly ornate but lacks originality.

The fourth and fifth century kingdoms of Chin, Sung, and Ch'i are known for the abundance and superior quality of their folk yüeh-fu ballads. In the succeeding dynasties, Liang and Ch'en rulers and courtiers were preoccupied with the imitation of folksongs of previous periods. Their poems are generally lyrical in content and ornate in form. Gradually the folk and the literati traditions converged, and specific prosodic regulation started to take shape. Some well-known poets of this phase include Emperor Wu of Liang (r. 502-549), Emperor Chien-wen of Liang (r. 552), Chiang Yen,* Wu Chün 吳均 (469-520),

Hsü Ling 徐陵 (507-583), and Chiang Tsung.* Pao Chao* must be singled out for his innovation of using Han models rather than those of the early Southern Dynasties. Unlike his contemporaries, he employed the less rigid *yüeh-fu* forms of the Han and achieved greater flexibility.

By the T'ang dynasty, although the music of the original corpus had almost all been lost, *yüeh-fu* poetry came of age. Imitation became freedom, and the prototypes were often merely used as symbolic structures with which literary *yüeh-fu* poets tried to invoke certain sentiments of the past and the folk. In other words, at the beginning of the dynasty literary *yüeh-fu* poems strictly followed the ancient models but had gained almost total independence at the end.

The so-called "Ch'u T'ang ssu chieh" 唐初四傑 (Four Geniuses of Early T'ang)—Wang Po,* Yang Chiung,* Lu Chao-lin,* and Lo Pin-wang*—tried, without deviating from the model of the folk *yüeh-fu* poems, to blend the effeminacy of the southern style with the masculinity of the northern. Later, Shen Ch'üan-ch'i* and Sung Chih-wen (see Shen Ch'üan-ch'i) carried on the experiment, accommodating and elaborating the original themes by employing the newly introduced regulated-verse (see *shih*) form. In the early eighth century Kao Shih* brought another new element to *yüeh-fu* by injecting certain frontier and martial motifs. Thus his subsequent *yüeh-fu* dealt with personal sentiments while also embodying heroic feelings. Wang Wei,* Ts'en Shen,* Ts'ui Hao 崔顥 (d. 754), and Wang Ch'ang-ling* followed Kao's innovation.

Li Po's* *yüeh-fu* included poems on immortals, poems reminiscing on the past, and poems about love. In Tu Fu's* long narrative poems, *yüeh-fu* turned realistic, often reflecting the hardships of the common people.

By the late T'ang, the *yüeh-fu* had undergone another change at the hands of Han Yü,* Chia Tao,* and Meng Chiao.* Both its diction and its prosody became rigid and esoteric. The distinction between *yüeh-fu* and *shih** became insignificant. By the time

of Po Chü-i* and Yüan Chen,* the so-called "*hsin yüeh-fu*" 新樂府 (*new yüeh-fu*) had appeared. They were relatively free in form and content and had little formal relationship to earlier *yüeh-fu*. Strictly speaking, this development marked the end of *yüeh-fu*, even though the term was used in a very broad sense to include those poetic works of subsequent periods which were accompanied by music, particularly *tz'u* and *ch'ü*.*

STUDIES:

Chou, Ying-hsiung. "The Wooden-Tongued Bell: The Use of Literature and Poetry-Collecting in Han China." Unpublished Ph.D. dissertation, University of California, San Diego, 1977.

Diény, Jean-Pierre. *Aux origines de la poésie classique en Chine, Étude sur la poésie lyrique a l'epoque des Han.* Leiden, 1968.

———. *Les dix-neuf poems anciens.* Paris, 1963.

Evans, Marilyn Jane Coutant. "Popular Songs of the Southern Dynasties: A Study in Chinese Poetic Style." Unpublished Ph.D. dissertation, Yale University, 1966.

Frankel, Hans H. "The Chinese Ballad 'Southeast Fly the Peacocks,' " *HJAS*, 34 (1974), 248-271.

———. "The Formulaic Language of the Chinese Ballad 'Southeast Fly the Peacocks,' " *BHIP*, 39.2 (October 1969), 219-244.

———. "*Yüeh-fu* Poetry," in *Literary Genres*, pp. 69-107.

Frodsham, *Anthology*, pp. 1-8, 99-110.

Fujiwara, Sosui 藤原楚水. *Kanshi kayō gakufu rōei sen* 漢詩歌謠樂府朗詠選. 2v. Tokyo, 1977.

Hawkes, David. Review of Jean-Pierre Diény, *Aux origines de la poésie classique en Chine, TP,* 55 (1969), 151-157.

Hsiao, Ti-fei 蕭滌非. *Han Wei Liu-ch'ao yüeh-fu wen-hsüeh shih* 漢魏六朝樂府文學史. Chungking, 1944.

Hsieh, Sheau-mann. "The Folk Songs of the Southern Dynasties (318-589 A.D.)." Unpublished Ph.D. dissertation, University of California, Los Angeles, 1973.

Hsü, Ch'eng-yü 徐澄宇. *Chang Wang yüeh-fu* 張王樂府. Shanghai, 1957.

———, ed. *Yüeh-fu ku-shih* 樂府古詩. Shanghai, 1955.

Huang, Chieh 黃節, ed. *Han Wei yüeh-fu feng chien* 漢魏樂府風箋. Rpt. Hong Kong, 1961.

Kuo, Mao-ch'ien 郭茂倩. *Yüeh-fu shih chi* 樂府詩集. 4v. Peking, 1979.

Lo, Ken-tse 羅根澤. *Yüeh-fu wen-hsüeh shih*樂府文學史. Peking, 1931.

Loewe, Michael. "The Office of Music, *c.* 114-7 B.C.," *BSOAS*, 36 (1973), 340-351.

Lu, Kan-ju 陸侃如. *Yüeh-fu ku-tz'u k'ao* 樂府古辭考. Shanghai, 1926.

Masuda, Kiyohide 增田清秀. "Chū Tō shijin no gakufu" 初唐詩人の樂府, *Chūgoku bungakuhō*, 21 (1966), 109-136.

———. *Gakufu no rekishiteki kenkyū* 中唐詩人樂府. Tokyo, 1975.

Nakatsuhama, Wataru 中津濱涉. *Gakufu* 樂府. Tokyo, 1969.

———. *Gakufu shishū no kenkyū* 樂府詩集の研究. Tokyo, 1970.

Nienhauser, William H., Jr. " 'Twelve Poems Propagating the Music Bureau Ballad': A Series of *Yüeh-fu* by Yüan Chieh," in *Critical Essays*, pp. 135-146.

P'an Ch'ung-kuei 潘重規, ed. *Yüeh-fu shih ts'ui-chien* 樂府詩粹箋. Hong Kong, 1963.

South, M. T. "Li Ho and the New *Yüeh-fu* Movement," *JOSA*, 4.2 (December 1966), 49-61.

Suzuki, Shūji 鈴木修次. *Kan Gi shi no kenkyū* 漢魏詩の研究, Tokyo, 1962, pp. 42-54.

Suzuki, Toraō 鈴木虎雄. "Kambu no gakufu to saigai kakyoku" 漢賦の樂府と塞外歌曲, in *Shina bungaku kenkyū* 支那文學研究, Tokyo, 1962, pp. 42-54.

Waley, Arthur. *One Hundred and Seventy Chinese Poems*. London, 1919.

Wang, Yün-hsi 王運熙. *Liu-ch'ao yüeh-fu yü min-ko* 六朝樂府與民歌. Shanghai, 1961.

———. *Yüeh-fu shih lun-ts'ung* 樂府詩論叢. Shanghai, 1962.

Watson, *Lyricism*.

Williams, Gary Shelton. "A Study of the Oral Nature of the Han *yüeh-fu*." Unpublished Ph.D. dissertation, University of Washington, 1973.

Yü, Kuan-ying 余冠英, ed. *Han Wei Liu-ch'ao shih hsüan* 漢魏六朝詩選. Peking, 1961.

———. *Han Wei Liu-ch'ao shih lun-ts'ung* 漢魏六朝詩論叢. Shanghai, 1962.

———. *Yüeh-fu shih hsüan* 樂府詩選. Rpt. Hong Kong, n.d. (preface to first ed. dated 1950; postface to revised ed. dated 1954.)

Yüeh-fu shih yen-chiu lun-wen chi 樂府詩研究論文集. Tso-chia ch'u-pan-she pien-chi-pu 作家出版社編輯部, ed. Peking, 1957.

　　　　　　　　　　　　　　　　—YHC

Yüeh-fu shih-chi 樂府詩集 (Collection of Music-Bureau Poems) in one hundred *chüan* is a comprehensive anthology of *yüeh-fu* poetry dating from mythical times through the T'ang dynasty. It was compiled by Kuo Mao-ch'ien 郭茂倩 in the twelfth century. The poems are classified in twelve categories:

1) *Chiao-miao ko tz'u* 郊廟歌辭 (hymns for suburban and ancestral temple rituals, *ch.* 1-12);

2) *Yen-she ko tz'u* 燕射歌辭 (state banquet songs, *ch.* 13-15);

3) *Ku-ch'ui ch'ü tz'u* 鼓吹曲辭 (songs accompanied by drums and wind instruments, *ch.* 16-20);

4) *Heng-ch'ui ch'ü tz'u* 橫吹曲辭 (songs accompanied by horizontal flutes, *ch.* 21-25);

5) *Hsiang-ho ko tz'u* 相和歌辭 (matching songs, *ch.* 26-43);

6) *Ch'ing-shang ch'ü-tz'u* 清商曲辭 (songs in the tunes *ch'ing* and *shang*, *ch.* 44-51);

7) *Wu-ch'ü ko tz'u* 舞曲歌辭 (dance songs, *ch.* 52-56);

8) *Ch'in-ch'ü ko tz'u* 琴曲歌辭 (songs for the lute, *ch.* 57-60);

9) *Tsa-ch'ü ko tz'u* 雜曲歌辭 (miscellaneous songs, *ch.* 61-78);

10) *Chin-tai ch'ü tz'u* 近代曲辭 (songs of recent times, *ch.* 79-82);

11) *Tsa ko-yao tz'u* 雜歌謠辭 (miscellaneous songs and airs, *ch.* 83-89);

12) *Hsin yüeh-fu tzu* 新樂府辭 (new *yüeh-fu* poems, *ch.* 90-100).

This classification is based on the musical setting of the poems which has long since been lost.

Within each category, poems are grouped according to tune titles. Thus in *ch.* 35, which is the tenth installment of *Hsiang-ho ko tz'u*, is found the third section of *Ch'ing-tiao ch'ü* 清調曲. The section begins with a folk ballad, "Ch'ang-an yu hsieh-hsieh hsing" 長安有斜邪行, which is followed by literary imitations all bearing the same title and arranged in chronological order followed by two other groups of literary *yüeh-fu* poems under the collective titles of "San-fu yen shih" 三婦豔詩 and "Chung-fu chih liu-huang" 中婦織流黃, which also treat the same domestic situation described in the original ballad. Altogether more than 160 literary sources are quoted. The editor seems to have valued these introductions as highly as the original ballads, for he occasionally incorporates them into the introductions, making it difficult to identify the folk ballads and giving the impression that his main interest is the imitations rather than the original ballads.

Since *yüeh-fu* ballads were oral in origin and were set to music, variant texts are provided in the anthology. Two versions of "Ku han hsing" 苦寒行, for instance, are given in *ch.* 33, one accompanied by music from Chin and the other without musical accompaniment. Notes are also given in the introduction to indicate certain musical devices. However, on occasion the words and the music—which was also transcribed in characters—are intermingled, as in the case of "Shih liu" 石留 (*ch.* 16).

The collection has been criticized for including poems that are not properly *yüeh-fu* poetry. Ancient-style poetry (see *shih*), and epigrams are extensively represented, along with the imitations. Yet from a literary point of view, the collectiion provides an excellant corpus with which to study the interrelationship between the folk and literati traditions.

Not much is known about the editor, Kuo Mao-ch'ien. His grandfather, Kuo Pao 郭褒, was a well-known official from Hsü-ch'eng 須城 in Yün-chou 鄆州 (modern Tung-ping hsien 東平縣, Shantung). His father's name was Kuo Yüan-chung 源中. Kuo Mao-ch'ien was also credited with another anthology, entitled *Tsa-t'i shih* 雜體詩, which complemented the *Yüeh-fu shih-chi*. Unfortunately it has long since been lost.

EDITIONS:

Yüeh-fu shih-chi. 100 *chüan. SPTK.* Based on Yüan editions; transmitted by Mao Chin. Some errors in classification, tune titles, and attributes of the poems.

———. 100 *chüan.* Rpt. in 4v., Peking, 1979. Primarily based on Sung editions. Has emendations and author/title indexes. The best and most widely available edition.

STUDIES:

Masuda, Kiyohide 增田清秀. "Kaku Mosen on *Gakufu shishū* hensan" 郭茂倩の樂府詩集編纂, *Tōhōgaku*, 3 (1952), 61-69.

Nakatsuhama, Wataru 中津濱涉. *Gakufu shishū no kenkyū* 樂府詩集の研究. Tokyo, 1970. Includes the Sung-edition based text and an author and title index, an index of secondary sources, and an excellent bibliographical study of secondary sources.

—YHC

Yüeh-fu tsa-lu 樂府雜錄 (Miscellaneous Notes on Songs, preface 894) is the first comprehensive work about musical entertainments in Chinese history. Not much is known about the author, Tuan An-chieh 段安節 (*tzu*, T'ai-i 太儀, *c.* 830-*c.* 900). There is a short note about him in the official biography of his father, Tuan Ch'eng-shih (see *Yu-yang tsa-tsu*), in which he was said to be a Director of Studies in the Directorate of Education in Ch'ang-an from 894 until 898. He is said to have been a connoisseur of music and a talented composer. According to the *Chin-hua-tzu tsa-pien* 金華子雜編, written by a contemporary, Tuan was married to the daughter of the famous poet Wen T'ing-yün.* Tuan composed another work about musical instruments, musicians, musical-plays, and theory, called the *P'i-p'a lu* 琵琶錄, but this is possibly an excerpt or an enlargement of a segment of the *Yüeh-fu tsa-lu.* Except for the *Chiao-fang chi** and the *Chieh-ku lu* 羯鼓錄, two other brief but important T'ang sources on musical history and theater, these two works are the only surviving complete treatises left on the T'ang.

Written in the prosperous T'ang capital Ch'ang-an during the decline of the T'ang Empire, the *Yüeh-fu tsa-lu* is limited mainly to contemporary music (beginning with the K'ai-yüan period).

The work consists of the following six main sections, each with several subdivisions of different length in which many episodes are interwoven:

(1) music sections; (2) singing, dancing, performance; (3) musical instruments and musicians; (4) musical plays and their origins; (5) music theory; and (6) music institutions. The first part is dedicated to ceremonial and ritual music, to musical performances held at the imperial court, to celebrations for ministers and high oficials, to sacrifices to heaven, and to other

festivals. The arrangement of musical instruments and persons taking part in the ceremonies are stated, and descriptions of the musical instruments, orchestras, and clothing of the musicians and dancers are given. Similar expositions about military music, cult music, music of dramatic and acrobatic show-pieces, and dance follow in the same section. Part two begins with a long treatise about singing, dancing, and performance. Famous singers of the eighth and ninth century are recalled by name, techniques of singing and breathing are explained, and something is said about the different kinds of dancing and role-types. The following section limns the origins and techniques of musical instruments. In part four a brief history of some musical plays are given. The penultimate section contains short classifications of keys and modes, and the last one gives brief information about the locations and organization of music institutions.

EDITIONS:

Yüeh-fu tsa-lu, in *Chung-kuo ku-tien hsi-ch'ü lun-chu chi-ch'eng*, v. 1, Peking, 1959, pp. 31-89. A modern, punctuated edition with variora and critical notes; includes a review of earlier editions.

TRANSLATIONS:

Gimm, Martin. *Das Yüeh-fu tsa-lu des Tuan-chieh: Studien auf Geschichte von Musik, Schauspiel und Tanz in der T'ang-Dynastie*. Wiesbaden, 1966. An annotated translation and study.

STUDIES:

Gimm, *Studien*.

Kishibe, Shigeo 岸邊成雄. *Tōdai ongaku no rekishiteki kenkyū* 唐代音樂の歴史的研究. 2v. Tokyo, 1960 and 1961.

—YHC

Yün-chi ch'i-ch'ien 雲笈七籤 (The Bookcase of the Clouds with the Seven Labels) is one of the major Taoist encyclopedias. Compiled by Chang Chün-fang 張君房 (*fl.* 1008-1025), this vast work of 120 *chüan* was praised by the authors of the *Ssu-k'u ch'üan-shu tsung-mu t'i-yao* (see Chi Yün) as "an anthology of the [*Tao-tsang**] that, with its clear classification, its concise yet complete examples, its rational organization in which

nothing is omitted, remains valid until the present day."

The intention of the author, as expressed in the undated preface, seems indeed to have been the compilation of a compendium to the *Taoist Canon* which he himself had edited. This was the *Ta Sung t'ien-kung pao-tsang* 大宋天宮寶藏 compiled under imperial auspices during the reigns of Emperors T'ai-tsung (976-997) and Chen-tsung (997-1022). It comprised 4565 *chüan* and was presented to the throne in 1019. Chang Chün-fang stresses the fact that the system of classification adopted for this *Canon* followed that adopted by the T'ang: The scriptures were divided into seven groups (*ch'i-pu* 七部), the Three Caverns (*san-tung* 三洞) and Four Supplements (*ssu-fu* 四輔). The expression "Seven Labels" in the title of the *Yün-chi ch'i-ch'ien* refers to this subdivision into seven parts.

Chang Chün-fang (*chin-shih*, 1004-1008) served as an official in the capital (his hometown) in different capacities. Author of a few collections of "remarkable stories," none of which survive in their authentic form, he became, thanks to the patronage of Wang Ch'in-jo 王欽若, editor of the *Tao-tsang* in 1013.

The work on the *Canon* had not been progressing satisfactorily. The problem seems to have been that much of the earlier Taoist literature had been lost during the troubles following the T'ang. At the same time, Taoism had evolved considerably during the late T'ang and the Five Dynasties, and many new works had appeared. The pro-Taoist policy of the early Sung emperors also provoked a great output of Taoist writings. The old classificatory system of the T'ang *Canon* was linked to the different scriptural traditions of the Six Dynasties, the texts of which were in Sung times already lost. The newer works no longer fit the mold of the ancient traditions. After several unsuccessful attempts to put the new wine into the old bottles, it was decided to reorganize the T'ang *Canon* rather than change the whole system in order to adapt it to the religious trends of the modern era. What was left of the old *Canons* had been, it appears, mostly preserved in Southern China, in various centers such as Soochow and the T'ien-t'ai Mountains. These collections, together with those of the Imperial Library and of the sanctuary at Po-chou 亳州 (Lao-tzu's birthplace), were all brought to Hangchow, where the editing and compilation was to take place. Thus the new *Canon* was made out of still extant collections of Six Dynasties and T'ang works. The same is true for the *Yün-chi ch'i-ch'ien.*

The *Yün-chi ch'i-ch'ien* poses, however, a number of problems. In his preface Chang Chün-fang surprisingly mentions Manichean works among those that entered into the compilation of the *Canon.* This has drawn the attention of historians of Manicheism, but the results of their investigations have been disappointing, as the *Yün-chi ch'i-ch'ien* in its present form contains no identifiable Manichean material. Another, far more important question is that, in spite of the title and the intention of the author as expressed in the preface, the extant *Yün-chi ch'i-ch'ien* is not divided into seven parts; it does not even contain the slightest trace of such an arrangement. The organization of subject matter is, despite the praise of the *Ssu-ku t'i-yao,* rather confused. There appears to be a division into sections (*pu*), but these are not always clearly indicated. John Lagerwey has recently identified 37 sections. The first is devoted to philosophical definitions of *Tao* and *Te.* Then follow a number of sections on cosmogony and the revelation of the sacred scriptures. Sections 7 to 11 deal with Heaven and Earth, the stars, and holy places. Sections 12 to 26, covering *chüan* 29 to 86 (almost half of the encyclopedia!), deal with *Yang-sheng* 養生 (Tending Life) techniques, including alchemy. Sections 27 to 32 contain doctrinal and philosophical treatises; sections 33 to 35, poetry. The last two sections are devoted to hagiography.

These topics do not exhaust the array of different aspects of Taoism as contained in the *Canon.* Most remarkable is the total absence of the liturgical forms of Taoism. The *Yün-chi ch'i-ch'ien* does not contain any ritual for retreats (*chai* 齋) or offerings (*chiao* 醮); it has no petitions (*chang* 章), no memorials (*shu* 疏), and no other written documents for oblation, and it contains only the merest handful of talismans, charts, and diagrams. Books of the liturgical tradition did, for sure, occupy a very large place in the *Canon* edited by Chang Chün-fang. The inevitable conclusion must therefore be that the *Yün-chi ch'i-ch'ien,* in its present form, cannot be considered as an anthology of the Sung *Canon.*

While it seems improbable that the present work is not descended from the original one, it is certain that the text has undergone changes. The original *Yün-chi ch'i-ch'ien* had 120 *chüan,* while the present versions have 122. Moreover, several *chüan* are divided into two parts (*shang* and *hsia*), for no apparent reason. This makes the total count of *chüan* even higher. The standard version of the *Yün-chi ch'i-ch'ien* is that of the Ming Taoist Canon (*Cheng-t'ung Tao-tsang* 正統道藏), reproduced in the *SPTK.* A later Ming edition by Chang Hsüan 張萱 (1558-1641), despite of a number of textual variants, is on the whole similar to the *Tao-tsang* edition. The *Yün-chi ch'i-ch'ien* was already included in the Taoist *Canon* compiled by Ch'üan-chen Masters in 1244. A single fascicle of this edition survives (library of the Palace Museum in Taipei), which enables us to see that the chapter division of this edition was the same as that in the Ming *Tao-tsang.*

It appears therefore impossible, at the present stage, to explain the discrepancies between the preface and the actual encyclopedia. But there are strong indications that the latter corresponds, by and large, to Chang's work. The encyclopedia contains no texts dating later than Chen-tsung's reign. The source material comes almost exclusively from Six Dynasties and T'ang works. Many texts are quoted *in extenso,* while other citations are abridged or eventually made into new compositions. A few Five Dynasties works are included. From the Sung there are a few prefaces by Chen-tsung as well as the complete account of the manifestations of the divine protector of the dynasty, I-sheng pao-te chen-chün 翊聖保德眞君, by Wang Ch'in-jo,

Chang's patron. Chang evokes his memory in the preface: "the late . . . Wang Chin-jo considered . . . that your servant was capable of accomplishing this task." The *Yün-chi ch'i-ch'ien* must therefore have been presented to the throne after 1025, the date of Wang's death, and the emperor to whom it was presented was Jen-tsung (r. 1023-1064). The latter was far less a patron of Taoism than Chen-tsung. Chang no doubt took into account the fact that the times had changed while compiling his work. Presenting the encyclopedia as the emperor's "bedside companion," he obviously must have left out all that was neither timely nor of interest to the ruler. This explains the specific character of the *Yün-chi ch'i-ch'ien*: a handbook to the mystical and *yang-sheng* Taoism of the T'ang, the religion of Li Po,* Li Shang-yin,* and even Han Yü.* The *Yün-chi ch'i-ch'ien* provides a key to the understanding of the arts and the literature of this period.

EDITIONS:

Schipper, K. M. *Index du Yunji qiqian*. Paris, 1981.

Yün-chi ch'i-ch'ien 雲笈七籤, 122 *ch.*, in *Tao-tsang,* * nr. 1032 (fasc. 677-702), Shanghai, 1926; rpt. Taipei, 1977. Earliest extant text.

———, in *Ssu-k'u ch'üan-shu* 四庫全書 (see Chi Yün). Reproduces the Ch'ing-chen Kuan 清 真 edition prepared with a table of contents by Chang Hsüan 張萱 (1558-1641). Derived directly from the *Tao-tsang* printing, this edition offers occasional variant readings—there are also copyist errors and corrections. Therefore, collation of this edition with that immediately above is essential.

———. 122 *ch.* Ch'ing-chen Kuan edition, Chang Hsüan, ed., rpt. *SPTK*. The second printing of the *SPTK* in 1929 reproduces the *Tao-tsang* text.

———, in *Tao-tsang chi-yao* 道藏輯要 , P'eng Wen-ch'in 彭文勤 and Ho Lung-hsiang 賀龍驤 , eds., Chengtu, 1906; rpt. Taipei, 1971. Table of contents printed separately in the introductory volumes.

———, in *Tao-tsang ching-hua* 道藏精華 , Hsiao T'ien-shih 蕭天石 , ed., Taipei, 1976.

STUDIES:

Chavannes, E. and P. Pelliot. "Un traité manichéen retrouvé en Chine," *JA*, (1911) and (1913), 499-617 and 261-392.

Fujino, Iwatomo 藤野岩友. "*Unkyū shichisen* in mieru sankon shichihaku" 雲笈七籤 に 見へる 三魂七魄 , *Jōnan kangaku*, 12 (1970), 45-51.

Lagerwey, J. "Le Yun-ji qi-qian, structure et sources," in K. M. Schipper, *Index du Yunji qiqian*, pp. xix-lxii.

Sun K'e-k'uan 孫克寬 . *Sung-Yüan tao-chiao chih fa-chan* 宋元道教之發展 . Taichung, 1965.

—KS

Yung-lo ta-tien hsi-wen san-chung 永樂大典 戲文三種 (Three "Play-texts" from the *Eternal Joy Grand Repository*) refers to three *hsi-wen* 戲文 or *nan-hsi** plays that survive from a group of thirty-three originally contained in the collectanea *Yung-lo ta-tien* (see *lei-shu*). These three are probably the earliest reliable survivals of the *nan-hsi* genre, and thus of particular interest to the historian of Chinese drama. They are entitled *Chang Hsieh Chuang-yüan* 張協狀元 (Top Graduate Chang Hsieh), *Ts'o li-shen* 錯立身 (In the Wrong Career) and *Hsiao Sun-t'u* 小孫屠 (Little Butcher Sun). These plays may not be typical of *nan-hsi* in all respects. *Hsiao Sun-t'u* and *Ts'o li-shen* are adaptations of *tsa-chü** dramas, and *Chang Hsieh Chuang-yüan* may have been written as a conscious parody of the typical treatment of wronged love in the *nan-hsi* tradition (cf. the plots of Chao Chen-wü and Wang K'uei in *nan-hsi*).

The dating of these plays is uncertain, but all three were almost certainly composed before the end of the Yüan. Only *Chang Hsieh Chuang-yüan* might have been written during the late Southern Sung dynasty. It is the longest and most interesting in form of the three. Student Chang of Szechwan, on his way to the capital to take the imperial examinations, is attacked and robbed by a highwayman. He finds refuge with an orphaned girl called P'in-nü 貧女 (Poor Girl) in a temple and persuades her to marry him. He reaches the capital and takes the examinations, coming out Top Graduate. Grand Councilor Wang Te-yung 王德用 presses him to marry his daughter, Wang Sheng-hua 王勝花 . He refuses. P'in-nü makes the arduous journey to the capital, but Chang, in his new-found glory, disowns her, and has her chased from the yamen. Later, on his way to take up a government post in Szechwan, he seeks out P'in-nü at the old temple, hacks her down with a sword, and leaves her for dead. Meanwhile Sheng-hua dies of chagrin, and Wang Te-yung seeks revenge. He has himself appointed Commissioner over the region where Chang holds office. By chance, he encounters P'in-nü, who has been saved by friends, and, seeing in her the image of his Sheng-hua, adopts her as his foster-daughter. On the wedding day, P'in-nü bitterly denounces Chang, he attempts some self-justifications, and the two are at last happily reconciled, to the joy of all concerned!

Ts'o li-shen is also known by its fuller title *Huan-men tzu-ti ts'o li-shen* 宦門子弟錯立身 (Grandee's Son Takes the Wrong Career). It concerns the love affair of the young Jurchen student and nobleman Wan-yen Shou-ma 完顏壽馬 and the actress Wang Chin-pang 王金榜; because of his father's opposition to the match, Wan-yen runs away to join Wang's family troupe and lead the life of an itinerant performer. Later, his father, on a tour of government inspection in a city, calls for actors to entertain. The troupe turns out to be none other than that his son has joined. Overjoyed to be reunited with him, he gives his blessing to the pair's marriage.

This play gives valuable insights into Yüan theater conditions. The setting is northern, and the play is most likely an adaptation of the Yüan *tsa-chü* of the same title by the Jurchen Li Chih-fu 李直夫 (thirteenth century). A likely dating of this adaptation would be the late thirteenth or early fourteenth century.

The third play, *Hsiao Sun-t'u*, is a murder story. Butcher Sun Pi-kuei's 孫必貴 brother Sun Pi-ta 孫必達 marries the evil courtesan Li Ch'iung-mei 李瓊梅. She and her paramour, court clerk Chu Chieh 朱傑, kill her maidservant, disguise the corpse as Ch'iung-mei, and decamp together. On Chu's instigation, Pi-ta is accused of the murder; under torture he confesses, but the butcher Pi-kuei contrives to have the crime attributed to himself instead and is executed. The gods, moved by his act, restore him to life. The two brothers meet Ch'iung-mei and frighten a confession out of her. Then they locate Chu, and with the help of the maidservant's ghost, march the pair off to court. There the famous judge Pao Cheng 包拯 sentences them to death and recompenses the Sun brothers with Chu's property.

These plays were composed by *shu-hui*,* and it has been suggested that they were written and performed by young amateur actors of respectable families, but the matter is in some doubt.

EDITIONS:
Yung-lo ta-tien (1403-1407) (remnant volumes). Peking, 1960, fol. 13991, pp. 1a-13b, 13b-54b and 54b-60a.
"*Yung-lo ta-tien*" *hsi-wen san-chung chiao-chu* 永樂大典戲文三種校注. Ch'ien Nan-yang 錢南揚, coll. and annot. Peking, 1979.

TRANSLATIONS:
Dolby, *Eight*, pp. 30-52; a translation of *Ts'o li-shen*.
———, *History*, pp. 28-33 and 83-84; the prologues of all three plays.
Idema and West, *Chinese Theater*, pp. 205-235.

STUDIES:
Hu, Chi 胡忌. *Sung Chin tsa-chü k'ao* 宋金雜劇考, Shanghai, 1957, pp. 60-61 and passim.
Idema, Wilt. "The *Wen-ching yüan-yang hui* and the *Chia-men* of Yüan-Ming *Ch'uan-ch'i*, TP, 67 (1981), 91-106.
T'an, Cheng-pi 譚正璧. "*Huan-men tzu-ti ts'o li-shen* so-shu Sung Yüan hsi-wen er-shih-chiu chung k'ao" 宦門子弟立身所述宋元戲文二十九種考, and "*Yung-lo ta-tien* so-shou Sung Yüan hsi-wen san-shih-san chung k'ao" 永樂大典所收宋元戲文三十三種考, in his *Hua-pen yü ku-chü* 話本與古劇, Shanghai, 1957, pp. 205-220 and 221-240.

—WD

Name Index

This is an index to actual people—major literary characters are in the Subject Index. Only the texts of the essays and the entries have been indexed, not the bibliographies. For some individuals birth and death dates are in dispute or not certainly known; the index gives the dates that seem most reliable. A boldface number in the cited pages means there is an entry for that person, starting on that page.

990

Title Index

A boldface number shows the page on which the entry for that title begins.

Subject Index

A boldface number shows the page on which the entry for that subject begins.

treatises on, 121; forensic (see rhetoric, judicial), 123; in poetry, 122; in prose, 122; judicial, 123; Latin treatises on, 124; literary, 121, 123; of political action, 728; ornamental, 123; ornamental (see rhetoric, literary), 121; persuasive, 121; stages of similar to Western rhetoric, 121; study of, 896; Western, 123, 126, as a methodological model, 123

rhetoricians, 98, 618

rhyme, according to vernacular rhyme schemes in *ta-ku*, 741; categories in, 350, 370; handbooks, 86, 361; in binomes, 324; in poetry, 217; in prose, 102, 658; internal, 825; southern, 371; tables, 370; use in drama, 211

rhyme-prose (see *fu*)

rhythm, 58, 72, 324; colloquial language, incorporated into *ku-wen*, 398; in prose, 93, 95, 124; poetic, 218

riddles, 78, 83, 389, 483, 708; as Warrings States genre, 348; lantern, 78

ritual, 95, 310, 311, 326; court, 960, 961; manuals, Buddhist, 10; Mao-shan, 487; masters, Taoist, 150; music, 268; shamanic, 379; songs, 365; texts, 98, 102, 311, 312, 342, Taoist, 142, 148, 150, 764; verse, 72

role types (see also *chiao-se*), 14, 15, 20, 21, 22, 273, 274, 321, 329, 958, 959; in *ch'uan-ch'i* (romance), 354; dramatic, 774, 775; vary according to type of drama, 273

sacred geography, Taoist, 146

sacred mountains, 160, 250

salons, literary, 266, 267, 516; of the Liang dynasty, 585

San-Chang (Three Poets Named Chang, see Chang Tsai), 221

san-ch'ü (see *ch'ü*), 26, 36, 163, 190, 217, 218, 235, 275, 321, 329, 345, 350, 351, 375, 382, 386, 387, 467, 510, 511, 540, 541, 611, 612, 643, 676, 700, 819, 857, 914; Confucianization of, 386; criticism of, 55

san-hsien, 515, 741, 742, 747

San-kuo (Three Kingdoms) cycle, 906

San-lun School (of Buddhism), 3, 6

San-t'ung; 480; *San-t'ung ti-tzu* (Disciple of the Three Caverns), 480

san-wen (free prose), 94, 99, 106, 107, 656, 759

Sanskrit, 9, 103, 143, 684; Buddhist anagogic and pedagogic literature in, translations of, 947; mantras, 66; works in, 5

sao (lamentations), 58, 61, 95, 489, 575, 590, 682, 871; mode, 347; style, 348; tradition, 61, 212

sastra (Buddhist scholastic commentary), 197

satire, 21, 100, 104, 211, 285, 318, 405, 414, 462, 463, 464, 483, 536, 580, 654, 663, 906; political, 861

sayings, 6; by Ch'an Masters, 6, 201; popular, 179

scholars, Buddhist, 475; Confucian, 585, 586, 592, 778, 834, 835, 836, 841; Japanese, 392; Marxist, 318; modern, 955; Mohist, 860, 861; of ancient-text versions of the classics (see also *ku-wen*), 613; Taoist, 149, 677; Western, 616

scholarship, 524; Buddhist, 4; classical, 218; Han, methodology of, 149; linguistic, 216, 219; of the Ch'ing dynasty, 811; on drama, 869; philological, 228; Taoist, 146, 147

School of Han Learning (see *Han-hsüeh p'ai*)

School of Poetic Meter (see Shen Ching), 435, 858

schools, poetic, 261; of Sung poetry (during the Ch'ing dynasty), 738; of T'ang poetry (during the Ch'ing dynasty), 738

scriptures, pre-Sung Taoist, 149; Taoist, 144, 147, 148, modeled on Buddhist sutras, 142

serialized fiction, in newspapers, 45

Seven Masters of the Chien-an Era (see Ch'en Lin), 466, 878

seven-syllable poetry, 217, 488; early, 212

sexual relations, Neo-Confucian view of, 179

sexual rites, Taoist, 140, 142

Sha Wu-ching (Sha Monk), 414, 415

shamanism, 347, 379, 537, 671; literature of, 50; Manchu, 307; motifs, 348; ritual, popular verses of, 347, texts, 593

shan-ko, 382, **672**, 673

shan-shui shih (landscape poetry), 428, 610, 767

Shang dynasty, 100, 107, 256, 257, 295, 296, 297, 311, 379, 385; capital of, 384, 385; fictionalized histories of, 370; rulers, 121

Shang-ch'ing (Upper Empyrean) School of Taoism, 481, 719, 720; Pantheon, 821; patriarchs, 147, 160; Revelations, 141, 142, 155, 764; Scriptures, 142, 479; tradition, 146, 155, 157, Taoist ritual of, 396

Shanghai, Library, 812; Museum, 849

Shansi, drama companies of, 771; Southern, as home of the *chu-kung-tiao*, 332

Shantung, 964; bandits, in fiction, 711, 712, 713, 714, 715; *K'uai-shu* (Shantung Storytelling), 742

Shen-hsiao scriptures, 154, 155; lineage of, 154

shen-hua (myth), 77

shen-yün (spirit-resonance) theory of poetry, 322, 679, 755, 876; School of Poetry (early Ch'ing dynasty), 839, 840

sheng (male lead or young male), 18, 19, 20, 21, 273, 354, 636

WILLIAM H. NIENHAUSER, JR., Editor and Compiler, is Professor of Chinese Language and Literature at the University of Wisconsin.

CHARLES HARTMAN, Associate Editor for Poetry, is Associate Professor and Director of the Chinese Studies Program at the State University of New York, Albany.

Y. W. MA, Associate Editor for Fiction, is Professor of Chinese Literature at the University of Hawaii.

STEPHEN H. WEST, Associate Editor for Drama, is Professor of Oriental Studies at the University of Arizona.

Copy editor: Lynn Lightfoot
Book designer: Sharon Sklar
Jacket designer: Sharon Sklar
Production Coordinators: John Vint and Harriet Curry
Typeface: Baskerville
Typesetter: Impressions, Inc.
Printer: Malloy Lithographing
Paper: 50 lb. Glatfelter Natural
Binder: John Dekker & Sons, Inc.
Cover material: Holliston, Kingston Natural Finish